KB244856

반 서 연
전남대 의예과 2025년 입학
광주 숭덕고 졸

"단어는 암기가 아니라 문맥에서 쓰임을 보고, 정답은 감이 아니라 단서로 찾는다!"

■ 시험 시간에 맞춘 루틴으로 졸음과 이별하자!

나는 영어 시간만 되면 졸음이 쏟아져서, 점심 직후엔 무조건 스탠딩 책상 앞에 서는 규칙을 만들었어. 거기서 단어와 구문을 정리한 영어 노트를 펼쳐서 빠르게 복습하고, 눈이 풀리려 하면 짧게 제자리걸음으로 몸을 깨웠지.

그리고 매일 12시부터 2시까지는 '영어 전용 시간'으로 고정했어. 실제 시험과 같은 시간에 기출과 모의고사 문항을 풀고, 조금이라도 멍해지면 끝까지 문제를 붙잡아 해설 없이 근거를 찾는 연습을 반복했지. 이 과정에서 틀린 문제는 표시해 두고, 왜 틀렸는지를 한 줄로 요약해 적고 나서 나중에 다시 확인했어. 그렇게 몇 주를 보내니 그 시간대에는 영어에 최적화된 느낌이 들었어. 수능 당일에 컨디션이 완벽하진 않았지만, 다행히 평소 루틴 덕분에 크게 흔들리지 않았고, 끝까지 집중을 유지할 수 있었어.

■ 문맥 속에서 살아 있는 단어를 외우자!

나는 하루에 30~40개의 단어를 외우며 꾸준히 공부했지만, 막상 문제를 풀 때는 여전히 단어가 잘 기억나지 않았어. 그래서 단순히 단어의 뜻만 외우는 것이 아니라, 문맥 속에서 단어가 어떻게 쓰이는지에 집중하는 것으로 전략을 바꿨지. 문제를 풀다가 모르는 단어가 나오면 노트에 따로 정리했고 의미별로 예문까지 함께 적어 두었어. 그 예문을 직접 소리 내어 읽으며 발음과 뉘앙스까지 확인했지.

학습한 다음 날에는 반드시 복습하고, 복습이 끝나면 몇 번 복습했는지를 늘 체크하면서 반복 학습을 관리했어. 뿐만 아니라 주말에는 일주일 동안 정리한 단어를 모아 스스로 퀴즈를 내며 점검했지. 이런 식으로 단어를 단순 암기가 아닌 실전 연습과 연결시키니, 학습할 때도 전처럼 큰 부담을 느끼지 않을 수 있었어.

또, 이렇게 공부하니 지문 속에서 단어를 볼 때 문맥과 연결되어 쉽게 뜻을 생각해 낼 수 있었어. 결국 단어 암기가 무의미한 단순 반복 학습이 아니라, 실제로 독해에 도움이 되는 학습임을 깨달을 수 있었지.

■ 직감이 아닌 확신을 원한다면 역시 자이스토리!

연습 때와 다르게 실전에서 점수의 변동이 심했는데, 그건 내가 문제를 '감'으로 풀었기 때문이었어. 그래서 문제 풀이의 확신을 얻기 위해 자이스토리의 해설지를 참고했지. 자이스토리 해설은 단순 해석이 아니라 지문 자체를 분석해 줘서 핵심이 한눈에 들어와. 특히 정답의 근거가 되는 문장에 '단서'가 표시되어 있어서, 왜 정답 선택지가 맞는지 논리적으로 확인할 수 있었어.

나는 문제를 풀고 나서 맞든 틀리든 지문에서 근거 문장을 직접 표시했고, 해설의 단서와 대조하며 놓친 부분을 점검했어. 그걸 반복하다 보니 "그냥 이게 답 같아"가 아니라 근거를 찾아 추론하는 습관이 자리 잡았지. 덕분에 긴장되는 시험장에서 풀이 과정을 헷갈리지 않았고, 모의고사와 수능에서도 안정적인 점수를 받을 수 있었어.

■ 끝까지 버티는 힘이 성적 향상으로 이어진다!

나는 모든 과목 중에서 영어를 가장 싫어했지만, 기출 분석과 오답 정리를 꾸준히 하면서 늘 내 발목을 붙잡던 약점들을 극복할 수 있었어. 수험 생활에서 중요한 건 오늘 해야 할 공부를 성실히 해내는 것이라고 생각해. 과거의 후회나 미래의 불안을 뒤로 하고, 눈앞의 문제를 하나씩 풀어나갔더니 결국 성적 향상으로 이어졌거든. 특히 하기 싫은 과목일수록 더 정직하게 노력한 만큼 결과가 나왔어.

후배들에게 꼭 말하고 싶은 건, '나는 원래 못한다'라고 단정 짓지 말라는 거야. 누구나 처음엔 부족하지만, 매일 꾸준한 노력이 쌓이다 보면 반드시 성장할 수 있어.

수능은 끝이 있는 레이스니까, 끝까지 버티며 완주하는 자신을 믿고 공부했으면 해.

결국 막막하게 느껴졌던 날들이 모두 지나고, 환하게 웃을 수 있는 날들이 분명 올 거야.

***My Story* Xi Story** [전국연합 모의고사 고1 영어]

자이스토리 33개년 역사

- 수능 난이도 **상** 빨간색
- 수능 난이도 **중** 검정색
- 수능 난이도 **하** 파란색

2025
11. 13
7년 만에 응시자가 최대였던 역대급 수능, 칸트를 너무 많이 사랑했다! 국어의 과학 지문, 칸트 지문으로 초반부터 완전 난감 ㅠㅠ. 영어에서도 칸트, 홉스 지문이 최고 오답률, 윤리에서도 칸트 문제!! 수학에서도 고난도 문항들이 많이 출제되었지만, 이번 입시 전략 최대 변수는 사탐런의 난이도 불균형으로 인한 유불리 발생이 아닐까.

2024
11. 14
축축하고 어색한 수능 날씨! 국어, 수학 난이도는 그냥저냥 했는데 영어는 까탈스러움. 선택과목별 난이도 편차가 커서 표준점수 영향력이 커질 듯. 의대 증원으로 21년만에 최대로 폭발한 최상위권 N수생, 과탐 응시자는 줄고 사과탐 혼합 응시는 늘고, 수능 등급을 짐작하기 너무나 어렵다 ㅠㅠ

2023
11. 16
킬러를 없앤다고 했는데, 국어·영어는 매력적 오답들을 지뢰밭처럼 쫙 깔아 놨네ㅠㅠ 수학은 킬러 문제 대신에 무늬만 준킬러 문제들을 우중충하게 많이 깔아 놓고ㅠㅠ 서울대가 과탐Ⅱ 과목 필수 응시를 폐지해서 표준 점수가 요동치지 않을까? 이과생들의 문과 침공이 또 다른 입시 변수가 될까?

2022
11. 17
따뜻했지만 가슴은 쿵쿵! 떨렸던 1교시 국어, 휴~ 그렇게 어렵진 않았어. 수학은 킬러 문항은 없었지만 까다로운 문제가 많아서 등급이~ ㅠㅠ. 영어는 듣기 속도가 평소보다 빨라서 귀가 빨간 토끼처럼 되어버렸네. 통합 수능 2년차, n수생들이 많아서 입시 전략 짜기 머리가 뽀개질듯!

2021
11. 18
창문을 열어도 춥지 않던 따뜻한 수능날이었어. 선택과목이 생겨서 안 그래도 혼란스러운 수학은 빈칸추론 문제의 등장으로 우리의 머리를 뜨겁게 달구는데... 마음을 다잡으며 풀기 시작한 영어는 듣기 뒷부분이 마치 독해처럼 길고 어려워서 채 식지 않은 열이 더욱 활활 타올랐어 @_@!

2020
12. 03
코로나 때문에 플라스틱 칸막이 장벽을 마주하고 치러진 수능. 이러한 수험생들의 고충을 고려해서인지 대체로 평이하게 나왔어! 그렇지만 수학 가형 30번 문제는 까다로웠다. 마스크를 끼고, 쉬는 시간마다 창문을 열어 환기를 해서 춥고, 방호복까지 등장한 수능이었지만, 처음 겪는 멘붕 상황에서도 무사히 수능을 치른 것에 엄지 척! 올려 주고 싶어 :)

2019
11. 14
별밭에 누워 너무 맑고 초롱한 눈으로, 8년 만에 바뀐 샤프로 수능을 보면 점수가 잘 나올까? 다행히 BIS비율 관련 지문을 제외하곤 국어 난이도는 평이했어. 그러나 역시 수능은 수능! 수학 나형의 30번 문제, 좀 당황스럽더라. 국어와 영어는 까다롭지 않지만 수학으로 변별력을 키운 2020 수능, 작은 실수가 뼈 때릴 듯!

2018
11. 15
국어 너.... 좀 낯설다? 중국 천문학은 뭐고, 《출생기》는 또 뭐야? 국어는 독서와 문학 모두 낯섦의 결정체였어. 역대급 난이도의 국어를 풀고 나니 수학은 그래도 평이했어. 근데 작년보다 훨씬 어려워진 영어 때문에 또 다시 긴장 백배였지. 일명 "국어 쇼크, 역대 최저 등급 컷!" but, 내가 어려웠으면 남도 어려웠을 것이니 마음 편히 먹으면 좋은 결과가 있을 듯^^

2017
11. 23
어서 와~ 수능 연기는 처음이지? 일주일 동안 마음을 다잡고 힘겹게 수능 시험을 맞이했는데 날씨도 마음도 추운 시험 날이었어. 국어의 낯선 시와 긴 독서 지문, 수학은 그래프 유형 추론 문제, 어려워진 탐구 영역. 여진 올까 불안한데 문제까지 어려웠지. 올해 수능은 우리들의 정신력과 의지로 헤쳐 낸 《강 건너간 노래》였어.

2016
11. 17
지문을 다 읽었는데 기억이 안 난다ㅠ 생소한 주제의 제시문과 복합 유형까지! 1교시 국어 영역은 길고 낯설었다. 2교시, 세트 문제가 없어지고, 언어적 독해력을 묻는 문제도 출제된 수학(나형), 안 그래도 이미 쿠크다스처럼 깨진 내 정신은 이제 먼지가 되어 사라짐;; 덕분에 상위권 변별력은 커졌으나 우리는 그 누구랑 다르게 오직 실력으로 당당히 대학 가자!!

2015
11. 12
수능 날인데 날씨가 따뜻했다. 평가원에서는 포근한 난이도 출제를 발표하셨다. 하지만 EBS 체감 연계율이 하락한 영어와 국어에서 수험생들은 당황했다. 수학 A형에서는 귀납적 추론 문제 때문에 중하위권 수험생들의 심장이 요동쳤다. 모의평가보다 상승한 난이도로 '매운맛 수능'이 된 2016 수능!

2014
11. 13
입시 한파가 수험생들을 꽁꽁 얼리고ㅠ.ㅠ 낯선 지문으로 까다롭게 출제된 국어 A·B형 때문에 수능 체감 난이도 급상승! 무난한 난이도였던 수학에서는 실수와의 싸움이 등급을 결정하고~ '쉬운 영어' 방침에 따라 변별력이 떨어진 영어의 등급 컷은 하늘을 찌를 듯... 들쭉날쭉한 난이도로 수험생들을 당황시킨 2015 수능!

2013
11. 07
출제 위원도 수험생도 떨렸던 첫 수준별 수능!! 국어 A형의 과학 지문이 최상위권을 나누다... 수학 A·B형은 모두 주관식이 최고난도 문항으로 출제되고ㅠ.ㅠ 영어 B형에 상위권 학생들이 몰려 대입 당락의 변수가 될 전망!! 고난도 문제들은 EBS 연계와 전혀 무관했던 2014 수능~ 상위권 수험생들의 입시 경쟁이 치열할 터!

2012
11. 08
수준별 A·B형 체제로 개편되기 전의 마지막 수능 - 변별력 있는 고난도 문제가 여러 개 나와 상위권의 수학 실력을 제대로 세분화시키고... 빈칸 추론 유형 때문에 난이도가 급상승한 외국어가 또 한 번 수험생들의 발목을 잡았다고 -_-

2011
11. 10
쉬운 수능이었지만 복병은 존재~ 비문학 지문이 까다로웠던 언어 때문에 1교시부터 쩔쩔 매다! 수리 가형은 조금 어려웠지만, 난이도 조절에 실패해서 너무 쉬웠던 외국어는 점수가 대폭 상승?? 변별력을 잃은 수능 때문에 논술이 더더욱 중요해지고~

2010
11. 18
EBS와 연계 출제되었다고 하지만 체감 난이도는 더욱 더 상승↑ 비문학 지문 때문에 시간이 부족했던 언어와 최상위권 변별력 확보를 위해 확 어려워진 수리 영역~!! 외국어마저 어려운 어휘와 고난도 독해가 출제되어, EBS만 믿고 공부한 수험생들 제대로 배신 당하다...

2009
11. 12
2009년을 휩쓴 신종 인플루엔자 때문에 공부하기도, 시험보기도 힘들었던 수험생들을 위해 언어와 수리는 몸풀기 난이도로 출제! 하지만 오후엔 강력 외국어 펀치를 날리고, 이어지는 들쑥날쑥 난이도의 사과탐 펀치... 이래저래 원서 접수로 머리가 뽀개질 2010 대학입시!!!

2008
11. 13
표준점수와 백분위가 다시 부활한 09수능! 언어와 외국어, 사·과탐은 대체로 평이하게 출제되었으나 ~ 수험생들 간의 변별력 확보를 위해서인지 유독 까다로운 문항이 많았던 수리 가형과 수리 나형 때문에 체감 난이도 급상승↑ 수리 영역이 주요 변수로 작용하다!

2007
11. 15
등급제가 처음으로 적용된 08수능! 언어와 수리 나형은 어렵게, 수리 가형, 사·과탐, 외국어는 평이한 수준으로 출제돼 등급 블랭크를 없애기 위한 등급 간 변별력 확보는 성공~ 하지만 등급 내 동점자의 대거 발생으로 단 1점 차이로 희비가 엇갈리다!

2006
11. 16
수리 나형과 외국어는 만만~, 언어와 사·과탐은 지난해보다 유독 까다롭고 어려웠던 07수능! 결국 언어와 사·과탐 점수가 당락의 변수로 작용하다. 선택과목 간 난이도 조절 실패로, 휴~ 앞으로는 재수도 힘들다는데...

2005
11. 23
2006 수능 기상도 '맑다가 차차 흐림'- "너무 쉬웠어. 하하~"(언어 영역 종료 후)→"머릴 얻어맞은 느낌이야."(수리 영역 종료 후)→"그냥 찍었어."(외국어 영역 종료 후)→"망했어!!"(탐구 영역 종료 후)

2004
11. 17
♪♫외로워도 슬퍼도 나는 안 울어~. 언어 듣기에 느닷없이 등장한 캔디 주제곡은 일종의 복선이었을까…. 수험생들을 1교시는 웃게, 2·3교시는 내리 울게 만들었던 2005 수능, 그래도 모의평가 수준으로 평이하게 출제된 데다 후폭 효과 덕이었는지 중·상위권 인플레 또 다시 야기.

2003
11. 05
대체로 교과서에 충실한 평이한 수준의 문제 출제가 이루어졌으나, 예상 지문 출제와 사상 첫 복수 정답 인정 논란으로 말도 많고 탈도 많던 2004 수능, 재수생의 연이은 강세로 고교 4학년 시대 가속화 되다!

2002
11. 06
너무 쉬웠던 2001 수능과 너무 어려웠던 2002 수능 사이의 적정선을 유지하며 널뛰기 논란을 일순간 잠재우는 듯 했으나, 고3의 학력 수준을 고려하지 않은 문제 출제로 난이도 조절 실패~

2001
11. 07
터무니없이 어려운 문제에 수험생들 쩔쩔~. 작년과는 반대로 언어와 수리가 오히려 점수 하락을 주도했으며, 쉬운 수능에 눈높이가 맞춰진 수험생들의 체감 난이도 상승으로 1, 2교시 이후 시험 중도 포기가 속출했다. 난이도 조절 大실패! 수능 평균 66점 하락↓

2000
11. 15
수능 만점자 66명, 풍년이로세! 수능 무용론이 나돌 정도로 변별력 상실 지속~ 변별력을 잃은 언어와 수리가 점수밭으로 작용하며 널뛰기식 난이도가 도마 위에 올랐다.

1999
11. 17
변별력을 아예 상실하다! 유독 깐깐했던 언어 영역을 제외하고 대체로 작년보다 쉽게 출제되면서 또다시 중·상위권 인플레 현상 야기. 1명의 수능 만점자 배출과 함께 300점 이상을 25만까지 늘린 2000 수능!!

1998
11. 18
쉽게 낸다는 애초 발표와는 달리 수리가 어렵고 까다롭게 출제되는 바람에 수험생들 배신감에 부들부들~. 그러나 나머지 영역이 총점의 하락폭을 상쇄시켜 평균 27점 상승↑ 수능에서 첫 만점자가 탄생하였으나, 쉽기로 소문난 99 수능 하마터면 만점자가 쏟아질 뻔!—;

1997
11. 19
교과서 내에서 자주 접해본 평이한 수준의 문제와 기출과 유사한 유형의 다수 출제로 평균 42점 상승↑ 변별력 논란을 일으키며, 상·하위권이 좁았던 기존의 항아리형에서 중·하위권이 비대한 꽃병형 점수대 분포로 변화!

1996
11. 13
1교시 언어가 예상보다 쉬워 내쉬던 안도의 한숨을 여지없이 끊어버린 수리와 사·과탐의 연이은 高난이도 출제는 재수생들을 두 번 죽이는 일이었다! 수능 사적으로 볼 때, 바야흐로 이 시기는 수리 주관식 문제와 총점 400점이 처음 도입되고, 영어 듣기가 17문항으로 늘어난 수능 과도기 시점.

1995
11. 22
영역별 난이도 예상과 달라 당황~ 수리&외국어=easy, 언어&사·과탐=hard 특히 생소한 지문으로 어렵게 1교시 언어와 통합 교과 소재의 高난이도 사·과탐이 수능 총점 초토화~! 지난해보다 평균 7점 down↓ 96 수능 시험 0점 지난해 3배!

1994
11. 23
수능 연 1회 시행의 시발점이었으나, 수능 高난이도 연속 행진 계속! 10문항이 늘어난 수리와 외국어는 무난했지만, 의외의 복병이었던 사·과탐의 난이도가 특히 높아 점수를 마구 갉아먹다.

영어는 항상 1등급입니다.

고교학점제 실시!
내신 5등급제 실시!

입시변수가 다양해졌지만, 영어 실력 향상은
언제나 최고의 결과를 보장합니다.

자이스토리는 수능 영어에 대비하기 위해
최신 3개년 전국연합학력평가 모의고사 12회분을
동일하게 수록하여
완벽한 수능 실전 훈련을 할 수 있도록 하였습니다.

듣기 영역의 딕테이션 배속 조절 유튜브 QR코드 파일과
독해 영역의 동영상 강의까지 제공하여
영어 1등급으로 가는 최고의 지름길을 안내합니다.

문제를 풀고 난 이후에는
정답의 근거와 오답 함정까지 알려주는 입체 첨삭 해설을 통해
모든 문제를 완전히 이해하면서 공부할 수 있습니다.

이 책의 마지막 페이지를 넘길 때쯤
여러분은 이미 영어 1등급에 도달해 있을 것입니다.

- 대한민국 No.1 수능 문제집 자이스토리 -

🍀 내신+수능 1등급 완성 학습 계획표 [12일]

★ 최근 3개년 학력평가를 수록하였습니다.

★ 실전처럼 정해진 시간에 맞춰 꾸준히 풀면 영어 1등급을 받을 수 있습니다.

Day	회차	틀린 문제 / 헷갈리는 문제 번호 적기	날짜	복습 날짜
1	**1** 회 - Dictation - 어휘 Review Test		월　일	월　일
2	**2** 회 - Dictation - 어휘 Review Test		월　일	월　일
3	**3** 회 - Dictation - 어휘 Review Test		월　일	월　일
4	**4** 회 - Dictation - 어휘 Review Test		월　일	월　일
5	**5** 회 - Dictation - 어휘 Review Test		월　일	월　일
6	**6** 회 - Dictation - 어휘 Review Test		월　일	월　일
7	**7** 회 - Dictation - 어휘 Review Test		월　일	월　일
8	**8** 회 - Dictation - 어휘 Review Test		월　일	월　일
9	**9** 회 - Dictation - 어휘 Review Test		월　일	월　일
10	**10** 회 - Dictation - 어휘 Review Test		월　일	월　일
11	**11** 회 - Dictation - 어휘 Review Test		월　일	월　일
12	**12** 회 - Dictation - 어휘 Review Test		월　일	월　일

• 나는 _____ 대학교 _____ 학과 _____ 학번이 된다.

• 磨斧作針 (마부작침) - 도끼를 갈아 바늘을 만든다. (아무리 어려운 일이라도 끈기 있게 노력하면 이룰 수 있음을 비유하는 말)

🍀 집필진 · 감수진 선생님들

🌸 자이스토리는 내신 + 수능 준비를 가장 효과적으로
할 수 있도록 수능, 모의평가, 학력평가 기출문제를
개념별, 유형별, 난이도별로 수록하였습니다.
그리고 명강의로 소문난 학교·학원 선생님들께서 명쾌한
해설을 입체 첨삭으로 집필하셨습니다.

[집필진]

김현아	서울 가락고등학교	이탁균	서울 대일외국어고등학교	
박형우	안산 경안고등학교	이혜은	서울 잠실고등학교	
신수진	서울 한영외국어고등학교	정유진	시흥 은행고등학교	
윤혜경	부천 소사고등학교	한규리	안산 성안고등학교	
이아영	오산 매홀고등학교	수경 English Lab.		

중요·핵심 문제 동영상 강의
자이스토리 유튜브 채널
Blair Lee(블쌤영어), 홍민석

[특별 감수진]

강민석	수원 이의고등학교	신대한	용인 한국외국어대학교부설 고등학교	황윤하	서울 석관고등학교
강영석	전주 전주영생고등학교			김정원	부산 영어의정원
권수정	포항 유성여자고등학교	오가영	서울 경희고등학교	신인철	부산 오아시스영어학원
서유경	서울 경희여자고등학교	이가영	부산 해운대고등학교	천지현	부산 연세바른영어
송도원	전북 전북여자고등학교	이지은	수원 수원외국어고등학교	Jennifer Kim	김해 일타수학원

[감수진]

강가연	광주 정점학원	남현욱	서울 스카이영어학원	이인혁	구리 프리미엄영어학원
강승원	서울 (영등포)장학학원	문명기	서울 (강동)올인영어학원	이지영	부산 모멘텀입시영어학원
강영호	양주 상승영어공부방	문정아	화성 (동탄)SDH어학원	이진희	광주 이마스터학원
강준구	울산 갑영어전문학원	민수진	서울 대치다원교육	이현규	전주 이현규영어전문학원
계지숙	포항 Happy Helen English	박계리	안양 글로리영어교습소	이현정	진주 니키잉글리쉬
고수희	양주 이지듀터힉원	박민영	부산 스마일영어	이현지	대구 리즈영어학원
공혜진	대구 삼성영어셀레나제니퍼학원	박수진	용인 서주연영어학원	이혜정	부산 로엠어학원
권선희	거제 월그로우어학원	박일진	김해 루체테어학원(율하캠퍼스)	임은희	광명 유니스영어
권수현	대구 호우재영어	배상돈	광주 뉴욕영어학원	임충일	포항 이동이앤앰 학원
권엘리사	안동 가온영어학원	배인홍	대구 프란영수학원	전수지	강릉 에리카영어학원
권유주	서울 유주쌤영어	백성희	서울 대치동시크릿	전채원	서울 (동작)미래탐구
권정숙	과천 에밀리권영어	백재민	대구 에소테리카영어학원	정도희	서울 대치청담학원
김광희	대전 외대타임즈학원	서은진	부산 투애티(toAt)거제어학원	정석환	고양 이안의학원
김기원	대구 베가영어학원	서창준	화성 (동탄)메타영어	정예슬	대전 소로영어
김기형	대전 상승학원	성낙경	서울 (성북)학림학원	정온유	전주 다온영어전문학원
김남형	대전 연세잉글리시	성지현	창원 JH English	정재식	수원 마스터제이학원
김다래	부산 김다래영어전문	송연주	고양 루멘영어교습소	조윤선	서울 쉘리영어학원
김다예	서울 대치써밋학원	신세현	대전 힐탑학원	주정아	무안 주정아영어
김득원	안성 역사적사명기숙학원/평촌 RYUSTUDY	안준형	제주 위드유학원	지선근	서울 세이지잉글리쉬영어학원
		엄수현	서울 엔콕학원(종암관)	진보라	대구 진보라영어학원
김상욱	울산 울산입시전략연구소	엄여은	울산 준쌤영어	차한솔	사천 월그로우어학원
김상호	포항 스카이학원	오다예	광주 이지스터디학원	최민우	서울 다원학원
김아늑	안양 (평촌)공감영어수학	유형숙	수원 다이애나영어 교습소	최은정	오창 오창비상아이비츠종합학원
김예림	수원 제이원학원	유형주	서울 마크영어학원	최재병	평촌 Pax 어학원
김예은	세종 KU영어	윤수빈	서울 The Open청담어학원	최해정	용인 HAAS하스학원
김예지	창원 케이트영어	윤용배	대전 이룸학원	최현희	봉담 프라임영어전문학원
김원선	구미 정도학원	이다니엘	울산 반석성균관학원	하정완	인천 송도정탑학원
김유미	창원 PSH어학원	이동훈	대구 이투엠영어	한지현	용인 유캔영어학원
김윤한	광주 비비드영어학원	이수민	파주 (운정)올라영어	현명숙	안산 링키영어
김자경	서울 월곡올림포스학원	이슬	화성 (동탄)리듀입시영어학원	홍문식	시흥 유니스영어학원
김지은	서울 Exodus 영어	이운영	천안 도치쌤의영어창고	홍웅기	서울 (송파)베토영어학원
김지인	서울 Emily English(서울영어도서관)	이위동	서울 (강서)에듀라인학원	황보훈	제주 이루다잉글리쉬학원
김학수	용인 CL PAMUS어학원	이윤석	인천 일등예감학원	황의정	인천 (송도)캐런영어학원
나성혜	성남 (분당)아카데미아어학원				

🍀 차 례

🍀 등급컷

[자이스토리 전국연합 모의고사 고1 영어] 등급컷

❖ 영어 영역은 절대평가 기준으로 9등급으로 구분됩니다.

〈영어 영역 등급 분할 원점수〉

등급	1등급	2등급	3등급	4등급	5등급	6등급	7등급	8등급	9등급
분할기준 (원점수)	100~90	89~80	79~70	69~60	59~50	49~40	39~30	29~20	19~0

*고1 학력평가 대비 학습 전략

구분	대비 학습 전략	문제 구성
3월	중등 과정에서 배운 내용과 비교했을 때 지문이 길어지고 어려운 표현이 많아진다. 문제 자체의 난이도는 높지 않으므로, 긴 지문과 고1 수준에 맞는 어휘를 많이 섭해 대비하도록 한다.	• 듣기 17문항 　(1~17번) • 어법 · 어휘 3문항 　(29~30번, 42번) • 독해 25문항 　(그 외 전 문항)
6월	3월에 비해 소재가 다양해지고, 길이도 늘어난다. 듣기 문제 또한 점차 까다롭게 출제된다. 그러므로 평소 다양한 소재의 지문을 접함으로써 낯선 지문에 대한 거부감을 줄여야 한다.	
9월	1등급을 가르는 난이도 최상의 어려운 지문이 독해 문제에 등장할 수 있다. 소재가 어려운 지문은 글의 구조가 오히려 간단하여 정답을 쉽게 찾을 수 있으므로, 겁을 먹지 않도록 연습해야 한다.	
11월	고1의 마지막 학력평가이므로 지문, 문제가 모두 어렵게 출제된다. 어법 문제는 문장 구조를 완벽히 분석한 후 어법의 적절성을 파악하며 풀어야 한다. 독해 문항 유형별 접근법을 떠올리며 침착하게 지문을 읽고 문제를 푸는 연습을 해야 한다.	

🍀 내신+수능 1등급을 위한 최고의 실전 모의고사

1 최신 3개년 학력평가 기출 모의고사 12회

최신 3개년 학력평가를 집중 학습할 수 있도록 월별로
구분해서 최신 연도를 제일 우선 수록하였습니다.
시간을 제한해서 풀어보고 채점하여 자신의 영어 실력 위치를
확인하고, 동영상 강의를 통해 틀린 문제를 정확히 알고
넘어갈 수 있습니다.

2 듣기 만점을 위한 Dictation

듣기 파일을 다시 들으면서 핵심 단어나 표현을 받아쓰는
문제를 통해 듣기 만점을 위한 연습을 할 수 있습니다.
듣기 어려운 발음을 별도로 표시했기 때문에 듣기 실력
향상에 큰 도움이 될 것입니다.

☺: 듣기 어려운 발음 표시

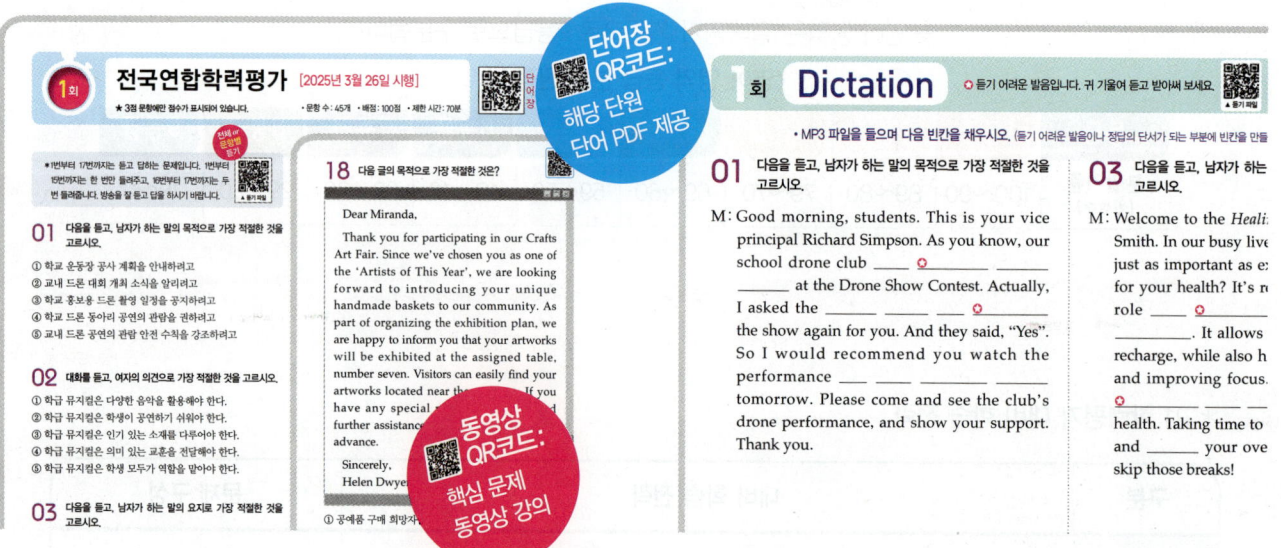

3 문제를 통한 어휘 학습 – 어휘 Review Test

학교 시험과 수능을 위해 꼭 학습해야 하는 어휘와 표현들을
다양한 문제 유형을 통해 연습하고 기억할 수 있습니다.
• 단어나 표현에 알맞은 우리말 뜻 찾기 유형
• 빈칸에 알맞은 단어를 〈보기〉에서 찾아 쓰기 유형
• 헷갈리는 두 어휘 중 의미에 맞는 어휘 고르기 유형
• 각 회차별 모의고사 다음에 수록

4 특별부록: 휴대용 단어장, QR코드 단어장

이 책에 수록된 중요 핵심 어휘를 모의고사 회차별로 정리해
놓은 단어장으로, 휴대하기 편리하게 제작하였습니다.
QR코드 단어장을 제공하여 전체 및 회차별 단어장을 pdf
파일로 손쉽게 확인할 수 있습니다.
단어, 품사, 뜻을 함께 수록하여 언제, 어디서든 암기할 수
있습니다.

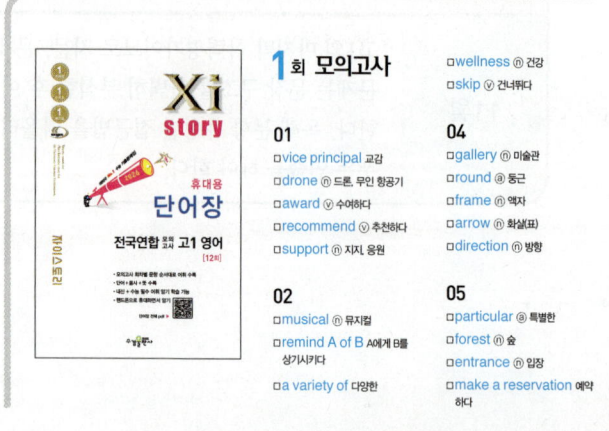

⑤ 입체 첨삭 해설!

글의 주제
지문의 내용을 한 눈에 파악할 수 있도록 주제를 제시하였습니다.

직독직해
의미 중심의 문장별 끊어 읽기 표시와 해석을 달아주어 바로바로 해석할 수 있도록 돕습니다.

핵심 문장
글의 핵심 문장을 표시하였습니다.

왜 정답
정답이 되는 핵심 이유와 문제풀이를 알기 쉽고 자세하게 수록하였습니다.

단서
문제를 푸는 데 핵심이 되는 어구나 문장을 표시했습니다.

구문 풀이
해석과 지문 이해에 기본이 되는 구문 설명을 직접 첨삭하여 문법과 독해 실력 모두를 키울 수 있습니다.

어휘 풀이
필수 어휘와 어려운 어휘의 뜻을 정리하여 독해를 하면서 어휘의 뜻도 자연스럽게 익히고 어휘 실력 또한 키울 수 있게 합니다.

글의 흐름
고난도 지문의 경우, 글의 전개 방식을 한눈에 파악할 수 있도록 도표로 정리하여 수록하였습니다.

선택지 첨삭 해설
정확한 정답을 확인할 수 있도록 선택지를 꼼꼼하게 분석하여 설명했습니다.

배경 지식
지문과 관련 있는 알아두면 유용한 배경 지식을 수록하였습니다.

---

23 정답 ② ✽ 아이들이 수학적 이해를 발달시키는 방법

Every day, / children explore and construct / relationships among objects. //
매일 / 아이들은 탐구하고 구성한다 / 사물 사이의 관계들을 //

Frequently, / these relationships focus on / how much or how many of something exists. // 간접의문문
빈번히 / 이러한 관계들은 ~에 초점을 맞춘다 / 무언가가 얼마만큼 혹은 몇 개 존재하는지 //
핵심 문장 단서1 아이들은 사물 사이의 관계들을 수자와 양으로 초점을 맞춤

Thus, / children count — "One cookie, / two shoes, / three candles on the birthday cake, / four children in the sandbox." //
따라서 / 아이들은 센다 / "쿠키 하나 / 신발 두 개 / 생일 케이크 위에 초 세 개 / 모래놀이통에 아이 네 명" //

Children compare — "Which has more? // Which has fewer? // Will there be enough?" //   few의 비교급
아이들은 비교한다 / "무엇이 더 많지 / 무엇이 더 적지 / 충분할까" //

Children calculate — "How many will fit? // Now, I have five. // I need one more." //
아이들은 계산한다 / "몇 개가 알맞을까 / 나는 지금 다섯 개가 있어 / 하나 더 필요하네" //

In all of these instances, / children are developing a notion of quantity. // 단서2 아이들은 일상에서 양의 개념을 발달시킴
이 모든 예시에서 / 아이들은 양의 개념을 발달시키는 중이다 //

Children reveal and investigate mathematical concepts / through their own activities or experiences, /
아이들은 수학적 개념을 밝히고 연구한다 / 그들만의 활동이나 경험을 통해 /
단서3 아이들은 경험과 활동을 통해 수학 개념을 밝히고 연구함
의문형용사(how many)+명사(crackers)

such as figuring out / how many crackers to take at snack time / or sorting shells into piles. //   병렬
알아내는 것이나와 같은 / 간식 시간에 몇 개의 크래커를 가져갈지 / 혹은 조개껍질들을 더미로 분류하는 것과 같은) //

• explore ⓥ 탐구하다   • construct ⓥ 구성하다   • object ⓝ 사물
• frequently 🄰 빈번히   • exist ⓥ 존재하다
• compare ⓥ 비교하다   • calculate ⓥ 계산하다
• fit ⓥ 적합하다, 알맞다   • develop ⓥ 발달시키다
• notion ⓝ 개념   • quantity ⓝ 양   • reveal ⓥ 밝히다
• investigate ⓥ 조사하다, 연구하다   • mathematical ⓐ 수학적인
• figure out ~을 알아내다   • sort ⓥ 분류하다   • shell ⓝ 조개껍질
• pile ⓝ (수북이 쌓여 있는) 더미   • count ⓥ (수를) 세다
• advantage ⓝ 이점

매일, 아이들은 사물 사이의 관계를 탐구하고 구성한다. 빈번히, 이러한 관계들은 무언가가 얼마만큼 혹은 몇 개 존재하는지에 초점을 맞춘다. 따라서, 아이들은 센다. "쿠키 하나, 신발 두 개, 생일 케이크 위에 초 세 개, 모래놀이통에 아이 네 명." 아이들은 비교한다. "무엇이 더 많지? 무엇이 더 적지? 충분할까?" 아이들은 계산한다. "몇 개가 알맞을까? 나는 지금 다섯 개가 있어. 하나 더 필요하네." 이 모든 예시에서, 아이들은 양의 개념을 발달시키는 중이다. 아이들은 간식 시간에 몇 개의 크래커를 가져갈지 알아내는 것 혹은 조개껍질들을 더미로 분류하는 것과 같은, 그들만의 활동이나 경험을 통해 수학적 개념을 밝히고 연구한다.

다음 글의 주제로 가장 적절한 것은?
① difficulties of children in learning how to count 아이들이 숫자를 세는 법을 배우는 어려움
　숫자 세는 법을 배우는 아이들의 어려움   세는 것은 나와 있지만 그 어려움은 제시되지 않음
② how children build mathematical understanding 아이들이
　아이들이 수학적 이해를 발달시키는 방법   경험과 활동을 통해 수학 발달시킨다고 했음
③ why fingers are used in counting objects 사물을 세는 내용은 나오지만
　사물을 세는 데 손가락이 사용되는 이유   손가락을 사용하는 것에 대한 언급은 없음
④ importance of early childhood education 유아
　유아 교육의 중요성   교육의 중요성에 대한 내용이 아님
⑤ advantages of singing number song
　숫자 노래를 부르는 것의 이점   숫자 노래를 부르는 것에 대한 내용은 없음

왜 정답? ★★ [정답률 82%]

단서 동사에 밑줄이 있으므로
발상 주어를 찾아 그 수가 일치하는지 확인한다.
해결 that이 이끄는 관계대명사절을 제외하면 문장의 핵심 주어는 A general strategy로 단수이다. 따라서 동사는 are가 아니라 단수 동사인 is가 와야 한다.
개념 주어를 꾸미는 수식어구와 상관없이 핵심 주어의 수에 동사의 수를 일치시킨다.

왜 오답?

① 아이들이 사물의 관계를 탐구할 때 숫자를 세는 것에 초점을 맞춘다고 했지만, 거기서 겪는 어려움은 언급되지 않았다. (🄳❷ 이유: 어려움에 관한 글이다.)
③ 아이들이 숫자를 셀 때 손가락을 사용한다는 내용은 제시되지 않았다.   주의
④ 유아 교육의 중요성을 설명하는 글이 아니다.
⑤ 아이들이 수학적 개념을 일상의 경험과 활동을 통해 탐구한다고 설명했지만, 숫자 노래를 부르는 내용은 나오지 않았다.   함정

선택지 순서대로 제시되지 않았다.

✱ 글의 흐름

주제	패션은 우리의 삶에 기여하고 우리가 중요한 사회적 가치를 개발하고 나타내는 수단을 제공함
전개 ①	패션은 아름답고 유용하며 창의성과 취향을 드러냄
전개 ②	패션을 통해 자아 존중과 타인의 즐거움에 대한 관심을 보여줄 수 있음
전개 ③	패션은 다른 정체성의 시도와 친교적 기능을 제공함

✱ [주어와 동사의 수 일치] 해결하기   KEY
• 수식어구를 제외하고 주어를 찾아 동사의 수를 일치시킨다.
• 주어와 동사의 수 일치를 묻는 문제의 대부분은 동사 바로 앞에 핵심 주어가 위치하지 않는다.

✱ to부정사의 형용사적 용법   어법 특강

– to부정사의 세 가지 용법 중 하나로, to부정사가 형용사처럼 (대명사를 수식하거나 「be+to부정사」 형태로 주어를 보충 설명하는) 역할을 한다. 이때 to부정사는 '~하는, ~할' 등으로 해석된다.

• They had no time to change the schedule.
(그들은 일정을 바꿀 시간이 없었다.) 명사(time)를 수식하는 to부정사

• I have some pictures to show Luke.
(나는 Luke에게 보여줄 몇 장의 사진들이 있다.) 명사(pictures)를 수식하는 to부정사

– 「be+to부정사」, 형태로 주어를 보충 설명할 때에는 예정, 의무, 운명, 가능, 의지나 의도를 나타낸다.

• We are to leave for Canada tomorrow.
(우리는 내일 캐나다로 떠날 예정이다.) 명사(time)를 수식하는 to부정사

✱ 텔레비전 수신료(受信料)   배경 지식

수신료(受信料)는 텔레비전과 같은 영상 매체를 수신하는 대가로 지불하는 요금을 말한다. 각국의 공영방송에서 방송재원 확보를 위해 국민을 대상으로 징수하는 것이다. 우리나라의 공영방송인 KBS는 1963년부터 수신료를 징수하고 있다. 처음에는 수신료가 월 100원에서 출발했고 꾸준히 인상됐다.

수신료는 KBS 이사회가 심의·의결한 후 방송위원회를 거쳐서 국회의 승인을 얻어 확정한다. 국내 거주 중 집에 수상기가 있는 사람은 모두 수신료를 납부해야 한다. 가정용 수상기는 세대별로 1대분을, 일반용(사무실·영업장소) 수상기는 소지한 대수에 따라 수신료를 부과한다.

정답률
교육청 자료, 기타 기관 공지 자료와 내부 검토 과정을 거쳐 제시됩니다.

단서
문제 풀이의 핵심이 되는 단서를 꼭 짚어 설명합니다.

발상
핵심 단서로 문제 풀이 방법을 구체적으로 설명합니다.

해결
찾아야 하는 것들을 다 찾은 뒤 적용하여 해결합니다.

개념
문제 풀이에 필요한 개념을 다시 한 번 확인합니다.

꿀팁
문제를 쉽고 빠르게 풀 수 있는 특별한 꿀팁입니다.

주의
단서를 잘못 이용할 가능성이 있을 때, 올바른 풀이로 나아갈 수 있도록 합니다.

함정
빠지기 쉬운 함정을 체크해 주고 해결할 수 있는 방법을 제시하였습니다.

KEY: 문제 속 어법 설명
해당 어법 사항이 문제로 출제됐을 때 정답을 찾는 가장 핵심적인 방법을 설명했습니다.

어법 특강
핵심 어법 사항을 한 번 더 짚어 주어 심화학습을 돕습니다.

왜 오답
오답 선택지와 매력적 오답을 상세히 분석하여 오답의 함정에 빠지지 않도록 하였습니다.

매력적 오답
오답을 정답이라고 착각하게 되는 이유에 대해 철저하게 분석하고 대책까지 제시합니다.

매력적 오답 이유
매력적 오답이 되는 이유를 자세히 설명합니다.

✿ **동영상 강의 QR코드**: 독해 문항에는 동영상 강의로 이어지는 QR코드 수록

✿ **단어장 PDF QR코드**: 회차마다 단어 PDF 파일로 이어지는 QR코드 수록

✿ **듣기 파일 QR코드**: 각 회차마다 수록된 QR코드를 통해 전체 듣기, 문항별 듣기 파일을 선택해 들을 수 있습니다.

— **듣기 파일 다운로드**: www.book-sk.kr

🍀 전국연합학력평가 고1 영어 활용법+α

❶ 연습은 실전처럼, 실전은 연습처럼!

- 모의고사를 풀 때는 반드시 실전처럼 시간을 재면서 풀어야 합니다. 영어 시험 시간인 70분에 맞추어 지문을 읽고 정답을 찾는 연습을 하세요.
- 쉬운 유형의 문제는 최대한 빨리 정답을 찾고 넘어가야 고난도 유형의 문제를 풀 시간을 벌 수 있습니다.
- 철저한 훈련을 통해 자신에게 맞는 시간 분배 기술을 습득하세요.

❷ 듣기 실력을 키우자!

- 유튜브로 연결되는 QR코드를 통해 전체 듣기, 문항별 듣기를 선택해 들을 수 있습니다.
- 틀린 문항은 단서가 들릴 때까지 반복해 정답을 확인하세요.
- 각 회차가 끝난 후 듣기 파일을 다시 한 번 들으면서 꼼꼼하게 받아쓰기를 해보세요. 딕테이션은 듣기 실력을 향상시키는 가장 효과적인 방법입니다.

❸ 독해 문항에 제공되는 동영상 강의를 활용하자!

- 모든 독해 문항에 동영상 강의로 연결되는 QR코드를 제공합니다.
- 헷갈리거나 단서를 정확하게 찾지 못한 문제는 동영상 강의를 통해 자신이 놓친 부분을 꼭 점검하세요.

❹ 정확한 근거로 문제를 풀어 답을 고르자!

- 독해 문제를 풀 때 어림짐작으로 답을 고르는 학생들이 꽤 많은데, 이는 수능을 대비하는 올바른 자세가 아닙니다.
- 선택지를 가리고 지문에서 정답의 단서를 찾는 연습을 통해 정확한 근거로 문제를 푸는 습관을 가지는 것이 좋습니다.
- 어려운 유형 또는 정답률이 낮은 문제에는 단계별 해설이 제공됩니다. 혼자서 문제를 풀 때도 떠올릴 수 있도록 단계별 해설을 완벽하게 익히세요.

❺ QR 코드 단어장, 휴대용 단어장, 어휘 Review Test로 어휘를 꼼꼼히 외우자!

- 공부한 후에는 그 지문에 나온 단어들을 바로바로 모두 암기한다는 생각으로 공부해야 합니다.
- 각 회차마다 다양한 유형의 문제들로 출제된 어휘 문제들을 풀면서 주요 어휘를 완벽하게 외우세요.
- 휴대용 단어장으로 어휘를 외울 수 있어 오래 기억할 수 있습니다.

*3월 전국연합학력평가

[회별 45문항, 제한 시간 70분]

★ 최근 연도부터 차례대로 수록하였습니다.

1회 　모의고사 — 2025년 시행

2회 　모의고사 — 2024년 시행

3회 　모의고사 — 2023년 시행

출제 범위	중학교 영어 전범위
난이도	하 : 12~14문항　　중 : 14~16문항 상 : 7~9문항　　최상 : 8~10문항

출제 경향
· **듣기** 17문항 (1~17번), **어법 · 어휘** 3문항 (29~30번, 42번),
　독해 25문항 (그 외 전 문항)

3월 대비 학습 전략
중등 과정에서 배운 내용과 비교했을 때 지문이 길어지고 어려운 표현이
많아진다. 문제 자체의 난이도는 높지 않으므로, 긴 지문과 고1 수준에 맞는
어휘를 많이 접해 대비하도록 한다.

전국연합학력평가 [2025년 3월 26일 시행]

★ 3점 문항에만 점수가 표시되어 있습니다.

• 문항 수: 45개   • 배점: 100점   • 제한 시간: 70분

 단어장

*1번부터 17번까지는 듣고 답하는 문제입니다. 1번부터 15번까지는 한 번만 들려주고, 16번부터 17번까지는 두 번 들려줍니다. 방송을 잘 듣고 답을 하시기 바랍니다.

▲ 듣기 파일

01 다음을 듣고, 남자가 하는 말의 목적으로 가장 적절한 것을 고르시오.

① 학교 운동장 공사 계획을 안내하려고
② 교내 드론 대회 개최 소식을 알리려고
③ 학교 홍보용 드론 촬영 일정을 공지하려고
④ 학교 드론 동아리 공연의 관람을 권하려고
⑤ 교내 드론 공연의 관람 안전 수칙을 강조하려고

02 대화를 듣고, 여자의 의견으로 가장 적절한 것을 고르시오.

① 학급 뮤지컬은 다양한 음악을 활용해야 한다.
② 학급 뮤지컬은 학생이 공연하기 쉬워야 한다.
③ 학급 뮤지컬은 인기 있는 소재를 다루어야 한다.
④ 학급 뮤지컬은 의미 있는 교훈을 전달해야 한다.
⑤ 학급 뮤지컬은 학생 모두가 역할을 맡아야 한다.

03 다음을 듣고, 남자가 하는 말의 요지로 가장 적절한 것을 고르시오.

① 건강을 지키기 위해서 규칙적인 운동이 필수적이다.
② 바쁜 일상에서 휴식을 취하는 것은 건강에 중요하다.
③ 집중력을 높이는 것은 업무 수행 능력을 향상시킨다.
④ 운동 부족을 보완하려면 적절한 식이 요법이 필요하다.
⑤ 다양한 인간관계가 스트레스를 줄이는 데 도움이 된다.

04 대화를 듣고, 그림에서 대화의 내용과 일치하지 않는 것을 고르시오.

05 대화를 듣고, 남자가 할 일로 가장 적절한 것을 고르시오.

① 숲지도 다운로드 하기
② 산책 장소 찾아보기
③ 숲 입장권 구매하기
④ 식당 메뉴 찾아보기
⑤ 식당 예약하기

06 대화를 듣고, 여자가 지불할 금액을 고르시오. [3점]

① $13   ② $20   ③ $23   ④ $30   ⑤ $33

07 대화를 듣고, 남자가 휴대 전화를 수리받지 못한 이유를 고르시오.

① 수리점의 위치를 찾지 못해서
② 예약 없이 수리점을 방문해서
③ 수학 시험을 준비하느라 바빠서
④ 수리점에서 오래 기다려야 해서
⑤ 버스에서 휴대 전화를 잃어버려서

08 대화를 듣고, Future Generation Talk Show에 관해 언급되지 않은 것을 고르시오.

① 개최 장소   ② 강연자
③ 강연 주제   ④ 시작 시간
⑤ 온라인 시청 가능 여부

09 Science Day 행사에 관한 다음 내용을 듣고, 일치하지 않는 것을 고르시오.

① 이번 주 토요일에 진행된다.
② 학생들이 직접 로봇을 작동해 볼 수 있다.
③ 선생님들이 오전에 실험 부스를 운영한다.
④ QR 코드를 스캔하여 참가 신청을 할 수 있다.
⑤ 참가자들에게 점심을 제공한다.

10 다음 표를 보면서 대화를 듣고, 여자가 수강할 운동 수업을 고르시오.

Exercise Classes

	Class	Fee	Time	Exercise Type	Level
①	A	$25	9:00 a.m.	Dancing	Beginner
②	B	$35	10:00 a.m.	Dancing	Advanced
③	C	$35	10:00 a.m.	Tennis	Beginner
④	D	$35	2:00 p.m.	Boxing	Beginner
⑤	E	$45	10:00 a.m.	Boxing	Advanced

11 대화를 듣고, 여자의 마지막 말에 대한 남자의 응답으로 가장 적절한 것을 고르시오.

① I'll ask the teacher if I can change my topic.
② I record myself talking and watch it later.
③ I'm looking forward to your presentation.
④ I need more time to finish my slides.
⑤ I haven't decided what to wear.

12 대화를 듣고, 남자의 마지막 말에 대한 여자의 응답으로 가장 적절한 것을 고르시오.

① Thanks. But I'm not hungry now.
② I agree. Printing it out is such a waste.
③ Of course not. I'll help you at any time.
④ Great idea! It'll catch the students' attention.
⑤ No worries. I like the menu of our school cafeteria.

13 대화를 듣고, 여자의 마지막 말에 대한 남자의 응답으로 가장 적절한 것을 고르시오.

Man: _____

① Right. I'll try to go to bed earlier and get more sleep.
② I'm sorry. I didn't know you had a hard time sleeping.
③ Absolutely! I believe you'll do better next time.
④ Sure. I'll do my best to stay awake longer.
⑤ I see. I'll try to come back home in time.

14 대화를 듣고, 남자의 마지막 말에 대한 여자의 응답으로 가장 적절한 것을 고르시오. [3점]

Woman: _____

① Reading books can also be a good hobby.
② You had to practice a lot to win the game.
③ How about going out with me this Saturday?
④ Just bring your racket and some comfortable clothes.
⑤ If you don't have a hobby, you can get more stressed.

15 다음 상황 설명을 듣고, Kevin이 Ms. Tyler에게 할 말로 가장 적절한 것을 고르시오. [3점]

Kevin: _____

① Isn't it fortunate that the rain stopped yesterday?
② Could you teach us about the stars today?
③ Is it okay if we change the camp site?
④ Can we reschedule the camp for another day?
⑤ How can we gather more volunteers for the camp?

[16~17] 다음을 듣고, 물음에 답하시오.

16 여자가 하는 말의 주제로 가장 적절한 것은?

① useful tips for safe world travel
② necessary items for city travelers
③ famous historical cities in the world
④ importance of learning photo techniques
⑤ attractive photo spots around the world

17 언급된 도시가 아닌 것은?

① New York   ② Rome   ③ Paris
④ London   ⑤ Sydney

*이제 듣기 문제가 끝났습니다. 18번부터는 문제지의 지시에 따라 답을 하시기 바랍니다.

18 다음 글의 목적으로 가장 적절한 것은?

Dear Miranda,

Thank you for participating in our Crafts Art Fair. Since we've chosen you as one of the 'Artists of This Year', we are looking forward to introducing your unique handmade baskets to our community. As part of organizing the exhibition plan, we are happy to inform you that your artworks will be exhibited at the assigned table, number seven. Visitors can easily find your artworks located near the entrance. If you have any special requirements or need further assistance, feel free to contact us in advance.

Sincerely,
Helen Dwyer

① 공예품 구매 희망자를 소개하려고
② 비상시 박람회장 대피 동선을 안내하려고
③ 작품이 전시될 지정 테이블을 알려 주려고
④ 올해의 공예가 선정 투표 방식을 공지하려고
⑤ 박람회에 참여할 새로운 공예가를 모집하려고

19 다음 글에 드러난 'I'의 심경 변화로 가장 적절한 것은?

The shed is cold and damp, the air thick with the smell of old wood and earth. It's dark, and I can't make out what's moving in the shadows. "Who's there?" I ask, my voice shaking with fear. The shadow moves closer, and my heart is beating fast — until the figure steps into a faint beam of light breaking through a crack in the wall. A rabbit. A laugh escapes my lips as it stares at me with wide, curious eyes. "You scared me," I say, feeling much better. The rabbit pauses for a moment, then hops away, disappearing back into the shadows. I'm left smiling. I start to feel at ease.

*shed: 헛간

① envious → hopeful
② anxious → angry
③ frightened → relieved
④ curious → regretful
⑤ excited → disappointed

20 다음 글에서 필자가 주장하는 바로 가장 적절한 것은?

Improving your gestural communication involves more than just knowing when to nod or shake hands. It's about using gestures to complement your spoken messages, adding layers of meaning to your words. Open-handed gestures, for example, can indicate honesty, creating an atmosphere of trust. You invite openness and collaboration when you speak with your palms facing up. This simple yet powerful gesture can make others feel more comfortable and willing to engage in conversation. But be careful of the trap of over-gesturing. Too many hand movements can distract from your message, drawing attention away from your words. Imagine a speaker whose hands move quickly like birds, their message lost in the chaos of their gestures. Balance is key. Your gestures should highlight your words, not overshadow them.

① 메시지를 잘 전달하기 위해서 열린 마음을 지녀야 한다.
② 효과적인 의사소통을 위해 몸짓을 적절히 사용해야 한다.
③ 청중의 반응을 파악하기 위해 그들의 몸짓에 주목해야 한다.
④ 전달하고자 하는 것을 감추기보다 직접적으로 표현해야 한다.
⑤ 상대방을 설득하기 위해서는 메시지를 반복적으로 강조해야 한다.

21 밑줄 친 start down this slippery slope이 다음 글에서 의미하는 바로 가장 적절한 것은? [3점]

Assuming gene editing in humans proves to be safe and effective, it might seem logical, even preferable, to correct disease-causing mutations at the earliest possible stage of life, *before* harmful genes begin causing serious problems. Yet once it becomes possible to transform an embryo's mutated genes into "normal" ones, there will certainly be temptations to upgrade normal genes to superior versions. Should we begin editing genes in unborn children to lower their lifetime risk of heart disease or cancer? What about giving unborn children beneficial features, like greater strength and increased mental abilities, or changing physical characteristics, like eye and hair color? The pursuit for perfection seems almost natural to human nature, but if we start down this slippery slope, we may not like where we end up.

*mutation: 돌연변이 **embryo: 배아

① allow genetic alterations to upgrade humans
② stick to the traditional beliefs in human nature
③ resist the temptation to change genes in humans
④ fail to reduce the risk of suffering from diseases
⑤ consider more about the moral issues of genetics

22 다음 글의 요지로 가장 적절한 것은?

The science we learn in grade school is a collection of certainties about the natural world — the earth goes around the sun, DNA carries the information of an organism, and so on. Only when you start to learn the practice of science do you realize that each of these "facts" was hard won through a succession of logical inferences based upon many observations or experiments. The process of science is less about collecting pieces of knowledge than it is about reducing the uncertainties in what we know. Our uncertainties can be greater or lesser for any given piece of knowledge depending upon where we are in that process — today we are quite certain of how an apple will fall from a tree, but our understanding of the turbulent fluid flow remains a work in progress after more than a century of effort.

*inference: 추론 **turbulent fluid flow: 난류 유동

① 과학은 현재의 지식에 대한 불확실함을 줄이는 과정이다.
② 관찰과 실험 과정에서 우연히 얻어진 과학적 사실이 많다.
③ 학생들에게 다양한 연구 방법을 가르치는 것이 중요하다.
④ 과학 연구에서는 정확한 실험 과정 설계가 핵심이다.
⑤ 과학은 분산된 지식을 수집하여 통합하는 학문이다.

23 다음 글의 주제로 가장 적절한 것은?

There is a wealth of evidence that when parents, teachers, supervisors, and coaches are perceived as involved and caring, people feel happier and more motivated. And it is not just those people with power — we need to feel valued and respected by peers and coworkers. Thus, when the need for relatedness is met, motivation and internalization are fueled, provided that support for autonomy and competence are also there. If we are trying to motivate others, a caring relationship is a crucial basis from which to begin. And when we are trying to motivate ourselves, doing things to enhance a sense of connectedness to others can be crucial to long-term persistence. So exercise with a friend, call someone when you have a difficult decision to make, and be there as a support for others as they take on challenges.

*autonomy: 자율성 **persistence: 지속

① ways of getting out of dependent relationships
② necessity of independent decision-making for happier life
③ key factors required for boosting a competitive atmosphere
④ challenges in maintaining lasting bonds with family members
⑤ importance of building connected relationships in motivation

Modern brain-scanning techniques such as fMRI (functional Magnetic Resonance Imaging) have revealed that reading aloud lights up many areas of the brain. There is intense activity in areas associated with pronunciation and hearing the sound of the spoken response, which strengthens the connective structures of your brain cells for more brainpower. This leads to an overall improvement in concentration. Reading aloud is also a good way to develop your public speaking skills because it forces you to read each and every word — something people don't often do when reading quickly, or reading in silence. Children, in particular, should be encouraged to read aloud because the brain is wired for learning through connections that are created by positive stimulation, such as singing, touching, and reading aloud.

*stimulation: 자극

① Reading Aloud: Improving Brainpower and Speaking Skills
② Reading Practices: Shortcuts to Academic Achievements
③ Improve Your Writing Skills Through Reading Aloud
④ How Your Brain Changes When You Read in Silence
⑤ Techniques for Faster and More Effective Reading

The above graph shows how often people in America consumed fast food in 2023, sorted according to frequency of consumption. ① More than 50 percent of individuals consumed fast food once a week or more frequently. ② The most highly reported pattern of consumption was a few times a week, which was 36 percent of the total. ③ The second most highly reported pattern was a few times a month, accounting for 18 percent of the total. ④ The percentage of people who ate fast food once every couple of months was more than that of those who consumed it daily. ⑤ The combined share of those who rarely or never ate fast food was less than 10 percent.

26 Robert E. Lucas, Jr.에 관한 다음 글의 내용과 일치하지 <u>않는</u> 것은?

   Robert E. Lucas, Jr. was born on September 15, 1937, in Yakima, Washington. During World War II, his family moved to Seattle, where he graduated from Roosevelt High School. At the University of Chicago, he majored in history. After taking economic history courses at University of California, Berkeley, he developed an interest in economics. He earned a doctoral degree in economics from the University of Chicago in 1964. He taught at Carnegie Mellon University from 1963 to 1974 before returning to the University of Chicago to become a professor of economics. He was known as a very influential economist and, in 1995, he was awarded the Nobel Prize in Economic Sciences.

① 제2차 세계대전 중에 그의 가족이 Seattle로 이주했다.
② 경제사를 수강한 후에 경제학에 대한 흥미를 키웠다.
③ University of Chicago에서 경제학 박사 학위를 받았다.
④ 1963년부터 1974년까지 University of Chicago에서 가르쳤다.
⑤ 1995년에 노벨상을 수상했다.

27 Blackwood Zoo에 관한 다음 안내문의 내용과 일치하지 <u>않는</u> 것은?

Welcome to Blackwood Zoo

   Get ready to explore! You can watch amazing animals on our 10km walking path.

Hours of Operation
• Every day, all year round!
• 9:30 a.m. - 4:30 p.m. (Last admission at 3:30 p.m.)

Ticket Prices
• Age 13 - 64: $30
• Age 3 - 12: $20
• Others: Free

Seasonal Note
Since the weather is still cold, some animals like snakes and turtles will stay only indoors.

※Free shuttle bus departs from Blackwood Subway Station every 30 minutes.

① 10km의 보행로에서 동물들을 볼 수 있다.
② 운영 시간은 오후 3시 30분까지이다.
③ 3세부터 12세까지의 티켓 가격은 20달러이다.
④ 날씨가 여전히 추워서 일부 동물은 실내에만 머무를 것이다.
⑤ 무료 셔틀버스가 30분마다 출발한다.

28 Sock DIY Workshop에 관한 다음 안내문의 내용과 일치하는 것은?

Sock DIY Workshop

Join us for a fun and creative Sock DIY (Do It Yourself) Workshop for all ages!

When & Where
· Saturday, April 19th, from 1 p.m. to 3 p.m.
· The community hall, Clanton Center

Workshop Program

Time	DIY Item	Things to Do
1 p.m.-2 p.m.	Toys	Create stuffed toys with socks
2 p.m.-3 p.m.	Flowerpot Covers	Transform socks into decorative covers for small flowerpots

What Participants Should Prepare
· Used but clean socks

Participation Fee
· $5 per person (including the cost for materials)

※For more details, visit the Clanton Center website or call us at 555-123-4567.

① 4월 19일 토요일 오후 1시부터 4시까지 열린다.
② Clanton Center의 커뮤니티 홀에서 진행된다.
③ 참가자는 오후 2시부터 양말로 장난감을 만든다.
④ 참가자는 사용하지 않은 깨끗한 양말을 준비해야 한다.
⑤ 참가비는 재료비를 제외하고 1인당 5달러이다.

29 다음 글의 밑줄 친 부분 중, 어법상 틀린 것은?

Routines enable athletes to evaluate competition conditions. For example, bouncing a ball in a volleyball service routine ① supplies the server with information about the ball, the floor, and the state of her muscles. This information can then be used to ② properly prepare for her serve. Routines also enable athletes to adjust and fine-tune their preparations ③ based on those evaluations or in pursuit of a particular competitive goal. This adaptation can involve adjustment to the conditions, rivals, competitive situation, or internal influences ④ what can affect performance. Just like adjusting a race-car engine to the conditions of the track, air temperature, and weather, routines adjust all competitive components ⑤ to achieve proper performance.

*component: 구성 요소

30 다음 글의 밑줄 친 부분 중, 문맥상 낱말의 쓰임이 적절하지 않은 것은? [3점]

Promotion deals with consumer psychology. We can't ① force people to think one way or another, and the clever marketer knows that promotion is used to provide information in the most clear, honest, and simple fashion possible. By doing so, the possibility of increasing sales goes up. Gone are the days when promotions were done in order to ② fool the consumer into purchasing something. The long-term effect of getting a consumer to buy something they did not really want or need wasn't good. In fact, consumers fooled once can do ③ damage to sales as they relate their experience to others. Instead, marketers now know that their goal is to ④ identify the consumers who are most likely to appreciate a good or service, and to promote that good or service in a way that makes the value clear to the consumer. Therefore, marketers must know where the ⑤ uninterested consumers are, and how to reach them.

[31~34] 다음 빈칸에 들어갈 말로 가장 적절한 것을 고르시오.

31

Plato argued that when you see something that strikes you as beautiful, you are really just seeing a partial reflection of true beauty, just as a painting or even a photograph only captures part of the real thing. True beauty, or what Plato calls the Form of Beauty, has no particular color, shape, or size. Rather, it is a(n) _____ idea, like the number five. You can make drawings of the number five in blue or red ink, big or small, but the number five itself is none of those things. It has no physical form. Think of the idea of a triangle, for example. Although it has no particular color or size, it somehow lies within each and every triangle you see. Plato thought the same was true of beauty. The Form of Beauty somehow lies within each and every beautiful thing you see.

① abstract   ② practical   ③ imperfect
④ visualized   ⑤ changeable

32

As you listen to your child in an emotional moment, be aware that _____ usually works better than asking questions to get a conversation rolling. You may ask your child "Why do you feel sad?" and she may not have a clue. As a child, she may not have an answer on the tip of her tongue. Maybe she's feeling sad about her parents' arguments, or because she feels overtired, or she's worried about a piano recital. But she may or may not be able to explain any of this. And even when she does come up with an answer, she might be worried that the answer is not good enough to justify the feeling. Under these circumstances, a series of questions can just make a child silent. It's better to simply reflect what you notice. You can say, "You seem a little tired today," or, "I noticed that you frowned when I mentioned the recital," and wait for her response.

① giving quick advice
② pushing her for answers
③ sharing simple observations
④ telling your own life stories
⑤ leaving her alone to cool down

33

Our skin conducts electricity more or less efficiently, depending on our emotions. We know that when we're emotionally stimulated — stressed, sad, any intense emotion, really — our bodies sweat a tiny bit, so little we might not even notice. And when those tiny drops of sweat appear, our skin gets more electrically conductive. This change in sweat gland activity happens completely without your conscious mind having much say in the matter. If you feel emotionally intense, you're going to notice an increase in sweat gland activity. This is particularly useful from a scientific viewpoint, because it allows us to put an objective value on a subjective state of mind. We can actually _____ by tracking how your body subconsciously sweats, by running a bit of electricity through your skin. We can then turn the subjective, subconscious experience of emotional intensity into an objective number by figuring out how good your skin gets at transferring an electrical current. [3점]

*sweat gland: 땀샘

① limit reactions of hormones
② control the electrical current
③ improve your skin conditions
④ measure your emotional state
⑤ diversify emotional experiences

34

Plants can communicate, although not in the same way we do. Some express their discontent through scents. You know that smell that hangs in the air after you've mowed the lawn? Yeah, that's actually an SOS. Some plants use sound. Yes, sound, though at a frequency that we can't hear. Researchers experimented with plants and microphones to see if they could record any trouble calls. They found that plants produce a high-frequency clicking noise when stressed and can make different sounds for different stressors. The sound a plant makes when it's not getting watered differs from the one it'll make when a leaf is cut. However, it's worth noting that experts don't think plants are crying out in pain. It's more likely that these reactions are knee-jerk survival actions. Plants are living organisms, and their main objective is to survive. Scents and sounds are their tools for _____.

[3점]   *scent: 냄새 **mow: (잔디를) 깎다 ***knee-jerk: 자동적인

① defending against things that might harm them
② showing their support for neighboring plants
③ hiding their pains and dissatisfaction
④ sharing nutrients with other plants
⑤ changing their genetic structure

35 다음 글에서 전체 흐름과 관계 없는 문장은?

What does it mean for a character to be a hero as opposed to a villain? In artistic and entertainment descriptions, it's essential for the author to establish a positive relationship between a protagonist and the audience. ① In order for tragedy or misfortune to draw out an emotional response in viewers, the character must be adjusted so as to be recognizable as either friend or enemy. ② Likewise, the line between friends and enemies is not clear in reality. ③ Whether the portrayal is fictional or documentary, we must feel that the protagonist is someone whose actions benefit us; the protagonist is, or would be, a worthy companion or valued ally. ④ Violent action films are often filled with dozens of incidental deaths of minor characters that draw out little response in the audience. ⑤ In order to feel strong emotions, the audience must be emotionally invested in a character as either ally or enemy.

*villain: 악당 **protagonist: 주인공

[36~37] 주어진 글 다음에 이어질 글의 순서로 가장 적절한 것을 고르시오.

36

Let's assume that at least some animals are capable of thinking despite lacking a language.

(A) This doesn't imply that squirrels lack concepts, simply that they don't need them for this concrete form of thinking. For us to be able to say that an animal has concepts, we have to show not just that she's capable of thinking, but also that she has certain specific abilities.

(B) To do this, in principle she doesn't need a concept of branch nor a concept of tree. It might be enough for her to have, for example, the ability to think in images; to make a mental map of the tree where she can imagine and try out different routes.

(C) This doesn't necessarily mean that they possess concepts, for some forms of thought may be nonconceptual. We can imagine, for instance, a squirrel who is planning how to get from the branch she's currently standing on to a branch from the tree in front. [3점]

*squirrel: 다람쥐

① (A) — (C) — (B)   ② (B) — (A) — (C)
③ (B) — (C) — (A)   ④ (C) — (A) — (B)
⑤ (C) — (B) — (A)

37

Cartilage is extremely important for the healthy functioning of a joint, especially if that joint bears weight, like your knee.

(A) This squeezing of joint fluid into and out of the cartilage helps it respond to the off-and-on pressure of walking without breaking under the pressure.

(B) The cartilage in your left knee then "drinks in" synovial fluid, in much the same way that a sponge soaks up liquid when put in water. When you take another step and transfer the weight back onto your left leg, much of the fluid squeezes out of the cartilage.

(C) Imagine for a moment that you're looking into the inner workings of your left knee as you walk down the street. When you shift your weight from your left leg to your right, the pressure on your left knee is released. [3점]

*cartilage: 연골 **synovial fluid: 윤활액

① (A) — (C) — (B)　　② (B) — (A) — (C)
③ (B) — (C) — (A)　　④ (C) — (A) — (B)
⑤ (C) — (B) — (A)

[38~39] 글의 흐름으로 보아, 주어진 문장이 들어가기에 가장 적절한 곳을 고르시오.

38

Piaget argued that children's understanding of morality is like their understanding of those water glasses: we can't say that it is innate or kids learn it directly from adults.

Piaget put the same amount of water into two different glasses: a tall narrow glass and a wide glass, then asked kids to compare two glasses. (①) Kids younger than six or seven usually say that the tall narrow glass now holds more water, because the level is higher. (②) And when they are ready, they figure out the conservation of volume for themselves just by playing with cups of water. (③) Rather, it is self-constructed as kids play with other kids. (④) Taking turns in a game is like pouring water back and forth between glasses. (⑤) Once kids have reached the age of five or six, then playing games and working things out together will help them learn about fairness far more effectively than any teaching from adults.

*innate: 타고난 **conservation: 보존

39

But all this wisdom about how to deal with heat, accumulated over centuries of practical experience, is all too often ignored.

The rise of air-conditioning accelerated the construction of sealed boxes, where the building's only airflow is through the filtered ducts of the air-conditioning unit. It doesn't have to be this way. Look at any old building in a hot climate, whether it's in Sicily or Marrakesh or Tehran. (①) Architects understood the importance of shade, airflow, light colors. (②) They oriented buildings to capture cool breezes and block the worst heat of the afternoon. (③) They built with thick walls and white roofs and transoms over doors to encourage airflow. (④) Anyone who has ever spent a few minutes in a mudbrick house in Tucson, or walked on the narrow streets of old Seville, knows how well these construction methods work. (⑤) In this sense, air-conditioning is not just a technology of personal comfort; it is also a technology of forgetting.

*accumulate: 축적하다 **duct: (배)관 ***transom: 채광창

In the course of trying to solve a problem with an invention, you may encounter a brick wall of resistance when you try to think your way logically through the problem. Such logical thinking is a linear type of process, which uses our reasoning skills. This works fine when we're operating in the area of what we know or have experienced. However, when we need to deal with new information, ideas, and viewpoints, linear thinking will often come up short. On the other hand, creativity by definition involves the application of new information to old problems and the conception of new viewpoints and ideas. For this you will be most effective if you learn to operate in a nonlinear manner; that is, use your creative brain. Stated differently, if you think in a linear manner, you'll tend to be conservative and keep coming up with techniques which are already known. This, of course, is just what you don't want.   *linear: 선형의 **conservative: 보수적인

↓

> ___(A)___ thinking works well with familiar problems but falls short in dealing with new ideas, for which creative thinking is needed to come up with ___(B)___ solutions.

	(A)		(B)
①	Logical	—	innovative
②	Flexible	—	instant
③	Logical	—	proven
④	Flexible	—	superior
⑤	Logical	—	collaborative

Some researchers view spoken languages as incomplete devices for capturing precise differences. They think numbers represent the most neutral language of description. However, when our language of description is changed to numbers, we do not move toward greater (a) accuracy. Numbers are no more appropriate 'pictures of the world' than words, music, or painting. While useful for specific purposes (e.g. census taking, income distribution), they (b) include information of enormous value. For example, the future lives of young students are tied to their scores on national tests. In effect, whether they can continue with their education, where, and at what cost depends importantly on a handful of numbers. These numbers do not account for the (c) quality of schools they have attended, whether they have been tutored, have supportive parents, have test anxiety, and so on. Finally, putting aside the many ways in which statistical results can be manipulated, there are ways in which turning people's lives into numbers is (d) morally insulating. Statistics on crime, homelessness, or the spread of a disease say nothing of people's suffering. We read the statistics as reports on events at a distance, thus allowing us to (e) escape without being disturbed. Statistics are human beings with the tears wiped off. Quantify with caution.

*statistical: 통계의 **manipulate: 조작하다 ***insulating: 차단하는

41 윗글의 제목으로 가장 적절한 것은?

① Numbers Don't Tell Us Everything
② Human Stories Uncovered by the Numbers
③ Data: A Framework for Understanding Humans
④ The Limitations of Language in Conveying Truth
⑤ The Advantages of Quantifying Human Experiences

42 밑줄 친 (a)~(e) 중에서 문맥상 낱말의 쓰임이 적절하지 <u>않은</u> 것은? [3점]

① (a)   ② (b)   ③ (c)   ④ (d)   ⑤ (e)

(A)

Jack, an Arkansas farmer, was unhappy because he couldn't make enough money from his farm. He worked hard for many years, but things didn't improve. He sold his farm to his neighbor, Victor, who was by no means wealthy. Hoping for a fresh start, he left for the big city to find better opportunities. Years passed, but Jack still couldn't find the fortune he was looking for. Tired and broke, (a) he returned to the area where his old farm was.

*broke: 무일푼의

(B)

"How did you do all this?" he asked. And he continued, "When you bought the farm, you barely had any money. How did you get so rich?" Victor smiled and said, "I owe it all to (b) you. There were diamonds on this land — acres and acres of diamonds! I got rich because I discovered those diamonds." "Diamonds?" Jack said in disbelief. And he said, "I knew every part of that land, and there were no diamonds!" *acres of: 대량의

(C)

Victor reached into his pocket and carefully pulled out something small and shiny. Holding it between (c) his fingers, he let it catch the light. He said, "This is a diamond." Jack was amazed and said, "I saw so many rocks like that and thought they were useless. They made farming so hard!" Victor laughed and said, "(d) You didn't know what diamonds look like. Sometimes, treasures are hidden right in front of us."

(D)

One day, he drove past his old land and was shocked by what he saw. Victor, the man who had bought the farm with very little money, now seemed to be living a life of great success. He had torn down the farmhouse and built a massive house in its place. New buildings, trees, and flowers adorned the well-kept property. Jack could hardly believe that (e) he had ever worked on this same land. Curious, he stopped to talk to Victor.

*adorn: 꾸미다

---

43 주어진 글 (A)에 이어질 내용을 순서에 맞게 배열한 것으로 가장 적절한 것은?

① (B) — (D) — (C)   ② (C) — (B) — (D)
③ (C) — (D) — (B)   ④ (D) — (B) — (C)
⑤ (D) — (C) — (B)

44 밑줄 친 (a)~(e) 중에서 가리키는 대상이 나머지 넷과 다른 것은?

① (a)   ② (b)   ③ (c)   ④ (d)   ⑤ (e)

45 윗글에 관한 내용으로 적절하지 않은 것은?

① Jack은 자신의 농장에서 충분한 돈을 벌지 못했다.
② Jack은 자신의 이웃인 Victor에게서 농장을 샀다.
③ Victor는 다이아몬드를 발견해서 부자가 되었다.
④ Victor는 자신의 주머니에서 작고 반짝이는 것을 꺼냈다.
⑤ Victor는 농가가 있던 자리에 거대한 집을 지었다.

• MP3 파일을 들으며 다음 빈칸을 채우시오. (듣기 어려운 발음이나 정답의 단서가 되는 부분에 빈칸을 만들었습니다.)

01 다음을 듣고, 남자가 하는 말의 목적으로 가장 적절한 것을 고르시오.

M: Good morning, students. This is your vice principal Richard Simpson. As you know, our school drone club _____ ✿ _____ _____ _____ at the Drone Show Contest. Actually, I asked the _____ _____ _____ ✿ _____ the show again for you. And they said, "Yes". So I would recommend you watch the performance ____ ____ _____ _____ tomorrow. Please come and see the club's drone performance, and show your support. Thank you.

02 대화를 듣고, 여자의 의견으로 가장 적절한 것을 고르시오.

W: Ryan, did you enjoy the musical "Tigers" yesterday?

M: Yes, I loved it. I can't believe we got tickets for such a popular show.

W: Yes, we were lucky. By the way, it _____ _____ of the class musical that we have to prepare for the next month's school festival.

M: You read my mind! I think we should look for a musical with a variety of music.

W: Well, there might be something even more important than that.

M: Should we give _____ _____ _____ ✿ _____ _____?

W: Not necessarily. Do you remember what we did last year?

M: Yes. We focused on preparing a musical that was easy to perform.

W: Right. But not everyone ✿ _____. I think everyone should have a _____ for the class musical.

M: That's a good point.

03 다음을 듣고, 남자가 하는 말의 요지로 가장 적절한 것을 고르시오.

M: Welcome to the *Healing Tip Podcast*. I'm Dr. Smith. In our busy lives, what do you think is just as important as exercising or eating well for your health? It's rest. Rest plays a crucial role _____ ✿ _____ _____ _____ _____. It allows your body to heal and recharge, while also helping your mind relax and improving focus. That's why I want to ✿ _____ _____ _____ rest is for your health. Taking time to rest can _____ stress and _____ your overall wellness. So, don't skip those breaks!

04 대화를 듣고, 그림에서 대화의 내용과 일치하지 않는 것을 고르시오.

W: Hi, Jayden, you know what? I visited the Dream Gallery with my mom yesterday.

M: Oh, I've always wanted to visit there. Did you take any pictures?

W: Sure. Look at this.

M: Is the person _____ __ ✿ _____ your mom?

W: Yes, it is. She really loved the painting on the left side of the wall.

M: Oh, the painting of flowers? That's nice. I also like the other painting.

W: You mean the painting of umbrellas in the _____ _____?

M: Yes, it _____ ____ ____. I can see a person sitting on the right side of the picture. Who's the person?

W: The man wearing glasses, right? He's the manager of the gallery.

M: I see. What's _____ ✿ _____ _____ on the right wall?

W: It shows the direction to the next area.

M: Oh, the gallery must be huge!

05 대화를 듣고, 남자가 할 일로 가장 적절한 것을 고르시오.

W: Honey, the flowers are really beautiful these days. Why don't we take a walk this weekend?

M: Wow, that sounds great. Do you have _____ ✪_____ _____ in mind?

W: Yes, I'd like to visit the Grand Forest. I've ✪_____ _____ the map of the forest.

M: That's nice. Do we have to buy _____ _____?

W: Yes. We can buy tickets online. I'll buy two tickets in the afternoon.

M: Great. Let's have a nice lunch there, too. There's a restaurant called Treehouse Pasta in the Grand Forest.

W: Nice. Do we have to make a reservation?

M: Yes. I'll make the reservation _____ _____.

W: Then, I'll look up the menu of the restaurant.

M: Thanks.

06 대화를 듣고, 여자가 지불할 금액을 고르시오.

M: Hello. How can I help you today?

W: Hi. I'm here to buy some _____ for my sister's shoes.

M: Great. We have those over here. They are five dollars each.

W: She would love the decorations with this _____ ✪_____, so I'll take two of them.

M: Wonderful. Do you need anything else?

W: Oh, I've just _____ _____ _____ _____ for her. How much is it?

M: It's ten dollars.

W: I'll buy it. And I'd like them ✪_____, please.

M: We charge for gift-wrapping. It costs three dollars. Would that be okay with you?

W: Yes, that's fine.

M: Then, I'll gift-wrap two decorations and one bracelet together in one box.

W: Okay. Here's my credit card.

07 대화를 듣고, 남자가 휴대 전화를 수리받지 못한 이유를 고르시오.

W: Hi, Brian. Why didn't you answer my text message yesterday? I wanted to ask about the math exam.

M: Hi, Sarah. I'm really sorry. I _____ ____ ____ _____ yesterday, so I couldn't read it.

W: Oh, no! What happened to it?

M: Well, I dropped it _____ ✪_____ ____ the bus. And now, it doesn't work at all.

W: Why didn't you get it fixed?

M: I wanted to, but I couldn't.

W: Was it because you couldn't find a _____ _____? There's one right by the bus stop near our school.

M: I went there to get it fixed, but I couldn't.

W: Oh, did you have to wait too long?

M: No, I didn't. Actually, I didn't know I had to make a reservation ____ _____. So I just went back home.

W: Ah! That's too bad!

08

대화를 듣고, Future Generation Talk Show에 관해 언급되지 <u>않은</u> 것을 고르시오.

[Cell phone rings.]

M: Hi, Kelly. What's up?

W: Hey, Robert. Do you have time on Friday?

M: Sure.

W: Have you heard about the Future Generation Talk Show?

M: Oh, you mean the talk show that _____ _____ _____ _____ Southern University?

W: Yes, that's right. Professor Peter Johnson is coming to talk.

M: The famous Peter Johnson? What's the topic of the talk show?

W: It's about the _____ ✪_____ _____ _____ and how it's _____ the future.

M: Sounds interesting. Can I watch the talk show online?

W: No. There's no _____ ✪_____ _____. But if you go there, you can ask questions directly to Professor Johnson.

M: Great. I can go in person. Can we go together?

W: Sure! I'll text you the details of the talk show right now.

09

Science Day 행사에 관한 다음 내용을 듣고, 일치하지 <u>않는</u> 것을 고르시오.

W: Hello, students! This is your science teacher Jane Brown. I have some good news. This Saturday we're having Science Day at our school. In the morning, _____ _____ will teach you how to make a computer program. You can also ✪_____ _____ _____ by yourself in the school hall. In the afternoon, your science teachers will run some ✪_____ _____ for you. It's a good chance to experiment with what you've learned from the textbooks. You can sign up for Science Day by scanning the QR codes on the school board. For the participants, lunch will be _____. Come and enjoy Science Day!

10

다음 표를 보면서 대화를 듣고, 여자가 수강할 운동 수업을 고르시오.

M: Sweetie, what are you doing?

W: I'm looking at the schedule for exercise classes. Would you like to help me choose?

M: Sure. What's your ✪_____ for it?

W: Well, I don't want to spend more than forty dollars.

M: Okay. Then, forget about this one. What about class time?

W: As you know, I have things to do in the afternoon.

M: In that case, let's _____ _____ _____ _____. Now you have dancing and tennis left.

W: I heard the tennis class is held outside. I don't like _____ _____.

M: Okay. Then, we have only two exercise classes left. Which level is good for you?

W: Since I've already taken the ✪_____ _____, I'll take the other one this time.

11

대화를 듣고, 여자의 마지막 말에 대한 남자의 응답으로 가장 적절한 것을 고르시오.

W: Hi, Daniel. Are you ready for your presentation tomorrow?

M: Hi, Tina. Not really. I've _____ my slides, but I ✪_____ _____ _____ _____ yet.

W: How do you usually practice it?

M: _____

12

대화를 듣고, 남자의 마지막 말에 대한 여자의 응답으로 가장 적절한 것을 고르시오.

M: Ashley, do you remember the digital poster we made to upload _____ _____ _____?

W: Yes, of course. It was about _____ ✪_____, right?

M: Exactly. Let's print it out and put it on the wall in our school cafeteria.

W: _____

13 대화를 듣고, 여자의 마지막 말에 대한 남자의 응답으로 가장 적절한 것을 고르시오.

W: Chris, you've been looking so tired these days.

M: Yeah, Mom. I'm studying for my first high school exam. I really want to do well.

W: I understand, but I'm worried about you. Have you had any _____ ✪ _____ your time?

M: Well, I don't have enough of it. I've been staying up late studying these days.

W: Staying up late won't help you much, Chris.

M: But I have so much to do, Mom.

W: I see your point, but staying up too late might actually hurt _____ _____ ____ _____ _____.

M: Maybe you're right, but I thought studying would be more helpful to me than sleeping.

W: Not if you're too tired. If you don't sleep enough, it'll hurt your _____ _____ ✪ _____.

M: _____

14 대화를 듣고, 남자의 마지막 말에 대한 여자의 응답으로 가장 적절한 것을 고르시오.

M: Hi, Cindy! What are you doing this weekend?

W: I'm going to play badminton with my friends.

M: You play _____ ✪ _____ _____.

W: It's my new hobby. It helps me reduce stress.

M: How nice! I've been looking for something to reduce stress.

W: Well, you don't have to think too hard. Just think of something that makes you happy.

M: Hmm…. But _____ _____ ____ _____ right away.

W: Then, why don't you come and play badminton with me this Saturday? You'll like it, too, I think.

M: Really? Is it okay if I join you?

W: Of course, it is! We meet ____ ____ _____ _____ every Saturday morning.

M: Thanks a lot! Do I need to ✪ _____ _____?

W: _____

15 다음 상황 설명을 듣고, Kevin이 Ms. Tyler에게 할 말로 가장 적절한 것을 고르시오.

M: Kevin is the president of the Starlight Club in the school. For weeks, the club has been preparing _____ ✪ _____ _____ at the school yard with the club teacher, Ms. Tyler. They expected that the sky _____ _____ _____ on camp-night. But today, there's a ✪ _____ _____ in the weather forecast, and it says it's going to rain during camp-night. It means the camp cannot go on ____ _____. Kevin wants to ask Ms. Tyler if they can change the camp date to another day. In this situation, what would Kevin most likely say to Ms. Tyler?

Kevin: _____

[16~17] 다음을 듣고, 물음에 답하시오.

W: Hello! Everyone. I'm Jasmine, a _____ ✪ _____, and I'm excited to share some wonderful places to take photos around the world. The first place is Times Square in New York. It is full of energy, with its tall buildings and _____ _____. Next, Rome amazed me with its _____ ✪ _____ _____, like the Colosseum. It made me feel like traveling back in time! And when you visit London, you shouldn't miss Buckingham Palace. It's a perfect place for ✪ _____ _____. Lastly, in Sydney, the Opera House was great for taking beautiful sunset photos. Traveling with a camera is such a joy, and I can't wait to share more travel places with you. Now let's take a look at the photos of these places.

• 제한시간 20분 • 맞은 개수 ___ / 40

＊ 다음 영어는 우리말 뜻을, 우리말은 영어 단어를 〈보기〉에서 찾아 쓰시오.

01 faint _____

02 massive _____

03 logically _____

04 necessary _____

05 emphasize _____

06 적절히 _____

07 증진[촉진]하다 _____

08 실용적인 _____

09 개조, 변경 _____

10 영향을 미치다 _____

─────────[보기]─────────
평가하다	alteration
거대한	practical
희미한	earn
강조하다	affect
논리적으로	boost
필수적인	properly

＊ 다음 우리말에 알맞은 영어 표현을 찾아 연결하시오.

11 허물다 ·   · put aside

12 제쳐 두다 ·   · cross out

13 빼다, 지우다 ·   · tear down

14 ~에 발언권이 많다 ·   · distract from

15 ~에 집중이 안 되게 하다 ·   · have much say in

＊ 다음 우리말과 같은 표현이 되도록 알맞은 단어를 〈보기〉에서 찾아 쓰시오.

─────────────────[보기]─────────────────
recital / overall / morality / assistance / frequently / appreciate
influential / viewpoints / pursuit / correct / stimulation / circumstances

16 이러한 상황에서는 ➡ under these _____

17 매우 영향력 있는 경제학자 ➡ a very _____ economist

18 특정 경쟁 목표를 추구하여 ➡ in _____ of a particular competitive goal

19 일주일에 한 번 또는 더 자주 ➡ once a week or more _____

20 도덕성에 대한 아이들의 이해 ➡ children's understanding of _____

21 새로운 관점과 아이디어의 구상 ➡ the conception of new _____ and ideas

22 노래 부르기와 같은 긍정적인 자극 ➡ positive _____ such as singing

23 상품이나 서비스의 진가를 인정하다 ➡ _____ a good or service

24 당신의 전반적인 웰빙을 유지하는 것 ➡ maintaining your _____ well-being

25 질병을 유발하는 돌연변이를 교정하는 것 ➡ to _____ disease-causing mutations

* 다음 우리말 표현에 알맞은 단어를 고르시오.

26 객관적인 값을 부여하는 것 ➜ to put a(n) (objective / subjective) value

27 허구적이든 사실이든 ➜ (fictional / functional) or documentary

28 직접 몇 개의 로봇을 작동하다 ➜ (operate / deliberate) some robots by oneself

29 또래와 직장 동료들에게서 존중받는 ➜ respected by (pears / peers) and coworkers

30 여러분의 뇌세포의 결합 구조 ➜ the (consistent / connective) structures of your brain cells

* 다음 문장의 빈칸에 알맞은 단어를 〈보기〉에서 찾아 쓰시오.

───────────── [보기] ─────────────

compliment / intense / nodded / partial / accelerated / fortunate

imply / discontent / justify / complement / state / ally

31 어제 비가 그쳐서 다행이지 않나요?

➜ Isn't it _____ that the rain stopped yesterday?

32 발음과 연관된 영역에서 강렬한 활동이 있다.

➜ There is _____ activity in areas associated with pronunciation.

33 몇몇은 냄새를 통해 자신들의 불만을 표현한다.

➜ Some express their _____ through scents.

34 그 대답은 그 감정을 정당화하기에는 충분하지 않다.

➜ The answer is not good enough to _____ the feeling.

35 우리는 실제로 여러분의 감정적 상태를 측정할 수 있다.

➜ We can actually measure your emotional _____.

36 이것은 다람쥐가 개념이 부족하다는 것을 의미하는 것이 아니다.

➜ This doesn't _____ that squirrels lack concepts.

37 냉방 설비의 부상은 밀폐된 구조물의 건설을 가속화했다.

➜ The rise of air-conditioning _____ the construction of sealed boxes.

38 주인공은 가치 있는 동료나 소중한 협력자이고, 혹은 그렇게 될 것이다.

➜ The protagonist is, or would be, a worthy companion or valued _____.

39 여러분은 실제로는 진정한 아름다움의 부분적인 반영을 보고 있을 뿐이다.

➜ You are really just seeing a(n) _____ reflection of true beauty.

40 이는 여러분의 말로 전하는 메시지를 보완하기 위해 몸짓을 사용하는 것에 대한 것이다.

➜ It's about using gestures to _____ your spoken messages.

*1번부터 17번까지는 듣고 답하는 문제입니다. 1번부터 15번까지는 한 번만 들려주고, 16번부터 17번까지는 두 번 들려줍니다. 방송을 잘 듣고 답을 하시기 바랍니다.

▲ 듣기 파일

01 다음을 듣고, 남자가 하는 말의 목적으로 가장 적절한 것을 고르시오.

① 학교 체육관 공사 일정을 알리려고
② 학교 수업 시간표 조정을 안내하려고
③ 학교 통학 시 대중교통 이용을 권장하려고
④ 학교 방과 후 수업 신청 방식을 설명하려고
⑤ 학교 셔틀버스 운행 시간 변경을 공지하려고

02 대화를 듣고, 여자의 의견으로 가장 적절한 것을 고르시오.

① 전기 자전거 이용 전에 배터리 상태를 점검하여야 한다.
② 전기 자전거 운행에 관한 규정이 더 엄격해야 한다.
③ 전기 자전거의 속도 규정에 대한 논의가 필요하다.
④ 전기 자전거 구입 시 가격을 고려해야 한다.
⑤ 전기 자전거 이용 시 헬멧을 착용해야 한다.

03 다음을 듣고, 여자가 하는 말의 요지로 가장 적절한 것을 고르시오.

① 학업 목표를 분명히 설정하는 것이 필요하다.
② 친구와의 협력은 학교생활의 중요한 덕목이다.
③ 과제 제출 마감 기한을 확인하고 준수해야 한다.
④ 적절한 휴식은 성공적인 과업 수행의 핵심 요소이다.
⑤ 할 일의 목록을 활용하는 것이 시간 관리에 유용하다.

04 대화를 듣고, 그림에서 대화의 내용과 일치하지 않는 것을 고르시오.

05 대화를 듣고, 남자가 할 일로 가장 적절한 것을 고르시오.

① 따뜻한 옷 챙기기
② 체스 세트 가져가기
③ 읽을 책 고르기
④ 간편식 구매하기
⑤ 침낭 준비하기

06 대화를 듣고, 여자가 지불할 금액을 고르시오. [3점]

① $15   ② $20   ③ $27   ④ $30   ⑤ $33

07 대화를 듣고, 남자가 체육 대회 연습을 할 수 없는 이유를 고르시오.

① 시험공부를 해야 해서
② 동아리 면접이 있어서
③ 축구화를 가져오지 않아서
④ 다리가 완전히 회복되지 않아서
⑤ 가족 식사 모임에 참석해야 해서

08 대화를 듣고, Science Open Lab Program에 관해 언급되지 않은 것을 고르시오.

① 지원 가능 학년
② 실험 재료 구입 필요성
③ 지원서 제출 기한
④ 참가 인원수
⑤ 시상 여부

09 Triwood High School Volunteer Program에 관한 다음 내용을 듣고, 일치하지 않는 것을 고르시오.

① 노인을 도와주는 봉사 활동이다.
② 봉사자는 대면으로 활동한다.
③ 스마트폰 사용 방법 교육을 한다.
④ 봉사자는 매주 토요일에 세 시간씩 참여한다.
⑤ 지원자는 이메일로 참가 신청서를 보내야 한다.

10 다음 표를 보면서 대화를 듣고, 여자가 주문할 휴대용 선풍기를 고르시오.

Portable Fan

	Model	Number of Speed Options	Color	LED Display	Price
①	A	1	blue	×	$15
②	B	3	white	○	$26
③	C	3	yellow	×	$31
④	D	4	pink	×	$37
⑤	E	5	green	○	$42

11 대화를 듣고, 남자의 마지막 말에 대한 여자의 응답으로 가장 적절한 것을 고르시오.

① I can help you find it.
② I already bought a new one.
③ I had it before biology class.
④ You should report it to the police.
⑤ It was a birthday gift from my dad.

12 대화를 듣고, 여자의 마지막 말에 대한 남자의 응답으로 가장 적절한 것을 고르시오.

① Thank you. Everything looks delicious.
② Yes. I have an appointment this Saturday.
③ You're welcome. I made it with my dad's recipe.
④ Sounds good. What time did you make a reservation?
⑤ That's too bad. Why don't we try another restaurant?

13 대화를 듣고, 남자의 마지막 말에 대한 여자의 응답으로 가장 적절한 것을 고르시오. [3점]

Woman: _____

① No problem. You can find other projects at the organization.
② Sure. Let's choose one from your old children's books.
③ Congratulations. You finally made your first audiobook.
④ I hope so. You're going to be a wonderful writer.
⑤ Exactly. Kids grow faster than you think.

14 대화를 듣고, 여자의 마지막 말에 대한 남자의 응답으로 가장 적절한 것을 고르시오.

Man: _____

① Well, let's do the presentation together.
② Cheer up! I know you did your best.
③ Yes, I got a good grade on science.
④ Wow! It was a really nice presentation.
⑤ Right. I have already finished the project.

15 다음 상황 설명을 듣고, Robert가 Michelle에게 할 말로 가장 적절한 것을 고르시오. [3점]

Robert: _____

① When can I use the library?
② Where can I find the library?
③ How can I join the reading club?
④ Why do you want to go to the library?
⑤ What time does the lost and found open?

[16~17] 다음을 듣고, 물음에 답하시오.

16 남자가 하는 말의 주제로 가장 적절한 것은?

① useful foods to relieve coughs
② importance of proper food recipes
③ various causes of cough symptoms
④ traditional home remedies for fever
⑤ connection between weather and cough

17 언급된 음식 재료가 아닌 것은?

① ginger   ② lemon   ③ pineapple
④ honey   ⑤ banana

*이제 듣기 문제가 끝났습니다. 18번부터는 문제지의 지시에 따라 답을 하시기 바랍니다.

18 다음 글의 목적으로 가장 적절한 것은?

Dear Ms. Jane Watson,

I am John Austin, a science teacher at Crestville High School. Recently I was impressed by the latest book you wrote about the environment. Also my students read your book and had a class discussion about it. They are big fans of your book, so I'd like to ask you to visit our school and give a special lecture. We can set the date and time to suit your schedule. Having you at our school would be a fantastic experience for the students. We would be very grateful if you could come.

Best regards,
John Austin

① 환경 보호의 중요성을 강조하려고
② 글쓰기에서 주의할 점을 알려 주려고
③ 특강 강사로 작가의 방문을 요청하려고
④ 작가의 팬 사인회 일정 변경을 공지하려고
⑤ 작가가 쓴 책의 내용에 관하여 문의하려고

19 다음 글에 드러난 Sarah의 심경 변화로 가장 적절한 것은?

Marilyn and her three-year-old daughter, Sarah, took a trip to the beach, where Sarah built her first sandcastle. Moments later, an enormous wave destroyed Sarah's castle. In response to the loss of her sandcastle, tears streamed down Sarah's cheeks and her heart was broken. She ran to Marilyn, saying she would never build a sandcastle again. Marilyn said, "Part of the joy of building a sandcastle is that, in the end, we give it as a gift to the ocean." Sarah loved this idea and responded with enthusiasm to the idea of building another castle — this time, even closer to the water so the ocean would get its gift sooner!

① sad → excited
② envious → anxious
③ bored → joyful
④ relaxed → regretful
⑤ nervous → surprised

20 다음 글에서 필자가 주장하는 바로 가장 적절한 것은?

Magic is what we all wish for to happen in our life. Do you love the movie *Cinderella* like me? Well, in real life, you can also create magic. Here's the trick. Write down all the real-time challenges that you face and deal with. Just change the challenge statement into positive statements. Let me give you an example here. If you struggle with getting up early in the morning, then write a positive statement such as "I get up early in the morning at 5:00 am every day." Once you write these statements, get ready to witness magic and confidence. You will be surprised that just by writing these statements, there is a shift in the way you think and act. Suddenly you feel more powerful and positive.

① 목표한 바를 꼭 이루려면 생각을 곧바로 행동으로 옮겨라.
② 자신감을 얻으려면 어려움을 긍정적인 진술로 바꿔 써라.
③ 어려운 일을 해결하려면 주변 사람에게 도움을 청하라.
④ 일상에서 자신감을 향상하려면 틈틈이 마술을 배워라.
⑤ 실생활에서 마주하는 도전을 피하지 말고 견뎌 내라.

21 밑줄 친 push animal senses into Aristotelian buckets가 다음 글에서 의미하는 바로 가장 적절한 것은? [3점]

Consider the seemingly simple question *How many senses are there?* Around 2,370 years ago, Aristotle wrote that there are five, in both humans and animals — sight, hearing, smell, taste, and touch. However, according to the philosopher Fiona Macpherson, there are reasons to doubt it. For a start, Aristotle missed a few in humans: the perception of your own body which is different from touch and the sense of balance which has links to both touch and vision. Other animals have senses that are even harder to categorize. Many vertebrates have a different sense system for detecting odors. Some snakes can detect the body heat of their prey. These examples tell us that "senses cannot be clearly divided into a limited number of specific kinds," Macpherson wrote in *The Senses*. Instead of trying to push animal senses into Aristotelian buckets, we should study them for what they are.　　*vertebrate: 척추동물 **odor: 냄새

① sort various animal senses into fixed categories
② keep a balanced view to understand real senses
③ doubt the traditional way of dividing all senses
④ ignore the lessons on senses from Aristotle
⑤ analyze more animals to find real senses

22 다음 글의 요지로 가장 적절한 것은?

When we think of leaders, we may think of people such as Abraham Lincoln or Martin Luther King, Jr. If you consider the historical importance and far-reaching influence of these individuals, leadership might seem like a noble and high goal. But like all of us, these people started out as students, workers, and citizens who possessed ideas about how some aspect of daily life could be improved on a larger scale. Through diligence and experience, they improved upon their ideas by sharing them with others, seeking their opinions and feedback and constantly looking for the best way to accomplish goals for a group. Thus we all have the potential to be leaders at school, in our communities, and at work, regardless of age or experience.　　*diligence: 근면

① 훌륭한 리더는 고귀한 목표를 위해 희생적인 삶을 산다.
② 위대한 인물은 위기의 순간에 뛰어난 결단력을 발휘한다.
③ 공동체를 위한 아이디어를 발전시키는 누구나 리더가 될 수 있다.
④ 다른 사람의 의견을 경청하는 자세는 목표 달성에 가장 중요하다.
⑤ 근면하고 경험이 풍부한 사람들은 경제적으로 성공할 수 있다.

23 다음 글의 주제로 가장 적절한 것은?

Crop rotation is the process in which farmers change the crops they grow in their fields in a special order. For example, if a farmer has three fields, he or she may grow carrots in the first field, green beans in the second, and tomatoes in the third. The next year, green beans will be in the first field, tomatoes in the second field, and carrots will be in the third. In year three, the crops will rotate again. By the fourth year, the crops will go back to their original order. Each crop enriches the soil for the next crop. This type of farming is sustainable because the soil stays healthy.　　*sustainable: 지속 가능한

① advantage of crop rotation in maintaining soil health
② influence of purchasing organic food on farmers
③ ways to choose three important crops for rich soil
④ danger of growing diverse crops in small spaces
⑤ negative impact of crop rotation on the environment

24 다음 글의 제목으로 가장 적절한 것은?

Working around the whole painting, rather than concentrating on one area at a time, will mean you can stop at any point and the painting can be considered "finished." Artists often find it difficult to know when to stop painting, and it can be tempting to keep on adding more to your work. It is important to take a few steps back from the painting from time to time to assess your progress. Putting too much into a painting can spoil its impact and leave it looking overworked. If you find yourself struggling to decide whether you have finished, take a break and come back to it later with fresh eyes. Then you can decide whether any areas of your painting would benefit from further refinement.

*tempting: 유혹하는 **refinement: 정교하게 꾸밈

① Drawing Inspiration from Diverse Artists
② Don't Spoil Your Painting by Leaving It Incomplete
③ Art Interpretation: Discover Meanings in a Painting
④ Do Not Put Down Your Brush: The More, the Better
⑤ Avoid Overwork and Find the Right Moment to Finish

25 다음 도표의 내용과 일치하지 않는 것은?

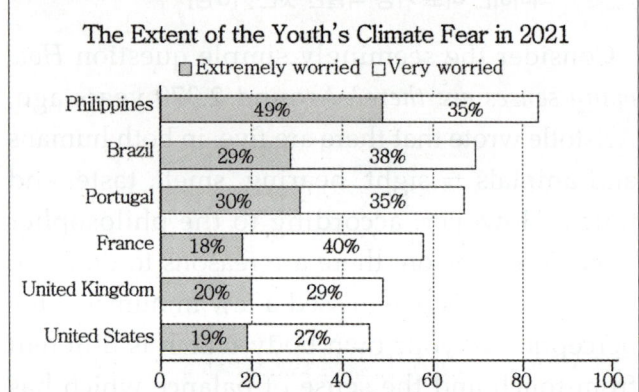

The above graph shows the extent to which young people aged 16-25 in six countries had fear about climate change in 2021. ① The Philippines had the highest percentage of young people who said they were extremely or very worried, at 84 percent, followed by 67 percent in Brazil. ② More than 60 percent of young people in Portugal said they were extremely worried or very worried. ③ In France, the percentage of young people who were extremely worried was higher than that of young people who were very worried. ④ In the United Kingdom, the percentage of young generation who said that they were very worried was 29 percent. ⑤ In the United States, the total percentage of extremely worried and very worried youth was the smallest among the six countries.

26 Jaroslav Heyrovsky에 관한 다음 글의 내용과 일치하지 <u>않는</u> 것은?

Jaroslav Heyrovsky was born in Prague on December 20, 1890, as the fifth child of Leopold Heyrovsky. In 1901 Jaroslav went to a secondary school called the Akademicke Gymnasium. Rather than Latin and Greek, he showed a strong interest in the natural sciences. At Czech University in Prague he studied chemistry, physics, and mathematics. From 1910 to 1914 he continued his studies at University College, London. Throughout the First World War, Jaroslav served in a military hospital. In 1926, Jaroslav became the first Professor of Physical Chemistry at Charles University in Prague. He won the Nobel Prize in chemistry in 1959.

① 라틴어와 그리스어보다 자연 과학에 강한 흥미를 보였다.
② Czech University에서 화학, 물리학 및 수학을 공부했다.
③ 1910년부터 1914년까지 런던에서 학업을 이어 나갔다.
④ 제1차 세계 대전이 끝난 후 군 병원에 복무했다.
⑤ 1959년에 노벨 화학상을 수상했다.

27 Spring Tea Class for Young People에 관한 다음 안내문의 내용과 일치하지 <u>않는</u> 것은?

Spring Tea Class for Young People

Join us for a delightful Spring Tea Class for young people, where you'll experience the taste of tea from various cultures around the world.

Class Schedule
• Friday, April 5 (4:30 p.m. – 6:00 p.m.)
• Saturday, April 6 (9:30 a.m. – 11:00 a.m.)

Details
• We will give you tea and snacks.
• We offer special tips for hosting a tea party.

Participation Fee
• Age 13 – 15: $25 per person
• Age 16 – 18: $30 per person

Note
If you have any food allergy, you should email us in advance at youth@seasonteaclass.com.

① 수강생은 전 세계 다양한 문화권의 차를 경험할 수 있다.
② 금요일 수업은 오후에 1시간 30분 동안 진행된다.
③ 수강생에게 차와 간식을 제공할 것이다.
④ 15세 이하의 수강생은 30달러의 참가비를 내야 한다.
⑤ 음식 알레르기가 있는 수강생은 이메일을 미리 보내야 한다.

28

Clothes Upcycling Contest 2024에 관한 다음 안내문의 내용과 일치하는 것은?

Clothes Upcycling Contest 2024

Are you passionate about fashion and the environment? Then we have a contest for you!

- **Participants**
  – Anyone living in Lakewood, aged 11 to 18
- **How to participate**
  – Take before and after photos of your upcycled clothes.
  – Email the photos at lovelw@lwplus.com.
  – Send in the photos from April 14 to May 12.
- **Winning Prize**
  – A $100 gift card to use at local shops
  – The winner will be announced on our website on May 30.

For more details, visit our website www. lovelwplus.com.

① Lakewood에 사는 사람이면 누구든지 참가할 수 있다.
② 참가자는 출품 사진을 직접 방문하여 제출해야 한다.
③ 참가자는 5월 14일까지 출품 사진을 제출할 수 있다.
④ 우승 상품은 지역 상점에서 쓸 수 있는 기프트 카드이다.
⑤ 지역 신문을 통해 우승자를 발표한다.

29

다음 글의 밑줄 친 부분 중, 어법상 틀린 것은? [3점]

It would be hard to overstate how important meaningful work is to human beings — work ① that provides a sense of fulfillment and empowerment. Those who have found deeper meaning in their careers find their days much more energizing and satisfying, and ② to count their employment as one of their greatest sources of joy and pride. Sonya Lyubomirsky, professor of psychology at the University of California,

has conducted numerous workplace studies ③ showing that when people are more fulfilled on the job, they not only produce higher quality work and a greater output, but also generally earn higher incomes. Those most satisfied with their work ④ are also much more likely to be happier with their lives overall. For her book *Happiness at Work*, researcher Jessica Pryce-Jones conducted a study of 3,000 workers in seventy-nine countries, ⑤ finding that those who took greater satisfaction from their work were 150 percent more likely to have a happier life overall.

*numerous: 수많은

30

다음 글의 밑줄 친 부분 중, 문맥상 낱말의 쓰임이 적절하지 <u>않은</u> 것은? [3점]

The rate of speed at which one is traveling will greatly determine the ability to process detail in the environment. In evolutionary terms, human senses are adapted to the ① speed at which humans move through space under their own power while walking. Our ability to distinguish detail in the environment is therefore ideally ② suited to movement at speeds of perhaps five miles per hour and under. The fastest users of the street, motorists, therefore have a much more limited ability to process details along the street — a motorist simply has ③ enough time or ability to appreciate design details. On the other hand, pedestrian travel, being much slower, allows for the ④ appreciation of environmental detail. Joggers and bicyclists fall somewhere in between these polar opposites; while they travel faster than pedestrians, their rate of speed is ordinarily much ⑤ slower than that of the typical motorist.

*distinguish: 구별하다 **pedestrian: 보행자

31

Every species has certain climatic requirements — what degree of heat or cold it can endure, for example. When the climate changes, the places that satisfy those requirements change, too. Species are forced to follow. All creatures are capable of some degree of _____. Even creatures that appear immobile, like trees and barnacles, are capable of dispersal at some stage of their life — as a seed, in the case of the tree, or as a larva, in the case of the barnacle. A creature must get from the place it is born — often occupied by its parent — to a place where it can survive, grow, and reproduce. From fossils, scientists know that even creatures like trees moved with surprising speed during past periods of climate change.

*barnacle: 따개비 **dispersal: 분산 ***fossil: 화석

① endurance   ② movement
③ development   ④ transformation
⑤ communication

32

No respectable boss would say, "I make it a point to discourage my staff from speaking up, and I maintain a culture that prevents disagreeing viewpoints from ever getting aired." If anything, most bosses even say that they are pro-dissent. This idea can be found throughout the series of conversations with corporate, university, and nonprofit leaders, published weekly in the business sections of newspapers. In the interviews, the featured leaders are asked about their management techniques, and regularly claim to continually encourage _____ from more junior staffers. As Bot Pittman remarked in one of these conversations: "I want us to listen to these dissenters because they may intend to tell you why we can't do something, but if you listen hard, what they're really telling you is what you must do to get something done." [3점] *dissent: 반대

① unconditional loyalty
② positive attitude
③ internal protest
④ competitive atmosphere
⑤ outstanding performance

33

One of the most striking characteristics of a sleeping animal or person is that they do not respond normally to environmental stimuli. If you open the eyelids of a sleeping mammal the eyes will not see normally — they _____. Some visual information apparently gets in, but it is not normally processed as it is shortened or weakened; same with the other sensing systems. Stimuli are registered but not processed normally and they fail to wake the individual. Perceptual disengagement probably serves the function of protecting sleep, so some authors do not count it as part of the definition of sleep itself. But as sleep would be impossible without it, it seems essential to its definition. Nevertheless, many animals (including humans) use the intermediate state of drowsiness to derive some benefits of sleep without total perceptual disengagement. [3점]

*stimuli: 자극 **disengagement: 이탈 ***drowsiness: 졸음

① get recovered easily
② will see much better
③ are functionally blind
④ are completely activated
⑤ process visual information

34

A number of research studies have shown how experts in a field often experience difficulties when introducing newcomers to that field. For example, in a genuine training situation, Dr. Pamela Hinds found that people expert in using mobile phones were remarkably less accurate than novice phone users in judging how long it takes people to learn to use the phones. Experts can become insensitive to how hard a task is for the beginner, an effect referred to as the 'curse of knowledge'. Dr. Hinds was able to show that as people acquired the skill, they then began to underestimate the level of difficulty of that skill. Her participants even underestimated how long it had taken themselves to acquire that skill in an earlier session. Knowing that experts forget how hard it was for them to learn, we can understand the need to _____, rather than making assumptions about how students 'should be' learning. [3점]

*novice: 초보

① focus on the new functions of digital devices
② apply new learning theories recently released
③ develop varieties of methods to test students
④ forget the difficulties that we have had as students
⑤ look at the learning process through students' eyes

35 다음 글에서 전체 흐름과 관계 <u>없는</u> 문장은?

A group of psychologists studied individuals with severe mental illness who experienced weekly group music therapy, including singing familiar songs and composing original songs. ① The results showed that the group music therapy improved the quality of participants' life, with those participating in a greater number of sessions experiencing the greatest benefits. ② Focusing on singing, another group of psychologists reviewed articles on the efficacy of group singing as a mental health treatment for individuals living with a mental health condition in a community setting. ③ The findings showed that, when people with mental health conditions participated in a choir, their mental health and wellbeing significantly improved. ④ The negative effects of music were greater than the psychologists expected. ⑤ Group singing provided enjoyment, improved emotional states, developed a sense of belonging and enhanced self-confidence.

*therapy: 치료 **efficacy: 효능

[36~37] 주어진 글 다음에 이어질 글의 순서로 가장 적절한 것을 고르시오.

36

In many sports, people realized the difficulties and even impossibilities of young children participating fully in many adult sport environments.

(A) As examples, baseball has T ball, football has flag football and junior soccer uses a smaller and lighter ball and (sometimes) a smaller field. All have junior competitive structures where children play for shorter time periods and often in smaller teams.

(B) In a similar way, tennis has adapted the court areas, balls and rackets to make them more appropriate for children under 10. The adaptations are progressive and relate to the age of the child.

(C) They found the road to success for young children is unlikely if they play on adult fields, courts or arenas with equipment that is too large, too heavy or too fast for them to handle while trying to compete in adult-style competition. Common sense has prevailed: different sports have made adaptations for children.

*prevail: 널리 퍼지다

① (A) — (C) — (B)
② (B) — (A) — (C)
③ (B) — (C) — (A)
④ (C) — (A) — (B)
⑤ (C) — (B) — (A)

37

With no horses available, the Inca empire excelled at delivering messages on foot.

(A) When a messenger neared the next hut, he began to call out and repeated the message three or four times to the one who was running out to meet him. The Inca empire could relay messages 1,000miles (1,610km) in three or four days under good conditions.

(B) The messengers were stationed on the royal roads to deliver the Inca king's orders and reports coming from his lands. Called Chasquis, they lived in groups of four to six in huts, placed from one to two miles apart along the roads.

(C) They were all young men and especially good runners who watched the road in both directions. If they caught sight of another messenger coming, they hurried out to meet them. The Inca built the huts on high ground, in sight of one another. [3점]

*excel: 탁월하다 **messenger: 전령

① (A) — (C) — (B)　　② (B) — (A) — (C)
③ (B) — (C) — (A)　　④ (C) — (A) — (B)
⑤ (C) — (B) — (A)

[38~39] 글의 흐름으로 보아, 주어진 문장이 들어가기에 가장 적절한 곳을 고르시오.

38

Research in the 1980s and 1990s, however, demonstrated that the "tongue map" explanation of how we taste was, in fact, totally wrong.

The tongue was mapped into separate areas where certain tastes were registered: sweetness at the tip, sourness on the sides, and bitterness at the back of the mouth. (①) As it turns out, the map was a misinterpretation and mistranslation of research conducted in Germany at the turn of the twentieth century. (②) Today, leading taste researchers believe that taste buds are not grouped according to specialty. (③) Sweetness, saltiness, bitterness, and sourness can be tasted everywhere in the mouth, although they may be perceived at a little different intensities at different sites. (④) Moreover, the mechanism at work is not place, but time. (⑤) It's not that you taste sweetness at the tip of your tongue, but rather that you register that perception *first*.

*taste bud: 미뢰

39

Environmental factors can also determine how the animal will respond during the treatment.

No two animals are alike. (①) Animals from the same litter will display some of the same features, but will not be exactly the same as each other; therefore, they may not respond in entirely the same way during a healing session. (②) For instance, a cat in a rescue center will respond very differently than a cat within a domestic home environment. (③) In addition, animals that experience healing for physical illness will react differently than those accepting healing for emotional confusion. (④) With this in mind, every healing session needs to be explored differently, and each healing treatment should be adjusted to suit the specific needs of the animal. (⑤) You will learn as you go; healing is a constant learning process.

*litter: (한 배에서 태어난) 새끼들

The mind has parts that are known as the conscious mind and the subconscious mind. The subconscious mind is very fast to act and doesn't deal with emotions. It deals with memories of your responses to life, your memories and recognition. However, the conscious mind is the one that you have more control over. You think. You can choose whether to carry on a thought or to add emotion to it and this is the part of your mind that lets you down frequently because — fueled by emotions — you make the wrong decisions time and time again. When your judgment is clouded by emotions, this puts in biases and all kinds of other negativities that hold you back. Scared of spiders? Scared of the dark? There are reasons for all of these fears, but they originate in the conscious mind. They only become real fears when the subconscious mind records your reactions.

⬇

> While the controllable conscious mind deals with thoughts and ___(A)___, the fast-acting subconscious mind stores your responses, ___(B)___ real fears.

	(A)		(B)
①	emotions	—	forming
②	actions	—	overcoming
③	emotions	—	overcoming
④	actions	—	avoiding
⑤	moralities	—	forming

[41~42] 다음 글을 읽고, 물음에 답하시오.

Norms are everywhere, defining what is "normal" and guiding our interpretations of social life at every turn. As a simple example, there is a norm in Anglo society to say *Thank you* to strangers who have just done something to (a) help, such as open a door for you, point out that you've just dropped something, or give you directions. There is no law that forces you to say *Thank you*. But if people don't say *Thank you* in these cases it is marked. People expect that you will say it. You become responsible. (b) Failing to say it will be both surprising and worthy of criticism. Not knowing the norms of another community is the (c) central problem of cross-cultural communication. To continue the *Thank you* example, even though another culture may have an expression that appears translatable (many don't), there may be (d) similar norms for its usage, for example, such that you should say *Thank you* only when the cost someone has caused is considerable. In such a case it would sound ridiculous (i.e., unexpected, surprising, and worthy of criticism) if you were to thank someone for something so (e) minor as holding a door open for you.

41 윗글의 제목으로 가장 적절한 것은?

① Norms: For Social Life and Cultural Communication
② Don't Forget to Say "Thank you" at Any Time
③ How to Be Responsible for Your Behaviors
④ Accept Criticism Without Hurting Yourself
⑤ How Did Diverse Languages Develop?

42 밑줄 친 (a)~(e) 중에서 문맥상 낱말의 쓰임이 적절하지 않은 것은?

① (a)　② (b)　③ (c)　④ (d)　⑤ (e)

(A)

Long ago, when the world was young, an old Native American spiritual leader Odawa had a dream on a high mountain. In his dream, Iktomi, the great spirit and searcher of wisdom, appeared to (a) <u>him</u> in the form of a spider. Iktomi spoke to him in a holy language.

(B)

Odawa shared Iktomi's lesson with (b) <u>his</u> people. Today, many Native Americans have dream catchers hanging above their beds. Dream catchers are believed to filter out bad dreams. The good dreams are captured in the web of life and carried with the people. The bad dreams pass through the hole in the web and are no longer a part of their lives.

(C)

When Iktomi finished speaking, he spun a web and gave it to Odawa. He said to Odawa, "The web is a perfect circle with a hole in the center. Use the web to help your people reach their goals. Make good use of their ideas, dreams, and visions. If (c) <u>you</u> believe in the great spirit, the web will catch your good ideas and the bad ones will go through the hole." Right after Odawa woke up, he went back to his village.

(D)

Iktomi told Odawa about the cycles of life. (d) <u>He</u> said, "We all begin our lives as babies, move on to childhood, and then to adulthood. Finally, we come to old age, where we must be taken care of as babies again." Iktomi also told (e) <u>him</u> that there are good and bad forces in each stage of life. "If we listen to the good forces, they will guide us in the right direction. But if we listen to the bad forces, they will lead us the wrong way and may harm us," Iktomi said.

43 주어진 글 (A)에 이어질 내용을 순서에 맞게 배열한 것으로 가장 적절한 것은?

① (B) — (D) — (C) 　② (C) — (B) — (D)
③ (C) — (D) — (B) 　④ (D) — (B) — (C)
⑤ (D) — (C) — (B)

44 밑줄 친 (a)~(e) 중에서 가리키는 대상이 나머지 넷과 <u>다른</u> 것은?

① (a)　② (b)　③ (c)　④ (d)　⑤ (e)

45 윗글에 관한 내용으로 적절하지 <u>않은</u> 것은?

① Odawa는 높은 산에서 꿈을 꾸었다.
② 많은 미국 원주민은 드림캐처를 현관 위에 건다.
③ Iktomi는 Odawa에게 거미집을 짜서 주었다.
④ Odawa는 잠에서 깨자마자 자신의 마을로 돌아갔다.
⑤ Iktomi는 Odawa에게 삶의 순환에 대해 알려 주었다.

• MP3 파일을 들으며 다음 빈칸을 채우시오. (듣기 어려운 발음이나 정답의 단서가 되는 부분에 빈칸을 만들었습니다.)

01 다음을 듣고, 남자가 하는 말의 목적으로 가장 적절한 것을 고르시오.

M : Good afternoon, students! _____ ___ _____ _____ _____, Jack Eliot. Due to the heavy rain last night, there's some damage on the road and the _____ _____ is not good. So we decided to make some ✪_____ to the school shuttle bus schedule. From tomorrow, _____ ___ _____ _____ the bus schedule will be delayed by 15 minutes. We want to make sure all of you are safe. This bus schedule change will continue for one week. We appreciate your understanding and ✪_____. Thank you for your attention!

02 대화를 듣고, 여자의 의견으로 가장 적절한 것을 고르시오.

W : Brian, ___ _____ _____ you are thinking of buying an electric bicycle.
M : Yes, that's right.
W : That's good. But be careful when you ride it.
M : Yeah, I know _____ _____ _____. On my way here I saw a man riding an electric bicycle without wearing a helmet.
W : Some riders don't even follow basic ✪_____ _____.
M : What do you mean by that?
W : These days many people ride electric bicycles on sidewalks.
M : Yes, it's so dangerous.
W : Right. There should be _____ _____ _____ riding electric bicycles.
M : I totally agree with you.

03 다음을 듣고, 여자가 하는 말의 요지로 가장 적절한 것을 고르시오.

W : Hello, this is your student counselor, Susan Smith. You might be worried about your new school life as a freshman. You _____ ___ _____ ___ _____ to do in the beginning of the year. Today, I'm going to give you a tip about _____ _____. Make a to-do list! Write down the tasks you have to do on a list and _____ _____ what you finish, one by one. By doing this, you won't miss the things you need to do. Using a to-do list will help you manage your time ✪_____. Good luck to you and don't forget to start today.

04 대화를 듣고, 그림에서 대화의 내용과 일치하지 않는 것을 고르시오.

M : Hi, Amy. I heard that _____ _____ the English Newspaper Club.
W : Yes, Tom. I went to the club room yesterday and _____ ___ _____ ___ ___. Look.
M : Wow, the place looks nice. I like the lockers on the left.
W : Yes, they're good. We also have a ✪_____ mirror on the wall.
M : It looks cool. What's that on the bookshelf?
W : Oh, that's the trophy my club won for 'Club of the Year'.
M : You must be very _____ ___ ___. There's also a computer on the right side of the room.
W : Yeah, we use the computer when we need it.
M : Great. I can see a newspaper on the table.
W : Yes, it was published last December.

05 대화를 듣고, 남자가 할 일로 가장 적절한 것을 고르시오.

W: Mike, I think we've got most of the camping ✪_____ ready now.

M: Yeah, the tent, sleeping bags, and cooking tools _____ _____ _____.

W: Perfect. I bought some easy-to-cook meals and snacks for us.

M: Great. What about some _____ _____? It might get cold at night.

W: _____ _____ some warm jackets for us, too. Anything else we need to consider?

M: We need something fun for the camping night. I already packed some books to read.

W: How about playing board games?

M: Nice. I have a chess set at home.

W: Cool, can you bring it?

M: Of course! _____ _____ ____ with me.

06 대화를 듣고, 여자가 지불할 금액을 고르시오.

M: Hello, what can I _____ _____ _____ today?

W: Hi! I want to buy some fruit and ✪_____. What's fresh today?

M: We just got some apples in.

W: How much are they?

M: They are ten dollars for one bag.

W: Fantastic! I'll take two bags of apples.

M: Okay, _____ _____ do you need?

W: I'd like to buy some carrots, too.

M: The carrots are five dollars for one bag. How many do you need?

W: I need two bags of carrots.

M: Okay, you need two bags of apples and two bags of carrots.

W: Right. And I have a coupon. I can _____ ____ _____ with this, right?

M: Yes. You can get a ten percent discount off the total price.

W: Good. Here's the coupon and my credit card.

07 대화를 듣고, 남자가 체육 대회 연습을 할 수 없는 이유를 고르시오.

W: Hey, Jake! How was your math test yesterday?

M: Better than I expected.

W: That's great. Let's go and practice for Sports Day.

M: I'm so sorry but I can't make it.

W: Come on, Jake! Sports Day is _____ _____ _____ _____.

M: I know. _____ _____ ____ _____ my soccer shoes.

W: Then, why can't you practice today? Do you have a club interview?

M: No, I already _____ _____ _____ last week.

W: Then, does your leg still hurt?

M: Not really, it's okay, now. Actually, I have to attend a family dinner ✪_____ tonight for my mother's birthday.

W: Oh, that's important! Family always comes first. Are you available tomorrow, then?

M: Sure. _____ _____ _____ for the ✪_____ practice.

08 대화를 듣고, Science Open Lab Program에 관해 언급되지 않은 것을 고르시오.

W: Hey, Chris. Have you heard about the Science Open Lab Program?

M: Yes, I heard about it. But I don't know what it is ✪_____.

W: In that program, we can _____ any science ✪_____ we want.

M: That sounds pretty cool. Do you want to join the program?

W: Sure, it's only for _____ _____ ____. Let's join it together.

M: Great! Do we need to buy some _____ for experiments?

W: No, they'll prepare everything for us. We just _____ ____ _____ the application form online.

M: When is the _____ _____ _____?

W: It's tomorrow. We need to hurry.

M: Oh, I see. Is there any special prize?

W: Yes. I heard they're giving out prizes for the most creative projects.

M: Perfect! I'm so excited.

09 Triwood High School Volunteer Program에 관한 다음 내용을 듣고, 일치하지 <u>않는</u> 것을 고르시오.

W: Hello, students! Are you _____ _____ _____ to help others? Then, I recommend you to join Triwood High School Volunteer Program to help ✿_____ _____. You're supposed to help the senior citizens face-to-face. You teach them how to use their smartphones for things such as sending text messages or taking pictures. You will also teach seniors how to use ✿_____ apps. The program will _____ _____ _____ for two hours every Saturday. If you are _____ ___ _____ our program, please send us an application form through email.

10 다음 표를 보면서 대화를 듣고, 여자가 주문할 휴대용 선풍기를 고르시오.

M: Sophie, what are you looking for?
W: I'm trying to choose _____ _____ _____ ✿_____ _____ as a gift for my friend Cathy.
M: Oh, let me help you. How many speed options do you think she would want?
W: She would like it if the fan has more than two options.
M: Okay, then, what color do you _____ _____ _____?
W: Cathy's _____ _____ was white. I want to choose a different color.
M: Good idea. Do you want an LED display to show the _____ _____ _____?
W: Hmm, I don't think she will need it.
M: You're left with two options. Which one do you prefer?
W: Well, I'll take the cheaper one.

11 대화를 듣고, 남자의 마지막 말에 대한 여자의 응답으로 가장 적절한 것을 고르시오.

M: What's wrong, Jane? You look so upset.
W: I lost my ✿_____! I have been searching for it _____ _____ ✿_____, but I can't find it.
M: When did you _____ _____ ___?
W: _____

12 대화를 듣고, 여자의 마지막 말에 대한 남자의 응답으로 가장 적절한 것을 고르시오.

W: Honey, what do you _____ ___ _____ for lunch this Saturday?
M: I was thinking we should try the new Italian ✿_____.
W: Hmm… I heard that it's hard to make a ✿_____ there these days.
M: _____

13 대화를 듣고, 남자의 마지막 말에 대한 여자의 응답으로 가장 적절한 것을 고르시오.

M: Mom! I've started to _____ ✿_____ for kids.
W: That's great! How did you _____ _____ _____ that?
M: My teacher told me that a local ✿_____ is looking for students to record audiobooks.
W: Fantastic! Are you having fun with it?
M: Well, actually, I'm _____ _____ my voice acting.
W: Oh? Is that so?
M: Yes, it's ___ _____ _____ to get the right tone for kids.
W: I'm sure you'll get better with practice soon.
M: Thanks. I'm trying my best.
W: That's wonderful. Anything I can help you with?
M: Can you _____ a good book for my audiobook recording?
W: _____

14 대화를 듣고, 여자의 마지막 말에 대한 남자의 응답으로 가장 적절한 것을 고르시오.

W: Hi, Fred. What _____ _____ ____ for our history project?

M: Actually, I was thinking about it. Why don't we _____ ____ _____ for the project?

W: Okay. Good idea. We have the research part, the visual ✪ _____ part, and the presentation part.

M: Hmm, is there any part you want to take on?

W: Well, I would like to do the research. I've been _____ _____ _____ about history.

M: Excellent. You are good at gathering ✪ _____ information.

W: Thanks. Can you handle the visual material?

M: Okay. I'll _____ _____ ____ ____. I have done it before.

W: All right. Then, the only part left is the presentation.

M: _____

15 다음 상황 설명을 듣고, Robert가 Michelle에게 할 말로 가장 적절한 것을 고르시오.

W: Robert and Michelle are attending their high school ✪ _____. After _____ _____, the teacher begins to explain student clubs, school activities, and school ✪ _____. Robert is focusing very carefully on the explanation. However, while _____ _____ _____ _____ about the school library, Robert _____ ____ ____. Trying to find his pen, Robert misses important information about ____ _____ _____ of the library, so now, Robert wants to ask Michelle when the library is open. In this situation, what would Robert most likely say to Michelle?

Robert: _____

[16~17] 다음을 듣고, 물음에 답하시오.

M: Hello, listeners. Thank you for _____ ____ to our Happy Radio Show. Are you taking good care of your _____ in the early spring? Today, I want to _____ some foods that can reduce the ✪ _____ ____ ____ _____. Ginger is a popular _____ _____ for coughs. A cup of hot ginger tea can be helpful for reducing your cough. Lemon is a rich source of vitamin C. Lemon tea can help you ✪ _____ your cough. Surprisingly, pineapple is another excellent food to help relieve a cough. When you are _____ _____ a cough, eating bananas also helps to _____ _____ ____ the symptoms more easily. These foods are rich in vitamins and they are recommended for people suffering from a cough. I hope you have a healthy week.

* 다음 영어는 우리말 뜻을, 우리말은 영어 단어를 〈보기〉에서 찾아 쓰시오.

01 feature _____

02 conscious _____

03 intensity _____

04 ridiculous _____

05 fulfillment _____

06 연관성 _____

07 감사하다 _____

08 먹이 _____

09 과소평가하다 _____

10 구조 _____

[보기]

의식적인	underestimate
성취감	spiritual
강도	structure
계속되다	prey
우스꽝스러운	connection
특징	appreciate

* 다음 우리말에 알맞은 영어 표현을 찾아 연결하시오.

11 ~을 가능하게 하다 • · look for

12 ~에 참여하다 • · get involved in

13 ~을 없애다 • · keep in mind

14 명심하다 • · allow for

15 ~을 찾다 • · get rid of

* 다음 우리말과 같은 표현이 되도록 알맞은 단어를 〈보기〉에서 찾아 쓰시오.

[보기]

acquired / interpretations / evolutionary / inspiration / accurate / genuine
treatment / distinguish / definition / perception / appropriate / relay

16 진화론적 관점에서 ➔ in _____ terms

17 다양한 예술가로부터 영감을 끌어내기 ➔ drawing _____ from diverse artists

18 수면 자체의 정의 ➔ the _____ of sleep itself

19 사람이 기술을 습득했을 때 ➔ as people _____ the skill

20 어린아이에게 더 적합한 ➔ more _____ for children

21 사회적 생활에 대한 우리의 해석 ➔ our _____ of social life

22 놀랍도록 덜 정확한 ➔ remarkably less _____

23 1,000마일(1,610km) 정도 메시지를 이어 가다 ➔ _____ messages 1,000 miles

24 세세한 것을 구별하는 우리의 능력 ➔ our ability to _____ detail

25 너 자신의 몸에 대한 인식 ➔ the _____ of your own body

26 훨씬 더 제한된 능력 ➡ a much more (limited / abundant) ability

27 일련의 대담을 통해서 ➡ throughout the series of (conversations / competitions)

28 참여자의 삶의 질 ➡ the (quality / quantity) of participants' life

29 자신감을 강화하였다 ➡ (reduced / enhanced) self-confidence

30 동물의 특정한 필요 ➡ the (specific / diverse) needs of the animal

* 다음 문장의 빈칸에 알맞은 단어를 〈보기〉에서 찾아 쓰시오.

─────────────[보기]─────────────

satisfy / rotate / criticism / constant / insensitive / forces
enthusiasm / witness / sustainable / categorize / expected / discussion

31 전문가는 한 과업이 초보자에게 얼마나 어려운지에 대해 무감각해질 수 있다.

➡ Experts can become _____ to how hard a task is for the beginner.

32 그러한 요건을 충족시키는 장소도 역시 변한다.

➡ The places that _____ those requirements change, too.

33 3년 차에 작물은 다시 순환할 것이다.

➡ In year three, the crops will _____ again.

34 치료는 끊임없는 학습의 과정이다.

➡ Healing is a(n) _____ learning process.

35 여러분이 '감사합니다'라고 말하도록 강요하는 법은 없다.

➡ There is no law that _____ you to say *Thank you.*

36 Sarah는 이 생각이 마음에 들었고, 열정적으로 반응했다.

➡ Sarah loved this idea and responded with _____.

37 또한 저의 학생들은 당신의 책을 읽었고 그것에 대해 토론 수업을 하였습니다.

➡ Also my students read your book and had a class _____ about it.

38 일단 여러분이 이러한 진술을 적는다면, 마법과 자신감을 목격할 준비를 하라.

➡ Once you write these statements, get ready to _____ magic and confidence.

39 다른 동물들은 훨씬 더 범주화하기 어려운 감각을 가지고 있다.

➡ Other animals have senses that are even harder to _____.

40 음악의 부정적인 효과는 심리학자가 예상했던 것보다 더 컸다.

➡ The negative effects of music were greater than the psychologists _____.

전체 or 문항별 듣기

*1번부터 17번까지는 듣고 답하는 문제입니다. 1번부터 15번까지는 한 번만 들려주고, 16번부터 17번까지는 두 번 들려줍니다. 방송을 잘 듣고 답을 하시기 바랍니다.

▲ 듣기 파일

01 다음을 듣고, 남자가 하는 말의 목적으로 가장 적절한 것을 고르시오.

① 아이스하키부의 우승을 알리려고
② 아이스하키부 훈련 일정을 공지하려고
③ 아이스하키부 신임 감독을 소개하려고
④ 아이스하키부 선수 모집을 안내하려고
⑤ 아이스하키부 경기의 관람을 독려하려고

02 대화를 듣고, 여자의 의견으로 가장 적절한 것을 고르시오.

① 과다한 항생제 복용을 자제해야 한다.
② 오래된 약을 함부로 폐기해서는 안 된다.
③ 약을 복용할 때는 정해진 시간을 지켜야 한다.
④ 진료 전에 자신의 증상을 정확히 확인해야 한다.
⑤ 다른 사람에게 처방된 약을 복용해서는 안 된다.

03 대화를 듣고, 두 사람의 관계를 가장 잘 나타낸 것을 고르시오.

① 관람객 – 박물관 관장 ② 세입자 – 건물 관리인
③ 화가 – 미술관 직원 ④ 고객 – 전기 기사
⑤ 의뢰인 – 건축사

04 대화를 듣고, 그림에서 대화의 내용과 일치하지 <u>않는</u> 것을 고르시오.

05 대화를 듣고, 남자가 할 일로 가장 적절한 것을 고르시오.

① 티켓 디자인하기 ② 포스터 게시하기
③ 블로그 개설하기 ④ 밴드부원 모집하기
⑤ 콘서트 장소 대여하기

06 대화를 듣고, 여자가 지불할 금액을 고르시오. [3점]

① $70 ② $90 ③ $100 ④ $110 ⑤ $120

07 대화를 듣고, 남자가 지갑을 구매하지 <u>못한</u> 이유를 고르시오.

① 해당 상품이 다 팔려서
② 브랜드명을 잊어버려서
③ 계산대의 줄이 길어서
④ 공항에 늦게 도착해서
⑤ 면세점이 문을 닫아서

08 대화를 듣고, Youth Choir Audition에 관해 언급되지 <u>않은</u> 것을 고르시오.

① 지원 가능 연령 ② 날짜 ③ 심사 기준
④ 참가비 ⑤ 지원 방법

09 2023 Career Week에 관한 다음 내용을 듣고, 일치하지 <u>않는</u> 것을 고르시오.

① 5일 동안 열릴 것이다.
② 미래 직업 탐색을 돕는 프로그램이 있을 것이다.
③ 프로그램 참가 인원에 제한이 있다.
④ 특별 강연이 마지막 날에 있을 것이다.
⑤ 등록은 5월 10일에 시작된다.

10 다음 표를 보면서 대화를 듣고, 여자가 구입할 프라이팬을 고르시오.

Frying Pans

	Model	Price	Size (inches)	Material	Lid
①	A	$30	8	Aluminum	○
②	B	$32	9.5	Aluminum	○
③	C	$35	10	Stainless Steel	×
④	D	$40	11	Aluminum	×
⑤	E	$70	12.5	Stainless Steel	○

11 대화를 듣고, 남자의 마지막 말에 대한 여자의 응답으로 가장 적절한 것을 고르시오.

① I don't think I can finish editing it by then.
② I learned it by myself through books.
③ This short movie is very interesting.
④ You should make another video clip.
⑤ I got an A⁺ on the team project.

12 대화를 듣고, 여자의 마지막 말에 대한 남자의 응답으로 가장 적절한 것을 고르시오.

① All right. I'll come pick you up now.
② I'm sorry. The library is closed today.
③ No problem. You can borrow my book.
④ Thank you so much. I'll drop you off now.
⑤ Right. I've changed the interior of my office.

13 대화를 듣고, 남자의 마지막 말에 대한 여자의 응답으로 가장 적절한 것을 고르시오.

Woman: _____

① Try these tomatoes and cucumbers.
② I didn't know peppers are good for skin.
③ Just wear comfortable clothes and shoes.
④ You can pick tomatoes when they are red.
⑤ I'll help you grow vegetables on your farm.

14 대화를 듣고, 여자의 마지막 말에 대한 남자의 응답으로 가장 적절한 것을 고르시오. [3점]

Man: _____

① You're right. I'll meet her and apologize.
② I agree with you. That's why I did it.
③ Thank you. I appreciate your apology.
④ Don't worry. I don't think it's your fault.
⑤ Too bad. I hope the two of you get along.

2023. 3
3회

15 다음 상황 설명을 듣고, John이 Ted에게 할 말로 가장 적절한 것을 고르시오. [3점]

John: _____

① How can we find the best sunrise spot?
② Why do you go mountain climbing so often?
③ What time should we get up tomorrow morning?
④ When should we come down from the mountain top?
⑤ Where do we have to stay in the mountain at night?

[16~17] 다음을 듣고, 물음에 답하시오.

16 여자가 하는 말의 주제로 가장 적절한 것은?

① indoor sports good for the elderly
② importance of learning rules in sports
③ best sports for families to enjoy together
④ useful tips for winning a sports game
⑤ history of traditional family sports

17 언급된 스포츠가 <u>아닌</u> 것은?

① badminton　　　② basketball
③ table tennis　　　④ soccer
⑤ bowling

＊이제 듣기 문제가 끝났습니다. 18번부터는 문제지의 지시에 따라 답을 하시기 바랍니다.

18 다음 글의 목적으로 가장 적절한 것은?

To whom it may concern,

I am a resident of the Blue Sky Apartment. Recently I observed that the kid zone is in need of repairs. I want you to pay attention to the poor condition of the playground equipment in the zone. The swings are damaged, the paint is falling off, and some of the bolts on the slide are missing. The facilities have been in this terrible condition since we moved here. They are dangerous to the children playing there. Would you please have them repaired? I would appreciate your immediate attention to solve this matter.

Yours sincerely,

Nina Davis

① 아파트의 첨단 보안 설비를 홍보하려고
② 아파트 놀이터의 임시 폐쇄를 공지하려고
③ 아파트 놀이터 시설의 수리를 요청하려고
④ 아파트 놀이터 사고의 피해 보상을 촉구하려고
⑤ 아파트 공용 시설 사용 시 유의 사항을 안내하려고

19 다음 글에 드러난 'I'의 심경 변화로 가장 적절한 것은?

On a two-week trip in the Rocky Mountains, I saw a grizzly bear in its native habitat. At first, I felt joy as I watched the bear walk across the land. He stopped every once in a while to turn his head about, sniffing deeply. He was following the scent of something, and slowly I began to realize that this giant animal was smelling me! I froze. This was no longer a wonderful experience; it was now an issue of survival. The bear's motivation was to find meat to eat, and I was clearly on his menu.

*scent: 냄새

① sad → angry
② delighted → scared
③ satisfied → jealous
④ worried → relieved
⑤ frustrated → excited

20 다음 글에서 필자가 주장하는 바로 가장 적절한 것은?

It is difficult for any of us to maintain a constant level of attention throughout our working day. We all have body rhythms characterised by peaks and valleys of energy and alertness. You will achieve more, and feel confident as a benefit, if you schedule your most demanding tasks at times when you are best able to cope with them. If you haven't thought about energy peaks before, take a few days to observe yourself. Try to note the times when you are at your best. We are all different. For some, the peak will come first thing in the morning, but for others it may take a while to warm up.

*alertness: 기민함

① 부정적인 감정에 에너지를 낭비하지 말라.
② 자신의 신체 능력에 맞게 운동량을 조절하라.
③ 자기 성찰을 위한 아침 명상 시간을 확보하라.
④ 생산적인 하루를 보내려면 일을 균등하게 배분하라.
⑤ 자신의 에너지가 가장 높은 시간을 파악하여 활용하라.

21 밑줄 친 The divorce of the hands from the head가 다음 글에서 의미하는 바로 가장 적절한 것은? [3점]

If we adopt technology, we need to pay its costs. Thousands of traditional livelihoods have been pushed aside by progress, and the lifestyles around those jobs removed. Hundreds of millions of humans today work at jobs they hate, producing things they have no love for. Sometimes these jobs cause physical pain, disability, or chronic disease. Technology creates many new jobs that are certainly dangerous. At the same time, mass education and media train humans to avoid low-tech physical work, to seek jobs working in the digital world. The divorce of the hands from the head puts a stress on the human mind. Indeed, the sedentary nature of the best-paying jobs is a health risk — for body and mind.

*chronic: 만성의 **sedentary: 주로 앉아서 하는

① ignorance of modern technology
② endless competition in the labor market
③ not getting along well with our coworkers
④ working without any realistic goals for our career
⑤ our increasing use of high technology in the workplace

22 다음 글의 요지로 가장 적절한 것은?

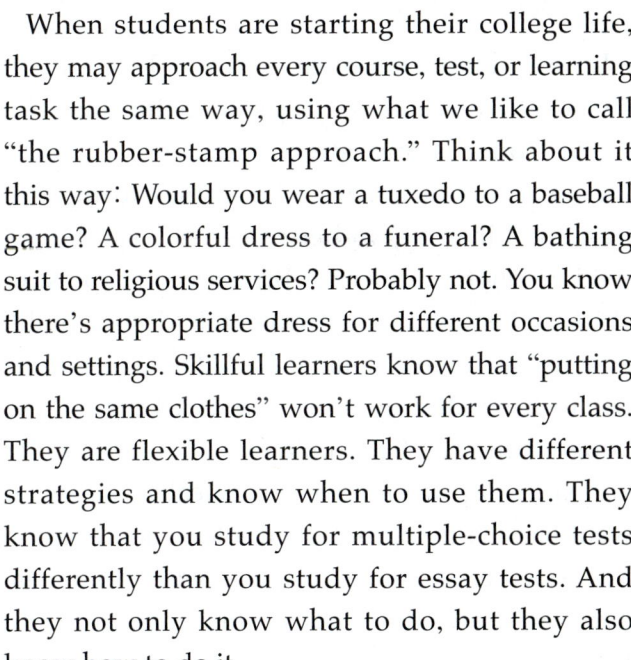

When students are starting their college life, they may approach every course, test, or learning task the same way, using what we like to call "the rubber-stamp approach." Think about it this way: Would you wear a tuxedo to a baseball game? A colorful dress to a funeral? A bathing suit to religious services? Probably not. You know there's appropriate dress for different occasions and settings. Skillful learners know that "putting on the same clothes" won't work for every class. They are flexible learners. They have different strategies and know when to use them. They know that you study for multiple-choice tests differently than you study for essay tests. And they not only know what to do, but they also know how to do it.

① 숙련된 학습자는 상황에 맞는 학습 전략을 사용할 줄 안다.
② 선다형 시험과 논술 시험은 평가의 형태와 목적이 다르다.
③ 문화마다 특정 행사와 상황에 맞는 복장 규정이 있다.
④ 학습의 양보다는 학습의 질이 학업 성과를 좌우한다.
⑤ 학습 목표가 명확할수록 성취 수준이 높아진다.

23 다음 글의 주제로 가장 적절한 것은?

As the social and economic situation of countries got better, wage levels and working conditions improved. Gradually people were given more time off. At the same time, forms of transport improved and it became faster and cheaper to get to places. England's industrial revolution led to many of these changes. Railways, in the nineteenth century, opened up now famous seaside resorts such as Blackpool and Brighton. With the railways came many large hotels. In Canada, for example, the new coast-to-coast railway system made possible the building of such famous hotels as Banff Springs and Chateau Lake Louise in the Rockies. Later, the arrival of air transport opened up more of the world and led to tourism growth.

① factors that caused tourism expansion
② discomfort at a popular tourist destination
③ importance of tourism in society and economy
④ negative impacts of tourism on the environment
⑤ various types of tourism and their characteristics

24 다음 글의 제목으로 가장 적절한 것은?

Success can lead you off your intended path and into a comfortable rut. If you are good at something and are well rewarded for doing it, you may want to keep doing it even if you stop enjoying it. The danger is that one day you look around and realize you're so deep in this comfortable rut that you can no longer see the sun or breathe fresh air; the sides of the rut have become so slippery that it would take a superhuman effort to climb out; and, effectively, you're stuck. And it's a situation that many working people worry they're in now. The poor employment market has left them feeling locked in what may be a secure, or even well-paying — but ultimately unsatisfying — job.   *rut: 틀에 박힌 생활

① Don't Compete with Yourself
② A Trap of a Successful Career
③ Create More Jobs for Young People
④ What Difficult Jobs Have in Common
⑤ A Road Map for an Influential Employer

25 다음 도표의 내용과 일치하지 <u>않는</u> 것은?

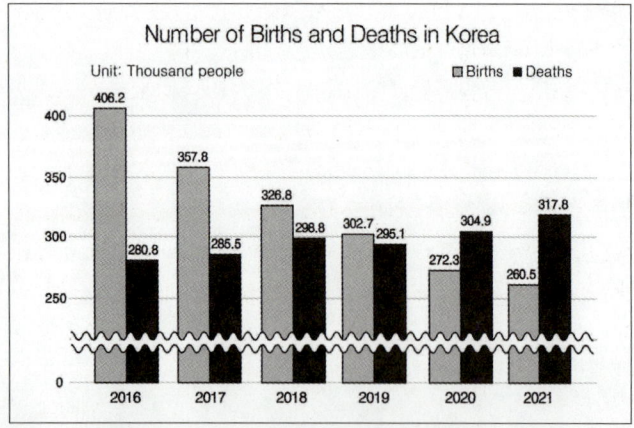

The above graph shows the number of births and deaths in Korea from 2016 to 2021. ① The number of births continued to decrease throughout the whole period. ② The gap between the number of births and deaths was the largest in 2016. ③ In 2019, the gap between the number of births and deaths was the smallest, with the number of births slightly larger than that of deaths. ④ The number of deaths increased steadily during the whole period, except the period from 2018 to 2019. ⑤ In 2021, the number of deaths was larger than that of births for the first time.

26 Lilian Bland에 관한 다음 글의 내용과 일치하지 <u>않는</u> 것은?

Lilian Bland was born in Kent, England in 1878. Unlike most other girls at the time she wore trousers and spent her time enjoying adventurous activities like horse riding and hunting. Lilian began her career as a sports and wildlife photographer for British newspapers. In 1910 she became the first woman to design, build, and fly her own airplane. In order to persuade her to try a slightly safer activity, Lilian's dad bought her a car. Soon Lilian was a master driver and ended up working as a car dealer. She never went back to flying but lived a long and exciting life nonetheless. She married, moved to Canada, and had a kid. Eventually, she moved back to England, and lived there for the rest of her life.

① 승마와 사냥 같은 모험적인 활동을 즐겼다.
② 스포츠와 야생 동물 사진작가로 경력을 시작했다.
③ 자신의 비행기를 설계하고 제작했다.
④ 자동차 판매원으로 일하기도 했다.
⑤ 캐나다에서 생의 마지막 기간을 보냈다.

27 Call for Articles에 관한 다음 안내문의 내용과 일치하지 <u>않는</u> 것은?

Call for Articles

Do you want to get your stories published? *New Dream Magazine* is looking for future writers! This event is open to anyone aged 13 to 18.

Articles

• Length of writing: 300 – 325 words
• Articles should also include high-quality color photos.

Rewards

• Five cents per word
• Five dollars per photo

Notes

• You should send us your phone number together with your writing.
• Please email your writing to us at article@ndmag.com.

① 13세에서 18세까지의 누구나 참여할 수 있다.
② 기사는 고화질 컬러 사진을 포함해야 한다.
③ 사진 한 장에 5센트씩 지급한다.
④ 전화번호를 원고와 함께 보내야 한다.
⑤ 원고를 이메일로 제출해야 한다.

28 Greenhill Roller Skating에 관한 다음 안내문의 내용과 일치하는 것은?

Greenhill Roller Skating

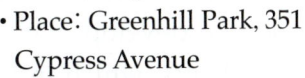

Join us for your chance to enjoy roller skating!

• Place: Greenhill Park, 351 Cypress Avenue
• Dates: Friday, April 7 – Sunday, April 9
• Time: 9 a.m. – 6 p.m.
• Fee: $8 per person for a 50-minute session

Details

– Admission will be on a first-come, first-served basis with no reservations.
– Children under the age of 10 must be accompanied by an adult.
– We will lend you our roller skates for free.

Contact the Community Center for more information at 013-234-6114.

① 오전 9시부터 오후 9시까지 운영한다.
② 이용료는 시간 제한 없이 1인당 8달러이다.
③ 입장하려면 예약이 필요하다.
④ 10세 미만 어린이는 어른과 동행해야 한다.
⑤ 추가 요금을 내면 롤러스케이트를 빌려준다.

29 다음 글의 밑줄 친 부분 중, 어법상 <u>틀린</u> 것은?

[3점]

The most noticeable human characteristic projected onto animals is ① <u>that</u> they can talk in human language. Physically, animal cartoon characters and toys ② <u>made</u> after animals are also most often deformed in such a way as to resemble humans. This is achieved by ③ <u>showing</u> them with humanlike facial features and deformed front legs to resemble human hands. In more recent animated movies the trend has been to show the animals in a more "natural" way. However, they still use their front legs ④ <u>like</u> human hands (for example, lions can pick up and lift small objects with one paw), and they still talk with an appropriate facial expression. A general strategy that is used to make the animal characters more emotionally appealing, both to children and adults, ⑤ <u>are</u> to give them enlarged and deformed childlike features.

*deform: 변형하다 **paw: (동물의) 발

30

다음 글의 밑줄 친 부분 중, 문맥상 낱말의 쓰임이 적절하지 <u>않은</u> 것은? [3점]

The major philosophical shift in the idea of selling came when industrial societies became more affluent, more competitive, and more geographically spread out during the 1940s and 1950s. This forced business to develop ① <u>closer</u> relations with buyers and clients, which in turn made business realize that it was not enough to produce a quality product at a reasonable price. In fact, it was equally ② <u>essential</u> to deliver products that customers actually wanted. Henry Ford produced his best-selling T-model Ford in one color only (black) in 1908, but in modern societies this was no longer ③ <u>possible</u>. The modernization of society led to a marketing revolution that ④ <u>strengthened</u> the view that production would create its own demand. Customers, and the desire to ⑤ <u>meet</u> their diverse and often complex needs, became the focus of business. *affluent: 부유한

[31~34] 다음 빈칸에 들어갈 말로 가장 적절한 것을 고르시오.

31

People differ in how quickly they can reset their biological clocks to overcome jet lag, and the speed of recovery depends on the _____ of travel. Generally, it's easier to fly westward and lengthen your day than it is to fly eastward and shorten it. This east-west difference in jet lag is sizable enough to have an impact on the performance of sports teams. Studies have found that teams flying westward perform significantly better than teams flying eastward in professional baseball and college football. A more recent study of more than 46,000 Major League Baseball games found additional evidence that eastward travel is tougher than westward travel. *jet lag: 시차로 인한 피로감

① direction   ② purpose   ③ season
④ length   ⑤ cost

32

If you want the confidence that comes from achieving what you set out to do each day, then it's important to understand _____. Over-optimism about what can be achieved within a certain time frame is a problem. So work on it. Make a practice of estimating the amount of time needed alongside items on your 'things to do' list, and learn by experience when tasks take a greater or lesser time than expected. Give attention also to fitting the task to the available time. There are some tasks that you can only set about if you have a significant amount of time available. There is no point in trying to gear up for such a task when you only have a short period available. So schedule the time you need for the longer tasks and put the short tasks into the spare moments in between. *gear up: 준비를 갖추다, 대비하다

① what benefits you can get
② how practical your tasks are
③ how long things are going to take
④ why failures are meaningful in life
⑤ why your leisure time should come first

33

In Lewis Carroll's *Through the Looking-Glass*, the Red Queen takes Alice on a race through the countryside. They run and they run, but then Alice discovers that they're still under the same tree that they started from. The Red Queen explains to Alice: *"here*, you see, it takes all the running you can do, to keep in the same place." Biologists sometimes use this Red Queen Effect to explain an evolutionary principle. If foxes evolve to run faster so they can catch more rabbits, then only the fastest rabbits will live long enough to make a new generation of bunnies that run even faster — in which case, of course, only the fastest foxes will catch enough rabbits to thrive and pass on their genes. Even though they might run, the two species _____. [3점]

*thrive: 번성하다

① just stay in place
② end up walking slowly
③ never run into each other
④ won't be able to adapt to changes
⑤ cannot run faster than their parents

34

Everything in the world around us was finished in the mind of its creator before it was started. The houses we live in, the cars we drive, and our clothing — all of these began with an idea. Each idea was then studied, refined and perfected before the first nail was driven or the first piece of cloth was cut. Long before the idea was turned into a physical reality, the mind had clearly pictured the finished product. The human being designs his or her own future through much the same process. We begin with an idea about how the future will be. Over a period of time we refine and perfect the vision. Before long, our every thought, decision and activity are all working in harmony to bring into existence what we _____. [3점]

*refine: 다듬다

① didn't even have the potential to accomplish
② have mentally concluded about the future
③ haven't been able to picture in our mind
④ considered careless and irresponsible
⑤ have observed in some professionals

35

다음 글에서 전체 흐름과 관계 없는 문장은?

Whose story it is affects *what* the story is. Change the main character, and the focus of the story must also change. If we look at the events through another character's eyes, we will interpret them differently. ① We'll place our sympathies with someone new. ② When the conflict arises that is the heart of the story, we will be praying for a different outcome. ③ Consider, for example, how the tale of Cinderella would shift if told from the viewpoint of an evil stepsister. ④ We know Cinderella's kingdom does not exist, but we willingly go there anyway. ⑤ *Gone with the Wind* is Scarlett O'Hara's story, but what if we were shown the same events from the viewpoint of Rhett Butler or Melanie Wilkes?

*sympathy: 공감

[36~37] 주어진 글 다음에 이어질 글의 순서로 가장 적절한 것을 고르시오.

36

In the Old Stone Age, small bands of 20 to 60 people wandered from place to place in search of food. Once people began farming, they could settle down near their farms.

(A) While some workers grew crops, others built new houses and made tools. Village dwellers also learned to work together to do a task faster.

(B) For example, toolmakers could share the work of making stone axes and knives. By working together, they could make more tools in the same amount of time.

(C) As a result, towns and villages grew larger. Living in communities allowed people to organize themselves more efficiently. They could divide up the work of producing food and other things they needed.

*dweller: 거주자

① (A) — (C) — (B)　　② (B) — (A) — (C)
③ (B) — (C) — (A)　　④ (C) — (A) — (B)
⑤ (C) — (B) — (A)

37

Natural processes form minerals in many ways. For example, hot melted rock material, called magma, cools when it reaches the Earth's surface, or even if it's trapped below the surface. As magma cools, its atoms lose heat energy, move closer together, and begin to combine into compounds.

(A) Also, the size of the crystals that form depends partly on how rapidly the magma cools. When magma cools slowly, the crystals that form are generally large enough to see with the unaided eye.

(B) During this process, atoms of the different compounds arrange themselves into orderly, repeating patterns. The type and amount of elements present in a magma partly determine which minerals will form.

(C) This is because the atoms have enough time to move together and form into larger crystals. When magma cools rapidly, the crystals that form will be small. In such cases, you can't easily see individual mineral crystals. [3점]

*compound: 화합물

① (A) — (C) — (B)　　② (B) — (A) — (C)
③ (B) — (C) — (A)　　④ (C) — (A) — (B)
⑤ (C) — (B) — (A)

[38~39] 글의 흐름으로 보아, 주어진 문장이 들어가기에 가장 적절한 곳을 고르시오.

38

Bad carbohydrates, on the other hand, are simple sugars.

All carbohydrates are basically sugars. (①) Complex carbohydrates are the good carbohydrates for your body. (②) These complex sugar compounds are very difficult to break down and can trap other nutrients like vitamins and minerals in their chains. (③) As they slowly break down, the other nutrients are also released into your body, and can provide you with fuel for a number of hours. (④) Because their structure is not complex, they are easy to break down and hold few nutrients for your body other than the sugars from which they are made. (⑤) Your body breaks down these carbohydrates rather quickly and what it cannot use is converted to fat and stored in the body.

*carbohydrate: 탄수화물　**convert: 바꾸다

39

> It was also found that those students who expected the lecturer to be warm tended to interact with him more.

People commonly make the mistaken assumption that because a person has one type of characteristic, then they automatically have other characteristics which go with it. (①) In one study, university students were given descriptions of a guest lecturer before he spoke to the group. (②) Half the students received a description containing the word 'warm', the other half were told the speaker was 'cold'. (③) The guest lecturer then led a discussion, after which the students were asked to give their impressions of him. (④) As expected, there were large differences between the impressions formed by the students, depending upon their original information of the lecturer. (⑤) This shows that different expectations not only affect the impressions we form but also our behaviour and the relationship which is formed. [3점]

40

다음 글의 내용을 한 문장으로 요약하고자 한다. 빈칸 (A), (B)에 들어갈 말로 가장 적절한 것은?

To help decide what's risky and what's safe, who's trustworthy and who's not, we look for *social evidence*. From an evolutionary view, following the group is almost always positive for our prospects of survival. "If everyone's doing it, it must be a sensible thing to do," explains famous psychologist and best selling writer of *Influence*, Robert Cialdini. While we can frequently see this today in product reviews, even subtler cues within the environment can signal trustworthiness. Consider this: when you visit a local restaurant, are they busy? Is there a line outside or is it easy to find a seat? It is a hassle to wait, but a line can be a powerful cue that the food's tasty, and these seats are in demand. More often than not, it's good to adopt the practices of those around you.

*subtle: 미묘한 **hassle: 성가신 일

↓

> We tend to feel safe and secure in ____(A)____ when we decide how to act, particularly when faced with ____(B)____ conditions.

	(A)		(B)
①	numbers	—	uncertain
②	numbers	—	unrealistic
③	experiences	—	unrealistic
④	rules	—	uncertain
⑤	rules	—	unpleasant

Chess masters shown a chess board in the middle of a game for 5 seconds with 20 to 30 pieces still in play can immediately reproduce the position of the pieces from memory. Beginners, of course, are able to place only a few. Now take the same pieces and place them on the board randomly and the (a) difference is much reduced. The expert's advantage is only for familiar patterns — those previously stored in memory. Faced with unfamiliar patterns, even when it involves the same familiar domain, the expert's advantage (b) disappears.

The beneficial effects of familiar structure on memory have been observed for many types of expertise, including music. People with musical training can reproduce short sequences of musical notation more accurately than those with no musical training when notes follow (c) unusual sequences, but the advantage is much reduced when the notes are ordered randomly. Expertise also improves memory for sequences of (d) movements. Experienced ballet dancers are able to repeat longer sequences of steps than less experienced dancers, and they can repeat a sequence of steps making up a routine better than steps ordered randomly. In each case, memory range is (e) increased by the ability to recognize familiar sequences and patterns.

*expertise: 전문 지식 **sequence: 연속, 순서
***musical notation: 악보

41 윗글의 제목으로 가장 적절한 것은?

① How Can We Build Good Routines?
② Familiar Structures Help Us Remember
③ Intelligence Does Not Guarantee Expertise
④ Does Playing Chess Improve Your Memory?
⑤ Creative Art Performance Starts from Practice

42 밑줄 친 (a)~(e) 중에서 문맥상 낱말의 쓰임이 적절하지 않은 것은?

① (a)   ② (b)   ③ (c)   ④ (d)   ⑤ (e)

(A)

Once upon a time, there was a king who lived in a beautiful palace. While the king was away, a monster approached the gates of the palace. The monster was so ugly and smelly that the guards froze in shock. He passed the guards and sat on the king's throne. The guards soon came to their senses, went in, and shouted at the monster, demanding that (a) <u>he</u> get off the throne.

*throne: 왕좌

(B)

Eventually the king returned. He was wise and kind and saw what was happening. He knew what to do. He smiled and said to the monster, "Welcome to my palace!" He asked the monster if (b) <u>he</u> wanted a cup of coffee. The monster began to grow smaller as he drank the coffee.

(C)

The king offered (c) <u>him</u> some take-out pizza and fries. The guards immediately called for pizza. The monster continued to get smaller with the king's kind gestures. (d) <u>He</u> then offered the monster a full body massage. As the guards helped with the relaxing massage, the monster became tiny. With another act of kindness to the monster, he just disappeared.

(D)

With each bad word the guards used, the monster grew more ugly and smelly. The guards got even angrier — they began to brandish their swords to scare the monster away from the palace. But (e) <u>he</u> just grew bigger and bigger, eventually taking up the whole room. He grew more ugly and smelly than ever.

*brandish: 휘두르다

43 주어진 글 (A)에 이어질 내용을 순서에 맞게 배열한 것으로 가장 적절한 것은?

① (B) — (D) — (C) ② (C) — (B) — (D)
③ (C) — (D) — (B) ④ (D) — (B) — (C)
⑤ (D) — (C) — (B)

2023. 3
3회

44 밑줄 친 (a)~(e) 중에서 가리키는 대상이 나머지 넷과 다른 것은?

① (a)   ② (b)   ③ (c)   ④ (d)   ⑤ (e)

45 윗글에 관한 내용으로 적절하지 <u>않은</u> 것은?

① 왕이 없는 동안 괴물이 궁전 문으로 접근했다.
② 왕은 미소를 지으며 괴물에게 환영한다고 말했다.
③ 왕의 친절한 행동에 괴물의 몸이 계속 더 작아졌다.
④ 경비병들은 괴물을 마사지해 주기를 거부했다.
⑤ 경비병들은 겁을 주어 괴물을 쫓아내려 했다.

• MP3 파일을 들으며 다음 빈칸을 채우시오. (듣기 어려운 발음이나 정답의 단서가 되는 부분에 빈칸을 만들었습니다.)

01 다음을 듣고, 남자가 하는 말의 목적으로 가장 적절한 것을 고르시오.

M : Hello, Villeford High School students. This is
✪_____ Aaron Clark. As a ____ ____ of
the Villeford ice hockey team, I'm very excited
about the upcoming National High School Ice
Hockey League. As you all know, the first
game _____ ___ _____ in the Central Rink
at 6 p.m. this Saturday. I want as many of you
as possible to _____ ____ _____ our team
to victory. I've seen them put in an _____
_____ of effort to win the league. It will
help them play better just to see you there
cheering for them. I really hope to see you at
the ✪_____. Thank you.

02 대화를 듣고, 여자의 의견으로 가장 적절한 것을 고르시오.

W : Honey, are you okay?

M : I'm afraid I've ✪_____ ____ _____. I've got
a ✪_____ _____.

W : Why don't you go see a doctor?

M : Well, I don't think it's _____. I've found
some medicine in the cabinet. I'll take it.

W : You shouldn't take that medicine. That's what
I ____ _____ last week.

M : My symptoms are _____ ____ _____.

W : Honey, you shouldn't take medicine
_____ for others.

M : It's just a cold. I'll get better if I take your
medicine.

W : It could be dangerous to take someone else's
✪_____.

M : Okay. Then I'll go see a doctor this afternoon.

03 대화를 듣고, 두 사람의 관계를 가장 잘 나타낸 것을 고르시오.

W : Hi, Mr. Thomson. How are your ✪_____
_____?

M : You arrived at the right time. I have something
to tell you.

W : Okay. What is it?

M : Well, I'm _____ that we _____ ____
_____ the exhibition room for your
paintings.

W : May I ask why?

M : Sure. We have some ✪_____ _____
there.

W : I see. Then where are you going to exhibit my
works?

M : Our gallery is going to exhibit your paintings
in the main hall.

W : Okay. Can I see the hall now?

M : Sure. _____ _____ ___.

04 대화를 듣고, 그림에서 대화의 내용과 일치하지 않는 것을 고르시오.

M : Hi, Grace. What are you _____ ___ ____
your phone?

W : Hi, James. It's a photo I took when I did some
volunteer work. We painted pictures on a
_____ ✪_____.

M : Let me see. Wow, I like the whale with the
flower pattern.

W : I like it, too. ____ ___ ____ _____ the house
under the whale?

M : It's beautiful. What are these two chairs for?

W : You can take a picture sitting there. The
painting becomes the background.

M : Oh, I see. Look at this tree! It has _____
_____.

W : That's right. We named it the Love Tree.

M : The butterfly on the _____ ✪_____ is lovely,
too.

W : I hope a lot of people enjoy the painting.

05 대화를 듣고, 남자가 할 일로 가장 적절한 것을 고르시오.

M: Hi, Stella. How are you doing these days?

W: Hi, Ryan. I've _____ _____ _____ my granddad with his concert. He made a rock band with his friends.

M: There must be a lot of things to do.

W: Yeah. I ✪_____ ___ _____ for the concert yesterday.

M: What about posters and tickets?

W: Well, I've _____ _____ _____ a poster.

M: Then I think I can help you.

W: Really? How?

M: Actually, I have a _____ _____. I think I can upload the poster there.

W: That's great!

M: Just send the poster to me, and I'll post it online.

W: Thanks a lot.

06 대화를 듣고, 여자가 지불할 금액을 고르시오.

M: Good morning. How may I help you?

W: Hi. I want to buy a coffee pot.

M: Okay. You _____ _____ _____ _____ coffee pots.

W: I like this one. How much is it?

M: It _____ ✪_____ $60, but it's now on sale for $50.

W: Okay, I'll buy it. I'd also like to buy this _____ ✪_____.

M: Actually, it comes in two sizes. This smaller one is $20 and a bigger one is $30.

W: The smaller one would be easier to _____ _____. I'll buy two smaller ones.

M: All right. Is there _____ _____ you need?

W: No, that's all. Thank you.

M: Okay. How would you like to pay?

W: I'll pay by credit card. Here you are.

07 대화를 듣고, 남자가 지갑을 구매하지 못한 이유를 고르시오.

[Cell phone rings.]

W: Hi, Brian.

M: Hi, Mom. I'm ___ _____ to get on the plane.

W: Okay. By the way, did you _____ ___ the ✪_____ _____ _____ in the airport?

M: Yes, but I couldn't buy the wallet you asked me to buy.

W: Did you forget the brand name?

M: No. I remembered that. I _____ ___ _____.

W: Then did you arrive late at the airport?

M: No, I had enough time to shop.

W: Then why couldn't you buy the wallet?

M: Actually, because they were all _____ _____.

W: Oh, really?

M: Yeah. The wallet must be very popular.

W: Okay. Thanks for checking anyway.

08 대화를 듣고, Youth Choir Audition에 관해 언급되지 않은 것을 고르시오.

M: Lucy, look at this.

W: Wow. It's about the Youth Choir Audition.

M: Yes. It's open ___ _____ ✪_____ 13 to 18.

W: I'm _____ ___ _____ the choir. When is it?

M: April 2nd, from 9 a.m. to 5 p.m.

W: The place for the audition is the Youth Training Center. It's really _____ _____ _____.

M: I think you should leave early in the morning.

W: That's no problem. Is there an ✪_____ _____?

M: No, it's free.

W: Good. I'll apply for the audition.

M: Then you should fill out an ✪_____ _____ on this website.

W: All right. Thanks.

09

2023 Career Week에 관한 다음 내용을 듣고, 일치하지 않는 것을 고르시오.

W: Hello, Rosehill High School students! I'm your _____ ✪ _____, Ms. Lee. I'm so happy to announce a special event, the 2023 Career Week. It'll be held from May 22nd for five days. There will be many programs to help you _____ _____ future jobs. Please kindly note that the _____ ___ ✪ _____ for each program ___ _____ ___ 20. A special lecture on future career choices _____ ___ _____ on the first day. Registration begins on May 10th. For more information, please visit our school website. I hope you can come and enjoy the 2023 Career Week!

10

다음 표를 보면서 대화를 듣고, 여자가 구입할 프라이팬을 고르시오.

M: Jessica, what are you doing?
W: I'm trying to buy ____ ___ _____ five frying pans.
M: Let me see. This frying pan seems _____ _____.
W: Yeah. I don't want to spend more than $50.
M: Okay. And I think 9 to 12-inch frying pans will work for most of your cooking.
W: I think so, too. An 8-inch frying pan seems too small for me.
M: What about the ✪ _____? Stainless steel pans are good for fast cooking.
W: I know, but _____ ___ _____. I'll buy an aluminum pan.
M: Then you have two options left. Do you need a lid?
W: Of course. A lid keeps the oil _____ ✪ _____. I'll buy this one.
M: Good choice.

11

대화를 듣고, 남자의 마지막 말에 대한 여자의 응답으로 가장 적절한 것을 고르시오.

M: Have you finished your team's short-movie project?
W: ____ ✪ ____. I'm still editing the video clip.
M: Oh, you edit? How ____ ____ _____ to do that?
W: _____

12

대화를 듣고, 여자의 마지막 말에 대한 남자의 응답으로 가장 적절한 것을 고르시오.

[Cell phone rings.]
W: Daddy, are you still working now?
M: No, Emma. I'm _____ ___ ____ ___ my car and drive home.
W: Great. Can you _____ ___ ___ ✪ _____? I'm at the City Library near your office.
M: _____

13 대화를 듣고, 남자의 마지막 말에 대한 여자의 응답으로 가장 적절한 것을 고르시오.

M: Claire, how's your farm doing?

W: Great! I ✿_____ some cherry tomatoes and cucumbers last weekend. Do you want some?

M: Of course. I'd like some very much.

W: Okay. I'll _____ _____ _____ tomorrow.

M: Thanks. Are you going to the farm this weekend too?

W: Yes. The peppers are almost _____ ____ ____ _____.

M: Can I go with you? I'd like to _____ _____ your farm and help you pick the peppers.

W: Sure. It ✿_____ ____ _____ to work on the farm together.

M: Sounds nice. Is there anything I need to prepare?

W: _____

14 대화를 듣고, 여자의 마지막 말에 대한 남자의 응답으로 가장 적절한 것을 고르시오.

W: Daniel, what's wrong?

M: Hi, Leila. I _____ ____ ✿_____ with Olivia.

W: Was it _____?

M: I'm not sure, but I think I made a mistake.

W: So that's why you have a _____ _____.

M: Yeah. I want to _____ _____ _____ her, but she's still angry at me.

W: Did you say you're sorry to her?

M: Well, I _____ _____ saying that I'm sorry.

W: I don't think it's a good idea to _____ _____ ✿_____ through a text message.

M: Do you think so? Now I know why I haven't received any response from her yet.

W: I think it'd be best to go and talk to her in person.

M: _____

15 다음 상황 설명을 듣고, John이 Ted에게 할 말로 가장 적절한 것을 고르시오.

M: Ted and John are _____ ✿_____. They are climbing Green Diamond Mountain together. Now they _____ _____ the campsite near the mountain top. After climbing the mountain all day, they have a relaxing time at the campsite. While drinking coffee, Ted ✿_____ ____ John that they watch the sunrise at the mountain top the next morning. John thinks it's a good idea. So, now John wants to ask Ted _____ _____ _____ _____ wake up to see the sunrise. In this situation, what would John most likely say to Ted?

John: _____

[16~17] 다음을 듣고, 물음에 답하시오.

W: Good morning, everyone. Do you spend a lot of time with your family? One of the best ways to spend time with your family is to enjoy sports together. Today, I will share some of the best sports that _____ _____ _____ _____. The first one is badminton. The whole family can enjoy the sport with ✿_____ _____. The second one is basketball. You can easily find a _____ ✿_____ near your house. The third one is table tennis. It can be played ✿_____ anytime. The last one is bowling. Many families have a great time playing it together. When you go home today, how about playing one of _____ _____ with your family?

✱ 다음 영어는 우리말 뜻을, 우리말은 영어 단어를 〈보기〉에서 찾아 쓰시오.

01 sore _____

02 shift _____

03 sizable _____

04 careless _____

05 compound _____

06 전망 _____

07 가정 _____

08 표면 _____

09 다가오는 _____

10 생계 수단 _____

[보기]

큰	assumption
변화	livelihood
아픈	upcoming
화합물	prospect
정직한	surface
부주의한	income

✱ 다음 우리말에 알맞은 영어 표현을 찾아 연결하시오.

11 가지고 다니다 ·   · take up

12 ~을 차지하다 ·   · run into

13 정착하다 ·   · cope with

14 ~와 마주치다 ·   · settle down

15 ~을 처리하다 ·   · carry around

✱ 다음 우리말과 같은 표현이 되도록 알맞은 단어를 〈보기〉에서 찾아 쓰시오.

[보기]

equipment / skillful / orderly / demand / expertise / traditional
sympathy / adventurous / outcome / habitat / uncertain / beneficial

16 자연 서식지 ➔ native _____

17 유익한 효과 ➔ _____ effects

18 숙련된 학습자 ➔ _____ learners

19 다른 결과 ➔ a different _____

20 그 자체의 수요 ➔ its own _____

21 불확실한 상황 ➔ _____ conditions

22 놀이터 설비 ➔ playground _____

23 모험적인 활동 ➔ _____ activities

24 전통적인 가족 스포츠 ➔ _____ family sports

25 많은 유형의 전문 지식 ➔ many types of _____

26 위치를 재현하다 ➜ (restrict / **reproduce**) the position

27 이곳저곳을 돌아다니다 ➜ (**wander** / surrender) from place to place

28 방울토마토를 좀 수확하다 ➜ (seed / **harvest**) some cherry tomatoes

29 궁전 문으로 접근하다 ➜ (**approach** / detach) the gates of the palace

30 다양한 미래 직업들을 탐색하다 ➜ (**explore** / export) various future jobs

* 다음 문장의 빈칸에 알맞은 단어를 〈보기〉에서 찾아 쓰시오.

---[보기]---

constant / wage / quality / additional / appropriate / savage
quantity / description / sensible / kindness / apology / motivation

---

31 임금 수준과 근로 여건이 개선되었다.

➜ _____ levels and working conditions improved.

32 곰의 동기는 먹을 고기를 찾는 것이었다.

➜ The bear's _____ was to find meat to eat.

33 더 최근의 연구는 추가적인 증거를 발견했다.

➜ A more recent study found _____ evidence.

34 그것들은 여전히 적절한 표정을 지으며 이야기한다.

➜ They still talk with a(n) _____ facial expression.

35 모든 사람이 그것을 하고 있다면, 그것은 해야 할 분별 있는 일인 것임이 틀림없다.

➜ If everyone's doing it, it must be a(n) _____ thing to do.

36 대학생들은 초청 강사에 대한 설명을 들었다.

➜ University students were given _____ of a guest lecturer.

37 그 괴물에게 또 한 번의 친절한 행동을 베풀자, 그는 바로 사라졌다.

➜ With another act of _____ to the monster, he just disappeared.

38 합리적인 가격에 양질의 제품을 생산하는 것으로는 충분하지 않았다.

➜ It was not enough to produce a(n) _____ product at a reasonable price.

39 문자로 사과하는 것은 좋은 생각 같지 않다.

➜ I don't think it's a good idea to express your _____ through a text message.

40 근무일 내내 꾸준한 수준의 주의 집중을 유지하기는 어렵다.

➜ It is difficult to maintain a(n) _____ level of attention throughout our working day.

연세 국궁부

연세대학교 스포츠 동아리

전통 활쏘기의 매력 속으로!

우리나라의 전통 활쏘기를 이르는 말인 국궁은 생활체육 중 하나이며, 국궁을 통해 스트레스 해소와 심신단련, 전통의 매력을 동시에 느낄 수 있습니다.

연세 국궁부는 국궁의 기초부터 심화 과정까지 차근차근 가르쳐줌은 물론, 동아리의 공용 장비를 자유롭게 이용할 수도 있습니다. 현재 70여 명의 부원이 매주 자율적으로 활쏘기 연습에 참여해 국궁을 연마하고, 동아리 국궁대회를 개최하고 있습니다.

그 밖에도 매 홀수 달마다 자체 대회인 '사회'를 개최하여 부원들이 쌓아온 실력을 서로 겨룰 수 있는 기회를 마련합니다. 또한 국궁 연고전을 개최해 양교 궁사들 간의 화합을 도모하기도 하고, 14개의 서울 국궁 동아리가 모여 연합 교류전을 개최하는 등 외부 대회에도 적극적으로 참여하고 있습니다.

매년 다양한 궁도대회에서 대학부 1위를 차지하는 등 꾸준히 좋은 성적을 내고 있는 연세 국궁부의 일원이 되고 싶다면 매년 5월과 11월에 실시되는 신입부원 모집에 관심을 가져보세요.

*6월 전국연합학력평가

[회별 45문항, 제한 시간 70분]

★ 최근 연도부터 차례대로 수록하였습니다.

4회　모의고사 ─ 2025년 시행

5회　모의고사 ─ 2024년 시행

6회　모의고사 ─ 2023년 시행

출제 범위	고1 6월 수준
난이도	**하** : 11~13문항　**중** : 15~17문항 **상** : 7~9문항　**최상** : 8~10문항

출제 경향
- 듣기 17문항 (1~17번), **어법 · 어휘** 3문항 (29~30번, 42번),
  독해 25문항 (그 외 전 문항)

6월 대비 학습 전략
3월에 비해 소재가 다양해지고, 길이도 늘어난다. 듣기 문제 또한 점차 까다롭게 출제된다. 그러므로 평소 다양한 소재의 지문을 접함으로써 낯선 지문에 대한 거부감을 줄여야 한다.

전국연합학력평가 [2025년 6월 4일 시행]

★ 3점 문항에만 점수가 표시되어 있습니다.

· 문항 수: 45개 · 배점: 100점 · 제한 시간: 70분

단어장

전체 or 문항별 듣기

*1번부터 17번까지는 듣고 답하는 문제입니다. 1번부터 15번까지는 한 번만 들려주고, 16번부터 17번까지는 두 번 들려줍니다. 방송을 잘 듣고 답을 하시기 바랍니다.

▲ 듣기 파일

01 다음을 듣고, 여자가 하는 말의 목적으로 가장 적절한 것을 고르시오.

① 학생회관 리모델링 일정을 공지하려고
② 새로운 학습 자료를 제공하려고
③ 학생용 프린터 설치를 알리려고
④ 학생회장 선출 방법을 안내하려고
⑤ 프린터 고장 시 해결 방법을 설명하려고

02 대화를 듣고, 남자의 의견으로 가장 적절한 것을 고르시오.

① 단어를 소리내어 말하는 것이 암기에 효과적이다.
② 말하기와 쓰기는 언어 학습에서 필수적인 요소이다.
③ 뇌 기능의 효율성을 높이려면 충분한 휴식이 필요하다.
④ 문화를 이해하면 그 나라의 언어를 더 쉽게 배울 수 있다.
⑤ 언어 학습 과정에서의 실수는 장기 기억 형성에 도움이 된다.

03 다음을 듣고, 남자가 하는 말의 요지로 가장 적절한 것을 고르시오.

① 햇빛을 쬐는 것은 신체와 정신의 건강에 도움이 된다.
② 자외선 차단제를 바르는 것은 피부 노화를 예방한다.
③ 건강을 위해 다양한 영양소를 고루 섭취해야 한다.
④ 몸과 마음이 건강하면 삶의 만족도가 높아진다.
⑤ 야외 활동 시 안전 수칙을 준수해야 한다.

04 대화를 듣고, 그림에서 대화의 내용과 일치하지 않는 것을 고르시오.

05 대화를 듣고, 남자가 할 일로 가장 적절한 것을 고르시오.

① 시식용 사탕 고르기
② 가격표 붙이기
③ 홍보 포스터 게시하기
④ 스피커 점검하기
⑤ 음악 재생 목록 만들기

06 대화를 듣고, 여자가 지불할 금액을 고르시오. [3점]

① $80   ② $90   ③ $100   ④ $110   ⑤ $120

07 대화를 듣고, 여자가 버스킹 공연에 참여할 수 없는 이유를 고르시오.

① 기타 연주를 연습해야 해서
② 아르바이트를 해야 해서
③ 테니스 수업을 받아야 해서
④ 오디션을 준비해야 해서
⑤ 대중 앞 공연이 긴장되어서

08 대화를 듣고, Fireworks Festival 자원봉사에 관해 언급되지 않은 것을 고르시오.

① 기간
② 지원 가능 연령
③ 준비물
④ 활동 내용
⑤ 신청 기한

09 2025 Talent Show에 관한 다음 내용을 듣고, 일치하지 않는 것을 고르시오.

① 학교 강당에서 개최될 것이다.
② 모든 학생이 참가할 수 있다.
③ 3명의 교사가 심사할 것이다.
④ 모든 참가자는 열쇠고리를 받을 것이다.
⑤ 공연 막바지에 댄스 파티가 있을 것이다.

10 다음 표를 보면서 대화를 듣고, 두 사람이 구매할 책가방을 고르시오.

School Backpacks

	Model	Price	Shape	Color	Waterproof
①	A	$50	Round	Black	×
②	B	$55	Square	Black	×
③	C	$60	Square	White	○
④	D	$65	Square	Black	○
⑤	E	$75	Round	White	○

11 대화를 듣고, 남자의 마지막 말에 대한 여자의 응답으로 가장 적절한 것을 고르시오. [3점]

① I see. Then you should leave now to go see a doctor.
② Good idea. I can put you in another group next class.
③ Too bad. You should have taken some medicine first.
④ Never mind. I hope you do better on the final exam.
⑤ Thank you. I'll go to the nurse's office right now.

12 대화를 듣고, 여자의 마지막 말에 대한 남자의 응답으로 가장 적절한 것을 고르시오.

① No. I made all these cakes by myself.
② Sure. I'm looking forward to my 30th birthday.
③ Actually, I don't mind if you eat my carrot cake.
④ Not really. It's hard to remember all the anniversaries.
⑤ Yes, I'd like a heart-shaped cake with a message on it.

13 대화를 듣고, 여자의 마지막 말에 대한 남자의 응답으로 가장 적절한 것을 고르시오.

Man: _____

① I see. You've always preferred dogs over cats.
② Okay. I'll ask him if you can look after his cat.
③ Sorry. I don't have time to take care of your cat.
④ No problem. I'll take his pet to the animal hospital.
⑤ I agree. I know for sure he's a great pet caretaker.

14 대화를 듣고, 남자의 마지막 말에 대한 여자의 응답으로 가장 적절한 것을 고르시오. [3점]

Woman: _____

① You're right. That's how I found the book.
② Well, I think the food will be delivered soon.
③ Thanks. I guess I haven't lost my chef skills.
④ Really? I didn't know that you loved to cook.
⑤ I know. That's the reason I quit being a chef.

2025.6
4회

15 다음 상황 설명을 듣고, Chloe가 호텔 직원에게 할 말로 가장 적절한 것을 고르시오.

Chloe: _____

① What's the best tourist attraction near the hotel?
② Would it be possible to change to another room?
③ Could you check the refrigerator in my room?
④ Is there any way to get some cool water?
⑤ Can you turn off the air conditioner?

[16~17] 다음을 듣고, 물음에 답하시오.

16 남자가 하는 말의 주제로 가장 적절한 것은?

① native plants of various countries
② wild plants and their medical uses
③ endangered flowers across the world
④ roles of flowers in national ceremonies
⑤ national flowers with symbolic meanings

17 언급된 국가가 아닌 것은?

① Philippines ② Denmark ③ Germany
④ France   ⑤ United States

*이제 듣기 문제가 끝났습니다. 18번부터는 문제지의 지시에 따라 답을 하시기 바랍니다.

18 다음 글의 목적으로 가장 적절한 것은?

Dear Dog Owners,

My name is Lily Paxton, and I'm the town's Pet Program Coordinator. As part of our goal to make the community more dog-friendly, we recently opened a new dog park. The park was designed to provide an enjoyable experience for both dogs and owners. There are big grassy areas where your dogs can run, jump, and play. We have separate spaces for small dogs and big dogs, to ensure safety. You'll also find lots of benches and areas for resting and staying cool. We hope you will have a wonderful time with your dogs in this newly opened park.

Regards,

Lily Paxton, Pet Program Coordinator

① 새로 만든 반려견 공원의 개장을 홍보하려고
② 동물 보호 정책에 대한 의견을 구하려고
③ 유기견 보호 자원봉사자를 모집하려고
④ 반려견 공원 운영 시간의 변경을 안내하려고
⑤ 반려견 훈련 프로그램에의 참여를 권유하려고

19 다음 글에 드러난 Maya의 심경 변화로 가장 적절한 것은?

Maya waited in line to check in for her flight. Her expectations about her European backpacking trip were really high. She had been looking forward to the trip for a year. She couldn't wait to visit museums in Madrid and see the Eiffel Tower at night in Paris. As she stood in line, she could feel those experiences were finally so close. When she approached the counter, the airline employee asked to see her passport. Maya reached into her pocket but felt nothing. She realized she had left her passport at home. Her plans were ruined. She was heartbroken, knowing she could not board the flight and had to delay her dream trip.

① excited → frustrated
② joyful → indifferent
③ terrified → relaxed
④ worried → satisfied
⑤ bored → curious

20 다음 글에서 필자가 주장하는 바로 가장 적절한 것은?

People often ask me, "What surprises you most about habits?" One thing that continually astonishes me is the degree to which we're influenced by sheer convenience. The amount of effort, time, or decision making required by an action has a huge influence on habit formation. To a truly remarkable extent, we're more likely to do something if it's convenient, and less likely if it's not. For this reason, we should pay close attention to the convenience of any activity we want to make into a habit. Putting a wastebasket next to our front door made mail sorting slightly more convenient, and I stopped procrastinating with this chore. Many people report that they do a much better job of staying close to distant family members now that tools like group chats make it easy to stay in touch.   *sheer: 순전한 **procrastinate: 미루다

① 불필요한 자극을 유발하는 작업 환경을 개선해야 한다.
② 생활방식 개선을 위해 규칙적인 생활 습관을 길러야 한다.
③ 목표를 신속하게 달성하려면 구체적인 계획을 세워야 한다.
④ 반복적인 업무의 편의를 위해 디지털 도구를 사용해야 한다.
⑤ 습관으로 만들고 싶은 행동의 편리성에 주의를 기울여야 한다.

It is common sense that people's inner beliefs may drive their external behavior. If you're attracted to a certain person, you should be more likely to socialize with that person. If you favor a brand of toothpaste, you're more likely to buy it. Of course, our internal thoughts don't *always* predict our public behavior, but, overall, what we do obviously reflects what we think. But beliefs and behaviors are also related in a more remarkable way. It turns out that <u>the arrow is as likely to point in the reverse direction</u>. As social psychologist David Myers observes, "If social psychology has taught us anything during the last 25 years, it is that we are likely not only to think ourselves into a way of acting but also to act ourselves into a way of thinking."

① actions can be entirely separate from beliefs
② our behaviors can also shape what we believe
③ our opinions can be dependent on our emotions
④ behaviors can clearly reflect one's surroundings
⑤ what we think can matter more than what we do

22 다음 글의 요지로 가장 적절한 것은?

Imagine following the spirit of a silence vow into daily life. Challenge yourself to spend an entire day saying only what you absolutely must say. It's been widely observed by behavioral psychology experts — and anyone who's ever been on a first date — that we too often tend to treat "conversation" as a game of waiting for our own turn to speak. We miss what's being said because we're mentally rehearsing our next utterance. What if you could eliminate the idea that the next available mini-silence is your next opening to express whatever is in your head? What if you were limited to, say, fifty spoken words tomorrow? I think you'd listen quite differently. You'd attend quite carefully to every word you heard. You'd be attuned to what you must respond to. You might discover that the less you say, the more you hear.

*vow: 서약 **utterance: 발언 ***attune: 맞추다

2025. 6
4회

① 말을 적게 하면 상대방의 말을 경청할 수 있다.
② 첫 만남에서는 언행에 더욱 신중할 필요가 있다.
③ 불필요한 대화를 줄이면 스트레스가 감소한다.
④ 침묵은 의사소통의 효율성을 저해할 수 있다.
⑤ 몸짓 언어는 효과적인 대화에 도움이 된다.

23 다음 글의 주제로 가장 적절한 것은?

Science is concerned with accumulating and understanding observations of the physical world. That understanding alone solves no problems. Individual people have to act on that understanding for it to help solve problems. For instance, science has found that regular exercise can lower your risk of heart disease. Knowing this fact is interesting, but it will do nothing for your personal health unless you act on it and actually exercise. And that's the hard part. Reading an article about exercise is easy. Getting into an actual routine of regular exercise is harder. In this sense, science really solves *no* problems at all. Problems are only solved when people take the knowledge provided by science and use it. In fact, many of humanity's biggest problems are caused by lack of action, and not lack of knowledge.

*accumulate: 축적하다

① advantages of putting strategic plans into action
② danger of acting against the wisdom of the crowd
③ difficulty in sharing scientific knowledge with the public
④ problems with lacking specific knowledge about exercising
⑤ need to act on scientific understanding in solving problems

24 다음 글의 제목으로 가장 적절한 것은?

We think we're being logical, objective, and rational — and therefore accurate in our analysis, judgment, and decisions. So we think that if other people are logical, objective, and rational, they will agree with us and see what we see. But the opposite is the case. Every human brain is different. Everyone's life experience is different. Everyone's desires and knowledge are different. You might think you're being realistic — that is, that your ideas match reality, but that's impossible. It's only your interpretation of reality, which will always be different from someone else's. When two nations play each other in the World Cup, the fans of each country criticize the referees for missing all the infractions that the other team commits. Without fail, each fan base believes that the referees are biased against their team.

*infraction: 위반

① Open to Interpretation: Everyone Sees Reality Differently
② Efforts Made to Fill the Gap Between Real and Ideal
③ One Single Reality: What We All Agree Upon
④ Why Sports Fans Judge Their Team's Play Objectively
⑤ Knowledge: The Key to Interpreting the World Accurately

25 다음 도표의 내용과 일치하지 <u>않는</u> 것은?

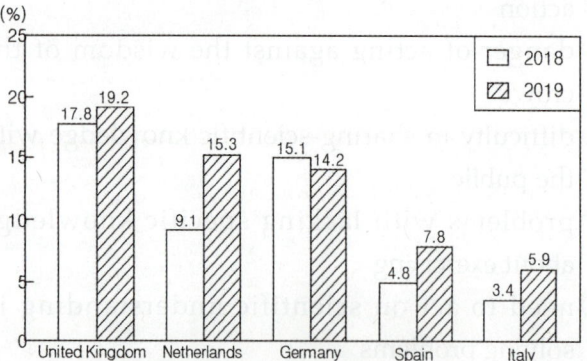

Online Share of Retail Trade in Selected European Countries in 2018 and 2019

The graph above shows the online share of retail trade in selected European countries in 2018 and 2019. ① In 2019, the United Kingdom recorded the highest online share of retail trade, reaching 19.2 percent. ② The Netherlands showed the largest increase in its online share of retail trade among the countries from 2018 to 2019, with a jump of over 6 percentage points. ③ In 2018, Germany had a higher online share of retail trade than the Netherlands, whereas, in 2019, Germany fell behind the Netherlands. ④ In 2018, Germany's online share of retail trade was over four times higher than that of Spain. ⑤ Among the five countries, Italy recorded the lowest online share of retail trade in both 2018 and 2019.

26 Edward O. Wilson에 관한 다음 글의 내용과 일치하지 <u>않는</u> 것은?

Edward O. Wilson was born in Birmingham, Alabama, in 1929. In his early childhood, he became interested in nature and spent much time in the outdoors. At age seven, he was partially blinded in a fishing accident; his reduced sight led Wilson to the study of ants. He could not observe larger animals from a distance. Instead, he concentrated on smaller creatures he could study up close. After studying evolutionary biology at the University of Alabama, Wilson transferred to Harvard University, where he became a professor in 1956. He never received a Nobel Prize — the prize didn't recognize research in the field of evolutionary biology. However, he was awarded the Crafoord Prize in 1990. Wilson, known to some as the "modern-day Darwin", died at the age of 92 in Massachusetts.

① 어린 시절에 자연에 관심을 갖게 되었다.
② 7세에 낚시 사고를 겪었다.
③ 1956년에 Harvard 대학 교수가 되었다.
④ 진화 생물학 분야에서 Nobel Prize를 수상했다.
⑤ Massachusetts에서 92세에 사망했다.

27 Houseplant Heaven Pop-up Shop에 관한 다음 안내문의 내용과 일치하지 <u>않는</u> 것은?

Houseplant Heaven Pop-up Shop

Enjoy a special plant shopping experience! Explore beautiful houseplants, and bring some green into your home.

When: October 11 - 13, 10 a.m. - 8 p.m.

Where: Tasty Cup Cafe

Details

- Indoor plants are available for purchase.
- If you buy 2 plants, you will get a 50% discount on coffee.

Activities

- Take pictures in a photo zone filled with unique plants.
- Decorate eco-friendly pots made from recycled glass.

※ Outside food and drinks are not allowed.

① 3일간 진행된다.
② 실내 식물이 구매 가능하다.
③ 식물을 2개 사면 커피를 무료로 받을 것이다.
④ 친환경 화분을 장식하는 활동이 있다.
⑤ 외부 음식과 음료는 허용되지 않는다.

28 2025 Summer Cartoon Festival에 관한 다음 안내문의 내용과 일치하는 것은?

2025 Summer Cartoon Festival

It's the 8th annual Summer Cartoon Festival! The festival drew a lot of visitors last year. Why not be one of them this year?

Dates: July 5 - 6

Time: 9 a.m. - 6 p.m.

Place: Merryville Park

Featured Events

- Cartoon drawing classes for beginners only
- Face painting by cartoonists
- Parade of costumed characters

Notes

- All visitors will receive character stickers.
- For a more detailed timetable and other information, check out www.SummerCartoonFest.com.

① 처음으로 개최되는 축제이다.
② 오전 9시부터 오후 7시까지 진행된다.
③ 상급자를 위한 만화 그리기 수업이 있다.
④ 페이스 페인팅 행사가 있다.
⑤ 방문객 중 일부만 캐릭터 스티커를 받을 것이다.

29 다음 글의 밑줄 친 부분 중, 어법상 <u>틀린</u> 것은? [3점]

Studies of experts provide insight into ① <u>what</u> it means to have deep and flexible understanding. Experts in a particular domain are people who have deep, richly interconnected ideas about the world. They are not just good thinkers or people who are ② <u>exceptionally</u> smart. Rather, experts ③ <u>having</u> knowledge in a specific domain — such as chess, chemistry, or tennis — and are not generalists. However, experts do not just know "a bunch of facts." In fact, having expertise in a topic means ④ <u>that</u> knowledge is organized into coherent frameworks, and the expert understands the inter-relationship between facts and can distinguish which ideas are most central. This kind of deep but organized understanding allows for greater flexibility in learning and ⑤ <u>facilitates</u> application across multiple contexts.

*coherent: 일관성 있는

30 다음 글의 밑줄 친 부분 중, 문맥상 낱말의 쓰임이 적절하지 <u>않은</u> 것은?

It is natural for people to observe happenings and then seek explanations for why those happenings occurred. But sometimes the reasoning is ① <u>wrong</u> because of one or more misconceptions. One of these is the *ecological fallacy*, where an argument claims that there is a causal relationship between two things merely because they occur ② <u>together</u>. For example, in the 1950s it was found that crime rates were the highest in neighborhoods where immigrants were most numerous. Some people used this "co-occurrence" to argue that immigrants were a ③ <u>cause</u> of crime. But a careful analysis of this situation revealed that immigrants were forced to live in neighborhoods where crime rates were already ④ <u>low</u>; they could not afford more expensive housing in safer neighborhoods. Immigrants themselves committed very few of the crimes. Unless you analyze the claim carefully, you would ⑤ <u>misinterpret</u> the relationship and thereby construct a faulty belief.　*immigrant: 이민자

[31~34] 다음 빈칸에 들어갈 말로 가장 적절한 것을 고르시오.

31

In everyday life, we use ＿＿＿＿＿＿ to predict where we should pay attention. Different environments create different expectations. This was profoundly illustrated by the scientist Jared Diamond in his book *Guns, Germs, and Steel*. He describes an adventure wandering through the New Guinea jungle with native New Guineans. He relates that these natives tend to perform poorly at tasks Westerners have been trained to do since childhood. But they are hardly stupid. They can detect the most subtle changes in the jungle, good for following the tracks of a predator or for finding the way back home. They know which insects to leave alone, know where food exists, can build and tear down shelters with ease. Diamond, who had never spent time in such places, has no ability to pay attention to these things. Were he to be tested on such tasks, he also would perform poorly. [3점]

*profoundly: 심오하게 **subtle: 미묘한

① close cooperation
② previous experience
③ survival instinct
④ modern technology
⑤ parental advice

32

Most entrepreneurs put in tremendous amounts of time and effort in creating and launching new products and services and then make the mistake of overpricing them. They have created something they care deeply about, it's theirs, and this powerful sense of ownership distorts their perception of value which causes them to overprice their products. While many of them are quick to realize that their initial prices are too high, not all these people are happy or willing to drop their prices to make their products more attractive. And this can be a very costly mistake that may lead to the failure of their new business. When you launch a new product or service, your priority should be to get sufficient market adoption as soon as possible and you should be ready to ＿＿＿＿＿＿＿＿＿ to achieve this aim. Once you have strong sales volumes, you can increase your prices to maximize your profits.　*entrepreneur: 기업가 **tremendous: 엄청난

① sacrifice your initial prices and profits
② upgrade your products and service
③ maintain the overpricing strategy
④ switch to a brand-new business
⑤ seek out consumer reviews

33

In most respects, humans are one of a relatively small number of species that evolved a very different strategy of _____. Like apes and elephants, we mature at a leisurely pace, grow large bodies, and have few babies but devote much time and energy to raising them well. This unusual strategy succeeds because while apes and elephants produce fewer babies than mice, a larger percentage of their offspring survive to then reproduce. A house mouse can become a mother when she is just five weeks old, has four to ten pups per litter, and can have a new litter every two months over the course of her approximately twelve-month life. However, the vast majority of her pups die young. In contrast, a chimp or elephant mother does not reproduce until she is at least twelve years old, and she gives birth to only one infant every five or six years over the next thirty or so years. About half of these offspring make it to becoming parents. [3점]

*ape: 유인원 **offspring: 자손 ***litter: 한 배에서 난 새끼

① making use of fewer resources for reproduction
② investing more energy to reproduce more slowly
③ hiding their intentions to get what they really want
④ passing down shared social values to their offspring
⑤ living separately from their family units at an early age

34

When scientists make an important new discovery or experimentally prove some hypothesis, they do not, in general, keep that information to themselves so that they alone can consider its meaning and derive additional theories from it. Instead, they publish their results and make their data available for inspection. This makes it possible for other scientists to reconsider their data and possibly refute their conclusions. More important, though, it makes it possible for other scientists to use that data to construct new hypotheses and perform new experiments. The assumption is that society as a whole will end up knowing more if information is spread as widely as possible, rather than being limited to a few people. In a strict sense, every scientist _____.

*derive: 도출하다 **refute: 반박하다

① pursues only new discoveries
② sticks to their own research ideas
③ is restricted from using certain data
④ ignores the data against their theories
⑤ depends on the work of other scientists

35 다음 글에서 전체 흐름과 관계 없는 문장은?

In the 1930s, the British psychologist Sir Frederic Bartlett asked people to listen to folktales from other countries and then recall these stories at a later date. As you might guess, unfamiliar stories were not remembered as well as familiar stories. ① Surprisingly, however, errors in memory were not random. ② Rather, subjects often rewrote similar parts of the stories in their own minds — particularly the parts that made the least sense to them. ③ To attract a wide audience, stories should focus on topics that interest many people. ④ Bartlett concluded that when facing problems, humans draw upon mental schemata, or shelves of stored knowledge in our brains, to fill in any minor gaps in our memories. ⑤ Therefore, remembering is an imaginative process that involves building upon past experiences.

*folktale: 민간 설화

36

History, people often say, repeats itself. And looking at the historical records of the ancient civilizations, some things do seem to happen again and again.

(A) If so, archaeology would be pretty boring; one thing would happen again and again. But that's not what archaeologists see. Some civilizations end suddenly, like the Aztec and Inca, conquered by invaders in the 1520s AD.

(B) Civilizations expand, get overextended, and then collapse as in the cases of Rome, which went under in 476 AD, and the British Empire, which fell apart more than a thousand years later in the post-World War II era. But is this always the case?

(C) Those empires never had the chance to collapse as a result of overexpansion. So in the case of civilizations, "history repeats itself" seems to be an oversimplification. [3점]

*archaeology: 고고학 **invader: 침입자 ***empire: 제국

① (A) — (C) — (B)　　② (B) — (A) — (C)
③ (B) — (C) — (A)　　④ (C) — (A) — (B)
⑤ (C) — (B) — (A)

37

Stanford psychology professor Dr. Carol Dweck is the internationally recognized pioneer of the concept of "growth mindset" as a way to continually grow, learn, and persevere in our efforts.

(A) These kids end up taking on tougher things, and feel better about themselves. "Emphasizing effort gives a child a variable that they can control," Dweck has explained.

(B) In contrast, Dweck found, kids who are praised not for their smarts but for their effort develop what Dweck calls a "growth mindset." They learn that their effort is what led to their success, and if they continue to try, over time they'll improve and achieve more things.

(C) Dweck found that kids who are told they're "smart" actually underperform in future tasks, by choosing easier tasks to avoid evidence that they are not smart, which Dweck calls having a "fixed mindset."　　*persevere: 인내하다 **variable: 변수

① (A) — (C) — (B)　　② (B) — (A) — (C)
③ (B) — (C) — (A)　　④ (C) — (A) — (B)
⑤ (C) — (B) — (A)

38

Partly this was the obvious convenience of being able to exit more quickly.

To monitor our surroundings is to focus on what's outside of ourselves: what we see, hear, smell, feel, and perhaps even taste. But sometimes what really marks a place is something less specific — a *feeling* within us. (①) An interesting example emerged from a study of subway passenger behavior. (②) Researchers trying to understand why people sit where they sit or stand where they stand in subway and metro trains examined the factors that shape the way riders used and navigated that space in different situations. (③) One of their findings involved the reasons many riders like to plant themselves close to the train's doors. (④) But it was shaped partly by a more abstract sensation — the desire to avoid the sometimes uncomfortable feeling of accidentally making eye contact with seated passengers. (⑤) We can't see feelings — but they're very real, and they influence our experience of the world.

39

But if we sink just our face in a bowl of water, while the whole of the rest of our body is in the dry air, the diving reflex is triggered.

We have a 'diving reflex', like other marine mammals. (①) This means that special nerve endings on our faces, around the mouth and nose, trigger this reflex only when the facial region goes under water. (②) If we are in the water, with our head out in the air, there is no diving reflex. (③) It automatically closes down the airway, reducing the risk of swallowing water, and it narrows the small air-passages in the lungs. (④) At the same time the heart rate is slowed down to half speed and blood is shunted to the vital organs, protecting them from the effects of the brief stop in breathing. (⑤) By contrast, if a chimpanzee or a gorilla found itself in water with its face below the surface, it would panic, its heart would race and it would quickly drown. [3점]

*reflex: 반사 **trigger: 유발하다 ***shunt: 방향을 돌리다

There is a natural assumption of truth, or a truth bias when humans communicate with one another. In other words, when we're listening to others or reading their words, our automatic assumption is that the other person is telling the truth. This usually works out fine. If you ask someone where the restroom is located or if it's raining outside, you can safely assume that most people will not lie in their responses. Imagine how difficult it would be to converse with someone if you assumed that *everything* they were telling you was false! Indeed, questioning the truth of a statement and then choosing not to believe it requires additional mental steps. For the most part, humans are "cognitive misers," which means we typically don't expend more mental effort than seems necessary in a given situation. It makes sense then, that when we see something online, even if it is fake, our default is to believe it, at least at first.

*expend: 들이다 **default: 기본값

↓

> We humans are unlikely to ___(A)___ the truth of information we receive, due to our tendency to ___(B)___ mental effort.

	(A)		(B)
①	doubt	—	save
②	trust	—	maintain
③	judge	—	add
④	doubt	—	increase
⑤	trust	—	reduce

[41~42] 다음 글을 읽고, 물음에 답하시오.

Paying with plastic fundamentally changes the way we spend money, altering the calculus of our financial decisions. When you buy something with cash, the purchase involves an actual (a) loss — your wallet is literally lighter. Credit cards, however, make the purchase abstract, so that you don't really feel the downside of spending money. Brain-imaging experiments suggest that paying with credit cards actually (b) reduces activity in the insula, a brain region associated with negative feelings. As George Loewenstein, a neuroeconomist at Carnegie Mellon, says, "The nature of credit cards ensures that your brain is anesthetized against the pain of payment." Spending money doesn't feel (c) bad, so you spend more money.

Consider this experiment: Drazen Prelec and Duncan Simester, two business professors at MIT, organized a real-life, sealed-bid auction for tickets to a Boston Celtics game. Half the participants in the auction were informed that they had to pay with cash; the other half were told they had to pay with credit cards. Prelec and Simester then averaged the bids for the two different groups. It turns out that the average credit card bid was *twice* as (d) high as the average cash bid. When people used their credit cards, their bids were much more (e) careful. They no longer felt the need to limit their expenses.

*calculus: 계산법 **anesthetize: 마비시키다 ***bid: 입찰

41 윗글의 제목으로 가장 적절한 것은?

① Once Set, Spending Habits Seldom Change
② Why Do We Spend More with Credit Cards?
③ Credit Cards: A Safer Way to Pay than Cash
④ Paying with Plastic: The Secret to Saving Money
⑤ Using Cash Leads to Taking More Financial Risks

42 밑줄 친 (a) ~(e) 중에서 문맥상 낱말의 쓰임이 적절하지 <u>않은</u> 것은? [3점]

① (a) ② (b) ③ (c) ④ (d) ⑤ (e)

[43~45] 다음 글을 읽고, 물음에 답하시오.

(A)

The sun shone in the cloudless sky as Becky, a retired teacher, walked to the fruit market. Across town, Dana was riding a bus towards the museum for a job interview. Just before reaching her stop, Dana noticed the sky had suddenly darkened. Her heart sank — she had no umbrella. As (a) she stepped off the bus next to the market, where Becky had just finished shopping, raindrops began to fall.

(B)

Dana thanked her, took the umbrella, and opened it. She saw a small card tied to the handle. It read: "Cover each other." She was touched by the message. She hurried to the museum, arriving dry and comfortable, and performed well in her interview. The Museum CEO was impressed by Dana and offered (b) her the Event Manager position, her dream job. Throughout the years ahead, she often thought back to Becky's kind gesture.

(C)

Inspired by the memory, Dana created a museum event called "Cover Each Other" with paintings of people supporting others. She donated half of the money from ticket sales to families who lost their homes to natural disasters. Dana kept Becky's message framed in (c) her office as a reminder that one kind gesture could change someone's life. The kindness of one stranger had shaped her path, and she made sure it continued to shape the world.

(D)

Dana felt panic. She didn't want to show up to her interview soaked. She looked around but couldn't find any stores nearby to buy an umbrella, and she didn't have time to search around. Just then, Becky approached (d) her, holding an open umbrella in one hand and a closed one in the other. "Take this," (e) she said with a smile. Dana's eyes widened. "Are you sure?" Becky nodded. "I always carry an extra on rainy days."

*soaked: 흠뻑 젖은

43 주어진 글 (A)에 이어질 내용을 순서에 맞게 배열한 것으로 가장 적절한 것은?

① (B) — (D) — (C) ② (C) — (B) — (D)
③ (C) — (D) — (B) ④ (D) — (B) — (C)
⑤ (D) — (C) — (B)

44 밑줄 친 (a) ~ (e) 중에서 가리키는 대상이 나머지 넷과 다른 것은?

① (a) ② (b) ③ (c) ④ (d) ⑤ (e)

45 윗글에 관한 내용으로 적절하지 않은 것은?

① Becky는 과일 시장으로 걸어갔다.
② 작은 카드는 Dana가 받은 우산 손잡이에 매여 있었다.
③ Dana는 Becky의 친절한 행동을 종종 떠올렸다.
④ Dana는 티켓 판매금 전액을 기부했다.
⑤ Dana는 우산을 구매할 가게를 찾을 수 없었다.

2025.6
4회

• MP3 파일을 들으며 다음 빈칸을 채우시오. (듣기 어려운 발음이나 정답의 단서가 되는 부분에 빈칸을 만들었습니다.)

01 다음을 듣고, 여자가 하는 말의 목적으로 가장 적절한 것을 고르시오.

W : Good morning, everyone. I'm your student council president, Kelly Green. Many students have _____ _____ there are no printers available for them to use. ___ _____ _____ _____, next week we will set up several new printers in the student council room. Students _____ ___ _____ ___ ____ the printers for homework, projects, or any other school tasks. We hope this will help you do your work more ⭐_____ and make your school life easier. Thank you.

02 대화를 듣고, 남자의 의견으로 가장 적절한 것을 고르시오.

M : Anna, I see you're studying Spanish.

W : Hi, Mr. Brown. Yeah, _____ _____ really into it these days.

M : I've noticed. Do you feel like you're improving a lot?

W : Hmm... Well, remembering words is really hard. I forget them quickly.

M : I see. How about _____ _____ _____ ____ _____? It can be an effective way to remember them.

W : Does it really help? I feel more comfortable just ⭐_____ _____.

M : When you speak out loud, you use different parts of your brain, and that helps you remember words better.

W : But I always thought saying words out loud would make it harder to focus.

M : Not at all. Studies show that it can help you stay more focused on the task.

W : Really? Then, maybe I should _____ ___ ___ _____.

03 다음을 듣고, 남자가 하는 말의 요지로 가장 적절한 것을 고르시오.

M : Hello, listeners! This is Thomas White's *Living Well*. What do you do to stay healthy? Maybe you exercise regularly and eat healthy food. Those are both great habits. But I have one more simple tip for you. Go outside and ____ _____ _____! Sunlight is important for your body and mind. Getting sunlight can prevent you from getting sick and _____ _____ ⭐_____. It's an easy way to help you stay healthy _____ ⭐_____ _____ _____. I'll be right back with more after the break.

04 대화를 듣고, 그림에서 대화의 내용과 일치하지 않는 것을 고르시오.

M : Jenny, how was the pajama party yesterday?

W : It was great, Dad. Here, _____ ___ _____ at this photo.

M : Let's see. Oh, I like the pajama party banner next to the clock.

W : Yeah, it's really eye-catching, isn't it?

M : It is. And here you are standing in your striped pajamas.

W : I ⭐_____ love these pajamas. They look so cute.

M : And the girl making a V-sign with her fingers is your friend Mia, right?

W : That's right. Do you see the pillows on the bed? We had a pillow fight!

M : It _____ _____ so much fun. By the way, what are those three stars on the wall?

W : Oh, those are stickers. They _____ _____ _____.

M : I see. Sounds like you had an amazing time at the pajama party.

W : Definitely! I'll never forget it.

05 대화를 듣고, 남자가 할 일로 가장 적절한 것을 고르시오.

W: Brian, I think we're almost ready for our candy shop's opening event.

M: That's right. What do we have left to do?

W: Well, let's see. Is the background music playlist ready?

M: Yes, I chose some cheerful songs and _____ __ _____.

W: Great! What about the bluetooth speakers?

M: I tested them and they're working fine. _____ _____ _____ the sample candies for ✪_____ __ ____?

W: Yeah. Look! I put them in these pretty little baskets.

M: Thanks! They look nice.

W: And all the other candies are nicely placed around the shop.

M: Wait, how about the price tags?

W: Oh, we almost forgot. _____ ____ ____ _____ __ the candy boxes?

M: Of course. I'll do it right away.

06 대화를 듣고, 여자가 지불할 금액을 고르시오.

M: Welcome to Lake Boat Tours. How can I help you?

W: Hello. I'd like to buy some tickets for today.

M: We have daytime tickets and sunset tickets. Which would you like?

W: We'd like sunset tickets, please. How much are they?

M: It's $30 for adults and $20 for children. _____ _____ _____ do you want?

W: Two adult tickets and one child ticket, please.

M: Okay. And, we _____ _____ for $10 per person. Would you like them?

W: Yes. Snacks for all three of us, please.

M: Alright. Do you _____ _____ ____?

W: No, that's it.

M: So, that's two adults and one child for the sunset tour, all with snacks.

W: Perfect. Here's my credit card.

07 대화를 듣고, 여자가 버스킹 공연에 참여할 수 없는 이유를 고르시오.

M: Hey, Alicia. I saw a video of you playing the guitar ____ _____ _____ _____. It was great.

W: Thanks, Oliver. Your singing videos are fantastic, too.

M: I have an idea. There's a busking event this Sunday. How about performing together?

W: This Sunday? I'd really love to, but I can't.

M: Why not? Do you feel nervous about ✪_____ ___ _____?

W: Not really, but I already have another plan on Sunday.

M: Oh, do you still take tennis lessons every Sunday?

W: Not anymore. Do you remember I _____ ___ _____ for a part-time job?

M: Of course. ____ ____ ____ ___?

W: Yes, so I have to start working the part-time job this Sunday.

M: I see. Maybe we can try for another time.

2025.6

4회

08 대화를 듣고, Fireworks Festival 자원봉사에 관해 언급되지 <u>않은</u> 것을 고르시오.

W: Jay, did you hear about the Fireworks Festival?

M: Yeah, I heard _____ _____ _____ _____ _____.

W: I'm thinking of volunteering there. Take a look at this poster about it.

M: The volunteer period is for two days, June 14th and 15th.

W: That's right. Would you like to join?

M: _____ _____ _____. But can just anyone _____ _____ _____ _____ _____?

W: Only people over 18 can apply. So, we're both good.

M: I see. What exactly will we do during the festival?

W: It says we'll check tickets, run activity booths, or take photos for the festival website.

M: Sounds interesting. And look! We have to ✪_____ _____ _____ _____ _____.

W: Really? We don't have much time. Let's do it right now.

09 2025 Talent Show에 관한 다음 내용을 듣고, 일치하지 <u>않는</u> 것을 고르시오.

W: Hello, everyone! This is Ms. Westwood, your vice principal. I'm excited to announce the 2025 Talent Show! It'll take place in our school auditorium on June 20th at 6 p.m. All students are welcome to participate and ✪_____ their unique talent, whether it's singing, dancing, or acting. Three wonderful teachers will be the judges, and there will be _____ _____ _____ _____ _____. Every participant will receive a free T-shirt with _____ _____ _____ _____ _____. At the end of the show, we'll have a short dance party. For more details, please check out our school website. Thank you.

10 다음 표를 보면서 대화를 듣고, 두 사람이 구매할 책가방을 고르시오.

W: Honey, we need to buy Robert a backpack for school.

M: Right, _____ _____ _____ one online.

W: [Clicking Sound] Wow, there are so many options. What should we consider first?

M: Well, let's _____ _____ ✪_____.

W: We already spent a lot on his other school supplies. I'd like to _____ _____ _____ $70.

M: All right. What shape should we get him, a square one?

W: Yeah, it's better for carrying school supplies. Then, what about the color?

M: White ones get dirty easily, so we should go with a black one.

W: Sounds good. And does it _____ _____ _____ ✪_____?

M: Definitely. It'll be useful on rainy days.

W: Then, this is the one. Let's buy it.

11 대화를 듣고, 남자의 마지막 말에 대한 여자의 응답으로 가장 적절한 것을 고르시오.

M: Ms. Adams, I'm not feeling well. I _____ _____ _____ ✪_____.

W: Oh, sorry to hear that, Jack. Have you _____ _____ _____?

M: Yes, I took some _____ _____ _____, but I don't think I can stay in class.

W: _____

12 대화를 듣고, 여자의 마지막 말에 대한 남자의 응답으로 가장 적절한 것을 고르시오.

W: Welcome to Emily's Cake Shop. How can I help you today?

M: I'd like to order a cake. _____ _____ my first wedding anniversary.

W: Congratulations on your anniversary! Do you have a _____ _____ _____ _____?

M: _____

13 대화를 듣고, 여자의 마지막 말에 대한 남자의 응답으로 가장 적절한 것을 고르시오.

W: Dad, look at the cat over there!

M: Oh, it's so cute.

W: I've wanted a cat for a long time. Can we get one?

M: You know, raising a cat isn't easy, Rebecca.

W: I understand. But I promise I'd love it _____ _____ ___ _____.

M: It's not just about love. It's about _____ _____ ✿ _____.

W: Trust me, Dad. I know I can handle it.

M: Hmm... Then, how about practicing first? Uncle Tony is looking for someone to take care of his cat during his business trip.

W: That sounds great! If I do a good job with his cat, will you let me get my own cat?

M: I'll definitely think about it if you _____ _____ _____ ___ _____ ____.

W: Thanks, Dad. Please tell Uncle Tony that I want to do it.

M: _____

14 대화를 듣고, 남자의 마지막 말에 대한 여자의 응답으로 가장 적절한 것을 고르시오.

M: Grandma, look what I found in the garage. It's an old cookbook.

W: Oh, I _____ _____ _____ for years.

M: It says here, "Recipes for Fine Dishes."

W: That's the cookbook I wrote when I was a chef before you were born.

M: Really? You were a professional chef?

W: Yeah, I _____ ___ _____ ___ a restaurant. Look! These were my special dishes.

M: Wow, they look fantastic! Did you create all the recipes in the book?

W: Yes. I really loved cooking and was _____ ___ ___ back then.

M: You're still good at cooking!

W: Do you really think so?

M: Of course! I've always thought your food _____ _____.

W: _____

15 다음 상황 설명을 듣고, Chloe가 호텔 직원에게 할 말로 가장 적절한 것을 고르시오.

W: Chloe is _____ _____ ✿ _____ _____ and staying at a hotel in Cairo, Egypt. After some ✿ _____, she goes back to her hotel room. It's hot outside, so she decides to turn on the air conditioner, but it doesn't work. She calls the hotel clerk to _____ ____ _____. He explains that it can be fixed tomorrow. It's _____ _____ ____ _____ without the air conditioning, and Chloe wants to know if she can stay in another room. In this situation, what would Chloe most likely say to the hotel clerk?

Chloe: _____

[16~17] 다음을 듣고, 물음에 답하시오.

M: Hello, class! Last time, we learned about the national flags of various countries. Today, we'll talk about different countries' national flowers and what they ✿ _____. First, the Philippines' national flower is jasmine. Because it means good luck, people often give big necklaces made of this flower _____ _____ _____ _____. Next, Denmark's flower is the daisy and it represents happiness. Children express happiness by making daisy chains during their traditional games. In France, the national flower is the iris. ✿ _____ _____, French people have thought of this flower as a symbol of perfection. Lastly, the United States uses the rose as its national flower. Americans _____ ____ a symbol of love. So you can find many roses in American weddings. Now, let's watch a short video to look at these flowers up close.

• 제한시간 20분 • 맞은 개수 ___ / 40

✻ 다음 영어는 우리말 뜻을, 우리말은 영어 단어를 〈보기〉에서 찾아 쓰시오.

01 pioneer _____

02 sacrifice _____

03 overseas _____

04 inspection _____

05 waterproof _____

06 ~을 통틀어 _____

07 상징하다 _____

08 저지르다 _____

09 연례의, 매년의 _____

10 어울리다, 교류하다 _____

[보기]

점검	symbolize
사건	throughout
해외의	complain
방수의	socialize
선구자	annual
희생하다	commit

✻ 다음 우리말에 알맞은 영어 표현을 찾아 연결하시오.

11 해체되다 •   • make use of

12 일리가 있다 •   • make sense

13 ~을 사용하다 •   • be dependent on

14 ~에 의존하다 •   • stay in touch

15 연락을 유지하다 •   • fall apart

✻ 다음 우리말과 같은 표현이 되도록 알맞은 단어를 〈보기〉에서 찾아 쓰시오.

[보기]

analysis / approximately / endangered / accidentally / contexts / intentions
bias / wander / obvious / abstract / nerve / distort

16 진실 편향 ➡ a truth _____

17 명확한 편리함 ➡ the _____ convenience

18 약 12개월의 생애 ➡ the course of _____ twelve-month life

19 구매를 추상화시키다 ➡ make the purchase _____

20 그들의 의도를 숨기는 것 ➡ hiding their _____

21 우연히 눈이 마주치는 것 ➡ _____ making eye contact

22 다양한 맥락에 걸친 적용 ➡ application across multiple _____

23 우리의 분석에 있어서 정확한 ➡ accurate in our _____

24 우리의 얼굴에 있는 특수 신경 말단 ➡ special _____ endings on our faces

25 가치에 대한 그들의 인식을 왜곡하다 ➡ _____ their perception of value

26 신용카드의 본질 ➜ the (mature / **nature**) of credit cards

27 그들의 초기 가격 ➜ their (**initial** / impartial) prices

28 잘못된 믿음을 형성하다 ➜ (destruct / **construct**) a faulty belief

29 생각을 없애다 ➜ (**eliminate** / illuminate) the idea

30 무엇을 의미하는지에 대한 통찰 ➜ (**insight** / foresight) into what it means

* 다음 문장의 빈칸에 알맞은 단어를 〈보기〉에서 찾아 쓰시오.

———— [보기] ————

rational / addressing / downside / exceptionally / emphasizing / transferred
criticize / typically / showcase / fundamentally / sufficient / collapse

31 Wilson은 Harvard 대학으로 옮겼다.
➜ Wilson _____ to Harvard University.

32 문명은 서기 476년에 멸망한 로마의 경우처럼 붕괴한다.
➜ Civilizations _____ as in the cases of Rome, which went under in 476 AD.

33 우리는 우리가 논리적이고 객관적이며 합리적이라고 생각한다.
➜ We think we're being logical, objective, and _____.

34 당신은 실제로 돈을 소비하는 것의 부정적인 면을 느끼지 못한다.
➜ You don't really feel the _____ of spending money.

35 그들은 단순히 생각을 잘하는 사람이거나 유난히 똑똑한 사람이 아니다.
➜ They are not just good thinkers or people who are _____ smart.

36 각 나라의 팬들은 모든 반칙을 놓친 것에 대해 심판들을 비난한다.
➜ The fans of each country _____ the referees for missing all the infractions.

37 모든 학생이 참가해서 그들의 독특한 재능을 마음껏 뽐낼 수 있습니다.
➜ All students are welcome to participate and _____ their unique talent.

38 노력을 강조하는 것은 아이에게 그들이 통제할 수 있는 변수를 제공한다.
➜ _____ effort gives a child a variable that they can control.

39 당신의 우선순위는 가능한 한 빨리 충분한 시장 점유를 확보하는 것이어야 한다.
➜ Your priority should be to get _____ market adoption as soon as possible.

40 우리는 필요한 것처럼 보이는 것보다 더 많은 정신적인 노력을 전형적으로 기울이지 않는다.
➜ We _____ don't expend more mental effort than seems necessary.

전국연합학력평가 [2024년 6월 4일 시행]

★ 3점 문항에만 점수가 표시되어 있습니다.

• 문항 수 : 45개 • 배점 : 100점 • 제한 시간 : 70분

 단어장

전체 *or* 문항별 듣기

▲ 듣기 파일

*1번부터 17번까지는 듣고 답하는 문제입니다. 1번부터 15번까지는 한 번만 들려주고, 16번부터 17번까지는 두 번 들려줍니다. 방송을 잘 듣고 답을 하시기 바랍니다.

01 다음을 듣고, 여자가 하는 말의 목적으로 가장 적절한 것을 고르시오.

① 친환경 제품 사용을 홍보하려고
② 음식 대접에 대한 감사를 표하려고
③ 간식이 마련되어 있음을 안내하려고
④ 휴식 시간이 변경되었음을 공지하려고
⑤ 구내식당 메뉴에 관한 의견을 구하려고

02 대화를 듣고, 남자의 의견으로 가장 적절한 것을 고르시오.

① 인공 지능에서 얻은 정보를 맹목적으로 믿어서는 안 된다.
② 출처를 밝히지 않고 타인의 표현을 인용해서는 안 된다.
③ 인공 지능의 도움을 통해 과제물의 질을 높일 수 있다.
④ 과제를 할 때 본인의 생각이 들어가는 것이 중요하다.
⑤ 기술의 변화에 맞추어 작업 방식을 바꿀 필요가 있다.

03 다음을 듣고, 여자가 하는 말의 요지로 가장 적절한 것을 고르시오.

① 소셜 미디어는 원만한 대인관계 유지에 도움이 된다.
② 온라인에서는 자아가 다양한 모습으로 표출될 수 있다.
③ 소셜 미디어는 자존감에 부정적인 영향을 줄 수 있다.
④ 친밀한 관계일수록 상대의 언행에 쉽게 영향을 받는다.
⑤ 유명인 사생활 보호의 중요성은 종종 간과된다.

04 대화를 듣고, 그림에서 대화의 내용과 일치하지 <u>않는</u> 것을 고르시오.

05 대화를 듣고, 남자가 할 일로 가장 적절한 것을 고르시오.

① 과학 캠프 지원하기
② 참가 실험 결정하기
③ 체크리스트 작성하기
④ 실험 계획서 보여주기
⑤ 자기 소개 영상 촬영하기

06 대화를 듣고, 여자가 지불할 금액을 고르시오. [3점]

① $50   ② $55   ③ $60   ④ $65   ⑤ $70

07 대화를 듣고, 남자가 마술쇼에 갈 수 <u>없는</u> 이유를 고르시오.

① 록 콘서트에 가야 해서
② 다른 학교 축제에 가야 해서
③ 가족 중 아픈 사람이 있어서
④ 동아리 축제를 준비해야 해서
⑤ 삼촌 생일 파티에 참석해야 해서

08 대화를 듣고, Victory Marathon에 관해 언급되지 <u>않은</u> 것을 고르시오.

① 행사 날짜   ② 신청 방법   ③ 출발 지점
④ 참가비   ⑤ 예상 참가 인원

09 Violet Hill Mentorship에 관한 다음 내용을 듣고, 일치하지 <u>않는</u> 것을 고르시오.

① 다음 주 금요일에 개최될 예정이다.
② 대학 생활에 관한 조언이 제공된다.
③ 신청 시 질문을 미리 제출해야 한다.
④ 신청 마감일은 다음 주 화요일이다.
⑤ 전공별 참가 가능한 인원은 20명이다.

10 다음 표를 보면서 대화를 듣고, 두 사람이 구입할 무선 진공 청소기를 고르시오.

Cordless Vacuum Cleaner

	Model	Battery Life	Price	Wet Cleaning	Color
①	A	1 hour	$300	×	Red
②	B	2 hours	$330	×	White
③	C	2 hours	$370	○	Red
④	D	3 hours	$390	○	White
⑤	E	3 hours	$410	○	Black

11 대화를 듣고, 남자의 마지막 말에 대한 여자의 응답으로 가장 적절한 것을 고르시오.

① Fine. Let's talk about it over dinner.
② Okay. Be more responsible next time.
③ Great. I already ordered some pet food.
④ Too bad. I hope your cat gets well soon.
⑤ Sorry. I can't take care of your cat tonight.

12 대화를 듣고, 여자의 마지막 말에 대한 남자의 응답으로 가장 적절한 것을 고르시오.

① I can't accept late assignments.
② You did an excellent job this time.
③ Upload your work to our school website.
④ Try to do your homework by yourself.
⑤ We can finish it before the next class.

13 대화를 듣고, 남자의 마지막 말에 대한 여자의 응답으로 가장 적절한 것을 고르시오. [3점]

Woman: _____
① Yes. I can give you the phone number of the clinic I visited.
② I agree. Last evening's badminton match was awesome.
③ No problem. I'll teach you how to serve this time.
④ Too bad. I hope you recover from your knee injury soon.
⑤ You're right. Maybe I should start taking badminton lessons.

14 대화를 듣고, 여자의 마지막 말에 대한 남자의 응답으로 가장 적절한 것을 고르시오. [3점]

Man: _____
① Sure. It seems like a perfect place for bears.
② Great. Let's think about the club name first.
③ My pleasure. I can always give you a ride.
④ I agree. It's hard to give up using plastics.
⑤ No worries. I'll get my bike repaired.

15 다음 상황 설명을 듣고, Laura가 Tony에게 할 말로 가장 적절한 것을 고르시오.

Laura: _____
① I don't like visiting a hospital for medical checkups.
② I appreciate you taking me to the doctor today.
③ You'd better take a break for a few days.
④ You should finish your work before the deadline.
⑤ I'm afraid I can't reduce your workload right now.

[16~17] 다음을 듣고, 물음에 답하시오.

16 남자가 하는 말의 주제로 가장 적절한 것은?

① relationships between media and voters
② common ways of promoting school policy
③ guidelines for student election campaigns
④ requirements for becoming a candidate
⑤ useful tips for winning school debates

17 언급된 매체가 아닌 것은?

① social media   ② poster
③ pamphlet   ④ school newspaper
⑤ school website

＊이제 듣기 문제가 끝났습니다. 18번부터는 문제지의 지시에 따라 답을 하시기 바랍니다.

18 다음 글의 목적으로 가장 적절한 것은?

Dear Reader,

We always appreciate your support. As you know, our service is now available through an app. There has never been a better time to switch to an online membership of *TourTide Magazine*. At a 50% discount off your current print subscription, you can access a full year of online reading. Get new issues and daily web pieces at TourTide.com, read or listen to *TourTide Magazine* via the app, and get our members-only newsletter. You'll also gain access to our editors' selections of the best articles. Join today!

Yours,

TourTide Team

① 여행 일정 지연에 대해 사과하려고
② 잡지 온라인 구독을 권유하려고
③ 무료 잡지 신청을 홍보하려고
④ 여행 후기 모집을 안내하려고
⑤ 기사에 대한 독자 의견에 답변하려고

19 다음 글에 드러난 'I'의 심경 변화로 가장 적절한 것은?

As I walked from the mailbox, my heart was beating rapidly. In my hands, I held the letter from the university I had applied to. I thought my grades were good enough to cross the line and my application letter was well-written, but was it enough? I hadn't slept a wink for days. As I carefully tore into the paper of the envelope, the letter slowly emerged with the opening phrase, "It is our great pleasure..." I shouted with joy, "I am in!" As I held the letter, I began to make a fantasy about my college life in a faraway city.

① relaxed → upset
② anxious → delighted
③ guilty → confident
④ angry → grateful
⑤ hopeful → disappointed

20 다음 글에서 필자가 주장하는 바로 가장 적절한 것은?

Having a messy room can add up to negative feelings and destructive thinking. Psychologists say that having a disorderly room can indicate a disorganized mental state. One of the professional tidying experts says that the moment you start cleaning your room, you also start changing your life and gaining new perspective. When you clean your surroundings, positive and good atmosphere follows. You can do more things efficiently and neatly. So, clean up your closets, organize your drawers, and arrange your things first, then peace of mind will follow.

① 자신의 공간을 정돈하여 긍정적 변화를 도모하라.
② 오랜 시간 고민하기보다는 일단 행동으로 옮겨라.
③ 무질서한 환경에서 창의적인 생각을 시도하라.
④ 장기 목표를 위해 단기 목표를 먼저 설정하라.
⑤ 반복되는 일상을 새로운 관점으로 관찰하라.

21 밑줄 친 luxury real estate가 다음 글에서 의미하는 바로 가장 적절한 것은? [3점]

The soil of a farm field is forced to be the perfect environment for monoculture growth. This is achieved by adding nutrients in the form of fertilizer and water by way of irrigation. During the last fifty years, engineers and crop scientists have helped farmers become much more efficient at supplying exactly the right amount of both. World usage of fertilizer has tripled since 1969, and the global capacity for irrigation has almost doubled; we are feeding and watering our fields more than ever, and our crops are loving it. Unfortunately, these luxurious conditions have also excited the attention of certain agricultural undesirables. Because farm fields are loaded with nutrients and water relative to the natural land that surrounds them, they are desired as luxury real estate by every random weed in the area.

*monoculture: 단일 작물 재배 **irrigation: (논,밭에)물을 댐; 관개

① a farm where a scientist's aid is highly required
② a field abundant with necessities for plants
③ a district accessible only for the rich
④ a place that is conserved for ecology
⑤ a region with higher economic value

22 다음 글의 요지로 가장 적절한 것은?

When it comes to helping out, you don't have to do much. All you have to do is come around and show that you care. If you notice someone who is lonely, you could go and sit with them. If you work with someone who eats lunch all by themselves, and you go and sit down with them, they will begin to be more social after a while, and they will owe it all to you. A person's happiness comes from attention. There are too many people out in the world who feel like everyone has forgotten them or ignored them. Even if you say hi to someone passing by, they will begin to feel better about themselves, like someone cares.

① 사소한 관심이 타인에게 도움이 될 수 있다.
② 사람마다 행복의 기준이 제각기 다르다.
③ 선행을 통해 자신을 되돌아볼 수 있다.
④ 원만한 대인 관계는 경청에서 비롯된다.
⑤ 현재에 대한 만족이 행복의 필수조건이다.

23 다음 글의 주제로 가장 적절한 것은?

We often try to make cuts in our challenges and take the easy route. When taking the quick exit, we fail to acquire the strength to compete. We often take the easy route to improve our skills. Many of us never really work to achieve mastery in the key areas of life. These skills are key tools that can be useful to our career, health, and prosperity. Highly successful athletes don't win because of better equipment; they win by facing hardship to gain strength and skill. They win through preparation. It's the mental preparation, winning mindset, strategy, and skill that set them apart. Strength comes from struggle, not from taking the path of least resistance. Hardship is not just a lesson for the next time in front of us. Hardship will be the greatest teacher we will ever have in life.

① characteristics of well-equipped athletes
② difficulties in overcoming life's sudden challenges
③ relationship between personal habit and competence
④ risks of enduring hardship without any preparation
⑤ importance of confronting hardship in one's life

24 다음 글의 제목으로 가장 적절한 것은?

Your behaviors are usually a reflection of your identity. What you do is an indication of the type of person you believe that you are — either consciously or nonconsciously. Research has shown that once a person believes in a particular aspect of their identity, they are more likely to act according to that belief. For example, people who identified as "being a voter" were more likely to vote than those who simply claimed "voting" was an action they wanted to perform. Similarly, the person who accepts exercise as the part of their identity doesn't have to convince themselves to train. Doing the right thing is easy. After all, when your behavior and your identity perfectly match, you are no longer pursuing behavior change. You are simply acting like the type of person you already believe yourself to be.

① Action Comes from Who You Think You Are
② The Best Practices for Gaining More Voters
③ Stop Pursuing Undesirable Behavior Change!
④ What to Do When Your Exercise Bores You
⑤ Your Actions Speak Louder than Your Words

25 다음 도표의 내용과 일치하지 않는 것은?

Electronic Waste Collection and Recycling Rate
by Region in 2016 and 2019

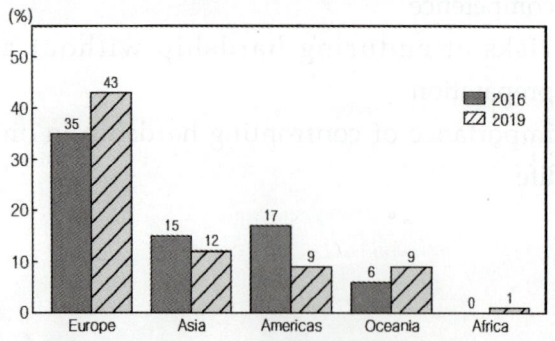

The above graph shows the electronic waste collection and recycling rate by region in 2016 and 2019. ① In both years, Europe showed the highest electronic waste collection and recycling rates. ② The electronic waste collection and recycling rate of Asia in 2019 was lower than in 2016. ③ The Americas ranked third both in 2016 and in 2019, with 17 percent and 9 percent respectively. ④ In both years, the electronic waste collection and recycling rates in Oceania remained under 10 percent. ⑤ Africa had the lowest electronic waste collection and recycling rates in both 2016 and 2019, showing the smallest gap between 2016 and 2019.

26 Fritz Zwicky에 관한 다음 글의 내용과 일치하지 않는 것은?

Fritz Zwicky, a memorable astrophysicist who coined the term 'supernova', was born in Varna, Bulgaria to a Swiss father and a Czech mother. At the age of six, he was sent to his grandparents who looked after him for most of his childhood in Switzerland. There, he received an advanced education in mathematics and physics. In 1925, he emigrated to the United States and continued his physics research at California Institute of Technology (Caltech). He developed numerous theories that have had a profound influence on the understanding of our universe in the early 21st century. After being appointed as a professor of astronomy at Caltech in 1942, he developed some of the earliest jet engines and holds more than 50 patents, many in jet propulsion.

*patent: 특허(권) **propulsion: 추진(력)

① 불가리아의 Varna에서 태어났다.
② 스위스에서 수학과 물리학 교육을 받았다.
③ 미국으로 이주하여 연구를 이어갔다.
④ 우주 이해에 영향을 미친 수많은 이론을 발전시켰다.
⑤ 초창기 제트 엔진을 개발한 후 교수로 임용되었다.

27 Gourmet Baking Competition에 관한 다음 안내문의 내용과 일치하지 <u>않는</u> 것은?

Gourmet Baking Competition

Get out your cookbooks and dust off your greatest baking recipes.

When & Where
• 5 p.m. - 7 p.m. Saturday, August 3rd
• Gourmet Baking Studio

Registration
• Register online at www.bakeoff.org by July 25th.
• Anyone can participate in the competition.

Categories
• Pies, Cakes, and Cookies
• Each person can only enter one category.

Prizes & Gifts
• Prizes will be given to the top three in each category.
• Souvenirs will be given to every participant.

① 8월 3일 토요일에 개최된다.
② 온라인으로 참가 신청이 가능하다.
③ 누구나 참가할 수 있다.
④ 참가자 한 명이 여러 부문에 참여할 수 있다.
⑤ 모든 참가자에게 기념품이 제공될 것이다.

28 Winter Sports Program에 관한 다음 안내문의 내용과 일치하는 것은?

Winter Sports Program

Winter is coming! Let's have some fun together!

Time & Location
• Every Sunday in December from 1 p.m. to 3 p.m.
• Grand Blue Ice Rink

Lesson Details
• Ice Hockey, Speed Skating, and Figure Skating
• Participants must be 8 years of age or older.

Fee
• Ice Hockey: $200
• Speed Skating / Figure Skating: $150

Notice
• Skates and helmets will be provided for free.
• You should bring your own gloves.
※ For more information, visit www.wintersports.com.

① 오후 2시에서 4시 사이에 실시된다.
② 네 종목의 강좌가 개설된다.
③ 참가 연령에 제한은 없다.
④ 모든 종목 강좌의 수강료는 같다.
⑤ 장갑은 각자 가져와야 한다.

29 다음 글의 밑줄 친 부분 중, 어법상 틀린 것은?
[3점]

The hunter-gatherer lifestyle, which can ① <u>be described</u> as "natural" to human beings, appears to have had much to recommend it. Examination of human remains from early hunter-gatherer societies ② <u>has</u> suggested that our ancestors enjoyed abundant food, obtainable without excessive effort, and suffered very few diseases. If this is true, it is not clear why so many humans settled in permanent villages and developed agriculture, growing crops and domesticating animals: cultivating fields was hard work, and it was in farming villages ③ <u>what</u> epidemic diseases first took root. Whatever its immediate effect on the lives of humans, the development of settlements and agriculture ④ <u>undoubtedly</u> led to a high increase in population density. This period, known as the New Stone Age, was a major turning point in human development, ⑤ <u>opening</u> the way to the growth of the first towns and cities, and eventually leading to settled "civilizations."

*remains: 유적, 유해 **epidemic: 전염병의

30 다음 글의 밑줄 친 부분 중, 문맥상 낱말의 쓰임이 적절하지 않은 것은? [3점]

Many human and non-human animals save commodities or money for future consumption. This behavior seems to reveal a preference of a ① delayed reward over an immediate one: the agent gives up some immediate pleasure in exchange for a future one. Thus the discounted value of the future reward should be ② greater than the un-discounted value of the present one. However, in some cases the agent does not wait for the envisioned occasion but uses their savings ③ prematurely. For example, early in the year an employee might set aside money to buy Christmas presents but then spend it on a summer vacation instead. Such cases could be examples of ④ weakness of will. That is, the agents may judge or resolve to spend their savings in a certain way for the greatest benefit but then act differently when temptation for immediate pleasure ⑤ disappears.

*envision: 계획하다

[31~34] 다음 빈칸에 들어갈 말로 가장 적절한 것을 고르시오.

31

The costs of _____ are well-documented. Martin Luther King Jr. lamented them when he described "that lovely poem that didn't get written because someone knocked on the door." Perhaps the most famous literary example happened in 1797 when Samuel Taylor Coleridge started writing his poem *Kubla Khan* from a dream he had but then was visited by an unexpected guest. For Coleridge, by coincidence, the untimely visitor came at a particularly bad time. He forgot his inspiration and left the work unfinished. While there are many documented cases of sudden disruptions that have had significant consequences for professionals in critical roles such as doctors, nurses, control room operators, stock traders, and pilots, they also impact most of us in our everyday lives, slowing down work productivity and generally increasing stress levels.

*lament: 슬퍼하다

① misunderstandings　② interruptions
③ inequalities　④ regulations
⑤ arguments

32

There's a lot of scientific evidence demonstrating that focused attention leads to _____. In animals rewarded for noticing sound (to hunt or to avoid being hunted for example), we find much larger auditory centers in the brain. In animals rewarded for sharp eyesight, the visual areas are larger. Brain scans of violinists provide more evidence, showing dramatic growth and expansion in regions of the cortex that represent the left hand, which has to finger the strings precisely, often at very high speed. Other studies have shown that the hippocampus, which is vital for spatial memory, is enlarged in taxi drivers. The point is that the physical architecture of the brain changes according to where we direct our attention and what we practice doing.

*cortex: (대뇌) 피질(皮質) **hippocampus: (대뇌 측두엽의) 해마

① improved decision making
② the reshaping of the brain
③ long-term mental tiredness
④ the development of hand skills
⑤ increased levels of self-control

33

How did the human mind evolve? One possibility is that _____ caused our brains to evolve the way they did. A human tribe that could out-think its enemies, even slightly, possessed a vital advantage. The ability of your tribe to imagine and predict where and when a hostile enemy tribe might strike, and plan accordingly, gives your tribe a significant military advantage. The human mind became a weapon in the struggle for survival, a weapon far more decisive than any before it. And this mental advantage was applied, over and over, within each succeeding generation. The tribe that could out-think its opponents was more likely to succeed in battle and would then pass on the genes responsible for this mental advantage to its offspring. You and I are the descendants of the winners. [3점]

① physical power to easily hunt prey
② individual responsibility in one's inner circle
③ instinctive tendency to avoid natural disasters
④ superiority in the number of one's descendants
⑤ competition and conflicts with other human tribes

34

To find the hidden potential in teams, instead of brainstorming, we're better off shifting to a process called brainwriting. The initial steps are solo. You start by asking everyone to generate ideas separately. Next, you pool them and share them anonymously among the group. To preserve independent judgment, each member evaluates them on their own. Only then does the team come together to select and refine the most promising options. By _____ before choosing and elaborating them, teams can surface and advance possibilities that might not get attention otherwise. This brainwriting process makes sure that all ideas are brought to the table and all voices are brought into the conversation. It is especially effective in groups that struggle to achieve collective intelligence. [3점]

*anonymously: 익명으로 **surface: 드러내다

① developing and assessing ideas individually
② presenting and discussing ideas out loud
③ assigning different roles to each member
④ coming to an agreement on these options
⑤ skipping the step of judging these options

35 다음 글에서 전체 흐름과 관계 없는 문장은?

Simply giving employees a sense of agency — a feeling that they are in control, that they have genuine decision-making authority — can radically increase how much energy and focus they bring to their jobs. ① One 2010 study at a manufacturing plant in Ohio, for instance, carefully examined assembly-line workers who were empowered to make small decisions about their schedules and work environment. ② They designed their own uniforms and had authority over shifts while all the manufacturing processes and pay scales stayed the same. ③ It led to decreased efficiency because their decisions were not uniform or focused on meeting organizational goals. ④ Within two months, productivity at the plant increased by 20 percent, with workers taking shorter breaks and making fewer mistakes. ⑤ Giving employees a sense of control improved how much self-discipline they brought to their jobs.

*radically: 급격하게 **shift: (근무) 교대

36

As businesses shift some core business activities to digital, such as sales, marketing, or archiving, it is assumed that the impact on the environment will be less negative.

(A) When we store bigger data on clouds, increased carbon emissions make our green clouds gray. The carbon footprint of an email is smaller than mail sent via a post office, but still, it causes four grams of CO_2, and it can be as much as 50 grams if the attachment is big.

(B) However, digital business activities can still threaten the environment. In some cases, the harm of digital businesses can be even more hazardous. A few decades ago, offices used to have much more paper waste since all documents were paper based.

(C) When workplaces shifted from paper to digital documents, invoices, and emails, it was a promising step to save trees. However, the cost of the Internet and electricity for the environment is neglected. A recent *Wired* report declared that most data centers' energy source is fossil fuels. [3점]

① (A) — (C) — (B) ② (B) — (A) — (C)
③ (B) — (C) — (A) ④ (C) — (A) — (B)
⑤ (C) — (B) — (A)

37

Problems often arise if an exotic species is suddenly introduced to an ecosystem.

(A) The grey had the edge because it can adapt its diet; it is able, for instance, to eat green acorns, while the red can only digest mature acorns. Within the same area of forest, grey squirrels can destroy the food supply before red squirrels even have a bite.

(B) Britain's red and grey squirrels provide a clear example. When the grey arrived from America in the 1870s, both squirrel species competed for the same food and habitat, which put the native red squirrel populations under pressure.

(C) Greys can also live more densely and in varied habitats, so have survived more easily when woodland has been destroyed. As a result, the red squirrel has come close to extinction in England. *edge: 우위 **acorn: 도토리

① (A) — (C) — (B) ② (B) — (A) — (C)
③ (B) — (C) — (A) ④ (C) — (A) — (B)
⑤ (C) — (B) — (A)

38

> Farmers, on the other hand, could live in the same place year after year and did not have to worry about transporting young children long distances.

Growing crops forced people to stay in one place. Hunter-gatherers typically moved around frequently, and they had to be able to carry all their possessions with them every time they moved. (①) In particular, mothers had to carry their young children. (②) As a result, hunter-gatherer mothers could have only one baby every four years or so, spacing their births so that they never had to carry more than one child at a time. (③) Societies that settled down in one place were able to shorten their birth intervals from four years to about two. (④) This meant that each woman could have more children than her hunter-gatherer counterpart, which in turn resulted in rapid population growth among farming communities. (⑤) An increased population was actually an advantage to agricultural societies, because farming required large amounts of human labor.   *counterpart: (대응 관계에 있는) 상대

39

> By comparison, birds with the longest childhoods, and those that migrate with their parents, tend to have the most efficient migration routes.

Spending time as children allows animals to learn about their environment. Without childhood, animals must rely more fully on hardware, and therefore be less flexible. (①) Among migratory bird species, those that are born knowing how, when, and where to migrate — those that are migrating entirely with instructions they were born with — sometimes have very inefficient migration routes. (②) These birds, born knowing how to migrate, don't adapt easily. (③) So when lakes dry up, forest becomes farmland, or climate change pushes breeding grounds farther north, those birds that are born knowing how to migrate keep flying by the old rules and maps. (④) Childhood facilitates the passing on of cultural information, and culture can evolve faster than genes. (⑤) Childhood gives flexibility in a changing world. [3점]

40 다음 글의 내용을 한 문장으로 요약하고자 한다. 빈칸 (A), (B)에 들어갈 말로 가장 적절한 것은?

Over the last several decades, scholars have developed standards for how best to create, organize, present, and preserve digital information for future generations. What has remained neglected for the most part, however, are the needs of people with disabilities. As a result, many of the otherwise most valuable digital resources are useless for people who are deaf or hard of hearing, as well as for people who are blind, have low vision, or have difficulty distinguishing particular colors. While professionals working in educational technology and commercial web design have made significant progress in meeting the needs of such users, some scholars creating digital projects all too often fail to take these needs into account. This situation would be much improved if more projects embraced the idea that we should always keep the largest possible audience in mind as we make design decisions, ensuring that our final product serves the needs of those with disabilities as well as those without.

⬇

The needs of people with disabilities have often been ___(A)___ in digital projects, which could be changed by adopting a(n) ___(B)___ design.

	(A)		(B)
①	overlooked	—	inclusive
②	accepted	—	practical
③	considered	—	inclusive
④	accepted	—	abstract
⑤	overlooked	—	abstract

[41~42] 다음 글을 읽고, 물음에 답하시오.

All humans, to an extent, seek activities that cause a degree of pain in order to experience pleasure, whether this is found in spicy food, strong massages, or stepping into a too-cold or too-hot bath. The key is that it is a 'safe threat'. The brain perceives the stimulus to be painful but ultimately (a) non-threatening. Interestingly, this could be similar to the way humor works: a 'safe threat' that causes pleasure by playfully violating norms. We feel uncomfortable, but safe. In this context, where (b) survival is clearly not in danger, the desire for pain is actually the desire for a reward, not suffering or punishment. This reward-like effect comes from the feeling of mastery over the pain. The closer you look at your chilli-eating habit, the more remarkable it seems. When the active ingredient of chillies — capsaicin — touches the tongue, it stimulates exactly the same receptor that is activated when any of these tissues are burned. Knowing that our body is firing off danger signals, but that we are actually completely safe, (c) produces pleasure. All children start off hating chilli, but many learn to derive pleasure from it through repeated exposure and knowing that they will never experience any real (d) joy. Interestingly, seeking pain for the pain itself appears to be (e) uniquely human. The only way scientists have trained animals to have a preference for chilli or to self-harm is to have the pain always directly associated with a pleasurable reward.

41 윗글의 제목으로 가장 적절한 것은?

① The Secret Behind Painful Pleasures
② How 'Safe Threat' Changes into Real Pain
③ What Makes You Stronger, Pleasure or Pain?
④ How Does Your Body Detect Danger Signals?
⑤ Recipes to Change Picky Children's Eating Habits

42 밑줄 친 (a)~(e) 중에서 문맥상 낱말의 쓰임이 적절하지 <u>않은</u> 것은?

① (a)　　② (b)　　③ (c)　　④ (d)　　⑤ (e)

(A)

An airplane flew high above the deep blue seas far from any land. Flying the small plane was a student pilot who was sitting alongside an experienced flight instructor. As the student looked out the window, (a) she was filled with wonder and appreciation for the beauty of the world. Her instructor, meanwhile, waited patiently for the right time to start a surprise flight emergency training exercise.

(B)

Then, the student carefully flew low enough to see if she could find any ships making their way across the surface of the ocean. Now the instructor and the student could see some ships. Although the ships were far apart, they were all sailing in a line. With the line of ships in view, the student could see the way to home and safety. The student looked at (b) her in relief, who smiled proudly back at her student.

(C)

When the student began to panic, the instructor said, "Stay calm and steady. (c) You can do it." Calm as ever, the instructor told her student, "Difficult times always happen during flight. The most important thing is to focus on your flight in those situations." Those words encouraged the student to focus on flying the aircraft first. "Thank you, I think (d) I can make it," she said, "As I've been trained, I should search for visual markers."

(D)

When the plane hit a bit of turbulence, the instructor pushed a hidden button. Suddenly, all the monitors inside the plane flashed several times then went out completely! Now the student was in control of an airplane that was flying well, but (e) she had no indication of where she was or where she should go. She did have a map, but no other instruments. She was at a loss and then the plane shook again.

*turbulence: 난(亂)기류

43 주어진 글 (A)에 이어질 내용을 순서에 맞게 배열한 것으로 가장 적절한 것은?

① (B) — (D) — (C) ② (C) — (B) — (D)
③ (C) — (D) — (B) ④ (D) — (B) — (C)
⑤ (D) — (C) — (B)

44 밑줄 친 (a)~(e) 중에서 가리키는 대상이 나머지 넷과 다른 것은?

① (a) ② (b) ③ (c) ④ (d) ⑤ (e)

45 윗글에 관한 내용으로 적절하지 않은 것은?

① 교관과 교육생이 소형 비행기에 타고 있었다.
② 배들은 서로 떨어져 있었지만 한 줄을 이루고 있었다.
③ 교관은 어려운 상황에서는 집중이 가장 중요하다고 말했다.
④ 비행기 내부의 모니터가 깜박이다가 다시 정상 작동했다.
⑤ 교육생은 지도 이외의 다른 도구는 가지고 있지 않았다.

• MP3 파일을 들으며 다음 빈칸을 채우시오. (듣기 어려운 발음이나 정답의 단서가 되는 부분에 빈칸을 만들었습니다.)

01 다음을 듣고, 여자가 하는 말의 목적으로 가장 적절한 것을 고르시오.

W: [Chime bell rings.] Attention, everyone! Our CEO, Mr. Wayne, has prepared a snack bar to _____ ____ _____ on last month's project. Please come down to the lobby and enjoy some delicious snacks. _____ ___ _____ until 4 p.m. You'll be ⭐_____ by the amazing _____, from crispy fries and hot dogs to fresh lemonade and coffee. It'd be great if you could bring your own _____ cups for the drinks. See you there.

02 대화를 듣고, 남자의 의견으로 가장 적절한 것을 고르시오.

M: Hi, Pamela. Did you finish your history ⭐_____?

W: Yes, Dad. I finished it _____ _____ with the help of AI.

M: Really? Do you mean you used an ⭐_____ -intelligence website?

W: Yeah. I _____ ___ ____ _____ and AI gave me the answers right away.

M: Well, is it a good idea to do your homework that way?

W: Why not? It saves ___ ____ ___ _____ and gives me just the information I need.

M: I used to think so, too. But after trying it a couple of times, I _____ ____ AI sometimes uses false information as well.

W: Really? I didn't know that.

M: Yeah, you shouldn't blindly trust the answers from AI.

W: Okay. I'll _____ _____ ___ _____ next time.

03 다음을 듣고, 여자가 하는 말의 요지로 가장 적절한 것을 고르시오.

W: Hello, listeners. This is Kelly Watson's *Love Yourself*. _____ ____ _____ _____ about your social media use? Social media _____ _____ stay connected with others easily. However, it can _____ _____ _____ yourself with others, too. For example, a celebrity's post about going on a ⭐_____ trip may make you jealous. _____ making such comparisons _____ _____ _____ looking at yourself the way you truly are. You might think, "Why can't I have a better life?" and feel small about yourself. As you can see, social media can have a negative effect on your ⭐_____. I'll be right back with some tips for healthy social media use.

04 대화를 듣고, 그림에서 대화의 내용과 일치하지 <u>않는</u> 것을 고르시오.

W: Honey, I love this park!

M: Me, too. This park is so cool. But, oh, look! What's that in the tree?

W: It's _____ ____ kite _____ ____ the tree's branches.

M: I guess some kids _____ _____ without their kite.

W: By the same tree, a woman is walking her dog. They look so lovely.

M: _____ _____ the little girl beside her?

W: You mean the girl holding balloons in her hand?

M: Right. She's ⭐_____. And look there! _____ ____ _____ a basket full of flowers on the picnic mat?

W: Yes, right. It adds a touch of romance to the scene.

M: I think so, too. Oh, there's a ⭐_____. Next to it, a man is playing the violin.

W: The melody is beautiful. I'm glad we came here.

05 대화를 듣고, 남자가 할 일로 가장 적절한 것을 고르시오.

M: Hey, Alice. I _____ ____ the science camp next week. What about you?

W: Me, too. But I didn't know that there were so many things to do before the camp.

M: Right. _____ ____ _____ to go over my checklist together?

W: Hmm, let's see. Did you upload your introduction video to the website?

M: Yes, I _____ ____ _____ my interest in science. Oh, hey, _____ ____ _____ which ✪_____ to work on?

W: Yes. I decided to participate in a biology experiment.

M: Me, too. Wasn't it difficult to make a plan for your experiment?

W: Actually, I _____ _____ _____ _____ because I've never written a plan for a biology experiment before.

M: I'll show you mine after class. Maybe you can get some ideas.

W: Really? That'd be great. See you soon.

06 대화를 듣고, 여자가 지불할 금액을 고르시오.

W: Hi, I'm looking for a backpack for my niece. She's going on a camping trip this summer.

M: Great. We have this blue backpack that has _____ _____.

W: It looks stylish and ✪_____. How much is it?

M: It's $50, but we have a special discount only on backpacks today. Every backpack is 10% off.

W: That's a _____ _____! I'll take it.

M: I'm sure your niece will love it. Do you need anything else?

W: Yes. I like this camping hat. How much is it?

M: It's $10, not on sale, ✪_____.

W: That's okay. I'll _____ ____ ____ _____.

M: _____ _____ for them would be a total of $5. Would you like gift wrapping?

W: Yes, please. _____ ____ _____ _____.

07 대화를 듣고, 남자가 마술쇼에 갈 수 없는 이유를 고르시오.

W: Hi, Chris. How was your weekend?

M: Hello, Martha. I _____ ____ ___ _____ _____ and had fun. How about you?

W: _____ _____ _____ for tomorrow's club festival.

M: Oh, what kind of activity are you preparing for the festival?

W: Our club members are ✪_____ a magic show. Come and watch us at 4 p.m. tomorrow ___ ____ ____ _____.

M: I'd love to, but I can't make it.

W: Why? It'd be nice to have you there.

M: I'm sorry, but I have to attend my uncle's birthday party.

W: Oh, I understand. I _____ _____ have a wonderful time with your family.

M: Thank you, I will.

08 대화를 듣고, Victory Marathon에 관해 언급되지 <u>않은</u> 것을 고르시오.

W: Hey, Alex. Have you seen the ⭐_____ for the Victory Marathon?

M: Not yet, but I'm _____ _____ _____. When's the event?

W: It's on Saturday, July 13th.

M: Nice. Where will the race start?

W: It will start at William Stadium.

M: Oh, great. How much _____ ___ _____ to participate?

W: It costs $30.

M: That's ⭐_____. How many participants are they expecting?

W: Last year, there were around 5,000. They say they _____ _____ _____ _____ this year.

M: I didn't know that many people love marathons. _____ ___!

W: Great. I look forward to running with you.

09 Violet Hill Mentorship에 관한 다음 내용을 듣고, 일치하지 <u>않는</u> 것을 고르시오.

M: Good morning, students of Violet Hill High School. This is your principal speaking. I'm _____ _____ _____ that the annual Violet Hill Mentorship _____ ___ _____ next Friday. Our school ⭐_____ who are now majoring in English literature, bioengineering, and theater and film will be _____ _____ _____ on university life. To register for this event, visit our school website and submit two questions you would like to _____ _____ ___ _____. The deadline for ⭐_____ is next Tuesday, so don't wait too long. And remember, the _____ number of participants for each major is 30 people. For more information, visit our school website.

10 다음 표를 보면서 대화를 듣고, 두 사람이 구입할 무선 진공청소기를 고르시오.

M: Honey, look. This website's Summer Sale _____ _____ _____.

W: Oh, great. Why don't we buy a new _____ vacuum cleaner?

M: Sure. There are five bestsellers shown here.

W: Let's _____ _____ _____ first.

M: I think it should be at least two hours so that we don't have to _____ _____ ___ _____.

W: I agree. But let's not spend more than $400 on a vacuum cleaner.

M: Fine. Oh, _____ ___ _____ also have a wet cleaning function.

W: I'd love that. With that function, we can ⭐_____ save a lot of time.

M: Okay. What about the color? The white one looks better to me.

W: Right. It'll match the color tone of our living room.

M: Perfect. So, let's buy this one.

W: Great.

11 대화를 듣고, 남자의 마지막 말에 대한 여자의 응답으로 가장 적절한 것을 고르시오.

M: Mom, I want to have a cat. Have you ever thought about us _____ ___ _____?

W: Sweetie, having a pet _____ a lot of ⭐_____.

M: I'm _____ _____ for it. Mom, we could at least consider it.

W: _____

12 대화를 듣고, 여자의 마지막 말에 대한 남자의 응답으로 가장 적절한 것을 고르시오.

W: Jake, I _____ forgot about the math assignment. When's the ⭐_____?

M: You need to _____ _____ by next Tuesday.

W: Phew, I still _____ _____ _____. Where should I submit it?

M: _____

13 대화를 듣고, 남자의 마지막 말에 대한 여자의 응답으로 가장 적절한 것을 고르시오.

M: Hey, Cindy. Have you been playing a lot of badminton these days?

W: No, I've been _____ some pain in my knee since a badminton match last weekend.

M: I'm sorry to hear that. Did you go see a doctor?

W: Yes, I _____ ___ _____ _____ yesterday.

M: I hope you feel better soon. _____ _____ ____, have you ever taken a badminton lesson?

W: No, I haven't. Why are you asking?

M: In my experience, that _____ ___ _____ can come from bad ✪_____. A lesson might reduce the risk of any further injury.

W: Well, ___ _____ ___ _____ need those lessons.

M: Cindy, if you want to keep playing badminton _____ _____ _____, it's important to learn from an instructor to develop the right posture.

W: _____

14 대화를 듣고, 여자의 마지막 말에 대한 남자의 응답으로 가장 적절한 것을 고르시오.

W: Mike, don't you think _____ _____ is kind of scary?

M: Right. The ✪_____ seems higher than ever.

W: I heard it's putting a number of animals in danger these days.

M: Right. Maybe one day we _____ ___ _____ ___ see polar bears anymore.

W: That's not good. What can we do?

M: Use less plastic, plant more trees. Small things matter.

W: And maybe we can ride bikes _____ ___ always asking for rides.

M: Yeah. Making a Tree-Planting Day at school can also be helpful.

W: ✪_____. Then, why don't we make our own school club to ____ ___ ____ _____?

M: _____

15 다음 상황 설명을 듣고, Laura가 Tony에게 할 말로 가장 적절한 것을 고르시오.

W: Laura and Tony are close coworkers. Laura notices that Tony has been looking _____ tired and _____ recently. One day, she asks Tony if he's not been feeling well lately, but Tony says he's _____ __ _____ _____ from work. Laura knows that Tony sometimes works even on weekends without taking a break or getting any rest. However, this time, she is really worried about him and wants him to take at least __ _____ ___ _____ ____. In this situation, what would Laura most likely say to Tony?

Laura: _____

[16~17] 다음을 듣고, 물음에 답하시오.

M: Hello, Lincoln High School. This is David Newman, your current student ✪_____, and I'm speaking to you today to ____ ____ _____ about the _____ _____ for next year's student representative. _____ can now begin their campaigns, following these _____. First, they can share short promotional video clips on their social media, but the video clips must not be longer than 3 minutes. Second, candidates can _____ _____ only in allowed areas, and it's important to keep the size to A3 or smaller, as larger posters _____ ___ _____ without warning. Third, the use of pamphlets is allowed, but they must only be _____ within the school campus. Lastly, there will be an online debate broadcast on our school website among the candidates three days before the election. It's important to be _____ toward the other candidates during the debate. Let's make this election a success.

✽ 다음 영어는 우리말 뜻을, 우리말은 영어 단어를 〈보기〉에서 찾아 쓰시오.

01 curious _____

02 capacity _____

03 route _____

04 permanent _____

05 offspring _____

06 소화하다 _____

07 쾌락 _____

08 밀도 _____

09 진화하다 _____

10 조기에 _____

┌─── [보기] ───┐

길	evolve
영구적인	digest
과제	prematurely
궁금한	density
능력	candidate
자손	pleasure

✽ 다음 우리말에 알맞은 영어 표현을 찾아 연결하시오.

11 지나가다 •   • set aside

12 ~을 확보하다 •   • pass by

13 발사하다 •   • be loaded with

14 ~으로 가득 차다 •   • settle down

15 정착하다 •   • fire off

✽ 다음 우리말과 같은 표현이 되도록 알맞은 단어를 〈보기〉에서 찾아 쓰시오.

┌─── [보기] ───┐

literary / destructive / commodities / vital / succeeding / assembly
frequently / migrate / punishment / threaten / extinction / agricultural

16 조립 라인 근로자들 ➡ _____-line workers

17 다음 세대에 걸쳐 ➡ within each _____ generation

18 물건이나 돈을 저축하다 ➡ save _____ or money

19 공간 기억에 중요한 ➡ _____ for spatial memory

20 자주 이동했다 ➡ moved around _____

21 멸종 위기에 이르다 ➡ come close to _____

22 환경을 위협하다 ➡ _____ the environment

23 가장 유명한 문학적 사례 ➡ the most famous _____ example

24 부모와 함께 이동하다 ➡ _____ with their parents

25 고통이나 처벌 ➡ suffering or _____

26 저항이 가장 적은 길 ➡ the path of least (registration / resistance)

27 중요한 역할을 담당하는 전문가들 ➡ professionals in (critical / trivial) roles

28 당신의 정체성의 반영 ➡ a(n) (reflection / inflection) of your identity

29 방이 지저분한 것 ➡ having a (mossy / messy) room

30 과도한 노력 없이 ➡ without (excessive / successive) effort

* 다음 문장의 빈칸에 알맞은 단어를 〈보기〉에서 찾아 쓰시오.

─── [보기] ───

authority / interruptions / flexibility / exotic / refine / convince
instruments / preserve / separately / profound / remarkable / hazardous

31 유년기는 변화하는 세상에서 유연성을 제공한다.
➡ Childhood gives _____ in a changing world.

32 방해로 인한 대가는 잘 기록되어 있다.
➡ The costs of _____ are well-documented.

33 먼저 모든 사람에게 개별적으로 아이디어를 내도록 요청한다.
➡ You start by asking everyone to generate ideas _____.

34 그들은 그들 자신의 유니폼을 디자인했고 근무 교대에 대한 권한을 가졌다.
➡ They designed their own uniforms and had _____ over shifts.

35 디지털 비즈니스가 끼치는 해악이 훨씬 더 위험할 수 있다.
➡ The harm of digital businesses can be even more _____.

36 그녀는 지도는 가지고 있었지만, 다른 도구는 가지고 있지 않았다.
➡ She did have a map, but no other _____.

37 칠리를 먹는 습관을 자세히 들여다볼수록 이는 더욱 분명하게 드러난다.
➡ The closer you look at your chilli-eating habit, the more _____ it seems.

38 독립적인 판단을 유지하기 위해, 각 구성원이 스스로 그 아이디어를 평가한다.
➡ To _____ independent judgment, each member evaluates them on their own.

39 외래종이 갑자기 생태계에 유입되면 문제가 종종 발생한다.
➡ Problems often arise if a(n) _____ species is suddenly introduced to an ecosystem.

40 그러고 나서야 팀이 함께 모여 가장 유망한 옵션을 선택하고 다듬는다.
➡ Only then dose the team come together to select and _____ the most promising options.

*1번부터 17번까지는 듣고 답하는 문제입니다. 1번부터 15번까지는 한 번만 들려주고, 16번부터 17번까지는 두 번 들려줍니다. 방송을 잘 듣고 답을 하시기 바랍니다.

▲ 듣기 파일

01 다음을 듣고, 여자가 하는 말의 목적으로 가장 적절한 것을 고르시오.

① 체육대회 종목을 소개하려고
② 대회 자원봉사자를 모집하려고
③ 학생 회장 선거 일정을 공지하려고
④ 경기 관람 규칙 준수를 당부하려고
⑤ 학교 홈페이지 주소 변경을 안내하려고

02 대화를 듣고, 남자의 의견으로 가장 적절한 것을 고르시오.

① 산책은 창의적인 생각을 할 수 있게 돕는다.
② 식사 후 과격한 운동은 소화를 방해한다.
③ 지나친 스트레스는 집중력을 감소시킨다.
④ 독서를 통해 창의력을 증진할 수 있다.
⑤ 꾸준한 운동은 기초체력을 향상시킨다.

03 대화를 듣고, 두 사람의 관계를 가장 잘 나타낸 것을 고르시오.

① 고객 – 우체국 직원
② 투숙객 – 호텔 지배인
③ 여행객 – 여행 가이드
④ 아파트 주민 – 경비원
⑤ 손님 – 옷가게 주인

04 대화를 듣고, 그림에서 대화의 내용과 일치하지 않는 것을 고르시오.

05 대화를 듣고, 남자가 할 일로 가장 적절한 것을 고르시오.

① 초대장 보내기
② 피자 주문하기
③ 거실 청소하기
④ 꽃다발 준비하기
⑤ 스마트폰 사러 가기

06 대화를 듣고, 여자가 지불할 금액을 고르시오. [3점]

① $54 ② $60 ③ $72 ④ $76 ⑤ $80

07 대화를 듣고, 남자가 록 콘서트에 갈 수 없는 이유를 고르시오.

① 일을 하러 가야 해서
② 피아노 연습을 해야 해서
③ 할머니를 뵈러 가야 해서
④ 친구의 개를 돌봐야 해서
⑤ 과제를 아직 끝내지 못해서

08 대화를 듣고, Eco Day에 관해 언급되지 않은 것을 고르시오.

① 행사 시간
② 행사 장소
③ 참가비
④ 준비물
⑤ 등록 방법

09 Eastville Dance Contest에 관한 다음 내용을 듣고, 일치하지 않는 것을 고르시오.

① 처음으로 개최되는 경연이다.
② 모든 종류의 춤이 허용된다.
③ 춤 영상을 8월 15일까지 업로드 해야 한다.
④ 학생들은 가장 좋아하는 영상에 투표할 수 있다.
⑤ 우승팀은 상으로 상품권을 받게 될 것이다.

10

다음 표를 보면서 대화를 듣고, 두 사람이 구입할 정수기를 고르시오.

Water Purifiers

	Model	Price	Water Tank Capacity (liters)	Power-saving Mode	Warranty
①	A	$570	4	×	1 year
②	B	$650	5	○	1 year
③	C	$680	5	×	3 years
④	D	$740	5	○	3 years
⑤	E	$830	6	○	3 years

11

대화를 듣고, 남자의 마지막 말에 대한 여자의 응답으로 가장 적절한 것을 고르시오.

① Great. We don't have to wait in line.
② All right. We can come back later.
③ Good job. Let's buy the tickets.
④ No worries. I will stand in line.
⑤ Too bad. I can't buy that car.

12

대화를 듣고, 여자의 마지막 말에 대한 남자의 응답으로 가장 적절한 것을 고르시오.

① Yes. You can register online.
② Sorry. I can't see you next week.
③ Right. I should go to his office now.
④ Fantastic! I'll take the test tomorrow.
⑤ Of course. I can help him if he needs my help.

13

대화를 듣고, 여자의 마지막 말에 대한 남자의 응답으로 가장 적절한 것을 고르시오. [3점]

Man: _____
① I agree. You can save a lot by buying secondhand.
② Great idea! Our message would make others smile.
③ Sorry. I forgot to write a message in the book.
④ Exactly. Taking notes during class is important.
⑤ Okay. We can arrive on time if we leave now.

14

대화를 듣고, 남자의 마지막 말에 대한 여자의 응답으로 가장 적절한 것을 고르시오. [3점]

Woman: _____
① Why not? I can bring some food when we go camping.
② I'm sorry. That fishing equipment is not for sale.
③ I don't think so. The price is most important.
④ Really? I'd love to meet your family.
⑤ No problem. You can use my equipment.

2023. 6

6회

15

다음 상황 설명을 듣고, Violet이 Peter에게 할 말로 가장 적절한 것을 고르시오.

Violet: _____
① Will you join the science club together?
② Is it okay to use a card to pay for the drinks?
③ Why don't we donate our books to the library?
④ How about going to the cafeteria to have lunch?
⑤ Can you borrow the books for me with your card?

[16~17] 다음을 듣고, 물음에 답하시오.

16

남자가 하는 말의 주제로 가장 적절한 것은?

① different causes of sleep disorders
② various ways to keep foods fresh
③ foods to improve quality of sleep
④ reasons for organic foods' popularity
⑤ origins of popular foods around the world

17

언급된 음식이 <u>아닌</u> 것은?

① kiwi fruits ② milk ③ nuts
④ tomatoes ⑤ honey

＊이제 듣기 문제가 끝났습니다. 18번부터는 문제지의 지시에 따라 답을 하시기 바랍니다.

18 다음 글의 목적으로 가장 적절한 것은?

ACC Travel Agency Customers:

Have you ever wanted to enjoy a holiday in nature? This summer is the best time to turn your dream into reality. We have a perfect travel package for you. This travel package includes special trips to Lake Madison as well as massage and meditation to help you relax. Also, we provide yoga lessons taught by experienced instructors. If you book this package, you will enjoy all this at a reasonable price. We are sure that it will be an unforgettable experience for you. If you call us, we will be happy to give you more details.

① 여행 일정 변경을 안내하려고
② 패키지 여행 상품을 홍보하려고
③ 여행 상품 불만족에 대해 사과하려고
④ 여행 만족도 조사 참여를 부탁하려고
⑤ 패키지 여행 업무 담당자를 모집하려고

19 다음 글에 드러난 'I'의 심경 변화로 가장 적절한 것은?

When I woke up in our hotel room, it was almost midnight. I didn't see my husband nor daughter. I called them, but I heard their phones ringing in the room. Feeling worried, I went outside and walked down the street, but they were nowhere to be found. When I decided I should ask someone for help, a crowd nearby caught my attention. I approached, hoping to find my husband and daughter, and suddenly I saw two familiar faces. I smiled, feeling calm. Just then, my daughter saw me and called, "Mom!" They were watching the magic show. Finally, I felt all my worries disappear.

① anxious → relieved
② delighted → unhappy
③ indifferent → excited
④ relaxed → upset
⑤ embarrassed → proud

20 다음 글에서 필자가 주장하는 바로 가장 적절한 것은?

Research shows that people who work have two calendars: one for work and one for their personal lives. Although it may seem sensible, having two separate calendars for work and personal life can lead to distractions. To check if something is missing, you will find yourself checking your to-do lists multiple times. Instead, organize all of your tasks in one place. It doesn't matter if you use digital or paper media. It's okay to keep your professional and personal tasks in one place. This will give you a good idea of how time is divided between work and home. This will allow you to make informed decisions about which tasks are most important.

① 결정한 것은 반드시 실행하도록 노력하라.
② 자신이 담당한 업무에 관한 전문성을 확보하라.
③ 업무 집중도를 높이기 위해 책상 위를 정돈하라.
④ 좋은 아이디어를 메모하는 습관을 길러라.
⑤ 업무와 개인 용무를 한 곳에 정리하라.

21 밑줄 친 become unpaid ambassadors가 다음 글에서 의미하는 바로 가장 적절한 것은?

Why do you care how a customer reacts to a purchase? Good question. By understanding post-purchase behavior, you can understand the influence and the likelihood of whether a buyer will repurchase the product (and whether she will keep it or return it). You'll also determine whether the buyer will encourage others to purchase the product from you. Satisfied customers can become unpaid ambassadors for your business, so customer satisfaction should be on the top of your to-do list. People tend to believe the opinions of people they know. People trust friends over advertisements any day. They know that advertisements are paid to tell the "good side" and that they're used to persuade them to purchase products and services. By continually monitoring your customer's satisfaction after the sale, you have the ability to avoid negative word-of-mouth advertising.

① recommend products to others for no gain
② offer manufacturers feedback on products
③ become people who don't trust others' words
④ get rewards for advertising products overseas
⑤ buy products without worrying about the price

22 다음 글의 요지로 가장 적절한 것은?

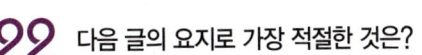

The promise of a computerized society, we were told, was that it would pass to machines all of the repetitive drudgery of work, allowing us humans to pursue higher purposes and to have more leisure time. It didn't work out this way. Instead of more time, most of us have less. Companies large and small have off-loaded work onto the backs of consumers. Things that used to be done for us, as part of the value-added service of working with a company, we are now expected to do ourselves. With air travel, we're now expected to complete our own reservations and check-in, jobs that used to be done by airline employees or travel agents. At the grocery store, we're expected to bag our own groceries and, in some supermarkets, to scan our own purchases.

*drudgery: 고된 일

① 컴퓨터 기반 사회에서는 여가 시간이 더 늘어난다.
② 회사 업무의 전산화는 업무 능률을 향상시킨다.
③ 컴퓨터화된 사회에서 소비자는 더 많은 일을 하게 된다.
④ 온라인 거래가 모든 소비자들을 만족시키기에는 한계가 있다.
⑤ 산업의 발전으로 인해 기계가 인간의 일자리를 대신하고 있다.

23 다음 글의 주제로 가장 적절한 것은?

We tend to believe that we possess a host of socially desirable characteristics, and that we are free of most of those that are socially undesirable. For example, a large majority of the general public thinks that they are more intelligent, more fair-minded, less prejudiced, and more skilled behind the wheel of an automobile than the average person. This phenomenon is so reliable and ubiquitous that it has come to be known as the "Lake Wobegon effect," after Garrison Keillor's fictional community where "the women are strong, the men are good-looking, and all the children are above average." A survey of one million high school seniors found that 70% thought they were above average in leadership ability, and only 2% thought they were below average. In terms of ability to get along with others, *all* students thought they were above average, 60% thought they were in the top 10%, and 25% thought they were in the top 1%!

*ubiquitous: 도처에 있는

① importance of having a positive self-image as a leader
② our common belief that we are better than average
③ our tendency to think others are superior to us
④ reasons why we always try to be above average
⑤ danger of prejudice in building healthy social networks

24 다음 글의 제목으로 가장 적절한 것은?

Few people will be surprised to hear that poverty tends to create stress: a 2006 study published in the American journal *Psychosomatic Medicine*, for example, noted that a lower socioeconomic status was associated with higher levels of stress hormones in the body. However, richer economies have their own distinct stresses. The key issue is time pressure. A 1999 study of 31 countries by American psychologist Robert Levine and Canadian psychologist Ara Norenzayan found that wealthier, more industrialized nations had a faster pace of life — which led to a higher standard of living, but at the same time left the population feeling a constant sense of urgency, as well as being more prone to heart disease. In effect, fast-paced productivity creates wealth, but it also leads people to feel time-poor when they lack the time to relax and enjoy themselves.

*prone: 걸리기 쉬운

① Why Are Even Wealthy Countries Not Free from Stress?
② In Search of the Path to Escaping the Poverty Trap
③ Time Management: Everything You Need to Know
④ How Does Stress Affect Human Bodies?
⑤ Sound Mind Wins the Game of Life!

25 다음 도표의 내용과 일치하지 <u>않는</u> 것은?

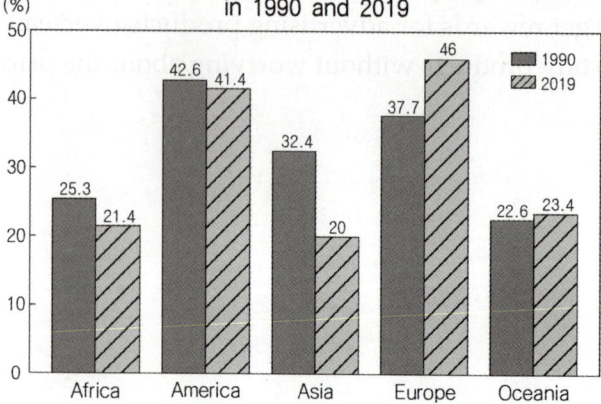

Share of Forest Area in Total Land Area by Region in 1990 and 2019

The above graph shows the share of forest area in total land area by region in 1990 and 2019. ① Africa's share of forest area in total land area was over 20% in both 1990 and 2019. ② The share of forest area in America was 42.6% in 1990, which was larger than that in 2019. ③ The share of forest area in Asia declined from 1990 to 2019 by more than 10 percentage points. ④ In 2019, the share of forest area in Europe was the largest among the five regions, more than three times that in Asia in the same year. ⑤ Oceania showed the smallest gap between 1990 and 2019 in terms of the share of forest area in total land area.

26 Gary Becker에 관한 다음 글의 내용과 일치하지 <u>않는</u> 것은?

Gary Becker was born in Pottsville, Pennsylvania in 1930 and grew up in Brooklyn, New York City. His father, who was not well educated, had a deep interest in financial and political issues. After graduating from high school, Becker went to Princeton University, where he majored in economics. He was dissatisfied with his economic education at Princeton University because "it didn't seem to be handling real problems." He earned a doctor's degree in economics from the University of Chicago in 1955. His doctoral paper on the economics of discrimination was mentioned by the Nobel Prize Committee as an important contribution to economics. Since 1985, Becker had written a regular economics column in *Business Week*, explaining economic analysis and ideas to the general public. In 1992, he was awarded the Nobel Prize in economic science.

*discrimination: 차별

① New York City의 Brooklyn에서 자랐다.
② 아버지는 금융과 정치 문제에 깊은 관심이 있었다.
③ Princeton University에서의 경제학 교육에 만족했다.
④ 1955년에 경제학 박사 학위를 취득했다.
⑤ *Business Week*에 경제학 칼럼을 기고했다.

27 2023 Drone Racing Championship에 관한 다음 안내문의 내용과 일치하지 <u>않는</u> 것은?

2023 Drone Racing Championship

Are you the best drone racer? Then take the opportunity to prove you are the one!

When & Where
• 6 p.m. – 8 p.m., Sunday, July 9
• Lakeside Community Center

Requirements
• Participants: High school students only
• Bring your own drone for the race.

Prize
• $500 and a medal will be awarded to the winner.

Note
• The first 10 participants will get souvenirs.

For more details, please visit www.droneracing.com or call 313-6745-1189.

① 7월 9일 일요일에 개최된다.
② 고등학생만 참가할 수 있다.
③ 자신의 드론을 가져와야 한다.
④ 상금과 메달이 우승자에게 수여될 것이다.
⑤ 20명의 참가자가 기념품을 받을 것이다.

28 Summer Scuba Diving One-day Class에 관한 다음 안내문의 내용과 일치하는 것은?

Summer Scuba Diving One-day Class

Join our summer scuba driving lesson for beginners, and become an underwater explorer!

Schedule
- 10:00 – 12:00 Learning the basics
- 13:00 – 16:00 Practicing diving skills in a pool

Price
- Private lesson: $150
- Group lesson (up to 3 people): $100 per person
- Participants can rent our diving equipment for free.

Notice
- Participants must be 10 years old or over.
- Participants must register at least 5 days before the class begins.

For more information,
please go to www.ssdiver.com.

① 오후 시간에 바다에서 다이빙 기술을 연습한다.
② 그룹 수업의 최대 정원은 4명이다.
③ 다이빙 장비를 유료로 대여할 수 있다.
④ 연령에 관계없이 참가할 수 있다.
⑤ 적어도 수업 시작 5일 전까지 등록해야 한다.

29 다음 글의 밑줄 친 부분 중, 어법상 틀린 것은? [3점]

Although praise is one of the most powerful tools available for improving young children's behavior, it is equally powerful for improving your child's self-esteem. Preschoolers believe what their parents tell ① them in a very profound way. They do not yet have the cognitive sophistication to reason ② analytically and reject false information. If a preschool boy consistently hears from his mother ③ that he is smart and a good helper, he is likely to incorporate that information into his self-image. Thinking of himself as a boy who is smart and knows how to do things ④ being likely to make him endure longer in problem-solving efforts and increase his confidence in trying new and difficult tasks. Similarly, thinking of himself as the kind of boy who is a good helper will make him more likely to volunteer ⑤ to help with tasks at home and at preschool.

*profound: 뜻 깊은 **sophistication: 정교화(함)

30 다음 글의 밑줄 친 부분 중, 문맥상 낱말의 쓰임이 적절하지 않은 것은?

Advertisers often displayed considerable facility in ① adapting their claims to the market status of the goods they promoted. Fleischmann's yeast, for instance, was used as an ingredient for cooking homemade bread. Yet more and more people in the early 20th century were buying their bread from stores or bakeries, so consumer demand for yeast ② increased. The producer of Fleischmann's yeast hired the J. Walter Thompson advertising agency to come up with a different marketing strategy to ③ boost sales. No longer the "Soul of Bread," the Thompson agency first turned yeast into an important source of vitamins with significant health ④ benefits. Shortly thereafter, the advertising agency transformed yeast into a natural laxative. ⑤ Repositioning yeast helped increase sales.

*laxative: 완하제(배변을 쉽게 하는 약·음식·음료)

[31~34] 다음 빈칸에 들어갈 말로 가장 적절한 것을 고르시오.

31

Individuals who perform at a high level in their profession often have instant credibility with others. People admire them, they want to be like them, and they feel connected to them. When they speak, others listen — even if the area of their skill has nothing to do with the advice they give. Think about a world-famous basketball player. He has made more money from endorsements than he ever did playing basketball. Is it because of his knowledge of the products he endorses? No. It's because of what he can do with a basketball. The same can be said of an Olympic medalist swimmer. People listen to him because of what he can do in the pool. And when an actor tells us we should drive a certain car, we don't listen because of his expertise on engines. We listen because we admire his talent. _____ connects. If you possess a high level of ability in an area, others may desire to connect with you because of it.

*endorsement: (유명인의 텔레비전 등에서의 상품) 보증 선전

① Patience ② Sacrifice ③ Honesty
④ Excellence ⑤ Creativity

32

Think of the brain as a city. If you were to look out over a city and ask "where is the economy located?" you'd see there's no good answer to the question. Instead, the economy emerges from the interaction of all the elements — from the stores and the banks to the merchants and the customers. And so it is with the brain's operation: it doesn't happen in one spot. Just as in a city, no neighborhood of the brain _____. In brains and in cities, everything emerges from the interaction between residents, at all scales, locally and distantly. Just as trains bring materials and textiles into a city, which become processed into the economy, so the raw electrochemical signals from sensory organs are transported along superhighways of neurons. There the signals undergo processing and transformation into our conscious reality. [3점] *electrochemical: 전기화학의

① operates in isolation
② suffers from rapid changes
③ resembles economic elements
④ works in a systematic way
⑤ interacts with another

33

Someone else's body language affects our own body, which then creates an emotional echo that makes us feel accordingly. As Louis Armstrong sang, "When you're smiling, the whole world smiles with you." If copying another's smile makes us feel happy, the emotion of the smiler has been transmitted via our body. Strange as it may sound, this theory states that _____. For example, our mood can be improved by simply lifting up the corners of our mouth. If people are asked to bite down on a pencil lengthwise, taking care not to let the pencil touch their lips (thus forcing the mouth into a smile-like shape), they judge cartoons funnier than if they have been asked to frown. The primacy of the body is sometimes summarized in the phrase "I must be afraid, because I'm running." [3점] *lengthwise: 길게 **frown: 얼굴을 찡그리다

① language guides our actions
② emotions arise from our bodies
③ body language hides our feelings
④ what others say affects our mood
⑤ negative emotions easily disappear

34

_____ boosts sales. Brian Wansink, Professor of Marketing at Cornell University, investigated the effectiveness of this tactic in 1998. He persuaded three supermarkets in Sioux City, Iowa, to offer Campbell's soup at a small discount: 79 cents rather than 89 cents. The discounted soup was sold in one of three conditions: a control, where there was no limit on the volume of purchases, or two tests, where customers were limited to either four or twelve cans. In the unlimited condition shoppers bought 3.3 cans on average, whereas in the scarce condition, when there was a limit, they bought 5.3 on average. This suggests scarcity encourages sales. The findings are particularly strong because the test took place in a supermarket with genuine shoppers. It didn't rely on claimed data, nor was it held in a laboratory where consumers might behave differently. [3점] *tactic: 전략

① Promoting products through social media
② Reducing the risk of producing poor quality items
③ Restricting the number of items customers can buy
④ Offering several options that customers find attractive
⑤ Emphasizing the safety of products with research data

35 다음 글에서 전체 흐름과 관계 없는 문장은?

Although technology has the potential to increase productivity, it can also have a negative impact on productivity. For example, in many office environments workers sit at desks with computers and have access to the internet. ① They are able to check their personal e-mails and use social media whenever they want to. ② This can stop them from doing their work and make them less productive. ③ Introducing new technology can also have a negative impact on production when it causes a change to the production process or requires workers to learn a new system. ④ Using technology can enable businesses to produce more goods and to get more out of the other factors of production. ⑤ Learning to use new technology can be time consuming and stressful for workers and this can cause a decline in productivity.

[36~37] 주어진 글 다음에 이어질 글의 순서로 가장 적절한 것을 고르시오.

36

Up until about 6,000 years ago, most people were farmers. Many lived in different places throughout the year, hunting for food or moving their livestock to areas with enough food.

(A) For example, priests wanted to know when to carry out religious ceremonies. This was when people first invented clocks — devices that show, measure, and keep track of passing time.

(B) There was no need to tell the time because life depended on natural cycles, such as the changing seasons or sunrise and sunset. Gradually more people started to live in larger settlements, and some needed to tell the time.

(C) Clocks have been important ever since. Today, clocks are used for important things such as setting busy airport timetables — if the time is incorrect, aeroplanes might crash into each other when taking off or landing! [3점]

① (A) — (C) — (B)　　② (B) — (A) — (C)
③ (B) — (C) — (A)　　④ (C) — (A) — (B)
⑤ (C) — (B) — (A)

37

Managers are always looking for ways to increase productivity, which is the ratio of costs to output in production. Adam Smith, writing when the manufacturing industry was new, described a way that production could be made more efficient, known as the "division of labor."

(A) Because each worker specializes in one job, he or she can work much faster without changing from one task to another. Now 10 workers can produce thousands of pins in a day — a huge increase in productivity from the 200 they would have produced before.

(B) One worker could do all these tasks, and make 20 pins in a day. But this work can be divided into its separate processes, with a number of workers each performing one task.

(C) Making most manufactured goods involves several different processes using different skills. Smith's example was the manufacture of pins: the wire is straightened, sharpened, a head is put on, and then it is polished.

*ratio: 비율

① (A) — (C) — (B)　　② (B) — (A) — (C)
③ (B) — (C) — (A)　　④ (C) — (A) — (B)
⑤ (C) — (B) — (A)

38

Yet we know that the face that stares back at us from the glass is not the same, cannot be the same, as it was 10 minutes ago.

Sometimes the pace of change is far slower. (①) The face you saw reflected in your mirror this morning probably appeared no different from the face you saw the day before — or a week or a month ago. (②) The proof is in your photo album: Look at a photograph taken of yourself 5 or 10 years ago and you see clear differences between the face in the snapshot and the face in your mirror. (③) If you lived in a world without mirrors for a year and then saw your reflection, you might be surprised by the change. (④) After an interval of 10 years without seeing yourself, you might not at first recognize the person peering from the mirror. (⑤) Even something as basic as our own face changes from moment to moment.

*peer: 응시하다

39

As children absorb more evidence from the world around them, certain possibilities become much more likely and more useful and harden into knowledge or beliefs.

According to educational psychologist Susan Engel, curiosity begins to decrease as young as four years old. By the time we are adults, we have fewer questions and more default settings. As Henry James put it, "Disinterested curiosity is past, the mental grooves and channels set." (①) The decline in curiosity can be traced in the development of the brain through childhood. (②) Though smaller than the adult brain, the infant brain contains millions more neural connections. (③) The wiring, however, is a mess; the lines of communication between infant neurons are far less efficient than between those in the adult brain. (④) The baby's perception of the world is consequently both intensely rich and wildly disordered. (⑤) The neural pathways that enable those beliefs become faster and more automatic, while the ones that the child doesn't use regularly are pruned away. [3점]

*default setting: 기본값 **groove: 고랑 ***prune: 가지치기하다

2023.6
6회

Nearly eight of ten U.S. adults believe there are "good foods" and "bad foods." Unless we're talking about spoiled stew, poison mushrooms, or something similar, however, no foods can be labeled as either good or bad. There are, however, combinations of foods that add up to a healthful or unhealthful diet. Consider the case of an adult who eats only foods thought of as "good" — for example, raw broccoli, apples, orange juice, boiled tofu, and carrots. Although all these foods are nutrient-dense, they do not add up to a healthy diet because they don't supply a wide enough variety of the nutrients we need. Or take the case of the teenager who occasionally eats fried chicken, but otherwise stays away from fried foods. The occasional fried chicken isn't going to knock his or her diet off track. But the person who eats fried foods every day, with few vegetables or fruits, and loads up on supersized soft drinks, candy, and chips for snacks has a bad diet.

⬇

Unlike the common belief, defining foods as good or bad is not ____(A)____ ; in fact, a healthy diet is determined largely by what the diet is ____(B)____ .

	(A)		(B)
①	incorrect	—	limited to
②	appropriate	—	composed of
③	wrong	—	aimed at
④	appropriate	—	tested on
⑤	incorrect	—	adjusted to

[41~42] 다음 글을 읽고, 물음에 답하시오.

Early hunter-gatherer societies had (a) <u>minimal</u> structure. A chief or group of elders usually led the camp or village. Most of these leaders had to hunt and gather along with the other members because the surpluses of food and other vital resources were seldom (b) <u>sufficient</u> to support a full-time chief or village council. The development of agriculture changed work patterns. Early farmers could reap 3–10 kg of grain from each 1 kg of seed planted. Part of this food/energy surplus was returned to the community and (c) <u>limited</u> support for nonfarmers such as chieftains, village councils, men who practice medicine, priests, and warriors. In return, the nonfarmers provided leadership and security for the farming population, enabling it to continue to increase food/energy yields and provide ever larger surpluses.

With improved technology and favorable conditions, agriculture produced consistent surpluses of the basic necessities, and population groups grew in size. These groups concentrated in towns and cities, and human tasks (d) <u>specialized</u> further. Specialists such as carpenters, blacksmiths, merchants, traders, and sailors developed their skills and became more efficient in their use of time and energy. The goods and services they provided brought about an (e) <u>improved</u> quality of life, a higher standard of living, and, for most societies, increased stability.

*reap: (농작물을) 베어들이다 **chieftain: 수령, 두목

41 윗글의 제목으로 가장 적절한 것은?

① How Agriculture Transformed Human Society
② The Dark Shadow of Agriculture: Repetition
③ How Can We Share Extra Food with the Poor?
④ Why Were Early Societies Destroyed by Agriculture?
⑤ The Advantages of Large Groups Over Small Groups in Farming

42 밑줄 친 (a)~(e) 중에서 문맥상 낱말의 쓰임이 적절하지 <u>않은</u> 것은? [3점]

① (a)   ② (b)   ③ (c)   ④ (d)   ⑤ (e)

(A)

A nurse took a tired, anxious soldier to the bedside. "Jack, your son is here," the nurse said to an old man lying on the bed. She had to repeat the words several times before the old man's eyes opened. Suffering from the severe pain because of heart disease, he barely saw the young uniformed soldier standing next to him. (a) He reached out his hand to the soldier.

(B)

Whenever the nurse came into the room, she heard the soldier say a few gentle words. The old man said nothing, only held tightly to (b) him all through the night. Just before dawn, the old man died. The soldier released the old man's hand and left the room to find the nurse. After she was told what happened, she went back to the room with him. The soldier hesitated for a while and asked, "Who was this man?"

(C)

She was surprised and asked, "Wasn't he your father?" "No, he wasn't. I've never met him before," the soldier replied. She asked, "Then why didn't you say something when I took you to (c) him?" He said, "I knew there had been a mistake, but when I realized that he was too sick to tell whether or not I was his son, I could see how much (d) he needed me. So, I stayed."

(D)

The soldier gently wrapped his fingers around the weak hand of the old man. The nurse brought a chair so that the soldier could sit beside the bed. All through the night the young soldier sat there, holding the old man's hand and offering (e) him words of support and comfort. Occasionally, she suggested that the soldier take a rest for a while. He politely said no.

43 주어진 글 (A)에 이어질 내용을 순서에 맞게 배열한 것으로 가장 적절한 것은?

① (B) — (D) — (C) ② (C) — (B) — (D)
③ (C) — (D) — (B) ④ (D) — (B) — (C)
⑤ (D) — (C) — (B)

44 밑줄 친 (a)~(e) 중에서 가리키는 대상이 나머지 넷과 다른 것은?

① (a) ② (b) ③ (c) ④ (d) ⑤ (e)

45 윗글에 관한 내용으로 적절하지 않은 것은?

① 노인은 심장병으로 극심한 고통을 겪고 있었다.
② 군인은 간호사를 찾기 위해 병실을 나갔다.
③ 군인은 노인과 이전에 만난 적이 있다고 말했다.
④ 간호사는 군인이 앉을 수 있도록 의자를 가져왔다.
⑤ 군인은 잠시 쉬라는 간호사의 제안을 정중히 거절하였다.

• MP3 파일을 들으며 다음 빈칸을 채우시오. (듣기 어려운 발음이나 정답의 단서가 되는 부분에 빈칸을 만들었습니다.)

01 다음을 듣고, 여자가 하는 말의 목적으로 가장 적절한 것을 고르시오.

W: Good afternoon, everybody. This is your _____ ★_____ _____, Monica Brown. Our school's ★_____ e-sports competition will be held on the last day of the semester. For the competition, we need some volunteers ____ _____ ____ ____ computers. If you're interested in helping us make the competition successful, please fill out the _____ _____ _____ and email it to me. For more information, please visit our school website. I hope many of you will join us. Thank you for listening.

02 대화를 듣고, 남자의 의견으로 가장 적절한 것을 고르시오.

M: Hannah, how's your design project going?
W: Hey, Aiden. I'm still working on it, but I'm not making _____ ★_____.
M: Can you tell me what the problem is?
W: Hmm... [Pause] It's hard to think of _____ _____. I feel like I'm _____ my time.
M: I understand. Why don't you take a walk?
W: How can that help me ___ _____ my creativity?
M: It will actually make your brain _____ _____. Then you'll see things differently.
W: But I don't have time for that.
M: You don't need a lot of time. Even a short walk will help you to _____ ___ _____ creative ideas.
W: Then I'll try it. Thanks for the tip.

03 대화를 듣고, 두 사람의 관계를 가장 잘 나타낸 것을 고르시오.

W: Excuse me. Could you please tell me where I can put this box?
M: Right here ___ _____ _____. How can I help you today?
W: I'd like to send this to Jeju Island.
M: Sure. Are there any ★_____ _____ in the box?
W: No, there are only _____ in it.
M: Then, there should be no problem.
W: I see. What's the fastest way to send it?
M: You can send the package by _____ _____, but there's ____ _____.
W: That's okay. I want it to be _____ as soon as possible. When will it arrive in Jeju if it goes out today?
M: If you send it today, it will be there by this Friday.
W: Oh, Friday will be great. I'll do the _____ _____.

04

대화를 듣고, 그림에서 대화의 내용과 일치하지 <u>않는</u> 것을 고르시오.

M : Kayla, I heard you _____ ✪ _____ on the street last weekend.

W : It was amazing! I've got a picture here. Look!

M : Oh, you're wearing the hat I gave you.

W : Yeah, I really like it.

M : Looks great. This boy playing the guitar next to you must be your brother Kevin.

W : You're right. He played _____ __ _____.

M : Cool. Why did you leave the _____ _____ _____?

W : That's for the _____. If they like _____ ✪ _____, they give us some money.

M : Oh, and you set up two speakers!

W : I did. I _____ _____ them.

M : I see. And did you design that poster on the wall?

W : Yeah. My brother and I worked on it together.

M : It sounds like you really had a lot of fun!

05

대화를 듣고, 남자가 할 일로 가장 적절한 것을 고르시오.

W : Honey, are we ready for Jake's birthday party tomorrow?

M : I sent the _____ _____ last week. What about other things?

W : I'm not sure. Let's check.

M : We are _____ a lot of _____. How about the dinner menu?

W : I _____ _____ yet.

M : We won't have much time to cook, so let's just order pizza.

W : Okay. I'll do it tomorrow. What about _____ _____?

M : Oh, you mean the smartphone? I forgot to get it!

W : That's alright. Can you go to the ✪ _____ _____ and buy it now?

M : No problem. I'll do it right away.

W : Good. Then, I'll clean up the living room while you're out.

06

대화를 듣고, 여자가 지불할 금액을 고르시오.

M : Good morning! How can I help you?

W : Hi. I'm _____ _____ a blanket and some cushions _____ _____ _____.

M : Okay. We've got some _____ _____. Would you like to have a look?

W : Yes. How much is this green blanket?

M : That's $40.

W : Oh, I love the color green. Can you also show me some cushions that _____ ✪ _____ _____ this blanket?

M : Sure! How about these?

W : They look good. I need two of them. How much are they?

M : The cushions are $20 _____.

W : Okay. I'll take one green blanket and two cushions. Can I use _____ _____?

M : Sure. It will give you 10% _____ _____ _____.

W : Thanks! Here's my credit card.

07

대화를 듣고, 남자가 록 콘서트에 갈 수 <u>없는</u> 이유를 고르시오.

W : Hello, Justin. What are you doing?

M : Hi, Ellie. I'm doing my project for _____ _____.

W : Can you go to _____ ✪ _____ _____ with me this Saturday? My sister gave me two tickets!

M : I'd love to! [Pause] But I'm afraid I _____.

W : Do you have to work that day?

M : No, I don't work _____ _____.

W : Then, why not? I thought you really like ✪ _____ _____.

M : Of course I do. But I have to _____ _____ _____ my friend's dog this Saturday.

W : Oh, really? Is your friend _____ _____?

M : He's visiting his grandmother that day.

W : Okay, no problem. I'm sure I can find _____ _____ to go with me.

08 대화를 듣고, Eco Day에 관해 언급되지 <u>않은</u> 것을 고르시오.

W: Scott, did you see this Eco Day poster?

M: No, not yet. Let me see. *[Pause]* It's an event for _____ ___ _____ while walking around a park.

W: Why don't we do it together? It's next Sunday from 10 a.m. to 5 p.m.

M: _____ good. I've been thinking a lot about the ✿_____ _____.

W: Me, too. Also, the event will be held in Eastside Park. You know, we _____ _____ to go there.

M: That's great. Oh, look at this. We have to bring our _____ ✿_____ and small bags for the trash.

W: No problem. ___ _____ _____. I can bring some for you as well.

M: Okay, thanks. Do we have to sign up for the event?

W: Yes. The poster says we _____ ____ ____ online.

M: Let's do it right now. I'm _____ _____ ____ it.

09 Eastville Dance Contest에 관한 다음 내용을 듣고, 일치하지 <u>않는</u> 것을 고르시오.

M: Hello, Eastville High School students. This is your P.E. teacher, Mr. Wilson. I'm pleased to let you know that we're _____ _____ _____ Eastville Dance Contest. Any Eastville students who love dancing _____ ✿_____ ___ the contest as a team. All kinds of dance _____ _____. If you'd like to ✿_____, please upload your team's dance video to our school website by August 15th. Students _____ _____ for their favorite video from August 16th to 20th. The winning team will receive a ✿_____ as a _____. Don't miss this _____ ✿_____ to show off your talents!

10 다음 표를 보면서 대화를 듣고, 두 사람이 구입할 정수기를 고르시오.

M: Honey, we need a water purifier for our new house.

W: You're right. Let's _____ _____ online.

M: Good idea. *[Clicking Sound]* Look! These are the _____ _____.

W: I see. What's _____ ✿_____?

M: Well, I don't want to spend more than 800 dollars.

W: Okay, how about the water tank ✿_____?

M: I think the five-liter tank would be perfect for us.

W: I think so, too. And I like the ones with a power-saving _____.

M: Okay, then we can _____ ✿_____. Now, there are just two options left.

W: Let's look at _____ ✿_____. The longer, the better.

M: I agree. We should order this model.

11 대화를 듣고, 남자의 마지막 말에 대한 여자의 응답으로 가장 적절한 것을 고르시오.

M: Let's get inside. I'm so _____ to see this ✿_____ _____.

W: Look over there. So many people are already _____ ___ _____ to buy tickets.

M: ✿_____, I bought our tickets in advance.

W: _____

12 대화를 듣고, 여자의 마지막 말에 대한 남자의 응답으로 가장 적절한 것을 고르시오.

W: Hi, Chris. Did you check _____ _____ for the history test we took last week?

M: Yes. But I think there's _____ ✿_____ with my grade.

W: Don't you think you should go ask Mr. Morgan about it?

M: _____

13 대화를 듣고, 여자의 마지막 말에 대한 남자의 응답으로 가장 적절한 것을 고르시오.

M: Mom, did you write this note?

W: What's that?

M: I found this in the book you gave me.

W: Oh, the one I _____ for you at the ✪_____ _____ last week?

M: Yes. At first I thought it was ____ _____, but it wasn't. It's a note with a message!

W: What does it say?

M: It says, "I hope you enjoy this book."

W: _____ _____! That really brings a smile to my face.

M: Yeah, mom. I love this message so much.

W: Well, then, why don't we leave a note ____ _____ ✪_____ this book later?

M: _____

14 대화를 듣고, 남자의 마지막 말에 대한 여자의 응답으로 가장 적절한 것을 고르시오.

M: Do you have ____ _____ for this weekend, Sandy?

W: Hey, Evan. I'm planning to go camping with my family.

M: I've never gone before. Do you ____ _____ _____?

W: Yes. Two or three times a month at least.

M: That's cool. Why do you like it so much?

W: I like spending time ____ _____ with my family. It makes ____ _____ _____ to them.

M: I understand. It's like a _____ _____, right?

W: Yes, you're right. Camping _____ ____ ✪_____ all my stress, too.

M: Sounds interesting. I'd love to try it.

W: If you go camping with your family, you'll see what I mean.

M: I wish I could, but I don't have _____ ✪_____ for it.

W: _____

15 다음 상황 설명을 듣고, Violet이 Peter에게 할 말로 가장 적절한 것을 고르시오.

W: Violet and Peter are _____. They're doing their _____ _____ ✪_____ together. On Saturday morning, they meet at the _____ _____. They decide to find the books they need in _____ ✪_____ of the library. Violet finds two useful books and tries to check them out. Unfortunately, she _____ _____ that she didn't bring her library card. At that _____, Peter _____ ____ to Violet. So, Violet wants to ask Peter to check out the books for her because she knows he has his library card. In this situation, what would Violet most likely say to Peter?

Violet: _____

2023.6
6회

[16~17] 다음을 듣고, 물음에 답하시오.

M: Hello, everyone. I'm Shawn Collins, a doctor at Collins Sleep Clinic. Sleep is one of the most ✪_____ _____ of our daily lives. So today, I'm _____ ____ _____ the best foods for helping you sleep better. First, kiwi fruits _____ a high level of hormones that help ____ _____ _____ more quickly, sleep longer, and wake up less during the night. Second, milk is rich in vitamin D and it ✪_____ ____ _____ ____ _____. If you drink a cup of milk before you go to bed, it will definitely help you get a good night's sleep. Third, nuts can help to produce the hormone that controls your ✪_____ _____ _____ and _____ _____ for the body to sleep at the right time. The last one is honey. Honey helps you sleep well because it reduces the hormone that keeps the brain awake! Now, I'll show you some _____ _____ _____ using these foods.

* 다음 영어는 우리말 뜻을, 우리말은 영어 단어를 〈보기〉에서 찾아 쓰시오.

01 vital _____

02 severe _____

03 interval _____

04 livestock _____

05 repetitive _____

06 주장 _____

07 분배 _____

08 직업 _____

09 진짜의 _____

10 박사 학위의 _____

[보기]

가축	pond
간격	claim
극심한	genuine
생동감	division
필수적인	doctoral
반복적인	profession

* 다음 우리말에 알맞은 영어 표현을 찾아 연결하시오.

11 ~을 뽐내다 •   • major in

12 ~에서는 •   • show off

13 미리 사전에 •   • sign up for

14 ~에 등록하다 •   • in advance

15 ~을 전공하다 •   • in terms of

* 다음 우리말과 같은 표현이 되도록 알맞은 단어를 〈보기〉에서 찾아 쓰시오.

[보기]

standard / consistent / priest / combination / semester / support
cognitive / infant / agriculture / separate / fictional / prejudice

16 편견의 위험성 ➜ danger of _____

17 지속적인 흑자 ➜ _____ surpluses

18 음식들의 조합 ➜ _____ of foods

19 인지적 정교함 ➜ the _____ sophistication

20 농업의 발전 ➜ the development of _____

21 두 개의 별도의 달력 ➜ two _____ calendars

22 더 높은 생활 수준 ➜ a higher _____ of living

23 학기의 마지막 날 ➜ the last day of the _____

24 지지와 위로의 말 ➜ words of _____ and comfort

25 Garrison Keillor의 허구적인 공동체 ➜ Garrison Keillor's _____ community

* 다음 우리말 표현에 알맞은 단어를 고르시오.

26 잠시 머뭇거리다 ➡ (meditate / hesitate) for a while

27 더 많은 증거를 흡수하다 ➡ (absorb / reject) more evidence

28 무급 대사가 되다 ➡ become unpaid (opponent / ambassador)

29 그 정보를 통합하다 ➡ (incorporate / invalidate) that information

30 희소성이 판매를 장려한다 ➡ (scarcity / abundance) encourages sales

* 다음 문장의 빈칸에 알맞은 단어를 〈보기〉에서 찾아 쓰시오.

┌──────────────── [보기] ────────────────┐
│ disordered / application / harden / stability / pace / desirable │
│ express / labeled / gradually / volume / poverty / active │
└──┘

31 그것이 실제로 당신의 뇌를 더 활발하게 만들어 줄 것이다.
➡ It will actually make your brain more _____.

32 때때로 변화의 속도는 훨씬 더 느리다.
➡ Sometimes the _____ of change is far slower.

33 어떤 음식도 좋고 나쁨으로 분류될 수 없다.
➡ No foods can be _____ as either good or bad.

34 구매량에 제한이 없었다.
➡ There was no limit on the _____ of purchases.

35 특정한 가능성들은 지식이나 믿음으로 굳어진다.
➡ Certain possibilities _____ into knowledge or beliefs.

36 우리는 사회적으로 바람직한 특성들을 많이 지니고 있다.
➡ We possess a host of socially _____ characteristics.

37 세상에 대한 아기의 인식은 상당히 무질서하다.
➡ The baby's perception of the world is wildly _____.

38 점점 더 많은 사람들이 더 큰 정착지에서 살기 시작했다.
➡ _____ more people started to live in larger settlements.

39 그들이 제공한 재화와 서비스는 향상된 안정성을 가져왔다.
➡ The goods and services they provided brought about increased _____.

40 가난이 스트레스를 만드는 경향이 있다는 것을 듣고 놀랄 사람은 거의 없을 것이다.
➡ Few people will be surprised to hear that _____ tends to create stress.

연세문학회

연세대학교 문예 창작 동아리

윤동주가 동아리 선배라고?!

〈연세문학회〉는 윤동주, 정현종, 기형도, 나희덕, 마광수, 성석제, 원재길,
황경신, 우상호 등 유명한 문인들을 배출한 문예 창작 동아리입니다.

1941년 윤동주 시인이 만든 〈문우〉에서 출발하여
1958년 정현종 시인에 의해 〈연세문학회〉라는 현재의 이름을 얻었습니다.

매주 문학에 열정을 가진 학우들이 모여
시, 소설, 독서, 합평 분야별로 창작 활동을 합니다.
학우들이 직접 쓴 작품을 함께 읽으며 창조적 비평을 진행하고,
학기 말에는 학우들의 작품을 수합하여 정기 문집 《연세문학》을 발간합니다.
또한 합동 합평회를 통해 다른 학교의 문학 동아리와 교류하기도 합니다.

〈연세문학회〉는 연세 대학교의 문학청년들이
마음껏 창작의 나래를 펼치는 드넓은 '광장'입니다.

전공과 관계없이, 문학을 사랑하는 학우라면 〈연세문학회〉의 문을 두드리세요!

★**9월** 전국연합학력평가

[회별 45문항, 제한 시간 70분]

★ 최근 연도부터 차례대로 수록하였습니다.

7회 **모의고사** ― 2025년 시행

8회 **모의고사** ― 2024년 시행

9회 **모의고사** ― 2023년 시행

출제 범위	고1 9월 수준
난이도	하 : 11~13문항 중 : 15~17문항 상 : 7~9문항 최상 : 8~10문항

출제 경향
• 듣기 17문항 (1~17번), **어법·어휘** 3문항 (29~30번, 42번), 독해 25문항 (그 외 전 문항)

9월 대비 학습 전략
1등급을 가르는 난이도 최상의 어려운 지문이 독해 문제에 등장할 수 있다. 소재가 어려운 지문은 글의 구조가 오히려 간단하여 정답을 쉽게 찾을 수 있으므로, 겁을 먹지 않도록 연습해야 한다.

전체 or 문항별 듣기

*1번부터 17번까지는 듣고 답하는 문제입니다. 1번부터 15번까지는 한 번만 들려주고, 16번부터 17번까지는 두 번 들려줍니다. 방송을 잘 듣고 답을 하시기 바랍니다.

▲ 듣기 파일

01 다음을 듣고, 여자가 하는 말의 목적으로 가장 적절한 것을 고르시오.

① 학부모 간담회 참석을 독려하려고
② 학부모 상담 기간 연기를 안내하려고
③ 교직원 회의 시간 변경에 대한 협조를 요청하려고
④ 학부모 간담회를 위한 교직원 주차 장소 변경을 알리려고
⑤ 지역 주민 행사를 위한 주말 교내 주차 허용을 공지하려고

02 대화를 듣고, 남자의 의견으로 가장 적절한 것을 고르시오.

① 환경을 위해 친환경 가방을 가능한 오래 사용해야 한다.
② 가방 구입 시 디자인과 실용성을 동시에 고려해야 한다.
③ 윤리적인 소비를 위해 친환경 제품을 선택해야 한다.
④ 환경을 위해 일회용 봉투의 사용을 줄여야 한다.
⑤ 쇼핑할 때 할인 혜택을 잘 활용해야 한다.

03 다음을 듣고, 여자가 하는 말의 요지로 가장 적절한 것을 고르시오.

① 이해가 선행되어야 학습 효과가 극대화된다.
② 학생을 가르칠 때 큰 소리로 말해 집중시켜야 한다.
③ 발표 시 핵심어를 반복하여 말하는 것이 효과적이다.
④ 수업에서 이해한 내용을 빠른 시간 내에 복습해야 한다.
⑤ 배운 내용을 소리내어 설명하는 것이 기억에 도움이 된다.

04 대화를 듣고, 그림에서 대화의 내용과 일치하지 않는 것을 고르시오.

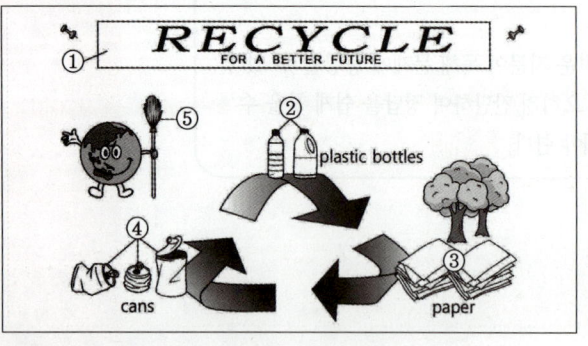

05 대화를 듣고, 남자가 할 일로 가장 적절한 것을 고르시오.

① 바닥 보호용 천 가져오기
② 문자 메시지 보내기
③ 벽화 디자인 선택하기
④ 간식 구입하기
⑤ 페인트와 붓 주문하기

06 대화를 듣고, 여자가 지불할 금액을 고르시오. [3점]

① $25   ② $35   ③ $40   ④ $45   ⑤ $50

07 대화를 듣고, 남자가 학교 영화제에 갈 수 없는 이유를 고르시오.

① 가족 여행을 가야 해서
② 결혼식에 참석해야 해서
③ 축제 행사를 진행해야 해서
④ 학교 과제를 제출해야 해서
⑤ 아르바이트 면접을 봐야 해서

08 대화를 듣고, Topas Beachcombing에 관해 언급되지 않은 것을 고르시오.

① 날짜   ② 등록 방법   ③ 준비물
④ 참가 인원   ⑤ 참가비

09 Time Travel VR Experience에 관한 다음 내용을 듣고, 일치하지 않는 것을 고르시오.

① VR을 통해 한국 석기 시대를 경험한다.
② 9월 한 달간 진행된다.
③ 어린이를 위한 VR 체험 구역이 있다.
④ 전문가 가이드를 현장에서 신청할 수 있다.
⑤ 입장료는 무료이다.

10
다음 표를 보면서 대화를 듣고, 남자가 주문할 스마트 배낭을 고르시오.

Smart Backpacks

	Model	Price	Size	Safety Feature	Charging Port
①	A	$75	13 inches	×	Internal
②	B	$85	15 inches	○	External
③	C	$90	16 inches	○	Internal
④	D	$95	16 inches	×	External
⑤	E	$110	17 inches	○	External

11
대화를 듣고, 남자의 마지막 말에 대한 여자의 응답으로 가장 적절한 것을 고르시오.

① Yes, the repairman is on the way with a spare tire.
② Of course, I filled up the tank at the gas station.
③ No, I can't find the entrance to the building.
④ Don't worry. You can use my tire.
⑤ I did. I got here just in time.

12
대화를 듣고, 여자의 마지막 말에 대한 남자의 응답으로 가장 적절한 것을 고르시오.

① That effect in the theater makes your experience special.
② I prefer to follow the fixed time schedule at work.
③ Right, the theater has set up comfortable chairs.
④ Really? I haven't watched movies with friends at home.
⑤ Exactly! At home you can watch movies whenever you want.

13
대화를 듣고, 남자의 마지막 말에 대한 여자의 응답으로 가장 적절한 것을 고르시오. [3점]

Woman: _____
① Sure. I'll recommend a list of courses you might like.
② Okay. Choose a course you think you'll score well in.
③ Cheer up! You'll make up with Henry soon.
④ Well, the time to choose courses is over.
⑤ No worries. I think you did your best!

14
대화를 듣고, 여자의 마지막 말에 대한 남자의 응답으로 가장 적절한 것을 고르시오. [3점]

Man: _____
① Good decision. I'm sure you'll do a good job.
② Yes. Let's remove the kitchen table for more space.
③ I don't think so. I could never do something like that.
④ Exactly. You'd rather work harder to earn more money.
⑤ No way. You should stick to your usual spending habits.

15
다음 상황 설명을 듣고, Liam이 Sophia에게 할 말로 가장 적절한 것을 고르시오.

Liam: _____
① Can I borrow your mini oven to practice baking cookies?
② Are you using the recipe for cookies that I gave you?
③ Do you want to learn how to bake cookies together?
④ Where will you buy a mini oven to use at home?
⑤ How do you make your cookies taste so good?

[16~17] 다음을 듣고, 물음에 답하시오.

16
여자가 하는 말의 주제로 가장 적절한 것은?

① tips for using outdoor items for camping
② essential items for observing wild animals
③ practical items made from natural surroundings
④ costs of upgrading tools for wildlife observation
⑤ tools that were inspired by wild animals' behaviors

17
언급된 물건이 아닌 것은?

① a notebook   ② a camera   ③ a raincoat
④ a flashlight   ⑤ a map

---

*이제 듣기 문제가 끝났습니다. 18번부터는 문제지의 지시에 따라 답을 하시기 바랍니다.

18 다음 글의 목적으로 가장 적절한 것은?

Dear Principal Jones,

I hope this message finds you well. As student council president, I am reaching out to discuss an important matter regarding our school library's current operating hours. At present, the library closes at 5 p.m., which many students feel limits their ability to fully use its resources for study and research after regular class hours. This is particularly challenging for those preparing for college entrance exams or working on academic projects that demand a quiet and resourceful environment. Therefore, I'd like to ask you to extend the library's operating hours to 7 p.m. This change would greatly benefit students by providing additional time to focus on their academic goals. I hope you will consider this proposal as a step toward improving our academic environment and better supporting our needs.

Sincerely,

Eric Park

Student Council President

① 신간 도서 구입을 건의하려고
② 도서관 프로그램 확대를 부탁하려고
③ 도서관 운영 시간 연장을 요청하려고
④ 도서 대출 시스템 개선에 감사하려고
⑤ 도서관 열람실 공간 확대를 제안하려고

19 다음 글에 드러난 'I'의 심경 변화로 가장 적절한 것은?

I glanced at the clock on the wall. 10:00. That meant the casting director would call very soon with the results of my first audition for a musical part in *The Wizard of Oz*. I felt shaky all over, chewing my thumbnail and jiggling my feet.

Finally, the telephone rang. While I was coming round, Dad answered. I heard him say, "Ahh, thank you. I'll let her know ..." As I got to the bottom of the stairs, he was just putting the phone down. "That was *The Wizard of Oz*. You're second senior munchkin," he announced. I got a little rush of excitement, knowing I was in — that whatever happened I could be involved in one of the productions.

① puzzled → calm
② bored → confused
③ nervous → pleased
④ satisfied → regretful
⑤ confident → disappointed

20 다음 글에서 필자가 주장하는 바로 가장 적절한 것은?

Inefficient teachers overlook the potential power of the opening minutes of class. Often, if students are quiet enough and if there are many pressing demands on a teacher's time at that moment, more than ten minutes can disappear before class starts. It's no wonder that students are late for class; they have little reason to be on time. You can use the first ten minutes to get your class off to a great start, or you can choose to waste this time. The first minutes set the tone for the rest of the class. If you are prepared for class and have taught your students an opening routine, they can use this brief time to make mental and emotional transitions from the last class or subject and prepare to focus on learning new material. In summary, you should establish an opening routine to develop your class with an effective start.

① 학생의 적극적인 참여를 위해 포용적 수업 분위기를 형성하라.
② 수업을 효과적으로 전개하기 위해 시작 루틴을 마련하라.
③ 학습 동기를 부여할 수 있는 창의적인 수업 자료를 개발하라.
④ 적절한 학습량 조절을 통해 학습 부담을 줄여라.
⑤ 학생이 스스로 학습 루틴을 만들도록 장려하라.

21

밑줄 친 There will be many who will follow you가 다음 글에서 의미하는 바로 가장 적절한 것은?

Many atoms in your body are nearly as old as the universe itself. When you breathe, for example, only some of the atoms that you inhale are exhaled in your next breath. The remaining atoms are taken into your body to become part of you, and they later leave your body by various means. You don't "own" the atoms that make up your body; you borrow them. We all share from the same atom pool because atoms forever travel around, within, and among us. Atoms cycle from person to person as we breathe and as our sweat is evaporated. We recycle atoms on a grand scale. The origin of the lightest atoms goes back to the origin of the universe, and most heavier atoms are older than the Sun and Earth. There are atoms in your body that have existed since the first moments of time, recycling throughout the universe among limitless forms, both nonliving and living. You're the present caretaker of the atoms in your body. <u>There will be many who will follow you.</u>

*evaporate: 증발시키다

① Atoms will become part of other forms after you
② Atoms will remain unique and cannot be shared
③ Atoms will follow their original forms
④ Atoms will never be taken by a new form
⑤ Atoms will disappear completely after your lifetime

22

다음 글의 요지로 가장 적절한 것은?

The act of gardening itself is a fantastic form of physical activity. It involves a range of motions, from digging and planting to watering and harvesting. These activities help improve strength, flexibility, and endurance. You might not realize it, but small tasks like weeding or turning compost can burn many calories. Gardening is particularly beneficial for those who find traditional exercise challenging. It's a low-impact way to stay active and fit, making it accessible for people of all ages and physical abilities. Besides physical health, gardening has profound mental health benefits. Tending to plants can be incredibly calming and meditative. It allows you to focus on the present moment, reducing stress and anxiety. The repetitive tasks involved in gardening can induce a state of mindfulness, similar to meditation. Studies have shown that spending time in nature, even in a small garden, can elevate mood, improve cognition, and reduce depression symptoms. The sense of accomplishment from watching your plants grow and thrive can also boost self-esteem and overall well-being.

*compost: 퇴비

① 야외 활동을 통해 협동심과 자존감을 높일 수 있다.
② 취미 활동을 지속적으로 할 수 있는 동기가 필요하다.
③ 원예 활동은 신체적 건강과 더불어 정신적 건강에 이롭다.
④ 실내에서 식물을 기르는 것은 집중력 향상에 도움이 된다.
⑤ 원예 활동은 연령에 관계없이 다양한 사람들이 즐길 수 있다.

For many centuries, humans have taken advantage of tools that translate and bring into our perception natural phenomena that we can't perceive with our senses. In some cases, this consists of simply amplifying signals that feed into our normal sensory inputs (e.g., telescopes can bring into clear view that which is too far away for our eyes to perceive on their own). Other instruments turn signals that we cannot perceive into ones that we can observe. Some of these take the form of expanding the reach of our current senses, such as creating visible images based on the ultraviolet spectrum of light or changing sounds that are normally outside the range of what human ears can hear into audible signals. Alternatively, some instruments measure properties for which we have no sensory capacity at all and change them into that which we can observe. *amplify: 확장하다 **audible: 들을 수 있는

① difficulties in replacing human senses with tools
② the tools that increase the ability of human senses
③ human senses that inspire the inventing of scientific tools
④ differences between visual and auditory senses in humans
⑤ the power of human imagination in discovering the universe

Many opponents of animal experimentation argue that not only is modern medicine not the only cause for the decline in mortality, many medical advances that did contribute to human health were not the result of animal experimentation. Defenders of research have claimed that since there is a strong correlation between the practice of animal experimentation and medical advancement, the former caused the latter. Opponents of research reject this inference. After all, we have independent reasons to expect these phenomena to be correlated. Since the law prescribes that all new drugs, prosthetic devices, and surgical techniques be tried on animals before they are used in humans, we will subsequently find that all medical advances are correlated with prior experimentation on animals. Consequently, the correlation between animal experimentation and medical discovery is the result of legal necessity, not evidence that animal experimentation led to medical advances. Moreover, several influential physicians have offered historical evidence that animal experimentation has not been as responsible for biomedical discovery as defenders suggest. They claim that clinical discoveries played a more substantial role than animal researchers have led us to believe. *prosthetic: 보철의

① Bio-medicine: Unlocking New Frontiers in Health Care
② Is Medicine Advanced by Experimenting on Animals?
③ Refer to Historical Evidence to Solve Medical Issues
④ Why Aren't There Strict Laws for Animal Adoption?
⑤ Medical Advances for Extending Human Life Span

25 다음 도표의 내용과 일치하지 <u>않는</u> 것은?

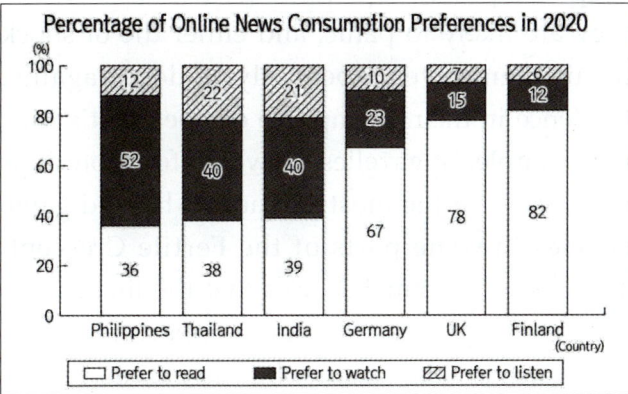

Percentage of Online News Consumption Preferences in 2020

(%)

	Philippines	Thailand	India	Germany	UK	Finland
Prefer to listen	12	22	21	10	7	6
Prefer to watch	52	40	40	23	15	12
Prefer to read	36	38	39	67	78	82

(Country)

☐ Prefer to read　■ Prefer to watch　▨ Prefer to listen

The graph above shows the percentage of online news consumption preferences in three ways for six countries in 2020. ① In Germany, the UK and Finland, reading was the most preferred way of consuming online news, with its percentage over 60 percent across the three countries. ② The interesting point is that the Philippines, Thailand and India all preferred to watch online news the most. ③ In terms of preference to watching online news, the Philippines showed the highest percentage and Finland showed the lowest preference among all six countries. ④ Four out of ten preferred to watch online news in both Thailand and India, and that percentage was more than three times as high as that of Finland. ⑤ For listening, the least preferred way of consuming online news, the percentage of people who preferred it in Finland was a third of that of Thailand.

26 Roger Payne에 관한 다음 글의 내용과 일치하지 <u>않는</u> 것은?

Roger Payne was born in Manhattan in 1935. He studied biology at Harvard University and eventually earned his Ph.D. from Cornell University in 1961. In 1967, he discovered that humpback whales make long and complex sounds. They're known as "whale songs," and he showed that whales use them to communicate. Then in 1970, he released an album *Songs of the Humpback Whale*, which became a surprise hit and helped start the global "Save the Whales" movement. The following year, he founded Ocean Alliance to protect whales and the earth's oceans, and he used new, safe methods to study whales without harming them. Over his career, he led more than 100 research trips worldwide, including the Voyage of the Odyssey from 2000 to 2005, which studied ocean pollution. His work helped make laws that protect marine mammals, which finally led to the global ban on commercial whaling in 1986.　*humpback whale: 혹등고래

① 하버드 대학교에서 생물학을 공부했다.
② 혹등고래가 길고 복잡한 소리를 낸다는 것을 발견했다.
③ 그의 앨범 *Songs of the Humpback Whale*은 인기를 얻지 못했다.
④ 고래와 지구의 해양을 보호하기 위해 Ocean Alliance를 설립했다.
⑤ 그의 연구는 해양 포유류를 보호하는 법 제정에 도움을 주었다.

27 Father-Daughter Sock Hop에 관한 다음 안내문의 내용과 일치하지 <u>않는</u> 것은?

Father-Daughter Sock Hop

We are excited to bring you the 5th annual Father-Daughter Sock Hop — an incredibly special evening for fathers and daughters to dance!

When & Where
· September 12th(Friday), from 6 p.m. to 9 p.m.
· Maple Creek Community Center

Participation Fee
· $25 per pair
· $5 per each additional daughter
· No refund for cancellations on the day of the event

Notice
· A pair of socks will be given out as a gift to every participant.
· Take pictures at the photo zone.

Registration
· Register online at www.maplecreekcity.org.

① 9월 12일 금요일에 개최된다.
② 한 쌍당 참가비는 $25이다.
③ 행사 당일 취소 시 환불이 가능하다.
④ 모든 참가자에게 선물이 제공된다.
⑤ 포토존에서 사진을 찍을 수 있다.

28 2025 Library Bookmark Design Contest에 관한 다음 안내문의 내용과 일치하는 것은?

2025 Library Bookmark Design Contest

The 6th annual Library Bookmark Design Contest is now open! Show your creativity and design skills.

Participation
· Participants need to be between the ages of 5-12.

Guidelines
· Create a bookmark by hand using markers or crayons.
· Designs must fit the slogan "Find Your Voice."
· Do not use commercialized character images in your design.

Submission
· Limit one entry per participant.
· Entries should be submitted via email to contest@srpls.org by October 4th.

Prizes
· 1st place: $50 gift card, 2nd place: $30 gift card
· Winners' bookmarks will be printed and given to visitors.

※ For more information, please visit our website at www.sherrillpubliclibrary.org.

① 여덟 번째 열리는 대회이다.
② 13세 이상이면 누구나 참가할 수 있다.
③ 상업용 캐릭터 이미지를 사용할 수 있다.
④ 출품작은 참가자당 두 개로 제한된다.
⑤ 수상자의 책갈피는 인쇄되어 방문객에게 제공될 것이다.

---

29 다음 글의 밑줄 친 부분 중, 어법상 틀린 것은?
[3점]

Big mammalian herbivore species react to danger from predators or humans in different ways. Some species are nervous, fast, and programmed for instant flight when they perceive a threat. Other species are slower, less nervous, seek protection in herds, ① stand their ground when threatened, and don't run until necessary. Naturally, the nervous species are difficult to keep in captivity. If ② putting into an enclosure, they are likely to panic, and either die of shock or hit themselves repeatedly to death against the fence in their attempts to escape. That's true, for example, of gazelles, ③ which for thousands of years were the most frequently hunted game species in some parts of the Fertile Crescent. There is no mammal species that the first settled peoples of that area had more opportunity ④ to domesticate than gazelles. But no gazelle species has ever been domesticated. Just imagine trying to herd an animal that runs away, blindly hits ⑤ itself against walls, can leap up to nearly 30 feet, and can run at a speed of 50 miles per hour!

*herbivore: 초식동물 **herd: 무리

---

30 다음 글의 밑줄 친 부분 중, 문맥상 낱말의 쓰임이 적절하지 않은 것은?

For a species born in a time when resources were limited and dangers were great, our natural tendency to share and cooperate is ① complicated when resources are plenty and outside dangers are few. When we have less, we tend to be more open to sharing what we have. Certain nomadic tribes don't have much, yet they are happy to share because it is in their ② interest to do so. If you happen upon them in your travels, they will open up their homes and give you their food and hospitality. It's not just because they are nice people; it's because their ③ survival depends on sharing, for they know that they may be the travelers in need of food and shelter another day. Ironically, the ④ more we have, the bigger our fences, the more sophisticated our security to keep people away and the less we want to share. Our desire for more, combined with our ⑤ increased physical interaction with the "common folk," starts to create a disconnection or blindness to reality.

*nomadic: 유목의 **hospitality: 환대

31

Whether we feel happy or sad, content or discontent, is not determined merely by each individual successive moment of life experience — a good thing happens and I'm happy, a bad thing happens and I'm sad. While our experiences affect our mood, we are not blown in a completely new direction by each gust of wind. As humans, we adjust — to new information and events both good and bad — and return to our personal default level of well-being. There will be highs and lows, but over time, like water seeking its own level, we are pulled toward our baseline — back *up* after bad news and back *down* after good. The euphoria of first love fades, and so does the despair of a break-up. This tendency is best seen with little kids and their toy joy: When they get what they've longed for, they believe they will be happy for the rest of their lives. And for the first few minutes of the rest of their lives, they are. But then the kids — like adults — _____.

*euphoria: (극도의) 행복감

① adapt   ② regret   ③ explore
④ struggle   ⑤ celebrate

32

Although you may put off going to sleep in order to squeeze more activities into your day, eventually your need for sleep becomes overwhelming and you are forced to get some sleep. This daily drive for sleep appears to be due, in part, to a compound known as adenosine. This natural chemical builds up in your blood as time awake increases. While you sleep, your body breaks down the adenosine. Thus, this molecule may be what your body uses to keep track of lost sleep and to trigger sleep when needed. An accumulation of adenosine and other factors might explain why, after several nights of less than optimal amounts of sleep,

you build up a sleep debt that you must make up by sleeping longer than normal. Because of such built-in molecular feedback, you can't become accustomed to getting less sleep than your body needs. Eventually, a lack of sleep _____. [3점]

*compound: 화합물 **accumulation: 축적

① takes away your energy
② causes mood swings
③ catches up with you
④ breaks down natural chemicals
⑤ triggers adenosine to disappear

2025. 9
7회

33

One of the things that makes uncertainty difficult for members of the public to appreciate is that _____.
Take, for example, the distance between Earth and the sun: 1.49597×10^8 km, as measured at one point during the year. This seems relatively precise; after all, using six significant digits means I know the distance to an accuracy of one part in a million or so. However, if the next digit is uncertain, that means the uncertainty in knowing the precise Earth-sun distance is larger than the distance between New York and Chicago! Whether or not the quoted number is "precise" therefore depends on what I'm intending to do with it. If I care only about what minute the sun will rise tomorrow, then the number quoted here is fine. If I want to send a satellite to orbit just above the sun, however, then I would need to know distances more accurately. [3점]

*significant digit: 유효 숫자

① the significance of uncertainty is relative
② the relativity of time is difficult to recognize
③ all measurements have the same level of uncertainty
④ measurements of distance do not depend on intention
⑤ specific numbers make people believe without question

34

Richard Heinberg, an American journalist, argues that in building the renewable energy infrastructure to stop global warming, we are actually involved in one of the greatest change projects in human history. In addition to solar panels and wind turbines, we have to build an alternative transport infrastructure, farming procedures and industrial processes. This transformation cannot happen without fossil fuels. For instance, production of concrete structures and steel elements require amounts of energy that is only possible to produce with fossil energy. Production of solar panels requires scarce and expensive minerals which must be excavated, again requiring the use of fossil fuels. Thus, the harder we push towards a renewable energy system, the faster _____. This is not only expensive, but also an undermining factor for our efforts to cut global emissions. Heinberg remarks that the cost of building this new energy infrastructure is seldom counted in transition proposals, which tend to focus just on energy supply requirements. [3점]   *excavate: 발굴하다

① we are taking full advantage of renewable energy sources
② we have to use fossil energy for the construction process
③ we invest in more natural resources for the environment
④ we are able to decrease the rate of global warming
⑤ alternative energy markets become competitive

35 다음 글에서 전체 흐름과 관계 <u>없는</u> 문장은?

Humans for centuries have dreamed of machines that could become intelligent and make human-like decisions. There have been myths about robots, automatons, and artificial beings since ancient Greece (e.g., the myth of Pandora, who released ills upon the world). ① Likewise, literature throughout history has dreamed of creating human-like creatures and thinking machines (e.g., Mary Shelley's *Frankenstein*). ② In 1950, British mathematician Alan Turing asked whether machines could think and reason like humans and then developed the Turing test to measure a machine's intelligence and whether the machines can think autonomously. ③ A few years later, MIT professor John McCarthy coined "artificial intelligence," replacing the previously used expression "automata studies." ④ But artificial intelligence didn't stop there; its first major appearance was in a movie where feeling artificial intelligence replaced human characters with robots. ⑤ Since then, artificial intelligence has become the study and practice of "making intelligent machines" that are programmed to think like humans — endowed by their creators with reasoning and learning.

*automaton: 자동 장치 **endow: 부여하다

[36~37] 주어진 글 다음에 이어질 글의 순서로 가장 적절한 것을 고르시오.

36

The desert tortoise has a simple solution for coping with Death Valley's extreme heat: It avoids it.

(A) But to stay supplied with water through its extended hibernation, the reptile relies on something else — its highly sophisticated bladder. Unlike most animals, the tortoise's bladder acts as a holding tank, allowing it to reabsorb water back into its body. Incredibly, a desert tortoise can go a full year without taking in any freshwater at all.

(B) The slow-moving creature hibernates during the winter and stays in its tunnel for much of the summer, meaning that it spends more than 90 percent of its life immobile. In fact, the tortoise usually only surfaces after a good rain. Then, it gets to work. The tortoise stocks up on water by eating plants and digging holes to collect rain.

(C) And because its bladder is so important to a tortoise's survival, park rangers often remind visitors not to stop and help the slow-movers across the road. Tortoises become so terrified when people pick them up that they empty their bladders, losing their precious water reserves. [3점]   *hibernation: 동면 **bladder: 방광

① (A) — (C) — (B)   ② (B) — (A) — (C)
③ (B) — (C) — (A)   ④ (C) — (A) — (B)
⑤ (C) — (B) — (A)

37

Imagine you are pedalling your bicycle on a level road. You stop pedalling: no force is now acting to move you forward. What happens?

(A) One of these is friction in the wheels rubbing on the axles. Another is air resistance, which you can feel, pushing you backwards as you and the bicycle move forwards. When you apply these ideas to something around you, like a cart, you can see what could be generating friction: mainly the axles rubbing on the body as they rotate.

(B) You gradually slow down. How could you slow down more suddenly, in a shorter distance? By putting the brakes on. Because the brakes change your movement, making you slow down more suddenly, they must be exerting a force on the bicycle and you, as they grip and rub on the wheel-rims.

(C) This is the force called friction, which tends to slow down moving things by acting in the direction opposite to movement, that is backwards. Even without the brakes on, there are other friction forces acting on you and your bicycle, which also slow you down.

*axle: (바퀴의) 축 **rim: 테두리

① (A) — (C) — (B)
② (B) — (A) — (C)
③ (B) — (C) — (A)
④ (C) — (A) — (B)
⑤ (C) — (B) — (A)

[38~39] 글의 흐름으로 보아, 주어진 문장이 들어가기에 가장 적절한 곳을 고르시오.

38

Nonlinear editing, on the other hand, is like using a word processing program.

All editing systems are now nonlinear computer-based systems that allow random access to any video shot or scene without having to fast forward or fast reverse to find it. Nonlinear systems can create a range of special effects, such as slow motion, wipes and dissolves. (①) Another highlight of a digital nonlinear system is its random access process that makes it easy for an editor to find desired shots or scenes without having to spend time fast forwarding or rewinding videotape. (②) With nonlinear editing, shots or scenes can be easily added or removed anywhere in the program, and the computer adjusts the program length automatically. (③) Linear editing was like composing a paper on a typewriter. (④) If a mistake was made or new information needed to be added the whole piece had to be retyped. (⑤) If a mistake is made, it is easily deleted and fixed with a few keystrokes, and new information can be added easily.

*linear: 선형의

39

A person who always tries to prevent harm but never does, is not generally thought of as morally good.

A morally good person is one who does morally bad actions significantly less often than most and does morally good ones significantly more often than most. In judging a person not only her actions but also her intentions and motives are relevant. (①) A morally good person must intend to do morally good actions and intend to avoid morally bad ones. (②) A person who unintentionally prevents harm to others and does not harm them simply because things do not turn out as she intends is not morally good. (③) Although this kind of situation generally occurs only in slapstick movies, it is worth mentioning to avoid the false impression that it is the actual consequences of a person's actions that count toward her being judged morally good or bad. (④) But actual consequences are important. (⑤) Of such a person, it may be said that she means well; but, contrary to Kant, some results are necessary before she is regarded as morally good. [3점]

❖ 정답 및 해설 190 ~ 196p

Vision is influenced by our preconceptions about reality. In viewing a scene, we establish unconscious hierarchies that reflect our functional relationship to objects and our momentary priorities. For example, when visualizing a hammer in our mind's eye, we tend to "see" it in profile or at some other "ready for use" angle. One would probably not visualize a hammer as seen from the top so that the handle is hidden by the hammer's head. The functional relationship we have with objects creates visual expectations that interfere with our ability to see "like a camera." The camera, like the human eye, sees only shapes and colors. It documents the world impartially through a lens that is similar to the eye. When we look at them carefully, photographs are often surprising because they don't interpret confusing details but simply serve them up to us with a mechanical indifference. And because of their flatness, photographs often contain areas that appear as unrecognizable colors and shapes.

⬇

Our visual perception is shaped by an established hierarchy based on functional relationships, which ___(A)___ our ability to see objects as they truly are, unlike the ___(B)___ perspective of a camera.

	(A)		(B)
①	enhances	—	accurate
②	simplifies	—	fixed
③	interrupts	—	objective
④	enhances	—	neutral
⑤	interrupts	—	inconsistent

[41~42] 다음 글을 읽고, 물음에 답하시오.

"May I help you?" are the worst four words that a retail salesperson can utter because they don't encourage the customer to talk and put them on the defensive. The four words usually draw out a negative response that stops cold a sales transaction. Examples of (a) <u>better</u> questions to use when approaching customers are "Is there anything in particular that you are looking for?" and "Are you shopping for a gift?" If a fashion salesperson approached you with "May I help you?" chances are you would feel the salesperson didn't (b) <u>care</u>. This line is a rote approach that is so overused by untrained and uninterested salespeople. In fact, most of us shudder in horror on hearing these words. The very meaning of the question "May I help you?" (c) <u>rejects</u> that the customer is in trouble of some sort and needs rescuing. This almost always puts the customer on the defense. "No, thank you" is usually the immediate response, even if the customer is actually in need of assistance. The subconscious thought by the customer is often "I'm smart enough to figure out what I want, and I don't need your help!"

If customers feel pressured or cornered, then salespeople won't make any sales. The approach has to promote a (d) <u>comfortable</u> environment that makes customers feel there is no rush. Furthermore, if customers just want to look around, they should feel that it is all right to do so. In situations where customers really do want to look around on their own, salespeople should give customers their business cards and keep themselves (e) <u>accessible</u> in case customers have questions or concerns.

*shudder: 몸서리치다

41 윗글의 제목으로 가장 적절한 것은?

① Breaking the Ice: Building Trust with Customers
② To Be a Smart Consumer or Not
③ Why "May I Help You?" Fails
④ How "Buy One Get One" Opens Your Wallet
⑤ The Closer to Customers, the More Money You Make

42 밑줄 친 (a)~(e) 중에서 문맥상 낱말의 쓰임이 적절하지 않은 것은? [3점]

① (a)　　② (b)　　③ (c)　　④ (d)　　⑤ (e)

[43~45] 다음 글을 읽고, 물음에 답하시오.

(A)

While the cafeteria was full of high school students on that afternoon, Dave was thirsty. We sat near yet away from him, fixing our hair and worrying about the test next period we hadn't studied for. (a) He was far away from our world, yet forced to be a part of it.

(B)

Although it was clear that they were from very different worlds, for one moment, they'd shared a real understanding. As I walked away from my lunch table that day, I looked at Dave. I thought he and the dollar were very much alike. They both weren't accepted where the world said they were supposed to be. But just as the dollar had found a place in a warm-hearted senior's pocket, I was sure (b) he would eventually find his, too.

(C)

But for some reason, he decided against it. He wasn't leaving until he got a drink. With a determined expression, (c) he kept aimlessly pushing the dollar bill into the machine. Just then a popular senior boy stood up from his seat, and walked over to the boy. (d) He calmly explained how the machine often had trouble accepting dollar bills. After that, he pulled some coins from his pocket and put them into the machine. Dave gave him his dollar and chose a flavor of fruit juice. Then the two walked off in different directions.

(D)

He stood at the drink machine with purpose, fumbling through his fake leather wallet for some change. He came up with a wrinkled dollar bill, and nervously glanced back at his table where other students in (e) his class were sitting. Dave tried to make the machine accept his money. After he failed a few times, some students began to laugh at him. He started shaking, and tears began to form in his eyes. I saw him turn to sit down, looking like he had given up.　*fumble: 더듬어 찾다

43 주어진 글 (A)에 이어질 내용을 순서에 맞게 배열한 것으로 가장 적절한 것은?

① (B) ― (D) ― (C)　　② (C) ― (B) ― (D)
③ (C) ― (D) ― (B)　　④ (D) ― (B) ― (C)
⑤ (D) ― (C) ― (B)

44 밑줄 친 (a)~(e) 중에서 가리키는 대상이 나머지 넷과 다른 것은?

① (a)　　② (b)　　③ (c)　　④ (d)　　⑤ (e)

45 윗글에 관한 내용으로 적절하지 않은 것은?

① 그날 오후 식당은 고등학생들로 가득 찼다.
② 'I'는 Dave와 그 달러가 비슷하다고 생각했다.
③ 상급생은 주머니에서 동전을 꺼냈다.
④ Dave와 상급생은 같은 방향으로 떠났다.
⑤ Dave의 눈에 눈물이 맺히기 시작했다.

• MP3 파일을 들으며 다음 빈칸을 채우시오. (듣기 어려운 발음이나 정답의 단서가 되는 부분에 빈칸을 만들었습니다.)

01 다음을 듣고, 여자가 하는 말의 목적으로 가장 적절한 것을 고르시오.

W: Hello, this is Karen Smith, the principal of Sunnyfield High School. I would like to inform all staff about an important plan for next week's Parent-Teacher Meeting. _____ _____ _____ _____ on campus, all teachers and staff should park at the nearby community center on Wednesday. It is only a five-minute walk from the school. This plan will ⭐ _____ that parents attending the meeting have easy access to parking. Your cooperation will greatly _____ ____ _____ this event a smooth and successful experience. Thank you in advance for your cooperation with ____ _____ _____.

02 대화를 듣고, 남자의 의견으로 가장 적절한 것을 고르시오.

M: Lisa. What are you looking at?

W: I'm planning to buy this eco-bag. Isn't it cute?

M: It is, but _____ ____ _____ _____ several eco-bags?

W: Yes, I do. But this one is limited edition!

M: Well, _____ ____ _____ more bags, wouldn't it be better to use the ones you already have?

W: I know what you mean. But I thought eco-bags were ⭐ _____-friendly.

M: That's true, but the point is even eco-bags need to be reused as long as possible.

W: Oh, that _____ _____.

M: If you use one eco-bag for a long time, it will be much better for the environment.

W: Okay. I'll try to use the bags I already have.

03 다음을 듣고, 여자가 하는 말의 요지로 가장 적절한 것을 고르시오.

W: Hi, everyone! Welcome back to Smart Study Tips. Has your mind _____ _____ _____ during a test, even though you studied very hard? Here's a simple but ⭐ _____ tip. Explaining what you've learned out loud can help you remember better. Just pretend you're a teacher and explain what you've learned in your own words. You can even _____ ___ _____ in front of a mirror. Try it. You'll be surprised how well it works!

04 대화를 듣고, 그림에서 대화의 내용과 일치하지 않는 것을 고르시오.

M: Hey, Lucy! Look at this recycling poster. What do you notice first?

W: The title at the top really stands out. It says "RECYCLE FOR A BETTER FUTURE."

M: Right! And below it, there's the big recycling symbol with _____ _____ _____ __ ⭐ _____.

W: That makes it clear that this is about recycling. On the top arrow, there are plastic bottles.

M: Yeah, there are! Oh, look! Below the trees, there is paper, which students often waste.

W: Right. And beside one of the bottom arrows, there are three cans. Cans are ____ _____ _____ to recycle.

M: Exactly. Look at this. There's an Earth holding a flower. That's a fun way to remind us that we can ____ ___ ___.

W: I agree! This poster does a great job of _____ recycling.

05 대화를 듣고, 남자가 할 일로 가장 적절한 것을 고르시오.

W: Ryan, I'm excited to paint designs on the walls of the community center tomorrow!

M: Me too, Emily. It's going to ✪ _____ up the neighborhood.

W: Are we all set? Let's go over the preparations.

M: Okay. I've selected designs to put on each wall. What about the paint and brushes?

W: I ordered them yesterday and they will be delivered this evening.

M: Good. What else do we need to do?

W: Oh! I guess we also need _____ ____ _____ the ground from paint.

M: I've already picked them up from the art center. Did you buy snacks for the volunteers?

W: Yes, I did. One last thing. Do we need to remind all volunteers to _____ _____ _____? Their clothes might get dirty.

M: I think we do. I'll send a text message to them right away.

W: Perfect. The ✪ _____ will love the finished walls!

06 대화를 듣고, 여자가 지불할 금액을 고르시오.

M: Hello! Welcome to Central Park Bike Rentals. How can I help you today?

W: Hi, we'd like to rent some bikes.

M: How many bikes _____ ____ _____ ___ ✪ _____ today?

W: We'll need one adult bike and one child bike.

M: Sure! Adult bikes are 15 dollars per hour, and children's bikes are 10 dollars _____ _____. How long will you be renting them for?

W: We'll need them for two hours.

M: _____ ____. So, that's one adult bike for two hours and one child bike for two hours.

W: That's right. We want to rent helmets too.

M: Bike rentals include helmets for safety. You should wear them while riding the bikes in the park.

W: Okay, can I use this "GO Green" coupon today?

M: Sure, you can ____ __ ____ _____ on the total price.

W: Great! Here's my credit card.

07 대화를 듣고, 남자가 학교 영화제에 갈 수 없는 이유를 고르시오.

W: Hey, Alex. Are you coming to the School Film Festival this Saturday?

M: I wish I could, but I have to _____ ___ _____ _____.

W: Oh, no, why? I thought you were really looking forward to it.

M: I was! But something came up, so I can't make it.

W: That's too bad. You don't have your part-time job this weekend, right?

M: No, I've ____ ____ _____ ____.

W: Hmm, then maybe you're busy with some schoolwork?

M: No, I already finished my big ✪ _____ this week.

W: So, why can't you come?

M: I'm going to my cousin's wedding and the place is really far. It'll take _____ ____ _____ ____ to get there and back.

W: Oh, sorry to hear that. But family events like that are important.

M: Yeah, they are. I'll definitely check out the next school film festival.

❖ 정답 200p

회 **135**

08

대화를 듣고, Topas Beachcombing에 관해 언급되지 않은 것을 고르시오.

M: Hey, Emma, _____ _____ _____ _____?
W: Hi. I'm reading a post about the Topas Beachcombing activity.
M: What is that? I've never _____ ___ ___.
W: It's an activity where you go along the beach and collect garbage and make _____ _____ ___ _____ with it.
M: Great! When is it?
W: This Saturday, the 25th of September, at 10 a.m. on Sunset Beach.
M: Oh, it's near my house. How can I join the activity?
W: You can sign up on their website.
M: Do I need to bring anything?
W: Yes, we'll need gloves and a bag for the garbage.
M: No problem. Is there a ✪ _____ _____?
W: No, it's free.
M: Perfect! It sounds meaningful and fun.

09

Time Travel VR Experience에 관한 다음 내용을 듣고, 일치하지 않는 것을 고르시오.

M: Hello, everyone! I'm excited to tell you about the Time Travel VR Experience happening at the Natural History Museum. This event will _____ _____ _____ the Stone Age of Korea in an amazing way using ✪ _____ _____. It will run for the whole month of September 2025 in the Asian Gallery on the second floor. With a VR headset, you'll _____ _____ ___ _____ to see how people lived in the Stone Age of Korea and learn about their daily life. For children, there will also be a fun and interactive VR section. Expert guides will be available only for those who _____ ___ _____ ___ _____ online. There is no entrance fee and you can enjoy all the activities free of charge.

10

다음 표를 보면서 대화를 듣고, 남자가 주문할 스마트 배낭을 고르시오.

W: Hey, John. What are you looking at?
M: You know I'm planning to _____ _____, so I'm checking out smart backpacks. Want to help me pick one?
W: Sure, let me see. *[Pause]* The prices are different.
M: Yeah, but I don't want to spend more than 100 dollars.
W: Got it. Let's _____ _____ _____.
M: I usually carry a laptop, so it should be at least 15 inches.
W: There's also an option with a _____ ✪ _____. Do you need that?
M: Definitely. It will help keep my belongings safe while traveling. That narrows it down to just two models.
W: Now, how about a charging port? I think an external port _____ ___ _____ _____.
M: Sounds great. I'll pick the one with an external port. I'll order it right now.

11

대화를 듣고, 남자의 마지막 말에 대한 여자의 응답으로 가장 적절한 것을 고르시오.

[Cell phone rings.]
M: Hey, Daisy. It's Jacob. Are you almost here? I'm waiting on the street near my house.
W: Sorry, Jacob. ___ _____ ___ _____ with my car tire. Can you _____ ___ _____ _____?
M: Sure. Did you call someone to _____ ___?
W: _____

12

대화를 듣고, 여자의 마지막 말에 대한 남자의 응답으로 가장 적절한 것을 고르시오.

W: Danny, do you _____ ___ _____ _____ at home or going to the theater?
M: I sometimes go to the theater with friends, but I watch most movies at home.
W: So do I. Home is _____ _____ because I don't need to follow the _____ _____.
M: _____

13 대화를 듣고, 남자의 마지막 말에 대한 여자의 응답으로 가장 적절한 것을 고르시오.

M: Hello, Ms. Taylor.
W: Hi, Luke. _____ _____ _____ in my office?
M: I'm not sure about which courses to pick for next year. I'm thinking of taking the same courses as my friend, Henry.
W: I understand why you feel that way. However, it's not a good idea to just follow your friend _____ _____ what's best for you.
M: But, I don't even know where to begin. Can you give me _____ ✪ _____ ?
W: What do you enjoy doing?
M: Umm. I guess I like creating video clips.
W: That is the starting point. You can choose courses _____ ____ _____.
M: Ah! I see. Could you help me find courses that fit me?
W: _____

14 대화를 듣고, 여자의 마지막 말에 대한 남자의 응답으로 가장 적절한 것을 고르시오.

W: Kevin, what are you writing about?
M: Hi, Eva. I'm writing about the money-saving challenge I completed.
W: The money-saving challenge? What's that?
M: It's a challenge where you try to reduce your spending and do not buy ✪ _____ _____ for a set time. I did it for a month.
W: Really? Wasn't it so hard?
M: Not that much. I spent money on things I really needed.
W: Why ____ ____ _____ to do that?
M: At first, it was just to save money. But it also made me realize that I have wasted money on too many extra things.
W: Oh, I see. So it's about cutting out unnecessary spending?
M: Exactly. And I found free ways to have fun. For example, _____ _____ ___ _____, instead of eating out!
W: That sounds _____ ____ _____. I'll do the same!
M: _____

15 다음 상황 설명을 듣고, Liam이 Sophia에게 할 말로 가장 적절한 것을 고르시오.

M: Liam and Sophia are college students and friends. Liam ✪ _____ _____ how to bake cookies in a cooking class and wants to practice the recipe at home. However, he doesn't have a mini oven, and he cannot _____ ____ _____ _____ right now. He remembers that Sophia has a mini oven at home and often brings _____ _____ _____ to class. So, he wants to ask her if she can _____ ____ her mini oven. In this situation, what would Liam most likely say to Sophia?
Liam: _____

2025.9
7회

[16~17] 다음을 듣고, 물음에 답하시오.

W: Hello, nature lovers! If you're planning to observe wild animals ____ _____ _____ _____ _____, here are must-have items to make your experience enjoyable. First, bring a notebook to record interesting ✪ _____ about the animals you spot, such as their behavior or appearance. Second, don't forget to carry a camera. It's a great way to capture special moments and share them with others later. Next, a raincoat will keep you dry and comfortable ____ _____ ____ _____ _____, allowing you to stay focused on your adventure. Lastly, bring a map to help you navigate unfamiliar areas and avoid getting lost. _____ _____ ✪ _____ will ensure that you have a safe and enjoyable experience while exploring the natural surroundings of wild animals.

• 제한시간 20분 • 맞은 개수 ___ / 40

* 다음 영어는 우리말 뜻을, 우리말은 영어 단어를 〈보기〉에서 찾아 쓰시오.

01 frontier _____

02 extend _____

03 alliance _____

04 sophisticated _____

05 arrangement _____

06 절망 _____

07 중요한 _____

08 목적 없이 _____

09 내구력 _____

10 사망률 _____

[보기]

정교한	assignment
과제	aimlessly
배정	despair
연장하다	substantial
동맹, 연합	mortality
경계, 지평	endurance

* 다음 우리말에 알맞은 영어 표현을 찾아 연결하시오.

11 ~에 들어가다 •   • feed into

12 분위기를 잡다 •   • have access to

13 ~을 따라잡다 •   • catch up with

14 ~에 접근하다 •   • set the tone

15 갑자기 멈추다 •   • stop cold

* 다음 우리말과 같은 표현이 되도록 알맞은 단어를 〈보기〉에서 찾아 쓰시오.

[보기]

cancellations / rush / mammals / scarce / interactive / alternative
capture / overlook / interest / motives / observations / attempts

16 흥분의 물결 ➡ _____ of excitement

17 관찰을 기록하다 ➡ record _____

18 희귀하고 값비싼 광물들 ➡ _____ and expensive minerals

19 잠재력을 간과하다 ➡ _____ the potential power

20 그녀의 의도와 동기 ➡ her intentions and _____

21 그들의 탈출하려는 시도에서 ➡ in their _____ to escape

22 대체 교통 기반 시설 ➡ _____ transport infrastructure

23 특별한 순간을 포착하기 ➡ to _____ special moments

24 해양 포유류를 보호하는 법 ➡ laws that protect marine _____

25 재밌고 상호작용 하는 VR 구역 ➡ a fun and _____ VR section

26 길들일 기회 ➡ more opportunity to (dedicate / domesticate)

27 온라인 뉴스 소비 선호도 ➡ online news (consumption / consultation) preferences

28 세상을 공평하게 기록하다 ➡ document the world (incidentally / impartially)

29 확립된 위계에 의해 형성된 ➡ shaped by an established (anarchy / hierarchy)

30 즉각적인 비행을 하도록 프로그램화된 ➡ programmed for (instant / ignorant) flight

* 다음 문장의 빈칸에 알맞은 단어를 〈보기〉에서 찾아 쓰시오.

┌─────────────────── [보기] ───────────────────┐
preconceptions / directions / exerting / meditative / coined / utter
alternatively / quoted / immobile / preferred / grand / composing
└──┘

31 그러면 여기 인용된 숫자로 괜찮다.
➡ Then the number _____ here is fine.

32 그러고 나서 둘은 다른 방향으로 떠났다.
➡ Then the two walked off in different _____.

33 우리는 거대한 규모로 원자를 재순환시킨다.
➡ We recycle atoms on a(n) _____ scale.

34 선형 편집은 타자기로 글을 작성하는 것과 같았다.
➡ Linear editing was like _____ a paper on a typewriter.

35 그것들이 자전거와 당신에게 힘을 가하고 있어야 한다.
➡ They must be _____ a force on the bicycle and you.

36 시각은 현실에 대한 우리의 선입견에 의해 영향을 받는다.
➡ Vision is influenced by our _____ about reality.

37 그것은 그 생의 90퍼센트 이상을 움직이지 않은 채로 보낸다.
➡ It spends more than 90 percent of its life _____.

38 식물을 돌보는 것은 믿을 수 없을 정도로 고요하고 명상적일 수 있다.
➡ Tending to plants can be incredibly calming and _____.

39 MIT 교수인 John MacCarthy는 '인공지능'이라는 표현을 만들어냈다.
➡ MIT professor John McCarthy _____ "artificial intelligence."

40 "도와드릴까요?"는 소매 판매원이 말할 수 있는 최악의 네 단어이다.
➡ "May I help you?" are the worst four words that a retail salesperson can _____.

*1번부터 17번까지는 듣고 답하는 문제입니다. 1번부터 15번까지는 한 번만 들려주고, 16번부터 17번까지는 두 번 들려줍니다. 방송을 잘 듣고 답을 하시기 바랍니다.

▲ 듣기 파일

01 다음을 듣고, 여자가 하는 말의 목적으로 가장 적절한 것을 고르시오.

① 축제 기간 연장을 요청하려고
② 신설된 지하철 노선을 홍보하려고
③ 축제 당일의 지하철 연장 운행을 안내하려고
④ 축제 방문객에게 안전 수칙 준수를 당부하려고
⑤ 축제 기간 중 도심 교통 통제 구간을 공지하려고

02 대화를 듣고, 남자의 의견으로 가장 적절한 것을 고르시오.

① 불규칙한 수면 습관은 청소년의 뇌 발달을 방해한다.
② 스마트폰의 화면 밝기를 조절하여 눈을 보호해야 한다.
③ 취침 전 스마트폰 사용을 줄여야 수면의 질이 높아진다.
④ 집중력 향상을 위해 디지털 기기 사용을 최소화해야 한다.
⑤ 일정한 시간에 취침하는 것이 생체 리듬 유지에 도움을 준다.

03 다음을 듣고, 남자가 하는 말의 요지로 가장 적절한 것을 고르시오.

① 과도한 컴퓨터 사용은 스트레스 지수를 증가시킨다.
② 컴퓨터 관련 취미 활동은 IT 활용 능력을 향상시킨다.
③ 직업을 선택할 때 자신의 흥미와 적성을 고려해야 한다.
④ 다양한 악기 연주를 배우는 것은 인생을 풍요롭게 만든다.
⑤ 직업과 관련 없는 취미 활동이 스트레스 감소에 도움이 된다.

04 대화를 듣고, 그림에서 대화의 내용과 일치하지 않는 것을 고르시오.

05 대화를 듣고, 여자가 할 일로 가장 적절한 것을 고르시오.

① 선물 준비하기
② 온라인 초대장 보내기
③ 음식 주문하기
④ 초대 손님 명단 확인하기
⑤ 전시 부스 설치하기

06 대화를 듣고, 남자가 지불할 금액을 고르시오. [3점]

① $63   ② $70   ③ $81   ④ $86   ⑤ $90

07 대화를 듣고, 여자가 이번 주말에 등산을 갈 수 없는 이유를 고르시오.

① 아르바이트를 해야 해서
② 학교 시험공부를 해야 해서
③ 폭우로 인해 등산로가 폐쇄되어서
④ 경연을 위한 춤 연습을 해야 해서
⑤ 주문한 등산 장비가 도착하지 않아서

08 대화를 듣고, Lakestate Apartment Yoga Program에 관해 언급되지 않은 것을 고르시오.

① 대상 연령   ② 운영 요일   ③ 모집 인원
④ 등록 방법   ⑤ 등록 준비물

09 Global Food Market에 관한 다음 내용을 듣고, 일치하지 않는 것을 고르시오.

① 학교 주차장에서 열린다.
② 이틀간 진행된다.
③ 8개 국가의 음식을 즐길 수 있다.
④ 음식마다 가격이 다르다.
⑤ 채식주의자를 위한 메뉴가 있다.

10
다음 표를 보면서 대화를 듣고, 남자가 주문할 디지털 텀블러를 고르시오.

Digital Tumblers

	Model	Price	Size	Water Intake Display	Color
①	A	$35	350ml	×	White
②	B	$40	470ml	×	Gold
③	C	$45	470ml	○	Black
④	D	$55	550ml	○	White
⑤	E	$65	550ml	○	Gold

11
대화를 듣고, 여자의 마지막 말에 대한 남자의 응답으로 가장 적절한 것을 고르시오.

① If it's too dry inside, you can easily get a cold.
② When you cough, you should cover your mouth.
③ You need to wash your hands not to get a cold.
④ It's really important to keep yourself warm.
⑤ Drinking water can make your skin soft.

12
대화를 듣고, 남자의 마지막 말에 대한 여자의 응답으로 가장 적절한 것을 고르시오.

① Awesome. The new bookshelf looks good in your room.
② Right. Then, shall we sell them at a used bookstore?
③ I see. Can you borrow them from the library?
④ Okay. I'll buy you books in a good condition.
⑤ I'm sorry. I haven't finished the book yet.

13
대화를 듣고, 여자의 마지막 말에 대한 남자의 응답으로 가장 적절한 것을 고르시오. [3점]

Man: _____

① I'll clarify each group member's specific role.
② I'll collect more data for our group research.
③ I should challenge myself for the competition.
④ I need to change the topic of our group project.
⑤ I'll let you know how to analyze data effectively.

14
대화를 듣고, 남자의 마지막 말에 대한 여자의 응답으로 가장 적절한 것을 고르시오. [3점]

Woman: _____

① Trust me. When we eat makes a big difference.
② Okay. I'll check my meals to get in better shape.
③ Thank you for your tip. But I don't think I can do it.
④ Of course. I'll make sure to follow your workout routine.
⑤ Sure. That's why I didn't succeed at keeping a balanced diet.

15
다음 상황 설명을 듣고, Julia가 Sophie에게 할 말로 가장 적절한 것을 고르시오.

Julia: _____

① Could you help me assemble my desk?
② Can you share where you bought your desk?
③ How about choosing a new computer together?
④ Why don't you repair the furniture by yourself?
⑤ Do you have any ideas for decorating my room?

[16~17] 다음을 듣고, 물음에 답하시오.

16
여자가 하는 말의 주제로 가장 적절한 것은?

① material trends in the fashion industry
② benefits of making clothes from nature
③ tips to purchase natural material clothes
④ development of clothes washing methods
⑤ proper ways to wash natural material clothes

17
언급된 소재가 <u>아닌</u> 것은?

① cotton   ② silk   ③ leather
④ linen   ⑤ wool

*이제 듣기 문제가 끝났습니다. 18번부터는 문제지의 지시에 따라 답을 하시기 바랍니다.

18 다음 글의 목적으로 가장 적절한 것은?

To whom it may concern,

I am writing to express my deep concern about the recent change made by Pittsburgh Train Station. The station had traditional ticket offices with staff before, but these have been replaced with ticket vending machines. However, individuals who are unfamiliar with these machines are now experiencing difficulty accessing the railway services. Since these individuals heavily relied on the staff assistance to be able to travel, they are in great need of ticket offices with staff in the station. Therefore, I am urging you to consider reopening the ticket offices. With the staff back in their positions, many people would regain access to the railway services. I look forward to your prompt attention to this matter and a positive resolution.

Sincerely,
Sarah Roberts

① 승차권 발매기 수리를 의뢰하려고
② 기차표 단체 예매 방법을 문의하려고
③ 기차 출발 시간 지연에 대해 항의하려고
④ 기차역 직원의 친절한 도움에 감사하려고
⑤ 기차역 유인 매표소 재운영을 요구하려고

19 다음 글에 드러난 Jeevan의 심경 변화로 가장 적절한 것은?

All the actors on the stage were focused on their acting. Then, suddenly, Arthur fell into the corner of the stage. Jeevan immediately approached Arthur and found his heart wasn't beating. Jeevan began CPR. Jeevan worked silently, glancing sometimes at Arthur's face. He thought, "Please, start breathing again, please." Arthur's eyes were closed. Moments later, an older man in a grey suit appeared, swiftly kneeling beside Arthur's chest. "I'm Walter Jacobi. I'm a doctor." He announced with a calm voice. Jeevan wiped the sweat off his forehead. With combined efforts, Jeevan and Dr. Jacobi successfully revived Arthur. Arthur's eyes slowly opened. Finally, Jeevan was able to hear Arthur's breath again, thinking to himself, "Thank goodness. You're back."

① thrilled → bored   ② ashamed → confident
③ hopeful → helpless   ④ surprised → indifferent
⑤ desperate → relieved

20 다음 글에서 필자가 주장하는 바로 가장 적절한 것은?

As the parent of a gifted child, you need to be aware of a certain common parent trap. Of course you are a proud parent, and you should be. While it is very easy to talk nonstop about your little genius and his or her remarkable behavior, this can be very stressful on your child. It is extremely important to limit your bragging behavior to your very close friends, or your parents. Gifted children feel pressured when their parents show them off too much. This behavior creates expectations that they may not be able to live up to, and also creates a false sense of self for your child. You want your child to be who they are, not who they seem to be as defined by their incredible achievements. If not, you could end up with a driven perfectionist child or perhaps a drop-out, or worse.

① 부모는 자녀를 다른 아이와 비교하지 말아야 한다.
② 부모는 자녀의 영재성을 지나치게 자랑하지 말아야 한다.
③ 영재교육 프로그램에 대한 맹목적인 믿음을 삼가야 한다.
④ 과도한 영재교육보다 자녀와의 좋은 관계 유지에 힘써야 한다.
⑤ 자녀의 독립성을 기르기 위해 자기 일은 스스로 하게 해야 한다.

21 밑줄 친 "hanging out with the winners"가 다음 글에서 의미하는 바로 가장 적절한 것은?

One valuable technique for getting out of helplessness, depression, and situations which are predominantly being run by the thought, "I can't," is to choose to be with other persons who have resolved the problem with which we struggle. This is one of the great powers of self-help groups. When we are in a negative state, we have given a lot of energy to negative thought forms, and the positive thought forms are weak. Those who are in a higher vibration are free of the energy from their negative thoughts and have energized positive thought forms. Merely to be in their presence is beneficial. In some self-help groups, this is called "hanging out with the winners." The benefit here is on the psychic level of consciousness, and there is a transfer of positive energy and relighting of one's own latent positive thought forms.

*latent: 잠재적인

① staying with those who sacrifice themselves for others
② learning from people who have succeeded in competition
③ keeping relationships with people in a higher social position
④ spending time with those who need social skill development
⑤ being with positive people who have overcome negative states

22 다음 글의 요지로 가장 적절한 것은?

Our emotions are thought to exist because they have contributed to our survival as a species. Fear has helped us avoid dangers, expressing anger helps us scare off threats, and expressing positive emotions helps us bond with others. From an evolutionary perspective, an emotion is a kind of "program" that, when triggered, directs many of our activities (including attention, perception, memory, movement, expressions, etc.). For example, fear makes us very attentive, narrows our perceptual focus to threatening stimuli, will cause us either to face a situation (fight) or avoid it (flight), and may cause us to remember an experience more acutely (so that we avoid the threat in the future). Regardless of the specific ways in which they activate our systems, the specific emotions we possess are thought to exist because they have helped us (as a species) survive challenges within our environment long ago. If they had not helped us adapt and survive, they would not have evolved with us.

① 과거의 경험이 현재의 감정에 영향을 미친다.
② 문명의 발달에 따라 인간의 감정은 다양화되어 왔다.
③ 감정은 인간이 생존하도록 도와왔기 때문에 존재한다.
④ 부정적인 감정은 긍정적인 감정보다 더 오래 기억된다.
⑤ 두려움의 원인을 파악함으로써 두려움을 없앨 수 있다.

By improving accessibility of the workplace for workers that are typically at a disadvantage in the labour market, AI can improve inclusiveness in the workplace. AI-powered assistive devices to aid workers with visual, speech or hearing difficulties are becoming more widespread, improving the access to, and the quality of work for people with disabilities. For example, speech recognition solutions for people with dysarthric voices, or live captioning systems for deaf and hard of hearing people can facilitate communication with colleagues and access to jobs where inter-personal communication is necessary. AI can also enhance the capabilities of low-skilled workers, with potentially positive effects on their wages and career prospects. For example, AI's capacity to translate written and spoken word in real-time can improve the performance of non-native speakers in the workplace. Moreover, recent developments in AI-powered text generators can instantly improve the performance of lower-skilled individuals in domains such as writing, coding or customer service.

*dysarthric: (신경 장애로 인한) 구음(構音) 장애의

① jobs replaced by AI in the labour market
② ethical issues caused by using AI in the workplace
③ necessity of using AI technology for language learning
④ impacts of AI on supporting workers with disadvantages
⑤ new designs of AI technology to cure people with disabilities

Whales are highly efficient at carbon storage. When they die, each whale sequesters an average of 30 tons of carbon dioxide, taking that carbon out of the atmosphere for centuries. For comparison, the average tree absorbs only 48 pounds of CO_2 a year. From a climate perspective, each whale is the marine equivalent of thousands of trees. Whales also help sequester carbon by fertilizing the ocean as they release nutrient-rich waste, in turn increasing phytoplankton populations, which also sequester carbon — leading some scientists to call them the "engineers of marine ecosystems." In 2019, economists from the International Monetary Fund (IMF) estimated the value of the ecosystem services provided by each whale at over $2 million USD. They called for a new global program of economic incentives to return whale populations to preindustrial whaling levels as one example of a "nature-based solution" to climate change. Calls are now being made for a global whale restoration program, to slow down climate change.

*sequester: 격리하다 **phytoplankton: 식물성 플랑크톤

① Saving Whales Saves the Earth and Us
② What Makes Whales Go Extinct in the Ocean
③ Why Is Overpopulation of Whales Dangerous?
④ Black Money: Lies about the Whaling Industry
⑤ Climate Change and Its Effect on Whale Habitats

25 다음 도표의 내용과 일치하지 <u>않는</u> 것은?

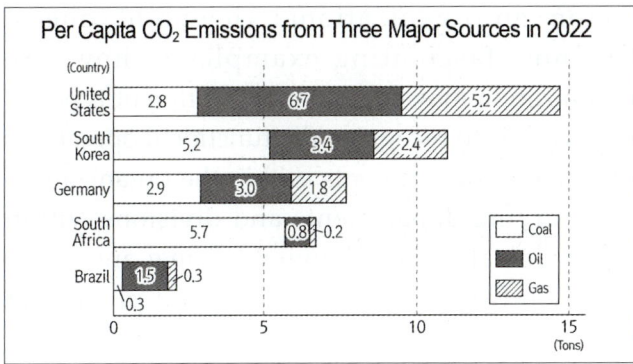

Per Capita CO₂ Emissions from Three Major Sources in 2022

The above graph shows per capita CO_2 emissions from coal, oil, and gas by countries in 2022. ① The United States had the highest total per capita CO_2 emissions, even though its emissions from coal were the second lowest among the five countries shown. ② South Korea's total per capita CO_2 emissions were over 10 tons, ranking it the second highest among the countries shown. ③ Germany had lower CO_2 emissions per capita than South Korea in all three major sources respectively. ④ The per capita CO_2 emissions from coal in South Africa were over three times higher than those in Germany. ⑤ In Brazil, oil was the largest source of CO_2 emissions per capita among its three major sources, just as it was in the United States and Germany.

*per capita: 1인당

26 Émilie du Châtelet에 관한 다음 글의 내용과 일치하지 <u>않는</u> 것은?

Émilie du Châtelet, a French mathematician and physicist, was born in Paris in 1706. During her childhood, with her father's support, she was able to get mathematical and scientific education that most women of her time did not receive. In 1737, she submitted her paper on the nature of fire to a contest sponsored by the French Academy of Sciences, and it was published a year later. In her book, *Institutions de Physique*, Émilie du Châtelet explained the ideas of space and time in a way that is closer to what we understand in modern relativity than what was common during her time. Her most significant achievement was translating Isaac Newton's *Principia* into French near the end of her life. Émilie du Châtelet's work was not recognized in her time, but she is now remembered as a symbol of the Enlightenment and the struggle for women's participation in science.

① 어린 시절에 수학과 과학 교육을 받았다.
② 불의 속성에 관한 그녀의 논문이 1737년에 출간되었다.
③ *Institutions de Physique*에서 공간과 시간의 개념을 설명했다.
④ 아이작 뉴턴의 *Principia*를 프랑스어로 번역했다.
⑤ 이룩한 업적은 당대에 인정받지 못했다.

27 2024 Young Inventors Robot Competition에 관한 다음 안내문의 내용과 일치하지 <u>않는</u> 것은?

2024 Young Inventors Robot Competition

Join us for an exciting day of the Young Inventors Robot Competition!

□ **Categories**
  – Participants can compete in one of the following categories:
  • Robot Design   • Robot Coding
  • Robot Remote Control

□ **Date and Time**
  – September 28, 2024, 10 a.m. to 3 p.m.

□ **Location**
  – Computer Lab, Oakwood University

□ **Registration**
  – From August 1 to August 10, 2024
  – Open to high school students
  – Online registration only
    (www.younginventors.edu)

□ **Awards**
  – In each competition category, three participants will be honored.
  • 1st place: $300   • 2nd place: $200
  • 3rd place: $100

※ For more information, visit our website.

① 세 가지 분야 중 하나에 참가할 수 있다.
② 9월 28일에 5시간 동안 열린다.
③ 고등학생이 등록할 수 있다.
④ 등록은 온라인으로만 가능하다.
⑤ 수상자는 각 분야당 한 명이다.

28 Saintville Art Week Stamp Tour에 관한 다음 안내문의 내용과 일치하는 것은?

Saintville Art Week Stamp Tour

The 8th annual Saintville Art Week Stamp Tour is back this year! Anyone can participate in our event. Join us and enjoy exhibitions and new collections.

□ **When:** The first week of October, 2024

□ **Where:** Saintville Arts District

□ **How:**

　Step 1. Take a stamp tour map from the Saintville Arts Center.

　Step 2. Get stamps from at least 3 out of 5 spots and receive your gift.

　– You can choose either an umbrella or a mug with printed artwork on it for your gift.

※ For more information, please visit our website at www.SaintvilleArtsCenter.com.

① 참가 대상에 제한이 있다.

② 10월 둘째 주에 진행된다.

③ Saintville Arts Center에서 스탬프 투어 지도를 받는다.

④ 적어도 다섯 곳에서 도장을 받아야 선물을 받는다.

⑤ 선물로 가방과 머그잔 중 하나를 고를 수 있다.

29 다음 글의 밑줄 친 부분 중, 어법상 틀린 것은?

From an organizational viewpoint, one of the most fascinating examples of how any organization may contain many different types of culture ① is to recognize the functional operations of different departments within the organization. The varying departments and divisions within an organization will inevitably view any given situation from their own biased and prejudiced perspective. A department and its members will acquire "tunnel vision" which disallows them to see things as others see ② them. The very structure of organizations can create conflict. The choice of ③ whether the structure is "mechanistic" or "organic" can have a profound influence on conflict management. A mechanistic structure has a vertical hierarchy with many rules, many procedures, and many levels of management ④ involved in decision making. Organic structures are more horizontal in nature, ⑤ which decision making is less centralized and spread across the plane of the organization.

*hierarchy: 위계

30 다음 글의 밑줄 친 부분 중, 문맥상 낱말의 쓰임이 적절하지 않은 것은? [3점]

An excellent alternative to calming traffic is removing it. Some cities ① reserve an extensive network of lanes and streets for bikes, pedestrians, and the occasional service vehicle. This motivates people to travel by bike rather than by car, making streets safer for everyone. As bicycles become more ② popular in a city, planners can convert more automobile lanes and entire streets to accommodate more of them. Nevertheless, even the most bikeable cities still ③ require motor vehicle lanes for taxis, emergency vehicles, and delivery trucks. Delivery vehicles are frequently a target of animus, but they are actually an essential component to making cities greener. A tightly packed delivery truck is a far more ④ inefficient transporter of goods than several hybrids carrying a few shopping bags each. Distributing food and other goods to neighborhood vendors ⑤ allows them to operate smaller stores close to homes so that residents can walk, rather than drive, to get their groceries.

*animus: 반감, 미움

31

You hear again and again that some of the greatest composers were misunderstood in their own day. Not everyone could understand the compositions of Beethoven, Brahms, or Stravinsky in their day. The reason for this initial lack of acceptance is unfamiliarity. The musical forms, or ideas expressed within them, were completely new. And yet, this is exactly one of the things that makes them so great. Effective composers have their own ideas. Have you ever seen the classic movie *Amadeus*? The composer Antonio Salieri is the "host" of this movie; he's depicted as one of the most famous non-great composers — he lived at the time of Mozart and was completely overshadowed by him. Now, Salieri wasn't a bad composer; in fact, he was a very good one. But he wasn't one of the world's great composers because his work wasn't _____. What he wrote sounded just like what everyone else was composing at the time.

① simple ② original
③ familiar ④ conventional
⑤ understandable

32

Every time a new medium comes along — whether it's the invention of the printed book, or TV, or SNS — and you start to use it, it's like you are putting on a new kind of goggles, with their own special colors and lenses. Each set of goggles you put on makes you see things differently. So when you start to watch television, before you absorb the message of any particular TV show — whether it's *Wheel of Fortune* or *The Wire* — you start to see the world as being shaped like television itself. That's why Marshall McLuhan said that every time a new medium comes along — a new way for humans to communicate — it has buried in it a message. It is gently guiding us to _____.
The way information gets to you, McLuhan argued, is more important than the information itself. TV teaches you that the world is fast; that it's about surfaces and appearances. [3점]

① see the world according to a new set of codes
② ignore unfamiliar messages from new media
③ maintain steady focus and clear understanding
④ interpret information through a traditional lens
⑤ enjoy various media contents with one platform

33

Concepts are vital to human survival, but we must also be careful with them because concepts open the door to essentialism. They _____. Stuart Firestein opens his book, *Ignorance*, with an old proverb, "It is very difficult to find a black cat in a dark room, especially when there is no cat." This statement beautifully sums up the search for essences. History has many examples of scientists who searched fruitlessly for an essence because they used the wrong concept to guide their hypotheses. Firestein gives the example of luminiferous ether, a mysterious substance that was thought to fill the universe so that light would have a medium to move through. The ether was a black cat, writes Firestein, and physicists had been theorizing in a dark room, and then experimenting in it, looking for evidence of a cat that did not exist. [3점]

① encourage us to see things that aren't present
② force scientists to simplify scientific theories
③ let us think science is essential and practical
④ drive physicists to explore philosophy
⑤ lead us to ignore the unknown

34

While social media attention is potentially an instrument to achieve ends like elite celebrity, some content creators desire ordinary fame as a social end in itself. Not unlike reality television stars, social media celebrities are often criticized for not having skills and talents associated with traditional, elite celebrity, such as acting or singing ability. This criticism highlights the fact that digital content creators face real barriers to crossing over to the sphere of elite celebrity. However, the criticism also misses the point that the phenomenon of ordinary celebrity _____. The elite celebrity is symbolized by the metaphor of the star, characterized by mystery and hierarchical distance and associated with naturalized qualities of talent and class. The ordinary celebrity attracts attention through regular and frequent interactions with other ordinary people. Achieving ordinary fame as a social media celebrity is like doing well at a game, because in this sphere, fame is nothing more nor less than relatively high scores on attention scales, the metrics of subscribers, followers, Likes, or clicks built into social media applications. [3점]

*sphere: 영역 **metric: 측정 기준

① shifts to that of elite celebrity
② disappears gradually over time
③ focuses solely on talent and class
④ reconstructs the meaning of fame
⑤ restricts interactions with the public

35 다음 글에서 전체 흐름과 관계 없는 문장은?

Why do we have the illusion that cramming for an exam is the best learning strategy? Because we are unable to differentiate between the various sections of our memory. Immediately after reading our textbook or our class notes, information is fully present in our mind. ① It sits in our conscious working memory, in an active form. ② We feel as if we know it, because it is present in our short-term storage space ... but this short-term section has nothing to do with the long-term memory that we will need in order to recall the same information a few days later. ③ After a few seconds or minutes, working memory already starts disappearing, and after a few days, the effect becomes enormous: unless you retest your knowledge, memory vanishes. ④ Focusing on exploring new topics rather than reviewing the same material over and over again can improve your academic performance. ⑤ To get information into long-term memory, it is essential to study the material, then test yourself, rather than spend all your time studying.

*cram: 벼락 공부를 하다

[36~37] 주어진 글 다음에 이어질 글의 순서로 가장 적절한 것을 고르시오.

36

The discovery of mirror neurons has profoundly changed the way we think of a fundamental human capacity, learning by observation.

(A) You may not see the tongue stick out each time you stick yours out at your newborn, but if you do it many times, the tongue will come out more often than if you do something different. Babies babble and later start to imitate the sounds their parents produce.

(B) As children we learn a lot by observing what our parents and friends do. Newborns, in the first week of life, have an inborn tendency to stick out their tongue if their parents stick out theirs. Such imitation is not perfect.

(C) Later still, they play with vacuum cleaners and hammers in imitation of their parents. Our modern cultures, in which we write, speak, read, build spaceships and go to school, can work only because we are not restricted to the behavior we are born with or learn by trial and error. We can learn a lot by simply watching others.

*babble: 옹알이하다

① (A) — (C) — (B)   ② (B) — (A) — (C)
③ (B) — (C) — (A)   ④ (C) — (A) — (B)
⑤ (C) — (B) — (A)

37

Have you ever been surprised to hear a recording of your own voice? You might have thought, "Is that really what my voice sounds like?"

(A) There are two pathways through which we perceive our own voice when we speak. One is the route through which we perceive most external sounds, like waves that travel from the air through the outer, middle and inner ear.

(B) But because our vocal cords vibrate when we speak, there is a second internal path. Vibrations are conducted through our bones and stimulate our inner ears directly. Lower frequencies are emphasized along this pathway. That makes your voice sound deeper and richer to yourself than it may sound to other people.

(C) Maybe your accent is more pronounced in the recording than you realized, or your voice is higher than it seems to your own ears. This is of course quite a common experience. The explanation is actually fairly simple. [3점]

*vocal cords: 성대 **frequency: 주파수

① (A) — (C) — (B)　　② (B) — (A) — (C)
③ (B) — (C) — (A)　　④ (C) — (A) — (B)
⑤ (C) — (B) — (A)

[38~39] 글의 흐름으로 보아, 주어진 문장이 들어가기에 가장 적절한 곳을 고르시오.

38

"Homologous" traits, in contrast, may or may not have a common function, but they descended from a common ancestor and hence have some common structure that indicates their being "the same" organ.

Biologists distinguish two kinds of similarity. (①) "Analogous" traits are ones that have a common function but arose on different branches of the evolutionary tree and are in an important sense not "the same" organ. (②) The wings of birds and the wings of bees are both used for flight and are similar in some ways because anything used for flight has to be built in those ways, but they arose independently in evolution and have nothing in common beyond their use in flight. (③) The wing of a bat and the front leg of a horse have very different functions, but they are all modifications of the forelimb of the ancestor of all mammals. (④) As a result, they share nonfunctional traits like the number of bones and the ways they are connected. (⑤) To distinguish analogy from homology, biologists usually look at the overall architecture of the organs and focus on their most useless properties.

39

Thus, as global warming raises the temperature of marine waters, it is self-evident that the amount of dissolved oxygen will decrease.

Seawater contains an abundance of dissolved oxygen that all marine animals breathe to stay alive. (①) It has long been established in physics that cold water holds more dissolved oxygen than warm water does — this is one reason that cold polar seas are full of life while tropical oceans are blue, clear, and relatively poorly populated with living creatures. (②) This is a worrisome and potentially disastrous consequence if allowed to continue to an ecosystem-threatening level. (③) Now scientists have analyzed data indicating that the amount of dissolved oxygen in the oceans has been declining for more than a half century. (④) The data show that the ocean oxygen level has been falling more rapidly than the corresponding rise in water temperature. (⑤) Falling oxygen levels in water have the potential to impact the habitat of marine organisms worldwide and in recent years this has led to more frequent anoxic events that killed or displaced populations of fish, crabs, and many other organisms. [3점]

*dissolved: 용해된 **anoxic: 산소 결핍의

Capuchins — New World Monkeys that live in large social groups — will, in captivity, trade with people all day long, especially if food is involved. *I give you this rock and you give me a treat to eat.* If you put two monkeys in cages next to each other, and offer them both slices of cucumber for the rocks they already have, they will happily eat the cucumbers. If, however, you give one monkey grapes instead — grapes being universally preferred to cucumbers — the monkey that is still receiving cucumbers will begin to throw them back at the experimenter. Even though she is still getting "paid" the same amount for her effort of sourcing rocks, and so her particular situation has not changed, the comparison to another makes the situation unfair. Furthermore, she is now willing to abandon all gains — the cucumbers themselves — to communicate her displeasure to the experimenter.

⬇

According to the passage, if the Capuchin monkey realizes the ___(A)___ in rewards compared to another monkey, she will ___(B)___ her rewards to express her feelings about the treatment, despite getting exactly the same rewards as before.

	(A)		(B)
①	benefit	—	protect
②	inequality	—	share
③	abundance	—	yield
④	inequality	—	reject
⑤	benefit	—	display

[41~42] 다음 글을 읽고, 물음에 답하시오.

Higher education has grown from an elite to a mass system across the world. In Europe and the USA, (a) <u>increased</u> rates of participation occurred in the decades after the Second World War. Between 2000 and 2014, rates of participation in higher education almost doubled from 19% to 34% across the world among the members of the population in the school-leaving age category (typically 18—23). The dramatic expansion of higher education has been marked by a wider range of institutions of higher learning and a more diverse demographic of students.

Changes from an elite system to a mass higher education system are associated with political needs to build a (b) <u>specialised</u> workforce for the economy. In theory, the expansion of higher education to develop a highly skilled workforce should diminish the role of examinations in the selection and control of students, initiating approaches to assessment which (c) <u>block</u> lifelong learning: assessment *for* learning and a focus on feedback for development. In reality, socio-political changes to expand higher education have set up a 'field of contradictions' for assessment in higher education. Mass higher education requires efficient approaches to assessment, such as examinations and multiple-choice quizzes, with minimalist, (d) <u>impersonal</u>, or standardised feedback, often causing students to focus more on grades than feedback. In contrast, the relatively small numbers of students in elite systems in the past (e) <u>allowed</u> for closer relationships between students and their teachers, with formative feedback shaping the minds, academic skills, and even the characters of students. *demographic: 인구집단

41 윗글의 제목으로 가장 적절한 것은?

① Is It Possible to Teach Without Assessment?
② Elite vs. Public: A History of Modern Class Society
③ Mass Higher Education and Its Reality in Assessment
④ Impacts of Mass Higher Education on Teachers' Status
⑤ Mass Higher Education Leads to Economic Development

42 밑줄 친 (a)~(e) 중에서 문맥상 낱말의 쓰임이 적절하지 <u>않은</u> 것은? [3점]

① (a)　② (b)　③ (c)　④ (d)　⑤ (e)

[43~45] 다음 글을 읽고, 물음에 답하시오.

(A)

Once upon a time in the Iranian city of Shiraz, there lived the famous poet Sheikh Saadi. Like most other poets and philosophers, he led a very simple life. A rich merchant of Shiraz was preparing for his daughter's wedding and invited (a) <u>him</u> along with a lot of big businessmen of the town. The poet accepted the invitation and decided to attend.

(B)

The host personally led the poet to his seat and served out chicken soup to him. After a moment, the poet suddenly dipped the corner of his coat in the soup as if he fed it. All the guests were now staring at (b) <u>him</u> in surprise. The host said, "Sir, what are you doing?" The poet very calmly replied, "Now that I have put on expensive clothes, I see a world of difference here. All that I can say now is that this feast is meant for my clothes, not for me."

(C)

Seeing all this, the poet quietly left the party and went to a shop where he could rent clothes. There he chose a richly decorated coat, which made him look like a new person. With this coat, he entered the party and this time was welcomed with open arms. The host embraced him as (c) <u>he</u> would do to an old friend and complimented him on the clothes he was wearing. The poet did not say a word and allowed the host to lead (d) <u>him</u> to the dining room.

(D)

On the day of the wedding, the rich merchant, the host of the wedding, was receiving the guests at the gate. Many rich people of the town attended the wedding. They had come out in their best clothes. The poet wore simple clothes which were neither grand nor expensive. He waited for someone to approach him but no one gave (e) <u>him</u> as much as even a second glance. Even the host did not greet him and looked away.

43 주어진 글 (A)에 이어질 내용을 순서에 맞게 배열한 것으로 가장 적절한 것은?

① (B) — (D) — (C)　② (C) — (B) — (D)
③ (C) — (D) — (B)　④ (D) — (B) — (C)
⑤ (D) — (C) — (B)

44 밑줄 친 (a)~(e) 중에서 가리키는 대상이 나머지 넷과 <u>다른</u> 것은?

① (a)　② (b)　③ (c)　④ (d)　⑤ (e)

45 윗글에 관한 내용으로 적절하지 <u>않은</u> 것은?

① 시인은 상인의 초대를 받아들였다.
② 상인은 시인의 외투 자락을 수프에 담갔다.
③ 시인은 옷을 빌릴 수 있는 가게로 갔다.
④ 결혼식 날 상인은 입구에서 손님을 맞이했다.
⑤ 마을의 많은 부유한 사람들이 결혼식에 참석했다.

• MP3 파일을 들으며 다음 빈칸을 채우시오. (듣기 어려운 발음이나 정답의 단서가 되는 부분에 빈칸을 만들었습니다.)

01 다음을 듣고, 여자가 하는 말의 목적으로 가장 적절한 것을 고르시오.

W: Hello! I'm Olivia Parker from Pineview City Subway. I _____ ___ _____ for this Saturday's fireworks festival. Many people are expected to visit and enjoy the festival late into the night. For _____ _____ and visitor safety, we're ☆_____ ____ _____ _____ of the subway on the day of the festival. The subway will run for an extra two hours after the regular last train from the festival area stations. For a comfortable and safe journey from the event, we encourage you to _____ _____ ___ our extended subway services. We hope you enjoy this fantastic festival with convenience. Thank you!

02 대화를 듣고, 남자의 의견으로 가장 적절한 것을 고르시오.

M: Hi, Emma. What's up? You look tired.

W: Hey, David. I always feel tired. ☆_____ _____ I sleep many hours, ___ _____ __ _____ ____ any good sleep.

M: That's too bad. Is there anything you do before you go to bed?

W: I usually read webtoons on my smartphone ____ ___ ___ _____.

M: Ah, that's the problem. Having too much screen time right before bed is not good.

W: Really? But I'm so _____ _____ _____ _____ on my phone at night!

M: Long exposure to the screen light can make your brain stay awake.

W: I never knew using smartphones had a negative impact on sleep.

M: Reducing your smartphone use before going to bed will increase the quality of your sleep.

W: Okay, I can give it a try.

03 다음을 듣고, 남자가 하는 말의 요지로 가장 적절한 것을 고르시오.

M: Hello, listeners! Welcome to your *Daily Tips*. Today, I'll tell you a helpful way to _____ _____ _____. Recent research shows that having hobbies completely unrelated to your job can significantly reduce stress. For example, if you work in IT, _____ _____ _____ that are far from the digital field. Playing the guitar might be a good option ☆_____ _____ _____ computer games. Let's enjoy hobbies that are different from our work! That'll be the best way to get a refreshing break. Remember, a well-chosen hobby can be a powerful tool for stress relief. _____ ___ tomorrow for more helpful daily tips!

04 대화를 듣고, 그림에서 대화의 내용과 일치하지 <u>않는</u> 것을 고르시오.

M: Hey, Amy. Here is the new recording studio for our band. How do you like it?

W: Wow, these two speakers are impressive!

M: Yes, they are. The sound ☆_____ ___ _____.

W: Also, the long desk between the speakers looks great.

M: Yeah. And on the desk, there is a microphone. We can use it ____ _____ _____ _____.

W: Nice. Oh, this chair looks comfortable. It could be helpful for long recordings.

M: Agreed. And _____ _____ _____ _____ _____ gives the room a cozy feeling, doesn't it?

W: Yes, and I like the flower patterns on the rug.

M: I like it, too. How about the poster on the wall?

W: It's cool. This studio feels like where _____ _____ _____ _____!

M: I'm glad you like this place.

W: Absolutely. I can't wait to start recording here.

05 대화를 듣고, 여자가 할 일로 가장 적절한 것을 고르시오.

W: Tony, I'm so excited for our Go-Green event!

M: Me too. The event is almost here. _____ _____ ___ ___ _____ our preparations together?

W: Okay. I think the exhibition booths are very important for our event. How are they going?

M: Almost ready. I'm _____ _____ _____ _____ _____ this afternoon. What about the welcome gifts?

W: I've already prepared some eco-friendly bags.

M: Perfect! What's next?

W: We need to confirm the list of guests for the ceremony.

M: I double-checked the list. But I haven't sent the online invitation cards, yet.

W: No problem. I'll ✪_____ _____ ___ right away. How about the food and drinks?

M: I've scheduled food and drink services and I'll _____ ___ _____ ___ _____ _____.

W: Nice! I'm confident our event will be a great success.

06 대화를 듣고, 남자가 지불할 금액을 고르시오.

W: Welcome to the Riverside Camping store. How can I help you?

M: I'm looking for a camping table for my family. Can you _____ ___ ?

W: Sure. How about this one? It's light and easy to fold, so it's our best-selling product.

M: It looks good. How much is it?

W: It _____ ___ ___ _____. The small one is 30 dollars and the large one is 50 dollars.

M: I'll buy the large one. Are there folding chairs, too?

W: Yep. These folding chairs ✪_____ ___ _____ with the table. They're 10 dollars each.

M: Sounds good. I'll buy four of those chairs.

W: Okay. That's one large camping table and four chairs.

M: That's right. _____ __ _____ _____ _____ _____ now?

W: Of course. You can get a 10% discount on the total price.

M: Perfect. Here's my credit card.

07 대화를 듣고, 여자가 이번 주말에 등산을 갈 수 <u>없는</u> 이유를 고르시오.

W: Lately, the weather has been lovely. This is __ _____ _____ _____ _____.

M: Indeed. Oh, would you like to go mountain climbing together?

W: Sounds awesome. I have all the climbing equipment.

M: Great. How about this upcoming weekend? I'll find a nice mountain for us.

W: Hold on, this weekend? I don't think I _____ _____ ___ _____.

M: Really? All school tests are finally done, so I thought this weekend would be good for us.

W: Sorry, but I have something important to do this weekend.

M: Do you have a part-time job?

W: No. Actually, I need to practice dancing for the entire weekend.

M: Ah, for the dance ✪_____ _____ _____ _____?

W: Yes. Surprisingly, I _____ ___ _____ the first round, and it's the finals next Monday.

M: That's fantastic! I wish you the best of luck.

08 대화를 듣고, Lakestate Apartment Yoga Program에 관해 언급되지 <u>않은</u> 것을 고르시오.

W: Grandpa, _____ _____ _____ _____ _____ . It's a Lakestate Apartment Yoga Program poster.

M: Wow, a new program for the residents. I've always wanted to join a yoga program.

W: I know, and this one is only for those aged 60 and above.

M: That's perfect for me. [Pause] Oh, it says _____ _____ _____ _____ every Tuesday and Friday.

W: It'll be a good time for you. You're an early bird.

M: Yes, I am. How do I register?

W: You just need to _____ _____ _____ _____ _____ at the apartment fitness center.

M: Okay, I think I'll go right now.

W: Good. But don't forget to take your ID card with you.

M: Oh, do I need that _____ _____ ✪ _____ ?

W: Yes. It says that on the poster. Would you like me to go with you?

M: That would be lovely.

09 Global Food Market에 관한 다음 내용을 듣고, 일치하지 <u>않는</u> 것을 고르시오.

W: Good morning! This is Allison _____ _____ _____ ✪ _____ . I'm happy to announce the Global Food Market right here at Westhill High School. Get ready for a _____ _____ _____ _____ _____ in the school parking lot. Our Global Food Market will take place for two days, on September 25th and 26th. You can enjoy food from eight different countries, including Mexico and France. And there's no need to worry about prices. Every single dish is only five dollars. Wait! You don't eat meat? No problem! We also have _____ _____ _____ . So, join us at the Global Food Market. It's not just about food, but _____ _____ _____ _____ _____ _____ ✪ _____ . Don't miss this chance to taste the world!

10 다음 표를 보면서 대화를 듣고, 남자가 주문할 디지털 텀블러를 고르시오.

W: Honey, what are you looking at?

M: I'm looking at digital tumblers. They _____ _____ _____ on an LED screen. Would you like to help me choose one?

W: Sure, let me see. [Pause] The price ✪ _____ _____ _____ .

M: Hmm, I don't want to pay more than 60 dollars.

W: That sounds reasonable. Look, there are various sizes to choose from.

M: Less than 400ml would be too small for me.

W: Alright. Oh, _____ _____ _____ _____ . Do you need the water intake display? It'll show you how much water you drink in a day.

M: That sounds smart. _____ _____ _____ _____ . Then, I have just two options left.

W: What color do you like? You have too many black items and they're boring.

M: Okay. I'll go with the one that's not black. Then, I'll order this one.

W: Great idea!

11 대화를 듣고, 여자의 마지막 말에 대한 남자의 응답으로 가장 적절한 것을 고르시오.

W: I easily _____ _____ _____ these days.

M: That's too bad. It's a good idea to _____ _____ ✪ _____ in your room.

W: Oh, how does that _____ _____ _____ _____ ?

M: _____

12 대화를 듣고, 남자의 마지막 말에 대한 여자의 응답으로 가장 적절한 것을 고르시오.

M: Mom, the bookshelf in my room _____ _____ _____ _____ . There's no space for new ones.

W: Well, how about ✪ _____ _____ _____ _____ you don't read anymore?

M: But some of them are in _____ _____ _____ to throw away.

W: _____

13 대화를 듣고, 여자의 마지막 말에 대한 남자의 응답으로 가장 적절한 것을 고르시오.

W: Hey, Peter. How's your group project going?

M: Hello, Ms. Adams. It's my first time as a leader, so it's quite challenging.

W: I thought your group was working well together.

M: Yes. We're all ✪ _____ _____ _____ _____ , but progress is slow.

W: Well, what are you all working on at this moment?

M: Everyone is _____ ___ _____ _____ as much as possible.

W: Hmm, did you assign individual tasks to each member?

M: Oh, we haven't discussed it yet. We're not exactly _____ _____ _____ _____ .

W: That's crucial. Otherwise, it can _____ ___ ✪ _____ _____ in a group project.

M: That makes sense. That's why our progress is not that fast.

W: Then, as the leader, what do you think you should do now?

M: _____

14 대화를 듣고, 남자의 마지막 말에 대한 여자의 응답으로 가장 적절한 것을 고르시오.

M: Hey, Emily! You're looking great these days.

W: Thanks, Isaac. I've been trying hard to _____ ___ _____ _____ .

M: Good for you! I'm trying to get fit, too. But it's ✪ _____ .

W: Haven't you been _____ _____ ___ _____ lately?

M: Yeah, but I don't see a big difference. What's your secret?

W: Well, I started being careful about when I eat.

M: You mean like not eating right before bed?

W: _____ ____ . I noticed I was eating a lot at night. So now I don't eat after 7 p.m.

M: Hmm... I don't know if _____ _____ ____ ____ me in better shape.

W: _____

15 다음 상황 설명을 듣고, Julia가 Sophie에게 할 말로 가장 적절한 것을 고르시오.

M: Julia is a college student, living in the dormitory. Recently, she ordered a new computer desk. _____ _____ the desk, she realized that the desk was a DIY product. It means she needs to put the pieces together ___ _____ ____ _____ . However, it was ✪ _____ to assemble it by herself. Julia knows that Sophie, her best friend, is _____ ___ _____ DIY furniture and enjoys it. So, Julia wants to ask Sophie to help her with the desk. In this situation, what would Julia most likely say to Sophie?

Julia: _____

[16~17] 다음을 듣고, 물음에 답하시오.

W: Hello, *Family-Life* subscribers! These days, many people are looking for clothes made from natural materials for their family. Today, I'd like to introduce some tips for how to _____ _____ _____ _____ _____ . First, for cotton, like 100% cotton t-shirts, you should hand-wash in cool water to _____ ✪ _____ ___ ✪ _____ . Second, silk should be washed separately and quickly to keep its shape and color. Also, when you dry silk clothes such as blouses, avoid direct sunlight and dry them in the shade. Third, _____ ____ ___ _____ _____ to wash. For example, to wash linen jackets, use vinegar instead of fabric softener. Lastly, for wool, the best way is to wash ___ _____ ___ _____ . If you have to wash wool sweaters, use special wool washing soap. Apply these tips so you can keep and enjoy natural clothes for a longer time!

✱ 다음 영어는 우리말 뜻을, 우리말은 영어 단어를 〈보기〉에서 찾아 쓰시오.

01 initiate _____

02 wrinkle _____

03 overlap _____

04 procedure _____

05 transportation _____

06 영향 _____

07 습기 _____

08 은유 _____

09 상당히 _____

10 줄어들다 _____

[보기]

교통	moisture
겹치다	significantly
구독자	metaphor
시작하다	complicated
주름이 생기다	shrink
절차	impact

✱ 다음 우리말에 알맞은 영어 표현을 찾아 연결하시오.

11 ~을 이용하다 •　　　　　　　　　• stare at

12 ~을 바라보다 •　　　　　　　　　• be aware of

13 ~의 자리에 (함께) 있다 •　　　　　　• end up with

14 결국 ~로 끝나다 •　　　　　　　　• take advantage of

15 ~을 알다[주의하다] •　　　　　　　• be in one's presence

✱ 다음 우리말과 같은 표현이 되도록 알맞은 단어를 〈보기〉에서 찾아 쓰시오.

[보기]

nonfunctional / impersonal / organizational / demographic / mechanistic / experimenter
overshadowed / evolutionary / disastrous / restoration / assistive / breathe

16 조직의 관점에서 ➔ from a(n) _____ viewpoint

17 AI 동력의 보조 장치들 ➔ AI-powered _____ devices

18 진화 계보의 다른 가지 ➔ different branches of the _____ tree

19 살아남기 위해 호흡하다 ➔ _____ to stay alive

20 그에 의해 완전히 가려진 ➔ completely _____ by him

21 더 다양한 학생 인구 집단 ➔ a more diverse _____ of students

22 세계적인 고래 복원 프로그램 ➔ a global whale _____ program

23 비개인적이거나 표준화된 피드백 ➔ _____, or standardised feedback

24 뼈의 개수와 같은 비기능적 형질 ➔ _____ traits like the number of bones

25 구조가 '기계적'인지 또는 '유기적'인지 ➔ whether the structure is "_____" or "organic"

26 세탁하기에 민감한 소재 ➡ a (sensible / sensitive) material to wash

27 의식의 정신적 수준 ➡ the (physic / psychic) level of consciousness

28 새로운 일련의 방식에 따라 ➡ according to a new set of (codes / nodes)

29 각각의 모든 세 가지 주요한 원천에서 ➡ in all three major sources (respectively / relatively)

30 그가 입고 있는 옷에 대해 그에게 칭찬했다 ➡ (complimented / complemented) him on the clothes he was wearing

* 다음 문장의 빈칸에 알맞은 단어를 〈보기〉에서 찾아 쓰시오.

─────────── [보기] ───────────
unfamiliarity / facilitate / contradiction / caption / hypotheses / enlightenment
energized / regain / embraced / tendency / force / displaced

31 현재 그녀는 계몽주의의 상징으로 기억된다.

➡ She is now remembered as a symbol of the _____.

32 그들은 가설을 이끄는 개념을 잘못 사용했다.

➡ They used the wrong concept to guide their _____.

33 이러한 초기의 수용 부족의 이유는 낯섦이다.

➡ The reason for this initial lack of acceptance is _____.

34 사회 정치적 변화는 모순의 장을 조성해 왔다.

➡ Socio-political changes have set up a field of _____.

35 혼주는 그가 오랜 친구에게 하듯이 그를 껴안았다.

➡ The host _____ him as he would do to an old friend.

36 그것들은 과학 이론을 단순화하도록 과학자들을 강요한다.

➡ They _____ scientists to simplify scientific theories.

37 그것은 평생학습을 촉진하는 평가로의 접근 방법을 시작한다.

➡ It initiates approaches to assessment which _____ lifelong learning.

38 갓난아기들은 자신의 혀를 내미는 선천적인 성향을 갖고 있다.

➡ Newborns have an inborn _____ to stick out their tongue.

39 더 높은 진동에 있는 사람들은 긍정적인 사고 형태를 활기 띠게 했다.

➡ Those who are in a higher vibration have _____ positive thought forms.

40 이것은 물고기 개체군을 쫓아낸 더 빈번한 산소 결핍 사건을 초래해 왔다.

➡ This has led to more frequent anoxic events that _____ populations of fish.

전체 or 문항별 듣기

*1번부터 17번까지는 듣고 답하는 문제입니다. 1번부터 15번까지는 한 번만 들려주고, 16번부터 17번까지는 두 번 들려줍니다. 방송을 잘 듣고 답을 하시기 바랍니다.

▲ 듣기 파일

01 다음을 듣고, 남자가 하는 말의 목적으로 가장 적절한 것을 고르시오.

① 강당의 천장 수리 기간을 공지하려고
② 콘서트 관람 규칙 준수를 요청하려고
③ 학교 축제에서 공연할 동아리를 모집하려고
④ 폭우에 대비한 교실 시설 관리를 당부하려고
⑤ 학교 록 밴드 공연의 장소 변경을 안내하려고

02 대화를 듣고, 여자의 의견으로 가장 적절한 것을 고르시오.

① 달리기를 할 때 적합한 신발을 신어야 한다.
② 운동을 한 후에 충분한 물을 섭취해야 한다.
③ 야외 활동 전에 일기예보를 확인하는 것이 좋다.
④ 달리기 전 스트레칭은 통증과 부상을 예방해 준다.
⑤ 초보자의 경우 달리는 거리를 점진적으로 늘려야 한다.

03 대화를 듣고, 두 사람의 관계를 가장 잘 나타낸 것을 고르시오.

① 관객 – 영화감독
② 연극 배우 – 시나리오 작가
③ 잡지 기자 – 의상 디자이너
④ 토크쇼 진행자 – 영화 평론가
⑤ 배우 지망생 – 연기 학원 강사

04 대화를 듣고, 그림에서 대화의 내용과 일치하지 않는 것을 고르시오.

05 대화를 듣고, 여자가 할 일로 가장 적절한 것을 고르시오.

① 관객용 의자 배치하기
② 마이크 음향 점검하기
③ 공연 포스터 붙이기
④ 무대 조명 설치하기
⑤ 배터리 구매하기

06 대화를 듣고, 남자가 지불할 금액을 고르시오. [3점]

① $37　　② $45　　③ $55　　④ $60　　⑤ $80

07 대화를 듣고, 여자가 스키 여행을 갈 수 없는 이유를 고르시오.

① 카페에서 일해야 해서
② 숙소를 예약하지 못해서
③ 역사 시험 공부를 해야 해서
④ 수술받은 고양이를 돌봐야 해서
⑤ 캐나다에 사는 친척을 방문해야 해서

08 대화를 듣고, Street Photography Contest에 관해 언급되지 않은 것을 고르시오.

① 참가 대상　　② 주제　　③ 심사 기준
④ 제출 마감일　　⑤ 우승 상품

09 Twin Stars Chocolate Day에 관한 다음 내용을 듣고, 일치하지 않는 것을 고르시오.

① 11월 12일 오후에 열린다.
② 초콜릿의 역사에 관한 강의가 진행된다.
③ 초콜릿 5개를 만든다.
④ 사전 등록 없이 참가할 수 있다.
⑤ 등록비에 재료비가 포함된다.

10

다음 표를 보면서 대화를 듣고, 두 사람이 주문할 실내 사이클링 자전거를 고르시오.

Indoor Cycling Bikes

	Model	Price	Color	Foldable	Customer Rating
①	A	$100	White	×	★★★★
②	B	$150	Black	×	★★★
③	C	$190	Black	○	★★★★
④	D	$250	Black	○	★★★★★
⑤	E	$320	White	×	★★★★★

11

대화를 듣고, 여자의 마지막 말에 대한 남자의 응답으로 가장 적절한 것을 고르시오.

① Sure. I'll send you a link to the website.
② It would look better in a different color.
③ Sorry. I forgot to bring your sweater.
④ You need your receipt to return it.
⑤ My brother bought it on sale, too.

12

대화를 듣고, 남자의 마지막 말에 대한 여자의 응답으로 가장 적절한 것을 고르시오.

① Let's take the leftovers home.
② I prefer fried chicken over pizza.
③ I don't want to go out for lunch today.
④ I'll call the restaurant and check our order.
⑤ The letter was delivered to the wrong address.

13

대화를 듣고, 여자의 마지막 말에 대한 남자의 응답으로 가장 적절한 것을 고르시오.

Man: _____

① You're right. I won't skip meals anymore.
② Thank you for the lunch you prepared for me.
③ You need to check when the cafeteria is open.
④ Trust me. I can teach you good table manners.
⑤ No problem. We'll finish the science project on time.

14

대화를 듣고, 남자의 마지막 말에 대한 여자의 응답으로 가장 적절한 것을 고르시오. [3점]

Woman: _____

① No. It isn't difficult for me to learn Spanish.
② I'm glad you finally passed the vocabulary test.
③ Exactly. Learning a language starts with repetition.
④ It's very helpful to use a dictionary while writing.
⑤ You should turn in your homework by this afternoon.

15

다음 상황 설명을 듣고, Brian이 Melissa에게 할 말로 가장 적절한 것을 고르시오. [3점]

Brian: _____

① Let's clean the classroom after art class.
② Did you remove the stickers from the board?
③ Please turn off the heater when you leave the room.
④ When is the final date to sign up for the design class?
⑤ Will you design stickers that encourage energy saving?

[16~17] 다음을 듣고, 물음에 답하시오.

16

남자가 하는 말의 주제로 가장 적절한 것은?

① advantages of renting houses in cities
② reasons tourists prefer visiting old cities
③ ways cities deal with overtourism problems
④ correlation between cities' sizes and overtourism
⑤ how cities face their aging transportation systems

17

언급된 도시가 아닌 것은?

① Barcelona　　② Amsterdam　　③ London
④ Venice　　⑤ Paris

*이제 듣기 문제가 끝났습니다. 18번부터는 문제지의 지시에 따라 답을 하시기 바랍니다.

18 다음 글의 목적으로 가장 적절한 것은?

Dear Professor Sanchez,
My name is Ellis Wight, and I'm the director of the Alexandria Science Museum. We are holding a Chemistry Fair for local middle school students on Saturday, October 28. The goal of the fair is to encourage them to be interested in science through guided experiments. We are looking for college students who can help with the experiments during the event. I am contacting you to ask you to recommend some students from the chemistry department at your college who you think are qualified for this job. With their help, I'm sure the participants will have a great experience. I look forward to hearing from you soon.
　　Sincerely,
　　Ellis Wight

① 과학 박물관 내 시설 이용 제한을 안내하려고
② 화학 박람회 일정이 변경된 이유를 설명하려고
③ 중학생을 위한 화학 실험 특별 강연을 부탁하려고
④ 중학교 과학 수업용 실험 교재 집필을 의뢰하려고
⑤ 화학 박람회에서 실험을 도울 대학생 추천을 요청하려고

19 다음 글에 드러난 'I'의 심경 변화로 가장 적절한 것은?

Gregg and I had been rock climbing since sunrise and had had no problems. So we took a risk. "Look, the first bolt is right there. I can definitely climb out to it. Piece of cake," I persuaded Gregg, minutes before I found myself pinned. It wasn't a piece of cake. The rock was deceptively barren of handholds. I clumsily moved back and forth across the cliff face and ended up with nowhere to go...but down. The bolt that would save my life, if I could get to it, was about two feet above my reach. My arms trembled from exhaustion. I looked at Gregg. My body froze with fright from my neck down to my toes. Our rope was tied between us. If I fell, he would fall with me.

*barren of: ~이 없는

① joyful → bored
② confident → fearful
③ nervous → relieved
④ regretful → pleased
⑤ grateful → annoyed

20 다음 글에서 필자가 주장하는 바로 가장 적절한 것은?

We are always teaching our children something by our words and our actions. They learn from seeing. They learn from hearing and from *overhearing*. Children share the values of their parents about the most important things in life. Our priorities and principles and our examples of good behavior can teach our children to take the high road when other roads look tempting. Remember that children do not learn the values that make up strong character simply by being *told* about them. They learn by seeing the people around them *act* on and *uphold* those values in their daily lives. Therefore show your child good examples of life by your action. In our daily lives, we can show our children that we respect others. We can show them our compassion and concern when others are suffering, and our own self-discipline, courage and honesty as we make difficult decisions.

① 자녀를 타인과 비교하는 말을 삼가야 한다.
② 자녀에게 행동으로 삶의 모범을 보여야 한다.
③ 칭찬을 통해 자녀의 바람직한 행동을 강화해야 한다.
④ 훈육을 하기 전에 자녀 스스로 생각할 시간을 주어야 한다.
⑤ 자녀가 새로운 것에 도전할 때 인내심을 가지고 지켜봐야 한다.

21 밑줄 친 fall silently in the woods가 다음 글에서 의미하는 바로 가장 적절한 것은? [3점]

Most people have no doubt heard this question: If a tree falls in the forest and there is no one there to hear it fall, does it make a sound? The correct answer is no. Sound is more than pressure waves, and indeed there can be no sound without a hearer. And similarly, scientific communication is a two-way process. Just as a signal of any kind is useless unless it is perceived, a published scientific paper (signal) is useless unless it is both received *and* understood by its intended audience. Thus we can restate the axiom of science as follows: A scientific experiment is not complete until the results have been published *and understood*. Publication is no more than pressure waves unless the published paper is understood. Too many scientific papers fall silently in the woods.

*axiom: 자명한 이치

① fail to include the previous study
② end up being considered completely false
③ become useless because they are not published
④ focus on communication to meet public demands
⑤ are published yet readers don't understand them

22 다음 글의 요지로 가장 적절한 것은?

We all negotiate every day, whether we realise it or not. Yet few people ever learn *how* to negotiate. Those who do usually learn the traditional, win-lose negotiating style rather than an approach that is likely to result in a win-win agreement. This old-school, adversarial approach may be useful in a one-off negotiation where you will probably not deal with that person again. However, such transactions are becoming increasingly rare, because most of us deal with the same people repeatedly — our spouses and children, our friends and colleagues, our customers and clients. In view of this, it's essential to achieve successful results for ourselves and maintain a healthy relationship with our negotiating partners at the same time. In today's interdependent world of business partnerships and long-term relationships, a win-win outcome is fast becoming the *only* acceptable result. *adversarial: 적대적인

① 협상 상대의 단점뿐 아니라 장점을 철저히 분석해야 한다.
② 의사소통 과정에서 서로의 의도를 확인하는 것이 바람직하다.
③ 성공적인 협상을 위해 다양한 대안을 준비하는 것이 중요하다.
④ 양측에 유리한 협상을 통해 상대와 좋은 관계를 유지해야 한다.
⑤ 원만한 인간관계를 위해 상호독립성을 인정하는 것이 필요하다.

23 다음 글의 주제로 가장 적절한 것은?

The interaction of workers from different cultural backgrounds with the host population might increase productivity due to positive externalities like knowledge spillovers. This is only an advantage up to a certain degree. When the variety of backgrounds is too large, fractionalization may cause excessive transaction costs for communication, which may lower productivity. Diversity not only impacts the labour market, but may also affect the quality of life in a location. A tolerant native population may value a multicultural city or region because of an increase in the range of available goods and services. On the other hand, diversity could be perceived as an unattractive feature if natives perceive it as a distortion of what they consider to be their national identity. They might even discriminate against other ethnic groups and they might fear that social conflicts between different foreign nationalities are imported into their own neighbourhood.

*externality: 외부 효과 **fractionalization: 분열

① roles of culture in ethnic groups
② contrastive aspects of cultural diversity
③ negative perspectives of national identity
④ factors of productivity differences across countries
⑤ policies to protect minorities and prevent discrimination

24 다음 글의 제목으로 가장 적절한 것은?

We think we are shaping our buildings. But really, our buildings and development are also shaping us. One of the best examples of this is the oldest-known construction: the ornately carved rings of standing stones at Göbekli Tepe in Turkey. Before these ancestors got the idea to erect standing stones some 12,000 years ago, they were hunter-gatherers. It appears that the erection of the multiple rings of megalithic stones took so long, and so many successive generations, that these innovators were forced to settle down to complete the construction works. In the process, they became the first farming society on Earth. This is an early example of a society constructing something that ends up radically remaking the society itself. Things are not so different in our own time.   *ornately: 화려하게 **megalithic: 거석의

① Buildings Transform How We Live!
② Why Do We Build More Than We Need?
③ Copying Ancient Buildings for Creativity
④ Was Life Better in Hunter-gatherer Times?
⑤ Innovate Your Farm with New Constructions

25 다음 도표의 내용과 일치하지 않는 것은?

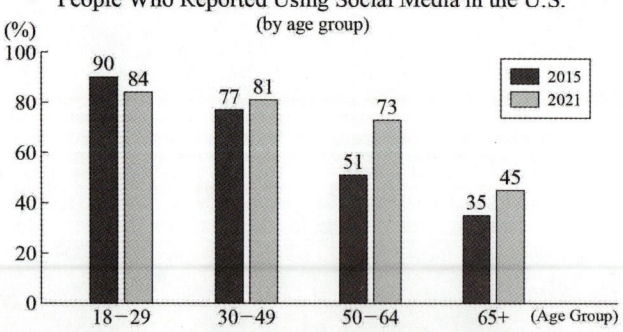

People Who Reported Using Social Media in the U.S. (by age group)

The graph above shows the percentages of people in different age groups who reported using social media in the United States in 2015 and 2021. ① In each of the given years, the 18-29 group had the highest percentage of people who said they used social media. ② In 2015, the percentage of people who reported using social media in the 30-49 group was more than twice that in the 65 and older group. ③ The percentage of people who said they used social media in the 50-64 group in 2021 was 22 percentage points higher than that in 2015. ④ In 2021, except for the 65 and older group, more than four-fifths of people in each age group reported using social media. ⑤ Among all the age groups, only the 18-29 group showed a decrease in the percentage of people who reported using social media from 2015 to 2021.

26 Bill Evans에 관한 다음 글의 내용과 일치하지 않는 것은?

American jazz pianist Bill Evans was born in New Jersey in 1929. His early training was in classical music. At the age of six, he began receiving piano lessons, later adding flute and violin. He earned bachelor's degrees in piano and music education from Southeastern Louisiana College in 1950. He went on to serve in the army from 1951 to 1954 and played flute in the Fifth Army Band. After serving in the military, he studied composition at the Mannes School of Music in New York. Composer George Russell admired his playing and hired Evans to record and perform his compositions. Evans became famous for recordings made from the late-1950s through the 1960s. He won his first Grammy Award in 1964 for his album *Conversations with Myself*. Evans' expressive piano works and his unique harmonic approach inspired a whole generation of musicians.

① 6세에 피아노 수업을 받기 시작했다.
② Southeastern Louisiana 대학에서 학위를 취득했다.
③ 군 복무 이후 뉴욕에서 작곡을 공부했다.
④ 작곡가 George Russell을 고용했다.
⑤ 1964년에 자신의 첫 번째 그래미상을 수상했다.

Silversmithing Class

Kingston Club is offering a fine jewelry making class. Don't miss this great chance to make your own jewelry!

When & Where
· Saturday, October 21, 2023 (2 p.m. to 4 p.m.)
· Kingston Club studio

Registration
· Available only online
· Dates: October 1 – 14, 2023
· Fee: $40 (This includes all tools and materials.)
· Registration is limited to 6 people.

Note
· Participants must be at least 16 years old.
· No refund for cancellation on the day of the class

① 두 시간 동안 진행된다.
② 10월 1일부터 등록할 수 있다.
③ 등록 인원은 6명으로 제한된다.
④ 참가 연령에 제한이 없다.
⑤ 수업 당일 취소 시 환불이 불가하다.

2023 Ocean Awareness Film Contest

Join our 7th annual film contest and show your knowledge of marine conservation.

□ **Theme**
– Ocean Wildlife / Ocean Pollution (Choose one of the above.)

□ **Guidelines**
– Participants: High school students
– Submission deadline: September 22, 2023
– The video must be between 10 and 15 minutes.
– All entries must be uploaded to our website.
– Only one entry per person

□ **Prizes**
· 1st place: $100   · 2nd place: $70
· 3rd place: $50
(Winners will be announced on our website.)
For more information,
please visit www.oceanawareFC.com.

① 세 가지 주제 중 하나를 선택해야 한다.
② 중학생이 참가할 수 있다.
③ 영상은 10분을 넘길 수 없다.
④ 1인당 두 개까지 출품할 수 있다.
⑤ 수상자는 웹사이트에 공지될 것이다.

2023. 9
9회

There is a reason the title "Monday Morning Quarterback" exists. Just read the comments on social media from fans discussing the weekend's games, and you quickly see how many people believe they could play, coach, and manage sport teams more ① <u>successfully</u> than those on the field. This goes for the boardroom as well. Students and professionals with years of training and specialized degrees in sport business may also find themselves ② <u>being given</u> advice on how to do their jobs from friends, family, or even total strangers without any expertise. Executives in sport management ③ <u>have</u> decades of knowledge and experience in their respective fields. However, many of them face criticism from fans and community members telling ④ <u>themselves</u> how to run their business. Very few people tell their doctor how to perform surgery or their accountant how to prepare their taxes, but many people provide feedback on ⑤ <u>how</u> sport organizations should be managed.

*boardroom: 이사회실

30 다음 글의 밑줄 친 부분 중, 문맥상 낱말의 쓰임이 적절하지 <u>않은</u> 것은? [3점]

While moving is difficult for everyone, it is particularly stressful for children. They lose their sense of security and may feel disoriented when their routine is disrupted and all that is ① <u>familiar</u> is taken away. Young children, ages 3–6, are particularly affected by a move. Their understanding at this stage is quite literal, and it is ② <u>easy</u> for them to imagine beforehand a new home and their new room. Young children may have worries such as "Will I still be me in the new place?" and "Will my toys and bed come with us?" It is important to establish a balance between validating children's past experiences and focusing on helping them ③ <u>adjust</u> to the new place. Children need to have opportunities to share their backgrounds in a way that ④ <u>respects</u> their past as an important part of who they are. This contributes to building a sense of community, which is essential for all children, especially those in ⑤ <u>transition</u>.

[31~34] 다음 빈칸에 들어갈 말로 가장 적절한 것을 고르시오.

31

Many people are terrified to fly in airplanes. Often, this fear stems from a lack of control. The pilot is in control, not the passengers, and this lack of control instills fear. Many potential passengers are so afraid they choose to drive great distances to get to a destination instead of flying. But their decision to drive is based solely on emotion, not logic. Logic says that statistically, the odds of dying in a car crash are around 1 in 5,000, while the odds of dying in a plane crash are closer to 1 in 11 million. If you're going to take a risk, especially one that could possibly involve your well-being, wouldn't you want the odds in your favor? However, most people choose the option that will cause them the least amount of _____. Pay attention to the thoughts you have about taking the risk and make sure you're basing your decision on facts, not just feelings.

*instill: 스며들게 하다

① anxiety   ② boredom   ③ confidence
④ satisfaction   ⑤ responsibility

32

The famous primatologist Frans de Waal, of Emory University, says humans downplay similarities between us and other animals as a way of maintaining our spot at the top of our imaginary ladder. Scientists, de Waal points out, can be some of the worst offenders — employing technical language to _____. They call "kissing" in chimps "mouth-to-mouth contact"; they call "friends" between primates "favorite affiliation partners"; they interpret evidence showing that crows and chimps can make tools as being somehow qualitatively different from the kind of toolmaking said to define humanity. If an animal can beat us at a cognitive task — like how certain bird species can remember the precise locations of thousands of seeds — they write it off as instinct, not intelligence. This and so many more tricks of language are what de Waal has termed "linguistic castration." The way we use our tongues to disempower animals, the way we invent words to maintain our spot at the top. [3점]

*primatologist: 영장류학자 **affiliation: 제휴

① define human instincts
② overestimate chimps' intelligence
③ distance the other animals from us
④ identify animals' negative emotions
⑤ correct our misconceptions about nature

33

A key to engagement and achievement is providing students with _____. My scholarly work and my teaching have been deeply influenced by the work of Rosalie Fink. She interviewed twelve adults who were highly successful in their work, including a physicist, a biochemist, and a company CEO. All of them had dyslexia and had had significant problems with reading throughout their school years. While she expected to find that they had avoided reading and discovered ways to bypass it or compensate with other strategies for learning, she found the opposite. "To my surprise, I found that these dyslexics were enthusiastic readers...they rarely avoided reading. On the contrary, they sought out books." The pattern Fink discovered was that all of her subjects had been passionate in some personal interest. The areas of interest included religion, math, business, science, history, and biography. What mattered was that they read voraciously to find out more.

*dyslexia: 난독증 **voraciously: 탐욕스럽게

① examples from official textbooks
② relevant texts they will be interested in
③ enough chances to exchange information
④ different genres for different age groups
⑤ early reading experience to develop logic skills

34

For many people, *ability* refers to intellectual competence, so they want everything they do to reflect how smart they are — writing a brilliant legal brief, getting the highest grade on a test, writing elegant computer code, saying something exceptionally wise or witty in a conversation. You could also define ability in terms of a particular skill or talent, such as how well one plays the piano, learns a language, or serves a tennis ball. Some people focus on their ability to be attractive, entertaining, up on the latest trends, or to have the newest gadgets. However ability may be defined, a problem occurs when _____. The performance becomes the *only* measure of the person; nothing else is taken into account. An outstanding performance means an outstanding person; an average performance means an average person. Period. [3점]

① it is the sole determinant of one's self-worth
② you are distracted by others' achievements
③ there is too much competition in one field
④ you ignore feedback about a performance
⑤ it is not accompanied by effort

35 다음 글에서 전체 흐름과 관계 <u>없는</u> 문장은? [3점]

Sensory nerves have specialized endings in the tissues that pick up a particular sensation. If, for example, you step on a sharp object such as a pin, nerve endings in the skin will transmit the pain sensation up your leg, up and along the spinal cord to the brain. ① While the pain itself is unpleasant, it is in fact acting as a protective mechanism for the foot. ② That is, you get used to the pain so the capacity with which you can avoid pain decreases. ③ Within the brain, nerves will connect to the area that controls speech, so that you may well shout 'ouch' or something rather less polite. ④ They will also connect to motor nerves that travel back down the spinal cord, and to the muscles in your leg that now contract quickly to lift your foot away from the painful object. ⑤ Sensory and motor nerves control almost all functions in the body — from the beating of the heart to the movement of the gut, sweating and just about everything else.　*spinal cord: 척수 **gut: 장

36

Maybe you've heard this joke: "How do you eat an elephant?" The answer is "one bite at a time."

(A) Common crystal habits include squares, triangles, and six-sided hexagons. Usually crystals form when liquids cool, such as when you create ice cubes. Many times, crystals form in ways that do not allow for perfect shapes. If conditions are too cold, too hot, or there isn't enough source material, they can form strange, twisted shapes.

(B) So, how do you "build" the Earth? That's simple, too: one atom at a time. Atoms are the basic building blocks of crystals, and since all rocks are made up of crystals, the more you know about atoms, the better. Crystals come in a variety of shapes that scientists call *habits*.

(C) But when conditions are right, we see beautiful displays. Usually, this involves a slow, steady environment where the individual atoms have plenty of time to join and fit perfectly into what's known as the *crystal lattice*. This is the basic structure of atoms that is seen time after time. [3점]

① (A) — (C) — (B)　　② (B) — (A) — (C)
③ (B) — (C) — (A)　　④ (C) — (A) — (B)
⑤ (C) — (B) — (A)

37

When you pluck a guitar string it moves back and forth hundreds of times every second.

(A) The vibration of the wood creates more powerful waves in the air pressure, which travel away from the guitar. When the waves reach your eardrums they flex in and out the same number of times a second as the original string.

(B) Naturally, this movement is so fast that you cannot see it — you just see the blurred outline of the moving string. Strings vibrating in this way on their own make hardly any noise because strings are very thin and don't push much air about.

(C) But if you attach a string to a big hollow box (like a guitar body), then the vibration is amplified and the note is heard loud and clear. The vibration of the string is passed on to the wooden panels of the guitar body, which vibrate back and forth at the same rate as the string.　　*pluck: (현악기를) 뜯다 **amplify: 증폭시키다

① (A) — (C) — (B)　　② (B) — (A) — (C)
③ (B) — (C) — (A)　　④ (C) — (A) — (B)
⑤ (C) — (B) — (A)

38

> Other individuals prefer integrating work and family roles all day long.

Boundaries between work and home are blurring as portable digital technology makes it increasingly possible to work anywhere, anytime. Individuals differ in how they like to manage their time to meet work and outside responsibilities. (①) Some people prefer to separate or segment roles so that boundary crossings are minimized. (②) For example, these people might keep separate email accounts for work and family and try to conduct work at the workplace and take care of family matters only during breaks and non-work time. (③) We've even noticed more of these "segmenters" carrying two phones — one for work and one for personal use. (④) Flexible schedules work well for these individuals because they enable greater distinction between time at work and time in other roles. (⑤) This might entail constantly trading text messages with children from the office, or monitoring emails at home and on vacation, rather than returning to work to find hundreds of messages in their inbox. [3점]

*entail: 수반하다

39

> However, do not assume that a product is perfectly complementary, as customers may not be completely locked in to the product.

A "complementary good" is a product that is often consumed alongside another product. (①) For example, popcorn is a complementary good to a movie, while a travel pillow is a complementary good for a long plane journey. (②) When the popularity of one product increases, the sales of its complementary good also increase. (③) By producing goods that complement other products that are already (or about to be) popular, you can ensure a steady stream of demand for your product. (④) Some products enjoy perfect complementary status — they *have* to be consumed together, such as a lamp and a lightbulb. (⑤) For example, although motorists may seem required to purchase gasoline to run their cars, they can switch to electric cars.

It's not news to anyone that we judge others based on their clothes. In general, studies that investigate these judgments find that people prefer clothing that matches expectations — surgeons in scrubs, little boys in blue — with one notable exception. A series of studies published in an article in June 2014 in the *Journal of Consumer Research* explored observers' reactions to people who broke established norms only slightly. In one scenario, a man at a black-tie affair was viewed as having higher status and competence when wearing a red bow tie. The researchers also found that valuing uniqueness increased audience members' ratings of the status and competence of a professor who wore red sneakers while giving a lecture. The results suggest that people judge these slight deviations from the norm as positive because they suggest that the individual is powerful enough to risk the social costs of such behaviors.

⬇

A series of studies show that people view an individual ___(A)___ when the individual only slightly ___(B)___ the norm for what people should wear.

	(A)		(B)
①	positively	—	challenges
②	negatively	—	challenges
③	indifferently	—	neglects
④	negatively	—	meets
⑤	positively	—	meets

[41~42] 다음 글을 읽고, 물음에 답하시오.

Claims that local food production cut greenhouse gas emissions by reducing the burning of transportation fuel are usually not well founded. Transport is the source of only 11 percent of greenhouse gas emissions within the food sector, so reducing the distance that food travels after it leaves the farm is far (a) <u>less</u> important than reducing wasteful energy use on the farm. Food coming from a distance can actually be better for the (b) <u>climate</u>, depending on how it was grown. For example, field-grown tomatoes shipped from Mexico in the winter months will have a smaller carbon footprint than (c) <u>local</u> winter tomatoes grown in a greenhouse. In the United Kingdom, lamb meat that travels 11,000 miles from New Zealand generates only one-quarter the carbon emissions per pound compared to British lamb because farmers in the United Kingdom raise their animals on feed (which must be produced using fossil fuels) rather than on clover pastureland.

When food does travel, what matters most is not the (d) <u>distance</u> traveled but the travel mode (surface versus air), and most of all the load size. Bulk loads of food can travel halfway around the world by ocean freight with a smaller carbon footprint, per pound delivered, than foods traveling just a short distance but in much (e) <u>larger</u> loads. For example, 18-wheelers carry much larger loads than pickup trucks so they can move food 100 times as far while burning only one-third as much gas per pound of food delivered.

*freight: 화물 운송

41 윗글의 제목으로 가장 적절한 것은?

① Shorten the Route, Cut the Cost
② Is Local Food Always Better for the Earth?
③ Why Mass Production Ruins the Environment
④ New Technologies: What Matters in Agriculture
⑤ Reduce Food Waste for a Smaller Carbon
   Footprint

42 밑줄 친 (a)~(e) 중에서 문맥상 낱말의 쓰임이 적절하지 않은 것은?

① (a)　　② (b)　　③ (c)　　④ (d)　　⑤ (e)

[43~45] 다음 글을 읽고, 물음에 답하시오.

(A)

Long ago, an old man built a grand temple at the center of his village. People traveled to worship at the temple. So the old man made arrangements for food and accommodation inside the temple itself. He needed someone who could look after the temple, so (a) <u>he</u> put up a notice: Manager needed.

(B)

When that young man left the temple, the old man called him and asked, "Will you take care of this temple?" The young man was surprised by the offer and replied, "I have no experience caring for a temple. I'm not even educated." The old man smiled and said, "I don't want any educated man. I want a qualified person." Confused, the young man asked, "But why do (b) <u>you</u> consider me a qualified person?"

(C)

The old man replied, "I buried a brick on the path to the temple. I watched for many days as people tripped over that brick. No one thought to remove it. But you dug up that brick." The young man said, "I haven't done anything great. It's the duty of every human being to think about others. (c) <u>I</u> only did my duty." The old man smiled and said, "Only people who know their duty and perform it are qualified people."

(D)

Seeing the notice, many people went to the old man. But he returned all the applicants after interviews, telling them, "I need a qualified person for this work." The old man would sit on the roof of (d) <u>his</u> house every morning, watching people go through the temple doors. One day, (e) <u>he</u> saw a young man come to the temple.

43 주어진 글 (A)에 이어질 내용을 순서에 맞게 배열한 것으로 가장 적절한 것은?

① (B) — (D) — (C)　　② (C) — (B) — (D)
③ (C) — (D) — (B)　　④ (D) — (B) — (C)
⑤ (D) — (C) — (B)

44 밑줄 친 (a)~(e) 중에서 가리키는 대상이 나머지 넷과 다른 것은?

① (a)　　② (b)　　③ (c)　　④ (d)　　⑤ (e)

45 윗글에 관한 내용으로 적절하지 않은 것은?

① 노인은 마을 중심부에 사원을 지었다.
② 젊은이가 사원을 나설 때 노인이 그를 불렀다.
③ 젊은이는 노인의 제안에 놀랐다.
④ 노인은 사원으로 통하는 길에 묻혀있던 벽돌을 파냈다.
⑤ 공고를 보고 많은 사람들이 노인을 찾아갔다.

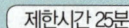
• MP3 파일을 들으며 다음 빈칸을 채우시오. (듣기 어려운 발음이나 정답의 단서가 되는 부분에 빈칸을 만들었습니다.)

01 다음을 듣고, 남자가 하는 말의 목적으로 가장 적절한 것을 고르시오.

M: Attention, Fargo High School students. This is your music teacher, Mr. Nelson. Our school rock band _____ ★ _____ ____ hold its concert in the auditorium today. I'm sure you've been looking forward to the concert. Unfortunately, the rain yesterday caused a ★_____ ___ ____ _____ of the auditorium. The _____ _____ to be fixed, so we decided to change the location of the concert. The rock band will now perform in the _____ _____. The time for the concert hasn't changed. I hope you'll enjoy the _____.

02 대화를 듣고, 여자의 의견으로 가장 적절한 것을 고르시오.

W: Simon, are you doing anything after school?

M: Nothing special. What about you?

W: I'm planning to go for a run in the park. It's a _____ ★ _____.

M: The _____ ___ _____ for running. Can I go with you?

W: Why not? [Pause] Wait! You're wearing slippers. Those aren't good for running.

M: It's okay. I can run in slippers.

W: No way. Slippers aren't _____ _____ _____. You can get hurt if you run in them.

M: You mean I need to put on running shoes?

W: You got it. You need ____ _____ ____ _____ shoes for running.

M: All right. I'll go home and change.

03 대화를 듣고, 두 사람의 관계를 가장 잘 나타낸 것을 고르시오.

M: Good morning, Ms. Clapton. It's nice to meet you.

W: Nice to meet you, too. I'm a fan of _____ _____.

M: You won many _____ at the film festival this year. Congratulations!

W: Thank you. I was lucky to work with a great director ____ _____ _____.

M: The clothes and ★ _____ in the movie are _____. How do you start your costume designs?

W: I read the _____ ___ _____ _____ the characters. Then I research the characters' _____.

M: That sounds like a lot of work. Which of the costumes from this film is your favorite?

W: It's hard to pick just one because I love all of my designs.

M: I totally understand. Thank you for _____ _____ _____ with the readers of our magazine.

W: It was my pleasure.

04 대화를 듣고, 그림에서 대화의 내용과 일치하지 <u>않는</u> 것을 고르시오.

W: Come look at the new reading room in the library.

M: Wow! It's much better than I thought.

W: _____ _____. I like the rug in the center of the room.

M: The ✪_____ _____ of the rug makes the room feel warm.

W: I agree. I think putting the sofa between two plants was a good idea.

M: Right. We can sit there and read for hours.

W: There's a round clock on the wall.

M: I have the same clock at home. Oh, the _____ _____ ____ _____ is full of books.

W: We can read the books at the long table.

M: Yeah, it looks like a good place to read. The ____ _____ on the table will make it easy to focus.

W: _____ ✪_____ is important for reading.

M: I can't wait to start using the reading room.

05 대화를 듣고, 여자가 할 일로 가장 적절한 것을 고르시오.

M: Kelly, the school musical is tomorrow. _____ ____ ____ _____ the final checklist together?

W: Let's do it. What's first? [Pause] Oh, the posters. We put them up around school last week.

M: Right. Do we have _____ _____ for the ✪_____ microphones?

W: Yeah. I bought them yesterday. We should check that the microphones work well with the sound system.

M: I did that this morning. They _____ _____.

W: How about the stage lights?

M: They work perfectly. I think everyone will love the lighting design you made.

W: Really? Thanks. It looks like we've finished everything.

M: No, wait. The chairs for the _____ _____ _____ _____ yet.

W: You're right! I'll go take care of that now.

M: The musical is going to ____ _____.

06 대화를 듣고, 남자가 지불할 금액을 고르시오.

W: Welcome to Libby's Flowers. How can I help you?

M: I'd like to order a rose basket for my parents' _____ ✪_____.

W: All right. Our rose baskets come in two sizes.

M: What are the options?

W: The _____ _____ is 30 dollars, and the large size is 50 dollars.

M: Hmm.... I think the bigger one is better.

W: Good choice. So, you'll get one rose basket in the large size. By the way, we're giving a 10-percent discount on ____ _____ this week.

M: Excellent! When will my order ____ _____?

W: It'll be ready around 11 a.m. If you can't pick it up, we _____ ____ _____ _____. It's 10 dollars.

M: Oh, great. I'd like it to be delivered. Here's my credit card.

07 대화를 듣고, 여자가 스키 여행을 갈 수 <u>없는</u> 이유를 고르시오.

M: You seem busy this morning, Olivia.

W: I am. I had to see Professor Martin about my _____ _____.

M: Oh, I see. Do you remember that our club's ____ _____ ____ this weekend?

W: Yeah. I heard that a nice ski resort has been booked for the trip.

M: I _____ _____ _____. I'm so excited to go skiing at a nice resort.

W: I bet it'll be great, but I don't think I can go this time.

M: Why? You don't work at the cafe ____ _____ _____, do you?

W: No, I don't. But I need to take care of my cat. She's _____ _____ _____.

M: Isn't there anyone else who can look after your cat?

W: No one but me. My parents are visiting ✪_____ ____ _____. They won't be back for two weeks.

M: I'm sorry that you can't join us.

W: Me, too. _____ _____ this weekend.

08 대화를 듣고, Street Photography Contest에 관해 언급되지 <u>않은</u> 것을 고르시오.

W: What are you doing, Tim?

M: I'm looking at the Street Photography Contest website.

W: I've heard about that. It's a contest _____ _____ _____, right?

M: Actually, it's open to high school students, too. Why don't you try it?

W: Really? Maybe I will. Does the contest have ____ ⭐ _____?

M: Sure. This _____ ⭐ _____ is Daily Life.

W: That sounds interesting. When is _____ _____?

M: You have to submit your photographs by September 15.

W: That's _____ _____ I expected.

M: You should hurry and choose your photos. The winner will _____ ____ _____ as a prize.

W: Okay! Wish me luck.

09 Twin Stars Chocolate Day에 관한 다음 내용을 듣고, 일치하지 <u>않는</u> 것을 고르시오.

M: Hello, listeners. I'm Charlie Anderson from the Twin Stars Chocolate Museum. I'm _____ ____ _____ the Twin Stars Chocolate Day, a _____ _____ to create your own delicious chocolates. It'll be held on November 12 from 1 p.m. to 4 p.m. First, you'll listen to a _____ _____ the history of chocolate. Then you'll have a chance to taste our _____ _____ ⭐ _____. At the end of the event, you'll make five chocolates yourself. If you want to take part in the event, you must register in advance. You can sign up on our website until November 1. The _____ ____ is 20 dollars, which includes the cost ____ ⭐ _____. Don't miss this sweet opportunity!

10 다음 표를 보면서 대화를 듣고, 두 사람이 주문할 실내 사이클링 자전거를 고르시오.

M: Honey, what are you looking at?

W: I'm looking at _____ _____ _____. Would you like to choose one together?

M: Sure, let me see. [Pause] The price _____ by model.

W: I don't want to pay more than 300 dollars. That's too expensive.

M: I agree. Which color do you like?

W: I prefer a dark color because it _____ _____ _____ our living room.

M: Okay. Then we ⭐ _____ _____ a white one. What do you think about the _____ ____?

W: We definitely need that. It'll take up less ⭐ _____ _____.

M: We have just two options left. Which one should we get?

W: I think we should go with the one with a _____ _____ _____. The reviews are based ____ _____ customers' experiences.

M: Sounds good. Let's order this one.

11 대화를 듣고, 여자의 마지막 말에 대한 남자의 응답으로 가장 적절한 것을 고르시오.

W: Jason, is that ____ ____ ⭐ _____? It looks good on you.

M: Thanks. I _____ it online. It was on sale.

W: I'd _____ ____ buy the same one ____ ____ _____. Can you tell me where you got it?

M: _____

12 대화를 듣고, 남자의 마지막 말에 대한 여자의 응답으로 가장 적절한 것을 고르시오.

M: Becky, did you order ____ _____ for dinner?

W: Yes. I _____ _____ about an hour ago.

M: An hour ago? ⭐ _____ _____ _____ less than 40 minutes.

W: _____

13 대화를 듣고, 여자의 마지막 말에 대한 남자의 응답으로 가장 적절한 것을 고르시오.

W: I haven't seen you in the cafeteria this week. Where have you been?
M: I've been in _____ _____ working on _____ _____ project.
W: Does that mean you've _____ _____ lunch?
M: Yeah. This project is really important _____ _____ _____.
W: You _____ _____ that. It's not good for your health.
M: Don't worry. I always have ____ ____ _____ when I get home.
W: That's the problem. _____ ✪ _____ makes you _____ later.
M: I hadn't thought of that. Then what should I do?
W: It's simple. You _____ _____ regularly to stay healthy.
M: _____

14 대화를 듣고, 남자의 마지막 말에 대한 여자의 응답으로 가장 적절한 것을 고르시오.

M: Excuse me, Ms. Lopez. Can I ask you something?
W: Sure, Tony. What can I do for you?
M: I want ____ ____ _____ ____ Spanish, but I don't know _____ ____ _____.
W: You seem to do well during class. Do you study when you're at home?
M: I do all _____ _____ and try to learn 20 _____ _____ every day.
W: That's a good start. Do you also _____ _____ those words ✪ _____?
M: Do I need to do that? That sounds like it'll take a lot of time.
W: It does. _____ _____ you're still ____ _____, you have to put in _____ _____ ____ _____ _____ to new words.
M: I see. So are you _____ _____ I practice them over and over?
W: _____

15 다음 상황 설명을 듣고, Brian이 Melissa에게 할 말로 가장 적절한 것을 고르시오.

W: Brian is a class leader. He is ✪ _____ _____ _____ _____ and saving energy. Recently, he's noticed that his classmates don't turn the lights off when they leave the classroom. Brian thinks this is _____ ✪ _____. He wants to make _____ _____ _____ his classmates to save energy by turning off the lights. He tells this idea to his classmate Melissa, _____ _____ _____ it's a good idea. Brian knows Melissa is ____ _____ _____, so he wants to ask her to _____ _____ _____ _____ their classmates to save energy. In this situation, what would Brian most likely say to Melissa?
Brian: _____

[16~17] 다음을 듣고, 물음에 답하시오.

M: Good afternoon, everyone. Last time, we learned that ✪ _____ happens when there are too many visitors _____ _____ _____ _____. Today, we'll learn how cities deal with the problems caused _____ ✪ _____. First, some cities limit the number of hotels so there are _____ _____ ____ _____ to stay. In Barcelona, building new hotels is not allowed in the city center. Second, other cities _____ _____ _____ from popular sites. For instance, Amsterdam encourages tourists to visit less-crowded areas. Third, many cities have _____ ____ _____ _____. For example, Venice has tried to _____ _____ _____ by stopping large cruise ships from docking on the island. Similarly, Paris has focused on reducing tourism to certain parts of the city by having car-restricted areas. Now, let's watch some video clips.

· 제한시간 20분 · 맞은 개수 ___ / 40

* 다음 영어는 우리말 뜻을, 우리말은 영어 단어를 〈보기〉에서 찾아 쓰시오.

01 atom _____

02 scrub _____

03 grand _____

04 integrate _____

05 respective _____

06 인식 _____

07 고막 _____

08 유일한 _____

09 지루함 _____

10 목초지 _____

[보기]

원자	sole
각자의	refund
수술복	boredom
개선하다	eardrum
웅장한	awareness
통합하다	pastureland

* 다음 우리말에 알맞은 영어 표현을 찾아 연결하시오.

11 ~을 파내다 ·   · pass on

12 ~을 전달하다 ·   · dig up

13 ~에서 생겨나다 ·   · take into account

14 ~을 고려하다 ·   · stem from

15 ~을 나타내다 ·   · refer to

* 다음 우리말과 같은 표현이 되도록 알맞은 단어를 〈보기〉에서 찾아 쓰시오.

[보기]

flavor / bypass / successive / script / correlation / hollow
excessive / intended / compassion / wireless / surgery / leak

16 커다란 속이 빈 상자 ➔ a big _____ box

17 천장의 누수 ➔ a(n) _____ in the ceiling

18 그것을 우회할 방법들 ➔ ways to _____ it

19 그것의 의도된 독자 ➔ its _____ audience

20 과도한 거래 비용 ➔ _____ transaction costs

21 많은 잇따른 세대 ➔ many _____ generations

22 우리의 연민과 걱정 ➔ our _____ and concern

23 우리의 가장 인기 있는 맛 ➔ our most popular _____

24 무선 마이크에 쓸 여분의 배터리 ➔ extra batteries for the _____ microphones

25 도시의 규모와 관광 사이의 상관관계 ➔ _____ between cities' sizes and tourism

26 사원에서 예배를 드리다 ➔ (disrespect / worship) at the temple

27 꾸준한 흐름을 보장하다 ➔ ensure a (steady / greedy) stream

28 작곡을 공부하다 ➔ study (opposition / composition)

29 반복에서 시작하다 ➔ start with (repetition / reputation)

30 적은 저장 공간을 차지하다 ➔ take up less (storage / shortage) space

* 다음 문장의 빈칸에 알맞은 단어를 〈보기〉에서 찾아 쓰시오.

─────────────── [보기] ───────────────

passionate / rare / distinction / bulk / leftover / disoriented

sensory / fright / alongside / norm / dock / accommodation

31 그러한 거래는 점점 더 드물어지고 있다.

➔ Such transactions are becoming increasingly _____.

32 감각 신경은 특화된 말단을 조직에 가지고 있다.

➔ _____ nerves have specialized endings in the tissues.

33 내 몸은 목에서부터 발끝까지 공포로 얼어붙었다.

➔ My body froze with _____ from my neck down to my toes.

34 그들은 안도감을 잃고 혼란스럽게 느낄 수도 있다.

➔ They lose their sense of security and may feel _____.

35 사람들은 규범으로부터 이러한 약간의 일탈들을 긍정적으로 판단한다.

➔ People judge these slight deviations from the _____ as positive.

36 그것은 다른 제품과 함께 종종 소비되는 제품이다.

➔ It is a product that is often consumed _____ another product.

37 노인은 음식과 숙소를 준비했다.

➔ The old man made arrangements for food and _____.

38 그는 환경 문제와 에너지 절약에 열정적이다.

➔ He is _____ about environmental issues and saving energy.

39 대량의 적재된 식품은 세계의 절반을 해상 화물 운송으로 이동할 수 있다.

➔ _____ loads of food can travel halfway around the world by ocean freight.

40 그것들은 직장에서의 시간과 다른 역할에서의 시간 사이에 더 큰 구별을 가능하게 한다.

➔ They enable greater _____ between time at work and time in other roles.

여로

KAIST 여행 동아리

인싸들의 핫플레이스를 찾아가다!

이 절로 나오는 멋진 풍경, 인싸들의 핫플레이스 그리고 평소에 쉽게 접하지 못한 음식들을 찾아가는 여행을 하고 싶으시다고요?

저희는 매학기마다 조별로 힐링, 레저, 이색, 즉석 등 다양한 컨셉을 테마로 하여 여행을 떠납니다! 평소에 지인들과 다니던 일반적인 여행과는 달리, 여행 조원들 간의 활발한 의견 교류 및 회의 그리고 전체 정기모임을 통한 부원들의 피드백을 통해 더 재밌고 특별한 여행을 기획할 수 있습니다. 또한 여행을 다녀오면 카드뉴스와 기사를 작성해 유용한 여행 정보를 KAIST 학내 구성원들과 공유하여 많은 사람들이 이를 활용할 수 있도록 노력하고 있습니다

공부하느라 스트레스도 많이 받고 몸과 정신이 지친다고 느껴질때, 유쾌하고 멋진 사람들과 여행을 떠나고 싶으시다면 KAIST 여행 동아리 '여로'에 합류하세요.

여행을 사랑하고 다양한 사람들과 어울리기를 좋아하는 학생 여러분, 여행 가방 나누어 들고, 특별한 추억이 될 '여로'와 함께 걸어요.

[https://www.facebook.com/Yeoro.kaist]

*11월 전국연합학력평가

[회별 45문항, 제한 시간 70분]

★ 최근 연도부터 차례대로 수록하였습니다.

10회 **모의고사** ─ 2024년 시행

11회 **모의고사** ─ 2023년 시행

12회 **모의고사** ─ 2022년 시행

출제 범위	고1 11월 수준
난이도	**하** : 11~13문항 **중** : 14~16문항 **상** : 8~10문항 **최상** : 8~10문항

출제 경향
• **듣기** 17문항 (1~17번), **어법 · 어휘** 3문항 (29~30번, 42번),
　독해 25문항 (그 외 전 문항)

11월 대비 학습 전략
고1의 마지막 학력평가이므로 지문, 문제가 모두 어렵게 출제된다. 어법 문제는 문장 구조를 완벽히 분석한 후 어법의 적절성을 파악하며 풀어야 한다. 독해 문항 유형별 접근법을 떠올리며 침착하게 지문을 읽고 문제를 푸는 연습을 해야 한다.

전국연합학력평가 [2024년 10월 15일 시행]

★ 3점 문항에만 점수가 표시되어 있습니다.

• 문항 수: 45개 • 배점: 100점 • 제한 시간: 70분

 단어장

---

*1번부터 17번까지는 듣고 답하는 문제입니다. 1번부터 15번까지는 한 번만 들려주고, 16번부터 17번까지는 두 번 들려줍니다. 방송을 잘 듣고 답을 하시기 바랍니다.

▲ 듣기 파일

01 다음을 듣고, 남자가 하는 말의 목적으로 가장 적절한 것을 고르시오.

① 중간고사 실시 일정의 변경을 알리려고
② 시험 문제 이의 제기 기간을 공지하려고
③ 분실한 스마트 시계를 찾아가도록 안내하려고
④ 시험 중 전자 기기를 소지하지 않도록 당부하려고
⑤ 전자 기기를 활용한 시험 방식에 대해 설명하려고

02 대화를 듣고, 여자의 의견으로 가장 적절한 것을 고르시오.

① 자녀들이 스스로 인터넷 사용 시간을 조절하도록 교육해야 한다.
② 온라인에 자녀의 사진을 올릴 때 그 위험성을 인식해야 한다.
③ 사진을 영구적으로 보존하려면 온라인에 업로드해야 한다.
④ 부모는 자녀의 올바른 소셜 미디어 사용을 지도해야 한다.
⑤ 온라인 범죄에 노출될 경우 경찰에 즉시 신고해야 한다.

03 다음을 듣고, 여자가 하는 말의 요지로 가장 적절한 것을 고르시오.

① 여러 기관의 통계 자료 활용은 발표의 신뢰도를 높여 준다.
② 좋은 발표의 핵심은 청중의 수준에 맞는 주제 선정에 있다.
③ 대화를 나눌 때 매력적인 화법은 좋은 인상을 남길 수 있다.
④ 청중의 흥미를 유지하기 위해 지속적인 주의 환기가 필요하다.
⑤ 성공적인 발표를 위해 흥미로운 도입부로 시작하는 게 중요하다.

04 대화를 듣고, 그림에서 대화의 내용과 일치하지 <u>않는</u> 것을 고르시오.

05 대화를 듣고, 남자가 할 일로 가장 적절한 것을 고르시오.

① 카메라 빌려 오기
② 영상 촬영하기
③ 단체 티셔츠 주문하기
④ 연습 일정 안내하기
⑤ 구매 사이트 주소 보내기

06 대화를 듣고, 여자가 지불할 금액을 고르시오. [3점]

① $50　　② $55　　③ $63　　④ $66　　⑤ $70

07 대화를 듣고, 남자가 등산을 갈 수 <u>없는</u> 이유를 고르시오.

① 사전 교육 프로그램에 참여해야 해서
② 등산 스틱을 구매하지 못해서
③ 인턴십 면접 일정과 겹쳐서
④ 감기가 아직 낫지 않아서
⑤ 여동생을 돌봐야 해서

08 대화를 듣고, Art and Humanities Tour에 관해 언급되지 <u>않은</u> 것을 고르시오.

① 목적
② 운영 프로그램
③ 날짜
④ 모집 인원
⑤ 등록비

09 Sports Complex Opening Ceremony에 관한 다음 내용을 듣고, 일치하지 <u>않는</u> 것을 고르시오.

① 이번 주 금요일에 열릴 것이다.
② 1층에서는 가족 미니 게임이 있을 것이다.
③ 2층에서는 탁구 메달리스트들이 경기를 할 것이다.
④ 연간 회원권의 반값 할인이 행사 당일에만 제공될 것이다.
⑤ 예약은 웹사이트에서만 가능하다.

10
다음 표를 보면서 대화를 듣고, 두 사람이 구매할 향신료 분쇄기를 고르시오.

Spice Grinder

	Model	Price	Operation	Capacity	Adjustability
①	A	$20	Manual	60g	×
②	B	$25	Automatic	65g	○
③	C	$35	Automatic	72g	○
④	D	$40	Automatic	73g	×
⑤	E	$55	Manual	75g	○

11
대화를 듣고, 남자의 마지막 말에 대한 여자의 응답으로 가장 적절한 것을 고르시오.

① A DJ unexpectedly mixed and played my requested songs.
② My family and I went camping together once in a while.
③ It wasn't as good as when you were there last year.
④ The festival will be more exciting than before.
⑤ The food there was too expensive to enjoy.

12
대화를 듣고, 여자의 마지막 말에 대한 남자의 응답으로 가장 적절한 것을 고르시오.

① Certainly. Delivery food is not preferred due to health issues.
② That's strange. Check if the address on the app is correct.
③ No worries. I think you can deliver the package tomorrow.
④ I see. I'll leave the plate outside when we're done.
⑤ That sounds nice. I'll go with the cheaper one.

13
대화를 듣고, 남자의 마지막 말에 대한 여자의 응답으로 가장 적절한 것을 고르시오. [3점]

Woman: _____

① Absolutely. I'll start first thing tomorrow.
② Sorry. The pill you've taken has a side effect.
③ Good choice. Let's sign up for the cooking class.
④ Unbelievable. Your smoothies are already sold out.
⑤ Sure. I don't think carrots ease my stomach issues.

14
대화를 듣고, 여자의 마지막 말에 대한 남자의 응답으로 가장 적절한 것을 고르시오. [3점]

Man: _____

① Right. That's why I always like to pay separately.
② No problem. Tipping more than 10% isn't too much.
③ Really? I could recommend a nice restaurant in Rome.
④ Exactly. Italy is also a country where tipping is common.
⑤ No way. You should ask politely if the tip could be removed.

15
다음 상황 설명을 듣고, Mr. Jang이 Mina에게 할 말로 가장 적절한 것을 고르시오.

Mr. Jang: _____

① I'm here for you to finish the project.
② Believe in yourself and take advanced math.
③ You could set up a booth for a curriculum fair.
④ Advanced math must be a tough choice for you.
⑤ Focus on preparing for the exam to pass advanced math.

[16~17] 다음을 듣고, 물음에 답하시오.

16
여자가 하는 말의 주제로 가장 적절한 것은?

① skills to control AI technology in job fields
② ways to protect job fields from AI invasion
③ effects of AI technology on various job fields
④ newly emerging high-paying job fields due to AI
⑤ integration of job fields in response to the rise of AI

17
언급된 직업 분야가 아닌 것은?

① customer service　　② legal fields
③ financial sectors　　④ marketing fields
⑤ graphic design

＊이제 듣기 문제가 끝났습니다. 18번부터는 문제지의 지시에 따라 답을 하시기 바랍니다.

18 다음 글의 목적으로 가장 적절한 것은?

To the State Education Department,

I am writing with regard to the state's funding for the construction project at Fort Montgomery High School. Our school needs additional spaces to provide a fully functional Art and Library Media Center to serve our students in a more meaningful way. Despite submitting all required documentation for funding to your department in April 2024, we have not yet received any notification from your department. A delay in the process can carry considerable consequences related to the school's budgetary constraints and schedule. Therefore, in order to proceed with our project, we request you notify us of the review result regarding the submitted documentation. I look forward to hearing from you.

Respectfully,

Clara Smith

Principal, Fort Montgomery High School

① 제출 서류의 마감 기한 연장을 요청하려고
② 교내 미디어 센터의 리모델링을 제안하려고
③ 학교 프로젝트에 배정된 예산을 확인하려고
④ 학교 공간 조성을 위한 공모전을 홍보하려고
⑤ 제출 서류에 대한 검토 결과 통지를 요구하려고

19 다음 글에 드러난 'I'의 심경 변화로 가장 적절한 것은?

As I waited outside the locker room after a hard-fought basketball game, the coach called out to me, "David, walk with me." I figured he was going to tell me something important. He was going to select me to be the captain of the team, the leader I had always wanted to be. My heart was racing with anticipation. But when his next words hit my ears, everything changed. "We're going to have to send you home," he said coldly. "I don't think you are going to make it." I couldn't believe his decision. I tried to hold it together, but inside I was falling apart. A car would be waiting tomorrow morning to take me home. And just like that, it was over.

① hopeful → frustrated　② confident → jealous
③ anxious → grateful　④ relaxed → indifferent
⑤ bored → annoyed

20 다음 글에서 필자가 주장하는 바로 가장 적절한 것은?

For many of us, making time for exercise is a continuing challenge. Between work commitments and family obligations, it often feels like there's no room in our packed schedules for a dedicated workout. But what if the workout came to you, right in the midst of your daily routine? That's where the beauty of integrating mini-exercises into household chores comes into play. Let's be realistic; chores are inevitable. Whether it's washing dishes or taking out the trash, these tasks are an essential part of daily life. But rather than viewing chores as purely obligatory activities, why not seize these moments as opportunities for physical activity? For instance, practice squats or engage in some wall push-ups as you wait for your morning kettle to boil. Incorporating quick exercises into your daily chores can improve your health.

① 간단한 운동일지라도 강도를 점진적으로 높여야 한다.
② 집안일을 간단한 운동을 병행할 기회로 활용해야 한다.
③ 집안일을 할 때 동선을 고려하여 효율을 높여야 한다.
④ 자신이 즐길 수 있는 운동을 찾아 꾸준히 해야 한다.
⑤ 몸에 무리를 주지 않으려면 집안일을 줄여야 한다.

When we see something, we naturally and automatically break it up into shapes, colors, and concepts that we have learned through education. We recode what we see through the lens of everything we know. We reconstruct memories rather than retrieving the video from memory. This is a useful trait. It's a more efficient way to store information—a bit like an optimal image compression algorithm such as JPG, rather than storing a raw bitmap image file. People who lack this ability and remember everything in perfect detail struggle to generalize, learn, and make connections between what they have learned. But representing the world as abstract ideas and features comes at a cost of seeing the world as it is. Instead, we see the world through our assumptions, motivations, and past experiences. The discovery that our memories are reconstructed through abstract representations rather than played back like a movie completely undermined the legal primacy of eyewitness testimony. Seeing is not believing.

*retrieve: 상기하다 **primacy: 우위성

① Abstract ideas are hard to explain without relevant images.
② It takes longer to retrieve unconsciously encoded information.
③ Beliefs formed from repeated experiences do not easily change.
④ Our memories fall short of an objective representation of the world.
⑤ Comprehension of facts precedes the formation of abstract concepts.

In his Cornell laboratory, David Dunning conducted experimental tests of eyewitness testimony and found evidence that a careful deliberation of facial features and a detailed discussion of selection procedures can actually be a sign of an *inaccurate* identification. It's when people find themselves unable to explain why they recognize the person, saying things like "his face just popped out at me," that they tend to be accurate more often. Sometimes our first, immediate, automatic reaction to a situation is the truest interpretation of what our mind is telling us. That very first impression can also be more accurate about the world than the deliberative, reasoned self-narrative can be. In his book *Blink*, Malcolm Gladwell describes a variety of studies in psychology and behavioral economics that demonstrate the superior performance of relatively unconscious first guesses compared to logical step-by-step justifications for a decision.

2024. 10
10회

① 논리적인 근거가 부족한 판단은 진실을 왜곡할 수 있다.
② 인간의 표정은 무의식적인 감정 상태를 가장 잘 반영한다.
③ 사람을 정확하게 식별하기 위해서는 상황에 대한 정보가 중요하다.
④ 목격자 진술은 사건 직후보다 일정 시간이 지난 뒤 더 명확해진다.
⑤ 무의식적인 최초의 반응이 신중히 판단한 결과보다 정확할 수 있다.

Many forms of research lead naturally to quantitative data. A study of happiness might measure the number of times someone smiles during an interaction, and a study of memory might measure the number of items an individual can recall after one, five, and ten minutes. Asking people how many times in a year they are sad will also yield quantitative data, but it might not be reliable. Respondents' recollections may be inaccurate, and their definitions of 'sad' could vary widely. But asking "How many times in the past year were you sad enough to call in sick to work?" prompts a concrete answer. Similarly, instead of asking people to rate how bad a procrastinator they are, ask, "How many of your utility bills are you currently late in paying, even though you can afford to pay them?" Questions that seek concrete responses help make abstract concepts clearer and ensure consistency from one study to the next.   *procrastinator: 미루는 사람

① risks of overgeneralizing results from the collected data
② usefulness of answering abstract questions with numbers
③ effect of sample size on enhancing the reliability of research
④ limitations of measuring and quantifying various human emotions
⑤ importance of specific questions to attain reliable quantitative data

The evolution of AI is often associated with the concept of singularity. Singularity refers to the point at which AI exceeds human intelligence. After that point, it is predicted that AI will repeatedly improve itself and evolve at an accelerated pace. When AI becomes self-aware and pursues its own goals, it will be a conscious being, not just a machine. AI and human consciousness will then begin to evolve together. Our consciousness will evolve to new dimensions through our interactions with AI, which will provide us with intellectual stimulation and inspire new insights and creativity. Conversely, our consciousness also has a significant impact on the evolution of AI. The direction of AI's evolution will depend greatly on what values and ethics we incorporate into AI. We need to see our relationship with AI as a mutual coexistence of conscious beings, recognizing its rights and supporting the evolution of its consciousness.

① An Unsolvable Dilemma: Is AI Friend or Enemy?
② The History of Humans' Resistance Against Machines
③ Upcoming Future: AI as a Human Partner for Co-evolution
④ AI World Without Human Intelligence Is Staring You in the Face
⑤ How AI Makes Human-to-Human Relationships More Meaningful

25 다음 도표의 내용과 일치하지 않는 것은?

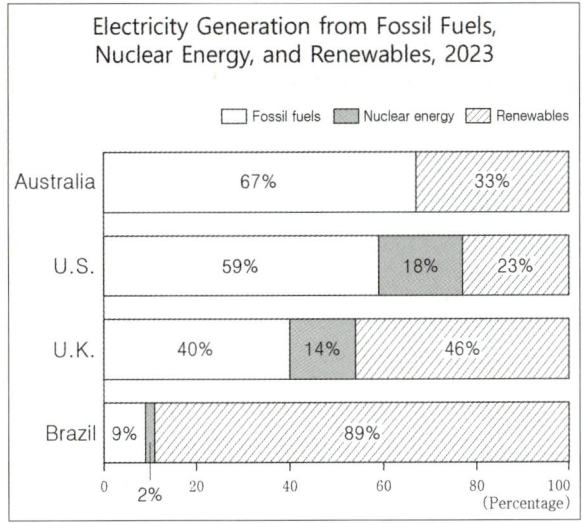

Electricity Generation from Fossil Fuels, Nuclear Energy, and Renewables, 2023

	Fossil fuels	Nuclear energy	Renewables
Australia	67%		33%
U.S.	59%	18%	23%
U.K.	40%	14%	46%
Brazil	9% 2%		89%

The above graph shows the electricity generation from fossil fuels, nuclear energy, and renewables in four countries in 2023. ① Australia's electricity generation only comes from fossil fuels and renewables, and the percentage of fossil fuels is more than twice that of renewables. ② In terms of electricity generation from nuclear energy, the U.S. shows the highest percentage among all four countries. ③ The percentage of electricity generation from fossil fuels in the U.S. is higher than that in the U.K., which is also true for renewables. ④ In the U.K., the percentage of electricity generated from nuclear energy is less than a third of that generated from renewables. ⑤ Brazil's percentage of electricity generated from renewables is 10 percentage points larger than that of Australia and the U.K. combined.

26 Douglas Kirkland에 관한 다음 글의 내용과 일치하지 않는 것은?

Douglas Kirkland, known for his highly artistic portraits of Hollywood celebrities, was born in Toronto, Canada. When he was young, he eagerly awaited the weekly arrival of *Life* magazine and discussed the photographs the magazine contained with his father. Believing that he would have better career prospects, Kirkland moved to the United States after graduating from high school and found work at a photography studio. When *Look* magazine hired him at age 24, he became their second-youngest photographer ever. His photos taken of Marilyn Monroe in 1961 became iconic almost instantly. Kirkland spent his weeks shooting day-to-day life across the United States and his weekends in exotic locations. His photo essays could run up to a dozen pages and were seen by more than half of all Americans.

① 어린 시절에 *Life* 잡지에 실린 사진에 대해 아버지와 토의했다.
② 고등학교 졸업 후 미국으로 이주하여 일자리를 찾았다.
③ 고용될 당시 *Look* 잡지사의 역대 사진 작가 중 가장 어렸다.
④ 1961년에 찍은 Marilyn Monroe 사진은 거의 즉시 상징적인 것이 되었다.
⑤ 전체 미국인들 중 절반이 넘는 이들이 그의 포토 에세이를 보았다.

27 Yummy Paws: Pet Food Cooking Class에 관한 다음 안내문의 내용과 일치하지 않는 것은?

Yummy Paws: Pet Food Cooking Class

Join us for an exciting pet food cooking class where you will learn how to create healthy and delicious pumpkin biscuits for your furry friends!

When: 2:00 p.m.-4:00p.m., Every Sunday, December, 2024

Where: Green Park Community Center, Room 5

Registration
· Register online at www.yummypawsclass.com.
· Limited to 10 participants for each class

Fee
· $30 per participant (Full payment is required when registering.)
· The fee includes all ingredients.

Note
· Additional recipes available for free
· For safety reasons, no pets are allowed.
· For a refund, cancel at least 48 hours before the class.

① 12월에 일요일마다 2시간씩 진행된다.
② 각 수업당 참여 인원이 10명으로 제한된다.
③ 수업료는 등록 시 전액 지불해야 한다.
④ 추가 레시피는 별도로 구매해야 한다.
⑤ 환불을 위해서는 수업 48시간 전까지 취소해야 한다.

28 2024 K-Pop Cover Dance Contest에 관한 다음 안내문의 내용과 일치하는 것은?

2024 K-Pop Cover Dance Contest

Good news for K-Pop fans in Canada! It's time for your dance team to show your talents at this contest!

When & Where

· Date: November 29th, 2024
· Time: 7 p.m.-9 p.m.
· Location: So Merry Theatre

Judging Criteria: Cooperation, Artistic Skill, Costume

Prize
· Top 3 teams will receive a $200 gift certificate.
· The winning team will have the chance to visit Korea's top management agencies.

Application
· A cover dance video should not be more than 4 minutes long.
· Submit the video, along with your application, via our website by November 3rd.
For more information, visit www.2024kpopcontest.com.

① 2일 동안 진행된다.
② 심사 기준에 관객 호응이 포함된다.
③ 상위 열 팀은 200달러 상품권을 받을 것이다.
④ 커버 댄스의 영상 길이는 4분이 넘어야 한다.
⑤ 신청서와 함께 영상을 웹사이트를 통해 제출해야 한다.

29 다음 글의 밑줄 친 부분 중, 어법상 틀린 것은?

Digital technologies are essentially related to metaphors, but digital metaphors are different from linguistic ① ones in important ways. Linguistic metaphors are passive, in the sense that the audience needs to choose to actively enter the world proposed by metaphor. In the Shakespearean metaphor "time is a beggar," the audience is unlikely to understand the metaphor without cognitive effort and without further ② engaging Shakespeare's prose. Technological metaphors, on the other hand, are active (and often imposing) in the sense that they are realized in digital artifacts that are actively doing things, forcefully ③ changing a user's meaning horizon. Technological creators cannot generally afford to require their potential audience to wonder how the metaphor works; normally the selling point is ④ what the usefulness of the technology is obvious at first glance. Shakespeare, on the other hand, is beloved in part because the meaning of his works is not immediately obvious and ⑤ requires some thought on the part of the audience.

30 다음 글의 밑줄 친 부분 중, 문맥상 낱말의 쓰임이 적절하지 않은 것은? [3점]

Herbert Simon won his Nobel Prize for recognizing our limitations in information, time, and cognitive capacity. As we lack the resources to compute answers independently, we ① distribute the computation across the population and solve the answer slowly, generation by generation. Then all we have to do is socially learn the right answers. You don't need to understand how your computer or toilet works; you just need to be able to use the interface and flush. All that needs to be ② transmitted is which button to push — essentially how to interact with technologies rather than how they work. And so instead of holding ③ less information than we have mental capacity for and indeed need to know, we could dedicate our large brains to a small piece of a giant calculation. We understand things well enough to ④ benefit from them, but all the while we are making small calculations that contribute to a larger whole. We are just doing our part in a larger computation for our societies' ⑤ collective brains.

31

The best defence most species of octopus have is to stay hidden as much as possible and do their own hunting at night. So to find one in full view in the shallows in daylight was a surprise for two Australian underwater photographers. Actually, what they saw at first was a flounder. It was only when they looked again that they saw a medium-sized octopus, with all eight of its arms folded and its two eyes staring upwards to _____. An octopus has a big brain, excellent eyesight and the ability to change colour and pattern, and this one was using these assets to turn itself into a completely different creature. Many more of this species have been found since then, and there are now photographs of octopuses that could be said to be transforming into sea snakes. And while they mimic, they hunt — producing the spectacle of, say, a flounder suddenly developing an octopodian arm, sticking it down a hole and grabbing whatever's hiding there.

*flounder: 넙치 **mimic: 모방하다

① get a broad view
② create the illusion
③ capture the moment
④ find its hiding spot
⑤ mark its territory

32

How much we suffer relates to _____. When 1500m runners push themselves into extreme pain to win a race — their muscles screaming and their lungs exploding with oxygen deficit, they don't psychologically suffer much. In fact, ultra-marathon runners — those people who are crazy enough to push themselves beyond the normal boundaries of human endurance, covering distances of 50-100km or more over many hours, talk about making friends with their pain. When a patient has paid for some form of passive back pain therapy and the practitioner pushes deeply into a painful part of a patient's back to mobilise it, the patient calls that good pain if he or she believes this type of deep pressure treatment will be of value, even though the practitioner is pushing right into the patient's sore tissues.

① how long we have been in pain
② how we frame the pain in our mind
③ how fast we can recover from past pain
④ what part of our body we train regularly
⑤ what treatment we receive from experts

33

When I worked for a large electronics company that manufactured laser and ink-jet printers, I soon discovered why there are often three versions of many consumer goods. If the manufacturer makes only one version of its product, people who bought it might have been willing to spend more money, so the company is losing some income. If the company offers two versions, one with more features and more expensive than the other, people will compare the two models and still buy the less expensive one. But if the company introduces a third model with even more features and more expensive than the other two, sales of the second model go up; many people like the features of the most expensive model, but not the price. The middle item has more features than the least expensive one, and it is less expensive than the fanciest model. They buy the middle item, unaware that they have been _____. [3점]

① manipulated by the presence of the higher-priced item
② persuaded by a high-volume, low-margin strategy
③ tricked to keep purchasing unnecessary products
④ fooled by the wrong information on the price
⑤ exposed to a discounted price repeatedly

34

On-screen, climate disaster is everywhere you look, but the scope of the world's climate transformation may just as quickly eliminate the climate-fiction genre — indeed eliminate any effort to tell the story of warming, which could grow too large and too obvious even for Hollywood. You can tell stories 'about' climate change while it still seems a marginal feature of human life. But when the temperature rises by three or four more degrees, hardly anyone will be able to feel isolated from its impacts. And so as climate change expands across the horizon, _____. Why watch or read climate fiction about the world you can see plainly out your own window? At the moment, stories illustrating global warming can still offer an escapist pleasure, even if that pleasure often comes in the form of horror. But when we can no longer pretend that climate suffering is distant — in time or in place — we will stop pretending about it and start pretending within it. [3점]

① it may resolve on its own
② it may cease to be a story
③ a forgotten genre will be reborn
④ its impact will be overestimated
⑤ the story's plot will become complex

35 다음 글에서 전체 흐름과 관계 없는 문장은?

Today, the water crisis is political — which is to say, not inevitable or beyond our capacity to fix — and, therefore, functionally elective. ① That is one reason it is nevertheless distressing: an abundant resource made scarce through governmental neglect and indifference, bad infrastructure and contamination, and careless urbanization. ② There is no need for a water crisis, in other words, but we have one anyway, and aren't doing much to address it. ③ Some cities lose more water to leaks than they deliver to homes: even in the United States, leaks and theft account for an estimated loss of 16 percent of freshwater; in Brazil, the estimate is 40 percent. ④ The numerical comparison of available resources seems to exaggerate the real-world water shortage problem that we face. ⑤ Seen in both cases, as everywhere, the selective scarcity clearly highlights have-and-have-not inequities, leaving 2.1 billion people without safe drinking water and 4.5 billion without proper sanitation worldwide.

*elective: 선택의

[36~37] 주어진 글 다음에 이어질 글의 순서로 가장 적절한 것을 고르시오.

36

As individuals, our ability to thrive depended on how well we navigated relationships in a group. If the group valued us, we could count on support, resources, and probably a mate.

(A) And, crucially, they are meant to make that motivation feel like it is coming from within. If we realized, on a conscious level, that we were responding to social pressure, our performance might come off as grudging or cynical, making it less persuasive.

(B) If it didn't, we might get none of these merits. It was a matter of survival, physically and genetically. Over millions of years, the pressure selected for people who are sensitive to and skilled at maximizing their standing.

(C) The result was the development of a tendency to unconsciously monitor how other people in our community perceive us. We process that information in the form of self-esteem and such related emotions as pride, shame, or insecurity. These emotions compel us to do more of what makes our community value us and less of what doesn't. [3점]   *grudging: 투덜대는

① (A) — (C) — (B)　　　② (B) — (A) — (C)
③ (B) — (C) — (A)　　　④ (C) — (A) — (B)
⑤ (C) — (B) — (A)

37

Conventional medicine has long believed that depression is caused by an imbalance of neurotransmitters in the brain.

(A) However, there is a major problem with this explanation. This is because the imbalance of substances in the brain is a consequence of depression, not its cause. In other words, depression causes a decrease in brain substances such as serotonin and noradrenaline, not a decrease in brain substances causes depression.

(B) If it is not consciousness itself, then the root cause of depression is also a distortion of our state of consciousness: a consciousness that has lost its sense of self and the meaning of life. Such a disease of consciousness may manifest itself in the form of depression.

(C) In this revised cause-and-effect, the key is to reframe depression as a problem of consciousness. Our consciousness is a more fundamental entity that goes beyond the functioning of the brain. The brain is no more than an organ of consciousness.

*neurotransmitter: 신경 전달 물질 **manifest: (명백히) 나타내다

① (A) — (C) — (B)   ② (B) — (A) — (C)
③ (B) — (C) — (A)   ④ (C) — (A) — (B)
⑤ (C) — (B) — (A)

[38~39] 글의 흐름으로 보아, 주어진 문장이 들어가기에 가장 적절한 곳을 고르시오.

38

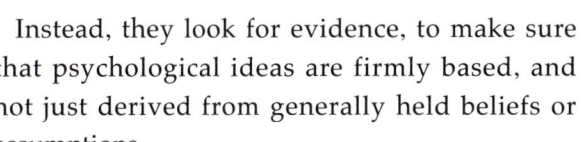

Instead, they look for evidence, to make sure that psychological ideas are firmly based, and not just derived from generally held beliefs or assumptions.

The common accounts of human nature that float around in society are generally a mixture of assumptions, tales and sometimes plain silliness. However, psychology is different. (①) It is the branch of science that is devoted to understanding people: how and why we act as we do; why we see things as we do; and how we interact with one another. (②) The key word here is 'science.' (③) Psychologists don't depend on opinions and hearsay, or the generally accepted views of society at the time, or even the considered opinions of deep thinkers. (④) In addition to this evidence-based approach, psychology deals with fundamental processes and principles that generate our rich cultural and social diversity, as well as those shared by all human beings. (⑤) These are what modern psychology is all about.

2024.10
10회

39

Such a system can only hope to be stable if only a smaller number of collective ways of being may emerge.

Life is what physicists might call a 'high-dimensional system,' which is their fancy way of saying that there's a lot going on. (①) In just a single cell, the number of possible interactions between different molecules is enormous. (②) For example, it is only a limited number of tissues and body shapes that may result from the development of a human embryo. (③) In 1942, the biologist Conrad Waddington called this drastic narrowing of outcomes *canalization*. (④) The organism may switch between a small number of well-defined possible states, but can't exist in random states in between them, rather as a ball in a rough landscape must roll to the bottom of one valley or another. (⑤) We'll see that this is true also of health and disease: there are many causes of illness, but their manifestations at the physiological and symptomatic levels are often strikingly similar. [3점]

*embryo: 배아 **physiological: 생리적인

Punishing a child may not be effective due to what Álvaro Bilbao, a neuropsychologist, calls 'trick-punishments.' A trick-punishment is a scolding, a moment of anger or a punishment in the most classic sense of the word. Instead of discouraging the child from doing something, it encourages them to do it. For example, Hugh learns that when he hits his little brother, his mother scolds him. For a child who feels lonely, being scolded is much better than feeling invisible, so he will continue to hit his brother. In this case, his mother would be better adopting a different strategy. For instance, she could congratulate Hugh when he has not hit his brother for a certain length of time. The mother clearly cannot allow the child to hit his little brother, but instead of constantly pointing out the negatives, she can choose to reward the positives. In this way, any parent can avoid trick-punishments.

A trick-punishment ___(A)___ the unwanted behavior of a child, which implies that parents should focus on ___(B)___ the attention to negatives while rewarding positive behaviors.

	(A)	(B)
①	reinforces	reducing
②	reinforces	maximizing
③	discourages	attracting
④	discourages	lowering
⑤	controls	increasing

[41~42] 다음 글을 읽고, 물음에 답하시오.

From an early age, we assign purpose to objects and events, preferring this reasoning to random chance. Children assume, for instance, that pointy rocks are that way because they don't want you to sit on them. When we encounter something, we first need to (a) determine what sort of thing it is. Inanimate objects and plants generally do not move and can be evaluated from physics alone. However, by attributing intention to animals and even objects, we are able to make fast decisions about the (b) likely behaviour of that being. This was essential in our hunter-gatherer days to avoid being eaten by predators.

The anthropologist Stewart Guthrie made the point that survival in our evolutionary past meant that we interpret ambiguous objects as agents with human mental characteristics, as those are the mental processes which we understand. Ambiguous events are caused by such agents. This results in a perceptual system strongly (c) resistant towards anthropomorphism. Therefore, we tend to assume intention even where there is none. This would have arisen as a survival mechanism. If a lion is about to attack you, you need to react (d) quickly, given its probable intention to kill you. By the time you have realized that the design of its teeth and claws could kill you, you are dead. So, assuming intent, without detailed design analysis or understanding of the physics, has (e) saved your life.

*ambiguous: 모호한 **anthropomorphism: 의인화

41 윗글의 제목으로 가장 적절한 것은? [3점]

① Agency Detection: Inherited from Survival Mechanism
② How Humans' Perceptual System Is Operated for Hunting
③ Hiding Intentions: The Unique Trait of Human Mentality
④ Our Ambiguous Intention Makes Understanding Confusing
⑤ How We Interpret Animate and Inanimate Objects Differently

42 밑줄 친 (a)~(e) 중에서 문맥상 낱말의 쓰임이 적절하지 <u>않은</u> 것은?

① (a)　② (b)　③ (c)　④ (d)　⑤ (e)

[43~45] 다음 글을 읽고, 물음에 답하시오.

(A)

Once long ago, deep in the Himalayas, there lived a little panda. He was as ordinary as all the other pandas. He was completely white from head to toe. His two big ears, his four furry feet and his cute round nose were all frosty white, leaving (a) <u>him</u> feeling ordinary and sad. Unlike the cheerful and contented pandas around him, he desired to be distinctive, special, and unique.

(B)

The little panda changed his path and hurried to the nearest berry bush, greedily eating a mouthful of juicy red berries. However, they were so bitter he couldn't swallow even one. At dusk, he finally got home and slowly climbed his favorite bamboo tree. There, he discovered a strange black and red flower with a sweet scent that tempted (b) <u>him</u> to eat all its blossoms.

(C)

Driven by the desire for uniqueness, the little panda sought inspiration from (c) <u>his</u> distant cousin, a giant white panda covered with heavenly black patches. But the cousin revealed the patches were from an unintended encounter with mud, and he disliked them. Disappointed, the little panda walked home. On his way, he met a red-feathered peacock, who explained (d) <u>he</u> turned red from eating wild berries.

(D)

The following morning, under sunny skies, the little panda felt remarkably better. During breakfast, he found the other pandas chatting enthusiastically and asked why. They burst into laughter, exclaiming, "Look at yourself!" Glancing down, he discovered his once white fur was now stained jet black and glowing red. He was overjoyed and realized that, rather than by imitating others, (e) <u>his</u> wishes can come true from unexpected places and genuine experiences.

43 주어진 글 (A)에 이어질 내용을 순서에 맞게 배열한 것으로 가장 적절한 것은?

① (B) — (D) — (C)　② (C) — (B) — (D)
③ (C) — (D) — (B)　④ (D) — (B) — (C)
⑤ (D) — (C) — (B)

44 밑줄 친 (a)~(e) 중에서 가리키는 대상이 나머지 넷과 <u>다른</u> 것은?

① (a)　② (b)　③ (c)　④ (d)　⑤ (e)

45 윗글의 'little panda'에 관한 내용으로 적절하지 <u>않은</u> 것은?

① 다른 판다들과는 달리 특별해지기를 갈망했다.
② 베리가 너무 써서 한 개도 삼킬 수 없었다.
③ 집에 돌아오는 길에 검고 붉은 꽃을 발견하였다.
④ 그의 사촌은 자신의 검은 반점을 싫어했다.
⑤ 다른 판다들이 왜 신나게 수다를 떠는지 물어보았다.

• MP3 파일을 들으며 다음 빈칸을 채우시오. (듣기 어려운 발음이나 정답의 단서가 되는 부분에 빈칸을 만들었습니다.)

01 다음을 듣고, 남자가 하는 말의 목적으로 가장 적절한 것을 고르시오.

[Chime bell rings.]

M: Hello, Bronx High School students. This is your vice principal, Jeremy Wilson. As you know, _____ _____ _____ will start next Tuesday. I'd like to announce that you should not carry any ✪_____ _____ while taking the exam including smart watches or wireless earphones. If you're found with an electronic device, even if it's in your bag, it'll be _____ __ ✪_____. This will result in a penalty that affects your test score. So please make sure that you don't have any electronic devices with you during the exam. I _____ _____ _____ good luck.

02 대화를 듣고, 여자의 의견으로 가장 적절한 것을 고르시오.

W: Brandon, what are you so focused on?

M: Hi, Chloe! I'm looking at pictures of my kids to post on social media.

W: _____ _____? Posting their pictures on social media?

M: Yes. I'm just sharing our joyful moments online.

W: I understand, but when posting your kids' photos online, you should be _____ ___ ___ _____.

M: Risks? What do you mean by that?

W: You know, the photos you post could be seen by anyone.

M: Is it a big problem?

W: Of course. The photos could ✪_____ be used for ✪_____ _____.

M: Oh, no. I've never thought of that.

W: That's why you should be mindful of the risks when sharing your children's photos online.

M: Thanks for your advice. I'll be careful.

03 다음을 듣고, 여자가 하는 말의 요지로 가장 적절한 것을 고르시오.

W: Hello, students. I'm Megan, a public speaking instructor. Imagine you're sitting in an audience at a presentation. And the speaker begins _____ ___ _____ _____. Quickly, you would lose interest. So, for a successful presentation, it's important to start with an interesting opening. An engaging opening ✪_____ _____ and _____ _____. It also serves as a hook and makes the audience eager to hear more. For example, a challenging question or a _____ ✪_____ can be used. Once again, remember that an attractive beginning is the key to a good presentation. Keep it in mind. Thank you.

04 대화를 듣고, 그림에서 대화의 내용과 일치하지 않는 것을 고르시오.

M: Honey, look at this picture. How about this _____ _____ _____ for while we're away?

W: [Pause] Looks good! Is that a photo booth?

M: Yes. We can take photos with our dogs before we leave them there.

W: Lovely! Oh, can you see the dog?

M: Where? [Pause] Ah. It's on the slide. It looks fun.

W: I also like the ✪_____ _____.

M: Me, too. Dogs can have fun running through it. Oh, can you guess what that ✪_____ thing is?

W: Sure. It must be a doggy pool. By the way, where can our dogs eat?

M: Look under the tree!

W: Aha! There are _____ _____ _____. Dogs can easily get their food.

M: Right. How do you feel about this center?

W: I'm delighted to find such a good place.

05 대화를 듣고, 남자가 할 일로 가장 적절한 것을 고르시오.

W: Hurray! We've finally completed all of our dance moves for the flash mob.

M: Excellent! Now all we have to do is practice together.

W: What do you think about recording a video to get a _____ _____ ___ ___ _____?

M: Good idea! Could we ask someone to help us?

W: Well... I know someone who is good _____ ___ _____.

M: Okay. Then, is there anything I can help with?

W: Hold on. Umm... *[Pause]* I forgot to order our group T-shirts.

M: You mean the ones we chose together last week?

W: Right. _____ ____ ____ _____ for me?

M: Of course! Please let me know the website. Then, I'll order the T-shirts ✪_____.

W: Great! Thanks for your help.

M: It's always my pleasure.

06 대화를 듣고, 여자가 지불할 금액을 고르시오.

W: Hello, can I buy some essential oils?

M: Absolutely. Depending on _____ _____, we have many options.

W: Could you recommend good oils for _____ ✪_____ and skin troubles?

M: Okay. For sound sleep, I recommend lavender or chamomile oils. They're on special offer. They're $15 each.

W: I'll take one of each. Both scents are my favorites.

M: Good choice. And, for your skin troubles, you can try geranium oil.

W: I've heard geranium is effective ____ _____ _____. How much is it?

M: It's $20.

W: Reasonable. I'll buy two bottles of geranium.

M: Alright. So, one lavender, one chamomile and two geranium oils, correct?

W: Exactly. And I have a 10% discount coupon.

M: Let me see... *[Pause]* Sorry, but it's no longer ✪_____.

W: I see. Here's my credit card.

07 대화를 듣고, 남자가 등산을 갈 수 <u>없는</u> 이유를 고르시오.

[Cell phone rings.]

M: Hello, Emma. Are you okay? I heard you _____ ___ _____ last weekend.

W: Thanks, Ben. But I'm better now.

M: Good to hear that. By the way, I bought those _____ _____ _____ you recommended.

W: Perfect. Now, we can go hiking this Saturday!

M: Well. *[Pause]* That's the reason I called.

W: Oh. Please don't tell me you need to look after your younger sister, again.

M: Not this time.

W: Then why can't you go?

M: Actually, I got a message from the internship I ✪_____ _____, and I'm in.

W: Congratulations! You've waited for this chance for so long!

M: Thanks. But that means I have to attend a ✪_____ _____ every weekend. It starts from this Saturday.

W: Every weekend? I understand. Let's make it some other time.

08 대화를 듣고, Art and Humanities Tour에 관해 언급되지 <u>않은</u> 것을 고르시오.

W: Justin, what are you looking at?

M: Hi, Gabriela. Look at this poster. It says the Art and Humanities Tour is coming up.

W: Great. What does it say?

M: It's the first annual tour. And its purpose is to _____ ____ ____ ____ _____ of the novelist, *Mark Twain*.

W: Sounds interesting. Let me see. *[Pause]* In the program, there will be a guided museum tour and a visit to ____ _____.

M: Excellent. It says it's on October 27th. The weather should be perfect around that time.

W: It also mentions anyone can participate, but ✪_____ students get ✪_____.

M: Cool! How about going together?

W: Definitely! By the way, I can't see the registration fee.

M: Well... *[Pause]* There, at the bottom. It says $10 per person.

W: I can _____ _____. Let's register right now.

M: Fantastic!

09 Sports Complex Opening Ceremony에 관한 다음 내용을 듣고, 일치하지 <u>않는</u> 것을 고르시오.

M: Hello. This is Grayson, presenter at the public Sports Complex Opening Ceremony. I'm excited to announce that the _____ _____ will be held this Friday. We have various events on each floor. On the first floor, there will be family mini games such as a ✪_____ race. It'll be fun for the whole family. On the second floor, table tennis medalists will play games. Most ✪_____, special promotions will be available at the entrance. ____ _____ _____ for annual membership will continue until the following Friday. Come and enjoy the ceremony. Reservations are only available through our website. See you then.

10 다음 표를 보면서 대화를 듣고, 두 사람이 구매할 향신료 분쇄기를 고르시오.

W: Honey, our spice grinder is broken, so we need to buy a new one.

M: Really? Hold on. I'm checking online. *[Tapping sound]* Come and see.

W: Oh, there are five models to choose from. What do you think is a reasonable price?

M: I think it should be under $50.

W: Okay. Since we used to have a _____ _____, I'd prefer to get an ✪_____ one this time.

M: Great idea. It'll be much more convenient. Anything else that we should consider?

W: Well... It should have a big _____ _____.

M: Good point. You want it to be able to hold at least 70g, right?

W: Right. Now, we have two options left.

M: I think we should buy the one with the ✪_____ _____.

W: Excellent. Let's go with that one.

11 대화를 듣고, 남자의 마지막 말에 대한 여자의 응답으로 가장 적절한 것을 고르시오.

M: Hey, Cindy. Are you going to the DJ Music Festival this weekend?

W: ✪_____! I can't wait. Last year, the festival was awesome. You couldn't make it, right?

M: Yeah, I was ____ ____ _____ _____. Anyway, why was it so fun?

W: _____

12 대화를 듣고, 여자의 마지막 말에 대한 남자의 응답으로 가장 적절한 것을 고르시오.

W: Luca, I'll bring the food we ordered inside. *[Door opening sound]* There's no food in front of the door.

M: What? Did you check the _____ ✪_____ on the app?

W: Sure. The app says the food ____ _____. But it's not here.

M: _____

13 대화를 듣고, 남자의 마지막 말에 대한 여자의 응답으로 가장 적절한 것을 고르시오.

W: Hi, Liam.
M: What's wrong, Jenny? You look sick.
W: I have trouble ✪_____ _____ these days. So, I got a medical check-up.
M: What did the doctor say?
W: Nothing special. I was ✪_____ some medicine, but I don't think it's working.
M: That's unfortunate. Do you remember I had the same symptoms last month?
W: Right. You were sick for a long time. How did you get better?
M: My mother started making me a healthy smoothie every morning. It really helped.
W: Healthy smoothie? What's in it?
M: It's made of carrots, cabbages and apples. It could help _____ _____ _____ _____.
W: Sounds great. Actually, I'm also thinking of eating more fruit and vegetables _____ _____ _____ _____ _____.
M: Well, now you know what you need to do.
W: _____

14 대화를 듣고, 여자의 마지막 말에 대한 남자의 응답으로 가장 적절한 것을 고르시오.

M: Amy. I enjoyed the class today. How about you?
W: Same here! I especially liked the part on American ✪_____ _____.
M: Yeah. It's an interesting idea that you can tip if you like the service.
W: You know, I went to New York recently.
M: Right. Did you have to give a tip?
W: I was asked for a tip whenever I got the bill.
M: Ah! It's for real!
W: I know. One time I was _____ _____, though.
M: Oh, what happened?
W: At this restaurant, the waiters were so rude and the food was awful. People there were giving tips _____ _____ about the service.
M: You did, too? In that case, as we learned, you shouldn't have tipped.
W: What else could I do? When in Rome, do as the ✪_____ _____.
M: _____

15 다음 상황 설명을 듣고, Mr. Jang이 Mina에게 할 말로 가장 적절한 것을 고르시오.

M: Mina is a first-year high school student. She has to select subjects for next year, and she is considering taking ✪_____ _____. However, she doubts whether she could do well in the course. For advice, she visits Mr. Jang, her basic math teacher last semester. While Mina shares her concern, Mr. Jang remembers how _____ Mina's math project was in his class. He also knows she _____ ___ _____ _____ last semester. So, Mr. Jang wants to tell Mina that she should stop ✪_____ _____ and choose advanced math. In this situation, what would Mr. Jang most likely say to Mina?
Mr. Jang: _____

[16~17] 다음을 듣고, 물음에 답하시오.

W: Hello, students. According to a global institute research, about 70% of companies around the world will use _____ _____ by 2030. So, today we'll discuss various job fields that could be affected by AI technology. First, let's talk about customer service. In this sector, AI chatbots can provide speedy, ✪_____ _____ to customers' questions, which ✪_____ _____ human's workload. Second, legal fields will be greatly influenced as well. AI will help perform many tasks that legal assistants usually handle such as _____ _____ and case management. Next, AI is also making an impact on financial sectors. It can monitor banking systems and provide detailed financial advice. Lastly, in graphic design, editing pictures used to take _____ ___ _____. But now, AI makes it easy for anyone to create realistic images. Like these, AI has the _____ to be among the most influential technologies across many job fields. Now, let's watch a video.

• 제한시간 20분 • 맞은 개수 ___ / 40

* 다음 영어는 우리말 뜻, 우리말은 영어 단어를 〈보기〉에서 찾아 쓰시오.

01 trait _____

02 automatic _____

03 humanities _____

04 commitment _____

05 manifestation _____

06 향 _____

07 유효한 _____

08 소화시키다 _____

09 우선순위 _____

10 잠재적으로 _____

[보기]	
최적의	potentially
자동의	digest
전념	valid
인문학	eager
발현	scent
특성	priority

* 다음 우리말에 알맞은 영어 표현을 찾아 연결하시오.

11 (그 결과) ~가 되다 •   • contribute to

12 ~에 기여하다 •   • be willing to

13 ~에 참여하다 •   • engage in

14 (~을 살) 여유가 있다 •   • result in

15 기꺼이 ~하려고 하다 •   • afford to

* 다음 우리말과 같은 표현이 되도록 알맞은 단어를 〈보기〉에서 찾아 쓰시오.

[보기]
ambiguous / cynical / encounter / broad / testimony / mutual
sanitation / constraint / passive / genuine / identification / electronic

16 넓은 시야 ➤ _____ view

17 전자 기기 ➤ _____ device

18 상호 공존 ➤ _____ coexistence

19 예산 제약 ➤ budgetary _____

20 모호한 사물 ➤ _____ objects

21 목격자 증언 ➤ eyewitness _____

22 적절한 위생 ➤ proper _____

23 부정확한 식별 ➤ inaccurate _____

24 의도치 않은 접촉 ➤ unintended _____

25 수동적 등 통증 치료 ➤ _____ back pain therapy

26 인간의 지능을 넘어서다 ➡ (exceed / proceed) human intelligence

27 우수성을 보여주다 ➡ (frustrate / demonstrate) the superior performance

28 우리의 큰 두뇌를 바치다 ➡ (dedicate / vindicate) our large brains

29 상당한 결과를 초래하다 ➡ carry (considerate / considerable) consequences

30 기후 고통이 멀리 있다고 가장하다 ➡ (prevent / pretend) that climate suffering is distant

* 다음 문장의 빈칸에 알맞은 단어를 〈보기〉에서 찾아 쓰시오.

─── [보기] ───

legal / enthusiastically / strategy / reconstruct / reinforces / manipulated
psychologically / yield / fundamental / instantly / anticipation / substances

31 나의 심장이 기대감으로 빠르게 뛰었다.
➡ My heart was racing with _____.

32 그들은 정신적으로 많이 고통받지 않는다.
➡ They don't _____ suffer much.

33 우리의 의식은 보다 근본적인 실체이다.
➡ Our consciousness is a more _____ entity.

34 우울증은 뇌의 물질들의 감소를 유발한다.
➡ Depression causes a decrease in brain _____.

35 그는 다른 판다들이 신나게 수다를 떨고 있는 것을 발견했다.
➡ He found the other pandas chatting _____.

36 그의 어머니는 다른 전략을 채택하는 것이 나을 것이다.
➡ His mother would be better adopting a different _____.

37 트릭 처벌은 아이의 바람직하지 못한 행동을 강화한다.
➡ A trick-punishment _____ the unwanted behavior of a child.

38 그들은 더 비싼 가격의 제품의 존재에 의해 조종되어왔다.
➡ They have been _____ by the presence of the higher-priced item.

39 우리는 기억에서 영상을 생각해 내기보다 기억을 재구성한다.
➡ We _____ memories rather than retrieving the video from memory.

40 그가 1961년에 찍은 Marilyn Monroe 사진은 거의 즉시 상징적인 것이 되었다.
➡ His photos taken of Marilyn Monroe in 1961 became iconic almost _____.

전국연합학력평가 [2023년 12월 19일 시행]

★ 3점 문항에만 점수가 표시되어 있습니다.

• 문항 수: 45개 • 배점: 100점 • 제한 시간: 70분

 단어장

▲ 듣기 파일

*1번부터 17번까지는 듣고 답하는 문제입니다. 1번부터 15번까지는 한 번만 들려주고, 16번부터 17번까지는 두 번 들려줍니다. 방송을 잘 듣고 답을 하시기 바랍니다.

01 다음을 듣고, 남자가 하는 말의 목적으로 가장 적절한 것을 고르시오.

① 로봇 프로그램 만족도 조사 참여를 독려하려고
② 관람객을 위한 안내 로봇 서비스를 소개하려고
③ 전시 작품 해설 서비스 중단을 안내하려고
④ 오디오 가이드 대여 장소를 공지하려고
⑤ 전시관 온라인 예약 방법을 설명하려고

02 대화를 듣고, 여자의 의견으로 가장 적절한 것을 고르시오.

① 번역 프로그램으로 번역한 글은 검토가 필요하다.
② 읽기 학습을 통해 쓰기 능력을 향상시킬 수 있다.
③ 글을 인용할 때는 출처를 명확히 밝혀야 한다.
④ 예상 독자를 고려하여 글을 작성해야 한다.
⑤ 번역기 사용은 외국어 학습에 효과적이다.

03 대화를 듣고, 두 사람의 관계를 가장 잘 나타낸 것을 고르시오.

① 광고 제작자 – 사진작가
② 이사업체 직원 – 의뢰인
③ 고객 – 에어컨 설치 기사
④ 트럭 운전사 – 물류 창고 직원
⑤ 구매자 – 중고 물품 개인 판매자

04 대화를 듣고, 그림에서 대화의 내용과 일치하지 않는 것을 고르시오.

05 대화를 듣고, 남자가 할 일로 가장 적절한 것을 고르시오.

① 스티커 준비하기
② 안내문 게시하기
③ 급식 메뉴 선정하기
④ 설문 조사 실시하기
⑤ 우수 학급 시상하기

06 대화를 듣고, 남자가 매달 지불할 금액을 고르시오.

① $20 ② $27 ③ $30 ④ $36 ⑤ $40

07 대화를 듣고, 여자가 토크 쇼를 방청하러 갈 수 없는 이유를 고르시오.

① 가족 모임에 가야 해서
② 아르바이트를 해야 해서
③ 책 사인회를 준비해야 해서
④ 화학 프로젝트를 해야 해서
⑤ 친구 결혼식에 참석해야 해서

08 대화를 듣고, Polar Bear Swim에 관해 언급되지 않은 것을 고르시오.

① 행사 날짜
② 제출 서류
③ 최대 참가 인원
④ 기념품
⑤ 참가비

09 Walk in the Snow에 관한 다음 내용을 듣고, 일치하지 않는 것을 고르시오.

① 1일 투어 프로그램이다.
② 하이킹에 관심이 있는 누구든 참여할 수 있다.
③ 장비를 무료로 대여할 수 있다.
④ 학생에게 등록비 할인을 해 준다.
⑤ 참여하려면 사전에 등록해야 한다.

10 다음 표를 보면서 대화를 듣고, 두 사람이 선택할 달력을 고르시오.

Calendar

	Product	Price	Format	Recyclable Paper	Theme
①	A	$8	standing desk	×	modern art
②	B	$10	standing desk	○	classic art
③	C	$12	standing desk	○	movie
④	D	$16	wall	○	nature
⑤	E	$22	wall	×	animal

11 대화를 듣고, 여자의 마지막 말에 대한 남자의 응답으로 가장 적절한 것을 고르시오.

① I covered the worrying state of marine life.
② I sent an article to the biology department.
③ Whatever you did, let's not speak about it.
④ I spent lots of time preparing the speech.
⑤ The article was mainly read by students.

12 대화를 듣고, 남자의 마지막 말에 대한 여자의 응답으로 가장 적절한 것을 고르시오.

① Take care. The weather is freezing cold.
② Good news. Thanks for letting me know.
③ Hurry up. The bus is leaving very soon.
④ Seriously? I'd better try walking, then.
⑤ Really? I was on the shuttle bus, too.

13 대화를 듣고, 여자의 마지막 말에 대한 남자의 응답으로 가장 적절한 것을 고르시오. [3점]

Man: _____

① Definitely. That's why I got a refund for the app.
② Sorry. I should have repaired my tablet PC earlier.
③ Exactly. Documents were filed in alphabetical order.
④ I see. I'll give it some thought before buying this app.
⑤ Don't worry. I still have a few more days for the free trial.

14 대화를 듣고, 남자의 마지막 말에 대한 여자의 응답으로 가장 적절한 것을 고르시오. [3점]

Woman: _____

① Good idea. Let's learn how to read sign language.
② You're right. That's because I wanted to help him.
③ Okay. Wish me luck in getting this volunteer work.
④ Trust me. I bet you'll be selected as a note-taker.
⑤ Wonderful. Thank you for taking notes for me in class.

15 다음 상황 설명을 듣고, Tony가 Kate에게 할 말로 가장 적절한 것을 고르시오. [3점]

2023.11
11회

Tony: _____

① Why don't we post a review of this bakery?
② Let's give her the baker of the month award.
③ We'd better check if we're on the waiting list.
④ We should come later when the repairs are done.
⑤ How about finding a different bakery for the list?

[16~17] 다음을 듣고, 물음에 답하시오.

16 여자가 하는 말의 주제로 가장 적절한 것은?

① fruits that can pose a risk to dogs' health
② ways to help dogs develop a taste for fruits
③ tips for protecting garden fruits from animals
④ reasons fruits should be included in dogs' diets
⑤ stories that use fruits and vegetables as characters

17 언급된 과일이 아닌 것은?

① grapes ② cherries ③ avocados
④ grapefruits ⑤ cranberries

*이제 듣기 문제가 끝났습니다. 18번부터는 문제지의 지시에 따라 답을 하시기 바랍니다.

18 다음 글의 목적으로 가장 적절한 것은?

Dear Ms. MacAlpine,

I was so excited to hear that your brand is opening a new shop on Bruns Street next month. I have always appreciated the way your brand helps women to feel more stylish and confident. I am writing in response to your ad in the Bruns Journal. I graduated from the Meline School of Fashion and have worked as a sales assistant at LoganMart for the last five years. During that time, I've developed strong customer service and sales skills, and now I would like to apply for the sales position in your clothing store. I am available for an interview at your earliest convenience. I look forward to hearing from you. Thank you for reading my letter.

Yours sincerely,
Grace Braddock

① 영업 시작일을 문의하려고
② 인터뷰 일정을 변경하려고
③ 디자인 공모전에 참가하려고
④ 제품 관련 문의에 답변하려고
⑤ 의류 매장 판매직에 지원하려고

19 다음 글에 드러난 'I'의 심경 변화로 가장 적절한 것은?

I had never seen a beach with such white sand or water that was such a beautiful shade of blue. Jane and I set up a blanket on the sand while looking forward to our ten days of honeymooning on an exotic island. "Look!" Jane waved her hand to point at the beautiful scene before us — and her gold wedding ring went flying off her hand. I tried to see where it went, but the sun hit my eyes and I lost track of it. I didn't want to lose her wedding ring, so I started looking in the area where I thought it had landed. However, the sand was so fine and I realized that anything heavy, like gold, would quickly sink and might never be found again.

① excited → frustrated ② pleased → jealous
③ nervous → confident ④ annoyed → grateful
⑤ relaxed → indifferent

20 다음 글에서 필자가 주장하는 바로 가장 적절한 것은?

Unfortunately, many people don't take personal responsibility for their own growth. Instead, they simply run the race laid out for them. They do well enough in school to keep advancing. Maybe they manage to get a good job at a well-run company. But so many think and act as if their learning journey ends with college. They have checked all the boxes in the life that was laid out for them and now lack a road map describing the right ways to move forward and continue to grow. In truth, that's when the journey really begins. When school is finished, your growth becomes voluntary. Like healthy eating habits or a regular exercise program, you need to commit to it and devote thought, time, and energy to it. Otherwise, it simply won't happen — and your life and career are likely to stop progressing as a result.

① 성공 경험을 위해 달성 가능한 목표를 수립해야 한다.
② 체계적인 경력 관리를 위해 전문가의 도움을 받아야 한다.
③ 건강을 위해 꾸준한 운동과 식습관 관리를 병행해야 한다.
④ 졸업 이후 성장을 위해 자발적으로 배움을 실천해야 한다.
⑤ 적성에 맞는 직업을 찾기 위해 학교 교육에 충실해야 한다.

21 밑줄 친 our brain and the universe meet가 다음 글에서 의미하는 바로 가장 적절한 것은? [3점]

Many people take the commonsense view that color is an objective property of things, or of the light that bounces off them. They say a tree's leaves are green because they reflect green light — a greenness that is just as real as the leaves. Others argue that color doesn't inhabit the physical world at all but exists only in the eye or mind of the viewer. They maintain that if a tree fell in a forest and no one was there to see it, its leaves would be colorless — and so would everything else. They say there is no such *thing* as color; there are only the people who see it. Both positions are, in a way, correct. Color is objective *and* subjective — "the place," as Paul Cézanne put it, "where <u>our brain and the universe meet</u>." Color is created when light from the world is registered by the eyes and interpreted by the brain.

① we see things beyond the range of perception
② objects appear different by the change of light
③ your perspectives and others' reach an agreement
④ our mind and physical reality interact with each other
⑤ structures of the human brain and the universe are similar

22 다음 글의 요지로 가장 적절한 것은?

When writing a novel, research for information needs to be done. The thing is that some kinds of fiction demand a higher level of detail: crime fiction, for example, or scientific thrillers. The information is never hard to find; one website for authors even organizes trips to police stations, so that crime writers can get it right. Often, a polite letter will earn you permission to visit a particular location and record all the details that you need. But remember that you will drive your readers to boredom if you think that you need to pack everything you discover into your work. The details that matter are those that reveal the human experience. The crucial thing is telling a story, finding the characters, the tension, and the conflict — not the train timetable or the building blueprint.

① 작품의 완성도는 작가의 경험의 양에 비례한다.
② 작가의 상상력은 가장 훌륭한 이야기 재료이다.
③ 소설에서 사건 전개에 대한 묘사는 구체적일수록 좋다.
④ 소설을 쓸 때 독자의 관심사를 먼저 고려하는 것이 중요하다.
⑤ 소설에 포함될 세부 사항은 인간의 경험을 드러내는 것이어야 한다.

23 다음 글의 주제로 가장 적절한 것은?

Nearly everything has to go through your mouth to get to the rest of you, from food and air to bacteria and viruses. A healthy mouth can help your body get what it needs and prevent it from harm — with adequate space for air to travel to your lungs, and healthy teeth and gums that prevent harmful microorganisms from entering your bloodstream. From the moment you are created, oral health affects every aspect of your life. What happens in the mouth is usually just the tip of the iceberg and a reflection of what is happening in other parts of the body. Poor oral health can be a cause of a disease that affects the entire body. The microorganisms in an unhealthy mouth can enter the bloodstream and travel anywhere in the body, posing serious health risks.

*microorganism: 미생물

① the way the immune system fights viruses
② the effect of unhealthy eating habits on the body
③ the difficulty in raising awareness about oral health
④ the importance of oral health and its impact on the body
⑤ the relationship between oral health and emotional well-being

24 다음 글의 제목으로 가장 적절한 것은?

Kids tire of their toys, college students get sick of cafeteria food, and sooner or later most of us lose interest in our favorite TV shows. The bottom line is that we humans are easily bored. But why should this be true? The answer lies buried deep in our nerve cells, which are designed to reduce their initial excited response to stimuli each time they occur. At the same time, these neurons enhance their responses to things that change — especially things that change quickly. We probably evolved this way because our ancestors got more survival value, for example, from attending to what was moving in a tree (such as a puma) than to the tree itself. Boredom in reaction to an unchanging environment turns down the level of neural excitation so that new stimuli (like our ancestor's hypothetical puma threat) stand out more. It's the neural equivalent of turning off a front door light to see the fireflies.

*neural: 신경의 **hypothetical: 가정(假定)의, 가설상의
***equivalent: (~와) 같은 것, 대응물

① The Brain's Brilliant Trick to Overcome Fear
② Boredom: Neural Mechanism for Detecting Change
③ Humans' Endless Desire to Pursue Familiar Experiences
④ The Destruction of Nature in Exchange for Human Survival
⑤ How Humans Changed the Environment to Their Advantage

25 다음 도표의 내용과 일치하지 않는 것은?

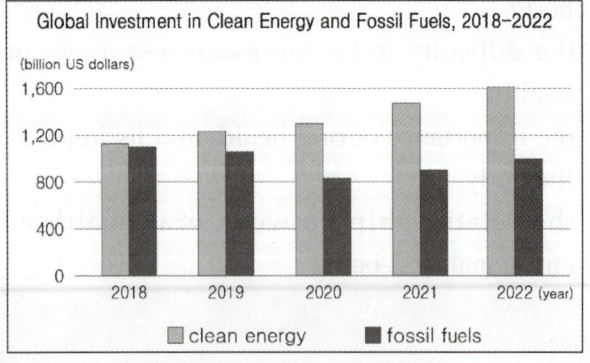

The above graph shows global energy investment in clean energy and in fossil fuels between 2018 and 2022. ① Since 2018 global energy investment in clean energy continued to rise, reaching its highest level in 2022. ② The investment gap between clean energy and fossil fuels in 2020 was larger than that in 2019. ③ Investment in fossil fuels was highest in 2018 and lowest in 2020. ④ In 2021, investment in clean energy exceeded 1,200 billion dollars, while investment in fossil fuels did not. ⑤ In 2022, the global investment in clean energy was more than double that of fossil fuels.

26 Frederick Douglass에 관한 다음 글의 내용과 일치하지 않는 것은?

Frederick Douglass was born into slavery at a farm in Maryland. His full name at birth was Frederick Augustus Washington Bailey. He changed his name to Frederick Douglass after he successfully escaped from slavery in 1838. He became a leader of the Underground Railroad — a network of people, places, and routes that helped enslaved people escape to the north. He assisted other runaway slaves until they could safely get to other areas in the north. As a slave, he had taught himself to read and write and he spread that knowledge to other slaves as well. Once free, he became a well-known abolitionist and strong believer in equality for all people including Blacks, Native Americans, women, and recent immigrants. He wrote several autobiographies describing his experiences as a slave. In addition to all this, he became the first African-American candidate for vice president of the United States.

*abolitionist: 노예제 폐지론자

① Maryland에서 노예로 태어났다.
② 노예들이 탈출하는 것을 돕는 조직의 리더가 되었다.
③ 다른 노예들로부터 읽고 쓰는 법을 배웠다.
④ 노예로서의 자신의 경험을 묘사한 자서전을 썼다.
⑤ 미국의 첫 아프리카계 미국인 부통령 후보가 되었다.

2023 Australian Gateball Championships

The Diamond Coast is getting set to welcome the Australian Gateball Championships. Join this great outdoor competition and be the winner this year!

When & Where
• December 19 — 22, 2023
• Diamond Coast Performance Centre

Schedule of Matches
• Doubles matches (9 a.m. — 11 a.m.)
• Team matches (1 p.m. — 3 p.m.)

Prizes
• Every participant will receive a certificate for entry.
• Champions are awarded a medal.

Note
• Participation is free.
• Visit www.australiangateball.com for registration.
(Registration on site is not available.)

① 4일 동안 신행된나.
② 복식 경기는 오전에 열린다.
③ 모든 참가자는 참가 증서를 받는다.
④ 참가비는 무료이다.
⑤ 현장에서 등록하는 것이 가능하다.

The Amazing Urban Adventure Quest

Explore Central Park while solving clues and completing challenges! Guided by your smartphone, make your way among the well-known places in the park.

When & How
• Available 365 days a year (from sunrise to sunset)
• Start when you want.
• Get a stamp at each checkpoint.

Adventure Courses
• East Side: Starts at Twilight Gardens (no age limit)
• West Side: Starts at Strawberry Castle (over 15 years old)

Registration & Cost
• Sign up online at www.urbanquest.com.
• $40 for a team of 2 – 5 people
• Save 20% with discount code: CENTRALQUEST

① 참여하는 동안 스마트폰 사용은 금지된다.
② 일 년 내내 일몰 후 참여할 수 있다.
③ 서편 코스는 나이 제한이 없다.
④ 1인딩 40달러의 요금이 든다.
⑤ 할인받을 수 있는 코드가 있다.

2023.11
11회

29 다음 글의 밑줄 친 부분 중, 어법상 틀린 것은? [3점]

Some countries have proposed tougher guidelines for determining brain death when transplantation — transferring organs to others — is under consideration. In several European countries, there are legal requirements which specify ① <u>that</u> a whole team of doctors must agree over the diagnosis of death in the case of a potential donor. The reason for these strict regulations for diagnosing brain death in potential organ donors ② <u>is</u>, no doubt, to ease public fears of a premature diagnosis of brain death for the purpose of obtaining organs. But it is questionable whether these requirements reduce public suspicions as much as they create ③ <u>them</u>. They certainly maintain mistaken beliefs that diagnosing brain death is an unreliable process ④ <u>lack</u> precision. As a matter of consistency, at least, criteria for diagnosing the deaths of organ donors should be exactly the same as for those for ⑤ <u>whom</u> immediate burial or cremation is intended.

*diagnosis: 진단 **donor: 기증자 ***cremation: 화장(火葬)

30 다음 글의 밑줄 친 부분 중, 문맥상 낱말의 쓰임이 적절하지 않은 것은?

The term minimalism gives a negative impression to some people who think that it is all about sacrificing valuable possessions. This insecurity naturally stems from their ① <u>attachment</u> to their possessions. It is difficult to distance oneself from something that has been around for quite some time. Being an emotional animal, human beings give meaning to the things around them. So, the question arising here is that if minimalism will ② <u>hurt</u> one's emotions, why become a minimalist? The answer is very simple; the assumption of the question is fundamentally ③ <u>wrong</u>. Minimalism does not hurt emotions. You might feel a bit sad while getting rid of a useless item but sooner than later, this feeling will be ④ <u>maintained</u> by the joy of clarity. Minimalists never argue that you should leave every convenience of the modern era. They are of the view that you only need to ⑤ <u>eliminate</u> stuff that is unused or not going to be used in the near future.

[31~34] 다음 빈칸에 들어갈 말로 가장 적절한 것을 고르시오.

31

A remarkable characteristic of the visual system is that it has the ability of _____. Psychologist George M. Stratton made this clear in an impressive self-experiment. Stratton wore reversing glasses for several days, which literally turned the world upside down for him. In the beginning, this caused him great difficulties: just putting food in his mouth with a fork was a challenge for him. With time, however, his visual system adjusted to the new stimuli from reality, and he was able to act normally in his environment again, even seeing it upright when he concentrated. As he took off his reversing glasses, he was again confronted with problems: he used the wrong hand when he wanted to reach for something, for example. Fortunately, Stratton could reverse the perception, and he did not have to wear reversing glasses for the rest of his life. For him, everything returned to normal after one day.

*reverse: 뒤집다, 반전시키다

① adapting itself
② visualizing ideas
③ assessing distances
④ functioning irregularly
⑤ operating independently

32

Participants in a study were asked to answer questions like "Why does the moon have phases?" Half the participants were told to search for the answers on the internet, while the other half weren't allowed to do so. Then, in the second part of the study, all of the participants were presented with a new set of questions, such as "Why does Swiss cheese have holes?" These questions were unrelated to the ones asked during the first part of the study, so participants who used the internet had absolutely no advantage over those who hadn't. You would think that both sets of participants would be equally sure or unsure about how well they could answer the new questions. But those who used the internet in the first part of the study rated themselves as more knowledgeable than those who hadn't, even about questions they hadn't searched online for. The study suggests that having access to unrelated information was enough to _____.

*phase: (달의) 상(相)

① improve their judgment skills
② pump up their intellectual confidence
③ make them endure challenging situations
④ lead to a collaboration among the participants
⑤ motivate them to pursue in-depth knowledge

33

Anthropologist Gregory Bateson suggests that we tend to understand the world by _____. Take platypuses. We might zoom in so closely to their fur that each hair appears different. We might also zoom out to the extent where it appears as a single, uniform object. We might take the platypus as an individual, or we might treat it as part of a larger unit such as a species or an ecosystem. It's possible to move between many of these perspectives, although we may need some additional tools and skills to zoom in on individual pieces of hair or zoom out to entire ecosystems. Crucially, however, we can only take up one perspective at a time. We can pay attention to the varied behavior of individual animals, look at what unites them into a single species, or look at them as part of bigger ecological patterns. Every possible perspective involves emphasizing certain aspects and ignoring others. [3점]

*anthropologist: 인류학자 **platypus: 오리너구리

① using our experiences as a guide
② breaking the framework of old ideas
③ adding new information to what we know
④ focusing in on particular features within it
⑤ considering both bright and dark sides of it

34

Plato's realism includes all aspects of experience but is most easily explained by considering the nature of mathematical and geometrical objects such as circles. He asked the question, what is a circle? You might indicate a particular example carved into stone or drawn in the sand. However, Plato would point out that, if you looked closely enough, you would see that neither it, nor indeed any physical circle, was perfect. They all possessed flaws, and all were subject to change and decayed with time. So how can we talk about perfect circles if we cannot actually see or touch them? Plato's extraordinary answer was that the world we see is a poor reflection of a deeper unseen reality of *Forms*, or *universals*, where perfect cats chase perfect mice in perfect circles around perfect rocks. Plato believed that the *Forms* or *universals* are the true reality that exists in _____. [3점]

① observable phenomena of the physical world
② our experiences shaped by external influences
③ an overlapping area between emotion and reason
④ an invisible but perfect world beyond our senses
⑤ our perception affected by stereotype or generalization

35 다음 글에서 전체 흐름과 관계 <u>없는</u> 문장은?

In statistics, the law of large numbers describes a situation where having more data is better for making predictions. According to it, the more often an experiment is conducted, the closer the average of the results can be expected to match the true state of the world. ① For instance, on your first encounter with the game of roulette, you may have beginner's luck after betting on 7. ② But the more often you repeat this bet, the closer the relative frequency of wins and losses is expected to approach the true chance of winning, meaning that your luck will at some point fade away. ③ Each number's symbolic meanings can be interpreted in various ways and are promising in situations that may change unexpectedly. ④ Similarly, car insurers collect large amounts of data to figure out the chances that drivers will cause accidents, depending on their age, region, or car brand. ⑤ Both casinos and insurance industries rely on the law of large numbers to balance individual losses.

[36~37] 주어진 글 다음에 이어질 글의 순서로 가장 적절한 것을 고르시오.

36

The adolescent brain is not fully developed until its early twenties. This means the way the adolescents' decision-making circuits integrate and process information may put them at a disadvantage.

(A) On the other hand, the limbic system matures earlier, playing a central role in processing emotional responses. Because of its earlier development, it is more likely to influence decision-making. Decision-making in the adolescent brain is led by emotional factors more than the perception of consequences.

(B) Due to these differences, there is an imbalance between feeling-based decision-making ruled by the more mature limbic system and logical-based decision-making by the not-yet-mature prefrontal cortex. This may explain why some teens are more likely to make bad decisions.

(C) One of their brain regions that matures later is the prefrontal cortex, which is the control center, tasked with thinking ahead and evaluating consequences. It is the area of the brain responsible for preventing you from sending off an initial angry text and modifying it with kinder words. [3점]

*integrate: 통합하다 **limbic system: 대뇌변연계
***prefrontal cortex: 전전두엽 피질

① (A) — (C) — (B)　　② (B) — (A) — (C)
③ (B) — (C) — (A)　　④ (C) — (A) — (B)
⑤ (C) — (B) — (A)

37

Despite the remarkable progress in deep-learning based facial recognition approaches in recent years, in terms of identification performance, they still have limitations. These limitations relate to the database used in the learning stage.

(A) To counteract this problem, researchers have developed models for face aging or digital de-aging. It is used to compensate for the differences in facial characteristics, which appear over a given time period.

(B) If the selected database does not contain enough instances, the result may be systematically affected. For example, the performance of a facial biometric system may decrease if the person to be identified was enrolled over 10 years ago.

(C) The factor to consider is that this person may experience changes in the texture of the face, particularly with the appearance of wrinkles and sagging skin. These changes may be highlighted by weight gain or loss.

*biometric: 생체 측정의 **sagging: 처진

① (A) — (C) — (B) ② (B) — (A) — (C)
③ (B) — (C) — (A) ④ (C) — (A) — (B)
⑤ (C) — (B) — (A)

[38~39] 글의 흐름으로 보아, 주어진 문장이 들어가기에 가장 적절한 곳을 고르시오.

38

Leaving the contribution of that strategy to one side, the danger of creating more uniform crops is that they are more at risk when it comes to disasters.

The decline in the diversity of our food is an entirely human-made process. The biggest loss of crop diversity came in the decades that followed the Second World War. (①) In an attempt to save millions from extreme hunger, crop scientists found ways to produce grains such as rice and wheat on an enormous scale. (②) And thousands of traditional varieties were replaced by a small number of new super-productive ones. (③) The strategy worked spectacularly well, at least to begin with. (④) Because of it, grain production tripled, and between 1970 and 2020 the human population more than doubled. (⑤) Specifically, a global food system that depends on just a narrow selection of plants has a greater chance of not being able to survive diseases, pests and climate extremes.

*pest: 해충

39

A few years ago, Cuba altered that uniform style, modernizing it and perhaps conforming to other countries' style; interestingly, the national team has declined since that time.

Between 1940 and 2000, Cuba ruled the world baseball scene. They won 25 of the first 28 World Cups and 3 of 5 Olympic Games. (①) The Cubans were known for wearing uniforms covered in red from head to toe, a strong contrast to the more conservative North American style featuring grey or white pants. (②) Not only were their athletic talents superior, the Cubans appeared even stronger from just the colour of their uniforms. (③) A game would not even start and the opposing team would already be scared. (④) The country that ruled international baseball for decades has not been on top since that uniform change. (⑤) Traditions are important for a team; while a team brand or image can adjust to keep up with present times, if it abandons or neglects its roots, negative effects can surface.

*conservative: 보수적인

40 다음 글의 내용을 한 문장으로 요약하고자 한다. 빈칸 (A), (B)에 들어갈 말로 가장 적절한 것은? [3점]

Many of the first models of cultural evolution drew noticeable connections between culture and genes by using concepts from theoretical population genetics and applying them to culture. Cultural patterns of transmission, innovation, and selection are conceptually likened to genetic processes of transmission, mutation, and selection. However, these approaches had to be modified to account for the differences between genetic and cultural transmission. For example, we do not expect the cultural transmission to follow the rules of genetic transmission strictly. If two biological parents have different forms of a cultural trait, their child is not necessarily equally likely to acquire the mother's or father's form of that trait. Further, a child can acquire cultural traits not only from its parents but also from nonparental adults and peers; thus, the frequency of a cultural trait in the population is relevant beyond just the probability that an individual's parents had that trait.

*mutation: 돌연변이 **relevant: 유의미한

⬇

Early cultural evolution models used the ___(A)___ between culture and genes but had to be revised since cultural transmission allows for more ___(B)___ factors than genetic transmission.

　　　(A)　　　　　　(B)
① similarity　—　diverse
② similarity　—　limited
③ difference　—　flexible
④ difference　—　complicated
⑤ interaction　—　credible

[41~42] 다음 글을 읽고, 물음에 답하시오.

A ball thrown into the air is acted upon by the initial force given it, persisting as inertia of movement and tending to carry it in the same straight line, and by the constant pull of gravity downward, as well as by the resistance of the air. It moves, accordingly, in a (a) curved path. Now the path does not represent the working of any particular force; there is simply the (b) combination of the three elementary forces mentioned; but in a real sense, there is something in the total action besides the isolated action of three forces, namely, their joint action. In the same way, when two or more human individuals are together, their mutual relationships and their arrangement into a group are things which would not be (c) concealed if we confined our attention to each individual separately. The significance of group behavior is greatly (d) increased in the case of human beings by the fact that some of the tendencies to action of the individual are related definitely to other persons, and could not be aroused except by other persons acting as stimuli. An individual in complete (e) isolation would not reveal their competitive tendencies, their tendencies towards the opposite sex, their protective tendencies towards children. This shows that the traits of human nature do not fully appear until the individual is brought into relationships with other individuals.

*inertia: 관성 **arouse: 유발하다

41 윗글의 제목으로 가장 적절한 것은?

① Common Misunderstandings in Physics
② Collaboration: A Key to Success in Relationships
③ Interpersonal Traits and Their Impact on Science
④ Unbalanced Forces Causing Objects to Accelerate
⑤ Human Traits Uncovered by Interpersonal Relationships

42 밑줄 친 (a)~(e) 중에서 문맥상 낱말의 쓰임이 적절하지 않은 것은? [3점]

① (a)　　② (b)　　③ (c)　　④ (d)　　⑤ (e)

[43~45] 다음 글을 읽고, 물음에 답하시오.

(A)

There once lived a man in a village who was not happy with his life. He was always troubled by one problem or another. One day, a saint with his guards stopped by his village. Many people heard the news and started going to him with their problems. The man also decided to visit the saint. Even after reaching the saint's place in the morning, (a) he didn't get the opportunity to meet him till evening.

(B)

But the saint also asked if the man could do a small job for him. He told the man to take care of a hundred camels in his group that night, saying "When all hundred camels sit down, you can go to sleep." The man agreed. The next morning when the saint met that man, (b) he asked if the man had slept well. Tired and sad, the man replied that he couldn't sleep even for a moment.

(C)

In fact, the man tried very hard but couldn't make all the camels sit at the same time because every time (c) he made one camel sit, another would stand up. The saint told him, "You realized that no matter how hard you try, you can't make all the camels sit down. If one problem is solved, for some reason, another will arise like the camels did. So, humans should enjoy life despite these problems."

(D)

When the man got to meet the saint, (d) he confessed that he was very unhappy with life because problems always surrounded him, like workplace tension or worries about his health. (e) He said, "Please give me a solution so that all the problems in my life will end and I can live peacefully." The saint smiled and said that he would answer the request the next day.

43 주어진 글 (A)에 이어질 내용을 순서에 맞게 배열한 것으로 가장 적절한 것은?

① (B) — (D) — (C)　　② (C) — (B) — (D)
③ (C) — (D) — (B)　　④ (D) — (B) — (C)
⑤ (D) — (C) — (B)

44 밑줄 친 (a)~(e) 중에서 가리키는 대상이 나머지 넷과 다른 것은?

① (a)　　② (b)　　③ (c)　　④ (d)　　⑤ (e)

45 윗글에 관한 내용으로 적절하지 않은 것은?

① 많은 사람들이 자신들의 문제를 가지고 성자에게 갔다.
② 성자는 자신을 위해 작은 일을 해 줄 수 있는지 남자에게 물었다.
③ 성자는 남자가 낙타를 모두 재우면 잠을 자러 가도 좋다고 했다.
④ 성자는 문제가 있어도 인생을 즐겨야 한다고 말했다.
⑤ 성자는 남자의 요청에 대한 답을 다음 날 말해 주기로 했다.

• MP3 파일을 들으며 다음 빈칸을 채우시오. (듣기 어려운 발음이나 정답의 단서가 되는 부분에 빈칸을 만들었습니다.)

01 다음을 듣고, 남자가 하는 말의 목적으로 가장 적절한 것을 고르시오.

M: Hello, visitors. This is Scott Wolfman from the Edison Convention Center management office. We're _____ _____ _____ ___ make sure that visitors have a wonderful experience in our convention center. _____ _____ _____ _____ _____, our center provides a robot guide service. The robot offers guided-tours of our ✿ _____. Foreign languages, such as Chinese and Spanish, are available. And if you _____ _____ _____, the robot will accompany you to where you want to go. So, please feel free to ask our friendly robot guide, and ✿ ____ _____ help you. I hope this service makes your experience even better. Thank you.

02 대화를 듣고, 여자의 의견으로 가장 적절한 것을 고르시오.

W: Kevin, what are you doing?

M: Mom, I'm writing a letter to my ✿ _____ child in Congo.

W: That's why you're writing in French. Your French has _____ _____ _____ _____.

M: Actually, I got help from a translation program.

W: I see. [Pause] Did you check the translated text before copying it?

M: No, I didn't. Do you think I have to?

W: Yes. _____ _____ _____ the translation.

M: Well, I think the translation program does a better job than I can.

W: Not exactly. The translation could have meanings different from what you intended.

M: Hmm, you may be right. The translated text often loses the meaning of my original writing.

W: See? When translating a text _____ _____ _____ _____, you need to check the results.

M: Okay. Thanks for your advice.

03 대화를 듣고, 두 사람의 관계를 가장 잘 나타낸 것을 고르시오.

[Cell phone rings.]

M: Hello. This is Johnny. ✿ _____ _____ _____ each other on the online marketplace.

W: Oh, hi. You have more questions about the air conditioner, right?

M: Yes. Could you tell me _____ _____ _____ _____ using it?

W: I bought it a year ago. It works well and is like new as you can see from the photo.

M: Then why do you want to sell it?

W: Because I _____ _____ ___ _____. I'm moving to a place with a built-in air conditioner.

M: I see. I'd like to buy it, then. It's $400, correct?

W: That's right. When can you pick it up?

M: Maybe tomorrow. I need to find a truck to _____ ___ ___ _____.

W: Okay. Let me know when you're ready.

M: Thanks. I'll call you again.

04
대화를 듣고, 그림에서 대화의 내용과 일치하지 <u>않는</u> 것을 고르시오.

W : Hi, Benjamin. _____ _____ _____ your work for the student lounge design contest?

M : Yes. I'm confident that I'm going to win. Here's my design for it.

W : Awesome. Is that a hanging plant ____ _____ ____ _____ _____?

M : Yes. The plant will give a fresh feel to the lounge. What do you think about the banner on the wall?

W : I love it. The slogan "TO THE WORLD" goes well with the world map.

M : I hope this place _____ _____ _____ ____.

W : That's cool. And the two cushions on the sofa make the atmosphere cozier.

M : You're right. Check out the square-shaped table as well.

W : Good. It can be useful. Most of all, students will _____ _____ ✪ _____ _____ under the clock.

M : You bet!

05
대화를 듣고, 남자가 할 일로 가장 적절한 것을 고르시오.

M : Ms. Kim, Empty Your Plate Day is coming. How's the preparation going?

W : _____ _____ _____ on the lunch menu for that day.

M : You did! How did you do that?

W : I did ___ _____ ___ students' favorite foods.

M : Good idea! Can I _____ _____ _____ _____?

W : Actually, Mr. Han, I'm not sure how to motivate students to participate.

M : How about an award for the class with the fewest leftovers?

W : Sounds great. But _____ _____ ____ _____ that class?

M : You could give a sticker to the students who leave nothing on their plates. And then, you can find the class with the most stickers.

W : Excellent. Could you prepare some stickers for me?

M : Sure. I'll do that for you.

W : Thanks. Then I'll put a notice on the ✪ _____ board.

06
대화를 듣고, 남자가 매달 지불할 금액을 고르시오.

W : Welcome to Boom Telecom. How can I help you?

M : Hi. I'm thinking of changing my internet provider. What service plans do you have?

W : Okay. We have the ✪ _____ plan that's $20 per month. And the Supreme plan, which is faster, is $30 _____ _____.

M : I prefer the faster one.

W : Alright. We also have an OTT service for an extra $10 per month. What do you think?

M : Awesome. I'd like that as well.

W : Excellent choice. Then you'll have the Supreme plan with the OTT service, right?

M : Correct. Can I _____ ___ _____?

W : I'm afraid that the 10% discount promotion is over.

M : That's a shame. But I'll take it anyway.

W : Thank you. Please _____ ____ _____ _____ with your payment information.

M : Okay. *[Writing sound]* Here you are.

07
대화를 듣고, 여자가 토크 쇼를 방청하러 갈 수 <u>없는</u> 이유를 고르시오.

[Cell phone rings.]

M : Hi, Isabella.

W : Hi, Lorenzo. Did you finish your part-time job?

M : Yes. I'm on my way to a meeting for a ✪ _____ project. What's up?

W : Your favorite talk show is *The Alice Mitchell Show*, right?

M : Yeah, I'm a big fan of hers. ____ ____ _____ ____ her book signing event.

W : I knew it! I got two tickets for her talk show. It's next Saturday evening.

M : Whoa! Can you please _____ ____ ____?

W : Actually, I'm not available that day. The tickets are all yours.

M : Wait, why can't you go? Is it because of the family gathering ____ _____ _____?

W : No, that's in two weeks. Next Saturday I have to attend my friend's wedding.

M : Oh, I see. Then I'll take the tickets with pleasure. Thank you so much.

08 대화를 듣고, Polar Bear Swim에 관해 언급되지 않은 것을 고르시오.

W: Michael, look at this poster. The Polar Bear Swim will be held soon.

M: I know! I've been really _____ _____ ____ ____. [Pause] It's on December 23rd.

W: Yeah. We can enjoy winter sea-swimming.

M: How nice! To join this event, ____ _____ _____ ____ a medical check-up paper.

W: I think it's a good policy for everyone's health since the water is icy cold.

M: I agree. By the way, it says that there's a limit of 100 people.

W: Oh, we must hurry. Look! ✪_____ starts this Saturday.

M: I'll set a reminder on my phone.

W: Great idea. And the entry fee is just $15.

M: Yes. And all entry fees will be ✪_____ ____ _____.

W: Cool. Let's have some icy fun while doing a good deed.

09 Walk in the Snow에 관한 다음 내용을 듣고, 일치하지 않는 것을 고르시오.

W: Hello, listeners! Are you a winter person? Then, Walk in the Snow might just be the adventure for you. It's a one-day tour program at Great White Mountain. _____ ____ _____ _____, anyone who is interested in hiking can participate in the tour. Participants are required to bring their own snowshoes and poles. But ✪_____ is also available to rent for a small fee. The registration fee is $10, and we offer discounts to students. Don't forget that you must register ____ _____ ____ _____. For more information, please visit our website, www.walkinthesnow.com. Thank you.

10 다음 표를 보면서 대화를 듣고, 두 사람이 선택할 달력을 고르시오.

M: Honey, what are you looking at?

W: It's a ✪_____ for a new calendar. _____ _____ ____ _____ one together?

M: Great. How much do you want to spend?

W: I think more than $20 is not reasonable.

M: Agreed. How about trying a new format _____ ____ ____ _____ _____? We've only used wall calendars so far.

W: Good idea. Let's pick the standing desk format, then.

M: Okay. And I prefer one that's _____ ____ ✪_____ _____.

W: Me, too. It's more eco-friendly than those that cannot be recycled.

M: Then, _____ _____ _____ ____. Now, we have two options left. Which one do you prefer?

W: I think the classic art theme doesn't match our interior design.

M: Good point. Then, let's choose this one.

11 대화를 듣고, 여자의 마지막 말에 대한 남자의 응답으로 가장 적절한 것을 고르시오.

W: Congratulations, Lucas! ____ _____ _____ _____ _____ to speak at the National ✪_____.

M: Thanks. It's a real honor. I think ____ _____ __ _____ in the newspaper made a strong impression.

W: I'm so proud of you. What ____ ____ ____ write about?

M: _____

12 대화를 듣고, 남자의 마지막 말에 대한 여자의 응답으로 가장 적절한 것을 고르시오.

M: Claire, why are you ✪_____? It's pretty cold outside.

W: Hey, Jamie. I ran to be in time for class. It's ____ ____ ____ _____ from the subway station to our college, don't you think?

M: Yes, but the shuttle bus began running last week. You can _____ ____ _____.

W: _____

13 대화를 듣고, 여자의 마지막 말에 대한 남자의 응답으로 가장 적절한 것을 고르시오.

W: Good morning, Pablo.

M: Hi, Eva. Look at my new tablet PC.

W: Wow. How do you like it?

M: _____ _____ a brand new world to me. But I have a small problem.

W: What is it? Maybe I _____ ___ ___ _____.

M: This file works well on my laptop, but it won't open on my tablet.

W: Did you ✪_____ a file-reading app? You need one to open the file on a tablet.

M: I already did that a week ago.

W: Then, I'll _____ ___ ____ _____. *[Tapping sound]* I got it. The free ✪_____ _____ of this app is over.

M: Oh, _____ ____ it doesn't work. Do you think I should pay for this app?

W: Well, it depends on you. You can consider it if you need this app.

M: _____

14 대화를 듣고, 남자의 마지막 말에 대한 여자의 응답으로 가장 적절한 것을 고르시오.

M: Hi, Naomi. What are you up to?

W: Hi. I'm _____ ____ _____ _____. Didn't you say you're volunteering?

M: Yes. I'm working as a note-taker.

W: You mean helping students with hearing difficulties?

M: Right. It helps deaf students understand the class better.

W: Interesting. _____ ____ tell me more?

M: I type everything during class, even jokes. The more detailed, the more understandable.

W: It sounds like a unique and ✪_____ experience.

M: Yeah. Are you thinking about joining?

W: Absolutely. But can I _____ ___ the middle of the semester?

M: It could be possible. I heard one member _____ ___ ____ _____ ____.

W: Lucky me. Is the position still available?

M: Hmm, I'm not sure, but if you ask the student volunteer center, you'll _____ ___ _____ ✪_____.

W: _____

15 다음 상황 설명을 듣고, Tony가 Kate에게 할 말로 가장 적절한 것을 고르시오.

M: Tony and Kate are members of the bread lovers club. They plan to go on a bakery tour every month. ___ _____ ___ _____ of places to visit, they're sharing their ideas about must-visit bakeries. Kate ✪_____ a bakery whose bread she thinks is super delicious. However, Tony finds out that the baker there quit and since then there have been _____ ___ _____ complaining about the bread ✪_____ _____ _____. So, he wants to suggest that they choose a better bakery for their where-to-go list. In this situation, what would Tony most likely say to Kate?

Tony: _____

[16~17] 다음을 듣고, 물음에 답하시오.

W: Hello, students. Last time, we learned why it's good for us to eat fruits and ✪_____. But what's good for us isn't always good for animals. Today, let's find out what fruits to avoid when feeding dogs. First, grapes are known to be _____ _____ to dogs. You should be careful because even a single grape can _____ _____ _____ _____. Now, let's take a look at cherries. If a dog swallows their seeds, the dog is likely to _____ _____ _____. Next, if your dog doesn't eat avocados, it would be for the best. That's because eating large amounts of avocados can make your dog sick. Finally, don't let your dog _____ ___ _____. The fruit contains so much acid that some dogs can _____ ✪_____ _____. Now, you may understand why some fruits are _____ ___ ___ _____ to dogs. I hope this information will help you and your dog in living a happy life.

2023.11
11회

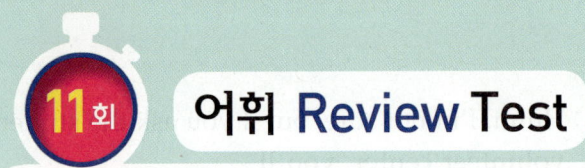

✱ 다음 영어는 우리말 뜻을, 우리말은 영어 단어를 〈보기〉에서 찾아 쓰시오.

01 sponsor _____

02 exhibition _____

03 accompany _____

04 translation _____

05 equipment _____

06 형식, 형태 _____

07 짐을 싣다 _____

08 자신감 있는 _____

09 분위기 _____

10 체험의 _____

[보기]

후원하다	load
장비	format
번역	immediately
동행하다	trial
인상	atmosphere
전시회	confident

✱ 다음 우리말에 알맞은 영어 표현을 찾아 연결하시오.

11 ~을 설명하다 •   • account for

12 ~에 영향을 받다 •   • regardless of

13 ~와 관계없이 •   • conform to

14 ~을 제출하다 •   • hand in

15 ~에 순응하다 •   • be subject to

✱ 다음 우리말과 같은 표현이 되도록 알맞은 단어를 〈보기〉에서 찾아 쓰시오.

[보기]

geometrical / remarkable / recognition / appreciate / transmission / regulation
extraordinary / difficulty / assumption / premature / commonsense / significance

16 전파의 문화적 방식 ➜ cultural patterns of _____

17 그룹 행동의 중요성 ➜ the _____ of group behavior

18 엄격한 규정 ➜ strict _____

19 상식적인 견해 ➜ the _____ view

20 비범한 대답 ➜ a(n) _____ answer

21 얼굴 인식 ➜ facial _____

22 그 질문의 가정 ➜ the _____ of the question

23 너무 이른 진단 ➜ a(n) _____ diagnosis

24 청각 장애 ➜ hearing _____

25 기하학적인 대상 ➜ _____ objects

* 다음 우리말 표현에 알맞은 단어를 고르시오.

26 그 유니폼 스타일을 바꾸다 ➡ (alter / elder) that uniform style

27 정보를 통합하고 처리하다 ➡ (cooperate / integrate) and process information

28 다른 도망친 노예들을 돕다 ➡ (resist / assist) other runaway slaves

29 그들의 반응을 강화하다 ➡ (enhance / hence) their responses

30 물리적인 세계에 존재하지 않는다 ➡ doesn't (inhibit / inhabit) the physical world

* 다음 문장의 빈칸에 알맞은 단어를 〈보기〉에서 찾아 쓰시오.

─────────────── [보기] ───────────────

otherwise / insurance / diversity / guidelines / adjust / crucially
advantage / frequency / initial / combination / permission / perception

31 언급된 세 가지 기본적인 힘의 결합이 존재할 뿐이다.

➡ There is simply the _____ of the three elementary forces mentioned.

32 집단의 문화적인 특성의 빈도는 유의미하다.

➡ The _____ of a cultural trait in the population is relevant.

33 팀 브랜드나 이미지는 현시대를 따르기 위해 조정될 수 있다.

➡ A team brand or image can _____ to keep up with present times.

34 농작물 다양성의 가장 큰 손실은 수십 년 동안 나타났다.

➡ The biggest loss of crop _____ came in the decades.

35 카지노와 보험 산업 모두 대수의 법칙에 의존한다.

➡ Both casinos and _____ industries rely on the law of large numbers.

36 그러나 결정적으로 우리는 한 번에 하나의 관점만 취할 수 있다.

➡ _____, however, we can only take up one perspective at a time.

37 일부 국가는 뇌사를 결정하는 것에 대한 더 엄격한 지침을 제안했다.

➡ Some countries have proposed tougher _____ for determining brain death.

38 다행히 Stratton은 지각을 뒤집을 수 있었다.

➡ Fortunately, Stratton could reverse the _____.

39 인터넷을 사용한 참가자들은 이점이 전혀 없었다.

➡ Participants who used the internet had absolutely no _____.

40 종종 정중한 편지는 여러분에게 허가를 얻어 줄 것이다.

➡ Often, a polite letter will earn you _____.

*1번부터 17번까지는 듣고 답하는 문제입니다. 1번부터 15번까지는 한 번만 들려주고, 16번부터 17번까지는 두 번 들려줍니다. 방송을 잘 듣고 답을 하시기 바랍니다.

▲ 듣기 파일

01 다음을 듣고, 남자가 하는 말의 목적으로 가장 적절한 것을 고르시오.

① 얼음으로 덮인 일부 등산로 폐쇄를 공지하려고
② 등산객에게 야간 산행의 위험성을 경고하려고
③ 겨울 산행을 위한 안전 장비를 안내하려고
④ 긴급 제설에 필요한 작업자를 모집하려고
⑤ 일출 명소인 전망대를 소개하려고

02 대화를 듣고, 남자의 의견으로 가장 적절한 것을 고르시오.

① 조리법을 있는 그대로 따를 필요는 없다.
② 요리 도구를 정기적으로 소독해야 한다.
③ 설탕 섭취는 단기 기억력을 향상시킨다.
④ 열량이 높은 음식은 건강에 좋지 않다.
⑤ 신선한 재료는 요리의 풍미를 높인다.

03 대화를 듣고, 두 사람의 관계를 가장 잘 나타낸 것을 고르시오.

① 음악 평론가 – 방송 연출가
② 작곡가 – 게임 제작자
③ 독자 – 웹툰 작가
④ 삽화가 – 소설가
⑤ 영화감독 – 배우

04 대화를 듣고, 그림에서 대화의 내용과 일치하지 않는 것을 고르시오.

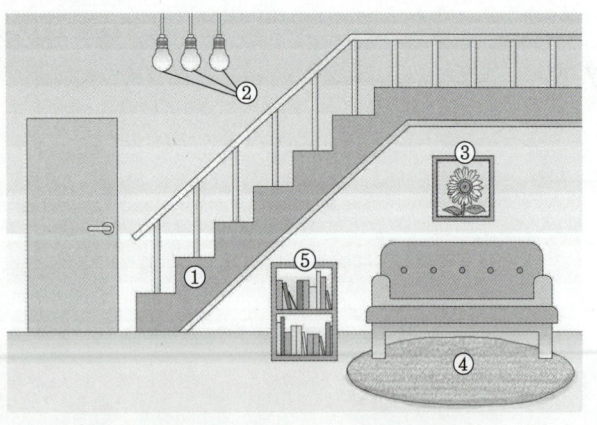

05 대화를 듣고, 남자가 할 일로 가장 적절한 것을 고르시오.

① 음료 구매하기
② 연필 준비하기
③ 의자 설치하기
④ 마이크 점검하기
⑤ 스케치북 가져오기

06 대화를 듣고, 여자가 지불할 금액을 고르시오. [3점]

① $17   ② $22   ③ $35   ④ $37   ⑤ $39

07 대화를 듣고, 남자가 얼음낚시를 갈 수 없는 이유를 고르시오.

① 손목을 다쳐서
② 병원에 입원해야 해서
③ 직장에 출근해야 해서
④ 기상 여건이 나빠져서
⑤ 친구와 농구를 해야 해서

08 대화를 듣고, Kids' Pottery Class에 관해 언급되지 않은 것을 고르시오.

① 날짜
② 장소
③ 수강 인원
④ 수강료
⑤ 등록 방법

09 2022 Online Whistling Championship에 관한 다음 내용을 듣고, 일치하지 않는 것을 고르시오.

① 좋아하는 어떤 노래든 선택할 수 있다.
② 12월 4일까지 동영상을 업로드해야 한다.
③ 녹음 시 마이크의 에코 효과를 반드시 꺼야 한다.
④ 운영진의 심사에 의해 수상자들이 결정될 것이다.
⑤ 결과는 웹사이트에 발표될 것이다.

10

다음 표를 보면서 대화를 듣고, 두 사람이 선택할 커튼을 고르시오.

Curtains

	Product	Price	Care Instruction	Blackout	Color
①	A	$70	machine washable	×	navy
②	B	$80	machine washable	○	brown
③	C	$90	dry cleaning only	○	ivory
④	D	$95	machine washable	○	gray
⑤	E	$110	dry cleaning only	×	white

11

대화를 듣고, 남자의 마지막 말에 대한 여자의 응답으로 가장 적절한 것을 고르시오.

① I've been waiting for 30 minutes.
② I've enjoyed this ride very much.
③ You're standing in the correct line.
④ I have enough time to wait for you.
⑤ You may end the construction in a year.

12

대화를 듣고, 여자의 마지막 말에 대한 남자의 응답으로 가장 적절한 것을 고르시오.

① No way. I don't know who's lost.
② Okay. Let's see if he needs our help.
③ Exactly. Just stop crying like a child.
④ Sure. He loves walking around the park.
⑤ Thanks. We were worried about our son.

13

대화를 듣고, 남자의 마지막 말에 대한 여자의 응답으로 가장 적절한 것을 고르시오. [3점]

Woman: _____

① Great. I believe my previous offer will benefit your company.
② I'm sorry. Your interview has been delayed to next Wednesday.
③ Good. Your effort will give a good impression on the interviewer.
④ Excellent. The second candidate's work experience caught my eye.
⑤ No worries. You can purchase nice clothes for the upcoming party.

14

대화를 듣고, 여자의 마지막 말에 대한 남자의 응답으로 가장 적절한 것을 고르시오.

Man: _____

① Please wait. I'll be back with the shoes in a minute.
② Hurry up. You don't have enough time to do this.
③ Of course. You can get a refund for these shoes.
④ Don't worry. The color doesn't matter to me.
⑤ Sorry. The red ones are already sold out.

15

다음 상황 설명을 듣고, Amelia가 Jacob 교수에게 할 말로 가장 적절한 것을 고르시오. [3점]

Amelia: _____

① Could you extend the deadline for the assignment?
② Would it be possible to change our appointment?
③ Why don't you join my final psychology project?
④ Do you want to meet at the information center?
⑤ How about visiting the doctor for a checkup?

[16~17] 다음을 듣고, 물음에 답하시오.

16

여자가 하는 말의 주제로 가장 적절한 것은?

① ways to stop the spread of false information
② methods of delivering messages in the past
③ modes of communication in modern times
④ types of speeches according to purposes
⑤ means to survive in prehistoric times

17

언급된 수단이 아닌 것은?

① drum   ② smoke   ③ pigeon
④ flag   ⑤ horse

> *이제 듣기 문제가 끝났습니다. 18번부터는 문제지의 지시에 따라 답을 하시기 바랍니다.

2022.11
12회

Dear Mr. Krull,

I have greatly enjoyed working at Trincom Enterprises as a sales manager. Since I joined in 2015, I have been a loyal and essential member of this company, and have developed innovative ways to contribute to the company. Moreover, in the last year alone, I have brought in two new major clients to the company, increasing the company's total sales by 5%. Also, I have voluntarily trained 5 new members of staff, totaling 35 hours. I would therefore request your consideration in raising my salary, which I believe reflects my performance as well as the industry average. I look forward to speaking with you soon.

Kimberly Morss

① 부서 이동을 신청하려고
② 급여 인상을 요청하려고
③ 근무 시간 조정을 요구하려고
④ 기업 혁신 방안을 제안하려고
⑤ 신입 사원 연수에 대해 문의하려고

19 다음 글에 드러난 'I'의 심경 변화로 가장 적절한 것은?

On one beautiful spring day, I was fully enjoying my day off. I arrived at the nail salon, and muted my cellphone so that I would be disconnected for the hour and feel calm and peaceful. I was so comfortable while I got a manicure. As I left the place, I checked my cellphone and saw four missed calls from a strange number. I knew immediately that something bad was coming, and I called back. A young woman answered and said that my father had fallen over a stone and was injured, now seated on a bench. I was really concerned since he had just recovered from his knee surgery. I rushed getting into my car to go see him.

① nervous → confident   ② relaxed → worried
③ excited → indifferent   ④ pleased → jealous
⑤ annoyed → grateful

20 다음 글에서 필자가 주장하는 바로 가장 적절한 것은?

You already have a business and you're about to launch your blog so that you can sell your product. Unfortunately, here is where a 'business mind' can be a bad thing. Most people believe that to have a successful business blog promoting a product, they have to stay strictly 'on the topic.' If all you're doing is shamelessly promoting your product, then who is going to want to read the latest thing you're writing about? Instead, you need to give some useful or entertaining information away for free so that people have a reason to keep coming back. Only by doing this can you create an interested audience that you will then be able to sell to. So, the best way to be successful with a business blog is to write about things that your audience will be interested in.

① 인터넷 게시물에 대한 윤리적 기준을 세워야 한다.
② 블로그를 전문적으로 관리할 인력을 마련해야 한다.
③ 신제품 개발을 위해 상업용 블로그를 적극 활용해야 한다.
④ 상품에 대한 고객들의 반응을 정기적으로 분석할 필요가 있다.
⑤ 상업용 블로그는 사람들이 흥미 있어 할 정보를 제공해야 한다.

21 밑줄 친 challenge this sacred cow가 다음 글에서 의미하는 바로 가장 적절한 것은? [3점]

Our language helps to reveal our deeper assumptions. Think of these revealing phrases: When we accomplish something important, we say it took "blood, sweat, and tears." We say important achievements are "hard-earned." We recommend a "hard day's work" when "day's work" would be enough. When we talk of "easy money," we are implying it was obtained through illegal or questionable means. We use the phrase "That's easy for you to say" as a criticism, usually when we are seeking to invalidate someone's opinion. It's like we all automatically accept that the "right" way is, inevitably, the harder one. In my experience this is hardly ever questioned. What would happen if you do challenge this sacred cow? We don't even pause to consider that something important and valuable could be made easy. What if the biggest thing keeping us from doing what matters is the false assumption that it has to take huge effort?   *invalidate: 틀렸음을 입증하다

① resist the tendency to avoid any hardship
② escape from the pressure of using formal language
③ doubt the solid belief that only hard work is worthy
④ abandon the old notion that money always comes first
⑤ break the superstition that holy animals bring good luck

22 다음 글의 요지로 가장 적절한 것은?

The old saying is that "knowledge is power," but when it comes to scary, threatening news, research suggests the exact opposite. Frightening news can actually rob people of their inner sense of control, making them less likely to take care of themselves and other people. Public health research shows that when the news presents health-related information in a pessimistic way, people are actually less likely to take steps to protect themselves from illness as a result. A news article that's intended to warn people about increasing cancer rates, for example, can result in fewer people choosing to get screened for the disease because they're so terrified of what they might find. This is also true for issues such as climate change. When a news story is all doom and gloom, people feel depressed and become less interested in taking small, personal steps to fight ecological collapse.

① 두려움을 주는 뉴스는 사람들이 문제에 덜 대처하게 할 수 있다.
② 정보를 전달하는 시기에 따라 뉴스의 영향력이 달라질 수 있다.
③ 지속적인 환경 문제 보도가 사람들의 인식 변화를 가져온다.
④ 정보 제공의 지연은 정확한 문제 인식에 방해가 될 수 있다.
⑤ 출처가 불분명한 건강 정보는 사람들에게 유익하지 않다.

23 다음 글의 주제로 가장 적절한 것은?

The most remarkable and unbelievable consequence of melting ice and rising seas is that together they are a kind of time machine, so real that they are altering the duration of our day. It works like this: As the glaciers melt and the seas rise, gravity forces more water toward the equator. This changes the shape of the Earth ever so slightly, making it fatter around the middle, which in turns slows the rotation of the planet similarly to the way a ballet dancer slows her spin by spreading out her arms. The slowdown isn't much, just a few thousandths of a second each year, but like the barely noticeable jump of rising seas every year, it adds up. When dinosaurs lived on the Earth, a day lasted only about twenty-three hours.

① cause of rising temperatures on the Earth
② principles of planets maintaining their shapes
③ implications of melting ice on marine biodiversity
④ way to keep track of time without using any device
⑤ impact of melting ice and rising seas on the length of a day

Have you ever brought up an idea or suggestion to someone and heard them immediately say "No, that won't work."? You may have thought, "He/she didn't even give it a chance. How do they know it won't work?" When you are right about something, you close off the possibility of another viewpoint or opportunity. Being right about something means that "it is the way it is, period." You may be correct. Your particular way of seeing it may be true with the facts. However, considering the other option or the other person's point of view can be beneficial. If you see their side, you will see something new or, at worse, learn something about how the other person looks at life. Why would you think everyone sees and experiences life the way you do? Besides how boring that would be, it would eliminate all new opportunities, ideas, invention, and creativity.

① The Value of Being Honest
② Filter Out Negative Points of View
③ Keeping Your Word: A Road to Success
④ Being Right Can Block New Possibilities
⑤ Look Back When Everyone Looks Forward

25 다음 도표의 내용과 일치하지 않는 것은?

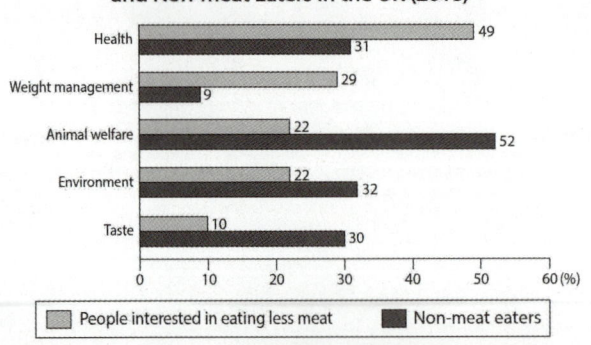

Reasons for People Interested in Eating Less Meat and Non-meat Eaters in the UK (2018)

Health — 49 / 31
Weight management — 29 / 9
Animal welfare — 22 / 52
Environment — 22 / 32
Taste — 10 / 30

People interested in eating less meat ▮ Non-meat eaters
※ allowed to choose multiple reasons

The graph above shows the survey results on reasons for people interested in eating less meat and those eating no meat in the UK in 2018. ① For the group of people who are interested in eating less meat, health is the strongest motivator for doing so. ② For the group of non-meat eaters, animal welfare accounts for the largest percentage among all reasons, followed by environment, health, and taste. ③ The largest percentage point difference between the two groups is in animal welfare, whereas the smallest difference is in environment. ④ The percentage of non-meat eaters citing taste is four times higher than that of people interested in reducing their meat consumption citing taste. ⑤ Weight management ranks the lowest for people who don't eat meat, with less than 10 percent.

Margaret Knight was an exceptionally prolific inventor in the late 19th century; journalists occasionally compared her to Thomas Edison by nicknaming her "a woman Edison." From a young age, she built toys for her older brothers. After her father died, Knight's family moved to Manchester. Knight left school in 1850, at age 12, to earn money for her family at a nearby textile factory, where she witnessed a fellow worker injured by faulty equipment. That led her to create her first invention, a safety device for textile equipment, but she never earned money from the invention. She also invented a machine that cut, folded and glued flat-bottomed paper bags and was awarded her first patent in 1871 for it. It eliminated the need for workers to assemble them slowly by hand. Knight received 27 patents in her lifetime and entered the National Inventors Hall of Fame in 2006. *prolific: 다작(多作)의 **patent: 특허

① 기자들이 '여자 Edison'이라는 별명을 지어 주었다.
② 가족을 위해 돈을 벌려고 학교를 그만두었다.
③ 직물 장비에 쓰이는 안전장치를 발명하여 많은 돈을 벌었다.
④ 밑이 평평한 종이 가방을 자르고 접고 붙이는 기계를 발명했다.
⑤ 2006년에 국립 발명가 명예의 전당에 입성했다.

27 E-Waste Recycling Day에 관한 다음 안내문의 내용과 일치하지 <u>않는</u> 것은?

E-Waste Recycling Day

E-Waste Recycling Day is an annual event in our city. Bring your used electronics such as cell phones, tablets, and laptops to recycle. Go green!

When
Saturday, December 17, 2022
8:00 a.m. – 11:00 a.m.

Where
Lincoln Sports Center

Notes
· Items NOT accepted: light bulbs, batteries, and microwaves
· All personal data on the devices must be wiped out in advance.
· This event is free but open only to local residents.

Please contact us at 986-571-0204 for more information.

① 3시간 동안 진행된다.
② Lincoln 스포츠 센터에서 열린다.
③ 전자레인지는 허용되지 않는 품목이다.
④ 기기 속 모든 개인 정보는 미리 삭제되어야 한다.
⑤ 거주 지역에 상관없이 참가할 수 있다.

---

28 Undersea Walking Activity에 관한 다음 안내문의 내용과 일치하는 것은?

Undersea Walking Activity

Enjoy a fascinating underwater walk on the ocean floor. Witness wonderful marine life on foot!

Age Requirement
10 years or older

Operating Hours
from Tuesday to Sunday
9:00 a.m. – 4:00 p.m.

Price
$30 (insurance fee included)

What to Bring
swim suit and towel

Notes
· Experienced lifeguards accompany you throughout the activity.
· With a special underwater helmet, you can wear glasses during the activity.
· Reservations can be made on-site or online at www.seawalkwonder.com.

① 연중무휴로 운영된다.
② 가격에 보험료는 포함되어 있지 않다.
③ 숙련된 안전 요원이 활동 내내 동행한다.
④ 특수 수중 헬멧 착용 시 안경을 쓸 수 없다.
⑤ 현장 예약은 불가능하다.

---

29 다음 글의 밑줄 친 부분 중, 어법상 <u>틀린</u> 것은?
[3점]

You may have seen headlines in the news about some of the things machines powered by artificial intelligence can do. However, if you were to consider all the tasks ① <u>that</u> AI-powered machines could actually perform, it would be quite mind-blowing! One of the key features of artificial intelligence ② <u>is</u> that it enables machines to learn new things, rather than requiring programming specific to new tasks. Therefore, the core difference between computers of the future and ③ <u>those</u> of the past is that future computers will be able to learn and self-improve. In the near future, smart virtual assistants will know more about you than your closest friends and family members ④ <u>are</u>. Can you imagine how that might change our lives? These kinds of changes are exactly why it is so important ⑤ <u>to recognize</u> the implications that new technologies will have for our world.

30

다음 글의 밑줄 친 부분 중, 문맥상 낱말의 쓰임이 적절하지 <u>않은</u> 것은? [3점]

Plant growth is controlled by a group of hormones called auxins found at the tips of stems and roots of plants. Auxins produced at the tips of stems tend to accumulate on the side of the stem that is in the shade. Accordingly, the auxins ① <u>stimulate</u> growth on the shaded side of the plant. Therefore, the shaded side grows faster than the side facing the sunlight. This phenomenon causes the stem to bend and appear to be growing ② <u>towards</u> the light. Auxins have the ③ <u>opposite</u> effect on the roots of plants. Auxins in the tips of roots tend to limit growth. If a root is horizontal in the soil, the auxins will accumulate on the lower side and interfere with its development. Therefore, the lower side of the root will grow ④ <u>faster</u> than the upper side. This will, in turn, cause the root to bend ⑤ <u>downwards</u>, with the tip of the root growing in that direction.

[31~34] 다음 빈칸에 들어갈 말로 가장 적절한 것을 고르시오.

31

To demonstrate how best to defeat the habit of delaying, Dan Ariely, a professor of psychology and behavioral economics, performed an experiment on students in three of his classes at MIT. He assigned all classes three reports over the course of the semester. The first class had to choose three due dates for themselves, up to and including the last day of class. The second had no deadlines — all three papers just had to be submitted by the last day of class. In his third class, he gave students three set deadlines over the course of the semester. At the end of the semester, he found that students with set deadlines received the best grades, the students with no deadlines had the worst, and those who could choose their own deadlines fell somewhere in the middle. Ariely concludes that _____ — whether by the professor or by students who recognize their own tendencies to delay things — improves self-control and performance.

① offering rewards
② removing obstacles
③ restricting freedom
④ increasing assignments
⑤ encouraging competition

32

The best way in which innovation changes our lives is by _____. The main theme of human history is that we become steadily more specialized in what we produce, and steadily more diversified in what we consume: we move away from unstable self-sufficiency to safer mutual interdependence. By concentrating on serving other people's needs for forty hours a week — which we call a job — you can spend the other seventy-two hours (not counting fifty-six hours in bed) relying on the services provided to you by other people. Innovation has made it possible to work for a fraction of a second in order to be able to afford to turn on an electric lamp for an hour, providing the quantity of light that would have required a whole day's work if you had to make it yourself by collecting and refining sesame oil or lamb fat to burn in a simple lamp, as much of humanity did in the not so distant past.
[3점]   *a fraction of a second: 아주 짧은 시간 **refine: 정제하다

① respecting the values of the old days
② enabling people to work for each other
③ providing opportunities to think creatively
④ satisfying customers with personalized services
⑤ introducing and commercializing unusual products

33

If you've ever made a poor choice, you might be interested in learning how to break that habit. One great way to trick your brain into doing so is to sign a "Ulysses Contract." The name of this life tip comes from the Greek myth about Ulysses, a captain whose ship sailed past the island of the Sirens, a tribe of dangerous women who lured victims to their death with their irresistible songs. Knowing that he would otherwise be unable to resist, Ulysses instructed his crew to stuff their ears with cotton and tie him to the ship's mast to prevent him from turning their ship towards the Sirens. It worked for him and you can do the same thing by _____. For example, if you want to stay off your cellphone and concentrate on your work, delete the apps that distract you or ask a friend to change your password!

*lure: 유혹하다 **mast: 돛대

① letting go of all-or-nothing mindset
② finding reasons why you want to change
③ locking yourself out of your temptations
④ building a plan and tracking your progress
⑤ focusing on breaking one bad habit at a time

34

Our homes aren't just ecosystems, they're unique ones, hosting species that are adapted to indoor environments and pushing evolution in new directions. Indoor microbes, insects, and rats have all evolved the ability to survive our chemical attacks, developing resistance to antibacterials, insecticides, and poisons. German cockroaches are known to have developed a distaste for glucose, which is commonly used as bait in roach traps. Some indoor insects, which have fewer opportunities to feed than their outdoor counterparts, seem to have developed the ability to survive when food is limited. Dunn and other ecologists have suggested that as the planet becomes more developed and more urban, more species will _____. Over a long enough time period, indoor living could drive our evolution, too. Perhaps my indoorsy self represents the future of humanity. [3점]

*glucose: 포도당 **bait: 미끼

① produce chemicals to protect themselves
② become extinct with the destroyed habitats
③ evolve the traits they need to thrive indoors
④ compete with outside organisms to find their prey
⑤ break the boundaries between wildlife and humans

35 다음 글에서 전체 흐름과 관계 없는 문장은?

Developing a personal engagement with poetry brings a number of benefits to you as an individual, in both a personal and a professional capacity. ① Writing poetry has been shown to have physical and mental benefits, with expressive writing found to improve immune system and lung function, diminish psychological distress, and enhance relationships. ② Poetry has long been used to aid different mental health needs, develop empathy, and reconsider our relationship with both natural and built environments. ③ Poetry is also an incredibly effective way of actively targeting the cognitive development period, improving your productivity and scientific creativity in the process. ④ Poetry is considered to be an easy and useful means of expressing emotions, but you fall into frustration when you realize its complexity. ⑤ In short, poetry has a lot to offer, if you give it the opportunity to do so.

*cognitive: 인지적인

[36~37] 주어진 글 다음에 이어질 글의 순서로 가장 적절한 것을 고르시오.

36

Things are changing. It has been reported that 42 percent of jobs in Canada are at risk, and 62 percent of jobs in America will be in danger due to advances in automation.

(A) However, what's difficult to automate is the ability to creatively solve problems. Whereas workers in "doing" roles can be replaced by robots, the role of creatively solving problems is more dependent on an irreplaceable individual.

(B) You might say that the numbers seem a bit unrealistic, but the threat is real. One fast food franchise has a robot that can flip a burger in ten seconds. It is just a simple task but the robot could replace an entire crew.

(C) Highly skilled jobs are also at risk. A supercomputer, for instance, can suggest available treatments for specific illnesses in an automated way, drawing on the body of medical research and data on diseases.

① (A) — (C) — (B) ② (B) — (A) — (C)
③ (B) — (C) — (A) ④ (C) — (A) — (B)
⑤ (C) — (B) — (A)

37

Each beech tree grows in a particular location and soil conditions can vary greatly in just a few yards. The soil can have a great deal of water or almost no water. It can be full of nutrients or not.

(A) This is taking place underground through the roots. Whoever has an abundance of sugar hands some over; whoever is running short gets help. Their network acts as a system to make sure that no trees fall too far behind.

(B) However, the rate is the same. Whether they are thick or thin, all the trees of the same species are using light to produce the same amount of sugar per leaf. Some trees have plenty of sugar and some have less, but the trees equalize this difference between them by transferring sugar.

(C) Accordingly, each tree grows more quickly or more slowly and produces more or less sugar, and thus you would expect every tree to be photosynthesizing at a different rate. [3점]

*photosynthesize: 광합성하다

① (A) — (C) — (B) ② (B) — (A) — (C)
③ (B) — (C) — (A) ④ (C) — (A) — (B)
⑤ (C) — (B) — (A)

38

Nevertheless, language is enormously important in human life and contributes largely to our ability to cooperate with each other in dealing with the world.

Should we use language to understand mind or mind to understand language? (①) Analytic philosophy historically assumes that language is basic and that mind would make sense if proper use of language was appreciated. (②) Modern cognitive science, however, rightly judges that language is just one aspect of mind of great importance in human beings but not fundamental to all kinds of thinking. (③) Countless species of animals manage to navigate the world, solve problems, and learn without using language, through brain mechanisms that are largely preserved in the minds of humans. (④) There is no reason to assume that language is fundamental to mental operations. (⑤) Our species *homo sapiens* has been astonishingly successful, which depended in part on language, first as an effective contributor to collaborative problem solving and much later, as collective memory through written records. [3점]

*appreciate: (제대로) 인식하다

39

If we could magically remove the glasses, we would find the two water bodies would not mix well.

Take two glasses of water. Put a little bit of orange juice into one and a little bit of lemon juice into the other. (①) What you have are essentially two glasses of water but with a completely different chemical makeup. (②) If we take the glass containing orange juice and heat it, we will still have two different glasses of water with different chemical makeups, but now they will also have different temperatures. (③) Perhaps they would mix a little where they met; however, they would remain separate because of their different chemical makeups and temperatures. (④) The warmer water would float on the surface of the cold water because of its lighter weight. (⑤) In the ocean we have bodies of water that differ in temperature and salt content; for this reason, they do not mix.

2022.11
12회

40 다음 글의 내용을 한 문장으로 요약하고자 한다. 빈칸 (A), (B)에 들어갈 말로 가장 적절한 것은?

One of the most powerful tools to find meaning in our lives is reflective journaling — thinking back on and writing about what has happened to us. In the 1990s, Stanford University researchers asked undergraduate students on spring break to journal about their most important personal values and their daily activities; others were asked to write about only the good things that happened to them in the day. Three weeks later, the students who had written about their values were happier, healthier, and more confident about their ability to handle stress than the ones who had only focused on the good stuff. By reflecting on how their daily activities supported their values, students had gained a new perspective on those activities and choices. Little stresses and hassles were now demonstrations of their values in action. Suddenly, their lives were full of meaningful activities. And all they had to do was reflect and write about it — positively reframing their experiences with their personal values.

*hassle: 귀찮은 일

⬇

Journaling about daily activities based on what we believe to be ____(A)____ can make us feel that our life is meaningful by ____(B)____ our experiences in a new way.

	(A)		(B)
①	factual	—	rethinking
②	worthwhile	—	rethinking
③	outdated	—	generalizing
④	objective	—	generalizing
⑤	demanding	—	describing

[41~42] 다음 글을 읽고, 물음에 답하시오.

Mike May lost his sight at the age of three. Because he had spent the majority of his life adapting to being blind — and even cultivating a skiing career in this state — his other senses compensated by growing (a) stronger. However, when his sight was restored through a surgery in his forties, his entire perception of reality was (b) disrupted. Instead of being thrilled that he could see now, as he'd expected, his brain was so overloaded with new visual stimuli that the world became a frightening and overwhelming place. After he'd learned to know his family through touch and smell, he found that he couldn't recognize his children with his eyes, and this left him puzzled. Skiing also became a lot harder as he struggled to adapt to the visual stimulation.

This (c) confusion occurred because his brain hadn't yet learned to see. Though we often tend to assume our eyes function as video cameras which relay information to our brain, advances in neuroscientific research have proven that this is actually not the case. Instead, sight is a collaborative effort between our eyes and our brains, and the way we process (d) visual reality depends on the way these two communicate. If communication between our eyes and our brains is disturbed, our perception of reality is altered accordingly. And because other areas of May's brain had adapted to process information primarily through his other senses, the process of learning how to see was (e) easier than he'd anticipated.

41 윗글의 제목으로 가장 적절한 것은?

① Eyes and Brain Working Together for Sight
② Visualization: A Useful Tool for Learning
③ Collaboration Between Vision and Sound
④ How to Ignore New Visual Stimuli
⑤ You See What You Believe

42 밑줄 친 (a)~(e) 중에서 문맥상 낱말의 쓰임이 적절하지 <u>않은</u> 것은?

① (a) ② (b) ③ (c) ④ (d) ⑤ (e)

[43~45] 다음 글을 읽고, 물음에 답하시오.

(A)

On my daughter Marie's 8th birthday, she received a bunch of presents from her friends at school. That evening, with her favorite present, a teddy bear, in her arms, we went to a restaurant to celebrate her birthday. Our server, a friendly woman, noticed my daughter holding the teddy bear and said, "My daughter loves teddy bears, too." Then, we started chatting about (a) <u>her</u> family.

(B)

When Marie came back out, I asked her what she had been doing. She said that she gave her teddy bear to our server so that she could give it to (b) <u>her</u> daughter. I was surprised at her sudden action because I could see how much she loved that bear already. (c) <u>She</u> must have seen the look on my face, because she said, "I can't imagine being stuck in a hospital bed. I just want her to get better soon."

(C)

I felt moved by Marie's words as we walked toward the car. Then, our server ran out to our car and thanked Marie for her generosity. The server said that (d) <u>she</u> had never had anyone doing anything like that for her family before. Later, Marie said it was her best birthday ever. I was so proud of her empathy and warmth, and this was an unforgettable experience for our family.

(D)

The server mentioned during the conversation that her daughter was in the hospital with a broken leg. (e) <u>She</u> also said that Marie looked about the same age as her daughter. She was so kind and attentive all evening, and even gave Marie cookies for free. After we finished our meal, we paid the bill and began to walk to our car when unexpectedly Marie asked me to wait and ran back into the restaurant.

43 주어진 글 (A)에 이어질 내용을 순서에 맞게 배열한 것으로 가장 적절한 것은?

① (B) ― (D) ― (C)   ② (C) ― (B) ― (D)
③ (C) ― (D) ― (B)   ④ (D) ― (B) ― (C)
⑤ (D) ― (C) ― (B)

44 밑줄 친 (a)~(e) 중에서 가리키는 대상이 나머지 넷과 <u>다른</u> 것은?

① (a) ② (b) ③ (c) ④ (d) ⑤ (e)

45 윗글에 관한 내용으로 적절하지 <u>않은</u> 것은?

① Marie는 테디 베어를 팔에 안고 식당에 갔다.
② 'I'는 Marie의 갑작스러운 행동에 놀랐다.
③ 종업원은 Marie의 관대함에 고마워했다.
④ 종업원은 자신의 딸이 팔이 부러져서 병원에 있다고 말했다.
⑤ 종업원은 Marie에게 쿠키를 무료로 주었다.

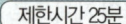

• MP3 파일을 들으며 다음 빈칸을 채우시오. (듣기 어려운 발음이나 정답의 단서가 되는 부분에 빈칸을 만들었습니다.)

01 다음을 듣고, 남자가 하는 말의 목적으로 가장 적절한 것을 고르시오.

[Chime bell rings.]

M : Good morning. This is Ethan Cooper from the Reindeer Mountain maintenance office. Last night, we had 20cm of heavy snow. Most of the snow _____ _____ _____ _____ _____ _____ in the morning, but some of it froze in the shade. For hikers' safety, _____ _____ _____ _____ _____ _____ covered with ice. At this moment, Sunrise Trail and Lakeview Trail are ★ _____ _____ _____. I'll make an announcement later when the trails are ready to be reopened. Until then, keep in mind that Sunrise Trail and Lakeview Trail are closed. Thank you.

02 대화를 듣고, 남자의 의견으로 가장 적절한 것을 고르시오.

M : Honey, what are you doing?

W : I'm looking for the measuring spoons. Do you know where they are?

M : _____ ____ _____ _____ ★ _____. Why do you need them?

W : The recipe says four teaspoons of sugar.

M : Dear, you don't have to follow the recipe as it is.

W : What do you mean?

M : A recipe is just an example. You don't need to add _____ _____ _____ ____ ★ _____ as stated in the recipe.

W : Hmm. Right. Sometimes the food is too sweet when I cook based on the recipe instructions.

M : See? You don't need to ★ _____ _____ _____ _____.

W : Okay. I'll remember that.

03 대화를 듣고, 두 사람의 관계를 가장 잘 나타낸 것을 고르시오.

[Door knocks.]

W : Can I come in?

M : Yes. Oh, Ms. Smith. Did you read the email I sent?

W : I did. I liked your game scenario. _____ _____ _____ _____ were very mysterious. How did you create the characters?

M : Actually, old science fiction movies ★ _____ ____ ____ _____ those characters.

W : Interesting. Now, could you describe the main character more specifically? It'll be helpful when I compose _____ _____ _____ for the character.

M : Well, he's a thrill seeker. So, a strong, bold, and rhythmic sound would suit him.

W : Okay. Do you need anything else?

M : I also want you to make some background music.

W : Of course. When do you need them?

M : By December 21st. I'd like to _____ _____ ____ _____ _____ _____ _____ by then.

W : All right. Then I'll talk to you later.

04 대화를 듣고, 그림에서 대화의 내용과 일치하지 <u>않는</u> 것을 고르시오.

M: Hi, Chelsea. Did you finish your art assignment?

W: Oh, my dream room drawing? Yes. Here's the picture.

M: Wow, it's so creative. There is a staircase next to the door.

W: Yes. I've always dreamed of a room with two floors. Look at _____ _____ _____ _____ _____ _____ ✪ _____ .

M: They look very stylish. And I like the flower picture above the sofa. It'll bring warmth to your room.

W: Thanks. Check out the square-shaped ✪ _____ _____ _____ _____ .

M: It goes well with this place. Oh, there is a bookshelf by the sofa.

W: You're right. I want to _____ ____ _____ _____ _____ .

M: That's a good idea.

05 대화를 듣고, 남자가 할 일로 가장 적절한 것을 고르시오.

W: Jamie, is the cartoon artist on her way?

M: Yes. She'll arrive at our studio in an hour.

W: Perfect. Let's check if we have everything ready for our talk show.

M: Okay. I ____ ____ __ _____ ____ _____ _____ yesterday.

W: Great. And I bought a drink and put it on the table.

M: Good. Did you prepare a pencil? The artist said _____ _____ ✪ _____ ____ ___ during the live show.

W: Oh, she told me that she'll bring her own pencil.

M: She did? Then we don't need it.

W: Yeah. By the way, where's the sketchbook?

M: Oops. __ _____ ___ ___ ___ _____ . I'll go get it right now.

W: Fine. Then I'll check the microphones.

M: Thanks.

06 대화를 듣고, 여자가 지불할 금액을 고르시오.

M: Welcome to Crispy Fried Chicken. What would you like to order?

W: What kind of chicken do you have?

M: We only have two kinds. Fried chicken is $15 and barbecue chicken is $20.

W: I'll have one fried and one barbecue chicken.

M: Okay. Would you like _____ _____ _____ _____ _____ _____ ? They're our most popular side dish.

W: How much are they?

M: One basket of potato chips is $2.

W: Then I'll get one basket.

M: _____ _____ ___ ____ ?

W: Yes. And can I use this coupon for a free soda?

M: Of course. You can grab ____ _____ _____ _____ ✪ _____ .

W: Great. Here's my credit card.

07 대화를 듣고, 남자가 얼음낚시를 갈 수 <u>없는</u> 이유를 고르시오.

[Cell phone rings.]

W: Leo, I'm sorry I missed your call. What's up?

M: Well, I just called to tell you that I can't go ice fishing with you this weekend.

W: Oh, no. I heard the weather will be perfect this weekend.

M: I'm sorry. I really wish I could go.

W: Didn't you say _____ ____ _____ _____ this weekend?

M: I am. It's not because of work. Actually, I hurt my wrist.

W: That's terrible. Are you okay?

M: Don't worry. I'll be fine.

W: How did you get injured?

M: I was playing basketball with a friend and ✪ _____ ___ _____ .

W: Did you go to the hospital?

M: I did. The doctor told me that _____ ___ _____ ___ _____ _____ .

W: That's good. I hope you feel better soon.

08 대화를 듣고, Kids' Pottery Class에 관해 언급되지 않은 것을 고르시오.

M: Honey, look at this flyer about Kids' Pottery Class.

W: Okay. Let's take a look.

M: I think our little Austin would love to _____ _____ _____ _____ ☆ _____.

W: I think so, too. It says that the class is held on October 8th. We can take him there on that day.

M: Great. And it's held in Pottery Village. _____ _____ _____ _____ from our home.

W: That's so close. And check out the price. The class costs only $15.

M: That's reasonable. We should sign up. How can we register for the class?

W: It says you can _____ _____ _____ _____ _____ to register online.

M: Okay. Let's do it right away.

09 2022 Online Whistling Championship에 관한 다음 내용을 듣고, 일치하지 않는 것을 고르시오.

W: Hello, listeners. The most interesting music competition is back! You can now sign up for the 2022 Online Whistling Championship. You can select any song that you like, but note that _____ _____ _____ _____ _____ _____ is limited to three minutes. To enter the competition, you must upload your video on our website by December 4th. When recording your whistling, _____ _____ _____ _____ _____ ☆ _____ _____ on the microphone. Winners will be decided _____ _____ _____ _____. The result will be announced on our website. We look forward to your enthusiastic participation.

10 다음 표를 보면서 대화를 듣고, 두 사람이 선택할 커튼을 고르시오.

M: Honey, I'm looking at a shopping site to choose curtains for our bedroom. But there are too many options to consider.

W: Okay. Let's pick one together.

M: I don't think we should spend more than $100.

W: I agree. Let's drop this one. And some of them _____ _____ _____ _____ _____.

M: Fantastic. We won't have to pay for dry cleaning all the time.

W: Good for us. Let's cross out this one then. What about a blackout option?

M: We definitely need it. It'll completely block sunlight, _____ _____ _____ _____ ☆ _____. And which color do you like?

W: I don't mind _____ _____ _____ _____ _____.

M: Okay. Then we narrowed it down to one.

W: Well then, let's choose this one.

11 대화를 듣고, 남자의 마지막 말에 대한 여자의 응답으로 가장 적절한 것을 고르시오.

M: Excuse me. Is this really the line for the rollercoaster?

W: Yes. This is the line for the ride.

M: Oh, no. I can't believe it. There are so many people standing in line. _____ _____ _____ _____ _____ _____?

W: _____

12 대화를 듣고, 여자의 마지막 말에 대한 남자의 응답으로 가장 적절한 것을 고르시오.

W: Chris, what are you looking at?

M: A little boy is ☆ _____ _____ _____ _____ _____ _____. He's all by himself.

W: Oh, I see him, too. We should ask him if he's lost.

M: _____

13 대화를 듣고, 남자의 마지막 말에 대한 여자의 응답으로 가장 적절한 것을 고르시오.

M : Hi, Ava.

W : Hi, Samuel. Are you all set for the job interview?

M : I'm still working on it. I've come up with ____ _____ ____ _____ the interviewer might ask.

W : Good job. Preparing answers to those questions will help you for the interview.

M : But I think I'm not ready.

W : Hmm. Have you thought about how you'll make a good first impression?

M : Could you be more specific?

W : You know a smile makes you look confident. Also, people usually dress up ____ _____ ____ ✪_____ _____.

M : That's a good point.

W : I believe you'll get a good interview result with a proper presentation of yourself.

M : Okay. Then I'm going to _____ _____ ____ _____ ____ ____ _____ _____.

W : _____

14 대화를 듣고, 여자의 마지막 말에 대한 남자의 응답으로 가장 적절한 것을 고르시오.

W : Excuse me.

M : Yes, ma'am. How can I help you?

W : How much are those shoes?

M : They're $60. But today only, we're offering a 30% discount.

W : That's a good price. Do you have a size six?

M : Sure. Here they are. Take a seat here and try them on.

W : Thank you. *[Pause]* Well, these shoes _____ ____ _____ ✪_____ _____ _____. Can I get a size six and a half?

M : I'm sorry. That size in this color is sold out.

W : Do you have _____ _____ ___ __ _____ _____?

M : Let me check. *[Typing sounds]* We have ____ ____ _____ ___ _____.

W : A green pair sounds good. I want to try them on.

M : _____

15 다음 상황 설명을 듣고, Amelia가 Jacob 교수에게 할 말로 가장 적절한 것을 고르시오.

M : Amelia is a high school student. She is working on a psychology project. She thinks that an interview with an expert in the field will make her project even better. She emails Professor Jacob, who is a ✪_____ _____ _____. Even though he's busy, she manages to set up an interview with him. Unfortunately, on that morning, she eats a sandwich and feels sick. She knows this interview is important, and difficult to set up again. But she can't go meet him because of ____ ✪_____ _____. So she wants to ask him ___ ___ _____ _____ _____ _____. In this situation, what would Amelia most likely say to Professor Jacob?

Amelia : _____

2022.11
12회

[16~17] 다음을 듣고, 물음에 답하시오.

W : Good morning, students. These days we can easily send messages to each other using phones or computers. However, communication has not always been as simple as it is today. Here are a few ways people in the past _____ ___ _____ _____ _____. First, some tribes used a special drum. They were able to send warnings or important information ____ _____ ____ ✪_____ ___ _____. Next, other people used smoke to send messages over long distances. For example, our ancestors used smoke ____ _____ _____ _____ _____. Third, a pigeon was a reliable means of communication. It always found its way home with messages attached to its legs. Finally, a horse was one of the most efficient ways to communicate. The horse with a messenger on its back delivered mail more _____ _____ ✪_____. Now you may understand the ways of sending messages back in the old days. Then let's take a look in detail at each communication method.

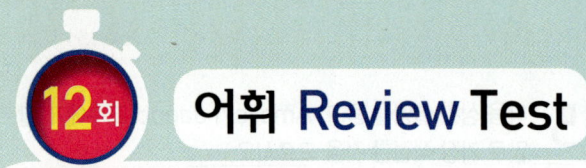
✱ 다음 영어는 우리말 뜻을, 우리말은 영어 단어를 〈보기〉에서 찾아 쓰시오.

01 cite _____

02 tribe _____

03 equator _____

04 immune _____

05 temptation _____

06 심한 _____

07 미신 _____

08 호의적인 _____

09 목격하다 _____

10 보수, 관리 _____

[보기]	
부족	aid
유혹	severe
적도	witness
면역의	favorable
숙련된	superstition
언급하다	maintenance

✱ 다음 우리말에 알맞은 영어 표현을 찾아 연결하시오.

11 ~을 이용하다 •   • draw on

12 ~을 방해하다 •   • keep track of

13 삭제하다 •   • manage to

14 ~을 기록하다 •   • interfere with

15 간신히 ~하다 •   • wipe out

✱ 다음 우리말과 같은 표현이 되도록 알맞은 단어를 〈보기〉에서 찾아 쓰시오.

[보기]

lung / experienced / unstable / motivator / distaste / empathy
reflective / collective / renowned / consequence / indoorsy / textile

16 집단 기억 ➡ _____ memory

17 공감과 따뜻함 ➡ _____ and warmth

18 성찰적 일기 쓰기 ➡ _____ journaling

19 숙련된 안전 요원 ➡ _____ lifeguards

20 가장 강력한 동기 ➡ the strongest _____

21 불안정한 자급자족 ➡ _____ self-sufficiency

22 믿을 수 없는 결과 ➡ unbelievable _____

23 포도당에 대한 혐오감 ➡ a(n) _____ for glucose

24 가까이에 있는 직물 공장 ➡ a nearby _____ factory

25 유명한 심리학 교수 ➡ _____ psychology professor

26 필요를 없애다 ➡ (elaborate / eliminate) the need

27 이 차이를 균등하게 하다 ➡ (equalize / utilize) this difference

28 세계를 항해하다 ➡ (obligate / navigate) the world

29 과제의 마감일을 연장하다 ➡ (extend / shorten) the deadline for the assignment

30 적들의 공격을 알리다 ➡ (signal / ignore) attacks from enemies

* 다음 문장의 빈칸에 알맞은 단어를 〈보기〉에서 찾아 쓰시오.

[보기]

perspective / loyal / attentive / abundance / welfare / engagement
accumulate / challenge / function / means / illegal / irreplaceable

---

31 그녀는 저녁 내내 매우 친절하고 세심했다.

➡ She was so kind and _____ all evening.

32 비둘기는 믿을 수 있는 통신의 수단이었다.

➡ A pigeon was a reliable _____ of communication.

33 옥신은 줄기의 옆면에 축적하는 경향이 있다.

➡ Auxins tend to _____ on the side of the stem.

34 그것은 불법적이거나 의심스러운 수단을 통해 얻어졌다.

➡ It was obtained through _____ and questionable means.

35 풍부한 당을 가진 누구든 일부를 건네준다.

➡ Whoever has a(n) _____ of sugar hands some over.

36 그 역할은 대체 불가능한 개인에 더 의존한다.

➡ The role is more dependent on a(n) _____ individual.

37 저는 이 회사의 충성스럽고 필수적인 구성원이었습니다.

➡ I have been a(n) _____ and essential member of this company.

38 우리는 종종 우리의 눈이 비디오카메라로서 기능한다고 가정하는 경향이 있다.

➡ We often tend to assume our eyes _____ as video cameras.

39 학생들은 그 활동들과 선택들에 대해 새로운 관점을 얻었다.

➡ Students had gained a new _____ on those activities and choices.

40 시와의 개인적 관계를 발전시키는 것은 많은 이점을 가져다준다.

➡ Developing a personal _____ with poetry brings a number of benefits.

1회 모의고사 ───────── 문제편 p. 10~21

01 ④ 02 ⑤ 03 ② 04 ③ 05 ⑤ 06 ③ 07 ② 08 ④ 09 ③ 10 ②
11 ② 12 ④ 13 ① 14 ④ 15 ④ 16 ⑤ 17 ③ 18 ③ 19 ③ 20 ②
21 ① 22 ① 23 ⑤ 24 ① 25 ④ 26 ④ 27 ② 28 ② 29 ④ 30 ⑤
31 ① 32 ③ 33 ④ 34 ① 35 ② 36 ⑤ 37 ⑤ 38 ③ 39 ⑤ 40 ①
41 ① 42 ② 43 ④ 44 ③ 45 ②

2회 모의고사 ───────── 문제편 p. 28~39

01 ⑤ 02 ② 03 ⑤ 04 ⑤ 05 ② 06 ③ 07 ⑤ 08 ④ 09 ④ 10 ③
11 ③ 12 ⑤ 13 ② 14 ① 15 ① 16 ① 17 ④ 18 ③ 19 ① 20 ②
21 ① 22 ③ 23 ① 24 ⑤ 25 ③ 26 ④ 27 ④ 28 ④ 29 ② 30 ③
31 ② 32 ⑤ 33 ③ 34 ⑤ 35 ④ 36 ④ 37 ③ 38 ① 39 ② 40 ①
41 ① 42 ④ 43 ⑤ 44 ④ 45 ②

3회 모의고사 ───────── 문제편 p. 46~57

01 ⑤ 02 ⑤ 03 ③ 04 ⑤ 05 ② 06 ② 07 ① 08 ③ 09 ④ 10 ②
11 ② 12 ① 13 ③ 14 ① 15 ③ 16 ③ 17 ④ 18 ③ 19 ② 20 ⑤
21 ⑤ 22 ① 23 ③ 24 ① 25 ⑤ 26 ⑤ 27 ③ 28 ④ 29 ⑤ 30 ④
31 ① 32 ③ 33 ① 34 ② 35 ④ 36 ④ 37 ② 38 ④ 39 ⑤ 40 ①
41 ② 42 ③ 43 ④ 44 ④ 45 ④

4회 모의고사 ───────── 문제편 p. 66~77

01 ③ 02 ① 03 ① 04 ⑤ 05 ② 06 ④ 07 ② 08 ③ 09 ④ 10 ④
11 ① 12 ⑤ 13 ② 14 ③ 15 ② 16 ⑤ 17 ③ 18 ① 19 ① 20 ⑤
21 ② 22 ① 23 ⑤ 24 ① 25 ④ 26 ④ 27 ③ 28 ④ 29 ③ 30 ④
31 ② 32 ① 33 ② 34 ⑤ 35 ③ 36 ② 37 ⑤ 38 ④ 39 ③ 40 ①
41 ② 42 ⑤ 43 ④ 44 ⑤ 45 ④

5회 모의고사 ───────── 문제편 p. 84~95

01 ③ 02 ① 03 ③ 04 ⑤ 05 ④ 06 ③ 07 ⑤ 08 ② 09 ⑤ 10 ④
11 ① 12 ③ 13 ⑤ 14 ② 15 ③ 16 ③ 17 ④ 18 ② 19 ② 20 ①
21 ② 22 ① 23 ⑤ 24 ① 25 ③ 26 ⑤ 27 ④ 28 ⑤ 29 ③ 30 ⑤
31 ② 32 ② 33 ⑤ 34 ① 35 ③ 36 ③ 37 ② 38 ③ 39 ④ 40 ①
41 ① 42 ④ 43 ⑤ 44 ② 45 ④

6회 모의고사 ───────── 문제편 p. 102~113

01 ② 02 ① 03 ① 04 ④ 05 ⑤ 06 ③ 07 ④ 08 ③ 09 ⑤ 10 ④
11 ① 12 ③ 13 ② 14 ⑤ 15 ⑤ 16 ③ 17 ④ 18 ② 19 ① 20 ⑤
21 ① 22 ③ 23 ② 24 ① 25 ④ 26 ④ 27 ⑤ 28 ⑤ 29 ④ 30 ②
31 ④ 32 ① 33 ④ 34 ③ 35 ④ 36 ② 37 ⑤ 38 ② 39 ⑤ 40 ②
41 ① 42 ③ 43 ④ 44 ④ 45 ③

7회 모의고사 ───────── 문제편 p. 122~133

01 ④ 02 ① 03 ⑤ 04 ④ 05 ② 06 ④ 07 ② 08 ④ 09 ④ 10 ②
11 ① 12 ⑤ 13 ① 14 ① 15 ① 16 ② 17 ④ 18 ③ 19 ③ 20 ②
21 ③ 22 ③ 23 ② 24 ② 25 ⑤ 26 ③ 27 ③ 28 ⑤ 29 ② 30 ⑤
31 ② 32 ① 33 ① 34 ② 35 ④ 36 ② 37 ⑤ 38 ⑤ 39 ⑤ 40 ③
41 ③ 42 ③ 43 ⑤ 44 ④ 45 ④

8회 모의고사 ───────── 문제편 p. 140~151

01 ③ 02 ③ 03 ⑤ 04 ④ 05 ② 06 ③ 07 ④ 08 ③ 09 ④ 10 ④
11 ① 12 ② 13 ① 14 ① 15 ① 16 ⑤ 17 ③ 18 ⑤ 19 ⑤ 20 ②
21 ⑤ 22 ③ 23 ④ 24 ① 25 ④ 26 ② 27 ⑤ 28 ③ 29 ⑤ 30 ④
31 ② 32 ① 33 ① 34 ④ 35 ④ 36 ② 37 ④ 38 ③ 39 ② 40 ④
41 ③ 42 ③ 43 ⑤ 44 ③ 45 ②

9회 모의고사 ───────── 문제편 p. 158~169

01 ⑤ 02 ① 03 ③ 04 ⑤ 05 ① 06 ③ 07 ④ 08 ③ 09 ④ 10 ④
11 ① 12 ④ 13 ① 14 ③ 15 ⑤ 16 ③ 17 ③ 18 ⑤ 19 ② 20 ②
21 ⑤ 22 ④ 23 ② 24 ① 25 ④ 26 ④ 27 ④ 28 ⑤ 29 ④ 30 ②
31 ① 32 ③ 33 ② 34 ① 35 ② 36 ② 37 ③ 38 ⑤ 39 ⑤ 40 ①
41 ② 42 ⑤ 43 ④ 44 ③ 45 ④

10회 모의고사 ───────── 문제편 p. 178~189

01 ④ 02 ② 03 ⑤ 04 ⑤ 05 ③ 06 ⑤ 07 ① 08 ④ 09 ④ 10 ③
11 ① 12 ② 13 ① 14 ⑤ 15 ② 16 ③ 17 ④ 18 ⑤ 19 ① 20 ②
21 ④ 22 ⑤ 23 ⑤ 24 ③ 25 ③ 26 ③ 27 ④ 28 ⑤ 29 ④ 30 ③
31 ② 32 ② 33 ① 34 ② 35 ④ 36 ③ 37 ① 38 ④ 39 ② 40 ①
41 ① 42 ③ 43 ② 44 ④ 45 ③

11회 모의고사 ───────── 문제편 p. 196~207

01 ② 02 ① 03 ⑤ 04 ④ 05 ① 06 ⑤ 07 ⑤ 08 ④ 09 ③ 10 ③
11 ① 12 ② 13 ④ 14 ③ 15 ④ 16 ① 17 ⑤ 18 ⑤ 19 ① 20 ④
21 ④ 22 ⑤ 23 ④ 24 ② 25 ④ 26 ③ 27 ⑤ 28 ⑤ 29 ④ 30 ④
31 ① 32 ② 33 ④ 34 ④ 35 ④ 36 ④ 37 ③ 38 ⑤ 39 ④ 40 ①
41 ⑤ 42 ③ 43 ④ 44 ② 45 ③

12회 모의고사 ───────── 문제편 p. 214~225

01 ① 02 ① 03 ② 04 ④ 05 ⑤ 06 ④ 07 ① 08 ④ 09 ④ 10 ②
11 ① 12 ② 13 ③ 14 ① 15 ② 16 ② 17 ④ 18 ② 19 ② 20 ⑤
21 ③ 22 ① 23 ⑤ 24 ① 25 ④ 26 ③ 27 ⑤ 28 ③ 29 ④ 30 ④
31 ③ 32 ② 33 ③ 34 ③ 35 ④ 36 ③ 37 ⑤ 38 ⑤ 39 ③ 40 ②
41 ① 42 ⑤ 43 ④ 44 ③ 45 ④

  **판매량 1위, 만족도 1위, 추천도서 1위!!**

쉬운 개념 이해와 정확한 **연산력**을 키운다 !!

★ **수력충전**이 꼭 필요한 학생들

- 계산력이 약해서 시험에서 실수가 잦은 학생
- 개념 이해가 어려워 자신감이 없는 학생
- 부족한 단원을 빠르게 보충하려는 학생

- 스스로 원리를 터득하기 원하는 학생
- 수학의 전체적인 흐름을 잡기 원하는 학생
- 선행 학습을 하고 싶은 학생

1 쉬운 개념 이해와 다양한 문제의 풀이를 따라가면서 수학의 연산 원리를 이해하는 교재!!

2 매일매일 반복하는 연산학습으로 기본 개념을 자연스럽고 완벽하게 이해하는 교재!!

3 단원별, 유형별 다양한 문제 접근 방법으로 부족한 부분의 문제를 집중 학습할 수 있는 교재!!

─────────────────────────────── ★ **수력충전** 시리즈

초등 수력충전 [기본]

초등 수학 1-1, 2 / 초등 수학 2-1, 2
초등 수학 3-1, 2 / 초등 수학 4-1, 2
초등 수학 5-1, 2 / 초등 수학 6-1, 2

중등 수력충전

중등 수학 1-1, 2
중등 수학 2-1, 2
중등 수학 3-1, 2

고등 수력충전

공통수학 1, 공통수학 2
대수 / 미적분 I / 확률과 통계

Xistory stands for e**X**tra **I**ntensive story for the University Entrance Examination.
Xistory는 e**X**tra **I**ntensive story의 약자로 [**특별한 수능 단련 이야기**]라는 의미입니다.

대한민국 No.1 수능 기출 문제집 – 자이스토리

국어
- 국어 기본 (고1)
- 언어(문법) 기본 (고1)
- 언어와 매체 실전 (고3)
- 화법과 언어 (고2)
- 화법과 작문 실전 (고3)
- 독서 기본 (고1)
- 독서와 작문 (고2)
- 독서 실전 (고3)
- 문학 기본 (고1)
- 문학 완성 (고2)
- 문학 실전 (고3)
- 수능 국어 개념어 총정리
- 고등 국어 문법 총정리 ★
- 전국연합 모의고사 고1 국어 ★
- 전국연합 모의고사 고2 국어 ★
- 연도별 모의고사 고3 국어 (언어와 매체)
- 연도별 모의고사 고3 국어 (화법과 작문)

영어
- 독해 기본 (고1) ★
- 독해 완성 (고2) ★
- 독해 실전 (고3) ★
- 고난도 영어 독해
- 고등 영문법 기본
- 어법·어휘 기본 (고1) ★
- 어법·어휘 완성 (고2)
- 어법·어휘 실전 (고3)
- 듣기 기본 (고1 전국연합 모의고사 24회)
- 듣기 완성 (고2 전국연합 모의고사 24회)
- 듣기 실전 (고3 수능 대비 모의고사 35회)
- 전국연합 모의고사 고1 영어
- 전국연합 모의고사 고2 영어
- 연도별 모의고사 고3 영어

수학
- 공통수학 1 ★
- 공통수학 2 ★
- 고2 대수
- 고2 미적분 I
- 고2 확률과 통계
- 고3 수학 I ★
- 고3 수학 II ★
- 고3 미적분
- 고3 확률과 통계
- 고3 기하
- 전국연합 모의고사 고1 수학 (공통수학)
- 연도별 모의고사 고3 수학
- 내신 핵심 기출 1000제 (공통수학 1)
- 내신 핵심 기출 1000제 (공통수학 2)

사회
- 통합사회 1, 2 ★
- 내신 한국사 1, 2 ★
- 고2 사회와 문화
- 고2 세계시민과 지리
- 고2 현대사회와 윤리
- 고2 세계사
- 사회·문화 ★
- 한국지리
- 세계지리
- 윤리와 사상
- 생활과 윤리 ★
- 수능 한국사
- 동아시아사
- 전국연합 모의고사 통합사회 (고1, 2)

과학
- 통합과학 1, 2 ★
- 개념 화학 I
- 개념 생명과학 I
- 개념 물리학 I
- 개념 지구과학 I
- 고2 화학
- 고2 생명과학
- 고2 물리학
- 고2 지구과학
- 화학 I ★
- 화학 II
- 생명과학 I ★
- 생명과학 II
- 물리학 I ★
- 지구과학 I ★
- 지구과학 II
- 전국연합 모의고사 통합과학 (고1, 2)

★ 는 강남인강 강의교재
는 2026 신간 교재

edu.ingang.go.kr
Xistory
강남구청 인터넷 수능방송 공인인시

자이스토리는...
수능 문제 은행 최고의 교재입니다.

수능 공부는 자이스토리가 제일 중요합니다. 자이스토리에 수록된 수능 기출문제는 일반 문제와 달리 출제위원들이 심혈을 기울여 만든 고품격의 문제들이면서, 수능에 또다시 출제될 수 있기 때문입니다. 그래서 일반 문제집 10권을 푸는 것보다 자이스토리를 한 번 더 푸는 게 훨씬 효과적입니다.

자이스토리는...
수능 유형 분석이 쉽고 빠릅니다.

자이스토리는 수능 문제와 평가원 모의고사 문제를 유형별, 단원별로 수록했습니다. 문제를 풀면서 답을 구하는 과정을 통해 출제자의 의도와 유형을 쉽게 파악할 수 있습니다. 더불어 자주 출제되는 유형, 정답을 빨리 찾는 방법, 매력적인 오답을 피하는 방법 등도 자연스럽게 체득할 수 있습니다.

자이스토리는...
수능 문제를 수험생 스스로 예측합니다.

단원별, 유형별, 난이도별로 분류된 자이스토리를 차례대로 풀어 가면 난이도의 흐름, 출제 빈도의 흐름, 신유형 문제의 출제 변화 양상 등을 쉽게 파악할 수 있습니다. 그래서 '이번 수능에는 이런 문제들이 반드시 출제될 거야.'라는 예측을 수험생 스스로 할 수 있습니다.

[검색] 수경출판사 · 자이스토리　　 ID: xistory_insta

등록번호 제2013-000088호　**발행처** (주)수경출판사　**발행인** 박영란　**발행일** 2026년 1월 30일 (제3쇄)
홈페이지 www.book-sk.co.kr　**대표전화** 02-333-6080　**구입문의** 02-333-7812　**팩스** 02-333-7197
주소 서울시 영등포구 양평로 21길 26 (양평동 5가) IS비즈타워 807호 (우07207)
내용문의 02-333-6414　**편집책임** 윤재희/고은미/정의인/김민주　**디자인** 박지영/전찬우
마케팅 임순규/손형관/서정훈/김민주　**제작물류** 조인호/류혜리/임영훈

자이스토리 · 전국연합 모의고사 고1 영어

53740

9 791162 409046

ISBN 979-11-6240-904-6

정가 19,500원

🍀 차 례

pdf 파일

1회 모의고사

12

- □ upload ⓥ 올리다, 업로드하다
- □ social media 소셜 미디어
- □ waste ⓝ 쓰레기
- □ cafeteria ⓝ (구내)식당
- □ attention ⓝ 관심

13

- □ have trouble -ing ~하는 데 어려움을 겪다
- □ manage ⓥ 관리하다
- □ stay up late (늦게까지) 자지 않고 있다
- □ focus ⓝ 집중력
- □ memory ⓝ 기억력

14

- □ badminton ⓝ 배드민턴
- □ hobby ⓝ 취미
- □ reduce ⓥ 줄이다
- □ prepare ⓥ 준비하다
- □ comfortable ⓐ 편한

15

- □ prepare ⓥ 준비하다
- □ expect ⓥ 예상하다, 기대하다
- □ sudden ⓐ 갑작스러운
- □ weather forecast 일기 예보
- □ as planned 예정대로
- □ fortunate ⓐ 다행인
- □ volunteer ⓝ 자원봉사자

16~17

- □ photographer ⓝ 사진작가
- □ sidewalk ⓝ 보도, 인도
- □ amaze ⓥ 놀라게 하다
- □ historical ⓐ 역사적인
- □ miss ⓥ 놓치다
- □ once-in-a-lifetime ⓐ 일생에 한 번 뿐인
- □ sunset ⓝ 일몰
- □ necessary ⓐ 필요한
- □ traveler ⓝ 여행자
- □ importance ⓝ 중요성

18

- □ introduce ⓥ 소개하다
- □ handmade ⓐ 수공예의
- □ organize ⓥ 조직하다
- □ exhibition plan 전시 배치도
- □ inform ⓥ 알리다
- □ requirement ⓝ 요구 사항
- □ further ⓐ 추가적인
- □ assistance ⓝ 도움

19

- □ damp ⓐ 습기 찬
- □ thick ⓐ (공기가) 짙은
- □ make out 알아보다, 식별하다
- □ shadow ⓝ 그림자
- □ shaking ⓐ 떨리는
- □ figure ⓝ 형체, 형상
- □ faint ⓐ 희미한
- □ beam ⓝ 빛줄기
- □ crack ⓝ 틈새

- □ escape ⓥ (웃음 등이) 새어 나오다
- □ stare at ~을 바라보다
- □ hop ⓥ 깡충 뛰다
- □ at ease 편안한

20

- □ gestural ⓐ 몸짓의
- □ nod ⓥ 고개를 끄덕이다
- □ complement ⓥ 보완하다
- □ layer ⓝ 겹
- □ indicate ⓥ 나타내다, 보여 주다
- □ honesty ⓝ 정직함
- □ atmosphere ⓝ 분위기
- □ collaboration ⓝ 협력
- □ palm ⓝ 손바닥
- □ willing to 기꺼이 ~ 하는
- □ engage in ~에 참여하다
- □ over-gesturing ⓝ 과도한 몸짓
- □ distract from ~에 집중이 안 되게 하다
- □ chaos ⓝ 혼돈
- □ overshadow ⓥ 가리다

21

- □ gene editing 유전자 편집
- □ logical ⓐ 합리적인
- □ preferable ⓐ 바람직한
- □ correct ⓥ 교정하다
- □ transform ⓥ 변형하다, 바꾸다
- □ temptation ⓝ 유혹
- □ superior ⓐ 우수한
- □ characteristics ⓝ 특징

- □ pursuit ⓝ 추구
- □ slippery ⓐ 미끄러운
- □ slope ⓝ 경사
- □ end up 결국 ~하게 되다
- □ alteration ⓝ 개조, 변경
- □ stick to ~을 고수하다
- □ belief ⓝ 믿음, 신념
- □ moral ⓐ 도덕적인

22

- □ grade school 초등학교
- □ certainty ⓝ 확실함, 확실한 것
- □ carry ⓥ 담고 있다
- □ organism ⓝ 유기체
- □ practice ⓝ 실제
- □ succession ⓝ 연속
- □ logical ⓐ 논리적인
- □ observation ⓝ 관찰
- □ uncertainty ⓝ 불확실함
- □ in progress 진행 중인

23

- □ a wealth of 수많은
- □ supervisor ⓝ 상사
- □ perceive ⓥ 여기다, 인식하다
- □ motivate ⓥ 동기를 부여하다
- □ value ⓥ 소중히 여기다
- □ peer ⓝ 또래, 동료
- □ relatedness ⓝ 관계성
- □ internalization ⓝ 내면화
- □ fuel ⓥ 자극하다, 연료를 공급하다
- □ competence ⓝ 유능함, 능숙함

- □ crucial ⓐ 중요한
- □ enhance ⓥ 강화하다, 향상시키다
- □ a sense of connectedness 유대감
- □ take on ~에 맞서다

24

- □ technique ⓝ 기법, 기술
- □ light up 밝히다
- □ intense ⓐ 강렬한
- □ associated with ~과 연관된
- □ pronunciation ⓝ 발음
- □ strengthen ⓥ 강화시키다
- □ connective structure 결합 구조
- □ cell ⓝ 세포
- □ overall ⓐ 전반적인
- □ concentration ⓝ 집중력
- □ in silence 조용히
- □ in particular 특히
- □ encourage ⓥ 장려하다
- □ wire ⓥ 연결하다

25

- □ consume ⓥ 먹다
- □ sort ⓥ 분류하다
- □ frequency ⓝ 빈도
- □ frequently ⓐⓓ 자주
- □ account for ~을 차지하다
- □ percentage ⓝ 비율
- □ combine ⓥ 합치다

- □ share ⓝ 몫
- □ rarely ⓐⓓ 거의 ~ 않는

26

- □ move ⓥ 이주하다
- □ major ⓥ 전공하다
- □ earn ⓥ 받다
- □ doctoral degree 박사 학위
- □ economics ⓝ 경제학
- □ influential ⓐ 영향력 있는
- □ award ⓥ 수여하다
- □ Economic Sciences 경제학

27

- □ explore ⓥ 탐험하다
- □ amazing ⓐ 놀라운
- □ walking path 보행로
- □ operation ⓝ 운영
- □ admission ⓝ 입장
- □ seasonal ⓐ 계절에 따른
- □ indoors ⓐⓓ 실내에
- □ depart ⓥ 출발하다

28

- □ stuffed toy 봉제 인형
- □ transform ⓥ 변형하다, 바꾸다
- □ decorative ⓐ 장식의
- □ flowerpot ⓝ 화분
- □ participation fee 참가비
- □ material ⓝ 재료
- □ detail ⓝ 세부 사항

29

- □ routine ⓝ 루틴, 일상의 과정
- □ enable ⓥ ~할 수 있게 하다
- □ athlete ⓝ 운동선수
- □ evaluate ⓥ 평가하다
- □ competition ⓝ 경기, 경쟁
- □ condition ⓝ 조건
- □ bounce ⓥ (공을) 튕기다
- □ supply ⓥ 제공하다
- □ properly ⓐⓓ 적절히
- □ adjust ⓥ 조절하다, 조정하다
- □ fine-tune ⓥ 미세하게 조정하다
- □ in pursuit of ~을 추구하여
- □ adaptation ⓝ 적응
- □ internal ⓐ 내적인
- □ influence ⓝ 영향
- □ affect ⓥ 영향을 미치다
- □ performance ⓝ 수행
- □ achieve ⓥ 해내다

30

- □ promotion ⓝ 프로모션, 홍보
- □ deal with ~을 다루다
- □ consumer ⓝ 소비자
- □ psychology ⓝ 심리
- □ one way or another 어떤 한 방식으로
- □ fashion ⓝ 방식, 방법
- □ possibility ⓝ 가능성
- □ sales ⓝ 매출, 판매
- □ fool ⓥ 속이다
- □ purchase ⓥ 구매하다

- □ long-term ⓐ 장기적인
- □ relate ⓥ 전하다
- □ experience ⓝ 경험
- □ identify ⓥ 확인하다
- □ appreciate ⓥ 진가를 인정하다
- □ reach ⓥ 도달하다

31

- □ strike ⓥ 인상을 주다
- □ partial ⓐ 부분적인
- □ reflection ⓝ 반영
- □ capture ⓥ 포착하다, 담아내다
- □ idea ⓝ 관념
- □ physical ⓐ 물리적인, 구체적인
- □ each and every 각각의 모든
- □ somehow ⓐⓓ 어떻게든
- □ abstract ⓐ 추상적인
- □ practical ⓐ 실용적인
- □ imperfect ⓐ 불완전한
- □ visualized ⓐ 시각화된

32

- □ be aware that ~을 인식하다
- □ have a clue 짐작하다
- □ on the tip of one's tongue 당장 떠오르지 않는, 혀 끝에서 맴도는
- □ argument ⓝ 말다툼, 논쟁
- □ overtired ⓐ 극도로 지친
- □ recital ⓝ 연주회

- □ justify ⓥ 정당화하다
- □ circumstances ⓝ 상황, 환경
- □ a series of 연속된
- □ frown ⓥ (얼굴을) 찡그리다
- □ mention ⓥ 얘기를 꺼내다
- □ push ~ for … ~에게 …을 요구하다
- □ observation ⓝ 관찰
- □ cool down 식히다, 진정시키다

33

- □ conduct ⓥ 전도하다, 전달하다
- □ electricity ⓝ 전기
- □ more or less 꽤, 다소
- □ efficiently ⓐⓓ 효율적으로
- □ drop ⓝ 방울
- □ conscious mind 의식(적 마음)
- □ have much say in ~에 발언권이 많다[영향력이 크다]
- □ intense ⓐ 강렬한
- □ viewpoint ⓝ 관점
- □ objective ⓐ 객관적인
- □ subjective ⓐ 주관적인
- □ track ⓥ 추적하다
- □ subconscious ⓐ 잠재의식의
- □ intensity ⓝ 강도
- □ figure out 계산하다
- □ transfer ⓥ 전달하다
- □ electrical current 전류

34

- □ communicate ⓥ 의사소통을 하다
- □ discontent ⓝ 불만
- □ frequency ⓝ 주파수
- □ researcher ⓝ 연구자
- □ experiment ⓥ 실험하다
- □ survival ⓐ 살아남기 위한
- □ organism ⓝ 유기체
- □ objective ⓝ 목표
- □ defend ⓥ 지키다, 방어하다
- □ neighboring ⓐ 인접한, 이웃한
- □ dissatisfaction ⓝ 불만
- □ nutrient ⓝ 영양소
- □ genetic ⓐ 유전적인

35

- □ as opposed to ~와 대비되는
- □ essential ⓐ 필수적인
- □ establish ⓥ 수립하다
- □ positive ⓐ 긍정적인
- □ tragedy ⓝ 비극
- □ misfortune ⓝ 불행
- □ draw out 끌어내다
- □ recognizable ⓐ 알아볼 수 있는, 인식할 수 있는
- □ portrayal ⓝ 묘사
- □ fictional ⓐ 허구의, 가상의
- □ documentary ⓐ 사실을 기록한, 사실적인
- □ companion ⓝ 동료
- □ valued ⓐ 소중한, 가치 있는

- □ ally ⓝ 협력자
- □ dozens of 많은, 수십의
- □ incidental ⓐ 부수적인

36

- □ assume ⓥ 가정하다
- □ capable ⓐ ~할 수 있는
- □ despite prep ~에도 불구하고
- □ lack ⓥ 부족하다
- □ imply ⓥ 의미하다
- □ concept ⓝ 개념
- □ concrete ⓐ 구체적인
- □ specific ⓐ 특정한
- □ in principle 원칙적으로
- □ possess ⓥ 가지고 있다, 소유하다
- □ nonconceptual ⓐ 비(非)개념적인
- □ currently ⓐd 현재

37

- □ joint ⓝ 관절
- □ bear ⓥ 지탱하다
- □ weight ⓝ 무게, 체중
- □ squeeze ⓥ 압착하다
- □ respond ⓥ 반응하다
- □ off-and-on ⓐ 반복적인
- □ soak up 흡수하다
- □ transfer ⓥ 옮기다, 이동하다
- □ look into ~을 들여다보다
- □ shift ⓥ 옮기다
- □ pressure ⓝ 압력
- □ release ⓥ 풀다

38

- □ argue ⓥ 주장하다
- □ morality ⓝ 도덕(성)
- □ amount ⓝ 양
- □ narrow ⓐ 좁은
- □ level ⓝ 수위, 높이
- □ volume ⓝ 부피
- □ self-constructed ⓐ 스스로 구성해 낸
- □ reach ⓥ ~에 이르다
- □ fairness ⓝ 공평함

39

- □ air-conditioning ⓝ 냉방 설비
- □ accelerate ⓥ 가속화하다
- □ box ⓝ 구조물
- □ airflow ⓝ 공기 흐름
- □ unit ⓝ 장치
- □ architect ⓝ 건축가
- □ breeze ⓝ 산들바람
- □ comfort ⓝ 안락

40

- □ invention ⓝ 발명품
- □ encounter ⓥ 맞닥뜨리다, 직면하다
- □ resistance ⓝ 저항
- □ logically ⓐd 논리적으로
- □ reasoning ⓝ 추론
- □ viewpoint ⓝ 관점
- □ by definition 정의상
- □ application ⓝ 적용

2회 모의고사

□ task ⓝ 과업
□ one by one 하나씩
□ manage ⓥ 관리하다
□ efficiently ⓐⓓ 효율적으로

04
□ club ⓝ 동아리
□ locker ⓝ 사물함
□ star-shaped ⓐ 별 모양의
□ bookshelf ⓝ 책장
□ trophy ⓝ 상패
□ publish ⓥ 발행하다

05
□ camping supplies 캠핑용품
□ sleeping bag 침낭
□ cooking tool 요리 도구
□ easy-to-cook meal 간편식
□ clothes ⓝ 옷
□ pack ⓥ (짐을) 챙기다
□ consider ⓥ 고려하다

06
□ vegetable ⓝ 채소
□ fantastic ⓐ 굉장한
□ need ⓥ 필요하다
□ discount ⓝ 할인
□ price ⓝ 가격
□ credit card 신용카드

07
□ expect ⓥ 기대하다
□ already ⓐⓓ 이미
□ attend ⓥ 참여하다
□ available ⓐ 참석이 가능한
□ make up for ~을 보충하다 [보상하다]

08
□ lab ⓝ 실험실
□ exactly ⓐⓓ 정확히
□ design ⓥ 설계하다
□ pretty ⓐⓓ 꽤
□ join ⓥ 참여하다
□ experiment ⓝ 실험
□ material ⓝ 재료
□ prepare ⓥ 준비하다
□ application form 지원서
□ deadline ⓝ 기한, 마감 시간
□ prize ⓝ 상
□ give out ~을 주다
□ creative ⓐ 창의적인

09
□ look for ~을 찾다
□ recommend ⓥ 추천하다
□ volunteer ⓝ 봉사 활동
□ senior ⓐ 노인의
□ citizen ⓝ 시민
□ face-to-face ⓐⓓ 대면(으로)
□ text message 문자 메시지
□ take picture 사진을 찍다
□ various ⓐ 다양한

□ require ⓥ 요구하다
□ participate ⓥ 참여하다
□ be interested in ~에 관심이 있다
□ application ⓝ 지원

10
□ portable ⓐ 휴대용의
□ fan ⓝ 선풍기
□ prefer ⓥ 선호하다

11
□ search for ~을 찾다
□ biology ⓝ 생물학

12
□ reservation ⓝ 예약
□ recipe ⓝ 요리법

13
□ get involved in ~에 참여하다[관여하다]
□ organization ⓝ 단체
□ struggle ⓥ 고군분투하다
□ challenging ⓐ 도전적인
□ tone ⓝ 어조
□ recommend ⓥ 추천하다

14
□ divide ⓥ 나누다
□ research ⓝ 조사
□ visual material 시각 자료
□ presentation ⓝ 발표

□take on ~을 맡다
□collect ⓥ 모으다
□article ⓝ (신문 등의) 기사
□gather ⓥ 모으다
□necessary ⓐ 필요한
□information ⓝ 정보
□handle ⓥ 다루다

15

□attend ⓥ 참석하다
□orientation ⓝ 설명회
□greetings ⓝ 인사
□explain ⓥ 설명하다
□facility ⓝ 시설
□explanation ⓝ 설명
□library ⓝ 도서관
□miss ⓥ 놓치다
□opening hours 개방 시간
□lost and found 분실물 센터

16~17

□tune in to ~을 열심히 듣다
□recommend ⓥ 추천하다
□cough ⓝ 기침
□reduce ⓥ 줄이다
□symptom ⓝ 증상
□ginger ⓝ 생강
□remedy ⓝ 치료법
□rich ⓐ 풍부한
□source ⓝ 공급원
□relieve ⓥ 완화하다
□suffer ⓥ 고생하다
□get rid of ~을 없애다

□healthy ⓐ 건강한
□connection ⓝ 연관성

18

□science ⓝ 과학
□recently ⓐd 최근에
□impressed ⓐ 감명을 받은
□environment ⓝ 환경
□discussion ⓝ 토론
□lecture ⓝ 강의
□suit ⓥ 맞추다
□experience ⓝ 경험
□grateful ⓐ 감사한

19

□sandcastle ⓝ 모래성
□enormous ⓐ 거대한
□destroy ⓥ 부수다
□stream ⓥ 흐르다
□ocean ⓝ 바다
□respond ⓥ 반응하다
□enthusiasm ⓝ 열정
□regretful ⓐ 후회하는

20

□magic ⓝ 마법, 마술
□challenge ⓝ 어려움, 도전
□statement ⓝ 진술
□positive ⓐ 긍정적인
□struggle ⓥ 어려움을 겪다
□witness ⓥ 목격하다
□confidence ⓝ 자신감
□surprise ⓥ 놀라게 하다

□shift ⓝ 변화
□powerful ⓐ 강력한

21

□seemingly ⓐd 겉보기에
□sense ⓝ 감각
□sight ⓝ 시각
□philosopher ⓝ 철학자
□doubt ⓥ 의심하다
□perception ⓝ 인식
□balance ⓝ 균형
□vision ⓝ 시각
□categorize ⓥ 분류하다
□detect ⓥ 감지하다
□prey ⓝ 먹잇감
□divide ⓥ 나누다
□specific ⓐ 특정한
□bucket ⓝ 양동이

22

□historical ⓐ 역사적인
□importance ⓝ 중요성
□far-reaching ⓐ 광범위한
□influence ⓝ 영향력
□noble ⓐ 고귀한
□possess ⓥ 가지다, 소유하다
□aspect ⓝ 측면
□improve ⓥ 개선하다
□scale ⓝ 규모
□share ⓥ 공유하다
□seek ⓥ 찾다, 구하다
□opinion ⓝ 의견
□constantly ⓐd 끊임없이

□accomplish ⓥ 성취하다
□thus ⓐd 그러므로
□potential ⓝ 잠재력
□community ⓝ 공동체
□regardless of ~와 관계없이

23
□crop rotation 윤작
□process ⓝ 과정
□field ⓝ 밭
□order ⓝ 순서
□rotate ⓥ 순환하다
□original ⓐ 원래의
□enrich ⓥ 비옥하게 하다
□soil ⓝ 토양
□type ⓝ 유형
□maintain ⓥ 유지하다
□organic ⓐ 유기농의
□impact ⓝ 영향

24
□concentrate ⓥ 집중하다
□keep on v-ing 계속 ~하다
□from time to time 때때로
□assess ⓥ 평가하다
□progress ⓝ 진행 상황, 진전
□spoil ⓥ 망치다
□impact ⓝ 영향(력)
□overwork ⓥ 과하게 작업하다
□struggle ⓥ 어려움을 겪다, 분투하다
□benefit ⓥ 득을 보다
□inspiration ⓝ 영감

□incomplete ⓐ 미완성의, 불완전한
□interpretation ⓝ 해석, 이해

25
□extent ⓝ 정도
□youth ⓝ 청소년, 젊은 사람들
□fear ⓝ 두려움
□climate change 기후 변화
□extremely ⓐd 극도로
□generation ⓝ 세대

26
□Prague ⓝ 프라하(체코의 수도)
□secondary school 중등학교
□show interest in ~에 흥미를 보이다
□chemistry ⓝ 화학
□physics ⓝ 물리학
□mathematics ⓝ 수학
□throughout ⓟrep 내내
□serve ⓥ 복무하다
□military ⓐ 군대의

27
□delightful ⓐ 즐거운
□experience ⓥ 경험하다
□various ⓐ 다양한
□host ⓥ (파티 등을) 주최하다
□in advance 미리

28
□passionate ⓐ 열정적인
□environment ⓝ 환경
□contest ⓝ 대회
□upcycled ⓐ 업사이클된
□winning prize 우승 상품
□local ⓐ 지역의
□announce ⓥ 발표하다

29
□overstate ⓥ 과장해서 말하다
□meaningful ⓐ 의미 있는
□human being 인간
□provide ⓥ 제공하다
□fulfillment ⓝ 성취감
□empowerment ⓝ 권한
□career ⓝ 직업, 경력
□energizing ⓐ 활기찬
□count ~ as … ~을 …라고 여기다
□employment ⓝ 직업, 고용
□source ⓝ 원천
□pride ⓝ 자부심
□conduct ⓥ 수행하다
□psychology ⓝ 심리
□workplace ⓝ 업무 현장, 직장
□output ⓝ 성과
□generally ⓐd 일반적으로
□income ⓝ 수입
□overall ⓐd 전반적으로
□satisfaction ⓝ 만족

30

- □ rate ⓝ 빠르기
- □ travel ⓥ 이동하다
- □ determine ⓥ 결정하다
- □ ability ⓝ 능력
- □ process ⓥ 처리하다
- □ evolutionary ⓐ 진화의
- □ ideally ⓐⓓ 이상적으로
- □ suited ⓐ 맞추어진
- □ motorist ⓝ 운전자
- □ limited ⓐ 제한된
- □ appreciate ⓥ 감상하다
- □ allow for ~을 가능하게 하다 [허락하다]
- □ polar ⓐ 극과 극의
- □ opposite ⓝ 반대의 것
- □ ordinarily ⓐⓓ 보통
- □ typical ⓐ 전형적인

31

- □ climatic ⓐ 기후의
- □ requirement ⓝ 요건
- □ endure ⓥ 견디다
- □ satisfy ⓥ 충족시키다
- □ species ⓝ 종(種)
- □ force ⓥ 강요하다
- □ creature ⓝ 생명체
- □ be capable of ~을 할 수 있다
- □ immobile ⓐ 움직이지 않는
- □ larva ⓝ 유충
- □ occupy ⓥ 점유하다
- □ survive ⓥ 생존하다

- □ reproduce ⓥ 번식하다
- □ endurance ⓝ 인내
- □ transformation ⓝ 변형

32

- □ respectable ⓐ 존경할 만한
- □ make it a point 반드시 ~하도록 하다
- □ discourage ⓥ 못하게 하다
- □ speak up 자유롭게 의견을 내다
- □ maintain ⓥ 유지하다
- □ viewpoint ⓝ 관점
- □ get aired 공공연히 알려지다
- □ if anything 오히려
- □ boss ⓝ 상사
- □ conversation ⓝ 대담, 대화
- □ corporate ⓝ 기업
- □ nonprofit ⓐ 비영리인
- □ publish ⓥ 발행하다, 출판하다
- □ section ⓝ 구역, (신문의) ~란
- □ feature ⓥ (기사로) 다루다
- □ management ⓝ 경영
- □ techniques ⓝ 기법
- □ regularly ⓐⓓ 어김없이, 규칙적으로
- □ claim ⓥ 주장하다
- □ continually ⓐⓓ 계속해서
- □ remark ⓥ 말하다

33

- □ striking ⓐ 두드러진
- □ characteristic ⓝ 특징

- □ respond ⓥ 반응하다
- □ environmental ⓐ 환경의
- □ eyelid ⓝ 눈꺼풀
- □ mammal ⓝ 포유류
- □ visual ⓐ 시각의
- □ apparently ⓐⓓ 분명히
- □ process ⓥ 처리하다
- □ shorten ⓥ 짧아지다
- □ weaken ⓥ 약해지다
- □ essential ⓐ 필수적인
- □ nevertheless ⓐⓓ 그럼에도 불구하고
- □ derive ⓥ 얻다
- □ perceptual ⓐ 지각의
- □ activate ⓥ 활성화하다

34

- □ research ⓝ 연구
- □ expert ⓝ 전문가 ⓐ 능숙한
- □ field ⓝ 분야, 영역
- □ difficulty ⓝ 어려움
- □ newcomer ⓝ 초보
- □ genuine ⓐ 실제의
- □ remarkably ⓐⓓ 놀랍게도
- □ accurate ⓐ 정확한
- □ insensitive ⓐ 무감각한
- □ acquire ⓥ 습득하다
- □ underestimate ⓥ 과소평가하다
- □ session ⓝ 기간, 시간
- □ assumption ⓝ 추정, 가정

35

□ psychologist ⓝ 심리학자

□ severe ⓐ 심각한

□ mental ⓐ 정신적인

□ illness ⓝ 병, 질환

□ compose ⓥ 작곡하다

□ improve ⓥ 개선하다

□ participant ⓝ 참가자

□ session ⓝ 활동, 기간

□ benefit ⓝ 이점

□ review ⓥ 검토하다

□ treatment ⓝ 치료

□ setting ⓝ 환경

□ finding ⓝ 결과

□ choir ⓝ 합창단

□ wellbeing ⓝ 행복

□ significantly ⓐ 상당히

□ state ⓝ 상태

□ enhance ⓥ 강화하다

36

□ realize ⓥ 깨닫다

□ impossibility ⓝ 불가능

□ field ⓝ 경기장

□ competitive ⓐ 경쟁적인

□ structure ⓝ 구조

□ period ⓝ 기간

□ racket ⓝ 라켓

□ appropriate ⓐ 적절한

□ progressive ⓐ 점진적인

□ relate to ~와 관련되다

□ arena ⓝ 경기장

□ equipment ⓝ 장비

□ handle ⓥ 다루다

□ compete ⓥ 경쟁하다

□ common sense
(일반인들의) 공통된 견해, 상식

□ adaptation ⓝ 조정

37

□ available ⓐ 구할 수 있는

□ empire ⓝ 제국

□ on foot 걸어서

□ near ⓥ 다가가다

□ relay ⓥ 이어가다

□ under good condition
좋은 상황에서, 사정이 좋으면

□ station ⓥ 배치하다

□ royal ⓐ 왕의, 왕실의

□ order ⓝ 명령

□ hut ⓝ 오두막

□ place ⓥ 배치하다

□ apart ⓐ 떨어져

□ along ⓟⓡⓔⓟ ~을 따라

□ especially ⓐ 특히

□ direction ⓝ 방향

□ catch sight of ~을 찾아내다

38

□ demonstrate ⓥ 보여주다

□ explanation ⓝ 설명

□ map ⓥ (지도에) 구획하다

□ separate ⓐ 개별적인, 별개의

□ register ⓥ 등록하다

□ tip ⓝ 끝

□ sourness ⓝ 신맛

□ bitterness ⓝ 쓴맛

□ misinterpretation ⓝ 오해

□ mistranslation ⓝ 오역

□ conduct ⓥ 수행하다

□ turn ⓝ 전환기

□ leading ⓐ 선도적인

□ specialty ⓝ 특화된 분야

□ perceive ⓥ 지각하다

□ intensity ⓝ 강도

□ mechanism ⓝ 기제

□ at work 작동 중인

39

□ factor ⓝ 요인

□ determine ⓥ 결정하다

□ respond ⓥ 반응하다

□ treatment ⓝ 치료

□ alike ⓐ 비슷한, 같은

□ display ⓥ 보이다

□ feature ⓝ 특징

□ therefore ⓐ 그런 까닭에

□ entirely ⓐ 완전히

□ healing session 치료 활동

□ rescue center 구조 센터

□ domestic ⓐ 가정의

□ illness ⓝ 질병

□ react ⓥ 반응하다

□ confusion ⓝ 동요, 혼란

□ with ~ in mind ~을 염두에
두고

□ explore ⓥ 탐구하다

□ specific ⓐ 특정한, 구체적인

□ constant ⓐ 끊임없는

□ process ⓝ 과정

3회 모의고사

□ indoors ⓐⓓ 실내에서
□ elderly ⓐ 나이가 지긋한
□ useful ⓐ 유용한
□ traditional ⓐ 전통적인

18

□ resident ⓝ 거주자
□ recently ⓐⓓ 최근에
□ observe ⓥ 알다, 목격하다
□ repair ⓝ 수리
□ attention ⓝ 주의
□ condition ⓝ 상태
□ playground ⓝ 놀이터
□ equipment ⓝ 설비
□ swing ⓝ 그네
□ damage ⓥ 손상하다
□ fall off 떨어져 나가다
□ slide ⓝ 미끄럼틀
□ facility ⓝ 시설
□ terrible ⓐ 형편없는
□ appreciate ⓥ 감사하다
□ immediate ⓐ 즉각적인
□ solve ⓥ (문제 등을) 해결하다

19

□ grizzly bear 회색곰
□ native ⓐ 자연의
□ habitat ⓝ 서식지
□ sniff ⓥ (코를) 킁킁거리다
□ realize ⓥ 깨닫다
□ giant ⓐ 거대한
□ freeze ⓥ 얼어붙다
□ issue ⓝ 문제

□ survival ⓝ 생존
□ motivation ⓝ 동기
□ clearly ⓐⓓ 분명히

20

□ maintain ⓥ 유지하다
□ constant ⓐ 일정한
□ attention ⓝ 주의 (집중)
□ characterise ⓥ 특징으로 하다
□ peaks and valleys 정점과 저점
□ achieve ⓥ 이루다
□ confident ⓐ 자신감 있는
□ benefit ⓝ 이익, 혜택
□ demanding ⓐ (일이) 힘든
□ task ⓝ 과업, 작업
□ cope with ～을 처리하다

21

□ adopt ⓥ 받아들이다, 채택하다
□ traditional ⓐ 전통적인
□ livelihood ⓝ 생계 수단
□ progress ⓝ 발전
□ remove ⓥ 없애다
□ physical ⓐ 육체의
□ disability ⓝ 장애
□ mass ⓐ 대중의
□ avoid ⓥ 피하다
□ divorce ⓝ 단절, 이혼
□ indeed ⓐⓓ 실제로, 참으로
□ risk ⓝ 위험 (요소)
□ ignorance ⓝ 무지, 무식

□ endless ⓐ 끝없는
□ labor ⓝ 노동
□ realistic ⓐ 현실적인

22

□ approach ⓥ 접근하다
□ tuxedo ⓝ 턱시도
□ funeral ⓝ 장례식
□ bathing suit 수영복
□ religious ⓐ 종교적인
□ appropriate ⓐ 적합한, 알맞은
□ occasion ⓝ 행사
□ setting ⓝ 상황
□ skillful ⓐ 숙련된, 능숙한
□ flexible ⓐ 유연한
□ strategy ⓝ 전략
□ multiple-choice test 선다형 시험

23

□ economic ⓐ 경제의
□ wage ⓝ 임금, 급료
□ condition ⓝ 여건, 조건
□ gradually ⓐⓓ 점차
□ transport ⓝ 운송, 수송
□ industrial ⓐ 산업의
□ revolution ⓝ 혁명
□ railway ⓝ 철도
□ open up ～을 가능하게 하다
□ seaside ⓐ 해안가의
□ coast-to-coast ⓐ 대륙 횡단의
□ arrival ⓝ 출현

31

□differ ⓥ 다르다
□reset ⓥ 재설정하다
□biological ⓐ 생물체의
□overcome ⓥ 극복하다
□recovery ⓝ 회복
□westward ad 서쪽으로
□lengthen ⓥ 연장하다
□eastward ad 동쪽으로
□sizable ⓐ 큰
□impact ⓝ 영향
□significantly ad 상당히
□additional ⓐ 추가의
□evidence ⓝ 증거
□tough ⓐ 힘든
□purpose ⓝ 목적

32

□set out ~에 착수하다
□over-optimism ⓝ 지나친 낙관주의
□certain ⓐ 특정한
□estimate ⓥ 추산하다, 어림잡다
□alongside prep ~와 함께
□task ⓝ 과제
□fit ⓥ 맞추다
□available ⓐ 이용 가능한
□significant ⓐ 상당한
□spare ⓐ 남겨둔
□benefit ⓝ 이익
□practical ⓐ 실용적인
□leisure ⓝ 여가

33

□countryside ⓝ 시골
□biologist ⓝ 생물학자
□evolutionary ⓐ 진화의
□principle ⓝ 원리
□evolve ⓥ 진화하다
□generation ⓝ 세대
□bunny ⓝ 토끼
□pass on ~을 물려주다
□gene ⓝ 유전자
□run into ~와 마주치다
□adapt ⓥ 적응하다

34

□creator ⓝ 창조자
□clothing ⓝ 의복
□nail ⓝ 못
□drive ⓥ (못 · 말뚝 등을) 박다
□physical ⓐ 물리적인
□reality ⓝ 실체
□process ⓝ 과정
□decision ⓝ 결정
□harmony ⓝ 조화
□existence ⓝ 존재
□potential ⓝ 잠재력
□accomplish ⓥ 완성하다
□careless ⓐ 부주의한
□irresponsible ⓐ 무책임한
□observe ⓥ 탐색하다
□professional ⓝ 전문직 (종사자)

35

□interpret ⓥ 해석하다
□sympathy ⓝ 공감
□conflict ⓝ 갈등
□arise ⓥ 발생하다
□outcome ⓝ 결과
□tale ⓝ 이야기
□shift ⓥ 바꾸다
□viewpoint ⓝ 관점
□evil ⓐ 사악한
□stepsister ⓝ 의붓자매
□exist ⓥ 존재하다
□willingly ad 기꺼이

36

□band ⓝ 무리
□wander ⓥ 돌아다니다
□settle down 정착하다
□crop ⓝ 농작물
□toolmaker ⓝ 도구 제작자
□axe ⓝ 도끼
□community ⓝ 공동체
□organize ⓥ 조직하다
□efficiently ad 효율적으로
□divide ⓥ 나누다

37

□natural ⓐ 자연의
□mineral ⓝ 광물
□melt ⓥ 녹이다, 녹다
□material ⓝ 물질
□surface ⓝ 표면
□trap ⓥ 가두다

☐ **atom** ⓝ 원자
☐ **crystal** ⓝ 결정(체)
☐ **rapidly** ⓐⓓ 빨리
☐ **unaided** ⓐ 도움 없는
☐ **arrange** ⓥ 배열하다
☐ **orderly** ⓐ 질서 있는
☐ **element** ⓝ 원소
☐ **determine** ⓥ 결정하다
☐ **individual** ⓐ 개별의

38

☐ **complex** ⓐ 복합의
☐ **compound** ⓝ 화합물
☐ **nutrient** ⓝ 영양소
☐ **chain** ⓝ 사슬
☐ **release** ⓥ 방출하다
☐ **provide** ⓥ 제공하다
☐ **fuel** ⓝ 연료
☐ **structure** ⓝ 구조
☐ **store** ⓥ 저장하다

39

☐ **interact** ⓥ 소통하다
☐ **commonly** ⓐⓓ 흔히
☐ **assumption** ⓝ 가정
☐ **automatically** ⓐⓓ 자동적으로
☐ **description** ⓝ 설명, 묘사
☐ **contain** ⓥ 포함하다
☐ **discussion** ⓝ 토론
☐ **impression** ⓝ 인상
☐ **expectation** ⓝ 기대
☐ **behaviour** ⓝ 행동

40

☐ **risky** ⓐ 위험한
☐ **trustworthy** ⓐ 신뢰할 수 있는
☐ **evidence** ⓝ 증거
☐ **evolutionary** ⓐ 진화의
☐ **prospect** ⓝ 전망
☐ **sensible** ⓐ 분별 있는
☐ **psychologist** ⓝ 심리학자
☐ **cue** ⓝ 신호
☐ **signal** ⓥ 나타내다
☐ **local** ⓐ 지역의, 현지의
☐ **tasty** ⓐ 맛있는
☐ **adopt** ⓥ 따르다, 채택하다
☐ **practice** ⓝ 행동, 관행
☐ **uncertain** ⓐ 불확실한
☐ **unrealistic** ⓐ 비현실적인

41~42

☐ **master** ⓝ 달인
☐ **reproduce** ⓥ 재현하다
☐ **randomly** ⓐⓓ 무작위로
☐ **expert** ⓝ 전문가
☐ **advantage** ⓝ 유리함
☐ **familiar** ⓐ 익숙한
☐ **previously** ⓐⓓ 이전에
☐ **face** ⓥ 직면하다
☐ **domain** ⓝ 분야
☐ **beneficial** ⓐ 유익한
☐ **structure** ⓝ 구조
☐ **observe** ⓥ 관찰하다
☐ **accurately** ⓐⓓ 정확하게
☐ **note** ⓝ 음표

☐ **order** ⓥ 배열하다
☐ **guarantee** ⓥ 보장하다
☐ **experienced** ⓐ 숙련된
☐ **range** ⓝ 범위
☐ **recognize** ⓥ 인식하다

43~45

☐ **approach** ⓥ 접근하다
☐ **smelly** ⓐ 냄새가 나는
☐ **guard** ⓝ 경비병
☐ **shock** ⓝ 충격
☐ **demand** ⓥ 요구하다
☐ **wise** ⓐ 현명한
☐ **offer** ⓥ 제안하다
☐ **immediately** ⓐⓓ 즉시
☐ **call for** ~을 시키다
☐ **gesture** ⓝ 행동
☐ **tiny** ⓐ 매우 작은
☐ **kindness** ⓝ 친절(한 행위)
☐ **sword** ⓝ 칼
☐ **eventually** ⓐⓓ 결국, 마침내
☐ **take up** ~을 차지하다

4회 모의고사

01
- student council 학생회
- complain ⓥ 불평하다
- set up 설치하다
- task ⓝ 과제, 업무
- efficiently 교 효율적으로

02
- notice ⓥ 알아채다
- improve ⓥ 향상시키다
- effective ⓐ 효과적인
- memorize ⓥ 암기하다
- focus ⓥ 집중하다
- study ⓝ 연구

03
- regularly 교 규칙적으로
- prevent ⓥ 예방하다
- anxiety ⓝ 불안
- physically 교 신체적으로
- mentally 교 정신적으로

04
- banner ⓝ 현수막
- eye-catching ⓐ 눈에 띄는
- striped ⓐ 줄무늬의
- pillow fight 베개 싸움
- glow ⓥ 빛나다

05
- playlist ⓝ 재생 목록
- cheerful ⓐ 신나는
- sample ⓝ (시식용) 샘플, 견본
- customer ⓝ 고객, 손님
- place ⓥ 배치하다, 진열하다
- price tag 가격표

06
- tour ⓝ 여행, 관광
- daytime ⓝ 낮 시간
- sunset ⓝ 일몰
- credit card 신용카드

07
- perform ⓥ 공연하다
- nervous ⓐ 긴장한
- in public 사람들[대중] 앞에서
- interview ⓝ 면접
- part-time job 아르바이트

08
- fireworks ⓝ 불꽃놀이
- volunteer ⓥ 자원봉사하다
  ⓝ 자원봉사자
- period ⓝ 기간
- apply ⓥ 지원하다
- exactly 교 정확히
- run ⓥ 운영하다
- activity booth 체험 부스
- sign up 신청하다

09
- vice principal 교감
- talent show 장기자랑
- auditorium ⓝ 강당
- participate ⓥ 참가하다
- showcase ⓥ 뽐내다,
  선보이다
- judge ⓝ 심사위원
- prize ⓝ 상
- performance ⓝ 공연
- participant ⓝ 참가자
- symbol ⓝ 상징
- detail ⓝ 자세한 내용[세부 사항]

10
- backpack ⓝ 책가방
- option ⓝ 선택지
- consider ⓥ 고려하다
- budget ⓝ 예산
- school supplies 학용품
- square ⓐ 사각형의
- waterproof ⓐ 방수의
- useful ⓐ 유용한

11
- headache ⓝ 두통
- medicine ⓝ 약
- leave ⓥ 떠나다, 나가다
- go see a doctor 병원에
  가다

12

☐ **order** ⓥ 주문하다

☐ **celebrate** ⓥ 기념하다

☐ **anniversary** ⓝ 기념일

☐ **specific** ⓐ 특정한, 구체적인

☐ **heart-shaped** ⓐ 하트 모양의

13

☐ **raise** ⓥ 키우다, 기르다

☐ **effort** ⓝ 노력

☐ **responsibility** ⓝ 책임

☐ **handle** ⓥ 감당하다

☐ **business trip** 출장

☐ **look after** ~을 돌보다

☐ **caretaker** ⓝ 관리인, 돌보는 사람

14

☐ **garage** ⓝ 차고

☐ **cookbook** ⓝ 요리책

☐ **recipe** ⓝ 레시피, 조리법

☐ **fine** ⓐ 고급의

☐ **dish** ⓝ 요리

☐ **chef** ⓝ 요리사

☐ **professional** ⓐ 전문적인

☐ **create** ⓥ 만들어 내다

☐ **quit** ⓥ 그만두다

15

☐ **overseas** ⓐ 해외의

☐ **sightseeing** ⓝ 관광

☐ **air conditioner** 에어컨

☐ **clerk** ⓝ (호텔) 직원

☐ **fix** ⓥ 고치다

☐ **tourist attraction** 관광지, 관광 명소

☐ **possible** ⓐ 가능한

☐ **refrigerator** ⓝ 냉장고

16~17

☐ **national flag** 국기

☐ **various** ⓐ 여러 가지의, 다양한

☐ **national flower** 국화

☐ **symbolize** ⓥ 상징하다

☐ **necklace** ⓝ 목걸이

☐ **guest** ⓝ 손님

☐ **represent** ⓥ 나타내다, 상징하다

☐ **happiness** ⓝ 행복

☐ **express** ⓥ 표현하다

☐ **chain** ⓝ 목걸이

☐ **iris** ⓝ 붓꽃

☐ **throughout** ⓟⓡⓔⓟ ~을 통틀어

☐ **symbol** ⓝ 상징

☐ **perfection** ⓝ 완벽함

☐ **consider** ⓥ 여기다, 간주하다

☐ **endangered** ⓐ 멸종 위기의

18

☐ **coordinator** ⓝ 코디네이터

☐ **community** ⓝ 지역 사회

☐ **recently** ⓐⓓ 최근에

☐ **grassy area** 잔디밭

☐ **separate** ⓐ 별도의

☐ **ensure** ⓥ 보장하다

☐ **newly** ⓐⓓ 새롭게

19

☐ **check in** (비행기) 탑승 수속을 하다

☐ **expectation** ⓝ 기대

☐ **look forward to** ~을 기대하다

☐ **approach** ⓥ 다가가다

☐ **passport** ⓝ 여권

☐ **ruin** ⓥ 망치다

☐ **heartbroken** ⓐ 상심한

☐ **board** ⓥ 탑승하다

☐ **indifferent** ⓐ 무관심한

20

☐ **astonish** ⓥ 놀라게 하다

☐ **degree** ⓝ 정도

☐ **convenience** ⓝ 편리성

☐ **decision making** 의사 결정

☐ **remarkable** ⓐ 놀라운

☐ **extent** ⓝ 정도

☐ **chore** ⓝ 일, 잡일

☐ **stay in touch** 연락을 유지하다

21

☐ **common sense** 상식

☐ **belief** ⓝ 신념

☐ **drive** ⓥ 이끌다

☐ **external** ⓐ 외적인

☐ **behavior** ⓝ 행동

☐ **socialize** ⓥ 어울리다, 교류하다

☐ **internal** ⓐ 내적인, 내면의

☐ **obviously** ⓐⓓ 분명히

□ reflect ⓥ 반영하다

□ remarkable ⓐ 놀랄 만한, 놀라운

□ likely ⓐ ~할 가능성이 있는

□ reverse ⓐ 반대의

□ direction ⓝ 방향

□ entirely ⓐⓓ 완전히

□ separate ⓐ 분리된

□ be dependent on ~에 의존하다

□ surroundings ⓝ (주변) 환경

□ matter ⓥ 중요하다

22

□ spirit ⓝ 정신

□ challenge ⓥ 도전하다

□ observe ⓥ 관찰하다

□ behavioral ⓐ 행동의

□ psychology ⓝ 심리학

□ expert ⓝ 전문가

□ treat ⓥ 여기다

□ rehearse ⓥ 연습하다

□ eliminate ⓥ 제거하다

□ attend ⓥ 귀[주의]를 기울이다

23

□ observation ⓝ 관찰

□ physical ⓐ 물리적인, 신체적인

□ lower ⓥ 낮추다

□ risk ⓝ 위험

□ personal ⓐ 개인의

□ act on ~을 행동으로 옮기다

□ article ⓝ 기사

□ humanity ⓝ 인류

□ strategic ⓐ 전략적인

□ act against ~을 거슬러 행동하다

□ lack ⓝ 부족

24

□ logical ⓐ 논리적인

□ objective ⓐ 객관적인

□ rational ⓐ 합리적인

□ accurate ⓐ 정확한

□ analysis ⓝ 분석

□ agree ⓥ 동의하다

□ opposite ⓝ 반대

□ the case 사실

□ realistic ⓐ 현실적인

□ match ⓥ 일치하다

□ interpretation ⓝ 해석

□ criticize ⓥ 비난하다

□ referee ⓝ 심판

□ commit ⓥ 저지르다

□ biased ⓐ 편파적인, 편향된

□ interpret ⓥ 해석하다

25

□ share ⓝ 점유율, 몫

□ retail ⓝ 소매

□ trade ⓝ 거래

□ record ⓥ 기록하다

□ reach ⓥ 도달하다

□ increase ⓝ 증가

□ fall behind 뒤처지다

26

□ outdoors ⓝ 야외

□ partially ⓐⓓ 부분적으로

□ blinded ⓐ 실명한, 눈이 먼

□ observe ⓥ 관찰하다

□ from a distance 멀리서

□ concentrate ⓥ 집중하다

□ creature ⓝ 생물

□ evolutionary ⓐ 진화의

□ biology ⓝ 생물학

□ transfer ⓥ 옮기다, 이동하다

□ recognize ⓥ 인정하다

□ award ⓥ 수여하다

27

□ houseplant ⓝ 실내 식물

□ explore ⓥ 구경하다, 둘러보다

□ available ⓐ 이용 가능한

□ purchase ⓝ 구매

□ unique ⓐ 독특한

□ eco-friendly ⓐ 친환경적인

□ recycle ⓥ 재활용하다

□ allow ⓥ 허용하다

28

□ annual ⓐ 연례의, 매년의

□ featured ⓐ 주요한

□ drawing ⓝ 그림 그리기

□ beginner ⓝ 초급자

□ costumed ⓐ 의상을 갖춰 입은

□ receive ⓥ 받다

□ detailed ⓐ 자세한

□ check out 확인하다

4회

□ publish ⓥ 발표하다
□ inspection ⓝ 점검
□ construct ⓥ 세우다
□ assumption ⓝ 가정
□ end up -ing 결국 ~하게 되다
□ sense ⓝ 의미
□ pursue ⓥ 추구하다
□ stick to ~을 고수하다

35

□ psychologist ⓝ 심리학자
□ recall ⓥ 기억해 내다
□ random ⓐ 무작위의
□ particularly ⓐ 특히
□ audience ⓝ 청중
□ face ⓥ 직면하다
□ draw upon ~을 활용하다
□ minor ⓐ 사소한
□ gap ⓝ 틈
□ imaginative ⓐ 상상의

36

□ ancient ⓐ 고대의
□ civilization ⓝ 문명
□ seem ⓥ ~처럼 보이다
□ conquer ⓥ 정복하다
□ expand ⓥ 확장하다
□ collapse ⓥ 붕괴하다
□ go under 멸망하다, 가라앉다
□ fall apart 해체되다
□ era ⓝ 시기
□ oversimplification
　ⓝ 지나친 단순화

37

□ internationally
　ⓐ 국제적으로
□ recognized ⓐ 인정받는
□ pioneer ⓝ 선구자
□ effort ⓝ 노력
□ end up -ing 결국 ~하게 되다
□ take on ~을 받아들이다, 맡다
□ tough ⓐ 힘든
□ emphasize ⓥ 강조하다
□ control ⓥ 통제하다
□ continue ⓥ 계속[지속]하다
□ improve ⓥ 발전하다
□ underperform ⓥ 기대에 못
　미치는 성과를 내다
□ evidence ⓝ 증거

38

□ obvious ⓐ 명확한
□ convenience ⓝ 편리함
□ surroundings ⓝ 주변
□ mark ⓥ 특징짓다
□ specific ⓐ 구체적인
□ emerge ⓥ 나타나다
□ passenger ⓝ 승객
□ behavior ⓝ 행동
□ examine ⓥ 조사하다
□ factor ⓝ 요인
□ shape ⓥ 형성하다
□ navigate ⓥ 탐색하다
□ findings ⓝ 연구 결과
□ involve ⓥ ~와 관련이 있다
□ abstract ⓐ 추상적인
□ sensation ⓝ 느낌

□ desire ⓝ 욕구
□ accidentally ⓐ 우연히
□ influence ⓥ ~에 영향을
　미치다

39

□ sink ⓥ 가라앉히다
□ marine ⓐ 해양의
□ mammal ⓝ 포유류
□ nerve ⓝ 신경
□ region ⓝ 부위, 지역
□ automatically ⓐ 자동으로
□ airway ⓝ 기도
□ risk ⓝ 위험
□ swallow ⓥ 삼키다
□ narrow ⓥ 좁히다
□ passage ⓝ 통로
□ lung ⓝ 폐
□ heart rate 심박수
□ vital ⓐ 중요한
□ organ ⓝ 장기
□ brief ⓐ 짧은
□ below prep ~의 아래에
□ panic ⓥ 당황하다
□ drown ⓥ 익사하다

40

□ assumption ⓝ 가정
□ bias ⓝ 편향
□ in other words 다시 말해
□ automatic ⓐ 자동적인
□ work out 잘 작동하다,
　잘 풀리다
□ assume ⓥ 가정하다

5회 모의고사

□ envelope ⓝ 봉투
□ emerge ⓥ 나타나다
□ phrase ⓝ 문구
□ faraway ⓐ 거리가 먼

20

□ messy ⓐ 지저분한
□ destructive ⓐ 파괴적인
□ disorderly ⓐ 무질서한
□ indicate ⓥ 나타내다
□ disorganized ⓐ 체계적이지 못한
□ mental state 정신 상태
□ tidy ⓥ 정돈하다
□ gain ⓥ 얻다
□ surroundings ⓝ 주변 환경
□ atmosphere ⓝ 분위기
□ neatly ⓐⓓ 단정하게

21

□ soil ⓝ 토양
□ nutrient ⓝ 영양분
□ fertilizer ⓝ 비료
□ capacity ⓝ 능력
□ agricultural ⓐ 농업의
□ undesirable ⓝ 원하지 않는 것
□ be loaded with ~으로 가득 차다
□ real estate 부동산
□ weed ⓝ 잡초
□ abundant ⓐ 풍부한

22

□ care ⓥ 관심을 보이다
□ social ⓐ 사교적인, 사회적인
□ owe ⓥ 빚지다
□ ignore ⓥ 무시하다
□ pass by 지나가다

23

□ route ⓝ 경로, 길
□ acquire ⓥ 획득하다
□ compete ⓥ 경쟁하다
□ mastery ⓝ 숙달
□ prosperity ⓝ 번영
□ equipment ⓝ 장비
□ hardship ⓝ 고난
□ mindset ⓝ 마음가짐
□ struggle ⓝ 투쟁, 분투
□ resistance ⓝ 저항
□ confront ⓥ 직면하다

24

□ reflection ⓝ 반영
□ identity ⓝ 정체성
□ indication ⓝ 암시
□ consciously ⓐⓓ 의식적으로
□ vote ⓥ 투표하다
□ claim ⓥ 주장하다
□ convince ⓥ 설득하다
□ pursue ⓥ 추구하다

25

□ electronic waste 전자 폐기물
□ recycling ⓝ 재활용

□ region ⓝ 지역
□ respectively ⓐⓓ 각각
□ gap ⓝ 격차

26

□ coin ⓥ (새로운 낱말 · 어구를) 만들다
□ advanced ⓐ 진보된
□ emigrate ⓥ (타국으로) 이주하다
□ numerous ⓐ 수많은
□ profound ⓐ 심오한
□ influence ⓝ 영향
□ appoint ⓥ 임명하다
□ astronomy ⓝ 천문학

27

□ dust off 먼지를 털다; 방치했던 것을 오랜만에 꺼내다
□ competition ⓝ 대회
□ souvenir ⓝ 기념품

28

□ provide ⓥ 제공하다
□ for free 무료로

29

□ hunter-gatherer ⓝ 수렵 채집인
□ examination ⓝ 조사
□ abundant ⓐ 풍부한
□ obtainable ⓐ 획득할 수 있는
□ excessive ⓐ 지나친, 과도한
□ permanent ⓐ 영구적인

□domesticate ⓥ 길들이다,
　재배하다

□cultivate ⓥ 경작하다

□take root 뿌리를 내리다

□immediate ⓐ 즉각적인

□density ⓝ 밀도

□civilization ⓝ 문명

30

□commodity ⓝ 상품

□consumption ⓝ 소비

□reveal ⓥ 드러내다

□preference ⓝ 선호

□delay ⓥ 지연하다

□reward ⓝ 보상

□agent ⓝ 행위자

□prematurely 🔠 조기에

□set aside ~을 확보하다

□judge ⓥ 판단하다

□resolve ⓥ 결심하다

□temptation ⓝ 유혹

31

□document ⓥ 기록하다

□literary ⓐ 문학적인

□coincidence ⓝ 우연

□untimely ⓐ 시기가 적절하지
　않은

□particularly 🔠 특히

□inspiration ⓝ 영감

□sudden ⓐ 갑작스러운

□disruption ⓝ 방해

□significant ⓐ 상당한

□consequence ⓝ 결과

□critical ⓐ 중요한

□impact ⓥ 영향을 끼치다

□productivity ⓝ 생산성

32

□evidence ⓝ 증거

□demonstrate ⓥ 보여주다

□attention ⓝ 주의 집중

□auditory ⓐ 청각의

□sharp ⓐ 예리한

□eyesight ⓝ 시력

□dramatic ⓐ 극적인

□expansion ⓝ 확장

□represent ⓥ 나타내다

□precisely 🔠 정확하게

□vital ⓐ 중요한

□spatial ⓐ 공간의

□enlarge ⓥ 확대하다

□physical ⓐ 신체적인

□architecture ⓝ 건축, 설계

□direct ⓥ 지시하다

33

□evolve ⓥ 진화하다

□possibility ⓝ 가능성

□tribe ⓝ 부족

□out-think ⓥ ~보다 우수한
　생각을 하다

□slightly 🔠 약간

□possess ⓥ 소유하다

□vital ⓐ 중요한

□predict ⓥ 예측하다

□hostile ⓐ 적대적인

□accordingly 🔠 그에 맞춰

□decisive ⓐ 결정적인

□succeeding ⓐ 다음의

□opponent ⓝ 반대자

□offspring ⓝ 자손

□descendant ⓝ 후손

34

□potential ⓝ 잠재력

□shift ⓥ 바꾸다

□initial ⓐ 초기의

□generate ⓥ 발생하다

□separately 🔠 따로, 별도로

□pool ⓥ 모으다

□preserve ⓥ 보존하다

□judgment ⓝ 판단

□evaluate ⓥ 평가하다

□refine ⓥ 다듬다

□promising ⓐ 유망한

□elaborate ⓥ 정교하게 말하다

□advance ⓥ 발전시키다

□struggle to ~ ~하기 위해
　애쓰다

□collective ⓐ 집단적인

□intelligence ⓝ 지능

35

□agency ⓝ 행위자

□genuine ⓐ 진정한

□authority ⓝ 권한

□examine ⓥ 살펴보다

□assembly ⓝ 조립

□empower ⓥ (권한을)
　부여하다

□scale ⓝ 규모

□ efficiency ⓝ 효율성
□ uniform ⓐ 똑같은
□ organizational ⓐ 조직의
□ productivity ⓝ 생산성
□ self-discipline ⓝ 자기 통제력

36

□ shift ⓥ 전환하다
□ archive ⓥ 보관하다
□ assume ⓥ 추정하다
□ store ⓥ 저장하다
□ carbon ⓝ 탄소
□ emission ⓝ 배출
□ footprint ⓝ 발자국
□ via ⓟⓡⓔⓟ ~을 통하여
□ attachment ⓝ 첨부
□ threaten ⓥ 위협하다
□ harm ⓝ 해
□ hazardous ⓐ 위험한
□ promising ⓐ 유망한
□ neglect ⓥ 소홀히 하다
□ declare ⓥ 선언하다
□ fossil fuel 화석 연료

37

□ arise ⓥ 생기다
□ exotic ⓐ 이국적인
□ species ⓝ 종
□ introduce ⓥ 도입하다
□ adapt ⓥ 적응하다
□ digest ⓥ 소화하다
□ mature ⓐ 익은

□ compete ⓥ 경쟁하다
□ native ⓐ 토종의
□ densely ⓐⓓ 밀집하게
□ varied ⓐ 다양한
□ habitat ⓝ 서식지
□ extinction ⓝ 멸종

38

□ transport ⓥ 이동시키다
□ distance ⓝ 거리
□ crop ⓝ 농작물
□ typically ⓐⓓ 보통, 일반적으로
□ frequently ⓐⓓ 자주, 빈번하게
□ possession ⓝ 소유
□ space ⓥ 간격을 두다
□ birth ⓝ 출산
□ settle down 정착하다
□ shorten ⓥ 단축하다
□ interval ⓝ 간격
□ rapid ⓐ 빠른
□ labor ⓝ 노동력

39

□ migrate ⓥ 이동하다
□ route ⓝ 경로
□ adapt ⓥ 적응하다
□ breeding ⓝ 번식
□ farther ⓐⓓ 더 멀리
□ facilitate ⓥ 촉진하다
□ passing on 전달, 대물림
□ evolve ⓥ 진화하다
□ gene ⓝ 유전자
□ flexibility ⓝ 유연성

40

□ scholar ⓝ 학자
□ organize ⓥ 정리하다
□ present ⓥ 제시하다
□ preserve ⓥ 보존하다
□ neglect ⓥ 소홀히 하다
□ disability ⓝ 장애
□ deaf ⓐ 귀먹은
□ blind ⓐ 눈이 먼
□ distinguish ⓥ 구별하다
□ embrace ⓥ 포용하다
□ ensure ⓥ 반드시 ~ 하게 하다

41~42

□ seek ⓥ 찾다
□ pleasure ⓝ 쾌락
□ perceive ⓥ 인식하다
□ stimulus ⓝ 자극
□ ultimately ⓐⓓ 궁극적으로
□ violate ⓥ 침해하다
□ norm ⓝ 표준
□ suffering ⓝ 고통
□ punishment ⓝ 처벌
□ mastery ⓝ 숙달
□ remarkable ⓐ 놀라운
□ stimulate ⓥ 자극시키다
□ receptor ⓝ 수용체
□ activate ⓥ 활성화시키다
□ tissue ⓝ (세포) 조직
□ fire off 발사하다
□ derive ⓥ 끌어내다
□ exposure ⓝ 노출
□ preference ⓝ 선호

6회 모의고사

6회

10

- □ purifier ⓝ 정화 장치
- □ budget ⓝ 예산
- □ capacity ⓝ 용량, 능력
- □ electricity ⓝ 전기
- □ warranty ⓝ (상품 등의) 보증 (기간)

11

- □ auto ⓝ 자동차
- □ in advance 미리, 사전에

12

- □ register ⓥ 등록하다
- □ fantastic ⓐ 엄청난, 환상적인

13

- □ secondhand ⓐ 중고의
- □ bookmark ⓝ 책갈피
- □ resell ⓥ 되팔다
- □ arrive ⓥ 도착하다

14

- □ nature ⓝ 자연
- □ close ⓐ 가까운
- □ relieve ⓥ 줄이다, 없애다
- □ equipment ⓝ 장비

15

- □ assignment ⓝ 과제
- □ section ⓝ 구역, 부분
- □ useful ⓐ 유용한
- □ realize ⓥ 깨닫다

- □ donate ⓥ 기부하다
- □ cafeteria ⓝ 구내식당

16~17

- □ essential ⓐ 필수적인
- □ daily ⓐ 매일의
- □ introduce ⓥ 소개하다
- □ contain ⓥ 함유하다
- □ calm ⓥ 진정하다
- □ definitely ⓐⓓ 확실히
- □ produce ⓥ 생성하다
- □ internal ⓐ 내부의
- □ signal ⓝ 신호
- □ reduce ⓥ 감소하다
- □ disorder ⓝ 장애
- □ origin ⓝ 기원

18

- □ include ⓥ 포함하다
- □ meditation ⓝ 명상
- □ instructor ⓝ 강사
- □ book ⓥ 예약하다
- □ reasonable ⓐ 합리적인
- □ unforgettable ⓐ 잊지 못할

19

- □ midnight ⓝ 자정
- □ nowhere ⓐⓓ 아무 데도 (없다)
- □ crowd ⓝ 군중, 무리
- □ approach ⓥ 다가가다
- □ suddenly ⓐⓓ 갑자기
- □ familiar ⓐ 익숙한, 친숙한
- □ calm ⓐ 침착한

- □ disappear ⓥ 사라지다
- □ indifferent ⓐ 무관심한
- □ embarrassed ⓐ 당황한

20

- □ personal ⓐ 개인적인
- □ sensible ⓐ 실용적인
- □ separate ⓐ 별도의
- □ distraction ⓝ 주의산만
- □ multiple ⓐ 많은
- □ organize ⓥ 정리하다
- □ media ⓝ 매체, 수단
- □ professional ⓐ 직업의
- □ divide ⓥ 나누다
- □ informed ⓐ 정보에 입각한

21

- □ react ⓥ 반응하다
- □ behavior ⓝ 행동
- □ influence ⓝ 영향
- □ likelihood ⓝ 가능성
- □ repurchase ⓥ 재구매하다
- □ determine ⓥ 알아내다
- □ encourage ⓥ 권장하다
- □ satisfied ⓐ 만족한
- □ ambassador ⓝ 대사
- □ persuade ⓥ 설득하다
- □ monitor ⓥ 추적 관찰하다
- □ word-of-mouth ⓐ 구두의, 구전의
- □ gain ⓝ 이득, 대가
- □ manufacturer ⓝ 제조업체, 제조사

□ reward ⓝ 보상
□ overseas ⓐⓓ 해외에서

22

□ promise ⓝ 약속
□ repetitive ⓐ 반복적인
□ pursue ⓥ 추구하다
□ purpose ⓝ 목적
□ leisure ⓝ 여가
□ off-load ⓥ 떠넘기다
□ consumer ⓝ 소비자
□ value-added ⓐ 부가가치의
□ reservation ⓝ 예약
□ agent ⓝ 직원
□ grocery ⓝ 식료품

23

□ possess ⓥ 지니다, 소유하다
□ desirable ⓐ 바람직한
□ characteristic ⓝ 특성, 특징
□ majority ⓝ 다수
□ general ⓐ 일반적인
□ intelligent ⓐ 지적인
□ fair-minded ⓐ 공정한
□ prejudiced ⓐ 편견이 있는
□ automobile ⓝ 자동차
□ average ⓐ 평균의
□ phenomenon ⓝ 현상
□ reliable ⓐ 믿을 만한
□ fictional ⓐ 허구적인
□ senior ⓝ (고등학교의) 졸업반 학생
□ self-image ⓝ 자아상

□ tendency ⓝ 경향
□ superior ⓐ (~보다) 우월한
□ prejudice ⓝ 편견

24

□ poverty ⓝ 가난
□ socioeconomic ⓐ 사회 경제적인
□ status ⓝ 지위
□ associate ⓥ 연상하다, 연관짓다
□ distinct ⓐ 뚜렷한
□ pressure ⓝ 압박
□ psychologist ⓝ 심리학자
□ wealthy ⓐ 부유한
□ industrialized ⓐ 산업화된
□ pace ⓝ 속도
□ standard ⓝ 수준, 기준
□ constant ⓐ 지속적인
□ urgency ⓝ 촉박함
□ lack ⓥ 부족하다
□ trap ⓝ 덫, 함정

25

□ share ⓝ 몫, 점유율
□ region ⓝ 지역
□ decline ⓥ 감소하다

26

□ financial ⓐ 금융의
□ political ⓐ 정치의
□ major in ~을 전공하다
□ economics ⓝ 경제학

□ dissatisfy ⓥ 불만을 느끼게 하다
□ handle ⓥ 다루다
□ earn ⓥ 얻다, 취득하다
□ doctor's degree 박사 학위
□ doctoral ⓐ 박사 학위의
□ mention ⓥ 언급하다
□ contribution ⓝ 기여
□ regular ⓐ 정기적인, 규칙적인
□ analysis ⓝ 분석

6회

27

□ opportunity ⓝ 기회
□ prove ⓥ 증명하다
□ requirement ⓝ 필요 요건
□ award ⓥ 수여하다
□ participant ⓝ 참가자
□ souvenir ⓝ 기념품

28

□ underwater ⓐ 수중의
□ explorer ⓝ 탐험가
□ private ⓐ 개인을 위한
□ rent ⓥ 대여하다
□ equipment ⓝ 장비
□ register ⓥ 등록하다

29

□ praise ⓝ 칭찬
□ equally ⓐⓓ 동등하게
□ self-esteem ⓝ 자존감
□ preschooler ⓝ 미취학 아동
□ cognitive ⓐ 인지적인

□ reason ⓥ 추론하다
□ analytically ⓐⓓ 분석적으로
□ reject ⓥ 거부[거절]하다
□ consistently ⓐⓓ 지속적으로
□ incorporate ⓥ 통합하다
□ self-image ⓝ 자아상
□ endure ⓥ 지속하다, 견디다

30
□ display ⓥ 보여주다, 전시하다
□ considerable ⓐ 상당한
□ facility ⓝ 재능, 시설
□ adapt ⓥ 조절하다
□ claim ⓝ 주장
□ status ⓝ 지위
□ promote ⓥ 홍보하다
□ yeast ⓝ 효모
□ ingredient ⓝ 재료
□ demand ⓝ 수요, 요구
□ hire ⓥ 고용하다
□ strategy ⓝ 전략
□ boost ⓥ 촉진하다
□ significant ⓐ 상당한
□ thereafter ⓐⓓ 그 후에
□ transform ⓥ 바꾸다
□ reposition ⓥ 이미지 전환을 꾀하다

31
□ individual ⓝ 개인
□ profession ⓝ 직업
□ instant ⓐ 즉각적인

□ credibility ⓝ 신뢰
□ admire ⓥ 존경하다
□ advice ⓝ 조언
□ knowledge ⓝ 지식
□ certain ⓐ 특정한
□ expertise ⓝ 전문 지식[기술]
□ talent ⓝ 재능
□ patience ⓝ 인내심, 참을성
□ sacrifice ⓝ 희생

32
□ economy ⓝ 경제
□ emerge ⓥ 나타나다
□ interaction ⓝ 상호 작용
□ element ⓝ 요소
□ merchant ⓝ 상인
□ operation ⓝ 작용, 작동
□ resident ⓝ 거주자
□ scale ⓝ 정도, 규모
□ distantly ⓐⓓ 멀리서
□ textile ⓝ 직물
□ raw ⓐ 가공되지 않은
□ sensory ⓐ 감각의
□ organ ⓝ (체내의) 장기
□ transport ⓥ 전하다, 이동하다
□ superhighway ⓝ 초고속도로
□ undergo ⓥ 겪다
□ conscious ⓐ 의식적인
□ isolation ⓝ 독립, 분리
□ resemble ⓥ 유사하다
□ systemic ⓐ 체계적인

33
□ echo ⓝ 메아리
□ accordingly ⓐⓓ 그에 따라
□ transmit ⓥ 전달하다
□ via ⓟⓡⓔⓟ ~을 통하여
□ theory ⓝ 이론
□ mood ⓝ 기분, 분위기
□ judge ⓥ 판단하다
□ disappear ⓥ 사라지다

34
□ boost ⓥ 증가시키다, 촉진하다
□ investigate ⓥ 조사하다
□ effectiveness ⓝ 효과
□ persuade ⓥ 설득하다
□ condition ⓝ 조건
□ control ⓝ 통제 집단
□ volume ⓝ 용량, 양
□ on average 평균적으로
□ scarce ⓐ 부족한, 드문
□ scarcity ⓝ 희소성
□ particularly ⓐⓓ 특히
□ genuine ⓐ 진짜의
□ claimed ⓐ 주장된
□ laboratory ⓝ 실험실
□ restrict ⓥ 제한하다

35
□ potential ⓝ 잠재력
□ productivity ⓝ 생산성
□ access ⓝ 접근
□ introduce ⓥ 도입하다

□factor ⓝ 요소, 요인
□decline ⓝ 감소

36

□livestock ⓝ 가축
□priest ⓝ 성직자
□religious ⓐ 종교적인
□invent ⓥ 발명하다
□device ⓝ 장치
□gradually ⓐ 점점
□settlement ⓝ 정착지
□timetable ⓝ 시간표
□aeroplane ⓝ 비행기

37

□productivity ⓝ 생산성
□output ⓝ 산출량
□efficient ⓐ 효율적인
□division ⓝ 분배
□specialize in ~을 전문으로 하다
□separate ⓐ 별개의
□manufactured ⓐ 제작된
□straighten ⓥ 펴다
□polish ⓥ 다듬다

38

□stare ⓥ 쳐다보다, 응시하다
□pace ⓝ 속도
□reflect ⓥ 비추다
□proof ⓝ 증거
□interval ⓝ 간격

□recognize ⓥ 알아보다
□moment ⓝ 순간

39

□absorb ⓥ 흡수하다
□possibility ⓝ 가능성
□harden ⓥ 굳어지다
□psychologist ⓝ 심리학자
□curiosity ⓝ 호기심
□mental ⓐ 정신의
□channel ⓝ 경로
□decline ⓝ 감소
□trace ⓥ (원인을) 추적하다
□infant ⓐ 유아의
□neural ⓐ 신경의
□wiring ⓝ 연결, 배선
□mess ⓝ 엉망
□efficient ⓐ 효율적인
□perception ⓝ 인식
□consequently ⓐ 결과적으로
□intensely ⓐ 매우
□wildly ⓐ 상당히, 극도로
□disordered ⓐ 무질서한

40

□spoiled ⓐ 상한
□stew ⓝ 스튜(고기와 채소를 넣고 천천히 끓인 요리)
□poison ⓝ 독
□label ⓥ 분류하다
□combination ⓝ 조합
□boiled ⓐ 끓인, 삶은

□tofu ⓝ 두부
□nutrient ⓝ 영양소
□occasionally ⓐ 가끔
□otherwise ⓐ 그렇지 않으면
□load ⓥ 채우다, 싣다
□supersized ⓐ 초대형의
□soft drink (청량) 음료
□appropriate ⓐ 적절한

6회

41~42

□minimal ⓐ 최소한의
□structure ⓝ 구조
□chief ⓝ 우두머리, 족장
□elder ⓝ 원로, 어른
□surplus ⓝ 잉여, 흑자
□vital ⓐ 필수적인
□sufficient ⓐ 충분한
□council ⓝ 의회
□agriculture ⓝ 농업
□grain ⓝ 곡물
□priest ⓝ 성직자, 사제
□warrior ⓝ 전사
□favorable ⓐ 유리한
□consistent ⓐ 지속적인
□necessity ⓝ 필수품
□concentrate ⓥ 집중하다
□efficient ⓐ 효율적인
□standard ⓝ 기준, 수준
□stability ⓝ 안정성
□shadow ⓝ 그림자
□repetition ⓝ 반복

7회 모의고사

09

- virtual reality 가상현실
- interactive ⓐ 상호작용하는
- available ⓐ 이용 가능한
- free of charge 무료로

10

- belonging ⓝ 소지품
- narrow down 좁히다
- charging port 충전 포트
- external ⓐ 외부의
- internal ⓐ 내부의

11

- repairman ⓝ 수리공
- spare ⓐ 여분의
- fill up ~을 가득 채우다
- entrance ⓝ 입구
- in time 제시간에

12

- prefer ⓥ 선호하다
- comfortable ⓐ 편안한
- effect ⓝ 효과
- set up 설치하다

13

- consider ⓥ 고려하다
- guidance ⓝ 안내, 지도
- score ⓥ 성적을 받다
- make up with ~와 화해하다

14

- challenge ⓝ 도전
- complete ⓥ 완수하다
- unnecessary ⓐ 불필요한
- realize ⓥ 깨닫다
- rewarding ⓐ 보람 있는
- remove ⓥ (어떤 곳에서) 치우다
- stick to ~을 고수하다

15

- recently ⓐⓓ 최근에
- recipe ⓝ 요리법
- afford ⓥ 지불할 능력이 있다
- freshly ⓐⓓ 갓 ~한

16~17

- countryside ⓝ 시골
- must-have ⓐ 필수적인
- observation ⓝ 관찰
- spot ⓥ 발견하다
- behavior ⓝ 행동
- appearance ⓝ 외형
- capture ⓥ 포착하다
- adventure ⓝ 모험
- navigate ⓥ 길을 찾다
- necessity ⓝ 필수품
- surroundings ⓝ 환경, 주변
- outdoor ⓐ 야외의
- essential ⓐ 필수적인
- practical ⓐ 실용적인
- wildlife ⓝ 야생동물
- inspire ⓥ 영감을 주다

18

- reach out 연락하다
- current ⓐ 현재의
- operating hour 운영 시간
- resource ⓝ 자원
- entrance ⓝ 입학
- academic ⓐ 학문의, 학업의
- extend ⓥ 연장하다
- proposal ⓝ 제안

19

- glance ⓥ 흘끗 보다
- casting director 섭외 감독
- chew ⓥ 씹다
- jiggle ⓥ 가볍게 흔들다
- rush ⓝ 물결
- production ⓝ 작품

20

- inefficient ⓐ 비효율적인
- overlook ⓥ 간과하다
- potential ⓐ 잠재적인
- demand ⓝ 요구
- disappear ⓥ 사라지다
- get ~ off to a great start ~을 순조롭게 시작하다
- set the tone 분위기를 잡다
- brief ⓐ 짧은
- transition ⓝ 변화
- material ⓝ 자료
- establish ⓥ 설립하다, 마련하다

21

□ **atom** ⓝ 원자
□ **inhale** ⓥ 흡입하다
□ **exhale** ⓥ 내뱉다
□ **means** ⓝ 수단, 방법
□ **make up** ~을 구성하다
□ **cycle** ⓥ 순환하다
□ **sweat** ⓝ 땀
□ **grand** ⓐ 거대한
□ **scale** ⓝ 규모
□ **limitless** ⓐ 제한 없는
□ **caretaker** ⓝ 관리인

22

□ **dig** ⓥ 파다
□ **harvest** ⓥ 수확하다
□ **flexibility** ⓝ 유연성
□ **endurance** ⓝ 내구력
□ **beneficial** ⓐ 이익을 가져오는
□ **incredibly** ⓐⓓ 믿을 수 없게
□ **meditative** ⓐ 명상의
□ **anxiety** ⓝ 불안감
□ **mindfulness** ⓝ 마음 돌봄
□ **meditation** ⓝ 명상
□ **elevate** ⓥ 증진시키다
□ **cognition** ⓝ 인지
□ **depression** ⓝ 우울함
□ **accomplishment**
  ⓝ 성취감
□ **thrive** ⓥ 번성하다, 번영하다
□ **boost** ⓥ 높이다
□ **self-esteem** ⓝ 자아존중감

23

□ **translate** ⓥ 바꾸다
□ **perception** ⓝ 지각
□ **feed into** ~에 들어가다
□ **sensory** ⓐ 감각의
□ **telescope** ⓝ 망원경
□ **ultraviolet** ⓐ 자외(선)의
□ **property** ⓝ 속성
□ **capacity** ⓝ 수용
□ **difficulty** ⓝ 어려움
□ **replace A with B** A를 B로
  대체하다
□ **inspire** ⓥ 영감을 주다
□ **visual** ⓐ 시각의
□ **auditory** ⓐ 청각의
□ **imagination** ⓝ 상상

24

□ **opponent** ⓝ 반대자
□ **mortality** ⓝ 사망률
□ **advance** ⓝ 발전, 진보
□ **contribute** ⓥ 기여하다
□ **defender** ⓝ 옹호자
□ **correlation** ⓝ 상관관계
□ **inference** ⓝ 추론
□ **prescribe** ⓥ 규정하다
□ **surgical** ⓐ 외과의
□ **evidence** ⓝ 증거
□ **biomedical** ⓐ 생물 의학의
□ **substantial** ⓐ 중요한
□ **unlock** ⓥ 열다
□ **frontier** ⓝ 경계, 지평
□ **refer to** ~을 참고하다
□ **strict** ⓐ 엄격한

□ **adoption** ⓝ 입양
□ **extend** ⓥ 연장하다
□ **life span** 수명

25

□ **consumption** ⓝ 소비
□ **preference** ⓝ 선호(도)
□ **consume** ⓥ 소비하다
□ **least** ⓐⓓ 가장 적게

26

□ **biology** ⓝ 생물학
□ **eventually** ⓐⓓ 마침내, 결국
□ **complex** ⓐ 복잡한
□ **communicate**
  ⓥ 의사소통하다
□ **release** ⓥ 발표하다, 출시하다
□ **movement** ⓝ (사회적) 운동
□ **found** ⓥ 설립하다
□ **alliance** ⓝ 동맹, 연합
□ **career** ⓝ 경력, 생애
□ **pollution** ⓝ 오염
□ **marine** ⓐ 해양의
□ **mammal** ⓝ 포유류
□ **ban** ⓝ 금지
□ **commercial** ⓐ 상업적인
□ **whaling** ⓝ 고래 포획

27

□ **annual** ⓐ 연례의, 매년의
□ **participation** ⓝ 참가, 참여
□ **fee** ⓝ 요금
□ **additional** ⓐ 추가의
□ **refund** ⓝ 환불

□ cancellation ⓝ 취소
□ participant ⓝ 참가자
□ registration ⓝ 등록

28

□ creativity ⓝ 창의성
□ slogan ⓝ 슬로건, 구호
□ commercialized ⓐ 상업화된
□ submission ⓝ 제출
□ limit ⓥ 제한하다
□ entry ⓝ 출품작
□ submit ⓥ 제출하다

29

□ mammalian ⓐ 포유류의
□ species ⓝ 종
□ react ⓥ 반응하다
□ predator ⓝ 포식자
□ instant ⓐ 즉각적인
□ perceive ⓥ 인지하다, 감지하다
□ threat ⓝ 위협
□ protection ⓝ 보호
□ captivity ⓝ 사육, 감금
□ enclosure ⓝ 우리, 울타리
□ panic ⓥ 공황 상태에 빠지다
□ repeatedly ⓐ 반복적으로
□ attempt ⓝ 시도
□ frequently ⓐ 빈번하게
□ opportunity ⓝ 기회
□ domesticate ⓥ 길들이다, 사육하다

□ blindly ⓐ 맹목적으로
□ leap ⓥ 뛰어오르다

30

□ resource ⓝ 자원
□ tendency ⓝ 경향
□ cooperate ⓥ 협력하다
□ complicated ⓐ 복잡한
□ plenty ⓐ 풍부한
□ interest ⓝ 이익
□ survival ⓝ 생존
□ depend on ~에 달려있다
□ shelter ⓝ 안식처
□ ironically ⓐ 역설적으로
□ sophisticated ⓐ 정교한
□ desire ⓝ 욕망
□ combine A with B A를 B와 결합하다
□ interaction ⓝ 상호작용
□ disconnection ⓝ 단절

31

□ content ⓐ 만족하는
□ discontent ⓐ 불만족하는
□ determined ⓐ 결정되는
□ merely ⓐ 단지
□ successive ⓐ 연속적인
□ affect ⓥ 영향을 미치다
□ adjust ⓥ 적응하다
□ default ⓝ 기본값
□ well-being ⓝ 행복, 안녕
□ baseline ⓝ 기준선
□ fade ⓥ 사라지다, 희미해지다
□ despair ⓝ 절망

□ tendency ⓝ 경향
□ long for ~을 갈망하다
□ adapt ⓥ 적응하다
□ regret ⓥ 후회하다
□ struggle ⓥ 고군분투하다

32

□ put off 미루다, 연기하다
□ eventually ⓐ 결국
□ overwhelming ⓐ 압도적인
□ drive ⓝ 욕구, 충동
□ chemical ⓝ 화학물질
□ build up 쌓이다
□ break down 분해하다
□ molecule ⓝ 분자
□ trigger ⓥ 유발하다
□ optimal ⓐ 최적의
□ debt ⓝ 빚
□ make up 보충하다
□ built-in ⓐ 내재된
□ lack ⓝ 부족, 결핍
□ take away 뺏다
□ swing ⓝ (기분의) 변화
□ catch up with ~을 따라잡다

33

□ uncertainty ⓝ 불확실성
□ appreciate ⓥ 이해하다, 진가를 알다
□ relatively ⓐ 상대적으로
□ precise ⓐ 정확한, 정밀한
□ digit ⓝ 자릿수
□ accuracy ⓝ 정확도
□ quoted ⓐ 인용된

□depend on ~에 달려 있다
□intend ⓥ 의도하다
□satellite ⓝ (인공)위성
□orbit ⓥ 궤도를 돌다
□accurately ⓐⓓ 정확하게
□significance ⓝ 중요성
□relative ⓐ 상대적인
□intention ⓝ 의도

34
□renewable energy 재생 가능 에너지
□infrastructure ⓝ 사회 기반 시설
□alternative ⓐ 대안의
□procedure ⓝ 절차
□transformation ⓝ 변화, 변혁
□fossil fuel 화석 연료
□steel ⓝ 강철
□element ⓝ 요소
□require ⓥ 필요로 하다
□scarce ⓐ 희귀한
□mineral ⓝ 광물
□undermining ⓐ 약화시키는
□effort ⓝ 노력
□emission ⓝ 배출(물)
□remark ⓥ 말하다, 언급하다
□transition ⓝ 전환
□supply ⓝ 공급
□take advantage of ~을 활용하다
□construction ⓝ 건설
□competitive ⓐ 경쟁력 있는

35
□intelligent ⓐ 지능적인
□decision ⓝ 결정
□myth ⓝ 신화
□literature ⓝ 문학
□mathematician ⓝ 수학자
□reason ⓥ 추론하다
□measure ⓥ 측정하다
□intelligence ⓝ 지능
□autonomously ⓐⓓ 자율적으로
□coin ⓥ (신조어를) 만들다
□previously ⓐⓓ 이전에
□appearance ⓝ 등장
□practice ⓝ 실행, 실제
□reasoning ⓝ 추론

36
□cope with ~에 대처하다
□extreme ⓐ 극심한
□avoid ⓥ 피하다
□reptile ⓝ 파충류
□rely on ~에 의존하다
□sophisticated ⓐ 정교한
□reabsorb ⓥ 재흡수하다
□take in ~을 섭취하다
□freshwater ⓝ 담수
□creature ⓝ 생물
□immobile ⓐ 움직이지 않는
□surface ⓥ 표면으로 나오다
□stock up on ~을 비축하다
□survival ⓝ 생존
□ranger ⓝ 경비대원, 순찰대원
□reserves ⓝ 비축물

37
□level ⓐ 평평한
□force ⓝ 힘
□act ⓥ 작용하다
□friction ⓝ 마찰
□rub ⓥ 문지르다
□resistance ⓝ 저항
□generate ⓥ 발생시키다
□rotate ⓥ 회전하다
□gradually ⓐⓓ 점차적으로
□exert ⓥ (힘을) 가하다
□grip ⓥ 꽉 잡다

38
□nonlinear ⓐ 비선형의
□random ⓐ 임의의
□scene ⓝ 장면
□reverse ⓥ 되감다
□highlight ⓝ 주요 특징
□editor ⓝ 편집자
□remove ⓥ 제거하다
□adjust ⓥ 조정하다
□automatically ⓐⓓ 자동적으로
□compose ⓥ 작성하다, 구성하다
□retype ⓥ 다시 타이핑하다
□delete ⓥ 삭제하다
□keystroke ⓝ 키 입력

39
□prevent ⓥ 막다, 예방하다
□harm ⓝ 해, 손해
□morally ⓐⓓ 도덕적으로

□ significantly @d 상당히, 훨씬

□ judge ⓥ 판단하다

□ intention ⓝ 의도

□ motive ⓝ 동기

□ relevant ⓐ 관련된

□ intend ⓥ 의도하다

□ unintentionally @d 의도치 않게

□ occur ⓥ 발생하다

□ impression ⓝ 인상

□ actual ⓐ 실제의

□ consequence ⓝ 결과

□ count ⓥ 중요하다

□ contrary to ~와는 반대로

□ necessary ⓐ 필요한

□ regard ⓥ 여기다, 간주하다

40

□ preconception ⓝ 선입견

□ establish ⓥ 확립하다

□ unconscious ⓐ 무의식적인

□ hierarchy ⓝ 위계

□ reflect ⓥ 반영하다

□ functional ⓐ 기능적인

□ momentary ⓐ 순간적인

□ priority ⓝ 우선순위

□ visualize ⓥ 마음속에 그리다

□ tend to-v ~하는 경향이 있다

□ profile ⓝ 옆모습

□ interfere with ~을 방해하다

□ document ⓥ 기록하다

□ impartially @d 공정하게

□ interpret ⓥ 해석하다

□ mechanical ⓐ 기계적인

□ indifference ⓝ 무관심

□ unrecognizable ⓐ 알아볼 수 없는

□ perspective ⓝ 관점

□ enhance ⓥ 향상시키나

□ neutral ⓐ 중립적인

41~42

□ retail ⓝ 소매

□ utter ⓥ (말을) 하다

□ encourage ⓥ 장려하다

□ defensive ⓐ 방어적인

□ stop cold 갑자기 멈추다

□ transaction ⓝ 거래

□ approach ⓥ 접근하다

□ rote ⓐ 기계적인

□ overused ⓐ 남용되는

□ immediate ⓐ 즉각적인

□ assistance ⓝ 도움, 지원

□ subconscious ⓐ 잠재의식의

□ figure out 알아내다

□ promote ⓥ 촉진하다, 조성하다

□ furthermore @d 게다가

□ accessible ⓐ 접근 가능한

43~45

□ period ⓝ 교시

□ force ⓥ 강요하다

□ understanding ⓝ 이해

□ alike ⓐ 비슷한, 닮은

□ accept ⓥ 받아들이다

□ determined ⓐ 단호한, 결심이 굳은

□ expression ⓝ 표정

□ aimlessly @d 목적 없이, 아무렇게나

□ direction ⓝ 방향

□ wrinkled ⓐ 구겨진

□ nervously @d 초조하게

□ glance ⓥ 힐끗 보다

□ give up 포기하다

8회 모의고사

01
- announcement ⓝ 안내
- fireworks ⓝ 불꽃놀이
- transportation ⓝ 교통
- extend ⓥ 연장하다
- operational hours 운영(운행) 시간
- regular ⓐ 정규의
- journey ⓝ 이동, 여행
- take advantage of ~을 이용하다
- convenience ⓝ 편의

02
- screen time 스크린 타임 (스마트폰을 사용하는 시간)
- exposure ⓝ 노출
- stay awake 깨어 있다
- impact ⓝ 영향
- reduce ⓥ 줄이다
- increase ⓥ 높이다
- quality ⓝ 질

03
- helpful ⓐ 도움이 되는, 유익한
- relieve ⓥ 완화하다
- significantly ⓐⓓ 상당히
- reduce ⓥ 줄이다
- might A rather than B B보다는 A일 수도 있다

04
- impressive ⓐ 인상적인
- direction ⓝ 지시
- comfortable ⓐ 편안한
- cozy ⓐ 아늑한

05
- preparation ⓝ 준비
- exhibition ⓝ 전시
- setup ⓝ 설치
- eco-friendly ⓐ 친환경의
- confirm ⓥ 확인하다
- ceremony ⓝ 의식, 식
- double-check ⓥ 다시 확인하다
- deal with ~을 처리하다
- reusable ⓐ 재사용할 수 있는
- confident ⓐ 자신감 있는, 확신하는

06
- recommend ⓥ 추천하다
- fold ⓥ 접다
- discount ⓝ 할인

07
- indeed ⓐⓓ 정말
- equipment ⓝ 장비

- option ⓝ 선택
- refreshing ⓐ 상쾌한
- well-chosen ⓐ 잘 선택된, 적절한

- upcoming ⓐ 다가오는
- practice ⓥ 연습하다
- entire ⓐ 전체의
- competition ⓝ 경연
- mention ⓥ 언급하다

08
- resident ⓝ 거주자
- register ⓥ 등록하다
- application ⓝ 신청(서)
- ID card 신분증 (=identity card)

09
- student council 학생회
- announce ⓥ 알리다
- journey ⓝ 여행
- vegetarian ⓝ 채식주의자
- celebration ⓝ 기념
- diversity ⓝ 다양성

10
- temperature ⓝ 온도
- differ ⓥ 다르다
- reasonable ⓐ 타당한
- function ⓝ 기능
- intake ⓝ 섭취

11
- catch a cold 감기에 걸리다
- moisture ⓝ 습기
- relate to ~와 관련되다
- cough ⓥ 기침하다

12

□ bookshelf ⓝ 책장
□ throw away 버리다
□ condition ⓝ 상태

13

□ challenging ⓐ 어려운
□ motivate ⓥ 동기를 부여하다
□ progress ⓝ 진전
□ assign ⓥ 맡기다
□ task ⓝ 일, 과제
□ crucial ⓐ 중대한
□ overlap ⓥ 겹치다
□ clarify ⓥ 명확히 하다
□ topic ⓝ 주제
□ analyze ⓥ 분석하다

14

□ fit ⓐ 건강한
□ tough ⓐ 힘든
□ lately ⓐ 최근에
□ difference ⓝ 차이
□ careful ⓐ 조심하는
□ notice ⓥ 알아차리다
□ workout ⓝ 운동
□ succeed ⓥ 성공하다
□ balanced ⓐ 균형 잡힌

15

□ college ⓝ 대학
□ dormitory ⓝ 기숙사
□ recently ⓐ 최근에
□ complicated ⓐ 복잡한

□ assemble ⓥ 조립하다
□ furniture ⓝ 가구
□ decorate ⓥ 장식하다

16~17

□ subscriber ⓝ 구독자
□ natural material 천연 재료
□ properly ⓐ 적절히, 제대로
□ hand-wash ⓥ 손빨래하다
□ shrink ⓥ 줄어들다
□ wrinkle ⓥ 주름이 생기다
□ separately ⓐ 별도로
□ direct sunlight 직사광선
□ sensitive ⓐ 민감한
□ vinegar ⓝ 식초
□ trend ⓝ 동향
□ proper ⓐ 적절한

18

□ concern ⓝ 우려
□ traditional ⓐ 전통적인
□ vending machine
　자동판매기
□ assistance ⓝ 도움
□ urge ⓥ 촉구하다
□ regain ⓥ 되찾다
□ prompt ⓐ 신속한
□ resolution ⓝ 해결

19

□ immediately ⓐ 즉시
□ glance ⓥ 흘긋 보다
□ swiftly ⓐ 신속하게
□ kneel ⓥ 무릎을 꿇다

□ combined ⓐ 합쳐진
□ effort ⓝ 노력
□ revive ⓥ 소생시키다
□ thrilled ⓐ 흥분한
□ desperate ⓐ 간절한

20

□ be aware of ~을 알다
　[주의하다]
□ nonstop ⓐ 연속적으로
□ remarkable ⓐ 놀라운
□ bragging ⓐ 자랑하는
□ expectation ⓝ 기대
□ incredible ⓐ 엄청난
□ achievement ⓝ 업적
□ end up with 결국 ~로 끝나다
□ driven ⓐ 지나친
□ perfectionist ⓝ 완벽주의자
□ drop-out ⓝ 학업 중단자,
　중퇴자

21

□ technique ⓝ 기술
□ helplessness ⓝ 무력감
□ depression ⓝ 우울감
□ predominantly ⓐ 현저히
□ resolve ⓥ 해결하다
□ self-help ⓝ 자조, 자립
□ energize ⓥ 활기를 북돋우다
□ be in one's presence
　~의 자리에 (함께) 있다
□ psychic ⓐ 정신의
□ transfer ⓝ 이동
□ relight ⓥ 재점화하다

22

- □ contribute ⓥ 기여하다
- □ species ⓝ 종
- □ bond ⓥ 유대감을 형성하다
- □ evolutionary ⓐ 진화론적인
- □ direct ⓥ 지시하다
- □ attentive ⓐ 주의를 기울이는
- □ narrow ⓥ 좁히다
- □ stimuli ⓝ 자극
- □ acutely ⓓ 강렬하게

23

- □ accessibility ⓝ 접근성
- □ disadvantage ⓝ 불리함
- □ labour ⓝ 노동
- □ inclusiveness ⓝ 포괄성
- □ assistive ⓐ 도움이 되는
- □ recognition ⓝ 인지
- □ caption ⓝ 자막
- □ facilitate ⓥ 촉진하다
- □ capability ⓝ 능력
- □ potentially ⓓ 잠재적으로
- □ wage ⓝ 임금
- □ prospect ⓝ 전망
- □ domain ⓝ 영역
- □ ethical ⓐ 윤리적인
- □ necessity ⓝ 필요성
- □ support ⓥ 지원하다
- □ disadvantage ⓝ 불리한 점, 약점
- □ cure ⓥ 치료하다

24

- □ storage ⓝ 저장
- □ atmosphere ⓝ 대기
- □ comparison ⓝ 비교
- □ absorb ⓥ 흡수하다
- □ marine ⓐ 해양의
- □ equivalent ⓝ (~에) 상응하는 것
- □ fertilize ⓥ 비옥하게 하다
- □ release ⓥ 내보내다
- □ estimate ⓥ 추정하다
- □ incentive ⓝ 장려책
- □ preindustrial ⓐ 산업화 이전의
- □ restoration ⓝ 복원
- □ extinct ⓐ 멸종된
- □ overpopulation ⓝ 과밀 (과잉 밀집)
- □ industry ⓝ 산업
- □ habitat ⓝ 서식지

25

- □ emission ⓝ 배출량
- □ rank ⓥ (순위를) 차지하다
- □ major ⓐ 주요한
- □ respectively ⓓ 각각

26

- □ physicist ⓝ 물리학자
- □ submit ⓥ 제출하다
- □ sponsor ⓥ 후원하다
- □ publish ⓥ 출판하다
- □ relativity ⓝ 상대성

- □ significant ⓐ 주요한
- □ symbol ⓝ 상징
- □ enlightenment ⓝ 계몽주의
- □ struggle ⓝ 투쟁
- □ participation ⓝ 참여

27

- □ competition ⓝ 대회
- □ participant ⓝ 참가자
- □ category ⓝ 분야
- □ remote ⓐ 원격의
- □ registration ⓝ 등록
- □ honor ⓥ 수여하다

28

- □ annual ⓐ 매년의
- □ participate ⓥ 참가하다
- □ exhibition ⓝ 전시

29

- □ organizational ⓐ 조직의
- □ viewpoint ⓝ 관점
- □ fascinating ⓐ 매력적인
- □ functional ⓐ 기능상의
- □ operation ⓝ 운영
- □ varying ⓐ 가지각색의
- □ division ⓝ (조직의) 분과
- □ inevitably ⓓ 필연적으로
- □ prejudiced ⓐ 편견이 있는
- □ acquire ⓥ 습득하다
- □ disallow ⓥ 허가하지 않다
- □ conflict ⓝ 갈등
- □ mechanistic ⓐ 기계적인

□ organic ⓐ 유기적인
□ profound ⓐ 깊은
□ management ⓝ 관리
□ vertical ⓐ 수직의
□ procedure ⓝ 절차
□ horizontal ⓐ 수평의

30

□ alternative ⓝ 대안
□ reserve ⓥ 마련하다
□ extensive ⓐ 광범위한
□ lane ⓝ 길, 도로
□ pedestrian ⓝ 보행자
□ vehicle ⓝ 교통 수단
□ occasional ⓐ 가끔의
□ motivate ⓥ 동기를 부여하다
□ automobile ⓝ 자동차
□ accommodate ⓥ 수용하다
□ frequently ⓐⓓ 자주
□ distribute ⓥ 나누어주다
□ neighborhood ⓝ 이웃
□ vendor ⓝ 상점
□ operate ⓥ 운영하다
□ resident ⓝ 거주자

31

□ misunderstand ⓥ 진가를
  못 알아보다
□ composition ⓝ 작품
□ initial ⓐ 초기의
□ lack ⓝ 부족
□ acceptance ⓝ 수용
□ unfamiliarity ⓝ 낯섦
□ host ⓝ 주인공

□ depict ⓥ 묘사하다
□ composer ⓝ 작곡가
□ overshadow ⓥ 가리다
□ original ⓐ 독창적인
□ conventional ⓐ 관습적인

32

□ medium ⓝ 매체
□ invention ⓝ 발명
□ absorb ⓥ 흡수하다
□ communicate ⓥ 소통하다
□ surface ⓝ 표면
□ appearance ⓝ 겉모습
□ code ⓝ 규칙, 방식
□ interpret ⓥ 해석하다

33

□ concept ⓝ 개념
□ vital ⓐ 필수적인
□ essentialism ⓝ 본질주의
□ proverb ⓝ 속담
□ statement ⓝ 진술
□ essence ⓝ 본질
□ fruitlessly ⓐⓓ 헛되이
□ hypothesis ⓝ 가설(pl.
  hypotheses)
□ luminiferous ⓐ 발광의,
  빛을 내는
□ mysterious ⓐ 신비로운
□ substance ⓝ 물질
□ theorize ⓥ 이론을 세우다
□ simplify ⓥ 단순하게 만들다
□ philosophy ⓝ 철학

34

□ potentially ⓐⓓ 잠재적으로
□ instrument ⓝ 도구
□ end ⓝ 목적
□ celebrity ⓝ 유명인, 명성
□ criticize ⓥ 비판하다
□ highlight ⓥ 강조하다
□ barrier ⓝ 장애물
□ phenomenon ⓝ 현상
□ symbolize ⓥ 상징하다
□ metaphor ⓝ 은유
□ characterize ⓥ 특징짓다
□ hierarchical ⓐ 계층적인
□ scale ⓝ 척도
□ shift ⓥ 전환하다
□ gradually ⓐⓓ 점차
□ solely ⓐⓓ 오로지, 단지
□ restrict ⓥ 제한하다

35

□ illusion ⓝ 착각
□ cram ⓥ 벼락치기를 하다
□ strategy ⓝ 전략
□ differentiate ⓥ 구분하다
□ present ⓐ 존재하는
□ conscious ⓐ 의식적인
□ enormous ⓐ 엄청난
□ vanish ⓥ 사라지다
□ material ⓝ 자료
□ academic ⓐ 학업적인
□ performance ⓝ 성취
□ essential ⓐ 필수적인

36

- □ discovery ⓝ 발견
- □ profoundly ⓐⓓ 완전히
- □ fundamental ⓐ 근본적인
- □ capacity ⓝ 능력
- □ observation ⓝ 관찰
- □ newborn ⓝ 신생아
- □ stick out ~을 내밀다
- □ imitate ⓥ 모방하다
- □ inborn ⓐ 선천적인
- □ tendency ⓝ 성향
- □ restrict ⓥ 제한하다
- □ behavior ⓝ 행동
- □ trial and error 시행착오

37

- □ pathway ⓝ 경로
- □ route ⓝ 경로
- □ perceive ⓥ 인지하다
- □ external ⓐ 외부의
- □ travel ⓥ 이동하다
- □ vibrate ⓥ 진동하다
- □ internal ⓐ 내부의
- □ conduct ⓥ 전하다
- □ stimulate ⓥ 자극하다
- □ emphasize ⓥ 강조하다
- □ pronounced ⓐ 강조된
- □ fairly ⓐⓓ 꽤

38

- □ trait ⓝ 형질
- □ descend ⓥ 내려오다
- □ ancestor ⓝ 조상

- □ hence ⓐⓓ 이런 이유로
- □ structure ⓝ 구조
- □ indicate ⓥ 나타내다
- □ organ ⓝ 기관
- □ distinguish ⓥ 구별하다
- □ similarity ⓝ 유사성
- □ arise ⓥ 생겨나다
- □ independently ⓐⓓ ~와 관계없이
- □ modification ⓝ 수정
- □ forelimb ⓝ 앞다리
- □ mammal ⓝ 포유류
- □ nonfunctional ⓐ 비기능적
- □ architecture ⓝ 구성
- □ property ⓝ 특성

39

- □ marine ⓐ 해양의
- □ self-evident ⓐ 자명한
- □ abundance ⓝ 풍부함
- □ breathe ⓥ 호흡하다
- □ established ⓐ 확립된
- □ polar ⓐ 극지의
- □ tropical ⓐ 열대의
- □ worrisome ⓐ 걱정스러운
- □ potentially ⓐⓓ 잠재적으로
- □ disastrous ⓐ 처참한
- □ consequence ⓝ 결과
- □ analyze ⓥ 분석하다
- □ potential ⓝ 잠재력
- □ organism ⓝ 생물(체)
- □ displace ⓥ 쫓아내다

40

- □ captivity ⓝ 감금
- □ trade ⓥ 거래하다
- □ cucumber ⓝ 오이
- □ universally ⓐⓓ 일반적으로
- □ experimenter ⓝ 실험자
- □ source ⓥ 모으다
- □ comparison ⓝ 비교
- □ abandon ⓥ 포기하다
- □ communicate ⓥ 전달하다
- □ displeasure ⓝ 불쾌함

41~42

- □ participation ⓝ 참여
- □ decade ⓝ 10년
- □ typically ⓐⓓ 일반적으로
- □ dramatic ⓐ 극적인
- □ expansion ⓝ 확대
- □ range ⓝ 범주
- □ institution ⓝ 기관
- □ specialised ⓐ 전문화된
- □ workforce ⓝ 노동력
- □ diminish ⓥ 줄어들다
- □ initiate ⓥ 시작하다
- □ approach ⓝ 접근법
- □ development ⓝ 발달
- □ socio-political ⓐ 사회 정치적인
- □ contradiction ⓝ 모순
- □ assessment ⓝ 평가
- □ minimalist ⓐ 최소한의
- □ impersonal ⓐ 비개인적인
- □ standardised ⓐ 표준화된

□ relatively ⓐⓓ 비교적으로
□ character ⓝ 성격
□ class ⓝ 계급
□ status ⓝ 지위

43~45

□ philosopher ⓝ 철학자
□ merchant ⓝ 상인
□ businessman ⓝ 사업가
□ attend ⓥ 참석하다
□ personally ⓐⓓ 직접
□ dip ⓥ 담그다
□ stare at ~을 바라보다
□ a world of 막대한, 엄청난
□ rent ⓥ 대여하다
□ embrace ⓥ 껴안다
□ compliment ⓥ 칭찬하다
□ grand ⓐ 거창한, 웅장한
□ approach ⓥ 접근하다
□ glance ⓝ 눈길
□ greet ⓥ 맞이하다

9회 모의고사

01
□ hold ⓥ 열다, 개최하다
□ auditorium ⓝ 강당
□ look forward to ~을 고대하다
□ leak ⓝ 누수, 새는 곳
□ ceiling ⓝ 천장
□ perform ⓥ 공연하다
□ theater ⓝ 극장

02
□ route ⓝ 길, 경로
□ design ⓥ 만들다, 설계하다

03
□ article ⓝ (신문 · 잡지의) 기사
□ award ⓝ 상
□ talented ⓐ 뛰어난
□ impressive ⓐ 인상적인
□ costume ⓝ 의상
□ script ⓝ 대본
□ background ⓝ 배경

04
□ center ⓝ 중앙, 한가운데
□ striped ⓐ 줄무늬가 있는
□ bookshelf ⓝ 책꽂이
□ lighting ⓝ 조명

05
□ extra ⓐ 추가의
□ wireless ⓐ 무선의
□ terrific ⓐ 아주 좋은
□ audience ⓝ 관객
□ arrange ⓥ 배열하다
□ fantastic ⓐ 환상적인

06
□ anniversary ⓝ 기념일
□ regular ⓐ 보통의
□ purchase ⓝ 구매
□ delivery ⓝ 배달, 배송

07
□ book ⓥ 예약하다
□ recover ⓥ 회복하다
□ surgery ⓝ 수술
□ relative ⓝ 친척

08
□ theme ⓝ 주제
□ deadline ⓝ 마감 기한
□ expect ⓥ 예상하다
□ receive ⓥ 받다
□ prize ⓝ 상품, 경품

09
□ introduce ⓥ 소개하다
□ opportunity ⓝ 기회
□ lecture ⓝ 강의, 강연
□ taste ⓥ 맛보다
□ flavor ⓝ 맛

□register ⓥ 등록하다
□registration ⓝ 등록
□ingredient ⓝ 재료

10
□indoor ⓐ 실내(용)의
□differ ⓥ 다르다
□foldable ⓐ 접을 수 있는
□definitely ⓐⓓ 분명히, 절대로
□take up 차지하다
□storage ⓝ 저장, 보관
□rating ⓝ 평가, 순위
□actual ⓐ 실제의

11
□on sale 할인 중인
□receipt ⓝ 영수증
□return ⓥ 돌려주다, 반품하다

12
□order ⓥ 주문하다
□delivery ⓝ 배달, 배송
□leftover ⓝ 남은 음식

13
□cafeteria ⓝ 구내식당
□skip ⓥ 거르다, 빼먹다
□grade ⓝ 성적
□overeat ⓥ 과식하다
□regularly ⓐⓓ 규칙적으로
□manner ⓝ 예의, 태도
□on time 제시간에

14
□improve ⓥ 향상하다
□repeatedly ⓐⓓ 반복해서
□effort ⓝ 노력
□suggest ⓥ 제안하다
□vocabulary ⓝ 어휘
□repetition ⓝ 반복

15
□passionate ⓐ 열정적인
□environmental ⓐ 환경의
□notice ⓥ 알아차리다
□careless ⓐ 부주의한
□remind ⓥ 상기하다
□encourage ⓥ 장려하다
□remove ⓥ 제거하다
□board ⓝ 게시판
□heater ⓝ 난방(기)

16~17
□overtourism ⓝ 과잉 관광
□particular ⓐ 특정한
□destination ⓝ 목적지
□limit ⓥ 제한하다
□allow ⓥ 허용하다
□promote ⓥ 홍보하다
□site ⓝ 장소, 위치
□access ⓝ 접근
□reduce ⓥ 줄이다
□overall ⓐⓓ 전반적으로
□dock ⓥ 정박하다
□rent ⓥ 빌리다

□correlation ⓝ 상관관계
□transportation ⓝ 교통 (수단)

18
□director ⓝ 책임자, 관리자
□chemistry ⓝ 화학
□local ⓐ 지역의
□goal ⓝ 목표
□experiment ⓝ 실험
□contact ⓥ 연락하다
□recommend ⓥ 추천하다
□department ⓝ (대학의) 학과
□look forward to ~을 고대하다

19
□risk ⓝ 위험
□definitely ⓐⓓ 분명히
□persuade ⓥ 설득하다
□pin ⓥ 꼼짝 못하게 하다
□deceptively ⓐⓓ 속을 정도로, 믿을 수 없게
□handhold ⓝ 손으로 잡을 곳
□clumsily ⓐⓓ 서투르게
□cliff ⓝ 절벽
□reach ⓝ (닿을 수 있는) 거리[범위]
□tremble ⓥ 떨(리)다
□exhaustion ⓝ 기진맥진
□fright ⓝ 공포, 놀람
□fearful ⓐ 두려운
□regretful ⓐ 후회하는

20

□ action ⓝ 행동
□ overhear ⓥ 우연히 듣다
□ value ⓝ 가치
□ priority ⓝ 우선순위
□ tempting ⓐ 솔깃한
□ uphold ⓥ 유지하다
□ respect ⓥ 존중하다
□ compassion ⓝ 연민
□ concern ⓝ 걱정
□ suffer ⓥ 고통받다
□ self-discipline ⓝ 자제력
□ honesty ⓝ 정직함

21

□ indeed ⓐⓓ 정말로
□ hearer ⓝ 듣는 사람
□ process ⓝ 과정
□ signal ⓝ 신호
□ useless ⓐ 쓸모없는
□ perceive ⓥ 감지하다
□ receive ⓥ 수신하다, 받다
□ intended ⓐ 의도된
□ audience ⓝ 관객, 독자
□ restate ⓥ 다시 말하다
□ experiment ⓝ 실험
□ publication ⓝ 출판
□ previous ⓐ 이전의
□ demand ⓝ 요구

22

□ negotiate ⓥ 협상하다
□ realise ⓥ 알아차리다

□ traditional ⓐ 전통적인
□ approach ⓝ 접근(법)
□ agreement ⓝ 합의, 동의
□ one-off ⓐ 단 한 번의
□ transaction ⓝ 거래
□ rare ⓐ 드문
□ repeatedly ⓐⓓ 반복적으로
□ spouse ⓝ 배우자
□ essential ⓐ 매우 중요한
□ maintain ⓥ 유지하다
□ interdependent ⓐ 상호 의존적인
□ acceptable ⓐ 받아들일 수 있는

23

□ interaction ⓝ 상호작용
□ productivity ⓝ 생산성
□ spillover ⓝ 여파, 파급
□ degree ⓝ 정도
□ excessive ⓐ 과도한
□ transaction ⓝ 거래
□ diversity ⓝ 다양성
□ labour ⓝ 노동
□ tolerant ⓐ 관대한
□ multicultural ⓐ 다문화의
□ region ⓝ 지역
□ perceive ⓥ 인식하다
□ unattractive ⓐ 매력적이지 않은
□ feature ⓝ 특징
□ distortion ⓝ 왜곡
□ discriminate ⓥ 차별하다
□ ethnic ⓐ 민족의

□ conflict ⓝ 갈등
□ nationality ⓝ 국적
□ import ⓥ 수입하다, 유입하다
□ contrastive ⓐ 대조하는
□ perspective ⓝ 관점

24

□ development ⓝ 개발
□ construction ⓝ 건축(물)
□ carve ⓥ 조각하다
□ ancestor ⓝ 조상
□ erect ⓐ (똑바로) 세우다
□ successive ⓐ 연속적인
□ innovator ⓝ 혁신가
□ settle down 정착하다
□ radically ⓐⓓ 근본적으로
□ transform ⓥ 바꾸다

25

□ given ⓐ 주어진, 정해진
□ among ⓟⓡⓔⓟ ~ 중에서
□ decrease ⓝ 감소

26

□ receive ⓥ 받다
□ bachelor's degree 학사 학위
□ military ⓝ 군대
□ composition ⓝ 작곡
□ admire ⓥ 감탄하다
□ hire ⓥ 고용하다
□ expressive ⓐ 표현적인
□ harmonic ⓐ 화성의
□ approach ⓝ 접근

27

- □ available ⓐ 이용할 수 있는
- □ material ⓝ 재료
- □ registration ⓝ 등록
- □ limit ⓥ 제한하다
- □ participant ⓝ 참가자
- □ refund ⓝ 환불
- □ cancellation ⓝ 취소

28

- □ awareness ⓝ 인식
- □ annual ⓐ 연례의
- □ knowledge ⓝ 지식
- □ marine ⓐ 해양의
- □ conservation ⓝ 보존
- □ pollution ⓝ 오염
- □ submission ⓝ 제출
- □ entry ⓝ 출품[응모]작

29

- □ exist ⓥ 존재하다
- □ professional ⓝ 전문가
- □ degree ⓝ 학위
- □ expertise ⓝ 전문 지식
- □ executive ⓝ 경영진, 간부
- □ decade ⓝ 10년
- □ respective ⓐ 각자의
- □ criticism ⓝ 비판, 비난
- □ surgery ⓝ 수술
- □ accountant ⓝ 회계사
- □ organization ⓝ 조직

30

- □ particularly ⓐⓓ 특히
- □ security ⓝ 안도감, 안심
- □ disoriented ⓐ 혼란에 빠진
- □ disrupt ⓥ 방해하다
- □ take away ~을 제거하다
- □ literal ⓐ 융통성이 없는, 문자 그대로의
- □ beforehand ⓐⓓ 미리
- □ establish ⓥ 확고히 하다, 설립하다
- □ validate ⓥ 인정하다
- □ contribute ⓥ 기여하다
- □ transition ⓝ 변화

31

- □ terrified ⓐ 두려워하는
- □ stem from ~에서 생겨나다
- □ passenger ⓝ 승객
- □ potential ⓐ 잠재적인
- □ destination ⓝ 목적지
- □ base ⓥ 근거하다
- □ solely ⓐⓓ 오로지
- □ logic ⓝ 논리
- □ statistically ⓐⓓ 통계적으로
- □ odds ⓝ (어떤 일이 있을) 가능성
- □ boredom ⓝ 지루함
- □ responsibility ⓝ 책임감

32

- □ downplay ⓥ 경시하다
- □ similarity ⓝ 유사성
- □ imaginary ⓐ 상상에만 존재하는

- □ ladder ⓝ 사다리
- □ offender ⓝ 범죄자
- □ contact ⓝ 접촉
- □ primate ⓝ 영장류
- □ interpret ⓥ 해석하다
- □ evidence ⓝ 증거
- □ crow ⓝ 까마귀
- □ qualitatively ⓐⓓ 질적으로
- □ define ⓥ 정의하다
- □ humanity ⓝ 인류
- □ beat ⓥ 이기다
- □ cognitive ⓐ 인지적인
- □ precise ⓐ 정확한
- □ instinct ⓝ 본능
- □ intelligence ⓝ 지능
- □ linguistic ⓐ 언어(학)의
- □ castration ⓝ 거세
- □ overestimate ⓥ 과대평가하다
- □ misconception ⓝ 오해

33

- □ engagement ⓝ 참여
- □ achievement ⓝ 성취
- □ scholarly ⓐ 학문적인
- □ physicist ⓝ 물리학자
- □ biochemist ⓝ 생화학자
- □ significant ⓐ 중요한, 상당한
- □ bypass ⓥ 우회하다
- □ compensate ⓥ 보완하다
- □ strategy ⓝ 전략
- □ enthusiastic ⓐ 열성적인
- □ rarely ⓐⓓ 좀처럼 ~않는

□seek ⓥ 찾다
(seek-sought-sought)

□subject ⓝ 실험대상자, 대상

□passionate ⓐ 열정적인

34

□refer to ~을 나타내다

□intellectual ⓐ 지적인

□competence ⓝ 능력, 능숙함

□brilliant ⓐ 훌륭한

□legal ⓐ 법률과 관련된

□brief ⓝ 업무 (보고서)

□elegant ⓐ 우아한, 정연한

□exceptionally ⓐⓓ 각별히

□witty ⓐ 재치 있는

□gadget ⓝ 기기, 장치

□measure ⓝ 척도, 기준

□take into account ~을 고려하다

□outstanding ⓐ 뛰어난

□sole ⓐ 유일한

□determinant ⓝ 결정 요인

□accompany ⓥ 동반하다

35

□sensory ⓐ 감각의

□nerve ⓝ 신경

□ending ⓝ 끝, 말단

□tissue ⓝ (세포로 이루어진) 조직

□sensation ⓝ 감각

□transmit ⓥ 전달하다

□protective ⓐ 보호하는

□mechanism ⓝ 방법, 메커니즘

□capacity ⓝ 능력, 용량

□polite ⓐ 공손한

□muscle ⓝ 근육

□contract ⓥ 수축하다

□function ⓝ 기능

□sweating ⓝ 발한

36

□hexagon ⓝ 육각형

□condition ⓝ 조건

□twisted ⓐ 뒤틀린

□atom ⓝ 원자

□display ⓝ 배열

□steady ⓐ 안정적인, 꾸준한

□individual ⓐ 개별적인

37

□string ⓝ 줄, 끈

□vibration ⓝ 진동

□pressure ⓝ 압력

□eardrum ⓝ 고막

□flex ⓥ 굽히다

□blurred ⓐ 흐릿한

□outline ⓝ 윤곽, 개요

□hardly ⓐⓓ 거의 ~ 않다

□hollow ⓐ (속이) 빈

□pass on ~을 전달하다

□panel ⓝ 판

38

□integrate ⓥ 통합하다

□boundary ⓝ 경계(선)

□blur ⓥ 흐릿해지다

□portable ⓐ 휴대용의

□responsibility ⓝ 책임(감)

□separate ⓥ 분리하다

□segment ⓥ 분할하다

□minimize ⓥ 최소화하다

□conduct ⓥ 수행하다

□flexible ⓐ 유연한

□distinction ⓝ 구별, 차이

□constantly ⓐⓓ 거듭, 지속적으로

□inbox ⓝ 받은 편지함

39

□assume ⓥ 가정하다

□complementary ⓐ (상호) 보완적인

□lock ⓥ 고정하다, 잠그다

□alongside ⓟⓡⓔⓟ ~와 함께

□pillow ⓝ 베개

□journey ⓝ 여행

□popularity ⓝ 인기

□complement ⓥ 보완하다

□ensure ⓥ 보장하다

□steady ⓐ 꾸준한

□stream ⓝ 흐름, 연속

□status ⓝ 상태

□motorist ⓝ 운전자

□gasoline ⓝ 휘발유

40

□investigate ⓥ 조사하다

□judgment ⓝ 판단

□expectation ⓝ 예상, 기대

10회 모의고사

□ capture ⓥ 사로잡다

□ attention ⓝ 관심

□ serve ⓥ 역할을 하다

□ hook ⓝ 후크 (청중의 흥미를
이끄는 문장)

□ eager ⓐ ~하고 싶어 하는

□ challenging ⓐ 어려운,
도전적인

□ statistic ⓝ 통계

□ attractive ⓐ 매력적인

04

□ daycare center 돌봄 센터

□ slide ⓝ 미끄럼틀

□ star-patterned ⓐ 별 무늬의

□ bone-shaped ⓐ 뼈 모양의

□ dispenser ⓝ 지급기

□ delighted ⓐ 기쁜

05

□ complete ⓥ 완성하다

□ flash mob 플래시몹

□ record ⓥ 기록하다

□ understanding ⓝ 이해

□ forget ⓥ 잊어버리다

□ choose ⓥ 선택하다

□ immediately ⓐⒹ 즉시

06

□ need ⓝ 필요

□ option ⓝ 선택(할 수 있는 것),
선택권

□ disorder ⓝ 장애

□ sound sleep 숙면

□ scent ⓝ 향

□ effective ⓐ 효과적인

□ sensitive ⓐ 민감한

□ reasonable ⓐ 합리적인

□ discount ⓝ 할인

□ valid ⓐ 유효한

07

□ catch a cold 감기에 걸리다

□ stick ⓝ 막대기

□ recommend ⓥ 추천하다

□ look after 돌보다

□ apply ⓥ 지원하다

□ attend ⓥ 참여[참석]하다

08

□ humanities ⓝ 인문학

□ annual ⓐ 연례의

□ purpose ⓝ 목적

□ explore ⓥ 탐구하다

□ novelist ⓝ 소설가

□ birthplace ⓝ 출생지

□ senior ⓐ 고학년의, 연장자의

□ priority ⓝ 우선순위

□ registration fee 등록비

□ afford ⓥ (~을 살 · 할 금전적 ·
시간적) 여유가 되다

09

□ opening ceremony
개장식

□ hold ⓥ 개최하다

□ floor ⓝ 층

□ table tennis 탁구

□ importantly ⓐⒹ 중요하게

□ available ⓐ 이용 가능한

□ entrance ⓝ 입구

□ continue ⓥ 계속되다

□ following ⓐ 다음의

□ reservation ⓝ 예약

10

□ broken ⓐ 고장 난

□ reasonable ⓐ 합리적인

□ manual ⓐ 수동의

□ automatic ⓐ 자동의

□ convenient ⓐ 편리한

□ consider ⓥ 고려하다

□ storage ⓝ 저장

□ capacity ⓝ 용량

□ adjustability ⓝ 조절 기능

11

□ awesome ⓐ (매우) 재미있는,
굉장한

□ unexpectedly ⓐⒹ 예상치
못하게

12

□ bring ⓥ 가져오다

□ order ⓥ 주문하다

□ delivery ⓝ 배달

□ status ⓝ 상태

□ arrive ⓥ 도착하다

13

- □ digest ⓥ 소화시키다
- □ medical check-up 건강 검진
- □ prescribe ⓥ 처방하다
- □ unfortunate ⓐ 안타까운, 불운한
- □ symptom ⓝ 증상
- □ relieve ⓥ 완화하다
- □ stomach ⓝ 위장
- □ rely on ~에 의존하다
- □ ease ⓥ 편하게 해 주다

14

- □ especially ⓐⓓ 특히
- □ ask for 요청하다
- □ bill ⓝ 청구서
- □ puzzled ⓐ 당황스러운
- □ rude ⓐ 무례한
- □ complain ⓥ 불평하다
- □ politely ⓐⓓ 정중하게
- □ remove ⓥ 빼다, 제거하다

15

- □ select ⓥ 선택하다
- □ subject ⓝ 과목
- □ advanced ⓐ 고급의
- □ doubt ⓥ 의문을 갖다
- □ advice ⓝ 조언
- □ semester ⓝ 학기
- □ concern ⓝ 걱정
- □ creative ⓐ 창의적인

16~17

- □ institute ⓝ 기관
- □ affect ⓥ 영향을 미치다
- □ speedy ⓐ 신속한
- □ personalized ⓐ 개인화된
- □ significantly ⓐⓓ 크게, 상당히
- □ reduce ⓥ 감소시키다
- □ workload ⓝ 업무량
- □ influence ⓥ 영향을 미치다
- □ assistant ⓝ 비서
- □ handle ⓥ 다루다
- □ contract ⓝ 계약
- □ impact ⓝ 영향
- □ monitor ⓥ 모니터링[감시]하다
- □ provide ⓥ 제공하다
- □ edit ⓥ 편집하다
- □ realistic ⓐ 사실적인
- □ potential ⓝ 잠재력
- □ influential ⓐ 영향력 있는

18

- □ funding ⓝ 재정 지원
- □ construction ⓝ 건축, 건설
- □ additional ⓐ 추가적인
- □ functional ⓐ 기능을 하는
- □ submit ⓥ 제출하다
- □ documentation ⓝ 서류
- □ notification ⓝ 통지
- □ considerable ⓐ 상당한
- □ consequence ⓝ 결과
- □ budgetary ⓐ 예산의
- □ constraint ⓝ 제약
- □ notify A of B A에게 B를 통지하다

19

- □ hard-fought ⓐ 치열히 싸운
- □ figure ⓥ 생각하다
- □ race ⓥ 빠르게 뛰다
- □ anticipation ⓝ 기대감
- □ fall apart 무너지다

20

- □ commitment ⓝ 전념, 헌신
- □ obligation ⓝ 의무
- □ dedicated ⓐ 전념[헌신]하는
- □ integrate ⓥ 통합하다
- □ chore ⓝ 일
- □ come into play 작동하다
- □ realistic ⓐ 현실적인
- □ inevitable ⓐ 피할 수 없는
- □ seize ⓥ 잡다
- □ engage in ~을 시작하다
- □ incorporate ⓥ 포함하다

21

- □ automatically ⓐⓓ 자동적으로
- □ break up 해체하다
- □ concept ⓝ 개념
- □ recode ⓥ 재부호화하다
- □ reconstruct ⓥ 재구성하다
- □ trait ⓝ 특성
- □ store ⓥ 저장하다
- □ optimal ⓐ 최적의
- □ compression ⓝ 압축
- □ raw ⓐ 날것의, 가공되지 않은
- □ generalize ⓥ 일반화하다

□make connections
　between ~ 사이를 연결하다
□represent ⓥ 재현하다
□abstract ⓐ 추상적인
□assumption ⓝ 가정
□undermine ⓥ 손상시키다
□legal ⓐ 법적인
□eyewitness ⓝ 목격자
□testimony ⓝ 증언
□relevant ⓐ 관련 있는
□fall short of ~이 부족하다
□comprehension ⓝ 이해
□precede ⓥ (~보다) 먼저
　일어나다

22

□conduct ⓥ 수행하다
□deliberation ⓝ 숙고
□feature ⓝ 특징
□inaccurate ⓐ 부정확한
□identification ⓝ 식별
□recognize ⓥ 알아채다
□accurate ⓐ 정확한
□immediate ⓐ 즉각적인
□automatic ⓐ 자동적인
□interpretation ⓝ 해석
□impression ⓝ 인상
□reasoned ⓐ 논리적인
□self-narrative ⓝ 자기 서사
□demonstrate ⓥ 보여 주다
□superior ⓐ 우수한
□relatively ⓐⓓ 상대적으로
□unconscious ⓐ 무의식의

□logical ⓐ 논리적인
□justification ⓝ 정당화

23

□quantitative ⓐ 양적인
□measure ⓥ 측정하다
□recall ⓥ 회상하다
□yield ⓥ 산출하다
□reliable ⓐ 신뢰할 만한
□recollection ⓝ 회상
□inaccurate ⓐ 부정확한
□vary ⓥ 다르다
□prompt ⓥ 유발[촉구]하다
□concrete ⓐ 구체적인
□rate ⓥ 평가하다
□utility bill 공과금 고지서
□afford to (~을 살) 여유가 있다
□seek ⓥ 요구하다, 찾다
□abstract ⓐ 추상적인
□ensure ⓥ 보장하다
□consistency ⓝ 일관성
□overgeneralize ⓥ 지나치게
　일반화하다
□enhance ⓥ 높이다
□attain ⓥ 얻다

24

□evolution ⓝ 진화
□singularity ⓝ 특이점
□exceed ⓥ 넘어서다, 능가하다
□intelligence ⓝ 지능
□predict ⓥ 예측하다
□accelerate ⓥ 가속하다

□pursue ⓥ 추구하다
□conscious ⓐ 의식이 있는
□insight ⓝ 통찰력
□significant ⓐ 상당한
□direction ⓝ 방향
□incorporate ⓥ 통합시키다
□mutual ⓐ 상호의
□coexistence ⓝ 공존
□recognize ⓥ 인식하다
□unsolvable ⓐ 해결할 수 없는
□resistance ⓝ 저항
□upcoming ⓐ 다가오는
□stare in the face 노려보다

10회

25

□generation ⓝ 생산
□fossil ⓝ 화석
□fuel ⓝ 연료
□nuclear ⓐ 핵의
□renewables ⓝ 재생 가능
　에너지
□combine ⓥ 합치다, 결합하다

26

□artistic ⓐ 예술적인
□portrait ⓝ 인물 사진
□celebrity ⓝ 유명 인사
□eagerly ⓐⓓ 간절히
□await ⓥ 기다리다
□contain ⓥ 포함하다
□prospect ⓝ 전망
□hire ⓥ 고용하다
□iconic ⓐ 상징적인

□ instantly ⓐⓓ 즉시
□ exotic ⓐ 이국적인
□ run up to ~에 달하다

27

□ furry ⓐ 털이 많은
□ register ⓥ 등록하다
□ limit ⓥ 제한하다
□ participant ⓝ 참가자
□ payment ⓝ 지불
□ require ⓥ 요구하다
□ ingredient ⓝ 재료
□ additional ⓐ 추가적인
□ available ⓐ 이용 가능한
□ safety ⓝ 안전
□ refund ⓝ 환불

28

□ talent ⓝ 재능
□ contest ⓝ 대회
□ judge ⓥ 심사하다
□ criterion ⓝ 기준 (pl. criteria)
□ cooperation ⓝ 협동
□ costume ⓝ 의상
□ gift certificate 상품권
□ management agency
　매니지먼트 회사[기획사]
□ application ⓝ 신청
□ submit ⓥ 제출하다

29

□ essentially ⓐⓓ 근본적으로
□ metaphor ⓝ 은유

□ linguistic ⓐ 언어적인
□ passive ⓐ 수동적인
□ propose ⓥ 제시하다
□ beggar ⓝ 구걸하는 사람
□ cognitive ⓐ 인지적인
□ engage ⓥ 사로잡다
□ prose ⓝ 산문
□ imposing ⓐ 강요[강압]적인
□ artifact ⓝ 인공물
□ forcefully ⓐⓓ 강력하게
□ horizon ⓝ 지평선
□ selling point 매력, 장점
□ at first glance 첫눈에
□ immediately ⓐⓓ 즉각적으로

30

□ limitation ⓝ 한계
□ cognitive ⓐ 인지적인
□ capacity ⓝ 능력
□ independently
　ⓐⓓ 독립적으로
□ distribute ⓥ 분배하다
□ computation ⓝ 계산
□ generation ⓝ 세대
□ flush ⓥ (변기의) 물을 내리다
□ transmit ⓥ 전달하다
□ essentially ⓐⓓ 근본적으로
□ dedicate ⓥ 바치다, 헌신하다
□ calculation ⓝ 계산
□ benefit ⓥ 이득을 얻다
□ contribute to ~에 기여하다
□ collective ⓐ 집합적인

31

□ defence ⓝ 방어
□ species ⓝ (생물의) 종
□ shallows ⓝ 얕은 곳
□ fold ⓥ 접다
□ stare ⓥ 응시하다
□ eyesight ⓝ 시력
□ asset ⓝ 이점, 자산
□ creature ⓝ 생물체
□ transform ⓥ 변신하다
□ spectacle ⓝ 광경
□ octopodian ⓐ 문어와 같은
□ stick ⓥ 찔러 넣다
□ grab ⓥ 움켜잡다
□ broad ⓐ 넓은
□ illusion ⓝ 착시[착각]
□ territory ⓝ 영토, 지역

32

□ suffer ⓥ 고통받다
□ explode ⓥ 폭발하다
□ deficit ⓝ 부족, 결핍
□ psychologically
　ⓐⓓ 정신적으로
□ boundary ⓝ 경계
□ endurance ⓝ 인내력
□ distance ⓝ 거리
□ passive ⓐ 수동적인
□ therapy ⓝ 치료
□ practitioner ⓝ 의사
□ mobilise ⓥ 풀어주다,
　움직이게 하다
□ pressure ⓝ 압박
□ treatment ⓝ 치료법

□ sore ⓐ 아픈

□ tissue ⓝ (근육) 조직

□ frame ⓥ 구성하다

□ expert ⓝ 전문가

33

□ manufacture
　ⓥ 생산[제조]하다

□ goods ⓝ 상품

□ be willing to-v 기꺼이
　~하려고 하다

□ income ⓝ 수입

□ feature ⓝ 기능

□ fancy ⓐ 고급의

□ unaware ⓐ 알지 못하는

□ manipulate ⓥ 조종하다

□ presence ⓝ 존재

□ high-volume ⓐ 대량의

□ low-margin ⓐ 가격이 싼,
　수익이 적은

□ trick ⓥ 속이다

□ unnecessary ⓐ 불필요한

□ fool ⓥ 속이다

□ repeatedly ⓐ 반복적으로

34

□ disaster ⓝ 재난

□ scope ⓝ 범위

□ transformation ⓝ 변화

□ indeed ⓐ 실제로

□ eliminate ⓥ 없애다

□ obvious ⓐ 명백한

□ marginal ⓐ 주변적인

□ isolated ⓐ 고립된

□ impact ⓝ 영향

□ expand ⓥ 확장하다

□ horizon ⓝ 지평선

□ plainly ⓐ 뚜렷하게

□ escapist ⓐ 현실 도피(주의)의

□ pretend ⓥ 가장하다

□ suffering ⓝ 고통

□ distant ⓐ 먼

□ resolve ⓥ 해결하다

□ cease ⓥ 멈추다, 중단하다

□ reborn ⓐ 다시 태어난

□ overestimated
　ⓐ 과대평가된

□ plot ⓝ 줄거리

□ complex ⓐ 복잡한

35

□ inevitable ⓐ 피할 수 없는

□ capacity ⓝ 능력

□ functionally ⓐ 기능적으로

□ distressing ⓐ 괴로움을 주는

□ abundant ⓐ 풍족한

□ scarce ⓐ 부족한

□ neglect ⓝ 소홀함

□ indifference ⓝ 무관심

□ contamination ⓝ 오염

□ urbanization ⓝ 도시화

□ address ⓥ (문제 등을) 다루다

□ leak ⓝ 누수

□ theft ⓝ 도난

□ account for ~을 차지하다

□ estimate ⓝ 추정(치)

□ numerical ⓐ 수치[숫자]의

□ exaggerate ⓥ 과장하다

□ shortage ⓝ 부족

□ selective ⓐ 선택적인

□ inequity ⓝ 불평등

□ sanitation ⓝ 위생

36

□ thrive ⓥ 성공하다

□ navigate ⓥ 다루다, 길을 찾다

□ value ⓥ 가치 있게 여기다

□ count on ~을 기대하다

□ mate ⓝ 짝

□ crucially ⓐ 결정적으로

□ conscious ⓐ 의식적인

□ cynical ⓐ 냉소적인

□ persuasive ⓐ 설득력 있는

□ merit ⓝ 이점

□ physically ⓐ 신체적으로

□ genetically ⓐ 유전적으로

□ select for ~을 선택하다

□ sensitive ⓐ 민감한

□ skilled ⓐ 능숙한

□ maximize ⓥ 최대화하다

□ standing ⓝ 지위

□ tendency ⓝ 경향

□ unconsciously
　ⓐ 무의식적으로

□ perceive ⓥ 인식하다

□ self-esteem ⓝ 자존감

□ pride ⓝ 자존심

□ shame ⓝ 수치심

□ insecurity ⓝ 불안

□ compel ⓥ 강요하다

37

- □ conventional ⓐ 전통적인
- □ depression ⓝ 우울증
- □ cause ⓥ 발생시키다
- □ imbalance ⓝ 불균형
- □ explanation ⓝ 설명
- □ substance ⓝ 물질
- □ consequence ⓝ 결과
- □ decrease ⓝ 감소
- □ root ⓝ 근본
- □ distortion ⓝ 왜곡
- □ revise ⓥ 수정하다
- □ cause-and-effect ⓝ 인과 관계
- □ reframe ⓥ 재구성하다
- □ fundamental ⓐ 근본적인
- □ entity ⓝ 실체
- □ organ ⓝ (인체의) 기관[장기]

38

- □ evidence ⓝ 증거
- □ firmly ⓐⓓ 확고하게
- □ derive from ~로부터 도출하다
- □ assumption ⓝ 가정
- □ account ⓝ 설명
- □ float ⓥ 떠돌다
- □ plain ⓐ 순전한
- □ silliness ⓝ 어리석음
- □ branch ⓝ 분야
- □ devote ⓥ 전념[헌신]하다
- □ hearsay ⓝ 소문
- □ fundamental ⓐ 근본적인
- □ principle ⓝ 원리

- □ generate ⓥ 만들어 내다
- □ diversity ⓝ 다양성

39

- □ stable ⓐ 안정적인
- □ collective ⓐ 집합적인
- □ emerge ⓥ 나타나다
- □ dimensional ⓐ 차원적인
- □ cell ⓝ 세포
- □ molecule ⓝ 분자
- □ enormous ⓐ 거대한
- □ tissue ⓝ (근육) 조직
- □ drastic ⓐ 극적인
- □ outcome ⓝ 결과
- □ organism ⓝ 유기체
- □ switch ⓥ 바꾸다
- □ well-defined ⓐ 명확히 정의된
- □ state ⓝ 상태
- □ rough ⓐ 울퉁불퉁한
- □ landscape ⓝ 경관
- □ illness ⓝ 질병
- □ manifestation ⓝ 발현
- □ symptomatic ⓐ 증상적인
- □ strikingly ⓐⓓ 놀랍게도

40

- □ punish ⓥ 벌주다, 처벌하다
- □ trick ⓝ 트릭, 속임수
- □ scolding ⓝ 꾸짖음
- □ discourage ⓥ 단념[좌절]시키다
- □ invisible ⓐ 눈에 띄지 않는
- □ adopt ⓥ 채택하다

- □ strategy ⓝ 전략
- □ congratulate ⓥ 자랑스러워하다
- □ constantly ⓐⓓ 계속, 지속적으로
- □ point out 지적하다
- □ reward ⓥ 보상하다
- □ unwanted ⓐ 바람직하지 못한, 원치 않는
- □ imply ⓥ 시사하다
- □ reinforce ⓥ 강화하다
- □ maximize ⓥ 최대화하다
- □ lower ⓥ 낮추다

41~42

- □ assign ⓥ 부여하다
- □ prefer ⓥ 선호하다
- □ reasoning ⓝ 논리, 추론
- □ assume ⓥ 가정하다
- □ pointy ⓐ 뾰족한
- □ encounter ⓥ 마주치다
- □ determine ⓥ 결정하다
- □ inanimate ⓐ 무생물의
- □ evaluate ⓥ 평가하다
- □ physics ⓝ 물리
- □ attribute ~ to … ~을 …의 것으로 보다
- □ likely ⓐ ~할 것 같은
- □ hunter-gatherer ⓝ 수렵 채집인
- □ predator ⓝ 포식자
- □ anthropologist ⓝ 인류학자
- □ evolutionary ⓐ 진화상의
- □ agent ⓝ 행위자

11 회 모의고사

11회

□ format ⓝ 형식, 형태
□ instead of ~ 대신에
□ so far 지금까지
□ recyclable ⓐ 재활용 가능한
□ eco-friendly ⓐ 친환경의
□ cross out 선을 그어 지우다
□ match ⓥ 어울리다

11

□ National Assembly 국회
□ honor ⓝ 영광
□ impression ⓝ 인상
□ mostly ⓐⓓ 주로
□ cover ⓥ 보도하다
□ state ⓝ 상태
□ marine ⓐ 해양의
□ biology ⓝ 생물학

12

□ sweat ⓥ 땀을 흘리다
□ in time 제시간에

13

□ install ⓥ 설치하다
□ trial ⓐ 체험의
□ depend on ~에 달려 있다
□ alphabetical ⓐ 알파벳순의
□ give it some thought
  그것에 대해 좀 생각해 보다

14

□ hearing difficulty 청각 장애
□ deaf ⓐ 귀가 먹은, 농인의

□ in the middle of ~의
  도중에[중간에]
□ immediately ⓐⓓ 즉시
□ sign language 수어

15

□ must-visit ⓐ 꼭 방문해야 할
□ propose ⓥ 제안하다
□ review ⓝ 후기
□ complain ⓥ 불평하다

16~17

□ veggie ⓝ 채소
□ feed ⓥ 먹이를 주다
□ toxic ⓐ 독성이 있는
□ severe ⓐ 심각한
□ swallow ⓥ 삼키다
□ breathe ⓥ 숨을 쉬다
□ snack on ~을 간식으로 먹다
□ grapefruit ⓝ 자몽
□ contain ⓥ 포함하다, 함유하다
□ acid ⓝ (화학) 산
□ pose ⓥ (문제를) 일으키다

18

□ appreciate ⓥ 감사하다
□ confident ⓐ 자신감 있는
□ in response to ~에 대한
  응답으로
□ ad(= advertisement)
  ⓝ 광고
□ graduate ⓥ 졸업하다
□ at one's convenience
  편한 때에

19

□ shade ⓝ 색조
□ honeymoon ⓥ 신혼여행을
  하다
□ exotic ⓐ 이국적인
□ track ⓝ (이동하는) 길[방향]
□ land ⓥ (땅에) 떨어지다
□ fine ⓐ 고운

20

□ take responsibility for
  ~에 책임을 지다
□ advance ⓥ 발전하다
□ manage to (간신히) 해내다
□ well-run ⓐ 잘 운영되는
□ commit to ~에 전념하다
□ devote ~ to … ~을 …에
  쏟다[바치다]
□ otherwise ⓐⓓ 그렇지 않으면
□ career ⓝ 경력

21

□ commonsense
  ⓐ 상식적인
□ objective ⓐ 객관적인
□ property ⓝ 속성, 성질
□ bounce off 튕겨 나오다
□ reflect ⓥ 반사하다
□ inhabit ⓥ ~에 살다[존재하다]
□ physical ⓐ 물리적인
□ subjective ⓐ 주관적인

22

□ demand ⓥ 요구하다

□ crime fiction 범죄 소설

□ organize ⓥ 계획하다, 준비하다

□ get it right 제대로 이해하다

□ permission ⓝ 허가

□ drive ~ to ... ⓥ ~을 ...하게 만들다

□ boredom ⓝ 지루함

□ reveal ⓥ 드러내다

□ crucial ⓐ 중요한

□ tension ⓝ 긴장

□ conflict ⓝ 갈등

□ blueprint ⓝ 청사진

23

□ nearly ⓐ 거의

□ go through ~을 거쳐가다

□ adequate ⓐ 적당한

□ lung ⓝ 폐

□ gum ⓝ 잇몸

□ harmful ⓐ 해로운

□ bloodstream ⓝ 혈류

□ oral ⓐ 구강의

□ affect ⓥ 영향을 미치다

□ aspect ⓝ 측면

□ tip of the iceberg 빙산의 일각

□ reflection ⓝ 반영, 반사

□ entire ⓐ 전체의

□ pose ⓥ ~을 초래하다, 제기하다

□ immune system 면역 체계

24

□ tire of ~에 질리다[싫증이 나다]

□ get sick of ~에 싫증이 나다

□ cafeteria ⓝ 구내식당, 카페테리아

□ sooner or later 머지않아

□ the bottom line is ~ 요점은 ~이다

□ be designed to ~하도록 설계되다

□ initial ⓐ 초기의

□ response ⓝ 반응

□ stimulus ⓝ 자극(pl. stimuli)

□ occur ⓥ 발생하다

□ enhance ⓥ 강화하다

□ especially ⓐ 특히

□ value ⓝ 가치

□ threat ⓝ 위협

□ firefly ⓝ 반딧불이

□ brilliant ⓐ 영특한

□ detect ⓥ 감지하다

□ destruction ⓝ 파괴

25

□ investment ⓝ 투자, 투자액

□ fossil fuel 화석 연료

□ gap ⓝ 차이

26

□ slavery ⓝ 노예

□ successfully ⓐ 성공적으로

□ route ⓝ 길

□ enslave ⓥ 노예로 만들다

□ assist ⓥ 돕다

□ knowledge ⓝ 지식

□ well-known ⓐ 잘 알려진

□ equality ⓝ 평등

□ immigrant ⓝ 이민자

□ autobiography ⓝ 자서전

□ candidate ⓝ 후보자

□ vice president 부통령

27

□ get set 준비하다

□ competition ⓝ 대회, 경기

□ double match 복식 경기

□ participant ⓝ 참가자

□ certificate ⓝ 증서

□ award ⓥ (상을) 주다

28

□ urban ⓐ 도시의

□ clue ⓝ 단서

□ registration ⓝ 등록

□ sign up 등록하다

□ save ⓥ ~을 절약하다[아끼다]

□ discount ⓝ 할인

29

□ propose ⓥ 제안하다

□ tough ⓐ 엄격한, 힘든

□ transplantation ⓝ 이식

□ transfer ⓥ 전달하다, 옮기다

□ legal requirement 법적 요건

□ specify ⓥ 명시하다

□ potential ⓐ 잠재적인

11회

□ regulation ⓝ 규정, 규제

□ no doubt 의심할 바 없이, 틀림없는

□ ease ⓥ 완화하다

□ premature ⓐ 너무 이른

□ obtain ⓥ 확보하다

□ suspicion ⓝ 의심

□ belief ⓝ 믿음, 신념

□ unreliable ⓐ 믿을 수 없는

□ precision ⓝ 정확성

□ consistency ⓝ 일관성

□ criterion ⓝ 기준(pl. criteria)

□ burial ⓝ 매장

30

□ term ⓝ 용어

□ impression ⓝ 인상

□ sacrifice ⓥ 희생하다

□ possession ⓝ 소유물

□ insecurity ⓝ 불안

□ stem from ~에서 비롯되다

□ attachment ⓝ 애착

□ distance … from ~ …을 ~로부터 멀리 두다

□ hurt ⓥ 상하게 하다

□ assumption ⓝ 가정

□ fundamentally ⓐⓓ 근본적으로

□ get rid of ~을 제거하다

□ sooner than later 머지않아

□ clarity ⓝ 명료함

□ convenience ⓝ 편의

□ modern era 현대

□ be of the view that ~라는 견해를 갖다

□ eliminate ⓥ 없애다

31

□ remarkable ⓐ 두드러진

□ characteristic ⓝ 특징

□ visual system 시각 체계

□ adapt ⓥ 적응하다

□ psychologist ⓝ 심리학자

□ self-experiment ⓝ 자가 실험

□ literally ⓐⓓ 말 그대로

□ upside down 거꾸로

□ difficulty ⓝ 어려움

□ challenge ⓝ 도전

□ stimulus ⓝ 자극 (pl. stimuli)

□ concentrate ⓥ 집중하다

□ be confronted with ~에 직면하다

□ fortunately ⓐⓓ 다행히

□ perception ⓝ 지각

32

□ participant ⓝ 참가자

□ be allowed to ~하도록 허용되다

□ be unrelated to ~와 연관 되지 않다

□ absolutely ⓐⓓ 절대적으로

□ equally ⓐⓓ 동등하게

□ rate ⓥ 평가하다

□ knowledgeable ⓐ 유식한

□ suggest ⓥ 시사하다

□ have access to ~에 접근하다

□ judgment ⓝ 판단

□ pump up 부풀리다, 증대하다

□ intellectual ⓐ 지능의

□ confidence ⓝ 자신감

□ endure ⓥ 견디다

□ challenging ⓐ 힘든

□ collaboration ⓝ 협동

□ motivate ⓥ 동기를 부여하다

□ pursue ⓥ 추구하다

□ in-depth ⓐ 심도 있는, 면밀한

33

□ tend to ~하는 경향이 있다

□ fur ⓝ 털

□ to the extent where ~할 정도까지

□ uniform ⓐ 동일한, 획일적인

□ object ⓝ 개체

□ unit ⓝ 단위

□ species ⓝ 종(種)

□ ecosystem ⓝ 생태계

□ perspective ⓝ 관점

□ additional ⓐ 추가적인

□ individual ⓐ 개별의

□ entire ⓐ 전체의

□ crucially ⓐⓓ 결정적으로

□ varied ⓐ 다양한

□ behavior ⓝ 행동

□ unite ⓥ 통합하다

□ ecological ⓐ 생태학적인

□ emphasize ⓥ 강조하다

□ aspect ⓝ 측면

□ ignore ⓥ 무시하다, 외면하다
□ framework ⓝ 틀

34

□ realism ⓝ 실재론
□ geometrical ⓐ 기하학적인
□ nature ⓝ 본성
□ indicate ⓥ 가리키다
□ carve ⓥ 조각하다, 새기다
□ point out 지적하다
□ indeed ⓐⓓ 진실로, 진정
□ physical ⓐ 물리적인
□ flaw ⓝ 결함
□ be subject to ~에 영향을
　받다
□ decay ⓥ 부패하다, 쇠하다
□ extraordinary ⓐ 비범한
□ reflection ⓝ 반영, 반영물
□ unseen ⓐ 보이지 않는
□ exist ⓥ 존재하다
□ observable ⓐ 관찰 가능한
□ overlap ⓥ 겹치다
□ sense ⓝ 감각
□ stereotype ⓝ 고정관념
□ generalization ⓝ 일반화

35

□ statistics ⓝ 통계학
□ law of large numbers
　대수의 법칙
□ describe ⓥ 설명하다
□ prediction ⓝ 예측
□ conduct ⓥ 수행하다
□ average ⓝ 평균

□ state ⓝ 상태
□ encounter ⓝ 만남, 접함
□ relative ⓐ 상대적인
□ frequency ⓝ 빈도
□ approach ⓥ 접근하다
□ fade away 사라지다
□ symbolic ⓐ 상징적인
□ interpret ⓥ 해석하다
□ unexpectedly ⓐⓓ 예상치
　못하게
□ insurer ⓝ 보험사
□ figure out ~을 알아내다
□ balance ⓥ 균형을 맞추다

36

□ adolescent ⓐ 청소년기의
□ decision-making
　ⓝ 의사결정
□ circuit ⓝ 회로
□ process ⓥ 처리하다
□ put ~ at a disadvantage
　~을 불리하게 만들다
□ on the other hand 반면에
□ mature ⓥ 성숙해지다
　ⓐ 성숙한
□ influence ⓥ 영향을 미치다
□ factor ⓝ 요인
□ imbalance ⓝ 불균형
□ feeling-based ⓐ 감정에
　기반한
□ rule ⓥ 지배하다
□ logical-based ⓐ 논리에
　기반한
□ evaluate ⓥ 평가하다

□ initial ⓐ 초기의
□ modify ⓥ 수정하다

37

□ remarkable ⓐ 눈에 띄는,
　두드러진
□ progress ⓝ 발전, 진전
□ facial ⓐ 얼굴의
□ recognition ⓝ 인식
□ identification ⓝ 식별
□ performance ⓝ 성능
□ limitation ⓝ 한계
□ relate to ~와 관련이 있다
□ counteract ⓥ 대응하다
□ compensate for ~을
　보완하다
□ characteristic ⓝ 특징
□ instance ⓝ 사례, 예시
□ systematically
　ⓐⓓ 체계적으로
□ enroll ⓥ 등록하다
□ factor ⓝ 요인
□ texture ⓝ 질감
□ particularly ⓐⓓ 특히
□ appearance ⓝ 발현,
　나타나는 것
□ wrinkle ⓝ 주름
□ highlight ⓥ 강조하다

38

□ leave A to one side A를
　보류하다
□ contribution ⓝ 기여
□ strategy ⓝ 전략

□be at risk 위험에 처하다
□disaster ⑩ 재앙
□decline ⑩ 감소
□diversity ⑩ 다양성
□entirely ⓐⓓ 전적으로
□process ⑩ 과정
□extreme ⓐ 극심한
□hunger ⑩ 배고픔
□grain ⑩ 곡물
□enormous ⓐ 거대한
□scale ⑩ 규모
□traditional ⓐ 전통적인
□variety ⑩ 품종
□super-productive
　ⓐ 초생산적인
□spectacularly ⓐⓓ 극적으로,
　광장히
□specifically ⓐⓓ 특히
□depend on ~에 의존하다
□climate extreme 기후 위기

39

□alter ⓥ 바꾸다
□modernize ⓥ 현대화하다
□conform to ~에 순응하다
□interestingly ⓐⓓ 흥미롭게도
□decline ⓥ 쇠퇴하다
□rule ⓥ 지배하다
□contrast ⑩ 대조
□feature ⓥ ~을 특징으로 하다
□athletic ⓐ 운동의
□opposing team 상대 팀
□tradition ⑩ 전통
□adjust ⓥ 조정하다

□keep up with ~에 따르다
□abandon ⓥ 버리다
□neglect ⓥ 무시하다
□root ⑩ 뿌리, 기원
□effect ⑩ 영향

40

□evolution ⑩ 진화
□draw ⓥ 이끌어내다
□noticeable ⓐ 주목할 만한
□connection ⑩ 접점, 연결
□gene ⑩ 유전자
□concept ⑩ 개념
□theoretical population
　genetics 이론 집단 유전학
□apply ⓥ 적용하다
□transmission ⑩ 전파
□innovation ⑩ 혁신
□selection ⑩ 선택
□conceptually ⓐⓓ 개념적으로
□liken to ~와 유사하다
□mutation ⑩ 돌연변이
□modify ⓥ 수정하다
□account for ~을 설명하다
□strictly ⓐⓓ 엄격하게
□trait ⑩ 특성
□acquire ⓥ 습득하다
□further ⓐⓓ 더욱이
□nonparental ⓐ 부모가 아닌
□peer ⑩ 동료
□frequency ⑩ 빈도
□probability ⑩ 개연성, 확률
□revise ⓥ 수정하다, 개정하다
□credible ⓐ 믿을 만한

41~42

□persist ⓥ 지속하다
□tend to ~하는 경향이 있다
□constant ⓐ 지속적인
□downward ⓐⓓ 아래로
□resistance ⑩ 저항
□accordingly ⓐⓓ 그에 따라
□represent ⓥ 나타내다
□combination ⑩ 결합
□elementary ⓐ 기본적인
□besides ⓟⓡⓔⓟ ~ 외에
□isolated ⓐ 고립된
□joint ⓐ 공동의
□mutual ⓐ 상호의
□arrangement ⑩ 배치
□conceal ⓥ 감추다, 숨기다
□confine ⓥ 제한하다, 국한하다
□attention ⑩ 관심
□separately ⓐⓓ 개별적으로
□significance ⑩ 중요성
□tendency ⑩ 경향
□definitely ⓐⓓ 명백히
□stimulus ⑩ 자극 (pl. stimuli)
□competitive ⓐ 경쟁적인
□human nature 인간 본성

43~45

□saint ⑩ 성자
□guard ⑩ 경호인
□opportunity ⑩ 기회
□camel ⑩ 낙타
□reply ⓥ 답하다
□in fact 사실

12회 모의고사

12회

07

- □ miss ⓥ 놓치다
- □ off ⓐ 쉬는
- □ wrist ⓝ 손목
- □ injure ⓥ 부상을 입다
- □ sprain ⓥ (특히 손목·발목을) 삐다

08

- □ flyer ⓝ 전단지
- □ pottery ⓝ 도자기
- □ bowl ⓝ 그릇
- □ cost ⓥ (비용이) ~이다
- □ reasonable ⓐ 적정한, 합리적인
- □ sign up 참가하다, 등록하다
- □ register ⓥ 등록하다

09

- □ competition ⓝ (경연)대회
- □ sign up for ~에 참가하다
- □ whistling ⓝ 휘파람, 휘파람 불기
- □ championship ⓝ 선수권 대회
- □ note ⓥ 주목[주의]하다
- □ echo ⓝ (소리의) 울림
- □ look forward to ~을 기대하다
- □ enthusiastic ⓐ 열렬한

10

- □ option ⓝ 선택(권)
- □ consider ⓥ 고려하다

machine washable 기계 세탁할 수 있는

- □ cross out (줄을 그어) 지우다
- □ blackout ⓝ (창문에 치는) 암막, 빛 차단
- □ disturb ⓥ 방해하다
- □ except for ~을 제외하고는
- □ narrow ⓥ 좁히다

11

- □ ride ⓝ 놀이기구
- □ construction ⓝ 건설, 공사

12

- □ wander ⓥ 돌아다니다, 헤매다
- □ all by oneself (다른 사람 없이) 혼자

13

- □ come up with ~을 생각해 내다[찾아내다]
- □ impression ⓝ 인상
- □ specific ⓐ 구체적인
- □ confident ⓐ 자신감 있는
- □ dress up 옷을 갖춰 입다
- □ favorable ⓐ 호의적인
- □ presentation ⓝ 소개, 발표
- □ previous ⓐ 이전의
- □ candidate ⓝ 후보자, 지원자
- □ upcoming ⓐ 다가오는, 곧 있을

14

- □ try on ~을 입어[신어]보다
- □ tight ⓐ 꽉 끼는
- □ storage ⓝ 창고, 저장
- □ refund ⓝ 환불

15

- □ psychology ⓝ 심리학
- □ expert ⓝ 전문가
- □ field ⓝ 분야
- □ renowned ⓐ 유명한, 명성 있는
- □ manage to 간신히 ~하다
- □ set up 마련하다, 준비하다
- □ severe ⓐ 심한
- □ stomachache ⓝ 복통
- □ extend ⓥ 연장하다
- □ assignment ⓝ 과제
- □ appointment ⓝ 약속
- □ checkup 건강 진단

16~17

- □ tribe ⓝ 부족
- □ warning ⓝ 경고
- □ vary ⓥ 다르게 하다
- □ pitch ⓝ 음정
- □ beat ⓝ 박자
- □ distance ⓝ 거리
- □ ancestor ⓝ 조상
- □ signal ⓥ 알리다
- □ reliable ⓐ 믿을 수 있는
- □ means ⓝ 수단
- □ attach ⓥ 붙이다
- □ efficient ⓐ 효율적인

□ deliver ⓥ 전달하다

□ in detail 상세하게

□ spread ⓝ 확산

□ prehistoric ⓐ 선사 시대의

18

□ loyal ⓐ 충성스러운, 충실한

□ essential ⓐ 필수적인

□ innovative ⓐ 혁신적인

□ contribute ⓥ 기여하다

□ voluntarily ⓐd 자발적으로, 자원해서

□ total ⓥ 합계가 ~이 되다

□ request ⓥ 요청하다

□ consideration ⓝ 고려

□ reflect ⓥ 반영하다

□ performance ⓝ 성과

19

□ day off (근무를) 쉬는 날

□ mute ⓥ (소리를) 작게 하다, 음 소거하다

□ disconnect ⓥ 단절하다

□ calm ⓐ 침착한, 차분한

□ immediately ⓐd 즉시

□ fall over ~에 걸려 넘어지다

□ injured ⓐ 다친, 부상을 입은

□ concerned ⓐ 걱정되는

□ recover ⓥ 회복하다

□ surgery ⓝ 수술

□ indifferent ⓐ 무관심한

□ annoyed ⓐ 화난

20

□ launch ⓥ (새로운 일을) 시작하다[개시하다]

□ promote ⓥ 홍보하다

□ strictly ⓐd 엄격하게

□ shamelessly ⓐd 뻔뻔스럽게

□ give ~ away ~을 나누어 주다

□ entertaining ⓐ 재미있는, 즐거움을 주는

□ audience ⓝ 청중, 독자

21

□ reveal ⓥ 드러내다

□ assumption ⓝ 추정, 전제

□ accomplish ⓥ 성취하다

□ achievement ⓝ 성취, 성과

□ imply ⓥ 암시하다, 넌지시 나타내다

□ obtain ⓥ 얻다

□ illegal ⓐ 불법적인

□ questionable ⓐ 의심스러운

□ means ⓝ 수단

□ criticism ⓝ 비판, 비평

□ automatically ⓐd 자동으로, 무의식적으로

□ inevitably ⓐd 반드시, 불가피하게

□ challenge ⓥ 도전하다, 의문을 제기하다

□ sacred ⓐ 신성한

□ pause ⓥ 잠시 멈추다

□ valuable ⓐ 가치 있는

□ matter ⓥ 중요하다

□ false ⓐ 잘못된

□ tendency ⓝ 경향

□ hardship ⓝ 고난

□ solid ⓐ 확고한

□ abandon ⓥ 버리다

□ notion ⓝ 개념, 생각

□ superstition ⓝ 미신

22

□ saying ⓝ 속담, 격언

□ threatening ⓐ 위협적인

□ opposite ⓝ 반대

□ frightening ⓐ 두려움을 주는

□ inner ⓐ 내면의

□ pessimistic ⓐ 비관적인

□ take a slep 조치를 취하다

□ intend ⓥ 의도하다

□ rate ⓝ 비율

□ screen ⓥ (특정 질병이 있는지) 검진하다

□ terrified ⓐ 두려워하는, 겁이 난

□ be true for ~에 해당되다

□ climate ⓝ 기후

□ doom ⓝ 파멸, (불행한) 운명

□ gloom ⓝ 우울, 어둠

□ depressed ⓐ 우울한

□ ecological ⓐ 생태학적인

□ collapse ⓝ 붕괴

23

- □ remarkable ⓐ 놀라운, 주목할 만한
- □ unbelievable ⓐ 믿을 수 없는
- □ consequence ⓝ 결과
- □ alter ⓥ 바꾸다, 고치다
- □ duration ⓝ (지속되는) 기간
- □ glacier ⓝ 빙하
- □ gravity ⓝ 중력
- □ equator ⓝ (지구의) 적도
- □ rotation ⓝ 회전
- □ spread out (몸을) 뻗다
- □ barely ⓐⓓ 간신히, 거의 ~ 아니게
- □ noticeable ⓐ 알아차릴 수 있는, 뚜렷한
- □ add up 누적되다, 쌓이다
- □ dinosaur ⓝ 공룡
- □ last ⓥ 지속하다
- □ temperature ⓝ 온도
- □ principle ⓝ 원리
- □ maintain ⓥ 유지하다
- □ implication ⓝ 영향, 결과
- □ biodiversity ⓝ (균형 잡힌 환경을 위한) 생물의 다양성
- □ keep track of ~을 기록하다

24

- □ bring up (화제를) 꺼내다
- □ suggestion ⓝ 제안
- □ immediately ⓐⓓ 즉시
- □ close off ~을 차단하다[막다]
- □ possibility ⓝ 가능성

- □ viewpoint ⓝ 관점
- □ period ⓝ 마침표, 끝
- □ consider ⓥ 고려하다
- □ option ⓝ 선택(지)
- □ point of view 관점
- □ beneficial ⓐ 유익한, 이로운
- □ eliminate ⓥ 제거하다, 없애다
- □ invention ⓝ 발명
- □ honest ⓐ 정직한
- □ filter out (액체·빛 등에서) ~을 걸러내다
- □ block ⓥ 막다, 차단하다

25

- □ motivator ⓝ 동기 (요인)
- □ welfare ⓝ 복지
- □ account for (부분·비율을) 차지하다
- □ cite ⓥ 언급하다
- □ consumption ⓝ 섭취, 소비
- □ management ⓝ 관리
- □ rank ⓥ (순위를) 차지하다

26

- □ exceptionally ⓐⓓ 유난히, 특출나게
- □ inventor ⓝ 발명가
- □ journalist ⓝ 기자, 언론인
- □ occasionally ⓐⓓ 가끔
- □ nickname ⓥ 별명을 붙이다
- □ textile ⓝ 직물
- □ witness ⓥ 목격하다
- □ faulty ⓐ 결함이 있는
- □ equipment ⓝ 장비, 설비

- □ device ⓝ 장치
- □ flat-bottomed ⓐ 바닥이 평평한
- □ eliminate ⓥ 제거하다, 없애다
- □ assemble ⓥ 조립하다

27

- □ e-waste 전자 폐기물
- □ annual ⓐ 해마다의, 연례의
- □ electronics ⓝ 전자 제품
- □ accept ⓥ 받아들이다, 허용하다
- □ light bulb 전구
- □ microwave ⓝ 전자레인지
- □ wipe out ~을 완전히 없애다 [삭제하다]
- □ in advance 사전에, 미리
- □ resident ⓝ 거주자, 주민

28

- □ fascinating ⓐ 매력적인, 대단히 흥미로운
- □ witness ⓥ 목격하다
- □ marine life 해양 생물
- □ requirement ⓝ 요건, 필요조건
- □ insurance ⓝ 보험
- □ experienced ⓐ 경험 있는, 숙련된
- □ accompany ⓥ 동반하다, 동행하다
- □ underwater ⓐ 수중의

29

- □ power ⓥ 작동시키다, 동력을 공급하다
- □ artificial intelligence 인공 지능(AI)
- □ task ⓝ 과업, 작업
- □ perform ⓥ 수행하다
- □ mind-blowing ⓐ 놀라운, 감동적인
- □ feature ⓝ 특징, 특색
- □ core ⓐ 핵심적인
- □ virtual ⓐ 가상의
- □ assistant ⓝ 조수, 비서
- □ recognize ⓥ 인식하다
- □ implication ⓝ 영향, 결과

30

- □ tip ⓝ 끝 (부분)
- □ stem ⓝ (식물의) 줄기
- □ accumulate ⓥ 축적하다
- □ shade ⓝ 그늘
- □ accordingly ⓐⓓ 따라서, 그래서
- □ stimulate ⓥ 자극하다
- □ face ⓥ 직면하다, 마주하다
- □ phenomenon ⓝ 현상
- □ bend ⓥ 구부러지다, 휘어지다
- □ opposite ⓐ 반대의
- □ limit ⓥ 제한하다
- □ horizontal ⓐ 수평의
- □ soil ⓝ 토양
- □ interfere with ~을 방해하다
- □ development ⓝ 발달
- □ in turn 결국, 결과적으로

31

- □ demonstrate ⓥ 보여주다, 설명하다
- □ defeat ⓥ 패배시키다, 이기다
- □ delay ⓥ 미루다
- □ behavioral ⓐ 행동의, 행동에 관한
- □ assign ⓥ 맡기다, 배정하다
- □ due date 마감일, 만기일
- □ for oneself 스스로
- □ submit ⓥ 제출하다
- □ conclude ⓥ 결론을 내리다
- □ restrict ⓥ 제한하다
- □ recognize ⓥ 인식하다
- □ tendency ⓝ 경향, 성향
- □ performance ⓝ 수행, 성과
- □ reward ⓝ 보상
- □ obstacle ⓝ 장애물
- □ assignment ⓝ 과제
- □ competition ⓝ 경쟁

32

- □ innovation ⓝ 혁신
- □ theme ⓝ 주제
- □ steadily ⓐⓓ 꾸준히
- □ specialized ⓐ 전문화된
- □ diversified ⓐ 다양화된, 여러 가지의
- □ unstable ⓐ 불안정한
- □ self-sufficiency ⓝ 자급자족
- □ mutual ⓐ 서로의, 상호간의
- □ interdependence ⓝ 상호 의존

- □ concentrate ⓥ 집중하다
- □ rely ⓥ 의존하다, 믿다
- □ afford ⓥ (금전적·시간적) 여유[형편]가 되다
- □ sesame oil 참기름
- □ lamb ⓝ 어린 양
- □ humanity ⓝ 인류
- □ creatively ⓐⓓ 창의적으로
- □ personalized ⓐ 개인화된
- □ commercialize ⓥ 상품화하다

33

- □ trick ⓥ 속이다
- □ contract ⓝ 계약
- □ myth ⓝ 신화
- □ tribe ⓝ 부족
- □ victim ⓝ 희생자
- □ irresistible ⓐ 저항할 수 없는
- □ otherwise ⓐⓓ 그렇지 않으면
- □ resist ⓥ 저항하다
- □ instruct ⓥ 지시하다
- □ crew ⓝ (배·비행기의) 선원 [승무원]
- □ stuff ⓥ 채워 넣다
- □ temptation ⓝ 유혹
- □ concentrate ⓥ 집중하다
- □ distract ⓥ 주의를 산만하게 하다
- □ mindset ⓝ 사고방식
- □ track ⓥ 추적하다
- □ progress ⓝ 과정

34

□ecosystem ⓝ 생태계

□adapt ⓥ 적응하다

□evolution ⓝ 진화

□microbe ⓝ 미생물

□evolve ⓥ 진화하다

□resistance ⓝ 저항(력), 내성

□antibacterial ⓝ 항균제

□insecticide ⓝ 살충제

□cockroach ⓝ 바퀴벌레 (= roach)

□distaste ⓝ 혐오감, 불쾌감

□counterpart ⓝ 상대(방)

□ecologist ⓝ 생태학자

□urban ⓐ 도시의

□trait ⓝ 특성, 속성

□thrive ⓥ 번성하다, 번창하다

□indoorsy ⓐ 실내 생활을 좋아하는

□humanity ⓝ 인류

□extinct ⓐ 멸종된

□habitat ⓝ 서식지

35

□engagement ⓝ 관계

□poetry ⓝ (집합적으로) 시

□benefit ⓝ 이점, 혜택

□professional ⓐ 전문적인

□capacity ⓝ 능력, 용량

□expressive ⓐ 표현의, 표현적인

□immune ⓐ 면역의

□lung ⓝ 폐, 허파

□function ⓝ 기능

□diminish ⓥ 줄이다, 약화하다

□psychological ⓐ 심리적인

□distress ⓝ 고통

□enhance ⓥ (질을) 높이다, 향상하다

□aid ⓥ 지원하다, 돕다

□empathy ⓝ 공감 (능력)

□incredibly ⓐⓓ 믿을 수 없을 정도로

□target ⓥ 목표로 삼다, 겨냥하다

□productivity ⓝ 생산성

□frustration ⓝ 좌절감

36

□at risk 위험에 처한

□advance ⓝ 발전, 진전

□automation ⓝ 자동화

□automate ⓥ 자동화하다

□dependent ⓐ 의존하는

□irreplaceable ⓐ 대체할 수 없는

□unrealistic ⓐ 비현실적인

□threat ⓝ 위협

□flip ⓥ (휙) 뒤집다

□task ⓝ (해야 할) 일, 업무

□crew ⓝ (한 팀으로 일하는) 직원

□skilled ⓐ 숙련된

□draw on ~을 이용하다

37

□beech tree 너도밤나무

□soil ⓝ 흙, 토양

□vary ⓥ (상황에 따라) 달라지다

□nutrient ⓝ 영양분

□underground ⓐⓓ 지하에서

□abundance ⓝ 풍부(함)

□run short (~이) 부족하다

□plenty of 풍부한, 많은

□equalize ⓥ 균등하게 하다

□transfer ⓥ 전달하다, 옮기다

□accordingly ⓐⓓ 따라서, 그에 따라

□rate ⓝ 정도, 비율

38

□enormously ⓐⓓ 엄청나게, 대단히

□contribute ⓥ 기여하다

□cooperate ⓥ 협력하다

□deal with ~을 다루다

□analytic philosophy 분석 철학

□assume ⓥ 가정하다

□cognitive science 인지 과학

□rightly ⓐⓓ 당연히

□judge ⓥ 판단하다

□aspect ⓝ 측면

□fundamental ⓐ 근본적인, 기본적인

□countless ⓐ 셀 수 없이 많은

□navigate ⓥ 항해하다, 길을 찾다

□preserve ⓥ 보존하다

□operation ⓝ 작용, 작동

□astonishingly ⓐⓓ 놀라운 정도로

□contributor ⓝ 기여 요소, 원인 제공자

□ collaborative ⓐ 협력적인, 공동의

□ collective ⓐ 협력적인

39

□ magically ⓐⓓ 마법처럼

□ remove ⓥ 제거하다, 없애다

□ essentially ⓐⓓ 본질적으로

□ completely ⓐⓓ 완전히

□ chemical ⓐ 화학적인

□ makeup ⓝ 성질, 구성

□ contain ⓥ ~이 들어 있다

□ temperature ⓝ 온도

□ separate ⓐ 분리된, 따로 떨어진

□ float ⓥ (물이나 공기 위에) 떠 있다

□ differ ⓥ 다르다

□ salt content 염분

40

□ reflective ⓐ 성찰적인

□ journaling ⓝ 일기 쓰기

□ think back on ~을 돌이켜 보다

□ undergraduate ⓝ (대학) 학부생

□ value ⓝ 가치

□ handle ⓥ 다루다

□ reflect ⓥ 성찰하다, 숙고하다

□ support ⓥ 뒷받침하다

□ perspective ⓝ 관점

□ demonstration ⓝ 입증, (분명히) 보여줌

□ reframe ⓥ 재구성하다

□ worthwhile ⓐ 가치 있는

41~42

□ majority ⓝ 대다수, 대부분

□ adapt ⓥ 적응하다

□ cultivate ⓥ 경작하다, (관계를) 쌓다

□ state ⓝ 상태

□ compensate ⓥ 보상하다, 보충되다

□ entire ⓐ 전체의

□ perception ⓝ 인식

□ disrupt ⓥ 방해하다

□ thrilled ⓐ 감격한, 짜릿한

□ overload ⓥ (짐을) 너무 많이 싣다, 과부하가 걸리게 하다

□ stimulus ⓝ 자극(pl. stimuli)

□ overwhelming ⓐ 압도적인

□ recognize ⓥ 알아보다, 인식하다

□ puzzled ⓐ 혼란스러워하는

□ stimulation ⓝ 자극

□ confusion ⓝ 혼란, 혼동

□ assume ⓥ 가정하다

□ function ⓥ 기능하다

□ relay ⓥ 전달하다

□ neuroscientific ⓐ 신경 과학의

□ collaborative ⓐ 협력적인, 공동 작업의

□ alter ⓥ 바꾸다, 고치다

□ accordingly ⓐⓓ 그에 따라

□ anticipate ⓥ 예상하다, 기대하다

43~45

□ a bunch of 다수의, 많은

□ notice ⓥ 알아차리다

□ chat ⓥ 담소를 나누다

□ sudden ⓐ 갑작스러운

□ be stuck in ~에 갇히다

□ generosity ⓝ 관대함, 너그러움

□ empathy ⓝ 공감 (능력)

□ unforgettable ⓐ 잊을 수 없는

□ mention ⓥ 언급하다, 말하다

□ conversation ⓝ 대화

□ attentive ⓐ 주의를 기울이는, 세심한

□ unexpectedly ⓐⓓ 예상치 못하게, 갑자기

12회

판매량 1
만족도 1
평가도 1

Xistory stands for
eXtra Intensive story for
the University Entrance Examination.

Xi story

대한민국 **No.1** 수능 기출문제집

2026

해 설 편

전국연합 모의고사 고1 영어

자이스토리

수경출판사

🍀 차 례

1회 모의고사 — 문제편 p. 10~21
01④ 02⑤ 03② 04③ 05⑤ 06③ 07② 08④ 09③ 10②
11② 12④ 13④ 14④ 15④ 16⑤ 17③ 18③ 19③ 20②
21① 22① 23⑤ 24① 25④ 26④ 27② 28② 29④ 30⑤
31① 32③ 33④ 34① 35② 36⑤ 37⑤ 38③ 39⑤ 40①
41① 42② 43④ 44③ 45②

2회 모의고사 — 문제편 p. 28~39
01⑤ 02② 03⑤ 04⑤ 05② 06③ 07⑤ 08④ 09④ 10③
11③ 12⑤ 13② 14① 15① 16① 17④ 18③ 19① 20②
21① 22③ 23① 24⑤ 25③ 26④ 27④ 28④ 29② 30③
31② 32③ 33③ 34⑤ 35④ 36④ 37③ 38① 39② 40①
41① 42④ 43⑤ 44④ 45②

3회 모의고사 — 문제편 p. 46~57
01⑤ 02⑤ 03③ 04⑤ 05② 06② 07① 08③ 09④ 10②
11② 12① 13③ 14① 15③ 16③ 17④ 18③ 19② 20⑤
21⑤ 22④ 23① 24② 25⑤ 26⑤ 27④ 28④ 29⑤ 30④
31① 32③ 33① 34② 35④ 36④ 37② 38④ 39⑤ 40①
41② 42③ 43④ 44④ 45④

4회 모의고사 — 문제편 p. 66~77
01③ 02① 03① 04⑤ 05② 06④ 07② 08③ 09④ 10④
11① 12⑤ 13④ 14② 15② 16⑤ 17③ 18① 19① 20⑤
21② 22① 23⑤ 24① 25④ 26④ 27③ 28④ 29③ 30④
31② 32① 33② 34⑤ 35④ 36② 37⑤ 38④ 39③ 40①
41② 42⑤ 43④ 44⑤ 45④

5회 모의고사 — 문제편 p. 84~95
01③ 02① 03③ 04⑤ 05④ 06③ 07⑤ 08② 09⑤ 10④
11① 12④ 13⑤ 14② 15③ 16④ 17④ 18② 19② 20①
21② 22① 23④ 24① 25③ 26⑤ 27④ 28⑤ 29③ 30⑤
31② 32② 33③ 34① 35③ 36③ 37② 38③ 39④ 40①
41① 42④ 43⑤ 44② 45④

6회 모의고사 — 문제편 p. 102~113
01② 02① 03① 04④ 05④ 06③ 07④ 08④ 09⑤ 10④
11① 12③ 13② 14⑤ 15⑤ 16③ 17④ 18② 19① 20⑤
21① 22③ 23④ 24① 25④ 26④ 27⑤ 28⑤ 29④ 30②
31④ 32① 33④ 34③ 35④ 36② 37⑤ 38④ 39⑤ 40②
41① 42③ 43④ 44② 45③

7회 모의고사 — 문제편 p. 122~133
01④ 02① 03⑤ 04⑤ 05② 06④ 07② 08④ 09④ 10②
11① 12⑤ 13① 14① 15① 16② 17④ 18③ 19③ 20②
21② 22③ 23② 24② 25⑤ 26③ 27② 28⑤ 29② 30⑤
31① 32③ 33① 34② 35④ 36④ 37② 38⑤ 39⑤ 40③
41③ 42③ 43⑤ 44④ 45④

8회 모의고사 — 문제편 p. 140~151
01③ 02③ 03⑤ 04④ 05② 06③ 07④ 08③ 09④ 10④
11① 12② 13① 14① 15① 16⑤ 17③ 18⑤ 19⑤ 20②
21⑤ 22④ 23④ 24① 25④ 26② 27⑤ 28④ 29⑤ 30④
31② 32① 33① 34④ 35④ 36② 37④ 38⑤ 39② 40④
41④ 42③ 43⑤ 44③ 45②

9회 모의고사 — 문제편 p. 158~169
01⑤ 02① 03③ 04⑤ 05① 06③ 07④ 08③ 09④ 10④
11② 12④ 13① 14① 15⑤ 16③ 17③ 18⑤ 19② 20②
21⑤ 22④ 23② 24① 25④ 26④ 27④ 28⑤ 29④ 30②
31② 32③ 33② 34① 35② 36② 37③ 38⑤ 39⑤ 40①
41② 42⑤ 43④ 44③ 45④

10회 모의고사 — 문제편 p. 178~189
01④ 02② 03⑤ 04⑤ 05③ 06⑤ 07① 08④ 09④ 10③
11① 12② 13① 14⑤ 15② 16③ 17④ 18⑤ 19① 20②
21④ 22⑤ 23⑤ 24③ 25③ 26③ 27④ 28⑤ 29④ 30③
31② 32④ 33① 34⑤ 35④ 36④ 37① 38④ 39② 40①
41① 42③ 43② 44④ 45③

11회 모의고사 — 문제편 p. 196~207
01② 02① 03⑤ 04④ 05① 06⑤ 07⑤ 08④ 09③ 10③
11① 12④ 13④ 14⑤ 15⑤ 16① 17⑤ 18⑤ 19① 20④
21④ 22⑤ 23④ 24② 25⑤ 26③ 27⑤ 28⑤ 29④ 30④
31① 32④ 33④ 34④ 35③ 36④ 37③ 38⑤ 39④ 40①
41⑤ 42③ 43④ 44② 45③

12회 모의고사 — 문제편 p. 214~225
01① 02① 03② 04④ 05⑤ 06④ 07① 08③ 09④ 10②
11① 12④ 13① 14① 15② 16② 17④ 18② 19② 20⑤
21③ 22① 23⑤ 24① 25④ 26③ 27⑤ 28② 29④ 30④
31③ 32② 33④ 34④ 35④ 36③ 37⑤ 38⑤ 39③ 40②
41① 42⑤ 43④ 44③ 45④

01 정답 ④ ＊학교 드론 동아리 공연 관람 권유

M : Good morning, students.
남 : 좋은 아침입니다, 학생 여러분.

This is your vice principal Richard Simpson.
저는 교감인 Richard Simpson입니다.

As you know, our school drone club was awarded first prize at the Drone Show Contest.
아시다시피, 우리 학교 드론 동아리가 드론 쇼 대회에서 1등을 차지했습니다.

Actually, I asked the drone club **to perform** the show again for you.
〈asked의 목적격 보어(to부정사)〉
사실, 저는 드론 동아리에게 그 쇼를 다시 한 번 여러분을 위해 보여달라고 부탁했습니다.

And they said, "Yes".
그리고 그들이 "네"라고 답했습니다.

So I would **recommend you watch** the performance at the school field tomorrow.
〈주장, 요구, 명령, 제안을 나타내는 동사(+that)+주어(+should)+동사원형〉
단서 학교 운동장에서 드론 동아리의 공연이 열릴 것임을 안내함
그래서 저는 여러분에게 내일 학교 운동장에서 드론 동아리의 공연을 보기를 추천합니다.

Please come and see the club's drone performance, and show your support.
와서 드론 동아리의 공연을 보고, 응원해 주세요.

Thank you.
감사합니다.

- vice principal 교감
- drone ⓝ 드론, 무인 항공기
- award ⓥ 수여하다
- recommend ⓥ 추천하다
- support ⓝ 지지, 응원

다음을 듣고, 남자가 하는 말의 목적으로 가장 적절한 것을 고르시오.
① 학교 운동장 공사 계획을 안내하려고 운동장 공사는 언급되어 있지 않음
② 교내 드론 대회 개최 소식을 알리려고 대회가 아닌 공연이 개최될 예정임
③ 학교 홍보용 드론 촬영 일정을 공지하려고 촬영은 관련이 없는 내용임
④ 학교 드론 동아리 공연의 관람을 권하려고 학교 드론 동아리의 공연이 개최됨을 안내함
⑤ 교내 드론 공연의 관람 안전 수칙을 강조하려고 안전 수칙은 언급된 내용이 아님

> **왜 정답?** ✸✸✸ [정답률 88%]

학교 드론 동아리가 드론 쇼 대회에서 1등을 했고, 교감 선생님의 부탁으로 학생들을 대상으로 학교에서 공연하기로 예정되어 있다고 했다. 따라서 남자가 하는 말의 목적으로 가장 적절한 것은 ④이다.

> **왜 오답?**

① 학교 운동장에서 드론 동아리의 공연이 열릴 예정이지, 공사는 언급되어 있지 않다.
② 교내에서는 드론 공연을 하는 것이고 드론 대회는 이미 개최되었다. 함정
③ 학교 홍보용 드론 촬영은 관련이 없는 내용이다.
⑤ 드론 공연 관람 안전 수칙은 언급된 내용이 아니다.

02 정답 ⑤ ＊학급 뮤지컬 준비

W : Ryan, did you enjoy the musical "Tigers" yesterday?
여 : Ryan, 어제 뮤지컬 〈Tigers〉 재미있게 봤어?

M : Yes, I loved it. I can't believe we got tickets for **such a popular show**.
〈such+a(n)+형용사+명사〉
남 : 응, 정말 좋았어. 그렇게 인기 많은 공연의 티켓을 우리가 구했다는 게 믿기지 않아.

W : Yes, we were lucky. By the way, it reminded me of the class musical **that** we have to prepare for the next month's school festival.
〈목적격 관계대명사〉
여 : 맞아, 우리가 운이 좋았지. 그런데, 그것이 내게 다음 달 학교 축제에서 우리가 준비해야 하는 학급 뮤지컬을 상기시키더라.

M : You read my mind! I think we should look for a musical with a variety of music.
남 : 내 생각을 읽었네! 음악 종류가 다양한 뮤지컬을 찾아봐야 할 것 같아.

W : Well, there might be something **even** more important than that.
〈비교급 강조 부사〉
여 : 음, 그보다 훨씬 더 중요한 게 있을지도 몰라.

M : Should we give the audience a meaningful lesson?
남 : 관객에게 의미 있는 교훈을 줘야 할까?

W : Not necessarily. Do you remember **what** we did last year?
〈선행사를 포함한 관계대명사〉
여 : 꼭 그런 건 아니야. 작년에 우리가 뭐 했는지 기억나?

M : Yes. We focused on preparing a musical that was easy **to perform**.
〈부사적 용법(형용사 easy 수식)〉
남 : 응. 공연하기 쉬운 뮤지컬을 준비하는 데 집중했지.

W : Right. But not everyone participated. I think everyone should have a role for the class musical.
여 : 맞아. 근데 모두가 참여하지는 않았잖아. 난 모두가 학급 뮤지컬의 역할을 하나씩 맡아야 한다고 생각해.
단서 작년에는 모두가 참여하지 않았으나 이번에는 모두가 역할을 맡아야 한다고 생각함

M : That's a good point.
남 : 그거 좋은 지적이야.

- musical ⓝ 뮤지컬
- remind A of B A에게 B를 상기시키다
- a variety of 다양한
- audience ⓝ 관객, 청중
- meaningful ⓐ 의미 있는
- participate ⓥ 참가[참여]하다
- role ⓝ 역할

대화를 듣고, 여자의 의견으로 가장 적절한 것을 고르시오.
① 학급 뮤지컬은 다양한 음악을 활용해야 한다. 다양한 음악이 언급된 것으로 만든 오답
② 학급 뮤지컬은 학생이 공연하기 쉬워야 한다. 작년에는 공연하기 쉬운 뮤지컬을 고름
③ 학급 뮤지컬은 인기 있는 소재를 다루어야 한다. 어제 본 뮤지컬 공연이 인기 있는 작품이었다는 언급만 있음
④ 학급 뮤지컬은 의미 있는 교훈을 전달해야 한다. 뮤지컬을 통해 꼭 교훈을 줄 필요는 없다고 했음
⑤ 학급 뮤지컬은 학생 모두가 역할을 맡아야 한다. 일부가 아닌 모두가 역할을 맡아서 참여해야 한다고 했음

> **왜 정답?** ✸✸✸ [정답률 83%]

여자는 작년에 뮤지컬 공연을 준비할 때 모든 학급 구성원들이 참여하지는 않았다고 했다. 그러면서 이번에는 모두가 각자의 역할을 맡아서 참여해야 한다고 말했다. 따라서 여자의 의견으로 가장 적절한 것은 ⑤이다.

> **왜 오답?**

① 다양한 음악을 사용하는 것보다 더 중요한 것이 따로 있다고 했다.
② 작년에 이미 공연하기 쉬운 뮤지컬 작품을 골랐다.
③ 어제 본 뮤지컬 〈Tigers〉는 인기가 많은 작품이라고 했을 뿐이다.
④ 학급 뮤지컬을 통해 교훈을 전달하는 것은 중요하지만 꼭 그렇게 해야 하는 것은 아니라고 했다. **주의**

03 정답 ② ＊휴식의 중요성

M : Welcome to the *Healing Tip Podcast*.
남 : Healing Tip Podcast에 오신 것을 환영합니다.

I'm Dr. Smith.
저는 Smith 박사입니다.

In our busy lives, what do you think is just as important as
exercising or eating well for your health?
우리의 바쁜 일상 속에서, 건강을 위해 운동하거나 잘 먹는 것만큼 중요한 것이 무엇이라고 생각하시나요?

It's rest.
바로 휴식입니다.

Rest plays a crucial role in maintaining your overall well-
being. 단서1 휴식은 웰빙에 있어서 중요한 역할을 함
휴식은 여러분의 전반적인 웰빙을 유지하는 데 있어 매우 중요한 역할을 합니다.

It allows your body to heal and recharge, while also helping
your mind relax and improving focus.
그것은 몸이 치유되고 재충전될 수 있게 해줄 뿐만 아니라, 여러분의 마음을 진정시키고 집중력을 높이는 데도 도움이 됩니다.

That's why I want to emphasize how important rest is for
your health. 단서2 건강을 위해 휴식의 중요성을 강조함
그것이 여러분의 건강을 위해 얼마나 휴식이 중요한지 제가 강조하고 싶은 이유입니다.

Taking time to rest can prevent stress and boost your overall
wellness.
휴식을 취할 시간을 갖는 것은 스트레스를 예방하고 여러분의 전반적인 건강을 증진시킬 수 있습니다.

So, don't skip those breaks!
그러니, 그런 휴식 시간을 놓치지 마세요!

- podcast ⓝ 팟캐스트, 인터넷망을 통해 다양한 콘텐츠를 제공하는 서비스
- crucial ⓐ 중요한, 결정적인 ・ maintain ⓥ 유지하다
- overall ⓐ 전반적인 ・ well-being ⓝ (건강과) 행복, 웰빙
- recharge ⓥ 재충전하다 ・ emphasize ⓥ 강조하다
- prevent ⓥ 예방하다 ・ boost ⓥ 증진[촉진]하다
- wellness ⓝ 건강 ・ skip ⓥ 건너뛰다

다음을 듣고, 남자가 하는 말의 요지로 가장 적절한 것을 고르시오.
① 건강을 지키기 위해서 규칙적인 운동이 필수적이다.
　　　　　　　　　　　　　　운동이 언급되었으나 요지는 아님
② 바쁜 일상에서 휴식을 취하는 것은 건강에 중요하다.
　　　　　　　　　　　　휴식이 건강에 얼마나 중요한지 말하는 내용임
③ 집중력을 높이는 것은 업무 수행 능력을 향상시킨다.
　　　　　　　　　　휴식을 통해 집중력 향상이 가능하다고 한 것으로 만든 함정
④ 운동 부족을 보완하려면 적절한 식이 요법이 필요하다.
　　　　　　　　　　　잘 먹는 것이 중요하다고 언급했을 뿐임
⑤ 다양한 인간관계가 스트레스를 줄이는 데 도움이 된다.
　　　　　　　　　　　　　　인간관계에 대한 내용은 없음

왜 정답 ? ✿✿✿ [정답률 90%]

남자는 운동과 건강한 식습관만큼이나 중요한 것이 휴식이라고 설명하며, 건강을 위해 휴식이 중요한 이유와 휴식의 기능에 대해 설명했다. 따라서 남자가 하는 말의 요지로 가장 적절한 것은 ②이다.

왜 오답 ?

① 규칙적인 운동이 건강에 긍정적인 영향을 미치기는 하지만 이것이 요지는 아니다.
③ 휴식을 통해 집중력 향상을 불러옴으로써 업무 수행 능력이 향상된다고 언급하며 휴식의 효과를 설명한 내용이지 집중력이 핵심은 아니다.
④ 운동 부족 보완을 위한 식이 요법에 대한 내용은 언급되지 않았다.
⑤ 인간관계가 스트레스를 완화시킬 수 있다는 내용은 관련이 없다.

04 정답 ③ ＊Dream 미술관

W : Hi, Jayden, you know what? I visited the Dream Gallery
with my mom yesterday.
여 : 안녕, Jayden, 그거 알아? 내가 어제 엄마와 Dream 미술관에 다녀왔어.

M : Oh, I've always wanted to visit there. Did you take any
pictures?
남 : 오, 나 거기 항상 가보고 싶었는데. 사진 찍었어?

W : Sure. Look at this.
여 : 그럼. 이것 좀 봐.

M : Is the person wearing a striped-dress your mom?
남 : 줄무늬 원피스 입은 사람이 너희 엄마셔? ①의 단서 줄무늬 원피스를 입고 있는 사람은 엄마임

W : Yes, it is. She really loved the painting on the left side of the
wall.
여 : 응, 맞아. 엄마가 벽 왼쪽에 있는 그림을 정말 좋아하셨어.

M : Oh, the painting of flowers? That's nice. I also like the other
painting. ②의 단서 왼쪽에 꽃 그림이 있음
남 : 오, 꽃 그림 말하는 거야? 좋다. 난 다른 그림도 마음에 들어.

W : You mean the painting of umbrellas in the round frame?
여 : 둥근 액자에 있는 우산 그림 말하는 거야? ③의 단서 우산 그림의 액자는 사각형임

M : Yes, it caught my eye. I can see a person sitting on the right
side of the picture. Who's the person?
남 : 응, 눈에 확 띄더라. 그림 오른쪽에 앉아 있는 사람도 보이는데. 그 사람은 누구야?

W : The man wearing glasses, right? He's the manager of the
gallery. ④의 단서 안경 쓴 남자가 있음
여 : 안경 쓴 남자 말이지, 그렇지? 그분은 미술관 관리자야.

M : I see. What's the arrow sign on the right wall?
남 : 그렇구나. 오른쪽 벽에 있는 화살표 표시는 뭐야? ⑤의 단서 오른쪽 벽에 화살표 표시가 있음

W : It shows the direction to the next area.
여 : 그것은 다음 구역으로 가는 방향을 알려주는 거야.

M : Oh, the gallery must be huge!
남 : 오, 미술관이 정말 큰가 보구나!

- gallery ⓝ 미술관 ・ round ⓐ 둥근 ・ frame ⓝ 액자
- arrow ⓝ 화살(표) ・ direction ⓝ 방향

대화를 듣고, 그림에서 대화의 내용과 일치하지 않는 것을 고르시오.

오른쪽 벽에 있는 화살표는 다음 구역으로 가는 방향을 표시함
미술관 관리자는 안경을 쓰고 오른쪽에 앉아 있음
② 왼쪽에는 꽃 그림이 있음
엄마는 줄무늬 원피스를 입고 계심
우산 그림의 액자는 둥글지 않고 사각형임

왜 정답 ? ✿✿✿ [정답률 81%]

우산 그림의 액자가 둥글다고 했지만 그림에서 액자는 사각형이므로 ③은 대화의 내용과 일치하지 않는다.

왜 오답 ?

① 엄마는 줄무늬 원피스를 입고 계시다고 했다.
② 꽃 그림은 왼쪽에 걸려 있다고 했다.
④ 미술관 관리자는 안경을 쓰고 오른쪽에 앉아 있다고 했다.
⑤ 오른편 벽에 있는 화살표는 다음 구역으로 가는 방향을 표시한다고 했다.

W : Honey, the flowers are really beautiful these days. Why
don't we take a walk this weekend?
Why don't we+동사원형?: ~하는 게 어때?

여 : 여보, 요즘 꽃들이 정말 예뻐요. 이번 주말에 산책하러 갈래요?

M : Wow, that sounds great. Do you have any particular place
in mind?

남 : 와, 정말 좋아요. 특별히 생각해둔 장소가 있어요?

W : Yes, I'd like to visit the Grand Forest. I've already
②의 함정   현재완료
downloaded the map of the forest. ①의 함정

여 : 네, Grand Forest에 가고 싶어요. 이미 숲 지도도 다운로드 해놨어요.

M : That's nice. Do we have to buy entrance tickets?

남 : 좋네요. 우리 입장권을 사야 해요?

W : Yes. We can buy tickets online. I'll buy two tickets in the
afternoon. ③의 함정

여 : 네. 온라인으로 티켓을 살 수 있어요. 내가 오후에 두 장 살게요.

M : Great. Let's have a nice lunch there, too. There's a restaurant
앞에 주격 관계대명사와 be동사 생략
called Treehouse Pasta in the Grand Forest.

남 : 좋아요. 거기서 맛있는 점심도 먹읍시다. Grand Forest에 'Treehouse 파스타'라는
식당이 있어요.

W : Nice. Do we have to make a reservation?

여 : 좋아요. 우리 예약해야 해요?

M : Yes. I'll make the reservation right away.

남 : 네. 난 지금 바로 식당을 예약할게요. **단서** 남자가 지금 바로 식당 예약을 하겠다고 함

W : Then, I'll look up the menu of the restaurant. ④의 함정

여 : 그럼, 나는 식당 메뉴를 찾아볼게요.

M : Thanks.

남 : 고마워요.

- particular ⓐ 특별한   · forest ⓝ 숲   · entrance ⓝ 입장
- make a reservation 예약하다

대화를 듣고, 남자가 할 일로 가장 적절한 것을 고르시오.

① 숲지도 다운로드 하기 여자가 이미 다운로드 해놨음
② 산책 장소 찾아보기 여자가 이미 장소를 선정함
③ 숲 입장권 구매하기 여자가 온라인으로 구매하기로 함
④ 식당 메뉴 찾아보기 식당 메뉴는 여자가 찾아볼 예정임
⑤ 식당 예약하기 남자가 식당을 예약하기로 함

〉왜 정답 ? ✿✿❁ [정답률 84%]

두 사람은 주말에 Grand Forest에 산책을 가서 거기 있는 Treehouse 파스타에 방
문할 예정이다. 남자가 예약이 필요하다고 하면서 지금 바로 식당 예약을 하겠다고 했
으므로 남자가 할 일로 가장 적절한 것은 ⑤이다.

〉왜 오답 ?

① 숲지도는 여자가 이미 다운로드를 해놓은 상태이다.
② Grand Forest를 이미 산책 장소로 찾아놓았다.
③ 숲 입장권은 온라인으로 여자가 구매할 예정이다.
④ 식당의 메뉴는 여자가 검색해보기로 했다. 함정

---

06 정답 ③ ＊신발 장식과 팔찌 구입

M : Hello. How can I help you today?

남 : 안녕하세요. 오늘 무엇을 도와드릴까요?

W : Hi. I'm here to buy some decorations for my sister's shoes.

여 : 안녕하세요. 제 여동생의 신발 장식을 좀 사려고 왔어요.
= some decorations
M : Great. We have those over here. They are five dollars each.

남 : 좋습니다. 그것들은 여기 있습니다. 하나에 5달러입니다. **단서 1** 장식은 1개당 5달러

W : She would love the decorations with this frog character, so
I'll take two of them. **단서 2** 장식을 2개 구입함

여 : 여동생은 이 개구리 캐릭터 장식을 좋아할 거에요. 그래서 두 개 살게요.

M : Wonderful. Do you need anything else?

남 : 멋지네요. 다른 거 필요한 게 있으세요?

W : Oh, I've just noticed this cute bracelet for her. How much is
현재완료
it?

여 : 오, 여동생을 위한 이 귀여운 팔찌를 방금 발견했어요. 이거 얼마예요?

M : It's ten dollars. **단서 3** 팔찌는 1개당 10달러

남 : 10달러입니다. ┌ **단서 4** 팔찌를 구입함

W : I'll buy it. And I'd like them gift-wrapped, please.

여 : 그거 살게요. 그리고 선물 포장도 해주세요.

M : We charge for gift-wrapping. It costs three dollars. Would
that be okay with you? **단서 5** 선물 포장 비용은 3달러임

남 : 선물 포장에는 요금이 부과됩니다. 포장 비용은 3달러입니다. 괜찮으세요?

W : Yes, that's fine.

여 : 네, 괜찮아요.

M : Then, I'll gift-wrap two decorations and one bracelet
together in one box. **단서 6** 장식 두 개와 팔찌 하나를 선물 포장할 것임

남 : 그럼 장식 두 개와 팔찌 하나를 같이 한 박스에 포장해 드리겠습니다.

W : Okay. Here's my credit card.

여 : 네. 여기 제 카드 있습니다.

- decoration ⓝ 장식(품)   · frog ⓝ 개구리   · bracelet ⓝ 팔찌
- gift-wrap ⓥ 선물 포장하다   · charge ⓥ (요금을) 부과하다

대화를 듣고, 여자가 지불할 금액을 고르시오. [3점]

① $13   ② $20   ③ $23   ④ $30   ⑤ $33

(개구리 캐릭터 신발 장식 $5×2) + (팔찌 $10 1개) + $3(포장 비용) = $23

〉왜 정답 ? ✿✿❁ [정답률 88%]

여자는 하나에 5달러인 개구리 캐릭터 신발 장식 두 개와 10달러인 팔찌 한 개를 구매
했고 포장까지 요청했으므로 3달러가 추가되어 여자가 지불할 금액은 ③ '23달러'이다.

---

07 정답 ② ＊휴대 전화를 수리하지 못한 이유

W : Hi, Brian. Why didn't you answer my text message
yesterday? I wanted to ask about the math exam. ③의 함정

여 : 안녕, Brian. 어제 왜 내 문자에 답장 안 했어? 수학 시험에 대해 물어보려고 했거든.

M : Hi, Sarah. I'm really sorry. I broke my cell phone yesterday,
so I couldn't read it.

남 : 안녕, Sarah. 정말 미안해. 어제 휴대 전화가 고장 나서 문자를 볼 수가 없었어.
= your cell phone
W : Oh, no! What happened to it?

여 : 오, 안돼! 무슨 일이 있었어?
부사절에서 「주어+be동사」 생략
M : Well, I dropped it while getting off the bus. And now, it
doesn't work at all. ⑤의 함정

남 : 음, 내가 버스에서 내리다가 그것을 떨어뜨렸거든. 그래서 지금은 아예 작동을 안 해.
과거분사(get의 목적격 보어)
W : Why didn't you get it fixed?

여 : 고치러 가지 그랬어?

M : I wanted to, but I couldn't.

남 : 그러고 싶었는데, 못 갔어.
= a repair shop
W : Was it because you couldn't find a repair shop? There's one
right by the bus stop near our school. ①의 함정

여 : 수리점을 못 찾아서 그런 거야? 우리 학교 근처 버스 정류장 바로 옆에 하나 있잖아.

M : I went there to get it fixed, but I couldn't.

남 : 거기 고치러 갔는데, 결국 못 고쳤어.

W : Oh, did you have to wait too long? ④의 함정

여 : 오, 너무 오래 기다려야 했어?

M : No, I didn't. Actually, I didn't know I had to make a
reservation in advance. So I just went back home. **단서** 미리 예약하지 않고 수리점을 방문했음

남 : 아니. 사실, 미리 예약해야 하는지 몰랐거든. 그래서 그냥 집에 돌아왔어.

W : Ah! That's too bad!

여 : 아! 안타깝다!

- break ⓥ 고장 내다　• get off ~에서 내리다　• repair ⓝ 수리
- in advance 미리, 사전에

대화를 듣고, 남자가 휴대 전화를 수리받지 못한 이유를 고르시오.

① 수리점의 위치를 찾지 못해서 이미 수리점에 방문했음
② 예약 없이 수리점을 방문해서 예약하고 방문해야 하는지 몰랐음
③ 수학 시험을 준비하느라 바빠서 휴대 전화가 고장 나 수학 시험 관련 질문을 못 받음
④ 수리점에서 오래 기다려야 해서 사람이 많아서 돌아온 것은 아님
⑤ 버스에서 휴대 전화를 잃어버려서 휴대 전화는 분실된 게 아니라 고장 난 것임

왜 정답? ✿✿✿ [정답률 89%]

수학 시험에 대해서 여자가 질문하려고 남자에게 문자했으나 남자는 휴대 전화가 고장 나서 보지 못했다고 했다. 남자는 수리점을 방문했지만 예약 없이 갔기 때문에 수리를 받지 못하고 돌아왔다고 했으므로 정답은 ②이다.

왜 오답?

① 학교 근처 버스 정류장 옆에 있는 것을 알고 이미 다녀왔다.
③ 남자는 수학 시험 때문에 휴대 전화를 수리받지 못한 것이 아니다.
④ 수리점에 대기 인원이 많아서 못 고치고 되돌아온 것은 아니다.
⑤ 휴대 전화가 고장 났는데 수리하지 못해서 연락이 어려웠다고 했다.

- generation ⓝ 세대　• hold ⓥ 열다, 개최하다　• topic ⓝ 주제
- birth rate 출생률　• affect ⓥ 영향을 주다
- live streaming 실시간 스트리밍, 생중계　• in person 직접, 몸소
- detail ⓝ 자세한 내용[세부 사항]

대화를 듣고, Future Generation Talk Show에 관해 언급되지 않은 것을 고르시오.

① 개최 장소 the talk show that will be held at Southern University
② 강연자 Professor Peter Johnson is coming to talk.
③ 강연 주제 It's about the low birth rate issue and how it's affecting the future.
④ 시작 시간 언급되지 않음
⑤ 온라인 시청 가능 여부 There's no live streaming service.

왜 정답? ✿✿✿ [정답률 94%]

Future Generation Talk Show의 개최 장소, 강연자, 강연 주제, 온라인 시청 가능 여부는 언급되었지만, 시작 시간에 대해서는 언급하지 않았으므로 정답은 ④이다.

왜 오답?

① Southern 대학교에서 개최된다.
② Peter Johnson 교수님이 강연자이다.
③ 출생률 저하 문제와 그것이 미래에 주는 영향이 강연 주제이다.
⑤ 온라인 시청은 가능하지 않다.

---

08 정답 ④ ＊Future Generation Talk Show

[Cell phone rings.]
[휴대 전화가 울린다.]

M : Hi, Kelly. What's up?
남 : 안녕, Kelly. 무슨 일이야?

W : Hey, Robert. Do you have time on Friday?
여 : 안녕, Robert. 금요일에 시간 있어?

M : Sure.
남 : 물론이지.

W : Have you heard about the Future Generation Talk Show?
여 : Future Generation Talk Show에 대해 들어봤어?

M : Oh, you mean the talk show **that** will be held at Southern University? ①의 단서 개최 장소
주격 관계대명사
남 : 오, 그거 Southern 대학교에서 열리는 토크쇼 말하는 거야?

W : Yes, that's right. Professor Peter Johnson **is coming** to talk. ②의 단서 강연자
현재진행형(가까운 미래 표현 가능)
여 : 응, 맞아. Peter Johnson 교수님이 강연하러 오신대.

M : The famous Peter Johnson? What's the topic of the talk show?
남 : 그 유명한 Peter Johnson 교수님? 토크쇼 주제는 뭐야?

W : It's about the low birth rate issue and how it's affecting the future. ③의 단서 강연 주제
여 : 출생률 저하 문제와 그것이 미래에 어떤 영향을 주는지에 대한 이야기야.

M : Sounds interesting. Can I watch the talk show online?
남 : 흥미롭다. 그 토크쇼 온라인으로 볼 수 있어?

W : No. There's no live streaming service. But **if** you go there, you can ask questions directly to Professor Johnson. ⑤의 단서 온라인 시청 가능 여부
조건의 부사절 접속사
여 : 아니. 생중계 서비스는 없어. 그런데 거기 가면 Johnson 교수님께 직접 질문도 할 수 있어.

M : Great. I can go in person. Can we go together?
남 : 좋아. 난 직접 갈 수 있어. 우리 같이 갈까?

W : Sure! I'll text you the details of the talk show right now.
여 : 좋아! 지금 토크쇼에 대한 자세한 내용을 문자로 보낼게.

---

09 정답 ③ ＊Science Day 행사 안내

W : Hello, students!
여 : 안녕하세요, 학생 여러분!

This is your science teacher Jane Brown.
저는 여러분의 과학 선생님 Jane Brown입니다.

I have some good news.
좋은 소식이 좀 있어요.

This Saturday we're having Science Day at our school. ①의 단서 이번 주 토요일에 진행됨
이번 토요일에 우리 학교에서 Science Day 행사가 열립니다.

In the morning, coding experts will teach you **how to make** a computer program. how to-v: ~하는 법
오전에는 코딩 전문가들이 여러분에게 컴퓨터 프로그램 만드는 방법을 가르쳐 줄 거예요.

You can also operate some robots by yourself in the school hall. ②의 단서 학생들이 직접 로봇을 작동해 볼 수 있음
여러분은 학교 강당에서 직접 몇 개의 로봇을 작동해 볼 수도 있어요.

In the afternoon, your science teachers will run some experimental booths for you. ③의 단서 선생님들이 오후에 실험 부스를 운영함
오후에는 여러분의 과학 선생님들이 여러분을 위해 몇 개의 실험 부스를 운영할 예정이에요.

It's a good chance **to experiment** with **what** you've learned from the textbooks. 형용사적 용법(chance 수식)　선행사를 포함하는 관계대명사
여러분이 교과서에서 배운 내용을 실험해 볼 수 있는 좋은 기회랍니다.

You can sign up for Science Day by scanning the QR codes on the school board. ④의 단서 QR 코드를 스캔하여 참가 신청을 할 수 있음
학교 게시판에 있는 QR 코드를 스캔하면 Science Day 행사에 신청할 수 있어요.

For the participants, lunch will be provided. ⑤의 단서 참가자들에게 점심을 제공함
참가자들을 위해서 점심도 제공될 것입니다.

Come and enjoy Science Day!
Science Day에 와서 즐겨봐요!

- science ⓝ 과학　• expert ⓝ 전문가
- operate ⓥ 작동하다, 조작하다　• experimental booth 실험 부스
- textbook ⓝ 교과서

Science Day 행사에 관한 다음 내용을 듣고, 일치하지 <u>않는</u> 것을 고르시오.

① 이번 주 토요일에 진행된다.
  This Saturday we're having Science Day at our school.
② 학생들이 직접 로봇을 작동해 볼 수 있다.
  You can also operate some robots by yourself in the school hall.
③ 선생님들이 오전에 실험 부스를 운영한다.
  In the afternoon, your science teachers will run some experimental booths for you.
④ QR 코드를 스캔하여 참가 신청을 할 수 있다.
  You can sign up for Science Day by scanning the QR codes on the school board.
⑤ 참가자들에게 점심을 제공한다. For the participants, lunch will be provided.

➢왜 정답 ? ✱✱✸ [정답률 84%]

선생님들은 오후에 실험 부스를 운영한다고 (In the afternoon, your science teachers will run some experimental booths for you.) 했으므로 오전에 한다고 한 ③은 일치하지 않는다.

➢왜 오답 ?

① 이번 주 토요일에 진행된다고 했다.
② 학생들이 직접 로봇을 작동해 볼 수 있다고 했다.
④ QR 코드를 스캔하여 참가 신청을 할 수 있다고 했다.
⑤ 참가자들에게 점심을 제공한다고 했다.

다음 표를 보면서 대화를 듣고, 여자가 수강할 운동 수업을 고르시오.

Exercise Classes 운동 수업

	Class 수업	Fee 수업료	Time 시간	Exercise Type 운동 종류	Level 수준
①	A	$25	9:00 a.m.	Dancing 댄스	Beginner 초급반 이미
②	B	$35	10:00 a.m. 야외	Dancing	Advanced 수강함 초급 고급
③	C	$35	10:00 a.m. 운동 아니어 야함	Tennis 테니스	Beginner
④	D	$35 수업은 2:00 p.m. 불가함		Boxing 복싱	Beginner
⑤	E	$45	10:00 a.m.	Boxing	Advanced

40달러 이상임

➢왜 정답 ? ✱✱✸ [정답률 79%]

여자는 운동 수업을 고르는데 40달러 이상은 쓰고 싶지 않(⑤ 제외)고, 오후에 할 일이 있어서 오전 수업이어야 한다고(④ 제외) 했다. 또한, 야외 운동은 싫어서 실내 운동이 좋고(③ 제외) 초급반은 이미 들어서 다른 수업을 선택하겠다고(① 제외) 했으므로 여자가 수강할 운동 수업은 ②이다.

➢왜 오답 ?

① 초급반은 이미 들어서 제외시켜야 한다.
③ 야외 운동은 싫어서 실내 수업이어야 한다.
④ 오후에는 할 일이 있어서 오전 수업이어야 한다.
⑤ 40달러 이상은 쓰고 싶지 않다.

---

10 정답 ② ✱운동 수업 선택

M : Sweetie, what are you doing?
남 : 자기야, 뭐 하고 있어요?

W : I'm looking at the schedule for exercise classes. Would you like to help me choose?
여 : 운동 수업 시간표를 보고 있어요. 내가 고르는 걸 도와줄 수 있어요?

M : Sure. What's your budget for it?
남 : 물론이죠. 예산은 얼마 생각하고 있어요?

W : Well, I don't want to spend **more than** forty dollars. ~이상
여 : 음, 난 40달러 이상은 쓰고 싶지 않아요. [단서 1] 40달러 이상은 쓰고 싶지 않음(⑤ 제외)

M : Okay. Then, forget about this **one**. What about class time? =class
남 : 알겠어요. 그럼 이 수업은 제외해요. 수업 시간은?

W : As you know, I have things to do in the afternoon.
여 : 알다시피, 나는 오후에 할 일이 있어요. [단서 2] 오전 수업이어야 함 (④ 제외)

M : In that case, let's cross this one out. Now you have dancing and tennis left.
남 : 그렇다면 이 수업도 뺍시다. 이제 춤이랑 테니스 수업이 남았네요.

W : I heard the tennis class is held outside. I don't like outdoor sports. [단서 3] 실내 수업이어야 함 (③ 제외)
여 : 테니스 수업은 야외에서 한다고 들었어요. 나는 야외 운동은 좋아하지 않아요.

M : Okay. Then, we have only two exercise classes left. Which level is good for you?
남 : 알겠어요. 그럼 이제 운동 수업 두 개만 남았네요. 어떤 수준이 당신한테 좋을까요?

W : Since I've already taken the beginner's class, I'll take **the other** one this time. [단서 4] 초급반이 아니어야 함 (① 제외)
여 : 초급반은 이미 들었으니까 이번엔 다른 걸 들을게요. 두 개 중 나머지 하나

- **schedule** ⓝ 시간표 • **budget** ⓝ 예산
- **cross out** 빼다, 지우다 • **outdoor** ⓐ 야외의
- **beginner** ⓝ 초보자, 초급 단계

---

11 정답 ② ✱말하기 연습 방식

W : Hi, Daniel. Are you ready for your presentation tomorrow?
여 : 안녕, Daniel. 내일 발표 준비는 다 됐어?

M : Hi, Tina. Not really. **I've finished** my slides, but I **haven't practiced** my speech yet. 현재완료의 병렬 구조
남 : 안녕, Tina. 아니. 난 슬라이드는 다 만들었는데, 말하기 연습은 아직 안 했어.

W : How do you usually practice it? [단서] 평소 연습 방법에 대해 질문함
여 : 넌 그것을 보통 어떻게 연습해?

M : I record **myself** talking and watch it later. 재귀대명사
남 : 나는 내가 말하는 걸 녹화해서 나중에 그것을 봐.

- **presentation** ⓝ 발표, 프레젠테이션 • **tomorrow** ⓐⓓ 내일
- **slide** ⓝ 슬라이드, 발표 자료 • **practice** ⓥ 연습하다
- **speech** ⓝ 말하기 • **record** ⓥ 녹음[녹화]하다

대화를 듣고, 여자의 마지막 말에 대한 남자의 응답으로 가장 적절한 것을 고르시오.

① I'll ask the teacher if I can change my topic.
  내 주제를 바꿔도 되는지 선생님께 여쭤볼 거야. 발표 주제를 바꾸는 것은 언급되지 않음
② I record myself talking and watch it later.
  나는 내가 말하는 걸 녹화해서 나중에 그것을 봐. 자신의 말하기 연습 방식을 설명함
③ I'm looking forward to your presentation. 남자가 발표하는 것임
  난 네 발표가 기대돼.
④ I need more time to finish my slides. 슬라이드는 이미 다 만듦
  슬라이드를 다 끝내려면 난 시간이 좀 더 필요해.
⑤ I haven't decided what to wear. 복장은 관련 없는 내용임
  난 뭘 입을지 아직 결정 못 했어.

➢왜 정답 ? ✱✱✸ [정답률 76%]

남자가 발표를 위한 슬라이드는 만들었지만 말하기 연습은 아직 안 했다고 했고, 이에 대해 여자는 연습 방식에 관해 물었다. 따라서 남자는 ② '나는 내가 말하는 걸 녹화해서 나중에 그것을 봐.'라고 응답하는 것이 가장 적절하다.

➢왜 오답 ?

① 주제 교체는 언급된 내용이 아니다.
③ 발표가 기대된다는 말은 흐름상 적절하지 않다.
④ 슬라이드 제작은 이미 끝냈다고 말했다. 주의
⑤ 복장에 관한 이야기는 등장하지 않았다.

12 정답 ④ *음식물 쓰레기 포스터

앞에 목적격 관계대명사 생략

M : Ashley, do you remember the digital poster we made to upload on social media?
남 : Ashley, 우리가 소셜 미디어에 올리려고 만들었던 디지털 포스터 기억나?

= the digital poster

W : Yes, of course. It was about food waste, right?
여 : 응, 물론이지. 그것은 음식물 쓰레기에 관한 거였지, 맞지?

M : Exactly. Let's print it out and put it on the wall in our school cafeteria. **단서** 학생들이 음식물 쓰레기에 관한 포스터를 볼 수 있게 학교 식당 벽에 붙이자고 함
남 : 맞아. 그거 출력해서 학교 식당 벽에 붙이자.

W : **Great idea! It'll catch the students' attention.**
여 : 좋은 생각이야! 그게 학생들의 관심을 끌 거야.

- upload ⓥ 올리다, 업로드하다 · social media 소셜 미디어
- waste ⓝ 쓰레기 · cafeteria ⓝ (구내)식당 · attention ⓝ 관심

대화를 듣고, 남자의 마지막 말에 대한 여자의 응답으로 가장 적절한 것을 고르시오.

① Thanks. But I'm not hungry now. 배고픔 여부는 묻지 않음
 고마워. 근데 지금은 배가 안 고파.
② I agree. Printing it out is such a waste. 출력해서 붙일 예정임
 동의해. 그걸 출력하는 건 정말 낭비야.
③ Of course not. I'll help you at any time. not을 넣어 답변할 수 있는 맥락이 아님
 당연히 아니지. 언제든지 도와줄게.
④ Great idea! It'll catch the students' attention.
 좋은 생각이야! 그게 학생들의 관심을 끌 거야. 포스터가 갖는 효과에 대해 긍정적인 응답
⑤ No worries. I like the menu of our school cafeteria.
 걱정 마. 난 우리 학교 식당 메뉴가 좋아. 학교식당 메뉴는 언급되지 않음

> **왜** 정답 ? ✸✸✾ [정답률 75%]

남자는 음식물 쓰레기에 관련된 디지털 포스터를 만들어서 소셜 미디어에 올리려 했던 것을 말하면서, 그것을 출력해서 학교 식당 벽에 붙이자고 했다. 이에 여자는 ④ '좋은 생각이야! 그게 학생들의 관심을 끌 거야.'라고 응답하는 것이 가장 적절하다.

> **왜** 오답 ?

① 식당이 언급되긴 했지만 배고픔은 관련이 없는 내용이다.
② 출력해서 식당 벽에 붙이기로 했으므로 적절하지 않다.
③ not을 넣어 답변할 수 있는 맥락이 아니므로 적절하지 않다.
⑤ 학교 식당 메뉴는 언급되지 않았다.

13 정답 ① *수면 부족이 공부에 끼치는 역효과

현재완료 진행형

W : Chris, you've been looking so tired these days.
여 : Chris, 너 요즘 너무 피곤해 보여.

M : Yeah, Mom. I'm studying for my first high school exam. I really want to do well.
남 : 네, 엄마. 저는 고등학교 첫 시험을 위해 공부하고 있어요. 정말 잘 보고 싶어요.

W : I understand, but I'm worried about you. Have you had any trouble managing your time?
여 : 이해는 되지만 네가 걱정돼. 시간 관리를 하는 데 어려움을 겪고 있니?

M : Well, I don't have enough of it. I've been staying up late studying these days.
남 : 음, 시간이 부족해요. 요즘 공부하느라 늦게까지 자지 않고 있어요.

동명사구 주어

W : **Staying up late** won't help you much, Chris.
여 : 늦게까지 자지 않는 건 그다지 도움이 안 될 거야, Chris.

형용사적 용법

M : But I have so much **to do**, Mom. 남 : 하지만 할 일이 너무 많아요, 엄마.

W : I see your point, but staying up too late might actually hurt your chances of doing well.
여 : 네 말도 이해하지만, 너무 늦게까지 자지 않는 것은 시험을 잘 볼 기회를 실제로 놓치게 할 수 있어.

비교급 표현

M : Maybe you're right, but I thought studying would be **more helpful** to me **than** sleeping.
남 : 엄마 말씀이 맞을 수도 있어요, 하지만 저는 자는 것보다 공부하는 게 저에게 더 도움이 될 거라고 생각했어요.

W : Not if you're too tired. If you don't sleep enough, it'll hurt your focus and memory. **단서** 공부 시간을 확보하기 위해 잠을 충분히 못 자면 오히려 역효과가 날 수 있음
여 : 네가 너무 피곤하면 그렇지 않아. 잠을 충분히 못 자면 너의 집중력과 기억력이 떨어질 거야.

W : **Right. I'll try to go to bed earlier and get more sleep.**
남 : 알겠어요. 좀 더 일찍 자고 잠을 더 자도록 노력할게요.

- have trouble -ing ~하는 데 어려움을 겪다 · manage ⓥ 관리하다
- stay up late (늦게까지) 자지 않고 있다 · focus ⓝ 집중력
- memory ⓝ 기억력

대화를 듣고, 여자의 마지막 말에 대한 남자의 응답으로 가장 적절한 것을 고르시오.

Man :
① Right. I'll try to go to bed earlier and get more sleep. 수면 부족은 집중력과 기억력을 떨어뜨려 공부에 안 좋은 영향을 준다고 했음
 알겠어요. 좀 더 일찍 자고 잠을 더 자도록 노력할게요.
② I'm sorry. I didn't know you had a hard time sleeping. 여자가 잠을 잘 못 자는 것이 아님
 미안해요. 당신이 잠을 잘 못 자는 줄 몰랐어요.
③ Absolutely! I believe you'll do better next time. 여자가 시험을 보는 것이 아님
 물론이죠! 난 당신이 다음번에는 더 잘할 거라고 믿어요.
④ Sure. I'll do my best to stay awake longer. 잠이 부족한 게 문제인 상황임
 물론이죠. 더 오래 깨어 있으려고 최선을 다할게요.
⑤ I see. I'll try to come back home in time. 귀가 시간은 언급되지 않음
 알겠어요. 제시간에 집에 오도록 노력할게요.

> **왜** 정답 ? ✸✾✾ [정답률 90%]

남자는 첫 시험을 잘 보고 싶어서 수면 시간을 줄이고 공부하고 있다고 했다. 그런데 여자는 너무 늦게까지 자지 않으면 집중력과 기억력이 떨어질 것이라고 했으므로 이에 대한 남자의 응답으로 가장 적절한 것은 ① '알겠어요. 좀 더 일찍 자고 잠을 더 자도록 노력할게요.'이다.

> **왜** 오답 ?

② 여자가 잠을 잘 못 자는 것이 아니므로 적절하지 않은 내용이다.
③ 여자가 시험을 보는 것이 아니므로 흐름상 어색하다.
④ 공부하느라 수면 시간을 줄인 것이 문제인 상황이므로 적절하지 않다.
⑤ 잠 자는 시간이 짧은 상황에 대한 내용이므로 귀가 시간은 관련이 없다.

14 정답 ④ *스트레스를 줄이는 배드민턴

M : Hi, Cindy! What are you doing this weekend?
남 : 안녕, Cindy! 이번 주말에 뭐 할 거야?

W : I'm going to play badminton with my friends.
여 : 내 친구들이랑 배드민턴 칠 거야.

현재형(현재의 습관, 반복되는 일)

M : You **play** badminton quite often.
남 : 너 배드민턴 꽤 자주 치는구나.

help의 목적격 보어(동사원형)

W : It's my new hobby. It helps me **reduce** stress.
여 : 그게 내 새 취미거든. 내가 스트레스를 푸는 데 도움이 돼.

M : How nice! I've been looking for something to reduce stress.
남 : 정말 좋다! 나도 스트레스를 줄일 무언가를 찾고 있었어.

주격 관계대명사

W : Well, you don't have to think too hard. Just think of something **that** makes you happy.
여 : 음, 너무 어렵게 생각할 필요 없어. 그냥 너를 행복하게 해주는 걸 생각해 봐.

M : Hmm.... But nothing comes to mind right away.
남 : 음… 그런데 당장 떠오르는 게 없네.

why don't you + 동사원형: ~하는 게 어때?

W : Then, **why don't you come** and **play** badminton with me this Saturday? You'll like it, too, I think.
여 : 그럼 이번 토요일에 와서 나랑 같이 배드민턴 치는 게 어때? 너도 좋아할 거라고 생각해.

M : Really? Is it okay if I join you?
남 : 정말? 내가 같이 가도 괜찮아?

W : Of course, it is! We meet at the sports center every Saturday morning.
여 : 물론이지! 우리는 매주 토요일 아침에 스포츠 센터에서 만나.

M : Thanks a lot! Do I need to prepare anything?

남 : 정말 고마워! 내가 준비할 게 있을까? 단서 배드민턴을 함께 칠 때 필요한 준비물에 대해 질문함

W : **Just bring your racket and some comfortable clothes.**

여 : 그냥 네 라켓이랑 편한 옷을 좀 가져오면 돼.

- badminton ⓝ 배드민턴 · hobby ⓝ 취미 · reduce ⓥ 줄이다
- prepare ⓥ 준비하다 · comfortable ⓐ 편한

대화를 듣고, 남자의 마지막 말에 대한 여자의 응답으로 가장 적절한 것을 고르시오. [3점]

Woman: _____

① Reading books can also be a good hobby. 독서는 언급된 내용이 아님
독서도 좋은 취미가 될 수 있어.
② You had to practice a lot to win the game.
너는 경기에서 이기려면 많이 연습해야 했어. 경기에서 이기는 것에 대한 내용이 아님
③ How about going out with me this Saturday?
이번 토요일에 나랑 함께 외출하는 게 어때? 준비물에 관한 질문과 관련 없음
④ Just bring your racket and some comfortable clothes.
그냥 네 라켓이랑 편한 옷을 좀 가져오면 돼. 배드민턴을 칠 때 필요한 준비물에 대한 적절한 응답
⑤ If you don't have a hobby, you can get more stressed.
취미가 없으면 스트레스를 더 받을 수 있어. 스트레스 감소를 위해 취미를 만들려고 하는 중임

>왜 정답? ✿✿❀❀ [정답률 93%]

여자가 새 취미로 배드민턴을 친다고 하자, 남자는 자신도 스트레스를 줄일 수 있는 방법을 고민하고 있다고 했다. 그래서 여자는 함께 배드민턴을 치자고 했고, 남자가 필요한 준비물을 물었으므로 여자의 응답으로 가장 적절한 것은 ④ '그냥 네 라켓이랑 편한 옷을 좀 가져오면 돼.'이다.

>왜 오답?

① 독서는 언급된 내용이 아니다.
② 경기에서 이기기 위한 방법에 관한 대화가 아니다.
③ 준비물을 물어보았기 때문에 함께 외출하자는 말은 어색하다.
⑤ 취미가 없어서 새로 만들려는 상황이다.

---

15 정답 ④ *캠프 날짜 변경

M : Kevin is the president of the Starlight Club in the school.

남 : Kevin은 학교의 Starlight Club 회장이다.

For weeks, the club has been preparing the star-viewing
현재완료진행
camp-night at the school yard with the club teacher, Ms. Tyler.

몇 주 동안, 그 동아리는 동아리 담당 선생님인 Tyler 선생님과 함께 학교 운동장에서 열릴 별을 관측하는 캠프의 밤을 준비해 왔다.

They expected that the sky would be clear on camp-night.
목적어절을 이끄는 접속사
그들은 캠프 당일 밤에 하늘이 맑을 것이라고 기대하고 있었다.

But today, there's a sudden change in the weather forecast,
단서1 일기예보에 따르면 캠프 밤 당일에 비가 올 것임
and it says it's going to rain during camp-night.

하지만 오늘 갑자기 일기 예보가 바뀌어 캠프의 밤 동안에 비가 올 것이라고 한다.

It means the camp cannot go on as planned.
'~대로'
그것은 캠프를 예정대로 진행할 수 없다는 뜻이다.

Kevin wants to ask Ms. Tyler if they can change the camp
명사절을 이끄는 접속사
date to another day. 단서2 캠프 날짜를 다른 날로 바꿀 수 있는지 여쭤보고 싶음

Kevin은 Tyler 선생님께 캠프 날짜를 다른 날로 바꿀 수 있는지 여쭤보길 원한다.

In this situation, what would Kevin most likely say to Ms. Tyler?

이런 상황에서, Kevin이 Tyler 선생님께 할 말로 가장 적절한 것은 무엇인가?

Kevin: **Can we reschedule the camp for another day?**

Kevin: 캠프 날짜를 다른 날로 바꿀 수 있을까요?

* 상황 요약: 캠프 당일 밤에 비가 올 것이라 하여 다른 날로 바꾸고 싶은 상황

- prepare ⓥ 준비하다 · expect ⓥ 예상하다, 기대하다
- sudden ⓐ 갑작스러운 · weather forecast 일기 예보
- as planned 예정대로 · fortunate ⓐ 다행인
- volunteer ⓝ 자원봉사자

다음 상황 설명을 듣고, Kevin이 Ms. Tyler에게 할 말로 가장 적절한 것을 고르시오. [3점]

Kevin: _____

① Isn't it fortunate that the rain stopped yesterday?
어제 비가 그쳐서 다행이지 않나요? 비가 올 것이라고 했음
② Could you teach us about the stars today?
저희에게 오늘 별에 대해 가르쳐 주실 수 있나요? 별 관측 행사는 오늘 하는 것이 아님
③ Is it okay if we change the camp site? 장소가 아닌 날짜를 바꾸고 싶음
저희가 캠프 장소를 바꿔도 될까요?
④ Can we reschedule the camp for another day?
캠프 날짜를 다른 날로 바꿀 수 있을까요? 비가 예정되어 있어 날짜 변경이 필요한 상황임
⑤ How can we gather more volunteers for the camp?
캠프를 위해 자원봉사자를 더 모으려면 어떻게 할 수 있을까요? 자원봉사자는 언급되지 않음

>왜 정답? ✿✿✿❀ [정답률 86%]

Kevin은 학교 운동장에서 열릴 별 관측 캠프를 준비해 왔는데 행사 당일에 비가 온다는 예보를 접했다. 별을 관측하기 어려운 날씨인 만큼 Tyler 선생님께 행사를 다른 날로 바꿀 수 있는지 여쭤보고 싶다. 따라서 Kevin이 Tyler 선생님께 할 말로 가장 적절한 것은 ④ '캠프 날짜를 다른 날로 바꿀 수 있을까요?'이다.

>왜 오답?

① 비가 그친 게 아니고 올 것이라고 했다.
② 별을 관측하는 행사는 오늘 하는 것이 아니다.
③ 캠프 장소가 아닌 날짜를 조정하려는 상황이다.
⑤ 자원봉사자는 언급되지 않은 내용이다.

16~17 *전 세계의 매력적인 사진 명소들

W: Hello! // Everyone. //

여 : 안녕하세요 // 여러분 //

I'm Jasmine, a travel photographer, / and I'm excited / to
동격   부사적 용법(감정의 원인) 형용사적 용법(places 수식)
share some wonderful places / to take photos around the
world. // 16번 단서: 전 세계의 사진 찍기 좋은 장소들을 소개할 것임

저는 여행 사진작가 Jasmine입니다 / 그리고 정말 기대됩니다 / 좋은 몇몇 멋진 장소들을 여러분과 함께 나눌 수 있어 / 전 세계에서 사진 찍기에

The first place is Times Square / in New York. //

첫 번째 장소는 타임스스퀘어입니다 / 뉴욕의 // 17번①

It is full of energy, / with its tall buildings and busy
sidewalks. //

그곳은 활기가 넘칩니다 / 높은 빌딩들과 분주한 인도로 //

Next, / Rome amazed me / with its famous historical places,
전치사   17번②
/ like the Colosseum. //

다음으로 / 로마가 저를 놀라게 했습니다 / 유명한 역사적 장소들로 / 콜로세움 같은 //

It made me feel like traveling back in time! //

마치 시간 여행을 하는 기분이었죠 //

And when you visit London, / you shouldn't miss
Buckingham Palace. // 17번④

그리고 런던을 방문하게 된다면 / 버킹엄 궁전을 놓치지 마세요 //

It's a perfect place / for once-in-a-lifetime photos. //

그곳은 완벽한 장소랍니다 / 일생에 한 번뿐인 사진을 찍기에 //

Lastly, / in Sydney, / the Opera House was great / for taking
17번⑤
beautiful sunset photos. //

마지막으로 / 시드니에서는 / 오페라 하우스가 정말 좋았습니다 / 아름다운 일몰 사진을 찍기에 //

Traveling with a camera is such a joy, / and I can't wait / to
동명사구 주어
share more travel places with you. //

카메라와 함께 여행하는 건 정말 즐거운 일입니다 / 그리고 저는 기대됩니다 / 더 많은 여행지를 여러분께 소개해드리는 것이 //

Now let's take a look / at the photos of these places. //

이제 살펴봅시다 / 이 장소들의 사진을 //

- **photographer** ⓝ 사진작가 • **sidewalk** ⓝ 보도, 인도
- **amaze** ⓥ 놀라게 하다 • **historical** ⓐ 역사적인 • **miss** ⓥ 놓치다
- **once-in-a-lifetime** ⓐ 일생에 한 번 뿐인 • **sunset** ⓝ 일몰
- **necessary** ⓐ 필요한 • **traveler** ⓝ 여행자
- **importance** ⓝ 중요성

여: 안녕하세요! 여러분. 저는 여행 사진작가 Jasmine이고, 전 세계에서 사진 찍기 좋은 몇몇 멋진 장소들을 여러분과 함께 나눌 수 있어 정말 기대됩니다. 첫 번째 장소는 뉴욕의 타임스퀘어입니다. 그곳은 높은 빌딩들과 분주한 인도로 활기가 넘칩니다. 다음으로, 로마가 콜로세움 같은 유명한 역사적 장소들로 저를 놀라게 했습니다. 마치 시간 여행을 하는 기분이었죠! 그리고 런던을 방문하게 된다면, 버킹엄 궁전을 놓치지 마세요. 그곳은 일생에 한 번뿐인 사진을 찍기에 완벽한 장소랍니다. 마지막으로, 시드니에서는 오페라 하우스가 아름다운 일몰 사진을 찍기에 정말 좋았습니다. 카메라와 함께 여행하는 건 정말 즐거운 일이고, 저는 더 많은 여행지를 여러분께 소개해드리는 것이 기대됩니다. 이제 이 장소들의 사진을 살펴봅시다.

16 정답 ⑤

여자가 하는 말의 주제로 가장 적절한 것은?

① useful tips for safe world travel 안전에 관련된 내용은 없음
  안전한 세계 여행을 위한 유용한 팁
② necessary items for city travelers 필요한 물품들에 대한 내용이 아님
  도시 여행자들에게 필요한 물품들
③ famous historical cities in the world 역사적 도시들이 핵심은 아님
  세계의 유명한 역사적 도시들
④ importance of learning photo techniques
  사진 촬영 기술 습득의 중요성 촬영 기술 습득에 관련된 내용은 없음
⑤ attractive photo spots around the world
  전 세계의 매력적인 사진 명소들 전 세계의 사진 찍기 좋은 명소들을 소개함

>왜 정답? ✽✽✽ [정답률 91%]

여자는 여행 사진작가로서 전 세계의 사진 찍기 좋은 장소들을 언급하며 각 도시의 매력 포인트와 촬영 팁을 설명하고 있다. 따라서 여자가 하는 말의 주제로 가장 적절한 것은 ⑤ '전 세계의 매력적인 사진 명소들'이다.

>왜 오답?

① 여행을 위한 안전과 관련된 내용은 없다.
② 도시 여행자들이 필요한 물품들은 관련이 없는 내용이다.
③ 세계적으로 유명한 역사적 도시들 자체를 소개하려는 것이 아니다. 함정
④ 사진 촬영 기술을 습득하는 것이 중요하다는 내용은 언급되지 않았다.

17 정답 ③

언급된 도시가 아닌 것은?

① New York The first place is Times Square in New York.
  뉴욕
② Rome Next, Rome amazed me with its famous historical places, like the Colosseum.
  로마
③ Paris 언급되지 않음
  파리
④ London And when you visit London, you shouldn't miss Buckingham Palace.
  런던
⑤ Sydney Lastly, in Sydney, the Opera House was great for taking beautiful sunset photos.
  시드니

>왜 정답? ✽✽✽ [정답률 90%]

뉴욕, 로마, 런던, 시드니에 대해서는 언급했지만 파리에 대해서는 언급하지 않았으므로 정답은 ③ '파리'이다.

>왜 오답?

① 뉴욕은 높은 빌딩들과 분주한 인도로 활기가 넘치는 곳이라고 했다.
② 로마는 콜로세움 같은 유명한 역사적 장소들이 있다고 했다.
④ 런던을 방문하게 된다면 버킹엄 궁전을 꼭 가보라고 했다.
⑤ 시드니에서는 오페라 하우스에 방문해 아름다운 일몰 사진을 꼭 찍으라고 했다.

18 정답 ③ ＊작품 전시 안내

Dear Miranda, /
Miranda님께 /

Thank you / for participating in our Crafts Art Fair. //
감사합니다 / 우리의 Crafts Art Fair에 참여해 주셔서 //

Since we've chosen you / as one of the 'Artists of This Year', /
  ~로(서)
  look forward to -ing: ~ 하는 것을 기대하다
we are looking forward to introducing / your unique handmade baskets / to our community. //
우리가 당신을 선정했기에 / '올해의 예술가들' 중 한 명으로 / 소개하기를 기대하고 있습니다 / 당신의 독창적인 수공예 바구니를 / 우리 지역 사회에 //

'~의 일환으로'
As part of organizing the exhibition plan, / we are happy to inform you / that your artworks will be exhibited / at the
  목적어절 접속사
assigned table, number seven. // 단서 작품이 전시될 테이블 안내
전시 배치도를 조직하는 것의 일환으로 / 알려 드리게 되어 우리는 기쁩니다 / 당신의 작품이 전시될 예정임을 / 지정된 7번 테이블에 //

앞에 주격 관계대명사와 be동사가 생략됨
Visitors can easily find your artworks / located near the entrance. //
방문객들이 당신의 작품을 쉽게 찾을 수 있습니다 / 입구 근처에 위치한 //

If you have any special requirements / or need further assistance, / feel free to contact us / in advance. //
특별한 요구 사항이 있거나 / 추가적인 도움이 필요하시면 / 편히 연락해 주시기 바랍니다 / 미리 //

Sincerely, / Helen Dwyer /
진심을 담아 / Helen Dwyer /

- **introduce** ⓥ 소개하다 • **handmade** ⓐ 수공예의
- **organize** ⓥ 조직하다 • **exhibition plan** 전시 배치도
- **inform** ⓥ 알리다 • **requirement** ⓝ 요구 사항
- **further** ⓐ 추가적인 • **assistance** ⓝ 도움

Miranda님께,
우리의 Crafts Art Fair에 참여해 주셔서 감사합니다. 우리가 당신을 '올해의 예술가들' 중 한 명으로 선정했기에, 당신의 독창적인 수공예 바구니를 우리 지역 사회에 소개하기를 기대하고 있습니다. 전시 배치도를 조직하는 것의 일환으로, 우리는 당신의 작품이 지정된 7번 테이블에 전시될 예정임을 알려 드리게 되어 기쁩니다. 방문객들이 입구 근처에 위치한 당신의 작품을 쉽게 찾을 수 있습니다. 특별한 요구 사항이 있거나 추가적인 도움이 필요하시면, 편히 미리 연락해 주시기 바랍니다.
진심을 담아,
Helen Dwyer

다음 글의 목적으로 가장 적절한 것은?

① 공예품 구매 희망자를 소개하려고 판매가 아닌 전시에 관한 내용임
② 비상시 박람회장 대피 동선을 안내하려고 비상 대피 동선은 언급되지 않았음
③ 작품이 전시될 지정 테이블을 알려 주려고
④ 올해의 공예가 선정 투표 방식을 공지하려고 선정 투표 방식은 언급되지 않았음
⑤ 박람회에 참여할 새로운 공예가를 모집하려고
  이미 선정되어 작품이 전시될 예정임

>왜 정답? ✽✽✽ [정답률 84%]

올해의 예술가로 선정되어 작품이 전시될 예정이고 작품의 전시 위치를 안내하는 내용이므로 정답은 ③이다.

>왜 오답?

① 공예품 판매가 아닌 전시에 관한 글이다.
② 비상시 대피 동선은 언급되지 않았다.
④ 선정 투표 방식은 언급되지 않았다.
⑤ 편지를 받은 Miranda는 이미 올해의 예술가 중 한 명으로 선정되었다.

19 정답 ③ ★토끼의 등장

사이에 반복되는 be동사 is가 생략됨
The shed is cold and damp, / the air thick / with the smell of old wood and earth. //
헛간은 춥고 습기가 차 있고 / 공기에 짙다 / 오래된 나무와 흙냄새가 //

선행사를 포함하는 관계대명사
It's dark, / and I can't make out / what's moving in the shadows. //
어두워서 / 나는 알아볼 수 없다 / 그림자 속에서 움직이는 무언가를 //

"Who's there?" / I ask, / my voice shaking with fear. //　**단서 1** 두려움에 목소리가 떨림
"거기 누구세요" / 나는 묻는다 / 목소리가 두려움에 떨리며 //

현재분사구 (light 수식)
The shadow moves closer, / and my heart is beating fast / — until the figure steps into a faint beam of light / breaking through a crack in the wall. //
그림자가 점점 가까이 다가오고 / 나의 심장은 점점 빠르게 뛰고 있다 / 희미한 빛줄기 속으로 그 형체가 들어설 때 / 벽 틈새로 새어 들어온 //

A rabbit. // 토끼다 //

부사절 접속사 (시간)
A laugh escapes my lips / as it stares at me / with wide, curious eyes. //
웃음이 내 입술에서 새어 나온다 / 그것이 나를 바라볼 때 / 크고 호기심 가득한 눈으로 //

분사구문
"You scared me," / I say, / feeling much better. //
"너 때문에 놀랐잖아" / 나는 말한다 / 훨씬 나아진 기분을 느끼며 //

분사구문
The rabbit pauses for a moment, / then hops away, / disappearing back into the shadows. //
토끼는 잠시 멈칫하더니 / 이내 깡충 뛰어 / 그림자 속으로 다시 사라진다 //

I'm left smiling. // 나는 미소 지으며 남아 있다 //

I start to feel at ease. //　**단서 2** 놀랐던 마음이 진정되고 안도함
나의 마음이 편안해지기 시작한다 //

- damp ⓐ 습기 찬　　• thick ⓐ (공기가) 짙은
- make out 알아보다, 식별하다　　• shadow ⓝ 그림자
- shaking ⓐ 떨리는　　• figure ⓝ 형체, 형상　　• faint ⓐ 희미한
- beam ⓝ 빛줄기　　• crack ⓝ 틈새
- escape ⓥ (웃음 등이) 새어 나오다　　• stare at ~을 바라보다
- hop ⓥ 깡충 뛰다　　• at ease 편안한

헛간은 춥고 습기가 차 있고, 공기에 오래된 나무와 흙냄새가 짙다. 어두워서, 나는 그림자 속에서 움직이는 무언가를 알아볼 수 없다. "거기 누구세요?" 목소리가 두려움에 떨리며, 나는 묻는다. 그림자가 점점 가까이 다가오고, 나의 심장은 점점 빠르게 뛰고 있다. 그때, 벽 틈새로 새어 들어온 희미한 빛줄기 속으로 그 형체가 들어선다. 토끼다. 그것이 크고 호기심 가득한 눈으로 나를 바라볼 때, 웃음이 내 입술에서 새어 나온다. "너 때문에 놀랐잖아." 훨씬 나아진 기분을 느끼며, 나는 말한다. 토끼는 잠시 멈칫하더니, 이내 깡충 뛰어 그림자 속으로 다시 사라진다. 나는 미소 지으며 남아 있다. 나의 마음이 편안해지기 시작한다.

> 다음 글에 드러난 'I'의 심경 변화로 가장 적절한 것은?
> ① envious → hopeful　부러워서 심장이 빨리 뛰므로 두려움의 감정은 아님
> 　부러워하는 → 희망찬
> ② anxious → angry　정체를 알게 된 후 안도감을 느낌
> 　걱정스러운 → 화난
> ③ frightened → relieved　정체 모를 대상에 두려움을 느꼈으나 정체를 알고는 안도했음
> 　겁먹은 → 안도한
> ④ curious → regretful　후반부에 'I'가 아닌 토끼의 표정에 호기심이 묻어 있었음
> 　호기심 있는 → 후회하는
> ⑤ excited → disappointed　실망보다는 안도에 가까움
> 　흥분한 → 실망한

❓왜 정답? ❋❋❋ [정답률 84%]

전반부: 헛간에 있는데 정체 모를 존재가 다가와서 심장이 빠르게 뛰됨 ▶ '겁먹은'
후반부: 다가온 존재를 확인하니 토끼임을 알게 됨 ▶ '안도한'
따라서 'I'의 심경 변화로 가장 적절한 것은 ③ '겁먹은 → 안도한'이다.

❓왜 오답?

① 두려움을 느끼고 있으므로 부러운 감정을 느낀 것이 아니다.
② 다가오는 대상에 화가 난 것이 아니라 안도감을 느꼈다.
④ 후반부에 호기심을 드러낸 것은 'I'가 아니라 토끼였고, 후회하기보다는 안도했다.
⑤ 초반에 걱정하고 두려움에 떨다가 긴장이 풀린 것이지, 실망한 것은 아니다.

20 정답 ② ★적절한 몸짓의 효과

동명사 (전치사 than의 목적어)　　knowing의 목적어 (의문사+to부정사)
Improving your gestural communication involves / more than just knowing / when to nod or shake hands. //
몸짓을 사용하는 의사소통을 개선하는 것은 포함한다 / 단순히 아는 것 이상을 / 고개를 끄덕이거나 악수를 해야 할 때를 //

분사구문
It's about using gestures / to complement your spoken messages, / adding layers of meaning to your words. //
이는 몸짓을 사용하는 것에 대한 것이다 / 여러분의 말로 전하는 메시지를 보완하기 위해 / 여러분의 말에 여러 겹의 의미를 더하면서 //

분사구문
Open-handed gestures, / for example, / can indicate honesty, / creating an atmosphere of trust. //
손바닥을 보이는 동작은 / 예를 들어 / 정직함을 나타낸다 / 신뢰의 분위기를 만들며 //

with 분사구문
You invite openness and collaboration / when you speak with your palms facing up. //
여러분은 개방성과 협력을 끌어낸다 / 손바닥을 위로 향한 채로 이야기할 때 //

This simple yet powerful gesture can make / others feel more comfortable and willing to engage in conversation. //
이 간단하지만 강력한 몸짓은 만들 수 있다 / 상대방이 더 편안함을 느끼고 대화에 더 기꺼이 참여하고 싶도록 //　**단서** 적절한 몸짓은 상대방이 대화에 참여하게 함

명령문 동사
But be careful / of the trap of over-gesturing. //
하지만 주의하라 / 과도한 몸짓의 함정에 //

분사구문
Too many hand movements can distract / from your message, / drawing attention away from your words. //
너무 많은 손동작은 집중이 안 되게 한다 / (그들을) 여러분의 메시지에 / 여러분의 말로부터 (사람들의) 관심을 돌리게 해서 //

소유격 관계대명사
Imagine / a speaker / whose hands move quickly like birds, / their message lost in the chaos of their gestures. //
　　　　　　　　　　주어가 생략되지 않은 분사구문
상상해 보라 / 발표자를 / 손이 마치 새처럼 빠르게 움직이는 / 자신의 메시지가 몸짓의 혼돈 속에 사라져 버린 //

Balance is key. // 균형이 핵심이다 //

= your words
Your gestures should highlight your words, / not overshadow them. // 여러분의 몸짓은 여러분의 말을 강조해야지 / 말을 가려서는 안 된다 //

- gestural ⓐ 몸짓의　　• nod ⓥ 고개를 끄덕이다
- complement ⓥ 보완하다　　• layer ⓝ 겹
- indicate ⓥ 나타내다, 보여 주다　　• honesty ⓝ 정직함
- atmosphere ⓝ 분위기　　• collaboration ⓝ 협력
- palm ⓝ 손바닥　　• willing to 기꺼이 ~ 하는
- engage in ~에 참여하다　　• over-gesturing ⓝ 과도한 몸짓
- distract from ~에 집중이 안 되게 하다　　• chaos ⓝ 혼돈
- overshadow ⓥ 가리다

몸짓을 사용하는 의사소통을 개선하는 것은 단순히 고개를 끄덕이거나 악수를 해야 할 때를 아는 것 이상을 포함한다. 이는 여러분의 말로 전하는 메시지를 보완하기 위해 여러분의 말에 여러 겹의 의미를 더하면서 몸짓을 사용하는 것에 대한 것이다. 예를 들어 손바닥을 보이는 동작은 정직함을 나타내어 신뢰의 분위기를 만든다. 손바닥을 위로 향한 채로 이야기할 때 여러분은 개방성과 협력을 끌어낸다. 이 간단하지만 강력한 몸짓은 상대방이 더 편안함을 느끼고 대화에 더 기꺼이 참여하고 싶도록 만들 수 있다. 하지만 과도한 몸짓의 함정에 주의하라. 너무 많은 손동작은 여러분의 말로부터 (사람들의) 관심을 돌리게 해서 (그들을) 여러분의 메시지에 집중이 안 되게 한다. 손이 마치 새처럼 빠르게 움직여서 자신의 메시지가 몸짓의 혼돈 속에 사라져 버린 발표자를 상상해 보라. 균형이 핵심이다. 여러분의 몸짓은 여러분의 말을 강조해야지, 말을 가려서는 안 된다.

다음 글에서 필자가 주장하는 바로 가장 적절한 것은?

① 메시지를 잘 전달하기 위해서 열린 마음을 지녀야 한다.
　　열린 마음이 아니라 손바닥을 보이는 것이 언급되었음
② 효과적인 의사소통을 위해 몸짓을 적절히 사용해야 한다.
　　적절한 몸짓을 통해 말의 효과를 높일 수 있음
③ 청중의 반응을 파악하기 위해 그들의 몸짓에 주목해야 한다.
　　청중의 반응은 언급되지 않았음
④ 전달하고자 하는 것을 감추기보다 직접적으로 표현해야 한다.
　　직접적으로 표현하라는 것은 언급되지 않았음
⑤ 상대방을 설득하기 위해서는 메시지를 반복적으로 강조해야 한다.
　　메시지의 반복은 언급되지 않았음

> **왜 정답?** ✽✽✽ [정답률 90%]

적절한 몸짓은 의사소통을 원활하게 하지만, 부적절한 몸짓은 의사소통을 방해한다고 주장하므로 정답은 ②이다.

> **왜 오답?**

> 몸짓이라는 핵심어는 같지만, 주체가 다르다! **꿀팁**

① 손바닥을 보이는 것(Open-handed)이 언급되었을 뿐, 열린 마음은 언급되지 않았다.
③ 자신이 사용하는 몸짓에 관한 내용이지, 청중의 몸짓에 주목하라는 내용이 아니다.
④ 전달하려는 것을 직접적으로 표현하라는 주장이 아니다.
⑤ 상대방을 대화로 끌어들이기 위해 몸짓을 사용하는 것을 언급했지만, 상대방을 설득하기 위해 메시지를 반복적으로 강조하라는 것은 언급되지 않았다.

21 정답 ① ✽ 인간 유전자 편집

분사구문을 이끄는 현재분사 (주어와 if가 생략됨)　명사절 (Assuming의 목적어)
Assuming / gene editing in humans / proves to be safe and
　　　　　　　　　　　　　　주격 보어
effective, / it might seem logical, even preferable, / to correct
　　　　　　　　　　　　　　　　　　　　부사적 용법 (형용사 수식)
disease-causing mutations /
가정한다면 / 인간 유전자 편집이 / 안전하고 효과적이라고 입증된다고 / 합리적이고, 심지어 바람직해 보일 수도 있다 / 질병을 유발하는 돌연변이를 교정하는 것이 /

at the earliest possible stage of life, / *before* harmful genes begin
동명사 (begin의 목적어)
causing serious problems. //
생애의 가능한 한 가장 이른 단계에서 / 해로운 유전자가 심각한 문제를 일으키기 '전에' //

가주어　　　　　　　　　　　진주어
Yet once it becomes possible / to transform an embryo's mutated
genes into "normal" ones, / there will certainly be temptations /
to upgrade normal genes to superior versions. //
하지만 일단 가능해지면 / 배아의 돌연변이가 된 유전자를 '정상적인' 유전자로 변형하는 것이 / 유혹이 분명히 있을 것이다 / 정상적인 유전자를 더 우수한 버전으로 업그레이드하려는 //

　　　　　　　　　　　　　　　　　부사적 용법 (목적)
Should we begin / editing genes in unborn children / to lower
their lifetime risk of heart disease or cancer? //
우리가 시작해야 할까 / 태어나지 않은 아이들의 유전자를 편집하는 것을 / 심장병이나 암과 같은 질병에 대한 평생 위험을 낮추기 위해 //
단서 1 질병에 대한 위험을 낮춤

단서 2 유전자에 유익한 특성을 부여하거나 신체적 특징을 바꿀 수 있음
What about giving unborn children beneficial features, / like
　　　　　　　　　병렬 구조 (동명사)
greater strength and increased mental abilities, / or changing
physical characteristics, / like eye and hair color? //
유익한 특성을 태어나지 않은 아이들에게 부여하는 것은 어떤가 / 더 강한 체력이나 향상된 인지 능력 같은 / 또는 신체적 특징을 바꾸거나 / 눈이나 머리카락 색 같은 //

The pursuit for perfection seems almost natural to human
nature, / but if we start down this slippery slope, / we may not
　　　　　　의문사절
like where we end up. // **단서 3** 완벽을 계속 추구하면 좋지 않은 결과로 이어질 수 있음
완벽에 대한 추구는 인간의 본성에 거의 자연스러워 보이지만 / 만약 우리가 이 미끄러운 경사 길을 내려가기 시작한다면 / 우리는 결국 놓일 곳이 마음에 들지 않을 수도 있다 //

- gene editing 유전자 편집　　· logical ⓐ 합리적인
- preferable ⓐ 바람직한　　　· correct ⓥ 교정하다
- transform ⓥ 변형하다, 바꾸다　· temptation ⓝ 유혹
- superior ⓐ 우수한　　· characteristics ⓝ 특징　· pursuit ⓝ 추구
- slippery ⓐ 미끄러운　　· slope ⓝ 경사
- end up 결국 ~하게 되다　　· alteration ⓝ 개조, 변경
- stick to ~을 고수하다　　· belief ⓝ 믿음, 신념　· moral ⓐ 도덕적인

인간 유전자 편집이 안전하고 효과적이라고 입증된다고 가정한다면, 해로운 유전자가 심각한 문제를 일으키기 '전에' 생애의 가능한 한 가장 이른 단계에서 질병을 유발하는 돌연변이를 교정하는 것이 합리적이고, 심지어 바람직해 보일 수도 있다. 하지만 일단 배아의 돌연변이가 된 유전자를 '정상적인' 유전자로 변형하는 것이 가능해지면, 정상적인 유전자를 더 우수한 버전으로 업그레이드하려는 유혹이 분명히 있을 것이다. 우리가 심장병이나 암과 같은 질병에 대한 평생 위험을 낮추기 위해 태어나지 않은 아이들의 유전자를 편집하는 것을 시작해야 할까? 더 강한 체력이나 향상된 인지 능력 같은 유익한 특성을 태어나지 않은 아이들에게 부여하거나 또는 눈이나 머리카락 색 같은 신체적 특징을 바꾸는 것은 어떨까? 완벽에 대한 추구는 인간의 본성에 거의 자연스러워 보이지만, 만약 우리가 이 미끄러운 경사 길을 내려가기 시작한다면, 우리는 결국 놓일 곳이 마음에 들지 않을 수도 있다.

밑줄 친 start down this slippery slope이 다음 글에서 의미하는 바로 가장 적절한 것은? [3점]

① allow genetic alterations to upgrade humans
　　인간을 개선하기 위해 유전적 개조를 허용한다　유전적 발전을 위해 유전자 편집을 시도할 수 있음
② stick to the traditional beliefs in human nature
　　인간 본성에 대한 전통적인 믿음을 고수한다　인간의 본성에 대한 믿음은 언급되지 않음
③ resist the temptation to change genes in humans
　　인간의 유전자를 바꾸고자 하는 유혹에 저항한다　인간 유전자 개량에 대한 욕구와 반대됨
④ fail to reduce the risk of suffering from diseases
　　질병에 걸릴 위험을 줄이는 데 실패한다　질병에 걸릴 위험을 줄이고자 함
⑤ consider more about the moral issues of genetics
　　유전학의 도덕적 문제에 대해 더 많이 고려한다　유전자 개량의 도덕적 문제는 언급되지 않았음

> **왜 정답?** ✽✽✽ [정답률 62%]

- 질병에 대한 평생 위험을 낮추기 위해 유전자를 편집하는 것 **단서 1**
- 유익한 특성을 부여하거나 신체적 특징을 바꾸는 것 **단서 2**
- 완벽을 계속 추구하면 우리는 원치 않는 곳에 놓일 것임 **단서 3**

➡ 질병 예방과 우월한 신체적 특성을 갖추기 위해 유전자를 인위적으로 변형시키는 것이 어떤지를 묻다가, 이처럼 완벽을 추구하다 보면 우리는 결국 원치 않는 곳에 놓일 것이라는 부정적인 결말을 제시했다. '미끄러운 경사 길'은 한번 내려가기 시작하면 되돌아가기 힘들어지기 때문에 돌이킬 수 없는 문제를 시작하는 것, 즉 '유전자 변형 및 편집을 허용하는 것'과 같다.

▶ 따라서 '미끄러운 경사 길을 내려간다'는 것은 ① '인간을 개선하기 위해 유전적 개조를 허용한다'를 의미한다.

> **왜 오답?**

② 인간 본성에 대한 전통적인 믿음에 관한 글이 아니다.
③ 인간 유전자 편집에 대한 유혹에 저항하는 것이 아니라 계속 빠져드는 것에 해당한다. **함정**
④ 질병의 가능성을 낮추기 위해 유전자 변형을 해결책으로 거론하고 있다.
⑤ 유전학의 도덕적 문제는 언급되지 않았다.

22 정답 ① ✽ 과학을 통한 불확실성 축소

사이에 목적격 관계대명사가 생략됨
The science we learn in grade school / is a collection / of
certainties about the natural world / — the earth goes around
the sun, / DNA carries the information of an organism, and so
on. //
우리가 초등학교에서 배우는 과학은 / 모음인데 / 자연계에 대한 확실함의 / 즉 지구는 태양 주위를 돌고 / DNA는 유기체의 정보를 담고 있다는 것 등이다 /

only가 문두로 오면서 주어와 동사가 도치됨
Only when you start to learn the practice of science / do you
　　　　　　　　　　　　　　　　　　　　　　부사
realize / that each of these "facts" was hard won /
여러분이 과학의 실제를 배우기 시작할 때만 / 깨닫게 된다 / 이러한 각각의 '사실'이 어렵게 얻어졌다고 /

through a succession of logical inferences / based upon many
observations or experiments. //
연속적인 논리적 추론을 통해 / 많은 관찰이나 실험을 바탕으로 한 //

The process of science is / less about collecting pieces of
knowledge / than it is about reducing the uncertainties / in what
we know. // **단서** 과학의 과정은 지식의 불확실함을 줄이는 것임
= the process of science
선행사를 포함하는 관계대명사
과학의 과정은 ~이다 / 지식의 조각을 모으는 것보다는 / 불확실함을 줄이는 것에 대한 것 / 우
리가 알고 있는 것에서 /

Our uncertainties can be greater or lesser / for any given piece
of knowledge / depending upon where we are / in that process /
'~에 따라'
우리의 불확실함이 더 크거나 더 적을 수 있는데 / 주어진 어떤 지식의 조각에 대해서 / 우리가
지금 있는 곳에 따라 / 그 과정에서 /

— today we are quite certain / of how an apple will fall from
a tree, / but our understanding of the turbulent fluid flow /
전치사 of의 목적어 (간접의문문)
remains a work in progress / after more than a century of effort. //
즉 오늘날 우리는 꽤 확신하지만 / 사과가 나무에서 어떻게 떨어질지 / 난류 유동에 대한 우리
의 이해는 / 여전히 진행 중인 연구로 남아 있다 / 한 세기가 넘는 노력 후에도 //

- grade school 초등학교 · certainty ⓝ 확실함, 확실한 것
- carry ⓥ 담고 있다 · organism ⓝ 유기체 · practice ⓝ 실제
- succession ⓝ 연속 · logical ⓐ 논리적인
- observation ⓝ 관찰 · uncertainty ⓝ 불확실함
- in progress 진행 중인

우리가 초등학교에서 배우는 과학은 자연계에 대한 확실함의 모음인데, 즉 지
구는 태양 주위를 돌고, DNA는 유기체의 정보를 담고 있다는 것 등이다. 여러
분이 과학의 실제를 배우기 시작할 때만, 이러한 각각의 '사실'이 많은 관찰이나
실험을 바탕으로 한 연속적인 논리적 추론을 통해 어렵게 얻어졌다고 깨닫게 된
다. 과학의 과정은 지식의 조각을 모으는 것보다는 우리가 알고 있는 것에서 불
확실함을 줄이는 것에 대한 것이다. 그 과정에서 우리가 지금 있는 곳에 따라
주어진 어떤 지식의 조각에 대해서 우리의 불확실함이 더 크거나 더 적을 수 있
는데, 즉 오늘날 우리는 사과가 나무에서 어떻게 떨어질지 꽤 확신하지만, 난류
유동에 대한 우리의 이해는 한 세기가 넘는 노력 후에도 여전히 진행 중인 연구
로 남아 있다.

다음 글의 요지로 가장 적절한 것은?
① 과학은 현재의 지식에 대한 불확실함을 줄이는 과정이다.
과학 탐구를 통해 불확실함을 다소 감소시킬 수 있음
② 관찰과 실험 과정에서 우연히 얻어진 과학적 사실이 많다.
우연보다는 연속적인 추론을 통해 과학적 사실들을 발견함
③ 학생들에게 다양한 연구 방법을 가르치는 것이 중요하다.
다양한 연구 방법 교육의 필요성은 언급되지 않았음
④ 과학 연구에서는 정확한 실험 과정 설계가 핵심이다.
실험 과정 설계는 언급되지 않았음
⑤ 과학은 분산된 지식을 수집하여 통합하는 학문이다.
지식의 분산이 아니라 누적과 확장에 관한 내용임

> 왜 정답? ✱✱❊ [정답률 72%]
도입: 초등학교 때 접한 다양한 과학 지식은 연속적인 추론의 결과임
주장: 과학의 과정은 지식의 불확실성을 줄이는 것임 **단서**
예시: 만유인력(사과가 어떻게 떨어질지)은 충분히 연구되었기에 확실히 알고 있지만,
난류 유동처럼 아직 불확실해서 연구가 진행 중인 경우도 있음
▶ 과학은 탐구를 통해 지식의 불확실성을 줄이는 과정이라는 내용이므로 정답은 ①이
다.

> 왜 오답?
② 우연이 아닌 끊임없는 탐구와 연속적인 논리 추론을 통해 과학적 사실이 밝혀진다.
③ 다양한 연구 방법의 교육에 관한 내용이 아니다.
④ 실험 과정 설계의 정확한 방향성은 언급된 내용이 아니다.
⑤ 과학의 과정은 지식의 조각을 모으는 것보다는 지식의 불확실함을 줄이는 것이라고
했다. **주의**

---

23 정답 ⑤ ＊유대감의 효과

There is a wealth of evidence / that when parents, teachers,
유도부사   동격절 접속사
supervisors, and coaches / are perceived as involved and caring,
/ people feel happier and more motivated. // **단서 1** 배려를 받으면 동기가 부여됨
수많은 증거가 있다 / 부모, 교사, 상사, 그리고 코치가 / 관여되어 있고 배려한다고 여겨질 때
/ 사람들은 더 행복하고 더 동기가 부여된다는 //

And it is not just those people with power / — we need to feel
valued and respected / by peers and coworkers. //
그리고 그것이 단지 권력을 가진 사람들만은 아닌데 / 즉 우리는 소중히 여겨지고 존중받는다
는 느낌을 받을 필요가 있다 / 또래와 직장 동료들에게서도 //

Thus, / when the need for relatedness is met, / motivation and
internalization are fueled, / provided that support for autonomy
비인칭 독립분사구문 (= If we are provided that)
and competence are also there. // **단서 2** 관계성이 충족되면 동기와 내면화가 자극됨
따라서 / 관계성에 대한 욕구가 충족될 때 / 동기와 내면화는 자극된다 / 그리고 자율성과 유능
함에 대한 지원 또한 제공된다면 //

If we are trying to motivate others, / a caring relationship is a
crucial basis from which to begin. //
「전치사 + 관계대명사 + to부정사」(= which we can begin from)
만약 우리가 다른 사람들에게 동기를 부여하려고 한다면 / 배려하는 관계는 그곳에서 시작할
수 있는 중요한 기반이 된다 //

And when we are trying to motivate ourselves, / doing things to
재귀대명사 (재귀 용법)   동명사구 (주어)
enhance a sense of connectedness to others / can be crucial / to
long-term persistence. // **단서 3** 타인과의 유대감 강화는 동기부여에 중요함
그리고 우리가 스스로 동기를 부여하려고 할 때 / 타인과의 유대감을 강화하기 위한 일을 하는
것은 / 중요할 수 있다 / 장기적인 지속에 //

So exercise with a friend, / call someone when you have a
difficult decision to make, / and be there as a support for others
병렬 구조 (명령문 동사)   부사절 접속사 (시간)
/ as they take on challenges. //
그러니 친구와 함께 운동하라 / 당신이 어려운 결정을 내려야 할 때 누군가에게 전화하라 / 그
리고 그들을 위한 버팀목으로 그곳에 있어라 / 다른 사람들이 도전에 맞설 때 //

- a wealth of 수많은 · supervisor ⓝ 상사
- perceive ⓥ 여기다, 인식하다 · motivate ⓥ 동기를 부여하다
- value ⓥ 소중히 여기다 · peer ⓝ 또래, 동료
- relatedness ⓝ 관계성 · internalization ⓝ 내면화
- fuel ⓥ 자극하다, 연료를 공급하다 · competence ⓝ 유능함, 능숙함
- crucial ⓐ 중요한 · enhance ⓥ 강화하다, 향상시키다
- a sense of connectedness 유대감 · take on ~에 맞서다

부모, 교사, 상사, 그리고 코치가 관여되어 있고 배려한다고 여겨질 때, 사람들
은 더 행복하고 더 동기가 부여된다는 수많은 증거가 있다. 그리고 그것이 단지
권력을 가진 사람들만은 아닌데, 즉 우리는 또래와 직장 동료들에게서도 소중
히 여겨지고 존중받는다는 느낌을 받을 필요가 있다. 따라서, 관계성에 대한 욕
구가 충족될 때, 그리고 자율성과 유능함에 대한 지원 또한 제공된다면, 동기와
내면화는 자극된다. 만약 우리가 다른 사람들에게 동기를 부여하려고 한다면,
배려하는 관계는 그곳에서 시작할 수 있는 중요한 기반이 된다. 그리고 우리가
스스로 동기를 부여하려고 할 때, 타인과의 유대감을 강화하기 위한 일을 하는
것은 장기적인 지속에 중요할 수 있다. 그러니 친구와 함께 운동하라, 당신이
어려운 결정을 내려야 할 때 누군가에게 전화하라, 그리고 다른 사람들이 도전
에 맞설 때 그들을 위한 버팀목으로 그곳에 있어라.

다음 글의 주제로 가장 적절한 것은?
① ways of getting out of dependent relationships
의존적인 관계에서 벗어나는 방법들
의존의 긍정적 측면에 관한 내용임
② necessity of independent decision-making for happier
life 독립이 아닌 타인과의 관계를 통해 동기부여가 가능함
더 행복한 삶을 위한 독립적인 의사결정의 필요성
③ key factors required for boosting a competitive
atmosphere 경쟁보다는 관계 형성의 효과에 관한 내용임
경쟁적인 분위기를 조성하는 데 필요한 핵심 요소
④ challenges in maintaining lasting bonds with family
members 유대감 유지의 어려움은 언급되지 않았음
가족 구성원과의 지속적인 유대감을 유지하는 데 따른 어려움들
⑤ importance of building connected relationships in
motivation 유대감 형성이 동기부여에 긍정적 영향을 미침
동기부여에 있어 유대감 있는 관계 형성의 중요성

왜 정답? ✽✽❀ [정답률 80%]

- 배려를 받을 때 동기가 부여됨 **단서1**
- 관계성이 충족되면 동기와 내면화가 자극됨 **단서2**
- 타인과의 유대감 강화는 동기부여에 중요함 **단서3**

➡ 배려와 존중을 받을 때, 관계성이 충족될 때 동기가 부여되므로 타인과의 유대감을 강화하는 것이 동기부여에 중요하다는 내용이다.

▶ 따라서 글의 주제는 ⑤ '동기부여에 있어 유대감 있는 관계 형성의 중요성'이다.

왜 오답?

① 글의 내용은 타인에 대한 의존이 긍정적이라는 것에 가깝고, 의존적 관계에서 벗어나는 방법은 언급되지 않았다.

② 타인과의 관계보다 독립이 행복을 준다는 내용이 아니다.

③ 경쟁보다는 유대감 강화를 권장하는 내용이다.

④ 유대감 강화가 중요하다고는 했지만, 가족 구성원과 유대감을 유지하는 어려움은 언급되지 않았다.

---

24 정답 ① * 소리 내어 읽는 것의 효과

Modern brain-scanning techniques / **such as** fMRI (functional Magnetic Resonance Imaging) / have revealed / that **reading aloud lights** up many areas of the brain. // **단서1** 소리 내어 읽는 것은 두뇌를 깨움
현대의 뇌 스캐닝 기법은 / fMRI(기능적 자기 공명 영상)와 같은 / 드러냈다 / 소리 내어 읽는 것이 두뇌의 여러 영역을 밝힌다는 것을 //

There is intense activity in areas / **associated with pronunciation and hearing the sound of the spoken response, / which** strengthens the connective structures of your brain cells / for more brainpower. //
영역에서 강렬한 활동이 있으며 / 발음과 발화된 반응의 소리를 듣는 것과 연관된 / 이는 여러분의 뇌세포의 결합 구조를 강화시킨다 / 더 많은 뇌 능력을 위한 //

This leads / to an overall improvement in concentration. //
이것은 이어진다 / 전반적인 집중력 향상으로 //

Reading aloud is also a good way / **to develop** your public speaking skills / because **it** forces you to read each and every word / **단서2** 소리 내어 읽음으로써 말하기 능력이 향상됨
소리 내어 읽는 것은 좋은 방법인데 / 여러분의 대중 말하기 능력을 발전시키는 / 왜냐하면 그것은 여러분으로 하여금 하나도 빠짐없이 단어를 읽게 강제하기 때문인데
— something **people don't often do / when reading quickly, or reading in silence.** //
이는 사람들이 자주 하지 않는 일이다 / 빨리 읽거나 조용히 읽을 때 //

Children, in particular, should **be encouraged / to read** aloud / because the brain is wired for learning through connections / that are created by positive stimulation, / such as singing, touching, and reading aloud. //
특히 어린이는 장려되어야 한다 / 소리 내어 읽도록 / 뇌가 결합을 통한 학습에 대해 연결되어 있기 때문에 / 긍정적인 자극에 의해 만들어진 / 노래 부르기, 만지기, 소리 내어 읽기와 같은 //

- technique ⓝ 기법, 기술 · light up 밝히다 · intense ⓐ 강렬한
- associated with ~과 연관된 · pronunciation ⓝ 발음
- strengthen ⓥ 강화시키다 · connective structure 결합 구조
- cell ⓝ 세포 · overall ⓐ 전반적인 · concentration ⓝ 집중력
- in silence 조용히 · in particular 특히 · encourage ⓥ 장려하다
- wire ⓥ 연결하다

fMRI(기능적 자기 공명 영상)와 같은 현대의 뇌 스캐닝 기법은 소리 내어 읽는 것이 두뇌의 여러 영역을 밝힌다는 것을 드러냈다. 발음과 발화된 반응의 소리를 듣는 것과 연관된 영역에서 강렬한 활동이 있으며, 이는 더 많은 뇌 능력을 위한 여러분의 뇌세포의 결합 구조를 강화시킨다. 이것은 전반적인 집중력 향상으로 이어진다. 소리 내어 읽는 것은 여러분의 대중 말하기 능력을 발전시

키는 좋은 방법인데, 왜냐하면 그것은 여러분으로 하여금 하나도 빠짐없이 단어를 읽게 강제하기 때문인데, 이는 사람들이 빨리 읽거나 조용히 읽을 때 자주 하지 않는 일이다. 특히 어린이는 뇌가 노래 부르기, 만지기, 소리 내어 읽기와 같은 긍정적인 자극에 의해 만들어진 결합을 통한 학습에 대해 연결되어 있기 때문에 소리 내어 읽도록 장려되어야 한다.

다음 글의 제목으로 가장 적절한 것은?

① Reading Aloud: Improving Brainpower and Speaking Skills 소리 내어 읽으면 두뇌와 말하기 능력이 향상됨
소리 내어 읽기: 두뇌 능력과 말하기 능력 향상

② Reading Practices: Shortcuts to Academic Achievements
독서 습관: 학문적 성취를 위한 지름길 독서의 습관이 아닌 방법에 관한 내용임

③ Improve Your Writing Skills Through Reading Aloud
소리 내어 읽기를 통한 글쓰기 능력 향상 글쓰기 능력 향상은 언급되지 않았음

④ How Your Brain Changes When You Read in Silence 조용히
조용히 읽을 때 뇌가 어떻게 변하는지 읽으면 단어를 하나도 빠짐없이 읽지는 못한다고 했음

⑤ Techniques for Faster and More Effective Reading
더 빠르고 효과적인 독서를 위한 기법 빨리 읽으면 단어를 하나도 빠짐없이 읽지는 못한다고 했음

왜 정답? ✽✽❀ [정답률 82%]

- 소리 내어 읽는 것은 두뇌의 여러 영역을 밝힌다. **단서1**
- 소리 내어 읽는 것은 말하기 능력을 향상시킨다. **단서2**

➡ 소리 내어 읽는 것이 두뇌와 말하기 능력에 주는 긍정적 효과에 관한 글이다.

▶ 따라서 정답은 ① '소리 내어 읽기: 두뇌 능력과 말하기 능력 향상'이다.

왜 오답?

② 소리 내어 읽는 것이 뇌와 말하기 능력에 끼치는 긍정적 영향에 관한 내용이지, 독서가 학문적 성취에 끼치는 영향은 언급되지 않았다.

③ 소리 내어 읽는 것의 긍정적 효과가 글의 주제이지만, 그중에 글쓰기 능력 향상은 언급되지 않았다. **주의**

④ 조용히 읽으면 단어를 하나도 빠짐없이 읽는 것을 자주 하지 않는다고 했을 뿐이며, 조용히 읽는 것은 글의 주제가 아니다.

⑤ 빠르게 읽으면 단어를 하나도 빠짐없이 읽는 것을 자주 하지 않는다고 했을 뿐이며, 빠르고 효과적인 독서를 위한 기법은 언급되지 않았다.

---

25 정답 ④ * 미국인들의 패스트푸드 섭취 빈도

The above graph shows / **how often people in America consumed fast food in 2023, / sorted** according to frequency of consumption. //
위 그래프는 보여 준다 / 2023년 미국에서 사람들이 얼마나 자주 패스트푸드를 먹었는지를 / 빈도 순에 따라 / 주 1회 이상: 13%(매일)+36%(일주일에 몇 번)+16%(일주일에 한 번)=65% > 50%

① More than 50 percent of individuals / consumed fast food / once a week or more frequently. //
50퍼센트가 넘는 사람들은 / 패스트푸드를 먹었다 / 일주일에 한 번 또는 더 자주 //
일주일에 몇 번: 36% → 가장 큰 비중 차지

② The most highly reported pattern of consumption / was a few times a week, / **which** was 36 percent of the total. //
가장 많이 응답된 섭취 패턴은 / 일주일에 몇 번이었고 / 이는 전체의 36퍼센트였다 //
한 달에 몇 번: 18% → 두 번째로 큰 비중 차지

③ The second most highly reported pattern was a few times a month, / **accounting** for 18 percent of the total. //
두 번째로 가장 많이 응답된 패턴은 한 달에 몇 번이었으며 / 이는 전체의 18퍼센트를 차지했다 //

④ **The percentage** of people / who ate fast food once every couple of months / **was** more(→ less) / than **that** of those who consumed **it** daily. // **단서** 8%(두 달에 한 번) < 13%(매일)
사람들의 비율은 / 패스트푸드를 두 달에 한 번 먹었던 / 많았다(→ 적었다) / 패스트푸드를 매일 먹었던 사람들의 비율보다 //

⑤ The combined share of those who rarely or never ate fast food / was less than 10 percent. // 거의 혹은 전혀 먹지 않음: 5%+4%=9% < 10%
패스트푸드를 거의 혹은 전혀 먹지 않았던 사람들을 합친 몫은 / 10퍼센트 미만이었다 //

- consume ⓥ 먹다   · sort ⓥ 분류하다   · frequency ⓝ 빈도
- frequently ⓐⓓ 자주   · account for ~을 차지하다
- percentage ⓝ 비율   · combine ⓥ 합치다
- share ⓝ 몫   · rarely ⓐⓓ 거의 ~ 않는

위 그래프는 2023년 미국에서 사람들이 얼마나 자주 패스트푸드를 먹었는지를 빈도 순에 따라 보여 준다. ① 50퍼센트가 넘는 사람들은 패스트푸드를 일주일에 한 번 또는 더 자주 먹었다. ② 가장 많이 응답된 섭취 패턴은 일주일에 몇 번이었고, 이는 전체의 36퍼센트였다. ③ 두 번째로 가장 많이 응답된 패턴은 한 달에 몇 번이었으며, 이는 전체의 18퍼센트를 차지했다. ④ 패스트푸드를 두 달에 한 번 먹었던 사람들의 비율은 패스트푸드를 매일 먹었던 사람들의 비율보다 **많았다(→ 적었다)**. ⑤ 패스트푸드를 거의 혹은 전혀 먹지 않았던 사람들을 합친 몫은 10퍼센트 미만이었다.

다음 도표의 내용과 일치하지 않는 것은?

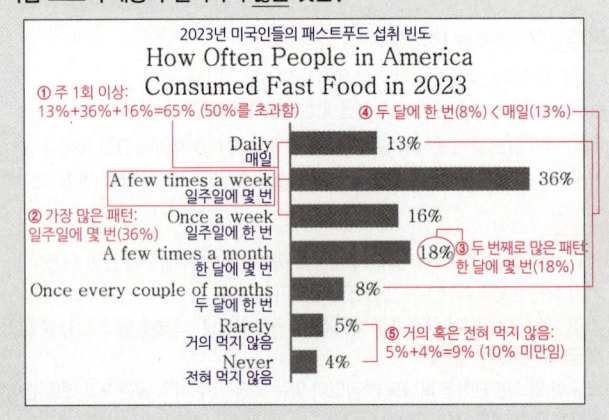

2023년 미국인들의 패스트푸드 섭취 빈도
How Often People in America Consumed Fast Food in 2023

- Daily 매일 — 13%
- A few times a week 일주일에 몇 번 — 36%
- Once a week 일주일에 한 번 — 16%
- A few times a month 한 달에 몇 번 — 18%
- Once every couple of months 두 달에 한 번 — 8%
- Rarely 거의 먹지 않음 — 5%
- Never 전혀 먹지 않음 — 4%

① 주 1회 이상: 13%+36%+16%=65% (50%를 초과함)
④ 두 달에 한 번(8%) < 매일(13%)
② 가장 많은 패턴: 일주일에 몇 번(36%)
③ 두 번째로 많은 패턴 한 달에 몇 번(18%)
⑤ 거의 혹은 전혀 먹지 않음: 5%+4%=9% (10% 미만임)

＞왜 정답 ? ❈❈❈ [정답률 88%]

두 달에 한 번 섭취하는 사람들은 8퍼센트이고 매일 섭취하는 사람은 13퍼센트이므로 매일 섭취하는 사람이 두 달에 한 번 섭취하는 사람들보다 많다. 따라서 ④이 도표의 내용과 일치하지 않는다.

＞왜 오답 ?   주의

① 주 1회 이상 섭취하는 사람은 일주일에 한 번, 일주일에 몇 번, 매일 먹는 사람들의 비율을 전부 합해야 하므로 총 65퍼센트, 즉 50퍼센트를 초과한다.
② 일주일에 몇 번 섭취하는 경우는 36퍼센트로 가장 큰 비중을 차지한다.
③ 두 번째로 가장 많이 응답된 패턴은 한 달에 몇 번 섭취하는 경우로 18퍼센트이다.
⑤ 거의 먹지 않거나 전혀 먹지 않는 사례는 총 9퍼센트이므로 10퍼센트 미만이다.

26 정답 ④ ＊Robert E. Lucas, Jr.의 생애

Robert E. Lucas, Jr. was born / on September 15, 1937, / in Yakima, Washington. //
Robert E. Lucas, Jr.는 태어났다 / 1937년 9월 15일 / Washington주 Yakima에서 //

계속적 용법의 관계부사
During World War II, / his family moved to Seattle, / where he graduated from Roosevelt High School. // ①의 단서 제2차 세계대전 중 Seattle로 이주함
제2차 세계대전 중에 / 그의 가족은 Seattle로 이주했고 / 그곳에서 그는 Roosevelt High School을 졸업했다 //

At the University of Chicago, / he majored in history. //
University of Chicago에서 / 그는 역사를 전공했다 //

= After he took
After taking economic history courses / at University of California, Berkeley, / he developed an interest in economics. //
경제사를 수강한 후 / University of California, Berkeley에서 / 그는 경제학에 대한 흥미를 키웠다 // ②의 단서 경제사 수강 후 경제학에 흥미를 키움

He earned a doctoral degree in economics / from the University of Chicago / in 1964. // ③의 단서 University of Chicago에서 경제학 박사 학위를 받음
그는 경제학 박사 학위를 받았다 / University of Chicago에서 / 1964년에 //

He taught at Carnegie Mellon University / from 1963 to 1974
= before he returned   부사적 용법 (목적)
/ **before returning** to the University of Chicago / **to become** a professor of economics. // ④의 단서 1963년부터 1974년까지 University of Chicago가 아닌 Carnegie Mellon University에서 가르침
그는 Carnegie Mellon University에서 가르쳤다 / 1963년부터 1974년까지 / University of Chicago로 돌아오기 전에 / 경제학 교수가 되기 위해 //

He was known as a very influential economist / and, in 1995, / he was awarded the Nobel Prize in Economic Sciences. //
그는 매우 영향력 있는 경제학자로 알려졌으며 / 1995년에 / 경제학에서 노벨상을 수상했다 // ⑤의 단서 1995년에 노벨상을 수상했음

- move ⓥ 이주하다   · major ⓥ 전공하다   · earn ⓥ 받다
- doctoral degree 박사 학위   · economics ⓝ 경제학
- influential ⓐ 영향력 있는   · award ⓥ 수여하다
- Economic Sciences 경제학

Robert E. Lucas, Jr.는 1937년 9월 15일 Washington주 Yakima에서 태어났다. 제2차 세계대전 중에, 그의 가족은 Seattle로 이주했고, 그곳에서 그는 Roosevelt High School을 졸업했다. 그는 University of Chicago에서 역사를 전공했다. University of California, Berkeley에서 경제사를 수강한 후, 그는 경제학에 대한 흥미를 키웠다. 그는 1964년에 University of Chicago에서 경제학 박사 학위를 받았다. University of Chicago로 돌아와 경제학 교수가 되기 전에, 그는 1963년부터 1974년까지 Carnegie Mellon University에서 가르쳤다. 그는 매우 영향력 있는 경제학자로 알려졌으며, 1995년에, 경제학에서 노벨상을 수상했다.

Robert E. Lucas, Jr.에 관한 다음 글의 내용과 일치하지 않는 것은?

① 제2차 세계대전 중에 그의 가족이 Seattle로 이주했다.
During World War II, his family moved to Seattle
② 경제사를 수강한 후에 경제학에 대한 흥미를 키웠다.
After taking economic history courses ~ developed an interest in economics.
③ University of Chicago에서 경제학 박사 학위를 받았다.
He earned a doctoral degree in economics from the University of Chicago
④ 1963년부터 1974년까지 University of Chicago에서 가르쳤다.
He taught at Carnegie Mellon University from 1963 to 1974
⑤ 1995년에 노벨상을 수상했다. in 1995, he was awarded the Nobel Prize

＞왜 정답 ? ❈❈❈ [정답률 81%]

Robert E. Lucas, Jr.는 Carnegie Mellon University에서 1963년부터 1974년까지 가르쳤다고 (He taught at Carnegie Mellon University from 1963 to 1974) 했으므로, 그 기간에 University of Chicago에서 가르쳤다고 한 ④이 글의 내용과 일치하지 않는다.

＞왜 오답 ?

① 제2차 세계대전 중에 그의 가족이 Seattle로 이주했다. (During World War II, his family moved to Seattle)
② 경제사를 수강한 후에 경제학에 대한 흥미를 키웠다. (After taking economic history courses ~ developed an interest in economics.)
③ University of Chicago에서 경제학 박사 학위를 받았다. (He earned a doctoral degree in economics from the University of Chicago)
⑤ 1995년에 노벨상을 수상했다. (in 1995, he was awarded the Nobel Prize)

27 정답 ② ＊Blackwood 동물원

Welcome to Blackwood Zoo /
Blackwood 동물원에 오신 것을 환영합니다 /
부사적 용법 (ready 수식)
Get ready / **to explore!** //
준비를 하세요 / 탐험할 //

You can watch amazing animals / on our 10km walking path. // ①의 단서 10km의 보행로로 동물 관람 가능
여러분은 놀라운 동물들을 볼 수 있습니다 / 10 km의 보행로에서 //

Hours of Operation / 운영 시간 /

- Every day / all year round! // 매일 / 1년 내내 //
- 9:30 a.m. - 4:30 p.m. / (Last admission at 3:30 p.m.) /
오전 9:30 ~ 오후 4:30 / (오후 3:30에 마지막 입장) / ②의 단서 마지막 입장이 3시 30분이고 운영은 4시 30분에 종료됨

Ticket Prices / 티켓 가격 /
- Age 13 - 64: $30 / 13세~64세: 30달러 /
- Age 3 - 12: $20 / **③의 단서** 3~12세는 20달러의 입장료를 내야 함
  3세~12세: 20달러 /
- Others: Free / 그 외: 무료 /

Seasonal Note / 계절에 따른 안내 /
부사절 접속사 (이유)
<mark>Since</mark> the weather is still cold, / some animals like snakes and
turtles / will stay only indoors. // **④의 단서** 추운 날씨로 인해 일부 동물은 실내에만 머무를 예정
날씨가 여전히 추워서 / 뱀과 거북이 같은 일부 동물은 / 실내에만 머무를 것입니다 //
현재시제 (규칙적인 사실, 반복되는 일정, 시간표 등)
※Free shuttle bus <mark>departs</mark> / from Blackwood Subway Station /
every 30 minutes. // **⑤의 단서** 무료 셔틀버스는 30분마다 출발
무료 셔틀버스는 출발합니다 / Blackwood 지하철역에서 / 30분마다 //

- explore ⓥ 탐험하다   - amazing ⓐ 놀라운
- walking path 보행로   - operation ⓝ 운영
- admission ⓝ 입장   - seasonal ⓐ 계절에 따른
- indoors ⓐⓓ 실내에   - depart ⓥ 출발하다

Blackwood 동물원에 오신 것을 환영합니다
탐험할 준비를 하세요! 여러분은 10km의 보행로에서 놀라운 동물들을 볼 수 있습니다.
운영 시간
- 매일, 1년 내내!
- 오전 9:30 ~ 오후 4:30 (오후 3:30에 마지막 입장)
티켓 가격
- 13세~64세: 30달러
- 3세~12세: 20달러
- 그 외: 무료
계절에 따른 안내
날씨가 여전히 추워서, 뱀과 거북이 같은 일부 동물은 실내에만 머무를 것입니다.
※ 무료 셔틀버스는 30분마다 Blackwood 지하철역에서 출발합니다.

> Blackwood Zoo에 관한 다음 안내문의 내용과 일치하지 <u>않는</u> 것은?
> ① 10km의 보행로에서 동물들을 볼 수 있다.
>   You can watch amazing animals on our 10km walking path.
> ② 운영 시간은 오후 3시 30분까지이다.
>   9:30 a.m. - 4:30 p.m. (Last admission at 3:30 p.m.)
> ③ 3세부터 12세까지의 티켓 가격은 20달러이다. Age 3 - 12: $20
> ④ 날씨가 여전히 추워서 일부 동물은 실내에만 머무를 것이다.
>   Since the weather is still cold, some animals ~ will stay only indoors.
> ⑤ 무료 셔틀버스가 30분마다 출발한다.
>   Free shuttle bus departs ~ every 30 minutes.

> **왜 정답?** ✽✽✽ [정답률 93%]
운영 시간은 오후 4시 30분까지라고 (9:30 a.m. - 4:30 p.m.) 했으므로 운영 시간이 오후 3시 30분까지라고 한 ②이 안내문의 내용과 일치하지 않는다.

> **왜 오답?**
① 10km의 보행로에서 동물들을 볼 수 있다. (You can watch amazing animals on our 10km walking path.)
③ 3세부터 12세까지의 티켓 가격은 20달러이다. (Age 3 - 12: $20)
④ 날씨가 여전히 추워서 일부 동물은 실내에만 머무를 것이다. (Since the weather is still cold, some animals ~ will stay only indoors.)
⑤ 무료 셔틀버스가 30분마다 출발한다. (Free shuttle bus departs ~ every 30 minutes.)

28 정답 ② ✽양말 DIY 워크숍

Sock DIY Workshop / 양말 DIY 워크숍 /
Join us / for a fun and creative Sock DIY(Do It Yourself)
Workshop / for all ages! //
함께하세요 / 재미있고 창의적인 양말 DIY(손수 만들기) 워크숍에 / 모든 연령대를 위한 //

When & Where / 일시 및 장소 / **①의 단서** 4월 19일 토요일 오후 1시에서 3시까지 진행됨
- Saturday, / April 19th, / from 1 p.m. to 3 p.m. /
  토요일 / 4월 19일 / 오후 1시부터 오후 3시까지 /
- The community hall, Clanton Center /
  커뮤니티 홀, Clanton Center / **②의 단서** Clanton Center의 커뮤니티 홀에서 열림

Workshop Program / 워크숍 프로그램 /

Time / 시간	DIY Item / DIY 품목	Things to Do / 할 일
③의 단서 양말로 장난감 만들기는 오후 1시에 시작 1 p.m. - 2 p.m. / 오후 1시 ~ 오후 2시	Toys / 장난감 /	과거분사 (toys 수식) Create <mark>stuffed</mark> toys / with socks / 봉제 인형 만들기 / 양말로 /
2 p.m. - 3 p.m. / 오후 2시 ~ 오후 3시	Flowerpot Covers / 화분 커버 /	Transform socks / into decorative covers / for small flowerpots / 양말을 변형하기 / 장식 커버로 / 소형 화분용 /

What Participants Should Prepare / 참가자가 준비해야 할 것 /
과거분사 (socks 수식)
- <mark>Used</mark> / but clean socks / **④의 단서** 사용했어도 깨끗하면 준비물로 가능함
  사용했지만 / 깨끗한 양말 /

Participation Fee / 참가비 /
'~당, ~마다'
- $5 <mark>per</mark> person / (including the cost for materials) /
  1인당 5달러 / (재료비를 포함함) / **⑤의 단서** 재료비를 포함해서 1인당 5달러
- For more details, / visit the Clanton Center website / or call us
  at 555-123-4567. //
  세부 사항은 / Clanton Center 웹사이트를 방문하거나 / 555-123-4567로 전화하세요 //

- stuffed toy 봉제 인형   - transform ⓥ 변형하다, 바꾸다
- decorative ⓐ 장식의   - flowerpot ⓝ 화분
- participation fee 참가비   - material ⓝ 재료
- detail ⓝ 세부 사항

양말 DIY 워크숍
모든 연령대를 위한 재미있고 창의적인 양말 DIY(손수 만들기) 워크숍에 함께하세요!
일시 및 장소
- 4월 19일 토요일, 오후 1시부터 오후 3시까지
- 커뮤니티 홀, Clanton Center
워크숍 프로그램

시간	DIY 품목	할 일
오후 1시 ~ 오후 2시	장난감	양말로 봉제 인형 만들기
오후 2시 ~ 오후 3시	화분 커버	양말을 소형 화분용 장식 커버로 변형하기

참가자가 준비해야 할 것
- 사용했지만 깨끗한 양말
참가비
- 1인당 5달러(재료비를 포함함)
※ 세부 사항은 Clanton Center 웹사이트를 방문하거나 555-123-4567로 전화하세요.

Sock DIY Workshop에 관한 다음 안내문의 내용과 일치하는 것은?

① 4월 19일 토요일 오후 1시부터 4시까지 열린다.
　　　　　　　Saturday, April 19th, from 1 p.m. to 3 p.m.
② Clanton Center의 커뮤니티 홀에서 진행된다.
　　　　　　　　The community hall, Clanton Center
③ 참가자는 오후 2시부터 양말로 장난감을 만든다.
　　　　　　　1 p.m.-2 p.m. / Create stuffed toys with socks
④ 참가자는 사용하지 않은 깨끗한 양말을 준비해야 한다.
　　　　　　　　　　　Used but clean socks
⑤ 참가비는 재료비를 제외하고 1인당 5달러이다.
　　　　　　$5 per person (including the cost for materials)

> 왜 정답 ? ✽✻✻ [정답률 87%]

행사의 진행 장소가 Clanton Center의 커뮤니티 홀이므로 (The community hall, Clanton Center) 안내문의 내용과 일치하는 것은 ②이다.

> 왜 오답 ?

① 4시가 아닌 3시까지 진행된다. (Saturday, April 19th, from 1 p.m. to 3 p.m.)
③ 오후 2시가 아닌 1시부터 양말로 장난감을 만든다. (1 p.m.-2 p.m. / Create stuffed toys with socks)
④ 사용했더라도 깨끗한 양말을 준비해야 한다. (Used but clean socks)
⑤ 참가비는 재료비를 포함해서 1인당 5달러이다. ($5 per person (including the cost for materials))

29 정답 ④ ✱ 루틴의 역할과 중요성

다음 글의 밑줄 친 부분 중, 어법상 틀린 것은?

　　　　　　enable A to-v: A가 ~할 수 있도록 하다
Routines enable athletes / to evaluate competition conditions. //
루틴은 운동선수가 ~할 수 있도록 해 준다 / 경기 조건을 평가하는 //
　　　　　　　　　　　　　　단수 주어
For example, bouncing a ball in a volleyball service routine /
　　단수 동사
① supplies the server / with information about the ball, the
floor, and the state of her muscles. //
예를 들어 / 배구 서브 루틴에서 공을 튕기는 것은 / 서브를 하는 선수에게 제공한다 / 공, 바닥, 그리고 자신의 근육 상태에 대한 정보를 //
　　　　　　　　　　　　　prepare를 수식하기 위해 to와 동사원형 사이에 삽입된 부사
This information / can then be used / to ② properly prepare for
her serve. //
이 정보는 / 그다음 사용될 수 있다 / 자신의 서브를 적절히 준비하기 위해 //
　　　　　　　　　　　　　　문장의 본동사
Routines also enable athletes / to adjust and fine-tune their
　　　　　　　　　　　　병렬 구조(부사구)
preparations / ③ based on those evaluations / or in pursuit of a
particular competitive goal. //
루틴은 또한 선수가 ~할 수 있게 해 준다 / 준비 상태를 조절하고 미세하게 조정하는 / 그러한 평가에 기반하거나 / 또는 특정 경쟁 목표를 추구하여 //
　　　　　　　　　　　　　　　　　　선행사
This adaptation can involve / adjustment to the conditions,
rivals, competitive situation, or internal influences / ④ what (→
선행사를 포함하지 않는 주격 관계대명사
that 또는 which) can affect performance. // 단서 선행사가 존재함
이러한 적응은 포함할 수 있다 / 조건, 경쟁 상대, 경기 상황, 또는 내적 영향에 대한 조정 / 수행에 영향을 미칠 수 있는 //
　　　　　동명사　　adjust A to B: A를 B에 맞게 조정하다
Just like adjusting a race-car engine / to the conditions of
the track, air temperature, and weather, / routines adjust all
competitive components / ⑤ to achieve proper performance. //
　　　　　　　　부사적 용법 (목적)
경주용 자동차 엔진을 조정하는 것과 마찬가지로 / 트랙, 기온, 그리고 날씨의 조건에 맞게 / 루틴은 경기의 모든 구성 요소를 조정한다 / 적절한 수행을 해내기 위해 //

- -
• routine ⓝ 루틴, 일상의 과정　• enable ⓥ ~할 수 있게 하다
• athlete ⓝ 운동선수　• evaluate ⓥ 평가하다
• competition ⓝ 경기, 경쟁　• condition ⓝ 조건
• bounce ⓥ (공을) 튕기다　• supply ⓥ 제공하다
• properly ⓐⓓ 적절히　• adjust ⓥ 조절하다, 조정하다
• fine-tune ⓥ 미세하게 조정하다　• in pursuit of ~을 추구하여
• adaptation ⓝ 적응　• internal ⓐ 내적인　• influence ⓝ 영향
• affect ⓥ 영향을 미치다　• performance ⓝ 수행
• achieve ⓥ 해내다

루틴은 운동선수가 경기 조건을 평가할 수 있도록 해준다. 예를 들어, 배구 서브 루틴에서 공을 튕기는 것은 서브를 하는 선수에게 공, 바닥, 그리고 자신의 근육 상태에 대한 정보를 제공한다. 그다음 이 정보는 자신의 서브를 적절히 준비하기 위해 사용될 수 있다. 루틴은 또한 그러한 평가에 기반하거나 또는 특정 경쟁 목표를 추구하여 선수가 준비 상태를 조절하고 미세하게 조정할 수 있게 해준다. 이러한 적응은 수행에 영향을 미칠 수 있는 조건, 경쟁 상대, 경기 상황, 또는 내적 영향에 대한 조정을 포함할 수 있다. 경주용 자동차 엔진을 트랙, 기온, 그리고 날씨의 조건에 맞게 조정하는 것과 마찬가지로, 루틴은 적절한 수행을 해내기 위해 경기의 모든 구성 요소를 조정한다.

> 왜 정답 ? ✽✽✻ [정답률 71%]

④ 선행사를 포함하는 관계대명사 what 앞에 선행사가 있다!

This adaptation can involve / adjustment to the conditions,
　　　　　　　　　　　　　　　　선행사
rivals, competitive situation, or internal influences / ④ what
선행사를 포함하지 않는 주격 관계대명사　　　　　　선행사가 있음
(→ that 또는 which) can affect performance. //

단서 선행사를 포함하는 관계대명사 what에 밑줄이 있으므로
발상 그 앞에는 선행사가 없을 것이다.
해결 그런데 what 앞에 관계사절 can affect performance의 주어 역할을 하는 선행사 the conditions ~ internal influences가 있다. 따라서 what을 주격 관계대명사 that 또는 which로 고쳐야 한다.
개념 관계대명사 what은 선행사를 포함하므로, 앞에 선행사가 있을 때는 who, which, that처럼 다른 관계대명사를 써야 한다.

> 왜 오답 ?

① 동사는 주어에 그 수를 일치시킨다.
　　　　　　　　　동명사 (단수 주어)
For example, / bouncing a ball in a volleyball service routine /
　　　단수 동사
① supplies the server / ~

supplies는 단수 동사이며, 문장의 주어가 동명사구 bouncing ~ routine이므로 마찬가지로 단수이다. 따라서 단수 동사 supplies가 알맞게 쓰였다.

② 부사는 준동사를 수식할 수 있다.
　　　　　　　　　　　　　　prepare를 수식하기 위해 to와 동사원형 사이에 삽입된 부사
This information can then be used / to ② properly prepare for
her serve. //

문맥상 서브를 '적절하게' 준비하는 것이므로 부사 properly가 준동사 to prepare를 수식하고 있다.

③ 분사구문은 부사구의 역할을 한다.
　　　　　　　　　　문장의 본동사
Routines also enable athletes / to adjust and fine-tune their
　　　　　　　　분사구문을 이끄는 과거분사　　　　　　병렬 구조 (부사구)
preparations / ③ [based on those evaluations] / or[in pursuit
of a particular competitive goal]. //

밑줄 친 based 외에도 문장에 본동사 enable이 이미 있다. 따라서 based는 분사구문을 이끄는 과거분사이며, 이 분사구문은 문장에 '그러한 평가에 기반하여'라는 뜻을 더해준다.
이는 등위접속사 or로 병렬 구조를 이루는 전치사구(in pursuit of ~ goal)와 마찬가지로 문장에 의미를 더하는 부사구의 역할을 한다. 따라서 과거분사 based는 알맞게 쓰였다.

⑤ 부사적 용법의 to부정사는 목적의 의미를 나타낼 수 있다.
　　　　　　　　　　　　　　　　　　　　　　　부사적 용법 (목적)
~ / routines adjust all competitive components / ⑤ to achieve
proper performance. //

이 문장에서 to achieve는 부사의 역할을 하며 앞 절에 '적절한 수행을 해내기 위해'라는 목적의 의미를 더해준다. 따라서 to achieve는 알맞게 쓰였다.

30 정답 ⑤ * 소비자 심리에 기반한 마케팅 전략

다음 글의 밑줄 친 부분 중, 문맥상 낱말의 쓰임이 적절하지 않은 것은? [3점]

Promotion deals with consumer psychology. //
프로모션은 소비자 심리를 다룬다 //

We can't ① force people / to think one way or another, /
우리가 사람들을 강요할 수는 없으며 / 어떤 한 방식으로 생각하도록 /

be used to-v: ~하는 데 사용되다
and the clever marketer knows that / promotion is used / to provide information / in the most clear, honest, and simple fashion possible. //
단서1 현명한 마케팅 담당자는 명확하게 정보를 제공하기 위해
프로모션을 사용함
현명한 마케팅 담당자는 알고 있다 / 프로모션이 사용된다는 것을 / 정보를 제공하기 위해 / 가능한 한 가장 명확하고 정직하며 단순한 방식으로 //

앞 문장의 내용   단수 주어   단수 동사
By doing so, / the possibility of increasing sales goes up. //
그렇게 함으로써 / 매출 증가의 가능성이 높아진다 //

gone을 강조하기 위해 주어와 동사가 도치됨   단서2 예전에는 프로모션으로 소비자를
속였지만 지금은 다름
Gone are the days when promotions were done / in order to ②
fool A into B: A를 속여서 B하게 하다
fool the consumer / into purchasing something. //
getting의 목적어와 목적격 보어 (to부정사)
프로모션이 행해지던 시대는 갔다 / 소비자를 속이기 위해 / 무언가를 구매하도록 //

단수 주어
The long-term effect of getting a consumer to buy something /
앞에 목적격 관계대명사가 생략됨   단수 동사
they did not really want or need / wasn't good. //
소비자가 물건을 구매하도록 하는 것의 장기적인 효과는 / 그들이 정말로 원하지 않았거나 필요로 하지 않았던 / 좋지 않았다 //

앞에 주격 관계대명사와 be동사가 생략됨
In fact, / consumers fooled once can do ③ damage to sales / as they relate their experience to others. //
사실 / 한 번 속은 소비자는 판매에 손해를 끼칠 수 있다 / 자신의 경험을 다른 사람에게 전하기 때문에 //
단서3 기만당한 소비자는 그 경험을 알릴 수 있으므로 판매에 손해를 끼침

Instead, / marketers now know that / their goal is / to ④ identify the consumers / who are most likely to appreciate a good or service, /
병렬 구조 (주격 보어로 쓰인 to부정사)
대신 / 마케팅 담당자들은 이제 알고 있다 / 목표가 되어야 한다는 것을 / 소비자를 확인하고 / 상품이나 서비스의 진가를 가장 인정할 것 같은 /

지시형용사   주격 관계대명사
and to promote that good or service / in a way that makes the value clear / to the consumer. //
단서4 상품과 서비스의 가치를 인정하는 소비자를
대상으로 마케팅을 진행해야 함
그 상품이나 서비스를 홍보하는 것이 / 가치를 명확하게 하는 방식으로 / 그 소비자에게 //

Therefore, / marketers must know / where the ⑤ uninterested(→
병렬 구조 (know의 목적어)
potential) consumers are, / and how to reach them. //
그러므로 / 마케팅 담당자는 알아야 한다 / 그 무관심한(→ 잠재적인) 소비자가 어디에 있는지 / 그리고 어떻게 그들에게 도달해야 하는지 //

- promotion ⓝ 프로모션, 홍보 • deal with ~을 다루다
- consumer ⓝ 소비자 • psychology ⓝ 심리
- one way or another 어떤 한 방식으로 • fashion ⓝ 방식, 방법
- possibility ⓝ 가능성 • sales ⓝ 매출, 판매 • fool ⓥ 속이다
- purchase ⓥ 구매하다 • long-term ⓐ 장기적인
- relate ⓥ 전하다 • experience ⓝ 경험 • identify ⓥ 확인하다
- appreciate ⓥ 진가를 인정하다 • reach ⓥ 도달하다

프로모션은 소비자 심리를 다룬다. 우리가 사람들을 어떤 한 방식으로 생각하도록 ① 강요할 수는 없으며, 현명한 마케팅 담당자는 프로모션이 가능한 한 가장 명확하고 정직하며 단순한 방식으로 정보를 제공하기 위해 사용된다는 것을 알고 있다. 그렇게 함으로써, 매출 증가의 가능성이 높아진다. 무언가를 구매하도록 소비자를 ② 속이기 위해 프로모션이 행해지던 시대는 갔다. 소비자가 정말로 원하지 않았거나 필요로 하지 않았던 물건을 구매하도록 하는 것의 장기적인 효과는 좋지 않았다. 사실, 한 번 속은 소비자는 자신의 경험을 다른 사람에게 전하기 때문에 판매에 ③ 손해를 끼칠 수 있다. 대신, 마케팅 담당자들은 상품이나 서비스의 진가를 가장 인정할 것 같은 소비자를 ④ 확인하고, 그 소비자에게 그 상품이나 서비스의 가치를 명확하게 하는 방식으로 홍보하는 것이 목표가 되어야 한다는 것을 이제 알고 있다. 그러므로, 마케팅 담당자는 그 ⑤ 무관심한(→ 잠재적인) 소비자가 어디에 있는지, 그리고 어떻게 그들에게 도달해야 하는지 알아야 한다.

⟩왜 정답? ✱✱✱ [정답률 68%]

⑤ uninterested 무관심한

그러므로, 마케팅 담당자는 그 ⑤ 무관심한(잠재적인) 소비자가 어디에 있는지, 그리고 어떻게 그들에게 도달해야 하는지 알아야 한다.

➡ 소비자를 속이던 과거와는 다르게 현대에는 정직한 마케팅, 즉 자신들의 상품과 서비스의 가치를 인정하는 '잠재적인' 소비자를 찾는 마케팅이 중요하므로 '무관심한' 소비자를 찾는 것은 문맥에 맞지 않는다.
▶ uninterested를 potential(잠재적인)과 같은 어휘로 바꿔야 함

⟩왜 오답?

① force 강요하다

우리가 사람들을 어떤 한 방식으로 생각하도록 ① 강요할 수는 없으며, 현명한 마케팅 담당자는 프로모션이 가능한 한 가장 명확하고 정직하며 단순한 방식으로 정보를 제공하기 위해 사용된다는 것을 알고 있다.

➡ 프로모션이 소비자 심리를 다루고, 명확하고 단순하게 정보를 제공하기 위해 사용되는 것이라고 했다. 즉, 프로모션은 소비자들에게 정보를 제공하여 그들이 심리를 바꾸도록 유도할 뿐이지, 그들이 특정 방식으로 생각하도록 '강요'할 수는 없다.
▶ force는 문맥에 맞음

② fool 속이다

무언가를 구매하도록 소비자를 ② 속이기 위해 프로모션이 행해지던 시대는 갔다.

➡ 앞에서 정직하게 정보를 제공하기 위해 프로모션이 사용된다고 했으므로, 예전처럼 구매자들을 '속이는' 프로모션이 행해지는 시대가 갔다는 표현은 적절하다.
▶ fool은 문맥에 맞음

③ damage 손해를 끼치다

사실, 한 번 속은 소비자는 자신의 경험을 다른 사람에게 전하기 때문에 판매에 ③ 손해를 끼칠 수 있다.

➡ 기만당한 소비자들이 다른 사람에게 자신의 경험을 공유하면 판매가 줄어들 것이므로, 판매에 '손해를 끼칠' 수 있다는 표현은 적절하다. ▶ damage는 문맥에 맞음

④ identify (정체 등을) 확인하다

대신, 마케팅 담당자들은 상품이나 서비스의 진가를 가장 인정할 것 같은 소비자를 ④ 확인하고, 그 소비자에게 그 상품이나 서비스의 가치를 명확하게 하는 방식으로 홍보하는 것이 목표가 되어야 한다는 것을 이제 알고 있다.

➡ 마케팅의 대상을 정해야 하므로, 자신들의 가치를 잘 알아줄 수 있는 소비자들을 '확인한다'는 표현은 적절하다. ▶ identify는 문맥에 맞음

31 정답 ① * Plato의 미(美)의 형상

주격 관계대명사 (something 수식)
Plato argued that / when you see something that strikes you as beautiful, / you are really just seeing a partial reflection of true beauty, /
Plato는 주장했다 / 여러분이 자신에게 아름답다는 인상을 주는 무언가를 볼 때 / 여러분은 실제로는 진정한 아름다움의 부분적인 반영을 보고 있을 뿐이라고 /

'마치 ~처럼'
just as a painting or even a photograph only captures / part of the real thing. //
마치 그림이나 사진조차 포착하는 것처럼 / 실재하는 것의 일부만을 //

동격
True beauty, / or what Plato calls the Form of Beauty, / has no particular color, shape, or size. //
단서1 아름다움은 특정한 형태를 가지고
있지는 않음
진정한 아름다움 / 즉, Plato가 미(美)의 형상(Form of Beauty)이라고 부르는 것은 / 특정한 색상, 모양, 혹은 크기를 갖고 있지 않다 //
= true beauty, the Form of Beauty
Rather, / it is a(n) abstract idea, / like the number five. //
오히려 / 그것은 추상적인 관념이다 / 숫자 5처럼 //

You can make drawings of the number five / in blue or red ink, / big or small, / but the number five **itself** is **none** of those things. //
재귀대명사 (강조 용법)   대명사
여러분은 숫자 5의 그림을 만들 수 있지만 / 파란색이나 빨간색 잉크로 / 크거나 작게 / 숫자 5 자체는 그런 것들 중 어느 것도 아니다 //

It has no physical form. // 단서2 숫자 5는 구체적인 형태가 없음
그것은 구체적인 형태를 가지고 있지 않다 //
명령문 동사
Think of the idea of a triangle, / for example. //
삼각형이라는 관념을 생각해 보라 / 예를 들어 //
= the idea of a triangle
Although **it** has no particular color or size, / it somehow lies / within each and every triangle / **you see**. //
앞에 목적격 관계대명사가 생략됨
그것은 특정한 색상이나 크기가 없을지라도 / 어떻게든 존재한다 / 각각의 모든 삼각형 속에 / 당신이 보는 //
앞에 목적어절 접속사 that이 생략됨
Plato thought / **the same** was true of beauty. //
Plato는 생각했다 / 아름다움도 마찬가지라고 //

The Form of Beauty somehow lies / within each and every beautiful thing / **you see**. //
앞에 목적격 관계대명사가 생략됨
미의 원형은 어떻게든 존재한다 / 각각의 모든 아름다운 것 속에 / 당신이 보는 //

- strike ⓥ 인상을 주다   • partial ⓐ 부분적인   • reflection ⓝ 반영
- capture ⓥ 포착하다, 담아내다   • idea ⓝ 관념
- physical ⓐ 물리적인, 구체적인   • each and every 각각의 모든
- somehow ⓐⓓ 어떻게든   • abstract ⓐ 추상적인
- practical ⓐ 실용적인   • imperfect ⓐ 불완전한
- visualized ⓐ 시각화된

Plato는 여러분이 자신에게 아름답다는 인상을 주는 무언가를 볼 때, 마치 그림이나 사진조차 실재하는 것의 일부만을 포착하는 것처럼, 여러분은 실제로는 진정한 아름다움의 부분적인 반영을 보고 있을 뿐이라고 주장했다. 진정한 아름다움, 즉, Plato가 미(美)의 형상(Form of Beauty)이라고 부르는 것은 특정한 색상, 모양, 혹은 크기를 갖고 있지 않다. 오히려, 그것은 숫자 5처럼 **추상적인** 관념이다. 여러분은 숫자 5의 그림을 파란색이나 빨간색 잉크로, 크거나 작게, 만들 수 있지만, 숫자 5 자체는 그런 것들 중 어느 것도 아니다. 그것은 구체적인 형태를 가지고 있지 않다. 예를 들어, 삼각형이라는 관념을 생각해 보라. 그것은 특정한 색상이나 크기가 없을지라도, 당신이 보는 각각의 모든 삼각형 속에 어떻게든 존재한다. Plato는 아름다움도 마찬가지라고 생각했다. 미의 원형은 당신이 보는 각각의 모든 아름다운 것 속에 어떻게든 존재한다.

다음 빈칸에 들어갈 말로 가장 적절한 것을 고르시오.

① abstract   미의 형상은 숫자와 같이 고정된 형태를 갖추고 있지 않음
추상적인
② practical   미의 형상의 실용성은 언급되지 않았음
실용적인
③ imperfect   미의 형상이 불완전하다는 것은 언급되지 않았음
불완전한
④ visualized   우리가 보는 것은 시각된 것이지만 미의 형상 자체는 추상적임
시각화된
⑤ changeable   미의 형상 자체가 바뀔 수 있는지는 언급되지 않았음
바뀔 수 있는

| 문제 풀이 순서 | ★★★ [정답률 52%]

1st 빈칸이 포함된 문장을 읽고, 빈칸에 들어갈 말에 대한 단서를 얻는다.

빈칸 문장	Rather, **it** is a(n) _____ idea, like the number five.
	오히려, 그것은 숫자 5처럼, _____ 관념이다.

➡ it이 숫자 5와 같은 '관념'이라고 했으므로, 단서
it이 무엇인지, 5라는 관념의 특징으로 어떤 것들이 언급되는지 살펴봐야 한다. 발상

2nd 글의 내용을 종합해서 빈칸에 들어갈 적절한 말을 찾는다.
- 미(美)의 형상은 특정한 색상, 모양, 혹은 크기가 없음 단서1
- 숫자 5는 구체적인 형태를 가지고 있지 않음 단서2

➡ Plato는 우리가 아름답다고 느끼는 것은 진정한 아름다움의 일부만을 반영하고, 진정한 아름다움인 '미의 형상'은 숫자 5라는 관념처럼 구체적인 형태나 크기가 없다고 했다.
▶ 따라서 it은 '미의 형상'을 가리키고, 이러한 관념의 특징은 구체적이지 않고 ① '추상적'이다.

| 선택지 분석 |
① 미의 형상은 구체적인 형태가 없으므로 추상적인 개념이다.
② 미의 형상의 개념과 추상성이 설명되었을 뿐, 어느 측면에서 실용적인지는 언급되지 않았다.
③ 미의 형상은 구체적인 형태가 없다는 점이 강조되었을 뿐, 불완전한지는 언급되지 않았다.
④ 우리가 보는 것, 즉 아름다움의 부분적인 반영은 시각화된 것이지만 미의 형상은 추상적이다.
⑤ 우리가 보는 것, 즉 아름다움의 부분적인 반영은 여러 형태로 나타나므로 바뀔 수 있지만, 미의 형상이 바뀔 수 있는지는 언급되지 않았다.

---

32 정답 ③   ＊대화를 지속하기 위해 질문보다는 관찰하기

명령문 동사
As you listen to your child / in an emotional moment, / **be aware** / that **sharing simple observations** usually works **better / than asking questions** / to get a conversation rolling. //
비교급   비교 대상
여러분이 자녀의 말을 들을 때 / 어떤 감정적인 순간에 놓인 / 인식하라 / 단순한 관찰 결과를 공유하는 것이 대개는 더 효과적임을 / 질문을 하는 것보다 / 대화가 계속 굴러가게 하기 위해 //

You may ask your child / "Why do you feel sad?" / and she may not have a clue. // 단서1 자녀는 감정의 원인을 묻는 말에 제대로 대답하지 못할 수도 있음
여러분이 자녀에게 물으면 / "왜 슬픈 기분이 드니"라고 / 그녀는 짐작조차 못 할 수도 있다 //

As a child, / she may not have an answer on the tip of her tongue. //
아이라서 / 그녀는 답이 당장 떠오르지 않을지도 모른다 //

Maybe / she's feeling sad / about her parents' arguments, / or because she feels overtired, / or she's worried about a piano recital. // 단서2 감정 상태와 원인 중 어떤 것도 대답하지 못할 수도 있음
어쩌면 / 그녀는 슬픔을 느끼고 있거나 / 부모님의 말다툼에 대해 / 혹은 그녀가 극도로 지쳤기 때문이거나 / 혹은 피아노 연주회를 걱정할지도 모른다 //

앞에 언급된 내용 (자신의 감정 상태와 그 원인)
But she may or may not be able to explain / any of **this**. //
그러나 그녀는 이것에 대해 설명할 수도 있고 설명하지 못할 수도 있다 / 어떤 것도 //

'비록 ~할 때라도'   강조 용법의 do동사
And / **even when** she **does** come up with an answer, / she might be worried / that the answer is not good enough to justify the feeling. //
그리고 / 그녀가 정말로 답이 떠오를 때조차도 / 걱정할 수도 있다 / 그 대답이 그 감정을 정당화하기에는 충분하지 않다고 //

Under these circumstances, / a series of questions can just make **a child silent**. //
사역동사 make의 목적어와 목적격 보어 (형용사)
이러한 상황에서는 / 연속된 질문들이 그저 자녀를 침묵하게 만들 수 있다 //

가주어   진주어
It's better / to simply reflect what you notice. // 단서3 감정을 알아차렸음을 보이는 것이 직접적인 질문보다 더 나음
더 낫다 / 여러분이 인지한 것을 단순히 나타내는 것이 //

병렬 구조 (직접 화법)
You can **say**, / "**You seem a little tired today**," / or, "**I noticed that you frowned / when I mentioned the recital**," / and **wait** for her response. //
병렬 구조 (문장의 동사)
여러분은 말할 수 있다 / "너 오늘 조금 피곤해 보이네" / 혹은 "네가 얼굴을 찡그린 것을 알아챘어 / 내가 연주회 얘기를 꺼냈을 때"라고 / 그리고 그녀의 반응을 기다려 볼 수 있다 //

- be aware that ~을 인식하다   • have a clue 짐작하다
- on the tip of one's tongue 당장 떠오르지 않는, 혀 끝에서 맴도는
- argument ⓝ 말다툼, 논쟁   • overtired ⓐ 극도로 지친
- recital ⓝ 연주회   • justify ⓥ 정당화하다

- circumstances ⓝ 상황, 환경　• a series of 연속된
- frown ⓥ (얼굴을) 찡그리다　• mention ⓥ 얘기를 꺼내다
- push ~ for … ~에게 …을 요구하다　• observation ⓝ 관찰
- cool down 식히다, 진정시키다

여러분이 어떤 감정적인 순간에 놓인 자녀의 말을 들을 때, 대화가 계속 굴러가게 하기 위해 질문을 하는 것보다 **단순한 관찰 결과를 공유하는 것**이 대개는 더 효과적임을 인식해라. 여러분이 자녀에게 "왜 슬픈 기분이 드니?"라고 물으면 그녀는 짐작조차 못 할 수도 있다. 아이라서, 그녀는 답이 당장 떠오르지 않지도 모른다. 어쩌면 그녀는 부모님의 말다툼에 대해 슬픔을 느끼고 있거나, 혹은 그녀가 극도로 지쳤기 때문이거나, 혹은 피아노 연주회를 걱정할지도 모른다. 그러나 그녀는 이것에 대해 설명할 수도 있고 어떤 것도 설명하지 못할 수도 있다. 그리고 그녀가 정말로 답이 떠오를 때조차도 그 대답이 그 감정을 정당화하기에는 충분하지 않다고 걱정할 수도 있다. 이러한 상황에서는 연속된 질문들이 그저 자녀를 침묵하게 만들 수 있다. 여러분이 인지한 것을 단순히 나타내는 것이 더 낫다. "너 오늘 조금 피곤해 보이네." 혹은 "내가 연주회 얘기를 꺼냈을 때 네가 얼굴을 찡그린 것을 알아챘어."라고 말하고, 그녀의 반응을 기다려 볼 수 있다.

다음 빈칸에 들어갈 말로 가장 적절한 것을 고르시오.

① giving quick advice 소년은 언급되지 않았음
　빠르게 조언하는 것
② pushing her for answers 대답을 억지로 요구하면 답을 듣기 더 어려움
　대답을 억지로 요구하는 것
③ sharing simple observations 자녀가 답변의 부담을 느낄 때는 계속 묻기보다는
　단순한 관찰 결과를 공유하는 것　부모가 감정을 인지했음을 알려 주는 것이 더 효과적임
④ telling your own life stories 이야기를 공유하는 것은 언급되지 않았음
　자신의 인생 이야기를 들려주는 것
⑤ leaving her alone to cool down 자녀를 혼자 두면 대화가 이어질 수 없음
　진정할 시간을 주며 혼자 두는 것

| 문제 풀이 순서 |　✱✱❀　[정답률 60%]

1st 빈칸이 포함된 문장을 읽고, 빈칸에 들어갈 말에 대한 단서를 얻는다.

| 빈칸 문장 | As you listen to your child in an emotional moment, be aware that ＿＿＿＿＿＿ usually works better than asking questions to get a conversation rolling.

여러분이 어떤 감정적인 순간에 놓인 자녀의 말을 들을 때, 대화가 계속 굴러가게 하기 위해 질문을 하는 것보다 ＿＿＿＿＿＿ 이 대개는 더 효과적임을 인식해라. |

➡ 자녀와의 대화를 지속하기 위해서 질문보다 '무엇'이 더 효과적이라고 했으므로, 단서 질문 외에 다른 방식이 언급되는지 확인해야 한다. 발상

2nd 글의 내용을 종합해서 빈칸에 들어갈 적절한 말을 찾는다.

- • 자녀가 감정의 원인을 묻는 말에 제대로 대답하지 못할 수도 있음 단서 1
- • 자녀는 감정 상태와 원인 중 어떤 것도 대답하지 못할 수도 있음 단서 2
- • 단순히 감정을 인지했음을 나타내는 것이 직접 감정을 묻는 것보다 나음 단서 3

➡ 자녀에게 감정 상태나 원인을 물을 때 제대로 된 답변을 얻지 못할 수도 있다. 이때 답을 얻기 위해 계속 묻기보다는, 단순하게 부모가 인지하는(관찰하는) 자녀의 감정을 말해주는 것이 더 낫다는 내용이다.

▶ 따라서 감정적인 순간에 놓인 자녀와 대화하려면 계속 질문하는 것보다 자녀의 감정에 관하여 ③ '단순한 관찰 결과를 공유하는 것'이 대개는 더 효과적이다.

| 선택지 분석 |

① 자녀의 감정 상태를 알기 위해 계속 질문하는 것은 언급되었지만, 빠르게 조언하는 것은 언급되지 않았다.
② 계속 질문하여 대답을 억지로 요구하는 것은 오히려 자녀가 침묵하게 한다.
③ 자녀의 감정에 관하여 계속 질문하여 자녀에게 부담을 주는 것보다는, 부모의 입장에서 자녀의 상태를 관찰한 결과를 말해주고 반응을 보는 것이 더 효과적이다.
④ 자신의 인생을 공유하는 것보다는, 부모가 관찰한 자녀의 감정 상태를 알려주는 것이 대화를 지속하는 데 더 도움이 된다.
⑤ 결국 자녀와 대화해야 하는데, 자녀를 혼자 두면 대화를 이어가기 어려울 것이다.

---

33 정답 ④ ＊땀으로 감정을 측정하기

동사 conducts를 수식하는 부사구
Our skin conducts electricity / more or less efficiently, / depending on our emotions. //
우리의 피부는 전기를 전도한다 / 꽤 효율적으로 / 우리의 감정에 따라 //

We know that when we're emotionally stimulated / — stressed, sad, any intense emotion, really / — our bodies sweat a tiny bit, / so little we might not even notice. // 단서 1 감정적 자극이 있을 때 피부는 땀을 분비함
그 정도로 적게
우리가 감정적으로 자극되었을 때 / 즉, 정말로 스트레스를 받거나, 슬프거나, 어떤 강렬한 감정일 때 / 우리 몸은 땀을 아주 약간 흘리는데 / 너무 적어서 알아차리지도 못할 정도이다 //

And when those tiny drops of sweat appear, / our skin gets more electrically conductive. // 단서 2 땀은 피부에 전기가 더 잘 흐르게 함
그리고 이 작은 땀방울이 나타날 때 / 우리의 피부는 전기적으로 더 전도력이 있는 상태가 된다 //

This change in sweat gland activity happens / completely
「without + 명사 + 분사」: ~이 …하지 않은 채
without your conscious mind having much say in the matter. //
이러한 땀샘 활동의 변화는 일어난다 / 여러분의 의식이 그 상황에 그다지 관여하지 않은 채 //

If you feel emotionally intense, / you're going to notice / an increase in sweat gland activity. //
만약 여러분이 감성적으로 강렬하게 느낀다면 / 여러분은 알아차릴 것이다 / 땀샘 활동의 증가를 //

= An increase in sweat gland activity
This is particularly useful / from a scientific viewpoint, / because it allows us to put an objective value / on a subjective state of mind. // 단서 3 감정과 땀샘 활동의 관계를 통해 마음 상태를 수치화할 수 있음
이는 특히 유용한데 / 과학적 관점에서 / 그것이 우리가 객관적인 값을 부여할 수 있게 해주기 때문이다 / 주관적인 마음 상태에 //

We can actually measure your emotional state / by tracking how your body subconsciously sweats, / by running a bit of electricity through your skin. //
tracking의 목적어 (간접의문문)
우리는 실제로 여러분의 감정적 상태를 측정할 수 있다 / 여러분의 신체가 의식하지 못한 채 어떻게 땀을 흘리는지를 추적함으로써 / 그리고 피부를 통해 약간의 전류를 흐르게 함으로써 //

We can then turn the subjective, subconscious experience of emotional intensity / into an objective number / by figuring out / how good your skin gets at transferring an electrical current. //
turn ~ into …: ~을 …로 바꾸다
figuring out의 목적어 (간접의문문)
우리는 그다음에 감정적 강도의 주관적이고, 잠재의식적인 경험을 바꿀 수 있다 / 객관적인 숫자로 / 계산함으로써 / 여러분의 피부가 전류를 얼마나 잘 전달하는지를 //

- conduct ⓥ 전도하다, 전달하다　• electricity ⓝ 전기
- more or less 꽤, 다소　• efficiently ⓐⓓ 효율적으로　• drop ⓝ 방울
- conscious mind 의식(적 마음)
- have much say in ~에 발언권이 많다[영향력이 크다]
- intense ⓐ 강렬한　• viewpoint ⓝ 관점　• objective ⓐ 객관적인
- subjective ⓐ 주관적인　• track ⓥ 추적하다
- subconscious ⓐ 잠재의식의　• intensity ⓝ 강도
- figure out 계산하다　• transfer ⓥ 전달하다
- electrical current 전류

우리의 피부는 우리의 감정에 따라, 전기를 꽤 효율적으로 전도한다. 우리가 감정적으로 자극되었을 때, 즉, 정말로 스트레스를 받거나, 슬프거나, 어떤 강렬한 감정일 때, 우리 몸은 땀을 아주 약간 흘리는데, 너무 적어서 알아차리지도 못할 정도이다. 그리고 이 작은 땀방울이 나타날 때, 우리의 피부는 전기적으로 더 전도력이 있는 상태가 된다. 이러한 땀샘 활동의 변화는 여러분의 의식이 그 상황에 그다지 관여하지 않은 채 일어난다. 만약 여러분이 감정적으로 강렬하게 느낀다면, 여러분은 땀샘 활동의 증가를 알아차릴 것이다. 이는 특히 과학적 관점에서 유용한데, 그것이 우리가 객관적인 값을 주관적인 마음 상태에 부여할 수 있게 해주기 때문이다. 우리는 실제로 여러분의 신체가 의식하지 못한 채 어떻게 땀을 흘리는지를 추적함으로써, 그리고 피부를 통해 약간의 전류를 흐르게 함으로써 **여러분의 감정 상태를 측정할** 수 있다. 그다음에 여러분의 피부가 전류를 얼마나 잘 전달하는지를 계산함으로써 우리는 감정적 강도의 주관적이고, 잠재의식적인 경험을 객관적인 숫자로 바꿀 수 있다.

다음 빈칸에 들어갈 말로 가장 적절한 것을 고르시오. [3점]

① limit reactions of hormones 호르몬은 언급되지 않았음
호르몬 반응을 제한하다
② control the electrical current 전류를 조절하는 것은 언급되지 않았음
전류를 조절하다
③ improve your skin conditions 피부 상태 자체의 개선은 전류의 결과가 아님
여러분의 피부 상태를 개선하다
④ measure your emotional state 땀의 전도력을 통해 감정 상태를 측정할 수 있음
여러분의 감정 상태를 측정하다
⑤ diversify emotional experiences 감정 경험의 다양화는 관련이 없음
감정 경험을 다양화하다

| 문제 풀이 순서 | ★★★ [정답률 54%]

1st 첫 문장과 빈칸이 포함된 문장을 읽고, 빈칸에 들어갈 말에 대한 단서를 얻는다.

첫 문장	Our skin conducts electricity more or less efficiently, depending on our emotions. 우리의 피부는 우리의 감정에 따라, 전기를 꽤 효율적으로 전도한다.
빈칸 문장	We can actually _____ by tracking how your body subconsciously sweats, by running a bit of electricity through your skin. 우리는 실제로 여러분의 신체가 의식하지 못한 채 어떻게 땀을 흘리는지를 추적함으로써, 그리고 피부를 통해 약간의 전류를 흐르게 함으로써 _____ 할 수 있다.

➡ 우리의 피부가 감정에 따라 전기를 흘려보낸다고 했다. 단서
땀도 물이기 때문에, 피부의 땀은 전류가 더 잘 흐르게 할 것이다. 땀이 나는 피부에 전류가 흐르면 감정에 관하여 '무엇'을 알아낼 수 있는지를 파악해야 한다. 발상

2nd 글의 내용을 종합해서 빈칸에 들어갈 적절한 말을 찾는다.
- 인간의 피부는 감정에 따라 전기가 흐르게 함 단서1
- 땀은 피부에 전기가 더 잘 흐르게 함 단서2
- 감정과 땀샘 활동의 관계를 통해 (주관적인) 마음 상태를 수치화할 수 있음 단서3

➡ 감정적인 자극이 강렬해지면 피부의 땀샘 활동이 증가하므로 전도성이 증가한다. 즉, 피부에 전기가 흐르는 정도를 측정하면 주관적인 감정 상태를 객관적으로 수치화할 수 있다.

▶ 따라서 땀이 분비되어 피부에 전기가 흐르면 ④ '감정 상태를 측정할' 수 있다.

| 선택지 분석 |
① 호르몬은 언급되지 않았다.
② 피부에 흐르는 전류를 조절하는 것은 언급되지 않았다.
③ 피부 상태를 좋게 만드는 것은 관련 없는 내용이다.
④ 감정에 따라 피부에 흐르는 땀의 양이 달라지므로 얼마나 전기가 더 잘 통하는지를 측정하여 감정 상태를 측정할 수 있다.
⑤ 감정적으로 자극받는 예시로 스트레스, 슬픔, 강렬한 감정이 언급되었지만, 감정 경험의 다양화와는 관련이 없다.

34 정답 ① ＊식물의 생존 기제

부사절 접속사 (양보)
Plants can communicate, / although not in the same way we = communicate
do. // 단서1 식물은 의사표현을 할 수 있음
식물은 의사소통을 할 수 있다 / 우리가 하는 방식과 같지는 않을지라도 //

Some express their discontent / through scents. //
몇몇은 자신들의 불만을 표현한다 / 냄새를 통해 // 단서2 몇몇 식물은 냄새로 불만을 표현함
지시형용사 관계대명사절 (smell 수식)
You know that smell / that hangs in the air / after you've mowed the lawn? //
여러분은 냄새를 알고 있는가 / 공기 중에 감도는 / 잔디를 깎고 난 후 //
S로 시작하지만 [es]로 발음
Yeah, / that's actually an SOS. //
그렇다 / 그것은 사실 일종의 SOS 신호다 //

Some plants use sound. // 단서3 어떤 식물은 소리로 의사소통할 수 있음
어떤 식물은 소리를 사용한다 //

Yes, / sound, / though at a frequency that we can't hear. //
그렇다 / 소리다 / 우리는 들을 수 없는 주파수에 있지만 //

부사적 용법 (목적)
Researchers experimented with plants and microphones / to see = researchers
/ if they could record any trouble calls. //
연구자는 식물과 마이크를 사용해 실험했다 / 알아보기 위해 / 식물이 곤경에 처했음을 알리는 소리를 녹음할 수 있는지 //

They found / that plants produce a high-frequency clicking noise / when stressed / and can make different sounds / for 부사절에서 「주어+be동사」 생략
different stressors. //
그들은 사실을 알아냈다 / 식물이 고주파수의 딸깍거리는 소리를 내며 / 스트레스를 받을 때 / 다른 소리를 낼 수 있다는 / 스트레스 요인에 따라 //

앞에 목적격 관계대명사가 생략됨
The sound a plant makes / when it's not getting watered / differs = the sound
from the one it'll make / when a leaf is cut. //
식물이 내는 소리는 / 물을 공급받지 못하고 있을 때 / 낼 소리와 다르다 / 잎이 잘릴 때 //

가주어 worth -ing: ~할 가치가 있는
However, / it's worth noting / that experts don't think / plants 진주어절 접속사
are crying out in pain. //
하지만 / 주목할 가치가 있다 / 전문가가 보지는 않는다는 것에 / 식물이 고통으로 울부짖고 있다고 //

It's more likely / that these reactions are knee-jerk survival actions. // 단서4 식물은 살아남기 위해 반응하는 경우가 있음
가능성이 더 크다 / 이러한 반응은 살아남기 위한 자동적인 행위일 //

Plants are living organisms, / and their main objective is to survive. //
식물은 살아 있는 유기체이며 / 그들의 주요 목표는 살아남는 것이다 //

Scents and sounds are their tools / for **defending against things that might harm them**. //
냄새와 소리는 그들의 도구이다 / 자신들에게 해를 끼칠 수도 있는 것들로부터 지키기 위한 //

- communicate ⓥ 의사소통을 하다 • discontent ⓝ 불만
- frequency ⓝ 주파수 • researcher ⓝ 연구자
- experiment ⓥ 실험하다 • survival ⓐ 살아남기 위한
- organism ⓝ 유기체 • objective ⓝ 목표
- defend ⓥ 지키다, 방어하다 • neighboring ⓐ 인접한, 이웃한
- dissatisfaction ⓝ 불만 • nutrient ⓝ 영양소
- genetic ⓐ 유전적인

우리가 하는 방식과 같지는 않을지라도, 식물은 의사소통을 할 수 있다. 몇몇은 냄새를 통해 자신들의 불만을 표현한다. 여러분은 잔디를 깎고 난 후 공기 중에 감도는 냄새를 알고 있는가? 그렇다. 그것은 사실 일종의 SOS 신호다. 어떤 식물은 소리를 사용한다. 그렇다, 우리는 들을 수 없는 주파수에 있지만, 소리다. 연구자는 식물이 곤경에 처했음을 알리는 소리를 녹음할 수 있는지 알아보기 위해 식물과 마이크를 사용해 실험했다. 그들은 식물이 스트레스를 받을 때 고주파수의 딸깍거리는 소리를 내며, 스트레스 요인에 따라 다른 소리를 낼 수 있다는 사실을 알아냈다. 식물이 물을 공급받지 못하고 있을 때 내는 소리와 잎이 잘릴 때 낼 소리가 다르다. 하지만, 전문가가 식물이 고통으로 울부짖고 있다고 보지는 않는다는 것에 주목할 가치가 있다. 이러한 반응은 살아남기 위한 자동적인 행위일 가능성이 더 크다. 식물은 살아 있는 유기체이며, 그들의 주요 목표는 살아남는 것이다. 냄새와 소리는 **자신들에게 해를 끼칠 수도 있는 것들로부터 지키기** 위한 그들의 도구이다.

다음 빈칸에 들어갈 말로 가장 적절한 것을 고르시오. [3점]

① defending against things that might harm them
자신들에게 해를 끼칠 수도 있는 것들로부터 지키기 위험을 받으면 방어를 위해 반응함
② showing their support for neighboring plants
인접한 식물들을 지지함을 보여주기 인접한 식물들은 언급되지 않았음
③ hiding their pains and dissatisfaction
고통과 불만을 숨기기 고통과 불만을 숨기지 않고 표출하며 방어함
④ sharing nutrients with other plants
다른 식물들과 영양소를 나누기 영양소를 나누는 것은 언급되지 않았음
⑤ changing their genetic structure 유전 구조 변화는 언급되지 않았음
유전 구조를 변화시키기

⟩ 왜 정답 ? ★★★ [정답률 68%]
빈칸 문장의 Scents and sounds는 식물이 살아남으려 할 때 보이는 반응이다. 식물들은 이러한 반응으로 자신이 곤경에 처했음을 알리고 의사소통한다. 따라서 냄새와 소리는 ① '자신들에게 해를 끼칠 수도 있는 것들로부터 지키기' 위한 식물들의 도구이다.

왜 오답?

② 식물이 위험에 처했을 때 인접한 식물들을 도와준다는 내용은 언급되지 않았다.

③ 식물들이 냄새와 소리를 통해 고통과 불만을 표현한다는 내용이지, 이를 숨긴다는 내용이 아니다.

④ 다른 식물들과 영양소를 나눈다는 것은 언급되지 않았다.

⑤ 유전 구조를 변화시키는 것은 언급되지 않았다.

---

35 정답 ② ＊감정적 반응의 조건

다음 글에서 전체 흐름과 관계 없는 문장은?

What does it mean / for a character to be a hero / as opposed to a villain? //
무슨 의미인가 / 등장인물이 영웅이라는 것은 / 악당과 대비되는 //

In artistic and entertainment descriptions, / it's essential for the author / to establish a positive relationship / between a protagonist and the audience. // **단서 1** 주인공과 관객 사이 긍정적인 관계가 필수적임
예술적이고 오락적인 묘사에서 / 작가에게 필수적이다 / 긍정적인 관계를 수립하는 것이 / 주인공과 관객 사이에 **단서 2** 등장인물이 확실히 인식되어야 관객으로부터 감정적인 반응을

① In order for tragedy or misfortune / to draw out an emotional response in viewers, / the character must be adjusted / so as to be recognizable as either friend or enemy. //
비극 또는 불행이 관객에게서 감정적 반응을 끌어내기 위해서 / 등장인물은 조정되어야 한다 / 친구 또는 적 둘 중의 하나로 인식될 수 있도록 //

② Likewise, / the line between friends and enemies / is not clear / in reality. //)
(마찬가지로 / 친구와 적 사이의 선이 / 명확하지 않다 / 현실에서는 //

③ Whether the portrayal is fictional or documentary, / we must feel / that the protagonist is someone / whose actions benefit us; /
묘사가 허구적이든 사실을 기록하든 간에 / 우리는 느껴야 한다 / 주인공은 누군가이며 / 행동이 우리에게 이로움을 주는 /

the protagonist is, or would be, / a worthy companion or valued ally. //
주인공은 ~이고, 혹은 그렇게 될 (존재일) 것이라고 / 가치 있는 동료나 소중한 협력자 /

④ Violent action films are often filled with / dozens of incidental deaths of minor characters / that draw out little response in the audience. // **단서 3** 비중이 적은 등장인물은 관객의 반응에 큰 영향을 미치지 않음
폭력적인 액션 영화는 흔히 가득 차 있다 / 비중이 적은 등장인물의 많은 부수적인 죽음으로 / 관객들에게서 반응을 거의 끌어내지 않는 //

⑤ In order to feel strong emotions, / the audience must be emotionally invested in a character / as either ally or enemy. //
강한 감정을 느끼기 위해 / 관객은 등장인물에게 감정적으로 깊이 연관되어 있어야 한다 / 협력자 또는 적 둘 중 하나로 // **단서 4** 등장인물과의 감정적 연관이 관객이 강한 감정을 느끼도록 유도함

- as opposed to ~와 대비되는 · essential ⓐ 필수적인
- establish ⓥ 수립하다 · positive ⓐ 긍정적인 · tragedy ⓝ 비극
- misfortune ⓝ 불행 · draw out 끌어내다
- recognizable ⓐ 알아볼 수 있는, 인식할 수 있는 · portrayal ⓝ 묘사
- fictional ⓐ 허구의, 가상의 · documentary ⓐ 사실을 기록한, 사실적인
- companion ⓝ 동료 · valued ⓐ 소중한, 가치 있는
- ally ⓝ 협력자 · dozens of 많은, 수십의 · incidental ⓐ 부수적인

등장인물이 악당과 대비되는 영웅이라는 것은 무슨 의미인가? 예술적이고 오락적인 묘사에서, 작가가 주인공과 관객 사이에 긍정적인 관계를 수립하는 것이 필수적이다. ① 비극 또는 불행이 관객에게서 감정적 반응을 끌어내기 위해서, 등장인물은 친구 또는 적 둘 중의 하나로 인식될 수 있도록 조정되어야 한다.

(② 마찬가지로, 친구와 적 사이의 선이 현실에서는 명확하지 않다.) ③ 묘사가 허구적이든 사실을 기록하든 간에, 주인공은 행동이 우리에게 이로움을 주는 누군가이며, 주인공은 가치 있는 동료나 소중한 협력자이고, 혹은 그렇게 될 (존재일) 것이라고 우리는 느껴야 한다. ④ 폭력적인 액션 영화는 흔히 관객들에게서 반응을 거의 끌어내지 않는 비중이 적은 등장인물의 많은 부수적인 죽음으로 가득 차 있다. ⑤ 강한 감정을 느끼기 위해, 관객은 협력자 또는 적 둘 중 하나로 등장인물에게 감정적으로 깊이 연관되어 있어야 한다.

왜 정답·오답? ★★★ [정답률 46%]

글의 앞부분: 영웅이 돋보이고 악당과 대비되기 위해서는 작가가 주인공과 관객 사이에 긍정적인 관계를 만드는 것이 중요하다는 내용임

① 비극 또는 불행이 관객에게서 감정적 반응을 끌어내려면, 등장인물은 친구 또는 적 둘 중의 하나로 인식되어야 함

▶ 주인공과 관객 간 긍정적인 관계를 형성하는 첫 단계를 설명하므로, ①은 무관한 문장이 아님

② 마찬가지로, 친구와 적 사이의 선이 현실에서는 명확하지 않음

▶ 영웅과 악당 간 대비를 설명하다가, 이와 마찬가지라고 하며 친구와 적 사이의 선이 현실에서 명확하지 않다고 설명하므로, ②은 무관한 문장임

③ 묘사가 허구적이든 사실을 기록하든, 주인공은 가치 있는 동료나 소중한 협력자로 느껴져야 함

▶ 주인공과 관객의 긍정적인 관계 형성이 구체적으로 어떻게 이루어져야 하는지 이어서 제시하므로, ③은 무관한 문장이 아님

④ 폭력적인 액션 영화는 흔히 관객들에게서 반응을 거의 끌어내지 않는 비중이 적은 등장인물의 많은 부수적인 죽음으로 가득 차 있음

▶ 주인공은 가치 있고 소중하지만, 비중이 적은 그 외 인물들의 죽음에는 주목하지 않음을 설명하므로, ④은 무관한 문장이 아님

⑤ 강한 감정을 느끼기 위해, 관객은 협력자 또는 적 둘 중 하나로 등장인물에게 감정적으로 깊이 연관되어 있어야 함

▶ ①에서 관객의 감정적 반응을 끌어내려면 등장인물이 친구나 적으로 인식되어야 한다고 했는데, 이와 비슷한 내용을 강조하며 글을 마무리하므로, ⑤은 무관한 문장이 아님

＊ 글의 흐름

1 도입: 작가가 주인공과 관객 사이에 긍정적인 관계를 수립하는 것이 필수적임

2 전개: 관객이 감정적으로 반응하려면 주인공은 이로운 친구나 명확한 적으로 인식되어야 함

3 부연: 폭력적인 액션 영화는 주인공을 제외하면 비중이 적은 등장인물의 많은 부수적인 죽음으로 가득 차 있음

4 결론: 강한 감정을 느끼기 위해, 관객은 협력자 또는 적 둘 중 하나로 등장인물에게 감정적으로 깊이 연관되어 있어야 함

---

36 정답 ⑤ ＊비개념적 사고와 동물의 인지 능력

Let's assume / that at least some animals are capable of thinking / despite lacking a language. //
가정해 보자 / 적어도 일부 동물은 사고할 수 있다고 / 언어가 부족함에도 불구하고 //

단서 1 다람쥐가 개념 없이도 상상을 통해 행동할 수 있다는 (B)의 내용

(A) This doesn't imply / that squirrels lack concepts, / simply that they don't need them / for this concrete form of thinking. //
＝squirrels ＝concepts
이것은 의미하는 것이 아니라 / 다람쥐가 개념이 부족하다는 것을 / 단지 다람쥐가 그것들이 필요하지 않다는 것을 의미한다 / 이 사고의 구체적인 형태를 위해 //

For us to be able to say / that an animal has concepts, / we have to show / not just that she's capable of thinking, / but also that she has certain specific abilities. //
우리가 말할 수 있기 위해서 / 동물이 개념을 가지고 있다고 / 우리는 보여 주어야 한다 / 그 동물이 사고할 수 있다는 것뿐만 아니라 / 어떤 특정한 능력을 가지고 있다는 것을 //

(B) To do this, / in principle / she doesn't need a concept of branch / nor a concept of tree. //

이것을 하기 위해서 / 원칙적으로 / 다람쥐는 나뭇가지의 개념이 필요하지 않고 / 또한 나무의 개념도 필요하지 않다 //

It might be enough for her to have, / for example, / the ability to think in images; / to make a mental map of the tree / where she can imagine and try out different routes. //

다람쥐가 가지고 있는 것으로 충분할 수도 있다 / 예를 들어 / 이미지로 생각하는 능력 / 즉, 나무에 대한 머릿속 지도를 만드는 능력만 / 다람쥐가 다양한 경로를 상상하고 시도해 볼 수 있는 //

(C) This doesn't necessarily mean / that they possess concepts, / for some forms of thought may be nonconceptual. //

이것이 반드시 의미하지는 않는데 / 그들이 개념을 가지고 있다고 / 왜냐하면 사고의 어떤 형태는 비(非)개념적일 수도 있기 때문이다 //

We can imagine, / for instance, / a squirrel who is planning how to get / from the branch she's currently standing on / to a branch from the tree in front. //

우리는 상상해 볼 수 있다 / 예를 들어 / 가는 방법을 계획하고 있는 다람쥐를 / 현재 서 있는 나뭇가지에서 / 앞쪽 나무의 나뭇가지로 //

- assume ⓥ 가정하다 · capable ⓐ ~할 수 있는
- despite prep ~에도 불구하고 · lack ⓥ 부족하다
- imply ⓥ 의미하다 · concept ⓝ 개념 · concrete ⓐ 구체적인
- specific ⓐ 특정한 · in principle 원칙적으로
- possess ⓥ 가지고 있다, 소유하다 · nonconceptual ⓐ 비(非)개념적인
- currently ad 현재

적어도 일부 동물은 언어가 부족함에도 불구하고 사고할 수 있다고 가정해 보자. (C) 이것이 그들이 개념을 가지고 있다고 반드시 의미하지는 않는데, 왜냐하면 사고의 어떤 형태는 비(非)개념적일 수도 있기 때문이다. 예를 들어, 우리는 현재 서 있는 나뭇가지에서 앞쪽 나무의 나뭇가지로 가는 방법을 계획하고 있는 다람쥐를 상상해 볼 수 있다. (B) 이것을 하기 위해서, 원칙적으로 다람쥐는 나뭇가지의 개념이 필요하지 않고 또한 나무의 개념도 필요하지 않다. 예를 들어, 다람쥐가 이미지로 생각하는 능력, 즉, 다람쥐가 다양한 경로를 상상하고 시도해 볼 수 있는 나무에 대한 머릿속 지도를 만드는 능력만 가지고 있는 것으로 충분할 수도 있다. (A) 이것은 다람쥐가 개념이 부족하다는 것을 의미하는 것이 아니라, 단지 다람쥐가 이 사고의 구체적인 형태를 위해 그것들이 필요하지 않다는 것을 의미한다. 우리가 동물이 개념을 가지고 있다고 말할 수 있기 위해서, 그 동물이 사고할 수 있다는 것뿐만 아니라 어떤 특정한 능력을 가지고 있다는 것을 우리는 보여 주어야 한다.

주어진 글 다음에 이어질 글의 순서로 가장 적절한 것을 고르시오. [3점]

① (A) — (C) — (B) 주어진 글에 (A)의 '이것'과 연결되는 내용이 없음
② (B) — (A) — (C) (B)의 '이것'은 (C)의 뒷부분에 있음
③ (B) — (C) — (A)
④ (C) — (A) — (B) (A)의 '이것'은 (B)의 뒷부분에 있음
⑤ (C) — (B) — (A) 일부 동물들은 언어 없이도 사고가 가능하다는 가정 — (C) 일부 사고는 비개념적 — (B) 다람쥐는 행동에 대한 개념이 없어도 이미지로 계획 가능 — (A) 개념 없이도 구체적인 사고가 가능

| 문제 풀이 순서 | ★★★ [정답률 52%]

1st 각 문단의 내용을 파악하고, 글의 논리적인 순서를 추론한다.

┌ **주어진 글:** 적어도 일부 동물은 언어가 부족함에도 불구하고 사고할 수 있다고 가정해 보자.

➡ **주어진 글 뒤:** 언어가 부족하지만 사고가 실제 이루어지는 상황이 제시될 것이다.

┌ **(A):** 이것(This)은 다람쥐가 개념이 부족하다는 것을 의미하는 것이 아니라, 단지 다람쥐가 이 사고의 구체적인 형태를 위해 그것들이 필요하지 않다는 것을 의미한다. 우리가 동물이 개념을 가지고 있다고 말할 수 있기 위해서, 그 동물이 사고할 수 있다는 것뿐만 아니라 어떤 특정한 능력을 가지고 있다는 것을 우리는 보여 주어야 한다.

➡ **(A) 앞:** 다람쥐는 개념이 필요하지 않다는 것과 관련된 This가 무엇인지 앞에 나와야 한다. ▶ 주어진 글에는 언어 없이도 사고할 수 있다는 내용 외에 어떠한 사례도 없으므로 (A) 앞에 올 수 없음

(A) 뒤: 동물의 행동에 개념이 필수적이지는 않고 동물이 개념을 가진다고 말하려면 사고 능력뿐 아니라 특정한 능력을 지녔음을 입증해야 한다는 내용으로 마무리되었으므로 글의 마지막일 가능성이 높다.

┌ **(B):** 이것(this)을 하기 위해서, 원칙적으로 다람쥐는 나뭇가지의 개념이 필요하지 않고 또한 나무의 개념도 필요하지 않다. 예를 들어, 다람쥐가 이미지로 생각하는 능력, 즉, 다람쥐가 다양한 경로를 상상하고 시도해 볼 수 있는 나무에 대한 머릿속 지도를 만드는 능력만 가지고 있는 것으로 충분할 수도 있다.

➡ **(B) 앞:** 나뭇가지나 나무와 관련된 this가 무엇인지 앞에 나와야 한다. ▶ 주어진 글에는 다람쥐나 나뭇가지 등 어떠한 사례도 없으므로 (B) 앞에 올 수 없음

(B) 뒤: 다람쥐가 이미지로 생각하는 능력만 있어도 충분하다는 내용을 (A)에서 This로 다시 언급하며, 이는 개념이 부족하다는 것이 아니라, 개념이 필요하지 않은 것이라는 내용으로 이어진다. ▶ (B) 뒤에 (A)가 와야 함 (순서: (B) → (A))

┌ **(C):** 이것이 그들(they)이 개념을 가지고 있다고 반드시 의미하지는 않는데, 왜냐하면 사고의 어떤 형태는 비(非)개념적일 수도 있기 때문이다. 예를 들어, 우리는 현재 서 있는 나뭇가지에서 앞쪽 나무의 나뭇가지로 가는 방법을 계획하고 있는 다람쥐를 상상해 볼 수 있다.

➡ **(C) 앞:** 개념을 가지지 않을 수도 있다는 they는 주어진 글에서 언어가 부족해도 사고할 수 있는 일부 동물들을 나타낸다. ▶ (C) 앞에 주어진 글이 와야 함 (순서: 주어진 글 → (C))

(C) 뒤: 다람쥐가 나뭇가지마다 이동하는 예시가 등장했으므로, (B)에서 다람쥐가 이동하기 위해 나뭇가지의 개념이 필요하지 않다는 내용으로 이어진다. ▶ (C) 뒤에 (B)가 와야 함 (순서: 주어진 글 → (C) → (B) → (A))

2nd 글이 한눈에 들어오도록 정리하여 정답을 확인한다.

주어진 글: 일부 동물은 언어가 부족하더라도 사고할 수 있다.
→ **(C):** 일부 사고는 비개념적일 수 있다.
→ **(B):** 다람쥐는 나뭇가지의 개념 없이도 이미지로 경로를 상상하여 이동할 수 있다.
→ **(A):** 개념 없이도 구체적인 사고를 할 수 있다.
▶ 주어진 글 다음에 이어질 글의 순서는 (C) → (B) → (A)이므로 정답은 ⑤임

37 정답 ⑤ ＊연골의 작동 원리와 중요성

Cartilage is extremely important / for the healthy functioning of a joint, / especially if that joint bears weight, / like your knee. //

연골은 아주 중요하며 / 관절의 건강한 기능에 / 특히 그 관절이 당신의 무게를 지탱한다면 그렇다 / 무릎처럼 //

(A) This squeezing of joint fluid into and out of the cartilage / helps it respond to the off-and-on pressure of walking / without breaking under the pressure. //

이러한 관절 윤활액의 연골 안팎으로의 압착은 / 연골이 걷는 것의 반복적인 압력에 반응할 수 있도록 돕는다 / 압력에 부서지지 않고 //

(B) The cartilage in your left knee / then "drinks in" synovial fluid, / in much the same way that a sponge soaks up liquid / when put in water. //

당신의 왼쪽 무릎의 연골은 / 그러면 윤활액을 '흡수'한다 / 거의 같은 방식으로 / 스펀지가 액체를 흡수하는 것과 / 물에 담겼을 때 //

When you take another step / and transfer the weight back onto your left leg, / much of the fluid squeezes out of the cartilage. //

당신이 또 다른 한 걸음을 내딛어 / 체중을 다시 왼쪽 다리로 옮길 때 / 윤활액의 상당 부분이 압착되어 연골 밖으로 나간다 //

(C) Imagine for a moment / that you're looking into the inner workings of your left knee / as you walk down the street. //
잠시 상상해 봐라 / 당신이 왼쪽 무릎의 내부 작동 방식을 들여다본다고 / 길을 걸으며 //

When you shift your weight / from your left leg to your right, / the pressure on your left knee is released. //
문장의 주어 / 수동태 동사
당신이 체중을 옮길 때 / 왼쪽 다리에서 오른쪽 다리로 / 당신의 왼쪽 무릎의 압력이 풀린다 //

- joint ⓝ 관절   - bear ⓥ 지탱하다   - weight ⓝ 무게, 체중
- squeeze ⓥ 압착하다   - respond ⓥ 반응하다
- off-and-on ⓐ 반복적인   - soak up 흡수하다
- transfer ⓥ 옮기다, 이동하다   - look into ~을 들여다보다
- shift ⓥ 옮기다   - pressure ⓝ 압력   - release ⓥ 풀다

연골은 관절의 건강한 기능에 아주 중요하며, 특히 그 관절이 당신의 무릎처럼 무게를 지탱한다면 그렇다. (C) 당신이 길을 걸으며 왼쪽 무릎의 내부 작동 방식을 들여다본다고 잠시 상상해 봐라. 당신이 왼쪽 다리에서 오른쪽 다리로 체중을 옮길 때, 당신의 왼쪽 무릎의 압력이 풀린다. (B) 그러면 당신의 왼쪽 무릎의 연골은 스펀지가 물에 담겼을 때 액체를 흡수하는 것과 거의 같은 방식으로 윤활액을 '흡수'한다. 당신이 또 다른 한 걸음을 내딛어 체중을 다시 왼쪽 다리로 옮길 때, 윤활액의 상당 부분이 압착되어 연골 밖으로 나간다. (A) 이러한 관절 윤활액의 연골 안팎으로의 압착은 연골이 걷는 것의 반복적인 압력에 부서지지 않고 반응할 수 있도록 돕는다.

(A)에서 윤활액의 역할을 설명했으므로 (B)에 이어져야 자연스러움
주어진 글 다음에 이어질 글의 순서로 가장 적절한 것을 고르시오. [3점]
① (A) — (C) — (B) 주어진 글에서 윤활액이 언급되지 않았으므로 (A)가 바로 올 수 없음
② (B) — (A) — (C) ┐
③ (B) — (C) — (A) ┘ then을 받을 만한 표현이 주어진 글에 없음
④ (C) — (A) — (B) 연골의 관절은 무게를 지탱함 — (C) 보행 시 한쪽 다리로 체중을 옮기면 반대쪽 무릎의 압력이 풀림 — (B) 연골이 윤활액을 흡수한 후, 내딛을 때 윤활액이 압착되어 연골 밖으로 나감 — (A) 윤활액의 압착 덕분에 연골이 보호됨
⑤ (C) — (B) — (A)

| **문제 풀이 순서** | ✱✱✲ [정답률 63%]

1st 각 문단의 내용을 파악하고, 글의 논리적인 순서를 추론한다.

주어진 글: 연골은 관절의 건강한 기능에 아주 중요하며, 특히 그 관절이 당신의 무릎처럼 무게를 지탱한다면 그렇다.

➡ **주어진 글 뒤:** 연골이 관절을 보호하는 원리를 설명할 것이다.

(A): 이러한(This) 관절 윤활액의 연골 안팎으로의 압착(squeezing)은 연골이 걷는 것의 반복적인 압력에 부서지지 않고 반응할 수 있도록 돕는다.

➡ **(A) 앞:** 연골을 보호하는 This squeezing이 무엇인지 앞에 언급되어야 한다.
▶ 주어진 글에는 연골의 중요성과 기능만 제시되었으므로 (A) 앞에 올 수 없음
(A) 뒤: 관절 윤활액의 압착 덕분에 연골이 부서지지 않고 반응할 수 있게 된다고 했으므로 연골이 보호되는 과정의 마지막, 다시 말해, 글의 마지막일 가능성이 높다.

(B): 그러면(then) 당신의 왼쪽 무릎의 연골은 스펀지가 물에 담겼을 때 액체를 흡수하는 것과 거의 같은 방식으로 윤활액을 '흡수'한다. 당신이 또 다른 한 걸음을 내딛어 체중을 다시 왼쪽 다리로 옮길 때, 윤활액의 상당 부분이 압착되어(squeezes) 연골 밖으로 나간다.

➡ **(B) 앞:** 다음 순서를 나타내는 then이 나왔으므로, 왼쪽 무릎의 연골이 윤활액을 흡수하기 이전 과정이 앞에 나와야 한다.
▶ 주어진 글에는 연골의 중요성과 기능만 제시되었으므로 (B) 앞에 올 수 없음
(B) 뒤: 연골 안으로 흡수된 윤활액이 압착되어 연골 밖으로 나가는 과정을 (A)에서 This squeezing으로 다시 언급했다.
▶ (B) 뒤에 (A)가 와야 함 (순서: (B) ➡ (A))

(C): 당신이 길을 걸으며 왼쪽 무릎의 내부 작동 방식을 들여다본다고 잠시 상상해 봐라. 당신이 왼쪽 다리에서 오른쪽 다리로 체중을 옮길 때, 당신의 왼쪽 무릎의 압력이 풀린다.

➡ **(C) 앞:** 주어진 글에서 연골이 관절에 중요하다고 했는데, 왼쪽 무릎의 내부 작동 방식을 예로 들며 이를 설명한다.
▶ (C) 앞에 주어진 글이 와야 함 (순서: 주어진 글 ➡ (C))
(C) 뒤: 왼쪽 무릎의 압력이 풀린다는 내용 뒤에, (B)의 then이 연골이 윤활액을 흡수한다는 내용을 받는다.
▶ (C) 뒤에 (B)가 와야 함 (순서: 주어진 글 ➡ (C) ➡ (B) ➡ (A))

2nd 글이 한눈에 들어오도록 정리하여 정답을 확인한다.

주어진 글: 연골은 무게를 지탱하는 무릎 관절의 기능에 아주 중요하다.
➡ **(C):** 걷는 동안 왼쪽 다리에서 오른쪽 다리로 체중을 옮기면 왼쪽 무릎의 압력이 줄어든다.
➡ **(B):** 그러면 왼쪽 무릎의 연골은 윤활액을 흡수하고, 다시 체중을 왼쪽 다리로 옮기면 이를 압착해 밖으로 내보낸다.
➡ **(A):** 윤활액의 압착 덕분에 연골이 반복적인 걷기 압력에도 견딜 수 있다.
▶ 주어진 글 다음에 이어질 글의 순서는 (C) ➡ (B) ➡ (A)이므로 정답은 ⑤임

38 정답 ③   ＊ 놀이를 통한 아이들의 도덕성 발달

글의 흐름으로 보아, 주어진 문장이 들어가기에 가장 적절한 곳을 고르시오.

단서 1 도덕성을 설명하기 위해 앞에서 물잔을 예로 듦
Piaget argued / that children's understanding of morality / is like their understanding of those water glasses: / we can't say / that it is innate or kids learn it directly from adults. //
Piaget는 주장했다 / 도덕에 대한 아이들의 이해는 / 그런 물잔에 대한 이해와 같은데 / 즉 우리가 말할 수 없다고 / 그것이 타고났다거나 혹은 아이들이 어른들로부터 직접 그것을 배운다고 //

Piaget put the same amount of water / into two different glasses: / a tall narrow glass and a wide glass, / then asked kids to compare two glasses. //
병렬 구조
Piaget는 똑같은 양의 물을 넣고 / 두 개의 서로 다른 유리잔에 / 키가 크고 폭이 좁은 유리잔과 넓은 유리잔 / 그런 다음 아이들에게 두 유리잔을 비교하라고 요청했다 //

(①) Kids younger than six or seven usually say / that the tall narrow glass now holds more water, / because the level is higher. // 단서 2 아이들은 상황을 단편적으로만 이해함
6세 혹은 7세보다 더 어린 아이들은 대개 말하는데 / 키가 크고 폭이 좁은 유리잔에 물이 더 많이 담겨 있다고 / 왜냐하면 수위가 더 높기 때문이다 // 단서 3 아이들은 놀이를 통해 개념을 이해함

(②) And when they are ready, / they figure out the conservation of volume for themselves / just by playing with cups of water. //
by -ing: ~함으로써
그리고 아이들이 준비가 되어 있을 때 / 그들은 부피의 보존을 스스로 알아낸다 / 물이 든 컵을 갖고 놂으로써 //
부사절 접속사 (~ 하면서) 단서 4 다른 아이들과 놀면서 도덕성을 깨달음

(③) Rather, / it is self-constructed / as kids play with other kids. //
오히려 / 그것은 아이들이 스스로 구성해 낸 것이다 / 다른 아이들과 놀면서 //
동명사구 주어
(④) Taking turns in a game is like / pouring water back and forth between glasses. //
게임을 순서대로 돌아가며 하는 것은 같다 / 물잔 사이를 왔다 갔다 하며 물을 붓는 것과 //
'일단 ~하면'
(⑤) Once kids have reached the age of five or six, / then playing games and working things out together will help / them
동명사구 주어
learn about fairness far more effectively / than any teaching
비교급 강조 부사
from adults. // 단서 5 함께 놀며 공평과 같은 가치를 배움
일단 아이들이 5세 혹은 6세에 이르면 / 함께 게임을 하고 문제를 해결해 나가는 것이 도움이 될 것이다 / 그들이 훨씬 더 효과적으로 공평함에 대해 배우는 데 / 어른들로부터의 그 어떤 가르침보다 //

- argue ⓥ 주장하다   - morality ⓝ 도덕(성)   - amount ⓝ 양
- narrow ⓐ 좁은   - level ⓝ 수위, 높이   - volume ⓝ 부피
- self-constructed ⓐ 스스로 구성해 낸   - reach ⓥ ~에 이르다
- fairness ⓝ 공평함

Piaget는 똑같은 양의 물을 키가 크고 폭이 좁은 유리잔과 넓은 유리잔, 두 개의 서로 다른 유리잔에 넣고 그런 다음 아이들에게 두 유리잔을 비교하라고 요청했다. (①) 6세 혹은 7세보다 더 어린 아이들은 키가 크고 폭이 좁은 유리잔에 물이 더 많이 담겨 있다고 대개 말하는데, 왜냐하면 수위가 더 높기 때문이다. (②) 그리고 아이들이 준비가 되어 있을 때, 그들은 물이 든 컵들을 갖고 놂으로써 부피의 보존을 스스로 알아낸다. (③ Piaget는 도덕성에 대한 아이들의 이해는 그런 물잔에 대한 이해와 같은데, 즉 우리가 그것이 타고났다거나 혹은 아이들이 어른들로부터 직접 그것을 배운다고 말할 수 없다고 주장했다.) 오히려 그것은 아이들이 다른 아이들과 놀면서 스스로 구성해 낸 것이다. (④) 게임을 순서대로 돌아가며 하는 것은 물잔 사이를 왔다 갔다 하며 물을 붓는 것과 같다. (⑤) 일단 아이들이 5세 혹은 6세에 이르면, 함께 게임을 하고 문제를 해결해 나가는 것이 어른들로부터의 그 어떤 가르침보다 그들이 훨씬 더 효과적으로 공평함에 대해 배우는 데 도움이 될 것이다.

│ 문제 풀이 순서 │ ★★★ [정답률 50%]

1st 주어진 문장을 해석하고, 앞뒤에 어떤 내용이 올지 생각한다.

Piaget argued that children's understanding of morality is like their understanding of those water glasses: we can't say that it is innate or kids learn it directly from adults.

Piaget는 도덕성에 대한 아이들의 이해는 그런 물잔에 대한 이해와 같은데, 즉 우리가 그것이 타고났다거나 혹은 아이들이 어른들로부터 직접 그것을 배운다고 말할 수 없다고 주장했다.

➡ **주어진 문장 앞:** those water glasses(그런 물잔)라고 했으므로, **단서** 아이들의 도덕성 이해도를 설명하는 예시로 '물잔'이 언급되고 다른 내용으로 전환되는 부분을 찾아야 한다. **발상**

2nd 각 선택지의 앞뒤 흐름이 매끄러운지 확인한다.

①의 앞 문장과 뒤 문장

┌ **앞 문장:** Piaget는 똑같은 양의 물을 키가 크고 폭이 좁은 유리잔과 넓은 유리잔, 두 개의 서로 다른 유리잔에 넣고 그런 다음 아이들에게 두 유리잔을 비교하라고 요청했다.

└ **뒤 문장:** 6세 혹은 7세보다 더 어린 아이들은 키가 크고 폭이 좁은 유리잔에 물이 더 많이 담겨 있다고 대개 말하는데, 왜냐하면 수위가 더 높기 때문이다.

➡ 아이들에게 모양이 다른 두 물잔을 비교하라고 요청했고, 6~7세보다 어린 아이들이 단순히 수위를 기준으로 물의 양을 판단했다는 결과가 앞으로 이어진다.
▶ 주어진 문장이 **①**에 들어갈 수 없음

②의 앞 문장과 뒤 문장

┌ **앞 문장:** ①의 뒤 문장과 같음

└ **뒤 문장:** 그리고 아이들이 준비가 되어 있을 때, 그들은 물이 든 컵들을 갖고 놂으로써 부피의 보존을 스스로 알아낸다.

➡ 아이들이 6~7세 이전에는 물의 양을 단순한 기준으로 판단했지만, 나중에 물잔을 갖고 놀면서 스스로 부피 보존의 개념을 알아낸다는 내용이 이어진다.
▶ 주어진 문장이 **②**에 들어갈 수 없음

③의 앞 문장과 뒤 문장

┌ **앞 문장:** ②의 뒤 문장과 같음

└ **뒤 문장:** 오히려(Rather) 그것(it)은 아이들이 다른 아이들과 놀면서 스스로 구성해 낸 것이다.

➡ 물잔 예시가 마무리되고 오히려 아이들이 it을 스스로 구성한다고 했는데, 이는 물잔이나 부피의 보존 자체를 가리키는 것이 아니므로 앞뒤 문장이 이어지지 않는다. 주어진 문장에 아이들의 도덕성 이해가 물잔 이해와 같다고 했으므로, it은 도덕성에 대한 이해를 가리킨다. ▶ 주어진 문장이 **③**에 들어가야 함

---

④의 앞 문장과 뒤 문장

┌ **앞 문장:** ③의 뒤 문장과 같음

└ **뒤 문장:** 게임을 순서대로 돌아가며 하는 것은 물잔 사이를 왔다 갔다 하며 물을 붓는 것과 같다.

➡ 아이들이 놀이를 통해 도덕성을 스스로 구성한 예를 들기 위해, 물잔 사이를 왔다 갔다 하며 물을 붓는 게임을 언급했다. ▶ 주어진 문장이 **④**에 들어갈 수 없음

⑤의 앞 문장과 뒤 문장

┌ **앞 문장:** ④의 뒤 문장과 같음

└ **뒤 문장:** 일단 아이들이 5세 혹은 6세에 이르면, 함께 게임을 하고 문제를 해결해 나가는 것이 어른들로부터의 그 어떤 가르침보다 그들이 훨씬 더 효과적으로 공평함에 대해 배우는 데 도움이 될 것이다.

➡ 게임의 순서를 지키는 것을 물잔 놀이를 통해 배운다는 점에 이어서, 공평함을 배우려면 어른의 가르침보다 놀이를 통해 배우는 것이 더 효과적이라는 내용으로 글이 마무리된다. ▶ 주어진 문장이 **⑤**에 들어갈 수 없음

39 정답 ⑤ ＊냉방 설비의 지혜

글의 흐름으로 보아, 주어진 문장이 들어가기에 가장 적절한 곳을 고르시오.

But / all this **wisdom** about how to deal with heat, / **accumulated over centuries of practical experience**, / **is** all too often ignored. //
불가산 명사 / 분사구문 / 단수 동사
그러나 / 열을 다루는 방법에 대한 이 모든 지혜는 / 수 세기의 실제적인 경험을 하면서 축적됐는데 / 너무 자주 간과된다 //

The rise of air-conditioning accelerated / the construction of sealed boxes, / **where** the building's only airflow is through the filtered ducts / of the air-conditioning unit. //
계속적 용법의 관계부사
냉방 설비의 부상은 가속화했는데 / 밀폐된 구조물의 건설을 / 그곳에서 건물의 유일한 공기 흐름은 여과된 배관을 통해서 이루어진다 / 냉방 설비 장치의 //

It doesn't have to be this way. //
그것이 이러한 방식일 필요는 없다 //

Look at any old building / in a hot climate, / **whether** it's in Sicily or Marrakesh or Tehran. //
부사절 접속사 (~이든 아니든)
오래된 아무 건물이나 보아라 / 더운 기후에 있는 / Sicily에 있든 Marrakesh에 있든 Tehran에 있든 간에 //

(①) Architects understood the importance / of shade, airflow, light colors. //
건축가들은 중요성을 이해했다 / 그늘, 공기 흐름, 밝은 색상의 //

(②) They oriented buildings / **to capture** cool breezes / and **block** the worst heat of the afternoon. //
부사적 용법 (목적)
그들은 건물을 향하게 했다 / 시원한 산들바람을 잡아 두고 / 오후의 가장 혹독한 열기를 막을 수 있도록 //

(③) They built with thick walls / and white roofs / and transoms over doors / **to encourage** airflow. //
부사적 용법 (목적)
그들은 두꺼운 벽 건물을 지었다 / 흰색 지붕과 / 문 위의 채광창을 / 공기 흐름을 촉진하기 위해서 //

(④) **Anyone** / who has ever spent a few minutes in a mudbrick house in Tucson, / or walked on the narrow streets of old Seville, / **knows** how well these construction methods work. //
핵심 주어 (단수) / 단수동사 / **단서 1** 전통적인 냉방 설비가 다양한 지역에서 사용되고 있고 잘 작동함
어느 누구든 / Tucson의 진흙 벽돌 집에서 몇 분을 보내 봤거나 / 옛 Seville의 좁은 길을 걸어 본 / 이 건설 방법이 얼마나 잘 작동하는지 안다 //

(⑤) In this sense, / air-conditioning is not just a technology of personal comfort; / it is also a technology of forgetting. //
이러한 의미에서 / 냉방 설비는 개인적인 안락의 기술일 뿐만 아니라 / 이것은 망각의 기술이다 //
단서 2 전통적으로 효과적인 냉방 설비를 망각한 채로 여전히 다른 냉방 설비가 발전함

- air-conditioning ⓝ 냉방 설비
- accelerate ⓥ 가속화하다
- box ⓝ 구조물
- airflow ⓝ 공기 흐름
- unit ⓝ 장치
- architect ⓝ 건축가
- breeze ⓝ 산들바람
- comfort ⓝ 안락

냉방 설비의 부상은 밀폐된 구조물의 건설을 가속화했는데, 그곳에서 건물의 유일한 공기 흐름은 냉방 설비 장치의 여과된 배관을 통해서 이루어진다. 그것이 이러한 방식일 필요는 없다. Sicily에 있든 Marrakesh에 있든 Tehran에 있든 간에, 더운 기후에 있는 오래된 아무 건물이나 보아라. (①) 건축가들은 그늘, 공기 흐름, 밝은 색상의 중요성을 이해했다. (②) 그들은 시원한 산들바람을 잡아 두고 오후의 가장 혹독한 열기를 막을 수 있도록 건물을 향하게 했다. (③) 그들은 공기 흐름을 촉진하기 위해서 두꺼운 벽과 흰색 지붕과 문 위의 채광창을 가지고 있는 건물을 지었다. (④) Tucson의 진흙 벽돌 집에서 몇 분을 보내 봤거나, 옛 Seville의 좁은 길을 걸어 본 어느 누구든 이 건설 방법이 얼마나 잘 작동하는지 안다. (⑤ 그러나 열을 다루는 방법에 대한 이 모든 지혜는, 수 세기의 실제적인 경험을 하면서 축적됐는데, 너무 자주 간과된다.) 이러한 의미에서, 냉방 설비는 개인적인 안락의 기술일 뿐만 아니라, 이것은 망각의 기술이다.

| 문제 풀이 순서 | ★★★ [정답률 48%]

1st 주어진 문장을 해석하고, 연결어, 지시어 등을 확인한다.

┌ But all this wisdom about how to deal with heat, accumulated over centuries of practical experience, is all too often ignored.
│ 그러나 열을 다루는 방법에 대한 이 모든 지혜는, 수 세기의 실제적인 경험을 하면서 축적됐는데, 너무 자주 간과된다.

➡ 주어진 문장 앞: 앞의 내용을 가리키는 all this wisdom이 있으므로, (단서) 열을 다루는 전통적인 방법들과 그 예시가 전부 주어진 문장 앞에 제시될 것이다. (발상)

➡ 주어진 문장 뒤: But과 ignored가 있으므로 (단서) 앞의 내용과는 다르게, 열을 다루는 전통적인 방법들이 간과된다는 내용이 뒤에 이어질 것이다. (발상)

2nd 각 선택지의 앞뒤 흐름이 매끄러운지 확인한다.

①의 앞 문장과 뒤 문장

┌ 앞 문장: Sicily에 있든 Marrakesh에 있든 Tehran에 있든 간에, 더운 기후에 있는 오래된 아무 건물이나 보아라.
└ 뒤 문장: 건축가들은 그늘, 공기 흐름, 밝은 색상의 중요성을 이해했다.

➡ 더운 기후의 건축에는 그늘 등 여러 요소의 중요성이 반영되어 있다는 흐름으로 앞뒤 내용이 이어진다. ▶ 주어진 문장이 ①에 들어갈 수 없음

②의 앞 문장과 뒤 문장

┌ 앞 문장: ①의 뒤 문장과 같음
└ 뒤 문장: 그들은 시원한 산들바람을 잡아 두고 오후의 가장 혹독한 열기를 막을 수 있도록 건물을 향하게 했다.

➡ 건축 요소 중 공기 흐름이 반영된 예시가 자연스럽게 연결되었다.
▶ 주어진 문장이 ②에 들어갈 수 없음

③의 앞 문장과 뒤 문장

┌ 앞 문장: ②의 뒤 문장과 같음
└ 뒤 문장: 그들은 공기 흐름을 촉진하기 위해서 두꺼운 벽과 흰색 지붕과 문 위의 채광창을 가지고 있는 건물을 지었다.

➡ 건축 요소 중 공기 흐름 및 밝은 색상과 그 외 요소가 반영된 예시가 자연스럽게 연결되었다. ▶ 주어진 문장에 ③에 들어갈 수 없음

④의 앞 문장과 뒤 문장

┌ 앞 문장: ③의 뒤 문장과 같음
└ 뒤 문장: Tucson의 진흙 벽돌 집에서 몇 분을 보내 봤거나, 옛 Seville의 좁은 길을 걸어 본 어느 누구든 이 건설 방법이 얼마나 잘 작동하는지 안다.

➡ 앞에 언급된 전통적인 냉방 설비의 예시에 이어서, 이러한 설비들이 여전히 잘 작동한다는 내용이 자연스럽게 연결되었다. ▶ 주어진 문장이 ④에 들어갈 수 없음

⑤의 앞 문장과 뒤 문장

┌ 앞 문장: ④의 뒤 문장과 같음
└ 뒤 문장: 이러한 의미에서, 냉방 설비는 개인적인 안락의 기술일 뿐만 아니라, 이것은 망각의 기술이다.

➡ In this sense가 있으므로 망각에 관한 내용이 앞에 있어야 하는데, 앞 문장에는 옛 냉방 설비가 충분히 잘 작동한다는 내용밖에 없어서 앞뒤 내용이 이어지지 않는다. 주어진 문장에 열을 다루는 지혜가 오래 축적되었지만 '간과된다'고 했으므로, 냉방 설비가 '망각의 기술'이라는 문장과 자연스럽게 연결된다.
▶ 주어진 문장이 ⑤에 들어가야 함

40 정답 ① ＊창의적 사고의 필요성

In the course / of trying to solve a problem with an invention, / you may encounter a brick wall of resistance / when you try to think your way logically through the problem. //
어떤 과정에서 / 발명품을 통해 문제를 해결하려고 하는 / 저항이라는 벽돌 벽에 맞닥뜨릴지도 모른다 / 여러분이 문제를 논리적으로 생각해 나가려고 애쓸 때 //

Such logical thinking is a linear type of process, / which uses our reasoning skills. // **단서 1** 논리적 사고는 선형적 과정임
계속적 용법의 주격 관계대명사
그러한 논리적 사고는 선형적 과정으로 / 우리의 추론 능력을 활용한다 //

= Logical thinking
This works fine / when we're operating / in the area of / what we know or have experienced. //
이는 잘 작동한다 / 우리가 작업할 때는 / ~의 영역에서 / 알고 있거나 경험해 본 //

However, / when we need to deal with new information, ideas, and viewpoints, / linear thinking will often come up short. //
그러나 / 우리가 새로운 정보, / 아이디어, 관점을 다뤄야 힐 때 / 선형적 사고로는 흔히 충분하지 않을 것이다 // **단서 2** 새로운 아이디어를 다룰 때 선형적(논리적) 사고는 불충분함

On the other hand, / creativity by definition involves / the application of new information to old problems / and the conception of new viewpoints and ideas. //
반면 / 창의성은 정의상 포함한다 / 기존 문제에 대한 새로운 정보의 적용과 / 새로운 관점과 아이디어의 구상을 //

앞 문장의 내용을 가리킴   부사절 접속사 (조건)
For this / you will be most effective / if you learn to operate in a nonlinear manner; / that is, use your creative brain. //
이를 위해서 / 여러분은 가장 효과적이 될 것이다 / 여러분이 비선형적 방식으로 작업하는 법을 배운다면 / 즉, 창의적인 뇌를 사용하는 법을 // **단서 3** 새로운 아이디어를 다룰 때는 비선형적(창의적) 사고가 효과적임
앞에 Being이 생략된 분사구문

Stated differently, / if you think in a linear manner, / you'll tend to be conservative / and keep coming up with techniques / which are already known. //
다시 말해 / 여러분이 선형적인 방식으로 사고하면 / 보수적으로 되고 / 기술을 계속 떠올리려 할 것이다 / 이미 알려진 //

선행사를 포함하는 관계대명사
This, of course, / is just what you don't want. //
이것이 물론 / 여러분이 원하지 않는 바로 그것이다 //

┌ → (A) **Logical** thinking works well with familiar problems / but falls short in dealing with new ideas, / for which creative thinking is needed / to come up with (B) **innovative** solutions. //
│ 전치사 + 계속적 용법의 관계대명사
│ 논리적 사고는 익숙한 문제에서는 잘 작동하지만 / 새로운 아이디어를 다루는 데에는 불충분한데 / 이를 위해서는 창의적 사고가 필요하다 / 혁신적인 해결책을 생각해 내는 데에 //

- invention ⑩ 발명품　　・encounter ⓥ 맞닥뜨리다, 직면하다
- resistance ⑩ 저항　　・logically ⓐⓓ 논리적으로
- reasoning ⑩ 추론　　・viewpoint ⑩ 관점　　・by definition 정의상
- application ⑩ 적용　　・conception ⑩ 구상
- effective ⓐ 효과적인　　・nonlinear ⓐ 비선형적
- manner ⑩ 방식　　・state ⓥ 말하다　　・innovative ⓐ 혁신적인
- flexible ⓐ 유연한　　・instant ⓐ 즉각적인　　・proven ⓐ 증명된
- superior ⓐ 우월한　　・collaborative ⓐ 협력하는

어떤 발명품을 통해 문제를 해결하려고 하는 과정에서, 여러분이 문제를 논리적으로 생각해 나가려고 애쓸 때 저항이라는 벽돌 벽에 맞닥뜨릴지도 모른다. 그러한 논리적 사고는 선형적 과정으로, 우리의 추론 능력을 활용한다. 이는 우리가 알고 있거나 경험해 본 영역에서 작업할 때는 잘 작동한다. 그러나 우리가 새로운 정보, 아이디어, 관점을 다뤄야 할 때 선형적 사고로는 흔히 충분하지 않을 것이다. 반면, 창의성은 정의상 기존 문제에 대한 새로운 정보의 적용과 새로운 관점과 아이디어의 구상을 포함한다. 이를 위해서 여러분이 비선형적 방식으로 작업하는 법, 즉, 창의적인 뇌를 사용하는 법을 배운다면 여러분은 가장 효과적이 될 것이다. 다시 말해, 여러분이 선형적인 방식으로 사고하면, 보수적으로 되고 이미 알려진 기술을 계속 떠올리려 할 것이다. 이것이 물론 여러분이 원하지 않는 바로 그것이다.

→ (A) 논리적 사고는 익숙한 문제에서는 잘 작동하지만, 새로운 아이디어를 다루는 데에는 불충분한데, 이를 위해서는 창의적 사고가 (B) 혁신적인 해결책을 생각해 내는 데에 필요하다.

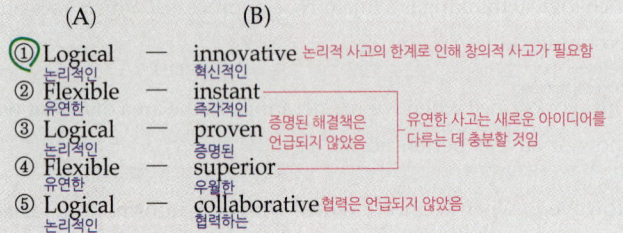

다음 글의 내용을 한 문장으로 요약하고자 한다. 빈칸 (A), (B)에 들어갈 말로 가장 적절한 것은?

	(A)	(B)
①	Logical 논리적인	innovative 혁신적인 — 논리적 사고의 한계로 인해 창의적 사고가 필요함
②	Flexible 유연한	instant 즉각적인
③	Logical 논리적인	proven 증명된 — 증명된 해결책은 언급되지 않았음
④	Flexible 유연한	superior 우월한 — 유연한 사고는 새로운 아이디어를 다루는 데 충분할 것임
⑤	Logical 논리적인	collaborative 협력하는 — 협력은 언급되지 않았음

왜 정답? ★★☆ [정답률 69%]

(A):
- 논리적 사고는 선형적 과정이다. 단서1
- 그러나 우리가 새로운 정보, 아이디어, 관점을 다뤄야 할 때 선형적 사고로는 흔히 충분하지 않을 것이다. 단서2
⇒ 선형적(논리적) 사고는 새로운 아이디어를 다뤄야 할 때는 충분하지 않을 것이라고 했음
▶ (A)에는 ①, ③, ⑤ Logical이 들어가야 함

(B):
- 이를 위해서 여러분이 비선형적 방식으로 작업하는 법, 즉, 창의적인 뇌를 사용하는 법을 배운다면 여러분은 가장 효과적이 될 것이다. 단서3
⇒ 선형적 사고로 해결할 수 없는 일, 즉 새로운(혁신적인) 해결책을 생각하려면 비선형적(창의적) 사고가 효과적이라고 했음
▶ (B)에는 ① innovative가 들어가야 하므로 정답은 ①임

왜 오답?
② 유연한 사고는 오히려 새로운 아이디어를 생각하는 데 효과적일 것이며, 즉각적인 해결책은 언급되지 않았다.
③ 증명된 해결책은 언급되지 않았다.
④ 유연한 사고는 오히려 새로운 아이디어를 생각하는 데 효과적일 것이며, 우월한 해결책은 언급되지 않았다.
⑤ 협력에 관한 해결책은 언급되지 않았다.

---

1 도입: 발명품으로 문제를 해결하려 할 때, 논리적 사고만으로는 저항에 부딪힘
2 전개: 선형적(논리적) 사고는 익숙한 작업에서는 효과적이지만 새로운 아이디어를 다룰 때는 불충분함
3 대조: 창의성은 새로운 아이디어와 관점을 적용하는 비선형적 사고를 포함함
4 부연: 새로운 아이디어를 다룰 때는 비선형적(창의적) 사고가 효과적임

41 ~ 42　★ 수량화의 문제점

view A as B: A를 B로 여기다
Some researchers view spoken languages / as incomplete devices / for capturing precise differences. //
일부 연구자는 발화된 언어를 여긴다 / 불완전한 도구로 / 정확한 차이를 포착하는 데에 //

They think / numbers represent / the most neutral language of description. //
그들은 생각한다 / 숫자가 나타낸다고 / 묘사의 가장 중립적인 언어를 //

However, / when our language of description is changed to numbers, / we do not move / toward greater (a) accuracy. //
그러나 / 우리의 묘사의 언어가 숫자로 바뀔 때 / 우리가 나아가지는 않는다 / 더 큰 정확성으로 //
41번 단서 1: 숫자로 묘사하는 것이 더 정확하지는 않음

Numbers are no more appropriate 'pictures of the world' / than words, music, or painting. // 41번 단서 2: 숫자가 세상을 묘사하는 최고의 방법은 아님
숫자가 더 적절한 '세상의 묘사'는 아니다 / 말, 음악, 또는 그림보다 //
부사절 접속사 (양보)
While useful for specific purposes (e.g. census taking, income distribution), / they (b) include(→ exclude) information of enormous value. // 42번 단서 1: 숫자에는 엄청난 가치(질적 및 심리적)를 지닌 정보가 없음
특정한 목적(예를 들어, 인구 조사, 소득 분포)에는 유용하지만 / 숫자는 엄청난 가치를 지닌 정보를 포함한다(→ 제외한다) //

For example, / the future lives of young students are tied / to their scores on national tests. //
예를 들어 / 어린 학생들의 미래의 삶은 매여 있다 / 그들의 전국 단위 시험 점수에 //
명사절 접속사 (~인지 아닌지)
In effect, / whether they can continue with their education, / where, / and at what cost / depends importantly on a handful of numbers. //
단수 동사
사실상 / 그들이 교육을 지속할 수 있는지 / 어디에서일지 / 그리고 얼마의 비용일지가 / 한 줌의 숫자에 중대하게 달려 있다 // 41번 단서 3, 42번 단서 2: 질적인 측면처럼 숫자가 설명할 수 없는 부분이 존재함

These numbers do not account for / the (c) quality of schools they have attended, / whether they have been tutored, / have supportive parents, / have test anxiety, and so on. //
이들 숫자는 설명하지 않는다 / 그들이 다닌 학교의 질 / 그들이 개인 교습을 받아 오는지 / 지지적인 부모가 있는지 / 시험 불안이 있는지 등의 여부를 //
분사구문을 이끄는 현재분사
Finally, / putting aside the many ways / in which statistical results can be manipulated, / there are ways / in which turning people's lives into numbers / is (d) morally insulating. //
전치사+관계대명사 (ways 수식)
마지막으로 / 많은 방식을 제쳐 두더라도 / 통계 결과가 조작될 수 있는 / 측면이 있다 / 사람들의 삶을 숫자로 바꾸는 것이 / 도덕적으로 차단하는 // 41번 단서 4: 삶을 수치화하면 도덕성이 차단됨

Statistics on crime, homelessness, or the spread of a disease say nothing / of people's suffering. //
범죄, 노숙자 문제, 질병의 확산에 관한 통계는 아무것도 말하지 않는다 / 사람들의 고통에 대해 //
전치사 (~처럼)
We read the statistics / as reports on events at a distance, / thus allowing us to (e) escape / without being disturbed. //
동명사의 수동태
우리는 그 통계를 읽는데 / 멀리 있는 사건에 대한 보고서처럼 / 그러므로 이것은 우리가 도망갈 수 있도록 해준다 / 동요되지 않고 //
「with + 명사 + 분사」; with 분사구문
Statistics are human beings / with the tears wiped off. //
통계는 인간이다 / 눈물이 닦인 //

Quantify with caution. //
수량화할 때는 신중해라 //

- **represent** ⓥ 나타내다, 표현하다 • **accuracy** ⓝ 정확성
- **census taking** 인구 조사 • **income distribution** 소득 분포
- **in effect** 사실상 • **test anxiety** 시험 불안 • **put aside** 제쳐 두다
- **way** ⓝ 방식, 측면 • **morally** ⓐⓓ 도덕적으로
- **homelessness** ⓝ 노숙자 문제 • **spread** ⓝ 확산
- **suffering** ⓝ 고통 • **disturb** ⓥ 동요시키다 • **wipe off** 닦아 내다
- **quantify** ⓥ 수량화하다 • **uncovered** ⓐ 드러난, 밝혀진
- **framework** ⓝ 체계 • **convey** ⓥ 전달하다

일부 연구자는 발화된 언어를 정확한 차이를 포착하는 데에 불완전한 도구로 여긴다. 그들은 숫자가 묘사의 가장 중립적인 언어를 나타낸다고 생각한다. 그러나, 우리의 묘사의 언어가 숫자로 바뀔 때, 우리가 더 큰 (a) 정확성으로 나아가지는 않는다. 숫자가 말, 음악, 또는 그림보다 더 적절한 '세상의 묘사'는 아니다. 특정한 목적(예를 들어, 인구 조사, 소득 분포)에는 유용하지만, 숫자는 엄청난 가치를 지닌 정보를 (b) 포함한다(→ 배제한다). 예를 들어, 어린 학생들의 미래의 삶은 그들의 전국 단위 시험 점수에 매여 있다. 사실상, 그들이 교육을 지속할 수 있는지, 어디에서일지, 그리고 얼마의 비용일지가 한 줌의 숫자에 중대하게 달려 있다. 이들 숫자는 그들이 다닌 학교의 (c) 질, 그들이 개인 교습을 받아 오는지, 지지적인 부모가 있는지, 시험 불안이 있는지 등의 여부를 설명하지 않는다. 마지막으로, 통계 결과가 조작될 수 있는 많은 방식을 제쳐 두더라도, 사람들의 삶을 숫자로 바꾸는 것이 (d) 도덕적으로 차단하는 측면이 있다. 범죄, 노숙자 문제, 질병의 확산에 관한 통계는 사람들의 고통에 대해 아무것도 말하지 않는다. 우리는 그 통계를 멀리 있는 사건에 대한 보고서처럼 읽는데, 그러므로 이것은 우리가 동요되지 않고 (e) 도망갈 수 있도록 해준다. 통계는 눈물이 닦인 인간이다. 수량화할 때는 신중해라.

41 정답 ①

윗글의 제목으로 가장 적절한 것은?

① Numbers Don't Tell Us Everything 숫자로 묘사할 수 없는 삶의 부분도 있음
숫자가 우리에게 모든 것을 말해주지는 않는다
② Human Stories Uncovered by the Numbers 인간의 삶의 모든 부분을
숫자로 드러난 인간의 이야기들 숫자로만 나타낼 수 없다는 것이 글의 내용임
③ Data: A Framework for Understanding Humans
데이터: 인간을 이해하기 위한 체계 작용하기에는 부족함
④ The Limitations of Language in Conveying Truth
진실을 전달하는 데 있어 언어의 한계 언어의 한계가 아니라 숫자의 한계에 관한 글임
⑤ The Advantages of Quantifying Human Experiences
인간의 경험을 수량화하는 것의 이점들 수량화의 이점은 언급되지 않음

〉왜 정답? ✹✹✤ [정답률 60%]

- 숫자로 묘사하는 것이 더 정확하지는 않다. [41번 단서 1]
- 숫자가 세상을 묘사하는 최고의 방법은 아니다. [41번 단서 2]
- 질적인 측면처럼 숫자로 설명할 수 없는 부분도 있다. [41번 단서 3]
- 삶을 수치화하면 도덕성이 차단되고 심리적인 측면을 파악할 수 없다. [41번 단서 4]

➡ 일부 연구자들은 숫자가 가장 중립적인 묘사 도구라고 여기지만, 숫자는 질적 및 심리적 정보를 담아내지 못하므로 모든 것을 설명하지는 못한다.

▶ 따라서 제목으로 가장 적절한 것은 ① '숫자가 우리에게 모든 것을 말해주지는 않는다'이다.

〉왜 오답?

② 인간의 이야기, 즉 삶의 모든 부분을 숫자로 나타낼 수는 없다는 것이 글의 주제이다.
③ 데이터는 인간을 이해하기 위한 체계 중 하나이지만 절대적인 도구는 아니다.
④ 언어의 한계가 아닌 숫자의 한계에 관한 내용이다.
⑤ 인간 경험을 수량화하는 것의 이점이 아닌 한계가 글의 주제이다.

42 정답 ②

밑줄 친 (a)~(e) 중에서 문맥상 낱말의 쓰임이 적절하지 않은 것은? [3점]

① (a) 숫자가 정확성의 향상을 보장하진 않음
정확성
② (b) 숫자는 질적 및 심리적 정보를 배제함
포함하다
③ (c) 질은 숫자로 표현할 수 없음
질
④ (d) 삶을 수치화하면 사회 문제에 대한 공감이 떨어지기에 도덕성과 멀어지게 함
도덕성
⑤ (e) 사회 문제에 관한 통계 결과에 감정적으로 동요되지 않고 멀어질 수 있게 함
도망가다

〉왜 정답? ✹✹✹ [정답률 29%]

② (b) include 포함하다

특정한 목적(예를 들어, 인구 조사, 소득 분포)에는 유용하지만, 숫자는 엄청난 가치를 지닌 정보를 (b) 포함한다.
배제한다

➡ 숫자는 삶의 질적 및 심리적 측면을 묘사할 수 없으므로, 숫자가 엄청난 가치를 가진 정보를 '포함한다'가 아니라 '배제한다'가 더 자연스럽다.

▶ include를 exclude(배제한다)와 같은 반의어로 바꿔야 함

〉왜 오답?

① (a) accuracy 정확성

그러나, 우리의 묘사의 언어가 숫자로 바뀔 때, 우리가 더 큰 (a) 정확성으로 나아가지는 않는다.

➡ 설명을 제공할 때, 숫자가 도움이 될 경우도 있지만 꼭 더 정확한 정보를 주는 것은 아니므로 '정확성'은 적절하다. ▶ accuracy는 문맥에 맞음

③ (c) quality 질

이들 숫자는 그들이 다닌 학교의 (c) 질, 그들이 개인 교습을 받아 오는지, 지지적인 부모가 있는지, 시험 불안이 있는지 등의 여부를 설명하지 않는다.

➡ 숫자로 '양'을 나타낼 수는 있지만 '질'을 설명할 수는 없으므로 문맥상 자연스럽다.

▶ quality는 문맥에 맞음

④ (d) morally 도덕적으로

마지막으로, 통계 결과가 조작될 수 있는 많은 방식을 제쳐 두더라도, 사람들의 삶을 숫자로 바꾸는 것이 (d) 도덕적으로 차단하는 측면이 있다.

➡ 삶을 수치화하면 그 삶에 대한 인간의 '도덕적인' 판단을 차단할 것이다.

▶ morally는 문맥에 맞음

⑤ (e) escape 도망가다

우리는 그 통계를 멀리 있는 사건에 대한 보고서처럼 읽는데, 그러므로 이것은 우리가 동요되지 않고 (e) 도망갈 수 있도록 해준다.

➡ 사회 문제에 관한 통계는 결과 외에 어떤 정보도 말하지 않기 때문에, 우리가 그 문제에 공감할 수 없게 되므로 감정적으로 동요되지 않고 '도망갈 수 있게 한다.

▶ escape는 문맥에 맞음

43~45 *알면 보물, 모르면 돌덩이

(A) Jack, / an Arkansas farmer, / was unhappy / because he
동격   45번 ① Jack은 자신의 농장에서 충분한 돈을 벌지 못했음
couldn't make enough money / from his farm. //
Jack은 / Arkansas주의 농부인 / 불행했다 / 충분한 돈을 벌지 못해 / 자신의 농장에서 //

He worked hard for many years, / but things didn't improve. //
여러 해 동안 열심히 일했지만 / 상황은 나아지지 않았다 //

He sold his farm / to his neighbor, Victor, / who was by no
means wealthy. // 45번 ② Jack은 자신의 이웃인 Victor에게 농장을 판매함
그는 자신의 농장을 팔았는데 / 자신의 이웃인 Victor에게 / 그는 결코 부유하지 않았다 //

Hoping for a fresh start, / he left for the big city / **to find** better opportunities. //
분사구문 · 부사적 용법(목적)
새로운 출발을 기대하며 / 그는 대도시로 떠났다 / 더 나은 기회를 찾아 //

Years passed, / but Jack still couldn't find the fortune / **he was looking for**. //
앞에 목적격 관계대명사가 생략됨
몇 년이 흘렀지만 / Jack은 여전히 부를 얻지 못했다 / 자신이 찾고 있던 //

Tired and broke, / (a) **he** returned to the area / **where** his old farm was. //
Being이 생략된 분사구문 · =Jack · 관계부사
43번 단서 1: 타지에서 실패 후 자신이 살던 곳으로 돌아옴
지치고 무일푼이 되어서 / 그는 지역으로 돌아왔다 / 자신의 옛 농장이 있던 //

* (A) 문단 요약: 농부인 Jack은 연속되는 실패 끝에 고향에 다시 돌아옴

(B) "How did you do all this?" / he asked. //
"어떻게 이 모든 걸 해냈어요" 라고 / 그가 물었다 //

And he continued, / "When you bought the farm, / you barely had any money. //
그리고 그는 계속해서 물었다 / "당신이 농장을 샀을 때 / 당신은 돈이 거의 없었잖아요 //

How did you get so rich?" //
어떻게 그렇게 부자가 되었죠"라고 //

Victor smiled and said, / "I owe it all to (b) **you**. //
=Jack
Victor는 미소를 지으며 / "그 모든 것이 다 당신 덕분이에요 //

There were diamonds on this land / — acres and acres of diamonds! //
이 땅에는 다이아몬드가 있었어요 / 대량의 다이아몬드가 //

I got rich / because I discovered those diamonds." //
43번 단서 2, 45번 ③ Victor는 다이아몬드를 발견하여 부자가 되었음
저는 부자가 되었어요 / 그 다이아몬드를 발견했기 때문에" //

"Diamonds?" / Jack said in disbelief. //
"다이아몬드요"라고 / Jack은 믿지 못하며 말했다 //

And he said, / "I knew every part of that land, / and there were no diamonds!" //
그리고 그는 말했다 / "제가 그 땅에 대해 전부 아는데 / 다이아몬드는 없었어요"라고 //

* (B) 문단 요약: Victor는 Jack의 옛 농장에서 다이아몬드를 발견해 부자가 되었다고 말함

(C) Victor reached into his pocket / and carefully pulled out something small and shiny. //
45번 ④ 주머니에서 작고 반짝이는 다이아몬드를 꺼냄
Victor는 자신의 주머니로 손을 뻗어 / 조심스럽게 작고 반짝이는 것을 꺼냈다 //

Holding it between (c) **his** fingers, / he let it catch the light. //
분사구문을 이끄는 현재분사 · =Victor's
그것을 자신의 손가락 사이에 잡고 / 그는 그것이 빛을 받도록 했다 //

He said, / "This is a diamond." //
그는 말했다 / "이것이 다이아몬드입니다"라고 //

Jack was amazed and said, / "I saw so many rocks like that / and thought **they** were useless. //
=many rocks
Jack은 놀라서 말했다 / "저는 그런 돌을 많이 봤는데 / 그것들이 쓸모가 없다고 생각했어요 //

They made farming so hard!" //
그것들이 농사짓는 걸 너무 힘들게 만들었어요"라고 //

Victor laughed and said, / "(d) **You** didn't know / what diamonds look like. //
=Jack
43번 단서 3: Victor는 다이아몬드를 알아보고 부자가 되었고, Jack은 그러지 못함
Victor는 웃으며 말했다 / "당신은 몰랐군요 / 다이아몬드가 어떻게 생겼는지 //

Sometimes, / treasures **are hidden** / right in front of us." //
수동태 동사
때때로 / 보물은 숨겨져 있으니까요 / 바로 우리 앞에"라고 //

* (C) 문단 요약: Jack과 달리 Victor는 다이아몬드를 알아봄

(D) One day, / he drove past his old land / and was shocked by what he saw. //
어느 날 / 그는 자신의 옛 땅을 운전해 지나가다가 / 그가 본 것에 깜짝 놀랐다 //

Victor, / the man who had bought the farm with very little money, / now seemed to be living a life of great success. //
동격
43번 단서 4: 농장을 팔고 나니 농장주는 부자가 되어 있었음
Victor가 / 아주 적은 돈으로 농장을 샀던 / 이제는 대단한 성공을 거둔 삶을 살고 있는 것처럼 보였다 //

He had torn down the farmhouse / and built a massive house in its place. //
45번 ⑤ 농가가 있던 자리에는 거대한 집이 생김
그는 농가를 허물었고 / 그것이 있던 자리에 거대한 집을 지었다 //

New buildings, trees, and flowers / adorned the well-kept property. //
새 건물들, 나무들, 그리고 꽃들이 / 잘 관리된 소유지를 꾸몄다 //

Jack could hardly believe / that (e) **he** had ever worked on this same land. //
=Jack
Jack은 도저히 믿을 수 없었다 / 자신이 예전에 이 똑같은 땅에서 일했던 것을 //

Curious, / he stopped to talk to Victor. //
Being이 생략된 분사구문
43번 단서 5: 부자가 된 비결을 알기 위해 질문함
궁금해서 / 그는 Victor에게 말을 걸기 위해 멈췄다 //

* (D) 문단 요약: Jack은 옛 농지가 크게 변한 것에 놀라서 Victor에게 말을 걺

- by no means 결코 ~이 아닌 • barely [ad] 거의 ~ 없이
- owe [v] 덕분이다 • disbelief [n] 믿지 않음, 불신 • treasure [n] 보물
- tear down 허물다 • massive [a] 거대한 • property [n] 소유지

(A) Arkansas주의 농부인 Jack은 자신의 농장에서 충분한 돈을 벌지 못해 불행했다. 여러 해 동안 열심히 일했지만, 상황은 나아지지 않았다. 그는 자신의 농장을 자신의 이웃인 Victor에게 팔았는데, 그는 결코 부유하지 않았다. 새로운 출발을 기대하며, 그는 더 나은 기회를 찾아 대도시로 떠났다. 몇 해가 흘렀지만, Jack은 여전히 자신이 찾고 있던 부를 얻지 못했다. 지치고 무일푼이 되어서, (a) 그는 자신의 옛 농장이 있던 지역으로 돌아왔다.

(D) 어느 날, 그는 자신의 옛 땅을 운전해 지나가다가 그가 본 것에 깜짝 놀랐다. 아주 적은 돈으로 농장을 샀던 Victor가 이제는 대단한 성공을 거둔 삶을 살고 있는 것처럼 보였다. 그는 농가를 허물었고 그것이 있던 자리에 거대한 집을 지었다. 새 건물들, 나무들, 그리고 꽃들이 잘 관리된 소유지를 꾸몄다. Jack은 (e) 자신이 예전에 이 똑같은 땅에서 일했던 것을 도저히 믿을 수 없었다. 궁금해서, 그는 Victor에게 말을 걸기 위해 멈췄다.

(B) "어떻게 이 모든 걸 해냈어요?"라고 그가 물었다. 그리고 그는 계속해서 "당신이 농장을 샀을 때, 당신은 돈이 거의 없었잖아요. 어떻게 그렇게 부자가 되었죠?"라고 물었다. Victor는 미소를 지으며, "그 모든 것이 다 (b) 당신 덕분이에요. 이 땅에는 다이아몬드가, 대량의 다이아몬드가 있었어요! 제가 부자가 된 것은 그 다이아몬드를 발견했기 때문이에요."라고 말했다. "다이아몬드요?"라고 Jack은 믿지 못하며 말했다. 그리고 그는 "제가 그 땅에 대해 전부 아는데, 다이아몬드는 없었어요!"라고 말했다.

(C) Victor는 자신의 주머니로 손을 뻗어 조심스럽게 작고 반짝이는 것을 꺼냈다. 그것을 (c) 자신의 손가락 사이에 잡고, 그는 그것이 빛을 받도록 했다. 그는 "이것이 다이아몬드입니다."라고 말했다. Jack은 놀라서 "저는 그런 돌을 많이 봤는데 그것들이 쓸모가 없다고 생각했어요. 그것들이 농사짓는 걸 너무 힘들게 만들었어요!"라고 말했다. Victor는 웃으며 "(d) 당신은 다이아몬드가 어떻게 생겼는지 몰랐군요. 때때로 보물은 바로 우리 앞에 숨겨져 있으니까요."라고 말했다.

43 정답 ④

주어진 글 (A)에 이어질 내용을 순서에 맞게 배열한 것으로 가장 적절한 것은?

① (B) — (D) — (C)
② (C) — (B) — (D) — Victor가 부자가 된 사실을 발견했다는 (D)가 (A) 바로 뒤에 이어짐
③ (C) — (D) — (B) — 부자가 된 비결을 밝히는 (C)가 가장 마지막에 옴
④ (D) — (B) — (C) — [(D) Jack은 자신이 팔았던 농장이 발전했음을 발견함 — (B) Victor가 농장에서 다이아몬드를 발견하여 부자가 되었음을 밝힘 — (C) Jack은 눈앞의 보물을 발견하지 못했으나 Victor는 이를 발견하여 부자가 되었음]
⑤ (D) — (C) — (B) — Jack이 농장에 다이아몬드가 없었다고 한 (B) 바로 뒤에 Victor가 다이아몬드를 직접 보여 주는 (C)가 와야 함

왜 정답 · 오답? ★★★ [정답률 79%]

(A): Jack은 농장에서 충분한 수입을 얻지 못해 Victor에게 농장을 팔고 대도시로 떠났지만 결국 실패하고 고향으로 돌아왔다.

➡ Jack이 고향으로 돌아온 후 어떤 일이 일어났는지에 주목한다.

(B): Jack이 Victor에게 어떻게 성공했는지 묻자, Victor는 농장 땅에서 다이아몬드를 발견해 부자가 되었다고 답했고, Jack은 그럴 리가 없다고 했다.

➡ Victor의 성공이 구체적으로 어떤 것인지 앞에 나와야 한다. 뒤에는 농장 땅에 다이아몬드가 있을 리 없다는 Jack의 말에 대한 Victor의 말이 이어져야 한다.

[(C): Victor는 Jack에게 실제 다이아몬드를 보여줬는데, Jack은 그것들이 보물임을 몰랐고 Victor는 때때로 보물이 우리 앞에 숨겨져 있다고 말했다.

➡ Jack이 농장 땅에 다이아몬드가 있을 리 없다고 한 (B)에 이어지는 내용으로, 눈앞의 보물을 알아보는 사람이 부자가 될 수 있다고 하며 글이 마무리된다.

[(D): Jack은 자신이 팔았던 농장이 Victor에 의해 멋지게 바뀐 것을 보고 놀라 Victor에게 말을 걸었다.

➡ Jack이 Victor에게 농장을 팔고 실패한 뒤에, 농장이 있던 지역으로 돌아왔다는 (A)에 이어지는 내용이다. Victor에게 어떻게 성공했는지 묻는 (B)가 뒤에 이어진다.
▶ 글의 순서는 ④ (D) ─ (B) ─ (C)임

44 정답 ③

밑줄 친 (a)~(e) 중에서 가리키는 대상이 나머지 넷과 다른 것은?
① (a)   ② (b)   ③(c)   ④ (d)   ⑤ (e)
 = Jack   = Jack   = Victor's   = Jack   = Jack

>왜 정답? ✱✱✱ [정답률 77%]
③ (c) his: 다이아몬드를 손가락 사이에 잡아 보여준 사람 ▶ Victor's

>왜 오답?
① (a) he: 무일푼이 되어서 옛 농장이 있던 지역으로 돌아온 사람 ▶ Jack
② (b) you: Victor가 부자가 될 수 있도록 도와준 사람 ▶ Jack
④ (d) You: 다이아몬드가 어떻게 생겼는지 몰랐던 사람 ▶ Jack
⑤ (e) he: 자신이 이 똑같은 땅에서 일했던 것을 믿지 못하는 사람 ▶ Jack

45 정답 ②

윗글에 관한 내용으로 적절하지 않은 것은?
① Jack은 자신의 농장에서 충분한 돈을 벌지 못했다.
    he couldn't make enough money from his farm
②Jack은 자신의 이웃인 Victor에게서 농장을 샀다.
    He sold his farm to his neighbor, Victor
③ Victor는 다이아몬드를 발견해서 부자가 되었다.
    I got rich because I discovered those diamonds
④ Victor는 자신의 주머니에서 작고 반짝이는 것을 꺼냈다.
    Victor reached into his pocket ~ pulled out something small and shiny.
⑤ Victor는 농가가 있던 자리에 거대한 집을 지었다.
    He had torn down the farmhouse and built a massive house in its place.

>왜 정답? ✱✱✱ [정답률 82%]
Jack이 Victor에게 농장을 판 것이므로 (He sold his farm to his neighbor, Victor) Jack이 자신의 이웃인 Victor에게서 농장을 샀다는 ②은 적절하지 않다.

>왜 오답?
① Jack은 자신의 농장에서 충분한 돈을 벌지 못했다. (he couldn't make enough money from his farm)
③ Victor는 다이아몬드를 발견해서 부자가 되었다. (I got rich because I discovered those diamonds)
④ Victor는 자신의 주머니에서 작고 반짝이는 것을 꺼냈다. (Victor reached into his pocket ~ pulled out something small and shiny.)
⑤ Victor는 농가가 있던 자리에 거대한 집을 지었다. (He had torn down the farmhouse and built a massive house in its place.)

1회 Dictation   문제 p. 22

01 was awarded first prize / drone club to perform / at the school field
02 reminded me / the audience a meaningful lesson / participated / role
03 in maintaining your overall well-being / emphasize how important / prevent / boost
04 wearing a striped-dress / round frame / caught my eye / the arrow sign
05 any particular place / already downloaded / entrance tickets / right away
06 decorations / frog character / noticed this cute bracelet / gift-wrapped
07 broke my cell phone / while getting off / repair shop / in advance
08 will be held at / low birth rate issue / affecting / live streaming service
09 coding experts / operate some robots / experimental booths / provided
10 budget / cross this one out / outdoor sports / beginner's class
11 finished / haven't practiced my speech
12 on social media / food waste
13 trouble managing / your chances of doing well / focus and memory
14 badminton quite often / nothing comes to mind / at the sports center / prepare anything
15 the star-viewing camp-night / would be clear / sudden change / as planned
[16~17] travel photographer / busy sidewalks / famous historical places / once-in-a-lifetime photos

1회 어휘 Review Test   문제 p. 26

01 희미한	15 distract from	29 peers
02 거대한	16 circumstances	30 connective
03 논리적으로	17 influential	31 fortunate
04 필수적인	18 pursuit	32 intense
05 강조하다	19 frequently	33 discontent
06 properly	20 morality	34 justify
07 boost	21 viewpoints	35 state
08 practical	22 stimulation	36 imply
09 alteration	23 appreciate	37 accelerated
10 affect	24 overall	38 ally
11 tear down	25 correct	39 partial
12 put aside	26 objective	40 complement
13 cross out	27 fictional	
14 have much say in	28 operate	

01 정답 ⑤ ＊학교 셔틀버스 운행 시간 변경 공지

M : Good afternoon, students!
남 : 학생 여러분, 안녕하세요!

This is your vice principal, Jack Eliot.
저는 Jack Eliot 교감입니다.

'~ 때문에'
Due to the heavy rain last night, there's some damage on the road and the road condition is not good.
어젯밤에 폭우로, 도로에 일부 피해가 있었고 도로 상태가 좋지 않습니다.

명사적 용법(decided의 목적어)
So we decided **to make** some rearrangements to the school shuttle bus schedule. **단서 1** 학교 셔틀버스 운행 시간을 재조정함
그래서 우리는 학교 셔틀버스 운행 시간을 재조정하기로 결정했습니다.

미래시제 수동태
From tomorrow, keep in mind that the bus schedule **will be delayed** by 15 minutes. **단서 2** 학교 셔틀버스 운행 시간이 15분 늦춰진다는 것을 알림
내일부터, 버스 운행 시간이 15분 지연될 예정이라는 점을 기억해 주세요.

We want to make sure all of you are safe.
모든 학생들이 안전하도록 하기 위함입니다.

This bus schedule change will continue for one week.
이 버스 일정 변동은 한 주 동안 계속될 것입니다.

We appreciate your understanding and cooperation.
여러분의 이해와 협조에 감사드립니다.

Thank you for your attention!
경청해 주셔서 감사합니다!

- vice principal 교감 · damage ⓝ 손상 · condition ⓝ 상태
- rearrangement ⓝ 재조정 · keep in mind 명심하다, ~을 기억해 두다
- delay ⓥ 지연시키다 · continue ⓥ 계속되다
- appreciate ⓥ 감사하다 · understanding ⓝ 이해
- cooperation ⓝ 협조

다음을 듣고, 남자가 하는 말의 목적으로 가장 적절한 것을 고르시오.
① 학교 체육관 공사 일정을 알리려고 학교 체육관에 관한 언급은 없음
② 학교 수업 시간표 조정을 안내하려고
학교 셔틀버스 일정을 조정하는 것이지 수업 시간표를 조정하는 것이 아님
③ 학교 통학 시 대중교통 이용을 권장하려고 학교 셔틀버스가 운행됨
④ 학교 방과 후 수업 신청 방식을 설명하려고 방과 후 수업에 관한 언급은 없음
⑤ 학교 셔틀버스 운행 시간 변경을 공지하려고
the bus schedule will be delayed by 15 minutes

＞왜 정답 ? ✽✽✽ [정답률 92%]
도로 상태가 좋지 않아서 학교 셔틀버스 운행 시간을 15분 늦추는 것으로 재조정했다는 사실을 알리고 있다. 따라서 남자가 하는 말의 목적으로 가장 적절한 것은 ⑤이다.

＞왜 오답 ?
① 학교 체육관에 관한 내용은 언급되지 않았다.
② 학교 셔틀버스 운행 시간이 조정되었으나 수업 시간표가 변동되지는 않았다. 주의
③ 학교 셔틀버스 운행 시간이 지연된다는 공지이며 대중교통을 이용하라는 내용은 없다.
④ 방과 후 수업에 관한 내용은 언급하지 않았다.

02 정답 ② ＊엄격한 전기 자전거 이용 규정의 필요성

목적어절 접속사
W : Brian, I heard **that** you are thinking of buying an electric bicycle.
여 : Brian, 나는 당신이 전기 자전거를 사려고 생각하는 중이라고 들었어요.

M : Yes, that's right.
남 : 네, 맞아요.

명령문
W : That's good. But **be careful** when you ride it.
여 : 잘됐네요. 그런데 자전거를 탈 때 조심해야 해요.

on one's way + 장소: ~로 가는(오는) 중인
M : Yeah, I know what you mean. **On my way here** I saw a man
지각동사의 목적격 보어(현재분사)
riding an electric bicycle without wearing a helmet.
남 : 네, 무슨 말인지 알죠. 여기 오는 길에 헬멧을 쓰지 않고 전기 자전거를 타고 있는 남자를 봤어요.

단서 1 자전거를 탈 때 기본 교통 규칙을 따르지 않는 사람들이 있음
W : Some riders don't even follow basic traffic rules.
여 : 일부 자전거를 타는 사람들은 기본 교통 규칙조차 따르지 않아요.

M : What do you mean by that?
남 : 그게 무슨 말인가요?

W : These days many people ride electric bicycles on sidewalks.
여 : 요즘 많은 사람들이 전기 자전거를 보행로로 타요.

M : Yes, it's so dangerous.
남 : 네, 정말 위험해요.

전치사의 목적어(동명사구)
W : Right. There should be stricter rules about **riding electric bicycles**. **단서 2** 전기 자전거를 타는 것에 관한 더 엄격한 규정이 있어야 함
여 : 맞아요. 전기 자전거를 타는 것에 관한 더 엄격한 규정이 있어야 해요.

M : I totally agree with you.
남 : 완전히 동의해요.

- electric bicycle 전기 자전거 · be careful 조심하다
- traffic rule 교통 법규 · sidewalk ⓝ 보행로, 인도
- dangerous ⓐ 위험한 · strict ⓐ 엄격한 · agree ⓥ 동의하다

대화를 듣고, 여자의 의견으로 가장 적절한 것을 고르시오.
① 전기 자전거 이용 전에 배터리 상태를 점검하여야 한다. 배터리에 대한 언급은 없음
② 전기 자전거 운행에 관한 규정이 더 엄격해야 한다.
There should be stricter rules about riding electric bicycles.
③ 전기 자전거의 속도 규정에 대한 논의가 필요하다. 속도 규정에 대한 언급은 없음
④ 전기 자전거 구입 시 가격을 고려해야 한다. 가격에 대한 언급은 없음
⑤ 전기 자전거 이용 시 헬멧을 착용해야 한다.
남자가 헬멧을 쓰지 않고 전기 자전거를 타는 남자를 봤다는 내용으로 만든 오답

＞왜 정답 ? ✽✽✽ [정답률 95%]
여자는 전기 자전거를 보행로에서 타며 기본 교통 규칙조차 따르지 않는 사람들이 있다고 말하며, 전기 자전거를 타는 것에 관한 더 엄격한 규정이 있어야 한다고 했다. 따라서 여자의 의견으로 가장 적절한 것은 ②이다.

＞왜 오답 ?
① 전기 자전거 배터리에 대한 언급은 없다.
③ 전기 자전거 운행 규정이 더 엄격해져야 한다고 말했을 뿐 속도 규정에 대해서는 언급하지 않았다.
④ 남자가 전기 자전거를 사는 것을 고려하고 있다고 했지만 가격은 말하지 않았다.
⑤ 남자가 헬멧을 쓰지 않고 전기 자전거를 타는 사람에 대해서 말했고 여자는 전기 자전거 운행 규정이 엄격해져야 한다고 말했다. 함정

03 정답 ⑤ *신입생을 위한 시간 관리 조언

W : Hello, this is your student counselor, Susan Smith.
동격
여 : 안녕하세요, 여러분의 학생 상담사인 Susan Smith입니다.

You might be worried about your new school life as a
'~로서'
freshman.
1학년으로서 여러분은 새로운 학교생활에 대해 걱정할 수도 있습니다.
You have a lot of things to do in the beginning of the year.
형용사적 용법(things 수식)
여러분은 연초에 해야 할 일이 많습니다.
Today, I'm going to give you a tip about time management.
[단서 1] 여자는 시간 관리에 관한 조언을 하려고 함
오늘은, 시간 관리에 관한 한 가지 조언을 드리겠습니다.
Make a to-do list! [단서 2] 할 일 목록을 만들라고 권함
할 일 목록을 만드세요!
앞에 목적격 관계대명사 생략
Write down the tasks you have to do on a list and check off
what you finish, one by one.
해야 할 일을 목록에 적어 두고, 끝내는 것을 하나씩 체크하세요.
'~함으로써'   앞에 목적격 관계대명사 생략
By doing this, you won't miss the things you need to do.
이렇게 함으로써, 여러분은 해야 할 일을 놓치지 않을 것입니다.

Using a to-do list will help you manage your time efficiently.
할 일 목록을 사용하는 것은 시간을 효율적으로 관리하도록 도울 것입니다.
명령문
Good luck to you and don't forget to start today.
여러분에게 행운을 빌며 오늘부터 시작하는 것을 잊지 마세요.

- counselor ⓝ 상담사 · freshman ⓝ 1학년
- beginning ⓝ 시작 · time management 시간 관리
- to-do list 할 일 목록 · task ⓝ 과업 · one by one 하나씩
- manage ⓥ 관리하다 · efficiently ⓐⓓ 효율적으로

다음을 듣고, 여자가 하는 말의 요지로 가장 적절한 것을 고르시오.
① 학업 목표를 분명히 설정하는 것이 필요하다. 학업 목표에 관한 내용은 언급하지 않음
② 친구와의 협력은 학교생활의 중요한 덕목이다. 시간 관리에 관한 조언을 하고 있음
③ 과제 제출 마감 기한을 확인하고 준수해야 한다. 과제 제출에 대한 내용은 없음
④ 적절한 휴식은 성공적인 과업 수행의 핵심 요소이다. 휴식의 필요성에 대한 언급은 없음
⑤ 할 일의 목록을 활용하는 것이 시간 관리에 유용하다. Make a to-do list!

> 왜 정답 ? ✿✿✿ [정답률 94%]
여자는 1학년 신입생들에게 시간 관리에 대한 조언을 하고 있으며 할 일 목록을
작성하면 해야 할 일을 놓치지 않고 시간을 효율적으로 관리할 수 있다고 말하고 있다.
따라서 여자가 하는 말의 요지는 ⑤이다.

> 왜 오답 ?
① 학업 목표를 설정하는 것에 대해 설명하지 않았다.
② 시간 관리에 관한 조언이며, 협력이나 학교생활의 중요한 덕목은 언급되지 않았다.
③ 할 일 목록을 작성하면 해야 할 일을 놓치지 않을 수 있다고 말했지만 과제 제출
마감 기한을 준수하는 것에 대해서는 언급하지 않았다.
④ 휴식의 필요성에 대해서는 언급하지 않았다.

04 정답 ⑤ *사진 속 영어 신문 동아리방 설명

M : Hi, Amy. I heard that you've joined the English Newspaper
목적어절 접속사
Club.
남 : 안녕, Amy. 네가 영어 신문 동아리에 가입했다고 들었어.
병렬 구조
W : Yes, Tom. I went to the club room yesterday and took a
picture of it. Look.
여 : 맞아, Tom. 어제 동아리방에 갔다가 사진을 찍었어. 봐봐. [①의 단서] 왼쪽에 사물함이 있음
M : Wow, the place looks nice. I like the lockers on the left.
남 : 와, 장소가 멋져 보여. 나는 왼쪽에 있는 사물함이 맘에 들어.
'~ 모양의'
W : Yes, they're good. We also have a star-shaped mirror on the
wall. [②의 단서] 벽에 별 모양의 거울이 있음
여 : 맞아, 사물함이 좋아. 우리는 벽에 별 모양 거울도 있어.

M : It looks cool. What's that on the bookshelf?
남 : 멋져 보여. 책장 위에 있는 건 뭐야? [③의 단서] 책장 위에 트로피가 있음
W : Oh, that's the trophy my club won for 'Club of the Year'.
여 : 오, 그건 우리 동아리가 '올해의 동아리'로 받은 트로피야.
강한 추측(~임이 틀림없다)   = the trophy
M : You must be very proud of it. There's also a computer on
the right side of the room. [④의 단서] 방의 오른쪽에 컴퓨터가 있음
남 : 굉장히 자랑스럽겠구나. 방의 오른쪽에 컴퓨터도 있네.
W : Yeah, we use the computer when we need it.
여 : 맞아, 우리는 필요할 때 컴퓨터를 사용해.
M : Great. I can see a newspaper on the table.
남 : 멋지구나. 탁자 위에 신문이 보여. [⑤의 단서] 탁자 위에 신문이 아닌 달력이 있음
과거시제 수동태
W : Yes, it was published last December.
여 : 응, 그건 지난 12월에 발행된 거야.

- club ⓝ 동아리 · locker ⓝ 사물함 · star-shaped ⓐ 별 모양의
- bookshelf ⓝ 책장 · trophy ⓝ 상패 · publish ⓥ 발행하다

대화를 듣고, 그림에서 대화의 내용과 일치하지 않는 것을 고르시오.

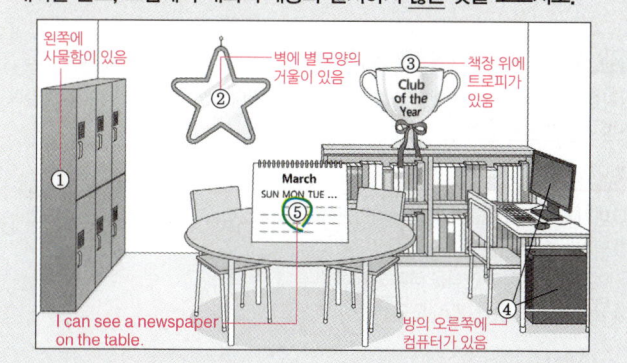

> 왜 정답 ? ✿❀❀ [정답률 93%]
남자는 탁자 위에 신문이 있다고 했는데, 탁자 위에는 달력이 있으므로 ⑤은 대화의
내용과 일치하지 않는다.

> 왜 오답 ?
① 왼쪽에 시물함이 있다고 했다.
② 벽에 별 모양의 거울이 있다고 했다.
③ 책장 위에 트로피가 있다고 했다.
④ 방의 오른쪽에 컴퓨터가 있다고 했다.

05 정답 ② *캠핑 준비

got의 목적격 보어(형용사)
W : Mike, I think we've got most of the camping supplies ready
now.
여 : Mike, 우리는 이제 캠핑용품 대부분을 준비한 것 같아요.
M : Yeah, the tent, sleeping bags, and cooking tools are all set.
남 : 네, 텐트, 침낭, 요리 도구가 모두 준비됐어요. ⑤의 함정
W : Perfect. I bought some easy-to-cook meals and snacks for
us.   ④의 함정
여 : 완벽해요. 우리를 위한 간편식과 간식을 좀 샀어요.
M : Great. What about some warm clothes? It might get cold at
night.
남 : 잘했어요. 따뜻한 옷은 좀 챙겼나요? 밤에 추워질 수도 있어요.
W : I've packed some warm jackets for us, too. Anything else
앞에 목적격 관계대명사 생략   ①의 함정
we need to consider?
여 : 우리가 입을 몇 벌의 따뜻한 재킷도 챙겼어요. 그 밖에 더 고려할 것이 있나요?
-thing으로 끝나는 대명사는 뒤에서 수식함
M : We need something fun for the camping night. I already
형용사적 용법(books 수식)   ③의 함정
packed some books to read.
남 : 캠핑하는 밤에 재미있을 무언가가 필요해요. 나는 이미 읽을 책을 몇 권 챙겼어요.

W : How about playing board games?
여 : 보드게임을 하는 것은 어때요?

M : Nice. I have a chess set at home. 남 : 좋아요. 집에 체스 세트가 있어요.

W : Cool, can you bring it? 여 : 멋져요, 가져올 수 있어요?

M : Of course! I'll take it with me. 단서 남자는 체스 세트를 가져온다고 함
남 : 물론이죠! 가져갈게요.

- camping supplies 캠핑용품 • sleeping bag 침낭
- cooking tool 요리 도구 • easy-to-cook meal 간편식
- clothes ⓝ 옷 • pack ⓥ (짐을) 챙기다 • consider ⓥ 고려하다

대화를 듣고, 남자가 할 일로 가장 적절한 것을 고르시오.
① 따뜻한 옷 챙기기 여자가 따뜻한 옷을 챙김
② 체스 세트 가져가기 I'll take it with me.
③ 읽을 책 고르기 남자는 이미 책을 골라서 챙김
④ 간편식 구매하기 여자가 간편식을 구매함
⑤ 침낭 준비하기 침낭은 텐트, 요리 도구와 함께 이미 준비됨

왜 정답? ✿✿✿ [정답률 95%]
남자는 집에 체스 세트가 있으며 캠핑을 위해 가져간다고 말했으므로 남자가 할 일로 가장 적절한 것은 ②이다.

왜 오답?
① 여자가 추워질 것을 대비해서 따뜻한 재킷을 챙겼다.
③ 남자는 이미 읽을 책을 골라서 짐을 쌌다.
④ 여자가 간편식과 간식을 이미 구매하였다.
⑤ 남자가 텐트, 침낭, 요리 도구가 준비되었다고 언급했다.

06 정답 ③ ＊식료품 쇼핑

M : Hello, what can I help you with today?
남 : 안녕하세요, 오늘은 무엇을 도와드릴까요?

W : Hi! I want to buy some fruit and vegetables. What's fresh today?
여 : 안녕하세요! 과일과 채소를 사고 싶어요. 오늘은 무엇이 신선한가요?

M : We just got some apples in. '도착하다'
남 : 방금 사과가 들어왔습니다.

W : How much are they? 여 : 사과는 얼마인가요?

M : They are ten dollars for one bag. 단서 1 사과 한 봉지에 10달러
남 : 한 봉지에 10달러예요.

W : Fantastic! I'll take two bags of apples. 단서 2 사과 두 봉지 구입
여 : 잘됐네요! 사과 두 봉지를 살게요.

M : Okay, what else do you need? '그 밖에'
남 : 알겠어요, 다른 필요하신 것이 있나요?

W : I'd like to buy some carrots, too. 여 : 당근도 사고 싶어요.

M : The carrots are five dollars for one bag. How many do you need? 단서 3 당근 한 봉지에 5달러
남 : 당근은 한 봉지에 5달러예요. 몇 봉지 필요하세요?

W : I need two bags of carrots. 단서 4 당근 두 봉지 구입
여 : 당근은 두 봉지가 필요해요.

M : Okay, you need two bags of apples and two bags of carrots.
남 : 알겠어요, 사과 두 봉지와 당근 두 봉지가 필요하시죠.

W : Right. And I have a coupon. I can get a discount with this, right? = the coupon
여 : 네. 그리고 쿠폰이 있어요. 이거로 할인받을 수 있죠?

M : Yes. You can get a ten percent discount off the total price. '할인을 받다'
남 : 네. 총액에서 10% 할인받으실 수 있어요. 단서 5 쿠폰으로 총액에서 10% 할인

W : Good. Here's the coupon and my credit card.
여 : 좋아요. 여기 쿠폰과 신용카드를 드릴게요.

- vegetable ⓝ 채소 • fantastic ⓐ 굉장한 • need ⓥ 필요하다
- discount ⓝ 할인 • price ⓝ 가격 • credit card 신용카드

대화를 듣고, 여자가 지불할 금액을 고르시오. [3점]
① $15 ② $20 ③ $27 ④ $30 ⑤ $33
(사과 한 봉지 $10×2) + (당근 한 봉지 $5×2) − $3(쿠폰 10퍼센트 할인)

왜 정답? ✿✿✿ [정답률 90%]
한 봉지에 10달러짜리 사과 두 봉지와 5달러짜리 당근 두 봉지를 구입하기로 하였으므로 총액은 30달러이다. 쿠폰을 쓰면 총액의 10%인 3달러를 할인받을 수 있으므로 여자가 지불할 금액은 ③ '27달러'이다.

07 정답 ⑤ ＊체육 대회 연습에 불참하는 이유

W : Hey, Jake! How was your math test yesterday?
여 : 안녕, Jake! 어제 수학 시험 어땠어?

M : Better than I expected. ①의 함정
남 : 예상했던 것보다 더 잘 봤어.

W : That's great. Let's go and practice for Sports Day.
여 : 잘됐네. 체육 대회를 위해 연습하러 가자.

M : I'm so sorry but I can't make it. '참석하다' 남 : 미안한데 난 참석할 수 없어.

W : Come on, Jake! Sports Day is just around the corner. '임박한'
여 : 이봐, Jake! 체육 대회가 얼마 안 남았어.

M : I know. That's why I brought my soccer shoes. ③의 함정
남 : 알아. 그래서 축구화도 가져왔어.

W : Then, why can't you practice today? Do you have a club interview?
여 : 그러면, 오늘 왜 연습을 못하니? 동아리 면접이 있니?

M : No, I already had the interview last week. ②의 함정
남 : 아니, 면접은 이미 지난주에 봤어.

W : Then, does your leg still hurt? 여 : 그러면, 아직 다리가 아픈 거니?
④의 함정

M : Not really, it's okay, now. Actually, I have to attend a family dinner gathering tonight for my mother's birthday.
남 : 그렇지 않아, 지금은 괜찮아. 사실, 오늘 밤 어머니 생신을 축하하는 가족 저녁 식사 모임에 참석해야 해. 단서 남자는 가족 식사 모임에 참석해야 함

W : Oh, that's important! Family always comes first. Are you available tomorrow, then?
여 : 오, 그건 중요하지! 가족이 언제나 우선이야. 그럼, 내일은 시간이 되니?

M : Sure. Let's make up for the missed practice. 과거분사(practice 수식)
남 : 물론이지. 놓친 연습을 보충하자.

- expect ⓥ 기대하다 • already ⓐⓓ 이미 • attend ⓥ 참여하다
- available ⓐ 참석이 가능한 • make up for ~을 보충하다[보상하다]

대화를 듣고, 남자가 체육 대회 연습을 할 수 없는 이유를 고르시오.
① 시험공부를 해야 해서 수학 시험을 이미 봄
② 동아리 면접이 있어서 동아리 면접은 지난주에 봄
③ 축구화를 가져오지 않아서 축구화를 가져옴
④ 다리가 완전히 회복되지 않아서 다리는 이제 괜찮음
⑤ 가족 식사 모임에 참석해야 해서 I have to attend a family dinner gathering

왜 정답? ✿✿✿ [정답률 95%]
남자는 오늘 밤 어머니 생신을 축하하는 가족 저녁 식사 모임에 참석해야 해서 체육 대회 연습을 할 수 없다고 했다. 따라서 정답은 ⑤이다.

왜 오답?
① 수학 시험이 어제 있었고 예상보다 잘 봤다고 말했다.
② 동아리 면접은 지난주에 봤다고 말했다.
③ 축구화를 가져왔다고 말했다.
④ 다리는 이제 괜찮다고 했다.

W : Hey, Chris. <mark>Have you heard</mark> about the Science Open Lab
     ^{현재완료}
    Program?
여 : 안녕, Chris. Science Open Lab Program에 대해 들어봤어?

M : Yes, I heard about it. But I don't know <u>what it is</u> exactly.
                                       ^{간접의문문(의문사+주어+동사)}
남 : 응, 들어봤어. 그런데 정확히 무슨 프로그램인지는 모르겠어.

W : In that program, we can design any science experiment <mark>we</mark>
    <mark>want</mark>.
    ^{앞에 목적격 관계대명사 생략}
여 : 그 프로그램에서는 우리가 원하는 어느 과학 실험이든 설계할 수 있어.

M : That sounds pretty cool. Do you want to join the program?
남 : 정말 멋지구나. 그 프로그램에 참여하고 싶어?

W : Sure, it's only for freshmen <mark>like</mark> us. Let's join it together.
                    ^{전치사(~ 같은)} **①의 단서** 지원 가능 학년
여 : 물론이야, 우리 같은 신입생만을 위한 프로그램이야. 같이 참여하자.

M : Great! Do we need to buy some materials for experiments?
남 : 좋아! 실험을 위해 재료들을 사야 할 필요가 있을까?

W : No, they'll prepare everything for us. We just need to send
    the application form online. **②의 단서** 실험 재료 구입 필요성
여 : 아니, 우리를 위해 모든 것을 준비해 줄 거야. 우리는 단지 온라인으로 지원서를 보내면
    돼.

M : When is the deadline for applying?
남 : 지원 제출 기한은 언제야?

W : It's tomorrow. We need to hurry. **③의 단서** 지원서 제출 기한
여 : 내일이야. 서둘러야 해.

M : Oh, I see. Is there any special prize?
남 : 오, 알겠어. 특별한 상이 있어?

W : Yes. I heard they're giving out prizes for <mark>the most creative</mark>
                                              ^{최상급}
    <mark>projects</mark>. **⑤의 단서** 시상 여부
여 : 응. 가장 창의적인 프로젝트에는 상을 준다고 들었어.

M : Perfect! I'm so excited.
남 : 완벽해! 너무 기대 돼.

- lab ⓝ 실험실   • exactly ⓐⓓ 정확히   • design ⓥ 설계하다
- pretty ⓐⓓ 꽤   • join ⓥ 참여하다   • experiment ⓝ 실험
- material ⓝ 재료   • prepare ⓥ 준비하다
- application form 지원서   • deadline ⓝ 기한, 마감 시간
- prize ⓝ 상   • give out ~을 주다   • creative ⓐ 창의적인

대화를 듣고, Science Open Lab Program에 관해 언급되지 **않은**
것을 고르시오.

① 지원 가능 학년 it's only for freshmen like us
② 실험 재료 구입 필요성 they'll prepare everything for us
③ 지원서 제출 기한 It's tomorrow.
④ 참가 인원수 언급되지 않음
⑤ 시상 여부 they're giving out prizes

＞왜 정답 ? ✱❀❀ [정답률 96%]

지원 가능 학년, 실험 재료 구입 필요성, 지원서 제출 기한, 시상 여부는 언급했지만,
참가 인원수는 언급하지 않았으므로 정답은 ④이다.

＞왜 오답 ?

① 신입생인 1학년만 지원이 가능하다.
② 실험 재료는 구입할 필요가 없다.
③ 지원서 제출 기한은 내일이다.
⑤ 가장 창의적인 프로젝트에 상을 준다.

W : Hello, students! Are you looking for a chance <mark>to help</mark> others?
                                        ^{형용사적 용법(a chance 수식)}
여 : 안녕하세요, 학생 여러분! 다른 사람들을 도울 기회를 찾고 있나요?

    ^{recommend의 목적격 보어(to부정사)}
    Then, I recommend you <mark>to join</mark> Triwood High School
    Volunteer Program to help senior citizens. **①의 단서** 어르신을
                                                 돕는 봉사 활동임
여 : 그렇다면, 저는 여러분이 Triwood 고등학교 봉사 프로그램에 참여하여 어르신들을
    돕는 것을 추천합니다.
    ^{be supposed to: ~하기로 되어 있다} **②의 단서** 봉사자는 대면으로 어르신을 도움
    You're <mark>supposed to help</mark> the senior citizens face-to-face.
여 : 여러분은 어르신들과 대면하여 도움을 줄 것입니다.

    You teach them how to use their smartphones for things
                               ^{~와 같은}   ^{병렬 구조}
    <u>such as sending</u> text messages or <u>taking</u> pictures.
여 : 여러분은 어르신들께 문자 메시지를 보내거나 사진 찍기와 같은 일들을 위해
    스마트폰을 사용하는 방법을 가르칩니다. **③의 단서** 스마트폰 사용 방법을 가르침

    You will also teach seniors how to use various apps.
여 : 여러분은 어르신들에게 다양한 앱을 사용하는 방법도 가르칠 것입니다.
    ^{require의 목적격 보어(to부정사)}
    The program will require volunteers <mark>to participate</mark> for two
    hours every Saturday. **④의 단서** 매주 토요일 두 시간씩 봉사에 참여함
여 : 이 프로그램은 봉사자들이 매주 토요일 두 시간 동안 참여하도록 요청할 것입니다.

    If you are interested in joining our program, please send us
    an application form through email.
여 : 저희 프로그램에 참여하는 데 관심이 있다면, 우리에게 이메일을 통해 참가 신청서를
    보내주십시오. **⑤의 단서** 지원자는 이메일로 참가 신청서를 보냄

- look for ~을 찾다   • recommend ⓥ 추천하다
- volunteer ⓝ 봉사 활동   • senior ⓐ 노인의   • citizen ⓝ 시민
- face-to-face ⓐⓓ 대면(으로)   • text message 문자 메시지
- take picture 사진을 찍다   • various ⓐ 다양한
- require ⓥ 요구하다   • participate ⓥ 참여하다
- be interested in ~에 관심이 있다   • application ⓝ 지원

Triwood High School Volunteer Program에 관한 다음 내용을
듣고, 일치하지 **않는** 것을 고르시오.

① 노인을 도와주는 봉사 활동이다. I recommend you ~ to help senior citizens.
② 봉사자는 대면으로 활동한다. You're supposed to help ~ face-to-face.
③ 스마트폰 사용 방법 교육을 한다.
    You teach them how to use their smartphones
④ 봉사자는 매주 토요일에 세 시간씩 참여한다.
    to participate for two hours every Saturday
⑤ 지원자는 이메일로 참가 신청서를 보내야 한다.
    please send us an application form through email

＞왜 정답 ? ✱❀❀ [정답률 94%]

이 프로그램은 봉사자들이 매주 토요일 두 시간 동안 참여하도록 요청할 것이라고
했으므로 (to participate for two hours every Saturday) 세 시간씩 참여한다고
한 ④은 일치하지 않는다.

＞왜 오답 ?

① 노인을 도와주는 봉사 활동이다.
② 봉사자는 대면으로 활동한다.
③ 스마트폰 사용 방법 교육을 한다.
⑤ 지원자는 이메일로 참가 신청서를 보내야 한다.

10 정답 ③ ✱선물할 휴대용 선풍기 고르기

M : Sophie, what are you looking for? 남 : Sophie, 무엇을 찾고 있니?

W : I'm trying to choose one of these portable fans as a gift for
「one 의 + 복수 명사」 : ~ 중 하나
my friend Cathy.

여 : 이 휴대용 선풍기 중에서 하나를 내 친구 Cathy를 위한 선물로 고르려고 해.

사역동사 let의 목적격 보어(동사원형)
M : Oh, let me help you. How many speed options do you think
she would want?

남 : 오, 도와줄게. 그녀가 몇 개의 풍속 옵션을 원할 것 같니?

W : She would like it if the fan has more than two options.

여 : 그녀는 선풍기에 두 개 이상의 풍속 옵션이 있으면 좋아할 거야. **단서 1** 풍속 옵션이 두 개
'~에 관해 생각하다' 이상이어야 함 (① 제외)
M : Okay, then, what color do you have in mind?

남 : 알겠어, 그럼 어떤 색을 생각하고 있어?

= portable fan
W : Cathy's old one was white. I want to choose a different
color. **단서 2** 하얀색이 아닌 색을 고르길 원함 (② 제외)

여 : Cathy의 이전 휴대용 선풍기는 하얀색이었어. 나는 다른 색을 고르고 싶어.

형용사적 용법(an LED display 수식)
M : Good idea. Do you want an LED display to show the
remaining battery power?

남 : 좋은 생각이야. 배터리 잔량을 보여주는 LED 디스플레이를 원하니?

W : Hmm, I don't think she will need it.

여 : 음, 그녀에게 그건 필요 없을 거야. **단서 3** LED 디스플레이가 필요하지 않음 (⑤ 제외)
= option
M : You're left with two options. Which one do you prefer?

남 : 두 가지 선택지가 남았구나. 어느 쪽이 더 좋아?
= option
W : Well, I'll take the cheaper one. **단서 4** 둘 중에 더 저렴한 것을 선택함 (④ 제외)

여 : 음, 더 저렴한 걸로 할게.

• portable ⓐ 휴대용의 • fan ⓝ 선풍기 • prefer ⓥ 선호하다

다음 표를 보면서 대화를 듣고, 여자가 주문할 휴대용 선풍기를
고르시오.

Portable Fan 휴대용 선풍기

	Model 모델	Number of Speed Options 풍속 옵션의 수	Color 색깔	LED Display LED 디스플레이	Price 가격
①	A	① 풍속 옵션이 두 개 미만임	blue 파란색	×	$15
②	B	3	white 하얀색임	○	$26
③	C	3	yellow 노란색	×	$31
④	D	4	pink 분홍색	× 남은 선택지 중 더 비쌈	$37
⑤	E	5	green 초록색	○ LED 디스플레이가 있음	$42

왜 정답? ✿✿✿ [정답률 93%]

풍속 옵션이 두 개 이상이고(① 제외), 하얀색이 아니며(② 제외), LED 디스플레이가
없고(⑤ 제외), 가격이 더 저렴한 제품은 (④ 제외) ③이다.

왜 오답?

① 풍속 옵션은 두 개 이상이어야 한다.
② 하얀색이 아닌 것을 고르고 싶다고 했다.
④ 선택할 수 있는 제품 중에서 더 저렴한 것으로 사길 원한다.
⑤ LED 디스플레이가 필요 없을 것이라고 했다.

11 정답 ③ ✱지갑을 분실한 Jane

M : What's wrong, Jane? You look so upset.

남 : 무슨 일이야, Jane? 기분이 매우 안 좋아 보여.
현재완료 진행형
W : I lost my purse! I have been searching for it for an hour, but
I can't find it.

여 : 지갑을 잃어버렸어! 한 시간 동안 찾고 있지만, 못 찾겠어.

M : When did you last have it? **단서** 마지막으로 언제 지갑을 가지고 있었는지 질문함

남 : 마지막으로 지갑을 가지고 있었던 게 언제야?

W : I had it before biology class.

여 : 나는 생물 수업 시간 전에 그것을 가지고 있었어.

• search for ~을 찾다 • biology ⓝ 생물학

대화를 듣고, 남자의 마지막 말에 대한 여자의 응답으로 가장 적절한
것을 고르시오.

① I can help you find it. 여자가 지갑을 잃어버림
나는 네가 그것을 찾는 것을 도울 수 있어.
② I already bought a new one. 지갑을 잃어버려서 찾는 상황임
나는 이미 새로운 것을 샀어.
③ I had it before biology class. 생물 수업 시간 전에 지갑을 가지고 있었음
나는 생물 수업 시간 전에 그것을 가지고 있었어.
④ You should report it to the police. 남자가 어떤 일을 해야 하는지 물어본 상황이 아님
너는 그걸 경찰에 신고해야 해.
⑤ It was a birthday gift from my dad. 지갑을 마지막으로 가지고 있었던 시점을 질문함
그것은 내 아빠로부터 받은 생일 선물이었어.

왜 정답? ✿✿✿ [정답률 73%]

지갑을 잃어버려서 찾고 있다는 여자의 말에 남자는 언제 마지막으로 지갑을 가지고
있었는지 물었다. 따라서 여자의 응답으로 가장 적절한 것은 ③ '나는 생물 수업 시간
전에 그것을 가지고 있었어.'이다.

왜 오답?

① 여자가 지갑을 잃어버린 상황이지, 남자가 물건을 분실한 상황이 아니다. **주의**
② 여자는 한 시간 동안 계속 지갑을 찾는 중이다.
④ 남자가 여자에게 본인이 어떤 일을 해야 하는지 질문하지 않았다.
⑤ 지갑을 마지막으로 가지고 있었던 시점에 대해 대답해야 한다.

12 정답 ⑤ ✱토요일 점심 식사 계획

'계획하다'
W : Honey, what do you have in mind for lunch this Saturday?

여 : 여보, 이번 토요일 점심에 무엇을 먹을 계획인가요?

M : I was thinking we should try the new Italian restaurant.

남 : 새로 생긴 이탈리아 식당을 가려 생각하던 중이었어요.
가주어 진주어
W : Hmm... I heard that it's hard to make a reservation there
these days. **단서** 남자가 가려는 식당이 요즘 예약하기 어렵다는 문제 상황을 말함

여 : 음… 요즘 그곳에 예약하는 것이 어렵다고 들었어요.

M : That's too bad. Why don't we try another restaurant?

남 : 아쉽네요. 다른 식당을 가는 건 어때요?

• reservation ⓝ 예약 • recipe ⓝ 요리법

대화를 듣고, 여자의 마지막 말에 대한 남자의 응답으로 가장 적절한
것을 고르시오.

① Thank you. Everything looks delicious. 식사를 하는 상황이 아님
고마워요. 모든 것이 맛있어 보여요.
② Yes. I have an appointment this Saturday. 토요일에 함께 점심을 먹으려고 함
네. 이번 토요일에 약속이 있어요.
③ You're welcome. I made it with my dad's recipe. 남자는 요리를 하지 않았음
천만에요. 저는 아빠의 요리법으로 이것을 만들었어요.
④ Sounds good. What time did you make a reservation? 여자는 식당을 예약하지 않았음
좋아요. 몇 시로 예약했어요?
⑤ That's too bad. Why don't we try another restaurant? 식당 예약이 어려운 문제 상황에 대한 해결책을 제시함
아쉽네요. 다른 식당을 가는 건 어때요?

왜 정답? ✿✿✿ [정답률 61%]

남자가 가려는 이탈리아 식당이 요즘 예약하기 어렵다는 문제 상황을 여자가
말했으므로 이에 대한 해결책을 제시한 ⑤ '아쉽네요. 다른 식당을 가는 건 어때요?'가
남자의 응답으로 가장 적절하다.

왜 오답?

① 대화에서 두 사람이 함께 식사를 하고 있는 상황이 아니다.
② 두 사람은 토요일에 함께 점심을 먹으려고 한다.
③ 남자가 직접 만든 요리를 먹고 있는 상황이 아니다.
④ 여자가 식당을 예약했다는 내용은 언급되지 않았다.

13 정답 ② ＊아이들을 위한 오디오 북 녹음

M : Mom! I've started to record audiobooks for kids.
단서1 아이들을 위한 오디오 북 녹음을 시작함
남 : 엄마! 저는 아이들을 위한 오디오 북 녹음을 시작했어요.

W : That's great! How did you get involved in that?
여 : 정말 좋네! 어떻게 그 일에 참여하게 되었니?

M : My teacher told me that a local organization is looking for
목적어절을 이끄는 접속사
students to record audiobooks.
형용사적 용법 (students 수식)
남 : 선생님께서 한 지역 단체가 오디오 북을 녹음할 학생을 찾고 있다고 저에게
말씀하셨어요.

W : Fantastic! Are you having fun with it?
여 : 멋지네! 재미있게 하고 있니?

M : Well, actually, I'm struggling with my voice acting.
남 : 음, 사실, 목소리 연기에 어려움을 겪고 있어요.

W : Oh? Is that so?
여 : 오? 그래?

M : Yes, it's a bit challenging to get the right tone for kids.
가주어　　　　　　　　진주어
남 : 네, 아이들에게 알맞은 어조를 내는 게 좀 어렵네요.

W : I'm sure you'll get better with practice soon.
여 : 연습하면서 곧 더 나아질 거라고 확신해.

M : Thanks. I'm trying my best.
남 : 감사해요. 최선을 다하고 있어요.

W : That's wonderful. Anything I can help you with?
앞에 목적격 관계대명사 생략
여 : 정말 멋지다. 내가 도와줄 만한 것이 있을까?

M : Can you recommend a good book for my audiobook
recording? 단서2 오디오 북 녹음을 위한 책 추천을 부탁함
남 : 오디오 북 녹음을 위해 좋은 책을 추천해 주실 수 있나요?

W : Sure. Let's choose one from your old children's books.
여 : 물론이야. 네 오래된 아동용 책 중에서 하나를 고르자.

• get involved in ~에 참여하다[관여하다]　• organization ⓝ 단체
• struggle ⓥ 고군분투하다　• challenging ⓐ 도전적인
• tone ⓝ 어조　• recommend ⓥ 추천하다

대화를 듣고, 남자의 마지막 말에 대한 여자의 응답으로 가장 적절한
것을 고르시오. [3점]

Woman: _____

① No problem. You can find other projects at the
organization. 다른 일을 하고 싶다고 말하지 않았음
문제없어. 너는 그 단체에서 다른 프로젝트를 찾을 수 있어.
② Sure. Let's choose one from your old children's books.
물론이야. 네 오래된 아동용 책 중에서 하나를 고르자.
③ Congratulations. You finally made your first audiobook.
축하해. 드디어 첫 오디오 북을 만들었네. 완성된 오디오 북을 들려주는 상황이 아님
④ I hope so. You're going to be a wonderful writer.
그랬으면 좋겠어. 너는 훌륭한 작가가 될 거야. 남자가 글을 쓰는 상황이 아님
⑤ Exactly. Kids grow faster than you think.
정확해. 아이들은 네가 생각하는 것보다 더 빨리 성장해. 아이들의 성장에 관한 내용은 말하지 않았음
─ 아이들을 위한 오디오 북을 녹음하기 위해 책을 추천해달라고 요청함

> 왜 정답 ? ✽✿✿ [정답률 94%]

남자가 아이들을 위해 오디오 북을 녹음하는 일을 시작했고 좋은 책을 추천해달라고
요청하고 있으므로 이에 대한 여자의 응답으로는 ② '물론이야. 네 오래된 아동용 책
중에서 하나를 고르자.'가 가장 적절하다.

> 왜 오답 ?

① 남자가 다른 일을 하고 싶다고 말하지 않았다.
③ 여자에게 완성된 오디오 북을 들려주는 상황이 아니다.
④ 남자가 글을 쓰고 있다는 내용은 전혀 언급되지 않았다.
⑤ 대화에서 아이들의 성장에 대한 내용은 나오지 않는다.

14 정답 ① ＊역사 프로젝트 역할 분담

W : Hi, Fred. What should we do for our history project?
여 : 안녕, Fred. 역사 프로젝트를 위해 무엇을 해야 할까?

M : Actually, I was thinking about it. Why don't we divide the
'~하는 건 어때?'
roles for the project? 단서1 역사 프로젝트를 위해 역할 분담을 제안함
남 : 사실, 나도 프로젝트에 대해 생각하고 있었어. 프로젝트를 위해 역할을 나누는 건
어떠니?

W : Okay. Good idea. We have the research part, the visual
material part, and the presentation part.
여 : 그래. 좋은 생각이야. 우리는 조사 부분, 시각 자료 부분, 그리고 발표 부분이 있어.

M : Hmm, is there any part you want to take on?
앞에 목적격 관계대명사 생략
남 : 음, 맡고 싶은 부분이 있어?

W : Well, I would like to do the research. I've been collecting
현재완료 진행형
news articles about history.
여 : 음, 나는 조사를 맡고 싶어. 역사에 관한 뉴스 기사를 모으고 있었거든.

M : Excellent. You are good at gathering necessary information.
'be good at -ing' ~하는 것을 잘하다
남 : 훌륭해. 너는 필요한 정보를 모으는 걸 잘하잖아.

W : Thanks. Can you handle the visual material?
여 : 고마워. 시각 자료를 맡을 수 있니?

M : Okay. I'll take care of it. I have done it before.
현재완료(경험)
남 : 좋아. 내가 맡을게. 전에 해본 적이 있어.

W : All right. Then, the only part left is the presentation.
과거분사(part 수식)
여 : 그래. 그럼, 유일하게 남은 부분은 발표네. 단서2 역할 분담 후에 발표 부분이 남음

M : Well, let's do the presentation together.
남 : 그럼, 발표는 같이 하자.

• divide ⓥ 나누다　• research ⓝ 조사　• visual material 시각 자료
• presentation ⓝ 발표　• take on ~을 맡다　• collect ⓥ 모으다
• article ⓝ (신문 등의) 기사　• gather ⓥ 모으다
• necessary ⓐ 필요한　• information ⓝ 정보　• handle ⓥ 다루다

대화를 듣고, 여자의 마지막 말에 대한 남자의 응답으로 가장 적절한
것을 고르시오.

Man: _____

① Well, let's do the presentation together.
그럼, 발표는 같이 하자. 역사 프로젝트의 역할을 분담한 후에 발표 부분이 남음
② Cheer up! I know you did your best. 여자가 위로받는 상황이 아님
힘내! 네가 최선을 다했다는걸 알아.
③ Yes, I got a good grade on science. 시험 성적에 관한 대화가 아님
응, 나는 과학에서 좋은 성적을 받았어.
④ Wow! It was a really nice presentation.
와! 정말 멋진 발표였어. 아직 발표하지 않았고 발표 부분을 누가 맡을 것인지 결정해야 함
⑤ Right. I have already finished the project.
맞아. 나는 이미 그 프로젝트를 끝냈어. 역사 프로젝트를 시작해야 하는 상황임

> 왜 정답 ? ✽✿✿ [정답률 92%]

역사 프로젝트를 하기 위해 두 사람이 역할을 분담하기로 결정했고 각자 하고 싶은
부분을 정하고 나니 발표 부분이 남았다고 여자가 말했다. 따라서 여자의 마지막 말에
대한 남자의 적절한 응답은 ① '그럼, 발표는 같이 하자.'이다.

> 왜 오답 ?

② 여자가 위로받는 상황이 아니라 프로젝트를 어떻게 할지 상의하는 상황이다.
③ 두 사람이 시험 성적에 관해 말하고 있는 것이 아니다.
④ 대화에서 발표를 들었다는 내용은 전혀 언급되지 않았다.
⑤ 역사 프로젝트를 시작하기 위해 역할을 분담하는 상황이다.

W : Robert and Michelle are attending their high school orientation. 단서 1 Robert와 Michelle이 고등학교 설명회에 참석 중인 상황

여 : Robert와 Michelle은 그들의 고등학교 설명회에 참석 중입니다.

After short greetings, the teacher begins to explain student clubs, school activities, and school facilities.

짧은 인사 후에, 선생님은 학생 동아리, 학교 활동, 그리고 학교 시설에 대하여 설명하기 시작합니다.

Robert is focusing very carefully on the explanation.

Robert는 매우 세심하게 설명에 집중하고 있습니다.

사이에 he is가 생략됨
However, while writing down important things about the school library, Robert drops his pen.

하지만, 학교 도서관에 대한 중요한 정보를 적어 내려가던 중에, Robert는 펜을 떨어뜨립니다.

분사구문 단서 2 Robert가 떨어진 펜을 찾는 동안 도서관 개방 시간에 대한 정보를 놓침
Trying to find his pen, Robert misses important information about the opening hours of the library, so now, Robert wants to ask Michelle when the library is open.
간접의문문(의문사+주어+동사) 단서 3 Robert가 Michelle에게 도서관이 열리는 시간을 묻고 싶음

펜을 찾으려고 하는 동안, Robert는 도서관 개방 시간에 대한 중요한 정보를 놓치고, 그래서 지금, Robert는 Michelle에게 도서관이 언제 열리는지 묻고 싶어 합니다.

In this situation, what would Robert most likely say to Michelle?

이 상황에서, Robert가 Michelle에게 할 말로 가장 적절한 것은 무엇인가요?

Robert: **When can I use the library?**

Robert: 도서관을 언제 이용할 수 있나요?

＊상황 요약: Robert가 Michelle에게 도서관이 언제 열리는지 물어보려는 상황

- attend ⓥ 참석하다 • orientation ⓝ 설명회 • greetings ⓝ 인사
- explain ⓥ 설명하다 • facility ⓝ 시설 • explanation ⓝ 설명
- library ⓝ 도서관 • miss ⓥ 놓치다 • opening hours 개방 시간
- lost and found 분실물 센터

다음 상황 설명을 듣고, Robert가 Michelle에게 할 말로 가장 적절한 것을 고르시오. [3점]

Robert: ＿＿＿＿＿＿＿＿＿＿＿＿＿＿＿＿＿

① When can I use the library? 도서관이 언제 열리는지 물어보고 싶음
　도서관을 언제 이용할 수 있나요?
② Where can I find the library? 도서관의 위치를 물어보는 상황이 아님
　도서관은 어디에 있나요?
③ How can I join the reading club?
　독서 동아리에 어떻게 가입할 수 있나요? 독서 동아리를 궁금해하는 내용은 언급되지 않음
④ Why do you want to go to the library?
　당신은 왜 도서관에 가고 싶나요? Michelle이 도서관에 가고 싶다는 언급은 없음
⑤ What time does the lost and found open?
　분실물 센터는 몇 시에 열리나요? 대화에 분실물 센터에 관한 내용은 전혀 없음

＞왜 정답 ? ✿✿✿ [정답률 92%]

고등학교 설명회를 듣던 중 Robert가 떨어진 펜을 찾으려다가 도서관 개방 시간에 대한 중요한 정보를 놓친 상황이다. Robert는 Michelle에게 도서관이 언제 열리는지 물어보고 싶어 한다고 했다. 따라서 Robert가 할 말로 가장 적절한 것은 ① '도서관을 언제 이용할 수 있나요?'이다.

＞왜 오답 ?

② Robert가 도서관의 위치를 질문하려는 상황이 아니다.
③ Robert가 독서 동아리를 궁금해한다는 내용은 언급되지 않았다.
④ Michelle이 Robert에게 도서관에 가고 싶다고 말하지 않았다.
⑤ 분실물 센터에 대한 내용은 전혀 나오지 않았고, Robert는 분실물 센터가 아닌 도서관 개방 시간을 알고 싶어 한다.

M : Hello, listeners. //

남 : 안녕하세요, 청취자 여러분 //

Thank you / for tuning in to our Happy Radio Show. //

감사합니다 / 저희 Happy Radio Show를 들어 주셔서 //

Are you taking good care of your health / in the early spring? //

여러분은 건강을 잘 챙기고 있으신가요 / 초봄에 //

주격 관계대명사
Today, I want to recommend some foods / that can reduce the symptoms of a cough. // 16번 단서: 기침 증상을 줄일 수 있는 음식들
추천할 것임
오늘은 음식 몇 가지를 추천하고 싶습니다 / 기침 증상을 줄일 수 있는 //

Ginger is a popular home remedy for coughs. // 17번①

생강은 기침을 위한 인기 있는 민간요법입니다 //

동명사구(전치사의 목적어)
A cup of hot ginger tea can be helpful / for reducing your cough. //

따뜻한 생강차 한 잔은 도움이 될 수 있습니다 / 기침을 줄이는 데 //

Lemon is a rich source of vitamin C. //

레몬은 비타민 C의 풍부한 원천입니다 //

help의 목적격 보어(동사원형)
Lemon tea can help you relieve your cough. // 17번②

레몬차는 기침을 완화하는 데 도움을 줄 수 있습니다 //

형용사적 용법(food 수식)
Surprisingly, / pineapple is another excellent food / to help relieve a cough. // 17번③

놀랍게도, / 파인애플은 또 다른 훌륭한 음식입니다 / 기침을 완화하는데 도움이 되는 //

동명사 주어
When you are suffering from a cough, / eating bananas also / helps to get rid of the symptoms more easily. // 17번⑤
단수 동사

여러분이 기침으로 고생할 때 / 바나나를 먹는 것도 / 증상을 더 쉽게 없애는 것을 돕습니다 //

= these foods 수동태 동사
These foods are rich in vitamins / and they are recommended for people / suffering from a cough. //
현재분사(people 수식)

이 음식들은 비타민이 풍부하며 / 사람들에게 추천됩니다 / 기침으로 고생하는 //

I hope you have a healthy week. //

건강한 한 주 되시길 바랍니다 //

- tune in to ~을 열심히 듣다 • recommend ⓥ 추천하다
- cough ⓝ 기침 • reduce ⓥ 줄이다 • symptom ⓝ 증상
- ginger ⓝ 생강 • remedy ⓝ 치료법 • rich ⓐ 풍부한
- source ⓝ 공급원 • relieve ⓥ 완화하다 • suffer ⓥ 고생하다
- get rid of ~을 없애다 • healthy ⓐ 건강한 • connection ⓝ 연관성

남 : 안녕하세요, 청취자 여러분. 저희 Happy Radio Show를 들어 주셔서 감사합니다. 초봄에 여러분은 건강을 잘 챙기고 있으신가요? 오늘은 기침 증상을 줄일 수 있는 음식 몇 가지를 추천하고 싶습니다. 생강은 기침을 위한 인기 있는 민간요법입니다. 따뜻한 생강차 한 잔은 기침을 줄이는 데 도움이 될 수 있습니다. 레몬은 비타민 C의 풍부한 원천입니다. 레몬차는 기침을 완화하는 데 도움을 줄 수 있습니다. 놀랍게도, 파인애플은 기침을 완화하는 데 도움이 되는 또 다른 훌륭한 음식입니다. 여러분이 기침으로 고생할 때 바나나를 먹는 것도 증상을 더 쉽게 없애는 것을 돕습니다. 이 음식들은 비타민이 풍부하며 기침으로 고생하는 사람들에게 추천됩니다. 건강한 한 주 되시길 바랍니다.

---

16 정답 ①

남자가 하는 말의 주제로 가장 적절한 것은?

① useful foods to relieve coughs recommend some foods that can
　기침을 완화하는 유용한 음식들 reduce the symptoms of a cough
② importance of proper food recipes
　적절한 음식 요리법의 중요성 음식 요리법에 대해서는 전혀 언급하지 않음
③ various causes of cough symptoms 기침 증상의 원인을 설명하지 않음
　기침 증상의 다양한 원인들
④ traditional home remedies for fever
　발열에 대한 전통적인 민간요법 기침에 대한 전통적인 민간요법을 설명함
⑤ connection between weather and cough
　날씨와 기침의 연관성 기침을 완화하는 음식에 관한 내용이지, 날씨에 관한 내용이 아님

왜 정답? ❀❀❀ [정답률 95%]

남자는 기침 증상을 줄이는 음식을 추천하고 싶다며, 생강, 레몬, 파인애플, 바나나를 소개했다. 따라서 남자가 하는 말의 주제로 가장 적절한 것은 ① '기침을 완화하는 유용한 음식들'이다.

왜 오답?

② 생강과 레몬을 소개하면서 이것들로 만든 차에 대한 내용이 나오지만, 음식 요리법이나 그 중요성에 대해서는 전혀 언급하지 않았다.

③ 기침 증상을 완화하는 음식들을 추천하는 내용이며, 기침의 원인에 대해서는 설명하지 않았다.

④ 생강이 기침에 인기 있는 민간요법이라고 언급했을 뿐, 발열과는 관련이 없다. 함정

⑤ 날씨와 기침이 어떤 연관이 있는지 언급하지 않았다.

17 정답 ④

언급된 음식 재료가 아닌 것은?

① ginger 생강 — Ginger is a popular home remedy for coughs.
② lemon 레몬 — Lemon tea can help you relieve your cough.
③ pineapple 파인애플 — pineapple is another excellent food to help relieve a cough
④ honey 꿀 — 언급되지 않음
⑤ banana 바나나 — eating bananas also helps to get rid of the symptoms

왜 정답? ❀❀❀ [정답률 90%]

생강, 레몬, 파인애플, 바나나에 대해서는 언급했지만 꿀에 대해서는 언급하지 않았으므로 정답은 ④ '꿀'이다.

왜 오답?

① 생강은 기침에 인기 있는 민간요법이라고 했다.

② 레몬은 비타민 C의 풍부한 원천이며 레몬차는 기침을 완화하는 데 도움을 줄 수 있다고 했다.

③ 파인애플은 기침을 완화하는 데 도움이 되는 또 다른 훌륭한 음식이라고 했다.

⑤ 바나나를 먹는 것도 기침 증상을 없애는 것을 도울 수 있다고 했다.

18 정답 ③ ✱작가에게 학교 특별 강연 요청하기

Dear Ms. Jane Watson, /
Jane Watson 씨께 /

I am John Austin, / a science teacher / at Crestville High School. //
(동격)
저는 John Austin입니다 / 과학 교사인 / Crestville 고등학교의 //

Recently / I was impressed / by the latest book you wrote / about the environment. //
앞에 목적격 관계대명사 생략
최근에 / 저는 감명받았습니다 / 당신이 쓴 최신 도서에 / 환경에 관해서 //

Also / my students read your book / and had a class discussion about it. //
또한 / 저의 학생들은 당신의 책을 읽었고 / 그것에 대한 수업 토론을 하였습니다 //

They are big fans of your book, / so I'd like to ask you / to visit our school / and give a special lecture. //
ask의 목적격 보어(to부정사)
단서 1 작가에게 학교를 방문하여 특별 강연을 해달라고 요청함
그들은 당신의 책을 아주 좋아합니다 / 그래서 저는 당신에게 요청드리고 싶습니다 / 우리 학교에 방문하여 / 특별 강연을 해 주시기를 //

We can set the date and time / to suit your schedule. //
우리는 날짜와 시간을 정할 수 있습니다 / 당신의 일정에 맞춰 //

Having you at our school / would be a fantastic experience / for the students. //
동명사 주어
단서 2 작가의 방문과 강연이 학생들에게 어떤 영향을 미칠지 설명함
당신이 우리 학교에 와 주신다면 / 멋진 경험이 될 것 같습니다 / 학생들에게 //

We would be very grateful / if you could come. //
주절이 앞에 온 가정법 과거 문장
우리는 정말 감사하겠습니다 / 당신이 와 주신다면 //

Best regards, John Austin /
John Austin 드림 /

- science ⓝ 과학 · recently ⓐ 최근에 · impressed ⓐ 감명을 받은
- environment ⓝ 환경 · discussion ⓝ 토론 · lecture ⓝ 강의
- suit ⓥ 맞추다 · experience ⓝ 경험 · grateful ⓐ 감사한

Jane Watson 씨께,
저는 Crestville 고등학교의 과학 교사 John Austin입니다. 최근에, 저는 환경에 관해 당신이 쓴 최신 도서에 감명받았습니다. 또한 저의 학생들은 당신의 책을 읽었고 그것에 대해 토론 수업을 하였습니다. 그들은 당신의 책을 아주 좋아하고, 그래서 저는 당신이 우리 학교에 방문하여 특별 강연을 해 주시기를 요청드리고 싶습니다. 우리는 당신의 일정에 맞춰 날짜와 시간을 정할 수 있습니다. 당신이 우리 학교에 와 주신다면 학생들에게 멋진 경험이 될 것 같습니다. 우리는 당신이 와 주신다면 정말 감사하겠습니다.
John Austin 드림

다음 글의 목적으로 가장 적절한 것은?

① 환경 보호의 중요성을 강조하려고
   작가가 환경에 관한 책을 썼다고 했으나, 환경 보호의 중요성을 강조하는 내용은 없음
② 글쓰기에서 주의할 점을 알려 주려고 작가의 책에 감명받았다며 칭찬하고 있음
③ 특강 강사로 작가의 방문을 요청하려고
   I'd like to ask you to visit our school and give a special lecture
④ 작가의 팬 사인회 일정 변경을 공지하려고
   팬 사인회나 일정 변경에 관한 내용은 없음
⑤ 작가가 쓴 책의 내용에 관하여 문의하려고 책의 내용에 대해 질문하지 않음

왜 정답? ❀❀❀ [정답률 94%]

작가에게 학교를 방문하여 특별 강연을 해달라고 요청하고 있고 작가의 방문이 학생들에게 멋진 경험이 될 것이라고 했기 때문에 글의 목적은 ③이다.

왜 오답?

① 작가가 쓴 최신 도서가 환경에 관한 책이라는 내용만 나와 있다. 함정

② 작가의 책에 감명받았다고 칭찬하고 있으며 글쓰기에서 주의할 점은 언급하지 않았다.

④ 작가의 팬 사인회와 그 일정 변경에 관한 내용은 없다.

⑤ 작가의 방문과 특별 강연을 요청할 뿐, 책의 내용에 대해서는 질문하지 않았다.

19 정답 ① ✱ 모래성 쌓기의 진정한 의미

Marilyn and her three-year-old daughter, Sarah, / took a trip to
동격
계속적용법의 관계부사(선행사: the beach)
the beach, / where Sarah built her first sandcastle. //
Marilyn과 세 살 된 딸 Sarah는 / 해변으로 여행을 떠났고 / 그곳에서 Sarah는 처음으로 모래성을 쌓았다 //

Moments later, / an enormous wave destroyed Sarah's castle. //
잠시 후 / 거대한 파도가 Sarah의 성을 무너뜨렸다 //

In response to the loss of her sandcastle, / tears streamed down Sarah's cheeks / and her heart was broken. //
단서 1 마음이 무너지고 눈물을 흘림
모래성을 잃은 것에 반응하여 / 눈물이 Sarah의 뺨을 타고 흘러내렸고 / 그녀의 마음은 무너졌다 //

She ran to Marilyn, / saying / she would never build a sandcastle again. //
분사구문을 이끄는 현재분사
그녀는 Marilyn에게 달려갔다 / 말하며 / 그녀가 다시는 모래성을 쌓지 않겠다고 //

Marilyn said, / "Part of the joy of building a sandcastle is / that, in the end, / we give it as a gift / to the ocean." //
단수 주어 / 단수 동사
Marilyn은 말했다 / "모래성을 쌓는 즐거움 중 일부는 / 결국에는 / 우리가 그것을 선물로 주는 것이란다 / 바다에게"라고 //
단서 2 모래성 쌓기에 대한 엄마 Marilyn의 생각을 매우 좋아함

Sarah loved this idea / and responded with enthusiasm / to the idea of building another castle —
병렬 구조
단서 3 또 다른 모래성을 만들 생각에 열정적으로 반응함
Sarah는 이 생각이 마음에 들었고 / 열정적으로 반응했다 / 또 다른 모래성을 만들 생각에 /

this time, / even closer to the water / so the ocean would get its gift sooner! //
비교급 강조 부사
이번에는 / 바다와 훨씬 더 가까운 곳에서 / 바다가 그 선물을 더 빨리 받을 수 있도록 //

- sandcastle ⓝ 모래성 · enormous ⓐ 거대한
- destroy ⓥ 부수다 · stream ⓥ 흐르다 · respond ⓥ 반응하다
- enthusiasm ⓝ 열정 · regretful ⓐ 후회하는

Marilyn과 세 살 된 딸 Sarah는 해변으로 여행을 떠났고, 그곳에서 Sarah는 처음으로 모래성을 쌓았다. 잠시 후, 거대한 파도가 Sarah의 성을 무너뜨렸다. 모래성을 잃은 것에 반응하여 눈물이 Sarah의 뺨을 타고 흘러내렸고, 그녀의

마음은 무너졌다. 그녀는 다시는 모래성을 쌓지 않겠다고 말하며 Marilyn에게 달려갔다. Marilyn은 "모래성을 쌓는 즐거움 중 일부는 결국에는 우리가 그것을 바다에게 선물로 주는 것이란다."라고 말했다. Sarah는 이 생각이 마음에 들었고 또 다른 모래성을 만들 생각에 이번에는 바다와 훨씬 더 가까운 곳에서 바다가 그 선물을 더 빨리 받을 수 있도록 하겠다며 열정적으로 반응했다.

다음 글에 드러난 Sarah의 심경 변화로 가장 적절한 것은?

① sad → excited her heart was broken → loved this idea and responded with
　슬픈 → 신이 난　enthusiasm
② envious → anxious 초반부에 슬퍼서 눈물을 흘리는 상황임
　부러워한 → 걱정하는
③ bored → joyful 모래성을 잃은 것에 마음이 무너졌다고 했기 때문에 지루한 감정이 아님
　지루한 → 즐거운
④ relaxed → regretful 안도하거나 후회하는 감정을 느낄 상황이 아님
　안도하는 → 후회하는
⑤ nervous → surprised 초조한 감정이나 놀란 감정이 표현되지 않음
　초조한 → 놀란

왜 정답? ✽✾✾ [정답률 95%]

전반부: 파도가 모래성을 무너뜨려서 마음이 무너짐 ▶ '슬픈'

후반부: 바다에 모래성을 선물로 주는 거라는 엄마의 생각이 마음에 들어 또 다른 모래성을 쌓는 것에 열정적으로 반응함 ▶ '신이 난'

따라서 Sarah의 심경 변화로 가장 적절한 것은 ① '슬픈 → 신이 난'이다.

왜 오답?

② 초반부에 모래성이 무너져서 눈물을 흘리며 슬퍼하는 상황이므로 부러워하는 감정이라고 볼 수 없다.

③ 모래성을 잃은 것에 반응하여 눈물을 흘리고 마음이 무너졌다는 내용이 나오기 때문에 지루한 감정이 아니다.

④ 초반부에 모래성이 무너진 것에 대해 안도하거나 후반부에 엄마의 말을 듣고 모래성을 쌓는 것에 대해 후회하고 있지 않다.

⑤ 내용에서 초조하거나 놀란 감정을 나타내는 표현이 나와 있지 않다.

---

20 정답 ② ✽긍정적인 진술이 가져오는 변화

　　　선행사를 포함하는 관계대명사
Magic is what we all wish for / to happen in our life. //
마법은 우리 모두 바라는 바이다 / 자신의 삶에서 일어나기를 //

Do you love the movie Cinderella / like me? //
여러분도 '신데렐라' 영화를 사랑하는가 / 나처럼 //

Well, / in real life, / you can also create magic. //
그러면 / 실제 삶에서 / 여러분도 마법을 만들 수 있다 //

Here's the trick. // 여기 그 요령이 있다 //

　　　　　　　　　　　　　　　목적격 관계대명사
Write down all the real-time challenges / that you face and deal with. //
모든 실시간의 어려움을 적어라 / 여러분이 직면하고 처리하는 //

　　　　　change A into B: A를 B로 바꾸다
Just change the challenge statement / into positive statements. //
단지 그 어려움에 관한 진술을 바꾸어라 / 긍정적인 진술로 //　단서1 어려움에 관한 진술을 긍정적인 진술로 바꿈

사역동사+목적어+목적격 보어(동사원형)
Let me give you / an example / here. //
여러분에게 제시하겠다 / 한 예시를 / 여기서 //

　　　　　　　　　동명사구(전치사의 목적어)
If you struggle with / getting up early in the morning, / then write a positive statement / such as "I get up early in the morning at 5:00 am every day." //
만약 여러분이 어려움을 겪는다면 / 아침 일찍 일어나는 것에 / 그러면 긍정적인 진술을 써라 / '나는 매일 일찍 아침 5시에 일어난다'와 같은 //

접속사(일단 ~하면)
Once you write these statements, / get ready to witness / magic and confidence. //
일단 여러분이 이러한 진술을 적는다면 / 목격할 준비를 하라 / 마법과 자신감을 //

　　　　　　　　　'~ 함으로써'
You will be surprised / that just by writing these statements, / there is a shift / in the way you think and act. //
여러분은 놀랄 것이다 / 단지 이러한 진술을 적음으로써 / 변화가 있다는 것에 / 여러분이 생각하고 행동하는 방식에 //　단서2 긍정적인 진술이 생각과 행동 방식에 변화를 가져옴

Suddenly you feel / more powerful and positive. //
어느 순간 여러분은 느끼게 된다 / 더 강력하고 긍정적이라고 //　단서3 자신이 더 강력하고 긍정적이라고 느낄 수 있음

• magic ⓝ 마법, 마술　• challenge ⓝ 어려움, 도전
• statement ⓝ 진술　• positive ⓐ 긍정적인
• struggle ⓥ 어려움을 겪다　• witness ⓥ 목격하다
• confidence ⓝ 자신감　• surprise ⓥ 놀라게 하다　• shift ⓝ 변화
• powerful ⓐ 강력한

마법은 우리 모두 자신의 삶에서 일어나기를 바라는 바이다. 여러분도 나처럼 '신데렐라' 영화를 사랑하는가? 그러면, 실제 삶에서, 여러분도 마법을 만들 수 있다. 여기 그 요령이 있다. 여러분이 직면하고 처리하는 모든 실시간의 어려움을 적어라. 그 어려움에 관한 진술을 긍정적인 진술로 바꾸어라. 여기서 여러분에게 한 예시를 제시하겠다. 만약 여러분이 아침 일찍 일어나는 것에 어려움을 겪는다면, 그러면 '나는 매일 일찍 아침 5시에 일어난다.'와 같은 긍정적인 진술을 써라. 일단 여러분이 이러한 진술을 적는다면, 마법과 자신감을 목격할 준비를 하라. 여러분은 단지 이러한 진술을 적음으로써 여러분이 생각하고 행동하는 방식에 변화가 있다는 것에 놀랄 것이다. 어느 순간 여러분은 더 강력하고 긍정적이라고 느끼게 된다.

다음 글에서 필자가 주장하는 바로 가장 적절한 것은?

① 목표한 바를 꼭 이루려면 생각을 곧바로 행동으로 옮겨라.
　　　　　　　　　　　　　　생각을 행동으로 옮기라는 내용은 없음
② 자신감을 얻으려면 어려움을 긍정적인 진술로 바꿔 써라.
　　Just change the challenge statement into positive statements.
③ 어려운 일을 해결하려면 주변 사람에게 도움을 청하라.
　　　　　　　　　　　　어려움에 직면했을 때 긍정적인 진술을 하라는 내용임
④ 일상에서 자신감을 향상하려면 틈틈이 마술을 배워라.
　　　　　　　　　　　　　　　마술을 배우라고 하지 않음
⑤ 실생활에서 마주하는 도전을 피하지 말고 견뎌 내라.
　　　　　　　　도전을 견뎌내는 인내와 관련된 내용은 없음

왜 정답? ✽✾✾ [정답률 91%]

요령: 실시간으로 직면하는 어려움을 긍정적인 진술로 바꾸기

예시: 아침에 일찍 일어나는 것이 어렵다면, '매일 일찍 아침 5시에 일어난다.'라고 적어보기

결과: 그렇게 행동할 자신감을 얻고, 생각과 행동 방식이 변화되어 스스로에 대해 긍정적으로 느낄 수 있음

▶ 긍정적인 진술을 통해 스스로를 더 강력하고 긍정적이라고 느낄 수 있는 변화와 자신감을 보게 될 것이라는 내용이므로 정답은 ②이다.

왜 오답?

① 목표를 이루기 위해 생각을 행동으로 옮기라는 내용은 언급되지 않았다.

③ 어려운 일에 직면했을 때 변화를 위해서 긍정적인 진술을 하는 방법이 제시되었다.

④ 이 글에서 마법은 어려움이 해결되고 변화가 일어나는 일을 비유적으로 표현한 것이지, 실제로 마술을 배우라는 의미가 아니다.

⑤ 도전을 피하지 말고 인내해야 한다는 내용은 언급되지 않았다.

---

21 정답 ① ✽동물의 수많은 감각

Consider / the seemingly simple question / How many senses are there? //
고려해 봐라 / 겉으로 보기에 단순한 질문을 / '얼마나 많은 감각이 존재하는가'라는 //

　　　　　　　　　　　　　　　　　　　목적어절을 이끄는 접속사
Around 2,370 years ago, / Aristotle wrote / that there are five, / in both humans and animals — / sight, hearing, smell, taste, and touch. //
　　　　　　　　　　both A and B: A와 B 둘 다
약 2,370년 전 / Aristotle은 썼다 / 다섯(감각)이 있다고 / 인간과 동물 둘 다에게 / 시각, 청각, 후각, 미각, 그리고 촉각 //　단서1 Aristotle은 인간과 동물에게 다섯(감각)이 있다고 기술함

　　　　　　　'~에 따르면'
However, / according to the philosopher Fiona Macpherson, / there are reasons to doubt it. //
　　　　　　　　　　　　　형용사적 용법(reasons 수식)
그러나 / 철학자 Fiona Macpherson에 따르면 / 그것을 의심할 이유가 존재한다 //

For a start, / Aristotle missed a few in humans: / the perception of your own body / which is different from touch / and the sense of balance / which has links to both touch and vision. //
　　　　　　　　　　　　　　　　　　　　　　병렬 구조
　　　　　　　　　　　　　　　주격 관계대명사
우선 / Aristotle은 인간에게서 몇 가지를 빠뜨렸는데 / 여러분 자신의 신체에 대한 인식과 촉각과는 다른 / 균형 감각 / 촉각과 시각 모두에 관련되어 있는 //　단서2 다른 동물들은 범주화하기

　　　　　　복수 선행사(senses)와 수 일치
Other animals have senses / that are even harder to categorize. //
　　　　　　　　　　　　　　　　훨씬 더 어려운 감각을 가짐
다른 동물들은 감각을 가지고 있다 / 범주화하기 훨씬 더 어려운 //

Many vertebrates have a different sense system / for **detecting** [동명사구(전치사의 목적어)] **odors**. //
많은 척추동물은 다른 감각 체계를 가지고 있다 / 냄새를 탐지하기 위한 //

Some snakes can detect / the body heat of their prey. //
어떤 뱀은 감지할 수 있다 / 그들의 먹잇감의 체열을 //

These examples tell us / **that** [목적어절을 이끄는 접속사] "senses cannot be clearly divided into a limited number of specific kinds," / Macpherson wrote in *The Senses*. // **단서 3** 감각은 특정한 종류로 명확하게 분류되지 않을 수 있음
이러한 사례는 우리에게 알려 준다 / '감각은 제한된 수의 특정한 종류로 명확하게 나누어지지 않을 수 있다'라는 것을 / Macpherson이 'The Senses'에서 쓰기를 //

Instead of [~ 대신에] trying to push animal senses / into Aristotelian buckets, / we should study them / for what they are. //
동물의 감각을 밀어 넣는 대신 / Aristotle의 양동이로 / 우리는 그것들을 연구해야 한다 / 그것들이 존재하는 그대로 //

- seemingly [ad] 겉보기에 · sense [n] 감각 · sight [n] 시각
- philosopher [n] 철학자 · doubt [v] 의심하다
- perception [n] 인식 · balance [n] 균형 · vision [n] 시각
- categorize [v] 분류하다 · detect [v] 감지하다 · prey [n] 먹잇감
- divide [v] 나누다 · specific [a] 특정한 · bucket [n] 양동이

'얼마나 많은 감각이 존재하는가?'라는 겉으로 보기에 단순한 질문을 고려해 봐라. 약 2,370년 전 Aristotle은 인간과 동물 둘 다에게 시각, 청각, 후각, 미각, 그리고 촉각의 다섯(감각)이 있다고 썼다. 그러나, 철학자 Fiona Macpherson에 따르면, 그것을 의심할 이유가 존재한다. 우선, Aristotle은 인간에게서 몇 가지를 빠뜨렸는데, 그것은 촉각과는 다른 여러분 자신의 신체에 대한 인식과, 촉각과 시각 모두에 관련되어 있는 균형 감각이었다. 다른 동물들은 훨씬 더 범주화하기 어려운 감각을 가지고 있다. 많은 척추동물은 냄새를 탐지하기 위한 다른 감각 체계를 가지고 있다. 어떤 뱀은 그들의 먹잇감의 체열을 감지할 수 있다. Macpherson이 'The Senses'에서 쓰기를, 이러한 사례는 우리에게 '감각은 제한된 수의 특정한 종류로 명확하게 나누어지지 않을 수 있다.'라는 것을 알려 준다. 동물의 감각을 Aristotle의 양동이로 밀어 넣는 대신, 우리는 그것들을 존재하는 그대로 연구해야 한다.

밑줄 친 push animal senses into Aristotelian buckets가 다음 글에서 의미하는 바로 가장 적절한 것은? [3점]

① sort various animal senses into fixed categories
다양한 동물의 감각을 고정된 범주로 분류하다 · Aristotle은 동물의 감각을 다섯 가지로 분류했음
② keep a balanced view to understand real senses 균형 잡힌 견해를
실제 감각을 이해하기 위해 균형 잡힌 견해를 유지한다 · 유지하라는 내용은 언급되지 않음
③ doubt the traditional way of dividing all senses
모든 감각을 나누는 전통적인 방식에 의문을 제기한다 · 전통적인 방식으로 나눈다는 의미임
④ ignore the lessons on senses from Aristotle 제시되지 않음
Aristotle의 감각에 대한 가르침을 무시한다
⑤ analyze more animals to find real senses 동물의 감각을 기존의 고정된
실제 감각을 찾기 위해 더 많은 동물을 분석한다 · 범주로 분류하는 것에서 벗어나야 한다는 내용임

왜 정답? ✿✿✿ [정답률 64%]

- Aristotle은 인간과 동물에게 다섯 가지 감각이 있다고 기술했음 **단서 1**
- 다른 동물들은 훨씬 더 범주화하기 어려운 감각을 가짐 **단서 2**
→ 감각은 특정한 종류로 명확하게 분류되지 않을 수 있음 **단서 3**
  ▶ '동물의 감각을 Aristotle의 양동이로 밀어 넣는 것'은 '동물의 감각을 Aristotle이 정한 다섯 가지 감각의 범주로 분류하는 것'을 의미하므로 ① '다양한 동물의 감각을 고정된 범주로 분류한다'는 것을 의미한다.

왜 오답?

② 균형 잡힌 견해를 유지하라는 내용은 이 글에서 다루어지지 않았다.
③ 감각을 나누는 전통적인 방식에서 벗어나 다양하고 복잡한 감각을 있는 그대로 연구해야 한다는 글의 내용과 부합하나, 밑줄 친 부분은 감각을 전통적인 방식으로 나누는 것을 의미한다. **함정**
④ Aristotle의 감각에 대한 가르침을 무시하라는 내용은 언급되지 않았다.
⑤ 동물의 감각이 범주화하기 어려울 만큼 훨씬 다양하고 복잡하다는 내용은 있지만, 더 많은 동물을 분석하라는 내용은 제시되지 않았다. **주의**

---

22 정답 ③ ＊우리가 지닌 리더가 될 수 있는 잠재력

When we think of leaders, / we may think of people / **such as** [~와 같은] Abraham Lincoln or Martin Luther King, Jr. //
우리가 리더에 대해 생각할 때 / 우리는 사람들에 대해 생각할지 모른다 / Abraham Lincoln 혹은 Martin Luther King, Jr.와 같은 //

If you consider / the historical importance and far-reaching influence / of these individuals, / leadership might seem / like a noble and high goal. //
만약 여러분이 고려한다면 / 역사적 중요성과 광범위한 영향력을 / 이러한 인물들의 / 리더십은 보일지도 모른다 / 고귀하고 높은 목표처럼 //

But like all of us, / these people started out as students, workers, and citizens /
그러나 우리 모두와 마찬가지로 / 이러한 인물들은 학생, 근로자, 그리고 시민으로 시작했다 / 주격 관계대명사 간접의문문(의문사+주어+동사)
who possessed ideas / about **how some aspect of daily life could be improved** / on a larger scale. // **단서 1** 위대한 리더들은 일상을 개선할 아이디어를 가진 학생, 근로자, 시민으로 시작함
생각을 가졌던 / 일상생활의 어느 측면이 어떻게 개선될 수 있는지에 대한 / 더 큰 규모로 //

Through diligence and experience, / they improved upon their ideas / **단서 2** 리더들은 근면함과 경험을 통해 본인의 생각을 발전시킴
근면함과 경험을 통해 / 이 사람들은 자신의 생각을 발전시켰다 / by v-ing: ~함으로써
by sharing them with others, / **seeking** their opinions and feedback / and constantly **looking** for the best way / **to** accomplish goals / for a group. // [병렬 구조] [형용사적 용법(way 수식)]
자신의 생각을 다른 사람들과 공유하고 / 그들의 의견과 반응을 구하며 / 끊임없이 가장 좋은 방법을 찾음으로써 / 목표를 성취할 수 있는 / 집단을 위한 // **단서 3** 우리 모두는 리더가 형용사적 용법(potential 수식) 될 수 있는 잠재력을 가짐

Thus we all have the potential / **to be leaders** at school, in our communities, and at work, / regardless of age or experience. //
그러므로 우리는 모두 잠재력을 가지고 있다 / 학교, 공동체, 그리고 일터에서 리더가 될 수 있는 / 나이나 경험에 관계없이 //

- historical [a] 역사적인 · importance [n] 중요성
- far-reaching [a] 광범위한 · influence [n] 영향력
- noble [a] 고귀한 · possess [v] 가지다, 소유하다 · aspect [n] 측면
- improve [v] 개선하다 · scale [n] 규모 · share [v] 공유하다
- seek [v] 찾다, 구하다 · opinion [n] 의견 · constantly [ad] 끊임없이
- accomplish [v] 성취하다 · thus [ad] 그러므로
- potential [n] 잠재력 · community [n] 공동체
- regardless of ~와 관계없이

우리가 리더에 대해 생각할 때, 우리는 Abraham Lincoln 혹은 Martin Luther King, Jr.와 같은 사람들에 대해 생각할지 모른다. 만약 여러분이 이러한 인물들의 역사적 중요성과 광범위한 영향력을 고려한다면, 리더십은 고귀하고 높은 목표처럼 보일지도 모른다. 그러나 우리 모두와 마찬가지로, 이러한 인물들은 일상생활의 어느 측면이 더 큰 규모로 어떻게 개선될 수 있는지에 대한 생각을 가졌던 학생, 근로자, 그리고 시민으로 시작했다. 근면함과 경험을 통해, 그들은 자신의 생각을 다른 사람들과 공유하고, 그들의 의견과 반응을 구하며, 끊임없이 집단을 위한 목표를 성취할 수 있는 가장 좋은 방법을 찾음으로써 자신의 생각을 발전시켰다. 그러므로 우리는 모두, 나이나 경험에 관계없이, 학교, 공동체, 그리고 일터에서 리더가 될 수 있는 잠재력을 가지고 있다.

다음 글의 요지로 가장 적절한 것은?

① 훌륭한 리더는 고귀한 목표를 위해 희생적인 삶을 산다.
리더가 희생적인 삶을 산다는 것은 언급되지 않음
② 위대한 인물은 위기의 순간에 뛰어난 결단력을 발휘한다.
자신의 생각을 발전시킨 사람들이 리더가 된 내용이 제시됨
③ 공동체를 위한 아이디어를 발전시키는 누구나 리더가 될 수 있다.
큰 규모에서 일상을 개선할 아이디어를 가진 사람이라면 누구나 리더가 될 잠재력을 가짐
④ 다른 사람의 의견을 경청하는 자세는 목표 달성에 가장 중요하다.
리더가 된 사람들이 다른 사람들의 의견과 반응을 구한다는 내용이 있긴 하지만 글의 중심 내용은 아님
⑤ 근면하고 경험이 풍부한 사람들은 경제적으로 성공할 수 있다.
경제적으로 성공하는 사람들에 대한 것은 언급되지 않음

왜 정답? ✿✿✿ [정답률 92%]

오해: 리더십은 고귀하고 높은 목표임

진실: 우리 모두와 마찬가지로, 위대한 리더들은 일상생활의 어느 측면이 더 큰 규모로 어떻게 개선될 수 있는지에 관한 생각을 가진 일반적인 사람(학생, 근로자, 시민)이었음 **단서 1**

부연: 그들은 근면함과 경험을 통해 본인의 생각을 발전시킴 **단서 2**

주장: 우리 모두 리더가 될 수 있는 잠재력을 가지고 있음 **단서 3**

▶ 평범한 학생, 근로자, 시민도 생각을 발전시켜 집단을 위한 목표를 성취할 수 있다면 위대한 리더가 될 수 있고 우리는 그렇게 할 수 있는 잠재력이 있다는 내용이므로 정답은 ③이다.

왜 오답?

① 리더가 희생적인 삶을 산다는 것은 언급되지 않았다.

② 리더는 본인의 생각을 발전시켜 집단을 위한 목표를 성취할 수 있는 가장 좋은 방법을 찾는다고 했다.

④ 위대한 리더가 다른 사람들과 생각을 공유하고 의견과 반응을 구한다는 내용이 나오지만, 이는 핵심 내용이 아니다. (✄ 이유: 경청하는 것은 생각을 발전시키는 과정의 일부일 뿐이다.)

⑤ 경제적으로 성공하는 사람들에 대한 것은 언급되지 않았다.

> 리더와 혼동하면 안 됨 **꿀 팁**

---

23 정답 ① ★2등급 대비 [정답률 78%]

★ 윤작의 장점

전치사+관계대명사
Crop rotation is the process / in which farmers change the crops
앞에 목적격 관계대명사 생략
/ they grow in their fields / in a special order. //
윤작은 과정이다 / 농부가 작물을 바꾸는 / 자신의 밭에서 재배하는 / 특별한 순서로 //

For example, / if a farmer has three fields, / he or she may grow / carrots in the first field, / green beans in the second, / and tomatoes in the third. //
예를 들면 / 만약 한 농부가 세 개의 밭을 가지고 있다면 / 그들은 재배할 수 있다 / 첫 번째 밭에는 당근을 / 두 번째 밭에는 녹색 콩을 / 세 번째 밭에는 토마토를 //
사이에 반복되는 will be가 생략됨
The next year, / green beans will be in the first field, / tomatoes in the second field, / and carrots will be in the third. //
그 다음 해에 / 첫 번째 밭에는 녹색 콩을 / 두 번째 밭에는 토마토를 / 세 번째 밭에는 당근을 재배할 것이다 //

In year three, / the crops will rotate again. //
3년 차에 / 작물은 다시 순환할 것이다 //

By the fourth year, / the crops will go back to their original order. //
4년째에 이르면 / 작물은 원래의 순서로 되돌아갈 것이다 //
Each+단수 명사+단수 동사   **단서 1** 작물을 바꿔서
Each crop enriches the soil / for the next crop. //   심으면 각각의 작물은
각각의 작물은 토양을 비옥하게 한다 / 다음 작물을 위한 //   다음 작물을 위한 토양을
                                                        비옥하게 함
This type of farming is sustainable / because the soil stays healthy. // **단서 2** 윤작은 토양이 건강하게 유지되어 지속 가능함
이 유형의 농업은 지속 가능하다 / 토양이 건강하게 유지되기 때문에 //

- crop rotation 윤작 · process ⓝ 과정 · field ⓝ 밭
- order ⓝ 순서 · rotate ⓥ 순환하다 · original ⓐ 원래의
- enrich ⓥ 비옥하게 하다 · soil ⓝ 토양 · type ⓝ 유형
- maintain ⓥ 유지하다 · organic ⓐ 유기농의 · impact ⓝ 영향

윤작은 농부가 자신의 밭에서 재배하는 작물을 특별한 순서로 바꾸는 과정이다. 예를 들면, 만약 한 농부가 세 개의 밭을 가지고 있다면, 그들은 첫 번째 밭에는 당근을, 두 번째 밭에는 녹색 콩을, 세 번째 밭에는 토마토를 재배할 수 있다. 그 다음 해에 첫 번째 밭에는 녹색 콩을, 두 번째 밭에는 토마토를, 세 번째 밭에는 당근을 재배할 것이다. 3년 차에 작물은 다시 순환할 것이다. 4년째에 이르면 작물은 원래의 순서로 되돌아 갈 것이다. 각각의 작물은 다음 작물을 위한 토양을 비옥하게 한다. 이 유형의 농업은 토양이 건강하게 유지되기 때문에 지속 가능하다.

다음 글의 주제로 가장 적절한 것은?

① advantage of crop rotation in maintaining soil health
토양 건강 유지에 있어서 윤작의 장점 — 윤작을 하면 토양이 건강하게 유지되어 지속 가능함

② influence of purchasing organic food on farmers
유기농 식품 구매가 농부에게 주는 영향 — 유기농 식품 구매에 대해 언급하지 않음

③ ways to choose three important crops for rich soil
비옥한 토양을 위해 세 가지 중요 작물을 선택하는 방법

④ danger of growing diverse crops in small spaces
작은 공간에서 다양한 작물을 재배하는 것의 위험성 — 작은 공간에서 다양한 작물을 재배한다는 것은 없음

⑤ negative impact of crop rotation on the environment
윤작이 환경에 미치는 부정적인 영향 — 윤작이 토양을 비옥하게 한다는 내용임

┗ 세 가지 작물이 예시로 나오기는 하지만 윤작의 방법을 설명하기 위해 제시됨

왜 2등급? 마지막 두 문장을 제외하면 전부 윤작의 정의와 과정에 관한 내용이기 때문에, 글을 처음부터 읽는다면 주제를 오해하기 쉬운 2등급 대비 문제이다. 윤작의 순기능이 언급되는 글의 마지막 부분에 집중해서 글의 주제를 파악해야 한다.

| 문제 풀이 순서 |

1st 글의 앞부분에서 글의 소재를 파악하고 이어질 내용을 예상한다.

┌ 윤작은 농부가 자신의 밭에서 재배하는 작물을 특별한 순서로 바꾸는
└ 과정이다. **단서**

➡ 글의 소재: 윤작(재배하는 작물의 순서를 바꾸는 과정)
윤작의 구체적인 방법이나 윤작의 장점이 이어질 것이다. **발상**

2nd 글의 나머지 부분에서 내용을 파악하고 정답을 찾는다.

┌ 작물을 바꿔서 심으면 각각의 작물은 다음 작물을 위한 토양을 비옥하게 함 **단서 1**
└ 윤작은 토양을 건강하게 유지하기 때문에 지속 가능함 **단서 2**

➡ 윤작을 하여 작물을 바꿔서 심으면 각 작물이 다음 작물이 심어질 토양을 비옥하게 하고, 토양이 건강하게 유지되어 농사가 지속 가능해짐

▶ 윤작의 장점을 설명하고 있는 이 글의 주제로 가장 적절한 것은 ① '토양 건강 유지에 있어서 윤작의 장점'이다.

| 선택지 분석 |

① **advantage of crop rotation in maintaining soil health**
토양 건강 유지에 있어서 윤작의 장점
윤작을 하면 토양의 건강이 유지되어 농사가 지속 가능하다는 장점을 설명하는 글이다.

② **influence of purchasing organic food on farmers**
유기농 식품 구매가 농부에게 주는 영향
유기농 식품 구매는 언급되지 않았다.

③ **ways to choose three important crops for rich soil**
비옥한 토양을 위해 세 가지 중요 작물을 선택하는 방법
윤작 방식을 설명하기 위해서 세 가지 작물을 예로 들었을 뿐이며, 세 가지 작물을 선택하는 방법에 관한 글이 아니다.

④ **danger of growing diverse crops in small spaces**
작은 공간에서 다양한 작물을 재배하는 것의 위험성
다양한 작물을 재배하는 내용이 나오긴 하지만, 작은 공간에서 재배한다는 내용은 제시되지 않았다.

⑤ **negative impact of crop rotation on the environment**
윤작이 환경에 미치는 부정적인 영향
윤작이 토양을 비옥하게 한다는 긍정적인 영향에 관한 글이기 때문에 부정적인 영향은 제시되지 않았다.

---

24 정답 ⑤ ★그림 작품 완성 시점의 판단

동명사 주어   ~보다는
Working around the whole painting, / rather than concentrating
                                              병렬 구조
on one area at a time, / will mean / you can stop at any point / and the painting can be considered "finished." //
전체 그림에 대해서 작업하는 것은 / 한 번에 한 영역에만 집중하기보다 / 의미할 것이다 / 여러분이 어떤 지점에서도 멈출 수 있고 / 그림이 '완성'된 것으로 간주될 수 있다는 것을 //
가목적어   진목적어   stop v-ing: ~하는 것을 그만두다
Artists often find it difficult / to know when to stop painting, /
가주어   진주어
and it can be tempting / to keep on adding more to your work. //
화가인 여러분은 종종 어렵다는 것을 발견하고 / 언제 그림을 멈춰야 할지 알기가 / 유혹을 느낄 수도 있다 / 자신의 그림에 계속해서 더 추가하고 싶은 //

가주어 진주어
It is important / **to take** a few steps back from the painting / from
부사적용법(목적)
time to time / **to assess** your progress. //
중요하다 / 그림에서 몇 걸음 뒤로 물러나는 것이 / 때때로 / 자신의 진행 상황을 평가하기
위해 // **단서 1** 자신의 진행 상황을 평가하기 위해 그림에서 몇 걸음 뒤로 물러나는 것이 중요함

Putting too much into a painting / can spoil its impact / and
주격 보어(과거분사)
leave it looking **overworked**. // **단서 2** 그림에 너무 많은 것을 넣으면 망칠 수 있음
한 그림에 너무 많은 것을 넣으면 / 그것의 영향력을 망칠 수 있고 / 그것이 과하게 작업된
것처럼 보이게 둘 수 있다 //

명사절 접속사
If you find yourself struggling / to decide **whether** you have
finished, / take a break / and come back to it later / with fresh
eyes. // **단서 3** 작업이 끝났는지 결정하는 것이 어렵다면 휴식을 취한 후에 그림을 다시 봄
만약 여러분이 자신이 어려움을 겪고 있음을 알게 된다면 / 끝냈는지를 결정하는 데 / 잠시
휴식을 취하고 / 나중에 그것(그림)으로 다시 돌아와라 / 새로운 눈으로 //

Then you can decide / whether any areas of your painting
would benefit / from further refinement. //
그러면 여러분은 결정할 수 있다 / 자신의 그림 어느 부분이 득을 볼지를 / 더 정교하게 꾸며서 //

- concentrate ⓥ 집중하다 • keep on v-ing 계속 ~하다
- from time to time 때때로 • assess ⓥ 평가하다
- progress ⓝ 진행 상황, 진전 • spoil ⓥ 망치다
- impact ⓝ 영향(력) • overwork ⓥ 과하게 작업하다
- struggle ⓥ 어려움을 겪다, 분투하다 • benefit ⓥ 득을 보다
- inspiration ⓝ 영감 • incomplete ⓐ 미완성의, 불완전한
- interpretation ⓝ 해석, 이해

한 번에 한 영역에만 집중하기보다 전체 그림에 대해서 작업하는 것은 여러분
이 어떤 지점에서도 멈출 수 있고 그림이 '완성'된 것으로 간주될 수 있다는 것
을 의미할 것이다. 화가인 여러분은 종종 언제 그림을 멈춰야 할지 알기 어렵다
는 것을 발견하고, 자신의 그림에 계속해서 더 추가하고 싶은 유혹을 느낄 수도
있다. 때때로 자신의 진행 상황을 평가하기 위해 그림에서 몇 걸음 뒤로 물러나
는 것이 중요하다. 한 그림에 너무 많은 것을 넣으면 그것의 영향력을 망칠 수
있고 그것이 과하게 작업된 것처럼 보이게 둘 수 있다. 만약 여러분이 끝났는지
를 결정하는 데 자신이 어려움을 겪고 있음을 알게 된다면, 잠시 휴식을 취하고
나중에 새로운 눈으로 그것(그림)으로 다시 돌아와라. 그러면 여러분은 더 정교
하게 꾸며서 자신의 그림 어느 부분이 득을 볼지를 결정할 수 있다.

다음 글의 제목으로 가장 적절한 것은?
그림에 너무 많은 것을 추가했을 때 망칠 수 있다는 내용임
① Drawing Inspiration from Diverse Artists
다양한 예술가들로부터 영감을 끌어내기
다양한 예술가에게 영감을 얻는 내용은 언급되지 않음
② Don't Spoil Your Painting by Leaving It Incomplete
너의 그림을 완성하지 않은 상태로 두어서 망치지 마라
③ Art Interpretation: Discover Meanings in a Painting
예술 해석: 그림 속의 의미를 발견해라   그림 속의 의미를 발견하는 내용은 제시되지 않음
④ Do Not Put Down Your Brush: The More, the Better
붓을 내려놓지 마라 : 다다익선   너무 많은 추가가 그림 작품에 해가 될 수 있음을 설명함
⑤ Avoid Overwork and Find the Right Moment to Finish
과한 작업을 피하고 마무리할 적절한 순간을 찾아라
적절한 시점에 과도한 작업을 멈추고 새로운 눈으로 작품을 다시 봐야 함

왜 정답? ✿✿ [정답률 67%]

- 작품의 진행 상황을 평가하기 위해서 본인 그림에서 몇 걸음 뒤로 물러나는 것이
  중요함 **단서 1**
- 한 그림에 너무 많은 것을 넣으면 작품의 영향력을 망칠 수 있고 과하게 작업된
  것처럼 보이게 둘 수 있음 **단서 2**
- 작업이 끝났는지 결정하는 데 어려움이 있다면 잠시 휴식을 취하고 새로운 눈으로
  그림을 바라봐야 함 **단서 3**
➡ 과도하게 그림 작품을 작업하지 않고 적절한 시점에 작업을 멈추는 것의 중요성과
  그 방법을 제시하고 있다.
▶ 따라서 정답은 ⑤ '과한 작업을 피하고 마무리할 적절한 순간을 찾아라'이다.

왜 오답?
① 다양한 예술가에게 영감을 얻는 내용은 언급되지 않았다.
② 너무 많은 것을 그림에 넣으면 안 된다는 내용이지 그림을 완성해야 한다는 내용이
   아니다.
③ 그림에서 의미를 발견하고 예술 작품을 해석하는 내용은 제시되지 않았다.
④ 그림에 너무 많은 것을 추가했을 때 작품의 영향력을 망치고 과하게 작업된 것처럼
   보이게 할 수 있다는 내용이므로, 글의 내용과 반대된다.

25 정답 ③ ＊젊은 사람들의 기후 변화에 대한 두려움

목적격 관계대명사(선행사: the extent)   '16세에서 25세 사이의'
The above graph shows / the extent to **which** young people **aged**
16-25 in six countries had fear / about climate change / in 2021. //
위 그래프는 보여준다 / 6개국의 16세에서 25세 사이 젊은 사람들이 두려움을 갖는 정도를 /
/ 기후 변화에 대해 / 2021년에 //

① The Philippines had the highest percentage / of young people
주격 관계대명사
who said they were extremely or very worried, / at 84 percent, /
분사구문을 이끄는 과거분사
followed by 67 percent in Brazil. // 필리핀이 가장 높음(49% + 35% = 84%),
브라질이 두 번째로 높음(29% + 38% = 67%)
필리핀은 비율이 가장 높았다 / 극도로 혹은 매우 걱정한다고 말한 젊은 사람들의 (비율이) /
84퍼센트로 / 브라질이 67퍼센트로 그 뒤를 이었다 //

② More than 60 percent of young people in Portugal said / they
were extremely worried or very worried. // 포르투갈(30% + 35% = 65%)은
60% 이상
포르투갈은 60퍼센트 이상의 젊은 사람들이 말했다 / 그들이 극도로 혹은 매우 걱정하고
있다고 //

복수 선행사(people)와 수 일치
③ In France, / the percentage of young people / who **were**
= the percentage
extremely worried / was higher(→ lower) / than **that** of young
people who were very worried. // **단서** 회색 막대(극도로 걱정하는 비율)가 하얀색
막대(매우 걱정하는 비율)보다 짧음
프랑스는 / 젊은 사람들의 비율이 / 극도로 걱정하는 / 더 높았다(→ 낮았다) / 매우 걱정하는
젊은 사람들의 비율보다 //

단수 주어
④ In the United Kingdom, / **the percentage** of young generation
단수 동사
/ who said that they were very worried / **was** 29 percent. //
영국은 / 젊은 세대의 비율이 / 매우 걱정한다고 말하는 / 29퍼센트였다 / 영국의 하얀색 막대는
29퍼센트임

⑤ In the United States, / the total percentage of extremely
worried and very worried youth / was the smallest among the
six countries. // 미국은 회색 막대와 하얀색 막대를 합한 길이가 가장 짧음
미국은 / 극도로 걱정하거나 매우 걱정하는 젊은 사람들의 총비율이 / 6개국 중에서 가장
작았다 //

- extent ⓝ 정도 • youth ⓝ 청소년, 젊은 사람들
- fear ⓝ 두려움 • climate change 기후 변화
- extremely 〔ad〕 극도로 • generation ⓝ 세대

위 그래프는 2021년 6개국의 16세에서 25세 사이 젊은 사람들이 기후 변화에
대해 두려움을 갖는 정도를 보여 준다. ① 필리핀은 극도로 혹은 매우 걱정한다
고 말한 젊은 사람들의 비율이 84퍼센트로 가장 높았으며, 브라질이 67퍼센트
로 그 뒤를 이었다. ② 포르투갈은 60퍼센트 이상의 젊은 사람들이 극도로 혹은
매우 걱정하고 있다고 말했다. ③ 프랑스는 극도로 걱정하는 젊은 사람들의 비
율이 매우 걱정하는 젊은 사람들의 비율보다 높았다(→ 낮았다). ④ 영국은 매
우 걱정한다고 말하는 젊은 세대의 비율이 29퍼센트였다. ⑤ 미국은 극도로 걱
정하거나 매우 걱정하는 젊은 사람들의 총비율이 6개국 중에서 가장 작았다.

다음 도표의 내용과 일치하지 않는 것은?

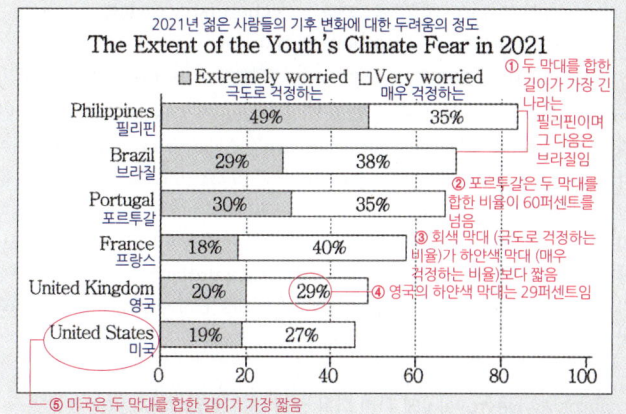

2021년 젊은 사람들의 기후 변화에 대한 두려움의 정도
The Extent of the Youth's Climate Fear in 2021
☐ Extremely worried ☐ Very worried
극도로 걱정하는   매우 걱정하는

① 두 막대를 합한 길이가 가장 긴 나라는 필리핀이며 그 다음은 브라질임
② 포르투갈은 두 막대를 합한 비율이 60퍼센트를 넘음
③ 회색 막대(극도로 걱정하는 비율)가 하얀색 막대(매우 걱정하는 비율)보다 짧음
④ 영국의 하얀색 막대는 29퍼센트임
⑤ 미국은 두 막대를 합한 길이가 가장 짧음

	Extremely worried	Very worried
Philippines 필리핀	49%	35%
Brazil 브라질	29%	38%
Portugal 포르투갈	30%	35%
France 프랑스	18%	40%
United Kingdom 영국	20%	29%
United States 미국	19%	27%

왜 정답? ✿✿✿ [정답률 85%]

프랑스에서 극도로 걱정하는 젊은 사람들의 비율은 18퍼센트이며 매우 걱정하는 젊은
사람들의 비율은 40퍼센트로, 극도로 걱정하는 젊은 사람들의 비율이 매우 걱정하는
젊은 사람들의 비율보다 작다. 따라서 도표의 내용과 일치하지 않는 것은 ③이다.

① 극도로 걱정하는 젊은 사람들의 비율(회색 막대)과 매우 걱정하는 젊은 사람들의 비율(하얀색 막대)의 합이 가장 큰 나라는 필리핀이고 두 번째로 큰 나라는 브라질이다.

② 포르투갈은 회색 막대와 하얀색 막대를 합한 비율이 65퍼센트이다.

④ 영국에서는 매우 걱정하는 젊은 사람들의 비율을 가리키는 하얀색 막대가 29퍼센트이다.

⑤ 미국은 극도로 걱정하는 젊은 사람들의 비율을 가리키는 회색 막대와 매우 걱정하는 젊은 사람들의 비율을 가리키는 하얀색 막대를 합한 길이가 가장 짧은 국가이다.

---

26 정답 ④ * Jaroslav Heyrovsky의 생애

Jaroslav Heyrovsky was born / in Prague on December 20, 1890, / as the fifth child of Leopold Heyrovsky. //
Jaroslav Heyrovsky는 태어났다 / 1890년 12월 20일 Prague에서 / Leopold Heyrovsky의 다섯째 자녀로 //

In 1901 / Jaroslav went to a secondary school / **called** the 〔과거분사(a secondary school 수식)〕 Akademicke Gymnasium. //
1901년에 / Jaroslav는 중등학교에 다녔다 / Akademicke Gymnasium이라고 불리는 //

Rather than Latin and Greek, / he showed a strong interest / in 〔'~보다는'〕 the natural sciences. // ①의 단서 라틴어와 그리스어보다 자연 과학에 강한 흥미를 보임
라틴어와 그리스어보다는 / 그는 강한 흥미를 보였다 / 자연 과학에 //

★ 주어가 대명사인 경우의 도치구문
주어가 대명사일 때, 〈방향·장소〉의 부사구와 보어가 문두에 오더라도 주어와 동사를 도치하지 않는다.

★ 주어와 동사가 도치되지 않음
At Czech University in Prague / he studied chemistry, physics, and mathematics. // ②의 단서 Czech University에서 화학, 물리학, 수학을 공부함
Prague에 있는 Czech University에서 / 그는 화학, 물리학 및 수학을 공부했다 //

From 1910 to 1914 / he continued his studies / at University College, London. // ③의 단서 1910년부터 1914년까지 런던의 University College에서 학업을 계속함
1910년부터 1914년까지 / 그는 학업을 이어 나갔다 / 런던의 University College에서 //

Throughout the First World War, / Jaroslav served in a military hospital. // ④의 단서 제1차 세계 대전 내내 군 병원에서 복무함
제1차 세계 대전 내내 / Jaroslav는 군 병원에 복무했다 //

In 1926, / Jaroslav became the first Professor of Physical Chemistry / at Charles University in Prague. //
1926년에 / Jaroslav는 최초의 물리화학 교수가 되었다 / Prague에 있는 Charles University에서 //

He won the Nobel Prize in chemistry / in 1959. //
그는 노벨 화학상을 수상했다 / 1959년에 // ⑤의 단서 1959년에 노벨 화학상을 수상함

· Prague ⓝ 프라하(체코의 수도)   · secondary school 중등학교
· show interest in ~에 흥미를 보이다   · chemistry ⓝ 화학
· physics ⓝ 물리학   · mathematics ⓝ 수학
· throughout prep 내내   · serve ⓥ 복무하다   · military ⓐ 군대의

Jaroslav Heyrovsky는 1890년 12월 20일 Prague에서 Leopold Heyrovsky의 다섯째 자녀로 태어났다. 1901년 Jaroslav는 Akademicke Gymnasium이라고 불리는 중등학교에 다녔다. 그는 라틴어와 그리스어보다는 자연 과학에 강한 흥미를 보였다. Prague에 있는 Czech University에서 그는 화학, 물리학 및 수학을 공부했다. 1910년부터 1914년까지 그는 런던의 University College에서 학업을 이어 나갔다. 제1차 세계 대전 내내 Jaroslav는 군 병원에 복무했다. 1926년에 Jaroslav는 Prague에 있는 Charles University 최초의 물리화학 교수가 되었다. 그는 1959년에 노벨 화학상을 수상했다.

Jaroslav Heyrovsky에 관한 다음 글의 내용과 일치하지 않는 것은?
① 라틴어와 그리스어보다 자연 과학에 강한 흥미를 보였다.
    Rather than Latin and Greek, he showed a strong interest in the natural sciences.
② Czech University에서 화학, 물리학 및 수학을 공부했다.
    At Czech University in Prague he studied chemistry, physics and mathematics.
③ 1910년부터 1914년까지 런던에서 학업을 이어 나갔다.
    From 1910 to 1914 he continued his studies at University College, London.
④ 제1차 세계 대전이 끝난 후 군 병원에 복무했다.
    Throughout the First World War, Jaroslav served in a military hospital.
⑤ 1959년에 노벨 화학상을 수상했다.
    He won the Nobel Prize in chemistry in 1959.

〉왜 정답 ? ✿✿✿ [정답률 87%]

제1차 세계 대전 내내 Jaroslav는 군 병원에 복무했다고 했으므로 (Throughout the First World War, Jaroslav served in a military hospital.) 제1차 세계 대전이 끝난 후 복무했다고 한 ④은 글의 내용과 일치하지 않는다.

〉왜 오답 ?

① 라틴어와 그리스어보다 자연 과학에 강한 흥미를 보였다. (Rather than Latin and Greek, he showed a strong interest in the natural sciences.)

② Czech University에서 화학, 물리학 및 수학을 공부했다. (At Czech University in Prague he studied chemistry, physics and mathematics.)

③ 1910년부터 1914년까지 런던에서 학업을 이어 나갔다. (From 1910 to 1914 he continued his studies at University College, London.)

⑤ 1959년에 노벨 화학상을 수상했다. (He won the Nobel Prize in chemistry in 1959.)

---

27 정답 ④ * 봄철 차 교실

Spring Tea Class for Young People /
청소년을 위한 봄철 차 교실 /

Join us for a delightful Spring Tea Class / for young people, / **where** you'll experience / the taste of tea / from various cultures 〔관계부사(선행사: Spring Tea Class)〕 around the world. // ①의 단서 수강생은 차 교실에서 전 세계 다양한 문화권의 차를 맛보는 경험을 함
즐거운 봄철 차 교실에 참여하세요 / 청소년을 위한 / 그곳에서 여러분은 경험을 할 것입니다 / 차를 맛보는 / 전 세계 다양한 문화권의 //

Class Schedule / 수업 일정 /
· Friday, April 5 (4:30 p.m.–6:00 p.m.) / ②의 단서 금요일 수업은 오후 4:30 ~ 오후 6:00에 진행됨
4월 5일 금요일 (오후 4:30 ~ 오후 6:00) /
· Saturday, April 6 (9:30 a.m.–11:00 a.m.) /
4월 6일 토요일 (오전 9:30 ~ 오전 11:00) /

Details / 세부 내용 /
· We will give you / tea and snacks. // ③의 단서 수강생에게 차와 간식을 제공함
우리는 여러분에게 드리겠습니다 / 차와 간식을 /
· We offer special tips / for **hosting** a tea party. // 〔동명사(전치사의 목적어)〕
우리는 특별한 조언을 제공합니다 / 차 모임 주최를 위한 //

Participation Fee / 참가비 /
· Age 13-15: $25 **per** person / ④의 단서 15세 이하의 수강생은 25달러의 참가비를 냄 〔'~당, ~마다'〕
13 ~ 15세: 1인당 25달러 /
· Age 16-18: $30 per person /
16 ~ 18세: 1인당 30달러 /

Note / 주의 사항 / ⑤의 단서 음식 알레르기가 있는 수강생은 이메일을 미리 보내야 함
If you have any food allergy, / you should email us in advance at youth@seasonteaclass.com. //
만약 여러분이 음식 알레르기가 있다면 / 저희에게 미리 youth@seasonteaclass.com으로 이메일을 보내야 합니다 //

· delightful ⓐ 즐거운   · experience ⓥ 경험하다
· various ⓐ 다양한   · host ⓥ (파티 등을) 주최하다
· in advance 미리

청소년을 위한 봄철 차 교실

청소년을 위한 즐거운 봄철 차 교실에 참여하세요. 그곳에서 여러분은 전 세계 다양한 문화권의 차를 맛보는 경험을 할 것입니다.

수업 일정
· 4월 5일 금요일 (오후 4:30 ~ 오후 6:00)
· 4월 6일 토요일 (오전 9:30 ~ 오전 11:00)

세부 내용
· 우리는 여러분에게 차와 간식을 드리겠습니다.
· 우리는 차 모임 주최를 위한 특별한 조언을 제공합니다.

참가비
• 13 ~ 15세: 1인당 25달러
• 16 ~ 18세: 1인당 30달러

주의 사항
만약 여러분이 음식 알레르기가 있다면 저희에게 미리
youth@seasonteaclass.com으로 이메일을 보내야 합니다.

> Spring Tea Class for Young People에 관한 다음 안내문의 내용과 일치하지 <u>않는</u> 것은?
> ① 수강생은 전 세계 다양한 문화권의 차를 경험할 수 있다.
> you'll experience the taste of tea from various cultures around the world
> ② 금요일 수업은 오후에 1시간 30분 동안 진행된다.
> Friday, April 5 (4:30 p.m. - 6:00 p.m.)
> ③ 수강생에게 차와 간식을 제공할 것이다.
> We will give you tea and snacks.
> ④ 15세 이하의 수강생은 30달러의 참가비를 내야 한다.
> Age 13 - 15: $25 per person
> ⑤ 음식 알레르기가 있는 수강생은 이메일을 미리 보내야 한다.
> If you have any food allergy, you should email us in advance

> 왜 정답 ? ❀❀❀ [정답률 95%]
13세에서 15세는 1인당 25달러(Age 13 - 15: $25 per person)라고 했으므로 15세 이하의 수강생은 30달러의 참가비를 내야 한다고 한 ④이 안내문의 내용과 일치하지 않는다.

> 왜 오답 ?
① 수강생은 전 세계 다양한 문화권의 차를 경험할 수 있다. (you'll experience the taste of tea from various cultures around the world)
② 금요일 수업은 오후에 1시간 30분 동안 진행된다. (Friday, April 5 (4:30 p.m. - 6:00 p.m.))
③ 수강생에게 차와 간식을 제공할 것이다. (We will give you tea and snacks.)
⑤ 음식 알레르기가 있는 수강생은 이메일을 미리 보내야 한다. (If you have any food allergy, you should email us in advance)

28 정답 ④ *의류 업사이클링 대회

Clothes Upcycling Contest 2024 / 2024 의류 업사이클링 대회 /

Are you passionate / about fashion and the environment? //
여러분은 열정이 있으신가요 / 패션과 환경에 대한 //

Then we have a contest for you! //
그렇다면 우리가 여러분을 위한 대회를 개최합니다 //

• **Participants** / 참가자 /
현재분사(Anyone 수식)
①의 단서 Lakewood에 사는 11세~18세 사람들이 참여 가능
- Anyone living in Lakewood, aged 11 to 18 /
Lakewood에 거주하는 11세에서 18세까지이면 누구나 /

• **How to participate** / 참여 방법 /
- Take before and after photos / of your upcycled clothes. //
전, 후 사진을 찍으세요 / 여러분의 업사이클된 옷의 //

- Email the photos at lovelw@lwplus.com. // ②의 단서 참가자는 출품 사진을 이메일로 보냄
사진은 lovelw@lwplus.com으로 이메일을 보내세요 //

- Send in the photos / from April 14 to May 12. //
사진은 보내세요 / 4월 14일부터 5월 12일까지 // ③의 단서 참가자는 5월 12일까지 출품 사진을 제출할 수 있음

• **Winning Prize** / 우승 상품 /
형용사적 용법(gift card 수식)
- A $100 gift card / to use at local shops / ④의 단서 우승 상품은 지역 상점에서 쓸 수 있는 100달러 기프트 카드임
100달러 기프트 카드 한 장 / 지역 상점에서 쓸 수 있는 /
미래시제 수동태
- The winner will be announced / on our website on May 30. //
우승자를 발표할 것입니다 / 우리 웹사이트에서 5월 30일에 // ⑤의 단서 웹사이트에서 우승자를 발표함

For more details, / visit our website www.lovelwplus.com. //
더 많은 정보를 위해서는 / 우리 웹사이트(www.lovelwplus.com)를 방문하세요 //

• passionate ⓐ 열정적인 • environment ⓝ 환경
• contest ⓝ 대회 • upcycled ⓐ 업사이클된
• winning prize 우승 상품 • local ⓐ 지역의
• announce ⓥ 발표하다

2024 의류 업사이클링 대회
여러분은 패션과 환경에 대한 열정이 있으신가요? 그렇다면 우리가 여러분을 위한 대회를 개최합니다!
• 참가자
- Lakewood에 거주하는 11세에서 18세까지이면 누구나
• 참여 방법
- 여러분의 업사이클된 옷의 전, 후 사진을 찍으세요.
- 사진은 lovelw@lwplus.com으로 이메일을 보내세요.
- 사진은 4월 14일부터 5월 12일까지 보내세요.
• 우승 상품
- 지역 상점에서 쓸 수 있는 100달러 기프트 카드 한 장
- 우승자를 우리 웹사이트에서 5월 30일에 발표할 것입니다.
더 많은 정보를 위해서는 우리 웹사이트(www.lovelwplus.com)를 방문하세요.

> Clothes Upcycling Contest 2024에 관한 다음 안내문의 내용과 일치하는 것은?
> ① Lakewood에 사는 사람이면 누구든지 참가할 수 있다.
> Anyone living in Lakewood, aged 11 to 18
> ② 참가자는 출품 사진을 직접 방문하여 제출해야 한다.
> Email the photos at lovelw@lwplus.com.
> ③ 참가자는 5월 14일까지 출품 사진을 제출할 수 있다.
> Send in the photos from April 14 to May 12.
> ④ 우승 상품은 지역 상점에서 쓸 수 있는 기프트 카드이다.
> A $100 gift card to use at local shops
> ⑤ 지역 신문을 통해 우승자를 발표한다.
> The winner will be announced on our website on May 30.

> 왜 정답 ? ❀❀❀ [정답률 92%]
우승 상품은 지역 상점에서 쓸 수 있는 100달러 기프트 카드 한 장이라고 했으므로 (A $100 gift card to use at local shops) 안내문의 내용과 일치하는 것은 ④이다.

> 왜 오답 ?
① Lakewood에 사는 11세에서 18세까지의 사람들이 참가할 수 있다. (Anyone living in Lakewood, aged 11 to 18)
② 직접 방문하는 것이 아니라 이메일을 통해 제출한다. (Email the photos at lovelw@lwplus.com.)
③ 5월 12일까지 출품 사진을 제출해야 한다. (Send in the photos from April 14 to May 12.)
⑤ 지역 신문이 아니라 웹사이트에서 우승자를 발표한다. (The winner will be announced on our website on May 30.)

29 정답 ② *의미 있는 일의 긍정적 영향

> 다음 글의 밑줄 친 부분 중, 어법상 틀린 것은? [3점]
가주어   진주어   간접의문문(의문사+주어+동사)
It would be hard to overstate how important meaningful
주격 관계대명사
work is / to human beings / — work ① that provides a sense of fulfillment and empowerment. //
과장해서 말하기도 어려울 것이다 / 의미 있는 일이 얼마나 중요한지를 / 인간에게 / 성취감과 권한을 제공하는 일 //
'~한 사람들'   동사
Those who have found deeper meaning in their careers / find
비교급 강조 부사
their days much more energizing and satisfying, /
자신의 직업에서 더 깊은 의미를 찾은 사람은 / 자신의 하루하루가 훨씬 더 활기차고 만족감을 준다는 것을 발견한다 /

and ② to count (→ count) their employment / as one of their
greatest sources of joy and pride. // 단서 접속사 and가 동사 find와 동사 count를 연결하는 병렬 구조임
그리고 자신의 직업을 꼽는다 / 기쁨과 자부심의 가장 큰 원천 중 하나로 /
동격
Sonya Lyubomirsky, professor of psychology at the University
of California, / has conducted numerous workplace studies / ③
현재분사
showing /
University of California의 심리학 교수인 Sonya Lyubomirsky는 / 수많은 업무 현장 연구를 수행했다 / 보여 주는 /

정답 및 해설 43

목적어절 접속사
that when people are more fulfilled on the job, / they **not only**
produce higher quality work and a greater output, / **but also**
not only A but also B: A뿐만 아니라 B도
generally earn higher incomes. //

사람이 직업에 더 많은 성취감을 느낄 때 / 그들은 더 질 높은 업무와 더 큰 성과를 만들어 낼
뿐만 아니라 / 일반적으로 더 높은 수입을 거둔다는 것을 //

사이에 who are 생략됨   be likely to ~: ~할 가능성이 있다
Those **most** satisfied with their work / ④ **are** also much more
likely to be happier / with their lives overall. //

자신의 일에 가장 만족하는 사람은 / 또한 더 행복해할 가능성이 훨씬 더 크다 / 전반적으로
자신의 삶에 //

For her book *Happiness at Work*, / researcher Jessica Pryce-Jones
conducted / a study of 3,000 workers in seventy-nine countries, /

자신의 저서 'Happiness at Work'를 위해 / 연구자 Jessica Pryce-Jones는 수행했다 /
79개 국가의 3,000명의 근로자에 대한 연구를 /

분사구문을 이끄는 현재분사
⑤ **finding** / that **those** who took greater satisfaction from their
복수 동사   복수 주어
work / **were** 150 percent more likely / to have a happier life
overall. //

그리고 알아냈다 / 자신의 일로부터 더 큰 만족감을 갖는 사람이 / 가능성이 150퍼센트 더
크다는 것을 / 전반적으로 더 행복한 삶을 살 //

- overstate ⓥ 과장해서 말하다 · meaningful ⓐ 의미 있는
- human being 인간 · provide ⓥ 제공하다
- fulfillment ⓝ 성취감 · empowerment ⓝ 권한
- career ⓝ 직업, 경력 · energizing ⓐ 활기찬
- count ~ as … ~을 …라고 여기다 · employment ⓝ 직업, 고용
- source ⓝ 원천 · pride ⓝ 자부심 · conduct ⓥ 수행하다
- psychology ⓝ 심리 · workplace ⓝ 업무 현장, 직장
- output ⓝ 성과 · generally ⓐⓓ 일반적으로 · income ⓝ 수입
- overall ⓐⓓ 전반적으로 · satisfaction ⓝ 만족

인간에게 의미 있는 일, 즉 성취감과 권한을 제공하는 일이 얼마나 중요한지는
아무리 강조해도 지나치지 않을 것이다. 자신의 직업에서 더 깊은 의미를 찾은
사람은 자신의 하루하루가 훨씬 더 활기차고 만족감을 준다는 것을 발견하고,
자신의 직업을 기쁨과 자부심의 가장 큰 원천 중 하나로 꼽는다. University of
California의 심리학 교수인 Sonya Lyubomirsky는 사람이 직업에 더 많은 성
취감을 느낄 때 그들은 더 질 높은 업무와 더 큰 성과를 만들어 낼 뿐만 아니라
일반적으로 더 높은 수입을 거둔다는 것을 보여 주는 수많은 업무 현장 연구를
수행했다. 자신의 일에 가장 만족하는 사람은 또한 전반적으로 자신의 삶에 더
행복해할 가능성이 훨씬 더 크다. 자신의 저서 'Happiness at Work'를 위해 연
구자 Jessica Pryce-Jones는 79개 국가의 3,000명의 근로자에 대한 연구를 수
행했고, 자신의 일로부터 더 큰 만족감을 갖는 사람이 전반적으로 더 행복한 삶
을 살 가능성이 150퍼센트 더 크다는 것을 알아냈다.

왜 정답? ★★❀ [정답률 75%]
② 접속사로 연결되는 두 요소가 병렬 구조를 이루어야 한다!

주어   첫 번째 동사
Those who have found deeper meaning in their careers / **find**
their days much more energizing and satisfying, / **and** ②
                                   등위접속사
두 번째 동사
to count (→ count) their employment / as one of their greatest
sources of joy and pride. //

단서 접속사 and 뒤에 나오는 to부정사에 밑줄이 있으므로
발상 to count와 병렬 구조를 이룰 만한 요소를 찾아본다.
해결 주어인 Those ~ their careers 뒤에 복수 현재형 동사 find가 있으므로
등위접속사 and로 연결되는 요소는 마찬가지로 복수 현재형 동사여야 한다.
따라서 부정사인 to count를 count로 고쳐야 어법상 알맞다.
개념 접속사 and, but, or로 연결되는 두 요소는 문장 성분이 같아야 한다.

왜 오답?
① that은 사물과 사람 모두를 선행사로 취할 수 있다.
It would be hard to overstate / how important meaningful
                                        that의 선행사주격 관계대명사
work is / to human beings / — work ① **that** provides a sense
                                              주어가 없는 불완전한 절
of fulfillment and empowerment. //

관계대명사는 주어나 목적어가 빠진 불완전한 절을 이끈다. 개념
밑줄 친 that 뒤에 오는 절은 주어가 없고 동사 provides가 곧바로 이어지는 불완전한
절이다. 단서
work를 선행사로 하는 주격 관계대명사 that이 알맞게 쓰였다.

③ 현재분사는 명사를 수식할 수 있다.
Sonya Lyubomirsky, professor of psychology at the University
of California, / has conducted numerous workplace studies /
현재분사(studies 수식)
③ **showing** /[that when people are more fulfilled on the job,
                          showing의 목적어절
/ they not only produce higher quality work and a greater
output, / but also generally earn higher incomes.]//

현재분사는 명사를 수식하는 역할을 한다. 현재분사가 한 단어일 때는 수식하는 명사
앞에 위치하고 구의 형태일 때는 수식하는 명사 뒤에 위치한다. 개념
showing 앞에 문장의 주어 Sonya Lyubomirsky와 동사 has conducted가
주어졌다. 단서
여기서 showing은 앞의 studies를 수식하고 that 뒤의 목적어절을 수반하는
현재분사이다.
따라서 현재분사 showing이 알맞게 쓰였다.

④ 동사는 주어에 그 수를 일치시킨다.
복수 주어 관계대명사절(who are가 생략됨)   복수 동사
Those most satisfied with their work / ④ **are** also much more
likely to be happier / with their lives overall. //

주어를 꾸미는 수식어구와 상관없이 핵심 주어의 수에 동사의 수를 일치시킨다. 개념
동사 are에 밑줄이 있으므로 단서 주어를 찾아서 수가 일치하는지 확인한다. 발상
주격 관계대명사 who와 be동사 are가 생략된 관계대명사절인 most satisfied
with their work를 제외하면 핵심 주어인 Those가 남는다. Those는 복수이므로
be동사도 복수형 동사인 are를 쓰는 것이 적절하다. 해결

⑤ 접속사와 주어를 생략하여 분사구문을 만들 수 있다.
전치사구: 제외하고 생각하기
For her book Happiness at Work, / researcher Jessica Pryce-
Jones conducted / a study of 3,000 workers in seventy-
분사구문을 이끄는 현재분사(= and she found)
nine countries, / ⑤ **finding** / [that those who took greater
                                        finding의 목적어절
satisfaction from their work / were 150 percent more likely / to
have a happier life overall.]//

두 문장의 주어가 같을 때, 접속사가 있는 문장에서 접속사와 주어를 생략하고 동사를
분사 형태로 바꾸어 분사구문을 만들 수 있다. 개념
주어 researcher Jessica Pryce-Jones와 동사 conducted를 포함하는 완전한
문장이 끝나고 콤마 뒤에 finding이 이어진다. 단서
finding의 목적어절은 그녀가 발견한 연구 결과를 설명하기 때문에 finding 앞에
생략된 주어는 she라는 것을 알 수 있다.
따라서 콤마 바로 뒤에 있던 접속사 and와 주어 she를 생략하고 동사 found를
현재분사로 바꾼 finding이 적절히 쓰였다.

30 정답 ③ ✽ 이동 속도와 세부 정보 처리의 관계

다음 글의 밑줄 친 부분 중, 문맥상 낱말의 쓰임이 적절하지 <u>않은</u> 것은? [3점]

The rate of speed at which one is traveling / will greatly
「전치사+관계대명사」 형용사적 용법(the ability 수식)
determine / the ability to process detail in the environment. //
사람이 이동하는 속도의 빠르기는 / 크게 결정할 것이다 / 환경 속 세세한 것을 처리하는
능력을 //
단서 1 인간의 이동 속도는 환경 속 세부 정보 처리 능력을 결정함

In evolutionary terms, / human senses are adapted to the ①
「전치사+관계대명사」
speed / at which humans move through space / under their own
접속사가 생략되지 않은 분사구문
power while walking. //
진화론적 관점에서 / 인간의 감각은 속도에 적응되어 있다 / 공간을 이동하는 / 그 자신의
힘으로 걸으며 /
형용사적 용법(Our ability 수식)
Our ability to distinguish detail / in the environment / is
therefore ideally ② suited to / movement at speeds of perhaps
five miles per hour and under. //
단서 2 환경 속 세부 정보 구별 능력은 우리가 스스로 이동하는 속도에 맞춰져 있음
세세한 것을 구별하는 우리의 능력은 / 환경 속에서 / 그래서 이상적으로 맞춰져 있다 / 대략
시속 5마일 또는 그 속도 이하의 이동에 //
단서 3 도로 위 운전자는 세부 정보를 처리하는 능력이 훨씬 더 제한됨
동격
The fastest users of the street, motorists, / therefore have a much
more limited ability / to process details along the street /
도로의 가장 빠른 사용자인 운전자들은 / 그러므로 훨씬 더 제한된 능력을 가지고 있고 /
도로를 따라 (이동하며) 세세한 것을 처리하는 /
— a motorist simply has ③ enough (→ little) time or ability / to
형용사적 용법
appreciate design details. //
운전자는 단지 충분한(→ 적은) 시간이나 능력이 있다 / 디자인의 세세한 것을 감상할 수 있는 //
On the other hand, / pedestrian travel, being much slower, /
allows for the ④ appreciation of environmental detail. //
반면에 / 보행자 이동은 훨씬 더 느려서 / 환경의 세세한 것을 감상할 수 있도록 허용해 준다 //
Joggers and bicyclists // fall somewhere in between these polar
opposites; /
조깅하는 사람과 자전거를 타는 사람은 / 이러한 극과 극 사이의 어딘가에 해당한다 /
while they travel faster than pedestrians, / their rate of speed is
비교급 강조 부사   = rate of speed
ordinarily much ⑤ slower / than that of the typical motorist. //
그들은 보행자보다 더 빨리 이동하지만 / 속도의 빠르기는 보통 훨씬 더 느리다 / 전형적인
운전자의 그것보다 //

- rate ⓝ 빠르기 · travel ⓥ 이동하다 · determine ⓥ 결정하다
- ability ⓝ 능력 · process ⓥ 처리하다 · evolutionary ⓐ 진화의
- ideally ⓐⓓ 이상적으로 · suited ⓐ 맞추어진 · motorist ⓝ 운전자
- limited ⓐ 제한된 · appreciate ⓥ 감상하다
- allow for ~을 가능하게 하다[허락하다] · polar ⓐ 극과 극의
- opposite ⓝ 반대의 것 · ordinarily ⓐⓓ 보통 · typical ⓐ 전형적인

사람이 이동하는 속도의 빠르기는 환경 속 세세한 것을 처리하는 능력을 크
게 결정할 것이다. 진화론적 관점에서, 인간의 감각은 그 자신의 힘으로 걸으
며 공간을 이동하는 ① 속도에 적응되어 있다. 환경 속에서 세세한 것을 구별하
는 우리의 능력은 그래서 대략 시속 5마일 또는 그 속도 이하의 이동에 이상적
으로 ② 맞추어져 있다. 그러므로 도로의 가장 빠른 사용자인 운전자는 도로를
따라서 (이동하며) 세세한 것을 처리하는 훨씬 더 제한된 능력을 가지고 있고,
그래서 운전자는 단지 디자인의 세세한 것을 감상할 수 있는 ③ 충분한(→ 적은)
시간이나 능력이 있다. 반면에 보행자 이동은 훨씬 더 느려서, 환경의 세세한
것을 ④ 감상할 수 있도록 허용해 준다. 조깅하는 사람과 자전거를 타는 사람은
이러한 극과 극 사이의 어딘가에 해당한다. 그들은 보행자보다 더 빨리 이동하
지만, 속도의 빠르기는 보통 전형적인 운전자의 그것보다 ⑤ 더 느리다.

왜 정답 ? ✽✽✽ [정답률 66%]

③ enough 충분한

그러므로 도로의 가장 빠른 사용자인 운전자는 도로를 따라서 (이동하며)
세세한 것을 처리하는 훨씬 더 제한된 능력을 가지고 있고, 그래서
운전자는 단지 디자인의 세세한 것을 감상할 수 있는 ③ ~~충분한~~ 시간이나
능력이 있다.
적은

➡ 도로 위 운전자는 인간이 걷는 속도보다 훨씬 빠르게 이동하기 때문에 세부 정보를
처리하는 능력이 제한된다고 했으므로, 운전자가 세세한 것을 감상할 수 있는
'충분한' 시간이나 능력이 있다는 것은 문맥에 맞지 않는다.

▶ enough를 little(적은)과 같은 반의어로 바꾸어야 함

왜 오답 ?

① speed 속도

진화론적 관점에서, 인간의 감각은 그 자신의 힘으로 걸으며 공간을
이동하는 ① 속도에 적응되어 있다.

➡ 사람이 이동하는 속도의 빠르기는 환경 속 세부 정보를 처리하는 능력을
결정한다고 했으므로, 인간의 감각은 이동하는 '속도'에 적응되어 있다는 표현은
적절하다.

▶ speed는 문맥에 맞음

② suited 맞추어진

환경 속에서 세세한 것을 구별하는 우리의 능력은 그래서 대략 시속 5마일
또는 그 속도 이하의 이동에 이상적으로 ② 맞추어져 있다.

➡ 이동 속도가 환경 속 세부 정보를 처리하는 능력을 결정한다고 했으므로, 인간이
스스로 이동하는 속도인 대략 시속 5마일 또는 그 속도 이하에 우리의 세부 정보
구별 능력이 '맞추어져' 있다는 표현은 적절하다.

▶ suited는 문맥에 맞음

④ appreciation 감상

반면에 보행자 이동은 훨씬 더 느려서, 환경의 세세한 것을 ④ 감상할 수
있도록 허용해 준다.

➡ 보행자의 이동 속도가 운전자보다 훨씬 더 느리기 때문에 주변을 둘러볼 시간을
충분히 가지므로, 환경의 세부 정보를 '감상'할 수 있도록 허용한다는 표현은
적절하다.

▶ appreciation은 문맥에 맞음

⑤ slower 더 느린

조깅하는 사람과 자전거를 타는 사람은 이러한 극과 극 사이의 어딘가에
해당한다. 그들은 보행자보다 더 빨리 이동하지만, 속도의 빠르기는 보통
전형적인 운전자의 그것보다 훨씬 ⑤ 더 느리다.

➡ 조깅하는 사람과 자전거를 타는 사람의 이동 속도는 보행자의 속도와 운전자의
속도 사이 어딘가에 있으므로, 운전자의 이동 속도 빠르기보다 '더 느리다'는 표현은
적절하다.

▶ slower는 문맥에 맞음

---

31 정답 ② ✽ 기후 변화에 따른 종의 이동

every+단수 명사+단수 동사
Every species has certain climatic requirements — / what degree
of heat or cold it can endure, for example. //
모든 종은 특정한 기후 요건을 가지고 있다 / 예를 들어 어느 정도의 더위나 추위를 견딜 수
있는지와 같은 //
주격 관계대명사(선행사: the places)
When the climate changes, / the places that satisfy those
requirements / change, too. //
단서 1 기후가 변할 때 종의 기후 요건을 충족시키는 장소도 변화함
기후가 변할 때 / 그러한 요건을 충족시키는 장소도 / 역시 변한다 //
Species are forced to follow. //
종은 따르도록 강요받는다 //
All creatures are capable of / some degree of **movement**. //
모든 생명체는 가능하다 / 어느 정도의 이동이 //
복수 주어   주격 관계대명사(선행사: creatures)
Even creatures that appear immobile, / like trees and barnacles,
복수 동사
/ are capable of dispersal / at some stage of their life — /
심지어 움직이지 않는 것처럼 보이는 생명체도 / 나무나 따개비처럼 / 분산할 수 있다 / 그들
일생의 어느 단계에서 /
단서 2 움직이지 않는 것처럼 보이는 생명체조차도 분산할 수 있음
as a seed, in the case of the tree, / or as a larva, in the case of the
barnacle. //
나무의 경우는 씨앗으로 / 따개비의 경우는 유충으로 //

A creature must get / from the place it is born — / often **occupied**
과거분사(the place 수식)
by its parent — / to a place **where** it can survive, grow, and
관계부사(선행사: a place)
reproduce. // 단서3 생물은 자신이 태어난 장소로부터 생존, 성장, 번식할 수 있는 장소로 이동해야 함
생명체는 이동해야 한다 / 자신이 태어난 장소로부터 / 종종 자신의 부모에 의해서 점유된 /
생존하고 성장하며 번식할 수 있는 장소로 //
From fossils, / scientists know / **that** even creatures like trees
목적어절 접속사
moved / with surprising speed / during past periods of climate
change. // 단서4 화석에도 생명체가 이동한 증거가 있음
화석으로부터 / 과학자들은 알고 있다 / 심지어 나무와 같은 생명체가 이동했다는 것을 /
놀라운 속도로 / 기후 변화의 과거 시기 동안 //

- climatic ⓐ 기후의 · requirement ⓝ 요건 · endure ⓥ 견디다
- satisfy ⓥ 충족시키다 · species ⓝ 종(種) · force ⓥ 강요하다
- creature ⓝ 생명체 · be capable of ~을 할 수 있다
- immobile ⓐ 움직이지 않는 · larva ⓝ 유충 · occupy ⓥ 점유하다
- survive ⓥ 생존하다 · reproduce ⓥ 번식하다
- endurance ⓝ 인내 · transformation ⓝ 변형

모든 종은, 예를 들자면 어느 정도의 더위나 추위를 견딜 수 있는지와 같은, 특정한 기후 요건을 가지고 있다. 기후가 변할 때, 그러한 요건을 충족시키는 장소도 역시 변한다. 종은 따르도록 강요받는다. 모든 생명체는 어느 정도의 **이동**이 가능하다. 심지어 나무나 따개비처럼 움직이지 않는 것처럼 보이는 생명체도, 나무의 경우는 씨앗으로, 따개비의 경우는 유충으로, 그들 일생의 어느 단계에서 분산할 수 있다. 생명체는 종종 자신의 부모에 의해서 점유된, 그래서 자신이 태어난 장소로부터 생존하고 성장하며 번식할 수 있는 장소로 이동해야 한다. 화석으로부터, 과학자들은 심지어 나무와 같은 생명체는 기후 변화의 과거 시기 동안 놀라운 속도로 이동했다는 것을 알고 있다.

> 다음 빈칸에 들어갈 말로 가장 적절한 것을 고르시오.
> ① endurance 생명체가 인내하며 한 장소에 머무는 것이 아니라 이동함
>   인내
> ② movement
>   이동   움직이지 않는 것처럼 보이는 생명체조차도 기후 요건에 맞는 장소로 이동할 수 있음
> ③ development 생명체의 발달이 아닌 생존, 성장, 번식을 위해 이동하는 내용이 나옴
>   발달
> ④ transformation 생명체가 변형된다는 내용이 아님
>   변형
> ⑤ communication 생명체의 의사소통을 다룬 내용이 아님
>   의사소통

| 문제 풀이 순서 | ★★★ [정답률 45%]

1st 먼저 빈칸 문장을 읽고, 빈칸에 들어갈 말을 예측한다.

| 빈칸 문장 | 모든 생명체는 어느 정도의 ＿＿＿＿＿＿ 이 가능하다.

➡ 모든 생명체가 어느 정도의 '무엇이' 가능하다고 했으므로, 단서
모든 생명체의 공통적인 특징이나 공통적으로 가능한 무언가를 찾아야 한다. 발상

2nd 글의 나머지 부분을 읽고, 모든 생명체가 가능한 것이 무엇인지 찾는다.
- 모든 종은 특정한 기후 요건을 가지고, 기후가 변할 때 종의 기후 요건을 충족시키는 장소도 변화함 단서1
- 움직이지 않는 것처럼 보이는 생명체조차도 일생의 어느 단계에서 분산을 통해 이동함 단서2
- 생물은 부모에 의해 점유된 태어난 장소로부터 생존, 성장, 번식할 수 있는 장소로 이동해야 함 단서3
- 기후가 변화했던 과거의 시기에 생명체가 놀라운 속도로 이동했다는 것을 화석으로부터 알 수 있음 단서4
➡ 움직이지 않는 듯한 생명체를 포함한 모든 생명체는 특정한 기후 요건을 가지고, 기후가 변화하면 이동한다.
▶ 따라서 빈칸에 들어갈 말은 ② '이동'이다.

| 선택지 분석 |

① **endurance** 인내
생명체가 기후가 바뀐 장소에 인내하며 머물지 않고 기후 요건에 맞는 장소로 이동한다.

② **movement** 이동
움직이지 않는 듯한 생명체를 포함하여 모든 종은 기후가 변화할 때 기후 요건을 충족시키는 장소로 이동한다고 했다.

③ **development** 발달
생명체의 발달이 아닌 생존, 성장, 번식을 위해 이동하는 내용이 나온다.

④ **transformation** 변형
나무와 따개비가 씨앗이나 유충의 상태일 때가 있다고 언급했지만, 이는 분산을 통한 이동의 예시일 뿐이므로 생명체의 변형에 관한 내용이 아니다.

⑤ **communication** 의사소통
모든 생명체가 어느 정도의 의사소통을 한다는 내용은 언급되지 않았다.

32 정답 ③ ＊부하 직원의 반대 의견 지지하기

No respectable boss would say, / "I make it a point to discourage
주격 관계대명사
my staff from speaking up, / and I maintain a culture / **that**
prevent A from -ing: A가 ~하는 것을 막다
prevents disagreeing viewpoints **from** ever **getting aired**." //
존경할 만한 상사라면 누구라도 말하지는 않을 것이다 / "나는 반드시 내 직원이 자유롭게 의견을 내지 못하도록 하고 / 나는 문화를 유지한다 / 동의하지 않는 관점이 언제든 공공연히 알려지는 것을 가로막는"라고 //
단서1 대부분의 상사는 반대 의견에 찬성한다고 말함
If anything, / most bosses even say / that they are pro-dissent. //
오히려 / 대부분의 상사는 심지어 말한다 / 자신은 반대에 찬성한다고 //
This idea can be found / throughout the series of conversations
과거분사(conversations 수식)
/ with corporate, university, and nonprofit leaders, / **published**
weekly in the business sections of newspapers. //
이러한 생각은 발견될 수 있다 / 일련의 대담을 통해서 / 기업, 대학, 그리고 비영리 (단체의) 리더와의 / 신문의 경제란에 매주 발행되는 //
단서2 리더들과의 대담에서 반대 의견을 찬성하는 생각이 발견됨
In the interviews, / the **featured** leaders / are asked about their
과거분사(leaders 수식)
management techniques, / and regularly claim / to continually
encourage / **internal protest** from more junior staffers. //
인터뷰에서 / (기사에) 다루어진 리더는 / 자신의 경영 기법에 대해 질문을 받고 / 어김없이 주장한다 / 계속해서 장려하고 있다고 / 내부적인 저항이 더 많은 부하 직원에게서 (나오기를) //
As Bot Pittman remarked / in one of these conversations: / "I
want us to listen to these dissenters / because they may intend
to tell you / **why we can't do something**, / 단서3 우리가 반대자에게
간접의문문(의문사+주어+동사)   귀 기울이기를 원함
Bot Pittman이 말한 것처럼 / 이러한 대화 중 하나에서 / "저는 우리가 이러한 반대자에게 귀 기울이기를 원합니다 / 왜냐하면 그들은 여러분에게 말하려고 의도할 수 있겠지만 / 우리가 무엇인가를 할 수 없는 이유를 /
but if you listen hard, / what they're really telling you / is what
you must do / to **get something done**." //
get+목적어+과거분사(수동의 의미)
그러나 만약에 여러분이 열심히 귀 기울이면 / 그들이 정말로 여러분에게 말하고 있는 것은 / 여러분이 무엇을 해야만 하는가이기 때문입니다 / 어떤 일이 이루어지도록 하기 위해서" //

- respectable ⓐ 존경할 만한 · make it a point 반드시 ~하도록 하다
- discourage ⓥ 못하게 하다 · speak up 자유롭게 의견을 내다
- maintain ⓥ 유지하다 · viewpoint ⓝ 관점
- get aired 공공연히 알려지다 · if anything 오히려 · boss ⓝ 상사
- conversation ⓝ 대담, 대화 · corporate ⓝ 기업
- nonprofit ⓐ 비영리인 · publish ⓥ 발행하다, 출판하다
- section ⓝ 구역, (신문의) ~란 · feature ⓥ (기사로) 다루다
- management ⓝ 경영 · techniques ⓝ 기법
- regularly ⓐd 어김없이, 규칙적으로 · claim ⓥ 주장하다
- continually ⓐd 계속해서 · remark ⓥ 말하다

존경할 만한 상사라면 누구라도 '나는 반드시 내 직원이 자유롭게 의견을 내지 못하도록 하고, 동의하지 않는 관점이 언제든 공공연히 알려지는 것을 가로막는 문화를 유지한다.'라고 말하지는 않을 것이다. 오히려, 대부분의 상사는 심지어 자신은 반대에 찬성한다고 말한다. 이러한 생각은 매주 발행되는 신문의 경제란

에 기업, 대학, 그리고 비영리 (단체의) 리더와의 일련의 대담을 통해서 발견될 수 있다. 인터뷰에서, (기사에) 다루어진 리더는 자신의 경영 기법에 대해 질문을 받고, <u>내부적인 저항</u>이 더 많은 부하 직원에게서 (나오기를) 계속해서 장려하고 있다고 어김없이 주장한다. Bot Pittman은 이러한 대담 중 하나에서 "저는 우리가 이러한 반대자에게 귀 기울이기를 원합니다. 왜냐하면 그들은 여러분에게 우리가 무엇인가를 할 수 없는 이유를 말하려고 의도할 수 있겠지만, 그러나 만약에 여러분이 열심히 귀 기울이면, 그들이 정말로 여러분에게 말하고 있는 것은 어떤 일이 이루어지도록 하기 위해서 여러분이 무엇을 해야만 하는가이기 때문입니다."라고 말했다.

다음 빈칸에 들어갈 말로 가장 적절한 것을 고르시오. [3점]

① unconditional loyalty 리더가 반대 의견에 귀 기울이는 내용이 나옴
무조건적인 충성
② positive attitude 직원의 태도를 다루고 있는 내용이 아님
긍정적인 태도
③ internal protest 리더가 반대자에게 귀를 기울이면 무엇을 해야 할지 알 수 있음
내부적인 저항
④ competitive atmosphere
경쟁적인 분위기 리더가 의견을 듣는 내용이지 직원들을 경쟁시키는 내용이 아님
⑤ outstanding performance 리더가 직원의 성과를 중요시한다는 내용은 나오지 않음
뛰어난 성과

| 문제 풀이 순서 | ★★★ [정답률 47%]

1st 먼저 빈칸 문장을 읽고, 빈칸에 들어갈 말을 예측한다.

| 빈칸 문장 | 인터뷰에서, (기사에) 다루어진 리더는 자신의 경영 기법에 대해 질문을 받고, _____ 이 더 많은 부하 직원에게서 (나오기를) 계속해서 장려하고 있다고 어김없이 주장한다. |

➡ 리더가 자신의 경영 기법에 대해 질문을 받고 더 많은 부하 직원에게서 '무엇'이 나오기를 계속 장려한다고 했으므로, **단서**
리더의 경영 기법에 대해 부하 직원들이 제기할 수 있는 것이 '무엇'인지 파악해야 한다. **발상**

2nd 글의 나머지 부분을 확인해서 정답을 찾는다.
- 존경할 만한 상사라면 직원들의 자유로운 의견과 동의하지 않는 관점을 가로막지 않는다.
- 대부분의 상사는 반대 의견에 찬성한다고 말하며 반대 의견을 지지하는 태도를 보인다. **단서 1**
- 신문 경제란에 실리는 리더들과의 일련의 대담에서는 반대 의견을 찬성하는 생각이 발견된다. **단서 2**
- Bot Pittman은 우리가 반대자에게 귀 기울이기를 원하며 반대자가 말하는 것은 어떤 일이 이루어지려면 무엇을 해야만 하는가에 대한 것이라고 한다. **단서 3**
▶ 즉, 리더가 직원들의 반대 의견에도 경청하기 때문에 이들에게서 ③ '내부적인 저항'이 나오기를 격려한다는 내용이다.

| 선택지 분석 |

① unconditional loyalty 무조건적인 충성
반대자에게 귀를 기울이면 무엇을 해야 하는지 알 수 있다고 했으므로 무조건적인 충성을 장려하는 내용은 아니다.

② positive attitude 긍정적인 태도
리더가 직원들의 긍정적인 태도를 장려하는 내용이 아니라 반대 의견을 듣고자 한다는 내용이다.

③ internal protest 내부적인 저항
리더는 직원들의 내부적인 저항이 나오기를 격려하고 반대 의견에 귀 기울여서 무엇을 해야 할지 알 수 있다.

④ competitive atmosphere 경쟁적인 분위기
경쟁적인 분위기는 반대 의견을 듣고자 하는 리더의 의지와 직접적인 관련이 없다.

⑤ outstanding performance 뛰어난 성과
리더가 의견의 다양성과 반대 의견을 듣는 것에 가치를 둔다는 내용이다.

---

33 정답 ③ ＊수면 중 환경 자극에 대한 감각 반응 감소

단수 주어
One of the most striking characteristics / of a sleeping animal or
단수동사
person / is that they do not respond normally / to environmental
stimuli. // **단서 1** 수면 중 사람이나 동물은 환경 자극에 정상적으로 반응하지 않음
가장 두드러진 특징 중 하나는 / 잠을 자고 있는 동물이나 사람의 / 그들이 정상적으로 반응하지 않는다는 것이다 / 환경의 자극에 **단서 2** 수면하는 포유류의 눈은 정상적으로 볼 수 없음
If you open the eyelids of a sleeping mammal / the eyes will not
see normally / — they **are functionally blind**. //
만약 당신이 잠을 자고 있는 포유류의 눈꺼풀을 열면 / 그 눈은 정상적으로 볼 수 없을 것인데 / 즉 그 눈은 기능적으로는 실명 상태이다 //

Some visual information apparently gets in, / but it is not
normally processed / as it is shortened or weakened; / same
with the other sensing systems. // **단서 3** 다른 감각 체계처럼 시각적 정보는 정상적으로 처리되지 않음
어떤 시각적 정보는 명백히 눈으로 들어오지만 / 그것은 정상적으로 처리되지 않는데 / 짧아지거나 약화되어서 / 이는 다른 감각 체계도 마찬가지다 //
병렬 구조
Stimuli are **registered** but / **not processed** normally / and they
fail to wake the individual. // **단서 4** 수면 중 자극은 등록되지만 정상적으로 처리가 안 되고 사람을 깨우지 못함
자극은 등록되지만 / 정상적으로 처리되지 않고 / 사람을 깨우는 데 실패한다 //

Perceptual disengagement probably / serves the function of
동명사구(전치사의 목적어)   count A as B: A를 B로 여기다[간주하다]
protecting sleep, / so some authors do not **count** it / **as** part of
the definition of sleep itself. //
지각 이탈은 추측하건대 / 수면을 보호하는 기능을 제공해서 / 어떤 저자는 그것을 여기지 않는다 / 수면 자체의 정의의 일부로 //
= perceptual disengagement
But as sleep would be impossible without it, / it seems essential
= the definition of sleep
to its definition. //
그러나 수면이 그것 없이는 불가능하기 때문에 / 그것(지각 이탈)은 그것(수면)의 정의에 필수적인 것으로 보여진다 //

Nevertheless, many animals (including humans) / use the
부사적 용법(목적)
intermediate state of drowsiness / to derive some benefits of
sleep / without total perceptual disengagement. //
그럼에도 (인간을 포함한) 많은 동물은 / 졸음이라는 중간 상태를 이용한다 / 수면의 일부 이득을 끌어내기 위해서 / 완전한 지각 이탈 없이 //

- striking ⓐ 두드러진   • characteristic ⓝ 특징
- respond ⓥ 반응하다   • environmental ⓐ 환경의
- eyelid ⓝ 눈꺼풀   • mammal ⓝ 포유류   • visual ⓐ 시각의
- apparently ⓐⓓ 분명히   • process ⓥ 처리하다
- shorten ⓥ 짧아지다   • weaken ⓥ 약해지다
- essential ⓐ 필수적인   • nevertheless ⓐⓓ 그럼에도 불구하고
- derive ⓥ 얻다   • perceptual ⓐ 지각의   • activate ⓥ 활성화하다

잠을 자고 있는 동물이나 사람의 가장 두드러진 특징 중 하나는 그들이 환경의 자극에 정상적으로 반응하지 않는다는 것이다. 만약 당신이 잠을 자고 있는 포유류의 눈꺼풀을 열면, 그 눈은 정상적으로 볼 수 없을 것인데, 즉 그 눈은 **기능적으로는 실명 상태이다**. 어떤 시각적 정보는 명백히 눈으로 들어오지만, 그것은 짧아지거나 약화되어서 정상적으로 처리되지 않는데, 이는 다른 감각 체계도 마찬가지다. 자극은 등록되지만 정상적으로 처리되지 않고 사람을 깨우는 데 실패한다. 지각 이탈은 추측하건대 수면을 보호하는 기능을 제공해서 어떤 저자는 그것을 수면 자체의 정의의 일부로 여기지 않는다. 그러나 수면이 그것 없이는 불가능하기 때문에 그것(지각 이탈)은 그것(수면)의 정의에 필수적인 것으로 보여진다. 그럼에도 (인간을 포함한) 많은 동물은 완전한 지각 이탈 없이 수면의 일부 이득을 끌어내기 위해서 졸음이라는 중간 상태를 이용한다.

다음 빈칸에 들어갈 말로 가장 적절한 것을 고르시오. [3점]

① get recovered easily 수면 중에는 시각이 정상적이지 않음
쉽게 회복한다
② will see much better 동물이 수면 상태일 때 시각적 정보 처리가 방해받음
훨씬 더 잘 보게 될 것이다
③ are functionally blind
기능적으로는 실명 상태이다 수면 중에는 시각적 정보가 들어오긴 하지만 정상적으로 처리되지 않음
④ are completely activated 시각적 정보가 제대로 처리되지 않음
완전히 활성화된다
⑤ process visual information
시각 정보를 처리한다 잠잘 때 시각 자극은 등록되지만 정상적으로 처리되지 않음

1st 먼저 빈칸 문장과 그 뒤 문장을 읽고, 빈칸에 들어갈 말을 예측한다.

빈칸 문장	만약 당신이 잠을 자고 있는 포유류의 눈꺼풀을 열면, 그 눈은 정상적으로 볼 수 없을 것인데, **단서2** 즉 그 눈은 _____.
빈칸 문장 뒤	어떤 시각적 정보는 명백히 눈으로 들어오지만, 그것은 짧아지거나 약화되어서 정상적으로 처리되지 않는데, 이는 다른 감각 체계도 마찬가지다. **단서3**

➡ 수면 상태의 눈은 정상적으로 기능하지 않고 이때 그 눈은 '어떠하다'라고 했으므로, **단서**
수면 상태의 눈이 '어떠한지'에 관한 다른 표현을 찾아봐야 한다. **발상**
빈칸 문장 뒤에서 모든 시각적 정보가 정상적으로 처리되지 않는다고 했으므로, 비슷한 내용이 빈칸에 들어갈 것이라는 걸 짐작할 수 있다.

2nd 글의 나머지 부분을 읽고, 수면 상태의 눈이 어떠한지 파악한다.

- 잠을 자고 있는 동물이나 사람의 가장 두드러진 특징 중 하나는 그들이 환경의 자극에 정상적으로 반응하지 않는다는 것이다. **단서1**
- 자극은 등록되지만 정상적으로 처리되지 않고 사람을 깨우는 데 실패한다. **단서4**

➡ 동물이나 사람은 잠을 잘 때 환경의 자극에 정상적으로 반응하지 않고, 자극이 등록되어도 정상적으로 처리되지 않는다. 이는 눈의 본래 기능을 하지 못하는 '실명 상태'와도 같다.

▶ 즉, 수면 상태에서 눈은 ③ '기능적으로는 실명 상태이다.'

| 선택지 분석 |

① **get recovered easily** 쉽게 회복한다
수면 중에 포유류의 눈이 쉽게 회복한다는 내용은 언급되지 않았다.

② **will see much better** 훨씬 더 잘 보게 될 것이다
눈이 훨씬 더 잘 보게 된다는 내용은 수면 중 정상적인 시각적 정보 처리가 방해받는다는 내용과 모순된다.

③ **are functionally blind** 기능적으로는 실명 상태이다
수면 중 포유류는 눈꺼풀을 열더라도 정상적으로 볼 수 없으며 시각적 정보가 들어오기는 하지만 정상적으로 처리되지 않는다고 했다.

④ **are completely activated** 완전히 활성화된다
수면하는 포유류의 눈이 완전히 활성화된다고 하는 것은 수면 중에는 시각적 정보가 제대로 처리되지 않는다는 내용과 대조된다.

⑤ **process visual information** 시각 정보를 처리한다
수면 중에 자극은 등록되지만 정상적으로 처리되지 않는다고 했다.

---

34 정답 ⑤ ＊전문가들이 초보자 교육에서 겪는 어려움

A number of research studies have shown / how experts in a field / often experience difficulties / **when introducing** newcomers to
사이에 they are 생략
that field. //
많은 조사 연구는 보여주었다 / 어떻게 한 분야의 전문가가 / 어려움을 종종 겪는지를 / 그 분야로 초보자를 입문시킬 때 //

For example, / in a genuine training situation, / Dr. Pamela
목적어절 접속사 사이에 who were 생략
Hinds found / **that people expert** in using mobile phones / were
remarkably less accurate than novice phone users /
예를 들어 / 실제 교육 상황에서 / Pamela Hinds 박사는 알아냈다 / 휴대 전화기를 사용하는 데 능숙한 사람들이 / 초보 휴대 전화기 사용자보다 놀랍도록 덜 정확하다는 것을 /

in judging / how long it takes people to learn to use the phones. //
판단하는 데 있어서 / 휴대 전화기 사용법을 배우는 것에 얼마나 오랜 시간이 걸리는지를 //

Experts can become insensitive / to how hard a task is for the
beginner, / an effect referred to as the 'curse of knowledge.' //
전문가는 무감각해질 수 있는데 / 한 과업이 초보자에게 얼마나 어려운지에 대해 / 즉 '지식의 저주'로 칭해지는 효과이다 // **단서1** 과업에 대한 초보자의 어려움에 대해 무감각해지는 전문가

Dr. Hinds was able to show / **that** as people acquired the skill, /
목적어절 접속사
they then began to underestimate / the level of difficulty of that
skill. // **단서2** 기술을 습득한 사람은 그 기술의 어려움을 과소평가함
Hinds 박사는 보여 줄 수 있었다 / 사람이 기술을 습득했을 때 / 그 이후에 과소평가하기 시작했다는 것을 / 그 기술의 어려움의 정도를 //

Her participants even underestimated / how long it had taken
themselves / to acquire that skill in an earlier session. //
그녀의 참가자는 심지어 과소평가했다 / 자신들이 얼마나 오래 걸렸는지를 / 이전 기간에 그 기술을 습득하는 데 // **단서3** 자신들이 기술을 습득하는 데 얼마나 오래 걸렸는지 과소평가함
분사구문을 이끄는 현재분사   to learn의 의미상 주어
Knowing that experts forget / how hard it was **for them** to learn,
/ we can understand the need / **to look at the learning process
through students' eyes**, /
전문가가 잊어버린다는 것을 안다면 / 자신이 학습하는 것이 얼마나 어려웠는지를 / 우리는 필요성을 이해할 수 있을 것이다 / 학생들의 눈을 통해 학습 과정을 바라봐야 할 (필요성) /
                ~보다는
rather than making assumptions / about how students 'should
be' learning. //
추정을 하기보다 / 학생이 어떻게 학습을 '해야 하는지'에 대한 //

- **research** ⓝ 연구 ・ **expert** ⓝ 전문가 ⓐ 능숙한
- **field** ⓝ 분야, 영역 ・ **difficulty** ⓝ 어려움 ・ **newcomer** ⓝ 초보
- **genuine** ⓐ 실제의 ・ **remarkably** ⓐⅾ 놀랍게도
- **accurate** ⓐ 정확한 ・ **insensitive** ⓐ 무감각한
- **acquire** ⓥ 습득하다 ・ **underestimate** ⓥ 과소평가하다
- **session** ⓝ 기간, 시간 ・ **assumption** ⓝ 추정, 가정

많은 조사 연구는 한 분야의 전문가가 그 분야로 초보자를 입문시킬 때 어떻게 어려움을 종종 겪는지를 보여주었다. 예를 들어, 실제 교육 상황에서 Pamela Hinds 박사는 휴대 전화기를 사용하는 데 능숙한 사람들이 휴대 전화기 사용법을 배우는 것에 얼마나 오랜 시간이 걸리는지를 판단하는 데 있어서, 초보 휴대 전화기 사용자보다 놀랍도록 덜 정확하다는 것을 알아냈다. 전문가는 한 과업이 초보자에게 얼마나 어려운지에 대해 무감각해질 수 있는데, 즉 '지식의 저주'로 칭해지는 효과이다. Hinds 박사는 사람이 기술을 습득했을 때 그 이후에 그 기술의 어려움의 정도를 과소평가하기 시작했다는 것을 보여 줄 수 있었다. 그녀의 참가자는 심지어 자신들이 이전 기간에 그 기술을 습득하는 데 얼마나 오래 걸렸는지를 과소평가했다. 전문가가 자신이 학습하는 것이 얼마나 어려웠는지를 잊어버린다는 것을 안다면, 우리는 학생이 어떻게 학습을 '해야 하는지'에 대한 (근거 없는) 추정을 하기보다 **학생들의 눈을 통해 학습 과정을 바라봐야 할** 필요성을 이해할 수 있을 것이다.

다음 빈칸에 들어갈 말로 가장 적절한 것을 고르시오. [3점]
① focus on the new functions of digital devices
디지털 기기의 새로운 기능에 주목해야 할   디지털 기기의 새로운 기능에 관한 내용이 아님
② apply new learning theories recently released
최근에 발표된 새로운 학습 이론을 적용해야 할   적용의 필요성에 대해 언급하지 않음
③ develop varieties of methods to test students
학생들을 평가하는 다양한 방법을 개발해야 할   평가하는 방법을 개발해야 한다는 내용이 없음
④ forget the difficulties that we have had as students
우리가 학생일 때 겪었던 어려움을 잊어야 할
⑤ look at the learning process through students' eyes   전문가가
학생들의 눈을 통해 학습 과정을 바라봐야 할   초보자의 입장에서 학습의 어려움을 이해해야 함
전문가가 초보자의 어려움에 대해 무감각해지는 것에서 문제가 발생함

| 문제 풀이 순서 | ★★★ [정답률 39%]

1st 먼저 빈칸 문장을 읽고, 빈칸에 들어갈 말을 예측한다.

빈칸 문장	전문가가 자신이 학습하는 것이 얼마나 어려웠는지를 잊어버린다는 것을 안다면, 우리는 학생이 어떻게 학습을 '해야 하는지'에 대한 (근거 없는) 추정을 하기보다 _____ 필요성을 이해할 수 있을 것이다.

➡ 전문가가 자신이 학습하며 겪은 어려움을 잊는다는 가정으로 문장이 시작되고, 학생이 어떻게 학습해야 하는지 추정하는 것보다는 '무엇'할 필요성이 있다고 했다. **단서**
학습의 어려움을 잊고 학생들에게 학습 방법을 가르치려 하는 것 대신, 학생의 입장이 된다거나 학생의 어려움을 이해해야 한다는 내용이 빈칸에 들어갈 것이다. **발상**

2nd 글의 나머지 부분을 읽고, 어떤 필요성에 대해 이야기하고 있는지 파악한다.

글의 앞부분	• 전문가는 한 과업이 초보자에게 얼마나 어려운지에 대해 무감각해질 수 있는데, 즉 '지식의 저주'로 칭해지는 효과이다. **단서 1**

➡ 전문가는 초보자의 어려움에 무감각해질 수 있다.
  ▶ 빈칸 문장에 제시된 가정과 일치하는 내용이다.

글의 뒷부분	• Hinds 박사는 사람이 기술을 습득했을 때 그 이후에 그 기술의 어려움의 정도를 과소평가하기 시작했다는 것을 보여 줄 수 있었다. **단서 2** • 그녀의 참가자는 심지어 자신들이 이전 기간에 그 기술을 습득하는 데 얼마나 오래 걸렸는지를 과소평가했다. **단서 3**

➡ Hinds 박사의 실험에서, 사람이 기술을 습득한 이후에 그 기술의 어려움은 물론이고 습득하는 데 필요한 기간을 과소평가한다고 했다.

➡ 전문가들은 초보자의 어려움을 이해하지 못하기 때문에, 그들이 어떻게 배워야 하는지 근거 없이 추정하려 할 수 있다.

3rd **2nd**에서 이해한 내용을 선택지에서 고른다.

➡ 전문가는 초보자의 어려움을 이해하지 못하기 때문에, 그들이 어떻게 기술을 습득해야 하는지를 추정하려 할 텐데, 그보다 먼저 그들의 입장을 이해해야 한다고 주장하는 글이다.
  ▶ 따라서 빈칸 문장에서는 초보자를 학생에 빗대었으므로, 전문가들은 ⑤ '학생들의 눈을 통해 학습 과정을 바라봐야 할' 필요성이 있다.

| 선택지 분석 |

① **focus on the new functions of digital devices**
  디지털 기기의 새로운 기능에 주목해야 할
휴대 전화기 사용법을 배우는 것을 예시로 들었을 뿐 디지털 기기의 새로운 기능에 관해 설명한 글이 아니다.

② **apply new learning theories recently released**
  최근에 발표된 새로운 학습 이론을 적용해야 할
새로운 학습 이론을 적용해야 할 필요성은 언급되지 않았다.

③ **develop varieties of methods to test students**
  학생들을 평가하는 다양한 방법을 개발해야 할
평가하는 방법을 개발해야 한다는 내용은 언급되지 않았다.

④ **forget the difficulties that we have had as students**
  우리가 학생일 때 겪었던 어려움을 잊어야 할
전문가가 초보자의 어려움에 대해 무감각해지는 것에서 문제가 발생하기 때문에 그러한 어려움을 잊는 것은 글의 내용과 모순된다.

⑤ **look at the learning process through students' eyes**
  학생들의 눈을 통해 학습 과정을 바라봐야 할
전문가가 초보자의 입장에서 학습의 어려움을 이해해야 한다는 내용의 글이다.

---

35 정답 ④ * 집단 음악 활동의 정신 건강 문제 개선

다음 글에서 전체 흐름과 관계 없는 문장은?

A group of psychologists studied / individuals with severe mental illness / **who** experienced weekly group music therapy, / including **singing** familiar songs and **composing** original songs. //
주격 관계대명사(선행사: individuals) / *병렬 구조*
한 심리학자 그룹이 연구했다 / 심각한 정신 질환이 있는 사람들을 / 집단 음악 치료를 매주 경험한 / 친숙한 노래 부르기와 독창적인 노래 작곡하기를 포함한 //

① The results showed / **that** the group music therapy improved the quality of participants' life, / **단서 1** 집단 음악 치료가 참여자의 삶의 질을 개선함
목적어절 접속사
그 연구 결과는 보여주었다 / 집단 음악 치료가 참여자의 삶의 질을 개선하였음을 /

with those participating in a greater number of sessions experiencing the greatest benefits. //
with+명사+현재분사: 명사가 ~한 채로, ~했기에 *현재분사구(those 수식)*
참여자가 (치료) 활동에 참여한 횟수가 많을수록 가장 큰 효과를 경험했기에 //

---

② **Focusing** on singing, / another group of psychologists reviewed articles / on the efficacy of group singing / as a mental health treatment /
분사구문을 이끄는 현재분사
노래 부르기에 초점을 두고 / 또 다른 그룹의 심리학자는 논문을 검토했다 / 집단 가창의 효능에 대한 / 정신 건강 치료로서 /

for individuals living with a mental health condition in a community setting. //
집단 생활의 환경에서 정신적인 건강 문제를 가지고 살고 있는 이들에게 미치는 //

③ The findings showed / **that**, **when** people with mental health conditions participated in a choir, / their mental health and wellbeing significantly improved. // **단서 2** 정신 건강 문제를 가진 사람이 합창단에 참여했을 때 정신 건강과 행복이 향상됨
목적어절 접속사 *부사절 접속사(시간)*
발견된 결과는 보여주었다 / 정신 건강 문제를 가진 사람이 합창단에 참여했을 때 / 그들의 정신 건강과 행복이 상당히 개선되었음을 //

④ The negative effects of music / were greater than the psychologists expected. //)
(음악의 부정적인 효과는 / 심리학자가 예상했던 것보다 더 컸다 //)

⑤ Group singing **provided** enjoyment, / **improved** emotional states, / **developed** a sense of belonging / and **enhanced** self-confidence. // **단서 3** 집단 가창은 정신적으로 여러 긍정적 효과를 가져옴
병렬 구조
집단 가창은 즐거움을 제공했고 / 감정 상태를 개선하였으며 / 소속감을 키웠고 / 자신감을 강화하였다 //

- psychologist ⓝ 심리학자 • severe ⓐ 심각한
- mental ⓐ 정신적인 • illness ⓝ 병, 질환 • compose ⓥ 작곡하다
- improve ⓥ 개선하다 • participant ⓝ 참가자
- session ⓝ 활동, 기간 • benefit ⓝ 이점 • review ⓥ 검토하다
- treatment ⓝ 치료 • setting ⓝ 환경 • finding ⓝ 결과
- choir ⓝ 합창단 • wellbeing ⓝ 행복 • significantly ⓐⓓ 상당히
- state ⓝ 상태 • enhance ⓥ 강화하다

한 심리학자 그룹이 친숙한 노래 부르기와 독창적인 작곡하기를 포함한 집단 음악 치료를 매주 경험한 심각한 정신 질환이 있는 사람들을 연구했다. ① 그 연구 결과는 참여자가 (치료) 활동에 참여한 횟수가 많을수록 가장 큰 효과를 경험했기에, 집단 음악 치료가 참여자의 삶의 질을 개선하였음을 보여주었다. ② 노래 부르기에 초점을 두고, 또 다른 그룹의 심리학자는 집단생활의 환경에서 정신적인 건강 문제를 가지고 살고 있는 이들에게 미치는 집단 가창의 효능에 대한 논문을 검토했다. ③ 발견된 결과는, 정신적인 건강 문제를 가진 사람이 합창단에 참여했을 때, 정신 건강과 행복이 상당히 개선되었음을 보여주었다. (④ 음악의 부정적인 효과는 심리학자가 예상했던 것보다 더 컸다.) ⑤ 집단 가창은 즐거움을 제공했고 감정 상태를 개선하였으며 소속감을 키웠고 자신감을 강화하였다.

왜 정답·오답? ★★★ [정답률 72%]

앞부분: 한 심리학자 그룹이 친숙한 노래 부르기와 독창적인 작곡하기를 포함한 집단 음악 치료를 매주 경험한 심각한 정신 질환이 있는 사람들을 연구했다.

➡ 집단 음악 치료가 정신 질환이 있는 사람들에 미치는 영향에 관한 글이다.

① 그 연구 결과는 참여자가 (치료) 활동에 참여한 횟수가 많을수록 가장 큰 효과를 경험했기에, 집단 음악 치료가 참여자의 삶의 질을 개선하였음을 보여주었다.

➡ 집단 음악 치료는 참여자의 삶의 질을 개선한다는 연구 결과가 이어진다.
  ▶ ①은 무관한 문장이 아님

② 노래 부르기에 초점을 두고, 또 다른 그룹의 심리학자는 집단생활의 환경에서 정신적인 건강 문제를 가지고 살고 있는 이들에게 미치는 집단 가창의 효능에 대한 논문을 검토했다.

➡ 집단적인 음악 활동이 정신 건강 문제를 가진 이들에게 미치는 영향에 대한 또 다른 연구가 자연스럽게 이어진다. ▶ ②은 무관한 문장이 아님

③ 발견된 결과는, 정신적인 건강 문제를 가진 사람이 합창단에 참여했을 때, 정신 건강과 행복이 상당히 개선되었음을 보여주었다.

➡ 정신 건강 문제를 가진 이들에게 미치는 집단 가창의 효능을 연구한 결과가 이어진다. ▶ ③은 무관한 문장이 아님

④ 음악의 부정적인 효과는 심리학자가 예상했던 것보다 더 컸다.

➡ 집단 가창이 정신 건강 문제가 있는 사람들에게 주는 긍정적인 효과를 이야기하다가, 음악의 부정적 효과를 이야기하므로 글의 흐름에 맞지 않는다. ▶ ④이 무관한 문장임

⑤ 집단 가창은 즐거움을 제공했고 감정 상태를 개선하였으며 소속감을 키웠고 자신감을 강화하였다.

➡ 집단 가창이 정신 상태에 미치는 긍정적인 효과를 다시 이어주는 적절한 흐름이다. ▶ ⑤은 무관한 문장이 아님

＊ 글의 흐름

연구	한 심리학자 그룹이 집단 음악 치료를 매주 경험한 심각한 정신 질환이 있는 사람들을 연구함
연구 결과	정신 질환이 있는 사람들이 집단 음악 치료를 받으면 삶의 질이 개선되었음
관련 논문	또 다른 그룹의 심리학자는 정신적인 건강 문제를 가지고 살고 있는 이들에게 미치는 집단 가창의 효능에 대한 논문을 검토함
논문의 결론	정신적인 건강 문제를 가진 사람이 합창단에 참여했을 때, 정신 건강과 행복이 상당히 개선되었음

36 정답 ④ ＊어린아이들을 위한 성인 스포츠 환경 조정

In many sports, people realized / the difficulties and even impossibilities / of young children / participating fully in many adult sport environments. //
많은 스포츠에서 사람들은 깨달았다 / 어렵고 심지어 불가능하다는 것을 / 어린아이들이 / 여러 성인 스포츠 환경에 완전히 참여하기란 //

(A) As examples, / baseball has T ball, / football has flag football / and junior soccer uses a smaller and lighter ball and (sometimes) a smaller field. //
예를 들자면 / 야구에는 티볼이 있고 / 풋볼에는 플래그 풋볼이 있고 / 유소년 축구는 더 작고 더 가벼운 공과 (가끔은) 더 작은 경기장을 사용한다 //

All have junior competitive structures / where children play / for shorter time periods and often in smaller teams. //
모두가 유소년 시합의 구조를 가진다 / 어린아이들이 경기하는 / 더 짧아진 경기 시간 동안 그리고 종종 더 작은 팀으로 //

(B) In a similar way, / tennis has adapted the court areas, balls and rackets / to make them more appropriate / for children under 10. //
비슷한 방식으로 / 테니스는 코트 면적, 공, 라켓을 조정했다 / 더 적합하도록 만들기 위해 / 10세 미만의 어린아이에게 //

The adaptations are progressive / and relate to the age of the child. //
이러한 조정은 점진적이고 / 어린이의 연령과 관련이 있다 //

(C) They found / the road to success for young children is unlikely / if they play on adult fields, courts or arenas / with equipment / that is too large, / too heavy / or too fast for them to handle / while trying to compete in adult-style competition. //
그들은 발견했다 / 어린아이들이 성공으로 가는 길이 있을 것 같지 않다는 것을 / 성인용 운동장, 코트 또는 경기장에서 운동한다면 / 장비를 가지고 / 너무 크거나 / 너무 무겁고 / 또는 너무 빨라서 그들(어린아이들)이 다룰 수 없는 / 성인 스타일의 시합에서 경쟁하려고 하면서 //

Common sense has prevailed: / different sports have made adaptations for children. //
이러한 공통된 견해가 널리 퍼졌기에 / 여러 스포츠는 어린아이들을 위한 조정을 했다 //

- realize ⓥ 깨닫다　・impossibility ⓝ 불가능　・field ⓝ 경기장
- competitive ⓐ 경쟁적인　・structure ⓝ 구조　・period ⓝ 기간
- racket ⓝ 라켓　・appropriate ⓐ 적절한
- progressive ⓐ 점진적인　・relate to ~와 관련되다
- arena ⓝ 경기장　・equipment ⓝ 장비　・handle ⓥ 다루다
- compete ⓥ 경쟁하다　・common sense (일반인들의) 공통된 견해, 상식
- adaptation ⓝ 조정

많은 스포츠에서 사람들은 어린아이들이 여러 성인 스포츠 환경에 완전히 참여하기란 어렵고 심지어 불가능하다는 것을 깨달았다. (C) 어린아이들이 너무 크거나 너무 무겁고 또는 너무 빨라서 그들(어린아이들)이 다룰 수 없는 장비를 가지고 성인 스타일의 시합에서 경쟁하려고 하면서 성인용 운동장, 코트 또는 경기장에서 운동한다면 그들(어린아이들)이 성공으로 가는 길이 있을 것 같지 않다는 것을 그들은 발견했다. 이러한 공통된 견해가 널리 퍼졌기에 여러 스포츠는 어린아이들을 위한 조정을 했다. (A) 예를 들자면, 야구에는 티볼이 있고, 풋볼에는 플래그 풋볼이 있고, 유소년 축구는 더 작고 더 가벼운 공과 (가끔은) 더 작은 경기장을 사용한다. 모두가 어린아이들이 더 짧아진 경기 시간 동안 그리고 종종 더 작은 팀으로 경기하는 유소년 시합의 구조를 가진다. (B) 비슷한 방식으로, 테니스는 코트 면적, 공, 라켓을 10세 미만의 어린아이에게 더 적합하도록 만들기 위해 조정했다. 이러한 조정은 점진적이고 어린아이의 연령과 관련이 있다.

주어진 글 다음에 이어질 글의 순서로 가장 적절한 것을 고르시오.

① (A) — (C) — (B)　(A)가 주어진 글에 관한 예시가 아님
② (B) — (A) — (C)　(B)가 '비슷한 방식으로'라는 접속사로 시작했지만, 주어진 글과 이어지지 않음
③ (B) — (C) — (A)
④ (C) — (A) — (B)
⑤ (C) — (B) — (A)

(C) 어린아이들이 성인 스포츠 환경에서 겪는 문제점을 해결하기 위해 여러 스포츠에서 어린아이들을 위한 조정을 함 — (A) 야구, 풋볼, 유소년 축구에서 어린아이들을 위해 조정함 — (B) 비슷한 방식으로 테니스에서도 어린아이들에게 적합하게 조정함
(B) 앞에는 다른 스포츠의 예시가 먼저 나와야 함

| 문제 풀이 순서 |　★★※ [정답률 73%]

1st 각 문단의 내용을 파악하고, 글의 논리적인 순서를 추론한다.

주어진 글: 많은 스포츠에서 사람들은 어린아이들이 여러 성인 스포츠 환경에 완전히 참여하기란 어렵고 심지어 불가능하다는 것을 깨달았다.

➡ 주어진 글 뒤: 어린아이들이 여러 성인 스포츠 환경에 완전히 참여하는 것이 어렵거나 불가능하다는 것을 사람들이 깨달았기 때문에 이를 해결하기 위한 방법이 이어질 것이다.

(A): 예를 들자면, 야구에는 티볼이 있고, 풋볼에는 플래그 풋볼이 있고, 유소년 축구는 더 작고 더 가벼운 공과 (가끔은) 더 작은 경기장을 사용한다. 모두가 어린아이들이 더 짧아진 경기 시간 동안 그리고 종종 더 작은 팀으로 경기하는 유소년 시합의 구조를 가진다.

➡ (A) 앞: (A)는 야구, 풋볼, 축구 등 대표적인 스포츠들이 유소년에 맞게 조정된 예시를 언급하고 있으므로, 앞에는 성인 스포츠가 유소년에 맞게 조정되었다는 등의 중심 문장이 직접 언급되어야 한다. ▶ 주어진 글 바로 뒤에 (A)가 올 수 없음
(A) 뒤: 다양한 스포츠가 어린아이들을 위해 조정된 것에 관한 부연 설명이 이어질 것이다.

(B): 비슷한 방식으로(In a similar way), 테니스는 코트 면적, 공, 라켓을 10세 미만의 어린아이에게 더 적합하도록 만들기 위해 조정했다. 이러한 조정은 점진적이고 어린아이의 연령과 관련이 있다.

➡ (B) 앞: In a similar way 뒤에 테니스가 어린아이에게 더 적합하도록 조정된 내용이 나오므로 앞에는 어린아이에게 더 적합하도록 조정된 다른 스포츠 예시가 언급되어야 한다.
▶ 어린아이들을 위해 적합하게 조정된 야구, 풋볼, 유소년 축구라는 예시가 언급된 (A)가 (B) 앞에 와야 함 (순서: (A) → (B))
(B) 뒤: 조정을 어떻게 했는지 설명하며 마무리했다. ▶ (B)가 마지막에 옴

50　자이스토리 전국연합학력평가 고1 영어

(C): 어린아이들이 너무 크거나 너무 무겁고 또는 너무 빨라서 그들(어린아이들)이 다룰 수 없는 장비를 가지고 성인 스타일의 시합에서 경쟁하려고 하면서 성인용 운동장, 코트 또는 경기장에서 운동한다면 그들(어린아이들)이 성공으로 가는 길이 있을 것 같지 않다는 것을 그들은(They) 발견했다. 이러한 공통된 견해가 널리 퍼졌기에 여러 스포츠는 어린아이들을 위한 조정을 했다.

➡ **(C) 앞:** They(그들은)가 가리키는 대상에 관한 내용이 있어야 한다.
  ▶ 주어진 글에서 They(그들은)가 가리키는 대상인 people(사람들은)이 나옴 (순서: 주어진 글 ➡ (C))
  (C) 뒤: 여러 스포츠가 어린아이들을 위해 조정됐다는 내용 뒤에는 이에 관한 예시로서 야구, 풋볼, 유소년 축구를 언급한 (A)가 이어질 것이다.
  ▶ (C) 뒤에 (A)가 이어져야 함 (순서: 주어진 글 ➡ (C) ➡ (A) ➡ (B))

2nd 글이 한눈에 들어오도록 정리하여 정답을 확인한다.

주어진 글: 어린아이들이 성인 스포츠 환경에 완전히 참여하기란 어렵고 심지어 불가능하다.
→ **(C):** 장비나 경기 환경이 어린아이들에게 적합하지 않다는 견해가 널리 퍼져서 여러 스포츠는 어린아이들을 위한 조정을 했다.
→ **(A):** 예를 들어 야구, 풋볼, 유소년 축구는 각각 어린아이들에게 적합하도록 조정을 했다.
→ **(B):** 비슷한 방식으로 테니스도 어린아이에게 더 적합하도록 조정을 했다.
  ▶ 주어진 글 다음에 이어질 글의 순서는 (C) ➡ (A) ➡ (B)이므로 정답은 ④임

37 정답 ③ ＊Inca 제국의 Chasquis 전령들

With no horses available, / the Inca empire excelled / at delivering messages on foot. // **단서 1** Inca 제국은 걸어서 메시지를 전달하는 데 탁월했음
구할 수 있는 말이 없어서 / Inca 제국은 탁월했다 / 걸어서 메시지를 전달하는 데 //

(A) When a messenger neared the next hut, / he began to call out and repeated the message three or four times / to the one who was running out to meet him. // 주격 관계대명사(선행사: the one) 부사적 용법(목적) **단서 2** 전령이 오두막을 향해 오는 내용이 앞에 와야 함
전령은 다음 오두막에 다가갈 때 / 소리치기 시작했고 메시지를 서너 번 반복했다 / 자신을 만나러 달려 나오고 있는 전령에게 //

The Inca empire could relay messages 1,000 miles (1,610 km) / in three or four days under good conditions. //
Inca 제국은 1,000마일(1,610km) 정도 메시지를 이어 갈 수 있었다 / 사정이 좋으면 사나흘 만에 //

(B) The messengers were stationed on the royal roads / to deliver the Inca king's orders and reports / coming from his lands. // **단서 3** 누가 걸어서 메시지를 전달했는지 설명함 현재분사구(orders and reports 수식)
전령들은 왕의 길에 배치되었다 / Inca 왕의 명령과 보고를 전달하기 위해 / 그의 영토에서 오는 //

Called Chasquis, / they lived in groups of four to six / in huts, placed from one to two miles apart along the roads. // 앞에 주격 관계대명사와 be동사 생략됨
Chasquis라고 불리는 / 그들은 네 명에서 여섯 명의 집단을 이루어 생활했다 / 길을 따라 1마일에서 2마일 간격으로 떨어져 배치된 오두막에서 //

(C) They were all young men / and especially good runners / who watched the road in both directions. // **단서 4** (C) 앞에 They(그들은)가 가리키는 대상이 나와야 함 주격 관계대명사(선행사: runners)
그들은 모두 젊은 남자였고 / 특히 잘 달리는 이들이었다 / 양방향으로 길을 주시하는 //

If they caught sight of another messenger coming, / they hurried out to meet them. //
그들은 다른 전령이 오는 것을 발견하면 / 그들을 맞이하기 위해 서둘러 나갔다 //

The Inca built the huts on high ground, / in sight of one another. //
Inca 사람들은 높은 지대에 오두막을 지었다 / 서로를 볼 수 있는 //

- **available** ⓐ 구할 수 있는 - **empire** ⓝ 제국 - **on foot** 걸어서
- **near** ⓥ 다가가다 - **relay** ⓥ 이어가다
- **under good condition** 좋은 상황에서, 사정이 좋으면
- **station** ⓥ 배치하다 - **royal** ⓐ 왕의, 왕실의 - **order** ⓝ 명령

- **hut** ⓝ 오두막 - **place** ⓥ 배치하다 - **apart** ⓐⓓ 떨어져
- **along** ⓟⓡⓔⓟ ~을 따라 - **especially** ⓐⓓ 특히 - **direction** ⓝ 방향
- **catch sight of** ~을 찾아내다

구할 수 있는 말이 없어서, Inca 제국은 걸어서 메시지를 전달하는 데 탁월했다. (B) 전령들은 Inca 왕의 명령과 그의 영토에서 오는 보고를 전달하기 위해 왕의 길에 배치되었다. Chasquis라고 불리는, 그들은 네 명에서 여섯 명의 집단을 이루어 길을 따라 1마일에서 2마일 간격으로 떨어져 배치된 오두막에서 생활했다. (C) 그들은 모두 젊은 남자였고, 양방향으로 길을 주시하는 특히 잘 달리는 이들이었다. 그들은 다른 전령이 오는 것을 발견하면 그들을 맞이하기 위해 서둘러 나갔다. Inca 사람들은 서로를 볼 수 있는 높은 지대에 오두막을 지었다. (A) 전령은 다음 오두막에 다가갈 때, 자신을 만나러 달려 나오고 있는 전령에게 소리치기 시작했고 메시지를 서너 번 반복했다. Inca 제국은 사정이 좋으면 사나흘 만에 1,000마일(1,610km) 정도 메시지를 이어 갈 수 있었다.

> **주어진 글 다음에 이어질 글의 순서로 가장 적절한 것을 고르시오. [3점]**
> ① (A) — (C) — (B) (A) 앞에 전령과 오두막에 대한 언급이 먼저 나와야 함
> ② (B) — (A) — (C) (A)의 끝에서 메시지 전달 속도를 설명하는데 (C)의 They(그들은)와 이어지지 않아서 어색함
> ③ (B) — (C) — (A) (B) 전령들이 왕의 길에 배치되었고 오두막에서 집단으로 생활함 — (C) 전령들은 잘 달리는 젊은 남자들이었고 다른 전령이 오는 것을 발견하면 서둘러 나감 — (A) 전령이 자신을 만나러 달려 나오는 다음 전령에게 소리치며 메시지를 서너 번 반복함
> ④ (C) — (A) — (B)
> ⑤ (C) — (B) — (A) (C)의 They(그들은)가 가리키는 대상이 누구인지 먼저 언급해야 함

| 문제 풀이 순서 | ★★★ [정답률 42%]

1st 각 문단의 내용을 파악하고, 글의 논리적인 순서를 추론한다.

주어진 글: 구할 수 있는 말이 없어서, Inca 제국은 걸어서 메시지를 전달하는 데 탁월했다.
➡ **주어진 글 뒤:** 걸어서 메시지를 전달하는 방법에 관한 내용이 이어질 것이다.

(A): 전령은 다음 오두막(the next hut)에 다가갈 때, 자신을 만나러 달려 나오고 있는 전령에게 소리치기 시작했고 메시지를 서너 번 반복했다. Inca 제국은 사정이 좋으면 사나흘 만에 1,000마일(1,610km) 정도 메시지를 이어 갈 수 있었다.
➡ **(A) 앞:** 정관사 the가 쓰였으므로, 오두막에 대한 설명이 앞에 언급되어야 하는데, 주어진 글에는 오두막에 관한 내용이 없다.
  ▶ 주어진 글 바로 뒤에 (A)가 올 수 없음
  (A) 뒤: 구체적인 메시지 전달 속도로 문장을 마무리했으므로, 주어진 글의 중심 문장인 'Inca 제국이 걸어서 메시지를 전달하는 데 탁월했다'를 정리하는 문단임을 유추할 수 있다.

(B): 전령들은 Inca 왕의 명령과 그의 영토에서 오는 보고를 전달하기 위해 왕의 길에 배치되었다. Chasquis라고 불리는, 그들은 네 명에서 여섯 명의 집단을 이루어 길을 따라 1마일에서 2마일 간격으로 떨어져 배치된 오두막에서 생활했다.
➡ **(B) 앞:** 명령과 보고를 전달하는 수단으로서 오두막마다 배치된 전령들이 언급되었다. 구할 수 있는 말이 없어서 Inca 제국이 전령들을 통해 메시지를 전달했음을 유추할 수 있다.
  ▶ (B) 앞에 주어진 글이 와야 함 (순서: 주어진 글 ➡ (B))
  (B) 뒤: 전령들에 대한 부연 설명이 이어질 것이다.

(C): 그들은(They) 모두 젊은 남자였고, 양방향으로 길을 주시하는 특히 잘 달리는 이들이었다. 그들은 다른 전령이 오는 것을 발견하면 그들을 맞이하기 위해 서둘러 나갔다. Inca 사람들은 서로를 볼 수 있는 높은 지대에 오두막을 지었다.
➡ **(C) 앞:** '그들(They)'이 가리키는 대상이 앞에 나와야 한다. 명령과 보고를 전달하기 위해 배치된 전령에 관한 내용이 (B)에 있다.
  ▶ (C) 앞에 (B)가 와야 함 (순서: 주어진 글 ➡ (B) ➡ (C))
  (C) 뒤: 전령들이 높은 지대에 오두막을 짓고 어떻게 활동했는지에 대한 부연 설명이 이어져야 한다.
  ▶ (A)에서 전령들의 메시지 전달 방법과 메시지 전달 속도에 대한 설명을 이어감 (순서: 주어진 글 ➡ (B) ➡ (C) ➡ (A))

주어진 글: Inca 제국은 구할 수 있는 말이 없어서 걸어서 메시지를 전달하는 데 탁월했다.

→ **(B):** Inca 왕의 명령과 그의 영토에서 오는 보고를 전달하기 위해 Chasquis라고 불리는 전령들이 왕의 길에 배치되었다.

→ **(C):** 전령들은 잘 달리는 젊은 남자들이었고 다른 전령이 오는 것을 발견하면 서둘러 나갔다.

→ **(A):** 전령이 자신을 만나러 달려 나오는 다음 전령에게 소리치며 메시지를 서너 번 반복하고, 사정이 좋으면 메시지는 사나흘 만에 1000마일 정도를 이어 갈 수 있었다.

▶ 주어진 글 다음에 이어질 글의 순서는 (B) → (C) → (A)이므로 정답은 ③임

---

38 정답 ① *잘못 알려진 혀 지도 이론

글의 흐름으로 보아, 주어진 문장이 들어가기에 가장 적절한 곳을 고르시오.

Research in the 1980s and 1990s, however, / demonstrated / that the "tongue map" explanation of how we taste / was, in fact, totally wrong. // **단서 1** 혀 지도가 틀렸음을 설명하는 내용 앞에 와야 함
그러나 1980년대와 1990년대의 연구는 / 보여 주었다 / 우리가 맛을 느끼는 방식에 대한 '혀 지도' 설명이 / 사실은 완전히 틀렸다는 것을 //

단서 2 혀가 특정 맛이 등록되는 개별적인 영역으로 구획됨   관계부사(선행사: areas)
The tongue was mapped into separate areas / where certain tastes were registered: / sweetness at the tip, / sourness on the sides, / and bitterness at the back of the mouth. //
혀는 개별적인 영역으로 구획되었는데 / 특정 맛이 등록되는 / 끝에는 단맛 / 측면에는 신맛 / 그리고 입의 뒤쪽에는 쓴맛이 있었다 //

(①) As it turns out, / the map was a misinterpretation and mistranslation / of research conducted in Germany at the turn of the twentieth century. // **단서 3** 그 지도(혀 지도)는 연구를 오해하고 오역한 것임
밝혀진 바와 같이 / 그 지도는 오해하고 오역한 것이었다 / 20세기 초입 독일에서 수행된 연구를 //

(②) Today, / leading taste researchers believe / that taste buds are not grouped according to specialty. // **단서 4** 미뢰는 맛을 느끼는 특화된 분야에 따라 분류되지 않음
오늘날 / 선도적인 미각 연구자는 믿는다 / 미뢰가 맛을 느끼는 특화된 분야에 따라 분류되지 않는다고 //

(③) Sweetness, saltiness, bitterness, and sourness / can be tasted everywhere in the mouth, / although they may be perceived / at a little different intensities at different sites. //
단맛, 짠맛, 쓴맛 그리고 신맛은 / 입안 어디에서나 느낄 수 있다 / 비록 그것들이 지각될지도 모르겠지만 / 여러 위치에서 조금씩 다른 강도로 //

(④) Moreover, the mechanism at work is not place, / but time. //
게다가, 작동 중인 기제는 위치가 아니라 / 시간이다 //

(⑤) It's not that you taste sweetness at the tip of your tongue, / but rather that you register that perception first. //
여러분은 혀끝에서 단맛을 느낀다기보다 / 오히려 그 지각(단맛)을 '가장 먼저' 등록하는 것이다 //

- **demonstrate** ⓥ 보여주다
- **explanation** ⓝ 설명
- **map** ⓥ (지도에) 구획하다
- **separate** ⓐ 개별적인, 별개의
- **register** ⓥ 등록하다
- **tip** ⓝ 끝
- **sourness** ⓝ 신맛
- **bitterness** ⓝ 쓴맛
- **misinterpretation** ⓝ 오해
- **mistranslation** ⓝ 오역
- **conduct** ⓥ 수행하다
- **turn** ⓝ 전환기
- **leading** ⓐ 선도적인
- **specialty** ⓝ 특화된 분야
- **perceive** ⓥ 지각하다
- **intensity** ⓝ 강도
- **mechanism** ⓝ 기제
- **at work** 작동 중인

혀는 특정 맛이 등록되는 개별적인 영역으로 구획되었는데, 즉, 끝에는 단맛, 측면에는 신맛, 그리고 입의 뒤쪽에는 쓴맛이 있었다. (① 그러나 1980년대와 1990년대의 연구는 우리가 맛을 느끼는 방식에 대한 '혀 지도' 설명이 사실은 완전히 틀렸다는 것을 보여주었다.) 밝혀진 바와 같이, 그 지도는 20세기 초입 독일에서 수행된 연구를 오해하고 오역한 것이었다. (②) 오늘날, 선도적인 미각 연구자는 미뢰가 맛을 느끼는 특화된 분야에 따라 분류되지 않는다고 믿는다. (③) 비록 그것들이 여러 위치에서 조금씩 다른 강도로 지각될지도 모르겠지만, 단맛, 짠맛, 쓴맛 그리고 신맛은 입안 어디에서나 느낄 수 있다. (④) 게다가, 작동 중인 기제는 위치가 아니라 시간이다. (⑤) 여러분은 혀끝에서 단맛을 느낀다기보다 오히려 그 지각(단맛)을 '가장 먼저' 등록하는 것이다.

| 문제 풀이 순서 | ✳✳✳ [정답률 54%]

1st 주어진 문장을 해석하고, 연결어, 지시어 등을 확인한다.

Research in the 1980s and 1990s, however, demonstrated that the "tongue map" explanation of how we taste was, in fact, totally wrong.
그러나 1980년대와 1990년 대의 연구는 우리가 맛을 느끼는 방식에 대한 '혀 지도' 설명이 사실은 완전히 틀렸다는 것을 보여주었다.

➡ 주어진 문장 앞: however(그러나)라고 했으므로 **단서**
앞에는 '혀 지도' 설명이 옳다고 여겨진 시기나 이 설명이 제시된 상황이 나와야 하고, 뒤에는 '혀 지도' 설명이 틀리다는 내용이 이어져야 한다. **발상**

2nd 찾은 단서를 생각하며 각 선택지의 앞뒤 흐름이 매끄러운지 확인한다.

① 의 앞 문장과 뒤 문장
앞 문장: 혀는 특정 맛이 등록되는 개별적인 영역으로 구획되었는데, 즉, 끝에는 단맛, 측면에는 신맛, 그리고 입의 뒤쪽에는 쓴맛이 있었다.
뒤 문장: 밝혀진 바와 같이, 그 지도(the map)는 20세기 초입 독일에서 수행된 연구를 오해하고 오역한 것이었다.

➡ 혀의 구역마다 느끼는 맛이 다르다는 것, 즉 '혀 지도'에 관한 내용에 이어서 그 지도(the map)가 오역된 것이라는 부정적인 내용이 나온다. 주어진 글의 tongue map이 ①의 뒤 문장에서 the map으로 다시 언급되었으며 혀 지도가 잘못되었다는 내용으로 전환되는 지점이므로 주어진 글이 ①에 오는 것이 적절하다.
▶ 주어진 문장이 ①에 들어가야 함

② 의 앞 문장과 뒤 문장
앞 문장: ①의 뒤 문장과 같음
뒤 문장: 오늘날, 선도적인 미각 연구자는 미뢰가 맛을 느끼는 특화된 분야에 따라 분류되지 않는다고 믿는다.

➡ 혀 지도에 관한 연구가 오역된 것이기 때문에, 오늘날에는 미뢰가 특정 맛을 느끼는 것으로 분류되지 않는다고 믿어진다는 내용으로 자연스럽게 이어졌다.
▶ 주어진 문장이 ②에 들어갈 수 없음

③ 의 앞 문장과 뒤 문장
앞 문장: ②의 뒤 문장과 같음
뒤 문장: 비록 그것들이 여러 위치에서 조금씩 다른 강도로 지각될지도 모르겠지만, 단맛, 짠맛, 쓴맛 그리고 신맛은 입안 어디에서나 느낄 수 있다.

➡ 미뢰가 특정 맛을 느끼는 것으로 분류되지 않는다는 설명에 이어서 다양한 맛을 입안 어디에서나 느낄 수 있다는 부연 설명이 자연스럽게 이어졌다.
▶ 주어진 문장이 ③에 들어갈 수 없음

- ④의 앞 문장과 뒤 문장

┌ 앞 문장: ③의 뒤 문장과 같음
└ 뒤 문장: 게다가, 작동 중인 기제는 위치가 아니라 시간이다.

➡ 미뢰가 특정 맛을 감지하는 것으로 분류될 수 없다는 내용에 이어서 혀가 맛을 느낄 때 작동하는 기제는 위치가 아닌 시간이라는 추가적인 정보가 자연스럽게 이어졌다. ▶ 주어진 문장이 ④에 들어갈 수 없음

- ⑤의 앞 문장과 뒤 문장

┌ 앞 문장: ④의 뒤 문장과 같음
│ 뒤 문장: 여러분은 혀끝에서 단맛을 느낀다기보다 오히려 그 지각(단맛)을
└ '가장 먼저' 등록하는 것이다.

➡ 작동 중인 기제가 시간이라는 앞의 내용을 구체적으로 설명하는 자연스러운 흐름이다. ▶ 주어진 문장이 ⑤에 들어갈 수 없음

3rd 글이 한눈에 들어오도록 정리하여 정답을 확인한다.

혀는 특정 맛이 등록되는 개별적인 영역으로 구획되었다.
(① 그러나 1980년대와 1990년대 연구는 '혀 지도'가 잘못된 설명임을 밝혔다.)
20세기 초 독일의 연구를 잘못 해석하여 그 지도가 생겨났다.
(②) 오늘날 미각 연구자들은 미뢰가 맛을 느끼는 특화된 분야로 분류되지 않는다고 믿는다.
(③) 맛은 위치와 관계없이 입안 전체에서 느낄 수 있으며, 각 위치에서 강도 차이가 있을 수 있다.
(④) 맛을 인지하는 기제는 위치가 아닌 시간이다.
(⑤) 단맛을 혀끝에서 느낀다기보다는 가장 먼저 인지하는 것이다.

39 정답 ② ＊동물의 특성과 필요에 따라 조정되어야 하는 치료

글의 흐름으로 보아, 주어진 문장이 들어가기에 가장 적절한 곳을 고르시오.

Environmental factors can also determine / how the animal will respond during the treatment. // 【단서 1】 치료 중에 다르게 반응하게 하는 다른 요인이 앞에 언급되어야 함
또한 환경적 요인은 결정할 수 있다 / 치료 중에 동물이 어떻게 반응할지를 //

No two animals are alike. //
어떤 두 동물도 똑같지 않다 //

(①) Animals from the same litter / will display some of the same features, / but will not be exactly the same as each other; /
한 배에서 태어난 동물은 / 똑같은 몇몇 특성을 보여 줄 수 있겠지만 / 서로 정확히 같지는 않을 것이다 /

therefore, they may not respond / in entirely the same way / during a healing session. // 【단서 2】 한 배에서 태어난 동물도 서로 다르므로 치료 중에 완전히 똑같은 방식으로 반응하지 않음
그런 까닭에, 그들은 반응하지 않을지도 모른다 / 완전히 똑같은 방식으로 / 치료 활동 중에 //

(②) For instance, / a cat in a rescue center will respond very differently / than a cat within a domestic home environment. // 【단서 3】 어떤 환경에 있는 고양이인지에 따라 다르게 반응함
예를 들어 / 구조 센터에 있는 고양이는 / 매우 다르게 반응할 것이다 / 가정집 환경 내에 있는 고양이와는 //

(③) In addition, / animals that experience healing for physical illness / will react differently / than those accepting healing for emotional confusion. //
게다가 / 신체적 질병의 치료를 받는 동물은 / 다르게 반응할 것이다 / 감정적 동요의 치료를 받는 동물과는 //

(④) With this in mind, / every healing session needs to be explored differently, / and each healing treatment should be adjusted / to suit the specific needs of the animal. //
이를 염두에 두어 / 모든 치료 활동은 다르게 탐구되어야 하고 / 각각의 치료법은 조정되어야 한다 / 동물의 특정한 필요에 맞도록 //

(⑤) You will learn as you go; / healing is a constant learning process. //
여러분은 직접 겪으면서 배우게 될 것이다 / 치료가 끊임없는 학습의 과정인 것을 //

- factor ⓝ 요인 • determine ⓥ 결정하다 • respond ⓥ 반응하다
- treatment ⓝ 치료 • alike ⓐ 비슷한, 같은 • display ⓥ 보이다
- feature ⓝ 특징 • therefore ⓐⓓ 그런 까닭에 • entirely ⓐⓓ 완전히
- healing session 치료 활동 • rescue center 구조 센터
- domestic ⓐ 가정의 • illness ⓝ 질병 • react ⓥ 반응하다
- confusion ⓝ 동요, 혼란 • with ~ in mind ~을 염두에 두고
- explore ⓥ 탐구하다 • specific ⓐ 특정한, 구체적인
- constant ⓐ 끊임없는 • process ⓝ 과정

어떤 두 동물도 똑같지 않다. (①) 한 배에서 태어난 동물은 똑같은 몇몇 특성을 보여 줄 수 있겠지만, 서로 정확히 같지는 않을 것이다. 그런 까닭에, 그들은 치료 활동 중에 완전히 똑같은 방식으로 반응하지 않을지도 모른다. (② 또한 환경적 요인은 치료 중에 동물이 어떻게 반응할지를 결정할 수 있다.) 예를 들어, 구조 센터에 있는 고양이는 가정집 환경 내에 있는 고양이와는 매우 다르게 반응할 것이다. (③) 게다가, 신체적 질병의 치료를 받는 동물은 감정적 동요의 치료를 받는 동물과는 다르게 반응할 것이다. (④) 이를 염두에 두어, 모든 치료 활동은 다르게 탐구되어야 하고, 각각의 치료법은 동물의 특정한 필요에 맞도록 조정되어야 한다. (⑤) 여러분은 치료가 끊임없는 학습의 과정인 것을 직접 겪으면서 배우게 될 것이다.

| 문제 풀이 순서 | ★★★ [정답률 26%]

1st 주어진 문장을 해석하고, 연결어, 지시어 등을 확인한다.

┌ Environmental factors can also determine how the animal
│ will respond during the treatment.
└ 또한 환경적 요인은 치료 중에 동물이 어떻게 반응할지를 결정할 수 있다.

➡ 주어진 문장 앞: also(또한)가 있으므로 단서
환경적 요인의 다른 역할이 앞에 언급되거나, 치료 중인 동물의 반응을 결정하는 다른 요인이 앞에 나올 것이다. 발상

2nd 찾은 단서를 생각하며 각 선택지의 앞뒤 흐름이 매끄러운지 확인한다.

- ①의 앞 문장과 뒤 문장

┌ 앞 문장: 어떤 두 동물도 똑같지 않다.
│ 뒤 문장: 한 배에서 태어난 동물은 똑같은 몇몇 특성을 보여 줄 수 있겠지만,
│ 서로 정확히 같지는 않을 것이다. 그런 까닭에, 그들은 치료 활동 중에
└ 완전히 똑같은 방식으로 반응하지 않을지도 모른다.

➡ 어떤 두 동물도 똑같지 않다는 문장 뒤에, 한 배에서 태어난 동물들도 서로 다른 까닭에, 치료 활동에 대한 반응도 완전히 똑같지 않다는 부연 설명이 자연스럽게 이어진다.
▶ 주어진 문장이 ①에 들어갈 수 없음

- ②의 앞 문장과 뒤 문장

┌ 앞 문장: ①의 뒤 문장과 같음
│ 뒤 문장: 예를 들어, 구조 센터에 있는 고양이는 가정집 환경 내에 있는
└ 고양이와는 매우 다르게 반응할 것이다.

➡ ②의 앞 문장은 한 배에서 태어난 동물들도 치료 활동에 대한 반응이 같지 않다는 내용, 즉 생물학적 요인에 관한 것이지만, ②의 뒤 문장은 고양이가 다른 환경 안에서 반응을 다르게 할 수 있다는 예시, 즉 환경적 요인에 관한 것이다. 두 문장이 이어지려면, 그 사이에 환경에 따라 동물의 치료에 대한 반응이 달라질 수 있다는 내용이 와야 한다.
▶ 주어진 문장이 ②에 들어가야 함

- ③의 앞 문장과 뒤 문장

앞 문장: ②의 뒤 문장과 같음

뒤 문장: 게다가, 신체적 질병의 치료를 받는 동물은 감정적 동요의 치료를 받는 동물과는 다르게 반응할 것이다.

➡ 환경적 요인에 이어서, 동물의 치료 반응에 영향을 미치는 요인으로서 신체적 질병의 치료와 감정적 동요의 치료를 받는 동물이 다르게 반응한다는 내용이 추가로 제시되었다.

▶ 주어진 문장이 ③에 들어갈 수 없음

- ④의 앞 문장과 뒤 문장

앞 문장: ③의 뒤 문장과 같음

뒤 문장: 이를(this) 염두에 두어, 모든 치료 활동은 다르게 탐구되어야 하고, 각각의 치료법은 동물의 특정한 필요에 맞도록 조정되어야 한다.

➡ 동물의 치료 반응이 달라지는 다양한 요인이 앞에 쭉 제시되었고, 이러한 요인들로 인해 동물의 치료 반응이 달라질 수 있다는 사실을 this로 가리키며 문장이 자연스럽게 이어졌다.

▶ 주어진 문장이 ④에 들어갈 수 없음

- ⑤의 앞 문장과 뒤 문장

앞 문장: ④의 뒤 문장과 같음

뒤 문장: 여러분은 치료가 끊임없는 학습의 과정인 것을 직접 겪으면서 배우게 될 것이다.

➡ 치료가 동물에 따라 다른 특정한 필요에 맞게 조정되어야 하므로 치료는 끊임없는 학습의 과정이라는 내용이 자연스럽게 이어진다.

▶ 주어진 문장이 ⑤에 들어갈 수 없음

3rd 글이 한눈에 들어오도록 정리하여 정답을 확인한다.

두 동물이 완전히 같을 수는 없다.
(①) 심지어 같은 배에서 태어난 동물들조차도 서로 다른 특성을 가지고, 치료에도 각기 다르게 반응할 수 있다.
(② 또한 환경적 요인은 치료 중에 동물이 어떻게 반응할지를 결정할 수 있다.)
예를 들어 구조 센터에 있는 고양이와 가정집 환경에 있는 고양이는 치료에 다르게 반응할 것이다.
(③) 동물이 신체적 질병이나 감정적 문제로 치료를 받을 때, 그 반응 역시 서로 다를 수 있다.
(④) 다른 반응을 고려하여 치료 활동이 다르게 탐구되고 동물의 필요에 맞추어 치료법이 개별적으로 조정되어야 한다.
(⑤) 치료는 끊임없는 학습의 과정이라는 것을 경험하고 배우게 될 것이다.

40 정답 ① ＊의식적 마음과 잠재의식적 마음의 다른 기능

The mind has parts / that are known as the conscious mind and the subconscious mind. //
복수 선행사 / 복수 동사(수 일치)
마음은 부분을 갖고 있다 / 의식적 마음과 잠재의식적 마음이라고 알려진 //

The subconscious mind is very fast to act / and doesn't deal with emotions. //
부사적 용법
잠재의식적 마음은 매우 빠르게 작동하며 / 감정을 다루지 않는다 //

It deals with / memories of your responses to life, your memories and recognition. //
'~을 다루다'
그것은 다룬다 / 여러분의 삶에 대한 반응의 기억, 기억 및 인식을 //

However, the conscious mind is the one / that you have more control over. // 단서 1 우리는 의식적 마음에 더 많은 통제력을 가짐
목적격 관계대명사(선행사: the one)
그러나 의식적 마음은 부분이다 / 여러분이 더 많은 통제력을 갖고 있는 //

You think. //
여러분은 생각한다 //

You can choose / whether to carry on a thought / or to add emotion to it / 단서 2 (의식적 마음에서는) 생각을 계속할지 그 생각에 감정을 더할지 선택할 수 있음
whether A or B: A인지 B인지
여러분은 선택할 수 있다 / 생각을 계속할지 / 또는 그 생각에 감정을 더할지를 /

and this is the part of your mind / that lets you down frequently / because — fueled by emotions / — you make the wrong decisions / time and time again. //
주격 관계대명사(선행사: the part)
과거분사가 이끄는 분사구문
그리고 이것은 마음의 부분이기도 하다 / 여러분을 빈번하게 낙담시키는 / 왜냐하면 감정에 북받쳐 / 잘못된 결정을 내리게 만들기 때문에 / 반복해서 //

When your judgment is clouded / by emotions, / this puts in biases and all kinds of other negativities / that hold you back. //
주격 관계대명사(선행사: negativities)
여러분의 판단력이 흐려질 때 / 감정에 의해 / 이것은 편견과 그 밖의 모든 종류의 부정성을 자리 잡게 만든다 / 여러분을 억제하는 //

Scared of spiders? //
거미를 무서워하는가 //

Scared of the dark? //
어둠을 무서워하는가 //

There are reasons for all of these fears, / but they originate in the conscious mind. //
이러한 두려움 전부 이유가 있지만 / 그것들은 의식적 마음에서 비롯된다 //

They only become real fears / when the subconscious mind records your reactions. // 단서 3 잠재의식적 마음이 반응을 기록할 때 실제 두려움이 됨
그것들은 오직 실제 두려움이 된다 / 잠재의식적 마음이 여러분의 반응을 기록할 때 //

→ While the controllable conscious mind deals with / thoughts and (A) emotions, / the fast-acting subconscious mind / stores your responses, / (B) forming real fears. //
'반면에'
분사구문
통제할 수 있는 의식적 마음은 다루지만 / 생각과 감정을 / 빠르게 작동하는 잠재의식적 마음이 / 여러분의 반응을 저장하고 / 이는 실제 두려움을 형성한다 //

- conscious ⓐ 의식적인 · subconscious ⓐ 잠재의식적인
- recognition ⓝ 인식 · frequently ⓐⓓ 자주, 빈번히
- judgment ⓝ 판단(력) · cloud ⓥ (기억력, 판단력 등을) 흐리게 하다
- bias ⓝ 편견 · negativity ⓝ 부정성 · fear ⓝ 두려움
- originate ⓥ 비롯되다 · controllable ⓐ 통제할 수 있는
- overcome ⓥ 극복하다

마음은 의식적 마음과 잠재의식적 마음이라고 알려진 부분을 갖고 있다. 잠재의식적 마음은 매우 빠르게 작동하며 감정을 다루지 않는다. 그것은 여러분의 삶에 대한 반응의 기억, 기억 및 인식을 다룬다. 그러나 의식적 마음은 여러분이 더 많은 통제력을 갖고 있는 부분이다. 여러분은 생각한다. 여러분은 생각을 계속할지 또는 그 생각에 감정을 더할지를 선택할 수 있다. 그리고 이것은 감정에 북받쳐 잘못된 결정을 반복해서 내리게 만들기 때문에 여러분을 빈번하게 낙담시키는 마음의 부분이기도 하다. 감정에 의해 여러분의 판단력이 흐려질 때 이것은 편견과 그 밖의 여러분을 억제하는 모든 종류의 부정성을 자리 잡게 만든다. 거미를 무서워하는가? 어둠을 무서워하는가? 이러한 두려움 전부 이유가 있지만 그것들은 의식적 마음에서 비롯된다. 그것들은 오직 잠재의식적 마음이 여러분의 반응을 기록할 때 실제 두려움이 된다.
→ 통제할 수 있는 의식적 마음은 생각과 (A) 감정을 다루지만, 빠르게 작동하는 잠재의식적 마음이 여러분의 반응을 저장하고, 이는 실제 두려움을 (B) 형성한다.

다음 글의 내용을 한 문장으로 요약하고자 한다. 빈칸 (A), (B)에 들어갈 말로 가장 적절한 것은?

	(A)	(B)	
①	emotions 감정	forming 형성하면서	의식적 마음은 생각에 감정을 더할 수 있으며 잠재의식적 마음은 반응을 저장하여 실제 두려움을 형성함
②	actions 행동	overcoming 극복하면서	의식적 마음이 행동을 다루는지 알 수 없음
③	emotions	overcoming	잠재의식적 마음이 실제 두려움을 극복한다는 언급이 없음
④	actions	avoiding 피하면서	잠재의식적 마음이 실제 두려움을 피한다는 내용이 없음
⑤	moralities 도덕성	forming	의식적 마음이 도덕성을 다루는지 이 글에서는 알 수 없음

✓왜 정답? ✹✹✿ [정답률 67%]

(A):

- 그러나 의식적 마음은 여러분이 더 많은 통제력을 갖고 있는 부분이다. 단서1
- 여러분은 생각을 계속할지 또는 그 생각에 감정을 더할지를 선택할 수 있다. 단서2

➡ 우리가 의식적 마음에 더 많은 통제력을 갖고 있고 생각을 계속할지 감정을 더할지 선택할 수 있다고 했기 때문에 통제할 수 있는 의식적 마음이 생각과 '감정(emotions)'을 다룬다.

(B):

- 그것들은 오직 잠재의식적 마음이 여러분의 반응을 기록할 때 실제 두려움이 된다. 단서3

➡ 잠재의식적 마음이 실제 두려움을 '형성하면서(forming)' 우리의 반응을 기록(=저장)한다.

▶ 요약문의 빈칸에는 각각 ① '감정'과 '형성하면서'가 들어가야 함

✓왜 오답?

② 이 글을 통해서는 의식적 마음이 행동을 다루는지 알 수 없다.

③ 잠재의식적 마음이 실제 두려움을 형성한다고 했지만 이를 극복하는지는 언급되지 않았다.

④ 잠재의식적 마음은 실제 두려움을 피하는 것이 아니라 반응을 기록하여 실제 두려움을 형성한다.

⑤ 이 글에서는 의식적 마음과 도덕성의 관계가 나오지 않는다.

＊ 글의 흐름

도입	마음은 의식적 마음과 잠재의식적 마음이라고 알려진 부분을 가지고 있음
전개	잠재의식적 마음은 매우 빠르게 작동하며 삶에 대한 반응의 기억, 기억 및 인식을 다루는 반면에, 의식적 마음은 생각을 계속할지 또는 그 생각에 감정을 더할지를 선택할 수 있음
부연	의식적 마음이 다루는 감정 때문에 잘못된 결정을 반복적으로 내리거나 판단력이 흐려져서 편견과 부정성을 자리 잡게 만들기도 함
마무리	잠재의식적 마음이 반응을 저장할 때 실제 두려움이 됨

41~42 ＊사회생활과 문화 간 의사소통에서 중요한 규범

Norms are everywhere, / defining what is "normal" / and guiding our interpretations of social life / at every turn. //

규범은 어디에나 존재한다 / 무엇이 '정상적'인지를 규정하고 / 사회적 생활에 대한 우리의 해석을 안내해 주며 / 모든 순간 //

41번 단서1: 규범은 무엇이 정상적인지 규정하고 사회생활에서 우리를 안내함

As a simple example, / there is a norm in Anglo society / to say Thank you to strangers / who have just done something to (a) help, /

간단한 예로 / Anglo 사회에 규범이 있다 / 낯선 사람에게 '감사합니다'라고 말하는 / 도움을 줄 수 있는 무언가를 이제 막 해준 /

such as open a door for you, / point out that you've just dropped something, / or give you directions. //

문을 열어 주거나 / 여러분이 물건을 방금 떨어뜨렸다는 것을 짚어 주거나 / 길을 알려주는 것과 같이 //

There is no law / that forces you to say Thank you. //

법은 없다 / 여러분이 '감사합니다'라고 말하도록 강요하는 //

But if people don't say Thank you / in these cases, / it is marked. //

하지만 사람들이 '감사합니다'라고 말하지 않으면 / 이런 상황에서 / 그것은 눈에 띄게 된다 //

People expect / that you will say it. //

사람들은 기대한다 / 여러분이 그렇게 말하기를 //

You become responsible. //

여러분은 책임을 지게 되는 것이다 //

(b) Failing to say it / will be both surprising and worthy of criticism. //

그렇게 말하지 못하는 것은 / (주변을) 놀라게 하기도 하고 비판을 받을 만하다 //

Not knowing the norms of another community / is the (c) central problem of cross-cultural communication. //

다른 집단의 규범을 모른다는 것은 / 문화 간 의사소통에서 중심적인 문제이다 //

41번 단서2: 다른 집단의 규범을 모르는 것은 문화 간 의사소통의 중심 문제임

To continue the Thank you example, / even though another culture may have an expression / that appears translatable / (many don't), /

'감사합니다'의 예를 이어 보자면 / 비록 또 다른 문화권이 어떤 표현을 가지고 있다 할지라도 / 번역할 수 있는 것처럼 보이는 / (다수는 그렇지 못하지만) /

there may be (d) similar(→ different) norms for its usage, / for example, / such that you should say Thank you / only when the cost someone has caused is considerable. //

그것의 사용법에 대해 유사한(→ 다른) 규범이 있을 수 있다 / 예를 들어 '감사합니다'라고 말해야 한다는 것처럼 / 누군가가 초래한 대가가 상당할 때만 //

42번 단서1: 다른 문화권에서는 누군가 초래한 대가가 상당할 때만 '감사합니다'라고 말함

In such a case / it would sound ridiculous / (i.e., unexpected, surprising, and worthy of criticism) / if you were to thank someone /

그 같은 상황에서 / 그것은 우스꽝스럽게 들릴 수 있을 것이다 / (즉, 예상치 못하게, 놀랍게, 비판을 받을 만하게) / 만약 여러분이 혹시라도 누군가에게 감사해한다면 /

for something so (e) minor / as holding a door open for you. //

아주 사소한 일에 대해 / 여러분을 위해 문을 잡아주는 것과 같이 //

42번 단서2: 사소한 일에 감사해하면 우스꽝스럽게 들릴 수 있음

- norm ⓝ 규범 · define ⓥ 규정하다 · interpretation ⓝ 해석
- point out ~을 짚어 주다 · give directions 길을 알려주다
- force ⓥ 강요하다 · marked ⓐ 눈에 띄는 · expect ⓥ 기대하다
- responsible ⓐ 책임이 있는 · worthy of ~을 받을 만한
- criticism ⓝ 비난 · central ⓐ 중심적인
- cross-cultural ⓐ 문화 간의 · translatable ⓐ 번역할 수 있는
- usage ⓝ 사용 · cost ⓝ 대가, 비용 · considerable ⓐ 상당한
- ridiculous ⓐ 우스꽝스러운 · i.e.(id est) 즉
- unexpected ⓐ 예상치 못한 · minor ⓐ 사소한

규범은 무엇이 '정상적'인지를 규정하고 모든 순간 사회적 생활에 대한 우리의 해석을 안내해 주며 어디에나 존재한다. 간단한 예로, 문을 열어 주거나, 여러분이 물건을 방금 떨어뜨렸다는 것을 짚어 주거나, 길을 알려주는 것과 같이 (a) 도움을 줄 수 있는 무언가를 이제 막 해준 낯선 사람에게 '감사합니다'라고 말하는 규범이 Anglo 사회에 있다. 여러분이 '감사합니다'라고 말하도록 강요하는 법은 없다. 하지만 이런 상황에서 사람들이 '감사합니다'라고 말하지 않으면 그것은 눈에 띄게 된다. 사람들은 여러분이 그렇게 말하기를 기대한다. 여러분은 책임을 지게 되는 것이다. 그렇게 말하지 (b) 못하는 것은 (주변을) 놀라게 하기도 하고 비판을 받을 만하다. 다른 집단의 규범을 모른다는 것은 문화 간 의사소통에서 (c) 중심적인 문제이다. '감사합니다'의 예를 이어 보자면, 비록 또 다른 문화권이 번역할 수 있는 것처럼 보이는 어떤 표현(다수는 그렇지 못하지만)을 가지고 있다 할지라도, 그것의 사용법에 대해, 예를 들어, 누군가가 초래한 대가가 상당할 때만 '감사합니다'라고 말해야 한다는 것처럼 (d) 유사한(→ 다른) 규범이 있을 수 있다. 그 같은 상황에서 만약 여러분이 혹시라도, 여러분을 위해 문을 잡아주는 것과 같이 아주 (e) 사소한 일에 대해 누군가에게 감사해한다면, 그것은 우스꽝스럽게(즉, 예상치 못하게, 놀랍게, 비판을 받을 만하게) 들릴 수 있을 것이다.

41 정답 ①

윗글의 제목으로 가장 적절한 것은?

① Norms: For Social Life and Cultural Communication
규범: 사회생활과 문화적 의사소통을 위한 것 / 사회생활과 문화적 의사소통을 위해 규범이 존재함

② Don't Forget to Say "Thank you" at Any Time
언제든지 '감사합니다'라고 말하는 것을 잊지 마라

③ How to Be Responsible for Your Behaviors
당신의 행동에 책임을 지는 방법 / 글 전체 내용이 행동에 책임을 지는 방법에 관해 설명하고 있다고 볼 수 없음

④ Accept Criticism Without Hurting Yourself
스스로 상처받지 않으면서 비판을 수용해라 / 비판을 수용하라는 내용에 관한 글이 아님

⑤ How Did Diverse Languages Develop?
다양한 언어는 어떻게 발전했을까? / 다양한 언어의 발전에 대해서는 전혀 언급하지 않음

└ 'Thank you' 사용법에 관한 규범이 예시로 내용에 나온 것을 이용한 함정임

왜 정답 ? ✖✖✧ [정답률 80%]

- 규범은 무엇이 '정상적'인지를 규정하고 모든 순간 사회적 생활에 대한 우리의 해석을 안내해 주며 어디에나 존재한다. `41번 단서1`
- 다른 집단의 규범을 모른다는 것은 문화 간 의사소통에서 중심적인 문제이다. `41번 단서2`

➡ 사회적 규범이 일상생활과 문화 간 소통에서 중요한 역할을 한다는 것을 설명하며, '감사합니다'라는 말의 사용법에 대해 문화마다 달라질 수 있는 규범을 예시로 제시하였다.

▶ 따라서 제목으로 적절한 것은 ① '규범: 사회생활과 문화적 의사소통을 위한 것'이다.

왜 오답 ?

② 언제든지 "Thank you"라고 말하라는 내용의 글이 아니다. (🎀 이유: 문화권에 따라 다른 "Thank you" 사용법이 예시로 나온 것으로 만든 오답이다.)
③ 행동에 책임을 지는 방법에 관해 설명하는 글이 아니다.
④ Anglo 사회에서 '감사합니다'를 말하지 못하면 비판을 받을 만하다는 내용이 나오지만, 글에서 비판을 수용하라는 생각을 중심적으로 전달하지는 않는다. 함정
⑤ 다양한 언어의 발전에 대해서는 전혀 언급하지 않았다.

42 정답 ④

밑줄 친 (a)~(e) 중에서 문맥상 낱말의 쓰임이 적절하지 <u>않은</u> 것은?
① (a) 낯선 사람이 도움이 되는 일을 해줌
　　 도움을 주다
② (b) 감사의 말을 못하는 것은 주변을 놀라게 하기도 하고 비판을 받을 만함
　　 못하는 것
③ (c) 다른 문화 규범을 모르는 것은 문화 간 의사소통에 중심적인 큰 문제가 될 수 있음
　　 중심적인
④ (d) 유사한 규범이 아닌 다른 규범이 있음
　　 유사한
⑤ (e) 문을 잡아주는 것은 사소한 작은 행동임
　　 사소한

왜 정답 ? ✖✖✧ [정답률 74%]

④ (d) similar 유사한

'감사합니다'의 예를 이어 보자면, 비록 또 다른 문화권이 번역할 수 있는 것처럼 보이는 어떤 표현(다수는 그렇지 못하지만)을 가지고 있다 할지라도, 그것의 사용법에 대해, 예를 들어, 누군가가 초래한 대가가 상당할 때만 '감사합니다'라고 말해야 한다는 것처럼 (d) ~~유사한~~ 규범이 있을 수 있다. 다른

➡ Anglo 사회에서는 사소한 도움을 받을 때 '감사합니다'를 말하는 것이 규범이지만 다른 문화권에서는 누군가가 초래한 대가가 상당할 때만 '감사합니다'를 말하므로 규범이 다르다. ▶ 유사한 규범이 아니라 다른 규범이 있을 수 있다는 내용이어야 하므로 similar를 different(다른)와 같은 어휘로 바꾸어야 한다.

왜 오답 ?

① (a) help 도움을 주다

간단한 예로, 문을 열어 주거나, 여러분이 물건을 방금 떨어뜨렸다는 것을 짚어 주거나, 길을 알려주는 것과 같이 (a) 도움을 줄 수 있는 무언가를 이제 막 해준 낯선 사람에게 '감사합니다'라고 말하는 규범이 Anglo 사회에 있다.

➡ 낯선 사람이 문을 열어주거나, 물건을 방금 떨어뜨렸다는 것을 짚어 주거나, 길을 알려주는 것은 '도움을 주는' 것이다. ▶ help는 문맥에 맞음

② (b) Failing 못하는 것

그렇게 말하지 (b) 못하는 것은 (주변을) 놀라게 하기도 하고 비판을 받을 만하다.

➡ 주변을 놀라게 하고 비판을 받게 될 경우는 감사하다고 말하지 '못했을' 때이다. ▶ Failing은 문맥에 맞음

- 다른 집단의 규범을 모른다는 것은 문화 간 의사소통에서 (c) 중심적인 문제이다.

➡ 다른 문화의 규범을 모르는 것은 문화 간 의사소통에서 '중심적' 문제가 될 수 있다. ▶ central은 문맥에 맞음

⑤ (e) minor 사소한

그 같은 상황에서 만약 여러분이 혹시라도, 여러분을 위해 문을 잡아주는 것과 같이 아주 (e) 사소한 일에 대해 누군가에게 감사해한다면, 그것은 우스꽝스럽게(즉, 예상치 못하게, 놀랍게, 비판을 받을 만하게) 들릴 수 있을 것이다.

➡ 문을 잡아주는 것은 누군가가 초래한 대가가 상당한 일이 아니라 '사소한' 일이므로 감사하면 우스꽝스럽게 들릴 수 있다. ▶ minor는 문맥에 맞음

43~45 ＊Iktomi의 교훈과 드림캐처

(A) Long ago, / when the world was young, / an old Native American spiritual leader Odawa / had a dream on a high mountain. // `45번①` Odawa는 높은 산에서 꿈을 꿈
오래전 / 세상이 생겨난 지 오래지 않을 무렵 / 아메리카 원주민의 늙은 영적 지도자인 Odawa는 / 높은 산에서 꿈을 꾸었다 //

　　　　　　동격
In his dream, / Iktomi, the great spirit and searcher of wisdom, / appeared to (a) him in the form of a spider. // ＝Odawa
자신의 꿈속에서 / 위대한 신령이자 지혜의 구도자인 Iktomi가 / 거미의 형태로 그에게 나타났다 //

`43번 단서1: Iktomi가 Odawa에게 성스러운 언어로 말함`
Iktomi spoke to him / in a holy language. //
Iktomi는 그에게 말했다 / 성스러운 언어로 //

＊(A) 문단 요약: Odawa가 산에서 꿈을 꾸었고 Iktomi가 나타나서 성스러운 언어로 말함

(B) Odawa shared Iktomi's lesson / with (b) his people. // ＝Odawa's
Odawa는 Iktomi의 교훈을 나누었다 / 그의 마을 사람들과 //
`43번 단서2: Odawa가 마을 사람들과 Iktomi의 교훈을 나눔`

Today, many Native Americans / have dream catchers hanging 현재분사(dream catchers 수식)
above their beds. // `45번②` 오늘날 많은 미국 원주민은 침대 위에 드림캐처를 걸어놓음
오늘날 많은 미국 원주민은 / 침대 위에 드림캐처를 건다 //

Dream catchers are believed / to filter out bad dreams. //
드림캐처는 믿어진다 / 나쁜 꿈을 걸러 준다고 //
　　　　　　　　　　　병렬 구조
The good dreams are captured in the web of life / and carried with the people. //
좋은 꿈은 인생이라는 거미집에 걸리고 / 사람들과 동반하게 된다 //
　　　　　　　　병렬 구조
The bad dreams pass through the hole in the web / and are no longer a part of their lives. //
나쁜 꿈은 거미집의 구멍 사이로 빠져나가고 / 더 이상 그들의 삶의 한 부분이 되지 못한다 //

＊(B) 문단 요약: Odawa는 Iktomi의 교훈을 부족에 전하였고, 오늘날 많은 미국 원주민들은 나쁜 꿈을 걸러내고 좋은 꿈을 담는 드림캐처를 침대 위에 걸어둠

동명사(finished의 목적어)
(C) When Iktomi finished speaking, / he spun a web / and gave it to Odawa. // `45번③` Iktomi는 Odawa에게 거미집을 짜서 줌
Iktomi가 말을 끝냈을 때 / 그는 거미집을 짜서 / Odawa에게 주었다 //

He said to Odawa, / "The web is a perfect circle / with a hole in the center. //
그가 Odawa에게 말했다 / "그 거미집은 완벽한 원이다 / 가운데 구멍이 뚫린 //

준사역동사 help의 목적격 보어(동사원형)
Use the web / to help your people reach their goals. //
거미집을 사용해라 / 너의 마을 사람들이 자신들의 목표에 도달할 수 있도록 //

Make good use of their ideas, dreams, and visions. //
그들의 생각, 꿈, 비전을 잘 활용해라 //

If (c) <u>you</u> believe in the great spirit, / the web will catch your
=Odawa
good ideas / and the bad <u>ones</u> will go through the hole." //
=ideas
만약 네가 위대한 신령을 믿는다면 / 그 거미집이 네 좋은 생각을 붙잡아 줄 것이고 / 나쁜
생각은 구멍을 통해 빠져 나갈 것이다"라고 //

43번 단서 3, 45번 ④ Odawa는 잠에서 깨어나자 자신의 마을로 돌아감

Right after Odawa woke up, / he went back to his village. //
Odawa는 잠에서 깨어나자마자 / 자기 마을로 되돌아갔다 //

*(C) 문단 요약: Iktomi가 말을 마친 후에 거미집을 짜서 Odawa에게 주었고 거미집의
용도를 설명함

45번 ⑤ Iktomi는 Odawa에게 삶의 순환에 대해 말함

(D) Iktomi told Odawa / about the cycles of life. //
Iktomi는 Odawa에게 말했다 / 삶의 순환에 관해서 //
=Iktomi
(d) <u>He</u> said, / "We all begin our lives as babies, / move on to
childhood, and then to adulthood. //
그는 말했다 / "우리는 모두 아기로 삶을 출발하고 / 유년기를 거쳐 그다음 성년기에 이르게
된다 //

계속적 용법의 관계부사(선행사: old age)

Finally, we come to old age, / <u>where</u> we must be taken care of /
as babies again." // **43번 단서 4: Iktomi가 Odawa에게 성스러운 언어로 말한 내용**
결국 우리는 노년기에 도달하고 / 거기서 우리는 보살핌을 받아야 한다 / 다시 아기처럼"
이라고 //
=Odawa   목적어절 접속사
Iktomi also told (e) <u>him</u> / <u>that</u> there are good and bad forces / in
each stage of life. // **43번 단서 5: Iktomi가 Odawa에게 성스러운 언어로 말한 내용**
또한 Iktomi는 그에게 말했다 / 좋고 나쁜 힘이 있다고 / 삶의 각 단계에는 //

"If we listen to the good forces, / they will guide us in the right
direction. //
"우리가 좋은 힘에 귀를 기울이면 / 그들은 우리를 올바른 방향으로 인도할 것이다 //

But if we listen to the bad forces, / they will lead us the wrong
way / and may harm us," / Iktomi said. //
하지만 만약 나쁜 힘에 귀를 기울이면 / 그들은 우리를 잘못된 길로 이끌고 / 우리를 해칠 수도
있다"라고 / Iktomi는 말했다 //

*(D) 문단 요약: Iktomi가 Odawa에게 삶의 순환에 관해 설명하며 삶의 각 단계에는
좋은 힘과 나쁜 힘이 있고 좋은 힘에 귀를 기울여야 한다고 말함

- Native American 미국 원주민 · spiritual ⓐ 영적인
- in the form of ~의 모양으로 · holy ⓐ 성스러운 · lesson ⓝ 교훈
- filter out ~을 걸러내다 · pass through ~을 통과하다
- spin ⓥ 짜다 (과거형 spun) · reach ⓥ 도달하다 · cycle ⓝ 순환
- guide ⓥ 인도하다 · harm ⓥ 해치다

(A) 오래전, 세상이 생겨난 지 오래지 않을 무렵, 아메리카 원주민의 늙은 영적 지도자인 Odawa는 높은 산에서 꿈을 꾸었다. 자신의 꿈속에서 위대한 신령이자 지혜의 구도자인 Iktomi가 거미의 형태로 (a) <u>그에게</u> 나타났다. Iktomi는 성스러운 언어로 그에게 말했다.

(D) Iktomi는 Odawa에게 삶의 순환에 관해서 말했다. (d) <u>그는</u> "우리는 모두 아기로 삶을 출발하고, 유년기를 거쳐 그다음 성년기에 이르게 된다. 결국 우리는 노년기에 도달하고, 거기서 우리는 다시 아기처럼 보살핌을 받아야 한다."라고 말했다. 또한 Iktomi는 삶의 각 단계에는 좋고 나쁜 힘이 있다고 (e) <u>그에게</u> 말했다. "우리가 좋은 힘에 귀를 기울이면 그들은 우리를 올바른 방향으로 인도할 것이다. 하지만 만약 나쁜 힘에 귀를 기울이면 그들은 우리를 잘못된 길로 이끌고 우리를 해칠 수도 있다."라고 Iktomi는 말했다.

(C) Iktomi가 말을 끝냈을 때, 그는 거미집을 짜서 Odawa에게 주었다. 그가 Odawa에게 말하기를, "그 거미집은 가운데 구멍이 뚫린 완벽한 원이다. 너의 마을 사람들이 자신들의 목표에 도달할 수 있도록 거미집을 사용해라. 그들의 생각, 꿈, 비전을 잘 활용해라. 만약 (c) <u>네가</u> 위대한 신령을 믿는다면 그 거미집이 네 좋은 생각을 붙잡아 줄 것이고 나쁜 생각은 구멍을 통해 빠져 나갈 것이다." Odawa는 잠에서 깨자마자 자기 마을로 되돌아갔다.

(B) Odawa는 Iktomi의 교훈을 (b) <u>그의</u> 마을 사람들과 나누었다. 오늘날 많은 미국 원주민은 침대 위에 드림캐처를 건다. 드림캐처는 나쁜 꿈을 걸러 준다고 믿어진다. 좋은 꿈은 인생이라는 거미집에 걸리고 사람들과 동반하게 된다. 나쁜 꿈은 거미집의 구멍 사이로 빠져나가고 더 이상 그들의 삶의 한 부분이 되지 못한다.

---

43 정답 ⑤

주어진 글 (A)에 이어질 내용을 순서에 맞게 배열한 것으로 가장 적절한 것은?

① (B) — (D) — (C) 주어진 글에 Iktomi가 준 교훈이 나오지 않기 때문에 (B)가 올 수 없음

② (C) — (B) — (D) 주어진 글에 Iktomi가 어떤 말을 했는지 나오지 않기 때문에 (C)가 올 수 없음

③ (C) — (D) — (B)

④ (D) — (B) — (C) 마을 사람들과 Iktomi의 교훈을 나누는 (B) 앞에 Odawa가 잠에서 깨어 마을로 돌아가는 (C)가 와야 함

⑤ (D) — (C) — (B) (D) Iktomi가 Odawa에게 가르침을 줌 — (C) Iktomi가 Odawa에게 거미집을 주고 용도를 설명함 — (B) Odawa는 Iktomi의 교훈을 마을 사람들과 나누고 오늘날 많은 미국 원주민은 드림캐처를 침대에 걸어둠

> **왜** 정답·오답 **?** ✱✿✿ [정답률 92%]

[(A): Odawa가 산에서 꿈을 꾸었고 Iktomi가 나타나서 성스러운 언어로 말했다.

➡ Iktomi가 Odawa에게 전한 이야기가 이어질 것이다.

[(B): Odawa는 Iktomi의 교훈을 부족에 전하였고, 오늘날 많은 미국 원주민들은 나쁜 꿈을 걸러내고 좋은 꿈을 담는 드림캐처를 침대 위에 걸어둔다.

➡ Iktomi가 준 교훈이 오늘날에 미친 영향을 설명하므로 글의 마무리 부분에 해당한다. Iktomi가 준 교훈의 내용과 드림캐처를 왜 걸어두게 되었는지가 앞에 와야 한다.

[(C): Iktomi가 말을 마친 후에 거미집을 짜서 Odawa에게 주었고 거미집의 용도를 설명하였다.

➡ Iktomi가 Odawa에게 어떤 말을 했는지가 앞에 와야 한다.

[(D): Iktomi가 Odawa에게 삶의 순환에 관해 설명하며 삶의 각 단계에는 좋은 힘과 나쁜 힘이 있고 좋은 힘에 귀를 기울여야 한다고 말했다.

➡ Iktomi가 나타나서 성스러운 언어로 이야기한 내용이므로 (A)의 바로 뒤에 이어진다.

▶ (A) Odawa가 산에서 꿈을 꾸었고 Iktomi가 나타나서 성스러운 언어로 이야기함 → (D) Iktomi가 Odawa에게 삶의 순환과, 좋고 나쁜 힘에 대해 설명함 → (C) Iktomi가 말을 마친 후에 거미집을 짜서 Odawa에게 주었고 거미집의 용도를 설명함 → (B) Odawa는 Iktomi의 교훈을 부족에 전하였고, 오늘날 많은 미국 원주민들은 나쁜 꿈을 걸러내고 좋은 꿈을 담는 드림캐처를 침대 위에 걸어두게 됨

▶ 글의 순서는 ⑤ (D) — (C) — (B)임

---

44 정답 ④

밑줄 친 (a)~(e) 중에서 가리키는 대상이 나머지 넷과 다른 것은?

① (a)　② (b)　③ (c)　④(d)　⑤ (e)
= Odawa　= Odawa's　= Odawa　= Iktomi　= Odawa

> **왜** 정답 **?** ✱✿✿ [정답률 87%]

④ (d) He: Odawa에게 삶의 순환에 관해 설명하고 있는 사람 ▶ Iktomi

> **왜** 오답 **?**

① (a) him: Iktomi가 거미의 형태로 찾아간 사람 ▶ Odawa

② (b) his: Iktomi의 교훈을 Odawa가 자신의 마을 사람들과 나눔 ▶ Odawa's

③ (c) you: Iktomi가 '너'라고 지칭하는 사람 ▶ Odawa

⑤ (e) him: Iktomi가 삶의 각 단계에는 좋고 나쁜 힘이 있다고 말한 대상 ▶ Odawa

45 정답 ②

윗글에 관한 내용으로 적절하지 <u>않은</u> 것은?

① Odawa는 높은 산에서 꿈을 꾸었다.
Odawa had a dream on a high mountain

② 많은 미국 원주민은 드림캐처를 현관 위에 건다.
Today, many Native Americans have dream catchers hanging above their beds.

③ Iktomi는 Odawa에게 거미집을 짜서 주었다.
he spun a web and gave it to Odawa

④ Odawa는 잠에서 깨자마자 자신의 마을로 돌아갔다.
Right after Odawa woke up, he went back to his village.

⑤ Iktomi는 Odawa에게 삶의 순환에 대해 알려주었다.
Iktomi told Odawa about the cycles of life.

▶왜 정답 ? ✽✽✽ [정답률 89%]

오늘날 많은 미국 원주민은 침대 위에 드림캐처를 건다고 했으므로 (Today, many Native Americans have dream catchers hanging above their beds.) 현관 위에 드림캐처를 건다는 ②은 적절하지 않다.

▶왜 오답 ?

① Odawa는 높은 산에서 꿈을 꾸었다. (Odawa had a dream on a high mountain)

③ Iktomi는 Odawa에게 거미집을 짜서 주었다. (he spun a web and gave it to Odawa)

④ Odawa는 잠에서 깨자마자 자신의 마을로 돌아갔다. (Right after Odawa woke up, he went back to his village.)

⑤ Iktomi는 Odawa에게 삶의 순환에 대해 알려주었다. (Iktomi told Odawa about the cycles of life.)

2회 Dictation
문제 p. 40

01 This is your vice principal / road condition / rearrangements / keep in mind that / cooperation

02 I heard that / what you mean / traffic rules / stricter rules about

03 have a lot of things / time management / check off / efficiently

04 you've joined / took a picture of it / star-shaped / proud of it

05 supplies / are all set / warm clothes / I've packed / I'll take it

06 help you with / vegetables / what else / get a discount

07 just around the corner / That's why I brought / had the interview / gathering / Let's make up / missed

08 exactly / design / experiment / freshmen like us / materials / need to send / deadline for applying

09 looking for a chance / senior citizens / various / require volunteers to participate / interested in joining

10 one of these portable fans / have in mind / old one / remaining battery power

11 purse / for an hour / last have it

12 have in mind / restaurant / reservation

13 record audiobooks / get involved in / organization / struggling with / a bit challenging / recommend

14 should we do / divide the roles / material / collecting news articles / necessary / take care of it

15 orientation / short greetings / facilities / writing down important things / drops his pen / the opening hours

[16~17] tuning in / health / recommend / symptoms of a cough / home remedy / relieve / suffering from / get rid of

---

2회 어휘 Review Test
문제 p. 44

01 특징	**15** look for	**29** enhanced
02 의식적인	**16** evolutionary	**30** specific
03 강도	**17** inspiration	**31** insensitive
04 우스꽝스러운	**18** definition	**32** satisfy
05 성취감	**19** acquired	**33** rotate
06 connection	**20** appropriate	**34** constant
07 appreciate	**21** interpretations	**35** forces
08 prey	**22** accurate	**36** enthusiasm
09 underestimate	**23** relay	**37** discussion
10 structure	**24** distinguish	**38** witness
11 allow for	**25** perception	**39** categorize
12 get involved in	**26** limited	**40** expected
13 get rid of	**27** conversations	
14 keep in mind	**28** quality	

3회 전국연합학력평가
[2023년 3월 시행]
문제편 p. 46~57

01 정답 ⑤ *아이스하키 경기 관람 독려

M : Hello, Villeford High School students.
남 : 안녕하세요, Villeford 고등학교 학생 여러분.

This is principal Aaron Clark.
저는 교장 Aaron Clark입니다.

'~로서'
As a big fan of the Villeford ice hockey team, I'm very excited about the upcoming National High School Ice Hockey League.
Villeford 아이스하키팀의 열렬한 팬으로서, 저는 다가오는 전국 고등학교 아이스하키 리그가 매우 기대됩니다.

미래시제 수동태
As you all know, the first game **will be held** in the Central Rink at 6 p.m. this Saturday.
여러분 모두가 알고 있다시피, 첫 경기가 이번 주 토요일 저녁 6시에 Central Rink에서 개최될 예정입니다.

I want as many of you as possible to come and cheer our team to victory. **단서 1** 경기를 보러 와서 응원하기를 바람
저는 우리 팀의 승리를 위해 최대한 많은 학생이 와서 응원하기를 바랍니다.

부사적 용법(목적)
I've seen them put in an incredible amount of effort **to win** the league.
저는 그들이 리그 우승을 위해 놀라울 정도의 노력을 기울이는 모습을 지켜보았습니다.

가주어   진주어
It will help them play better just **to see** you there cheering for them.
단지 여러분이 그곳에서 그들을 위해 응원하는 모습을 보는 것이 그들이 더 잘 경기하도록 도와줄 것입니다.

단서 2 학생들이 경기장에 와줄 것을 다시 한번 강조함
I really hope to see you at the rink.
저는 여러분들을 꼭 링크장에서 볼 수 있기를 바랍니다.

Thank you.
감사합니다.

- **principal** ⓝ 교장 - **upcoming** ⓐ 다가오는 - **cheer** ⓥ 응원하다
- **victory** ⓝ 승리, 성공 - **incredible** ⓐ 놀라울 정도의
- **amount** ⓝ 양 - **effort** ⓝ 노력

다음을 듣고, 남자가 하는 말의 목적으로 가장 적절한 것을 고르시오.
① 아이스하키부의 우승을 알리려고 아직 리그가 시작하지 않음
② 아이스하키부 훈련 일정을 공지하려고 훈련 일정을 공지하는 것이 아님
③ 아이스하키부 신임 감독을 소개하려고 신임 감독은 언급되지 않음
④ 아이스하키부 선수 모집을 안내하려고 선수를 새로 모집하는 것이 아님
⑤ 아이스하키부 경기의 관람을 독려하려고 학생들이 경기를 응원하러 오기를 바람

〉왜 정답 ? ✽✾✾ [정답률 87%]
곧 개최될 아이스하키 리그의 첫 경기에 대해 언급하며 열심히 훈련한 선수들을 위해 경기를 관람하러 오라고 권하는 내용이므로 정답은 ⑤이다.

〉왜 오답 ?
① 아이스하키 경기가 시작하는 단계이므로 우승을 알린다는 것은 적절하지 않다.
② 훈련 일정이 아니라 첫 경기 일정에 대해 언급했다. **주의**
③ 감독이 새로 오는 지는 알 수 없다.
④ 선수를 새로 모집하는 것이 아니다.

02 정답 ⑤ *남이 처방받은 약을 먹어도 될까?

W : Honey, are you okay?
여 : 여보, 괜찮아요?

M : I'm afraid I've caught a cold. I've got a sore throat.
남 : 나 감기에 걸린 것 같아요. 목이 아파요.

W : Why don't you go see a doctor?
여 : 병원에 가는 게 어때요?

뒤에 목적어절 접속사 that이 생략됨
M : Well, I **don't think** it's necessary. I've found some medicine in the cabinet. I'll take it.
남 : 음, 꼭 그래야 할 것 같지는 않아요. 내가 수납장에서 약을 좀 찾았어요. 그걸 먹을게요.

선행사를 포함하는 관계대명사
W : You shouldn't take that medicine. That's **what** I got prescribed last week.
여 : 그 약은 먹으면 안 돼요. 그건 내가 지난주에 처방받은 거잖아요.

= your symptoms
M : My symptoms are similar to **yours**.
남 : 내 증상은 당신의 증상과 비슷해요.

앞에 주격 관계대명사와 be동사가 생략됨
W : Honey, you shouldn't take medicine **prescribed** for others.
여 : 여보, 다른 사람들에게 처방된 약은 먹으면 안 돼요. **단서** 타인이 처방받은 약을 먹으려는 남자를 저지함

M : It's just a cold. I'll get better if I take your medicine.
남 : 단순히 감기인걸요. 당신의 약을 먹으면 나는 더 나아질 거예요.

가주어   진주어
W : **It** could be dangerous **to take** someone else's prescription.
여 : 다른 사람의 처방된 약을 먹는 것은 위험할 수 있어요.

M : Okay. Then I'll go see a doctor this afternoon.
남 : 알겠어요. 그러면 내가 오후에 병원에 갈게요.

- **sore** ⓐ 아픈 - **throat** ⓝ 목(구멍) - **necessary** ⓐ 필요한
- **medicine** ⓝ 약 - **cabinet** ⓝ 수납장 - **prescribe** ⓥ 처방하다
- **symptom** ⓝ 증상 - **prescription** ⓝ 처방전, 처방된 약

대화를 듣고, 여자의 의견으로 가장 적절한 것을 고르시오.
① 과다한 항생제 복용을 자제해야 한다. 항생제를 적당히 복용하라는 내용이 아님
② 오래된 약을 함부로 폐기해서는 안 된다. 약의 폐기가 아닌 복용에 관한 내용임
③ 약을 복용할 때는 정해진 시간을 지켜야 한다. 약 복용 시간과는 관련 없음
④ 진료 전에 자신의 증상을 정확히 확인해야 한다. 증상을 정확히 파악하라는 내용이 아님
⑤ 다른 사람에게 처방된 약을 복용해서는 안 된다. 증상이 비슷해도 타인이 처방받은 약은 먹으면 안 됨

〉왜 정답 ? ✽✾✾ [정답률 91%]
감기에 걸린 남자가 여자의 약을 먹으려고 하자, 여자는 증상이 비슷하더라도 다른 사람에게 처방된 약을 복용하는 것은 위험할 수 있다며 남자를 말리고 있다.
따라서 여자의 의견으로 가장 적절한 것은 ⑤이다.

〉왜 오답 ?
① 약 과다 복용이나 항생제에 관한 내용은 언급되지 않았다.
② 지난주에 처방받은 약이 언급된 것으로 만든 오답이다. **함정**
③ 약 복용 시간에 대해서는 언급하지 않았다.
④ 증상을 정확히 파악하라고 한 것이 아니라 직접 의사의 처방을 받아 약을 먹으라고 했다.

03 정답 ③ *작품 전시장 변경

W : Hi, Mr. Thomson. How are your preparations going?
여 : 안녕하세요, Thomson 씨. 준비는 어떻게 되어가나요?

형용사적 용법(something 수식)
M : You arrived at the right time. I have something **to tell** you.
남 : 딱 맞는 시간에 오셨네요. 당신에게 말씀드릴 게 있어요.

W : Okay. What is it?
여 : 알겠습니다. 무엇인가요?

M : Well, I'm afraid that we have to change the exhibition room for your paintings.
남 : 음, 안타깝게도 당신의 그림을 위한 전시 장소를 바꿔야 할 것 같아요.

W : May I ask why?

여 : 제가 이유를 여쭤봐도 될까요?

M : Sure. We have some electrical problems there.

남 : 물론이죠. 그곳에 전기 문제가 좀 있어요.

W : I see. Then where are you going to exhibit my works?

여 : 그렇군요. 그럼 제 작품들은 어디에 전시하실 건가요?

M : Our gallery is going to exhibit your paintings in the main hall. **단서** 남자의 미술관은 여자의 그림을 중앙 홀에 전시할 예정임

남 : 저희 미술관은 당신의 그림들을 중앙 홀에 전시할 예정이에요.

W : Okay. Can I see the hall now?

여 : 알겠습니다. 제가 지금 그 홀을 볼 수 있을까요?

M : Sure. Come with me.

남 : 물론이죠. 저와 함께 가시죠.

- preparation ⓝ 준비   • arrive ⓥ 도착하다   • exhibition ⓝ 전시
- electrical ⓐ 전기의   • exhibit ⓥ 전시하다

대화를 듣고, 두 사람의 관계를 가장 잘 나타낸 것을 고르시오.

① 관람객 – 박물관 관장 여자는 작품을 전시하려고 하는 화가임
② 세입자 – 건물 관리인 건물 임대는 언급되지 않음
③ 화가 – 미술관 직원 그림 전시 장소 변경에 관해 이야기하고 있음
④ 고객 – 전기 기사 전기 문제가 언급된 것으로 만든 오답
⑤ 의뢰인 – 건축사 건축을 의뢰하는 내용이 아님

> **왜 정답?** ✽❀❀ [정답률 87%]

여자의 그림이 전시될 예정이었던 장소에 전기 문제가 생겼다고 하며, 남자는 중앙 홀로 전시 장소를 바꿀 것이라고 했으므로 두 사람의 관계로 가장 적절한 것은 ③이다.

> **왜 오답?**

① 여자는 관람객이 아니라 작품을 전시할 화가이다.
② 건물 임대와 관련된 내용은 언급되지 않았다.
④ 전기 문제가 있다고 언급하긴 했지만, 수리를 위해 전기 기사가 온 상황은 아니다.
⑤ 건축을 의뢰하는 것과 관련된 내용은 언급되지 않았다. **함정**

04 정답 ⑤ ✽ Grace가 찍은 벽화 사진

M : Hi, Grace. What are you looking at on your phone?

남 : 안녕, Grace. 넌 휴대 전화에서 뭘 보고 있어?

앞에 목적격 관계대명사가 생략됨
W : Hi, James. It's a photo I took when I did some volunteer work. We painted pictures on a street wall.

여 : 안녕, James. 이것은 내가 자원봉사를 했을 때 찍은 사진이야. 우리는 거리의 벽에 그림을 그렸어. **①의 단서** 꽃무늬가 있는 고래가 있음

M : Let me see. Wow, I like the whale with the flower pattern.

남 : 어디 보자. 우아, 나는 꽃무늬가 있는 고래가 마음에 들어.

W : I like it, too. How do you like the house under the whale?

여 : 나도 그게 좋아. 고래 밑에 있는 집은 어때? **②의 단서** 고래 아래에 집이 있음

M : It's beautiful. What are these two chairs for?

남 : 아름다워. 이 의자 두 개는 무엇을 위한 거야? **③의 단서** 의자가 두 개 있음

W : You can take a picture sitting there. The painting becomes the background.

여 : 너는 거기에 앉아서 사진을 찍을 수 있어. 그림이 배경이 되는 거야.

M : Oh, I see. Look at this tree! It has heart-shaped leaves.

남 : 오, 그렇구나. 이 나무를 봐! 하트 모양의 나뭇잎이 있어. **④의 단서** 나무에는 하트 모양의 나뭇잎이 있음

목적어   목적격 보어
W : That's right. We named it the Love Tree.

여 : 맞아. 우리는 그것을 사랑 나무라고 이름 붙였어.

M : The butterfly on the tree branch is lovely, too.

남 : 나뭇가지 위에 있는 나비도 사랑스러워. **⑤의 단서** 나뭇가지 위에는 나비가 아니라 새가 있음

뒤에 목적어절 접속사 that이 생략됨
W : I hope a lot of people enjoy the painting.

여 : 나는 많은 사람들이 이 그림을 즐기면 좋겠어.

- volunteer work 자원봉사   • whale ⓝ 고래   • pattern ⓝ 무늬
- background ⓝ 배경   • heart-shaped ⓐ 하트 모양의
- branch ⓝ 나뭇가지

대화를 듣고, 그림에서 대화의 내용과 일치하지 않는 것을 고르시오.

꽃무늬가 있는 고래가 있음
나뭇가지 위에는 나비가 아니라 새가 있음
나무에는 하트 모양의 나뭇잎이 있음
고래 아래에 집이 있음
의자가 두 개 있음

> **왜 정답?** ✽❀❀ [정답률 89%]

남자는 나뭇가지 위에 있는 나비도 사랑스럽다고 했지만, 나뭇가지 위에는 새가 있으므로 ⑤은 대화의 내용과 일치하지 않는다.

> **왜 오답?**

① 꽃무늬가 있는 고래가 그려져 있다.
② 고래 아래에는 집이 그려져 있다.
③ 벽화를 배경으로 앉아서 사진을 찍을 수 있는 두 개의 의자가 있다.
④ 하트 모양의 나뭇잎이 달린 나무가 그려져 있다.

05 정답 ② ✽ Stella의 할아버지를 위한 콘서트 홍보하기

M : Hi, Stella. How are you doing these days?

남 : 안녕, Stella. 요즘 어떻게 지내?

be busy -ing ~하느라 바쁘다
W : Hi, Ryan. I've been busy helping my granddad with his concert. He made a rock band with his friends. **④의 함정**

여 : 안녕, Ryan. 나는 할아버지의 콘서트 준비를 도와드리느라 바빴어. 할아버지께서 친구분들과 록밴드를 만드셨거든.

강한 추측
M : There must be a lot of things to do.

남 : 할 일이 많겠네.

W : Yeah. I reserved a place for the concert yesterday. **⑤의 함정**

여 : 응. 어제는 콘서트 장소를 예약했어.

M : What about posters and tickets?

남 : 포스터와 티켓은?

현재완료(완료)
W : Well, I've just finished designing a poster.

여 : 음, 나는 포스터를 디자인하는 것을 방금 끝냈어.

M : Then I think I can help you.

남 : 그럼 내가 널 도와줄 수 있을 것 같아.

W : Really? How?

여 : 진짜? 어떻게?

M : Actually, I have a music blog. I think I can upload the poster there. **단서** 남자가 자신의 블로그에 콘서트 포스터를 게시하겠다고 함 **③의 함정**

남 : 사실, 나는 음악 블로그를 운영해. 거기에 내가 포스터를 게시할 수 있을 것 같아.

W : That's great!

여 : 좋아!

M : Just send the poster to me, and I'll post it online.

남 : 나에게 포스터를 보내만 주면 내가 온라인에 게시할게.

W : Thanks a lot.

여 : 정말 고마워.

- reserve ⓥ 예약하다   • upload ⓥ (온라인에) 올리다
- post ⓥ 게시하다

대화를 듣고, 남자가 할 일로 가장 적절한 것을 고르시오.
① 티켓 디자인하기 여자가 포스터 디자인을 끝냈다고 함
②포스터 게시하기 남자가 포스터를 자신의 블로그에 게시하겠다고 함
③ 블로그 개설하기 남자가 이미 운영하고 있음
④ 밴드부원 모집하기 밴드부원을 모집하는 것이 아님
⑤ 콘서트 장소 대여하기 여자가 이미 예약했음

왜 정답? ✿✿✿ [정답률 91%]
여자가 포스터 디자인을 끝냈다고 하자 남자는 자신의 음악 블로그에 그 포스터를 게시해 주겠다고 했으므로 정답은 ②이다.

왜 오답?
① 여자가 포스터 디자인을 끝냈다고는 했지만, 티켓도 디자인해야 하는지는 대화를 통해 알 수 없다. ──주의
③ 남자는 이미 음악 블로그를 운영하고 있었다.
④ 콘서트를 준비 중이므로 밴드부원을 모집한다는 것은 어색하다.
⑤ 콘서트 장소는 어제 예약했다고 했다.

06 정답 ② ＊커피포트와 텀블러 구입하기

M : Good morning. How may I help you?
남 : 좋은 아침입니다. 무엇을 도와드릴까요?

W : Hi. I want to buy a coffee pot.
여 : 안녕하세요. 저는 커피포트를 사고 싶습니다.

M : Okay. You can choose from these coffee pots.
남 : 알겠습니다. 이 커피포트들 중에서 고르시면 됩니다.

W : I like this one. How much is it?
여 : 저는 이것이 좋습니다. 얼마인가요? 단서 1 커피포트는 한 개에 50달러임

M : It was originally $60, but it's now on sale for $50.
남 : 그것은 원래는 60달러인데, 지금은 할인해서 50달러입니다.

W : Okay, I'll buy it. I'd also **like to buy** this red tumbler. would like to-v: ~하고 싶다
여 : 좋네요, 이것으로 살게요. 저는 이 빨간색 텀블러도 사고 싶습니다.

M : Actually, it comes in two sizes. This smaller **one** is $20 and a bigger one is $30. = red tumbler
남 : 사실, 그것은 두 가지 크기로 나옵니다. 이 작은 것은 20달러고 큰 것은 30달러입니다.

W : The smaller one would be easier to carry around. I'll buy two smaller ones. 단서 2 20달러인 작은 크기의 텀블러를 두 개 구입함
여 : 작은 것이 가지고 다니기에 더 편하겠네요. 저는 작은 것으로 두 개 살게요.

M : All right. Is there anything else you need?
남 : 좋습니다. 더 필요한 게 있으신가요?

W : No, that's all. Thank you.
여 : 아니요, 그것이 전부입니다. 감사합니다.

M : Okay. How would you like to pay?
남 : 알겠습니다. 계산은 어떻게 하시겠어요?

W : I'll pay by credit card. Here you are.
여 : 신용카드로 계산하겠습니다. 여기 있습니다.

• pot ⓝ 주전자 • originally ⓐ 원래 • tumbler ⓝ 텀블러
• carry around 가지고 다니다 • credit card 신용카드

대화를 듣고, 여자가 지불할 금액을 고르시오. [3점]
① $70 ②$90 ③ $100 ④ $110 ⑤ $120
$50(커피포트 한 개)＋$20×2(작은 텀블러 두 개)

왜 정답? ✿✿✿ [정답률 81%]
여자는 할인해서 50달러인 커피포트 한 개와 하나에 20달러인 작은 크기의 텀블러를 두 개 구입하겠다고 했으므로 여자가 지불할 금액은 ② '90달러'이다.

07 정답 ① ＊지갑을 살 수 없었던 이유

[Cell phone rings.]
[휴대 전화가 울린다.]

W : Hi, Brian.
여 : 안녕, Brian.

M : Hi, Mom. I'm in line **to get** on the plane. 부사적 용법(목적)
남 : 안녕하세요, 엄마. 저는 비행기에 타려고 줄 서 있어요.

W : Okay. By the way, did you drop by the duty free shop in the airport?
여 : 그렇구나. 그런데, 공항에 있는 면세점에는 들렀니?

M : Yes, but I couldn't buy the wallet **you asked** me to buy. 앞에 목적격 관계대명사가 생략됨 asked의 목적격 보어
남 : 네, 그런데 엄마가 제게 부탁하신 그 지갑은 살 수 없었어요.

W : Did you forget the brand name?
여 : 브랜드 이름을 잊어버렸니? ②의 함정

M : No. I remembered that. I took a memo.
남 : 아니요. 그건 기억했어요. 제가 기록해 두었거든요.

W : Then did you arrive late at the airport? ④의 함정
여 : 그러면 공항에 늦게 도착했어?

M : No, I had enough time **to shop**. 형용사적 용법(time 수식)
남 : 아니요, 쇼핑할 시간은 충분히 있었어요.

W : Then why couldn't you buy the wallet?
여 : 그러면 넌 왜 지갑을 사지 못한 거야?

M : Actually, because they were all sold out.
남 : 사실, 그것들이 다 팔렸기 때문이에요. 단서 지갑이 모두 팔려서 구입할 수 없었음

W : Oh, really?
여 : 오, 정말?

M : Yeah. The wallet **must** be very popular. 강한 추측
남 : 네. 그 지갑이 무척 인기가 많은 것이 분명해요.

W : Okay. Thanks for checking anyway.
여 : 알겠어. 어쨌든 확인해 줘서 고마워.

• drop by (잠깐) 들르다 • duty free shop 면세점 • airport ⓝ 공항
• wallet ⓝ 지갑 • actually ⓐ 사실 • popular ⓐ 인기 있는

대화를 듣고, 남자가 지갑을 구매하지 못한 이유를 고르시오.
①해당 상품이 다 팔려서 지갑이 다 팔렸다고 함
② 브랜드명을 잊어버려서 브랜드 이름은 기록해 두었다고 함
③ 계산대의 줄이 길어서 계산대 줄이 길었는지는 언급되지 않음
④ 공항에 늦게 도착해서 쇼핑할 시간은 충분히 있었음
⑤ 면세점이 문을 닫아서 면세점이 문을 닫아서 못산 것이 아님

왜 정답? ✿✿✿ [정답률 93%]
남자는 여자가 부탁한 지갑의 브랜드명도 기억하고 있었고 쇼핑할 시간도 충분했지만, 그 지갑이 다 팔려서 살 수 없었다고 했으므로 정답은 ①이다.

왜 오답?
② 지갑의 브랜드 이름은 기록해 두었다고 했다.
③ 계산대의 줄이 길었는지는 언급하지 않았다.
④ 쇼핑할 시간은 충분히 있었다고 했다.
⑤ 지갑이 다 팔렸다고 했으므로 면세점은 문을 열었음을 알 수 있다.

정답 ③ ＊합창단 오디션 지원하기 ──────

M : Lucy, look at this.
남 : Lucy, 이것 좀 봐.

W : Wow. It's about the Youth Choir Audition.
여 : 우아. Youth Choir Audition에 관한 것이구나.

M : Yes. It's open to anyone aged 13 to 18. ❶의 단서 지원 가능 연령
남 : 맞아. 13세부터 18세까지 누구나 지원할 수 있어.
　　앞에 주격 관계대명사와 be동사가 생략됨

W : I'm interested in joining the choir. When is it?
여 : 나는 합창단에 가입하는 것에 관심이 있어. 그건 언제야?

M : April 2nd, from 9 a.m. to 5 p.m. ❷의 단서 날짜
남 : 4월 2일 오전 9시부터 오후 5시까지야.
　　핵심 주어　　　　　　　　단수 동사

W : The place for the audition is the Youth Training Center. It's really far from here.
여 : 오디션 장소가 Youth Training Center네. 여기서 정말 멀어.

M : I think you should leave early in the morning.
남 : 나는 네가 아침 일찍 출발해야 한다고 생각해.

W : That's no problem. Is there an entry fee?
여 : 그건 문제없어. 참가비가 있어?

M : No, it's free. ❹의 단서 참가비
남 : 아니, 무료야.

W : Good. I'll apply for the audition.
여 : 좋아. 나는 이 오디션에 지원할 거야.

M : Then you should fill out an application form on this website.
남 : 그러면 너는 이 웹사이트에 있는 지원서 양식을 작성해야 해. ❺의 단서 지원 방법

W : All right. Thanks.
여 : 알겠어. 고마워.

- choir ⓝ 합창단　- audition ⓝ 오디션　- entry fee 참가비
- apply for ~에 지원하다　- fill out ~을 작성하다

대화를 듣고, Youth Choir Audition에 관해 언급되지 않은 것을 고르시오.

① 지원 가능 연령　It's open to anyone aged 13 to 18.
② 날짜　April 2nd
③ 심사 기준　언급되지 않음
④ 참가비　it's free
⑤ 지원 방법　Then you should fill out an application form on this website.

>왜 정답 ? ✽✽✽ [정답률 88%]

지원 가능 연령, 오디션 날짜, 참가비, 지원 방법은 언급되었지만, 심사 기준은 언급되지 않았으므로 정답은 ③이다.

>왜 오답 ?

① 13세부터 18세까지 누구나 지원할 수 있다고 했다.
② 오디션은 4월 2일 오전 9시부터 오후 5시까지 진행된다고 했다.
④ 참가비는 무료라고 했다.
⑤ 오디션에 지원하기 위해 웹사이트에 있는 지원서를 작성해야 한다고 했다.

09 **정답 ④** ＊2023 Career Week 안내 ──────

W : Hello, Rosehill High School students!
여 : 안녕하세요, Rosehill 고등학교 학생 여러분!

I'm your school counselor, Ms. Lee.
저는 여러분들의 학교 상담사인 Lee입니다.

I'm so happy to announce a special event, the 2023 Career Week. 저는 특별한 행사인 2023 Career Week를 알려드리게 되어 매우 기쁩니다.
　　　　부사적 용법(감정의 원인)

It'll be held from May 22nd for five days.
행사는 5월 22일부터 5일간 열릴 예정입니다. ❶의 단서 행사는 5일 동안 열림

There will be many programs to help you explore various future jobs. ❷의 단서 미래 직업 탐색을 돕는 프로그램들이 있을 것임
여러분들이 다양한 미래 직업들을 탐색하도록 돕는 많은 프로그램들이 있을 것입니다.
　　　　　　　　　　　　　　　　'~의 수(단수 취급)'
Please kindly note that the number of participants for each program is limited to 20. ❸의 단서 프로그램 참가 인원은 20명으로 제한됨
각 프로그램 참가자의 수는 20명으로 제한된다는 점을 주의하시기 바랍니다.
　　　단수 동사　　　　　　　　　　　　　　미래시제 수동태
A special lecture on future career choices will be presented on the first day. 단서 특별 강연은 첫째 날에 진행될 것임
미래 직업 선택에 관한 특별 강연이 첫째 날에 진행될 것입니다.

Registration begins on May 10th. ❺의 단서 등록은 5월 10일에 시작됨
등록은 5월 10일에 시작됩니다.

For more information, please visit our school website.
더 많은 정보를 원하시면, 우리 학교의 웹사이트를 방문하세요.
뒤에 목적격 접속사 that이 생략됨
I hope you can come and enjoy the 2023 Career Week!
저는 여러분들이 2023 Career Week에 와서 즐거운 시간을 보내시기를 바랍니다.

- counselor ⓝ 상담사　- announce ⓥ 알리다
- explore ⓥ 탐색하다, 탐험하다　- various ⓐ 다양한
- note ⓥ 주의하다, 기억하다　- participant ⓝ 참가자
- limit ⓥ 제한하다　- lecture ⓝ 강의, 강연　- registration ⓝ 등록

2023 Career Week에 관한 다음 내용을 듣고, 일치하지 않는 것을 고르시오.

① 5일 동안 열릴 것이다.　It'll be held from May 22nd for five days.
② 미래 직업 탐색을 돕는 프로그램이 있을 것이다.
　There will be many programs to help you explore various future jobs.
③ 프로그램 참가 인원에 제한이 있다.
　Please kindly note that the number of participants for each program is limited to 20.
④ 특별 강연이 마지막 날에 있을 것이다.
　A special lecture on future career choices will be presented on the first day.
⑤ 등록은 5월 10일에 시작된다.
　Registration begins on May 10th.

>왜 정답 ? ✽✽✽ [정답률 90%]

미래 직업 선택에 관한 특별 강연은 첫째 날에 진행될 것이라고(A special lecture on future career choices will be presented on the first day.) 했으므로 마지막 날에 있을 것이라고 한 ④이 2023 Career Week에 관한 내용과 일치하지 않는다.

>왜 오답 ?

① 5월 22일부터 5일간 열릴 예정이라고 했다.
② 미래 직업 탐색을 돕는 많은 프로그램이 있을 것이라고 했다.
③ 각 프로그램 참가자의 수는 20명으로 제한된다고 했다.
⑤ 등록은 5월 10일에 시작된다고 했다.

10 **정답 ②** ＊프라이팬 구매하기 ──────

M : Jessica, what are you doing?
남 : Jessica, 너 뭐 하고 있어?

W : I'm trying to buy one of these five frying pans.
여 : 나는 이 다섯 개의 프라이팬 중 한 개를 구입하려고 하고 있어.

M : Let me see. This frying pan seems pretty expensive.
남 : 어디 보자. 이 프라이팬은 꽤 비싸 보여.
　　　　　　　명사적 용법(want의 목적어)
W : Yeah. I don't want to spend more than $50.
여 : 맞아. 나는 50달러 이상을 쓰고 싶지는 않아. 단서 1 50달러 이하여야 함(⑤ 제외)

M : Okay. And I think 9 to 12-inch frying pans will work for most of your cooking. 단서 2 9~12인치 사이의 프라이팬(① 제외)
남 : 그래. 그리고 나는 9~12인치의 프라이팬이 대부분의 너의 요리에 맞을 것이라 생각해.

W : I think so, too. An 8-inch frying pan seems too small for me.
여 : 나도 그렇게 생각해. 8인치 프라이팬은 나한텐 너무 작아 보여.

M : What about the material? Stainless steel pans are good for fast cooking.

남 : 소재는 어때? 스테인리스강 프라이팬은 빠른 요리에 좋아. 단서 3 알루미늄 프라이팬(③ 제외)

W : I know, but they are heavier. I'll buy an aluminum pan.

여 : 나도 알아, 하지만 그것들은 더 무거워. 나는 알루미늄 팬을 사야겠어.

M : Then you have two options left. Do you need a lid?

남 : 그러면 남은 선택지가 두 개 있어. 넌 뚜껑이 필요해?

keep A from -ing: A가 ~하지 못하게 하다

W : Of course. A lid keeps the oil from splashing. I'll buy this one. 단서 4 뚜껑이 있는 프라이팬(④ 제외)

여 : 물론이지. 뚜껑은 기름이 튀는 것을 막아줘. 이거로 사야겠다.

M : Good choice

남 : 좋은 선택이야.

- pretty ⓐⓓ 꽤 • expensive ⓐ 비싼 • spend ⓥ (돈·시간을) 쓰다
- material ⓝ 소재, 재료 • aluminum ⓐ 알루미늄의
- option ⓝ 선택지 • lid ⓝ 뚜껑 • splash ⓥ 튀다

다음 표를 보면서 대화를 듣고, 여자가 구입할 프라이팬을 고르시오.

Frying Pans 프라이팬

	Model 모델	Price 가격	Size (inches) 크기(인치)	Material 소재	Lid 뚜껑
①	A	$30	8 9인치보다 작음	Aluminum 알루미늄	○
②	B	$32	9.5	Aluminum	○
③	C	$35	10	Stainless Steel 스테인리스강	×
④	D	$40	11	Aluminum	× 뚜껑이 없음
⑤	E	$70	12.5	Stainless Steel	○

50달러가 넘음 스테인리스강은 무거움

왜 정답 ? ✽✽✽ [정답률 91%]

여자는 50달러를 넘지 않고(⑤ 제외) 9~12인치 사이이며(① 제외) 알루미늄 소재로 된(③ 제외) 뚜껑이 있는(④ 제외) 프라이팬을 사기로 선택했으므로 정답은 ②이다.

왜 오답 ?

① 8인치 프라이팬은 너무 작아 보인다고 했다.
③ 스테인리스강 프라이팬은 무겁다고 했다.
④ 기름이 튀지 않도록 뚜껑이 필요하다고 했다.
⑤ 50달러 이상 쓰고 싶지 않다고 했다.

---

11 정답 ② ✽ 영상을 편집하고 있는 여자

현재완료(완료)

M : Have you finished your team's short-movie project?

남 : 당신 팀의 단편영화 프로젝트는 끝났나요?

W : Not yet. I'm still editing the video clip.

여 : 아직이요. 저는 아직 영상을 편집 중이에요.

M : Oh, you edit? How did you learn to do that?

남 : 오, 당신이 편집하나요? 편집하는 방법을 어떻게 배웠나요? 단서 남자는 여자에게 영상 편집을 어떻게 배웠는지 물어봄

W : I learned it by myself through books.

여 : 저는 책으로 직접 배웠어요.

- short-movie ⓝ 단편영화 • edit ⓥ 편집하다

대화를 듣고, 남자의 마지막 말에 대한 여자의 응답으로 가장 적절한 것을 고르시오.

① I don't think I can finish editing it by then.
저는 그때까지 편집을 끝낼 수 있을 것 같지 않아요. 편집 마감 기한에 관한 대화가 아님
② I learned it by myself through books.
저는 책으로 직접 배웠어요. 편집을 어떻게 배웠냐는 질문에 대한 대답
③ This short movie is very interesting.
이 단편영화는 매우 흥미로워요. 단편영화의 내용을 물어본 것이 아님
④ You should make another video clip.
당신은 또 다른 영상을 제작해야 해요. 여자가 남자에게 프로젝트를 준 것이 아님
⑤ I got an A⁺ on the team project.
저는 팀 프로젝트에서 A⁺를 받았어요. 아직 편집 중이므로 결과는 알 수 없음

왜 정답 ? ✽✽✽ [정답률 88%]

직접 영상을 편집 중인 여자에게 남자는 편집하는 방법을 어떻게 배웠냐고 물었으므로, 이에 대한 응답으로는 ② '저는 책으로 직접 배웠어요.'가 가장 적절하다.

왜 오답 ?

① 편집 마감 기한에 관한 대화가 아니다.
③ 단편영화의 내용은 물어보지 않았다.
④ 여자가 남자에게 영상 편집을 맡기는 내용이 아니다.
⑤ 프로젝트가 끝나지 않았으므로 성적은 알 수 없다. 함정

---

12 정답 ① ✽ 퇴근하는 아빠에게 요청하기

[Cell phone rings.] [휴대 전화가 울린다.]

W : Daddy, are you still working now?

여 : 아빠, 지금도 일하고 계세요?

be about to-v: 막 ~하려던 참이다

M : No, Emma. I'm about to get in my car and drive home.

남 : 아니야, Emma. 나는 막 차에 타서 집에 가려던 참이었어.

W : Great. Can you give me a ride? I'm at the City Library near your office. 단서 여자는 남자에게 차를 태워달라고 요청함

여 : 잘됐네요. 저를 태워주실 수 있나요? 저는 아빠의 사무실 근처 시립 도서관에 있어요.

M : All right. I'll come pick you up now.

남 : 좋아. 내가 지금 너를 태우러 갈게.

- give ~ a ride ~를 태워 주다 • borrow ⓥ 빌리다
- interior ⓝ 내부 (인테리어)

대화를 듣고, 여자의 마지막 말에 대한 남자의 응답으로 가장 적절한 것을 고르시오.

① All right. I'll come pick you up now. 차에 태워달라는 요청에 대한 대답
좋아. 내가 지금 너를 태우러 갈게.
② I'm sorry. The library is closed today. 도서관에 가자고 요청한 것이 아님
미안해. 도서관은 오늘 닫았어.
③ No problem. You can borrow my book. 도서관이 언급된 것으로 만든 오답
괜찮아. 너는 내 책을 빌려도 돼.
④ Thank you so much. I'll drop you off now. 차에 아직 타지 않았음
정말 고마워. 내가 지금 너를 내려줄게.
⑤ Right. I've changed the interior of my office. 사무실 안에서 나누는 대화가 아님
맞아. 나는 사무실 내부를 바꿨어.

왜 정답 ? ✽✽✽ [정답률 85%]

여자는 남자의 사무실 근처라고 하면서 막 집에 가려던 남자에게 차를 태워달라고 요청했으므로 남자는 ① '좋아. 내가 지금 너를 태우러 갈게.'라고 응답하는 것이 가장 적절하다.

왜 오답 ?

② 도서관에 같이 가자고 요청한 것이 아니다.
③ 도서관이 언급된 것으로 만든 오답으로, 남자의 책을 빌리려는 것이 아니다.
④ 아직 차에 타지 않았기 때문에 내려주겠다는 것은 어색하다.
⑤ 남자의 사무실에서 나누는 대화가 아니다.

---

13 정답 ③ ✽ Claire의 농장에 가고 싶은 남자

M : Claire, how's your farm doing?

남 : Claire, 요즘 농장 어때?

W : Great! I harvested some cherry tomatoes and cucumbers last weekend. Do you want some?

여 : 좋아! 나는 지난 주말에 방울토마토와 오이를 좀 수확했어. 좀 가져갈래?

M : Of course. I'd like some very much.

남 : 물론이지. 나는 정말 가져가고 싶어.

will bring의 간접목적어와 직접목적어

W : Okay. I'll bring you some tomorrow.

여 : 좋아. 내가 내일 좀 가져갈게.

M : Thanks. Are you going to the farm this weekend too?

남 : 고마워. 너는 이번 주말에도 농장에 갈 거야?

W : Yes. The peppers are almost ready to be picked.
여 : 응. 고추가 거의 수확될 준비가 됐어.

M : Can I go with you? I'd like to look around your farm and
   병렬 구조
   help you pick the peppers. 단서1 남자는 농장에 가서 고추를 따고 싶다고 함
남 : 내가 함께 가도 될까? 나는 네 농장을 둘러보고 고추 따는 것을 돕고 싶어.

W : Sure. It would be fun to work on the farm together.
여 : 물론이지. 농장에서 함께 일하면 재미있을 거야.

M : Sounds nice. Is there anything I need to prepare?
                          앞에 목적격 관계대명사가 생략됨
남 : 좋아. 내가 준비해야 할 것이 있는지 물어봄
   단서2 농장에 갈 때 준비할 것이 있는지 물어봄

W : **Just wear comfortable clothes and shoes.**
여 : 그냥 편한 옷과 신발만 착용하면 돼.

- harvest ⓥ 수확하다   - cherry tomato 방울토마토
- cucumber ⓝ 오이   - pepper ⓝ 고추   - pick ⓥ (과일 등을) 따다
- prepare ⓥ 준비하다   - comfortable ⓐ 편한   - vegetable ⓝ 채소

대화를 듣고, 남자의 마지막 말에 대한 여자의 응답으로 가장 적절한
것을 고르시오.
Woman : _____

① Try these tomatoes and cucumbers. 내일 가져오기로 함
  이 토마토와 오이를 먹어봐.
② I didn't know peppers are good for skin.
  고추가 피부에 좋은지 몰랐어.   고추의 효능은 언급되지 않음
③ Just wear comfortable clothes and shoes.
  그냥 편한 옷과 신발만 착용하면 돼.   농장에 갈 때 준비물을 물어본 것에 대한 대답
④ You can pick tomatoes when they are red.
  토마토가 빨갛게 익으면 따도 돼.   토마토를 따고 있는 상황이 아님
⑤ I'll help you grow vegetables on your farm.
  네가 농장에 채소를 기르는 것을 도와줄게. 남자의 농장에 채소를 기르는 것이 아님

▶왜 정답? ✿✿✿ [정답률 86%]

지난 주말에 농장에서 방울토마토와 오이를 수확했다는 여자에게 남자는 이번 주말에
자신도 함께 가서 고추 따는 것을 도와도 되는지 물어봤다.
여자가 허락하자 남자는 준비할 것이 있냐고 물어봤으므로, 이에 대한 여자의
응답으로는 ③ '그냥 편한 옷과 신발만 착용하면 돼'가 가장 적절하다.

▶왜 오답?

① 토마토와 오이는 여자가 내일 가져다주기로 했다.
② 고추의 효능에 대해서는 언급하지 않았다.
④ 토마토를 따면서 나누는 대화가 아니다.   주의
⑤ 남자가 여자의 농장에서 고추 따는 것을 도와주겠다고 했지, 여자가 남자의 농장에
  채소 기르는 것을 도와준다고는 하지 않았다.

---

14 정답 ① ＊Olivia와 다툰 Daniel

W : Daniel, what's wrong?
여 : Daniel, 무슨 일이야?

M : Hi, Leila. I had an argument with Olivia.
남 : 안녕, Leila. 나 Olivia와 언쟁을 했어.

W : Was it serious?
여 : 심각했어?

M : I'm not sure, but I think I made a mistake.
                 뒤에 목적어절 접속사 that이 생략됨
남 : 잘 모르겠어, 하지만 내가 실수했다고 생각해.

W : So that's why you have a long face.
                              '우울한 얼굴'
여 : 그래서 네가 우울한 얼굴을 하고 있구나.

M : Yeah. I want to get along with her, but she's still angry at
                      '~와 잘 지내다'
   me.
남 : 맞아. 나는 그녀와 잘 지내고 싶지만, 그녀는 아직도 나한테 화가 나 있어.

W : Did you say you're sorry to her?
         뒤에 목적어절 접속사 that이 생략됨
여 : 너는 그녀에게 미안하다고 말했어?

M : Well, I texted her saying that I'm sorry.
남 : 음, 나는 그녀에게 미안하다고 문자를 보냈어.

W : I don't think it's a good idea to express your apology
                    가주어   진주어
   through a text message. 단서1 문자 메시지로 사과하는 것은 적절한 방법이 아님
여 : 문자 메시지로 사과를 표현하는 것은 좋은 생각 같지 않아.

M : Do you think so? Now I know why I haven't received any
                                          현재 완료
   response from her yet.
남 : 너는 그렇게 생각해? 이제야 왜 내가 그녀한테서 아직 아무런 답장을 못 받았는지 알겠어.

W : I think it'd be best to go and talk to her in person.
여 : 나는 그녀에게 가서 직접 말하는 것이 가장 좋은 방법이라고 생각해.
   단서2 직접 가서 사과하는 것이 좋겠다고 제안함

M : **You're right. I'll meet her and apologize.**
남 : 네가 맞아. 내가 그녀를 만나서 사과할게.

- argument ⓝ 언쟁   - serious ⓐ 심각한, 진지한
- mistake ⓝ 실수, 잘못   - express ⓥ 표현하다   - apology ⓝ 사과
- receive ⓥ 받다   - response ⓝ 답장

대화를 듣고, 여자의 마지막 말에 대한 남자의 응답으로 가장 적절한
것을 고르시오. [3점]
Man : _____

① You're right. I'll meet her and apologize. 문자 메시지보다는 직접
  네가 맞아. 내가 그녀를 만나서 사과할게. 만나서 사과하는 것이 가장 좋은 방법이라고 함
② I agree with you. That's why I did it.
  나도 네게 동의해. 그래서 내가 그런 거야. 직접 만나서 사과하지 않았음
③ Thank you. I appreciate your apology.
  고마워. 사과해 줘서 고마워.   여자가 남자에게 사과한 것이 아님
④ Don't worry. I don't think it's your fault.
  걱정하지 마. 나는 네 잘못이라고 생각하지 않아. 여자가 잘못한 것이 아님
⑤ Too bad. I hope the two of you get along.
  안됐다. 너희 둘이 잘 지내기를 바랄게.   여자가 Olivia와 다툰 것이 아님

▶왜 정답? ✿✿✿ [정답률 90%]

Olivia와 싸운 뒤 문자 메시지로만 사과한 남자에게 여자는 직접 만나서 사과하라고
조언했다. 따라서 직접 사과하는 것이 가장 좋은 방법이라는 여자의 마지막 말에
남자는 ① '네가 맞아. 내가 그녀를 만나서 사과할게.'라고 응답하는 것이 가장
적절하다.

▶왜 오답?

② 남자는 아직 Olivia를 직접 만나 사과하지 않았다.
③ 남자가 여자의 사과를 받는 상황이 아니므로 적절하지 않다.
④ 여자가 자신의 잘못을 걱정하는 상황이 아니다.
⑤ 여자가 아니라 남자가 Olivia와 다툰 것이다.

---

15 정답 ③ ＊함께 등산한 Ted와 John

M : Ted and John are college freshmen.
남 : Ted와 John은 대학 신입생이다.

They are climbing Green Diamond Mountain together.
그들은 Green Diamond Mountain을 함께 등산하고 있다.
                      현재완료
Now they have reached the campsite near the mountain
top.
이제 그들은 산 정상 근처의 캠핑지에 도착했다.
              접속사가 생략되지 않은 분사구문
After climbing the mountain all day, they have a relaxing
time at the campsite.
하루 종일 산을 오른 후, 그들은 캠핑지에서 휴식 시간을 갖는다.
      접속사가 생략되지 않은 분사구문   목적어절 접속사
While drinking coffee, Ted suggests to John that they watch
the sunrise at the mountain top the next morning.
커피를 마시면서, Ted는 John에게 다음 날 아침 산 정상에서 해돋이를 보자고
제안한다.   단서1 Ted가 다음 날 아침 해돋이를 보고 제안함

John thinks it's a good idea. 단서2 John도 해돋이를 보고 싶음
John은 그것이 좋은 생각이라고 생각한다.
                              간접의문문
So, now John wants to ask Ted how early they should wake
up to see the sunrise.
그래서, 이제 John은 Ted에게 해돋이를 보려면 그들이 얼마나 일찍 일어나야 하는지
묻고 싶어 한다.   단서3 John은 해돋이를 보려면 얼마나 일찍 일어나야 하는지 궁금해함

In this situation, what would John most likely say to Ted?
이 상황에서, John이 Ted에게 할 말로 가장 적절한 것은 무엇인가?

John: **What time should we get up tomorrow morning?**
John: 우리 내일 아침 몇 시에 일어나야 해?

*상황 요약: Ted와 John은 내일 아침 일찍 해돋이를 보러 가기로 한 상황

- college ⓝ 대학 • freshman ⓝ 1학년 학생
- climb ⓥ 등산하다, 오르다 • reach ⓥ 도착하다
- campsite ⓝ 캠핑지 • top ⓝ 꼭대기 • relaxing ⓐ 편안한, 휴식의
- suggest ⓥ 제안하다 • sunrise ⓝ 해돋이 • spot ⓝ 지점, 장소

다음 상황 설명을 듣고, John이 Ted에게 할 말로 가장 적절한 것을 고르시오. [3점]

John: _____

① How can we find the best sunrise spot? 정상에서 해돋이를 보기로 함
우리는 어떻게 최고의 해돋이 장소를 찾을 수 있을까?
② Why do you go mountain climbing so often?
너는 등산을 왜 그렇게 자주 가니? 등산을 자주 하는 이유가 궁금해하는 것이 아님
③ What time should we get up tomorrow morning?
우리 내일 아침 몇 시에 일어나야 해? 아침에 해돋이를 보기 위해 언제 일어나야 하는지 궁금해하는 상황
④ When should we come down from the mountain top?
우리 산 정상에서 언제 내려와야 해? 내려오는 것보다 언제 올라갈지가 궁금한 상황
⑤ Where do we have to stay in the mountain at night?
우리 밤에는 산 어디에 머물러야 해? 산 정상 근처 캠핑지에서 머물

>왜 정답? ✿✿✿ [정답률 82%]

Ted와 John은 함께 산에 올라 휴식하고 있다. Ted가 John에게 다음 날 아침 정상에 올라 해돋이를 보자고 제안했고 John도 좋다고 생각한다.
John은 해돋이를 보려면 얼마나 일찍 일어나야 하는지 Ted에게 묻고 싶어 하므로
③ '우리 내일 아침 몇 시에 일어나야 해?'라고 말하는 것이 가장 적절하다.

>왜 오답?

① 두 사람은 산 정상에 올라 해돋이를 보기로 했다.
② 둘이 함께 등산한 상황일 뿐 얼마나 자주 다니는지 궁금해하는 상황이 아니다.
④ 산에서 내려와서 해돋이를 보러 가기로 한 것이 아니다.
⑤ 산 정상 근처 캠핑지에 머물기로 했다.

16~17 * 가족과 함께 하기 좋은 운동들

W: Good morning, everyone. //
여: 좋은 아침입니다, 여러분 //

Do you spend a lot of time / with your family? //
여러분은 많은 시간을 보내나요 / 가족들과 //

One of the best ways / to spend time with your family / is to
「one of+복수 명사」: ~ 중 하나   단수 동사
enjoy sports together. //
가장 좋은 방법 중 하나는 / 여러분의 가족과 함께 시간을 보내는 / 함께 스포츠를 즐기는 것입니다 //

Today, / I will share some of the best sports / that families
목적격 관계대명사
can play together. // 16번 단서: 가족과 함께 할 수 있는 스포츠들에 관해 이야기할 것임
오늘, / 저는 몇몇 가장 좋은 스포츠들을 공유해 드릴 것입니다 / 가족들이 함께 할 수 있는 //

The first one / is badminton. // 17번①
첫 번째는 / 배드민턴입니다 //

The whole family can enjoy the sport / with minimal
equipment. //
가족 전체가 스포츠를 즐길 수 있습니다 / 최소한의 장비로 //

The second one / is basketball. // 17번②
두 번째는 / 농구입니다 //

You can easily find a basketball court / near your house. //
여러분은 농구 코트를 쉽게 찾을 수 있습니다 / 집 근처에서 //

The third one / is table tennis. // 17번③
세 번째는 / 탁구입니다 //
수동태 동사
It can be played indoors / anytime. //
그것은 실내에서 할 수 있습니다 / 언제든 //

The last one / is bowling. // 17번⑤
마지막은 / 볼링입니다 //
분사구문
Many families have a great time / playing it together. //
많은 가족들이 좋은 시간을 보냅니다 / 그것을 함께 하며 //
부사절 접속사(시간)
When you go home today, / how about playing one of these
sports / with your family? //
여러분이 오늘 집에 가면 / 이 스포츠들 중 하나를 해보는 것은 어떤가요 / 여러분의 가족과 //

- share ⓥ 공유하다 • minimal ⓐ 최소한의 • equipment ⓝ 장비
- easily ⓐ𝖽 쉽게 • indoors ⓐ𝖽 실내에서 • elderly ⓐ 나이가 지긋한
- useful ⓐ 유용한 • traditional ⓐ 전통적인

여: 좋은 아침입니다, 여러분. 여러분은 가족들과 많은 시간을 보내나요? 여러분의 가족과 함께 시간을 보내는 가장 좋은 방법 중 하나는 함께 스포츠를 즐기는 것입니다. 오늘, 제가 가족들이 함께 할 수 있는 가장 좋은 스포츠들을 공유해 드리겠습니다. 첫 번째는 배드민턴입니다. 가족 전체가 최소한의 장비로 스포츠를 즐길 수 있습니다. 두 번째는 농구입니다. 여러분은 집 근처에서 농구 코트를 쉽게 찾을 수 있습니다. 세 번째는 탁구입니다. 탁구는 실내에서 언제든 할 수 있습니다. 마지막은 볼링입니다. 많은 가족들이 볼링을 함께 하며 좋은 시간을 보냅니다. 오늘 집에 가면, 여러분의 가족들과 이 스포츠들 중 하나를 해보는 것은 어떤가요?

16 정답 ③

여자가 하는 말의 주제로 가장 적절한 것은?

① indoor sports good for the elderly 어르신에게 국한된 내용이 아님
어르신들에게 좋은 실내 스포츠들
② importance of learning rules in sports 규칙에 관한 언급은 없음
스포츠에서 규칙을 배우는 것의 중요성
③ best sports for families to enjoy together
가족들이 함께 즐기기 가장 좋은 스포츠들 가족 모두가 함께 즐길 수 있는 스포츠들을 이야기함
④ useful tips for winning a sports game
스포츠 경기에서 이길 수 있는 유용한 조언들 경기에서 이기라는 것이 아님
⑤ history of traditional family sports
전통적인 가족 스포츠의 역사 전통적인 가족 스포츠들을 소개한 것이 아님

>왜 정답? ✿✿✿ [정답률 95%]

여자는 가족과 함께 시간을 보내는 좋은 방법은 함께 스포츠를 즐기는 것이라고 말하며 배드민턴, 농구, 탁구 등을 소개하고 있다. 따라서 여자가 하는 말의 주제는 ③ '가족들이 함께 즐기기 가장 좋은 스포츠들'이다.

>왜 오답?

① 어르신들만을 위한 스포츠를 추천한 것이 아니다.
② 스포츠 규칙에 관해서는 언급하지 않았다.
④ 함께 즐기는 스포츠를 소개한 것이지 이기라고 조언하는 것이 아니다.
⑤ 전통적인 가족 스포츠의 역사를 소개한 것이 아니다.

17 정답 ④

언급된 스포츠가 아닌 것은?

① badminton 최소한의 장비로 즐길 수 있음
배드민턴
② basketball 집 근처에서 쉽게 즐길 수 있음
농구
③ table tennis 실내에서 언제든 할 수 있음
탁구
④ soccer 언급되지 않음
축구
⑤ bowling 많은 가족이 함께 할 수 있음
볼링

>왜 정답? ✿✿✿ [정답률 95%]

가족들이 함께 할 수 있는 스포츠로 배드민턴, 농구, 탁구, 볼링을 소개했지만 ④ '축구'는 언급하지 않았다.

>왜 오답 ?

① 최소한의 장비로 즐길 수 있다고 했다.
② 집 근처에서 쉽게 즐길 수 있다고 했다.
③ 실내에서 언제든 할 수 있다고 했다.
⑤ 많은 가족들이 함께 할 수 있다고 했다.

18 정답 ③ * 놀이터 시설 수리 요청

To whom it may concern, / 관계자분께 /

I am a resident of the Blue Sky Apartment. //
저는 Blue Sky 아파트의 거주자입니다 //

Recently / I observed / **that** the kid zone is **in need of** repairs. //
최근에 / 저는 알게 되었습니다 / 아이들을 위한 구역이 수리가 필요하다는 것을 //
목적어절 접속사 '~을 필요로 하는'

I want you **to pay attention** / to the poor condition / of the
want의 목적격 보어(to부정사)
playground equipment in the zone. // 단서 1 놀이터의 설비가 열악해 수리가 필요함
저는 귀하께서 관심을 기울여 주시기를 바랍니다 / 열악한 상태에 / 그 구역 놀이터 설비의 //
부분 표현은 of 뒤의 명사에 수 일치
The swings are damaged, / the paint is falling off, / and **some of**
복수 동사
the bolts on the slide **are missing**. //
그네가 손상되었고 / 페인트가 떨어져 나가고 있고 / 미끄럼틀의 볼트 몇 개가 빠져 있습니다 //
현재완료(계속)
The facilities **have been** in this terrible condition / since we
moved here. //
(놀이터) 시설은 이렇게 형편없는 상태였습니다 / 우리가 이곳으로 이사 온 이후로 //
앞에 주격 관계대명사와 be동사가 생략됨
They are dangerous / to the children **playing** there. //
그것들은 위험합니다 / 거기서 노는 아이들에게 //

Would you please have them repaired? // 단서 2 놀이터 설비의 수리를 요청함
그것을 수리해 주시겠습니까 //
부사적 용법(목적)
I would appreciate your immediate attention / **to solve** this
matter. //
즉각적인 관심을 주시면 감사하겠습니다 / 이 문제를 해결하기 위해 //

Yours sincerely, Nina Davis / Nina Davis 드림 /

- resident ⓝ 거주자　　- recently ⓐ𝖽 최근에
- observe ⓥ 알다, 목격하다　　- repair ⓝ 수리　　- attention ⓝ 주의
- equipment ⓝ 설비　　- swing ⓝ 그네　　- damage ⓥ 손상하다
- fall off 떨어져 나가다　　- slide ⓝ 미끄럼틀　　- facility ⓝ 시설
- terrible ⓐ 형편없는　　- appreciate ⓥ 감사하다
- immediate ⓐ 즉각적인　　- solve ⓥ (문제 등을) 해결하다

관계자분께,
저는 Blue Sky 아파트의 거주자입니다. 최근에 저는 아이들을 위한 구역이 수리가 필요하다는 것을 알게 되었습니다. 저는 귀하께서 그 구역 놀이터 설비의 열악한 상태에 관심을 기울여 주시기를 바랍니다. 그네가 손상되었고, 페인트가 떨어져 나가고 있고, 미끄럼틀의 볼트 몇 개가 빠져 있습니다. (놀이터) 시설은 우리가 이곳으로 이사 온 이후로 이렇게 형편없는 상태였습니다. 그것들은 거기서 노는 아이들에게 위험합니다. 그것을 수리해 주시겠습니까? 이 문제를 해결하기 위해 즉각적인 관심을 주시면 감사하겠습니다.
Nina Davis 드림

다음 글의 목적으로 가장 적절한 것은?

① 아파트의 첨단 보안 설비를 홍보하려고　첨단 보안 설비는 언급되지 않음
② 아파트 놀이터의 임시 폐쇄를 공지하려고
놀이터에 수리가 필요하지 폐쇄되는 것은 아님
③ 아파트 놀이터 시설의 수리를 요청하려고
손상된 설비가 수리되어야 한다고 요청함
④ 아파트 놀이터 사고의 피해 보상을 촉구하려고
사고 예방을 위해서 수리를 요청하는 것임
⑤ 아파트 공용 시설 사용 시 유의 사항을 안내하려고
놀이터 이용의 유의 사항을 말하는 것이 아님

>왜 정답 ? ❀❀❀ [정답률 93%]

현재 놀이터의 그네와 미끄럼틀들이 일부 망가져 있고 페인트가 벗겨져 있는 등 시설이 열악하므로 놀이터 시설을 수리해달라고 요청하는 내용이다. 따라서 이 글의 목적으로 가장 적절한 것은 ③이다.

>왜 오답 ?

① 첨단 보안 설비는 언급되지 않았다.
② 놀이터를 임시 폐쇄하자는 글이 아니고 수리해야 한다는 내용이다.
④ 놀이터 사고가 발생하였는지는 알 수 없고, 예방 차원에서 수리를 요청하고 있다.
⑤ 유의 사항 안내가 아니라 수리를 요청하는 글이다.

19 정답 ② * 먹이를 찾고 있었던 곰

On a two-week trip / in the Rocky Mountains, / I saw a grizzly
bear / in its native habitat. // 단서 1 처음에는 곰을 보고 기분이 좋았음
2주간의 여행 중 / 로키산맥에서 / 나는 회색곰 한 마리를 보았다 / 자연 서식지에서 //
부사절 접속사(시간)　　watched의 목적격 보어
At first, / I felt joy / **as** I watched the bear / **walk** across the land. //
처음에 / 나는 기분이 좋았다 / 그 곰을 보았을 때 / 땅을 가로질러 걸어가는 //
'이따금'　　부사적 용법(목적)
He stopped **every once in a while** / **to turn** his head about, /
sniffing deeply. // 분사구문
그것은 이따금 멈춰 섰다 / 그것의 고개를 돌리기 위해 / 깊게 코를 킁킁거리며 //

He was following the scent of something, / and slowly I began
목적어절 접속사
to realize / **that** this giant animal was smelling me! // 단서 2 곰은 나를 찾고 있었음
그것은 무언가의 냄새를 따라가고 있었다 / 그리고 서서히 나는 깨닫기 시작했다 / 이 거대한 동물이 내 냄새를 맡고 있다는 것을 //

I froze. //
나는 얼어붙었다 //

This was no longer a wonderful experience; / it was now an
issue / of survival. // 단서 3 이제 생존의 문제가 됨
이것은 더는 멋진 경험이 아니었고 / 이제 문제였다 / 생존의 //
명사적 용법(주격 보어)　　형용사적 용법(meat 수식)
The bear's motivation was **to find** meat **to eat**, / and I was clearly
on his menu. //
그 곰의 동기는 먹을 고기를 찾는 것이었고 / 나는 분명히 그의 메뉴에 올라 있었다 //

- grizzly bear 회색곰　　- native ⓐ 자연의　　- habitat ⓝ 서식지
- sniff ⓥ (코를) 킁킁거리다　　- realize ⓥ 깨닫다　　- giant ⓐ 거대한
- freeze ⓥ 얼어붙다　　- issue ⓝ 문제　　- survival ⓝ 생존
- motivation ⓝ 동기　　- clearly ⓐ𝖽 분명히

로키산맥에서 2주간의 여행 중, 나는 자연 서식지에서 회색곰 한 마리를 보았다. 처음에 나는 그 곰이 땅을 가로질러 걸어가는 모습을 보았을 때 기분이 좋았다. 그것은 이따금 멈춰 서서 고개를 돌려 깊게 코를 킁킁거렸다. 그것은 무언가의 냄새를 따라가고 있었고, 나는 서서히 거대한 이 동물이 내 냄새를 맡고 있다는 것을 깨닫기 시작했다! 나는 얼어붙었다. 이것은 더는 멋진 경험이 아니었고, 이제 생존의 문제였다. 그 곰의 동기는 먹을 고기를 찾는 것이었고, 나는 분명히 그의 메뉴에 올라 있었다.

다음 글에 드러난 'I'의 심경 변화로 가장 적절한 것은?

① sad → angry　처음엔 기분이 좋았음
슬픔 → 화난
② delighted → scared　곰을 보고 기분이 좋았지만 먹이가 될 수도 있음을 알고 무서워함
기쁜 → 무서운
③ satisfied → jealous　곰을 질투한 것이 아님
만족하는 → 질투하는
④ worried → relieved　먹이가 될 수도 있는 것이 안도할 상황은 아님
걱정하는 → 안도하는
⑤ frustrated → excited　오히려 처음에 흥분하고 마지막에 좌절했다고 볼 수 있음
좌절한 → 흥분하는

>왜 정답 ? ❀❀❀ [정답률 85%]

전반부: 로키산맥에서 곰을 보고 기분이 좋았음 ▶ '기쁜', '만족하는'
후반부: 곰이 내 냄새를 따라오고 있다는 것을 깨달음 ▶ '무서운'
따라서 'I'의 심경 변화로 가장 적절한 것은 ② '기쁜 → 무서운'이다.

왜 오답 ?

① 처음에는 곰을 보고 기분이 좋았다.

③ 질투의 대상은 나오지 않았다.

④ 곰의 먹이가 될 수도 있는 상황이므로 안도하는 것이 아니다.

⑤ 반대로 처음에는 곰을 봐서 흥분했다가 먹이가 될 수 있음에 좌절했다고 볼 수 있다.

왜 오답 ?

① 부정적인 감정이 아니라 자신에게 맞지 않는 시간에는 에너지가 저점일 수 있다고 했다.

② 신체 리듬을 언급했을 뿐, 운동량을 조절하라는 내용은 없었다. 함정

③ 자기 성찰을 하는 것은 중요하지만 명상에 대한 내용은 없었다.

④ 오히려 힘든 작업을 가장 잘 처리할 수 있는 시간에 하라고 했다.

---

20 정답 ⑤ ＊에너지가 높은 시간 파악하기

It is difficult for any of us / to maintain a constant level of attention / throughout our working day. //
~은 우리 중 누구라도 어렵다 / 꾸준한 수준의 주의 집중을 유지하는 것 / 근무일 내내

We all have body rhythms / characterised by peaks and valleys of energy and alertness. //
우리는 모두 신체 리듬을 가지고 있다 / 에너지와 기민함의 정점과 저점으로 특징지어지는 //

You will achieve more, / and feel confident as a benefit, / if you schedule your most demanding tasks / at times when you are best able to cope with them. //
당신은 더 많은 것을 이루고 / 이익으로 자신감을 느낄 것이다 / 만약 당신이 가장 힘든 작업을 계획하면 / 그것들을 가장 잘 처리할 수 있는 시간에 //

If you haven't thought / about energy peaks before, / take a few days / to observe yourself. //
만약 당신이 생각해 본 적이 없다면 / 전에 에너지 정점에 관해 / 며칠을 사용해라 / 자신을 관찰하기 위해 //

단서 1 자신이 가장 좋은 상태인 때를 알라고 함
Try to note the times / when you are at your best. //
때를 알아차리도록 노력하라 / 당신이 가장 좋은 상태인 //

We are all different. //
우리는 모두 다르다 //

단서 2 사람마다 정점인 시간은 다름
For some, / the peak will come first thing / in the morning, / but for others / it may take a while / to warm up. //
어떤 사람에게는 / 정점은 제일 먼저 오는 것이다 / 아침에 / 하지만 다른 사람들에게는 / ~은 얼마간의 시간이 걸릴 수도 있다 / 준비하는 것 //

- maintain ⓥ 유지하다 · constant ⓐ 일정한
- attention ⓝ 주의 (집중) · characterise ⓥ 특징으로 하다
- peaks and valleys 정점과 저섬 · achieve ⓥ 이루다
- confident ⓐ 자신감 있는 · benefit ⓝ 이익, 혜택
- demanding ⓐ (일이) 힘든 · task ⓝ 과업, 작업
- cope with ~을 처리하다

우리 중 누구라도 근무일 내내 꾸준한 주의 집중을 유지하기는 어렵다. 우리 모두 에너지와 기민함의 정점과 저점을 특징으로 하는 신체 리듬을 가지고 있다. 가장 힘든 작업을 가장 잘 처리할 수 있는 시간에 그것을 하도록 계획을 잡으면, 더 많은 것을 이루고 이익으로 자신감을 느낄 것이다. 만약 전에 에너지 정점에 관해 생각해 본 적이 없다면, 며칠 동안 자신을 관찰하라. 자신이 가장 좋은 상태일 때를 알아차리도록 노력하라. 우리는 모두 다르다. 어떤 사람에게는 정점이 아침에 제일 먼저 오지만, 다른 사람에게는 준비하는 데 얼마간의 시간이 걸릴 수도 있다.

다음 글에서 필자가 주장하는 바로 가장 적절한 것은?
① 부정적인 감정에 에너지를 낭비하지 말라. 부정적인 감정은 글의 내용과 관련 없음
② 자신의 신체 능력에 맞게 운동량을 조절하라. 신체 리듬을 언급한 것으로 만든 오답
③ 자기 성찰을 위한 아침 명상 시간을 확보하라. 자기 성찰을 위해 명상을 하라는 내용은 없음
④ 생산적인 하루를 보내려면 일을 균등하게 배분하라. 일의 분배는 언급되지 않음
⑤ 자신의 에너지가 가장 높은 시간을 파악하여 활용하라. 자신이 가장 효율적인 시간을 파악해서 활용하라고 했음

왜 정답 ? ＊※※ [정답률 84%]
- 문제점: 언제나 꾸준한 주의 집중을 유지하는 어려움
- 해결책: 하루 중 자신이 가장 좋은 상태인 시간을 파악하기
▶ 자신의 에너지가 가장 높은 시간을 파악하여 활용하라는 것이므로 정답은 ⑤이다.

---

21 정답 ⑤ ＊기술의 발전으로 변하는 일자리

If we adopt technology, / we need to pay its costs. //
만약 우리가 기술을 받아들이면 / 우리는 그것의 비용을 치러야 한다 //

Thousands of traditional livelihoods have been pushed aside / by progress, / and the lifestyles around those jobs removed. //
수천 개의 전통적인 생계 수단이 밀려났다 / 발전에 의해 / 그리고 그 직업들 주변의 생활 방식이 없어졌다 //

Hundreds of millions of humans today work / at jobs they hate, / producing things they have no love for. //
오늘날 수억 명의 사람들이 일한다 / 그들이 싫어하는 직장에서 / 그들이 아무런 애정을 갖지 않는 것들을 생산하면서 //

Sometimes / these jobs cause / physical pain, disability, or chronic disease. //
때때로 / 이러한 일자리들은 유발한다 / 육체적 고통, 장애 또는 만성 질환을 //

Technology creates many new jobs / that are certainly dangerous. //
기술은 많은 새로운 일자리를 창출한다 / 확실히 위험한 //

At the same time, / mass education and media train humans / to avoid low-tech physical work, / to seek jobs working in the digital world. //
단서 1 과거와 다르게 인간이 육체노동을 적게 하는 직종에 많이 종사하게 됨
동시에 / 대중 교육과 대중 매체는 인간을 훈련시킨다 / 낮은 기술의 육체노동을 피하고 / 디지털 세계에서 일하는 직업을 찾도록 //

The divorce of the hands from the head puts a stress / on the human mind. //
머리로부터 손이 단절되는 것은 부담을 준다 / 인간의 정신에 //

Indeed, / the sedentary nature of the best-paying jobs / is a health risk / — for body and mind. //
단서 2 보수가 좋은 앉아서 일하는 직업은 건강에 부정적 영향을 미침
실제로 / 가장 보수가 좋은 직업의 주로 앉아서 하는 특성은 / 건강 위험 요소이다 / 신체와 정신에 //

- adopt ⓥ 받아들이다, 채택하다 · traditional ⓐ 전통적인
- livelihood ⓝ 생계 수단 · progress ⓝ 발전 · remove ⓥ 없애다
- physical ⓐ 육체의 · disability ⓝ 장애 · mass ⓐ 대중의
- avoid ⓥ 피하다 · divorce ⓝ 단절, 이혼
- indeed ⓐⓓ 실제로, 참으로 · risk ⓝ 위험 (요소)
- ignorance ⓝ 무지, 무식 · endless ⓐ 끝없는 · labor ⓝ 노동
- realistic ⓐ 현실적인

만약 우리가 기술을 받아들이면, 우리는 그것의 비용을 치러야 한다. 수천 개의 전통적인 생계 수단이 발전에 의해 밀려났으며, 그 직업과 관련된 생활 방식이 없어졌다. 오늘날 수억 명의 사람들이 자기가 싫어하는 직장에서 일하면서, 자신이 아무런 애정을 느끼지 못하는 것들을 생산한다. 때때로 이러한 일자리는 육체적 고통, 장애 또는 만성 질환을 유발한다. 기술은 확실히 위험한 많은 새로운 일자리를 창출한다. 동시에, 대중 교육과 대중 매체는 낮은 기술의 육체노동을 피하고 디지털 세계에서 일하는 직업을 찾도록 인간을 훈련시킨다. 머리로부터 손이 단절되는 것은 인간의 정신에 부담을 준다. 실제로, 가장 보수가 좋은 직업의 주로 앉아서 하는 특성은 신체와 정신에 건강 위험 요소이다.

밑줄 친 The divorce of the hands from the head가 다음 글에서 의미하는 바로 가장 적절한 것은? [3점]

① ignorance of modern technology
현대 기술의 무지
현대 기술의 무지가 아니라 변화에 관한 내용임
② endless competition in the labor market
노동 시장에서의 끝없는 경쟁
노동 시장에서의 경쟁에 관한 글이 아님
③ not getting along well with our coworkers
동료들과 잘 어울리지 못하는 것
동료들과의 관계는 언급되지 않음
④ working without any realistic goals for our career
우리의 경력을 위해 현실적 목표 없이 일하는 것
목표 설정을 하라는 것이 아님
⑤ our increasing use of high technology in the workplace
직장에서 우리의 증가하는 첨단 기술 사용
기술의 발전으로 육체노동을 피하게 됨

왜 정답? ★★★ [정답률 57%]

• 과거와 다르게 인간이 육체노동을 적게 하는 직종에 많이 종사하게 됨 단서1
• 보수가 좋은 앉아서 일하는 직업은 건강에 부정적 영향을 미침 단서2

➡ 기술의 발전으로 과거와는 다르게 육체노동을 적게 하는 직종이 많아지고, 앉아서만 일하다 보니 건강에 부정적인 영향을 미침
▶ 몸을 쓰지 않고 기술을 사용해 머리로 일한다는 것이므로 '머리로부터 손이 단절되는 것'은 ⑤ '직장에서 우리의 증가하는 첨단 기술 사용'을 의미한다.

왜 오답?

① 현대 기술의 무지가 아니라 변화에 관한 글이다.
② 노동 시장에서의 경쟁을 말하는 글이 아니다.
③ 동료들과의 관계에 관해서는 언급되지 않았다.
④ 현실적 목표를 세우라고 조언하는 글이 아니다.

---

22 정답 ① ★상황에 따른 학습 전략 활용하기

When students are starting their college life, / they may approach every course, test, or learning task / the same way, /
선행사를 포함하는 관계대명사
using what we like to call / "the rubber-stamp approach." //
학생들이 대학 생활을 시작할 때 / 그들은 모든 과목이나, 시험, 학습 과제에 접근할지도 모른다 / 똑같은 방식으로 / 우리가 부르고 싶은 방법을 이용하여 / '고무도장 방식'이라고 //

Think about it this way: / Would you wear a tuxedo / to a baseball game? //
그것을 이런 식으로 생각해 보라 / 여러분은 턱시도를 입겠는가 / 야구 경기에 //

A colorful dress / to a funeral? //
화려한 드레스를 (입겠는가) / 장례식에 //

A bathing suit / to religious services? //
수영복을 (입겠는가) / 종교적인 예식에 //

Probably not. //
아마 아닐 것이다 //
뒤에 목적어절 접속사 that이 생략됨
You know / there's appropriate dress / for different occasions and settings. //
여러분은 알고 있다 / 적합한 옷이 있음을 / 다양한 행사와 상황에 //
목적어절 접속사
Skillful learners know / that "putting on the same clothes" won't work / for every class. // 단서1 상황마다 적절한 복장이 있는 것처럼 수업마다 다른 학습 전략이 있음
숙련된 학습자는 알고 있다 / '같은 옷을 입는 것'이 효과가 없을 것임을 / 모든 수업에는 //

They are flexible learners. //
그들은 유연한 학습자이다 //
병렬 구조
They have different strategies / and know when to use them. //
그들은 다양한 전략을 갖고 있으며 / 그것들을 언제 사용해야 하는지 안다 //

They know / that you study for multiple-choice tests differently / than you study for essay tests. // 단서2 시험별로 적절한 학습 방법이 있음
그들은 안다 / 여러분이 선다형 시험은 다르게 공부한다는 것을 / 논술 시험을 위해 공부하는 것과는 //

---

not only A but also B : A뿐만 아니라 B도
And they not only know what to do, / but they also know / how to do it. //
그리고 그들은 무엇을 해야 하는지 알고 있을 뿐만 아니라 / 그들은 또한 알고 있다 / 그것을 어떻게 해야 하는지도 //

• approach ⓥ 접근하다 • tuxedo ⓝ 턱시도 • funeral ⓝ 장례식
• bathing suit 수영복 • religious ⓐ 종교적인
• appropriate ⓐ 적합한, 알맞은 • occasion ⓝ 행사
• setting ⓝ 상황 • skillful ⓐ 숙련된, 능숙한 • flexible ⓐ 유연한
• strategy ⓝ 전략 • multiple-choice test 선다형 시험

대학 생활을 시작할 때 학생들은 우리가 '고무도장 방식'이라고 부르고 싶은 방법을 이용하여, 모든 과목이나, 시험, 학습 과제를 똑같은 방식으로 접근할지도 모른다. 그것을 이런 식으로 생각해 보라. 여러분은 야구 경기에 턱시도를 입고 가겠는가? 장례식에 화려한 드레스를 입고 가겠는가? 종교적인 예식에 수영복을 입고 가겠는가? 아마 아닐 것이다. 다양한 행사와 상황마다 적합한 옷이 있음을 여러분은 알고 있다. 숙련된 학습자는 '같은 옷을 입는 것'이 모든 수업에 효과가 있지는 않을 것임을 알고 있다. 그들은 유연한 학습자이다. 그들은 다양한 전략을 갖고 있으며 그것을 언제 사용해야 하는지 안다. 그들은 선다형 시험은 논술 시험을 위해 공부하는 것과는 다르게 공부한다는 것을 안다. 그리고 그들은 무엇을 해야 하는지 알고 있을 뿐만 아니라, 그것을 어떻게 해야 하는지도 알고 있다.

다음 글의 요지로 가장 적절한 것은?

① 숙련된 학습자는 상황에 맞는 학습 전략을 사용할 줄 안다.
평가 방식에 맞는 학습 전략을 사용해야 함
② 선다형 시험과 논술 시험은 평가의 형태와 목적이 다르다.
두 시험을 위한 공부법이 다름
③ 문화마다 특정 행사와 상황에 맞는 복장 규정이 있다.
복장은 예시로 든 것일 뿐임
④ 학습의 양보다는 학습의 질이 학업 성과를 좌우한다.
학습의 양과 질을 비교한 글이 아님
⑤ 학습 목표가 명확할수록 성취 수준이 높아진다.
목표보다는 방법과 전략이 중요함

왜 정답? ★★☆ [정답률 85%]

• 문제점: 서로 다른 상황에 같은 방식(= 고무도장 방식)으로 접근하는 것
• 해결책: 상황마다 적절한 복장이 있는 것처럼 수업, 시험별로 더 적절한 방법을 사용하기 단서1, 단서2
▶ 상황에 맞는 학습 전략을 사용해야 한다는 것이므로 정답은 ①이다.

왜 오답?

② 서로 다른 시험에 맞는 학습 전략을 세워야 한다는 내용으로, 두 시험을 비교한 글이 아니다.
③ 복장 규정은 예시로 든 것이지 글의 요지는 아니다.
④ 학습의 양과 질이 성과를 좌우한다는 것은 언급되지 않았다.
⑤ 학습 목표가 아닌 적절한 전략이 성취 결과에 영향을 미친다고 했다.

---

23 정답 ① ★관광 산업의 성장 배경

'~함에 따라' 단서1 여러 국가들의 상황이 나아지면서 근로 여건이 개선됨
As the social and economic situation of countries got better, / wage levels and working conditions improved. //
국가들의 사회적, 경제적 상황이 더 나아지면서 / 임금 수준과 근로 여건이 개선되었다 //
수동태 동사
Gradually people were given / more time off. //
점차 사람들은 받게 되었다 / 더 많은 휴가를 // 단서2 사람들도 더 많은 휴가를 받게 됨
가주어
At the same time, / forms of transport improved / and it became faster and cheaper / to get to places. // 단서3 운송 형태가 개선되어 이동이 더 빠르고 저렴해짐
진주어
동시에 / 운송 형태가 개선되었고 / ~이 더 빠르고 더 저렴해졌다 / 장소를 이동하는 것 //

England's industrial revolution / led to many of these changes. //
영국의 산업 혁명이 / 이러한 변화 중 많은 것을 일으켰다 //

Railways, / in the nineteenth century, / opened up now famous seaside resorts / such as Blackpool and Brighton. //
철도는 / 19세기에 / 현재 유명한 해안가 리조트가 들어서게 했다 / Blackpool과 Brighton 같은

With the railways / came many large hotels. //
(전치사구가 앞에 오면서 주어와 동사가 도치됨)
철도가 생기면서 / 많은 대형 호텔이 생겨났다 //

In Canada, / for example, / the new coast-to-coast railway system made possible / the building of such famous hotels / as Banff Springs and Chateau Lake Louise in the Rockies. //
캐나다에서는 / 예를 들어 / 새로운 대륙 횡단 철도 시스템이 가능하게 했다 / 그런 유명한 호텔의 건설을 / 로키산맥의 Banff Springs와 Chateau Lake Louise 같은 //

Later, / the arrival of air transport / opened up more of the world / and led to tourism growth. //
(병렬 구조) **단서 4** 항공 운송은 관광 산업을 성장시킴
이후에 / 항공 운송의 출현은 / 세계의 더 많은 곳(으로 가는 길)을 열어 주었고 / 관광 산업의 성장을 이끌었다 //

- economic ⓐ 경제의 · wage ⓝ 임금, 급료
- condition ⓝ 여건, 조건 · gradually ⓐⓓ 점차
- transport ⓝ 운송, 수송 · industrial ⓐ 산업의
- revolution ⓝ 혁명 · railway ⓝ 철도
- open up ~을 가능하게 하다 · seaside ⓐ 해안가의
- coast-to-coast ⓐ 대륙 횡단의 · arrival ⓝ 출현 · factor ⓝ 요인
- expansion ⓝ 확장, 확대 · discomfort ⓝ 불편함
- destination ⓝ 목적지 · impact ⓝ 영향

국가들의 사회적, 경제적 상황이 더 나아지면서, 임금 수준과 근로 여건이 개선되었다. 점차 사람들은 더 많은 휴가를 받게 되었다. 동시에, 운송 형태가 개선되었고 장소를 이동하는 것이 더 빠르고 더 저렴해졌다. 영국의 산업 혁명이 이러한 변화 중 많은 것을 일으켰다. 19세기에, 철도로 인해 Blackpool과 Brighton 같은 현재 유명한 해안가 리조트가 들어서게 되었다. 철도가 생기면서 많은 대형 호텔이 생겨났다. 예를 들어, 캐나다에서는 새로운 대륙 횡단 철도 시스템이 로키산맥의 Banff Springs와 Chateau Lake Louise 같은 유명한 호텔의 건설을 가능하게 했다. 이후에 항공 운송의 출현은 세계의 더 많은 곳으로 가는 길을 열어 주었고 관광 산업의 성장을 이끌었다.

다음 글의 주제로 가장 적절한 것은?

① factors that caused tourism expansion
관광 확대를 야기한 요인들 사회적, 경제적 상황 개선으로 인한 관광 확대에 대한 내용임
② discomfort at a popular tourist destination
유명한 관광지에서의 불편함 불편함은 언급되지 않음
③ importance of tourism in society and economy
사회와 경제에서 관광의 중요성 관광의 중요성이 아닌 확대가 주제임
④ negative impacts of tourism on the environment
관광이 환경에 미치는 부정적 영향들 환경에 어떤 영향을 미쳤는지는 알 수 없음
⑤ various types of tourism and their characteristics
다양한 종류의 관광과 그 특징들 관광 산업 성장에 관한 내용임

＞왜 정답? ★★★ [정답률 49%]

- 국가들의 사회적, 경제적 상황이 나아지면서 임금 수준과 근로 여건이 개선되었다. **단서 1**
  → 개인들은 더 많은 휴가를 받게 됨 **단서 2**
- 운송 형태도 개선되어 이동이 더 빠르고 저렴해졌다. **단서 3**
  → 철도와 항공 운송의 출현이 관광 산업의 성장을 이끌었음 **단서 4**

⇒ 여러 국가의 상황이 나아지면서 발생한 연쇄적인 결과로 관광이 확대되었음
▶ 따라서 글의 주제로는 ① '관광 확대를 야기한 요인들'이 가장 적절하다.

＞왜 오답?

② 유명한 관광지에서 마주하게 되는 불편함에 대해서는 언급하지 않았다.
③ 관광의 중요성이 아닌 확대가 주제이다.
④ 환경에 미치는 부정적 영향에 대해서는 언급하지 않았다.
⑤ 관광의 종류가 아닌 관광 산업의 성장에 대한 내용이다. (▶◀ 이유: 해안가 리조트, 호텔 등은 예시일 뿐 관광의 종류와 특징을 설명하는 글이 아니다.)

---

24 정답 ② ＊성공이 불러올 수 있는 문제점

Success can lead you / off your intended path / and into a comfortable rut. // **단서 1** 성공은 틀에 박힌 편안한 생활로 이끌 수 있음
(전치사구의 병렬 구조)
성공은 여러분을 이끌 수 있다 / 여러분이 의도한 길에서 벗어나 / 틀에 박힌 편안한 생활로 //

If you are good at something / and are well rewarded for doing it, / you may want to keep doing it / even if you stop enjoying it. //
(부사절 접속사(양보))
여러분이 어떤 일을 잘하고 / 그것을 하는 것에 대한 보상을 잘 받는다면 / 계속 그것을 하고 싶을 수도 있다 / 그것을 즐기지 않게 되더라도 //

The danger is / that one day you look around and realize / you're so deep in this comfortable rut / that you can no longer see the sun / or breathe fresh air; /
(주격 보어절 접속사) (so ~ that ...: 너무 ~해서 ...하다)
위험한 점은 ~이다 / 어느 날 여러분이 주변을 둘러보고 깨닫게 된다는 것 / 자신이 틀에 박힌 이 편안한 생활에 너무나 깊이 빠져 있어서 / 더는 태양을 보거나 / 신선한 공기를 호흡할 수 없다는 것을 /

the sides of the rut / have become so slippery / that it would take a superhuman effort / to climb out; / and, effectively, you're stuck. // **단서 2** 틀에 박힌 생활에서 빠져나오려면 초인적인 노력이 필요함
(so ~ that ...: 너무 ~해서 ...하다)
그 틀에 박힌 생활의 양쪽 면이 / 너무나 미끄럽게 되어 / 초인적인 노력이 필요할 것이다 / 기어올라 나오려면 / 그리고 사실상 여러분이 꼼짝할 수 없다는 것을 //

And it's a situation / that many working people worry / they're in now. //
(동격절 접속사)
그리고 그것은 상황이다 / 많은 근로자가 걱정하는 / 현재 자신이 처해 있다고 //

The poor employment market / has left them feeling locked / in what may be a secure, or even well-paying / — but ultimately unsatisfying — job. // **단서 3** 안정적이지만 불만족스러운 일자리에 갇혀 있다고 느끼게 됨
(선행사를 포함하는 관계대명사)
열악한 고용 시장이 / 그들을 갇혀 있다고 느끼게 해 놓았다 / 안정적이거나 심지어 보수가 좋을 수도 있지만 / 궁극적으로는 만족스럽지 못한 일자리에 //

- lead ⓥ 이끌다 · intend ⓥ 의도하다 · path ⓝ 길
- reward ⓥ 보상하다 · realize ⓥ 깨닫다 · breathe ⓥ 호흡하다
- slippery ⓐ 미끄러운 · superhuman ⓐ 초인적인
- effectively ⓐⓓ 사실상, 실제로 · employment ⓝ 고용
- secure ⓐ 안정적인 · ultimately ⓐⓓ 궁극적으로
- unsatisfying ⓐ 만족스럽지 못한 · trap ⓝ 함정, 덫
- influential ⓐ 영향력 있는

성공은 여러분을 의도한 길에서 벗어나 틀에 박힌 편안한 생활로 이끌 수 있다. 여러분이 어떤 일을 잘하고 그것을 하는 것에 대한 보상을 잘 받는다면, 그것을 즐기지 않게 되더라도 계속 그것을 하고 싶을 수도 있다. 위험한 점은 어느 날 여러분이 주변을 둘러보고, 자신이 틀에 박힌 이 편안한 생활에 너무나 깊이 빠져 있어서 더는 태양을 보거나 신선한 공기를 호흡할 수 없으며, 그 틀에 박힌 생활의 양쪽 면이 너무나 미끄럽게 되어 기어올라 나오려면 초인적인 노력이 필요할 것이고, 사실상 자신이 꼼짝할 수 없다는 것을 깨닫게 된다는 것이다. 그리고 그것은 많은 근로자가 현재 자신이 처해 있다고 걱정하는 상황이다. 열악한 고용 시장이 그들을 안정적이거나 심지어 보수가 좋을 수도 있지만, 궁극적으로는 만족스럽지 못한 일자리에 갇혀 있다고 느끼게 해 놓았다.

다음 글의 제목으로 가장 적절한 것은?

① Don't Compete with Yourself 현실에 안주하지 말라는 내용임
자신과 경쟁하지 말라
② A Trap of a Successful Career
성공적인 커리어의 함정 성공적인 커리어를 가졌을 때 야기될 수 있는 문제점에 관한 내용임
③ Create More Jobs for Young People
젊은이들을 위한 더 많은 직업을 만들어라 직업이 부족하다는 내용이 아님
④ What Difficult Jobs Have in Common
어려운 직업들이 공통으로 갖는 것 어려운 직업들에 관한 내용은 언급되지 않음
⑤ A Road Map for an Influential Employer
영향력 있는 고용주를 위한 지침 영향력 있는 고용주가 되라는 내용이 아님

왜 정답? ✱✱❋ [정답률 71%]

> • 성공은 틀에 박힌 편안한 생활로 이끌 수 있음 **단서1**
> • 틀에 박힌 생활에서 빠져나오려면 초인적인 노력이 필요함 **단서2**
> • 안정적이지만 불만족스러운 일자리에 갇혀 있다고 느끼게 됨 **단서3**

➡ 성공적인 커리어로 인해 편안한 생활에 오히려 갇히게 된다는 내용이므로
정답은 ② '성공적인 커리어의 함정'이다.

왜 오답?

① 자신과 경쟁하지 말라는 내용이 아니다.
③ 젊은이들을 위한 더 많은 일자리를 만들라는 내용이 아니다.
④ 어려운 직업들에 대한 내용은 없다.
⑤ 고용주에게만 국한된 내용이 아니다.

---

25 정답 ⑤ ✱ 한국의 출생과 사망 인구

The above graph shows / the number of births and deaths / in
Korea / from 2016 to 2021. //
위 그래프는 보여준다 / 출생자 수와 사망자 수를 / 한국에서의 / 2016년부터 2021년까지 //

① The number of births continued to decrease / throughout the
whole period. //
출생자 수는 계속 감소했다 / 전체 기간 내내 //

_{단수 주어} _{단수 동사}
② The gap / between the number of births and deaths / was the
largest in 2016. //
차이는 / 출생자와 사망자 수 사이의 / 2016년에 가장 컸다 //

_{'~의 수'}
③ In 2019, / the gap / between the number of births and deaths
_{단수 동사}   _{= the number}
/ was the smallest, / with the number of births slightly larger /
than that of deaths. //
2019년에는 / 차이가 / 출생자와 사망자 수 사이의 / 가장 작았다 / 출생자 수가 약간 더 큰
채로 / 사망자의 수보다 //

_{전치사}
④ The number of deaths increased steadily / during the whole
period, / except the period from 2018 to 2019. //
사망자 수는 꾸준히 증가했다 / 전체 기간 동안 / 2018년과 2019년까지의 기간을 제외하고 //

_{= the number}
⑤ In 2021(→ 2020), / the number of deaths was larger / than that
of births / for the first time. // **단서** 2020년에도 사망자가 출생자보다 많았음
2021년(→ 2020년)에는 / 사망자 수가 더 컸다 / 출생자 수보다 / 처음으로 //

• birth ⓝ 출생   • decrease ⓥ 감소하다   • period ⓝ 기간
• gap ⓝ 차이   • slightly ⓐⓓ 약간   • increase ⓥ 증가하다
• steadily ⓐⓓ 꾸준히   • except ⓟⓡⓔⓟ ~을 제외하고

위 그래프는 2016년부터 2021년까지 한국에서의 출생자 수와 사망자 수를
보여준다. ① 출생자 수는 전체 기간 내내 계속 감소했다. ② 출생자 수와
사망자 수 사이의 차이는 2016년에 가장 컸다. ③ 2019년에는 출생자 수와
사망자 수 사이의 차이가 가장 작았는데, 출생자 수가 사망자 수보다 약간 더
컸다. ④ 사망자 수는 2018년과 2019년까지의 기간을 제외하고 전체 기간 동안
꾸준히 증가했다. ⑤ 2021년(→ 2020년)에는 처음으로 사망자 수가 출생자
수보다 더 컸다.

다음 도표의 내용과 일치하지 않는 것은?

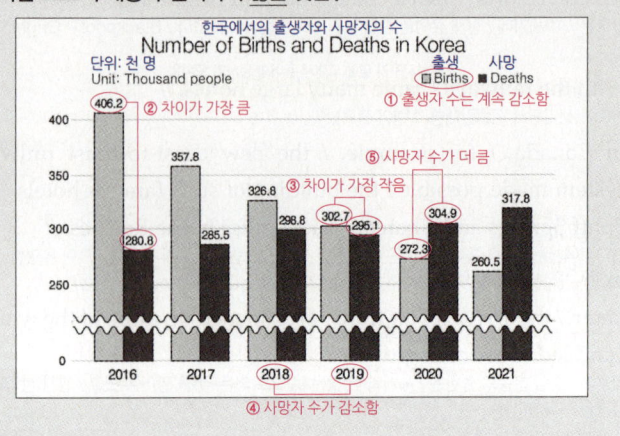

왜 정답? ✱✱❋ [정답률 77%]

사망자의 수가 출생자의 수보다 커지기 시작한 해는 2021년이 아니라 2020년이므로
도표의 내용과 일치하지 않는 것은 ⑤이다.

왜 오답?

① 2016년에서 2021년까지 출생자의 수는 계속 감소했다.
② 출생자 수와 사망자 수 사이의 차이는 2016년에 가장 컸다.
③ 2019년에는 출생자 수와 사망자 수 사이의 차이가 가장 작았는데, 출생자 수가
사망자 수보다 약간 더 컸다.
④ 사망자 수는 2018년에서 2019년 사이에만 소폭 줄었고, 이외에는 매년 증가했다.

---

26 정답 ⑤ ✱ Lilian Bland의 생애

Lilian Bland was born / in Kent, England / in 1878. //
Lilian Bland는 태어났다 / 영국 Kent에서 / 1878년에 //

_{spend+시간+-ing : ~하는 데 시간을 보내다}
Unlike most other girls at the time / she wore trousers / and
spent her time enjoying adventurous activities / like horse
riding and hunting. // **①의 단서** 승마와 사냥 같은 모험적인 활동을 즐김
그 당시 대부분의 다른 여자아이와 달리 / 그녀는 바지를 입었고 / 모험적인 활동을 즐기며
시간을 보냈다 / 승마와 사냥 같은 //

Lilian began her career / as a sports and wildlife photographer /
for British newspapers. // **②의 단서** 스포츠와 야생 동물 사진작가로 경력을 시작함
Lilian은 자신의 경력을 시작했다 / 스포츠와 야생 동물 사진작가로 / 영국 신문사의 //

In 1910 / she became the first woman / to design, build, and fly
her own airplane. // **③의 단서** 자신의 비행기를 설계하고 제작함
1910년에 / 그녀는 최초의 여성이 되었다 / 자신의 비행기를 설계하고, 제작하고, 비행한 //

_{'~하기 위해'}
In order to persuade her / to try a slightly safer activity, / Lilian's
dad bought her a car. //
그녀를 설득하기 위해 / 약간 더 안전한 활동을 하도록 / Lilian의 아버지는 그녀에게 자동차를
사주었다 //

_{end up -ing : 결국 ~하게 되다}
Soon Lilian was a master driver / and ended up working / as a
car dealer. // **④의 단서** 자동차 판매원으로도 일함
곧 Lilian은 뛰어난 운전자가 되었고 / 결국 일하게 되었다 / 자동차 판매원으로 //

_{병렬 구조}
She never went back to flying / but lived a long and exciting life
nonetheless. //
그녀는 결코 비행으로 돌아가지 않았지만 / 그렇더라도 오랫동안 흥미진진한 삶을 살았다 //

_{자동사}
She married, / moved to Canada, / and had a kid. //
그녀는 결혼하여 / 캐나다로 이주했고 / 아이를 낳았다 //

Eventually, / she moved back to England, / and lived there / for
the rest of her life. // **⑤의 단서** 캐나다가 아니라 영국에서 생의 마지막 기간을 보냄
결국 / 그녀는 영국으로 돌아와 / 거기서 보냈다 / 생의 마지막 기간을 //

- trousers ⓝ 바지　　• adventurous ⓐ 모험적인　　• activity ⓝ 활동
- wildlife ⓝ 야생 동물　　• persuade ⓥ 설득하다　　• slightly ⓐⓓ 약간
- dealer ⓝ 판매원　　• nonetheless ⓐⓓ 그렇더라도

Lilian Bland는 1878년 영국 Kent에서 태어났다. 그 당시 대부분의 다른 여자아이와 달리 그녀는 바지를 입었고, 승마와 사냥 같은 모험적인 활동을 즐기며 시간을 보냈다. Lilian은 영국 신문사의 스포츠와 야생 동물 사진작가로 자신의 경력을 시작했다. 1910년에 그녀는 자신의 비행기를 설계하고, 제작하고, 비행한 최초의 여성이 되었다. 약간 더 안전한 활동을 하도록 그녀를 설득하기 위해, Lilian의 아버지는 그녀에게 자동차를 사주었다. 곧 Lilian은 뛰어난 운전자가 되었고 결국 자동차 판매원으로 일하게 되었다. 그녀는 결코 비행을 다시 시작하지 않았지만, 그렇더라도 오랫동안 흥미진진한 삶을 살았다. 그녀는 결혼하여 캐나다로 이주했고, 아이를 낳았다. 결국 그녀는 영국으로 돌아와 거기서 생의 마지막 기간을 보냈다.

> **Lilian Bland에 관한 다음 글의 내용과 일치하지 <u>않는</u> 것은?**
> ① 승마와 사냥 같은 모험적인 활동을 즐겼다.
> spent her time enjoying adventurous activities like horse riding and hunting
> ② 스포츠와 야생 동물 사진작가로 경력을 시작했다.
> Lilian began her career as a sports and wildlife photographer
> ③ 자신의 비행기를 설계하고 제작했다.
> the first woman to design, build, and fly her own airplane
> ④ 자동차 판매원으로 일하기도 했다.
> Soon Lilian was a master driver and ended up working as a car dealer.
> ⑤ 캐나다에서 생의 마지막 기간을 보냈다.
> Eventually, she moved back to England, and lived there for the rest of her life.

⟩왜 정답 ? ✿✾✾ [정답률 92%]

Lilian은 결혼하여 캐나다로 이주했으나 생의 마지막은 영국에서 보냈다고 (Eventually, she moved back to England, and lived there for the rest of her life.) 했으므로 ⑤은 글의 내용과 일치하지 않는다.

⟩왜 오답 ?

① 승마와 사냥 같은 모험적인 활동을 즐겼다고 했다. (spent her time enjoying adventurous activities like horse riding and hunting)
② 스포츠와 야생 동물 사진작가로 경력을 시작했다고 했다. (Lilian began her career as a sports and wildlife photographer)
③ 자신의 비행기를 설계하고 제작했다고 했다. (the first woman to design, build, and fly her own airplane)
④ 자동차 판매원으로 일하기도 했다고 했다. (ended up working as a car dealer)

27 정답 ③ ✱ 기사 모집 공고문

Call for Articles /
기사 모집 /

Do you want / to get your stories **published**? //
목적격 보어(과거분사)
여러분은 원하나요 / 여러분의 이야기가 출간되기를 //

New Dream Magazine is looking for future writers! //
〈New Dream Magazine〉은 미래의 작가를 찾고 있습니다 //

This event is open to anyone / **aged** 13 to 18. //
앞에 주격 관계대명사와 be동사가 생략됨
이 행사는 모두에게 열려있습니다 / 13세에서 18세까지의 //
①의 단서 13세에서 18세까지 누구나 참여할 수 있음

Articles /
기사 /

• Length of writing: / 300 – 325 words /
원고의 길이 / 300~325단어 /

• Articles should also include / high-quality color photos. //
기사에는 또한 포함해야 합니다 / 고화질 컬러 사진을 // **②의 단서** 고화질 컬러 사진을 포함해야 함

Rewards /
사례금 /

• Five cents per word /
단어당 5센트 /

• Five dollars per photo / **③의 단서** 사진 한 장당 5달러의 사례금을 받음
사진당 5달러 /

Notes /
주의 사항 /

• You should send us / **your phone number** / together with your
간접목적어　　　직접 목적어
writing. // **④의 단서** 원고와 함께 전화번호를 보내야 함
여러분은 우리에게 보내야 합니다 / 여러분의 전화번호를 / 원고와 함께 //

• Please email your writing to us / at article@ndmag.com. //
여러분의 원고를 이메일로 우리에게 보내주세요 / article@ndmag.com으로 //
⑤의 단서 원고는 이메일로 제출해야 함

- article ⓝ 기사　　• publish ⓥ 출간하다　　• look for ~을 찾다
- length ⓝ 길이　　• include ⓥ 포함하다　　• reward ⓝ 사례금

기사 모집

여러분의 이야기가 출간되기를 원하시나요? 〈New Dream Magazine〉은 미래의 작가를 찾고 있습니다! 이 행사는 13세에서 18세까지 누구나 참여할 수 있습니다.

기사
• 원고 길이: 300~325단어
• 기사에는 또한 고화질 컬러 사진이 포함되어야 합니다.

사례금
• 단어당 5센트
• 사진당 5달러

주의 사항
• 여러분은 전화번호를 원고와 함께 보내야 합니다.
• 원고를 이메일 article@ndmag.com으로 보내세요.

> **Call for Articles에 관한 다음 안내문의 내용과 일치하지 <u>않는</u> 것은?**
> ① 13세에서 18세까지의 누구나 참여할 수 있다.
> This event is open to anyone aged 13 to 18.
> ② 기사는 고화질 컬러 사진을 포함해야 한다.
> Articles should also include high-quality color photos.
> ③ 사진 한 장에 5센트씩 지급한다.
> Five dollars per photo
> ④ 전화번호를 원고와 함께 보내야 한다.
> You should send us your phone number together with your writing.
> ⑤ 원고를 이메일로 제출해야 한다.
> Please email your writing to us at article@ndmag.com.

⟩왜 정답 ? ✿✾✾ [정답률 93%]

사례금은 사진당 5달러라고(Five dollars per photo) 했으므로 사진 한 장에 5센트씩 지급한다고 한 ③은 안내문의 내용과 일치하지 않는다.

⟩왜 오답 ?

① 13세에서 18세 사이라면 누구나 참여할 수 있다. (This event is open to anyone aged 13 to 18.)
② 기사는 고화질 컬러 사진을 포함해야 한다. (Articles should also include high-quality color photos.)
④ 원고를 보낼 때 전화번호를 함께 보내야 한다. (You should send us your phone number together with your writing.)
⑤ 원고 제출은 이메일로 하라고 했다. (Please email your writing to us at article@ndmag.com.)

28 정답 ④ ✱ 롤러스케이트장 홍보

Greenhill Roller Skating /
Greenhill 롤러스케이팅 /

Join us / for your chance **to enjoy** roller skating! //
형용사적 용법(chance 수식)
함께 해요 / 롤러스케이팅을 즐길 기회를 //

• Place: / Greenhill Park, 351 Cypress Avenue /
장소 / Greenhill Park, 351 Cypress Avenue /

• Dates: / Friday, April 7 – Sunday, April 9 /
일자 / 4월 7일 금요일~4월 9일 일요일 /

• Time: / 9 a.m. – 6 p.m. / **①의 단서** 운영 시간은 오전 9시부터 오후 6시까지임
시간 / 오전 9시~오후 6시 /

• Fee: / $8 per person / for a 50-minute session //
요금 / 1인당 8달러 / 50분 수업에 // **②의 단서** 입장료는 50분 기준 1인당 8달러임

Details /
세부 사항 /

– Admission will be on a first-come, first-served basis / with no reservations. // ❸의 단서 선착순 입장으로 별도의 예약은 불필요함
입장은 선착순입니다 / 예약 없이 //

– Children / under the age of 10 / must **be accompanied** by an adult. // ❹의 단서 10세 미만의 어린이는 어른 동행 필수임 *(수동태 동사)*
어린이는 / 10세 미만의 / 어른과 동행해야 합니다 //

– We will lend you our roller skates / for free. // ❺의 단서 롤러 스케이트 대여는 무료임
우리는 롤러스케이트를 빌려줍니다 / 무료로 //

Contact the Community Center / for more information / at 013-234-6114 //
커뮤니티 센터로 연락하세요 / 더 많은 정보를 위해서 / 013-234-6114로 //

- fee ⓝ 요금 • session ⓝ 수업 • admission ⓝ 입장
- first-come, first-served basis 선착순 • reservation ⓝ 예약
- accompany ⓥ 동행하다 • lend ⓥ 빌려주다
- contact ⓥ 연락하다

Greenhill 롤러스케이팅

롤러스케이팅을 즐길 기회를 함께 해요!
- 장소: Greenhill Park, 351 Cypress Avenue
- 일자: 4월 7일 금요일~4월 9일 일요일
- 시간: 오전 9시~오후 6시
- 요금: 50분 수업에 1인당 8달러

세부 사항
– 입장은 예약 없이 선착순입니다.
– 10세 미만의 어린이는 어른과 동행해야 합니다.
– 롤러스케이트는 무료로 빌려줍니다.
더 많은 정보를 위해서 커뮤니티 센터 013-234-6114로 연락하세요.

Greenhill Roller Skating에 관한 다음 안내문의 내용과 일치하는 것은?
① 오전 9시부터 오후 9시까지 운영한다. Time: 9 a.m. - 6 p.m.
② 이용료는 시간 제한 없이 1인당 8달러이다. $8 per person for a 50-minute session
③ 입장하려면 예약이 필요하다. Admission will be on a first-come, first-served basis with no reservations.
④ 10세 미만 어린이는 어른과 동행해야 한다. Children under the age of 10 must be accompanied by an adult.
⑤ 추가 요금을 내면 롤러스케이트를 빌려준다. We will lend you our roller skates for free.

왜 정답? ✱❀❀ [정답률 90%]
10세 미만 어린이는 어른과 동행해야 한다고(Children under the age of 10 must be accompanied by an adult.) 했으므로 안내문의 내용과 일치하는 것은 ④이다.

왜 오답?
① 오전 9시부터 오후 6시까지 운영한다고 했다. (Time: 9 a.m. - 6 p.m.)
② 입장료는 50분 수업에 1인당 8달러라고 했다. ($8 per person for a 50-minute session)
③ 선착순 입장이므로 예약은 필요 없다고 했다. (Admission will be on a first-come, first-served basis with no reservations.)
⑤ 롤러스케이트 대여는 무료로 가능하다고 했다. (We will lend you our roller skates for free.)

다음 글의 밑줄 친 부분 중, 어법상 틀린 것은? [3점]

The most noticeable human characteristic *(주어)* / projected onto animals / is ① that *(주격 보어절 접속사)* they can talk / in human language. //
가장 눈에 띄는 인간의 특징은 / 동물에게 투영된 / 동물들이 대화할 수 있다는 것이다 / 인간의 언어로 //

Physically, / animal cartoon characters and toys / ② made *(앞에 주격 관계대명사와 be동사가 생략됨 / 문장의 동사)* after animals / **are** also most often deformed / in such a way as to resemble humans. //
신체적으로 / 동물 만화 캐릭터와 장난감은 / 동물을 본떠 만들어진 / 또한 변형되는 경우가 가장 흔하다 / 인간을 닮게 하는 그런 방식으로 //

This is achieved by ③ **showing** *(전치사 / 동명사(전치사의 목적어))* them / with humanlike facial features / and deformed front legs / **to resemble** *(부사적 용법(목적))* human hands. //
이것은 그것들을 보여줌으로써 달성된다 / 인간과 같은 얼굴 특징과 / 변형된 앞다리로 / 사람의 손을 닮게 //

In more recent animated movies / the trend **has been** *(현재완료(계속))* to show the animals / in a more "natural" way. //
더 최근의 만화 영화에서 / 추세는 동물을 묘사하는 것이었다 / 더 '자연스러운' 방식으로 //

However, / they still use their front legs / ④ **like** *(전치사)* human hands / (for example, / lions can pick up and lift small objects, / with one paw), /
그러나 / 그것들은 여전히 앞다리를 사용한다 / 사람의 손처럼 / (예를 들어 / 사자가 작은 물체를 집어 들어 올릴 수 있는 것처럼 / 한 발로) /

and they still talk / with an appropriate facial expression. //
그리고 그것들은 여전히 이야기한다 / 적절한 표정을 지으며 //

A general strategy *(핵심 주어(단수))* / that is used to make the animal characters more emotionally appealing, / both to children and adults, / *(단서 핵심 주어가 단수이므로 동사도 단수 동사 is가 와야 함)*
일반적인 전략은 / 동물 캐릭터를 더 감정적으로 매력적이게 만들기 위해 이용되는 / 아이와 어른 모두에게 /

⑤ **are**(→ is) to give them / enlarged and deformed childlike features. //
그것들에게 부여하는 것이다 / 확대되고 변형된 어린이 같은 특징을 //

- noticeable ⓐ 눈에 띄는 • characteristic ⓝ 특징, 특성
- project ⓥ 투영하다 • physically 〔ad〕 신체적으로
- cartoon ⓝ 만화 • resemble ⓥ ~와 닮다 • achieve ⓥ 달성하다
- facial ⓐ 얼굴의 • feature ⓝ 특징 • animated ⓐ 만화 영화의
- appropriate ⓐ 적절한 • strategy ⓝ 전략
- emotionally 〔ad〕 감정적으로 • appealing ⓐ 매력적인
- enlarge ⓥ 확대하다 • childlike ⓐ 어린이 같은

동물에게 투영된 가장 눈에 띄는 인간의 특징은 동물이 인간의 언어로 대화할 수 있다는 점이다. 신체적으로도, 동물 만화 캐릭터와 동물을 본떠 만든 장난감은 또한 인간을 닮게 하는 방식으로 변형되는 경우가 가장 많다. 이것은 인간과 같은 얼굴 특징과 사람의 손을 닮게 변형된 앞다리를 가지고 있는 것으로 그것들을 보여줌으로써 달성된다. 더 최근의 만화 영화에서 추세는 동물을 더 '자연스러운' 방식으로 묘사하는 것이었다. 그러나 그것들은 (예를 들어 사자가 한 발로 작은 물체를 집어 들어 올릴 수 있는 것처럼) 여전히 사람의 손처럼 앞다리를 사용하고, 여전히 적절한 표정을 지으며 이야기한다. 동물 캐릭터를 아이와 어른 모두에게 더 감정적으로 매력적이게 만들기 위해 이용되는 일반적인 전략은 그것들에 확대되고 변형된 어린이 같은 특징을 부여하는 것이다.

왜 정답? ✽✽✽ [정답률 66%]

⑤ 주어는 단수인데 복수 동사가 쓰였다!

> 핵심 주어(단수)　　주격 관계대명사
> A general strategy / [that is used to make the animal characters more emotionally appealing, / both to children and adults,] / ⑤ are(→ is) to give them / enlarged and deformed childlike features. //
> 단수 동사　간접목적어
> 동사의 수는 주어의 수와 일치시켜야 함
> 직접목적어

(단서) 동사에 밑줄이 있으므로

(발상) 주어를 찾아 그 수가 일치하는지 확인한다.

(해결) that이 이끄는 관계대명사절을 제외하면 문장의 핵심 주어는 A general strategy로 단수이다. 따라서 동사는 are가 아니라 단수 동사인 is가 와야 한다.

(개념) 주어를 꾸미는 수식어구와 상관없이 핵심 주어의 수에 동사의 수를 일치시킨다.

왜 오답?

① 접속사 that 뒤에는 완전한 절이 온다.

> 문장의 주어
> The most noticeable human characteristic / projected onto animals / is ① that they can talk / in human language. //
> 문장의 동사
> 주격 보어절을 이끄는 접속사　완전한 1형식 문장

접속사로 쓰인 that은 완전한 절을 이끈다. (개념)
that 뒤에 주어 they, 자동사 can talk로 구성된 완전한 1형식 문장이 이어진다. (단서)
주격 보어절을 이끄는 접속사 that이 알맞게 쓰였다.

② 주격 관계대명사와 be동사는 함께 생략할 수 있다.

> Physically, / animal cartoon characters and toys / ② [made after animals] / are also most often deformed / in such a way as to resemble humans. //
> 선행사　which[that] are
> 문장의 동사

주격 관계대명사절의 동사가 be동사일 경우 주격 관계대명사와 함께 생략할 수 있다. (개념)
뒤에 문장의 진짜 동사 are deformed가 오므로 made는 주격 관계대명사절의 동사임을 알 수 있다. (단서)
동물을 본떠 '만들어진' 것이므로 수동태 동사 are made의 be동사 are와 주격 관계대명사 which[that]가 생략된 문장이다.

③ 전치사 뒤에는 명사에 해당하는 어구가 온다.

> 전치사　동명사
> This is achieved by ③ showing them / with humanlike facial features / and deformed front legs / to resemble human hands. //
> 수식어구(제외하고 생각하기)

전치사의 목적어로 동사가 올 때는 동명사의 형태로 온다. (개념)
showing은 전치사 by의 목적어 자리에 왔다. (단서)
'~함으로써'라는 의미를 완성하면서 전치사 by의 목적어로 동명사 showing은 알맞게 쓰였다.

④ like가 전치사로 쓰였다.

> 주어　　동사　　목적어　　전치사
> However, / they still use their front legs / ④ like human hands / (for example, / lions can pick up and lift small objects, / with one paw), / and they still talk / with an appropriate facial expression. //
> 제외하고 생각하기

like는 동사와 전치사로 쓰일 수 있는데, 앞에 동사 use가 왔다. (개념)
use와 like 사이에 접속사가 없으므로 like는 동사가 아니라 전치사로 쓰였다. (단서)
'사람의 손처럼'이라는 의미를 완성하는 전치사로 like는 알맞게 쓰였다.

30 정답 ④　✽고객의 수요 파악

다음 글의 밑줄 친 부분 중, 문맥상 낱말의 쓰임이 적절하지 않은 것은? [3점]

> 주어
> The major philosophical shift / in the idea of selling / came /
> 동사
> 주요한 철학적 변화가 / 판매 개념에 / 일어났다 /

when industrial societies became more affluent, / more competitive, / and more geographically spread out / during the 1940s and 1950s. //
산업 사회가 더 부유하게 되면서 / 더 경쟁적이고 / 더 지리적으로 퍼져 나가게 (되면서) / 1940년대와 1950년대 동안 /

> forced의 목적어와 목적격 보어(to부정사)
> This forced business to develop / ① closer relations with buyers and clients, /
> 이것은 기업이 발전시키게 했다 / 구매자 및 고객과 더 긴밀한 관계를 /
> 계속적 용법의 주격 관계대명사　　가주어　　진주어
> which in turn made business realize / that it was not enough to produce a quality product / at a reasonable price. //
> 그리고 이것은 결과적으로 기업이 깨닫게 했다 / 양질의 제품을 생산하는 것으로는 충분하지 않다는 것을 / 합리적인 가격에 //

(단서 1) 합리적인 가격에 양질의 제품을 생산하는 것으로는 충분하지 않음

> 가주어　　진주어
> In fact, / it was equally ② essential / to deliver products / that customers actually wanted. //
> 사실 / ~이 마찬가지로 매우 중요했다 / 제품을 내놓는 것 / 고객이 실제로 원하는 //

Henry Ford produced / his best-selling T-model Ford / in one color only (black) in 1908, / but in modern societies / this was no longer ③ possible. //
Henry Ford는 생산했다 / 자신의 가장 많이 팔렸던 T-모델 Ford를 / 1908년에 단 하나의 색상(검은색)으로만 / 하지만 현대 사회에서는 / 이것이 더 이상 가능하지 않았다 //

The modernization of society / led to a marketing revolution / that ④ strengthened(→ destroyed) the view / that production would create its own demand. //
사회의 현대화는 / 마케팅 혁명으로 이어졌다 / 견해를 강화하는(→ 파괴하는) / 생산이 그 자체의 수요를 창출할 것이라는 //

> 핵심 주어　　　　(단서 2) 이전과는 다른 곳에 기업은 집중함
> Customers, / and the desire to ⑤ meet / their diverse and often complex needs, / became the focus of business. //
> 동사
> 고객과 / 충족하고자 하는 욕망이 / 그들의 다양하고 흔히 복잡한 욕구를 / 기업의 초점이 되었다 //

- major ⓐ 주요한
- philosophical ⓐ 철학적인
- shift ⓝ 변화
- industrial ⓐ 산업의
- competitive ⓐ 경쟁적인
- geographically ⓐⓓ 지리적으로
- client ⓝ 고객
- quality ⓐ 질 좋은
- reasonable ⓐ 합리적인
- equally ⓐⓓ 마찬가지로
- essential ⓐ 매우 중요한
- modernization ⓝ 현대화
- revolution ⓝ 혁명
- strengthen ⓥ 강화하다
- demand ⓝ 수요
- desire ⓝ 욕망, 욕구
- diverse ⓐ 다양한
- complex ⓐ 복잡한

2023. 3
3회

산업 사회가 1940년대와 1950년대 동안 더 부유하고, 더 경쟁적이고, 더 지리적으로 퍼져 나가게 되면서 판매 개념에 주요한 철학적 변화가 일어났다. 이것은 기업이 구매자 및 고객과 ① 더 긴밀한 관계를 발전시키게 했고, 결과적으로 기업이 합리적인 가격에 양질의 제품을 생산하는 것으로는 충분하지 않다는 것을 깨닫게 했다. 사실, 고객이 실제로 원하는 제품을 내놓는 것이 마찬가지로 ② 매우 중요했다. 1908년에 Henry Ford는 자신의 가장 많이 팔렸던 T-모델 Ford를 단 하나의 색상(검은색)으로만 생산했지만, 현대 사회에서는 이것이 더 이상 ③ 가능하지 않았다. 사회의 현대화는 생산이 그 자체의 수요를 창출할 것이라는 견해를 ④ 강화하는(→ 파괴하는) 마케팅 혁명으로 이어졌다. 고객과 그들의 다양하고 흔히 복잡한 욕구를 ⑤ 충족하고자 하는 욕망이 기업의 초점이 되었다.

>왜 정답 ? ✱✱✱ [정답률 41%]

④ strengthened 강화하는

> 사회의 현대화는 생산이 그 자체의 수요를 창출할 것이라는 견해를 ④ 강화하는 마케팅 혁명으로 이어졌다.
> 파괴하는

→ 기존에는 생산이 수요를 창출할 것이라고 생각했지만, 현대 사회에서는 인식이 변화되어서 이전과 다른 마케팅 혁명이 일어났다고 했으므로 이전의 견해를 '강화한다'고 하는 것은 자연스럽지 않다.
  ▶ strengthened를 destroyed(파괴하는)와 같은 반의어로 바꿔야 함

>왜 오답 ?

① closer 더 긴밀한

> 이것은 기업이 구매자 및 고객과 ① 더 긴밀한 관계를 발전시키게 했고, 결과적으로 기업이 합리적인 가격에 양질의 제품을 생산하는 것으로는 충분하지 않다는 것을 깨닫게 했다.

→ 합리적인 가격에 양질의 제품을 생산하는 것만으로는 충분하지 않았으므로 기업은 고객과 '더 긴밀한' 관계를 발전시켜야 했을 것이다.
  ▶ closer는 문맥에 맞음

② essential 매우 중요한

> 사실, 고객이 실제로 원하는 제품을 내놓는 것이 마찬가지로 ② 매우 중요했다.

→ 좋은 가격에 좋은 제품을 생산하는 것으로는 충분하지 않다고 했으므로 고객의 요구와 수요를 고려하는 것은 '매우 중요했을' 것이다.
  ▶ essential은 문맥에 맞음

③ possible 가능한

> 1908년에 Henry Ford는 자신의 가장 많이 팔렸던 T-모델 Ford를 단 하나의 색상(검은색)으로만 생산했지만, 현대 사회에서는 이것이 더 이상 ③ 가능하지 않았다.

→ 잘 팔리는 자동차 모델을 한 색상으로 생산했던 과거와는 달리 고객의 요구가 중요해진 현대 사회는 그런 것이 '가능하지' 않았을 것이다.
  ▶ possible은 문맥에 맞음

⑤ meet 충족하다

> 고객과 그들의 다양하고 흔히 복잡한 욕구를 ⑤ 충족하고자 하는 욕망이 기업의 초점이 되었다.

→ 고객의 수요를 파악해서 이에 맞춘 마케팅을 하려고 한다고 했으므로 고객의 복잡한 욕구를 '충족하고자' 하는 것에 기업이 초점을 맞추었을 것이다.
  ▶ meet는 문맥에 맞음

74 자이스토리 전국연합학력평가 고1 영어

---

31 정답 ① ＊이동 방향에 따른 회복 속도의 차이

People differ / in how quickly they can reset their biological clocks / to overcome jet lag, / and the speed of recovery / depends on the **direction** of travel. //
부사적 용법(목적) · 결과절을 잇는 등위접속사
사람마다 서로 다르다 / 자신의 체내 시계를 얼마나 빨리 재설정할 수 있는지 / 시차로 인한 피로감을 극복하기 위해서 / 그리고 그 회복 속도는 / 이동 방향에 달려 있다 //

Generally, / it's easier / to fly westward and lengthen your day / than it is to fly eastward and shorten it. //
가주어 · 진주어의 병렬 구조
일반적으로 / ~이 더 쉽다 / 서쪽으로 비행하여 여러분의 하루를 연장하는 것 / 동쪽으로 비행하여 그것을 단축하는 것보다 //
단서 1 동쪽보다는 서쪽 비행이 피로감을 덜 느끼게 함
단서 2 방향에 따른 시차로 인한 피로감이 경기력에 영향을 줌

This east-west difference in jet lag / is sizable enough / to have an impact / on the performance of sports teams. //
시차로 인한 피로감에서 이러한 동서의 차이는 / 충분히 크다 / 영향을 미칠 만큼 / 스포츠 팀의 경기력에 //

Studies have found / that teams flying westward perform significantly better / than teams flying eastward / in professional baseball and college football. //
목적어절을 이끄는 접속사 · 현재분사구(teams 수식)
연구는 발견했다 / 서쪽으로 비행하는 팀이 상당히 더 잘한다는 것을 / 동쪽으로 비행하는 팀보다 / 프로 야구와 대학 미식축구에서 //

A more recent study / of more than 46,000 Major League Baseball games / found additional evidence / that eastward travel is tougher / than westward travel. //
동격절 접속사 · 비교 표현
더 최근의 연구는 / 46,000 경기가 넘는 메이저 리그 야구 경기에 대한 / 추가적인 증거를 발견했다 / 동쪽으로 이동하는 것이 더 힘들다는 것을 / 서쪽으로 이동하는 것보다 //

- differ ⓥ 다르다 · reset ⓥ 재설정하다 · biological ⓐ 생물체의
- overcome ⓥ 극복하다 · recovery ⓝ 회복
- westward ⓐ̲d̲ 서쪽으로 · lengthen ⓥ 연장하다
- eastward ⓐ̲d̲ 동쪽으로 · sizable ⓐ 큰 · impact ⓝ 영향
- significantly ⓐ̲d̲ 상당히 · additional ⓐ 추가의
- evidence ⓝ 증거 · tough ⓐ 힘든 · purpose ⓝ 목적

시차로 인한 피로감을 극복하기 위해서 자신의 체내 시계를 얼마나 빨리 재설정할 수 있는지는 사람마다 서로 다르며, 그 회복 속도는 이동 **방향**에 달려 있다. 일반적으로 동쪽으로 비행하여 여러분의 하루를 단축하는 것보다 서쪽으로 비행하여 여러분의 하루를 연장하는 것이 더 쉽다. 시차로 인한 피로감에서 이러한 동서의 차이는 스포츠 팀의 경기력에 영향을 미칠 만큼 충분히 크다. 연구에 따르면 서쪽으로 비행하는 팀이 동쪽으로 비행하는 팀보다 프로 야구와 대학 미식축구에서 상당히 더 잘한다. 46,000 경기가 넘는 메이저 리그 야구 경기에 대한 더 최근의 연구는 동쪽으로 이동하는 것이 서쪽으로 이동하는 것보다 더 힘들다는 추가적인 증거를 발견했다.

> 다음 빈칸에 들어갈 말로 가장 적절한 것을 고르시오.
>
> ① direction 동서의 차이는 방향을 의미함
>   방향
> ② purpose 목적이 아닌 방향이 중요함
>   목적
> ③ season 계절이 영향을 미친다는 내용은 없음
>   계절
> ④ length 길이가 아니라 방향이 중요하다고 했음
>   길이
> ⑤ cost 비용에 대한 내용은 없음
>   비용

>왜 정답 ? ✱✱✲ [정답률 60%]

빈칸 문장	시차로 인한 피로감을 극복하기 위해서 자신의 체내 시계를 얼마나 빨리 재설정할 수 있는지는 사람마다 서로 다르며, 그 회복 속도는 이동 ＿＿＿＿＿＿＿ 에 달려 있다.
빈칸 문장 뒤 예시	일반적으로 동쪽으로 비행하여 여러분의 하루를 단축하는 것보다 서쪽으로 비행하여 여러분의 하루를 연장하는 것이 더 쉽다. **단서 1**

→ 빈칸 문장: 시차로 인한 피로감을 회복하는 속도는 이동의 '무엇'에 달려 있다.
→ 빈칸 문장 뒤 예시: 동쪽으로 여행하는 것보다 서쪽으로 여행하여 하루를 연장하는 것이 더 쉽다.

▶ 지구의 자전 방향(서 → 동)과 반대로 여행하는 것이 더 낫다는 것이므로 회복 속도는 이동의 ① '방향'에 달려 있다.

> 왜 오답 ?

② 이동의 목적이 아닌 방향이 중요하다는 내용이다.
③ 계절이 영향을 미친다는 내용은 없었다.
④ 이동의 길이가 아니라 방향이 중요하다고 했다. 주의
⑤ 비용에 대한 내용은 나오지 않았으므로 적절하지 않다.

---

32 정답 ③ * 성취를 위한 시간 활용

If you want the confidence / that comes from achieving / what
(주격 관계대명사) *(선행사를 포함하는 관계대명사)*
you set out to do each day, / then it's important to understand /
(가주어) *(진주어)*
how long things are going to take. //
만약 여러분이 자신감을 원한다면 / 성취함으로써 얻게 되는 / 매일 하고자 착수하는 일을 /
그러면 아는 것이 중요하다 / 일이 얼마나 시간이 걸릴지 //
핵심 주어
Over-optimism about what can be achieved / within a certain
time frame / **is** a problem. // 단서1 정해진 시간 내에 할 수 있다고 지나치게 믿는 것은 문제임
(동사)
성취될 수 있는 것에 대한 지나친 낙관주의는 / 특정한 기간 내에 / 문제이다 //

So / work on it. // 단서2 시간이 얼마나 필요할지 추산하는 것을
그러므로 / 그것을 (개선하려고) 노력하라 // 습관화하라고 함

Make a practice / of estimating the amount of time needed /
alongside items on your 'things to do' list, /
습관화하라 / 필요한 시간의 양을 추산하는 것을 / '해야 할 일' 목록에 있는 것들과 함께 /
병렬 구조
and **learn** by experience / when tasks take a greater or lesser
time / than expected. //
그리고 경험에서 배우라 / 과제가 더 많거나 더 적은 시간이 걸릴 때 / 예상보다 //

Give attention / also to fitting the task / to the available time. //
주의를 기울여라 / 과제를 맞추는 것에도 / 이용 가능한 시간에 //
목적격 관계대명사
There are some tasks / that you can only set about / if you have
a significant amount of time available. //
몇몇 과제가 있다 / 여러분이 시작할 수 있는 / 상당한 양의 이용할 수 있는 시간이 있어야만 //
'무의미하다'
There is no point / in trying to gear up for such a task / when
you only have a short period available. //
무의미하다 / 그런 과제를 위해 준비하려고 애쓰는 것은 / 여러분에게 이용할 수 있는 짧은
시간밖에 없을 때 // 단서3 과제별로 시간을 배분하여
앞에 목적격 관계대명사가 생략됨 순서를 정하라고 함
So schedule the time / **you need** / for the longer tasks / and put
the short tasks / into the spare moments in between. //
그러므로 시간을 계획하라 / 여러분이 필요로 하는 / 시간이 더 오래 걸리는 과제를 위해 /
그리고 시간이 짧게 걸리는 과제를 배치하라 / 사이의 남는 시간에 //

- set out ~에 착수하다 · over-optimism ⓝ 지나친 낙관주의
- certain ⓐ 특정한 · estimate ⓥ 추산하다, 어림잡다
- alongside prep ~와 함께 · task ⓝ 과제 · fit ⓥ 맞추다
- available ⓐ 이용 가능한 · significant ⓐ 상당한
- spare ⓐ 남겨둔 · benefit ⓝ 이익 · practical ⓐ 실용적인
- leisure ⓝ 여가

만약 여러분이 매일 하고자 착수하는 일을 성취함으로써 얻게 되는 자신감을
원한다면 **일이 얼마나 시간이 걸릴지** 아는 것이 중요하다. 어떤 특정 기간
내에 성취될 수 있는 것에 대한 지나친 낙관주의는 문제이다. 그러므로 그것을
개선하려고 노력하라. '해야 할 일' 목록에 있는 것들과 함께, 필요한 시간의
양을 추산하는 것을 습관화하고, 과제가 예상보다 더 많거나 적은 시간이 걸릴
때 경험을 통해 배우라. 이용 가능한 시간에 과제를 맞추는 것에도 주의를
기울여라. 상당한 양의 이용할 수 있는 시간이 있어야만 시작할 수 있는 몇몇
과제가 있다. 여러분에게 이용할 수 있는 시간이 짧을 때 그런 과제를 위해
준비하려고 애쓰는 것은 무의미하다. 그러므로 시간이 더 오래 걸리는 과제를
위해 필요한 시간을 계획하고, 그 사이의 남는 시간에 시간이 짧게 걸리는
과제를 배치하라.

다음 빈칸에 들어갈 말로 가장 적절한 것을 고르시오.
① what benefits you can get 이익에 대한 내용이 아님
여러분이 어떤 이익을 얻을 수 있는지
② how practical your tasks are 과제가 아니라 시간을 실용적으로 쓰라고 함
여러분의 과제가 얼마나 실용적인지
③ how long things are going to take
일이 얼마나 시간이 걸릴지 소요될 시간을 추산하여 적절하게 배치하라고 함
④ why failures are meaningful in life
왜 실패가 인생에 있어서 의미 있는지 실패를 통해 배우라는 내용이 아님
⑤ why your leisure time should come first
왜 여러분의 여가 시간을 우선시해야 하는지 여가 시간에 한정된 내용이 아님

> 왜 정답 ? *** [정답률 57%]

빈칸 문장	만약 여러분이 매일 하고자 착수하는 일을 성취함으로써 얻게 되는 자신감을 원한다면 _____ 아는 것이 중요하다.

➡ **빈칸 문장:** 일을 성취하여 자신감을 얻으려면 '무엇을' 아는 것이 중요하다.
➡ **빈칸 문장 뒤:**
1 정해진 시간 내에 무언가를 성취할 수 있다고 믿는 지나친 낙관주의는 문제임 단서1
2 필요한 시간의 양을 추산하는 것을 습관화하라고 함 단서2
3 과제별로 필요한 시간을 배분하고 순서를 배치하라고 함 단서3
▶ 따라서 일을 성취하여 얻게 되는 자신감에는 ③ '일이 얼마나 시간이 걸릴지' 아는 것이 중요하다.

> 왜 오답 ?

① 얻을 수 있는 이익을 계산하라고 조언하는 글이 아니다.
② 과제의 실용성이 아니라 효율적인 시간의 사용을 강조하는 글이다.
④ 실패를 통해 배우라는 언급은 없었다.
⑤ 여가 시간이 아니라 과제마다 소요될 시간을 파악하라고 했다.

어법 특강

* 주어-동사 수 일치

- 문장의 주어가 명사구 혹은 명사절일 때 항상 단수 취급한다. to부정사구, 동명사
구나 의문사절, that절, whether절 등과 같은 명사절이 주어로 오는 경우 동사와
멀어질 수 있기 때문에 수 일치 여부를 쉽게 판단하기 힘들다. 따라서 항상 문장
을 전체적으로 파악해야 한다.

· Creating a list of goals **is** a good way to be a better student.
 (동명사구 주어) *(단수 동사)*
 (목표들의 목록을 만드는 것은 더 나은 학생이 되기 위한 좋은 방법이다.)

· Whether he will accept my offer **is** not certain yet.
 (명사절 주어) *(단수 동사)*
 (그가 나의 제안을 받아들일 지는 아직 확실하지 않다.)

· To overcome my emotional problems **is** difficult.
 (to부정사구 주어) *(단수 동사)*
 (나의 감정적인 문제들을 극복하는 것은 어렵다.)

---

33 정답 ① * 진화의 원리

In Lewis Carroll's *Through the Looking-Glass*, / the Red Queen
takes Alice / on a race through the countryside. //
Lewis Carroll의 〈Through the Looking-Glass〉에서 / 붉은 여왕은 Alice를 데리고 간다
/ 시골을 통과하는 한 경주에 //
목적어절 접속사
They run and they run, / but then Alice discovers / that they're
목적격 관계대명사
still under the same tree / that they started from. //
그들은 달리고 또 달리지만 / 그러다가 Alice는 발견한다 / 그들이 똑같은 나무 아래에 여전히
있음을 / 자신들이 출발했던 //
단서1 최선을 다해서 뛰어야 현재의 자리를 유지할 수 있음
The Red Queen explains to Alice: / "here, you see, / it takes all the
running you can do, / to keep in the same place." //
붉은 여왕은 Alice에게 설명한다 / "'여기서는' 보다시피 / 네가 할 수 있는 모든 뜀박질을 해야
한단다 / 같은 장소에 머물러 있으려면"이라고 //

Biologists sometimes use this Red Queen Effect / **to explain** an evolutionary principle. // 〔부사적 용법(목적)〕

생물학자들은 때때로 이 '붉은 여왕 효과'를 사용한다 / 진화 원리를 설명하기 위해 //

If foxes evolve to run faster / **so** they can catch more rabbits, / 〔부사절 접속사(목적)〕
then only the fastest rabbits will live long enough / to make a new generation of bunnies / **that** run even faster / 〔주격 관계대명사〕

만약 여우가 더 빨리 달리도록 진화한다면 / 더 많은 토끼를 잡기 위해 / 그러면 오직 가장 빠른 토끼만이 충분히 오래 산다 / 새로운 세대의 토끼를 낳게 되도록 / 훨씬 더 빨리 달리는 /

— in which case, / of course, / only the fastest foxes will catch enough rabbits / to thrive and pass on their genes. //

이 경우 / 물론 / 가장 빠른 여우만이 충분한 / 토끼를 잡을 것이다 / 번성하여 자신들의 유전자를 물려주도록 // 〔부사절 접속사(양보)〕

단서 2 토끼와 여우가 생존을 위해 함께 진화함

Even though they might run, / the two species **just stay in place**. //

그것들이 달린다 해도 / 그 두 종은 제자리에 머무를 뿐이다 //

- countryside ⓝ 시골 · biologist ⓝ 생물학자
- evolutionary ⓐ 진화의 · principle ⓝ 원리
- evolve ⓥ 진화하다 · generation ⓝ 세대 · bunny ⓝ 토끼
- pass on ~을 물려주다 · gene ⓝ 유전자 · run into ~와 마주치다
- adapt ⓥ 적응하다

Lewis Carroll의 〈Through the Looking-Glass〉에서 붉은 여왕은 Alice를 시골을 통과하는 한 경주에 데리고 간다. 그들은 달리고 또 달리지만, 그러다가 Alice는 자신들이 출발했던 나무 아래에 여전히 있음을 발견한다. 붉은 여왕은 Alice에게 "'여기서는' 보다시피 같은 장소에 머물러 있으려면 네가 할 수 있는 모든 뜀박질을 해야 한단다."라고 설명한다. 생물학자들은 때때로 이 '붉은 여왕 효과'를 사용해 진화 원리를 설명한다. 만약 여우가 더 많은 토끼를 잡기 위해 더 빨리 달리도록 진화한다면, 오직 가장 빠른 토끼만이 충분히 오래 살아 훨씬 더 빨리 달리는 새로운 세대의 토끼를 낳을 텐데, 물론 이 경우 가장 빠른 여우만이 충분한 토끼를 잡아 번성하여 자신들의 유전자를 물려줄 것이다. 그 두 종이 달린다 해도 그것들은 제자리에 머무를 뿐이다.

> **다음 빈칸에 들어갈 말로 가장 적절한 것을 고르시오. [3점]**
>
> ① just stay in place 여우와 토끼가 함께 진화하므로 제자리에 머무는 것처럼 보임
>   제자리에 머무를 뿐이다
> ② end up walking slowly 더 빨리 달리도록 진화한다고 했음
>   결국 천천히 걷게 된다
> ③ never run into each other
>   결코 서로 마주치지 않는다 양쪽 모두 달린다는 것이 부딪치지 않는다는 것을 말하기 위함이 아님
> ④ won't be able to adapt to changes
>   변화에 적응할 수 없을 것이다 오히려 변화에 적응해야 한다는 내용임
> ⑤ cannot run faster than their parents
>   그것들의 부모보다 빨리 달릴 수 없다 이전 세대보다 빨리 달리도록 진화한다고 함

⟩**왜 정답**? **★★★** [정답률 51%]

빈칸 문장 앞	만약 여우가 더 많은 토끼를 잡기 위해 더 빨리 달리도록 진화한다면, 오직 가장 빠른 토끼만이 충분히 오래 살아 훨씬 더 빨리 달리는 새로운 세대의 토끼를 낳을 텐데, 물론 이 경우 가장 빠른 여우만이 충분한 토끼를 잡아 번성하여 자신들의 유전자를 물려줄 것이다. **단서 2**
빈칸 문장	그 두 종이 달린다 해도 그것들은 .

➡ **빈칸 문장:** 더 빨리 달리도록 함께 진화한 여우와 토끼는 달린다고 해도 '어떠할' 것이다.

글의 앞부분	· 그들은 달리고 또 달리지만, 그러다가 Alice는 자신들이 출발했던 나무 아래에 여전히 있음을 발견한다. · 붉은 여왕은 Alice에게 "'여기서는' 보다시피 같은 장소에 머물러 있으려면 네가 할 수 있는 모든 뜀박질을 해야 한단다."라고 설명한다. **단서 1**

➡ **글의 앞부분:** 계속 달려도 여전히 출발점에 있음 = 같은 장소에라도 있으려면 최선을 다해 달려야 함

▶ 여우와 토끼가 이전 세대에 비해 더 빨라졌다고 해도 더 진화한 상대와 달리는 것이기 때문에 그들은 ① '제자리에 머무를 뿐이다'.

⟩**왜 오답**?

② 천천히 걷는 것이 아니라 최선을 다해서 뛰어야 한다고 했다.

③ 서로 마주치지 않기 위해 달리는 것이 아니다.

④ 생존을 위해서는 오히려 변화에 적응하여 진화해야 한다고 했다. ◀**주의**

⑤ 부모 세대보다 더 향상된 방향으로 진화한다고 했다.

34 정답 ② ＊성취를 위한 구상 ━━━━━

〔단수 주어〕 〔단수 동사〕
Everything in the world around us / **was** finished / in the mind of its creator / before it was started. //

우리 주변 세상의 모든 것은 / 완성되었다 / 그것을 만들어 낸 사람의 마음속에서 / 그것이 시작되기 전에 //

단서 1 모든 것은 마음속에서 구상된 후 세상에 나옴

〔뒤에 목적격 관계대명사가 생략됨〕
The houses we live in, / **the cars** we drive, / and our clothing / all of these began with an idea. //

우리가 사는 집 / 우리가 운전하는 자동차 / 그리고 우리의 옷 / 이 모든 것이 아이디어에서 시작했다 //

단서 2 우리가 실생활에서 접하는 것들도 모두 같은 과정을 거침

〔병렬 구조〕
Each idea was then **studied**, / **refined** and **perfected** / before the first nail was driven / or the first piece of cloth was cut. //

각각의 아이디어는 그런 다음 연구되고 / 다듬어지고 / 완성되었다 / 첫 번째 못이 박히거나 / 첫 번째 천 조각이 재단되기 전에 //

단서 3 물리적으로 성취를 이루기 전에 마음속에 명확한 그림이 존재해야 함

Long before / the idea was turned into a physical reality, / the mind had clearly pictured the finished product. //

훨씬 전에 / 그 아이디어가 물리적 실체로 바뀌기 / 마음은 완제품을 분명하게 그렸다 //

The human being designs / his or her own future / through much the same process. //

인간은 설계한다 / 자신의 미래를 / 거의 같은 과정을 통해 //

〔전치사 about의 목적어(간접의문문)〕
We begin with an idea / about **how the future will be**. //

우리는 아이디어로 시작한다 / 미래가 어떨지에 대한 //

Over a period of time / we refine and perfect the vision. //

일정 기간에 걸쳐서 / 우리는 그 비전을 다듬어 완성한다 //

Before long, / our every thought, decision and activity / are all working in harmony / **to bring** into existence / **what** we **have mentally concluded** / about the future. // 〔부사적 용법(목적)〕 〔to bring의 목적어〕

머지않아 / 우리의 모든 생각, 결정, 활동은 / 모두 조화롭게 작용하게 된다 / 생겨나게 하려고 / 우리가 머릿속에서 완성한 것을 / 미래에 대해 //

- creator ⓝ 창조자 · clothing ⓝ 의복 · nail ⓝ 못
- drive ⓥ (못·말뚝 등을) 박다 · physical ⓐ 물리적인
- reality ⓝ 실체 · process ⓝ 과정 · decision ⓝ 결정
- harmony ⓝ 조화 · existence ⓝ 존재 · potential ⓝ 잠재력
- accomplish ⓥ 완성하다 · careless ⓐ 부주의한
- irresponsible ⓐ 무책임한 · observe ⓥ 탐색하다
- professional ⓝ 전문직 (종사자)

우리 주변 세상의 모든 것은 시작되기 전에 그것을 만들어 낸 사람의 마음속에서 완성되었다. 우리가 사는 집, 우리가 운전하는 자동차, 우리의 옷, 이 모든 것이 아이디어에서 시작했다. 각각의 아이디어는 그런 다음, 첫 번째 못이 박히거나 첫 번째 천 조각이 재단되기 전에, 연구되고, 다듬어지고, 완성되었다. 그 아이디어가 물리적 실체로 바뀌기 훨씬 전에 마음은 완제품을 분명하게 그렸다. 인간은 거의 같은 과정을 통해 자신의 미래를 설계한다. 우리는 미래가 어떨지에 대한 아이디어로 시작한다. 일정 기간에 걸쳐서 우리는 그 비전을 다듬어 완성한다. 머지않아, 우리의 모든 생각, 결정, 활동은 우리가 **미래에 대해 머릿속에서 완성한** 것을 생겨나게 하려고 모두 조화롭게 작용하게 된다.

다음 빈칸에 들어갈 말로 가장 적절한 것을 고르시오. [3점]

① didn't even have the potential to accomplish
완성할 수 있는 잠재력조차 갖고 있지 못하다   머리로 미전을 떠올리면 실행이 가능함
② have mentally concluded about the future
미래에 대해 머릿속에서 완성하다   머릿속에서 구상한 것이 실제 이루어진다고 했음
③ haven't been able to picture in our mind
우리의 마음에 그려낼 수 없다   이 과정이 선행되어야 성취로 이어짐
④ considered careless and irresponsible
부주의하고 무책임하다 여겨지다   전혀 언급되지 않은 내용
⑤ have observed in some professionals   여러 직종을 탐색하는 것은 나오지 않음
여러 직종을 탐색해 보다

| 문제 풀이 순서 | ★★★ [정답률 56%]

1st 먼저 빈칸 문장을 읽고, 빈칸에 들어갈 말을 예측한다.

빈칸 문장 | 머지않아, 우리의 모든 생각, 결정, 활동은 우리가 _____ 것을 생겨나게 하려고 모두 조화롭게 작용하게 된다.

➡ 우리가 '어떻게 한' 것을 생겨나게 하려고 우리의 생각, 결정, 활동이 조화롭게 작용한다고 했으므로, 단서 그 과정을 파악해야 한다. 발상

2nd 글의 나머지 부분을 확인해서 정답을 찾는다.

글의 첫 번째 문장 | 우리 주변 세상의 모든 것은 시작되기 전에 그것을 만들어 낸 사람의 마음속에서 완성되었다. 단서 1

글의 두 번째 문장 | 우리가 사는 집, 우리가 운전하는 자동차, 우리의 옷, 이 모든 것이 아이디어에서 시작했다. 단서 2

➡ 우리 주변의 모든 것이 사람의 마음속에서, 아이디어에서 시작했다고 했다.
▶ 물리적인 실체가 되려면 마음에서 명확하게 그려내야 함

글의 네 번째 문장 | 그 아이디어가 물리적 실체로 바뀌기 훨씬 전에 마음은 완제품을 분명하게 그렸다. 단서 3

➡ 마음속에서 이미 완성된 아이디어가 물리적 실체로 바뀐다.
▶ 우리의 모든 생각, 결정, 활동은 우리가 ② '미래에 대해 머릿속에서 완성'한 것을 생겨나게 하려고 조화롭게 작용한다.

| 선택지 분석 |

① didn't even have the potential to accomplish
완성할 수 있는 잠재력조차 갖고 있지 못하다
완성될 잠재력이 없는 것을 실현한다는 것이 아니다.

② have mentally concluded about the future
미래에 대해 머릿속에서 완성하다
머릿속에서 먼저 구상하는 과정을 거쳐 성취가 일어난다고 했다.

③ haven't been able to picture in our mind
우리의 마음속에 그려낼 수 없다
마음속에 그려내는 과정이 선행되어야 성취로 이어진다고 했다.

④ considered careless and irresponsible
부주의하고 무책임하다고 여겨지다
부주의하고 무책임한 태도에 관한 내용은 언급되지 않았다.

⑤ have observed in some professionals
여러 직종을 탐색해 보다
직종을 탐색하는 것과 관련된 글이 아니다.

---

35 정답 ④ ＊관점에 따라 달라지는 해석

다음 글에서 전체 흐름과 관계 없는 문장은?

주어(단수 취급)   단수 동사   목적어
Whose story it is affects / *what* the story is. //
'누구의' 이야기인지가 영향을 미친다 / '무슨' 이야기인지에 //
동사원형 ~ and ...: ~해라, 그러면 ...할 것이다
Change the main character, / **and** the focus of the story must
also change. // 주인공을 바꿔라 / 그러면 이야기의 초점도 틀림없이 바뀔 것이다 //

If we look at the events / through another character's eyes, / we
will interpret them differently. // 단서 1 다른 등장인물의 관점에서 사건을 보면
다른 해석이 가능해짐
만약 우리가 사건을 본다면 / 다른 등장인물의 눈을 통해 / 우리는 그것을 다르게 해석할 것이다 //

① We'll place our sympathies / with someone new. //
우리는 공감할 것이다 / 새로운 누군가에게 //
주격 관계대명사(선행사: the conflict)
② When the conflict arises / **that** is the heart of the story, / we
will be praying for a different outcome. //
갈등이 발생할 때 / 이야기의 핵심인 / 우리는 다른 결과를 간절히 바랄 것이다 //

③ Consider, / for example, / how the tale of Cinderella would
사이에 it+be동사가 생략됨
shift / **if told** from the viewpoint / of an evil stepsister. //
생각해 보라 / 예를 들어 / 신데렐라 이야기가 어떻게 바뀔지 / 관점에서 이야기된다면 /
사악한 의붓자매의   단서 2 악인으로 여기던 등장인물의 관점에서
뒤에 목적어절 접속사 that이 생략됨   이야기를 바라보면 또 다른 해석이 가능함
④ We know / Cinderella's kingdom does not exist, / but we
willingly go there anyway. //
(우리는 안다 / 신데렐라의 왕국이 존재하지 않는다는 것을 / 하지만 어쨌든 기꺼이 그곳에
간다 //)

⑤ *Gone with the Wind* is Scarlett O'Hara's story, / but what if
수동태 동사   능동태의 직접목적어
we **were shown the same events** / from the viewpoint of Rhett
Butler or Melanie Wilkes? //
〈Gone with the Wind〉는 Scarlett O'Hara의 이야기이지만 / 만약 같은 사건이 우리에게
제시된다면 어떠할 것인가 / Rhett Butler나 Melanie Wilkes의 관점에서 //

- interpret ⓥ 해석하다   • sympathy ⓝ 공감   • conflict ⓝ 갈등
- arise ⓥ 발생하다   • outcome ⓝ 결과   • tale ⓝ 이야기
- shift ⓥ 바꾸다   • viewpoint ⓝ 관점   • evil ⓐ 사악한
- stepsister ⓝ 의붓자매   • exist ⓥ 존재하다   • willingly ⓐⓓ 기꺼이

'누구의' 이야기인지가 '무슨' 이야기인지에 영향을 미친다. 주인공을 바꾸면, 이야기의 초점도 틀림없이 바뀔 것이다. 만약 우리가 다른 등장인물의 눈을 통해 사건을 본다면, 우리는 그것을 다르게 해석할 것이다. ① 우리는 새로운 누군가에게 공감할 것이다. ② 이야기의 핵심인 갈등이 발생할 때, 우리는 다른 결과를 간절히 바랄 것이다. ③ 예를 들어, 신데렐라 이야기가 사악한 의붓자매의 관점에서 이야기된다면 어떻게 바뀔지 생각해 보라. (④ 우리는 신데렐라의 왕국이 존재하지 않는다는 것을 알지만, 어쨌든 기꺼이 그곳에 간다.) ⑤ 〈Gone with the Wind〉는 Scarlett O'Hara의 이야기이지만, 만약 같은 시간이 Rhett Butler나 Melanie Wilkes의 관점에서 우리에게 제시된다면 어떠할 것인가?

왜 정답 · 오답? ★★❀ [정답률 64%]

글의 앞부분: '누구의' 이야기인지가 '무슨' 이야기인지에 영향을 미친다. 주인공을 바꾸면, 이야기의 초점도 틀림없이 바뀔 것이다. 만약 우리가 다른 등장인물의 눈을 통해 사건을 본다면, 우리는 그것을 다르게 해석할 것이다.

➡ 등장인물에 따라 사건을 해석하는 시각이 바뀌기 때문에 주인공이 누구인지가 중요하다는 내용의 글이다.

① 우리는 새로운 누군가에게 공감할 것이다.

➡ 앞에서 다른 등장인물의 눈을 통해 사건을 보면 그것을 다르게 해석한다고 했으므로 그 새로운 누군가에 공감한다는 내용이 자연스럽게 이어진다.
▶ ①은 무관한 문장이 아님

② 이야기의 핵심인 갈등이 발생할 때, 우리는 다른 결과를 간절히 바랄 것이다.

➡ 다른 인물의 관점에서 보는 것이므로 기존과는 다른 결과를 바라는 것은 자연스러운 흐름이다.
▶ ②은 무관한 문장이 아님

③ 예를 들어(for example), 신데렐라 이야기가 사악한 의붓자매의 관점에서 이야기된다면 어떻게 바뀔지 생각해 보라.

➡ 앞의 내용에 대한 예시로 신데렐라의 의붓자매의 관점을 이야기하는 흐름은 자연스럽다.
▶ ③은 무관한 문장이 아님

④ 우리는 신데렐라의 왕국이 존재하지 않는다는 것을 알지만, 어쨌든 기꺼이 그곳에 간다.

➡ ③에서 언급된 신데렐라에만 국한된 내용으로, 등장인물에 따라 이야기를 다르게 해석한다는 글의 전체 흐름과는 관련이 없다.
▶ ④이 무관한 문장임

⑤ 〈Gone with the Wind〉는 Scarlett O'Hara의 이야기이지만, 만약 같은 사건이 Rhett Butler나 Melanie Wilkes의 관점에서 우리에게 제시된다면 어떠할 것인가?

➡ 또 다른 예시가 이어지면서 다른 등장인물의 관점에서 이야기를 본다면 어떨지 질문을 던지면서 글을 마무리하고 있다.
▶ ⑤은 무관한 문장이 아님

＊ 글의 흐름

도입	'누구의' 이야기인지가 '무슨' 이야기인지에 영향을 미침
주제	같은 사건이라도 등장인물마다 다르게 해석할 것임
예시 ①	신데렐라의 사악한 의붓자매의 관점에서 이야기된다면 신데렐라 이야기는 바뀔 것임
예시 ②	Rhett Butler나 Melanie Wilkes의 관점에서 제시된다면 〈Gone with the Wind〉도 마찬가지일 것임

36 정답 ④ ＊구석기 시대의 분업과 협업

In the Old Stone Age, / small bands of 20 to 60 people wandered / from place to place / in search of food. //
구석기 시대에는 / 20명에서 60명의 작은 무리가 돌아다녔다 / 이곳저곳을 / 식량을 찾아 //
Once people began farming, / they could settle down / near their farms. // 단서1 농사를 지으면서 정착하기 시작함
일단 사람들이 농사를 짓기 시작하면서 / 그들은 정착할 수 있었다 / 자신들의 농경지 근처에 //

부사절 접속사(대조)
(A) While some workers grew crops, / others built new houses / and made tools. // 단서2 분업에 대한 예시
어떤 노동자들은 농작물을 재배한 반면 / 다른 노동자들은 새로운 집을 짓고 / 도구를 만들었다 //
명사적 용법(learned의 목적어) 부사적 용법(목적)
Village dwellers also learned / to work together / to do a task faster. //
마을 거주자들은 또한 배웠다 / 함께 일하는 것을 / 더 빨리 일을 하기 위해 //
(B) For example, / toolmakers could share the work / of making stone axes and knives. // 단서3 협업에 대한 예시
예를 들어 / 도구 제작자들은 작업을 공유할 수 있었다 / 돌도끼와 돌칼을 만드는 //
By working together, / they could make more tools / in the same amount of time. //
함께 일함으로써 / 그들은 더 많은 도구를 만들 수 있었다 / 같은 시간 안에 //

(C) As a result, / towns and villages grew larger. // 단서4 정착의 결과
그 결과 / 도시와 마을이 더 커졌다 //
to부정사를 목적격 보어로 취하는 동사
Living in communities / allowed people to organize themselves / more efficiently. //
공동체에서 생활하는 것은 / 사람들이 스스로 조직하도록 했다 / 더 효율적으로 //
앞에 목적격 관계대명사가 생략됨
They could divide up the work / of producing food and other things / they needed. //
그들은 일을 나눌 수 있었다 / 식량과 다른 것들을 생산하는 / 그들이 필요로 한 //

- band ⓝ 무리 · wander ⓥ 돌아다니다 · settle down 정착하다
- crop ⓝ 농작물 · toolmaker ⓝ 도구 제작자 · axe ⓝ 도끼
- community ⓝ 공동체 · organize ⓥ 조직하다
- efficiently ⓐⓓ 효율적으로 · divide ⓥ 나누다

구석기 시대에는 20명에서 60명의 작은 무리가 식량을 찾아 이곳저곳을 돌아다녔다. 일단 농사를 짓기 시작하면서, 사람들은 자신들의 농경지 근처에 정착할 수 있었다. (C) 그 결과, 도시와 마을이 더 커졌다. 공동체 생활을 통해 사람들은 자신들을 더 효율적으로 조직할 수 있었다. 그들은 식량과 자신들에게 필요한 다른 것들을 생산하는 일을 나눌 수 있었다. (A) 어떤 노동자들은 농작물을 재배했고, 다른 노동자들은 새로운 집을 짓고 도구를 만들었다. 마을 거주자들은 또한 일을 더 빨리 하기 위해 함께 일하는 것도 배웠다. (B) 예를 들어, 도구 제작자들은 돌도끼와 돌칼을 만드는 작업을 공유할 수 있었다. 함께 일함으로써, 그들은 같은 시간 안에 더 많은 도구를 만들 수 있었다.

주어진 글 다음에 이어질 글의 순서로 가장 적절한 것을 고르시오.
① (A) — (C) — (B) 주어진 글에는 노동과 관련된 언급이 없음
② (B) — (A) — (C) ┐
③ (B) — (C) — (A) ┘ 주어진 글에는 도구 제작자를 예로 들 만한 내용이 나오지 않음
④ (C) — (A) — (B) ┐ 농경지 주변에 정착함 — (C) 그 결과 마을이 커졌고 일을 나눔 — (A) 일부는 농사를 지었고 일부는 도구를 만들었고, 협업을 배움 — (B) 예를 들어 돌도끼와 돌칼을 만드는 노동자들은 작업을 공유함
⑤ (C) — (B) — (A) 분업을 말한 뒤 협업을 말하고 다시 분업을 말하는 것은 어색함

| 문제 풀이 순서 | ★★★ [정답률 39%]

1st 각 문단의 내용을 파악하고, 글의 논리적인 순서를 추론한다.

주어진 글: 구석기 시대에는 20명에서 60명의 작은 무리가 식량을 찾아 이곳저곳을 돌아다녔다. 일단 농사를 짓기 시작하면서, 사람들은 자신들의 농경지 근처에 정착할 수 있었다. 단서

➡ 주어진 글 뒤: 농사로 시작된 정착 생활과 관련된 내용이 이어질 것이다. 발상

(A): 어떤 노동자들은(workers) 농작물을 재배했고, 다른 노동자들은 새로운 집을 짓고 도구를 만들었다. 마을 거주자들은 또한 일을 더 빨리 하기 위해 함께 일하는 것도 배웠다.

➡ (A) 앞: 노동자 또는 노동과 관련된 내용이 나와야 한다.
▶ 주어진 글에는 없으므로 바로 뒤에 (A)가 올 수 없음
(A) 뒤: 함께 일하는 것을 배웠다는 것과 관련된 내용이 이어질 것이다.

(B): 예를 들어(For example), 도구 제작자들은 돌도끼와 돌칼을 만드는 작업을 공유할 수 있었다. 함께 일함으로써, 그들은 같은 시간 안에 더 많은 도구를 만들 수 있었다.

➡ (B) 앞: For example(예를 들어)로 (A)에서 말한 마을 거주자들이 배운 함께 일하는 것의 예시가 이어진다.
▶ (B) 앞에 (A)가 와야 함 (순서: (A) → (B))

(B) 뒤: (A) 앞에 주어진 글이 아닌 다른 문단이 와야 하는데, (B)는 (A) 뒤에 왔으므로 남은 (C)가 (A) 앞 순서일 것이다.
▶ (B)가 마지막에 올 확률이 높음

(C): 그 결과(As a result), 도시와 마을이 더 커졌다. 공동체 생활을 통해 사람들은 자신들을 더 효율적으로 조직할 수 있었다. 그들은 식량과 자신들에게 필요한 다른 것들을 생산하는 일을 나눌 수 있었다.

➡ **(C) 앞:** 주어진 글에서 말한 정착의 결과로 도시와 마을이 커져 사람들이 효율적으로 조직될 수 있었다고 하는 흐름이 적절하다.
▶ (C) 앞에 주어진 글이 와야 함 (순서: 주어진 글 ➡ (C))
(C) 뒤: 사람들은 식량과 생필품 생산을 분업했다고 했으므로 이 두 가지 노동과 관련된 내용이 이어질 것이다.
▶ 두 종류의 노동자를 언급한 (A)가 이어져야 함
(순서: 주어진 글 ➡ (C) ➡ (A) ➡ (B))

2nd 글이 한눈에 들어오도록 정리하여 정답을 확인한다.

주어진 글: 농사를 지으면서 사람들이 정착할 수 있었다.
➡ **(C):** 공동체 생활을 통해 사람들은 더 효율적으로 조직하고 분업했다.
➡ **(A):** 분업하며 마을 거주자들은 함께 일하는 것도 배웠다.
➡ **(B):** 도구 제작자들은 함께 일하며 같은 시간에 더 많은 작업을 할 수 있었다.
▶ 주어진 글 다음에 이어질 글의 순서는 (C) ➡ (A) ➡ (B)이므로 정답은 ④임

37 정답 ② ＊마그마의 결정 형성

Natural processes form minerals / in many ways. //
자연 과정은 광물을 형성한다 / 많은 방법으로 //
_{앞에 주격 관계대명사와 be동사가 생략됨}
For example, / hot melted rock material, / called magma, / cools / when it reaches the Earth's surface, / or even if it's trapped / below the surface. //
예를 들어 / 뜨거운 용암 물질은 / 마그마라고 불리는 / 식는다 / 그것이 지구의 표면에 도달할 때 / 또는 심지어 갇혔을 때도 / 표면 아래에 //

As magma cools, / its atoms lose heat energy, / move closer together, / and begin to combine into compounds. //
병렬 구조
마그마가 식으면서 / 마그마의 원자는 열에너지를 잃고 / 서로 더 가까이 이동해 / 화합물로 결합하기 시작한다 //
단서 1 마그마가 식으면서 화합물로 결합함

(A) Also, / the size of the crystals / that form depends partly / on how rapidly the magma cools. //
핵심 주어(단수) **단수 동사**
단서 2 광물의 종류를 결정할 뿐만 아니라 결정의 크기에도 영향을 끼친다는 추가 내용
또한 / 결정의 크기는 / 형성되는 / 부분적으로는 달려있다 / 마그마가 얼마나 빨리 식느냐에 //
When magma cools slowly, / the crystals that form are generally large enough / to see with the unaided eye. //
주격 관계대명사절
마그마가 천천히 식으면 / 형성되는 결정은 일반적으로 충분히 크다 / 육안으로 볼 수 있을 만큼 //
단서 3 마그마가 식는 과정에서 원자가 배열되어 화합물이 형성됨

(B) During this process, / atoms of the different compounds arrange themselves / into orderly repeating patterns. //
이 과정 동안 / 서로 다른 화합물의 원자가 스스로를 배열한다 / 질서 있고 반복적인 패턴으로 //
앞에 주격 관계대명사와 be동사가 생략됨
The type and amount of elements / present in a magma / partly determine / which minerals will form. //
원소의 종류와 양이 / 마그마에 존재하는 / 부분적으로 결정한다 / 어떤 광물이 형성될지를 //

(C) This is because the atoms have enough time / to move together / and form into larger crystals. //
병렬 구조
이것은 원자가 충분한 시간을 가지기 때문이다 / 함께 이동하고 / 더 큰 결정을 형성할 //
When magma cools rapidly, / the crystals that form will be small. //
주격 관계대명사절
단서 4 천천히 식은 마그마의 결정이 큰 이유 설명함
마그마가 빠르게 식으면 / 형성되는 결정은 작을 것이다 //
In such cases, / you can't easily see individual mineral crystals. //
그런 경우에는 / 당신은 개별 광물 결정을 쉽게 볼 수 없다 //

• natural ⓐ 자연의 • mineral ⓝ 광물 • melt ⓥ 녹이다, 녹다
• atom ⓝ 원자 • crystal ⓝ 결정(체) • rapidly ⓐⓓ 빨리
• unaided ⓐ 도움 없는 • arrange ⓥ 배열하다
• orderly ⓐ 질서 있는 • element ⓝ 원소

자연 과정은 많은 방법으로 광물을 형성한다. 예를 들어, 마그마라고 불리는 뜨거운 용암 물질은 지구의 표면에 도달할 때, 또는 심지어 표면 아래에 갇혔을 때도 식는다. 마그마가 식으면서, 마그마의 원자는 열에너지를 잃고, 서로 더 가까이 이동해, 화합물로 결합하기 시작한다. (B) 이 과정 동안, 서로 다른 화합물의 원자가 질서 있고 반복적인 패턴으로 스스로 배열된다. 마그마에 존재하는 원소의 종류와 양이 어떤 광물이 형성될지를 부분적으로 결정한다. (A) 또한, 형성되는 결정의 크기는 부분적으로는 마그마가 얼마나 빨리 식느냐에 달려있다. 마그마가 천천히 식으면, 형성되는 결정은 일반적으로 육안으로 볼 수 있을 만큼 충분히 크다. (C) 이것은 원자가 함께 이동해 더 큰 결정을 형성할 충분한 시간을 가지기 때문이다. 마그마가 빠르게 식으면, 형성되는 결정은 작을 것이다. 그런 경우에는 당신은 개별 광물 결정을 쉽게 볼 수 없다.

주어진 글 다음에 이어질 글의 순서로 가장 적절한 것을 고르시오. [3점]
① (A) — (C) — (B) (B)의 과정을 먼저 거쳐야 (A), (C)의 설명이 나올 수 있음
② (B) — (A) — (C) 마그마는 식으면서 화합물로 결합함 → (B) 마그마가 배열되면서 어떤 광물이 형성될지 부분적으로 결정됨 → (A) 결정의 크기는 마그마가 식는 속도에 영향을 받으므로 천천히 식으면 결정이 큼 → (C) 빠르게 식으면 결정이 작음
③ (B) — (C) — (A) (B)처럼 진행된 후 (A)의 영향이 더해져 (C)의 결과가 나옴
④ (C) — (A) — (B) 적절한 순서와 정반대
⑤ (C) — (B) — (A) This로 가리키는 내용이 주어진 글에 없음

| **문제 풀이 순서** | ＊＊＊ [정답률 45%]

1st 각 문단의 내용을 파악하고, 글의 논리적인 순서를 추론한다.

주어진 글: 자연 과정은 많은 방법으로 광물을 형성한다. 예를 들어, 마그마라고 불리는 뜨거운 용암 물질은 지구의 표면에 도달할 때, 또는 심지어 표면 아래에 갇혔을 때도 식는다. 마그마가 식으면서, 마그마의 원자는 열에너지를 잃고, 서로 더 가까이 이동해, 화합물로 결합하기 시작한다. **단서**

➡ **주어진 글 뒤:** 마그마가 식으면서 어떤 화합물로 결합되고, 그 결과는 어떤지를 설명하는 내용이 이어질 것이다. **발상**

(A): 또한(Also), 형성되는 결정의 크기는 부분적으로 마그마가 얼마나 빨리 식느냐에 달려있다. 마그마가 천천히 식으면, 형성되는 결정은 일반적으로 육안으로 볼 수 있을 만큼 충분히 크다.

➡ **(A) 앞:** '또한(Also)'으로 결정의 크기가 마그마가 식는 속도에 달려있다는 내용이 이어지므로 앞에도 결정의 무언가를 좌우하는 요인이 있어야 한다.
▶ 주어진 글에는 결합한다는 내용만 있으므로 주어진 글이 (A) 바로 앞에 올 수 없음
(A) 뒤: 천천히 식는 경우에 대해 설명했으므로 빠르게 식는 경우에는 어떤지 이어서 설명할 것이다.

(B): 이 과정(this process) 동안, 서로 다른 화합물의 원자가 질서 있고 반복적인 패턴으로 스스로 배열된다. 마그마에 존재하는 원소의 종류와 양이 어떤 광물이 형성될지를 부분적으로 결정한다.

➡ **(B) 앞:** **1** '이 과정(this process)'이 무엇인지 나와야 한다.
2 주어진 글에서 말한 마그마가 식어서 화합물로 결합하는 과정을 말한다.
▶ (B) 앞에 주어진 글이 있어야 함 (순서: 주어진 글 ➡ (B))
(B) 뒤: 광물 형성에 영향을 주는 또 다른 요인이 올 것이다.
▶ 마그마의 식는 속도에 결정의 크기가 정해진다는 (A)가 (B) 뒤에 와야 함
(순서: 주어진 글 ➡ (B) ➡ (A))

(C): 이것(This)은 원자가 함께 이동해 더 큰 결정을 형성할 충분한 시간을 가지기 때문이다. 마그마가 빠르게 식으면, 형성되는 결정은 작을 것이다. 그런 경우에는 당신은 개별 광물 결정을 쉽게 볼 수 없다.

➡ (C) 앞: **1** '이것(This)'이 가리키는 것이 앞에 나와야 한다.
　2 마그마가 천천히 식으면 결정이 큰 이유를 설명하고 있으므로 This는 (A)의 내용을 가리킨다.
▶ (A)에 이어지는 내용임 (순서: 주어진 글 → (B) → (A) → (C))

2nd 글이 한눈에 들어오도록 정리하여 정답을 확인한다.

주어진 글: 마그마는 흐르면서 열에너지를 잃고, 화합물로 결합한다.
→ **(B):** 이 과정에서 마그마에 존재하는 원소의 종류와 양이 어떤 광물이 형성될지를 결정한다.
→ **(A):** 마그마의 식는 속도에 결정의 크기가 결정되는데, 천천히 식으면 큰 결정이 형성된다.
→ **(C):** 왜냐하면 큰 결정이 될 시간이 충분하기 때문이다. 마그마가 빠르게 식으면 형성되는 결정은 작아진다.
▶ 주어진 글 다음에 이어질 글의 순서는 (B) → (A) → (C)이므로 정답은 ②임

---

38 정답 ④ ＊좋은 탄수화물과 나쁜 탄수화물

글의 흐름으로 보아, 주어진 문장이 들어가기에 가장 적절한 곳을 고르시오.

Bad carbohydrates, / on the other hand, / are simple sugars. //
나쁜 탄수화물은 / 반면에 / 단당류이다 //　**단서 1** 나쁜 탄수화물에 대한 설명이 on the other hand로 이어짐

All carbohydrates are basically sugars. //
모든 탄수화물은 기본적으로 당이다 //

(①) Complex carbohydrates are the good carbohydrates / for your body. // 복합 탄수화물은 좋은 탄수화물이다 / 여러분의 몸에 //

(②) These complex sugar compounds / are very difficult to break down / and can trap other nutrients / _{전치사} like vitamins and minerals / in their chains. // **단서 2** 복합 탄수화물은 분해하기 어려운 구조임
이러한 복당류 화합물은 / 분해하기 매우 어렵고 / 다른 영양소를 가두어 둘 수 있다 / 비타민과 미네랄 같은 / 그것의 사슬 안에 //

(③) ^{'~하면서, ~함에 따라'} As they slowly break down, / the other nutrients are also released into your body, / and can provide you with fuel / for a number of hours. // **단서 3** 복합 탄수화물이 분해될 때 다른 영양소를 우리 몸에 줄 수 있음
그것들이 천천히 분해되면서 / 다른 영양소도 여러분의 몸으로 방출되고 / 여러분에게 연료를 공급할 수 있다 / 많은 시간 동안 //　**단서 4** 구조가 복잡하지 않다는 상반되는 내용이 이어짐

(④) Because their structure is not complex, / they are easy to break down / and hold few nutrients for your body / other than the sugars / ^{전치사+관계대명사} from which they are made. //
그것의 구조는 복잡하지 않기 때문에 / 그것은 분해되기 쉽고 / 여러분의 몸을 위한 영양소를 거의 가지고 있지 않다 / 당 외에 / 그것이 만들어지는 //

(⑤) Your body breaks down these carbohydrates / rather quickly / and ^{선행사를 포함하는 관계대명사} what it cannot use / is _{병렬 구조} converted to fat / and stored in the body. // 여러분의 몸은 이러한 탄수화물을 분해하고 / 상당히 빨리 / 그것(몸)이 사용할 수 없는 것은 / 지방으로 바뀌어 / 몸에 저장된다 //

- complex ⓐ 복합의　　· compound ⓝ 화합물
- nutrient ⓝ 영양소　　· chain ⓝ 사슬　　· release ⓥ 방출하다

모든 탄수화물은 기본적으로 당이다. (①) 복합 탄수화물은 몸에 좋은 탄수화물이다. (②) 이러한 복당류 화합물은 분해하기 매우 어렵고 비타민과 미네랄 같은 다른 영양소를 그것의 사슬 안에 가두어 둘 수 있다. (③) 그것들이 천천히 분해되면서, 다른 영양소도 여러분의 몸으로 방출되고, 많은 시간 동안 여러분에게 연료를 공급할 수 있다. (④ 반면에 나쁜 탄수화물은 단당류이다.) 그것의 구조는 복잡하지 않기 때문에, 그것은 분해되기 쉽고 그것이 만들어지는 당 외에 몸을 위한 영양소를 거의 가지고 있지 않다. (⑤) 여러분의 몸은 이러한 탄수화물을 상당히 빨리 분해하고 그것(몸)이 사용할 수 없는 것은 지방으로 바뀌어 몸에 저장된다.

| 문제 풀이 순서 | ★★☆ [정답률 61%]

1st 주어진 문장을 해석하고, 연결어, 지시어 등을 확인한다.

Bad carbohydrates, on the other hand, are simple sugars.
반면에 나쁜 탄수화물은 단당류이다.

➡ 주어진 문장 앞: 'on the other hand(반면에)'라고 했으므로 **단서** 앞에는 나쁜 탄수화물과 반대되는 내용이 와야 한다. **발상**

2nd 찾은 단서를 생각하며 각 선택지의 앞뒤 흐름이 매끄러운지 확인한다.

- ①의 앞 문장과 뒤 문장

앞 문장: 모든 탄수화물은 기본적으로 당이다.
뒤 문장: 복합 탄수화물은 몸에 좋은 탄수화물이다.

➡ 앞 문장에서 언급한 탄수화물 중 하나를 뒤 문장에서 설명하고 있다.
▶ 주어진 문장이 ①에 들어갈 수 없음

- ②의 앞 문장과 뒤 문장

앞 문장: ①의 뒤 문장과 같음
뒤 문장: 이러한(These) 복당류 화합물은 분해하기 매우 어렵고 비타민과 미네랄 같은 다른 영양소를 그것의 사슬 안에 가두어 둘 수 있다.

➡ 앞 문장의 '복합 탄수화물'을 '이러한' 복당류 화합물로 가리키며 분해하기 매우 어렵다는 설명을 이어간다.
▶ 주어진 문장이 ②에 들어갈 수 없음

- ③의 앞 문장과 뒤 문장

앞 문장: ②의 뒤 문장과 같음
뒤 문장: 그것들이(they) 천천히 분해되면서, 다른 영양소도 여러분의 몸으로 방출되고, 많은 시간 동안 여러분에게 연료를 공급할 수 있다.

➡ '복당류 화합물'을 they로 지칭하며 오랜 시간 동안 연료를 공급한다는 설명을 이어간다.
▶ 주어진 문장이 ③에 들어갈 수 없음

④의 앞 문장과 뒤 문장

앞 문장: ③의 뒤 문장과 같음
뒤 문장: 그것의(their) 구조는 복잡하지 않기 때문에, 그것은 분해되기 쉽고 그것이 만들어지는 당 외에 몸을 위한 영양소를 거의 가지고 있지 않다.

➡ 복합 탄수화물, 즉 복당류 화합물은 분해하기 매우 어렵다고 했는데, '그것의' 구조는 복잡하지 않고 분해되기 쉽다는 반대되는 내용이 이어진다.
▶ 단당류를 처음 언급한 주어진 문장이 ④에 들어가야 함

- ⑤의 앞 문장과 뒤 문장

> 앞 문장: ④의 뒤 문장과 같음
> 뒤 문장: 여러분의 몸은 이러한 탄수화물(these carbohydrates)을 상당히 빨리 분해하고 그것(몸)이 사용할 수 없는 것은 지방으로 바뀌어 몸에 저장된다.

➡ '이러한 탄수화물'은 주어진 문장과 ④의 뒤 문장에서 말한 분해하기 쉬운 단당류를 말한다.
▶ 주어진 문장이 ⑤에 들어갈 수 없음

3rd 글이 한눈에 들어오도록 정리하여 정답을 확인한다.

모든 탄수화물은 기본적으로 당이다.
(①) 복합 탄수화물은 몸에 좋은 탄수화물이다.
(②) 이러한 복당류 화합물은 분해하기 어렵고 다른 영양소를 안에 가두어 둔다.
(③) 그것들은 천천히 분해되면서, 많은 시간 동안 에너지를 공급할 수 있다.
(④ 반면에 나쁜 탄수화물은 단당류이다.)
그것의 구조는 복잡하지 않아 분해되기 쉽고 영양소를 거의 가지고 있지 않다.
(⑤) 몸은 이러한 탄수화물을 빨리 분해해 사용할 수 없는 것은 지방으로 바꿔 저장한다.

---

39 정답 ⑤ *기대가 행동에 미치는 영향

> 글의 흐름으로 보아, 주어진 문장이 들어가기에 가장 적절한 곳을 고르시오. [3점]

가주어 **진주어절 접속사** **주격 관계대명사**
It was also found / that those students who expected the lecturer to be warm / tended to interact with him more. //
~이 또한 밝혀졌다 / 그 강사가 따뜻할 것이라 기대한 학생들은 / 그와 더 많이 소통하는 경향이 있다(는 것이) /
단서 1 앞에 다른 결과가 밝혀져야 함

단서 2 사람들이 유형별로 분류될 수 있는 특성을 갖는다고 잘못된 가정을 함
People commonly make the mistaken assumption / that because a person has one type of characteristic, / then they automatically have other characteristics / which go with it. //
흔히 사람들은 잘못된 가정을 한다 / 어떤 사람이 한 가지 유형의 특성을 가지고 있기 때문에 / 그러면 자동적으로 다른 특성을 가지고 있다는 / 그것과 어울리는 //

부사절 접속사
(①) In one study, / university students were given / descriptions of a guest lecturer / before he spoke to the group. //
한 연구에서 / 대학생들은 들었다 / 한 강사에 대한 설명을 / 그(초청 강사)가 그 (대학생) 집단에게 강연을 하기 전에 //

전체의 절반
(②) Half the students received a description / containing the word 'warm', / **나머지 절반** the other half were told / the speaker was 'cold'. //
학생들의 절반은 설명을 들었고 / '따뜻'이라는 단어가 포함된 / 나머지 절반은 말을 들었다 / 그 강사가 '차갑다'는 //

「전치사+관계대명사」
(③) The guest lecturer then led a discussion, / after which the students were asked / to give their impressions of him. //
그리고 나서 그 초청 강사가 토론을 이끌었고 / 그 후에 학생들은 요청받았다 / 그(강사)에 대한 그들의 인상을 말해 달라고 //

(④) As expected, / there were large differences / between the **앞에 주격 관계대명사와 be동사가 생략됨** impressions formed **분사구문** by the students, / depending upon their original information of the lecturer. //
예상한 대로 / 큰 차이가 있었다 / 학생들에 의해 형성된 인상 간에는 / 그 강사에 대한 학생들의 최초 정보에 따라 //
단서 3 사전에 접한 정보에 따라서 강사에 대한 인상이 다르게 형성됨

not only A but also B: A뿐만 아니라 B도
(⑤) This shows / that different expectations / not only affect the impressions we form / but also our behaviour and the relationship / which is formed. // **단서 4** 인상에서 더 나아가 행동 및 형성되는 관계까지 영향을 준다는 설명이 이어짐
이것은 보여 준다 / 서로 다른 기대가 / 우리가 형성하는 인상에 영향을 미칠 뿐만 아니라 / 우리의 행동 및 관계에도 (영향을 미친다는 것을) / 형성되는 //

- interact ⓥ 소통하다 · commonly ⓐⓓ 흔히
- assumption ⓝ 가정 · automatically ⓐⓓ 자동적으로
- description ⓝ 설명, 묘사 · contain ⓥ 포함하다
- discussion ⓝ 토론 · impression ⓝ 인상
- expectation ⓝ 기대 · behaviour ⓝ 행동

흔히 사람들은 어떤 사람이 한 가지 유형의 특성을 가지고 있기 때문에, 그러면 자동적으로 그것과 어울리는 다른 특성을 가지고 있다는 잘못된 가정을 한다. (①) 한 연구에서, 대학생들은 초청 강사가 그 (대학생) 집단에게 강연을 하기 전에 그 강사에 대한 설명을 들었다. (②) 학생들의 절반은 '따뜻한'이라는 단어가 포함된 설명을 들었고, 나머지 절반은 그 강사가 '차갑다'는 말을 들었다. (③) 그리고 나서 그 초청 강사가 토론을 이끌었고, 그 후에 학생들은 그(강사)에 대한 그들의 인상을 말해 달라고 요청받았다. (④) 예상한 대로, 학생들에 의해 형성된 인상 간에는 그 강사에 대한 학생들의 최초 정보에 따라 큰 차이가 있었다. (⑤ 또한, 그 강사가 따뜻할 것이라 기대한 학생들은 그와 더 많이 소통하는 경향이 있다는 것이 밝혀졌다.) 이것은 서로 다른 기대가 우리가 형성하는 인상뿐만 아니라 우리의 행동 및 형성되는 관계에도 영향을 미친다는 것을 보여 준다.

| 문제 풀이 순서 | ★★★ [정답률 51%]

1st 주어진 문장을 해석하고, 연결어, 지시어 등을 확인한다.

> It was also found that those students who expected the lecturer to be warm tended to interact with him more.
> 또한, 그 강사가 따뜻할 것이라 기대한 학생들은 그와 더 많이 소통하는 경향이 있다는 것이 밝혀졌다.

➡ 주어진 문장 앞: '또한(also)'이라고 했으므로 **단서** 앞에 강사에 대한 학생들의 기대가 어땠는지 설명하는 내용이 와야 한다. **발상**

2nd 각 선택지의 앞뒤 흐름이 매끄러운지 확인한다.

- ①의 앞 문장과 뒤 문장

> 앞 문장: 흔히 사람들은 어떤 사람이 한 가지 유형의 특성을 가지고 있기 때문에, ~ 다른 특성을 가지고 있다는 잘못된 가정을 한다.
> 뒤 문장: 한 연구에서, 대학생들은 초청 강사가 그 (대학생) 집단에게 강연을 하기 전에 그 강사에 대한 설명을 들었다.

➡ 앞 문장의 주장을 뒷받침하는 연구가 뒤 문장에 이어진다.
▶ 주어진 문장이 ①에 들어갈 수 없음

- ②의 앞 문장과 뒤 문장

> 앞 문장: ①의 뒤 문장과 같음
> 뒤 문장: 학생들의 절반은 '따뜻한'이라는 단어가 포함된 설명을 들었고, 나머지 절반은 그 강사가 '차갑다'는 말을 들었다.

➡ 앞 문장의 연구에 관해, 학생들을 두 그룹으로 나누어 강사에 관해 반대되는 설명을 했다는 내용이 자연스럽게 이어진다. ▶ 주어진 문장이 ②에 들어갈 수 없음

- ③의 앞 문장과 뒤 문장

> 앞 문장: ②의 뒤 문장과 같음
> 뒤 문장: 그리고 나서 그 초청 강사가 토론을 이끌었고, 그 후에 학생들은 그(강사)에 대한 그들의 인상을 말해 달라고 요청받았다.

➡ 강의 후에 학생들에게 강사에 대한 인상이 어땠는지 묻는 흐름은 자연스럽다.
▶ 주어진 문장이 ③에 들어갈 수 없음

> **앞 문장:** ③의 뒤 문장과 같음
> **뒤 문장:** 예상한 대로, 학생들에 의해 형성된 인상 간에는 그 강사에 대한 학생들의 최초 정보에 따라 큰 차이가 있었다.

➡ 사전 정보에 따라 학생들이 느끼는 강사에 대한 인상에 차이가 있었다는 결과가 자연스럽게 이어진다. ▶ 주어진 문장이 ④에 들어갈 수 없음

⑤의 앞 문장과 뒤 문장

> **앞 문장:** ④의 뒤 문장과 같음
> **뒤 문장:** 이것은(This) 서로 다른 기대가 우리가 형성하는 인상뿐만 아니라 ~ 관계에도 영향을 미친다는 것을 보여 준다.

➡ 앞 문장에서는 '인상'에 대한 차이만 언급했으므로 '행동과 관계'와 관련된 내용이 빠져 있다. ▶ 강사가 따뜻할 것이라 기대한 학생들이 강사와 더 많이 소통했다는 내용의 주어진 문장이 ⑤에 들어가야 함

3rd 글이 한눈에 들어오도록 정리하여 정답을 확인한다.

사람들은 어떤 사람이 한 특성을 가지고 있으면 어울리는 다른 특성도 가지고 있을 거라는 잘못된 가정을 한다.
(①) 한 연구에서 대학생들은 강사가 강연을 하기 전에 그 강사에 대한 설명을 들었다.
(②) 학생들은 두 그룹으로 나뉘어서 반대되는 설명(따뜻하다 / 차갑다)을 들었다.
(③) 강사의 강연이 끝난 후에 학생들은 강사에 대한 인상을 말해 달라고 요청받았다.
(④) 학생들에 의해 형성된 인상 간에는 학생들이 받은 최초 정보에 따라 큰 차이가 있었다.
(⑤ 그 강사가 따뜻할 거라고 기대한 학생들은 그와 더 많이 소통하는 경향이 있었다.)
이것은 서로 다른 기대가 우리의 행동 및 형성되는 관계에도 영향을 미친다는 것을 보여 준다.

40 정답 ① *생존을 위한 집단행동

단서 1 안전성을 높이고 신뢰 대상을 찾기 위해 사회적 증거를 찾음
To help decide / what's risky and what's safe, / who's trustworthy and who's not, / we look for *social evidence*. //
결정하는 것을 돕기 위해 / 무엇이 위험하고 무엇이 안전한지 / 누구를 신뢰할 수 있고 누구를 신뢰할 수 없는지를 / 우리는 '사회적 증거'를 찾는다 //

단서 2 다른 사람들과 비슷한 것을 택하는 것이 더 안전한 선택임
From an evolutionary view, / following the group is almost always positive / for our prospects of survival. //
동명사구 주어(단수 취급) 단수 동사
진화의 관점에서 볼 때 / 집단을 따르는 것이 거의 항상 긍정적이다 / 우리의 생존 전망에 //

"If everyone's doing it, / it must be a sensible thing to do," /
강한 확신을 나타내는 조동사
explains / famous psychologist / and best selling writer of *Influence*, Robert Cialdini. //
"모든 사람이 그것을 하고 있다면 / 그것은 해야 할 분별 있는 일인 것이 틀림없다" 라고 / 설명한다 / 유명한 심리학자이자 / 〈Influence〉를 쓴 베스트셀러 작가인 Robert Cialdini는 //

부사절 접속사(대조)
While we can frequently see this today / in product reviews, / even subtler cues / within the environment / can signal trustworthiness. //
우리는 오늘날 이것을 자주 볼 수 있지만 / 상품 평에서 / 훨씬 더 미묘한 신호가 / 환경 내의 / 신뢰성을 나타낼 수 있다 //

Consider this: / when you visit a local restaurant, / are they busy? //
이것을 생각해 보라 / 여러분이 어떤 지역의 음식점을 방문할 때 / 그들이 바쁜가 //

Is there a line outside / or is it easy to find a seat? //
밖에 줄이 있는가 / 아니면 자리를 찾기가 쉬운가 //

가주어 진주어 동격절 접속사
It is a hassle to wait, / but a line can be a powerful cue / that the food's tasty, / and these seats are in demand. //
기다리는 것은 성가신 일이지만 / 줄은 강력한 신호일 수 있다 / 음식이 맛있고 / 이곳의 좌석은 수요가 많다는 //

'대개, 자주' 가주어 진주어
More often than not, / it's good to adopt the practices / of those around you. // 단서 3 주변 사람들의 결정을 따르는 것이 좋음
대개는 / 행동을 따르는 것이 좋다 / 당신의 주변에 있는 사람들의 //

> → We tend to feel safe and secure / in (A) **numbers** / when
> 「의문사 how + to부정사」 어떻게 ~할지
> we decide **how to act**, / particularly when **faced** with (B)
> 앞에 we are가 생략됨
> **uncertain** conditions. //
> 우리는 안전하고 안심된다고 느끼는 경향이 있다 / 수에서 / 어떻게 행동할지 결정할 때 / 특히 불확실한 상황에 직면할 때 //

- risky ⓐ 위험한 • trustworthy ⓐ 신뢰할 수 있는
- evidence ⓝ 증거 • evolutionary ⓐ 진화의
- prospect ⓝ 전망 • sensible ⓐ 분별 있는
- psychologist ⓝ 심리학자 • cue ⓝ 신호 • signal ⓥ 나타내다
- local ⓐ 지역의, 현지의 • tasty ⓐ 맛있는
- adopt ⓥ 따르다, 채택하다 • practice ⓝ 행동, 관행
- uncertain ⓐ 불확실한 • unrealistic ⓐ 비현실적인

무엇이 위험하고 무엇이 안전한지, 누구를 신뢰할 수 있고 누구를 신뢰할 수 없는지를 결정하는 것을 돕기 위해, 우리는 '사회적 증거'를 찾는다. 진화의 관점에서 볼 때, 집단을 따르는 것이 거의 항상 우리의 생존 전망에 긍정적이다. "모든 사람이 그것을 하고 있다면, 그것은 해야 할 분별 있는 일인 것이 틀림없다."라고 유명한 심리학자이자 〈Influence〉를 쓴 베스트셀러 작가인 Robert Cialdini는 설명한다. 오늘날 상품 평에서 이것을 자주 볼 수 있지만, 환경 내의 훨씬 더 미묘한 신호가 신뢰성을 나타낼 수 있다. 이것을 생각해보라. 여러분이 어떤 지역의 음식점을 방문할 때, 그들이 바쁜가? 밖에 줄이 있는가, 아니면 자리를 찾기가 쉬운가? 기다리는 것은 성가신 일이지만, 줄은 음식이 맛있고 이곳의 좌석은 수요가 많다는 강력한 신호일 수 있다. 대개는 주변에 있는 사람들의 행동을 따르는 것이 좋다.
→ 우리는 어떻게 행동할지 결정할 때, 특히 (B) **불확실한** 상황에 직면할 때 (A) **수**에서 안전하고 안심된다고 느끼는 경향이 있다.

> **다음 글의 내용을 한 문장으로 요약하고자 한다. 빈칸 (A), (B)에 들어갈 말로 가장 적절한 것은?**
>
> | | (A) | | (B) | |
> |---|---|---|---|---|
> | ① | numbers 수 | — | uncertain 불확실한 | 상황이 불확실할 때 많은 수의 사람들이 어떤 것을 하면 신뢰한다고 했음 |
> | ② | numbers | — | unrealistic 비현실적인 | 비현실적이 아닌 불확실한 경우에 대해서 말했음 |
> | ③ | experiences 경험 | — | unrealistic | 경험하지 않아도 주위 사람을 보며 따라 하라고 했음 |
> | ④ | rules 규칙 | — | uncertain | 얼마나 많은 사람들이 어떤 것을 하느냐에 신경 쓰라고 했음 |
> | ⑤ | rules | — | unpleasant 불쾌한 | 불쾌하기보다는 불확실해서 정보가 필요할 경우에 해당함 |

왜 정답? ★★★ [정답률 52%]
(A):

> • 진화의 관점에서 볼 때, 집단을 따르는 것이 거의 항상 우리의 생존 전망에 긍정적이다. 단서 2
> • 대개는 주변에 있는 사람들의 행동을 따르는 것이 좋다. 단서 3

➡ 우리의 생존에 긍정적인 것은 집단을 따르는 것이라고 했다. 즉 모든 사람이 어떤 일을 하고 있으면 그것은 해야 할 일이라는 것이다.
▶ 많은 '수'의 사람이 하면 해야 한다는 것이므로 (A)에는 ①, ②의 numbers가 들어가야 함

(B):

> 무엇이 위험하고 무엇이 안전한지, 누구를 신뢰할 수 있고 누구를 신뢰할 수 없는지를 결정하는 것을 돕기 위해, 우리는 '사회적 증거'를 찾는다. 단서 1

➡ 무엇이 안전한 선택인지, 누가 믿을 수 있는 사람인지 모른다는 것은 '불확실한' 상황이다.
　▶ (B)에는 ①, ④의 uncertain이 들어가는 것이 적절하므로 정답은 ①임

왜 오답?

② 비현실적이 아닌 불확실한 경우에 집단을 따르는 우리의 행동에 대해 말하고 있다.
③ 내가 직접 경험하지 않아도 주위 사람을 보며 따라 하라고 했다.
④ 규칙이 아니라 얼마나 많은 사람들이 어떤 것을 하느냐를 신경 쓰라고 했다.
⑤ 불쾌하기보다는 불확실해서 정보가 필요할 경우에 해당하므로 적절하지 않다.

＊ 글의 흐름

도입	진화의 관점에서 볼 때, 집단을 따르는 것이 거의 항상 생존 전망에 긍정적이다.
예시	상품 평에서도 그렇고, 어떤 음식점을 방문할 때와 같은 상황이 이런 경우이다.
부연	음식점이 바쁜지 등을 보면 사람이 많이 오는 맛있는 음식점인지 알 수 있다.
결론	대개는 주변 사람들의 행동을 따르는 것이 좋다.

41~42 ＊익숙함에 비례하는 기억의 범위

앞에 주격 관계대명사와 be동사가 생략됨
Chess masters / shown a chess board in the middle of a game /
능동태의 직접목적어
for 5 seconds / with 20 to 30 pieces still in play / can immediately
reproduce the position of the pieces / from memory. //
체스의 달인들은 / 체스판을 게임 중간에 본 / 5초 동안 / 20개에서 30개의 말들이 아직 놓여 있는 상태로 / 그 말들의 위치를 즉시 재현할 수 있다 / 기억으로부터 //

Beginners, / of course, / are able to place only a few. //
초보자들은 / 물론 / 겨우 몇 개만 위치시킬 수 있다 //

Now take the same pieces / and place them on the board
randomly / and the (a) difference is much reduced. //
이제 같은 말들을 가져다가 / 체스판에 무작위로 놓으면 / 그 차이는 크게 줄어든다 //

The expert's advantage / is only for familiar patterns / — those
= patterns
previously stored in memory. // 41번 단서 1: 전문성은 익숙한 패턴에 대한 기억에서 나옴
전문가의 유리함은 / 익숙한 패턴에 대해서만 있다 / 즉 이전에 기억에 저장된 패턴 //

앞에 Being이 생략됨 ＊
Faced with unfamiliar patterns, / even when it involves the
same familiar domain, / the expert's advantage (b) disappears. //
익숙하지 않은 패턴에 직면하면 / 같은 익숙한 분야와 관련 있는 경우라도 / 전문가의 유리함은 사라진다 //

핵심 주어(복수)　　　　　　　　　　　　　　　복수 동사
The beneficial effects / of familiar structure on memory / have
been observed for many types of expertise, / including music. //
유익한 효과는 / 익숙한 구조가 기억에 미치는 / 많은 유형의 전문 지식에서 관찰되어 왔다 / 음악을 포함하여 //
42번 단서 1: 익숙한 구조를 접할 때 전문 지식이 발휘됨

People with musical training can reproduce / short sequences of
비교 표현
musical notation / more accurately / than those with no musical
training / when notes follow (c) unusual(→ usual) sequences, /
음악 훈련을 받은 사람은 재현할 수 있다 / 짧은 연속된 악보를 / 더 정확하게 / 음악 훈련을 받지 않은 사람보다 / 음표가 특이한(→ 전형적인) 순서를 따를 때는 /

　　　　　　　　　　　　　　　　　　　　　수동태 동사
but the advantage is much reduced / when the notes are ordered
randomly. // 42번 단서 2: 음표가 무작위면 전문성의 발휘가 덜 됨
하지만 그 유리함이 훨씬 줄어든다 / 음표가 무작위로 배열되면 //

Expertise also improves memory / for sequences of (d)
movements. // 41번 단서 2: 전문성은 연속 동작에 대한 기억력을 향상시킴
전문 지식은 또한 기억을 향상시킨다 / 연속 동작에 대한 //

Experienced ballet dancers / are able to repeat longer sequences
of steps / than less experienced dancers, /
숙련된 발레 무용수가 / 더 긴 연속 스텝을 반복할 수 있다 / 경험이 적은 무용수보다 /

and they can repeat a sequence of steps / making up a routine /
앞에 주격 관계대명사와 be동사가 생략됨
better than steps ordered randomly. //
그리고 그들은 연속 스텝을 반복할 수 있다 / 정해진 춤 동작을 이루는 / 무작위로 배열된 스텝보다 더 잘 //

In each case, / memory range is (e) increased / by the ability to
형용사적 용법(ability 수식)
recognize familiar sequences and patterns. //
각각의 경우 / 기억의 범위는 늘어난다 / 익숙한 순서와 패턴을 인식하는 능력에 의해 //

- -

- master ⓝ 달인　　• reproduce ⓥ 재현하다
- randomly ⓐⓓ 무작위로　　• expert ⓝ 전문가
- advantage ⓝ 유리함　　• familiar ⓐ 익숙한
- previously ⓐⓓ 이전에　　• face ⓥ 직면하다　　• domain ⓝ 분야
- beneficial ⓐ 유익한　　• structure ⓝ 구조　　• observe ⓥ 관찰하다
- accurately ⓐⓓ 정확하게　　• note ⓝ 음표　　• order ⓥ 배열하다
- guarantee ⓥ 보장하다　　• experienced ⓐ 숙련된
- range ⓝ 범위　　• recognize ⓥ 인식하다

체스판을 게임 중간에 20개에서 30개의 말들이 아직 놓여 있는 상태로 5초 동안 본 체스의 달인들은 그 말들의 위치를 기억으로부터 즉시 재현할 수 있다. 물론 초보자들은 겨우 몇 개만 위치시킬 수 있다. 이제 같은 말들을 가져다가 체스판에 무작위로 놓으면 그 (a) 차이는 크게 줄어든다. 전문가의 유리함은 익숙한 패턴, 즉 이전에 기억에 저장된 패턴에 대해서만 있다. 익숙하지 않은 패턴에 직면하면, 같은 익숙한 분야와 관련 있는 경우라도 전문가의 유리함은 (b) 사라진다.
익숙한 구조가 기억에 미치는 유익한 효과는 음악을 포함하여 많은 유형의 전문 지식에서 관찰되어 왔다. 음표가 (c) 특이한(→ 전형적인) 순서를 따를 때는 음악 훈련을 받은 사람이 음악 훈련을 받지 않은 사람보다 짧은 연속된 악보를 더 정확하게 재현할 수 있지만, 음표가 무작위로 배열되면 그 유리함이 훨씬 줄어든다. 전문 지식은 또한 연속 (d) 동작에 대한 기억을 향상시킨다. 숙련된 발레 무용수가 경험이 적은 무용수보다 더 긴 연속 스텝을 반복할 수 있고, 무작위로 배열된 스텝보다 정해진 춤 동작을 이루는 연속 스텝을 더 잘 반복할 수 있다. 각각의 경우, 기억의 범위는 익숙한 순서와 패턴을 인식하는 능력에 의해 (e) 늘어난다.

41 정답 ②

윗글의 제목으로 가장 적절한 것은?

① How Can We Build Good Routines? 어떻게 하면 좋은 루틴을 형성할 수 있는가?
　루틴 형성에 초점을 두고 있지는 않음
② Familiar Structures Help Us Remember
　익숙한 구조가 우리가 기억하는 것을 돕는다　자주 접하는 익숙한 구조를 잘 기억할 수 있다는 내용
③ Intelligence Does Not Guarantee Expertise
　지능이 전문 지식을 보장하진 않는다　　지능과는 관련이 없는 내용임
④ Does Playing Chess Improve Your Memory?
　체스를 두는 것이 기억력을 향상시키는가?　체스는 중심 내용을 설명하기 위한 예시일 뿐임
⑤ Creative Art Performance Starts from Practice
　창의적인 예술 작업은 연습으로부터 시작한다　창의성보다는 반복이 초점임

왜 정답? ✿✿❀ [정답률 69%]

> • 전문가의 유리함은 익숙한 패턴, 즉 이전에 기억에 저장된 패턴에 대해서만 있다. 41번 단서 1
> • 전문 지식은 또한 연속 동작에 대한 기억을 향상시킨다. 41번 단서 2

➡ 전문가들은 자신에게 익숙한 패턴은 잘 기억하지만, 익숙하지 않은 경우에는 전문성을 발휘하기 어렵다고 했고, 전문 지식 또한 연속 동작에 대한 기억을 향상시킨다고 했다.
　▶ 따라서 제목으로는 ② '익숙한 구조가 우리가 기억하는 것을 돕는다'가 적절하다.

> **왜 오답?**

① 루틴을 형성하는 방법에 대해 초점을 둔 글이 아니라 익숙함이 갖는 영향력에 대한 글이다.

③ 지능보다는 반복적인 경험을 통한 패턴의 인식 능력이 전문성에 기여한다고 했다.

④ 체스는 전문가의 패턴 파악 능력에 대한 예시로 쓰였을 뿐 중심 내용은 아니다. 함정

⑤ 창의적인 예술 작업과는 관련이 없다.

42 정답 ③

> 밑줄 친 (a)~(e) 중에서 문맥상 낱말의 쓰임이 적절하지 <u>않은</u> 것은?
>
> ① (a) 익숙함이 사라지면 전문가와 일반인 간의 차이는 줄어들 것임
>   차이
> ② (b) 익숙함이라는 요인을 제거하면 전문가와 일반인 간의 격차는 사라짐
>   사라지다
> ③ (c) 전문가에게 익숙한 전형적인 패턴에 대한 설명임
>   특이한, 일반적이지 않은
> ④ (d) 전문 지식을 가지고 있으면 패턴화된 움직임을 더 잘 기억할 수 있음
>   동작
> ⑤ (e) 익숙한 것을 접할 경우 기억할 수 있는 범주가 늘어남
>   늘어나다

> **왜 정답?** ★★★ [정답률 50%]

③ (c) unusual 특이한

> 음표가 (c) ~~특이한~~ 전형적인 순서를 따를 때는 음악 훈련을 받은 사람이 음악 훈련을 받지 않은 사람보다 짧은 연속된 악보를 더 정확하게 재현할 수 있지만(but), 음표가 무작위로 배열되면 그 유리함이 훨씬 줄어든다.

➡ 음표가 무작위로 배열되는 것(= 익숙하지 않은 것)과 역접의 연결어 but으로 연결되고 있으므로 특이한 순서(= 익숙하지 않은 것)를 따르는 상황과 반대되는 상황이여야 자연스럽다.

▶ unusual을 usual(전형적인)과 같은 반의어로 바꿔야 함

> **왜 오답?**

① (a) difference 차이

> 이제 같은 말들을 가져다가 체스판에 무작위로 놓으면 그 (a) 차이는 크게 줄어든다. 전문가의 유리함은 익숙한 패턴, 즉 이전에 기억에 저장된 패턴에 대해서만 있다.

➡ 전문가의 유리함은 익숙한 패턴에 대해서만 있다는 설명이 이어진다. 앞에서 초보자들은 게임 중인 말의 위치를 겨우 몇 개만 기억해 낼 수 있다고 했으므로, 무작위로 놓으면 전문가와 초보자가 위치시키는 말들의 수 '차이'는 크게 줄어들 것이다.

▶ difference는 문맥에 맞음

② (b) disappears 사라지다

> 전문가의 유리함은 익숙한 패턴, 즉 이전에 기억에 저장된 패턴에 대해서만 있다. 익숙하지 않은 패턴에 직면하면, 같은 익숙한 분야와 관련 있는 경우라도 전문가의 유리함은 (b) 사라진다.

➡ 전문가는 익숙한 패턴에 대해서만 유리하다고 했으므로, 익숙하지 않은 패턴에 대해서는 이 유리함이 '사라질' 것이다.

▶ disappears는 문맥에 맞음

④ (d) movements 동작

> 전문 지식은 또한 연속 (d) 동작에 대한 기억을 향상시킨다. 숙련된 발레 무용수가 경험이 적은 무용수보다 더 긴 연속 스텝을 반복할 수 있고, 무작위로 배열된 스텝보다 정해진 춤 동작을 이루는 연속 스텝을 더 잘 반복할 수 있다.

➡ 숙련된 발레 무용수가 더 긴 연속 스텝을 반복할 수 있다고 했으므로 전문 지식은 연속 '동작에 대한 기억을 향상시킬 것이다.

▶ movements는 문맥에 맞음

⑤ (e) increased 늘어나다

> 각각의 경우, 기억의 범위는 익숙한 순서와 패턴을 인식하는 능력에 의해 (e) 늘어난다.

➡ 앞에서 더 긴 연속 스텝을 반복할 수 있다고 했으므로 기억의 범위는 익숙한 패턴을 인식하는 능력에 의해 '늘어날' 것이다.

▶ increased는 문맥에 맞음

─── 어법 특강

✱ 분사구문의 형태

– 분사구문은 「현재분사/과거분사/형용사 ~, 주어+동사 ~.」로 표현되며, 분사구문이 콤마 뒤에 오는 경우도 있다. 특히, 형용사나 과거분사로 시작하는 분사구문에 유의해야 한다. 이런 형태가 되는 이유는 앞에 being이나 having been이 보통 생략되기 때문이다.

• The rope burnt evenly, <u>indicating</u> the passage of time.
 → 의미상 주어인 the rope와 능동의 관계
 (그 밧줄은 시간의 경과를 보여주면서 균등하게 탔다.)

• (Being) <u>Sent</u> to the boarding school, I was 11 years od.
 → 의미상 주어인 I와 수동의 관계이고, being이 생략되어 sent만 남게 됨
 (기숙학교에 보내어졌을 때 나는 11살이었다.)

• (Being) <u>Tired</u> with hard work, he fell asleep with TV on.
 → 앞에 being이 생략되어 tired만 남게 됨
 (과로로 피곤해서 그는 TV를 켜놓은 채 잠이 들었다.)

43~45 ✱친절을 베풀어라

(A) Once upon a time, / there was a king / who lived in a beautiful palace. //
옛날 옛적에 / 한 왕이 있었다 / 아름다운 궁전에 사는 //

While the king was away, / a monster approached the gates of the palace. // **45번 ①** 왕이 없는 동안 괴물이 궁전 문으로 접근함
왕이 없는 동안 / 한 괴물이 궁전 문으로 접근했다 //

The monster was **so** ugly and smelly / **that** the guards froze in shock. //   so ~ that ...: 너무 ~해서 …하다
그 괴물이 너무 추하고 냄새가 나서 / 경비병들은 충격으로 얼어붙었다 //

He passed the guards / and sat on the king's throne. //
그(괴물)는 경비병들을 지나 / 왕의 왕좌에 앉았다 //   **43번** 단서 1: 경비병들이 괴물에게 왕좌에서 내려올 것을 요구했음

The guards soon **came to their senses**, / went in, / and shouted at the monster, / **demanding** that (a) **he get off** the throne. // '정신을 차리다'   분사구문을 이끄는 현재분사 = the monster 앞에 should가 생략됨
경비병들은 곧 정신을 차리고 / 안으로 들어가 / 그 괴물을 향해 소리쳤다 / 그에게 왕좌에서 내려올 것을 요구하며 //

✱(A) 문단 요약: 왕이 궁전을 비운 동안에 추하고 냄새나는 괴물이 왕좌에 앉았고, 경비병들이 괴물에게 왕좌에서 내려올 것을 요구함

(B) Eventually / the king returned. // **43번** 단서 2: 왕좌를 차지하고 경비병들과 대치 중인 상황에서 자리의 주인이 나타남
마침내 / 왕이 돌아왔다 //

병렬 구조
He **was** wise and kind / and **saw** what was happening. //
그는 현명하고 친절했으며 / 무슨 일이 일어나고 있는지 알아차렸다 //

knew의 목적어로 쓰인「의문사＋to부정사」
He knew / **what** to do. //
그는 알았다 / 무엇을 해야 할지 //

45번 ② 왕이 미소를 지으며 괴물에게 환영한다고 말함
He smiled and said to the monster, / "Welcome to my palace!" //
그는 미소를 지으며 그 괴물에게 말했다 / "나의 궁전에 온 것을 환영하오"라고 //

= the monster
He asked the monster / if (b) **he** wanted a cup of coffee. //
왕은 그 괴물에게 물었다 / 그가 커피 한 잔을 원하는지 //

The monster began to grow smaller / as he drank the coffee. //
괴물은 더 작아지기 시작했다 / 그 커피를 마시면서 //

*(B) 문단 요약: 돌아온 왕이 괴물에게 커피를 권했고 괴물은 작아짐

= the monster
(C) The king offered (c) **him** / some take-out pizza and fries. //
왕은 그에게 제안했다 / 약간의 테이크아웃 피자와 감자튀김을 // **43번** 단서 3: 현명한 왕은 괴물을 겁줘서 쫓아내지 않고 친절을 베풀었음

The guards immediately called for pizza. //
경비병들은 즉시 피자를 시켰다 //

45번 ③ 왕의 친절한 행동에 괴물의 몸이 계속 더 작아짐
The monster continued to get smaller / with the king's kind gestures. //
그 괴물은 몸이 계속 더 작아졌다 / 왕의 친절한 행동에 //

= the king   간접목적어   직접목적어
(d) **He** then offered **the monster** / **a full body massage**. //
그러고 나서 그는 그 괴물에게 제안했다 / 전신 마사지를 //

As the guards helped with the relaxing massage, / the monster became tiny. // **45번 ④** 경비병들이 편안한 마사지를 제공함
경비병들이 편안한 마사지를 도와주자 / 그 괴물은 매우 작아졌다 //

With another act of kindness to the monster, / he just disappeared. //
그 괴물에게 또 한 번의 친절한 행동을 베풀자 / 그는 바로 사라졌다 //

*(C) 문단 요약: 왕이 괴물에게 다양한 음식을 제공했고 마사지까지 해주며 친절을 베풀었더니 괴물이 사라짐

앞에 목적격 관계대명사가 생략됨
(D) With each bad word **the guards used**, / the monster grew more ugly and smelly. // **43번** 단서 4: 경비병들이 왕좌에 앉은 괴물을 몰아내려 함
경비병들이 나쁜 말을 사용할 때마다 / 그 괴물은 더 추해졌고, 더 냄새가 났다 //

비교급 강조 부사   부사적 용법(목적)
The guards got **even** angrier / — they began to brandish their swords / **to scare** the monster away / from the palace. //
경비병들은 한층 더 화가 났다 / 그들은 칼을 휘두르기 시작했다 / 그 괴물을 겁주어 쫓아내려고 / 궁전에서 //

= the monster   분사구문(결과)
45번 ⑤ 경비병들은 겁을 주어 괴물을 쫓아내려 함
But (e) **he** just grew bigger and bigger, / eventually **taking up the whole room**. //
하지만 그는 그저 점점 더 커져서 / 결국 방 전체를 차지했다 //

He grew more ugly and smelly / than ever. //
그는 더 추해졌고, 더 냄새가 났다 / 그 어느 때 보다 //

*(D) 문단 요약: 경비병들이 괴물을 겁주어서 쫓아내려고 위협하자 괴물은 더욱 추하고 더 냄새가 나게 되었고 크기도 더 커짐

- **approach** ⓥ 접근하다 · **smelly** ⓐ 냄새가 나는
- **guard** ⓝ 경비병 · **shock** ⓝ 충격 · **demand** ⓥ 요구하다
- **wise** ⓐ 현명한 · **offer** ⓥ 제안하다 · **immediately** ⓐ 즉시
- **call for** ~을 시키다 · **gesture** ⓝ 행동 · **tiny** ⓐ 매우 작은
- **kindness** ⓝ 친절(한 행위) · **sword** ⓝ 칼
- **eventually** ⓐ 결국, 마침내 · **take up** ~을 차지하다

(A) 옛날 옛적에, 아름다운 궁전에 사는 한 왕이 있었다. 왕이 없는 동안, 한 괴물이 궁전 문으로 접근했다. 그 괴물이 너무 추하고 냄새가 나서 경비병들은 충격으로 얼어붙었다. 그(괴물)는 경비병들을 지나 왕의 왕좌에 앉았다. 경비병들은 곧 정신을 차리고 안으로 들어가 그 괴물을 향해 소리치며 (a) 그에게 왕좌에서 내려올 것을 요구했다.
(D) 경비병들이 나쁜 말을 사용할 때마다, 그 괴물은 더 추해졌고, 더 냄새가 났다. 경비병들은 한층 더 화가 났다. 그들은 그 괴물을 겁주어 궁전에서 쫓아내려고 칼을 휘두르기 시작했다. 하지만 (e) 그는 그저 점점 더 커져서 결국 방 전체를 차지했다. 그는 그 어느 때보다 더 추해졌고, 더 냄새가 났다.

(B) 마침내 왕이 돌아왔다. 그는 현명하고 친절했으며 무슨 일이 일어나고 있는지 알아차렸다. 그는 무엇을 해야 할지 알았다. 그는 미소를 지으며 그 괴물에게 "나의 궁전에 온 것을 환영하오!"라고 말했다. 왕은 그 괴물에게 (b) 그가 커피 한 잔을 원하는지 물었다. 괴물은 그 커피를 마시면서 더 작아지기 시작했다.
(C) 왕은 (c) 그에게 약간의 테이크아웃 피자와 감자튀김을 제안했다. 경비병들은 즉시 피자를 시켰다. 그 괴물은 왕의 친절한 행동에 몸이 계속 더 작아졌다. 그러고 나서 (d) 그는 그 괴물에게 전신 마사지를 제안했다. 경비병들이 편안한 마사지를 도와주자 그 괴물은 매우 작아졌다. 그 괴물에게 또 한 번의 친절한 행동을 베풀자, 그는 바로 사라졌다.

43 정답 ④

주어진 글 (A)에 이어질 내용을 순서에 맞게 배열한 것으로 가장 적절한 것은?

① (B) — (D) — (C) 왕이 부재중일 때 괴물이 더 커졌다는 내용인 (D)가 먼저 나와야 함
② (C) — (B) — (D) 글의 순서와 정반대임
③ (C) — (D) — (B) 괴물이 사라진 (C)는 결말임
④ (D) — (B) — (C) ⌈(D) 괴물은 더욱 추하고 크기도 더 커지게 됨 — (B) 왕이 괴물에게 커피를 권했고 괴물은 작아짐 — (C) 왕이 괴물에게 친절을 더 베풀었더니 괴물이 사라짐⌋
⑤ (D) — (C) — (B) (B)에서 왕이 돌아온 것이 친절을 베푸는 (C)보다 먼저 나와야 함

> **왜 정답 · 오답 ?** ❀❀❀ [정답률 80%]

(A): 왕이 궁전을 비운 동안 추하고 냄새나는 괴물이 왕좌에 앉았고, 경비병들은 괴물에게 왕좌에서 내려올 것을 요구했다.

→ 경비병들이 괴물에게 왕좌에서 내려오라고 어떻게 요구했는지가 이어질 것이다.

(B): 돌아온 왕이 권한 커피를 마시면서 괴물은 더 작아졌다.

→ 왕이 돌아오기 전에, 왕이 없는 상태에서 진행되는 내용이 앞에 나와야 하고, 뒤에는 괴물이 작아진 후에 벌어진 일이 이어져야 한다.

(C): 왕이 괴물에게 다양한 음식을 제공했고 마사지까지 해주며 친절을 베풀었더니 괴물이 사라졌다.

→ 괴물이 사라졌다는 문장으로 끝나므로 이야기의 결말일 가능성이 크다.

(D): 경비병들이 괴물을 겁주어서 쫓아내려고 공격하자 괴물은 더욱 추하고 더 냄새가 나게 되었고 크기도 더 커졌다.

→ 경비병들이 괴물에게 왕좌에서 내려오라고 소리쳤다는 (A)에 이어지는 내용이다.
▶ (D) 경비병들이 괴물을 겁주어서 쫓아내려 하자 괴물은 더욱 추하고 냄새가 나며 크기도 더 커짐 → (B) 돌아온 왕이 괴물에게 커피를 권하자 괴물이 작아짐
→ (C) 왕이 괴물에게 음식과 마사지 등 친절을 더 베풀었더니 괴물이 사라짐
▶ 글의 순서는 ④ (D) — (B) — (C)임

44 정답 ④

밑줄 친 (a)~(e) 중에서 가리키는 대상이 나머지 넷과 다른 것은?

① (a)　　② (b)　　③ (c)　　④(d)　　⑤ (e)
= the monster　= the monster　= the monster　= the king　= the monster

> **왜 정답 ?** ❀❀❀ [정답률 79%]

④ (d) He: 괴물에게 전신 마사지를 제안한 사람 ▶ the king

정답 및 해설 **85**

＞왜 오답？

① (a) he: 왕좌에 앉아서 내려올 것을 요구받는 것 ▶ the monster
② (b) he: 왕이 친절하게 커피를 원하는지 물은 대상 ▶ the monster
③ (c) him: 테이크아웃 피자와 감자튀김을 제안한 대상 ▶ the monster
⑤ (e) he: 경비병들의 자극으로 몸이 커진 것 ▶ the monster

45 정답 ④

윗글에 관한 내용으로 적절하지 않은 것은?

① 왕이 없는 동안 괴물이 궁전 문으로 접근했다.
  While the king was away, a monster approached the gates of the palace.
② 왕은 미소를 지으며 괴물에게 환영한다고 말했다.
  He smiled and said to the monster, "Welcome to my palace!"
③ 왕의 친절한 행동에 괴물의 몸이 계속 더 작아졌다.
  The monster continued to get smaller with the king's kind gestures.
④ 경비병들은 괴물을 마사지해 주기를 거부했다.
  As the guards helped with the relaxing massage, the monster became tiny.
⑤ 경비병들은 겁을 주어 괴물을 쫓아내려 했다.
  they began to brandish their swords to scare the monster away from the palace

＞왜 정답？ ❋❋❋ [정답률 86%]

경비병들이 편안한 마사지를 제공하자 괴물은 더 작아졌다고(As the guards helped with the relaxing massage, the monster became tiny.) 했다. 따라서 괴물을 마사지해 줄 것을 거부했다는 ④이 글의 내용과 일치하지 않는다.

＞왜 오답？

① 왕이 없는 동안 괴물이 궁전 문으로 접근했다고 했다. (While the king was away, a monster approached the gates of the palace.)
② 왕은 미소를 지으며 괴물에게 환영한다고 말했다고 했다. (He smiled and said to the monster, "Welcome to my palace!")
③ 왕의 친절한 행동에 괴물의 몸이 계속 더 작아졌다고 했다. (The monster continued to get smaller with the king's kind gestures.)
⑤ 경비병들은 겁을 주어 괴물을 쫓아내려 했다고 했다. (they began to brandish their swords to scare the monster away from the palace)

3회 Dictation
문제 p. 58

01 principal / big fan / will be held / come and cheer / incredible amount / rink

02 caught a cold / sore throat / necessary / got prescribed / similar to yours / prescribed / prescription

03 preparations going / afraid / have to change / electrical problems / Come with me

04 looking at on / street wall / How do you like / heart-shaped leaves / tree branch

05 been busy helping / reserved a place / just finished designing / music blog

06 can choose from these / was originally / red tumbler / carry around / anything else

07 in line / drop by / duty free shop / took a memo / sold out

08 to anyone aged / interested in joining / far from here / entry fee / application form

09 school counselor / explore various / number of participants / is limited to / will be presented

10 one of these / pretty expensive / material / they are heavier / from splashing

11 Not yet / did you learn

12 about to get in / give me a ride

13 harvested / bring you some / ready to be picked / look around / would be fun

14 had an argument / serious / long face / get along with / texted her / express your apology

15 college freshmen / have reached / suggests to / how early they should

[16~17] families can play together / minimal equipment / basketball court / indoors / these sports

3회 어휘 Review Test
문제 p. 62

01 아픈	**15** cope with	**29** approach
02 변화	**16** habitat	**30** explore
03 큰	**17** beneficial	**31** Wage
04 부주의한	**18** skillful	**32** motivation
05 화합물	**19** outcome	**33** additional
06 prospect	**20** demand	**34** appropriate
07 assumption	**21** uncertain	**35** sensible
08 surface	**22** equipment	**36** description
09 upcoming	**23** adventurous	**37** kindness
10 livelihood	**24** traditional	**38** quality
11 carry around	**25** expertise	**39** apology
12 take up	**26** reproduce	**40** constant
13 settle down	**27** wander	
14 run into	**28** harvest	

01 정답 ③ ✱학생용 프린터 설치 안내

W : Good morning, everyone. 여 : 안녕하세요, 여러분.

I'm your student council president, Kelly Green.
저는 여러분의 학생회장인 Kelly Green입니다.

Many students **have complained** that there are no printers
available **for them** to use.
많은 학생들이 사용할 수 있는 프린터가 없다고 불만을 제기해 왔습니다.

To solve this problem, next week we will set up several new
printers in the student council room. ┌단서┐ 학생회실에 새 프린터가 설치될 것임을 안내함
이 문제를 해결하기 위해, 다음 주에 학생회실에 새 프린터 여러 대를 설치할 예정입니다.

Students will **be able to** use the printers for homework,
projects, or any other school tasks.
학생들은 숙제, 프로젝트나 다른 학교 과제를 위해 프린터를 사용할 수 있게 될 것입니다.

We hope this will help **you do** your work more efficiently
and make your school life easier.
이것이 여러분이 과제를 더 효율적으로 수행하도록 돕고, 학교생활을 더 편리하게 만들기를 바랍니다.

Thank you. 감사합니다.

- student council 학생회
- complain ⓥ 불평하다
- set up 설치하다
- task ⓝ 과제, 업무
- efficiently ⓐⓓ 효율적으로

> 다음을 듣고, 여자가 하는 말의 목적으로 가장 적절한 것을 고르시오.
> ① 학생회관 리모델링 일정을 공지하려고 학생회관 리모델링은 언급되지 않음
> ② 새로운 학습 자료를 제공하려고 새로운 학습 자료 제공은 언급되지 않음
> ③ 학생용 프린터 설치를 알리려고 학생회실 프린터 설치 계획을 안내함
> ④ 학생회장 선출 방법을 안내하려고 학생회장 선출 방법에 관한 내용이 아님
> ⑤ 프린터 고장 시 해결 방법을 설명하려고 프린터 고장은 언급되지 않았음

＞왜 정답? ✿✿✿ [정답률 96%]

학생들이 사용할 프린터가 없다는 불만이 있었기 때문에 다음 주에 학생회실에 새 프린터가 설치될 예정이라고 했다. 따라서 여자가 하는 말의 목적으로 가장 적절한 것은 ③이다.

＞왜 오답?

① 학생회관 리모델링은 언급되지 않았다.
② 과제를 위해 프린터를 사용할 수 있다고 했을 뿐, 새로운 학습 자료 제공은 언급되지 않았다.
④ 학생회장 선출 방법에 관한 내용이 아니다.
⑤ 프린터 고장은 언급되지 않았다.

02 정답 ① ✱단어 암기 방법 제안

M : Anna, I see you're studying Spanish.
남 : Anna, 너 스페인어 공부하고 있구나.

W : Hi, Mr. Brown. Yeah, I**'ve been** really into it these days.
여 : 안녕하세요, Brown 선생님. 네, 요즘 정말 푹 빠졌어요.

M : I've noticed. Do you feel like you're improving a lot?
남 : 난 알아챘어. 실력이 많이 늘고 있다고 느끼니?

W : Hmm... Well, **remembering** words is really hard. I forget
them quickly.
여 : 음... 단어 암기가 진짜 어려워요. 저는 단어들을 금방 잊어요.

M : I see. **How about saying** the words out loud? **It** can be an
effective way **to remember** them.
남 : 그렇구나. 단어를 소리내어 말해보는 건 어때? 그것들을 외우는 데 효과적인 방법일 수 있어. ┌단서┐ 단어를 소리내어 말하는 것이 암기에 효과적임

W : Does it really help? I feel **more comfortable** just memorizing
quietly.
여 : 정말 도움이 되나요? 저는 그냥 조용히 암기하는 게 더 편해요.

M : When you speak out loud, you use different parts of your
brain, and **that** helps you remember words better.
남 : 소리내어 말하면, 뇌의 다양한 부분이 활성화돼서 단어를 더 잘 외울 수 있어.

W : But I always thought **saying** words out loud would make **it**
harder **to focus**.
여 : 그런데 저는 항상 단어를 소리내어 말하면 오히려 집중하기 더 힘들다고 생각했어요.

M : Not at all. Studies show **that it** can help **you stay** more
focused on the task.
남 : 전혀 그렇지 않아. 연구에 따르면 오히려 과제에 더 집중하는 데 도움이 된대.

W : Really? Then, maybe I should give **it** a try.
여 : 정말요? 그럼 한 번 해봐야겠네요.

- notice ⓥ 알아채다
- improve ⓥ 향상시키다
- effective ⓐ 효과적인
- memorize ⓥ 암기하다
- focus ⓥ 집중하다
- study ⓝ 연구

> 대화를 듣고, 남자의 의견으로 가장 적절한 것을 고르시오.
> ① 단어를 소리내어 말하는 것이 암기에 효과적이다. 단어를 소리내어 말하면 암기에 도움이 됨
> ② 말하기와 쓰기는 언어 학습에서 필수적인 요소이다. 쓰기는 언급되지 않았음
> ③ 뇌 기능의 효율성을 높이려면 충분한 휴식이 필요하다. 휴식은 언급되지 않았음
> ④ 문화를 이해하면 그 나라의 언어를 더 쉽게 배울 수 있다. 문화는 언급되지 않았음
> ⑤ 언어 학습 과정에서의 실수는 장기 기억 형성에 도움이 된다. 실수나 장기 기억은 언급되지 않았음

＞왜 정답? ✿✿✿ [정답률 94%]

여자가 단어를 금방 잊어버린다고 하자, 남자는 단어를 소리내어 말하면 뇌의 다양한 부분이 활성화되어 암기에 효과적이라고 했다. 따라서 남자의 의견으로 가장 적절한 것은 ①이나.

＞왜 오답?

② 소리내어 말하기에 관한 내용이지, 쓰기에 관한 내용이 아니다.
③ 뇌의 활성화가 언급되었을 뿐, 뇌 기능의 효율성이나 휴식은 언급되지 않았다.
④ 문화는 언급되지 않았다.
⑤ 학습 과정에서의 실수나 장기 기억은 언급되지 않았다.

03 정답 ① ✱햇빛 쬐기의 이점

M : Hello, listeners!
남 : 안녕하세요, 청취자 여러분!

This is Thomas White's *Living Well*.
Thomas White의 '건강하게 살기'입니다.

What do you do **to stay healthy**?
여러분은 건강을 유지하기 위해 무엇을 하시나요?

Maybe you exercise regularly and eat healthy food.
규칙적으로 운동하고 건강한 음식을 드시겠죠.

Those are both great habits. 둘 다 좋은 습관입니다.

But I have one more simple tip for you.
그런데 여러분께 드릴 간단한 팁이 하나 더 있습니다.

Go outside and **get** some sunlight!
밖에 나가서 햇빛을 쬐세요!

Sunlight is important for your body and mind.
햇빛은 여러분의 몸과 마음 모두에 중요합니다.

Getting sunlight can **prevent you from getting** sick and can reduce anxiety.

prevent A from -ing: A가 ~하는 것을 막다

햇빛을 쬐는 것은 병에 걸리는 것을 예방하고 불안을 줄일 수 있습니다.

It's an easy way **to help** you **stay** healthy both physically and mentally.

형용사적 용법 (way 수식) *to help의 목적격 보어 (원형부정사와 to부정사 모두 가능)*

단서 햇빛을 쬐는 것은 신체적, 정신적 건강 유지에 도움이 됨

이는 신체적으로도 정신적으로도 건강을 유지하는 데 도움이 되는 쉬운 방법입니다.

I'll be right back with more after the break.

광고 후 더 많은 이야기와 함께 돌아오겠습니다.

- **regularly** (ad) 규칙적으로
- **prevent** (v) 예방하다
- **anxiety** (n) 불안
- **physically** (ad) 신체적으로
- **mentally** (ad) 정신적으로

> 다음을 듣고, 남자가 하는 말의 요지로 가장 적절한 것을 고르시오.
>
> ① 햇빛을 쬐는 것은 신체와 정신의 건강에 도움이 된다.
> ② 자외선 차단제를 바르는 것은 피부 노화를 예방한다. ← 자외선 차단제는 언급되지 않았음
> ③ 건강을 위해 다양한 영양소를 고루 섭취해야 한다. ← 영양소 섭취는 언급되지 않았음
> ④ 몸과 마음이 건강하면 삶의 만족도가 높아진다. ← 삶의 만족도는 언급되지 않았음
> ⑤ 야외 활동 시 안전 수칙을 준수해야 한다. ← 야외 활동 안전 수칙은 언급되지 않았음

> **왜 정답?** ✱✿✿ [정답률 94%]

남자는 햇빛을 쬐는 것이 질병 예방과 불안 감소에 도움이 되며, 신체적, 정신적 건강 유지에 도움이 된다고 설명한다. 따라서 남자가 하는 말의 요지로 가장 적절한 것은 ①이다.

> **왜 오답?**

② 자외선 차단제나 피부 노화는 언급되지 않았다.

③ 건강한 음식은 언급되었지만, 다양한 영양소 섭취는 언급되지 않았다. **함정**

④ 햇빛 쬐기가 신체적으로도 정신적으로도 건강 유지에 도움이 된다고 했을 뿐, 몸과 마음의 건강이 삶의 만족도 향상으로 이어진다는 내용이 아니다.

⑤ 안전 수칙은 언급되지 않았다.

---

04 정답 ⑤ ✱ 파자마 파티

M : Jenny, how was the pajama party yesterday?

남 : Jenny, 어제 파자마 파티 어땠어?

W : It was great, Dad. Here, take a look at this photo.

여 : 정말 좋았어요, 아빠. 여기, 이 사진 좀 보세요.

M : Let's see. Oh, I like the pajama party banner next to the clock. **①의 단서** 시계 옆에 파자마 파티 현수막이 있음

남 : 어디 보자. 오, 시계 옆에 있는 파자마 파티 현수막이 마음에 드네.

W : Yeah, it's really eye-catching, isn't it?

여 : 네, 정말 눈에 띄죠, 그렇지 않나요?

M : It is. And here you are standing in your striped pajamas. **②의 단서** Jenny는 줄무늬 파자마를 입고 서 있음

남 : 그렇네. 그리고 여기 너가 줄무늬 파자마를 입고 서 있구나.

W : I absolutely love these pajamas. They **look** so **cute**.

look (감각동사) + 주격 보어 (형용사)

여 : 이 파자마 정말 좋아요. 너무 귀엽잖아요.

M : And the **girl making** a V-sign with her fingers is your friend Mia, right? **③의 단서** 손가락으로 V자 표시하고 있는 여자아이가 있음

사이에 주격 관계대명사와 be동사가 생략됨

남 : 손가락으로 V자 표시하고 있는 여자아이는 네 친구 Mia야, 그렇지?

W : That's right. Do you see the pillows on the bed? We had a pillow fight! **④의 단서** 침대 위에 베개가 있음

여 : 맞아요. 침대 위에 베개가 보이나요? 우리 베개 싸움을 했어요!

M : It **must've been** so much fun. By the way, what are those three stars on the wall? **⑤의 단서** 벽에 별 세 개가 아니라 두 개가 붙어 있음

must have p.p.: ~했음이 틀림없다

남 : 정말 재미있었겠구나. 그런데 벽에 붙어 있는 별 세 개는 뭐니?

W : Oh, those are stickers. They glow in the dark.

여 : 아, 그것들은 스티커예요. 어둠 속에서 빛나요.

M : I see. Sounds like you had an amazing time at the pajama party.

남 : 그렇구나. 파자마 파티에서 정말 멋진 시간을 보낸 것 같네.

W : Definitely! I'll never forget it.

여 : 물론이요! 절대 잊지 못할 거예요.

- **banner** (n) 현수막
- **eye-catching** (a) 눈에 띄는
- **striped** (a) 줄무늬의
- **pillow fight** 베개 싸움
- **glow** (v) 빛나다

> 대화를 듣고, 그림에서 대화의 내용과 일치하지 **않는** 것을 고르시오.

> **왜 정답?** ✱✿✿ [정답률 94%]

벽에 별 스티커 세 개가 붙어 있다고 했지만, 그림에는 두 개가 붙어 있으므로 ⑤이 대화의 내용과 일치하지 않는다.

> **왜 오답?**

① 시계 옆에 파자마 파티 현수막이 있다.

② Jenny는 줄무늬 파자마를 입고 서 있다.

③ Jenny의 친구인 Mia는 손가락으로 V자 표시를 하고 있다.

④ 침대 위에 베개들이 있다.

---

05 정답 ② ✱ 사탕 가게 개업 행사 준비

W : Brian, I think we're almost ready for our candy shop's opening event.

여 : Brian, 사탕 가게 개업 행사 준비가 거의 끝난 것 같아.

M : That's right. What do we have **left** to do?

과거분사

남 : 맞아. 이제 뭐만 하면 되지?

W : Well, let's see. Is the background music playlist ready? **⑤의 함정**

여 : 음, 보자. 배경 음악 재생 목록은 준비됐어?

M : Yes, I chose some cheerful songs and made a playlist.

남 : 응, 신나는 노래들로 골라서 재생 목록을 만들었어.

W : Great! What about the bluetooth speakers? **④의 함정**

여 : 잘했어! 블루투스 스피커는 어때?

M : I tested **them** and they're working fine. Did you choose the sample candies **for customers** to try? **①의 함정**

= the bluetooth speakers *to try의 의미상 주어*

남 : 시험해 봤는데 잘 작동해. 손님들이 맛볼 시식용 사탕은 골랐어?

W : Yeah. Look! I put them in these pretty little baskets.

여 : 응. 봐봐! 예쁜 작은 바구니에 담았어.

M : Thanks! They look nice. 남 : 고마워! 보기 좋다.

W : And all the other candies **are** nicely **placed** around the shop.

수동태 동사

여 : 그리고 다른 사탕들도 가게에 예쁘게 진열해 놨어.

M : Wait, how about the price tags? 남 : 잠깐, 가격표는?

W : Oh, we almost forgot. Could you put them on the candy boxes? 여 : 아, 까먹을 뻔했네. 사탕 상자에 가격표 좀 붙여줄래?

M : Of course. I'll do it right away. **단서** 남자가 가격표를 바로 붙이겠다고 함

남 : 물론이지. 지금 바로 할게.

- playlist ⓝ 재생 목록 • cheerful ⓐ 신나는
- sample ⓝ (시식용) 샘플, 견본 • customer ⓝ 고객, 손님
- place ⓥ 배치하다, 진열하다 • price tag 가격표

대화를 듣고, 남자가 할 일로 가장 적절한 것을 고르시오.
① 시식용 사탕 고르기 여자가 이미 골라놓음
②가격표 붙이기 남자가 가격표를 붙이기로 함
③ 홍보 포스터 게시하기 홍보 포스터는 언급되지 않았음
④ 스피커 점검하기 남자가 이미 점검함
⑤ 음악 재생 목록 만들기 남자가 이미 만들어놓음

＞왜 정답？ ✽✾✾ [정답률 92%]

사탕 가게 개업 행사를 준비 중인데, 아직 사탕 상자에 가격표를 붙이지 않아서 남자가 바로 붙이겠다고 했으므로 정답은 ②이다.

＞왜 오답？

① 시식용 사탕은 여자가 이미 골라놓았다.
③ 홍보 포스터는 언급되지 않았다.
④ 스피커는 남자가 이미 점검했다.
⑤ 음악 재생 목록은 남자가 이미 만들어놓았다.

---

06 정답 ④ ＊Lake Boat Tours 티켓과 간식 구입

M : Welcome to Lake Boat Tours. How can I help you?
남 : Lake Boat Tours에 오신 걸 환영합니다. 무엇을 도와드릴까요?

W : Hello. I'd like to buy some tickets for today.
여 : 안녕하세요. 오늘 탈 수 있는 표를 사고 싶어요.

M : We have daytime tickets and sunset tickets. Which would you like?
남 : 낮 시간 티켓과 일몰 티켓이 있어요. 어떤 걸 원하시나요?

W : We'd like sunset tickets, please. How much are they? = sunset tickets
여 : 일몰 티켓으로 할게요. 얼마인가요?

M : It's $30 for adults and $20 for children. How many tickets do you want? 단서 1 어른 1인당 30달러, 어린이 1인당 20달러
남 : 어른은 30달러, 어린이는 20달러입니다. 몇 장을 원하시나요?

W : Two adult tickets and one child ticket, please.
여 : 어른 두 장, 어린이 한 장이요. 단서 2 어른 티켓 두 장, 어린이 티켓 한 장을 구매함

M : Okay. And, we offer snacks for $10 per person. Would you like them? = snacks 단서 3 간식은 1인당 10달러
남 : 네. 그리고, 간식은 1인당 10달러입니다. 드릴까요?

W : Yes. Snacks for all three of us, please.
여 : 네. 세 명 다 주세요. 단서 4 간식 세 개를 구매함

M : Alright. Do you need anything else?
남 : 알겠습니다. 다른 게 필요하신가요?

W : No, that's it.
여 : 아니요, 그게 다예요.

M : So, that's two adults and one child for the sunset tour, all with snacks.
남 : 그러면 일몰 투어 어른 두 명, 어린이 한 명, 전부 간식 포함이네요.

W : Perfect. Here's my credit card.
여 : 좋아요. 여기 제 신용카드입니다.

- tour ⓝ 여행, 관광 • daytime ⓝ 낮 시간 • sunset ⓝ 일몰
- credit card 신용카드

대화를 듣고, 여자가 지불할 금액을 고르시오. [3점]
① $80 ② $90 ③ $100 ④$110 ⑤ $120
$30×2(어른 티켓 두 장) + $20(어린이 티켓 한 장) + $10×3(간식 세 개)

＞왜 정답？ ✽✾✾ [정답률 82%]

여자는 하나에 30달러인 어른 티켓 두 장과 20달러인 어린이 티켓 한 장을 구매했고, 10달러인 간식 세 개를 구매했으므로 여자가 지불할 금액은 ④ '110달러'이다.

---

07 정답 ② ＊버스킹 공연 불참

M : Hey, Alicia. I saw a video of you playing the guitar on your social media. It was great.
동명사의 의미상 주어 동명사 (전치사 of의 목적어) ①의 함정
남 : 안녕, Alicia. 네가 기타 연주하는 영상을 소셜 미디어에서 봤어. 멋지더라.

W : Thanks, Oliver. Your singing videos are fantastic, too.
여 : 고마워, Oliver. 네 노래 영상도 훌륭하더라.

M : I have an idea. There's a busking event this Sunday. How about performing together?
How about -ing?: ~하는 게 어때? (권유)
남 : 좋은 생각이 있어. 이번 주 일요일에 버스킹 행사가 있거든. 같이 공연하는 거 어때?

W : This Sunday? I'd really love to, but I can't.
뒤에 perform together가 생략됨
여 : 이번 주 일요일? 정말 하고 싶은데, 못 해.

M : Why not? Do you feel nervous about performing in public?
동명사 (전치사 about의 목적어) ⑤의 함정
남 : 왜? 사람들 앞에서 공연하는 게 긴장돼서 그래?

W : Not really, but I already have another plan on Sunday.
여 : 그런 건 아닌데, 일요일에 이미 다른 일정이 있어.

M : Oh, do you still take tennis lessons every Sunday?
남 : 아, 아직도 일요일마다 테니스 수업 받니? ③의 함정

W : Not anymore. Do you remember I had an interview for a part-time job?
앞에 목적어절 접속사 that이 생략됨
여 : 이제 안 받아. 나 아르바이트 면접 봤던 거 기억나?

M : Of course. Did you get it? = a part-time job
남 : 당연하지. 합격했어?

W : Yes, so I have to start working the part-time job this Sunday.
단서 이번 주 일요일부터 아르바이트를 시작해야 함
여 : 응, 그래서 이번 주 일요일부터 아르바이트 시작해야 해.

M : I see. Maybe we can try for another time.
남 : 그렇구나. 아마 우린 다음에 시도할 수 있을 거야.

- perform ⓥ 공연하다 • nervous ⓐ 긴장한
- in public 사람들[대중] 앞에서 • interview ⓝ 면접
- part-time job 아르바이트

대화를 듣고, 여자가 버스킹 공연에 참여할 수 없는 이유를 고르시오.
① 기타 연주를 연습해야 해서 기타 연주 연습은 언급되지 않았음
②아르바이트를 해야 해서 이번 주 일요일부터 아르바이트를 시작해야 함
③ 테니스 수업을 받아야 해서 테니스 수업은 이제 안 받음
④ 오디션을 준비해야 해서 오디션은 언급되지 않았음
⑤ 대중 앞 공연이 긴장되어서 대중 앞 공연이 긴장되는 것은 아니라고 했음

＞왜 정답？ ✽✾✾ [정답률 91%]

남자가 여자에게 이번 주 일요일 버스킹 행사에서 같이 공연하자고 제안했지만, 여자는 이번 주 일요일부터 아르바이트를 시작해야 해서 참여하지 못한다고 했으므로 정답은 ②이다.

＞왜 오답？

① 여자가 기타를 연주하는 영상을 남자가 소셜 미디어에서 봤을 뿐이며, 기타 연주 연습 때문에 버스킹 공연에 참여할 수 없는 것은 아니다.
③ 테니스 수업은 더 이상 받지 않는다.
④ 오디션은 언급되지 않았다.
⑤ 대중 앞에서 공연하는 것은 긴장되지 않는다고 했다.

08 정답 ③ ＊불꽃놀이 축제 자원봉사 지원

W : Jay, did you hear about the Fireworks Festival?
여 : Jay, 불꽃놀이 축제 소식 들었어?

M : Yeah, I heard it's going to be amazing. *(it = the Fireworks Festival)*
남 : 응, 엄청 멋질 거라던데.

W : I'm thinking of volunteering there. Take a look at this poster about it. *(there = the Fireworks Festival)*
여 : 거기서 자원봉사를 하려고 생각 중이야. 이 포스터 좀 봐.

M : The volunteer period is for two days, June 14th and 15th. *(①의 단서 기간)*
남 : 자원봉사 기간은 6월 14일하고 15일, 이틀 동안이네.

W : That's right. Would you like to join?
여 : 맞아. 너도 같이 할래?

M : I'd love to. But can just anyone apply to be a volunteer? *(부사적 용법 (목적))*
남 : 나도 하고 싶지. 그런데 아무나 자원봉사자로 지원할 수 있어?

W : Only people over 18 can apply. So, we're both good. *(사이에 who[that] are 생략됨 ②의 단서 지원 가능 연령)*
여 : 18세 이상만 지원할 수 있어. 그러니까 우리 둘 다 괜찮아.

M : I see. What exactly will we do during the festival?
남 : 그렇구나. 축제 때 정확히 무슨 일을 하게 되는데?

W : It says we'll check tickets, run activity booths, or take photos for the festival website. *(④의 단서 활동 내용)*
여 : 표를 확인하거나 체험 부스를 운영하거나, 축제 웹사이트용 사진을 찍는대.

M : Sounds interesting. And look! We have to sign up by this Friday. *('~까지' ⑤의 단서 신청 기한)*
남 : 재밌겠다. 그리고 봐봐! 이번 주 금요일까지 신청해야 해.

W : Really? We don't have much time. Let's do it right now.
여 : 진짜? 시간이 많지 않네. 지금 바로 신청하자.

- fireworks ⓝ 불꽃놀이   • volunteer ⓥ 자원봉사하다 ⓝ 자원봉사자
- period ⓝ 기간   • apply ⓥ 지원하다   • exactly ⓐⓓ 정확히
- run ⓥ 운영하다   • activity booth 체험 부스   • sign up 신청하다

대화를 듣고, Fireworks Festival 자원봉사에 관해 언급되지 않은 것을 고르시오.

① 기간 for two days, June 14th and 15th
② 지원 가능 연령 Only people over 18 can apply.
③ 준비물 언급되지 않음
④ 활동 내용 check tickets, run activity booths, or take photos for the festival website
⑤ 신청 기한 We have to sign up by this Friday.

＞왜 정답？ ✽✿✿ [정답률 86%]

불꽃놀이 축제 자원봉사의 기간, 지원 가능 연령, 활동 내용, 신청 기한은 언급되었지만, 준비물은 언급하지 않았으므로 정답은 ③이다.

＞왜 오답？

① 6월 14일부터 15일까지 이틀 동안 진행된다.
② 18세 이상만 지원할 수 있다.
④ 표 확인, 체험 부스 운영, 축제 웹사이트용 사진 촬영을 한다.
⑤ 이번 주 금요일까지 신청해야 한다.

09 정답 ④ ＊2025 Talent Show 안내

W : Hello, everyone! This is Ms. Westwood, your vice principal.
여 : 여러분 안녕하세요! 저는 교감인 Westwood입니다.

I'm excited to announce the 2025 Talent Show! *(부사적 용법 (감정의 원인))*
저는 2025 Talent Show를 알리게 되어 기쁩니다!

It'll take place in our school auditorium on June 20th at 6 p.m. *(①의 단서 학교 강당에서 개최될 예정임)*
행사는 6월 20일 저녁 6시에 우리 학교 강당에서 개최될 예정입니다.

All students are welcome to participate and showcase their unique talent, whether it's singing, dancing, or acting. *(②의 단서 모든 학생이 참가할 수 있음 부사절 접속사 (~든 간에) it = talent)*
모든 학생이 참가해서 노래, 춤, 연기 어떤 것이든 독특한 재능을 마음껏 뽐낼 수 있습니다.

Three wonderful teachers will be the judges, and there will be prizes for the top performances. *(③의 단서 3명의 교사가 심사함)*
세 분의 훌륭한 선생님이 심사위원이 될 것이고, 최고의 공연을 위한 상이 있을 것입니다.

Every participant will receive a free T-shirt with our school symbol on it. *(every + 단수 명사 it = T-shirt ④의 단서 모든 참가자는 티셔츠를 받음)*
모든 참가자는 학교 로고가 있는 티셔츠를 무료로 받게 됩니다.

At the end of the show, we'll have a short dance party. *(⑥의 단서 공연이 끝날 무렵에는 짧은 댄스 파티가 열림)*
공연이 끝날 무렵, 짧은 댄스 파티가 열릴 것입니다.

For more details, please check out our school website. Thank you.
자세한 내용은 학교 홈페이지를 확인해 주세요. 감사합니다.

- vice principal 교감   • talent show 장기자랑
- auditorium ⓝ 강당   • participate ⓥ 참가하다
- showcase ⓥ 뽐내다, 선보이다   • judge ⓝ 심사위원   • prize ⓝ 상
- performance ⓝ 공연   • participant ⓝ 참가자
- symbol ⓝ 상징   • detail ⓝ 자세한 내용[세부 사항]

2025 Talent Show에 관한 다음 내용을 듣고, 일치하지 않는 것을 고르시오.

① 학교 강당에서 개최될 것이다. 학교 강당에서 개최될 예정임
② 모든 학생이 참가할 수 있다. 모든 학생이 참가해서 재능을 뽐낼 수 있음
③ 3명의 교사가 심사할 것이다. 3명의 교사가 심사함
④ 모든 참가자는 열쇠고리를 받을 것이다. 열쇠고리가 아닌 티셔츠를 받음
⑤ 공연 막바지에 댄스 파티가 있을 것이다. 공연이 끝날 무렵 짧은 댄스 파티가 열림

＞왜 정답？ ✽✿✿ [정답률 97%]

모든 참가자는 티셔츠를 받기로 되어 있으므로 열쇠고리를 받는다고 한 ④이 일치하지 않는다.

＞왜 오답？

① 학교 강당에서 개최될 예정이다.
② 모든 학생이 참가해서 재능을 뽐낼 수 있다.
③ 3명의 교사가 심사할 것이다.
⑤ 공연 막바지에 짧은 댄스 파티가 열릴 것이다.

10 정답 ④ ＊학교용 책가방 선택

W : Honey, we need to buy Robert a backpack for school. *(buy의 간접목적어와 직접목적어)*
여 : 여보, 우리 Robert에게 학교용 책가방을 사줘야겠어요.

M : Right, let's search for one online. *(one = a backpack)*
남 : 맞아요, 온라인으로 찾아보죠.

W : [Clicking Sound] Wow, there are so many options. What should we consider first?
여 : [클릭 소리] 와, 선택지가 정말 많네요. 무엇을 먼저 고려해야 할까요?

M : Well, let's start with budget.
남 : 음, 일단 예산부터 생각해 보죠.

W : We already spent a lot on his other school supplies. I'd like to keep it under $70. *(단서 1 70달러 미만이어야 함 ⑤ 제외)*
여 : 우린 이미 다른 학용품에 돈을 많이 썼어요. 70달러 미만으로 하고 싶어요.

M : All right. What shape should we get him, a square one? *(get의 간접목적어)*
남 : 알겠어요. 그에게 어떤 모양을 줘야 할까요, 사각형?

W : Yeah, it's better for carrying school supplies. Then, what about the color? *(단서 2 사각형 모양이어야 함 ① 제외)*
여 : 네, 학용품 넣기엔 그게 더 좋아요. 그럼 색깔은 어떡해요?

M : White ones get dirty easily, so we should go with a black
「get + 형용사」: ~한 상태가 되다
one. 단서 3 검은색이어야 함 (③ 제외)

남 : 흰색은 금방 더러워지니까, 검은색으로 골라야 해요.

W : Sounds good. And does it need to be waterproof?

여 : 좋아요. 방수 기능도 있어야 할까요?

M : Definitely. It'll be useful on rainy days.
단서 4 방수 기능이 있어야 함 (② 제외)

남 : 물론이죠. 비 오는 날에 유용할 거예요.

W : Then, this is the one. Let's buy it.

여 : 그럼, 이거로 해요. 구매합시다.

- backpack ⓝ 책가방 • option ⓝ 선택지 • consider ⓥ 고려하다
- budget ⓝ 예산 • school supplies 학용품 • square ⓐ 사각형의
- waterproof ⓐ 방수의 • useful ⓐ 유용한

다음 표를 보면서 대화를 듣고, 두 사람이 구매할 책가방을 고르시오.

School Backpacks 학교용 책가방
둥근 모양이 아닌 사각형 모양을 선호함

	Model 모델	Price 가격	Shape 모양	Color 색깔	Waterproof 방수 기능
①	A	$50	Round 둥근	Black 검은색	×
②	B	$55	Square 사각형의	Black	×
③	C	$60	Square	White 흰색	방수 기능이 있는 것을 선호함
④	D	$65	Square	Black	○
⑤	E	$75	Round	White	○

70달러 미만이어야 함 / 흰색이 아닌 검은색을 선호함

> 왜 정답 ? ✿✿✿ [정답률 93%]

가격이 70달러 미만이고(⑤ 제외), 사각형 모양이며(① 제외), 검은색에(③ 제외), 방수 기능이 있는(② 제외) 가방은 ④이다.

> 왜 오답 ?

① 사각형 모양 가방이 학용품을 넣기에 더 좋다고 했다.
② 방수 기능이 있어야 비 오는 날에 유용할 것이라고 했다.
③ 흰색은 금방 더러워지니까 검은색으로 골라야 한다고 했다.
⑤ 70달러 미만이어야 한다고 했다.

11 정답 ① ＊두통으로 인한 조퇴

M : Ms. Adams, I'm not feeling well. I have a bad headache.

남 : Adams 선생님, 저 몸이 안 좋아요. 두통이 심해요.

W : Oh, sorry to hear that, Jack. Have you taken some medicine?
현재완료 (완료)

여 : 저런, 안 됐다, Jack. 약은 먹었니?

M : Yes, I took some an hour ago, but I don't think I can stay in
class. 단서 약을 먹었는데도 수업에 계속 있기 힘들 것 같음

남 : 네, 한 시간 전에 먹었는데, 수업에 계속 있기 힘들 것 같아요.

W : I see. Then you should leave now to go see a doctor.
부사적 용법 (목적)

여 : 알겠어. 그럼 지금 나가서 병원에 가보는 게 좋겠다.

- headache ⓝ 두통 • medicine ⓝ 약 • leave ⓥ 떠나다, 나가다
- go see a doctor 병원에 가다

대화를 듣고, 남자의 마지막 말에 대한 여자의 응답으로 가장 적절한 것을 고르시오. [3점]
약을 먹었는데도 견디기 어렵다고 했으므로 병원에 가라고 조언함

① I see. Then you should leave now to go see a doctor.
알겠어. 그럼 지금 나가서 병원에 가보는 게 좋겠다.
② Good idea. I can put you in another group next class.
좋은 생각이야. 다음 시간에 다른 조로 바꿔 줄게. 조 교체는 언급되지 않았음
③ Too bad. You should have taken some medicine first.
아쉽네. 먼저 약을 먹었어야 했는데. 약은 이미 먹었음
④ Never mind. I hope you do better on the final exam.
괜찮아. 기말고사에서 더 잘하길 바랄게. 시험은 언급되지 않았음
⑤ Thank you. I'll go to the nurse's office right now.
고마워. 지금 바로 보건실에 갈게. 보건실은 언급되지 않았음

> 왜 정답 ? ✿✿✿ [정답률 77%]

두통이 심한 남자에게 여자는 약을 먹었는지 물었고, 남자는 한 시간 전에 약을 먹었는데도 수업에 계속 있기 힘들 것 같다고 했다. 따라서 여자는 ① '알겠어. 그럼 지금 나가서 병원에 가보는 게 좋겠다.'라고 응답하는 것이 가장 적절하다.

> 왜 오답 ?

② 조 교체는 언급되지 않았다.
③ 약은 이미 먹었다고 했다. ← 주의
④ 시험은 언급되지 않았다.
⑤ 보건실은 언급되지 않았다.

12 정답 ⑤ ＊기념일 케이크 주문

W : Welcome to Emily's Cake Shop. How can I help you today?

여 : Emily의 케이크 가게에 오신 걸 환영합니다. 오늘은 어떻게 도와드릴까요?

M : I'd like to order a cake. It's to celebrate my first wedding
would like to-v: ~하고 싶다
anniversary.

남 : 케이크를 주문하고 싶어요. 결혼 1주년을 기념하려고요.

W : Congratulations on your anniversary! Do you have a
have ~ in mind: ~을 생각하고 있다
specific design in mind? 단서 생각해 둔 케이크 디자인이 있는지 질문함

여 : 결혼기념일 축하해요! 생각해 둔 특정한 디자인이 있으신가요?

M : Yes, I'd like a heart-shaped cake with a message on it.
= a cake
남 : 네, 메시지가 적힌 하트 모양 케이크를 원해요.

- order ⓥ 주문하다 • celebrate ⓥ 기념하다
- anniversary ⓝ 기념일 • specific ⓐ 특정한, 구체적인
- heart-shaped ⓐ 하트 모양의

대화를 듣고, 여자의 마지막 말에 대한 남자의 응답으로 가장 적절한 것을 고르시오.

① No. I made all these cakes by myself. 남자가 케이크를 주문하는 상황임
아뇨. 제가 이 케이크들을 다 직접 만들었어요.
② Sure. I'm looking forward to my 30th birthday.
물론이죠. 저의 서른 번째 생일이 기대돼요. 생일은 언급되지 않았음
③ Actually, I don't mind if you eat my carrot cake.
사실, 제 당근 케이크를 드셔도 괜찮아요. 당근 케이크는 언급되지 않았음
④ Not really. It's hard to remember all the anniversaries.
그렇지 않아요. 모든 기념일을 기억하기는 어려워요. 기념일을 기억하는 것은 묻지 않았음
⑤ Yes, I'd like a heart-shaped cake with a message on it.
네, 메시지가 적힌 하트 모양 케이크를 원해요.
여자가 남자에게 생각해 둔 케이크 디자인이 있는지 물었음

> 왜 정답 ? ✿✿✿ [정답률 93%]

여자가 남자에게 결혼기념일 케이크로 생각해 둔 특정한 디자인이 있는지 물어봤으므로, 남자는 ⑤ '네, 메시지가 적힌 하트 모양 케이크를 원해요.'라고 응답하는 것이 가장 적절하다.

> 왜 오답 ?

① 남자가 케이크를 주문하는 상황이지, 직접 만든 것이 아니다.
② 결혼 1주년을 기념한다고 했지, 생일은 언급되지 않았다.
③ 당근 케이크는 언급되지 않았다.
④ 기념일을 기억하는 것은 묻지 않았다.

13 정답 ② ＊고양이 돌보기

W : Dad, look at the cat over there!

여 : 아빠, 저기 고양이 좀 봐요!

M : Oh, it's so cute.

남 : 오, 정말 귀엽네.

W : I've wanted a cat for a long time. Can we get one?
현재완료 (계속) = a cat
여 : 저 오래전부터 고양이를 키우고 싶었어요. 우리 한 마리 키우면 안 돼요?

M : You know, raising a cat isn't easy, Rebecca.
동명사구 (주어)
남 : 너도 알다시피, 고양이 키우는 게 쉽지 않단다, Rebecca.

W : I understand. But I promise I'd love it with all my heart.

여 : 알아요. 하지만 진심으로 아껴줄게요. 정말요.

M : It's not just about love. It's about effort and responsibility.
　　not just A (but) B: A뿐만 아니라 B도

남 : 사랑만으로 되는 게 아니란다. 노력과 책임도 필요해.

W : Trust me, Dad. I know I can handle it.

여 : 믿어주세요, 아빠. 저 잘할 수 있어요.

M : Hmm... Then, how about practicing first? Uncle Tony is looking for someone to take care of his cat during his business trip.
　　형용사적 용법 (someone 수식)

남 : 음... 그럼 먼저 연습해 보는 건 어때? Tony 아저씨가 출장 중에 고양이 돌봐줄 사람 찾고 있어.

W : That sounds great! If I do a good job with his cat, will you let me get my own cat?
　　부사절 접속사 (조건) / *let의 목적어와 목적격 보어 (원형부정사)*

여 : 좋아요! 제가 잘 돌보면, 제 고양이도 키우게 해주실 거예요?

M : I'll definitely think about it if you take good care of his cat.

남 : 아저씨의 고양이를 잘 돌보면 꼭 생각해 볼게. [단서] Tony 아저씨의 고양이를 돌보는 일을 하고 싶다고 말해달라고 함

W : Thanks, Dad. Please tell Uncle Tony that I want to do it.

여 : 감사해요, 아빠. Tony 아저씨에게 제가 하고 싶다고 말씀해 주세요.

M : **Okay. I'll ask him if you can look after his cat.**
　　명사절 접속사 (~인지 아닌지)

남 : 알겠어. 네가 고양이를 돌봐도 되는지 그에게 물어볼게.

- raise ⓥ 키우다, 기르다　　• effort ⓝ 노력　　• responsibility ⓝ 책임
- handle ⓥ 감당하다　　• business trip 출장　　• look after ~을 돌보다
- caretaker ⓝ 관리인, 돌보는 사람

대화를 듣고, 여자의 마지막 말에 대한 남자의 응답으로 가장 적절한 것을 고르시오.

Man : _____

① I see. You've always preferred dogs over cats. 고양이보다 강아지를 더 좋아한다는 것은 언급되지 않음
　그렇구나. 넌 항상 고양이보다 강아지를 더 좋아했지.

②Okay. I'll ask him if you can look after his cat. Tony 아저씨의
　알겠어. 네가 고양이를 돌봐도 되는지 그에게 물어볼게. 고양이를 돌봐도 되는지 물어보기로 함

③ Sorry. I don't have time to take care of your cat. 여자가 Tony 아저씨의 고양이를 돌보려는 상황임
　미안해. 네 고양이를 돌볼 시간이 없어.

④ No problem. I'll take his pet to the animal hospital. 동물병원은 언급되지 않았음
　문제없어. 그의 반려동물을 동물병원에 데려갈게.

⑤ I agree. I know for sure he's a great pet caretaker. Tony 아저씨가 반려동물을 잘 돌본다는 것은 언급되지 않음
　동의해. 그가 반려동물을 정말 잘 돌본다고 확신해.

왜 정답? ✹✿✿ [정답률 93%]

여자가 Tony 아저씨의 고양이를 돌보는 일을 하고 싶다고 이야기해달라고 부탁했으므로, 남자는 ② '알겠어. 네가 고양이를 돌봐도 되는지 그에게 물어볼게.'라고 응답하는 것이 가장 적절하다.

왜 오답?

① 여자가 고양이보다 강아지를 더 좋아한다는 것은 언급되지 않았다.

③ 여자가 Tony 아저씨의 고양이를 돌보려는 상황이므로 남자가 여자의 고양이를 돌볼 시간이 없다는 것은 적절하지 않다.

④ 동물병원은 언급되지 않았다.

⑤ Tony 아저씨가 반려동물을 잘 돌본다는 것은 언급되지 않았다.

---

14 정답 ③ ＊할머니의 오래된 요리책 ─────

M : Grandma, look what I found in the garage. It's an old cookbook.

남 : 할머니, 제가 차고에서 찾은 것 좀 보세요. 오래된 요리책이에요.

W : Oh, I haven't seen that for years.
　　현재완료 (계속)

여 : 오, 오랫동안 못 본 책이구나.

M : It says here, "Recipes for Fine Dishes."

남 : '고급 요리 레시피'라고 여기 적혀 있어요.

W : That's the cookbook I wrote when I was a chef before you were born.
　　앞에 목적격 관계대명사가 생략됨

여 : 그건 네가 태어나기 전에 내가 요리사였을 때 쓴 요리책이야.

M : Really? You were a professional chef?

남 : 정말요? 할머니가 전문 요리사였어요?

W : Yeah, I used to work in a restaurant. Look! These were my special dishes.
　　used to-v: ~하곤 했다

여 : 그래, 레스토랑에서 일했었지. 보렴! 이게 내가 만들었던 특별 요리들이야.

M : Wow, they look fantastic! Did you create all the recipes in the book?

남 : 와, 정말 맛있어 보여요! 이 책에 있는 레시피를 다 직접 만드신 거예요?

W : Yes. I really loved cooking and was good at it back then.
　　병렬 구조 (문장의 동사)

여 : 그래. 그때는 요리하는 걸 정말 좋아했고, 잘했지.

M : You're still good at cooking!
　　'~을 잘하다'

남 : 지금도 요리 잘하시잖아요!

W : Do you really think so?

여 : 정말 그렇게 생각하니?

M : Of course! I've always thought your food tastes amazing.
　　현재완료 (계속)

남 : 당연하죠! 할머니의 음식은 최고라고 항상 생각했어요. [단서] 할머니의 음식은 항상 최고였음

W : **Thanks. I guess I haven't lost my chef skills.**

여 : 고맙구나. 아직 내가 요리 실력을 잃지는 않았나 보구나.

- garage ⓝ 차고　　• cookbook ⓝ 요리책　　• recipe ⓝ 레시피, 조리법
- fine ⓐ 고급의　　• dish ⓝ 요리　　• chef ⓝ 요리사
- professional ⓐ 전문적인　　• create ⓥ 만들어 내다
- quit ⓥ 그만두다

대화를 듣고, 남자의 마지막 말에 대한 여자의 응답으로 가장 적절한 것을 고르시오. [3점]

Woman : _____

① You're right. That's how I found the book. 요리책을 어떻게 찾아냈는지를 묻지 않았음
　맞아. 그렇게 해서 그 책을 찾았단다.

② Well, I think the food will be delivered soon. 음식 배달은 언급되지 않았음
　음. 음식이 곧 배달될 것 같구나.

③Thanks. I guess I haven't lost my chef skills. 남자는 여자의 음식이
　고맙구나. 아직 내가 요리 실력을 잃지는 않았나 보구나. 최고라고 했고 여자가 고맙다고 답하는 상황임

④ Really? I didn't know that you loved to cook. 요리를 좋아하는 사람은 남자가 아니라 여자임
　정말? 네가 요리하는 걸 좋아하는 줄 몰랐구나.

⑤ I know. That's the reason I quit being a chef. 요리사를 그만둔 이유는 언급되지 않았음
　맞아. 그래서 내가 요리사 일을 그만두었단다.

왜 정답? ✹✹✿ [정답률 82%]

과거에 요리사였던 여자에게 남자는 여자의 음식이 항상 최고였다고 말했으므로, 여자는 ③ '고맙구나. 아직 내가 요리 실력을 잃지는 않았나 보구나.'라고 응답하는 것이 가장 적절하다.

왜 오답?

① 요리책을 어떻게 찾았는지를 묻지 않았다.

② 음식 배달은 언급되지 않았다.

④ 요리를 좋아하는 사람은 남자가 아니라 여자이다.

⑤ 요리사를 그만둔 이유는 언급되지 않았다.

---

15 정답 ② ＊호텔 방 교체 요청 ─────

W : Chloe is on an overseas trip and staying at a hotel in Cairo, Egypt.

여 : Chloe는 해외여행 중이고, 이집트 카이로의 호텔에 머물고 있다.

After some sightseeing, she goes back to her hotel room.

관광을 마치고, 그녀는 호텔 방으로 돌아온다.

It's hot outside, so she decides to turn on the air conditioner, but it doesn't work. [단서 1] 호텔 에어컨이 작동하지 않음

밖이 더워서 에어컨을 켜고자 하지만, 작동하지 않는다.

She calls the hotel clerk to get it fixed.
　　get의 목적어와 목적격 보어 (과거분사)

그녀는 그것이 고쳐지도록 호텔 직원에게 전화를 건다.

He explains that it can be fixed tomorrow. [단서 2] 내일 수리 가능
　　목적어절 접속사

그는 그것이 내일 수리될 수 있다고 설명한다.

too 형용사 to부정사: 너무 ~해서 …할 수 없다
It's **too hot to sleep** without the air conditioning, and Chloe
wants to know **if** she can stay in **another** room.
~인지 아닌지 / 특정되지 않은 다른 선택지 / 단서 3 다른 방으로 옮기고 싶음
에어컨 없이 자기엔 너무 덥고, Chloe는 다른 방으로 옮길 수 있는지 알고 싶어 한다.

In this situation, what would Chloe most likely say to the
hotel clerk?
이 상황에서, Chloe가 호텔 직원에게 할 말로 가장 적절한 것은 무엇인가?

Chloe: **Would it be possible to change to another room?**
Chloe: 다른 방으로 바꿀 수 있을까요?

* 상황 요약: 에어컨이 작동하지 않아 호텔 방을 바꾸려는 상황

- overseas ⓐ 해외의   · sightseeing ⓝ 관광
- air conditioner 에어컨   · clerk ⓝ (호텔) 직원   · fix ⓥ 고치다
- tourist attraction 관광지, 관광 명소   · possible ⓐ 가능한
- refrigerator ⓝ 냉장고

다음 상황 설명을 듣고, Chloe가 호텔 직원에게 할 말로 가장 적절한
것을 고르시오.
Chloe: _____
① What's the best tourist attraction near the hotel?
  호텔 근처에 가장 좋은 관광지는 어디인가요?   호텔 근처 관광지는 언급되지 않았음
② Would it be possible to change to another room?
  다른 방으로 바꿀 수 있을까요?   호텔 에어컨이 작동하지 않아 다른 방으로 옮기려는 상황임
③ Could you check the refrigerator in my room?
  제 방 냉장고 좀 확인해 주실 수 있나요?   냉장고는 언급되지 않았음
④ Is there any way to get some cool water?
  시원한 물 좀 받을 방법이 있을까요?   물이 필요한 것이 아니라 다른 방으로 옮기려고 함
⑤ Can you turn off the air conditioner?
  에어컨을 꺼 주실 수 있나요?   에어컨은 고장이 나서 작동하지 않음

왜 정답? ✿✿✿ [정답률 92%]

Chloe는 더운 날씨에 호텔 에어컨이 작동하지 않아서 수리를 요청했으나 내일 수리가
가능하다는 답변을 들었다. 에어컨 없이 자기엔 너무 더워서 다른 방으로 옮길 수 있는
지 알고 싶은 상황이다. 따라서 Chloe가 할 말로 가장 적절한 것은 ② '다른 방으로 바
꿀 수 있을까요?'이다.

왜 오답?

① 호텔 근처 관광지는 언급되지 않았다.
③ 냉장고는 언급되지 않았다.
④ 너무 더워서 물이 필요한 것이 아니라, 다른 방으로 옮기려는 상황이다.
⑤ 에어컨은 고장이 나서 작동하지 않는 상황이다.

16~17 * 나라별 국화와 상징적 의미

M : Hello, class! //
남 : 안녕하세요, 여러분 //

Last time, we learned / about the national flags of various
countries. //
우리는 지난 시간에 배웠습니다 / 여러 나라의 국기에 대해 //

Today, we'll talk / about different countries' national
flowers / and **what they symbolize**. //
전치사 about의 목적어 (간접의문문) / 16번 단서: 여러 나라의 국화와 그것들이 무엇을 상징하는지를 이야기할 것임
오늘은 이야기할 것입니다 / 여러 나라의 국화와 / 그것들이 무엇을 상징하는지에 대해 //

First, / the Philippines' national flower is jasmine. //
17번 ①
먼저 / 필리핀의 국화는 재스민입니다 //
= jasmine
Because **it** means good luck, / people often give / big
앞에 주격 관계대명사와 be동사가 생략됨
necklaces **made** of this flower / to welcome special guests. //
그것은 행운을 의미하기 때문에 / 사람들은 자주 줍니다 / 이 꽃으로 만든 커다란 목걸이
를 / 특별한 손님을 환영할 때 //

Next, / Denmark's flower is the daisy / and it represents
happiness. //
17번 ②
다음은 / 덴마크의 국화인 데이지고 / 그것은 행복을 상징합니다 //

by v-ing: ~함으로써
Children express happiness / **by making** daisy chains /
during their traditional games. //
아이들은 행복을 표현합니다 / 데이지 목걸이를 만들어서 / 전통 놀이를 할 때 //

In France, / the national flower is the iris. //
17번 ④
프랑스에서 / 국화는 붓꽃입니다 //

현재완료 (계속)
Throughout history, / French people **have thought** of this
flower / as a symbol of perfection. //
역사를 통틀어 / 프랑스인들은 이 꽃을 여겨왔습니다 / 완벽함의 상징으로 //

Lastly, / the United States uses the rose / as its national
17번 ⑤
flower. //
마지막으로 / 미국은 장미를 사용합니다 / 국화로 //

consider의 목적어와 목적격 보어 (명사구)
Americans consider **it / a symbol of love**. //
미국인들은 그것을 여깁니다 / 사랑의 상징으로 //

So / you can find many roses / in American weddings. //
그래서 / 장미를 많이 볼 수 있습니다 / 미국의 결혼식에서 //

부사적 용법 (목적)
Now, / let's watch a short video / **to look** at these flowers up
close. //
이제 / 짧은 영상을 함께 봅시다 / 이 꽃들을 가까이에서 살펴보기 위해 //

- national flag 국기   · various ⓐ 여러 가지의, 다양한
- national flower 국화   · symbolize ⓥ 상징하다
- necklace ⓝ 목걸이   · guest ⓝ 손님
- represent ⓥ 나타내다, 상징하다   · happiness ⓝ 행복
- express ⓥ 표현하다   · chain ⓝ 목걸이   · iris ⓝ 붓꽃
- throughout (prep) ~을 통틀어   · symbol ⓝ 상징
- perfection ⓝ 완벽함   · consider ⓥ 여기다, 간주하다
- endangered ⓐ 멸종 위기의

여: 안녕하세요, 여러분! 우리는 지난 시간에 여러 나라의 국기에 대해 배웠습니
다. 오늘은 여러 나라의 국화와 그것들이 무엇을 상징하는지에 대해 이야기할
것입니다. 먼저, 필리핀의 국화는 재스민입니다. 이 꽃은 행운을 의미하기 때
문에, 사람들은 이 꽃으로 만든 커다란 목걸이를 특별한 손님을 환영할 때 자주
줍니다. 다음은 덴마크의 국화인 데이지고 그것은 행복을 상징합니다. 아이들
은 전통 놀이를 할 때 데이지 목걸이를 만들어서 행복을 표현합니다. 프랑스에
서, 국화는 붓꽃입니다. 역사를 통틀어, 프랑스인들은 이 꽃을 완벽함의 상징으
로 여겨왔습니다. 마지막으로, 미국은 장미를 국화로 사용합니다. 미국인들은
그것을 사랑의 상징으로 여깁니다. 그래서 미국의 결혼식에서 장미를 많이 볼
수 있습니다. 이제, 이 꽃들을 가까이에서 살펴보기 위해 짧은 영상을 함께 봅
시다.

16 정답 ⑤

남자가 하는 말의 주제로 가장 적절한 것은?
① native plants of various countries   여러 나라의 자생 식물은 언급되지 않았음
  여러 나라의 자생 식물
② wild plants and their medical uses
  야생 식물과 그들의 의료적 활용   야생 식물의 의료적 활용은 언급되지 않음
③ endangered flowers across the world   멸종 위기 꽃은 언급되지 않았음
  전 세계의 멸종 위기 꽃들
④ roles of flowers in national ceremonies
  국가 행사에서 꽃의 역할   국가 행사에서 꽃의 역할은 언급되지 않았음
⑤ national flowers with symbolic meanings
  상징적 의미를 지닌 국화들   각 나라에서 국화가 무엇을 상징하는지를 소개함

왜 정답? ✿✿✿ [정답률 93%]

남자는 여러 나라의 국화들과 그것들이 무엇을 상징하는지를 설명하고 있다. 따라서
남자가 하는 말의 주제로 가장 적절한 것은 ⑤ '상징적 의미를 지닌 국화들'이다.

왜 오답?

① 여러 나라의 자생 식물은 언급되지 않았다.
② 야생 식물의 의료적 활용은 언급되지 않았다.
③ 전 세계의 멸종 위기 꽃은 언급되지 않았다.
④ 각 나라의 국화에 대한 내용이지, 국가 행사에서 꽃의 역할에 대한 내용이 아니다.

언급된 국가가 아닌 것은?
① Philippines 필리핀 the Philippines' national flower is jasmine
② Denmark 덴마크 Denmark's flower is the daisy
③ Germany 독일 언급되지 않음
④ France 프랑스 In France, the national flower is the iris.
⑤ United States 미국 the United States uses the rose as its national flower

›왜 정답? ✿✿✿ [정답률 94%]
필리핀, 덴마크, 프랑스, 미국은 언급했지만 독일은 언급하지 않았으므로 정답은 ③ '독일'이다.

›왜 오답?
① 필리핀의 국화 재스민은 행운을 의미한다.
② 덴마크의 국화 데이지는 행복을 상징한다.
④ 프랑스의 국화 붓꽃은 완벽함의 상징이다.
⑤ 미국의 국화 장미는 사랑의 상징이다.

---

18 정답 ① ＊새로운 반려견 공원 개장

Dear Dog Owners, / 친애하는 반려견 주인 여러분 /
My name is Lily Paxton, / and I'm the town's Pet Program Coordinator. //
제 이름은 Lily Paxton이며 / 저는 이 마을의 반려동물 프로그램 코디네이터입니다 //
형용사적 용법 (our goal 수식)   make의 목적어와 목적보어 (형용사)
As part of our goal / **to make the community more dog-friendly**, / we recently opened / a new dog park. // **단서** 새로운 반려견 공원 개장을 알림
목표의 일환으로 / 이 지역 사회를 더욱 반려견 친화적으로 만들기 위한 / 저희는 최근에 개장했습니다 / 새로운 반려견 공원을 //
부사적 용법 (목적)
The park was designed / **to provide** an enjoyable experience / for both dogs and owners. //
이 공원은 설계되었습니다 / 즐거운 경험을 제공하도록 / 반려견과 주인 모두에게 //
관계부사 (선행사: areas)
There are big grassy areas / **where** your dogs can run, jump, and play. //
넓은 잔디밭들이 있습니다 / 반려견들이 달리고, 점프하고, 놀 수 있는 //
We have separate spaces / for small dogs and big dogs, / to
부사적 용법 (목적)
ensure safety. //
저희는 별도의 공간을 마련했습니다 / 소형견과 대형견을 위한 / 안전을 보장하기 위해 //
You'll also find lots of benches and areas / for resting and staying cool. //
여러분들은 벤치들과 공간들도 많이 찾을 수 있을 것입니다 / 휴식을 취하고 시원하게 머물 수 있는 //
뒤에 목적어절 접속사 that이 생략됨
We hope / you will have a wonderful time with your dogs / in this newly opened park. //
저희는 바랍니다 / 여러분이 반려견과 함께 멋진 시간을 보내시길 / 새롭게 개장한 이 공원에서 //
Regards, Lily Paxton, Pet Program Coordinator /
Lily Paxton, 반려동물 프로그램 코디네이터 드림 /

- coordinator ⓝ 코디네이터   • community ⓝ 지역 사회
- recently ⓐⓓ 최근에   • grassy area 잔디밭   • separate ⓐ 별도의
- ensure ⓥ 보장하다   • newly ⓐⓓ 새롭게

친애하는 반려견 주인 여러분,
제 이름은 Lily Paxton이며, 저는 이 마을의 반려동물 프로그램 코디네이터입니다. 이 지역 사회를 더욱 반려견 친화적으로 만들기 위한 목표의 일환으로, 저희는 최근에 새로운 반려견 공원을 개장했습니다. 이 공원은 반려견과 주인 모두에게 즐거운 경험을 제공하도록 설계되었습니다. 반려견들이 달리고, 점프

하고, 놀 수 있는 넓은 잔디밭들이 있습니다. 안전을 보장하기 위해, 저희는 소형견과 대형견을 위한 별도의 공간을 마련했습니다. 여러분은 휴식을 취하고 시원하게 머물 수 있는 벤치들과 공간들도 많이 찾을 수 있을 것입니다. 저희는 새롭게 개장한 이 공원에서 여러분이 반려견과 함께 멋진 시간을 보내시길 바랍니다.

Lily Paxton, 반려동물 프로그램 코디네이터 드림

다음 글의 목적으로 가장 적절한 것은?
① 새로 만든 반려견 공원의 개장을 홍보하려고
  새로운 반려견 공원의 개장을 알리고 있음
② 동물 보호 정책에 대한 의견을 구하려고 동물 보호 정책은 언급되지 않았음
③ 유기견 보호 자원봉사자를 모집하려고 유기견 보호는 언급되지 않았음
④ 반려견 공원 운영 시간의 변경을 안내하려고 운영 시간은 언급되지 않았음
⑤ 반려견 훈련 프로그램에의 참여를 권유하려고
  반려견 훈련 프로그램은 언급되지 않았음

›왜 정답? ✿✿✿ [정답률 97%]
마을의 반려견 프로그램 코디네이터가 새로운 반려견 공원의 개장을 알리고 공원 시설을 소개하고 있는 내용이므로 정답은 ①이다.

›왜 오답?
② 동물 보호 정책은 언급되지 않았다.
③ 유기견 보호는 언급되지 않았다.
④ 반려견 공원의 운영 시간이 아니라, 시설에 관해서만 언급되었다.
⑤ 반려견 훈련 프로그램은 언급되지 않았다.

---

19 정답 ① ＊유럽 배낭여행 연기
부사적 용법 (목적)
Maya waited in line / **to check** in for her flight. //
Maya는 줄을 서서 기다리고 있었다 / 비행기 탑승 수속을 위해 //
복수 주어   **복수 동사**
Her expectations / about her European backpacking trip / **were** really high. // **단서1** 유럽 배낭여행에 대한 기대가 높음
그녀의 기대는 / 유럽 배낭여행에 대한 / 아주 높았다 //
She had been looking forward to the trip / for a year. //
그녀는 이 여행을 손꼽아 기다려 왔다 / 일 년 동안 //
can't wait to-v: 빨리 ~하고 싶다   병렬 구조
She **couldn't wait to visit** museums in Madrid / and **see** the Eiffel Tower / at night in Paris. //
그녀는 빨리 Madrid의 박물관들을 방문하고 / Eiffel Tower를 보고 싶었다 / 밤에 Paris에서 //
부사절 접속사 (시간)   앞에 목적어절 접속사 that이 생략됨
As she stood in line, / she could feel / **those experiences** were finally so close. //
줄을 서 있는 동안 / 그녀는 느꼈다 / 그 경험들이 마침내 정말 가까워졌다고 //
타동사 (뒤에 전치사 없이 목적어가 옴)
When she **approached** the counter, / the airline employee asked
명사적 용법 (목적어)
/ **to see** her passport. //
그녀가 카운터에 다가갔을 때 / 항공사 직원이 요청했다 / 그녀의 여권을 보자고 //
자동사 (뒤에 전치사가 필요함)
Maya **reached** into her pocket / but felt nothing. //
Maya는 주머니에 손을 넣었지만 / 아무것도 만져지지 않았다 //
과거완료 (realized보다 이전의 일)
She realized / she **had left** her passport at home. //
그녀는 깨달았다 / 여권을 집에 두고 온 것을 //
Her plans were ruined. // 그녀의 계획은 망쳐졌다 //
분사구문을 이끄는 현재분사
She was heartbroken, / **knowing** / she could not board the flight / and had to delay her dream trip. // **단서2** 여행을 연기해야 한다는 것을 깨닫고는
상심함
그녀는 상심했다 / 깨달으며 / 비행기에 탑승할 수 없고 / 꿈꿔왔던 여행을 연기해야 한다는 것을 //

- check in (비행기) 탑승 수속을 하다   • expectation ⓝ 기대
- look forward to ~을 기대하다   • approach ⓥ 다가가다
- passport ⓝ 여권   • ruin ⓥ 망치다   • heartbroken ⓐ 상심한
- board ⓥ 탑승하다   • indifferent ⓐ 무관심한

Maya는 비행기 탑승 수속을 위해 줄을 서서 기다리고 있었다. 유럽 배낭여행에 대한 그녀의 기대는 아주 높았다. 그녀는 일 년 동안 이 여행을 손꼽아 기다려 왔다. 그녀는 빨리 Madrid의 박물관들을 방문하고 Paris에서 밤에 Eiffel Tower를 보고 싶었다. 줄을 서 있는 동안, 그녀는 그 경험들이 마침내 정말 가까워졌다고 느꼈다. 그녀가 카운터에 다가갔을 때, 항공사 직원이 그녀의 여권을 보자고 요청했다. Maya는 주머니에 손을 넣었지만 아무것도 만져지지 않았다. 그녀는 여권을 집에 두고 온 것을 깨달았다. 그녀의 계획은 망쳐졌다. 그녀는 비행기에 탑승할 수 없고 꿈꿔왔던 여행을 연기해야 한다는 것을 깨달으며, 상심했다.

다음 글에 드러난 Maya의 심경 변화로 가장 적절한 것은?

① excited → frustrated 여행을 앞두고 신났지만 비행기에 탑승할 수 없어서 상심했음
   신나는 → 좌절한
② joyful → indifferent 비행기에 탑승할 수 없어서 무관심했던 것이 아님
   즐거운 → 무관심한
③ terrified → relaxed 여행을 앞두고 겁에 질렸던 것이 아님
   겁에 질린 → 편안한
④ worried → satisfied 비행기에 탑승할 수 없어서 상심함
   걱정하는 → 만족한
⑤ bored → curious 비행기 탑승 수속을 기다리면서 기대했음
   지루한 → 호기심 많은

❯왜 정답? ✽❀❀ [정답률 93%]

전반부: 비행기 탑승 수속을 기다리며 유럽 배낭여행을 기대함 ▶ '신나는'
후반부: 여권을 집에 놓고 와서 비행기에 탑승할 수 없음을 깨달음 ▶ '좌절한'
따라서 Maya의 심경 변화로 가장 적절한 것은 ① '신나는 → 좌절한'이다.

❯왜 오답?

② 비행기를 기다리면서 즐거워했지만 비행기에 탑승할 수 없게 되자 무관심했던 것이 아니라 상심했다. 함정
③ 유럽 여행에 관해 겁에 질리지 않고 기대하였다.
④ 후반부에서 유럽 여행을 가지 못하게 되어 만족감이 아닌 상심이 드러난다.
⑤ 비행기 탑승 수속을 기다리며 지루해하지 않고 여행을 기대했다.

---

⑳ 정답 ⑤ ✱습관 형성에 영향을 주는 행동의 편리성

People often ask me, / "What surprises you most about habits?" //
사람들은 종종 나에게 묻는다 / "습관에 관한 무엇이 당신을 가장 놀라게 하나요"라고 //
　　　　　주격 관계대명사 (One thing 수식)
One thing / **that** continually astonishes me / is the degree / **to**
전치사 + 관계대명사
which we're influenced by sheer convenience. //
한 가지는 / 나를 계속해서 놀라게 하는 / 정도이다 / 우리가 순전한 편리성에 의해 영향을 받는 //
'~의 양' cf) an amount of: 많은 ~　　　　　　　　　　과거분사구
The amount of effort, time, or decision making / **required by an**
action / has a huge influence / on habit formation. //
노력, 시간, 또는 의사 결정의 양이 / 행동에 의해 요구되는 / 큰 영향을 미친다 / 습관 형성에 //
　　　　to ~ extent: ~한 정도로　　be likely to-v: ~할 가능성이 있다
To a truly remarkable **extent**, / we're more **likely to do** something
부사절 접속사 (조건)
/ **if** it's convenient, / and less likely / if it's not. //
정말 놀라울 정도로 / 우리는 어떤 일을 더 자주 할 것이고 / 그 일이 편리하다면 / 덜 하게 될 것이다 / 그렇지 않다면 //
　　　　　　　　　단서 습관으로 만들고 싶은 행동의 편리성에 주의를 기울여야 함
For this reason, / we should pay close attention / to the
　　　　사이에 목적격 관계대명사가 생략됨
convenience of any **activity** / **we** want to make into a habit. //
이런 이유로 / 우리는 세심한 주의를 기울여야 한다 / 행동의 편리성에 / 습관으로 만들고 싶은 //
　　　　　　　　　　동명사구 주어
Putting a wastebasket / **next to our front door** / made mail sorting
slightly more convenient, / and I stopped / procrastinating with
this chore. //
쓰레기통을 두는 것이 / 현관문 옆에 / 우편물을 분류하는 일을 약간 더 편리하게 했고 / 나는 멈추었다 / 이 일을 미루는 것을 //
　　　　　목적어절 접속사　　　　　　　동명사 (전치사 of의 목적어)
Many people report / **that** they do a much better job / of **staying**
　　　　　　　　　　　　　　부사절 접속사 (~이기 때문에)
close to distant family members / **now that** tools like group
　　가목적어　　　진목적어
chats / make **it** easy / **to stay in touch**. //
많은 사람들은 말한다 / 일을 훨씬 더 잘한다고 / 멀리 사는 가족들과 더 가까이 지내는 / 그룹 채팅 같은 도구들이 / 쉽게 만들어 주기 때문에 / 연락을 유지하는 것을 //

- **astonish** ⓥ 놀라게 하다
- **convenience** ⓝ 편리성
- **remarkable** ⓐ 놀라운
- **stay in touch** 연락을 유지하다
- **degree** ⓝ 정도
- **decision making** 의사 결정
- **extent** ⓝ 정도
- **chore** ⓝ 일, 잡일

사람들은 종종 나에게, "습관에 관한 무엇이 당신을 가장 놀라게 하나요?"라고 묻는다. 나를 계속해서 놀라게 하는 한 가지는 우리가 순전한 편리성에 의해 영향을 받는 정도이다. 행동에 의해 요구되는 노력, 시간, 또는 의사 결정의 양이 습관 형성에 큰 영향을 미친다. 정말 놀라울 정도로, 우리는 어떤 일이 편리하다면 그것을 더 자주 할 것이고, 그렇지 않다면 덜 하게 될 것이다. 이런 이유로, 우리는 습관으로 만들고 싶은 행동의 편리성에 세심한 주의를 기울여야 한다. 현관문 옆에 쓰레기통을 두는 것이 우편물을 분류하는 일을 약간 더 편리하게 했고, 나는 이 일을 미루는 것을 멈추었다. 많은 사람들은 그룹 채팅 같은 도구들이 연락을 유지하는 것을 쉽게 만들어 주기 때문에 멀리 사는 가족들과 더 가까이 지내는 일을 훨씬 더 잘한다고 말한다.

다음 글에서 필자가 주장하는 바로 가장 적절한 것은?

① 불필요한 자극을 유발하는 작업 환경을 개선해야 한다.
   작업 환경이 불필요한 자극을 유발한다는 것은 언급되지 않았음
② 생활방식 개선을 위해 규칙적인 생활 습관을 길러야 한다.
   　　　　　　　　　　　생활방식 개선은 언급되지 않았음
③ 목표를 신속하게 달성하려면 구체적인 계획을 세워야 한다.
   　　　　　　　　　　　구체적인 계획을 세우는 것은 언급되지 않았음
④ 반복적인 업무의 편의를 위해 디지털 도구를 사용해야 한다.
   디지털 도구 활용에 관한 내용이 아님
⑤ 습관으로 만들고 싶은 행동의 편리성에 주의를 기울여야 한다.
   습관으로 만들고 싶은 행동의 편리성이 습관을 형성하는 데 영향을 미침

❯왜 정답? ✽❀❀ [정답률 86%]

어떤 일이나 행동이 편리하다면 그것을 더 자주 하게 되어 행동의 편리성이 습관 형성에 영향을 준다고 주장하므로 정답은 ⑤이다.

❯왜 오답?

① 작업 환경이 불필요한 자극을 유발하고 있다는 내용은 언급되지 않았다.
② 습관이 반복적으로 언급되지만, 생활방식 개선을 위해서 습관 형성을 해야 한다는 내용이 아니다. 주의
③ 목표 달성을 위해 구체적인 계획을 세우라는 내용이 아니다.
④ 그룹 채팅이 연락을 유지하기 쉽게 하는 수단으로 언급되었지, 반복적인 업무의 편의를 위한 도구로 언급되지는 않았다.

㉑ 정답 ② ✱신념과 행동의 관계

　가주어　　　　　　진주어절 접속사
It is common sense / **that** people's inner beliefs / may drive their
external behavior. // 단서1 내적 신념이 외적 행동을 이끎
상식이다 / 사람들의 내적 신념이 / 그들의 외적인 행동을 이끌 수 있다는 것은 //
　　　　　　　　　　　　　　　　　　　　　　추측 (~일 것이다)
If you're attracted to a certain person, / you **should** be more
likely to socialize / with that person. //
만약 당신이 어떤 사람에게 끌린다면 / 당신은 더 어울리려고 할 것이다 / 그 사람과 //
If you favor a brand of toothpaste, / you're more likely to buy
it. //
만약 당신이 한 브랜드의 치약을 선호한다면 / 당신이 그것을 구매할 가능성은 더 높다 //
Of course, / our internal thoughts / don't *always* predict our
public behavior, / but, overall, / **what** we do / obviously reflects
　　　　　선행사를 포함하는 관계대명사
what we think. //
물론 / 우리의 내적 사고가 / '항상' 공개적인 행동을 예측하지는 않지만 / 전반적으로 / 우리가 하는 것은 / 분명히 우리가 생각하는 바를 반영한다 //
But beliefs and behaviors / are also related / in a more
remarkable way. // 단서2 신념과 행동은 더 놀라운 방식으로도 관련됨
그러나 신념과 행동은 / 또한 관련이 있다 / 이보다 더 놀라운 방식으로 //
가주어　　　　　진주어절 접속사
It turns out / **that** the arrow / is as likely to point / in the reverse
direction. //
드러난다 / 화살이 / 가리킬 가능성이 그만큼 높다 / 반대 방향을 //

As social psychologist David Myers observes, / "If social psychology has taught us anything / during the last 25 years, /
사회심리학자 David Myers가 말한 바에 따르면 / "사회심리학이 우리에게 가르쳐준 것이 있다면 / 지난 25년간 /

it is that / we are likely / <mark>not only</mark> to think ourselves into a way of acting / <mark>but also</mark> to act ourselves into a way of thinking." //
not only A but also B: A뿐만 아니라 B도
그것은 바로 / 우리가 가능성이 있다는 것이다 / 우리가 생각하여 행동 방식에 이를 뿐만 아니라 / 우리가 또한 행동하여 사고 방식에 이를" // 단서3 반대로 행동이 사고 방식에 이르기도 함

- common sense 상식 • belief ⓝ 신념 • drive ⓥ 이끌다
- external ⓐ 외적인 • behavior ⓝ 행동
- socialize ⓥ 어울리다, 교류하다 • internal ⓐ 내적의, 내면의
- obviously ⓐⓓ 분명히 • reflect ⓥ 반영하다
- remarkable ⓐ 놀랄 만한, 놀라운 • likely ⓐ ~할 가능성이 있는
- reverse ⓐ 반대의 • direction ⓝ 방향 • entirely ⓐⓓ 완전히
- separate ⓐ 분리된 • be dependent on ~에 의존하다
- surroundings ⓝ (주변) 환경 • matter ⓥ 중요하다

사람들의 내적 신념이 그들의 외적인 행동을 이끌 수 있다는 것은 상식이다. 만약 당신이 어떤 사람에게 끌린다면, 당신은 그 사람과 더 어울리려고 할 것이다. 만약 당신이 한 브랜드의 치약을 선호한다면, 당신이 그것을 구매할 가능성은 더 높다. 물론, 우리의 내적 사고가 '항상' 공개적인 행동을 예측하지는 않지만, 전반적으로, 우리가 하는 것은 분명히 우리가 생각하는 바를 반영한다. 그러나 신념과 행동은 이보다 더 놀라운 방식으로도 관련이 있다. 화살이 반대 방향을 가리킬 가능성이 그만큼 높다는 것이 드러난다. 사회 심리학자 David Myers가 말한 바에 따르면, "지난 25년간 사회 심리학이 우리에게 가르쳐준 것이 있다면, 그것은 우리가 생각하여 행동 방식에 이를 뿐만 아니라 우리가 행동하여 사고 방식에 이를 가능성도 있다는 것이다."

밑줄 친 the arrow is as likely to point in the reverse direction이 다음 글에서 의미하는 바로 가장 적절한 것은? [3점]
① actions can be entirely separate from beliefs
행동은 신념과 완전히 분리될 수 있다   행동과 신념이 분리되는 것이 아니라 서로 영향을 미침
② our behaviors can also shape what we believe
우리의 행동이 우리가 믿는 바를 형성할 수도 있다   행동이 신념을 이끌 수 있음
③ our opinions can be dependent on our emotions
우리의 의견은 감정에 의존할 수 있다   감정은 언급되지 않았음
④ behaviors can clearly reflect one's surroundings
행동은 분명히 주변 환경을 반영할 수 있다   환경은 언급되지 않았음
⑤ what we think can matter more than what we do
우리가 생각하는 것이 우리가 하는 것보다 더 중요할 수 있다   중요성을 비교하는 내용이 아님

왜 정답? ✽✽✽ [정답률 69%]
- 신념이 행동을 이끌 수 있음 단서1
- 신념과 행동은 더 놀라운 방식으로도 관련됨 단서2
- 행동하여 사고 방식에 이르기도 함 단서3
➡ 신념이 행동을 이끌 수 있다는 상식을 제시했으나, But 이후로는 행동 또한 생각에 이르게 한다는 반대 방향의 관계를 제시했다.
▶ 따라서 '화살이 반대 방향을 가리킬 가능성이 그만큼 높다'는 것은 신념이 행동을 이끈다는 상식과 반대로 ② '우리의 행동이 우리가 믿는 바를 형성할 수도 있다'를 의미한다.

왜 오답?
① 행동과 신념이 완전히 분리되는 것이 아니라 서로 영향을 미칠 수 있다고 했다.
③ 끌리는 사람과 더 어울리려고 한다는 예시가 언급되었을 뿐, 우리의 의견이 감정에 의존한다는 내용이 아니다.
④ 환경은 언급되지 않았다.
⑤ 생각과 행동 중 어느 것이 먼저 시작되는지에 관한 내용이지, 어느 것이 다른 것보다 중요하다는 것은 언급되지 않았다. 주의

---

22 정답 ① ✱말수를 줄일 때 나오는 경청

Imagine / following the spirit of a silence vow / into daily life. //
상상해 보라 / 침묵 서약의 정신을 따르는 것을 / 일상생활로 //

Challenge yourself / to <mark>spend</mark> an entire day <mark>saying</mark> / only <mark>what</mark> you absolutely must say. //
spend 시간 -ing: ~하는 데 시간을 쓰다   선행사를 포함하는 관계대명사
스스로 도전해 보라 / 말하는 데 하루 온종일을 보내는 것에 / 반드시 말해야 할 것만 //

가주어
<mark>It</mark>'s been widely observed / by behavioral psychology experts / — and anyone who's ever been on a first date — /
널리 관찰되어 왔다 / 행동 심리학 전문가들에 의해 / 그리고 첫 데이트를 해 본 적이 있는 누구든지 /

진주어절 접속사   '~로서'
<mark>that</mark> we too often tend to treat / "conversation" <mark>as</mark> a game of waiting for our own turn <mark>to speak</mark>. //
형용사적 용법 (our own turn 수식)
우리가 너무나 자주 여기는 경향이 있다는 것이 / "대화"를 자신이 말할 차례를 기다리는 게임처럼 //

진행형 수동태 (be being 과거분사)
We miss / <mark>what's being said</mark> / because we're mentally rehearsing / our next utterance. //
우리는 놓친다 / 말해지고 있는 것을 / 머릿속으로 연습하느라 / 다음 발언을 //

'~라면 어떨까?'   동격절 접속사
<mark>What if</mark> you could eliminate the idea / <mark>that</mark> the next available mini-silence / is your next opening / <mark>to express</mark> whatever is in your head? //
형용사적 용법 (your next opening 수식)
만약 당신이 생각을 없앨 수 있다면 어떨까 / 그 다음에 오는 작은 침묵이 / 그 다음 시작이라는 / 당신의 머릿속에 있는 무엇이든지를 표현할 //

What if you were limited to, / say, / fifty spoken words / tomorrow? //
당신이 제한받는다면 어떨까 / 이를테면 / 말을 50단어로 / 내일 //

I think / you'd listen quite differently. //
나는 생각한다 / 당신이 매우 다르게 듣게 될 것이라고 //

앞에 목적격 관계대명사가 생략됨
You'd attend quite carefully / to every word <mark>you heard</mark>. //
당신은 매우 신중히 귀를 기울이게 될 것이다 / 당신이 듣는 모든 단어에 //

You'd be attuned / to what you must respond to. //
당신이 맞춰질 것이다 / 반드시 응답해야 할 것에 //

「the+비교급 ~, the+비교급 …」: 더 ~할수록 더 …하다
You might discover / that <mark>the less</mark> you say, / <mark>the more</mark> you hear. //
당신은 발견할지도 모른다 / 말을 줄일수록 / 더 많이 듣게 된다는 것을 // 단서 더 적게 말할수록 더 많이 들을 수 있음

- spirit ⓝ 정신 • challenge ⓥ 도전하다 • observe ⓥ 관찰하다
- behavioral ⓐ 행동의 • psychology ⓝ 심리학
- expert ⓝ 전문가 • treat ⓥ 여기다 • rehearse ⓥ 연습하다
- eliminate ⓥ 제거하다 • attend ⓥ 귀[주의]를 기울이다

일상생활에서 침묵 서약의 정신을 따르는 것을 상상해 보라. 반드시 말해야 할 것만 말하는 데 하루 온종일을 보내는 것에 스스로 도전해 보라. 우리가 너무나 자주 "대화"를 자신이 말할 차례를 기다리는 게임처럼 여기는 경향이 있다는 것이 행동 심리학 전문가들 — 그리고 첫 데이트를 해 본 적이 있는 누구든지 — 에 의해 널리 관찰되어 왔다. 우리는 다음 발언을 머릿속으로 연습하느라 말해지고 있는 것을 놓친다. 만약 당신이 그 다음에 오는 작은 침묵이 당신의 머릿속에 있는 무엇이든지를 표현할 그 다음 시작이라는 생각을 없앨 수 있다면 어떨까? 내일 당신이 말을, 이를테면, 50단어로 제한받는다면 어떨까? 나는 당신이 매우 다르게 듣게 될 것이라고 생각한다. 당신은 당신이 듣는 모든 단어에 매우 신중히 귀를 기울이게 될 것이다. 당신이 반드시 응답해야 할 것에 맞춰질 것이다. 당신은 말을 줄일수록, 더 많이 듣게 된다는 것을 발견할지도 모른다.

다음 글의 요지로 가장 적절한 것은?
① 말을 적게 하면 상대방의 말을 경청할 수 있다. 말을 줄이면 더 많이 듣게 됨
② 첫 만남에서는 언행에 더욱 신중할 필요가 있다. 신중한 언행은 언급되지 않았음
③ 불필요한 대화를 줄이면 스트레스가 감소한다.
불필요한 대화와 스트레스에 관한 내용이 아님
④ 침묵은 의사소통의 효율성을 저해할 수 있다.
침묵이 아니라 말을 줄이는 것에 관한 내용임
⑤ 몸짓 언어는 효과적인 대화에 도움이 된다. 몸짓 언어는 언급되지 않았음

왜 정답? ✿❀❀ [정답률 91%]

도입: 반드시 해야 할 말만 해 볼 것을 권유
문제 제기: 대화에서 다음 발언을 준비하느라 상대의 말을 놓치는 문제가 발생함
해결 방법: 말을 적게 하면 더 신중하게 듣고 더 많이 듣게 될 수 있음 `단서`
▶ 말을 줄이면 상대방의 말을 더 잘 듣게 된다는 내용이므로 정답은 ①이다.

왜 오답?

② 첫 만남에서 언행에 신중해야 한다는 것은 언급되지 않았다.
③ 불필요한 대화가 유발하는 스트레스에 관한 내용이 아니다.
④ 대화 중간의 작은 침묵이 언급되었지만, 침묵이 의사소통 효율성을 저해한다는 것이 요지는 아니다. `함정`
⑤ 몸짓 언어는 언급되지 않았다.

---

23 정답 ⑤ ＊문제 해결을 위한 과학 지식의 실천

> be concerned with: ~와 관련이 있다

Science **is concerned with** / accumulating and understanding observations / of the physical world. //
과학은 관련이 있다 / 관찰을 축적하고 이해하는 것과 / 물리적 세계에 대한 //

That understanding alone / solves no problems. //
그 이해 단독으로는 / 어떠한 문제도 해결하지 않는다 //

to help의 의미상 주어 (= that understanding)
Individual people / have to act on that understanding / **for it to**
부사적 용법(목적)
help solve problems. // `단서 1` 문제를 해결하려면 이해를 행동으로 옮겨야 함
개개인은 / 그 이해를 행동으로 옮겨야 한다 / 그것이 문제를 해결하는 것을 돕기 위해 //

목적어절 접속사
For instance, science has found / **that** regular exercise can lower / your risk of heart disease. //
예를 들어, 과학은 발견했다 / 규칙적인 운동이 낮출 수 있다는 것을 / 심장병의 위험을 //

동명사구 주어   단수 동사   = Knowing this fact
Knowing this fact is interesting, / but **it** will do nothing / for
부사절 접속사 (조건)
your personal health / **unless** you act on it and actually exercise. //
이러한 사실을 아는 것은 흥미롭지만 / 그것은 아무런 도움이 되지 않는다 / 당신의 개인 건강에 / 당신이 이를 행동으로 옮겨 실제로 운동하지 않는다면 //

앞 문장의 but 이후 내용을 가리킴
And **that**'s the hard part. //
그리고 바로 이 점이 어려운 부분이다 //

Reading an article about exercise / is easy. //
운동에 대한 기사를 읽는 것은 / 쉽다 //

Getting into an actual routine of regular exercise / is harder. //
규칙적인 운동의 실제적인 루틴을 형성하는 것은 / 더 어렵다 //

'조금도 ~ 아니다'
In this sense, / science really / solves *no* problems **at all**. //
이러한 점에서 / 과학은 사실 / 어떤 문제도 해결하지 않는다 //

과거분사구 (the knowledge 수식)   병렬 구조
Problems are only solved / when people **take** the knowledge / **provided by science** / and **use it**. // `단서 2` 지식을 활용해야만 문제가 해결됨
= the knowledge
문제는 해결된다 / 사람들이 지식을 취하고 / 과학에 의해 제공된 / 그것을 사용할 때만 //

In fact, / many of humanity's biggest problems are caused / by lack of action, / and not lack of knowledge. // `단서 3` 인류 문제 중 다수가 행동 부족에 의해 발생함
실제로 / 인류의 가장 큰 문제들 중 다수는 야기된다 / 행동의 부족에 의해 / 지식의 부족이 아니라 //

- observation ⓝ 관찰 ・physical ⓐ 물리적인, 신체적인
- lower ⓥ 낮추다 ・risk ⓝ 위험 ・personal ⓐ 개인의
- act on ~을 행동으로 옮기다 ・article ⓝ 기사 ・humanity ⓝ 인류
- strategic ⓐ 전략적인 ・act against ~을 거슬러 행동하다
- lack ⓝ 부족

과학은 물리적 세계에 대한 관찰을 축적하고 이해하는 것과 관련이 있다. 그 이해 단독으로는 어떠한 문제도 해결하지 않는다. 개개인은 그것이 문제를 해결하는 것을 돕기 위해 그 이해를 행동으로 옮겨야 한다. 예를 들어, 과학은 규칙적인 운동이 심장병의 위험을 낮출 수 있다는 것을 발견했다. 이러한 사실을 아는 것은 흥미롭지만, 당신이 이를 행동으로 옮겨 실제로 운동하지 않는다면 그것은 당신의 개인 건강에 아무런 도움이 되지 않는다. 그리고 바로 이 점이 어려운 부분이다. 운동에 대한 기사를 읽는 것은 쉽다. 규칙적인 운동의 실제적인 루틴을 형성하는 것은 더 어렵다. 이러한 점에서, 과학은 사실 어떤 문제도 해결하

지 않는다. 문제는 사람들이 과학에 의해 제공된 지식을 취하고 그것을 사용할 때만 해결된다. 실제로, 인류의 가장 큰 문제들 중 다수는 지식의 부족이 아니라, 행동의 부족에 의해 야기된다.

다음 글의 주제로 가장 적절한 것은?
① advantages of putting strategic plans into action
전략적 계획을 실행에 옮기는 것의 이점   전략적 계획은 언급되지 않았음
② danger of acting against the wisdom of the crowd
다수의 지혜를 거슬러 행동하는 것의 위험성   다수의 지혜는 언급되지 않았음
③ difficulty in sharing scientific knowledge with the public 과학 지식 공유의 어려움은 언급되지 않았음
대중과 과학 지식을 공유하는 것의 어려움
④ problems with lacking specific knowledge about exercising 지식의 부족이 아니라 행동의 부족에 의해 문제가 야기됨
운동에 대한 구체적인 지식 부족으로 생기는 문제들
⑤ need to act on scientific understanding in solving problems 과학적 이해를 행동으로 옮길 때 문제가 해결될 수 있음
문제를 해결하기 위해 과학적 이해를 행동으로 옮길 필요성

왜 정답? ❀❀❀ [정답률 83%]

- 문제를 해결하려면 이해를 행동으로 옮겨야 함 `단서 1`
- 지식을 활용해야만 문제가 해결됨 `단서 2`
- 지식 부족이 아닌 행동 부족으로 인류의 가장 큰 문제들 중 다수가 발생함 `단서 3`
➡ 이해나 지식을 행동으로 옮겨 활용해야 문제를 해결할 수 있다고 했으므로 ⑤ '문제를 해결하기 위해 과학적 이해를 행동으로 옮길 필요성'이 글의 주제이다.

왜 오답?

① 전략적 계획은 언급되지 않았다.
② 과학적 지식의 실천에 관한 내용이지 다수의 지혜에 관한 내용이 아니다.
③ 대중과 과학 지식을 공유하기 어렵다는 내용은 언급되지 않았다.
④ 운동은 실천의 예시로 들었을 뿐이며, 과학적 이해를 행동으로 옮기는 것에 관한 내용이다.

---

24 정답 ① ＊현실에 대한 해석의 차이

병렬 구조
We think / we're being **logical**, **objective**, and **rational** — and
병렬 구조
therefore **accurate** / in **our analysis, judgment, and decisions**. //
우리는 생각한다 / 우리가 논리적이고 객관적이며 합리적이고 / 그러므로 정확하다고 / 분석, 판단, 그리고 결정에 있어서 //

목적어절 접속사
So we think / **that** if other people are logical, objective, and
병렬 구조 (will에 연결됨)
rational, / they will **agree** with us / and **see** what we see. //
따라서 우리는 생각한다 / 다른 사람들이 논리적이고 객관적이며 합리적이라면 / 그들이 우리에게 동의하고 / 우리가 보는 것을 볼 것이라고 //

But the opposite is the case. // 하지만 그 반대가 사실이다 //

Every human brain is different. // 모든 사람의 뇌는 다르다 //

Everyone's life experience is different. // 모두의 인생 경험은 다르다 //

Everyone's desires and knowledge are different. //
모두의 욕망과 지식은 다르다 //

앞에 목적어절 접속사 that이 생략됨
You might think / **you're** being realistic / — that is, that your ideas match reality, / but that's impossible. // `단서 1` 당신의 생각이 현실과 일치하는 것은 불가능함
당신은 생각할 수 있다 / 당신이 현실적이라고 / 즉, 당신의 생각이 현실과 일치한다고 / 하지만 그것은 불가능하다 //

계속적 용법의 주격 관계대명사
It's only your interpretation of reality, / **which** will always be
뒤에 interpretation of reality가 생략됨
different from **someone else's**. // `단서 2` 당신의 현실에 관한 해석과 다른 사람의 해석은 다름
그것은 현실에 대한 당신의 해석일 뿐이며 / 다른 사람의 것과 항상 다를 것이다 //

복수 주어   복수 동사
When two nations play each other / in the World Cup, / the **fans** of each country **criticize** the referees / for missing all the
목적격 관계대명사 (all the infractions 수식)
infractions / **that** the other team commits. //
두 나라가 서로 경기를 할 때 / World Cup에서 / 각 나라의 팬들은 심판들을 비난한다 / 모든 반칙을 놓친 것에 대해 / 상대 팀이 저지르는 //

= certainly   each + 단수 명사   단수 동사
Without fail, / each fan base believes / that the referees are biased / against their team. //
어김없이 / 각 팬층은 믿는다 / 심판이 편파적이라고 / 자기 팀에 불리하게 //

• logical ⓐ 논리적인　•objective ⓐ 객관적인
• rational ⓐ 합리적인　•accurate ⓐ 정확한　•analysis ⓝ 분석
• agree ⓥ 동의하다　•opposite ⓝ 반대　•the case 사실
• realistic ⓐ 현실적인　•match ⓥ 일치하다
• interpretation ⓝ 해석　•criticize ⓥ 비난하다　•referee ⓝ 심판
• commit ⓥ 저지르다　•biased ⓐ 편파적인, 편향된
• interpret ⓥ 해석하다

우리는 우리가 논리적이고 객관적이며 합리적이고 — 그러므로 분석, 판단, 그리고 결정에 있어서 정확하다고 생각한다. 따라서 우리는 다른 사람들이 논리적이고 객관적이며 합리적이라면, 그들이 우리에게 동의하고 우리가 보는 것을 볼 것이라고 생각한다. 하지만 그 반대가 사실이다. 모든 사람의 뇌는 다르다. 모두의 인생 경험은 다르다. 모두의 욕망과 지식은 다르다. 당신은 당신이 현실적이라고 — 즉, 당신의 생각이 현실과 일치한다고 생각할 수 있지만, 그것은 불가능하다. 그것은 현실에 대한 당신의 해석일 뿐이며, 다른 사람의 것과 항상 다를 것이다. World Cup에서 두 나라가 서로 경기를 할 때, 각 나라의 팬들은 상대 팀이 저지르는 모든 반칙을 놓친 것에 대해 심판들을 비난한다. 어김없이, 각 팬층은 심판이 자기 팀에 불리하게 편파적이라고 믿는다.

다음 글의 제목으로 가장 적절한 것은?

① Open to Interpretation: Everyone Sees Reality Differently 생각이 현실과 일치하는 것은 불가능하며 사람마다 현실에 대한 해석이 다르다는 내용임
다양한 해석의 여지: 모든 사람은 현실을 다르게 본다
② Efforts Made to Fill the Gap Between Real and Ideal 현실과 이상 사이의 간극을 메우기 위한 노력 현실과 이상 사이의 간극은 언급되지 않았음
③ One Single Reality: What We All Agree Upon 현실에 대한 해석은 하나의 단일한 현실: 모두가 동의하는 것 단일하지 않고 사람마다 다르다는 내용임
④ Why Sports Fans Judge Their Team's Play Objectively 왜 스포츠 팬들은 자기 팀의 경기를 객관적으로 판단하는가
⑤ Knowledge: The Key to Interpreting the World Accurately 모두의 지식이 다르기 때문에 현실에 대한 해석이 서로 다르다는 내용임
지식: 세상을 정확하게 해석하는 비결
└ 스포츠 팬들이 자기 팀의 경기에 관해 객관적이지 못하다는 내용임

왜 정답? ✹✹✸ [정답률 84%]
• 당신의 생각이 현실과 일치하는 것은 불가능하다. 단서 1
• 당신의 현실에 관한 해석과 다른 사람의 현실에 관한 해석은 다르다. 단서 2
➡ 생각과 현실이 일치하지 않으며 사람마다 현실에 관해 다르게 해석한다는 내용이다.
▶ 따라서 정답은 ① '다양한 해석의 여지: 모든 사람은 현실을 다르게 본다'이다.

왜 오답?
② 현실과 이상 사이의 간극은 언급되지 않았다.
③ 현실에 대한 해석은 단일하지 않고 사람마다 다르다는 것이 글의 내용이다.
④ 스포츠 팬들은 자기 팀의 경기 때 객관적이지 않다는 것이 글의 내용이다.
⑤ 모두의 지식이 다르기 때문에 현실에 대한 해석도 서로 다르다. (✕ 이유: 지식은 세상을 정확하게 해석하는 비결이 될 수 없다는 것이 글의 내용이다.)

25 정답 ④ ＊소매 거래에서 온라인 점유율

The graph above shows / the online share of retail trade / in 과거분사 (European countries 수식) selected European countries in 2018 and 2019. //
위 그래프는 보여준다 / 소매 거래에서의 온라인 점유율을 / 선정된 유럽 국가들에서 2018년과 2019년에 //

① In 2019, / the United Kingdom recorded / the highest online 최상급 분사구문 share of retail trade, / reaching 19.2 percent. // 2019년: 영국 19.2% → 가장 높음
2019년에 / 영국은 기록하였다 / 소매 거래에서 가장 높은 온라인 점유율을 / 19.2퍼센트에 달하며 //

② The Netherlands showed the largest increase / in its online share of retail trade / among the countries / from 2018 to 2019, / with a jump of over 6 percentage points. // 네덜란드: 9.1% → 15.3% 6.2%p 증가하여 가장 큼
네덜란드는 가장 큰 증가를 보였다 / 소매 거래에서의 온라인 점유율이 / 국가들 중 / 2018년부터 2019년까지 / 6퍼센트포인트 넘게 증가하여 //

③ In 2018, / Germany had a higher online share of retail trade / 비교급 than the Netherlands, / whereas, in 2019, / Germany fell behind the Netherlands. // 2018년: 독일 15.1% ＞ 네덜란드 9.1%, 2019년: 독일 14.2% ＜ 네덜란드 15.3%
2018년에는 / 독일은 소매 거래에서 더 높은 온라인 점유율을 가졌으나 / 네덜란드보다 / 반면 2019년에는 / 독일은 네덜란드에 뒤쳐졌다 //

④ In 2018, / Germany's online share of retail trade / was over 배수사 + 비교급 + than: ~배 더 …한 (→ not over) four times higher / than that of Spain. //
2018년에 / 독일의 소매 거래에서의 온라인 점유율은 / 네 배 넘게 높았다(→ 높지 않았다) / 스페인의 그것보다 // 단서 2018년 독일의 점유율은 스페인의 네 배(4.8% × 4 = 19.2%)를 넘지 않음

⑤ Among the five countries, / Italy recorded / the lowest online share / of retail trade / in both 2018 and 2019. // 이탈리아: 2018년 3.4%, 2019년 5.9%
다섯 국가들 중 / 이탈리아는 기록하였다 / 가장 낮은 온라인 점유율을 / 소매 거래에서 / 2018년과 2019년 모두 //

• share ⓝ 점유율, 몫　•retail ⓝ 소매　•trade ⓝ 거래
• record ⓥ 기록하다　•reach ⓥ 도달하다　•increase ⓝ 증가
• fall behind 뒤처지다

위 그래프는 선정된 유럽 국가들에서 2018년과 2019년에 소매 거래에서의 온라인 점유율을 보여준다. ① 2019년에, 영국은 19.2퍼센트에 달하며, 소매 거래에서 가장 높은 온라인 점유율을 기록하였다. ② 네덜란드는 2018년부터 2019년까지 소매 거래에서의 온라인 점유율이 6퍼센트포인트 넘게 증가하여, 국가들 중 가장 큰 증가를 보였다. ③ 2018년에는, 독일은 네덜란드보다 소매 거래에서 더 높은 온라인 점유율을 가졌으나, 2019년에는, 독일은 네덜란드에 뒤처졌다. ④ 2018년에, 독일의 소매 거래에서의 온라인 점유율은 스페인의 그것보다 네 배 넘게 높았다(→ 높지 않았다). ⑤ 다섯 국가들 중, 이탈리아는 2018년과 2019년 모두 소매 거래에서 가장 낮은 온라인 점유율을 기록하였다.

다음 도표의 내용과 일치하지 않는 것은?

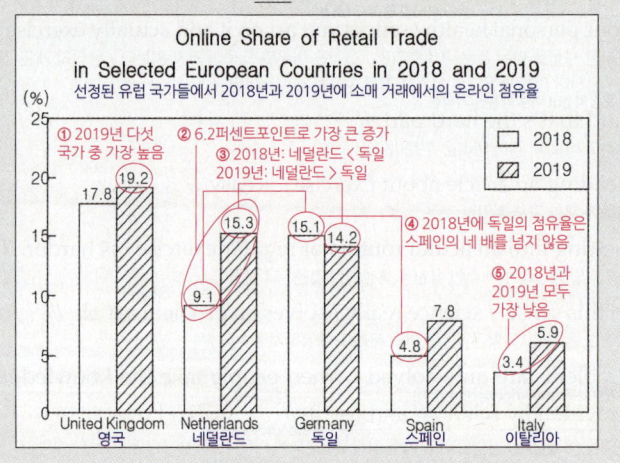

Online Share of Retail Trade in Selected European Countries in 2018 and 2019
선정된 유럽 국가들에서 2018년과 2019년에 소매 거래에서의 온라인 점유율

① 2019년 다섯 국가 중 가장 높음　② 6.2퍼센트포인트로 가장 큰 증가　③ 2018년: 네덜란드 ＜ 독일 2019년: 네덜란드 ＞ 독일　④ 2018년에 독일의 점유율은 스페인의 네 배를 넘지 않음　⑤ 2018년과 2019년 모두 가장 낮음

United Kingdom 영국 17.8 / 19.2　Netherlands 네덜란드 9.1 / 15.3　Germany 독일 15.1 / 14.2　Spain 스페인 4.8 / 7.8　Italy 이탈리아 3.4 / 5.9

왜 정답? ✹✸✸ [정답률 89%]
2018년에 독일의 소매 거래에서의 온라인 점유율은 15.1%로 스페인의 점유율인 4.8%의 네 배(4.8% × 4 = 19.2%)를 넘지 않는다. 따라서 ④이 도표의 내용과 일치하지 않는다.

왜 오답?
① 2019년 영국은 소매 거래에서의 온라인 점유율이 19.2퍼센트로 다른 나라들보다 높다.
② 네덜란드의 소매 거래에서의 온라인 점유율은 2018년부터 2019년까지 6.2퍼센트포인트 증가했으며, 다른 나라들보다 크게 증가했다.
③ 2018년 독일은 소매 거래에서의 온라인 점유율이 15.1%로 네덜란드 9.1%보다 높지만 2019년에는 14.2%로 네덜란드 15.3%보다 낮다.
⑤ 이탈리아는 소매 거래에서의 온라인 점유율이 2018년과 2019년에 각각 3.4%, 5.9%로 가장 낮다.

정답 ④ ＊Edward O. Wilson의 생애 ────────

Edward O. Wilson was born / in Birmingham, Alabama, in 1929. //
Edward O. Wilson은 태어났다 / 1929년 Alabama주 Birmingham에서 //

In his early childhood, / he became interested in nature and /
spent much time in the outdoors. // **①의 단서** 어린 시절에 자연에 관심을 갖게 됨
어린 시절에 / 그는 자연에 관심을 갖게 되었고 / 야외에서 많은 시간을 보냈다 //

At age seven, / he was partially blinded / in a fishing accident; / **②의 단서** 7살 때 낚시 사고를 겪음
과거분사 (sight 수식)
his **reduced** sight / led Wilson to the study of ants. //
7살 때 / 그는 부분적으로 실명했고 / 낚시 사고로 / 그의 좁아진 시야는 / Wilson을 개미 연구로 이끌었다 //

He could not observe / larger animals from a distance. //
그는 관찰할 수 없었다 / 멀리서 더 큰 동물을 //

Instead, / he concentrated / on smaller creatures / he could study
up close. //
대신, / 그는 집중했다 / 더 작은 생물에 / 그가 가까이에서 연구할 수 있는 //
접속사가 생략되지 않은 분사구문
After studying evolutionary biology / at the University of
계속적 용법의 관계부사
Alabama, / Wilson transferred to Harvard University, / **where**
he became a professor in 1956. // **③의 단서** 1956년에 Harvard 대학의 교수가 됨
진화 생물학을 공부한 후 / Alabama 대학에서 / Wilson은 Harvard 대학으로 옮겼고 / 그곳에서 1956년에 교수가 되었다 //
④의 단서 진화 생물학 분야에서 Nobel Prize를 받지 못함
He never received a Nobel Prize / — the prize didn't recognize
research / in the field of evolutionary biology. //
그는 Nobel Prize를 받지 못했다 / 그 상은 연구를 인정하지 않았다 / 진화생물학 분야의 //
수동태 동사
However, / he **was awarded** / the Craford Prize in 1990. //
그러나, / 그는 수상하였다 / 1990년에 Craford Prize를 //
삽입 구문 (Wilson에 관한 추가 정보)
Wilson, **known to some as the "modern-day Darwin"**, / died at
the age of 92 in Massachusetts. // **⑤의 단서** Massachusetts에서 92세에 사망함
몇몇에게 "현대의 Darwin"으로 알려진 Wilson은 / Massachusetts에서 92세에 사망했다 //

- outdoors ⓝ 야외   - partially ⓐᵈ 부분적으로
- blinded ⓐ 실명한, 눈이 먼   - observe ⓥ 관찰하다
- from a distance 멀리서   - concentrate ⓥ 집중하다
- creature ⓝ 생물   - evolutionary ⓐ 진화의
- biology ⓝ 생물학   - transfer ⓥ 옮기다, 이동하나
- recognize ⓥ 인정하다   - award ⓥ 수여하다

Edward O. Wilson은 1929년 Alabama주 Birmingham에서 태어났다. 어린 시절에, 그는 자연에 관심을 갖게 되었고 야외에서 많은 시간을 보냈다. 7살 때, 그는 낚시 사고로 부분적으로 실명했고; 그의 좁아진 시야는 Wilson을 개미 연구로 이끌었다. 그는 멀리서 더 큰 동물을 관찰할 수 없었다. 대신, 그는 가까이에서 연구할 수 있는 더 작은 생물에 집중했다. Alabama 대학에서 진화 생물학을 공부한 후, Wilson은 Harvard 대학으로 옮겼고, 그곳에서 1956년에 교수가 되었다. 그는 Nobel Prize를 받지 못했다 — 그 상은 진화생물학 분야의 연구를 인정하지 않았다. 그러나, 그는 1990년에 Craford Prize를 수상하였다. 몇몇에게 "현대의 Darwin"으로 알려진 Wilson은 Massachusetts에서 92세에 사망했다.

Edward O. Wilson에 관한 다음 글의 내용과 일치하지 <u>않는</u> 것은?

① 어린 시절에 자연에 관심을 갖게 되었다.
In his early childhood, he became interested in nature
② 7세에 낚시 사고를 겪었다.
At age seven, he was partially blinded in a fishing accident
③ 1956년에 Harvard 대학 교수가 되었다.
Wilson transferred to Harvard University, where he became a professor in 1956
④ 진화 생물학 분야에서 Nobel Prize를 수상했다.
He never received a Nobel Prize ~ in the field of evolutionary biology.
⑤ Massachusetts에서 92세에 사망했다.
Wilson ~ died at the age of 92 in Massachusetts.

＞왜 정답? ✿✿✿ [정답률 93%]

Edward O. Wilson은 Nobel Prize가 진화 생물학 분야의 연구를 인정하지 않아서 Nobel Prize를 받지 못했다고 했으므로(He never received a Nobel Prize ~ in the field of evolutionary biology.), 진화 생물학 분야에서 Nobel Prize를 수상했다고 한 ④은 글의 내용과 일치하지 않는다.

＞왜 오답?

① 어린 시절에 자연에 관심을 갖게 되었다. (In his early childhood, he became interested in nature)

② 7세에 낚시 사고를 겪었다. (At age seven, he was partially blinded in a fishing accident)

③ 1956년에 Harvard 대학 교수가 되었다. (Wilson transferred to Harvard University, where he became a professor in 1956)

⑤ Massachusetts에서 92세에 사망했다. (Wilson, ~ died at the age of 92 in Massachusetts.)

---

27 **정답 ③** ＊실내 식물을 파는 팝업 가게 안내
단기간 제품을 판매하고 운영을 종료하는 가게
Houseplant Heaven Pop-up Shop / 실내 식물 천국 팝업 숍 /

Enjoy / a special plant shopping experience! //
즐겨보세요 / 특별한 식물 쇼핑 경험을 //

Explore beautiful houseplants, / and bring some green into your
home. //
아름다운 실내 식물들을 구경하고 / 당신의 집으로 초록을 가져가세요 //

When: / October 11 – 13, 10 a.m. – 8 p.m. / **①의 단서** 3일간 진행됨
언제: / 10월 11 – 13일, 오전 10시 - 오후 8시 /

Where: / Tasty Cup Cafe / 어디서 / Tasty Cup Cafe /

Details / 세부 사항 /

- Indoor plants / are available for purchase. //
실내 식물이 구매 가능합니다 // **②의 단서** 실내 식물이 구매 가능함

- If you buy 2 plants, / you will get a 50% discount / on coffee. //
식물을 2개 사면 / 50% 할인받을 것입니다 / 커피를 // **③의 단서** 식물을 2개 사면 커피를 할인받음

Activities / 활동 /
과거분사구 (a photo zone 수식)
- Take pictures in a photo zone / filled with unique plants. //
포토존에서 사진을 찍으세요 / 독특한 식물로 가득 찬 //
과거분사구 (eco-friendly pots 수식)
- Decorate eco-friendly pots / made from recycled glass. //
친환경 화분들을 장식하세요 / 재활용 유리로 만든 // **④의 단서** 친환경 화분을 장식하는 활동이 있음
수동태 동사
※ Outside food and drinks / are not allowed. //
외부 음식과 음료는 / 허용되지 않습니다 // **⑤의 단서** 외부 음식과 음료는 허용되지 않음

- houseplant ⓝ 실내 식물   - explore ⓥ 구경하다, 둘러보다
- available ⓐ 이용 가능한   - purchase ⓝ 구매
- unique ⓐ 독특한   - eco-friendly ⓐ 친환경적인
- recycle ⓥ 재활용하다   - allow ⓥ 허용하다

실내 식물 천국 팝업 숍

특별한 식물 쇼핑 경험을 즐겨보세요! 아름다운 실내 식물들을 구경하고, 당신의 집으로 초록을 가져가세요.

언제: 10월 11 – 13일, 오전 10시 – 오후 8시
어디서: Tasty Cup Cafe
세부 사항
- 실내 식물이 구매 가능합니다.
- 식물을 2개 사면, 커피를 50% 할인 받을 것입니다.
활동
- 독특한 식물로 가득 찬 포토존에서 사진을 찍으세요.
- 재활용 유리로 만든 친환경 화분들을 장식하세요.
※ 외부 음식과 음료는 허용되지 않습니다.

Houseplant Heaven Popup Shop에 관한 다음 안내문의 내용과 일치하지 <u>않는</u> 것은?

① 3일간 진행된다. October 11 – 13

② 실내 식물이 구매 가능하다. Indoor plants are available for purchase.

③ 식물을 2개 사면 커피를 무료로 받을 것이다.
If you buy 2 plants, you will get a 50% discount on coffee.

④ 친환경 화분을 장식하는 활동이 있다.
Decorate eco-friendly pots made from recycled glass.

⑤ 외부 음식과 음료는 허용되지 않는다.
Outside food and drinks are not allowed.

❯왜 정답❓ ✽✾✾ [정답률 97%]

식물을 2개 사면 커피를 50% 할인받을 것이라고 (If you buy 2 plants, you will get a 50% discount on coffee.) 했으므로 커피를 무료로 받을 것이라고 한 ③이 안내문의 내용과 일치하지 않는다.

❯왜 오답❓

① 3일간 진행된다. (October 11 – 13)

② 실내 식물이 구매 가능하다. (Indoor plants are available for purchase.)

④ 친환경 화분을 장식하는 활동이 있다. (Decorate eco-friendly pots made from recycled glass.)

⑤ 외부 음식과 음료는 허용되지 않는다. (Outside food and drinks are not allowed.)

---

28 정답 ④ ✽2025 여름 만화 축제 안내

2025 Summer Cartoon Festival / 2025 여름 만화 축제 /

It's the 8th annual Summer Cartoon Festival! //
제8회 연례 여름 만화 축제입니다 // ①의 단서 8번째 열리는 연례 축제임

The festival drew / a lot of visitors last year. //
이 축제는 끌었습니다 / 작년에 많은 방문객을 //
'~하는 게 어떨까요?' = visitors

Why not be one of them this year? //
여러분도 올해 그 중 한 명이 되어보는 것은 어떨까요 //

Dates: / July 5 – 6 / 날짜 / 7월 5일 - 6일 /

Time: / 9 a.m. – 6 p.m. / ②의 단서 오전 9시부터 오후 6시까지 진행됨
시간 / 오전 9시 - 오후 6시 /

Place: / Merryville Park / 장소 / Merryville Park /

Featured Events / 주요 이벤트 /

• **Cartoon drawing classes for beginners only /**
초급자만을 위한 만화 그리기 수업 / ③의 단서 초급자만을 위한 만화 그리기 수업이 있음

• **Face painting by cartoonists /** ④의 단서 페이스 페인팅 행사가 있음
만화가에 의한 페이스 페인팅 /

• **Parade of costumed characters /** 의상을 갖춰 입은 캐릭터의 퍼레이드 /

Notes / 참고 사항 / ⑤의 단서 모든 방문객이 캐릭터 스티커를 받음

• **All visitors / will receive character stickers. //**
모든 방문객들은 / 캐릭터 스티커를 받을 것입니다 //

• **For a more detailed timetable and other information, / check out www.SummerCartoonFest.com. //**
더 자세한 시간표와 기타 정보를 위해서 / www.SummerCartoonFest.com을 확인하세요 //

• **annual** ⓐ 연례의, 매년의 • **featured** ⓐ 주요한
• **drawing** ⓝ 그림 그리기 • **beginner** ⓝ 초급자
• **costumed** ⓐ 의상을 갖춰 입은 • **receive** ⓥ 받다
• **detailed** ⓐ 자세한 • **check out** 확인하다

2025 여름 만화 축제

제8회 연례 여름 만화 축제입니다! 이 축제는 작년에 많은 방문객을 끌었습니다. 여러분도 올해 그 중 한 명이 되어보는 것은 어떨까요?

날짜: 7월 5일 – 6일

시간: 오전 9시 – 오후 6시

장소: Merryville Park
주요 이벤트
• 초급자만을 위한 만화 그리기 수업
• 만화가에 의한 페이스 페인팅
• 의상을 갖춰 입은 캐릭터의 퍼레이드
참고 사항
• 모든 방문객들은 캐릭터 스티커를 받을 것입니다.
• 더 자세한 시간표와 기타 정보를 위해서, www.SummerCartoonFest.com 을 확인하세요.

2025 Summer Cartoon Festival에 관한 다음 안내문의 내용과 일치하는 것은?

① 처음으로 개최되는 축제이다. It's the 8th annual Summer Cartoon Festival!

② 오전 9시부터 오후 7시까지 진행된다. Time: 9 a.m. – 6 p.m.

③ 상급자를 위한 만화 그리기 수업이 있다.
Cartoon drawing classes for beginners only

④ 페이스 페인팅 행사가 있다. Face painting by cartoonists

⑤ 방문객 중 일부만 캐릭터 스티커를 받을 것이다.
All visitors will receive character stickers.

❯왜 정답❓ ✽✾✾ [정답률 95%]

만화가에 의한 페이스 페인팅 행사(Face painting by cartoonists)가 있으므로 안내문의 내용과 일치하는 것은 ④이다.

❯왜 오답❓

① 8번째 열리는 연례 축제이다. (It's the 8th annual Summer Cartoon Festival!)

② 오전 9시부터 오후 6시까지 진행된다. (Time: 9 a.m. – 6 p.m.)

③ 초급자만을 위한 만화 그리기 수업이 있다. (Cartoon drawing classes for beginners only)

⑤ 모든 방문객이 캐릭터 스티커를 받을 것이다. (All visitors will receive character stickers.)

---

29 정답 ③ ✽전문가의 지식 구조

다음 글의 밑줄 친 부분 중, 어법상 틀린 것은? [3점]

간접의문문을 이끄는 의문사 가주어
Studies of experts / provide insight / into ① what it means / to
진주어 (to부정사)
have deep and flexible understanding. //
전문가에 대한 연구는 / 통찰을 제공한다 / 무엇을 의미하는지에 대한 / 깊고 유연한 이해를 갖는 것이 //

주격 관계대명사
Experts in a particular domain / are people / who have deep, richly interconnected ideas about the world. //
특정 분야의 전문가는 / 사람들이다 / 세상에 대해 깊고 풍부하게 상호 연결된 생각을 지닌 //

부사(smart 수식)
They are not / just good thinkers / or people who are ② exceptionally smart. //
그들은 아니다 / 단순히 생각을 잘하는 사람이거나 / 유난히 똑똑한 사람이 //

Rather, / experts ③ having (→ have) knowledge / in a specific
병렬 구조 (문장의 동사)
domain / — such as chess, chemistry, or tennis — / and are not
단서 experts에 대한 동사 자리임 등위접속사 (동사와 동사를 연결)
generalists. //
오히려 / 전문가는 지식을 가지고 있다 / 특정 분야에서 / 체스, 화학, 테니스와 같은 / 그리고 다방면의 지식을 가진 사람이 아니다 //

'많은'
However, / experts do not just know / "a bunch of facts." //
그러나 / 전문가는 알기만 하는 것은 아니다 / "많은 사실들"을 //

목적어절 접속사
In fact, / having expertise in a topic / means / that knowledge
목적어절의 첫 번째 문장
is organized into coherent frameworks, /
사실 / 한 주제에 대한 전문성이 있다는 것은 / 의미한다 / 지식이 일관된 틀로 조직되어 있고

목적어절의 두 번째 문장
and the expert understands the inter-relationship between facts / and can distinguish which ideas are most central. //
전문가가 사실 간의 상호 관계를 이해하고 / 어떤 아이디어가 가장 핵심적인지 구분할 수 있다는 것을 //

This kind of deep but organized understanding / allows for
과거분사 (understanding 수식)
greater flexibility in learning / and ⑤ facilitates application
병렬 구조
across multiple contexts. //
이러한 깊이 있으면서도 조직적인 이해는 / 학습에서 더 큰 유연성을 가능하게 하고 / 다양한 맥락에 걸쳐 적용을 촉진한다 //

- insight ⓝ 통찰 • flexible ⓐ 유연한 • domain ⓝ 분야
- interconnected ⓐ 상호 연결된 • exceptionally ⓪ 유난히
- generalist ⓝ 다방면의 지식을 가진 사람 • expertise ⓝ 전문성
- organize ⓥ 조직하다 • framework ⓝ 틀 • central ⓐ 핵심적인
- organized ⓐ 조직적인 • flexibility ⓝ 유연성
- application ⓝ 적용 • context ⓝ 맥락

전문가에 대한 연구는 깊고 유연한 이해를 가지는 것이 무엇을 의미하는지에 대한 통찰을 제공한다. 특정 분야의 전문가는 세상에 대해 깊고 풍부하게 상호 연결된 생각을 가진 사람들이다. 그들은 단순히 생각을 잘하는 사람이거나 유난히 똑똑한 사람이 아니다. 오히려, 전문가는 특정 분야 — 체스, 화학, 또는 테니스와 같은 — 에서 지식을 가지고 있고, 다방면의 지식을 가진 사람이 아니다. 그러나, 전문가는 "많은 사실"을 알기만 하는 것은 아니다. 사실, 한 주제에 대한 전문성이 있다는 것은 지식이 일관된 틀로 조직화되어 있고, 전문가가 사실 간의 상호 관계를 이해하고 어떤 아이디어가 가장 핵심적인지 구분할 수 있다는 것을 의미한다. 이러한 깊이 있으면서도 조직화된 이해는 학습에서의 더 큰 유연성을 가능하게 하고 다양한 맥락에 걸쳐 적용을 촉진한다.

> **왜 정답?** ✽✽❀ [정답률 64%]

③ 동사 자리에 준동사가 쓰였다!

Rather, / experts ③ ~~having~~ (→ have) knowledge / in a specific
동사가 와야 함 | *병렬 구조 (문장의 동사)*
domain / — such as chess, chemistry, or tennis — / and are not
삽입어구: 제외하고 생각하기 | *등위접속사 (동사와 동사를 연결)*
generalists.

Ⓒ 준동사 having에 밑줄이 있으므로
Ⓑ 동사 자리에 온 건 아닌지 확인한다.
Ⓗ 등위접속사 and 뒤에는 동사 are not이 알맞게 쓰였지만, and 앞에는 동사가 없다. 준동사 having은 문장에서 동사의 역할을 할 수 없으므로 having을 동사 have로 고쳐야 한다.
Ⓘ 주어와 동사는 문장의 필수 요소로서, 그중 하나라도 없으면 의미가 통하지 않으므로 문장이 될 수 없다.

> **왜 오답?**

① 간접의문문은 명사 역할을 한다.

Studies of experts / provide insight / into ① what it means / to
간접의문문을 이끄는 의문사 | *동사*
진주어 (to부정사) | *가주어*
have deep and flexible understanding. //

문맥상 '무엇을 의미하는지'를 뜻하므로, 의문사 what이 into의 목적어 역할을 하는 간접의문문을 알맞게 이끈다. 간접의문문은 「의문사 + 주어 + 동사」의 어순을 따른다.

② 부사는 형용사를 수식할 수 있다.

They are not / just good thinkers / or people who are ②
exceptionally smart. //
부사 (smart 수식)

문맥상 '유난히' 똑똑한 사람들에 대해 언급하고 있으므로 부사 exceptionally가 주격 보어 자리에 온 형용사 smart를 알맞게 수식하고 있다.

④ 접속사 that은 완전한 절을 이끈다.

In fact, / having expertise in a topic / means / ④ that [knowledge
목적어절 접속사
is organized into coherent frameworks], / and [the expert
목적어절의 첫 번째 문장
understands the inter-relationship between facts / and can
목적어절의 두 번째 문장
distinguish which ideas are most central]. //

목적어절 접속사 that이 knowledge is organized ~ frameworks와 the expert understands ~ central이라는 두 개의 완전한 절을 이끌고 있으므로 알맞게 쓰였다.

---

⑤ 등위접속사로 연결된 두 성분은 병렬 구조를 이룬다.

This kind of deep but organized understanding / allows for
문장의 주어
greater flexibility in learning / and ⑤ facilitates application
등위접속사 (동사와 동사를 연결) | *병렬 구조 (문장의 동사)*
across multiple contexts. //

동사 facilitates는 allows와 병렬 구조를 이루고 있다. 문장의 주어가 understanding으로 단수이므로 단수 동사의 형태로 온 것은 알맞다.

30 정답 ④ ＊인과 추론의 오류

다음 글의 밑줄 친 부분 중, 문맥상 낱말의 쓰임이 적절하지 않은 것은?

It is natural / for people / to observe happenings / and then seek
to observe와 seek의 의미상의 주어 | *진주어*
explanations / for why those happenings occurred. //
가주어 | *간접의문문*
당연하다 / 사람들이 / 사건들을 관찰하고 / 그 후 설명을 찾는 것은 / 왜 그런 사건들이 일어났는지에 대한 //

But sometimes / the reasoning is ① wrong / because of one or
more misconceptions. //
그러나 때로는 / 그 추론이 잘못된다 / 하나 또는 그 이상의 오해로 인해 //

One of these / is the ecological fallacy, / where an argument
단수 주어 | *단수 동사* | *관계부사*
claims / that there is a causal relationship between two things /
= misconceptions
merely because they occur ② together. //
그 중 하나는 / '생태학적 오류'이다 / 여기서 논지는 / 두 가지 사이에 인과관계가 있다는 것이다 / 그것들이 함께 발생한다는 이유만으로 //

For example, in the 1950s / it was found / that crime rates were
가주어 | *진주어절 접속사*
the highest / in neighborhoods / where immigrants were most
관계부사
numerous. //
예를 들어, 1950년대에 / 밝혀졌다 / 범죄율이 가장 높다는 것이 / 지역에서 / 이민자가 가장 많은 //

Some people used this "co-occurrence" / to argue / that
부사적 용법 (목적)
immigrants were a ③ cause of crime. //
일부 사람들은 이 "동시 발생"을 이용했다 / 주장하기 위해서 / 이민자들이 범죄의 원인이라고 //

But a careful analysis of this situation / revealed / that
immigrants were forced to live / in neighborhoods / where
관계부사
crime rates were already ④ low (→ high); /
그러나 이 상황에 대한 면밀한 분석은 / 밝혀냈다 / 이민자들이 거주할 수밖에 없었다는 것을 / 지역에서 / 이미 범죄율이 낮은(→ 높은) /

they could not afford more expensive housing / in safer
neighborhoods. // Ⓒ 이민자들은 안전한 지역에 살 여력이 없음
그들은 더 비싼 주택을 살 여력이 없었다 / 보다 안전한 지역의 //

Immigrants themselves / committed very few of the crimes. //
재귀대명사 (강조 용법)
이민자 자신들은 / 범죄를 거의 저지르지 않았다 //

Unless you analyze the claim carefully, / you would ⑤
부사절 접속사 (만약 ~하지 않는다면)
misinterpret the relationship / and thereby construct a faulty
병렬 구조 (문장의 동사)
belief. //
그 주장을 주의 깊게 분석하지 않으면 / 당신은 그 관계를 잘못 해석하고 / 그 결과 잘못된 믿음을 형성할 수 있다 //

- observe ⓥ 관찰하다 • happening ⓝ 사건
- explanation ⓝ 설명 • reasoning ⓝ 추론
- misconception ⓝ 오해 • ecological ⓐ 생태학적인
- fallacy ⓝ 오류 • argument ⓝ 논지, 주장 • causal ⓐ 인과적인
- merely ⓪ 단지 ~만으로 • crime rate 범죄율
- numerous ⓐ 많은 • co-occurrence ⓝ 동시 발생
- reveal ⓥ 밝혀내다 • afford ⓥ ~할 여력[여유]이 있다
- commit ⓥ 저지르다 • misinterpret ⓥ 잘못 해석하다, 오해하다
- construct ⓥ 구성하다, 형성하다 • faulty ⓐ 잘못된

사람들이 사건들을 관찰하고 나서 왜 그런 사건들이 일어났는지에 대한 설명을 찾는 것은 당연하다. 그러나 때로는 하나 또는 그 이상의 오해로 인해 그 추론이 ① 잘못된다. 그 중 하나는 '생태학적 오류'로, 여기서 논지는 두 가지가 ② 함께 발생한다는 이유만으로 두 가지 사이에 인과 관계가 있다는 것이다. 예를 들어, 1950년대에 범죄율이 이민자가 가장 많은 지역에서 가장 높다는 것이 밝혀졌다. 일부 사람들은 이민자들이 범죄의 ③ 원인이라고 주장하기 위해서 이러한 "동시 발생"을 이용했다. 그러나 이 상황에 대한 면밀한 분석은 이민자들이 이미 범죄율이 ④ 낮은(→ 높은) 지역에 거주할 수밖에 없었다는 것을 밝혀냈다; 그들은 보다 안전한 지역의 더 비싼 주택을 살 여력이 없었다. 이민자 자신들은 범죄를 거의 저지르지 않았다. 그 주장을 주의 깊게 분석하지 않으면, 당신은 그 관계를 ⑤ 잘못 해석하여 잘못된 믿음을 형성할 수 있다.

> **왜 정답?** ✽✽✽ [정답률 76%]

④ low 낮은

그러나 이 상황에 대한 면밀한 분석은 이민자들이 이미 범죄율이 ④ ~~낮은~~(높은) 지역에 거주할 수밖에 없었다는 것을 밝혀냈다. 그들은 보다 안전한 지역의 더 비싼 주택을 살 여력이 없었다.

➡ 이민자들은 안전한 지역의 비싼 주택을 살 여력이 없었다는 설명이 이어지므로 그들은 이미 범죄율이 '낮은' 지역이 아니라 '높은' 지역에 거주할 수밖에 없었던 것이다.
▶ low를 high(높은)와 같은 반의어로 바꿔야 함

> **왜 오답?**

① wrong 잘못된

그러나 때로는 하나 또는 그 이상의 오해로 인해 그 추론이 ① 잘못된다.

➡ 사람들은 사건을 관찰하고 나서 그것의 발생 원인을 찾는다는 앞 문장에 But으로 연결되므로 때로는 오해로 인해 그 추론이 '잘못된다'는 표현은 적절하다.
▶ wrong은 문맥에 맞음

② together 함께

그 중 하나는 '생태학적 오류'로, 여기서 논지는 두 가지가 ② 함께 발생한다는 이유만으로 두 가지 사이에 인과 관계가 있다는 것이다.

➡ 두 가지 사이에 인과 관계가 있다고 추론할 만한 상황은 두 가지가 '함께' 발생할 때이다. ▶ together는 문맥에 맞음

③ cause 원인

일부 사람들은 이민자들이 범죄의 ③ 원인이라고 주장하기 위해서 이러한 "동시 발생"을 이용했다.

➡ 높은 범죄율과 이민자 유입이 함께 발생할 때, 두 가지 사이에 인과 관계가 있다고 주장할 수도 있으므로, 이민자가 범죄의 '원인'이라고 주장할 것이다.
▶ cause는 문맥에 맞음

⑤ misinterpret 잘못 해석하다

그 주장을 주의 깊게 분석하지 않으면, 당신은 그 관계를 ⑤ 잘못 해석하여 잘못된 믿음을 형성할 수 있다.

➡ 생태학적 오류인 주장을 주의 깊게 분석하지 않으면, 두 사건 사이의 관계를 '잘못 해석하여' 잘못된 믿음을 형성할 것이다. ▶ misinterpret은 문맥에 맞음

31 정답 ② ✱ 경험에 기반한 주의 집중 ━━━━

In everyday life, / we use **previous experience** / to predict / where we should pay attention. //
일상생활에서 / 우리는 이전 경험을 사용한다 / 예측하기 위해 / 어디에 집중해야 할지를 //

Different environments create different expectations. //
다른 환경은 다른 기대를 만든다 //

This was profoundly illustrated / by the scientist Jared Diamond / in his book *Guns, Germs, and Steel*. //
이것은 깊이 있게 설명되었다 / 과학자 Jared Diamond에 의해 / 그의 저서인 *Guns, Germs, and Steel*에서 //

He describes an adventure / wandering through the New Guinea jungle / with native New Guineans. //
그는 모험을 묘사한다 / New Guinea 정글을 돌아다닌 / New Guinea 원주민들과 함께 //

He relates / that these natives / tend to perform poorly at tasks / Westerners have been trained to do / since childhood. //
그는 말한다 / 이 원주민들이 / 과업을 잘 수행하지 못하는 경향이 있다고 / 서구인들이 훈련받아 온 / 어린 시절부터 //

But they are hardly stupid. // 하지만 그들이 멍청한 것은 아니다 //

They can detect / the most subtle changes in the jungle, / good for / following the tracks of a predator / or for finding the way back home. //
그들은 감지할 수 있는데 / 정글에서 가장 미묘한 변화를 / 이는 유용하다 / 포식자의 흔적을 추적하거나 / 집으로 돌아오는 길을 찾는데 //

They know / which insects to leave alone, / know where food exists, / can build and tear down shelters with ease. //
그들은 알며 / 어느 곤충을 내버려 두어야 할지 / 어디에 음식이 있는지 알고 / 피난처를 쉽게 만들고 철거할 수 있다 //

Diamond, / who had never spent time in such places, / has no ability / to pay attention to these things. //
Diamond는 / 그러한 장소에서 시간을 보내본 적이 없는 / 능력이 없다 / 이러한 것들에 주의를 기울일 수 있는 //

Were he to be tested on such tasks, / he also would perform poorly. //
그가 그런 과업들에 대해 시험을 본다면 / 그 역시 잘하지 못할 것이다 //

- predict ⓥ 예측하다
- environment ⓝ 환경
- illustrate ⓥ 설명하다
- describe ⓥ 묘사하다
- wander ⓥ 돌아다니다, 방랑하다
- relate ⓥ 말하다, 이야기하다
- task ⓝ 과업
- detect ⓥ 감지하다
- predator ⓝ 포식자
- tear down 철거하다, 허물다
- shelter ⓝ 피난처
- cooperation ⓝ 협력
- instinct ⓝ 본능

일상생활에서, 우리는 어디에 집중해야 할지를 예측하기 위해 **이전 경험**을 사용한다. 다른 환경은 다른 기대를 만든다. 이것은 과학자 Jared Diamond에 의해 그의 저서인 *Guns, Germs, and Steel*에서 깊이 있게 설명되었다. 그는 New Guinea 정글을 New Guinea 원주민들과 함께 돌아다닌 모험을 묘사한다. 그는 서구인들이 어린 시절부터 훈련받아 온 과업을 이 원주민들이 잘 수행하지 못하는 경향이 있다고 말한다. 하지만 그들이 멍청한 것은 아니다. 그들은 정글에서 가장 미묘한 변화를 감지할 수 있는데, 이는 포식자의 흔적을 추적하거나 집으로 돌아오는 길을 찾는 데 유용하다. 그들은 어느 곤충을 내버려 두어야 할지 알며, 어디에 음식이 있는지 알고, 피난처를 쉽게 만들고 철거할 수 있다. 그러한 장소에서 시간을 보내본 적이 없는 Diamond는 이러한 것들에 주의를 기울일 수 있는 능력이 없다. 그가 그런 과업들에 대해 시험을 본다면, 그 역시 잘하지 못할 것이다.

다음 빈칸에 들어갈 말로 가장 적절한 것을 고르시오. [3점]
① close cooperation 긴밀한 협력은 언급되지 않음
긴밀한 협력
② previous experience 이전 경험에 따라 어디에 주의를 집중하는지가 달라짐
이전 경험
③ survival instinct 본능보다는 환경에 따라 달라지는 경험을 강조함
생존 본능
④ modern technology 현대 기술은 언급되지 않음
현대 기술
⑤ parental advice 부모의 조언은 언급되지 않음
부모의 조언

> **왜 정답?** ✽✽✽ [정답률 62%]

- New Guinea 원주민들은 서구인들에게 익숙한 과업을 잘 수행하지 못함 단서 1
- New Guinea 원주민들은 정글의 미묘한 변화를 감지할 수 있음 단서 2
- 다른 장소에서 성장한 Diamond는 이 원주민들과 같은 능력이 없음 단서 3

➡ New Guinea 원주민들은 서구인들이 어릴 때부터 훈련받아서 익숙한 과업을 잘 수행하지 못하지만, 정글에서 미묘한 변화에 주의를 기울이고 이를 감지할 수 있다. 반면에 Diamond는 정글에서 시간을 보낸 적이 없어서 New Guinea 원주민들과 같은 능력이 없다.

▶ 즉, 일상에서 어디에 집중할지 예측하기 위해 각자 성장한 환경 속에서 겪은 ② '이전 경험'을 사용한다는 것을 알 수 있다.

? 왜 오답 ?
① 어디에 집중할지 예측하기 위해 경험을 사용한다고 했을 뿐, 협력은 언급되지 않았다. 예시와 연관되더라도, 빈칸 문장에 더 집중하기! 꿀팁
③ 음식과 피난처가 언급되긴 했으나, <mark>생존 본능이 어디에 집중할지에 영향을 끼친다는 내용이 아니다.</mark>
④ 현대 기술이 어디에 집중할지에 영향을 끼친다는 내용은 언급되지 않았다.
⑤ 부모의 조언이 어디에 집중할지에 영향을 끼친다는 내용은 언급되지 않았다.

32 정답 ① ＊새로운 제품과 서비스의 초기 가격을 낮출 필요성

병렬 구조 (문장의 동사)
Most entrepreneurs / put in tremendous amounts of time and effort / in creating and launching new products and services / 동명사 (전치사 in의 목적어)
단서 1 새로운 제품과 서비스의 가격을 너무 비싸게 책정하는 실수를 함
and then make the mistake of overpricing them. //
대부분의 기업가들은 / 엄청난 시간과 노력을 들이며 / 새로운 제품과 서비스를 만들고 출시하는 데 / 그런 다음 그것들의 가격을 너무 비싸게 책정하는 실수를 저지른다 //

앞에 목적격 관계대명사가 생략됨
They have created / something they care deeply about, / it's theirs, /
그들은 만들었고 / 자신이 매우 소중히 여기는 무언가를 / 그것은 그들의 것이며 /

and this powerful sense of ownership / distorts their perception causes의 목적어와 목적격 보어 (to부정사)
of value / which causes them to overprice their products. //
이 강한 소유감은 / 가치에 대한 그들의 인식을 왜곡시켜 / 그들의 제품 가격을 너무 높게 책정하게 만든다 //

While many of them are quick to realize / that their initial prices are too high, /
그들 중에 많은 이들은 빠르게 깨닫기는 하지만 / 그들의 초기 가격이 너무 높다는 것을 /

make의 목적어와 목적격 보어 (형용사의 비교급)
not all these people / are happy or willing to drop their prices / to make their products more attractive. //
이 모든 사람들이 / 가격을 낮추는 것을 좋아하거나 내켜하지는 않는다 / 그들의 제품을 더 매력적으로 만들기 위해 //

앞의 내용을 가리키는 지시대명사   주격 관계대명사 (선행사: a very costly mistake)
And this can be a very costly mistake / that may lead to the failure / of their new business. // **단서 2** 가격을 낮추지 않는 것은 새로운 사업의 실패를 초래할 수도 있음
그리고 이것은 손해가 매우 큰 실수가 될 수 있다 / 실패를 초래할 수 있는 / 그들의 새로운 사업의 //

단서 3 새로운 제품과 서비스를 출시할 때 충분한 시장 점유를 우선순위로 두어야 함
When you launch a new product or service, / your priority should be to get sufficient market adoption / as soon as possible / 가능한 한 빨리
새로운 제품이나 서비스를 출시할 때 / 당신의 우선순위는 충분한 시장 점유를 확보하는 것이어야 하며 / 가능한 한 빨리 /

부사적 용법 (목적)
and you should be ready to / **sacrifice your initial prices and profits** / to achieve this aim. //
당신이 준비가 되어 있어야 한다 / 당신의 초기 가격과 수익을 희생할 / 이 목표를 달성하기 위해서 //

부사절 접속사 (조건)
Once you have strong sales volumes, / you can increase your prices / to maximize your profits. //
일단 당신이 높은 판매량을 확보하게 되면 / 당신은 가격을 인상할 수 있다 / 수익을 극대화하기 위해 //

- launch ⓥ 출시하다　• overprice ⓥ 과한 가격을 매기다
- distort ⓥ 왜곡하다　• perception ⓝ 인식　• initial ⓐ 초기의
- be willing to-v 기꺼이 ~하다　• costly ⓐ 손해가 큰, 비용이 많이 드는
- priority ⓝ 우선순위　• sufficient ⓐ 충분한　• volume ⓝ 양
- maximize ⓥ 극대화하다　• sacrifice ⓥ 희생하다
- strategy ⓝ 전략　• switch ⓥ 전환하다　• brand-new ⓐ 새로운

대부분의 기업가들은 새로운 제품과 서비스를 만들고 출시하는 데 엄청난 시간과 노력을 들이며, 그런 다음 그것들의 가격을 너무 비싸게 책정하는 실수를 저지른다. 그들은 자신이 매우 소중히 여기는 무언가를 만들었고, 그것은 그들의 것이며, 이 강한 소유감은 가치에 대한 그들의 인식을 왜곡시켜 그들의 제품 가격을 너무 높게 책정하게 만든다. 그들 중에 많은 이들은 그들의 초기 가격이 너무 높다는 것을 빠르게 깨닫기는 하지만, 이 모든 사람들이 그들의 제품을 더 매력적으로 만들기 위해 가격을 낮추는 것을 좋아하거나 내켜하지는 않는다. 그리고 이것은 그들의 새로운 사업의 실패를 초래할 수 있는 손해가 매우 큰 실수가 될 수 있다. 새로운 제품이나 서비스를 출시할 때, 당신의 우선순위는 가능한 한 빨리 충분한 시장 점유를 확보하는 것이어야 하며, 당신이 이 목표를 달성하기 위해서는 **당신의 초기 가격과 수익을 희생할** 준비가 되어 있어야 한다. 일단 당신이 높은 판매량을 확보하게 되면, 당신은 수익을 극대화하기 위해 가격을 인상할 수 있다.

2025.6
4회

다음 빈칸에 들어갈 말로 가장 적절한 것을 고르시오.
① sacrifice your initial prices and profits　새로운 제품과 서비스 사업에서
당신의 초기 가격과 수익을 희생할　처음부터 가격을 너무 높게 책정하면 실패를 초래할 수 있음
② upgrade your products and service
당신의 제품과 서비스를 개선할　제품과 서비스를 개선하는 것은 언급되지 않았음
③ maintain the overpricing strategy
가격을 높게 책정하는 전략을 유지할　초기 가격을 너무 비싸게 책정하면 안 된다고 했음
④ switch to a brand-new business
완전히 새로운 사업으로 전환할　완전히 새로운 사업으로 전환하는 것은 언급되지 않았음
⑤ seek out consumer reviews　소비자 평가는 언급되지 않았음
소비자 평가를 찾아볼

? 왜 정답 ? ✿✿✾ [정답률 63%]
• 대부분의 기업가들이 새로운 제품과 서비스의 가격을 너무 비싸게 책정하는 실수를 함 **단서 1**
• 초기 가격이 비싼 것을 알면서도 가격 인하를 꺼리면 사업의 실패를 초래할 수 있음 **단서 2**
• 새로운 제품·서비스를 출시할 때 충분한 시장 점유를 우선순위로 두어야 함 **단서 3**

➡ 대부분의 기업가들이 새로운 제품과 서비스를 출시할 때 초기 가격을 너무 높게 책정하고 가격 인하를 꺼리는데, 이는 사업의 실패를 초래할 수도 있으므로 충분한 시장 점유를 우선순위에 두어야 한다는 내용이다.
▶ 따라서 시장 점유를 충분히 달성하기 위해서는 ① '당신의 초기 가격과 수익을 희생할' 준비를 하고 가격을 낮춰야 한다.

? 왜 오답 ?
② 제품과 서비스를 개선하면 충분한 시장 점유를 확보할 수 있다는 내용이 아니다.
③ 초기 가격을 너무 비싸게 책정하면 안 된다고 했으므로 가격을 높게 책정하는 전략을 유지해서는 안 된다.
④ 새로운 사업을 시작하는 것은 언급되었으나, 완전히 새로운 사업으로 전환하는 것은 언급되지 않았다.
⑤ 소비자 평가는 언급되지 않았다.

33 정답 ② ＊인간의 번식 전략

In most respects, / humans are one of a relatively small number of species / '~ 중 하나'
대부분의 측면에서 / 인간은 비교적 소수의 종들 중 하나이다 /
주격 관계대명사 (선행사: species)
that evolved a very different strategy / of **investing more energy to reproduce more slowly**. //
매우 다른 전략을 진화시킨 / 더 많은 에너지를 투자하여 더 천천히 번식하는 //

Like apes and elephants, / we mature at a leisurely pace, / grow devote 목적어 to 동명사: ~을 …에 투자하다, 바치다
large bodies, / and have few babies / but devote much time and energy / to raising them well. // **단서 1** 인간은 새끼들을 적게 낳지만 잘 키우는 데 많은 시간과 에너지를 투자함
유인원과 코끼리와 마찬가지로 / 우리는 천천히 성숙하고 / 몸집을 크게 키우며 / 새끼들을 적게 낳지만 / 많은 시간과 에너지를 투자한다 / 그들을 잘 키우는 데 //

정답 및 해설 **103**

This unusual strategy succeeds / because while apes and elephants produce / fewer babies than mice, / a larger percentage of their offspring / survive to then reproduce. //
부사적 용법 (결과)
이 특이한 전략은 성공한다 / 왜냐하면 유인원과 코끼리는 낳지만 / 생쥐보다 더 적은 수의 새끼를 / 그들의 새끼 중 더 높은 비율이 / 살아남아서 번식한다 //

A house mouse can become a mother / when she is just five weeks old, / has four to ten pups per litter, / and can have a new
병렬 구조
litter every two months / over the course of her approximately twelve-month life. //
생쥐는 어미가 될 수 있으며 / 후 5주 만에 / 한 배에서 4마리에서 10마리의 새끼를 낳고 / 2개월마다 새로운 새끼들을 낳을 수 있다 / 약 12개월의 생애 동안 //

However, the vast majority of her pups die young. //
완전자동사 die와 함께 쓰인 유사 보어 (형용사)
그러나, 그의 새끼 대부분은 어릴 때 죽는다 //

In contrast, / a chimp or elephant mother does not reproduce
절과 절을 잇는 등위접속사
/ until she is at least twelve years old, / and she gives birth to only one infant / every five or six years / over the next thirty
= approximately   단서 2 침팬지와 코끼리는 생쥐보다 더 늦게 그리고 더 적게 자손을 번식함
or so years. //
반면 / 침팬지나 코끼리 어미는 번식을 하지 않으며 / 최소 12살이 될 때까지 / 단 한 마리의 새끼만 낳는다 / 5년 또는 6년마다 / 이후 30년 정도에 걸쳐 //

About half of these offspring / make it to becoming parents. //
동명사 (전치사 to의 목적어)
이러한 새끼 중 절반 정도가 / 부모가 되는 데 성공한다 //   단서 3 침팬지와 코끼리는 생쥐보다도 더 높은 비율의 자손이 생존하여 번식함

- respect ⓝ 측면   - relatively ⓐⓓ 비교적
- a small number of 소수의   - species ⓝ 종
- evolve ⓥ 진화시키다   - strategy ⓝ 전략   - mature ⓥ 성숙하다
- leisurely ⓐ 느긋한, 여유 있는   - pace ⓝ 속도   - raise ⓥ 키우다
- pup ⓝ 새끼   - approximately ⓐⓓ 약, 대략
- majority ⓝ 대부분, 다수   - give birth to ~을 낳다
- make it to ~에 이르다   - make use of ~을 사용하다
- reproduce ⓥ 번식하다   - intention ⓝ 의도
- pass down ~을 물려주다

대부분의 측면에서, 인간은 더 많은 에너지를 투자하여 더 천천히 번식하는 매우 다른 전략을 진화시킨 비교적 소수의 종들 중 하나이다. 유인원과 코끼리와 마찬가지로, 우리는 천천히 성숙하고, 몸집을 크게 키우며, 새끼들을 적게 낳지만 그들을 잘 키우는 데 많은 시간과 에너지를 투자한다. 유인원과 코끼리는 생쥐보다 더 적은 수의 새끼를 낳지만, 그들의 새끼 중 더 높은 비율이 살아남아서 번식하기 때문에 이 특이한 전략은 성공한다. 생쥐는 생후 5주 만에 어미가 될 수 있으며, 한 배에서 4마리에서 10마리의 새끼를 낳고, 약 12개월의 생애 동안 2개월마다 새로운 새끼들을 낳을 수 있다. 그러나, 그의 새끼 대부분은 어릴 때 죽는다. 반면, 침팬지나 코끼리 어미는 최소 12살이 될 때까지 번식을 하지 않으며, 이후 30년 정도에 걸쳐 5년 또는 6년마다 단 한 마리의 새끼만 낳는다. 이러한 새끼 중 절반 정도가 부모가 되는 데 성공한다.

다음 빈칸에 들어갈 말로 가장 적절한 것을 고르시오. [3점]
천천히 성숙하고 새끼를 적게 낳지만 양육에 더 많은 시간과 에너지를 투자함
① making use of fewer resources for reproduction
번식을 위해 더 적은 자원을 사용하는   번식과 자원량의 관계는 언급되지 않음
② investing more energy to reproduce more slowly
더 많은 에너지를 투자하여 더 천천히 번식하는
③ hiding their intentions to get what they really want
정말로 원하는 것을 얻기 위해 의도를 숨기는   의도를 숨기는 것은 언급되지 않음
④ passing down shared social values to their offspring
자손에게 공유된 사회적 가치를 물려주는   사회적 가치를 물려주는 전략은 언급되지 않음
⑤ living separately from their family units at an early age
어린 나이에 가족 단위로부터 분리되어 따로 사는   가족 단위로부터 분리하는 전략은 언급되지 않음

| 문제 풀이 순서 | ★★★ [정답률 54%]

1st 빈칸이 포함된 문장을 읽고, 빈칸에 들어갈 말에 대한 단서를 얻는다.

빈칸 문장 : In most respects, humans are one of a relatively small number of species that evolved a very different strategy of _____.
대부분의 측면에서, 인간은 _____ 매우 다른 전략을 진화시킨 비교적 소수의 종들 중 하나이다.

→ 인간이 매우 다른 전략을 진화시킨 소수의 종들 중 하나라고 했으므로 단서 인간이 다른 종과 다르게 '어떤' 전략을 진화시켰는지 확인해야 한다. 발상

2nd 글의 내용을 종합해서 빈칸에 들어갈 적절한 말을 찾는다.
- 인간은 유인원과 코끼리처럼 새끼들을 적게 낳지만 잘 키우는 데 많은 시간과 에너지를 들임 단서 1
- 침팬지와 코끼리는 생쥐에 비해 상대적으로 더 늦게 그리고 더 적게 새끼들을 번식함 단서 2
- 침팬지와 코끼리는 생쥐보다 더 높은 비율의 자손이 생존하여 번식함 단서 3
→ 인간은 침팬지와 코끼리처럼 늦은 나이에 적은 수의 새끼를 낳지만, 잘 키우는 데 많은 시간과 에너지를 들이므로 이들의 새끼가 생존하여 번식하는 비율은 생쥐의 그것보다 높다.
▶ 따라서 인간은 새끼들을 적게 낳으며 ② '더 많은 에너지를 투자하여 더 천천히 번식하는' 전략을 진화시켰다.

| 선택지 분석 |
① 인간은 번식을 위해 적은 자원이 아니라 오히려 많은 시간과 에너지를 들인다는 내용이다.
② 인간은 천천히 성숙하고 새끼를 적게 낳지만, 양육에 더 많은 시간과 에너지를 들인다.
③ 인간이 원하는 것을 얻기 위해서 의도를 숨기는 전략을 발전시켰다는 내용이 아니다.
④ 공유된 사회적 가치를 물려주는 것은 언급되지 않았다.
⑤ 가족 단위로부터 분리되어 사는 전략은 언급되지 않았다.

34 정답 ⑤ ＊과학자들의 정보 공유

When scientists make an important new discovery / or experimentally prove some hypothesis, / they do not, in general, keep that information to themselves /
과학자들은 중요한 새로운 발견할 때 / 또는 실험적으로 어떤 가설을 증명할 때 / 그들은, 일반적으로, 그 정보를 자기만 가지고 있지 않는다 /
부사절 접속사 (목적)
so that they alone can consider its meaning / and derive additional theories from it. //
그것의 의미를 혼자서 고려하고 / 그것으로부터 추가적인 이론을 도출할 수 있도록 //

= scientists   make의 목적어와 목적격 보어(형용사)
Instead, / they publish their results / and make their data available for inspection. //   단서 1 과학자들은 결과를 발표하여 데이터가 점검되도록 함
대신에 / 그들은 자신의 결과를 발표하고 / 그들의 데이터가 점검 가능하도록 한다 //

가목적어   to reconsider와 refute의 의미상 주어
This makes it possible / for other scientists to reconsider their
병렬 구조 (진목적어)
data / and possibly refute their conclusions. //
이것은 가능하게 한다 / 다른 과학자들이 그들의 데이터를 재고하게 하고 / 어쩌면 그들의 결론을 반박하는 것을 //   단서 2 다른 과학자들이 발표된 데이터를 재고하고 결론에 반박할 수 있음

'하지만'   가목적어
More important, / though, / it makes it possible for other
진목적어(명사적 용법의 to부정사)   부사적 용법 (목적)
scientists / to use that data / to construct new hypotheses and perform new experiments. //   단서 3 다른 과학자들은 이미 발표된 데이터를 활용할 수 있음
더 중요한 것은 / 하지만 / 이것이 다른 과학자들이 가능하도록 한다는 것이다 / 그 데이터를 사용하는 것을 / 새로운 가설들을 세우고 새로운 실험들을 수행하기 위하여 //

명사절 접속사 (주격 보어)
The assumption is / that society as a whole will end up knowing
'가능한 한 ~하게'
more / if information is spread as widely as possible, / rather
동명사의 수동태
than being limited to a few people. //
가정은 ~이다 / 사회 전체가 결국 더 많은 것을 알게 될 것이라는 것 / 만약 정보가 가능한 한 널리 확산되면 / 소수의 사람들에게 제한되기보다 //

In a strict sense, / every scientist **depends on the work of other scientists**. //
엄밀한 의미에서 / 모든 과학자는 다른 과학자들의 연구에 의존한다 //

- experimentally ⓐⓓ 실험적으로   - hypothesis ⓝ 가설
- in general 일반적으로   - publish ⓥ 발표하다
- inspection ⓝ 점검   - construct ⓥ 세우다
- assumption ⓝ 가정   - end up -ing 결국 ~하게 되다
- sense ⓝ 의미   - pursue ⓥ 추구하다   - stick to ~을 고수하다

과학자들은 중요한 새로운 발견을 하거나 실험적으로 어떤 가설을 증명할 때, 일반적으로, 그들은 그것의 의미를 혼자서 고려하고 그것으로부터 추가적인 이론을 도출할 수 있도록 그 정보를 자기만 가지고 있지 않는다. 대신에, 그들은 자신의 결과를 발표하고 그들의 데이터가 점검 가능하도록 한다. 이것은 다른 과학자들이 그들의 데이터를 재고하게 하고 어쩌면 그들의 결론을 반박하는 것을 가능하게 한다. 하지만, 더 중요한 것은 이것이 다른 과학자들이 새로운 가설들을 세우고 새로운 실험들을 수행하기 위하여 그 데이터를 사용하는 것을 가능하도록 한다는 것이다. 가정은 만약 정보가 소수의 사람들에게 제한되기보다 가능한 한 널리 확산되면 결국 사회 전체가 더 많은 것을 알게 될 것이라는 것이다. 엄밀한 의미에서, 모든 과학자는 **다른 과학자들의 연구에 의존한다.**

다음 빈칸에 들어갈 말로 가장 적절한 것을 고르시오.

① pursues only new discoveries
오직 새로운 발견만을 추구한다　새로운 발견만을 추구한다는 내용은 언급되지 않았음
② sticks to their own research ideas
그들 자신만의 연구 아이디어를 고수한다　과학자들은 이미 발표된 다른 자료를 활용한다고 했음
③ is restricted from using certain data
특정 데이터를 사용하는 데 제한받는다　연구 데이터가 확산되어 다른 과학자도 이를 사용한다는 내용임
④ ignores the data against their theories　발표된 데이터를 다른 과학자들이
그들의 이론에 맞서는 데이터를 무시한다　점검하고 반박하는 내용임
⑤ depends on the work of other scientists　과학자들이 결과를 발표하여
다른 과학자들의 연구에 의존한다　다른 과학자들에게 이를 점검받고, 다른
　　　　　　　　　　　　　　　　　　　　과학자들도 발표된 새로운 데이터를 활용함

| 문제 풀이 순서 | ★★★ [정답률 54%]

1st 첫 문장과 빈칸이 포함된 문장을 읽고, 빈칸에 들어갈 말에 대한 단서를 얻는다.

첫 문장	When scientists make an important new discovery or experimentally prove some hypothesis, they do not, in general, keep that information to themselves ~. 과학자들은 중요한 새로운 발견을 하거나 실험적으로 어떤 가설을 증명할 때, 일반적으로, 그들은 ~ 정보를 자기만 가지고 있지 않는다.
빈칸 문장	In a strict sense, every scientist _____. 엄밀한 의미에서, 모든 과학자는 _____.

➡ 과학자들이 새로운 발견을 하거나 어떤 가설을 실험적으로 증명할 때 그 정보를 자기만 가지고 있지 않는다고 했으므로, **단서**
과학자들이 서로 정보를 공유한다는 내용이 빈칸에 들어갈 것이다. **발상**

2nd 글의 내용을 종합해서 빈칸에 들어갈 적절한 말을 찾는다.

- 과학자들은 중요한 발견을 하거나 가설을 증명할 때 결과를 발표하여 데이터가 점검될 수 있도록 함 **단서1**
- 다른 과학자들이 발표된 데이터를 재고하고 결론을 반박할 수 있음 **단서2**
- 다른 과학자들은 이미 발표된 데이터를 활용할 수 있음 **단서3**

➡ 과학자들이 새로운 발견을 하거나 실험적으로 가설을 증명할 때 정보를 혼자만 아는 것이 아니라 공유함으로써 다른 과학자들이 그 데이터를 점검하거나 결론을 반박할 수 있게 하고, 새로운 가설을 세우거나 실험을 수행할 때 그 데이터를 활용할 수 있게 한다는 내용이다.

▶ 그러므로 모든 과학자는 ⑤ '다른 과학자들의 연구에 의존한다'고 볼 수 있다.

| 선택지 분석 |

① 새로운 발견의 결과를 발표하면 다른 과학자들이 이를 점검한다고 했지, 그들이 새로운 발견만을 추구한다는 내용이 아니다.
② 과학자들은 새로운 가설 설정과 실험에 다른 과학자가 발표한 데이터를 활용하므로, 자신만의 연구 아이디어를 고수하지 않는다.
③ 과학자들은 특정 데이터 사용에 제한을 받는 것이 아니라, 데이터를 공유한다.
④ 과학자들이 자신들의 이론에 맞서는 결과와 데이터를 무시하는 것이 아니라, 새로운 결과와 데이터를 점검하고 반박할 수 있다.
⑤ 과학자들은 데이터를 다른 과학자들과 공유하고, 다른 과학자들은 그 데이터를 활용할 수 있다는 내용이다.

---

35 정답 ③ ＊기억의 오류

다음 글에서 전체 흐름과 관계 없는 문장은?

In the 1930s, / the British psychologist Sir Frederic Bartlett /
ask ~ to부정사: ~에게 …을 요청하다
asked people / to listen to folktales from other countries and
　　　　　병렬 구조(to부정사)
then / recall these stories at a later date. // **단서1** 다른 나라의 민간 설화를 듣고
1930년대에 / 영국의 심리학자 Frederic Bartlett 경은 / 사람들에게 요청했다 / 다른 나라의　나중에 기억하는 실험을 함
민간 설화를 듣고 난 다음 / 나중에 이 이야기들을 기억해 내도록 //

As you might guess, / unfamiliar stories were not remembered /
　원급 비교
as well as familiar stories. //
당신이 아마 추측할 수 있듯이 / 낯선 이야기는 기억되지 않았다 / 익숙한 이야기만큼 잘 //

① Surprisingly, however, / errors in memory were not random. //
그러나 놀랍게도 / 기억의 오류들은 무작위적인 것이 아니었다 //　**단서2** 기억의 오류는
　　　　　　　　　　　　　　　　　　　　「not A rather B」: A가 아니라 B　무작위적인 것이 아님
② Rather, / subjects often rewrote / similar parts of the stories in
their own minds / — particularly the parts that made the least
　　　　　　　　　　　　　　　　　　　'이해가 되다'
sense to them. //
오히려 / 피험자들은 종종 다시 썼다 / 자신의 마음 속에서 이야기의 비슷한 부분 / 특히 그들에게 가장 이해가 되지 않는 부분을 //
　　　　　　　　　　　　　　　부사적 용법 (목적)
③ To attract a wide audience, / stories should focus on topics /
　　　　　　　　　　　　　　　　주격 관계대명사 (선행사: topics)
that interest many people. //)
(많은 청중을 끌어들이기 위해서 / 이야기들은 주제에 초점을 맞춰야 한다 / 많은 사람들의 흥미를 유발하는 //)
　　　　　　　　　　　　　　　　부사절에서 「주어 + be동사」 생략
④ Bartlett concluded / that when facing problems, / humans
draw upon mental schemata, or shelves of stored knowledge in
our brains, / to fill in any minor gaps in our memories. //
Bartlett은 결론을 내렸다 / 문제에 직면할 때 / 인간은 정신적 스키마타, 즉 뇌에 저장된 지식의 선반을 활용한다는 / 우리 기억의 사소한 틈을 메우기 위해 //　**단서3** 기억의 틈을 메우기
　　　　　　　　　　　　　　　　　　　　　　　　　위해 스키마타를 활용함
⑤ Therefore, remembering is an imaginative process / that
　　　　　　　　　　　　　　　　　주격 관계대명사 (선행사: an imaginative process)
involves building upon past experiences. //
따라서, 기억하는 것은 상상의 과정이다 / 과거의 경험을 기반으로 하는 것을 포함하는 //
　　　　　　　　　　　　　　　　단서4 기억하는 것은 과거의 경험에 기반한 상상의 과정임

- psychologist ⓝ 심리학자　　・ recall ⓥ 기억해 내다
- random ⓐ 무작위의　　・ particularly ⓐⓓ 특히
- audience ⓝ 청중　　・ face ⓥ 직면하다　　・ draw upon ~을 활용하다
- minor ⓐ 사소한　　・ gap ⓝ 틈　　・ imaginative ⓐ 상상의

1930년대에, 영국의 심리학자 Frederic Bartlett 경은 사람들에게 다른 나라의 민간 설화를 듣고 난 다음 나중에 이 이야기들을 기억해 내도록 요청했다. 당신이 아마 추측할 수 있듯이, 낯선 이야기는 익숙한 이야기만큼 잘 기억되지 않았다. ① 그러나 놀랍게도 기억의 오류들은 무작위적인 것이 아니었다. ② 오히려 피험자들은 자신의 마음 속에서 이야기의 비슷한 부분 — 특히 그들에게 가장 이해가 되지 않는 부분을 종종 다시 썼다. (③ 많은 청중을 끌어들이기 위해서, 이야기들은 많은 사람들의 흥미를 유발하는 주제에 초점을 맞춰야 한다.) ④ Bartlett은 문제에 직면할 때, 인간은 우리 기억의 사소한 틈을 메우기 위해 정신적 스키마타, 즉 뇌에 저장된 지식의 선반을 활용한다는 결론을 내렸다. ⑤ 따라서, 기억하는 것은 과거의 경험을 기반으로 하는 것을 포함하는 상상의 과정이다.

왜 정답·오답? ★★☆ [정답률 74%]

글의 앞부분: 영국의 심리학자 Bartlett가 피험자들에게 다른 나라 민간 설화를 들려주고 다시 떠올리도록 요청하는 실험을 하였고, 예상할 수 있듯이 피험자들에게 낯선 민간 설화는 익숙한 이야기만큼 잘 기억되지 않았음

① 그러나 놀랍게도 기억의 오류들은 무작위적인 것이 아니었음

▶ 예상과 다르게 기억의 오류들이 무작위적이 아니라는 내용이 자연스럽게 이어지므로 ①은 무관한 문장이 아님

② 오히려 피험자들은 자신의 마음 속에서 이야기의 비슷한 부분 — 특히 그들에게 가장 이해가 되지 않는 부분을 종종 다시 썼음

▶ ①의 내용을 부연 설명하므로 ②은 무관한 문장이 아님

③ 많은 청중을 끌어들이기 위해서, 이야기들은 많은 사람들의 흥미를 유발하는 주제에 초점을 맞춰야 함

▶ 이해가 되지 않는 부분을 오히려 다시 썼다는 내용 바로 뒤에, 흥미를 유발하는 주제에 관한 내용이 서로 이어지지 않으므로 ③이 무관한 문장임

④ Bartlett은 문제에 직면할 때, 인간은 기억의 사소한 틈을 메우기 위해 정신적 스키마타, 즉 뇌에 저장된 지식의 선반을 활용한다는 결론을 내림

▶ 기억의 오류에 대한 심리학자의 결론에 해당하므로 ④은 무관한 문장이 아님

⑤ 따라서, 기억하는 것은 과거의 경험을 기반으로 하는 것을 포함하는 상상의 과정임

▶ ④의 결론에 대한 부연 설명이므로 ⑤은 무관한 문장이 아님

＊ 글의 흐름

1 도입: 영국 심리학자 Bartlett은 피험자들에게 익숙하지 않은 이야기인 다른 나라 민간 설화를 들려주고 다시 떠올리도록 요청하는 실험을 함

2 전개: 피험자들은 익숙한 이야기만큼 낯선 이야기를 잘 기억하지는 못했지만, 기억의 오류는 무작위가 아니었음

3 부연: 피험자들은 이야기의 부분들을 생각 속에서 다시 썼고, Bartlett은 우리가 기억의 공백을 메우기 위해 스키마타를 활용한다는 결론을 내림

4 결론: 기억은 과거의 경험을 기반으로 한 상상의 과정임

---

36 정답 ② ＊역사적 반복의 예외가 나타나는 문명 붕괴

History, / people often say, / repeats itself. //
역사는 / 사람들이 종종 말하길 / 그 자체를 반복한다 //
삽입절 / 재귀대명사 (재귀 용법)

And looking at the historical records / of the ancient civilizations, / some things / do seem to happen again and again. //
분사구문 / 강조 용법의 do동사
그리고 역사적 기록들을 보면 / 고대 문명의 / 몇 가지 일들이 / 정말로 반복해서 일어나는 것처럼 보인다 //

(A) If so, / archaeology would be pretty boring; / one thing would happen again and again. //
만약 그렇다면 / 고고학은 꽤 지루할 것이다 / 한 가지 일이 반복해서 일어날 테니 말이다 //

But that's not what archaeologists see. // **단서 1** 역사가 항상 반복되는 것이 아니라 예외가 있음
선행사를 포함하는 관계대명사
하지만 그것은 고고학자들이 보는 것이 아니다 //

Some civilizations end suddenly, / like the Aztec and Inca, / conquered by invaders in the 1520s AD. //
과거분사구 (the Aztec and Inca 수식)
어떤 문명들은 갑작스럽게 끝난다 / Aztec과 Inca처럼 / 서기 1520년대에 침략자들에 의해 정복된 //

(B) Civilizations expand, / get overextended, / and then collapse / as in the cases of Rome, / which went under in 476 AD, /
문명은 확장하고 / 과도하게 확장되다가 / 결국 붕괴한다 / 로마의 경우와 / 서기 476년에 멸망한 /

and the British Empire, / which fell apart more than a thousand years later / in the post-World War II era. //
병렬 구조 (명사 + 관계사절) **단서 2** 주어진 글에서 언급된 고대 문명에서 반복해서 일어난 역사를 부연 설명함
대영제국의 사례에서처럼 / 천 년 이상 지난 후 해체된 / 제2차 세계 대전 이후에 //

But is this always the case? //
하지만 이것이 항상 그런가 //

(C) Those empires never had the chance / to collapse as a result of overexpansion. //
형용사적 용법 (the chance 수식) **단서 3** 침략으로 정복된 the Aztec and Inca를 가리킴
그러한 제국들은 기회조차 없었다 / 과도한 확장의 결과로 붕괴할 //

So in the case of civilizations, / "history repeats itself" / seems to be an oversimplification. //
그래서 문명의 경우에 / "역사는 그 자체를 반복한다"라는 말은 / 지나친 단순화로 보인다 //

---

106 자이스토리 전국연합학력평가 고1 영어

• ancient ⓐ 고대의 • civilization ⓝ 문명 • seem ⓥ ~처럼 보이다
• conquer ⓥ 정복하다 • expand ⓥ 확장하다
• collapse ⓥ 붕괴하다 • go under 멸망하다, 가라앉다
• fall apart 해체되다 • era ⓝ 시기
• oversimplification ⓝ 지나친 단순화

역사는, 사람들이 종종 말하길, 그 자체를 반복한다. 그리고 고대 문명의 역사적 기록들을 보면, 몇 가지 일들이 정말로 반복해서 일어나는 것처럼 보인다. (B) 문명은 서기 476년에 멸망한 로마의 경우와, 천 년 이상 지난 후 제2차 세계 대전 이후에 해체된 대영제국의 사례에서처럼 확장하고, 과도하게 확장되다가, 결국 붕괴한다. 하지만 이것이 항상 그런가? (A) 만약 그렇다면, 고고학은 꽤 지루할 것이다; 한 가지 일이 반복해서 일어날 테니 말이다. 하지만 그것은 고고학자들이 보는 것이 아니다. 어떤 문명들은, 서기 1520년대에 침략자들에 의해 정복된 Aztec과 Inca처럼 갑작스럽게 끝난다. (C) 그러한 제국들은 과도한 확장의 결과로 붕괴할 기회조차 없었다. 그래서 문명의 경우에, "역사는 그 자체를 반복한다"라는 말은 지나친 단순화로 보인다.

주어진 글 다음에 이어질 글의 순서로 가장 적절한 것을 고르시오. [3점]

① (A) — (C) — (B) (B)의 뒤에 이어지는 설명이 와야 함
② (B) — (A) — (C) 역사는 반복되는 것처럼 보임 — (B) 문명은 과도한 확장 끝에 붕괴함 — (A) 그러나 일부 문명은 갑자기 멸망하여 역사적 반복의 예외를 보임 — (C) 따라서 문명의 역사가 반복된다는 것은 지나치게 단순화한 주장임
③ (B) — (C) — (A) (C)의 Those empires는 (A)의 Aztec과 Inca를 가리킴
④ (C) — (A) — (B)
⑤ (C) — (B) — (A) 주어진 글에는 (C)의 Those empires가 가리킬 만한 대상이 없음

│ 문제 풀이 순서 │ ★★★ [정답률 70%]

1st 각 문단의 내용을 파악하고, 글의 논리적인 순서를 추론한다.

주어진 글: 역사는, 사람들이 종종 말하길, 그 자체를 반복한다. 그리고 고대 문명의 역사적 기록들을 보면, 몇 가지 일들이 정말로 반복해서 일어나는 것처럼 보인다.

➡ **주어진 글 뒤:** 사람들이 말하기로는 역사가 반복되고 고대 문명의 기록에서도 그런 것처럼 보인다고 했으므로, 이에 관한 예시나 반론이 뒤에 이어질 것이다.

(A): 만약 그렇다면(so), 고고학은 꽤 지루할 것이다; 한 가지 일이 반복해서 일어날 테니 말이다. 하지만 그것은 고고학자들이 보는 것이 아니다. 어떤 문명들은, 서기 1520년대에 침략자들에 의해 정복된 Aztec과 Inca처럼 갑작스럽게 끝난다.

➡ **(A) 앞:** so가 가리키는 내용, 즉 역사에서 구체적으로 무엇이 반복해서 일어나는지가 앞에 나와야 하는데, 주어진 글에는 역사가 반복되는 구체적인 사례가 없다.

▶ 주어진 글 바로 뒤에 (A)가 올 수 없음

(A) 뒤: 침략으로 정복된 Aztec과 Inca에 대한 부연 설명이 이어져야 한다.

(B): 문명은 서기 476년에 멸망한 로마의 경우와, 천 년 이상 지난 후 제2차 세계 대전 이후에 해체된 대영제국의 사례에서처럼 확장하고, 과도하게 확장되다가, 결국 붕괴한다. 하지만 이것이 항상 그런가?

➡ **(B) 앞:** 문명이 과도한 확장 끝에 붕괴하는 역사적 반복을 설명하고 그 예시로 로마와 대영제국을 제시한다.

▶ (B) 앞에 주어진 글이 와야 함 (순서: 주어진 글 → (B))

(B) 뒤: '하지만 이것이 항상 그런가?'라는 질문 뒤에 과도한 확장이 아닌 다른 원인으로 붕괴한 문명의 사례가 이어져야 하는데, (A)에 침략으로 정복된 Aztec과 Inca가 나온다.

▶ (B) 뒤에 (A)가 와야 함 (순서: 주어진 글 → (B) → (A))

(C): 그러한 제국들(Those empires)은 과도한 확장의 결과로 붕괴할 기회조차 없었다. 그래서 문명의 경우에, "역사는 그 자체를 반복한다"라는 말은 지나친 단순화로 보인다.

➡ **(C) 앞:** 과도한 확장으로 붕괴하지 않은 '그러한 제국들'이 앞에 나와야 한다.

▶ '그러한 제국들'은 침략으로 붕괴된 Aztec과 Inca를 가리키므로 (A) 뒤에 와야 함 (순서: 주어진 글 → (B) → (A) → (C))

(C) 뒤: 문명에서 역사가 반복된다는 말은 지나친 단순화라는 결론으로 글이 마무리된다.

2nd 글이 한눈에 들어오도록 정리하여 정답을 확인한다.

주어진 글: 역사는 반복되는 것처럼 보인다.
→ **(B)**: 문명은 팽창과 과도한 확장 끝에 붕괴한다.
→ **(A)**: 그러나 일부 문명은 갑자기 멸망하여 예외를 보인다.
→ **(C)**: 문명의 역사가 반복된다는 것은 지나친 단순화이다.
  ▶ 주어진 글 다음에 이어질 글의 순서는 (B) → (A) → (C)이므로 정답은 ②임

37 정답 ⑤ *노력에 대한 칭찬을 통한 성장 사고방식의 발달

Stanford psychology professor Dr. Carol Dweck / is the internationally recognized pioneer / of the concept of "growth mindset" / ~로서 **as** a way 형용사적 용법 (way 수식) **to** continually **grow**, **learn**, and **persevere** in our efforts. //
Stanford 심리학 교수인 Carol Dweck 박사는 / 국제적으로 인정받는 선구자이다 / "성장 사고방식" 개념으로 / 우리의 노력에서 지속적으로 성장하고, 배우며, 인내할 수 있는 방법인 //

단서 1 (B)에서 노력에 대한 칭찬으로 성장 사고방식을 발달시킨 아이들을 가리킴
(A) These kids / end up taking on tougher things, / and feel better about themselves. //
이 아이들은 / 결국 더 힘든 일을 받아들이고 / 스스로에 대해 더 좋은 느낌을 갖게 된다 //
동명사구 주어 단수 동사 목적격 관계대명사 (a variable 수식)
"**Emphasizing effort gives** a child a variable / **that** they can control," / Dweck has explained. //
"노력을 강조하는 것은 아이에게 변수를 제공한다 / 그들이 통제할 수 있는"이라고 / Dweck은 설명했다 //

'반대로' 선행사를 포함하는 관계대명사
(B) **In contrast**, Dweck found, / kids who are praised **not** for their smarts **but** for their effort / develop **what** Dweck calls a "growth mindset." // **단서 2** 똑똑함에 대해 칭찬받은 아이들에 대한 내용이 앞에 와야 함
반대로, Dweck은 발견했다 / 똑똑함이 아닌 노력에 대해 칭찬받는 아이들은 / Dweck이 "성장 사고방식"이라 부르는 것을 발달시킨다는 것을 //
목적어절 접속사 선행사를 포함하는 관계대명사 부사절 접속사 (조건)
They learn / **that** their effort is **what** led to their success, / and **if** they continue to try, / over time / they'll improve and achieve more things. //
그들은 배운다 / 그들의 노력이 성공으로 이르게 한 것임을 / 그리고 그들이 계속해서 노력한다면 / 시간이 지나면서 / 그들은 발전하고 더 많은 것을 성취하게 될 것이다 //

단서 3 똑똑하다는 칭찬을 들은 아이들에 관한 내용으로 (B)와 대조됨
(C) Dweck found / that kids who are told **they're "smart"** / 앞에 목적어절 접속사 that이 생략됨 actually underperform in future tasks, / by choosing easier tasks /
Dweck은 발견했는데 / "똑똑하다"라는 말을 듣는 아이들은 / 실제로 미래 과제에서 기대에 못 미치는 성과를 낸다는 것을 / 더 쉬운 과제를 선택함으로써 /
동격절 접속사 계속적 용법의 목적격 관계대명사
to avoid evidence / **that** they are not smart, / **which** Dweck calls having a "fixed mindset." //
증거를 피하기 위해 / 그들이 똑똑하지 않다는 / Dweck은 이를 "고정 사고방식"을 가진 것으로 부른다 //

- internationally [ad] 국제적으로 • recognized [a] 인정받는
- pioneer [n] 선구자 • effort [n] 노력 • end up -ing 결국 ~하게 되다
- take on ~을 받아들이다, 맡다 • tough [a] 힘든
- emphasize [v] 강조하다 • control [v] 통제하다
- continue [v] 계속[지속]하다 • improve [v] 발전하다
- underperform [v] 기대에 못 미치는 성과를 내다 • evidence [n] 증거

Stanford 심리학 교수인 Carol Dweck 박사는 우리의 노력에서 지속적으로 성장하고, 배우며, 인내할 수 있는 방법인 "성장 사고방식" 개념으로 국제적으로 인정받는 선구자이다. (C) Dweck은 "똑똑하다"라는 말을 듣는 아이들은 그들이 똑똑하지 않다는 증거를 피하기 위해 더 쉬운 과제를 선택함으로써 실제로 미래 과제에서 기대에 못 미치는 성과를 낸다는 것을 발견했는데, Dweck은 이를 "고정 사고방식"을 가진 것으로 부른다. (B) 반대로, Dweck은 똑똑함이 아닌 노력에 대해 칭찬받는 아이들은 Dweck이 "성장 사고방식"이라 부르는 것을 발달시킨다는 것을 발견했다. 그들은 그들의 노력이 성공으로 이르게 한 것임을 배우고, 그들이 계속해서 노력한다면, 시간이 지나면서 발전하고 더 많은 것을 성취하게 될 것이다. (A) 이 아이들은 결국 더 힘든 일을 받아들이고, 스스로에 대해 더 좋은 느낌을 갖게 된다. "노력을 강조하는 것은 아이에게 그들이 통제할 수 있는 변수를 제공한다."라고 Dweck은 설명했다.

주어진 글 다음에 이어질 글의 순서로 가장 적절한 것을 고르시오.

① (A) — (C) — (B) 주어진 글에는 (A)의 These kids를 가리키는 대상이 없음
② (B) — (A) — (C)
③ (B) — (C) — (A) 주어진 글에는 In contrast로 받을 내용이 없음
④ (C) — (A) — (B) 성장 사고방식의 장점을 설명하는 (A)가 (B) 뒤에 와야 함
⑤ (C) — (B) — (A) Dweck의 "성장 사고방식" 개념 — (C) 똑똑하다고 칭찬받는 아이들은 "고정 사고방식"을 가짐 — (B) 노력에 대해 칭찬받는 아이들은 "성장 사고방식"을 발달시킴 — (A) 성장 사고방식을 발달시킨 아이들의 특징

| 문제 풀이 순서 | ★★※ [정답률 65%]

1st 각 문단의 내용을 파악하고, 글의 논리적인 순서를 추론한다.

주어진 글: Stanford 심리학 교수인 Carol Dweck 박사는 우리의 노력에서 지속적으로 성장하고, 배우며, 인내할 수 있는 방법인 "성장 사고방식" 개념으로 국제적으로 인정받는 선구자이다.
⇒ **주어진 글 뒤**: Dweck이 밝혀낸 성장 사고방식 개념이 노력에 관한 것이라고 했는데, 이에 관하여 부연 설명이 이어질 것이다.

(A): 이 아이들(These kids)은 결국 더 힘든 일을 받아들이고, 스스로에 대해 더 좋은 느낌을 갖게 된다. "노력을 강조하는 것은 아이에게 그들이 통제할 수 있는 변수를 제공한다."라고 Dweck은 설명했다.
⇒ **(A) 앞**: These kids가 어떤 아이들을 가리키는지가 앞에 나와야 한다. 주어진 글에 성장 사고방식 개념이 언급되긴 하지만, 아이들은 언급되지 않았다.
  ▶ (A) 앞에 주어진 글이 올 수 없음
(A) 뒤: (A)는 성장 사고방식을 갖춘 아이들의 특징과 노력을 강조하는 것의 의의를 설명하고 있으므로 글의 마지막일 가능성이 높다.

(B): 반대로(In contrast), Dweck은 똑똑함이 아닌 노력에 대해 칭찬받는 아이들은 Dweck이 "성장 사고방식"이라 부르는 것을 발달시킨다는 것을 발견했다. 그들은 그들의 노력이 성공으로 이르게 한 것임을 배우고, 그들이 계속해서 노력한다면, 시간이 지나면서 발전하고 더 많은 것을 성취하게 될 것이다.
⇒ **(B) 앞**: 반대되는 내용을 나타내는 In contrast가 있으므로, 앞에는 똑똑함에 대해 칭찬받는 아이들이 언급되어야 한다. 노력에 대해 칭찬받는 아이들이 긍정적으로 언급되므로, 그와 반대인 아이들은 부정적으로 언급될 것이다.
  ▶ (B) 앞에 주어진 글과 (A)가 올 수 없음
(B) 뒤: 노력에 대한 칭찬이 성장 사고방식을 키우고, 이들은 시간이 지나면서 발전한다고 했으므로 (A)의 These kids는 성장 사고방식을 키운 아이들이다.
  ▶ (B) 뒤에 (A)가 와야 함 (순서: (B) → (A))

(C): Dweck은 "똑똑하다"라는 말을 듣는 아이들은 그들이 똑똑하지 않다는 증거를 피하기 위해 더 쉬운 과제를 선택함으로써 실제로 미래 과제에서 기대에 못 미치는 성과를 낸다는 것을 발견했는데, Dweck은 이를 "고정 사고방식"을 가진 것으로 부른다.
⇒ **(C) 앞**: 고정 사고방식과 관련된 개념이 먼저 제시되어야 한다. 주어진 글에서 노력에서 파생되는 성장 사고방식을 소개하고 이를 부연 설명하기에 앞서, (C)에서 노력이 아닌 똑똑함에서 파생되는 고정 사고방식을 먼저 설명하는 흐름이다.
  ▶ (C) 앞에 주어진 글이 와야 함 (순서: 주어진 글 → (C))
(C) 뒤: 고정 사고방식을 가진 아이들의 성과가 기대에 못 미친다는 부정적인 내용 바로 뒤에 성장 사고방식을 가진 아이들에 관한 내용이 (B)의 In contrast로 이어진다.
  ▶ (C) 뒤에 (B)가 와야 함 (순서: 주어진 글 → (C) → (B) → (A))

2nd 글이 한눈에 들어오도록 정리하여 정답을 확인한다.

주어진 글: Dweck은 성장 사고방식 개념을 제시하였다.
→ **(C)**: 똑똑하다고 칭찬받은 아이들은 고정 사고방식을 갖게 된다.
→ **(B)**: 반대로 노력에 관해 칭찬받은 아이들은 성장 사고방식을 발달시킨다.
→ **(A)**: 성장 사고방식을 발달시킨 아이들은 긍정적인 특성을 갖는다.
  ▶ 주어진 글 다음에 이어질 글의 순서는 (C) → (B) → (A)이므로 정답은 ⑤임

글의 흐름으로 보아, 주어진 문장이 들어가기에 가장 적절한 곳을 고르시오.

Partly this was the obvious convenience / of being able to exit more quickly. // 단서 1 승객들이 문 근처에 자리 잡기를 좋아하는 이성적인 이유
부분적으로 이것은 명확한 편리함 때문이었다 / 더 빨리 내릴 수 있다는 //

명사적 용법 (주어)   명사적 용법 (주격 보어)
To monitor our surroundings / is to focus on / what's outside
선행사를 포함하는 관계대명사
of ourselves: / what we see, hear, smell, feel, and perhaps even taste. //
우리 주변을 살피는 것은 / 집중하는 것이다 / 우리 자신 바깥에 있는 것에 / 우리가 보고, 듣고, 냄새 맡고, 느끼고, 어쩌면 맛보기도 하는 것 //

선행사를 포함하는 관계대명사   -thing으로 끝나는 대명사는 형용사가 뒤에서 수식함
But sometimes what really marks a place / is something less specific / — a *feeling* within us. //
그러나 때로는 어떤 장소를 진정으로 특징짓는 것은 / 덜 구체적인 것이다 / 우리 안에 있는 '감정' //

(①) An interesting example emerged / from a study of subway passenger behavior. //
흥미로운 예가 나왔다 / 지하철 승객 행동에 관한 연구에서 //

현재분사(Researchers 수식)
(②) Researchers trying to understand / why people sit where they sit / or stand where they stand / in subway and metro trains /
이해하려고 노력하는 연구자들은 / 왜 사람들이 그들이 앉는 곳에 앉거나 / 그들이 서는 곳에 서는지를 / 지하철이나 전철에서 //

주격 관계대명사 (선행사: the factors)   뒤에 관계부사 how가 생략됨
examined the factors / that shape / the way riders used and navigated that space / in different situations. //
요인들을 조사했다 / 형성하는 / 승객들이 그 공간을 사용하고 탐색하는 방식을 / 다양한 상황에서 //

단서 2 승객들이 기차의 문 근처에 자리 잡기를 좋아하는 이유를 연구함
(③) One of their findings / involved the reasons / many riders
자리 잡다
like to plant themselves close to the train's doors. //
연구 결과 중 하나는 / 이유들과 관련이 있었다 / 많은 승객들이 기차의 문 근처에 자리 잡기를 좋아하는 //

단서 3 승객들이 문 근처에 자리 잡기를 좋아하는 감정적인 이유
(④) But it was shaped partly / by a more abstract sensation /
그러나 이는 부분적으로 형성되었다 / 더 추상적인 느낌에 의해 /
형용사적 용법 (the desire 수식)
— the desire to avoid the sometimes uncomfortable feeling / of accidentally making eye contact with seated passengers. //
때때로 불편한 느낌을 피하려는 욕구 / 앉아 있는 승객들과 우연히 눈이 마주치는 //

(⑤) We can't see feelings / — but they're very real, / and they influence our experience of the world. //
우리는 감정들을 볼 수 없다 / 그러나 그것들은 매우 실재하고 / 그것들은 세상에 대한 우리의 경험에 영향을 미친다 //

- obvious ⓐ 명확한   - convenience ⓝ 편리함
- surroundings ⓝ 주변   - mark ⓥ 특징짓다
- specific ⓐ 구체적인   - emerge ⓥ 나타나다   - passenger ⓝ 승객
- behavior ⓝ 행동   - examine ⓥ 조사하다   - factor ⓝ 요인
- shape ⓥ 형성하다   - navigate ⓥ 탐색하다
- findings ⓝ 연구 결과   - involve ⓥ ~와 관련이 있다
- abstract ⓐ 추상적인   - sensation ⓝ 느낌   - desire ⓝ 욕구
- accidentally ⓐⓓ 우연히   - influence ⓥ ~에 영향을 미치다

우리 주변을 살피는 것은 우리 자신 바깥에 있는 것에 집중하는 것이다: 우리가 보고, 듣고, 냄새 맡고, 느끼고, 어쩌면 맛보기도 하는 것. 그러나 때로는 어떤 장소를 진정으로 특징짓는 것은 덜 구체적인 것 — 우리 안에 있는 '감정'이다. (①) 흥미로운 예가 지하철 승객 행동에 관한 연구에서 나왔다. (②) 지하철이나 전철에서 왜 사람들이 그들이 앉는 곳에 앉거나 그들이 서는 곳에 서는지를 이해하려고 노력하는 연구자들은 다양한 상황에서 승객들이 그 공간을 사용하고 탐색하는 방식을 형성하는 요인들을 조사했다. (③) 연구 결과 중 하나는 많은 승객들이 기차의 문 근처에 자리 잡기를 좋아하는 이유들과 관련이 있었다. (④ 부분적으로 이것은 더 빨리 내릴 수 있다는 명확한 편리함 때문이었다.) 그러나 이는 부분적으로 더 추상적인 느낌 — 앉아 있는 승객들과 우연히

눈이 마주치는 때때로 불편한 느낌을 피하려는 욕구에 의해 형성되었다. (⑤) 우리는 감정들을 볼 수 없다 — 그러나 그것들은 매우 실재하고, 그것들은 세상에 대한 우리의 경험에 영향을 미친다.

| 문제 풀이 순서 | ✿✿✿ [정답률 72%]

1st 주어진 문장을 해석하고, 지시어 등을 확인한다.

Partly this was the obvious convenience of being able to exit more quickly.
부분적으로 이것은 더 빨리 내릴 수 있다는 명확한 편리함 때문이었다.

➡ 주어진 문장 앞: this(이것)가 더 빨리 내리는 편리함 때문이라고 했으므로, 단서 무엇이 더 빨리 내릴 수 있는 편리함과 관련이 있는지 찾아야 한다. 발상

2nd 각 선택지의 앞뒤 흐름이 매끄러운지 확인한다.

①의 앞 문장과 뒤 문장
앞 문장: 그러나 때로는 어떤 장소를 진정으로 특징짓는 것은 덜 구체적인 것 — 우리 안에 있는 '감정'이다.
뒤 문장: 흥미로운 예가 지하철 승객 행동에 관한 연구에서 나왔다.
➡ 때로는 감정이 장소를 특징짓는다는 내용과 지하철 승객의 행동에 관한 연구 예시가 앞뒤로 이어진다. ▶ 주어진 문장이 ①에 들어갈 수 없음

②의 앞 문장과 뒤 문장
앞 문장: ①의 뒤 문장과 같음
뒤 문장: 지하철이나 전철에서 왜 사람들이 그들이 앉는 곳에 앉거나 그들이 서는 곳에 서는지를 이해하려고 노력하는 연구자들은 다양한 상황에서 승객들이 그 공간을 사용하고 탐색하는 방식을 형성하는 요인들을 조사했다.
➡ 지하철 승객의 행동에 관한 연구를 구체적으로 부연 설명한다.
▶ 주어진 문장이 ②에 들어갈 수 없음

③의 앞 문장과 뒤 문장
앞 문장: ②의 뒤 문장과 같음
뒤 문장: 연구 결과 중 하나는 많은 승객들이 기차의 문 근처에 자리 잡기를 좋아하는 이유들과 관련이 있었다.
➡ 지하철 승객의 행동에 관한 연구 결과가 승객들이 문 근처에 자리를 잡으려는 이유와 관련이 있음을 이어서 설명한다. ▶ 주어진 문장이 ③에 들어갈 수 없음

④의 앞 문장과 뒤 문장
앞 문장: ③의 뒤 문장과 같음
뒤 문장: 그러나(But) 이는 부분적으로 더(more) 추상적인 느낌 — 앉아 있는 승객들과 우연히 눈이 마주치는 때때로 불편한 느낌을 피하려는 욕구에 의해 형성되었다.
➡ 승객들이 문 근처에 자리를 잡으려는 이유가 이어져야 한다. 반대되는 내용을 나타내는 But과 비교급 표현인 more가 있으므로, 앞에 다른 이유가 먼저 제시되었을 것이다. 주어진 문장에 그 이유로서 더 빨리 내릴 수 있다는 명확한 편리함이 언급되었다. ▶ 주어진 문장이 ④에 들어가야 함

⑤의 앞 문장과 뒤 문장
앞 문장: ④의 뒤 문장과 같음
뒤 문장: 우리는 감정들을 볼 수 없다. — 그러나 그것들은 매우 실재하고, 그것들은 세상에 대한 우리의 경험에 영향을 미친다.
➡ 승객들이 문 근처에 자리를 잡으려는 감정적인 이유가 앞에 제시되었고, 이 감정이 실재하며 경험에 영향을 미친다는 내용으로 글이 마무리된다.
▶ 주어진 문장이 ⑤에 들어갈 수 없음

39 정답 ③ *인간의 잠수 반사

글의 흐름으로 보아, 주어진 문장이 들어가기에 가장 적절한 곳을 고르시오. [3점]

단서 1 얼굴만 물속에 있을 때 잠수 반사가 유발됨

But if we sink just our face / in a bowl of water, / while the whole of the rest of our body / is in the dry air, / the diving reflex is triggered. // 하지만 만약 우리가 얼굴만 가라앉히고 / 그릇의 물속에 / 나머지 몸 전체는 / 물기가 없는 공기 중에 있으면 / 잠수 반사가 유발된다 //

We have a 'diving reflex', / like other marine mammals. //
우리는 '잠수 반사'를 가지고 있다 / 다른 해양 포유류처럼 //

(①) This means / that special nerve endings on our faces, / around the mouth and nose, / trigger this reflex / only when the facial region goes under water. // 이것은 의미한다 / 얼굴에 있는 특수 신경 말단이 / 입과 코 주변의 / 이 반사를 유발한다는 것을 / 얼굴 부위가 물 아래에 들어갈 때만 //

(②) If we are in the water, / with our head out in the air, / there is no diving reflex. // **단서 2** 얼굴이 물 밖에 있다면 잠수 반사가 일어나지 않음
만약 우리가 물속에 있으면 / 머리는 공기 중에 있는 상태로 / 잠수 반사는 없다 //

(③) It automatically closes down the airway, / reducing the risk of swallowing water, / and it narrows the small air-passages in the lungs. // **단서 3** 잠수 반사가 일어났을 때 나타나는 신체적 변화
이것은 기도를 자동으로 닫아 / 물을 삼킬 위험을 줄이고 / 폐 속의 작은 공기 통로를 좁힌다 //

(④) At the same time / the heart rate is slowed down to half speed / and blood is shunted to the vital organs, /
동시에 / 심박수가 반반 속도로 느려지고 / 혈액이 중요한 장기들로 보내져 /
protecting them / from the effects of the brief stop in breathing. //
그것들을 보호한다 / 짧은 호흡 정지로 인한 영향으로부터 //

(⑤) By contrast, / if a chimpanzee or a gorilla found itself in water / with its face below the surface, / it would panic, / its heart would race / and it would quickly drown. //
반면 / 침팬지나 고릴라가 물속에 있는 자신을 발견하면 / 표면 아래에 얼굴이 있는 상태로 / 그것은 당황하여 / 그것의 심장이 빨리 뛰고 / 금방 익사할 것이다 //

- sink ⓥ 가라앉히다 • marine ⓐ 해양의 • mammal ⓝ 포유류
- nerve ⓝ 신경 • region ⓝ 부위, 지역
- automatically ⓐ 자동으로 • airway ⓝ 기도 • risk ⓝ 위험
- swallow ⓥ 삼키다 • narrow ⓥ 좁히다 • passage ⓝ 통로
- lung ⓝ 폐 • heart rate 심박수 • vital ⓐ 중요한
- organ ⓝ 장기 • brief ⓐ 짧은 • below prep ~의 아래에
- panic ⓥ 당황하다 • drown ⓥ 익사하다

우리는 다른 해양 포유류처럼 '잠수 반사'를 가지고 있다. (①) 이것은 입과 코 주변의 얼굴에 있는 특수 신경 말단이 얼굴 부위가 물 아래에 들어갈 때만 이 반사를 유발한다는 것을 의미한다. (②) 만약 우리가, 머리는 공기 중에 있는 상태로, 물속에 있으면 잠수 반사는 없다. (③ 하지만 만약 우리가 그릇의 물속에 얼굴만 가라앉히고, 나머지 몸 전체는 물기가 없는 공기 중에 있으면, 잠수 반사가 유발된다.) 이것은 기도를 자동으로 닫아, 물을 삼킬 위험을 줄이고, 폐 속의 작은 공기 통로를 좁힌다. (④) 동시에 심박수가 절반 속도로 느려지고 혈액이 중요한 장기들로 보내져, 짧은 호흡 정지로 인한 영향으로부터 그것들을 보호한다. (⑤) 반면, 침팬지나 고릴라가 표면 아래에 얼굴이 있는 상태로 물속에 있는 자신을 발견하면, 그것은 당황하여, 그것의 심장이 빨리 뛰고 금방 익사할 것이다.

| 문제 풀이 순서 | ★★❀ [정답률 69%]

1st 주어진 문장을 해석하고, 연결어 등을 확인한다.

But if we sink just our face in a bowl of water, while the whole of the rest of our body is in the dry air, the diving reflex is triggered.

하지만 만약 우리가 그릇의 물속에 얼굴만 가라앉히고, 나머지 몸 전체는 물기가 없는 공기 중에 있으면, 잠수 반사가 유발된다.

➡ **주어진 문장 앞:** 반대되는 내용을 나타내는 But과 잠수 반사가 유발되는 상황이 나오므로 **단서** 잠수 반사가 유발되지 않는 경우가 앞에 제시될 것이다. **발상**

2nd 각 선택지의 앞뒤 흐름이 매끄러운지 확인한다.

①의 앞 문장과 뒤 문장
- 앞 문장: 우리는 다른 해양 포유류처럼 '잠수 반사'를 가지고 있다.
- 뒤 문장: 이것은 입과 코 주변의 얼굴에 있는 특수 신경 말단이 얼굴 부위가 물 아래에 들어갈 때만 이 반사를 유발한다는 것을 의미한다.
➡ 우리가 다른 해양 포유류처럼 잠수 반사를 가지고 있다고 하며 어떤 상황에서 잠수 반사가 유발되는지를 이어서 설명한다. ▶ **주어진 문장이 ①에 들어갈 수 없음**

②의 앞 문장과 뒤 문장
- 앞 문장: ①의 뒤 문장과 같음
- 뒤 문장: 만약 우리가, 머리는 공기 중에 있는 상태로, 물속에 있으면 잠수 반사는 없다.
➡ 머리가 물 밖의 공기 중에 있고 몸만 물속에 있으면 잠수 반사가 일어나지 않는다고 하며, 잠수 반사가 유발되는 상황과 그렇지 않은 상황이 자연스럽게 연결된다.
▶ **주어진 문장이 ②에 들어갈 수 없음**

③의 앞 문장과 뒤 문장
- 앞 문장: ②의 뒤 문장과 같음
- 뒤 문장: 이것(It)은 기도를 자동으로 닫아, 물을 삼킬 위험을 줄이고, 폐 속의 작은 공기 통로를 좁힌다.
➡ It은 기도를 닫아 물을 삼킬 위험을 줄인다고 했는데, 앞 문장은 머리가 공기 중에 있는 상태를 설명하므로 앞뒤 문장이 이어지지 않는다. 얼굴만 물속에 가라앉히면 잠수 반사가 유발된다는 내용이 주어진 문장에 나오므로, It은 잠수 반사를 가리킨다. ▶ **주어진 문장이 ③에 들어가야 함**

④의 앞 문장과 뒤 문장
- 앞 문장: ③의 뒤 문장과 같음
- 뒤 문장: 동시에 심박수가 절반 속도로 느려지고 혈액이 중요한 장기들로 보내져, 짧은 호흡 정지로 인한 영향으로부터 그것들을 보호한다.
➡ 잠수 반사가 유발되었을 때 나타날 수 있는 신체적 변화를 이어서 설명한다.
▶ **주어진 문장이 ④에 들어갈 수 없음**

⑤의 앞 문장과 뒤 문장
- 앞 문장: ④의 뒤 문장과 같음
- 뒤 문장: 반면, 침팬지나 고릴라가 표면 아래에 얼굴이 있는 상태로 물속에 있는 자신을 발견하면, 그것은 당황하여, 그것의 심장이 빨리 뛰고 금방 익사할 것이다.
➡ 인간과 다르게 잠수 반사가 일어나지 않는 침팬지와 고릴라의 예시로 글이 마무리된다. ▶ **주어진 문장이 ⑤에 들어갈 수 없음**

40 정답 ① *정보에 대한 인간의 진실 편향

There is a natural assumption of truth, or a truth bias / when humans communicate with one another. // **단서 1** 인간은 소통할 때 진실 편향이 있음
진실에 대한 자연스러운 가정, 즉 진실 편향이 있다 / 인간이 서로 소통할 때 //

In other words, / when we're listening to others or reading their words, / our automatic assumption / is that the other person is telling the truth. // **단서 2** 자동적으로 상대방이 진실을 말하고 있다고 믿음
다시 말해 / 우리가 다른 사람의 말을 듣거나 그들의 글을 읽을 때 / 우리의 자동적인 가정은 / 상대방이 진실을 말하고 있다는 것이다 //

This usually works out fine. // 이는 보통 잘 작동한다 //

If you ask someone / where the restroom is located / or if it's raining outside, / you can safely assume / that most people will not lie / in their responses. //
만약 당신이 누군가에게 물어본다면 / 화장실이 어디 있는지나 / 밖에 비가 오고 있는지를 / 당신은 확신하며 가정할 수 있다 / 대부분의 사람들이 거짓말을 하지 않을 것이라고 / 그들의 응답에서 //

2025.6
4회

Imagine / how difficult **it** would be **to converse** with someone
/ if you assumed / **that** *everything* **they** were telling you / was
false! //

상해 보라 / 누군가와 대화하는 것이 얼마나 어려울지 / 만약 당신이 가정한다면 / 그들이 당
신에게 말하는 '모든 것'이 / 거짓이라고 //

Indeed, / **questioning** the truth of a statement and then **choosing**
not to believe it / **requires** additional mental steps. //

정말로 / 어떤 진술의 진실성에 의문을 제기하고 그것을 믿지 않는 것을 선택하는 것은 / 추가
적인 정신적인 단계를 요구한다 // 단서 3 진술의 진실성에 의문을 제기하고 믿지 않으면 추가적인
정신적 단계가 요구됨

For the most part, / humans are "cognitive misers," / **which**
means / we typically don't expend more mental effort / than
seems necessary in a given situation. // 단서 4 인간은 일반적으로 정신적 노력을
아끼려고 함

대부분의 경우 / 인간은 "인지적 구두쇠"이고 / 이는 의미한다 / 우리가 더 많은 정신적인 노
력을 전형적으로 기울이지 않는다는 것을 / 주어진 상황에서 필요한 것처럼 보이는 것보다 //

It makes sense then, / **that when** we see something online, / **even
if** it is fake, / our default is **to believe** it, / at least at first. //

그렇다면 일리가 있다 / 우리가 온라인에서 무언가를 볼 때 / 비록 그것이 가짜라고 해도 / 우
리의 기본값은 그것을 믿는 것이다 / 적어도 처음에는 //

→ We humans **are unlikely to** (A) **doubt** / the truth of
information **we receive**, / due to our tendency / to (B) **save**
mental effort. //

우리 인간은 의심하지 않으려 하는데 / 우리가 받는 정보의 진실성을 / 이는 우리의 경향 때
문이다 / 정신적 노력을 아끼려는 //

- assumption ⓝ 가정
- bias ⓝ 편향
- in other words 다시 말해
- automatic ⓐ 자동적인
- work out 잘 작동하다, 잘 풀리다
- assume ⓥ 가정하다
- response ⓝ 응답
- converse with ~와 대화하다
- indeed ⓐ 정말로
- statement ⓝ 진술
- additional ⓐ 추가적인
- cognitive ⓐ 인지적인
- miser ⓝ 구두쇠
- typically ⓐ 전형적으로, 일반적으로
- effort ⓝ 노력
- make sense 일리가 있다
- fake ⓐ 가짜의
- at least 적어도
- due to ~ 때문에
- tendency ⓝ 경향

인간이 서로 소통할 때 진실에 대한 자연스러운 가정, 즉 진실 편향이 있다. 다
시 말해, 우리가 다른 사람의 말을 듣거나 그들의 글을 읽을 때, 우리의 자동적
인 가정은 상대방이 진실을 말하고 있다는 것이다. 이는 보통 잘 작동한다. 만
약 당신이 누군가에게 화장실이 어디 있는지나 밖에 비가 오고 있는지를 물어
본다면, 당신은 대부분의 사람들이 그들의 응답에서 거짓말을 하지 않을 것이
라고 확신하며 가정할 수 있다. 만약 당신이 그들이 당신에게 말하는 '모든 것
이' 거짓이라고 가정한다면 누군가와 대화하는 것이 얼마나 어려울지 상상해 보
라! 정말로, 어떤 진술의 진실성에 의문을 제기하고 그것을 믿지 않는 것을 선
택하는 것은 추가적인 정신적인 단계를 요구한다. 대부분의 경우, 인간은 "인지
적 구두쇠"이고, 이는 우리가 주어진 상황에서 필요한 것처럼 보이는 것보다 더
많은 정신적인 노력을 전형적으로 기울이지 않는다는 것을 의미한다. 그렇다면
우리가 온라인에서 무언가를 볼 때, 비록 그것이 가짜라고 해도, 우리의 기본값
은, 적어도 처음에는, 그것을 믿는 것임이 일리가 있다.
→ 우리 인간은 우리가 받는 정보의 진실성을 (A) 의심하지 않으려 하는데, 이
는 정신적 노력을 (B) 아끼려는 우리의 경향 때문이다.

다음 글의 내용을 한 문장으로 요약하고자 한다. 빈칸 (A), (B)에 들어갈
말로 가장 적절한 것은?

	(A)		(B)	
①	doubt 의심하다	—	save 아끼다	정보의 진실성을 의심하지 않음으로써 정신적인 노력을 아끼려고 함
②	trust 신뢰하다	—	maintain 유지하다	정신적 노력을 유지하려는 것이 아니라 아끼려고 함
③	judge 판단하다	—	add 더하다	정신적 노력을 더하려는 것이 아니라 아끼려고 함
④	doubt	—	increase 증가시키다	정신적 노력을 증가시키는 것이 아니라 아끼려고 함
⑤	trust	—	reduce 줄이다	정보의 진실성을 신뢰하지 않으려고 한다는 것은 글의 내용과 반대됨

왜 정답? ✱✱✿ [정답률 62%]

(A):
- 인간은 소통할 때 진실 편향이 있다. 단서 1
- 인간은 자동적으로 상대방이 진실을 말하고 있다고 믿는다. 단서 2
→ 인간은 진실 편향이 있어서 소통할 때 정보의 진실을 믿는, 즉 '의심하지' 않는 경향
이 있다.
▶ (A)에는 ①, ④의 doubt가 들어가야 함

(B):
- 상대방의 진술에 의문을 제기하고 믿지 않으면 추가적인 정신적 단계가 요구된
다. 단서 3
- 인간은 일반적으로 정신적인 노력을 아끼려고 한다. 단서 4
→ 상대방의 진술을 의심하면 정신적인 노력이 더 들기 때문에, 정보가 진실이라고 믿
음으로써 그 노력을 '아끼려고' 한다.
▶ (B)에는 ①의 save가 들어가는 것이 적절하므로 정답은 ①임

왜 오답?

② 인간이 정신적 노력을 유지하려는 것이 아니라 아끼려는 것이다.
③, ④ 인간이 정신적 노력을 더하거나 증가시키려는 것이 아니라 아끼려는 것이다.
⑤ 인간이 정보의 진실성을 신뢰하려고 하지 않는다는 것은 글의 내용과 반대된다.

＊ 글의 흐름

1 도입: 인간은 다른 사람과 소통할 때 정보가 진실이라고 가정하는 진실 편향이 있음
2 전개: 진실 편향은 일반적으로 잘 작동하며, 일상적 질문에서 상대방의 응답을 의심
한다면 소통이 힘들어질 것임
3 부연: 상대의 진술을 의심하는 것은 추가적인 인지적 단계를 요구함
4 결론: 인간은 일반적으로 인지적 노력을 아끼려고 함

41~42 ＊신용카드 사용이 소비를 증가시키는 이유

Paying with plastic / fundamentally **changes** the way we spend
money, / **altering the calculus / of our financial decisions.** //

신용카드로 지불하는 것은 / 우리가 돈을 소비하는 방식을 근본적으로 바꾸며 / 계산법을 변화
시킨다 / 우리의 재정적 결정에 대한 //

When you buy something with cash, / the purchase involves an
actual (a) loss — / your wallet is literally lighter. //

당신이 무언가를 현금으로 구매할 때 / 그 구매는 실제 손실을 수반한다 / 당신의 지갑이 말 그
대로 더 가벼워진다 //

Credit cards, however, / make the purchase abstract, / **so that**
you don't really feel / the downside of spending money. //

하지만, 신용카드는 / 구매를 추상화시켜 / 당신은 실제로 느끼지 못한다 / 돈을 소비하는 것
의 부정적인 면을 // 41번 단서 1: 신용카드는 소비의 부정적인 면을 느끼지 못하게 함

Brain-imaging experiments suggest / that paying with credit
cards / actually (b) reduces activity / in the insula, / a brain
region associated with negative feelings. //

뇌 영상 실험은 보여준다 / 신용카드로 지불하는 것이 / 실제로 활동을 감소시킨다는 것을 / 뇌
섬엽에서의 / 부정적인 감정과 관련된 뇌 영역인 // 41번 단서 2: 신용카드 지불은 부정적
감정과 관련된 뇌 영역의 활동을 감소시킴

As **George Loewenstein**, / **a neuroeconomist at Carnegie Mellon**,
/ says, /

George Loewenstein이 / Carnegie Mellon의 신경경제학자인 / 말하듯이 /

"The nature of credit cards / ensures / that your brain is
anesthetized / against the pain of payment." //

신용카드의 본질은 / 확실하게 한다 / 당신의 뇌가 마비되는 것을 / 지불의 고통에 대해 //

Spending money / doesn't feel (c) bad, / so you spend more
money. // 41번 단서 3, 42번 단서 1: 신용카드는 돈을 더 많이 쓰게 만듦

돈을 쓰는 것이 / 나쁘게 느껴지지 않는다 / 그래서 당신은 더 많은 돈을 쓴다 //

Consider this experiment: /

이 실험을 생각해 보자 /

Drazen Prelec and Duncan Simester, / ^{동격}two business professors
at MIT, / organized a real-life, sealed-bid auction / for tickets to
a Boston Celtics game. //
Drazen Prelec과 Duncan Simester / MIT의 두 경영학 교수인 / 실제 봉인 입찰 경매를
준비했다 / Boston Celtics 경기 티켓을 위한 //
^{복수 주어}Half the participants in the auction / ^{복수 동사}were informed / that they
had to pay with cash; / the other half / were told / they had to
pay with credit cards. //
경매에 참여한 사람들 중 절반은 / 들었다 / 현금으로 지불해야 한다는 말을 / 나머지 절반은 /
들었다 / 신용카드로 지불해야 한다는 말을 //
Prelec and Simester / then averaged the bids / for the two
different groups. //
Prelec과 Simester는 / 그리고 나서 입찰가의 평균을 냈다 / 다른 두 집단의 //
^{가주어}It turns out / ^{진주어절 접속사}that the average credit card bid / ^{배수사+as+원급+as~: ~의 몇 배만큼 …한}was *twice* as (d)
high / as the average cash bid. // **41번** 단서 4: 평균 신용카드 입찰가가 현금
입찰가보다 두 배 높음
나타났다 / 평균 신용카드 입찰 금액이 / '두 배'만큼 높은 것으로 / 평균 현금 입찰금액의 //
When people used their credit cards, / their bids / were much
more (e) careful(→ reckless). //
사람들이 신용카드를 사용할 때 / 그들의 입찰은 / 훨씬 더 신중(→ 무모)했다 //
^{형용사적 용법 (the need 수식)}They no longer felt the need / to limit their expenses. //
그들은 더 이상 필요성을 느끼지 못했다 / 지출을 억제해야 할 //
42번 단서 2: 신용카드를 사용한 사람들은 지출을 억제해야 할 필요성을 느끼지 못함

- plastic ⓝ 신용카드   • fundamentally ⓐd 근본적으로
- alter ⓥ 바꾸다   • financial ⓐ 재정적인   • involve ⓥ 수반하다
- loss ⓝ 손실   • literally ⓐd 말 그대로   • abstract ⓐ 추상적인
- downside ⓝ 부정적인 면   • insula ⓝ 뇌섬엽   • region ⓝ 영역
- associated with ~와 관련된   • sealed-bid ⓝ 봉인 입찰
- auction ⓝ 경매   • inform ⓥ 알리다   • average ⓥ 평균을 내다
- expense ⓝ 지출

신용카드로 지불하는 것은 우리가 돈을 소비하는 방식을 근본적으로 바꾸며, 우리의 재정적 결정에 대한 계산법을 변화시킨다. 당신이 무언가를 현금으로 구매할 때, 그 구매는 실제 (a) 손실을 수반한다 — 당신의 지갑이 말 그대로 더 가벼워진다. 하지만, 신용카드는 구매를 추상화시켜, 당신은 돈을 소비하는 것의 부정적인 면을 실제로 느끼지 못한다. 뇌 영상 실험은 신용카드로 지불하는 것이 부정적인 감정과 관련된 뇌 영역인 뇌섬엽에서의 활동을 실제로 (b) 감소시킨다는 것을 보여준다. Carnegie Mellon의 신경경제학자 George Loewenstein이 말하듯이, "신용카드의 본질은 당신의 뇌가 지불의 고통에 대해 마비되는 것을 확실하게 한다." 돈을 쓰는 것이 (c) 나쁘게 느껴지지 않아서, 당신은 더 많은 돈을 쓴다.
이 실험을 생각해 보자: MIT의 두 경영학 교수인 Drazen Prelec과 Duncan Simester는 Boston Celtics 경기 티켓을 위한 실제 봉인 입찰 경매를 준비했다. 경매에 참여한 사람들 중 절반은 현금으로 지불해야 한다는 말을 들었고; 나머지 절반은 신용카드로 지불해야 한다는 말을 들었다. 그리고 나서 Prelec과 Simester는 다른 두 집단의 입찰가의 평균을 냈다. 평균 신용카드 입찰 금액은 평균 현금 입찰 금액의 '두 배'만큼 (d) 높은 것으로 나타났다. 사람들이 신용카드를 사용할 때, 그들의 입찰은 훨씬 더 (e) 신중(→ 무모)했다. 그들은 더 이상 지출을 억제해야 할 필요성을 느끼지 못했다.

41 정답 ②

윗글의 제목으로 가장 적절한 것은?
① Once Set, Spending Habits Seldom Change
한번 형성된 소비 습관은 좀처럼 변하지 않는다   소비 습관의 변화는 언급되지 않음
② Why Do We Spend More with Credit Cards? 신용카드를 사용할 때
왜 우리는 신용카드를 사용할 때 더 많이 지출할까?   더 많이 지출하게 되는 이유를 설명함
③ Credit Cards: A Safer Way to Pay than Cash
신용카드: 현금보다 더 안전한 결제 수단   결제 수단의 안전성은 언급되지 않음
④ Paying with Plastic: The Secret to Saving Money
신용카드 결제: 돈을 절약하는 비결   신용카드는 돈을 절약하는 것이 아니라 더 쓰게 만듦
⑤ Using Cash Leads to Taking More Financial Risks
현금 사용은 더 많은 재정적 위험으로 이어진다   현금 사용의 위험성은 언급되지 않음

>**왜 정답?** ✿✿❀ [정답률 77%]
- [신용카드는 소비의 부정적인 면을 느끼지 못하게 한다. **41번 단서 1**
- 신용카드 지불은 부정적 감정과 관련된 뇌 영역의 활동을 감소시킨다. **41번 단서 2**
- 신용카드는 돈을 더 많이 쓰게 만든다. **41번 단서 3**
- 평균 신용카드 입찰가가 현금 입찰가보다 두 배 높았다. **41번 단서 4**
➡ 신용카드로 지불하는 것은 돈을 소비하는 것의 부정적인 면을 느끼지 못하게 하여 현금으로 지불할 때보다 돈을 더 많이 쓰게 만든다고 했다.
▶ 따라서 제목으로 가장 적절한 것은 ② '왜 우리는 신용카드를 사용할 때 더 많이 지출할까?'이다.

>**왜 오답?**
① 소비 습관의 변화는 언급되지 않았다.
③ 신용카드가 현금보다 더 안전한 결제 수단이라는 것은 언급되지 않았다.
④ 신용카드는 돈을 절약하게 하지 않고 더 많이 쓰게 만든다는 것이 글의 주제이다.
⑤ 현금 사용이 더 많은 재정적 위험으로 이어진다는 것은 언급되지 않았다.

42 정답 ⑤

밑줄 친 (a)~(e) 중에서 문맥상 낱말의 쓰임이 적절하지 않은 것은? [3점]
① (a) 지갑이 더 가벼워지는 실제적인 손실을 수반함
손실
② (b) 신용카드 결제는 부정적인 감정과 관련된 뇌 부위의 활동을 감소시킴
감소시키다
③ (c) 뇌가 지불의 고통에 대해 마비되어 소비가 나쁘게 느껴지지 않음
나쁜
④ (d) 신용카드 입찰가가 현금 입찰가보다 평균적으로 두 배 높음
높은
⑤ (e) 신용카드를 사용한 사람들은 더 무모하게 입찰했음
신중한

>**왜 정답?** ✿✿❀ [정답률 72%]
⑤ (e) careful 신중한
[사람들이 신용카드를 사용할 때, 그들의 입찰은 훨씬 더 (e) ~~신중했다~~.
                                                    무모했다
➡ 신용카드는 돈을 더 많이 쓰게 만들며 지출을 억제할 필요성을 느끼지 못하게 만든다고 했으므로, 신용카드를 쓸 때 사람들의 입찰은 신중하지 않고 훨씬 더 '무모했을' 것이다. ▶ careful을 reckless(무모한)와 같은 반의어로 바꿔야 함

>**왜 오답?**
① (a) loss 손실
[당신이 무언가를 현금으로 구매할 때, 그 구매는 실제 (a) 손실을 수반한다.
➡ 현금 지불은 지갑이 더 가벼워지는 실제적인 '손실'을 수반한다.
▶ loss는 문맥에 맞음

② (b) reduces 감소시키다
[뇌 영상 실험은 신용카드로 지불하는 것이 부정적인 감정과 관련된 뇌 영역인 뇌섬엽에서의 활동을 실제로 (b) 감소시킨다는 것을 보여준다.
➡ 신용카드 지불은 돈을 쓰는 것의 단점을 느끼지 못하게 만든다고 했으므로, 부정적인 감정과 관련된 뇌 부위의 활동을 '감소시킬' 것이다. ▶ reduces는 문맥에 맞음

③ (c) bad 나쁜
[돈을 쓰는 것이 (c) 나쁘게 느껴지지 않아서, 당신은 더 많은 돈을 쓴다.
➡ 뇌가 지불의 고통에 대해 마비되어 소비가 '나쁘게' 느껴지지 않는다.
▶ bad는 문맥에 맞음

④ (d) high 높은
[평균 신용카드 입찰 금액은 평균 현금 입찰 금액의 '두 배'만큼 (d) 높은 것으로 나타났다.
➡ 신용카드는 더 많은 돈을 쓰게 만든다고 했으므로, 평균 신용카드 입찰가가 현금 입찰가보다 두 배 '높은' 것으로 나타났다는 것이 적절하다. ▶ high는 문맥에 맞음

(A) The sun shone / in the cloudless sky / as Becky, a retired teacher, walked to the fruit market. //
부사절 접속사 (시간)
45번 ① Becky가 과일 시장으로 걸어감
태양은 빛났다 / 구름 한 점 없는 하늘에서 / 퇴직한 교사인 Becky가 과일 시장으로 걸어갈 때 //

Across town, / Dana was riding a bus / towards the museum / for a job interview. //
도시를 가로질러 / Dana는 버스를 타고 가고 있었다 / 미술관으로 / 취업 면접을 위해 //

앞에 목적어절 접속사 that이 생략됨
Just before reaching her stop, / Dana noticed / the sky had suddenly darkened. //
그가 내릴 정류장에 다다르기 직전에 / Dana는 알아챘다 / 하늘이 갑자기 어두워진 것을 //

Her heart sank / — she had no umbrella. //
그녀는 가슴이 철렁했다 / 그녀는 우산이 없었다 //

= Dana   계속적 용법의 관계부사
As (a) she stepped off the bus / next to the market, / where Becky had just finished shopping, / raindrops began to fall. //
43번 단서 1: Dana가 버스에서 내렸을 때 비가 내리기 시작함
그녀가 버스에서 내렸을 때 / 시장 옆에서 / Becky가 장보기를 막 끝낸 / 빗방울이 떨어지기 시작했다 //

* (A) 문단 요약: Dana가 취업 면접을 보러 미술관에 가던 중 갑자기 비가 오기 시작했음

43번 단서 2: Dana는 Becky로부터 우산을 받고 고마워했음
병렬 구조
(B) Dana thanked her, / took the umbrella, / and opened it. //
Dana는 그녀에게 고마워했고 / 우산을 받아 / 그것을 펼쳤다 //

과거분사구 (a small card 수식)
She saw a small card / tied to the handle. //
45번 ② Dana가 받은 우산 손잡이에 작은 카드가 묶여 있었음
그녀는 작은 카드를 보았다 / 손잡이에 묶인 //

It read: "Cover each other." //
'~라고 적혀 있다'
그것에는 "서로를 감싸주세요"라고 적혀 있었다 //

She was touched by the message. // 그녀는 그 메시지에 감동받았다 //

병렬 구조
She hurried to the museum, / arriving dry and comfortable, / and performed well in her interview. //
그녀는 미술관에 서둘러 갔고 / 마른 채로 편안하게 도착해서 / 인터뷰에서 잘 해냈다 //

= Dana
The Museum CEO was impressed by Dana / and offered (b) her / the Event Manager position, her dream job. //
동격
미술관 CEO는 Dana에 의해 감명받았고 / 그녀에게 제시했다 / 그녀의 꿈의 직업인, 이벤트 매니저직을 //

Throughout the years ahead, / she often thought back / to Becky's kind gesture. //
45번 ③ Dana는 Becky의 친절한 행동을 종종 떠올렸음
향후 몇 년 동안 / 그녀는 종종 떠올렸다 / Becky의 친절한 행동을 //

* (B) 문단 요약: Dana는 인터뷰를 잘 해내고 이벤트 매니저직을 받은 뒤 종종 Becky의 친절한 행동을 떠올렸음

Being이 생략된 분사구문
(C) Inspired by the memory, / Dana created a museum event /
과거분사구 (a museum event 수식)   현재분사구 (people 수식)
called "Cover Each Other" / with paintings of people supporting others. //
43번 단서 3: Dana가 Becky의 친절한 행동에 영감을 받아서 미술관 행사를 엶
그 기억에 영감을 받아서 / Dana는 미술관 행사를 만들었다 / "서로를 감싸주세요"라는 / 다른 사람을 돕는 사람들의 그림들로 //

주격 관계대명사 (families 수식)
She donated / half of the money from ticket sales / to families / who lost their homes to natural disasters. //
45번 ④ Dana는 티켓 판매금의 절반을 기부함
그녀는 기부했다 / 티켓 판매로 얻은 돈의 절반을 / 가족들에게 / 자연재해로 그들의 집을 잃은 //

kept의 목적어와 목적격 보어 (과거분사)
Dana kept Becky's message framed / in (c) her office / as a reminder / that one kind gesture could change someone's life. //
동격절 접속사   = Dana's
Dana는 Becky의 메시지를 액자로 넣어두었다 / 그녀의 사무실에 / 상기시키는 것으로서 / 하나의 친절한 행동이 누군가의 삶을 바꿀 수 있음을 //

앞에 목적어절 접속사 that이 생략됨
The kindness of one stranger / had shaped her path, / and she made sure it continued to shape the world. //
낯선 한 사람의 친절이 / 그녀의 길을 만들었고 / 그녀는 그것이 계속해서 세상을 만들어가도록 했다 //

* (C) 문단 요약: Becky로부터 영감을 받은 Dana는 미술관 행사를 열어 기부하고 Becky의 메시지를 상기함

(D) Dana felt panic. // Dana는 당황했다 //
43번 단서 4: 면접에 가야 하는 Dana는 비를 맞고 싶지 않았음

She didn't want to show up / to her interview / soaked. //
분사구문
그녀는 나타나고 싶지 않았다 / 면접에 / 흠뻑 젖어서 //

형용사적 용법 (stores 수식)
She looked around but couldn't find any stores nearby / to buy
형용사적 용법 (time 수식)
an umbrella, / and she didn't have time / to search around. //
그녀는 주위를 둘러보았지만 어떤 가게도 근처에서 찾을 수 없었고 / 우산을 구매할 만한 / 시간도 없었다 / 주변을 찾아볼 //
45번 ⑤ Dana는 우산을 구매할 가게를 찾을 수 없었음

타동사 (뒤에 전치사 없이 목적어가 옴)   분사구문을 이끄는 현재분사
Just then, / Becky approached (d) her, / holding an open
= umbrella   = the other hand
umbrella in one hand / and a closed one in the other. //
바로 그때 / Becky가 그녀에게 다가왔다 / 한 손에는 펼친 우산을 들고서 / 다른 손에는 접힌 것을 //

= Becky
"Take this," / (e) she said with a smile. //
"이거 받아요" / 그녀가 미소를 지으며 말했다 //
43번 단서 5: Becky가 Dana에게 우산을 건넴

Dana's eyes widened. // Dana의 눈이 커졌다 //

"Are you sure?" // "정말이세요" //

Becky nodded. // Becky는 고개를 끄덕였다 //

"I always carry an extra / on rainy days." //
"저는 항상 여분 하나를 가지고 다녀요 / 비 오는 날에" //

* (D) 문단 요약: 우산 없이 비를 만나 당황한 Dana에게 Becky가 여분의 우산을 건넴

- retired ⓐ 퇴직한   - notice ⓥ 알아채다   - step off 내리다
- tie ⓥ 묶다   - touched ⓐ 감동한   - impressed ⓐ 감명받은
- offer ⓥ 제안하다   - inspired ⓐ 영감을 받은   - donate ⓥ 기부하다
- natural disaster 자연재해   - frame ⓥ 액자에 넣다
- shape ⓥ 형성하다   - nod ⓥ (고개를) 끄덕이다

(A) 퇴직한 교사인 Becky가 과일 시장으로 걸어갈 때, 태양은 구름 한 점 없는 하늘에서 빛났다. 도시를 가로질러, Dana는 취업 면접을 위해 버스를 타고 미술관으로 가고 있었다. 그녀가 내릴 정류장에 다다르기 직전에, Dana는 하늘이 갑자기 어두워진 것을 알아챘다. 그녀는 가슴이 철렁했다 — 그녀는 우산이 없었다. Becky가 장보기를 막 끝낸 시장 옆에서 (a) 그녀가 버스에서 내렸을 때, 빗방울이 떨어지기 시작했다.

(D) Dana는 당황했다. 그녀는 흠뻑 젖어서 면접에 나타나고 싶지 않았다. 그녀는 주위를 둘러보았지만 우산을 구매할 만한 어떤 가게도 근처에서 찾을 수 없었고, 주변을 찾아볼 시간도 없었다. 바로 그때, Becky가 한 손에는 펼친 우산을 다른 손에는 접힌 것을 들고서, (d) 그녀에게 다가왔다. "이거 받아요," (e) 그녀가 미소를 지으며 말했다. Dana의 눈이 커졌다. "정말이세요?" Becky는 고개를 끄덕였다. "저는 비 오는 날에 항상 여분 하나를 가지고 다녀요."

(B) Dana는 그녀에게 고마워했고, 우산을 받아, 그것을 펼쳤다. 그녀는 손잡이에 묶인 작은 카드를 보았다. 그것에는 "서로를 감싸주세요."라고 적혀 있었다. 그녀는 그 메시지에 감동받았다. 그녀는 미술관에 서둘러 갔고, 마른 채로 편안하게 도착해서, 인터뷰에서 잘 했어. 미술관 CEO는 Dana에 의해 감명받았고, (b) 그녀에게 그녀의 꿈의 직업인, 이벤트 매니저직을 제시했다. 향후 몇 년 동안, 그녀는 종종 Becky의 친절한 행동을 떠올렸다.

(C) 그 기억에 영감을 받아서, Dana는 다른 사람을 돕는 사람들의 그림들로 "서로를 감싸주세요"라는 미술관 행사를 만들었다. 그녀는 티켓 판매로 얻은 돈의 절반을 자연재해로 그들의 집을 잃은 가족들에게 기부했다. Dana는 하나의 친절한 행동이 누군가의 삶을 바꿀 수 있음을 상기시키는 것으로서 Becky의 메시지를 (c) 그녀의 사무실에 액자로 넣어두었다. 낯선 한 사람의 친절이 그녀의 길을 만들었고, 그녀는 그것이 계속해서 세상을 만들어가도록 했다.

43 정답 ④

주어진 글 (A)에 이어질 내용을 순서에 맞게 배열한 것으로 가장 적절한 것은?

① (B) — (D) — (C) 갑자기 비가 내리기 시작했다는 (A) 뒤에 Dana가 당황했다는 (D)가 이어져야 함
② (C) — (B) — (D) Becky의 친절한 행동에 영감을 받아 이를 실천했다는 (C)가 마지막에 와야 함
③ (C) — (D) — (B)
④ (D) — (B) — (C) (D) 비가 내려 당황한 Dana에게 Becky가 여분의 우산을 건네줌 — (B) 인터뷰를 잘 해내고 미술관 이벤트 매니저직을 받은 Dana가 Becky의 친절한 행동을 종종 떠올렸음 — (C) Dana는 미술관 행사를 열어 기부하고 Becky의 메시지를 상기했음
⑤ (D) — (C) — (B) Dana가 Becky로부터 우산을 받았다는 (D) 뒤에 Dana가 Becky에게 고마워했다는 (B)가 이어져야 함

> **왜** 정답 · 오답 ? ✽❀❀ [정답률 89%]

┌ **(A)**: Dana는 취업 면접을 위해 미술관에 가던 중 우산 없이 갑작스럽게
└ 비를 만났다.

➡ 우산이 없는 Dana에게 어떤 일이 일어났는지 주목한다.

┌ **(B)**: Dana는 Becky에게 고마워하며 우산을 받았고, 무사히 인터뷰를 마
│ 친 덕에 미술관 이벤트 매니저직을 맡게 된 Dana는 Becky의 친절한 행
└ 동을 종종 떠올린다.

➡ Dana가 고마워하는 내용 앞에 Becky가 Dana에게 우산을 건네주는 내용이 먼저
나와야 한다.

┌ **(C)**: Dana는 미술관 행사를 열어 기부하고 Becky의 메시지를 상기한다.

➡ Becky의 친절에 영감을 받은 Dana가 행사를 열어 기부하고, 친절한 행동이 누군
가의 삶을 바꿀 수 있다는 내용으로 글이 마무리된다.

┌ **(D)**: 우산이 없어서 당황한 Dana에게 Becky가 여분의 우산을 건넸다.

➡ Dana가 우산 없이 갑자기 비를 만났다는 (A)에 이어지는 내용이다. 우산을 받고
고마워했다는 (B)가 뒤에 이어진다.

▶ 글의 순서는 ④ (D) — (B) — (C)임

44 정답 ⑤

밑줄 친 (a)~(e) 중에서 가리키는 대상이 나머지 넷과 다른 것은?
① (a)　　② (b)　　③ (c)　　④ (d)　　⑤(e)
= Dana　　= Dana　　= Dana's　　= Dana　　= Becky

> **왜** 정답 ? ✽✽✽ [정답률 83%]
⑤ (e) she: 미소를 지으며 Dana에게 우산을 준 사람 ▶ Becky

> **왜** 오답 ?
① (a) she: 시장 옆에서 버스에서 내린 사람 ▶ Dana
② (b) her: 미술관 CEO에게 이벤트 매니저직을 제안받은 사람 ▶ Dana
③ (c) her: Becky의 메시지를 사무실 액자에 넣어둔 사람 ▶ Dana's
④ (d) her: Becky가 다가간 사람 ▶ Dana

45 정답 ④

윗글에 관한 내용으로 적절하지 <u>않은</u> 것은?
① Becky는 과일 시장으로 걸어갔다. Becky ~ walked to the fruit market.
② 작은 카드는 Dana가 받은 우산 손잡이에 매여 있었다.
　　　　　　　　　　　　She saw a small card tied to the handle.
③ Dana는 Becky의 친절한 행동을 종종 떠올렸다.
　　　　　　　　　she often thought back to Becky's kind gesture
④ Dana는 티켓 판매금 전액을 기부했다.
　　　　　　　　She donated half of the money from ticket sales
⑤ Dana는 우산을 구매할 가게를 찾을 수 없었다.
　　　　　　She ~ couldn't find any stores nearby to buy an umbrella

> **왜** 정답 ? ✽❀❀ [정답률 89%]
Dana가 티켓 판매금의 절반을 기부했으므로 (She donated half of the money
from ticket sales) 티켓 판매금 전액을 기부했다는 ④은 적절하지 않다.

> **왜** 오답 ?
① Becky는 과일 시장으로 걸어갔다. (Becky ~ walked to the fruit market.)
② 작은 카드는 Dana가 받은 우산 손잡이에 매여 있었다. (She saw a small card
tied to the handle.)
③ Dana는 Becky의 친절한 행동을 종종 떠올렸다. (she often thought back to
Becky's kind gesture)
⑤ Dana는 우산을 구매할 가게를 찾을 수 없었다. (She ~ couldn't find any
stores nearby to buy an umbrella)

4회 Dictation
문제 p. 78

01 complained that / To solve this problem / will be able to use /
efficiently

02 I've been / saying the words out loud / memorizing quietly /
give it a try

03 get some sunlight / can reduce anxiety /
both physically and mentally

04 take a look / absolutely / must've been / glow in the dark

05 made a playlist / Did you choose / customers to try /
Could you put them on

06 How many tickets / offer snacks / need anything else

07 on your social media / performing in public /
had an interview / Did you get it

08 it's going to be amazing / I'd love to / apply to be a volunteer /
sign up by this Friday

09 showcase / prizes for the top performances /
our school symbol on it

10 let's search for / start with budget / keep it under /
need to be waterproof

11 have a bad headache / taken some medicine / an hour ago

12 It's to celebrate / specific design in mind

13 with all my heart / effort and responsibility /
take good care of his cat

14 haven't seen that / used to work in / good at it /
tastes amazing

15 on an overseas trip / sightseeing / get it fixed /
too hot to sleep

[16~17] symbolize / to welcome special guests /
Throughout history / consider it

4회 어휘 Review Test
문제 p. 82

01 선구자
02 희생하다
03 해외의
04 점검
05 방수의
06 throughout
07 symbolize
08 commit
09 annual
10 socialize
11 fall apart
12 make sense
13 make use of
14 be dependent on

15 stay in touch
16 bias
17 obvious
18 approximately
19 abstract
20 intentions
21 accidentally
22 contexts
23 analysis
24 nerve
25 distort
26 nature
27 initial
28 construct

29 eliminate
30 insight
31 transferred
32 collapse
33 rational
34 downside
35 exceptionally
36 criticize
37 showcase
38 Emphasizing
39 sufficient
40 typically

01 정답 ③ *간식바 이용 안내

W : [Chime bell rings.] Attention, everyone!
여 : [차임벨이 울린다.] 모두 주목해 주세요!

Our CEO, Mr. Wayne, **has prepared** a snack bar **to celebrate**
(현재완료(완료)) (부사적 용법(목적))
our success on last month's project. 단서1 간식바를 준비함
우리의 CEO인 Wayne 씨가 지난달 프로젝트에 대한 우리의 성공을 축하하기 위해
간식바를 준비했습니다.

Please come down to the lobby and enjoy some delicious
snacks. 단서2 맛있는 간식을 즐기도록 권유함
로비로 내려오셔서 맛있는 간식을 즐기세요.

They'll be available until 4 p.m.
간식바는 오후 4시까지 이용이 가능합니다.

You'll be impressed by the amazing variety, **from** crispy
('~에서 ~까지')
fries and hot dogs **to** fresh lemonade and coffee.
바삭바삭한 감자튀김과 핫도그부터 신선한 레모네이드와 커피까지, 여러분은 놀랍도록
다양한 간식들에 감명받을 것입니다.

It'd be great **if** you could bring your own personal cups for
(부사절 접속사(조건))
the drinks.
음료를 담을 개인 컵을 가지고 오시면 좋습니다.

See you there. 간식바에서 뵙겠습니다.

- **prepare** ⓥ 준비하다 · **celebrate** ⓥ 축하하다
- **available** ⓐ (이용) 가능한 · **impressed** ⓐ 감명받은
- **variety** ⓝ 여러 가지 · **crispy** ⓐ 바삭바삭한 · **personal** ⓐ 개인의

다음을 듣고, 여자가 하는 말의 목적으로 가장 적절한 것을 고르시오.
① 친환경 제품 사용을 홍보하려고 친환경 제품을 홍보하는 내용이 아님
② 음식 대접에 대한 감사를 표하려고 감사를 표하는 내용은 없음
③ 간식이 마련되어 있음을 안내하려고 간식바 이용에 대해 안내했음
④ 휴식 시간이 변경되었음을 공지하려고 휴식 시간에 관한 내용은 없음
⑤ 구내식당 메뉴에 관한 의견을 구하려고 구내식당에 관한 내용이 아님

왜 정답? ✿✿✿ [정답률 97%]

CEO인 Wayne 씨가 성공을 축하하기 위해 간식바를 마련하였음을 알리며
사람들에게 와서 간식을 즐기도록 권유하고 있으므로 정답은 ③이다.

왜 오답?

① 친환경 제품은 언급되지 않았다.
② 대접에 감사하는 내용이 아니다.
④ 간식바를 이용할 수 있는 시간을 언급했을 뿐, 휴식 시간이 변경되었음을 알리는
것이 아니다.
⑤ 언급된 음식들은 구내식당이 아닌, 간식바의 메뉴들이다.

02 정답 ① *AI를 이용한 과제 수행

M : Hi, Pamela. Did you finish your history assignment?
남 : 안녕, Pamela. 역사 과제는 다 했니?

W : Yes, Dad. I finished it quite easily with the help of AI.
여 : 네, 아빠. AI의 도움으로 꽤 쉽게 끝냈어요.

M : Really? Do you mean you used an artificial-intelligence
website?
남 : 정말? 인공 지능 웹사이트를 이용했단 말이니?

W : Yeah. I typed in the questions and AI gave **me the answers**
(간접목적어) (직접목적어)
right away.
여 : 네. 제가 질문을 입력하면 AI가 바로 답변을 해줬어요.

M : Well, is **it** a good idea **to do** your homework that way?
(가주어) (진주어)
남 : 음, 그렇게 숙제하는 것이 과연 좋은 생각일까?

W : Why not? It **saves** a lot of time and **gives** me just the
(병렬 구조)
information I need.
(앞에 목적격 관계대명사가 생략됨)
여 : 왜 안 되나요? 시간도 많이 절약되고 제가 필요한 정보만 얻을 수 있잖아요.

M : I **used to think** so, too. But after trying it a couple of times, I
(used to-v: ~하곤 했다)
found out AI sometimes uses false information as well.
남 : 아빠도 그렇게 생각한 적이 있지. 그런데 몇 번 시도해 보니, AI도 가끔 허위 정보를
이용한다는 걸 알게 되었단다. 단서1 AI가 허위 정보를 사용할 수 있음

W : Really? I didn't know that.
여 : 그래요? 저는 그것을 몰랐어요.

M : Yeah, you shouldn't blindly trust the answers from AI.
남 : 그래, AI의 답변을 맹목적으로 믿어서는 안 된단다. 단서2 맹목적으로 AI를 믿으면 안 됨

W : Okay. I'll **keep** that **in mind** next time.
('~을 명심하다')
여 : 알겠어요. 다음번엔 명심하도록 할게요.

- **assignment** ⓝ 과제 · **AI(Artificial-Intelligence)** ⓝ 인공 지능
- **false** ⓐ 가짜인, 허위의 · **blindly** ⓐⓓ 맹목적으로

대화를 듣고, 남자의 의견으로 가장 적절한 것을 고르시오.
① 인공 지능에서 얻은 정보를 맹목적으로 믿어서는 안 된다.
AI의 답변을 맹목적으로 믿으면 안 된다고 함
② 출처를 밝히지 않고 타인의 표현을 인용해서는 안 된다.
출처나 인용에 관한 내용이 아님
③ 인공 지능의 도움을 통해 과제물의 질을 높일 수 있다.
과제물의 질에 관한 내용은 없음
④ 과제를 할 때 본인의 생각이 들어가는 것이 중요하다.
본인의 생각이 들어가야 한다는 내용은 없음
⑤ 기술의 변화에 맞추어 작업 방식을 바꿀 필요가 있다.
작업 방식에 대한 언급은 없음

왜 정답? ✿✿✿ [정답률 93%]

남자는 여자에게 AI가 허위 정보를 이용할 수도 있으므로 AI가 제공하는 정보를
맹목적으로 신뢰하지 말라고 조언하고 있다. 따라서 남자의 의견으로 가장 적절한
것은 ①이다.

왜 오답?

② 출처나 타인의 표현 인용에 관한 대화가 아니다.
③ 여자가 인공 지능이 과제에 도움이 되었다고 말했지만, 남자는 인공 지능을
맹목적으로 신뢰하지 말 것을 조언했다. 주의
④ 본인의 생각이 들어가야 하기 때문에 AI를 믿지 말라는 것이 아니다.
⑤ 작업 방식에 관한 내용은 언급되지 않았다.

어법 특강

＊ 가주어, 가목적어로 쓰이는 it

– 주어나 목적어 역할을 하는 to부정사가 길어질 경우,
가주어 또는 가목적어 it을 대신 쓰고 to부정사를 뒤로 보낸다.

- **It** is necessary **to master** at least one foreign language.
(적어도 한 개의 외국어를 마스터하는 것이 필요하다.)

- **It** is very dangerous **to swim** in this river.
(이 강에서 수영하는 것은 매우 위험하다.)

- Exercising hard every day will make **it** easier **to lose** weight.
(매일 열심히 운동하는 것은 살을 빼는 것을 더 쉽게 만들어줄 것이다.)

03 정답 ③ ＊소셜 미디어의 부정적인 영향

W : Hello, listeners. This is Kelly Watson's *Love Yourself*.
여 : 안녕하세요, 청취자 여러분. Kelly Watson의 Love Yourself입니다.

Have you ever thought about your social media use?
여러분은 소셜 미디어 사용에 대해 생각해 본 적이 있나요?

Social media lets you <mark>stay</mark> connected with others easily.
[사역동사 lets의 목적격 보어(동사원형)]
소셜 미디어는 여러분이 다른 사람들과 쉽게 연결되도록 해줍니다.

However, it can make you <mark>compare</mark> yourself with others, too.
[사역동사 make의 목적격 보어(동사원형)]
단서 1 소셜 미디어는 자신을 남들과 비교하게 함
하지만, 그것은 여러분이 다른 사람들과 자신을 비교하게 만들 수도 있습니다.

For example, a celebrity's post about going on a luxurious trip <mark>may make</mark> you jealous.
[문장의 동사]
예를 들어, 호화로운 여행을 떠나는 것에 관한 유명인의 게시물은 여러분을 질투하게 할지도 모릅니다.

Continuously <mark>making such comparisons stops you from looking</mark> at yourself the way you truly are.
[동명사구 주어] ['~가 ~하는 것을 막다']
단서 2 비교가 있는 그대로의 자신을 볼 수 없게 함
지속적으로 이러한 비교를 하는 것은 여러분이 진정으로 있는 그대로의 자기 자신을 바라보는 것을 막습니다.

You might <mark>think</mark>, "Why can't I have a better life?" and <mark>feel</mark> small about yourself.
[병렬 구조]
여러분은 "왜 나는 더 나은 삶을 살 수 없을까?"라고 생각하고 자신이 초라하다고 느낄지도 모릅니다.

As you can see, social media can <mark>have a</mark> negative <mark>effect on</mark> your self-esteem.
['~에 영향을 끼치다']
단서 3 소셜 미디어는 자존감에 부정적인 영향을 줌
보다시피, 소셜 미디어는 여러분의 자존감에 부정적인 영향을 미칠 수 있습니다.

I'll be right back with some tips for healthy social media use.
곧 건강한 소셜 미디어 사용을 위한 몇 가지 팁과 함께 돌아오겠습니다.

- compare ⓥ 비교하다
- luxurious ⓐ 호화로운
- feel small 초라한 기분이 들다, 풀이 죽다
- jealous ⓐ 질투하는
- continuously 〔ad〕 지속적으로
- comparison ⓝ 비교
- negative ⓐ 부정적인
- self-esteem ⓝ 자존감

> 다음을 듣고, 여자가 하는 말의 요지로 가장 적절한 것을 고르시오.
> ① 소셜 미디어는 원만한 대인관계 유지에 도움이 된다.
> 대인관계에 관한 언급은 없음
> ② 온라인에서는 자아가 다양한 모습으로 표출될 수 있다.
> 온라인상의 다양한 자아의 모습에 관한 내용이 아님
> ③ 소셜 미디어는 자존감에 부정적인 영향을 줄 수 있다.
> 소셜 미디어는 남들과 자신을 비교하도록 하여 자존감에 부정적인 영향을 미칠 수 있음
> ④ 친밀한 관계일수록 상대의 언행에 쉽게 영향을 받는다.
> 친밀한 관계 사이의 언행에 대한 내용이 아님
> ⑤ 유명인 사생활 보호의 중요성은 종종 간과된다.
> 유명인 사생활 보호에 대한 내용이 아님

왜 정답 ? ✿✿✿ [정답률 92%]

소셜 미디어의 사용은 다른 사람들과 자신을 비교하게 만들고 이러한 비교는 결국 자존감에 부정적인 영향을 끼친다고 말하고 있다. 따라서 여자가 하는 말의 요지로 가장 적절한 것은 ③이다.

왜 오답 ?

① 소셜 미디어의 부정적인 영향에 대해 말하고 있으며 대인관계에 관한 내용이 아니다. (➡ 이유: 소셜 미디어의 장점은 대화의 초반부에만 언급되었다.)
② 온라인상에서의 다양한 자아 표출에 관한 내용은 언급되지 않았다.
④ 친밀한 관계 사이의 언행은 언급되지 않았다.
⑤ 유명인의 게시물은 질투의 대상으로 언급되었을 뿐이다.

---

04 정답 ⑤ ＊평화로운 공원의 풍경

2024. 6
5회

W : Honey, I love this park! 여 : 여보, 이 공원 너무 맘에 들어요!

M : Me, too. This park is so cool. But, oh, look! What's that in the tree?
남 : 나도요. 이 공원은 너무 멋지네요. 그런데, 오, 봐요! 나무에 있는 저것은 뭐죠?

W : It's just a kite <mark>stuck</mark> in the tree's branches.
[과거분사(a kite 수식)]
여 : 그냥 나뭇가지에 꽂힌 연이네요. **①의 단서** 나뭇가지에 연이 꽂혀 있음

M : I guess some kids went home without their kite.
남 : 어떤 아이들이 자기들 연 없이 집에 갔군요.

W : <mark>By</mark> the same tree, a woman is walking her dog. They look so lovely.
['~옆에'] **②의 단서** 여자가 강아지를 산책시키고 있음
여 : 같은 나무 옆에, 한 여자가 그녀의 강아지를 산책시키고 있네요. 그들은 정말 사랑스러워 보여요.

M : What about the little girl beside her?
남 : 그 여자 옆에 있는 어린 소녀는 어때요?

W : You mean the girl <mark>holding</mark> balloons in her hand?
[현재분사(the girl 수식)]
여 : 손에 풍선을 들고 있는 소녀를 말하는 건가요? **③의 단서** 소녀는 풍선을 들고 있음

M : Right. She's adorable. And look there! Did you notice a basket <mark>full of flowers</mark> on the picnic mat?
[형용사구(a basket 수식)] **④의 단서** 꽃바구니가 소풍용 돗자리 위에 있음
남 : 맞아요. 그녀는 사랑스럽네요. 그리고 저기 봐요! 소풍용 돗자리 위에 꽃이 가득 담긴 바구니를 봤나요?

W : Yes, right. It adds a touch of romance to the scene.
여 : 네, 그렇네요. 이 장면에 로맨스의 느낌을 더하네요.

M : I think so, too. Oh, there's a fountain. Next to it, a man is playing the violin.
⑤의 단서 남자는 바이올린을 연주하는 것이 아니라 사진을 찍고 있음
남 : 나도 그렇게 생각해요. 아, 분수대가 있네요. 그 옆에 한 남자가 바이올린을 연주하고 있어요.

W : The melody is beautiful. I'm glad we came here.
여 : 멜로디가 아름답네요. 우리가 여기에 온 것이 다행이에요.

- branch ⓝ 나뭇가지
- add ⓥ 더하다
- scene ⓝ 장면
- fountain ⓝ 분수(대)

> 대화를 듣고, 그림에서 대화의 내용과 일치하지 않는 것을 고르시오.

남자는 바이올린을 연주하는 것이 아니라 사진을 찍고 있음
① 나뭇가지에 연이 꽂혀 있음
여자가 강아지를 산책시키고 있음 ②
③ 소녀가 풍선을 들고 있음
④
꽃으로 가득 찬 바구니가 돗자리 위에 있음
⑤

왜 정답 ? ✿✿✿ [정답률 95%]

분수 옆의 남자가 바이올린을 연주하고 있다고 했는데 그림 속의 남자는 사진기로 사진을 찍고 있으므로 ⑤가 대화의 내용과 일치하지 않는다.

왜 오답 ?

① 나뭇가지에 연이 꽂혀 있다.
② 여자가 강아지를 산책시키고 있다.
③ 소녀가 풍선을 들고 있다.
④ 꽃으로 가득 찬 바구니가 돗자리 위에 있다.

05 정답 ④ ★과학 캠프 전 체크리스트 확인

M : Hey, Alice. I applied for the science camp next week. What about you?

남 : 안녕, Alice. 나는 다음 주에 있는 과학 캠프에 지원했어. 넌?

W : Me, too. But I didn't know <u>that</u> there were so many things to do before the camp.
목적어절 접속사

여 : 나도. 그런데 캠프 전에 할 일이 이렇게 많은 줄 몰랐어.

M : Right. Would you like to go over my checklist together?

남 : 그러게. 나의 체크리스트를 같이 확인해 볼래?

W : Hmm, let's see. Did you upload your introduction video to the website? ⑤의 함정

여 : 흠, 한번 보자. 웹사이트에 자기 소개 영상을 올렸니?

M : Yes, I tried to show my interest in science. Oh, hey, have you picked <u>which</u> experiment <u>to work on</u>? ②의 함정
의문형용사 형용사적 용법(experiment 수식)

남 : 응, 내가 과학에 관심이 있다는 걸 보여주려고 노력했어. 아, 너는 어떤 실험을 할지 정했니?

W : Yes. I decided to participate in a biology experiment.

여 : 응. 나는 생물학 실험에 참가하기로 결정했어.

M : Me, too. Wasn't <u>it</u> difficult <u>to make</u> a plan for your experiment?
가주어 진주어

남 : 나도. 실험 계획을 세우는 것이 어렵진 않았니?

W : Actually, I <u>haven't</u> even <u>started</u> yet because <u>I've never written</u> a plan for a biology experiment before. 단서1 여자는 실험 계획서를 써본 적이 없다고 함
현재완료(완료) 현재완료(경험)

여 : 사실, 전에 생물학 실험 계획서를 써본 적이 없어서 아직 시작도 안 했어.

M : I'll show you mine after class. Maybe you can get some ideas. 단서2 남자는 여자에게 자신의 실험 계획서를 보여주겠다고 함

남 : 수업 끝나면 내 계획서를 보여줄게. 아마 아이디어를 얻을 수 있을 거야.

W : Really? That'd be great. See you soon. 여 : 정말? 너무 좋다. 이따 봐.

- introduction ⓝ 소개 • experiment ⓝ 실험
- participate in ~에 참여하다 • biology ⓝ 생물학

대화를 듣고, 남자가 할 일로 가장 적절한 것을 고르시오.

① 과학 캠프 지원하기 과학 캠프에 이미 지원함
② 참가 실험 결정하기 생물학 실험을 하기로 이미 결정함
③ 체크리스트 작성하기 체크리스트를 같이 확인하는 중임
④ 실험 계획서 보여주기 남자는 여자에게 자신의 실험 계획서를 보여주겠다고 함
⑤ 자기 소개 영상 촬영하기 자기 소개 영상은 이미 완성하여 업로드함

왜 정답? ★★※ [정답률 83%]

남자는 생물학 실험 계획서를 써본 적 없는 여자에게 수업 후 자신의 실험 계획서를 보여주겠다고 했으므로 남자가 여자를 위해 할 일로 가장 적절한 것은 ④이다.

왜 오답?

① 남자와 여자 모두 과학 캠프에 이미 지원했다.
② 남자와 여자 모두 생물학 실험을 하기로 결정했다.
③ 함께 체크리스트를 확인하는 상황이다.
⑤ 남자는 자기 소개 영상을 이미 업로드했다고 언급했다.

---

06 정답 ③ ★캠핑 배낭 및 모자 구입

W : Hi, I'm looking for a backpack for my niece. She<u>'s going</u> on a camping trip this summer.
가까운 미래를 대신하는 현재진행형

여 : 안녕하세요, 저는 조카에게 줄 배낭을 찾고 있어요. 그녀는 이번 여름에 캠핑을 갈 예정이에요.

M : Great. We have this blue backpack <u>that</u> has multiple pockets.
주격 관계대명사

남 : 좋아요. 여러 개의 주머니가 있는 이 파란색 배낭이 있습니다.

W : It looks stylish and functional. How much is it?

여 : 멋지고 실용적이네요. 가격이 얼마인가요?

M : It's $50, but we have a special discount only on backpacks today. Every backpack is 10% off. 단서2 모든 배낭은 10% 할인
단서1 파란색 배낭은 50달러

남 : 50달러이지만, 오늘은 배낭에만 특별 할인이 들어가요. 모든 배낭이 10% 할인됩니다.

W : That's a great deal! I'll take it.

여 : 좋은 가격이네요! 제가 살게요.

M : <u>I'm sure</u> your niece will love it. Do you need anything else?
뒤에 전치사 of와 명사절 접속사 that이 생략됨

남 : 조카가 분명 좋아할 거예요. 더 필요하신 건 없나요?

W : Yes. I like this camping hat. How much is it?

여 : 있어요. 이 캠핑 모자가 마음에 들어요. 얼마인가요?

M : It's $10, not on sale, <u>though</u>. 단서3 캠핑 모자는 10달러이며 할인이 없음
부사(그렇지만, 하지만)

남 : 10달러입니다, 하지만 할인은 없어요.

W : That's okay. I'll take it as well.

여 : 괜찮아요. 이것도 살게요.

M : Gift wrapping for them would be a total of $5. Would you like gift wrapping? 단서4 선물 포장은 총 5달러임

남 : 선물 포장은 총 5달러입니다. 선물 포장을 해드릴까요?

W : Yes, please. Here's my credit card.

여 : 네, 부탁드려요. 여기 제 신용카드입니다.

- niece ⓝ (여자) 조카 • multiple ⓐ 여러 개의
- functional ⓐ 기능적인 • discount ⓝ 할인

대화를 듣고, 여자가 지불할 금액을 고르시오. [3점]

① $50 ② $55 ③ $60 ④ $65 ⑤ $70

$50(파란색 배낭)*0.9(10% 할인) + $10(캠핑 모자) + $5(선물 포장비)

왜 정답? ★★※ [정답률 54%]

여자가 조카에게 사줄 파란색 배낭은 50달러인데 모든 배낭은 10% 할인을 하므로 45달러이며, 여자가 마음에 들어 한 캠핑 모자는 10달러이다. 여기에 선물 포장비는 총 5달러라고 했으므로 여자가 지불할 금액은 ③ '60달러'이다.

---

07 정답 ⑤ ★동아리 마술쇼 초대

W : Hi, Chris. How was your weekend?

여 : 안녕, Chris. 주말 잘 보냈니?

M : Hello, Martha. I went to a rock concert and had fun. How about you? ①의 함정

남 : 안녕, Martha. 나는 록 콘서트에 가서 재밌게 놀았어. 너는?

W : <u>I've been preparing</u> for tomorrow's club festival. ④의 함정
현재완료진행

여 : 나는 내일 있을 동아리 축제를 준비하고 있었어.

M : Oh, what kind of activity are you preparing for the festival?

남 : 오, 축제를 위해 어떤 활동을 준비하고 있니?

W : Our club members <u>are presenting</u> a magic show. Come and watch us at 4 p.m. tomorrow if you are available.
가까운 미래를 대신하는 현재진행형

여 : 우리 동아리원들은 마술쇼를 보여줄 거야. 시간이 되면 내일 오후 4시에 우리를 보러와.

M : I'd love to, but <u>I can't make it</u>.
갈 수 없음을 나타내는 표현

남 : 그러고 싶은데, 갈 수가 없어.

W : Why? <u>It</u>'d be nice <u>to have</u> you there.
가주어 진주어

여 : 왜? 네가 오면 좋을 텐데.

M : I'm sorry, but I have to attend my uncle's birthday party.
남 : 미안하지만, 나는 삼촌의 생일 파티에 참석해야 해. 단서 삼촌의 생일 파티에 참석해야 함

W : Oh, I understand. I hope you have a wonderful time with your family.
여 : 오, 이해해. 가족들과 함께 즐거운 시간 보내길 바랄게.

M : Thank you, I will.
남 : 고마워, 그렇게 할게.

- have fun 재밌게 놀다, 즐기다
- prepare for ~을 준비하다
- present ⓥ 보여주다
- attend ⓥ 참석하다

대화를 듣고, 남자가 마술쇼에 갈 수 없는 이유를 고르시오.

① 록 콘서트에 가야 해서 지난 주말에 다녀옴
② 다른 학교 축제에 가야 해서 다른 학교 축제에 관한 언급은 없음
③ 가족 중 아픈 사람이 있어서 가족 중 아픈 사람에 관한 언급은 없음
④ 동아리 축제를 준비해야 해서 동아리 축제 준비는 여자가 해야 함
⑤ 삼촌 생일 파티에 참석해야 해서 삼촌의 생일 파티에 참석해야 한다고 했음

＞왜 정답 ? ✽✾✾ [정답률 96%]

여자가 남자에게 시간이 되면 동아리 축제를 위해 준비한 마술쇼에 오라고 초대했지만, 남자는 삼촌 생일 파티에 참석해야 한다고 했으므로 정답은 ⑤이다.

＞왜 오답 ?

① 록 콘서트는 남자가 지난 주말에 다녀왔다.
② 다른 학교 축제에 가야 한다는 말은 언급되지 않았다.
③ 가족 중 아픈 사람이 있는 것이 아니라, 삼촌의 생일 파티가 있다.
④ 동아리 축제를 준비해야 하는 사람은 여자이다. 함정

---

08 정답 ② ✱ 마라톤 행사

W : Hey, Alex. Have you seen the announcement for the Victory Marathon?
여 : 안녕하세요, Alex. '승리 마라톤'에 대한 발표를 보셨나요?

M : Not yet, but I'm curious about it. When's the event?
남 : 아직 못 봤는데 궁금하네요. 행사는 언제 하나요?

W : It's on Saturday, July 13th. ①의 단서 여행 날짜
여 : 7월 13일 토요일이에요.

M : Nice. Where will the race start?
남 : 좋네요. 경주는 어디서 시작하나요?

W : It will start at William Stadium. ③의 단서 출발 지점
여 : William 경기장에서 시작합니다.

M : Oh, great. How much does it cost to participate?
남 : 오, 좋네요. 참가하는 데는 얼마가 드나요?

W : It costs $30. ④의 단서 참가비
여 : 30달러예요.

M : That's reasonable. How many participants are they expecting?
남 : 합리적이군요. 그들은 몇 명의 참가자를 예상하나요?

W : Last year, there were around 5,000. 뒤에 목적어절 접속사 that이 생략됨 They say they expect about the same this year. ⑤의 단서 예상 참가 인원
여 : 작년에는 약 5,000명 정도였어요. 올해도 비슷할 것으로 예상한다고 하네요.

M : I didn't know that many people love marathons. I'm in! 목적어절 접속사
남 : 많은 사람들이 마라톤을 사랑하는 줄 몰랐어요. 저도 참여할게요!
look forward to -ing: ~할 것을 기대하다
W : Great. I look forward to running with you.
여 : 좋습니다. 당신과 함께 뛰는 것이 기대가 되네요.

- announcement ⓝ 발표
- curious ⓐ 궁금한
- reasonable ⓐ 합리적인

대화를 듣고, Victory Marathon에 관해 언급되지 않은 것을 고르시오.

① 행사 날짜 It's on Saturday, July 13th.　② 신청 방법 언급되지 않음
③ 출발 지점 It will start at William Stadium　④ 참가비 It costs $30.
⑤ 예상 참가 인원
　Last year, there were around 5,000. They say they expect about the same this year.

＞왜 정답 ? ✽✾✾ [정답률 92%]

'승리 마라톤' 행사에 대해 말하면서 행사 날짜, 출발 지점, 참가비, 예상 참가 인원에 대해서는 언급했지만, 신청 방법은 언급하지 않았으므로 정답은 ②이다.

＞왜 오답 ?

① 행사 날짜는 7월 13일 토요일이다.
③ 출발 지점은 William 경기장이다.
④ 참가비는 30달러이다.
⑤ 예상 참가 인원은 작년과 같은 약 5,000명이다.

---

09 정답 ⑤ ✱ 멘토링 행사 안내

M : Good morning, students of Violet Hill High School.
남 : 좋은 아침입니다, Violet Hill 고등학교 학생 여러분.

This is your principal speaking. 저는 여러분의 교장 선생님입니다.
부사적 용법(이유)　목적어절 접속사
I'm delighted to announce that the annual Violet Hill
미래시제 수동태
Mentorship will be held next Friday. ①의 단서 다음 주 금요일에 열림
매년 열리는 Violet Hill 멘토링이 다음 주 금요일에 개최된다는 것을 발표하게 되어 기쁩니다.
주격 관계대명사
Our school graduates who are now majoring in English
literature, bioengineering, and theater and film will be
giving some tips on university life. ②의 단서 대학 생활에 관한 조언을 해 줌
현재 영문학, 생명공학, 연극영화학을 전공하고 있는 우리 학교 졸업생들이 대학 생활에 관한 조언을 해 줄 것입니다.
③의 단서 신청을 위해서는 질문을 미리 제출해야 함
To register for this event, visit our school website and submit
사이에 목적격 관계대명사가 생략됨
two questions you would like to ask them in advance.
이 행사에 등록하려면, 학교 웹사이트를 방문하여 그들에게 묻고 싶은 질문 두 가지를 미리 제출하세요.

The deadline for registration is next Tuesday, so don't wait
too long. ④의 단서 신청 마감일은 다음 주 화요일
등록 마감은 다음 주 화요일이니 너무 오래 기다리지는 마세요.
단수 주어
And remember, the maximum number of participants for
단수 동사
each major is 30 people. ⑤의 단서 전공별 참가 가능 인원은 30명임
그리고 전공별 최대 참여 인원은 30명임을 기억하세요.

For more information, visit our school website.
더 많은 내용을 알고 싶다면, 학교 웹사이트를 방문하세요.

- literature ⓝ 문학
- bioengineering ⓝ 생명공학
- register ⓥ 등록하다
- in advance 사전에, 미리

Violet Hill Mentorship에 관한 다음 내용을 듣고, 일치하지 않는 것을 고르시오.

① 다음 주 금요일에 개최될 예정이다. will be held next Friday
② 대학 생활에 관한 조언이 제공된다. giving some tips on university life
③ 신청 시 질문을 미리 제출해야 한다.
　To register ~ submit two questions ~ in advance
④ 신청 마감일은 다음 주 화요일이다.
　The deadline for registration is next Tuesday
⑤ 전공별 참가 가능한 인원은 20명이다. the maximum number ~ 30 people

＞왜 정답 ? ✽✾✾ [정답률 95%]

전공별 참가 가능한 최대 인원은 30명이라고 (the maximum number of participants for each major is 30 people) 했으므로 20명이라고 한 ⑤이 일치하지 않는다.

① 다음 주 금요일에 개최될 예정이다.
② 대학 생활에 관한 조언이 제공된다.
③ 신청 시 질문을 미리 제출해야 한다.
④ 신청 마감일은 다음 주 화요일이다.

10 정답 ④ ＊무선 진공 청소기 구입

M : Honey, look. This website's Summer Sale <mark>has</mark> just <mark>begun</mark>.   ^{현재완료}
남 : 여보, 이것 보세요. 이 웹사이트의 여름 세일이 이제 막 시작되었어요.

W : Oh, great. <mark>Why don't we buy</mark> a new cordless vacuum cleaner?   '~ 하는 게 어때?'
여 : 오, 좋아요. 우리 새 무선 진공 청소기를 사는 게 어때요?

M : Sure. There are five bestsellers <mark>shown</mark> here.   ^{과거분사(bestsellers 수식)}
남 : 물론이죠. 여기 다섯 개의 베스트셀러가 있네요.

W : Let's check the battery life first. 여 : 우선 배터리 수명을 확인해 봐요.

M : I think it should be at least two hours <mark>so that</mark> we don't have to charge it as often. **단서1** 배터리 수명은 최소 두 시간이어야 함 (① 제외)
남 : 충전을 자주 하지 않아도 되도록 최소 두 시간은 되어야 할 것 같아요.   '~하도록'

W : I agree. But <u>let's not spend</u> more than $400 on a vacuum cleaner. **단서2** 400달러 이상이면 안 됨 (⑤ 제외)   '~하지 말자'
여 : 동의해요. 하지만 진공 청소기에 400달러 이상은 쓰지 말아요.

M : Fine. Oh, some of these also have a wet cleaning function.
남 : 좋아요. 오, 이 중에 몇 개는 습식 세정 기능도 있네요.

W : I'd love that. With that function, we can definitely save a lot of time. **단서3** 습식 세정 기능이 있어야 함 (② 제외)
여 : 그거 마음에 드네요. 그 기능을 사용하면 확실히 많은 시간을 절약할 수 있어요.

M : Okay. What about the color? The white <mark>one</mark> looks better to me. **단서4** 흰색이어야 함 (③ 제외)   = vacuum cleaner
남 : 좋아요. 그럼 색상은요? 내가 보기에는 흰색이 더 좋아 보이네요.

W : Right. It'll match the color tone of our living room.
여 : 맞아요. 우리 거실의 색조와 잘 맞을 거예요.

M : Perfect. So, let's buy this one. 남 : 완벽해요. 그럼 이걸로 삽시다.

W : Great. 여 : 좋아요.

- cordless ⓐ 선이 없는, 무선의 · vacuum cleaner 진공 청소기
- battery life 배터리 수명 · at least 최소한 · charge ⓥ 충전하다
- function ⓝ 기능 · match ⓥ (색 등이) 맞다 · color tone 색조

다음 표를 보면서 대화를 듣고, 두 사람이 구입할 무선 진공 청소기를 고르시오.

배터리 수명이 두 시간 미만임
Cordless Vacuum Cleaner 무선 진공 청소기

	Model 모델	Battery Life 배터리 수명	Price 가격	Wet Cleaning 습식 세정	Color 색깔
①	A	1 hour	$300	×	Red 빨간색
②	B	2 hours	$330	×	White 흰색
③	C	2 hours	$370	○	Red
④	D	3 hours	$390	○	White
⑤	E	3 hours	$410	○	Black 검은색

습식 세정 기능이 없음
400달러가 넘음   색깔이 흰색이 아님

배터리 수명이 두 시간 이상이고 (① 제외), 습식 세정 기능이 있으며 (② 제외), 색깔이 흰색이고 (③ 제외), 가격이 400달러 이하인 제품은 (⑤ 제외) ④이다.

① 배터리 수명이 최소 두 시간이어야 한다.
② 습식 세정 기능이 있는 것이어야 한다.
③ 흰색을 선호한다.
⑤ 400달러 이하길 원한다.

11 정답 ① ＊반려동물 입양

M : Mom, I want to have a cat. Have you ever thought about <mark>us</mark> adopting a cat?   ^{동명사의 의미상 주어}
남 : 엄마, 저는 고양이를 키우고 싶어요. 우리가 고양이를 입양하는 것에 대해 생각해 보신 적이 있나요?

W : Sweetie, <mark>having a pet requires</mark> a lot of responsibility.   ^{동명사구 주어} ^{단수 동사}
여 : 얘야, 반려동물을 키우려면 많은 책임감이 필요하단다. **단서** 엄마에게 반려동물 입양을 고려해 보자고 함

M : I'm totally ready for it. Mom, we could at least consider it.
남 : 저는 완전히 준비되어 있어요. 엄마, 우리는 최소한 그것을 고려해 볼 수 있어요.

W : **Fine. Let's talk about it over dinner.**
여 : 좋아. 저녁 식사하면서 얘기해 보자.

- adopt ⓥ 입양하다 · require ⓥ 요구하다
- responsibility ⓝ 책임감

대화를 듣고, 남자의 마지막 말에 대한 여자의 응답으로 가장 적절한 것을 고르시오.

① Fine. Let's talk about it over dinner. 반려동물 입양을 얘기해 보자고 함
  좋아, 저녁 식사하면서 얘기해 보자.
② Okay. Be more responsible next time. 책임을 묻는 상황이 아님
  그래. 다음부터는 더욱 책임감을 가져라.
③ Great. I already ordered some pet food.
  좋아. 나는 이미 반려동물 사료를 주문했어. 반려동물 사료 주문에 대한 대화가 아님
④ Too bad. I hope your cat gets well soon. 고양이가 아픈 상황이 아님
  안됐구나. 너의 고양이가 빨리 낫기를 바랄게.
⑤ Sorry. I can't take care of your cat tonight.
  미안. 나는 오늘 밤 너의 고양이를 돌볼 수가 없어. 고양이를 돌봐달라고 부탁하지 않음

고양이를 반려동물로 입양하고 싶은 남자는 여자에게 적어도 이를 고려해 보자고 말하고 있다. 따라서 여자는 ① '좋아, 저녁 식사하면서 얘기해 보자.'라고 응답하는 것이 가장 적절하다.

② 남자에게 책임을 묻는 상황이 아니다.
③ 반려동물 사료 주문에 대한 대화가 아니다.
④ 남자는 고양이를 키우고 싶어 하는 상황이다.
⑤ 남자는 고양이를 돌봐달라고 부탁하지 않았다.

12 정답 ③ ＊수학 과제 제출

W : Jake, I completely forgot about the math assignment. When's the deadline?
여 : Jake, 나 수학 과제를 완전히 잊어버렸어. 마감일이 언제지?

M : You need to submit it <mark>by</mark> next Tuesday.   '~ 까지'
남 : 다음 주 화요일까지 제출해야 해. **단서** 과제를 어디에 제출해야 하는지 질문함

W : Phew, I still have some time. Where should I submit it?
여 : 휴, 아직 시간이 좀 남았네. 어디에 제출하면 될까?

M : **Upload your work to our school website.**
남 : 우리 학교 웹사이트에 네 과제를 업로드해.

- assignment ⓝ 과제 · completely ⓐⓓ 완전히
- deadline ⓝ 마감일 · submit ⓥ 제출하다

대화를 듣고, 여자의 마지막 말에 대한 남자의 응답으로 가장 적절한 것을 고르시오.

① I can't accept late assignments. 기한이 아직 지나지 않음
  기한이 지난 과제는 받아줄 수 없어.
② You did an excellent job this time. 여자가 무엇인가를 해낸 상황이 아님
  이번에는 정말 잘 해냈구나.
③ Upload your work to our school website.
  우리 학교 웹사이트에 네 과제를 업로드해. 어디에 과제를 제출해야 하는지 알려줌
④ Try to do your homework by yourself.
  너 스스로 과제를 해보려고 노력해 봐. 과제를 스스로 못하는 상황이 아님
⑤ We can finish it before the next class.
  다음 수업 전에 우리는 그것을 끝낼 수 있을 거야. 과제를 함께 하는 상황이 아님

왜 정답? ★★❀ [정답률 80%]

여자는 수학 과제 마감 기한이 아직 남았음에 안도하며 남자에게 수학 과제를 어디에 제출해야 하는지 질문하였다. 따라서 남자는 ③ '우리 학교 웹사이트에 네 과제를 업로드해.'라고 응답하는 것이 가장 적절하다.

왜 오답?

① 수학 과제의 마감 기한은 아직 지나지 않았다.
② 여자는 남자에게 과제 제출에 관한 정보를 물어보고 있다.
④ 여자가 과제를 스스로 못하고 있는 상황이 아니다.
⑤ 남자와 여자가 함께 과제를 하는 상황이 아니다.

왜 정답? ★★❀ [정답률 85%]

배드민턴 경기 이후에 무릎이 아프다고 하는 여자에게 남자는 부상 위험을 줄이고 바른 자세를 기르기 위해 강사에게 레슨을 받는 것이 중요하다고 얘기하고 있다. 따라서 여자의 응답으로 가장 적절한 것은 ⑤ '네 말이 맞아. 아마 나는 배드민턴 레슨을 받기 시작해야 할 것 같아.'이다.

왜 오답?

① 여자가 다니는 병원을 추천해 달라고 하지 않았다.
② 지난 저녁의 배드민턴 경기에 대해 말한 적이 없다.
③ 배드민턴 서브 방법을 묻는 상황이 아니다.
④ 남자가 아닌 여자가 무릎이 아프다고 했다.

---

13 정답 ⑤ * 배드민턴 레슨의 필요성

M : Hey, Cindy. Have you been playing a lot of badminton these days?
남 : 안녕, Cindy. 요즘 배드민턴을 많이 쳤니?

W : No, I've been experiencing some pain in my knee since a badminton match last weekend.
여 : 아니, 지난 주말 배드민턴 경기 이후로 무릎이 좀 아팠어.

M : I'm sorry to hear that. Did you go see a doctor?
남 : 유감이야. 병원은 다녀왔니?

W : Yes, I visited a local clinic yesterday.
여 : 응, 어제 동네 의원을 다녀왔어.

M : I hope you feel better soon. By the way, have you ever taken a badminton lesson?
남 : 너가 빨리 나았으면 좋겠어. 그나저나, 혹시 배드민턴 레슨을 받은 적이 있니?

W : No, I haven't. Why are you asking?
여 : 아니, 받은 적 없어. 왜 물어보는 거니?

M : In my experience, that kind of injury can come from bad posture. A lesson might reduce the risk of any further injury.
남 : 내 경험상, 그런 부상은 자세가 안 좋아서 올 수도 있어. 레슨을 받으면 더 이상의 부상 위험을 줄일 수 있지. **단서 1** 배드민턴 레슨이 부상 위험을 줄일 수 있음

W : Well, I thought I didn't need those lessons.
여 : 글쎄, 나는 그런 레슨이 필요하시 않다고 생각했어.

M : Cindy, if you want to keep playing badminton without any injuries, it's important to learn from an instructor to develop the right posture. **단서 2** 좋은 자세를 위해 강사에게 배우는 것이 중요함
남 : Cindy, 부상 없이 배드민턴을 계속 치고 싶다면, 올바른 자세를 기르기 위해 강사에게 배우는 게 중요해.

W : You're right. Maybe I should start taking badminton lessons.
여 : 네 말이 맞아. 아마 나는 배드민턴 레슨을 받기 시작해야 할 것 같아.

- experience ⓥ 겪다 · injury ⓝ 부상 · posture ⓝ 자세
- reduce ⓥ 줄이다 · risk ⓝ 위험 · clinic ⓝ 병원

대화를 듣고, 남자의 마지막 말에 대한 여자의 응답으로 가장 적절한 것을 고르시오. [3점]

Woman: _____

① Yes. I can give you the phone number of the clinic I visited. 병원을 추천해 달라는 내용이 아님
그래. 내가 방문한 병원의 전화번호를 줄 수 있어.
② I agree. Last evening's badminton match was awesome.
나도 동의해. 지난 저녁 배드민턴 경기는 정말 멋졌어. 지난 저녁의 배드민턴 경기에 대한 언급은 없음
③ No problem. I'll teach you how to serve this time.
문제없어. 이번엔 내가 서브하는 방법을 알려줄게. 배드민턴 서브 방법을 묻는 상황이 아님
④ Too bad. I hope you recover from your knee injury soon.
안됐구나. 너의 무릎 부상이 빨리 회복하길 바랄게. 남자가 아닌 여자가 무릎이 아프다고 했음
⑤ You're right. Maybe I should start taking badminton lessons. 배드민턴 레슨이 필요함을 인지함
네 말이 맞아. 아마 나는 배드민턴 레슨을 받기 시작해야 할 것 같아.

---

14 정답 ② * 기후 변화 예방을 위한 방법

W : Mike, don't you think climate change is kind of scary?
여 : Mike, 기후 변화가 좀 무섭다고 생각하지 않니?

M : Right. The temperature seems higher than ever.
남 : 맞아. 그 어느 때보다 기온이 더 높은 것 같아.

W : I heard it's putting a number of animals in danger these days.
여 : 기후 변화가 요즘 많은 동물들을 위험에 빠뜨리고 있다고 들었어.

M : Right. Maybe one day we won't be able to see polar bears anymore.
남 : 맞아. 아마 언젠가 우리는 북극곰을 더 이상 볼 수 없게 될지도 몰라.

W : That's not good. What can we do?
여 : 그것은 좋지 않아. 우리가 무엇을 할 수 있을까?

M : Use less plastic, plant more trees. Small things matter.
남 : 플라스틱을 덜 쓰고, 나무를 더 심어야지. 작은 것들이 중요해.

W : And maybe we can ride bikes instead of always asking for rides.
여 : 그리고 우리는 항상 차를 타는 대신 자전거를 탈 수도 있어.

M : Yeah. Making a Tree-Planting Day at school can also be helpful. **단서 1** 학교에서 '나무 심기의 날'을 만드는 것이 도움이 될 것이라고 함
남 : 맞아. 학교에서 '나무 심기의 날'을 만드는 것도 도움이 될 수 있어.

W : Absolutely. Then, why don't we make our own school club to put it into action? **단서 2** 동아리를 만들어서 실천하자고 제안함
여 : 그럼. 그러면, 우리가 학교 동아리를 만들어서 그것을 실천하는 건 어때?

M : Great. Let's think about the club name first.
남 : 좋아. 우선 동아리 이름부터 생각해 보자.

- climate change 기후 변화 · temperature ⓝ 온도
- polar bear 북극곰 · plant ⓥ 심다 · matter ⓥ 중요하다

대화를 듣고, 여자의 마지막 말에 대한 남자의 응답으로 가장 적절한 것을 고르시오. [3점]

Man: _____

① Sure. It seems like a perfect place for bears.
그럼. 곰을 위한 완벽한 장소인 것 같아. 곰을 위한 장소에 관한 대화가 아님
② Great. Let's think about the club name first.
좋아. 우선 동아리 이름부터 생각해 보자. 동아리 개설 제안에 대한 적절한 응답임
③ My pleasure. I can always give you a ride.
괜찮아. 나는 항상 너를 태워다줄 수 있어. 태워달라는 요청은 없었음
④ I agree. It's hard to give up using plastics.
동의해. 플라스틱 사용을 포기하는 것은 어려워. 플라스틱 사용을 포기하기 어렵다는 내용은 없었음
⑤ No worries. I'll get my bike repaired.
걱정하지 마. 나는 나의 자전거를 수리할 거야. 자전거 고장에 관한 대화가 아님

왜 정답? ★★❀ [정답률 83%]

기후 변화를 예방하는 방법들에 대한 의견을 나누는 도중 남자가 학교에서 '나무 심기의 날'을 만드는 것이 좋을 것이라고 언급했다. 이에 여자는 동아리를 만들어서 실천하는 게 어떤지 남자에게 제안하고 있으므로 남자의 응답으로 가장 적절한 것은 ② '좋아. 우선 동아리 이름부터 생각해 보자.'이다.

15 정답 ③ *과로하는 동료에 대한 걱정

W : Laura and Tony are close coworkers.
여 : Laura와 Tony는 가까운 동료이다.

Laura notices that Tony **has been looking** unusually tired
현재완료진행
and pale recently. 단서1 Tony가 최근 특히 피곤하고 창백해 보임
Laura는 Tony가 최근에 평소와 달리 피곤하고 창백해 보인다는 것을 알아차린다.
명사절 접속사(~인지)
One day, she asks Tony if he's not been feeling well lately,
뒤에 목적어절 접속사 that 생략
but **Tony says** he's just a bit tired from work.
어느 날, 그녀는 Tony에게 최근에 몸이 안 좋았는지 물어보지만, Tony는 단지 일
때문에 조금 피곤할 뿐이라고 말한다. 단서2 Tony는 주말에도 종종 쉬지 않고 일을 함
병렬 구조
Laura knows that Tony sometimes works even on weekends
without **taking a break** or **getting any rest**.
Laura는 Tony가 때때로 주말에도 휴식이나 쉬는 시간을 취하지 않고 일한다는 것을
알고 있다. 단서3 Laura는 Tony가 걱정되어
그가 며칠 쉬는 것을 원함
병렬 구조
However, this time, she **is** really worried about him and
wants의 목적격 보어(to부정사)
wants him **to take** at least a couple of days off.
하지만, 이번에 그녀는 그가 정말 걱정되고 그가 적어도 며칠 쉬기를 원한다.

In this situation, what would Laura most likely say to Tony?
이런 상황에서, Laura는 Tony에게 뭐라고 말하겠는가?
had better 동사 : ~하는 게 낫겠다
Laura: **You'd better take a break for a few days.**
Laura: 당신은 며칠 동안 쉬는 것이 좋겠습니다.

*상황 요약: 과로로 인하여 건강이 염려되는 Tony에게 휴식을 권유하는 상황

- coworker ⓝ 동료 · notice ⓥ 알아차리다
- unusually 🆎 평소와 달리 · pale ⓐ 창백한 · rest ⓝ 휴식

다음 상황 설명을 듣고, Laura가 Tony에게 할 말로 가장 적절한 것을
고르시오.

Laura: _____

① I don't like visiting a hospital for medical checkups.
저는 건강검진을 위해 병원을 방문하는 것을 좋아하지 않습니다. 건강검진에 대한 대화가 아님
② I appreciate you taking me to the doctor today.
오늘 병원에 데려다주셔서 감사합니다. 병원에 데려다줬다는 언급은 없음
③You'd better take a break for a few days.
당신은 며칠 동안 쉬는 것이 좋겠습니다. 건강이 염려되어 휴식을 권하고 있음
④ You should finish your work before the deadline.
마감일 전에 일을 끝내야 합니다. 마감일에 대한 언급은 없음
⑤ I'm afraid I can't reduce your workload right now.
죄송하지만 지금은 당신의 업무량을 줄일 수 없습니다. 업무량을 줄여달라는 요청은 없음

> 왜 정답 ? ❀❀❀ [정답률 84%]

Laura의 동료 Tony는 최근 유달리 피곤해 보였고, 주말에도 종종 쉬지 않고 일을
해서 Laura가 Tony에게 며칠 휴식할 것을 권유하려는 상황이다. 따라서 Laura가 할
말로 가장 적절한 것은 ③ '당신은 며칠 동안 쉬는 것이 좋겠습니다.'이다.

> 왜 오답 ?

① 건강검진에 관한 대화가 아니다.
② 병원에 데려다줬다는 언급은 없다.
④ 일의 마감 기한에 대한 언급은 없다.
⑤ 업무량을 줄여달라는 요청은 없다.

16~17 *학생 대표 선거 캠페인 지침

M : Hello, Lincoln High School. //
남 : 안녕하세요, Lincoln 고등학교입니다 //

This is David Newman, / your current student
representative, / and I'm speaking to you today / to let you
사역동사 let의 목적격 보어(동사원형)
know / about the upcoming election for next year's student
representative. //
저는 David Newman입니다 / 현재 학생 대표인 / 오늘 여러분께 말씀드립니다 /
알려드리기 위해 / 다가오는 내년 학생 대표 선거에 대해 //
분사구문을 이끄는 현재분사
Candidates can now begin their campaigns, / **following**
these instructions. // 16번 단서: 후보자들이 캠페인을 위해 따라야 할 지침들을
설명할 것임
후보자들은 이제 캠페인을 시작할 수 있습니다 / 이 지침들에 따라 //

First, / they can share / short promotional video clips / on
their social media, / but the video clips must not be longer
than 3 minutes. // 17번①
첫째 / 그들은 공유할 수 있습니다 / 짧은 홍보 동영상을 / 그들의 소셜 미디어에 / 하지만
그 동영상 클립은 3분을 초과해서는 안 됩니다 //

Second, / candidates can display posters / only in allowed
areas, / and it's important / to keep the size to A3 or smaller,
부사절 접속사(이유) 미래시제 수동태
/ as larger posters **will be removed** / without warning. //
둘째 / 후보자들은 포스터를 게시할 수 있습니다 / 허용된 지역에만 / 그리고 중요합니다
/ 포스터의 크기를 A3나 그 이하로 유지하는 것이 / 더 큰 포스터는 제거되기
때문입니다 / 예고 없이 //
17번③ 단수 동사 = pamphlets
Third, / the **use** of pamphlets **is** allowed, / but **they** must
only be distributed / within the school campus. //
셋째 / 팸플릿 사용은 허용됩니다 / 하지만 배포되어야 합니다 / 학교 캠퍼스 내에서만 //

Lastly, / there will be an online debate broadcast / on our
school website / among the candidates / three days before
the election. // 17번⑤
마지막으로 / 온라인 토론 방송이 있을 예정입니다 / 학교 웹사이트에서 / 후보자들 간 /
선거 3일 전에 //
가주어
It's important / **to be respectful** toward the other candidates
진주어
/ during the debate. //
중요합니다 / 다른 후보자들을 존중하는 것이 / 토론 중에는 //
make+목적어+목적격 보어
Let's **make this election a success**. //
이번 선거를 성공적으로 만들어 봅시다 //

- current ⓐ 현재의 · representative ⓝ 대표
- upcoming ⓐ 다가오는 · election ⓝ 선거
- candidate ⓝ 후보자 · promotional ⓐ 홍보의
- remove ⓥ 없애다 · distribute ⓥ 배부하다

남 : 안녕하세요, Lincoln 고등학교입니다. 저는 현재 학생 대표인 David
Newman이고 다가오는 내년 학생 대표 선거에 대해 알려드리기 위해 오
늘 여러분께 말씀드립니다. 이 지침들에 따라 후보자들은 이제 캠페인을
시작할 수 있습니다. 첫째, 짧은 홍보 동영상을 소셜 미디어에 공유할 수
있지만 그 동영상 클립은 3분을 초과해서는 안 됩니다. 둘째, 허용된 지역
에만 후보자들은 포스터를 게시할 수 있고 A3보다 더 큰 포스터는 예고 없
이 제거되기 때문에 포스터의 크기는 A3나 그 이하로 유지하는 것이 중요
합니다. 셋째, 팸플릿 사용이 허용되지만, 학교 캠퍼스 내에서만 배포되어
야 합니다. 마지막으로, 선거 3일 전에 학교 웹사이트에서 후보자들 간 온
라인 토론 방송이 있을 예정입니다. 토론 중에는 다른 후보자들을 존중하
는 것이 중요합니다. 이번 선거를 성공적으로 만들어 봅시다.

왜 정답? ✽✽❀ [정답률 83%]

- 성공한 운동선수들은 힘과 실력을 얻기 위해 고난에 맞섬으로써 승리한다. **단서 1**
- 힘은 맞서 싸우는 데서 나온다. **단서 2**
- 고난은 우리 인생에서 가장 위대한 스승이 될 것이다. **단서 3**

➡ 인생에서 어떤 것을 성취하기 위해서는 고난에 맞서 싸워야 한다고 했으므로 ⑤ '인생에서 고난을 직면하는 것의 중요성'이 글의 주제이다.

왜 오답?

✗ ① 잘 준비된 운동선수의 특징을 열거하는 글이 아니다. (◀━ 이유: 고난의 필요성에 대한 근거로서 성공한 운동선수를 예로 들었을 뿐이다.)

② 갑작스러운 난관을 극복하는 것이 어렵다는 내용은 없다.

③ 개인의 습관이 능력과 어떤 관계가 있는지 전혀 언급되지 않았다.

④ 고난의 필요성에 대한 글이지만 고난을 견뎌내는 것이 위험하다는 내용은 없다.

---

24 정답 ① ✱개인의 정체성과 행동의 관계

단서 1 행동은 정체성을 반영함
Your behaviors / are usually a reflection of your identity. //
당신의 행동은 / 대개 당신의 정체성을 반영한다 //

What you do / is an indication of the type of person / you believe that you are — / either consciously or nonconsciously. //
당신이 하는 행동은 / 어떤 사람인지를 나타낸다 / 당신이 스스로 그렇다고 믿고 있는 / 의식적으로든 무의식적으로든 //

Research has shown / that once a person believes in a particular aspect of their identity, / they are more likely to act / according to that belief. // **단서 2** 자신의 정체성에 따라 행동할 가능성이 높음
연구는 밝혔다 / 자신의 정체성의 특정 측면을 믿으면 / 그들은 행동할 가능성이 더 높다 / 그 믿음에 따라 //

For example, / people who identified as "being a voter" / were more likely to vote / than those who simply claimed / "voting" was an action they wanted to perform. //
예를 들어 / 자신을 "유권자"라고 느끼는 사람은 / 투표할 가능성이 더 높았다 / 단순히 주장하는 사람보다 / "투표"가 자신이 하고 싶은 행동이라고 //

Similarly, / the person who accepts exercise as the part of their identity / doesn't have to convince themselves / to train. //
마찬가지로 / 운동을 자신의 정체성의 일부로 받아들이는 사람은 / 스스로를 설득할 필요가 없다 훈련하라고 //

Doing the right thing is easy. // 옳은 일을 하는 것은 쉽다 //

After all, / when your behavior and your identity / perfectly match, / you are no longer pursuing behavior change. //
결국 / 자신의 행동과 정체성이 / 완벽하게 일치하면 / 더 이상 행동 변화를 추구하지 않아도 된다 //

You are simply acting / like the type of person / you already believe yourself to be. // **단서 3** 스스로가 그렇다고 믿는 사람의 유형처럼 행동함
당신은 행동하고 있을 뿐이다 / 어떤 유형의 사람처럼 / 당신 스스로가 그렇다고 이미 믿고 있는 //

- reflection ⓝ 반영 · identity ⓝ 정체성 · indication ⓝ 암시
- consciously ⓐⓓ 의식적으로 · vote ⓥ 투표하다
- claim ⓥ 주장하다 · convince ⓥ 설득하다 · pursue ⓥ 추구하다

당신의 행동은 대개 당신의 정체성을 반영한다. 당신이 하는 행동은 의식적으로든 무의식적으로든 당신이 스스로를 어떤 사람이라고 믿고 있는지를 나타낸다. 연구에 따르면 자신의 정체성의 특정 측면을 믿는 사람은 그 믿음에 따라 행동할 가능성이 더 높다. 예를 들어, 자신을 "유권자"라고 느끼는 사람은 단순히 "투표"가 자신이 하고 싶은 행동이라고 주장하는 사람보다 투표할 가능성이 더 높았다. 마찬가지로, 운동을 자신의 정체성의 일부로 받아들이는 사람은 훈련하라고 스스로를 설득할 필요가 없다. 옳은 일을 하는 것은 쉽다. 결국, 자신의 행동과 정체성이 완벽하게 일치하면 더 이상 행동 변화를 추구하지 않아도 된다. 당신은 그저 당신 스스로가 그렇다고 이미 믿고 있는 유형의 사람처럼 행동하고 있을 뿐이다.

다음 글의 제목으로 가장 적절한 것은?

① Action Comes from Who You Think You Are
자신의 정체성을 어떻게 인식하는지에 따라 행동하게 됨
행동은 당신이 자신을 어떤 사람으로 생각하는지로부터 나온다

② The Best Practices for Gaining More Voters
더 많은 유권자를 확보하기 위한 우수 사례
유권자 확보에 관한 내용이 아님

③ Stop Pursuing Undesirable Behavior Change!
바람직하지 않은 행동 변화를 추구하는 것을 멈추세요!
바람직하지 않은 행동 변화에 관한 언급은 없음

④ What to Do When Your Exercise Bores You
운동이 지루하게 느껴질 때 해야 할 일
운동이 지루해질 때 해야 하는 방법에 관한 글이 아님

⑤ Your Actions Speak Louder than Your Words
당신의 행동이 당신의 말보다 중요하다
행동이 말보다 중요하다는 내용이 아님

왜 정답? ✽✽❀ [정답률 76%]

- 당신의 행동은 대개 당신의 정체성을 반영한다. **단서 1**
- 자신의 정체성의 어떤 측면을 믿는 사람은 그에 따라 행동할 가능성이 높다. **단서 2**
- 스스로가 그렇다고 믿는 사람의 유형처럼 행동하게 된다. **단서 3**

➡ 행동은 자신이 인식하고 있는 자아를 반영하기 때문에 자신의 정체성을 어떻게 인식하는지에 따라 행동하게 된다는 글이므로 글의 제목으로 가장 적절한 것은 ① '행동은 당신이 자신을 어떤 사람으로 생각하는지로부터 나온다'이다.

왜 오답?

✗ ② 유권자 확보의 우수 사례에 관한 내용이 아니다. (◀━ 이유: 유권자는 정체성에 따른 행동의 예시로서 주어졌을 뿐이다.)

③ 바람직하지 않은 행동 변화에 대해 주의를 주거나 경고하는 글이 아니다.

④ 운동이 지루해질 때 어떻게 해야 하는지를 이야기하는 글이 아니다.

⑤ 행동이 말보다 더 중요하다는 내용이 아니다.

---

25 정답 ③ ✱지역별 전자 폐기물 수거율 및 재활용률

The above graph shows / the electronic waste collection and recycling rate / by region / in 2016 and 2019. //
위 도표는 보여준다 / 전자 폐기물 수거율 및 재활용률을 / 지역별 / 2016년과 2019년의 //

① In both years, / Europe showed / the highest electronic waste collection and recycling rates. // 2016년, 2019년 모두 유럽이 가장 높음
두 해 모두 / 유럽이 보였다 / 가장 높은 전자 폐기물 수거율 및 재활용률을 //

② The electronic waste collection and recycling rate of Asia in 2019 / was lower than in 2016. // 아시아: 2019년(12%) < 2016년(15%)
2019년 아시아의 전자 폐기물 수거율 및 재활용률은 / 2016년보다 낮았다 //

③ The Americas / ranked third both in 2016 and in 2019(→ second in 2016 and third in 2019), / with 17 percent and 9 percent respectively. // **단서** 아메리카: 2016년(17%, 전체 2위), 2019년(9%, 전체 3위)
(남·북·중앙) 아메리카는 / 2016년과 2019년 모두 3위(→ 2016년에는 2위, 2019년에는 3위)를 기록했으며 / 그 비율은 각각 17퍼센트와 9퍼센트였다 //

④ In both years, / the electronic waste collection and recycling rates in Oceania / remained under 10 percent. // 2016년(6%), 2019년(9%) 모두 10% 미만
두 해 모두 / 오세아니아의 전자 폐기물 수거율 및 재활용률은 / 10퍼센트 아래에 머물렀다 //

⑤ Africa / had the lowest electronic waste collection and recycling rates / in both 2016 and 2019, / showing the smallest gap between 2016 and 2019. // 2016년도, 2019년도 모두 막대가 가장 짧으며, 두 년도 간 차이는 1퍼센트포인트로 가장 낮음
아프리카는 / 가장 낮은 전자 폐기물 수거율 및 재활용률을 기록했다 / 2016년과 2019년 모두 / 그리고 두 해 사이의 비율 격차가 가장 적었다 //

- electronic waste 전자 폐기물 · recycling ⓝ 재활용
- region ⓝ 지역 · respectively ⓐⓓ 각각 · gap ⓝ 격차

위 도표는 2016년과 2019년의 지역별 전자 폐기물 수거율 및 재활용률을 보여준다. ① 두 해 모두 유럽이 가장 높은 전자 폐기물 수거율 및 재활용률을 보였다. ② 2019년 아시아의 전자 폐기물 수거율 및 재활용률은 2016년보다 낮았다. ③ (남·북·중앙) 아메리카는 2016년과 2019년 모두 3위(→ 2016년에는 2위, 2019년에는 3위)를 기록했으며, 그 비율은 각각 17퍼센트와 9퍼센트였다. ④ 오세아니아의 전자 폐기물 수거율 및 재활용률은 두 해 모두 10퍼센트 아래에 머물렀다. ⑤ 아프리카는 2016년과 2019년 모두 가장 낮은 전자 폐기물 수거율 및 재활용률을 기록했으며, 두 해 사이의 비율 격차가 가장 적었다.

다음 도표의 내용과 일치하지 않는 것은?

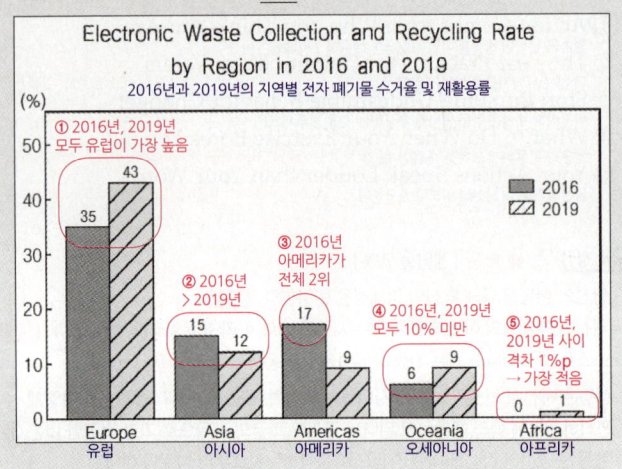

Electronic Waste Collection and Recycling Rate by Region in 2016 and 2019
2016년과 2019년의 지역별 전자 폐기물 수거율 및 재활용률

> 오내 정답 ? ✱❀❀ [정답률 89%]

아메리카의 전자 폐기물 수거율 및 재활용률은 2016년에 17%로 2위를 차지했으며 2019년에는 9%로 오세아니아와 공동 3위이다. 그러므로 2016년과 2019년 모두 3위를 기록했다고 한 ③이 도표의 내용과 일치하지 않는다.

> 오내 오답 ?

① 유럽은 2016년(35%), 2019년(43%) 모두 가장 높다.
② 아시아의 2019년 전자 폐기물 수거율 및 재활용률은 12%로, 2016년의 15%보다 적다.
④ 오세아니아의 2016년, 2019년 전자 폐기물 수거율 및 재활용률은 각각 6%, 9%로 모두 10% 미만이다.
⑤ 아프리카의 2016년과 2019년 사이의 전자 폐기물 수거율 및 재활용률은 가장 낮았고, 두 해의 격차는 1%p로 가장 적다.

26 정답 ⑤ ✱천체 물리학자 Fritz Zwicky

Fritz Zwicky, / a memorable astrophysicist who coined the term 'supernova', / was born in Varna, Bulgaria / to a Swiss father and a Czech mother. // ❶의 단서 불가리아 Varna에서 태어남
Fritz Zwicky는 / '초신성'이라는 용어를 만든 유명한 천체 물리학자인데 / 불가리아의 Varna에서 태어났다 / 스위스인 아버지와 체코인 어머니 사이에서 //

At the age of six, / he was sent to his grandparents / who looked after him / for most of his childhood in Switzerland. //
여섯 살이 되던 해 / 그는 조부모에게 보내졌다 / 그를 돌봐준 / 스위스에서 보낸 어린 시절의 대부분 동안 //

= In Switzerland
There, / he received an advanced education / in mathematics and physics. // ❷의 단서 스위스에서 수학과 물리학에 대한 교육을 받음
그곳에서 / 그는 고급 교육을 받았다 / 수학과 물리학에 대한 //

병렬 구조
In 1925, / he emigrated to the United States / and continued his physics research / at California Institute of Technology (Caltech). // ❸의 단서 미국으로 이주하여 연구를 계속함
1925년 / 미국으로 이주하여 / 물리학 연구를 이어갔다 / California Institute of Technology(Caltech)에서 //

He developed numerous theories / that have had a profound influence / on the understanding of our universe in the early 21st century. // ❹의 단서 우주 이해에 영향을 미친 수많은 이론을 발전시킴
그는 수많은 이론을 발전시켰다 / 지대한 영향을 미친 / 21세기 초 우주에 대한 이해에 //

❺의 단서 교수 임용이 된 후 제트 엔진을 개발함
After being appointed / as a professor of astronomy at Caltech in 1942, / he developed some of the earliest jet engines / and
= and many are in jet propulsion
holds more than 50 patents, / many in jet propulsion. //
임용된 후 / 1942년 Caltech의 천문학 교수로 / 그는 초창기 제트 엔진을 개발했고 / 50개 이상의 특허를 보유하고 있으며 / 이 중 많은 부분이 제트 추진 분야의 특허이다 //

• coin ⓥ (새로운 낱말·어구를) 만들다 • advanced ⓐ 진보된
• emigrate ⓥ (타국으로) 이주하다 • numerous ⓐ 수많은
• profound ⓐ 심오한 • influence ⓝ 영향 • appoint ⓥ 임명하다
• astronomy ⓝ 천문학

'초신성'이라는 용어를 만든 유명한 천체 물리학자 Fritz Zwicky는 불가리아의 Varna에서 스위스인 아버지와 체코인 어머니 사이에서 태어났다. 여섯 살이 되던 해, 그는 스위스에서 보낸 어린 시절의 대부분 동안 그를 돌봐준 조부모에게 보내졌다. 그곳에서, 그는 수학과 물리학에 대한 고급 교육을 받았다. 1925년 미국으로 이주하여 California Institute of Technology(Caltech)에서 물리학 연구를 이어갔다. 그는 21세기 초 우주에 대한 이해에 지대한 영향을 미친 수많은 이론을 발전시켰다. 1942년 Caltech의 천문학 교수로 임용된 후 그는 초창기 제트 엔진을 개발했고, 50개 이상의 특허를 보유하고 있으며, 이 중 많은 부분이 제트 추진 분야의 특허이다.

Fritz Zwicky에 관한 다음 글의 내용과 일치하지 않는 것은?

① 불가리아의 Varna에서 태어났다. born in Varna, Bulgaria
② 스위스에서 수학과 물리학 교육을 받았다.
There, he received an advanced education in mathematics and physics.
③ 미국으로 이주하여 연구를 이어갔다.
emigrated to the United States and continued his physics research
④ 우주 이해에 영향을 미친 수많은 이론을 발전시켰다.
He developed ~ on the understanding of our universe
⑤ 초창기 제트 엔진을 개발한 후 교수로 임용되었다. After being appointed as a professor of astronomy ~ he developed some of the earliest jet engines

> 오내 정답 ? ✱✱❀ [정답률 86%]

Fritz Zwicky는 Caltech의 천문학 교수로 임용된 후 초창기 제트 엔진을 개발했다고 했다. (After being appointed as a professor of astronomy ~ he developed some of the earliest jet engines) 따라서 개발 후 교수로 임용되었다는 ⑤은 글의 내용과 일치하지 않는다.

> 오내 오답 ?

① 불가리아의 Varna에서 태어났다. (born in Varna, Bulgaria)
② 스위스에서 수학과 물리학 교육을 받았다. (There, he received an advanced education in mathematics and physics.)
③ 미국으로 이주하여 연구를 이어갔다. (emigrated to the United States and continued his physics research)
④ 우주 이해에 영향을 미친 수많은 이론을 발전시켰다. (He developed ~ on the understanding of our universe)

27 정답 ④ ✱미식 베이킹 대회

Gourmet Baking Competition / 미식 베이킹 대회 /
병렬 구조
Get out your cookbooks / and dust off your greatest baking recipes. // 요리책을 꺼내 / 최고의 베이킹 레시피의 먼지를 털어내세요 //

When & Where / 일시 및 장소 /
• 5 p.m. -7 p.m. Saturday, August 3rd / ❶의 단서 8월 3일 토요일에 개최
8월 3일 토요일 오후 5시 - 오후 7시 /
• Gourmet Baking Studio / Gourmet Baking Studio /

Registration / 참가 신청 / ❷의 단서 온라인으로 신청
• Register online / at www.bakeoff.org by July 25th. //
온라인으로 신청하세요 / 7월 25일까지 www.bakeoff.org에서 //
• Anyone can participate / in the competition. //
누구나 참가할 수 있습니다 / 대회에 // ❸의 단서 누구나 참여 가능

Categories / 부문 /
• Pies, Cakes, and Cookies / 파이, 케이크, 쿠키 /
• Each person / can only enter one category. // ❹의 단서 참가자 한 명당 하나의 부문만 참가 가능
참가자 한 명당 / 하나의 부문만 참가할 수 있습니다 //

Prizes & Gifts / 상 및 선물 /
미래시제 수동태
• Prizes will be given / to the top three / in each category. //
상이 수여됩니다 / 최상위 3명에게는 / 각 부문별 //
• Souvenirs will be given / to every participant. //
기념품이 주어집니다 / 모든 참가자에게 // ❺의 단서 모든 참여자에게 기념품 수여

- dust off 먼지를 털다; 방치했던 것을 오랜만에 꺼내다
- competition ⓝ 대회 • souvenir ⓝ 기념품

미식 베이킹 대회

요리책을 꺼내 최고의 베이킹 레시피의 먼지를 털어내세요.

일시 및 장소
- 8월 3일 토요일 오후 5시 – 오후 7시
- Gourmet Baking Studio

참가 신청
- 7월 25일까지 www.bakeoff.org에서 온라인으로 신청하세요.
- 누구나 대회에 참가할 수 있습니다.

부문
- 파이, 케이크, 쿠키
- 참가자 한 명당 하나의 부문만 참가할 수 있습니다.

상 및 선물
- 각 부문별 최상위 3명에게는 상이 수여됩니다.
- 모든 참가자에게 기념품이 주어집니다.

Gourmet Baking Competition에 관한 다음 안내문의 내용과 일치하지 않는 것은?

① 8월 3일 토요일에 개최된다. Saturday, August 3rd
② 온라인으로 참가 신청이 가능하다. Register online at www.bakeoff.org
③ 누구나 참가할 수 있다. Anyone can participate in the competition.
④ 참가자 한 명이 여러 부문에 참여할 수 있다. Each person can only enter one category.
⑤ 모든 참가자에게 기념품이 제공될 것이다. Souvenirs will be given to every participant.

›왜 정답 ? ✽✽✽ [정답률 92%]

참가자 한 명당 한 부문에 참여할 수 있다고 (Each person can only enter one category.) 했으므로 참가자 한 명이 여러 부문에 참여할 수 있다고 한 ④이 안내문의 내용과 일치하지 않는다.

›왜 오답 ?

① 8월 3일 토요일에 개최된다. (Saturday, August 3rd)
② 온라인으로 참가 신청이 가능하다. (Register online at www.bakeoff.org)
③ 누구나 참가할 수 있다. (Anyone can participate in the competition.)
⑤ 모든 참가자에게 기념품이 제공될 것이다. (Souvenirs will be given to every participant.)

---

28 정답 ⑤ ✽ 겨울 스포츠 프로그램 ─────

Winter Sports Program / 겨울 스포츠 프로그램 /

Winter is coming! // 겨울이 옵니다 //

Let's have some fun together! // 같이 즐겨요 //

Time & Location / 시간 및 장소 /

- Every Sunday in December / from 1 p.m. to 3 p.m. /
  12월 매주 일요일 / 오후 1시부터 오후 3시까지 / ①의 단서 1시부터 3시임

- Grand Blue Ice Rink / Grand Blue Ice Rink /

Lesson Details / 강좌 세부 정보 /

- Ice Hockey, Speed Skating, and Figure Skating /
  아이스하키, 스피드 스케이팅, 피겨 스케이팅 / ②의 단서 종목은 3개

- Participants / must be 8 years of age or older. //
  참가자는 / 8세 이상이어야 합니다 // ③의 단서 참가 연령은 8세 이상

Fee / 수강료 /

- Ice Hockey: $200 / 아이스하키: $200 /

- Speed Skating / Figure Skating: $150 /
  스피드 스케이팅 / 피겨 스케이팅: $150 / ④의 단서 아이스하키와 스케이팅의 수강료가 다름

Notice / 주의 사항 /

- Skates and helmets / will be provided / for free. // 미래시제 수동태
  스케이트와 헬멧이 / 제공됩니다 / 무료로 //

- You should bring / your own gloves. // ⑤의 단서 장갑은 각자 가져와야 함
  가져와야 합니다 / 각자의 장갑을 //

※ For more information, / visit www.wintersports.com. //
더 많은 정보를 얻고자 한다면 / www.wintersports.com에 방문하세요 //

- provide ⓥ 제공하다 • for free 무료로

겨울 스포츠 프로그램

겨울이 옵니다! 같이 즐겨요!

시간 및 장소
- 12월 매주 일요일 오후 1시부터 오후 3시까지
- Grand Blue Ice Rink

강좌 세부 정보
- 아이스하키, 스피드 스케이팅, 피겨 스케이팅
- 참가자는 8세 이상이어야 합니다.

수강료
- 아이스하키: $200
- 스피드 스케이팅 / 피겨 스케이팅: $150

주의 사항
- 스케이트와 헬멧이 무료로 제공됩니다.
- 장갑은 각자 가져와야 합니다.

※ 더 많은 정보를 얻고자 한다면, www.wintersports.com에 방문하세요.

Winter Sports Program에 관한 다음 안내문의 내용과 일치하는 것은?

① 오후 2시에서 4시 사이에 실시된다. from 1 p.m. to 3 p.m.
② 네 종목의 강좌가 개설된다. Ice Hockey, Speed Skating, and Figure Skating
③ 참가 연령에 제한은 없다. Participants must be 8 years of age or older.
④ 모든 종목 강좌의 수강료는 같다. Ice Hockey: $200, Speed Skating / Figure Skating: $150
⑤ 장갑은 각자 가져와야 한다. You should bring your own gloves.

›왜 정답 ? ✽✽✽ [정답률 95%]

장갑이 각자 가져와야 한다고 (You should bring your own gloves.) 했으므로 안내문의 내용과 일치하는 것은 ⑤이다.

›왜 오답 ?

① 오후 1시에서 3시 사이에 실시된다. (from 1 p.m. to 3 p.m.)
② 아이스하키, 스피드 스케이팅, 피겨 스케이팅 총 세 종목이다. (Ice Hockey, Speed Skating, and Figure Skating)
③ 참가 연령은 8세 이상으로 제한되어 있다. (Participants must be 8 years of age or older.)
④ 아이스하키는 200달러이며 스피드 스케이팅과 피겨 스케이팅은 150달러이다. (Ice Hockey: $200, Speed Skating / Figure Skating: $150)

---

29 정답 ③ ✽ 인류 생활 방식의 변화와 문명의 탄생

다음 글의 밑줄 친 부분 중, 어법상 틀린 것은? [3점]

The hunter-gatherer lifestyle, / which can ① be described as 계속적 용법의 주격 관계대명사 / 수동태 동사
"natural" to human beings, / appears to have had much / to 주절의 동사
recommend it. //
수렵 채집 생활 방식은 / 인류에게 "자연스러운" 것으로 묘사될 수 있으며 / 많은 것(장점)이 있는 것으로 보인다 / 그것을 추천할 만한 //

Examination of human remains / from early hunter-gatherer 단수 주어
societies / ② has suggested / 단수 동사
유적 조사는 / 초기 수렵 채집 사회의 / 알려준다 /

목적어절 접속사
that our ancestors **enjoyed** abundant food, / obtainable without
병렬 구조
excessive effort, / and **suffered** very few diseases. //
인류의 조상들이 풍족한 식량을 누릴 수 있었고 / 과도한 노력 없이도 구할 수 있는 / 질병에
걸리는 일도 거의 없었다는 것을 //
가주어   진주어절을 이끄는 의문사
If this is true, / **it** is not clear / **why** so many humans settled
분사구문
in permanent villages / and developed agriculture, / **growing**
crops and domesticating animals: /
이것이 사실이라면 / 분명하지 않다 / 왜 그렇게 많은 인류가 영구적으로 마을에 정착하여 /
농업을 발달시켰는지는 / 농작물을 재배하고 동물을 기르면서 /
「it is[was] ~ that」강조 구문   단서 부사구를 강조하는
cultivating fields was hard work, / and **it was in farming villages**
「it is[was] ~ that」강조 구문
부사구
/ ③ ~~what~~(→ **that**) epidemic diseases first took root. //
밭을 경작하는 것은 힘든 일이었고 / 바로 농경 마을이었다 / 전염병이 처음 뿌리를 내린 곳은 //
부사절을 이끄는 복합 관계대명사   뒤에 be동사 생략
Whatever its immediate **effect** / on the lives of humans, / the
부사(동사 led 수식)
development of settlements and agriculture / ④ **undoubtedly**
본동사
led to / a high increase in population density. //
즉각적인 영향이 무엇이든 / 인간의 삶에 미치는 / 정착지와 농업의 발전은 / 의심의 여지 없이
이어졌다 / 인구 밀도의 높은 증가로 //
앞에 주격 관계대명사와 be동사 생략됨
This period, / **known as the New Stone Age**, / was a major
turning point in human development, /
이 시기는 / 신석기 시대로 알려진 / 인류 발전의 중요한 전환점으로 /
⑤ **opening** the way / to the growth of the first towns and cities,
병렬 구조(분사구문)
/ and eventually **leading** to settled "civilizations." //
길을 열었다 / 최초의 마을과 도시가 성장하도록 / 결국 정착된 "문명"으로 이어졌다 //

- hunter-gatherer ⓝ 수렵 채집인   • examination ⓝ 조사
- abundant ⓐ 풍부한   • obtainable ⓐ 획득할 수 있는
- excessive ⓐ 지나친, 과도한   • permanent ⓐ 영구적인
- domesticate ⓥ 길들이다, 재배하다   • cultivate ⓥ 경작하다
- take root 뿌리를 내리다   • immediate ⓐ 즉각적인
- density ⓝ 밀도   • civilization ⓝ 문명

수렵 채집 생활 방식은 인류에게 "자연스러운" 것으로 묘사될 수 있으며, 그것을 추천할 만한 많은 것(장점)이 있는 것으로 보인다. 초기 수렵 채집 사회의 유적 조사는 인류의 조상들이 과도한 노력 없이도 구할 수 있는 풍족한 식량을 누릴 수 있었고 질병에 걸리는 일도 거의 없었다는 것을 알려준다. 이것이 사실이라면, 왜 그렇게 많은 인류가 영구적으로 마을에 정착하여 농작물을 재배하고 동물을 기르면서 농업을 발달시켰는지는 분명하지 않다. 밭을 경작하는 것은 힘든 일이었고, 전염병이 처음 뿌리를 내린 곳은 농경 마을이었다. 인간의 삶에 미치는 즉각적인 영향이 무엇이든, 정착지와 농업의 발전은 의심의 여지 없이 인구 밀도의 높은 증가로 이어졌다. 신석기 시대로 알려진 이 시기는 인류 발전의 중요한 전환점으로, 최초의 마을과 도시가 성장하는 길을 열었고, 결국 정착된 "문명"으로 이어졌다.

왜 정답 ? **❋❋❋** [정답률 74%]
③ 부사구를 강조하는 「it is[was] ~ that」 강조 구문이다.

and로 연결되는 등위절: 제외하고 생각하기   「it is[was] ~ that」 강조 구문   강조를 받는 부사구
... cultivating fields was hard work, / and **it was in farming**
villages / ③ ~~what~~(→ **that**) epidemic diseases first took root. //
완전한 절을 이끄는 that 자리임

(단서) what에 밑줄이 있으므로

(발상) what이 의문사절이나 관계사절을 이끄는 것이 적절한지 확인해야 한다.

(해결) it was와 what 사이에 in farming villages라는 부사구가 왔고, what 뒤로는 주어 epidemic diseases와 동사 took root로 이루어진 완전한 절이 있다. 의문사절이나 관계사절을 이끄는 what은 불완전한 절만 이끌 수 있으므로, 여기에는 what 대신에, 부사구를 강조하는 「it is[was] ~ that」 강조 구문이 쓰이는 것이 적절하다. 따라서 what을 that으로 바꿔야 한다.

(개념) 「it is[was] ~ that」 강조 구문에서는 강조하고자 하는 어구를 it is[was]와 that 사이에 둔다.

왜 오답 ?

① 주어와 동사의 관계가 수동일 때 수동태 동사를 쓴다.
주어   계속적 용법의 주격 관계대명사   조동사의 수동태
The hunter-gatherer lifestyle, / **which can** ① **be described** as
본동사
"natural" to human beings, / **appears** to have had much / to
recommend it. //
관계사절의 수동태 동사인 be described에 밑줄이 있으므로 선행사와 동사가 수동의 관계인지 확인한다.
문맥상 관계사절의 선행사인 lifestyle이 인류에게 자연스러운 것으로 '묘사된다'는 것, 즉, 수동 관계를 나타낸다. (단서)
따라서 조동사 can 뒤에 be described가 오는 것은 어법상 적절하다.

② 동사는 주어에 그 수를 일치시킨다.
단수 주어
Examination of human remains / from early hunter-gatherer
societies / 단수 동사 ② **has suggested** / that our ancestors enjoyed
목적어절: 제외하고 생각하기
abundant food, / obtainable without excessive effort, / and
suffered very few diseases. //
문장의 동사는 주어에 그 수를 일치시킨다. (개념)
동사가 「has +과거분사」 형태이고 단수 동사인 has에 밑줄이 있으므로 문장의 주어 역시 단수인지 확인한다.
주어인 Examination은 단수이므로 단수 동사 has가 적절하게 쓰였다.

④ 부사는 동사를 수식할 수 있다.
부사절: 제외하고 생각하기
Whatever its immediate effect / on the lives of humans, / the
주어   부사(동사 led 수식)
development of settlements and agriculture / ④ **undoubtedly**
동사
led to / a high increase in population density. //
부사는 동사, 형용사, 부사, 문장 전체를 수식하는 수식어로서, 동사의 앞이나 뒤에서 그 동사를 수식할 수 있다. (개념)
부사인 undoubtedly에 밑줄이 있으므로 주변에 부사가 수식할 만한 문장 요소가 있는지 확인한다.
동사 led를 앞에서 수식하며 '의심의 여지 없이'라는 뜻을 더하는 부사 undoubtedly가 적절하게 쓰였다.

⑤ 분사구문의 현재분사는 능동의 의미를 나타낸다.
주어   본동사
This period, / known as the New Stone Age, / **was** a major
분사구문을 이끄는 현재분사
turning point in human development, / ⑤ **opening** the way
/ to the growth of the first towns and cities, / and eventually
leading to settled "civilizations."] //
주어(This period), 동사(was), 주격 보어(a major ~ development)의 완전한 절 뒤에 opening이 왔으므로, 분사구문을 이끄는 현재분사로 쓰였음을 알 수 있다.
분사구문의 생략된 주어는 This period(신석기 시대)이며 그 시기가 성장의 길을 '열었다'는 능동의 관계를 나타낸다. (단서)
따라서 현재분사 opening이 적절하게 쓰였다.
접속사가 이끄는 절의 접속사와 주어를 생략하고 동사를 분사로 바꾸어 분사구문을 만들 수 있다. 이때 주어와 동사의 관계가 능동이면 현재분사, 수동이면 「(being) + 과거분사」 형태로 쓴다. (개념)

30 정답 ⑤ ＊미래의 소비와 즉각적인 소비 사이의 갈등

다음 글의 밑줄 친 부분 중, 문맥상 낱말의 쓰임이 적절하지 않은 것은?
[3점]

Many human and non-human animals / save commodities or money / for future consumption. //
많은 인간과 인간이 아닌 동물은 / 물건이나 돈을 저축한다 / 미래의 소비를 위해 //

This behavior seems to reveal / a preference of a ① delayed reward / over an immediate **one**: / the agent gives up / some immediate pleasure / **in exchange for** a future **one**. //
이러한 행동은 드러내는 듯하다 / 지연된 보상을 선호하는 것을 / 즉각적인 보상보다 / 행위자는 포기한다 / 당장의 쾌락을 / 미래의 보상을 위해
단서 1 행위자는 미래의 보상을 위해 현재의 쾌락을 포기함

Thus / the discounted value of the future reward / should be ② greater / than the un-discounted value of the present **one**. //
그러므로 / 미래 보상의 하락된 가치는 / 더 커야만 한다 / 하락되지 않은 현재의 가치보다 //

However, / in some cases / the agent **does not wait** for the envisioned occasion / but **uses** their savings ③ prematurely. //
그러나 / 어떤 경우 / 행위자가 계획한 일을 기다리지 않고 / 그들의 저축을 조기에 사용한다 //

For example, / early in the year / an employee might **set aside** money / to buy Christmas presents / but then **spend** it / on a summer vacation instead. //
단서 2 행위자가 저축을 조기에 사용하는 경우이면서 약한 의지를 나타내는 예시임
예를 들어, / 연초에 / 한 직원이 자기 돈을 모아둘 수 있다 / 크리스마스 선물을 사기 위해 / 하지만 사용할 수 있다 / 여름 휴가에 대신 //

Such cases / could be examples of ④ weakness of will. //
이러한 사례는 / 의지의 약함의 예시가 될 수 있다 //

That is, / the agents may **judge or resolve** / **to spend** their savings in a certain way / for the greatest benefit /
즉, / 행위자는 판단하거나 결심할 수 있다 / 그들의 저축을 특정 방식으로 사용하기로 / 가장 큰 이익을 위해 /
단서 3 행위자는 저축 계획을 세워도 즉각적인 쾌락의 유혹이 생기면 다르게 행동할 수 있음

but then **act** differently / when temptation for immediate pleasure ⑤ disappears (→ appears). //
하지만 다르게 행동할 수도 있다 / 즉각적인 즐거움에 대한 유혹이 사라지면(→ 생기면) //

- commodity ⓝ 상품   - consumption ⓝ 소비
- reveal ⓥ 드러내다   - preference ⓝ 선호   - delay ⓥ 지연하다
- reward ⓝ 보상   - agent ⓝ 행위자   - prematurely ⓐⓓ 조기에
- set aside ~을 확보하다   - judge ⓥ 판단하다   - resolve ⓥ 결심하다
- temptation ⓝ 유혹

많은 인간과 인간이 아닌 동물은 물건이나 돈을 미래의 소비를 위해 저축한다. 이러한 행동은 즉각적인 보상보다 ① 지연된 보상을 선호하는 것을 드러내는 듯하다. 즉, 행위자는 미래의 보상을 위해 당장의 쾌락을 포기하는 것이다. 그러므로 미래 보상의 하락된 가치는 하락되지 않은 현재의 가치보다 ② 더 커야만 한다. 그러나, 어떤 경우 행위자가 계획한 일을 기다리지 않고 그들의 저축을 ③ 조기에 사용하는 경우도 있다. 예를 들어, 연초에 한 직원이 자기 돈을 크리스마스 선물을 사기 위해 모아두었지만 대신 여름 휴가에 사용할 수 있다. 이러한 사례는 의지의 ④ 약함의 예시가 될 수 있다. 즉, 행위자는 그들의 저축을 가장 큰 이익을 위해 특정 방식으로 사용하기로 판단하거나 결심했으나 즉각적인 즐거움에 대한 유혹이 ⑤ 사라지면(→ 생기면) 다르게 행동할 수도 있다.

＞왜 정답 ? ★★★ [정답률 42%]

⑤ disappears 사라지다

즉, 행위자는 그들의 저축을 가장 큰 이익을 위해 특정 방식으로 사용하기로 판단하거나 결심했으나 즉각적인 즐거움에 대한 유혹이 ⑤ ~~사라지면~~ 생기면 다르게 행동할 수도 있다.

➡ 저축을 가장 큰 이익을 위해 사용하려고 결정했으나 그와 다르게 행동하도록 하려면, 즉각적인 쾌락에 대한 유혹이 '사라지는' 것이 아니라 '생겨야' 할 것이다.
▶ disappears를 appears(생기다)와 같은 반의어로 바꿔야 함

＞왜 오답 ?

① delayed 지연된

많은 인간과 인간이 아닌 동물은 물건이나 돈을 미래의 소비를 위해 저축한다. 이러한 행동은 즉각적인 보상보다 ① 지연된 보상을 선호하는 것을 드러내는 듯하다.

➡ 미래의 소비를 위해 물건이나 돈을 저축하는 행위는 나중을 위한 것이므로 즉각적인 보상보다 '지연된' 보상을 선호하는 것을 의미한다.
▶ delayed는 문맥에 맞음

② greater 더 큰

즉, 행위자는 미래의 보상을 위해 당장의 쾌락을 포기하는 것이다. 그러므로 미래 보상의 하락된 가치는 하락되지 않은 현재의 가치보다 ② 더 커야만 한다.

➡ 미래의 가치가 현재의 가치보다 더 커야 행위자가 미래의 보상을 위해 당장의 쾌락을 포기하는 것이 설명되므로, 미래 보상의 하락된 가치는 하락되지 않은 현재의 가치보다 '더 커야만' 한다. ▶ greater는 문맥에 맞음

③ prematurely 조기에

그러나, 어떤 경우 행위자가 계획한 일을 기다리지 않고 그들의 저축을 ③ 조기에 사용하는 경우도 있다. 예를 들어, 연초에 한 직원이 자기 돈을 크리스마스 선물을 사기 위해 모아두었지만 대신 여름 휴가에 사용할 수 있다.

➡ 크리스마스 선물을 위해 저축한 돈을 여름 휴가에 사용하는 것은 행위자가 저축을 '조기에' 사용하는 경우이다. ▶ prematurely는 문맥에 맞음

④ weakness 약함

예를 들어, 연초에 한 직원이 자기 돈을 크리스마스 선물을 사기 위해 모아두었지만 대신 여름 휴가에 사용할 수 있다. 이러한 사례는 의지의 ④ 약함의 예시가 될 수 있다.

➡ 크리스마스 선물을 위해 저축한 돈을 여름 휴가에 사용하는 것은 크리스마스 때까지 지출을 참을 의지가 약한 것을 나타내므로, 의지의 '약함'의 예시가 된다.
▶ weakness는 문맥에 맞음

---

31 정답 ② ＊갑작스러운 방해의 대가

The costs of **interruptions** / are well-documented. //
방해로 인한 대가는 / 잘 기록되어 있다 //

Martin Luther King Jr. lamented them / **when** he described / **"that** lovely poem **that** didn't **get written** / **because** someone knocked on the door." //
단서 1 Martin Luther King Jr.는 갑자기 누가 문을 두드려 시를 완성하지 못함
Martin Luther King Jr.는 이를 슬퍼했다 / 그가 묘사했을 때 / "쓰여지지 못한 그 사랑스러운 시 / 누군가 문을 두드렸기 때문에" //

Perhaps / the most famous literary example happened in 1797 / when Samuel Taylor Coleridge **started** writing his poem / *Kubla Khan* / from a dream **he had** /
앞에 목적격 관계대명사 that이 생략됨
아마도 / 가장 유명한 문학적 사례는 1797년에 일어났던 일일 것이다 / Samuel Taylor Coleridge가 시를 쓰기 시작했는데 / *Kubla Khan*이라는 / 꿈에서 /

but then **was visited** by an unexpected guest. //
뜻밖의 손님이 찾아왔을 때 //

For Coleridge, by coincidence, / the untimely visitor came at a particularly bad time. //
공교롭게도 Coleridge에게 / 이 불청객은 특히 좋지 않은 시기에 찾아왔다 //

He forgot his inspiration / and left **the work unfinished**. //
그는 영감을 잊고 / 작품을 미완성로 남겼다 //
단서 2 Samuel Taylor Coleridge는 갑자기 손님이 찾아와서 작품을 끝내지 못함

부사절 접속사(대조)
While there are many documented cases of sudden disruptions
주격 관계대명사   단서3 심각한 결과를 초래한
/ **that** have had significant consequences /   갑작스러운 방해의 사례가 많음
갑작스러운 방해의 사례가 많이 기록되어 있지만 / 심각한 결과를 초래한 /
      '~와 같은'
for professionals in critical roles / **such as** doctors, nurses,
control room operators, stock traders, and pilots, /
중요한 역할을 담당하는 전문가들에게 / 의사, 간호사, 관제실 운영자, 주식 거래자, 조종사와
같은 /
they also impact most of us in our everyday lives, / **slowing**
            병렬 구조
down work productivity / and generally **increasing** stress levels. //
갑작스러운 방해는 일상 생활에서 대부분의 사람들에게도 영향을 미치고 / 업무 생산성을
떨어뜨리며 / 일반적으로 스트레스 수준을 높인다 //

- document ⓥ 기록하다
- coincidence ⓝ 우연
- particularly ⓐⓓ 특히
- sudden ⓐ 갑작스러운
- significant ⓐ 상당한
- critical ⓐ 중요한
- productivity ⓝ 생산성
- literary ⓐ 문학적인
- untimely ⓐ 시기가 적절하지 않은
- inspiration ⓝ 영감
- disruption ⓝ 방해
- consequence ⓝ 결과
- impact ⓥ 영향을 끼치다

방해로 인한 대가는 잘 기록되어 있다. Martin Luther King Jr.는 "누군가 문을 두드리는 바람에 쓰여지지 못한 사랑스러운 시"를 묘사하며 이를 슬퍼했다. 아마도 가장 유명한 문학적 사례는 1797년 Samuel Taylor Coleridge가 꿈을 꾸고 *Kubla Khan*이라는 시를 쓰기 시작했는데 뜻밖의 손님이 찾아왔을 때 일어났던 일일 것이다. 공교롭게도 Coleridge에게 이 불청객은 특히 좋지 않은 시기에 찾아왔다. 그는 영감을 잊고 작품을 미완성으로 남겼다. 의사, 간호사, 관제실 운영자, 주식 거래자, 조종사와 같은 중요한 역할을 담당하는 전문가들에게 심각한 결과를 초래한 갑작스러운 방해의 사례가 많이 기록되어 있지만, 갑작스러운 방해는 일상 생활에서 대부분의 사람들에게도 영향을 미쳐 업무 생산성을 떨어뜨리며 일반적으로 스트레스 수준을 높인다.

다음 빈칸에 들어갈 말로 가장 적절한 것을 고르시오.

① misunderstandings 오해에 대한 내용이 아님
  오해
②interruptions 방해의 대가를 여러 사례를 통해 설명하고 있음
  방해
③ inequalities 불평등에 대한 언급은 없음
  불평등
④ regulations 규제에 관한 내용이 아님
  규제
⑤ arguments 논쟁에 관한 내용이 아님
  논쟁

| **문제 풀이 순서** | ★★★ [정답률 58%]

1st 빈칸이 포함된 문장을 읽고, 빈칸에 들어갈 말에 대한 단서를 얻는다.

| 빈칸 문장 | The costs of _____ are well-documented.
___로 인한 대가는 잘 기록되어 있다. |

➡ '무엇'으로 인한 대가가 잘 기록되어 있다고 했으므로, **단서**
대가를 만드는 것이 '무엇'인지, 그리고 그것에 대한 어떤 기록이 있는지 알려줄
것이다. **발상**

2nd 글의 나머지 부분을 확인해서 정답을 찾는다.

예시 1 : Martin Luther King Jr. → 시를 쓰고 있을 때 누가 노크를 하여 시를
완성하지 못함 **단서1**
예시 2 : Samuel Taylor Coleridge → 시를 쓰고 있을 때 갑자기 손님이 찾아와서
영감을 잊고 작품을 끝내지 못함 **단서2**
갑작스러운 방해가 전문가들에게 심각한 결과를 초래한 사례들이 많이 기록되어
있음 **단서3**

➡ 예시로 제시된 두 인물 모두 작업 중에 누군가가 방해하여 작품을 끝내지 못했고,
이들과 비슷한 사례가 많이 기록되어 있다고 했다.

▶ 즉, ② '방해'의 대가인 업무 생산성 저하가 잘 기록되어 있다.

| **선택지 분석** |

① **misunderstandings** 오해
어떤 상황이나 관계에 대한 오해로 인한 대가가 아니다.

②**interruptions** 방해
갑작스러운 방해로 인해 대가를 치른 사례들이 많다고 했다.

③ **inequalities** 불평등
불평등의 대가는 언급되지 않았다.

④ **regulations** 규제
규제로 인한 대가가 발생한 상황이 아니다.

⑤ **arguments** 논쟁
논쟁으로 인한 대가가 발생했다는 내용은 없다.

---

32 정답 ② * 주의 집중과 뇌의 재구조화

                       현재분사(evidence 수식) 목적어절 접속사
There's a lot of scientific evidence / **demonstrating that** focused
attention leads / to **the reshaping of the brain**. //
과학적 증거는 많이 있다 / 주의 집중이 이어진다는 것을 보여주는 / 뇌의 재구조화로 //
             과거분사구(animals 수식)
In animals **rewarded for noticing sound** / (to hunt or to avoid
                              비교급 강조 부사
being hunted for example), / we find **much** larger auditory
centers in the brain. // 단서1 좋은 청각의 이점이 있는 동물은 뇌의 청각 중추가 큼
소리를 알아채는 것에 대한 보상을 받은 동물에서 / (예를 들어 사냥하거나 사냥감이 되는
것을 피하기 위해) / 우리는 뇌의 청각 중추가 훨씬 더 큰 것을 발견한다 //
             과거분사구(animals 수식)
In animals **rewarded for sharp eyesight**, / the visual areas are
larger. // 단서2 예리한 시력의 이점이 있는 동물은 뇌의 시각 영역이 큼
예리한 시력에 대한 보상을 받은 동물은 / 시각 영역이 더 크다 //
                            분사구문을 이끄는 현재분사
Brain scans of violinists provide more evidence, / **showing**
                              주격 관계대명사
dramatic growth and expansion / in regions of the cortex **that**
represent the left hand, / 단서3 바이올린 연주자는 왼손을 나타내는 피질 영역이
                      성장하고 확장됨
바이올린 연주자의 뇌 스캔 결과는 더 많은 증거를 제공하는데 / 극적인 성장과 확장을
보여준다 / 왼손을 나타내는 피질 영역의 /
계속적 용법의 주격 관계대명사
which has to **finger** the strings precisely, / often at very high
               '(손가락으로 악기를) 켜다'
speed. //
(그 왼손은) 현을 정확하게 켜야 한다 / 종종 매우 빠른 속도로 // 단서4 택시 운전사는 공간 기억에
                   목적어절 접속사   필수적인 해마가 확장됨
Other studies have shown / **that** the hippocampus, **which** is
                              계속적 용법의 주격 관계대명사
vital for spatial memory, / is enlarged in taxi drivers. //
다른 연구는 보여준다 / 공간 기억에 필수적인 해마가 / 택시 운전사에게서 확대되는 것을 //
          '요점은 ~이다'   주격 보어절 접속사
The point is / **that** the physical architecture of the brain changes
/ according to where we direct our attention / and what we
practice doing. // 단서5 어디에 주의를 집중하고 무엇을 연습하는지에 따라 뇌의 구조가 바뀜
요점은 / 뇌의 물리적 구조가 달라진다는 것이다 / 우리가 어디에 주의를 기울이고 무엇을
연습하느냐에 따라 //

- evidence ⓝ 증거
- attention ⓝ 주의 집중
- eyesight ⓝ 시력
- represent ⓥ 나타내다
- spatial ⓐ 공간의
- architecture ⓝ 건축, 설계
- demonstrate ⓥ 보여주다
- auditory ⓐ 청각의
- dramatic ⓐ 극적인
- precisely ⓐⓓ 정확하게
- enlarge ⓥ 확대하다
- direct ⓥ 지시하다
- sharp ⓐ 예리한
- expansion ⓝ 확장
- vital ⓐ 중요한
- physical ⓐ 신체적인

주의 집중이 **뇌의 재구조화**로 이어진다는 과학적 증거는 많이 있다. (예를 들어 사냥하거나 사냥감이 되는 것을 피하기 위해) 소리를 알아채는 것에 대한 보상을 받은 동물에서 우리는 뇌의 청각 중추가 훨씬 더 큰 것을 발견한다. 예리한 시력에 대한 보상을 받은 동물은 시각 영역이 더 크다. 바이올린 연주자의 뇌 스캔 결과는 더 많은 증거를 제공해서 종종 매우 빠른 속도로 현을 정확하게 켜야 하는 왼손을 나타내는 피질 영역의 극적인 성장과 확장을 보여준다. 다른 연구는 공간 기억에 필수적인 해마가 택시 운전사에게서 확대되는 것을 보여준다. 요점은 우리가 어디에 주의를 기울이고 무엇을 연습하느냐에 따라 뇌의 물리적 구조가 달라진다는 것이다.

다음 빈칸에 들어갈 말로 가장 적절한 것을 고르시오.

① improved decision making 의사 결정에 관한 내용이 아님
　향상된 의사 결정
②the reshaping of the brain 뇌의 구조가 변하게 됨
　뇌의 재구조화
③ long-term mental tiredness 정신적 피로에 관한 내용이 아님
　장기간의 정신적 피로
④ the development of hand skills 손 재주가 아닌 뇌의 구조가 발달함
　손 재주의 발달
⑤ increased levels of self-control 자기 통제력에 관한 내용이 아님
　증가된 자기 통제 수준

| 문제 풀이 순서 | ✳✳❀ [정답률 64%]

1st 빈칸이 포함된 문장을 읽고, 빈칸에 들어갈 말에 대한 단서를 얻는다.

빈칸 문장
There's a lot of scientific evidence demonstrating that focused attention leads to _____.
주의 집중이 _____로 이어진다는 과학적 증거는 많다.

➡ 주의 집중이 '무엇'으로 이어지는지에 대한 증거가 많다고 했으므로, (단서) 집중에 따라서 '무슨' 일이 일어나는지에 대한 과학적 증거들이 이어질 것이다. (발상)

2nd 글의 나머지 부분을 확인해서 정답을 찾는다.

증거**1**: 청각에 대한 보상이 큰 동물은 뇌의 청각 중추가 큼
증거**2**: 시력에 대한 보상이 큰 동물은 뇌의 시각 영역이 큼
증거**3**: 바이올린 연주자는 왼손을 나타내는 피질 영역이 성장하고 확장됨
증거**4**: 택시 운전사는 공간 기억에 필수적인 해마가 확대됨

➡ 주의를 집중하는 영역에 따라 그에 필요한 뇌의 부위가 커져서 뇌의 구조가 바뀐다는 과학적 증거들을 열거했다.
▶ 주의 집중으로 인해 뇌의 영역이나 구조가 변화한다, 즉 ② '뇌의 재구조화'로 이어진다는 과학적 증거가 많다.

| 선택지 분석 |

① improved decision making　향상된 의사 결정
주의 집중이 의사 결정을 향상되게 한다는 내용이 아니다.

②the reshaping of the brain　뇌의 재구조화
주의를 어디에 집중하고 연습하는지에 따라 뇌의 재구조화가 일어난다.

③ long-term mental tiredness　장기간의 정신적 피로
주의 집중이 장기간의 정신적 피로를 초래한다는 내용이 아니다.

④ the development of hand skills　손 재주의 발달
손 재주가 아닌 해당 부분의 뇌 구조가 발달한다는 내용이다.

⑤ increased levels of self-control　증가된 자기 통제 수준
주의 집중이 자기 통제 수준을 증가시킨다는 내용이 아니다.

33 정답 ⑤ ＊인간의 뇌가 진화한 이유 ──────

How did the human mind evolve? // 인간의 생각은 어떻게 진화했을까 //
One possibility is / that **competition and conflicts with other human tribes** / caused our brains to evolve the way they did. //
한 가지 가능성은 / 다른 인간 부족과의 경쟁과 갈등이 / 우리 두뇌가 그렇게 진화하도록 했다는 것이다 //
A human tribe that could out-think its enemies, even slightly, / possessed a vital advantage. // 단서**1** 적보다 더 우수한 생각을 하는 부족은 우위를 가짐
적보다 조금이라도 더 우수한 생각을 할 수 있는 인간 부족은 / 중요한 우위를 점했다 //

The ability of your tribe / to imagine and predict where and when a hostile enemy tribe might strike, / and plan accordingly, / gives your tribe / a significant military advantage. //
부족의 능력은 / 적대적인 적 부족이 언제 어디서 공격할지 상상하고 예측하며 / 그에 따라 계획을 세울 수 있는 / 부족에게 가져다준다 / 상당한 군사적 우위를 //

The human mind became a weapon / in the struggle for survival, / a weapon far more decisive than any before it. //
인간의 생각은 무기가 되었다 / 생존을 위한 투쟁에서 / 그 이전의 어떤 무기보다 훨씬 더 결정적인 무기인 // 단서**2** 인간의 생각은 생존을 위한 투쟁에서 가장 중요한 무기가 됨

And this mental advantage was applied, over and over, / within each succeeding generation. // 단서**3** 생각이 더 우수한 부족이 승리할 확률이 높고 그러한 유전자를 자손에게 물려줌
그리고 이러한 정신적 우위는 계속해서 적용되었다 / 다음 세대에 걸쳐 //
The tribe that could out-think its opponents / was more likely to succeed in battle / and would then pass on the genes / responsible for this mental advantage / to its offspring. //
상대보다 더 우수한 생각을 할 수 있는 부족은 / 전투에서 승리할 확률이 높았고 / 이러한 유전자를 물려주었다 / 정신적 우위를 담당하는 / 자손에게 //
You and I / are the descendants of the winners. //
당신과 나는 / 승자의 후손이다 //

- evolve ⓥ 진화하다　- possibility ⓝ 가능성　- tribe ⓝ 부족
- out-think ⓥ ~보다 우수한 생각을 하다　- slightly ⓐⓓ 약간
- possess ⓥ 소유하다　- vital ⓐ 중요한　- predict ⓥ 예측하다
- hostile ⓐ 적대적인　- accordingly ⓐⓓ 그에 맞춰
- decisive ⓐ 결정적인　- succeeding ⓐ 다음의
- opponent ⓝ 반대자　- offspring ⓝ 자손　- descendant ⓝ 후손

인간의 생각은 어떻게 진화했을까? 한 가지 가능성은 **다른 인간 부족과의 경쟁과 갈등**이 우리 두뇌가 그렇게 진화하도록 했다는 것이다. 적보다 조금이라도 더 우수한 생각을 할 수 있는 인간 부족은 중요한 우위를 점했다. 적대적인 적 부족이 언제 어디서 공격할지 상상하고 예측하며 그에 따라 계획을 세울 수 있는 능력은 부족에게 상당한 군사적 우위를 가져다준다. 인간의 생각은 생존을 위한 투쟁에서 그 이전의 어떤 무기보다 훨씬 더 결정적인 무기가 되었다. 그리고 이러한 정신적 우위는 다음 세대에 걸쳐 계속해서 적용되었다. 상대보다 더 우수한 생각을 할 수 있는 부족은 전투에서 승리할 확률이 높았고, 이러한 정신적 우위를 담당하는 유전자를 자손에게 물려주었다. 당신과 나는 승자의 후손이다.

다음 빈칸에 들어갈 말로 가장 적절한 것을 고르시오. [3점]

① physical power to easily hunt prey 신체 능력에 대한 언급 없음
　먹이를 쉽게 사냥할 수 있는 신체 능력
② individual responsibility in one's inner circle 책임에 관한 언급 없음
　내부 세력 안에서의 개인적 책임
③ instinctive tendency to avoid natural disasters 자연재해에 관한 언급 없음
　자연재해를 피하기 위한 본능적인 경향
④ superiority in the number of one's descendants 자손의 수에 대한 언급 없음
　자손의 수에서의 우위
⑤competition and conflicts with other human tribes
　다른 인간 부족과의 경쟁과 갈등
　정신적 우위를 가진 부족이 다른 부족과의 경쟁과 갈등에서 유리했고 이를 자손에게 물려줌

| 문제 풀이 순서 | ✳✳✳ [정답률 55%]

1st 빈칸이 포함된 문장 주변을 읽고, 빈칸에 들어갈 말에 대한 단서를 얻는다.

빈칸 앞 문장	How did the human mind evolve? 인간의 생각은 어떻게 진화했을까?
빈칸 문장	One possibility is that _____ caused our brains to evolve the way they did. 한 가지 가능성은 _____ 이 우리 두뇌가 그렇게 진화하도록 했다는 것이다.

➡ 빈칸 앞 문장에서 인간의 생각이 진화한 과정에 관하여 질문을 던졌고, 빈칸 문장은 우리 두뇌가 진화하도록 한 '무엇'이 한 가지 가능성이라고 했으므로, (단서) 우리 두뇌가 그렇게 진화하도록 한 것이 '무엇'인지 뒤에서 설명할 것이다. (발상)

2nd 글의 내용을 종합해서 빈칸에 들어갈 적절한 말을 찾는다.

- 적보다 조금이라도 더 우수한 생각을 할 수 있는 인간 부족은 중요한 우위를 점했다. **단서 1**
- 인간의 생각은 생존을 위한 투쟁에서 그 어떤 무기보다 훨씬 더 결정적인 무기가 되었다. **단서 2**
- 상대보다 더 우수한 생각을 할 수 있는 부족은 전투에서 승리할 확률이 높았고, 이러한 정신적 우위를 담당하는 유전자를 자손에게 물려주었다. **단서 3**
→ 적보다 더 뛰어난 생각을 할 수 있는 부족은 전투에서 승리할 확률이 높았고 생존에 유리했기 때문에, 이러한 유전자를 자손에게 물려주었다고 했다. 다른 부족보다 우수한 생각을 해야만 그들을 이기고 살아남았으므로 빈칸에는 다른 부족과의 경쟁이나 갈등에 관한 내용이 들어가야 한다.

3rd 글의 내용을 다시 한번 정리하며 이해한 중심 내용을 선택지에서 고른다.

우리의 뇌가 이렇게 진화하게 된 이유는 더 뛰어난 생각을 하는 인간 부족이 생존을 위한 투쟁에서 더 유리했고 그러한 유전자를 자손에게 물려주었기 때문이므로 빈칸에는 ⑤ '다른 인간 부족과의 경쟁과 갈등'이 들어가야 한다.

| 선택지 분석 |

① **physical power to easily hunt prey**
먹이를 쉽게 사냥할 수 있는 신체 능력
먹이 사냥을 위한 신체 능력이 아니라 뛰어난 정신적 능력이 우위를 가져다주었다.

② **individual responsibility in one's inner circle**
내부 세력 안에서의 개인적 책임
부족 내의 세력이나 개인적인 책임에 관한 내용은 언급되지 않았다.

③ **instinctive tendency to avoid natural disasters**
자연재해를 피하기 위한 본능적 경향
자연재해를 피하기 위한 본능에 관한 내용은 언급되지 않았다.

④ **superiority in the number of one's descendants**
자손의 수에서의 우위
자손의 수가 많은 것이 우리의 뇌를 진화하게 만든 것이 아니다.

⑤ **competition and conflicts with other human tribes**
다른 인간 부족과의 경쟁과 갈등
적과의 싸움에서 정신적 우위를 가진 부족이 유리했고 이러한 유전자로 진화할 수 있었다.

---

34 정답 ① ＊집단 지성을 위한 brainwriting 과정 ━━━━

To find the hidden potential in teams, / instead of brainstorming, / we're **better off** shifting to a process **called brainwriting**. //
팀의 숨겨진 잠재력을 찾으려면 / 브레인스토밍 대신 / 브레인라이팅이라는 과정으로 전환하는 것이 좋다 //
〔**단서 1** 팀의 잠재력을 찾는 과정으로 브레인라이팅이 제시됨〕

The initial steps are solo. //
초기 단계는 혼자서 진행한다 //
〔**단서 2** 개별적으로 아이디어를 냄〕

You start by asking everyone / to generate ideas separately. //
먼저 모든 사람에게 요청한다 / 개별적으로 아이디어를 내도록 //

Next, / you pool them / and share them anonymously among the group. //
그런 다음 / 아이디어를 모아 / 익명으로 그룹에 공유한다 //

To preserve independent judgment, / each member evaluates them on their own. // 〔**단서 3** 독립적으로 아이디어를 스스로 평가함〕
독립적인 판단을 유지하기 위해 / 각 구성원이 스스로 그 아이디어를 평가한다 //

Only then does the team come together / to select and refine the most promising options. // 〔**단서 4** 팀이 모여 옵션을 선택하고 다듬음〕
그러고 나서야 팀이 함께 모여 / 가장 유망한 옵션을 선택하고 다듬는다 //

By **developing and assessing ideas individually** / before choosing and elaborating them, / teams can surface and advance possibilities / that might not get attention otherwise. //
개별적으로 아이디어를 전개하고 평가함으로써 / 아이디어를 선택하고 구체화하기 전에 / 팀은 가능성을 드러내고 발전시킬 수 있다 / 다른 방법으로는 주목받지 못했을 //

This brainwriting process **makes sure** / **that** all ideas are brought to the table / and all voices are brought into the conversation. //
이 브레인라이팅 과정은 보장한다 / 모든 아이디어를 테이블에 올려놓고 / 모든 의견을 대화에 반영할 수 있도록 //

It is especially effective / in groups **that** struggle to achieve collective intelligence. //
특히 효과적이다 / 집단 지성을 달성하는 데 어려움을 겪는 그룹에서 //

- **potential** ⓝ 잠재력   • **shift** ⓥ 바꾸다   • **initial** ⓐ 초기의
- **generate** ⓥ 발생하다   • **separately** ⓐⓓ 따로, 별도로
- **pool** ⓥ 모으다   • **preserve** ⓥ 보존하다   • **judgment** ⓝ 판단
- **evaluate** ⓥ 평가하다   • **refine** ⓥ 다듬다   • **promising** ⓐ 유망한
- **elaborate** ⓥ 정교하게 말하다   • **advance** ⓥ 발전시키다
- **struggle to ~** ~하기 위해 애쓰다   • **collective** ⓐ 집단적인
- **intelligence** ⓝ 지능

팀의 숨겨진 잠재력을 찾으려면 브레인스토밍 대신 브레인라이팅이라는 과정으로 전환하는 것이 좋다. 초기 단계는 혼자서 진행한다. 먼저 모든 사람에게 개별적으로 아이디어를 내도록 요청한다. 그런 다음, 아이디어를 모아 익명으로 그룹에 공유한다. 독립적인 판단을 유지하기 위해 각 구성원이 스스로 그 아이디어를 평가한다. 그리고 나서야 팀이 함께 모여 가장 유망한 옵션을 선택하고 다듬는다. 아이디어를 선택하고 구체화하기 전에 **개별적으로 아이디어를 전개하고 평가함**으로써 팀은 다른 방법으로는 주목받지 못했을 가능성을 드러내고 발전시킬 수 있다. 이 브레인라이팅 과정은 모든 아이디어를 테이블에 올려놓고 모든 의견을 대화에 반영할 수 있도록 한다. 특히 집단 지성을 달성하는 데 어려움을 겪는 그룹에서 효과적이다.

다음 빈칸에 들어갈 말로 가장 적절한 것을 고르시오. [3점]
① developing and assessing ideas individually
개별적으로 아이디어를 전개하고 평가하기
② presenting and discussing ideas out loud
큰 소리로 아이디어를 발표하고 토론하기
③ assigning different roles to each member
각 구성원에게 다른 역할 할당하기
④ coming to an agreement on these options
이 옵션들에 대한 합의에 도달하기
⑤ skipping the step of judging these options
이 옵션들을 판단하는 단계 건너뛰기

〔① 아이디어를 선택하고 다듬기 전에는 개별적으로 아이디어를 전개하고 평가함〕
〔② 개별적으로 아이디어를 평가하는 것이 핵심임〕
〔③ 구성원의 역할 할당에 관한 내용이 아님〕
〔④ 옵션을 선택하고 다듬기 전에는 개별적으로 아이디어를 전개하고 평가해야 함〕
〔⑤ 개별적으로 평가하는 단계를 거쳐야 함〕

| 문제 풀이 순서 | ★★★ [정답률 46%]

1st 빈칸이 포함된 문장을 읽고, 빈칸에 들어갈 말에 대한 단서를 얻는다.

| 빈칸 문장 | By _____ before choosing and elaborating them, teams can surface and advance possibilities that might not get attention otherwise.
아이디어를 선택하고 구체화하기 전에 _____ 함으로써 팀은 다른 방법으로는 주목받지 못했을 가능성을 드러내고 발전시킬 수 있다. |

→ 아이디어를 선택하고 구체화하기 전에 '무엇'을 함으로써 팀이 가능성을 발전시킬 수 있다고 했으므로, 〔**단서**〕 아이디어를 선택하고 구체화하기 전의 과정이 빈칸 문장보다 앞에 나올 것이다. 〔**발상**〕

2nd **1st** 에서 찾은 단서를 염두에 두고, 빈칸 문장의 앞부분부터 확인한다.

- 팀의 잠재력을 찾으려면 브레인라이팅이라는 과정으로 전환하는 것이 좋다. **단서 1**
- 먼저 모든 사람에게 개별적으로 아이디어를 내도록 요청한다. **단서 2**
- 독립적인 판단을 유지하기 위해 각 구성원이 스스로 그 아이디어를 평가한다. **단서 3**
- 그러고 나서야 팀이 함께 모여 가장 유망한 옵션을 선택하고 다듬는다. **단서 4**

→ 개별적으로 아이디어를 내고 각 구성원이 스스로 그것을 평가하고 나서야 팀이 옵션을 선택하고 다듬는다(구체화한다)는 브레인라이팅 과정을 설명했다. 즉, 아이디어를 선택하고 다듬기 전의 과정은 개별적으로 아이디어를 내고 평가하는 것이다.

▶ 빈칸 문장은 〈아이디어를 구체화하고 선택하기 전에 ① '개별적으로 아이디어를 전개하고 평가함'으로써 팀은 다른 방법으로는 주목받지 못했을 가능성을 드러내고 발전시킬 수 있다.〉라는 내용이 되어야 한다.

3rd 글의 내용을 다시 한번 정리하며 정답이 맞는지 확인한다.

팀에서 개별적으로 낸 아이디어를 평가하고, 그중 유망한 옵션을 선택하고 다듬는 브레인라이팅 과정에 대한 글이다. 따라서 빈칸에는 ① '개별적으로 아이디어를 전개하고 평가하기'가 들어가는 것이 가장 적절하다.

| 선택지 분석 |

① **developing and assessing ideas individually**
개별적으로 아이디어를 전개하고 평가하기
아이디어를 선택하고 다듬기 전에는 개별적으로 아이디어를 전개하고 평가한다.

② **presenting and discussing ideas out loud**
큰 소리로 아이디어를 발표하고 토론하기
같이 모여 선택하기 전에 개별적으로 아이디어를 평가하는 것이 핵심이다.

③ **assigning different roles to each member**
각 구성원에게 다른 역할 할당하기
구성원의 역할 할당에 관한 내용이 아니다.

④ **coming to an agreement on these options**
이 옵션들에 대한 합의에 도달하기
옵션을 선택하고 다듬기 전에는 개별적으로 아이디어를 전개하고 평가해야 한다.

⑤ **skipping the step of judging these options**
이 옵션들을 판단하는 단계를 건너뛰기
각 구성원은 독립적인 판단을 위해서 개별적으로 평가하는 단계를 거친다.

---

35 정답 ③ ＊의사 결정 권한과 업무 생산성의 관계

다음 글에서 전체 흐름과 관계 없는 문장은?

Simply giving employees a sense of agency / — a feeling that they are in control, / that they have genuine decision-making authority — /
단순히 직원들에게 주인의식을 주는 것은 / (그들이 통제하고 있다는 느낌 / 진정한 의사 결정 권한이 있다는 느낌) /

can radically increase / how much energy and focus they bring to their jobs. // **단서 1** 직원들에게 주인의식을 주는 것은 그들이 업무에 쏟는 에너지와 집중력을 높임
급격하게 높일 수 있다 / 그들이 자신의 업무에 쏟는 에너지와 집중력을 //

① One 2010 study / at a manufacturing plant in Ohio, / for instance, / carefully examined assembly-line workers /
2010년의 한 연구는 / 오하이오주의 한 제조 공장에서 진행된 / 예를 들어 / 조립 라인 근로자를 주의 깊게 살펴보았다 /

who were empowered to make small decisions / about their schedules and work environment. // **단서 2** 직원들에게 결정 권한을 부여한 예시
작은 결정 권한을 부여받은 / 그들의 일정과 작업 환경에 대한 //

② They designed their own uniforms / and had authority over shifts / while all the manufacturing processes and pay scales stayed the same. //
그들은 그들 자신의 유니폼을 디자인했고 / 근무 교대에 대한 권한을 가졌다 / 모든 생산 과정과 임금 규모는 동일하게 유지된 반면에 //

③ It led to decreased efficiency / because their decisions were not uniform or focused on meeting organizational goals. //）
(그것은 효율성을 낮추는 결과를 낳았다 / 결정이 합치되거나 조직의 목표 달성에 초점이 맞춰지지 않았기 때문에 //)

④ Within two months, / productivity at the plant / increased by 20 percent, / with workers taking shorter breaks / and making fewer mistakes. // **단서 3** 생산성이 증가했음
두 달 만에 / 그 공장의 생산성은 / 20퍼센트 증가했다 / 직원들은 휴식 시간을 더 짧게 가졌고 / 실수를 더 적게 했다 //

⑤ Giving employees a sense of control / improved how much self-discipline they brought to their jobs. //
직원들에게 통제권을 쥐고 있다는 느낌을 주는 것이 / 그들이 업무에 끌어들이는 자기 통제력을 향상시켰다 // **단서 4** 주인의식이 업무에 대한 자기 통제력을 향상시킴

- agency ⓝ 행위자 • genuine ⓐ 진정한 • authority ⓝ 권한
- examine ⓥ 살펴보다 • assembly ⓝ 조립
- empower ⓥ (권한을) 부여하다 • scale ⓝ 규모
- efficiency ⓝ 효율성 • uniform ⓐ 똑같은
- organizational ⓐ 조직의 • productivity ⓝ 생산성
- self-discipline ⓝ 자기 통제력

단순히 직원들에게 주인의식(그들이 통제하고 있다는 느낌, 진정한 의사 결정 권한이 있다는 느낌)을 주는 것만으로도 그들이 자신의 업무에 쏟는 에너지와 집중력을 급격하게 높일 수 있다. ① 예를 들어, 오하이오주의 한 제조 공장에서 진행된 2010년의 한 연구는 그들의 일정과 작업 환경에 대한 작은 결정 권한을 부여받은 조립 라인 근로자를 주의 깊게 살펴보았다. ② 그들은 그들 자신의 유니폼을 디자인했고, 근무 교대에 대한 권한을 가진 반면에, 모든 생산 과정과 임금 규모는 동일하게 유지되었다. (③ 결정이 합치되거나 조직의 목표 달성에 초점이 맞춰지지 않았기 때문에 그것은 효율성을 낮추는 결과를 낳았다.) ④ 두 달 만에 직원들은 휴식 시간을 더 짧게 가졌고, 실수를 더 적게 하였으며, 그 공장의 생산성은 20퍼센트 증가했다. ⑤ 자신들이 통제권을 쥐고 있다는 느낌을 직원들에게 부여한 것이 그들이 업무에 끌어들이는 자기 통제력을 향상시켰다.

왜 정답·오답? ★★★ [정답률 58%]

첫 문장: 단순히 직원들에게 주인의식(그들이 통제하고 있다는 느낌, 진정한 의사 결정 권한이 있다는 느낌)을 주는 것만으로도 그들이 자신의 업무에 쏟는 에너지와 집중력을 급격하게 높일 수 있다.
➡ 직원에게 주인의식이 주어지면 업무에 대한 에너지와 집중력이 높아진다는 내용으로, 글의 주제문이다.

① 예를 들어, 오하이오주의 한 제조 공장에서 진행된 2010년의 한 연구는 그들의 일정과 작업 환경에 대한 작은 결정 권한을 부여받은 조립 라인 근로자를 주의 깊게 살펴보았다.
➡ 작은 결정 권한을 부여받은 한 공장 근로자들을 관찰한 연구를 소개하며 주제문을 뒷받침할 예시가 이어진다. ▶ ①은 무관한 문장이 아님

② 그들은 그들 자신의 유니폼을 디자인했고, 근무 교대에 대한 권한을 가진 반면에, 모든 생산 과정과 임금 규모는 동일하게 유지되었다.
➡ 앞에서 언급된 연구에 관한 부연 설명이 이어진다.
▶ ②은 무관한 문장이 아님

③ 결정이 합치되거나 조직의 목표 달성에 초점이 맞춰지지 않았기 때문에 그것은 효율성을 낮추는 결과를 낳았다.
➡ 주제문에 따르면 직원들에게 결정 권한을 주는 것이 긍정적인 효과를 불러온다고 했으므로, 효율성이 떨어졌다는 내용은 전체 글의 흐름에 맞지 않는다.
▶ ③이 무관한 문장임

④ 두 달 만에 직원들은 휴식 시간을 더 짧게 가졌고, 실수를 더 적게 하였으며, 그 공장의 생산성은 20퍼센트 증가했다.
➡ 직원들이 결정 권한을 부여받은 결과, 공장의 생산성이 증가했다고 하며 주제문을 뒷받침한다. ▶ ④은 무관한 문장이 아님

⑤ 자신들이 통제권을 쥐고 있다는 느낌을 직원들에게 부여한 것이 그들이 업무에 끌어들이는 자기 통제력을 향상시켰다.
➡ 직원들이 스스로 통제권(결정 권한)이 있다고 생각한 것이 업무에 대한 자기 통제력도 향상시키는 결과를 낳았다고 하며 주제문을 뒷받침한다.
▶ ⑤은 무관한 문장이 아님

＊ 글의 흐름

도입	직원들에게 주인의식을 주는 것만으로도 그들의 업무 능력을 높일 수 있음
연구	오하이오 주의 한 제조 공장에서 근로자에게 작은 결정 권한을 줬음
연구 결과	직원들의 업무 능력이 높아진 결과, 공장의 생산성도 증가함
부연	직원들이 통제권을 갖는다고 느낄 때 업무에서 자기 통제력이 높아짐

5회

정답 및 해설 **133**

단서1 디지털 비즈니스 활동이 환경에 덜 부정적인 영향을 미칠 거라 예상함

shift A to B: A를 B로 바꾸다
As businesses shift / some core business activities to digital, /
가주어   진주어(명사절 접속사)
such as sales, marketing, or archiving, / it is assumed that the
impact on the environment will be less negative. //
기업이 전환함에 따라 / 일부 핵심 비즈니스 활동을 디지털로 / 영업, 마케팅, 파일 보관
등과 같은 / 환경에 미치는 영향이 덜 부정적일 것으로 예상된다 //

과거분사
(A) When we store bigger data on clouds, / increased carbon
emissions make our green clouds gray. //
클라우드에 더 많은 데이터를 저장하면 / 증가된 탄소 배출량이 녹색 구름을 회색으로 변하게
만든다 // **단서2** (C)에서 언급된 '데이터 센터의 에너지원이 화석 연료인 것과 내용이 연결됨
과거분사구(mail 수식)
The carbon footprint of an email is smaller / than mail sent via a
post office, / but still, it causes four grams of CO_2, / and it can be
원급 비교
as much as 50 grams / if the attachment is big. //
이메일의 탄소 발자국은 더 적지만 / 우체국을 통해 보내는 우편물보다 / 여전히 4g의
이산화탄소를 유발하며 / 50g에 달할 수 있다 / 첨부 파일이 크면 //

(B) However, / digital business activities / can still threaten the
environment. // **단서3** 주어진 글의 내용과는 달리, 여전히 디지털 비즈니스 활동은 환경을 위협함
그러나 / 디지털 비즈니스 활동은 / 여전히 환경을 위협할 수 있다 //
In some cases, / the harm of digital businesses / can be even
more hazardous. //
경우에 따라서는 / 디지털 비즈니스가 끼치는 해악이 / 훨씬 더 위험할 수 있다 //
'~하곤 했다'
A few decades ago, / offices used to have much more paper
부사절 접속사(이유)
waste / since all documents were paper based. //
수십 년 전만 해도 / 사무실에서는 종이 폐기물이 훨씬 더 많았다 / 모든 문서가 종이로
작성되었기 때문에 // **단서4** (B)에서 언급된 종이의 디지털 전환은 나무를 보호하려는 조치였음
(C) When workplaces shifted from paper to digital documents,
형용사적 용법(step 수식)
invoices, and emails, / it was a promising step to save trees. //
직장에서 종이를 디지털 문서, (디지털) 송장, 이메일로 전환했을 때 / 그것은 나무를 보호할
수 있는 유망한 조치였다 //
However, / the cost of the Internet and electricity for the
environment / is neglected. //
하지만 / 인터넷과 전기가 환경에 입히는 손실은 / 간과되고 있다 //
목적어절 접속사
A recent *Wired* report declared / that most data centers' energy
source is fossil fuels. //
최근 Wired의 보고서는 말했다 / 대부분의 데이터 센터의 에너지원은 화석 연료라고 //

- shift ⓥ 전환하다 ・ archive ⓥ 보관하다 ・ assume ⓥ 추정하다
- store ⓥ 저장하다 ・ carbon ⓝ 탄소 ・ emission ⓝ 배출
- footprint ⓝ 발자국 ・ via prep ~을 통하여 ・ attachment ⓝ 첨부
- threaten ⓥ 위협하다 ・ harm ⓝ 해 ・ hazardous ⓐ 위험한
- promising ⓐ 유망한 ・ neglect ⓥ 소홀히 하다
- declare ⓥ 선언하다 ・ fossil fuel 화석 연료

기업이 영업, 마케팅, 파일 보관 등 일부 핵심 비즈니스 활동을 디지털로 전환함에 따라 환경에 미치는 영향이 덜 부정적일 것으로 예상된다. (B) 그러나 디지털 비즈니스 활동은 여전히 환경을 위협할 수 있다. 경우에 따라서는 디지털 비즈니스가 끼치는 해악이 훨씬 더 위험할 수 있다. 수십 년 전만 해도 사무실에서는 모든 문서가 종이로 작성되었기 때문에 종이 폐기물이 훨씬 더 많았다. (C) 직장에서 종이를 디지털 문서, (디지털) 송장, 이메일로 전환한 것은 나무를 보호할 수 있는 유망한 조치였다. 하지만 인터넷과 전기가 환경에 입히는 손실은 간과되고 있다. 최근 Wired의 보고서에 따르면 대부분의 데이터 센터의 에너지원은 화석 연료이다. (A) 클라우드에 더 많은 데이터를 저장할수록 탄소 배출량이 증가하여 녹색 구름을 회색으로 변하게 만든다. 이메일의 탄소 발자국은 우체국을 통해 보내는 우편물보다 적지만 여전히 4g의 이산화탄소를 유발하며 첨부 파일이 크면 50g에 달할 수 있다.

주어진 글 다음에 이어질 글의 순서로 가장 적절한 것을 고르시오. [3점]

① (A) ― (C) ― (B) (A)의 클라우드나 데이터 저장에 대한 언급은 주어진 글에 없음
② (B) ― (A) ― (C) (A)의 '탄소 배출량'에 대한 언급이 나온 이유는 (C)의 데이터 센터의
                     에너지원이 '화석 연료'이기 때문임
③ (B) ― (C) ― (A) 비즈니스 활동의 디지털 전환이 환경에 미치는 영향은 덜 부정적일
                     것으로 예상됨 ― (B) 디지털 비즈니스 활동은 여전히 환경을 위협함
④ (C) ― (A) ― (B) ― (C) 데이터 센터의 에너지원은 화석 연료임 ― (A) 더 많은
                     데이터를 저장할수록 탄소 배출량이 증가함
⑤ (C) ― (B) ― (A) (C)에서 언급된 종이 사용은 (B)에서 먼저 제시됨

| 문제 풀이 순서 | ✿✿✾ [정답률 61%]

1st 각 문단의 내용을 파악하고, 글의 논리적인 순서를 추론한다.

주어진 글: 기업이 영업, 마케팅, 파일 보관 등 일부 핵심 비즈니스 활동을
디지털로 전환함에 따라 환경에 미치는 영향이 덜 부정적일 것으로
예상된다.

➡ **주어진 글 뒤:** 비즈니스 활동의 디지털 전환이 환경에 미치는 영향에 관한 설명이
이어질 것이다.

(A): 클라우드에 더 많은 데이터를 저장할수록 탄소 배출량이 증가하여
녹색 구름을 회색으로 변하게 만든다. 이메일의 탄소 발자국은 우체국을
통해 보내는 우편물보다 적지만 여전히 4g의 이산화탄소를 유발하며 첨부
파일이 크면 50g에 달할 수 있다.

➡ **(A) 앞:** 데이터 저장과 탄소 배출량 사이의 관계가 앞에 제시되어야 한다.
  ▶ 주어진 글 바로 뒤에 (A)가 올 수 없음
  (A) 뒤: 디지털 비즈니스 활동이 탄소 배출을 증가시킨다는 구체적인 예시이므로
  (A)가 글의 마지막 부분일 가능성이 높다. ▶ (A)가 마지막에 올 확률이 높음

(B): 그러나(However) 디지털 비즈니스 활동은 여전히 환경을 위협할 수
있다. 경우에 따라서는 디지털 비즈니스가 끼치는 해악이 훨씬 더 위험할
수 있다. 수십 년 전만 해도 사무실에서는 모든 문서가 종이로 작성되었기
때문에 종이 폐기물이 훨씬 더 많았다.

➡ **(B) 앞:** 디지털 비즈니스 활동이 환경을 위협할 수 있다는 내용이 However로
이어지므로, 앞에는 비즈니스 활동의 디지털 전환이 환경에 미치는 영향이 덜
부정적이라고 한 주어진 글이 이어져야 한다.
  ▶ (B) 앞에 주어진 글이 와야 함 (순서: 주어진 글 ➡ (B))
  (B) 뒤: 문서가 종이에서 디지털로 전환되었다는 설명이 이어질 것이다.

(C): 직장에서 종이를 디지털 문서, (디지털) 송장, 이메일로 전환한 것은
나무를 보호할 수 있는 유망한 조치였다. 하지만 인터넷과 전기가 환경에
입히는 손실은 간과되고 있다. 최근 Wired의 보고서에 따르면 대부분의
데이터 센터의 에너지원은 화석 연료이다.

➡ **(C) 앞:** 수십 년 전만 해도 사무실에서 종이를 많이 사용했다고 언급한 (B)에
이어지는 내용이다. ▶ (C) 앞에 (B)가 와야 함 (순서: 주어진 글 ➡ (B) ➡ (C))
  (C) 뒤: 데이터 센터의 에너지원이 화석 연료라고 밝혔으므로, 데이터를
  저장할수록 탄소 배출량이 증가한다고 언급한 (A)가 이어져야 한다.
  ▶ (C) 뒤에 (A)가 이어져야 함 (순서: 주어진 글 ➡ (B) ➡ (C) ➡ (A))

2nd 글이 한눈에 들어오도록 정리하여 정답을 확인한다.

주어진 글: 디지털 비즈니스 활동이 환경에 미치는 영향은 덜 부정적일 것이라
예상된다.

➡ **(B):** 그러나 디지털 비즈니스 활동은 여전히 환경을 위협한다. 옛 사무실에서는
종이를 많이 사용했다.

➡ **(C):** 종이에서 디지털로 전환했지만, 인터넷과 전기가 환경에 입히는 손실이 있다.
데이터 센터의 에너지원은 화석 연료이다.

➡ **(A):** 디지털로 더 많은 데이터를 저장할수록 탄소 배출량이 증가한다. 첨부 파일이
큰 이메일의 경우 오히려 우편물보다 탄소 발자국은 더 많다.

  ▶ 주어진 글 다음에 이어질 글의 순서는 (B) ➡ (C) ➡ (A)이므로 정답은 ③임

37 정답 ② ＊외래종의 유입이 생태계에 미치는 영향

Problems often arise / if an exotic species is suddenly introduced / to an ecosystem. //
문제가 종종 발생한다 / 외래종이 갑자기 유입되면 / 생태계에 //

(A) The grey had the edge / because it can adapt its diet; / it is able, for instance, to eat green acorns, / while the red can only digest mature acorns. //
부사절 접속사 (대조)
단서 1 회색 다람쥐가 (붉은색 다람쥐보다) 먹이에 있어서 우위를 점함
회색 다람쥐는 우위를 점했다 / 먹이를 조절할 수 있기 때문에 / 예를 들어 회색 다람쥐는 설익은 도토리를 먹을 수 있다 / 반면 붉은 다람쥐는 다 익은 도토리만 소화할 수 있다 //

Within the same area of forest, / grey squirrels can destroy the food supply / before red squirrels even have a bite. //
숲의 같은 지역 내에서 / 회색 다람쥐는 식량 공급을 파괴할 수 있다 / 붉은 다람쥐가 한 입 먹기도 전에 //

(B) Britain's red and grey squirrels / provide a clear example. //
단서 2 외래종 유입으로 인한 문제의 예시를 제공
영국의 붉은색 다람쥐와 회색 다람쥐가 / 명확한 예를 제공한다 //

When the grey arrived from America in the 1870s, / both squirrel species competed / for the same food and habitat, / which put the native red squirrel populations under pressure. //
계속적 용법의 주격 관계대명사
1870년대 미국에서 회색 다람쥐가 왔을 때 / 두 다람쥐 종은 경쟁했고 / 동일한 먹이와 서식지를 놓고 / 이것이 토종의 붉은 다람쥐 개체군을 압박했다 //

(C) Greys can also live more densely and in varied habitats, / so have survived more easily / when woodland has been destroyed. //
병렬 구조(부사구)
앞에 주어 생략(Greys)
단서 3 회색 다람쥐가 생존에 더 강한 이유를 추가로 제시함
회색 다람쥐는 또한 더 밀집하며 다양한 서식지에서 살 수 있어서 / 더 쉽게 살아남았다 / 삼림이 파괴되었을 때 //

As a result, / the red squirrel has come close to extinction in England. //
단서 4 결국 붉은색 다람쥐는 멸종 위기에 처함
그 결과 / 붉은 다람쥐는 영국에서 거의 멸종 위기에 이르렀다 //

- arise ⓥ 생기다
- exotic ⓐ 이국적인
- species ⓝ 종
- introduce ⓥ 도입하다
- adapt ⓥ 적응하다
- digest ⓥ 소화하다
- mature ⓐ 익은
- compete ⓥ 경쟁하다
- native ⓐ 토종의
- densely ⓐ𝑑 밀집하게
- varied ⓐ 다양한
- habitat ⓝ 서식지
- extinction ⓝ 멸종

외래종이 갑자기 생태계에 유입되면 문제가 종종 발생한다. (B) 영국의 붉은색 다람쥐와 회색 다람쥐가 명확한 예를 제공한다. 1870년대 미국에서 회색 다람쥐가 왔을 때, 두 다람쥐 종은 동일한 먹이와 서식지를 놓고 경쟁했고, 이것이 토종의 붉은 다람쥐 개체군을 압박했다. (A) 회색 다람쥐는 먹이를 조절할 수 있기 때문에 우위를 점했다. 예를 들어 회색 다람쥐는 설익은 도토리를 먹을 수 있는 반면, 붉은 다람쥐는 다 익은 도토리만 소화할 수 있다. 숲의 같은 지역 내에서 회색 다람쥐는 붉은 다람쥐가 한 입 먹기도 전에 식량 공급을 파괴할 수 있다. (C) 회색 다람쥐는 또한 더 밀집하며 다양한 서식지에서 살 수 있어서 삼림이 파괴되었을 때 더 쉽게 살아남았다. 그 결과, 붉은 다람쥐는 영국에서 거의 멸종 위기에 이르렀다.

주어진 글 다음에 이어질 글의 순서로 가장 적절한 것을 고르시오.
(A)에서 얘기하고 있는 다람쥐에 대한 언급이 주어진 글에 없음
① (A) ― (C) ― (B)
외래종이 갑자기 유입되면 생태계에 문제가 발생함 ― (B) 영국의 토종 붉은색 다람쥐와 미국에서 유입된 회색 다람쥐의 예시 ― (A) 회색 다람쥐가
② (B) ― (A) ― (C)
먹이 조절에서 더 우위를 차지함 ― (C) 또한 회색 다람쥐가 삼림이 파괴되었을 때 더 쉽게 생존할 수 있으므로 결국 붉은 다람쥐는 멸종 위기에 처함
③ (B) ― (C) ― (A)
(C)의 '그 결과'로 나타나는 붉은색 다람쥐의 멸종 이유는 (A)에서 처음으로 제시됨
④ (C) ― (A) ― (B)
붉은색 다람쥐와 회색 다람쥐의 예를 처음으로 언급한 (B)가
⑤ (C) ― (B) ― (A)
맨 앞에 와야 함

| 문제 풀이 순서 | ★★☆ [정답률 71%]

1st 각 문단의 내용을 파악하고, 글의 논리적인 순서를 추론한다.

주어진 글: 외래종이 갑자기 생태계에 유입되면 문제가 종종 발생한다.

➡ **주어진 글 뒤:** 외래종이 유입되면 어떤 문제가 발생하는지에 대한 내용이 이어질 것이다.

(A): 회색 다람쥐는 먹이를 조절할 수 있기 때문에 우위를 점했다. 예를 들어 회색 다람쥐는 설익은 도토리를 먹을 수 있는 반면, 붉은 다람쥐는 다 익은 도토리만 소화할 수 있다. 숲의 같은 지역 내에서 회색 다람쥐는 붉은 다람쥐가 한 입 먹기도 전에 식량 공급을 파괴할 수 있다.

➡ **(A) 앞:** 회색 다람쥐와 붉은색 다람쥐에 관한 정보가 앞에 나와야 한다.
▶ 주어진 글 바로 뒤에 (A)가 올 수 없음
(A) 뒤: 붉은색 다람쥐가 불리하다는 내용이 이어지거나 그 결과가 제시될 것이다.

(B): 영국의 붉은색 다람쥐와 회색 다람쥐가 명확한 예(example)를 제공한다. 1870년대 미국에서 회색 다람쥐가 왔을 때, 두 다람쥐 종은 동일한 먹이와 서식지를 놓고 경쟁했고, 이것이 토종의 붉은 다람쥐 개체군을 압박했다.

➡ **(B) 앞:** 토종 붉은색 다람쥐와 외래종 회색 다람쥐가 어떤 경우의 예인지 제시되어야 하는데, 주어진 글에 외래종의 유입으로 인한 생태계 문제가 언급되었으므로 주어진 글에 이어지는 내용이다.
▶ (B) 앞에 주어진 글이 와야 함 (순서: 주어진 글 ➡ (B))
(B) 뒤: 회색 다람쥐가 어떻게 붉은 다람쥐를 압박했는지가 이어져야 한다. 구체적인 내용으로서 먹이 조절을 언급한 (A)가 이어질 수도 있지만, (C)의 내용도 확인해야 한다.

(C): 회색 다람쥐는 또한(also) 더 밀집하며 다양한 서식지에서 살 수 있어서 삼림이 파괴되었을 때 더 쉽게 살아남았다. 그 결과, 붉은 다람쥐는 영국에서 거의 멸종 위기에 이르렀다.

➡ **(C) 앞:** 또 다른 내용을 나타내는 also가 있으므로, 회색 다람쥐가 붉은 다람쥐보다 우위를 점한 첫 번째 이유로서 회색 다람쥐가 먹이를 조절할 수 있다고 언급한 (A)가 앞에 와야 한다.
▶ (C) 앞에 (A)가 와야 함 (순서: 주어진 글 ➡ (B) ➡ (A) ➡ (C))

2nd 글이 한눈에 들어오도록 정리하여 정답을 확인한다.

주어진 글: 외래종이 생태계에 유입되면 문제가 발생한다.
➡ **(B):** 그 예로, 영국의 토종 붉은색 다람쥐와 외래종 회색 다람쥐가 경쟁하였고 회색 다람쥐가 붉은색 다람쥐를 압박했다.
➡ **(A):** 먹이 조절에서 회색 다람쥐가 우위를 갖고 있으므로 회색 다람쥐는 붉은색 다람쥐의 식량 공급을 파괴할 수 있었다.
➡ **(C):** 또한 회색 다람쥐가 더 밀집하여 다양한 서식지에 살기 때문에 삼림이 파괴되었을 때 더 쉽게 생존한다. 그 결과 토종인 붉은색 다람쥐는 멸종 위기에 처했다.
▶ 주어진 글 다음에 이어질 글의 순서는 (B) ➡ (A) ➡ (C)이므로 정답은 ②임

38 정답 ③ ＊농업이 인구 증가에 미친 영향

글의 흐름으로 보아, 주어진 문장이 들어가기에 가장 적절한 곳을 고르시오.

Farmers, on the other hand, / could live in the same place year after year / and did not have to worry / about transporting young children long distances. //
병렬 구조
단서 1 반면 농부들은 같은 장소에서 오래 살 수 있었음
농부들은 반면에 / 매년 같은 장소에서 살 수 있었고 / 걱정을 하지 않아도 되었다 / 어린아이를 장거리 이동시켜야 하는 //

Growing crops / forced **people to stay** in one place. //
_{forced의 목적어와 목적격 보어(to부정사)}
농작물 재배는 / 사람들이 한곳에 머무르게 했다 //

Hunter-gatherers typically moved around frequently, / and they had to be able to carry all their possessions with them / every time they moved. //
수렵 채집인들은 일반적으로 자주 이동해야 했고 / 모든 소유물을 가지고 다닐 수 있어야 했다 / 이동할 때마다 //

(①) In particular, / mothers / had to carry their young children. //
특히 / 어머니들은 / 어린아이를 업고 이동해야 했다 //

단서 2 수렵 채집인 어머니들은 이동의 부담으로 출산 간격을 둠

(②) As a result, / hunter-gatherer mothers could have only one baby / every four years or so, / **spacing their births** / **so that** they never had to carry more than one child at a time. //
_{분사구문 (그래서) ~할 수 있도록}
그 결과 / 수렵 채집인 어머니들은 한 명의 아이만 낳을 수 있었고 / 대략 4년마다 / 출산 간격을 두었다 / 한 번에 한 명 이상의 아이를 업고 다닐 필요가 없도록 //

(③) **Societies** **that** settled down in one place / **were** able to shorten their birth intervals / from four years to about two. //
_{복수 주어 주격 관계대명사 복수 동사}
한곳에 정착하게 된 사회는 / 출산 간격을 단축할 수 있었다 / 4년에서 약 2년으로 //

단서 3 정착한 사회는 출산 간격을 단축할 수 있음

(④) This meant / **that** each woman could have more children / than her hunter-gatherer counterpart, / **which** in turn resulted in rapid population growth / among farming communities. //
_{목적어절 접속사 계속적 용법의 주격 관계대명사(앞 문장 전체 수식)}
이는 의미했다 / 여성 한 명이 더 많은 아이를 낳을 수 있다는 것을 / 수렵 채집인인 상대보다 / 그 결과 그것은 급격한 인구 증가를 야기했다 / 농경 사회에서 //

(⑤) An increased population was actually an advantage / to agricultural societies, / because farming required large amounts of human labor. //
인구 증가는 실제로 유리했다 / 농경 사회에 / 왜냐하면 농사는 많은 인간의 노동력을 필요로 했기 때문이다 //

- transport ⓥ 이동시키다 · distance ⓝ 거리 · crop ⓝ 농작물
- typically ⓐⓓ 보통, 일반적으로 · frequently ⓐⓓ 자주, 빈번하게
- possession ⓝ 소유 · space ⓥ 간격을 두다 · birth ⓝ 출산
- settle down 정착하다 · shorten ⓥ 단축하다 · interval ⓝ 간격
- rapid ⓐ 빠른 · labor ⓝ 노동력

농작물 재배는 사람들이 한곳에 머무르게 했다. 수렵 채집인들은 일반적으로 자주 이동해야 했고, 이동할 때마다 모든 소유물을 가지고 다닐 수 있어야 했다. (①) 특히, 어머니들은 어린아이를 업고 이동해야 했다. (②) 그 결과, 수렵 채집인 어머니들은 대략 4년마다 한 명의 아이만 낳을 수 있었고, 한 번에 한 명 이상의 아이를 업고 다닐 필요가 없도록 출산 간격을 두었다. (③ 반면, 농부들은 매년 같은 장소에서 살 수 있었고 어린아이를 장거리 이동시켜야 하는 걱정을 하지 않아도 되었다.) 한곳에 정착하게 된 사회는 출산 간격을 4년에서 약 2년으로 단축할 수 있었다. (④) 이는 여성 한 명이 수렵 채집인인 상대보다 더 많은 아이를 낳을 수 있다는 것을 의미했고, 그 결과 그것은 농경 사회에서 급격한 인구 증가를 야기했다. (⑤) 인구 증가는 실제로 농경 사회에 유리했는데, 왜냐하면 농사는 많은 인간의 노동력을 필요로 했기 때문이다.

| 문제 풀이 순서 | ★★★ [정답률 48%]

1st 주어진 문장을 해석하고, 연결어, 지시어 등을 확인한다.

Farmers, on the other hand, could live in the same place year after year and did not have to worry about transporting young children long distances.
_{반면,} 농부들은 매년 같은 장소에서 살 수 있었고 어린아이를 장거리 이동시켜야 하는 걱정을 하지 않아도 되었다.

➡ **주어진 문장 앞:** 반대되는 내용을 나타내는 on the other hand가 있으므로, **단서**
농부들과는 상황이 반대인 사람들이 언급될 것이다. **발상**
주어진 문장 뒤: 이동하지 않아도 되는 농부들의 상황에 대한 설명이 이어질 것이다.

2nd 각 선택지의 앞뒤 흐름이 자연스러운지 확인한다.

- ①의 앞 문장과 뒤 문장
앞 문장: 수렵 채집인들은 일반적으로 자주 이동해야 했고, 이동할 때마다 모든 소유물을 가지고 다닐 수 있어야 했다.
뒤 문장: 특히, 어머니들은 어린아이를 업고 이동해야 했다.

➡ 농부들과 상황이 반대인 사람들로 수렵 채집인들이 언급되었고, 이들이 자주 이동해야 해서 어머니들이 어린아이를 업고 이동해야 했다는 내용이 앞으로 이어진다. ▶ 주어진 문장이 ①에 들어갈 수 없음

- ②의 앞 문장과 뒤 문장
앞 문장: ①의 뒤 문장과 같음
뒤 문장: 그 결과, 수렵 채집인 어머니들은 대략 4년마다 한 명의 아이만 낳을 수 있었고, 한 번에 한 명 이상의 아이를 업고 다닐 필요가 없도록 출산 간격을 두었다.

➡ 수렵 채집인 어머니들은 아이를 업고 이동해야 했으므로 출산 간격을 둘 수밖에 없었다는 결과가 자연스럽게 이어진다. ▶ 주어진 문장이 ②에 들어갈 수 없음

- ③의 앞 문장과 뒤 문장
앞 문장: ②의 뒤 문장과 같음
뒤 문장: 한곳에 정착하게 된 사회는 출산 간격을 4년에서 약 2년으로 단축할 수 있었다.

➡ 자주 이동하는 수렵 채집인에 관한 앞 문장과 한곳에 정착하게 된 사회를 언급하는 뒤 문장이 서로 이어지지 않는다. 수렵 채집인에 관한 내용이 끝나고 on the other hand로 반대되는 부류인 농부들을 언급하는 주어진 문장이 여기에 와야 한다.
▶ 주어진 문장이 ③에 들어가야 함

- ④의 앞 문장과 뒤 문장
앞 문장: ③의 뒤 문장과 같음
뒤 문장: 이는 여성 한 명이 수렵 채집인인 상대보다 더 많은 아이를 낳을 수 있다는 것을 의미했고, 그 결과 그것은 농경 사회에서 급격한 인구 증가를 야기했다.

➡ 농경 사회에서 단축된 출산 간격은 수렵 채집 사회보다 출산이 많았다는 것을 의미했고, 이것이 급격한 인구 증가를 야기했다는 내용으로 자연스럽게 이어진다.
▶ 주어진 문장이 ④에 들어갈 수 없음

- ⑤의 앞 문장과 뒤 문장
앞 문장: ④의 뒤 문장과 같음
뒤 문장: 인구 증가는 실제로 농경 사회에 유리했는데, 왜냐하면 농사는 많은 인간의 노동력을 필요로 했기 때문이다.

➡ 농경 사회에서의 인구 증가가 실제로 노동력이 많이 필요했던 농경 사회에 유리했다는 내용이 자연스럽게 이어진다. ▶ 주어진 문장이 ⑤에 들어갈 수 없음

3rd 글이 한눈에 들어오도록 정리하여 정답을 확인한다.

농사는 사람들을 정착하게 했지만 수렵 채집인들은 자주 이동해야 했고 소유물을 가지고 다녀야 했다.
(①) 특히 수렵 채집인 어머니들은 어린아이를 업고 이동해야 했다.
(②) 그래서 수렵 채집인들은 여러 아이를 이동시킬 일이 없도록 출산 간격을 두었다.
(③ 반면, 농부들은 매년 같은 장소에서 살 수 있었고 어린아이를 장거리 이동시켜야 하는 걱정을 하지 않아도 되었다.)
한곳에 정착하게 된 사회는 출산 간격을 단축할 수 있었다.
(④) 이는 농경 사회에서 더 많은 출산을 의미했고, 급격한 인구 증가를 야기했다.
(⑤) 인구 증가는 실제로 농경 사회에 유리했는데, 농사는 많은 인간의 노동력을 필요로 했기 때문이다.

39 정답 ④ — ⭐ 1등급 대비 [정답률 39%]

*동물의 유연성 발달에 중요한 유년기

글의 흐름으로 보아, 주어진 문장이 들어가기에 가장 적절한 곳을 고르시오. [3점]

By comparison, / birds with the longest childhoods, / those **(=birds)**
that **(주격 관계대명사)** migrate with their parents, / tend to have the most
efficient migration routes. // **단서 1** 유년기가 길고 부모와 이동한 새는 가장 효율적인 이동 경로를 알고 있음
이에 비해 / 유년기가 가장 길고 / 부모와 함께 이동하는 새는 / 가장 효율적인 이동 경로를 가지고 있는 경향이 있다 //

Spending time as children **(동명사구 주어(단수 취급))** / allows **(단수 동사)** animals to learn about their
environment. //
유년기를 보내는 것은 / 동물에게 환경에 대해 배울 수 있게 한다 //

Without childhood, / animals must rely more fully on hardware, / and therefore be **(병렬 구조)** less flexible. //
유년기가 없으면 / 동물은 하드웨어에 더 많이 의존해야 한다 / 그러므로 유연성이 떨어질 수밖에 없다 //

(①) Among migratory bird species, / those **(복수 주어)** that are born knowing how, when, and where to migrate /
철새 중에서도 / 언제, 어디로, 어떻게 이동해야 하는지를 알고 태어나는 새들은 /
— those that are migrating entirely with instructions **(관계사절(instructions 수식))** / they were **(복수 동사)** born with — sometimes have very inefficient migration routes. //
즉 전적으로 지침에 따라 이동하는 새들은 / 태어날 때부터 주어진 / 때때로 매우 비효율적인 이동 경로를 가지고 있다 //

(②) These birds, born knowing how to migrate, **(앞에 주격 관계대명사와 be동사가 생략됨 / 분사구문)** / don't adapt easily. //
이동 방법을 알고 태어난 새들은 / 쉽게 적응하지 못한다 //

(③) So when lakes dry up, / forest becomes farmland, / or **(병렬 구조(부사절))** climate change pushes breeding grounds farther north, /
따라서 호수가 마르거나 / 숲이 농지로 바뀌거나 / 기후 변화로 번식지가 더 북쪽으로 밀려났을 때 /
those birds that **(주격 관계대명사)** are born knowing how to migrate / **단서 2** 이동하는 방법을 알고 태어난 새들은 기존의 경로로만 날아감 keep flying by the old rules and maps. //
이동하는 방법을 알고 태어난 새들은 / 기존의 규칙과 지도를 따라 계속 날아간다 //

(④) Childhood facilitates the passing on of cultural information, / and culture can evolve faster than genes. //
유년기는 문화적 정보의 전달을 촉진하며 / 문화는 유전자보다 더 빠르게 진화할 수 있다 // **단서 3** 유년기는 문화적 정보를 전달을 촉진함

(⑤) Childhood gives flexibility / in a changing world. //
유년기는 유연성을 제공한다 / 변화하는 세상에서 //

- migrate ⓥ 이동하다 · route ⓝ 경로 · adapt ⓥ 적응하다
- breeding ⓝ 번식 · farther ad 더 멀리 · facilitate ⓥ 촉진하다
- passing on 전달, 대물림 · evolve ⓥ 진화하다 · gene ⓝ 유전자
- flexibility ⓝ 유연성

동물은 유년기를 보내면서 환경에 대해 배울 수 있다. 유년기가 없으면, 동물은 하드웨어에 더 많이 의존해야 하므로 유연성이 떨어질 수밖에 없다. (①) 철새 중에서도 언제, 어디로, 어떻게 이동해야 하는지를 알고 태어나는 새들, 즉 전적으로 태어날 때부터 주어진 지침에 따라 이동하는 새들은 때때로 매우 비효율적인 이동 경로를 가지고 있다. (②) 이동 방법을 알고 태어난 새들은 쉽게 적응하지 못한다. (③) 따라서 호수가 마르거나 숲이 농지로 바뀌거나 기후 변화로 번식지가 더 북쪽으로 밀려났을 때, 이동하는 방법을 알고 태어난 새들은 기존의 규칙과 지도를 따라 계속 날아간다. (④ 이에 비해 유년기가 가장 길고 부모와 함께 이동하는 새는 가장 효율적인 이동 경로를 가지고 있는 경향이 있다.) 유년기는 문화적 정보의 전달을 촉진하며, 문화는 유전자보다 더 빠르게 진화할 수 있다. (⑤) 유년기는 변화하는 세상에서 유연성을 제공한다.

왜 1등급? 접속사 so로 시작하는 문장을 비롯하여, 주어진 문장의 birds를 가리키는 듯한 these birds로 시작하는 문장이 있어서 자칫하면 오답을 고르기 쉬운 1등급 대비 문제이다. 주어진 문장이 By comparison으로 시작하며 앞 문장과 대조되는 내용을 나타내므로, 유년기가 없는 동물(철새)에서 유년기가 있는 동물(부모와 함께 이동하는 새)로 내용의 흐름이 전환되는 부분을 찾아야 한다.

| 문제 풀이 순서 |

1st 주어진 문장을 해석하고, 연결어, 지시어 등을 확인한다.

> By comparison, birds with the longest childhoods, and those that migrate with their parents, tend to have the most efficient migration routes.
> 이에 비해 유년기가 가장 길고 부모와 함께 이동하는 새는 가장 효율적인 이동 경로를 가지고 있는 경향이 있다.

➡ **주어진 문장 앞:** 대조를 나타내는 By comparison이 있으므로, **단서** 효율적인 이동 경로를 가지지 못한 새에 관한 내용이 제시될 것이다. **발상**

2nd 각 선택지의 앞뒤 흐름이 매끄러운지 확인한다.

- ①의 앞 문장과 뒤 문장

앞 문장: 유년기가 없으면, 동물은 하드웨어에 더 많이 의존해야 하므로 유연성이 떨어질 수밖에 없다.
뒤 문장: 철새 중에서도 언제, 어디로, 어떻게 이동해야 하는지를 알고 태어나는 새들, 즉 전적으로 태어날 때부터 주어진 지침에 따라 이동하는 새들은 때때로 매우 비효율적인 이동 경로를 가지고 있다.

➡ 유년기가 없는 동물은 유연성이 떨어진다는 내용 바로 뒤에, 그 예시로서 태어날 때부터 주어진 지침에 따라 이동하는 일부 철새들은 매우 비효율적인 이동 경로를 가진다는 내용이 자연스럽게 이어진다. ▶ 주어진 문장이 ①에 들어갈 수 없음

- ②의 앞 문장과 뒤 문장

앞 문장: ①의 뒤 문장과 같음
뒤 문장: 이동 방법을 알고 태어난 새들은 쉽게 적응하지 못한다.

➡ 주어진 지침에 따라 이동하는 새들은 비효율적인 경로를 가지게 되고, 그러한 새들은 쉽게 적응하지 못하게 된다는 내용이 자연스럽게 이어진다.
▶ 주어진 문장이 ②에 들어갈 수 없음

- ③의 앞 문장과 뒤 문장

앞 문장: ②의 뒤 문장과 같음
뒤 문장: 따라서 호수가 마르거나 숲이 농지로 바뀌거나 기후 변화로 번식지가 더 북쪽으로 밀려났을 때, 이동하는 방법을 알고 태어난 새들은 기존의 규칙과 지도를 따라 계속 날아간다.

➡ 이동 방법을 알고 태어난 새들은 쉽게 적응하지 못하므로 환경이 바뀌어도 계속 기존의 이동 경로를 따라 날아간다는 내용으로 이어진다.
▶ 주어진 문장이 ③에 들어갈 수 없음

④의 앞 문장과 뒤 문장

앞 문장: ③의 뒤 문장과 같음
뒤 문장: 유년기는 문화적 정보의 전달을 촉진하며, 문화는 유전자보다 더 빠르게 진화할 수 있다.

➡ 이동 방법을 알고 태어난 새들은 기존의 방식대로 계속 날아간다는 내용과 유년기가 주는 장점에 관한 내용이 서로 이어지지 않는다. 비효율적인 이동 경로를 가지는 새들에 관한 내용이 끝나고, 반대되는 내용을 나타내는 By comparison으로 시작되며 효율적인 이동 경로를 가지는 새들을 언급하는 주어진 문장이 와야 한다.
▶ 주어진 문장이 ④에 들어가야 함

- ⑤의 앞 문장과 뒤 문장
┌ 앞 문장: ④의 뒤 문장과 같음
└ 뒤 문장: 유년기는 변화하는 세상에서 유연성을 제공한다.
➡ 문화적 정보의 전달을 촉진하고 빠르게 진화하기 때문에 유년기는 동물에게
  유연성을 제공한다는 내용이 자연스럽게 이어진다.
  ▶ 주어진 문장이 ⑤에 들어갈 수 없음

3rd 글이 한눈에 들어오도록 정리하여 정답을 확인한다.

동물은 유년기를 보내면서 환경에 대해 배우며, 유년기가 없으면 유연성이 떨어진다.
(①) 태어날 때 주어진 지침에 따라 이동하는 새들은 비효율적인 이동 경로를 가지고
있다.
(②) 이동 방법을 알고 태어난 새들은 적응하지 못한다.
(③) 이동 방법을 알고 태어난 새들은 환경이 변해도 기존 규칙과 지도를 따라 계속
날아간다.
(④ 이에 비해 유년기가 길고 부모와 함께 이동하는 새는 가장 효율적인 이동 경로를
안다.)
유년기는 문화적 정보의 전달을 촉진하며 문화는 유전자보다 빠르게 진화한다.
(⑤) 유년기는 변화하는 세상에서 유연성을 제공한다.

40 정답 ① *포괄적 디지털 디자인의 필요성

Over the last several decades, / scholars have developed
standards / for how best to create, organize, present, and
preserve digital information / for future generations. //
지난 수십 년 동안 / 학자들은 표준을 개발해 왔다 / 디지털 정보를 가장 잘 만들고, 정리하고,
제시하고, 보존하는 방법에 대한 / 미래 세대를 위해 //
What has remained neglected for the most part, / however, / are
the needs of people with disabilities. // **단서 1** 장애인의 요구는 여전히 무시되어 왔음
여전히 대부분 무시되어온 것은 / 그러나 / 장애가 있는 사람들의 요구이다 //

As a result, / many of the otherwise most valuable digital
resources are useless / for people who are deaf or hard of
hearing, /
그 결과 / 그렇지 않은 경우라면 가장 가치 있었을 디지털 자원 중 상당수가 무용지물이 되고
있다 / 청각 장애가 있거나 듣는 것이 힘든 사람에게 /
as well as for people who are blind, / have low vision, / or have
difficulty distinguishing particular colors. //
시각 장애가 있는 사람뿐만 아니라 / 시력이 낮거나 / 특정 색상을 구분하기 어려운 //
While professionals working in educational technology and
commercial web design / have made significant progress in
meeting the needs of such users, /
교육 기술 및 상업용 웹디자인에 종사하는 전문가들이 / 이러한 사용자의 요구를 충족시키는
데 상당한 진전을 이루었지만 /
some scholars creating digital projects / all too often fail to take
these needs into account. // **단서 2** 디지털 프로젝트에서 장애인의 요구를 고려하지
못하는 경우가 많음
디지털 프로젝트를 만드는 일부 학자들은 / 이러한 요구를 고려하지 못하는 경우가 너무 많다 //
단서 3 최대한 모두의 요구를 충족시킬 수 있는 디자인이 필요함
This situation would be much improved / if more projects
embraced the idea / that we should always keep the largest
possible audience in mind / as we make design decisions, /
이러한 상황은 훨씬 개선될 것이다 / 더 많은 프로젝트에서 생각을 받아들인다면 / 최대한
많은 사용자를 항상 염두에 두어야 한다고 / 디자인을 결정할 때 /
ensuring that our final product serves the needs of those with
disabilities / as well as those without. //
최종 제품이 장애가 있는 사람들의 요구를 충족시킬 수 있도록 하면서 / 장애가 없는 사람들의
요구뿐만 아니라 //

→ The needs of people with disabilities / have often been (A)
overlooked in digital projects, / which could be changed / by
adopting a(n) (B) **inclusive** design. //
장애가 있는 사람들의 요구는 / 디지털 프로젝트에서 종종 간과되어 왔으며 / 이것은
변화될 수 있다 / 포괄(포용)적인 디자인을 채택함으로써 //

• scholar ⓝ 학자   • organize ⓥ 정리하다   • present ⓥ 제시하다
• preserve ⓥ 보존하다   • neglect ⓥ 소홀히 하다
• disability ⓝ 장애   • deaf ⓐ 귀먹은   • blind ⓐ 눈이 먼
• distinguish ⓥ 구별하다   • embrace ⓥ 포용하다
• ensure ⓥ 반드시 ~ 하게 하다

지난 수십 년 동안 학자들은 미래 세대를 위해 디지털 정보를 가장 잘 만들고,
정리하고, 제시하고, 보존하는 방법에 대한 표준을 개발해 왔다. 그러나 대부분
의 경우 장애가 있는 사람들의 요구는 여전히 무시되어 왔다. 그 결과, 청각 장
애가 있거나 듣는 것이 힘든 사람, 시각 장애가 있거나 시력이 낮거나 특정 색
상을 구분하기 어려운 사람에게는 그렇지 않은 경우라면 가장 가치 있었을 디
지털 자원 중 상당수가 무용지물이 되고 있다. 교육 기술 및 상업용 웹 디자인
에 종사하는 전문가들은 이러한 사용자의 요구를 충족시키는 데 상당한 진전을
이루었지만, 디지털 프로젝트를 만드는 일부 학자들은 이러한 요구를 고려하지
못하는 경우가 너무 많다. 더 많은 프로젝트에서 디자인을 결정할 때 최대한 많
은 사용자를 항상 염두에 두고 최종 제품이 장애가 있는 사람들과 그렇지 않은
사람들 모두의 요구를 충족시킬 수 있도록 해야 한다는 생각을 받아들인다면 이
러한 상황은 훨씬 개선될 것이다.

→ 장애가 있는 사람들의 요구는 디지털 프로젝트에서 종종 (A) 간과되어 왔으
며, 이것은 (B) 포괄(포용)적인 디자인을 채택함으로써 변화될 수 있다.

> 다음 글의 내용을 한 문장으로 요약하고자 한다. 빈칸 (A), (B)에 들어갈
> 말로 가장 적절한 것은?
>
> | | (A) | | (B) |
> |---|---|---|---|
> | ① | overlooked 간과된 | — | inclusive 포괄적인 |
> | ② | accepted 수용된 | — | practical 실용적인 |
> | ③ | considered 고려된 | — | inclusive 포괄적인 |
> | ④ | accepted | — | abstract 추상적인 |
> | ⑤ | overlooked | — | abstract |
>
> 장애인의 요구는 간과되어 왔고 이를 수용할 수 있는 포괄적인 디자인이 필요함
> 장애인의 요구는 수용되지 않았으며 실용적인 디자인이 필요한 것이 아님
> 장애인의 요구는 고려되지 않았음
> 추상적인 디자인이 필요한 것이 아님

| 문제 풀이 순서 | ★★★ [정답률 55%]

1st 요약문을 통해 글에서 무엇을 찾아야 하는지 확인한다.

요약문	장애가 있는 사람들의 요구는 디지털 프로젝트에서 종종 (A) _____ 왔으며, 이것은 (B) _____ 디자인을 채택함으로써 변화될 수 있다.

➡ 글에서 찾아야 하는 것
(A): 장애가 있는 사람들의 요구가 디지털 프로젝트에서 종종 간과되어, 수용되어,
고려되어 왔는지
(B): 이것이 포괄적인, 실용적인, 추상적인 디자인을 채택함으로써 변화될 수
있는지

2nd 글의 내용을 파악하여 요약문을 완성한다.

┌ • 디지털 정보에 관한 표준 개발의 대부분의 경우 장애가 있는 사람들의 요구는
│   여전히 무시되어 왔음 **단서 1**
│ • 디지털 프로젝트를 만드는 일부 학자들은 이러한 요구를 고려하지 못하는 경우가
│   너무 많음 **단서 2**
│ • 더 많은 프로젝트에서 디자인을 결정할 때 최대한 많은 사용자를 항상 염두에
└   두어야 한다는 생각을 받아들인다면 이러한 상황은 훨씬 개선될 것임 **단서 3**
➡ 장애인의 요구가 '간과된' 것이므로 (A)에는 ①, ⑤ '간과된'이 들어가야 하고,
  최대한 많은 사용자를 '포함하는' 디자인이 필요한 것이므로 (B)에는 ①, ③
  '포괄적인'이 들어가야 한다.
  ▶ 따라서 정답은 ①임

도입	디지털 정보를 개발하는 데 있어서 장애인의 요구는 무시되어 왔음
전개	장애가 있는 사람들에게 디지털 자원은 무용지물이 되어 버림
부연	디지털 프로젝트에서는 여전히 장애인의 요구를 고려하지 못하는 경우가 많음
결론	디지털 프로젝트를 결정할 때 장애가 있는 사람들과 그렇지 않은 사람들 모두의 요구를 충족시킬 수 있도록 해야 함

| 선택지 분석 |

① overlooked — inclusive
　간과된　　　포괄적인
장애인의 요구는 간과되어 왔고 이를 수용할 수 있는 포괄적인 디자인이 필요하다.

② accepted — practical
　수용된　　　실용적인
장애인의 요구가 수용되지 않아, 포괄적인 디자인이 필요하다고 말하고 있다.

③ considered — inclusive
　고려된　　　포괄적인
장애인의 요구는 무시되었다.

④ accepted — abstract
　수용된　　　추상적인
장애인의 요구는 수용되지 않았고 추상적인 디자인이 필요한 것도 아니다.

⑤ overlooked — abstract
　간과된　　　추상적인
추상적인 디자인이 아닌 모두의 요구를 수용할 수 있는 포괄적인 디자인이 필요하다.

41~42 ※ 고통 속에서 쾌락을 느끼는 인간

주격 관계대명사
All humans, to an extent, / seek activities **that** cause a degree of
　'~하기 위해서'
pain / **in order to experience** pleasure, /
모든 인간은 어느 정도는 / 약간의 고통을 유발하는 활동을 추구한다 / 쾌락을 경험하기 위해 /

whether A or B: A든 B든
whether this is found in spicy food, strong massages, / **or**
stepping into a too-cold or too-hot bath. //
이것이 매운 음식 또는 강한 마사지에서 발견되든 / 너무 차갑거나 뜨거운 욕조에 들어가기 중
(어디에서 발견되든지 간에 말이다) //

The key is / that it is a 'safe threat'. //
핵심은 / 그것이 '안전한 위협'이라는 점이다 //

perceives의 목적어와 목적격 보어(to부정사)
The brain perceives **the stimulus to be** painful / but ultimately
(a) non-threatening. // 【41번】단서 1: 뇌에서 '안전한 위협'은 고통스럽지만 위협적이지 않은 것으로 인식함
뇌는 자극을 고통스러운 것으로 인식한다 / 하지만 궁극적으로 위협적이지 않은 것으로 //

관계부사절(the way 수식)
Interestingly, / this could be similar to the way **humor works**: / a
　　　　　주격 관계대명사
'safe threat' **that** causes pleasure / by playfully violating norms. //
흥미롭게도 / 이것은 유머가 작동하는 방식과 유사할 수 있다 / 즉 쾌락을 유발하는 '안전한
위협'과 규범을 장난스럽게 위반함으로써 //

We feel uncomfortable, / but safe. //
우리는 불편하지만 / 안전하다고 느낀다 //

관계부사(context 수식)
In this context, / **where** (b) survival is clearly not in danger, / the
desire for pain is actually the desire for a reward, / not suffering
or punishment. // 【41번】단서 2: 생존이 위험하지 않을 때 고통에 대한 욕구는 사실 보상에 대한 욕구임
이런 상황에서 / 생존이 위험하지 않은 / 고통에 대한 욕구는 실제로는 보상에 대한 욕구이다 /
고통이나 처벌이 아닌 //

This reward-like effect / comes from the feeling of mastery over
the pain. //
이러한 보상과 같은 효과는 / 고통에 대한 숙달된 느낌에서 비롯된다 //

'the 비교급 ~, the 비교급 …': '~할수록 더 …하다'
The closer you look at your chilli-eating habit, / **the more**
remarkable it seems. //
칠리를 먹는 습관을 자세히 들여다볼수록 / 이는 더욱 분명하게 드러난다 //

주격 관계대명사
When the active ingredient of chillies — capsaicin — touches
the tongue, / it stimulates exactly the same receptor / **that** is
activated / when any of these tissues are burned. //
칠리의 활성 성분인 캡사이신이 허에 닿으면 / 똑같은 수용체를 자극한다 / 활성화되는 / 피부
조직이 화상을 입었을 때 //

동명사(주어)　　　　　　　　　　　　　　　병렬 구조(know의 목적어절)
Knowing that our body is firing off danger signals, / but **that we
are actually completely safe,** / (c) produces pleasure. //
우리 몸이 위험 신호를 보내고 있음을 아는 것 / 하지만 실제로는 완전히 안전하다는 것을
아는 것은 / 쾌감이 생긴다 // 【41번】단서 3, 【42번】단서: 위험 신호를 받지만 실제로는 안전한 상황 속에서 고통은 쾌감을 줌

All children start off hating chilli, / but many learn to derive
　　　　　　　　　　　　　　　　　전치사 through의 목적어(동명사)
pleasure from it / through repeated exposure / and **knowing**
that they will never experience any real (d) joy(→ harm). //
모든 아이들은 처음에는 칠리를 싫어한다 / 하지만 그것에서 쾌락을 얻는 방법을 배우게 된다 /
반복적인 노출을 통해서 / 그리고 실질적인 기쁨을(→ 해를) 경험하지 않는다는 것을 통해서 //

동명사구 주어(단수 취급)　　　　　　단수 동사
Interestingly, / **seeking pain for the pain itself** / **appears** to be (e)
uniquely human. //
흥미롭게도 / 고통 그 자체를 위해 고통을 추구하는 것은 / 인간만이 할 수 있는 행동으로
보인다 //

관계부사절(the only way 수식)
The only way **scientists have trained animals** / to have a
preference for chilli or to self-harm / is to have **the pain** always
　　　　　　　　　　　　have의 목적어와 목적격 보어(과거분사)
directly **associated** with a pleasurable reward. //
과학자들이 동물을 훈련시키는 유일한 방법은 / 칠리를 선호하게 하거나 스스로에게 해를
가하도록 / 고통을 항상 즐거운 보상과 직접적으로 연관시키는 것이다 //

- seek ⓥ 찾다　　• pleasure ⓝ 쾌락　　• perceive ⓥ 인식하다
- stimulus ⓝ 자극　　• ultimately ⓐⓓ 궁극적으로
- violate ⓥ 침해하다　　• norm ⓝ 표준　　• suffering ⓝ 고통
- punishment ⓝ 처벌　　• mastery ⓝ 숙달
- remarkable ⓐ 놀라운　　• stimulate ⓥ 자극시키다
- receptor ⓝ 수용체　　• activate ⓥ 활성화시키다
- tissue ⓝ (세포) 조직　　• fire off 발사하다　　• derive ⓥ 끌어내다
- exposure ⓝ 노출　　• preference ⓝ 선호

모든 인간은 어느 정도는 쾌락을 경험하기 위해 약간의 고통을 유발하는 활동을 추구한다. 이것이 매운 음식 또는 강한 마사지, 너무 차갑거나 뜨거운 욕조에 들어가기 중 어디에서 발견되든지 간에 말이다. 핵심은 그것이 '안전한 위협'이라는 점이다. 뇌는 자극이 고통스럽지만 궁극적으로 (a) 위협적이지 않은 것으로 인식한다. 흥미롭게도 이것은 유머가 작동하는 방식, 즉 규범을 장난스럽게 위반함으로써 쾌락을 유발하는 '안전한 위협'과 유사할 수 있다. 우리는 불편하지만 안전하다고 느낀다. (b) 생존이 위험하지 않은 이런 상황에서 고통에 대한 욕구는 실제로는 고통이나 처벌이 아닌 보상에 대한 욕구이다. 이러한 보상과 같은 효과는 고통에 대한 숙달된 느낌에서 비롯된다. 칠리를 먹는 습관을 자세히 들여다볼수록 이는 더욱 분명하게 드러난다. 칠리의 활성 성분인 캡사이신이 허에 닿으면 피부 조직이 화상을 입었을 때 활성화되는 것과 똑같은 수용체를 자극한다. 우리 몸이 위험 신호를 보내고 있지만 실제로는 완전히 안전하다는 것을 알면 쾌감이 (c) 생긴다. 모든 아이들은 처음에는 칠리를 싫어하지만, 반복적인 노출과 실질적인 (d) 기쁨을(→ 해를) 경험하지 않는다는 것을 알게 됨을 통해 그것에서 쾌락을 얻는 방법을 배우게 된다. 흥미롭게도 고통 그 자체를 위해 고통을 추구하는 것은 인간만이 (e) 고유하게 할 수 있는 행동으로 보인다. 동물이 칠리를 선호하게 하거나 스스로에게 해를 가하도록 과학자들이 훈련시키는 유일한 방법은 고통을 항상 즐거운 보상과 직접적으로 연관시키는 것이다.

41 정답 ①

윗글의 제목으로 가장 적절한 것은?

① The Secret Behind Painful Pleasures
고통스러운 쾌락 뒤에 숨겨진 비밀　　　　고통 속에서 쾌락을 느끼는 이유를 설명함
② How 'Safe Threat' Changes into Real Pain
어떻게 '안전한 위협'이 실제 고통으로 바뀌는가　　'안전한 위협'이 언급된 것으로 만든 오답
③ What Makes You Stronger, Pleasure or Pain?
무엇이 당신을 더 강하게 만드는가, 쾌락인가, 고통인가?　　쾌락과 고통을 비교하는 것이 아님
④ How Does Your Body Detect Danger Signals?
당신의 몸은 어떻게 위험 신호를 감지하는가　　몸이 위험 신호를 감지하는 방법에 대한 내용이 아님
⑤ Recipes to Change Picky Children's Eating Habits
까다로운 아이들의 식습관을 바꾸는 요리법　　요리법을 소개하는 글이 아님

⑤ (e) uniquely 고유하게

ㄴ 흥미롭게도 고통 그 자체를 위해 고통을 추구하는 것은 인간만이 (e) 고유하게 할 수 있는 행동으로 보인다.

➡ 동물이 스스로에게 고통을 가하게 하는 방법은 보상의 직접적인 연관밖에 없다고 바로 뒤 문장에서 언급하고 있으므로, 이러한 행동은 인간만이 '고유하게' 할 수 있는 행동이라고 볼 수 있다. ▶ uniquely는 문맥에 맞음

43 ~ 45 *비행 중 비상 대처 훈련

(A) An airplane flew high / above the deep blue seas / far from any land. //
비행기가 높이 날고 있었다 / 깊고 푸른 바다 위를 / 육지에서 멀리 떨어진 //
현재분사가 문두로 오면서 주어와 동사가 도치됨   주격 관계대명사
Flying the small plane was a student pilot / who was sitting alongside an experienced flight instructor. // 45번 ① 교관과 교육생이 소형 비행기에 타고 있음
소형 비행기를 조종하고 있는 것은 한 파일럿 교육생이었다 / 노련한 비행 교관과 나란히 앉아 있는 //
부사절 접속사(시간)   = the student
As the student looked out the window, / (a) she was filled with wonder and appreciation / for the beauty of the world. //
교육생이 창문 밖을 바라볼 때 / 그녀는 경이로움과 감탄으로 가득 찼다 / 세상의 아름다움에 대한 //

Her instructor, / meanwhile, / waited patiently for the right time
형용사적 용법
/ to start a surprise flight emergency training exercise. //
비행 교관은 / 한편 / 적절한 때를 인내심을 가지고 기다리고 있었다 / 비행 중 돌발 비상 상황 대처 훈련을 시작할 // 43번 단서 1: 교관은 비상 상황 훈련을 시작할 적절한 때를 기다리고 있음

*(A) 문단 요약: 교관과 교육생이 평화롭게 비행하고 있는 상황

명사절 접속사
(B) Then, / the student carefully flew low enough / to see if she
find의 목적어와 목적격 보어(현재분사)
could find any ships / making their way across the surface of the ocean. // 43번 단서 2: 배가 보이는지 확인하기 위해 낮게 비행함
그런 다음 / 교육생은 충분히 낮게 조심히 비행하였다 / 배가 보이는지 확인할 수 있을 정도로 / 바다 표면을 가로지르는 //

Now the instructor and the student / could see some ships. //
이제 교관과 교육생은 / 배 몇 척을 볼 수 있었다 //

Although the ships were far apart, / they were all sailing in a line. // 45번 ② 배들은 서로 떨어져 있었지만 한 줄로 항해함
배들은 멀리 떨어져 있었지만 / 모두 한 줄을 이루고 항해하고 있었다 //

With the line of ships in view, / the student could see the way to home and safety. // 43번 단서 3: 안전하게 복귀하는 방법을 알아냄
배들이 줄을 지어있는 것이 보이자 / 교육생은 안전하게 복귀하는 길을 알 수 있었다 //
= the instructor 계속적 용법의 주격 관계대명사
The student looked at (b) her in relief, / who smiled proudly back at her student. //
교육생은 안도하며 그녀를 바라봤다 / 그녀도 교육생을 향해 자랑스럽게 웃어보였다 //

*(B) 문단 요약: 교육생은 바다 위의 배를 확인함으로써 안전하게 복귀하는 길을 찾음

(C) When the student began to panic, / the instructor said, /
= the student
"Stay calm and steady. / (c) You can do it." // 43번 단서 4: 교육생이 당황하기 시작함
교육생이 당황하기 시작하자 / 교관은 말했다 / "침착하세요 / 당신은 할 수 있습니다" //
앞에 Being이 생략됨
Calm as ever, / the instructor told her student, / "Difficult times always happen during flight. // The most important thing is / to focus on your flight / in those situations." // 45번 ③ 교관이 어려운 상황에서는 집중이 가장 중요하다고 말함
여느 때처럼 침착하게 / 교관은 교육생에게 말했다 / "비행 중에는 항상 어려운 상황이 발생합니다 // 가장 중요한 것은 / 비행에 집중하는 것입니다 / 그런 상황에서" //
encouraged의 목적어와 목적격 보어(to부정사)
Those words encouraged / the student to focus on flying the aircraft first. //
그 말은 용기를 주었다 / 교육생이 먼저 비행에 집중할 수 있게끔 //
= the student
"Thank you, / I think (d) I can make it," / she said, / "As I've been trained, / I should search for visual markers." //
"감사합니다 / 제가 해낼 수 있을 것 같아요"라고 / 그녀는 말했다 / "훈련받은 대로 / 저는 시각 표식을 찾아야겠어요" // 43번 단서 5: 교육생은 훈련받은 대로 시각 표식을 찾아야겠다고 함

*(C) 문단 요약: 당황한 교육생에게 교육관이 용기를 주었고 교육생은 해결책을 찾아냄

(왼쪽 단)

> **왜 정답?** ★★❀ [정답률 63%]

ㄴ • 뇌는 자극(안전한 위협)이 고통스럽지만 궁극적으로 위협적이지 않은 것으로 인식한다. 41번 단서 1
• 생존이 위험하지 않은 이런 상황에서 고통에 대한 욕구는 실제로는 고통이나 처벌이 아닌 보상에 대한 욕구이다. 41번 단서 2
• 우리 몸이 위험 신호를 보내고 있지만 실제로는 완전히 안전하다는 것을 알면 쾌감이 생긴다. 41번 단서 3

➡ '안전한 위협' 속에서 느끼는 고통은 위협적이지 않은 것으로 뇌가 인식하기 때문에, 이러한 고통에 대한 욕구는 실제로는 보상에 대한 욕구이다. 그래서 몸이 위험 신호(고통)를 보내더라도 실제로는 완전히 안전하다는 것을 앎으로써 쾌감이 생긴다는 내용이다.

▶ 따라서 제목으로 적절한 것은 ① '고통스러운 쾌락 뒤에 숨겨진 비밀'이다.

> **왜 오답?**

② 안전한 위협이 쾌감을 불러일으킨다는 글이다.
③ 인간을 더 강하게 만드는 것이 쾌락인지 고통인지를 비교하는 글이 아니다.
④ 우리의 몸이 위험 신호를 감지하는 방법이나 과정을 설명하는 글이 아니다.
⑤ 식습관이 까다로운 아이들이나 요리법에 관한 글이 아니다.

42 정답 ④

밑줄 친 (a)~(e) 중에서 문맥상 낱말의 쓰임이 적절하지 <u>않은</u> 것은?

① (a) 위협적이지 않은 안전한 위협임
   위협적이지 않은
② (b) 안전한 상황은 생존에 위험이 되지 않는 것임
   생존
③ (c) 고통을 느껴도 안전하다는 것을 알기 때문에 쾌감(보상)이 생김
   생산하다
④ (d) 해를 경험하지 않는다는 안전함을 알기 때문에 쾌감이 생김
   기쁨
⑤ (e) 인간만이 가질 수 있는 고유한 특성임
   고유하게

> **왜 정답?** ★★★ [정답률 50%]

④ (d) joy 기쁨

ㄴ 모든 아이들은 처음에는 칠리를 싫어하지만, 반복적인 노출과 실질적인
피해를
(d) 기쁨을 경험하지 않는다는 것을 알게 됨을 통해 그것에서 쾌락을 얻는 방법을 배우게 된다.

ㄴ 기쁨을 경험하지 않는 것이 아니라, 고통을 느껴도 실질적으로 피해를 경험하지 않는다는 안전함을 알기 때문에 쾌감이 생기는 것이므로 실질적인 '기쁨을' 경험하지 않는다는 것은 문맥에 맞지 않는다.

▶ joy를 harm(피해)과 같은 반의어로 바꾸어야 한다.

> **왜 오답?**

① (a) non-threatening 위협적이지 않은

ㄴ 뇌는 자극이 고통스럽지만 궁극적으로 (a) 위협적이지 않은 것으로 인식한다. ~ 우리는 불편하지만 안전하다고 느낀다.

➡ 우리는 '안전한 위협'이 있을 때 불편하지만 안전하다고 느낀다고 했으므로 뇌가 '안전한 위협'을 고통스럽지만 '위협적이지 않은' 것으로 인식할 것이다.

▶ non-threatening은 문맥에 맞음

② (b) survival 생존

ㄴ (b) 생존이 위험하지 않은 이런 상황에서(In this context) 고통에 대한 욕구는 실제로는 고통이나 처벌이 아닌 보상에 대한 욕구이다.

➡ this context란 안전한 위협을 느끼는 상황이므로 '생존'이 위험하지 않다.

▶ survival은 문맥에 맞음

③ (c) produce 생산하다

ㄴ 우리 몸이 위험 신호를 보내고 있지만 실제로는 완전히 안전하다는 것을 알면 쾌감이 (c) 생긴다.

➡ 매운 칠리를 먹으면 몸이 위험 신호를 보내지만 우리는 실제로 안전하다는 것을 알고 있으므로 쾌감이 '생긴다.' ▶ produce는 문맥에 맞음

(D) When the plane hit a bit of turbulence, / the instructor pushed a hidden button. // **43번** 단서 6: 난기류를 만나 비상 상황 훈련이 시작됨
비행기가 약간의 난기류를 만났을 때 / 교관은 숨겨진 버튼을 눌렀다 //

Suddenly, / all the monitors inside the plane flashed several times / then went out completely! // **45번 ④** 비행기 내부의 모니터가 깜박이다가 완전히 꺼짐
병렬 구조
갑자기 / 비행기 안의 모든 모니터가 여러 번 깜박이다가 / 완전히 꺼졌다 //

Now the student was in control of an airplane / that was flying well, / but (e) she had no indication / of where she was or where she should go. //
주격 관계대명사
= the student
이제 교육생은 비행기를 조종하고 있었다 / 잘 날고 있는 / 그러나 그녀는 알 수 없었다 / 자신이 어디에 있는지, 어디로 가야 하는지 // **45번 ⑤** 교육생은 지도 이외의 다른 도구는 가지고 있지 않음

She did have a map, / but no other instruments. //
교육생은 지도는 가지고 있었지만 / 다른 도구는 가지고 있지 않았다 //

She was at a loss / and then the plane shook again. //
그녀는 어쩔 줄 몰라 했고 / 그때 비행기가 다시 흔들렸다 //

　★(D) 문단 요약: 교관이 비상 상황 훈련을 시작하였고 교육생은 당황하게 됨

- flight instructor 비행 교관　· appreciation ⓝ 감상
- patiently ⓐ�d 인내심 있게　· panic ⓥ 당황하다
- indication ⓝ 표시　· instrument ⓝ 도구

(A) 비행기가 육지에서 멀리 떨어진 깊고 푸른 바다 위를 높이 날고 있었다. 소형 비행기를 조종하고 있는 것은 노련한 비행 교관과 나란히 앉아 있는 한 파일럿 교육생이었다. 교육생이 창문 밖을 바라볼 때, (a) 그녀는 세상의 아름다움에 대한 경이로움과 감탄으로 가득 찼다. 한편, 비행 교관은 비행 중 돌발 비상 상황 대처 훈련을 시작할 적절한 때를 인내심을 가지고 기다리고 있었다.

(D) 비행기가 약간의 난기류를 만났을 때, 교관은 숨겨진 버튼을 눌렀다. 갑자기, 비행기 안의 모든 모니터가 여러 번 깜박이다가 완전히 꺼졌다! 이제 교육생은 잘 날고 있는 비행기를 조종하고 있었지만, (e) 그녀는 자신이 어디에 있는지, 어디로 가야 하는지 알 방도가 없었다. 교육생은 지도는 가지고 있었지만, 다른 도구는 가지고 있지 않았다. 그녀는 어쩔 줄 몰라 했고 그때 비행기가 다시 흔들렸다.

(C) 교육생이 당황하기 시작하자 교관은 "침착하세요. (c) 당신은 할 수 있습니다." 여느 때처럼 침착한 교관은 교육생에게 "비행 중에는 항상 어려운 상황이 발생합니다. 그러한 상황에서는 비행에 집중하는 것이 가장 중요합니다."라고 말했다. 그 말이 교육생이 먼저 비행에 집중할 수 있게끔 용기를 주었다. "감사합니다. (d) 제가 해낼 수 있을 것 같아요."라고 그녀는 말했다. "훈련받은 대로, 저는 시각 표식을 찾아야겠어요."

(B) 그런 다음 교육생은 바다 표면을 가로지르는 배가 보이는지 확인할 수 있을 정도로 충분히 낮게 조심히 비행하였다. 이제 교관과 교육생은 배 몇 척을 볼 수 있었다. 배들은 멀리 떨어져 있었지만 모두 한 줄을 이루고 항해하고 있었다. 배들이 줄을 지어있는 것이 보이자, 교육생은 안전하게 복귀하는 길을 알 수 있었다. 교육생은 안도하며 (b) 그녀를 바라봤고, 그녀도 교육생을 향해 자랑스럽게 웃어보였다.

43 정답 ⑤

주어진 글 (A)에 이어질 내용을 순서에 맞게 배열한 것으로 가장 적절한 것은?

① (B) — (D) — (C) 주어진 글에서 안전하게 복귀해야 하는 비상 상황이 나오지 않음
② (C) — (B) — (D)　] 주어진 글에서 아직 교육생이 당황할 상황이 시작하지 않음
③ (C) — (D) — (B)　]
④ (D) — (B) — (C) (B)의 안전한 복귀를 위해서 생각해 낸 방법이 (C)에서 먼저 나옴
⑤ (D) — (C) — (B) (D) 비상 훈련 시작 - (C) 당황했지만 훈련받은 대로 시각 표식을 찾으려 함 - (B) 배를 확인함으로써 안전하게 복귀하는 길을 찾음

▶왜 정답·오답? ✽✽❀ [정답률 76%]

┌ (A): 비행 교관과 교육생이 소형 비행기를 운전하고 있는 중 교관이 곧 비행 중 돌발
└ 비상 상황 대처 훈련을 시작할 적절한 때를 기다리고 있다.
➡ 교관과 교육생이 비행 중이며 교관이 훈련을 위해 앞으로 할 행동에 주목한다.

[(B): 교육생이 바다의 배가 보이는지 확인하기 위해 낮게 비행하였고, 배들이 줄을 지어있는 것이 보이자, 교육생은 안전하게 복귀하는 길을 알 수 있었고 안도할 수 있었다.
➡ 바다의 배를 확인하게 된 이유와 안전하게 복귀하는 길을 찾아야 했던 상황이 앞에 나와야 한다. 안도할 수 있었다는 것으로 볼 때, 비상 상황이 끝나는 글의 마무리 부분임을 알 수 있다.

[(C): 교육생이 당황하기 시작했지만 교관은 교육생이 비행에 집중할 수 있게끔 용기를 주자 교육생은 훈련받은 대로 시각 표식을 찾아야겠다는 생각을 하게 되었다.
➡ 교육생이 당황하기 시작한 이유가 앞에 나와야 한다. 시각 표식을 찾아야겠다고 생각하여 바다의 배가 보이는지 확인한 것으로, (B)가 뒤에 이어질 것이다.

[(D): 난기류를 만나자 교관이 숨겨진 버튼을 눌렀고, 비행기 안의 모든 모니터가 꺼지자 교육생은 당황스러워했다.
➡ 비상 훈련을 시작할 때를 기다리는 (A)에 이어지는 내용으로, 교육생이 당황하기 시작했지만 교관이 용기를 주었다는 (C)가 뒤에 이어질 것이다.
　▶ (D) 난기류를 만나 교관이 비상 상황 훈련을 시작하였고 교육생은 당황하게 됨
　→ (C) 당황한 교육생에게 교관이 용기를 주었고 교육생은 해결책을 찾아냄→ (B) 교육생은 바다 위의 배를 확인함으로써 안전하게 복귀하는 길을 알아내고 안도감을 느낌
　▶ 글의 순서는 ⑤ (D) — (C) — (B)임

44 정답 ②

밑줄 친 (a)~(e) 중에서 가리키는 대상이 나머지 넷과 다른 것은?
① (a) ② (b) ③ (c) ④ (d) ⑤ (e)
= the student　= the instructor　= The student　= the student　= the student

▶왜 정답? ✽✽❀ [정답률 73%]

② (b) her: 교육생이 안도감을 느끼며 쳐다본 사람 ▶ the instructor

▶왜 오답?

① (a) she: 비행 중 세상의 아름다움에 대한 경이로움과 감탄을 느낀 사람
　　　　　　　　　　　　　　　　　　　　　　▶ the student
③ (c) You: 교관이 용기를 주고 있는 대상 ▶ The student
④ (d) I: 스스로 비상 상황에 대처할 수 있다고 믿는 사람 ▶ The student
⑤ (e) she: 꺼진 모니터 속 자신이 어디에 있는지 모른 채 비행기를 조종하고 있는 사람 ▶ the student

45 정답 ④

윗글에 관한 내용으로 적절하지 않은 것은?
① 교관과 교육생이 소형 비행기에 타고 있었다. Flying the small plane was a student pilot who was sitting alongside an experienced flight instructor.
② 배들은 서로 떨어져 있었지만 한 줄을 이루고 있었다.
　　　　Although the ships were far apart, they were all sailing in a line.
③ 교관은 어려운 상황에서는 집중이 가장 중요하다고 말했다.
　　　The most important thing is to focus on your flight in those situations.
④ 비행기 내부의 모니터가 깜박이다가 다시 정상 작동했다. Suddenly, all the monitors inside the plane flashed several times then went out completely!
⑤ 교육생은 지도 이외의 다른 도구는 가지고 있지 않았다.
　　　She did have a map, but no other instruments.

▶왜 정답? ✽✽❀ [정답률 74%]

비행기 내부의 모니터가 깜박이다가 완전히 꺼졌다고(all the monitors ~ then went out completely!) 했다. 따라서 비행기 내부의 모니터가 깜박이다가 다시 정상 작동했다는 ④은 적절하지 않다.

▶왜 오답?

① 교관과 교육생이 소형 비행기에 타고 있었다. (Flying the small plane was a student pilot ~ an experienced flight instructor.)
② 배들은 서로 떨어져 있었지만 한 줄을 이루고 있었다. (Although the ships were far apart, they were all sailing in a line.)
③ 교관은 어려운 상황에서는 집중이 가장 중요하다고 말했다. (The most important thing is to focus on your flight in those situations.)
⑤ 교육생은 지도 이외의 다른 도구는 가지고 있지 않았다. (She did have a map, but no other instruments.)

01 celebrate our success / They'll be available / impressed / variety / personal

02 assignment / quite easily / artificial / typed in the questions / a lot of time / found out / keep that in mind

03 Have you ever thought / lets you / make you compare / luxurious / Continuously / stops you from / self-esteem

04 just a / stuck in / went home / What about / adorable / Did you notice / fountain

05 applied for / Would you like / tried to show / have you picked / experiment / haven't even started yet

06 multiple pockets / functional / great deal / though / take it as well / Gift wrapping / Here's my credit card

07 went to a rock concert / I've been preparing / presenting / if you are available / hope you

08 announcement / curious about it / does it cost / reasonable / expect about the same / I'm in

09 delighted to announce / will be held / graduates / giving some tips / ask them in advance / registration / maximum

10 has just begun / cordless / check the battery life / charge it as often / some of these / definitely

11 adopting a cat / requires / responsibility / totally ready

12 completely / deadline / submit it / have some time

13 experiencing / visited a local clinic / By the way / kind of injury / posture / I thought I didn't / without any injuries

14 climate change / temperature / won't be able to / instead of / Absolutely / put it into action

15 unusually / pale / just a bit tired / a couple of days off

[16~17] representative / let you know / upcoming election / Candidates / instructions / display posters / will be removed / distributed / respectful

01 궁금한
02 능력
03 길
04 영구적인
05 자손
06 digest
07 pleasure
08 density
09 evolve
10 prematurely
11 pass by
12 set aside
13 fire off
14 be loaded with
15 settle down
16 assembly
17 succeeding
18 commodities
19 vital
20 frequently
21 extinction
22 threaten
23 literary
24 migrate
25 punishment
26 resistance
27 critical
28 reflection
29 messy
30 excessive
31 flexibility
32 interruptions
33 separately
34 authority
35 hazardous
36 instruments
37 remarkable
38 preserve
39 exotic
40 refine

01 정답 ②　＊e-스포츠 대회 자원봉사자 모집

W : Good afternoon, everybody.
여 : 안녕하세요, 여러분.

This is your student council president, Monica Brown.
저는 여러분들의 학생 회장 Monica Brown입니다.

Our school's annual e-sports competition 〔미래시제 수동태〕 will be held on the last day of the semester. 〔단서 1〕 학교의 연례 e-스포츠 대회가 열릴 것임
우리 학교의 연례 e-스포츠 대회가 학기의 마지막 날에 열립니다.

For the competition, we need some volunteers 〔형용사적 용법(volunteers 수식)〕 to help set up computers. 〔단서 2〕 컴퓨터 설치를 도울 자원봉사자가 필요함
이 대회를 위해, 우리는 컴퓨터 설치를 도와줄 자원봉사자들이 필요합니다.

If you 〔'~에 관심이 있다'〕 're interested in helping us 〔목적격 보어(원형부정사)〕 make the competition successful, please fill out the volunteer application form and email it to me.
저희가 대회를 성공적으로 진행할 수 있도록 돕는 데에 관심이 있으시다면, 자원봉사 신청서를 작성하여 저에게 이메일로 보내주시기 바랍니다.

For more information, please visit our school website.
더 많은 정보를 원하시면, 학교 웹사이트에 방문하세요.

I hope many of you will join us.
많은 분들이 저희와 함께 하기를 바랍니다.

Thank you for listening.
들어주셔서 감사합니다.

- council ⓝ 의회　• president ⓝ 회장　• annual ⓐ 연례의
- competition ⓝ 대회　• semester ⓝ 학기　• set up 설치하다
- application ⓝ 지원, 신청

다음을 듣고, 여자가 하는 말의 목적으로 가장 적절한 것을 고르시오.
① 체육대회 종목을 소개하려고 체육대회 종목을 소개하는 것이 아님
②대회 자원봉사자를 모집하려고 컴퓨터 설치를 도와줄 자원봉사자가 필요하다고 했음
③ 학생 회장 선거 일정을 공지하려고 학생 회장 선거에 대한 안내가 아님
④ 경기 관람 규칙 준수를 당부하려고 경기 관람 규칙은 언급되지 않음
⑤ 학교 홈페이지 주소 변경을 안내하려고 학교 홈페이지 주소 변경은 언급되지 않음

＞**왜** 정답？ ✽❀❀ [정답률 94%]
학교의 연례 e-스포츠 대회 개최 일정을 안내한 뒤, 대회에 필요한 컴퓨터 설치를 도울 자원봉사자를 구한다며 신청 방법을 설명하고 있으므로 정답은 ②이다.

＞**왜** 오답？
① 체육대회가 아니라 e-스포츠〔컴퓨터 게임을 일컫는 말! 꿀팁〕 대회이며, 종목을 소개하는 것이 아니다.
③ 자신을 학생 회장이라고 소개했을 뿐이다.
④ 경기 관람 규칙에 대한 내용은 언급되지 않았다.
⑤ 더 많은 정보를 위한 웹사이트를 언급했을 뿐, 주소 변경을 안내한 것이 아니다. 〔함정〕

02 정답 ①　＊창의적인 생각을 돕는 산책

M : Hannah, how's your design project going?
남 : Hannah, 디자인 프로젝트는 어떻게 되어가고 있니?

W : Hey, Aiden. I'm still working on it, but I'm not making much progress.
여 : 안녕, Aiden. 나는 아직 작업 중인데 진전이 별로 없어.

M : Can you tell me what the problem is?
남 : 무엇이 문제인지 말해줄 수 있어?

W : Hmm... It's hard 〔가주어 / 진주어〕 to think of creative ideas. I feel like I'm wasting my time. 〔단서 1〕 여자는 창의적인 아이디어를 생각해 내기가 어렵다고 함
여 : 흠… 창의적인 아이디어를 생각해 내기가 어려워. 나는 시간을 낭비하고 있는 것 같은 기분이야.

M : I understand. 〔'~하는 게 어때?'〕 Why don't you take a walk?
남 : 나는 이해해. 산책을 해보는 게 어때? 〔단서 2〕 남자는 여자에게 산책을 권함

W : How can 〔지시대명사〕 that help me to improve my creativity?
여 : 그게 내 창의력을 향상하는 데 어떻게 도움이 되는 거야?

M : It will actually 〔make+목적어+목적격 보어(형용사)〕 make your brain more active. Then you'll see things differently. 〔단서 3〕 산책은 뇌를 더 활발하게 만들어 줄 것임
남 : 그것이 실제로 너의 뇌를 더 활발하게 만들어 줄 거야. 그러면 넌 사물을 다르게 보게 될 거야.

W : But I don't have time for that.
여 : 하지만 난 그럴 시간이 없어.

M : You don't need a lot of time. Even a short walk will help you 〔'생각해 내다'〕 to come up with creative ideas.
남 : 넌 많은 시간이 필요하지 않아. 짧은 산책이라도 네가 창의적인 아이디어를 떠올리는 것을 도울 거야.

W : Then I'll try it. Thanks for the tip.
여 : 그럼 시도해 볼게. 조언 고마워.

- progress ⓝ 진전, 진행　• creative ⓐ 창의적인
- waste ⓥ 낭비하다　• improve ⓥ 향상하다
- creativity ⓝ 창의력　• active ⓐ 활발한

대화를 듣고, 남자의 의견으로 가장 적절한 것을 고르시오.
①산책은 창의적인 생각을 할 수 있게 돕는다. 산책은 뇌를 더 활발하게 만든다고 함
② 식사 후 과격한 운동은 소화를 방해한다. 소화와 관련된 대화가 아님
③ 지나친 스트레스는 집중력을 감소시킨다. 집중을 못 해서 고민 중인 것이 아님
④ 독서를 통해 창의력을 증진할 수 있다. 창의력 증진의 방법으로 독서가 아닌 산책을 추천함
⑤ 꾸준한 운동은 기초체력을 향상시킨다. 꾸준한 운동을 권장한 것이 아님

＞**왜** 정답？ ✽❀❀ [정답률 92%]
디자인 프로젝트를 위한 창의적인 아이디어를 생각해 내기가 어려운 여자에게 남자는 짧을지라도 산책은 뇌를 더 활발하게 한다며 산책을 권했다. 따라서 남자의 의견으로 가장 적절한 것은 ①이다.

＞**왜** 오답？
② 식사나 소화와 관련된 대화가 아니다.
③ 여자가 집중을 못 해서 스트레스를 받는 상황이 아니다.
④ 창의력 증진의 방법으로 독서가 아닌 산책을 추천했다.
⑤ 꾸준한 운동의 예로 산책을 든 것이 아니다.

03 정답 ①　＊제주도로 소포 발송하기

W : Excuse me. Could you please tell me 〔의문사+주어+동사(간접의문문)〕 where I can put this box?
여 : 실례합니다. 제가 이 상자를 어디에 놓을 수 있는지 알려주시겠어요?

M : Right here on this counter. How can I help you today?
남 : 바로 여기 이 카운터 위에요. 오늘은 어떻게 도와드릴까요?

W : I'd like to send this to Jeju Island.
여 : 저는 이걸 제주도로 보내고 싶어요. 〔단서 1〕 여자는 물건을 제주도로 보내고 싶음

M : Sure. Are there any breakable items in the box?
남 : 물론이죠. 박스 안에 깨지기 쉬운 물건이 있나요?

W : No, there are only clothes in it.
여 : 아니요, 옷만 들어있어요.

M : Then, there should be no problem.
남 : 그럼, 문제없겠네요.

2023.6
6회

W : I see. What's the fastest way **to send** it? <small>형용사적 용법(way 수식)</small>

여 : 그렇군요. 그것을 가장 빨리 보내는 방법은 무엇인가요?

M : You can send the package by express mail, but there's an extra charge. <small>단서 2 남자는 우편 발송 관련 비용을 안내함</small>

남 : 소포를 특급 우편으로 보낼 수 있지만, 추가 요금이 부과됩니다.

W : That's okay. I want it **to be delivered** <small>to부정사의 수동태</small> as soon as possible. <small>'가능한 한 빨리'</small> When will it arrive in Jeju if it goes out today?

여 : 괜찮아요. 저는 이것이 가능한 한 빨리 배송됐으면 합니다. 오늘 발송하면 제주도에 언제 도착하나요?

M : If you send it today, it will be there by this Friday.

남 : 오늘 보내시면, 이번 주 금요일까지 도착할 거예요.

W : Oh, Friday will be great. I'll do the express mail.

여 : 오, 금요일이면 좋습니다. 특급 우편으로 할게요.

- **breakable** ⓐ 깨지기 쉬운
- **package** ⓝ 소포, 상자
- **express** ⓐ 급행의, 속달의
- **charge** ⓝ 요금
- **arrive** ⓥ 도착하다

대화를 듣고, 두 사람의 관계를 가장 잘 나타낸 것을 고르시오.

① 고객 – 우체국 직원 <small>여자는 물건을 제주도로 발송하고자 하고 남자는 이를 도와줌</small>
② 투숙객 – 호텔 지배인 <small>여자가 제주도에 투숙하려는 것이 아님</small>
③ 여행객 – 여행 가이드 <small>여행과 관련된 상황이 아님</small>
④ 아파트 주민 – 경비원 <small>택배를 수령하는 상황이 아니라 발송하는 상황임</small>
⑤ 손님 – 옷가게 주인 <small>옷을 구매하는 상황이 아님</small>

ᐅ왜 정답? ✿✿✿ [정답률 90%]

여자가 옷을 제주도로 최대한 빨리 발송하고 싶다고 하자 남자는 소포 안에 깨지기 쉬운 물건이 있는지 확인한 뒤 특급 우편과 추가 비용이 있음을 안내했다. 따라서 두 사람의 관계로 가장 적절한 것은 ①이다.

ᐅ왜 오답?

② 여자가 제주도에 가서 투숙하려는 상황이 아니다.
③ 제주도는 물건을 보내고자 하는 도착지이지, 여행지가 아니다. <small>함정</small>
④ 아파트에서 택배를 수령하는 상황이 아니다.
⑤ 고객과 직원의 관계이긴 하지만, 옷가게에서의 대화가 아니다.

---

04 정답 ④ *버스킹을 한 Kayla

M : Kayla, I heard you went busking on the street last weekend.

남 : Kayla, 나는 네가 지난 주말에 길거리에서 버스킹을 했다고 들었어.

W : It was amazing! I've got a picture here. Look!

여 : 정말 멋졌어! 여기 사진 있어. 봐봐!

M : Oh, you're wearing the hat **I gave you**. <small>앞에 목적격 관계대명사가 생략됨</small>

남 : 오, 너는 내가 네게 준 모자를 쓰고 있네. <small>①의 단서 여자는 모자를 쓰고 있음</small>

W : Yeah, I really like it.

여 : 응, 정말 마음에 들어.

M : Looks great. This boy **playing the guitar** next to you must be your brother Kevin. <small>앞에 주격 관계대명사와 be동사가 생략됨</small> <small>②의 단서 옆에 기타를 연주하는 남자아이가 있음</small>

남 : 멋지다. 네 옆에서 기타를 연주하는 남자아이는 네 남동생 Kevin이겠구나.

W : You're right. He played **while** I sang. <small>부사절 접속사</small>

여 : 맞아. 내가 노래하는 동안 그가 연주했어.

M : Cool. Why did you leave the guitar case **open**? <small>leave의 목적격 보어(형용사)</small>

남 : 멋져. 너 기타 케이스는 왜 열어 둔 거야? <small>③의 단서 기타 케이스를 열어 둠</small>

W : That's for the audience. If they like our performance, they give **us** **some money**. <small>간접목적어 직접목적어</small>

여 : 그건 관객을 위해서야. 관객들이 우리 연주가 마음에 들면, 우리에게 돈을 좀 주거든.

M : Oh, and you set up two speakers! <small>④의 단서 스피커는 두 개가 아니라 한 개임</small>

남 : 아, 그리고 너는 스피커도 두 개 설치했네!

W : I did. I recently bought them.

여 : 그랬지. 나는 최근에 그것들을 샀어.

M : I see. And did you design that poster on the wall?

남 : 그렇구나. 그리고 벽에 걸린 저 포스터는 네가 디자인한 거야? <small>⑤의 단서 벽에 포스터가 걸려 있음</small>

W : Yeah. My brother and I worked on it together.

여 : 맞아. 내 남동생과 내가 함께 작업한 거야.

M : It sounds like you really had a lot of fun!

남 : 정말 재미있었던 것처럼 들려!

- **leave** ⓥ 그대로 두다
- **audience** ⓝ 관객, 청중
- **performance** ⓝ 연주, 공연
- **recently** ⓐⓓ 최근에

대화를 듣고, 그림에서 대화의 내용과 일치하지 않는 것을 고르시오.

ᐅ왜 정답? ✿✿✿ [정답률 90%]

남자는 여자에게 스피커가 두 개 설치된 것으로 보인다고 했지만, 그림에는 스피커가 한 개만 설치되어 있으므로 ④이 대화의 내용과 일치하지 않는다.

ᐅ왜 오답?

① 여자가 모자를 쓴 채로 버스킹을 하고 있다.
② 남자아이가 여자 옆에서 기타를 연주하고 있다.
③ 기타 케이스를 열어 두었다.
⑤ 벽에 포스터가 걸려 있다.

---

05 정답 ⑤ *Jake를 위한 생일 선물 준비

W : Honey, are we ready for Jake's birthday party tomorrow?

여 : 여보, 우리 내일 있을 Jake의 생일 파티는 준비됐나요?

M : I sent the invitation cards last week. What about other things? <small>①의 함정</small>

남 : 내가 지난주에 초대장을 보냈어요. 다른 것들은 어때요?

W : I'm not sure. Let's check.

여 : 잘 모르겠어요. 확인해 봅시다.

M : We are expecting a lot of guests. How about the dinner menu?

남 : 손님이 많이 올 것 같아요. 저녁 메뉴는 어때요?

W : I **haven't decided** yet. <small>현재완료</small>

여 : 아직 정하지 못했어요.

M : We won't have much time **to cook**, so let's just order pizza. <small>형용사적 용법(time 수식)</small>

남 : 우리는 요리할 시간이 별로 없으니까, 그냥 피자를 주문해요.

W : Okay. I'll do it tomorrow. What about the present? <small>②의 함정</small>

여 : 알았어요. 내가 내일 할게요. 선물은요?

M : Oh, you mean the smartphone? I forgot to get it!

남 : 아, 스마트폰 말하는 거예요? 내가 사는 걸 깜빡했어요!

W : That's alright. Can you **go** to the electronics store and **buy** it now? <small>병렬 구조</small> <small>단서 1 여자가 남자에게 스마트폰을 사 올 것을 요청함</small>

여 : 괜찮아요. 당신이 지금 전자 제품 매장에 가서 사 올 수 있어요?

M : No problem. I'll do it right away. <small>단서 2 남자는 바로 사러 가겠다고 했음</small>

남 : 그럼요. 지금 바로 사러 갈게요.

W : Good. Then, I'll clean up the living room **while** you're out. <small>③의 함정</small> <small>부사절 접속사</small>

여 : 좋아요. 그럼, 당신이 외출하는 동안 내가 거실을 청소할게요.

- invitation ⓝ 초대 ・ expect ⓥ 예상하다, 기대하다
- decide ⓥ 결정하다 ・ electronics ⓝ 전자 제품
- living room 거실

대화를 듣고, 남자가 할 일로 가장 적절한 것을 고르시오.
① 초대장 보내기 남자가 지난주에 보냄
② 피자 주문하기 여자가 내일 주문할 것임
③ 거실 청소하기 여자가 청소할 것임
④ 꽃다발 준비하기 언급되지 않음
⑤ 스마트폰 사러 가기 남자가 지금 사러 간다고 함

왜 정답? ✿✿✿ [정답률 91%]

Jake의 생일 파티를 준비하고 있는 상황이다. 여자가 남자에게 선물인 스마트폰이 준비됐는지 묻자, 남자는 깜빡했다고 하면서 지금 바로 사러 간다고 했으므로 정답은 ⑤이다.

왜 오답?

① 지난주에 이미 초대장을 보냈다.
② 여자가 내일 주문하기로 했다.
③ 남자가 스마트폰을 사러 간 동안 여자가 청소하기로 했다.
④ 꽃다발은 언급되지 않았다.

---

06 정답 ③ ＊담요와 쿠션 구매하기

M : Good morning! How can I help you?
남 : 좋은 아침입니다! 무엇을 도와드릴까요?

W : Hi. I'm **looking for** a blanket and some cushions for my sofa. '찾다, 구하다'
여 : 안녕하세요. 저는 소파에 놓을 담요와 쿠션을 찾고 있어요.

M : Okay. We've got some **on sale**. Would you like to have a look? '할인 중인'
남 : 알겠습니다. 할인 중인 것들이 있습니다. 한번 보시겠어요?

W : Yes. How much is this green blanket?
여 : 네. 이 녹색 담요는 얼마인가요?

M : That's $40. 단서1 녹색 담요는 40달러임
남 : 그건 40달러입니다.

W : Oh, I love the color green. Can you also show **me some** cushions **that** go well with this blanket? 간접목적어 / 직접목적어 / 주격 관계대명사
여 : 오, 저는 초록색이 맘에 드네요. 이 담요와 잘 어울리는 쿠션도 좀 보여주시겠어요?

M : Sure! How about these?
남 : 물론이죠! 이것들은 어떤가요?

W : They look good. I need two of them. How much are they?
여 : 좋아 보이네요. 그것들로 두 개 주세요. 얼마인가요?

M : The cushions are $20 each. 단서2 쿠션은 한 개에 20달러임
남 : 쿠션은 하나당 20달러입니다.

W : Okay. I'll take one green blanket and two cushions. Can I use this coupon? 단서3 40달러인 녹색 담요 한 개와 20달러인 쿠션 두 개를 구매하고 쿠폰을 사용함
여 : 알겠습니다. 저는 녹색 담요 하나와 쿠션 두 개를 구매할게요. 이 쿠폰을 사용할 수 있을까요?

M : Sure. It will give **you** 10% **off the total**. 단서4 10퍼센트를 할인받음 간접목적어 / 직접목적어
남 : 물론입니다. 총액에서 10퍼센트 할인을 받으시게 됩니다.

W : Thanks! Here's my credit card.
여 : 고맙습니다! 여기 제 신용카드가 있습니다.

- blanket ⓝ 담요 ・ go well with ~와 잘 어울리다

대화를 듣고, 여자가 지불할 금액을 고르시오. [3점]
① $54 ② $60 ③ $72 ④ $76 ⑤ $80
($40(녹색 담요 한 개)+$20*2(쿠션 두 개))*0.9(10% 할인)

왜 정답? ✿✿✿ [정답률 84%]

여자는 하나에 40달러인 녹색 담요 한 개와 개당 20달러인 쿠션 두 개를 구매했으므로 총 80달러를 지불해야 하는데, 총액의 10퍼센트가 할인되는 쿠폰을 사용했으므로 지불할 금액은 ③ '72달러'이다.

---

07 정답 ④ ＊콘서트에 갈 수 없는 Justin

W : Hello, Justin. What are you doing?
여 : 안녕, Justin. 뭐 하고 있어?

M : Hi, Ellie. I'm doing my project for art class. ⑤의 함정
남 : 안녕, Ellie. 나는 미술 수업 프로젝트를 하고 있어.

W : Can you go to a rock concert with me this Saturday? My sister gave **me two tickets**! 간접목적어 / 직접목적어
여 : 이번 주 토요일에 나랑 같이 록 콘서트에 갈 수 있어? 언니가 표를 두 장 줬거든!

M : I'd love **to**! But I'm afraid I **can't**. 뒤에 go to a rock concert가 생략됨
남 : 그러고 싶어! 하지만 그럴 수 없을 것 같아.

W : Do you have to work that day?
여 : 너는 그날 일해야 해?

M : No, I don't work on Saturdays. ①의 함정
남 : 아니, 나는 토요일에는 근무하지 않아.

W : Then, why not? I **thought** you really like rock music. 뒤에 목적어절 접속사 that이 생략됨
여 : 그럼, 왜 안 돼? 난 네가 록 음악을 정말 좋아한다고 생각했는데.

M : Of course I **do**. But I have to take care of my friend's dog this Saturday. 단서 대동사(= like) 이번 주 토요일에 친구의 개를 돌봐줘야 함
남 : 물론 좋아하지. 하지만 이번 주 토요일에는 친구의 개를 돌봐줘야 해.

W : Oh, really? Is your friend going somewhere?
여 : 아, 그래? 네 친구가 어디 가는 거야?

M : He **'s visiting** his grandmother that day. ③의 함정 가까운 미래를 대신하는 현재진행형
남 : 그 친구는 그날 할머니를 뵈러 가.

W : Okay, no problem. I'm sure I can find someone else to go with me.
여 : 그래, 괜찮아. 나는 나와 함께 갈 다른 사람을 찾을 수 있을 거야.

- take care of ~을 돌보다 ・ visit ⓥ 방문하다

대화를 듣고, 남자가 록 콘서트에 갈 수 없는 이유를 고르시오.
① 일을 하러 가야 해서 토요일에는 근무하지 않는다고 했음
② 피아노 연습을 해야 해서 언급되지 않음
③ 할머니를 뵈러 가야 해서 할머니를 뵈러 가는 건 남자의 친구임
④ 친구의 개를 돌봐야 해서 친구의 개를 돌봐줘야 한다고 했음
⑤ 과제를 아직 끝내지 못해서 과제 때문에 콘서트에 가지 못하는 것이 아님

왜 정답? ✿✿✿ [정답률 94%]

남자는 같이 록 콘서트에 가자는 여자에게 이번 주 토요일에는 할머니를 뵈러 가는 친구의 개를 돌봐줘야 한다고 말했다. 따라서 남자가 록 콘서트에 갈 수 없는 이유는 ④이다.

왜 오답?

① 남자는 토요일에 일을 하지 않는다고 했다.
② 피아노 연습은 대화에 언급되지 않았다.
③ 할머니를 뵈러 가는 사람은 남자에게 개를 돌봐달라고 부탁한 남자의 친구이다.
⑤ 남자가 현재 하고 있는 일이지, 토요일에 콘서트를 가지 못하는 이유가 아니다.
(▶◀ 이유: 과제 때문에 콘서트에 가지 못한다고 직접적으로 말하지 않았다.)

08 정답 ③ ＊환경의 날 행사 포스터 확인하기

W : Scott, did you see this Eco Day poster?
여 : Scott, 이 환경의 날 포스터 봤어?

M : No, not yet. Let me see. It's an event for picking up trash while walking around a park.
남 : 아니, 아직. 어디 보자. 공원을 산책하면서 쓰레기를 줍는 행사구나.
'~하는 게 어때?'
W : Why don't we do it together? It's next Sunday from 10 a.m. to 5 p.m. ①의 단서 행사 시간
여 : 우리 같이 하는 게 어때? 그건 다음 주 일요일 오전 10시부터 오후 5시까지야.
현재완료 진행형
M : Sounds good. I've been thinking a lot about the environment lately.
남 : 좋아. 나는 요즘 환경에 대해 많이 생각하고 있었어.

W : Me, too. Also, the event will be held in Eastside Park. You know, we often used to go there. ②의 단서 행사 장소
여 : 나도. 그리고, 이번 행사는 Eastside 공원에서 열릴 예정이야. 너도 알다시피, 우리는 자주 그곳에 가곤 했잖아.

M : That's great. Oh, look at this. We have to bring our own gloves and small bags for the trash. ④의 단서 준비물
남 : 잘됐다. 오, 이것 좀 봐. 우리는 쓰레기를 주울 장갑과 작은 봉투를 직접 가져가야 해.

W : No problem. I have extra. I can bring some for you as well.
여 : 문제없어. 나한테 여분이 있어. 내가 네 것도 가져갈게.

M : Okay, thanks. Do we have to sign up for the event?
남 : 좋아, 고마워. 우리가 이 행사에 등록해야 하는 건가?
뒤에 목적격 접속사 that이 생략됨
W : Yes. The poster says we can do it online. ⑤의 단서 등록 방법
여 : 응. 포스터에 온라인으로 할 수 있다고 쓰여 있어.
'기대하다'
M : Let's do it right now. I'm looking forward to it.
남 : 지금 바로 하자. 나 기대돼.

・ trash ⓝ 쓰레기 ・ environment ⓝ 환경 ・ lately ⓪ 최근에
・ sign up for ~에 등록[신청]하다

대화를 듣고, Eco Day에 관해 언급되지 않은 것을 고르시오.

① 행사 시간 It's next Sunday from 10 a.m. to 5 p.m.
② 행사 장소 the event will be held in Eastside Park
③ 참가비 언급되지 않음
④ 준비물 We have to bring our own gloves and small bags for the trash.
⑤ 등록 방법 The poster says we can do it online.

왜 정답？ ❋❋❋ [정답률 94%]

환경의 날 포스터에서 행사 시간, 행사 장소, 준비물, 등록 방법은 확인할 수 있었지만, 참가비는 확인할 수 없었으므로 정답은 ③이다.

왜 오답？

① 다음 주 일요일 오전 10시부터 오후 5시까지 열린다고 했다.
② 이번 행사는 Eastside 공원에서 열릴 예정이라고 했다.
④ 쓰레기를 줍는 데 쓸 장갑과 작은 봉투를 준비해야 한다고 했다.
⑤ 온라인으로 등록할 수 있다고 했다.

---

09 정답 ⑤ ＊제1회 Eastville 댄스 경연 대회

M : Hello, Eastville High School students.
남 : 안녕하세요, Eastville 고등학교 학생 여러분.

This is your P.E. teacher, Mr. Wilson.
저는 체육 선생님 Wilson입니다.
to let의 목적격 보어(원형부정사)
I'm pleased to let you know that we're hosting the first Eastville Dance Contest. ①의 단서 처음 개최되는 경연임
저는 제1회 Eastville 댄스 경연 대회를 개최한다는 소식을 여러분에게 알려드리게 되어 기쁩니다.

주격 관계대명사
Any Eastville students who love dancing can participate in the contest as a team.
춤추기를 좋아하는 Eastville 학생이라면 누구나 팀으로 경연 대회에 참가할 수 있습니다.

All kinds of dance are allowed. ②의 단서 모든 종류의 춤이 허용됨
모든 종류의 춤이 허용됩니다.
③의 단서 춤 영상을 8월 15일까지 업로드 해야 함
If you'd like to participate, please upload your team's dance video to our school website by August 15th.
참가를 원하시면, 8월 15일까지 학교 웹사이트에 여러분의 팀의 춤 영상을 업로드 해주세요.

Students can vote for their favorite video from August 16th to 20th. ④의 단서 학생들은 가장 좋아하는 영상에 투표할 수 있음
학생들은 8월 16일부터 20일까지 가장 좋아하는 영상에 투표할 수 있습니다.

The winning team will receive a trophy as a prize.
우승팀에게는 트로피가 상으로 수여됩니다. ⑤의 단서 우승팀은 상으로 트로피를 받게 됨
형용사적 용법(opportunity 수식)
Don't miss this great opportunity to show off your talents!
여러분의 재능을 뽐낼 이 좋은 기회를 놓치지 마세요!

・ P.E. ⓝ 체육(physical education) ・ host ⓥ 개최하다, 주최하다
・ participate ⓥ 참가하다 ・ allow ⓥ 허용하다 ・ vote ⓥ 투표하다
・ receive ⓥ 받다 ・ prize ⓝ 부상 ・ opportunity ⓝ 기회
・ show off ~을 뽐내다 ・ talent ⓝ 재능

Eastville Dance Contest에 관한 다음 내용을 듣고, 일치하지 않는 것을 고르시오.

① 처음으로 개최되는 경연이다. we're hosting the first Eastville Dance Contest
② 모든 종류의 춤이 허용된다. All kinds of dance are allowed.
③ 춤 영상을 8월 15일까지 업로드 해야 한다. please upload your team's dance video to our school website by August 15th
④ 학생들은 가장 좋아하는 영상에 투표할 수 있다. Students can vote for their favorite video
⑤ 우승팀은 상으로 상품권을 받게 될 것이다. The winning team will receive a trophy as a prize.

왜 정답？ ❋❋❋ [정답률 84%]

우승팀은 상으로 트로피를 받게 될 것이라고(The winning team will receive a trophy as a prize.) 했으므로 상품권을 받게 될 것이라고 한 ⑤가 일치하지 않는다.

왜 오답？

① 제1회 경연 대회라고 했다.
② 모든 종류의 춤이 허용된다고 했다.
③ 참가하려면 춤 영상을 8월 15일까지 업로드 하라고 했다.
④ 학생들은 가장 좋아하는 영상에 투표할 수 있다고 했다.

---

10 정답 ④ ＊정수기 선택하기

M : Honey, we need a water purifier for our new house.
남 : 여보, 우리는 새집에 정수기가 필요해요.

W : You're right. Let's order one online.
여 : 당신 말이 맞아요. 온라인으로 하나를 주문합시다.

M : Good idea. Look! These are the five bestsellers.
남 : 좋은 생각이에요. 봐요! 이것들이 가장 잘나가는 다섯 개의 상품이에요.

W : I see. What's our budget?
여 : 그렇군요. 우리 예산은 얼마나 돼요?

M : Well, I don't want to spend more than 800 dollars. 단서1 800달러가 넘지 않아야 함(⑤ 제외)
남 : 음, 나는 800달러 이상은 쓰고 싶지 않아요.

W : Okay, how about the water tank capacity? 단서2 물탱크는 5리터가 딱 맞음(① 제외)
여 : 좋아요, 물탱크 용량은요?

M : I think the five-liter tank would be perfect for us.
남 : 내 생각에는 5리터짜리 물탱크가 우리한테 딱 맞을 것 같아요.
부정대명사(= water purifiers)
W : I think so, too. And I like the ones with a power-saving mode. 단서3 절전 모드가 있는 모델을 구매하려고 함(③ 제외)
여 : 나도 그렇게 생각해요. 그리고 나는 절전 모드가 있는 것들이 좋아요.

M : Okay, then we can save electricity. Now, there are just two options left.
남 : 좋아요, 그러면 우리는 전기를 절약할 수 있겠네요. 이제, 두 개의 선택지만 남았어요.

「the+비교급 ~, the+비교급 ...」: ~할수록 더 ...하다
W : Let's look at the warranties. The longer, the better.
여 : 보증기간을 살펴봅시다. 길수록 더 좋잖아요.   단서 4 보증 기간이 더 긴 모델이 좋음(② 제외)

M : I agree. We should order this model.
남 : 동의해요. 우리는 이 모델을 주문해야겠네요.

- purifier ⓝ 정화 장치   - budget ⓝ 예산   - capacity ⓝ 용량, 능력
- electricity ⓝ 전기   - warranty ⓝ (상품 등의) 보증 (기간)

다음 표를 보면서 대화를 듣고, 두 사람이 구입할 정수기를 고르시오.

Water Purifiers 정수기

	Model 모델	Price 가격	Water Tank Capacity (liters) 물탱크 용량 (리터)	Power-saving Mode 절전 모드	Warranty 보증 기간
①	A	$570	4 물탱크 용량이 5리터가 아님	×	1 year
②	B	$650	5	○	1 year
③	C	$680	5	× 절전 모드 없음	3 years
④	D	$740	5	○	3 years
⑤	E	$830 800달러가 넘음	6	○	3 years 보증 기간이 짧음

✎왜 정답 ? ✳✳✳ [정답률 90%]
남자와 여자는 800달러는 넘지 않고(⑤ 제외), 물탱크 용량이 5리터이며(① 제외), 절전 모드가 있는(③ 제외) 것 중, 보증 기간이 더 긴(② 제외) 정수기를 선택했으므로 정답은 ④이다.

✎왜 오답 ?
① 물탱크의 용량이 4리터로, 5리터가 되지 않는다.
② 보증 기간이 1년으로 보증 기간이 3년인 타 모델들보다 짧다.
③ 절전 모드가 없다.
⑤ 800달러 이상 쓰고 싶지 않다고 했다.

11 정답 ①   * 자동차 전시회에 입장하기 ────────

부사적 용법 (감정의 원인)
M : Let's get inside. I'm so excited to see this auto show.
남 : 안으로 들어가자. 나는 이번 자동차 전시회를 보게 돼서 정말 기뻐.

부사적 용법(목적)
W : Look over there. So many people are already standing in line to buy tickets.
여 : 저기 봐봐. 벌써 정말 많은 사람들이 표를 사기 위해 줄을 서 있어.

M : Fortunately, I bought our tickets in advance.
남 : 다행히, 내가 미리 표를 구입했어.   단서 남자가 표를 미리 구입해 놓았음

W : **Great. We don't have to wait in line.**
여 : 좋아. 우린 줄 서서 기다리지 않아도 되겠네.

- auto ⓝ 자동차   - in advance 미리, 사전에

대화를 듣고, 남자의 마지막 말에 대한 여자의 응답으로 가장 적절한 것을 고르시오.
① Great. We don't have to wait in line.
좋아. 우린 줄 서서 기다리지 않아도 되겠네.   미리 표를 구입했기 때문에 줄을 서지 않아도 됨
② All right. We can come back later.
그래. 우리는 나중에 와도 돼.   바로 입장할 수 있는 상황임
③ Good job. Let's buy the tickets.
잘했어. 표를 사자.   미리 표를 구입함
④ No worries. I will stand in line.
걱정 마. 내가 줄을 설게.   줄을 서 있을 필요가 없음
⑤ Too bad. I can't buy that car.
이런. 나는 저 차를 살 수 없어.   차를 구매하는 상황이 아님

✎왜 정답 ? ✳✳✳ [정답률 77%]
자동차 전시회의 표를 구입하기 위해 많은 사람들이 줄을 서 있는 것을 알게 된 여자에게 남자는 미리 표를 구입했다고 말했다. 따라서 여자는 ① '좋아. 우린 줄 서서 기다리지 않아도 되겠네.'라고 응답하는 것이 가장 적절하다.

✎왜 오답 ?
② 표가 있어서 바로 입장할 수 있는 상황인데, 나중에 오자고 하는 것은 적절하지 않다.
③ 남자가 미리 표를 구입했다고 했으므로 표를 사자고 하는 것은 적절하지 않다. 주의
④ 표가 준비됐으므로 여자가 남자를 위해 줄을 설 필요는 없다.
⑤ 아직 전시회에 입장하지 않았기 때문에 적절한 응답이 아니다.

12 정답 ③   * 성적에 문제가 생긴 Chris ────────

앞에 목적격 관계대명사가 생략됨
W : Hi, Chris. Did you check your grade for the history test we took last week?
여 : 안녕, Chris. 너 지난주에 본 역사 시험 성적 확인했어?   단서 1 Chris는 성적에 문제가 있다고 생각함

-thing으로 끝나는 대명사는 뒤에서 수식함
M : Yes. But I think there's something wrong with my grade.
남 : 응. 그런데 내 생각에는 내 성적에 무언가 문제가 있는 것 같아.   단서 2 선생님께 가서 물어볼 것을 권함

W : Don't you think you should go ask Mr. Morgan about it?
여 : 네가 Morgan 선생님께 가서 그것에 관해 물어봐야 한다고 생각하지 않아?

M : **Right. I should go to his office now.**
남 : 맞아. 나는 지금 그의 사무실로 가야겠어.

- register ⓥ 등록하다   - fantastic ⓐ 엄청난, 환상적인

대화를 듣고, 여자의 마지막 말에 대한 남자의 응답으로 가장 적절한 것을 고르시오.
① Yes. You can register online.   수업을 등록하는 상황이 아님
그래. 넌 온라인으로 등록할 수 있어.
② Sorry. I can't see you next week.   두 사람이 만남을 약속하는 상황이 아님
미안해. 나는 다음 주에 너를 못 볼 것 같아.
③ Right. I should go to his office now.   선생님께 가서 물어보라는 말에 적절한 응답임
맞아. 나는 지금 그의 사무실로 가야겠어.
④ Fantastic! I'll take the test tomorrow.   시험은 지난주에 이미 봤음
엄청나! 나는 내일 시험을 볼 거야.
⑤ Of course. I can help him if he needs my help.   남자가 Morgan 선생님을 도와야 하는 상황이 아님
물론이지. 그가 내 도움이 필요하면 내가 도와줄 수 있어.

✎왜 정답 ? ✳✳✳ [정답률 76%]
Chris가 지난주에 본 역사 시험 성적에 문제가 있는 것 같다고 말하자, 여자는 Morgan 선생님께 가서 문의해 볼 것을 권유하였다. 따라서 남자는 ③ '맞아. 나는 지금 그의 사무실로 가야겠어.'라고 응답하는 것이 가장 적절하다.

✎왜 오답 ?
① 시험 성적이 나온 상황으로, 수업을 등록하는 상황이 아니다.
② 두 사람이 언제 만날지 일정을 정하는 상황이 아니다.
④ 시험은 지난주에 이미 봤고 성적이 나온 상황이므로 적절하지 않다.
⑤ Morgan 선생님께 성적 문의를 하러 가는 것이지, 그를 도와주려는 상황이 아니다.
(☞ 이유: 오히려 Morgan 선생님이 Chris에게 할 수 있는 응답이다.)

13 정답 ②   * 헌책에서 발견한 기분 좋은 메모 ────────

M : Mom, did you write this note?
남 : 엄마, 이 메모 엄마가 쓰신 거예요?

W : What's that?
여 : 그게 뭔데?

앞에 목적격 관계대명사가 생략됨
M : I found this in the book you gave me.
남 : 엄마가 제게 주신 책에서 이걸 발견했어요.

앞에 목적격 관계대명사가 생략됨
W : Oh, the one I bought for you at the secondhand bookstore last week?
여 : 아, 지난주에 내가 헌책방에서 네게 사준 것 말이니?

뒤에 목적어절 접속사 that이 생략됨
M : Yes. At first I thought it was a bookmark, but it wasn't. It's a note with a message!
남 : 맞아요. 처음에 저는 그것이 책갈피인 줄 알았는데, 아니었어요. 이건 메시지가 적힌 메모였어요!

W : What does it say?
여 : 뭐라고 적혀 있어?

2023. 6
6회

M : It says, "I hope you enjoy this book."
남 : "당신이 이 책을 즐기시길 바랍니다."라고 적혀 있어요.

W : How sweet! That really brings a smile to my face. 〔단서 1〕 메모는 미소를 짓게 해줌
여 : 정말 다정하구나! 그건 정말 내 얼굴에 미소를 정말 가져다주네.

M : Yeah, mom. I love this message so much.
남 : 맞아요, 엄마. 저는 이 메시지가 정말 마음에 들어요.

W : Well, then, why don't we leave a note if we resell this book later? 〔단서 2〕 책을 되팔 때 메모를 남길 것을 제안함
여 : 음, 그럼, 나중에 이 책을 되팔 때 우리도 메모를 남기는 건 어떨까?

M : Great idea! Our message would make others smile.
남 : 좋은 생각이에요! 우리의 메시지가 다른 사람들을 미소 짓게 할 거예요.

- secondhand ⓐ 중고의 · bookmark ⓝ 책갈피
- resell ⓥ 되팔다 · arrive ⓥ 도착하다

대화를 듣고, 여자의 마지막 말에 대한 남자의 응답으로 가장 적절한 것을 고르시오. [3점]

Man: _____

① I agree. You can save a lot by buying secondhand.
동의해요. 중고를 구입함으로써 많이 절약할 수 있어요. 헌책을 구입하고 있는 상황이 아님
② Great idea! Our message would make others smile.
좋은 생각이에요! 우리의 메시지가 다른 사람들을 미소 짓게 할 거예요.
③ Sorry. I forgot to write a message in the book.
죄송해요. 책에 메시지를 적는 것을 잊었어요. 책에 메시지는 나중에 적자고 함
④ Exactly. Taking notes during class is important.
정확해요. 수업 중에 필기하는 것은 중요해요. 필기하는 것과는 관련 없는 상황임
⑤ Okay. We can arrive on time if we leave now.
알았어요. 지금 출발하면 우리는 제시간에 도착할 수 있어요. 어디론가 이동하는 상황이 아님
└ 나중에 책을 되팔 때 메모를 남기자는 제안에 적절한 응답임

>왜 정답? ✽❀❀ [정답률 83%]

남자가 헌책에서 발견한 메모에 기분이 좋아진 그의 엄마는 책을 되팔 때 그들도 메모를 남기자고 했다. 따라서 이에 대한 남자의 응답으로 가장 적절한 것은 ② '좋은 생각이에요! 우리의 메시지가 다른 사람들을 미소 짓게 할 거예요.'이다.

>왜 오답?

① 헌책을 구입하면서 할 수 있는 응답이므로 적절하지 않다.
③ 나중에 책을 되팔 때 메시지를 적기로 한 것이므로 적절하지 않다.
④ 수업이나 필기와 관련된 대화가 아니다.
⑤ 어디로 이동하고 있는 상황이 아니다.

↑ 대화에서 leave는 떠나다가 아니라 메모를 남기다(leave a note)로 쓰임 〔꿀팁〕

〔14〕 정답 ⑤ ✽ 캠핑을 해보고 싶은 Evan ━━━━━

M : Do you have any plans for this weekend, Sandy?
남 : 이번 주말에 무슨 계획이 있니, Sandy?

W : Hey, Evan. I'm planning to go camping with my family.
여 : 안녕, Evan. 나는 가족들과 캠핑을 갈 계획이야.

M : I've never gone before. Do you go camping often?   현재완료(경험)
남 : 나는 한 번도 가본 적이 없어. 너는 캠핑 자주 가니?

W : Yes. Two or three times a month at least.   적어도, 최소한
여 : 응. 적어도 한 달에 두세 번은 가.

M : That's cool. Why do you like it so much?
남 : 멋지다. 너는 왜 그렇게 캠핑을 좋아해?

W : I like spending time in nature with my family. It makes me feel closer to them.   makes의 목적격 보어(원형부정사)
여 : 나는 가족과 함께 자연에서 시간을 보내는 게 좋아. 그건 내가 가족들과 더 가깝게 느끼도록 만들어.

M : I understand. It's like a family hobby, right?
남 : 이해해. 가족 취미 같은 거잖아, 맞지?

W : Yes, you're right. Camping helps me relieve all my stress, too.   helps의 목적격 보어(원형부정사)
여 : 응, 맞아. 캠핑은 또 내가 스트레스를 해소하도록 도와줘.

M : Sounds interesting. I'd love to try it.   〔단서 1〕 남자가 캠핑에 흥미를 느끼고 가보고 싶다고 말함
남 : 재미있겠다. 나도 한번 해보고 싶어.

W : If you go camping with your family, you'll see what I mean.   선행사를 포함하는 관계대명사
여 : 만약 네가 가족과 함께 캠핑을 가보면, 내 말이 무슨 뜻인지 알게 될 거야.

M : I wish I could, but I don't have any equipment for it.   〔단서 2〕 남자는 캠핑 장비가 없음
남 : 나도 그러고 싶지만, 나는 캠핑을 위한 장비가 하나도 없어.

W : No problem. You can use my equipment.
여 : 문제없어. 너는 내 장비를 사용해도 돼.

- nature ⓝ 자연 · close ⓐ 가까운 · relieve ⓥ 줄이다, 없애다
- equipment ⓝ 장비

대화를 듣고, 남자의 마지막 말에 대한 여자의 응답으로 가장 적절한 것을 고르시오. [3점]

Woman: _____

① Why not? I can bring some food when we go camping.   캠핑하러 가서 먹을 음식을 걱정하는 것이 아님
왜 안 되겠어? 우리가 캠핑 갈 때 내가 음식을 좀 가져갈게.
② I'm sorry. That fishing equipment is not for sale.   낚시가 아니라 캠핑과 관련된 대화임
미안해. 그 낚시 장비는 파는 게 아니야.
③ I don't think so. The price is most important.   남자가 캠핑 장비를
나는 그렇게 생각하지 않아. 가격이 제일 중요해.   구입하는 상황도 아니고, 가격이 중요하지 않다고 말한 것이 아님
④ Really? I'd love to meet your family.   남자가 여자를 초대한 상황이 아님
정말? 나는 너희 가족을 만나고 싶어.
⑤ No problem. You can use my equipment.
문제없어. 너는 내 장비를 사용해도 돼.   캠핑 장비가 없다는 남자에게 할 수 있는 적절한 응답임

>왜 정답? ✽❀❀ [정답률 89%]

주말에 가족들과 캠핑하러 간다는 여자에게 남자는 자신도 캠핑을 해보고 싶지만, 장비가 하나도 없다고 했다. 따라서 캠핑을 권하는 입장인 여자는 ⑤ '문제없어. 너는 내 장비를 사용해도 돼.'라고 응답하는 것이 가장 적절하다.

>왜 오답?

① 남자는 캠핑 장비가 없다고 했지, 함께 캠핑하러 갈 때 먹을 음식을 걱정하는 것이 아니다.
② 낚시가 아니라 캠핑과 관련된 대화를 나누었다.
③ 남자가 캠핑 장비를 구입하는 상황도 아니고, 가격이 중요하지 않다고 말한 것도 아니다.
④ 남자가 여자를 초대한 상황이 아니다.

〔15〕 정답 ⑤ ✽ 책을 대출하고 싶은 Violet ━━━━━

W : Violet and Peter are classmates.
여 : Violet과 Peter는 같은 반 친구이다.

They're doing their science group assignment together.
그들은 함께 과학 팀 과제를 하고 있다.

On Saturday morning, they meet at the public library.
토요일 아침, 그들은 공공 도서관에서 만난다.

They decide to find the books they need in different sections of the library.   앞에 목적격 관계대명사가 생략됨
그들은 도서관의 서로 다른 구역에서 필요한 책을 찾기로 결정한다.

Violet finds two useful books and tries to check them out.   병렬 구조
Violet은 유용한 책 두 권을 발견하고 그것들을 대출하려고 한다.

Unfortunately, she suddenly realizes that she didn't bring her library card.   목적어절 접속사   〔단서 1〕 Violet은 도서관 카드를 가져오지 않음
안타깝게도, 그녀는 자신이 도서관 카드를 가져오지 않았다는 것을 깨닫는다.

At that moment, Peter walks up to Violet.   〔단서 2〕 도서관 카드를 가지고 있는 Peter에게 책 대출을 부탁하려고 함
그 순간, Peter가 Violet에게 걸어온다.

So, Violet wants to ask Peter to check out the books for her because she knows he has his library card.   뒤에 목적어절 접속사 that이 생략됨
그래서, Violet은 Peter가 도서관 카드를 가지고 있다는 것을 알고 있기 때문에 그에게 책을 대출해 달라고 부탁하고 싶어 한다.

In this situation, what would Violet most likely say to Peter?
이 상황에서, Violet이 Peter에게 할 말로 가장 적절한 것은 무엇인가?

Violet: Can you borrow the books for me with your card?
Violet: 네 카드로 이 책들을 빌려줄 수 있어?

✽상황 요약: 도서관 카드를 두고 온 Violet은 Peter에게 그의 카드로 책을 빌려줄 수 있는지 물어보고 싶음

- assignment ⓝ 과제 ・ section ⓝ 구역, 부분 ・ useful ⓐ 유용한
- realize ⓥ 깨닫다 ・ donate ⓥ 기부하다 ・ cafeteria ⓝ 구내식당

다음 상황 설명을 듣고, Violet이 Peter에게 할 말로 가장 적절한 것을 고르시오.

Violet: _____

① Will you join the science club together?
같이 과학 동아리에 가입할래?   동아리에 가입하려고 도서관에 간 게 아님
② Is it okay to use a card to pay for the drinks?
음료수를 계산할 때 카드를 사용해도 괜찮아?   음료수를 구매하는 상황이 아님
③ Why don't we donate our books to the library?
도서관에 우리의 책을 기부하는 게 어때?   책을 기부하는 것이 아니라 대출하려는 상황임
④ How about going to the cafeteria to have lunch?
점심을 먹기 위해 구내식당에 가는 게 어때?   대출하려는 상황임
⑤ Can you borrow the books for me with your card?
네 카드로 이 책들을 빌려줄 수 있어?   Peter의 도서관 카드로 책을 대출하고자 함

> 왜 정답 ? ❋❋❋ [정답률 93%]

Peter와 함께 도서관에 간 Violet은 유용한 책 두 권을 발견했지만, 도서관 카드를 갖고 오지 않았다는 것을 깨달았다.
Peter가 도서관 카드를 가져왔다는 것을 아는 Violet은 그에게 책 대출을 부탁하려고 하는 상황이므로 정답은 ⑤ '네 카드로 이 책들을 빌려줄 수 있어?'이다.

> 왜 오답 ?

① 과학 과제를 위한 책을 빌리러 온 것이지, 과학 동아리에 가입하려고 도서관에 온 게 아니다. 주의

② Violet이 빌리려는 것은 도서관 대출 카드이다.

③ 과제에 필요한 책을 도서관에서 대출하려는 것이지 책을 기증하려는 것이 아니다.

④ 책을 대출하려는 상황에서 점심과 관련된 말을 하는 것은 자연스럽지 않다.

16~17 ＊숙면에 도움이 되는 음식들

M : Hello, everyone. //
남 : 안녕하세요, 여러분 //

I'm Shawn Collins, / a doctor at Collins Sleep Clinic. //
             동격
저는 Shawn Collins입니다 / Collins 수면 클리닉의 의사 //

Sleep is one of the most essential parts / of our daily lives. //
수면은 가장 필수적인 부분 중 하나입니다 / 우리 일상생활에서 //

So today, / I'm going to introduce the best foods / for helping
helping의 목적격 보어(원형부정사)
you sleep better. // 16번 단서: 수면에 도움이 되는 최고의 음식들을 소개할 것임
그래서 오늘 / 저는 최고의 음식을 소개해 드리려고 합니다 / 여러분이 더 잘 잘 수 있도록 도와주는 // 17번 ①

First, / kiwi fruits contain a high level of hormones / that
                                                          주격 관계대명사
                  병렬 구조(help의 목적격 보어)
help you fall asleep more quickly, sleep longer, and wake
up less / during the night. //
먼저 / 키위에는 높은 수준의 호르몬이 함유되어 있습니다 / 여러분이 더 빨리 잠들고, 더 오래 자고, 덜 깨도록 도와주는 / 밤에 //

Second, / milk is rich in vitamin D / and it calms the mind
and nerves. // 17번 ②
두 번째 / 우유는 비타민 D가 풍부하고 / 마음과 신경을 진정시킵니다 //

If you drink a cup of milk / before you go to bed, / it will
                         help의 목적격 보어(원형부정사)
definitely help / you get a good night's sleep. //
만약 여러분이 우유 한 잔을 마시면 / 잠자리에 들기 전에 / 그것은 확실히 도움이 될 것입니다 / 여러분이 숙면을 취하는 데 // 17번 ③

Third, / nuts can help / to produce the hormone / that
                        병렬 구조
controls your internal body clock / and sends signals / for
to sleep의 의미상 주어
the body to sleep at the right time. //
세 번째 / 견과류는 도와줄 수 있습니다 / 호르몬을 생성하도록 / 여러분의 체내 시계를 조절하고 / 신호를 보내는 / 신체가 제때 잠들도록 //

The last one is honey. //
마지막은 꿀입니다 // 17번 ⑤

Honey helps you sleep well / because it reduces the hormone
주격 관계대명사
/ that keeps the brain awake! //
꿀은 여러분이 잘 잠들도록 도와줍니다 / 그것이 호르몬을 감소시켜 주기 때문에 / 뇌를 깨어 있게 하는 //

                                            현재분사구(diet plans 수식)
Now, / I'll show you some delicious diet plans / using these
foods. //
이제 / 저는 여러분에게 맛있는 식단을 보여드리겠습니다 / 이 음식들을 활용한 //

- essential ⓐ 필수적인 ・ daily ⓐ 매일의 ・ introduce ⓥ 소개하다
- contain ⓥ 함유하다 ・ calm ⓥ 진정하다 ・ definitely ⓐⓓ 확실히
- produce ⓥ 생성하다 ・ internal ⓐ 내부의 ・ signal ⓝ 신호
- reduce ⓥ 감소하다 ・ disorder ⓝ 장애 ・ origin ⓝ 기원

남 : 안녕하세요, 여러분. 저는 Collins 수면 클리닉의 의사 Shawn Collins입니다. 수면은 우리 일상생활에서 가장 필수적인 부분 중 하나입니다. 그래서 오늘 저는 여러분이 더 잘 잘 수 있도록 도와주는 최고의 음식을 소개해 드리려고 합니다. 먼저, 키위에는 여러분이 더 빨리 잠들고, 더 오래 자고, 밤에 덜 깨는 데 도움이 되는 높은 수준의 호르몬이 함유되어 있습니다. 두 번째, 우유는 비타민 D가 풍부하여 마음과 신경을 진정시킵니다. 잠자리에 들기 전에 우유 한 잔을 마시면, 숙면을 취하는 데 확실히 도움이 될 것입니다. 세 번째, 견과류는 여러분의 체내 시계를 조절하고 신체가 제때 잠들도록 신호를 보내는 호르몬을 생성하는 데 도움이 될 수 있습니다. 마지막은 꿀입니다. 꿀은 뇌를 깨어 있게 하는 호르몬을 감소시키기 때문에 여러분이 잘 잠들도록 도와줍니다! 이제, 이 음식들을 활용한 맛있는 식단을 여러분에게 보여드리겠습니다.

16 정답 ③

남자가 하는 말의 주제로 가장 적절한 것은?

① different causes of sleep disorders 수면 장애의 원인은 언급되지 않음
수면 장애의 다양한 원인들
② various ways to keep foods fresh
음식을 신선하게 유지하는 다양한 방법들   음식들을 신선하게 유지하는 것과 관련 없는 내용
③ foods to improve quality of sleep
수면의 질을 향상하는 음식들   숙면을 돕는 음식들에 대해 소개함
④ reasons for organic foods' popularity
유기농 식품 인기의 이유   유기농 식품과 관련 없는 내용
⑤ origins of popular foods around the world
전 세계의 인기 있는 음식들의 기원   음식의 기원에 대해 말한 것이 아님

> 왜 정답 ? ❋❋❋ [정답률 95%]

수면 클리닉의 의사인 남자는 수면이 일상생활에서 가장 필수적인 부분 중 하나라고 강조한 후, 숙면에 도움이 되는 최고의 음식들을 소개하고 있다. 따라서 남자가 하는 말의 주제로 가장 적절한 것은 ③ '수면의 질을 향상하는 음식들'이다.

> 왜 오답 ?

① 수면 장애와 그 원인을 이야기한 것이 아니라, 숙면을 돕는 다양한 음식들을 소개했다.

② 언급된 음식들을 신선하게 유지하는 방법을 소개하는 내용이 아니다.

④ 유기농 식품과 그 인기 원인에 대해 말한 내용이 아니므로 적절하지 않다.

⑤ 여러 음식들의 기원을 소개하는 내용이 아니므로 적절하지 않다.

17 정답 ④

언급된 음식이 아닌 것은?

① kiwi fruits First, kiwi fruits contain a high level of hormones
키위
② milk Second, milk is rich in vitamin D
우유
③ nuts Third, nuts can help to produce the hormone
견과류
④ tomatoes 언급되지 않음
토마토
⑤ honey The last one is honey.
꿀

숙면에 도움이 되는 음식들로 키위, 우유, 견과류, 꿀을 소개했지만 ④ '토마토'는
언급하지 않았다.

>왜 오답 ?
① 키위 과일에는 빨리 잠들고, 오래 자고, 밤에 덜 깨도록 도와주는 호르몬이
  함유되어 있다.
② 우유에는 비타민 D가 풍부해서 마음과 신경을 진정시켜 준다.
③ 견과류는 신체가 제때 잠들도록 신호를 보내고 체내 시계를 조절하는 호르몬을
  생성하도록 도와준다.
⑤ 꿀은 뇌를 깨어 있게 하는 호르몬을 감소시켜 숙면에 도움이 된다.

18 정답 ② ✱패키지여행 상품 홍보

ACC Travel Agency Customers: /
ACC 여행사 고객님께 /
                현재완료(경험)
Have you ever **wanted** / to enjoy a holiday in nature? //
당신은 원했던 적이 있나요 / 자연 속에서 휴가를 즐기는 것을 //
                          turn A into B: A를 B로 바꾸다
This summer is the best time / to **turn** your dream **into** reality. //
이번 여름이 최고의 시간입니다 / 당신의 꿈을 현실로 바꿀 //

We have a perfect travel package / for you. // 단서 1 완벽한 패키지여행
우리에게는 완벽한 패키지여행 상품이 있습니다 / 당신을 위한 //   상품이 있다고 소개함

This travel package includes / special trips to Lake Madison / **as**
B as well as A: A뿐만 아니라 B도
well as massage and meditation / to help you relax. //
이 패키지여행 상품은 포함합니다 / Lake Madison으로의 특별한 여행을 / 마사지와
명상뿐만 아니라 / 당신이 쉬도록 돕는 //
                              앞에 주격 관계대명사와 be동사가 생략됨
Also, / we provide yoga lessons / **taught** by experienced
instructors. //
또한, / 우리는 요가 강의를 제공합니다 / 숙련된 강사로부터 배우는 //

If you book this package, / you will enjoy all this / at a reasonable
price. // 단서 2 합리적인 가격에 패키지여행을 이용할 수 있다고 함
만약 당신이 이 패키지를 예약한다면 / 당신은 이 모든 것을 즐길 것입니다 / 합리적인 가격에 //

We are sure / that it will be an unforgettable experience / for
you. //
우리는 확신합니다 / 그것이 잊지 못할 경험이 될 것이라고 / 당신에게 //

If you call us, / we will be happy to give you more details. //
우리에게 전화하시면 / 우리는 기꺼이 당신에게 더 많은 세부 사항을 알려드리겠습니다 //

• include ⓥ 포함하다   • meditation ⓝ 명상
• instructor ⓝ 강사   • book ⓥ 예약하다
• reasonable ⓐ 합리적인   • unforgettable ⓐ 잊지 못할

ACC 여행사 고객님께:
자연 속에서 휴가를 즐기는 것을 원한 적이 있습니까? 이번 여름이 당신의 꿈을
현실로 바꿀 최고의 시간입니다. 우리에게는 당신을 위한 완벽한 패키지여행
상품이 있습니다. 이 패키지여행 상품은 당신이 편히 쉴 수 있도록 돕는
마사지와 명상뿐만 아니라 Lake Madison으로의 특별한 여행도 포함합니다.
또한, 우리는 숙련된 강사의 요가 강의도 제공합니다. 만약 당신이 이 패키지를
예약한다면, 당신은 이 모든 것을 합리적인 가격에 즐길 것입니다. 우리는
그것이 당신에게 잊지 못할 경험이 될 것을 확신합니다. 우리에게 전화하시면,
우리는 당신에게 더 많은 세부 사항을 기꺼이 알려드리겠습니다.

다음 글의 목적으로 가장 적절한 것은?
① 여행 일정 변경을 안내하려고 여행 일정에 대한 언급은 없음
②패키지여행 상품을 홍보하려고 완벽한 패키지여행 상품을 합리적인 가격에 즐기라고 함
③ 여행 상품 불만족에 대해 사과하려고 고객의 불만족에 대해 사과하는 글이 아님
④ 여행 만족도 조사 참여를 부탁하려고 여행을 이미 다녀온 고객에게 쓴 글이 아님
⑤ 패키지여행 업무 담당자를 모집하려고 잠재적인 고객을 대상으로 한 글임

자연 속에서 즐길 수 있는 완벽한 패키지여행 상품이 있다고 소개하면서, 그것에
포함된 프로그램들과 합리적 가격을 설명하여 홍보하고 있으므로 정답은 ②이다.

>왜 오답 ?
① 여행 상품을 홍보하는 단계로 여행 일정 변경을 공지하는 것이 아니다.
③ 이미 여행을 다녀온 고객의 불만족에 대해 사과하는 것이 아니다.
④ 고객의 만족도 조사를 요청하는 글이 아니다.
⑤ 잠재적 고객을 대상으로 홍보하는 글이지 담당 직원을 모집하려는 글이 아니다.
  (▶ 이유: 직원을 모집하는 거라면 합리적인 가격은 언급할 이유가 없다.)

19 정답 ① ✱사라진 남편과 딸

When I woke up / in our hotel room, / it was almost midnight. //
내가 깨어났을 때 / 호텔 방에서 / 거의 자정이었다 //

I didn't see / my husband nor daughter. //
나는 보지 못했다 / 내 남편도 딸도 //

I called them, / but I heard their phones ringing / in the room. //
나는 그들에게 전화를 걸었지만 / 나는 그들의 전화가 울리는 것을 들었다 / 방에서 //
            분사구문
Feeling worried, / I went outside and walked down the street, /
but they were nowhere to be found. // 단서 1 걱정이 되어 남편과 딸을 찾아
걱정되어 / 나는 밖으로 나가 거리를 걸어 내려갔다 / 하지만 그들은 어디에도 없었다 // 다녔지만 찾을 수 없었음
                뒤에 목적어절 접속사 that이 생략됨
When I **decided** / I should ask someone for help, / a crowd
nearby caught my attention. //
내가 결정했을 때 / 누군가에게 도움을 요청해야겠다고 / 근처에 있던 군중이 내 주의를
끌었다 //
                              분사구문
I approached, / **hoping to find my husband and daughter**, / and
suddenly I saw two familiar faces. //
나는 다가갔다 / 남편과 딸을 찾기를 바라면서 / 그리고 갑자기 나는 익숙한 두 얼굴을 보았다 //
        분사구문
I smiled, / **feeling calm**. // 단서 2 남편과 딸을 보고 안도하며 미소를 지음
나는 미소를 지었다 / 안도감을 느끼며 //

Just then, / my daughter saw me / and called, "Mom!" //
바로 그때 / 나의 딸이 나를 보고 / "엄마"라고 불렀다 //

They were watching the magic show. //
그들은 마술쇼를 보고 있었다 //
                                felt의 목적격 보어(원형부정사)
Finally, / I felt all my worries **disappear**. // 단서 3 모든 걱정이 사라짐
마침내 / 나는 내 모든 걱정이 사라지는 것을 느꼈다 //

• midnight ⓝ 자정   • nowhere ⓐ 아무 데도 (없다)
• crowd ⓝ 군중, 무리   • approach ⓥ 다가가다
• suddenly ⓐ 갑자기   • familiar ⓐ 익숙한, 친숙한
• calm ⓐ 침착한   • disappear ⓥ 사라지다
• indifferent ⓐ 무관심한   • embarrassed ⓐ 당황한

내가 호텔 방에서 깨어났을 때는, 거의 자정이었다. 남편과 딸이 보이지
않았다. 나는 그들에게 전화를 걸었지만, 그들의 전화가 방에서 울리는 것을
들었다. 걱정돼서 나는 밖으로 나가 거리를 걸어 내려갔지만, 그들은 어디에도
없었다. 내가 누군가에게 도움을 요청하려고 했을 때, 근처에 있던 군중이 내
주의를 끌었다. 나는 남편과 딸을 찾기를 바라면서 다가갔고, 갑자기 낯익은
두 얼굴이 보였다. 나는 안도하며 미소를 지었다. 바로 그때, 딸이 나를 보고
"엄마!"라고 불렀다. 그들은 마술쇼를 보고 있었다. 마침내, 나는 내 모든
걱정이 사라지는 것을 느꼈다.

다음 글에 드러난 'I'의 심경 변화로 가장 적절한 것은?
①anxious → relieved 남편과 딸이 안 보여 걱정했지만, 찾은 후에는 안도했음
  걱정하는 → 안도하는
② delighted → unhappy 남편과 딸을 찾아 기쁜 것은 글의 후반부임
  기쁜 → 불행한
③ indifferent → excited 사라진 남편과 딸에 무관심하지 않았음
  무관심한 → 신난
④ relaxed → upset 남편과 딸을 찾았으므로 화난 것이 아님
  편안한 → 화난
⑤ embarrassed → proud 자랑스러울 만한 사건은 언급되지 않았음
  당황한 → 자랑스러운

다음 글에서 필자가 주장하는 바로 가장 적절한 것은?

① 결정한 것은 반드시 실행하도록 노력하라.
　　　　　결정한 사안에 대한 이행을 강조한 글이 아님
② 자신이 담당한 업무에 관한 전문성을 확보하라.
　　　　　업무를 할 때 전문성을 확보하라는 글이 아님
③ 업무 집중도를 높이기 위해 책상 위를 정돈하라.
　　　　　distractions로 만든 오답
④ 좋은 아이디어를 메모하는 습관을 길러라.
　　　　　메모의 중요성을 강조한 글이 아님
⑤ 업무와 개인 용무를 한 곳에 정리하라.
　　　　　두 개의 달력보다는 하나에 정리하라고 함

>왜 정답? ✽✿✿ [정답률 82%]

• **오해:** 달력을 업무 달력과 개인 달력으로 나누는 것이 실용적일 것이라고 생각함
• **해결:** 모든 일을 한 곳에 정리하면 시간이 어떻게 분배되는지 잘 알 수 있어서 더
나은 결정을 내리게 됨
▶ 업무와 개인 용무를 한 곳에 정리하라는 것이므로 정답은 ⑤이다.

>왜 오답?

① 결정한 사안은 꼭 실행하라고 주장하는 글이 아니다.
② 담당 업무에 관한 전문성 확보를 주장하는 글이 아니다.
③ 책상 위를 정돈하는 것과 업무 집중도 사이의 관계는 언급되지 않았다.
④ 메모하는 습관을 기르라고 이야기하는 글이 아니다.

---

20 정답 ⑤ ＊업무와 개인 용무를 한 곳에 정리하라

Research shows / that people who work have two calendars: /
　　　　　목적어절 접속사　주격 관계대명사절
one for work / and one for their personal lives. //
연구는 보여준다 / 일하는 사람들이 두 개의 달력을 가지고 있다는 것을 / 하나는 업무를 위한
달력이고 / 하나는 개인적인 삶을 위한 달력이다 //
Although it may seem sensible, / having two separate calendars
부사절 접속사(양보)　　　　　　　　　　　동명사구 주어
/ for work and personal life / can lead to distractions. //
비록 그것이 실용적으로 보일지라도 / 두 개의 별도의 달력을 갖는 것은 / 업무와 개인적인
삶을 위한 / 주의산만으로 이어질 수 있다 // **단서 1** 두 개의 달력을 갖는 것은 주의산만으로 이어짐

To check if something is missing, / you will find yourself /
checking your to-do lists multiple times. //
누락된 것이 있는지를 확인하기 위해 / 당신은 스스로를 발견할 것이다 / 할 일 목록을 여러 번
확인하는 //

Instead, / organize all of your tasks / in one place. //
대신, / 당신의 모든 일을 정리하라 / 한 곳에 // **단서 2** 모든 일을 한 곳에 정리할 것을 권함
가주어　　　　　진주어절 접속사
It doesn't matter / if you use digital or paper media. //
~은 중요하지 않다 / 당신이 디지털 또는 종이 매체를 사용하는지는 //
가주어　　　진주어
It's okay / to keep your professional and personal tasks / in one
place. //
~은 괜찮다 / 당신의 업무와 개인 일을 두는 것은 / 한 곳에 //
This will give you a good idea / of how time is divided / between
　　　　　　　　　　전치사의 목적어(간접의문문)
work and home. //
이것은 당신이 잘 알게 해줄 것이다 / 시간이 어떻게 쪼개지는지 / 일과 가정 사이에 //
　　　　　will allow의 목적어 보어　　　　　간접의문문
This will allow you / to make informed decisions / about which
tasks are most important. //
이것은 당신을 가능하게 할 것이다 / 정보에 입각한 결정을 하도록 / 어떤 일이 가장
중요한지에 대한 //

• personal ⓐ 개인적인　• sensible ⓐ 실용적인
• separate ⓐ 별도의　• distraction ⓝ 주의산만
• multiple ⓐ 많은　• organize ⓥ 정리하다
• media ⓝ 매체, 수단　• professional ⓐ 직업의
• divide ⓥ 나누다　• informed ⓐ 정보에 입각한

연구는 일하는 사람들이 두 개의 달력을 가지고 있다는 것을 보여준다: 하나는
업무를 위한 달력이고 하나는 개인적인 삶을 위한 달력이다. 비록 그것이
실용적으로 보일지라도, 업무와 개인적인 삶을 위한 두 개의 별도의 달력을
갖는 것은 주의를 산만하게 할 수 있다. 누락된 것이 있는지를 확인하기 위해,
당신은 할 일 목록을 여러 번 확인하는 것을 깨닫게 될 것이다. 대신, 당신의
모든 일을 한 곳에 정리하라. 당신이 디지털 매체를 사용하든 종이 매체를
사용하든 중요하지 않다. 당신의 업무와 개인 일을 한 곳에 두는 것은 괜찮다.
이것은 당신에게 일과 가정 사이에 시간이 어떻게 쪼개지는지에 대해 잘 알게
해줄 것이다. 이것은 어떤 일이 가장 중요한지에 대한 정보에 입각한 결정을
내리게 할 것이다.

---

21 정답 ① ＊고객 만족도 관리가 중요한 이유

　　　　　　　　　　　　　　간접의문문
Why do you care / how a customer reacts / to a purchase? //
당신은 왜 신경 쓰는가 / 고객이 어떻게 반응하는지를 / 구매품에 대해 //
Good question. //
좋은 질문이다 //
　by v-ing: ~함으로써
By understanding post-purchase behavior, / you can understand
the influence and the likelihood /
구매 후 행동을 이해함으로써 / 당신은 그 영향력과 가능성을 이해할 수 있다 /
of whether a buyer will repurchase the product / (and whether
she will keep it or return it). //
구매자가 제품을 재구매할지 / (그리고 그녀가 제품을 가질지 또는 반품할지) //
You'll also determine / whether the buyer will encourage others
　　　　　　　　　　명사절 접속사
/ to purchase the product from you. //
당신은 또한 알아낼 것이다 / 구매자가 다른 사람들에게 권장할지 / 당신으로부터 제품을
구매하도록 // **단서 1** 구매 후 행동을 통해 구매자가 다른 사람에게 제품을 추천할지 여부를 파악할 수 있음
Satisfied customers can become unpaid ambassadors / for your
business, / so customer satisfaction should be on the top / of
your to-do list. //
만족한 고객은 무급 대사가 될 수 있다 / 당신의 사업을 위한 / 따라서 고객 만족이 최상단에
있어야 한다 / 당신의 할 일 목록의 //
　　　　　　　　　　　　　앞에 목적격 관계대명사가 생략됨
People tend to believe / the opinions of people / they know. //
사람들은 믿는 경향이 있다 / 사람들의 의견을 / 그들이 아는 //
People trust friends / over advertisements / any day. //
사람들은 친구를 신뢰한다 / 광고보다 / 언제든 // **단서 2** 사람들은 광고보다 친구를 신뢰함
They know / that advertisements are paid / to tell the "good
　　　　　목적어절 접속사의 병렬 구조
side" / and that they're used / to persuade them / to purchase
　　　　　　　　　　　　　　부사적 용법(목적)
products and services. //
그들은 알고 있다 / 광고에는 돈이 쓰인다는 것을 / '좋은 면'을 말하기 위해 / 그리고 그것들이
사용된다는 것을 / 그들을 설득하기 위해 / 제품과 서비스를 구매하도록 //
By continually monitoring / your customer's satisfaction after
　　　　　　　　　　　　형용사적 용법(ability 수식)
the sale, / you have the ability / to avoid negative word-of-
mouth advertising. //
지속적으로 추적 관찰함으로써 / 판매 후 당신의 고객의 만족을 / 당신은 능력을 가진다 /
부정적인 입소문 광고를 피함 //

• react ⓥ 반응하다　• behavior ⓝ 행동　• influence ⓝ 영향
• likelihood ⓝ 가능성　• repurchase ⓥ 재구매하다
• determine ⓥ 알아내다　• encourage ⓥ 권장하다

- satisfied ⓐ 만족한　　　　• ambassador ⓝ 대사
- persuade ⓥ 설득하다　　　　• monitor ⓥ 추적 관찰하다
- word-of-mouth ⓐ 구두의, 구전의　　• gain ⓝ 이득, 대가
- manufacturer ⓝ 제조업체, 제조사　　• reward ⓝ 보상
- overseas [ad] 해외에서

당신은 왜 고객이 구매품에 어떻게 반응하는지를 신경 쓰는가? 좋은 질문이다. 구매 후 행동을 이해함으로써, 당신은 그 영향력과 구매자가 제품을 재구매할지 (그리고 그녀가 제품을 가질지 또는 반품할지)의 가능성을 이해할 수 있다. 당신은 구매자가 다른 사람들에게 당신으로부터 제품을 구매하도록 권장할지 여부 또한 알아낼 것이다. 만족한 고객은 당신의 사업을 위한 무급 대사가 될 수 있으므로, 고객 만족이 당신의 할 일 목록의 최상단에 있어야 한다. 사람들은 그들이 아는 사람들의 의견을 믿는 경향이 있다. 사람들은 언제든 광고보다 친구를 더 신뢰한다. 그들은 광고에는 '좋은 면'을 말하기 위해 돈이 쓰인다는 것과 그것들이 제품과 서비스를 구매하도록 그들을 설득하는 데 사용된다는 것을 알고 있다. 판매 후 고객의 만족을 지속적으로 추적 관찰함으로써, 당신은 부정적인 입소문 광고를 피할 능력을 가진다.

밑줄 친 become unpaid ambassadors가 다음 글에서 의미하는 바로 가장 적절한 것은?

① recommend products to others for no gain
　대가 없이 다른 사람에게 제품을 추천함　　만족한 고객은 다른 사람에게 제품을 추천함
② offer manufacturers feedback on products
　제조업체에 제품에 대한 피드백을 제공하다　제조업체에 직접 피드백을 제공하는 것이 아님
③ become people who don't trust others' words
　다른 사람의 말을 믿지 않는 사람이 되다　다른 구매자의 말을 듣지 않는다는 것이 아님
④ get rewards for advertising products overseas
　해외에서 제품 광고에 대한 보상을 받다　'무급'이라고 했으므로 보상을 받는 것이 아님
⑤ buy products without worrying about the price
　가격 걱정 없이 제품을 구매하다　가격에 구애받지 않는다는 내용은 언급되지 않음

▶왜 정답? ✱✱✿ [정답률 62%]

- 고객의 구매품에 대한 반응을 살펴야 함 → 고객이 다른 사람에게 제품 구매를 권장할지를 파악할 수 있음 단서1
- 사람들은 돈이 쓰인 광고보다 친구를 신뢰함 단서2

➡ 구매품에 만족한 고객은 다른 사람에게 제품을 추천할 것이고, 사람들은 광고보다 친구의 추천을 더 신뢰한다.
▶ '무급'은 '돈이 쓰이지 않은 친구의 말'을 의미하고, '대사'는 '제품 구매를 권장하는 사람'을 의미하므로 '무급 대사가 된다'는 것은 ① '대가 없이 다른 사람에게 제품을 추천하다'를 의미한다.

▶왜 오답?

② 구매자가 제조업체에 직접 피드백을 제공한다는 내용은 언급되지 않았다.
③ 만족한 고객은 말을 전하는 사람이므로 다른 사람의 말을 믿지 않는다는 것은 어색하다. ─주의
④ '무급'이라고 했으므로 보상을 받는다는 것은 적절하지 않으며, 해외와 관련된 내용은 언급되지 않았다.
⑤ 만족한 고객은 가격에 구애받지 않는다는 내용은 없다.

22 정답 ③ *늘어난 소비자의 일

핵심 주어(단수)　　　　삽입절　　단수 동사
The promise of a computerized society, / we were told, / was that it would pass to machines / all of the repetitive drudgery of work, /
컴퓨터화된 사회의 약속은 / 우리가 듣기로는 / 그것이 기계에 넘길 거라는 것이었다 / 모든 반복적인 고된 일을 /
분사구문을 이끄는 현재분사　　allowing의 목적격 보어
allowing us humans to pursue higher purposes / and to have more leisure time. //
우리 인간들로 하여금 더 높은 목적을 추구하게 하면서 / 그리고 더 많은 여가를 가질 수 있게 (하면서) //

It didn't work out this way. //
그것은 이런 식으로 되지는 않았다 //
뒤에 time이 생략됨
Instead of more time, / most of us have less. //
더 많은 시간 대신에 / 우리 대부분은 더 적은 시간을 가지고 있다 //

Companies large and small have off-loaded work / onto the backs of consumers. // 단서1 회사들은 고객들에게 일을 떠넘김
크고 작은 회사들은 일을 떠넘겼다 / 소비자들의 등에 //
　　　　　　　　주격 관계대명사
Things that used to be done for us, / as part of the value-added service of working with a company, / we are now expected to do ourselves. // 단서2 회사들이 서비스 차원으로 해주던 일도 이제는 우리가 스스로 하게 됨
우리를 위해 행해지던 일들은 / 회사와 함께 함으로써 받은 부가가치 서비스의 일환으로 / 우리는 이제 스스로가 하도록 기대된다 //

동격
With air travel, / we're now expected to complete / our own reservations and check-in, / jobs that used to be done / by airline employees or travel agents. //
항공 여행의 경우 / 이제는 우리가 완수하도록 기대된다 / 우리의 예약과 체크인을 / 행해지던 일인 / 항공사 직원이나 여행사 직원들에 의해 //

At the grocery store, / we're expected to bag our own groceries /
　　　　　　　　　　　병렬 구조
and, in some supermarkets, / to scan our own purchases. //
식료품점에서는 / 우리가 자신의 식료품을 봉지에 넣도록 기대된다 / 그리고 일부 슈퍼마켓에서는 / 자신이 구매한 물건을 스캔하도록 (기대된다) //

- promise ⓝ 약속　　• repetitive ⓐ 반복적인　　• pursue ⓥ 추구하다
- purpose ⓝ 목적　　• leisure ⓝ 여가　　• off-load ⓥ 떠넘기다
- consumer ⓝ 소비자　　• value-added ⓐ 부가가치의
- reservation ⓝ 예약　　• agent ⓝ 직원　　• grocery ⓝ 식료품

컴퓨터화된 사회의 약속은, 우리가 듣기로는, 그것이 모든 반복적인 고된 일을 기계에 넘겨, 우리 인간들이 더 높은 목적을 추구하고 더 많은 여가 시간을 가질 수 있게 해준다는 것이었다. 그것은 이런 식으로 되지는 않았다. 더 많은 시간 대신에, 우리 대부분은 더 적은 시간을 가지고 있다. 크고 작은 회사들은 일을 소비자들의 등에 떠넘겼다. 회사와 함께 함으로써 받은 부가가치 서비스의 일환으로, 우리를 위해 행해지던 것들을 이제 우리 스스로가 하도록 기대된다. 항공 여행의 경우, 항공사 직원이나 여행사 직원들에 의해 행해지던 일인 우리의 예약과 체크인을 이제는 우리가 완수하도록 기대된다. 식료품점에서는, 우리가 자신의 식료품을 봉지에 넣도록, 그리고 일부 슈퍼마켓에서는, 우리 자신이 구매한 물건을 스캔하도록 기대된다.

다음 글의 요지로 가장 적절한 것은?

① 컴퓨터 기반 사회에서는 여가 시간이 더 늘어난다.
　　　　　　　　　　　　　여가 시간이 더 적어졌다고 했음
② 회사 업무의 전산화는 업무 능률을 향상시킨다.
　　　　　　　업무 능률은 언급하지 않음
③ 컴퓨터화된 사회에서 소비자는 더 많은 일을 하게 된다.
　　　　　　　　　　　　　회사들이 일을 소비자에게 떠넘김
④ 온라인 거래가 모든 소비자들을 만족시키기에는 한계가 있다.
　　　　　　　　　　　온라인 거래에 국한된 내용이 아님
⑤ 산업의 발전으로 인해 기계가 인간의 일자리를 대신하고 있다.
　　　　　　　　　　오히려 인간의 일이 늘어났다는 내용임

▶왜 정답? ✱✱✱ [정답률 57%]

컴퓨터화된 사회에서 회사는 소비자에게 일을 떠넘겼고, 우리를 위해 행해지던 것들을 이제는 우리가 직접 하도록 기대된다. 단서1, 단서2
➡ 예시: ❶ 항공사나 여행사 직원의 일이었던 예약과 체크인을 우리가 함
❷ 상점에서 구매한 물건을 우리가 직접 봉지에 담거나 스캔함
▶ 컴퓨터화된 사회에서 소비자가 더 많은 일을 하게 되었다는 것이므로 정답은 ③이다.

▶왜 오답?

① 여가 시간이 더 늘어날 것을 기대했지만 그렇지 않다고 했다.
② 직원의 업무 능률이 늘었다는 것은 언급되지 않았다.
④ 온라인 거래만 이야기하는 글이 아니다.
⑤ 컴퓨터화된 사회의 문제점으로 인간의 일자리 감소를 이야기하는 글이 아니다.
　(▶ 이유: '컴퓨터화된 사회'로 떠올릴 수 있는 내용으로 만든 오답이다.)

23 정답 ② ＊Lake Wobegon 효과

We tend to believe / that we possess a host of socially desirable
병렬 구조(목적어절 접속사)   '다수의'
characteristics, / and that we are free of most of those / that are
주격 관계대명사
socially undesirable. //

우리는 믿는 경향이 있다 / 우리가 사회적으로 바람직한 특성들을 많이 지니고 있고 / 우리는
그것들의 대부분은 지니고 있지 않다고 / 사회적으로 바람직하지 않은 //

For example, / a large majority of the general public thinks /
예를 들어 / 대다수의 일반 대중들은 생각한다 /

that they are more intelligent, more fair-minded, less prejudiced,
/ and more skilled / behind the wheel of an automobile / than the
average person. // 단서 1 많은 사람들은 자신이 보통 사람보다 더 낫다고 생각함

그들이 더 지적이고, 더 공정하고, 덜 편견을 가지며 / 더 능숙하다고 / 자동차를 운전할 때 /
보통 사람보다 //
so ~ that ...: 너무 ~해서 …하다
This phenomenon is so reliable and ubiquitous / that it has come
to be known as the "Lake Wobegon effect," / after Garrison
Keillor's fictional community /

이 현상은 너무 신뢰할 수 있고 어디서나 볼 수 있어서 / 그것은 'Lake Wobegon 효과'라고
알려지게 되었다 / Garrison Keillor의 허구적인 공동체의 이름을 딴 /
관계부사
where "the women are strong, the men are good-looking, / and
all the children are above average." // 단서 2 리더십: 고등학생 100만 명 중
70퍼센트가 자신이 평균 이상이라고
'여성들은 강하고, 남성들은 잘생긴 / 그리고 모든 아이들은 평균 이상'인 //   생각했음

A survey of one million high school seniors found / that 70%
thought / they were above average in leadership ability, / and
뒤에 목적어절 접속사 that이 생략됨
only 2% thought / they were below average. //

고등학교 고학년 학생 100만 명을 대상으로 한 설문조사는 발견했다 / 70퍼센트는
생각했다는 것을 / 자신이 리더십 능력에 있어 평균 이상이라고 / 그리고 2퍼센트만이
생각했다는 것을 / 자신이 평균 이하라고 // 단서 3 다른 사람들과 잘 지내는 능력:
'~에 있어서'   '~와 잘 지내다'   모두 자신이 평균 이상이라고 생각했음
In terms of ability to get along with others, / all students thought
they were above average, / 60% thought they were in the top
10%, / and 25% thought they were in the top 1%! //

다른 사람들과 잘 지내는 능력에 있어서 / '모든' 학생들은 자신이 평균 이상이라고 생각했고 /
60퍼센트는 자신이 상위 10퍼센트에 속한다고 생각했으며 / 25퍼센트는 자신이 상위
1퍼센트에 속한다고 생각했다 //

- possess Ⓥ 지니다, 소유하다   - desirable ⓐ 바람직한
- characteristic Ⓝ 특성, 특징   - majority Ⓝ 다수
- general ⓐ 일반적인   - intelligent ⓐ 지적인
- fair-minded ⓐ 공정한   - prejudiced ⓐ 편견이 있는
- automobile Ⓝ 자동차   - average ⓐ 평균의
- phenomenon Ⓝ 현상   - reliable ⓐ 믿을 만한
- fictional ⓐ 허구적인   - senior Ⓝ (고등학교의) 졸업반 학생
- self-image Ⓝ 자아상   - tendency Ⓝ 경향
- superior ⓐ (~보다) 우월한   - prejudice Ⓝ 편견

우리는 우리가 사회적으로 바람직한 특성들을 많이 지니고 있고, 사회적으로
바람직하지 않은 특성들의 대부분은 지니고 있지 않다고 믿는 경향이 있다.
예를 들어, 대다수의 일반 대중들은 그들이 보통 사람보다 더 지적이고, 더
공정하고, 덜 편견을 가지며 자동차를 운전할 때 더 능숙하다고 생각한다. 이
현상은 너무 신뢰할 수 있고 어디서나 볼 수 있기 때문에 '여성들은 강하고,
남성들은 잘생겼으며, 모든 아이들은 평균 이상'인 Garrison Keillor의
허구적인 공동체의 이름을 따서 'Lake Wobegon 효과'라고 알려지게 되었다.
고등학교 고학년 학생 100만 명을 대상으로 한 설문조사에서 70퍼센트는
자신이 리더십 능력에 있어 평균 이상이라고 생각했고, 2퍼센트만이 자신이
평균 이하라고 생각했다는 것을 발견했다. 다른 사람들과 잘 지내는 능력에
있어서, '모든' 학생들은 자신이 평균 이상이라고 생각했고, 60퍼센트는 자신이
상위 10퍼센트에 속한다고 생각했으며, 25퍼센트는 자신이 상위 1퍼센트에
속한다고 생각했다!

다음 글의 주제로 가장 적절한 것은?

① importance of having a positive self-image as a leader
리더로서 긍정적인 자아상을 갖는 것의 중요성   리더의 자질을 설명하는 글이 아님
②our common belief that we are better than average
우리가 평균보다 우월하다는 우리의 공통된 믿음   대부분 스스로가 평균보다 낫다고 생각한다고 했음
③ our tendency to think others are superior to us
다른 사람이 우리보다 우월하다고 생각하는 우리의 경향   글의 주제와 정반대의 내용임
④ reasons why we always try to be above average
우리가 항상 평균 이상이 되려고 노력하는 이유   이미 평균 이상이라고 여기는 통념에 관한 글임
⑤ danger of prejudice in building healthy social networks
건강한 사회 연결망 구축에 있어 편견의 위험성
get along with others, prejudiced 등이 언급된 것으로 만든 오답

왜 정답? ✽✽❋ [정답률 71%]

대다수의 사람들은 그들이 보통 사람보다 더 지적이고, 더 공정하고, 덜 편견을
가지며 운전에 더 능숙하다고 생각함 단서 1

예시 1: 고등학교 고학년 학생 100만 명 중 70퍼센트가 자신의 리더십이 평균
이상이라고 생각함 단서 2

예시 2: 다른 사람들과 잘 지내는 능력에 있어서는 '모든' 학생들이 자신이 평균
이상이라고 생각함 단서 3

➡ 'Lake Wobegon 효과'를 대다수의 학생들이 리더십 능력에서 평균보다
우월하다고 믿는 예시를 들어 설명했다.
▶ 글의 주제는 ② '우리가 평균보다 우월하다는 우리의 공통된 믿음'이 적절하다.

왜 오답?

① 리더십은 예시로 제시되었을 뿐, 리더십의 자질을 설명하는 글이 아니다. 함정
③ 우리가 다른 사람보다 우월하다고 생각한다고 했으므로 글의 주제와는 정반대의
내용이다.
④ 사람들이 평균 이상이 되려고 노력하는 이유 등은 언급되지 않았다.
⑤ 건강한 사회 연결망 구축과 편견의 관계를 말한 글이 아니다.

---

24 정답 ① ＊부유한 국가가 갖는 스트레스
'거의 없는'   부사적 용법(감정의 원인)
Few people will be surprised / to hear that poverty tends to
명사절 접속사
create stress: /

놀랄 사람은 거의 없을 것이다 / 가난이 스트레스를 만드는 경향이 있다는 것을 듣고 /

a 2006 study published in the American journal Psychosomatic
앞에 주격 관계대명사와 be동사가 생략됨
Medicine, / for example, /

미국의 학술지 〈Psychosomatic Medicine〉에 발표된 2006년 연구는 / 예를 들어 /
동사
noted that a lower socioeconomic status was associated / with
명사절 접속사
higher levels of stress hormones in the body. //

더 낮은 사회 경제적 지위가 관련이 있다고 언급했다 / 체내의 더 높은 수치의 스트레스
호르몬과 //

However, / richer economies have their own distinct stresses. //

하지만 / 더 부유한 국가는 그들만의 뚜렷한 스트레스를 가지고 있다 // 단서 1 부유한 국가들도
그들만의 스트레스가 있음
The key issue is time pressure. //

핵심 쟁점은 시간 압박이다 //   단서 2 부유한 국가의 스트레스 요인은 시간 압박임
주어
A 1999 study / of 31 countries by American psychologist Robert
동사
Levine and Canadian psychologist Ara Norenzayan / found that
wealthier, more industrialized nations had a faster pace of life /

1999년 연구는 / 미국의 심리학자 Robert Levine과 캐나다의 심리학자 Ara Norenzayan
이 31개국을 대상으로 한 / 더 부유하고, 더 산업화된 국가들이 더 빠른 삶의 속도를 가지고
있다는 것을 알아냈다 / 단서 3 더 부유하고, 더 산업화된 국가들의 삶의 속도가 더 빠름
단서 4 빠른 삶의 속도는 촉박함을 느끼게 하고 심장병에 걸리기 쉽게 함
— which led to a higher standard of living, / but at the same
병렬 구조
time left the population feeling a constant sense of urgency, / as
병렬 구조(목적격 보어)
well as being more prone to heart disease. //

그리고 이것은 더 높은 생활 수준으로 이어졌지만 / 동시에 사람들에게 지속적인 촉박함을
느끼게 했다(는 것을) / 심장병에 걸리기 더 쉽게 했을 뿐만 아니라 //
'사실'
In effect, / fast-paced productivity creates wealth, / but it also
부사절 접속사(시간)   형용사적 용법(time 수식)
leads people to feel time-poor / when they lack the time / to
재귀대명사 (강조 용법)
relax and enjoy themselves. //

사실 / 빠른 속도의 생산력은 부를 창출하지만 / 그것은 또한 사람들이 시간이 부족하다고
느끼게 한다 / 그들이 시간이 없을 때 / 스스로 긴장을 풀고 즐겁게 지낼 //

- poverty ⓝ 가난　　· socioeconomic ⓐ 사회 경제적인
- status ⓝ 지위　　· associate ⓥ 연상하다, 연관짓다
- distinct ⓐ 뚜렷한　　· pressure ⓝ 압박
- psychologist ⓝ 심리학자　　· wealthy ⓐ 부유한
- industrialized ⓐ 산업화된　　· pace ⓝ 속도
- standard ⓝ 수준, 기준　　· constant ⓐ 지속적인
- urgency ⓝ 촉박함　　· lack ⓥ 부족하다　　· trap ⓝ 덫, 함정

가난이 스트레스를 유발하는 경향이 있다는 것을 듣고 놀랄 사람은 거의 없을 것이다: 예를 들어, 미국의 학술지 〈Psychosomatic Medicine〉에 발표된 2006년 연구는 더 낮은 사회 경제적 지위가 체내의 더 높은 수치의 스트레스 호르몬과 관련이 있다고 언급했다. 하지만, 더 부유한 국가는 그들만의 뚜렷한 스트레스를 가지고 있다. 핵심 쟁점은 시간 압박이다. 미국의 심리학자 Robert Levine과 캐나다의 심리학자 Ara Norenzayan이 31개국을 대상으로 한 1999년 연구는 더 부유하고, 더 산업화된 국가들이 더 빠른 삶의 속도를 가지고 있다는 것 — 그리고 이것이 더 높은 생활 수준으로 이어졌지만, 동시에 사람들에게 지속적인 촉박함을 느끼게 했을 뿐만 아니라 심장병에 걸리기 더 쉽게 했다는 것을 알아냈다. 사실, 빠른 속도의 생산력은 부를 창출하지만, 그것은 또한 사람들이 긴장을 풀고 즐겁게 지낼 시간이 없을 때 시간이 부족하다고 느끼게 한다.

다음 글의 제목으로 가장 적절한 것은?

① Why Are Even Wealthy Countries Not Free from Stress? 〔부유한 나라들은 시간 압박으로 스트레스를 받음〕
왜 부유한 나라들조차 스트레스에서 자유롭지 못한가?
② In Search of the Path to Escaping the Poverty Trap
빈곤의 덫에서 벗어날 수 있는 길을 찾아서　가난의 굴레에서 벗어나는 방법을 모색한 글이 아님
③ Time Management: Everything You Need to Know
시간 관리: 당신이 알아야 할 모든 것　시간 관리에 관해 설명한 글이 아님
④ How Does Stress Affect Human Bodies?
스트레스는 인체에 어떻게 영향을 미치는가?　stress, heart disease로 만든 오답
⑤ Sound Mind Wins the Game of Life!
건강한 마음이 인생의 게임에서 승리한다!　건강한 마음이 주는 이점을 이야기한 글이 아님

왜 정답? ✿✿✿ [정답률 68%]

- 부유한 국가들은 그들만의 뚜렷한 스트레스가 있다. 〔단서 1〕
- 부유한 국가의 스트레스 요인은 '시간 압박'이다. 〔단서 2〕
- 더 부유하고, 더 산업화된 국가들은 삶의 속도가 더 빠르다. 〔단서 3〕
- 빠른 삶의 속도는 촉박함을 느끼게 하고 심장병에 걸리기 쉽게 한다. 〔단서 4〕

➡ 부유한 국가의 스트레스 요인인 '시간 압박'과 '빠른 삶의 속도'에 관해 이야기하는 글이므로 글의 제목으로 가장 적절한 것은 ① '왜 부유한 나라들조차 스트레스에서 자유롭지 못한가?'이다.

왜 오답?

② 가난에서 벗어나는 방법을 설명한 글이 아니다.
③ 시간 관리의 중요성을 알리고 설명한 글이 아니다.
④ 빠른 삶의 속도가 심장병의 위험을 높였다는 것은 한 연구의 결과일 뿐, 이것이 글의 핵심은 아니다. 〔함정〕
⑤ 건강한 마음을 가지라고 조언하는 글이 아니다.

---

25 정답 ④　*산림 면적이 차지하는 비율

The above graph shows / the share of forest area / in total land area / by region / in 1990 and 2019. //
위 도표는 보여준다 / 산림 면적의 점유율을 / 총 토지 면적에서 / 지역별 / 1990년과 2019년의 //

① Africa's share of forest area in total land area / was over 20% / in both 1990 and 2019. // 〔아프리카: 1990년(25.3%), 2019년(21.4%)〕
아프리카의 전체 토지 면적에서 산림 면적의 점유율은 / 20퍼센트를 넘었다 / 1990년과 2019년에 모두 //

② The share of forest area in America / was 42.6% in 1990, / 〔아메리카: 1990년(42.6%) > 2019년(41.4%)〕
〔계속적 용법의 주격 관계대명사〕
which was larger than that in 2019. //
아메리카의 산림 면적 점유율은 / 1990년에 42.6퍼센트였고 / 이는 2019년의 그것보다 더 컸다 //

아시아: 1990년(32.4%) − 2019년(20%)=12.4%p
③ The share of forest area in Asia / declined from 1990 to 2019 / by more than 10 percentage points. //
아시아의 산림 면적 점유율은 / 1990년부터 2019년까지 감소했다 / 10퍼센트포인트 이상 //

④ In 2019, / the share of forest area in Europe / was the largest among the five regions, / more than three(→ two) times **that** in 〔= the share of forest area〕
Asia / in the same year. //
2019년 / 유럽의 산림 면적 점유율은 / 다섯 개 지역 중 가장 컸다 / 아시아의 그것의 세 배가 넘으며 / 같은 해에 // 〔단서〕 2019년: 유럽(46%)은 아시아(20%)의 3배(60%)보다 작음

⑤ Oceania showed the smallest gap / between 1990 and 2019 / 〔~에서는, ~에 관하여〕
in terms of the share of forest area in total land area. //
오세아니아는 가장 작은 차이를 보였다 / 1990년과 2019년 사이에 / 총 토지 면적에서 산림 면적의 점유율에 있어 // 오세아니아: 2019년(23.4%) − 1990년(22.6%)=0.8%p로 가장 작음

- share ⓝ 몫, 점유율　　· region ⓝ 지역　　· decline ⓥ 감소하다

위 도표는 1990년과 2019년의 지역별 총 토지 면적에서 산림 면적의 점유율을 보여준다. ① 아프리카의 전체 토지 면적에서 산림 면적의 점유율은 1990년과 2019년 둘 다 20퍼센트를 넘었다. ② 1990년 아메리카의 산림 면적 점유율은 42.6퍼센트였고, 이는 2019년의 점유율보다 더 컸다. ③ 아시아의 산림 면적 점유율은 1990년부터 2019년까지 10퍼센트포인트 이상 감소했다. ④ 2019년 유럽의 산림 면적 점유율은 다섯 개 지역 중 가장 컸고, 같은 해 아시아의 점유율의 세(→ 두) 배가 넘었다. ⑤ 오세아니아는 1990년과 2019년 사이에 총 토지 면적에서 산림 면적의 점유율에 있어 가장 작은 차이를 보였다.

다음 도표의 내용과 일치하지 않는 것은?

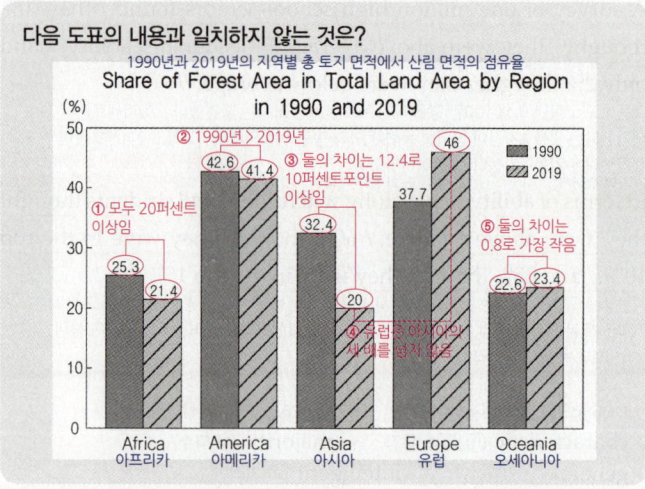

1990년과 2019년의 지역별 총 토지 면적에서 산림 면적의 점유율
Share of Forest Area in Total Land Area by Region in 1990 and 2019

왜 정답? ✿✿✿ [정답률 83%]

2019년 유럽의 산림 면적 점유율은 46퍼센트로 가장 크지만, 같은 해 아시아 점유율인 20퍼센트의 세 배인 60퍼센트보다는 작으므로 ④이 도표의 내용과 일치하지 않는다.

왜 오답?

① 아프리카의 산림 면적 점유율은 1990년에는 25.3퍼센트, 2019년에는 21.4퍼센트로, 모두 20퍼센트를 넘었다.
② 아메리카의 1990년 산림 면적 점유율은 42.6퍼센트로, 2019년의 41.4퍼센트보다 더 크다.
③ 아시아의 산림 면적 점유율은 1990년 32.4퍼센트에서 2019년 20퍼센트로, 12.4퍼센트포인트 감소했다.
⑤ 1990년과 2019년 오세아니아의 산림 면적 점유율의 차이는 0.8퍼센트포인트로, 가장 작다.

26 정답 ③ ＊Gary Becker의 생애

Gary Becker **was born** / in Pottsville, Pennsylvania in 1930 / and **grew up** / in Brooklyn, New York City. // `①의 단서` New York City의 Brooklyn에서 자람
└ 병렬 구조 ┘
Gary Becker는 태어났다 / 1930년 Pennsylvania 주 Pottsville에서 / 그리고 자랐다 / New York City의 Brooklyn에서 //
주격 관계대명사　　`②의 단서` 아버지는 금융과 정치 문제에 깊은 관심이 있었음
His father, / **who** was not well educated, / had a deep interest / in financial and political issues. //
그의 아버지는 / 교육을 제대로 받지 못한 / 깊은 관심이 있었다 / 금융과 정치 문제에 //
접속사가 생략되지 않은 분사구문
After graduating from high school, / Becker went to Princeton University, / **where** he majored in economics. //
계속적 용법의 관계부사
고등학교를 졸업한 후 / Becker는 Princeton University로 진학했다 / 그곳에서 그는 경제학을 전공했다 //

He was dissatisfied / with his economic education at Princeton University / because "it didn't seem to be handling real problems." // `③의 단서` Princeton University에서의 경제학 교육에 만족하지 못했음
그는 불만족스러웠다 / Princeton University에서의 경제학 교육이 / 왜냐하면 "그것이 현실적인 문제를 다루고 있는 것처럼 보이지 않았기" 때문에 //

He earned a doctor's degree in economics / from the University of Chicago in 1955. // `④의 단서` 1955년에 경제학 박사 학위를 취득함
그는 경제학 박사 학위를 취득했다 / 1955년에 University of Chicago에서 //
핵심 주어(단수)　　　　　　　　　　　단수 동사
His doctoral paper on the economics of discrimination / **was** mentioned by the Nobel Prize Committee / as an important contribution to economics. //
차별의 경제학에 대한 그의 박사 논문은 / 노벨상 위원회에 의해 언급되었다 / 경제학에 대한 중요한 기여로 //
`⑤의 단서` 〈Business Week〉에 경제학 칼럼을 기고함
Since 1985, / Becker had written a regular economics column / in *Business Week*, / explaining economic analysis and ideas / to the general public. //
1985년부터 / Becker는 정기적인 경제학 칼럼을 기고했다 / 〈Business Week〉에 / 경제학적 분석과 아이디어를 설명하는 / 일반 대중에게 //
수동태 동사
In 1992, / he **was awarded** the Nobel Prize in economic science. //
1992년에 / 그는 노벨경제학상을 수상했다 //

- financial ⓐ 금융의 · political ⓐ 정치의 · major in ~을 전공하다
- economics ⓝ 경제학 · dissatisfy ⓥ 불만을 느끼게 하다
- handle ⓥ 다루다 · earn ⓥ 얻다, 취득하다
- doctor's degree 박사 학위 · doctoral ⓐ 박사 학위의
- mention ⓥ 언급하다 · contribution ⓝ 기여
- regular ⓐ 정기적인, 규칙적인 · analysis ⓝ 분석

Gary Becker는 1930년 Pennsylvania 주 Pottsville에서 태어나 New York City의 Brooklyn에서 자랐다. 교육을 제대로 받지 못한 그의 아버지는 금융과 정치 문제에 깊은 관심이 있었다. 고등학교를 졸업한 후, Becker는 Princeton University로 진학했고, 그곳에서 그는 경제학을 전공했다. "Princeton University에서의 경제학 교육이 현실적인 문제를 다루고 있는 것처럼 보이지 않았기" 때문에 그는 그것에 불만족했다. 그는 1955년에 University of Chicago에서 경제학 박사 학위를 취득했다. 차별의 경제학에 대한 그의 박사 논문은 노벨상 위원회에 의해 경제학에 대한 중요한 기여로 언급되었다. 1985년부터, Becker는 〈Business Week〉에 경제학적 분석과 아이디어를 일반 대중에게 설명하는 경제학 칼럼을 정기적으로 기고했다. 1992년에, 그는 노벨경제학상을 수상했다.

Gary Becker에 관한 다음 글의 내용과 일치하지 **않는** 것은?

① New York City의 Brooklyn에서 자랐다.
grew up in Brooklyn, New York City
② 아버지는 금융과 정치 문제에 깊은 관심이 있었다.
His father ~ had a deep interest in financial and political issues.
③ Princeton University에서의 경제학 교육에 만족했다.
He was dissatisfied with his economic education at Princeton University
④ 1955년에 경제학 박사 학위를 취득했다.
He earned a doctor's degree in economics from the University of Chicago in 1955.
⑤ *Business Week*에 경제학 칼럼을 기고했다.
Becker had written a regular economics column in *Business Week*

＞왜 정답? ✿❀❀ [정답률 89%]
Gary Becker는 Princeton University에서의 경제학 교육이 현실적인 문제를 다루고 있는 것처럼 보이지 않았기 때문에 만족하지 못했다고 했다. (He was dissatisfied with his economic education at Princeton University) 따라서 ③이 글의 내용과 일치하지 않는다.

＞왜 오답?
① New York City의 Brooklyn에서 자랐다고 했다. (grew up in Brooklyn, New York City.)
② 아버지는 금융과 정치 문제에 깊은 관심이 있었다고 했다. (His father ~ had a deep interest in financial and political issues.)
④ 1955년에 University of Chicago에서 경제학 박사 학위를 취득했다고 했다. (He earned a doctor's degree in economics from the University of Chicago in 1955.)
⑤ 〈Business Week〉에 정기적인 경제학 칼럼을 기고했다고 했다. (Becker had written a regular economics column in *Business Week*.)

27 정답 ⑤ ＊2023 드론 레이싱 선수권 대회

2023 Drone Racing Championship /
2023 드론 레이싱 선수권 대회 /

Are you the best drone racer? //
당신은 최고의 드론 레이서인가요 //
형용사적 용법(opportunity 수식)
Then take the opportunity / **to prove** you are the one! //
그렇다면 기회를 잡으세요 / 여러분이 바로 그 사람이라는 것을 증명할 //

When & Where /
언제 & 어디서 /

· 6 p.m. – 8 p.m., / Sunday, July 9 / `①의 단서` 7월 9일 일요일에 개최됨
오후 6시부터 오후 8시까지 / 7월 9일 일요일 /

· Lakeside Community Center /
Lakeside Community Center /

Requirements /
필요 요건 /

· Participants: / High school students only /
참가자 / 고등학생만 / `②의 단서` 고등학생만 참가할 수 있음

· Bring your own drone / for the race. //
자신의 드론을 가지고 오세요 / 레이스를 위한 // `③의 단서` 자신의 드론을 가져와야 함

Prize / 상 /
미래시제 수동태
· $500 and a medal **will be awarded** / to the winner. //
500달러와 메달이 수여될 것입니다 / 우승자에게 // `④의 단서` 우승자에게는 상금과 메달이 수여됨

Note / 참고 사항 /
`⑤의 단서` 선착순 10명에게 기념품이 주어질 것임
· The first 10 participants will get souvenirs. //
선착순 10명의 참가자들은 기념품을 받게 될 것입니다 //

For more details, / please visit www.droneracing.com / or call 313-6745-1189. //
더 많은 세부 정보를 원하시면 / www.droneracing.com을 방문하시거나 / 313-6745-1189로 전화주세요 //

- opportunity ⓝ 기회 · prove ⓥ 증명하다
- requirement ⓝ 필요 요건 · award ⓥ 수여하다
- participant ⓝ 참가자 · souvenir ⓝ 기념품

2023 드론 레이싱 선수권 대회
당신은 최고의 드론 레이서인가요? 그렇다면 여러분이 바로 그 사람이라는 것을 증명할 기회를 잡으세요!
언제 & 어디서
· 오후 6시부터 오후 8시까지, 7월 9일 일요일
· Lakeside Community Center
필요 요건
· 참가자: 고등학생만
· 레이스를 위한 자신의 드론을 가지고 오세요.
상
· 500달러와 메달이 우승자에게 수여될 것입니다.

• 선착순 10명의 참가자들은 기념품을 받게 될 것입니다.
더 많은 세부 정보를 원하시면, www.droneracing.com을 방문하시거나
313-6745-1189로 전화주세요.

2023 Drone Racing Championship에 관한 다음 안내문의 내용과 일치하지 않는 것은?

① 7월 9일 일요일에 개최된다. *Sunday, July 9*
② 고등학생만 참가할 수 있다. *Participants: High school students only*
③ 자신의 드론을 가져와야 한다. *Bring your own drone for the race.*
④ 상금과 메달이 우승자에게 수여될 것이다.
⑤ 20명의 참가자가 기념품을 받을 것이다.
  $500 and a medal will be awarded to the winner.
  The first 10 participants will get souvenirs.

>왜 정답? ✽❀❀ [정답률 95%]

선착순 10명의 참가자들은 기념품을 받게 될 것이라고(The first 10 participants will get souvenirs.) 했으므로 20명의 참가자가 기념품을 받을 것이라고 한 ⑤이 안내문의 내용과 일치하지 않는다.

>왜 오답?

① 7월 9일 일요일에 개최된다. (Sunday, July 9)
② 고등학생만 참가할 수 있다. (Participants: High school students only)
③ 자신의 드론을 가져와야 한다. (Bring your own drone for the race.)
④ 상금 500달러와 메달이 우승자에게 수여될 것이다. ($500 and a medal will be awarded to the winner.)

28 정답 ⑤ ✽여름 스쿠버 다이빙 하루 수업

Summer Scuba Diving One-day Class /
여름 스쿠버 다이빙 하루 수업 /

<u>Join</u> our summer scuba driving lesson / for beginners, / and
병렬 구조
<u>become</u> an underwater explorer! //
우리의 여름 스쿠버 다이빙 수업에 참여하고 / 초보자를 위한 / 수중 탐험가가 되세요 //

Schedule /
일정 /

• 10:00 – 12:00 / Learning the basics /
10시에서 12시 / 기초 배우기 /

• 13:00 – 16:00 / Practicing diving skills in a pool /
13시에서 16시 / 수영장에서 다이빙 기술 연습하기 / **①의 단서** 다이빙 기술 연습은 수영장에서 함

Price /
가격 /

• Private lesson: / $150 /
개인 수업 / 150달러 /

• Group lesson (up to 3 people): / $100 per person /
그룹 수업 (3명까지) / 1인당 100달러 / **②의 단서** 그룹 수업은 최대 3명까지임

'무료로'
• Participants can rent our diving equipment / <u>for free.</u> //
참가자는 우리의 다이빙 장비를 대여할 수 있습니다 / 무료로 // **③의 단서** 다이빙 장비는 무료로 대여해 줌

Notice /
알림 /

• Participants must be 10 years old or over. //
참가자는 10세 이상이어야 합니다 // **④의 단서** 참가자의 연령은 10세 이상으로 제한됨

• Participants must register / at least 5 days before / the class begins. // **⑤의 단서** 수업 시작 5일 전까지는 등록해야 함
참가자는 등록해야 합니다 / 적어도 5일 전까지 / 수업이 시작하기 //

For more information, / please go to www.ssdiver.com. //
더 많은 정보를 원하시면 / www.ssdiver.com을 방문하세요 //

• underwater ⓐ 수중의   • explorer ⓝ 탐험가
• private ⓐ 개인을 위한   • rent ⓥ 대여하다
• equipment ⓝ 장비   • register ⓥ 등록하다

여름 스쿠버 다이빙 하루 수업

초보자를 위한 우리의 여름 스쿠버 다이빙 수업에 참여하고 수중 탐험가가 되세요!
일정
• 10시에서 12시 기초 배우기
• 13시에서 16시 수영장에서 다이빙 기술 연습하기
가격
• 개인 수업: 150달러
• 그룹 수업 (3명까지): 1인당 100달러
• 참가자는 우리의 다이빙 장비를 무료로 대여할 수 있습니다.
알림
• 참가자는 10세 이상이어야 합니다.
• 참가자는 적어도 수업 시작 5일 전까지 등록해야 합니다.
더 많은 정보를 원하시면, www.ssdiver.com을 방문하세요.

Summer Scuba Diving One-day Class에 관한 다음 안내문의 내용과 일치하는 것은?

① 오후 시간에 바다에서 다이빙 기술을 연습한다.
  Practicing diving skills in a pool
② 그룹 수업의 최대 정원은 4명이다.
  Group lesson (up to 3 people)
③ 다이빙 장비를 유료로 대여할 수 있다.
  Participants can rent our diving equipment for free.
④ 연령에 관계없이 참가할 수 있다.
  Participants must be 10 years old or over.
⑤ 적어도 수업 시작 5일 전까지 등록해야 한다.
  Participants must register at least 5 days before the class begins.

>왜 정답? ✽❀❀ [정답률 88%]

참가자는 적어도 수업 시작 5일 전까지 등록해야 한다고(Participants must register at least 5 days before the class begins.) 했으므로 안내문의 내용과 일치하는 것은 ⑤이다.

>왜 오답?

① 바다가 아니라 수영장에서 다이빙 기술을 연습한다고 했다. (Practicing diving skills in a pool)
② 그룹 수업은 3명까지라고 했다. (Group lesson (up to 3 people))
③ 참가자는 다이빙 장비를 무료로 대여할 수 있다고 했다. (Participants can rent our diving equipment for free.)
④ 참가자는 10세 이상이어야 한다고 했다. (Participants must be 10 years old or over.)

29 정답 ④ ✽아이를 향한 칭찬의 효과

다음 글의 밑줄 친 부분 중, 어법상 틀린 것은? [3점]

Although praise is one of the most powerful tools / available for
  = praise
improving young children's behavior, / <u>it</u> is equally powerful /
for improving your child's self-esteem. //
칭찬은 가장 강력한 도구 중 하나이지만 / 어린아이들의 행동을 개선하는 데 사용할 수 있는 / 그것은 똑같이 강력하다 / 여러분의 아이의 자존감을 향상시키는 데에도 //

선행사를 포함하는 관계대명사
Preschoolers believe / <u>what</u> their parents tell ① <u>them</u> / in a very
                                                    = preschoolers
profound way. //
미취학 아동들은 여긴다 / 그들의 부모가 그들에게 하는 말을 / 매우 뜻깊게 //

형용사적 용법(the cognitive sophistication 수식)
They do not yet have / the cognitive sophistication / <u>to reason</u> ②
to reason 수식
<u>analytically</u> / and <u>reject</u> false information. //
그들은 아직 가지고 있지 않다 / 인지적 정교함을 / 분석적으로 추론하는 / 그리고 잘못된 정보를 거부하는 //

목적어절 접속사
If a preschool boy consistently hears from his mother / ③ <u>that</u>
                                                    '~할 가능성이 높다'
he is smart and a good helper, / he <u>is likely to incorporate</u> that
information / into his self-image. //
만약 미취학 소년이 그의 어머니로부터 계속 듣는다면 / 그가 똑똑하고 좋은 조력자라는 것을 / 그는 그 정보를 통합시킬 가능성이 높다 / 그의 자아상으로 //

동명사 주어(단수 취급) **주격 관계대명사**
Thinking of himself as a boy / who is smart and knows how to
do things / ④being(→ is) likely to make him endure longer / in
단서 문장의 주어인 Thinking에 대한 동사가 없음
make의 목적격 보어 ①
problem-solving efforts /
스스로를 어떤 소년으로 생각하는 것은 / 똑똑하고 일을 어떻게 하는지 아는 / 그를 더 오래
지속하도록 만들 가능성이 높다 / 문제 해결 노력에 있어서 /
make의 목적격 보어 ②
and increase his confidence / in trying new and difficult tasks. //
그리고 그의 자신감을 증가시킬 (가능성이 높다) / 새롭고 어려운 일을 시도하는 것에 있어서 //
주어
Similarly, / thinking of himself as the kind of boy / who is a
동사
good helper / will make him more likely to volunteer / ⑤ to help
부사적 용법(목적)
with tasks / at home and at preschool. //
마찬가지로 / 자신을 그런 부류의 소년으로 생각하는 것은 / 좋은 조력자인 / 그를 더
자원하도록 만들 것이다 / 일을 돕기 위해 / 집에서와 유치원에서 //

- praise ⓝ 칭찬 • equally ⓐⓓ 동등하게 • self-esteem ⓝ 자존감
- preschooler ⓝ 미취학 아동 • cognitive ⓐ 인지적인
- reason ⓥ 추론하다 • analytically ⓐⓓ 분석적으로
- reject ⓥ 거부[거절]하다 • consistently ⓐⓓ 지속적으로
- incorporate ⓥ 통합하다 • self-image ⓝ 자아상
- endure ⓥ 지속하다, 견디다

칭찬은 어린아이들의 행동을 개선하는 데 사용할 수 있는 가장 강력한 도구
중 하나이지만, 그것은 아이의 자존감을 향상시키는 데에도 똑같이 강력하다.
미취학 아동들은 그들의 부모가 그들에게 하는 말을 매우 뜻깊게 여긴다.
그들은 분석적으로 추론하고 잘못된 정보를 거부할 수 있는 인지적 정교함을
아직 가지고 있지 않다. 만약 미취학 소년이 그의 어머니로부터 그가 똑똑하고
좋은 조력자라는 것을 계속 듣는다면, 그는 그 정보를 그의 자아상으로
통합시킬 가능성이 높다. 스스로를 똑똑하고 일을 어떻게 하는지 아는 소년으로
생각하는 것은 그가 문제 해결 노력에 있어 더 오래 지속하도록 하고, 새롭고
어려운 일을 시도하는 것에 있어 그의 자신감을 증가시킬 가능성이 높다.
마찬가지로, 자신을 좋은 조력자인 그런 부류의 소년으로 생각하는 것은 그가
집에서와 유치원에서 일을 돕기 위해 더 자원하도록 만들 것이다.

＞왜 정답？ ✱✱✱ [정답률 58%]

④ 문장에 동사가 없다!

동명사 주어 **선행사** **주격 관계대명사**
Thinking of himself as a boy / [who is smart and knows
단수 동사
how to do things] / ④ being(→ is) likely to make him
동사 자리임
endure longer / in problem-solving efforts / and increase
전치사구: 제외하고 생각하기   and로 연결: 제외하고 생각하기
his confidence / in trying new and difficult tasks. //

(단서) 밑줄이 동명사 being에 있으므로
(발상) 동명사가 쓰일 자리가 맞는지 확인해야 한다.
(해결) 그런데 문장의 주어 Thinking에 대한 동사 동사가 빠져 있다. 앞에 나온 is는
who가 이끄는 주격 관계대명사절의 동사이므로 being이 문장의 동사 자리에
쓰였음을 알 수 있다.
being과 같은 준동사는 동사 역할을 할 수 없으므로, 단수 주어 Thinking에
맞는 단수 동사 is로 고쳐야 한다.
(개념) 주어와 동사는 문장의 필수 요소로서, 둘 중 하나라도 없으면 의미가 통하지
않으므로 문장이 될 수 없다.

＞왜 오답？

① 대명사는 그것이 대신하는 명사에 수를 일치시킨다.

주어 **동사** **목적어절을 이끄는 관계대명사** **= preschoolers**
Preschoolers believe / what their parents tell ① them / in a
very profound way. //

대명사 them에 밑줄이 있으므로 그것이 대신하는 명사를 찾아 수 일치 여부를
확인한다.
문맥상 미취학 아동들은 그들의 부모가 '그들에게' 하는 말을 매우 뜻깊게 여기는
것이므로 preschoolers를 가리킨다.
따라서 복수 대명사 them은 어법상 적절하게 쓰였다.

---

② 부사는 준동사를 수식할 수 있다.

수식 받는 명사
They do not yet have / the cognitive sophistication / to
부사(to reason 수식)
reason ② analytically / and reject false information. //
형용사적 용법(the cognitive sophistication 수식)

부사 analytically에 밑줄이 있으므로 수식하는 대상을 찾아 부사의 수식을 받을 수
있는지를 확인한다.
문맥상 '분석적으로 추론하는' 인지적 정교함을 가지고 있지 않은 것이므로
to reason을 수식하고 있다.
to부정사는 준동사로, 부사의 수식을 받을 수 있으므로 analytically는 알맞게 쓰였다.

③ that이 목적어절을 이끌고 있다.

주어 **동사** 전치사구: 제외하고 생각하기
If a preschool boy consistently hears from his mother /
목적어절 접속사
[③ that he is smart and a good helper.] / he is likely to
완전한 2형식 문장
incorporate that information / into his self-image. //
주절: 제외하고 생각하기

명사절 접속사 that은 문장에서 명사 역할을 하는 절을 이끌며 '~하는 것'이라고
해석한다. (개념)
문장의 동사인 hears 뒤에 that이 왔고, that 뒤에는 주어(he), 동사(is), 주격
보어(smart and a good helper)를 갖춘 완전한 절이 이어진다.
따라서 that은 hears의 목적어절을 이끄는 명사절 접속사로 적절하게 쓰였다.

⑤ 부사적 용법의 to부정사가 쓰였다.

주어 관계대명사절: 제외하고 생각하기
Similarly, / thinking of himself as the kind of boy / who is
동사 **목적어** **목적격 보어**
a good helper / will make him more likely to volunteer / ⑤
부사적 용법(목적)
to help with tasks / at home and at preschool. //

주어(thinking ~ helper), 동사(will make), 목적어(him), 목적격 보어(more likely
to volunteer)를 갖춘 5형식 문장이므로, to help는 수식어인 형용사나 부사의
역할을 할 것이다.
문맥상 일을 '돕기 위해' 더 자원하도록 만든다는 것이므로 목적을 나타내는 부사적
용법으로 to help는 적절하게 쓰였다.

---

30 **정답 ②** ✱ 효모에서 천연 완하제로

다음 글의 밑줄 친 부분 중, 문맥상 낱말의 쓰임이 적절하지 **않은** 것은?

Advertisers often displayed considerable facility / in ① adapting
their claims / to the market status of the goods / they promoted. //
광고주들은 상당한 능력을 자주 보여주었다 / 그들의 주장을 조절하는 데 있어서 / 상품의
시장 지위에 맞게 / 그들이 홍보한 //
앞에 목적격 관계대명사가 생략됨
Fleischmann's yeast, / for instance, / was used as an ingredient /
단서 1 Fleischmann의 효모는 집에서 빵을
for cooking homemade bread. // 만드는 재료로 사용되었음
Fleischmann의 효모는 / 예를 들어 / 재료로 사용되었다 / 집에서 만든 빵을 요리하는 //
단서 2 20세기 초 사람들은 빵을 집에서 만들지 않고 가게에서 사게 됨
Yet / more and more people in the early 20th century / were
buying their bread from stores or bakeries, / so consumer
demand for yeast ② increased(→ decreased). //
하지만 / 20세기 초에 점점 더 많은 사람들이 / 가게나 빵집에서 빵을 사고 있었고 / 그래서
효모에 대한 소비자 수요는 증가했다(→ 감소했다) //
The producer of Fleischmann's yeast / hired the J. Walter
부사적 용법(목적)
Thompson advertising agency / to come up with a different
marketing strategy / to ③ boost sales. //
Fleischmann의 효모의 생산자는 / J. Walter Thompson 광고 대행사를 고용했다 / 다른
마케팅 전략을 고안하려고 / 판매를 촉진하기 위해서 //

2023. 6
6회

앞에 Being이 생략됨

No longer the "Soul of Bread," / the Thompson agency first turned yeast / into an important source of vitamins / with significant health ④ benefits. //
더 이상 "Soul of Bread"가 아니라 / Thompson 광고 대행사는 먼저 효모를 바꾸었다 / 비타민의 중요한 공급원으로 / 상당한 건강상의 이점이 있는 //

Shortly thereafter, / the advertising agency transformed yeast / into a natural laxative. //
그 직후 / 그 광고 대행사는 효모를 바꾸었다 / 천연 완하제로 //

helped의 목적어

⑤ Repositioning yeast / helped increase sales. //
효모의 이미지 전환을 꾀하는 것은 / 매출을 증가시키는 것을 도왔다 //

- display ⓥ 보여주다, 전시하다 · considerable ⓐ 상당한
- facility ⓝ 재능, 시설 · adapt ⓥ 조절하다 · claim ⓝ 주장
- status ⓝ 지위 · promote ⓥ 홍보하다 · yeast ⓝ 효모
- ingredient ⓝ 재료 · demand ⓝ 수요, 요구 · hire ⓥ 고용하다
- strategy ⓝ 전략 · boost ⓥ 촉진하다 · significant ⓐ 상당한
- thereafter ⓐⓓ 그 후에 · transform ⓥ 바꾸다
- reposition ⓥ 이미지 전환을 꾀하다

광고주들은 그들이 홍보한 상품의 시장 지위에 맞게 그들의 주장을 ① 조절하는 상당한 능력을 자주 보여주었다. 예를 들어, Fleischmann의 효모는 집에서 만든 빵을 요리하는 재료로 사용되었다. 하지만 20세기 초에 점점 더 많은 사람들이 가게나 빵집에서 빵을 사고 있었고, 그래서 효모에 대한 소비자 수요는 ② 증가했다(→ 감소했다). Fleischmann의 효모의 생산자는 판매를 ③ 촉진하기 위해서 다른 마케팅 전략을 고안하려고 J. Walter Thompson 광고 대행사를 고용했다. Thompson 광고 대행사는 먼저 효모를 더 이상 "Soul of Bread"가 아니라 상당한 건강상의 ④ 이점이 있는 비타민의 중요한 공급원으로 바꾸었다. 그 직후, 광고 대행사는 효모를 천연 완하제로 바꾸었다. 효모의 ⑤ 이미지 전환을 꾀하는 것은 매출을 증가시키는 것을 도왔다.

> 왜 정답 ? ★★★ [정답률 58%]

② increased 증가했다

예를 들어, Fleischmann의 효모는 집에서 만든 빵을 요리하는 재료로 사용되었다.
하지만 20세기 초에 점점 더 많은 사람들이 가게나 빵집에서 빵을 사고 있었고, 그래서 효모에 대한 소비자 수요는 ② 증가했다.
감소했다

➡ 효모는 집에서 빵을 요리하는 재료로 사용되었지만, 점점 많은 사람들이 빵을 가게에서 사면서 효모에 대한 소비자의 수요는 '증가한' 것이 아니라 '줄어들었을' 것이다. ▶ increased를 decreased(감소했다)와 같은 반의어로 바꿔야 함

> 왜 오답 ?

① adapting 조절하는

광고주들은 그들이 홍보한 상품의 시장 지위에 맞게 그들의 주장을 ① 조절하는 상당한 능력을 자주 보여주었다.

➡ 이어서 제시되는 광고 대행사가 Fleischmann의 효모를 비타민 공급원으로 바꾸고, 또 천연 완하제로 바꾸었다는 내용을 종합하면 광고주들이 그들의 주장을 '조절하는' 능력을 보여주었다는 것은 자연스럽다.
▶ adapting은 문맥에 맞음

③ boost 촉진하다

Fleischmann의 효모의 생산자는 판매를 ③ 촉진하기 위해서 다른 마케팅 전략을 고안하려고 J. Walter Thompson 광고 대행사를 고용했다.

➡ 마케팅 전략을 고안하기 위해 광고 대행사를 고용한 것은 판매를 '촉진하기' 위해서일 것이다.
▶ boost는 문맥에 맞음

---

④ benefits 이점

Thompson 광고 대행사는 먼저 효모를 더 이상 "Soul of Bread"가 아니라 상당한 건강상의 ④ 이점이 있는 비타민의 중요한 공급원으로 바꾸었다.

➡ 효모의 판매를 촉진하기 위한 새로운 마케팅 전략으로 효모를 건강상의 '이점'이 있는 비타민 공급원으로 홍보했다는 것은 어색하지 않다.
▶ benefits는 문맥에 맞음

⑤ Repositioning 이미지 전환을 꾀하는 것

그 직후, 광고 대행사는 효모를 천연 완하제로 바꾸었다. 효모의 ⑤ 이미지 전환을 꾀하는 것은 매출을 증가시키는 것을 도왔다.

➡ 효모를 비타민으로, 천연 완하제로 바꾼 것을 '이미지 전환을 꾀하는 것'이라고 말하는 것은 적절하다.
▶ Repositioning은 문맥에 맞음

31 정답 ④ *전문성이 주는 영향력

주격 관계대명사 | 단서 1 자신의 직업에 전문성이 있는 사람들은 즉각적인 신뢰를 얻음

Individuals / who perform at a high level in their profession / often have instant credibility with others. //
개인들은 / 자신의 직업에서 높은 수준으로 수행하는 / 흔히 다른 사람들에게 즉각적인 신뢰를 얻는다 //

People admire them, / they want to be like them, / and they feel connected to them. //
사람들은 그들을 존경하고 / 그들처럼 되고 싶어 하고 / 그들과 연결되어 있다고 느낀다 //

부사절 접속사(양보)

When they speak, / others listen / — even if the area of their skill / has nothing to do with the advice / they give. //
~와 관련이 없다 | 앞에 목적격 관계대명사가 생략됨
그들이 말할 때 / 다른 사람들은 경청한다 / 비록 그들의 기술 분야가 / 조언과 관련이 없을지라도 / 그들이 주는 //
단서 2 조언과 관련되지 않은 분야라도 전문성이 있으면 사람들은 경청함

Think about a world-famous basketball player. //
세계적으로 유명한 농구선수에 대해 생각해 보라 //

대동사(=made) | 분사구문

He has made more money from endorsements / than he ever did / playing basketball. //
그는 광고로부터 더 많은 돈을 벌었다 / 그가 그간 벌었던 것보다 / 농구를 하면서 //

앞에 목적격 관계대명사가 생략됨

Is it because of his knowledge / of the products he endorses? //
그것이 그의 지식 때문일까 / 그가 광고하는 제품에 대한 //

No. //
아니다 //

선행사를 포함하는 관계대명사

It's because of what he can do / with a basketball. //
그것은 그가 할 수 있는 것 때문이다 / 농구로 //

The same can be said / of an Olympic medalist swimmer. //
같은 것이 말해질 수 있다 / 올림픽 메달리스트 수영 선수에도 //

선행사를 포함하는 관계대명사

People listen to him / because of what he can do in the pool. //
사람들은 그의 말을 경청한다 / 그가 수영장에서 할 수 있는 것 때문에 //

앞에 직접목적어절 접속사 that이 생략됨

And when an actor tells us / we should drive a certain car, / we don't listen / because of his expertise on engines. //
그리고 어떤 배우가 우리에게 말할 때 / 우리가 특정 자동차를 운전해야 한다고 / 우리는 경청하는 것이 아니다 / 엔진에 대한 그의 전문 지식 때문에 //

We listen / because we admire his talent. //
우리는 경청한다 / 우리가 그의 재능을 존경하기 때문에 //

Excellence connects. //
탁월함이 연결된다 //
단서 3 사람들은 전문성이 있는 사람에게 연결되고 싶어 함

If you possess a high level of ability in an area, / others may desire to connect with you / because of it. //
만약 당신이 어떤 분야에서 높은 수준의 능력을 갖추고 있다면 / 다른 사람들은 당신과 연결되기를 원할 수도 있다 / 그것 때문에 //

- individual ⓝ 개인　• profession ⓝ 직업　• instant ⓐ 즉각적인
- credibility ⓝ 신뢰　• admire ⓥ 존경하다　• advice ⓝ 조언
- knowledge ⓝ 지식　• certain ⓐ 특정한
- expertise ⓝ 전문 지식[기술]　• talent ⓝ 재능
- patience ⓝ 인내심, 참을성　• sacrifice ⓝ 희생

자신의 직업에서 높은 수준으로 수행하는 사람들은 흔히 다른 사람들에게 즉각적인 신뢰를 얻는다. 사람들은 그들을 존경하고, 그들처럼 되고 싶어 하고, 그들과 연결되어 있다고 느낀다. 그들이 말할 때, 다른 사람들은 비록 그들의 기술 분야가 그들이 주는 조언과 관련이 없을지라도 경청한다. 세계적으로 유명한 농구선수에 대해 생각해 보라. 그는 그가 농구를 하면서 그간 벌었던 것보다 광고로부터 더 많은 돈을 벌었다. 그것이 그가 광고하는 제품에 대한 그의 지식 때문일까? 아니다. 그것은 그가 농구로 할 수 있는 것 때문이다. 올림픽 메달리스트 수영 선수도 마찬가지이다. 사람들은 그가 수영장에서 할 수 있는 것 때문에 그의 말을 경청한다. 그리고 어떤 배우가 우리에게 특정 자동차를 운전해야 한다고 말할 때, 우리는 엔진에 대한 그의 전문 지식 때문에 경청하는 것은 아니다. 우리는 그의 재능을 존경하기 때문에 경청한다. **탁월함**이 연결된다. 만약 당신이 어떤 분야에서 높은 수준의 능력을 갖추고 있다면, 다른 사람들은 그것 때문에 당신과 연결되기를 원할 수도 있다.

> **다음 빈칸에 들어갈 말로 가장 적절한 것을 고르시오.**
> ① Patience 인내심 때문에 존경을 받는 것이 아님
> 　인내심
> ② Sacrifice 희생이 중요하다는 것이 아님
> 　희생
> ③ Honesty 정직함이 중요하다는 것이 아님
> 　정직함
> ④ Excellence 특정 분야에서 보여준 전문성이 신뢰로 연결됨
> 　탁월함
> ⑤ Creativity 창의성은 언급되지 않음
> 　창의성

왜 정답? *** [정답률 57%]

빈칸 문장	＿＿＿이 연결된다.
빈칸 문장 뒤	만약 당신이 어떤 분야에서 높은 수준의 능력을 갖추고 있다면, 다른 사람들은 그것 때문에 당신과 연결되기를 원할 수도 있다. 단서 3

➡ **빈칸 문장:** '무엇'이 언결된다.
➡ **빈칸 문장 뒤:** 높은 수준의 능력을 갖춤 ➡ 사람들은 연결되기를 원함
　▶ 따라서 빈칸은 '높은 수준'과 같은 맥락일 것임

| 글의 앞부분 | • 자신의 직업에서 높은 수준으로 수행하는 사람들은 흔히 다른 사람들에게 즉각적인 신뢰를 얻는다. 단서 1
 • 그들이 말할 때, 다른 사람들은 비록 그들의 기술 분야가 그들이 주는 조언과 관련이 없을지라도 경청한다. 단서 2 |

➡ 특정 분야에서 높은 수준으로 수행하는 능력은 이와 상관없는 분야에 대한 신뢰로 이어진다.
　▶ 따라서 ④ '탁월함'이 다른 분야로도 연결되는 것이다.

왜 오답?

① 인내심 때문에 존경받는다는 내용이 아니다.
② 희생의 중요성을 강조하는 내용이 아니다.
③ 정직함과 관련된 내용은 언급되지 않았다.
⑤ 창의성과는 관련 없는 내용이다.

---

32 정답 ① *도시처럼 상호 작용하는 뇌

Think of the brain as a city. //
뇌를 도시라고 생각해 보라 //

If you were to **look out** over a city / and **ask** "where is the economy located?" / you'd **see** / there's no good answer to the question. //
<small>병렬 구조 / 뒤에 목적어절 접속사 that이 생략됨</small>
만약 당신이 도시를 내다보며 / "경제가 어디에 위치해 있나요"라고 묻는다면 / 당신은 알게 될 것이다 / 그 질문에 대한 좋은 답이 없다는 것을 //

Instead, / the economy emerges / from the interaction of all the elements / — **from** the stores and the banks / **to** the merchants and the customers. // 단서 1 도시의 경제는 모든 요소의 상호 작용으로부터 나타남
<small>from A to B: A에서 B까지</small>
대신 / 경제는 나타난다 / 모든 요소의 상호 작용으로부터 / 상점과 은행에서 / 상인과 고객에 이르기까지 //

And so it is with the brain's operation: / it doesn't happen in one spot. // 단서 2 도시와 마찬가지로 뇌의 작동도 한 곳에서 일어나지 않음
그리고 그것은 뇌의 작동도 그러하다 / 그것은 한 곳에서 일어나지 않는다 //

Just as in a city, / no neighborhood of the brain **operates in isolation**. //
도시에서처럼 / 뇌의 어떤 지역도 독립적으로 작동하지 않는다 //

In brains and in cities, / everything emerges / from the interaction between residents, / at all scales, / locally and distantly. // 단서 3 뇌와 도시는 짧든 멀든 내부 요소의 상호 작용으로부터 나타남
뇌와 도시 안에서 / 모든 것은 나타난다 / 거주자들 간의 상호 작용으로부터 / 모든 규모에서 / 근방에서든 원거리에서든 //

Just as trains bring materials and textiles into a city, / **which** become processed into the economy, /
<small>계속적 용법의 주격관계대명사</small>
기차가 자재와 직물을 도시로 들여오는 것처럼 / 그리고 그것은 경제 속으로 처리된다 /

so **the raw electrochemical signals** from sensory organs / **are** transported / along superhighways of neurons. //
<small>핵심 주어(복수) / 복수 동사</small>
감각 기관으로부터의 가공되지 않은 전기화학적 신호는 / 전해진다 / 뉴런의 초고속도로를 따라서 //

There / the signals undergo processing and transformation / into our conscious reality. //
거기서 / 신호는 처리와 변형을 겪는다 / 우리의 의식적인 현실로 //

- economy ⓝ 경제　• emerge ⓥ 나타나다
- interaction ⓝ 상호 작용　• element ⓝ 요소
- merchant ⓝ 상인　• operation ⓝ 작용, 작동
- resident ⓝ 거주자　• scale ⓝ 정도, 규모　• distantly ⓐⓓ 멀리에서
- textile ⓝ 직물　• raw ⓐ 가공되지 않은　• sensory ⓐ 감각의
- organ ⓝ (체내의) 장기　• transport ⓥ 전하다, 이동하다
- superhighway ⓝ 초고속도로　• undergo ⓥ 겪다
- conscious ⓐ 의식적인　• isolation ⓝ 독립, 분리
- resemble ⓥ 유사하다　• systemic ⓐ 체계적인

뇌를 도시라고 생각해 보라. 만약 당신이 도시를 내다보며 "경제가 어디에 위치해 있나요?"라고 묻는다면, 그 질문에 대한 좋은 답이 없다는 것을 알게 될 것이다. 대신, 경제는 상점과 은행에서 상인과 고객에 이르기까지 모든 요소의 상호 작용으로부터 나타난다. 그리고 그것은 뇌의 작동도 그러하다: 그것은 한 곳에서 일어나지 않는다. 도시에서처럼, 뇌의 어떤 지역도 **독립적으로 작동하지** 않는다. 뇌와 도시 안에서, 모든 것은, 모든 규모에서, 근거리에서든 원거리에서든, 거주자들 간의 상호 작용으로부터 나타난다. 기차가 자재와 직물을 도시로 들여오고, 그것이 경제 속으로 처리되는 것처럼, 감각 기관으로부터의 가공되지 않은 전기화학적 신호는 뉴런의 초고속도로를 따라서 전해진다. 거기서 신호는 처리와 우리의 의식적인 현실로 변형을 겪는다.

<small>2023.6</small>
<small>6회</small>

다음 빈칸에 들어갈 말로 가장 적절한 것을 고르시오. [3점]

① operates in isolation 도시처럼 뇌의 모든 지역과 신호들은 상호 작용함
독립적으로 작동하다
② suffers from rapid changes 급격한 변화와 고통에 대한 언급은 없음
급격한 변화로 고통받다
③ resembles economic elements 앞에 no가 있으므로 반대 내용이 됨
경제적 요소들과 유사하다
④ works in a systematic way 작동 방식이 체계적인지는 알 수 없음
체계적인 방식으로 작동하다
⑤ interacts with another 앞에 no가 있으므로 반대 내용이 됨
다른 요소와 상호 작용하다

| 문제 풀이 순서 | ★★★ [정답률 48%]

1st 먼저 빈칸 문장을 읽고, 빈칸에 들어갈 말에 대한 단서를 얻는다.

| 빈칸 문장 | Just as in a city, no neighborhood of the brain ____.
도시에서처럼, 뇌의 어떤 지역도 ____ 않는다. |

➡ 빈칸 문장 앞에 도시의 어떤 측면에 대한 설명이 있을 것이고, 빈칸 문장 뒤에서 그것이 왜 뇌와 비슷한지 설명할 것이다.
뇌의 어떤 지역도 '어떻지 않다'라고 했으므로, 빈칸 문장 앞부분을 통해 추론해야 한다.

2nd 나머지 부분을 읽고, 도시와 뇌가 어떻게 비슷한지 확인하여 정답을 찾는다.

| 글의 앞부분 | 만약 당신이 도시를 내다보며 "경제가 어디에 위치해 있나요?"라고 묻는다면, 그 질문에 대한 좋은 답이 없다는 것을 알게 될 것이다.
대신, 경제는 상점과 은행에서 상인과 고객에 이르기까지 모든 요소의 상호 작용으로부터 나타난다. 단서 1 |

➡ 도시의 경제는 한 곳에서 작용하는 것이 아님 → 상점과 은행, 상인과 고객 등 모든 요소의 상호 작용에서 나타남
▶ 뇌도 여러 요소의 상호 작용으로 작동할 것임

| 빈칸 문장 앞 | 그리고 그것은 뇌의 작동도 그러하다: 그것은 한 곳에서 일어나지 않는다. 단서 2 |
| 빈칸 문장 뒤 | 뇌와 도시 안에서, 모든 것은, 모든 규모에서, 근거리에서든 원거리에서든, 거주자들 간의 상호 작용으로부터 나타난다. 단서 3 |

➡ 뇌의 작동도 한 곳에서 일어나지 않음 → 모든 것들의 상호 작용에서 나타남
▶ 빈칸 앞에 no가 있으므로, 뇌의 어떤 지역도 ① '독립적으로 작동하지' 않는다고 해야 적절하다.

| 선택지 분석 |

① operates in isolation
독립적으로 작동하지 (않는다)
도시에서처럼, 뇌의 모든 지역과 신호들은 서로 상호 작용하므로 독립적으로 작동하지 않는 것이다.

② suffers from rapid changes
급격한 변화로 고통받지 (않는다)
도시가 급격한 변화로부터 자유롭다는 등의 언급은 없었기 때문에 적절하지 않다.

③ resembles economic elements
경제적 요소들과 유사하지 (않다)
도시와 뇌가 비슷하기 때문에, 도시의 경제적 요소들과 뇌의 지역은 유사하다고 볼 수 있지만, 빈칸 앞에 no가 있으므로 글과 반대 내용이 된다.

④ works in a systematic way
체계적인 방식으로 작동하지 (않는다)
체계적이지 않은 것이 상호 작용하는 것인지를 판단할 근거는 제시되지 않았다.

⑤ interacts with another
다른 요소와 상호 작용하지 (않는다)
빈칸 앞에 no가 있으므로 글과 반대 내용이 된다.

---

33 정답 ② ＊신체로부터 비롯되는 감정

계속적 용법의 주격 관계대명사
Someone else's body language affects our own body, / which then creates an emotional echo / that makes us feel accordingly. //
다른 사람의 몸짓 언어는 우리 자신의 신체에 영향을 미친다 / 그리고 그것은 그 후 감정적인 메아리를 만들어 낸다 / 우리가 그에 따라 느끼도록 하는 / 단서 1 다른 사람의 몸짓 언어 → 우리의 신체에 영향 → 그에 따른 감정을 느낌

As Louis Armstrong sang, / "When you're smiling, / the whole world smiles with you." //
Louis Armstrong이 노래했듯이 / "당신이 미소 지을 때 / 전 세계가 당신과 함께 미소 짓는다" //

동명사 주어(단수 취급) 단수 동사 makes의 목적격 보어(원형부정사)
If copying another's smile makes us feel happy, / the emotion of the smiler has been transmitted / via our body. //
만약 다른 사람의 미소를 따라 하는 것이 우리를 행복하게 한다면 / 그 미소 짓는 사람의 감정은 전달된 것이다 / 우리의 신체를 통해 // 단서 2 다른 사람의 감정이 우리의 신체를 통해 전달됨

「형용사+as+주어+동사」: 양보를 나타내는 as 구문 목적어절 접속사
Strange as it may sound, / this theory states / that emotions arise from our bodies. //
이상하게 들릴지 모르지만 / 이 이론은 말한다 / 감정이 우리 신체에서 발생한다고 //

For example, / our mood can be improved / by simply lifting up the corners of our mouth. // 단서 3 입꼬리만 올려도 기분이 좋아짐
예를 들어 / 우리의 기분은 좋아질 수 있다 / 단순히 입꼬리를 올림으로써 //

분사구문을 이끄는 현재분사 not to let의 목적격 보어(원형부정사)
If people are asked / to bite down on a pencil lengthwise, / taking care not to let the pencil touch their lips / (thus forcing the mouth into a smile-like shape), /
만약 사람들이 요구받으면 / 연필을 긴 방향으로 꽉 물라고 / 연필이 그들의 입술에 닿지 않도록 조심하면서 / (그리하여 강제로 입을 미소 짓는 것과 같은 모양이 되도록) //

현재완료 수동태
they judge cartoons funnier / than if they have been asked to frown. //
그들은 만화를 더 재미있다고 판단한다 / 그들이 인상을 찌푸리라고 요구받았을 때보다 //

The primacy of the body is sometimes summarized / in the phrase / "I must be afraid / because I'm running." //
신체가 우선함은 때때로 요약된다 / 구절로 / "나는 두려운 것이 분명하다 / 왜냐하면 나는 도망치고 있기 때문이다"라는 //

- echo ⓝ 메아리   - accordingly ⓐⓓ 그에 따라
- transmit ⓥ 전달하다   - via ⓟⓡⓔⓟ ~을 통하여   - theory ⓝ 이론
- mood ⓝ 기분, 분위기   - judge ⓥ 판단하다
- disappear ⓥ 사라지다

다른 사람의 몸짓 언어는 우리 자신의 신체에 영향을 미치며, 그것은 그 후 우리가 그에 따라 느끼도록 하는 감정적인 메아리를 만들어 낸다. Louis Armstrong이 노래했듯이, "당신이 미소 지을 때, 전 세계가 당신과 함께 미소 짓는다." 만약 다른 사람의 미소를 따라 하는 것이 우리를 행복하게 한다면, 그 미소 짓는 사람의 감정은 우리의 신체를 통해 전달될 것이다. 이상하게 들릴지 모르지만, 이 이론은 **감정이 우리 신체에서 발생한다**고 말한다. 예를 들어, 우리의 기분은 단순히 입꼬리를 올리는 것으로 좋아질 수 있다. 만약 사람들이 연필을 긴 방향으로 꽉 물라고 요구받으면, 연필이 그들의 입술에 닿지 않도록 조심하면서 (그리하여 강제로 입을 미소 짓는 것과 같은 모양이 되도록), 그들은 인상을 찌푸리라고 요구받았을 때보다 만화를 더 재미있다고 판단한다. 신체가 우선함은 "나는 두려운 것이 분명하다, 왜냐하면 나는 도망치고 있기 때문이다."라는 구절로 때때로 요약된다.

다음 빈칸에 들어갈 말로 가장 적절한 것을 고르시오. [3점]

① language guides our actions
언어가 우리의 행동을 안내한다   언어가 아니라 신체가 우리의 감정에 영향을 미친다고 했음
② emotions arise from our bodies
감정은 우리 신체에서 발생한다   억지로 입꼬리를 올려도 기분이 좋아질 수 있음
③ body language hides our feelings
몸짓 언어는 우리의 감정을 숨긴다   몸짓 언어는 감정을 이끈다고 볼 수 있음
④ what others say affects our mood   다른 사람의 말이 아니라 몸짓 언어가
다른 사람의 말은 우리의 기분에 영향을 미친다   영향을 미치는 것임
⑤ negative emotions easily disappear
부정적인 감정들은 쉽게 사라진다   부정적인 감정이 쉽게 사라지는지는 알 수 없음

왜 정답? ★★☆ [정답률 61%]

빈칸 문장	이상하게 들릴지 모르지만, 이 이론은 ____________ 고 말한다.
빈칸 문장 뒤 예시	예를 들어(For example), 우리의 기분은 단순히 입꼬리를 올리는 것으로 좋아질 수 있다. 단서 3

➡ **빈칸 문장:** 어떤 이론이 등장했고, 그 이론의 내용을 파악해야 한다.
➡ **빈칸 문장 뒤 예시:** 진짜 웃지 않고 단순히 입꼬리만 올려도 기분이 좋아질 수 있다.

빈칸 문장 앞 예시	만약 다른 사람의 미소를 따라 하는 것이 우리를 행복하게 한다면, ~ 감정은 우리의 신체를 통해 전달된 것이다. 단서 2

➡ 신체 변화(미소 짓는 것)가 감정(행복함)을 발생시킨 것
▶ 따라서 빈칸에는 ② '감정은 우리 신체에서 발생한다'가 적절하다.

왜 오답?

① 신체가 감정에 영향을 끼친다는 내용의 글로, 언어가 우리 행동에 미치는 영향을 설명한 글이 아니다.
③ 다른 사람의 몸짓 언어를 따라 함으로써 그 사람의 감정을 전달받았다고 했으므로 글과 반대되는 내용이다. 주의
④ 우리의 기분에 영향을 미치는 요인으로 다른 사람의 말이 아니라 몸짓 언어를 따라하는 것을 들었다.
⑤ 미소 짓는 것을 통해 부정적인 감정을 없앨 수 있다는 내용이 아니다.

34 정답 ③ *희소성이 판매를 장려한다!

앞에 목적격 관계대명사가 생략됨
Restricting the number of items / customers can buy / boosts sales. //
품목의 개수를 제한하는 것은 / 고객이 구입할 수 있는 / 매출을 증가시킨다 //

동격
Brian Wansink, / Professor of Marketing at Cornell University, / investigated the effectiveness of this tactic / in 1998. //
Brian Wansink는 / Cornell University의 마케팅 교수인 / 이 전략의 효과를 조사했다 / 1998년에 //

persuaded의 목적격 보어
He persuaded three supermarkets in Sioux City, Iowa, / to offer Campbell's soup at a small discount: / 79 cents rather than 89 cents. //
그는 Iowa 주 Sioux City에 있는 세 개의 슈퍼마켓을 설득했다 / Campbell의 수프를 약간 할인하여 제공하도록 / 89센트가 아닌 79센트로 //

수동태 동사 / 관계부사
The discounted soup was sold / in one of three conditions: / a control, / where there was no limit on the volume of purchases, /
할인된 수프는 판매되었다 / 세 가지 조건 중 하나의 조건으로 / 하나의 대조군 / 구매량에 제한이 없는 /

관계부사
or two tests, / where customers were limited to either four or twelve cans. // 단서 1 세 개의 조건이 제시됨 (구매량에 제한이 없거나, 4개로 제한되거나, 12개로 제한됨)
또는 두 개의 실험군/ 고객이 4개 또는 12개의 캔으로 제한되는 //

부사절 접속사(대조)
In the unlimited condition / shoppers bought 3.3 cans on average, / whereas in the scarce condition, / when there was a limit, / they bought 5.3 on average. // 단서 2 구매량에 제한이 없을 때보다 구매량에 제한이 있을 때 더 많이 구입함
무제한 조건에서 / 구매자들은 평균 3.3캔을 구입했다 / 반면 희소 조건에서는 / 제한이 있던 / 그들은 평균 5.3캔을 구입했다 //

뒤에 목적어절 접속사가 생략됨
This suggests / scarcity encourages sales. // 단서 3 희소성이 판매를 장려함
이것은 보여준다 / 희소성이 판매를 장려한다는 것을 //

The findings are particularly strong / because the test took place in a supermarket / with genuine shoppers. //
이 결과는 특히 강력하다 / 왜냐하면 이 실험은 슈퍼마켓에서 진행되었기 때문이다 / 진짜 구매자들이 있는 //

부정어(nor)로 인한 주어, 동사 도치
It didn't rely on claimed data, / nor was it held in a laboratory / where consumers might behave differently. //
관계부사
그것은 주장된 데이터에 의존하지 않았고 / 실험실에서 이루어진 것도 아니었다 / 소비자들이 다르게 행동할지도 모르는 //

• boost ⓥ 증가시키다, 촉진하다 • investigate ⓥ 조사하다
• effectiveness ⓝ 효과 • persuade ⓥ 설득하다
• condition ⓝ 조건 • control ⓝ 통제 집단 • volume ⓝ 용량, 양
• on average 평균적으로 • scarce ⓐ 부족한, 드문
• scarcity ⓝ 희소성 • particularly ad 특히 • genuine ⓐ 진짜의
• claimed ⓐ 주장된 • laboratory ⓝ 실험실 • restrict ⓥ 제한하다

고객이 구입할 수 있는 품목의 개수를 제한하는 것은 매출을 증가시킨다. Cornell University의 마케팅 교수인 Brian Wansink는 1998년에 이 전략의 효과를 조사했다. 그는 Iowa 주 Sioux City에 있는 세 개의 슈퍼마켓이 Campbell의 수프를 약간 할인하여 제공하도록 설득했다: 89센트가 아닌 79센트로. 할인된 수프는 세 가지 조건 중 하나의 조건으로 판매되었다: 구매량에 제한이 없는 하나의 대조군, 또는 고객이 4개의 캔으로 제한되거나 12개의 캔으로 제한되는 두 개의 실험군. 무제한 조건에서 구매자들은 평균 3.3캔을 구입했던 반면, 제한이 있던 희소 조건에서는, 평균 5.3캔을 구입했다. 이것은 희소성이 판매를 장려한다는 것을 보여준다. 이 실험은 진짜 구매자들이 있는 슈퍼마켓에서 진행되었기 때문에 그 결과는 특히 강력하다. 그것은 주장된 데이터에 의존하지 않았고, 소비자들이 다르게 행동할지도 모르는 실험실에서 이루어진 것도 아니었다.

다음 빈칸에 들어갈 말로 가장 적절한 것을 고르시오. [3점]

① Promoting products through social media
소셜 미디어를 통해 제품을 홍보하는 것 — 소셜 미디어는 언급되지 않았음
② Reducing the risk of producing poor quality items
품질이 낮은 제품을 생산할 위험성을 줄이는 것 — 질 좋은 제품이 매출을 증가시킨다는 내용이 아님
③ Restricting the number of items customers can buy
고객이 구입할 수 있는 품목의 개수를 제한하는 것 — 고객이 구입할 수 있는 개수를 제한함
④ Offering several options that customers find attractive
고객이 매력적으로 여기는 여러 옵션을 제공하는 것 — 구매 수량을 제한한 것이 매력적인 선택권인지 알 수 없음
⑤ Emphasizing the safety of products with research data
연구 자료와 함께 제품의 안전성을 강조하는 것 — 제품의 안전성에 관해서는 이야기하지 않음

왜 정답? ★★☆ [정답률 62%]

빈칸 문장	____________ 은 매출을 증가시킨다.

➡ **빈칸 문장:** '무엇'은 매출을 증가시킨다.
➡ **Brian Wansink 교수의 실험 결과:**
그룹 1: 수프 구매 수량에 제한이 없음 → 평균 3.3캔을 구입함
그룹 2, 3: 수프 구매가 4캔 또는 12캔으로 제한됨 → 평균 5.3캔을 구입함
▶ 희소성이 판매를 장려한 것이므로 ③ '고객이 구입할 수 있는 품목의 개수를 제한하는 것'이 매출을 증가시킨 것이다.

왜 오답?

① 소셜 미디어를 통해 제품을 홍보하여 매출을 증가시킨 것이 아니다.
② 제품 품질 관리를 통해 매출을 증가시켰다는 내용이 아니다.
④ 구매 수량에 제한을 둔 것을 매력적인 구매 옵션으로 보기는 어렵다.
(이유: 무제한으로 구매할 수 있는 것은 매력적인 옵션으로 볼 수 있지만, 4개로 제한하는 것까지 매력적인 옵션으로 볼 수 없다.)
⑤ 제품의 안정성은 언급되지 않았다.

35 정답 ④ *기술이 생산성에 미치는 부정적인 영향

다음 글에서 전체 흐름과 관계 없는 문장은?

부사절 접속사(양보) / 형용사적 용법(potential 수식)
Although technology has the potential / to increase productivity, / it can also have a negative impact / on productivity. //
기술은 잠재력을 가지고 있지만 / 생산성을 높일 수 있는 / 그것은 또한 부정적인 영향을 미칠 수 있다 / 생산성에 //
— 핵심문장, 단서 1 기술은 생산성에 부정적 영향을 미칠 수 있음

병렬 구조
For example, / in many office environments / workers sit at desks with computers / and have access to the internet. //
예를 들어 / 많은 사무실 환경에서 / 직원들은 컴퓨터가 있는 책상에 앉고 / 인터넷에 접속할 수 있다 //

① They are able to **check** their personal e-mails / and **use** social media / **whenever** they want to. //
<small>복합관계부사(= every time)</small>
<small>병렬 구조</small>
그들은 개인 이메일을 확인할 수 있고 / 소셜 미디어를 사용할 수 있다 / 그들이 원할 때마다 //

② This can **stop** them from doing their work / and **make** them less productive. //
<small>병렬 구조</small>
이것은 그들이 일을 하는 것을 막고 / 그들이 덜 생산적이게 만들 수 있다 //

<small>단서 2 새로운 기술로 생산 공정이 바뀌거나, 직원이 시스템을 새로 배워야 할 수도 있음</small>

③ Introducing new technology can also have a negative impact on production / when it **causes** a change to the production process / or **requires** workers to learn a new system. //
<small>병렬 구조</small>
새로운 기술을 도입하는 것은 또한 생산에 부정적인 영향을 미칠 수 있다 / 그것이 생산 공정에 변화를 야기할 때 / 또는 직원들에게 새로운 시스템을 배우도록 요구(할 때) //

④ Using technology can enable businesses **to produce** more goods / and **to get** more / out of the other factors of production. //)
<small>병렬 구조</small>
(기술을 사용하는 것은 기업이 더 많은 제품을 생산하게 할 수 있다 / 그리고 더 많은 것을 얻게 (할 수 있다) / 다른 생산 요소들로부터 //)

⑤ Learning to use new technology / can be time consuming and stressful for workers / and this can cause a decline in productivity. // <small>단서 3 새로운 기술 사용법을 배우는 것은 결국 생산성 저하를 야기할 수 있음</small>
새로운 기술을 사용하는 것을 배우는 것은 / 직원들에게 시간이 오래 걸리고 스트레스를 줄 수 있다 / 그리고 이것은 생산성 저하를 야기할 수 있다 //

- potential ⓝ 잠재력   - productivity ⓝ 생산성
- access ⓝ 접근   - introduce ⓥ 도입하다
- factor ⓝ 요소, 요인   - decline ⓝ 감소

기술은 생산성을 높일 수 있는 잠재력을 가지고 있지만, 또한 생산성에 부정적인 영향을 미칠 수 있다. 예를 들어, 많은 사무실 환경에서 직원들은 컴퓨터가 있는 책상에 앉아 인터넷에 접속할 수 있다. ① 그들은 원할 때마다 개인 이메일을 확인하고 소셜 미디어를 사용할 수 있다. ② 이것은 그들이 일을 하는 것을 막고 그들의 생산성을 떨어뜨릴 수 있다. ③ 또한 새로운 기술을 도입하는 것은 생산 공정에 변화를 야기하거나 직원들에게 새로운 시스템을 배우도록 요구할 때 생산에 부정적인 영향을 미칠 수 있다. (④ 기술을 사용하는 것은 기업이 더 많은 제품을 생산하고 다른 생산 요소들로부터 더 많은 것을 얻게 할 수 있다.) ⑤ 새로운 기술을 사용하는 것을 배우는 것은 직원들에게 시간이 오래 걸리고 스트레스를 줄 수 있으며 이것은 생산성 저하를 야기할 수 있다.

왜 정답·오답? ★★❋ [정답률 63%]

앞부분: 기술은 생산성을 높일 수 있는 잠재력을 가지고 있지만, 또한 생산성에 부정적인 영향을 미칠 수 있다. 예를 들어, 많은 사무실 환경에서 직원들은 컴퓨터가 있는 책상에 앉아 인터넷에 접속할 수 있다.

➡ 기술이 생산성에 미치는 부정적인 영향을 이야기하는 글이다.

① 그들은 원할 때마다 개인 이메일을 확인하고 소셜 미디어를 사용할 수 있다.

➡ 사무실 컴퓨터로 업무가 아닌 개인적인 용무를 보는 직원들의 행동이 이어진다.
▶ ①은 무관한 문장이 아님

② 이것(This)은 그들이 일을 하는 것을 막고 그들의 생산성을 떨어뜨릴 수 있다.

➡ 사무실 컴퓨터로 개인적인 용무를 보는 것을 This로 가리키며, 이것이 직원들의 생산성을 떨어뜨릴 수 있다는 결과가 자연스럽게 이어진다.
▶ ②은 무관한 문장이 아님

---

③ **또한(also)** 새로운 기술을 도입하는 것은 생산 공정에 변화를 야기하거나 직원들에게 새로운 시스템을 배우도록 요구할 때 생산에 부정적인 영향을 미칠 수 있다.

➡ also로 앞 문장의 내용과 같은 맥락의 주장을 이어간다.
▶ ③은 무관한 문장이 아님

④ 기술을 사용하는 것은 기업이 더 많은 제품을 생산하고 다른 생산 요소들로부터 더 많은 것을 얻게 할 수 있다.

➡ 계속 기술이 생산성에 미치는 부정적인 영향을 이야기하다가, 기술이 생산성을 높인다는 긍정적인 영향을 이야기하므로 전체 글의 흐름에 맞지 않는다.
▶ ④이 무관한 문장임

⑤ 새로운 기술을 사용하는 것을 배우는 것은 직원들에게 시간이 오래 걸리고 스트레스를 줄 수 있으며 이것은 생산성 저하를 야기할 수 있다.

➡ 기술이 생산성에 미치는 부정적인 영향을 다시 이어가는 적절한 흐름이다.
▶ ⑤은 무관한 문장이 아님

* 글의 흐름

도입	기술은 생산성을 높일 수 있는 잠재력을 가짐과 동시에 생산성에 부정적인 영향을 미칠 수도 있음
예시 ①	사무실 컴퓨터로 직원들이 개인 용무를 보는 것은 생산성을 떨어뜨림
예시 ②	생산 공정에 변화를 주는 새로운 기술은 생산성에 부정적인 영향을 미침
예시 ③	새로운 기술 사용법을 배우는 것은 직원들에게 스트레스를 주고 생산성 저하를 야기함

36 정답 ② * 시계가 필요했던 사람들

Up until about 6,000 years ago, / most people were farmers. //
약 6,000년 전까지 / 대부분의 사람들은 농부였다 //

Many lived in different places / throughout the year, / **hunting** for food / or **moving** their livestock / to areas with enough food. // <small>단서 1 과거 사람들은 일 년 내내 장소를 옮기면서 살았음</small>
<small>병렬 구조</small>
많은 사람들은 여러 장소에서 살았다 / 일 년 내내 / 식량을 찾아다니거나 / 그들의 가축을 옮기면서 / 충분한 먹이가 있는 지역으로 //

(A) For example, / priests wanted to know / **when to carry out** religious ceremonies. // <small>단서 2 (B)에서 언급된 시간을 알아야 했던 사람들의 예시</small>
<small>to know의 목적어(의문사+to부정사)</small>
예를 들어 / 성직자들은 알고 싶었다 / 언제 종교적인 의식을 수행해야 하는지 //

This was when people first invented clocks / — devices **that** show, measure, and keep track of passing time. //
<small>주격 관계대명사</small>
이때가 사람들이 시계를 처음으로 발명한 때이다 / 시간을 보여주고, 측정하고, 흐르는 시간을 추적하는 장치인 //

(B) There was no need to tell the time / **because** life depended on natural cycles, / such as the changing seasons or sunrise and sunset. //
<small>부사절 접속사(이유)</small>
시간을 알 필요가 없었다 / 왜냐하면 삶은 자연적인 주기에 달려있었기 때문에 / 변화하는 계절이나 일출과 일몰 같은 // <small>단서 3 정착하게 되면서 시간을 알아야 했던 사람들이 생겨남</small>

Gradually more people started to live in larger settlements, / and some needed to tell the time. //
점점 더 많은 사람들이 더 큰 정착지에서 살기 시작했다 / 그리고 어떤 사람들은 시간을 알 필요가 있었다 //

(C) Clocks have been important **ever since.** //   '이후로 줄곧'

시계는 그 이후로도 중요했다 //   **단서 4** (A)에서 시계가 발명된 이후로 줄곧 시계는 중요했음

Today, / clocks are used for important things / such as setting busy airport timetables / — if the time is incorrect / aeroplanes might crash into each other / **when taking off or landing**! //   분사구문

오늘날 / 시계는 중요한 일에 사용된다 / 바쁜 공항 시간표를 설정하는 것과 같은 / 만약 시간이 부정확하다면 / 비행기는 서로 충돌할지도 모른다 / 이륙하거나 착륙할 때 //

- **livestock** ⓝ 가축　　・**priest** ⓝ 성직자　　・**religious** ⓐ 종교적인
- **invent** ⓥ 발명하다　　・**device** ⓝ 장치　　・**gradually** ⓐ 점점
- **settlement** ⓝ 정착지　　・**timetable** ⓝ 시간표

약 6,000년 전까지, 대부분의 사람들은 농부였다. 많은 사람들은 식량을 찾아다니거나 가축을 충분한 먹이가 있는 지역으로 옮기며 일 년 내내 여러 장소에서 살았다. (B) 변화하는 계절이나 일출과 일몰 같은, 자연적인 주기에 삶이 달려있기 때문에 시간을 알 필요가 없었다. 점점 더 많은 사람들이 더 큰 정착지에서 살기 시작했고, 어떤 사람들은 시간을 알 필요가 있었다. (A) 예를 들어, 성직자들은 언제 종교적인 의식을 수행해야 하는지 알고 싶었다. 이때 사람들이 시간을 보여주고, 측정하고, 흐르는 시간을 추적하는 장치인 시계를 처음으로 발명했다. (C) 시계는 그 이후로도 중요했다. 오늘날, 시계는 바쁜 공항 시간표를 설정하는 것과 같은 중요한 일에 사용된다 — 만약 시간이 부정확하다면, 비행기는 이륙하거나 착륙할 때 서로 충돌할지도 모른다!

> • 시간을 알 필요가 있었던 성직자의 예시가 뒷받침하는 일반적 진술인 (B)가 (A)앞에 있어야 함
>
> **주어진 글 다음에 이어질 글의 순서로 가장 적절한 것을 고르시오. [3점]**
>
> ① (A) — (C) — (B)
> ② (B) — (A) — (C)   과거 사람들은 여러 장소를 이동하며 살았음–(B) 사람들이 정착하면서 시간을 알 필요가 있게 됨–(A) 이때 시계가 발명됨–(C) 그 이후로 오늘날까지 시계는 중요함
> ③ (B) — (C) — (A)   (A)는 (B)의 시간을 알 필요가 있었던 사람들의 예시임
> ④ (C) — (A) — (B)
> ⑤ (C) — (B) — (A)   오늘날까지 시계는 중요하다는 (C)는 글의 결말임

| 문제 풀이 순서 | ✽✽✽ [정답률 82%]

1st 각 문단의 내용을 파악하고, 글의 논리적인 순서를 추론한다.

> **주어진 글:** 약 6,000년 전까지, 대부분의 사람들은 농부였다. 많은 사람들은 식량을 찾아다니거나 가축을 충분한 먹이가 있는 지역으로 옮기며 일 년 내내 여러 장소에서 살았다. **단서**

➡ **주어진 글 뒤:** 여러 장소를 옮겨 다니며 살았던 과거의 사람들에 관해 구체적으로 설명한 뒤, 오늘날에는 어떤지가 이어질 것이다. **발상**

> **(A):** 예를 들어(For example), 성직자들은 언제 종교적인 의식을 수행해야 하는지 알고 싶었다. 이때 사람들이 시간을 보여주고, 측정하고, 흐르는 시간을 추적하는 장치인 시계를 처음으로 발명했다.

➡ **(A) 앞:** '언제' 종교 의식을 해야 하는지 알고 싶었던 성직자의 예시가 For example로 이어지므로, 앞에 '언제'와 관련된 내용이 와야 한다.
　▶ 주어진 글 바로 뒤에 (A)가 올 수 없음
　(A) 뒤: '시계'가 처음 등장했으므로 시계와 관련된 내용이 이어질 것이다.

> **(B):** 변화하는 계절이나 일출과 일몰 같은, 자연적인 주기에 삶이 달려있기 때문에 시간을 알 필요가 없었다. 점점 더 많은 사람들이 더 큰 정착지에서 살기 시작했고, 어떤 사람들은 시간을 알 필요가 있었다.

➡ **(B) 앞:** 자연 주기에 삶이 달려있다는 것은 주어진 글에서 언급한 일 년 내내 옮겨 다니며 살았던 것을 의미하므로 주어진 글에 이어지는 내용이다.
　▶ (B) 앞에 주어진 글이 와야 함 (순서: 주어진 글 → (B))
　(B) 뒤: 시간을 알 필요가 있는 사람들의 예시로 성직자를 말한 (A)가 이어져야 한다.
　▶ (B) 뒤에는 (A)가 이어져야 함 (순서: 주어진 글 → (B) → (A))

(C): 시계는 **그 이후로도(ever since)** 중요했다. 오늘날, 시계는 바쁜 공항 시간표를 설정하는 것과 같은 중요한 일에 사용된다 — 만약 시간이 부정확하다면, 비행기는 이륙하거나 착륙할 때 서로 충돌할지도 모른다!

➡ **(C) 앞:** 시계가 발명된 이후로 줄곧 중요했던 것이므로 시계가 처음 발명됐다고 언급한 (A)에 이어지는 내용이다.
　▶ (C) 앞에는 (A)가 와야 함 (순서: 주어진 글 → (B) → (A) → (C))
　(C) 뒤: 오늘날까지 시계는 매우 중요한 역할을 하고 있다면서 글을 마무리하고 있으므로 (C)는 마지막에 와야 한다.

2nd 글이 한눈에 들어오도록 정리하여 정답을 확인한다.

주어진 글: 과거 많은 사람들은 일 년 내내 여러 장소를 옮겨 다니며 살았다.

➡ **(B):** 그들은 자연적인 주기에 의존하여 살았기 때문에 시간을 알 필요가 없었지만, 정착하기 시작하면서 시간을 알아야 했던 사람들이 생겨났다.

➡ **(A):** 예를 들어 성직자들은 언제 종교 의식을 해야 하는지 알아야 했고, 이때 시계가 처음으로 발명되었다.

➡ **(C):** 시계가 발명된 이후로 오늘날까지 시계는 매우 중요한 역할을 하고 있다.

▶ 주어진 글 다음에 이어질 글의 순서는 (B) → (A) → (C)이므로 정답은 ②임

37 정답 ⑤　＊노동의 분업을 통한 생산성 증대

Managers are always looking for ways / **to increase** productivity, / **which** is the ratio of costs to output in production. //   계속적 용법의 주격 관계대명사 / 형용사적 용법(ways 수식)

관리자들은 항상 방법을 찾고 있다 / 생산성을 높일 수 있는 / 그리고 그 생산성은 생산에서 비용 대비 생산량의 비율이다 //   **단서 1** Adam Smith는 '노동의 분업'으로 더 효율적인 생산이 가능하다고 설명함

Adam Smith, / **writing when the manufacturing industry was new,** / described a way / **that** production could be made more efficient, / **known** as the "division of labor." //   분사구문 / 관계부사 / 앞에 주격 관계대명사와 be동사가 생략됨

Adam Smith는 / 제조 산업이 새로 등장했을 때 저술한 / 방식을 설명했다 / 생산이 더 효율적으로 될 수 있는 / '노동의 분업'으로 알려진 //

단서 2 (B)의 마지막에 언급된 한 가지 작업만 하는 노동자에 이어지는 내용임

(A) Because each worker specializes in one job, / he or she can work much faster / without changing from one task to another. //

각 노동자는 한 가지 작업을 전문으로 하기 때문에 / 그 또는 그녀는 훨씬 더 빠르게 일할 수 있다 / 한 작업에서 다른 작업으로 변경하지 않고도 //

Now 10 workers can produce / thousands of pins in a day / — a huge increase in productivity / from the 200 / **they would have produced before.** //   앞에 목적격 관계대명사가 생략됨

이제 10명의 노동자가 생산할 수 있다 / 하루에 수천 개의 핀을 / 이는 생산성 측면에서 크게 증가한 것이다 / 200개로부터 / 이전에 그들이 생산했던 //   병렬 구조

(B) One worker could **do** all these tasks, / and **make** 20 pins in a day. //   **단서 3** 분업이 적용되지 않은 (C)에 이어지는 내용임

한 명의 노동자가 이 모든 작업들을 할 수 있었고 / 하루에 20개의 핀을 만들 수도 있었다 //

But this work can be divided / into its separate processes, / with **a number of** workers each performing one task. //   '많은, 다수의'

그러나 이 일은 분리될 수 있다 / 별개의 과정으로 / 많은 노동자가 각각 한 가지 작업을 수행하면서 //

(C) **Making** most manufactured goods / **involves** several different processes / using different skills. //   동명사 주어(단수 취급) / 단수 동사

대부분의 공산품을 만드는 것은 / 여러 가지 다른 과정을 포함한다 / 다른 기술을 사용하는 //

Smith's example was the manufacture of pins: / the wire is straightened, / sharpened, / a head is put on, / and then it is polished. //   **단서 4** Smith의 '노동의 분업'을 설명하는 예로서 핀의 공정을 소개함

Smith의 예는 핀의 제조였다 / 철사는 곧게 펴지고 / 뾰족해지고 / 상부가 놓이고 / 그러고 나서 그것이 다듬어진다 //

- productivity ⓝ 생산성　　• output ⓝ 산출량　　• efficient ⓐ 효율적인
- division ⓝ 분배　　• specialize in ~을 전문으로 하다　　• separate ⓐ 별개의
- manufactured ⓐ 제작된　　• straighten ⓥ 펴다　　• polish ⓥ 다듬다

관리자들은 항상 생산성을 높일 수 있는 방법을 찾고 있는데, 생산성은 생산에서 비용 대비 생산량의 비율이다. 제조 산업이 새로 등장했을 때 저술한 Adam Smith는 '노동의 분업'으로 알려진 생산이 더 효율적으로 될 수 있는 방식을 설명했다. (C) 대부분의 공산품을 만드는 것은 다른 기술을 사용하는 여러 가지 다른 과정을 포함한다. Smith의 예는 핀의 제조였다. 철사는 곧게 펴지고, 뾰족해지고, 상부가 놓이고, 그리고 나서 그것이 다듬어진다. (B) 한 명의 노동자가 이 모든 작업들을 할 수 있었고, 하루에 20개의 핀을 만들 수도 있었다. 그러나 이 일은 많은 노동자가 각각 한 가지 작업을 수행하면서 별개의 과정으로 분리될 수 있다. (A) 각 노동자는 한 가지 작업을 전문으로 하기 때문에, 그 또는 그녀는 한 작업에서 다른 작업으로 변경하지 않고도 훨씬 더 빠르게 일할 수 있다. 이제 10명의 노동자가 하루에 수천 개의 핀을 생산할 수 있다. 이는 이전에 그들이 생산했던 200개로부터 생산성 측면에서 크게 증가한 것이다.

(A)의 한 가지 작업은 (B)의 마지막에 나온 별개의 과정으로 분리된 작업임

주어진 글 다음에 이어질 글의 순서로 가장 적절한 것을 고르시오.

① (A) ― (C) ― (B)
② (B) ― (A) ― (C)
③ (B) ― (C) ― (A)
④ (C) ― (A) ― (B)
⑤ (C) ― (B) ― (A)

(B)의 'all these tasks(이 모든 작업들)'가 가리키는 것이 앞에 있어야 함

Adam Smith는 '노동의 분업'을 설명함 – (C) Smith는 다양한 작업들이 필요한 핀 제조를 말함 – (B) 한 명이 모든 작업을 할 수도 있지만, 한 명이 하나의 작업을 할 수도 있음 – (A) 10명이 200개를 만들던 것이 수천 개로 증가함

| 문제 풀이 순서 | ★★★ [정답률 62%]

1st 각 문단의 내용을 파악하고, 글의 논리적인 순서를 추론한다.

주어진 글: 관리자들은 항상 생산성을 높일 수 있는 방법을 찾고 있는데, 생산성은 생산에서 비용 대비 생산량의 비율이다. 제조 산업이 새로 등장했을 때 저술한 Adam Smith는 '노동의 분업'으로 알려진 생산이 더 효율적으로 될 수 있는 방식을 설명했다. **단서**

➡ **주어진 글 뒤:** Adam Smith가 설명한 '노동의 분업'에 대한 구체적인 설명이 이어질 것이다. **발상**

(A): 각 노동자는 한 가지 작업을 전문으로 하기 때문에, 그 또는 그녀는 한 작업에서 다른 작업으로 변경하지 않고도 훨씬 더 빠르게 일할 수 있다. 이제 10명의 노동자가 하루에 수천 개의 핀을 생산할 수 있다. 이는 이전에 그들이 생산했던 200개로부터 생산성 측면에서 크게 증가한 것이다.

➡ **(A) 앞:** 어떤 과정을 거쳐 이러한 결과가 나왔는지가 언급되어야 한다.
▶ 주어진 글 바로 뒤에 (A)가 올 수 없음
(A) 뒤: 생산성이 크게 증가한 결과에 해당하므로 글의 결론일 가능성이 높다.
▶ (A)가 마지막에 올 확률이 높음

(B): 한 명의 노동자가 이 모든 작업들(all these tasks)을 할 수 있었고, 하루에 20개의 핀을 만들 수도 있었다. 그러나 이 일은 많은 노동자가 각각 한 가지 작업을 수행하면서 별개의 과정으로 분리될 수 있다.

➡ **(B) 앞:** 1 어떤 노동자인지,
2 어떤 작업들인지가 언급되어야 한다.
▶ (B) 앞에는 주어진 글과 (A) 모두 올 수 없으므로 (C)가 올 가능성이 높음
(B) 뒤: 많은 노동자가 각각 한 가지 작업을 수행하는 것을 (A)에서 한 가지 작업을 전문으로 하는 것으로 이야기했으므로 (A)가 이어지는 것이 적절하다.
▶ (A)가 (B) 뒤에 와야 함 (순서: (B) → (A))

(C): 대부분의 공산품을 만드는 것은 다른 기술을 사용하는 여러 가지 다른 과정을 포함한다. Smith의 예는 핀의 제조였다. 철사는 곧게 펴지고, 뾰족해지고, 상부가 놓이고, 그리고 나서 그것이 다듬어진다.

➡ **(C) 앞:** 주어진 글에서 말한 Adam Smith의 '노동의 분업'을 설명하는 예시로 핀의 제조가 등장했다.
▶ 주어진 글에 이어지는 내용임 (순서: 주어진 글 → (C))
(C) 뒤: 철사를 펴고, 뾰족하게 만들고, 상부를 놓아 다듬는 과정을 '이 모든 작업들'이라고 한 (B)가 이어져야 한다.
▶ (C) 뒤에 (B)가 이어져야 함 (순서: 주어진 글 → (C) → (B) → (A))

2nd 글이 한눈에 들어오도록 정리하여 정답을 확인한다.

주어진 글: Adam Smith는 생산의 효율성을 높이는 방법으로 '노동의 분업'을 설명했다.
➡ **(C):** Smith는 그 예로 철사를 펴고, 뾰족하게 만들고, 상부를 놓아 다듬어야 하는 핀의 제조를 제시했다.
➡ **(B):** 이 모든 작업들은 한 사람이 할 수도 있지만, 한 사람이 하나의 작업만 하는 별개의 과정으로 분리될 수 있다.
➡ **(A):** 한 가지 작업만 전문으로 하면 다른 작업으로 변경하지 않고 더 빠르게 작업할 수 있고, 생산성이 크게 증가한다.
▶ 주어진 글 다음에 이어질 글의 순서는 (C) → (B) → (A)이므로 정답은 ⑤임

38 정답 ② ＊느리지만 계속 일어나는 변화

글의 흐름으로 보아, 주어진 문장이 들어가기에 가장 적절한 곳을 고르시오.

Yet we know / **that** the face / **that** stares back at us from the glass / is not the same, / cannot be the same, / as it was 10 minutes ago. //
목적어절 접속사 / 주격 관계대명사
단서 1 거울 속 얼굴이 10분 전 얼굴과 같지 않다는 것이
Yet(그러나)으로 연결됨
그러나 우리는 안다 / 얼굴 / 거울로부터 우리를 쳐다보는 / 같지 않다는 것을 / 같을 리가 없다(는 것을) / 10분 전에 그랬던 것과 //

Sometimes / the pace of change / is **far** slower. //
비교급 강조 부사
때때로 / 변화의 속도는 / 훨씬 더 느리다 //

(①) The face **you saw** / reflected in your mirror this morning / probably appeared no different / from the face **you saw** the day before / — or a week or a month ago. //
앞에 목적격 관계대명사가 생략됨
단서 2 오늘 아침 거울에 비친 얼굴이
일주일이나 한 달 전과 다르지 않아 보임
당신이 본 얼굴은 / 오늘 아침 당신의 거울 속에 비친 / 아마도 다르지 않은 것처럼 보였을 것이다 / 당신이 그 전날 본 얼굴과 / 또는 일주일이나 한 달 전에 //

단서 3 5년 또는 10년 전에 찍힌 사진 속에 지금의 얼굴과는 다르다는 증거가 있음
(②) The proof is in your photo album: / Look at a photograph **taken** of yourself 5 or 10 years ago / and you see clear differences / between the face in the snapshot and the face in your mirror. //
앞에 주격 관계대명사와 be동사가 생략됨
증거는 당신의 사진 앨범에 있다 / 5년 또는 10년 전에 찍힌 당신의 사진을 보라 / 그러면 당신은 명확한 차이를 보게 될 것이다 / 스냅사진 속의 얼굴과 거울 속 얼굴 사이의 //

(③) If you **lived** in a world without mirrors for a year / and then **saw** your reflection, / you might be surprised / by the change. //
병렬 구조
만약 당신이 일 년간 거울이 없는 세상에 살고 / 그 이후 당신의 (거울에) 비친 모습을 본다면 / 당신은 깜짝 놀랄지도 모른다 / 그 변화 때문에 //

(④) After an interval of 10 years / without seeing yourself, / you might not at first recognize / the person **peering** from the mirror. //
앞에 주격 관계대명사와 be동사가 생략됨
10년의 기간이 지난 후에는 / 당신 자신을 보지 않고 / 당신은 아마 처음에는 알아보지 못할지도 모른다 / 거울에서 쳐다보고 있는 그 사람을 //

(⑤) Even something **as basic as** our own face / changes from moment to moment. //
원급 비교
심지어 우리 자신의 얼굴같이 아주 기본적인 것조차도 / 순간순간 변한다 //

- stare ⓥ 쳐다보다, 응시하다   • pace ⓝ 속도   • reflect ⓥ 비추다
- proof ⓝ 증거   • interval ⓝ 간격   • recognize ⓥ 알아보다

때때로 변화의 속도는 훨씬 더 느리다. (①) 오늘 아침 거울 속에 비친 당신이 본 얼굴은 아마도 당신이 그 전날 또는 일주일이나 한 달 전에 본 얼굴과 다르지 않은 것처럼 보였을 것이다. (② 그러나 우리는 거울로부터 우리를 쳐다보는 얼굴이 10분 전에 그랬던 것과 같지 않고, 같을 수 없다는 것을 안다.) 증거는 당신의 사진 앨범에 있다: 5년 또는 10년 전에 찍힌 당신의 사진을 보면 당신은 스냅사진 속의 얼굴과 거울 속 얼굴 사이의 명확한 차이를 보게 될 것이다. (③) 만약 당신이 일 년간 거울이 없는 세상에 살고 그 이후 (거울에) 비친 당신의 모습을 본다면, 당신은 그 변화 때문에 깜짝 놀랄지도 모른다. (④) 당신 자신을 보지 않고 10년의 기간이 지난 후, 당신은 거울에서 쳐다보고 있는 그 사람을 처음에는 알아보지 못할지도 모른다. (⑤) 심지어 우리 자신의 얼굴같이 아주 기본적인 것조차도 순간순간 변한다.

| 문제 풀이 순서 | ★★★ [정답률 43%]

1st 주어진 문장을 해석하고, 연결어, 지시어 등을 확인한다.

> Yet we know that the face that stares back at us from the glass is not the same, cannot be the same, as it was 10 minutes ago.
> 그러나 우리는 거울로부터 우리를 쳐다보는 얼굴이 10분 전에 그랬던 것과 같지 않고, 같을 수 없다는 것을 안다.

➡ 주어진 문장 앞: 'Yet(그러나)'이라고 했으므로 **단서**
앞에는 거울에 비친 얼굴이 이전과 같다는 내용이 와야 한다. **발상**

2nd 찾은 단서를 생각하며 각 선택지의 앞뒤 흐름이 매끄러운지 확인한다.

- ①의 앞 문장과 뒤 문장

> 앞 문장: 때때로 변화의 속도는 훨씬 더 느리다.
> 뒤 문장: 오늘 아침 거울 속에 비친 당신이 본 얼굴은 아마도 당신이 그 전날 또는 일주일이나 한 달 전에 본 얼굴과 다르지 않은 것처럼 보였을 것이다.

➡ 앞 문장의 예시를 뒤 문장에서 제시했다.
▶ 주어진 문장이 ①에 들어갈 수 없음

- ②의 앞 문장과 뒤 문장

> 앞 문장: ①의 뒤 문장과 같음
> 뒤 문장: 증거는 당신의 사진 앨범에 있다: 5년 또는 10년 전에 찍힌 당신의 사진을 보면 당신은 스냅사진 속의 얼굴과 거울 속 얼굴 사이의 명확한 차이를 보게 될 것이다.

➡ 앞 문장(과거 = 오늘)과 뒤 문장(과거 ≠ 오늘)이 서로 상반된 이야기를 하고 있으므로, 역접의 연결어 Yet으로 현재의 얼굴과 과거의 얼굴이 같을 수 없다는 것을 안다고 한 주어진 문장이 와야 한다.
▶ 주어진 문장이 ②에 들어가야 함

- ③의 앞 문장과 뒤 문장

> 앞 문장: ②의 뒤 문장과 같음
> 뒤 문장: 만약 당신이 일 년간 거울이 없는 세상에 살고 그 이후 (거울에) 비친 당신의 모습을 본다면, 당신은 그 변화 때문에 깜짝 놀랄지도 모른다.

➡ 과거에 찍힌 사진으로 얼굴이 변한 것을 볼 수 있는 것처럼, 일 년 동안 거울을 보지 않다가 거울을 보면 변화 때문에 깜짝 놀랄 것이라는 흐름은 자연스럽다.
▶ 주어진 문장이 ③에 들어갈 수 없음

- ④의 앞 문장과 뒤 문장

> 앞 문장: ③의 뒤 문장과 같음
> 뒤 문장: 당신 자신을 보지 않고 10년의 기간이 지난 후, 당신은 거울에서 쳐다보고 있는 그 사람을 처음에는 알아보지 못할지도 모른다.

➡ 시간이 지날수록 변화와 차이는 커질 것이라는 앞 문장과 같은 맥락의 내용이 이어진다.
▶ 주어진 문장이 ④에 들어갈 수 없음

- ⑤의 앞 문장과 뒤 문장

> 앞 문장: ④의 뒤 문장과 같음
> 뒤 문장: 심지어 우리 자신의 얼굴같이 아주 기본적인 것조차도 순간순간 변한다.

➡ 앞서 이야기해 온 바와 같이 변화의 속도가 때로는 매우 느리더라도, 자신의 얼굴같이 기본적인 것도 사실은 순간순간 변하고 있음을 재확인하며 글을 마무리한다.
▶ 주어진 문장이 ⑤에 들어갈 수 없음

3rd 글이 한눈에 들어오도록 정리하여 정답을 확인한다.

때때로 변화의 속도는 훨씬 더 느리다.
(①) 오늘 아침 당신의 얼굴은 하루, 일주일, 한 달 전에 본 얼굴과 같아 보였을 것이다.
(② 그러나 현재의 얼굴은 10분 전의 얼굴과 같을 수 없다.)
과거에 찍힌 사진을 보면 얼굴이 명확히 다른 것을 보게 될 것이다.
(③) 만약 일 년 만에 거울을 본다면, 변화 때문에 놀랄 것이다.
(④) 10년 만에 거울을 본다면, 자신을 처음에는 알아보지 못할지도 모른다.
(⑤) 우리의 얼굴같이 아주 기본적인 것도 순간순간 변한다.

39 정답 ⑤ ＊뇌의 발달과 함께 줄어드는 호기심

글의 흐름으로 보아, 주어진 문장이 들어가기에 가장 적절한 곳을 고르시오. [3점]

> '~함에 따라' **단서 1** 아이들이 흡수한 증거는 지식이나 믿음으로 굳어짐
> As children absorb more evidence / from the world around them, / certain possibilities become much more likely and more useful / and harden into knowledge or beliefs. // **병렬 구조**
> 아이들이 더 많은 증거를 흡수함에 따라 / 그들 주변의 세상으로부터 / 특정한 가능성들이 훨씬 더 커지게 되고 더 유용하게 되며 / 지식이나 믿음으로 굳어진다 //

According to educational psychologist Susan Engel, / curiosity begins to decrease / **원급 비교** as young as four years old. //
교육 심리학자 Susan Engel에 따르면 / 호기심은 줄어들기 시작한다 / 네 살 정도의 어린 나이에 //

뒤에 관계부사 when이 생략됨
By the time we are adults, / we have fewer questions and more default settings. //
우리가 어른이 될 무렵 / 우리의 질문은 더 적어지고 기본값은 더 많아진다 //

As Henry James put it, / "Disinterested curiosity is past, / the mental grooves and channels set." //
Henry James가 말했듯이 / "흥미를 유발하지 않는 호기심은 지나가고 / 정신의 고랑과 경로가 자리 잡는다" //

조동사가 포함된 수동태
(①) The decline in curiosity can be traced / in the development of the brain / through childhood. // **단서 2** 아이들의 뇌가 발달하면서 호기심은 감소함
호기심 감소의 원인은 찾을 수 있다 / 뇌의 발달에서 / 유년 시절을 통한 //

부사절 접속사(양보)
(②) Though smaller than the adult brain, / the infant brain contains millions more neural connections. //
비록 성인의 뇌보다 작지만 / 유아의 뇌는 수백만 개 더 많은 신경 연결을 가지고 있다 //

(③) The wiring, / however, / is a mess; / 핵심 주어(복수) the lines of communication between infant neurons / are far less efficient / than between those in the adult brain. //

연결 상태는 / 그러나 / 엉망이다 / 유아의 뉴런 간의 전달 선은 / 훨씬 덜 효율적이다 / 성인 뇌의 뉴런 간의 전달 선보다 //

단서 3 유아의 뇌의 뉴런 간 전달은 성인보다 덜 효율적임

단서 4 아기는 세상을 매우 풍부하면서도 무질서하게 인식함

(④) The baby's perception of the world / is consequently both intensely rich / and wildly disordered. //

세상에 대한 아기의 인식은 / 결과적으로 매우 풍부하면서도 / 상당히 무질서하다 //

(⑤) The neural pathways / 주격 관계대명사 that enable those beliefs / become faster and more automatic, / 부사절 접속사 while the ones / that the child doesn't use regularly / are pruned away. //

신경 경로들은 / 그러한 믿음을 가능하게 하는 / 더 빠르고 더 자동적으로 이루어지게 된다 / 반면에 어떤 경로들은 / 아이가 주기적으로 사용하지 않는 / 가지치기 된다 //

단서 5 어떤 믿음을 가능하게 하는 신경 경로는 더 빠르게 이루어지고, 그렇지 않은 신경 경로는 점점 사라짐

- absorb ⓥ 흡수하다   • possibility ⓝ 가능성
- harden ⓥ 굳어지다   • psychologist ⓝ 심리학자
- curiosity ⓝ 호기심   • mental ⓐ 정신의   • channel ⓝ 경로
- decline ⓝ 감소   • trace ⓥ (원인을) 추적하다   • infant ⓐ 유아의
- neural ⓐ 신경의   • wiring ⓝ 연결, 배선   • mess ⓝ 엉망
- efficient ⓐ 효율적인   • perception ⓝ 인식
- consequently 〔ad〕 결과적으로   • intensely 〔ad〕 매우
- wildly 〔ad〕 상당히, 극도로   • disordered ⓐ 무질서한

교육 심리학자 Susan Engel에 따르면, 호기심은 네 살 정도의 어린 나이에 줄어들기 시작한다. 우리가 어른이 될 무렵, 질문은 더 적어지고 기본값은 더 많아진다. Henry James가 말했듯이, "흥미를 유발하지 않는 호기심은 지나가고, 정신의 고랑과 경로가 자리 잡는다." (①) 호기심의 감소는 유년 시절을 통한 뇌의 발달에서 원인을 찾을 수 있다. (②) 비록 성인의 뇌보다 작지만, 유아의 뇌는 수백만 개 더 많은 신경 연결을 가지고 있다. (③) 그러나 연결 상태는 엉망이다; 유아의 뉴런 간의 전달 선은 성인 뇌의 뉴런들 간의 전달 선보다 훨씬 덜 효율적이다. (④) 결과적으로 세상에 대한 아기의 인식은 매우 풍부하면서도 상당히 무질서하다. (⑤ 아이들이 그들 주변의 세상으로부터 더 많은 증거를 흡수함에 따라, 특정한 가능성들이 훨씬 더 커지게 되고 더 유용하게 되며 지식이나 믿음으로 굳어진다.) 그러한 믿음을 가능하게 하는 신경 경로는 더 빠르고 자동적으로 이루어지게 되는 반면, 아이가 주기적으로 사용하지 않는 경로는 가지치기 된다.

| 문제 풀이 순서 | ★★★ [정답률 33%]

1st 주어진 문장을 해석하고, 연결어, 지시어 등을 확인한다.

> As children absorb more evidence from the world around them, certain possibilities become much more likely and more useful and harden into knowledge or beliefs.
> 아이들이 그들 주변의 세상으로부터 더 많은 증거를 흡수함에 따라, 특정한 가능성들이 훨씬 더 커지게 되고 더 유용하게 되며 지식이나 믿음으로 굳어진다. **단서**

➡ **주어진 문장 앞:** 아이들이 더 많은 증거를 흡수하는 이유가 제시될 것이다. **발상**

2nd 각 선택지의 앞뒤 흐름이 매끄러운지 확인한다.

- ①의 앞 문장과 뒤 문장

> **앞 문장:** Henry James가 말했듯이, "흥미를 유발하지 않는 호기심은 지나가고, 정신의 고랑과 경로가 자리 잡는다."
> **뒤 문장:** 호기심의 감소는 유년 시절을 통한 뇌의 발달에서 원인을 찾을 수 있다.

➡ 앞에서 Henry James가 주장한 호기심이 나이가 들수록 줄어드는 원인을 뒤 문장에서 언급한다.
▶ 주어진 문장이 ①에 들어갈 수 없음

- ②의 앞 문장과 뒤 문장

> **앞 문장:** ①의 뒤 문장과 같음
> **뒤 문장:** 비록 성인의 뇌보다 작지만, 유아의 뇌는 수백만 개 더 많은 신경 연결을 가지고 있다.

➡ 앞 문장에서 처음 언급한 '유년 시절의 뇌'를 뒤 문장에서 부연 설명한다.
▶ 주어진 문장이 ②에 들어갈 수 없음

- ③의 앞 문장과 뒤 문장

> **앞 문장:** ②의 뒤 문장과 같음
> **뒤 문장:** 그러나(however) 연결 상태는 엉망이다; 유아의 뉴런 간의 전달 선은 성인 뇌의 뉴런들 간의 전달 선보다 훨씬 덜 효율적이다.

➡ 앞 문장에서 유아의 뇌는 신경 연결이 많다고 한 것에 그 연결 상태는 엉망이라는 설명이 역접의 연결어 however로 자연스럽게 이어진다.
▶ 주어진 문장이 ③에 들어갈 수 없음

- ④의 앞 문장과 뒤 문장

> **앞 문장:** ③의 뒤 문장과 같음
> **뒤 문장:** 결과적으로(consequently) 세상에 대한 아기의 인식은 매우 풍부하면서도 상당히 무질서하다.

➡ 유아의 뇌에는 신경 연결이 많지만, 상태는 엉망인 것의 결과로(consequently) 세상을 풍부하면서도 무질서하게 인식한다는 내용이 이어진다.
▶ 주어진 문장이 ④에 들어갈 수 없음

- ⑤의 앞 문장과 뒤 문장

> **앞 문장:** ④의 뒤 문장과 같음
> **뒤 문장:** 그러한 믿음(those beliefs)을 가능하게 하는 신경 경로는 더 빠르고 자동적으로 이루어지게 되는 반면, 아이가 주기적으로 사용하지 않는 경로는 가지치기된다.

➡ 그러한 믿음: 주어진 문장에서 말한 아이들이 흡수하여 생성한 지식이나 믿음 세상을 풍부하면서 무질서하게 인식하면서 굳어진 믿음을 더 심화하는 신경 경로는 더 빨라지고, 그렇지 않은 신경 경로는 사라지는 것이 호기심의 감소라는 것이다.
▶ 주어진 문장이 ⑤에 들어가야 함

3rd 글이 한눈에 들어오도록 정리하여 정답을 확인한다.

호기심은 어린 나이에 줄어들기 시작하는데, 흥미를 유발하지 않는 호기심은 줄어든다.
(①) 유년 시절 뇌의 발달로 호기심은 줄어든다.
(②) 유아의 뇌는 성인의 뇌보다 작지만 수백만 개 더 많은 신경 연결을 가진다.
(③) 그러나 연결 상태는 엉망이라 뉴런 간의 연결은 훨씬 덜 효율적이다.
(④) 결과적으로 아기는 세상을 매우 풍부하면서 무질서하게 인식한다.
(⑤ 그렇게 인식한 증거 중에 특정 증거들은 지식이나 믿음으로 굳어진다.)
그 믿음을 강화하는 신경 경로는 더 빨라지고, 그렇지 않은 신경 경로는 없어지는 과정을 통해 호기심은 줄어든다.

40 정답 ② * 좋은 식단인가 나쁜 식단인가

뒤에 목적어절 접속사 that이 생략됨
Nearly eight of ten U.S. adults <mark>believe</mark> / there are "good foods" and "bad foods." //
미국 성인 10명 중 거의 8명이 믿는다 / '좋은 음식'과 '나쁜 음식'이 있다고 //

= If not
<mark>Unless</mark> we're talking / about spoiled stew, poison mushrooms, or something similar, / however, / no foods can be labeled / as either good or bad. //
단서 1 어떤 음식도 좋거나 나쁘다고 분류될 수 없음
우리가 이야기하고 있지 않는 한 / 상한 스튜, 독버섯, 또는 이와 유사한 것에 대해 / 하지만 / 어떤 음식도 분류될 수 없다 / 좋거나 나쁘다고 //

주격 관계대명사 '결국 ~이 되다'
There are, however, / combinations of foods / <mark>that add up to</mark> a healthful or unhealthful diet. //
단서 2 음식들의 조합이 건강에 좋거나 좋지 않은 식단을 만듦
하지만 ~이 있다 / 음식들의 조합이 (있다) / 결국 건강에 좋거나 건강에 좋지 않은 식단이 되는 //

주격 관계대명사
Consider the case of an adult / <mark>who</mark> eats only foods / <mark>thought of</mark> as "good" / — for example, / raw broccoli, apples, orange juice, boiled tofu, and carrots. //
앞에 주격 관계대명사와 be동사가 생략됨
어느 성인의 경우를 생각해 보라 / 어떤 음식만 먹는 / '좋은' 음식이라고 생각되는 / 예를 들어 / 생브로콜리, 사과, 오렌지 주스, 삶은 두부와 당근과 같은 //

부사절 접속사(양보)
<mark>Although</mark> all these foods are nutrient-dense, / they do not add up to a healthy diet / because they don't supply a wide enough variety of the nutrients / <mark>we need</mark>. //
앞에 목적격 관계대명사가 생략됨
비록 이 모든 음식들이 영양이 풍부하지만 / 그것들은 결국 건강한 식단이 되지 않는다 / 그것들이 충분히 다양한 영양소를 공급하지 않기 때문에 / 우리가 필요로 하는 //

주격 관계대명사
Or take the case of the teenager / <mark>who</mark> occasionally <mark>eats</mark> fried chicken, / but otherwise <mark>stays</mark> away from fried foods. //
병렬 구조
또는 한 십 대의 경우를 예로 들어보자 / 튀긴 닭을 가끔 먹지만 / 그렇지 않으면 튀긴 음식을 멀리하는 //

The occasional fried chicken / isn't going to knock his or her diet off track. //
가끔 먹는 튀긴 닭은 / 그나 그녀의 식단을 궤도에서 벗어나게 하지 않을 것이다 //

핵심 주어(단수)
But <mark>the person</mark> / who <mark>eats</mark> fried foods every day, / with few vegetables or fruits, / and <mark>loads</mark> upon supersized soft drinks, candy, and chips / for snacks / <mark>has</mark> a bad diet. //
병렬 구조 *단수 동사*
하지만 그 사람은 / 튀긴 음식을 매일 먹는 / 채소나 과일을 거의 먹지 않으면서 / 그리고 초대형 음료, 사탕, 그리고 감자칩으로 배를 가득 채우는 / 간식으로 / 나쁜 식단을 가지고 있다 //

전치사 *동명사 주어(단수 취급)*
→ <mark>Unlike</mark> the common belief, / <mark>defining</mark> foods as good or bad / <mark>is</mark> not (A) **appropriate**; / in fact, / a healthy diet is determined / largely by <mark>what</mark> the diet is (B) **composed of**. //
단수 동사 *선행사를 포함하는 관계대명사*
일반적인 믿음과 달리 / 음식을 좋거나 나쁘다고 정의하는 것은 / 적절하지 않다 / 사실 / 건강에 좋은 식단은 결정된다 / 대체로 그 식단이 무엇으로 구성되는지에 의해 //

- spoiled ⓐ 상한
- stew ⓝ 스튜(고기와 채소를 넣고 천천히 끓인 요리)
- poison ⓝ 독
- label ⓥ 분류하다
- combination ⓝ 조합
- boiled ⓐ 끓인, 삶은
- tofu ⓝ 두부
- nutrient ⓝ 영양소
- occasionally ⓐ 가끔
- otherwise ⓐ 그렇지 않으면
- load ⓥ 채우다, 싣다
- supersized ⓐ 초대형의
- soft drink (청량) 음료
- appropriate ⓐ 적절한

미국 성인 10명 중 거의 8명이 '좋은 음식'과 '나쁜 음식'이 있다고 믿는다. 하지만, 우리가 상한 스튜, 독버섯, 또는 이와 유사한 것에 대해 이야기하고 있지 않는 한, 어떤 음식도 좋고 나쁨으로 분류될 수 없다. 하지만, 결국 건강에 좋은 식단이나 건강에 좋지 않은 식단이 되는 음식들의 조합이 있다. '좋은' 음식이라고 생각되는 음식만 먹는 성인의 경우를 생각해 보라 — 예를 들어, 생브로콜리, 사과, 오렌지 주스, 삶은 두부와 당근. 비록 이 모든 음식들은 영양이 풍부하지만, 그것들은 우리가 필요로 하는 충분히 다양한 영양소를 공급하지 않기 때문에 결국 건강한 식단이 되지 않는다. 또는 튀긴 닭을 가끔 먹지만, 그렇지 않으면 튀긴 음식을 멀리하는 한 십 대의 경우를 예로 들어보자. 가끔 먹는 튀긴 닭은 그나 그녀의 식단을 궤도에서 벗어나게 하지 않을 것이다. 하지만 채소나 과일을 거의 먹지 않으면서 매일 튀긴 음식을 먹고, 간식으로 초대형 음료, 사탕, 그리고 감자칩으로 배를 가득 채우는 사람은 나쁜 식단을 가지고 있다.

→ 일반적인 믿음과 달리, 음식을 좋고 나쁨으로 정의하는 것은 (A) **적절하지 않다**; 사실, 건강에 좋은 식단은 대체로 그 식단이 무엇으로 (B) **구성되는지**에 의해 결정된다.

음식의 좋고 나쁨을 정의하는 것이 옳은 것은 아님
내용을 한 문장으로 요약하고자 한다. 빈칸 (A), (B)에 들어갈 말로 가장 적절한 것은?

	(A)		(B)
①	incorrect 틀린	—	limited to 제한되는
②	appropriate 적절한	—	composed of 구성되는 → 식단이 건강한지 여부는 음식 자체가 아니라 음식의 조합에 좌우됨
③	wrong 잘못된	—	aimed at 목표하는 → 식단의 목표는 언급되지 않음
④	appropriate 적절한	—	tested on 검사되는 → 식단을 검사한 것이 아님
⑤	incorrect 틀린	—	adjusted to 조절되는

왜 정답? ★★★ [정답률 59%]

(A):

> 하지만, 우리가 상한 스튜, 독버섯, 또는 이와 유사한 것에 대해 이야기하고 있지 않는 한, 어떤 음식도 좋고 나쁨으로 분류될 수 없다. **단서 1**

➡ 어떤 음식도 좋고 나쁨으로 분류될 수 '없음'
▶ 음식을 좋고 나쁨으로 정의하는 것은 '적절하지' **않은** 것이므로 (A)에는 ②, ④ appropriate가 들어가야 함
꿀팁 (A) 앞에 부정어 not이 있으므로 주의해야 함!

(B):

> 하지만, 결국 건강에 좋은 식단이나 건강에 좋지 않은 식단이 되는 음식들의 조합이 있다. **단서 2**

➡ 식단이 좋고 나쁜지는 식단을 구성하는 음식들의 조합에 달려있다.
▶ 식단을 '구성하는' 음식에 의해 식단이 건강한지가 결정되는 것이므로 (B)에는 ② composed of가 들어가야 함

왜 오답?

① 음식이 좋거나 나쁘다고 정의하는 것이 틀리지 '않다'고 하는 것은 글의 내용과 반대이다.
③ 목표에 맞춰 식단을 짜야 건강한 식단이 되는 것이 아니다.
④ 식단을 검사하는 것에 따라 식단이 건강한지가 좌우되는 것이 아니다.
⑤ 어떤 음식들을 얼마나 먹는지로 식단을 '조절한다'고 볼 수 있지만, 음식 자체를 좋고 나쁨으로 정의하는 것은 옳지 않다.

* 글의 흐름

도입	많은 사람이 좋은 음식과 나쁜 음식이 있다고 믿음
반박	음식이 좋고 나쁘다고 분류되는 것이 아니라 음식의 조합에 의해 식단이 건강한지가 결정됨
예시 ①	좋은 음식이라고 생각되는 음식만 먹는 것은 다양한 영양소를 갖추고 있지 않기 때문에 건강한 식단이 아님
예시 ②	튀긴 음식을 먹는다고 해도 자주 먹지 않으면 건강한 식단이 될 수도 있음

Early hunter-gatherer societies / had (a) <u>minimal</u> structure. //
초기 수렵 채집 사회는 / 최소한의 구조만 가지고 있었다 //

A chief or group of elders / usually led the camp or village. //
추장이나 장로 그룹이 / 주로 캠프나 마을을 이끌었다 //

Most of these leaders / had to hunt and gather / along with the other members /
대부분의 이러한 지도자들은 / 사냥과 채집을 해야 했다 / 다른 구성원들과 함께 /
부사절 접속사(이유)
<u>because</u> the surpluses of food and other vital resources / were
'거의 ~않는'
<mark>seldom</mark> (b) sufficient / to support a full-time chief or village
council. // **41번** 단서 1: 초기 수렵 채집 사회에는 잉여 식량과 자원이
충분하지 않았음
왜냐하면 식량과 기타 필수 자원의 잉여분이 / 거의 충분하지 않았기 때문에 / 전임 추장이나 마을 의회를 지원할 만큼 //

The development of agriculture / changed work patterns. //
농업의 발전은 / 작업 패턴을 변화시켰다 // **41번** 단서 2: 농업의 발전으로 작업 패턴이 변화함

Early farmers could reap 3–10 kg of grain / from each 1 kg of
앞에 주격 관계대명사와 be동사가 생략됨
seed <u>planted</u>. //
수동태 동사
초기 농부들은 / 3kg에서 10kg의 곡물을 수확할 수 있었다 / 심은 씨앗 1kg마다 //

Part of this food/energy surplus <mark>was returned</mark> to the community
/ and (c) <u>limited</u>(→ provided) support for nonfarmers /
이 식량/에너지 잉여분의 일부는 지역 사회에 환원되었고 / 비농민에 대한 지원을 제한했다
(→ 제공했다) /
주격 관계대명사
such as chieftains, village councils, men <u>who</u> practice medicine,
priests, and warriors. // **41번** 단서 3: 농업의 발전으로 생긴 잉여분이 사회에 환원되어
비농민들에게 제공됨
족장, 마을 의회, 의술가, 사제, 전사와 같은 /
'~에 대한 반응으로'
<mark>In return</mark>, / the nonfarmers provided leadership and security /
분사구문을 이끄는 현재분사
for the farming population, / <mark>enabling</mark> it to continue to increase
food/energy yields / and provide ever larger surpluses. //
그 대가로 / 비농민들은 리더십과 안보를 제공하였다 / 농업 인구에게 / 그들이 식량/에너지
생산량을 지속적으로 늘릴 수 있게 하면서 / 그리고 항상 더 많은 잉여를 제공할 (수 있게
하면서) //
42번 단서: 비농민들은 농민들이 지속해서 잉여를
전치사구 제공할 수 있도록 리더십과 안보를 제공함
<mark>With improved technology and favorable conditions</mark>, /
agriculture produced consistent surpluses of the basic
완전자동사
necessities, / and population groups <u>grew</u> in size. //
개선된 기술과 유리한 조건으로 / 농업은 기본 생필품의 지속적인 흑자를 창출했고 / 인구
집단은 규모가 커졌다 //

These groups concentrated in towns and cities, / and human
tasks (d) <u>specialized</u> further. //
이러한 집단은 마을과 도시에 집중되었고 / 인간의 업무는 더욱 전문화되었다 //

Specialists such as carpenters, blacksmiths, merchants, traders,
and sailors / developed their skills / and became more efficient /
in their use of time and energy. // **41번** 단서 4: 지원을 받은 비농민들은 여러
분야에서 전문가가 됨
목수, 대장장이, 상인, 무역업자, 선원과 같은 전문가들은 / 그들의 기술을 발전시키고 / 더
효율적으로 되었다 / 그들의 시간과 에너지 사용에 //
앞에 목적격 관계대명사가 생략됨
The goods and services <mark>they provided</mark> brought about / an (e)
<u>improved</u> quality of life, / a higher standard of living, / and, <mark>for</mark>
삽입구
<mark>most societies</mark>, increased stability. //
그들이 제공한 재화와 서비스는 가져왔다 / 향상된 삶의 질 / 더 높은 생활 수준 / 그리고
대부분의 사회에 향상된 안정성을 //

- minimal @ 최소한의 · structure ⓝ 구조
- chief ⓝ 우두머리, 족장 · elder ⓝ 원로, 어른
- surplus ⓝ 잉여, 흑자 · vital @ 필수적인 · sufficient @ 충분한
- council ⓝ 의회 · agriculture ⓝ 농업 · grain ⓝ 곡물
- priest ⓝ 성직자, 사제 · warrior ⓝ 전사 · favorable @ 유리한
- consistent @ 지속적인 · necessity ⓝ 필수품
- concentrate ⓥ 집중하다 · efficient @ 효율적인
- standard ⓝ 기준, 수준 · stability ⓝ 안정성
- shadow ⓝ 그림자 · repetition ⓝ 반복

초기 수렵 채집 사회는 (a) 최소한의 구조만 가지고 있었다. 추장이나 장로 그룹이 주로 캠프나 마을을 이끌었다. 식량과 기타 필수 자원의 잉여분이 전임 추장이나 마을 의회를 지원할 만큼 거의 (b) 충분하지 않았기 때문에 대부분의 이러한 지도자들은 다른 구성원들과 함께 사냥과 채집을 해야 했다. 농업의 발전은 작업 패턴을 변화시켰다. 초기 농부들은 심은 씨앗 1kg마다 3kg에서 10kg의 곡물을 수확할 수 있었다. 이 식량/에너지 잉여분의 일부는 지역 사회에 환원되었고 족장, 마을 의회, 의술가, 사제, 전사와 같은 비농민에 대한 지원을 (c) 제한했다(→ 제공했다). 그 대가로, 비농민들은 농업 인구에게 리더십과 안보를 제공하여, 그들이 식량/에너지 생산량을 지속적으로 늘리고 항상 더 많은 잉여를 제공할 수 있게 하였다. 개선된 기술과 유리한 조건으로, 농업은 기본 생필품의 지속적인 흑자를 창출했고, 인구 집단은 규모가 커졌다. 이러한 집단은 마을과 도시에 집중되었고, 인간의 업무는 더욱 (d) 전문화되었다. 목수, 대장장이, 상인, 무역업자, 선원과 같은 전문가들은 기술을 발전시키고 자신의 시간과 에너지 사용을 더 효율적으로 하게 되었다. 그들이 제공한 재화와 서비스는 (e) 향상된 삶의 질, 더 높은 생활 수준, 그리고, 대부분의 사회에 향상된 안정성을 가져왔다.

41 정답 ①

윗글의 제목으로 가장 적절한 것은?
농업의 발달로 발생한 잉여 자원/에너지를 활용하여 비농민들은 다양한 분야에서 전문가가 됨
① How Agriculture Transformed Human Society
농업이 인간 사회를 변화시킨 방법
② The Dark Shadow of Agriculture: Repetition
농업의 어두운 그림자: 반복 농업의 긍정적인 측면을 이야기함
③ How Can We Share Extra Food with the Poor?
어떻게 하면 우리는 남은 식량을 가난한 사람들과 나눌 수 있을까?
④ Why Were Early Societies Destroyed by Agriculture?
왜 초기 사회는 농업으로 인해 파괴되었는가? 언급되지 않음
⑤ The Advantages of Large Groups Over Small Groups in Farming 농업의 규모를 비교한 글이 아님
농업에서 대규모 집단이 소규모 집단에 비해 갖는 이점들
잉여 식량을 가난한 사람들과 나누자고 하는 글이 아님

왜 정답? ✱✱✲ [정답률 67%]

- 초기 수렵 사회에서는 식량과 기타 자원의 잉여분이 충분하지 않았기 때문에 대부분의 지도자들은 다른 구성원들과 함께 사냥과 채집을 해야 했다. **단서 1**
- 농업의 발전은 작업 패턴을 변화시켰다. **단서 2**
- 식량/에너지 잉여분은 지역 사회에 환원되어 비농민에게 제공되었다. **단서 3**
- 다양한 분야의 비농민 전문가들은 기술을 발전시키고 더 효율적으로 시간과 에너지를 사용하게 되었다. **단서 4**

➡ 초기 수렵 사회에는 식량과 자원이 남지 않음 → 농업으로 잉여분이 생김 → 남은 자원은 사회에 환원되어 비농민들에게 제공됨 → 비농민들은 다양한 기술을 발전시켜 여러 분야에서 전문가가 됨

▶ 따라서 글의 제목으로 가장 적절한 것은 ① '농업이 인간 사회를 변화시킨 방법'이다.

왜 오답?
② 농업의 부정적 측면이 아니라 긍정적인 영향을 이야기한 글이다.
③ 잉여 자원은 가난한 사람이 아니라 비농민에게 제공되었다고 했다.
(▸ 이유: 비농민이 가난한지는 글에 언급되지 않았다.)
④ 초기 사회가 파괴되었다거나 그 원인을 이야기한 글이 아니다.
⑤ 농업에 있어 집단의 규모가 클수록 유리하다고 주장한 글이 아니다.

42 정답 ③

밑줄 친 (a)~(e) 중에서 문맥상 낱말의 쓰임이 적절하지 <u>않은</u> 것은? [3점]
① (a) 이후 농업의 발전으로 사회의 규모가 증가함
최소한의
② (b) 지도자들도 사냥과 채집을 해야 했음
충분한
③ (c) 비농민들이 그 대가로 리더십과 안보를 제공함
제한했다
④ (d) 전문가들이 생겨 기술을 발전시킬 수 있음
전문화되었다
⑤ (e) 사회에 더 나은 안전성을 가져왔음
향상된

＞왜 정답 ? ★★☆ [정답률 63%]

③ (c) limited 제한했다

> 이 식량/에너지 잉여분의 일부는 지역 사회에 환원되었고 족장, 마을 의회, 의술가, 사제, 전사와 같은 비농민에 대한 지원을 (c) 계획했다. (제공했다)
> 그 대가로(In return), 비농민들은 농업 인구에게 리더십과 안보를 제공하여, 그들이 식량/에너지 생산량을 지속적으로 늘리고 항상 더 많은 잉여를 제공할 수 있게 하였다.

➡ **결과:** 비농민들이 리더십과 안보를 제공하여, 농민들이 더 많은 잉여를 만들도록 함
원인: 자원의 잉여분을 비농민에게 '제공'한 것
▶ limited를 provided(제공했다)와 같은 반의어로 바꿔야 함

＞왜 오답 ?

① (a) minimal 최소한의

> 초기 수렵 채집 사회는 (a) 최소한의 구조만 가지고 있었다. 추장이나 장로 그룹이 주로 캠프나 마을을 이끌었다.

➡ 중간 지도자 없이 추장이나 장로가 마을을 이끌었다는 것은 사회가 '최소한의' 구조만 가졌기 때문일 것이다.
▶ minimal은 문맥에 맞음

② (b) sufficient 충분한

> 식량과 기타 필수 자원의 잉여분이 전임 추장이나 마을 의회를 지원할 만큼 거의 (b) 충분하지 않았기 때문에 대부분의 이러한 지도자들은 다른 구성원들과 함께 사냥과 채집을 해야 했다.

➡ 남는 자원이 '충분하지' 않았기 때문에 지도자들까지 사냥과 채집을 해야 했을 것이다.
▶ sufficient는 문맥에 맞음

④ (d) specialized 전문화되었다

> 이러한 집단은 마을과 도시에 집중되었고, 인간의 업무는 더욱 (d) 전문화되었다. 목수, 대장장이, 상인, 무역업자, 선원과 같은 전문가들은 기술을 발전시키고 자신의 시간과 에너지 사용을 더 효율적으로 하게 되었다.

➡ 다양한 분야의 전문가들이 등장했으므로 인간의 업무는 더욱 '전문화된' 것이다.
▶ specialized는 문맥에 맞음

⑤ (e) improved 향상된

> 그들이 제공한 재화와 서비스는 (e) 향상된 삶의 질, 더 높은 생활 수준, 그리고, 대부분의 사회에 향상된 안정성을 가져왔다.

➡ '향상된' 삶의 질 = 더 높은 생활 수준, 향상된 안정성
▶ improved는 문맥에 맞음

43 ~ 45   ＊노인 곁에 머물렀던 군인

(A) A nurse took a tired, anxious soldier / to the bedside. //
한 간호사가 피곤하고 불안해하는 군인을 데려갔다 / 침대 곁으로 //

앞에 주격 관계대명사와 be동사가 생략됨
"Jack, / your son is here," / the nurse said to an old man / **lying** on the bed. //
"Jack 씨 / 당신의 아들이 왔어요"라고 / 간호사가 한 노인에게 말했다 / 침대에 누워있는 //

She had to repeat the words several times / before the old man's eyes opened. //
그녀는 그 말을 여러 번 반복해야 했다 / 그 노인의 눈이 떠지기 전에 //

분사구문을 이끄는 현재분사
Suffering from the severe pain / because of heart disease, / he barely saw / the young uniformed soldier / standing next to him. // 『45번①』 노인은 심장병으로 극심한 고통을 겪고 있었음
극심한 고통을 겪고 있어 / 심장병 때문에 / 그는 간신히 보았다 / 제복을 입은 젊은 군인이 / 그의 옆에 서 있는 것을 //
= The old man
(a) He reached out his hand / to the soldier. //
그는 손을 뻗었다 / 그 군인에게 // 『43번』 단서 1: 노인은 군인에게 손을 뻗었음

＊(A) 문단 요약: 간호사가 젊은 군인을 심장병으로 병원 침대에 누워있는 노인에게 데려감

복합관계부사 『43번』 단서 2: 군인은 계속해서 노인의 손을 잡고 위로의 말을 건넴
(B) **Whenever** the nurse came into the room, / she heard / the soldier say a few gentle words. //
간호사가 병실에 들어올 때마다 / 그녀는 들었다 / 그 군인이 부드러운 몇 마디의 말을 하는 것을 //

앞에 being이 생략됨   = the soldier
The old man said nothing, / only **held** tightly to (b) **him** / all through the night. //
노인은 아무 말도 하지 않았다 / 그에게 손이 꼭 쥐어진 채로 / 밤새도록 //

Just before dawn, / the old man died. //
동트기 직전에 / 그 노인은 죽었다 //

병렬 구조   부사적 용법(목적)
The soldier **released** the old man's hand / and **left** the room / **to find** the nurse. // 『45번②』 군인은 간호사를 찾기 위해 병실을 나감
그 군인은 노인의 손을 놓고 / 병실을 나갔다 / 간호사를 찾기 위해 //

선행사를 포함하는 관계대명사
After she was told **what** happened, / she went back to the room with him. //
그녀는 무슨 일이 있었는지 들은 후 / 그녀는 그와 함께 병실로 돌아갔다 //

병렬 구조
The soldier **hesitated** for a while / and **asked**, "Who was this man?" // 『43번』 단서 3: 노인이 죽자, 군인은 간호사에게 노인이 누구였는지 물어봄
군인은 잠시 머뭇거리고는 / "그 남자는 누구였나요"라고 물었다 //

＊(B) 문단 요약: 군인은 말이 없는 노인의 곁을 지켰고, 노인이 죽은 뒤 간호사에게 그가 누구였는지 물어봄

『43번』 단서 4: 간호사는 노인이 군인의 아버지가 아니었음을 듣고 놀람
(C) She was surprised and asked, / "Wasn't he your father?" //
그녀는 깜짝 놀라서 물었다 / "그가 당신의 아버지가 아니었나요" //

현재완료(경험)
"No, / he wasn't. // I've never **met** him before," / the soldier replied. // 『45번③』 군인은 노인과 이전에 만난 적이 없다고 말함
"아니요 / 그는 아니었어요 // 저는 그를 이전에 만난 적이 없어요"라고 / 군인이 대답했다 //

부사절 접속사
She asked, / "Then why didn't you say something / **when** I took you to (c) **him**?" //
= the old man
그녀는 물었다 / "그러면 왜 아무 말도 하지 않았나요 / 내가 당신을 그에게 데리고 갔을 때"라고 //

뒤에 목적어절 접속사 that이 생략됨
He said, / "I **knew** there had been a mistake, / but when I realized / **that** he was too sick to tell whether or not I was his
목적어절 접속사   = the old man
son, / I could see / how much (d) **he** needed me. // So, I stayed." //
그가 말했다 / "저는 실수가 있었다는 것을 알았습니다 / 하지만 제가 알게 되었을 때 / 그가 너무 위독해서 제가 그의 아들인지 아닌지 구별할 수 없다는 것을 / 저는 알 수 있었습니다 / 그가 얼마나 저를 필요로 하는지 // 그래서, 저는 머물렀습니다"라고 //

＊(C) 문단 요약: 놀란 간호사는 왜 진작 말하지 않았냐고 물었고, 군인은 노인이 자신을 필요로 하는 것을 느껴 머물렀다고 말함

(D) The soldier gently wrapped his fingers / around the weak hand of the old man. // 『43번』 단서 5: 노인이 뻗은 손을 군인이 부드럽게 감쌈
그 군인은 손가락으로 부드럽게 감쌌다 / 노인의 병약한 손을 //

'~하도록'
The nurse brought a chair / **so that** the soldier could sit / beside the bed. // 『45번④』 간호사는 군인이 앉을 수 있도록 의자를 가져옴
간호사는 의자를 가져왔다 / 군인이 앉을 수 있도록 / 침대 옆에 //

All through the night / the young soldier sat there, / **holding**
병렬 구조
the old man's hand / and **offering** (e) **him** words of support and comfort. //
= the old man
밤새 / 젊은 군인은 거기에 앉아 있었다 / 노인의 손을 잡고 / 그에게 지지와 위로의 말을 건네면서 //

Occasionally, / she suggested **that** the soldier take a rest for a while. //
목적어절 접속사

가끔 / 그녀는 군인에게 잠시 쉬라고 제안했다 //

He politely said no. // `45번 ⑤` 군인은 잠시 쉬라는 간호사의 제안을 정중히 거절함

그는 정중하게 거절했다 //

*(D) 문단 요약: 군인은 침대 옆 의자에 앉아 노인에게 쉬지 않고 밤새도록 지지와 위로의 말을 건넴

- anxious ⓐ 불안해하는 · suffer ⓥ 고통받다 · severe ⓐ 극심한
- barely 〔ad〕 간신히, 겨우 · gentle ⓐ 부드러운, 온화한
- tightly 〔ad〕 꽉, 단단히 · hesitate ⓥ 망설이다 · wrap ⓥ 감싸다
- weak ⓐ (병)약한 · support ⓝ 지지 · comfort ⓝ 위로, 위안
- occasionally 〔ad〕 가끔 · politely 〔ad〕 정중하게

(A) 한 간호사가 피곤하고 불안해하는 군인을 침대 곁으로 데려갔다. "Jack 씨, 당신 아들이 왔어요."라고 간호사가 침대에 누워있는 한 노인에게 말했다. 그 노인이 눈을 뜨기 전에 그녀는 그 말을 여러 번 반복해야 했다. 심장병 때문에 극심한 고통을 겪고 있어, 그는 제복을 입은 젊은 군인이 그의 옆에 서 있는 것을 간신히 보았다. (a) 그는 손을 그 군인에게 뻗었다.

(D) 그 군인은 노인의 병약한 손을 손가락으로 부드럽게 감쌌다. 간호사는 군인이 침대 옆에 앉을 수 있도록 의자를 가져왔다. 밤새 젊은 군인은 거기에 앉아, 노인의 손을 잡고 (e) 그에게 지지와 위로의 말을 건넸다. 가끔, 그녀는 군인에게 잠시 쉬라고 제안했다. 그는 정중하게 거절했다.

(B) 간호사가 병실에 들어올 때마다, 그녀는 그 군인이 부드러운 몇 마디의 말을 하는 것을 들었다. 밤새도록 (b) 그에게 손이 꼭 쥐어진 채로 노인은 아무 말도 하지 않았다. 동트기 직전에, 그 노인은 죽었다. 그 군인은 노인의 손을 놓고 간호사를 찾기 위해 병실을 나갔다. 그녀는 무슨 일이 있었는지 들은 후, 그와 함께 병실로 돌아갔다. 군인은 잠시 머뭇거리고는 "그 남자는 누구였나요?"라고 물었다.

(C) 그녀는 깜짝 놀라서 물었다. "그가 당신의 아버지가 아니었나요?" "아니요, 그는 아니었어요. 저는 그를 이전에 만난 적이 없어요."라고 군인이 대답했다. 그녀는 물었다, "그러면 내가 당신을 (c) 그에게 데리고 갔을 때 왜 아무 말도 하지 않았나요?" 그가 말했다, "저는 실수가 있었다는 것을 알았지만, 그가 너무 위독해서 제가 그의 아들인지 아닌지 구별할 수 없다는 걸 알게 되었을 때, 저는 (d) 그가 얼마나 저를 필요로 하는지 알 수 있었습니다. 그래서, 저는 머물렀습니다."

43 정답 ④

주어진 글 (A)에 이어질 내용을 순서에 맞게 배열한 것으로 가장 적절한 것은?

① (B) — (D) — (C) ┐ 노인이 죽은 (B) 뒤에 노인에게 말은 건네는 (D)가 올 수 없음
② (C) — (B) — (D) ┘
③ (C) — (D) — (B) ┐
④ (D) — (B) — (C) │ (D) 군인은 노인 곁을 밤새 지킴 – (B) 노인이 죽고, 군인은 간호사에게 그가 누구였는지 물어봄 – (C) 간호사는 그 사실에 놀람
⑤ (D) — (C) — (B) ┘ 노인이 죽은 (B) 뒤에 군인이 왜 그의 곁에 머물렀는지 설명하는 (C)가 와야 함

> **왜** 정답·오답 **?** ✿✿✿ [정답률 82%]

(A): 한 간호사가 젊은 군인을 심장병 때문에 극심한 고통을 겪으며 침대에 누워있는 노인에게 데려갔고, 그를 본 노인은 손을 뻗었다.

➡ 노인을 본 군인이 어떤 행동을 하는지 이어질 것이다.

(B): 밤새도록 군인은 말이 없는 노인의 곁을 지켰고, 노인이 죽은 뒤 군인은 간호사에게 그가 누구였는지 물었다.

➡ 뒤에 간호사의 대답이 이어질 것이다.

(C): 놀란 간호사는 왜 진작 말하지 않았냐고 물었고, 군인은 노인이 자신을 필요로 하는 것을 느껴 머물렀다고 말했다.

➡ 군인의 물음에 대한 답이므로 (B)에 이어지는 내용이며, 글의 마무리 부분에 해당한다.

(D): 군인은 노인의 손을 잡고 밤새 쉬지 않고 지지와 위로의 말을 건넸다.

➡ 노인이 군인에게 손을 뻗은 (A)에 이어지는 내용으로, 밤새 노인의 곁을 지켰다는 (B)가 뒤에 이어질 것이다.

▶ (D) 군인은 침대 옆 의자에 앉아 노인 곁을 밤새 지킴 → (B) 동트기 전 노인이 죽고, 군인은 간호사를 찾아가 그가 누구였는지 물어봄 → (C) 간호사는 놀라 왜 그의 아들이 아님을 밝히지 않았는지 물었고, 군인은 그가 자신을 필요로 하는 것을 느껴 머물렀다고 말함

▶ 글의 순서는 ④ (D) → (B) → (C)임

44 정답 ②

밑줄 친 (a)~(e) 중에서 가리키는 대상이 나머지 넷과 다른 것은?

① (a)　　②(b)　　③ (c)　　④ (d)　　⑤ (e)
= The old man　= the soldier　= the old man　= the old man　= the old man

> **왜** 정답 **?** ✿✿✿ [정답률 69%]

② (b) him: 노인의 손을 꼭 쥔 사람 ▶ the soldier

> **왜** 오답 **?**

① (a) He: 군인에게 손을 뻗은 사람 ▶ The old man
③ (c) him: 간호사가 군인을 데리고 간 대상 ▶ the old man
④ (d) he: 군인을 필요로 했던 사람 ▶ the old man
⑤ (e) him: 군인이 지지와 위로의 말을 건넨 사람 ▶ the old man

45 정답 ③

윗글에 관한 내용으로 적절하지 않은 것은?

① 노인은 심장병으로 극심한 고통을 겪고 있었다.
　Suffering from the severe pain because of heart disease
② 군인은 간호사를 찾기 위해 병실을 나갔다.
　The soldier released the old man's hand and left the room to find the nurse.
③ 군인은 노인과 이전에 만난 적이 있다고 말했다.
　"I've never met him before,"
④ 간호사는 군인이 앉을 수 있도록 의자를 가져왔다.
　The nurse brought a chair so that the soldier could sit beside the bed.
⑤ 군인은 잠시 쉬라는 간호사의 제안을 정중히 거절하였다.
　He politely said no.

> **왜** 정답 **?** ✿✿✿ [정답률 79%]

군인은 노인과 이전에 만난 적이 없다고("I've never met him before,") 했다. 따라서 군인은 노인과 이전에 만난 적이 있다고 한 ③은 적절하지 않다.

> **왜** 오답 **?**

① 노인은 심장병으로 극심한 고통을 겪고 있었다. (Suffering from the severe pain because of heart disease)
② 노인이 죽자, 군인은 간호사를 찾기 위해 병실을 나갔다. (The soldier released the old man's hand and left the room to find the nurse.)
④ 간호사는 군인이 앉을 수 있도록 의자를 가져왔다. (The nurse brought a chair so that the soldier could sit beside the bed.)
⑤ 군인은 잠시 쉬라는 간호사의 제안을 정중히 거절하였다. (He politely said no.)

01 student council president / annual / to help set up / volunteer application form

02 much progress / creative ideas / wasting / to improve / more active / come up with

03 on this counter / breakable items / clothes / express mail / an extra charge / delivered / express mail

04 went busking / while I sang / guitar case open / audience / our performance / recently bought

05 invitation cards / expecting / guests / haven't decided / the present / electronics store

06 looking for / for my sofa / on sale / go well with / each / this coupon / off the total

07 art class / a rock concert / can't / on Saturdays / rock music / take care of / going somewhere / someone else

08 picking up trash / Sounds / environment lately / often used / own gloves / I have extra / can do it / looking forward to

09 hosting the first / can participate in / are allowed / participate / can vote / trophy / prize / great opportunity

10 order one / five bestsellers / our budget / capacity / mode / save electricity / the warranties

11 excited / auto show / standing in line / Fortunately

12 your grade / something wrong

13 bought / secondhand bookstore / a bookmark / How sweet / if we resell

14 any plans / go camping often / in nature / me feel closer / family hobby / helps me relieve / any equipment

15 classmates / science group assignment / public library / different sections / suddenly realizes / moment / walks up

[16~17] essential parts / going to introduce / contain / you fall asleep / calms the mind and nerves / internal body clock / sends signals / delicious diet plans

01 필수적인
02 극심한
03 간격
04 가축
05 반복적인
06 claim
07 division
08 profession
09 genuine
10 doctoral
11 show off
12 in terms of
13 in advance
14 sign up for

15 major in
16 prejudice
17 consistent
18 combination
19 cognitive
20 agriculture
21 separate
22 standard
23 semester
24 support
25 fictional
26 hesitate
27 absorb
28 ambassador

29 incorporate
30 scarcity
31 active
32 pace
33 labeled
34 volume
35 harden
36 desirable
37 disordered
38 Gradually
39 stability
40 poverty

2023.6
6회

01 정답 ④ ＊교직원 주차 장소 변경 안내

W : Hello, this is Karen Smith, the principal of Sunnyfield High School.
여 : 안녕하세요, 저는 Sunnyfield 고등학교 교장 Karen Smith입니다.
I would like to inform all staff about an important plan for
= want　　　inform ~ about ~ : ~에게 …을 알리다
next week's Parent-Teacher Meeting.
다음 주 학부모-교사 간담회를 위한 중요한 계획을 모든 교직원께 안내하고자 합니다.
'~로 인해'
Due to limited parking on campus, all teachers and staff
should park at the nearby community center on Wednesday.
학교 내 제한된 주차 공간으로 인해, 수요일에는 모든 교사와 직원들께서 인근 커뮤니티 센터에 주차해 주시기 바랍니다. **[단서]** 학부모 간담회를 위해 교직원들이 다른 곳에 주차할 것을 요청함
It is only a five-minute walk from the school.
그곳은 학교에서 도보로 단 5분 거리에 있습니다.
　　　　　　목적어절 접속사　　　현재분사구 (parents 수식)
This plan will ensure that parents attending the meeting
have easy access to parking.
이 계획은 간담회에 참석하시는 학부모님들이 주차장에 쉽게 접근하는 것을 보장할 것입니다.
'~하는 것을 돕다'
Your cooperation will greatly assist in making this event a
smooth and successful experience.
여러분의 협조가 이번 행사를 원활하고 성공적인 경험으로 만드는 데 큰 도움이 될 것입니다.
Thank you in advance for your cooperation with the parking arrangements.
주차 배정에 관한 여러분의 협조에 미리 감사드립니다.

- inform ⓥ 안내하다 · staff ⓝ 직원 · ensure ⓥ 보장하다
- have access to ~에 접근하다 · cooperation ⓝ 협조
- assist ⓥ 돕다 · smooth ⓐ 원활한 · in advance 미리
- arrangement ⓝ 배정, 배치

다음을 듣고, 여자가 하는 말의 목적으로 가장 적절한 것을 고르시오.
① 학부모 간담회 참석을 독려하려고 학부모가 아니라 교직원들을 위한 안내임
② 학부모 상담 기간 연기를 안내하려고 학부모 상담은 언급되지 않음
③ 교직원 회의 시간 변경에 대한 협조를 요청하려고 교직원 회의는 언급되지 않음
④ 학부모 간담회를 위한 교직원 주차 장소 변경을 알리려고 교직원들이 학교 밖 인근 커뮤니티 센터에 주차하도록 안내함
⑤ 지역 주민 행사를 위한 주말 교내 주차 허용을 공지하려고 지역 주민 행사는 언급되지 않음

＞왜 정답? ✱✿✿ [정답률 87%]
학부모-교사 간담회에 참석하는 학부모들이 학교에 쉽게 주차할 수 있도록, 교직원들에게 수요일에는 인근 커뮤니티 센터에 주차할 것을 요청하는 안내이다. 따라서 여자가 하는 말의 목적으로 가장 적절한 것은 ④이다.

＞왜 오답?
① 학부모가 아니라 교직원들을 대상으로 하는 안내이다. **주의**
② 학부모 상담은 언급되지 않았다.
③ 교직원 회의가 아니라 학부모-교사 간담회에 관한 안내이다.
⑤ 커뮤니티 센터가 언급되긴 했으나, 지역 주민 행사를 위한 안내가 아니라 학부모-교사 간담회에 관한 안내이다. 함정

02 정답 ① ＊친환경 가방을 친환경적으로 쓰는 방법

M : Lisa. What are you looking at? 남 : Lisa, 뭐 보고 있어?
W : I'm planning to buy this eco-bag. Isn't it cute?
여 : 이 친환경 가방을 사려고 하는 중이야. 귀엽지 않아?
뒤에 반복되는 cute가 생략됨
M : It is, but don't you already have several eco-bags?
남 : 그렇긴 한데, 너 이미 친환경 가방을 여러 개 가지고 있지 않아?
have several eco-bags를 대신함
W : Yes, I do. But this one is limited edition!
여 : 맞아, 있어. 근데 이건 한정판이잖아!
　　　　　instead of -ing: ~하는 대신에
M : Well, instead of buying more bags, wouldn't it be better to
앞에 목적격 관계대명사가 생략됨
use the ones you already have?
남 : 음, 가방을 더 사는 것 대신에 이미 가지고 있는 것들을 쓰는 게 더 낫지 않을까?
W : I know what you mean. But I thought eco-bags were environmentally-friendly.
여 : 무슨 말인지 알아. 근데 난 친환경 가방이 친환경적인 줄 알았어.
M : That's true, but the point is even eco-bags need to be reused
'가능한 한 오래'
as long as possible. **[단서 1]** 친환경 가방은 오래 재사용되어야 함
남 : 그건 맞지만, 중요한 건 친환경 가방도 가능한 한 오래 재사용되어야 한다는 거야.
W : Oh, that makes sense. 여 : 아, 일리가 있네.
부사절 접속사 (조건)
M : If you use one eco-bag for a long time, it will be much better
for the environment. **[단서 2]** 친환경 가방 하나를 오래 쓰는 것이 환경에 더 좋음
남 : 친환경 가방 하나를 오랫동안 사용하면, 환경에 훨씬 더 좋을 거야.
앞에 목적격 관계대명사가 생략됨
W : Okay. I'll try to use the bags I already have.
여 : 알겠어. 내가 이미 가지고 있는 가방들을 써보도록 할게.

- eco-bag ⓝ 친환경 가방 · limited edition 한정판
- environmentally-friendly ⓐ 친환경적인 · reuse ⓥ 재사용하다

대화를 듣고, 남자의 의견으로 가장 적절한 것을 고르시오.
① 환경을 위해 친환경 가방을 가능한 오래 사용해야 한다. 친환경 가방 하나를 오래 사용해야 함
② 가방 구입 시 디자인과 실용성을 동시에 고려해야 한다. 가방의 디자인과 실용성은 언급되지 않음
③ 윤리적인 소비를 위해 친환경 제품을 선택해야 한다. 윤리적인 소비는 언급되지 않음
④ 환경을 위해 일회용 봉투의 사용을 줄여야 한다. 일회용 봉투는 언급되지 않음
⑤ 쇼핑할 때 할인 혜택을 잘 활용해야 한다. 할인 혜택은 언급되지 않음

＞왜 정답? ✱✿✿ [정답률 96%]
이미 여러 친환경 가방을 갖고 있는 여자가 친환경 가방을 하나 더 사려고 하자, 남자는 친환경 가방 하나를 오래 사용해야 환경에 좋다고 했다. 따라서 남자의 의견으로 가장 적절한 것은 ①이다.

＞왜 오답?
② 가방의 디자인과 실용성은 언급되지 않았다.
③ 윤리적인 소비는 언급되지 않았다.
④ 일회용 봉투는 언급되지 않았다.
⑤ 할인 혜택은 언급되지 않았다.

03 정답 ⑤ ＊배운 내용을 잘 기억하는 방법

W : Hi, everyone! 여 : 안녕하세요, 여러분!
Welcome back to Smart Study Tips.
Smart Study Tips에 돌아오신 것을 환영합니다.
　　　　현재완료 (경험)　　　　　　　　　　　　부사절 접속사 (양보)
Has your mind ever gone blank during a test, even though
you studied very hard?
혹시 열심히 공부했는데도 시험 중에 머리가 텅 비었던 적이 있나요?
Here's a simple but effective tip.
여기 간단하지만 효과적인 팁이 있습니다.
동명사 주어
Explaining what you've learned out loud can help you
help의 목적격 보어 (원형부정사)
remember better. **[단서]** 배운 내용을 큰 소리로 설명하면 더 잘 기억하게 됨
배운 내용을 큰 소리로 설명하는 것은 더 잘 기억하도록 도울 수 있습니다.

Just **pretend** you're a teacher and **explain** what you've learned in your own words.
병렬 구조
여러분이 선생님이라고 상상하고 배운 내용을 여러분의 말로 설명해 보세요.
You can even talk to **yourself** in front of a mirror.
재귀대명사 (재귀 용법)
심지어 거울 앞에서 혼자 말해도 괜찮습니다.

Try it. You'll be surprised how well it works!
한번 해보세요. 효과가 얼마나 좋은지 깜짝 놀라실 거예요!

- go blank (머리가) 텅 비다   - effective ⓐ 효과적인
- pretend ⓥ ~라고 상상하다

다음을 듣고, 여자가 하는 말의 요지로 가장 적절한 것을 고르시오.

① 이해가 선행되어야 학습 효과가 극대화된다. 이해의 선행은 언급되지 않았음
② 학생을 가르칠 때 큰 소리로 말해 집중시켜야 한다. 교사를 위한 팁이 아님
③ 발표 시 핵심어를 반복하여 말하는 것이 효과적이다. 핵심어를 반복하는 것은 언급되지 않았음
④ 수업에서 이해한 내용을 빠른 시간 내에 복습해야 한다. 빠른 시간 내에 복습하는 것은 언급되지 않았음
⑤ 배운 내용을 소리내어 설명하는 것이 기억에 도움이 된다. 배운 내용을 큰 소리로 설명하면 더 잘 기억하게 된다는 내용임

⟩왜 정답? ✽✾✾ [정답률 92%]

배운 내용을 큰 소리로 설명하면 더 잘 기억하게 된다는 내용이므로 정답은 ⑤이다.

⟩왜 오답?

① 이해가 선행되어야 한다는 것은 언급되지 않았다.
② 선생님이라고 상상하고 큰 소리로 말하라고 했을 뿐, 교사를 위한 팁이 아니다. *함정*
③ 핵심어를 반복하는 것은 언급되지 않았다.
④ 빠른 시간 내에 복습하는 것은 언급되지 않았다.

---

04 정답 ⑤ ✽재활용 장려 포스터

M : Hey, Lucy! Look at this recycling poster. What do you notice first?
남 : 안녕, Lucy! 이 재활용 포스터 좀 봐. 제일 먼저 뭐가 눈에 띄니?

W : The title at the top really stands out. It says "RECYCLE FOR A BETTER FUTURE." **①의 단서** 맨 위에 제목이 있음
여 : 맨 위 제목이 매우 눈에 띄네. "더 나은 미래를 위해 재활용하세요"라고 쓰여 있어.

M : Right! And below it, there's the big recycling symbol with three arrows **forming a triangle**. *현재분사구 (three arrows 수식)*
남 : 맞아! 그리고 그 밑에는 세 개의 화살표가 삼각형을 이루는 큰 재활용 마크가 있네.

W : That makes **it** clear **that** this is about recycling. On the top arrow, there are plastic bottles. **②의 단서** 위쪽 화살표에 플라스틱병이 있음
가목적어 진목적어절 접속사
여 : 그것은 이게 재활용에 관한 것이라는 걸 명확하게 하네. 위쪽 화살표에는 플라스틱병이 있네.

M : Yeah, there are! Oh, look! Below the trees, there is paper, **which** students often waste. **③의 단서** 나무 그림 아래에 종이가 있음
계속적 용법의 목적격 관계대명사
남 : 맞아, 그러네! 오, 봐봐! 나무 밑에는 종이가 있는데 학생들이 자주 낭비하는 거야.

W : Right. And beside one of the bottom arrows, there are three cans. Cans are an important item **to recycle**. *형용사적 용법 (item 수식)*
여 : 맞아. 그리고 아래쪽 화살표 옆에는 캔 세 개가 있네. 캔은 재활용해야 할 중요한 품목이야. **④의 단서** 캔 세 개가 아래쪽 화살표 옆에 그려져 있음   **⑤의 단서** 지구는 꽃이 아닌 빗자루를 들고 있음

M : Exactly. Look at this. There's an Earth holding a flower. That's a fun way to remind us that we can make a difference.
남 : 바로 그거야. 이것 좀 봐. 꽃을 들고 있는 지구가 있네. 우리가 변화를 만들 수 있다는 걸 우리에게 상기시키는 재밌는 방법이야.

W : I agree! This poster does a great job of promoting recycling.
여 : 나도 동의해! 이 포스터는 재활용을 잘 장려하고 있어.

- notice ⓥ 알아차리다   - stand out 눈에 띄다   - recycle ⓥ 재활용하다
- arrow ⓝ 화살표   - remind ⓥ 상기시키다   - promote ⓥ 장려하다

대화를 듣고, 그림에서 대화의 내용과 일치하지 않는 것을 고르시오.

① 맨 위에 제목이 있음
⑤ 꽃이 아니라 빗자루를 들고 있음
② 위쪽 화살표에는 플라스틱병이 있음
나무 아래에는 종이가 있음
아래쪽 화살표 옆에는 캔이 세 개 있음
plastic bottles
cans   paper

⟩왜 정답? ✽✾✾ [정답률 95%]

지구가 꽃을 들고 있다고 했지만, 그림에는 지구가 빗자루를 들고 있으므로, 그림에서 대화의 내용과 일치하지 않는 것은 ⑤이다.

⟩왜 오답?

① 맨 위에 제목이 있다.
② 위쪽 화살표에 플라스틱병이 있다.
③ 나무 아래에 종이가 있다.
④ 아래쪽 화살표 옆에 캔 세 개가 있다.

---

05 정답 ② ✽벽화 봉사 준비

W : Ryan, I'm excited to paint designs on the walls of the community center tomorrow!
여 : Ryan, 내일 커뮤니티 센터 벽에 그림을 그릴 생각에 신나!

M : Me too, Emily. It's going to brighten up the neighborhood.
남 : 나도 그래, Emily. 그것이 동네에 활기를 줄 거야.

W : Are we all set? Let's go over the preparations.
여 : 우리 준비는 다 되었지? 준비 사항을 점검해 보자.

M : Okay. I**'ve selected** designs **to put** on each wall. What about the paint and brushes? *현재완료 (완료)   형용사적 용법 (designs 수식)*
남 : 좋아. 각 벽에 그릴 디자인은 골랐어. 페인트와 붓은 어때?

W : I ordered **them** yesterday and **they** will **be delivered** this evening. **⑤의 함정** *= paint and brushes   수동태 동사*
여 : 내가 어제 주문했고 오늘 저녁에 배송될 거야.

M : Good. What else do we need to do?
남 : 좋아. 그밖에 무엇을 해야 하지?

W : Oh! I guess we also need sheets **to protect** the ground from paint. *형용사적 용법 (sheets 수식)*
여 : 아! 페인트로부터 바닥을 보호할 천도 필요할 것 같아.

M : I've already picked them up from the art center. Did you buy snacks for the volunteers? **①의 함정**
남 : 내가 이미 아트 센터에서 가져왔어. 자원봉사자들을 위한 간식은 샀어?

W : Yes, I did. One last thing. Do we need to remind all volunteers **to bring** extra clothes? Their clothes might get dirty. *remind의 목적격 보어 (to부정사)   ④의 함정*
여 : 응, 샀어. 마지막으로 한 가지. 모든 자원봉사자에게 여별 옷을 가져오라고 알려야 할까? 그들의 옷이 더러워질 수도 있어. **단서** 남자는 자원봉사자에게 문자 메시지를 보낼 것임

M : I think we do. I'll send a text message to them right away.
남 : 그래야 할 것 같아. 바로 그들에게 문자 메시지를 보낼게.

W : Perfect. The residents will love the finished walls!
여 : 완벽해. 주민들이 완성된 벽을 정말 좋아할 거야!

- brighten up 밝히다, 활기를 주다   - neighborhood ⓝ 이웃, 동네
- preparation ⓝ 준비 사항   - deliver ⓥ 배송하다   - ground ⓝ 땅
- remind ⓥ 상기시키다   - extra ⓐ 여분의   - resident ⓝ 주민

> 대화를 듣고, 남자가 할 일로 가장 적절한 것을 고르시오.
> ① 바닥 보호용 천 가져오기 남자가 이미 아트 센터에서 가져옴
> ② 문자 메시지 보내기 I'll send a text message to them right away.
> ③ 벽화 디자인 선택하기 남자가 이미 골랐음
> ④ 간식 구입하기 여자가 이미 샀음
> ⑤ 페인트와 붓 주문하기 여자가 어제 주문했음

왜 정답? ✿❀❀ [정답률 90%]

여자가 자원봉사자들에게 여분의 옷이 필요하다고 알려야 할지 물어보자, 남자가 바로 문자 메시지를 보내겠다고 했으므로 정답은 ②이다.

왜 오답?

① 남자가 이미 아트 센터에서 바닥 보호용 천을 가져왔다.
③ 남자가 이미 벽화 디자인을 골랐다.
④ 여자가 이미 자원봉사자를 위한 간식을 샀다.
⑤ 여자가 어제 페인트와 붓을 주문했다.

---

06 정답 ④ ＊공원 자전거 대여

M: Hello! Welcome to Central Park Bike Rentals. How can I help you today?
남: 안녕하세요! 센트럴 파크 자전거 대여점에 오신 것을 환영합니다. 오늘은 어떻게 도와드릴까요?

W: Hi, we'd like to rent some bikes. = want
여: 안녕하세요, 저희는 자전거를 빌리고 싶어요.

M: How many bikes would you like to rent today?
남: 오늘 자전거 몇 대를 빌리고 싶으신가요?

W: We'll need one adult bike and one child bike.
여: 성인용 자전거 한 대와 어린이용 자전거 한 대가 필요해요.

M: Sure! Adult bikes are 15 dollars per hour, and children's bikes are 10 dollars per hour. How long will you be renting them for? **단서 1** 한 시간에 성인용은 15달러, 어린이용은 10달러
남: 알겠습니다! 성인용 자전거는 시간당 15달러이고, 어린이용 자전거는 시간당 10달러입니다. 얼마나 오래 대여하시나요?

W: We'll need them for two hours. **단서 2** 두 시간 동안 대여
여: 두 시간 동안 필요해요.

M: Got it. So, that's one adult bike for two hours and one child bike for two hours.
남: 알겠습니다. 그러면 성인용 자전거 한 대 두 시간, 어린이용 자전거 한 대 두 시간이군요.

W: That's right. We want to rent helmets too.
여: 맞아요. 저희는 헬멧도 빌리고 싶어요.

M: Bike rentals include helmets for safety. You should wear them while riding the bikes in the park.
남: 자전거 대여에는 안전을 위해 헬멧이 포함되어 있습니다. 공원에서 자전거를 타실 때 꼭 착용하셔야 합니다.

W: Okay, can I use this "GO Green" coupon today?
여: 알겠습니다, 오늘 이 "GO Green" 쿠폰을 사용할 수 있나요?

M: Sure, you can get a 10% discount on the total price.
남: 네, 총액에서 10% 할인받으실 수 있습니다. **단서 3** 총액의 10% 할인

W: Great! Here's my credit card.
여: 좋아요! 여기 제 신용카드입니다.

• rent ⓥ 대여하다 • include ⓥ 포함하다 • discount ⓝ 할인
• credit card 신용카드

> 대화를 듣고, 여자가 지불할 금액을 고르시오. [3점]
> ① $25 ② $35 ③ $40 ④ $45 ⑤ $50
> ($15+$10)×2(성인용, 어린이용 자전거 한 대씩 두 시간) - $5(쿠폰 10% 할인)

왜 정답? ✿❀❀ [정답률 88%]

성인용 자전거는 한 시간에 15달러, 어린이용은 한 시간에 10달러고 모두 두 시간씩 대여하므로 전체 금액은 50달러이다. 여기에 총액의 10퍼센트가 할인되는 쿠폰을 사용했으므로 여자가 지불할 금액은 ④ '45달러'이다.

---

07 정답 ② ＊학교 영화제 불참 이유

W: Hey, Alex. Are you coming to the School Film Festival this Saturday? 가까운 미래를 대신하는 현재진행형
여: 안녕, Alex. 이번 토요일에 학교 영화제에 올 거야?

M: I wish I could, but I have to miss it this time.
남: 가고 싶긴 한데, 이번에는 못 갈 것 같아.

W: Oh, no, why? I thought you were really looking forward to it. 뒤에 목적어절 접속사 that이 생략됨
여: 아, 안 돼, 왜? 너 되게 기대하고 있는 줄 알았는데.

M: I was! But something came up, so I can't make it.
남: 기대했었지! 그런데 일이 생겨서 못 가게 됐어.

W: That's too bad. You don't have your part-time job this weekend, right?
여: 너무 아쉽다. 이번 주말에 아르바이트는 없어, 그렇지?

M: No, I've got the weekend off. ⑤의 함정
남: 아니, 주말은 쉬어.

W: Hmm, then maybe you're busy with some schoolwork?
여: 음, 그러면 아마도 학교 과제 때문에 바쁜 건가?

M: No, I already finished my big assignments this week.
남: 아니, 이번 주에 큰 과제들은 이미 끝냈어. ④의 함정

W: So, why can't you come?
여: 그럼 왜 못 오는 거야? **단서** 사촌의 결혼식에 참석해야 함

M: I'm going to my cousin's wedding and the place is really far. It'll take almost the whole day to get there and back. 가주어 진주어
남: 사촌 결혼식에 가야 하는데 장소가 너무 멀어. 왕복하려면 거의 하루 종일 걸려.

W: Oh, sorry to hear that. But family events like that are important.
여: 아, 안타깝다. 그래도 그런 가족 행사는 중요하지.

M: Yeah, they are. I'll definitely check out the next school film festival.
남: 맞아, 중요하지. 다음번 학교 영화제는 꼭 보러 갈 거야.

• look forward to ~을 기대하다 • assignment ⓝ 과제
• definitely 분명히, 확실히

> 대화를 듣고, 남자가 학교 영화제에 갈 수 없는 이유를 고르시오.
> ① 가족 여행을 가야 해서 가족 여행은 언급되지 않았음
> ② 결혼식에 참석해야 해서 I'm going to my cousin's wedding
> ③ 축제 행사를 진행해야 해서 행사 진행은 언급되지 않았음
> ④ 학교 과제를 제출해야 해서 학교 과제는 이미 마쳤음
> ⑤ 아르바이트 면접을 봐야 해서 주말에는 아르바이트를 쉰다고 했음

왜 정답? ✿❀❀ [정답률 93%]

여자는 토요일에 학교 영화제가 있다고 하며 남자에게 올 것인지 물어봤는데, 남자는 사촌 결혼식에 가야 한다고 했다. 따라서 정답은 ②이다.

왜 오답?

① 사촌 결혼식 장소까지 왕복하는 데 오래 걸린다고 했을 뿐, 가족 여행은 언급되지 않았다. 주의
③ 행사 진행은 언급되지 않았다.
④ 학교 과제는 이미 마쳤다고 했다.
⑤ 주말에는 아르바이트를 쉰다고 했으며, 면접은 언급되지 않았다.

08 정답 ④ ＊Topas Beachcombing 활동

M : Hey, Emma, what are you reading?
남 : 안녕, Emma. 뭐 읽고 있어?

W : Hi. I'm reading a post about the Topas Beachcombing activity.
여 : 안녕. Topas Beachcombing 활동에 관한 글을 읽고 있어.

M : What is that? I've never **heard** of it.
　현재완료 (경험)
남 : 그게 뭐야? 난 들어본 적이 없어.

W : It's an activity **where** you go along the beach and collect
　　　　　관계부사
garbage and make **something useful or creative** with it.
-thing으로 끝나는 대명사는 형용사가 뒤에서 수식함
여 : 해변을 따라 걸으면서 쓰레기를 줍고, 그것으로 유용하거나 창의적인 것을 만드는 활동이야.

M : Great! When is it?
남 : 멋진데! 언제 하는데?

W : This Saturday, the 25th of September, at 10 a.m. on Sunset Beach. ❶의 단서 날짜
여 : 이번 토요일, 9월 25일 오전 10시에 Sunset 해변에서 해.
　전치사 (~에서 가까이)

M : Oh, it's **near** my house. How can I join the activity?
남 : 오, 우리 집 근처네. 어떻게 참여할 수 있어?

W : You can sign up on their website. ❷의 단서 등록 방법
여 : 그들의 웹사이트에서 신청할 수 있어.
　부정대명사

M : Do I need to bring **anything**?
남 : 무언가를 가져가야 하니?

W : Yes, we'll need gloves and a bag for the garbage. ❸의 단서 준비물
여 : 응, 장갑이랑 쓰레기를 담을 봉지가 필요해.

M : No problem. Is there a participation fee?
남 : 문제없어. 참가비는 있어?

W : No, it's free. ❺의 단서 참가비
여 : 아니, 무료야.

M : Perfect! It sounds meaningful and fun.
남 : 완벽하네! 의미 있고 재미있을 것 같아.

- garbage ⓝ 쓰레기　• creative ⓐ 창의적인　• sign up 신청하다
- participation fee 참가비　• meaningful ⓐ 의미 있는

대화를 듣고, Topas Beachcombing에 관해 언급되지 **않은** 것을 고르시오.
① 날짜 the 25th of September
② 등록 방법 You can sign up on their website.
③ 준비물 gloves and a bag for the garbage
④ 참가 인원 언급되지 않음
⑤ 참가비 it's free

왜 정답? ✲✿✿ [정답률 96%]
Topas Beachcombing에 대해 말하면서 날짜, 등록 방법, 준비물, 참가비는 언급했지만 참가 인원은 언급하지 않았으므로 정답은 ④이다.

왜 오답?
① 날짜는 9월 25일이다. (the 25th of September)
② 등록은 웹사이트를 통해서 하면 된다. (You can sign up on their website.)
③ 장갑과 쓰레기를 담을 봉지를 준비해야 한다. (gloves and a bag for the garbage)
⑤ 참가비는 따로 없다. (it's free)

09 정답 ④ ＊VR (Virtual Reality) 체험 행사 안내

M : Hello, everyone!
남 : 여러분, 안녕하세요!

I'm excited to tell you about the Time Travel VR Experience
앞에 주격 관계대명사와 be동사가 생략됨
happening at the Natural History Museum.
제가 자연사 박물관에서 열리는 시간 여행 VR 체험을 소개하게 되어 기쁩니다.
　　　　let의 목적어와 목적격 보어 (원형부정사)
This event will let **you experience** the Stone Age of Korea in
an amazing way using virtual reality. ❶의 단서 VR을 통한 한국 석기 시대 경험
이 행사는 가상현실을 사용하는 놀라운 방식으로 한국의 구석기 시대를 체험할 수 있게 해줄 것입니다.

It will run for the whole month of September 2025 in the
Asian Gallery on the second floor. ❷의 단서 9월 한 달간 진행되는 체험 활동
행사는 2025년 9월 한 달 내내 2층 아시아관에서 진행됩니다.

With a VR headset, you'll **travel** back in time to see how
　　　　　　　　　　└ 병렬 구조 (문장의 동사) ┐
people lived in the Stone Age of Korea and **learn** about their
daily life.
VR 헤드셋을 착용하면, 시간을 거슬러 가서 한국 구석기 시대 사람들이 어떻게 살았는지를 보고 그들의 일상생활을 배울 수 있습니다.

For children, there will also be a fun and interactive VR
section. ❸의 단서 어린이를 위한 VR 체험 구역
어린이들을 위해, 재미있고 상호작용할 수 있는 VR 구역도 마련되어 있습니다.
　　　　　　　　　　　　　　　　'~한 사람들'
Expert guides will be available only for **those who** made a
reservation in advance online. ❹의 단서 전문가 가이드는 온라인 사전 예약이 필요함
전문가 가이드는 온라인으로 사전 예약한 분들만 이용하실 수 있습니다.

There is no entrance fee and you can enjoy all the activities
free of charge. ❺의 단서 입장료는 무료
입장료는 없으며 모든 활동을 무료로 즐기실 수 있습니다.

- virtual reality 가상현실　• interactive ⓐ 상호작용하는
- available ⓐ 이용 가능한　• free of charge 무료로

Time Travel VR Experience에 관한 다음 내용을 듣고, 일치하지 **않는** 것을 고르시오.
① VR을 통해 한국 석기 시대를 경험한다. experience the Stone Age of Korea ~ using virtual reality
② 9월 한 달간 진행된다. the whole month of September
③ 어린이를 위한 VR 체험 구역이 있다. For children, ~ interactive VR section.
④ 전문가 가이드를 현장에서 신청할 수 있다. Expert guides ~ only for those who made a reservation in advance online.
⑤ 입장료는 무료이다. There is no entrance fee

왜 정답? ✲✿✿ [정답률 89%]
전문가 가이드는 온라인으로 사전 예약한 분들만 이용할 수 있다고 했으므로 (Expert guides ~ only for those who made a reservation in advance online.) 일치하지 않는 것은 ④이다.

왜 오답?
① VR을 통해 한국 석기 시대를 경험한다. (experience the Stone Age of Korea ~ using virtual reality)
② 9월 한 달간 진행된다. (the whole month of September)
③ 어린이를 위한 VR 체험 구역이 있다. (For children, ~ interactive VR section.)
⑤ 입장료는 무료이다. (There is no entrance fee)

W : Hey, John. What are you looking at?
여 : 안녕, John. 뭐 보고 있어?

> *앞에 목적어철 접속사 that이 생략됨*

M : You know I'm planning to travel abroad, so I'm checking
out smart backpacks. Want to help me pick one?

> *앞에 Do you가 생략됨*

남 : 알다시피 나 해외여행 가려고 계획 중이잖아, 그래서 스마트 배낭을 알아보고 있어. 하나 고르는 걸 도와줄래?

W : Sure, let me see. [Pause] The prices are different.
여 : 좋아, 보자. [잠시 후] 가격이 다 다르네.

M : Yeah, but I don't want to spend more than 100 dollars.
남 : 응, 근데 100달러 넘게 쓰고 싶지 않아. **단서 1** 100달러 미만이어야 함 (⑤ 제외)

W : Got it. Let's check the size.
여 : 알겠어. 크기를 확인해 보자. **단서 2** 15인치 이상이어야 함 (① 제외)

M : I usually carry a laptop, so it should be at least 15 inches.
남 : 나는 보통 노트북을 들고 다니니까, 최소한 15인치는 되어야 해.

W : There's also an option with a safety feature. Do you need that?

> *= option with a safety feature*

여 : 안전 기능 옵션도 있네. 그게 필요할까?

> *부사절에서 「주어+be동사」 생략*

M : Definitely. It will help keep my belongings safe while traveling. That narrows it down to just two models.
남 : 당연하지. 여행할 때 내 물건을 안전하게 지키는 데 도움이 될 거야. 그럼 이제 두 모델로 좁혀지네. **단서 3** 안전 기능이 있어야 함 (④ 제외)

W : Now, how about a charging port? I think an external port would be more convenient.
여 : 자, 충전 포트는 어때? 난 외부 포트가 더 편리할 것 같아.

M : Sounds great. I'll pick the one with an external port. I'll order it right now. **단서 4** 외부 충전 포트가 있는 것 (③ 제외)
남 : 좋은데. 외부 포트가 있는 걸로 고를게. 지금 바로 이걸 주문해야겠다.

- **belonging** ⓝ 소지품
- **narrow down** 좁히다
- **charging port** 충전 포트
- **external** ⓐ 외부의
- **internal** ⓐ 내부의

다음 표를 보면서 대화를 듣고, 남자가 주문할 스마트 배낭을 고르시오.

Smart Backpacks 스마트 배낭

15인치 이상이어야 함

	Model 제품	Price 가격	Size 크기	Safety Feature 안전 기능	Charging Port 충전 포트
①	A	$75	13 inches	×	Internal 내부
②	B	$85	15 inches	○	External 외부
③	C	$90	16 inches	○	Internal
④	D	$95	16 inches	× 안전 기능이 있어야 함	External
⑤	E	$110	17 inches	○	External

100달러 미만이어야 함   외부 충전 포트가 있어야 함

왜 정답? ✿✿✿ [정답률 93%]

가격이 100달러 미만이고 (⑤ 제외), 크기가 15인치 이상이며 (① 제외) 안전 기능이 있는 것 중 (④ 제외) 외부 충전 포트가 있는 것을 주문하겠다고 했으므로 (③ 제외) 정답은 ②이다.

왜 오답?

① 크기가 15인치 이상이어야 한다. (it should be at least 15 inches)
③ 외부 충전 포트가 있는 것을 골랐다. (I'll pick the one with an external port.)
④ 안전 기능이 있어야 한다고 했다. (Definitely. It will ~ safe while traveling.)
⑤ 100달러 넘게 쓰고 싶지 않다고 했다. (I don't want to spend more than 100 dollars)

[Cell phone rings.]
[휴대 전화가 울린다.]

> *현재진행시제*

M : Hey, Daisy. It's Jacob. Are you almost here? I'm waiting on the street near my house.
남 : 안녕, Daisy. Jacob이야. 거의 다 왔어? 나 집 근처 길가에서 기다리고 있어.

W : Sorry, Jacob. I had a problem with my car tire. Can you wait a bit more? **단서 1** 타이어에 문제가 있어서 수리가 필요함
여 : 미안, Jacob. 차 타이어에 문제가 있었어. 조금만 더 기다릴 수 있어?

M : Sure. Did you call someone to fix it?
남 : 물론이지. 그걸 고칠 누군가를 불렀니? **단서 2** 타이어를 고칠 사람을 불렀는지 물어봄

W : **Yes, the repairman is on the way with a spare tire.**
여 : 응, 수리공이 예비 타이어를 가지고 오는 중이야.

- **repairman** ⓝ 수리공
- **spare** ⓐ 여분의
- **fill up** ~을 가득 채우다
- **entrance** ⓝ 입구
- **in time** 제시간에

대화를 듣고, 남자의 마지막 말에 대한 여자의 응답으로 가장 적절한 것을 고르시오. 남자는 여자에게 타이어를 고칠 누군가를 불렀는지 물어봄

① Yes, the repairman is on the way with a spare tire.
  응, 수리공이 예비 타이어를 가지고 오는 중이야.
② Of course, I filled up the tank at the gas station. 기름이 부족한 상황이 아님
  물론, 주유소에서 기름을 가득 채웠어.
③ No, I can't find the entrance to the building. 타이어 문제 때문에 늦은 상황임
  아니, 건물 입구를 찾을 수가 없어.
④ Don't worry. You can use my tire. 여자의 차 타이어에 문제가 있는 상황임
  걱정하지 마. 내 타이어를 써도 돼.
⑤ I did. I got here just in time. 약속에 늦은 상황임
  했어. 막 제시간에 도착했어.

왜 정답? ✿✿✿ [정답률 89%]

여자의 차 타이어에 문제가 있어서 남자는 그것을 고칠 누군가를 불렀는지 물어봤다. 따라서 여자의 응답으로 가장 적절한 것은 ① '응, 수리공이 예비 타이어를 가지고 오는 중이야.'이다.

왜 오답?

② 기름이 부족한 것은 언급되지 않았다.
③ 길을 잃은 것이 아니라 타이어에 문제가 생겨서 약속에 늦는 상황이다.
④ 여자의 타이어에 문제가 생겼으므로 여자가 '내 타이어를 써도 된다'라는 것은 어색하다.
⑤ 타이어에 문제가 생겨 약속 장소에 아직 도착하지 못한 상황이다.

W : Danny, do you prefer watching movies at home or going to the theater?
여 : Danny, 너는 집에서 영화 보는 걸 좋아해, 아니면 영화관에 가는 걸 좋아해?

M : I sometimes go to the theater with friends, but I watch most movies at home.
남 : 난 가끔 친구들이랑 영화관에 가는데, 대부분의 영화는 집에서 봐.

> *앞의 말에 대한 동의를 나타냄*

W : **So do I.** Home is more comfortable because I don't need to follow the theater's schedule. **단서** 집에서는 시간표를 따르지 않고도 영화를 볼 수 있음
여 : 나도 그래. 영화관의 시간표를 따를 필요가 없어서 집이 더 편해.

M : **Exactly! At home you can watch movies whenever you want.**
남 : 맞아! 집에서는 원하는 때에 언제든 영화를 볼 수 있지.

- **prefer** ⓥ 선호하다
- **comfortable** ⓐ 편안한
- **effect** ⓝ 효과
- **set up** 설치하다

대화를 듣고, 여자의 마지막 말에 대한 남자의 응답으로 가장 적절한 것을 고르시오.

① That effect in the theater makes your experience special.
영화관에서의 그 효과가 관람 경험을 특별하게 해. 영화관의 효과는 언급되지 않았음
② I prefer to follow the fixed time schedule at work.
나는 직장에서 정해진 시간표를 따르는 것을 선호해. 직장은 언급되지 않았음
③ Right, the theater has set up comfortable chairs.
맞아, 그 영화관은 편안한 의자를 설치해 두었어. 영화관의 시설에 관한 대화가 아님
④ Really? I haven't watched movies with friends at home.
정말? 나는 집에서 친구들과 함께 영화를 본 적이 없어. 친구들과 가끔 영화를 보러 간다고 했음
⑤ Exactly! At home you can watch movies whenever you want. 영화관과는 다르게 집에서는 언제든지 영화를 볼 수 있음
맞아! 집에서는 원하는 때에 언제든 영화를 볼 수 있지.

> 왜 정답 ? ✷✷❀ [정답률 70%]

남자가 대부분의 영화를 집에서 본다고 했고, 여자가 집에서는 영화관처럼 시간표를 따를 필요가 없어서 편하다고 했다. 따라서 남자는 이 말에 동의하며 ⑤ '맞아! 집에서는 원하는 때에 언제든 영화를 볼 수 있지.'라고 응답하는 것이 가장 적절하다.

> 왜 오답 ?

① 영화관의 효과는 언급되지 않았다.
② 영화관의 시간표가 언급되었을 뿐, 직장은 언급되지 않았다.
③ 영화관의 시설에 관한 대화가 아니다.
④ 남자는 친구들과 가끔 영화관에 간다고 했으며, 집에서 영화를 보는 장점에 관한 응답으로 어울리지 않는다.

---

13 정답 ① ✻ 과목 선택 상담

M : Hello, Ms. Taylor.
남 : 안녕하세요, Taylor 선생님.

W : Hi, Luke. What brings you in my office?
여 : 안녕, Luke. 무슨 일로 내 사무실에 왔니?

M : I'm not sure about **which** courses **to pick** for next year. I'm thinking of **taking** the same courses as my friend, Henry.
전치사 about의 목적어 (의문사 + to부정사) 전치사 of의 목적어 (동명사)
남 : 내년을 위해 어떤 과목을 선택해야 할지 잘 모르겠어요. 제 친구 Henry랑 같은 과목을 들을까 생각 중이에요

W : I understand **why you feel that way**. However, **it**'s not a good idea **to** just **follow** your friend without considering what's best for you.
understand의 목적어 (간접의문문) 가주어 진주어 (to부정사)
여 : 너가 왜 그렇게 느끼는지는 이해해. 그런데, 무엇이 네게 가장 좋은지 고려하지 않고 단순히 친구를 따라가는 건 좋은 생각이 아니야.

M : But, I don't even know **where to begin**. Can you give me some guidance?
know의 목적어 (의문사 + to부정사)
남 : 하지만 어디서부터 시작해야 할지조차 모르겠어요. 지도를 해주실 수 있나요?

W : What do you **enjoy doing**? 단서1 자신이 좋아하는 것을 알아야 함
여 : 네가 좋아하는 일이 뭐니?
enjoy[like] -ing: ~하는 것을 좋아하다

M : Umm. I guess I **like creating** video clips.
남 : 음. 동영상을 만드는 걸 좋아하는 것 같아요.

W : That is the starting point. You can choose courses related to that. 단서2 자신이 좋아하는 것과 관련된 과목을 선택하도록 조언함
여 : 그게 시작점이야. 그것과 관련된 과목을 선택할 수 있지. 단서3 남자는 자신에게 맞는 과목을 찾는 것을 도와달라고 함

M : Ah! I see. Could you help me find courses that fit me?
남 : 아! 알겠어요. 제게 맞는 과목을 찾는 것을 도와주실 수 있나요?

W : **Sure. I'll recommend a list of courses you might like.**
여 : 물론이지. 네가 좋아할 만한 과목 목록을 추천해 줄게.

- consider ⓥ 고려하다   - guidance ⓝ 안내, 지도
- score ⓥ 성적을 받다   - make up with ~와 화해하다

대화를 듣고, 남자의 마지막 말에 대한 여자의 응답으로 가장 적절한 것을 고르시오. [3점]

Woman: _____
남자는 자신에게 맞는 과목을 찾을 수 있도록 도움을 요청했음
① Sure. I'll recommend a list of courses you might like.
물론이지. 네가 좋아할 만한 과목 목록을 추천해 줄게.
② Okay. Choose a course you think you'll score well in.
알았어. 네가 성적을 잘 받을 것 같은 과목을 선택해라. 관심사를 기준으로 과목을 선택하라고 조언함
③ Cheer up! You'll make up with Henry soon.
힘내! 너는 곧 Henry와 화해할 거야. Henry와 사이가 나쁜 상황이 아님
④ Well, the time to choose courses is over.
음, 과목을 선택할 시간은 끝났어. 내년에 들을 과목을 고민하는 중임
⑤ No worries. I think you did your best! 무언가 마무리된 상황이 아님
걱정하지 마. 나는 네가 최선을 다했다고 생각해!

> 왜 정답 ? ✷❀❀ [정답률 88%]

내년에 어떤 수업을 들어야 할지 고민하는 남자가 단순히 친구와 같은 과목을 들으려 하자, 여자는 스스로가 좋아하는 것을 찾아서 그것과 관련된 과목을 골라야 한다고 조언하는 내용이다. 남자가 자신에게 맞는 과목을 찾는 것을 도와줄 수 있는지 여자에게 물어봤으므로 여자의 응답으로 가장 적절한 것은 ① '물론이지. 네가 좋아할 만한 과목 목록을 추천해 줄게.'이다.

> 왜 오답 ?

② 여자는 성적을 잘 받을 수 있는지가 아니라, 좋아하는 것을 기준으로 과목을 선택해야 한다고 조언했다.
③ Henry와 같은 과목을 들을지 생각 중이라고 했을 뿐, 현재 둘 사이가 나쁘다는 것은 언급되지 않았다.
④ 내년에 들을 과목을 고민한다고 했을 뿐, 과목 선택 기한은 언급되지 않았다.
⑤ 성적이 발표되거나 과목 선택을 마친 것처럼 무언가 마무리된 상황이 아니다.

---

14 정답 ① ✻ 절약 챌린지

W : Kevin, what are you writing about? 여 : Kevin, 뭐 쓰고 있어?
앞에 목적격 관계대명사가 생략됨
M : Hi, Eva. I'm writing about the money-saving challenge **I completed**.
남 : 안녕, Eva. 내가 완수한 절약 챌린지에 대해 쓰고 있어.

W : The money-saving challenge? What's that?
여 : 절약 챌린지? 그게 뭐야?

M : It's a challenge **where** you try to reduce your spending and do not buy unnecessary things for a set time. I did **it** for a month.
관계부사 (= in which) = a challenge
남 : 정해진 시간 동안 지출을 줄이고 불필요한 물건을 사지 않는 챌린지야. 나는 한 달 동안 했어.

W : Really? Wasn't it so hard? 여 : 정말? 엄청 힘들지 않았어?

M : Not that much. I spent money on things **I really needed**.
앞에 목적격 관계대명사가 생략됨
남 : 그렇게 힘들진 않았어. 꼭 필요한 것에만 돈을 썼거든.

W : Why did you decide **to do** that?
명사적 용법 (decide의 목적어)
여 : 왜 그런 걸 하기로 한 거야?

M : At first, it was just to save money. But it also made me realize **that** I have wasted money on too many extra things.
목적어절 접속사
남 : 처음엔 단순히 돈을 아끼기 위해서였어. 그런데 그건 내가 불필요한 것들에 돈을 너무 많이 낭비했다는 걸 깨닫게 하기도 해.

W : Oh, I see. So it's about **cutting** out unnecessary spending?
동명사 (전치사 about의 목적어)
여 : 아, 그렇구나. 그러니까 불필요한 지출을 줄이는 거네?

M : Exactly. And I found free ways to have fun. For example, cooking more at home, instead of eating out!
남 : 맞아. 그리고 돈을 쓰지 않고도 즐거움을 누리는 방법을 찾았어. 예를 들어 외식 대신 집에서 요리를 더 하는 거지!

W : That sounds difficult but rewarding. I'll do the same!
여 : 어렵지만 보람은 있겠다. 나도 할래! 단서 여자도 절약 챌린지를 하겠다고 함

M : **Good decision. I'm sure you'll do a good job.**
남 : 좋은 결정이야. 네가 잘 해낼 거라고 확신해.

- challenge ⓝ 도전 · complete ⓥ 완수하다
- unnecessary ⓐ 불필요한 · realize ⓥ 깨닫다
- rewarding ⓐ 보람 있는 · remove ⓥ (어떤 곳에서) 치우다
- stick to ~을 고수하다

대화를 듣고, 여자의 마지막 말에 대한 남자의 응답으로 가장 적절한 것을 고르시오. [3점]

Man: _____

① Good decision. I'm sure you'll do a good job.
좋은 결정이야. 네가 잘 해낼 거라고 확신해.　절약 챌린지를 하겠다는 여자를 응원함
② Yes. Let's remove the kitchen table for more space.
맞아. 더 많은 공간을 위해 부엌 식탁을 치우자.　공간을 넓히는 것은 언급되지 않았음
③ I don't think so. I could never do something like that.
글쎄. 나는 절대 그런 건 못했을 거야.　남자는 이미 절약 챌린지를 마쳤음
④ Exactly. You'd rather work harder to earn more money.
맞아. 차라리 더 열심히 일해서 돈을 더 벌어야.　돈을 더 벌어야 한다는 것은 언급되지 않았음
⑤ No way. You should stick to your usual spending habits. 소비 습관을 지키는 것은 무관함
안 돼. 네 평소 소비 습관을 지켜야 해.

> **왜 정답?** ✽✽❀ [정답률 84%]

남자가 낭비를 줄이는 절약 챌린지를 마쳤다고 했으며 여자도 절약 챌린지를 하겠다고 했다. 따라서 남자의 응답으로 가장 적절한 것은 ① '좋은 결정이야. 네가 잘 해낼 거라고 확신해.'이다.

> **왜 오답?**

② 공간을 넓히는 것은 언급되지 않았다.
③ 남자는 이미 절약 챌린지를 마쳤다.
④ 낭비를 줄이는 것에 관한 내용이지, 돈을 더 벌어야 한다는 것은 언급되지 않았다.
⑤ 일정 기간 동안 낭비하는 소비 습관을 바꾸는 챌린지이므로 평소 소비 습관을 지키는 것과는 무관하다.

---

15 정답 ① ＊미니 오븐 빌리기

M : Liam and Sophia are college students and friends.
남 : Liam과 Sophia는 대학생이자 친구이다.

Liam recently learned **how to bake** cookies in a cooking
class and wants to practice the recipe at home.
learned의 목적어 (의문사 + to부정사)
Liam은 최근 요리 수업에서 쿠키 굽는 법을 배웠고 집에서 그 요리법을 연습하고 싶어 한다.

However, he doesn't have a mini oven, and he cannot afford
to buy one right now.
그러나, 그는 미니 오븐이 없고, 지금 당장 하나를 살 형편이 되지 않는다.

He remembers that Sophia **has** a mini oven at home and
often **brings** freshly **baked** cookies to class.
병렬 구조 / 과거분사 (cookies 수식)
그는 Sophia가 집에 미니 오븐을 가지고 있고 갓 구운 쿠키를 종종 수업에 가져오는 것을 기억한다.

So, he wants **to ask** her if she can lend him her mini oven.
명사적 용법 (wants의 목적어)　단서 미니 오븐을 빌리고 싶어 함
그래서, 그는 그녀가 미니 오븐을 그에게 빌려줄 수 있는지 묻고 싶어 한다.

In this situation, what would Liam most likely say to
Sophia?
이 상황에서, Liam이 Sophia에게 할 말로 가장 적절한 것은 무엇인가?

Liam: Can I borrow your mini oven to practice baking cookies?
Liam: 내가 쿠키를 굽는 연습을 할 수 있도록 네 미니 오븐을 빌릴 수 있을까?

> ＊상황 요약: Liam이 Sophia에게 미니 오븐을 빌릴 수 있는지 물어보려는 상황

- recently ⓐⓓ 최근에 · recipe ⓝ 요리법
- afford ⓥ 지불할 능력이 있다 · freshly ⓐⓓ 갓 ~한

다음 상황 설명을 듣고, Liam이 Sophia에게 할 말로 가장 적절한 것을 고르시오.

Liam: _____

① Can I borrow your mini oven to practice baking cookies?
Sophia에게 미니 오븐을 빌릴 수 있는지 물어보려고
내가 쿠키를 굽는 연습을 할 수 있도록 네 미니 오븐을 빌릴 수 있을까?
② Are you using the recipe for cookies that I gave you? Liam이
내가 너한테 준 쿠키 요리법을 쓰고 있니?　Sophia에게 요리법을 알려주었는지는 알 수 없음
③ Do you want to learn how to bake cookies together?
쿠키 굽는 법을 같이 배워보고 싶니?　Sophia는 이미 쿠키를 구울 수 있음
④ Where will you buy a mini oven to use at home?
집에서 쓸 미니 오븐을 어디에서 살 거야?　Sophia는 이미 미니 오븐을 갖고 있음
⑤ How do you make your cookies taste so good?
너는 어떻게 쿠키를 그렇게 맛있게 만들 수 있니?　쿠키 요리법을 묻는 상황이 아님

> **왜 정답?** ✽✽❀ [정답률 86%]

Liam은 쿠키 굽는 연습을 하고 싶지만 오븐을 살 수 있는 형편이 아니다. 친구인 Sophia는 미니 오븐을 가지고 있기 때문에 그것을 빌려서 쿠키를 굽고 싶어 한다. 따라서 Liam이 Sophia에게 할 말로 가장 적절한 것은 ① '내가 쿠키를 굽는 연습을 할 수 있도록 네 미니 오븐을 빌릴 수 있을까?'이다.

> **왜 오답?**

② Liam이 Sophia에게 요리법을 알려주었는지는 알 수 없다.
③ Sophia는 이미 쿠키를 구울 수 있다.
④ Sophia는 이미 미니 오븐을 갖고 있다.
⑤ Sophia에게 쿠키 요리법을 묻는 상황이 아니다.

16~17 ＊야생동물 관찰을 위한 필수 준비물

W : Hello, nature lovers! //
여 : 안녕하세요, 자연을 사랑하는 여러분! //

부사절 접속사 (조건)
If you're planning to observe wild animals / on your next
형용사적 용법 (items 수식)
countryside walk, / here are must-have items / **to make** your
experience enjoyable. // 16번 단서: 야생동물 관찰 시 필요한 준비물들을 소개함
야생동물을 관찰할 계획이라면 / 다음 시골 산책에서 / 필수 준비물들이 있습니다 / 당신의 경험을 즐겁게 만들어 줄 //

17번① 형용사적 용법 (a notebook 수식)
First, / bring a notebook / **to record** interesting observations
앞에 목적격 관계대명사가 생략됨
/ about the animals **you spot**, / such as their behavior or
appearance. //
첫째 / 공책을 챙기세요 / 흥미로운 관찰을 기록할 / 발견한 동물들의 / 행동이나 외형 같은 //

명사적 용법 (forget의 목적어)
Second, / don't forget **to carry** a camera. // 17번②
둘째 / 카메라를 가져가는 것을 잊지 마세요 //

형용사적 용법 (way 수식)
It's a great way / **to capture** special moments / and **share**
them with others later. //
그것은 좋은 방법입니다 / 특별한 순간들을 포착하고 / 나중에 다른 사람들과 공유할 수 있는 //

17번③ '~의 경우에'
Next, / a raincoat will keep you dry and comfortable / **in
case of** unexpected rain, / **allowing** you to stay focused on
분사구문을 이끄는 현재분사
your adventure. //
다음으로 / 우비는 여러분이 젖지 않고 편안하도록 지켜 주어 / 갑자기 비가 올 경우 / 모험에 집중할 수 있게 해줍니다 //

17번⑤ help의 목적어와 목적격 보어 (원형부정사)
Lastly, / bring a map / to help **you navigate** unfamiliar areas
/ and avoid getting lost. //
마지막으로 / 지도를 챙기세요 / 익숙하지 않은 지역에서 길을 찾고 / 길을 잃는 것을 피하도록 //

목적어절 접속사
Preparing these necessities will ensure / **that** you have a
부사절에서「주어+be동사」 생략
safe and enjoyable experience / **while exploring** the natural
surroundings of wild animals. //
이러한 필수품들을 준비하는 것은 보장할 것입니다 / 안전하고 즐거운 경험을 갖는 것을 / 야생동물이 사는 자연환경을 탐험하면서도 //

- countryside ⓝ 시골
- must-have ⓐ 필수적인
- observation ⓝ 관찰
- spot ⓥ 발견하다
- behavior ⓝ 행동
- appearance ⓝ 외형
- capture ⓥ 포착하다
- adventure ⓝ 모험
- navigate ⓥ 길을 찾다
- necessity ⓝ 필수품
- surroundings ⓝ 환경, 주변
- outdoor ⓐ 야외의
- essential ⓐ 필수적인
- practical ⓐ 실용적인
- wildlife ⓝ 야생동물
- inspire ⓥ 영감을 주다

여: 안녕하세요, 자연을 사랑하는 여러분! 다음 시골 산책에서 야생동물을 관찰할 계획이라면, 당신의 경험을 즐겁게 만들어 줄 필수 준비물들이 있습니다. 첫째, 발견한 동물들의 행동이나 외형 같은 흥미로운 관찰을 기록할 공책을 챙기세요. 둘째, 카메라를 가져가는 것을 잊지 마세요. 그것은 특별한 순간들을 포착하고 나중에 다른 사람들과 공유할 수 있는 좋은 방법입니다. 다음으로, 갑자기 비가 올 경우 우비는 여러분이 젖지 않고 편안하도록 지켜 주어, 모험에 집중할 수 있게 해줍니다. 마지막으로, 익숙하지 않은 지역에서 길을 찾고 길을 잃는 것을 피하도록 지도를 챙기세요. 이러한 필수품들을 준비하는 것은 야생동물이 사는 자연환경을 탐험하면서도 안전하고 즐거운 경험을 갖는 것을 보장할 것입니다.

16 정답 ②

여자가 하는 말의 주제로 가장 적절한 것은?
① tips for using outdoor items for camping 캠핑용 야외용품은 무관함
  캠핑용 야외용품을 사용하기 위한 조언
②essential items for observing wild animals
  야생동물 관찰을 위한 필수품 야생동물 관찰에 필요한 물품을 소개함
③ practical items made from natural surroundings
  자연환경에서 만들어진 실용적인 물품들 자연환경에서 만들어진 것에 대한 내용이 아님
④ costs of upgrading tools for wildlife observation
  야생동물 관찰을 위한 도구 업그레이드 비용 도구 업그레이드 비용은 언급되지 않음
⑤ tools that were inspired by wild animals' behaviors
  야생동물의 행동에서 영감을 받은 도구들 야생동물의 행동으로부터의 영감은 언급되지 않음

> **왜 정답?** ✿✿✿ [정답률 90%]

야생동물 관찰 경험을 즐겁게 만들어 줄 필수 준비물들을 소개하는 내용이다. 따라서 여자가 하는 말의 주제로 가장 적절한 것은 ② '야생동물 관찰을 위한 필수품'이다.

> **왜 오답?**

① 야생동물 관찰을 위한 필수품에 관한 내용이며, 캠핑용 야외용품은 무관하다.
③ 야생동물 관찰을 위한 필수품에 관한 내용이지, 자연환경에서 만들어진 물품에 관한 내용이 아니다.
④ 도구 업그레이드나 그 비용은 언급되지 않았다.
⑤ 야생동물 관찰을 위한 필수품에 관한 내용이지, 야생동물에서 영감을 받은 도구에 관한 내용이 아니다.

17 정답 ④

언급된 물건이 아닌 것은?
① a notebook bring a notebook
  공책
② a camera don't forget to carry a camera
  카메라
③ a raincoat a raincoat will keep you dry and comfortable
  우비
④a flashlight 언급되지 않음
  손전등
⑤ a map bring a map
  지도

> **왜 정답?** ✿✿✿ [정답률 96%]

야생동물 관찰의 필수품으로 공책, 카메라, 우비, 지도에 대해서는 언급했지만, 손전등에 대해서는 언급하지 않았으므로 정답은 ④ '손전등'이다.

> **왜 오답?**

① 동물들을 관찰한 내용을 기록할 공책을 챙기라고 했다.
② 특별한 순간들을 포착하고 공유하기 위해 카메라를 가져가라고 했다.
③ 우비는 갑자기 비가 와도 모험에 집중할 수 있게 해준다고 했다.
⑤ 익숙하지 않은 지역에서 길을 찾을 수 있도록 지도를 챙기라고 했다.

18 정답 ③ ＊도서관 운영 시간 연장 요청

2025. 9
7회

Dear Principal Jones, / Jones 교장 선생님께 /
I hope / this message finds you well. //
저는 바랍니다 / 이 메시지가 당신에게 잘 전달되기를 //
As student council president, / I am reaching out / **to discuss** (부사적 용법 (목적))
an important matter / **regarding** our school library's current ('~에 관하여')
operating hours. //
학생회장으로서 / 저는 연락드립니다 / 중요한 문제를 논의하고자 / 우리 학교 도서관의 현재 운영 시간에 관한 //
At present, / the library closes at 5 p.m., / **which many students** (계속적 용법의 주격 관계대명사) (삽입절)
feel limits their ability / **to fully use** its resources for study and (관계사절의 동사) (형용사적 용법 (ability 수식))
research / after regular class hours. //
현재 / 도서관은 오후 5시에 문을 닫는데 / 이는 많은 학생이 느끼기에 능력을 제한합니다 / 학습과 연구를 위해 도서관 자원을 충분히 사용할 수 있는 / 정규 수업 시간 이후 //
This is particularly challenging for those / **preparing** for college
entrance exams / or **working** on academic projects / **that** demand (병렬 구조) (주격 관계대명사 (선행사: projects))
a quiet and resourceful environment. //
이것은 특히 그들에게 어렵습니다 / 대학 입학 시험을 준비하거나 / 학업 연구과제를 수행하는 / 조용하고 자료가 풍부한 환경을 요하는 //
Therefore, / I'd like to ask **you** / **to extend** the library's operating (ask의 목적어와 목적격 보어 (to부정사))
hours to 7 p.m. // 단서 도서관 운영 시간 연장을 요청함
그러므로 / 저는 당신에게 요청드리고 싶습니다 / 도서관 운영 시간을 오후 7시까지 연장해 주시기를 //
This change would greatly benefit students / **by providing** (by -ing: ~함으로써)
additional time / **to focus** on their academic goals. // (형용사적 용법 (time 수식))
이러한 변화는 학생들에게 크게 이익이 될 것입니다 / 추가시간을 제공함으로써 / 그들의 학업 목표에 집중하기 위한 //
I hope you will consider this proposal / as a step / toward
improving our academic environment / and better supporting
our needs. //
저는 이 제안을 당신이 고려 해주시기를 바랍니다 / 단계로써 / 우리의 학업 환경을 개선하고 / 우리의 필요성을 더 잘 지지해주는 //
Sincerely, / 진심을 담아 /
Eric Park / Student Council President / Eric Park / 학생회장 /

- reach out 연락하다
- current ⓐ 현재의
- operating hour 운영 시간
- resource ⓝ 자원
- entrance ⓝ 입학
- academic ⓐ 학문의, 학업의
- extend ⓥ 연장하다
- proposal ⓝ 제안

Jones 교장 선생님께,
저는 이 메시지가 당신에게 잘 전달되기를 바랍니다. 학생회장으로서 저는 우리 학교 도서관의 현재 운영 시간에 관한 중요한 문제를 논의하고자 연락드립니다. 현재, 도서관은 오후 5시에 문을 닫는데, 이는 많은 학생이 느끼기에, 정규 수업 시간 이후 학습과 연구를 위해 도서관 자원을 충분히 사용할 수 있는 능력을 제한합니다. 이것은 특히 대학 입학 시험을 준비하거나 조용하고 자료가 풍부한 환경을 요하는 학업 연구과제를 수행하는 그들에게 어렵습니다. 그러므로, 저는 도서관 운영 시간을 오후 7시까지 연장해 주시기를 당신에게 요청드리고 싶습니다. 이러한 변화는 그들의 학업 목표에 집중하기 위한 추가시간을 제공함으로써 학생들에게 크게 이익이 될 것입니다. 저는 우리의 학업 환경을 개선하고 우리의 필요성을 더 잘 지지해주는 단계로써 이 제안을 당신이 고려 해주시기를 바랍니다.
진심을 담아, Eric Park 학생회장

다음 글의 목적으로 가장 적절한 것은?
① 신간 도서 구입을 건의하려고 신간 도서 구입은 언급되지 않음
② 도서관 프로그램 확대를 부탁하려고 프로그램 확대는 언급되지 않음
③ 도서관 운영 시간 연장을 요청하려고 도서관 운영 시간을 연장할 것을 요청함
④ 도서 대출 시스템 개선에 감사하려고 도서 대출 시스템은 언급되지 않음
⑤ 도서관 열람실 공간 확대를 제안하려고 공간 확대는 언급되지 않음

왜 정답? ✾✾✾ [정답률 96%]
학업 목표에 집중할 추가시간을 위해 도서관의 운영 시간 연장을 요청하므로 글의 목적은 ③이다.

왜 오답?
① 신간 도서 구입은 언급되지 않았다.
② 도서관 프로그램이 아닌, 운영 시간 연장을 요청하고 있다.
④ 도서 대출 시스템은 언급되지 않았다.
⑤ 열람실 공간 확대는 언급되지 않았다.

19 정답 ③ ＊뮤지컬 배역 오디션 결과

I glanced at the clock / on the wall. //
나는 시계를 흘끗 보았다 / 벽에 있는 //

10:00. // 10시였다 //
뒤에 목적어절 접속사 that이 생략됨
That meant / the casting director would call very soon / with the results of my first audition / for a musical part in The Wizard of Oz. //
그것은 의미했다 / 섭외 감독이 전화할 것이라는 걸 / 나의 첫 번째 오디션 결과로 / '오즈의 마법사' 뮤지컬 배역에 대한 //
병렬 구조 (분사구문)
I felt shaky all over, / chewing my thumbnail and jiggling my feet. // **단서 1** 오디션 결과를 기다리며 긴장함
나는 온몸이 떨렸고 / 엄지손톱을 물어뜯고 발을 흔들어댔다 //

Finally, the telephone rang. // 마침내 전화기가 울렸다 //

While I was coming round, / Dad answered. //
내가 안절부절못하는 사이 / 아빠가 전화를 받았다 //

I heard him say, / "Ahh, thank you. / I'll let her know …" //
나는 그가 말하는 것을 들었다 / "아, 감사합니다. / 그녀에게 알려주겠습니다"라고 //
부사절 접속사 (시간)
As I got to the bottom of the stairs, / he was just putting the phone down. //
내가 계단을 다 내려갔을 때 / 그는 막 전화기를 내려놓고 있었다 //

"That was The Wizard of Oz. // "오즈의 마법사'였어. //

You're second senior munchkin," / he announced. //
너는 둘째 상급 먼치킨이야'라고 / 그가 알려주었다 //
분사구문을 이끄는 현재분사
I got a little rush of excitement, / knowing / I was in /
흥분감이 약간 밀려왔다 / 알게 되어 / 내가 참여한다는 것 / 앞에 목적어절 접속사 that이 생략됨
목적어절(I was in)을 구체적으로 설명
— that whatever happened / I could be involved in one of the productions. // **단서 2** 배역을 따냈다는 소식을 듣고 흥분감이 밀려옴
복합관계대명사 (= no matter what)
즉 어떤 일이 있었더라도 / 내가 작품들 중 하나에 참여할 수 있다는 것을 //

• glance ⓥ 흘끗 보다   • casting director 섭외 감독   • chew ⓥ 씹다
• jiggle ⓥ 가볍게 흔들다   • rush ⓝ 물결   • production ⓝ 작품

나는 벽에 있는 시계를 흘끗 보았다. 10시였다. 그것은 섭외 감독이 '오즈의 마법사' 뮤지컬 배역에 대한 나의 첫 번째 오디션 결과로 전화할 것이라는 걸 의미했다. 나는 온몸이 떨렸고, 엄지손톱을 물어뜯고 발을 흔들어댔다. 마침내 전화기가 울렸다. 내가 안절부절못하는 사이, 아빠가 전화를 받았다. 나는 그가, "아, 감사합니다. 그녀에게 알려주겠습니다 …"라고 말하는 것을 들었다. 내가 계단을 다 내려갔을 때, 그는 막 전화기를 내려놓고 있었다. "'오즈의 마법사'였어. 너는 둘째 상급 먼치킨이야."라고 그가 알려주었다. 내가 참여한다는 것 즉 어떤 일이 있었더라도 내가 작품들 중 하나에 참여할 수 있다는 것을 알게 되어 흥분감이 약간 밀려왔다.

다음 글에 드러난 'I'의 심경 변화로 가장 적절한 것은?
① puzzled → calm 결과를 듣고 침착하지는 않았음
   당황한 → 침착한
② bored → confused 결과를 기다리며 지루하지는 않았음
   지루한 → 혼란스러운
③ nervous → pleased I felt shaky → I got a little rush of excitement
   긴장한 → 기쁜
④ satisfied → regretful 결과를 기다리며 만족하지는 않았음
   만족한 → 후회하는
⑤ confident → disappointed 결과를 기다리며 자신감 있지는 않았음
   자신감 있는 → 실망한

왜 정답? ✾✾✾ [정답률 90%]
전반부: 온몸을 떨며 오디션 결과 전화를 기다림 ▶ '긴장한'
후반부: 뮤지컬에 참여하게 되었다는 소식을 들었음 ▶ '기쁜'
따라서 'I'의 심경 변화로 가장 적절한 것은 ③ '긴장한 → 기쁜'이다.

왜 오답?
① 오디션 결과를 듣고 침착했던 것은 아니다.
② 오디션 결과를 기다리며 지루했던 것은 아니다.
④ 오디션 결과를 기다리며 만족했던 것은 아니다.
⑤ 오디션 결과를 기다리며 자신감 있던 것은 아니다.

20 정답 ② ＊수업 시작의 중요성

Inefficient teachers overlook / the potential power of the opening minutes of class. //
비효율적인 교사들은 간과한다 / 수업 시작 몇 분의 잠재적인 힘을 //
병렬 구조 (부사절 접속사 (조건))
Often, / if students are quiet enough / and if there are many pressing demands / on a teacher's time at that moment, / more than ten minutes can disappear / before class starts. // 문장의 주어
종종 / 학생들이 충분히 조용하고 / 긴급한 요구가 많으면 / 그 순간 교사의 시간에 대한 / 10분 이상이 사라질 수 있다 / 수업이 시작되기 전에 //
가주어   진주어절 접속사   '거의 없는'
It's no wonder / that students are late for class; / they have little reason to be on time. //
놀라운 일이 아니다 / 학생들이 수업에 늦는 것은 / 그들이 제시간에 올 이유가 거의 없다 //
부사적 용법 (목적)   명사적 용법 (choose의 목적어)
You can use the first ten minutes / to get your class off to a great start, / or you can choose to waste this time. //
당신은 첫 10분을 사용하거나 / 훌륭한 시작으로 당신의 수업을 출발시키도록 / 당신은 이 시간을 낭비하도록 선택할 수 있다 //

The first minutes set the tone / for the rest of the class. // **단서 1** 수업 첫 몇 분이 수업의 분위기를 정함
첫 몇 분이 분위기를 설정한다 / 나머지 수업의 //

If you are prepared for class / and have taught your students an opening routine, /
당신이 수업 준비가 되어 있고 / 시작 루틴을 학생들에게 가르쳤다면 /
= your students
they can use this brief time / to make mental and emotional transitions from the last class or subject / and prepare to focus on learning new material. //
병렬 구조 (목적)   명사적 용법 (prepare의 목적어)
그들은 이 짧은 시간을 사용할 수 있다 / 지난 수업 또는 과목으로부터 정신적, 감정적 변화를 만들고 / 새로운 자료를 배우는 것에 집중하려고 준비하기 위해 //

In summary, / you should establish an opening routine / to develop your class with an effective start. // **단서 2** 효과적인 수업을 위해 수업 시작 루틴을 마련해야 함
요약하자면 / 시작 루틴을 마련해야 한다 / 효과적인 출발로 수업을 전개하기 위한 //

• inefficient ⓐ 비효율적인   • overlook ⓥ 간과하다
• potential ⓐ 잠재적인   • demand ⓝ 요구
• disappear ⓥ 사라지다
• get ~ off to a great start ~을 순조롭게 시작하다
• set the tone 분위기를 잡다   • brief ⓐ 짧은
• transition ⓝ 변화   • material ⓝ 자료
• establish ⓥ 설립하다, 마련하다

비효율적인 교사들은 수업 시작 몇 분의 잠재적인 힘을 간과한다. 종종, 학생들이 충분히 조용하고 그 순간 교사의 시간에 대한 긴급한 요구가 많으면, 수업이 시작되기 전에 10분 이상이 사라질 수 있다. 학생들이 수업에 늦는 것은 놀라운 일이 아니다. 그들이 제시간에 올 이유가 거의 없다. 당신은 훌륭한 시작으로 당신의 수업을 출발시키도록 첫 10분을 사용하거나 당신은 이 시간을 낭비하도록 선택할 수 있다. 첫 몇 분이 나머지 수업의 분위기를 설정한다. 당신이 수업 준비가 되어 있고 시작 루틴을 학생들에게 가르쳤다면, 그들은 지난 수업 또는 과목으로부터 정신적, 감정적 변화를 만들고 새로운 자료를 배우는 것에 집중하려고 준비하기 위해 이 짧은 시간을 사용할 수 있다. 요약하자면, 효과적인 출발로 수업을 전개하기 위한 시작 루틴을 마련해야 한다.

다음 글에서 필자가 주장하는 바로 가장 적절한 것은?

① 학생의 적극적인 참여를 위해 포용적 수업 분위기를 형성하라.
　　　　　포용적 수업 분위기 형성에 관한 내용이 아님
② 수업을 효과적으로 전개하기 위해 시작 루틴을 마련하라.
　　　　　시작 루틴을 통해 수업을 효과적으로 시작할 수 있음
③ 학습 동기를 부여할 수 있는 창의적인 수업 자료를 개발하라.
　　　　　창의적 수업 자료 개발에 관한 내용이 아님
④ 적절한 학습량 조절을 통해 학습 부담을 줄여라. 학습 부담은 언급되지 않았음
⑤ 학생이 스스로 학습 루틴을 만들도록 장려하라.
　　　　　학생의 학습 루틴에 관한 내용이 아님

왜 정답? ✸✸✸ [정답률 94%]

수업의 첫 몇 분이 가진 잠재력을 이해하고 수업 시작 루틴을 마련한다면 수업의 효율성이 높아진다는 내용이므로 정답은 ②이다.

왜 오답?

① 첫 몇 분이 나머지 수업의 분위기를 조성한다고 했을 뿐, 포용적 수업 분위기를 형성하라는 내용이 아니다.
③ 학생들의 새로운 자료 학습이 언급되었을 뿐, 창의적 수업 자료를 개발하라는 내용이 아니다.
④ 학습 부담은 언급되지 않았다.
⑤ 교사들이 수업 시작 루틴을 마련해야 한다고 했을 뿐, 학생이 스스로 학습 루틴을 만들어야 한다는 내용이 아니다.

---

21 정답 ① ✷ 원자의 끊임없는 순환

as 형용사/부사 원급 as …: …만큼이나 ~한
Many atoms in your body / are nearly **as** old **as** the universe itself. //
당신의 몸에 있는 많은 원자는 / 거의 우주 자체만큼이나 오래되었다 //

목적격 관계대명사
When you breathe, / for example, / only some of the atoms **that** you inhale / are exhaled / in your next breath. //
당신이 숨을 쉴 때 / 예를 들어 / 당신이 들이마신 원자 중 일부만이 / 내뱉어진다 / 당신의 다음 숨에서 //

부사적 용법 (결과)
The remaining atoms are taken into your body / **to become** part of you, / and they later leave your body / by various means. //
남아있는 원자는 당신의 몸으로 들어가 / 당신의 일부가 되고 / 이후 그것들은 당신의 몸을 떠난다 / 다양한 방법으로 //
[단서 1] 원자는 몸에 들어온 이후에 떠남

주격 관계대명사
You don't "own" the atoms / **that** make up your body; / you borrow **them**. //
= the atoms
당신은 원자를 '소유'하지 않는다 / 당신의 몸을 구성하는 / 당신은 그것들을 빌린다 //

We all share from the same atom pool / because atoms forever
병렬 구조 (전치사)
travel **around**, **within**, and **among** us. //
우리 모두는 같은 원자풀로부터 공유한다 / 원자는 영원히 우리 주변과 내부, 그리고 우리 사이를 이동하기 때문에 //

병렬 구조 (as가 이끄는 부사절)
Atoms cycle from person to person / **as we breathe** and **as our sweat is evaporated**. //
[단서 2] 원자는 사람들 사이를 순환함
원자는 사람에서 사람으로 순환한다 / 우리가 숨을 쉬고 땀이 증발하면서 //

We recycle atoms on a grand scale. //
우리는 거대한 규모로 원자를 재순환시킨다 //

The origin of the lightest atoms goes back / to the origin of the universe, / and most heavier atoms are older than the Sun and Earth. //
가장 가벼운 원자의 기원은 거슬러 올라가며 / 우주의 기원으로 / 대부분의 더 무거운 원자는 태양과 지구보다 오래되었다 //

주격 관계대명사
There are atoms in your body / **that** have existed since the first moments of time, /
당신의 몸에 원자가 있으며 / 태초부터 존재해 온 /
분사구문을 이끄는 현재분사
recycling throughout the universe / among limitless forms, both nonliving and living. // [단서 3] 원자는 다양한 형태로 재순환하며 우주에 존재함
우주 전체에 걸쳐 재순환한다 / 제한 없는 형태, 즉 비생물체와 생물체 가운데 //

You're the present caretaker / of the atoms in your body. //
당신은 현재 관리인이다 / 몸속 원자의 // [단서 4] 현재의 관리인에게서 떠나 다른 관리인으로 옮겨갈 것임
대명사 (많은 것[사람])
There will be **many** / who will follow you. //
많은 것[사람]들이 있을 것이다 / 당신의 뒤를 이을 //

- atom ⓝ 원자
- inhale ⓥ 흡입하다
- exhale ⓥ 내뱉다
- means ⓝ 수단, 방법
- make up ~을 구성하다
- cycle ⓥ 순환하다
- sweat ⓝ 땀
- grand ⓐ 거대한
- scale ⓝ 규모
- limitless ⓐ 제한 없는
- caretaker ⓝ 관리인

당신의 몸에 있는 많은 원자는 거의 우주 자체만큼이나 오래되었다. 당신이 숨을 쉴 때, 예를 들어, 당신이 들이마신 원자 중 일부만이 당신의 다음 숨에서 내뱉어진다. 남아있는 원자는 당신의 몸으로 들어가 당신의 일부가 되고, 이후 그것들은 다양한 방법으로 당신의 몸을 떠난다. 당신은 당신의 몸을 구성하는 원자를 '소유'하지 않는다. 당신은 그것들을 빌린다. 원자는 영원히 우리 주변과 내부, 그리고 우리 사이를 이동하기 때문에 우리 모두는 같은 원자풀로부터 공유한다. 원자는 우리가 숨을 쉬고 땀이 증발하면서 사람에서 사람으로 순환한다. 우리는 거대한 규모로 원자를 재순환시킨다. 가장 가벼운 원자의 기원은 우주의 기원으로 거슬러 올라가며, 대부분의 더 무거운 원자는 태양과 지구보다 오래되었다. 태초부터 존재해 온 원자가 당신의 몸에 있으며 제한 없는 형태, 즉 비생물체와 생물체 가운데 우주 전체에 걸쳐 재순환한다. 당신은 몸속 원자의 현재 관리인이다. 당신의 뒤를 이을 많은 것[사람]들이 있을 것이다.

밑줄 친 There will be many who will follow you가 다음 글에서 의미하는 바로 가장 적절한 것은?
원자들은 순환하며 또 다른 형태 속에 존재하게 될 것임

① Atoms will become part of other forms after you
　원자들은 당신 이후의 다른 형태의 일부가 될 것이다
② Atoms will remain unique and cannot be shared
　원자들은 고유한 상태로 남을 것이며 공유될 수 없다　원자들은 남아 있지 않고 순환하며 공유됨
③ Atoms will follow their original forms
　원자들은 원래 형태를 따를 것이다　원자들은 원래 형태를 따르지 않고 끊임없이 형태를 바꿈
④ Atoms will never be taken by a new form
　원자들은 새로운 형태에 결코 흡수되지 않을 것이다　원자들은 계속 새로운 형태로 흡수됨
⑤ Atoms will disappear completely after your lifetime
　원자들은 당신의 생애 후에 완전히 사라질 것이다　원자들은 사라지지 않고 순환함

왜 정답? ✸✸✸ [정답률 74%]

- 원자는 몸에 들어온 이후에 떠남 [단서 1]
- 원자는 사람들 사이를 순환함 [단서 2]
- 원자는 다양한 형태로 재순환하며 우주에 존재함 [단서 3]
- 원자가 현재의 관리인을 떠나 다른 관리인으로 옮겨갈 것임 [단서 4]

➡ 원자는 우리 몸에 들어왔다가 떠나며 사람들 사이를 순환하고, 다양한 형태로 재순환하며 우주에 존재한다. 즉, 현재 관리인에게 있는 원자는 결국 다른 관리인으로 옮겨갈 것이다.

▶ 따라서 '당신의 뒤를 이을 많은 것[사람]들이 있을 것이다'라는 것은 ① '원자들은 당신 이후의 다른 형태의 일부가 될 것이다'를 의미한다.

왜 오답?

② 원자는 고유한 상태로 남지 않고 순환하며 공유될 것이다.
③ 원자들은 원래의 형태를 따르지 않고 형태를 변화하며 존재한다.
④ 원자들은 끊임없이 새로운 형태에 흡수되어 우주에 존재한다.
⑤ 인간의 생애가 끝나도 그 안의 원자는 새로운 형태로 순환한다.

The act of gardening itself / is a fantastic form of physical activity. //
원예 행위 그 자체는 / 신체 활동의 환상적인 형태이다 //

It involves a range of motions, / **from digging and planting** / **to watering and harvesting**. //
_{from A to B: A에서 B까지}
그것은 다양한 움직임을 포함한다 / 파기와 심기에서 / 물 주기와 수확하기까지 이르는 //

These activities help **improve** / strength, flexibility, and endurance. //
_{help의 목적어}
이런 활동들은 향상시키는 것을 돕는다 / 강인함, 유연성과 내구력을 //

You might not realize it, / but small tasks like weeding or turning compost / can burn many calories. //
당신은 그것을 인식하지 못할 수도 있으나 / 잡초 뽑기나 퇴비 뒤섞기와 같은 작은 과업들은 / 많은 칼로리를 태울 수 있다 //

Gardening is particularly beneficial / for **those who** find traditional exercise challenging. //
_{'~한 사람들'}
원예는 특히 이롭다 / 전통적 운동이 힘들다고 생각하는 사람들에게 //

It's a low-impact way / to stay active and fit, / making **it** accessible / for people of all ages and physical abilities. //
_{= a low-impact way to stay active and fit}
그것은 부담을 주지 않는 방법이어서 / 활동적이고 건강하게 유지하기에 / 접근할 수 있게 만든다 / 모든 연령대 및 신체 능력을 지닌 사람들이 //

Besides physical health, / gardening has profound mental health benefits. // `단서` 원예의 신체적 및 정신적 이점
_{전치사 (~ 외에도)}
신체적 건강 외에도 / 원예는 충분한 정신적 건강 이점이 있다 //

Tending to plants can be incredibly calming and meditative. //
식물을 돌보는 것은 믿을 수 없을 정도로 고요하고 명상적일 수 있다 //

It allows **you to focus** on the present moment, / reducing stress and anxiety. //
_{allows의 목적어와 목적격 보어 (to부정사)}
그것은 당신이 현재 순간에 집중하게 하면서 / 스트레스와 불안감을 줄인다 //

The repetitive tasks **involved in gardening** can induce / a state of mindfulness, / similar to meditation. //
_{앞에 주격 관계대명사와 be동사가 생략됨}
원예와 관련한 반복적인 과업은 유도한다 / 마음 돌봄의 상태를 / 명상과 유사한 //

Studies have shown / **that spending** time in nature, / even in a small garden, / can **elevate** mood, **improve** cognition, and **reduce** depression symptoms. //
_{목적어절 접속사 동명사 (목적어절의 주어)}
_{병렬 구조 (목적어절의 동사)}
연구는 보여왔다 / 자연에서 시간을 보내는 것이 / 심지어 작은 정원이더라도 / 기분을 돋우고, 인지를 개선하며, 우울 증상을 줄일 수 있음을 //

The sense of accomplishment / from watching your plants **grow** and **thrive** / can also **boost** self-esteem and overall well-being. //
_{문장의 주어 / watching의 목적격 보어 / 문장의 동사}
성취감은 / 당신의 식물들이 성장하고 잘 자라는 것을 지켜본 것에서 온 / 또한 자아존중감과 전반적 행복을 높일 수 있다 //

- dig ⓥ 파다 • harvest ⓥ 수확하다 • flexibility ⓝ 유연성
- endurance ⓝ 내구력 • beneficial ⓐ 이익을 가져오는
- incredibly ⓐ 믿을 수 없게 • meditative ⓐ 명상의
- anxiety ⓝ 불안감 • mindfulness ⓝ 마음 돌봄
- meditation ⓝ 명상 • elevate ⓥ 증진시키다
- cognition ⓝ 인지 • depression ⓝ 우울함
- accomplishment ⓝ 성취감 • thrive ⓥ 번성하다, 번영하다
- boost ⓥ 높이다 • self-esteem ⓝ 자아존중감

원예 행위 그 자체는 신체 활동의 환상적인 형태이다. 그것은 파기와 심기에서 물 주기와 수확하기까지 이르는 다양한 움직임을 포함한다. 이런 활동들은 강인함, 유연성과 내구력을 향상시키는 것을 돕는다. 당신은 그것을 인식하지 못할 수도 있으나 잡초 뽑기나 퇴비 뒤섞기와 같은 작은 과업들은 많은 칼로리를 태울 수 있다. 원예는 특히 전통적 운동이 힘들다고 생각하는 사람들에게 이롭다. 그것은 활동적이고 건강하게 유지하기에 부담을 주지 않는 방법이어서 모든 연령대 및 신체 능력을 지닌 사람들이 접근할 수 있게 만든다. 신체적 건강 외에도, 원예는 충분한 정신적 건강 이점이 있다. 식물을 돌보는 것은 믿을 수 없을 정도로 고요하고 명상적일 수 있다. 그것은 당신이 현재 순간에 집중하게 하면서 스트레스와 불안감을 줄인다. 원예와 관련한 반복적인 과업은 명상과 유사한 마음 돌봄의 상태를 유도한다. 연구는 심지어 작은 정원이더라도 자연에서 시간을 보내는 것이 기분을 돋우고, 인지를 개선하며, 우울 증상을 줄일 수 있음을 보여왔다. 당신의 식물들이 성장하고 잘 자라는 것을 지켜본 것에서 온 성취감은 또한 자아존중감과 전반적 행복을 높일 수 있다.

다음 글의 요지로 가장 적절한 것은?

① 야외 활동을 통해 협동심과 자존감을 높일 수 있다.
_{원예 활동의 이점에 관한 내용임}
② 취미 활동을 지속적으로 할 수 있는 동기가 필요하다.
_{동기 부여의 필요성에 관한 내용이 아님}
③ 원예 활동은 신체적 건강과 더불어 정신적 건강에 이롭다.
_{원예 활동이 갖는 신체적 및 정신적 이점들을 소개함}
④ 실내에서 식물을 기르는 것은 집중력 향상에 도움이 된다.
_{실내에서 식물을 기르는 것은 언급되지 않았음}
⑤ 원예 활동은 연령에 관계없이 다양한 사람들이 즐길 수 있다.
_{원예의 이점 중 일부에만 해당함}

> **왜 정답?** ✿✿✿ [정답률 92%]
원예 활동이 주는 신체적 이점들을 나열하다가, 정신적 건강에 주는 이점들도 있다고 하며 예시를 소개하는 글이므로 정답은 ③이다.

> **왜 오답?**
① 야외 활동이 아니라 원예 활동의 이점에 관한 내용이다.
② 취미 활동을 지속하기 위한 동기부여가 필요하다는 내용이 아니다.
④ 원예 활동은 실내가 아닌 실외 활동이며, 집중력 향상 이외에도 여러 이점을 예로 들었다. 주의
⑤ 원예 활동은 모든 연령대의 사람들이 접근할 수 있다고 했을 뿐, 그 외에도 원예 활동의 다양한 이점을 소개하고 있다. 함정

---

23 정답 ② * 인간의 감각을 확장하는 도구들

For many centuries, / humans have taken advantage of tools / **that** translate and bring into our perception natural phenomena / **that** we can't perceive with our senses. // `단서 1` 인간은 지각할 수 없는 현상을 지각하기 위해 도구를 이용함
_{주격 관계대명사 / 목적격 관계대명사}
수 세기 동안 / 인간은 도구들을 이용해 왔다 / 자연 현상을 바꾸고 우리의 지각으로 가져오는 / 우리의 감각으로는 지각할 수 없는 //

In some cases, / this consists of simply amplifying / signals that feed into our normal sensory inputs / `단서 2` 감각 신호를 확장하는 도구
어떤 경우에는 / 이것은 단순히 확장하는 것으로 구성된다 / 우리의 일반적인 감각 입력으로 들어오는 신호를 /

(e.g., telescopes can bring **into clear view** / **that which** is **too** far away / for our eyes **to perceive** on their own). //
_{전치사구 / 목적어 주격 관계대명사 / '너무 ~해서 …할 수 없는'}
(예: 망원경은 명확한 시야로 가져올 수 있다 / 너무 멀어서 / 우리 눈이 그 자체로 지각할 수 없는 것을) //

Other instruments **turn** signals / **that** we cannot perceive / **into ones** that we can observe. // `단서 3` 인지할 수 없는 신호를 관찰하도록 돕는 도구
_{turn A into B: A를 B로 바꾸다 / 목적격 관계대명사 / = signals}
다른 도구들은 신호를 바꾼다 / 우리가 인지할 수 없는 / 우리가 관찰할 수 있는 것으로 //

Some of these take the form of expanding / the reach of our current senses, / such as **creating** visible images / based on the ultraviolet spectrum of light /
이러한 도구 중 일부는 확장하는 형태를 취한다 / 우리의 현재 감각 범위를 / 가시 이미지를 생성하거나 / 빛의 자외선 스펙트럼을 기반으로 /

or **changing** sounds / that are normally outside the range / of what human ears can hear / into audible signals. //
_{병렬 구조 (동명사)}
소리를 바꾸는 것과 같이 / 보통은 범위 밖에 있는 / 인간의 귀가 들을 수 있는 것의 / 들을 수 있는 신호로 //

Alternatively, / some instruments **measure** properties / for which we have no sensory capacity at all / and **change** them / into **that which** we can observe. //
_{병렬 구조 / 대명사 목적격 관계대명사}
아니면 / 일부 도구들은 속성을 측정하고 / 우리가 전혀 감각 수용 능력이 없는 / 그것들을 바꾼다 / 이를 우리가 관찰할 수 있는 것으로 //

- translate ⓥ 바꾸다
- perception ⓝ 지각
- feed into ~에 들어가다
- sensory ⓐ 감각의
- telescope ⓝ 망원경
- ultraviolet ⓐ 자외(선)의
- property ⓝ 속성
- capacity ⓝ 수용
- difficulty ⓝ 어려움
- replace A with B A를 B로 대체하다
- inspire ⓥ 영감을 주다
- visual ⓐ 시각의
- auditory ⓐ 청각의
- imagination ⓝ 상상

수 세기 동안, 인간은 우리의 감각으로는 지각할 수 없는 자연 현상을 바꾸고 우리의 지각으로 가져오는 도구들을 이용해 왔다. 어떤 경우에는, 이것은 우리의 일반적인 감각 입력으로 들어오는 신호를 단순히 확장하는 것(예: 망원경은 너무 멀어서 우리 눈이 그 자체로 지각할 수 없는 것을 명확한 시야로 가져올 수 있다)으로 구성된다. 다른 도구들은 우리가 인지할 수 없는 신호를 우리가 관찰할 수 있는 것으로 바꾼다. 이러한 도구 중 일부는 우리의 현재 감각 범위를 확장하는 빛의 자외선 스펙트럼을 기반으로 가시 이미지를 생성하거나 보통은 인간의 귀가 들을 수 있는 것의 범위 밖에 있는 소리를 들을 수 있는 신호로 바꾸는 것과 같이 형태를 취한다. 아니면, 일부 도구들은 우리가 전혀 감각 수용 능력이 없는 속성을 측정하고 이를 우리가 관찰할 수 있는 것으로 그것들을 바꾼다.

다음 글의 주제로 가장 적절한 것은?

① difficulties in replacing human senses with tools
인간의 감각을 도구로 대체하는 것의 어려움 인간의 감각 대체가 아니라 확장에 관한 내용임
②the tools that increase the ability of human senses
인간의 감각 능력을 향상시키는 도구들 도구를 통해 감각 능력을 향상시킴
③ human senses that inspire the inventing of scientific tools 도구 발명은 언급되지 않았음
과학 도구 발명에 영감을 주는 인간의 감각들
④ differences between visual and auditory senses in humans 시각과 청각의 차이점은 언급되지 않았음
인간의 시각과 청각의 차이점
⑤ the power of human imagination in discovering the universe 상상력은 언급되지 않았음
우주를 발견하는 데 있어서 인간 상상력의 힘

왜 정답? ✹✹❀ [정답률 80%]

- 인간은 지각할 수 없는 현상을 지각하기 위해 도구를 이용함 단서 1
- 감각 신호를 확장하는 도구 단서 2
- 인지할 수 없는 감각 신호를 관찰하도록 돕는 도구 단서 3

➡ 인간의 감각 신호를 확장하거나 인지할 수 없는 감각 신호를 관찰하도록 돕는 도구들을 예로 들었다. 이러한 도구들은 모두 인간의 감각 능력을 향상시킨다.

▶ 따라서 정답은 ② '인간의 감각 능력을 향상시키는 도구들'이다.

왜 오답?

① 인간의 감각을 대체하는 것이 아니라, 확장하는 도구에 관한 내용이다.
③ 인간의 감각을 확장하는 도구들의 예시가 나왔을 뿐, 과학 도구 발명에 관한 내용이 아니다. 주의
④ 인간의 시각과 청각의 차이점은 언급되지 않았다.
⑤ 인간의 상상력은 언급되지 않았다.

---

24 정답 ② ✳동물 실험과 의학적 발전의 인과관계

Many opponents of animal experimentation argue / that not
                                              목적어절 접속사
only is modern medicine not the only cause for the decline in
부정어구가 문두로 가면서 주어와 동사가 도치됨 '유일한 ~이 아닌'
mortality, /
많은 동물 실험 반대자들은 주장한다 / 현대 의학이 사망률 감소의 유일한 원인이 아닐 뿐만 아니라 / 단서 1 동물 실험 반대자들은 많은 의학적 발전이 동물 실험의 결과가 아니었다고 주장함
                                                강조 용법의 do동사
many medical advances / that did contribute to human health /
were not the result of animal experimentation. //
많은 의학적 발전이 / 인간 건강에 기여했던 / 동물 실험의 결과가 아니었다고 //
                          현재완료 (계속)   부사절 접속사 (이유)
Defenders of research have claimed / that since there is a strong
correlation /
연구 옹호자들은 주장해왔다 / 강한 상관관계가 있기 때문에 / 단서 2 동물 실험 옹호자들은 동물 실험이 의학적 발전을 초래했다고 주장함
between the practice of animal experimentation and medical
= the practice ~ experimentation   = medical advancement
advancement, / the former caused the latter. //
동물 실험 실행과 의학적 발전 사이에 / 전자가 후자를 초래했다고 //

Opponents of research reject this inference. //
연구 반대자들은 이 추론을 거부한다 //
                                                      형용사적 용법 (reasons 수식)
After all, / we have independent reasons / to expect these
                                    expect의 목적격 보어
phenomena to be correlated. //
결국 / 우리는 독립적인 이유를 가진다 / 이러한 현상들이 상관관계가 있을 것이라고 예상하게 하는 //
                                        요구 및 명령을 나타내는 동사
Since the law prescribes / that all new drugs, prosthetic devices,
                                        앞에 should가 생략됨
and surgical techniques be tried on animals / before they are
used in humans, /
법이 규정하기 때문에 / 모든 신약들, 보철 장치들 그리고 외과 기술들이 동물에게 시험 되어야 한다고 / 인간에게 사용되기 전에 /

we will subsequently find / that all medical advances are
correlated / with prior experimentation on animals. //
우리는 그 결과로서 알게 될 것이다 / 모든 의학적 발전들이 상관관계가 있다는 것을 / 이전의 동물 실험과 //

Consequently, / the correlation between animal experimentation
and medical discovery is the result of legal necessity, / not
                      동격절 접속사
evidence / that animal experimentation led to medical advances. //
따라서 / 동물 실험과 의학적 발견 간의 상관관계는 법적 필요성의 결과이지 / 증거가 아니다 / 동물 실험이 의학적 발전을 이끌었다는 //

Moreover, / several influential physicians have offered
                                  동격절 접속사
historical evidence / that animal experimentation has not been
as 형용사/부사 as ⋯ : ⋯만큼이나 ~한
as responsible for biomedical discovery / as defenders suggest. //
게다가 / 몇몇 영향력 있는 의사들은 역사적 증거를 제시해 왔다 / 동물 실험이 생의학적 발견의 원인이 아니었다는 / 옹호자들이 주장하는 것만큼 //

They claim / that clinical discoveries played a more substantial
role / than animal researchers have led us to believe. //
그들은 주장한다 / 임상적 발견들이 더 중요한 역할을 했다고 / 동물 연구자들이 우리가 믿게 해 온 것보다 //

- opponent ⓝ 반대자
- mortality ⓝ 사망률
- advance ⓝ 발전, 진보
- contribute ⓥ 기여하다
- defender ⓝ 옹호자
- correlation ⓝ 상관관계
- inference ⓝ 추론
- prescribe ⓥ 규정하다
- surgical ⓐ 외과의
- evidence ⓝ 증거
- biomedical ⓐ 생물 의학의
- substantial ⓐ 중요한
- unlock ⓥ 열다
- frontier ⓝ 경계, 지평
- refer to ~을 참고하다
- strict ⓐ 엄격한
- adoption ⓝ 입양
- extend ⓥ 연장하다
- life span 수명

많은 동물 실험 반대자들은 현대 의학이 사망률 감소의 유일한 원인이 아닐 뿐만 아니라, 인간 건강에 기여했던 많은 의학적 발전이 동물 실험의 결과가 아니었다고 주장한다. 연구 옹호자들은 동물 실험 실행과 의학적 발전 사이에 강한 상관관계가 있기 때문에 전자가 후자를 초래했다고 주장해왔다. 연구 반대자들은 이 추론을 거부한다. 결국, 우리는 이러한 현상들이 상관관계가 있을 것이라고 예상하게 하는 독립적인 이유를 가진다. 법이 모든 신약들, 보철 장치들 그리고 외과 기술들이 인간에게 사용되기 전에 동물에게 시험 되어야 한다고 규정하기 때문에, 우리는 그 결과로서 모든 의학적 발전들이 이전의 동물 실험과 상관관계가 있다는 것을 알게 될 것이다. 따라서, 동물 실험과 의학적 발견 간의 상관관계는 법적 필요성의 결과이지, 동물 실험이 의학적 발전을 이끌었다는 증거가 아니다. 게다가, 몇몇 영향력 있는 의사들은 동물 실험이 옹호자들이 주장하는 것만큼 생의학적 발견의 원인이 아니었다는 역사적 증거를 제시해 왔다. 그들은 임상적 발견들이 동물 연구자들이 우리가 믿게 해 온 것보다 더 중요한 역할을 했다고 주장한다.

다음 글의 제목으로 가장 적절한 것은?
동물 실험과 의학 발전의 인과관계에 대해 상반되는 주장을 소개함

① Bio-medicine: Unlocking New Frontiers in Health Care
생명 의학: 의료의 새로운 지평을 열다 생명 의학을 통한 의료 발전에 관한 내용이 아님
②Is Medicine Advanced by Experimenting on Animals?
의학은 동물 실험을 통해 발전하는가?
③ Refer to Historical Evidence to Solve Medical Issues
의학 문제 해결을 위해 역사적 증거를 참고하라 의학 문제 해결은 언급되지 않았음
④ Why Aren't There Strict Laws for Animal Adoption?
왜 동물 입양에 대한 엄격한 법이 없는가? 동물 입양은 언급되지 않았음
⑤ Medical Advances for Extending Human Life Span
인간 수명 연장을 위한 의학의 발전 인간 수명 연장은 언급되지 않았음

25 정답 ⑤ ＊국가별 온라인 뉴스 소비 방식 선호도 비교

The graph above shows / the percentage of online news consumption preferences in three ways / for six countries in 2020. //

위 그래프는 보여준다 / 세 가지 방식의 온라인 뉴스 소비 선호도 비율을 / 2020년 여섯 개 국가에서 //

독일(67%), 영국(78%), 핀란드(82%): 읽기가 가장 선호되고 모두 60%가 넘음
① In Germany, the UK and Finland, / reading was the most preferred way of consuming online news, / with its percentage over 60 percent / across the three countries. //
과거분사 (way 수식)

독일, 영국 그리고 핀란드에서 / 읽기는 온라인 뉴스를 소비하는 가장 선호되는 방식이었으며 / 그것의 비율이 60퍼센트가 넘었다 / 세 나라 모두에서 //

주격 보어절 접속사 필리핀(52%), 태국(40%), 인도(40%) : 보기를 가장 선호함
② The interesting point is / that the Philippines, Thailand and India all preferred to watch online news the most. //

흥미로운 점은 ~이다 / 필리핀, 태국 그리고 인도 모두가 온라인 뉴스 보기를 가장 선호했다는 것 //

'~의 측면에서, ~에 관하여' 보기 선호도: 필리핀(52%) 가장 높음, 핀란드(12%) 가장 낮음
③ In terms of preference to watching online news, / the Philippines showed the highest percentage / and Finland showed the lowest preference / among all six countries. //

온라인 뉴스 보기에 대한 선호도 측면에서 / 필리핀이 가장 높은 비율을 보였고 / 핀란드가 가장 낮은 선호도를 보였다 / 모든 여섯 개 나라 중에서 //

④ Four out of ten preferred to watch online news / in both Thailand and India, / and that percentage was more than three times as high as that of Finland. // 보기 선호도: 40%(태국, 인도) > 12%(핀란드)×3

열 명 중 네 명이 온라인 뉴스 보기를 선호했고 / 태국과 인도 둘 다에서 / 그 비율은 핀란드의 그것보다 세 배 이상 높았다 //

동격 단서 핀란드(6%)가 태국(22%)의 삼분의 일(약 7.3%)보다 적음
⑤ For listening, / the least preferred way of consuming online news, / the percentage of people who preferred it in Finland / was(→ was less than) a third of that of Thailand. //

듣기에서는 / 온라인 뉴스를 소비하는 가장 덜 선호되는 방법인 / 핀란드에서 그것을 선호하는 사람들의 비율은 / 태국의 그것의 삼분의 일이었다(→ 보다 적었다) //

· consumption ⓝ 소비   · preference ⓝ 선호(도)
· consume ⓥ 소비하다   · least ⓐⓓ 가장 적게

위 그래프는 2020년 여섯 개 국가에서 세 가지 방식의 온라인 뉴스 소비 선호도 비율을 보여준다. ① 독일, 영국 그리고 핀란드에서 읽기는 온라인 뉴스를 소비하는 가장 선호되는 방식이었으며 세 나라 모두에서 그것의 비율이 60퍼센트가 넘었다. ② 흥미로운 점은 필리핀, 태국 그리고 인도 모두 온라인 뉴스 보기를 가장 선호했다는 것이다. ③ 온라인 뉴스 보기에 대한 선호도 측면에서, 필리핀이 가장 높은 비율을 보였고, 핀란드가 모든 여섯 개 나라 중에서 가장 낮은 선호도를 보였다. ④ 태국과 인도 둘 다에서 열 명 중 네 명이 온라인 뉴스 보기를 선호했고, 그 비율은 핀란드의 그것보다 세 배 이상 높았다. ⑤ 온라인 뉴스를 소비하는 가장 덜 선호되는 방법인 듣기에서는, 핀란드에서 그것을 선호하는 사람들의 비율은 태국의 그것의 삼분의 일이었다(→ 보다 적었다).

다음 도표의 내용과 일치하지 않는 것은?

⑤ 핀란드(6%)가 태국(22%)의 삼분의 일(약 7.3%)보다 적음

Percentage of Online News Consumption Preferences in 2020
2020년 온라인 뉴스 소비 선호도 비율

② 모두 보기를 가장 선호함

③ 보기 선호도: 필리핀(52%)이 가장 높고 핀란드(12%)가 가장 낮음

④ 40%(태국, 인도) > 12%×3 핀란드의 세 배

① 모두 읽기를 가장 선호하고 그 비율이 60% 이상임

	Philippines 필리핀	Thailand 태국	India 인도	Germany 독일	UK 영국	Finland 핀란드 (Country) 국가
Prefer to read 읽기를 선호	36	38	39	67	78	82
Prefer to watch 보기를 선호	52	40	40	23	15	12
Prefer to listen 듣기를 선호	12	22	21	10	7	6

☐ Prefer to read 읽기를 선호   ■ Prefer to watch 보기를 선호   ▨ Prefer to listen 듣기를 선호

> **왜 정답 ?** ★★☆ [정답률 82%]

핀란드에서 온라인 뉴스 듣기 선호도는 6퍼센트이므로 태국(22퍼센트)의 삼분의 일(약 7.3퍼센트)보다 적다. 따라서 ⑤가 도표의 내용과 일치하지 않는다.

> **왜 오답 ?**

① 독일, 영국, 핀란드의 읽기 선호 비율은 각각 67%, 78%, 82%로, 모두 60% 이상이다.

② 필리핀, 태국, 인도의 보기·선호 비율은 각각 52%, 40%, 40%로, 각 국가에서 가장 선호도가 높다.

③ 여섯 국가의 보기 선호 비율 중 필리핀(52%)은 가장 높고, 핀란드(12%)는 가장 낮다.

④ 태국과 인도 모두 보기 선호 비율이 40%이므로 핀란드의 세 배(12%×3=36%)가 넘는다.

26 정답 ③ ＊Roger Payne의 생애

Roger Payne was born in Manhattan in 1935. //
Roger Payne은 1935년에 맨해튼에서 태어났다 // ①의 단서 하버드 대학교에서 생물학을 공부했음

He studied biology at Harvard University / and eventually earned his Ph.D. / from Cornell University in 1961. //

그는 하버드 대학교에서 생물학을 공부했고 / 마침내 박사 학위를 받았다 / 1961년에 코넬 대학교에서 //

목적어절 접속사
In 1967, / he discovered / that humpback whales make long and complex sounds. // ②의 단서 흑등고래가 길고 복잡한 소리를 낸다는 것을 발견함

1967년에 / 그는 발견했다 / 흑등고래가 길고 복잡한 소리를 낸다는 것을 //

목적어절 접속사
They're known as "whale songs," / and he showed that whales use them / to communicate. // 부사적 용법 (목적)

그것들은 "고래 노래"라고 알려져 있고 / 그는 고래들이 그것들을 사용한다는 것을 보여줬다 / 의사소통하기 위해 // ③의 단서 그의 앨범 Songs of the Humpback Whale은 놀라운 인기를 얻었음

계속적 용법의 주격 관계대명사
Then in 1970, / he released an album *Songs of the Humpback Whale*, / which became a surprise hit / and helped start the global "Save the Whales" movement. //

그 후 1970년에 / 그는 Songs of the Humpback Whale 앨범을 발표했는데 / 그것은 놀라운 인기를 얻었고 / 전 세계적인 "Save the Whales" 운동을 시작하는 것을 도왔다 //

부사적 용법 (목적)
The following year, / he founded Ocean Alliance / to protect whales and the earth's oceans, / ④의 단서 고래와 지구의 해양을 보호하기 위해 Oceans Alliance를 설립했음

다음 해에 / 그는 Ocean Alliance를 설립했고 / 고래와 지구의 해양을 보호하기 위해 /

and he used new, safe methods / to study whales without harming them. //

새롭고 안전한 방법을 사용했다 / 그들을 해치지 않고 고래를 연구하는 //

분사구문을 이끄는 현재분사
Over his career, / he led more than 100 research trips worldwide, / including the Voyage of the Odyssey from 2000 to 2005, / which studied ocean pollution. //

그의 경력 동안 / 그는 전세계적으로 100회 이상의 연구 탐사를 이끌었고 / 여기에는 2000년에서 2005년까지의 Voyage of the Odyssey를 포함한다 / 해양 오염을 연구한 //

His work helped make laws / that protect marine mammals, /

계속적 용법의 주격 관계대명사

which finally led to the global ban on commercial whaling in 1986. // ⑤의 단서 그의 연구는 해양 포유류를 보호하는 법 제정에 도움을 주었음

그의 연구는 법을 제정하는 것을 도왔는데 / 해양 포유류를 보호하는 / 이는 결국 1986년 상업적 고래 포획에 관한 세계적인 금지를 이끌었다 //

- biology ⓝ 생물학 · eventually [ad] 마침내, 결국
- complex ⓐ 복잡한 · communicate ⓥ 의사소통하다
- release ⓥ 발표하다, 출시하다 · movement ⓝ (사회적) 운동
- found ⓥ 설립하다 · alliance ⓝ 동맹, 연합 · career ⓝ 경력, 생애
- pollution ⓝ 오염 · marine ⓐ 해양의 · mammal ⓝ 포유류
- ban ⓝ 금지 · commercial ⓐ 상업적인
- whaling ⓝ 고래 포획

Roger Payne은 1935년에 맨해튼에서 태어났다. 그는 하버드 대학교에서 생물학을 공부했고, 마침내 1961년에 코넬 대학교에서 박사 학위를 받았다. 1967년에 그는 혹등고래가 길고 복잡한 소리를 낸다는 것을 발견했다. 그것들은 "고래 노래"라고 알려져 있고, 그는 고래들이 의사소통하기 위해 그것들을 사용한다는 것을 보여줬다. 그 후 1970년에 그는 *Songs of the Humpback Whale* 앨범을 발표했는데, 그것은 놀라운 인기를 얻었고 전 세계적인 "Save the Whales" 운동을 시작하는 것을 도왔다. 다음 해에 그는 고래와 지구의 해양을 보호하기 위해 Ocean Alliance를 설립했고, 그들을 해치지 않고 고래를 연구하는 새롭고 안전한 방법을 사용했다. 그의 경력 동안 그는 전 세계적으로 100회 이상의 연구 탐사를 이끌었고, 여기에는 해양 오염을 연구한 2000년에서 2005년까지의 Voyage of the Odyssey를 포함한다. 그의 연구는 해양 포유류를 보호하는 법을 제정하는 것을 도왔는데, 이는 결국 1986년 상업적 고래 포획에 관한 세계적인 금지를 이끌었다.

Roger Payne에 관한 다음 글의 내용과 일치하지 않는 것은?

① 하버드 대학교에서 생물학을 공부했다.
　He studied biology at Harvard University
② 혹등고래가 길고 복잡한 소리를 낸다는 것을 발견했다.
　he discovered that humpback whales make long and complex sounds
③ 그의 앨범 *Songs of the Humpback Whale*은 인기를 얻지 못했다.
　he released an album ~, which became a surprise hit
④ 고래와 지구의 해양을 보호하기 위해 Ocean Alliance를 설립했다.
　he founded Ocean Alliance to protect whales and the earth's oceans
⑤ 그의 연구는 해양 포유류를 보호하는 법 제정에 도움을 주었다.
　His work helped make laws that protect marine mammals

왜 정답? ✽❀❀ [정답률 97%]

Roger Payne은 1970년에 *Songs of the Humpback Whale* 앨범을 발표했고, 이는 놀라운 인기를 얻었다고 (he released an album ~, which became a surprise hit) 했으므로, 앨범이 인기를 얻지 못했다고 한 ③이 글의 내용과 일치하지 않는다.

왜 오답?

① 하버드 대학교에서 생물학을 공부했다. (He studied biology at Harvard University)
② 혹등고래가 길고 복잡한 소리를 낸다는 것을 발견했다. (he discovered that humpback whales make long and complex sounds)
④ 고래와 지구의 해양을 보호하기 위해 Ocean Alliance를 설립했다. (he founded Ocean Alliance to protect whales and the earth's oceans)
⑤ 그의 연구는 해양 포유류를 보호하는 법 제정에 도움을 주었다. (His work helped make laws that protect marine mammals)

27 정답 ③ ✽Father-Daughter Sock Hop

Father-Daughter Sock Hop /
Father-Daughter Sock Hop /

부사적 용법 (감정의 원인)

We are excited **to bring** you / the 5th annual Father-Daughter Sock Hop / — an incredibly special evening for fathers and daughters to dance! //

우리는 당신을 모시게 되어 기쁩니다 / 제5회 연례 Father-Daughter Sock Hop에 / 아빠와 딸이 춤을 추는 매우 특별한 저녁인 //

When & Where / 언제 & 어디서 /

- September 12th(Friday), / from 6 p.m. to 9 p.m. /
  9월 12일(금요일) / 저녁 6시에서 9시까지 / ①의 단서 9월 12일 금요일에 개최됨
- Maple Creek Community Center /
  Maple Creek 커뮤니티 센터 /

Participation Fee / 참가비 /

- $25 per pair / ②의 단서 한 쌍당 참가비는 25달러
  한 쌍당 25달러 /
- $5 per each additional daughter /
  추가되는 딸 1명당 5달러 /
- No refund for cancellations / on the day of the event /
  취소 시 환불 불가 / 행사 당일 / ③의 단서 행사 당일 취소 시 환불은 불가능함

Notice / 공지사항 /

미래시제 수동태 ④의 단서 모든 참가자에게 선물로 양말 한 켤레가 제공됨

- A pair of socks **will be given out** / as a gift to every participant. //
  양말 한 켤레가 제공될 것입니다 / 모든 참가자에게 선물로 //
- Take pictures at the photo zone. // ⑤의 단서 포토존에서 사진을 찍을 수 있음
  포토존에서 사진을 찍으세요 //

Registration / 등록 /

- Register online / at www.maplecreekcity.org. //
  온라인으로 등록하세요 / www.maplecreekcity.org에서 //

- annual ⓐ 연례의, 매년의 · participation ⓝ 참가, 참여
- fee ⓝ 요금 · additional ⓐ 추가의 · refund ⓝ 환불
- cancellation ⓝ 취소 · participant ⓝ 참가자
- registration ⓝ 등록

Father-Daughter Sock Hop

우리는 당신을 아빠와 딸이 춤을 추는 매우 특별한 저녁인 제5회 연례 Father-Daughter Sock Hop에 모시게 되어 기쁩니다!

언제 & 어디서

- 9월 12일(금요일), 저녁 6시에서 9시까지
- Maple Creek 커뮤니티 센터

참가비

- 한 쌍당 25달러
- 추가되는 딸 1명당 5달러
- 행사 당일 취소 시 환불 불가

공지사항

- 양말 한 켤레가 모든 참가자에게 선물로 제공될 것입니다.
- 포토존에서 사진을 찍으세요.

등록

- www.maplecreekcity.org에서 온라인으로 등록하세요.

Father-Daughter Sock Hop에 관한 다음 안내문의 내용과 일치하지 않는 것은?

① 9월 12일 금요일에 개최된다. September 12th(Friday)
② 한 쌍당 참가비는 $25이다. $25 per pair
③ 행사 당일 취소 시 환불이 가능하다.
　No refund for cancellations on the day of the event
④ 모든 참가자에게 선물이 제공된다.
　A pair of socks will be given out as a gift to every participant.
⑤ 포토존에서 사진을 찍을 수 있다. Take pictures at the photo zone.

왜 정답? ✽❀❀ [정답률 95%]

행사 당일 취소 시 환불이 불가능하다고 (No refund for cancellations on the day of the event) 했으므로 행사 당일 취소 시 환불이 가능하다고 한 ③이 안내문의 내용과 일치하지 않는다.

왜 오답?

① 9월 12일 금요일에 개최된다. (September 12th(Friday))
② 한 쌍당 참가비는 $25이다. ($25 per pair)
④ 모든 참가자에게 선물이 제공된다. (A pair of socks will be given out as a gift to every participant.)
⑤ 포토존에서 사진을 찍을 수 있다. (Take pictures at the photo zone.)

28

정답 ⑤ ＊도서관 책갈피 디자인 대회

2025 Library Bookmark Design Contest /
2025 도서관 책갈피 디자인 대회 /

The 6th annual Library Bookmark Design Contest is now open! //
①의 단서 여섯 번째 열리는 대회임
제6회 연례 Library Bookmark Design Contest가 지금 열립니다 //

Show your creativity and design skills. //
여러분의 창의성과 디자인 기술을 보여주세요 //

Participation / 참가 /

• **Participants need to be between the ages of 5-12. //**
②의 단서 5세에서 12세 사이여야 참가할 수 있음
참가자는 5세에서 12세 사이여야 합니다 //

Guidelines / 지침 /
분사구문
• **Create a bookmark by hand / using markers or crayons. //**
손으로 책갈피를 만드세요 / 마커 또는 크레용을 사용하여 //

• **Designs must fit the slogan "Find Your Voice." //**
디자인은 "Find Your Voice" 슬로건에 적합해야 합니다 //
부정 명령문 동사
• **Do not use / commercialized character images / in your**
design. // ③의 단서 상업용 캐릭터 이미지를 사용할 수 없음
사용하지 마세요 / 상업용 캐릭터 이미지들을 / 디자인에 //

Submission / 제출 /

• **Limit one entry per participant. //** ④의 단서 출품작은 참가자당 한 개로 제한됨
참가자당 한 개의 출품작으로 제한합니다 //
수동태 동사
• **Entries should be submitted / via email to contest@srpls.org**
by October 4th. //
출품작은 제출되어야 합니다 / 10월 4일까지 이메일(contest@srpls.org)로 //

Prizes / 시상 /

• **1st place: $50 gift card, / 2nd place: $30 gift card /**
1등: 50달러 선물 카드 / 2등: 30달러 선물 카드 /
⑤의 단서 수상자의 책갈피는 인쇄되어
미래시제 수동태 방문객에게 제공될 것임
• **Winners' bookmarks will be printed / and given to visitors. //**
수상자의 책갈피는 인쇄되어 / 방문객에게 제공될 것입니다 //

※ **For more information, / please visit our website at www.**
sherrillpubliclibrary.org. //
더 많은 정보를 위해 / 웹사이트 www.sherrillpubliclibrary.org를 방문하세요 //

• creativity ⓝ 창의성　　• slogan ⓝ 슬로건, 구호
• commercialized ⓐ 상업화된　　• submission ⓝ 제출
• limit ⓥ 제한하다　　• entry ⓝ 출품작　　• submit ⓥ 제출하다

2025 Library Bookmark Design Contest
제6회 연례 Library Bookmark Design Contest가 지금 열립니다! 여러분의 창의성과 디자인 기술을 보여주세요.
참가
• 참가자는 5세에서 12세 사이여야 합니다.
지침
• 마커 또는 크레용을 사용하여 책갈피를 만드세요.
• 디자인은 "Find Your Voice" 슬로건에 적합해야 합니다.
• 디자인에 상업용 캐릭터 이미지들을 사용하지 마세요.
제출
• 참가자당 한 개의 출품작으로 제한합니다.
• 출품작은 10월 4일까지 이메일(contest@srpls.org)로 제출되어야 합니다.
시상
• 1등: 50달러 선물 카드, 2등: 30달러 선물 카드
• 수상자의 책갈피는 인쇄되어 방문객에게 제공될 것입니다.
※ 더 많은 정보를 위해, 웹사이트 www.sherrillpubliclibrary.org를 방문하세요.

2025 Library Bookmark Design Contest에 관한 다음 안내문의 내용과 일치하는 것은?

① 여덟 번째 열리는 대회이다. The 6th annual Library Bookmark Design Contest
② 13세 이상이면 누구나 참가할 수 있다. between the ages of 5-12
③ 상업용 캐릭터 이미지를 사용할 수 있다. Do not use commercialized character images
④ 출품작은 참가자당 두 개로 제한된다. Limit one entry per participant.
⑤ 수상자의 책갈피는 인쇄되어 방문객에게 제공될 것이다. Winners' bookmarks will be printed and given to visitors.

〉왜 정답 ? ❊❊❊ [정답률 94%]

수상자의 책갈피는 인쇄되어 방문객에게 제공될 것이라고 했으므로(Winners' bookmarks will be printed and given to visitors) 안내문의 내용과 일치하는 것은 ⑤이다.

〉왜 오답 ?

① 여섯 번째 열리는 대회이다. (The 6th annual Library Bookmark Design Contest)
② 참가자는 5세에서 12세 사이여야 한다. (between the ages of 5-12)
③ 상업용 캐릭터 이미지를 사용할 수 없다. (Do not use commercialized character images)
④ 출품작은 참가자당 한 개로 제한된다. (Limit one entry per participant.)

정답 ② ＊큰 포유류의 초식동물 종을 길들이기 어려운 이유

다음 글의 밑줄 친 부분 중, 어법상 틀린 것은? [3점]

Big mammalian herbivore species react to danger / from predators or humans / in different ways. //
큰 포유류의 초식동물 종은 위험에 대해 반응한다 / 포식자나 인간으로부터의 / 다른 방식으로 //

Some species are nervous, fast, and programmed for instant flight / when they perceive a threat. //
어떤 종들은 긴장하고, 빠르고, 즉각적인 비행을 하도록 프로그램화되어 있다 / 그들이 위험을 감지할 때 //
복수 주어
Other species are slower, less nervous, / seek protection in
병렬 구조 (복수 동사)
herds, / ① stand their ground when threatened, / and don't run until necessary. //
다른 종들은 더 느리고, 덜 긴장하고 / 무리 속에서 보호를 찾고 / 위협을 받았을 때 그들의 자리를 지키고 / 필요할 때까지 도망가지 않는다 //

Naturally, / the nervous species are difficult to keep in captivity. //
자연스럽게 / 긴장하는 동물 종들은 갇힌 상태를 유지하기 어렵다 //
접속사가 생략되지 않은 분사구문　주절의 주어 (분사구문의 주어와 같음)
If ② putting (→ put) into an enclosure, / they are likely to panic, / and either die of shock or hit themselves repeatedly to death
단서 우리 안에 '넣어지는' 것이므로 수동 관계임
against the fence / in their attempts to escape. //
만약 우리 안에 넣어지면 / 그들은 패닉에 빠져 / 충격으로 죽거나 반복적으로 울타리에 부딪혀 죽을 가능성이 있다 / 탈출하려는 시도로 //
선행사　계속적 용법의 주격 관계대명사
That's true, for example, of gazelles, / ③ which for thousands of
복수 동사　전치사구
years were the most frequently hunted game species / in some parts of the Fertile Crescent. //
예를 들어 이것은 가젤에 해당하는데 / 이들은 수천 년 동안 가장 빈번하게 사냥된 사냥감 종이었다 / 비옥한 초승달 지대의 일부 지역에서 //
목적격 관계대명사
There is no mammal species / that the first settled peoples of that
형용사적 용법 (opportunity 수식)
area / had more opportunity ④ to domesticate / than gazelles. //
포유류는 없다 / 그 지역에 처음으로 정착한 인간들이 / 길들일 기회가 더 많았던 / 가젤보다 //

But no gazelle species has ever been domesticated. //
그러나 어떤 가젤 종도 지금까지 길들여진 적이 없다 //

Just imagine trying to herd <u>an animal</u>(선행사) / <u>that</u>(주격 관계대명사) runs away, blindly hits ⑤ <u>itself</u>(재귀대명사 (재귀 용법)) against walls, / can leap up to nearly 30 feet, / and can run at a speed of 50 miles per hour! //

동물을 무리 지으려고 노력하는 것을 상상해보라 / 도망가고, 자신을 맹목적으로 벽에 부딪히고 / 거의 30피트까지 뛰어오를 수 있고 / 시속 50마일 속도로 달릴 수 있는 //

- mammalian ⓐ 포유류의 • species ⓝ 종 • react ⓥ 반응하다
- predator ⓝ 포식자 • instant ⓐ 즉각적인
- perceive ⓥ 인지하다, 감지하다 • threat ⓝ 위협
- protection ⓝ 보호 • captivity ⓝ 사육, 감금
- enclosure ⓝ 우리, 울타리 • panic ⓥ 공황 상태에 빠지다
- repeatedly ⓐⅆ 반복적으로 • attempt ⓝ 시도
- frequently ⓐⅆ 빈번하게 • opportunity ⓝ 기회
- domesticate ⓥ 길들이다, 사육하다 • blindly ⓐⅆ 맹목적으로
- leap ⓥ 뛰어오르다

큰 포유류의 초식동물 종은 포식자나 인간으로부터의 위험에 대해 다른 방식으로 반응한다. 어떤 종은 그들이 위험을 감지할 때 긴장하고, 빠르고, 즉각적인 비행을 하도록 프로그램화되어 있다. 다른 종들은 더 느리고, 덜 긴장하고, 무리 속에서 보호를 찾고, 위협을 받았을 때 그들의 자리를 지키고 필요할 때까지 도망가지 않는다. 자연스럽게, 긴장하는 동물 종들은 갇힌 상태를 유지하기 어렵다. 만약 우리 안에 넣어지면, 그들은 패닉에 빠져 충격으로 죽거나 탈출하려는 시도로 반복적으로 울타리에 부딪혀 죽을 가능성이 있다. 예를 들어 이것은 가젤에 해당하는데, 이들은 수천 년 동안 비옥한 초승달 지대의 일부 지역에서 가장 빈번하게 사냥된 사냥감 종이었다. 그 지역에 처음으로 정착한 인간들이 가젤보다 길들일 기회가 더 많았던 포유류는 없다. 그러나 어떤 가젤 종도 지금까지 길들여진 적이 없다. 도망가고, 자신을 맹목적으로 벽에 부딪히고, 거의 30피트까지 뛰어오를 수 있고, 시속 50마일 속도로 달릴 수 있는 동물을 무리 지으려고 노력하는 것을 상상해보라!

왜 정답? ★★★ [정답률 48%]

② 주절의 주어와 분사의 관계가 수동이다!

If ② <u>putting</u>(→ put) into an enclosure, / they are likely to panic, ~ //
  (접속사가 생략되지 않은 분사구문) (주절의 주어 (분사구문의 주어와 같음))
  주어와 수동 관계이므로 과거분사가 와야 함

- **단서** 접속사 If가 생략되지 않은 분사구문이다. 분사구문의 생략된 주어는 주절의 주어인 they(= the nervous species)이다.
- **발상** the nervous species와 putting의 능동 및 수동 관계를 살펴본다.
- **해결** putting과 전치사구 into an enclosure 사이에 목적어가 없고, 문맥상으로도 the nervous species가 우리 안에 '넣어지는' 것이기 때문에 수동 관계를 나타낸다. 따라서 현재분사 putting을 과거분사 put으로 고쳐야 한다.
- **개념** 분사구문에서 주어와 동사의 관계가 능동이면 현재분사를, 수동이면 과거분사를 사용한다.

왜 오답?

① 동사는 주어에 그 수를 일치시킨다.

<u>Other species</u>(복수 주어) are slower, less nervous, / <u>seek</u> protection in herds, ① <u>stand</u> their ground when threatened, / and <u>don't run</u> until necessary. //
  ├─ 병렬 구조 (복수 동사) ─┤

문장의 주어는 복수 명사인 Other species이다. 문장의 동사인 are, seek, stand, don't run이 병렬 구조를 이루고 있으며 이들은 모두 복수형이므로 stand 또한 알맞게 쓰였다.

③ 계속적 용법의 관계대명사는 콤마 뒤에서 선행사를 수식한다.

That's true, for example, of <u>gazelles</u>, / ③ <u>which</u> for thousands of years <u>were</u> the most frequently hunted game species ~ //
  (선행사) (계속적 용법의 주격 관계대명사) (복수 동사)
  전치사구: 제외하고 생각하기

which가 콤마 뒤에 쓰여 선행사 gazelles에 대해 부가적인 설명을 덧붙이므로, 계속적 용법의 주격 관계대명사 which가 알맞게 쓰였다.

---

④ to부정사는 형용사적 용법으로 쓰여 명사를 수식할 수 있다.

~ had more opportunity ④ <u>to domesticate</u> / than gazelles. //
  (형용사적 용법 (opportunity 수식))

to domesticate가 바로 앞의 명사 opportunity를 수식하여 '길들일 기회'라는 뜻을 나타내므로, 형용사적 용법의 to부정사가 알맞게 쓰였다.

⑤ 주어와 목적어가 같을 때 목적어 자리에 재귀대명사를 쓴다.

Just imagine trying to herd <u>an animal</u>(선행사) / <u>that</u>(주격 관계대명사) runs away, blindly hits ⑤ <u>itself</u>(재귀대명사 (재귀 용법)) against walls, ~ //

관계사절의 주어는 선행사인 an animal이다. 문맥상 an animal이 벽에 부딪히는 대상은 자기 자신이므로, 즉 주어와 목적어가 같으므로 재귀 용법의 재귀대명사 itself가 알맞게 쓰였다.

30 정답 ⑤ ＊적게 가질수록 더 나누는 경향 ────

다음 글의 밑줄 친 부분 중, 문맥상 낱말의 쓰임이 적절하지 <u>않은</u> 것은?

For a species born in a time / <u>when</u>(관계부사) resources were limited and dangers were great, / our natural tendency <u>to share and cooperate</u>(형용사적 용법 (tendency 수식)) is ① <u>complicated</u> / when resources are plenty and outside dangers are few. //
단서 1 자원이 많고 위험이 적어지면 오히려 나누고 협력하려는 성향이 복잡해짐
시기에 태어난 종에게 있어 / 자원이 제한적이고 위험이 컸던 / 나누고 협력하려는 우리의 타고난 성향은 복잡하다 / 자원이 풍부하고 외부의 위험이 거의 없을 때 //

When we have less, / we tend to be more open / to sharing <u>what</u>(선행사를 포함하는 관계대명사) we have. //
우리가 더 적게 가질 때 / 더 개방적이 되는 경향이 있다 / 우리가 가진 것을 나누는 데 //

Certain nomadic tribes don't have much, / <u>yet</u>(동위접속사 (하지만)) they are happy to share / because it is in their ② <u>interest</u> to <u>do so</u>(= share).(부사적 용법 (감정의 원인)) //
특정 유목 부족은 많은 것을 가지고 있지 않지만 / 그들은 기꺼이 나누려고 한다 / 그렇게 하는 것이 그들의 이익에 부합하기 때문에 //

If you happen upon them in your travels, / they will open up their homes / and give you their food and hospitality. //
만약 당신이 여행 중 그들을 우연히 만나면 / 그들은 자신의 집을 열고 / 당신에게 음식과 환대를 제공할 것이다 //

It's not just because they are nice people; / it's because their ③ <u>survival</u> depends on sharing, /
이는 그들이 좋은 사람이어서만이 아니다 / 이는 그들의 생존이 나누는 것에 달려 있기 때문인데 /

단서 2 처지가 바뀌면 생존에 위협이 있으므로 특정 유목 부족은 기꺼이 나눔
<u>for</u>(동위접속사 (왜냐하면)) they know that they may be the travelers / in need of food and shelter another day. //
왜냐하면 그들은 여행자가 될 수 있음을 알기 때문이다 / 또 다른 날 그들이 음식과 거처가 필요한 //

Ironically, the ④ <u>more</u> we have, / the <u>bigger</u> our fences, / the <u>more</u> sophisticated our security to keep people away / and the <u>less</u> we want to share. //
  (the 비교급 ~, the 비교급 …: 더 ~할수록 더 …하다) (병렬 구조)
단서 3 더 많이 가질수록 사람들을 멀리 두고 덜 나누려고 함
아이러니하게도, 우리가 더 많이 가질수록 / 우리의 울타리는 더 커지고 / 사람들을 멀리 두기 위한 우리의 보안은 더 정교해지며 / 우리는 더 적게 나누기를 원하게 된다 //

<u>Our desire</u>(단수 주어) for more, / combined with our ⑤ <u>increased</u>(→ decreased) physical interaction with the "common folk," / <u>starts</u>(단수 동사) to create / a disconnection or blindness to reality. //
우리의 더 많은 것에 대한 욕망은 / "일반 대중"과의 늘어난(→ 줄어든) 실재적인 상호작용과 결합되어서 / 만들어내기 시작한다 / 현실에 대한 단절이나 눈멀음을 //

- resource ⓝ 자원 • tendency ⓝ 경향 • cooperate ⓥ 협력하다
- complicated ⓐ 복잡한 • plenty ⓝ 풍부한 • interest ⓝ 이익
- survival ⓝ 생존 • depend on ~에 달려있다 • shelter ⓝ 안식처
- ironically ⓐⅆ 역설적으로 • sophisticated ⓐ 정교한
- desire ⓝ 욕망 • combine A with B A를 B와 결합하다
- interaction ⓝ 상호작용 • disconnection ⓝ 단절

자원이 제한적이고 위험이 컸던 시기에 태어난 종에게 있어, 자원이 풍부하고 외부의 위험이 거의 없을 때 나누고 협력하려는 우리의 타고난 성향은 ① 복잡하다. 우리가 더 적게 가질 때, 우리가 가진 것을 나누는 데 더 개방적이 되는 경향이 있다. 특정 유목 부족은 많은 것을 가지고 있지 않지만, 그렇게 하는 것이 그들의 ② 이익에 부합하기 때문에 그들은 기꺼이 나누려고 한다. 만약 당신이 여행 중 그들을 우연히 만나면, 그들은 자신의 집을 열고 당신에게 음식과 환대를 제공할 것이다. 이는 그들이 좋은 사람이어서만이 아니다. 이는 그들의 ③ 생존이 나누는 것에 달려 있기 때문인데, 왜냐하면 그들은 또 다른 날 그들이 음식과 거처가 필요한 여행자가 될 수 있음을 알기 때문이다. 아이러니하게도, 우리가 ④ 더 많이 가질수록, 우리의 울타리는 더 커지고, 사람들을 멀리 두기 위한 우리의 보안은 더 정교해지며, 우리는 더 적게 나누기를 원하게 된다. 우리의 더 많은 것에 대한 욕망은 "일반 대중"과의 ⑤ 늘어난(→ 줄어든) 실재적인 상호작용과 결합되어서, 현실에 대한 단절이나 눈멀음을 만들어내기 시작한다.

▷왜 정답? ★★★❋ [정답률 61%]

⑤ increased 늘어난

┌ 우리의 더 많은 것에 대한 욕망은 "일반 대중"과의 ⑤ ~~늘어난~~ (줄어든) 실재적인 상호
└ 작용과 결합되어서, 현실에 대한 단절이나 눈멀음을 만들어내기 시작한다.

➡ 앞 문장에서 더 많이 가질수록 사람들을 멀리 두려 한다고 했다. 따라서 더 많은 것에 대한 욕망은 일반 대중과의 '늘어난' 상호작용이 아니라 '줄어든' 상호작용과 결합될 것이다.

▶ increased를 decreased(줄어든)와 같은 반의어로 바꿔야 함

▷왜 오답?

① complicated 복잡한

┌ 자원이 제한적이고 위험이 컸던 시기에 태어난 종에게 있어, 자원이 풍부하
│ 고 외부의 위험이 거의 없을 때 나누고 협력하려는 우리의 타고난 성향은
└ ① 복잡하다.

➡ 자원이 제한적이고 위험이 크다면 생존을 위해 가진 것을 나누려 하지만, 자원이 풍부하고 위험이 작다면 나눔과 협력의 동기가 예전처럼 단순하지 않고 '복잡할' 것이다. ▶ complicated는 문맥에 맞음

② interest 이익

┌ 특정 유목 부족은 많은 것을 가지고 있지 않지만, 그렇게 하는 것이 그들의
└ ② 이익에 부합하기 때문에 그들은 기꺼이 나누려고 한다.

➡ 가진 것이 적더라도 기꺼이 나누는 것은 그렇게 하는 것이 그들에게 '이익'이 되기 때문일 것이다. ▶ interest는 문맥에 맞음

③ survival 생존

┌ 이는 그들이 좋은 사람이어서만이 아니다. 이는 그들의 ③ 생존이 나누는
│ 것에 달려 있기 때문인데, 왜냐하면 그들은 또 다른 날 그들이 음식과 거처
└ 가 필요한 여행자가 될 수 있음을 알기 때문이다.

➡ 자원이 부족한 환경에서 나눔은 단순히 친절의 문제가 아니라, 언젠가 자신도 도움을 받아야 하는 상황에 처할 수 있기 때문에 필요한 '생존' 전략이다.

▶ survival은 문맥에 맞음

④ more 더 많이

┌ 아이러니하게도, 우리가 ④ 더 많이 가질수록, 우리의 울타리는 더 커지고,
│ 사람들을 멀리 두기 위한 우리의 보안은 더 정교해지며, 우리는 더 적게 나
└ 누기를 원하게 된다.

➡ 적게 가질 때 더 많이 나누던 것과 다르게, '더 많이' 가질수록 오히려 덜 나눈다는 아이러니한 상황을 설명하고 있다. ▶ more는 문맥에 맞음

---

31 정답 ① ＊적응하며 행복의 기준선으로 돌아오는 인간

명사절 접속사 (주어절을 이끎)
Whether we feel happy or sad, content or discontent, / is not determined / merely by each individual successive moment of life experience /
우리가 행복하거나 슬프거나, 만족스럽거나 불만족스러운 것은 / 결정되지 않는다 / 단지 삶의 경험의 각각의 개별적인 연속적인 순간에 의해 /

— a good thing happens and I'm happy, / a bad thing happens and I'm sad. //
좋은 일이 일어나면 행복하고 / 나쁜 일이 일어나면 슬픈 것처럼 //

부사절 접속사 (대조)
While our experiences affect our mood, / we are not blown in a completely new direction / by each gust of wind. //
우리의 경험은 우리의 기분에 영향을 미치지만 / 우리는 완전히 새로운 방향으로 날아가지 않는다 / 각 돌풍에 의해 //

As humans, we adjust / — to new information and events both good and bad — / and return to our personal default level of well-being. // **단서 1** 인간은 새로운 정보와 사건에 적응하고 원래의 기본 행복 수준으로 돌아감
인간으로서 우리는 적응하고 / 좋을 뿐 아니라 나쁘기도 한 새로운 정보와 사건들에 / 우리의 개인적인 기본 행복 수준으로 돌아간다 //

'높고 낮음, 기복' **단서 2** 기복이 있어도 결국 기준선으로 돌아옴
There will be **highs and lows**, / but over time, like water seeking its own level, / we are pulled toward our baseline /
기복은 있을 것이지만 / 시간이 지나면서 고유한 수위를 찾는 물처럼 / 우리는 우리의 기준선으로 끌려가는데 /

— back *up* after bad news / and back *down* after good. //
즉, 나쁜 소식 후에는 다시 '올라'오고 / 좋은 소식 후에는 다시 '내려'온다 //

도치 구문 (so + 동사 + 주어)
The euphoria of first love fades, / and **so does the despair of a break-up**. // **단서 3** 강렬한 감정은 결국 사라짐
첫사랑의 행복감은 사라지고 / 결별의 절망도 그렇다 //

This tendency is best seen / with little kids and their toy joy: /
이 경향은 가장 잘 보여진다 / 어린 아이들과 그들의 장난감 기쁨에서 /

뒤에 목적어절 접속사가 생략됨
When they get what they've longed for, / **they believe** they will be happy / for the rest of their lives. //
그들은 간절히 원하던 것을 얻을 때 / 행복할 것이라고 믿는다 / 그들의 남은 인생 동안 //

뒤에 반복되는 happy가 생략됨
And for the first few minutes / of the rest of their lives, / they **are**. //
그리고 처음 몇 분 동안 / 그들의 남은 인생의 / 그들은 그렇다 //

But then the kids / — like adults — / **adapt**. //
하지만 그리고 나서 아이들은 / 어른들처럼 / 적응한다 //

- content ⓐ 만족하는 · discontent ⓐ 불만족하는
- determined ⓐ 결정되는 · merely ⓐⓓ 단지
- successive ⓐ 연속적인 · affect ⓥ 영향을 미치다
- adjust ⓥ 적응하다 · default ⓝ 기본값
- well-being ⓝ 행복, 안녕 · baseline ⓝ 기준선
- fade ⓥ 사라지다, 희미해지다 · despair ⓝ 절망
- tendency ⓝ 경향 · long for ~을 갈망하다 · adapt ⓥ 적응하다
- regret ⓥ 후회하다 · struggle ⓥ 고군분투하다

우리가 행복하거나 슬프거나, 만족스럽거나 불만족스러운 것은 좋은 일이 일어나면 행복하고, 나쁜 일이 일어나면 슬픈 것처럼 단지 삶의 경험의 각각의 개별적인 연속적인 순간에 의해 결정되지 않는다. 우리의 경험은 우리의 기분에 영향을 미치지만, 우리는 각 돌풍에 의해 완전히 새로운 방향으로 날아가지 않는다. 인간으로서 우리는 좋을 뿐 아니라 나쁘기도 한 새로운 정보와 사건들에 적응하고 우리의 개인적인 기본 행복 수준으로 돌아간다. 기복은 있을 것이지만, 시간이 지나면서 고유한 수위를 찾는 물처럼 우리는 우리의 기준선으로 끌려가는데 즉, 나쁜 소식 후에는 다시 '올라'오고 좋은 소식 후에는 다시 '내려'온다. 첫사랑의 행복감은 사라지고, 결별의 절망도 그렇다. 이 경향은 어린 아이들과 그들의 장난감 기쁨에서 가장 잘 보여진다. 그들은 간절히 원하던 것을 얻을 때, 그들의 남은 인생 동안 행복할 것이라고 믿는다. 그리고 그들의 남은 인생의 처음 몇 분 동안, 그들은 그렇다. 하지만 그리고 나서 어른들처럼 아이들은 적응한다.

다음 빈칸에 들어갈 말로 가장 적절한 것을 고르시오.

① adapt 행복을 겪은 후 기준선으로 돌아가는 것은 적응하는 과정임
적응하다
② regret 후회는 언급되지 않았음
후회하다
③ explore 탐험은 언급되지 않았음
탐험하다
④ struggle 기준선으로 자연스럽게 돌아가는 경향에 관한 내용임
고군분투하다
⑤ celebrate 축하는 언급되지 않았음
축하하다

| 문제 풀이 순서 | ★★★ [정답률 53%]

1st 빈칸이 포함된 문장과 그 앞의 예시를 읽고, 빈칸에 들어갈 말에 대한 단서를 얻는다.

예시	This tendency is best seen with little kids and their toy joy: When they get what they've longed for, they believe they will be happy for the rest of their lives. And for the first few minutes of the rest of their lives, they are. 이 경향은 어린 아이들과 그들의 장난감 기쁨에서 가장 잘 보여진다. 그들은 간절히 원하던 것을 얻을 때, 그들의 남은 인생 동안 행복할 것이라고 믿는다. 그리고 그들의 남은 인생의 처음 몇 분 동안, 그들은 그렇다.
빈칸 문장	But then the kids — like adults — _____. 하지만 그리고 나서 어른들처럼 아이들은 _____

➡ 아이들의 장난감 기쁨을 예로 들며, 아이들이 원하던 장난감을 얻으면 처음에는 행복해도 그 뒤에는 어른들처럼 '무엇'을 한다고 했으므로, [단서] 어른들은 행복 뒤에 '무엇'을 하는지 파악해야 한다. [발상]

2nd 글의 내용을 종합해서 빈칸에 들어갈 적절한 말을 찾는다.

• 인간은 새로운 사건에 적응하고 원래의 기본 행복 수준으로 돌아옴 [단서1]
• 감정 기복이 있어도 시간이 지나면 기준선으로 돌아옴 [단서2]
• 강렬한 감정은 결국 사라짐 [단서3]

➡ 인간은 어떤 강렬한 감정이나 경험을 하더라도 결국에는 '익숙해져' 원래의 감정 상태인 기준선으로 돌아오는 경향이 있다.

▶ 따라서 아이들은 장난감을 얻고 처음에는 행복하다가 다시 원래의 상태로 돌아가기 때문에, 어른들처럼 ① '적응한다.'

| 선택지 분석 |

① 인간의 감정은 결국 기준선으로 돌아온다고 했으므로, 장난감에 대한 아이들의 행복이 사라지고 원래 상태로 돌아오는 것은 적응하는 과정이다.
② 장난감을 얻은 행복 이후에 기준선으로 돌아가므로, 후회하는 것이 아니다.
③ 장난감을 얻은 행복 이후에 기준선으로 돌아가므로, 탐험하는 것이 아니다.
④ 행복 이후에 자연스럽게 기준선으로 돌아가는 경향이므로, 고군분투한다는 것은 어울리지 않는다.
⑤ 아이들이 장난감을 얻은 직후에 축하했을 수도 있지만, 그 이후에 감정이 원래대로 돌아오는 경향이 핵심 내용이므로 어울리지 않는다.

32 정답 ③ ＊아데노신으로 인해 조정되는 수면 욕구

부사절 접속사 (양보)
Although you may put off going to sleep / in order to squeeze more activities into your day, / eventually your need for sleep becomes overwhelming / and you are forced to get some sleep. //
비록 당신은 잠자는 것을 미룰 수 있지만 / 하루에 더 많은 활동을 밀어 넣기 위해 / 결국 당신의 수면에 대한 필요는 압도적이게 되고 / 잠을 잘 수밖에 없게 된다 //

'~ 때문에'
This daily drive for sleep / appears to be **due**, in part, **to** a
과거분사구 (compound 수식)
compound / **known as adenosine**. //
이러한 매일의 수면 욕구는 / 부분적으로 화합물 때문으로 보인다 / 아데노신이라고 알려진 /
서술적 용법의 형용사 (명사 뒤에서 수식)
This natural chemical builds up in your blood / as time **awake** increases. // [단서1] 깨어 있는 시간이 길어질수록 혈액에 아데노신이 쌓임
이 자연 화학물질은 당신의 혈액 속에 쌓인다 / 깨어 있는 시간이 증가할수록 //

부사절 접속사 (시간)
While you sleep, / your body breaks down the adenosine. //
당신이 자는 동안 / 당신의 몸은 아데노신을 분해한다 // [단서2] 잠을 자야 아데노신이 분해됨
선행사를 포함하는 관계대명사 '추적하다'
Thus, / this molecule may be **what** your body uses / to **keep track of** lost sleep / and to trigger sleep when needed. //
따라서 / 이 분자는 당신의 몸이 사용하는 것일지도 모른다 / 놓쳐버린 수면을 추적하고 / 필요할 때 수면을 유도하는 데 //

An accumulation of adenosine and other factors might explain /
아데노신의 축적과 다른 요인들은 설명할 수도 있다 /
explain의 목적어절을 이끄는 의문사
why, after several nights of less than optimal amounts of sleep, / you build up a sleep debt / that you must make up / by sleeping longer than normal. // [단서3] 수면 빚은 더 오래 잠으로써 보충해야 함
왜 당신이 최적의 수면량에 미치지 못한 며칠 밤 후에 / 수면 빚을 쌓는지를 / 보충해야 하는 / 평소보다 더 오래 잠으로써 //

be[become] accustomed to -ing: ~에 익숙해지다
Because of such built-in molecular feedback, / you can't **become accustomed to getting** less sleep / than your body needs. //
이러한 내재된 분자적 피드백 때문에 / 당신은 더 적은 잠을 자는 것에 익숙해질 수 없다 / 당신의 몸이 필요한 것보다 // [단서4] 내재된 신체 작용 때문에 필요량보다 적게 자는 것에 익숙해질 수 없음
Eventually, a lack of sleep **catches up with you**. //
결국 수면 부족은 당신을 따라잡는다 //

• put off 미루다, 연기하다 • eventually ⓐⓓ 결국
• overwhelming ⓐ 압도적인 • drive ⓝ 욕구, 충동
• chemical ⓝ 화학물질 • build up 쌓이다 • break down 분해하다
• molecule ⓝ 분자 • trigger ⓥ 유발하다 • optimal ⓐ 최적의
• debt ⓝ 빚 • make up 보충하다 • built-in ⓐ 내재된
• lack ⓝ 부족, 결핍 • take away 뺏다 • swing ⓝ (기분의) 변화
• catch up with ~을 따라잡다

비록 당신은 하루에 더 많은 활동을 밀어 넣기 위해 잠자는 것을 미룰 수 있지만, 결국 당신의 수면에 대한 필요는 압도적이게 되고 잠을 잘 수밖에 없게 된다. 이러한 매일의 수면 욕구는 부분적으로 아데노신이라고 알려진 화합물 때문으로 보인다. 이 자연 화학물질은 깨어 있는 시간이 증가할수록 당신의 혈액 속에 쌓인다. 당신이 자는 동안, 당신의 몸은 아데노신을 분해한다. 따라서, 이 분자는 당신의 몸이 놓쳐버린 수면을 추적하고 필요할 때 수면을 유도하는 데 사용하는 것일지도 모른다. 아데노신의 축적과 다른 요인들은 왜 당신이 최적의 수면량에 미치지 못한 며칠 밤 후에 평소보다 더 오래 잠으로써 보충해야 하는 수면 빚을 쌓는지를 설명할 수도 있다. 이러한 내재된 분사적 피드백 때문에, 당신은 당신의 몸이 필요한 것보다 더 적은 잠을 자는 것에 익숙해질 수 없다. 결국 수면 부족은 **당신을 따라잡는다**.

다음 빈칸에 들어갈 말로 가장 적절한 것을 고르시오. [3점]
① takes away your energy 수면 부족의 영향을 피할 수 없다는 것이 핵심 내용임
당신의 에너지를 뺏는다
② causes mood swings 기분 변화는 언급되지 않았음
기분 변화를 유발한다
③ catches up with you 수면 부족은 피할 수 없으며 결국 그 대가를 치르게 됨
당신을 따라잡는다
④ breaks down natural chemicals 수면 부족이 아니라 수면이 아데노신을 분해함
천연 화학 물질을 분해한다
⑤ triggers adenosine to disappear 수면 부족은 아데노신을 축적함
아데노신이 사라지도록 유발한다

| 문제 풀이 순서 | ★★★ [정답률 27%]

1st 빈칸이 포함된 문장을 읽고, 빈칸에 들어갈 말에 대한 단서를 얻는다.

빈칸 문장	Eventually, a lack of sleep _____. 결국 수면 부족은 _____

➡ 수면 부족의 결과를 나타내는 결론 문장에 해당하므로 [단서] 수면 부족이 끼치는 영향을 파악하고 이를 한 문장으로 종합해야 한다. [발상]

2nd 글의 내용을 종합해서 빈칸에 들어갈 적절한 말을 찾는다.

• 깨어 있는 동안 아데노신이 계속 쌓여 수면 욕구가 증가함 [단서1]
• 잠을 자야 아데노신이 분해됨 [단서2]
• 아데노신의 축적(수면 빚)은 더 오래 잠으로써 보충해야 함 [단서3]
• 내재된 신체 작용 때문에 필요량보다 적게 자는 것에 익숙해질 수 없음 [단서4]

2025.9
7회

정답 및 해설 **189**

➡️ 사람은 잠을 안 잘수록 아데노신이 쌓이고 잠을 자야 이를 분해할 수 있는데, 이러한 수면 빚은 더 오래 잠으로써 보충해야 한다. 이러한 신체 작용은 내재된 것이므로 사람은 필요량보다 적게 자는 것에 익숙해질 수 없다.

▶ 따라서, 수면 부족의 영향에서 벗어날 수 없으므로 결국 수면 부족은 ③ '당신을 따라잡는다.'

| 선택지 분석 |
꿀팁: 수면 부족에 관한 일반적인 상식보단 지문에 근거해서 답을 고르기! 함정

① 수면 부족이 에너지를 뺏은 것은 사실이지만, 이는 수면 부족의 영향 중 일부일 뿐이며 수면 부족이 가져오는 신체 작용은 내재된 것이어서 피할 수 없다는 점이 핵심 내용이다.

② 수면 부족이 기분 변화를 일으킨다는 것은 언급되지 않았다.

③ 수면 부족이 누적되면 결국 피할 수 없이 그 대가를 치르게 된다는 내용이다.

④ 천연 화학 물질(아데노신)을 분해하는 것은 수면 부족이 아니라 수면의 역할이므로, 글의 내용과 반대된다.

⑤ 아데노신이 사라지도록 유발하는 것은 수면의 역할이며, 수면 부족은 오히려 아데노신을 쌓이게 하므로 글의 내용과 반대된다.

33 정답 ① ＊측정값의 불확실성이 갖는 의미의 상대성

one of + 복수 명사: ~중 하나 (one에 수 일치)   to appreciate의 의미상 주어
One of the things that makes uncertainty difficult **for members of the public** to appreciate / **is** that **the significance of uncertainty is relative**. //
단수 동사
대중이 불확실성을 이해하기 어렵게 만드는 것들 중 하나는 / 불확실성의 중요성이 상대적이라는 것이다 //

Take, for example, the distance between Earth and the sun: / 1.49597×10⁸ km, as measured at one point during the year. //
지구와 태양 사이의 거리의 예를 들어보자 / 즉 연중 한 지점에서 측정된 1.49597×10⁸ km //
= 1.49597×10⁸ km
This seems relatively precise; / after all, using six significant digits **means** / I know the distance to an accuracy of one part in a million or so. //
뒤에 목적어절 접속사가 생략됨
이것은 상대적으로 정확해 보이지만 / 결국, 여섯 자리의 유효 숫자를 사용하는 것은 의미한다 / 백만 분의 일 정도의 정확도로 그 거리를 알고 있다는 것을 //

However, if the next digit is uncertain, / that means the uncertainty in knowing the precise Earth-sun distance / is larger than the distance between New York and Chicago! //
하지만, 만약 다음 숫자가 불확실하다면 / 그것은 지구와 태양의 정확한 거리를 아는 것에 있어서의 불확실성이 / 뉴욕과 시카고의 거리보다 더 크다는 것을 의미한다 //
명사절 접속사 (~인지 아닌지)
Whether or not the quoted number is "precise" / therefore depends on / **what I'm intending to do with it**. //
간접의문문
인용된 숫자가 '정확한지' 아닌지는 / 따라서 ~에 따라 다르다 / 내가 그것으로 무엇을 하려고 하느냐 //
단서 1 숫자의 정확성 여부는 그것을 사용하려는 의도에 달려있음

If I care only about / what minute the sun will rise tomorrow, / then the number quoted here is fine. //
단서 2 일출 시각 예상은 여섯 자리 숫자 정도로도 괜찮음
만약 내가 관심이 있다면 / 내일 태양이 몇 분에 뜰지에만 / 여기에 인용된 숫자로 괜찮다 //
형용사적 용법 (satellite 수식)
If I want to send a satellite **to orbit** just above the sun, however, / then I would need to know distances more accurately. //
하지만 만약 내가 태양 주위에 궤도를 돌 위성을 보내고 싶다면 / 나는 더 정확하게 거리를 알 필요가 있을 것이다 //
단서 3 태양 주위를 돌 위성을 보내려면 더 정확한 수치가 필요함

- uncertainty ⓝ 불확실성
- appreciate ⓥ 이해하다, 진가를 알다
- relatively ⓐⓓ 상대적으로
- precise ⓐ 정확한, 정밀한
- digit ⓝ 자릿수
- accuracy ⓝ 정확도
- quoted ⓐ 인용된
- depend on ~에 달려 있다
- intend ⓥ 의도하다
- satellite ⓝ (인공)위성
- orbit ⓥ 궤도를 돌다
- accurately ⓐⓓ 정확하게
- significance ⓝ 중요성
- relative ⓐ 상대적인
- intention ⓝ 의도

대중이 불확실성을 이해하기 어렵게 만드는 것들 중 하나는 **불확실성의 중요성이 상대적이라는 것이다.** 지구와 태양 사이의 거리, 즉 연중 한 지점에서 측정된 1.49597×10⁸ km의 예를 들어보자. 이것은 상대적으로 정확해 보이지만,

---

결국, 여섯 자리의 유효 숫자를 사용하는 것은 백만 분의 일 정도의 정확도로 그 거리를 알고 있다는 것을 의미한다. 하지만, 만약 다음 숫자가 불확실하다면, 그것은 지구와 태양의 정확한 거리를 아는 것에 있어서의 불확실성이 뉴욕과 시카고의 거리보다 더 크다는 것을 의미한다! 따라서, 인용된 숫자가 '정확한지' 아닌지는 내가 그것으로 무엇을 하려고 하느냐에 따라 다르다. 만약 내가 내일 태양이 몇 분에 뜰지에만 관심이 있다면, 여기에 인용된 숫자로 괜찮다. 하지만 만약 내가 태양 주위에 궤도를 돌 위성을 보내고 싶다면, 나는 더 정확하게 거리를 알 필요가 있을 것이다.

모든 측정의 불확실성 수준이 같다는 것은 반대되는 내용임
다음 빈칸에 들어갈 말로 가장 적절한 것을 고르시오. [3점]
① the significance of uncertainty is relative
불확실성의 중요성은 상대적이다   불확실성의 정도는 의도에 따라 상대적임
② the relativity of time is difficult to recognize
시간의 상대성은 인지하기 어렵다   시간의 상대성에 관한 내용이 아님
③ all measurements have the same level of uncertainty
모든 측정값은 동일한 수준의 불확실성을 가진다
④ measurements of distance do not depend on intention
거리 측정은 의도에 따라 달라지지 않는다
⑤ specific numbers make people believe without question
구체적인 숫자는 사람들이 이의 없이 믿게 만든다   구체적인 숫자의 신뢰성이 아닌 중요성에 관한 내용임
거리 측정이 의도에 따라 달라지지 않는다는 것은 반대되는 내용임

| 문제 풀이 순서 | ★★★ [정답률 43%]

1st 빈칸이 포함된 문장을 읽고, 빈칸에 들어갈 말에 대한 단서를 얻는다.

빈칸 문장	One of the things that makes uncertainty difficult for members of the public to appreciate is that _____ 대중이 불확실성을 이해하기 어렵게 만드는 것들 중 하나는

➡️ 대중이 불확실성을 이해하기 어렵게 하는 원인을 묻고 있으므로 단서 불확실성을 이해하기 어려운 문제 상황이나 예시를 통해 그 원인을 파악해야 한다. 발상

2nd 글의 내용을 종합해서 빈칸에 들어갈 적절한 말을 찾는다.
- 어떤 숫자를 정확하다고 할 수 있는지는 그것을 사용하려는 의도에 따라 달라짐 단서 1
- 일출 시각 예상은 여섯 자리 숫자 정도로도 괜찮음 단서 2
- 태양 주위를 돌 위성을 보내려면 더 정확한 수치가 필요함 단서 3

➡️ 같은 측정값이라도 어떤 목적으로 사용하느냐에 따라 그 값이 정확한 정도가 달라진다.
▶ 따라서, ① '불확실성의 중요성은 상대적이기' 때문에 대중이 불확실성을 이해하기 어려운 것이다.

| 선택지 분석 |
① 측정값의 불확실성이 갖는 중요성은 그 측정값을 사용하려는 의도에 따라 달라진다.
② 시간의 상대성은 언급되지 않았다.
③ 의도에 따라 요구되는 정확성의 정도가 다르다고 했으므로, 모든 측정값의 불확실성이 동일하다는 것은 반대되는 내용이다.
④ 의도에 따라 요구되는 정확성의 정도가 다르다고 했으므로, 거리 측정이 의도에 따라 달라지지 않는다는 것은 반대되는 내용이다.
⑤ 구체적인 숫자의 신뢰성이 아닌 중요성에 관한 내용이다.

34 정답 ② ＊재생 가능 에너지를 위해 화석 연료가 필요한 역설

동격
Richard Heinberg, an American journalist, argues / that in building the renewable energy infrastructure / to stop global warming, /
미국인 저널리스트인 Richard Heinberg는 주장한다 / 재생 가능 에너지 기반 시설을 구축할 때 / 지구 온난화를 막기 위해 /

we are actually involved / in one of the greatest change projects in human history. //
우리는 실제로 관여하는 것이라고 / 인류 역사상 가장 큰 변화 프로젝트 중 하나에 //

In addition to solar panels and wind turbines, / we have to build / an alternative transport infrastructure, farming procedures and industrial processes. //
'~에 더하여'
태양광 패널과 풍력 터빈에 더하여 / 우리는 구축해야 한다 / 대체 교통 기반 시설, 농업 절차 그리고 산업 프로세스를 //

단서 1 재생 가능 에너지로의 전환은 화석 연료 없이는 불가능함
This transformation cannot happen / without fossil fuels. //
이 변화는 일어날 수 없다 / 화석 연료 없이는 //

For instance, / production of concrete structures and steel elements / require amounts of energy / that is only possible to produce with fossil energy.
주격 관계대명사
단서 2 건축을 위한 콘크리트와 강철 생산에 화석 에너지가 필요함
예를 들어, / 콘크리트 구조물과 강철 요소의 생산은 / 에너지의 양을 필요로 한다 / 화석 에너지로만 생산 가능한 //

Production of solar panels requires / scarce and expensive minerals / which must be excavated, / again requiring the use of fossil fuels. //
분사구문
단서 3 태양광 패널 생산을 위한 광물 채굴에도 화석 연료가 필요함
태양광 패널의 생산은 필요로 하며, / 희귀하고 값비싼 광물들을 / 발굴되어져야 하는 / 이는 또한 화석 연료 사용을 필요로 한다 //

Thus, the harder we push / towards a renewable energy system, / the faster we have to use fossil energy / for the construction process. //
the 비교급, the 비교급: ~할수록 더 …하다
따라서, 우리가 더 세게 밀고 나아갈수록 / 재생 가능 에너지 시스템을 향하여 / 더 빠르게 우리는 화석 에너지를 사용해야 한다 / 건설 과정에서 //

not only A but also B: A뿐만 아니라 B도
This is not only expensive, / but also an undermining factor for our efforts / to cut global emissions. //
이는 단지 비용이 많이 들 뿐만 아니라 / 우리의 노력을 저해하는 요인이 된다 / 전 세계적 배기가스를 줄이려는 //

Heinberg remarks / that the cost of building this new energy infrastructure / is seldom counted in transition proposals, /
Heinberg는 언급하는데 / 이러한 새로운 에너지 기반 시설을 구축하는 비용이 / 전환 제안에서 거의 계산되지 않는다고 /
계속적 용법의 주격 관계대명사
which tend to focus just on energy supply requirements. //
이는 에너지 공급 요구 사항에만 집중하는 경향이 있다 //

- renewable energy 재생 가능 에너지
- infrastructure ⓝ 사회 기반 시설   • alternative ⓐ 대안의
- procedure ⓝ 절차   • transformation ⓝ 변화, 변혁
- fossil fuel 화석 연료   • steel ⓝ 강철   • element ⓝ 요소
- require ⓥ 필요로 하다   • scarce ⓐ 희귀한
- mineral ⓝ 광물   • undermining ⓐ 약화시키는   • effort ⓝ 노력
- emission ⓝ 배출(물)   • remark ⓥ 말하다, 언급하다
- transition ⓝ 전환   • supply ⓝ 공급
- take advantage of ~을 활용하다   • construction ⓝ 건설
- competitive ⓐ 경쟁력 있는

미국인 저널리스트인 Richard Heinberg는 지구 온난화를 막기 위해 재생 가능 에너지 기반 시설을 구축할 때, 우리는 실제로 인류 역사상 가장 큰 변화 프로젝트 중 하나에 관여하는 것이라고 주장한다. 태양광 패널과 풍력 터빈에 더하여 우리는 대체 교통 기반 시설, 농업 절차 그리고 산업 프로세스를 구축해야 한다. 이 변화는 화석 연료 없이는 일어날 수 없다. 예를 들어, 콘크리트 구조물과 강철 요소의 생산은 화석 에너지로만 생산 가능한 에너지의 양을 필요로 한다. 태양광 패널의 생산은 발굴되어져야 하는 희귀하고 값비싼 광물들을 필요로 하며, 이는 또한 화석 연료 사용을 필요로 한다. 따라서, 우리가 재생 가능 에너지 시스템을 향하여 더 세게 밀고 나아갈수록, 더 빠르게 우리는 건설 과정에서 화석 에너지를 사용해야 한다. 이는 단지 비용이 많이 들 뿐만 아니라, 전 세계적 배기가스를 줄이려는 우리의 노력을 저해하는 요인이 된다. Heinberg는 이러한 새로운 에너지 기반 시설을 구축하는 비용이 전환 제안에서 거의 계산되지 않는다고 언급하는데, 이는 에너지 공급 요구 사항에만 집중하는 경향이 있다.

재생 가능 에너지 시스템이 구축되면서 화석 연료 사용도 빨라진다는 내용임
다음 빈칸에 들어갈 말로 가장 적절한 것을 고르시오. [3점]
① we are taking full advantage of renewable energy sources 에너지 전환의 긍정적인 결과가 아니라 과정의 폐해를 강조함
우리는 재생 가능 에너지원을 최대한 활용하고 있다
② we have to use fossil energy for the construction process
우리는 건설 과정에서 화석 에너지를 사용해야 한다
③ we invest in more natural resources for the environment
우리는 환경을 위해 더 많은 천연자원에 투자한다   천연자원이 아니라 화석 연료에 더 투자하게 될 것임
④ we are able to decrease the rate of global warming
우리는 지구 온난화의 속도를 줄일 수 있다
⑤ alternative energy markets become competitive
대체 에너지 시장이 경쟁력을 갖추게 된다   대체 에너지 시장의 경쟁력은 언급되지 않았음
에너지 전환 과정에서 지구 온난화를 늦추는 것이 아니라 부추길 수 있음

>왜 정답? ✱✱❂ [정답률 57%]
- 재생 가능 에너지로의 전환은 화석 연료 없이는 불가능함 단서 1
- 기반 시설 건축에 필요한 콘크리트와 강철 생산에 화석 에너지가 쓰임 단서 2
- 태양광 패널 생산에 필요한 광물 채굴에도 화석 연료가 쓰임 단서 3
➡ 화석 에너지에서 재생 가능 에너지로 전환하는 과정에서, 건축과 자재 생산을 위해 오히려 화석 연료가 필수적으로 쓰인다.
▶ 따라서 재생 가능 에너지 시스템 구축을 더 추진할수록, 더 빠르게 ② '우리는 건설 과정에서 화석 에너지를 사용해야 한다.'

>왜 오답?
① 재생 가능 에너지 시스템으로 전환하는 과정의 폐해를 강조할 뿐, 전환이 완료된 결과는 언급되지 않았다.
③ 재생 가능 에너지로 전환하면서 화석 연료에 더 투자하게 될 뿐, 천연자원에 더 투자하진 않을 것이다.
④ 재생 가능 에너지로 전환하면서 배기가스 배출량 감축을 위한 노력을 저해할 수 있다고 했으므로 오히려 지구 온난화를 부추길 수 있다.
⑤ 대체 에너지 시장의 경쟁력은 언급되지 않았다.

35 정답 ④ ✱인공지능의 발전 과정

다음 글에서 전체 흐름과 관계 없는 문장은?

Humans for centuries have dreamed of machines / that could become intelligent and make human-like decisions. //
주격 관계대명사
인간은 수 세기 동안 기계를 꿈꿔왔다 / 지능적이게 될 수 있고 인간과 같은 결정을 내릴 수 있는 //

단서 1 인간은 고대부터 지능을 가진 기계에 대한 상상을 해옴
There have been myths / about robots, automatons, and artificial beings / since ancient Greece / (e.g., the myth of Pandora, / who released ills upon the world). //
주격 관계대명사
신화가 존재해 왔다 / 로봇, 자동 장치, 인공 생명체에 대한 / 고대 그리스 이래로 / (예를 들면, 판도라의 신화와 같은 / 세상에 재앙을 풀어놓은) //

① Likewise, literature throughout history / has dreamed of creating human-like creatures and thinking machines / (e.g., Mary Shelley's *Frankenstein*). //
병렬 구조
단서 2 문학 작품에서도 지능을 가진 기계에 대한 상상이 이어짐
마찬가지로 역사를 통틀어 문학은 / 인간과 같은 생명체와 사고하는 기계를 창조하는 꿈을 꿔 왔다 / (예를 들면, Mary Shelley의 '프랑켄슈타인'과 같은) //

② In 1950, British mathematician Alan Turing asked / whether machines could think and reason like humans /
명사절 접속사(ask의 목적어절)
1950년, 영국의 수학자 Alan Turing은 물었고 / 기계가 인간처럼 사고하고 추론할 수 있는지 /
단서 3 상상에 머물던 개념이 과학적 연구(튜링 테스트)의 대상으로 전환됨
and then developed the Turing test / to measure a machine's intelligence / and whether the machines can think autonomously. //
그 다음에 튜링 테스트를 개발했다 / 기계의 지능을 측정하기 위해 / 그리고 기계가 자율적으로 사고할 수 있는지를 //
단서 4 이어서 '인공지능'이라는 학문적 용어가 정립됨

③ A few years later, / MIT professor John McCarthy coined "artificial intelligence," / replacing the previously used expression "automata studies." //
과거분사구 (the expression 수식)
몇 년 후 / MIT 교수 John McCarthy는 '인공지능'이라는 표현을 만들어냈다 / 이전에 사용된 '자동 장치 연구'라는 표현을 대체해 //

④ But artificial intelligence didn't stop there; / its first major
appearance was in a movie / **where** feeling artificial intelligence
_{관계부사}
replaced human characters **with** robots. //)
_{replace A with B: A를 B로 대체하다}
(하지만 인공지능은 거기서 멈추지 않았다 / 그것의 첫 번째 주요 등장은 영화에서였다 / 감정
을 느끼는 인공지능이 인간 등장인물을 로봇으로 대체한 //)

⑤ Since then, / artificial intelligence has become the study and
practice of "making intelligent machines" /
그 이후로 / 인공지능은 "지능적인 기계 만들기"에 대한 연구와 실행이 되었다 /
_{주격 관계대명사}
that are programmed to think like humans / — endowed by
their creators with reasoning and learning. //
인간처럼 사고하도록 프로그램화된 / 즉, 그들의 창조자들에 의해 추론과 학습 능력을 부여
받은 //

- intelligent ⓐ 지능적인
- decision ⓝ 결정
- myth ⓝ 신화
- literature ⓝ 문학
- mathematician ⓝ 수학자
- reason ⓥ 추론하다
- measure ⓥ 측정하다
- intelligence ⓝ 지능
- autonomously ⓐⓓ 자율적으로
- coin ⓥ (신조어를) 만들다
- previously ⓐⓓ 이전에
- appearance ⓝ 등장
- practice ⓝ 실행, 실제
- reasoning ⓝ 추론

인간은 수 세기 동안 지능적이게 될 수 있고 인간과 같은 결정을 내릴 수 있
는 기계를 꿈꿔왔다. 고대 그리스 이래로 로봇, 자동 장치, 인공 생명체에 대한
신화가 존재해 왔다 (예를 들면, 세상에 재앙을 풀어놓은 판도라의 신화와 같
은). ① 마찬가지로 역사를 통틀어 문학은 인간과 같은 생명체와 사고하는 기
계를 창조하는 꿈을 꿔왔다. (예를 들면, Mary Shelley의 '프랑켄슈타인'과 같
은) ② 1950년, 영국의 수학자 Alan Turing은 기계가 인간처럼 사고하고 추론
할 수 있는지 물었고, 그 다음에 기계의 지능과 기계가 자율적으로 사고할 수
있는지를 측정하기 위해 튜링 테스트를 개발했다. ③ 몇 년 후, MIT 교수 John
McCarthy는 이전에 사용된 '자동 장치 연구'라는 표현을 대체해 '인공지능'이
라는 표현을 만들어냈다. (④ 하지만 인공지능은 거기서 멈추지 않았다; 그것의
첫 번째 주요 등장은 감정을 느끼는 인공지능이 인간 등장인물을 로봇으로 대
체한 영화에서였다.) ⑤ 그 이후로, 인공지능은 인간처럼 사고하도록 프로그램
화된 즉, 그들의 창조자들에 의해 추론과 학습 능력을 부여받은 "지능적인 기계
만들기"에 대한 연구와 실행이 되었다.

왜 정답 · 오답? ★★★ [정답률 59%]

글의 앞부분: 인간은 지능을 가진 기계를 상상해왔고 고대에서부터 관련된 신화가
존재해왔음

① 문학에서도 인간과 같은 생명체와 사고하는 기계를 창조하는 꿈을 꿔왔음 (예: 프
랑켄슈타인)
▶ 신화 속 상상처럼 문학 작품에서도 비슷한 상상이 있었다는 내용으로 이어지므
로 ①은 무관한 문장이 아님

② 영국의 수학자 Alan Turing은 기계가 인간처럼 사고할 수 있는지를 측정하기 위
해 튜링 테스트를 개발했음
▶ 상상의 영역에 있던 인공지능이 과학적 탐구의 대상으로 전환되는 과정을 설명
하고 있으므로 ②은 무관한 문장이 아님

③ 몇 년 후, MIT 교수 John McCarthy는 '인공지능'이라는 용어를 만들어냈음
▶ 튜링의 연구에 이어 '인공지능'이라는 공식적인 학문 용어가 등장하는 역사적 사
실을 설명하며 흐름을 이어가므로 ③은 무관한 문장이 아님

④ 하지만 인공지능은 거기서 멈추지 않았고, 그것의 첫 주요 등장은 감정을 느끼는
인공지능이 인간을 대체하는 영화에서였음
▶ 인공지능 개념의 발전 과정이 서술되다가 갑자기 감정을 느끼는 인공지능이 실
제로 활용된 사례를 언급하며 주제에서 벗어나므로, ④이 무관한 문장임

⑤ 그 이후로, 인공지능은 '지능적인 기계 만들기'에 대한 연구와 실행을 뜻하게 되었
음
▶ '인공지능'이라는 용어가 만들어진 이후 그것이 어떤 의미로 정립되었는지를 설
명하며 글을 마무리하므로, ⑤은 무관한 문장이 아님

★ 글의 흐름

1 도입: 인간은 신화와 문학을 통해 오랫동안 지능을 가진 기계를 꿈꿔왔음
2 전개: 상상의 개념이 튜링 테스트를 통해 과학적 탐구의 대상이 되었고, '인공지능'
이라는 학문적 용어로도 정립됨
3 결론: 그 후 인공지능은 인간처럼 사고하는 지능적인 기계를 만드는 구체적인 연구
및 실행 분야로 발전함

36 정답 ② ★방광에 물을 오래 저장하는 사막거북

The desert tortoise has a simple solution / for coping with
Death Valley's extreme heat: / It avoids it. //
사막거북은 간단한 해결책을 가지고 있는데 / Death Valley의 극심한 더위를 극복하기
위해 / 그것은 더위를 피하는 것이다 //

_{부사적 용법 (목적)} _{주격 보어 (과거분사)}
(A) But **to stay supplied** with water / through its extended
hibernation, / the reptile relies on something else / — its highly
sophisticated bladder. // 단서 1 (B)에서 나열된 수분 비축 방법들과는 다른 방법을 가리킴
하지만 수분이 공급된 채로 지내기 위해 / 그것의 장기간에 걸친 동면 동안 / 이 파충류는 다른
것에 의존한다 / 즉, 그것의 매우 정교한 방광이다 //

Unlike most animals, / the tortoise's bladder acts as a holding
tank, / _{분사구문을 이끄는 현재분사}**allowing** it to reabsorb water back into its body. //
대부분의 동물과 달리 / 거북의 방광은 보관 탱크로서의 역할을 하며 / 그것이 그것의 몸으로
물을 다시 흡수할 수 있게 한다 //

_{without -ing: ~ 없이, ~하지 않고}
Incredibly, / a desert tortoise can go a full year / **without taking**
in any freshwater at all. // 단서 2 주어진 글의 The desert tortoise를 가리킴
놀랍게도 / 사막거북은 1년 내내 살아갈 수 있다 / 담수를 전혀 섭취하지 않고도 //

(B) The slow-moving creature hibernates during the winter /
and stays in its tunnel for much of the summer, / _{분사구문을 이끄는 현재분사}**meaning** that
it spends more than 90 percent of its life immobile. //
그 느리게 움직이는 생명체는 겨울에는 동면하고 / 대부분의 여름에는 그것의 굴 속에서 보내
는데 / 이는 그 생의 90퍼센트 이상을 움직이지 않은 채로 보낸다는 것을 의미한다 //

In fact, / the tortoise usually only surfaces / after a good rain. //
사실 / 거북은 보통 밖으로 나온다 / 충분한 비가 온 후에만 //

Then, it gets to work. // 그 다음에 그것은 활동을 시작한다 //
_{병렬 구조 (by의 목적어)}
The tortoise stocks up on water / by **eating** plants / and **digging**
_{형용사적 용법 (holes 수식)}
holes **to collect** rain. //
거북은 물을 비축한다 / 식물을 먹고 / 빗물을 모으기 위한 구멍을 팜으로써 //

(C) And because its bladder is so important / to a tortoise's
survival, / 단서 3 (A)에서 처음 언급된 '방광'을 부연 설명함
그리고 그것의 방광이 매우 중요하기 때문에 / 거북의 생존에 /

park rangers often remind visitors / not to stop and help the
slow-movers / across the road. //
공원 순찰대원들은 종종 방문객들에게 상기시킨다 / 멈추어 그 느리게 움직이는 것을 도와주
지 않을 것을 / 도로를 건너도록 //

Tortoises become **so terrified** / when people pick them up /
_{so + 형용사 + that …: 너무 ~해서 …하다} _{분사구문을 이끄는 현재분사}
that they empty their bladders, / **losing** their precious water
reserves. //
거북은 너무 겁을 먹어 / 사람들이 그들을 들어 올릴 때 / 그들의 방광을 비워버리고 / 소중한
저장된 물을 잃게 된다 //

- cope with ~에 대처하다
- extreme ⓐ 극심한
- avoid ⓥ 피하다
- reptile ⓝ 파충류
- rely on ~에 의존하다
- sophisticated ⓐ 정교한
- reabsorb ⓥ 재흡수하다
- take in ~을 섭취하다
- freshwater ⓝ 담수
- creature ⓝ 생물
- immobile ⓐ 움직이지 않는
- surface ⓥ 표면으로 나오다
- stock up on ~을 비축하다
- survival ⓝ 생존
- ranger ⓝ 경비대원, 순찰대원
- reserves ⓝ 비축물

사막거북은 Death Valley의 극심한 더위를 극복하기 위해 간단한 해결책을 가지고 있는데 그것은 더위를 피하는 것이다. (B) 그 느리게 움직이는 생명체는 겨울에는 동면하고 대부분의 여름에는 그것의 굴 속에서 보내는데 이는 그 생의 90퍼센트 이상을 움직이지 않은 채로 보낸다는 것을 의미한다. 사실, 거북은 보통 충분한 비가 온 후에만 밖으로 나온다. 그 다음에 그것은 활동을 시작한다. 거북은 식물을 먹고, 빗물을 모으기 위한 구멍을 팜으로써 물을 비축한다. (A) 하지만 그것의 장기간에 걸친 동면 동안 수분이 공급된 채로 지내기 위해, 이 파충류는 다른 것에 의존한다. 즉, 그것의 매우 정교한 방광이다. 대부분의 동물과 달리, 거북의 방광은 보관 탱크로서의 역할을 하며, 그것이 그것의 몸으로 물을 다시 흡수할 수 있게 한다. 놀랍게도, 사막거북은 1년 내내 담수를 전혀 섭취하지 않고도 살아갈 수 있다. (C) 그리고 그것의 방광이 거북의 생존에 매우 중요하기 때문에, 공원 순찰대원들은 종종 방문객들에게 멈추어 그 느리게 움직이는 것을 도로를 건너도록 도와주지 않을 것을 상기시킨다. 거북은 사람들이 그들을 들어 올릴 때 너무 겁을 먹어 그들의 방광을 비워버리고, 소중한 저장된 물을 잃게 된다.

(C): 그리고 그것의 방광(its bladder)이 거북의 생존에 매우 중요하기 때문에, 공원 순찰대원들은 종종 방문객들에게 멈추어 그 느리게 움직이는 것을 도로를 건너도록 도와주지 않을 것을 상기시킨다. 거북은 사람들이 그들을 들어 올릴 때 너무 겁을 먹어 그들의 방광을 비워버리고, 소중한 저장된 물을 잃게 된다.

➡ (C) 앞: its bladder라고 했으므로, bladder가 앞에 먼저 언급되었을 것이다. (A)에 bladder가 처음으로 언급되었으므로, its는 (B)에 언급된 사막거북을 가리킨다.
▶ (C) 앞에 (A)가 와야 함 (순서: 주어진 글 ➡ (B) ➡ (A) ➡ (C))
(C) 뒤: 방광의 중요성과 관련된 주의사항으로 글이 마무리된다.

2nd 글이 한눈에 들어오도록 정리하여 정답을 확인한다.

주어진 글: 사막거북의 더위 극복법은 더위를 피하는 것이다.
➡ (B): 생의 대부분을 움직이지 않지만, 활동할 때는 물을 비축한다.
➡ (A): 움직이지 않을 때는 물을 저장하기 위해 정교한 방광에 의존한다.
➡ (C): 이들을 들어 올리면 방광을 비우므로 그러지 않도록 주의해야 한다.
▶ 주어진 글 다음에 이어질 글의 순서는 (B) ➡ (A) ➡ (C)이므로 정답은 ②임

주어진 글 다음에 이어질 글의 순서로 가장 적절한 것을 고르시오. [3점]

① (A) ― (C) ― (B) · 주어진 글에는 (A)의 장기간에 걸친 동면에 대한 언급이 없음
② (B) ― (A) ― (C) · 사막 거북은 더위를 피함으로써 더위를 극복함 ― (B) 생의 대부분을 움직이지 않지만 활동할 때는 물을 비축함 ― (A) 움직이지 않을 때는 물을 저장하기 위해 정교한 방광에 의존함 ― (C) 이들을 들어 올리면 방광을 비우므로 그러지 않도록 주의해야 함
③ (B) ― (C) ― (A)
④ (C) ― (A) ― (B) · (A)에 처음 언급된 방광을 (C)에서 부연 설명함
⑤ (C) ― (B) ― (A)

| 문제 풀이 순서 | ✱✱❀ [정답률 62%]

1st 각 문단의 내용을 파악하고, 글의 논리적인 순서를 추론한다.

주어진 글: 사막거북은 Death Valley의 극심한 더위를 극복하기 위해 간단한 해결책을 가지고 있는데 그것은 더위를 피하는 것이다.
➡ 주어진 글 뒤: 사막거북이 더위를 피하는 구체적인 방법이 제시될 것이다.

(A): 하지만(But) 그것의 장기간에 걸친 동면 동안 수분이 공급된 채로 지내기 위해, 이 파충류는 다른 것(something else)에 의존한다. 즉, 그것의 매우 정교한 방광이다. 대부분의 동물과 달리, 거북의 방광은 보관 탱크로서의 역할을 하며, 그것이 그것의 몸으로 물을 다시 흡수할 수 있게 한다. 놀랍게도, 사막거북은 1년 내내 담수를 전혀 섭취하지 않고도 살아갈 수 있다.

➡ (A) 앞: 반대되는 내용을 나타내는 but과, 이미 언급된 것과는 다른 대상을 나타내는 something else가 쓰였으므로, 방광 외에 사막거북이 수분과 관련하여 이용하는 다른 방법이 앞에 먼저 언급되어야 한다.
▶ 주어진 글에는 사막거북이 더위를 피한다고만 했으므로 (A) 앞에 올 수 없음
(A) 뒤: 방광의 중요한 기능인 수분 재흡수가 언급되었으므로, 이에 관한 부연 설명이 이어질 것이다.

(B): 그 느리게 움직이는 생명체(The slow-moving creature)는 겨울에는 동면하고 대부분의 여름에는 그것의 굴 속에서 보내는데 이는 그 생의 90퍼센트 이상을 움직이지 않은 채로 보낸다는 것을 의미한다. 사실, 거북은 보통 충분한 비가 온 후에만 밖으로 나온다. 그 다음에 그것은 활동을 시작한다. 거북은 식물을 먹고, 빗물을 모으기 위한 구멍을 팜으로써 물(water)을 비축한다.

➡ (B) 앞: 정관사 the가 쓰인 The slow-moving creature로 시작하므로, 느리게 움직이는 생물이 (B)의 바로 앞에서 처음으로 언급되었을 것이다. 주어진 글이 사막거북에 대한 소개로 시작되며, (B)의 첫 문장은 사막거북이 더위를 피하는 구체적인 방법에 해당하므로 자연스럽게 이어진다.
▶ (B) 앞에 주어진 글이 와야 함 (순서: 주어진 글 ➡ (B))
(B) 뒤: 동면 동안 물을 비축하는 여러 방법이 소개되었는데, 사막거북은 이러한 방법들이 아닌 방광에 의지한다는 내용이 (A)에 나온다.
▶ (B) 뒤에 (A)가 와야 함 (순서: 주어진 글 ➡ (B) ➡ (A))

37 정답 ③ ＊자전거의 속도를 늦추는 다양한 마찰력의 원리

Imagine you are pedalling your bicycle / on a level road. //
자전거 페달을 밟고 있다고 상상해 보아라 / 수평의 도로에서 //
<small>형용사적 용법 (force 수식)</small>
You stop pedalling: / no force is now acting / **to move** you forward. //
당신은 페달을 밟는 것을 멈추고 / 어떠한 힘도 이제 작용하지 않는다 / 당신을 앞으로 나아가게 하는 //
What happens? // 그러면 어떻게 될까 //

<small>현재분사구 (the wheels 수식)</small>
(A) One of these is friction in the wheels / **rubbing on the axles.** //
이들 중 하나는 바퀴의 마찰이다 / 축에 닿는 // **단서 1** (C)의 other friction forces의 예시
<small>계속적 용법의 목적격 관계대명사 (air resistance 수식)</small>
Another is air resistance, / **which** you can feel, / **pushing you backwards** / as you and the bicycle move forwards. //
또 다른 하나는 공기 저항으로 / 이는 당신이 느낄 수 있다 / 당신을 뒤쪽으로 미는 / 당신과 자전거가 앞쪽으로 움직일 때 //
When you apply these ideas / to something around you, like a cart, / you can see **what could be generating friction:** /
<small>간접의문문 (see의 목적어)</small>
이러한 개념을 적용하면 / 카트와 같은 당신 주변에 있는 어떤 것에 / 당신은 무엇이 마찰력을 발생시킬 수 있을지 알 수 있다 /
<small>현재분사구 (the axles 수식)</small>
mainly the axles **rubbing on the body** as they rotate. //
주로 회전하면서 본체에 닿는 축들과 같이 //
(B) You gradually slow down. // 당신은 서서히 느려진다 //
How could you slow down more suddenly, / in a shorter distance? //
단서 2 주어진 글의 질문에 대한 대답
당신은 더 갑자기 속도를 줄이려면 어떻게 해야 할까 / 더 짧은 거리 안에서 //
By putting the brakes on. // 브레이크를 작동시키면 된다 //
<small>분사구문</small>
Because the brakes change your movement, / **making you slow down more suddenly**, / they must be exerting a force on the bicycle and you, / as they grip and rub on the wheel-rims. //
브레이크는 당신의 움직임을 변화시켜 / 당신을 더 갑자기 느려지게 하기 때문에 / 그것들이 자전거와 당신에게 힘을 가하고 있어야 한다 / 바퀴 테두리를 잡고 닿으면서 //
<small>계속적 용법의 주격 관계대명사</small>
(C) This is the force called friction, / **which** tends to slow down moving things / by acting in the direction opposite to movement, / that is backwards. // **단서 3** (B)의 a force를 가리킴
이것이 마찰력이라고 불리는 힘이며 / 그 힘은 움직이는 물체를 느리게 하는 경향이 있다 / 움직임의 반대 방향으로 작용함으로써 / 즉 뒤쪽으로 //
Even without the brakes on, / there are other friction forces /
<small>앞에 주격 관계대명사와 be동사가 생략됨　계속적 용법의 주격 관계대명사</small>
acting on you and your bicycle, / **which** also slow you down. //
심지어 브레이크를 작동시키지 않아도 / 다른 마찰력이 존재하며 / 당신과 당신의 자전거에 작용하는 / 이것은 또한 당신을 느리게 한다 //

- level ⓐ 평평한
- friction ⓝ 마찰
- generate ⓥ 발생시키다
- gradually ⓐⓓ 점차적으로
- grip ⓥ 꽉 잡다
- force ⓝ 힘
- rub ⓥ 문지르다
- rotate ⓥ 회전하다
- exert ⓥ (힘을) 가하다
- act ⓥ 작용하다
- resistance ⓝ 저항

자전거 페달을 수평의 도로에서 밟고 있다고 상상해 보아라. 당신은 페달을 밟는 것을 멈추고 당신을 앞으로 나아가게 하는 어떠한 힘도 이제 작용하지 않는다. 그러면 어떻게 될까? (B) 당신은 서서히 느려진다. 당신은 더 짧은 거리 안에서 더 갑자기 속도를 줄이려면 어떻게 해야 할까? 브레이크를 작동시키면 된다. 브레이크는 당신의 움직임을 변화시켜 당신을 더 갑자기 느려지게 하기 때문에, 그것들이 바퀴 테두리를 잡고 닿으면서 자전거와 당신에게 힘을 가하고 있어야 한다. (C) 이것이 마찰력이라고 불리는 힘이며, 그 힘은 움직임의 반대 방향, 즉 뒤쪽으로 작용함으로써 움직이는 물체를 느리게 하는 경향이 있다. 심지어 브레이크를 작동시키지 않아도 당신과 당신의 자전거에 작용하는 다른 마찰력이 존재하며, 이것은 또한 당신을 느리게 한다. (A) 이들 중 하나는 축에 닿는 바퀴의 마찰이다. 또 다른 하나는 당신과 자전거가 앞쪽으로 움직일 때 당신을 뒤쪽으로 미는 공기 저항으로 이는 당신이 느낄 수 있다. 카트와 같은 당신 주변에 있는 어떤 것에 이러한 개념을 적용하면, 주로 회전하면서 본체에 닿는 축들과 같이, 당신은 무엇이 마찰력을 발생시킬 수 있을지 알 수 있다.

(A)의 these가 가리키는 대상이 (B)에 없음

주어진 글 다음에 이어질 글의 순서로 가장 적절한 것을 고르시오.

① (A) — (C) — (B) 주어진 글의 질문에 대한 답이 (A)에 없음
② (B) — (A) — (C)
③ (B) — (C) — (A)
④ (C) — (A) — (B)
⑤ (C) — (B) — (A)

자전거를 타다가 페달 밟기를 멈추면 어떻게 되는가? → (B) 서서히 느려지게 되고, 브레이크를 작동할 때 바퀴에 가해지는 힘이 있음 → (C) 이것이 마찰력이며 이때 다른 마찰력들도 존재함 → (A) 주변 물체에 마찰의 개념을 적용하면 마찰력의 요인들을 알 수 있음

(C)의 This가 가리키는 힘이 주어진 글에 없음

| 문제 풀이 순서 | ★★❋ [정답률 67%]

1st 각 문단의 내용을 파악하고, 글의 논리적인 순서를 추론한다.

주어진 글: 자전거 페달을 수평의 도로에서 밟고 있다고 상상해 보아라. 당신은 페달을 밟는 것을 멈추고 당신을 앞으로 나아가게 하는 어떠한 힘도 이제 작용하지 않는다. 그러면 어떻게 될까(What happens)?

➡ **주어진 글 뒤:** What happens?에 대한 질문의 답변, 즉 자전거를 타고 가는 중에 페달 밟기를 멈추면 어떤 일이 일어나는지가 이어져야 한다.

(A): 이들 중 하나(One of these)는 축에 닿는 바퀴의 마찰이다. 또 다른 하나는 당신과 자전거가 앞쪽으로 움직일 때 당신을 뒤쪽으로 미는 공기 저항으로 이는 당신이 느낄 수 있다. 카트와 같은 당신 주변에 있는 어떤 것에 이러한 개념을 적용하면, 주로 회전하면서 본체에 닿는 축들과 같이, 당신은 무엇이 마찰력을 발생시킬 수 있을지 알 수 있다.

➡ **(A) 앞:** these가 가리키는 대상이 앞에 나와야 한다. 이는 마찰과 관련이 있어야 하는데, 주어진 글에는 마찰이 언급되지 않았다. 또한 주어진 글의 질문에 대한 답변이 (A)에 있지 않다. ▶ (A) 앞에 주어진 글이 올 수 없음
(A) 뒤: 주변 물체에 마찰의 개념을 적용하면 마찰력의 요인을 알 수 있다고 하며 글을 마무리하고 있으므로, 글의 마지막 부분일 가능성이 높다.

(B): 당신은 서서히 느려진다(You gradually slow down.). 당신은 더 짧은 거리 안에서 더 갑자기 속도를 줄이려면 어떻게 해야 할까? 브레이크를 작동시키면 된다. 브레이크는 당신의 움직임을 변화시켜 당신을 더 갑자기 느려지게 하기 때문에, 그것들이 바퀴 테두리를 잡고 닿으면서 자전거와 당신에게 힘을 가하고 있어야 한다.

➡ **(B) 앞:** 첫 문장(You gradually slow down.)은 주어진 글의 마지막 질문에 대한 가장 직접적인 대답이다.
▶ (B) 앞에 주어진 글이 와야 함 (순서: 주어진 글 → (B))
(B) 뒤: 브레이크가 가하는 힘을 부연 설명하는 내용이 이어질 것이다.

(C): 이것(This)이 마찰력이라고 불리는 힘이며, 그 힘은 움직임의 반대 방향, 즉 뒤쪽으로 작용함으로써 움직이는 물체를 느리게 하는 경향이 있다. 심지어 브레이크를 작동시키지 않아도 당신과 당신의 자전거에 작용하는 다른 마찰력(other friction forces)이 존재하며, 이것은 또한 당신을 느리게 한다.

➡ **(C) 앞:** This는 (B)의 마지막에 언급된 브레이크가 가하는 힘을 가리킨다.
▶ (C) 앞에 (B)가 와야 함 (순서: 주어진 글 → (B) → (C))
(C) 뒤: 다른 마찰력이 존재한다고 했는데, (A)에 바퀴의 마찰과 공기 저항이라는 다른 마찰력이 언급되었다.
▶ (C) 뒤에 (A)가 와야 함 (순서: 주어진 글 → (B) → (C) → (A))

2nd 글이 한눈에 들어오도록 정리하여 정답을 확인한다.

주어진 글: 자전거 페달을 밟고 있다가 멈추면 어떻게 될까?
➡ **(B):** 서서히 느려진다. 브레이크를 사용하면 더 빨리 멈추는데, 이때 작용하는 힘이 있다.
➡ **(C):** 이는 마찰력이며, 이외에 다른 마찰력들도 존재한다.
➡ **(A):** 주변 물체에 마찰의 개념을 적용하면 마찰력의 요인을 알 수 있다.
▶ 주어진 글 다음에 이어질 글의 순서는 (B) → (C) → (A)이므로 정답은 ③임

---

38 정답 ⑤ ＊비선형 미디어 편집 시스템의 특징

글의 흐름으로 보아, 주어진 문장이 들어가기에 가장 적절한 곳을 고르시오.

Nonlinear editing, / on the other hand, / is like using a word processing program. // 단서1 비선형 편집과 반대되는 개념이 앞에 나올 것임
비선형 편집은 / 반면 / 워드 프로세싱 프로그램을 사용하는 것과 같다 //

All editing systems are now nonlinear computer-based systems / **that** allow random access to any video shot or scene / [주격 관계대명사]
모든 편집 시스템은 이제 비선형 컴퓨터 기반 시스템이다 / 어떤 비디오 숏이나 장면으로의 임의적 접근을 가능하게 하는 /

without having to fast forward or fast reverse / to find **it**. // [= any video shot or scene]
빨리 감기나 빨리 되감기를 할 필요 없이 / 어떤 비디오 화면이나 장면을 찾기 위해 //

Nonlinear systems can create **a range of** special effects, / [다양한]
비선형 시스템은 다양한 특수 효과를 만들 수 있다 /

such as slow motion, **wipes** and **dissolves**. // [차량 와이퍼로 훑는 것처럼 화면을 전환하는 효과] [두 장면을 겹치며 화면을 전환하는 효과]
슬로 모션, 와이프 그리고 디졸브 같은 //

(①) Another highlight of a digital nonlinear system is its random access process / that makes **it** easy **for an editor** **to find** / [가목적어] [의미상 주어] [진목적어]
desired shots or scenes /
디지털 비선형 시스템의 또 다른 주요 특징은 그것의 임의적 접근 과정이다 / 편집자가 찾는 것을 쉽게 해주는 / 원하는 숏이나 장면을 /

without having to spend time / fast forwarding or rewinding videotape. //
시간을 들일 필요 없이 / 비디오테이프를 빨리 감거나 되감는 데 //

(②) With nonlinear editing, / shots or scenes can be easily added or removed / anywhere in the program, / and the computer adjusts the program length automatically. //
비선형 편집으로는 / 숏이나 장면을 쉽게 추가하거나 삭제할 수 있으며 / 프로그램의 어디에나 / 컴퓨터가 프로그램의 길이를 자동으로 조정한다 //

(③) Linear editing was like composing a paper on a typewriter. //
선형 편집은 타자기로 글을 작성하는 것과 같았다 //

(④) **If** a mistake was made or new information needed to be added / **the whole piece** had to be retyped. // 단서2 선형 편집은 수정하려면 전체를 다시 작성해야 함 [부사절 접속사 (조건)] [주절의 주어]
만약 실수가 생겼거나 새로운 정보가 추가되어야 할 필요가 있다면 / 전체를 다시 작성해야 했다 //

단서 3 수정하기 쉬운 것은 선형 편집이 아니라 비선형 편집임

(⑤) If a mistake is made, / it is easily deleted and fixed / with a few keystrokes, / and new information can be added easily. //
만약 실수가 생기면 / 그것은 쉽게 삭제되고 수정될 수 있으며 / 몇 번의 키 입력으로 / 새로운 정보가 쉽게 추가될 수 있다 //

- nonlinear ⓐ 비선형의 · random ⓐ 임의의 · scene ⓝ 장면
- reverse ⓥ 되감다 · highlight ⓝ 주요 특징 · editor ⓝ 편집자
- remove ⓥ 제거하다 · adjust ⓥ 조정하다
- automatically ⓐⓓ 자동적으로 · compose ⓥ 작성하다, 구성하다
- retype ⓥ 다시 타이핑하다 · delete ⓥ 삭제하다
- keystroke ⓝ 키 입력

모든 편집 시스템은 이제 어떤 비디오 화면이나 장면을 찾기 위해 빨리 감기나 빨리 되감기를 할 필요 없이 어떤 비디오 숏이나 장면으로의 임의적 접근을 가능하게 하는 비선형 컴퓨터 기반 시스템이다. 비선형 시스템은 슬로 모션, 와이프 그리고 디졸브 같은 다양한 특수 효과를 만들 수 있다. (①) 디지털 비선형 시스템의 또 다른 주요 특징은 편집자가 비디오테이프를 빨리 감거나 되감는 데 시간을 들일 필요 없이 원하는 숏이나 장면을 찾는 것을 쉽게 해주는 그것의 임의적 접근 과정이다. (②) 비선형 편집으로는 숏이나 장면을 프로그램의 어디에나 쉽게 추가하거나 삭제할 수 있으며, 컴퓨터는 프로그램의 길이를 자동으로 조정한다. (③) 선형 편집은 타자기로 글을 작성하는 것과 같았다. (④) 만약 실수가 생겼거나 새로운 정보가 추가되어야 할 필요가 있다면, 전체를 다시 작성해야 했다. (⑤ 비선형 편집은, 반면, 워드 프로세싱 프로그램을 사용하는 것과 같다.) 만약 실수가 생기면 그것은 몇 번의 키 입력으로 쉽게 삭제되고 수정될 수 있으며, 새로운 정보가 쉽게 추가될 수 있다.

| 문제 풀이 순서 | ★★★ [정답률 40%]

1st 주어진 문장을 해석하고, 핵심 단서를 파악한다.

Nonlinear editing, on the other hand, is like using a word processing program.
비선형 편집은, 반면, 워드 프로세싱 프로그램을 사용하는 것과 같다.

➡ **주어진 문장 앞:** 반대되는 내용을 나타내는 on the other hand가 있으므로, **단서** 비선형 편집과 반대되는 개념이 앞에 나올 것이다. **발상**

2nd 각 선택지의 앞뒤 흐름이 매끄러운지 확인한다.

①의 앞 문장과 뒤 문장

앞 문장: 모든 편집 시스템은 이제 ~ 어떤 비디오 숏이나 장면으로의 임의적 접근을 가능하게 하는 비선형 컴퓨터 기반 시스템이다.
뒤 문장: 디지털 비선형 시스템의 또 다른 주요 특징은 편집자가 비디오테이프를 빨리 감거나 되감는 데 시간을 들일 필요 없이 원하는 숏이나 장면을 찾는 것을 쉽게 해주는 그것의 임의적 접근 과정이다.

➡ 편집 시스템은 이제 비선형 시스템이라고 하며, 비선형 시스템의 특징을 이어서 설명한다. ▶ 주어진 문장이 ①에 들어갈 수 없음

②의 앞 문장과 뒤 문장

앞 문장: ①의 뒤 문장과 같음
뒤 문장: 비선형 편집으로는 숏이나 장면을 프로그램의 어디에나 쉽게 추가하거나 삭제할 수 있으며, 컴퓨터는 프로그램의 길이를 자동으로 조정한다.

➡ 비선형 편집의 장점을 이어서 설명한다. ▶ 주어진 문장이 ②에 들어갈 수 없음

③의 앞 문장과 뒤 문장

앞 문장: ②의 뒤 문장과 같음
뒤 문장: 선형 편집은 타자기로 글을 작성하는 것과 같았다(was).

➡ 현대의 방식인 비선형 편집을 설명하다가, 내용을 전환하기 위해 과거시제를 사용하며 과거의 방식인 선형 편집을 언급한다. ▶ 주어진 문장이 ③에 들어갈 수 없음

④의 앞 문장과 뒤 문장

앞 문장: ③의 뒤 문장과 같음
뒤 문장: 만약 실수가 생겼거나 새로운 정보가 추가되어야 할 필요가 있다면, 전체를 다시 작성해야 했다.

➡ 타자기 작업은 글을 수정하기 어렵다는 단점을 언급하며, 선형 편집의 특징을 이어서 부연 설명한다. ▶ 주어진 문장이 ④에 들어갈 수 없음

⑤의 앞 문장과 뒤 문장

앞 문장: ④의 뒤 문장과 같음
뒤 문장: 만약 실수가 생기면 그것은 몇 번의 키 입력으로 쉽게 삭제되고 수정될 수 있으며, 새로운 정보가 쉽게 추가될 수 있다.

➡ 선형 편집은 수정이 어렵다고 했는데, 갑자기 수정이 쉽다는 내용이 등장했다. 비선형 편집은 워드 프로세싱 프로그램 같다는 내용이 주어진 문장에 있고, 선형 편집과 반대로 비선형 편집은 쉽게 수정할 수 있다는 흐름이 되어야 한다.
▶ 주어진 문장이 ⑤에 들어가야 함

39 정답 ⑤ *의도와 결과 둘 다로 판단되는 도덕적 선함 —

글의 흐름으로 보아, 주어진 문장이 들어가기에 가장 적절한 곳을 고르시오. [3점]

문장의 주어 주격 관계대명사
A person / who always tries to prevent harm but never does, /
문장의 본동사
is not generally thought of / as morally good. //
사람은 / 항상 해를 예방하려고 하지만 결코 그렇게 하지 못하는 / 일반적으로 생각되지 않는다 / 도덕적으로 선하다고 //

주격 관계대명사
A morally good person / is one / who does morally bad actions
= actions
significantly less often than most / and does morally good ones
significantly more often than most. //
도덕적으로 선한 사람은 / 사람이다 / 도덕적으로 나쁜 행동을 대부분의 사람들보다 훨씬 덜 자주 하고 / 도덕적으로 선한 행동을 대부분의 사람들보다 훨씬 더 자주 하는 //
in -ing: ~할 때는, ~하는 데 있어서
In judging a person / not only her actions / but also her intentions
not only A but also B: A뿐만 아니라 B도
and motives are relevant. //
사람을 판단할 때는 / 그녀의 행동뿐 아니라 / 그녀의 의도와 동기 또한 관련이 있다 //
(①) A morally good person must intend to do / morally good actions / and intend to avoid / morally bad ones. //
도덕적으로 선한 사람은 하려고 의도해야 하고 / 도덕적으로 선한 행동을 / 피하려고 의도해야 한다 / 도덕적으로 나쁜 행동은 //
문장의 주어 주격 관계대명사
(②) A person / who unintentionally prevents harm to others / and does not harm them / simply because things do not turn out
문장의 본동사
as she intends / is not morally good. //
사람은 / 다른 사람에게 해를 의도하지 않게 예방하고 / 그들에게 해를 끼치지 않은 / 단지 그녀가 의도한대로 일이 일어나지 않았기 때문에 / 도덕적으로 선하지 않다 //
(③) Although this kind of situation / generally occurs only in slapstick movies, / it is worth mentioning / to avoid the false impression /
이런 종류의 상황은 / 일반적으로 슬랩스틱 영화에서만 발생하지만 / 언급할 가치가 있다 / 잘못된 인상을 피하기 위해 /
it ~ that 강조 구문
that it is the actual consequences of a person's actions that count
동격절 접속사
/ toward her being judged / morally good or bad. //
중요한 것은 한 사람의 행동의 실제 결과라는 / 그녀가 판단되는 것에 / 도덕적으로 선하거나 나쁜지 //
(④) But actual consequences are important. //
하지만 실제 결과는 중요하다 // **단서 1** 도덕성 판단에는 실제 결과가 중요함

(⑤) Of such a person, / **it** may be said **that** she means well; / but, contrary to Kant, / some results are necessary / before she is regarded as morally good. // **단서 2** 의도가 선하더라도 도덕적으로 선하려면 결과가 필요함
_{가주어} _{진주어절 접속사}

그런 사람에 대해 / 그녀가 선한 의도를 가지고 있다고 말할 수 있지만 / Kant와 달리 / 어떤 결과가 필요하다 / 그녀가 도덕적으로 선하다고 간주되기 전에 //

- prevent ⓥ 막다, 예방하다 · harm ⓝ 해, 손해
- morally ⓐⓓ 도덕적으로 · significantly ⓐⓓ 상당히, 훨씬
- judge ⓥ 판단하다 · intention ⓝ 의도 · motive ⓝ 동기
- relevant ⓐ 관련된 · intend ⓥ 의도하다
- unintentionally ⓐⓓ 의도치 않게 · occur ⓥ 발생하다
- impression ⓝ 인상 · actual ⓐ 실제의 · consequence ⓝ 결과
- count ⓥ 중요하다 · contrary to ~와는 반대로
- necessary ⓐ 필요한 · regard ⓥ 여기다, 간주하다

도덕적으로 선한 사람은 대부분의 사람들보다 도덕적으로 나쁜 행동을 훨씬 덜 자주 하고, 도덕적으로 선한 행동을 훨씬 더 자주 하는 사람이다. 사람을 판단할 때는 그녀의 행동뿐 아니라 그녀의 의도와 동기 또한 관련이 있다. (①) 도덕적으로 선한 사람은 도덕적으로 선한 행동을 하려고 의도해야 하고, 도덕적으로 나쁜 행동은 피하려고 의도해야 한다. (②) 다른 사람에게 해를 의도하지 않게 예방하고 단지 그녀가 의도한대로 일이 일어나지 않았기 때문에 그들에게 해를 끼치지 않은 사람은 도덕적으로 선하지 않다. (③) 이런 종류의 상황은 일반적으로 슬랩스틱 영화에서만 발생하지만, 그녀가 도덕적으로 선하거나 나쁜지 판단되는 것에 중요한 것은 한 사람의 행동의 실제 결과라는 잘못된 인상을 피하기 위해 언급할 가치가 있다. (④) 하지만 실제 결과는 중요하다. ⑤ 항상 해를 예방하려고 하지만 결코 그렇게 하지 못하는 사람은 일반적으로 도덕적으로 선하다고 생각되지 않는다.) 그런 사람에 대해, 그녀가 선한 의도를 가지고 있다고 말할 수 있지만, Kant와 달리, 그녀가 도덕적으로 선하다고 간주되기 전에 어떤 결과가 필요하다.

| 문제 풀이 순서 | ★★★ [정답률 38%]

1st 주어진 문장을 해석하고, 앞뒤에 어떤 내용이 올지 생각한다.

A person who always tries to prevent harm but never does, is not generally thought of as morally good.

항상 해를 예방하려고 하지만 결코 그렇게 하지 못하는 사람은 일반적으로 도덕적으로 선하다고 생각되지 않는다.

➡ **주어진 문장 앞:** 해를 예방하려고 시도는 하지만 실천하지 못하는 사람은 도덕적으로 선하다고 여겨지지 않는다고 했으므로, **단서** 실천이나 결과의 중요성이 등장하는 부분과 이어져야 한다. **발상**

2nd 각 선택지의 앞뒤 흐름이 매끄러운지 확인한다.

①의 앞 문장과 뒤 문장
┌ **앞 문장:** 사람을 판단할 때는 그녀의 행동뿐 아니라 그녀의 의도와 동기 또한 관련이 있다.
└ **뒤 문장:** 도덕적으로 선한 사람은 도덕적으로 선한 행동을 하려고 의도해야 하고, 도덕적으로 나쁜 행동은 피하려고 의도해야 한다.

➡ 도덕성 판단에 행동뿐 아니라 의도나 동기도 중요하다는 내용이 앞뒤로 이어진다.
▶ 주어진 문장이 ①에 들어갈 수 없음

②의 앞 문장과 뒤 문장
┌ **앞 문장:** ①의 뒤 문장과 같음
└ **뒤 문장:** 다른 사람에게 해를 의도하지 않게 예방하고 단지 그녀가 의도한대로 일이 일어나지 않았기 때문에 그들에게 해를 끼치지 않은 사람은 도덕적으로 선하지 않다.

➡ 결과적으로는 해를 끼치지 않았더라도 선한 의도가 없으면 도덕적으로 선하다고 판단하지 않는다는 내용이므로 앞 문장을 뒷받침한다.
▶ 주어진 문장이 ②에 들어갈 수 없음

③의 앞 문장과 뒤 문장
┌ **앞 문장:** ②의 뒤 문장과 같음
└ **뒤 문장:** 이런 종류의 상황(this kind of situation)은 일반적으로 슬랩스틱 영화에서만 발생하지만, 그녀가 도덕적으로 선하거나 나쁜지 판단되는 것에 중요한 것은 한 사람의 행동의 실제 결과라는 잘못된 인상을 피하기 위해 언급할 가치가 있다.

➡ this kind of situation은 ③의 앞 문장에 나온 상황을 가리킨다. 도덕성 판단에 실제 결과만 중요한 것이 아니라는 인상을 심기 위해 이 상황을 언급할 가치가 있다고 부연 설명한다. ▶ 주어진 문장이 ③에 들어갈 수 없음

④의 앞 문장과 뒤 문장
┌ **앞 문장:** ③의 뒤 문장과 같음
└ **뒤 문장:** 하지만 실제 결과는 중요하다.

➡ 앞 문장에서 실제 결과만 중요한 것이 아니라고 했으나, 실제 결과는 중요하다고 하며 반대되는 내용을 제시하는 흐름이다. ▶ 주어진 문장이 ④에 들어갈 수 없음

⑤의 앞 문장과 뒤 문장
┌ **앞 문장:** ④의 뒤 문장과 같음
└ **뒤 문장:** 그런 사람(such a person)에 대해, 그녀가 선한 의도를 가지고 있다고 말할 수 있지만, Kant와 달리, 그녀가 도덕적으로 선하다고 간주되기 전에 어떤 결과가 필요하다.

➡ such a person이 가리키는 사람은 선한 의도를 가진다고 말할 수 있다고 했는데, 앞에는 선한 의도가 없는 사람만 언급되었다. 선한 의도가 있지만 결과가 없는 사람의 사례는 주어진 문장에 있다. ▶ 주어진 문장이 ⑤에 들어가야 함

40 정답 ③ ＊우리가 카메라처럼 보지 못하는 이유

Vision is influenced / by our preconceptions about reality. //
시각은 영향을 받는다 / 현실에 대한 우리의 선입견에 의해 //

_{in -ing: ~할 때}
In viewing a scene, / we establish unconscious hierarchies / **that** reflect / our functional relationship to objects / and our momentary priorities. //
_{주격 관계대명사}

한 장면을 볼 때 / 우리는 무의식적인 위계를 확립한다 / 반영하는 / 우리의 사물과의 기능적 관계와 / 우리의 순간적인 우선순위를 //

_{부사절에서 「주어+be동사」가 생략됨}
For example, / **when visualizing** a hammer in our mind's eye, / we tend to "see" it / in profile or at some other "ready for use" angle. //
예를 들어 / 우리 마음의 눈으로 망치를 시각화할 때 / 우리는 망치를 "보는" 경향이 있다 / 옆모습이나 "사용 준비 완료" 각도에서 //

_{부사절 접속사 (목적)}
One would probably not visualize / a hammer as seen from the top / **so that** the handle is hidden / by the hammer's head. //
아마 시각화하지 않을 것이다 / 망치가 위에서 보여진 모습으로 / 손잡이가 가려지도록 / 망치 머리에 //

_{앞에 목적격 관계대명사가 생략됨}
The functional relationship **we have** with objects / creates visual expectations / **that** interfere with our ability / to see "like a camera." // **단서 1** 사물과의 기능적 관계는 우리가 카메라처럼 보는 능력을 방해함
_{주격 관계대명사}

우리가 가진 사물과의 기능적인 관계는 / 시각적 기대를 만든다 / 우리의 능력을 방해하는 / "카메라처럼" 보는 //

The camera, like the human eye, / sees only shapes and colors. //
카메라는 인간의 눈처럼 / 오직 형태와 색깔만을 본다 //

It documents the world impartially / through a lens / **that** is similar to the eye. // **단서 2** 카메라는 세상을 공평하게 기록함
_{주격 관계대명사}

그것은 세상을 공평하게 기록한다 / 렌즈를 통해 / 눈과 비슷한 //

_{= photographs}
When we look at **them** carefully, / photographs are often surprising / 우리가 사진들을 주의 깊게 들여다볼 때 / 종종 놀라게 된다 /

because they don't interpret confusing details / but simply serve
_{= details}
them up to us / with a mechanical indifference. //
그것들은 혼란을 주는 세부 사항들을 해석하는 것이 아니라 / 우리에게 그것들을 단순히 제공해주기 때문에 / 기계적인 무관심으로 // ┐ **단서 3** 사진(카메라)은 기계적인 무관심으로 대상을 보여줌

And because of their flatness, / photographs often contain areas
주격 관계대명사
/ **that** appear as unrecognizable colors and shapes. //
그리고 그것들의 평면성 때문에 / 사진들은 종종 영역을 포함한다 / 알아보기 어려운 색과 형
태들로 보이는 //

Our visual perception is shaped / by an established hierarchy
/ based on functional relationships, /
우리의 시각적 인식은 형성되며 / 확립된 위계에 의해 / 기능적 관계에 기반한 /
형용사적 용법 (ability 수식)
which (A) **interrupts** our ability **to see** objects as they truly
are, / unlike the (B) **objective** perspective of a camera. //
이는 사물을 있는 그대로 보는 능력을 방해한다 / 카메라의 객관적인 시각과는 달리 //

- preconception ⓝ 선입견 • establish ⓥ 확립하다
- unconscious ⓐ 무의식적인 • hierarchy ⓝ 위계
- reflect ⓥ 반영하다 • functional ⓐ 기능적인
- momentary ⓐ 순간적인 • priority ⓝ 우선순위
- visualize ⓥ 마음속에 그리다 • tend to-v ~하는 경향이 있다
- profile ⓝ 옆모습 • interfere with ~을 방해하다
- document ⓥ 기록하다 • impartially ⓐⓓ 공정하게
- interpret ⓥ 해석하다 • mechanical ⓐ 기계적인
- indifference ⓝ 무관심 • unrecognizable ⓐ 알아볼 수 없는
- perspective ⓝ 관점 • enhance ⓥ 향상시키다
- neutral ⓐ 중립적인

시각은 현실에 대한 우리의 선입견에 의해 영향을 받는다. 한 장면을 볼 때, 우
리는 우리의 사물과의 기능적 관계와 우리의 순간적인 우선순위를 반영하는 무
의식적인 위계를 확립한다. 예를 들어, 우리 마음의 눈으로 망치를 시각화할
때, 우리는 망치를 옆모습이나 "사용 준비 완료" 각도에서 "보는" 경향이 있다.
손잡이가 망치 머리에 가려지도록 망치가 위에서 보여진 모습으로 아마 시각화
하지 않을 것이다. 우리가 가진 사물과의 기능적인 관계는 "카메라처럼" 보는
우리의 능력을 방해하는 시각적 기대를 만든다. 카메라는 인간의 눈처럼 오직
형태와 색깔만을 본다. 그것은 눈과 비슷한 렌즈를 통해 세상을 공평하게 기록
한다. 우리가 사진들을 주의 깊게 들여다볼 때, 그것들은 혼란을 주는 세부 사
항들을 해석하는 것이 아니라 기계적인 무관심으로 우리에게 그것들을 단순히
제공해주기 때문에 종종 놀라게 된다. 그리고 그것들의 평면성 때문에 사진들은
종종 알아보기 어려운 색과 형태들로 보이는 영역을 포함한다.
→ 우리의 시각적 인식은 기능적 관계에 기반한 확립된 위계에 의해 형성되며,
이는 카메라의 (B) **객관적인** 시각과는 달리 사물을 있는 그대로 보는 능력을
(A) **방해한다.**

다음 글의 내용을 한 문장으로 요약하고자 한다. 빈칸 (A), (B)에 들어갈
말로 가장 적절한 것은?

	(A)		(B)
①	enhances 향상시킨다	—	accurate 기능적 관계는 객관적 인식을 향상시키지 않음 정확한
②	simplifies 단순화한다	—	fixed 시각적 인식이 사물을 보는 능력을 단순화하지 않음 고정된
③	interrupts 방해한다	—	objective 우리의 시각적 인식은 '객관적인' 카메라와 객관적인 달리 사물을 있는 그대로 보는 능력을 '방해함'
④	enhances 향상시킨다	—	neutral 기능적 관계는 객관적 인식을 향상시키지 않음 중립적인
⑤	interrupts	—	inconsistent 카메라의 시각은 일관성 있음 일관성 없는

왜 정답? ★★★ [정답률 45%]

(A):
┌ 우리가 가진 사물과의 기능적 관계는 카메라처럼 보는 우리의 능력을 방해한
└ 다. 단서 1
→ 우리의 시각적 인식은 사물을 있는 그대로 보는 능력을 방해한다.
  ▶ (A)에는 ③, ⑤ interrupts가 들어가야 함

(B):
┌ 카메라는 세상을 공평하게 기록한다. 단서 2
└ (카메라로 찍은) 사진은 기계적인 무관심으로 세부사항을 보여준다. 단서 3
→ 카메라의 시각은 주관이나 편견 없이 대상을 있는 그대로 본다.
  ▶ (B)에는 ③ objective, ④ neutral이 들어가야 하므로 정답은 ③임

왜 오답?

① 우리의 시각적 인식은 사물을 있는 그대로 보는 능력을 향상시키지 않는다.
② 사물을 있는 그대로 보는 능력을 단순화한다는 것은 언급되지 않았다.
④ 우리의 시각적 인식은 사물을 있는 그대로 보는 능력을 향상시키지 않는다.
⑤ 일관성이 없는 것은 인간의 시각에 해당하며, 카메라의 시각은 오히려 일관성이 있
다.

★ 글의 흐름

1 주제: 인간의 시각은 현실에 대한 선입견, 즉 기능적 관계에 의해 영향을 받음
2 예시: 망치를 떠올릴 때 사용하기 좋은 각도로 생각하는 경향이 있음
3 대조: 인간의 주관적 시각과 달리 카메라는 세상을 기계적으로 기록하는 객관적인
시각을 가짐

41~42 ★소매 판매에 "도와드릴까요?"라는 표현이 잘못된 이유
목적격 관계대명사
"May I help you?" / are the worst four words / **that** a retail
salesperson can utter / 41번 단서 1: "도와드릴까요?"는 고객을 방어적으로 만드는
최악의 표현임
"도와드릴까요?"는 / 최악의 네 단어이다 / 소매 판매원이 말할 수 있는 /
encourage의 목적어와 목적격 보어 (to부정사)
because they don't encourage **the customer to talk** / and put
them on the defensive. //
고객이 말을 하도록 하지 않고 / 그들이 방어적이게 하기 때문에 //

The four words usually draw out a negative response / that
stops cold a sales transaction. //
그 네 단어는 부정적인 반응을 주로 끌어낸다 / 판매 거래를 완전히 막는 //
부사절에서「주어+be동사」생략
Examples of (a) better questions to use / **when approaching**
목적격 관계대명사 (선행사: anything)
customers / are "Is there anything in particular **that** you are
looking for?" / and "Are you shopping for a gift?" //
사용할 수 있는 더 나은 질문들의 예들로는 / 고객에게 다가갈 때 / "특별히 당신이 찾고 계신
어떤 것이 있나요"와 / "당신은 선물을 위한 쇼핑을 하고 있나요"가 있다 //

If a fashion salesperson approached you with / "May I help
chances are (that): ~일 가능성이 있다
you?" / **chances are** you would feel / the salesperson didn't (b)
care. //
만약 패션 판매원이 당신에게 다가온다면 / "도와드릴까요"로 / 당신은 느낄 가능성이 있다 /
그 판매원이 신경 쓰지 않는다고 //
= "May I help you?" 주격 관계대명사
This line is a rote approach / **that** is so overused / by untrained
and uninterested salespeople. // 41번 단서 2: "도와드릴까요?"는 훈련되지 않고
무관심한 판매원의 기계적인 접근 방식임
이 문장은 기계적인 접근 방식이다 / 매우 지나치게 사용되는 / 훈련되지 않고 무관심한 판매
원들에 의해 //

In fact, / most of us shudder in horror / on hearing these words. //
실제로 / 우리 대부분은 기겁하여 몸서리친다 / 이 단어들을 들을 때 //

The very meaning of the question "May I help you?" / (c)
rejects(→ implies) that the customer is in trouble of some sort
and needs rescuing. // 42번 단서: "도와드릴까요?"는 고객이 실제로 문제에 처했음을 암시함
"도와드릴까요?"라는 이 질문의 진짜 의미는 / 고객이 어떤 종류의 곤경에 처해 있고 구출될
필요가 있다는 것을 부인한다(→ 내포한다) //

This almost always puts the customer on the defense. //
이는 거의 항상 그 고객이 방어적이게 한다 //
부사절 접속사 (양보)
"No, thank you" is usually the immediate response, / **even if** the
customer is actually in need of assistance. //
"아니요, 괜찮습니다"는 주로 즉각적인 반응이다 / 그 고객이 실제로 도움이 필요할지라도 //

The subconscious thought by the customer is often / "I'm **smart**
형용사 + enough + to부정사: …할 만큼 충분히 ~한
enough to figure out what I want, / and I don't need your help!" //
고객의 잠재의식적인 생각은 종종 / ~이다 / "나는 내가 원하는 것을 알 만큼 충분히 현명해 / 그
래서 나는 당신의 도움이 필요하지 않아" //

If customers feel pressured or cornered, / then salespeople won't make any sales. // **41번** 단서 3: 고객이 압박감을 느끼면 판매로 이어지지 않음

만약 고객들이 압박과 궁지에 몰림을 느낀다면 / 그러면 판매원들은 어떤 판매도 못할 것이다 //

The approach has to promote / a (d) comfortable environment
주격 관계대명사
that makes customers feel / there is no rush. //

그 접근 방식은 조장해야 한다 / 고객들이 느끼게 만드는 편안한 환경을 / 서두름이 없다고 //

Furthermore, / if customers just want to look around, / they
가주어   진주어 (do so = look around)
should feel / that **it** is all right **to do so**. //

게다가 / 만약 고객들이 그저 둘러보길 원한다면 / 그들은 느껴야만 한다 / 그렇게 하는 것이 괜찮다는 것을 //

In situations **where** customers really **do** want / to look around
관계부사   강조의 do
on their own, /

고객들이 정말로 원하는 상황들에서는 / 혼자 둘러보길 /

salespeople should give customers their business cards /
                                                     '~인 경우에 대비해서'
and keep themselves (e) accessible / **in case** customers have questions or concerns. //

판매원들은 고객들에게 그들의 명함을 주고 / 그들 스스로를 접근할 수 있는 상태로 유지해야 한다 / 고객들이 질문이나 걱정이 있을 경우를 대비하여 //

- retail ⓝ 소매 · utter ⓥ (말을) 하다 · encourage ⓥ 장려하다
- defensive ⓐ 방어적인 · stop cold 갑자기 멈추다
- transaction ⓝ 거래 · approach ⓥ 접근하다 · rote ⓐ 기계적인
- overused ⓐ 남용되는 · immediate ⓐ 즉각적인
- assistance ⓝ 도움, 지원 · subconscious ⓐ 잠재의식의
- figure out 알아내다 · promote ⓥ 촉진하다, 조성하다
- furthermore ⓐⓓ 게다가 · accessible ⓐ 접근 가능한

"도와드릴까요?"는 고객이 말을 하도록 하지 않고, 그들이 방어적이게 하기 때문에 소매 판매원이 말할 수 있는 최악의 네 단어이다. 그 네 단어는 판매 거래를 완전히 막는 부정적인 반응을 주로 끌어낸다. 고객에게 다가갈 때 사용할 수 있는 (a) **더 나은** 질문들의 예들로는 "특별히 당신이 찾고 계신 어떤 것이 있나요?"와 "당신은 선물을 위한 쇼핑을 하고 있나요?"가 있다. 만약 패션 판매원이 "도와드릴까요?"로 당신에게 다가온다면, 당신은 그 판매원이 (b) **신경 쓰지 않**는다고 느낄 가능성이 있다. 이 문장은 훈련되지 않고 무관심한 판매원들에 의해 매우 지나치게 사용되는 기계적인 접근 방식이다. 실제로, 우리 대부분은 이 단어들을 들을 때 기겁하여 몸서리친다. "도와드릴까요?"라는 이 질문의 진짜 의미는 고객이 어떤 종류의 곤경에 처해 있고 구출될 필요가 있다는 것을 (c) 부인한다(→ **내포한다**). 이는 거의 항상 그 고객이 방어적이게 한다. 그 고객이 실제로 도움이 필요할지라도 "아니요, 괜찮습니다"는 주로 즉각적인 반응이다. 고객의 잠재의식적인 생각은 종종 "나는 내가 원하는 것을 알 만큼 충분히 현명해, 그래서 나는 당신의 도움이 필요하지 않아!"이다. 만약 고객들이 압박과 궁지에 몰림을 느낀다면, 그러면 판매원들은 어떤 판매도 못할 것이다. 그 접근 방식은 고객들이 서두름이 없다고 느끼게 만드는 (d) **편안한** 환경을 조장해야 한다. 게다가, 만약 고객들이 그저 둘러보길 원한다면, 그들은 그렇게 하는 것이 괜찮다는 것을 느껴야만 한다. 고객들이 정말로 혼자 둘러보길 원하는 상황들에서는, 고객들이 질문이나 걱정이 있을 경우를 대비하여, 판매원들은 고객들에게 그들의 명함을 주고 그들 스스로를 (e) **접근할 수 있**는 상태로 유지해야 한다.

41 정답 ③

윗글의 제목으로 가장 적절한 것은?

① Breaking the Ice: Building Trust with Customers
어색함 깨기: 고객과의 신뢰 구축   신뢰 구축보다는 특정 표현의 문제점에 관한 내용임
② To Be a Smart Consumer or Not   판매원의 전략에 관한 내용임
현명한 소비자가 될 것인가 말 것인가
③ Why "May I Help You?" Fails
왜 "도와드릴까요?"가 실패하는가   '도와드릴까요?'라는 표현의 악영향과 대안을 설명함
④ How "Buy One Get One" Opens Your Wallet   '하나 사면 하나 더'와
어떻게 '하나 사면 하나 더'가 당신의 지갑을 여는가   같은 마케팅 전략은 언급되지 않았음
⑤ The Closer to Customers, the More Money You Make
고객에게 더 가까이 다가갈수록, 더 많은 돈을 번다
고객이 판매원에게 접근할 수 있도록 하는 전략을 설명함

왜 정답? ★★☆ [정답률 81%]

- "도와드릴까요?(May I help you?)"는 고객을 방어적으로 만든다. **41번 단서 1**
- 이 표현은 훈련되지 않은 판매원들이 사용하는 기계적인 접근 방식이다. **41번 단서 2**
- 고객에게 압박감을 주어 결국 판매 실패로 이어진다. **41번 단서 3**

➡ "도와드릴까요?(May I help you?)"라는 표현이 고객에게 미치는 악영향을 설명하고 그 대안을 설명하는 내용이다.

▶ 따라서 글의 제목으로 가장 적절한 것은 ③ '왜 "도와드릴까요?"가 실패하는가'이다.

왜 오답?

① 고객과의 신뢰 구축이 아니라, 특정 표현의 문제점과 그 대안이 핵심 내용이다.
② 소비자의 선택이 아니라, 판매원의 전략에 관한 내용이다.
④ '하나 사면 하나 더'와 같은 구체적인 판매 전략은 언급되지 않았다.
⑤ 고객에게 접근하라는 것이 아니라, 고객을 막는 특정 표현을 삼가고 고객이 판매원에게 접근할 수 있는 전략을 취하라는 내용이다.

42 정답 ③

밑줄 친 (a)~(e) 중에서 문맥상 낱말의 쓰임이 적절하지 않은 것은? [3점]

① (a) May I help you? 대신 사용할 수 있는 더 나은 질문의 예시를 제시함
더 나은
② (b) 기계적인 질문은 판매원이 고객에게 신경 쓰지 않는다는 느낌을 줌
신경 쓰다
③ (c) 이 질문은 고객이 곤경에 처했다는 의미를 내포하므로 고객을 방어적으로 만듦
부인하다
④ (d) 고객을 압박하지 않는 편안한 환경을 만들어야 한다고 조언함
편안한
⑤ (e) 도움이 필요할 경우를 대비해 판매원이 접근 가능한 상태로 있어야 함
접근할 수 있는

왜 정답? ★★★ [정답률 53%]

③ (c) rejects 부인한다

"도와드릴까요?"라는 이 질문의 진짜 의미는 고객이 어떤 종류의 곤경에 처해 있고 구출될 필요가 있다는 것을 (c) 부인한다.
                                   내포한다

➡ 이 질문은 고객이 혼자서 해결할 수 없는 곤경에 처해 있고 도움이 필요하다는 의미를 '부인하는' 것이 아니라 '내포하기' 때문에, 고객이 방어적으로 변한다는 내용이 되어야 한다.

▶ rejects를 implies(내포한다)와 같은 어휘로 바꿔야 함

왜 오답?

① (a) better 더 나은

고객에게 다가갈 때 사용할 수 있는 (a) 더 나은 질문들의 예들로는 "특별히 당신이 찾고 계신 어떤 것이 있나요?"와 "당신은 선물을 위한 쇼핑을 하고 있나요?"가 있다.

➡ 앞에서 "도와드릴까요?"는 소매 판매원이 말할 수 있는 최악의 네 단어라고 했으므로 그것보다 '더 나은' 두 가지 질문을 제시하고 있다. ▶ better는 문맥에 맞음

② (b) care 신경 쓰다

만약 패션 판매원이 "도와드릴까요?"로 당신에게 다가온다면, 당신은 그 판매원이 (b) 신경 쓰지 않는다고 느낄 가능성이 있다.

➡ 이어지는 문장에서 훈련되지 않고 무관심한 판매원이 사용하는 기계적인 접근이라고 했으므로, 고객은 판매원이 '신경 쓰지' 않는다고 느낄 것이다.

▶ care는 문맥에 맞음

④ (d) comfortable 편안한

그 접근 방식은 고객들이 서두름이 없다고 느끼게 만드는 (d) 편안한 환경을 조장해야 한다.

➡ 고객이 압박감을 느끼면 판매가 이뤄지지 않는다고 했으므로, 판매원은 '편안한' 환경을 조장해야 한다. ▶ comfortable은 문맥에 맞음

⑤ (e) accessible 접근할 수 있는

┌ 고객들이 정말로 혼자 둘러보길 원하는 상황들에서는, 고객들이 질문이나
│ 걱정이 있을 경우를 대비하여, 판매원들은 고객들에게 그들의 명함을 주고
└ 그들 스스로를 (e) 접근할 수 있는 상태로 유지해야 한다.

➡ 고객이 혼자 둘러보길 원하더라도, 도움이 필요할 때를 대비하여 고객들이 언제든지 판매원에게 '접근할 수 있도록' 해야 한다는 내용이다.

▶ accessible은 문맥에 맞음

43 ~ 45 ＊ 예상치 못한 친절에서 비롯된 Dave에 대한 이해

(A) While the cafeteria was full of high school students on that afternoon, / Dave was thirsty. // 〔45번 ①〕 그날 오후 식당은 고등학생들로 가득 참
그날 오후 식당이 고등학생들로 가득 차 있었던 동안 / Dave는 목이 말랐다 //

We sat near yet away from him, / fixing our hair and worrying about the test next period *we hadn't studied for.* //
〔분사구문〕 〔목적격 관계사절 (the test 수식)〕
우리는 가까이 앉아 있었지만 그와는 먼 곳에 앉아 있었고 / 머리를 매만지며 다음 교시에 있을 시험을 걱정했다 / 공부하지 않았던 //

(a) He was far away from our world, / yet forced to be a part of it. // = Dave
그는 우리 세계와는 동떨어져 있었지만 / 억지로 그 안의 일부가 되어야만 했다 //

＊ (A) 문단 요약: Dave는 목이 말랐고, 다른 학생들과 어울리지 못하고 있었음

(B) Although it was clear / that they were from very different 〔가주어〕 〔진주어절 접속사〕
worlds, / for one moment, / they'd shared a real understanding. //
비록 분명했지만 / 그들이 매우 다른 세상에서 온 것은 / 어느 한순간 / 그들은 진실한 이해를 나누었다 // 〔43번 단서 1: 다른 세상에서 온 둘(Dave와 상급생)이서 진실한 이해를 나눔〕

As I walked away from my lunch table that day, / I looked at Dave. // 그날 점심 테이블에서 떠나며 / 나는 Dave를 바라보았다 //

I thought / he and the dollar were very much alike. //
나는 생각했다 / 그와 그 달러가 많이 비슷하다고 // 〔45번 ②〕 '나'는 Dave와 그 달러가 비슷하다고 생각함

They both weren't accepted / where the world said / they were 〔관계부사〕
supposed to be. //
그들 둘 다 받아들여지지 않았다 / 세상이 말한 곳에서 / 그들이 있어야 할 자리라고 //

But just as the dollar had found a place / in a warm-hearted senior's pocket, / I was sure (b) he would eventually find his, = Dave = his place
too. //
하지만 그 달러가 자리를 찾았듯 / 마음씨 따뜻한 상급생의 주머니 속에서 / 나는 그 역시 결국 그의 자리를 찾을 거라고 확신했다 //

＊ (B) 문단 요약: 글쓴이는 결국 제자리를 찾은 달러처럼 Dave도 그럴 것이라고 확신함

(C) But for some reason, / he decided against it. // 〔43번 단서 2: Dave는 포기하지 않기로 함〕
하지만 무슨 이유에서인지 / 그는 그렇게 하지 않기로 했다 //

He wasn't leaving / until he got a drink. // 〔부사절 접속사 (~까지)〕
그는 떠나지 않고 있었다 / 음료를 얻을 때까지 //

With a determined expression, / (c) he kept aimlessly pushing = Dave
the dollar bill into the machine. //
단호한 표정을 지으며 / 그는 그 달러 지폐를 자판기에 계속 아무렇게나 밀어 넣었다 //

Just then / a popular senior boy stood up from his seat, / and walked over to the boy. // 〔43번 단서 3: 인기 많은 상급생이 자리에서 일어나 Dave에게 다가감〕
바로 그때 / 한 인기 많은 상급생이 자리에서 일어나더니 / 그 소년에게 다가갔다 //

(d) He calmly explained / how the machine often had trouble = a popular senior boy
accepting dollar bills. // 〔43번 단서 4: 상급생은 Dave에게 자판기가 지폐를 자주 인식하지 못함을 설명해 줌〕
그는 차분히 설명해 주었다 / 자판기가 얼마나 자주 지폐를 잘 인식하지 못하는지 //

After that, / he pulled some coins from his pocket / and put 〔병렬 구조(동사)〕
them into the machine. // 〔45번 ③〕 상급생은 주머니에서 동전을 꺼냈음
그 후 / 그는 자신의 주머니에서 동전을 꺼내 / 자판기에 넣었다 //

Dave gave him his dollar / and chose a flavor of fruit juice. // 〔병렬 구조(동사)〕
Dave는 자신의 달러를 그에게 주었고 / 과일 주스 맛을 골랐다 //

Then the two walked off / in different directions. //
그러고 나서 그들은 떠났다 / 다른 방향으로 // 〔45번 ④〕 Dave와 상급생은 다른 방향으로 떠남

＊ (C) 문단 요약: 포기하지 않던 Dave를 한 상급생이 동전으로 도와주고 각자 갈 길을 감

(D) He stood at the drink machine with purpose, / fumbling 〔분사구문을 이끄는 현재분사〕
through his fake leather wallet for some change. //
그는 목적을 가지고 음료 자판기 앞에 섰고 / 인조 가죽 지갑에서 잔돈을 더듬어 찾았다 //

He came up with a wrinkled dollar bill, / and nervously glanced back at his table / where other students in (e) his class were 〔관계부사〕 = Dave's
sitting. //
그는 구겨진 1달러 지폐를 꺼내어 / 테이블을 불안하게 돌아보았다 / 그의 학급의 다른 학생들이 앉아 있는 //

Dave tried to make the machine accept his money. // 〔make의 목적어와 목적격 보어 (원형부정사)〕
Dave는 자판기에 돈이 들어가게 하려고 노력했다 // 〔43번 단서 5: Dave는 돈을 넣기 위해 애씀〕

After he failed a few times, / some students began to laugh at him. //
그가 여러 번 실패한 후 / 몇몇 학생들은 그를 비웃기 시작했다 //

He started shaking, / and tears began to form in his eyes. //
그는 떨기 시작했고 / 눈에 눈물이 맺히기 시작했다 // 〔45번 ⑤〕 Dave의 눈에 눈물이 맺히기 시작함

I saw him turn to sit down, / looking like he had given up. // 〔지각동사 saw의 목적어와 목적격 보어 (원형부정사)〕
나는 그가 자리에 앉으려고 돌아서는 모습을 보았는데 / 그는 포기했던 듯 보였다 //

＊ (D) 문단 요약: Dave는 자판기 이용에 어려움을 겪고 다른 학생들이 비웃자 포기하는 듯 보였음

- period ⓝ 교시 · force ⓥ 강요하다 · understanding ⓝ 이해
- alike ⓐ 비슷한, 닮은 · accept ⓥ 받아들이다
- determined ⓐ 단호한, 결심이 굳은 · expression ⓝ 표정
- aimlessly ⓐⒹ 목적 없이, 아무렇게나 · direction ⓝ 방향
- wrinkled ⓐ 구겨진 · nervously ⓐⒹ 초조하게
- glance ⓥ 힐끗 보다 · give up 포기하다

(A) 그날 오후 식당이 고등학생들로 가득 차 있었던 동안, Dave는 목이 말랐다. 우리는 가까이 앉아 있었지만 그와는 먼 곳에 앉아 있었고, 머리를 매만지며 다음 교시에 있을 공부하지 않았던 시험을 걱정했다. (a) 그는 우리 세계와는 동떨어져 있었지만, 억지로 그 안의 일부가 되어야만 했다.

(D) 그는 목적을 가지고 음료 자판기 앞에 섰고, 인조 가죽 지갑에서 잔돈을 더듬어 찾았다. 그는 구겨진 1달러 지폐를 꺼내어, (e) 그의 학급의 다른 학생들이 앉아 있는 테이블을 불안하게 돌아보았다. Dave는 자판기에 돈이 들어가게 하려고 노력했다. 그가 여러 번 실패한 후, 몇몇 학생들은 그를 비웃기 시작했다. 그는 떨기 시작했고, 눈에 눈물이 맺히기 시작했다. 나는 그가 자리에 앉으려고 돌아서는 모습을 보았는데, 그는 포기했던 듯 보였다.

(C) 하지만 무슨 이유에서인지 그는 그렇게 하지 않기로 했다. 그는 음료를 얻을 때까지 떠나지 않고 있었다. 단호한 표정을 지으며, (c) 그는 그 달러 지폐를 자판기에 계속 아무렇게나 밀어 넣었다. 바로 그때 한 인기 많은 상급생이 자리에서 일어나더니, 그 소년에게 다가갔다. (d) 그는 자판기가 얼마나 자주 지폐를 잘 인식하지 못하는지 차분히 설명해 주었다. 그 후 그는 자신의 주머니에서 동전을 꺼내 자판기에 넣었다. Dave는 자신의 달러를 그에게 주었고 과일 주스 맛을 골랐다. 그러고 나서 그들은 다른 방향으로 떠났다.

(B) 비록 그들이 매우 다른 세상에서 온 것은 분명했지만, 어느 한순간 그들은 진실한 이해를 나누었다. 그날 점심 테이블에서 떠나며 나는 Dave를 바라보았다. 나는 그와 그 달러가 많이 비슷하다고 생각했다. 세상이 그들이 있어야 할 자리라고 말한 곳에서 그들 둘 다 받아들여지지 않았다. 하지만 그 달러가 마음씨 따뜻한 상급생의 주머니 속에서 자리를 찾았듯, 나는 (b) 그 역시 결국 그의 자리를 찾을 거라고 확신했다.

43 정답 ⑤

주어진 글 (A)에 이어질 내용을 순서에 맞게 배열한 것으로 가장 적절한 것은?

① (B) — (D) — (C) 소감이 나온 (B)가 사건의 시작이 서술된 (D)보다 먼저 올 수 없음
② (C) — (B) — (D) 사건의 해결이 나온 (C)가 문제 상황인 (B)보다 먼저 나올 수 없음
③ (C) — (D) — (B) ┐
④ (D) — (B) — (C) ┘ (D)의 문제 상황 바로 뒤에 사건의 해결인 (C)가 와야 함
⑤ (D) — (C) — (B) (A) Dave는 목이 말랐음 - (D) Dave는 자판기 이용에 어려움을 겪음 - (C) 상급생의 도움으로 자판기에서 음료를 뽑아 마심 - (B) 글쓴이는 Dave가 달러처럼 그의 자리를 찾을 것이라고 확신함

2025.9
7회

[(A): Dave는 목이 말랐고, 다른 학생들과 어울리지 못하고 있었다.

➡ Dave가 목을 축이기 위해 취할 행동이 이어질 것이다.

[(B): 글쓴이는 일련의 사건을 보며, 처음에는 거부당했지만 결국 제자리를 찾은 달러처럼 Dave도 그럴 것이라고 확신했다.

➡ 모든 상황을 지켜본 뒤에 '1'가 느낀 점이기에 마지막에 올 것이다.

[(C): 포기하지 않던 Dave를 한 상급생이 동전으로 도와주고 각자 다른 방향으로 갔다.

➡ Dave가 자판기에서 음료를 뽑아서 마시기 위해 어떤 노력을 했는지가 앞에 설명되어야 하고, 문제 상황이 끝났으므로 (B)가 (C) 뒤에 올 것이다.

[(D): Dave는 자판기에 돈을 넣으려다 실패하고 다른 학생들이 비웃자, 포기하려 했다.

➡ 목을 축이기 위해 한 행동을 설명하는 첫 부분이기에 (A) 뒤에 이어져야 한다.
▶ 글의 순서는 ⑤ (D) — (C) — (B)임

44 정답 ④

밑줄 친 (a)~(e) 중에서 가리키는 대상이 나머지 넷과 다른 것은?
① (a)   ② (b)   ③ (c)   ④ (d)   ⑤ (e)
= Dave   = Dave   = Dave   = a popular senior boy   = Dave's

>왜 정답? ✱✱✿ [정답률 76%]
④ (d) He: 자판기가 지폐를 잘 인식하지 못한다고 Dave에게 차분히 설명해 준 사람
▶ a popular senior boy

>왜 오답?
① (a) He: 다른 학생들의 세계와 동떨어져 있던 사람 ▶ Dave
② (b) he: 결국 자신의 자리를 찾을 것이라고 '1'가 확신한 사람 ▶ Dave
③ (c) he: 단호한 표정으로 자판기에 지폐를 계속 밀어 넣던 사람 ▶ Dave
⑤ (e) his: 그의 반 학생들이 앉아 있던 테이블을 돌아본 사람 ▶ Dave's

45 정답 ④

윗글에 관한 내용으로 적절하지 않은 것은?
① 그날 오후 식당은 고등학생들로 가득 찼다.
   the cafeteria was full of high school students on that afternoon
② '1'는 Dave와 그 달러가 비슷하다고 생각했다.
   I thought he and the dollar were very much alike.
③ 상급생은 주머니에서 동전을 꺼냈다. he pulled some coins from his pocket
④ Dave와 상급생은 같은 방향으로 떠났다.
   Then the two walked off in different directions.
⑤ Dave의 눈에 눈물이 맺히기 시작했다. tears began to form in his eyes

>왜 정답? ✱✱✿ [정답률 85%]
상급생이 Dave를 도와준 후, 그 둘은 각자 다른 방향으로 떠났으므로 (Then the two walked off in different directions.) 같은 방향으로 떠났다는 ④은 적절하지 않다.

>왜 오답?
① 그날 오후 식당은 고등학생들로 가득 찼다. (the cafeteria was full of high school students on that afternoon)
② '1'는 Dave와 그 달러가 비슷하다고 생각했다. (I thought he and the dollar were very much alike.)
③ 상급생은 주머니에서 동전을 꺼냈다. (he pulled some coins from his pocket)
⑤ Dave의 눈에 눈물이 맺히기 시작했다. (tears began to form in his eyes)

7회 Dictation
문제 p. 134

01 Due to limited parking / ensure / assist in making / the parking arrangements
02 don't you already have / instead of buying / environmentally / makes sense
03 ever gone blank / effective / talk to yourself
04 three arrows forming a triangle / an important item / make a difference / promoting
05 brighten / sheets to protect / bring extra clothes / residents
06 would you like to rent / per hour / Got it / get a 10% discount
07 miss it this time / got the weekend off / assignments / almost the whole day
08 what are you reading / heard of it / something useful or creative / participation fee
09 let you experience / virtual reality / travel back in time / made a reservation in advance
10 travel abroad / check the size / safety feature / would be more convenient
11 I had a problem / wait a bit more / fix it
12 prefer watching movies / more comfortable / theater's schedule
13 What brings you / without considering / some guidance / related to that
14 unnecessary things / did you decide / cooking more at home / difficult but rewarding
15 recently learned / afford to buy one / freshly baked cookies / lend him
[16~17] on your next countryside walk / observations / in case of unexpected rain / Preparing these necessities

7회 어휘 Review Test
문제 p. 138

01 경계, 지평
02 연장하다
03 동맹, 연합
04 정교한
05 배정
06 despair
07 substantial
08 aimlessly
09 endurance
10 mortality
11 feed into
12 set the tone
13 catch up with
14 have access to

15 stop cold
16 rush
17 observations
18 scarce
19 overlook
20 motives
21 attempts
22 alternative
23 capture
24 mammals
25 interactive
26 domesticate
27 consumption
28 impartially

29 hierarchy
30 instant
31 quoted
32 directions
33 grand
34 composing
35 exerting
36 preconceptions
37 immobile
38 meditative
39 coined
40 utter

01 정답 ③ ＊지하철 연장 운행 안내

W : Hello!
여 : 안녕하세요!

I'm Olivia Parker from Pineview City Subway.
저는 Pineview City 지하철의 Olivia Parker입니다.

I have an announcement for this Saturday's fireworks festival.
이번 토요일의 불꽃놀이 축제에 대한 안내가 있습니다.

Many people **are expected** to visit and enjoy the festival late into the night. (수동태 동사)
많은 사람들이 늦은 밤까지 축제를 방문하고 즐길 것으로 예상됩니다.

For smooth transportation and visitor safety, we're extending the operational hours of the subway on the day of the festival. 단서 축제 당일 지하철 운행 시간을 연장할 것임을 알림
원활한 교통과 방문객의 안전을 위해, 축제 당일 지하철 운행 시간을 연장합니다.

The subway **will run** for an extra two hours after the regular last train from the festival area stations. (완전자동사)
축제 지역 정류장에서 마지막 정규 열차 이후 두 시간 동안 추가로 지하철을 운행할 예정입니다.

For a comfortable and safe journey from the event, we encourage you **to take** advantage of our **extended** subway services. (encourage의 목적격 보어(to부정사)) (과거분사(subway services 수식))
행사에서 편안하고 안전한 이동을 위해 연장된 지하철 서비스를 이용할 것을 권해드립니다.

We hope you enjoy this fantastic festival with convenience.
이 환상적인 축제를 편하게 즐기시기 바랍니다.

Thank you! 감사합니다!

- announcement ⓝ 안내 • fireworks ⓝ 불꽃놀이
- transportation ⓝ 교통 • extend ⓥ 연장하다
- operational hours 운영(운행) 시간 • regular ⓐ 정규의
- journey ⓝ 이동, 여행 • take advantage of ~을 이용하다
- convenience ⓝ 편의

다음을 듣고, 여자가 하는 말의 목적으로 가장 적절한 것을 고르시오.

① 축제 기간 연장을 요청하려고 축제 기간을 연장한다는 내용은 없음
② 신설된 지하철 노선을 홍보하려고 지하철 노선이 신설되었다는 언급은 없음
③ 축제 당일의 지하철 연장 운행을 안내하려고
축제 당일 지하철이 연장 운행됨을 안내했음
④ 축제 방문객에게 안전 수칙 준수를 당부하려고 안전 수칙에 대한 언급은 없음
⑤ 축제 기간 중 도심 교통 통제 구간을 공지하려고
축제 동안 도심 교통을 통제한다는 언급은 없음

＞왜 정답 ？ ✿✿✿ [정답률 90%]

많은 사람들이 늦은 밤까지 축제를 방문할 것이라 예상되기 때문에, 축제 당일에 지하철 운행 시간을 연장할 예정임을 알리고 있다. 따라서 여자가 하는 말의 목적으로 가장 적절한 것은 ③이다.

＞왜 오답 ？

① 축제 기간 연장을 요청하는 것이 아니라, 지하철 운행 시간을 연장한다는 내용이다.
② 기존 지하철의 운행 시간을 조정한다고 했다.
④ 안전한 이동을 위해 연장된 지하철 서비스 이용을 바란다고 했으나, 안전 수칙은 언급되지 않았다.
⑤ 지하철을 연장 운행한다는 안내이지, 교통 통제에 대한 안내가 아니다. (함정)

---

02 정답 ③ ＊취침 전 스마트폰 사용

M : Hi, Emma. What's up? You look tired.
남 : 안녕, Emma. 어떻게 지내? 피곤해 보인다.

W : Hey, David. I always feel tired. Even though I sleep many hours, I **guess** I don't get any good sleep. (뒤에 목적어절 접속사 that이 생략됨)
여 : 안녕, David. 나는 항상 피곤해. 많은 시간을 자도, 푹 잠들지 못하는 것 같아.

M : That's too bad. Is there anything **you do** before you go to bed? (앞에 목적격 관계대명사가 생략됨)
남 : 안타깝네. 자기 전에 네가 하는 일이 있어?

W : I usually read webtoons on my smartphone for a few hours.
여 : 보통 스마트폰으로 몇 시간 동안 웹툰을 읽어.

M : Ah, that's the problem. **Having** too much screen time right before bed is not good. (동명사 주어) 단서 1 취침 전 스마트폰 사용이 문제라고 지적함
남 : 아, 그게 문제야. 자기 직전에 너무 오래 화면을 보는 건 좋지 않아.

W : Really? But I'm so **used to spending** time on my phone at night! (be used to v-ing: ~하는 데 익숙하다)
여 : 정말? 하지만 나는 밤에 스마트폰을 사용하는 게 너무 익숙해!

M : Long exposure to the screen light can make your brain stay awake. 단서 2 화면의 빛을 오래 보면 뇌가 깨어 있게 됨
남 : 화면의 빛에 오래 노출되는 것은 뇌가 깨어 있게 할 수 있어.

W : I never **knew** using smartphones had a negative impact on sleep. (뒤에 목적어절 접속사 that이 생략됨)
여 : 나는 스마트폰 사용이 수면에 부정적인 영향을 미친다는 걸 전혀 몰랐어.

M : **Reducing** your smartphone use before going to bed will increase the quality of your sleep. (동명사(주어)) 단서 3 취침 전 스마트폰 사용을 줄이면 수면의 질이 높아짐
남 : 자기 전에 스마트폰 사용을 줄이는 것은 수면의 질을 높일 거야.

W : Okay, I can **give it a try**. ('시도하다')
여 : 알겠어, 시도해 볼게.

- screen time 스크린 타임(스마트폰을 사용하는 시간) • exposure ⓝ 노출
- stay awake 깨어 있다 • impact ⓝ 영향 • reduce ⓥ 줄이다
- increase ⓥ 높이다 • quality ⓝ 질

대화를 듣고, 남자의 의견으로 가장 적절한 것을 고르시오.

① 불규칙한 수면 습관은 청소년의 뇌 발달을 방해한다.
수면이 뇌 발달을 방해한다는 내용은 없음
② 스마트폰의 화면 밝기를 조절하여 눈을 보호해야 한다.
화면 밝기 조절을 통해 눈을 보호해야 한다는 언급은 없음
③ 취침 전 스마트폰 사용을 줄여야 수면의 질이 높아진다.
자기 전에 스마트폰 사용을 줄이는 것이 수면의 질을 높일 것이라고 했음
④ 집중력 향상을 위해 디지털 기기 사용을 최소화해야 한다.
집중력 향상에 대한 언급은 없음
⑤ 일정한 시간에 취침하는 것이 생체 리듬 유지에 도움을 준다.
일정한 시간에 취침해야 한다는 내용은 없음

＞왜 정답 ？ ✿✿✿ [정답률 96%]

남자는 자기 전에 스마트폰 화면을 오래 보는 것은 뇌를 깨어 있게 할 수 있으므로, 취침 전 스마트폰 사용을 줄이는 것이 수면의 질을 높일 것이라고 했다. 따라서 남자의 의견으로 가장 적절한 것은 ③이다.

＞왜 오답 ？

① 자기 전에 스마트폰을 오래 보는 것이 뇌를 깨어 있게 한다고는 했으나, 청소년의 뇌 발달을 방해한다는 언급은 없다.
② 자기 전에 스마트폰 화면을 오래 보는 것에 대해서만 말했을 뿐, 눈 건강에 대한 언급은 없다.
④ 자기 전에 디지털 기기 사용을 줄여야 한다고는 했지만, 집중력 향상을 위한 것이 아니라 수면의 질을 높이기 위한 것이다. (주의)
⑤ 자기 전에 스마트폰 사용을 줄여야 한다는 내용일 뿐, 일정한 시간에 취침해야 한다는 내용이 아니다.

03 정답 ⑤ *직업과 관련이 없는 취미 활동 하기

M : Hello, listeners! Welcome to your *Daily Tips*.
남 : 안녕하세요, 청취자 여러분! '일일 팁'에 오신 것을 환영합니다.

형용사적 용법(way 수식)
Today, I'll tell you a helpful way **to relieve** your stress.
오늘은, 스트레스를 해소하는 데 도움이 되는 방법을 알려드리겠습니다.

목적어절 접속사   동명사구 주어(that절의 주어)
Recent research shows **that** having hobbies completely
unrelated to your job can significantly reduce stress.
최근 연구에 따르면, 직업과 전혀 관련 없는 취미를 가지는 것이 스트레스를 상당히 줄일
수 있다고 합니다. [단서] 직업과 관련 없는 취미를 갖는 것이 스트레스를 줄여줌

주격 관계대명사
For example, if you work in IT, consider exploring activities
that are far from the digital field.
예를 들어, IT 분야에서 일하는 경우, 디지털 분야와는 거리가 먼 활동을 탐색해 보세요.

동명사구 주어
Playing the guitar might be a good option rather than
playing computer games.
컴퓨터 게임을 하는 것 대신에 기타를 연주하는 것이 좋은 선택이 될 수 있습니다.

주격 관계대명사
Let's enjoy hobbies **that** are different from our work!
우리의 일과는 다른 취미를 즐깁시다!

형용사적 용법(the best way 수식)
That'll be the best way **to get** a refreshing break.
그것이 상쾌한 휴식을 취하는 최고의 방법이 될 것입니다.

Remember, a well-chosen hobby can be a powerful tool for
stress relief.
적절한 취미는 스트레스 해소를 위한 강력한 도구가 될 수 있다는 점을 기억하세요.
'(라디오, 텔레비전 프로그램을) 청취하다'
Tune in tomorrow for more helpful daily tips!
더 많은 유익한 일일 팁을 위해 내일도 청취해 주세요!

- helpful ⓐ 도움이 되는, 유익한 • relieve ⓥ 완화하다
- significantly ⓐᵈ 상당히 • reduce ⓥ 줄이다
- might A rather than B B보다는 A일 수도 있다 • option ⓝ 선택
- refreshing ⓐ 상쾌한 • well-chosen ⓐ 잘 선택된, 적절한

다음을 듣고, 남자가 하는 말의 요지로 가장 적절한 것을 고르시오.
① 과도한 컴퓨터 사용은 스트레스 지수를 증가시킨다.
                                          과도한 컴퓨터 사용에 대한 언급은 없음
② 컴퓨터 관련 취미 활동은 IT 활용 능력을 향상시킨다.
                        IT 활용 능력 향상에 대한 언급은 없음
③ 직업을 선택할 때 자신의 흥미와 적성을 고려해야 한다.
                            직업 선택에 관한 내용은 없음
④ 다양한 악기 연주를 배우는 것은 인생을 풍요롭게 만든다.
                        악기 연주를 배우는 것에 관한 내용이 아님
⑤ 직업과 관련 없는 취미 활동이 스트레스 감소에 도움이 된다.
   직업과 전혀 관련 없는 취미를 가지는 것이 스트레스를 상당히 줄일 수 있다고 했음

왜 정답 ? ✱✱✱ [정답률 94%]
남자는 스트레스 해소에 도움이 되는 방법을 알려준다고 하며, 직업과 전혀 관련 없는
취미를 가지는 것이 스트레스를 상당히 줄일 수 있다는 연구 결과를 소개했다. 따라서
남자가 하는 말의 요지로 가장 적절한 것은 ⑤이다.

왜 오답 ?
① IT 분야에서 일하는 경우를 예로 들었지만, 과도한 컴퓨터 사용은 언급되지 않았다.
② 컴퓨터 관련 취미 활동은 직업과 관련 있는 취미의 예시일 뿐이며, 이것이 IT 활용
   능력을 향상시킨다는 내용이 아니다.
③ 직업과 관련 없는 취미 활동을 찾으라는 내용이지, 직업을 선택할 때 고려해야 할
   사항을 알려주는 것이 아니다.
④ 직업과 관련 없는 취미의 예시로서 기타 연주가 제시되었을 뿐, 다양한 악기 연주를
   배우는 것은 언급되지 않았다.

04 정답 ④ *새로운 녹음 스튜디오

M : Hey, Amy. Here is the new recording studio for our band.
     How do you like it?
남 : 안녕, Amy. 여기가 우리 밴드를 위한 새로운 녹음 스튜디오야. 어때?

W : Wow, these two speakers are impressive!
여 : 와, 이 두 스피커가 인상적이야!   ①의 단서 방에 스피커 두 대가 있음

M : Yes, they are. The sound quality is excellent.
남 : 맞아, 정말 그래. 음질이 훌륭해.

주격 보어(형용사)
W : Also, the long desk between the speakers looks **great**.
여 : 그리고, 스피커 사이에 있는 긴 책상이 멋지네. ②의 단서 스피커 사이에 긴 책상이 있음

M : Yeah. And on the desk, there is a microphone. We can use it
     to give recording directions. ③의 단서 책상 위에 마이크가 있음
남 : 응. 그리고 책상 위에, 마이크가 있어. 녹음 지시를 주는 데 사용할 수 있지.

주격 보어(형용사)
W : Nice. Oh, this chair looks **comfortable**. It could be helpful
     for long recordings.
여 : 좋네. 오, 이 의자는 편안해 보여. 장시간의 녹음에 유용하겠어.

간접목적어   직접목적어
M : Agreed. And the rug under the chair gives **the room a cozy
     feeling**, doesn't it?
남 : 동감이야. 그리고 의자 아래 러그가 방에 아늑한 느낌을 줘, 그렇지 않니?

W : Yes, and I like the flower patterns on the rug.
여 : 응, 그리고 러그의 꽃무늬도 마음에 들어. ④의 단서 의자 아래 러그는
                                          꽃무늬가 아니라 체크무늬임
M : I like it, too. How about the poster on the wall?
남 : 나도 그걸 좋아해. 벽에 있는 포스터는 어때? ⑤의 단서 벽에 포스터가 있음

W : It's cool. This studio feels like where music truly comes
     alive! 여 : 멋져. 이 스튜디오는 음악이 정말로 활기를 띠는 곳 같아!

M : I'm glad you like this place. 남 : 네가 이곳을 마음에 들어 해서 기뻐.

W : Absolutely. I can't wait to start recording here.
여 : 물론이야. 여기서 녹음을 시작하고 싶어!

- impressive ⓐ 인상적인 • direction ⓝ 지시
- comfortable ⓐ 편안한   • cozy ⓐ 아늑한

대화를 듣고, 그림에서 대화의 내용과 일치하지 **않는** 것을 고르시오.

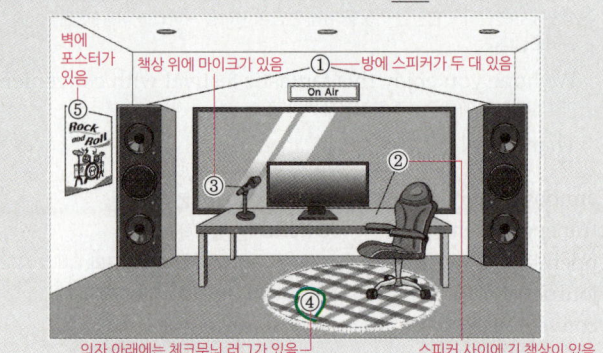

왜 정답 ? ✱✱✱ [정답률 85%]
의자 아래 러그가 꽃무늬라고 했지만, 그림에는 체크무늬 러그가 있으므로 ④이
대화의 내용과 일치하지 않는다.

왜 오답 ?
① 방에 스피커가 두 대 있다고 했다.
② 스피커 사이에 긴 책상이 있다고 했다.
③ 책상 위에 마이크가 있다고 했다.
⑤ 벽에 포스터가 있다고 했다.

05 정답 ② *Go-Green 행사 준비

W : Tony, I'm so excited for our Go-Green event!
여 : Tony, 나 우리의 Go-Green 행사가 너무 기대돼!
                                                '~을 점검하다'
M : Me too. The event is almost here. Why don't we **go over** our
     preparations together?
남 : 나도 그래. 행사가 거의 다가왔네. 준비 상황을 함께 점검해 보는 건 어때?
     뒤에 목적어절 접속사 that이 생략됨
W : Okay. I **think** the exhibition booths are very important for
     our event. How are they going?
여 : 좋아. 전시 부스가 우리 행사에 정말 중요하다고 생각해. 진행 상황은 어때?

M : Almost ready. I'm working on the booth setup this afternoon. What about the welcome gifts? ⑤의 함정
남 : 거의 준비됐어. 오늘 오후에 부스 설치 작업을 할 거야. 환영 선물은 어때?
현재완료(완료)
W : I've already **prepared** some eco-friendly bags. ①의 함정
여 : 이미 친환경 가방을 몇 개 준비해 놨어.

M : Perfect! What's next? 남 : 완벽해! 다음으로 할 일은 뭐야?

W : We need to confirm the list of guests for the ceremony.
여 : 식을 위한 초대 손님 명단을 확인해야 해.

M : I double-checked the list. But I haven't sent the online invitation cards, yet. ④의 함정
남 : 나는 명단을 다시 확인했어. 하지만 온라인 초대장을 아직 보내지 않았어.

W : No problem. I'll deal with it right away. How about the food and drinks? 단서 여자가 온라인 초대장을 바로 보내겠다고 함
여 : 문제없어. 내가 바로 처리할게. 음식과 음료는 어때?
현재완료(완료)
M : I've **scheduled** food and drink services and I'll serve the guests with reusable dishes. ③의 함정
남 : 음식과 음료 서비스는 예약했고 손님들에게 재사용할 수 있는 식기를 제공할 거야.

W : Nice! I'm confident our event will be a great success.
여 : 좋네! 우리 행사가 큰 성공을 거둘 거라고 확신해.

- preparation ⓝ 준비 · exhibition ⓝ 전시 · setup ⓝ 설치
- eco-friendly ⓐ 친환경의 · confirm ⓥ 확인하다
- ceremony ⓝ 의식, 식 · double-check ⓥ 다시 확인하다
- deal with ~을 처리하다 · reusable ⓐ 재사용할 수 있는
- confident ⓐ 자신감 있는, 확신하는

> 대화를 듣고, 여자가 할 일로 가장 적절한 것을 고르시오.
> ① 선물 준비하기 선물은 이미 여자가 준비함
> ② 온라인 초대장 보내기 여자가 온라인 초대장을 바로 보내겠다고 했음
> ③ 음식 주문하기 남자가 음식과 음료 서비스를 예약했음
> ④ 초대 손님 명단 확인하기 남자가 손님 명단을 다시 확인했음
> ⑤ 전시 부스 설치하기 남자가 오후에 전시 부스 설치 작업을 하겠다고 했음

왜 정답? ❁❁❁ [정답률 82%]
Go-Green 행사를 준비하는 상황에서 남자가 아직 온라인 초대장을 보내지 않았다고 하자, 여자가 바로 처리할 것이라고 했으므로 정답은 ②이다.

왜 오답?
① 여자가 친환경 가방을 이미 선물로 준비했다.
③ 남자가 음식과 음료 서비스를 예약했다고 했다.
④ 초대 손님 명단은 남자가 이미 확인했다.
⑤ 오늘 오후에 남자가 전시 부스 설치 작업을 할 것이라고 했다. 함정

06 정답 ③ ＊캠핑 테이블과 의자 구입

W : Welcome to the Riverside Camping store. How can I help you?
여 : Riverside 캠핑 상점에 오신 것을 환영합니다. 무엇을 도와드릴까요?
= a camping table
M : I'm looking for a camping table for my family. Can you recommend **one**?
남 : 가족을 위한 캠핑 테이블을 찾고 있어요. 하나 추천해 주실 수 있나요?

W : Sure. How about this one? It's light and easy to fold, so it's our best-selling product.
여 : 물론이죠. 이 제품은 어때요? 가볍고 접기 쉬워서, 가장 많이 팔리는 제품이에요.

M : It looks good. How much is it?
남 : 좋아 보이네요. 가격은 얼마인가요?

W : It comes in two sizes. The small one is 30 dollars and the large one is 50 dollars. 단서1 작은 테이블은 30달러이고, 큰 테이블은 50달러임
여 : 두 가지 사이즈가 있어요. 작은 것은 30달러, 큰 것은 50달러입니다.

단서2 큰 테이블을 한 개 구매함
M : I'll buy the large one. Are there folding chairs, too?
남 : 큰 걸로 살게요. 접이식 의자도 있나요?
'~와 잘 어울리다'
W : Yep. These folding chairs might **go well with** the table. They're 10 dollars each. 단서3 접이식 의자는 개당 10달러임
여 : 네. 이 접이식 의자가 테이블과 잘 어울릴 것 같아요. 각각 10달러입니다.

M : Sounds good. I'll buy four of those chairs.
남 : 좋네요. 그 의자 네 개를 살게요. 단서4 접이식 의자를 네 개 구매함

W : Okay. That's one large camping table and four chairs.
여 : 알겠습니다. 큰 캠핑 테이블 하나와 의자 네 개네요.

M : That's right. Can I use this discount coupon now?
남 : 맞아요. 이 할인 쿠폰 지금 사용할 수 있나요?

W : Of course. You can get a 10% discount on the total price.
여 : 물론이죠. 전체 가격에서 10% 할인받을 수 있어요. 단서5 쿠폰으로 전체 가격에서 10% 할인받을 수 있음

M : Perfect. Here's my credit card.
남 : 완벽해요. 여기 제 신용카드입니다.

- recommend ⓥ 추천하다 · fold ⓥ 접다 · discount ⓝ 할인

> 대화를 듣고, 남자가 지불할 금액을 고르시오. [3점]
> ① $63 ② $70 ③ $81 ④ $86 ⑤ $90
> $50(큰 캠핑용 테이블 1개) + $10 × 4(10달러짜리 접이식 의자 4개) − $9(쿠폰 10% 할인)

왜 정답? ❁❁❁ [정답률 91%]
남자는 하나에 50달러인 큰 캠핑용 테이블 한 개와 10달러인 접이식 의자 네 개를 구매했으므로 전체 금액은 90달러이다. 여기에 10% 할인 쿠폰을 사용했으므로 남자가 지불할 금액은 ③ '81달러'이다.

07 정답 ④ ＊등산을 갈 수 없는 여자
현재완료(계속)
W : Lately, the weather **has been** lovely. This is a perfect time for climbing.
여 : 요즘, 날씨가 너무 좋네요. 등산하기에 완벽한 시기예요.

M : Indeed. Oh, would you like to go mountain climbing together?
남 : 정말 그렇네요. 오, 함께 산에 갈까요?

W : Sounds awesome. I have all the climbing equipment. ⑥의 함정
여 : 좋아요. 저는 등산 장비를 다 갖추고 있어요.

M : Great. How about this upcoming weekend? I'll find a nice mountain for us.
남 : 훌륭해요. 이번 주말은 어때요? 우리에게 좋은 산을 찾아볼게요.

W : Hold on, this weekend? I don't think I can make it then.
여 : 잠깐만요, 이번 주말이요? 저는 그때 안 될 것 같아요.

M : Really? All school tests are finally done, so I thought this weekend would be good for us. ②의 함정
남 : 정말요? 모든 학교 시험이 마침내 끝났으니까, 이번 주말이 우리에게 좋을 것이라고 생각했어요.
-thing으로 끝나는 대명사는 형용사가 뒤에서 수식함
W : Sorry, but I have **something important** to do this weekend.
여 : 죄송하지만, 이번 주말에 중요한 일이 있어요.

M : Do you have a part-time job? ①의 함정
남 : 아르바이트가 있나요?

W : No. Actually, I need to practice dancing for the entire weekend. 단서1 주말 내내 춤 연습을 해야 함
여 : 아니요. 사실, 주말 내내 춤 연습을 해야 해요.
뒤에 목적격 관계대명사가 생략됨
M : Ah, for the dance **competition** you mentioned before?
남 : 아, 전에 말했던 춤 경연을 위해서요?
make it: 성공하다
W : Yes. Surprisingly, I **made it** through the first round, and it's the finals next Monday. 단서2 다음 주 월요일에 춤 경연 결승전이 있음
여 : 네. 놀랍게도, 저는 1차전을 통과했고, 다음 주 월요일에 결승전이 있어요.

M : That's fantastic! I wish you the best of luck.
남 : 정말 대단해요! 행운을 빌어요.

- indeed [ad] 정말 · equipment [n] 장비 · upcoming [a] 다가오는
- practice [v] 연습하다 · entire [a] 전체의 · competition [n] 경연
- mention [v] 언급하다

대화를 듣고, 여자가 이번 주말에 등산을 갈 수 <u>없는</u> 이유를 고르시오.

① 아르바이트를 해야 해서 이번 주말에 아르바이트가 있는 것은 아님
② 학교 시험공부를 해야 해서 모든 학교 시험이 끝남
③ 폭우로 인해 등산로가 폐쇄되어서 폭우나 등산로 폐쇄에 관한 언급은 없음
④ 경연을 위한 춤 연습을 해야 해서 여자는 춤 경연을 위해 주말 내내 춤 연습을 해야 함
⑤ 주문한 등산 장비가 도착하지 않아서 여자는 등산 장비를 다 갖췄다고 했음

>왜 정답? ✱✱✱ [정답률 97%]

남자는 모든 학교 시험이 끝난 이번 주말에 등산을 가자고 했는데, 여자는 다음 주 월요일에 있을 춤 경연 결승전을 위해 주말 내내 춤 연습을 해야 한다고 했다. 따라서 정답은 ④이다.

>왜 오답?

① 아르바이트 때문이 아니라 주말 내내 춤 연습을 해야 하기 때문이라고 했다.
② 이번 주말이 되기 전에 모든 학교 시험이 끝난다고 했다.
③ 폭우나 등산로 폐쇄는 언급되지 않았다.
⑤ 여자는 등산 장비를 다 갖추고 있다고 했다.

08 정답 ③ ＊아파트 요가 프로그램 등록

W : Grandpa, take a look at this. It's a Lakestate Apartment Yoga Program poster. '~을 보다'
여 : 할아버지, 이거 한 번 보세요. Lakestate 아파트 요가 프로그램 포스터예요.

M : Wow, a new program for the residents. I've always wanted to join a yoga program. 현재완료(계속)
남 : 와, 주민들을 위한 새로운 프로그램이구나. 난 항상 요가 프로그램에 참여하고 싶었어.

W : I know, and this one is only for those aged 60 and above. 사이에 주격 관계대명사와 be동사가 생략됨 ①의 단서 대상 연령
여 : 알죠, 그리고 이 프로그램은 60세 이상만을 위한 거예요.

M : That's perfect for me. [Pause] Oh, it says it's held at 8 a.m. every Tuesday and Friday. ②의 단서 운영 요일
남 : 나한테 딱 맞는구나. [잠시 후] 아, 매주 화요일과 금요일 오전 8시에 진행된다고 적혀 있네.

W : It'll be a good time for you. You're an early bird. '일찍 일어나는 사람'
여 : 그건 할아버지에게 좋은 시간이 될 거예요. 할아버지는 일찍 일어나는 분이시잖아요.

M : Yes, I am. How do I register? 남 : 그렇지. 어떻게 등록하니?

W : You just need to fill out an application form at the apartment fitness center. ④의 단서 등록 방법
여 : 아파트 피트니스 센터에서 신청서를 작성하기만 하면 돼요.

M : Okay, I think I'll go right now. 남 : 알겠어, 지금 바로 가야겠다.

W : Good. But don't forget to take your ID card with you. ⑤의 단서 등록 준비물
여 : 좋아요. 하지만 신분증 가져가는 걸 잊지 마세요.

M : Oh, do I need that for the registration? = ID card
남 : 아, 등록할 때 그것이 필요하니?

W : Yes. It says that on the poster. Would you like me to go with you? 여 : 네. 포스터에 그렇게 적혀 있어요. 같이 가 드릴까요?

M : That would be lovely. 남 : 그거 좋지.

- resident [n] 거주자 · register [v] 등록하다
- application [n] 신청(서) · ID card 신분증(= identity card)

대화를 듣고, Lakestate Apartment Yoga Program에 관해 언급되지 <u>않은</u> 것을 고르시오.

① 대상 연령 for those aged 60 and above ② 운영 요일 every Tuesday and Friday
③ 모집 인원 언급되지 않음 ④ 등록 방법 fill out an application form
⑤ 등록 준비물 don't forget to take your ID card with you

>왜 정답? ✱✱✱ [정답률 93%]

Lakestate 아파트 요가 프로그램의 대상 연령, 운영 요일, 등록 방법, 등록 준비물은 언급했지만, 모집 인원은 언급하지 않았으므로 정답은 ③이다.

>왜 오답?

① 대상 연령은 60세 이상이다.
② 매주 화요일과 금요일에 운영된다.
④ 등록하려면 신청서를 작성하면 된다.
⑤ 등록하려면 신분증을 챙겨가야 한다.

09 정답 ④ ＊Global Food Market 행사 소개

W : Good morning! This is Allison from the student council.
여 : 좋은 아침입니다! 저는 학생회의 Allison입니다.

I'm happy to announce the Global Food Market right here at Westhill High School. 부사적 용법(happy 수식)
Westhill 고등학교에서 열리는 Global Food Market을 알려드리게 되어 기쁩니다.

Get ready for a delicious journey around the world in the school parking lot. ①의 단서 학교 주차장에서 열림
학교 주차장에서 세계를 맛보는 여행을 준비하세요.

Our Global Food Market will take place for two days, on September 25th and 26th. '열리다, 개최되다' ②의 단서 이틀간 열림
우리 Global Food Market은 9월 25일과 26일, 이틀간 열릴 것입니다.

You can enjoy food from eight different countries, including Mexico and France. ③의 단서 8개 국가의 음식을 즐길 수 있음
멕시코와 프랑스를 포함해 8개 국가의 음식을 즐길 수 있습니다.

And there's no need to worry about prices. 형용사적 용법(need 수식)
가격은 걱정하지 않으셔도 됩니다.

Every single dish is only five dollars. every + 단수 명사 + 단수 동사 ④의 단서 모든 요리는 5달러임
모든 요리는 단돈 5달러입니다.

Wait! You don't eat meat? No problem!
잠깐! 고기를 먹지 않으신다고요? 괜찮아요!

We also have menus for vegetarians. ⑤의 단서 채식주의자를 위한 메뉴도 있음
채식주의자들을 위한 메뉴도 있습니다.

So, join us at the Global Food Market.
그러니, Global Food Market에 꼭 참여하세요.

It's not just about food, but a celebration of culture and diversity. 음식뿐만 아니라, 문화와 다양성을 기념하는 행사입니다.

Don't miss this chance to taste the world! 형용사적 용법(chance 수식)
세계를 맛볼 이 기회를 놓치지 마세요!

- student council 학생회 · vegetarian [n] 채식주의자
- celebration [n] 기념 · diversity [n] 다양성

Global Food Market에 관한 다음 내용을 듣고, 일치하지 <u>않는</u> 것을 고르시오.

① 학교 주차장에서 열린다. in the school parking lot
② 이틀간 진행된다. take place for two days
③ 8개 국가의 음식을 즐길 수 있다. You can enjoy food from eight different countries
④ 음식마다 가격이 다르다. Every single dish is only five dollars.
⑤ 채식주의자를 위한 메뉴가 있다. We also have menus for vegetarians.

>왜 정답? ✱✱✱ [정답률 96%]

모든 요리는 단돈 5달러라고 했으므로(Every single dish is only five dollars.) 음식마다 가격이 다르다고 한 ④은 일치하지 않는다.

>왜 오답?

① 학교 주차장에서 행사가 열린다.
② 9월 25일과 26일, 이틀 동안 진행된다.
③ 멕시코와 프랑스를 포함해 8개 국가의 음식을 즐길 수 있다.
⑤ 채식주의자를 위한 메뉴도 있다.

10 정답 ④ ＊디지털 텀블러 구입

W : Honey, what are you looking at? 여 : 여보, 뭐 보고 있어요?

M : I'm looking at digital tumblers. They show the temperature on an LED screen. Would you like to help me **choose** one?
help의 목적격 보어(원형부정사)
남 : 디지털 텀블러를 보고 있어요. LED 화면에 온도가 표시되네요. 하나 고르는 것을 도와줄래요?

W : Sure, let me see. *[Pause]* The price differs by model.
여 : 물론이죠, 어디 봐요. *[잠시 후]* 모델에 따라 가격이 다르네요.

M : Hmm, I don't want to pay more than 60 dollars.
남 : 흠, 60달러 이상은 지불하고 싶지 않아요. **단서 1** 60달러 이하여야 함 (⑤ 제외)

W : That sounds **reasonable**. Look, there are various sizes to choose from.
주격 보어(형용사)
여 : 그거 합리적이네요. 봐요, 고를 수 있는 다양한 크기가 있어요.

M : Less than 400ml would be too small for me.
남 : 400ml보다 작은 것은 제게 너무 작을 것 같아요. **단서 2** 400ml 이상이어야 함 (① 제외)

W : Alright. Oh, there's a new function. Do you need the water intake display? It'll show you how much water you drink in a day.
여 : 그래요. 오, 새로운 기능이 있네요. 물 섭취량 표시가 필요해요? 당신이 하루에 물 얼마나 마시는지 보여줄 거예요.

M : That sounds smart. I'd love to have **it**. Then, I have just two options left.
= water intake display
단서 3 물 섭취량 표시가 있는 것이 좋음 (② 제외)
남 : 똑똑하네요. 그게 있었으면 좋겠어요. 그러면 선택지가 두 개 남았네요.

W : What color do you like? You have too many black items and they're boring.
여 : 어떤 색이 좋아요? 당신은 검은색 물건을 너무 많이 가지고 있고 그것들은 지루해요.

M : Okay. I'll go with the one **that**'s not black. Then, I'll order this one.
주격 관계대명사
단서 4 검은색이 아닌 모델 (③ 제외)
남 : 알겠어요. 검은색이 아닌 걸로 할게요. 그럼, 이걸 주문할게요.

W : Great idea! 여 : 좋은 생각이에요!

- temperature ⓝ 온도 ・ differ ⓥ 다르다
- reasonable ⓐ 타당한 ・ function ⓝ 기능 ・ intake ⓝ 섭취

다음 표를 보면서 대화를 듣고, 남자가 주문할 디지털 텀블러를 고르시오.

Digital Tumblers 디지털 텀블러

	Model 모델	Price 가격	Size 크기	Water Intake Display 물 섭취량 표시	Color 색
①	A	$35	350ml	×	White 흰색
②	B	$40	470ml	×	Gold 금색
③	C	$45	470ml	○	Black 검은색
④	D	$55	550ml	○	White
⑤	E	$65	550ml	○	Gold

400ml보다 작음
물 섭취량 표시가 없음
60달러 이상임
검은색은 제외함

> 왜 정답 ? ✽✽✽ [정답률 90%]

가격이 60달러 이하이고(⑤ 제외), 크기가 400ml보다 크며(① 제외), 물 섭취량 표시가 있는 것(② 제외) 중, 검은색이 아닌 제품(③ 제외)은 ④이다.

> 왜 오답 ?

① 400ml 이하는 너무 작을 것 같다고 했다.
② 물 섭취량 표시가 있는 것이 좋겠다고 했다.
③ 검은색이 아닌 것을 고른다고 했다.
⑤ 60달러 이상은 지불하고 싶지 않다고 했다.

---

11 정답 ① ＊습도와 감기의 관계

W : I easily catch a cold these days.
여 : 요즘 저는 감기에 잘 걸려요.

M : That's too bad. It's a good idea to keep some moisture in your room. **단서** 방에 습기를 유지하는 것이 좋음
남 : 안타깝네요. 방에 습기를 유지하는 게 좋을 것 같아요.
= to keep some moisture in your room

W : Oh, how does **that** relate to a cold?
여 : 아, 그게 감기와 어떻게 관련이 있나요?

M : **If it's too dry inside, you can easily get a cold.**
남 : 실내가 너무 건조하면, 감기에 쉽게 걸릴 수 있어요.

- catch a cold 감기에 걸리다 ・ moisture ⓝ 습기
- relate to ~와 관련되다 ・ cough ⓥ 기침하다

2024. 9
8회

대화를 듣고, 여자의 마지막 말에 대한 남자의 응답으로 가장 적절한 것을 고르시오.

① If it's too dry inside, you can easily get a cold.
실내가 너무 건조하면, 감기에 쉽게 걸릴 수 있어요. 방의 습도와 감기의 연관성을 설명하고 있음
② When you cough, you should cover your mouth.
당신은 기침할 때, 입을 가려야 해요. 기침에 관한 내용이 아님
③ You need to wash your hands not to get a cold.
감기에 걸리지 않으려면 당신은 손을 씻어야 해요. 손을 씻어야 한다는 언급은 없음
④ It's really important to keep yourself warm.
몸을 따뜻하게 유지하는 것이 정말 중요해요. 몸을 따뜻하게 유지하는 것에 관한 언급은 없음
⑤ Drinking water can make your skin soft.
물을 마시면 피부가 부드러워질 수 있어요. 피부가 부드러워지는 것에 관한 언급은 없음

> 왜 정답 ? ✽✽✽ [정답률 63%]

요즘 감기에 잘 걸린다는 여자에게 남자는 방에 습기를 유지하는 것이 좋다고 했고, 이에 대해 여자는 방의 습도와 감기의 관계를 물었다. 따라서 남자는 ① '실내가 너무 건조하면, 감기에 쉽게 걸릴 수 있어요.'라고 응답하는 것이 가장 적절하다.

> 왜 오답 ?

② 요즘 감기에 잘 걸린다고 했을 뿐이지, 기침에 관한 내용이 아니다.
③ 실내 습도와 감기의 연관성을 묻는 것이지, 손을 씻는 것에 관한 내용이 아니다. 주의
④ 몸을 따뜻하게 유지하는 것은 언급되지 않았다.
⑤ 물을 마시는 것, 또는 피부가 부드러워지는 것은 언급되지 않았다.

---

12 정답 ② ＊읽지 않는 책들을 처분하기

M : Mom, the bookshelf in my room is full of books. There's no space for new **ones**.
부정대명사(= books)
남 : 엄마, 제 방 책장이 책으로 가득 찼어요. 새로운 책들을 넣을 공간이 없어요.

W : Well, how about throwing away **the books** you don't read anymore?
뒤에 목적격 관계대명사가 생략됨
여 : 그럼, 더 이상 읽지 않는 책들은 버리는 건 어때?
단서 일부 책들이 버리기에는 상태가 너무 좋음

M : But some of them are in too good condition to throw away.
남 : 하지만 그중 일부는 버리기에는 너무 좋은 상태예요.

W : **Right. Then, shall we sell them at a used bookstore?**
여 : 그래. 그럼, 그것들을 중고 서점에 팔아볼까?

- bookshelf ⓝ 책장 ・ throw away 버리다 ・ condition ⓝ 상태

대화를 듣고, 남자의 마지막 말에 대한 여자의 응답으로 가장 적절한 것을 고르시오.

① Awesome. The new bookshelf looks good in your room.
멋지다. 새 책장이 네 방에 잘 어울리네. 새 책장에 관한 내용이 아님
② Right. Then, shall we sell them at a used bookstore?
그래. 그럼, 그것들을 중고 서점에 팔아볼까? 상태가 좋은 책을 처분하는 방법을 제시함
③ I see. Can you borrow them from the library?
알겠어. 도서관에서 그것들을 빌릴 수 있어? 책을 빌린다는 내용이 아님
④ Okay. I'll buy you books in a good condition.
알겠어. 상태가 좋은 책들을 네게 사줄게. 책을 사달라는 내용이 아님
⑤ I'm sorry. I haven't finished the book yet.
미안해. 아직 그 책을 다 읽지 못했어. 책을 아직 다 읽지 못했다는 내용이 아님

왜 정답 ? ★★★ [정답률 78%]

책장이 가득 차서 새로운 책을 넣을 공간이 없다는 남자의 말에 여자는 더 이상 읽지 않는 책들을 버리는 건 어떠냐고 했다. 그러자 남자는 일부 책들이 버리기에는 상태가 너무 좋다고 했으므로, 여자는 책을 버리는 것 대신에 ② '그래. 그럼 그것들을 중고 서점에 팔아볼까?'라고 응답하는 것이 가장 적절하다.

왜 오답 ?

① 책장이 책으로 가득 찼다고 했지, 새 책장에 관한 내용이 아니다.
③ 도서관에서 책을 빌린다는 것은 언급되지 않았다.
④ 상태가 좋은 책들을 사달라는 내용이 아니다.
⑤ 책을 아직 다 읽지 못했다는 것은 언급되지 않았다.

---

13 정답 ① ＊그룹 프로젝트에서 역할 배정의 중요성

W : Hey, Peter. How's your group project going?
여 : 안녕, Peter. 그룹 프로젝트는 어떻게 진행되고 있니?

M : Hello, Ms. Adams. It's my first time as a leader, so it's quite challenging.
남 : 안녕하세요, Adams 선생님. 제가 리더인 건 처음이라서, 꽤 어렵네요.

W : I thought your group was working well together.
여 : 나는 네 그룹이 함께 잘하고 있다고 생각했는데.

M : Yes. We're all motivated and working hard, but progress is slow.
남 : 네. 우리 모두는 의욕이 있고 열심히 하고 있지만, 진행이 느려요.

W : Well, what are you all working on at this moment?
여 : 그러면, 지금 너희는 모두 무엇을 하고 있니?

M : Everyone is focusing on gathering data as much as possible.
남 : 모든 사람이 가능한 한 많은 자료를 모으는 데 집중하고 있어요.

W : Hmm, did you assign individual tasks to each member?
여 : 음, 각 구성원에게 개별적인 과제를 배정했니?

M : Oh, we haven't discussed it yet. We're not exactly sure who does what.
남 : 아, 아직 그것을 논의하지 않았어요. 누가 무엇을 하는지 확실하지 않아요.

W : That's crucial. Otherwise, it can lead to overlapping tasks in a group project.
여 : 그건 중요해. 그렇지 않으면, 그룹 프로젝트에서 그것은 중복 작업으로 이어질 수 있어.

M : That makes sense. That's why our progress is not that fast.
남 : 그 말이 맞네요. 그래서 우리의 진행이 그렇게 빠르지는 않았군요.

W : Then, as the leader, what do you think you should do now?
여 : 그러면, 리더로서, 지금 너는 무엇을 해야 한다고 생각하니?

M : I'll clarify each group member's specific role.
남 : 전 각 그룹 구성원의 구체적인 역할을 명확히 할 거예요.

- challenging ⓐ 어려운 · motivate ⓥ 동기를 부여하다
- progress ⓝ 진전 · assign ⓥ 맡기다 · task ⓝ 일, 과제
- crucial ⓐ 중대한 · overlap ⓥ 겹치다 · clarify ⓥ 명확히 하다
- topic ⓝ 주제 · analyze ⓥ 분석하다

대화를 듣고, 여자의 마지막 말에 대한 남자의 응답으로 가장 적절한 것을 고르시오. [3점]

Man: _____

① I'll clarify each group member's specific role.
전 각 그룹 구성원의 구체적인 역할을 명확히 할게요.
② I'll collect more data for our group research.
전 우리 그룹의 조사를 위해 더 많은 자료를 수집할 거예요.
③ I should challenge myself for the competition.
전 경쟁을 위해 도전할 거예요.
④ I need to change the topic of our group project.
전 우리 그룹 프로젝트의 주제를 바꿔야 해요.
⑤ I'll let you know how to analyze data effectively.
전 자료를 효과적으로 분석하는 방법을 선생님께 알려드릴게요.

왜 정답 ? ★★★ [정답률 62%]

본인이 리더로 있는 그룹 프로젝트의 진행이 느리다는 남자의 말에 여자는 각 구성원에게 개별적 과제를 배정했는지를 물어보면서 중복 작업을 막기 위해서 역할 배정은 중요하다고 했다. 따라서 리더로서 이제 무엇을 할 것인지 묻는 여자의 물음에 남자는 ① '전 각 그룹 구성원의 구체적인 역할을 명확히 할 거예요.'라고 응답하는 것이 가장 적절하다.

왜 오답 ?

② 이미 모든 구성원이 많은 자료를 모으는 데 집중하고 있어서 중복 작업이 발생할 수 있다고 했으므로, 더 많은 자료를 수집하지는 않을 것이다.
③ 경쟁을 위해 도전해야 한다는 내용이 아니다.
④ 프로젝트의 주제를 바꿔야 한다는 내용이 아니다.
⑤ 여자가 남자에게 리더로서 해야 할 일을 물어봤으므로, 남자가 자료 분석 방법을 알려준다는 것은 적절하지 않다.

---

14 정답 ① ＊좋은 몸 상태를 위한 조언

M : Hey, Emily! You're looking great these days.
남 : 안녕, Emily! 너 요즘 정말 좋아 보인다.

W : Thanks, Isaac. I've been trying hard to get in better shape.
여 : 고마워, Isaac. 더 좋은 몸 상태를 만들기 위해 열심히 노력하고 있어.

M : Good for you! I'm trying to get fit, too. But it's tough.
남 : 잘하고 있네! 나도 건강해지려고 하는 중이야. 하지만 힘들어.

W : Haven't you been working out a lot lately?
여 : 최근에 많이 운동하지 않았어?

M : Yeah, but I don't see a big difference. What's your secret?
남 : 응, 하지만 큰 차이를 못 느끼겠어. 네 비결은 뭐야?

W : Well, I started being careful about when I eat.
여 : 음, 내가 언제 먹는지를 신경 쓰기 시작했어.

M : You mean like not eating right before bed?
남 : 자기 직전에 먹지 않는 것처럼 말이지?

W : Kind of. I noticed I was eating a lot at night. So now I don't eat after 7 p.m.
여 : 그런 셈이지. 나는 내가 밤에 많이 먹고 있었다는 걸 알았어. 그래서 이제 오후 7시 이후로는 먹지 않아.

M : Hmm... I don't know if that's enough to get me in better shape.
남 : 음… 그게 나를 더 좋은 몸 상태로 만들기에 충분한지 모르겠어.

W : Trust me. When we eat makes a big difference.
여 : 믿어봐. 언제 먹는지가 큰 차이를 만들어.

- fit ⓐ 건강한 · tough ⓐ 힘든 · lately ⓐⓓ 최근에
- difference ⓝ 차이 · careful ⓐ 조심하는
- notice ⓥ 알아차리다 · workout ⓝ 운동
- succeed ⓥ 성공하다 · balanced ⓐ 균형 잡힌

대화를 듣고, 남자의 마지막 말에 대한 여자의 응답으로 가장 적절한 것을 고르시오. [3점]

Woman: _____

① Trust me. When we eat makes a big difference.
믿어봐. 언제 먹는지가 큰 차이를 만들어.
② Okay. I'll check my meals to get in better shape.
알겠어. 더 나은 몸매를 위해 식사를 점검해볼게.
③ Thank you for your tip. But I don't think I can do it.
조언 고마워. 하지만 내가 할 수 있을지 잘 모르겠어.
④ Of course. I'll make sure to follow your workout routine.
물론이지. 네 운동 루틴을 꼭 따를게.
⑤ Sure. That's why I didn't succeed at keeping a balanced diet.
맞아. 그래서 균형 잡힌 식단을 유지하는 데 성공하지 못했어.

왜 정답 ? ★★★ [정답률 65%]

남자는 건강해지려고 운동하지만 큰 차이를 못 느낀다고 하며 여자에게 좋은 몸 상태를 만드는 비결이 무엇인지 물어보았고, 여자는 언제 먹는지를 신경 쓰기 시작했다고 했다. 이것에 대해 의문을 품는 남자에게 해줄 여자의 응답으로 가장 적절한 것은 ① '믿어봐. 언제 먹는지가 큰 차이를 만들어.'이다.

206 자이스토리 전국연합학력평가 고1 영어

> **왜 오답 ?**

② 언제 먹는지를 신경 쓰라는 내용이지, 무엇을 먹는지를 신경 쓰라는 내용이 아니다.

③ 좋은 몸 상태를 만드는 비결을 물어본 사람은 남자이며, 여자가 조언을 주는 상황이다.

④ 좋은 몸 상태를 만드는 비결로서 운동 루틴은 언급되지 않았다.

⑤ 균형 잡힌 식단을 유지하는 데 실패했다는 내용이 아니다.

---

15 정답 ① * DIY 책상 조립을 위해 도움 요청하기

M : Julia is a college student, <mark>living in the dormitory.</mark>
〈현재분사 가 이끄는 분사구문〉

남 : Julia는 대학생이고, 기숙사에 살고 있다.

Recently, she ordered a new computer desk.

최근에, 그녀는 새로운 컴퓨터 책상을 주문했다.

「upon -ing」: ~하자마자   목적어절 접속사
<mark>Upon receiving</mark> the desk, she realized <mark>that</mark> the desk was a DIY product. **단서 1** 구매한 컴퓨터 책상이 DIY 제품임

책상을 받자마자, 그녀는 그것이 DIY 제품이라는 것을 깨달았다.
뒤에 목적어절 접속사 that이 생략됨
It <mark>means</mark> she needs to put the pieces together to build the desk.

그것은 그녀가 책상을 만들기 위해 부품들을 조립해야 한다는 것을 의미한다.

However, it was complicated to assemble it by herself.

하지만, 그녀 혼자서 조립하기에는 복잡했다. **단서 2** 혼자서 조립하기에는 복잡함

동명사(전치사 at의 목적어)   = assembling DIY furniture
Julia knows that Sophie, her best friend, is good at <mark>assembling DIY furniture</mark> and enjoys <mark>it</mark>.

Julia는 그녀의 가장 친한 친구인 Sophie가 DIY 가구 조립을 잘하고 즐긴다는 것을 알고 있다. **단서 3** Julia의 친구인 Sophie는 DIY 가구 조립을 잘하고 좋아함

So, Julia wants to ask Sophie to help her with the desk.

그래서 Julia는 Sophie에게 책상 조립을 도와달라고 요청하고 싶어 한다.
단서 4 Julia는 Sophie에게 책상 조립을 도와달라고 요청하고 싶어 함
In this situation, what would Julia most likely say to Sophie?

이 상황에서, Julia가 Sophie에게 할 말로 가장 적절한 것은 무엇인가?

Julia: **Could you help me assemble my desk?**

Julia: 내가 책상을 조립하는 것을 도와줄 수 있니?

*상황 요약: Julia가 DIY를 잘하는 Sophie에게 도움을 요청하고자 하는 상황

- college ⓝ 대학   - dormitory ⓝ 기숙사   - recently ⓐⓓ 최근에
- complicated ⓐ 복잡한   - assemble ⓥ 조립하다
- furniture ⓝ 가구   - decorate ⓥ 장식하다

다음 상황 설명을 듣고, Julia가 Sophie에게 할 말로 가장 적절한 것을 고르시오.

Julia: _____

① Could you help me assemble my desk?
내가 책상을 조립하는 것을 도와줄 수 있니? DIY 조립을 좋아하는 Sophie에게 도움을 요청함
② Can you share where you bought your desk?
네가 책상을 어디서 샀는지 알려줄 수 있니? Sophie가 책상을 샀다는 언급은 없음
③ How about choosing a new computer together?
새 컴퓨터를 함께 고르는 건 어때? 새 컴퓨터를 고른다는 언급은 없음
④ Why don't you repair the furniture by yourself?
왜 가구를 직접 수리하지 않니? 가구 수리에 관한 내용이 아님
⑤ Do you have any ideas for decorating my room?
내 방을 꾸미기 위한 아이디어가 있니? 방을 꾸민다는 언급은 없음

> **왜 정답 ?** **✲✲** [정답률 81%]

Julia가 산 새로운 컴퓨터 책상은 DIY 제품이고, 혼자서 조립하기에는 너무 복잡해서 DIY 조립을 잘하고 좋아하는 Sophie에게 도움을 요청하려는 상황이다. 따라서 Julia가 할 말로 가장 적절한 것은 ① '내가 책상을 조립하는 것을 도와줄 수 있니?'이다.

> **왜 오답 ?**

② Sophie가 책상을 샀다는 것은 언급되지 않았다.

③ 새 컴퓨터를 고르는 것은 언급되지 않았다.

④ DIY 가구 조립에 관한 내용이지, 가구 수리에 관한 내용이 아니다. **주의**

⑤ 방을 꾸민다는 것은 언급되지 않았다.

16~17 * 천연 소재 옷 세탁법

W : Hello, *Family-Life* subscribers! //

여 : 안녕하세요, *Family-Life* 구독자 여러분 //

사이에 주격 관계대명사와 be동사가 생략됨
These days, / many people are looking for <mark>clothes / made</mark> from natural materials / for their family. //

요즘 / 많은 사람들이 옷을 찾고 있습니다 / 천연 소재로 만든 / 가족을 위해 //

Today, I'd like to introduce some tips / for how to properly wash natural material clothes. // **16번** 단서: 천연 소재 옷을 올바르게 세탁하는 방법에 대한 팁을 소개할 것임

오늘은, 몇 가지 팁을 소개하고자 합니다 / 천연 소재 옷을 올바르게 세탁하는 방법에 대한 //

17번 ①
First, / for cotton, / like 100% cotton t-shirts, / you should
부사적 용법(목적)
hand-wash in cool water / <mark>to avoid</mark> shrinking or wrinkling. //

첫 번째로 / 면직물은 / 100% 면 티셔츠와 같은 / 찬물에 손세탁해야 합니다 / 수축이나 주름을 방지하기 위해 //

Second, / silk should be washed separately and quickly / <mark>to</mark>
부사적 용법(목적)
<mark>keep</mark> its shape and color. // **17번 ②**

둘째 / 실크는 별도로 빠르게 세탁되어야 합니다 / 모양과 색상을 유지하기 위해 //

Also, / when you dry silk clothes / such as blouses, / <mark>avoid</mark>
병렬 구조(명령문)
direct sunlight and <mark>dry</mark> them in the shade. //

또한 / 실크 옷을 건조할 때는 / 블라우스와 같은 / 직사광선을 피하고 그늘에서 말리세요 //

형용사적 용법(material 수식)
Third, / linen is a sensitive material <mark>to wash</mark>. // **17번 ④**

셋째 / 리넨은 세탁하기에 민감한 소재입니다 //

For example, / to wash linen jackets, / use vinegar / instead of fabric softener. //

예를 들어 / 리넨 재킷을 세탁할 때는 / 식초를 사용하세요 / 섬유 유연제 대신 //

명사적 용법(주격 보어)
Lastly, / for wool, / the best way is <mark>to wash</mark> / as little as possible. // **17번 ⑤**

마지막으로 / 모직물은 / 세탁하는 것이 가장 좋습니다 / 가능한 한 적게 //

부사절 접속사(조건)
<mark>If</mark> you have to wash wool sweaters, / use special wool washing soap. //

모직물 스웨터를 세탁해야 한다면 / 특별한 모직물 세탁비누를 사용하세요 //

Apply these tips / so you can keep and enjoy natural clothes / for a longer time! //

이 팁들을 적용하세요 / 천연 소재의 옷을 유지하고 즐기도록 / 오랫동안 //

- subscriber ⓝ 구독자   - natural material 천연 재료
- properly ⓐⓓ 적절히, 제대로   - hand-wash ⓥ 손빨래하다
- shrink ⓥ 줄어들다   - wrinkle ⓥ 주름이 생기다
- separately ⓐⓓ 별도로   - direct sunlight 직사광선
- sensitive ⓐ 민감한   - vinegar ⓝ 식초   - trend ⓝ 동향
- proper ⓐ 적절한

여 : 안녕하세요, *Family-Life* 구독자 여러분! 요즘 많은 사람들이 가족을 위해 천연 소재 옷을 찾고 있습니다. 오늘은 천연 소재 옷을 올바르게 세탁하는 방법에 대한 몇 가지 팁을 소개하고자 합니다. 첫 번째로, 100% 면 티셔츠와 같은 면직물은 수축이나 주름을 방지하기 위해 찬물에 손세탁해야 합니다. 둘째, 실크는 모양과 색상을 유지하기 위해 별도로 빠르게 세탁되어야 합니다. 또한, 블라우스와 같은 실크 옷을 건조할 때는 직사광선을 피하고 그늘에서 말리세요. 셋째, 리넨은 세탁하기에 민감한 소재입니다. 예를 들어, 리넨 재킷을 세탁할 때는 섬유 유연제 대신 식초를 사용하세요. 마지막으로, 모직물은 가능한 한 적게 세탁하는 것이 가장 좋습니다. 모직물 스웨터를 세탁해야 한다면, 특별한 모직물 세탁비누를 사용하세요. 오랫동안 천연 소재의 옷을 유지하고 즐기도록 이 팁들을 적용하세요!

2024. 9
8회

16 정답 ⑤

여자가 하는 말의 주제로 가장 적절한 것은?

① material trends in the fashion industry 소재의 동향에 관한 내용이 아님
패션 산업에서 소재의 동향
② benefits of making clothes from nature
자연으로부터 옷을 만드는 것의 이점 천연 소재의 이점에 관한 내용이 아님
③ tips to purchase natural material clothes
천연 소재의 옷을 구매하는 팁 천연 소재 옷을 구매하는 팁에 관한 언급은 없음
④ development of clothes washing methods
의류 세탁 방법의 발전 의류 세탁 방법의 발전에 관한 내용이 아님
⑤ proper ways to wash natural material clothes
천연 소재 의류를 세탁하는 적절한 방법
I'd like to introduce some tips for how to properly wash natural material clothes

왜 정답? ✹✹✶ [정답률 84%]

여자는 천연 소재의 옷을 세탁하는 방법에 대한 팁을 소개하고 있으며, 면직물, 실크, 리넨, 모직물 소재의 옷을 세탁하는 방법과 주의할 점을 알려주고 있다. 따라서 여자가 하는 말의 주제로 가장 적절한 것은 ⑤ '천연 소재 의류를 세탁하는 적절한 방법'이다.

왜 오답?

① 패션 산업 또는 소재의 동향에 관한 것은 언급되지 않았다.
② 가족들을 위해 천연 소재의 옷을 찾는다는 내용이 있지만, 이런 옷의 이점이 핵심 주제는 아니다.
③ 천연 소재 옷의 세탁에 관한 내용이지, 천연 소재 옷의 구매에 관한 내용이 아니다.
④ 의류 세탁 방법이 소개되긴 하지만, 세탁 방법의 발전에 관한 내용은 아니다.

17 정답 ③

언급된 소재가 아닌 것은?

① cotton 면직물 for cotton
② silk 실크 silk should be washed separately and quickly
③ leather 가죽 언급되지 않음
④ linen 리넨 linen is a sensitive material to wash
⑤ wool 모직물 for wool

왜 정답? ✹✶✶ [정답률 94%]

면직물, 실크, 리넨, 모직물에 대해서는 언급했지만 가죽에 대해서는 언급하지 않았으므로 정답은 ③ '가죽'이다.

왜 오답?

① 면직물 제품은 찬물에 손세탁하는 것이 좋다고 했다.
② 실크는 별도로 빠르게 세탁되어야 한다고 했다.
④ 리넨은 세탁하기에 민감한 소재라고 했다.
⑤ 모직물은 가능한 한 적게 세탁하는 것이 가장 좋다고 했다.

18 정답 ⑤ ＊기차역 유인 매표소 재운영 요구

To whom it may concern, /
관계자분께 /

I am writing / to express 부사적 용법(목적) my deep concern / about the recent
앞에 주격 관계대명사와 be동사가 생략됨
change / made by Pittsburgh Train Station. //
저는 글을 쓰고 있습니다 / 저의 깊은 우려를 표하기 위해 / 최근의 변경에 대해 / Pittsburgh Train Station에 의한 //

The station had traditional ticket offices with staff before, / but
현재완료 수동태
these have been replaced with ticket vending machines. //
이전에는 역에 직원이 있는 전통적인 매표소가 있었지만 / 이것들은 승차권 발매기로 대체되었습니다 //

However, / individuals who 복수 주어 주격 관계대명사 are unfamiliar with these machines /
복수 동사
are now experiencing difficulty / accessing the railway services. //
그러나 / 이러한 기계에 익숙하지 않은 사람들은 / 현재 어려움을 겪고 있습니다 / 철도 서비스에 접근하는 데 //

Since 부사절 접속사(이유) these individuals heavily relied on the staff assistance / to
be in need of: ~을 필요로 하다
be able to travel, / they are in great need of / ticket offices with
staff in the station. //
이 사람들은 직원의 도움에 크게 의존했기 때문에 / 이동할 수 있기 위해 / 그들은 매우 필요로 합니다 / 역 내에 직원이 있는 매표소를 //

Therefore, I am urging you urging의 목적어와 목적격 보어(to부정사) / to consider reopening the ticket
offices. 단서 매표소 재운영 고려를 촉구함
그러므로 저는 당신에게 촉구합니다 / 매표소 재운영을 고려할 것을 //
「with + 명사 + 형용사」, 주어 + would + 동사원형」: with 가정법
With the staff back in their positions, / many people would
regain access / to the railway services. //
직원이 그들의 자리로 돌아오면 / 많은 사람이 접근을 다시 얻을 것입니다 / 철도 서비스에 대한 //

I look forward to your prompt attention to this matter / and a
positive resolution. //
저는 이 문제에 대한 당신의 신속한 관심을 기대합니다 / 그리고 긍정적인 해결을 //

Sincerely, / Sarah Roberts /
진심을 담아 / Sarah Roberts /

- concern ⓝ 우려
- traditional ⓐ 전통적인
- vending machine 자동판매기
- assistance ⓝ 도움
- urge ⓥ 촉구하다
- regain ⓥ 되찾다
- prompt ⓐ 신속한
- resolution ⓝ 해결

관계자분께,
저는 Pittsburgh Train Station에 의한 최근의 변경에 대해 저의 깊은 우려를 표하기 위해 글을 쓰고 있습니다. 이전에는 역에 직원이 있는 전통적인 매표소가 있었지만, 이것들은 승차권 발매기로 대체되었습니다. 그러나 이러한 기계에 익숙하지 않은 사람들은 현재 철도 서비스에 접근하는 데 어려움을 겪고 있습니다. 이 사람들은 이동할 수 있기 위해 직원의 도움에 크게 의존했기 때문에, 그들은 역 내에 직원이 있는 매표소를 매우 필요로 합니다. 그러므로 저는 당신에게 매표소 재운영을 고려할 것을 촉구합니다. 직원이 그들의 자리로 돌아오면 많은 사람이 철도 서비스에 대한 접근을 다시 얻을 것입니다. 저는 이 문제에 대한 당신의 신속한 관심과 긍정적인 해결을 기대합니다.
진심을 담아, Sarah Roberts

다음 글의 목적으로 가장 적절한 것은?

① 승차권 발매기 수리를 의뢰하려고 수리에 대한 언급은 없음
② 기차표 단체 예매 방법을 문의하려고 단체 예매 방법에 관한 내용이 아님
③ 기차 출발 시간 지연에 대해 항의하려고 출발 시간 지연에 관한 언급은 없음
④ 기차역 직원의 친절한 도움에 감사하려고 직원의 도움에 감사하는 내용이 아님
⑤ 기차역 유인 매표소 재운영을 요구하려고
기차역 유인 매표소 재운영을 고려할 것을 촉구함

왜 정답? ✹✶✶ [정답률 92%]

기계에 익숙하지 않은 사람들이 승차권 발매기 사용을 어려워하고 있다며 유인 매표소 재운영을 요구하고 있으므로 글의 목적은 ⑤이다.

왜 오답?

① 매표소가 승차권 발매기로 대체되었다고는 했지만, 수리는 언급되지 않았다.
② 기차표 단체 예매에 관한 내용이 아니다.
③ 기차 출발 시간이 지연되었다는 것은 언급되지 않았다.
④ 기차역 직원의 친절한 도움은 언급되지 않았다.

19 정답 ⑤ ＊무대에서 쓰러진 Arthur의 소생

All the actors on the stage / were focused on their acting. //
무대 위의 모든 배우가 / 그들의 연기에 집중하고 있었다 //

Then, suddenly, / Arthur fell into the corner of the stage. //
그 때 갑자기 / Arthur가 무대의 한쪽 구석에 쓰러졌다 //

Jeevan immediately approached Arthur / and found 뒤에 목적어절 접속사 that이 생략됨 his heart
wasn't beating. //
Jeevan이 즉각 Arthur에게 다가갔고 / 그의 심장이 뛰지 않는 것을 알아차렸다 //

Jeevan began CPR. //
Jeevan은 CPR을 시작했다 //

Jeevan worked silently, / glancing sometimes at Arthur's face. 분사구문 //
Jeevan은 조용히 작업했다 / 때때로 Arthur의 얼굴을 흘긋 보며 //

He thought, / "Please, start breathing again, please." //
그는 생각했다 / '제발, 다시 숨쉬기를 시작해요, 제발'이라고 **단서 1** Arthur가 다시 숨쉬기를 간절히 바람

Arthur's eyes were closed. //
Arthur의 눈은 감겨 있었다 //

Moments later, / an older man in a grey suit appeared, / swiftly
kneeling beside Arthur's chest. // 분사구문
잠시 뒤 / 회색 정장 차림의 한 노인이 나타났고 / Arthur의 가슴 옆에 재빠르게 무릎을 꿇었다 //

"I'm Walter Jacobi. // I'm a doctor." //
"저는 Walter Jacobi입니다 // 저는 의사입니다" //

He announced with a calm voice. //
그는 차분한 목소리로 전했다 //

Jeevan wiped the sweat off his forehead. //
Jeevan은 그의 이마에서 땀을 닦아냈다 //

With combined efforts, / Jeevan and Dr. Jacobi successfully revived Arthur. //
협력하여 / Jeevan과 Dr. Jacobi는 Arthur를 성공적으로 소생시켰다 //

Arthur's eyes slowly opened. //
Arthur의 눈이 천천히 떠졌다 // **단서 2** Arthur가 깨어나서 안도함

Finally, / Jeevan was able to hear Arthur's breath again, /
thinking to himself, / "Thank goodness. // You're back." // 분사구문
마침내 / Jeevan은 Arthur의 숨을 다시 들을 수 있었고 / 자신에게 되뇌었다 / '다행이다 // 깨어났구나'라고 //

- immediately ad 즉시   · glance ⓥ 흘긋 보다
- swiftly ad 신속하게   · kneel ⓥ 무릎을 꿇다
- combined ⓐ 합쳐진   · effort ⓝ 노력   · revive ⓥ 소생시키다
- thrilled ⓐ 흥분한   · desperate ⓐ 간절한

무대 위의 모든 배우가 그들의 연기에 집중하고 있었다. 그 때 갑자기 Arthur가 무대의 한쪽 구석에 쓰러졌다. Jeevan이 즉각 Arthur에게 다가갔고 그의 심장이 뛰지 않는 것을 알아차렸다. Jeevan은 CPR을 시작했다. Jeevan은 때때로 Arthur의 얼굴을 흘긋 보며 조용히 작업했다. 그는 '제발, 다시 숨쉬기를 시작해요, 제발.'이라고 생각했다. Arthur의 눈은 감겨 있었다. 잠시 뒤, 회색 정장 차림의 한 노인이 나타났고, Arthur의 가슴 옆에 재빠르게 무릎을 꿇었다. "저는 Walter Jacobi입니다. 저는 의사입니다." 그는 차분한 목소리로 전했다. Jeevan은 그의 이마에서 땀을 닦아냈다. 협력하여, Jeevan과 Dr. Jacobi는 Arthur를 성공적으로 소생시켰다. Arthur의 눈이 천천히 떠졌다. 마침내 Jeevan은 Arthur의 숨을 다시 들을 수 있었고, '다행이다. 깨어났구나.'라고 자신에게 되뇌었다.

다음 글에 드러난 Jeevan의 심경 변화로 가장 적절한 것은?

① thrilled → bored 지루할 만한 상황이 아님
흥분한 → 지루한
② ashamed → confident 수치를 느낄 일이 아님
수치스러운 → 자신만만한
③ hopeful → helpless 결국 Arthur는 소생되었기에 무력함을 느끼지 않음
희망에 찬 → 무력한
④ surprised → indifferent 후반에 무관심함을 느끼지 않음
놀란 → 무관심한
⑤ **desperate → relieved** Please, start breathing → Thank goodness
간절한 → 안도한

왜 정답? ❋❋❋ [정답률 87%]

전반부: 심장이 뛰지 않는 Arthur에게 CPR을 하면서 다시 숨쉬기를 바람 ▶ '간절한'
후반부: 의사의 도움으로 Arthur가 다시 소생되었음 ▶ '안도한'

따라서 Jeevan의 심경 변화로 가장 적절한 것은 ⑤ '간절한 → 안도한'이다.

왜 오답?
① 다시 숨을 쉬기 시작한 Arthur를 보며 느낀 감정은 지루함이 아니다.
② 쓰러진 Arthur에게 심폐 소생술을 하며 느낀 감정은 수치가 아니다.
③ 결국 의사의 도움으로 Arthur는 소생되었기에 무력감을 느끼지 않았다.
④ 마지막에 의사의 도움으로 Arthur는 의식을 되찾았고, 다행이라 생각했기에 무관심을 느낀 것이 아니다.

---

20 정답 ② ＊지나친 영재 자랑을 자제할 필요성

As the parent of a gifted child, / you need to be aware of a certain common parent trap. //
영재의 부모로서 / 당신은 어떤 흔한 부모의 덫을 주의할 필요가 있다 //

Of course / you are a proud parent / and you should **be**. //
뒤에 반복되는 a proud parent가 생략됨
물론 / 당신은 자랑스러워하는 부모이고 / 그리고 그래야 한다 //

While **it** is very easy **to talk** nonstop / about your little genius and his or her remarkable behavior, / this can be very stressful on your child. //
가주어   진주어
쉬지 않고 말하는 것은 매우 쉬우나 / 당신의 작은 천재와 그 또는 그녀의 놀라운 행동에 대해서 / 이것은 당신의 아이에게 매우 스트레스가 될 수 있다 //

It is extremely important / **to limit** your bragging behavior / to your very close friends, / or your parents. //
가주어   진주어   **단서** 영재인 자녀를 주변에 자랑하는 것을 제한해야 함
매우 중요하다 / 당신의 자랑하는 행동을 제한하는 것이 / 당신의 아주 가까운 친구나 / 당신의 부모에게로 //

Gifted children feel pressured / when their parents **show** them **off** too much. //
'~을 자랑하다'
영재는 부담을 느낀다 / 그들의 부모가 지나치게 그들을 자랑할 때 //

This behavior creates expectations / **that** they may not be able to **live up to**, / and also creates a false sense of self for your child. //
목적격 관계대명사
'~에 부응하다'
이러한 행동은 기대를 만들고 / 그들이 부응할 수 없을지도 모르는 / 또한 당신의 자녀에게 있어 잘못된 자의식을 만든다 //

You want your child to be **who they are**, / not **who they seem to be** / as defined by their incredible achievements. //
보어 역할을 하는 간접의문문
당신은 당신의 자녀가 있는 그대로의 그들이기를 바란다 / 보이는 누군가가 아니라 / 그들의 엄청난 업적에 의해서 규정지어진 대로 //

If not, / you could end up with / a driven perfectionist child / or perhaps a drop-out, / or worse. //
그렇지 않으면 / 당신은 결국 마주하게 될 것이다 / 지나친 완벽주의자 아이 / 또는 아마도 학업 중단자이거나 / 그보다 더 안 좋은 것을 //

- be aware of ~을 알다[주의하다]   · nonstop ad 연속적으로
- remarkable ⓐ 놀라운   · bragging ⓐ 자랑하는
- expectation ⓝ 기대   · incredible ⓐ 엄청난
- achievement ⓝ 업적   · end up with 결국 ~로 끝나다
- driven ⓐ 지나친   · perfectionist ⓝ 완벽주의자
- drop-out ⓝ 학업 중단자, 중퇴자

영재의 부모로서, 당신은 어떤 흔한 부모의 덫을 주의할 필요가 있다. 물론, 당신은 자랑스러워하는 부모이고, 그리고 그래야 한다. 당신의 작은 천재와 그 또는 그녀의 놀라운 행동에 대해서 쉬지 않고 말하는 것은 매우 쉬우나, 이것은 당신의 아이에게 매우 스트레스가 될 수 있다. 당신의 자랑하는 행동을 당신의 아주 가까운 친구나, 당신의 부모에게로 제한하는 것이 매우 중요하다. 영재는 그들의 부모가 지나치게 그들을 자랑할 때 부담을 느낀다. 이러한 행동은 그들이 부응할 수 없을지도 모르는 기대를 만들고, 또한 당신의 자녀에게 있어 잘못된 자의식을 만든다. 당신은 당신의 자녀가 그들의 엄청난 업적에 의해서 규정지어진 대로 보이는 누군가가 아니라 있는 그대로의 그들이기를 바란다. 그렇지 않으면, 당신은 결국 지나친 완벽주의자 아이 또는 아마도 학업 중단자이거나 그보다 더 안 좋은 것을 마주하게 될 것이다.

다음 글에서 필자가 주장하는 바로 가장 적절한 것은?

① 부모는 자녀를 다른 아이와 비교하지 말아야 한다.
자녀를 다른 아이와 비교하지 말라는 내용이 아님
② 부모는 자녀의 영재성을 지나치게 자랑하지 말아야 한다.
영재인 자녀를 둔 부모들은 주변에 지나치게 자랑하는 것을 제한해야 함
③ 영재교육 프로그램에 대한 맹목적인 믿음을 삼가야 한다.
영재교육 프로그램에 대한 언급은 없음
④ 과도한 영재교육보다 자녀와의 좋은 관계 유지에 힘써야 한다.
자녀와 좋은 관계를 유지하는 것에 관한 언급은 없음
⑤ 자녀의 독립성을 기르기 위해 자기 일은 스스로 하게 해야 한다.
자녀의 독립성을 기르는 것에 관한 언급은 없음

영재인 자녀를 부모가 지나치게 자랑하면 그것은 그들에게 부담이 될 수 있고, 잘못된 자의식을 만들 수 있다며 이를 제한해야 한다고 주장하고 있다. 따라서 정답은 ②이다.

왜 오답 ?

① 영재인 자녀를 지나치게 자랑하면 안 된다는 내용이지, 다른 아이들과 비교하면 안 된다는 내용이 아니다.

③ 영재교육 프로그램은 언급되지 않았다.

④ 과도한 영재교육이나 자녀와의 좋은 관계 유지는 언급되지 않았다.

⑤ 자녀의 독립성을 기르는 것은 언급되지 않았다.

---

21 정답 ⑤ ✱부정에서 벗어나기 위해 긍정과 어울리기

단수 주어
One valuable technique / for getting out of / helplessness,
주격 관계대명사
depression, / and situations which are predominantly being run
/ by the thought, "I can't," /
한 가지 유용한 기술은 / ~에서 벗어나기 위한 / 무력함, 우울감 / 그리고 현저히 지배하는
상황 / '나는 할 수 없다'는 생각에 의해 /
단서 1 우리가 처한 문제를 해결한 사람들과 함께 있으면 부정적 감정과 상황에서 벗어날 수 있음
단수 동사
is to choose to be with other persons / who have resolved the
「전치사 + 관계대명사」   주격 관계대명사
problem / with which we struggle. //
타인과 함께 있기로 선택하는 것이다 / 문제를 해결해 본 / 우리가 분투하고 있는 //

This is one of the great powers of self-help groups. //
이것은 자조 집단의 큰 힘 중 하나이다 //
부사절 접속사(시간)   **현재완료(계속)**
When we are in a negative state, / we have given a lot of energy
/ to negative thought forms, / and the positive thought forms
are weak. //
우리가 부정적인 상태에 있을 때 / 우리는 많은 에너지를 투입해 왔고 / 부정적인 사고 형태에
/ 긍정적인 사고 형태는 약하다 //
'긍정적인 기운을 내는'
Those who are in a higher vibration / are free of the energy from
their negative thoughts / and have energized positive thought
forms. //
더 높은 진동에 있는(긍정적인 기운을 내는) 사람들은 / 그들의 부정적인 사고에서 나오는
에너지가 없고 / 긍정적인 사고 형태를 활기 띠게 했다 //
명사적 용법(주어)   = those who are in a higher vibration
Merely / to be in their presence / is beneficial. //
단지 / 그들이 있는 자리에 있기만 하는 것도 / 유익하다 //
단서 2 더 높은 진동에 있는 사람들과 함께 있기만 해도 도움이 됨
In some self-help groups, / this is called "hanging out with the
winners." //
일부 자조 집단에서 / 이것은 '승자들과 어울리기'라고 불린다 //

The benefit here / is on the psychic level of consciousness, / and
병렬 구조
there is a transfer of positive energy / and relighting of one's
own latent positive thought forms. //
여기에서의 이점은 / 의식의 정신적 수준에 있으며 / 긍정적인 에너지의 전달과 / 자신의
잠재적인 긍정적인 사고 형태의 재점화가 있다 //

- technique ⓝ 기술 • helplessness ⓝ 무력감
- depression ⓝ 우울감 • predominantly ⓐⓓ 현저히
- resolve ⓥ 해결하다 • self-help ⓝ 자조, 자립
- energize ⓥ 활기를 북돋우다
- be in one's presence ~의 자리에 (함께) 있다 • psychic ⓐ 정신의
- transfer ⓝ 이동 • relight ⓥ 재점화하다

무력함, 우울감, 그리고 '나는 할 수 없다'는 생각에 의해 현저히 지배당하는 상황에서 벗어나기 위한 한 가지 유용한 기술은 우리가 분투하고 있는 문제를 해결해 본 타인과 함께 있기로 선택하는 것이다. 이것은 자조 집단의 큰 힘 중 하나이다. 우리가 부정적인 상태에 있을 때, 우리는 부정적인 사고 형태에 많은 에너지를 투입해 왔고 긍정적인 사고 형태는 약하다. 더 높은 진동에 있는 사람들은 그들의 부정적인 사고에서 나오는 에너지가 없고, 긍정적인 사고 형태를 활기 띠게 했다. 단지 그들이 있는 자리에 있기만 하는 것도 유익하다. 일부 자조 집단에서 이것은 '승자들과 어울리기'라고 불린다. 여기에서의 이점은 의식의 정신적 수준에 있으며, 긍정적인 에너지의 전달과 자신의 잠재적인 긍정적인 사고 형태의 재점화가 있다.

밑줄 친 "hanging out with the winners"가 다음 글에서 의미하는 바로 가장 적절한 것은?

① staying with those who sacrifice themselves for others
타인을 위해 자신을 희생하는 사람들과 함께하기   타인을 위해 희생한다는 언급은 없음

② learning from people who have succeeded in competition
경쟁에서 성공한 사람들로부터 배우기   경쟁에서 성공한 사람들에 관한 내용이 아님

③ keeping relationships with people in a higher social
position
높은 사회적 지위에 있는 사람들과 관계를 유지하기   높은 사회적 지위에 있는 사람들과 관계를 유지하라는 내용이 아님

④ spending time with those who need social skill
development   사회적 기술 발달이 필요한 사람들에 대한 언급이 없음
사회적 기술 발달이 필요한 사람들과 시간 보내기

⑤being with positive people who have overcome negative
states   One valuable technique ~ with which we struggle.
부정적인 상태를 극복한 긍정적인 사람들과 함께하기

• 우리가 분투하고 있는 문제를 해결해 본 타인과 함께 있기로 선택하는 것은
부정적인 감정과 상황에서 벗어나는 유용한 방법임 **단서 1**

• 더 높은 진동에 있는 사람들과 함께하기만 해도 유익함 **단서 2**

➡ 부정적 감정과 상황에서 벗어나기 위해 우리가 처한 부정적 상황을 이미 해결한
사람과 함께 있는 것은 유용하고 유익한 방법이다.

▶ '승자'는 '어려움을 이미 극복한 긍정적인 사람'을 의미하고, '어울리는 것'은
그러한 사람들과 '함께 하는 것'을 의미하므로 '승자들과 함께하는 것'은
⑤ '부정적인 상태를 극복한 긍정적인 사람들과 함께하기'를 의미한다.

왜 오답 ?

① 타인을 위해 자신을 희생하는 사람들은 언급되지 않았다.

② 부정적 상황을 해결한 사람과 어울려야 한다는 것이지, 경쟁에서 이긴
사람들로부터 배우라는 내용이 아니다.

③ 높은 사회적 지위에 있는 사람들과 관계를 유지하는 것은 언급되지 않았다.

④ 사회적 기술 발달이 필요한 사람들은 언급되지 않았다.

a higher vibration은 높은 사회적 지위가 아니라 더
높은 진동에 있는(긍정적인 기운을 내는) 것을 의미함 꿀팁

---

22 정답 ③ ✱생존에 도움이 되는 감정

수동태 동사   **단서 1** 감정은 생존에 기여했기 때문에 존재한다고 여겨짐
Our emotions are thought to exist / because they have
contributed to our survival / as a species. //
우리의 감정은 존재한다고 여겨진다 / 그것들이 우리의 생존에 기여해 왔기 때문에 / 종으로서 //
첫 번째 절의 주어(명사)   두 번째 절의 주어(동명사구)
Fear has helped us avoid dangers, / expressing anger helps us
세 번째 절의 주어(동명사구)
scare off threats, / and expressing positive emotions helps us
bond with others. //
두려움은 우리가 위험을 피하는 데 도움을 주어 왔고 / 분노를 표현하는 것은 우리가 위협을
쫓아내도록 돕고 / 긍정적인 감정을 표현하는 것은 우리가 다른 사람과 유대하도록 돕는다 //
단수 주어
From an evolutionary perspective, / an emotion is a kind of
주격 관계대명사 삽입구 단수 동사
"program" / that, when triggered, / directs many of our activities /
진화적 관점에서 / 감정은 일종의 '프로그램'이다 / 유발될 때 / 우리의 많은 활동을 지시하는 /
(including attention, perception, memory, movement,
expressions, etc.) //
(주의, 지각, 기억, 움직임, 표현 등을 포함하는) //
For example, / fear makes us very attentive, / narrows our
perceptual focus to threatening stimuli, / will cause us either to
병렬 구조
face a situation (fight) or avoid it (flight), /
「either A or B」 A 또는 B (중 하나)
예를 들어 / 두려움은 우리를 매우 주의 깊게 만들고 / 우리의 지각의 초점을 위협적인
자극으로 좁히고 / 우리로 하여금 상황을 정면으로 대하거나 (싸우거나) 그것을 피하도록
(도피하도록) 하며 /
and may cause us / to remember an experience more acutely /
(so that we avoid the threat in the future). //
우리로 하여금 ~하도록 할 수도 있다 / 경험을 더 강렬하게 기억(하도록) / (그래서 우리가
미래에 위협을 피하도록) //

Regardless of the specific ways **in which** they activate our
「전치사 + 관계대명사」
systems, / the specific emotions **we possess** / are thought to exist /
앞에 목적격 관계대명사가 생략됨
그것들이 우리의 시스템을 활성화하는 구체적인 방식과는 관계없이 / 우리가 소유한 특정한
감정은 / 존재한다고 여겨진다 /

because they have helped us / (as a species) survive challenges /
within our environment long ago. // 단서2 감정은 힘든 상황에 생존하도록
도움을 줬기 때문에 존재한다고 여겨짐
그것들이 우리에게 도움을 주어 왔기 때문에 / (종으로서) 힘든 상황에서 생존하도록 /
오래전에 우리의 환경 내에서 /
If they **had not helped** us adapt and survive, / they **would not**
가정법 과거완료
have evolved with us. //
만약 그것들이 우리가 적응하고 생존하도록 도움을 주지 않았었더라면 / 그것들은 우리와
함께 진화해 오지 않았을 것이다 //

- contribute ⓥ 기여하다 · species ⓝ 종
- bond ⓥ 유대감을 형성하다 · evolutionary ⓐ 진화론적인
- direct ⓥ 지시하다 · attentive ⓐ 주의를 기울이는
- narrow ⓥ 좁히다 · stimuli ⓝ 자극 · acutely ⓐⓓ 강렬하게

우리의 감정은 그것들이 종으로서 우리의 생존에 기여해 왔기 때문에 존재한다고 여겨진다. 두려움은 우리가 위험을 피하는 데 도움을 주어 왔고, 분노를 표현하는 것은 우리가 위험을 쫓아내도록 돕고, 긍정적인 감정을 표현하는 것은 우리가 다른 사람과 유대하도록 돕는다. 진화적 관점에서, 감정은 유발될 때 (주의, 지각, 기억, 움직임, 표현 등을 포함하는) 우리의 많은 활동을 지시하는 일종의 '프로그램'이다. 예를 들어, 두려움은 우리를 매우 주의 깊게 만들고, 우리의 지각의 초점을 위협적인 자극으로 좁히고, 우리로 하여금 상황을 정면으로 대하거나 (싸우거나) 그것을 피하도록 (도피하도록) 하며, 우리로 하여금 경험을 더 강렬하게 기억하도록 (그래서 우리가 미래에 위협을 피하도록) 할 수도 있다. 그것들이 우리의 시스템을 활성화하는 구체적인 방식과는 관계없이, 우리가 소유한 특정한 감정은 그것들이 오래전에 우리의 환경 내에서 우리가 (종으로서) 힘든 상황에서 생존하도록 도움을 주어 왔기 때문에 존재한다고 여겨진다. 만약 그것들이 우리가 적응하고 생존하도록 도움을 주지 않았었더라면 그것들은 우리와 함께 진화해 오지 않았을 것이다.

다음 글의 요지로 가장 적절한 것은?
① 과거의 경험이 현재의 감정에 영향을 미친다.
　　과거의 경험이 현재의 감정에 영향을 미친다는 내용이 아님
② 문명의 발달에 따라 인간의 감정은 다양화되어 왔다.
　　　　감정이 다양하여 관한 내용이 아님
③ 감정은 인간이 생존하도록 도와왔기 때문에 존재한다.
　　감정은 생존에 도움을 줬기 때문에 존재한다고 여겨짐
④ 부정적인 감정은 긍정적인 감정보다 더 오래 기억된다.
　　어떤 감정이 더 오래 기억되는지에 관한 내용이 아님
⑤ 두려움의 원인을 파악함으로써 두려움을 없앨 수 있다.
　　　　두려움을 없애는 것에 관한 내용이 아님

왜 정답? ✸✸✸ [정답률 91%]
주장: 감정은 생존에 기여했기 때문에 존재한다고 여겨짐 단서1 단서2
예시: 두려움은 우리를 주의 깊게 만들고, 지각의 초점을 좁혀 위협적인 자극에 집중하고, 상황에 맞서거나 피하도록 하고, 경험을 더 강렬하게 기억하도록 할 수 있음
▶ 감정은 인간의 생존에 도움을 주었기에 지금까지 존재한다는 내용이므로 정답은 ③이다.

왜 오답?
① 먼 과거의 힘든 상황에서 감정이 생존에 도움을 줬기에 현재까지도 존재한다는 것이지, 과거의 경험이 현재의 감정에 영향을 미친다는 내용이 아니다.
② 인간의 생존에 도움을 준 감정인 두려움, 분노, 긍정적인 감정이 언급되었을 뿐, 감정의 다양화에 관한 내용이 아니다.
④ 어떤 감정이 더 오래 기억되는지에 관한 내용이 아니다.
⑤ 두려움은 생존에 도움을 준 감정의 예시로 제시되었을 뿐, 두려움을 없애는 것에 관한 내용이 아니다.

23 정답 ④ *불리한 조건의 노동자들을 돕는 AI

단서 AI는 노동 시장에서 불리한 노동자의 일터에서의 접근성을 향상시킴
By improving accessibility of the workplace / for workers / that
are typically at a disadvantage in the labour market, / AI can
improve inclusiveness in the workplace. //
일터로의 접근성을 향상시킴으로써 / 노동자를 위한 / 노동 시장에서 일반적으로 불리한
위치에 있는 / AI는 일터에서 포괄성을 향상시킬 수 있다 //
복수 주어
AI-powered assistive **devices** / to aid workers with visual,
speech or hearing difficulties /
AI 동력의 보조 장치들이 / 시각, 발화 또는 청각 장애가 있는 노동자들을 돕기 위한 /
복수 동사　　　　　　　　　　　분사구문을 이끄는 현재분사
are becoming more widespread, / **improving the access to**, and
병렬 구조(work를 전치사의 목적어로 받음)
the quality of work / for people with disabilities. //
더 널리 보급되어 / 업무 접근성과 업무의 질을 향상시키고 있다 / 장애를 지닌 사람들의 //

For example, / speech recognition solutions / for people with
dysarthric voices, / or live captioning systems / for deaf and
hard of hearing people /
예를 들어 / 발화 인식 솔루션이나 / 구음 장애가 있는 사람들을 위한 / 실시간 자막 시스템은 /
청각 장애인과 난청인을 위한 /
관계부사
can facilitate communication with colleagues and access to jobs
/ **where** inter-personal communication is necessary. //
동료와의 의사소통과 일에 대한 접근을 용이하게 할 수 있다 / 대인 의사소통이 필요한 //

AI can also enhance the capabilities of low-skilled workers,
/ with potentially positive effects / on their wages and career
prospects. //
AI는 또한 저숙련 노동자들의 능력을 향상시킬 수 있다 / 잠재적으로 긍정적인 영향과 함께 /
그들의 임금과 경력 전망에 //
형용사적 용법(capacity 수식)
For example, / AI's capacity **to translate** written and spoken
word in real-time / can improve the performance of non-native
speakers / in the workplace. //
예를 들어 / 문자 언어와 음성 언어를 실시간으로 번역하는 AI의 능력은 / 비원어민의 수행을
향상시킬 수 있다 / 일터에서 //

Moreover, / recent developments in AI-powered text generators
/ can instantly improve the performance of lower-skilled
individuals /
게다가 / 최근의 AI 동력의 텍스트 생성기의 발전은 / 저숙련된 개인의 수행을 즉시 향상시킬
수 있다 /
'~와 같은'
in domains **such as** writing, coding or customer service. //
글쓰기, 코딩, 고객 서비스와 같은 영역에서 //

- accessibility ⓝ 접근성 · disadvantage ⓝ 불리함
- labour ⓝ 노동 · inclusiveness ⓝ 포괄성
- assistive ⓐ 도움이 되는 · recognition ⓝ 인지
- caption ⓝ 자막 · facilitate ⓥ 촉진하다 · capability ⓝ 능력
- potentially ⓐⓓ 잠재적으로 · wage ⓝ 임금 · prospect ⓝ 전망
- domain ⓝ 영역 · ethical ⓐ 윤리적인 · necessity ⓝ 필요성
- support ⓥ 지원하다 · disadvantage ⓝ 불리한 점, 약점
- cure ⓥ 치료하다

노동 시장에서 일반적으로 불리한 위치에 있는 노동자를 위한 일터로의 접근성을 향상시킴으로써, AI는 일터에서 포괄성을 향상시킬 수 있다. 시각, 발화 또는 청각 장애가 있는 노동자들을 돕기 위한 AI 동력의 보조 장치들이 더 널리 보급되어, 장애를 지닌 사람들의 업무 접근성과 업무의 질을 향상시키고 있다. 예를 들어, 구음 장애가 있는 사람들을 위한 발화 인식 솔루션이나 청각 장애인과 난청인을 위한 실시간 자막 시스템은 동료와의 의사소통과 대인 의사소통이 필요한 일에 대한 접근을 용이하게 할 수 있다. AI는 또한 그들의 임금과 경력 전망에 잠재적으로 긍정적인 영향과 함께 저숙련 노동자들의 능력을 향상시킬 수 있다. 예를 들어, 문자 언어와 음성 언어를 실시간으로 번역하는 AI의 능력은 일터에서 비원어민의 수행을 향상시킬 수 있다. 게다가, 최근의 AI 동력의 텍스트 생성기의 발전은 글쓰기, 코딩, 고객 서비스와 같은 영역에서 저숙련된 개인의 수행을 즉시 향상시킬 수 있다.

다음 글의 주제로 가장 적절한 것은?
AI가 불리한 조건을 가진 노동자에게 도움을 줄 수 있다는 내용임

① jobs replaced by AI in the labour market
노동 시장에서 AI에 의해 대체된 직업들　　AI가 직업을 대체한다는 언급은 없음
② ethical issues caused by using AI in the workplace
직장에서 AI를 사용하는 것으로 인한 윤리적 문제　　AI의 윤리적 문제에 관한 내용이 아님
③ necessity of using AI technology for language learning
언어 학습을 위한 AI 기술 사용의 필요성　　언어 학습에 대한 언급은 없음
④ impacts of AI on supporting workers with disadvantages
불리한 조건을 가진 근로자를 지원하는 AI의 영향
⑤ new designs of AI technology to cure people with disabilities　장애를 치료하는 AI 기술에 대한 언급은 없음
장애를 가진 사람을 치료하기 위한 AI 기술의 새로운 설계

왜 정답? ✶✶✶ [정답률 74%]

- AI는 노동 시장에서 불리한 위치에 있는 노동자들의 접근성을 향상시킴으로써, 일터에서 포괄성을 향상시킬 수 있음 [단서]
- 예시 1: 발화 인식 솔루션과 실시간 자막 시스템 → 구음 장애 및 청각 장애가 있는 사람들도 의사소통이 필요한 일에 접근할 수 있게 함
- 예시 2: 실시간 번역 AI → 비원어민의 수행을 향상시킴
- 예시 3: AI 텍스트 생성기의 발전 → 저숙련된 개인의 수행을 향상시킴

➡ 노동 시장에서 불리한 조건을 가진 근로자를 위해 AI가 할 수 있는 역할을 설명하고 있다.

▶ 따라서 글의 주제는 ④ '불리한 조건을 가진 근로자를 지원하는 AI의 영향'이다.

왜 오답?

① AI가 노동 시장에서 근로자에게 도움을 줄 수 있다고 했을 뿐, 노동 시장에서 AI가 직업을 대체한다는 것은 언급되지 않았다.
② 직장에서 AI를 사용하는 것으로 인한 윤리적 문제에 관한 내용이 아니다.
③ AI를 사용한 언어 학습은 언급되지 않았다.
⑤ 장애를 치료한다는 것은 언급되지 않았다. (🎀 이유: AI가 불리한 조건을 가진 사람들의 업무 수행을 도울 수 있다는 것만 언급되었을 뿐이다.)

24 정답 ① ＊기후 변화 해결책이 될 수 있는 고래

Whales are highly efficient / at carbon storage. //
고래는 매우 효율적이다 / 탄소 저장에 //　　[단서 1] 고래는 탄소 저장에 효율적임

When they die, / each whale sequesters an average of 30 tons of carbon dioxide, / taking that carbon out of the atmosphere for centuries. //
분사구문을 이끄는 현재분사
그들이 죽을 때 / 각각의 고래는 평균 30톤의 이산화 탄소를 격리하며 / 수 세기 동안 대기로부터 그 탄소를 빼내어 둔다 //

For comparison, / the average tree absorbs / only 48 pounds of CO₂ a year. //
비교하자면 / 평균적인 나무는 흡수한다 / 연간 48파운드의 이산화 탄소만을 //

From a climate perspective, / each whale is / the marine equivalent of thousands of trees. //
기후의 관점에서 / 각각의 고래는 ~이다 / 수천 그루의 나무에 상응하는 바다에 사는 것 //

Whales also help sequester carbon / by fertilizing the ocean / as they release nutrient-rich waste, / in turn increasing phytoplankton populations, /
고래는 또한 탄소를 격리하는 데 도움을 주는데 / 바다를 비옥하게 함으로써 / 영양이 풍부한 배설물을 내보내면서 / 결과적으로 식물성 플랑크톤 개체를 증가시키고 /
계속적 용법의 주격 관계대명사　　분사구문을 이끄는 현재분사
which also sequester carbon / — leading some scientists to call them / the "engineers of marine ecosystems." //
이는 또한 탄소를 격리한다 / 그리하여 몇몇 과학자들은 그들을 부르게 되었다 / '해양 생태계의 기술자'라고 //

In 2019, economists from the International Monetary Fund (IMF) / estimated the value of the ecosystem services / provided
앞에 주격 관계대명사와 be동사가 생략됨
by each whale / at over $2 million USD. //
2019년 국제 통화 기금(IMF)의 경제학자들은 / 생태계 서비스의 가치를 추정했다 / 각각의 고래에 의해서 제공되는 / 미화 200만 달러가 넘게 //

---

call for: ~을 요구하다
They called for / a new global program of economic incentives / to return whale populations to preindustrial whaling levels / as
[단서 2] 고래는 기후 변화에 대한 자연 기반 해결책임
one example of a "nature-based solution" / to climate change. //
그들은 요구했다 / 새로운 글로벌 경제적 인센티브 프로그램을 / 고래 개체수를 산업화 이전의 고래잡이 수준으로 되돌리기 위한 / '자연 기반 해결책'의 한 예로서 / 기후 변화에 대한 //
수동태의 현재진행형
Calls are now being made / for a global whale restoration program, / to slow down climate change. //
요구가 현재 제기되고 있다 / 세계적인 고래 복원 프로그램에 대한 / 기후 변화를 늦추기 위해 //
[단서 3] 기후 변화를 늦추기 위해 세계적인 고래 복원 프로그램에 대한 요구가 제기됨

- storage ⓝ 저장　　• atmosphere ⓝ 대기　　• comparison ⓝ 비교
- absorb ⓥ 흡수하다　　• marine ⓐ 해양의
- equivalent ⓝ (~에) 상응하는 것　　• fertilize ⓥ 비옥하게 하다
- release ⓥ 내보내다　　• estimate ⓥ 추정하다
- incentive ⓝ 장려책　　• preindustrial ⓐ 산업화 이전의
- restoration ⓝ 복원　　• extinct ⓐ 멸종된
- overpopulation ⓝ 과밀(과잉 밀집)　　• industry ⓝ 산업
- habitat ⓝ 서식지

고래는 탄소 저장에 매우 효율적이다. 그들이 죽을 때, 각각의 고래는 평균 30톤의 이산화 탄소를 격리하며, 수 세기 동안 대기로부터 그 탄소를 빼내어 둔다. 비교하자면, 평균적인 나무는 연간 48파운드의 이산화 탄소만을 흡수한다. 기후의 관점에서 각각의 고래는 수천 그루의 나무에 상응하는 바다에 사는 것이다. 고래는 또한 영양이 풍부한 배설물을 내보내면서 바다를 비옥하게 함으로써 탄소를 격리하는 데 도움을 주는데, 결과적으로 식물성 플랑크톤 개체를 증가시키고 이는 또한 탄소를 격리한다. 그리하여 몇몇 과학자들은 그들을 '해양 생태계의 기술자'라고 부르게 되었다. 2019년 국제 통화 기금(IMF)의 경제학자들은 각각의 고래에 의해서 제공되는 생태계 서비스의 가치를 미화 200만 달러가 넘게 추정했다. 그들은 기후 변화에 대한 '자연 기반 해결책'의 한 예로서 고래 개체수를 산업화 이전의 고래잡이 수준으로 되돌리기 위한 새로운 글로벌 경제적 인센티브 프로그램을 요구했다. 기후 변화를 늦추기 위해 세계적인 고래 복원 프로그램에 대한 요구가 현재 제기되고 있다.

다음 글의 제목으로 가장 적절한 것은?

① Saving Whales Saves the Earth and Us
고래를 구하는 것은 지구와 우리를 구한다　　고래는 기후 변화에 대한 자연 기반 해결책임
② What Makes Whales Go Extinct in the Ocean
고래가 바다에서 멸종하도록 하는 것　　고래의 멸종 이유에 관한 내용이 아님
③ Why Is Overpopulation of Whales Dangerous?
고래의 과밀이 왜 위험한가?　　고래의 과밀에 대한 언급은 없음
④ Black Money: Lies about the Whaling Industry
검은 돈: 고래잡이 산업에 대한 거짓　　고래잡이 산업이 핵심 내용은 아님
⑤ Climate Change and Its Effect on Whale Habitats
기후 변화와 그것이 고래 서식지에 미치는 영향
고래 서식지에 기후 변화가 미치는 영향에 관한 언급은 없음

왜 정답? ✶✶✶ [정답률 79%]

- 고래는 탄소 저장에 매우 효율적이다. [단서 1]
- 고래는 기후 변화에 대한 자연 기반 해결책이다. [단서 2]
- 기후 변화를 늦추기 위해 세계적인 고래 복원 프로그램에 대한 요구가 제기되고 있다. [단서 3]

➡ 고래는 탄소 저장에 매우 효율적이며 기후 변화에 대한 자연 기반 해결책이므로, 기후 변화를 늦추기 위해 고래 복원 프로그램이 요구되고 있다는 내용의 글이다.

▶ 따라서 정답은 ① '고래를 구하는 것은 지구와 우리를 구한다'이다.

왜 오답?

② 고래가 멸종되는 원인에 관한 내용이 아니다.
③ 고래의 과밀이 위험한 이유는 언급되지 않았고, 오히려 기후 변화를 늦추기 위해 고래 개체수를 늘려야 한다는 내용이다.
④ 고래잡이 산업에 대한 거짓과 검은 돈(부정한 이득)은 언급되지 않았다.
⑤ 고래가 기후 변화 문제의 해결책이 될 수 있다고 했을 뿐, 기후 변화가 고래 서식지에 미치는 영향은 언급되지 않았다. 주의

25 정답 ④ *2022년 국가별 1인당 이산화 탄소 배출량

The above graph shows / per capita CO_2 emissions / from coal, oil, and gas by countries in 2022. //
위 그래프는 보여 준다 / 1인당 이산화 탄소 배출량을 / 2022년의 국가별 석탄, 석유, 천연가스에서 나온 //

미국은 총배출량(14.7)이 가장 높으며, 석탄에서 나온 배출량(2.8)은 두 번째로 낮음
① The United States had the highest total per capita CO_2 emissions, / even though its emissions from coal were the second lowest / among the five countries shown. //
미국은 가장 높은 1인당 이산화 탄소 총배출량을 가졌다 / 석탄에서 나온 배출량은 두 번째로 낮았음에도 불구하고 / 보여진 다섯 개의 국가 중 //

② South Korea's total per capita CO_2 emissions / were over 10 tons, / ranking it the second highest / among the countries shown. //
분사구문을 이끄는 현재분사 = South Korea
한국의 총배출량(11톤)은 10톤을 넘고, 두 번째로 높음
한국의 1인당 이산화 탄소 총배출량은 / 10톤이 넘고 / 두 번째로 높은 순위를 차지했다 / 보여진 국가 중 //

③ Germany had lower CO_2 emissions per capita / than South Korea / in all three major sources respectively. //
독일은 더 낮은 1인당 이산화 탄소 배출량을 가졌다 / 한국보다 / 각각의 모든 세 가지 주요한 원천에서 //
└ 독일은 모든 세 가지 원천의 1인당 이산화 탄소 배출량이 한국보다 더 낮음

복수 주어
④ The per capita CO_2 emissions from coal / in South Africa / were over three times higher than(→ nearly twice as high as) those in Germany. //
복수 동사 = the per capita CO_2 emissions from coal
단서 남아프리카 공화국의 석탄에서 나온 배출량(5.7)은 독일의 석탄에서 나온 배출량(2.9)의 세 배를 넘지 않음
석탄으로부터의 1인당 이산화 탄소 배출량은 / 남아프리카 공화국의 / 독일의 그것보다 세 배보다 더 높았다(→ 거의 두 배 높았다) //

⑤ In Brazil, / oil was the largest source of CO_2 emissions per capita / among its three major sources, / just as it was in the United States and Germany. //
= oil
브라질, 미국에선 석유의 1인당 이산화 탄소 배출량 비중이 가장 큼
브라질에서 / 석유는 1인당 이산화 탄소 배출량의 가장 큰 원천이었다 / 세 가지 주요한 원천 중에서 / 그것은 미국과 독일에서도 마찬가지였다 //

- emission ⓝ 배출량   - rank ⓥ (순위를) 차지하다
- major ⓐ 주요한   - respectively ⓐⓓ 각각

위 그래프는 2022년의 국가별 석탄, 석유, 천연가스에서 나온 1인당 이산화 탄소 배출량을 보여 준다. ① 석탄에서 나온 배출량은 보여진 다섯 개의 국가 중 두 번째로 낮았음에도 불구하고, 미국은 가장 높은 1인당 이산화 탄소 총배출량을 가졌다. ② 한국의 1인당 이산화 탄소 총배출량은 10톤이 넘고, 보여진 국가 중 두 번째로 높은 순위를 차지했다. ③ 독일은 한국보다 각각의 모든 세 가지 주요한 원천에서 더 낮은 1인당 이산화 탄소 배출량을 가졌다. ④ 남아프리카 공화국의 석탄으로부터의 1인당 이산화 탄소 배출량은 독일의 그것보다 세 배보다 더 높았다(→ 거의 두 배 높았다). ⑤ 브라질에서 석유는 브라질의 세 가지 주요한 원천 중 1인당 이산화 탄소 배출량의 가장 큰 원천이었고, 그것은 미국과 독일에서도 마찬가지였다.

다음 도표의 내용과 일치하지 않는 것은?

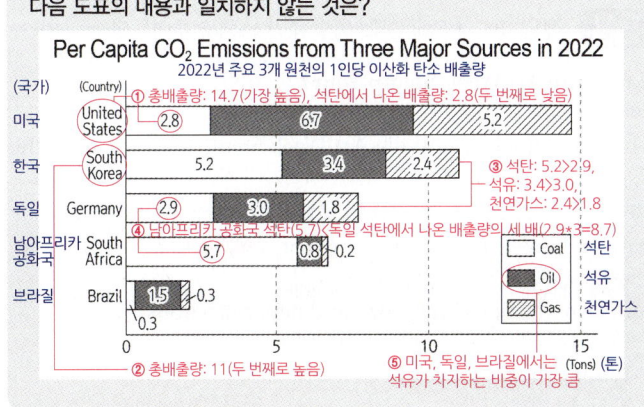

Per Capita CO_2 Emissions from Three Major Sources in 2022
2022년 주요 3개 원천의 1인당 이산화 탄소 배출량

남아프리카 공화국의 석탄에서 나온 1인당 이산화 탄소 배출량은 5.7톤으로, 독일의 석탄에서 나온 1인당 이산화 탄소 배출량인 2.9톤의 세 배인 8.7톤보다 적다. 따라서 ④이 도표의 내용과 일치하지 않는다.

왜 오답?
① 미국의 1인당 이산화 탄소 총배출량은 14.7톤이므로 전체 중 가장 높고, 석탄에서 나온 배출량은 2.8톤으로 브라질(0.3톤)에 이어 두 번째로 낮다.
② 한국의 1인당 이산화 탄소 총배출량은 11톤이므로 10톤을 넘고, 전체 중 미국에 이어 두 번째로 높다.
③ 석탄(5.2>2.9), 석유(3.4>3.0), 천연가스(2.4>1.8)에서 나온 이산화 탄소 배출량은 독일이 한국보다 모두 더 낮다.
⑤ 브라질, 미국, 독일 모두 세 가지 원천 중 석유에서 나온 이산화 탄소 배출량이 차지하는 비중이 가장 크다.

26 정답 ② *Émilie du Châtelet의 생애

동격
Émilie du Châtelet, / a French mathematician and physicist, / was born in Paris in 1706. //
Émilie du Châtelet는 / 프랑스 수학자이자 물리학자인 / 1706년에 파리에서 태어났다 //

During her childhood, / with her father's support, / she was able to get mathematical and scientific education / that most women of her time did not receive. //
목적격 관계대명사
①의 단서 어린 시절 수학과 과학 교육을 받음
어린 시절에 / 아버지의 도움으로 / 그녀는 수학과 과학 교육을 받을 수 있었다 / 당대 대부분의 여성들은 받지 못했던 //

In 1737, / she submitted her paper on the nature of fire / to a contest sponsored by the French Academy of Sciences, / and it was published a year later. //
= her paper
②의 단서 1737년에 제출되었고 1년 후인 1738년에 출간됨
1737년에 / 그녀는 불의 속성에 관한 논문을 제출했으며 / French Academy of Sciences에 의해 후원되는 대회에 / 그것은 1년 후에 출간되었다 //

In her book, *Institutions de Physique*, / Émilie du Châtelet explained the ideas of space and time / in a way that is closer to what we understand in modern relativity / than what was common during her time. //
주격 관계대명사
선행사를 포함하는 관계대명사
선행사를 포함하는 관계대명사
③의 단서 그녀의 책 *Institutions de Physique*에서 공간과 시간의 개념을 설명함
그녀의 책 *Institutions de Physique*에서 / Émilie du Châtelet는 공간과 시간의 개념을 설명했다 / 현대의 상대성 이론에서 우리가 이해하는 것에 더 가까운 방식으로 / 당대에 일반적이었던 것보다 //

④의 단서 아이작 뉴턴의 *Principia*를 프랑스어로 번역함
Her most significant achievement / was translating Isaac Newton's *Principia* into French / near the end of her life. //
그녀의 가장 주요한 성과는 / 아이작 뉴턴의 *Principia*를 프랑스어로 번역한 것이었다 / 그녀의 말년 무렵 //

⑤의 단서 그녀의 업적은 당대에 인정받지 못함
Émilie du Châtelet's work was not recognized in her time, / but she is now remembered / as a symbol of the Enlightenment and the struggle for women's participation in science. //
Émilie du Châtelet의 업적은 당대에 인정받지 못했지만 / 현재 그녀는 기억된다 / 계몽주의와 여성의 과학 분야 참여를 위한 투쟁의 상징으로 //

- physicist ⓝ 물리학자   - submit ⓥ 제출하다
- sponsor ⓥ 후원하다   - publish ⓥ 출판하다
- relativity ⓝ 상대성   - significant ⓐ 주요한   - symbol ⓝ 상징
- enlightenment ⓝ 계몽주의   - struggle ⓝ 투쟁
- participation ⓝ 참여

프랑스 수학자이자 물리학자인 Émilie du Châtelet는 1706년에 파리에서 태어났다. 어린 시절에 아버지의 도움으로 그녀는 당대 대부분의 여성들은 받지 못했던 수학과 과학 교육을 받을 수 있었다. 1737년에 그녀는 불의 속성에 관한 논문을 French Academy of Sciences에 의해 후원되는 대회에 제출했으며, 그것은 1년 후에 출간되었다. 그녀의 책 *Institutions de Physique*에서 Émilie du Châtelet는 당대에 일반적이었던 것보다 현대의 상대성 이론에서 우리가 이해하는 것에 더 가까운 방식으로 공간과 시간의 개념을 설명했다. 그녀의 가장 주요한 성과는 그녀의 말년 무렵 아이작 뉴턴의 *Principia*를 프랑스어로 번역한 것이었다. Émilie du Châtelet의 업적은 당대에 인정받지 못했지만, 현재 그녀는 계몽주의와 여성의 과학 분야 참여를 위한 투쟁의 상징으로 기억된다.

왜 정답? ✻✻✻ [정답률 76%]

Émilie du Châtelet는 대회에 불의 속성에 관한 논문을 1737년에 제출했으며, 1년 후인 1738년에 그 논문이 출간되었다고 했다. (it was published a year later) 따라서 ②이 글의 내용과 일치하지 않는다.

왜 오답?

① 어린 시절에 수학과 과학 교육을 받았다. (During her childhood ~ she was able to get mathematical and scientific education)
③ 그녀의 책 *Institutions de Physique*에서 공간과 시간의 개념을 설명했다. (In her book ~ explained the ideas of space and time)
④ 아이작 뉴턴의 *Principia*를 프랑스어로 번역했다. (translating Issac Newton's *Principia* into French)
⑤ 이룩한 업적은 당대에 인정받지 못했다. (Émilie du Châtelet's work was not recognized in her time)

---

27 정답 ⑤　*2024 Young Inventors 로봇 대회*

2024 Young Inventors Robot Competition /
2024 Young Inventors 로봇 대회 /

Join us / for an exciting day / of the Young Inventors Robot Competition! //
우리와 함께하세요 / 신나는 날에 / Young Inventors 로봇 대회의 //

□ **Categories** / 분야 /

- Participants can compete / in one of the following categories: /
　　　　　　　　　　　　　　　　　　'다음에 나오는'
참가자들은 참가할 수 있습니다 / 다음 분야 중 하나에 　**①의 단서** 세 가지 분야 중 하나에
　　　　　　　　　　　　　　　　　　　　참가할 수 있음
　• Robot Design /　• Robot Coding /　• Robot Remote Control /
　로봇 디자인 / 로봇 코딩 / 로봇 원격 조종 /

□ **Date and Time** / 날짜와 시간 /

- September 28, 2024, 10 a.m. to 3 p.m. / **②의 단서** 9월 28일에 오전 10시부터
2024년 9월 28일, 오전 10시부터 오후 3시까지 / 오후 3시까지 5시간 동안 열림

□ **Location** / 장소 /

- Computer Lab, Oakwood University /
Oakwood University 컴퓨터실 /

□ **Registration** / 등록 /

- From August 1 to August 10, 2024 /
2024년 8월 1일부터 8월 10일까지 /

- Open to high school students / **③의 단서** 고등학생이 등록할 수 있음
고등학생이 등록 가능 /
　　　　　　　　④의 단서 온라인 등록만 가능함
- Online registration only (www.younginventors.edu) /
온라인 등록만 가능 (www.younginventors.edu) /

□ **Awards** / 시상 /
　　　　　　　　　　　　　　　　　　　미래시제 수동태
- In each competition category, / three participants will be honored. // **⑤의 단서** 각 분야에서 세 명의 참가자가 수상함
각 경쟁 분야에서 / 세 명의 참가자가 수상할 것입니다 //

　• 1st place: $300 /　• 2nd place: $200 /　• 3rd place: $100 /
　1등: 300달러 / 2등: 200달러 / 3등: 100달러 /

※ For more information, / visit our website. //
더 많은 정보를 원하시면 / 저희 웹사이트를 방문하세요 //

• competition ⓝ 대회　　• participant ⓝ 참가자
• category ⓝ 분야　　• remote ⓐ 원격의　• registration ⓝ 등록
• honor ⓥ 수여하다

2024 Young Inventors 로봇 대회

Young Inventors 로봇 대회의 신나는 날에 우리와 함께하세요!
□ 분야
– 참가자들은 다음 분야 중 하나에 참가할 수 있습니다.
• 로봇 디자인 • 로봇 코딩 • 로봇 원격 조종
□ 날짜와 시간
– 2024년 9월 28일, 오전 10시부터 오후 3시까지
□ 장소
– Oakwood University 컴퓨터실
□ 등록
– 2024년 8월 1일부터 8월 10일까지
– 고등학생이 등록 가능
– 온라인 등록만 가능 (www.younginventors.edu)
□ 시상
– 각 경쟁 분야에서 세 명의 참가자가 수상할 것입니다.
• 1등: 300달러 • 2등: 200달러 • 3등: 100달러
※더 많은 정보를 원하시면, 저희 웹사이트를 방문하세요.

왜 정답? ✻✻✻ [정답률 92%]

수상자는 각 분야당 세 명이라고 (In each competition category, three participants will be honored.) 했으므로 수상자는 각 분야당 한 명이라고 한 ⑤이 안내문의 내용과 일치하지 않는다.

왜 오답?

① 세 가지 분야 중 하나에 참가할 수 있다. (Participants can compete in one of the following categories)
② 9월 28일에 5시간 동안 열린다. (September 28, 2024, 10 a.m. to 3 p.m.)
③ 고등학생이 등록할 수 있다. (Open to high school students)
④ 등록은 온라인으로만 가능하다. (Online registration only)

---

28 정답 ③　*Saintville 예술 주간 스탬프 투어*

Saintville Art Week Stamp Tour /
Saintville 예술 주간 스탬프 투어 /

The 8th annual / Saintville Art Week Stamp Tour / is back this year! //
해마다 열리는 8번째 / Saintville 예술 주간 스탬프 투어가 / 올해도 돌아왔습니다 //

Anyone can participate in our event. // **①의 단서** 누구나 행사에 참가할 수 있음
누구나 우리의 행사에 참가할 수 있습니다 //
　　　　　　병렬 구조(동사)　　　　병렬 구조(목적어)
Join us and enjoy exhibitions and new collections. //
우리와 함께하여 전시와 새로운 컬렉션을 즐겨 보세요 //

□ **When:** The first week of October, 2024 /
언제: 2024년 10월 첫째 주 / **②의 단서** 2024년 10월 첫째 주에 진행됨

□ **Where:** Saintville Arts District /
어디서: Saintville Arts District /

□ **How:** / 어떻게: /
③의 단서 Saintville Arts Center에서 스탬프 투어 지도를 받음
Step 1. Take a stamp tour map / from the Saintville Arts Center. //
1단계: 스탬프 투어 지도를 받으세요 / Saintville Arts Center에서 //

Step 2. Get stamps from at least 3 out of 5 spots / and receive ④의 단서 5곳 중 3곳에서 도장을 받으면 선물을 받을 수 있음
your gift. //
2단계: 다섯 곳 중 적어도 세 곳에서 도장을 받고 / 선물을 받으세요 //
「either A or B」: A 혹은 B (중 하나)
- You can choose / either an umbrella or a mug / with printed
artwork on it / for your gift. // ⑤의 단서 우산 혹은 머그잔 중 하나를 선물로 고를 수 있음
선택할 수 있습니다 / 우산이나 머그잔 중 하나를 / 예술 작품이 인쇄된 / 선물로 //

※ For more information, / please visit our website at www.
SaintvilleArtsCenter.com. //
더 많은 정보를 원하시면 / 저희 웹사이트 www.SaintvilleArtsCenter.com을 방문해
주세요 //

- annual ⓐ 매년의   • participate ⓥ 참가하다
- exhibition ⓝ 전시

Saintville 예술 주간 스탬프 투어

해마다 열리는 8번째 Saintville 예술 주간 스탬프 투어가 올해도 돌아왔습니다! 누구나 우리의 행사에 참가할 수 있습니다. 우리와 함께하여 전시와 새로운 컬렉션을 즐겨 보세요.
□ 언제: 2024년 10월 첫째 주
□ 어디서: Saintville Arts District
□ 어떻게:
1단계: Saintville Arts Center에서 스탬프 투어 지도를 받으세요.
2단계: 다섯 곳 중 적어도 세 곳에서 도장을 받고 선물을 받으세요.
– 예술 작품이 인쇄된 우산이나 머그잔 중 하나를 선물로 선택할 수 있습니다.
※ 더 많은 정보를 원하시면, 저희 웹사이트 www.SaintvilleArtsCenter.com 을 방문해 주세요.

Saintville Art Week Stamp Tour에 관한 다음 안내문의 내용과 일치하는 것은?
① 참가 대상에 제한이 있다. Anyone can participate in our event.
② 10월 둘째 주에 진행된다. The first week of October, 2024
③Saintville Arts Center에서 스탬프 투어 지도를 받는다.
    Take a stamp tour map from the Saintville Arts Center.
④ 적어도 다섯 곳에서 도장을 받아야 선물을 받는다.
    Get stamps from at least 3 out of 5 spots and receive your gift.
⑤ 선물로 가방과 머그잔 중 하나를 고를 수 있다.
    You can choose either an umbrella or a mug with printed artwork on it for your gift.

왜 정답? ✿✿✿ [정답률 91%]

참가 방법 중 첫 번째 단계가 Saintville Arts Center에서 스탬프 투어 지도를 받는 것이므로 (Take a stamp tour map from the Saintville Arts Center.) 안내문의 내용과 일치하는 것은 ③이다.

왜 오답?

① 참가 대상에 제한이 없다. (Anyone can participate in our event.)
② 10월 첫째 주에 진행된다. (The first week of October, 2024)
④ 다섯 곳 중 적어도 세 곳에서 도장을 받아야 선물을 받는다. (Get stamps from at least 3 out of 5 spots and receive your gift.)
⑤ 우산과 머그잔 중 하나를 선물로 고를 수 있다. (You can choose either an umbrella or a mug with printed artwork on it for your gift.)

---

29 정답 ⑤ ＊조직의 구조에 따른 갈등 관리

다음 글의 밑줄 친 부분 중, 어법상 틀린 것은?

단수 주어 「one of +복수 명사」: ~ 중 하나
From an organizational viewpoint, / one of the most fascinating
examples / of how any organization may contain / many
different types of culture /
조직의 관점에서 / 가장 매력적인 예시 중 하나는 / 어떻게 어느 조직이 포함할 수 있는지에 대한 / 많은 다른 문화 유형들을 /
단수 동사
① is to recognize the functional operations / of different
departments within the organization. //
기능적 운영을 인식하는 것이다 / 조직 내 다른 부서들의 //

The varying departments and divisions / within an organization
과거분사(situation 수식)
/ will inevitably view any given situation / from their own
「과거분사(perspective 수식)」
biased and prejudiced perspective. //
다양한 부서와 과는 / 조직 내 / 필연적으로 어떤 주어진 상황이라도 볼 것이다 / 그들 자신만의 편향적이고 편파적인 관점에서 //

주격 관계대명사   = things
A department and its members will acquire "tunnel vision" /
which disallows them to see things / as others see ② them. //
                          접속사(~대로)
한 부서와 그 구성원들은 '터널 시야 현상'을 갖게 될 것이다 / 그들이 (상황을) 볼 수 없게 하는 / 다른 이들이 그것들을 보는 대로 //
~ 자체, 바로 그 ㄱ
The very structure of organizations / can create conflict. //
조직의 구조 자체가 / 갈등을 만들어낼 수 있다 //
        명사절 접속사(~인지 아닌지)
The choice of ③ whether the structure is "mechanistic"
or "organic" / can have a profound influence / on conflict
management. //
구조가 '기계적'인지 또는 '유기적'인지의 선택은 / 깊은 영향을 미칠 수 있다 / 갈등 관리에 //

A mechanistic structure has a vertical hierarchy / with many
rules, many procedures, and many levels of management / ④
과거분사
involved in decision making. //
기계적 구조는 수직적 위계를 갖는다 / 많은 규칙, 많은 절차 그리고 많은 수준의 관리를 가진 / 의사결정에 포함된 //

Organic structures are more horizontal in nature, / ⑤ which(→
관계부사   병렬 구조
where) decision making is less centralized / and spread across
the plane of the organization. // 단서 관계대명사는 완전한 절을 이끌 수 없음
유기적 구조는 본래 더 수평적이고 / 여기서는 의사결정이 덜 중앙 집중화되고 / 조직 전반에 걸쳐 펼쳐진다 //

- organizational ⓐ 조직의   • viewpoint ⓝ 관점
- fascinating ⓐ 매력적인   • functional ⓐ 기능상의
- operation ⓝ 운영   • varying ⓐ 가지각색의
- division ⓝ (조직의) 분과   • inevitably ⓐⓓ 필연적으로
- prejudiced ⓐ 편견이 있는   • acquire ⓥ 습득하다
- disallow ⓥ 허가하지 않다   • conflict ⓝ 갈등
- mechanistic ⓐ 기계적인   • organic ⓐ 유기적인
- profound ⓐ 깊은   • management ⓝ 관리
- vertical ⓐ 수직의   • procedure ⓝ 절차   • horizontal ⓐ 수평의

조직의 관점에서, 어떤 조직이 어떻게 많은 다른 문화 유형들을 포함할 수 있는지에 대한 가장 매력적인 예시 중 하나는 조직 내 다른 부서들의 기능적 운영을 인식하는 것이다. 조직 내 다양한 부서와 과는 필연적으로 어떤 주어진 상황이라도 그들 자신만의 편향적이고 편파적인 관점에서 볼 것이다. 한 부서와 그 구성원들은 그들을 다른 이들이 그것들을 보는 대로 볼 수 없게 하는 '터널 시야 현상'을 갖게 될 것이다. 조직의 구조 자체가 갈등을 만들어낼 수 있다. 구조가 '기계적'인지 또는 '유기적'인지의 선택은 갈등 관리에 깊은 영향을 미칠 수 있다. 기계적 구조는 많은 규칙, 많은 절차 그리고 의사결정에 포함된 많은 수준의 관리를 가진 수직적 위계를 갖는다. 유기적 구조는 본래 더 수평적이고, 여기서는 의사결정이 덜 중앙 집중화되고, 조직 전반에 걸쳐 펼쳐진다.

⟩왜 정답? ★★★ [정답률 48%]

⑤ 관계대명사 뒤에 완전한 절이 왔다!

선행사
Organic structures are more horizontal in nature, / ⑤ which(→
관계부사 자리임
where) decision making is less centralized / and spread across
완전한 수동태 문장
the plane of the organization. //

병렬 구조

단서 밑줄이 관계대명사 which에 있으므로

발상 뒤에 주어나 목적어가 빠진 불완전한 절이 이어질 것이다.

해결 그런데 which 뒤에 주어 decision making, 동사 is, 그리고 과거분사 less
centralized와 spread가 병렬 구조를 이루는 완전한 수동태 문장이 이어진다.
이 문장은 nature라는 장소를 부연 설명한다. 따라서 관계대명사 which를
완전한 절을 이끄는 관계부사 where 또는 in which 등으로 바꿔야 한다.

개념 관계대명사는 앞에 수식받는 명사인 선행사가 있어야 하며, 불완전한 절을
이끈다.

⟩왜 오답?

① 동사는 주어에 그 수를 일치시킨다.

전치사구: 제외하고 생각하기   단수 주어
From an organizational viewpoint, / one of the most
fascinating examples / of how any organization may contain
전치사구: 제외하고 생각하기
many different types of culture /
단수 동사
is to recognize the functional operations of different
departments within the organization. //

be동사 is에 밑줄이 있으므로 주어도 마찬가지로 단수인지, 다른 동사는 없는지
확인한다.
문장에 다른 동사는 없으며 핵심 주어는 단수 명사인 one이므로 단수 동사가 와야
한다. 따라서 단수 동사 is가 알맞게 쓰였다.
「one of + 복수 명사」 구조에서 핵심 주어는 단수 명사인 one이다. **개념**

② 대명사는 그것이 대신하는 명사에 수를 일치시킨다.

주격 관계대명사   목적격 보어   to see의 목적어(복수 명사) = things
A department and its members will acquire "tunnel vision" /
[which disallows them to see things [as others see ② them.]]//
접속사(~대로)
대명사 them에 밑줄이 있으므로 **단서**
그것이 대신하는 명사를 찾아 수 일치 여부를 확인한다. **발상**
관계사절의 목적격 보어인 to see의 목적어는 복수 명사인 things이다.
'~대로'라는 의미의 접속사 as 뒤에도 마찬가지로 동사 see와 목적어 them이 있다.
의미상 them이 가리키는 것은 things이므로, 복수 대명사 them이 알맞게 쓰였다.

③ whether는 명사절을 이끈다.

명사절 접속사   주어   동사   주격 보어
The choice of ③ [whether the structure is "mechanistic" or
"organic"] / can have a profound influence on conflict
management. //

명사절 접속사 whether가 이끄는 절은 완전한 문장을 이루며, 문장에서 주어,
목적어, 보어의 역할을 한다. **개념**
whether가 이끄는 절이 전치사 of의 목적어로 쓰였으며, 주어는 the structure,
동사는 is, 주격 보어는 "mechanistic" or "organic"이므로 완전한 2형식 문장을
이룬다. 의미상으로도 '구조가 '기계적'인지 또는 '유기적'인지'를 나타내므로 명사절
접속사 whether가 알맞게 쓰였다.

④ 분사는 형용사처럼 명사를 수식할 수 있다.

본동사   전치사구
A mechanistic structure has a vertical hierarchy /[with many
rules, many procedures, and many levels of management ④
과거분사(levels of management 수식)
involved in decision making.]//

과거분사는 형용사처럼 명사를 수식하며, 수동의 의미를 나타낸다. **개념**
문장의 본동사는 has이고 '~을 가진다'라는 의미로 쓰였다. 전치사 with의 목적어로
many rules, many procedures, many levels of management가 왔으며,
involved는 이 중에서 levels of management를 수식한다. 해석상으로도
'의사결정에 포함된 많은 수준의 관리'라는 수동의 의미를 나타내므로 과거분사
involved가 알맞게 쓰였다.

30 정답 ④ ★도로의 친환경적인 역할

다음 글의 밑줄 친 부분 중, 문맥상 낱말의 쓰임이 적절하지 않은 것은?
[3점]

동명사(전치사 to의 목적어)   동명사(주격 보어)
An excellent alternative / to calming traffic / is removing it. //
훌륭한 대안은 / 교통을 진정시키는 / 그것을 제거하는 것이다 //

Some cities ① reserve / an extensive network of lanes and streets
/ for bikes, pedestrians, and the occasional service vehicle. //
몇몇 도시는 마련해 둔다 / 광범위한 망의 도로와 거리를 / 자전거, 보행자, 그리고 수시
서비스 차량을 위한 //

This motivates people / to travel by bike rather than by car, /
분사구문
making streets safer for everyone. //
이것은 사람들에게 동기를 부여한다 / 자동차보다 자전거로 이동을 하도록 / 그래서 거리를
모두에게 더 안전하게 만든다 //

As bicycles become more ② popular in a city, / planners
can convert more automobile lanes and entire streets / to
부사적 용법(목적)   = bicycles
accommodate more of them. //
자전거가 도시에서 더 인기가 많아지면 / 도시 계획자들은 더 많은 자동차 도로와 전체 거리를
전환할 수 있다 / 더 많은 자전거를 수용할 수 있도록 //

Nevertheless, / even the most bikeable cities / still ③ require
motor vehicle lanes / for taxis, emergency vehicles, and delivery
trucks. //
그럼에도 불구하고 / 가장 자전거를 타기 좋은 도시들조차도 / 여전히 자동차 도로를 필요로
한다 / 택시, 긴급 차량, 그리고 배달 트럭을 위한 //

= delivery vehicles
Delivery vehicles are frequently a target of animus, / but they
are actually an essential component / to making cities greener. //
배달 차량은 자주 반감의 대상이지만 / 그것들은 실제로 필수 구성요소이다 / 도시를 더
친환경적으로 만드는 (데 있어서) // **단서 1** 배달 차량은 도시를 더 친환경적으로 만드는 데 필수적임

비교급 강조 부사
A tightly packed delivery truck / is a far more ④ inefficient(→
efficient) transporter of goods / than several hybrids carrying a
hybrids를 수식하는 현재분사구
few shopping bags each. // **단서 2** 짐이 빽빽하게 들어찬 트럭과 몇 개의 쇼핑백을 실은
하이브리드 차량을 비교
짐이 빽빽하게 들어찬 배달 트럭은 / 훨씬 더 비효율적인(→ 효율적인) 상품 운송 수단이다 /
각각 몇 개의 쇼핑백을 실은 여러 하이브리드 차량보다 //

동명사(주어)
Distributing food and other goods to neighborhood vendors /
= vendors   '그래서 ~하도록'
⑤ allows them to operate smaller stores close to homes / so that
residents can walk, rather than drive, to get their groceries. //
음식과 다른 상품을 동네 상인에게 배포하는 것은 / 그들이 집에 가까운 더 작은 상점을 운영할
수 있게 하고 / 그 결과 주민들은 식료품을 사기 위해 운전하기보다는 걸어갈 수 있다 //

- - - - - - - - - - - - - - - -

- alternative ⓝ 대안   - reserve ⓥ 마련하다
- extensive ⓐ 광범위한   - lane ⓝ 길, 도로   - pedestrian ⓝ 보행자
- vehicle ⓝ 교통 수단   - occasional ⓐ 가끔의
- motivate ⓥ 동기를 부여하다 - automobile ⓝ 자동차
- accommodate ⓥ 수용하다   - frequently ⓐⓓ 자주
- distribute ⓥ 나누어주다   - neighborhood ⓝ 이웃
- vendor ⓝ 상점   - operate ⓥ 운영하다   - resident ⓝ 거주자

교통을 진정시키는 훌륭한 대안은 그것을 제거하는 것이다. 몇몇 도시는 자전거, 보행자, 그리고 수시 서비스 차량을 위한 광범위한 망의 도로와 거리를 ① 마련해 둔다. 이것은 사람들이 자동차보다 자전거로 이동을 하도록 동기를 부여하여 거리를 모두에게 더 안전하게 만든다. 자전거가 도시에서 더 ② 인기가 많아지면, 계획자들은 더 많은 자동차 도로와 전체 거리를 더 많은 자전거를 수용할 수 있도록 전환할 수 있다. 그럼에도 불구하고, 가장 자전거를 타기 좋은 도시들조차도 여전히 택시, 긴급 차량, 그리고 배달 트럭을 위한 자동차 도로를 ③ 필요로 한다. 배달 차량은 자주 반감의 대상이지만, 그것들은 실제로 도시를 더 친환경적으로 만드는 필수 구성요소이다. 짐이 빽빽하게 들어찬 배달 트럭은 각각 몇 개의 쇼핑백을 실은 여러 하이브리드 차량보다 훨씬 더 ④ 비효율적인(→ 효율적인) 상품 운송 수단이다. 음식과 다른 상품을 동네 상인에게 배포하는 것은 그들이 집에 가까운 더 작은 상점을 운영 ⑤ 할 수 있게 하고 그 결과 주민들은 식료품을 사기 위해 운전하기보다는 걸어갈 수 있다.

왜 정답? ★★☆ [정답률 74%]

④ inefficient 비효율적인

[짐이 빽빽하게 들어찬 배달 트럭은 각각 몇 개의 쇼핑백을 실은 여러 하이브리드 차량보다 훨씬 더 ④ ~~비효율적인~~(효율적인) 상품 운송 수단이다.

➡ 앞 문장에서 배달 트럭은 더 친환경적인 도시를 만드는 데 필수 요소라고 했으므로, 짐이 빽빽하게 들어찬 배달 트럭은 짐을 적게 실은 여러 하이브리드 차량보다 더 '비효율적인' 상품 운송 수단이 아니라 '효율적인' 상품 운송 수단이다.

▶ inefficient를 efficient(효율적인)와 같은 반의어로 바꿔야 함

왜 오답?

① reserve 마련하다

[몇몇 도시는 자전거, 보행자, 그리고 수시 서비스 차량을 위한 광범위한 망의 도로와 거리를 ① 마련해 둔다. 이것은 사람들이 자동차보다 자전거로 이동을 하도록 동기를 부여하여 거리를 모두에게 더 안전하게 만든다.

➡ 사람들이 자동차보다 자전거로 이동하도록 한다는 것은 자전거, 보행자, 서비스 차량을 위한 도로와 거리를 '마련한' 결과일 것이다. ▶ reserve는 문맥에 맞음

② popular 인기 있는

[자전거가 도시에서 더 ② 인기가 많아지면, 계획자들은 더 많은 자동차 도로와 전체 거리를 더 많은 자전거를 수용할 수 있도록 전환할 수 있다.

➡ 자전거의 '인기가 많아져서' 계획자들이 더 많은 자전거를 수용하도록 도로와 거리를 진환한다는 깃은 자연스럽다. ▶ popular는 문맥에 맞음

③ require 필요로 하다

[그럼에도 불구하고, 가장 자전거를 타기 좋은 도시들조차도 여전히 택시, 긴급 차량, 그리고 배달 트럭을 위한 자동차 도로를 ③ 필요로 한다.

➡ 자전거의 인기가 많은 도시에서도 여전히 다양한 차량을 위한 자동차 도로를 '필요로 한다'고 하는 것은 적절하다. ▶ require는 문맥에 맞음

⑤ allows 할 수 있게 하다

[음식과 다른 상품을 동네 상인에게 배포하는 것은 그들이 집에 가까운 더 작은 상점을 운영 ⑤ 할 수 있게 하고 그 결과 주민들은 식료품을 사기 위해 운전하기보다는 걸어갈 수 있다.

➡ 주민들이 가까운 상점으로 걸어가도록 하려면, 동네 상인에게 상품을 배포하여 각각의 생활 변경에 작은 상점을 운영'할 수 있게 하면' 된다.
▶ allows는 문맥에 맞음

---

31 정답 ② ＊위대한 작곡가의 특징

You hear again and again / that some of the greatest composers / were misunderstood / in their own day. //
여러분은 몇 번이고 듣는다 / 몇몇 가장 위대한 작곡가들이 / 진가를 인정받지 못했다고 / 그들의 시대에 //

Not everyone could understand / the compositions of Beethoven, Brahms, or Stravinsky / in their day. //
모든 사람이 이해할 수 있었던 것은 아니었다 / 베토벤, 브람스, 스트라빈스키의 곡들을 / 그들의 시대에 //

The reason / for this initial lack of acceptance / is unfamiliarity. //
이유는 / 이러한 초기의 수용 부족의 / 낯섦이다 //

The musical forms, / or ideas expressed within them, / were completely new. //
음악적 형식 / 또는 그 안에 표현된 생각은 / 완전히 새로운 것이었다 //

And yet, / this is exactly one of the things / that makes them so great. // 단서 1 작곡가들을 위대하게 만드는 것은 완전히 새로운 음악적 형식 또는 그 속의 생각임
그럼에도 불구하고 / 이것이 바로 ~인 것들 중 하나이다 / 그들을 그토록 위대하게 만드는 //

Effective composers have their own ideas. //
유능한 작곡가는 그들 자신만의 생각을 갖는다 //

Have you ever seen / the classic movie *Amadeus*? //
당신은 본 적이 있는가 / 고전 영화 *Amadeus*를 //

The composer Antonio Salieri is the "host" of this movie; / he's depicted / as one of the most famous non-great composers /
작곡가 Antonio Salieri가 이 영화의 '주인공'이다 / 그는 묘사된다 / 가장 유명한 위대하지 않은 작곡가 중 한 명으로 / 단서 2 위대하지 않은 작곡가로 묘사되는 Salieri

— he lived at the time of Mozart / and was completely overshadowed by him. //
그는 모차르트 시대에 살았고 / 그에 의해 완전히 가려졌다 //

Now, Salieri wasn't a bad composer; / in fact, / he was a very good one. //
자, Salieri는 형편없는 작곡가가 아니었다 / 사실 / 그는 매우 훌륭한 작곡가였다 //

But he wasn't one of the world's great composers / because his work wasn't original. //
하지만 그는 세계의 위대한 작곡가 중 한 명은 아니었다 / 그의 작품이 독창적이지 않았기 때문에 //

What he wrote / sounded just like / what everyone else was composing at the time. // 단서 3 Salieri가 작곡한 것은 당시 모든 사람이 작곡한 것과 비슷했음
그가 쓴 곡은 / 마치 ~처럼 들렸다 / 그 당시 모든 다른 사람들이 작곡했던 것 //

- misunderstand ⓥ 진가를 못 알아보다 · composition ⓝ 작품
- initial ⓐ 초기의 · lack ⓝ 부족 · acceptance ⓝ 수용
- unfamiliarity ⓝ 낯섦 · host ⓝ 주인공 · depict ⓥ 묘사하다
- composer ⓝ 작곡가 · overshadow ⓥ 가리다
- original ⓐ 독창적인 · conventional ⓐ 관습적인

여러분은 몇몇 가장 위대한 작곡가들이 그들의 시대에 진가를 인정받지 못했다고 몇 번이고 듣는다. 그들의 시대에 베토벤, 브람스, 스트라빈스키의 곡들을 모든 사람이 이해할 수 있었던 것은 아니었다. 이러한 초기의 수용 부족의 이유는 낯섦이다. 음악적 형식, 또는 그 안에 표현된 생각은 완전히 새로운 것이었다. 그럼에도 불구하고 이것이 바로 그들을 그토록 위대하게 만드는 것들 중 하나이다. 유능한 작곡가는 그들 자신만의 생각을 갖는다. 당신은 고전 영화 *Amadeus*를 본 적이 있는가? 작곡가 Antonio Salieri가 이 영화의 '주인공'이다. 그는 가장 유명한 위대하지 않은 작곡가 중 한 명으로 묘사된다. 그는 모차르트 시대에 살았고 그에 의해 완전히 가려졌다. 자, Salieri는 형편없는 작곡가가 아니었다. 사실, 그는 매우 훌륭한 작곡가였다. 하지만 그의 작품이 **독창적이지 않았기** 때문에 그는 세계의 위대한 작곡가들 중 한 명은 아니었다. 그가 쓴 곡은 마치 그 당시 모든 다른 사람들이 작곡했던 것처럼 들렸다.

> **다음 빈칸에 들어갈 말로 가장 적절한 것을 고르시오.**
> ① simple 그의 작품이 단순하지 않았다는 내용이 아님
> 단순한
> ② original 작품이 독창적이지 않았기 때문에 위대한 작곡가 중 한 명이 될 수 없었음
> 독창적인
> ③ familiar 그의 작품은 오히려 익숙했음
> 익숙한
> ④ conventional 그의 작품은 오히려 관습적이었음
> 관습적인
> ⑤ understandable 그의 작품이 이해하기 어려웠다는 내용이 아님
> 이해하기 쉬운

1st 빈칸이 포함된 문장 주변을 읽고, 빈칸에 들어갈 말에 대한 단서를 얻는다.

빈칸 문장	But he wasn't one of the world's great composers because his work wasn't _____.
	하지만 그의 작품이 _____ 않았기 때문에 그는 세계의 위대한 작곡가들 중 한 명은 아니었다.
빈칸 뒤 문장	What he wrote sounded just like what everyone else was composing at the time.
	그가 쓴 곡은 마치 그 당시 모든 다른 사람들이 작곡했던 것처럼 들렸다. 단서 3

➡ 빈칸 문장은 그의 작품이 '어떻지' 않았기 때문에 세계의 위대한 작곡가들 중 한 명이 아니었다고 했고, 빈칸 뒤 문장에서 그 이유가 그가 쓴 곡이 당시에 다른 사람들이 작곡했던 것과 유사했기 때문이라고 했다. 단서
여기서 '그'는 누구인지, 그리고 세계의 위대한 작곡가들은 '어떤' 사람들인지 언급될 것이다. 발상

2nd 글의 내용을 종합해서 빈칸에 들어갈 적절한 말을 찾는다.

- 완전히 새로운 음악적 형식, 또는 그 안에 표현된 생각은 작곡가들을 위대하게 만드는 것들 중 하나이다. 단서 1
- 작곡가 Antonio Salieri는 가장 유명한 위대하지 않은 작곡가 중 한 명으로 묘사된다. 단서 2

➡ 작곡가들을 위대하게 만드는 것은 '완전히 새로운' 음악적 형식 또는 그 안에 표현된 생각이라고 했으며, Salieri는 유명하지만 '위대하지는 않은' 작곡가로 묘사된다고 했다. 따라서 빈칸에는 Salieri의 작품이 '완전히 새롭지는' 않았다는 것에 관한 표현이 들어가야 한다.
▶ Salieri의 작품은 ② '독창적이지' 않았기 때문에 그는 세계의 위대한 작곡가들 중 한 명이 아니었다.

| 선택지 분석 |

① **simple** 단순한
곡의 단순함에 관한 내용이 아니라, 곡의 독창성에 관한 내용이다.

② **original** 독창적인
위대한 작곡가들은 완전히 새로운 음악적 형식과 생각이 있다고 했으므로, Salieri가 위대한 작곡가가 될 수 없었던 것은 작품에 독창성이 없었기 때문이다.

③ **familiar** 익숙한
Salieri의 곡은 오히려 익숙했기 때문에 그는 위대한 작곡가가 될 수 없었다. 빈칸 앞에 not이 있기 때문에 정답이 될 수 없다.

④ **conventional** 관습적인
Salieri의 곡은 오히려 관습적이었기 때문에 그는 위대한 작곡가가 될 수 없었다. 빈칸 앞에 not이 있기 때문에 정답이 될 수 없다.

⑤ **understandable** 이해하기 쉬운
곡을 이해하기 쉬운지에 관한 내용이 아니라, 곡의 독창성에 관한 내용이다.

32 정답 ① ＊새로운 매체가 관점에 미치는 영향

Every time a new medium comes along / — whether it's the
   　　　　　　　　　'나타나다'　　부사절 접속사(~이든)
invention of the printed book, or TV, or SNS — / and you start
to use it, /
새로운 매체가 나타날 때마다 / 인쇄된 책의 발명이든 텔레비전의 발명이든 SNS의 발명이든 / 그리고 여러분이 그것을 쓰기 시작할 때마다 /

it's like you are putting on a new kind of goggles, / with their
own special colors and lenses. //
여러분은 새 고글을 쓰는 것과 같다 / 고유의 색깔과 렌즈를 가진 //

　　　　　　　　　　　　앞에 목적격 관계대명사가 생략됨　　makes의 목적격 보어(원형부정사)
Each set of goggles / you put on / makes you see things
differently. // 단서 1 어떤 고글(매체)을 쓰는지에 따라 세상을 다르게 바라봄
각각의 고글은 / 여러분이 쓰는 / 세상을 다른 방식으로 바라보게 한다 //
　　　부사절 접속사(시간)
So when you start to watch television, / before you absorb the
message of any particular TV show / — whether it's *Wheel of
Fortune* or *The Wire* — /
그러므로 여러분이 텔레비전을 보기 시작하면 / 특정 텔레비전 프로그램의 메시지를 흡수하기 이전에 / 그것이 *Wheel of Fortune*이든 *The Wire*든 /

you start to see the world / as being shaped like television itself. //
세상을 바라보게 된다 / 텔레비전 그 자체처럼 형성된 것으로 //
단서 2 새로운 매체가 나타날 때마다 그 안에 메시지가 담겨 있음　　목적어절 접속사
That's why Marshall McLuhan said / that every time a
　　　　　　　　　　　　　　　　　　　　to부정사의 의미상 주어
new medium comes along / — a new way for humans to
형용사적 용법(a new way 수식)
communicate — / it has buried in it a message. //
이러한 이유로 Marshall McLuhan이 말한 것이다 / 새로운 매체가 나타날 때마다 / 즉, 인간이 의사소통하는 새로운 방식이 나타날 때마다 / 그 안에 메시지가 담겨 있다고 //

It is gently guiding us / to **see the world according to a new set
of codes**. //
그것(새로운 매체)은 자연스럽게 우리가 ~하게 한다 / 새로운 일련의 방식에 따라 세상을 바라보게 //
　　　　　　　　관계부사절　　　　　삽입절
The way information gets to you, / McLuhan argued, / is more
important than the information itself. //
정보가 여러분에게 도달하는 방식이 / McLuhan은 주장했다 / 정보 자체보다 더 중요하다고 //
　　　　　　　　　　　　　목적어절 접속사
TV teaches you / that the world is fast; / that it's about surfaces
and appearances. //
텔레비전은 우리에게 가르친다 / 세상은 빠르고 / 중요한 것은 표면과 겉모습이라고 //

- **medium** ⓝ 매체 · **invention** ⓝ 발명 · **absorb** ⓥ 흡수하다
- **communicate** ⓥ 소통하다 · **surface** ⓝ 표면
- **appearance** ⓝ 겉모습 · **code** ⓝ 규칙, 방식 · **interpret** ⓥ 해석하다

인쇄된 책의 발명이든 텔레비전의 발명이든 SNS의 발명이든, 새로운 매체가 나타나 여러분이 그것을 쓰기 시작할 때마다 여러분은 고유의 색깔과 렌즈를 가진 새 고글을 쓰는 것과 같다. 여러분이 쓰는 각각의 고글은 세상을 다른 방식으로 바라보게 한다. 그러므로 여러분이 텔레비전을 보기 시작하면, 그것이 *Wheel of Fortune*이든 *The Wire*든, 특정 텔레비전 프로그램의 메시지를 흡수하기 이전에 세상을 텔레비전 그 자체처럼 형성된 것으로 바라보게 된다. 이러한 이유로 Marshall McLuhan이 새로운 매체, 즉, 인간이 의사소통하는 새로운 방식이 나타날 때마다 그 안에 메시지가 담겨 있다고 말한 것이다. 그것은 자연스럽게 우리가 **새로운 일련의 방식에 따라 세상을 바라보게** 한다. McLuhan은 정보가 여러분에게 도달하는 방식이 정보 자체보다 더 중요하다고 주장했다. 텔레비전은 우리에게 세상은 빠르고, 중요한 것은 표면과 겉모습이라고 가르친다.

다음 빈칸에 들어갈 말로 가장 적절한 것을 고르시오. [3점]

① see the world according to a new set of codes
　새로운 일련의 방식에 따라 세상을 바라보다 　　새로운 매체가 등장할 때마다 세상을 다르게 바라보게 됨
② ignore unfamiliar messages from new media 　　새로운 미디어의
　새로운 미디어에서 온 익숙하지 않은 메시지를 무시하다 메시지를 무시한다는 내용이 아님
③ maintain steady focus and clear understanding
　꾸준한 집중력과 명확한 이해를 유지하다 　매체가 집중력과 이해에 도움이 된다는 내용이 아님
④ interpret information through a traditional lens
　전통적인 렌즈를 통해 정보를 해석하다 　전통적인 방식으로 정보를 이해한다는 내용이 아님
⑤ enjoy various media contents with one platform
　하나의 플랫폼으로 다양한 미디어 콘텐츠를 즐기다 　다양한 미디어 콘텐츠를 즐긴다는 언급은 없음

1st 빈칸이 포함된 문장을 읽고, 빈칸에 들어갈 말에 대한 단서를 얻는다.

빈칸 문장	It is gently guiding us to _____.
	그것은 자연스럽게 우리가 _____ 하게 한다.

➡ It이 자연스럽게 우리가 '무엇'하게 한다고 했으므로, 단서
It이 무엇을 가리키는지, 그리고 그것이 우리가 '무엇'을 하게 하는지를 파악해야 한다. 발상

2nd 글의 나머지 부분을 읽고, 빈칸에 들어갈 적절한 말을 찾는다.

- 여러분이 쓰는 각각의 고글은 세상을 다른 방식으로 바라보게 한다. **단서 1**
- 이러한 이유로 Marshall McLuhan이 새로운 매체, 즉, 인간이 의사소통하는 새로운 방식이 나타날 때마다 그 안에 메시지가 담겨 있다고 말한 것이다. **단서 2**

➡ 글의 첫 문장에서 매체를 고글에 비유하였으므로, 각각의 매체가 세상을 다른 방식으로 바라보게 한다는 내용이다. 또한 빈칸 바로 앞 문장에서 새로운 매체가 나타날 때마다 그 안에 메시지가 담겨 있다고 했으므로, 빈칸 문장의 It은 '새로운 매체'를 가리킨다.
따라서 빈칸에는 새로운 매체가 세상을 새로운 방식으로 바라보게 한다는 내용이 들어가야 한다.

▶ 새로운 매체는 자연스럽게 우리가 ① '새로운 일련의 방식에 따라 세상을 바라보게' 한다.

| 선택지 분석 |

① **see the world according to a new set of codes**
새로운 일련의 방식에 따라 세상을 바라보다
각각의 매체가 세상을 다른 방식으로 바라보게 하므로, 새로운 매체는 세상을 새로운 방식으로 바라보게 한다는 내용이다.

② **ignore unfamiliar messages from new media**
새로운 미디어에서 온 익숙하지 않은 메시지를 무시하다
특정 텔레비전 프로그램의 메시지를 흡수하는 것이 언급되긴 했으나, 메시지를 무시한다는 것은 언급되지 않았다.

③ **maintain steady focus and clear understanding**
꾸준한 집중력과 명확한 이해를 유지하다
매체가 집중력과 이해를 유지하게 한다는 것은 언급되지 않았다.

④ **interpret information through a traditional lens**
기존의 렌즈를 통해 정보를 해석하다
새로운 매체는 우리가 기존의 렌즈(관점)가 아닌 새로운 관점으로 세상을 바라보게 한다.

⑤ **enjoy various media contents with one platform**
하나의 플랫폼으로 다양한 미디어 콘텐츠를 즐기다
하나의 플랫폼이 아닌 다양한 플랫폼이 언급되며, 이를 통해 다양한 콘텐츠를 즐긴다는 것은 언급되지 않았다.

---

33 정답 ① ＊과학에서 개념을 다룰 때 주의할 점

Concepts are vital to human survival, / but we must also be careful with **them** (=concepts) / because concepts open the door to essentialism. //
개념은 인간의 생존에 필수적이지만 / 우리는 또한 그것들을 주의해야 한다 / 개념이 본질주의로 향하는 문을 열기 때문에 //

They **encourage us** / **to see things that aren't present**. //
그것들은 우리를 부추긴다 / 존재하지 않는 것들을 보도록 //

Stuart Firestein opens his book, *Ignorance*, / with an old proverb, / "**It** (가주어) is very difficult **to find** (진주어) a black cat in a dark room, / especially when there is no cat." // **단서 1** 고양이가 없는 어두운 방에서 검은 고양이를 찾는 것은 매우 어려움
Stuart Firestein은 그의 책인 *Ignorance*를 시작한다 / 옛 속담으로 / "어두운 방에서 검은 고양이를 찾는 것은 매우 어렵다 / 특히 고양이가 없을 때"라는 //

This statement beautifully **sums up** / the search for essences. //
이 말은 훌륭하게 요약한다 / 본질에 대한 탐구를 // '~을 요약하다'

History has many examples of scientists / **who** (주격 관계대명사) searched fruitlessly for an essence / because they used the wrong concept / **to guide** (형용사적 용법(concept 수식)) their hypotheses. // **단서 2** 잘못된 개념을 사용하여 헛되이 본질을 찾았던 과학자들
역사는 과학자들의 많은 예를 가지고 있다 / 헛되이 본질을 탐색했던 / 잘못된 개념을 사용했기 때문에 / 가설을 이끄는 //

Firestein gives the example of **luminiferous ether**, / **a mysterious substance** (동격) / that was thought to fill the universe / **so that** ('~하도록') light would have a medium to move through. //
Firestein은 발광 에테르의 예를 제시한다 / 신비한 물질인 / 우주를 가득 채워줄 것이라 여겨진 / 빛이 통과할 수 있는 매개체를 갖도록 //

The ether was a black cat, / writes Firestein, / and physicists **had been theorizing** (과거완료 진행형)(=a dark room) in a dark room, / and then experimenting in **it**, / **looking** (분사구문을 이끄는 현재분사) for evidence of a cat that did not exist. //
에테르는 검은 고양이였고 / Firestein이 쓰기를 / 물리학자들은 어두운 방에서 이론을 세우고 / 그리고 나서 그 안에서 실험을 하고 있었던 것이었다 / 존재하지 않았던 고양이라는 증거를 찾으며 // **단서 3** 에테르는 존재하지 않기에 찾을 수 없는 검은 고양이와 같음

- concept ⓝ 개념   • vital ⓐ 필수적인   • essentialism ⓝ 본질주의
- proverb ⓝ 속담   • statement ⓝ 진술   • essence ⓝ 본질
- fruitlessly ⓐⓓ 헛되이   • hypothesis ⓝ 가설(*pl.* hypotheses)
- luminiferous ⓐ 발광의, 빛을 내는   • mysterious ⓐ 신비로운
- substance ⓝ 물질   • theorize ⓥ 이론을 세우다
- simplify ⓥ 단순하게 만들다   • philosophy ⓝ 철학

개념은 인간의 생존에 필수적이지만, 개념이 본질주의로 향하는 문을 열기 때문에 우리는 또한 그것들을 주의해야 한다. 그것들은 존재하지 않는 것들을 보도록 우리를 부추긴다. Stuart Firestein은 "어두운 방에서 검은 고양이를 찾는 것은 특히 고양이가 없을 때 매우 어렵다."라는 옛 속담으로 그의 책, *Ignorance*를 시작한다. 이 말은 본질에 대한 탐구를 훌륭하게 요약한다. 역사는 가설을 이끄는 잘못된 개념을 사용했기 때문에 헛되이 본질을 탐색했던 과학자들의 많은 예를 가지고 있다. Firestein은 빛이 통과할 수 있는 매개체를 갖도록 우주를 가득 채워줄 것이라 여겨진 신비한 물질인 발광 에테르의 예를 제시한다. Firestein이 쓰기를, 에테르는 검은 고양이였고, 물리학자들은 어두운 방에서 이론을 세우고, 그리고 나서 존재하지 않았던 고양이라는 증거를 찾으며, 그 안에서 실험을 하고 있었던 것이었다.

다음 빈칸에 들어갈 말로 가장 적절한 것을 고르시오. [3점]

① **encourage us to see things that aren't present**
존재하지 않는 것들을 보도록 우리를 부추긴다 — 잘못된 개념은 존재하지 않는 본질을 찾기 위한 헛된 노력으로 이어질 수 있다는 내용임

② **force scientists to simplify scientific theories**
과학 이론을 단순화하도록 과학자들을 강요한다 — 과학 이론의 단순화에 대한 언급은 없음

③ **let us think science is essential and practical**
우리가 과학이 필수적이고 실용적이라고 생각하게 한다 — 과학이 필수적이고 실용적이라는 내용이 아님

④ **drive physicists to explore philosophy**
물리학자들이 철학을 탐구하도록 한다 — 철학을 탐구하게 한다는 내용이 아님

⑤ **lead us to ignore the unknown**
미지의 것을 무시하도록 우리를 이끈다 — 개념이 미지의 것을 무시하게 한다는 내용이 아님

| 문제 풀이 순서 | ★★★ [정답률 53%]

1st 빈칸이 포함된 문장과 앞 문장을 읽고, 빈칸에 들어갈 말에 대한 단서를 얻는다.

빈칸 앞 문장	Concepts are vital to human survival, but we must also be careful with them because concepts open the door to essentialism. 개념은 인간의 생존에 필수적이지만, 개념이 본질주의로 향하는 문을 열기 때문에 우리는 또한 그것들을 주의해야 한다.
빈칸 문장	They _____. 그것들은 _____

➡ 빈칸 문장 앞에서 개념(Concepts)이 필수적이지만 주의해야 한다고 했고, 빈칸 문장은 그것들을(They)은 '어떠하다'라고 했다. **단서**
They는 앞 문장의 Concepts를 나타내므로, 구체적으로 개념의 어떤 점을 주의해야 하는지가 뒤에 이어질 것이다. **발상**

2nd 글의 나머지 부분을 읽고, 글을 정리하면서 빈칸에 들어갈 내용을 찾는다.

- "어두운 방에서 검은 고양이를 찾는 것은 특히 고양이가 없을 때 매우 어렵다." **단서 1**
- 역사는 가설을 이끄는 잘못된 개념을 사용했기 때문에 헛되이 본질을 탐색했던 과학자들의 많은 예를 가지고 있다. **단서 2**
- 에테르는 검은 고양이였다. **단서 3**

➡ 검은 고양이의 속담과 에테르라는 예시를 통해, 잘못된 개념은 존재하지 않는 것을 찾도록 하므로 주의해야 한다고 말하고 있다. 따라서 빈칸에는 ① '존재하지 않는 것들을 보도록 우리를 부추긴다'가 들어가야 한다.

① encourage us to see things that aren't present
존재하지 않는 것들을 보도록 우리를 부추긴다
잘못된 개념은 존재하지 않는 본질을 찾기 위한 헛된 노력으로 이어질 수 있다는 내용이다.

② force scientists to simplify scientific theories
과학 이론을 단순화하도록 과학자들을 강요한다
잘못된 개념 때문에 잘못된 이론을 세웠다는 비유를 들었지만, 과학 이론을 단순화하는 것은 언급되지 않았다.

③ let us think science is essential and practical
우리가 과학이 필수적이고 실용적이라고 생각하게 한다
개념이 인간의 생존에 필수적이라고 했을 뿐, 과학이 필수적이고 실용적이라고 생각하게 한다는 내용이 아니다.

④ drive physicists to explore philosophy
물리학자들이 철학을 탐구하도록 한다
본질주의가 언급되긴 하지만, 물리학자가 철학을 탐구한다는 것은 언급되지 않았다.

⑤ lead us to ignore the unknown
미지의 것을 무시하도록 우리를 이끈다
Firestein의 책 제목이 Ignorance일 뿐, 무언가를 무시하는 것은 언급되지 않았다.

34 정답 ④ * 엘리트 명성과 다른 평범한 명성

While social media attention is potentially an instrument / to
형용사적 용법(instrument 수식)
achieve ends like elite celebrity, / some content creators desire
ordinary fame / as a social end in itself. //
소셜 미디어 관심은 잠재적으로 도구인 반면 / 엘리트 명성과 같은 목적을 달성하기 위한 / 일부 콘텐츠 제작자들은 평범한 명성을 원한다 / 사회적 목적 그 자체로서 //

Not unlike reality television stars, / social media celebrities are
often criticized / for not having skills and talents /
리얼리티 텔레비전 스타들과 다르지 않게 / 소셜 미디어 유명인들은 종종 비판을 받는다 / 기술과 재능을 가지고 있지 않다는 이유로 /
앞에 주격 관계대명사와 be동사가 생략됨
associated with traditional, elite celebrity, / such as acting or
singing ability. //
단서1 소셜 미디어 유명인들은 엘리트 명성에 관련된 기술이 없다는 이유로 비판을 받음
전통적인 엘리트 명성과 관련된 / 연기나 가창력과 같은 //
동격절 접속사
This criticism highlights the fact / that digital content creators
face real barriers / to crossing over to the sphere of elite celebrity. //
이러한 비판은 사실을 강조한다 / 디지털 콘텐츠 제작자들이 실질적인 장벽에 직면하고 있다는 / 엘리트 명성의 영역으로 넘어가는 데 있어서 //
'~라는 점을 놓치다'
However, / the criticism also misses the point / that the
phenomenon of ordinary celebrity reconstructs the meaning of
fame. //
그러나 / 이 비판은 또한 ~라는 점을 놓친다 / 평범한 명성 현상이 명성의 의미를 재구성한다는 //

The elite celebrity is symbolized by the metaphor of the star,
/ characterized by mystery and hierarchical distance / and
병렬 구조
associated with naturalized qualities of talent and class. //
엘리트 유명인은 스타라는 은유로 상징되고 / 신비로움과 계층적 거리로 특징지어지며 / 타고난 자질의 재능과 계층에 연관되어 있다 //
단서2 평범한 명성은 평범한 사람들과의 상호작용으로 관심을 끌어들임
The ordinary celebrity attracts attention / through regular and
frequent interactions / with other ordinary people. //
평범한 유명인은 관심을 끈다 / 정기적이고 빈번한 상호작용을 통해 / 다른 평범한 사람들과의 //
동명사구 주어(단수)   단수 동사
Achieving ordinary fame as a social media celebrity / is like
doing well at a game, /
소셜 미디어 유명인으로서 평범한 명성을 얻는 것은 / 게임에서 잘하는 것과 같은데 /
'그 이상도 그 이하도 아닌'
because in this sphere, / fame is nothing more nor less / than
relatively high scores on attention scales, /
왜냐하면 이 영역에서 / 명성은 그 이상도 그 이하도 아니기 때문이다 / 관심 척도에서 상대적으로 높은 점수 /
단서3 소셜 미디어 유명인의 영역에서 명성은 그저 관심 척도에서 높은 점수를 받는 것임
the metrics of subscribers, followers, Likes, or clicks / built into
'내장된'
social media applications. //
즉, 구독자, 팔로워, 좋아요 또는 클릭의 측정 기준(에서) / 소셜 미디어 애플리케이션에 내장된 //

- potentially ad 잠재적으로   · instrument n 도구   · end n 목적
- celebrity n 유명인, 명성   · criticize v 비판하다
- highlight v 강조하다   · barrier n 장애물
- phenomenon n 현상   · symbolize v 상징하다
- metaphor n 은유   · characterize v 특징짓다
- hierarchical a 계층적인   · scale n 척도   · shift v 전환하다
- gradually ad 점차   · solely ad 오직, 단지   · restrict v 제한하다

소셜 미디어 관심은 잠재적으로 엘리트 명성과 같은 목적을 달성하기 위한 도구인 반면, 일부 콘텐츠 제작자들은 사회적 목적 그 자체로서 평범한 명성을 원한다. 리얼리티 텔레비전 스타들과 다르지 않게, 소셜 미디어 유명인들은 연기나 가창력과 같은 전통적인 엘리트 명성과 관련된 기술과 재능을 가지고 있지 않다는 이유로 종종 비판을 받는다. 이러한 비판은 디지털 콘텐츠 제작자들이 엘리트 명성의 영역으로 넘어가는 데 있어 실질적인 장벽에 직면하고 있다는 사실을 강조한다. 그러나 이 비판은 또한 평범한 명성 현상이 명성의 의미를 재구성한다는 점을 놓친다. 엘리트 유명인은 스타라는 은유로 상징되고, 신비로움과 계층적 거리로 특징지어지며, 타고난 자질의 재능과 계층에 연관되어 있다. 평범한 유명인은 다른 평범한 사람들과의 정기적이고 빈번한 상호작용을 통해 관심을 끈다. 소셜 미디어 유명인으로서 평범한 명성을 얻는 것은 게임에서 잘하는 것과 같은데, 왜냐하면 이 영역에서 명성은 관심 척도, 즉, 소셜 미디어 애플리케이션에 내장된 구독자, 팔로워, 좋아요 또는 클릭의 측정 기준에서 상대적으로 높은 점수 그 이상도 그 이하도 아니기 때문이다.

다음 빈칸에 들어갈 말로 가장 적절한 것을 고르시오. [3점]
① shifts to that of elite celebrity 평범한 명성 현상이 엘리트 명성 현상으로 전환한다는 내용이 아님
엘리트 유명인의 그것으로 전환한다
② disappears gradually over time
시간이 지남에 따라 점진적으로 사라진다   평범한 명성 현상이 점차 사라진다는 언급은 없음
③ focuses solely on talent and class
재능과 계층에만 집중한다   재능과 계층에 집중하는 것은 엘리트 명성에 해당함
④ reconstructs the meaning of fame
명성의 의미를 재구성한다   평범한 명성 현상이 엘리트 명성과는 다르다는 것이 글의 핵심 내용임
⑤ restricts interactions with the public
대중과의 상호작용을 제한한다   평범한 명성은 오히려 대중과의 상호작용이 필요함

| 문제 풀이 순서 | ★★★ [정답률 38%]

1st 빈칸이 포함된 문장을 읽고, 빈칸에 들어갈 말에 대한 단서를 얻는다.

빈칸 문장	However, the criticism also misses the point that the phenomenon of ordinary celebrity _____. 그러나 이 비판은 또한 평범한 명성 현상이 _____ 라는 점을 놓친다.

➡ '이 비판'은 평범한 명성 현상이 '무엇을 한다'는 점을 놓친다고 했으므로, 단서 '이 비판'이 무엇을 가리키는지, 또한 평범한 명성 현상이 어떤 특성을 가지고 있다고 표현하는지에 주목하여 글을 읽어야 한다. 발상

2nd 글의 내용을 종합해서 빈칸에 들어갈 적절한 말을 찾는다.

- 소셜 미디어 유명인들은 연기나 가창력과 같은 전통적인 엘리트 명성과 관련된 기술과 재능을 가지고 있지 않다는 이유로 종종 비판을 받는다. 단서1
- 평범한 유명인은 다른 평범한 사람들과의 정기적이고 빈번한 상호작용을 통해 관심을 끈다. 단서2
- 소셜 미디어 유명인으로서 평범한 명성을 얻는 것은 게임에서 잘하는 것과 같은데, 왜냐하면 이 영역에서 명성은 관심 척도에서 상대적으로 높은 점수 그 이상도 그 이하도 아니기 때문이다. 단서3
➡ 빈칸 문장의 '이 비판'은 소셜 미디어 유명인들이 엘리트 명성과 관련된 기술과 재능이 없다는 이유로 받는 비판이다. 또한 평범한 명성을 얻는 것은 엘리트 명성과는 다르게 다른 평범한 사람들과의 상호작용이 필요하고, 이 영역에서 명성은 관심 척도에서 상대적으로 높은 점수라고 했다.

3rd 글의 내용을 다시 한번 정리하며 이해한 중심 내용을 선택지에서 고른다.

소셜 미디어 유명인들은 엘리트 명성에서 필요한 만큼의 기술과 재능이 없다는 '비판'을 받지만, 엘리트 명성과는 다르게 평범한 명성에 있어서 '인기'는 관심 척도에서 높은 점수를 받는 것뿐이라는 내용이다. 엘리트 명성이 형성한 인기의 의미와 평범한 명성에 있어서 인기의 의미가 다른 것이므로 빈칸에는 ④ '명성의 의미를 재구성한다'가 들어가야 한다.

| 선택지 분석 |

① **shifts to that of elite celebrity** 엘리트 유명인의 그것으로 전환한다
엘리트 명성과 평범한 명성의 차이점을 설명하는 내용이다.

② **disappears gradually over time** 시간이 지남에 따라 점진적으로 사라진다
평범한 명성 현상이 시간이 지남에 따라 사라진다는 것은 언급되지 않았다.

③ **focuses solely on talent and class** 재능과 계층에만 집중한다
재능과 계층에 집중하는 것은 엘리트 명성에 해당하며, 평범한 명성은 관심 척도의 높은 점수에 집중한다.

④ **reconstructs the meaning of fame** 명성의 의미를 재구성한다
평범한 명성에서 인기의 의미는 엘리트 명성에서 다루는 인기의 의미와는 다르므로, 평범한 명성은 인기의 의미를 재구성한다.

⑤ **restricts interactions with the public** 대중과의 상호작용을 제한한다
평범한 명성은 오히려 대중과의 상호작용이 필수적이며, 이것이 제한된 것은 엘리트 명성에 해당한다.

35 정답 ④ ＊학습에 사용되는 기억의 종류와 특징

다음 글에서 전체 흐름과 관계 없는 문장은?

Why do we have the illusion / that cramming for an exam / is the best learning strategy? //
왜 우리는 착각을 하는 것일까 / 시험을 위해 벼락 공부를 하는 것이 / 최고의 학습 전략이라는 //

Because we are unable to differentiate / between the various sections of our memory. //
우리가 구별할 수 없기 때문이다 / 우리의 기억의 다양한 구획을 //

Immediately after reading our textbook or our class notes, / information is fully present in our mind. //
우리의 교과서나 수업 노트를 읽은 직후에는 / 정보가 우리 머릿속에 완전히 존재한다 //

단서 1 정보는 우리의 의식적인 작업 기억에 자리함
① It sits in our conscious working memory, / in an active form. //
그것은 우리의 의식적인 작업 기억에 자리한다 / 활동적인 형태로 //

② We feel as if we know it, / because it is present in our short-term storage space ... / but this short-term section has nothing to do with the long-term memory / **단서 2** 정보를 알고 있는 것처럼 느끼지만 단기 저장 공간은 장기 기억과 무관함
우리는 마치 우리가 그것을 알고 있는 것처럼 느낀다 / 그것은 우리의 단기 저장 공간에 존재하기 때문이다 / 하지만 이 단기 구획은 장기 기억과는 아무런 관련이 없다 /

that we will need / in order to recall the same information / a few days later. //
우리가 필요로 할 / 같은 정보를 기억하기 위해 / 며칠 후 //

③ After a few seconds or minutes, / working memory already starts disappearing, / and after a few days, / the effect becomes enormous: /
몇 초 또는 몇 분 후 / 작업 기억은 이미 사라지기 시작하고 / 며칠 후 / 그 영향은 엄청나게 된다 /

단서 3 점차 작업 기억이 사라지기 시작하고 테스트를 하지 않으면 기억은 사라짐
unless you retest your knowledge, / memory vanishes. //
여러분이 자신의 지식을 다시 테스트하지 않으면 / 기억은 사라진다 //

④ Focusing on exploring new topics / rather than reviewing the same material over and over again / can improve your academic performance. //)
(새로운 주제를 탐구하는 데 집중하는 것이 / 같은 자료를 반복해서 다시 복습하는 것보다 / 여러분의 학업 성취를 향상시킬 수 있다 //)

⑤ To get information into long-term memory, / it is essential / to study the material, / then test yourself, / rather than spend all your time studying. // **단서 4** 정보를 장기 기억에 넣으려면 학습과 테스트가 필수적임
정보를 장기 기억에 넣으려면 / ~이 필수적이다 / 자료를 공부하는 것 / 그리고 나서 스스로를 테스트하는 것 / 여러분의 모든 시간을 공부하는 데에 쓰기보다는 //

- illusion ⓝ 착각 · cram ⓥ 벼락치기를 하다 · strategy ⓝ 전략
- differentiate ⓥ 구분하다 · present ⓐ 존재하는
- conscious ⓐ 의식적인 · enormous ⓐ 엄청난
- vanish ⓥ 사라지다 · material ⓝ 자료 · academic ⓐ 학업적인
- performance ⓝ 성취 · essential ⓐ 필수적인

왜 우리는 시험을 위해 벼락 공부를 하는 것이 최고의 학습 전략이라는 착각을 하는 것일까? 우리가 우리의 기억의 다양한 구획을 구별할 수 없기 때문이다. 우리의 교과서나 수업 노트를 읽은 직후에는 정보가 우리 머릿속에 완전히 존재한다. ① 그것은 우리의 의식적인 작업 기억에 활동적인 형태로 자리한다. ② 그것은 우리의 단기 저장 공간에 존재하기 때문에 우리는 마치 우리가 그것을 알고 있는 것처럼 느끼지만, 이 단기 구획은 며칠 후 같은 정보를 기억하기 위해 우리가 필요로 할 장기 기억과는 아무런 관련이 없다. ③ 몇 초 또는 몇 분 후, 작업 기억은 이미 사라지기 시작하고, 며칠 후 그 영향은 엄청나게 되어, 여러분이 자신의 지식을 다시 테스트하지 않으면 기억은 사라진다. (④ 같은 자료를 반복해서 다시 복습하는 것보다 새로운 주제를 탐구하는 데 집중하는 것이 여러분의 학업 성취를 향상시킬 수 있다.) ⑤ 정보를 장기 기억에 넣으려면, 여러분의 모든 시간을 공부하는 데에 쓰기보다는 자료를 공부하고 나서 스스로를 테스트하는 것이 필수적이다.

왜 정답·오답? ★★✿ [정답률 81%]

글의 앞부분: 왜 우리는 시험을 위해 벼락 공부를 하는 것이 최고의 학습 전략이라는 착각을 하는 것일까? 우리가 우리의 기억의 다양한 구획을 구별할 수 없기 때문이다. 우리의 교과서나 수업 노트를 읽은 직후에는 정보가 우리 머릿속에 완전히 존재한다.

➡ 벼락 공부가 최고의 학습 전략이라는 착각을 하는 이유는 우리가 기억의 다양한 구획을 구별할 수 없기 때문이며, 실제로 자료를 읽은 직후에는 정보가 우리 머릿속에 완전히 존재한다는 내용이다.

① 그것은(It)은 우리의 의식적인 작업 기억에 활동적인 형태로 자리한다.

➡ It은 앞 문장의 information을 가리킨다. 자료를 읽은 직후에 정보가 머리에 완전히 존재한다는 내용 뒤에, 의식적인 작업 기억에 활동적인 형태로 자리한다는 부연 설명이 이어진다. ▶ ①은 무관한 문장이 아님

② 그것은 우리의 단기 저장 공간에 존재하기 때문에 우리는 마치 우리가 그것을 알고 있는 것처럼 느끼지만, 이 단기 구획은 며칠 후 같은 정보를 기억하기 위해 우리가 필요로 할 장기 기억과는 아무런 관련이 없다.

➡ 정보는 단기 저장 공간(작업 기억)에 활동적인 형태로 자리하기 때문에 우리가 그 정보를 알고 있는 것처럼 느끼지만, 이는 장기 기억과 무관하다고 설명한다. ▶ ②은 무관한 문장이 아님

③ 몇 초 또는 몇 분 후, 작업 기억은 이미 사라지기 시작하고, 며칠 후 그 영향은 엄청나게 되어, 여러분이 자신의 지식을 다시 테스트하지 않으면 기억은 사라진다.

➡ 작업 기억이 장기 기억과는 무관하므로, 자신의 지식을 다시 테스트하지 않으면 작업 기억이 점차 사라진다는 내용이 자연스럽게 이어진다. ▶ ③은 무관한 문장이 아님

④ 같은 자료를 반복해서 다시 복습하는 것보다 새로운 주제를 탐구하는 데 집중하는 것이 여러분의 학업 성취를 향상시킬 수 있다.

➡ 작업 기억은 다시 테스트하지 않으면 사라진다는 내용이 이어지다가, 새로운 주제를 탐구하는 데 집중한다는 내용이 뒤에 오는 것은 전체 글의 흐름에 맞지 않는다. ▶ ④이 무관한 문장임

⑤ 정보를 장기 기억에 넣으려면, 여러분의 모든 시간을 공부하는 데에 쓰기보다는 자료를 공부하고 나서 스스로를 테스트하는 것이 필수적이다.

➡ 지식을 다시 테스트하지 않으면 작업 기억이 점차 사라진다고 했으므로, 장기 기억에 정보를 넣으려면 공부하고 나서 스스로 테스트하는 것이 필수라는 내용이 자연스럽게 이어진다. ▶ ⑤은 무관한 문장이 아님

* 글의 흐름

도입	우리는 기억의 구획을 구별할 수 없기 때문에 벼락 공부가 최고의 학습 전략이라는 착각을 함
전개	자료를 읽은 직후에는 정보가 머릿속에 완전히 존재함(정보가 작업 기억에 활동적인 형태로 자리하여 우리가 그것을 알고 있다고 착각하는 것임)
부연	작업 기억은 장기 기억과 무관하기 때문에, 정보를 다시 테스트하지 않으면 기억은 점차 사라짐
결론	정보를 장기 기억에 넣으려면 자료를 공부한 후 스스로 테스트하는 것이 필수적임

36 정답 ② * 관찰과 모방에 의한 학습

The discovery of mirror neurons has profoundly changed /
동격   동명사구
the way we think of a fundamental human capacity, / learning
by observation. // 단서1 관찰에 의한 학습이라는 소재를 소개함
거울 뉴런의 발견은 완전히 바꾸어 놓았다 / 근본적인 인간의 능력에 대해 우리가
생각하는 방식을 / 관찰에 의한 학습이라는 //

(A) You may not see the tongue stick out / each time you stick
= your tongue
yours out at your newborn, / 단서2 혀를 내미는 것이 앞에 언급되어야 함
당신은 (아기의) 혀가 내밀어 나오는 것을 보지 못할 수도 있지만 / 당신의 갓난아기에게
당신의 것(혀)을 내밀 때마다 /

but if you do it many times, / the tongue will come out more
often / than if you do something different. //
만약 당신이 그것을 여러 번 한다면 / (아기의) 혀가 더 자주 나올 것이다 / 당신이 다른 것을
할 때보다 //
앞에 목적격 관계대명사가 생략됨
Babies babble and later start to imitate the sounds / their parents
produce. // 단서3 아기들은 옹알이 이후에 소리를 모방함
아기들은 옹알이하고 이후에 소리를 모방하기 시작한다 / 그들의 부모가 내는 //
선행사를 포함하는 관계대명사
(B) As children / we learn a lot / by observing what our parents
and friends do. // 단서4 주어진 글에 나온 관찰에 의한 학습과 연결됨
어린이일 때 / 우리는 많이 배운다 / 우리의 부모와 친구들이 하는 것을 관찰하면서 //

Newborns, in the first week of life, / have an inborn tendency /
형용사적 용법(tendency 수식)
to stick out their tongue / if their parents stick out theirs. //
갓난아기들은 생의 첫 주에 / 선천적인 성향을 갖고 있다 / 자신의 혀를 내미는 / 그들의
부모가 그들의 것(혀)을 내밀면 / 단서5 갓난아기들은 혀를 내미는 성향을 가짐

Such imitation is not perfect. //
그러한 모방은 완벽하지 않다 //

(C) Later still, / they play with vacuum cleaners and hammers /
in imitation of their parents. // 단서6 (A)의 마지막 문장에서 언급되는 Babies가
they와 연결됨
이후에도 여전히 / 그들은 진공청소기와 망치를 갖고 논다 / 부모들을 흉내 내어 //
「전치사+관계대명사」
Our modern cultures, / in which we write, speak, read, build
spaceships and go to school, /
우리의 현대 문화는 / 쓰고 말하고 읽고 우주선을 만들고 학교에 가는 /

can work only because we are not restricted to the behavior / we
앞에 목적격 관계대명사가 생략됨
are born with or learn by trial and error. //
단지 행동에 국한되지 않기 때문에 작동할 수 있다 / 우리가 가지고 태어나는 또는 시행착오를
통해 배우는 //

We can learn a lot / by simply watching others. //
우리는 많이 배울 수 있다 / 그저 다른 사람들을 관찰하는 것을 통해 //

- discovery ⓝ 발견   · profoundly ⓐ 완전히
- fundamental ⓐ 근본적인   · capacity ⓝ 능력
- observation ⓝ 관찰   · newborn ⓝ 신생아
- stick out ~을 내밀다   · imitate ⓥ 모방하다   · inborn ⓐ 선천적인
- tendency ⓝ 성향   · restrict ⓥ 제한하다   · behavior ⓝ 행동
- trial and error 시행착오

거울 뉴런의 발견은 관찰에 의한 학습이라는 근본적인 인간의 능력에 대해 우리가 생각하는 방식을 완전히 바꾸어 놓았다. (B) 어린이일 때 우리는 우리의 부모와 친구들이 하는 것을 관찰하면서 많이 배운다. 갓난아기들은 생의 첫 주에 그들의 부모가 그들의 것(혀)을 내밀면 자신의 혀를 내미는 선천적인 성향을 갖고 있다. 그러한 모방은 완벽하지 않다. (A) 당신은 당신의 갓난아기에게 당신의 것(혀)을 내밀 때마다 (아기의) 혀가 내밀어 나오는 것을 보지 못할 수도 있지만, 만약 당신이 그것을 여러 번 한다면 당신이 다른 것을 할 때보다 (아기의) 혀가 더 자주 나올 것이다. 아기들은 옹알이하고 이후에 그들의 부모가 내는 소리를 모방하기 시작한다. (C) 이후에도 여전히, 그들은 부모들을 흉내 내어 진공청소기와 망치를 갖고 논다. 쓰고 말하고 읽고 우주선을 만들고 학교에 가는 우리의 현대 문화는 단지 우리가 가지고 태어나는 또는 시행착오를 통해 배우는 행동에 국한되지 않기 때문에 작동할 수 있다. 우리는 그저 다른 사람들을 관찰하는 것을 통해 많이 배울 수 있다.

주어진 글에는 혀에 관한 언급이 없음
주어진 글 다음에 이어질 글의 순서로 가장 적절한 것을 고르시오.
① (A) ─ (C) ─ (B) 거울 뉴런이 발견되어, 관찰에 의한 학습에 대한 관점이 바뀜 ─ (B)
② (B) ─ (A) ─ (C) 아기가 혀를 내미는 것을 따라 하는 것처럼, 관찰을 통해 학습함
③ (B) ─ (C) ─ (A) ─ (A) 특정 행동을 반복하면 그 행동을 더 자주 모방함 ─ (C) 인간은 다른
④ (C) ─ (A) ─ (B) 사람들을 관찰하며 많이 배움
⑤ (C) ─ (B) ─ (A)
(C)의 they가 가리키는 대상이 주어진 글에 없음
혀를 내미는 모방을 이어서 언급하는 (A)가 (B) 뒤에 이어져야 함

| 문제 풀이 순서 | ★★❀ [정답률 77%]

1st 각 문단의 내용을 파악하고, 글의 논리적인 순서를 추론한다.

주어진 글: 거울 뉴런의 발견은 관찰에 의한 학습이라는 근본적인 인간의 능력에 대해 우리가 생각하는 방식을 완전히 바꾸어 놓았다.

➡ 주어진 글 뒤: 관찰에 의한 학습과 연결되는 내용이 나올 것이다.

(A): 당신은 당신의 갓난아기에게 당신의 것(혀)을 내밀 때마다 (아기의) 혀가 내밀어 나오는 것을 보지 못할 수도 있지만, 만약 당신이 그것을 여러 번 한다면 당신이 다른 것을 할 때보다 (아기의) 혀가 더 자주 나올 것이다. 아기들(Babies)은 옹알이하고 이후에 그들의 부모가 내는 소리를 모방하기 시작한다.

➡ (A) 앞: 아기들이 부모들의 행동을 모방해 혀를 내민다는 설명과, 한계가 있다는 내용이 앞에 나와야 한다. 주어진 글에는 관찰에 의한 학습만 언급되었을 뿐, 혀가 언급되지 않았다.
▶ 주어진 글 바로 뒤에 (A)가 올 수 없음
(A) 뒤: 아기들이 성장하면서 보여주는 모방 행동들을 나열했으므로, (A) 뒤에도 아기의 다른 모방 행동이 이어질 것이다.

(B): 어린이일 때 우리는 우리의 부모와 친구들이 하는 것을 관찰하면서 많이 배운다(learn a lot by observing). 갓난아기는 생의 첫 주에 그들의 부모가 그들의 것(혀)을 내밀면 자신의 혀(tongue)를 내미는 선천적인 성향을 갖고 있다. 그러한 모방은 완벽하지 않다.

➡ (B) 앞: 어린이가 주변을 관찰하면서 많이 배운다고 했으므로, 관찰에 의한 학습을 처음 언급한 주어진 글이 앞에 와야 한다.
▶ 순서: 주어진 글 → (B)
(B) 뒤: 모방이 완벽하지는 않다고 했으므로, 매번 모방에 성공하는 것은 아니라는 내용의 (A)가 뒤에 와야 한다.
▶ 순서: 주어진 글 → (B) → (A)

(C): 이후에도 여전히, 그들(they)은 부모들을 흉내 내어 진공청소기와 망치를 갖고 논다. 쓰고 말하고 읽고 우주선을 만들고 학교에 가는 우리의 현대 문화는 단지 우리가 가지고 태어나는 또는 시행착오를 통해 배우는 행동에 국한되지 않기 때문에 작동할 수 있다. 우리는 그저 다른 사람들을 관찰하는 것을 통해 많이 배울 수 있다.

➡ (C) 앞: 부모들을 흉내 내어 물건을 갖고 노는 they(그들)가 누구인지 앞에 나와야 하므로, 아기들의 단계적인 모방 행동을 언급한 (A)가 앞에 와야 한다.
▶ 순서: 주어진 글 → (B) → (A) → (C)

주어진 글: 거울 뉴런의 발견은 관찰에 의한 학습에 대한 우리의 관점을 바꿨다.
→ **(B):** 우리는 주변의 행동을 관찰하며 배우고, 신생아는 불완전하지만 혀 내밀기를 모방한다.
→ **(A):** 특정 행동이 반복되면 그 행동을 더 자주 모방하며, 아기는 점차 소리도 모방한다.
→ **(C):** 나중에는 다른 행동들도 모방하며, 이처럼 우리는 다른 사람들을 관찰하며 많이 배운다.
▶ 주어진 글 다음에 이어질 글의 순서는 (B) → (A) → (C)이므로 정답은 ②임

37 정답 ④ ＊녹음된 자기 목소리가 다르게 들리는 이유

현재완료(경험)
Have you ever been surprised / to hear a recording of your own voice? //
당신은 놀랐던 적이 있는가 / 당신의 음성 녹음을 듣고 //
'(아마) ~했을지도 모른다'
You might have thought, / "Is that really what my voice sounds like?" //
당신은 생각했을지도 모른다 / '내 목소리가 정말 이렇게 들리는가'라고 //

(A) There are two pathways / 「전치사+관계대명사」 through which we perceive our own voice / when we speak. // **단서 1** (C)의 마지막 문장에 언급된 The explanation과 연결됨
두 가지 경로가 있다 / 우리 자신의 목소리를 인지하는 데는 / 우리가 말할 때 //
단서 2 첫 번째 경로를 소개함 「전치사+관계대명사」
One is the route / through which we perceive most external sounds, / like waves that travel from the air / through the outer, middle and inner ear. // 주격 관계대명사
하나는 경로이다 / 우리가 대부분의 외부의 소리를 인지하는 / 공기로부터 이동하는 파동처럼 / 외이, 중이, 내이를 통하는 //

(B) But because our vocal cords vibrate when we speak, / there is a second internal path. // **단서 3** 두 번째 경로를 소개함
그러나 우리가 말할 때 우리의 성대가 진동하기 때문에 / 두 번째 내부의 경로가 있다 //
병렬 구조
Vibrations are conducted through our bones / and stimulate our inner ears directly. //
진동은 뼈를 통해 전해지고 / 우리의 내이를 직접 자극한다 //
= second internal path
Lower frequencies are emphasized / along this pathway. //
낮은 주파수는 두드러진다 / 이 경로를 따라 //
= your voice
That makes your voice sound deeper and richer to yourself / than it may sound to other people. //
그것은 당신의 목소리가 당신 자신에게 더 깊고 풍부하게 들리게 한다 / 다른 사람에게 들릴 수 있는 것보다 //

(C) Maybe your accent is more pronounced in the recording / than you realized, / or your voice is higher / than it seems to your own ears. // **단서 4** 주어진 글에서 언급한 자신의 음성 녹음을 듣고 놀란 이유가 이어짐
어쩌면 녹음에서는 당신의 억양이 더 강조되거나 / 당신이 인식한 것보다 / 당신의 목소리가 더 높다 / 당신의 귀에 들리는 것 같은 것보다 //
This is of course quite a common experience. //
이것은 당연히 꽤 흔한 경험이다 //
The explanation is actually fairly simple. //
이 설명은 사실 꽤 간단하다 // **단서 5** 녹음된 자기 목소리가 다르게 들리는 이유가 뒤에 이어질 것임

- **pathway** ⓝ 경로 - **route** ⓝ 경로 - **perceive** ⓥ 인지하다
- **external** ⓐ 외부의 - **travel** ⓥ 이동하다 - **vibrate** ⓥ 진동하다
- **internal** ⓐ 내부의 - **conduct** ⓥ 전하다 - **stimulate** ⓥ 자극하다
- **emphasize** ⓥ 강조하다 - **pronounced** ⓐ 강조된 - **fairly** ⓪ 꽤

당신은 당신의 음성 녹음을 듣고 놀랐던 적이 있는가? 당신은 '내 목소리가 정말 이렇게 들리는가?'라고 생각했을지도 모른다. (C) 어쩌면 녹음에서는 당신이 인식한 것보다 당신의 억양이 더 강조되거나, 당신의 목소리가 당신의 귀에 들리는 것 같은 것보다 더 높다. 이것은 당연히 꽤 흔한 경험이다. 이 설명은 사실 꽤 간단하다. (A) 우리가 말할 때 우리 자신의 목소리를 인지하는 데는 두 가지 경로가 있다. 하나는 외이, 중이, 내이를 통하는 공기로부터 이동하는 파동처럼

우리가 대부분의 외부의 소리를 인지하는 경로이다. (B) 그러나 우리가 말할 때 우리의 성대가 진동하기 때문에 두 번째 내부의 경로가 있다. 진동은 뼈를 통해 전해지고, 우리의 내이를 직접 자극한다. 낮은 주파수는 이 경로를 따라 두드러진다. 그것은 당신의 목소리가 다른 사람에게 들릴 수 있는 것보다 당신 자신에게 더 깊고 풍부하게 들리게 한다.

> **주어진 글 다음에 이어질 글의 순서로 가장 적절한 것을 고르시오. [3점]**
> ① (A) — (C) — (B) 주어진 글의 현상을 (C)에서 부연 설명함
> ② (B) — (A) — (C) 두 번째 경로를 소개하는 (B)가 주어진 글 바로 뒤에 이어질 수 없음
> ③ (B) — (C) — (A) 자신의 음성 녹음을 들으면 목소리가 다르다고 생각함 — (C) 녹음된 목소리는 억양이 더 강조되거나 더 높게 들림 — (A) 목소리를 인지하는
> ④ (C) — (A) — (B) 경로는 두 가지가 있으며 첫 번째는 외부의 소리를 인지하는 경로임 — (B) 두 번째는 내부의 경로이며 이를 통해 자신의 목소리를 더 풍부하게 들음
> ⑤ (C) — (B) — (A) 첫 번째 경로를 소개한 (A)가 두 번째 경로를 소개한 (B)보다 앞에 와야 함

| **문제 풀이 순서 |** ✸✸✸ [정답률 78%]

1st 각 문단의 내용을 파악하고, 글의 논리적인 순서를 추론한다.

주어진 글: 당신은 당신의 음성 녹음을 듣고 놀랐던 적이 있는가? 당신은 '내 목소리가 정말 이렇게 들리는가?'라고 생각했을지도 모른다.

→ **주어진 글 뒤:** 녹음된 자신의 목소리가 원래의 목소리와 다르게 들리는 이유를 부연 설명할 것이다.

(A): 우리가 말할 때 우리 자신의 목소리를 인지하는(perceive) 데는 두 가지 경로가 있다. 하나(One)는 외이, 중이, 내이를 통하는 공기로부터 이동하는 파동처럼 우리가 대부분의 외부의 소리를 인지하는 경로이다.

→ **(A) 앞:** 자신의 목소리를 인지하는 경로를 설명하므로, 자신의 목소리를 인지하는 것에 관한 내용이 먼저 와야 한다. 주어진 글에는 녹음된 목소리가 실제 목소리와 다르게 들린다는 의문점만 제시되었으므로 (A)와 이어질 수 없다.
▶ 주어진 글 바로 뒤에 (A)가 올 수 없음
(A) 뒤: One이라고 했으므로 두 번째 경로에 대한 설명이 이어질 것이다.

(B): 그러나 우리가 말할 때 우리의 성대가 진동하기 때문에 두 번째 내부의 경로(second internal path)가 있다. 진동은 뼈를 통해 전해지고, 우리의 내이를 직접 자극한다. 낮은 주파수는 이 경로를 따라 두드러진다. 그것은 당신의 목소리가 다른 사람에게 들릴 수 있는 것보다 당신 자신에게 더 깊고 풍부하게 들리게 한다.

→ **(B) 앞:** second internal path가 등장했으므로, 목소리를 인지하는 두 가지 경로를 언급하며 첫 번째 경로를 소개한 (A)가 앞에 와야 한다.
▶ 순서: (A) → (B)
(B) 뒤: 두 경로에 대한 설명이 마무리되었으므로 글의 마지막일 가능성이 높다.

(C): 어쩌면 녹음에서는 당신이 인식한(realized) 것보다 당신의 억양이 더 강조되거나, 당신의 목소리가 당신의 귀에 들리는 것 같은 것보다 더 높다. 이것은 당연히 꽤 흔한 경험이다. 이 설명은 사실 꽤 간단하다.

→ **(C) 앞:** 녹음된 자신의 목소리가 낯설게 느껴지는 현상을 소개하는 내용이 있어야 하므로, 녹음된 목소리가 다르게 들린 경험을 묻는 주어진 글이 앞에 와야 한다.
▶ 순서: 주어진 글 → (C)
(C) 뒤: 녹음된 자신의 목소리가 자신이 인식한 목소리와 왜 다른지에 대한 설명이 이어져야 하므로, 자신의 목소리를 인지하는 경로를 설명한 (A)가 뒤에 이어져야 한다.
▶ 순서: 주어진 글 → (C) → (A) → (B)

2nd 글이 한눈에 들어오도록 정리하여 정답을 확인한다.

주어진 글: 녹음된 목소리가 실제 목소리와 다르게 들려서 놀란 적이 있는가?
→ **(C):** 녹음된 목소리에서 억양이 강조되거나 더 높게 느껴졌을 수도 있다.
→ **(A):** 목소리를 인지하는 두 가지 경로 중 첫 번째는 대부분의 외부 소리를 듣는 경로이다.
→ **(B):** 두 번째인 내부 경로에서 낮은 주파수가 두드러지기에 자신의 목소리가 더 깊고 풍부하게 들리게 된다.
▶ 주어진 글 다음에 이어질 글의 순서는 (C) → (A) → (B)이므로 정답은 ④임

2024. 9
8회

글의 흐름으로 보아, 주어진 문장이 들어가기에 가장 적절한 곳을 고르시오.

home=same, logous(logos)=relation
"**Homologous**" traits, / in contrast, / may or may not have a common function, 단서1 상동 형질은 공통적인 기능은 없을 수 있으나 공통적인 조상과 구조를 가짐
'상동' 형질은 / 대조적으로 / 공통된 기능이 있을 수도 없을 수도 있으나 /
but they descended from a common ancestor / and hence have some common structure / that indicates their being "the same" organ. //
주격 관계대명사 동명사 being의 의미상 주어
그것들은 공통의 조상으로부터 내려왔으므로 / 어떠한 공통된 구조를 가진다 / 그들이 '동일한' 기관임을 보여주는 //

Biologists distinguish two kinds of similarity. //
생물학자들은 두 종류의 유사성을 구별한다 // 단서2 두 가지 유사성이 나올 것임
ana=according to 주격 관계대명사
(①) "**Analogous**" traits are ones / that have a common function
병렬 구조
/ but arose on different branches of the evolutionary tree / and
병렬 구조
are in an important sense not "the same" organ. //
'상사' 형질은 형질이다 / 공통된 기능을 가지지만 / 진화 계보의 다른 가지에서 생겨났고 / 중요한 면에서 '동일한' 기관이 아닌 //
단서3 상사 형질은 공통 기능은 가지지만 진화 계보의 다른 가지에서 생겨남
(②) The wings of birds and the wings of bees / are both used for flight / and are similar in some ways / because anything used
과거분사구(anything 수식)
for flight has to be built / in those ways, / 단서4 상사 형질의 예시
새의 날개들과 벌의 날개들은 / 둘 다 비행에 쓰이고 / 일부 방식에서 유사하지만 / 비행에 쓰이는 것은 어떤 것이든 만들어져야 하기 때문에 / 그러한 방식으로 /
but they arose independently in evolution / and have nothing in common / beyond their use in flight. //
그것들은 진화상에 별개로 생겨났고 / 공통점이 없다 / 비행에서 그것들의 쓰임 외에는 //
(③) The wing of a bat and the front leg of a horse / have very different functions, / but they are all modifications / of the forelimb of the ancestor of all mammals. // 단서5 상동 형질의 예시
박쥐의 날개와 말의 앞다리는 / 매우 다른 기능들을 가지나 / 그것들은 모두 변형된 것이다 / 모든 포유류의 조상의 앞다리가 //
= The wing of a bat and the front leg of a horse
(④) As a result, / they share nonfunctional traits / like the number of bones / and the ways they are connected. //
그 결과 / 그들은 비기능적 형질을 공유한다 / 뼈의 개수와 같은 / 그리고 그것들이 연결된 방식과 (같은) //
(⑤) To distinguish analogy from homology, / biologists usually
병렬 구조
look at the overall architecture of the organs / and focus on their most useless properties. //
상사성과 상동성을 구별하기 위해 / 생물학자들은 주로 그 기관의 전체적인 구성을 살펴보고 / 그들의 가장 쓰임이 없는 특성에 집중한다 //

- trait ⓝ 형질 · descend ⓥ 내려오다 · ancestor ⓝ 조상
- hence ⓪ 이런 이유로 · structure ⓝ 구조 · indicate ⓥ 나타내다
- organ ⓝ 기관 · distinguish ⓥ 구별하다 · similarity ⓝ 유사성
- arise ⓥ 생겨나다 · independently ⓪ ~와 관계없이
- modification ⓝ 수정 · forelimb ⓝ 앞다리
- mammal ⓝ 포유류 · nonfunctional ⓐ 비기능적
- architecture ⓝ 구성 · property ⓝ 특성

생물학자들은 두 종류의 유사성을 구별한다. (①) '상사' 형질은 공통된 기능을 가지는 것들이지만, 진화 계보의 다른 가지에서 생겨났고 중요한 면에서 '동일한' 기관이 아닌 형질이다. (②) 새의 날개들과 벌의 날개들은 둘 다 비행에 쓰이고 비행에 쓰이는 것은 어떤 것이든 그러한 방식으로 만들어져야 하기 때문에 일부 방식에서 유사하지만, 그것들은 진화상에 별개로 생겨났고, 비행에서 그것들의 쓰임 외에는 공통점이 없다. (③ 대조적으로, '상동' 형질은 공통된 기능이 있을 수도 없을 수도 있으나 그것들은 공통의 조상으로부터 내려왔으므로 그들이 '동일한' 기관임을 보여주는 어떠한 공통된 구조를 가진다.) 박쥐의 날개와

말의 앞다리는 매우 다른 기능들을 가지나, 그것들은 모든 포유류의 조상의 앞다리가 모두 변형된 것들이다. (④) 그 결과, 그들은 뼈의 개수와 그것들이 연결된 방식과 같은 비기능적 형질을 공유한다. (⑤) 상사성과 상동성을 구별하기 위해, 생물학자들은 주로 그 기관의 전체적인 구성을 살펴보고 그들의 가장 쓰임이 없는 특성에 집중한다.

| 문제 풀이 순서 | ★★❀ [정답률 62%]

1st 주어진 문장을 해석하고, 앞뒤에 어떤 내용이 올지 생각한다.

"Homologous" traits, in contrast, may or may not have a common function, but they descended from a common ancestor and hence have some common structure that indicates their being "the same" organ.
대조적으로, '상동' 형질은 공통된 기능이 있을 수도 없을 수도 있으나 그것들은 공통의 조상으로부터 내려왔으므로 그들이 '동일한' 기관임을 보여주는 어떤 공통된 구조를 가진다.

➡ 주어진 문장 앞: 반대되는 내용을 나타내는 in contrast가 있으므로, 단서 상동 형질과 반대되는 형질이 앞에 언급될 것이다. 발상
➡ 주어진 문장 뒤: 상동 형질을 가지는 예시가 이어질 것이다.

2nd 각 선택지의 앞뒤 흐름이 매끄러운지 확인한다.

- ①의 앞 문장과 뒤 문장
앞 문장: 생물학자들은 두 종류의 유사성을 구별한다.
뒤 문장: '상사' 형질은 공통된 기능을 가지는 것들이지만, 진화 계보의 다른 가지에서 생겨났고 중요한 면에서 '동일한' 기관이 아닌 형질이다.
➡ 두 종류의 유사성을 구별한다는 내용에 이어서, 첫 번째 종류의 유사성인 '상사' 형질을 설명한다. ▶ 주어진 문장이 ①에 들어갈 수 없음

- ②의 앞 문장과 뒤 문장
앞 문장: ①의 뒤 문장과 같음
뒤 문장: 새의 날개들과 벌의 날개들은 둘 다 비행에 쓰이고 비행에 쓰이는 것은 어떤 것이든 그러한 방식으로 만들어져야 하기 때문에 일부 방식에서 유사하지만, 그것들은 진화상에 별개로 생겨났고, 비행에서 그것들의 쓰임 외에는 공통점이 없다.
➡ '상사' 형질의 예시로서 새의 날개들과 벌의 날개들을 언급하며, 비행이라는 기능적 측면에서는 공통적이지만, 그 외에는 공통점이 없다고 설명한다.
▶ 주어진 문장이 ②에 들어갈 수 없음

③의 앞 문장과 뒤 문장
앞 문장: ②의 뒤 문장과 같음
뒤 문장: 박쥐의 날개와 말의 앞다리는 매우 다른 기능들을 가지나, 그것들은 모든 포유류의 조상의 앞다리가 모두 변형된 것이다.
➡ 다른 기능을 가지지만 포유류의 조상의 앞다리가 변형된 박쥐의 날개와 말의 앞다리는 '상사' 형질의 예시가 아닌 '상동' 형질의 예시이다. 따라서 상동 형질의 개념을 언급하는 주어진 문장은 여기에 와야 한다.
▶ 주어진 문장이 ③에 들어가야 함

- ④의 앞 문장과 뒤 문장
앞 문장: ③의 뒤 문장과 같음
뒤 문장: 그 결과, 그들(They)은 뼈의 개수와 그것들이 연결된 방식과 같은 비기능적 형질을 공유한다.
➡ '상동' 형질은 동일한 기관임을 보여주는 어떤 공통된 구조를 가진다고 했으므로, 앞 문장에서 언급된 박쥐의 날개와 말의 앞다리가 비기능적 형질을 공유한다는 내용으로 자연스럽게 연결된다. ▶ 주어진 문장이 ④에 들어갈 수 없음

- ⑤의 앞 문장과 뒤 문장

앞 문장: ④의 뒤 문장과 같음
뒤 문장: 상사성과 상동성을 구별하기 위해, 생물학자들은 주로 그 기관의 전체적인 구성을 살펴보고 그들의 가장 쓰임이 없는 특성에 집중한다.

➡ 상사성과 상동성에 대한 설명이 끝난 후에 두 개념을 모두 언급하며, 생물학자들이 이들을 구별하는 방법을 설명하는 내용이 자연스럽게 이어진다.
▶ 주어진 문장이 ⑤에 들어갈 수 없음

3rd 글이 한눈에 들어오도록 정리하여 정답을 확인한다.

생물학자들은 두 종류의 유사성을 구별한다.
(①) '상사' 형질은 공통된 기능을 가지는 것들이지만, 조상이 다르고 동일한 구조를 가지지 않는다.
(②) 새와 벌의 날개들은 기능 외에는 공통점이 없고 진화상 별개로 생겨났다.
(③ 대조적으로, '상동' 형질은 공통된 기능이 없을 수도 있지만, 공통의 조상과 구조를 가진다.)
박쥐의 날개와 말의 앞다리는 기능이 다르지만 모두 포유류의 조상의 앞다리가 변형된 것들이다.
(④) 그 결과, 그들은 비기능적 형질을 공유한다.
(⑤) 생물학자들은 기관의 가장 쓰임이 없는 특성에 집중하여 상사성과 상동성을 구별한다.

39 정답 ② ＊지구 온난화로 인한 용존 산소량의 감소

글의 흐름으로 보아, 주어진 문장이 들어가기에 가장 적절한 곳을 고르시오. [3점]

> Thus, / as global warming raises the temperature of marine waters, / **it** is self-evident / **that** the amount of dissolved oxygen will decrease. //
> (가주어 / 진주어절 접속사)
> 따라서 / 지구 온난화가 해양 수온을 높임에 따라 / ~이 자명하다 / 용존 산소의 양이 감소할 것 //

Seawater contains an abundance of dissolved oxygen / **that** all marine animals breathe to stay alive. //
목적격 관계대명사
해수는 다량의 용존 산소를 포함한다 / 모든 해양 동물이 살아있기 위해 호흡하는 //
(①) **It** has long been established / in physics / **that** cold water holds more dissolved oxygen / than warm water does / — this is one reason / that cold polar seas are full of life /
(가주어 / 진주어절 접속사)
단서 1 차가운 물이 따뜻한 물보다 더 많은 용존 산소를 보유함
오랫동안 확립되어 왔다 / 물리학에서 / 차가운 물이 더 많은 용존 산소를 보유하고 있다는 사실은 / 따뜻한 물이 보유하고 있는 것보다 / 이는 하나의 이유이다 / 차가운 극지의 바다는 생명으로 가득한 /
부사절 접속사(대조)
while tropical oceans are blue, clear, / and relatively poorly populated with living creatures. //
반면 열대 해양은 푸르고 맑고 / 생물이 상대적으로 적게 서식하는 //
단서 2 걱정스럽고 잠재적으로 파괴적인 결과 This는 주어진 문장의 '지구 온난화'를 가리킴
(②) This is a worrisome / and potentially disastrous consequence / **if allowed to continue** / to an ecosystem-threatening level. //
접속사가 생략되지 않은 분사구문
이는 걱정스럽고 / 잠재적으로 파괴적인 결과다 / 만약 계속되도록 허용된다면 / 생태계를 위협하는 수준까지 //
(③) Now scientists have analyzed data / **indicating that** the amount of dissolved oxygen in the oceans **has been declining** / for more than a half century. //
현재분사(data 수식) 목적어절 접속사
현재완료 진행형
현재 과학자들은 데이터를 분석해 왔다 / 해양에서 용존 산소의 양이 감소해 왔다는 것을 보여 주는 / 반세기가 넘는 기간 동안 //

(④) The data show / **that** the ocean oxygen level **has been falling** more rapidly / than the corresponding rise in water temperature. //
목적어절 접속사 현재완료 진행형
이 데이터는 보여 준다 / 해양 산소 농도가 더 빠르게 감소해 오고 있음을 / 상응하는 수온 상승보다 //
(⑤) **Falling oxygen levels in water** have the potential / to impact the habitat of marine organisms worldwide /
동명사구 주어
감소하는 수중 산소 농도는 가능성을 갖고 있으며 / 세계적으로 해양 생물의 서식지에 영향을 끼칠 /
and in recent years this has led to more frequent anoxic events / **that** killed or displaced / populations of fish, crabs, and many other organisms. //
주격 관계대명사
최근에 이것은 더 빈번한 산소 결핍 사건을 초래해 왔다 / 죽이거나 쫓아낸 / 물고기, 게, 그리고 많은 다른 생물의 개체군을 //

- marine ⓐ 해양의 · self-evident ⓐ 자명한
- abundance ⓝ 풍부함 · breathe ⓥ 호흡하다
- established ⓐ 확립된 · polar ⓐ 극지의 · tropical ⓐ 열대의
- worrisome ⓐ 걱정스러운 · potentially ⓐⁿ 잠재적으로
- disastrous ⓐ 처참한 · consequence ⓝ 결과
- analyze ⓥ 분석하다 · potential ⓝ 잠재력
- organism ⓝ 생물(체) · displace ⓥ 쫓아내다

해수는 모든 해양 동물이 살아있기 위해 호흡하는 다량의 용존 산소를 포함한다. (①) 따뜻한 물이 보유하고 있는 것보다 차가운 물이 더 많은 용존 산소를 보유하고 있다는 사실은 물리학에서 오랫동안 확립되어 왔으며, 이는 열대 해양은 푸르고 맑고 생물이 상대적으로 적게 서식하는 반면 차가운 극지의 바다는 생명으로 가득한 하나의 이유이다. (② 따라서 지구 온난화가 해양 수온을 높임에 따라 용존 산소의 양이 감소할 것은 자명하다.) 만약 생태계를 위협하는 수준까지 계속되도록 허용된다면 이는 걱정스럽고 잠재적으로 파괴적인 결과다. (③) 현재 과학자들은 해양에서 용존 산소의 양이 반세기가 넘는 기간 동안 감소해 왔다는 것을 보여 주는 데이터를 분석해 왔다. (④) 이 데이터는 해양 산소 농도가 상응하는 수온 상승보다 더 빠르게 감소해 오고 있음을 보여 준다. (⑤) 감소하는 수중 산소 농도는 세계적으로 해양 생물의 서식지에 영향을 끼칠 가능성을 갖고 있으며 최근에 이것은 물고기, 게, 그리고 많은 다른 생물의 개체군을 죽이거나 쫓아낸 더 빈번한 산소 결핍 사건을 초래해 왔다.

| 문제 풀이 순서 | ★★★ [정답률 36%]

1st 주어진 문장을 해석하고, 연결어, 지시어 등을 확인한다.

> Thus, as global warming raises the temperature of marine waters, it is self-evident that the amount of dissolved oxygen will decrease.
> 따라서 지구 온난화가 해양 수온을 높임에 따라 용존 산소의 양이 감소할 것은 자명하다.

➡ 주어진 문장 앞: 결과를 나타내는 Thus가 있으므로, **단서** 온도와 용존 산소량의 관계가 앞에 언급될 것이다. **발상**
주어진 문장 뒤: 용존 산소량이 감소하는 현상을 부연 설명할 것이다.

2nd 각 선택지의 앞뒤 흐름이 매끄러운지 확인한다.
- ①의 앞 문장과 뒤 문장

앞 문장: 해수는 모든 해양 동물이 살아있기 위해 호흡하는 다량의 용존 산소를 포함한다.
뒤 문장: 따뜻한 물이 보유하고 있는 것보다 차가운 물이 더 많은 용존 산소를 보유하고 있다는 사실은 물리학에서 오랫동안 확립되어 왔으며, 이는 열대 해양은 푸르고 맑고 생물이 상대적으로 적게 서식하는 반면 차가운 극지의 바다는 생명으로 가득한 하나의 이유이다.

➡ 해수는 용존 산소를 포함한다는 사실을 소개한 뒤에, 수온과 용존 산소량의 관계에 대한 설명이 자연스럽게 이어진다. ▶ 주어진 문장이 ①에 들어갈 수 없음

②의 앞 문장과 뒤 문장

앞 문장: ①의 뒤 문장과 같음

뒤 문장: 만약 생태계를 위협하는 수준까지 계속되도록 허용한다면 이(This)는 걱정스럽고 잠재적으로 파괴적인 결과다.

➡ 걱정스럽고 파괴적인 결과를 낳은 This가 무엇인지 앞에 나와야 하는데, ①의 뒤 문장에는 생태계를 위협할 만한 현상이 언급되지 않았다. 해양 수온이 높아지면서 용존 산소량이 감소한다고 언급한 주어진 문장이 여기에 와야 한다.

▶ 주어진 문장이 ②에 들어가야 함

- **③의 앞 문장과 뒤 문장**

앞 문장: ②의 뒤 문장과 같음

뒤 문장: 현재 과학자들은 해양에서 용존 산소의 양이 반세기가 넘는 기간 동안 감소해 왔다는 것을 보여 주는 데이터를 분석해 왔다.

➡ 용존 산소량이 감소하는 현상이 파괴적인 결과이므로, 과학자들이 해양의 용존 산소량 감소에 관한 데이터를 분석했다는 내용은 자연스럽게 연결된다.

▶ 주어진 문장이 ③에 들어갈 수 없음

- **④의 앞 문장과 뒤 문장**

앞 문장: ③의 뒤 문장과 같음

뒤 문장: 이 데이터(The data)는 해양 산소 농도가 상응하는 수온 상승보다 더 빠르게 감소해 오고 있음을 보여 준다.

➡ 해양 용존 산소량이 감소해 왔다는 데이터를 부연 설명한다.

▶ 주어진 문장이 ④에 들어갈 수 없음

- **⑤의 앞 문장과 뒤 문장**

앞 문장: ④의 뒤 문장과 같음

뒤 문장: 감소하는 수중 산소 농도는 세계적으로 해양 생물의 서식지에 영향을 끼칠 가능성을 갖고 있으며 최근에 이것은 물고기, 게, 그리고 많은 다른 생물의 개체군을 죽이거나 쫓아낸 더 빈번한 산소 결핍 사건을 초래해 왔다.

➡ 해양 용존 산소량의 감소에 관한 데이터에 이어서, 이것이 생태계에 미치는 영향을 설명하므로 서로 자연스럽게 연결된다. ▶ 주어진 문장이 ⑤에 들어갈 수 없음

3rd 글이 한눈에 들어오도록 정리하여 정답을 확인한다.

해수는 모든 해양 동물이 살아가기 위해 호흡하는 다량의 용존 산소를 포함한다. (①) 해수에는 다량의 용존 산소가 있으며 수온이 낮을수록 용존 산소량이 많다. (② 따라서 지구 온난화는 용존 산소량을 감소시킨다.) 용존 산소량 감소가 위협적인 수준까지 계속되면 걱정스럽고 파괴적인 결과로 이어진다. (③) 현재 과학자들은 해양 용존 산소량이 감소해 왔다는 데이터를 분석해 왔다. (④) 이 데이터는 해양 산소 농도가 상응하는 수온 상승보다 더 빠르게 감소해 오고 있음을 보여 준다. (⑤) 감소하는 수중 산소 농도는 해양 생태계에 영향을 끼친다.

40 정답 ④ ＊불평등을 느끼는 Capuchin의 보상 거부

Capuchins / — New World Monkeys / **that** live in large social groups / — will, in captivity, trade with people all day long, / especially if food is involved. //
Capuchin은 / New World Monkey인 / 대규모의 사회 집단으로 서식하는 / 갇힌 상태에서 온종일 사람들과 거래를 할 것인데 / 특히 먹이가 연관된다면 (그러할 것이다) //

I give you this rock / and you *give me a treat* to eat. //
'내가 너에게 이 돌을 주고 / 너는 나에게 먹을 간식을 준다' //

If you **put** two monkeys in cages / next to each other, / and **offer** them both slices of cucumber / for the rocks they already have, / they will happily eat the cucumbers. //
만약 당신이 두 마리의 원숭이들을 우리에 넣고 / 나란히 있는 / 오이 조각을 둘 모두에게 주면 / 그들이 이미 가지고 있는 돌의 대가로 / 그들은 그 오이를 기쁘게 먹을 것이다 //

If, however, you give one monkey grapes instead / — **grapes** being universally preferred to cucumbers — / the monkey **that** is still receiving cucumbers / will begin to throw them back at the experimenter. // **단서 1** 한 원숭이에게만 포도를 주고 다른 원숭이에게는 오이를 주면, 오이를 받은 원숭이는 실험자에게 불만을 표함
하지만 만약 당신이 한 원숭이에게는 포도를 대신 준다면 / 일반적으로 포도는 오이보다 더 선호되는데 / 여전히 오이를 받은 원숭이는 / 그것들을 실험자에게 던지기 시작할 것이다 //

Even though she is still getting "paid" the same amount / for her effort of sourcing rocks, / and so her particular situation has not changed, / the comparison to another / makes the situation unfair. // **단서 2** 보상을 받는 상황은 바뀌지 않아도, 비교가 상황을 부당하게 만듦
비록 그녀가 같은 양을 여전히 '받고' / 돌을 모은 그녀의 수고에 대한 대가로 / 그래서 그녀의 특정한 상황이 변화가 없더라도 / 다른 원숭이와의 비교는 / 그 상황을 부당하게 만든다 //

Furthermore, / she is now willing to abandon all gains / — the cucumbers **themselves** — / to communicate her displeasure to the experimenter. // **단서 3** 원숭이는 불쾌함을 전달하기 위해 받은 보상을 기꺼이 포기함
게다가 / 그녀는 모든 얻은 것들을 이제 기꺼이 포기한다 / 즉, 오이 자체를 / 실험자에게 그녀의 불쾌함을 전달하기 위해 //

→ According to the passage, / if the Capuchin monkey realizes the (A) **inequality** / in rewards compared to another monkey, /
이 글에 따르면 / 만약 Capuchin 원숭이가 불평등을 알아차린다면 / 다른 원숭이와 비교하여 보상에서의 /

she will (B) **reject** her rewards / **to express** her feelings / about the treatment, / **despite** getting exactly the same rewards as before. //
그녀는 그녀의 보상을 거부할 것이다 / 그녀의 감정을 표현하기 위해 / 대우에 대한 / 이전과 정확히 똑같은 보상을 받더라도 //

- captivity ⓝ 감금 · trade ⓥ 거래하다 · cucumber ⓝ 오이
- universally 國 일반적으로 · experimenter ⓝ 실험자
- source ⓥ 모으다 · comparison ⓝ 비교 · abandon ⓥ 포기하다
- communicate ⓥ 전달하다 · displeasure ⓝ 불쾌함

대규모의 사회 집단으로 서식하는 New World Monkey인 Capuchin은 갇힌 상태에서 온종일 사람들과 거래를 할 것인데 특히 먹이가 연관된다면 그러할 것이다. '내가 너에게 이 돌을 주고 너는 나에게 먹을 간식을 준다.' 만약 당신이 두 마리의 원숭이들을 나란히 있는 우리에 넣고 그들이 이미 가지고 있는 돌의 대가로 오이 조각을 둘 모두에게 주었을 때 그들은 그 오이를 기쁘게 먹을 것이다. 하지만 만약 당신이 한 원숭이에게는 포도를 대신 준다면, 일반적으로 포도는 오이보다 더 선호되는데, 여전히 오이를 받은 원숭이는 그것들을 실험자에게 던지기 시작할 것이다. 비록 그녀가 돌을 모은 그녀의 수고에 대한 대가로 같은 양을 여전히 '받고', 그래서 그녀의 특정한 상황이 변화가 없더라도, 다른 원숭이와의 비교는 그 상황을 부당하게 만든다. 게다가, 그녀는 실험자에게 그녀의 불쾌함을 전달하기 위해 모든 얻은 것들, 즉, 오이 자체를 이제 기꺼이 포기한다.
→ 이 글에 따르면, 만약 Capuchin 원숭이가 다른 원숭이와 비교하여 보상에서의 (A) **불평등**을 알아차린다면, 그녀는 이전과 정확히 똑같은 보상을 받더라도 대우에 대한 그녀의 감정을 표현하기 위해 그녀의 보상을 (B) **거부**할 것이다.

다음 글의 내용을 한 문장으로 요약하고자 한다. 빈칸 (A), (B)에 들어갈 말로 가장 적절한 것은?

	(A)		(B)	
①	benefit 이익	—	protect 보호하다	다른 원숭이와 비교하여 보상의 이익을 알아차리는 내용이 아님
②	inequality 불평등	—	share 공유하다	보상을 공유한다는 언급은 없음
③	abundance 풍부함	—	yield 양보하다	다른 원숭이와 비교하여 보상의 풍부함을 알아차리는 내용이 아님
④	inequality 불평등	—	reject 거부하다	다른 원숭이와 비교하여 보상의 불평등을 알아차리면 불쾌함을 표현하기 위해 보상을 거부한다는 내용임
⑤	benefit 이익	—	display 보여주다	대우에 대한 감정을 표현하기 위해 보상을 보여준다는 내용이 아님

왜 정답 ? ★★☆ [정답률 60%]

(A):

- 하지만 만약 당신이 한 원숭이에게는 포도를 대신 준다면, 일반적으로 포도는 오이보다 더 선호되는데, 여전히 오이를 받은 원숭이는 그것들을 실험자에게 던지기 시작할 것이다. 단서 1
- 그래서 그녀의 특정한 상황이 변화가 없더라도, 다른 원숭이와의 비교는 그 상황을 부당하게 만든다. 단서 2

➡ 한 원숭이에게는 오이보다 더 선호되는 포도를, 다른 원숭이에게는 오이를 준다면, 다른 원숭이와 비교가 되는 부당한 상황이 만들어진다.

▶ 원숭이들의 보상이 '불평등한' 것이므로 (A)에는 ②, ④의 inequality가 들어가야 함

(B):

- 게다가, 그녀는 실험자에게 그녀의 불쾌함을 전달하기 위해 모든 얻은 것들, 즉, 오이 자체를 이제 기꺼이 포기한다. 단서 3

➡ 불평등한 상황임을 인지한 원숭이는 불쾌함을 표시하기 위해 보상 자체를 기꺼이 포기할, 즉, '거부할' 것이다.

▶ (B)에는 ④의 reject가 들어가는 것이 적절하므로 정답은 ④임

왜 오답 ?

① 다른 원숭이와 비교하여 보상에서의 이익을 알아차린다는 내용이 아니다.
② 원숭이들이 실험자로부터 보상을 받거나 이를 거부하는 것만 언급되었을 뿐, 보상을 공유하는 것은 언급되지 않았다.
③ 보상의 풍부함에 관한 내용이 아니다. (▶◀ 이유: 보상의 종류가 다르기 때문에 발생하는 불평등에 관한 내용이다.)
⑤ 원숭이들이 감정을 표현하기 위해 보상을 보여준다는 내용이 아니다.

＊ 글의 흐름

도입	Capuchin은 갇힌 상태에서는 (특히 먹이와 연관된) 거래를 계속할 것임
실험 ①	두 원숭이에게 거래의 보상으로 똑같이 오이를 준다면 만족하고 받을 것임
실험 ②	하지만 한 쪽에 오이보다 더 좋은 보상을 준다면 오이를 받은 원숭이는 불만을 표현할 것임
결론	보상을 받는 상황은 같아도 비교가 상황을 불평등하게 만들기 때문에 보상을 포기하면서까지 불쾌함을 표시할 것임

41~42 ＊고등 교육의 확대에 따른 평가 방식의 변화 ──

Higher education **has grown** / **from** an elite **to** a mass system / 현재완료(계속) from A to B: A에서 B로
across the world. // 41번 단서 1: 고등 교육이 엘리트에서 대중 체제로 변화함
고등 교육은 성장해 왔다 / 엘리트에서 대중 체제로 / 전 세계에 걸쳐 //

In Europe and the USA, / (a) underlined{increased} rates of participation
완전자동사
occurred / in the decades / after the Second World War. //
유럽과 미국에서는 / 증가된 참여율이 나타났다 / 수십 년 동안 / 2차 세계 대전 이후 //

Between 2000 and 2014, / rates of participation in higher
완전자동사
education almost **doubled** / from 19% to 34% across the world /
2000년과 2014년 사이에 / 고등 교육 참여율은 거의 두 배가 되었다 / 전 세계에 걸쳐
19%에서 34%로 /

among the members of the population / in the school-leaving
age category (typically 18–23). //
집단 구성원 사이에서의 / 졸업 연령 범주 (대체로 18세에서 23세) 내 //

The dramatic expansion of higher education / **has been marked** 현재완료 수동태
/ by a wider range of institutions of higher learning / and a more 병렬 구조
diverse demographic of students. //
고등 교육의 극적인 확대는 / 특징지어져 왔다 / 더 광범위한 고등 학습 기관과 / 더 다양한
학생 인구 집단으로 //
핵심 주어(복수)
Changes from an elite system to a mass higher education system
복수동사(수동태)
/ **are associated** with political needs / **to build** a (b) specialised
형용사적 용법(needs 수식)
workforce / for the economy. //
엘리트 체제에서 대중 고등 교육 체제로의 변화는 / 정치적 필요성과 관련이 있다 / 전문화된
노동력을 구축하려는 / 경제를 위한 //

In theory, / the expansion of higher education / **to develop** 부사적 용법(목적)
a highly skilled workforce / should diminish the role of
examinations / in the selection and control of students, /
이론적으로 / 고등 교육의 확대는 / 고도로 숙련된 노동력을 개발하기 위한 / 시험의 역할을
감소시킬 것이다 / 학생의 선발과 통제에 있어 / 41번 단서 2: 이론적으로는 고등 교육 확대가
시험의 역할을 감소시킬 것임
분사구문
initiating approaches to assessment / **which** (c) block(→ 주격 관계대명사
facilitate) lifelong learning: / assessment *for* learning and a focus
on feedback for development. // 42번 단서: 학습을 위한 평가와 발달을
위한 피드백은 평생학습을 가능하게 함
평가로의 접근 방법을 시작하면서 / 평생학습을 막는(→ 가능하게 하는) / 즉, 학습을 '위한'
평가와 발달을 위한 피드백에 집중을 (시작하면서) //

In reality, / socio-political changes / to expand higher education
/ have set up a 'field of contradictions' / for assessment in higher
education. // 41번 단서 3: 실제로는 고등 교육의 평가에 모순이 있음
실제로는 / 사회 정치적 변화는 / 고등 교육을 확대하기 위한 / '모순의 장'을 조성해 왔다 /
고등 교육에서의 평가에 있어 //

Mass higher education requires / efficient approaches to
assessment, / such as examinations and multiple-choice quizzes,
/ with minimalist, (d) impersonal, or standardised feedback, /
대중 고등 교육은 필요로 하며 / 평가로의 효율적인 접근 방법을 / 시험과 선다형 퀴즈와 같은 /
최소한이거나 비개인적이거나 표준화된 피드백을 갖춘 /
분사구문을 이끄는 현재분사   causing의 목적격 보어(to부정사)
often **causing** students **to focus** more on grades than feedback. //
이는 종종 학생이 피드백보다 성적에 더 집중하게 만든다 //
41번 단서 4: 대중 고등 교육은 학생들이 피드백보다 성적에 더 집중하게 함
In contrast, / the relatively small numbers of students / in
elite systems in the past / (e) allowed for closer relationships /
between students and their teachers, /
대조적으로 / 상대적으로 적은 학생의 수는 / 과거에 엘리트 체제의 / 더 긴밀한 관계를
허용했다 / 학생과 그들의 선생님 사이의 /
「with + 명사 + 현재분사」: ~이 …하면서
with formative feedback shaping / the minds, academic skills,
and even the characters of students. //
형성적 피드백이 형성하면서 / 학생의 마음, 학업 기술, 그리고 심지어 학생의 성격을 //

- participation ⓝ 참여 · decade ⓝ 10년
- typically ⓐᵈ 일반적으로 · dramatic ⓐ 극적인
- expansion ⓝ 확대 · range ⓝ 범주 · institution ⓝ 기관
- specialised ⓐ 전문화된 · workforce ⓝ 노동력
- diminish ⓥ 줄어들다 · initiate ⓥ 시작하다
- approach ⓝ 접근법 · development ⓝ 발달
- socio-political ⓐ 사회 정치적인 · contradiction ⓝ 모순
- assessment ⓝ 평가 · minimalist ⓐ 최소한의
- impersonal ⓐ 비개인적인 · standardised ⓐ 표준화된
- relatively ⓐᵈ 비교적으로 · character ⓝ 성격
- class ⓝ 계급 · status ⓝ 지위

고등 교육은 전 세계에 걸쳐 엘리트에서 대중 체제로 성장해 왔다. 유럽과 미국에서는 2차 세계 대전 이후 수십 년 동안 (a) 증가된 참여율이 나타났다. 2000년과 2014년 사이에 졸업 연령 범주 (대체로 18세에서 23세) 내 집단 구성원 사이에서의 고등 교육 참여율은 전 세계에 걸쳐 19%에서 34%로 거의 두 배가 되었다. 고등 교육의 극적인 확대는 더 광범위한 고등 학습 기관과 더 다양한 학생 인구 집단으로 특징지어져 왔다.

엘리트 체제에서 대중 고등 교육 체제로의 변화는 경제를 위한 (b) 전문화된 노동력을 구축하려는 정치적 필요성과 관련이 있다. 이론적으로, 고도로 숙련된 노동력을 개발하기 위한 고등 교육의 확대는 평생학습을 (c) 막는(→ 가능하게 하는) 평가로의 접근 방법, 즉, 학습을 '위한' 평가와 발달을 위한 피드백에 집중을 시작하면서, 학생의 선발과 통제에 있어 시험의 역할을 감소시킬 것이다. 실제로는 고등 교육을 확대하기 위한 사회 정치적 변화는 고등 교육에서의 평가에 있어 '모순의 장'을 조성해 왔다. 대중 고등 교육은 최소한이거나 (d) 비개인적이거나 표준화된 피드백을 갖춘, 시험과 선다형 퀴즈와 같은, 평가로의 효율적인 접근 방법을 필요로 하며, 이는 종종 학생이 피드백보다 성적에 더 집중하게 만든다. 대조적으로, 과거에 엘리트 체제의 상대적으로 적은 학생의 수는 형성적 피드백이 학생의 마음, 학업 기술, 그리고 심지어 학생의 성격을 형성하면서, 학생과 그들의 선생님 사이의 더 긴밀한 관계를 (e) 허용했다.

41 정답 ③

윗글의 제목으로 가장 적절한 것은?

① Is It Possible to Teach Without Assessment?
평가 없는 교육이 가능할까? · 평가 없는 교육에 대한 언급은 없음
② Elite vs. Public: A History of Modern Class Society
엘리트 대 대중: 현대 계급 사회의 역사 · 계급 사회에 관한 내용이 아님
③ Mass Higher Education and Its Reality in Assessment
대중 고등 교육과 그 평가의 현실 · 고등 교육의 대중화에 따른 평가의 현실에 관한 내용임
④ Impacts of Mass Higher Education on Teachers' Status
대중 고등 교육이 교사의 지위에 미치는 영향 · 교사의 지위에 대한 언급은 없음
⑤ Mass Higher Education Leads to Economic Development
대중 고등 교육이 경제 발전으로 이어진다 · 경제 발전은 글의 핵심 내용이 아님

왜 정답? ★★❋ [정답률 64%]

- 고등 교육은 전 세계에 걸쳐 엘리트에서 대중 체제로 성장해 왔다. **41번 단서 1**
- 이론적으로, 고등 교육의 확대는 학생의 선발과 통제에 있어 시험의 역할을 감소시킬 것이다. **41번 단서 2**
- 실제로는 고등 교육을 확대하기 위한 사회 정치적 변화는 고등 교육에서의 평가에 있어 '모순의 장'을 조성해 왔다. **41번 단서 3**
- 대중 고등 교육은 학생들이 피드백보다 성적에 집중하게 한다. **41번 단서 4**

➡ 고등 교육은 대중 체제로 성장해 왔는데, 이론적으로는 대중 고등 교육의 확대가 평가를 위한 시험의 역할을 감소시켰어야 했다. 하지만 실제로는 고등 교육이 확대되면서 학생들이 피드백보다 성적에 집중하게 되는 모순이 발생했다.
▶ 따라서 제목으로 적절한 것은 ③ '대중 고등 교육과 그 평가의 현실'이다.

왜 오답?

① 평가 없는 교육은 언급되지 않았다.
② 고등 교육이 엘리트 중심에서 대중 체제로 성장해 왔다는 것일 뿐, 계급 사회의 역사에 관한 내용이 아니다.
④ 마지막 문장에서 학생과 교사의 관계가 언급되지만, 교사의 지위는 언급되지 않았다.
⑤ 대중 고등 교육 체제로의 변화가 경제를 위한 것은 맞지만, 글의 핵심 내용은 대중 고등 교육 체제로 변화하면서 고등 교육의 평가에 모순이 발생했다는 것이다.

> 꿀팁 글의 내용과 일치하더라도 핵심 주제가 맞는지 다시 한번 확인하기!

42 정답 ③

밑줄 친 (a)~(e) 중에서 문맥상 낱말의 쓰임이 적절하지 않은 것은?

[3점]

① (a) 고등 교육이 점차 대중 체제로 확대됨
증가된
② (b) 대중 고등 교육 체제로의 변화는 전문화된 노동력을 구축하려는 것임
전문화된
③ (c) 발달을 위한 피드백과 배움을 위한 평가는 평생학습을 촉진함
막는
④ (d) 개별화되지 않고 최소한이고 표준화된 피드백은 비개인적이라 할 수 있음
비개인적인
⑤ (e) 학생의 마음, 학습 기술, 성격을 형성하는 형성적 피드백은 사제간 더 가까운 관계를 가능하게 함
허용했다

왜 정답? ★★★ [정답률 41%]

③ (c) block 막는

┌ 이론적으로, 고도로 숙련된 노동력을 개발하기 위한 고등 교육의 확대는 평생학습을 (c) ~~block~~(가능하게 하는) 평가로의 접근 방법, 즉, 학습을 '위한' 평가와 발달을 위한 피드백에 집중을 시작하면서, 학생의 선발과 통제에 있어 시험의 역할을 감소시킬 것이다.

➡ '학습을 위한 평가'와 '발달을 위한 피드백'을 평가로의 접근 방법이라고 언급했는데, 이들은 모두 평생학습을 '막는' 것이 아니라 '가능하게 하는' 방법이다.
▶ block을 facilitate(가능하게 하는)와 같은 반의어로 바꿔야 함

왜 오답?

① (a) increased 증가된

┌ 고등 교육은 전 세계에 걸쳐 엘리트에서 대중 체제로 성장해 왔다. 유럽과 미국에서는 2차 세계 대전 이후 수십 년 동안 (a) 증가된 참여율이 나타났다.

➡ 고등 교육이 엘리트에서 대중 체제로 성장해 왔다는 것은 더 많은 사람들이 고등 교육에 참여했다는 것이므로, (고등 교육의) '증가된' 참여율이 나타났다는 것은 적절하다.
▶ increased는 문맥에 맞음

② (b) specialised 전문화된

┌ 엘리트 체제에서 대중 고등 교육 체제로의 변화는 경제를 위한 (b) 전문화된 노동력을 구축하려는 정치적 필요성과 관련이 있다. 이론적으로, 고도로 숙련된 노동력을 개발하기 위한 고등 교육의 확대는 ~

➡ 바로 뒤 문장에 고도로 숙련된 인력을 개발하기 위한 고등 교육의 확대가 언급된다. 따라서 대중 고등 교육 체제로의 변화는 경제를 위해 '전문화된' 노동력을 구축하려는 것이다. ▶ specialised는 문맥에 맞음

④ (d) impersonal 비개인적인

┌ 대중 고등 교육은 최소한이거나 (d) 비개인적이거나 표준화된 피드백을 갖춘, 시험과 선다형 퀴즈와 같은, 평가로의 효율적인 접근 방법을 필요로 하며, 이는 종종 학생이 피드백보다 성적에 더 집중하게 만든다.

➡ 효율에 초점이 맞춰진 선다형 퀴즈, 즉, 최소한이고 표준화된 피드백을 제공하는 평가는 학생 개인에게 맞춰진 피드백을 제공하지 않으므로 '비개인적'이다.
▶ impersonal은 문맥에 맞음

⑤ (e) allowed 허용했다

┌ 대조적으로, 과거에 엘리트 체제의 상대적으로 적은 학생의 수는 형성적 피드백이 학생의 마음, 학업 기술, 그리고 심지어 학생의 성격을 형성하면서, 학생과 그들의 선생님 사이의 더 긴밀한 관계를 (e) 허용했다.

➡ 과거의 엘리트 체제에서는 학생의 수가 적어서 선생님이 학생들을 개별적으로 평가할 수 있었을 것이다. 그렇기에 형성적 피드백이 가능했으므로, 학생과 선생님 사이의 더 긴밀한 관계를 '허용했다'는 것은 적절하다. ▶ allowed는 문맥에 맞음

43 ~ 45 ＊부자의 결혼식에 초대받은 시인의 일침

(A) Once upon a time / in the Iranian city of Shiraz, / there lived the famous poet Sheikh Saadi. //
옛날 옛적에 / 이란의 도시 Shiraz에 / 유명한 시인 Sheikh Saadi가 살았다 //

lead a life: 생활을 하다
Like most other poets and philosophers, / he led a very simple life. //
대부분의 다른 시인들과 철학자들처럼 / 그는 매우 검소한 생활을 했다 //

A rich merchant of Shiraz / was preparing for his daughter's wedding / and invited (a) him / along with a lot of big businessmen of the town. //
병렬 구조(동사) / = the poet
Shiraz의 부유한 상인은 / 그의 딸의 결혼식을 준비하고 있었고 / 그를 초대했다 / 그 마을의 많은 큰 사업가들과 함께 //

The poet accepted the invitation / and decided to attend. //
43번 단서 1, 45번 ① 시인은 상인의 결혼식 초대를 수락했음
그 시인은 초대를 수락했고 / 참석하기로 결정했다 //

*(A) 문단 요약: 검소한 삶을 사는 유명한 시인 Sheikh Saadi는 부유한 상인의 딸의 결혼식에 초대받아 참석하기로 결정함

(B) The host personally led the poet to his seat / and served out chicken soup to him. //
혼주는 직접 시인을 그의 자리로 안내했고 / 그에게 닭고기 수프를 내주었다 //

After a moment, / the poet suddenly dipped the corner of his coat in the soup / as if he fed it. //
as if 가정법 과거   45번 ② 시인은 외투 자락을 수프에 담갔음
잠시 후에 / 시인은 갑자기 그의 외투 자락을 수프에 담갔다 / 마치 음식을 먹이듯 //

all + 복수 명사 + 복수 동사   = the poet
All the guests were now staring at (b) him in surprise. //
모든 손님이 바로 그를 놀라서 바라보고 있었다 //

The host said, / "Sir, what are you doing?" //
혼주가 말했다 / "선생님, 뭐 하는 겁니까" //

'~이므로'
The poet very calmly replied, / "Now that I have put on expensive clothes, / I see a world of difference here. //
시인은 매우 침착하게 대답했다 / "내가 비싼 옷을 입으니 / 이곳에서 엄청난 차이를 봅니다 //

All that I can say now / is that this feast is meant for my clothes, / not for me." //
내가 지금 할 수 있는 모든 말은 / 이 진수성찬이 내 옷을 위한 것이라는 것뿐입니다 / 나를 위한 것이 아니라" //

*(B) 문단 요약: 시인은 외투 자락을 수프에 담갔고, 왜 그러냐는 질문에 진수성찬이 옷을 위한 것일 뿐, 자신을 위한 것이 아니라고 했음

분사구문
(C) Seeing all this, / the poet quietly left the party / and went to a shop where he could rent clothes. //
43번 단서 2, 45번 ③ 시인은 파티를 떠나 옷을 빌릴 수 있는 가게로 감
이 모든 것을 보고 / 시인은 조용히 파티를 떠나 / 옷을 빌릴 수 있는 가게로 갔다 //

계속적 용법의 주격 관계대명사
There he chose a richly decorated coat, / which made him look like a new person. //
made의 목적격 보어(원형부정사)
그곳에서 그는 화려하게 장식된 외투를 골랐고 / 그것은 그를 새로운 사람처럼 보이게 만들었다 //

With this coat, / he entered the party / and this time was welcomed with open arms. //
43번 단서 3: 화려한 외투를 입고 파티에 가니 환영을 받음
이 외투를 입고 / 그는 파티에 들어갔고 / 이번에는 두 팔 벌려 환영을 받았다 //

The host embraced him / as (c) he would do to an old friend / and complimented him / on the clothes he was wearing. //
= the host   앞에 목적격 관계대명사가 생략됨
혼주는 그를 껴안았고 / 그가 오랜 친구에게 하듯이 / 그에게 칭찬했다 / 그가 입고 있는 옷에 대해 //

allowed의 목적격 보어(to부정사)
The poet did not say a word / and allowed the host to lead (d) him to the dining room. //
= the poet
시인은 한마디도 하지 않고 / 혼주가 그를 식당으로 안내하도록 허락했다 //

*(C) 문단 요약: 시인은 파티를 떠난 뒤에 화려한 옷을 빌려 입고 다시 파티에 가는데, 이번에는 환영받았음

43번 단서 4, 45번 ④ 결혼식 날에 부유한 상인은 입구에서 손님을 맞이하고 있었음
동격
(D) On the day of the wedding, / the rich merchant, the host of the wedding, / was receiving the guests at the gate. //
결혼식 날 / 결혼식의 혼주인 부유한 상인은 / 입구에서 손님을 맞이하고 있었다 //

Many rich people of the town attended the wedding. //
마을의 많은 부유한 사람들이 결혼식에 참석했다 //
= Many rich people   45번 ⑥ 마을의 많은 부유한 사람들이 결혼식에 참석함
They had come out / in their best clothes. //
그들은 나왔다 / 자신의 가장 좋은 옷차림으로 //

「neither A nor B」: A도 B도 아닌
The poet wore simple clothes / which were neither grand nor expensive. //
주격 관계대명사
시인은 소박한 옷을 입었다 / 거창하지도 비싸지도 않은 //

He waited for someone to approach him / but no one gave (e) him as much as even a second glance. //
= the poet   43번 단서 5: 소박한 옷을 입고 간 시인에게 아무도 눈길을 주지 않음
그는 누군가가 자신에게 다가오기를 기다렸지만 / 아무도 그에게 단 일 초의 눈길도 주지 않았다 //

Even the host did not greet him / and looked away. //
혼주조차도 그에게 인사하지 않고 / 눈길을 돌렸다 //

*(D) 문단 요약: 결혼식 날에 시인은 소박한 옷을 입고 갔는데, 혼주를 포함하여 아무도 눈길을 주지 않았음

- philosopher ⓝ 철학자 · merchant ⓝ 상인
- businessman ⓝ 사업가 · attend ⓥ 참석하다
- personally 〔ad〕 직접 · dip ⓥ 담그다 · stare at ~을 바라보다
- a world of 막대한, 엄청난 · rent ⓥ 대여하다 · embrace ⓥ 껴안다
- compliment ⓥ 칭찬하다 · grand ⓐ 거창한, 웅장한
- approach ⓥ 접근하다 · glance ⓝ 눈길 · greet ⓥ 맞이하다

(A) 옛날 옛적에 이란의 도시 Shiraz에 유명한 시인 Sheikh Saadi가 살았다. 대부분의 다른 시인들과 철학자들처럼 그는 매우 검소한 생활을 했다. Shiraz의 부유한 상인은 그의 딸의 결혼식을 준비하고 있었고 (a) 그를 그 마을의 많은 큰 사업가들과 함께 초대했다. 그 시인은 초대를 수락했고 참석하기로 결정했다.
(D) 결혼식 날, 결혼식의 혼주인 부유한 상인은 입구에서 손님을 맞이하고 있었다. 마을의 많은 부유한 사람들이 결혼식에 참석했다. 그들은 자신의 가장 좋은 옷차림으로 나왔다. 시인은 거창하지도 비싸지도 않은 소박한 옷을 입었다. 그는 누군가가 자신에게 다가오기를 기다렸지만 아무도 (e) 그에게 단 일 초의 눈길도 주지 않았다. 혼주조차도 그에게 인사하지 않고 눈길을 돌렸다.
(C) 이 모든 것을 보고 시인은 조용히 파티를 떠나 그가 옷을 빌릴 수 있는 가게로 갔다. 그곳에서 그는 화려하게 장식된 외투를 골랐고, 그것은 그를 새로운 사람처럼 보이게 만들었다. 이 외투를 입고, 그는 파티에 들어갔고 이번에는 두 팔 벌려 환영을 받았다. 혼주는 (c) 그가 오랜 친구에게 하듯이 그를 껴안았고, 그가 입고 있는 옷에 대해 그에게 칭찬했다. 시인은 한마디도 하지 않고 혼주가 (d) 그를 식당으로 안내하도록 허락했다.
(B) 혼주는 직접 시인을 그의 자리로 안내했고 그에게 닭고기 수프를 내주었다. 잠시 후에 시인은 마치 음식을 먹이듯 그의 외투 자락을 수프에 갑자기 담갔다. 모든 손님이 바로 (b) 그를 놀라서 바라보고 있었다. 혼주가 말했다. "선생님, 뭐 하는 겁니까?" 시인은 매우 침착하게 대답했다. "내가 비싼 옷을 입으니, 이곳에서 엄청난 차이를 봅니다. 내가 지금 할 수 있는 모든 말은 이 진수성찬이 내 옷을 위한 것이지, 나를 위한 것이 아니라는 것뿐입니다."

43 정답 ⑤

주어진 글 (A)에 이어질 내용을 순서에 맞게 배열한 것으로 가장 적절한 것은?
① (B) — (D) — (C) 혼주가 시인을 자리로 안내했다는 (B)보다 혼주가 결혼식장 입구에서 손님을 맞이했다는 (D)가 먼저 와야 함
② (C) — (B) — (D) 결혼식에 참석하기로 결정했다는 (A) 바로 뒤에 파티를 떠났다는 (C)가 오는 것은 어색함
③ (C) — (D) — (B)
④ (D) — (B) — (C) 혼주가 눈길조차 주지 않았다는 (D) 뒤에 혼주가 직접 시인을 자리로 안내했다는 (B)가 오는 것은 어색함
⑤ (D) — (C) — (B) (D) 시인은 소박한 옷을 입고 갔더니 모두가 무시함 — (C) 화려한 옷을 입고 다시 파티에 갔더니 환영받음 — (B) 시인은 외투 자락을 수프에 담갔고, 진수성찬이 옷을 위한 것일 뿐이며 자신을 위한 것이 아니라고 말함

왜 정답·오답? ✱✱✱ [정답률 69%]

[(A): 검소한 삶을 사는 Sheikh Saadi라는 유명한 시인은 부유한 상인의 딸의 결혼식에 초대받아 참석하기로 결정했다.

➡ 앞으로 결혼식에서 어떤 일이 생겼는지를 확인해야 한다.

[(B): 자리로 안내받고 치킨 수프를 대접받은 시인은 외투 자락을 수프에 담갔고, 왜 그러냐는 질문에 진수성찬이 옷을 위한 것일 뿐, 자신을 위한 것이 아니라고 했다.

➡ 결혼식장에 들어갔다는 내용이 앞에 있어야 하고, 시인이 옷을 위한 것일 뿐인 결혼식에 일침을 가하며 글이 마무리된다.

[(C): 시인은 파티를 떠난 뒤에 화려한 옷을 빌려 입고 다시 파티에 갔는데, 이번에는 환영받았다.

➡ 파티를 떠났다는 내용이 있으므로 파티(결혼식)에 참석했다는 내용이 앞에 있어야 한다.

[(D): 결혼식 날에 시인은 소박한 옷을 입고 갔는데, 혼주를 포함하여 아무도 눈길을 주지 않았다.

➡ 결혼식 당일 시인이 소박한 옷을 입고 갔을 때 겪은 일이므로 (A) 다음에 오는 내용이고, 뒤에는 파티를 떠났다는 내용이 이어져야 한다.

▶ (A) Sheikh Saadi라는 유명한 시인이 부유한 상인의 딸의 결혼식에 초대받고 그곳에 가기로 결정함 → (D) 결혼식에 소박한 옷을 입고 가자, 혼주를 포함한 모두가 무시함 → (C) 시인은 파티를 떠나 화려한 옷을 빌려 입고 다시 파티에 갔는데, 이번에는 환영받음 → (B) 시인은 외투 자락을 수프에 담갔고, 왜 그러냐는 물음에 진수성찬이 옷을 위한 것이지, 나를 위한 것은 아니라고 말했음
▶ 글의 순서는 ⑤ (D) — (C) — (B)임

44 정답 ③

밑줄 친 (a)~(e) 중에서 가리키는 대상이 나머지 넷과 다른 것은?
① (a)   ② (b)   ③(c)   ④ (d)   ⑤ (e)
= the poet = the poet = the host = the poet = the poet

>왜 정답? ✽✽✽ [정답률 72%]
③ (c) he: 오랜 친구에게 하듯 시인을 껴안은 사람 ▶ the host

>왜 오답?
① (a) him: 상인이 자신의 딸의 결혼식에 초대한 사람 ▶ the poet
② (b) him: 모든 손님이 놀라서 바라본 사람 ▶ the poet
④ (d) him: 혼주가 식당으로 안내한 사람 ▶ the poet
⑤ (e) him: 소박한 옷을 입고 가서 누구의 시선도 받지 못한 사람 ▶ the poet

45 정답 ②

윗글에 관한 내용으로 적절하지 않은 것은?
① 시인은 상인의 초대를 받아들였다. The poet accepted the invitation
② 상인은 시인의 외투 자락을 수프에 담갔다.
the poet suddenly dipped the corner of his coat in the soup
③ 시인은 옷을 빌릴 수 있는 가게로 갔다.
the poet quietly left the party and went to a shop where he could rent clothes
④ 결혼식 날 상인은 입구에서 손님을 맞이했다. On the day of the wedding,
the rich merchant, the host of the wedding, was receiving the guests at the gate.
⑤ 마을의 많은 부유한 사람들이 결혼식에 참석했다.
Many rich people of the town attended the wedding.

>왜 정답? ✽✽✽ [정답률 76%]
시인이 스스로 자신의 외투 자락을 수프에 담근 것이므로 (the poet suddenly dipped the corner of his coat in the soup) 상인이 시인의 외투 자락을 수프에 담갔다는 ②은 적절하지 않다.

>왜 오답?
① 시인은 상인의 초대를 받아들였다. (The poet accepted the invitation)
③ 시인은 옷을 빌릴 수 있는 가게로 갔다. (the poet quietly left the party and went to a shop where he could rent clothes)
④ 결혼식 날 상인은 입구에서 손님을 맞이했다. (On the day of the wedding, the rich merchant, the host of the wedding, was receiving the guests at the gate.)
⑤ 마을의 많은 부유한 사람들이 결혼식에 참석했다. (Many rich people of the town attended the wedding.)

8회 Dictation 문제 p. 152

01 have an announcement / smooth transportation / extending the operational hours / take advantage of
02 Even though / I guess I don't get / for a few hours / used to spending time
03 relieve your stress / consider exploring activities / rather than playing / Tune in
04 quality is excellent / to give recording directions / the rug under the chair / music truly comes alive
05 Why don't we go over / working on the booth setup / deal with it / serve the guests with reusable dishes
06 recommend one / comes in two sizes / might go well / Can I use this discount coupon
07 a perfect time for climbing / can make it then / competition you mentioned before / made it through
08 take a look at this / it's held at 8 a.m. / fill out an application form / for the registration
09 from the student council / delicious journey around the world / menus for vegetarians / a celebration of culture and diversity
10 show the temperature / differs by model / there's a new function / I'd love to have it
11 catch a cold / keep some moisture / relate to a cold
12 is full of books / throwing away the books / too good condition
13 motivated and working hard / focusing on gathering data / sure who does what / lead to overlapping tasks
14 get in better shape / tough / working out a lot / Kind of / that's enough to get
15 Upon receiving / to build the desk / complicated / good at assembling
[16~17] properly wash natural material clothes / avoid shrinking or wrinkling / linen is a sensitive material / as little as possible

8회 어휘 Review Test 문제 p. 156

01 시작하다
02 주름이 생기다
03 겹치다
04 절차
05 교통
06 impact
07 moisture
08 metaphor
09 significantly
10 shrink
11 take advantage of
12 stare at
13 be in one's presence
14 end up with
15 be aware of
16 organizational
17 assistive
18 evolutionary
19 breathe
20 overshadowed
21 demographic
22 restoration
23 impersonal
24 nonfunctional
25 mechanistic
26 sensitive
27 psychic
28 codes
29 respectively
30 complimented
31 enlightenment
32 hypotheses
33 unfamiliarity
34 contradiction
35 embraced
36 force
37 facilitate
38 tendency
39 energized
40 displaced

01 정답 ⑤ *콘서트 장소 변경 공지

M : Attention, Fargo High School students.
남 : 주목해 주세요, Fargo 고등학교 학생 여러분.

This is your music teacher, Mr. Nelson.
저는 여러분의 음악 교사 Nelson입니다.

Our school rock band **was supposed to** hold its concert in the auditorium today.
'~하기로 되어 있다'
우리 학교 록 밴드는 오늘 강당에서 콘서트를 열기로 했습니다.

I'm sure you've been looking forward to the concert.
저는 여러분이 그 콘서트를 고대해 왔음을 확신합니다.

Unfortunately, the rain yesterday caused a leak in the ceiling of the auditorium.
불행히도, 어제 온 비가 강당의 천장에 누수를 야기했습니다.

The ceiling needs to be fixed, **so** we decided to change the 등위접속사
location of the concert. 단서 1 천장 수리로 인해 콘서트 장소가 변경됨
천장이 수리되어야 해서, 우리는 콘서트 장소를 변경하기로 결정했습니다.

The rock band will now perform in the school theater.
록 밴드는 이제 학교 극장에서 공연할 예정입니다.

The time for the concert **hasn't changed**. 현재완료(완료)
콘서트의 시간은 변경되지 않았습니다. 단서 2 콘서트는 학교 극장에서 열릴 예정임

I hope you'll enjoy the performance.
저는 여러분이 공연을 즐기기를 바랍니다.

- hold ⓥ 열다, 개최하다 • auditorium ⓝ 강당
- look forward to ~을 고대하다 • leak ⓝ 누수, 새는 곳
- ceiling ⓝ 천장 • perform ⓥ 공연하다 • theater ⓝ 극장

다음을 듣고, 남자가 하는 말의 목적으로 가장 적절한 것을 고르시오.
① 강당의 천장 수리 기간을 공지하려고 수리 기간은 언급하지 않음
② 콘서트 관람 규칙 준수를 요청하려고 콘서트 관람 규칙은 언급하지 않음
③ 학교 축제에서 공연할 동아리를 모집하려고 동아리를 모집하는 것이 아님
④ 폭우에 대비한 교실 시설 관리를 당부하려고 시설 관리를 당부한 것이 아님
⑤ 학교 록 밴드 공연의 장소 변경을 안내하려고 폭우로 인해 공연 장소가 변경되었음

>왜 정답? ✿✿✿ [정답률 94%]
학교 록 밴드 공연 장소였던 강당이 천장 누수로 수리가 필요해, 콘서트 장소를 학교 극장으로 변경한다고 공지하고 있으므로 정답은 ⑤이다.

>왜 오답?
① 강당의 천장을 수리하는 것은 맞지만, 수리 기간을 공지하는 것은 아니다. 함정
② 콘서트 관람 규칙 준수를 당부하는 것이 아니다.
③ 학교 축제에서 공연할 동아리를 모집하는 것이 아니다.
④ 폭우에 대비한 시설 관리를 당부하는 것이 아니다.

02 정답 ① *슬리퍼를 신고 달리려는 Simon

W : Simon, are you doing anything after school?
여 : Simon, 너 방과 후에 뭐 해?
-thing으로 끝나는 대명사는 형용사가 뒤에서 수식함
M : **Nothing special**. What about you?
남 : 딱히 없어. 너는?

W : I'm planning to go for a run in the park. It's a five-kilometer route.
여 : 나는 공원에 달리기를 하러 갈 예정이야. 5킬로미터 길이야.

M : The weather is perfect for running. Can I go with you?
남 : 달리기 하기에 완벽한 날씨네. 나도 너와 같이 가도 돼?

W : Why not? [Pause] Wait! You're wearing slippers. Those aren't good for running.
여 : 왜 안 되겠어? [잠시 후] 잠깐! 너 슬리퍼 신고 있잖아. 그건 달리기에 좋지 않아.

M : It's okay. I can run in slippers.
남 : 괜찮아. 나 슬리퍼 신고 뛸 수 있어.

W : No way. Slippers **aren't designed** for running. You can get 수동태 동사
hurt if you run in them. 단서 1 슬리퍼를 신고 달리면 다칠 수 있다고 함
여 : 안 돼. 슬리퍼는 달리기를 위해 만들어진 게 아니야. 넌 그거 신고 달리다가 다칠 수 있어.

뒤에 목적어절 접속사 that이 생략됨
M : You **mean** I need to put on running shoes?
남 : 내가 러닝화를 신어야 한다는 말이니?

W : You got it. You need to wear the right shoes for running.
여 : 그래. 넌 달리기에 맞는 신발을 신어야 해. 단서 2 달리기에 맞는 신발을 신으라고 함

M : All right. I'll go home and change.
남 : 알았어. 나는 집에 가서 갈아 신을게.

- route ⓝ 길, 경로 • design ⓥ 만들다, 설계하다

대화를 듣고, 여자의 의견으로 가장 적절한 것을 고르시오.
① 달리기를 할 때 적합한 신발을 신어야 한다. 달리기에 맞는 신발을 신으라고 함
② 운동을 한 후에 충분한 물을 섭취해야 한다. 물을 많이 마시라고는 하지 않음
③ 야외 활동 전에 일기예보를 확인하는 것이 좋다. 일기예보를 확인하라고 하지 않음
④ 달리기 전 스트레칭은 통증과 부상을 예방해 준다. 스트레칭의 효과에 대한 언급은 없음
⑤ 초보자의 경우 달리는 거리를 점진적으로 늘려야 한다. 초보자의 달리기 거리에 대한 내용이 아님

>왜 정답? ✿✿✿ [정답률 98%]
여자와 함께 공원을 달리기로 한 남자가 슬리퍼를 신고 간다고 하자, 여자는 슬리퍼를 신고 달리면 다칠 수 있다고 하면서 맞는 신발을 신으라고 했으므로 정답은 ①이다.

>왜 오답?
② 달리기 후에 충분한 물을 섭취하라고 한 것이 아니다.
③ 달리기 전에 일기예보를 확인하라고 한 것이 아니다.
④ 슬리퍼를 신고 달리면 다칠 수 있다고 했지, 스트레칭을 하라고 한 것이 아니다.
⑤ 남자가 초보자인지 알 수 없고, 달리는 거리를 조금씩 늘리라고도 하지 않았다.

03 정답 ③ *Clapton 씨와의 인터뷰

M : Good morning, Ms. Clapton. It's nice to meet you.
남 : 안녕하세요, Clapton 씨. 만나서 반갑습니다.

W : Nice to meet you, too. I'm a fan of your articles.
여 : 저도 만나서 반갑습니다. 저는 당신이 쓴 기사들을 매우 좋아해요.

M : You won many awards at the film festival this year. Congratulations!
남 : 올해 영화제에서 많은 상을 받으셨죠. 축하드립니다!

W : Thank you. I was lucky to work with a great director and talented actors.
여 : 감사합니다. 훌륭한 감독님과 뛰어난 배우분들과 함께 작업할 수 있어서 행운이었어요.

M : The clothes and accessories in the movie are impressive.
How do you start your costume designs? 단서 1 여자는 의상을 디자인하는 사람임
남 : 영화 속 의상과 액세서리들이 인상적입니다. 의상 디자인을 어떻게 시작하시나요?

부사적 용법(목적)
W : I read the script **to fully understand** the characters. Then I research the characters' backgrounds.
여 : 저는 인물을 완전히 이해하기 위해 대본을 읽습니다. 그리고 인물들의 배경을 조사합니다.

M : That sounds like a lot of work. Which of the costumes from this film is your favorite?
남 : 작업량이 많을 것 같아요. 이번 영화의 의상 중 어느 것을 가장 좋아하시나요?

가주어 진주어 부사절 접속사(이유)
W : **It's** hard **to pick** just one **because** I love all of my designs.
여 : 모든 의상이 마음에 들어서 딱 하나만 고르기가 어렵네요.

M : I totally understand. Thank you for sharing your story with the readers of our magazine. 단서2 남자는 잡지사의 기자임

남 : 전적으로 이해합니다. 우리 잡지의 독자들에게 당신의 이야기를 들려주셔서 감사합니다.

W : It was my pleasure.

여 : 저도 즐거웠습니다.

• article ⓝ (신문·잡지의) 기사　• award ⓝ 상　• talented ⓐ 뛰어난
• impressive ⓐ 인상적인　• costume ⓝ 의상　• script ⓝ 대본
• background ⓝ 배경

대화를 듣고, 두 사람의 관계를 가장 잘 나타낸 것을 고르시오.

① 관객 – 영화감독 관객이 영화감독을 인터뷰하는 것이 아님
② 연극 배우 – 시나리오 작가 연극이 아니라 영화와 관련된 대화임
③ 잡지 기자 – 의상 디자이너 잡지 기자가 의상 디자이너를 인터뷰하고 있음
④ 토크쇼 진행자 – 영화 평론가 토크쇼에 나간 상황이 아님
⑤ 배우 지망생 – 연기 학원 강사 연기를 배우거나 가르치는 것이 아님

＞왜 정답 ? ✿✿✿ [정답률 92%]

잡지 기자인 남자가 영화제에서 수상한 의상 디자이너인 여자에게 여러 가지 질문을 하고, 여자는 이에 답을 해주고 있는 상황이므로 두 사람의 관계를 가장 잘 나타낸 것은 ③이다.

＞왜 오답 ?

① 영화에 관한 대화는 맞지만, 관객과 영화감독이 나누는 대화가 아니다.
(↪ 이유: 영화감독이라면 의상 디자인에 대해서만 말하지 않았을 것이다.)
② 연극과 관련된 상황은 언급되지 않았다.
④ 영화 평론가가 토크쇼에 나간 상황이 아니다.
⑤ 연기를 배우거나 가르치는 상황이 아니다.

---

04 정답 ⑤ ＊열람실 살펴보기

W : Come look at the new reading room in the library.

여 : 와서 도서관의 새로운 열람실을 봐봐.

M : Wow! It's much better than I thought. 비교급 강조 부사

남 : 우아! 내가 생각했던 것보다 훨씬 더 좋다.

W : Same here. I like the rug in the center of the room. ①의 단서 방 중앙에 러그가 있음

여 : 그러게. 나는 방 중앙에 있는 러그가 마음에 들어.

M : The striped pattern of the rug makes the room feel warm. makes의 목적격 보어(원형부정사)

남 : 러그의 줄무늬가 방을 따뜻하게 느껴지도록 만드네. ①의 단서 러그는 줄무늬임

W : I agree. I think putting the sofa between two plants was a good idea. 동명사 주어(단수 취급) 단수 동사 ②의 단서 두 개의 식물 사이에 소파가 있음

여 : 동의해. 나는 두 개의 식물 사이에 소파를 둔 것은 좋은 아이디어였다고 생각해.

M : Right. We can sit there and read for hours.

남 : 맞아. 우리는 저기 앉아서 몇 시간 동안 책을 읽을 수 있겠어.

W : There's a round clock on the wall. ③의 단서 벽에 원형 시계가 있음

여 : 벽에 원형 시계가 있네.

M : I have the same clock at home. Oh, the bookshelf under the clock is full of books. '~로 가득하다' ④의 단서 시계 아래 책꽂이에 책이 가득함

남 : 나는 집에 똑같은 시계가 있어. 오, 시계 아래에 있는 책꽂이가 책으로 가득하네.

W : We can read the books at the long table.

여 : 우리는 긴 탁자에서 책을 읽을 수 있겠다.

M : Yeah, it looks like a good place to read. The two lamps on the table will make it easy to focus. 형용사적 용법(place 수식) 가목적어 진목적어 ⑤의 단서 탁자 위에 램프는 한 개임

남 : 응, 책 읽기에 좋은 장소 같아 보여. 탁자 위에 있는 램프 두 개가 집중하기 쉽게 만들어 줄 거야.

W : Good lighting is important for reading.

여 : 좋은 조명은 독서에 중요하지.

M : I can't wait to start using the reading room.

남 : 나는 빨리 열람실 사용을 시작하고 싶어.

• center ⓝ 중앙, 한가운데　• striped ⓐ 줄무늬가 있는
• bookshelf ⓝ 책꽂이　• lighting ⓝ 조명

대화를 듣고, 그림에서 대화의 내용과 일치하지 않는 것을 고르시오.

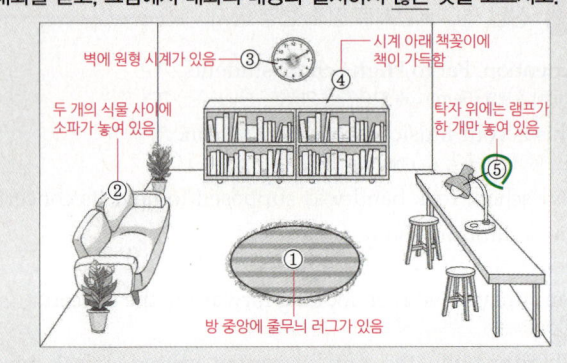

벽에 원형 시계가 있음 ③
시계 아래 책꽂이에 책이 가득함
④
두 개의 식물 사이에 소파가 놓여 있음
탁자 위에는 램프가 한 개만 놓여 있음 ⑤
①
방 중앙에 줄무늬 러그가 있음

＞왜 정답 ? ✿✿✿ [정답률 86%]

남자는 여자에게 탁자 위에 램프가 두 개 있다고 했지만, 그림에는 램프가 한 개만 놓여 있으므로 ⑤가 대화의 내용과 일치하지 않는다.

＞왜 오답 ?

① 방 중앙에 줄무늬 러그가 놓여 있다.
② 두 개의 식물 사이에 소파가 놓여 있다.
③ 벽에는 원형 시계가 걸려 있다.
④ 시계 아래에 있는 책꽂이에는 책이 가득 차 있다.

---

05 정답 ① ＊학교 뮤지컬을 위한 준비

M : Kelly, the school musical is tomorrow. Shall we go over the final checklist together? '~을 점검[검토]하다'

남 : Kelly, 학교 뮤지컬이 내일이야. 우리 최종 체크 리스트를 같이 검토해 볼까?

W : Let's do it. What's first? [Pause] Oh, the posters. We put them up around school last week. 'put-put-put'

여 : 해보자. 첫 번째가 뭐지? [잠시 후] 오, 포스터네. 우리 지난주에 그것들을 학교 근처에 붙였잖아.

M : Right. Do we have extra batteries for the wireless microphones? ⑤의 함정

남 : 맞아. 우리 무선 마이크에 쓸 여분의 배터리는 있어?

W : Yeah. I bought them yesterday. We should check that the microphones work well with the sound system. 목적어절 접속사 ②의 함정

여 : 응. 내가 어제 샀어. 우리는 마이크가 음향 시스템하고 잘 작동하는지 점검해야 해.

M : I did that this morning. They sound terrific.

남 : 그건 내가 오늘 아침에 했어. 소리가 아주 좋아.

W : How about the stage lights? ④의 함정

여 : 무대 조명은 어때?

M : They work perfectly. I think everyone will love the lighting design you made. 앞에 목적격 관계대명사가 생략됨

남 : 그것들은 완벽하게 작동해. 나는 모두 네가 만든 조명 디자인을 좋아할 거라고 생각해.

W : Really? Thanks. It looks like we've finished everything.

여 : 정말? 고마워. 우리 모든 걸 끝낸 것 같아.

M : No, wait. The chairs for the audience haven't been arranged yet. 현재완료 수동태 단서1 관객용 의자가 아직 배치되지 않음

남 : 아니, 잠깐만. 관객용 의자가 아직 배치되지 않았어.

W : You're right! I'll go take care of that now.

여 : 네가 맞아! 내가 지금 가서 처리할게. 단서2 여자가 지금 처리할 것임

M : The musical is going to be fantastic.

남 : 뮤지컬은 아주 멋질 거야.

• extra ⓐ 추가의　• wireless ⓐ 무선의　• terrific ⓐ 아주 좋은
• audience ⓝ 관객　• arrange ⓥ 배열하다　• fantastic ⓐ 환상적인

대화를 듣고, 여자가 할 일로 가장 적절한 것을 고르시오.
① 관객용 의자 배치하기 관객용 의자가 아직 배치되지 않음
② 마이크 음향 점검하기 남자가 아침에 점검함
③ 공연 포스터 붙이기 지난주에 같이 붙임
④ 무대 조명 설치하기 이미 설치되어 잘 작동함
⑤ 배터리 구매하기 여자가 어제 구매함

> 왜 정답 ? ✱❀❀ [정답률 90%]
관객용 의자가 아직 배치되지 않았다는 남자의 말에, 여자가 지금 가서 처리하겠다고
했으므로 정답은 ①이다.

> 왜 오답 ?
② 마이크 음향은 남자가 아침에 점검했다.
③ 공연 포스터는 지난주에 이미 붙였다.
④ 무대 조명은 이미 설치되어 남자가 작동을 확인했다.
⑤ 배터리는 여자가 어제 구매했다.

06 정답 ③ ✱장미꽃 바구니 구매하기

W : Welcome to Libby's Flowers. How can I help you?
여 : Libby의 꽃집에 오신 걸 환영합니다. 무엇을 도와드릴까요?
M : I'd like to order a rose basket for my parents' wedding
anniversary.
　　　would like to-v: ~하고 싶다
남 : 저는 부모님의 결혼기념일을 위해 장미꽃 바구니를 주문하고 싶습니다.
W : All right. Our rose baskets come in two sizes.
여 : 좋아요. 저희 장미꽃 바구니는 두 가지 크기로 나옵니다.
M : What are the options?
남 : 어떤 선택지들이 있나요?
W : The regular size is 30 dollars, and the large size is 50 dollars.
여 : 보통 크기는 30달러이고, 큰 크기는 50달러입니다. 단서1 큰 바구니는 50달러임
M : Hmm.... I think the bigger one is better.
남 : 음…. 더 큰 것이 더 좋을 것 같아요. 단서2 큰 바구니 한 개를 구매함
W : Good choice. So, you'll get one rose basket in the large size.
By the way, we're giving a 10 percent discount on all
purchases this week. 단서3 10퍼센트 할인이 제공됨
여 : 좋은 선택이에요. 그러면 큰 크기의 장미꽃 바구니를 하나 하시는 거죠. 그런데, 저희가
이번 주에는 모든 구매에 10퍼센트 할인을 제공해 드리고 있어요.
M : Excellent! When will my order be ready?
남 : 좋네요! 제 주문은 언제 준비가 되나요?
　　　　　　　　　구동사(동사＋대명사 목적어＋부사)
W : It'll be ready around 11 a.m. If you can't pick it up, we offer
a delivery service. It's 10 dollars. 단서4 배달은 10달러임
여 : 오전 11시까지 준비될 것입니다. 찾으러 오지 못하신다면, 저희가 배달 서비스를 제공해
드려요. 그건 10달러입니다.
　　　　　　　　　　to부정사의 수동태 단서5 배달을 원함
M : Oh, great. I'd like it to be delivered. Here's my credit card.
남 : 오, 좋네요. 저는 그것이 배달되기를 원합니다. 여기 제 신용카드입니다.

- anniversary ⓝ 기념일 - regular ⓐ 보통의
- purchase ⓝ 구매 - delivery ⓝ 배달, 배송

대화를 듣고, 남자가 지불할 금액을 고르시오. [3점]
① $37 ② $45 ③ $55 ④ $60 ⑤ $80
$50(큰 바구니 한 개)×0.9(10퍼센트 할인)＋$10(배달비)

> 왜 정답 ? ✱✱❀ [정답률 83%]
남자는 50달러인 큰 장미꽃 바구니 하나를 구입하였고 10퍼센트를 할인받았다.
여기에 추가로 10달러인 배달 서비스를 이용했으므로 지불할 금액은 ③ '55달러'이다.

배달 서비스에는
할인이 적용되지 않음!

07 정답 ④ ✱스키 여행을 갈 수 없는 Olivia

M : You seem busy this morning, Olivia.
남 : 너 오늘 아침에 바빠 보인다, Olivia.
W : I am. I had to see Professor Martin about my history test.
여 : 나 바빠. 역사 시험에 관해서 Martin 교수님을 만나야 했거든. ③의 함정
　　　　　　　　　　목적어절 접속사
M : Oh, I see. Do you remember that our club's ski trip is this
weekend?
남 : 오, 그랬구나. 넌 우리 동아리의 스키 여행이 이번 주말인 거 기억하지?
　　　　　　　　　　현재완료 수동태
W : Yeah. I heard that a nice ski resort has been booked for the
trip. ②의 함정
여 : 응. 이번 여행을 위해 좋은 스키 리조트가 예약되었다고 들었어.
　　　　　　　　　　　　　　부사적 용법(감정의 원인)
M : I didn't know that. I'm so excited to go skiing at a nice
resort.
남 : 난 그건 몰랐어. 좋은 리조트에 스키를 타러 간다니 너무 신나.
W : I bet it'll be great, but I don't think I can go this time.
여 : 정말 좋을 거야. 그런데 나는 이번에는 갈 수 없을 것 같아.
M : Why? You don't work at the cafe on the weekends, do you?
남 : 왜? 너 주말에는 카페에서 일하지 않잖아, 안 그래? ①의 함정
　　　　　　　　　　　　　　　'~을 돌보다'
W : No, I don't. But I need to take care of my cat. She's recovering
from surgery. 단서 수술에서 회복 중인 고양이를 돌봐야 함
여 : 아니, 일 안 해. 그런데 나는 내 고양이를 돌봐줘야 해. 수술에서 회복 중이거든.
　　　　　　　　　　　　　주격 관계대명사
M : Isn't there anyone else who can look after your cat?
남 : 네 고양이를 돌봐줄 다른 누군가가 없어?
　　　　　　　　　　　　　가까운 미래를 대신하는 현재진행형
W : No one but me. My parents are visiting relatives in Canada.
They won't be back for two weeks. ⑤의 함정
여 : 나밖에 없어. 우리 부모님은 캐나다에 친척을 만나러 가시거든. 그들은 2주 동안
돌아오지 않으실 거야.
M : I'm sorry that you can't join us.
남 : 네가 우리랑 같이 가지 못하다니 유감이야.
W : Me, too. Have fun this weekend.
여 : 나도 그래. 주말 재미있게 보내.

- book ⓥ 예약하다 - recover ⓥ 회복하다
- surgery ⓝ 수술 - relative ⓝ 친척

대화를 듣고, 여자가 스키 여행을 갈 수 없는 이유를 고르시오.
① 카페에서 일해야 해서 주말에는 일을 하지 않음
② 숙소를 예약하지 못해서 숙소는 예약함
③ 역사 시험 공부를 해야 해서 역사 시험이 언급된 것으로 만든 오답
④ 수술받은 고양이를 돌봐야 해서 수술받은 고양이를 돌봐야 함
⑤ 캐나다에 사는 친척을 방문해야 해서 캐나다에 사는 친척은 부모님이 방문함

> 왜 정답 ? ✱❀❀ [정답률 94%]
여자는 수술에서 회복 중인 고양이를 돌봐야 해서 스키 여행을 갈 수 없다고 했으므로
정답은 ④이다.

> 왜 오답 ?
① 여자는 주말에는 카페 일을 하지 않는다고 했다.
② 숙소는 좋은 곳으로 예약되었다고 했다.
③ 역사 시험과 관련해서 교수님과 면담했다고 했을 뿐이다. 주의
⑤ 캐나다에 사는 친척을 방문하는 사람은 여자의 부모님이다.

08 정답 ③ ✱거리 사진 대회 참가하기

W : What are you doing, Tim?
여 : 너 뭐 하고 있어, Tim?
M : I'm looking at the Street Photography Contest website.
남 : 나는 거리 사진 대회 웹사이트를 보고 있어.

W : I've heard about that. It's a contest for college students, right?

여 : 나도 그거 들었어. 대학생을 위한 대회라는데, 맞지?

M : Actually, it's open to high school students, too. **Why don't you** try it? ①의 단서 참가 대상

남 : 사실, 고등학생에게도 열려 있어. 너도 해보지 않을래?

W : Really? Maybe I will. Does the contest have a theme?

여 : 정말? 나도 해볼 수도 있겠네. 대회에 주제가 있어?

M : Sure. This year's theme is Daily Life. ②의 단서 주제

남 : 물론이지. 올해의 주제는 '일상생활'이야.

W : That sounds interesting. When is the deadline?

여 : 재미있게 들린다. 마감 기한이 언제야?

M : You have to submit your photographs by September 15.

남 : 너는 9월 15일까지 사진들을 제출해야 해. ④의 단서 제출 마감일

W : That's **sooner than** I expected.
　　　비교급 비교

여 : 그건 내 예상보다 더 빠르네.

M : You should hurry and choose your photos. The winner will receive a laptop as a prize. ⑤의 단서 우승 상품

남 : 너는 서둘러서 사진을 골라야겠다. 우승자는 상품으로 휴대용 컴퓨터를 받을 거래.

W : Okay! Wish me luck.

여 : 알았어! 행운을 빌어줘.

· theme ⓝ 주제　　· deadline ⓝ 마감 기한　　· expect ⓥ 예상하다
· receive ⓥ 받다　　· prize ⓝ 상품, 경품

대화를 듣고, Street Photography Contest에 관해 언급되지 않은 것을 고르시오.

① 참가 대상　it's open to high school students, too
② 주제　This year's theme is Daily Life.
③ 심사 기준　언급되지 않음
④ 제출 마감일　You have to submit your photographs by September 15.
⑤ 우승 상품　The winner will receive a laptop as a prize.

>왜 정답 ? ✽✽✽ [정답률 89%]

거리 사진 대회의 참가 대상, 주제, 제출 마감일, 우승 상품은 언급되었지만, 심사 기준은 언급되지 않았으므로 정답은 ③이다.

>왜 오답 ?

① 대학생뿐만 아니라 고등학생도 참가할 수 있다고 했다.
② 올해의 주제는 '일상생활'이라고 했다.
④ 사진은 9월 15일까지 제출해야 한다고 했다.
⑤ 우승 상품은 휴대용 컴퓨터라고 했다.

09　정답 ④　✽Twin Stars 초콜릿의 날 안내

M : Hello, listeners.

남 : 안녕하세요, 청취자 여러분.

I'm Charlie Anderson from the Twin Stars Chocolate Museum.

저는 Twin Stars 초콜릿 박물관의 Charlie Anderson입니다.

I'm happy **to introduce** the Twin Stars Chocolate Day, a
　　　　　부사적 용법(감정의 원인)
special opportunity **to create** your own delicious chocolates.
　　　　　형용사적 용법(opportunity 수식)

저는 여러분만의 맛있는 초콜릿을 만들 특별한 기회인 Twin Stars 초콜릿의 날을 소개하게 되어 기쁩니다.

It'll be held on November 12 from 1 p.m. to 4 p.m. ①의 단서 11월 12일 오후에 열림
미래시제 수동태

그것은 11월 12일 오후 1시부터 오후 4시까지 개최됩니다.

First, you'll listen to a lecture about the history of chocolate.

먼저, 여러분은 초콜릿의 역사에 관한 강의를 들을 것입니다. ②의 단서 초콜릿의 역사에 관한 강의가 진행됨

Then you'll have a chance **to taste** our most popular flavors.
　　　　　형용사적 용법(chance 수식)

그리고 여러분은 우리의 가장 인기 있는 맛들을 맛볼 기회를 가질 것입니다.

At the end of the event, you'll make five chocolates yourself.

행사의 마지막에, 여러분은 스스로 5개의 초콜릿을 만들 것입니다. ③의 단서 초콜릿 5개를 만듦

If you want to **take part in** the event, you must register **in**
'~에 참가하다'　　　　　　　　　　　'사전에, 미리'
advance. ④의 단서 참가하려면 사전 등록을 해야 함

만약 이 행사에 참가하기를 원하신다면, 여러분은 사전에 등록해야 합니다.

You can sign up on our website until November 1.

우리의 웹사이트에서 11월 1일까지 등록하실 수 있습니다.
　　　　　　　　　　　　　계속적 용법의 주격 관계대명사
The registration fee is 20 dollars, **which** includes the cost of ingredients. ⑤의 단서 등록비에 재료비가 포함됨

등록비는 20달러로, 그것은 재료의 가격을 포함합니다.

Don't miss this sweet opportunity!

이 달콤한 기회를 놓치지 마세요!

· introduce ⓥ 소개하다　　· opportunity ⓝ 기회
· lecture ⓝ 강의, 강연　　· taste ⓥ 맛보다　　· flavor ⓝ 맛
· register ⓥ 등록하다　　· registration ⓝ 등록
· ingredient ⓝ 재료

Twin Stars Chocolate Day에 관한 다음 내용을 듣고, 일치하지 않는 것을 고르시오.

① 11월 12일 오후에 열린다.　It'll be held on November 12 from 1 p.m. to 4 p.m.
② 초콜릿의 역사에 관한 강의가 진행된다.
　you'll listen to a lecture about the history of chocolate
③ 초콜릿 5개를 만든다.
　you'll make five chocolates yourself
④ 사전 등록 없이 참가할 수 있다.
　you must register in advance
⑤ 등록비에 재료비가 포함된다.
　The registration fee ~ includes the cost of ingredients.

>왜 정답 ? ✽✽✽ [정답률 94%]

행사에 참가하려면 사전에 등록해야 한다고(If you want to take part in the event, you must register in advance.) 했으므로 사전 등록 없이 참가할 수 있다고 한 ④가 일치하지 않는다.

>왜 오답 ?

① 11월 12일 오후 1시부터 4시까지 열린다고 했다.
② 초콜릿의 역사에 관한 강의가 진행된다고 했다.
③ 참가자가 직접 초콜릿 5개를 만들 것이라고 했다.
⑤ 등록비 20달러에 재료비가 포함되어 있다고 했다.

10　정답 ④　✽실내 사이클링 자전거 구매하기

M : Honey, what are you looking at?

남 : 여보, 뭘 보고 있어요?

W : I'm looking at indoor cycling bikes. Would you like to choose one together?

여 : 실내 사이클링 자전거를 보고 있어요. 같이 하나 고를래요?

M : Sure, let me see. [Pause] The price differs by model.

남 : 그럼요, 어디 봐요. [잠시 후] 가격이 모델마다 다르네요.

W : I don't want to pay more than 300 dollars. That's too expensive. 단서 1 300달러가 넘지 않아야 함(⑤ 제외)

여 : 나는 300달러 이상은 쓰고 싶지 않아요. 그건 너무 비싸요.

M : I agree. Which color do you like?

남 : 동의해요. 당신은 어떤 색이 좋아요?

W : I prefer a dark color because it **goes well with** our living
　　　　　　　　　　　　　　　　　　　'~와 잘 어울리다'
room.

여 : 나는 우리 거실이랑 잘 어울리기 때문에 어두운색이 좋아요.

M : Okay. Then we shouldn't get a white one. What do you think about the foldable one? 단서 2 어두운색을 선호함(① 제외)

남 : 좋아요. 그러면 우리는 흰색은 사면 안 되겠어요. 접을 수 있는 자전거는 어떻게 생각해요? 단서 3 접을 수 있는 자전거여야 함(② 제외)

W : We definitely need that. It'll take up less storage space.

여 : 우리는 그게 꼭 필요해요. 그게 저장 공간을 덜 차지할 거예요.

M : We have just two options <u>left</u>. Which one should we get?

과거분사(options 수식)

남 : 우리는 선택지가 2개만 남았네요. 우린 어떤 걸 사야 할까요? **단서 4** 고객 평점이 높아야 함(③ 제외)

W : I think we should go with the one with a higher customer rating. The reviews <mark>are based on</mark> actual customers' experiences.

'~에 기초하다'

여 : 고객 평점이 더 높은 걸 사야 한다고 생각해요. 후기는 실제 고객의 경험을 바탕으로 하니까요.

M : Sounds good. Let's order this one.

남 : 좋아요. 이걸로 주문합시다.

- indoor ⓐ 실내(용)의 • differ ⓥ 다르다 • foldable ⓐ 접을 수 있는
- definitely ⓐd 분명히, 절대로 • take up 차지하다
- storage ⓝ 저장, 보관 • rating ⓝ 평가, 순위 • actual ⓐ 실제의

다음 표를 보면서 대화를 듣고, 두 사람이 주문할 실내 사이클링 자전거를 고르시오.

Indoor Cycling Bikes 실내 사이클링 자전거

	Model 모델	Price 가격	Color 색	Foldable 접을 수 있는	Customer Rating 고객 평점
①	A	$100	White 흰색 *어두운 색이 아님*	×	★★★★
②	B	$150	Black 검은색	× *접을 수 없음*	★★★
③	C	$190	Black	○	★★★★
④	D	$250	Black	○	★★★★★
⑤	E	$320 *300달러가 넘음*	White	×	★★★★★ *고객 평점이 낮음*

> **왜 정답?** ✱✿✿ [정답률 92%]

남자와 여자는 300달러를 넘지 않고(⑤ 제외), 흰색이 아니며(① 제외), 접을 수 있는(② 제외) 자전거 중, 고객 평점이 더 높은(③ 제외) 자전거를 선택했으므로 정답은 ④이다.

> **왜 오답?**

① 어두운색을 선호하기 때문에 흰색은 사지 않기로 했다.
② 접을 수가 없다.
③ 고객 평점이 5점보다 낮다.
⑤ 300달러 이상 쓰고 싶지 않다고 했다.

11 정답 ① ＊새 스웨터를 산 Jason

W : Jason, is that a new sweater? It looks good on you.

여 : Jason, 그거 새 스웨터야? 너한테 잘 어울린다.

단서 1 남자는 스웨터를 온라인에서 샀다고 함

M : Thanks. I bought it online. It was on sale.

남 : 고마워. 나는 온라인에서 샀어. 할인하고 있었어.

= sweater

W : I'd love to buy the same <u>one</u> for my brother. Can you tell me *간접의문문* <mark>where you got it?</mark> **단서 2** 스웨터를 어디에서 샀는지 말해 달라고 함

여 : 나도 똑같은 것을 내 남동생에게 사주고 싶어. 그것을 어디에서 샀는지 말해줄 수 있어?

M : **Sure. I'll send you a link to the website.**

남 : 물론이지. 내가 웹사이트 링크를 네게 보내줄게.

- on sale 할인 중인 • receipt ⓝ 영수증
- return ⓥ 돌려주다, 반품하다

대화를 듣고, 여자의 마지막 말에 대한 남자의 응답으로 가장 적절한 것을 고르시오.

① Sure. I'll send you a link to the website.
물론이지. 내가 웹사이트 링크를 네게 보내줄게. *스웨터를 구매한 곳을 알려줄 수 있는지 물어봄*
② It would look better in a different color.
그게 다른 색이면 더 잘 어울릴 것 같아. *스웨터의 색을 추천해 달라고는 하지 않았음*
③ Sorry. I forgot to bring your sweater.
미안해. 내가 네 스웨터를 가져오는 걸 깜빡했어. *스웨터를 가져다주는 상황은 아님*
④ You need your receipt to return it.
그걸 반품하려면 넌 영수증이 필요해. *새 스웨터를 반품하는 상황이 아님*
⑤ My brother bought it on sale, too.
내 남동생도 할인할 때 그걸 샀어. *웹사이트를 물어본 것에 맞지 않는 응답*

> **왜 정답?** ✱✿✿ [정답률 92%]

여자는 남자가 온라인으로 산 스웨터를 보고 자기 남동생에게도 사주고 싶다고 하면서 구매한 곳을 말해줄 수 있는지 물었다. 따라서 남자는 ① '물론이지. 내가 웹사이트 링크를 네게 보내줄게.'라고 응답하는 것이 가장 적절하다.

> **왜 오답?**

② 여자는 스웨터를 구매한 웹사이트를 물어본 것이지, 남동생에게 어울릴 스웨터의 색을 물어본 것이 아니다. *함정*
③ 남자가 여자에게 스웨터를 가져다줘야 하는 상황이 아니다.
④ 스웨터가 맘에 들지 않아 반품하는 상황이 아니다.
⑤ 스웨터를 구매한 웹사이트를 묻는 말에 어울리지 않는 응답이다.

12 정답 ④ ＊피자를 주문한 Becky

M : Becky, did you order our food for dinner?

남 : Becky, 우리가 저녁으로 먹을 음식 주문했어?

W : Yes. I ordered pizza about an hour ago.

여 : 응. 나는 한 시간 전에 피자를 주문했어. **단서** 보통 40분 걸리는 배달이 한 시간째 안 오는 상황임

M : An hour ago? Delivery usually takes <mark>less than</mark> 40 minutes.

남 : 한 시간 전에? 보통 배달은 40분보다 더 적게 걸리는데. *비교급 비교*

W : **I'll call the restaurant and check our order.**

여 : 내가 식당에 전화해서 우리의 주문을 확인해 볼게.

- order ⓥ 주문하다 • delivery ⓝ 배달, 배송
- leftover ⓝ 남은 음식

대화를 듣고, 남자의 마지막 말에 대한 여자의 응답으로 가장 적절한 것을 고르시오.

① Let's take the leftovers home. *음식은 아직 배달되지 않음*
남은 음식은 집에 가져가자.
② I prefer fried chicken over pizza.
난 피자보다 프라이드치킨이 더 좋아. *어떤 음식을 더 좋아하는지 물어본 것이 아님*
③ I don't want to go out for lunch today.
나는 오늘 점심 먹으러 나가고 싶지 않아. *점심이 아니라 저녁 시간대임*
④ I'll call the restaurant and check our order.
내가 식당에 전화해서 우리의 주문을 확인해 볼게. *배달이 늦어지고 있는 상황임*
⑤ The letter was delivered to the wrong address.
그 편지는 잘못된 주소로 배송됐어. *편지에 관한 내용이 아님*

> **왜 정답?** ✱✿✿ [정답률 83%]

저녁 식사로 주문한 피자가 1시간이 지나도 오지 않는 상황이다. 보통 배달은 40분 이상 걸리지 않는다는 남자의 말에 여자는 ④ '내가 식당에 전화해서 우리의 주문을 확인해 볼게.'라고 응답하는 것이 가장 적절하다.

> **왜 오답?**

① 피자는 아직 배달되지 않았으므로 음식이 남았다는 것은 적절하지 않다.
② 어떤 음식을 좋아하는지 물어본 것이 아니다.
③ 점심이 아니라 저녁으로 먹을 음식에 대한 대화이다. *함정*
⑤ 편지가 아니라 피자 배달을 기다리는 상황이다.

13 정답 ① ＊성적보다 중요한 규칙적인 식사

W : I haven't seen you in the cafeteria this week. Where have you been?

여 : 나 이번 주에 너를 구내식당에서 못 봤어. 너 어디 있었어?

분사구문

M : I've been in the library <mark>working on my science project</mark>.

남 : 나는 과학 프로젝트를 준비하면서 도서관에 있었어.

현재완료 진행형

W : Does that mean you<mark>'ve been skipping</mark> lunch?

여 : 너는 점심을 거르고 있었다는 말이야?

M : Yeah. This project is really important for my grade.

남 : 응. 이 프로젝트가 내 성적에 정말 중요하거든.

W : You shouldn't do that. It's not good for your health.

여 : 너 그러면 안 돼. 그건 건강에 안 좋아.

2023.9

9회

M : Don't worry. I always have a big dinner when I get home.
부사절 접속사

남 : 걱정하지 마. 나는 항상 집에 가면 저녁을 많이 먹거든.

W : That's the problem. Skipping meals makes you overeat later.
makes의 목적어와 목적격 보어(원형부정사)
단서 1 식사를 거르는 것은 과식을 유발함

여 : 그게 문제야. 식사를 거르는 것은 네가 나중에 과식하게 만들어.

M : I hadn't thought of that. Then what should I do?

남 : 그건 생각하지 못했어. 그러면 난 어떻게 해야 해?

W : It's simple. You should eat regularly to stay healthy.
부사적 용법(목적)
단서 2 건강을 유지하려면 규칙적으로 먹어야 한다고 말함

여 : 간단해. 건강을 유지하려면 넌 규칙적으로 먹어야 해.

M : **You're right. I won't skip meals anymore.**

남 : 네 말이 맞아. 나 더 이상 식사를 거르지 않을게.

- cafeteria Ⓝ 구내식당　　· skip Ⓥ 거르다, 빼먹다　　· grade Ⓝ 성적
- overeat Ⓥ 과식하다　　· regularly [ad] 규칙적으로
- manner Ⓝ 예의, 태도　　· on time 제시간에

> 대화를 듣고, 여자의 마지막 말에 대한 남자의 응답으로 가장 적절한 것을 고르시오.
>
> Man: _____
>
> ① You're right. I won't skip meals anymore.
> 네 말이 맞아. 나 더 이상 식사를 거르지 않을게.　규칙적으로 먹어야 한다고 했음
> ② Thank you for the lunch you prepared for me.
> 나를 위해 네가 준비한 점심 고마워.　점심을 준비해 준 것이 아님
> ③ You need to check when the cafeteria is open.
> 너는 구내식당이 언제 문을 여는지 확인해야 해.　식당이 문을 닫았던 것이 아님
> ④ Trust me. I can teach you good table manners.
> 날 믿어. 내가 좋은 식사 예절을 가르쳐 줄 수 있어.　식사 예절에 대한 대화가 아님
> ⑤ No problem. We'll finish the science project on time.
> 문제없어. 우리는 제시간에 과학 프로젝트를 끝낼 거야.　같이 과학 프로젝트를 하는 것이 아님

왜 정답? ✽❀❀ [정답률 89%]

점심을 거르고 있었다는 남자에게 여자는 규칙적으로 식사를 해야 과식하지 않고 건강할 수 있다고 말했다. 따라서 이에 대한 응답으로 ① '네 말이 맞아. 나 더 이상 식사를 거르지 않을게.'라고 하는 것이 가장 적절하다.

왜 오답?

② 여자가 남자를 위해 점심을 준비해 준 상황이 아니다.

③ 식당이 문을 닫아서 남자가 식사를 거르고 있었던 것이 아니다.

(▶◀ 이유: 남자는 과학 프로젝트 준비 때문에 식사를 거르고 있었다.)

④ 식사 예절에 대해 대화를 나누고 있는 상황이 아니다.

⑤ 여자도 과학 프로젝트를 하고 있는지는 알 수 없으며, 과학 프로젝트가 아니라 식사에 관한 대화이다.

---

14 정답 ③ ✽반복 연습에서 시작하는 언어 학습

M : Excuse me, Ms. Lopez. Can I ask you something?

남 : 실례합니다, Lopez 씨. 뭐 좀 여쭤봐도 될까요?

W : Sure, Tony. What can I do for you?

여 : 물론이지, Tony. 내가 무엇을 도와줄까?

M : I want to do better in Spanish, but I don't know how to improve.
how to-v: ~하는 방법
단서 1 남자는 스페인어를 더 잘하는 방법이 궁금함

남 : 저는 스페인어를 더 잘하고 싶은데, 더 잘하는 방법을 모르겠어요.

W : You seem to do well during class. Do you study when you're at home?

여 : 너는 수업 중에는 잘하는 것 같아. 집에 있을 때 공부하니?

M : I do all my homework and try to learn 20 new words every day.
병렬 구조

남 : 저는 숙제를 다 하고 매일 새로운 단어를 20개씩 익히려고 해요.

W : That's a good start. Do you also practice saying those words repeatedly?

여 : 좋은 시작이네. 너는 그 단어들을 반복해서 말하는 것도 연습하니?

M : Do I need to do that? That sounds like it'll take a lot of time.

남 : 그걸 해야 하나요? 그건 시간이 오래 걸릴 것처럼 들려요.

W : It does. But since you're still a beginner, you have to put in more effort to get used to new words.
= takes a lot of time　부사절 접속사(이유)
부사적 용법(목적)
단서 2 시간이 걸리더라도 단어를 반복해서 말하는 연습을 하라고 함

여 : 그렇지. 하지만 너는 아직 초보자니까, 새로운 단어에 익숙해지려면 더 많은 노력을 기울여야 해.

M : I see. So are you suggesting that I practice them over and over?
목적어절 접속사
단서 3 여자의 제안을 확인하며 되물음

남 : 알겠습니다. 그러니까 제가 그것들을 반복해서 연습하라고 제안하시는 거죠?

W : **Exactly. Learning a language starts with repetition.**

여 : 정확해. 언어를 배우는 건 반복에서부터 시작해.

- improve Ⓥ 향상하다　　· repeatedly [ad] 반복해서　　· effort Ⓝ 노력
- suggest Ⓥ 제안하다　　· vocabulary Ⓝ 어휘　　· repetition Ⓝ 반복

> 대화를 듣고, 남자의 마지막 말에 대한 여자의 응답으로 가장 적절한 것을 고르시오. [3점]
>
> Woman: _____
>
> ① No. It isn't difficult for me to learn Spanish.
> 아니. 스페인어를 배우는 건 나한테는 어렵지 않아.　여자의 스페인어 학습과는 관련 없는 내용임
> ② I'm glad you finally passed the vocabulary test.
> 네가 마침내 어휘 시험에 통과해서 나는 기뻐.　어휘 시험을 봤다는 언급은 없음
> ③ Exactly. Learning a language starts with repetition.
> 정확해. 언어를 배우는 건 반복에서부터 시작해.　새로운 단어를 반복해서 연습할 것을 제안함
> ④ It's very helpful to use a dictionary while writing.
> 글쓰기를 할 때 사전을 사용하는 것은 매우 유용해.　글쓰기에 대한 언급은 없음
> ⑤ You should turn in your homework by this afternoon.
> 너는 오늘 오후까지 과제를 제출해야 해.　과제 제출에 대한 대화가 아님

왜 정답? ✽✽❀ [정답률 80%]

스페인어를 잘하는 방법에 대한 조언을 구하는 남자에게 여자는 새로운 단어를 반복해서 연습할 것을 제안했다. 따라서 그 제안을 확인하며 묻는 남자에게 여자는 ③ '정확해. 언어를 배우는 건 반복에서부터 시작해.'라고 응답하는 것이 적절하다.

왜 오답?

① 남자가 여자에게 스페인어 학습이 어려운지 물어본 것이 아니다.

② 남자가 어휘 시험을 봤는지는 대화를 통해 알 수 없다.

④ 스페인어로 글을 쓸 때 유용한 방법을 물어본 것이 아니다. ─주의

⑤ 과제 제출 기한을 물어본 것이 아니다.

---

15 정답 ⑤ ✽불을 끄지 않는 반 친구들

W : Brian is a class leader.

여 : Brian은 반장이다.

He is passionate about environmental issues and saving energy.

그는 환경 문제와 에너지 절약에 열정적이다.

Recently, he's noticed that his classmates don't turn the lights off when they leave the classroom.
목적어절 접속사
부사절 접속사

최근에, 그는 반 친구들이 교실을 떠날 때 불을 끄지 않는다는 것을 알게 되었다.
뒤에 목적어절 접속사가 생략됨

Brian thinks this is very careless.

Brian은 이것이 매우 부주의하다고 생각한다.

He wants to make stickers that remind his classmates to save energy by turning off the lights.
주격 관계대명사
by v-ing: ~함으로써
단서 1 에너지 절약을 상기하는 스티커를 만들고 싶음

그는 불을 꺼서 에너지를 절약하는 것을 반 친구들에게 상기하는 스티커를 만들기 원한다.

He tells this idea to his classmate Melissa, and she agrees it's a good idea.
뒤에 목적어절 접속사가 생략됨

그는 이 아이디어를 반 친구 Melissa에게 말하고, 그녀는 그것이 좋은 아이디어라고 동의한다.
뒤에 목적어절 접속사가 생략됨

Brian knows Melissa is a great artist, so he wants to ask her to design stickers that encourage their classmates to save energy.
to ask의 목적어와 목적격 보어(to부정사)
단서 2 Melissa에게 스티커 디자인을 부탁하고 싶음

Brian은 Melissa가 뛰어난 예술가라는 것을 알고, 그래서 그는 그녀에게 반 친구들이 에너지를 절약하도록 장려하는 스티커를 디자인해 달라고 부탁하고 싶다.

In this situation, what would Brian most likely say to Melissa?

이 상황에서, Brian이 Melissa에게 할 말로 가장 적절한 것은 무엇인가?

Brian: **Will you design stickers that encourage energy saving?**

Brian: 에너지 절약을 장려하는 스티커를 디자인해 줄래?

*상황 요약: Brian은 반 친구들의 에너지 절약을 장려하기 위한 스티커를 제작하고 싶은데, Melissa가 그 스티커를 디자인해 줬으면 함

- passionate ⓐ 열정적인
- environmental ⓐ 환경의
- notice ⓥ 알아차리다
- careless ⓐ 부주의한
- remind ⓥ 상기하다
- encourage ⓥ 장려하다
- remove ⓥ 제거하다
- board ⓝ 게시판
- heater ⓝ 난방(기)

다음 상황 설명을 듣고, Brian이 Melissa에게 할 말로 가장 적절한 것을 고르시오. [3점]

Brian: _____

① Let's clean the classroom after art class. 교실이 더럽다는 것이 아님
미술 수업 후에 교실을 청소하자.
② Did you remove the stickers from the board? 스티커를 제작하려는 상황임
게시판에 있는 스티커 네가 떼었니?
③ Please turn off the heater when you leave the room. 난방이 아니라 불을 끄지 않는 상황임
방을 나갈 때 난방을 꺼줘.
④ When is the final date to sign up for the design class? 디자인 수업 등록에 관한 상황이 아님
디자인 수업에 등록할 수 있는 마지막 날이 언제야?
⑤ Will you design stickers that encourage energy saving? 에너지 절약 스티커 디자인을 부탁하려고 함
에너지 절약을 장려하는 스티커를 디자인해 줄래?

〉왜 정답? ✿✿✿ [정답률 89%]

Brian은 교실을 나가면서 불을 끄지 않는 반 친구들을 보고, 에너지 절약을 장려하는 스티커를 만들고 싶어 한다. 이것이 좋은 생각이라고 생각하는 뛰어난 예술가인 Melissa에게 그 스티커의 디자인을 부탁하고 싶은 상황이므로 ⑤ '에너지 절약을 장려하는 스티커를 디자인해 줄래?'라고 말하는 것이 가장 적절하다.

〉왜 오답?

① 교실이 더러워서 청소하려고 하는 상황이 아니다.
② 스티커를 제작하고자 하는 것이지, 스티커 제거와 관련된 상황이 아니다.
③ 반 친구들은 난방이 아니라 불을 끄지 않고 교실을 떠난다고 했다. (▸◂ 이유: 난방을 켜놓는 것도 에너지 낭비이지만, 난방과 관련된 내용은 언급되지 않았다.)
④ 디자인 수업 등록에 관해 묻고자 하는 상황이 아니다.

16~17 *과잉 관광 문제 해결하기

M : Good afternoon, / everyone. //
남 : 안녕하세요 / 여러분 //

Last time, / we learned / **that** overtourism happens / **when** there are too many visitors / to a particular destination. //
목적어절 접속사 / 부사절 접속사
지난 시간에 / 우리는 배웠습니다 / 과잉 관광이 발생한다는 것을 / 너무 많은 관광객이 있을 때 / 특정 목적지에 //

Today, / we'll learn / **how cities deal with the problems** / 간접의문문
caused by overtourism. // 16번 단서: 도시들이 과잉 관광 문제에 어떻게
과거분사(problems 수식) 대처하는지 이야기할 것임
오늘 / 우리는 배울 것입니다 / 어떻게 도시들이 문제에 대처하는지 / 과잉 관광으로 야기된 //

First, / some cities limit the number of hotels / so there are fewer places / **for visitors** to stay. //
to stay의 의미상 주어
첫 번째로 / 어떤 도시들은 호텔의 수를 제한합니다 / 그래서 장소가 더 적어집니다 / 관광객이 머물 //

In Barcelona, / **building new hotels is not allowed** / in the city center. // 17번①
동명사구 주어(단수 취급) / 단수 동사
Barcelona에서는 / 새로운 호텔을 짓는 것이 허용되지 않습니다 / 도심에 //

Second, / other cities promote areas / away from popular sites. //
두 번째로 / 다른 도시들은 지역을 홍보합니다 / 유명한 곳에서 멀리 떨어진 //

For instance, / Amsterdam encourages tourists / to visit less-crowded areas. // 17번②
예를 들어 / Amsterdam은 관광객들에게 장려합니다 / 덜 붐비는 장소를 방문할 것을 //

Third, / many cities have tried to limit access. //
세 번째로 / 많은 도시들은 접근을 제한하고자 했습니다 //

For example, / Venice has tried to reduce tourism overall / 17번④
by **stopping large cruise ships** / **from docking** on the island. //
stop A from v-ing: A가 ~하는 것을 막다
예를 들어 / Venice는 관광산업을 전반적으로 줄이고자 했습니다 / 많은 대형 크루즈 선박들을 막음으로써 / 그 섬에 정박하는 것에서 //

Similarly, / Paris has focused on reducing tourism / to 17번⑤
certain parts of the city / **by having** car-restricted areas. //
by v-ing: ~함으로써
마찬가지로 / Paris는 관광산업을 줄이는 데에 집중했습니다 / 도시의 특정 구역에 / 자동차 제한 구역을 두어서 //

Now, / let's watch some video clips. //
이제 / 영상을 봅시다 //

- overtourism ⓝ 과잉 관광
- particular ⓐ 특정한
- destination ⓝ 목적지
- limit ⓥ 제한하다
- allow ⓥ 허용하다
- promote ⓥ 홍보하다
- site ⓝ 장소, 위치
- access ⓝ 접근
- reduce ⓥ 줄이다
- overall ⓐⓓ 전반적으로
- dock ⓥ 정박하다
- rent ⓥ 빌리다
- correlation ⓝ 상관관계
- transportation ⓝ 교통 (수단)

남 : 안녕하세요, 여러분. 지난 시간에 우리는 특정 목적지에 너무 많은 관광객이 있을 때 과잉 관광이 발생한다는 것을 배웠습니다. 오늘 우리는 어떻게 도시들이 과잉 관광으로 야기된 문제에 대처하는지 배울 것입니다. 첫 번째로, 어떤 도시들은 호텔의 수를 제한하고, 그래서 관광객들이 머물 장소가 더 적어집니다. Barcelona에서는 도심에 새로운 호텔을 짓는 것이 허용되지 않습니다. 두 번째로, 다른 도시들은 유명한 곳에서 멀리 떨어진 지역을 홍보합니다. 예를 들어, Amsterdam은 관광객들에게 덜 붐비는 지역을 방문할 것을 장려합니다. 세 번째로, 많은 도시들은 접근을 제한하고자 했습니다. 예를 들어, Venice는 많은 대형 크루즈 선박들이 그 섬에 정박하는 것을 막음으로써 관광산업을 전반적으로 줄이고자 했습니다. 마찬가지로, Paris는 자동차 제한 구역을 두어서 도시의 특정 구역에 관광산업을 줄이는 데에 집중했습니다. 이제, 영상을 봅시다.

16 정답 ③

남자가 하는 말의 주제로 가장 적절한 것은?

① advantages of renting houses in cities 도시에서 집을 빌리는 것의 이점 도시에서 집을 빌리는 것에 대한 언급은 없음
② reasons tourists prefer visiting old cities
여행객들이 오래된 도시 방문을 선호하는 이유 여행객들이 오래된 도시를 방문한다는 언급은 없음
③ ways cities deal with overtourism problems 여러 도시들이 과잉
도시들이 과잉 관광 문제에 대처하는 방법 관광 문제에 대처하는 방법을 소개함
④ correlation between cities' sizes and overtourism
도시의 규모와 과잉 관광 사이의 상관관계 도시의 규모와 과잉 관광의 연관성은 언급되지 않음
⑤ how cities face their aging transportation systems
도시들이 그들의 노후화된 교통 시스템에 대처하는 방법 노후화된 교통 시스템은 언급하지 않음

〉왜 정답? ✿✿✿ [정답률 84%]

도시들이 과잉 관광으로 야기된 문제에 어떻게 대처하는지를 여러 도시를 예로 들며 이야기했다. 따라서 남자가 하는 말의 주제는 ③ '도시들이 과잉 관광 문제에 대처하는 방법'이다.

〉왜 오답?

① 도시에서 집을 빌리는 것의 이점은 언급하지 않았다.
② 여행객들이 오래된 도시 방문을 선호한다는 언급은 없다.
④ 도시 규모와 과잉 관광의 연관성은 담화를 통해 알 수 없다.
⑤ 도시들이 노후화된 교통 시스템에 어떻게 대처하고 있는지에 관한 내용이 아니다.

17 정답 ③

언급된 도시가 <u>아닌</u> 것은?

① Barcelona 새로운 호텔 건설이 허용되지 않음
② Amsterdam 관광객에게 덜 붐비는 지역의 방문을 권장함
③ London 언급되지 않음
④ Venice 대형 크루즈 선박의 정박을 막음
⑤ Paris 자동차 제한 구역을 둠

>왜 정답? ✿❀❀ [정답률 93%]

과잉 관광 문제에 대처하고 있는 도시의 예로 Barcelona, Amsterdam, Venice, Paris를 소개했지만 ③ London은 언급하지 않았다.

>왜 오답?

① Barcelona는 도심에 새로운 호텔을 건설하는 것을 막았다고 했다.
② Amsterdam은 관광객들이 덜 붐비는 지역에 가도록 장려했다고 했다.
④ Venice는 대형 크루즈 선박의 정박을 막았다고 했다.
⑤ Paris는 자동차 제한 구역을 두었다고 했다.

18 정답 ⑤ ＊화학 박람회를 위한 대학생 모집

Dear Professor Sanchez, /
Sanchez 교수님께 /

My name is Ellis Wight, / and I'm the director of the Alexandria Science Museum. //
제 이름은 Ellis Wight이고 / 저는 Alexandria 과학 박물관의 관장입니다 //

We are holding a Chemistry Fair / for local middle school students / on Saturday, October 28. //
저희는 화학 박람회를 개최합니다 / 지역 중학교 학생들을 위한 / 10월 28일 토요일에 //

The goal of the fair is to encourage them to be interested in science / through guided experiments. //
이 박람회의 목적은 그들을 장려하는 것입니다 / 과학에 관심을 갖도록 / 안내되는 실험을 통해 //

We are looking for college students / who can help with the experiments / during the event. // **단서1** 박람회에서 실험을 도와줄 대학생을 모집 중임
저희는 대학생을 모집합니다 / 실험을 도와줄 수 있는 / 행사 기간 동안 //

I am contacting you to ask you / to recommend some students from the chemistry department at your college / who you think are qualified for this job. // **단서2** 일을 도와줄 수 있는 화학과 학생을 추천해 달라고 함
저는 교수님께 요청을 드리고자 연락드립니다 / 귀교의 화학과 학생 몇 명을 추천해 줄 것을 / 교수님께서 생각하기에 이 일에 적합한 //

With their help, I'm sure / the participants will have a great experience. //
그들의 도움으로 / 저는 확신합니다 / 참가자들이 훌륭한 경험을 하게 될 것을 //

I look forward to hearing from you soon. //
교수님으로부터 곧 연락이 오기를 고대하겠습니다 //

Sincerely, Ellis Wight /
Ellis Wight 드림 /

- director ⓝ 책임자, 관리자
- chemistry ⓝ 화학
- local ⓐ 지역의
- goal ⓝ 목표
- experiment ⓝ 실험
- contact ⓥ 연락하다
- recommend ⓥ 추천하다
- department ⓝ (대학의) 학과
- look forward to ~을 고대하다

Sanchez 교수님께,
제 이름은 Ellis Wight이며, Alexandria 과학 박물관의 관장입니다. 저희는 10월 28일 토요일에 지역 중학교 학생을 위한 화학 박람회를 개최합니다. 이 박람회의 목적은 안내되는 실험을 통해 학생들이 과학에 관심을 갖도록 장려하는 것입니다. 저희는 행사 기간 동안 실험을 도와줄 수 있는 대학생을 모집하고자 합니다. 저는 교수님께서 이 일에 적합하다고 생각하시는 귀교의

화학과 학생 몇 명을 추천해 달라는 요청을 드리고자 연락드립니다. 저는 그 학생들의 도움으로 참가자들이 훌륭한 경험을 하게 될 것을 확신합니다. 교수님으로부터 곧 연락이 오기를 고대하겠습니다.
Ellis Wight 드림

다음 글의 목적으로 가장 적절한 것은?

① 과학 박물관 내 시설 이용 제한을 안내하려고 시설 이용이 제한되는 것이 아님
② 화학 박람회 일정이 변경된 이유를 설명하려고 일정은 변경되지 않음
③ 중학생을 위한 화학 실험 특별 강연을 부탁하려고
④ 중학교 과학 수업용 실험 교재 집필을 의뢰하려고 특별 강연을 부탁하는 것이 아님 교재 집필에 관해서는 언급되지 않음
⑤ 화학 박람회에서 실험을 도울 대학생 추천을 요청하려고
실험을 도울 대학생을 추천해 달라고 함

>왜 정답? ✿❀❀ [정답률 90%]

중학생을 위한 화학 박람회에서 실험 진행을 도와줄 대학생을 모집 중이라고 하면서, Sanchez 교수가 재직 중인 대학교의 화학과 학생 몇 명을 추천해 달라고 요청하고 있으므로 정답은 ⑤이다.

>왜 오답?

① 과학 박물관에서는 박람회가 개최될 뿐, 시설 이용이 제한된다는 언급은 없다.
② 화학 박람회 일정 변경은 언급하지 않았다.
③ 안내되는 실험이 있다고만 언급했을 뿐, 이에 관한 강연을 부탁하는 것은 아니다.
④ 교재 집필은 전혀 언급되지 않았다. 함정

19 정답 ② ＊암벽 등반 중에 생긴 일

Gregg and I had been rock climbing since sunrise / and had had no problems. // **단서1** 아무런 문제없이 암벽 등반을 하고 있었음
과거완료 진행시제 ／ 과거완료
Gregg와 나는 일출 이후에 암벽 등반을 해왔고 / 아무런 문제가 없었다 //

So we took a risk. //
그래서 우리는 위험을 감수했다 //

"Look, the first bolt is right there. //
"봐, 첫 번째 볼트가 바로 저기에 있어 //

I can definitely climb out to it. //
나는 분명히 거기까지 올라갈 수 있어 //

Piece of cake," / I persuaded Gregg, / minutes before I found myself pinned. // **단서2** '식은 죽 먹기'라고 하면서 자신만만해 함
'식은 죽 먹기' ／ 재귀대명사(목적어) 목적격 보어(과거분사)
식은 죽 먹기야'라고 / 나는 Gregg를 설득했다 / 내가 꼼짝 못 하다는 것을 알게 되기 몇 분 전에 //

It wasn't a piece of cake. //
그것은 식은 죽 먹기가 아니었다 //

The rock was deceptively barren of handholds. //
그 바위는 믿을 수 없게도 손으로 잡을 곳이 없었다 //

I clumsily moved back and forth / across the cliff face / and ended up with nowhere to go...but down. //
병렬 구조
나는 서투르게 앞뒤로 움직여 보았다 / 절벽 면을 가로질러 / 그리고 결국 아래쪽밖에는 갈 곳이 없게 되었다 //

The bolt / that would save my life, / if I could get to it, / was about two feet / above my reach. // **단서3** 목숨을 구해줄 볼트가 손에 닿지 않음
주격 관계대명사 ／ 삽입절
볼트는 / 내 목숨을 구해줄 / 만약 내가 거기까지 갈 수 있다면 / 약 2피트 위에 있었다 / 내 손이 닿을 수 있는 곳에서 //

My arms trembled from exhaustion. //
내 팔은 기진맥진하여 떨렸다 //

I looked at Gregg. //
나는 Gregg를 쳐다보았다 //

My body froze with fright / from my neck down to my toes. // **단서4** 몸이 공포로 얼어붙음
내 몸은 공포로 얼어붙었다 / 목에서부터 발끝까지 //

Our rope was tied between us. //
수동태 동사
우리 사이에 밧줄이 묶여 있었다 //

If I fell, / he would fall with me. //
가정법 과거
내가 떨어지면 / 그도 나와 함께 떨어질 것이다 //

- **risk** ⓝ 위험　　· **definitely** [ad] 분명히　　· **persuade** ⓥ 설득하다
- **pin** ⓥ 꼼짝 못하게 하다　　· **deceptively** [ad] 속을 정도로, 믿을 수 없게
- **handhold** ⓝ 손으로 잡을 곳　　· **clumsily** [ad] 서투르게
- **cliff** ⓝ 절벽　　· **reach** ⓝ (닿을 수 있는) 거리[범위]
- **tremble** ⓥ 떨(리)다　　· **exhaustion** ⓝ 기진맥진
- **fright** ⓝ 공포, 놀람　　· **fearful** ⓐ 두려운　　· **regretful** ⓐ 후회하는

Gregg와 나는 일출 이후에 암벽 등반을 해왔고 아무런 문제가 없었다.
그래서 우리는 위험을 감수했다. "봐, 첫 번째 볼트가 바로 저기에 있어.
나는 분명히 거기까지 올라갈 수 있어. 식은 죽 먹기야."라고 나는 Gregg를
설득했고, 얼마 지나지 않아 나는 내가 꼼짝 못 한다는 것을 알게 되었다.
그것은 식은 죽 먹기가 아니었다. 그 바위는 믿을 수 없게도 손으로 잡을
곳이 없었다. 나는 서투르게 절벽 면을 앞뒤로 가로질러 보았지만, 갈 곳이
없었다…아래쪽밖에는. 만약 내가 거기까지 갈 수 있다면, 내 목숨을 구해줄
볼트는 손이 닿을 수 있는 곳에서 약 2피트 위에 있었다. 내 팔은 기진맥진하여
떨렸다. 나는 Gregg를 쳐다보았다. 내 몸은 목에서부터 발끝까지 공포로
얼어붙었다. 우리 사이에 밧줄이 묶여 있었다. 내가 떨어지면, 그도 나와 함께
떨어질 것이다.

다음 글에 드러난 'I'의 심경 변화로 가장 적절한 것은?

① joyful → bored　떨어질지도 모르는 상황임
　즐거운 → 지루한
②(정답) confident → fearful　처음에는 자신만만했지만, 공포로 얼어붙음
　자신감 있는 → 두려운
③ nervous → relieved　안심할 상황이 아님
　불안한 → 안심한
④ regretful → pleased　오히려 반대의 상황임
　후회하는 → 즐거운
⑤ grateful → annoyed　감사하거나 화를 낸 상황이 아님
　감사하는 → 화가 난

왜 정답? ✾✾✾ [정답률 74%]

전반부: 식은 죽 먹기라고 하며 위험을 감수함 ▶ '즐거운' 또는 '자신감 있는'
후반부: 볼트는 손에 닿지 않고, 공포로 몸이 얼어붙음 ▶ '두려운'
따라서 I의 심경 변화는 ② '자신감 있는 → 두려운'이다.

왜 오답?

① 처음엔 즐거웠지만, 목숨이 위태로운 상황이므로 지루한 것이 아니다.
③(✘) 안심할 상황은 언급되지 않았다. (▶ 이유: Gregg와 나 사이에 밧줄이 있는 것은
　서로를 지켜주는 것이 아니라, 한 명이 떨어지면 같이 떨어지는 더 위험한 상황을
　암시하는 것이므로 안심했다고 볼 수 없다.)
④ 정답과 정반대의 심경 변화라고 할 수 있다.
⑤ 감사하거나 화가 날 상황은 없었다.

---

20 정답 ②　✾ 행동으로 삶의 모범을 보이기

**We are always teaching our children something / by our words
and our actions. //**
우리는 항상 우리의 자녀에게 무언가를 가르치고 있다 / 우리의 말과 행동으로 //

동명사(전치사의 목적어)
They learn from seeing. //　단서 1 우리의 자녀는 보는 것으로 배움
그들은 보는 것으로부터 배운다 //

They learn from hearing / and from overhearing. //
그들은 듣는 것으로부터 배우고 / '우연히 듣는 것'으로부터 (배운다) //

**Children share the values of their parents / about the most
important things in life. //**
아이들은 그들 부모의 가치를 공유한다 / 인생에서 가장 중요한 것에 대해 //

**Our priorities and principles / and our examples of good
behavior / can teach our children / to take the high road / when
other roads look tempting. //**
명사적 용법(목적격 보어)　'확실한 길, 올바른 길'
우리의 우선순위와 원칙 / 그리고 훌륭한 행동에 대한 본보기는 / 우리의 자녀에게 가르칠 수
있다 / 올바른 길로 가도록 / 다른 길이 유혹적으로 보일 때 //

목적어절 접속사　　　　　　　　주격 관계대명사
Remember / that children do not learn the values / that make up
by v-ing: ~함으로써
strong character / simply by being told about them. //
기억하라 / 아이들은 가치를 배우지 않는다 / 확고한 인격을 구성하는 / 단순히 그것들에 대해
'들음'으로써 //

seeing의 목적격 보어(원형부정사)
**They learn / by seeing the people around them / act on and
uphold those values / in their daily lives. //**
그들은 배운다 / 그들 주변 사람들을 봄으로써 / 그러한 가치를 좇아 '행동'하고 '유지'하는 것을
/ 그들의 일상생활에서 //

**Therefore / show your child / good examples of life / by your
action. //**　단서 2 자녀에게 행동으로 삶의 모범을 보이라고 함
그러므로 / 여러분의 자녀에게 보여라 / 삶의 모범을 / 여러분의 행동으로 //

show의 간접목적어　　　직접목적어절 접속사
**In our daily lives, / we can show our children / that we respect
others. //**
우리의 일상생활에서 / 우리는 우리의 자녀에게 보여줄 수 있다 / 우리가 타인을 존중하는 것을 //

부사절 접속사(시간)
**We can show them / our compassion and concern / when others
are suffering, / and our own self-discipline, courage and honesty**
병렬 구조
/ as we make difficult decisions. //
부사절 접속사(시간)
우리는 그들에게 보여줄 수 있다 / 우리의 연민과 걱정을 / 다른 사람이 괴로워할 때 / 그리고
우리 자신의 자제력, 용기 그리고 정직을 / 우리가 어려운 결정을 할 때 //

- **action** ⓝ 행동　　· **overhear** ⓥ 우연히 듣다　　· **value** ⓝ 가치
- **priority** ⓝ 우선순위　　· **tempting** ⓐ 솔깃한
- **uphold** ⓥ 유지하다　　· **respect** ⓥ 존중하다
- **compassion** ⓝ 연민　　· **concern** ⓝ 걱정　　· **suffer** ⓥ 고통받다
- **self-discipline** ⓝ 자제력　　· **honesty** ⓝ 정직함

우리는 항상 우리의 자녀에게 말과 행동으로 무언가를 가르치고 있다. 그들은
보는 것으로부터 배운다. 그들은 듣거나 '우연히 듣는 것'으로부터 배운다.
아이들은 인생에서 가장 중요한 것에 대해 그들 부모의 가치를 공유한다.
우리의 우선순위와 원칙 그리고 훌륭한 행동에 대한 본보기는 우리의
자녀에게 다른 길이 유혹적으로 보일 때 올바른 길로 가도록 가르칠 수 있다.
아이들은 확고한 인격을 구성하는 가치를 단순히 그것에 대해 '들음'으로써
배우지 않는다는 것을 기억하라. 그들은 그들 주변 사람들이 그들의
일상생활에서 그러한 가치를 좇아 '행동'하고 '유지'하는 것을 봄으로써 배운다.
그러므로 여러분의 자녀에게 여러분의 행동으로 삶의 모범을 보여라. 우리의
일상생활에서, 우리는 우리 자녀에게 우리가 타인을 존중하는 것을 보여줄 수
있다. 우리는 그들에게 다른 사람이 괴로워할 때 우리의 연민과 걱정을, 그리고
우리가 어려운 결정을 할 때 우리 자신의 자제력, 용기 그리고 정직을 보여줄
수 있다.

다음 글에서 필자가 주장하는 바로 가장 적절한 것은?

① 자녀를 타인과 비교하는 말을 삼가야 한다.　자녀를 타인과 비교하지 말라는 글이 아님
②(정답) 자녀에게 행동으로 삶의 모범을 보여야 한다.
　아이들은 보는 것으로부터 배운다고 했음
③ 칭찬을 통해 자녀의 바람직한 행동을 강화해야 한다.
　칭찬하라는 내용이 아님
④ 훈육을 하기 전에 자녀 스스로 생각할 시간을 주어야 한다.
　훈육이 아니라 본보기가 되라는 내용임
⑤ 자녀가 새로운 것에 도전할 때 인내심을 가지고 지켜봐야 한다.
　자녀가 새로운 것에 도전한다는 내용은 없음

왜 정답? ✾✾✾ [정답률 95%]

· **오해:** 아이들이 단순히 '들음'으로써 배운다고 생각함
· **해결:** 아이들은 어떤 행동을 하고 그것을 유지하는 것을 '봄'으로써 배움
▶ 아이들이 볼 수 있게 행동으로 삶의 모범을 보이라고 주장하고 있으므로 정답은
②이다.

왜 오답?

① 자녀를 타인과 비교하지 말라고 주장하는 글이 아니다.
③ 자녀를 칭찬하라는 내용은 언급되지 않았다.
④ 자녀를 훈육하라는 것이 아니라 자녀에게 본보기가 되라는 내용이다.
⑤ 자녀가 새로운 것에 도전한다거나 인내심을 가지라는 내용은 없었다.

'틀림없이'
Most people have **no doubt** heard / this question: / If a tree falls
절과 절을 연결하는 등위접속사   목적격 보어(원형부정사)
in the forest / **and** there is no one there / to hear it **fall**, / does it
make a sound? //
대부분의 사람들은 틀림없이 들어봤을 것이다 / 이 질문을 / 만약 숲에서 나무가 쓰러진다면 /
그리고 거기에 아무도 없다면 / 그것이 쓰러지는 것을 들을 / 그것은 소리를 내는 것일까 //

The correct answer is no. // **단서1** 듣는 사람이 없는 숲에서 쓰러지는 나무는
소리를 내지 않음
정답은 '아니요'이다 //

Sound is more than pressure waves, / and indeed there can be
no sound / without a hearer. // **단서2** 듣는 사람이 없다면 소리는 있을 수 없음
소리는 압력파 이상이고 / 정말로 소리는 있을 수 없다 / 듣는 사람 없이는 //

And similarly, / scientific communication is a two-way process. //
그리고 마찬가지로 / 과학적 의사소통은 양방향 과정이다 //
단서3 마찬가지로 출판된 과학 논문도 독자에 의해 이해되지 않으면 쓸모가 없음
Just as a signal of any kind is useless / **unless** it is perceived, /
부사절 접속사(조건)
a published scientific paper (signal) is useless / **unless** it is both
received *and* understood / by its intended audience. //
어떠한 종류의 신호든 쓸모가 없는 것처럼 / 그것이 감지되지 않으면 / 출판된 과학
논문(신호)도 쓸모가 없다 / 수신되거나 '그리고' 이해되지 않으면 / 의도된 독자에 의해 //

Thus we can restate / the axiom of science / as follows: / A
scientific experiment is not complete / until the results **have**
현재완료 수동태
been published *and understood*. //
따라서 우리는 재진술할 수 있다 / 과학의 자명한 이치를 / 다음과 같이 / 과학 실험은
완성되지 않는다 / 결과가 출판되고 '그리고 이해될' 때까지 //
'~에 지나지 않는'
Publication is **no more than** pressure waves / unless the
published paper is understood. //
출판은 압력파에 지나지 않는다 / 출판된 논문이 이해되지 않으면 //

Too many scientific papers / fall silently in the woods. //
너무 많은 과학 논문이 / 소리 없이 숲속에서 쓰러진다 //

- **indeed** ⓐ 정말로 • **hearer** ⓝ 듣는 사람 • **process** ⓝ 과정
- **signal** ⓝ 신호 • **useless** ⓐ 쓸모없는 • **perceive** ⓥ 감지하다
- **receive** ⓥ 수신하다, 받다 • **intended** ⓐ 의도된
- **audience** ⓝ 관객, 독자 • **restate** ⓥ 다시 말하다
- **experiment** ⓝ 실험 • **publication** ⓝ 출판
- **previous** ⓐ 이전의 • **demand** ⓝ 요구

대부분의 사람들은 틀림없이 이 질문을 들어봤을 것이다. 만약 숲에서 나무가
쓰러지고 그것이 쓰러지는 것을 들을 사람이 아무도 없다면, 그것은 소리를
내는 것일까? 정답은 '아니요'이다. 소리는 압력파 이상이며, 정말로 듣는 사람
없이는 소리가 있을 수 없다. 그리고 마찬가지로, 과학적 의사소통은 양방향
과정이다. 어떠한 종류의 신호든 그것이 감지되지 않으면 쓸모가 없는 것처럼,
출판된 과학 논문(신호)도 그것이 의도된 독자에 의해 수신되거나 '그리고'
이해되지 않으면 쓸모가 없다. 따라서 우리는 과학의 자명한 이치를 다음과
같이 재진술할 수 있다. 과학 실험은 결과가 출판되고 '그리고 이해될' 때까지
완성되지 않는다. 출판된 논문이 이해되지 않으면 출판은 압력파에 지나지
않는다. 너무 많은 과학 논문이 소리 없이 숲속에서 쓰러진다.

밑줄 친 fall silently in the woods가 다음 글에서 의미하는 바로 가장
적절한 것은? [3점]
① fail to include the previous study 이전 연구를 포함하는지는 언급되지 않음
이전 연구를 포함하는 데 실패한다
② end up being considered completely false
결국 완전히 잘못된 것으로 간주된다   맞고 틀림을 판단하는 것이 아님
③ become useless because they are not published
그것들이 출판되지 않기 때문에 쓸모없어진다   출판되지 않아서 쓸모없는 것이 아님
④ focus on communication to meet public demands
대중의 요구를 충족하기 위해 소통에 집중한다   communication이 언급된 것으로 만든 오답
⑤ are published yet readers don't understand them
출판되었으나 독자들이 그것들을 이해하지 못한다   독자가 이해하지 못하면 쓸모없어짐

왜 정답? ★★★ [정답률 50%]

- 아무도 없는 숲에서 나무는 소리 없이 쓰러짐 **단서1**
- 듣는 사람이 없다면 소리도 없음 **단서2**

➡ 나무와 마찬가지로 출판된 과학 논문도 그것을 읽고 이해할 사람이 없다면
쓸모없는 것임 **단서3**
▶ '소리 없이 숲속에서 쓰러진다'는 것은 '듣는 사람이 없어 쓸모없어진다는
것'을 의미하므로 ⑤ '출판되었으나 독자들이 그것들을 이해하지 못한다'는 것을
의미한다.

왜 오답?
① 이전 연구를 포함한다는 언급은 없었다.
② 쓸모가 없어진다는 것이지 논문이 과학적으로 맞거나 틀리는지를 판단하는 것이
아니다.
③ 출판되지 않아서 쓸모없어지는 것이 아니라, 출판된 후에 이해하는 사람이 없을 때
쓸모없어지는 것이다. **주의**
④ communication이 언급된 것으로 만든 오답으로, 대중과 소통해야 한다는
내용이 아니다.

We all negotiate every day, / whether we realise it or not. //
우리는 모두 매일 협상한다 / 우리가 그것을 알든 모르든지 간에 //
준부정어(거의 ~ 않는)   how to-v: ~하는 법
Yet / **few** people ever learn / *how to negotiate*. //
하지만 / 이제까지 배운 사람은 거의 없다 / '어떻게' 협상하는지를 //
= learn how to negotiate
Those who **do** / usually learn the traditional, win-lose
negotiating style / rather than an approach / **that** is likely to
주격 관계대명사
result in / a win-win agreement. //
(협상 방식을) 배우는 사람들은 / 대개 전통적인, 한쪽만 이기는 협상 방식을 배운다 /
접근법보다는 / 도출할 가능성이 있는 / 양쪽이 이기는 합의를 //

This old-school, adversarial approach may be useful / in a one-
관계부사   지시형용사
off negotiation / **where** you will probably not deal with **that**
person again. //
이 구식의 적대적인 접근법은 아마 유용할지도 모른다 / 일회성 협상에서 / 여러분이 아마 그
사람을 다시 상대하지 않을 //

However, / such transactions are becoming increasingly rare, /
부사절 접속사(이유)
because most of us deal with the same people repeatedly /
그러나 / 이러한 거래는 점점 더 드물어지고 있다 / 우리의 대부분이 동일한 사람들을
반복적으로 상대하기 때문에 //

— our spouses and children, our friends and colleagues, our
customers and clients. // **단서1** 성공적인 결과를
얻으면서 상대방과도 좋은
배우자와 자녀, 우리의 친구와 동료, 고객과 의뢰인 같은 // 관계를 유지하는 것이 중요함
가주어   진주어
In view of this, / **it**'s essential / **to achieve** successful results
for ourselves / and **maintain** a healthy relationship with our
병렬 구조
negotiating partners / at the same time. //
이러한 관점에서 / ~이 매우 중요하다 / 우리 자신을 위해 성공적인 결과를 얻어내는 것이 /
그리고 우리의 협상 파트너들과 건전한 관계를 유지하는 것이 / 동시에 //

In today's interdependent world / of business partnerships and
long-term relationships, / a win-win outcome is **fast** becoming /
형용사와 부사의 형태가 같음
the *only* acceptable result. // **단서2** 양쪽이 모두 이기는 성과만 받아들여지고 있음
오늘날의 상호 의존적인 세계에서 / 사업 협력과 장기적인 관계의 / 양쪽이 이기는 성과는
빠르게 되어가고 있다 / '유일하게' 받아들일 수 있는 결과가 //

- **negotiate** ⓥ 협상하다 • **realise** ⓥ 알아차리다
- **traditional** ⓐ 전통적인 • **approach** ⓝ 접근(법)
- **agreement** ⓝ 합의, 동의 • **one-off** ⓐ 단 한 번의
- **transaction** ⓝ 거래 • **rare** ⓐ 드문 • **repeatedly** ⓐ 반복적으로
- **spouse** ⓝ 배우자 • **essential** ⓐ 매우 중요한
- **maintain** ⓥ 유지하다 • **interdependent** ⓐ 상호 의존적인
- **acceptable** ⓐ 받아들일 수 있는

우리는 그것을 알든지 모르든지 간에, 모두 매일 협상한다. 하지만 이제까지
'어떻게' 협상하는지를 배운 사람은 거의 없다. (협상 방식을) 배우는 사람들은
대개 양쪽이 이기는 합의를 도출할 가능성이 있는 접근법보다는 전통적인,
한쪽만 이기는 협상 방식을 배운다. 이 구식의 적대적인 접근법은 아마
여러분이 그 사람을 다시 상대하지 않을 일회성 협상에서 유용할지도 모른다.
그러나, 우리 대부분은 배우자와 자녀, 친구와 동료, 고객과 의뢰인같이 동일한

사람들을 반복적으로 상대하기 때문에, 이러한 거래는 점점 더 드물어지고 있다. 이러한 관점에서, 우리 자신을 위해 성공적인 결과를 얻어내는 동시에 협상 파트너들과 건전한 관계를 유지하는 것이 매우 중요하다. 오늘날 사업 협력과 장기적인 관계의 상호 의존적인 세계에서, 양측이 이기는 성과는 '유일하게' 받아들일 수 있는 결과가 빠르게 되어가고 있다.

다음 글의 요지로 가장 적절한 것은?
① 협상 상대의 단점뿐 아니라 장점을 철저히 분석해야 한다.
협상 상대를 철저하게 분석하라는 언급은 없음
② 의사소통 과정에서 서로의 의도를 확인하는 것이 바람직하다.
서로의 의도를 확인하라는 내용이 아님
③ 성공적인 협상을 위해 다양한 대안을 준비하는 것이 중요하다.
다양한 대안의 필요성을 제시하지 않았음
④ 양측에 유리한 협상을 통해 상대와 좋은 관계를 유지해야 한다.
양쪽이 이기는 성과만이 받아들여짐
⑤ 원만한 인간관계를 위해 상호독립성을 인정하는 것이 필요하다.
interdependent가 언급된 것으로 만든 오답

왜 정답? ✸✸✸ [정답률 87%]
• **구식 협상**: 한쪽만 이김, 일회성 협상에 유용함
• **오늘날 협상**: 양쪽이 모두 이겨서 좋은 관계를 유지하는 것이 중요함 **단서 1**, **단서 2**
▶ 양측에 유리한 협상을 통해 상대와 좋은 관계를 유지해야 한다는 것이므로 정답은 ④이다.

왜 오답?
① 협상 상대를 분석하라고 이야기하는 글이 아니다.
② 의사소통 과정에서 서로의 의도를 확인해야 한다는 내용이 아니다.
③ 성공적인 협상이 필요하다고 하는 것은 맞지만, 다양한 대안을 준비하라는 것이 아니다. (이유: 일반적으로 '성공적인 협상'하면 떠올릴 수 있는 내용으로 만든 오답이다.)
⑤ 글에서 언급된 interdependent에서 떠올릴 수 있는 '상호독립성'으로 만든 오답이다.

23 정답 ② ✳ 매력적이지만은 않은 문화적 다양성

단서 1 다양한 문화적 배경을 가진 노동자들과 현지 주민이 상호작용하면 생산성이 증가될 수 있음
The **interaction** of workers / from different cultural backgrounds
핵심 주어
/ with the host population / **might increase** productivity / due to
본동사
positive externalities / like knowledge spillovers. //
노동자들의 상호작용은 / 다른 문화적 배경으로부터의 / 현지 주민과의 / 생산성을 증가시킬 수 있다 / 긍정적인 외부 효과로 인해 / 지식 피급과 같은 //

This is only an advantage / up to a certain degree. //
이것은 장점일 뿐이다 / 어느 정도까지만 //

When the variety of backgrounds is too large, / fractionalization
may cause excessive transaction costs / for communication, /
계속적 용법의 주격 관계대명사
which may lower productivity. // **단서 2** 배경의 다양성이 너무 크면 오히려
생산성이 저하될 수 있음
배경의 다양성이 너무 크면 / 분열은 과도한 거래 비용을 초래할 수 있다 / 의사소통에 대해 / 그리고 이것은 생산성을 저하시킬 수 있다 //

not only A but also B: A뿐만 아니라 B도
Diversity **not only** impacts the labour market, / **but** may **also**
affect the quality of life / in a location. //
다양성은 노동 시장에 영향을 줄 뿐만 아니라 / 삶의 질에도 영향을 미칠 수 있다 / 한 지역의 //

A tolerant native population may value / a multicultural city or
전치사
region / **because of** an increase / in the range of available goods
and services. // **단서 3** 관용적인 원주민은 다문화 도시를 가치 있게 여길 것임
관용적인 원주민은 가치 있게 여길 수 있다 / 다문화 도시나 지역을 / 증가로 인해 / 이용 가능한 재화와 서비스의 범위의 //
단서 4 다양성은 그것을 국가 정체성의 왜곡으로
생각하는 원주민들에게는 매력적이지 않음
On the other hand, / diversity **could be perceived** / as an
조동사가 포함된 수동태
unattractive feature / if natives perceive **it** / as a distortion / of
선행사가 포함된 관계대명사   = diversity
what they consider to be their national identity. //
반면에 / 다양성은 인식될 수 있다 / 매력적이지 않은 특징으로 / 만약 원주민들이 그것을 인식한다면 / 왜곡으로 / 그들의 국가 정체성이리고 그들이 생각히는 것에 대한 //

They might even discriminate / against other ethnic groups / and
목적어절 접속사
they might fear / **that** social conflicts between different foreign
nationalities are imported / into their own neighbourhood. //
그들은 심지어 차별할 수도 있다 / 다른 민족 집단을 / 그리고 그들은 두려워할 수도 있다 / 다른 외국 국적들 간의 사회적 갈등이 유입되는 것을 / 그들 주변으로 //

• interaction ⓝ 상호작용 • productivity ⓝ 생산성
• spillover ⓝ 여파, 파급 • degree ⓝ 정도 • excessive ⓐ 과도한
• transaction ⓝ 거래 • diversity ⓝ 다양성 • labour ⓝ 노동
• tolerant ⓐ 관대한 • multicultural ⓐ 다문화의
• region ⓝ 지역 • perceive ⓥ 인식하다
• unattractive ⓐ 매력적이지 않은 • feature ⓝ 특징
• distortion ⓝ 왜곡 • discriminate ⓥ 차별하다
• ethnic ⓐ 민족의 • conflict ⓝ 갈등 • nationality ⓝ 국적
• import ⓥ 수입하다, 유입하다 • contrastive ⓐ 대조하는
• perspective ⓝ 관점

다른 문화적 배경으로부터의 노동자들과 현지 주민의 상호작용은 지식 파급과 같은 긍정적인 외부 효과로 인해 생산성을 증가시킬 수 있다. 이것은 어느 정도까지만 장점일 뿐이다. 배경의 다양성이 너무 크면, 분열은 의사소통에 대한 과도한 거래 비용을 초래하는데, 이는 생산성을 저하시킬 수 있다. 다양성은 노동 시장에 영향을 줄 뿐만 아니라 한 지역의 삶의 질에도 영향을 미칠 수 있다. 관용적인 원주민은 이용 가능한 재화와 서비스의 범위의 증가로 인해 다문화 도시나 지역을 가치 있게 여길 수 있다. 반면에, 원주민들이 다양성을 그들의 국가 정체성이라고 생각하는 것에 대한 왜곡으로 인식한다면 다양성은 매력적이지 않은 특징으로 인식될 수 있다. 그들은 심지어 다른 민족 집단을 차별할 수도 있고 그들은 다른 외국 국적들 간의 사회적 갈등이 그들 주변으로 유입되는 것을 두려워할 수도 있다.

다음 글의 주제로 가장 적절한 것은?
① roles of culture in ethnic groups 특정 인종에 국한된 내용이 아님
인종 집단 내에서 문화의 역할
② contrastive aspects of cultural diversity
문화적 다양성의 대조적 측면   문화적 다양성이 갖는 장단점을 이야기함
③ negative perspectives of national identity
국가적 정체성의 부정적 관점   국가적 정체성의 왜곡은 특정 원주민의 예시일 뿐임
④ factors of productivity differences across countries
국가 간 생산성 차이의 요인   국가 간 생산성의 차이에 관한 글이 아님
⑤ policies to protect minorities and prevent discrimination
소수 집단을 보호하고 차별을 예방하기 위한 정책   소수 집단을 보호해야 한다는 글이 아님

왜 정답? ✸✸✸ [정답률 63%]

• 다양한 문화적 배경을 가진 노동자들과 현지 주민이 상호작용하면 생산성이 향상됨 **단서 1**
➡ **예시**: 관용적인 원주민은 다문화 지역을 가치 있게 여길 것임 **단서 3**
• 다양성이 너무 큰 경우에는 생산성이 저하됨 **단서 2**
➡ **예시**: 다양성을 국가 정체성의 왜곡으로 생각하는 원주민은 다양성을 매력적이게 보지 않음 **단서 4**

▶ 문화적 다양성이 초래할 수 있는 긍정적, 부정적 현상을 예시를 들어 설명하고 있으므로 글의 주제로 가장 적절한 것은 ② '문화적 다양성의 대조적 측면'이다.

왜 오답?
① 다양한 문화적 배경을 이야기했으므로 특정 인종 집단 내에서 문화의 역할을 말한 것이 아니다.
③ 국가적 정체성을 부정적으로 바라보는 것은 다양성을 왜곡으로 인식하는 원주민의 관점일 뿐이다. **함정**
④ 국가 간 생산성 차이나 그 요인을 설명한 글이 아니다.
⑤ 원주민, 다양성 등이 언급된 것으로 만든 오답으로, 소수 집단 보호를 이야기하는 글이 아니다.

24 정답 ① *건축물이 우리 삶에 미치는 영향

뒤에 목적어절 접속사 that이 생략됨
We **think** / we are shaping our buildings. //
우리는 생각한다 / 우리가 건물을 형성하고 있다고 //

But really, / our buildings and development are also shaping
us. // 단서1 건물과 개발이 우리를 형성함
그러나 실제로 / 우리의 건물과 개발도 우리를 형성하고 있다 //

핵심 주어   단수 동사
One of the best examples of this / **is** the oldest-known
construction: / the ornately carved rings of standing stones / at
Göbekli Tepe in Turkey. //
이것의 가장 좋은 예 중 하나는 / 가장 오래된 것으로 알려진 건축물이다 / 화려하게 조각된
입석의 고리 / 튀르키예의 Göbekli Tepe에 있는 //

부사절 접속사(시간)   형용사적 용법(idea 수식)
Before these ancestors got the idea / **to erect** standing stones /
some 12,000 years ago, / they were hunter-gatherers. //
이 조상들이 아이디어를 얻기 전에 / 입석을 세우는 / 약 12,000년 전에 / 그들은 수렵
채집인이었다 // 단서2 튀르키예의 조상들은 입석을 세우기 전에는 수렵 채집인이었음

It appears / that the erection of the multiple rings of megalithic
              so ~ that ...: 너무 ~해서 …하다
stones / took **so** long, / and **so** many successive generations, /
~으로 보인다 / 거석으로 된 여러 개의 고리를 세우는 것이 / 너무 오랜 시간이 걸렸고 / 너무
많은 잇따른 세대를 거쳤어야 해서 /

(앞의 so와 연결됨)   부사적 용법(목적)
that these innovators were forced to settle down / **to complete**
the construction works. //
이 혁신가들은 정착해야만 했다 / 건설 작업을 완료하기 위해 //
단서3 입석을 세우는 과정에서 정착했고 최초의 농업 사회가 형성됨

In the process, / they became the first farming society / on Earth. //
그 과정에서 / 그들은 최초의 농업 사회가 되었다 / 지구상에서 //
                            현재분사(society 수식)
This is an early example / of a society **constructing** something /
주격 관계대명사
that ends up radically remaking the society itself. //
이것은 초기 예이다 / 무언가를 건설하는 사회의 / 결국 사회 그 자체를 근본적으로
재구성하는 // 단서4 무언가를 건설 = 사회 자체를 재구성하는 것

Things are not so different / in our own time. //
상황은 그렇게 다르지 않다 / 우리 시대에도 //

- development ⓝ 개발   - construction ⓝ 건축(물)
- carve ⓥ 조각하다   - ancestor ⓝ 조상   - erect ⓥ (똑바로) 세우다
- successive ⓐ 연속적인   - innovator ⓝ 혁신가
- settle down 정착하다   - radically ⓐⓓ 근본적으로
- transform ⓥ 바꾸다

우리는 우리가 건물을 형성하고 있다고 생각한다. 그러나 실제로, 우리의
건물과 개발도 또한 우리를 형성하고 있다. 이것의 가장 좋은 예 중 하나는
가장 오래된 것으로 알려진 건축물인 튀르키예의 Göbekli Tepe에 있는
화려하게 조각된 입석의 고리이다. 이 조상들이 약 12,000년 전에 입석을
세우는 아이디어를 얻기 전에, 그들은 수렵 채집인이었다. 거석으로 된 여러
개의 고리를 세우는 것이 너무 오랜 시간이 걸렸고 너무 많은 잇따른 세대를
거쳤어야 해서 이 혁신가들은 건설 작업을 완료하기 위해 정착해야만 했던
것으로 보인다. 그 과정에서, 그들은 지구상에서 최초의 농업 사회가 되었다.
이것은 결국 사회 자체를 근본적으로 재구성하는 무언가를 건설하는 사회의
초기 예이다. 우리 시대에도 상황은 그렇게 다르지 않다.

다음 글의 제목으로 가장 적절한 것은?

① Buildings Transform How We Live!
건물이 우리가 사는 방식을 바꾼다!   건물이나 개발이 우리를 형성한다고 함
② Why Do We Build More Than We Need?
왜 우리는 우리가 필요한 것보다 더 지을까?   필요보다 많은 건물을 짓는다는 언급은 없음
③ Copying Ancient Buildings for Creativity
창의성을 위해 고대 건물을 모방하기   창의성과 관련된 글이 아님
④ Was Life Better in Hunter-gatherer Times?
수렵 채집 시대의 삶은 더 좋았을까?   hunter-gatherers가 언급된 것으로 만든 오답
⑤ Innovate Your Farm with New Constructions
새로운 건축물로 당신의 농장을 혁신하라   농장을 혁신하라는 글이 아님

> 왜 정답? ❖❖❖ [정답률 65%]

우리가 건물을 형성하는 것처럼 건물과 개발도 우리를 형성함 단서1
1 튀르키예의 조상들은 입석을 세우기 전에는 수렵 채집인이었음 단서2
2 그들은 입석을 세우면서 정착해야 했고, 최초의 농업 사회가 형성됨 단서3
3 무언가를 건설한 것이 사회 자체를 재구성한 것의 초기 예시임 단서4
▶ 튀르키예를 예로 들어 사회에서 건축물이 가지는 의미는 사회 자체의 재구성임을
설명했으므로 정답은 ① '건물이 우리가 사는 방식을 바꾼다!'이다.

> 왜 오답?

② 필요 이상으로 많은 건축물을 짓는다는 언급은 없다.
③ 창의성을 위해 고대 건물을 모방한다는 내용이 아니다.
④ 수렵 채집 시대가 더 살기 좋았을지 알아보는 글이 아니다.
  (이유: 수렵 채집 사회에서 농경 사회가 된 튀르키예의 예시가 제시됐을 뿐, 둘
  중 언제 더 살기 좋았는지는 설명하지 않았다.)
⑤ 새로운 건축물로 혁신하는 것은 맞지만, 농장에만 국한된 내용이 아니다.

25 정답 ④ *미국의 소셜 미디어 사용 비율

The graph above shows / the percentages of people in different
                      주격 관계대명사
age groups / **who** reported using social media / in the United
States / in 2015 and 2021. //
위 그래프는 보여준다 / 다양한 연령 집단에서 사람들의 비율을 / 소셜 미디어를 사용한다고
보고한 / 미국에서 / 2015년과 2021년에 //
                                    18-29 집단: 두 해 모두 가장 높음
① In each of the given years, / the 18-29 group had the highest
                            뒤에 목적어절 접속사 that이 생략됨
percentage of people / who **said** they used social media. //
주어진 각각의 해에서 / 18세에서 29세 집단에서 사람들의 비율이 가장 높았다 / 그들이 소셜
미디어를 사용한다고 말한 //

② In 2015, / the percentage of people / who reported using social
                            = the percentage of people who reported using social media
media / in the 30-49 group / was more than twice / **that** in the 65
and older group. // 2015년: 30-49 집단(77%) > 65 이상 집단(35%) x2
2015년에 / 사람들의 비율은 / 소셜 미디어를 사용한다고 보고한 / 30세에서 49세 집단에서
/ 두 배보다 컸다 / 65세 이상 집단에서의 그것보다 //

③ The percentage of people / who said they used social media
/ in the 50-64 group in 2021 / was 22 percentage points higher /
than that in 2015. // 50-64 집단: 2021년(73%) - 2015년(51%) = 22%p
사람들의 비율은 / 그들이 소셜 미디어를 사용한다고 말한 / 2021년에 50세에서 64세
집단에서 / 22퍼센트포인트 더 높았다 / 2015년의 그것보다 //

                                            분수 표현
④ In 2021, / except for the 65 and older group(→ 50 and older
groups), / more than **four-fifths** of people / in each age group /
reported using social media. // 단서 2021년에 50세에서 64세 집단(73%)도 80퍼센트
                                미만임
2021년에 / 65세(→ 50세) 이상 집단을 제외하고 / 5분의 4가 넘는 사람들이 / 각 연령
집단에서 / 소셜 미디어를 사용한다고 보고했다 //

⑤ Among all the age groups, / only the 18-29 group showed
a decrease / in the percentage of people / who reported using
social media / from 2015 to 2021. // 18-29 집단: 90%(2015)에서 84%(2021)로
                                    감소함
모든 연령 집단 중에서 / 18세에서 29세 집단만이 감소를 보였다 / 사람들의 비율에서 / 소셜
미디어를 사용한다고 보고한 / 2015년에서 2021년까지 //

- given ⓐ 주어진, 정해진   - among ⓟⓡⓔⓟ ~ 중에서
- decrease ⓝ 감소

위 그래프는 2015년과 2021년에 미국에서 소셜 미디어를 사용한다고 보고한
다양한 연령 집단에서 사람들의 비율을 보여준다. ① 주어진 각각의 해에서
18세에서 29세 집단에서 소셜 미디어를 사용한다고 말한 사람들의 비율이
가장 높았다. ② 2015년에 30세에서 49세 집단에서 소셜 미디어를 사용한다고
보고한 사람들의 비율은 65세 이상 집단에서의 비율의 두 배보다 컸다.
③ 2021년에 50세에서 64세 집단에서 소셜 미디어를 사용한다고 말한 사람들의
비율은 2015년의 비율보다 22퍼센트포인트 더 높았다. ④ 2021년에 65세(→
50세) 이상 집단을 제외한 각 연령 집단에서 5분의 4가 넘는 사람들이 소셜
미디어를 사용한다고 보고했다. ⑤ 모든 연령 집단 중에서 18세에서 29세
집단만이 2015년에서 2021년까지 소셜 미디어를 사용한다고 보고한 사람들의
비율에서 감소를 보였다.

다음 도표의 내용과 일치하지 않는 것은?

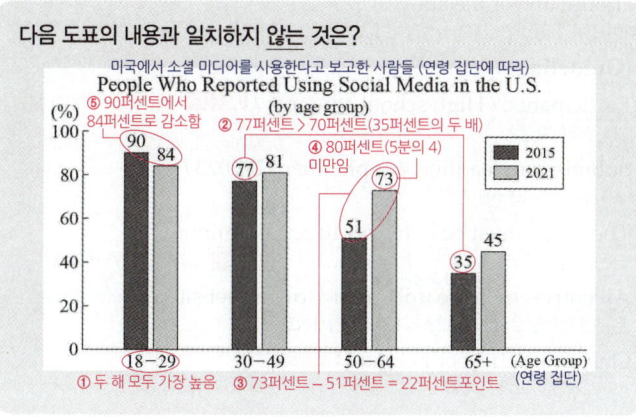

미국에서 소셜 미디어를 사용한다고 보고한 사람들 (연령 집단에 따라)
People Who Reported Using Social Media in the U.S.
(by age group)

⑤ 90퍼센트에서 84퍼센트로 감소함
② 77퍼센트 > 70퍼센트(35퍼센트의 두 배)
④ 80퍼센트(5분의 4) 미만임
① 두 해 모두 가장 높음
③ 73퍼센트 − 51퍼센트 = 22퍼센트포인트

> **왜 정답?** ❋❋❋ [정답률 81%]

2021년 50세에서 64세 집단의 수치는 73퍼센트로 전체의 5분의 4인 80퍼센트가 되지 않으므로 65세 이상 집단만 5분의 4가 넘지 않는다고 한 ④이 도표의 내용과 일치하지 않는다.

> **왜 오답?**

① 18세에서 29세 집단의 비율은 2015년에는 90퍼센트, 2021년에는 84퍼센트로 두 해 모두 가장 높다.

② 2015년 30세에서 49세 집단은 77퍼센트로, 65세 이상 집단의 35퍼센트의 두 배인 70퍼센트보다 높다.

③ 50세에서 64세 집단의 2021년 비율은 73퍼센트로, 2015년의 51퍼센트보다 22퍼센트포인트 더 높다.

⑤ 18세에서 29세 집단만 유일하게 2015년에서 2021년까지의 비율이 감소했다.

26 정답 ④ ＊Bill Evans의 생애

American jazz pianist Bill Evans was born / in New Jersey in 1929. //
미국인 재즈 피아니스트 Bill Evans는 태어났다 / New Jersey에서 1929년에 //

His early training was in classical music. //
그의 초기 교육은 클래식 음악이었다 //

At the age of six, / he began receiving piano lessons, / later adding flute and violin. // <분사구문> ①의 단서 6세에 피아노 수업을 받기 시작함
6세에 / 그는 피아노 수업을 받기 시작했고 / 나중에 플루트와 바이올린을 더했다 //

He earned bachelor's degrees / in piano and music education / from Southeastern Louisiana College in 1950. //
그는 학사 학위를 취득했다 / 피아노와 음악 교육에서 / 1950년에 Southeastern Louisiana 대학에서 // ②의 단서 Southeastern Louisiana 대학에서 학사 학위를 취득함

He **went** on to serve in the army / from 1951 to 1954 / and **played** flute in the Fifth Army Band. // <병렬 구조>
그는 군 복무를 하며 / 1951년에서 1954년까지 / 제5군악대에서 플루트를 연주했다 //

After serving in the military, / he studied composition / at the Mannes School of Music / in New York. // <접속사가 생략되지 않은 분사구문> ③의 단서 군 복무 이후 New York에서 작곡을 공부함
군 복무 이후 / 그는 작곡을 공부했다 / Mannes School of Music에서 / New York에 있는 //

Composer George Russell admired **his** playing / and hired Evans / to record and perform **his** compositions. // ④의 단서 작곡가 George Russell이 Evans를 고용함 = Evans' / = George Russell's
작곡가 George Russell은 그의 연주에 감탄하여 / Evans를 고용했다 / 자신의 곡을 녹음하고 연주하도록 하기 위해 //

Evans became famous for recordings / **made** from the late-1950s through the 1960s. // <앞에 주격 관계대명사와 be동사가 생략됨>
Evans는 음반으로 유명해졌다 / 1950년대 후반부터 1960년대 동안에 만들어진 //

He won his first Grammy Award in 1964 / for his album *Conversations with Myself.* // ⑤의 단서 1964년에 첫 번째 그래미상을 수상함
그는 1964년에 자신의 첫 번째 그래미상을 수상했다 / 자신의 앨범 〈Conversations with Myself〉로 //

Evans' expressive piano works / and his unique harmonic approach / inspired a whole generation of musicians. //
Evans의 표현이 풍부한 피아노 작품과 / 그의 독특한 화성적 접근은 / 전 세대의 음악가들에게 영감을 주었다 //

- - - - - - - - -

- receive ⓥ 받다
- bachelor's degree 학사 학위
- military ⓝ 군대
- composition ⓝ 작곡
- admire ⓥ 감탄하다
- harmonic ⓐ 화성의
- approach ⓝ 접근

미국인 재즈 피아니스트 Bill Evans는 New Jersey에서 1929년에 태어났다. 그의 초기 교육은 클래식 음악이었다. 6세에 그는 피아노 수업을 받기 시작해서, 나중에 플루트와 바이올린을 더했다. 그는 1950년에 Southeastern Louisiana 대학에서 피아노와 음악 교육에서 학사 학위를 취득했다. 그는 1951년에서 1954년까지 군 복무를 하며 제5군악대에서 플루트를 연주했다. 군 복무 이후 그는 New York에 있는 Mannes School of Music에서 작곡을 공부했다. 작곡가 George Russell은 그의 연주에 감탄하여 자신의 곡을 녹음하고 연주하도록 하기 위해 Evans를 고용했다. Evans는 1950년대 후반부터 1960년대 동안에 만들어진 음반으로 유명해졌다. 그는 자신의 앨범 〈Conversations with Myself〉로 1964년에 자신의 첫 번째 그래미상을 수상했다. Evans의 표현이 풍부한 피아노 작품과 그의 독특한 화성적 접근은 전 세대의 음악가들에게 영감을 주었다.

Bill Evans에 관한 다음 글의 내용과 일치하지 않는 것은?

① 6세에 피아노 수업을 받기 시작했다.
At the age of six, he began receiving piano lessons

② Southeastern Louisiana 대학에서 학위를 취득했다.
He earned bachelor's degrees ~ from Southeastern Louisiana College in 1950.

③ 군 복무 이후 뉴욕에서 작곡을 했다.
After serving in the military, he studied composition ~ in New York.

④ 작곡가 George Russell을 고용했다.
Composer George Russell admired his playing and hired Evans

⑤ 1964년에 자신의 첫 번째 그래미상을 수상했다.
He won his first Grammy Award in 1964

> **왜 정답?** ❋❋❋ [정답률 85%]

George Russell이 Evans의 연주에 감탄하여 그를 고용했다고 (Composer George Russell admired his playing and hired Evans) 했으므로 Evans가 George Russell을 고용했다고 한 ④이 글의 내용과 일치하지 않는다.

> **왜 오답?**

① 6세에 피아노 수업을 받기 시작했다. (At the age of six, he began receiving piano lessons)

② Southeastern Louisiana 대학에서 피아노와 음악 교육 학사 학위를 취득했다. (He earned bachelor's degrees ~ Southeastern Louisiana College in 1950.)

③ 군 복무 이후 뉴욕에서 작곡을 공부했다. (After serving in the military, he studied composition at the Mannes School of Music in New York.)

⑤ 1964년에 자신의 첫 번째 그래미상을 수상했다. (He won his first Grammy Award in 1964)

27 정답 ④ ＊은공예 수업 안내

Silversmithing Class /
은공예 수업 /

Kingston Club is offering / a fine jewelry making class. //
Kingston Club은 제공합니다 / 정교한 보석 만들기 수업을 //

Don't miss this great chance / **to make** your own jewelry! // <형용사적 용법(chance 수식)>
이 좋은 기회를 놓치지 마세요 / 여러분만의 보석을 만들 //

When & Where / 언제 & 어디에서 /

- Saturday, October 21, 2023 / (2 p.m. to 4 p.m.) / ①의 단서 두 시간 동안 진행됨
2023년 10월 21일 토요일 / (오후 2시부터 오후 4시까지) /

- Kingston Club studio /
Kingston Club 스튜디오 /

Registration / 등록 /

- Available only online / 온라인으로만 가능 /

- Dates: October 1 – 14, 2023 / [②의 단서] 10월 1일부터 등록할 수 있음
날짜: 2023년 10월 1일부터 14일 /
- Fee: $40 (This includes all tools and materials.) /
비용: 40달러 (이것은 모든 도구와 재료를 포함합니다) / 수동태 동사
- Registration is limited to 6 people. // [③의 단서] 등록 인원은 6명으로 제한됨
등록은 6명으로 제한됩니다 //

Note /
유의 사항 /

- Participants must be at least 16 years old. //
참가자는 16세 이상이어야 합니다 // [④의 단서] 16세 이상만 참가할 수 있음
- No refund / for cancellation on the day of the class /
환불 불가 / 수업 당일 취소에 대한 / [⑤의 단서] 수업 당일 취소 시 환불되지 않음

- -
- available ⓐ 이용할 수 있는 · material ⓝ 재료
- registration ⓝ 등록 · limit ⓥ 제한하다
- participant ⓝ 참가자 · refund ⓝ 환불 · cancellation ⓝ 취소
- -

은공예 수업
Kingston Club은 정교한 보석 만들기 수업을 제공합니다. 여러분만의 보석을 만들 이 좋은 기회를 놓치지 마세요!
언제 & 어디에서
· 2023년 10월 21일 토요일(오후 2시부터 오후 4시까지)
· Kingston Club 스튜디오
등록
· 온라인으로만 가능
· 날짜: 2023년 10월 1일부터 14일
· 비용: 40달러 (이것은 모든 도구와 재료를 포함합니다.)
· 등록은 6명으로 제한됩니다.
유의 사항
· 참가자는 16세 이상이어야 합니다.
· 수업 당일 취소 시 환불 불가

> Silversmithing Class에 관한 다음 안내문의 내용과 일치하지 <u>않는</u> 것은?
> ① 두 시간 동안 진행된다. 2 p.m. to 4 p.m.
> ② 10월 1일부터 등록할 수 있다. Dates: October 1 – 14, 2023
> ③ 등록 인원이 6명으로 제한된다. Registration is limited to 6 people.
> ④ 참가 연령에 제한이 없다. Participants must be at least 16 years old.
> ⑤ 수업 당일 취소 시 환불이 불가하다.
> No refund for cancellation on the day of the class

➢**왜 정답 ?** ✽❀❀ [정답률 96%]
참가자는 16세 이상이어야 하므로(Participants must be at least 16 years old.) 참가 연령에 제한이 없다고 한 ④이 안내문의 내용과 일치하지 않는다.

➢**왜 오답 ?**
① 오후 2시부터 4시까지 두 시간 동안 진행된다. (2 p.m. to 4 p.m.)
② 10월 1일부터 등록이 시작된다. (Dates: October 1 – 14, 2023)
③ 등록 인원이 6명으로 제한된다. (Registration is limited to 6 people.)
⑤ 수업 당일 취소에 대한 환불은 불가하다. (No refund ~ on the day of the class)

28 정답 ⑤ ✽2023 해양 인식 영상 대회 ━━━━━━

2023 Ocean Awareness Film Contest /
2023 해양 인식 영상 대회 /
병렬 구조
<u>Join</u> our 7th annual film contest / and <u>show</u> your knowledge / of marine conservation. //
우리의 일곱 번째 연례 영상 대회에 참가하세요 / 그리고 여러분의 지식을 보여주세요 / 해양 보존에 관한 //

□ **Theme /** 주제 /
- Ocean Wildlife / Ocean Pollution / [①의 단서] 주제는 두 가지임
해양 야생 생물 / 해양 오염 /

(Choose one of the above.) //
(위에서 하나를 선택하세요) //

□ **Guidelines /** 지침 /
- Participants: / High school students / [②의 단서] 고등학생만 참가할 수 있음
참가자 / 고등학생 /
- Submission deadline: / September 22, 2023 /
제출 기한 / 2023년 9월 22일 /
- The video must be between 10 and 15 minutes. //
영상은 10분에서 15분 사이여야 합니다 / [③의 단서] 영상은 10분에서 15분 사이여야 함
조동사가 포함된 수동태
- All entries must be uploaded / to our website. //
모든 출품작은 업로드되어야 합니다 / 우리 웹사이트에 //
- Only one entry per person / [④의 단서] 1인당 하나만 출품할 수 있음
1인당 오직 하나의 출품작 /

□ **Prizes /** 상금 /
· 1st place / $100 / · 2nd place: / $70 / · 3rd place: / $50 /
1등 / 100달러 / 2등 / 70달러 / 3등 / 50달러 /
미래시제 수동태
(Winners will be announced / on our website.) //
(수상자는 공지될 것입니다 / 우리 웹사이트에) // [⑥의 단서] 수상자는 웹사이트에 공지됨

For more information, / please visit www.oceanawareFC.com. //
더 많은 정보를 위해 / www.oceanawareFC.com을 방문하세요 //

- -
- awareness ⓝ 인식 · annual ⓐ 연례의 · knowledge ⓝ 지식
- marine ⓐ 해양의 · conservation ⓝ 보존 · pollution ⓝ 오염
- submission ⓝ 제출 · entry ⓝ 출품[응모]작
- -

2023 해양 인식 영상 대회
우리의 일곱 번째 연례 영상 대회에 참가하여 해양 보존에 관한 여러분의 지식을 보여주세요.
□ 주제
– 해양 야생 생물 / 해양 오염
  (위에서 하나를 선택하세요.)
□ 지침
– 참가자: 고등학생
– 제출 기한: 2023년 9월 22일
– 영상은 10분에서 15분 사이여야 합니다.
– 모든 출품작은 우리 웹사이트에 업로드되어야 합니다.
– 1인당 오직 하나의 출품작
□ 상금
· 1등: 100달러 · 2등: 70달러 · 3등: 50달러
  (수상자는 우리 웹사이트에 공지될 것입니다.)
더 많은 정보를 위해 www.oceanawareFC.com을 방문하세요.

> 2023 Ocean Awareness Film Contest에 관한 다음 안내문의 내용과 일치하는 것은?
> ① 세 가지 주제 중 하나를 선택해야 한다.
> Theme: Ocean Wildlife / Ocean Pollution
> ② 중학생이 참가할 수 있다.
> Participants: High school students
> ③ 영상은 10분을 넘길 수 없다.
> The video must be between 10 and 15 minutes.
> ④ 1인당 두 개까지 출품할 수 있다.
> Only one entry per person
> ⑤ 수상자는 웹사이트에 공지될 것이다.
> Winners will be announced on our website.

➢**왜 정답 ?** ✽❀❀ [정답률 94%]
수상자는 웹사이트에 공지될 것이라고(Winners will be announced on our website.) 했으므로 안내문의 내용과 일치하는 것은 ⑤이다.

➢**왜 오답 ?**
① 선택해야 하는 주제는 두 가지만 제시되었다. (Theme: Ocean Wildlife / Ocean Pollution)
② 고등학생만 참가할 수 있다. (Participants: High school students)
③ 영상은 10분에서 15분 사이여야 하므로 10분을 넘겨야 한다. (The video must be between 10 and 15 minutes.) 주의
④ 1인당 한 개만 출품할 수 있다. (Only one entry per person)

29 정답 ④ ＊Monday Morning Quarterback

다음 글의 밑줄 친 부분 중, 어법상 틀린 것은?

There is a <mark>reason</mark> / the title "Monday Morning Quarterback"
뒤에 관계부사 why가 생략됨
exists. //
이유가 있다 / 'Monday Morning Quarterback'이라는 이름이 존재하는 //

Just read the comments on social media / from fans <mark>discussing</mark>
현재분사(fans 수식)
the weekend's games, /
소셜 미디어의 댓글만 읽어 보아라 / 주말 경기에 대해 토론하는 팬들의 /

and you quickly see / <mark>how many people believe</mark> / they could
간접의문문
play, coach, and manage sport teams / more ① <mark>successfully</mark> /
than those on the field. //
동사(could play, coach, manage)를 수식하는 부사
그러면 여러분은 금방 알 수 있다 / 얼마나 많은 사람들이 믿는지 / 자신이 경기를 뛰고,
감독하고, 스포츠팀을 관리할 수 있다고 / 더 성공적으로 / 경기장에 있는 사람들보다 //

This goes for the boardroom as well. //
이것은 이사회실에서도 마찬가지이다 //

Students and professionals / with years of training and
specialized degrees / in sport business / may also find <mark>themselves</mark>
목적격(재귀대명사)
목적격 보어(진행형 수동태)
② <mark>being given</mark> advice /
학생들과 전문가들은 / 수년간의 훈련을 받고 전문적인 학위를 가진 / 스포츠 사업에서 / 또한
충고를 듣고 있는 자신을 발견할지도 모른다 /

on how to do their jobs / from friends, family, or even total
strangers / without any expertise. //
어떻게 자신의 일을 해야 하는지에 대한 / 친구들, 가족, 혹은 심지어 완전히 낯선
사람들로부터 / 전문 지식이 전혀 없는 //

<mark>Executives</mark> in sport management / ③ <mark>have</mark> decades of knowledge
핵심 주어(복수) *복수 동사*
and experience / in their respective fields. //
스포츠 경영 임원진들은 / 수십 년의 지식과 경험을 가지고 있다 / 자신의 각 분야에서 //

However, / many of them face criticism / from fans and
단서 telling의 행위자와 대상이 서로 다름
community members / telling ④ themselves(→ them) / how to
run their business. //
현재분사(fans and community members 수식)
하지만 / 그들 중 많은 사람들이 비난에 직면한다 / 팬들과 지역 사회 구성원들로부터의 /
그들에게 알려주는 / 그들의 사업 운영 방식을 //

Very few people tell <mark>their doctor</mark> / <mark>how to perform surgery</mark> / or
간접목적어 *직접목적어*
<mark>their accountant</mark> / <mark>how to prepare their taxes</mark>, /
간접목적어 *직접목적어*
자신의 의사에게 알려 주는 사람은 거의 없다 / 수술하는 방법을 / 또는 회계사(에게) / 자신의
세금을 준비하는 방법을 /

but many people provide feedback / <mark>on</mark> ⑤ <mark>how</mark> sport
전치사 *간접의문문*
<mark>organizations should be managed</mark>. //
그러나 많은 사람들이 피드백을 제공한다 / 스포츠 조직이 어떻게 관리되어야 하는지에 대한 //

- exist ⓥ 존재하다 · professional ⓝ 전문가 · degree ⓝ 학위
- expertise ⓝ 전문 지식 · executive ⓝ 경영진, 간부
- decade ⓝ 10년 · respective ⓐ 각자의
- criticism ⓝ 비판, 비난 · surgery ⓝ 수술
- accountant ⓝ 회계사 · organization ⓝ 조직

'Monday Morning Quarterback'이라는 이름이 존재하는 이유가 있다.
주말 경기에 대해 토론하는 팬들의 소셜 미디어의 댓글만 읽어봐도 여러분은
자신이 경기장에 있는 사람들보다 더 성공적으로 경기를 뛰고, 감독하고,
스포츠팀을 관리할 수 있다고 얼마나 많은 사람들이 믿는지 금방 알 수 있다.
이것은 이사회실에서도 마찬가지이다. 스포츠 사업에서 수년간의 훈련을 받고
전문적인 학위를 가진 학생들과 전문가들 또한 친구들, 가족, 혹은 전문 지식이
전혀 없는 심지어 완전히 낯선 사람들로부터 어떻게 자신의 일을 해야 하는지에
대한 충고를 듣고 있는 자신을 발견할지도 모른다. 스포츠 경영 임원진들은
자신의 각 분야에서 수십 년의 지식과 경험을 가지고 있다. 하지만, 그들
중 많은 사람들이 그들에게 그들의 사업 운영 방식을 알려주는 팬들과 지역
사회 구성원들로부터의 비난에 직면한다. 자신의 의사에게 수술하는 방법을
알려주거나 자신의 회계사에게 자신의 세금을 준비하는 방법을 알려주는
사람은 거의 없지만, 많은 사람들이 스포츠 조직이 어떻게 관리되어야 하는지에
대한 피드백은 제공한다.

＞왜 정답? ＊＊＊ [정답률 38%]

④ telling의 행위자와 대상이 다르다!

However, / many of them face criticism / from fans and
telling의 대상
community members / [telling ④ themselves(→ them) /
telling의 행위자 *현재분사* *many of them을 가리켜야 함*
how to run their business]. //

단서 밑줄이 재귀대명사 themselves에 있고 앞에 telling이 있으므로
발상 재귀적 용법의 재귀대명사로 맞게 쓰였는지 확인해야 한다.
해결 그런데 문맥상 현재분사 telling의 행위자는 '팬들과 지역 사회 구성원들'이고
telling의 대상은 '그들 중 많은 사람들'로 같지 않다. 따라서 재귀대명사가
아니라 일반 대명사인 them으로 고쳐야 어법상 적절하다.
개념 동사의 행위가 주어에게 가해질 때(주어 = 목적어) 목적어로 재귀대명사를 쓴다.

＞왜 오답?

① 부사는 동사를 수식할 수 있다.

and로 연결된 절: 제외하고 생각하기
Just read the comments on social media / from fans
discussing the weekend's games, / and you quickly see
/ how many people believe / they could play, coach, and
manage sport teams / more ① successfully / than those on
부사 *동사(구)*
the field.

부사 successfully에 밑줄이 있으므로 수식하는 대상을 찾아 부사의 수식을 받을 수
있는지를 확인한다.
문맥상 '더 성공적으로 경기를 뛰고, 감독하고, 스포츠팀을 관리한다'는 것이므로
동사구 could play, coach, and manage를 수식하고 있다.
부사는 동사를 수식할 수 있으므로 successfully는 적절하게 쓰였다.

② 수동의 관계에는 「be+p.p.」 형태를 사용한다.

주어
Students and professionals / with years of training and
specialized degrees / in sport business / may also find
농사
themselves ② being given advice / on how to do their jobs
목적격 보어
/ from friends, family, or even total strangers / without any
목적어
expertise. //
전치사구: 제외하고 생각하기

밑줄이 수동의 의미를 나타내는 being given에 있으니까, 수식을 하는 명사와의
관계가 수동일 것이다.
밑줄 친 being given은 may find의 목적격 보어 자리에 왔다. find는 지각동사와
마찬가지로 진행 중인 순간을 나타내기 위해 목적격 보어 자리에 현재분사를 쓸 수
있다.
따라서 충고를 '듣고 있는' 자신을 발견한다는 의미로 being given이 목적격 보어
자리에 온 것은 적절하다.

③ 동사는 주어에 그 수를 일치시킨다.

핵심 주어(복수) *수식어구*
Executives in sport management / ③ have decades of
복수 동사
knowledge and experience / in their respective fields. //
목적어

동사 have에 밑줄이 있으므로 주어를 찾아 수 일치 여부를 확인한다.
문장의 핵심 주어는 Executives로 복수 명사이므로 동사도 복수 동사인 have가
알맞게 쓰였다.
주어를 꾸미는 수식어구와 상관없이 핵심 주어의 수에 동사의 수를 일치시킨다. **개념**

2023.9
9회

⑤ 간접의문문은 명사 역할을 한다.

> but으로 연결된 절: 제외하고 생각하기
> Very few people tell their doctor / how to perform surgery /
> or their accountant / how to prepare their taxes, / but **many**
> _{주어}
> **people** _{동사}**provide** _{목적어}feedback / _{전치사}**on** ⑤ _{전치사의 목적어(간접의문문)}**how** sport organizations
> should be managed. //

의문문이 문장의 일부로 명사절의 역할을 할 때 이를 간접의문문이라고 하는데,
간접의문문은 「의문사+주어+동사」의 어순을 갖는다. [개념]
의문사 how가 전치사 on 뒤의 목적어 자리에서 명사절을 이끌고 있다.
「의문사(how) + 주어(sport organizations) + 동사(should be managed)」가
간접의문문의 어순에 알맞게 쓰였다.

---

30 정답 ② *이사가 힘든 아이들

다음 글의 밑줄 친 부분 중, 문맥상 낱말의 쓰임이 적절하지 않은 것은?
[3점]

_{부사절 접속사(대조)}
While moving is difficult for everyone, / it is particularly
stressful for children. //
이사는 모두에게 힘들지만 / 그것은 아이들에게 특히 스트레스가 많은 일이다 //

They lose their sense of security / and may feel disoriented /
_{부사절 접속사} _{주격 관계대명사}
when their routine is disrupted / and all **that** is ① familiar is
taken away. //
그들은 안도감을 잃고 / 혼란스러움을 느낄 수도 있다 / 그들의 일상이 무너질 때 / 그리고
익숙한 모든 것이 사라질 때 //

Young children, ages 3–6, / are particularly affected / by a move. //
3세에서 6세 사이의 어린아이들은 / 특히 영향을 받는다 / 이사에 의해 //

Their understanding at this stage / is quite literal, / and **it** is ②
_{가주어}
_{to imagine의 의미상 주어} _{진주어}
easy(→ difficult) **for them** / **to imagine** beforehand / a new home
> 단서 이해력에 융통성이 없는 시기임
and their new room. //
이 시기에 그들의 이해력은 / 꽤 융통성이 없다 / 그리고 ~은 그들에게 쉽다(→ 어렵다) / 미리
상상하는 것은 / 새로운 집과 자신의 새로운 방을 //

Young children may have worries / such as "Will I still be me in
the new place?" / and "Will my toys and bed come with us?" //
어린아이들은 걱정들을 가질지도 모른다 / "내가 새로운 곳에서 여전히 나일까"와 같은 /
그리고 "내 장난감과 침대가 우리와 함께 갈까"(와 같은) //

_{가주어} _{진주어}
It is important **to establish** a balance / between validating
_{helping의 목적어와 목적격 보어(원형부정사)}
children's past experiences / and focusing on helping **them** / ③
adjust to the new place. //
균형을 잡는 것이 중요하다 / 아이들의 과거 경험을 인정하는 것 사이에서 / 그들을 돕는 데
집중하는 것과 / 새로운 곳에 적응하도록 //

_{형용사적 용법(opportunities 수식)}
Children need to have opportunities / **to share** their backgrounds
_{주격 관계대명사}
/ in a way **that** ④ respects their past / as an important part / of
_{간접의문문}
who they are. //
아이들은 기회를 가질 필요가 있다 / 자신의 배경을 공유할 / 자신의 과거를 존중하는
방식으로 / 중요한 부분으로서 / 자신이 누구인지에 대한 //

_{계속적 용법의 주격 관계대명사}
This contributes / to building a sense of community, / **which**
= children
is essential for all children, / especially **those** in ⑤ transition. //
이것은 기여한다 / 공동체 의식을 형성하는 데 / 이는 모든 아이들에게 매우 중요하다 / 특히
변화를 겪는 아이들(에게) //

- **particularly** ⓐ𝖽 특히 · **security** ⓝ 안도감, 안심
- **disoriented** ⓐ 혼란에 빠진 · **disrupt** ⓥ 방해하다
- **take away** ~을 제거하다 · **literal** ⓐ 융통성이 없는, 문자 그대로의
- **beforehand** ⓐ𝖽 미리 · **establish** ⓥ 확고히 하다, 설립하다
- **validate** ⓥ 인정하다 · **contribute** ⓥ 기여하다
- **transition** ⓝ 변화

이사는 모두에게 힘들지만, 아이들에게 특히 스트레스가 많은 일이다.
그들은 안도감을 잃고 그들의 일상이 무너지고 ① 익숙한 모든 것이 사라질
때 혼란스러움을 느낄 수도 있다. 3세에서 6세 사이의 어린아이들은 이사에
특히 영향을 받는다. 이 시기에 그들의 이해력은 꽤 융통성이 없고, 그들이
새로운 집과 자신의 새로운 방을 미리 상상하는 것은 ② 쉽다(→ 어렵다).
어린아이들은 "내가 새로운 곳에서 여전히 나일까?"와 "내 장난감과 침대가
우리와 함께 갈까?"와 같은 걱정들을 가질지도 모른다. 아이들의 과거 경험을
인정하는 것과 그들이 새로운 곳에 ③ 적응하도록 돕는 데 집중하는 것
사이에서 균형을 잡는 것이 중요하다. 아이들은 자신이 누구인지에 대한 중요한
부분으로서 자신의 과거를 ④ 존중하는 방식으로 자신의 배경을 공유할 기회를
가질 필요가 있다. 이것은 공동체 의식을 형성하는 데 기여하고, 이는 모든
아이들, 특히 ⑤ 변화를 겪는 아이들에게 매우 중요하다.

> **왜 정답?** ✱✱✱ [정답률 63%]

② **easy** 쉬운

> 이 시기에 그들의 이해력은 꽤 융통성이 없어서, 그들이 새로운 집과
> 자신의 새로운 방을 미리 상상하는 것은 ② ~~쉽다~~.
> 어렵다

→ 아이들의 이해력에 융통성이 없는 시기라고 했으므로, 새로운 집이나 방을
상상하는 것이 '쉽다'고 하는 것은 문맥에 맞지 않는다.
▶ easy를 difficult(어려운)와 같은 반의어로 바꿔야 함

> **왜 오답?**

① **familiar** 익숙한

> 이사는 모두에게 힘들지만, 아이들에게 특히 스트레스가 많은 일이다.
> 그들은 안도감을 잃고 그들의 일상이 무너지고 ① 익숙한 모든 것이
> 사라질 때 혼란스러움을 느낄 수도 있다.

→ 이사는 아이들에게 특히 스트레스라고 했으므로, 이사로 인해 '익숙한' 모든 것이
사라질 때 아이들은 혼란스러움을 느낄 것이다.
▶ familiar는 문맥에 맞음

③ **adjust** 적응하다

> 어린아이들은 "내가 새로운 곳에서 여전히 나일까?"와 "내 장난감과
> 침대가 우리와 함께 갈까?"와 같은 걱정들을 가질지도 모른다.
> 아이들의 과거 경험을 인정하는 것과 그들이 새로운 곳에 ③
> 적응하도록 돕는 데 집중하는 것 사이에서 균형을 잡는 것이 중요하다.

→ 아이들은 과거로부터 변하는 것을 혼란스러워하여 걱정하므로 이사 가기 전의
경험은 인정하고, 새로운 곳에는 '적응하도록' 돕는 것이 중요할 것이다.
▶ adjust는 문맥에 맞음

④ **respects** 존중하다

> 아이들은 자신이 누구인지에 대한 중요한 부분으로서 자신의 과거를
> ④ 존중하는 방식으로 자신의 배경을 공유할 기회를 가질 필요가 있다.

→ 앞에서 아이들의 과거 경험을 인정하는 것도 중요하다고 했으므로, 아이들은
자신의 과거를 '존중하는' 방식으로 자신의 배경을 공유할 기회를 가져야 할 것이다.
▶ respects는 문맥에 맞음

⑤ **transition** 변화

> **이것(This)**은 공동체 의식을 형성하는 데 기여하고, 이는 모든 아이들,
> 특히 ⑤ 변화를 겪는 아이들에게 매우 중요하다.

→ 앞 문장의 내용을 '이것'이라고 하면서, 배경을 공유할 기회를 가지는 것은 이사로
인해 '변화'를 겪는 아이들에게 중요하다고 하는 흐름은 적절하다.
▶ transition은 문맥에 맞음

31 정답 ① ＊감정에 근거한 두려움

Many people are terrified / to fly in airplanes. //
부사적 용법(감정의 원인)
많은 사람들은 두려워한다 / 비행기를 타는 것을 //

Often, / this fear stems / from a lack of control. //
종종 / 이 두려움은 비롯된다 / 통제력의 부족에서 //

The pilot is in control, / not the passengers, / and this lack of control instills fear. //
조종사는 통제를 하지만 / 승객은 그렇지 않으며 / 이러한 통제력의 부족은 두려움을 스며들게 한다 //

Many potential passengers are so afraid / they choose to drive great distances / to get to a destination / instead of flying. //
so ~ (that) ...: 너무 ~해서 …하다 / *부사적 용법(목적)* / *that이 생략됨*
많은 잠재적인 승객들은 너무 두려워서 / 그들은 먼 거리를 운전하는 것을 선택한다 / 목적지에 도착하기 위해 / 비행하는 대신 //

But their decision to drive / is based solely on emotion, / not logic. //
형용사적 용법(decision 수식) / **단서1** 비행기를 타는 것이 무서워 운전을 하는 것은 논리가 아닌 감정에 근거한 결정임
그러나 운전을 하기로 한 그들의 결정은 / 오직 감정에 근거한다 / 논리가 아닌 //

Logic says / that statistically, / the odds of dying in a car crash / are around 1 in 5,000, / while the odds of dying in a plane crash / are closer to 1 in 11 million. //
목적어절 접속사 / *핵심 주어(복수)* / *복수 동사* / **단서2** 통계적으로 자동차 사고로 사망할 확률이 비행기 사고로 사망할 확률보다 훨씬 높음
논리는 말한다 / 통계적으로 / 자동차 사고로 사망할 확률은 / 약 5,000분의 1이고 / 반면 비행기 사고로 사망할 확률은 / 1,100만분의 1에 더 가깝다고 //

If you're going to take a risk, / especially one that could possibly involve / your well-being, / wouldn't you want the odds / in your favor? //
= risk / *주격 관계대명사* / *'~에게 유리하게'*
만약 여러분이 위험을 감수할 것이라면 / 특히 포함할 수 있는 것이라면 / 여러분의 안녕을 / 여러분은 확률을 원하지 않겠는가 / 여러분에게 유리한 //

However, / most people choose the option / that will cause them / the least amount of anxiety. //
주격 관계대명사 / *간접목적어* / *직접목적어*
그러나 / 대부분의 사람들은 선택지를 고른다 / 그들에게 야기할 수 있는 / 최소한의 불안감을 //

Pay attention / to the thoughts you have / about taking the risk / and make sure / you're basing your decision on facts, / not just feelings. //
앞에 목적격 관계대명사가 생략됨 / **단서3** 감정이 아니라 사실에 근거해서 결정을 내리고 있는지 확인하라고 함
주의를 기울여라 / 여러분이 가지고 있는 생각에 / 위험을 감수하는 것에 대해 / 그리고 확인하라 / 여러분이 결정을 사실에 근거하고 있는지 / 단지 감정이 아니라 //

- terrified ⓐ 두려워하는
- stem from ~에서 생겨나다
- passenger ⓝ 승객
- potential ⓐ 잠재적인
- destination ⓝ 목적지
- base ⓥ 근거하다
- solely ⓐ𝒹 오로지
- logic ⓝ 논리
- statistically ⓐ𝒹 통계적으로
- odds ⓝ (어떤 일이 있을) 가능성
- boredom ⓝ 지루함
- responsibility ⓝ 책임감

많은 사람들은 비행기를 타는 것을 두려워한다. 종종, 이 두려움은 통제력의 부족에서 비롯된다. 조종사는 통제를 하지만, 승객은 그렇지 않으며, 이러한 통제력의 부족은 두려움을 스며들게 한다. 많은 잠재적인 승객들은 너무 두려워서 그들은 비행기를 타는 대신 목적지에 도착하기 위해 먼 거리를 운전하는 것을 선택한다. 그러나 운전을 하기로 한 그들의 결정은 논리가 아닌 오직 감정에 근거한다. 논리에 따르면 통계적으로 자동차 사고로 사망할 확률은 약 5,000분의 1이고, 반면 비행기 사고로 사망할 확률은 1,100만분의 1에 더 가깝다고 한다. 만약 여러분이 위험을 감수할 것이라면, 특히 여러분의 안녕을 혹시 포함할 수 있는 위험을 감수할 것이라면, 여러분에게 유리한 확률을 원하지 않겠는가? 그러나 대부분의 사람들은 그들에게 최소한의 **불안감**을 야기할 수 있는 선택을 한다. 위험을 감수하는 것에 대해 여러분이 가지고 있는 생각에 주의를 기울이고 여러분이 결정을 단지 감정이 아닌 사실에 근거하고 있는지 확인하라.

다음 빈칸에 들어갈 말로 가장 적절한 것을 고르시오.

① **anxiety** 확률보다 두려움에 근거하여 자동차를 탐
불안감
② boredom 지루함과는 관련 없는 내용임
지루함
③ confidence 자신감을 최소화한다는 내용이 아님
자신감
④ satisfaction 최소한의 만족감을 주는 선택이 아님
만족감
⑤ responsibility 책임감과는 관련 없는 내용임
책임감

왜 정답? ＊＊❀ [정답률 61%]

빈칸 문장
그러나(However) 대부분의 사람들은 그들에게 최소한의 _____ 을 야기할 수 있는 선택을 한다.

➡ **빈칸 문장:** 사람들은 '무엇'을 최소화하는 선택을 한다.

글의 앞부분
- 비행기를 타는 것이 두려워 먼 거리를 운전하는 선택을 함
  = 감정에 근거한 결정 **단서1**
- 자동차 사고로 사망할 확률 ＞ 비행기 사고로 사망할 확률 **단서2**

➡ 논리적으로는 비행기로 사망할 확률이 더 낮음에도 사람들은 단지 두려운 감정 때문에 자동차 운전을 선택한다.

마지막 문장
단지 감정이 아니라 사실에 근거한 결정을 하고 있는지 확인해야 함 **단서3**

➡ 감정이 아니라 사실에 근거한 결정을 해야 한다.
▶ 많은 사람들이 논리가 아니라 감정, 즉 ① '불안감'을 최소화하는 선택을 한다는 것이다.

왜 오답?
② 지루함을 줄이기 위한 선택을 한다는 내용이 아니다.
③ 자신감을 줄이기 위한 선택을 한다는 내용이 아니다.
④ 논리가 아니라 감정에 근거한 결정은 오히려 각자의 만족감을 최대화하려는 결정이라고 볼 수 있다. **주의**
⑤ 책임감과 관련된 내용이 아니다.

---

32 정답 ③ ＊동물에 대한 인간의 언어 사용

The famous primatologist / Frans de Waal, of Emory University, says /
뒤에 목적어절 접속사 that이 생략됨
유명한 영장류학자 / Emory 대학의 Frans de Waal은 말한다 /

humans downplay similarities / between us and other animals / as a way of maintaining our spot / at the top of our imaginary ladder. //
단서1 인간은 상상 속의 높은 위치를 유지하기 위해 동물이 가진 인간과의 유사성을 경시함
인간은 유사성을 경시한다고 / 우리와 다른 동물들 사이의 / 우리의 위치를 유지하는 방법으로 / 우리의 상상 속 사다리의 꼭대기에서 //

Scientists, / de Waal points out, / can be some of the worst offenders / — employing technical language / to distance the other animals from us. //
삽입절 / *부사적 용법(목적)*
과학자들은 / de Waal은 지적한다 / 최악의 범죄자들 중 일부일 수 있다고 / 기술적인 언어를 사용하는 / 우리와 다른 동물들 사이에 거리를 두기 위해 //

They call / "kissing" in chimps / "mouth-to-mouth contact"; / they call / "friends" between primates / "favorite affiliation partners"; /
그들은 부른다 / 침팬지의 '키스'를 / '입과 입의 접촉'이라고 / 그들은 부른다 / 영장류 사이의 '친구'를 / '좋아하는 제휴 파트너'라고 /

they interpret evidence / **showing** that crows and chimps can 현재분사(evidence 수식)

make tools / as being somehow qualitatively different / from the

kind of toolmaking / **said** to define humanity. // 앞에 주격 관계대명사와 be동사가 생략됨

그들은 증거를 해석한다 / 까마귀와 침팬지가 도구를 만들 수 있다는 것을 보여주는 / 아무래도 질적으로 다르다고 / 그 종류의 도구 제작과는 / 인류를 정의한다고 하는 //

단서3 동물의 지능이 인간보다 우세하면 본능으로 치부함

If an animal can beat us / at a cognitive task / — like **how** certain 전치사 like의 목적어절을 이끄는 의문사

bird species can remember / the precise locations of thousands '치부하다'

of seeds / — they **write** it **off** instinct, / not intelligence. //

만약 동물이 우리를 이길 수 있다면 / 인지적인 과업에서 / 특정 종의 새들이 기억할 수 있는 방식처럼 / 수천 개의 씨앗의 정확한 위치를 / 그들은 그것을 본능으로 치부한다 / 지능이 아니라 //

This and so many more tricks of language / are **what** de Waal 선행사를 포함하는 관계대명사

has termed / "linguistic castration." //

이것과 더 많은 언어적 수법은 / de Waal이 명명한 것이다 / '언어적 거세'라고 //

부사적 용법(목적)

The way we use our tongues / **to disempower** animals, / the way

we invent words / to maintain our spot at the top. //

우리가 우리의 언어를 사용하는 방식 / 동물로부터 힘을 빼앗기 위해 / 우리가 단어들을 만드는 방식 / 꼭대기에서 우리의 위치를 유지하기 위해 //

단서4 우리는 동물로부터 힘을 빼앗고 우리의 높은 위치를 유지하는 방식으로 언어를 사용

- downplay ⓥ 경시하다 • similarity ⓝ 유사성
- imaginary ⓐ 상상에만 존재하는 • ladder ⓝ 사다리
- offender ⓝ 범죄자 • contact ⓝ 접촉 • primate ⓝ 영장류
- interpret ⓥ 해석하다 • evidence ⓝ 증거 • crow ⓝ 까마귀
- qualitatively ad 질적으로 • define ⓥ 정의하다
- humanity ⓝ 인류 • beat ⓥ 이기다 • cognitive ⓐ 인지적인
- precise ⓐ 정확한 • instinct ⓝ 본능 • intelligence ⓝ 지능
- linguistic ⓐ 언어(학)의 • castration ⓝ 거세
- overestimate ⓥ 과대평가하다 • misconception ⓝ 오해

Emory 대학의 유명한 영장류학자 Frans de Waal은 인간은 상상 속 사다리의 꼭대기에서 우리의 위치를 유지하는 방법으로 우리와 다른 동물들 사이의 유사성을 경시한다고 말한다. de Waal은 과학자들이 **우리와 다른 동물들 사이에 거리를 두기** 위해 기술적인 언어를 사용하는 최악의 범죄자들 중 일부일 수 있다고 지적한다. 그들은 침팬지의 '키스'를 '입과 입의 접촉'이라고 부르고, 영장류 사이의 '친구'를 '좋아하는 제휴 파트너'라고 부르며, 그들은 까마귀와 침팬지가 도구를 만들 수 있다는 것을 보여주는 증거를 인류를 정의한다고 하는 종류의 도구 제작과는 아무래도 질적으로 다르다고 해석한다. 만약 동물이, 특정 종의 새들이 수천 개의 씨앗의 정확한 위치를 기억할 수 있는 방식처럼, 인지적인 과업에서 우리를 이길 수 있다면, 그들은 그것을 지능이 아니라 본능으로 치부한다. 이것과 더 많은 언어적 수법은 de Waal이 '언어적 거세'라고 명명한 것이다. 우리가 동물로부터 힘을 빼앗기 위해 우리의 언어를 사용하는 방식이며, 우리가 꼭대기에서 우리의 위치를 유지하기 위해 단어들을 만드는 방식이다.

다음 빈칸에 들어갈 말로 가장 적절한 것을 고르시오. [3점]

① define human instincts 인간의 본능을 정의하기 위해 언어를 사용하는 것 아님
  인간의 본능을 정의하다
② overestimate chimps' intelligence 침팬지는 예시로 제시되었음
  침팬지의 지능을 과대평가하다
③ distance the other animals from us 인간과 동물 사이에 거리를 두기 위해
  우리와 다른 동물들 사이에 거리를 두다 기술적인 언어를 사용함
④ identify animals' negative emotions
  동물의 부정적 감정을 밝히다 동물의 감정을 밝히기 위해 언어를 사용하는 것이 아님
⑤ correct our misconceptions about nature
  자연에 관한 우리의 오해를 바로잡다 자연에 관한 우리의 오해는 언급되지 않음

| 문제 풀이 순서 | ★★★ [정답률 47%]

1st 먼저 빈칸 문장을 읽고, 빈칸에 들어갈 말을 예측한다.

빈칸 문장 | de Waal은 과학자들이 _____ 위해 기술적인 언어를 사용하는 최악의 범죄자들 중 일부일 수 있다고 지적한다.

➡ 과학자들이 '무엇을' 위해 기술적인 언어를 사용하는 범죄자라고 했으므로, **단서** 부정적인 목적으로 언어를 사용한다는 내용이 이어질 것이다. **발상**

2nd 글의 나머지 부분을 확인해서 정답을 찾는다.

- 인간은 상상 속의 높은 위치를 유지하기 위해 동물이 가진 인간과의 유사성을 경시함 **단서1**
  예시 **1**: 침팬지의 키스 → 입과 입의 접촉
  예시 **2**: 영장류 사이의 친구 → 좋아하는 제휴 파트너
  예시 **3**: 까마귀와 침팬지의 도구 제작 능력 → 인류의 도구 제작 능력과 질적으로 다름 **단서2**
- 동물이 인간보다 우세한 경우에는 지능이 아니라 본능으로 치부함 **단서3**

➡ 우리는 동물의 힘을 빼앗고 우리가 그들보다 우세한 위치에 있다는 것을 유지하기 위한 방법으로 언어를 사용한다는 것이다. **단서4**
▶ 즉, 과학자들은 ③ '우리와 다른 동물들 사이에 거리를 두기' 위해 기술적인 언어를 사용하는 범죄자일 수 있다.

| 선택지 분석 |

① **define human instincts**
  인간의 본능을 정의하다
인간의 본능을 정의하는 것이 아니라 인간이 동물보다 우세함을 주장하기 위해 언어를 사용한다는 것이다.

② **overestimate chimps' intelligence**
  침팬지의 지능을 과대평가하다
침팬지의 지능을 오히려 낮게 평가하기 위해 언어를 사용한다는 것이다.

③ **distance the other animals from us**
  우리와 다른 동물들 사이에 거리를 두다
인간과 동물 사이에 거리를 두기 위해 기술적인 언어를 사용한다고 했다.

④ **identify animals' negative emotions**
  동물의 부정적 감정을 밝히다
동물의 부정적 감정은 언급되지 않았다.

⑤ **correct our misconceptions about nature**
  자연에 관한 우리의 오해를 바로잡다
자연을 오해하는 것이 아니라 일부러 경시한다고 했다.

---

33 정답 ② ＊관심 분야에서는 읽기를 피하지 않는다!

A key to engagement and achievement / **is** providing students / 핵심 주어 단수 동사

with **relevant texts they will be interested in**. //

참여와 성취의 핵심은 / 학생들에게 제공하는 것이다 / 그들이 관심 있어 할 적절한 글을 //

My scholarly work and my teaching / **have been** deeply

influenced / by the work of Rosalie Fink. // 현재완료(계속)

나의 학문적인 연구와 나의 수업은 / 깊이 영향을 받아왔다 / Rosalie Fink의 연구에 //

주격 관계대명사

She interviewed twelve adults / **who** were highly successful in

their work, / **including** a physicist, a biochemist, and a company 분사 형태의 전치사

CEO. //

그녀는 열두 명의 성인들과 면담했다 / 그들의 직업에서 매우 성공한 / 물리학자, 생화학자 그리고 회사의 최고 경영자를 포함해 //

앞의 had보다 더 이전 시점을 나타내는 과거완료

All of them had dyslexia / and **had had** significant problems

with reading / throughout their school years. //

그들 모두가 난독증이 있었고 / 읽기에 상당한 문제를 겪어 왔다 / 그들의 학령기 내내 //

부사절 접속사(대조) 목적어절 접속사

While she expected to find / **that** they had avoided reading / 형용사적 용법(ways 수식) to bypass와 병렬 구조

and discovered ways / **to bypass** it / or **compensate** with other

strategies / for learning, / she found the opposite. //

그녀는 알아낼 것을 예상했으나 / 그들이 읽기를 피했고 / 방법을 발견했을 것이라고 / 그것을 우회하거나 / 다른 전략들로 보완할 / 학습에 있어 / 그녀는 정반대를 알아냈다 //

단서1 난독증이 있는 사람들은 읽기를 피하거나 회피할 거라고 예상했지만, 결과는 정반대였음

"To my surprise, / I found / that these dyslexics were enthusiastic

readers... / they rarely avoided reading. //

"놀랍게도 / 나는 알아냈다 / 이런 난독증이 있는 사람들이 열성적인 독자인 것을… / 그들은 좀처럼 읽기를 피하지 않았다 //

On the contrary, / they sought out books." //

이에 반하여 / 그들은 책을 찾았다" //

단서2 그들은 책을 찾아서 읽었음

The pattern **Fink discovered** / was **that** all of her subjects had

앞에 목적격 관계대명사가 생략됨   주격 보어절 접속사

been passionate / in some personal interest. //

Fink가 발견한 패턴은 / 그녀의 실험대상자 모두가 열정적이었다는 것이었다 / 어떤 개인적인
관심사에 //

단서 3 실험대상자는 모두 개인적인 관심사에 열정적이었음

The areas of interest included / religion, math, business, science,

history, and biography. //

관심 분야는 포함했다 / 종교, 수학, 상업, 과학, 역사 그리고 생물학을 //

부사적 용법(목적)

What mattered was that they read voraciously / **to find** out

more. // **단서 4** 관심사에 관해 더 알기 위해 열심히 읽음

중요한 것은 그들이 탐욕스럽게 읽었다는 것이다 / 더 많이 알아내기 위해 //

- engagement ⓝ 참여   - achievement ⓝ 성취
- scholarly ⓐ 학문적인   - physicist ⓝ 물리학자
- biochemist ⓝ 생화학자   - significant ⓐ 중요한, 상당한
- bypass ⓥ 우회하다   - compensate ⓥ 보완하다
- strategy ⓝ 전략   - enthusiastic ⓐ 열성적인
- rarely ⓐⓓ 좀처럼 ~않는   - seek ⓥ 찾다(seek-sought-sought)
- subject ⓝ 실험대상자, 대상   - passionate ⓐ 열정적인

참여와 성취의 핵심은 학생들에게 **그들이 관심 있어 할 적절한 글**을 제공하는
것이다. 나의 학문적인 연구와 나의 수업은 Rosalie Fink의 연구에 깊이 영향을
받아왔다. 그녀는 물리학자, 생화학자 그리고 회사의 최고 경영자를 포함해
그들의 직업에서 매우 성공한 열두 명의 성인들과 면담했다. 그들 모두가
난독증이 있었고 그들의 학령기 내내 읽기에 상당한 문제를 겪어 왔다. 그녀는
그들이 학습에 있어 읽기를 피했고 그것을 우회하거나 다른 전략들로 보완할
방법을 발견했으리라고 예상했으나, 정반대를 알아냈다. "놀랍게도,
나는 이런 난독증이 있는 사람들이 열성적인 독자인 것을… 그들이 좀처럼
읽기를 피하지 않았다는 것을 알아냈다. 이에 반하여, 그들은 책을 찾았다."
Fink가 발견한 패턴은 그녀의 실험대상자 모두가 어떤 개인적인 관심사에
열정적이었다는 것이었다. 관심 분야는 종교, 수학, 상업, 과학, 역사 그리고
생물학을 포함했다. 중요한 것은 그들이 더 많이 알아내기 위해 탐욕스럽게
읽었다는 것이다.

다음 빈칸에 들어갈 말로 가장 적절한 것을 고르시오.

① examples from official textbooks
공인 교과서에서 나온 예시   공인 교과서에서 나온 예시가 핵심이라는 언급은 없음
② relevant texts they will be interested in
그들이 관심 있어 할 적절한 글   관심 분야에는 열정적으로 읽음
③ enough chances to exchange information
정보를 교환할 충분한 기회   정보를 교환할 기회를 주라는 것이 아님
④ different genres for different age groups
다양한 연령 집단에 대한 다양한 장르   다양한 연령 집단과 관련된 내용이 아님
⑤ early reading experience to develop logic skills
논리 기술을 발전시키기 위한 초기의 읽기 경험   초기의 읽기 경험이 중요하다는 내용이 아님

왜 정답? ✱✱✿ [정답률 62%]

빈칸 문장	참여와 성취의 핵심은 학생들에게 _____을 제공하는 것이다.

➡ **빈칸 문장**: 학생들에게 '무엇'을 제공하는 것이 참여와 성취의 핵심이다.
➡ **Rosalie Fink의 연구**
　가정: 난독증이 있는 사람들은 읽기를 피하거나 우회할 것임 **단서 1**
　결과: 그들은 오히려 책을 찾아서 읽었음 **단서 2**
　원인: 그들은 모두 각자의 관심사에 더 알기 위해 열정적으로 읽음 **단서 3**, **단서 4**
　▶ '관심 분야에는 열정적이므로, 참여와 성취의 핵심은 학생들에게 ② '그들이 관심
　있어 할 적절한 글'을 제공하는 것이다.

왜 오답?

① 공인 교과서에서 나온 예시가 핵심이라는 언급은 없다.
③ 학생들에게 서로 정보를 교환할 기회를 주라는 것이 아니다.
④ 다양한 연령 집단과 관련된 내용이 아니다. (▶ 이유: 물리학자, 생물학자 등이
　언급되기는 했지만, 연령과 관련 없는 내용이다.)
⑤ 읽기와 관련된 내용은 맞지만, 성공하기 위해 초기 읽기 경험이 중요하다고 말하는
　글이 아니다. **함정**

---

34 정답 ① ✱능력이 유일한 척도가 될 때

For many people, / *ability* refers to intellectual competence, / so

앞에 목적격 관계대명사가 생략됨   명사적 용법(목적격 보어)

they want everything **they do** / **to reflect** how smart they are /

많은 사람들에게 / '능력'은 지적 능력을 의미한다 / 그래서 그들은 자신이 하는 모든 것을
원한다 / 자신이 얼마나 똑똑한지를 보여주기를 /

— **writing** a brilliant legal brief, / **getting** the highest grade on

a test, / **writing** elegant computer code, / **saying** something

병렬 구조

exceptionally wise or witty / in a conversation. //

예컨대 훌륭한 법률 보고서를 작성하는 것 / 시험에서 최고의 성적을 받는 것 / 정연한 컴퓨터
코드를 작성하는 것 / 비범하게 현명하거나 재치 있는 말을 하는 것 / 대화에서 //

'~에 관하여'

You could also define ability / **in terms of** a particular skill

or talent, / such as how well one **plays** the piano, / **learns** a

병렬 구조

language, / or **serves** a tennis ball. //

여러분은 또한 능력을 정의할 수도 있다 / 특정한 기술이나 재능의 관점에서 / 누군가가
피아노를 얼마나 잘 치는지 / 언어를 얼마나 잘 배우는지 / 또는 테니스공을 얼마나 잘
서브하는지와 같은 //

Some people focus on their ability / **to be** attractive, entertaining,

/ up on the latest trends, / or **to have** the newest gadgets. //

병렬 구조

어떤 사람들은 그들의 능력에 초점을 맞춘다 / 매력적이고 재미있으며 / 최신 유행에 맞추거나
/ 최신 기기를 가질 수 있는 //

복합 관계부사(= No matter how)   **단서 1** 능력은 어떻게 정의되든 문제가 발생함

However ability may be defined / a problem occurs / when **it is**

the sole determinant of one's self-worth. //

능력이 어떻게 정의되든지 / 문제가 발생한다 / 그것이 자신의 가치의 유일한 결정 요소일 때 //

The performance becomes the *only* measure of the person; /

'~을 고려하다'

nothing else is **taken into account**. // **단서 2** 누군가의 수행이 유일한 척도가 되어

다른 것은 고려되지 않음

수행이 그 사람의 '유일한' 척도가 된다 / 그 외 어느 것도 고려되지 않는다 //

An outstanding performance means / an outstanding person; /

an average performance means / an average person. //

뛰어난 수행은 의미한다 / 뛰어난 사람을 / 평범한 수행은 의미한다 / 평범한 사람을 //

단서 3 단순히 뛰어난 수행은 뛰어난 사람을, 평범한 수행은 평범한 사람을 의미하게 됨

Period. //

끝 //

- refer to ~을 나타내다   - intellectual ⓐ 지적인
- competence ⓝ 능력, 능숙함   - brilliant ⓐ 훌륭한
- legal ⓐ 법률과 관련된   - brief ⓝ 업무 (보고서)
- elegant ⓐ 우아한, 정연한   - exceptionally ⓐⓓ 각별히
- witty ⓐ 재치 있는   - gadget ⓝ 기기, 장치
- outstanding ⓐ 뛰어난   - sole ⓐ 유일한
- determinant ⓝ 결정 요인   - accompany ⓥ 동반하다

많은 사람들에게 '능력'은 지적 능력을 의미하므로 그들은 자신이 하는 모든
것이 자신이 얼마나 똑똑한지를 보여주기를 원한다. 예컨대, 훌륭한 법률
보고서를 작성하는 것, 시험에서 최고의 성적을 받는 것, 정연한 컴퓨터 코드를
작성하는 것, 대화에서 비범하게 현명하거나 재치 있는 말을 하는 것이다.
여러분은 또한 피아노를 얼마나 잘 치는지, 언어를 얼마나 잘 배우는지,
테니스공을 얼마나 잘 서브하는지와 같은 특정한 기술이나 재능의 관점에서
능력을 정의할 수도 있다. 어떤 사람들은 매력적이고, 재미있고, 최신 유행에
맞추거나, 최신 기기를 가질 수 있는 그들의 능력에 초점을 맞춘다. 능력이
어떻게 정의되든지, 그것이 자신의 가치의 유일한 결정 요소일 때 문제가
발생한다. 수행이 그 사람의 '유일한' 척도가 되며, 다른 어느 것도 고려되지
않는다. 뛰어난 수행은 뛰어난 사람을 의미하고, 평범한 수행은 평범한 사람을
의미한다. 끝.

다음 빈칸에 들어갈 말로 가장 적절한 것을 고르시오. [3점]

① it is the sole determinant of one's self-worth
그것이 자신의 가치의 유일한 결정 요소이다   능력이 유일한 척도일 때 문제가 발생함
② you are distracted by others' achievements
여러분은 다른 사람의 성취에 의해 주의가 분산된다   주의가 분산된다는 언급은 없음
③ there is too much competition in one field
한 분야에 너무 많은 경쟁이 있다   너무 많은 경쟁이 있다는 내용이 아님
④ you ignore feedback about a performance
여러분은 수행에 대한 피드백을 무시한다   수행에 대한 피드백을 무시한다는 내용은 없음
⑤ it is not accompanied by effort
그것이 노력을 수반하지 않는다   능력이 노력을 수반하지 않을 때 문제가 발생한다는 내용이 아님

빈칸 문장	능력이 어떻게 정의되든지, _____일 때 문제가 발생한다.
빈칸 문장 뒤 예시	수행이 그 사람의 '유일한' 척도가 되며, 다른 어느 것도 고려되지 않는다.

➡ **빈칸 문장:** 능력은 어떻게 정의되든, '어떨 때' 문제가 발생한다. 단서1
➡ **빈칸 문장 뒤:** 수행 = 그 사람을 판단하는 유일한 척도 = 그 사람의 능력 단서2
　▶ 다른 요소는 고려하지 않고, 수행만으로 사람을 정의한다고 했으므로 ① '그것이 자신의 가치의 유일한 결정 요소'일 때 문제가 발생하는 것이다.

> **왜 오답?**

🎀 ② 다른 사람의 성취에 의해 주의가 분산되면 문제가 발생한다는 언급은 없다.
　(🎀 이유: 앞에 언급된 여러 능력들은 다른 사람의 성취로 제시된 것이 아니다.)
③ 한 분야에 너무 많은 경쟁이 있으면 문제가 발생한다는 내용의 글이 아니다.
④ 수행에 대한 피드백을 무시하면 문제가 발생한다고는 하지 않았다.
⑤ 능력이 노력을 수반해야 한다고 말하는 글이 아니다.

---

35 정답 ② ＊특화된 말단 조직을 가진 감각 신경

다음 글에서 전체 흐름과 관계 없는 문장은? [3점]

Sensory nerves have specialized[과거분사(endings 수식)] endings / in the tissues / that[주격 관계대명사] pick up a particular sensation. //
감각 신경은 특화된 말단을 가지고 있다 / 조직에 / 특정 감각을 포착하는 //

[단서1 신경 말단이 통증을 발, 다리, 척수, 뇌로 전달함]
If, for example, / you step on a sharp object / such as a pin, / nerve endings in the skin will transmit the pain sensation / up your leg, / up and along the spinal cord / to the brain. //
만약 예를 들어 / 여러분이 날카로운 물체를 밟는다면 / 핀과 같이 / 피부의 신경 말단이 통증 감각을 전달할 것이다 / 여러분의 다리 위로 / 그리고 척수를 따라 위로 / 뇌까지 //

① While[부사절 접속사(대조)] the pain itself[강조 용법의 재귀대명사] is unpleasant, / it is in fact acting / as a protective mechanism / for the foot. //
[단서2 통증은 발을 보호하는 메커니즘으로 작용하는 것임]
통증 자체는 불쾌하지만 / 그것은 사실은 작용하고 있다 / 보호하는 메커니즘으로 / 발을 //

② That is, / you get used to the pain / so[결과 절을 잇는 등위접속사] the capacity with which[전치사+관계대명사] you can avoid pain / decreases. //
['즉, 다시 말해']
(즉 / 여러분은 그 고통에 익숙해져서 / 고통을 피할 수 있는 능력이 / 감소하게 된다 //)

③ Within the brain, / nerves will connect to the area / that[주격 관계대명사＊] controls speech, / so that[그래서 ~하도록] you may well shout 'ouch' / or something rather less polite. //
[단서3 뇌의 신경이 언어를 통제해서 아픔을 말로 표현함]
뇌 안에서 / 신경은 부분에 연결될 것이다 / 언어를 통제하는 / 그래서 여러분은 '아야'라고 외칠 것이다 / 또는 다소 덜 공손한 무언가를 //

④ They will also connect to motor nerves / that travel back down the spinal cord, /
그것들은 또한 운동신경에 연결될 것이다 / 척수를 타고 내려오는 /
and to the muscles in your leg / that now contract quickly / to lift[부사적 용법(목적)] your foot away / from the painful object. //
그리고 여러분의 다리 근육에 / 이제 재빨리 수축하는 / 발을 떼어 들어 올리기 위해 / 고통을 주는 물체로부터 //
[단서4 운동신경은 다리 근육까지 연결돼서 발을 들어 올리게 함]

⑤ Sensory and motor nerves control / almost all functions in the body / — from[from A to B: A에서 B까지] the beating of the heart / to the movement of the gut, sweating and just about everything else. //
감각 신경과 운동 신경은 통제한다 / 신체의 거의 모든 기능을 / 심장의 박동에서부터 / 장의 운동, 발한과 그 밖에 모든 것에까지 //

- sensory ⓐ 감각의　　- nerve ⓝ 신경　　- ending ⓝ 끝, 말단
- tissue ⓝ (세포로 이루어진) 조직　　- sensation ⓝ 감각
- transmit ⓥ 전달하다　　- protective ⓐ 보호하는
- mechanism ⓝ 방법, 메커니즘　　- capacity ⓝ 능력, 용량

- polite ⓐ 공손한　　- muscle ⓝ 근육　　- contract ⓥ 수축하다
- function ⓝ 기능　　- sweating ⓝ 발한

감각 신경은 특정 감각을 포착하는 특화된 말단을 조직에 가지고 있다. 예를 들어, 만약 여러분이 핀과 같이 날카로운 물체를 밟는다면, 피부의 신경 말단이 통증 감각을 여러분의 다리 위로, 그리고 척수를 따라 위로 뇌까지 전달할 것이다. ① 통증 자체는 불쾌하지만, 그것은 사실 발을 보호하는 메커니즘으로 작용하고 있다. (② 즉, 여러분은 그 고통에 익숙해져서 고통을 피할 수 있는 능력이 감소하게 된다.) ③ 뇌 안에서, 신경은 언어를 통제하는 부분에 연결될 것이고, 그래서 여러분은 '아야' 또는 다소 덜 공손한 무언가를 외칠 것이다. ④ 그것들은 또한 척수를 타고 내려오는 운동신경에 연결될 것이고, 이제 고통을 주는 물체로부터 발을 떼어 들어올리기 위해 재빨리 수축하는 여러분의 다리 근육에 연결될 것이다. ⑤ 감각 신경과 운동 신경은 심장의 박동에서부터 장의 운동, 발한과 그 밖에 모든 것에 이르기까지 신체의 거의 모든 기능을 통제한다.

> **왜 정답·오답?** ✭✭✭ [정답률 41%]

> **앞부분:** 감각 신경은 특정 감각을 포착하는 특화된 말단을 조직에 가지고 있다. 예를 들어, 만약 여러분이 핀과 같이 날카로운 물체를 밟는다면, 피부의 신경 말단이 통증 감각을 여러분의 다리 위로, 그리고 척수를 따라 위로 뇌까지 전달할 것이다.

➡ 감각 신경의 말단이 통증을 포착하여 전달하는 과정을 이야기하는 글이다.

> ① 통증 자체는 불쾌하지만, 그것은 사실 발을 보호하는 메커니즘으로 작용하고 있다.

➡ 핀을 밟았을 때의 통증은 사실 발을 보호하는 메커니즘이라고 이야기하는 흐름은 자연스럽다.
　▶ ①은 무관한 문장이 아님

> ② 즉(That is), 여러분은 그 고통에 익숙해져서 고통을 피할 수 있는 능력이 감소하게 된다.

➡ 핀을 밟았을 때의 고통에 익숙해져 그 고통을 잘 피할 수 없게 되면, 계속 핀을 밟게 될 것이므로 발을 보호하는 메커니즘이라는 앞 문장과의 흐름에 맞지 않는다.
　▶ ②이 무관한 문장임

> ③ 뇌 안에서, 신경은 언어를 통제하는 부분에 연결될 것이고, 그래서 여러분은 '아야' 또는 다소 덜 공손한 무언가를 외칠 것이다.

➡ 핀을 밟은 통증이 뇌로 전달되었을 때, 뇌 안에서 일어나는 신경 작용에 대한 설명이 이어진다.
　▶ ③은 무관한 문장이 아님

> ④ 그것들은 또한 척수를 타고 내려오는 운동신경에 연결될 것이고, 이제 고통을 주는 물체로부터 발을 떼어 들어올리기 위해 재빨리 수축하는 여러분의 다리 근육에 연결될 것이다.

➡ 앞 문장에 이어서 통증은 뇌를 거쳐 척수를 타고 내려와 다리 근육에 연결된다며 순서에 따라 자연스럽게 설명한다.
　▶ ④은 무관한 문장이 아님

> ⑤ 감각 신경과 운동 신경은 심장의 박동에서부터 장의 운동, 발한과 그 밖에 모든 것에 이르기까지 신체의 거의 모든 기능을 통제한다.

➡ 감각 신경과 운동 신경이 신체 거의 모든 기능을 통제한다고 정리하면서 글을 마무리하고 있다.
　▶ ⑤은 무관한 문장이 아님

도입	감각 신경의 말단 조직은 특정 감각을 포착하는 데 특화됨
예시	날카로운 핀을 밟으면 피부의 신경 말단이 통증 감각을 다리, 척수, 뇌 순서로 전달함
과정(뇌)	뇌에서는 언어 통제 부분에 연결되어 아픔을 언어로 표현하게 함
과정(운동신경)	통증은 척수를 타고 내려와 다리 근육에 연결되어 발을 핀에서 떼게 함
결론	감각 신경과 운동 신경은 신체의 거의 모든 기능을 통제함

36 정답 ② * 환경에 영향을 받는 결정(結晶) 형성

Maybe you've heard this joke: / "How do you eat an
elephant?" // 단서 1 질문 형태의 농담으로 글을 시작함
아마 여러분은 이 농담을 들어본 적이 있을 것이다 / "당신은 코끼리를 어떻게 먹는가" //

The answer is "one bite at a time." //
정답은 '한 번에 한 입'이다 //

(A) Common crystal habits include / squares, triangles, and six-
sided hexagons. // 단서 2 (B)에서 과학자들이 언급한 습성에 이어지는 내용임
일반적인 결정 습성은 포함한다 / 사각형, 삼각형, 그리고 육면의 육각형을 //

Usually crystals form / when liquids cool, / such as when you
create ice cubes. // 부사절 접속사(시간)
보통 결정이 형성된다 / 액체가 차가워질 때 / 여러분이 얼음 조각을 만들 때와 같이 //

Many times, / crystals form / in ways / that do not allow for
perfect shapes. // 주격 관계대명사
많은 경우 / 결정은 형성된다 / 방식으로 / 완벽한 모양을 허용하지 않는 //

If conditions are too cold, / too hot, / or there isn't enough source
material, / they can form strange, twisted shapes. //
조건이 너무 차갑거나 / 너무 뜨겁거나 / 혹은 원천 물질이 충분하지 않으면 / 그것들은
이상하고 뒤틀린 모양을 형성할 수 있다 //

(B) So, / how do you "build" the Earth? //
그렇다면 / 여러분은 어떻게 지구를 '건설'하는가 // 단서 3 질문 형태의 다른 농담이 제시됨

That's simple, too: / one atom at a time. //
그것은 또한 간단하다 / 한 번에 하나의 원자이다 //

Atoms are the basic building blocks of crystals, / and since
all rocks are made up of crystals, / the more you know about
atoms, / the better. // 부사절 접속사(이유) * / the 비교급 S V, the 비교급 (S V): ~할수록 더욱 …하다
원자는 결정의 기본 구성 요소이고 / 모든 암석은 결정으로 이루어져 있기 때문에 / 여러분이
원자에 대해 더 많이 알수록 / 더 좋다 //

Crystals come in a variety of shapes / that scientists call habits. // 목적격 관계대명사
결정은 다양한 모양으로 나온다 / 과학자들이 '습성'이라고 부르는 //

(C) But when conditions are right, / we see beautiful displays. //
하지만 조건이 맞을 때 / 우리는 아름다운 배열을 본다 // 단서 4 (A)의 조건이 안 좋을 때와 상반된 내용이 But으로 연결됨

Usually, / this involves a slow, steady environment / where the
individual atoms have plenty of time / to join and fit perfectly
into / what's known as the crystal lattice. // 관계부사 형용사적 용법(time 수식) 선행사를 포함하는 관계대명사 '결정격자'
보통 / 이것은 느리고 안정적인 환경을 수반한다 / 개별적인 원자들이 충분한 시간을 가지는 /
결합하고 완벽하게 들어맞는 / '결정격자'라고 알려진 것에 //

This is the basic structure of atoms / that is seen time after time. // 주격 관계대명사
이것은 원자의 기본적인 구조이다 / 반복하여 보여지는 //

- hexagon ⑩ 육각형　　· condition ⑩ 조건　　· twisted ⓐ 뒤틀린
- atom ⑩ 원자　　· display ⑩ 배열　　· steady ⓐ 안정적인, 구준한
- individual ⓐ 개별적인

아마 여러분은 이 농담을 들어본 적이 있을 것이다. "당신은 코끼리를 어떻게 먹는가?" 정답은 '한 번에 한 입'이다. (B) 그렇다면, 여러분은 어떻게 지구를 '건설'하는가? 그것은 또한 간단하다. 한 번에 하나의 원자이다. 원자는 결정의 기본 구성 요소이고, 모든 암석은 결정으로 이루어져 있기 때문에, 여러분이 원자에 대해 더 많이 알수록 더 좋다. 결정은 과학자들이 '습성'이라고 부르는 다양한 모양으로 나온다.
(A) 일반적인 결정 습성은 사각형, 삼각형, 육면의 육각형을 포함한다. 보통 여러분이 얼음 조각을 만들 때와 같이 액체가 차가워질 때 결정이 형성된다. 많은 경우, 결정은 완벽한 모양을 허용하지 않는 방식으로 형성된다. 조건이 너무 차갑거나, 너무 뜨겁거나, 혹은 원천 물질이 충분하지 않으면 그것들은 이상하고 뒤틀린 모양을 형성할 수 있다. (C) 하지만 조건이 맞을 때, 우리는 아름다운 배열을 본다. 보통, 이것은 개별적인 원자들이 결합하고 '결정격자'라고 알려진 것에 완벽하게 들어맞는 충분한 시간을 가지는 느리고 안정적인 환경을 수반한다. 이것은 반복하여 보이는 원자의 기본적인 구조이다.

주어진 글 다음에 이어질 글의 순서로 가장 적절한 것을 고르시오. [3점]

① (A) — (C) — (B)　(B)의 질문 형태 농담은 주어진 글에 이어져야 함
② (B) — (A) — (C)　코끼리를 어떻게 먹는가에 대한 정답(한 번에 한 입) — (B) 지구를 구성하는 원자는 결정의 기본 구성 요소임 — (A) 결정은 환경이 맞지 않으면 이상한 모양을 형성함 — (C) 환경 조건이 좋으면 결정격자를 형성함
③ (B) — (C) — (A)
④ (C) — (A) — (B)　환경 조건이 좋지 않은 (A)가 먼저 나온 뒤
⑤ (C) — (B) — (A)　But으로 조건이 좋은 (C)가 연결되어야 함

| 문제 풀이 순서 | ✱✱❄ [정답률 77%]

1st 각 문단의 내용을 파악하고, 글의 논리적인 순서를 추론한다.

주어진 글: 아마 여러분은 이 농담을 들어본 적이 있을 것이다. "당신은 코끼리를 어떻게 먹는가?" 정답은 '한 번에 한 입'이다. 단서

➡ **주어진 글 뒤:** 농담을 제시해 글을 시작한 이유나 배경을 설명할 것이다. 발상

(A): 일반적인 결정 습성은 사각형, 삼각형, 육면의 육각형을 포함한다. 보통 여러분이 얼음 조각을 만들 때와 같이 액체가 차가워질 때 결정이 형성된다. 많은 경우, 결정은 완벽한 모양을 허용하지 않는 방식으로 형성된다. 조건이 너무 차갑거나, 너무 뜨겁거나, 혹은 원천 물질이 충분하지 않으면 그것들은 이상하고 뒤틀린 모양을 형성할 수 있다.

➡ **(A) 앞:** 결정 습성에 대한 설명이 나오기 전에, 결정에 관한 내용이 언급되어야 한다.
▶ 주어진 글 바로 뒤에 (A)가 올 수 없음
(A) 뒤: 조건이 좋지 않은 상황을 이야기했으므로, 반대로 조건이 좋을 때는 결정이 어떻게 형성되는지에 대한 설명이 이어질 것이다.

(B): 그렇다면, 여러분은 어떻게 지구를 '건설'하는가? 그것은 또한 간단하다. 한 번에 하나의 원자이다. 원자는 결정의 기본 구성 요소이고, 모든 암석은 결정으로 이루어져 있기 때문에, 여러분이 원자에 대해 더 많이 알수록 더 좋다. 결정은 과학자들이 '습성'이라고 부르는 다양한 모양으로 나온다.

➡ **(B) 앞:** 주어진 글의 질문과 유사한 질문이 제시되었다.
▶ 주어진 글에 이어지는 내용임 (순서: 주어진 글 ➡ (B))
(B) 뒤: 결정과 결정 습성을 처음으로 언급했으므로, 이에 관해 부연 설명하는 (A)가 이어질 것이다.
▶ (B) 뒤에 (A)가 이어져야 함 (순서: 주어진 글 ➡ (B) ➡ (A))

2023.9
9회

➡ **(C) 앞:** 역접의 연결어 But으로 조건이 맞을 때 결정 배열이 아름답다는 내용이 이어졌으므로, 앞에는 조건이 맞지 않을 때의 결정 모양에 관해 이야기한 (A)가 와야 한다.
▶ (A)에 이어지는 내용임 (순서: 주어진 글 → (B) → (A) → (C))
(C) 뒤: 앞의 내용을 정리하며 결정격자는 보이는 원자의 기본적인 구조라고 하며 글을 마무리했다.

2nd 글이 한눈에 들어오도록 정리하여 정답을 확인한다.

주어진 글: 코끼리를 어떻게 먹는가? 한 번에 한 입씩.
→ **(B):** 지구도 한 번에 하나의 원자로 건설할 수 있는데, 원자는 결정을 구성하고, 결정은 암석을 구성한다.
→ **(A):** 결정은 주로 액체가 차가워질 때 형성되는데, 환경 조건이 맞지 않으면 결정 모양이 이상해진다.
→ **(C):** 하지만 조건이 맞으면 결정은 아름답게 배열되며 이러한 결정격자는 보이는 원자의 기본 구조이다.
▶ 주어진 글 다음에 이어질 글의 순서는 (B) → (A) → (C)이므로 정답은 ②임

37 정답 ③ * 기타가 소리를 내는 원리

When you pluck a guitar string / it moves back and forth / hundreds of times every second. //
여러분이 기타 줄을 뜯을 때 / 그것은 이리저리 움직인다 / 매초 수백 번 //

단서 1 (C)의 나무판의 진동을 가리킴
(A) The vibration of the wood / creates more powerful waves / in the air pressure, / which travel away from the guitar. //
계속적 용법의 주격 관계대명사
그 나무의 진동은 / 더 강력한 파동을 만들어 낸다 / 공기의 압력에 / 그리고 그것은 기타로부터 멀리 퍼진다 //
부사절 접속사
When the waves reach your eardrums / they flex in and out / the same number of times a second / as the original string. //
그 파동이 여러분의 고막에 도달할 때 / 그것들은 굽이쳐 들어가고 나온다 / 초당 동일한 횟수로 / 원래의 줄과 //

단서 2 주어진 글에서 말한 기타 줄의 움직임을 가리킴
so ~ that ...: 너무 ~해서 ...하다
(B) Naturally, / this movement is so fast that you cannot see it / — you just see / the blurred outline of the moving string. //
당연히 / 이 움직임은 너무 빨라서 여러분은 그것을 볼 수 없다 / 여러분은 그저 본다 / 움직이는 줄의 흐릿한 윤곽만 //
현재분사(Strings 수식)
Strings vibrating in this way on their own / make hardly any noise / because strings are very thin / and don't push much air about. //
병렬 구조
이렇게 스스로 진동하는 줄들은 / 거의 어떤 소리도 나지 않는다 / 왜냐하면 줄이 매우 가늘고 / 많은 공기를 밀어내지 못하기 때문이다 //
부사절 접속사(조건)
(C) But if you attach a string / to a big hollow box / (like a guitar body), / then the vibration is amplified / and the note is heard loud and clear. // **단서 3** (B)의 마지막과 반대되는 내용이 But으로 연결됨
하지만 여러분이 줄을 달면 / 커다란 속이 빈 상자에 / (기타 몸통 같은) / 그러면 그 진동은 증폭되어 / 그 음이 크고 선명하게 들린다 //
2어동사의 수동태는 동사만 be p.p.로 바꾸고 부사나 전치사는 그대로 씀
The vibration of the string is passed on / to the wooden panels of the guitar body, / which vibrate back and forth / at the same rate as the string. //
계속적 용법의 주격 관계대명사
그 줄의 진동은 전달된다 / 기타 몸통의 나무판으로 / 그리고 그것은 이리저리 떨린다 / 줄과 같은 속도로 //

- string ⓝ 줄, 끈 • vibration ⓝ 진동 • pressure ⓝ 압력
- eardrum ⓝ 고막 • flex ⓥ 굽히다 • blurred ⓐ 흐릿한
- outline ⓝ 윤곽, 개요 • hardly ⓐⓓ 거의 ~ 않다
- hollow ⓐ (속이) 빈 • pass on ~을 전달하다 • panel ⓝ 판

주어진 글 다음에 이어질 글의 순서로 가장 적절한 것을 고르시오.
① (A) — (C) — (B) ← 주어진 글과 (B)에는 (A)의 나무를 가리킬 만한 내용이 없음
② (B) — (A) — (C)
③ (B) — (C) — (A) ← 기타 줄은 빠르게 움직임 — (B) 이 움직임은 소리가 나지 않는데, 줄이 너무 가늘어서 공기를 밀어내지 못하기 때문임 — (C) 하지만 기타 몸통의 나무판처럼 속이 빈 상자에 줄을 달면 진동이 증폭되어 소리가 잘 들림 — (A) 그 나무의 진동이 파동을 만들고, 그 파동이 고막에 들리는 것임
④ (C) — (A) — (B)
⑤ (C) — (B) — (A)
← (C)와 주어진 글은 But으로 연결될 수 없음

| **문제 풀이 순서** | ★★☆ [정답률 68%]

1st 각 문단의 내용을 파악하고, 글의 논리적인 순서를 추론한다.

주어진 글: 여러분이 기타 줄을 뜯을 때 그것은 매초 수백 번 이리저리 움직인다. 단서

➡ **주어진 글 뒤:** 빠르게 움직이는 기타 줄과 관련된 내용이 이어질 것이다. 발상

(A): 그 나무(the wood)의 진동은 공기의 압력에 더 강력한 파동을 만들어 내어 기타로부터 멀리 퍼진다. 그 파동이 여러분의 고막에 도달할 때 원래의 줄과 초당 동일한 횟수로 굽이쳐 들어가고 나온다.

➡ **(A) 앞:** '그 나무'라고 했으므로 앞에 어떤 나무가 언급되어야 한다.
▶ 주어진 글 바로 뒤에 (A)가 올 수 없음
(A) 뒤: 파동이 고막에 도달했다고 했는데, 그 파동이 고막 이후에 어디로 가는지를 설명하지 않는다면 (A)가 글의 결론일 것이다.
▶ (A)가 마지막에 올 확률이 높음

(B): 당연히, 이 움직임(this movement)은 너무 빨라서 여러분은 그것을 볼 수 없다. 여러분은 그저 움직이는 줄의 흐릿한 윤곽만 본다. 이렇게 스스로 진동하는 줄들은 거의 소리가 나지 않는데, 이는 줄이 매우 가늘고 많은 공기를 밀어내지 못하기 때문이다.

➡ **(B) 앞:** ① '이 움직임(this movement)'이 무엇을 가리키는지 앞에 나와야 한다.
② 너무 빠르게 움직여서 움직임을 볼 수 없다고 했으므로, 주어진 글에서 말한 매초 수백 번 움직이는 기타 줄의 움직임을 말하는 것이다.
▶ 주어진 글에 이어지는 내용임 (순서: 주어진 글 → (B))
(B) 뒤: (A)의 '그 나무'를 가리킬 내용이 (B)에 없으므로 (A)가 이어질 수는 없다.
▶ (C)가 이어질 확률이 높음

(C): 하지만(But) 여러분이 (기타 몸통 같은) 커다란 속이 빈 상자에 줄을 달면, 그 진동은 증폭되어 그 음이 크고 선명하게 들린다. 그 줄의 진동은 기타 몸통의 나무판으로 전달되어 줄과 같은 속도로 이리저리 떨린다.

➡ **(C) 앞:** 소리가 잘 들린다는 내용이 역접의 연결어 But으로 이어지므로, 앞에는 소리가 잘 들리지 않는다고 설명한 (B)가 와야 한다.
▶ 순서: 주어진 글 → (B) → (C)
(C) 뒤: 기타 몸통, 즉 나무판의 진동을 (A)에서 '그 나무의 진동'으로 가리켜 설명을 이어갔다. ▶ (A)가 이어져야 함 (순서: 주어진 글 → (B) → (C) → (A))

주어진 글: 기타 줄을 뜯으면 그것은 매우 빠르게 움직인다.

→ **(B):** 그 움직임은 너무 빨라서 볼 수 없는데, 이렇게 스스로 진동하는 줄은 가늘고 공기를 밀어내지 못하기 때문에 소리가 거의 나지 않는다.

→ **(C):** 하지만 커다란 속이 빈 상자에 줄을 연결하면 진동이 증폭되어 소리가 커지며, 그 진동이 기타 몸통의 나무판까지 전달되어 떨린다.

→ **(A):** 나무판의 진동은 더 강력한 파동을 만들어 내어 퍼지고 고막에까지 도달한다.

▶ 주어진 글 다음에 이어질 글의 순서는 (B) → (C) → (A)이므로 정답은 ③임

---

38 정답 ⑤ * 직장과 가정의 경계에서 보이는 차이

글의 흐름으로 보아, 주어진 문장이 들어가기에 가장 적절한 곳을 고르시오. [3점]

> Other individuals prefer / integrating work and family roles / all day long. // 단서1 앞에는 직장과 가정의 역할을 통합하는 것을 선호하지 않는 사람들이 나와야 함
> 다른 사람들은 선호한다 / 직장과 가정의 역할을 통합하는 것을 / 하루 종일 //

Boundaries between work and home are blurring / as portable digital technology makes **it** / **increasingly possible** / to work anywhere, anytime. //
직장과 가정의 경계가 흐릿해지고 있다 / 휴대용 디지털 기술이 ~을 만듦에 따라 / 점차 가능하게 / 언제, 어디서나 작업하는 것을 //

Individuals differ / in **how they like to manage their time** / to meet work and outside responsibilities. //
사람들은 차이가 있다 / 자신의 시간을 관리하기를 바라는 방식에 / 직장과 외부의 책임을 수행하기 위해 //

(①) Some people prefer / to separate or segment roles / **so that** boundary crossings are minimized. //
어떤 사람들은 선호한다 / 역할을 분리하거나 분할하는 것을 / 경계 교차 지점이 최소화되도록 //

(②) For example, / these people might **keep** separate email accounts / for work and family /
예를 들어 / 이러한 사람들은 별개의 이메일 계정을 유지할지도 모른다 / 직장과 가정을 위한 /

and **try to conduct** work at the workplace / and **take care of** family matters / only during breaks and non-work time. //
그리고 직장에서 일을 수행하려고 할지도 모른다 / 그리고 가정사를 처리할지도 모른다 / 휴식 시간과 일을 하지 않는 시간 동안에만 //

(③) We've even noticed / **more of these "segmenters"** / **carrying** two phones / — one for work / and one for personal use. //
우리는 심지어 알게 되었다 / 더 많은 이러한 '분할자들'이 / 두 개의 전화기를 가지고 다니는 것을 / 하나는 업무용 / 그리고 하나는 개인용인 //

(④) Flexible schedules work well / for these individuals / **because** they enable greater distinction / between time at work / and time in other roles. // 단서2 직장과 다른 역할을 잘 구분하는 사람들에 관한 설명이 앞에서부터 이어졌음
유연근로시간제는 잘 적용된다 / 이런 사람들에게 / 그것들이 더 큰 구별을 가능하게 하기 때문에 / 직장에서의 시간 사이에 / 다른 역할에서의 시간과 //

(⑤) This might entail / constantly **trading** text messages with children / from the office, /
이것은 수반할지도 모른다 / 아이들과 문자 메시지를 지속적으로 주고받는 것을 / 직장에서 /

or **monitoring** emails at home and on vacation, / rather than **returning** to work **to find** / hundreds of messages in their inbox. //
또는 집에서 그리고 휴가 중에 이메일을 확인하는 것을 / 직장으로 돌아가서 발견하는 것 대신에 / 받은 편지함에서 수백 개의 메시지를 // 단서3 직장과 가정의 역할이 통합된 사람에 관한 설명임

- integrate ⓥ 통합하다   • boundary ⓝ 경계(선)
- blur ⓥ 흐릿해지다   • portable ⓐ 휴대용의
- responsibility ⓝ 책임(감)   • separate ⓥ 분리하다
- segment ⓥ 분할하다   • minimize ⓥ 최소화하다
- conduct ⓥ 수행하다   • flexible ⓐ 유연한
- distinction ⓝ 구별, 차이   • constantly ⓐⓓ 거듭, 지속적으로
- inbox ⓝ 받은 편지함

휴대용 디지털 기술이 언제, 어디서나 작업하는 것을 점차 가능하게 함에 따라 직장과 가정의 경계가 흐릿해지고 있다. 사람들이 직장과 외부의 책임을 수행하기 위해 자신의 시간을 관리하기를 바라는 방식에는 차이가 있다. (①) 어떤 사람들은 경계 교차 지점이 최소화되도록 역할을 분리하거나 분할하는 것을 선호한다. (②) 예를 들어, 이러한 사람들은 직장과 가정을 위한 별개의 이메일 계정을 유지하고 직장에서 일을 수행하며 휴식 시간과 일을 하지 않는 시간 동안에만 가정사를 처리하려고 할지도 모른다. (③) 우리는 더 많은 이러한 '분할자들'이 하나는 업무용이고 하나는 개인용인 두 개의 전화기를 가지고 다니고 있음을 심지어 알게 되었다. (④) 유연근로시간제는 이런 사람들에게 잘 적용되는데, 왜냐하면 직장에서의 시간과 다른 역할에서의 시간 사이에 더 큰 구별을 가능하게 하기 때문이다. (⑤ 다른 사람들은 하루 종일 직장과 가정의 역할을 통합하는 것을 선호한다.) 이것은 직장으로 돌아가서 받은 편지함에서 수백 개의 메시지를 발견하는 것 대신 직장에서 아이들과 문자 메시지를 지속적으로 주고받거나 집에서 그리고 휴가 중에 이메일을 확인하는 것을 수반할지도 모른다.

| 문제 풀이 순서 | ★★★ [정답률 29%]

1st 주어진 문장을 해석하고, 연결어, 지시어 등을 확인한다.

> Other individuals prefer integrating work and family roles all day long.
> 다른 사람들은 하루 종일 직장과 가정의 역할을 통합하는 것을 선호한다.

➡ **주어진 문장 앞:** Other individuals(다른 사람들)라고 했으므로 단서 앞에는 직장과 가정의 역할을 통합하는 것을 선호하지 않는 사람들이 언급되어야 한다. 발상

2nd 찾은 단서를 생각하며 각 선택지의 앞뒤 흐름이 매끄러운지 확인한다.

- ①의 앞 문장과 뒤 문장

> **앞 문장:** 사람들이 직장과 외부의 책임을 수행하기 위해 자신의 시간을 관리하기를 바라는 방식에는 차이가 있다.
> **뒤 문장:** 어떤 사람들은 경계 교차 지점이 최소화되도록 역할을 분리하거나 분할하는 것을 선호한다.

➡ 앞 문장에는 직장과 가정의 역할을 통합하는 것을 선호하지 않는 사람들은 언급되지 않았고, 뒤 문장에서 역할을 분리하는 것을 선호하는 사람들에 대해 언급을 시작하고 있다.
▶ 주어진 문장이 ①에 들어갈 수 없음

- ②의 앞 문장과 뒤 문장

> **앞 문장:** ①의 뒤 문장과 같음
> **뒤 문장:** 예를 들어(For example), 이러한 사람들은 직장과 가정을 위한 별개의 이메일 계정을 유지하고 직장에서 일을 수행하며 휴식 시간과 일을 하지 않는 시간 동안에만 가정사를 처리하려고 할지도 모른다.

➡ 앞 문장에서 말한 역할을 분리하는 것을 선호하는 사람들에 대한 예시가 이어진다.
▶ 주어진 문장이 ②에 들어갈 수 없음

2023.9
9회

- ③의 앞 문장과 뒤 문장

> **앞 문장:** ②의 뒤 문장과 같음
> **뒤 문장:** 우리는 더 많은 이러한(these) '분할자들'이 하나는 업무용이고 하나는 개인용인 두 개의 전화기를 가지고 다니고 있음을 심지어 알게 되었다.

➡ 역할을 분리하는 것을 선호하는 '분할자들'에 대한 설명이 이어진다.
▶ 주어진 문장이 ③에 들어갈 수 없음

- ④의 앞 문장과 뒤 문장

> **앞 문장:** ③의 뒤 문장과 같음
> **뒤 문장:** 유연근로시간제는 이런(these) 사람들에게 잘 적용되는데, 왜냐하면 직장에서의 시간과 다른 역할에서의 시간 사이에 더 큰 구별을 가능하게 하기 때문이다.

➡ 직장과 다른 역할에서의 시간을 구별하는 것은 두 가지 역할을 분리하고자 하는 사람들에게 잘 적용되는 것이므로 앞 문장과 같은 사람들에 관해 이야기하고 있다.
▶ 주어진 문장이 ④에 들어갈 수 없음

-⑤의 앞 문장과 뒤 문장

> **앞 문장:** ④의 뒤 문장과 같음
> **뒤 문장:** 이것(This)은 직장으로 돌아가서 받은 편지함에서 수백 개의 메시지를 발견하는 것 대신 직장에서 아이들과 문자 메시지를 지속적으로 주고받거나 집에서 그리고 휴가 중에 이메일을 확인하는 것을 수반할지도 모른다.

➡ 직장에서 아이들과 문자를 주고받고, 집에서 업무 이메일을 확인하는 것은 직장과 가정의 역할을 통합하는 것의 예시이다.
따라서 직장과 가정의 역할을 통합하는 것을 선호하는 사람들이 처음 언급된 주어진 문장이 ⑤에 오는 것이 적절하다.
▶ 주어진 문장이 ⑤에 들어가야 함

3rd 글이 한눈에 들어오도록 정리하여 정답을 확인한다.

휴대용 디지털 기술로 언제, 어디서나 작업할 수 있게 되자 직장과 가정의 경계가 흐릿해졌고 사람마다 직장과 그 외의 자신의 시간을 관리하는 방식에는 차이가 생겼다.
(①) 어떤 사람들은 역할을 분리하는 것을 선호한다.
(②) 이들은 직장과 가정에서 별개의 이메일 계정을 사용하거나, 직장에서는 업무를 하지 않는 시간에만 가정사를 처리한다.
(③) 이런 분할자들은 심지어 직장용과 개인용 전화기를 가지고 다닌다.
(④) 이런 사람들에게는 직장과 그 외 시간을 더 확실히 구별하는 유연근로시간제가 잘 적용된다.
(⑤ 다른 사람들은 직장과 가정의 일을 통합하기를 선호한다.)
이들은 직장에서 아이들과 문자를 주고받고, 집에서 업무 이메일을 확인한다.

> **어법 특강**
>
> **✱ 가주어, 가목적어로 쓰이는 it**
> – 주어나 목적어 역할을 하는 to부정사가 길어질 경우, 가주어 또는 가목적어 it을 대신 쓰고 to부정사를 뒤로 보낸다.
> • It is necessary to master at least one foreign language.
> (적어도 한 개의 외국어를 마스터하는 것이 필요하다.)
> • It is very dangerous to swim in this river.
> (이 강에서 수영하는 것은 매우 위험하다.)
> • Exercising hard every day will make it easier to lose weight.
> (매일 열심히 운동하는 것은 살을 빼는 것을 더 쉽게 만들어줄 것이다.)

---

39 정답 ⑤ ✱보완재의 정의와 특징

> 글의 흐름으로 보아, 주어진 문장이 들어가기에 가장 적절한 곳을 고르시오.

> However, / do not assume **that** a product is perfectly complementary, / **as** customers may not be completely locked in / to the product. //
> **단서 1** 앞에는 완벽하게 보완적인 제품이 제시되어야 함
> 그러나 / 어떤 제품이 완벽하게 보완적이라고 가정하지 마라 / 고객들이 완전히 고정되어 있지 않을 수 있으므로 / 그 제품에 //

A "complementary good" is a product / **that** is often consumed / alongside another product. //
'보완재'는 제품이다 / 종종 소비되는 / 다른 제품과 함께 //

(①) For example, / popcorn is a complementary good to a movie, / **while** a travel pillow is a complementary good / for a long plane journey. //
예를 들어 / 팝콘은 영화에 대한 보완재다 / 한편 여행 베개는 보완재이다 / 긴 비행기 여행에 대한 //

(②) When the popularity of one product increases, / the **sales** of its complementary good also **increase**. //
한 제품의 인기가 높아지면 / 그것의 보완재 판매량도 늘어난다 //

(③) By producing goods / **that** complement other products / **that** are already (or about to be) popular, / you can ensure a steady stream / of demand for your product. //
제품을 생산함으로써 / 다른 제품을 보완하는 / 이미 인기가 있는 (또는 곧 있을) / 여러분은 꾸준한 흐름을 보장할 수 있다 / 여러분의 제품에 대한 수요의 //

(④) Some products enjoy perfect complementary status / — they *have* to be consumed together, / such as a lamp and a lightbulb. // **단서 2** 램프와 전구처럼 일부 제품은 완벽한 보완적 상태에 있음
일부 제품들은 완벽한 보완적 상태를 누리고 있고 / 그것들은 함께 소비되어야 한다 / 램프와 전구와 같이 //

(⑤) For example, / **although** motorists may seem required to purchase gasoline / **to run** their cars, / they can switch to electric cars. // **단서 3** 운전에 휘발유가 필요해 보일지라도 전기 자동차로 바꿀 수 있음
예를 들어 / 비록 운전자들이 휘발유를 구매할 필요가 있는 것처럼 보일지라도 / 자신의 차를 운전하기 위해 / 그들은 전기 자동차로 바꿀 수 있다 //

• assume ⓥ 가정하다   • complementary ⓐ (상호) 보완적인
• lock ⓥ 고정하다, 잠그다   • alongside prep ~와 함께
• pillow ⓝ 베개   • journey ⓝ 여행   • popularity ⓝ 인기
• complement ⓥ 보완하다   • ensure ⓥ 보장하다
• steady ⓐ 꾸준한   • stream ⓝ 흐름, 연속   • status ⓝ 상태
• motorist ⓝ 운전자   • gasoline ⓝ 휘발유

'보완재'는 종종 다른 제품과 함께 소비되는 제품이다. (①) 예를 들어, 팝콘은 영화에 대한 보완재인 한편, 여행 베개는 긴 비행기 여행에 대한 보완재이다. (②) 한 제품의 인기가 높아지면 그것의 보완재 판매량도 늘어난다. (③) 여러분은 이미 인기가 있는 (또는 곧 있을) 다른 제품을 보완하는 제품을 생산함으로써 여러분의 제품에 대한 꾸준한 수요 흐름을 보장할 수 있다. (④) 일부 제품들은 완벽한 보완적 상태를 누리고 있고, 그것들은 램프와 전구와 같이 함께 소비되어야' 한다. (⑤ 그러나 고객들이 그 제품에 완전히 고정되어 있지 않을 수 있으므로, 어떤 제품이 완벽하게 보완적이라고 가정하지 마라.) 예를 들어, 비록 운전자들이 자신의 차를 운전하기 위해 휘발유를 구매할 필요가 있는 것처럼 보일지라도, 그들은 전기 자동차로 바꿀 수 있다.

1st 주어진 문장을 해석하고, 연결어, 지시어 등을 확인한다.

> However, do not assume that a product is perfectly complementary, as customers may not be completely locked in to the product.
> 그러나 고객들이 그 제품에 완전히 고정되어 있지 않을 수 있으므로, 어떤 제품이 완벽하게 보완적이라고 가정하지 마라.

➡ 주어진 문장 앞: However(그러나)라고 했으므로 단서
앞에는 어떤 제품이 완벽하게 보완적이라는 내용이 올 것이다. 발상

2nd 찾은 단서를 생각하며 각 선택지의 앞뒤 흐름이 매끄러운지 확인한다.

- ①의 앞 문장과 뒤 문장

> 앞 문장: '보완재'는 종종 다른 제품과 함께 소비되는 제품이다.
> 뒤 문장: 예를 들어(For example), 팝콘은 영화에 대한 보완재인 한편, 여행 베개는 긴 비행기 여행에 대한 보완재이다.

➡ 앞 문장에서 언급한 다른 제품과 함께 소비되는 제품인 보완재의 예시가 뒤 문장에 이어진다.
▶ 주어진 문장이 ①에 들어갈 수 없음

- ②의 앞 문장과 뒤 문장

> 앞 문장: ①의 뒤 문장과 같음
> 뒤 문장: 한 제품의 인기가 높아지면 그것의 보완재 판매량도 늘어난다.

➡ 앞에서 보완재의 정의와 예시를 말한 뒤, 보완재의 특징을 이어서 말하는 흐름은 자연스럽다.
▶ 주어진 문장이 ②에 들어갈 수 없음

- ③의 앞 문장과 뒤 문장

> 앞 문장: ②의 뒤 문장과 같음
> 뒤 문장: 여러분은 이미 인기가 있는 (또는 곧 있을) 다른 제품을 보완하는 제품을 생산함으로써 여러분의 제품에 대한 꾸준한 수요 흐름을 보장할 수 있다.

➡ 앞에서 어떤 제품의 인기가 높아지면 그 보완재 판매량이 늘어난다고 한 뒤, 이를 활용하여 꾸준한 수요 흐름을 보장할 수 있다고 말하는 흐름은 자연스럽다.
▶ 주어진 문장이 ③에 들어갈 수 없음

- ④의 앞 문장과 뒤 문장

> 앞 문장: ③의 뒤 문장과 같음
> 뒤 문장: 일부 제품들은 완벽한 보완적 상태를 누리고 있고, 그것들은 램프와 전구와 같이 함께 소비'되어야' 한다.

➡ 꾸준한 수요 흐름을 보장할 수 있는 예시로 완벽한 보완적 상태를 누리는 램프와 전구를 제시했다.
▶ 주어진 문장이 ④에 들어갈 수 없음

- ⑤의 앞 문장과 뒤 문장

> 앞 문장: ④의 뒤 문장과 같음
> 뒤 문장: 예를 들어(For example), 비록 운전자들이 자신의 차를 운전하기 위해 휘발유를 구매할 필요가 있는 것처럼 보일지라도, 그들은 전기 자동차로 바꿀 수 있다.

➡ 앞 문장: 램프와 전구(= 완벽한 보완적 상태)는 함께 소비되어야 함
뒤 문장: 자동차(= 휘발유와 보완적 상태) 운전자는 전기 자동차를 탈 수 있음
앞 문장과는 달리 뒤 문장에서는 완벽한 보완적 상태로 보이지만, 실제로는 그렇지 않은 사례를 이야기했으므로 어떤 제품이 완벽하게 보완적이라고 가정하지 말라고 한 주어진 문장이 ⑤에 와야 한다.
▶ 주어진 문장이 ⑤에 들어가야 함

3rd 글이 한눈에 들어오도록 정리하여 정답을 확인한다.

보완재는 다른 제품과 함께 소비되는 제품이다.
(①) 예를 들어, 팝콘은 영화에 대한, 여행 베개는 긴 비행기 여행에 대한 보완재이다.
(②) 한 제품의 인기가 높아지면 그것의 보완재 판매량도 늘어난다.
(③) 이미 인기가 있는 제품의 보완 제품을 생산하면 꾸준한 수요를 보장할 수 있다.
(④) 일부 제품들은 램프와 전구처럼 완벽한 보완적 상태를 누리고 있다.
(⑤ 그러나 고객이 제품에 완전히 고정되지 않을 수 있으므로, 완벽한 보완적 상태를 가정해서는 안 된다.)
예를 들어, 자동차와 휘발유가 완벽히 보완적 상태로 보일지라도 운전자들이 전기자동차로 바꾸는 일이 발생할 수 있다.

40 정답 ① ＊약간의 일탈을 긍정적으로 판단하기

가주어 / 진주어절 접속사 / '~에 근거하여'
It's not news to anyone / that we judge others / based on their clothes. //
~은 누구에게도 새로운 일이 아니다 / 우리가 다른 사람들을 판단하는 것은 / 그들의 의복에 근거하여 //

주격 관계대명사 / 목적어절 접속사
In general, / studies that investigate these judgments find / that people prefer clothing / that matches expectations / — surgeons in scrubs, little boys in blue / — with one notable exception. //
일반적으로 / 이러한 판단을 조사하는 연구는 발견한다 / 사람들이 옷을 선호한다는 것을 / 예상에 맞는 / 수술복을 입은 외과 의사, 파란 옷을 입은 남자아이와 같이 / 하나의 눈에 띄는 예외가 있는 //

앞에 주격 관계대명사와 be동사가 생략됨
A series of studies / published in an article / in June 2014 / in the *Journal of Consumer Research* / explored observers' reactions / to people who broke established norms only slightly. //
일련의 연구는 / 기사에 실린 / 2014년 6월에 / 〈Journal of Consumer Research〉에 / 관찰자들의 반응을 탐구했다 / 확립된 규범을 아주 약간 어긴 사람들에 대한 //

접속사가 생략되지 않은 분사구문✱
In one scenario, / a man at a black-tie affair was viewed / as having higher status and competence / when wearing a red bow tie. // 단서1 정장 행사에서 빨간 나비넥타이를 맴 → 더 높은 지위와 능력 가진 것으로 보여짐
한 시나리오에서는 / 정장 차림의 행사에서 한 남자가 보여졌다 / 더 높은 지위와 능력을 갖춘 것으로 / 빨간 나비넥타이를 맸을 때 //

단서2 빨간 운동화를 신은 교수 → 지위와 역량에 대한 평가가 높아짐
목적어절 접속사
The researchers also found / that valuing uniqueness increased audience members' ratings / of the status and competence of a professor / who wore red sneakers / while giving a lecture. //
주격 관계대명사 / 접속사가 생략되지 않은 분사구문✱
연구자들은 또한 발견했다 / 독특함을 중시하는 것이 청중들의 평가를 높였다는 것을 / 교수의 지위와 역량에 대한 / 빨간 운동화를 신은 / 강의를 하는 동안 //

목적어절 접속사
The results suggest / that people judge these slight deviations from the norm / as positive / 단서3 사람들은 규범에서 살짝 일탈한 것을 긍정적으로 봄
그 결과들은 시사한다 / 사람들이 규범으로부터 이러한 약간의 일탈들을 판단한다는 것을 / 긍정적으로 //

목적어절 접속사
because they suggest / that the individual is powerful enough / to risk the social costs / of such behaviors. //
왜냐하면 그것들은 시사하기 때문이다 / 그 사람이 충분히 강하다는 것을 / 사회적 비용을 감수할 만큼 / 그러한 행동으로 인한 //

> 목적어절 접속사
> → A series of studies show / that people view an individual (A) **positively** / when the individual only slightly (B) **challenges** the norm for what people should wear. // 간접의문문
> 일련의 연구는 나타낸다 / 사람들이 한 사람을 긍정적으로 본다는 것을 / 그 사람이 아주 약간 도전할 때 / 사람들이 무엇을 착용해야 하는지에 대한 규범에 //

- investigate ⓥ 조사하다　　• judgment ⓝ 판단
- expectation ⓝ 예상, 기대　　• surgeon ⓝ 외과 의사
- scrub ⓝ 수술복　　• notable ⓐ 눈에 띄는　　• exception ⓝ 예외
- explore ⓥ 탐구하다　　• observer ⓝ 관찰자　　• norm ⓝ 규범, 기준
- affair ⓝ (공식적인) 일　　• competence ⓝ 능숙함, 능력
- rating ⓝ 평가, 순위　　• deviation ⓝ 일탈
- indifferently 졘 무관심하게　　• neglect ⓥ 무시하다

우리가 다른 사람들을 그들의 의복에 근거하여 판단하는 것은 누구에게도 새로운 일이 아니다. 일반적으로, 이러한 판단을 조사하는 연구는 사람들이 수술복을 입은 외과 의사, 파란 옷을 입은 남자아이와 같이 예상에 맞지만 하나의 눈에 띄는 예외가 있는 옷을 선호한다는 것을 발견한다. 〈Journal of Consumer Research〉의 2014년 6월 기사에 실린 일련의 연구는 확립된 규범을 아주 약간 어긴 사람들에 대한 관찰자들의 반응을 탐구했다. 한 시나리오에서는, 정장 차림의 행사에서 한 남자가 빨간 나비넥타이를 맸을 때 더 높은 지위와 능력을 갖춘 것으로 보여졌다. 연구자들은 독특함을 중시하는 것이 강의를 하는 동안 빨간 운동화를 신은 교수의 지위와 역량에 대한 청중들의 평가를 높였다는 것을 또한 발견했다. 그 결과들은 사람들이 규범으로부터 이러한 약간의 일탈들을 긍정적으로 판단한다는 것을 시사하는데, 왜냐하면 그것들은 그 사람이 그러한 행동으로 인한 사회적 비용을 감수할 만큼 충분히 강하다는 것을 시사하기 때문이다.
→ 일련의 연구는 사람들이 무엇을 착용해야 하는지에 대한 규범에 한 사람이 아주 약간 (B) 도전할 때 사람들이 그 사람을 (A) 긍정적으로 본다는 것을 나타낸다.

다음 글의 내용을 한 문장으로 요약하고자 한다. 빈칸 (A), (B)에 들어갈 말로 가장 적절한 것은?

	(A)		(B)	
①	positively 긍정적으로	—	challenges 도전하다	규범에 약간 일탈하는 것은 긍정적으로 봄
②	negatively 부정적으로	—	challenges	규범에 도전하는 사람들을 긍정적으로 봄
③	indifferently 무관심하게	—	neglects	규범을 무시하는 사람들에게 무관심하다는 내용이 아님
④	negatively	—	meets 지키다	규범을 지키는 사람들을 부정적으로 본다는 언급은 없음
⑤	positively	—	meets	규범을 지키는 사람들을 긍정적으로 본다는 언급은 없음

| 문제 풀이 순서 | ★★★ [정답률 54%]

1st 요약문을 통해 글에서 무엇을 찾아야 하는지 확인한다.

요약문	일련의 연구는 사람들이 무엇을 착용해야 하는지에 대한 규범에 한 사람이 아주 약간 (B)_____ 때 사람들이 그 사람을 (A)_____ 본다는 것을 나타낸다.

→ 글에서 찾아야 하는 것
(B): 무엇을 착용해야 하는지에 대한 규범에 한 사람이 아주 약간 도전할, 무시할, 지킬 때
(A): 사람들이 그 사람을 긍정적으로, 부정적으로, 무관심하게 보는지

2nd 글의 내용을 파악하여 요약문을 완성한다.

확립된 규범을 아주 약간 어긴 사람들에 대한 반응을 탐구함
예시 1: 정장 차림의 행사에서 빨간 나비넥타이를 맨 남자
　　　　→ 더 높은 지위와 능력을 갖춘 것으로 보여짐 단서 1
예시 2: 빨간 운동화를 신고 강의한 교수
　　　　→ 지위와 역량에 대한 평가가 높아짐 단서 2

→ 약간의 일탈이 그 행동으로 인한 사회적 비용을 감수할 만큼 강하다는 것을 시사하기 때문에 사람들은 이를 긍정적으로 본다. 단서 3
▶ 무엇을 착용할지 규범에 약간 벗어난, 즉 '도전한' 것이므로 (B)에는 ①, ② challenges가 들어가야 하고, 이에 사람들의 평가가 '긍정적'이었으므로 (A)에는 ①, ⑤ positively가 들어가야 함

3rd 글의 흐름을 정리하면서 정답이 맞는지 다시 한번 확인한다.

연구 내용	확립된 규범을 아주 약간 어긴 사람들에 대한 관찰자들의 반응을 탐구했다.
연구 결과 ①	정장 차림의 행사에서 빨간 나비넥타이를 한 사람이 더 높은 지위와 능력을 갖춘 것으로 여겨졌다.
연구 결과 ②	강의를 하는 동안 빨간 운동화를 신은 교수의 지위와 역량에 대해 청중들은 높이 평가했다.
결론	약간의 일탈은 그 행동으로 인한 사회적 비용을 감수할 만큼 강하다는 것을 시사하기 때문에 긍정적으로 판단된다.

→ 일련의 연구는 사람들이 무엇을 착용해야 하는지에 대한 규범에 한 사람이 아주 약간 (B) 도전할 때 사람들이 그 사람을 (A) 긍정적으로 본다는 것을 나타낸다.

| 선택지 분석 |

① positively — challenges
긍정적으로 — 도전하다
규범에 약간의 일탈로 도전하는 사람들을 긍정적으로 본다고 했다.

② negatively — challenges
부정적으로 — 도전하다
규범에 도전하는 사람들을 부정적으로 본다는 것은 글의 내용과 정반대이다.

③ indifferently — neglects
무관심하게 — 무시하다
규범을 무시하는 사람들에게 무관심하다는 내용의 글이 아니다.

④ negatively — meets
부정적으로 — 지키다
규범을 지키는 사람들을 부정적으로 보는지는 언급되지 않았다.

⑤ positively — meets
긍정적으로 — 지키다
규범을 지키는 사람들을 긍정적으로 보는지도 언급되지 않았다.

어법 특강

✱ **분사구문**
– 분사가 이끄는 어구가 부사절을 대신할 때 이 어구를 분사구문이라고 하며, 부사절을 분사구문으로 바꿀 때는,
　1. 주절의 주어와 부사절의 주어가 같은 경우 주어를 생략한다.
　2. 주절의 시제와 일치할 때 현재분사로, 주절의 시제보다 앞설 때는 having p.p.의 형태로, 수동태일 때는 (being/having been)+p.p. 형태로 바꾼다.
　3. 내용상 밝혀야 할 때를 제외하고, 부사절 접속사를 생략한다.
• I sat down at a table, ~~while I put~~ my bag on the seat beside me,
　= I sat down at a table, putting my bag on the seat beside me,
　(내 가방을 내 옆의 의자 위에 올려놓으면서, 나는 테이블에 앉았다.)
• You should measure your feet, when ~~you buy~~ new shoes.
　= You should measure your feet, when buying new shoes.
　의미를 명확하게 하기 위해 접속사를 그대로 둔 형태
　(새 신발을 살 때, 너는 네 발 크기를 측정해야 한다.)

41~42 ✱식품 생산 과정에서 환경을 보호하는 진정한 방법
핵심 주어(복수)　동격절 접속사
Claims / that local food production cut greenhouse gas emissions
by v-ing: ~함으로써　　　　　　　　　　　　　　　　복수 동사
/ by reducing the burning of transportation fuel / are usually not
well founded. // **41번** 단서 1: 지역 음식 생산이 온실가스 배출을 줄였음을 뒷받침하는 근거는 충분하지 않음
주장들은 / 지역 음식 생산이 온실가스 배출을 줄였다는 / 운송 연료의 연소를 줄임으로써 / 대개 근거가 충분하지 않다. //

Transport is the source / of only 11 percent of greenhouse gas emissions / within the food sector, /
운송은 원천이다 / 온실가스 배출의 11퍼센트만을 차지하는 / 식품 부문 내에서 /
동명사 주어(단수 취급)✱　　　　　목적격 관계대명사
so reducing the distance / that food travels / after it leaves the
단수 동사✱　비교급 강조 부사
farm / is far (a) less important / than reducing wasteful energy
use / on the farm. // **41번** 단서 2: 음식의 이동 거리를 줄이는 것보다 생산지에서 낭비되는 에너지를 줄이는 것이 더 중요함
그래서 거리를 줄이는 것은 / 식품이 이동하는 / 그것이 농장을 떠난 후 / 훨씬 덜 중요하다 / 낭비되는 에너지 사용을 줄이는 것보다 / 농장에서 //

Food coming from a distance / can actually be better / for the (b)
climate, / depending on how it was grown. //
'~에 따라' *전치사의 목적어 역할을 하는 간접의문문*
먼 곳에서 오는 식품은 / 실제로 더 좋을 수 있다 / 기후에 / 그것이 어떻게 재배되었느냐에 따라 //

For example, / field-grown tomatoes / shipped from Mexico in
the winter months / will have a smaller carbon footprint / than
앞에 주격 관계대명사와 be동사가 생략됨
(c) local winter tomatoes / grown in a greenhouse. //
예를 들어 / 밭에서 재배된 토마토는 / 겨울에 멕시코로부터 수송된 / 더 적은 탄소 발자국을
가질 것이다 / 현지의 겨울 토마토보다 / 온실에 재배된 //
주격 관계대명사
In the United Kingdom, / lamb meat that travels 11,000 miles
from New Zealand / generates only one-quarter the carbon
emissions per pound / compared to British lamb /
영국에서 / 뉴질랜드에서 11,000마일을 이동하는 양고기는 / 파운드당 탄소 배출량의 4분의
1만 발생시킨다 / 영국의 양고기에 비해 /
부사절 접속사(이유)
because farmers in the United Kingdom raise their animals / on
조동사가 포함된 수동태   *분사구문*
feed / (which must be produced using fossil fuels) / rather than
on clover pastureland. //
왜냐하면 영국의 농부들이 자신의 동물들을 기르기 때문에 / 사료로 / (화석 연료를 사용하여
생산되어야만 하는) / 클로버 목초지에서가 아닌 //
강조 용법의 do동사   *선행사를 포함하는 관계대명사*
When food does travel, / what matters most is not the (d)
not A but B: A가 아니라 B
distance traveled / but the travel mode (surface versus air), /
and most of all the load size. // **42번** 단서 1: 식품 이동에 가장 중요한 것은
이동 거리가 아니라 적재량의 규모임
식품이 정말 이동할 때 / 가장 중요한 것은 / 이동 거리가 아니라 / 이동 방식 (지상 대 공중) /
그리고 무엇보다 적재량의 규모이다 //

Bulk loads of food can travel / halfway around the world / by
ocean freight / with a smaller carbon footprint, / per pound
과거분사(pound 수식)
delivered, /
대량의 적재된 식품은 이동할 수 있다 / 세계의 절반을 / 해상 화물 운송으로 / 더 적은 탄소
발자국으로 / 배달된 파운드당 /
현재분사(foods 수식)
than foods / traveling just a short distance / but in much (e)
larger(→ smaller) loads. //
식품에 비해 / 단지 단거리를 이동하지만 / 훨씬 더 많은(→ 더 적은) 적재량인 //
42번 단서 2: 대형트럭이 픽업트럭보다 훨씬 더 많은 적재량을 운반해 연료 연소를 줄임
For example, / 18-wheelers carry much larger loads / than pickup
trucks / so they can move food / 100 times as far / while burning
접속사가 생략되지 않은 분사구문
only one-third as much gas / per pound of food delivered. //
예를 들어 / 18륜 대형트럭은 훨씬 더 많은 적재량을 운반한다 / 픽업트럭보다 / 그래서
그것들은 식품을 이동시킬 수 있다 / 100배 멀리 / 오직 3분의 1의 가스만 연소하면서 /
배달된 식품의 파운드당 //

- claim ⓝ 주장   - production ⓝ 생산
- greenhouse gas 온실가스   - emission ⓝ 방출, 배출
- transportation ⓝ 운송, 수송   - found ⓥ 근거를 부여하다, 설립하다
- sector ⓝ 부문   - wasteful ⓐ 낭비하는   - climate ⓝ 기후
- carbon ⓝ 탄소   - footprint ⓝ 발자국   - lamb ⓝ ((동물)) 양
- fossil ⓝ 화석   - pastureland ⓝ 목초지   - bulk ⓝ 큰 규모
- route ⓝ 길, 경로   - mass ⓐ 대량의   - agriculture ⓝ 농업

지역 음식 생산이 운송 연료의 연소를 줄임으로써 온실가스 배출을 줄였다는
주장들은 대개 근거가 충분하지 않다. 운송은 식품 부문 내에서 온실가스
배출의 11퍼센트만을 차지하는 원천이라서, 식품이 농장을 떠난 후 이동하는
거리를 줄이는 것은 농장에서 낭비되는 에너지 사용을 줄이는 것보다 훨씬
(a) 덜 중요하다. 먼 곳에서 오는 식품은 그것이 어떻게 재배되었느냐에 따라
실제로 (b) 기후에 더 좋을 수 있다. 예를 들어, 겨울에 멕시코로부터 수송된
밭에서 재배된 토마토는 온실에서 재배된 (c) 현지의 겨울 토마토보다 탄소
발자국이 더 적을 것이다. 영국에서는, 영국의 농부들이 클로버 목초지에서가
아닌 (화석 연료를 사용하여 생산되어야 하는) 사료로 자신의 동물들을 기르기
때문에 뉴질랜드에서 11,000마일을 이동하는 양고기는 영국의 양고기에 비해
파운드당 탄소 배출량의 4분의 1만 발생시킨다.
식품이 이동할 때, 가장 중요한 것은 이동 (d) 거리가 아니라 이동 방식 (지상
대 공중), 그리고 무엇보다 적재량의 규모이다. 대량의 적재된 식품은 단지
단거리를 이동하지만 훨씬 (e) 더 많은(→ 더 적은) 적재량인 식품에 비해

배달된 파운드당 탄소 발자국이 더 적은 해상 화물 운송으로 세계의 절반을
이동할 수 있다. 예를 들어, 18륜 대형트럭은 픽업트럭보다 훨씬 더 많은
적재량을 운반하므로 배달된 식품 파운드당 오직 3분의 1의 가스만 연소하면서
100배 멀리 식품을 이동시킬 수 있다.

41 정답 ②

윗글의 제목으로 가장 적절한 것은?
① Shorten the Route, Cut the Cost — 경로가 아니라 적재량이 중요하다는 내용임
   경로를 줄이고 비용을 절감하라
② Is Local Food Always Better for the Earth?
   지역 음식은 항상 지구에 더 좋을까? — 지역 음식이 환경에 좋지만은 않다는 내용임
③ Why Mass Production Ruins the Environment
   대량 생산이 환경을 파괴하는 이유 — 대량 생산의 환경 파괴와는 관련 없는 내용임
④ New Technologies: What Matters in Agriculture
   새로운 기술: 농업에서 중요한 것 — 농업에 새로운 기술이 중요하다는 내용이 아님
⑤ Reduce Food Waste for a Smaller Carbon Footprint
   더 적은 탄소 발자국을 위해 음식물 쓰레기를 줄여라 — 음식물 쓰레기는 언급되지 않음

〉왜 정답? ★★❀ [정답률 60%]

- 지역 음식 생산이 온실가스 배출을 줄였다는 근거는 충분하지 않음 **41번 단서 1**
- 음식의 이동 거리를 줄이는 것보다 생산지에서 낭비되는 에너지 사용을
  줄이는 것이 더 중요함 **41번 단서 2**

➡ 탄소 발자국 배출량
   예시 1: 멕시코 밭에서 재배되어 수송된 토마토 〈 온실에서 재배된 현지 토마토
   예시 2: 11,000마일을 이동한 뉴질랜드 양
              〈 화석 연료를 사용하여 생산되는 사료로 기른 현지 양
   ▶ 현지에서 식품을 생산하는 것보다 멀리에서 이동한 식품이 환경에 더 좋을
   수 있다는 것이므로 제목으로 가장 적절한 것은 ② '지역 음식은 항상 지구에 더
   좋을까?'이다.

〉왜 오답?
① 이동 거리가 아니라 적재량이 중요하다는 글이며, 가격과 관련된 내용도 아니다. 확정
③ 대량 생산이 아니라 대량 적재가 환경에 더 좋다는 내용이다.
④ 새로운 기술이 중요하다는 언급은 없다.
⑤ 더 적은 탄소 배출을 위해 음식물 쓰레기를 줄이라는 글이 아니다.
   (▶ 이유: 탄소 배출하면 떠오르는 쓰레기 배출로 만든 오답이다.)

42 정답 ⑤

밑줄 친 (a)~(e) 중에서 문맥상 낱말의 쓰임이 적절하지 않은 것은? [3점]
① (a) 이동 거리는 현지에서 낭비되는 에너지 줄이는 것보다 중요하지 않음
     덜
② (b) 먼 곳에도 온 식품이 오히려 환경에 좋을 수 있음
     기후
③ (c) 멕시코에서 온 토마토가 현지의 토마토보다 탄소 발자국이 더 적을 수 있음
     현지의
④ (d) 이동 거리가 아니라 이동 방식과 적재량이 중요함
     거리
⑤ (e) 대량으로 적재된 식품과 적재량이 적은 식품을 비교하고 있음
     더 많은

〉왜 정답? ★★★ [정답률 42%]

⑤ (e) larger 더 많은

더 적은
대량의 적재된 식품은 단지 단거리를 이동하지만(but) 훨씬 (e) 더 많은
적재량인 식품에 비해 배달된 파운드당 탄소 발자국이 더 적은 해상
화물 운송으로 세계의 절반을 이동할 수 있다.

➡ 식품을 이동할 때 이동 거리보다 이동 방식과 적재량이 중요하다는 것을 설명하는
부분이다.
따라서 세계의 절반을 이동하는 대량의 적재량을 배달하는 것이 탄소 발자국을 더
적게 남기는 것으로 비교되어야 하는 것은 단거리를 이동하는 '더 적은' 적재량을
배달하는 것이다.
▶ larger을 smaller(더 적은)와 같은 반의어로 바꿔야 함

2023. 9
9회

① (a) less 덜

> 운송은 식품 부문 내에서 온실가스 배출의 11퍼센트만을 차지하는 원천이라서, 식품이 농장을 떠난 후 이동하는 거리를 줄이는 것은 농장에서 낭비되는 에너지 사용을 줄이는 것보다 훨씬 (a) 덜 중요하다.

➡ 운송이 온실가스 배출에 미치는 영향력이 크지 않으므로, 식품의 이동 거리를 줄이는 것은 농장에서 낭비되는 에너지 사용을 줄이는 것보다 훨씬 '덜' 중요할 것이다.

▶ less는 문맥에 맞음

② (b) climate 기후

> 먼 곳에서 오는 식품은 그것이 어떻게 재배되었느냐에 따라 실제로 (b) 기후에 더 좋을 수 있다.

➡ 이동 거리가 온실가스 배출에 크게 중요하지 않다고 했으므로 먼 곳에서 오는 식품이라도 재배 방식에 따라 '기후'에, 즉 환경에 더 좋을 수도 있을 것이다.

▶ climate는 문맥에 맞음

③ (c) local 현지의

> 예를 들어, 겨울에 멕시코로부터 수송된 밭에서 재배된 토마토는 온실에서 재배된 (c) 현지의 겨울 토마토보다 탄소 발자국이 더 적을 것이다.

➡ 먼 곳에서 오는 식품이라도 재배 방식에 따라 기후에 더 좋을 수 있는 예시가 언급되었다. 먼 멕시코에서 온 토마토가 '현지의' 토마토보다 탄소 발자국이 더 적을 수 있다는 흐름은 적절하다.

> 온실에서 재배된 경우 = 재배할 때 낭비되는 에너지가 많음 (꿀팁)

▶ local은 문맥에 맞음

④ (d) distance 거리

> 식품이 이동할 때, 가장 중요한 것은 이동 (d) 거리가 아니라 이동 방식(지상 대 공중), 그리고 무엇보다 적재량의 규모이다. ~ 예를 들어, 18륜 대형트럭은 픽업트럭보다 훨씬 더 많은 적재량을 운반하므로 배달된 식품 파운드당 오직 3분의 1의 가스만 연소하면서 100배 멀리 식품을 이동시킬 수 있다.

➡ 식품을 이동할 때 '거리'보다 적재량이 더 중요하다는 예시가 이어진다.

▶ distance는 문맥에 맞음

어법 특강

✱ 주어–동사 수 일치

– 문장의 주어가 명사구 혹은 명사절일 때 항상 단수 취급한다. to부정사구, 동명사구나 의문사절, that절, whether절 등과 같은 명사절이 주어로 오는 경우 동사와 멀어질 수 있기 때문에 수 일치 여부를 쉽게 판단하기 힘들다. 따라서 항상 문장을 전체적으로 파악해야 한다.

• **Creating a list of goals is** a good way to be a better student.
  동명사구 주어 / 단수 동사
  (목표들의 목록을 만드는 것은 더 나은 학생이 되기 위한 좋은 방법이다.)

• **Whether he will accept my offer is** not certain yet.
  명사절 주어 / 단수 동사
  (그가 나의 제안을 받아들일 지는 아직 확실하지 않다.)

• **To overcome my emotional problems is** difficult.
  to부정사구 주어 / 단수 동사
  (나의 감정적인 문제들을 극복하는 것은 어렵다.)

---

43 ~ 45 ✱ 사원 관리인이 될 자격

(A) Long ago, / an old man built a grand temple / at the center of his village. // 〔45번 ①〕 노인은 마을 중심부에 사원을 지음
옛날에 / 한 노인이 큰 사원을 지었다 / 마을 중심부에 //

People traveled / **to worship** at the temple. // 부사적 용법(목적)
사람들이 멀리서 왔다 / 사원에서 예배를 드리기 위해 //

So the old man made arrangements / for food and accommodation / inside the temple **itself**. // 강조 용법의 재귀대명사
그래서 노인은 준비했다 / 음식과 숙소를 / 사원 그 안에 //

He needed someone / **who** could look after the temple, / so (a) 주격 관계대명사
he put up a notice: / Manager needed. // = the old man
그는 사람이 필요했다 / 사원을 관리할 수 있는 / 그래서 그는 공고를 붙였다 / '관리자 구함'이라는 // 〔43번〕 단서 1: 노인은 사원 관리자를 구하는 공고를 붙임

✱(A) 문단 요약: 사원을 지은 노인은 그것을 관리할 사람이 필요해 구인 공고를 붙임

(B) When **that** young man left the temple, / the old man called him and asked, / "Will you take care of this temple?" // 지시형용사
그 젊은이가 사원을 나섰을 때 / 노인이 그를 불러 질문했다 / "이 사원의 관리를 맡아 주겠소" // 〔43번〕 단서 2, 〔45번 ②〕 젊은이가 사원을 나설 때 그를 불러서 질문함

The young man **was** surprised / by the offer / and **replied**, / "I have no experience / **caring** for a temple. // 병렬 구조 / 현재분사(experience 수식)
젊은이는 놀랐다 / 그 제안에 / 그리고 대답했다 / "저는 경험이 없습니다 / 사원을 관리하는 // 〔45번 ③〕 젊은이는 노인의 제안에 놀람

I'm not even educated."//
저는 심지어 교육도 받지 못했습니다."//

The old man smiled and said, / "I don't want any educated man. //
노인은 미소를 지으며 말했다 / "나는 교육을 받은 사람이 필요한 게 아니오 //

I want a qualified person." //
나는 자격 있는 사람을 원하오"라고 // 앞에 Being이 생략됨

Confused, / the young man asked, / "But why do (b) **you** consider me / a qualified person?" // consider A (as) B: A를 B라고 여기다 / = the old man
당황하여 / 젊은이는 물었다 / "그런데 당신은 왜 저를 여기시나요 / 자격이 있는 사람이라고" 라고 // 〔43번〕 단서 3: 젊은이는 노인에게 질문을 함

✱(B) 문단 요약: 노인이 젊은이에게 사원 관리를 부탁하자 젊은이는 놀라 왜 자신을 자격 있는 사람이라고 여기는지 물음

(C) The old man replied, / "I buried a brick / on the path to the temple. // 〔43번〕 단서 4: 노인이 대답함
노인은 대답했다 / "나는 벽돌 한 개를 묻었소 / 사원으로 통하는 길에 //

I watched for many days / as people tripped over / that brick. //
나는 여러 날 동안 지켜보았소 / 사람들이 발이 걸려 넘어지는 것을 / 그 벽돌에 // 명사적 용법(thought의 목적어)

No one thought / **to remove** it. //
아무도 생각을 하지 않았소 / 그것을 치울 //

But you dug up / that brick." // 〔45번 ④〕 젊은이가 벽돌을 파냄
하지만 당신은 파냈소 / 그 벽돌을" //

The young man said, / "I haven't done **anything great**. // -thing으로 끝나는 대명사는 형용사가 뒤에서 수식함
젊은이는 말했다 / "저는 대단한 일을 한 것이 아닙니다 //

It's the duty of every human being / **to think** about others. // 가주어 / 진주어
~은 모든 인간의 의무입니다 / 타인을 생각하는 것은 // = the young man

(c) **I** only did my duty." //
저는 제 의무를 다했을 뿐입니다" //

The old man smiled and said, / "Only **people who** know their duty and perform it / **are** qualified people." // 핵심 주어(복수) / 주격 관계대명사 / 복수 동사
노인은 미소를 지으며 말했다 / "자신의 의무를 알고 그것을 수행하는 사람만이 / 자격이 있는 사람이오"라고 //

✱(C) 문단 요약: 노인이 길에 묻어둔 벽돌을 치운 사람이 젊은이뿐이었고, 노인은 타인을 생각하는 의무를 다하는 사람만이 자격 있는 사람이라고 함

(D) **Seeing the notice**, / many people went to the old man. // 분사구문
공고를 보고 / 많은 사람들이 노인을 찾아갔다 // 〔43번〕 단서 5, 〔45번 ⑤〕 공고를 보고 많은 사람들이 노인을 찾아감

But he returned / all the applicants / after interviews, / **telling them**, / "I need a qualified person for this work." // 분사구문
그러나 그는 돌려보냈다 / 모든 지원자들을 / 면접 후에 / 그들에게 말하면서 / "나는 이 일에 자격을 갖춘 사람이 필요합니다"라고 //

The old man would sit / on the roof of (d) his house / every
　　분사구문을 이끄는 현재분사　　목적격 보어(원형부사) 　　= the old man's
morning, / watching people / go through the temple doors. //
노인은 앉아 있곤 했다 / 그의 집 지붕에 / 매일 아침 / 사람들을 지켜보면서 / 사원의 문을
통과하는 것을 //　　　　43번 단서 6: 노인은 사원에 온 한 젊은이를 발견함
　　　　　　　= the old man　목적격 보어(원형부사)
One day, / (e) he saw a young man / come to the temple. //
어느 날 / 그는 한 젊은이를 보았다 / 사원으로 오는 //

*(D) 문단 요약: 노인은 면접을 보러 온 사람들을 돌려보냈고, 매일 아침 사람들을
지켜보다가 한 젊은이가 오는 것을 보게 됨

- grand ⓐ 웅장한, 큰　　　• temple ⓝ 사원, 절　　• worship ⓥ 예배하다
- arrangement ⓝ 준비　　• accommodation ⓝ 숙소, 거처
- look after ~을 관리하다[돌보다]　　• offer ⓝ 제안
- qualified ⓐ 자격이 있는　　• bury ⓥ 묻다　　• brick ⓝ 벽돌
- path ⓝ 길, 경로　　• trip over ~에 발이 걸려 넘어지다
- remove ⓥ 제거하다　　• dig up ~을 파내다　　• duty ⓝ 의무
- applicant ⓝ 지원자

(A) 옛날에, 한 노인이 마을 중심부에 큰 사원을 지었다. 사람들이 사원에서
예배를 드리기 위해 멀리서 왔다. 그래서 노인은 사원 안에 음식과 숙소를
준비했다. 그는 사원을 관리할 수 있는 사람이 필요했고, 그래서 (a) 그는
'관리자 구함'이라는 공고를 붙였다.

(D) 공고를 보고 많은 사람들이 노인을 찾아갔다. 그러나 그는 면접 후에
그들에게 "나는 이 일에 자격을 갖춘 사람이 필요합니다."라고 말하며, 모든
지원자들을 돌려보냈다. 노인은 사람들이 사원의 문을 통과하는 것을 지켜보며
매일 아침 (d) 그의 집 지붕에 앉아 있곤 했다. 어느 날 (e) 그는 한 젊은이가
사원으로 오는 것을 보았다.

(B) 젊은이가 사원을 나설 때, 노인이 그를 불러 "이 사원의 관리를 맡아
주겠소?"라고 질문했다. 젊은이는 그 제안에 놀라서 "저는 사원을 관리한
경험이 없고, 심지어 교육도 받지 못했습니다."라고 대답했다. 노인은 미소
지으며 "나는 교육을 받은 사람이 필요한 게 아니오. 나는 자격 있는 사람을
원하오."라고 말했다. 당황하여, 젊은이는 "그런데 (b) 당신은 왜 저를 자격이
있는 사람이라고 여기시나요?"라고 물었다.

(C) 노인은 대답했다. "나는 사원으로 통하는 길에 벽돌 한 개를 묻었소.
나는 여러 날 동안 사람들이 그 벽돌에 발이 걸려 넘어지는 것을 지켜보았소.
아무도 그것을 치울 생각을 하지 않았소. 하지만 당신은 그 벽돌을 파냈소."
젊은이는 "저는 대단한 일을 한 것이 아닙니다. 타인을 생각하는 것은 모든
인간의 의무입니다. (c) 저는 제 의무를 다했을 뿐입니다."라고 말했다. 노인은
미소를 지으며 "자신의 의무를 알고 그 의무를 수행하는 사람만이 자격이 있는
사람이오."라고 말했다.

43 정답 ④

**주어진 글 (A)에 이어질 내용을 순서에 맞게 배열한 것으로 가장 적절한
것은?**
① (B) — (D) — (C)
② (C) — (B) — (D)　←공고를 보고 사람들이 왔다는 (D)가 가장 먼저 와야 함
③ (C) — (D) — (B)
④ (D) — (B) — (C)　(D) 공고를 보고 온 사람들을 돌려보낸 노인이 한 젊은이가 사원에
　　　　　　　　　　오는 걸 발견함 — (B) 노인은 젊은이에게 사원 관리를 제안했고,
⑤ (D) — (C) — (B)　젊은이는 이유를 물음 — (C) 노인은 그가 의무를 수행한 유일한
　　　　　　　　　　사람이라고 대답함
젊은이가 질문한 (B)가 노인이 대답한 (C) 앞에 와야 함

>왜 정답 · 오답 ? ✸❀❀ [정답률 87%]

(A): 사원 관리자를 찾기 위해 노인이 구인 공고를 올렸다.

➡ 공고에 대한 사람들의 반응이 이어질 것이다.

(B): 노인이 한 젊은이에게 자격 있는 사람이라며 사원 관리를 제안하자
젊은이는 놀라 그 이유를 물었다.

➡ 한 젊은이가 등장했다는 내용이 앞에 있어야 하고, 뒤에는 젊은이의 질문에 대한
노인의 답이 이어질 것이다.

(C): 사원으로 오는 길에 묻은 벽돌을 파낸 사람은 젊은이뿐이며, 이처럼 타인을
생각하는 의무를 다하는 사람만이 사원 관리인으로서 자격 있는 사람이라고
노인이 대답했다.

➡ 젊은이가 질문한 (B)에 이어지는 내용이고, 어떤 사람이 자격 있는 사람인지를
설명하는 글의 마무리 부분이다.

(D): 공고를 보고 온 사람들은 돌려보내고 사원에 오는 사람들을 지켜보던
노인이 한 젊은이가 사원에 오는 것을 보게 됐다.

➡ 공고를 붙였다는 (A)에 이어지는 내용이고, 뒤에는 노인이 젊은이에게 사원
관리직을 제안하는 (B)가 이어져야 한다.
▶ (D) 공고를 보고 온 사람들을 돌려보낸 노인이 한 젊은이가 사원에 오는 것을
발견함 → (B) 노인은 그 젊은이에게 사원 관리를 제안했고, 젊은이는 이유를 물음
→ (C) 노인은 그가 의무를 수행한 유일한 사람이라고 대답함
▶ 글의 순서는 ④ (D) → (B) → (C)임

44 정답 ③

밑줄 친 (a)~(e) 중에서 가리키는 대상이 나머지 넷과 다른 것은?
① (a)　② (b)　③ (c)　④ (d)　⑤ (e)
= the old man　= the old man　= the young man　= the old man's　= the old man

>왜 정답 ? ✸❀❀ [정답률 87%]
③ (c) I: 그저 의무를 다했을 뿐이라고 말한 사람 ▶ the young man

>왜 오답 ?
① (a) he: 사원 관리자를 구하는 구인 공고를 붙인 사람 ▶ the old man
② (b) you: 젊은이를 자격 있는 사람이라고 여긴 사람 ▶ the old man
④ (d) his: 매일 아침 집 지붕에 앉아 있던 사람 ▶ the old man's
⑤ (e) he: 한 젊은이가 사원으로 오는 것을 본 사람 ▶ the old man

45 정답 ④

윗글에 관한 내용으로 적절하지 않은 것은?
① 노인은 마을 중심부에 사원을 지었다.
　　　　　　　　an old man built a grand temple at the center of his village
② 젊은이가 사원을 나설 때 노인이 그를 불렀다.
　　　　　　When that young man left the temple, the old man called him
③ 젊은이는 노인의 제안에 놀랐다.
　　　　　　The young man was surprised by the offer
④ 노인은 사원으로 통하는 길에 묻혀있던 벽돌을 파냈다.
　　　　　　　　But you dug up that brick.
⑤ 공고를 보고 많은 사람들이 노인을 찾아갔다.
　　Seeing the notice, many people went to the old man.

>왜 정답 ? ✸❀❀ [정답률 83%]
노인은 젊은이에게 '하지만 당신은 그 벽돌을 파냈소.(But you dug up that
brick.)'라고 이야기했다. 따라서 벽돌을 파낸 것은 젊은이이므로 노인이 벽돌을
파냈다고 한 ④은 적절하지 않다.

>왜 오답 ?
① 노인은 마을 중심부에 사원을 지었다. (an old man built a grand temple at
the center of his village)
② 젊은이가 사원을 나설 때 노인이 그를 불렀다. (When that young man left the
temple, the old man called him)
③ 젊은이는 노인의 제안에 놀랐다. (The young man was surprised by the
offer)
⑤ 공고를 보고 많은 사람들이 노인을 찾아갔다. (Seeing the notice, many
people went to the old man.)

01 was supposed to / leak in the ceiling / ceiling needs / school theater / performance

02 five-kilometer route / weather is perfect / designed for running / to wear the right

03 your articles / awards / and talented actors / accessories / impressive / script to fully understand / backgrounds / sharing your story

04 Same here / striped pattern / bookshelf under the clock / two lamps / Good lighting

05 Shall we go over / extra batteries / wireless / sound terrific / audience haven't been arranged / be fantastic

06 wedding anniversary / regular size / all purchases / be ready / offer a delivery service

07 history test / ski trip is / didn't know that / on the weekends / recovering from surgery / relatives in Canada / Have fun

08 for college students / a theme / year's theme / the deadline / sooner than / receive a laptop

09 happy to introduce / special opportunity / lecture about / most popular flavors / registration fee / of ingredients

10 indoor cycling bikes / differs / goes well with / shouldn't get / foldable one / storage space / higher customer rating / on actual

11 a new sweater / bought / love to / for my brother

12 our food / ordered pizza / Delivery usually takes

13 the library / my science / been skipping / for my grade / shouldn't do / a big dinner / Skipping meals / overeat / should eat

14 to do better in / how to improve / my homework / new words / practice saying / repeatedly / But since / a beginner / more effort to get used / suggesting that

15 passionate about environmental issues / very careless / stickers that remind / and she agrees / a great artist / design stickers that encourage

[16~17] overtourism / to a particular destination / by overtourism / fewer places for visitors / promote areas away / tried to limit access / reduce tourism overall

01 원자

02 수술복

03 웅장한

04 통합하다

05 각자의

06 awareness

07 eardrum

08 sole

09 boredom

10 pastureland

11 dig up

12 pass on

13 stem from

14 take into account

15 refer to

16 hollow

17 leak

18 bypass

19 intended

20 excessive

21 successive

22 compassion

23 flavor

24 wireless

25 correlation

26 worship

27 steady

28 composition

29 repetition

30 storage

31 rare

32 Sensory

33 fright

34 disoriented

35 norm

36 alongside

37 accommodation

38 passionate

39 Bulk

40 distinction

01 정답 ④ ＊시험 중 전자 기기 소지 금지 안내

[Chime bell rings.]
[차임벨이 울린다.]

M : Hello, Bronx High School students.
남 : 안녕하세요, Bronx 고등학교 학생 여러분.

This is your vice principal, Jeremy Wilson.
저는 교감 Jeremy Wilson입니다.

As you know, our mid-term exam will start next Tuesday.
여러분도 아시다시피, 중간고사가 다음 주 화요일에 시작될 예정입니다.

목적어절 접속사
I'd like to announce **that** you should not carry any electronic
~을 포함하여
devices while taking the exam **including** smart watches or
wireless earphones. **단서1** 시험 중 전자 기기를 소지하지 않도록 안내함
시험을 치르는 동안은 스마트 시계나 무선 이어폰을 포함하여 어떤 전자 기기도 소지하지 말아야 한다는 점을 알려드립니다.

수동태   양보의 부사절 접속사
If you **'re found** with an electronic device, **even if** it's in your
수동태
bag, it'll **be regarded** as cheating.
여러분이 전자 기기를 소지하고 있는 것이 발견되면, 가방에 있어도 부정행위로 간주될 것입니다.

주격 관계대명사
This will result in a penalty **that** affects your test score.
이로 인해 여러분의 시험 점수에 영향을 미치는 처벌을 받게 될 것입니다.

So please make sure that you don't have any electronic
devices with you during the exam. **단서2** 시험 중 전자 기기를 소지하지 않도록 다시 당부함
따라서 시험 동안에는 어떤 전자 기기도 소지하지 않도록 주의해 주세요.

I wish you all good luck.
모두 행운을 빕니다.

- vice principal 교감
- mid-term ⓐ 중간의
- announce ⓥ 알리다
- electronic device 전자 기기
- wireless ⓐ 무선의
- regard ⓥ 간주하다
- cheating ⓝ 부정행위
- result in (그 결과) ~가 되다
- penalty ⓝ 처벌

다음을 듣고, 남자가 하는 말의 목적으로 가장 적절한 것을 고르시오.
① 중간고사 실시 일정의 변경을 알리려고 중간고사 일정을 변경한다는 내용이 아님
② 시험 문제 이의 제기 기간을 공지하려고 시험 문제에 대한 내용이 아님
③ 분실한 스마트 시계를 찾아가도록 안내하려고 스마트 시계를 언급한 것으로 만든 오답
④ 시험 중 전자 기기를 소지하지 않도록 당부하려고 시험 중 전자 기기를 소지하지 않도록 안내함
⑤ 전자 기기를 활용한 시험 방식에 대해 설명하려고 시험 방식에 대한 언급은 없음

＞왜 정답? ＊❀❀ [정답률 97%]
시험 중 전자 기기를 소지하면 부정행위로 처리되어 시험 점수에 영향을 미칠 수 있으므로 시험 중에는 전자 기기를 소지하지 않아야 함을 당부하고 있다. 따라서 남자가 하는 말의 목적으로 가장 적절한 것은 ④이다.

＞왜 오답?
① 중간고사의 일정이 언급되었으나 그것을 변경한다는 내용이 아니다.
② 시험 문제 이의 제기 기간을 공지하는 내용이 아니다.
③ 스마트 시계를 포함한 전자 기기의 소지를 금지한다는 내용이지, 분실한 스마트 시계를 찾아가라는 내용이 아니다.
⑤ 시험 중 전자 기기를 소지하지 말라는 내용이지, 전자 기기를 활용하는 시험에 대한 내용이 아니다. 함정

02 정답 ② ＊자녀 사진을 온라인에 올리는 것의 위험성

W : Brandon, what are you so focused on?
여 : Brandon, 뭐에 그렇게 집중하고 있나요?

형용사적 용법 (pictures of my kids 수식)
M : Hi, Chloe! I'm looking at pictures of my kids **to post** on social media.
남 : 안녕하세요, Chloe! 소셜 미디어에 올릴 제 자녀들의 사진들을 보고 있어요.

W : For real? Posting their pictures on social media?
여 : 정말요? 그들의 사진을 소셜 미디어에 올리는 건가요?

M : Yes. I'm just sharing our joyful moments online.
남 : 네. 저는 그냥 우리의 즐거운 순간들을 온라인에 공유하고 있어요.

W : I understand, but when posting your kids' photos online, you should be aware of the risks. **단서1** 자녀의 사진을 온라인에 게시할 때는 위험을 인지해야 함
여 : 이해합니다만, 당신 자녀들의 사진을 온라인에 게시할 때는 그 위험들을 인지해야 합니다.

M : Risks? What do you mean by that?
남 : 위험들이요? 그게 무슨 뜻인가요?

앞에 목적격 관계대명사 생략   수동태
W : You know, the photos **you post** could **be seen** by anyone.
여 : 그게요, 당신이 게시하는 사진은 누구에게나 보여질 수 있어요.

M : Is it a big problem?
남 : 그것이 큰 문제인가요?

수동태
W : Of course. The photos could potentially **be used** for criminal purposes. **단서2** 사진이 범죄 목적으로 사용될 수 있음
여 : 물론이죠. 그 사진들은 잠재적으로 범죄 목적으로 사용될 수 있어요.

M : Oh, no. I've never thought of that.
남 : 오, 저런. 그런 생각은 한 번도 해본 적이 없어요.

W : That's why you should be mindful of the risks when sharing your children's photos online. **단서3** 위험을 인지하고 있어야 함을 다시 강조함
여 : 그렇기 때문에 당신 자녀들의 사진을 온라인에 공유할 때 위험을 염두에 두어야 해요.

M : Thanks for your advice. I'll be careful.
남 : 조언해 주셔서 감사합니다. 조심할게요.

- focused ⓐ 집중한
- post ⓥ 올리다, 게시하다
- joyful ⓐ 즐거운
- aware ⓐ 인지하고 있는
- potentially ⓐⓓ 잠재적으로
- criminal ⓐ 범죄의
- purpose ⓝ 목적
- mindful ⓐ ~을 염두에 두는
- risk ⓝ 위험

대화를 듣고, 여자의 의견으로 가장 적절한 것을 고르시오.
① 자녀들이 스스로 인터넷 사용 시간을 조절하도록 교육해야 한다. 자녀의 인터넷 사용 문제에 대한 내용이 아님
② 온라인에 자녀의 사진을 올릴 때 그 위험성을 인식해야 한다. 자녀의 사진을 온라인에 게시할 때는 위험을 인지해야 한다고 함
③ 사진을 영구적으로 보존하려면 온라인에 업로드해야 한다. 사진을 영구적으로 보관하는 방법에 대한 내용이 아님
④ 부모는 자녀의 올바른 소셜 미디어 사용을 지도해야 한다. 자녀의 소셜 미디어 사용에 대한 내용이 아님
⑤ 온라인 범죄에 노출될 경우 경찰에 즉시 신고해야 한다. 온라인 범죄에 노출 시 경찰에 신고하라는 언급은 없음

＞왜 정답? ❀❀❀ [정답률 97%]
여자는 남자에게 자녀의 사진을 온라인에 게시하면 누구나 볼 수 있으므로 범죄 목적으로 사용될 수 있는 위험을 인지하고 있어야 한다고 말했다. 따라서 여자의 의견으로 가장 적절한 것은 ②이다.

＞왜 오답?
① 자녀의 인터넷 사용 시간에 대한 내용이 아니라, 자녀 사진을 온라인에 게시하는 것에 대한 내용이다.
③ 자녀 사진의 온라인 게시가 위험하다는 내용이지, 사진을 영구적으로 보존하는 방법에 대한 내용이 아니다.
④ 자녀 사진을 온라인 소셜 미디어에 게시하는 것이 위험하다는 내용이지, 자녀의 올바른 소셜 미디어 사용에 대한 내용이 아니다.
⑤ 온라인에 게시된 자녀의 사진이 범죄에 이용될 수 있다는 내용이지, 온라인 범죄에 노출될 경우 경찰에 신고하라는 내용이 아니다. 주의

03 정답 ⑤ ＊성공적인 발표의 열쇠

W : Hello, students.
여 : 안녕하세요, 학생 여러분.

I'm Megan, a public speaking instructor.
저는 대중 연설 강사 Megan입니다.

뒤에 목적어절 접속사 that 생략
Imagine you're sitting in an audience at a presentation.
여러분이 발표에서 청중석에 앉아 있다고 상상해 보세요.

And the speaker begins with a boring introduction.
그리고 발표자가 지루한 도입으로 시작합니다.

Quickly, you would lose interest.
빠르게, 여러분은 흥미를 잃게 될 것입니다.

가주어   명사적 용법(진주어)
So, for a successful presentation, it's important to start with
an interesting opening. 단서1 성공적인 발표는 흥미로운 오프닝으로 시작하는 것이 중요함
따라서 성공적인 발표를 위해서는 흥미로운 오프닝으로 시작하는 것이 중요합니다.

병렬 구조
An engaging opening captures attention and creates
interest. 단서2 매력적인 오프닝은 관심과 흥미를 유발함
매력적인 오프닝은 관심을 사로잡고 흥미를 유발합니다.

It also serves as a hook and makes the audience eager to
hear more.
그것은 또한 후크 역할을 하며 청중이 더 듣고 싶어 하게 만듭니다.

수동태
For example, a challenging question or a surprising statistic
can be used.
예를 들어, 어려운 질문이나 놀라운 통계가 사용될 수 있습니다.

목적어절 접속사
Once again, remember that an attractive beginning is the
key to a good presentation. 단서3 매력적인 시작은 좋은 발표의 열쇠임
다시 한 번, 매력적인 시작이 좋은 발표의 열쇠라는 것을 기억하세요.

Keep it in mind. Thank you.
그것을 명심하세요. 감사합니다.

- instructor ⓝ 강사 ・ audience ⓝ 청중 ・ introduction ⓝ 도입
- interest ⓝ 흥미 ・ successful ⓐ 성공적인
- engaging ⓐ 매력적인 ・ capture ⓥ 사로잡다
- attention ⓝ 관심 ・ serve ⓥ 역할을 하다
- hook ⓝ 후크 (청중의 흥미를 이끄는 문장) ・ eager ⓐ ~하고 싶어 하는
- challenging ⓐ 어려운, 도전적인 ・ statistic ⓝ 통계
- attractive ⓐ 매력적인

다음을 듣고, 여자가 하는 말의 요지로 가장 적절한 것을 고르시오.

① 여러 기관의 통계 자료 활용은 발표의 신뢰도를 높여 준다.
발표의 신뢰도에 대한 언급은 없음
② 좋은 발표의 핵심은 청중의 수준에 맞는 주제 선정에 있다.
발표 주제 선정에 대한 내용은 없음
③ 대화를 나눌 때 매력적인 화법은 좋은 인상을 남길 수 있다.
매력적인 화법에 대한 내용이 아님
④ 청중의 흥미를 유지하기 위해 지속적인 주의 환기가 필요하다.
지속적인 주의 환기에 대한 언급은 없음
⑤ 성공적인 발표를 위해 흥미로운 도입부로 시작하는 게 중요하다.
성공적인 발표를 위해 흥미로운 도입부로 시작하는 것이 중요하다고 했음

왜 정답? ✿✿✿ [정답률 91%]

여자는 발표의 시작이 지루하면 청중의 흥미를 잃게 하므로 성공적인 발표를 위해서는 청중들의 관심을 사로잡고 흥미를 유발하는 도입부가 중요하다고 말했다. 따라서 여자의 의견으로 가장 적절한 것은 ⑤이다.

왜 오답?

① 흥미로운 발표 도입부를 위해 통계 자료를 사용할 수 있다는 것이 예시로 언급되었을 뿐, 발표의 신뢰도에 대한 내용은 언급되지 않았다.
② 좋은 발표의 핵심은 흥미로운 도입부라는 내용이지, 청중의 수준에 맞는 주제 선정에 대한 내용은 없다.
③ 흥미로운 도입부가 성공적인 발표를 만든다는 내용이지, 매력적인 화법에 대한 내용이 아니다.
④ 청중의 흥미를 발표의 도입부에서 유발하는 것이 중요하다는 내용이지, 지속적으로 청중의 주의를 환기시켜야 한다는 것은 언급되지 않았다.

---

04 정답 ⑤ ＊반려견 돌봄 센터

M : Honey, look at this picture. How about this doggy daycare
center for while we're away?
남 : 여보, 이 사진 좀 봐요. 우리가 없는 동안을 위해 이 반려견 돌봄 센터는 어때요?

W : [Pause] Looks good! Is that a photo booth? ①의 단서 사진 부스가 있음
여 : [잠시 후] 좋아 보여요! 저것은 사진 부스예요?

M : Yes. We can take photos with our dogs before we leave them
there.
남 : 맞아요. 반려견을 거기에 맡기기 전에 우리의 반려견과 함께 사진을 찍을 수 있어요.

W : Lovely! Oh, can you see the dog?
여 : 너무 좋아요! 오, 개가 보이나요?

②의 단서 개가 미끄럼틀 위에 있음
M : Where? [Pause] Ah. It's on the slide. It looks fun.
남 : 어디요? [잠시 후] 아. 미끄럼틀 위에 있네요. 재밌어 보이네요.

W : I also like the star-patterned tunnel. ③의 단서 별 무늬 터널이 있음
여 : 별 무늬 터널도 마음에 드네요.

have fun -ing: 즐겁게 ~하다
M : Me, too. Dogs can have fun running through it. Oh, can you
선행사를 포함하는 관계대명사
guess what that bone-shaped thing is? ④의 단서 뼈 모양의 수영장이 있음
남 : 나도 그래요. 개들은 터널을 즐겁게 뛰어다닐 수 있겠네요. 오, 저 뼈 모양의 것이 뭔지 알아요?

W : Sure. It must be a doggy pool. By the way, where can our
dogs eat?
여 : 물론이죠. 강아지 수영장인가 봐요. 그런데 우리 강아지들은 어디서 먹을 수 있나요?

M : Look under the tree!
남 : 나무 아래를 봐요!

W : Aha! There are three food dispensers. Dogs can easily get
their food. ⑤의 단서 사진에 사료 지급기는 두 개 있음
여 : 아하! 세 개의 사료 지급기가 있네요. 개들이 쉽게 사료를 먹을 수 있겠어요.

M : Right. How do you feel about this center?
남 : 맞네요. 이 센터에 대해 어떻게 생각해요?

부사적 용법
W : I'm delighted to find such a good place.
여 : 이렇게 좋은 곳을 찾아서 기뻐요.

- daycare center 돌봄 센터 ・ slide ⓝ 미끄럼틀
- star-patterned ⓐ 별 무늬의 ・ bone-shaped ⓐ 뼈 모양의
- dispenser ⓝ 지급기 ・ delighted ⓐ 기쁜

대화를 듣고, 그림에서 대화의 내용과 일치하지 않는 것을 고르시오.

왜 정답? ✿✿✿ [정답률 92%]

나무 아래에 개 사료 지급기가 세 개 있다고 했지만(There are three food dispensers.) 그림에는 사료 지급기가 두 개밖에 없으므로 ⑤이 대화의 내용과 일치하지 않는다.

왜 오답?

① 사진 부스가 있다고 했다.
② 미끄럼틀 위에 개가 있다고 했다.
③ 별 무늬 터널이 있다고 했다.
④ 뼈 모양의 수영장이 있다고 했다.

05 정답 ③ ＊플래시몹 행사 준비

W : Hurray! We've finally **completed** all of our dance moves for the flash mob.
현재완료(완료)

여 : 만세! 우리는 드디어 플래시몹을 위한 모든 춤 동작을 완성했어요.

M : Excellent! Now all we have to do is practice together.

남 : 훌륭해요! 이제 우리는 함께 연습만 하면 됩니다.

W : What do you think about **recording** a video to get a better understanding of the moves? ②의 함정
동명사

여 : 동작을 더 잘 이해하기 위해 동영상을 찍는 것에 대해 어떻게 생각하나요?

M : Good idea! Could we ask someone **to help us**?
ask의 목적격 보어

남 : 좋은 생각이에요! 누군가에게 우리를 도와달라고 부탁할 수 있을까요?

W : Well... I know someone **who** is good with a camera. ①의 함정
주격 관계대명사

여 : 음… 저는 카메라를 잘 다루는 사람을 알고 있어요.

M : Okay. Then, is there anything **I can help with**?
앞에 목적격 관계대명사가 생략됨

남 : 알겠습니다. 그럼 제가 도와드릴 일이 있나요?

W : Hold on. Umm... [Pause] I **forgot to order** our group T-shirts.
forget+to부정사: (미래에) ~해야 할 것을 잊어버리다

여 : 잠깐만요. 음… [잠시 후] 우리 단체 티셔츠를 주문하는 걸 깜빡했네요.

M : You mean the ones **we chose together last week**?
앞에 목적격 관계대명사가 생략됨

남 : 지난주에 우리가 함께 선택한 티셔츠들을 말하는 건가요?

W : Right. Could you do that for me?

여 : 네. 혹시 그걸 해주실 수 있나요?

M : Of course! Please **let** me **know** the website. Then, I'll order the T-shirts immediately. 단서 남자가 티셔츠를 주문하겠다고 함
사역동사 목적격 보어(동사원형) ⑤의 함정

남 : 물론이죠! 웹사이트를 알려주세요. 그럼 바로 티셔츠를 주문할게요.

W : Great! Thanks for your help.

여 : 좋아요! 도와줘서 고마워요.

M : It's always my pleasure.

남 : 언제든지요.

- complete ⓥ 완성하다
- flash mob 플래시몹
- record ⓥ 기록하다
- understanding ⓝ 이해
- forget ⓥ 잊어버리다
- choose ⓥ 선택하다
- immediately ⓪ 즉시

대화를 듣고, 남자가 할 일로 가장 적절한 것을 고르시오.
① 카메라 빌려 오기 카메라를 빌려야 하는 상황이 아님
② 영상 촬영하기 영상 촬영은 여자가 아는 다른 사람에게 부탁하기로 함
③ 단체 티셔츠 주문하기 남자가 단체 티셔츠를 주문하기로 함
④ 연습 일정 안내하기 연습 일정에 대한 언급은 없음
⑤ 구매 사이트 주소 보내기 여자가 남자에게 알려줘야 함

> **왜** 정답? ＊＊＊ [정답률 94%]

플래시몹 행사를 위해 선택했던 단체 티셔츠 주문을 여자가 깜빡 잊어버렸다고 하자, 남자가 자신에게 구매 사이트를 알려주면 즉시 주문하겠다고 했으므로 남자가 할 일로 가장 적절한 것은 ③이다.

> **왜** 오답?

① 카메라를 빌려야 한다는 내용은 언급되지 않았다.
② 영상 촬영은 여자가 아는 사람에게 부탁할 예정이다.
④ 연습 일정을 안내해야 한다는 내용은 언급되지 않았다.
⑤ 여자가 남자에게 구매 사이트 주소를 보내야 한다.

06 정답 ⑤ ＊에센셜 오일 구입

W : Hello, can I buy some essential oils?

여 : 안녕하세요, 에센셜 오일을 좀 구매할 수 있을까요?

M : Absolutely. **Depending on** your needs, we have many options. 남 : 물론이죠. 필요에 따라 다양한 선택지가 있습니다.
'~에 따라서'

W : Could you recommend good oils for sleep disorder and skin troubles?

여 : 수면 장애와 피부 트러블에 좋은 오일을 추천해 주시겠어요? 단서 1 라벤더와 카모마일 오일은 각각 15달러

M : Okay. For sound sleep, I recommend lavender or chamomile oils. They're **on special offer**. They're $15 each.
'특별 할인 중인'

남 : 알겠습니다. 숙면을 위해 라벤더 오일이나 카모마일 오일을 추천합니다. 특별 할인 중입니다. 개당 15달러입니다. 단서 2 각 한 병씩 구매함

W : I'll take one of each. Both scents are my favorites.

여 : 각각 하나씩 가져갈게요. 두 향 모두 제가 가장 좋아하는 향입니다.

M : Good choice. And, for your skin troubles, you can try geranium oil.

남 : 좋은 선택입니다. 그리고 피부 트러블에 대해서는 제라늄 오일을 사용해 보세요.

W : **I've heard** geranium is effective for sensitive skin. How much is it?
뒤에 목적어절 접속사 that 생략

여 : 제라늄이 민감한 피부에 효과적이라고 들었습니다. 가격이 얼마인가요?

M : It's $20. 단서 3 제라늄 오일은 개당 20달러

남 : 20달러입니다.

W : Reasonable. I'll buy two bottles of geranium.

여 : 합리적이네요. 제라늄 두 병을 살게요. 단서 4 제라늄 오일을 두 병 구입함

M : Alright. So, one lavender, one chamomile and two geranium oils, correct?

남 : 알겠습니다. 라벤더 하나, 카모마일 하나, 제라늄 오일 두 개 맞죠?

W : Exactly. And I have a 10% discount coupon.

여 : 맞아요. 그리고 10% 할인 쿠폰이 있습니다.

M : Let me see... [Pause] Sorry, but it's **no longer** valid.
'더 이상 ~ 하지 않은'

남 : 한번 볼게요… [잠시 후] 죄송하지만, 이 쿠폰은 더 이상 유효하지 않습니다.

W : I see. Here's my credit card. 단서 5 할인 쿠폰이 유효하지 않음

여 : 그렇군요. 여기 제 신용카드입니다.

- need ⓝ 필요
- option ⓝ 선택(할 수 있는 것), 선택권
- disorder ⓝ 장애
- sound sleep 숙면
- scent ⓝ 향
- effective ⓐ 효과적인
- sensitive ⓐ 민감한
- reasonable ⓐ 합리적인
- discount ⓝ 할인
- valid ⓐ 유효한

대화를 듣고, 여자가 지불할 금액을 고르시오. [3점]
① $50　② $55　③ $63　④ $66　⑤$70
$15×2(라벤더와 카모마일 오일 1병씩) + $20×2(제라늄 오일 2병) = $70 (쿠폰 할인 없음)

> **왜** 정답? ＊＊※ [정답률 76%]

여자는 15달러인 라벤더와 카모마일 오일을 각 1병씩 구입했으며, 20달러인 제라늄 오일 2병을 구입했으므로 전체 금액은 70달러이다. 10% 할인 쿠폰을 사용하려 했으나 유효기간이 지나 사용하지 못했으므로 여자가 지불할 금액은 ⑤ '70달러'이다.

07 정답 ① ＊등산을 갈 수 없는 남자

[Cell phone rings.] [휴대 전화가 울린다.]

M : Hello, Emma. Are you okay? **I heard** you caught a cold last weekend. 남 : 안녕하세요, Emma. 괜찮아요? 지난 주말에 감기에 걸렸다고 들었어요.
뒤에 목적어절 접속사 that 생략 ④의 함정

W : Thanks, Ben. But I'm better now.

여 : 고마워요, Ben. 하지만 이제 괜찮아졌어요.

M : Good to hear that. By the way, I bought those new hiking sticks **you recommended**. ②의 함정
앞에 목적격 관계대명사 생략

남 : 반가운 소식이네요. 그나저나, 당신이 추천해준 그 새로운 등산 스틱을 샀어요.

W : Perfect. Now, we can go hiking this Saturday!

여 : 좋아요. 이제 이번 토요일에 하이킹을 갈 수 있겠네요!

M : Well. [Pause] That's the reason **I called**.
앞에 관계부사 why가 생략됨

남 : 음. [잠시 후] 그래서 전화드린 거예요.

W : Oh. Please don't tell me you need to look after your younger sister, again. ⑤의 함정

여 : 오. 제발 다시는 여동생을 돌봐야 한다고 말하지 마세요.

M : Not this time. 남 : 이번에는 그렇지 않아요.

W : Then why can't you go? 여 : 그럼 왜 못 가나요?

M : Actually, I got a message from the internship I applied for, ^{앞에 목적격 관계대명사 생략} and I'm in. ^{③의 함정}

남 : 사실, 제가 지원한 인턴십에서 메시지를 받았고 합격했어요.

W : Congratulations! You've waited for this chance for so long!

여 : 축하해요! 당신은 이 기회를 오랫동안 기다렸잖아요.

M : Thanks. But that means I have to attend a pre-training program every weekend. It starts from this Saturday. ^{뒤에 목적어절 접속사 that 생략} 단서 사전 교육 프로그램에 참여해야 함

남 : 감사해요. 하지만 매주 주말에 사전 교육 프로그램에 참여해야 해요. 이번 주 토요일부터 시작해요.

W : Every weekend? I understand. Let's make it some other time. 여 : 매주 주말이요? 이해해요. 다음에 갑시다.

- catch a cold 감기에 걸리다 • stick ⓝ 막대기
- recommend ⓥ 추천하다 • look after 돌보다
- apply ⓥ 지원하다 • attend ⓥ 참여[참석]하다

대화를 듣고, 남자가 등산을 갈 수 없는 이유를 고르시오.

① 사전 교육 프로그램에 참여해야 해서
남자는 합격한 인턴십의 사전 교육 프로그램에 참여해야 함
② 등산 스틱을 구매하지 못해서 남자는 등산 스틱을 구매했음
③ 인턴십 면접 일정과 겹쳐서 면접 일정이 아니라 사전 교육 프로그램 일정이 겹침
④ 감기가 아직 낫지 않아서 여자가 지난 주말에 감기에 걸렸다고 했음
⑤ 여동생을 돌봐야 해서 이번에는 여동생을 돌봐야 하는 것이 이유가 아님

> 왜 정답 ? ★★★ [정답률 46%]

이번 주 토요일에 함께 등산을 갈 예정이었지만, 남자는 지원한 인턴십에서 합격 메시지를 받았고 이번 주 토요일부터 매주 주말 사전 교육 프로그램에 참여해야 한다고 했다. 따라서 정답은 ①이다.

> 왜 오답 ?

② 남자는 여자가 추천한 등산 스틱을 구매했다.
③ 인턴십 면접 일정이 아니라 사전 교육 프로그램 일정이 겹친 것이다.
④ 여자가 지난 주말에 감기에 걸렸음을 알 수 있다.
⑤ 남자는 이번에는 여동생을 돌봐야 하지 않는다고 했다.

08 정답 ④ ＊예술과 인문학 투어 등록

W : Justin, what are you looking at?
여 : Justin, 뭘 보고 있어요?

M : Hi, Gabriela. Look at this poster. It says the Art and Humanities Tour is coming up. 남 : 안녕하세요, Gabriela. 이 포스터 좀 보세요. 예술과 인문학 투어가 곧 시작될 것이라고 나와 있어요.

W : Great. What does it say? 여 : 좋아요. 뭐라고 적혀 있나요?

M : It's the first annual tour. And its purpose is to explore the ^{명사적 용법} life and times of the novelist, Mark Twain. ①의 단서 목적

남 : 첫 번째 연례 투어라고 하네요. 그리고 그 목적은 소설가 Mark Twain의 삶과 시대를 탐구하는 것이에요.

W : Sounds interesting. Let me see. [Pause] In the program, there will be a guided museum tour and a visit to his birthplace.

여 : 흥미롭군요. 어디 봅시다. [잠시 후] 이 프로그램에서는 가이드 박물관 투어와 그의 출생지 방문이 있을 예정이군요. ②의 단서 운영 프로그램

M : Excellent. It says it's on October 27th. The weather should be perfect around that time. ③의 단서 날짜

남 : 좋아요. 10월 27일이라고 나와 있네요. 그즈음에는 날씨가 완벽할 거예요.

W : It also mentions anyone can participate, but senior-year students get priority. ^{뒤에 목적어절 접속사 that 생략}

여 : 또한 누구나 참여할 수 있지만 고학년 학생들이 우선이라고 언급되어 있어요.

M : Cool! How about going together?
남 : 멋지네요! 같이 가는 건 어때요?

W : Definitely! By the way, I can't see the registration fee.
여 : 물론이죠! 그런데 등록비가 보이지 않네요. ⑤의 단서 등록비

M : Well... [Pause] There, at the bottom. It says $10 per person.
남 : 음… [잠시 후] 저기, 맨 아래에 있어요. 1인당 10달러라고 적혀 있어요.

W : I can afford that. Let's register right now.
여 : 저는 그것을 살 여유가 있어요. 지금 바로 등록합시다.

M : Fantastic! 남 : 좋습니다!

- humanities ⓝ 인문학 • annual ⓐ 연례의 • purpose ⓝ 목적
- explore ⓥ 탐구하다 • novelist ⓝ 소설가
- birthplace ⓝ 출생지 • senior ⓐ 고학년의, 연장자의
- priority ⓝ 우선순위 • registration fee 등록비
- afford ⓥ (~을 살·할 금전적·시간적) 여유가 되다

대화를 듣고, Art and Humanities Tour에 관해 언급되지 않은 것을 고르시오.

① 목적 its purpose is to explore the life and times of the novelist, Mark Twain
② 운영 프로그램 there will be a guided museum tour and a visit to his birthplace
③ 날짜 it's on October 27th
④ 모집 인원 언급되지 않음
⑤ 등록비 It says $10 per person.

> 왜 정답 ? ★★※ [정답률 79%]

예술과 인문학 투어의 목적, 운영 프로그램, 날짜, 등록비는 각각 언급되었지만, 모집 인원에 대해서는 언급하지 않았으므로 정답은 ④이다.

> 왜 오답 ?

① 목적은 소설가 Mark Twain의 삶과 시대를 탐구하는 것이다.
② 운영 프로그램에는 가이드 박물관 투어와 그의 출생지 방문이 있다.
③ 날짜는 10월 27일이다.
⑤ 등록비는 한 사람당 10달러이다.

09 정답 ④ ＊종합 운동장 개장 행사

M : Hello. This is Grayson, presenter at the public Sports Complex Opening Ceremony.

남 : 안녕하세요. 공공 종합 운동장 개장식의 발표자 Grayson입니다.

I'm excited to announce that the opening ceremony will be ^{부사적 용법} ^{목적어절 접속사} held this Friday. ^{수동태} ①의 단서 이번 주 금요일에 열림

이번 주 금요일에 개장식이 개최된다는 소식을 전하게 되어 기쁩니다.

We have various events on each floor.
각 층마다 다양한 이벤트가 준비되어 있습니다.

On the first floor, there will be family mini games such as a ^{'~와 같은'} three-legged race. ②의 단서 1층에는 가족 미니 게임이 열림

1층에서는 3각 경기와 같은 가족 미니 게임이 열립니다.

It'll be fun for the whole family. 온 가족이 즐길 수 있습니다.

On the second floor, table tennis medalists will play games.
2층에서는 탁구 메달리스트들이 경기를 할 것입니다. ③의 단서 2층에는 탁구 메달리스트들의 경기가 있음

Most importantly, special promotions will be available at the entrance. 가장 중요한 것은 입구에서 특별 프로모션이 진행된다는 점입니다.

A half-price discount for annual membership will continue ^{'~까지'} until the following Friday. ④의 단서 연간 회원권의 반값 할인은 다음 주 ^{금요일까지임}

연간 회원권에 대한 반값 할인은 다음 주 금요일까지 계속됩니다.

Come and enjoy the ceremony. 오셔서 행사를 즐기세요.

Reservations are only available through our website.
예약은 웹사이트를 통해서만 가능합니다. ⑤의 단서 예약은 웹사이트에서만 가능

See you then. 그럼 그때 뵙겠습니다.

- opening ceremony 개장식 • hold ⓥ 개최하다 • floor ⓝ 층
- table tennis 탁구 • importantly ⓐⓓ 중요하게
- available ⓐ 이용 가능한 • entrance ⓝ 입구
- continue ⓥ 계속되다 • following ⓐ 다음의
- reservation ⓝ 예약

Sports Complex Opening Ceremony에 관한 다음 내용을 듣고, 일치하지 <u>않는</u> 것을 고르시오.

① 이번 주 금요일에 열릴 것이다. the opening ceremony will be held this Friday
② 1층에서는 가족 미니 게임이 있을 것이다.
On the first floor, there will be family mini games
③ 2층에서는 탁구 메달리스트들이 경기를 할 것이다.
On the second floor, table tennis medalists will play games.
④ 연간 회원권의 반값 할인이 행사 당일에만 제공될 것이다.
A half-price discount for annual membership will continue until the following Friday.
⑤ 예약은 웹사이트에서만 가능하다.
Reservations are only available through our website.

> 왜 정답 ? ✱✱❀ [정답률 88%]

연간 회원권의 반값 할인은 다음 주 금요일까지 계속된다고 (A half-price discount for annual membership will continue until the following Friday.) 했으므로, 행사 당일에만 제공된다고 한 ④이 일치하지 않는 내용이다.

> 왜 오답 ?

① 이번 주 금요일에 열린다고 했다.
② 1층에서는 가족 미니 게임을 할 수 있다고 했다.
③ 2층에서는 탁구 메달리스트들이 경기를 한다고 했다.
⑤ 예약은 웹사이트에서만 가능하다고 했다.

---

10 정답 ③ ✱향신료 분쇄기 구입

W : Honey, our spice grinder is broken, so we need to buy a new one. 여 : 여보, 우리 향신료 분쇄기가 고장 나서 새로 사야 해요.

M : Really? Hold on. I'm checking online. [Tapping sound] Come and see.
남 : 정말요? 잠깐만요. 온라인으로 확인하고 있어요. [두드리는 소리] 와서 보세요.

W : Oh, there are five models to choose from. What do you think is a reasonable price?
형용사적 용법(five models 수식)
여 : 오, 다섯 가지 모델 중에서 선택할 수 있어요. 합리적인 가격은 얼마라고 생각해요?

M : I think it should be under $50. 단서1 50달러 미만이어야 함 (⑤ 제외)
남 : 50달러 미만이어야 한다고 생각해요.

W : Okay. Since we used to have a manual grinder, I'd prefer to get an automatic one this time. 단서2 자동 방식이어야 함 (① 제외)
'used to-v: ~하곤 했다'
여 : 알겠어요. 예전에는 수동 그라인더가 있었기 때문에 이번에는 자동 그라인더를 구입하고 싶어요.

M : Great idea. It'll be much more convenient. Anything else that we should consider?
비교급 강조 / 목적격 관계대명사
남 : 좋은 생각이에요. 훨씬 더 편리할 것 같아요. 우리가 고려해야 할 다른 것이 있나요?

W : Well... It should have a big storage capacity.
여 : 음… 저장 용량이 커야 해요.

M : Good point. You want it to be able to hold at least 70g, right? 단서3 최소 70g의 저장 용량이어야 함 (② 제외)
want의 목적격 보어(to부정사) / '최소한'
남 : 좋은 생각이에요. 최소 70g을 담을 수 있기를 원하죠, 그렇죠?

W : Right. Now, we have two options left.
여 : 맞아요. 이제 두 가지 옵션이 남았네요.

M : I think we should buy the one with the adjustability setting. 단서4 조절 기능이 있어야 함 (④ 제외)
남 : 조절 기능이 있는 것을 사야 할 것 같아요.

W : Excellent. Let's go with that one. 여 : 좋아요. 그걸로 해요.

- broken ⓐ 고장 난 • reasonable ⓐ 합리적인
- manual ⓐ 수동의 • automatic ⓐ 자동의
- convenient ⓐ 편리한 • consider ⓥ 고려하다 • storage ⓝ 저장
- capacity ⓝ 용량 • adjustability ⓝ 조절 기능

다음 표를 보면서 대화를 듣고, 두 사람이 구매할 향신료 분쇄기를 고르시오.

Spice Grinder 향신료 분쇄기

	Model 모델	Price 가격	Operation 작동	Capacity 용량	Adjustability 조절 기능
①	A	$20	Manual 자동이 아닌 수동임	60g	×
②	B	$25	Automatic 수동의 자동의	65g 저장 용량이 70g 이하임	○
③	C	$35	Automatic	72g	○
④	D	$40	Automatic	73g 조절 기능이 없음	×
⑤	E	$55 50달러 이상임	Manual	75g	○

> 왜 정답 ? ✱❀✱ [정답률 90%]

가격이 50달러 미만이고 (⑤ 제외), 작동 방식은 자동이어야 하며 (① 제외), 저장 용량이 최소 70g 이상인 것 (② 제외) 중, 조절 기능이 있는 제품(④ 제외)은 ③이다.

> 왜 오답 ?

① 작동 방식은 수동이 아닌 자동이 좋다고 했다.
② 저장 용량이 최소 70g 이상인 것을 원했다.
④ 조절 기능이 있는 것을 원했다.
⑤ 50달러 미만인 가격이 좋다고 했다.

---

11 정답 ① ✱DJ 뮤직 페스티벌

M : Hey, Cindy. Are you going to the DJ Music Festival this weekend?
남 : 안녕, Cindy. 이번 주말에 DJ 뮤직 페스티벌에 갈 거야?

W : Definitely! I can't wait. Last year, the festival was awesome. You couldn't make it, right? 단서1 작년에 축제가 굉장했음
'참석하다'
여 : 물론이지! 정말 기대돼. 작년에는 축제가 정말 재밌었어. 너는 참석하지 못했지, 맞지?

M : Yeah, I was on my family trip. Anyway, why was it so fun? 단서2 작년에 축제가 왜 재미있었는지 물어봄
남 : 맞아, 가족 여행 중이었어. 어쨌든 왜 그렇게 재미있었어?

W : **A DJ unexpectedly mixed and played my requested songs.**
여 : DJ가 예상치 못하게 내가 요청한 노래를 믹싱해서 재생했어.

- awesome ⓐ (매우) 재미있는, 굉장한 • unexpectedly ⓐⓓ 예상치 못하게

대화를 듣고, 남자의 마지막 말에 대한 여자의 응답으로 가장 적절한 것을 고르시오.

① A DJ unexpectedly mixed and played my requested songs. 작년 페스티벌이 재미있었던 이유에 대해 설명하고 있음
DJ가 예상치 못하게 내가 요청한 노래를 믹싱해서 재생했어.
② My family and I went camping together once in a while. 가족과의 캠핑에 대한 내용이 아님
우리 가족과 나는 가끔씩 함께 캠핑을 갔어.
③ It wasn't as good as when you were there last year. 좋지 않았던 경험에 대한 내용이 아님
작년에 네가 거기 있었을 때만큼 좋지 않았어.
④ The festival will be more exciting than before. 이번에 있을 축제에 대한 생각을 물어본 것이 아님
축제는 이전보다 더 흥미진진할 거야.
⑤ The food there was too expensive to enjoy. 페스티벌의 음식에 대한 언급은 없음
그곳의 음식은 너무 비싸서 즐길 수 없었어.

> 왜 정답 ? ✱✱❀ [정답률 68%]

이번 주말에 DJ 뮤직 페스티벌에 참석하는 여자는 작년에도 매우 재미있었다고 남자에게 말했다. 이에 작년에 참석하지 못한 남자는 왜 재밌었는지를 물었다. 따라서 여자는 ① 'DJ가 예상치 못하게 내가 요청한 노래를 믹싱해서 재생했어.'라고 응답하는 것이 가장 적절하다.

> 왜 오답 ?

② 뮤직 페스티벌에 대한 것이지 가족과의 캠핑에 대한 내용이 아니다.
③ 남자는 작년에 뮤직 페스티벌을 가지 못했으며, 작년 페스티벌이 좋지 않았다는 말은 여자가 말한 내용과 상반되는 내용이다. 주의
④ 작년 축제가 왜 재미있었는지를 묻는 것이지, 이번 축제에 대해 묻는 것이 아니다.
⑤ 페스티벌의 음식에 관한 내용은 대화 속에 언급되지 않았다.

12 정답 ② ＊주문한 음식의 배달 상태

W: Luca, I'll bring the food <u>we ordered</u> inside. *[Door opening sound]* There's no food in front of the door.
앞에 목적격 관계대명사 생략

여 : Luca, 주문한 음식을 안으로 가져올게요. *[문 여는 소리]* 문 앞에 음식이 없어요.

M: What? Did you check the delivery status on the app?

남 : 뭐라고요? 앱에서 배달 상태를 확인했나요?

W: Sure. The app says the food <u>has arrived</u>. But it's not here.
현재완료(완료)

단서 앱에서는 음식이 배달 완료
되었다고 했으나 도착하지 않음

여 : 물론이죠. 앱에 음식이 도착했다고 나와 있어요. 하지만 여기 없어요.

M: **That's strange. Check if the address on the app is correct.**

남 : 이상하네요. 앱의 주소가 맞는지 확인해 보세요.

・ bring ⓥ 가져오다 ・ order ⓥ 주문하다 ・ delivery ⓝ 배달
・ status ⓝ 상태 ・ arrive ⓥ 도착하다

> 대화를 듣고, 여자의 마지막 말에 대한 남자의 응답으로 가장 적절한 것을 고르시오.
> ① Certainly. Delivery food is not preferred due to health issues.
> 배달 음식과 건강의 관계에 대한 내용이 아님
> 물론이죠. 건강 문제로 인해 배달 음식은 선호되지 않아요.
> ②That's strange. Check if the address on the app is correct.
> 배달 주소를 제대로 확인해 보도록 제안함
> 이상하네요. 앱의 주소가 맞는지 확인해 보세요.
> ③ No worries. I think you can deliver the package tomorrow.
> 택배를 보내야 하는 상황이 아님
> 걱정하지 마세요. 내일 당신이 택배를 배달할 수 있을 것 같습니다.
> ④ I see. I'll leave the plate outside when we're done.
> 알겠어요. 다 먹으면 접시를 밖에 두겠습니다.
> 음식이 도착하지 않았음
> ⑤ That sounds nice. I'll go with the cheaper one.
> 좋네요. 더 저렴한 걸로 할게요.
> 음식 가격에 대한 언급은 없음

> **왜** 정답 ？ ★★⊛ [정답률 83%]

여자가 앱에서 주문한 음식을 가지러 문 앞으로 나갔으나 음식이 없자 남자가 여자에게 배달 상태를 확인했냐고 했다. 이에 여자는 앱에 음식이 도착했다고 나와 있다고 말했으므로 남자는 ② '이상하네요. 앱의 주소가 맞는지 확인해 보세요.'라고 응답하는 것이 가장 적절하다.

> **왜** 오답 ？

① 배달 음식의 건강 문제에 대한 내용은 언급되지 않았다.
③ 보내야 할 택배가 있는 것이 아니다.
④ 주문한 음식을 아직 받지 못했으며, 다 먹은 접시는 언급되지 않았다.
⑤ 주문한 음식을 찾고 있는 상황이지, 가격을 언급하며 음식을 고르는 내용이 아니다.

13 정답 ① ＊위장 문제에 도움이 되는 음식

W: Hi, Liam. 여 : 안녕하세요, Liam.

M: What's wrong, Jenny? You look sick.

남 : 무슨 일이에요, Jenny? 아파 보이네요.

have trouble -ing: ~하는 데 어려움을 겪다

W: I <u>have trouble digesting</u> food these days. So, I got a medical check-up. 여 : 요즘 음식 소화가 잘 안 돼요. 그래서 건강 검진을 받았어요.

M: What did the doctor say? 남 : 의사가 뭐라고 했나요?

수동태

W: Nothing special. I <u>was prescribed</u> some medicine, but I don't think it's <u>working</u>.
효과가 있다

여 : 특별한 건 없어요. 약을 좀 처방받았는데 효과가 없는 것 같아요.

M: That's unfortunate. Do you remember I had the same symptoms last month?

남 : 안타깝네요. 저도 지난달에 같은 증상이 있었던 것 기억하시나요?

W: Right. You were sick for a long time. How did you get better? 여 : 맞아요. 오랫동안 아팠잖아요. 어떻게 나아졌어요?

동명사(start의 목적어)

M: My mother started <u>making</u> me a healthy smoothie every morning. It really helped.

남 : 어머니께서 매일 아침 저에게 건강한 스무디를 만들어 주시기 시작하셨어요. 그게 정말 도움이 되었어요.

W: Healthy smoothie? What's in it?

여 : 건강한 스무디? 그것에 뭐가 들어 있어요?

'~로 만들어지다'

M: It<u>'s made of</u> carrots, cabbages and apples. It could help <u>relieve</u> your stomach problems.
앞에 to 생략(help의 목적어)

남 : 당근, 양배추, 사과로 만들어졌습니다. 당신의 위장 문제를 완화하는 데 도움이 될 수 있어요.

W: Sounds great. Actually, I'm also thinking of eating more fruit and vegetables <u>instead of</u> relying on medicine.
'~ 대신에'

여 : 좋네요. 사실 저도 약에 의존하는 대신에 과일과 채소를 더 많이 먹을까 생각 중이에요.

know의 목적어(간접의문문)

M: Well, now you know <u>what you need to do.</u>
단서 과일과 채소를 더 많이 먹는 것을 고려 중임

남 : 음, 이제 무엇을 해야 하는지 알게 되었군요.

W: **Absolutely. I'll start first thing tomorrow.**

여 : 물론이죠. 내일 제일 먼저 시작하려고 합니다.

・ digest ⓥ 소화시키다 ・ medical check-up 건강 검진
・ prescribe ⓥ 처방하다 ・ unfortunate ⓐ 안타까운, 불운한
・ symptom ⓝ 증상 ・ relieve ⓥ 완화하다 ・ stomach ⓝ 위장
・ rely on ~에 의존하다 ・ ease ⓥ 편하게 해 주다

> 대화를 듣고, 남자의 마지막 말에 대한 여자의 응답으로 가장 적절한 것을 고르시오. [3점]
> Woman:
> ①Absolutely. I'll start first thing tomorrow.
> 물론이죠. 내일 제일 먼저 시작하려고 합니다.
> 여자는 과일과 채소를 더 많이 먹는 것을 생각하고 있다고 했음
> ② Sorry. The pill you've taken has a side effect.
> 죄송합니다. 복용하신 약에 부작용이 있습니다.
> 약의 부작용에 대한 언급은 없음
> ③ Good choice. Let's sign up for the cooking class.
> 좋은 선택입니다. 요리 수업에 등록합시다.
> 요리 수업에 대한 내용이 아님
> ④ Unbelievable. Your smoothies are already sold out.
> 믿을 수가 없어요. 당신의 스무디는 이미 매진되었습니다.
> 스무디 판매에 대한 언급은 없음
> ⑤ Sure. I don't think carrots ease my stomach issues.
> 물론이죠. 당근은 제 위장 문제를 편하게 해 주지 않는 것 같아요.
> 당근은 위장 문제에 도움이 됨

> **왜** 정답 ？ ★★⊛ [정답률 82%]

소화 불량을 겪고 있는 여자에게 남자는 과일과 채소가 들어간 건강 스무디가 도움이 되었다고 말했다. 여자는 자신도 사실 과일과 채소를 더 많이 먹을 생각임을 밝혔으며, 그럼 이제 무엇을 해야 할지 알고 있겠다는 남자의 말에 여자의 응답으로 가장 적절한 것은 ① '물론이죠. 내일 제일 먼저 시작하려고 합니다.'이다.

> **왜** 오답 ？

② 여자는 약을 먹고 효과가 없다고 언급했을 뿐, 약의 부작용에 대한 내용이 아니다.
③ 요리 수업을 함께 등록하자는 내용이 아니다.
④ 남자가 언급한 스무디의 판매에 대한 언급은 없다.
⑤ 당근은 위장 문제 완화에 도움이 되는 것으로 언급되었다.

14 정답 ⑤ ＊미국의 팁 문화에 대한 의견

M: Amy. I enjoyed the class today. How about you?

남 : Amy. 오늘 수업 즐거웠어요. 당신은요?

W: Same here! I especially liked the part on American tipping culture.

여 : 저도 마찬가지예요! 특히 미국 팁 문화에 대한 부분이 마음에 들었습니다.

가주어 진주어절을 이끄는 접속사 부사절 접속사(조건)

M: Yeah. <u>It</u>'s an interesting idea <u>that</u> you can tip <u>if</u> you like the service.

남 : 맞아요. 서비스가 마음에 든다면 팁을 줄 수 있는 것은 흥미로운 생각이에요.

W: You know, I went to New York recently.

여 : 아시다시피, 최근에 저는 뉴욕을 다녀왔습니다.

M: Right. Did you have to give a tip?

남 : 맞아요. 팁을 줘야 했나요?

수동태 복합관계부사

W: I <u>was asked</u> for a tip <u>whenever</u> I got the bill.

여 : 청구서를 받을 때마다 팁을 달라는 요청을 받았습니다.

M: Ah! It's for real!

남 : 아! 진짜군요!

W: I know. One time I was quite puzzled, though.

여 : 알아요. 하지만 한 번은 꽤 당황스러웠습니다.

M: Oh, what happened?

남 : 오, 무슨 일이 있었나요?

W : At this restaurant, the waiters were so rude and the food was awful. People there were giving tips while complaining about the service. 단서 1 서비스에 불만이 있어도 팁을 주었다고 함

여 : 이 식당에서는 웨이터들이 너무 무례하고 음식도 끔찍했습니다. 사람들은 서비스에 대해 불평하면서 팁을 주고 있었어요.

M : You did, too? In that case, as we learned, you shouldn't have tipped. 단서 2 남자는 그런 경우 팁을 주지 말아야 한다고 함
should not have p.p.: ~하지 말았어야 했다

남 : 당신도 그랬나요? 그렇다면, 우리가 배운 것처럼 팁을 주지 말아야 했어요.
단서 3 여자는 어쩔 수 없이 그 나라의 방식을 따라야 했다고 함

W : What else could I do? When in Rome, do as the Romans do.

여 : 제가 다른 무엇을 할 수 있었을까요? 로마에 가면 로마법을 따라야 해요.

M : No way. You should ask politely if the tip could be removed. 남 : 말도 안 돼요. 팁을 뺄 수 있는지 정중하게 물어봐야 합니다.

- especially (ad) 특히　· ask for 요청하다　· bill (n) 청구서
- puzzled (a) 당황스러운　· rude (a) 무례한　· complain (v) 불평하다
- politely (ad) 정중하게　· remove (v) 빼다, 제거하다

대화를 듣고, 여자의 마지막 말에 대한 남자의 응답으로 가장 적절한 것을 고르시오. [3점]

Man : _____

① Right. That's why I always like to pay separately. 맞아요. 그래서 저는 항상 따로 계산하는 것을 좋아합니다. 따로 계산하는 방식에 대한 내용이 아님

② No problem. Tipping more than 10% isn't too much. 팁을 문제없어요. 10% 이상 팁을 주는 것은 과하지 않아요. 얼마나 줘야 하는지에 대한 내용이 아님

③ Really? I could recommend a nice restaurant in Rome. 정말요? 로마에 있는 멋진 레스토랑을 추천해 드릴 수 있습니다. 로마의 레스토랑에 대한 내용이 아님

④ Exactly. Italy is also a country where tipping is common. 맞아요. 이탈리아는 팁을 주는 것이 흔한 나라이기도 합니다.

⑤ No way. You should ask politely if the tip could be removed. 남자는 서비스가 별로인 레스토랑에서는 팁을 주지 않아야 한다고 주장함 말도 안 돼요. 팁을 뺄 수 있는지 정중하게 물어봐야 합니다.
└ 이탈리아가 아닌 미국의 팁 문화에 대한 내용임

> 왜 정답 ? ❋❋❋ [정답률 62%]

여자가 미국에 있을 때 서비스가 좋지 않아도 팁을 준 것에 대해 말하자 남자는 그런 경우 팁을 주지 말아야 한다고 답했다. 어쩔 수 없이 '로마에서는 로마의 방식을 따라야 한다'고 말하는 여자에게 남자의 응답으로 가장 적절한 것은 ⑤ '말도 안 돼요. 팁을 뺄 수 있는지 정중하게 물어봐야 합니다.'라고 자신의 의견을 말하는 것이다.

> 왜 오답 ?

① 팁을 주는 것에 대한 내용이지, 계산하는 방식에 대한 내용이 아니다.

② 서비스가 별로인 곳에서 팁을 줘야 하는지에 대한 내용이지, 팁을 얼마나 줘야 하는지에 대한 내용이 아니다.

③ 여자가 미국의 레스토랑에서 경험한 팁 문화에 대한 내용이지, 로마의 레스토랑에 대한 내용이 아니다.

④ 이탈리아가 아닌 미국의 팁 문화에 대한 내용이며, 여자는 '로마에 가면 로마법을 따라야 한다'는 속담을 인용했을 뿐이다.

15 　정답 ②　＊과목 선택에 대한 조언 ────

M : Mina is a first-year high school student.

남 : 미나는 고등학교 1학년이다.

She has to select subjects for next year, and she is considering taking advanced math. 단서 1 선택 과목으로 고급 수학을 고려하고 있음
동명사 목적어

그녀는 내년에 과목을 선택해야 하는데 고급 수학을 듣는 것을 고려하고 있다.
명사절 접속사(~인지 아닌지)

However, she doubts whether she could do well in the course. 하지만 그녀는 이 수업에서 잘 할 수 있을지 의문이다.

For advice, she visits Mr. Jang, her basic math teacher last semester. 조언을 구하기 위해 지난 학기 기초 수학 선생님인 장 선생님을 방문한다.
부사절 접속사(시간)

While Mina shares her concern, Mr. Jang remembers how creative Mina's math project was in his class. 목적어 역할을 하는 간접의문문

미나가 자신의 걱정을 공유하는 동안 장 선생님은 자신의 수업에서 미나의 수학 프로젝트가 얼마나 창의적이었는지 기억한다. 단서 2 미나의 수학 프로젝트는 창의적이었음
뒤에 목적절 접속사 that 생략

He also knows she got a good grade last semester. 단서 3 지난 학기 성적이 좋음

또한 장 선생님은 미나가 지난 학기에 좋은 성적을 받았다는 것도 알고 있다.

So, Mr. Jang wants to tell Mina that she should stop doubting herself and choose advanced math. 병렬 구조

그래서 장 선생님은 미나에게 자신을 의심하지 말고 고급 수학을 선택하라고 말하고 싶어 한다. 단서 4 미나에게 자신을 의심하지 말고 고급 수학을 선택하도록 하고 싶어 함

In this situation, what would Mr. Jang most likely say to Mina? 이 상황에서, 장 선생님이 미나에게 할 말로 가장 적절한 것은 무엇인가?

Mr. Jang: Believe in yourself and take advanced math.

장 선생님: 네 자신을 믿고 고급 수학을 수강해.

★ 상황 요약: 미나에게 고급 수학을 선택하라고 말하고 싶은 상황

- select (v) 선택하다　· subject (n) 과목　· advanced (a) 고급의
- doubt (v) 의문을 갖다　· advice (n) 조언　· semester (n) 학기
- concern (n) 걱정　· creative (a) 창의적인

다음 상황 설명을 듣고, Mr. Jang이 Mina에게 할 말로 가장 적절한 것을 고르시오.

Mr. Jang: _____

① I'm here for you to finish the project. 네가 프로젝트를 끝낼 수 있게 도와줄게. 미나가 해야 할 프로젝트에 대한 언급은 없음

② Believe in yourself and take advanced math. 너 자신을 믿고 고급 수학을 수강해. 고급 수학을 선택하라고 조언하고 싶음

③ You could set up a booth for a curriculum fair. 너는 교육과정 박람회를 위한 부스를 설치할 수 있어. 교육과정 박람회에 대한 언급은 없음

④ Advanced math must be a tough choice for you. 고급 수학은 네게 어려운 선택임에 틀림없어. 고급 수학을 선택하라고 말하고 싶은 상황임

⑤ Focus on preparing for the exam to pass advanced math. 고급 수학 시험을 통과하기 위해 시험 준비에 집중해. 고급 수학 시험에 대한 언급은 없음

> 왜 정답 ? ❋❋❋ [정답률 82%]

선택 과목으로 고급 수학을 고려하고 있는 미나가 장 선생님에게 조언을 구하고 있으며, 장 선생님은 미나가 기초 수학에서 잘 해냈기 때문에 자신을 믿고 고급 수학을 선택하라고 말하고 싶은 상황이다. 따라서 장 선생님이 할 말로 가장 적절한 것은 ② '네 자신을 믿고 고급 수학을 수강해.'이다.

> 왜 오답 ?

① 미나가 지금 끝내야 하는 프로젝트는 언급되지 않았다.

③ 교육과정 박람회에 대한 내용이 아니다.

④ 고급 수학을 권하고 싶은 것이지 어려운 것이라고 말하는 상황이 아니다.

⑤ 고급 수학 과목 선택에 대한 내용이지, 시험 준비에 대한 내용이 아니다. 주의

16~17 　＊AI 기술이 다양한 직업 분야에 미치는 영향 ───

W : Hello, students. // 여 : 안녕하세요, 학생 여러분 //
'~에 따르면'

According to a global institute research, / about 70% of companies around the world / will use AI technology by 2030. //

글로벌 기관의 연구에 따르면 / 전 세계 기업의 약 70%가 / 2030년까지 AI 기술을 사용할 것이라고 합니다 //

So, today / we'll discuss various job fields / that could be affected by AI technology. // 주격 관계대명사 수동태 16번 단서: AI 기술의 영향을 받는 다양한 직업 분야를 논의할 것임

그래서, 오늘은 / 다양한 직업 분야에 대해 논의해 보겠습니다 / AI 기술의 영향을 받을 수 있는 //

First, / let's talk about customer service. // 17번 ①

첫 번째로 / 고객 서비스에 대해 이야기해 보겠습니다 //

In this sector, / AI chatbots can provide speedy, personalized responses to customers' questions, / which significantly reduces human's workload. // 계속적 용법의 주격 관계대명사

이 분야에서 / AI 챗봇은 고객의 질문에 신속하고 개인화된 응답을 제공할 수 있고 / 인간의 업무량을 크게 줄입니다 // 17번 ② 수동태

Second, / legal fields will be greatly influenced as well. //

둘째 / 법률 분야도 큰 영향을 받게 됩니다 //
목적격 관계대명사

AI will help perform many tasks / that legal assistants usually handle / such as contract analysis and case management. //

AI는 많은 업무를 수행하는 데 도움이 될 것입니다 / 법률 비서가 주로 담당하는 / 계약 분석, 사례 관리와 같은 //

Next, / AI is also making an impact on financial sectors. //
다음으로 / AI는 금융 부문에도 영향을 미치고 있습니다 // **17번 ③**

It can monitor banking systems / and provide detailed financial advice. //
그것은 은행 시스템을 모니터링하고 / 자세한 재무 조언을 제공할 수 있습니다 //

Lastly, / in graphic design, / ~~동명사 주어~~ editing pictures used to take years of practice. // **17번 ⑤**
마지막으로 / 그래픽 디자인에서는 / 사진을 편집하는 데 수년간의 연습이 필요하곤 했습니다 //

But now, / AI makes it easy / ~~가목적어~~ ~~to부정사의 의미상 주어~~ ~~진목적어~~ for anyone to create realistic images. //
하지만 이제 / AI는 쉽게 해줍니다 / 누구나 사실적인 이미지를 만들 수 있게 //

Like these, / AI has the potential / ~~형용사적 용법(the potential 수식)~~ to be among the most influential technologies / across many job fields. //
이처럼 / AI는 잠재력을 가지고 있습니다 / 가장 영향력 있는 기술 중 하나가 될 수 있는 / 다양한 직업 분야에서 //

Now, / let's watch a video. // 이제 / 동영상을 시청해 보겠습니다 //

- institute ⓝ 기관 · affect ⓥ 영향을 미치다 · speedy ⓐ 신속한
- personalized ⓐ 개인화된 · significantly ⓐ 크게, 상당히
- reduce ⓥ 감소시키다 · workload ⓝ 업무량
- influence ⓥ 영향을 미치다 · assistant ⓝ 비서
- handle ⓥ 다루다 · contract ⓝ 계약 · impact ⓝ 영향
- monitor ⓥ 모니터링[감시]하다 · provide ⓥ 제공하다
- edit ⓥ 편집하다 · realistic ⓐ 사실적인 · potential ⓝ 잠재력
- influential ⓐ 영향력 있는

여: 안녕하세요, 학생 여러분. 글로벌 기관의 연구에 따르면 2030년까지 전 세계 기업의 약 70%가 AI 기술을 사용할 것이라고 합니다. 그래서, 오늘은 AI 기술의 영향을 받을 수 있는 다양한 직업 분야에 대해 논의해 보겠습니다. 첫 번째로, 고객 서비스에 대해 이야기해 보겠습니다. 이 분야에서 AI 챗봇은 고객의 질문에 신속하고 개인화된 응답을 제공할 수 있어 인간의 업무량을 크게 줄입니다. 둘째, 법률 분야도 큰 영향을 받게 됩니다. AI는 계약 분석, 사례 관리 등 법률 비서가 주로 담당하는 많은 업무를 수행하는 데 도움이 될 것입니다. 다음으로, AI는 금융 부문에도 영향을 미치고 있습니다. 그것은 은행 시스템을 모니터링하고 자세한 재무 조언을 제공할 수 있습니다. 마지막으로, 그래픽 디자인에서는 사진을 편집하는 데 수년간의 연습이 필요하곤 했습니다. 하지만 이제 AI는 누구나 쉽게 사실적인 이미지를 만들 수 있게 해줍니다. 이처럼 AI는 다양한 직업 분야에서 가장 영향력 있는 기술 중 하나가 될 수 있는 잠재력을 가지고 있습니다. 이제 동영상을 시청해 보겠습니다.

16 정답 ③

여자가 하는 말의 주제로 가장 적절한 것은?
① skills to control AI technology in job fields
직업 분야에서 AI 기술을 통제하는 기술 — AI 기술 통제에 대한 언급은 없음
② ways to protect job fields from AI invasion
AI 침략으로부터 직업 분야를 보호하는 방법 — AI로부터 직업 분야를 보호하는 내용이 아님
③ effects of AI technology on various job fields
AI 기술이 다양한 직업 분야에 미치는 영향
④ newly emerging high-paying job fields due to AI
AI로 인해 새롭게 떠오르는 고임금 직업 분야 — 새로 떠오르는 직업 분야를 소개하는 것이 아님
⑤ integration of job fields in response to the rise of AI
AI의 부상에 대응한 직업 분야 통합 — 직업 통합에 대한 언급은 없음
~~we'll discuss various job fields that could be affected by AI technology~~

>왜 정답? ✱✱✻ [정답률 89%]
여자는 고객 서비스, 법률 분야, 금융 부문, 그래픽 디자인과 같은 다양한 직업 분야에서 AI 기술이 미칠 영향과 변화를 소개하고 있다. 따라서 여자가 하는 말의 주제로 가장 적절한 것은 ③ 'AI 기술이 다양한 직업 분야에 미치는 영향'이다.

>왜 오답?
① AI 기술을 통제할 수 있는 기술을 소개하는 내용이 아니다.
② AI의 침략으로부터 직업 분야를 보호해야 한다는 내용이 아니다.
④ AI가 여러 직업 분야에 미친 영향을 소개한 것이지, AI로 인해 새로 생긴 직업은 언급되지 않았다.

⑤ AI의 발전에 따라 그것이 다양한 직업 분야에 미치는 영향을 설명한 것이지, 다양한 직업 통합에 대한 언급은 없다.

17 정답 ④

언급된 직업 분야가 아닌 것은?
First, let's talk about customer service.
① customer service 고객 서비스
② legal fields 법률 분야 Second, legal fields will be greatly influenced as well.
③ financial sectors 금융 부문 Next, AI is also making an impact on financial sectors.
④ marketing fields 마케팅 분야 언급되지 않음
⑤ graphic design 그래픽 디자인 Lastly, in graphic design, editing pictures used to take years of practice.

>왜 정답? ✱✻✻ [정답률 95%]
고객 서비스, 법률 분야, 금융 부문, 그래픽 디자인 직업 분야에 대해서는 언급했지만 마케팅 분야에 대해서는 언급하지 않았으므로 정답은 ④ '마케팅 분야'이다.

>왜 오답?
① 고객 서비스 분야에서는 AI 챗봇 덕분에 인간의 업무량을 줄일 수 있다고 했다.
② 법률 분야에서는 AI가 법률 비서가 주로 담당하는 많은 업무를 수행할 것이라고 했다.
③ 금융 부문에서 은행 시스템 모니터링과 재무 조언이 가능해진다고 했다.
⑤ 그래픽 디자인 분야에서 사진 편집이 쉬워져 누구나 이미지를 만들 수 있다고 했다.

18 정답 ⑤ ✱서류 검토 결과 통지 요구

To the State Education Department, / 주 교육부 귀중 /
I am writing / ~~'~와 관련하여'~~ with regard to the state's funding / for the construction project at Fort Montgomery High School. //
저는 편지를 씁니다 / 주 예산과 관련하여 / Fort Montgomery 고등학교의 건축 프로젝트를 위한 //
Our school needs additional spaces / ~~형용사적 용법 (spaces 수식)~~ to provide a fully functional Art and Library Media Center / ~~부사적 용법 (목적)~~ to serve our students / in a more meaningful way. //
저희 학교는 추가 공간이 필요합니다 / 완전하게 제 기능을 하는 Art and Library Media Center를 제공하기 위한 / 학생들을 만족시키기 위해 / 보다 의미 있는 방식으로 //
~~전치사 + 동명사~~ Despite submitting all required documentation for funding / to your department / in April 2024, / we have not yet received / any notification from your department. //
재정 지원에 필요한 모든 서류를 제출했음에도 불구하고 / 귀하의 부서로 / 2024년 4월에 / 저희는 아직 받지 못했습니다 / 귀하의 부서로부터 어떠한 통지도 //
A delay in the process / can carry considerable consequences / related to the school's budgetary constraints and schedule. //
과정상 지연은 / 상당한 결과를 초래할 수 있습니다 / 학교의 예산 제약 및 일정과 관련하여 //
~~in order to + 동사원형; ~하기 위해~~ ~~뒤에 목적어절 접속사 that 생략~~ Therefore, / in order to proceed with our project, / we request you / notify us of the review result / ~~'~와 관련하여'~~ regarding the submitted documentation. // **단서** 제출한 서류에 대한 검토 결과를 통지해달라고 요청함
그러므로 / 저희의 프로젝트를 진행하기 위해 / 요청합니다 / 검토 결과를 저희에게 통지해 줄 것을 / 제출 서류와 관련한 //
~~look forward to ~ing; ~을 고대하다~~ I look forward to hearing from you. // 귀하로부터의 답변을 고대합니다 //
Respectfully, Clara Smith / Clara Smith 드림 /
Principal, Fort Montgomery High School /
Fort Montgomery 고등학교 교장 /

- funding ⓝ 재정 지원 · construction ⓝ 건축, 건설
- additional ⓐ 추가적인 · functional ⓐ 기능을 하는
- submit ⓥ 제출하다 · documentation ⓝ 서류
- notification ⓝ 통지 · considerable ⓐ 상당한
- consequence ⓝ 결과 · budgetary ⓐ 예산의
- constraint ⓝ 제약 · notify A of B A에게 B를 통지하다

주 교육부 귀중,

저는 Fort Montgomery 고등학교의 건축 프로젝트를 위한 주 예산과 관련하여 편지를 씁니다. 저희 학교는 보다 의미있는 방식으로 학생들을 만족시키기 위해 완전하게 제 기능을 하는 Art and Library Media Center를 제공하기 위한 추가 공간이 필요합니다. 2024년 4월에 귀하의 부서로 예산에 필요한 모든 서류를 제출했음에도 불구하고, 저희는 아직 귀하의 부서로부터 어떠한 통지도 받지 못했습니다. 과정상 지연은 학교의 예산 제한 및 일정과 관련하여 상당한 결과를 초래할 수 있습니다. 그러므로, 저희의 프로젝트를 진행하기 위해 제출 서류와 관련한 검토 결과를 저희에게 통지해 줄 것을 요청합니다. 귀하로부터의 답변을 고대합니다.

Fort Montgomery 고등학교 교장, Clara Smith 드림

다음 글의 목적으로 가장 적절한 것은?
① 제출 서류의 마감 기한 연장을 요청하려고 마감 기한에 관한 내용이 아님
② 교내 미디어 센터의 리모델링을 제안하려고 리모델링은 언급되지 않음
③ 학교 프로젝트에 배정된 예산을 확인하려고 예산을 확인하는 내용이 아님
④ 학교 공간 조성을 위한 공모전을 홍보하려고 공모전은 언급되지 않음
⑤ 제출 서류에 대한 검토 결과 통지를 요구하려고
　제출 서류에 관련한 검토 결과를 통지해 줄 것을 요청함

왜 정답? ✽✽✾ [정답률 73%]

건축 프로젝트를 위한 예산 지원을 받기 위해 필요한 서류를 제출했음에도 아직 아무런 통지를 받지 못했기에 제출 서류와 관련한 검토 결과 통지를 요청하고 있으므로 글의 목적은 ⑤이다.

왜 오답?

① 이미 서류는 제출하였으므로 마감 기한에 대한 연장을 요청하는 것이 아니다.
② 교내 미디어 센터의 리모델링은 언급되지 않았다.
③ 건축 프로젝트를 위한 예산을 지원받는 과정에서 제출 서류의 검토 결과를 요청할 뿐, 배정된 예산을 확인하는 것이 글의 목적은 아니다. 함정
④ 학교 공간 조성을 위한 공모전은 언급되지 않았다.

---

19 정답 ① ✽농구 코치의 충격적인 통보

As I waited outside the locker room / after a hard-fought basketball game, / the coach called out to me, / "David, walk with me." //
내가 라커룸 밖에서 기다릴 때 / 치열하게 싸운 농구 경기 후에 / 코치가 나를 크게 불렀다 / "David, 나와 함께 걷자"라며 //

뒤에 목적어절 접속사 that 생략
I figured / he was going to tell me / something important. //
나는 생각했다 / 그가 나에게 말해 줄 거라고 / 무언가 중요한 것을 //

select의 목적격 보어 (to부정사)
He was going to select me to be the captain of the team, / the
관계대명사절 (the leader 수식)
leader I had always wanted to be. //
그가 나를 팀의 주장으로 뽑을 것으로 (생각했다) / 내가 항상 되기를 원했던 리더인 //

My heart was racing / with anticipation. // 단서 1 팀의 주장이 될 것으로 기대
나의 심장이 빠르게 뛰었다 / 기대감으로 //

But when his next words hit my ears, / everything changed. //
그러나 그의 다음 말이 내 귀를 쳤을 때 / 모든 것이 변했다 //

"We're going to have to send you home," / he said coldly. //
"우리는 너를 집으로 보내야만 해"라고 / 그가 차갑게 말했다 //

해내다
"I don't think you are going to make it." //
"나는 네가 해낼 거라고 생각하지 않아" //

I couldn't believe his decision. //
나는 그의 결정을 믿을 수 없었다 //
마음을 추스르다
I tried to hold it together, / but inside I was falling apart. // 단서 2 코치의 말을 듣고 좌절함
나는 마음을 가다듬으려고 했지만 / 내면에서 나는 산산이 무너지고 있었다 //

형용사적 용법 (A car 수식)
A car would be waiting tomorrow morning / to take me home. //
내일 아침에 차가 기다리고 있을 것이다 / 나를 집에 데려갈 //

And just like that, / it was over. // 그리고 그렇게 / 끝이 났다 //

• hard-fought ⓐ 치열히 싸운　• figure ⓥ 생각하다
• race ⓥ 빠르게 뛰다　• anticipation ⓝ 기대감　• fall apart 무너지다

내가 치열하게 싸운 농구 경기 후에 라커룸 밖에서 기다릴 때, 코치가 "David, 나와 함께 걷자."라며 나를 크게 불렀다. 나는 그가 나에게 무언가 중요한 것을 말해 줄 거라고 생각했다. 그는 내가 항상 되기를 원했던 리더인 팀의 주장으로 나를 뽑으려 할 것이라고 (생각했다). 나의 심장이 기대감으로 빠르게 뛰었다. 그러나 그의 다음 말이 내 귀를 쳤을 때, 모든 것이 변했다. "우리는 너를 집으로 보내야만 해."라고 그가 차갑게 말했다. "나는 네가 해낼 거라고 생각하지 않아." 나는 그의 결정을 믿을 수 없었다. 나는 마음을 가다듬으려고 했지만, 내면에서 나는 산산이 무너지고 있었다. 내일 아침에 나를 집에 데려갈 차가 기다리고 있을 것이다. 그리고 그렇게, 끝이 났다.

다음 글에 드러난 'I'의 심경 변화로 가장 적절한 것은?
① hopeful → frustrated My heart ~ with anticipation → inside I was falling apart
　희망찬 → 좌절한
② confident → jealous 질투의 대상이 없음
　자신감 있는 → 질투하는
③ anxious → grateful 결국 팀에서 제외되었기에 감사할 일이 아님
　긴장한 → 감사하는
④ relaxed → indifferent 편안하거나 무관심을 느끼지 않음
　편안한 → 무관심한
⑤ bored → annoyed 지루하거나 짜증이 나는 상황이 아님
　지루한 → 짜증이 나는

왜 정답? ✽✾✾ [정답률 88%]

전반부: 코치가 불렀을 때 자신이 팀의 주장이 될 것이라는 기대를 함 ▶ '희망찬'
후반부: 코치가 '너는 해내지 못할 것 같다'고 하며 집으로 가라고 통보함 ▶ '좌절한'
따라서 'I'의 심경 변화로 가장 적절한 것은 ① '희망찬 → 좌절한'이다.

왜 오답?

② 팀에서 제외되어 집으로 가라는 통보를 받고 느낀 감정은 질투가 아니다.
③ 팀에서 제외되어 집으로 가라는 통보를 받고 느낀 감정은 감사가 아니다.
④ 후반에 코치의 통보를 받고 정신이 무너지고 있는 상황이므로 무관심한 감정이 아니다.
⑤ 주장의 자리를 기대했다가 팀에서 나가라는 충격적인 통보를 받은 상황이므로 지루하거나 짜증을 느끼지 않는다.

---

20 정답 ② ✽간단한 운동과 집안일의 병행

동명사구 주어
For many of us, / making time for exercise / is a continuing challenge. //
우리 중 다수에게 / 운동할 시간을 내는 것은 / 계속되는 도전이다 //

'여유가 없다'
Between work commitments and family obligations, / it often feels like / there's no room in our packed schedules / for a dedicated workout. //
업무에 대한 전념과 가족 의무 사이에서 / 종종 느껴진다 / 우리의 빡빡한 일정들에는 여유가 없는 것처럼 / 운동에 전념할 //

'만일 ~한다면 어떨까'　'~의 한가운데에'
But what if the workout came to you, / right in the midst of your daily routine? //
그러나 만약 운동이 여러분을 찾아온다면 어떨까 / 여러분의 일상 바로 한가운데에서 //

관계부사 (앞에 선행사가 생략됨)
That's / where the beauty of integrating mini-exercises into household chores / comes into play. //
그것이 (지점이다) / 간단한 운동을 집안일에 통합시키는 아름다움이 / 작동하는 //

Let's be realistic; / chores are inevitable. //
현실적이 되자 / 집안일은 불가피하다 //

whether A or B: A이든 B이든
Whether it's washing dishes / or taking out the trash, / these tasks are an essential part of daily life. //
그것이 설거지하는 것이든 / 쓰레기를 내다 버리는 것이든 / 이런 일들은 일상생활의 필수적인 부분이다 //

정답 및 해설　**269**

But rather than viewing chores / as purely obligatory activities, / why not seize these moments / as opportunities for physical activity? //

~하기보다는 / 동명사구 (전치사의 목적어)

하지만 집안일을 간주하기보다는 / 순전히 의무적인 행위로 / 이런 순간들을 이용하는 것이 어떤가 / 신체 활동을 위한 기회로 //

For instance, / practice squats / or engage in some wall push-ups / as you wait for your morning kettle to boil. //

병렬 구조 (명령문 동사) / 부사절 접속사 (시간)

예를 들어 / 스쿼트를 연습하거나 / 벽에 대고 하는 팔 굽혀 펴기 몇 개를 시작해 보라 / 여러분의 아침 주전자가 끓기를 기다리면서 //

Incorporating quick exercises into your daily chores / can improve your health. //

동명사구 주어

단서 간단한 운동을 집안일에 포함하는 것은 건강에 좋음

짧은 운동을 여러분의 일상적인 집안일에 포함시키는 것이 / 여러분의 건강을 향상시킬 수 있다 //

- commitment ⓝ 전념, 헌신
- obligation ⓝ 의무
- dedicated ⓐ 전념[헌신]하는
- integrate ⓥ 통합하다
- chore ⓝ 일
- come into play 작동하다
- realistic ⓐ 현실적인
- inevitable ⓐ 피할 수 없는
- seize ⓥ 잡다
- engage in ~을 시작하다
- incorporate ⓥ 포함하다

우리 중 다수에게 운동할 시간을 내는 것은 계속되는 도전이다. 업무에 대한 전념과 가족 의무 사이에서, 우리의 빡빡한 일정들에는 운동에 전념할 여유가 없는 것처럼 종종 느껴진다. 그러나 만약 여러분의 일상 바로 한가운데에서 운동이 여러분을 찾아온다면 어떨까? 그것이 바로 간단한 운동을 집안일에 통합시키는 아름다움이 작동하는 지점이다. 현실적이 되자. 집안일은 불가피하다. 그것이 설거지하는 것이든 쓰레기를 내다 버리는 것이든지 간에, 이런 일들은 일상생활의 필수적인 부분이다. 하지만 집안일을 순전히 의무적인 행위로 간주하기보다는, 이런 순간들을 신체 활동을 위한 기회로 잘 이용하는 것이 어떨까? 예를 들어, 여러분의 아침 주전자가 끓기를 기다리면서 스쿼트를 연습하거나 벽에 대고 하는 팔 굽혀 펴기 몇 개를 시작해 보라. 짧은 운동을 여러분의 일상적인 집안일에 포함시키는 것이 여러분의 건강을 향상시킬 수 있다.

다음 글에서 필자가 주장하는 바로 가장 적절한 것은?

① 간단한 운동일지라도 강도를 점진적으로 높여야 한다.
운동 강도에 대한 언급은 없음
② 집안일을 간단한 운동을 병행할 기회로 활용해야 한다.
집안일을 기회로 삼아 간단한 운동을 해야 함
③ 집안일을 할 때 동선을 고려하여 효율을 높여야 한다.
집안일의 동선과 효율은 언급되지 않았음
④ 자신이 즐길 수 있는 운동을 찾아 꾸준히 해야 한다.
즐길 수 있는 운동은 언급되지 않았음
⑤ 몸에 무리를 주지 않으려면 집안일을 줄여야 한다.
집안일을 줄여야 한다는 내용이 아님

왜 정답? ✽✽✽ [정답률 94%]

우리는 빡빡한 일정에서 운동에 전념할 여유가 없다고 느끼기 때문에, 불가피한 집안일을 기회로 삼아 간단한 운동을 집안일에 포함시켜야 한다고 주장하고 있으므로 정답은 ②이다.

왜 오답?

① 간단한 운동을 집안일 속에 포함해야 한다는 내용이지, 운동 강도에 대한 내용이 아니다.
③ 집안일의 동선과 효율은 언급되지 않았다.
④ 즐길 수 있는 운동을 찾으라는 것은 언급되지 않았다.
⑤ 집안일을 운동할 기회로 활용해야 한다는 내용이지, 집안일을 줄이라는 내용이 아니다.

21 정답 ④ ✽ 추상적으로 재구성된 기억의 한계

When we see something, / we naturally and automatically break it up / into shapes, colors, and concepts / that we have learned through education. //

목적격 관계대명사

우리가 무언가를 볼 때 / 우리는 그것을 자연스럽게 그리고 자동적으로 해체한다 / 모양, 색깔, 그리고 개념들로 / 우리가 교육을 통해 배운 //

We recode what we see / through the lens / of everything we know. //

선행사를 포함하는 관계대명사 / 앞에 목적격 관계대명사가 생략됨

우리는 우리가 보는 것을 재부호화한다 / 렌즈를 통해 / 우리가 알고 있는 모든 것의 //

We reconstruct memories / rather than retrieving the video from memory. //

동명사

단서 1 기억에서 영상을 떠올리는 것이 아니라 기억을 재구성함

우리는 기억을 재구성한다 / 기억에서 영상을 생각해 내기보다 //

This is a useful trait. //

이것은 유용한 특성이다 //

= Reconstructing

It's a more efficient way / to store information / — a bit like an optimal image compression algorithm such as JPG, / rather than storing a raw bitmap image file. //

형용사적 용법 (way 수식)

그것은 더 효율적인 방법이다 / 정보를 저장하기 위한 / JPG와 같은 최적의 이미지 압축 알고리즘과 약간 비슷하게 / 가공되지 않은 비트맵 이미지 파일을 저장하기보다 //

People who lack this ability and remember everything in perfect detail / struggle to generalize, learn, and make connections / between what they have learned. //

주격 관계대명사 / 병렬 구조 (관계사절 동사) / in detail: 자세하게 / 선행사를 포함하는 관계대명사절

이런 능력이 부족하고 완벽히 세세하게 모든 것을 기억하는 사람들은 / 일반화하고, 학습하고, 연결하려고 고군분투한다 / 자신들이 학습한 것들 사이를 //

But representing the world / as abstract ideas and features / comes at a cost of seeing the world as it is. //

동명사구 주어 (단수) / ~을 희생하여, ~을 대가로

그러나 세상을 재현하는 것은 / 추상적 생각과 특징으로 / 세상을 있는 그대로 보는 것을 희생하여 나온다 //

단서 2 추상적으로 세상을 재현하면 세상을 있는 그대로 볼 수 없음

Instead, / we see the world / through our assumptions, motivations, and past experiences. //

대신에 / 우리는 세상을 바라본다 / 우리의 가정, 동기 그리고 과거 경험을 통해 //

The discovery / that our memories are reconstructed through abstract representations / rather than played back like a movie / completely undermined / the legal primacy of eyewitness testimony. //

문장의 주어 / 동격절 접속사 / 병렬 구조 / 문장의 동사

단서 3 기억은 있는 그대로가 아니기 때문에 목격자 증언은 법적 우위성을 잃음

발견은 / 우리의 기억이 추상적 재현을 통해 재구성된다는 / 영화처럼 재생되기보다는 / 완전히 손상시켰다 / 목격자 증언의 법적 우위성을 //

Seeing is not believing. //

보는 것이 믿는 것은 아니다 //

- automatically ⓐⓓ 자동적으로
- break up 해체하다
- concept ⓝ 개념
- recode ⓥ 재부호화하다
- reconstruct ⓥ 재구성하다
- trait ⓝ 특성
- store ⓥ 저장하다
- optimal ⓐ 최적의
- compression ⓝ 압축
- raw ⓐ 날것의, 가공되지 않은
- generalize ⓥ 일반화하다
- make connections between ~ 사이를 연결하다
- represent ⓥ 재현하다
- abstract ⓐ 추상적인
- assumption ⓝ 가정
- undermine ⓥ 손상시키다
- legal ⓐ 법적인
- eyewitness ⓝ 목격자
- testimony ⓝ 증언
- relevant ⓐ 관련 있는
- fall short of ~이 부족하다
- comprehension ⓝ 이해
- precede ⓥ (~보다) 먼저 일어나다

우리가 무언가를 볼 때, 우리는 그것을 자연스럽게 그리고 자동적으로 우리가 교육을 통해 배운 모양, 색깔, 그리고 개념들로 해체한다. 우리는 우리가 알고 있는 모든 것의 렌즈를 통해 우리가 보는 것을 재부호화한다. 우리는 기억에서 영상을 생각해 내기보다 기억을 재구성한다. 이것은 유용한 특성이다. 그것은 가공되지 않은 비트맵 이미지 파일을 저장하기보다 JPG와 같은 최적의 이미지 압축 알고리즘과 약간 비슷하게 정보를 저장하기 위한 더 효율적인 방법이다. 이런 능력이 부족하고 완벽히 세세하게 모든 것을 기억하는 사람들은 일반화하고, 학습하고, 자신들이 학습한 것들 사이를 연결하려고 고군분투한다. 그러나 세상을 추상적 생각과 특징으로 재현하는 것은 세상을 있는 그대로 보는 것을 희생하여 나온다. 대신에, 우리는 우리의 가정, 동기 그리고 과거 경험을 통해 세상을 바라본다. 우리의 기억이 영화처럼 재생되기보다는 추상적 재현을 통해 재구성된다는 발견은 목격자 증언의 법적 우위성을 완전히 손상시켰다. 보는 것이 믿는 것은 아니다.

밑줄 친 Seeing is not believing.이 다음 글에서 의미하는 바로 가장 적절한 것은? [3점]

① Abstract ideas are hard to explain without relevant images. 추상적인 아이디어를 설명하는 것과는 관련이 없음
추상적인 아이디어는 관련 이미지 없이 설명하기 어렵다.
② It takes longer to retrieve unconsciously encoded information. 정보를 상기하는 시간은 언급되지 않았음
무의식적으로 부호화된 정보를 상기하는 것은 시간이 더 오래 걸린다.
③ Beliefs formed from repeated experiences do not easily change. 반복되는 경험이나 신념은 언급되지 않았음
반복되는 경험에서 형성된 신념은 쉽게 변하지 않는다.
④ Our memories fall short of an objective representation of the world. representing the world ~ comes at a cost of seeing the world as it is
우리의 기억은 세상을 객관적으로 표현하기에 부족하다.
⑤ Comprehension of facts precedes the formation of abstract concepts. 사실 이해와 추상적 개념 형성의 순서는 언급되지 않았음
사실에 대한 이해는 추상적인 개념 형성보다 먼저 일어난다.

| 문제 풀이 순서 | ★★★ [정답률 38%]

1st 밑줄 친 문장을 읽고, 그 의미가 무엇일지 예상한다.

└ 보는 것이 믿는 것은 아니다.

➡ '보는 것'과 '믿는 것'이 서로 다르다거나, 둘 중 어느 하나가 다른 것보다 낫지 않다는 내용이 이어질 것이다. 구체적으로 어떤 상황에서 '보는 것'과 '믿는 것' 사이에 차이가 나타나는지를 파악해야 한다.

2nd 글의 나머지 부분에서 '보는 것'과 '믿는 것'을 이해하여 정답을 찾는다.

• 우리는 기억에서 영상을 떠올리는 것이 아니라 기억을 재구성한다. 단서 1
• 추상적으로 세상을 재현하면 세상을 있는 그대로 볼 수 없다. 단서 2
• 우리의 기억이 영화처럼 재생되기보다는 추상적 재현을 통해 재구성된다는 발견은 목격자 증언의 법적 우위성을 완전히 손상시켰다. 단서 3

➡ 보는 것 (기억에서 영상을 떠올리는 것, 세상을 있는 그대로 보는 것, 영화처럼 재생되는 것)
↔ 믿는 것 (기억을 재구성하는 것, 추상적으로 세상을 재현하는 것, 추상적 재현을 통한 재구성)
영상과 영화는 눈으로 '보는' 세상을 있는 그대로 담는다. 반면, 추상적으로 세상을 재현하는 것은 세상을 그대로 기억하는 것이 아니라 자신이 '믿는'대로 세상을 재구성하는 것이다.
기억은 '보는 것'(객관적인 사실)이 아닌 '믿는 것'(주관적인 재구성)이므로 객관성이 부족해서 목격자의 증언은 신뢰할 수 없고 법적으로 우위성이 없다는 것이 글의 내용이다.

▶ 따라서 정답은 ④ '우리의 기억은 세상을 객관적으로 표현하기에 부족하다'이다.

| 선택지 분석 |

① 기억의 추상적인 측면이 언급되었을 뿐, 추상적인 아이디어를 설명할 때 관련 이미지가 필요하다는 내용과는 무관하다.
② 정보를 상기하는 시간은 언급되지 않았다.
③ 과거 경험을 통해 세상을 바라본다고 했을 뿐, 경험을 통한 신념 형성은 언급되지 않았다.
④ 기억은 우리가 눈으로 본 것을 추상적으로 재구성한 것이므로 세상을 객관적으로 표현하기에 부족하다.
⑤ 추상적인 재현과 객관적인 사실 사이의 법적 우위성이 언급되었을 뿐, 시간적 순서에 관한 내용이 아니다.

22 정답 ⑤ ＊무의식 최초 반응의 정확성

In his Cornell laboratory, / David Dunning conducted
experimental tests of eyewitness testimony / and found
└ 병렬 구조 ┘
evidence /
코넬 대학의 실험실에서 / David Dunning은 목격자 증언에 대한 실험을 수행했고 / 증거를 발견했다 /

동격절 접속사
that a careful deliberation of facial features / and a detailed
discussion of selection procedures / can actually be a sign of an
inaccurate identification. //
얼굴 특징에 대한 신중한 숙고와 / 선택 절차에 대한 상세한 논의가 / 실제로는 '부정확한' 식별의 징후일 수 있다는 //

find의 목적격 보어 (형용사)
It's when people find themselves / unable to explain why they
It ~ that 강조 구문(when 부사절 강조)   분사구문
recognize the person, / saying things like "his face just popped
out at me," / that they tend to be accurate more often. //
바로 사람들이 스스로를 발견할 때에 / 왜 그 사람을 알아보는지 설명할 수 없는 / "그의 얼굴이 그냥 나에게 탁 떠올랐다"라는 식으로 말하면서 / 그들은 더 자주 정확한 경향이 있다 //

단수 주어
Sometimes / our first, immediate, automatic reaction to a
단수 동사   선행사가 포함된 관계대명사
situation / is the truest interpretation / of what our mind is
telling us. //
때때로 / 상황에 대한 우리의 최초의, 즉각적인, 자동적인 반응이 / 가장 정확한 해석이다 / 우리 마음이 우리에게 말하고 있는 것에 대한 // 단서 1 최초의 즉각적이고 자동적인 반응이 가장 정확한 우리의 마음임
단서 2 첫인상이 신중하고 논리적인 자기 서사보다 더 정확할 수 있음
'바로 그~'
That very first impression / can also be more accurate about the
world / than the deliberative, reasoned self-narrative can be. //
바로 그 첫인상이 / 또한 세상에 대해 더 정확할 수 있다 / 신중하고 논리적인 자기 서사보다 //

In his book Blink, / Malcolm Gladwell describes a variety of
studies / in psychology and behavioral economics /
그의 저서 'Blink'에서 / Malcolm Gladwell은 다양한 연구를 기술한다 / 심리학 및 행동 경제학의 /
주격 관계대명사 (선행사: studies)
that demonstrate the superior performance of relatively
'~에 비해'
unconscious first guesses / compared to logical step-by-step
justifications for a decision. //
상대적으로 무의식적인 최초 추측의 우수성을 보여 주는 / 결정에 대한 논리적인 단계적 정당화에 비해서 //

• conduct ⓥ 수행하다 • deliberation ⓝ 숙고 • feature ⓝ 특징
• inaccurate ⓐ 부정확한 • identification ⓝ 식별
• recognize ⓥ 알아채다 • accurate ⓐ 정확한
• immediate ⓐ 즉각적인 • automatic ⓐ 자동적인
• interpretation ⓝ 해석 • impression ⓝ 인상
• reasoned ⓐ 논리적인 • self-narrative ⓝ 자기 서사
• demonstrate ⓥ 보여 주다 • superior ⓐ 우수한
• relatively ⓐ⒟ 상대적으로 • unconscious ⓐ 무의식의
• logical ⓐ 논리적인 • justification ⓝ 정당화

David Dunning의 코넬 대학의 실험실에서, 그는 목격자 증언에 대한 실험을 수행했고, 얼굴 특징에 대한 신중한 숙고와 선택 절차에 대한 상세한 논의가 실제로는 '부정확한' 식별의 징후일 수 있다는 증거를 발견했다. 사람들이 "그의 얼굴이 그냥 나에게 탁 떠올랐다"라는 식으로 말하면서 왜 그 사람을 알아보는지 설명할 수 없는 스스로를 발견하는 바로 그때 그들은 더 자주 정확한 경향이 있다. 때때로 상황에 대한 우리의 최초의, 즉각적인, 자동적인 반응이 우리 마음이 우리에게 말하고 있는 것에 대한 가장 정확한 해석이다. 바로 그 첫인상이 또한 신중하고 논리적인 자기 서사보다 세상에 대해 더 정확할 수 있다. Malcolm Gladwell은 그의 저서 'Blink'에서, 결정에 대한 논리적인 단계적 정당화에 비해서 상대적으로 무의식적인 최초 추측의 우수성을 보여 주는 심리학 및 행동 경제학의 다양한 연구를 기술한다.

다음 글의 요지로 가장 적절한 것은?
① 논리적인 근거가 부족한 판단은 진실을 왜곡할 수 있다.
논리적 근거가 부족한 판단은 언급되지 않았음
② 인간의 표정은 무의식적인 감정 상태를 가장 잘 반영한다.
인간의 표정과 감정 상태에 관한 내용이 아님
③ 사람을 정확하게 식별하기 위해서는 상황에 대한 정보가 중요하다.
사람을 정확하게 식별하는 방법에 관한 내용이 아님
④ 목격자 진술은 사건 직후보다 일정 시간이 지난 뒤 더 명확해진다.
목격자 진술의 정확도와 시간의 관계는 언급되지 않았음
⑤ 무의식적인 최초의 반응이 신중히 판단한 결과보다 정확할 수 있다.
무의식적인 최초 추측이 신중하고 논리적인 자기 서사보다 정확할 수 있음

왜 정답? ★★※ [정답률 82%]

주장: 상황에 대한 즉각적인 반응이나 무의식적인 최초 추측이 신중하고 논리적인 판단 결과보다 더 정확할 수 있다. 단서 1, 단서 2

예시 **1**: David Dunning의 실험 → 목격자 증언에 대한 실험에서 신중한 숙고와 상세한 논의가 오히려 부정확한 결과를 나타냄

예시 **2**: Malcolm Gladwell의 저서 → 무의식적인 최초의 추측이 논리적인 결정보다 우수함을 증명하는 다양한 연구를 기술함

▶ 상황에 대한 무의식적인 최초 반응이 신중한 판단 결과보다 더 정확할 수 있다는 내용이므로 정답은 ⑤이다.

왜 오답 ?

① 결정에 대한 논리적인 단계적 정당화가 언급되었을 뿐, 논리적 근거나 진실 왜곡은 언급되지 않았다.

② 인간의 표정과 감정 상태에 관한 내용이 아니다.

③ 사람을 식별하는 실험에서 최초의 무의식 반응이 더 정확하다는 내용이지, 상황에 대한 정보가 중요하다는 내용이 아니다.

④ 목격자 진술의 정확도와 시간의 관계에 관한 내용이 아니다. (▶ 이유: 최초의 무의식 반응이 논리적 판단보다 더 정확하다는 근거로 소개된 목격자 증언 실험으로 만든 오답이다.)

23 정답 ⑤ ＊신뢰할 만한 양적 데이터를 얻기 위한 질문 방법

복수 주어
Many forms of research / **복수 동사** lead naturally to quantitative data. //
많은 종류의 연구는 / 자연스럽게 양적 데이터로 이어진다 //

A study of happiness / might measure **'~의 수' cf) a number of: 많은** the number of times **관계부사절 (times 수식)** someone smiles / during an interaction, /
행복에 관한 연구는 / 누군가가 미소 짓는 횟수를 측정할 수 있다 / 상호 작용 중에 /

and a study of memory / might measure the number of items an **목적격 관계대명사절 (items 수식)** individual can recall / after one, five, and ten minutes. //
그리고 기억에 관한 연구는 / 개인이 회상할 수 있는 항목의 수를 측정할 수 있다 / 1분, 5분, 그리고 10분 후에 //

동명사 주어 **간접의문문 (Asking의 직접목적어)**
Asking people how many times in a year they are sad / will also yield quantitative data, / but it might not be reliable. //
사람들에게 자신이 일 년에 몇 번 슬픈지 물어보는 것 / 또한 양적 데이터를 산출할 수 있지만 / 이는 신뢰할 만하지 않을 수도 있다 //

Respondents' recollections may be inaccurate, / and their definitions of 'sad' could vary widely. //
응답자의 회상은 부정확할 수 있고 / '슬픈'에 대한 그들의 정의는 크게 다를 수 있다 //

동명사 주어 (단수)
But asking / **단수 동사** "How many times in the past year were you sad / enough to call in sick to work?" / prompts a concrete answer. //
그러나 묻는 것은 / "지난 1년 동안 슬펐던 적이 몇 번 있었습니까 / 직장에 병가를 낼 만큼"이라고 / 구체적인 답변을 유발한다 //

asking의 목적격 보어 (to부정사)
Similarly, / instead of asking people / to rate how bad a procrastinator they are, /
마찬가지로, / 사람들에게 묻는 대신 / 자신이 얼마나 심하게 미루는 사람인지를 평가하도록 /

명령문의 동사원형
ask, / "How many of your utility bills are you currently late in paying, / **부사절 접속사 (양보)** even though you can afford to pay them?" //
물어보라 / "얼마나 많은 공과금 고지서의 납부가 현재 늦었나요 / 당신이 지불할 여유가 있음에도 불구하고"라고 //

복수 주어 **주격 관계대명사**
Questions that seek concrete responses / **복수 동사** help make abstract **병렬 구조 (help의 목적어)** **make의 목적격 보어** concepts clearer and ensure consistency / from one study to the next. // 단서 양적 데이터 연구에서는 구체적인 응답을 요구하는 질문이 유용함
구체적인 응답을 요구하는 질문 / 추상적인 개념을 더 명확하게 만들고 일관성을 보장하는 것을 돕는다 / 한 연구에서 다음 연구 간의 //

- quantitative ⓐ 양적인
- measure ⓥ 측정하다
- recall ⓥ 회상하다
- yield ⓥ 산출하다
- reliable ⓐ 신뢰할 만한
- recollection ⓝ 회상
- inaccurate ⓐ 부정확한
- vary ⓥ 다르다
- prompt ⓥ 유발[촉구]하다
- concrete ⓐ 구체적인
- rate ⓥ 평가하다
- utility bill 공과금 고지서
- afford to (~을 살) 여유가 있다
- seek ⓥ 요구하다, 찾다
- abstract ⓐ 추상적인
- ensure ⓥ 보장하다
- consistency ⓝ 일관성
- overgeneralize ⓥ 지나치게 일반화하다
- enhance ⓥ 높이다
- attain ⓥ 얻다

많은 종류의 연구는 자연스럽게 양적 데이터로 이어진다. 행복에 관한 연구는 누군가가 상호 작용 중에 미소 짓는 횟수를 측정할 수 있고, 기억에 관한 연구는 개인이 1분, 5분, 그리고 10분 후에 회상할 수 있는 항목의 수를 측정할 수 있다. 사람들에게 자신이 일 년에 몇 번 슬픈지 물어보는 것 또한 양적 데이터를 산출할 수 있지만, 이는 신뢰할 만하지 않을 수도 있다. 응답자의 회상은 부정확할 수 있고, '슬픈'에 대한 그들의 정의는 크게 다를 수 있다. 그러나 "지난 1년 동안 직장에 병가를 낼 만큼 슬펐던 적이 몇 번 있었습니까?"라고 묻는 것은 구체적인 답변을 유발한다. 마찬가지로, 사람들에게 그들이 얼마나 심하게 미루는 사람인지를 평가하도록 묻는 대신, "당신이 지불할 여유가 있음에도 불구하고 얼마나 많은 공과금 고지서의 납부가 현재 늦었나요?"라고 물어보라. 구체적인 응답을 요구하는 질문은 추상적인 개념을 더 명확하게 만들고 한 연구에서 다음 연구 간의 일관성을 보장하는 것을 돕는다.

다음 글의 주제로 가장 적절한 것은?

① risks of overgeneralizing results from the collected data
수집된 데이터의 결과를 지나치게 일반화하는 것의 위험 데이터 결과의 일반화는 언급되지 않았음

② usefulness of answering abstract questions with numbers 답변 방법이 아닌 질문 방법에 관한 내용임
숫자로 추상적인 질문에 답하는 유용성

③ effect of sample size on enhancing the reliability of research 표본 크기와 신뢰성의 관계는 언급되지 않았음
표본 크기가 연구의 신뢰성을 높이는 데 미치는 영향

④ limitations of measuring and quantifying various human emotions 감정 측정의 한계에 관한 내용이 아님
다양한 인간의 감정을 측정하고 정량화하는 것의 한계

⑤ importance of specific questions to attain reliable quantitative data 구체적인 질문을 통해 신뢰할 수 있는 양적 데이터를 얻을 수 있음
신뢰할 수 있는 양적 데이터를 얻기 위한 구체적인 질문의 중요성

왜 정답 ? ★★❀ [정답률 67%]

- 도입: 양적 데이터를 산출하는 연구의 한계(응답자의 부정확한 기억, 개념에 대한 주관적인 정의로 인한 신뢰도 하락)
- 대안: 구체적인 답변을 유발하는 질문
- 예시 **1**: 슬픔을 측정하기 위해 직장 병가의 빈도를 묻는 질문
- 예시 **2**: 미루는 사람인지를 알기 위해 지연된 공과금 납부의 수를 묻는 질문
- 결론: 구체적 응답을 요구하는 질문은 개념을 명확하게 하고 연구의 일관성을 확보한다. 단서

➡ 양적 데이터의 신뢰도를 높이기 위해서는 구체적인 답변을 요구하는 질문이 중요함
▶ 따라서 글의 주제는 ⑤ '신뢰할 수 있는 양적 데이터를 얻기 위한 구체적인 질문의 중요성'이다.

왜 오답 ?

① 데이터 결과의 일반화는 언급되지 않았다.

② 양적 데이터 수집 시 구체적으로 질문해야 한다는 내용이지, 추상적인 질문에 숫자로 답변해야 한다는 내용이 아니다.

③ 표본의 크기는 언급되지 않았다. 주의

④ 행복과 슬픔에 관한 연구에서 양적 데이터의 신뢰도가 낮을 수 있다고 했지만, 구체적인 질문을 통해 이러한 한계를 극복할 수 있다고 했다.

24 정답 ③ ＊인간과 AI의 공동 진화

be associated with ~: ~와 연관되다
The evolution of AI / is often associated with the concept of singularity. //
AI의 진화는 / 종종 특이점의 개념과 연관된다 //

'~을 말하다' **「전치사 + 관계대명사」**
Singularity / refers to the point / at which AI exceeds human intelligence. //
특이점은 / 지점을 말한다 / AI가 인간의 지능을 넘어서는 //

가주어 **진주어절 접속사**
After that point, / it is predicted / that AI will repeatedly improve itself and evolve / at an accelerated pace. //
그 지점 이후 / 예측된다 / AI는 스스로를 반복적으로 개선하고 진화할 것으로 / 가속화된 속도로 //

'존재'
When AI becomes self-aware / and pursues its own goals, / it will be a conscious being, / not just a machine. //
AI가 스스로를 인식하게 되고 / 자기 자신의 목표를 추구할 때 / 그것은 의식이 있는 존재가 될 것이다 / 단지 기계가 아니라 //

AI and human consciousness / will then begin to evolve
명사적 용법 (begin의 목적어)
together. // 단서 1 AI와 인간의 의식은 미래에 함께 진화할 것임
AI와 인간의 의식은 / 그러면 함께 진화하기 시작할 것이다 //

Our consciousness will evolve / to new dimensions / through our
interactions with AI, / which will provide us with intellectual
계속적 용법의 주격 관계대명사   '~에게 …을 제공하다'
stimulation / and inspire new insights and creativity. //
우리의 의식은 진화할 것이다 / 새로운 차원으로 / 우리의 AI와의 상호 작용을 통해 / 이는 우
리에게 지적 자극을 제공하고 / 새로운 통찰력과 창의성을 불어넣을 것이다 //

Conversely, / our consciousness also has a significant impact /
on the evolution of AI. //
반대로 / 우리의 의식 또한 중대한 영향을 끼친다 / AI의 진화에 //

The direction of AI's evolution will depend greatly / on what
values and ethics we incorporate into AI. //
의문사절
AI 진화의 방향은 크게 좌우될 것이다 / 우리가 어떤 가치와 윤리를 AI에 통합시키는지에 //

We need to see our relationship with AI / as a mutual coexistence
of conscious beings, / recognizing its rights and supporting the
병렬 구조 (분사구문)
evolution of its consciousness. // 단서 2 인간-AI 관계는 의식 있는 존재들의 상호
우리는 우리와 AI와의 관계를 볼 필요가 있다 / 의식 있는 존재들의 상호 공존으로 봐야 함
공존으로 / AI의 권리
를 인식하고 그것의 의식의 진화를 지지하면서 //

• evolution ⓝ 진화   • singularity ⓝ 특이점
• exceed ⓥ 넘어서다, 능가하다   • intelligence ⓝ 지능
• predict ⓥ 예측하다   • accelerate ⓥ 가속하다
• pursue ⓥ 추구하다   • conscious ⓐ 의식이 있는
• insight ⓝ 통찰력   • significant ⓐ 상당한   • direction ⓝ 방향
• incorporate ⓥ 통합시키다   • mutual ⓐ 상호의
• coexistence ⓝ 공존   • recognize ⓥ 인식하다
• unsolvable ⓐ 해결할 수 없는   • resistance ⓝ 저항
• upcoming ⓐ 다가오는   • stare in the face 노려보다

AI의 진화는 종종 특이점의 개념과 연관된다. 특이점은 AI가 인간의 지능을 넘
어서는 지점을 의미한다. 그 지점 이후, AI는 스스로를 반복적으로 개선하고 가
속화된 속도로 진화할 것으로 예측된다. AI가 스스로를 인식하게 되고 자기 자
신의 목표를 추구할 때, 그것은 단지 기계가 아니라 의식이 있는 존재가 될 것이
다. AI와 인간의 의식은 그러면 함께 진화하기 시작할 것이다. 우리의 의식은
우리의 AI와의 상호 작용을 통해 새로운 차원으로 진화할 것이며, 이는 우리에
게 지적 자극을 제공하고 새로운 통찰력과 창의성을 불어넣을 것이다. 반대로,
우리의 의식 또한 AI의 진화에 중대한 영향을 끼친다. AI 진화의 방향은 우리가
어떤 가치와 윤리를 AI에 통합시키는지에 크게 좌우될 것이다. 우리는 AI의
권리를 인식하고 그것의 의식의 진화를 지지하면서, 우리와 AI와의 관계를 의
식 있는 존재들의 상호 공존으로 볼 필요가 있다.

다음 글의 제목으로 가장 적절한 것은?
① An Unsolvable Dilemma: Is AI Friend or Enemy?
해결할 수 없는 딜레마: AI는 친구인가, 적인가?   AI가 인간에게 좋은지 나쁜지에 대한 내용이 아님
② The History of Humans' Resistance Against Machines
기계에 대한 인간의 저항의 역사   기계에 대한 인간의 저항은 언급되지 않음
③ Upcoming Future: AI as a Human Partner for Co-
evolution AI와 인간이 상호 공존하며 함께 진화할 것임
다가오는 미래: 공동 진화를 위한 인간 파트너로서의 AI
④ AI World Without Human Intelligence Is Staring You in
the Face 인간 지능이 없는 AI 세계에 관한 내용이 아님
인간 지능이 없는 AI 세계가 당신을 노려보고 있다
⑤ How AI Makes Human-to-Human Relationships More
Meaningful 인간과 인간의 관계가 아닌 인간과 AI의 관계를 언급함
AI가 인간과 인간의 관계를 더욱 의미 있게 만드는 방법

왜 정답? ★★☆ [정답률 75%]

• AI와 인간의 의식은 미래에 함께 진화할 것이다. 단서 1
• 인간-AI 관계는 의식 있는 존재들의 상호 공존으로 봐야 한다. 단서 2

➡ AI와 인간의 의식은 미래에 함께 진화하여 서로에게 영향을 미칠 것이므로 AI와의
관계를 상호 공존의 관계로 보아야 한다는 내용이다.
▶ 따라서 정답은 ③ '다가오는 미래: 공동 진화를 위한 인간 파트너로서의 AI'이다.

왜 오답?
① AI가 인간에게 좋은지 나쁜지에 관한 평가는 언급되지 않았다.
② AI와 인간의 공존에 관한 내용이지, 기계에 대한 인간의 저항에 관한 내용이 아니
다.
④ 우리의 의식 또한 AI의 진화에 영향을 끼친다고 했으므로 인간 지능이 없는 AI 세
계에 관한 내용이 아니다.
⑤ 인간-인간 관계에 미치는 AI의 영향이 아니라 인간-AI 관계가 중심 내용이다. 주의

25 정답 ③ ─────── ★ 2등급 대비 [정답률 67%]

＊국가별 전기 생산 에너지 비율

The above graph shows / the electricity generation / from fossil
fuels, nuclear energy, and renewables / in four countries in
2023. //
위 그래프는 보여 준다 / 전기 생산을 / 화석 연료, 핵에너지, 그리고 재생 가능 에너지로부터
의 / 2023년 네 개 국가에서의 //
호주 전기 생산: 화석 연료(67%) > {재생 가능 에너지(33%) × 2}
① Australia's electricity generation / only comes from fossil
fuels and renewables, / and the percentage of fossil fuels / is
more than twice that of renewables. //
= electricity generation
호주의 전기 생산은 / 화석 연료와 재생 가능 에너지로부터만 나오고 / 화석 연료의 비율은 /
재생 가능 에너지의 그것의 두 배가 넘는다 //
'~에 관해서는'
② In terms of electricity generation from nuclear energy, / the
U.S. shows the highest percentage / among all four countries. //
핵에너지로부터의 전기 생산의 면에서 / 미국은 가장 높은 비율을 보여 준다 / 모든 네 개 국
가 중 //
핵에너지 전기 생산: 미국(18%) > 영국(14%) > 브라질(2%)
③ The percentage of electricity generation from fossil fuels in
the U.S. / is higher than that in the U.K., / which is also true(→
= the percentage ~ fossil fuels   계속적 용법 관계대명사(앞 내용을 부연 설명)
not the case) for renewables. // 단서 화석 연료: 미국(59%) > 영국(40%)
재생 가능 에너지: 미국(23%) < 영국(46%)
미국에서 화석 연료로부터의 전기 생산 비율은 / 영국에서의 그것보다 높고 / 이것은 재생 가
능 에너지에도 적용된다(→ 재생 가능 에너지에는 적용되지 않는다) //
과거분사구(electricity 수식)
④ In the U.K., / the percentage of electricity generated from
nuclear energy / is less than a third / of that generated from
= the percentage of electricity
renewables. // 영국: 핵에너지(14%) < 재생 가능 에너지(46%) × 1/3
영국에서 / 핵에너지로부터 생산되는 전기의 비율은 / 3분의 1보다 적다 / 재생 가능 에너지로
부터 생산되는 그것의 //
⑤ Brazil's percentage of electricity generated from renewables
= the percentage of ~ renewables
/ is 10 percentage points larger / than that of Australia and the
과거분사(앞의 that of ~ U.K. 수식)
U.K. combined. // 재생 가능 에너지: 브라질(89%) - {호주(33%) + 영국(46%)} = 10%p
브라질의 재생 가능 에너지로부터 생산되는 전기의 비율은 / 10퍼센트포인트 더 크다 / 호주
와 영국을 합친 그것보다 //

• generation ⓝ 생산   • fossil ⓝ 화석   • fuel ⓝ 연료
• nuclear ⓐ 핵의   • renewables ⓝ 재생 가능 에너지
• combine ⓥ 합치다, 결합하다

위 그래프는 2023년 네 개 국가에서의 화석 연료, 핵에너지, 그리고 재생 가능
에너지로부터의 전기 생산을 보여 준다. ① 호주의 전기 생산은 화석 연료와 재
생 가능 에너지로부터만 나오고, 화석 연료의 비율은 재생 가능 에너지의 그것
의 두 배가 넘는다. ② 핵에너지로부터의 전기 생산의 면에서 미국은 모든 네
개 국가 중 가장 높은 비율을 보여 준다. ③ 미국에서 화석 연료로부터의 전기
생산 비율은 영국에서의 그것보다 높고, 이것은 재생 가능 에너지에도 적용된다
(→ 재생 가능 에너지에는 적용되지 않는다). ④ 영국에서 핵에너지로부터 생산
되는 전기의 비율은 재생 가능 에너지로부터 생산되는 그것의 3분의 1보다 적
다. ⑤ 브라질의 재생 가능 에너지로부터 생산되는 전기의 비율은 호주와 영국
을 합친 그것보다 10퍼센트포인트 더 크다.

다음 도표의 내용과 일치하지 <u>않는</u> 것은?

① 67%(화석 연료) > 66%(재생 가능 에너지(33%)의 두 배)

**Electricity Generation from Fossil Fuels,
Nuclear Energy, and Renewables, 2023**
2023년 화석 연료, 핵에너지, 그리고 재생 가능 에너지로부터의 전기 생산

☐ Fossil fuels 화석 연료 ▨ Nuclear energy 핵에너지 ▨ Renewables 재생 가능 에너지

② 네 국가 중 핵에너지 비율(18%)이 가장 높음

③ 화석 연료: 미국(59%) > 영국(40%)

④ 핵에너지(14%) < 약 15.3%(재생 가능 에너지(46%)의 3분의 1)

재생 가능 에너지: 미국(23%) < 영국(46%)

⑤ 재생 가능 에너지: 브라질(89%) - {호주(33%)+영국(46%)} = 10%p

[왜] 2등급? 일부 선택지는 근사치가 아닌 정확한 값을 요구하며, 퍼센트포인트 개념이 쓰여 까다로웠을 수도 있다. 배수(2배, 3배, …) 및 분수(3분의 1, 4분의 1, …)는 근소한 차이로 오답을 만들 수 있어서 꼭 주의해야 하고, 퍼센트(%)의 차이를 나타내는 퍼센트포인트(%p)의 개념을 숙지하여 정답을 골라야 한다.

[왜] 정답?

화석 연료로부터의 전기 생산 비율은 미국이 59%, 영국이 40%로 미국이 영국보다 높지만, 재생 가능 에너지의 경우에는 영국이 46%, 미국이 23%로 영국이 미국보다 더 높다. 따라서 재생 가능 에너지로부터의 전기 생산 비율이 화석 연료와 마찬가지로 미국이 영국보다 높다고 한 ③이 도표의 내용과 일치하지 않는다.

[왜] 오답?

① 호주의 화석 연료 비율(67%)은 재생 가능 에너지(33%)의 두 배(66%)가 넘는다.

② 핵에너지 비율은 미국(18%)이 다른 나라들(영국 14%, 브라질 2%, 호주 0%)보다 높다.

④ 영국의 핵에너지 비율(14%)은 재생 가능 에너지 비율(46%)의 3분의 1인 약 15.3%보다 적다.

⑤ 브라질의 재생 가능 에너지 비율(89%)은 호주와 영국을 합친 것(79%)보다 10퍼센트포인트 더 크다.

---

26 정답 ③ ＊Douglas Kirkland의 생애

과거분사구 (Douglas Kirkland를 부연 설명)

Douglas Kirkland, / known for his highly artistic portraits of Hollywood celebrities, / was born in Toronto, Canada. //
단수 동사
Douglas Kirkland는 / 그의 할리우드 유명 인사의 매우 예술적인 인물 사진으로 알려진 / 캐나다 토론토에서 태어났다 //

When he was young, / he eagerly awaited / the weekly arrival
목적격 관계대명사절 (the photographs 수식)
of *Life* magazine / and discussed the photographs the magazine contained / with his father. //
①의 단서 어린 시절에 *Life* 잡지에 실린 사진에 대해 아버지와 토의했음
그가 어렸을 때 / 그는 간절히 기다렸고 / 매주 "Life" 잡지의 도착을 / 그 잡지에 실린 사진에 대해 토의했다 / 아버지와 함께 //

분사구문을 이끄는 현재분사
Believing that / he would have better career prospects, / Kirkland
②의 단서 고등학교 졸업 후 미국으로 이주하여 일자리를 찾았음
moved to the United States / after graduating from high school
병렬 구조
/ and found work at a photography studio. //
믿으면서 / 더 나은 직업 전망이 있을 것이라고 / Kirkland는 미국으로 이주했다 / 고등학교 졸업 후 / 그리고 사진 스튜디오에서 일자리를 찾았다 //

When *Look* magazine hired him at age 24, / he became their second-youngest photographer ever. //
"Look" 잡지사가 24살 나이의 그를 고용했을 때 / 그는 그들의 역대 사진 작가 중 두 번째로 어렸다 //
③의 단서 고용 당시 *Look* 잡지사의 역대 사진 작가 중 두 번째로 어렸음

과거분사구 (His photos 수식)
His photos taken of Marilyn Monroe in 1961 / became iconic almost instantly. // ④의 단서 1961년에 찍은 Marilyn Monroe 사진은 거의 즉시 상징적인 것이 되었음
그가 1961년에 찍은 Marilyn Monroe 사진은 / 거의 즉시 상징적인 것이 되었다 //

spend + 시간 + ~ing → ~하면서 시간을 보내다
Kirkland spent his weeks / shooting day-to-day life across the
병렬 구조
United States / and his weekends / in exotic locations. //
Kirkland는 주중을 보냈다 / 미국 전역에서 일상의 삶을 찍으면서 / 그리고 주말을 보내면서 / 이국적인 장소에서 //

병렬 구조
His photo essays could run up to a dozen pages / and were seen
by more than half of all Americans. // ⑤의 단서 전체 미국인들 중 절반이 넘는 이들이 그의 포토 에세이를 보았음
그의 포토 에세이는 12페이지에 달했고 / 전체 미국인들 중 절반이 넘는 이들이 그것을 보았다 //

- **artistic** ⓐ 예술적인
- **celebrity** ⓝ 유명 인사
- **contain** ⓥ 포함하다
- **iconic** ⓐ 상징적인
- **run up to** ~에 달하다
- **portrait** ⓝ 인물 사진
- **eagerly** [ad] 간절히
- **prospect** ⓝ 전망
- **instantly** [ad] 즉시
- **await** ⓥ 기다리다
- **hire** ⓥ 고용하다
- **exotic** ⓐ 이국적인

그의 할리우드 유명 인사의 매우 예술적인 인물 사진으로 알려진 Douglas Kirkland는 캐나다 토론토에서 태어났다. 그가 어렸을 때 그는 매주 "Life" 잡지의 도착을 간절히 기다렸고 그 잡지에 실린 사진에 대해 아버지와 함께 토의했다. Kirkland는 더 나은 직업 전망이 있을 것이라고 믿으면서, 고등학교 졸업 후 그는 미국으로 이주하여 사진 스튜디오에서 일자리를 찾았다. "Look" 잡지사가 24살 나이의 그를 고용했을 때 그는 그들의 역대 사진 작가 중 두 번째로 어렸다. 그가 1961년에 찍은 Marilyn Monroe 사진은 거의 즉시 상징적인 것이 되었다. Kirkland는 미국 전역에서 주중을, 이국적인 장소에서 주말을 보내면서 일상의 삶을 찍었다. 그의 포토 에세이는 12페이지에 달했고 전체 미국인들 중 절반이 넘는 이들이 그것을 보았다.

Douglas Kirkland에 관한 다음 글의 내용과 일치하지 <u>않는</u> 것은?

① 어린 시절에 *Life* 잡지에 실린 사진에 대해 아버지와 토의했다.
discussed the photographs the magazine contained with his father
② 고등학교 졸업 후 미국으로 이주하여 일자리를 찾았다.
Kirkland moved to the United States ~ found work
③ 고용될 당시 *Look* 잡지사의 역대 사진 작가 중 가장 어렸다.
When *Look* magazine hired him ~ second-youngest photographer ever
④ 1961년에 찍은 Marilyn Monroe 사진은 거의 즉시 상징적인 것이 되었다.
His photos taken of Marilyn Monroe in 1961 became iconic almost instantly.
⑤ 전체 미국인들 중 절반이 넘는 이들이 그의 포토 에세이를 보았다.
His photo essays ~ were seen by more than half of all Americans.

[왜] 정답? ✽❀❀ [정답률 93%]

Douglas Kirkland가 24살 나이에 "Look" 잡지사에 고용되었을 때, 그는 그들의 역대 사진 작가 중 두 번째로 어렸다고(their second-youngest photographer ever) 했으므로 가장 어렸다고 한 ③은 글의 내용과 일치하지 않는다.

[왜] 오답?

① 어린 시절에 *Life* 잡지에 실린 사진에 대해 아버지와 토의했다. (discussed the photographs the magazine contained with his father)

② 고등학교 졸업 후 미국으로 이주하여 사진 스튜디오에서 일자리를 찾았다. (Kirkland moved to the United States ~ found work)

④ 1961년에 찍은 Marilyn Monroe 사진은 거의 즉시 상징적인 것이 되었다. (His photos taken of Marilyn Monroe in 1961 became iconic almost instantly.)

⑤ 전체 미국인들 중 절반이 넘는 이들이 그의 포토 에세이를 보았다. (His photo essays ~ were seen by more than half of all Americans.)

---

27 정답 ④ ＊반려동물 먹이 요리 교실

Yummy Paws: Pet Food Cooking Class /
냠냠 발: 반려동물 먹이 요리 교실 /

관계부사 (cooking class 수식)
Join us / for an exciting pet food cooking class / where you will learn / how to create healthy and delicious pumpkin biscuits / for your furry friends! //
참여하세요 / 신나는 반려동물 먹이 요리 교실에 / 당신이 배울 수 있는 / 건강하고 맛있는 호박 비스킷을 만드는 방법을 / 여러분의 털북숭이 친구를 위해 //

When: / 2:00 p.m.–4:00 p.m., Every Sunday, December, 2024 /
언제 / 2024년 12월 매주 일요일 오후 2시-4시 / ①의 단서 12월에 일요일마다 2시간씩 진행

Where: / Green Park Community Center, Room 5 /
어디서 / Green Park Community Center, 5호실 /

Registration / 등록 /

• Register online / at www.yummypawsclass.com. //
온라인으로 등록하세요 / www.yummypawsclass.com에서 //

• Limited to 10 participants / for each class /
참여 인원을 10명으로 제한 / 각 수업당 / ②의 단서 수업당 인원은 10명으로 제한함

Fee / 수업료 /

• $30 per participant / (Full payment is required / when registering.) // ③의 단서 등록 시 전액 지불해야 함
참가자당 30달러 / (전액 지불해야 합니다 / 등록 시) //

• The fee includes / all ingredients. //
수업료는 포함합니다 / 모든 재료를 //

Note / 유의 사항 /

• Additional recipes / available for free /
추가 레시피는 / 무료로 이용 가능 / ④의 단서 추가 레시피는 무료로 이용 가능함

• For safety reasons, / no pets are allowed. //
안전상의 이유로 / 반려동물 출입이 허용되지 않습니다 //

• For a refund, / cancel at least 48 hours before the class. //
환불을 위해서는 / 최소한 수업 48시간 전까지 취소하세요 // ⑤의 단서 환불을 위해서는 수업 48시간 전까지 취소해야 함

• furry ⓐ 털이 많은 • register ⓥ 등록하다 • limit ⓥ 제한하다
• participant ⓝ 참가자 • payment ⓝ 지불 • require ⓥ 요구하다
• ingredient ⓝ 재료 • additional ⓐ 추가적인
• available ⓐ 이용 가능한 • safety ⓝ 안전 • refund ⓝ 환불

냠냠 발: 반려동물 먹이 요리 교실

여러분의 털북숭이 친구를 위해 건강하고 맛있는 호박 비스킷을 만드는 방법을 배울 수 있는 신나는 반려동물 먹이 요리 교실에 참여하세요!

언제: 2024년 12월 매주 일요일 오후 2시–4시
어디서: Green Park Community Center, 5호실
등록
• www.yummypawsclass.com에서 온라인으로 등록하세요.
• 각 수업당 참여 인원을 10명으로 제한
수업료
• 참가자당 30달러(등록 시 전액 지불해야 합니다.)
• 수업료는 모든 재료를 포함합니다.
유의 사항
• 추가 레시피는 무료로 이용 가능
• 안전상의 이유로 반려동물 출입이 허용되지 않습니다.
• 환불을 위해서는 최소한 수업 48시간 전까지 취소하세요.

Yummy Paws: Pet Food Cooking Class에 관한 다음 안내문의 내용과 일치하지 않는 것은?
① 12월에 일요일마다 2시간씩 진행된다. 2:00 p.m.-4:00 p.m., Every Sunday, December
② 각 수업당 참여 인원이 10명으로 제한된다. Limited to 10 participants for each class
③ 수업료는 등록 시 전액 지불해야 한다. Full payment is required when registering.
④ 추가 레시피는 별도로 구매해야 한다. Additional recipes available for free
⑤ 환불을 위해서는 수업 48시간 전까지 취소해야 한다. For a refund, cancel at least 48 hours before the class.

왜 정답? ✱✱✱ [정답률 96%]
추가 레시피는 무료로 이용 가능하다고 (Additional recipes available for free) 했으므로, 추가 레시피는 별도로 구매해야 한다는 ④이 안내문의 내용과 일치하지 않는다.

왜 오답?
① 12월에 매주 일요일 2시에서 4시로 2시간씩 진행된다. (2:00 p.m.-4:00 p.m., Every Sunday, December)

---

② 각 수업당 참여 인원이 10명으로 제한된다. (Limited to 10 participants for each class)
③ 수업료는 등록 시에 전액 지불해야 한다. (Full payment is required when registering.)
⑤ 환불을 위해서는 최소한 수업 48시간 전까지 취소해야 한다. (For a refund, cancel at least 48 hours before the class.)

28 정답 ⑤ ＊K-Pop 커버 댄스 대회

2024 K-Pop Cover Dance Contest / 2024 K-Pop 커버 댄스 대회 /
Good news / for K-Pop fans in Canada! //
희소식 / 캐나다의 K-Pop 팬을 위한 //
  to부정사의 의미상 주어
It's time / for your dance team / to show your talents / at this contest! //
시간입니다 / 여러분의 댄스 팀이 / 재능을 보여줄 수 있는 / 이 대회에서 //

When & Where / 언제 & 어디서 /

• Date: / November 29th, 2024 / ①의 단서 하루만 진행됨
날짜 / 2024년 11월 29일 /

• Time: / 7 p.m.–9 p.m. / 시간 / 오후 7시-9시 /

• Location: / So Merry Theatre / 장소 / So Merry Theatre /

Judging Criteria: / Cooperation, Artistic Skill, Costume /
심사 기준 / 협동, 예술적 기술, 무대의상 / ②의 단서 심사 기준에 관객 호응은 없음

Prize / 상품 /

• Top 3 teams will receive / a $200 gift certificate. //
상위 세 팀은 받을 것입니다 / 200달러 상품권을 // ③의 단서 상위 세 팀만 상품권을 받음
                                                    형용사적 용법 (the chance 수식)
• The winning team will have the chance / to visit Korea's top management agencies. //
우승 팀은 기회를 가질 것입니다 / 한국의 최고 매니지먼트 회사를 방문할 //

Application / 신청 /

• A cover dance video / should not be more than 4 minutes long. // ④의 단서 영상 길이는 4분이 넘지 않아야 함
커버 댄스의 영상 길이는 / 4분이 넘지 않아야 합니다 //
                                                    '~을 통해서'
• Submit the video, / along with your application, / via our website / by November 3rd. // ⑤의 단서 신청서와 함께 영상을 웹사이트에 제출해야 함
영상을 제출하세요 / 신청서와 함께 / 우리 웹사이트를 통해 / 11월 3일까지 //

For more information, / visit www.2024kpopcontest.com. //
더 많은 정보를 위해서 / www.2024kpopcontest.com에 방문하세요 //

• talent ⓝ 재능 • contest ⓝ 대회 • judge ⓥ 심사하다
• criterion ⓝ 기준 (pl. criteria) • cooperation ⓝ 협동
• costume ⓝ 의상 • gift certificate 상품권
• management agency 매니지먼트 회사[기획사] • application ⓝ 신청
• submit ⓥ 제출하다

2024 K-Pop 커버 댄스 대회

캐나다의 K-Pop 팬을 위한 희소식! 이 대회에서 여러분의 댄스팀이 재능을 보여 줄 때입니다!
언제 & 어디서
• 날짜: 2024년 11월 29일
• 시간: 오후 7시 – 9시
• 장소: So Merry Theatre
심사 기준: 협동, 예술적 기술, 무대의상
상품
• 상위 세 팀은 200달러 상품권을 받을 것입니다.
• 우승 팀은 한국의 최고 매니지먼트 회사를 방문할 기회를 가질 것입니다.
신청
• 커버 댄스의 영상 길이는 4분이 넘지 않아야 합니다.
• 신청서와 함께 영상을 11월 3일까지 우리 웹사이트를 통해 제출하세요.
더 많은 정보를 위해서 www.2024kpopcontest.com에 방문하세요.

2024 K-Pop Cover Dance Contest에 관한 다음 안내문의 내용과 일치하는 것은?

① 2일 동안 진행된다. November 29th, 2024
② 심사 기준에 관객 호응이 포함된다. Judging Criteria: Cooperation, Artistic Skill, Costume
③ 상위 열 팀은 200달러 상품권을 받을 것이다. Top 3 teams will receive a $200 gift certificate.
④ 커버 댄스의 영상 길이는 4분이 넘어야 한다. A cover dance video should not be more than 4 minutes long.
⑤ 신청서와 함께 영상을 웹사이트를 통해 제출해야 한다. Submit the video, along with your application, via our website

왜 정답? [정답률 86%]

신청하려면 신청서와 함께 커버 영상을 웹사이트를 통해 제출해야 하므로(Submit the video, along with your application, via our website) 안내문의 내용과 일치하는 것은 ⑤이다.

왜 오답?

① 하루 동안 진행된다. (November 29th, 2024)
② 심사 기준은 협동, 예술적 기술, 무대의상이므로 관객 호응은 포함되지 않는다. (Judging Criteria: Cooperation, Artistic Skill, Costume)
③ 상위 세 팀만 200달러 상품권을 받을 것이다. (Top 3 teams will receive a $200 gift certificate.)
④ 커버 댄스의 영상 길이는 4분이 넘지 않아야 한다. (A cover dance video should not be more than 4 minutes long.)

29 정답 ④ *디지털 은유와 언어적 은유의 차이

다음 글의 밑줄 친 부분 중, 어법상 틀린 것은?

Digital technologies are essentially related to metaphors, / but digital metaphors are different from linguistic ① ones / in important ways. //
(= metaphors)
디지털 기술은 근본적으로 은유와 관련되어 있지만 / 디지털 은유는 언어적 은유와 다르다 / 중요한 면에서 //

Linguistic metaphors are passive, / in the sense that the audience needs to choose / to actively enter the world / proposed by metaphor. //
('~라는 점에서', 과거분사구 (the world 수식))
언어적 은유는 수동적이다 / 독자가 선택할 필요가 있다는 점에서 / 세계에 적극적으로 들어가도록 / 은유에 의해 제시된 //

In the Shakespearean metaphor "time is a beggar," / the audience is unlikely to understand the metaphor /
"시간은 구걸하는 자다"라는 셰익스피어의 은유에서 / 독자는 은유를 이해할 것 같지 않다 /

without cognitive effort / and without further ② engaging Shakespeare's prose. //
(병렬 구조, 부사, 동명사)
인지적인 노력 없이는 / 그리고 셰익스피어의 산문을 더 끌어들이지 않고는 //

Technological metaphors, / on the other hand, / are active (and often imposing) /
기술적 은유는 / 반면에 / 능동적이다 (그리고 종종 강요적이다) /

in the sense that they are realized / in digital artifacts that are actively doing things, / forcefully ③ changing a user's meaning horizon. //
(수동태, 주격 관계대명사, 분사구문을 이끄는 현재분사)
그것이 실현된다는 점에서 / 능동적으로 일을 하는 디지털 인공물에서 / 사용자의 의미의 지평을 강력하게 바꾸면서 //

Technological creators / cannot generally afford / to require their potential audience / to wonder how the metaphor works; /
(require의 목적격 보어 (to부정사))
기술적인 창작자는 / 일반적으로 여유가 없다 / 그들의 잠재적인 독자에게 요구할 / 어떻게 은유가 작용하는지 궁금해하도록 /

normally the selling point is / ④ what(→ that) the usefulness of the technology / is obvious at first glance. //
(명사절 접속사 (보어 역할); 단서 뒤에 완전한 문장이 왔으므로 명사절 접속사 that 자리임)
일반적으로 매력은 ~이다 / 기술의 유용성이 / 첫눈에 분명하다는 것 //

Shakespeare, / on the other hand, / is beloved / in part / because the meaning of his works is not immediately obvious / and ⑤ requires some thought on the part of the audience. //
(수동태 동사, 단수 주어, 병렬 구조 (단수 동사))
셰익스피어는 / 반면에 / 사랑받는다 / 부분적으로는 / 그의 작품의 의미가 즉각적으로 분명하지 않고 / 독자 측에서 어느 정도의 생각을 요구하기 때문에 //

- essentially (ad) 근본적으로
- metaphor (n) 은유
- linguistic (a) 언어적인
- passive (a) 수동적인
- propose (v) 제시하다
- beggar (n) 구걸하는 사람
- cognitive (a) 인지적인
- engage (v) 사로잡다
- prose (n) 산문
- imposing (a) 강요[강압]적인
- artifact (n) 인공물
- forcefully (ad) 강력하게
- horizon (n) 지평선
- selling point 매력, 장점
- at first glance 첫눈에
- immediately (ad) 즉각적으로

디지털 기술은 근본적으로 은유와 관련되어 있지만, 디지털 은유는 중요한 면에서 언어적 은유와 다르다. 언어적 은유는 독자가 은유에 의해 제시된 세계에 적극적으로 들어가도록 선택할 필요가 있다는 점에서 수동적이다. "시간은 구걸하는 자다"라는 셰익스피어의 은유에서 독자는 인지적인 노력 없이는 그리고 셰익스피어의 산문을 더 끌어들이지 않고는 은유를 이해할 것 같지 않다. 반면에 기술적 은유는 사용자의 의미의 지평을 강력하게 바꾸면서 능동적으로 일을 하는 디지털 인공물에서 그것이 실현된다는 점에서 능동적이다. (그리고 종종 강요적이다.) 기술적인 창작자는 일반적으로 그들의 잠재적인 독자에게 어떻게 은유가 작용하는지 궁금해하도록 요구할 여유가 없고, 일반적으로 매력은 기술의 유용성이 첫눈에 분명하다는 것이다. 반면에 셰익스피어는 부분적으로는 그의 작품의 의미가 즉각적으로 분명하지 않고 독자 측에서 어느 정도의 생각을 요구하기 때문에 사랑받는다.

왜 정답? [정답률 66%]

④ 관계대명사 what 뒤에 완전한 절이 왔다!

~ normally the selling point is / ④ what(→ that) the usefulness of the technology is obvious at first glance. //
(주어, 동사, 명사절 접속사 that 필요, 완전한 2형식 문장)

(단서) 밑줄이 선행사를 포함하는 관계대명사 what에 있으므로
(발상) 주격과 목적격 관계대명사 뒤에는 주어나 목적어가 빠진 불완전한 절이 와야 한다.
(해결) 하지만 what 뒤에 주어(the usefulness of the technology), 동사(is), 보어(obvious)가 이어지며 완전한 2형식 문장을 이룬다. 따라서 what을 명사절 접속사 that으로 바꿔야 한다.
(개념) 선행사를 포함하는 관계대명사 what은 불완전한 절을 이끈다.

왜 오답?

① 대명사는 앞에서 반복되는 명사를 찾아 수를 일치시킨다.

Digital technologies are essentially related to metaphors, / but digital metaphors are different from linguistic ① ones / in important ways. //
(복수 주어, 복수 동사, = metaphors)

문맥상 linguistic ones는 digital metaphors와는 다른 유형인 linguistic metaphors를 가리킨다. 따라서 metaphors를 대신하여 복수 대명사 ones가 알맞게 쓰였다.

② 전치사 뒤에는 명사에 해당하는 어구가 온다.

~ without cognitive effort / and without further ② engaging Shakespeare's prose. //
(전치사, 부사, 동명사)

전치사 without 뒤에 명사에 해당하는 동명사 engaging이 알맞게 쓰였다.

③ 분사구문의 현재분사는 능동의 의미를 나타낸다.

Technological metaphors, / on the other hand, / are active (and often imposing) / in the sense that they are realized / in digital artifacts that are actively doing things, / forcefully ③ changing a user's meaning horizon. //

주절의 주어는 Technological metaphors이며 이것이 '강력하게 사용자의 의미의 지평을 변화시켰다(forcefully changing a user's meaning horizon)'는 능동의 의미이므로, 현재분사 changing이 알맞게 쓰였다.

⑤ 동사는 주어에 그 수를 일치시킨다.

~ because the meaning of his works is not immediately obvious / and ⑤ requires some thought on the part of the audience. //

because로 시작하는 부사절에서 단수 동사인 is와 requires가 병렬 구조를 이루고 있다. 수 일치를 해야 하는 핵심 주어는 단수인 the meaning이므로 requires는 알맞게 쓰였다.

30 정답 ③ ＊집단 지성을 통한 문제 해결

다음 글의 밑줄 친 부분 중, 문맥상 낱말의 쓰임이 적절하지 않은 것은? [3점]

Herbert Simon won his Nobel Prize / for recognizing our limitations / in information, time, and cognitive capacity. //
Herbert Simon은 그의 노벨상을 받았다 / 우리의 한계를 인지한 것으로 / 정보, 시간, 그리고 인지적인 능력에서 //

As we lack the resources / to compute answers independently, / we ① distribute the computation across the population / and solve the answer slowly, / generation by generation. //
우리는 자원이 부족하기 때문에 / 독립적으로 해답을 계산하기 위한 / 우리는 전체 인구에 걸쳐 계산을 분배하고 / 해답을 천천히 풀어낸다 / 세대에 걸쳐 //

Then / all we have to do / is socially learn the right answers. //
그러면 / 우리가 해야 하는 모든 것은 / 올바른 해답을 사회적으로 배우는 것이다 //

단서 1 우리는 해답만 사회적으로 배우게 됨

You don't need to understand / how your computer or toilet works; / you just need to be able to use the interface and flush. //
여러분은 이해할 필요가 없다 / 여러분의 컴퓨터 혹은 변기가 어떻게 작동하는지 / 여러분은 단지 (컴퓨터의) 인터페이스를 사용할 수 있고 (변기의) 물을 내릴 수 있기만 하면 된다 //

All that needs to be ② transmitted / is which button to push / — essentially how to interact with technologies / rather than how they work. //
단서 2 우리는 기술과 상호 작용하는 방법만 알면 됨
전달될 필요가 있는 모든 것은 / 어떤 버튼을 눌러야 하는지 / 근본적으로 기술과 상호 작용하는 방법이다 / 어떻게 그것들이 작동하는지보다는 /

And so instead of holding ③ less(→ more) information / than we have mental capacity for / and indeed need to know, /
그렇다면 더 적은(→ 더 많은) 정보를 가지는 것 대신에 / 우리가 정신적 수용을 할 수 있는 것보다 / 그리고 정말로 알아야 할 필요가 있는 것보다 /

we could dedicate our large brains / to a small piece of a giant calculation. //
우리는 우리의 큰 두뇌를 바칠 수 있다 / 거대한 계산의 작은 조각에 //

We understand things / well enough to ④ benefit from them, / but all the while / we are making small calculations / that contribute to a larger whole. //
우리는 사물을 이해한다 / 그것들로부터 이득을 얻기에 충분히 잘 / 하지만 그러면서 / 우리는 작은 계산을 하고 있다 / 더 큰 전체에 기여하는 //

We are just doing our part / in a larger computation / for our societies' ⑤ collective brains. //
우리는 단지 우리의 역할을 하고 있는 것이다 / 더 큰 계산에서 / 우리 사회의 집합적인 두뇌를 위한 //

- limitation ⓝ 한계 · cognitive ⓐ 인지적인 · capacity ⓝ 능력
- independently ⓐⓓ 독립적으로 · distribute ⓥ 분배하다
- computation ⓝ 계산 · generation ⓝ 세대
- flush ⓥ (변기의) 물을 내리다 · transmit ⓥ 전달하다
- essentially ⓐⓓ 근본적으로 · dedicate ⓥ 바치다, 헌신하다
- calculation ⓝ 계산 · benefit ⓥ 이득을 얻다
- contribute to ~에 기여하다 · collective ⓐ 집합적인

Herbert Simon은 정보, 시간, 그리고 인지적인 능력에서 우리의 한계를 인지한 것으로 그의 노벨상을 받았다. 우리는 독립적으로 해답을 계산하기 위한 자원이 부족하기 때문에 우리는 전체 인구에 걸쳐 계산을 ① 분배하고 세대에 걸쳐 해답을 천천히 풀어낸다. 그러면 우리가 해야 하는 모든 것은 올바른 해답을 사회적으로 배우는 것이다. 여러분은 여러분의 컴퓨터 혹은 변기가 어떻게 작동하는지 이해할 필요가 없고 여러분은 단지 인터페이스를 사용할 수 있고 (변기의) 물을 내릴 수 있기만 하면 된다. ② 전달될 필요가 있는 모든 것은 어떤 버튼을 눌러야 하는지, 근본적으로 어떻게 그것들이 작동하는지보다는 기술과 상호 작용하는 방법이다. 그렇다면 우리가 정신적 수용을 할 수 있는 것과 정말로 알아야 할 필요가 있는 것보다 ③ 더 적은(→ 더 많은) 정보를 가지는 것 대신에 우리는 우리의 큰 두뇌를 거대한 계산의 작은 조각에 바칠 수 있다. 우리는 그것들로부터 ④ 이득을 얻기에 충분할 정도로 사물을 잘 이해하지만 그러면서 우리는 더 큰 전체에 기여하는 작은 계산을 하고 있다. 우리는 우리 사회의 ⑤ 집합적인 두뇌를 위한 더 큰 계산에서 단지 우리의 역할을 하고 있는 것이다.

＞왜 정답? ✱✱✽ [정답률 75%]

③ less 더 적은

그렇다면 우리가 정신적 수용을 할 수 있는 것보다 정말로 알아야 할 필요가 있는 것보다 ③ 더 적은(더 많은) 정보를 가지는 것 대신에 우리는 우리의 큰 두뇌를 거대한 계산의 작은 조각에 바칠 수 있다.

➡ 인간은 인지적인 한계로 인해 세대에 걸쳐 해답을 내므로, 올바른 해답을 사회적으로 배워야 한다고 했다. 즉, 기술의 원리는 몰라도 기술을 사용하는 방법만 알면 된다는 것이다. 이처럼 우리는 모든 것을 알 필요가 없으므로, 우리가 알아야 하는 정보량보다 '더 적은' 정보가 아니라 '더 많은' 정보를 가지지 않고 작은 계산에 두뇌를 할애할 수 있다. ▶ less를 more(더 많은)와 같은 반의어로 바꿔야 함

＞왜 오답?

① distribute 분배하다

우리는 독립적으로 해답을 계산하기 위한 자원이 부족하기 때문에 우리는 전체 인구에 걸쳐 계산을 ① 분배하고 세대에 걸쳐 해답을 천천히 풀어낸다.

➡ 독립적으로 계산하는 것이 아닌, 전체 인구에 걸쳐서 복잡한 계산을 끌어낸다는 의미이므로, 계산을 '분배한다'라는 표현은 적절하다. ▶ distribute는 문맥에 맞음

② transmitted 전달되는

② 전달될 필요가 있는 모든 것은 어떤 버튼을 눌러야 하는지, 근본적으로 어떻게 그것들이 작동하는지보다는 기술과 상호 작용하는 방법이다.

➡ 우리는 올바른 해답을 사회적으로 배우기 때문에, 우리에게 '전달될' 필요가 있는 정보라는 표현은 적절하다. ▶ transmitted는 문맥에 맞음

④ benefit 이득을 얻다

우리는 그것들로부터 ④ 이득을 얻기에 충분할 정도로 사물을 잘 이해하지만 그러면서 우리는 더 큰 전체에 기여하는 작은 계산을 하고 있다.

➡ 우리가 기술과 상호 작용하는 방법을 알고 이를 이용할 수 있으므로, 사물로부터 '이득을 얻기에' 충분할 정도로 사물을 잘 이해한다는 표현은 적절하다.
▶ benefit은 문맥에 맞음

⑤ collective 집합적인

우리는 우리 사회의 ⑤ **집합적인** 두뇌를 위한 더 큰 계산에서 단지 우리의 역할을 하고 있는 것이다.

→ 더 큰 계산은 '개별적인' 두뇌가 아닌 우리 사회의 '집합적인' 두뇌를 위해 사회 전체적으로 이루어진다. ▶ collective는 문맥에 맞음

31 정답 ② *변신술로 사냥하는 문어

The best defence / <u>most species of octopus have</u>(목적격 관계대명사절 (defence 수식)) / is to stay hidden <u>as much as possible</u>('가능한 한 ~하게') / and do their own hunting at night. //

최고의 방어는 / 대부분의 문어 종(種)이 가진 / 가능한 한 많이 숨어 있는 것과 / 밤에 그들 자신의 사냥을 하는 것이다 //

So / <u>to find one</u>(명사적 용법 (주어) = octopus) in full view in the shallows in daylight / <u>was</u>(단수 동사) a surprise / for two Australian underwater photographers. //

그래서 / 낮에 얕은 곳에서 전체가 보이는 문어를 발견한 것은 / 놀라운 일이었다 / 두 명의 호주 수중 사진작가들에게 //

Actually, / what they saw at first / was a flounder. //

사실 / 그들이 처음에 봤던 것은 / 넙치였다 (단서 1 처음에는 문어가 아니라 넙치를 발견했음)

<u>It</u> was <u>only when they looked again</u> / <u>that</u> they saw a medium-sized octopus, / <u>with all eight of its arms folded</u>(병렬 구조 (with 분사구문)) / and <u>its two eyes staring upwards</u> / to **create the illusion**. // (It ~ that … 강조 구문 (only when ~ again 강조))

오직 그들이 다시 봤을 때서야 / 그들은 중간 크기의 문어를 보았고 / 그것의 여덟 개의 모든 팔이 접혀 있었고 / 그것의 두 눈이 위쪽으로 응시하고 있었다 / 착시를 만들기 위해 // (단서 2 문어는 색깔과 패턴을 바꿔 다른 생물체로 변신할 수 있음)

An octopus has a big brain, excellent eyesight and the ability to change colour and pattern, / and this one was using these assets / <u>to turn</u>(부사적 용법 (목적)) itself into a completely different creature. //

문어는 큰 뇌, 뛰어난 시력과 색깔과 패턴을 바꾸는 능력을 지니고 있고 / 이것은 이러한 이점을 사용하고 있었다 / 스스로를 완전히 다른 생물체로 바꾸기 위해 //

Many more of this species / <u>have been found</u>(현재완료 수동태) since then, / and there are now photographs of octopuses / <u>that</u>(주격 관계대명사) could be said to be transforming into sea snakes. //

이 종의 더 많은 것들이 / 그때 이후로 발견되어 왔으며 / 지금은 문어의 사진이 있다 / 바다뱀으로 변신하는 중이라고 말해질 수 있는 //

And while they mimic, they hunt / — <u>producing</u>(분사구문을 이끄는 현재분사) the spectacle of, / say, / (단서 3 문어는 다른 생물체를 모방하는 동안에 사냥함)

그리고 그들이 모방하는 동안에 그들은 사냥을 한다 / 이것은 광경을 만들어낸다 / 말하자면 /

a flounder / suddenly <u>developing</u> an octopodian arm, / <u>sticking</u> it down a hole / and <u>grabbing</u> whatever's hiding there. // (병렬 구조 (a flounder를 수식하는 현재분사))

넙치가 / 갑자기 문어 다리 같은 팔을 펼치며 / 그것을 구멍으로 찔러 넣어 / 그곳에 숨어 있는 무엇이든지 움켜잡는 // (단서 4 넙치로 변신한 채 갑자기 다리를 꺼내 사냥함)

- defence ⓝ 방어 · species ⓝ (생물의) 종 · shallows ⓝ 얕은 곳
- fold ⓥ 접다 · stare ⓥ 응시하다 · eyesight ⓝ 시력
- asset ⓝ 이점, 자산 · creature ⓝ 생물체 · transform ⓥ 변신하다
- spectacle ⓝ 광경 · octopodian ⓐ 문어와 같은
- stick ⓥ 찔러 넣다 · grab ⓥ 움켜잡다 · broad ⓐ 넓은
- illusion ⓝ 착시[착각] · territory ⓝ 영토, 지역

대부분의 문어 종(種)이 가진 최고의 방어는 가능한 한 많이 숨어 있는 것과 밤에 그들 자신의 사냥을 하는 것이다. 그래서 낮에 얕은 곳에서 전체가 보이는 문어를 발견한 것은 두 명의 호주 수중 사진작가들에게는 놀라운 일이었다. 사실 그들이 처음 봤던 것은 넙치였다. 오직 그들이 다시 봤을 때서야 그들은 중간 크기의 문어를 보았고 **착시를 만들기** 위해 그것의 여덟 개의 모든 팔이 접혀 있었고 그것의 두 눈이 위쪽으로 응시하고 있었다. 문어는 큰 뇌, 뛰어난 시력과 색깔과 패턴을 바꾸는 능력을 지니고 있고, 이것은 스스로를 완전히 다른 생물체로 바꾸기 위해 이러한 이점을 사용하고 있었다. 이 종의 더 많은 것들이 그때 이후로 발견되어 왔으며 지금은 바다뱀으로 변신하는 중이라고 말해질 수 있는 문어의 사진이 있다. 그리고 그들이 모방하는 동안에 그들은 사냥을 한다. 이것은 말하자면 넙치가 갑자기 문어 다리 같은 팔을 펼치며 그것을 구멍으로 찔러 넣어 그곳에 숨어 있는 무엇이든지 움켜잡는 광경을 만들어낸다.

| 문제 풀이 순서 | ★★★ [정답률 40%]

1st 빈칸이 포함된 문장과 그 앞 문장을 읽고, 빈칸에 들어갈 말에 대한 단서를 얻는다.

빈칸 문장 앞	Actually, what they saw at first was a flounder. 단서 1
	사실 그들이 처음에 봤던 것은 넙치였다. 단서 1
빈칸 문장	It was only when they looked again that they saw a medium-sized octopus, with all eight of its arms folded and its two eyes staring upwards to _____.
	오직 그들이 다시 봤을 때서야 그들은 중간 크기의 문어를 보았고 _____ 위해 그것의 여덟 개의 모든 팔이 접혀 있었고 그것의 두 눈이 위쪽으로 응시하고 있었다.

→ 그들이 처음에는 넙치를 봤지만, 문어가 '무엇'을 하기 위해 자신의 모든 팔을 접고 두 눈을 위쪽으로 응시하고 있었다고 했으므로, 단서 빈칸 문장에 나온 문어는 넙치를 모방했음을 알 수 있다. 발상 나머지 글을 읽으며 문어가 '어떤' 상황에서 '왜' 넙치를 모방했는지 파악해야 한다.

2nd 글의 내용을 종합해서 빈칸에 들어갈 적절한 말을 찾는다.

- 문어는 다른 생물체로 변신할 수 있음 단서 2
- 문어는 다른 생물체를 모방하는 동안에 사냥함 단서 3
- 넙치로 변신한 채 갑자기 다리를 꺼내 사냥함 단서 4

→ 문어는 다른 생명체를 모방할 수 있고, 모방하는 동안에 사냥한다고 했다. 예를 들어, 넙치로 변신하여 먹잇감이 '착각하게' 한 채로, 갑자기 다리를 꺼내 사냥하는 방식이다.

▶ 즉, 문어는 사냥할 때 자신이 다른 생명체로 보이도록 ② '착시를 만들기' 위해 넙치처럼 모든 팔을 접고 두 눈이 위쪽으로 응시하고 있던 것이다.

| 선택지 분석 |

① 문어의 두 눈이 위쪽으로 응시하고 있던 것은 시야를 확보하기 위한 것이 아니라 넙치를 모방한 것이다.
② 다른 생명체인 넙치를 모방하여 먹잇감이 착각하도록 하기 위함이었다.
③ 문어의 사냥 과정에서 순간을 포착하여 사냥한다는 내용이 아니다.
④ 문어가 넙치를 모방한 상태에서 먹잇감이 숨어 있는 곳에 다리를 찔러넣어 움켜잡는다고 했을 뿐, 넙치를 모방한 것 자체가 은신처를 찾기 위한 행동은 아니다.
⑤ 문어가 사냥하기 위해 모방을 한다는 내용이지, 영토를 표시한다는 것은 언급되지 않았다.

32 정답 ② *고통 인식의 주관성

How much we suffer / relates to **how we frame the pain in our mind**. //

우리가 얼마나 고통받는지는 / 우리가 고통을 우리의 마음에서 어떻게 구성하는지와 관련된다 //

When 1500m runners push <u>themselves</u>(재귀대명사 (재귀 용법)) / into extreme pain / to win a race / — <u>their muscles screaming</u> / and <u>their lungs exploding with oxygen deficit</u>, / they don't psychologically suffer much. // (병렬 구조 (주어가 생략되지 않은 분사구문)) (단서 1 달리기 선수는 극심한 육체적 고통에도 정신적으로는 덜 고통받음)

1500미터 달리기 선수가 스스로를 밀어붙일 때 / 극심한 고통으로 / 경주에서 이기기 위해 / 그들의 근육이 비명을 지르고 / 그들의 폐가 산소 부족으로 폭발하면서 / 그들은 정신적으로 많이 고통받지 않는다 //

In fact, / **ultra-marathon runners** / — those people **who** are crazy
<small>복수 주어 / 주격 관계대명사</small>
enough to push themselves / beyond the normal boundaries of
human endurance, /
사실 / 울트라 마라톤 선수들은 / 즉, 스스로를 밀어붙일 만큼 충분히 열정적인 사람들은 / 인
간 인내력의 정상적 경계를 넘어서 /
<small>분사구문을 이끄는 현재분사</small>
covering distances of 50-100km or more over many hours, / **talk**
<small>복수 동사</small>
about making friends with their pain. // 단서 2 고통과 친구가 되는 울트라
마라톤 선수
많은 시간 동안 50에서 100킬로미터 혹은 그 이상의 거리를 가지만 / 그들의 고통과 친구가
되는 것에 대해 이야기한다 //

When a patient has paid / for some form of passive back pain
therapy / and the practitioner pushes deeply / into a painful part
of a patient's back / to mobilise it, /
한 환자가 돈을 지불했고 / 특정 형태의 수동적 등 통증 치료에 / 의사가 깊게 눌렀을 때 / 환자
등의 아픈 부분을 / 그것을 풀어 주기 위해 / 단서 3 치료가 가치 있다고 생각하는 환자는
그에 따른 고통도 좋은 것으로 느낌
<small>calls의 목적어와 목적격 보어</small>
the patient calls **that good pain** / if he or she believes / this type
<small>of + 추상 명사 → 형용사</small>
of deep pressure treatment will be **of value**, / even though the
practitioner is pushing / right into the patient's sore tissues. //
환자는 그것을 좋은 아픔이라고 부른다 / 만약 그 또는 그녀가 믿는다면 / 이러한 종류의 깊은
압박 치료법이 가치가 있을 것이라고 / 비록 의사가 누르고 있을지라도 / 환자의 아픈 조직을
직접적으로 //

- suffer ⓥ 고통받다　· explode ⓥ 폭발하다　· deficit ⓝ 부족, 결핍
- psychologically [ad] 정신적으로　· boundary ⓝ 경계
- endurance ⓝ 인내력　· distance ⓝ 거리　· passive ⓐ 수동적인
- therapy ⓝ 치료　· practitioner ⓝ 의사
- mobilise ⓥ 풀어주다, 움직이게 하다　· pressure ⓝ 압박
- treatment ⓝ 치료법　· sore ⓐ 아픈　· tissue ⓝ (근육) 조직
- frame ⓥ 구성하다　· expert ⓝ 전문가

우리가 얼마나 고통받는지는 <u>우리가 고통을 우리의 마음에서 어떻게 구성하는</u>
<u>지</u>와 관련된다. 1500미터 달리기 선수가 경주에서 이기기 위해 그들의 근육이
비명을 지르고 그들의 폐가 산소 부족으로 폭발하면서, 스스로를 극심한 고통
으로 밀어붙일 때, 그들은 정신적으로 많이 고통받지 않는다. 사실 울트라 마라
톤 선수들은 즉, 인간 인내력의 정상적 경계를 넘어서 스스로를 밀어붙일 만큼
충분히 열정적인 사람들은 많은 시간 동안 50에서 100킬로미터 혹은 그 이상의
거리를 가지만 그들의 고통과 친구가 되는 것에 대해 이야기한다. 한 환자가 특
정 형태의 수동적 능 봉승 지료에 논을 지물했고 의사가 그것을 쑬어 수기 위해
환자 등의 아픈 부분을 깊게 눌렀을 때, 비록 의사가 환자의 아픈 조직을 직접
적으로 누르고 있을지라도, 만약 그 또는 그녀가 이러한 종류의 깊은 압박 치료
법이 가치가 있을 것이라고 믿는다면, 환자는 그것을 좋은 아픔이라고 부른다.

> 다음 빈칸에 들어갈 말로 가장 적절한 것을 고르시오.
> ① how long we have been in pain 지속 시간과 고통의 관계는 언급되지 않았음
> 　우리가 얼마나 오래 고통스러워했는지
> ② how we frame the pain in our mind 우리가 고통을 어떻게 인식하느냐에
> 　우리가 고통을 우리의 마음에서 어떻게 구성하는지 따라 고통의 정도가 달라짐
> ③ how fast we can recover from past pain
> 　과거의 고통에서 얼마나 빨리 회복할 수 있는지 고통의 회복은 언급되지 않았음
> ④ what part of our body we train regularly 신체 부위별 훈련에 따른
> 　우리가 어떤 신체 부위를 규칙적으로 훈련하는지 고통은 언급되지 않았음
> ⑤ what treatment we receive from experts
> 　전문가로부터 어떤 치료를 받는지 치료법과 고통의 관계는 언급되지 않았음

| 문제 풀이 순서 | ★★★ [정답률 58%]

1st 빈칸이 포함된 문장을 읽고, 빈칸에 들어갈 말에 대한 단서를 얻는다.

| 빈칸 문장 | How much we suffer relates to _____.
우리가 얼마나 고통받는지는 _____ 와 관련된다.

➡ '우리가 얼마나 고통받는지(고통의 정도)'는 '무엇'과 관련된다고 했다. 단서
빈칸 문장이 글의 맨 앞에 있으므로 주제문일 가능성이 높다. 글의 나머지 부분에서
'무엇'에 따라 고통의 정도가 달라지는지를 구체적으로 설명하거나 예시를 제시할
것이다. 발상

2nd 글의 나머지 부분을 읽고, 글의 내용을 종합해서 빈칸에 들어갈 내용을 찾는다.

- 1500m 달리기 선수가 경주에서 스스로를 극심한 고통으로 밀어붙여도 그들은 정신적으로 많이 고통받지 않는다. 단서 1
- 울트라 마라톤 선수들은 많은 시간 동안 먼 거리를 달리면서도 그들의 고통과 친구가 되는 것에 대해 이야기한다. 단서 2
- 환자가 압박 치료법이 가치가 있을 것이라고 믿는다면, 압박 시 느끼는 아픔을 좋은 아픔이라고 생각한다. 단서 3

➡ 1500m 달리기 선수, 울트라 마라톤 선수, 환자를 예시로 들며 '가치가 있다'라고 생각하는 일에 따르는 고통은 아무렇지 않은 것으로, 심지어 좋은 고통으로도 여긴다고 했다. 즉, 우리가 고통을 어떻게 인식하고 받아들이는지에 따라 극심한 고통도 긍정적으로 여길 수 있다는 내용이다.

▶ 우리가 얼마나 고통받는지는 ② '우리가 고통을 우리의 마음에서 어떻게 구성하는지'와 관련된다.

| 선택지 분석 |
① 고통의 지속 기간에 따라 고통의 정도가 달라진다는 내용이 아니다.
② 우리가 고통을 마음에서 어떻게 인식하는지에 따라 고통의 정도가 달라진다는 내용이다.
③ 과거의 고통이나 고통의 회복은 언급되지 않았다.
④ 어떤 신체 부위를 훈련하는지에 따라 고통의 정도가 달라진다는 내용이 아니다.
⑤ 압박 치료법이 가치가 있다고 느끼면 그에 따른 고통을 긍정적으로 여긴다고 했을 뿐, 어떤 치료법을 받는지에 따라 고통의 정도가 달라진다는 내용이 아니다.

2024.10
10회

33　정답 ①　⭐ 2등급 대비 [정답률 48%]

＊가격을 이용한 소비자 심리 조작

When I worked for a large electronics company / **that**
<small>주격 관계대명사</small>
manufactured laser and ink-jet printers, / I soon discovered /
why there are often three versions of many consumer goods. //
내가 큰 전자 회사에서 일했을 때 / 레이저와 잉크젯 프린터를 생산했던 / 나는 곧 발견했다 /
많은 소비 상품의 세 가지 버전이 종종 있는 이유를 //
<small>부사절 접속사 (조건)</small>
If the manufacturer makes / only one version of its product, /
<small>주격 관계대명사 / might have p.p.: ~했을지도 모른다</small>
people **who** bought it / **might have been** willing to spend more
money, / so the company is losing some income. //
만약 생산자가 만든다면 / 그 제품의 오직 한 가지 버전만 / 그것을 구매했던 사람들은 / 기꺼
이 더 많은 돈을 쓰려고 했을 수도 있어서 / 회사는 일부 수입을 잃을 것이다 //
단서 1 두 개의 버전이 제공되면 덜 비싼 모델을 구입함
If the company offers two versions, / **one** with more features
<small>one: 하나 the other: 나머지 하나</small>
and more expensive than **the other**, / people will compare the
two models / and still buy the less expensive one. //
만약 그 회사가 두 버전을 제공하는데 / 하나가 다른 것보다 더 많은 기능과 더 비싼 가격을 가
진다면 / 사람들은 두 모델을 비교하고 / 여전히 덜 비싼 것을 살 것이다 //
<small>비교급 강조 부사</small>
But / if the company introduces a third model / with **even** more
features and more expensive than the other two, / **sales** of the
<small>복수 주어 / 복수 동사</small>
second model **go** up; /
하지만 / 만약 그 회사가 세 번째 모델을 출시한다면 / 나머지 두 개보다 훨씬 더 많은 기능과
더 비싼 가격을 가진 / 두 번째 모델의 판매가 증가하는데 /

many people like the features of the most expensive model, /
but not the price. // 단서 2 세 번째 모델이 제공되면 그보다는 덜 비싼 중간 모델을 구입함
왜냐하면 많은 사람들은 가장 비싼 모델의 기능을 좋아하지만 / 그것의 가격을 좋아하지는 않
기 때문이다 // 단서 3 가장 싼 모델보다는 기능이 많고 가장 비싼 모델보다는 가격이 덜 비싼
중간 제품을 사게 됨
The middle item has more features / than the least expensive
one, / and it is less expensive than the fanciest model. //
중간 제품은 더 많은 기능이 있고 / 가장 저렴한 제품보다 / 가장 고급 모델보다는 덜 비싸다 //
<small>being이 생략된 분사구문 / 현재완료 수동태</small>
They buy the middle item, / **unaware** that / they **have been**
manipulated by the presence of the higher-priced item. //
그들은 중간 제품을 구입한다 / 알지 못한 채 / 자신이 더 비싼 가격의 제품의 존재에 의해 조
종되었다는 것을 //

- manufacture ⓥ 생산[제조]하다　　・goods ⓝ 상품
- be willing to-v 기꺼이 ~하려고 하다　　・income ⓝ 수입
- feature ⓝ 기능　　・fancy ⓐ 고급의　　・unaware ⓐ 알지 못하는
- manipulate ⓥ 조종하다　　・presence ⓝ 존재
- high-volume ⓐ 대량의　　・low-margin ⓐ 가격이 싼, 수익이 적은
- trick ⓥ 속이다　　・unnecessary ⓐ 불필요한　　・fool ⓥ 속이다
- repeatedly ⓐⓓ 반복적으로

내가 레이저와 잉크젯 프린터를 생산했던 큰 전자 회사에서 일했을 때 나는 많은 소비 상품의 세 가지 버전이 종종 있는 이유를 곧 발견했다. 만약 생산자가 그 제품의 오직 한 가지 버전만 만든다면 그것을 구매했던 사람들은 기꺼이 더 많은 돈을 쓰려고 했을 수도 있어서 회사는 일부 수입을 잃을 것이다. 만약 그 회사가 두 버전을 제공하는데 한 버전이 나머지보다 더 많은 기능과 더 비싼 가격을 가진다면, 사람들은 두 모델을 비교하고 여전히 덜 비싼 것을 살 것이다. 하지만 만약 그 회사가 나머지 두 개보다 훨씬 더 많은 기능과 더 비싼 가격을 가진 세 번째 모델을 출시한다면 두 번째 모델의 판매가 증가하는데, 왜냐하면 많은 사람들은 가장 비싼 모델의 기능을 좋아하지만 그것의 가격을 좋아하지는 않기 때문이다. 중간 제품은 가장 저렴한 제품보다 더 많은 기능이 있고 가장 고급 모델보다는 덜 비싸다. 그들은 자신이 **더 비싼 가격의 제품의 존재에 의해 조종되었다**는 것을 알지 못한 채 중간 제품을 구입한다.

다음 빈칸에 들어갈 말로 가장 적절한 것을 고르시오. [3점]

① manipulated by the presence of the higher-priced item
더 비싼 세 번째 제품의 존재로 인해 중간 제품을 사도록 소비자들의 결정이 유도됨
더 비싼 가격의 제품의 존재에 의해 조종된
② persuaded by a high-volume, low-margin strategy
싼 가격으로 대량 판매하는 전략에 의해 설득된　싼 가격으로 대량 판매하는 전략은 언급되지 않았음
③ tricked to keep purchasing unnecessary products
불필요한 제품을 계속 구매하도록 속은　소비자들이 반복해서 불필요한 제품을 구매하는 내용은 없음
④ fooled by the wrong information on the price
잘못된 가격 정보에 속아 넘어간　잘못된 가격 정보는 언급되지 않았음
⑤ exposed to a discounted price repeatedly
할인된 가격에 반복적으로 노출된　제품 가격의 할인은 언급되지 않았음

왜 2등급? 일반적으로 알려진 잘못된 소비 습관들(박리다매에 현혹되는 것, 불필요한 제품 구매)이 선택지에 있어서 선입견으로 답을 고르기 쉬운 2등급 대비 문제이다. 세 가지 제품이 등장하기 때문에 제품 간 '비교'가 정답의 단서임을 파악해야 한다.

| 문제 풀이 순서 |

1st 빈칸이 포함된 문장과 그 앞 문장을 읽고, 빈칸에 들어갈 말에 대한 단서를 얻는다.

빈칸 문장 앞	The middle item has more features than the least expensive one, and it is less expensive than the fanciest model. 중간 제품은 가장 저렴한 제품보다 더 많은 기능이 있고 가장 고급 모델보다는 덜 비싸다. **단서3**
빈칸 문장	They buy the middle item, unaware that they have been _____. 그들은 자신이 _____ 것을 알지 못한 채 중간 제품을 구입한다.

➡ 중간(두 번째) 제품은 가장 저렴한 모델보다 기능은 더 많지만 가장 비싼 모델보다는 가격이 저렴하다고 했다. **단서** 소비자들이 '무엇'을 알지 못한 채 중간 제품을 선택하게 되는지 살펴봐야 한다. **발상**

2nd 글의 나머지 부분을 읽고, 빈칸에 들어갈 적절한 말을 찾는다.

┌ 기능 및 가격: 모델 A < 모델 B ⇨ 덜 비싼 '모델 A'를 선택 **단서1**
└ 기능 및 가격: 모델 A < 모델 B < 모델 C ⇨ 중간인 '모델 B'의 판매가 증가함 **단서2**

➡ 선택지가 두 가지(모델 A와 B)뿐일 때는 덜 비싼 모델 A가 선택된다. 하지만 세 가지(모델 A, B, C)일 때는 A보다는 많은 기능과 C보다는 저렴한 가격으로 인해 앞의 경우에서 선택되지 않았던 모델 B의 판매가 증가한다.

▶ 더 비싼 모델 C의 존재로 인해 처음에는 선택되지 않았던 모델 B가 선택을 더 많이 받게 되는 것이므로, 소비자들은 ① '더 비싼 가격의 제품의 존재에 의해 조종된' 것을 모른 채 중간 제품을 구매하는 것이다.

| 선택지 분석 |

① 더 비싼 세 번째 제품의 존재로 인해 중간 제품을 사도록 소비자들의 결정이 조종되는 것이다.
② 제품별 가격 비교는 언급되었지만, 대량 판매는 언급되지 않았다.
③ 세 가지 모델이 있을 때 소비자들이 중간 제품을 선택하게 된다고 했을 뿐, 소비자들이 반복해서 불필요한 제품을 구매하게 된다는 내용이 아니다.
④ 가격 비교를 통해 중간 제품을 사도록 조종된다는 것이지, 제품의 가격 자체를 속인다는 내용이 아니다.
⑤ 제품 가격의 할인은 언급되지 않았다.

---

34 정답 ② ＊기후 변화 픽션의 소멸

On-screen, / climate disaster is everywhere you look, / but
　　　　　　　　　　　　　　　　　　　　관계부사절 (everywhere 수식)
the scope of the world's climate transformation / may just as
quickly eliminate the climate-fiction genre / **단서1** 세계의 기후 변화는 기후 픽션 장르를 없앨 것임
영화상 / 기후 재난은 여러분이 보는 어디에나 있지만 / 세계의 기후 변화의 범위는 / 그것만큼이나 빠르게 기후 픽션 장르를 없앨지도 모르고 /
　　　　　　　　　　　　　　　　　형용사적 용법 (any effort 수식)
— indeed eliminate any effort / to tell the story of warming,
　계속적 용법의 주격 관계대명사
/ which could grow too large and too obvious / even for
Hollywood. //
실제로 노력도 없애 버린다 / 온난화 이야기를 하고자 하는 / 그것은 너무 커지고 너무 명백해질 것이다 / 할리우드에서조차 //

You can tell stories 'about' climate change / while it still seems
a marginal feature of human life. // **단서2** 기후 변화의 영향을 별로 느끼지 못할 때는 그것에 대한 이야기를 할 수 있음
여러분은 기후 변화에 관한 이야기를 할 수 있을 것이다 / 기후 변화가 여전히 인간 삶의 주변적인 특징처럼 보이는 동안에 //

But when the temperature rises / by three or four more degrees,
　　　　　　　　　　　　　　　　　　　　　　　과거분사
'거의 ~하지 않다'
/ hardly anyone will be able to feel isolated / from its impacts. //
하지만 기온이 상승할 때는 / 3도 혹은 4도 이상 / 아무도 고립되었다고 느낄 수 없을 것이다 / 그것의 영향으로부터 //

And so as climate change expands across the horizon, / it may
cease to be a story. //
그리고 기후 변화가 지평선을 넘어 확장될 때 / 그것은 이야기가 되기를 멈출 것이다 //
　　　　　　　　　　　　　　　　　　　　　목적격 관계대명사절
Why watch or read climate fiction / about the world you can see
plainly out your own window? // **단서3** 현실에서 바로 볼 수 있는 기후 변화에 대한 픽션은 볼 필요 없음
왜 기후 픽션을 보거나 읽는가 / 당신이 자신의 창문 밖으로 뚜렷하게 볼 수 있는 세상에 대한 //
　　　　　　　　　　　　　　　　현재분사구 (stories 수식)
At the moment, / stories illustrating global warming / can still
　　　　　　　　　　　　　　　　　　　　　지시형용사
offer an escapist pleasure, / even if that pleasure often comes /
in the form of horror. //
지금 당장은 / 지구 온난화를 묘사하는 이야기가 / 현실 도피적인 즐거움을 여전히 제공할 수 있다 / 비록 그 즐거움이 종종 올지라도 / 공포의 형태로 //
　　　　　　　　　　　　　　　　　　목적어절 접속사
But when we can no longer pretend / that climate suffering is
　　　　　　　　　　　　　　　　　　　　　stop -ing: ~하는 것을 멈추다
distant / — in time or in place / — we will stop pretending about
　　　　　　　　　　　병렬 구조
it / and start pretending within it. //
하지만 우리가 더 이상 가장할 수 없을 때 / 기후 고통이 멀리 있다고 / 시간적으로 또는 장소적으로 / 우리는 그것에 대해 가장하는 것을 멈추고 / 그것 내에서 가장하기 시작할 것이다 //

- disaster ⓝ 재난　　・scope ⓝ 범위　　・transformation ⓝ 변화
- indeed ⓐⓓ 실제로　　・eliminate ⓥ 없애다　　・obvious ⓐ 명백한
- marginal ⓐ 주변적인　　・isolated ⓐ 고립된　　・impact ⓝ 영향
- expand ⓥ 확장하다　　・horizon ⓝ 지평선
- plainly ⓐⓓ 뚜렷하게　　・escapist ⓐ 현실 도피(주의)의
- pretend ⓥ 가장하다　　・suffering ⓝ 고통　　・distant ⓐ 먼
- resolve ⓥ 해결하다　　・cease ⓥ 멈추다, 중단하다
- reborn ⓐ 다시 태어난　　・overestimated ⓐ 과대평가된
- plot ⓝ 줄거리　　・complex ⓐ 복잡한

영화상 기후 재난은 여러분이 보는 어디에나 있지만, 세계의 기후 변화의 범위는 그것만큼이나 빠르게 기후 픽션 장르를 없앨지도 모르고 실제로 온난화 이야기를 하고자 하는 노력도 없애 버리는데, 그것은 할리우드에서조차 너무 커지고 너무 명백해질 것이다. 기후 변화가 여전히 인간 삶의 주변적인 특징처럼 보이는 동안에 여러분은 그것에 '관한' 이야기를 할 수 있을 것이다. 하지만 기온이 3도 혹은 4도 이상 상승할 때는 아무도 그것의 영향으로부터 고립되었다고 느낄 수 없을 것이다. 그리고 기후 변화가 지평선을 넘어 확장될 때, **그것은 이야기가 되기를 멈출 것이다.** 왜 여러분 자신의 창문 밖으로 뚜렷하게 볼 수 있는 세상에 대한 기후 픽션을 보거나 읽겠는가? 비록 그 즐거움이 종종 공포의 형태로 올지라도 지금 당장은 지구 온난화를 묘사하는 이야기가 현실 도피적인 즐거움을 여전히 제공할 수 있다. 하지만 우리가 더 이상 기후 고통이 시간적으로 또는 장소적으로 멀리 있다고 가장할 수 없을 때 우리는 그것에 대해 가장하는 것을 멈추고 그것 내에서 가장하기 시작할 것이다.

다음 빈칸에 들어갈 말로 가장 적절한 것을 고르시오. [3점]

① it may resolve on its own 저절로 해결될 수 있는 것은 아님
그것은 저절로 해결될지도 모른다
② it may cease to be a story 기후 변화가 현실이 되면 그것은 더 이상
그것은 이야기가 되기를 멈출 것이다 허구(이야기)가 아님
③ a forgotten genre will be reborn 기후 픽션 장르가 없어질 것이라는 내용임
잊혀진 장르가 다시 태어날 것이다
④ its impact will be overestimated 기후 변화가 실제보다 과대평가된다는 내용은 없음
그것의 영향은 과대평가될 것이다
⑤ the story's plot will become complex
이야기의 줄거리가 복잡해질 것이다 기후 변화 상황이 복잡해진다는 내용이 아님

| 문제 풀이 순서 | ★★★ [정답률 37%]

1st 빈칸이 포함된 문장과 그 앞 문장을 읽고, 빈칸에 들어갈 말에 대한 단서를 얻는다.

빈칸 문장 앞	But when the temperature rises by three or four more degrees, hardly anyone will be able to feel isolated from its impacts. 하지만 기온이 3도 혹은 4도 이상 상승할 때는 아무도 그것의 영향으로부터 고립되었다고 느낄 수 없을 것이다.
빈칸 문장	And so as climate change expands across the horizon, _____. 그리고 기후 변화가 지평선을 넘어 확장될 때,

➡ 기온이 3~4도 오르면 모두가 그 영향을 느낄 것이라고 했고, 단서 기후 변화가 지평선을 넘어 확장된다면, 즉 기후 변화가 세계적으로 확장된다면 '어떤' 일이 일어날지를 나머지 글에서 확인해야 한다. 발상

2nd 글의 내용을 종합해서 빈칸에 들어갈 내용을 찾는다.

• 세계의 기후 변화는 빠르게 기후 픽션 장르를 없앨지도 모른다. 단서1
• 기후 변화가 인간 삶의 주변적이라면 그것에 '관한' 이야기를 할 수 있다. 단서2
• 사람들이 기후 변화를 현실에서 명백하게 볼 수 있다면 왜 기후 픽션을 보거나 읽겠는가? 단서3

➡ 세계의 기후 변화(현실) ↔ 기후 픽션 장르(이야기, 허구)
기후 변화가 우리의 삶에서 '주변적'이라는 것은 현실과는 거리가 멀기 때문에 허구적인 이야기로 만들 수 있다는 것이다. 그러나, 기후 변화가 현실이 되면 그것은 더 이상 허구적인 이야기가 아니기 때문에 기후 픽션을 볼 이유가 없을 것이다.
▶ 따라서 기후 변화가 지평선을 넘어 확장될 때, ② '그것(기후 변화)은 이야기가 되기를 멈출 것이고' 현실이 될 것이다.

| 선택지 분석 |

① 기후 변화가 저절로 해결될 수 있다는 내용이 아니다.
② 기후 변화가 점점 더 현실이 되면 그것은 더 이상 허구의 이야기가 아니게 된다.
③ 앞으로 기후 변화를 다루는 픽션 장르는 없어질 것이라는 내용이지, 잊혀진 장르가 다시 태어난다는 내용이 아니다.
④ 기후 변화가 현실이 되면서 픽션이 없어질 것이라는 내용이지, 기후 변화의 영향이 과장되었다는 내용이 아니다. 픽션의 특징 중 허구와 과장을 구별하기! 꿀팁
⑤ 기후 변화 픽션의 줄거리, 즉 기후 변화 상황이 복잡해진다는 내용이 아니다.

---

35 정답 ④ ⭐ 2등급 대비 [정답률 41%]

＊무관심과 부주의로 커진 물 위기

다음 글에서 전체 흐름과 관계 없는 문장은?

Today, / the water crisis is political / — **which** is to say, / not inevitable or beyond our capacity to fix — / and, therefore, functionally elective. // 단서1 물 위기는 정치적이며 선택적임
주격 관계대명사
오늘날 / 물 위기는 정치적이다 / 즉 ~ 이다 / 피할 수 없는 것이 아니며 우리의 바로잡을 수 있는 능력을 넘어서지 않는 / 따라서 기능적으로 선택적이다 //

① **That** is one reason / **it** is nevertheless distressing: / an abundant resource / **made scarce** / **through governmental neglect and indifference, bad infrastructure and contamination, and careless urbanization.** // 단서2 풍족한 자원이 여러 정치적 무관심으로 부족하게 됨
지시대명사(앞 문장 전체) = the water crisis 과거분사구(an abundant resource 수식)
그것이 한 가지 이유이다 / 그럼에도 불구하고 그것이 괴로운 / 즉, 풍족한 자원이 / 부족하게 되었다 / 정부의 소홀함과 무관심, 열악한 사회 기반 시설과 오염, 부주의한 도시화를 통해 //

② There is no need for a water crisis, / in other words, / but we have one anyway, / and aren't doing much **to address** it. //
부사적 용법(목적)
물 위기가 있어야 할 필요가 없다 / 다시 말해서 / 하지만 우리는 그것을 겪고 있고 / 그것을 해결하기 위해 많은 일을 하고 있지 않다 // 단서3 물 위기를 해결하려는 노력이 부족함

③ Some cities lose more water to leaks / than they deliver to homes: / even in the United States, / leaks and theft account for an estimated loss of 16 percent of freshwater; / in Brazil, the estimate is 40 percent. // 단서4 누수로 인해 물 손실을 겪고 있는 도시들
일부 도시들은 누수로 인해 더 많은 물을 잃는다 / 그들이 주택으로 공급하는 것보다 / 즉, 미국에서조차 / 누수와 도난은 담수의 16퍼센트의 추정된 손실을 차지하고 / 브라질에서는 그 추정치가 40퍼센트이다 //

④ The numerical comparison of available resources / seems to exaggerate the real-world water shortage problem / that we face. //)
단수 주어 단수 동사 목적격 관계대명사
(가용 자원의 수치 비교는 / 실제 세계의 물 부족 문제를 과장하는 것처럼 보인다 / 우리가 직면한 //)

⑤ **Seen in both cases,** / as everywhere, / the selective scarcity / clearly highlights have-and-have-not inequities, /
분사구문(앞에 Being이 생략됨) 단서5 모든 곳에서 선택적인 물 부족은 불평등을 나타냄
양쪽의 경우에서 보여지듯이 / 모든 곳에서처럼 / 선택적 부족 / 분명히 가진 자와 가지지 못한 자의 불평등을 분명히 강조하고 있다 /

leaving 2.1 billion people without safe drinking water / and 4.5 billion without proper sanitation / worldwide. //
병렬 구조
이것은 21억 명을 안전한 식수가 없는 채로 둔다 / 그리고 45억 명을 적절한 위생이 없는 채로 (둔다) / 전 세계적으로 //

• inevitable ⓐ 피할 수 없는 • capacity ⓝ 능력
• functionally ⓐᵈ 기능적으로 • distressing ⓐ 괴로움을 주는
• abundant ⓐ 풍족한 • scarce ⓐ 부족한 • neglect ⓝ 소홀함
• indifference ⓝ 무관심 • contamination ⓝ 오염
• urbanization ⓝ 도시화 • address ⓥ (문제 등을) 다루다
• leak ⓝ 누수 • theft ⓝ 도난 • account for ~을 차지하다
• estimate ⓝ 추정(치) • numerical ⓐ 수치[숫자]의
• exaggerate ⓥ 과장하다 • shortage ⓝ 부족
• selective ⓐ 선택적인 • inequity ⓝ 불평등 • sanitation ⓝ 위생

오늘날, 물 위기는 피할 수 없는 것이 아니며 우리의 바로잡을 수 있는 능력을 넘어서지 않는, 즉 정치적인 것이고 따라서 기능적으로 선택적이다. ① 그것은 그럼에도 불구하고 그것이 괴로운 한 가지 이유이다. 즉, 풍족한 자원이 정부의 소홀함과 무관심, 열악한 사회 기반 시설과 오염, 부주의한 도시화를 통해 부족하게 되었다. ② 다시 말해서 물 위기가 있어야 할 필요가 없지만 어쨌든 우리는 그것을 겪고 있고 그것을 해결하기 위해 많은 일을 하고 있지 않다. ③ 일부 도시들은 그들이 주택으로 공급하는 것보다 누수로 인해 더 많은 물을 잃는다. 즉, 미국에서조차 누수와 도난은 담수의 16퍼센트의 추정된 손실을 차지하고 브라질에서는 그 추정치가 40퍼센트이다. (④ 가용 자원의 수치 비교는 우리

가 직면한 실제 세계의 물 부족 문제를 과장하는 것처럼 보인다.) ⑤ 양쪽의 경우에서 보여지듯이 모든 곳에서처럼 선택적 부족이 가진 자와 가지지 못한 자의 불평등을 분명히 강조하고, 이것은 전 세계적으로 21억 명을 안전한 식수가 없고 45억 명을 적절한 위생이 없는 채로 둔다.

왜 2등급? 물 부족 문제의 원인이 인간이라는 점을 다양한 문장으로 표현하여 무관한 문장을 구분하기 어려운 2등급 대비 문제이다. 정답 문장과 그 앞 문장이 서로 연결되는 것처럼 보이지만, 결국 글의 주제와는 확연히 어긋나므로 이를 잘 파악해야 한다.

왜 정답·오답?

- **글의 앞부분:** 오늘날 물 위기는 정치적이고 선택적이므로, 피할 수 있고 바로잡을 수 있는 문제라고 말함
- ① 풍족한 자원이 정부의 무관심, 사회의 부주의를 통해 부족하게 되었기 때문에, 물 위기가 선택적임에도 불구하고 괴로운 것임
  - ▶ 물 위기가 정치적이고 선택적임에도 발생하는 이유, 즉 정부의 무관심과 사회의 부주의를 나열하므로, ①은 무관한 문장이 아님
- ② 물 위기가 있을 필요가 없고, 그것을 겪고 있음에도 이를 해결하기 위한 노력이 부족함
  - ▶ 물 위기가 필연적이지 않지만 우리는 그것을 겪고 있으며, 우리의 해결 노력이 부족하다는 문제를 제기하므로, ②은 무관한 문장이 아님
- ③ 일부 도시들은 그들이 주택으로 공급하는 것보다 누수로 인해 더 많은 물을 잃음
  - ▶ 미국과 브라질의 예를 들며, 누수나 도난과 같이 충분히 해결할 수 있는 원인에 의해 물을 잃어버리고 있음을 설명하므로, ③은 무관한 문장이 아님
- ④ 가용 자원의 수치 비교는 우리가 직면한 실제 물 부족 문제를 과장하는 것처럼 보임
  - ▶ 물 위기의 원인과 문제 상황이 이어지다가, 가용 자원의 수치 비교가 물 부족 문제를 과장하는 것처럼 보인다는 내용은 전체 글의 흐름과 맞지 않으므로, ④이 무관한 문장임
- ⑤ 선택적 부족이 가진 자와 가지지 못한 자의 불평등을 분명히 강조하며 많은 세계 인구에 과로 관련된 문제를 초래함
  - ▶ 이러한 선택적인 물 위기는 빈부격차를 심화시키며, 전 세계적으로 많은 이들에게 물 관련 문제를 초래한다는 내용이 자연스럽게 이어지므로, ⑤은 무관한 문장이 아님

＊글의 흐름

1. **도입:** 물 위기는 정치적이고 선택적인 문제임
2. **전개:** 정부의 무관심과 사회의 부주의로 인해 물 부족이라는 문제가 일어나고 있으며 우리의 해결 노력이 부족함
3. **부연(예시):** 미국, 브라질 등 일부 도시에서 누수로 많은 물이 손실됨
4. **결론:** 물 부족의 선택적 현상은 빈부격차를 심화시키며 전 세계적으로 물 관련 문제를 초래함

---

36 정답 ③ ★ 1등급 대비 [정답률 36%]

＊사회적 압박이 개인에 미치는 영향

As individuals, / our ability **to thrive** / depended on **how well we navigated relationships in a group.** //
형용사적 용법 (our ability 수식) / 간접의문문
개인으로서 / 성공하려는 우리의 능력은 / 우리가 집단 내에서 관계를 얼마나 잘 다루는지에 달려 있었다 //

If the group valued us, / we could count on / support, resources, and probably a mate. //
If 가정법 과거
만약 그 집단이 우리를 가치 있게 여긴다면 / 우리는 기대할 수 있을 것이다 / 지원, 자원, 그리고 아마도 짝을 //
단서 1 집단이 개인을 가치 있게 여기면 그 개인은 이점을 얻음

(A) And, crucially, / they are meet to make / **that motivation feel** like it is coming from within. //
make의 목적어와 목적격 보어(원형부정사)
단서 2 they와 that motivation이 가리키는 대상이 (A) 앞에 나와야 함
그리고 결정적으로 / 그것들은 만들도록 되어있다 / 그 동기가 내부에서 나오고 있는 것처럼 느끼게 //

If we realized, / on a conscious level, / **that** we were responding to social pressure, / our performance might **come off as** grudging or cynical, / **making it less persuasive.** //
목적어절 접속사 / '~처럼 느껴지다' / 분사구문
우리가 깨닫는다면 / 의식적인 수준에서 / 우리가 사회적 압박에 반응하고 있었다는 것을 / 우리의 행동은 투덜대거나 냉소적인 것으로 나타날 수 있다 / 그것(그 동기)를 설득력이 떨어지게 만들면서 //

(B) **If it didn't,** / **we might get** none of these merits. //
If 가정법 과거 *단서 3* it은 주어진 글의 the group을 가리킴
만약 그렇지 않다면 / 우리는 그러한 이점들 중 아무것도 얻지 못할 것이다 //

It was a matter of survival, / physically and genetically. //
그것은 생존의 문제였다 / 신체적으로 그리고 유전적으로 //

Over millions of years, / the pressure selected for people / **who are sensitive to** and **skilled at** maximizing their standing. //
주격 관계대명사 / 병렬 구조
수백만 년 동안 / 그러한 압박은 사람들을 선택했다 / 자신의 지위를 최대화하는 데 민감하고 능숙한 //
단서 4 사회적 압박은 자신의 지위를 높이는 인간을 선택함

(C) The result was the development of a tendency / **to** unconsciously **monitor** / how other people in our community perceive us. //
형용사적 용법 (a tendency 수식)
그 결과는 경향의 발달이었다 / 무의식적으로 관찰하는 / 우리 공동체의 다른 사람들이 우리를 어떻게 인식하는지 //
단서 5 (B)에서 언급한 사회적 압박의 결과가 제시됨

We process that information / in the form of self-esteem / and such related emotions as pride, shame, or insecurity. //
우리는 그 정보를 처리한다 / 자존감의 형태로 / 그리고 자존심, 수치심 또는 불안 같은 관련된 감정(의 형태로) //

These emotions compel us / **to do more of what** makes our community value us / and **less of what** doesn't. //
compel의 목적격 보어 (to부정사) / 병렬 구조('비교급 + of + 선행사를 포함하는 관계대명사')
이러한 감정들은 우리에게 강요한다 / 우리의 공동체가 우리를 가치 있게 여기도록 만드는 것을 더 많이 하고 / 그렇지 않은 것을 덜 하도록 //

- thrive ⓥ 성공하다
- navigate ⓥ 다루다, 길을 찾다
- value ⓥ 가치 있게 여기다
- count on ~을 기대하다
- mate ⓝ 짝
- crucially ⓐ결정적으로
- conscious ⓐ 의식적인
- cynical ⓐ 냉소적인
- persuasive ⓐ 설득력 있는
- merit ⓝ 이점
- physically ⓐ신체적으로
- genetically ⓐ유전적으로
- select for ~을 선택하다
- sensitive ⓐ 민감한
- skilled ⓐ 능숙한
- maximize ⓥ 최대화하다
- standing ⓝ 지위
- tendency ⓝ 경향
- unconsciously ⓐ 무의식적으로
- perceive ⓥ 인식하다
- self-esteem ⓝ 자존감
- pride ⓝ 자존심
- shame ⓝ 수치심
- insecurity ⓝ 불안
- compel ⓥ 강요하다

개인으로서 성공하려는 우리의 능력은 우리가 집단 내에서 관계를 얼마나 잘 다루는지에 달려 있었다. 만약 그 집단이 우리를 가치 있게 여긴다면 우리는 지원, 자원, 그리고 아마도 짝을 기대할 수 있을 것이다. (B) 만약 그렇지 않다면, 우리는 그러한 이점들 중 아무것도 얻지 못할 것이다. 그것은 신체적으로 그리고 유전적으로 생존의 문제였다. 수백만 년 동안 그러한 압박은 자신의 지위를 최대화하는 데 민감하고 능숙한 사람들을 선택했다. (C) 그 결과는 우리 공동체의 다른 사람들이 우리를 어떻게 인식하는지 무의식적으로 관찰하는 경향의 발달이었다. 우리는 자존감 그리고 자존심, 수치심 또는 불안 같은 관련된 감정의 형태로 그 정보를 처리한다. 이러한 감정들은 우리에게 우리의 공동체가 우리를 가치 있게 여기도록 만드는 것을 더 많이 하고 그렇지 않은 것을 덜 하도록 강요한다. (A) 그리고 결정적으로 그것들은 그 동기가 내부에서 나오고 있는 것처럼 그것을 느끼게 만들도록 되어 있다. 우리가 사회적 압박에 반응하고 있었다는 것을 의식적인 수준에서 깨닫는다면, 우리의 행동은 그것(그 동기)을 설득력이 떨어지게 만들면서 투덜대거나 냉소적인 것으로 나타날 수 있다.

주어진 글 다음에 이어질 글의 순서로 가장 적절한 것을 고르시오. [3점]

- ① (A) — (C) — (B) (A)의 '그 동기'에 대한 언급이 주어진 글에 없음
- ② (B) — (A) — (C) (B)에서 언급된 내용의 결과를 (C)에서 설명하고 있음
- ③ (B) — (C) — (A) 집단이 개인을 가치 있게 여기면 그 개인은 이점을 얻음 - (B) 그렇지 않으면 그런 이점은 없으며 생존하지 못함 - (C) 그 결과, 타인의 인식을 관찰하는 경향을 발전시키면서 자존감 등의 감정들이 나타나고 집단에 가치 있는 행동을 하도록 만들어짐 - (A) 그 감정들로 인해 자신이 하는 행동의 동기가 내적인 것처럼 느끼게 함
- ④ (C) — (A) — (B)
- ⑤ (C) — (B) — (A) (B)는 주어진 글과 반대되는 경우이므로 주어진 글 바로 뒤에 와야 함

왜 1등급? 주어진 글과 연결되는 문단은 쉽게 찾을 수 있지만, 이후 문단의 지시어와 대응하는 확실한 단어를 찾기 어렵고, 내용의 인과 관계를 자세히 살펴봐야 하는 1등급 대비 문제이다.

| 문제 풀이 순서 |

1st 각 문단의 내용을 파악하고, 글의 논리적인 순서를 추론한다.

┌ **주어진 글:** 개인으로서 성공하려는 우리의 능력은 우리가 집단 내에서 관계를 얼마나 잘 다루는지에 달려 있었다. 만약(If) 그 집단이 우리를 가치 있게 여겼다면 우리는 지원, 자원, 그리고 아마도 짝을 기대할 수 있었을 것이다.

➡ **주어진 글 뒤:** 집단 내 관계 형성과 개인의 성공이 어떤 관련이 있는지를 설명할 것이다. If 가정법 문장이 집단 내에서 가치 있다고 인정받는 경우를 소개하므로 이와 반대되는 경우가 뒤에 이어질 수도 있다.

┌ **(A):** 그리고 결정적으로 그것들(they)은 그 동기(that motivation)가 내부에서 나오고 있는 것처럼 그것을 느끼게 만들도록 되어있다. 우리가 사회적 압박에 반응하고 있었다는 것을 의식적인 수준에서 깨닫는다면, 우리의 행동은 그것(그 동기)을 설득력이 떨어지게 만들면서 투덜대거나 냉소적인 것으로 나타날 수 있다.

➡ **(A) 앞:** they와 that motivation이 가리키는 내용이 앞에 나와야 한다.
▶ 주어진 글 바로 뒤에 (A)가 올 수 없음
(A) 뒤: they나 that motivation에 관해 추가적인 내용이 나오지 않는다면 마무리에 해당할 가능성이 높다. ▶ (A)가 마지막에 올 확률이 높음

┌ **(B):** 만약 그렇지 않았다면(If it didn't), 우리는 그러한 이점들(these merits) 중 아무것도 얻지 못했을 것이다. 그것은 신체적으로 그리고 유전적으로 생존의 문제였다. 수백만 년 동안 그러한 압박은 자신의 지위를 최대화하는 데 민감하고 능숙한 사람들을 선택했다.

➡ **(B) 앞:** it과 these merits가 가리키는 대상이 앞에 나와야 한다. 주어진 글에 집단 내에서 가치 있다고 '인정받으면' 지원, 자원, 짝이라는 '이점'을 기대할 수 있다는 내용이 있으므로, it didn't는 the group didn't value us에 해당하고 지원, 자원, 짝이라는 이점들이 these merits에 해당함을 알 수 있다.
▶ (B) 앞에 주어진 글이 와야 함 (순서: 주어진 글 → (B))
(B) 뒤: 집단 내에서 가치 있다고 인정받는 것은 생존과 직결되고, 인정받아야 한다는 압박은 사람들이 지위를 최대화하도록 했으므로, 이러한 경향의 결과가 뒤에 이어질 것이다.

┌ **(C):** 그 결과(the result)는 우리 공동체의 다른 사람들이 우리를 어떻게 인식하는지 무의식적으로 관찰하는 경향의 발달이었다. 우리는 자존감 그리고 자존심, 수치심 또는 불안 같은 관련된 감정의 형태로 그 정보를 처리한다. 이러한 감정들(these emotions)은 우리에게 우리의 공동체가 우리를 가치 있게 여기도록 만드는 것을 더 많이 하고 그렇지 않은 것을 덜 하도록 강요한다.

➡ **(C) 앞:** (B)에서 사람들이 인정받아야 하는 압박을 받았다고 했는데, 이는 다른 사람들의 시선을 관찰하는 경향이 발달하는 결과(the result)로 이어졌다.
▶ (C) 앞에 (B)가 와야 함 (순서: 주어진 글 → (B) → (C))
(C) 뒤: 우리가 인정을 얻어야 한다는 압박을 통해 느끼는 감정들(these emotions)이 집단에서 가치 있게 행동하도록 강요한다고 했다. 이는 (A)에서 그 감정들(they)이 집단에서 가치 있게 행동할 동기(the motivation)가 내부에서 나오는 것처럼 느끼게 한다는 내용과 연결된다.
▶ (C) 뒤에 (A)가 와야 함 (순서: 주어진 글 → (B) → (C) → (A))

2nd 글이 한눈에 들어오도록 정리하여 정답을 확인한다.

주어진 글: 개인의 성공은 집단 내 관계 형성에 달려 있어서 집단이 우리를 가치 있게 여기면 이점들을 얻을 수 있다.

➡ **(B):** 그렇지 않으면 그런 이점들을 얻을 수 없었으며, 생존과 직결되는 이러한 압박은 지위를 최대화하도록 했다.

➡ **(C):** 그 결과로 다른 사람들의 시선을 무의식적으로 관찰하는 경향을 발전시켜 왔고, 이에 따른 감정들은 우리가 집단에서 가치 있는 행동을 하도록 만든다.

➡ **(A):** 그러한 감정들은 그 동기가 우리의 내부에서 나온 것처럼 느끼게 만들며, 만약 사회적 압박에 의해 행동한다고 우리가 의식적으로 인식하면 투덜대거나 냉소적인 태도가 나타날 수 있다.

▶ 주어진 글 다음에 이어질 글의 순서는 (B) → (C) → (A)이므로 정답은 ③임

---

37 정답 ① ＊우울증의 원인이 되는 의식의 왜곡

Conventional medicine / has long believed / **that** depression **is caused** / by an imbalance of neurotransmitters in the brain. //
명사절 접속사 / 수동태 동사
전통적인 의학은 / 오랫동안 믿어 왔다 / 우울증이 발생한다고 / 뇌의 신경 전달 물질의 불균형으로 인해 //
┗ 단서 1 우울증에 대한 전통적 의학 해석 소개

(A) However, / there is a major problem / with this explanation. //
그러나 / 중대한 문제가 있다 / 이 설명에는 //   단서 2 this explanation은 주어진 글의 내용임

This is because / the imbalance of substances in the brain / is a consequence of depression, / not its cause. // 단서 3 뇌 속 물질의 불균형은 우울증의 원인이 아니라 결과임
이것은 왜냐하면 / 뇌 속 물질의 불균형은 / 우울증의 결과이다 / (우울증의) 원인이 아니라 //

In other words, / depression causes a decrease in brain substances / such as serotonin and noradrenaline, / not a decrease in brain substances causes depression. //
다시 말해서 / 우울증이 뇌의 물질의 감소를 유발하는 것이지 / 세로토닌이나 노르아드레날린과 같은 / 뇌의 물질의 감소가 우울증을 유발하는 것이 아니다 //

(B) **If** it is not consciousness **itself**, / then the root cause of depression / is also a distortion of our state of consciousness: /
부사절 접속사 (조건) / 재귀대명사 (강조 용법)
만약 그것이 의식 그 자체가 아니라면 / 우울증의 근본 원인 / 역시 우리의 의식 상태의 왜곡이며 /
┗ 단서 4 우울증이 의식의 문제임을 부연 설명함

a consciousness / **that** has lost its sense of self and the meaning of life. //
주격 관계대명사
즉, 의식이다 / 자아감과 삶의 의미를 상실한 //

Such a disease of consciousness / may manifest **itself** / in the form of depression. //
재귀대명사 (재귀 용법)
그러한 의식의 질환이 / 명백히 나타날 수 있다 / 우울증의 형태로 //

(C) In this revised cause-and-effect, / the key is **to reframe** depression / as a problem of consciousness. //
명사적 용법 (주격 보어)
이 수정된 인과 관계에서 / 핵심은 우울증을 재구성하는 것이다 / 의식의 문제로 //
┗ 단서 5 (A)의 인과 관계(원인: 우울증, 결과: 뇌의 물질의 감소)를 가리킴

Our consciousness is a more fundamental entity / **that** goes beyond the functioning of the brain. //
주격 관계대명사
우리의 의식은 보다 근본적인 실체이다 / 뇌의 기능을 넘어서는 //

The brain / is **no more than** an organ of consciousness. //
'단지 ~일 뿐이다'
뇌는 / 의식의 기관에 지나지 않는다 //   단서 6 뇌는 의식의 기관일 뿐이라는 내용이 (B)와 연결됨

- conventional ⓐ 전통적인   - depression ⓝ 우울증
- cause ⓥ 발생시키다   - imbalance ⓝ 불균형
- explanation ⓝ 설명   - substance ⓝ 물질
- consequence ⓝ 결과   - decrease ⓝ 감소   - root ⓝ 근본
- distortion ⓝ 왜곡   - revise ⓥ 수정하다
- cause-and-effect ⓝ 인과 관계   - reframe ⓥ 재구성하다
- fundamental ⓐ 근본적인   - entity ⓝ 실체
- organ ⓝ (인체의) 기관[장기]

전통적인 의학은 우울증이 뇌의 신경 전달 물질의 불균형으로 인해 발생한다고 오랫동안 믿어 왔다. (A) 그러나 이 설명에는 중대한 문제가 있다. 이것은 왜냐하면 뇌 속 물질의 불균형은 우울증의 원인이 아니라 그것의 결과이기 때문이다. 다시 말해서, 우울증이 세로토닌이나 노르아드레날린과 같은 뇌의 물질의 감소를 유발하는 것이지 뇌의 물질의 감소가 우울증을 유발하는 것이 아니다. (C) 이 수정된 인과 관계에서, 핵심은 우울증을 의식의 문제로 재구성하는 것이다. 우리의 의식은 뇌의 기능을 넘어서는 보다 근본적인 실체이다. 뇌는 의식의 기관에 지나지 않는다. (B) 만약 그것이 의식 그 자체가 아니라면, 우울증의 근본 원인 역시 우리의 의식 상태의 왜곡이며 즉, 자아감과 삶의 의미를 상실한 의식이다. 그러한 의식의 질환이 우울증의 형태로 명백히 나타날 수 있다.

2024. 10
10회

정답 및 해설 **283**

주어진 글 다음에 이어질 글의 순서로 가장 적절한 것을 고르시오.

① (A) — (C) — (B)
② (B) — (A) — (C)
③ (B) — (C) — (A)
④ (C) — (A) — (B)
⑤ (C) — (B) — (A)

전통 의학은 우울증이 뇌 속 물질의 불균형의 원인이라고 했음 - (A) 이와 반대로 뇌 속 물질의 불균형은 우울증의 원인이 아니라 결과임 - (C) 우울증은 의식의 문제이며 뇌는 의식의 기관일 뿐임 - (B) 우울증의 근본 원인은 왜곡된 의식 상태임

의식에 대한 언급이 없는 주어진 글이 (B) 바로 앞에 올 수 없음

(C)의 '이 수정된 인과 관계'가 주어진 글에 없음

| 문제 풀이 순서 | ★★★ [정답률 42%]

1st 각 문단의 내용을 파악하고, 글의 논리적인 순서를 추론한다.

주어진 글: 전통적인(Conventional) 의학은 우울증이 뇌의 신경 전달 물질의 불균형으로 인해 발생한다고 오랫동안 믿어 왔다.

➡ **주어진 글 뒤:** 우울증과 뇌의 신경 전달 물질 불균형의 인과 관계가 현대에서는 어떻게 바뀌었는지를 설명할 것이다.

(A): 그러나 이 설명(this explanation)에는 중대한 문제가 있다. 이것은 왜냐하면 뇌 속 물질의 불균형은 우울증의 원인이 아니라 그것의 결과이기 때문이다. 다시 말해서, 우울증이 세로토닌이나 노르아드레날린과 같은 뇌의 물질의 감소를 유발하는 것이지 뇌의 물질의 감소가 우울증을 유발하는 것이 아니다.

➡ **(A) 앞:** this explanation이 무엇인지 앞에 나와야 한다. 주어진 글에 우울증이 뇌 속 물질 불균형의 결과라는 전통적인 설명이 나왔는데, (A)는 이 설명과 반대되는 인과 관계가 사실이라고 했다.
  ▶ (A) 앞에 주어진 글이 와야 함 (순서: 주어진 글 → (A))
(A) 뒤: 새롭게 수정된 인과 관계에 대한 부연 설명이 이어질 것이다.

(B): 만약 그것(it)이 의식 그 자체가 아니라면, 우울증의 근본 원인 역시 우리의 의식 상태의 왜곡이며 즉, 자아감과 삶의 의미를 상실한 의식이다. 그러한 의식의 질환이 우울증의 형태로 명백히 나타날 수 있다.

➡ **(B) 앞:** 의식 그 자체가 아니라는 it이 무엇인지 앞에 나와야 한다.
  ▶ 주어진 글과 (A) 바로 뒤에 (B)가 올 수 없음
(B) 뒤: 왜곡된 의식 상태로 우울증이 발생한다는 부연 설명을 끝으로 글이 마무리된다.

(C): 이 수정된 인과 관계(this revised cause-and-effect)에서, 핵심은 우울증을 의식의 문제로 재구성하는 것이다. 우리의 의식은 뇌의 기능을 넘어서는 보다 근본적인 실체이다. 뇌는 의식의 기관에 지나지 않는다.

➡ **(C) 앞:** this revised cause-and-effect가 가리키는 것이 앞에 나와야 한다. 전통적인 인과 관계를 수정한 내용이 (A)에 제시되었다.
  ▶ (C) 앞에 (A)가 와야 함 (순서: 주어진 글 → (A) → (C))
(C) 뒤: 우울증은 의식의 문제이며 뇌는 의식의 기관일 뿐, 의식이 근본적인 실체라고 했다. 따라서 (B)에서 의식 그 자체가 아니라는 it은 '뇌'에 해당한다. 즉, 뇌는 의식의 기관일 뿐이므로, 우울증의 원인은 뇌가 아니라 의식에 있다는 것이다.
  ▶ (C) 뒤에 (B)가 와야 함 (순서: 주어진 글 → (A) → (C) → (B))

2nd 글이 한눈에 들어오도록 정리하여 정답을 확인한다.

주어진 글: 전통 의학에서는 우울증의 원인이 뇌의 신경 전달 물질의 불균형이다.
→ **(A):** 사실 뇌 물질의 감소는 우울증의 원인이 아니라 결과이다.
→ **(C):** 우울증은 의식의 문제이며 뇌는 의식의 기관일 뿐, 의식이 근본적인 실체이다.
→ **(B):** 우울증의 근본 원인은 왜곡된 의식 상태이다.
  ▶ 주어진 글 다음에 이어질 글의 순서는 (A) → (C) → (B)이므로 정답은 ①임

---

38 정답 ④ ＊심리학도 과학이다

글의 흐름으로 보아, 주어진 문장이 들어가기에 가장 적절한 곳을 고르시오.

Instead, / they look for evidence, / to make sure / that
psychological ideas are firmly **based**, / and not just **derived** /
from generally **held** beliefs or assumptions. //
병렬 구조 / 과거분사
단서 1 그들(심리학자들)은 증거를 찾으려고 함
대신에 / 그들은 증거를 찾는다 / 확인하기 위해 / 심리학적 개념이 확고하게 기반을 두고 있는지 / 단지 도출된 것이 아니라 / 일반적으로 받아들여지는 신념이나 가정으로부터 //

The common accounts of human nature / **that** float around
in society / **are** generally a mixture of assumptions, tales and
sometimes plain silliness. //
복수 주어 / 주격 관계대명사 / 복수 동사
인간 본성에 대한 흔한 설명은 / 사회에 떠도는 / 일반적으로 가정, 이야기, 그리고 때로는 순전한 어리석음의 혼합이다 //

However, / psychology is different. //
그러나 / 심리학은 다르다 // 단서 2 인간 본성에 대한 흔한 설명과 심리학의 차이점이 이어질 것임

(①) **It** is the branch of science / that is devoted to **understanding**
people: / how and why we act as we do; / why we see things as
we do; / and how we interact with one another. //
=psychology / 동명사
단서 3 심리학은 과학의 분야임
그것은 과학의 분야이다 / 사람들을 이해하는 데 전념하는 / 즉 우리가 어떻게 그리고 왜 행동하는 대로 행동하는지 / 우리가 왜 보는 대로 사물을 보는지 / 그리고 우리가 어떻게 서로 상호작용하는지 //

(②) The key word here is 'science.' //
여기서 핵심어는 '과학'이다 //

(③) Psychologists don't depend on / opinions and hearsay, / or
the generally accepted views of society at the time, / or even the
considered opinions of deep thinkers. //
단서 4 심리학자들이 의존하지 않는 것을 나열함
심리학자들은 의존하지 않는다 / 의견과 소문 / 혹은 당대의 사회에서 일반적으로 받아들여지는 견해 / 혹은 심지어 심오한 사상가들의 숙고된 의견에 //
단서 5 증거에 기반한다는 내용이 앞에 언급되어야 함

(④) **In addition to** this evidence-based approach, / psychology
deals with fundamental processes and principles /
'~에 더하여'
이러한 증거 기반 접근법에 더하여 / 심리학은 근본적인 과정과 원리를 다룬다 /
주격 관계대명사 / '~뿐만 아니라'
that generate our rich cultural and social diversity, / **as well as**
those **shared by all human beings**. //
과거분사구 (those 수식)
우리의 풍부한 문화적 사회적 다양성을 만들어 내는 / 모든 인간에 의해 공유되는 것들뿐만 아니라 //

(⑤) These are / what modern psychology is all about. //
이것들은 / 현대 심리학이 무엇인지 보여 주는 것이다 //

• evidence ⓝ 증거   • firmly ⓐⓓ 확고하게
• derive from ~로부터 도출하다   • assumption ⓝ 가정
• account ⓝ 설명   • float ⓥ 떠돌다   • plain ⓐ 순전한
• silliness ⓝ 어리석음   • branch ⓝ 분야
• devote ⓥ 전념[헌신]하다   • hearsay ⓝ 소문
• fundamental ⓐ 근본적인   • principle ⓝ 원리
• generate ⓥ 만들어 내다   • diversity ⓝ 다양성

사회에 떠도는 인간 본성에 대한 흔한 설명은 일반적으로 가정, 이야기, 그리고 때로는 순전한 어리석음의 혼합이다. 그러나, 심리학은 다르다. (①) 그것은 사람들을 이해하는, 즉 우리가 어떻게 그리고 왜 행동하는 대로 행동하는지, 우리가 왜 보는 대로 사물을 보는지, 그리고 우리가 어떻게 서로 상호작용하는지를 이해하는 데 전념하는 과학 분야이다. (②) 여기서 핵심어는 '과학'이다. (③) 심리학자들은 의견과 소문, 혹은 당대의 사회에서 일반적으로 받아들여지는 견해, 혹은 심지어 심오한 사상가들의 숙고된 의견에 의존하지 않는다. (④ 대신에 그들은 심리학적 개념이 단지 일반적으로 받아들여지는 신념이나 가정에서 도출된 것이 아니라, 확고하게 기반을 두고 있는지 확신하기 위해 증거를 찾는다.) 이러한 증거 기반 접근법에 더하여 심리학은 모든 인간에 의해 공유되는 근본적인 과정과 원리뿐만 아니라, 우리의 풍부한 문화적 사회적 다양성을 만들어 내는 것들을 다룬다. (⑤) 이것들은 현대 심리학이 무엇인지 보여 준다.

1st 주어진 문장을 해석하고 핵심 내용과 연결어, 지시어 등을 확인한다.

Instead, they look for evidence, to make sure that psychological ideas are firmly based, and not just derived from generally held beliefs or assumptions.

대신에 그들은 심리학적 개념이 단지 일반적으로 받아들여지는 신념이나 가정에서 도출된 것이 아니라, 확고하게 기반을 두고 있는지 확신하기 위해 증거를 찾는다.

➡ **주어진 문장 앞:** 대조를 나타내는 Instead와 대명사 they가 있으므로, **단서** they가 가리키는 대상, 그리고 주어진 문장과 대조되는 내용이 앞에 언급될 것이 다. **발상**

주어진 문장 뒤: 증거에 기반한 심리학을 부연 설명할 것이다.

2nd 각 선택지의 앞뒤 흐름이 매끄러운지 확인한다.

① 의 앞 문장과 뒤 문장

앞 문장: 사회에 떠도는 인간 본성에 대한 흔한 설명은 일반적으로 가정, 이야기, 그리고 때로는 순전한 어리석음의 혼합이다, 그러나, 심리학은 다르다.

뒤 문장: 그것은 사람들을 이해하는, 즉 우리가 어떻게 그리고 왜 행동하는 대로 행동하는지, 우리가 왜 보는 대로 사물을 보는지, 그리고 우리가 어떻게 서로 상호작용하는지를 이해하는 데 전념하는 과학 분야이다.

➡ 일반적인 인간 본성에 대한 설명들과 심리학은 다르다고 말했으며, 바로 이어서 심리학은 과학 분야임을 강조했다. ▶ 주어진 문장이 ①에 들어갈 수 없음

② 의 앞 문장과 뒤 문장

앞 문장: ①의 뒤 문장과 같음

뒤 문장: 여기서 핵심어는 '과학'이다.

➡ 심리학이 과학 분야임을 설명한 앞 문장의 내용을 다시 강조한다.
▶ 주어진 문장이 ②에 들어갈 수 없음

③ 의 앞 문장과 뒤 문장

앞 문장: ②의 뒤 문장과 같음

뒤 문장: 심리학자들은 의견과 소문, 혹은 당대의 사회에서 일반적으로 받아들여지는 견해, 혹은 심지어 심오한 사상가들의 숙고된 의견에 의존하지 않는다.

➡ 심리학은 과학이므로 심리학자들이 과학적이지 않은 것들에 의존하지 않는다는 설명이 이어진다. ▶ 주어진 문장이 ③에 들어갈 수 없음

④ 의 앞 문장과 뒤 문장

앞 문장: ③의 뒤 문장과 같음

뒤 문장: 이러한 증거 기반 접근법에 더하여 심리학은 모든 인간에 의해 공유되는 근본적인 과정과 원리뿐만 아니라, 우리의 풍부한 문화적 사회적 다양성을 만들어 내는 것들을 다룬다.

➡ ④의 앞 문장에 나열된 과학적이지 않은 것들은 this evidence-based approach와 이어질 수 없다. 주어진 문장에서 they는 과학적이지 않은 것들에 의존하는 '대신에' '증거'를 찾는다고 했으므로, they는 심리학자에 해당한다. 따라서 주어진 문장은 심리학자들이 과학적이지 않은 것들에 의존하지 않는다는 ④의 앞 문장과 증거 기반 접근법이 언급된 ④의 뒤 문장을 적절히 이어준다.
▶ 주어진 문장이 ④에 들어가야 함

⑤ 의 앞 문장과 뒤 문장

앞 문장: ④의 뒤 문장과 같음

뒤 문장: 이것들은 현대 심리학이 무엇인지 보여 준다.

➡ 증거 기반의 심리학에 대한 부연 설명 후에 이것이 바로 현대 심리학이라고 하며 글을 마무리한다. ▶ 주어진 문장이 ⑤에 들어갈 수 없음

---

39 정답 ② ✪ 2등급 대비 [정답률 26%]

＊생명 체계의 운하화 이론

글의 흐름으로 보아, 주어진 문장이 들어가기에 가장 적절한 곳을 고르시오. [3점]

Such a system / can only hope to be stable / if only a smaller number of collective ways of being / may emerge. //

이러한 시스템은 / 오직 안정적이기를 기대할 수 있다 / 더 적은 수의 존재의 집합적인 방식이 / 나타날 때만 //
단서 1 존재의 집합적인 방식이 제한되어야만 안정적임

선행사를 포함하는 관계대명사
Life is / what physicists might call a 'high-dimensional system,'
계속적 용법의 주격 관계대명사   목적어절 접속사
/ which is their fancy way of saying / that there's a lot going on. //

생명은 / 물리학자들이 '고차원 시스템'이라고 부를 수 있는 것이다 / 이는 그들의 말하는 멋진 방식이다 / 많은 일이 발생하고 있다고 //
단서 2 하나의 세포에서도 가능한 상호 작용의 수가 매우 큼

(①) In just a single cell, / the number of possible interactions
                                          '~의 수'
between different molecules / is enormous. //
                              단수 동사

단 하나의 세포 내에서도 / 여러 분자 간의 가능한 상호 작용의 수는 / 매우 크다 //

(②) For example, / it is only a limited number of tissues and
body shapes / that may result from the development of a human
         it ~ that 강조 구문
embryo. // **단서 3** 인간 배아로부터 나올 수 있는 조직과 형태는 제한되어 있음

예를 들어 / 오직 제한된 수의 조직과 신체 형태이다 / 인간 배아의 발달로부터 나올 수 있는 것은 //

          called의 목적어와 목적격 보어 (명사)
(③) In 1942, / the biologist Conrad Waddington called / this
drastic narrowing of outcomes / canalization. //

1942년에 / 생물학자 Conrad Waddington이 불렀다 / 이러한 극적인 결과의 제한을 / '운하화'라고 //
단서 4 Conrad가 이 극적인 결과의 제한을 '운하화'라고 함

(④) The organism may switch / between a small number of well-defined possible states, / but can't exist / in random states in between them, /

유기체는 바뀔 수 있다 / 적은 수의 명확하게 정의된 가능한 상태 사이에서 / 하지만 존재할 수 없다 / 그것들 사이에 있는 무작위의 상태로 /

rather as a ball in a rough landscape must roll / to the bottom of one valley or another. //

오히려 울퉁불퉁한 경관에 있는 공이 반드시 굴러가야 하는 것처럼 / 이 계곡 혹은 또 다른 계곡의 바닥으로 //

          목적어절 접속사 be true of: ~에도 적용된다
(⑤) We'll see / that this is true also of health and disease: / there are many causes of illness, /

우리는 알게 될 것이다 / 이것이 건강과 질병에도 적용된다는 것을 / 즉 질병에는 많은 원인이 있다 /

          복수 주어
but their manifestations at the physiological and symptomatic
    복수 동사
levels / are often strikingly similar. //

하지만 그것들의 생리적이고 증상적인 수준에서의 발현은 / 종종 놀랍도록 유사하다 //

- stable ⓐ 안정적인   · collective ⓐ 집합적인
- emerge ⓥ 나타나다   · dimensional ⓐ 차원적인   · cell ⓝ 세포
- molecule ⓝ 분자   · enormous ⓐ 거대한   · tissue ⓝ (근육) 조직
- drastic ⓐ 극적인   · outcome ⓝ 결과   · organism ⓝ 유기체
- switch ⓥ 바꾸다   · well-defined ⓐ 명확히 정의된
- state ⓝ 상태   · rough ⓐ 울퉁불퉁한   · landscape ⓝ 경관
- illness ⓝ 질병   · manifestation ⓝ 발현
- symptomatic ⓐ 증상적인   · strikingly ⓐ 놀랍게도

생명은 물리학자들이 '고차원 시스템'이라고 부를 수 있는 것인데 이는 많은 일이 발생하고 있다고 말하는 그들의 멋진 방식이다. (①) 단 하나의 세포 내에서도 여러 분자 간의 가능한 상호 작용의 수는 매우 크다. (② 이러한 시스템은 더 적은 수의 존재의 집합적인 방식이 나타날 때만 오직 안정적이기를 기대할 수 있다.) 예를 들어 인간 배아의 발달로부터 나올 수 있는 것은 오직 제한된 수의 조직과 신체 형태이다. (③) 1942년에 생물학자 Conrad Waddington은

2024.10 10회

이러한 극적인 결과의 제한을 '운하화'라고 불렀다. (④) 오히려 울퉁불퉁한 경관에 있는 공이 이 계곡 혹은 또 다른 계곡의 바닥으로 반드시 굴러가야 하는 것처럼, 유기체는 적은 수의 명확하게 정의된 가능한 상태 사이에서 바뀔 수 있지만 그것들 사이에 있는 무작위의 상태로 존재할 수는 없다. (⑤) 우리는 이것이 건강과 질병에도 적용된다는 것을 알게 될 것이다. 즉 질병의 많은 원인이 있지만, 그것들의 생리적이고 증상적인 수준에서의 발현은 종종 놀랍도록 유사하다.

2등급? 전반적으로 지문의 어휘 수준이 높고, 주어진 문장의 Such a system과 연결될 만한 함정들이 골고루 있어서 헷갈릴 수 있는 2등급 대비 문제이다. 수량을 나타내는 표현이 갑자기 전환되는 부분을 잘 찾으면 정답을 쉽게 고를 수 있다.

| 문제 풀이 순서 |

1st 주어진 문장을 해석하고 핵심 내용과 연결어, 지시어 등을 확인한다.

Such a system can only hope to be stable if only a smaller number of collective ways of being may emerge.
이러한 시스템은 더 적은 수의 존재의 집합적인 방식이 나타날 때만 오직 안정적이기를 기대할 수 있다.

➡ **주어진 문장 앞:** 앞의 내용을 다시 언급하는 Such a system과 존재의 집합적 방식이 적은 경우에만 시스템이 안정적임을 강조하는 only가 있으므로 [단서] 그 시스템이 무엇인지, 그리고 시스템이 불안정한 상황과 그 원인이 먼저 나올 것이다. [발상]

2nd 각 선택지의 앞뒤 흐름이 매끄러운지 확인한다.

①의 앞 문장과 뒤 문장
- **앞 문장:** 생명은 물리학자들이 '고차원 시스템'이라고 부를 수 있는 것인데 이는 많은 일이 발생하고 있다고 말하는 그들의 멋진 방식이다.
- **뒤 문장:** 단 하나의 세포 내에서도 여러 분자 간의 가능한 상호 작용의 수는 매우 크다.

➡ 주어진 문장에서 언급된 Such a system이 생명이라는 '고차원 시스템'임을 알 수 있다. 시스템이 무엇인지와 그 특징이 모두 나왔지만, 생명은 많은 일이 발생하는 고차원 시스템이라는 내용과 단 하나의 세포에도 분자 간 상호 작용이 많다는 내용이 자연스럽게 이어지므로 다음 내용도 살펴봐야 한다.
▶ 주어진 문장이 ①에 들어갈 수 없음

②의 앞 문장과 뒤 문장
- **앞 문장:** ①의 뒤 문장과 같음
- **뒤 문장:** 예를 들어 인간 배아의 발달로부터 나올 수 있는 것은 오직 제한된 수의 조직과 신체 형태이다.

➡ 하나의 세포에도 분자 간 상호 작용의 수가 매우 '크다'라는 앞 문장의 내용과 인간 배아의 발달에서 '제한된' 수의 조직과 신체 형태가 나온다는 뒤 문장의 내용이 서로 이어지지 않는다. 제한적인 수가 앞에 나와야 하는데, 주어진 문장에서 존재의 집합적 방식의 수가 '적을' 때만 '이러한 시스템'이 안정적이라고 했다. 따라서 경우의 수가 많은(불안정한) 고차원 시스템(생명)에서 존재가 안정적으로 구성되려면 경우의 수가 제한적이어야 한다는 흐름으로 적절하게 두 내용을 이어준다.
▶ 주어진 문장이 ②에 들어가야 함

③의 앞 문장과 뒤 문장
- **앞 문장:** ②의 뒤 문장과 같음
- **뒤 문장:** 1942년에 생물학자 Conrad Waddington은 이러한 극적인 결과의 제한을 '운하화'라 불렀다.

➡ 인간 배아에서 나올 수 있는 결과의 제한성에 대해서 한 생물학자가 '운하화' 이론이라고 이름을 붙였다는 내용으로 이어진다. ▶ 주어진 문장이 ③에 들어갈 수 없음

④의 앞 문장과 뒤 문장
- **앞 문장:** ③의 뒤 문장과 같음
- **뒤 문장:** 오히려 울퉁불퉁한 경관에 있는 공이 이 계곡 혹은 또 다른 계곡의 바닥으로 반드시 굴러가야 하는 것처럼, 유기체는 적은 수의 명확하게 정의된 가능한 상태 사이에서 바뀔 수 있지만 그것들 사이에 있는 무작위의 상태로 존재할 수는 없다.

➡ '운하화'를 '계곡에서 굴러가는 공'에 비유하여 설명한다.
▶ 주어진 문장이 ④에 들어갈 수 없음

⑤의 앞 문장과 뒤 문장
- **앞 문장:** ④의 뒤 문장과 같음
- **뒤 문장:** 우리는 이것이 건강과 질병에도 적용된다는 것을 알게 될 것이다. 즉 질병의 많은 원인이 있지만, 그것들의 생리적이고 증상적인 수준에서의 발현은 종종 놀랍도록 유사하다.

➡ 생명의 '운하화'가 우리의 건강과 질병에도 적용된다는 점을 부연 설명한다.
▶ 주어진 문장이 ⑤에 들어갈 수 없음

40 정답 ① ＊트릭 처벌의 부작용과 대안

Punishing a child may not be effective / **due to** what **Álvaro Bilbao**, a neuropsychologist, calls 'trick-punishments.' //
동명사 (주어)　　　~ 때문에　　동격
아이를 벌주는 것은 효과적이지 않을 수 있다 / 신경심리학자 Álvaro Bilbao가 '트릭 처벌'이라고 부르는 것으로 인해 //

A trick-punishment is / a scolding, a moment of anger / or a punishment / in the most classic sense of the word. //
트릭 처벌은 / 꾸짖음, 순간의 화 / 혹은 처벌이다 / (처벌이라는) 단어의 가장 전형적인 의미에서의 //

Instead of discouraging the child from doing something, / it encourages **them to do it**. //
encourages의 목적어와 목적격 보어 (to부정사)
[단서 1] 트릭 처벌은 행동을 단념시키는 대신 오히려 장려함
아이가 무언가를 하는 것을 단념시키는 대신 / 트릭 처벌은 그들이 그것을 하도록 장려한다. //

For example, / Hugh learns / **that** when he hits his little brother, / his mother scolds him. //
목적어절 접속사
예를 들어 / Hugh는 배운다 / 그가 자신의 남동생을 때릴 때 / 그의 어머니가 그를 꾸짖는다는 것을 //

For a child **who feels lonely**, / **being scolded** is **much** better / than feeling invisible, / so he will continue to hit his brother. //
주격 관계대명사절　　동명사 주어 (수동태)　　비교급 강조
외로움을 느끼는 아이에게는 / 꾸중을 듣는 것이 훨씬 낫다 / 눈에 띄지 않는다고 느끼는 것보다 / 그래서 그는 그의 남동생을 때리는 것을 계속할 것이다 //

In this case, / his mother would **be better adopting** a different strategy. //
be better -ing: ~하는 것이 낫다
이 경우에 / 그의 어머니는 다른 전략을 채택하는 것이 나을 것이다 //

For instance, / she could congratulate Hugh / when he has not hit his brother / for a certain length of time. //
예를 들어 / 그녀는 Hugh를 자랑스러워해 줄 수 있다 / 그가 그의 남동생을 때리지 않았을 때 / 일정 기간 동안 //
[단서 2] 어머니는 그가 남동생을 때리지 않았을 때 자랑스러워해 줄 수 있음

The mother clearly cannot allow the child to hit his little brother, / but instead of constantly **pointing** out the negatives, / she can choose to reward the positives. //
동명사
[단서 3] 부정적인 면을 계속 지적하는 대신 긍정적인 면을 보상해야 함
어머니는 분명 아이가 그의 남동생을 때리는 것을 내버려둘 수 없지만 / 그녀는 부정적 측면을 계속 지적하는 대신에 / 긍정적 측면을 보상하는 것을 선택할 수 있다 //

In this way, / any parent can avoid trick-punishments. //
이렇게 / 어느 부모도 트릭 처벌을 피할 수 있다 //

A trick-punishment / (A) **reinforces** the unwanted behavior of a child, / which implies / that parents should focus on / (B) **reducing** the attention to negatives / while rewarding positive behaviors. //

계속적 용법의 주격 관계대명사 / 목적어절 접속사

트릭 처벌은 / 아이의 바람직하지 못한 행동을 강화하는데 / 이는 시사한다 / 부모가 집중해야 한다는 것을 / 부정적 측면에 관한 관심을 줄이는 데 / 긍정적인 행동을 보상하면서 //

- punish ⓥ 벌주다, 처벌하다 · trick ⓝ 트릭, 속임수
- scolding ⓝ 꾸짖음 · discourage ⓥ 단념[좌절]시키다
- invisible ⓐ 눈에 띄지 않는 · adopt ⓥ 채택하다
- strategy ⓝ 전략 · congratulate ⓥ 자랑스러워하다
- constantly ⓐⓓ 계속, 지속적으로 · point out 지적하다
- reward ⓥ 보상하다 · unwanted ⓐ 바람직하지 못한, 원치 않는
- imply ⓥ 시사하다 · reinforce ⓥ 강화하다
- maximize ⓥ 최대화하다 · lower ⓥ 낮추다

아이를 벌주는 것은 신경심리학자 Álvaro Bilbao가 '트릭 처벌'이라고 부르는 것으로 인해 효과적이지 않을 수 있다. 트릭 처벌은 꾸짖음, 순간의 화 혹은 (처벌이라는) 단어의 가장 전형적인 의미에서의 처벌이다. 아이가 무언가를 하는 것을 단념시키는 대신 트릭 처벌은 그들이 그것을 하도록 장려한다. 예를 들어 Hugh는 그가 자신의 남동생을 때릴 때 그의 어머니가 그를 꾸짖는다는 것을 배운다. 외로움을 느끼는 아이에게는 꾸중을 듣는 것이 눈에 띄지 않는다고 느끼는 것보다 훨씬 나아서 그는 그의 남동생을 때리는 것을 계속할 것이다. 이 경우에, 그의 어머니는 다른 전략을 채택하는 것이 보다 나을 것이다. 예를 들어 그녀는 Hugh가 그의 남동생을 일정 기간 동안 때리지 않았을 때 그를 자랑스러워해 줄 수 있다. 어머니는 분명 아이가 그의 남동생을 때리는 것을 내버려둘 수 없기 때문에 그녀는 부정적 측면을 계속 지적하는 대신에 긍정적 측면을 보상하는 것을 선택할 수 있다. 이렇게 어느 부모도 트릭 처벌을 피할 수 있다.

→ 트릭 처벌은 아이의 바람직하지 못한 행동을 (A) **강화하는데**, 이는 부모가 긍정적인 행동을 보상하면서 부정적 측면에 관한 관심을 (B) **줄이는** 데 집중해야 한다는 것을 시사한다.

다음 글의 내용을 한 문장으로 요약하고자 한다. 빈칸 (A), (B)에 들어갈 말로 가장 적절한 것은?

	(A)		(B)	
①	reinforces 강화하다	—	reducing 줄이는 것	트릭 처벌은 아이의 길못된 행동을 강화하므로 부정적인 측면에 주목하기보다 긍정적인 측면을 보상해야 한다는 내용임
②	reinforces	—	maximizing 최대화하는 것	아이의 부정적인 행동에 대한 주목은 줄여야 함
③	discourages 단념시키다	—	attracting 끌어모으는 것	트릭 처벌은 아이의 잘못된 행동을 단념시키지 못함
④	discourages	—	lowering 낮추는 것	
⑤	controls 통제하다	—	increasing 증가시키는 것	트릭 처벌은 아이의 잘못된 행동을 통제하지 못함

왜 정답? ★★★ [정답률 47%]

- 트릭 처벌은 아이가 무언가를 하는 것을 단념시키는 대신 오히려 그들이 그것을 하도록 장려한다. 단서 1
- Hugh의 예시: Hugh가 외로움을 느끼는 아이라면 어머니의 꾸중을 듣는 것이 훨씬 나아서 남동생을 때리는 것을 계속할 것이다.

➡ 트릭 처벌은 아이의 잘못된 행동을 단념시키는 대신 오히려 그것을 계속하도록 장려한다는 점을 Hugh의 예시로 설명하고 있다.

▶ 트릭 처벌은 아이의 행동을 오히려 장려하여 '강화'하므로 (A)에는 ①, ②의 reinforces가 들어가야 함

- 어머니는 Hugh가 그의 남동생을 일정 기간 때리지 않았을 때 그를 자랑스러워해 줄 수 있다. 단서 2
- 부정적 측면을 계속 지적하는 대신에 긍정적 측면을 보상하는 것을 선택할 수 있다. 단서 3

➡ 아이의 행동을 막기 위해서 부정적인 측면을 지적하지 말고, 즉 관심을 줄이고 긍정적인 측면을 보상하는 전략을 채택해야 한다고 말하고 있다.

▶ (B)에는 ①의 reducing이나 ④의 lowering이 들어가는 것이 적절하므로 정답은 ①임

왜 오답?

② 트릭 처벌이 아이의 부정적인 행동을 강화하기 때문에 부정적 행동에 대한 주목은 줄여야 하는 것이지 최대화하면 안 된다.

③ 트릭 처벌은 아이의 부정적인 행동을 단념시키는 것이 아니라 오히려 강화시킨다.

④ 트릭 처벌은 아이의 부정적인 행동을 단념시키지 못하고 오히려 강화시킨다.

⑤ 트릭 처벌은 부정적인 행동을 통제할 수 없고, 부정적인 행동을 향한 관심은 증가시키는 것이 아니라 줄여야 한다.

41~42 ✱ 생존을 위한 행위 감지 메커니즘

From an early age, / we assign purpose to objects and events, / **preferring** this reasoning / **to** random chance. //

분사구문을 이끄는 현재분사 / prefer A to B: A를 B보다 선호하다

어릴 때부터 / 우리는 사물과 사건에 목적을 부여하며 / 이러한 논리를 선호한다 / 무작위적인 우연보다 //

Children assume, / for instance, / **that** pointy rocks are that way / because they don't want **you to sit** on them. //

목적어절 접속사 / want의 목적어와 목적격 보어

아이들은 가정한다 / 예를 들어 / 뾰족한 돌은 그렇게 생겼다고 / 아이들이 그 위에 앉기를 원치 않기 때문에 //

When we encounter something, / we first need to (a) **determine** / what sort of thing it is. //

간접의문문

우리가 무언가를 마주칠 때 / 우리는 먼저 결정할 필요가 있다 / 그것이 어떤 종류의 것인지 //

Inanimate objects and plants / generally do not move / and can be evaluated from physics alone. //

무생물과 식물은 / 일반적으로 움직이지 않으며 / 물리적 현상만으로 평가될 수 있다 //

However, / **by attributing** intention to animals and even objects, / we are able to make fast decisions / about the (b) **likely** behaviour of that being. //

by -ing: ~함으로써

41번 단서 1: 동물 및 사물에 의도를 부여하여 그것의 예상 행동을 빨리 판단할 수 있음

그러나 / 동물과 심지어 사물도 의도가 있다고 생각함으로써 / 우리는 빠른 결정을 내릴 수 있다 / 그 존재가 할 것 같은 행동에 대해 //

This was essential / in our hunter-gatherer days / to avoid **being eaten** by predators. //

avoid의 목적어 (동명사의 수동태)

이는 필수적이었다 / 우리의 수렵 채집 시절에 / 포식자에게 잡아먹히는 것을 피하기 위해 //

The anthropologist Stewart Guthrie made the point / **that** survival in our evolutionary past meant / that we interpret ambiguous objects /

동격절 접속사

인류학자 Stewart Guthrie는 주장했다 / 우리의 진화상 과거에서 생존이 의미한다고 / 우리가 모호한 사물을 해석하는 것을 /

as agents with human mental characteristics, / **as** those are the mental processes **which** we understand. //

전치사 (~로서) / 접속사 (이유) / 목적격 관계대명사

인간의 정신적 특성을 가진 행위자로 / 그것들(인간의 정신적 특성)이 우리가 이해하는 정신 과정이기 때문에 //

41번 단서 2: 생존을 위해 모호한 대상을 의도를 가진 행위자로 해석하는 경향을 발전시킴

Ambiguous events are caused / by such agents. //

모호한 사건은 발생한다 / 이러한 행위자에 의해 //

42번 단서 1: 행위자(사물)에 의해 사건이 발생한다고 생각함

This **results in** a perceptual system / strongly (c) **resistant(→ biased)** towards anthropomorphism. //

'그 결과 ~가 되다' / 앞에 주격 관계대명사와 be동사가 생략됨

이는 지각 체계로 귀결된다 / 의인화에 강하게 저항하는(→ 편향된) //

Therefore, / we tend to assume intention / even where there is none. //

41번 단서 3, 42번 단서 2: 인간은 모든 것에서 의도를 가정하려는 경향을 지님

그러므로 / 우리는 의도를 가정하는 경향이 있다 / 의도가 없는 곳에서도 //

This **would have arisen** as a survival mechanism. //

would have p.p.: ~ 했었을 것이다

이는 발생해 왔을 것이다 / 생존 메커니즘으로 //

If a lion **is about to attack** you, / you need to react (d) **quickly**, / **given** its probable intention to kill you. //

be about to ~: 막 ~하려 하다 / '~을 고려하면'

만약 사자가 당신을 막 공격하려 한다면 / 당신은 빠르게 반응할 필요가 있다 / 당신을 죽이려는 그것의 가능한 의도를 고려하여 //

By the time you have realized / **that** the design of its teeth and claws / could kill you, / you are dead. //

'~ 할 즈음' / 목적어절 접속사

당신이 깨달았을 즈음 / 그것의 이빨과 발톱의 구조가 / 당신을 죽일 수 있다는 것을 / 당신은 죽어 있다 //

So, / assuming intent, / without detailed design analysis or understanding of the physics, / has (e) saved your life. //
동명사 (주어) — assuming
단수 동사 — has

따라서 / 의도를 부여하는 것이 / 상세한 구조 분석 또는 물리적 현상의 이해 없이 / 당신의 목숨을 구해 왔다 //

- assign ⓥ 부여하다
- prefer ⓥ 선호하다
- reasoning ⓝ 논리, 추론
- assume ⓥ 가정하다
- pointy ⓐ 뾰족한
- encounter ⓥ 마주치다
- determine ⓥ 결정하다
- inanimate ⓐ 무생물의
- evaluate ⓥ 평가하다
- physics ⓝ 물리
- attribute ~ to ... ~을 …의 것으로 보다
- likely ⓐ ~할 것 같은
- hunter-gatherer ⓝ 수렵 채집인
- predator ⓝ 포식자
- anthropologist ⓝ 인류학자
- evolutionary ⓐ 진화상의
- agent ⓝ 행위자
- perceptual ⓐ 지각의
- resistant ⓐ 저항하는
- claw ⓝ 발톱
- intent ⓝ 의도

어릴 때부터 우리는 사물과 사건에 목적을 부여하며, 무작위적인 우연보다 이러한 논리를 선호한다. 예를 들어 뾰족한 돌은 아이들이 그 위에 앉기를 원치 않기 때문에 그것이 그렇게 생겼다고 그들(아이들)은 가정한다. 우리가 무언가를 마주칠 때 우리는 먼저 그것이 어떤 종류의 것인지 (a) 결정할 필요가 있다. 무생물과 식물은 일반적으로 움직이지 않으며 물리적 현상만으로 평가될 수 있다. 그러나 동물과 심지어 사물도 의도가 있다고 생각함으로써 우리는 그 존재가 (b) 할 것 같은 행동에 대해 빠른 결정을 내릴 수 있다. 이는 우리의 수렵 채집 시절에 포식자에게 잡아먹히는 것을 피하기 위해 필수적이었다. 인류학자 Stewart Guthrie는 인간의 정신적 특성이 우리가 이해하는 정신 과정이기 때문에, 우리의 진화상 과거에서 생존이란 우리가 모호한 사물을 인간의 정신적 특성을 가진 행위자로 해석하는 것을 의미한다고 주장했다. 모호한 사건은 이러한 행위자에 의해 발생한다. 이는 의인화에 강하게 (c) 저항하는(→편향된) 지각 체계로 귀결된다. 그러므로, 우리는 의도가 없는 곳에서도 의도를 가정하는 경향이 있다. 이는 생존 메커니즘으로 발생해 왔을 것이다. 만약 사자가 당신을 막 공격하려 한다면 당신을 죽이려는 그것의 가능한 의도를 고려하여 당신은 (d) 빠르게 반응할 필요가 있다. 당신이 그것의 이빨과 발톱의 구조가 당신을 죽일 수 있다는 것을 깨달았을 즈음 당신은 죽어 있다. 따라서 상세한 구조 분석 또는 물리적 현상의 이해 없이 의도를 부여하는 것이 당신의 목숨을 (e) 구해 왔다.

41 정답 ①

윗글의 제목으로 가장 적절한 것은? [3점]

인간은 생존을 위해 행위자에 의도를 부여하여 판단하는 경향을 발전시켰음
① Agency Detection: Inherited from Survival Mechanism
행위자 감지: 생존 메커니즘으로부터 물려받은 것
② How Humans' Perceptual System Is Operated for Hunting 사냥을 위한 인간의 지각 체계에 관한 내용이 아님
사냥을 위해 인간의 지각 체계가 어떻게 작동하는가
③ Hiding Intentions: The Unique Trait of Human Mentality
의도 숨기기: 인간 정신의 독특한 특성 │ 의도를 숨기는 것이 인간의 특성이라는 내용이 아님
④ Our Ambiguous Intention Makes Understanding Confusing 모호한 의도로 인한 혼돈은 언급되지 않았음
우리의 모호한 의도가 이해를 혼란스럽게 만든다
⑤ How We Interpret Animate and Inanimate Objects Differently 생물과 무생물을 구분하는 방법에 관한 내용이 아님
우리는 어떻게 생물과 무생물을 다르게 해석하는가

왜 정답? ★★★ [정답률 46%]

- 동물 및 사물에 의도를 부여하여 그 존재의 예상 행동을 빨리 판단할 수 있음 **41번 단서 1**
- 진화상 과거에서 생존이란 모호한 사물을 인간의 정신적 특성을 가진 행위자로 해석하는 것 **41번 단서 2**
- 우리는 의도가 없는 곳에서도 의도를 가정하는 경향이 있음 **41번 단서 3**

➡ 인간은 동물 및 사물, 즉 의도가 없을 듯한 존재들도 의도를 가진 행위자로 해석하여 그들의 행동을 빠르게 예측했다. 이러한 경향이 생존에 유리했기 때문에 인간은 모든 것에 의도를 부여하여 판단하는 특성을 가지게 되었다는 내용이다.

▶ 따라서 정답은 ① '행위자 감지: 생존 메커니즘으로부터 물려받은 것'이다.

왜 오답?

② 사냥을 위한 인간의 지각 체계를 설명하는 내용이 아니다.

③ 의도를 숨기는 것이 인간의 특성이라는 내용이 아니다.

④ 우리가 모호한 사물에 의도를 부여한다는 내용이지, 우리의 의도가 모호하다거나 그로 인해서 인간의 이해가 혼란스러워진다는 내용이 아니다.

⑤ 무생물과 식물의 경우 물리적 현상만으로 평가될 수 있다고 했지만, 글의 중심 내용은 무생물과 생물을 구분하는 방법이 아니라 생존을 위해 모호한 사물에 의도를 부여하여 행위자로 해석하는 경향을 발전시켰다는 것이다. **주의**

42 정답 ③

밑줄 친 (a)~(e) 중에서 문맥상 낱말의 쓰임이 적절하지 않은 것은?

① (a) 우리가 무엇을 마주치면 그것의 종류를 결정해야 함
결정하다
② (b) 동물과 사물에게 의도를 부여하면서 그것들이 할 것 같은 행동을 예측함
할 것 같은
③ (c) 우리의 지각 체계는 의인화하는 데 편향되도록 발전해 옴
저항하는
④ (d) 공격을 당할 때 그것의 의도를 고려하여 빠르게 반응해야 함
빠르게
⑤ (e) 의도를 부여하는 성향은 우리의 목숨을 구해왔음
구하다

왜 정답? ★★★ [정답률 55%]

③ (c) **resistant** 저항하는

이는 의인화에 강하게 (c) 저항하는(→편향된) 지각 체계로 귀결된다.

➡ 우리는 모호한 사물을 의도를 가진 행위자로 해석하는 성향, 즉 사물을 의인화하는 성향을 발전시켰다고 했다. 따라서 인간의 지각 체계는 의인화에 '저항하는' 것이 아니라 '편향된' 것이다.

▶ resistant를 biased(편향된)와 같은 반의어로 바꿔야 함

왜 오답?

① (a) **determine** 결정하다

우리가 무언가를 마주칠 때 우리는 먼저 그것이 어떤 종류의 것인지 (a) 결정할 필요가 있다.

➡ 글의 앞부분에서 우리는 사물과 사건에 목적을 부여한다고 했으므로, 우리가 무언가를 마주칠 때 그것이 어떤 종류의 것인지 먼저 '결정하는' 것은 적절하다.

▶ determine은 문맥에 맞음

② (b) **likely** 할 것 같은

그러나 동물과 심지어 사물도 의도가 있다고 생각함으로써 우리는 그 존재가 (b) 할 것 같은 행동에 대해 빠른 결정을 내릴 수 있다.

➡ 어떤 존재에 의도가 있다고 생각하면 그 존재가 '할 것 같은' 행동에 대해 빠른 결정(예측)을 내릴 수 있다. ▶ likely는 문맥에 맞음

④ (d) **quickly** 빠르게

만약 사자가 당신을 막 공격하려 한다면 당신을 죽이려는 그것의 가능한 의도를 고려하여 당신은 (d) 빠르게 반응할 필요가 있다.

➡ 뒤 문장에서 사자가 공격하려 할 때 사자의 이빨과 발톱의 구조를 이해할 즈음이면 우리는 이미 죽었을 것이라고 했으므로, 우리는 사자를 만났을 때 그것의 의도를 고려하여 '빠르게' 반응해야 한다. ▶ quickly는 문맥에 맞음

⑤ (e) **saved** 구해 왔다

따라서 상세한 구조 분석 또는 물리적 현상의 이해 없이 의도를 부여하는 것이 당신의 목숨을 (e) 구해 왔다.

➡ 앞 문장에서 사자가 공격할 때 그것의 의도를 고려하여 빠르게 반응할 수 있다고 했으므로, 이해 없이 의도를 부여하는 것이 결국 우리의 목숨을 '구해 왔다'라는 것은 적절하다. ▶ saved는 문맥에 맞음

43~45 ☆ 2등급 대비

*특별해지고 싶었던 판다의 깨달음

(A) Once long ago, / deep in the Himalayas, / there lived a little panda. //

옛날에 / 히말라야 산맥 깊숙한 곳에 / 작은 판다가 살았다 //

He was **as** ordinary **as** all the other pandas. //
그는 다른 모든 판다들만큼 평범했다 //

He was completely white / from head to toe. //
그는 전부 하얬다 / 머리부터 발끝까지 //

His two big ears, his four furry feet and his cute round nose / were all frosty white, / **leaving** (a) **him feeling** ordinary and sad. //
그의 두 개의 큰 귀, 네 개의 털 많은 발, 그리고 귀여운 둥근 코는 / 모두 서리처럼 하얘서 / 그가 평범하고 슬프게 느끼게 하였다 //

Unlike the cheerful and contented pandas around him, / he desired to be distinctive, special, and unique. //
그의 주위에 있는 명랑하고 만족스러운 판다들과 달리 / 그는 특이하고 특별하며 독특해지기를 갈망했다 //

* (A) 문단 요약: 평범한 작은 판다는 특별해지길 원했음

(B) The little panda changed his path / and hurried to the nearest berry bush, / greedily **eating a mouthful of juicy red berries**. //
작은 판다는 경로를 바꾸어 / 가장 가까운 베리 덤불로 서둘러 가서 / 탐욕스럽게 한입 가득 즙이 많은 빨간 베리를 먹었다 //

However, / they were **so** bitter / he **couldn't** swallow even one. //
하지만 / 그것들은 너무 써서 / 그는 한 개도 삼킬 수 없었다 //

At dusk, / he finally got home / and slowly climbed his favorite bamboo tree. //
해질 무렵 / 그는 마침내 집에 도착했고 / 그가 가장 좋아하는 대나무에 천천히 올라갔다 //

There, / he discovered a strange black and red flower / with a sweet scent / **that** tempted (b) **him to eat** all its blossoms. //
그곳에서 / 그는 기묘한 검고 붉은 꽃을 발견하였다 / 달콤한 향기를 가진 / 그가 그것의 모든 꽃을 먹도록 유혹하는 //

* (B) 문단 요약: 베리를 먹는 것에 실패한 작은 판다는 집에 돌아와 검고 붉은 꽃을 발견함

(C) **Driven by the desire for uniqueness**, / the little panda sought inspiration / from (c) **his distant cousin**, / **a giant white panda covered with heavenly black patches**. //
독특함에 대한 열망에 사로잡혀 / 작은 판다는 영감을 찾으려 했다 / 그의 먼 사촌으로부터 / 멋진 검은 반점으로 뒤덮인 거대한 흰 판다인 //

But the cousin revealed / the patches were from an unintended encounter with mud, / and he disliked **them**. //
그러나 사촌은 밝혔다 / 그 반점이 진흙과 의도치 않게 접촉한 결과이며 / 그는 그것(반점)을 싫어한다고 //

Disappointed, / the little panda walked home. //
실망한 채로 / 작은 판다는 집으로 걸어갔다 //

On his way, / he met a red-feathered peacock, / **who** explained / (d) **he** turned red from eating wild berries. //
가는 길에 / 그는 붉은 깃털을 가진 공작새를 만났는데 / 그 공작새는 설명했다 / 그가 야생 베리를 먹어서 붉게 변했다고 //

* (C) 문단 요약: 독특함에 대한 열망에 사로잡힌 작은 판다는 야생 베리를 먹고 붉게 변했다는 공작새를 만남

(D) The following morning, / under sunny skies, / the little panda felt remarkably better. //
다음 날 아침 / 맑은 하늘 아래에서 / 작은 판다는 기분이 매우 좋아졌다 //

During breakfast, / he found the other pandas **chatting** enthusiastically / and asked why. //
아침 식사 중에 / 그는 다른 판다들이 신나게 수다를 떨고 있는 것을 발견하고 / 이유를 물어보았다 //

They **burst into laughter**, / **exclaiming**, "Look at yourself!" //
그들은 웃음을 터뜨리며 / "네 자신을 좀 봐"라고 외쳤다 //

Glancing down, / he discovered / his once white fur / was now stained jet black and glowing red. //
아래를 흘긋 보고 / 그는 발견했다 / 한때 하얬던 자신의 털이 / 이제 새까맣고 빛나는 붉은색으로 얼룩져 있다는 것을 //

He was overjoyed / and realized **that**, / rather than by imitating others, / (e) **his** wishes can come true / from unexpected places and genuine experiences. //
그는 매우 기뻤고 / 깨달았다 / 남들을 모방하기보다는 / 그의 소원이 실현될 수 있음을 / 예상치 못한 곳과 진정한 경험으로부터 //

* (D) 문단 요약: 검고 붉게 변한 작은 판다는 진정한 특별함에 대해 깨달음

- ordinary ⓐ 평범한 · furry ⓐ 털이 많은 · frosty ⓐ 서리가 내리는
- cheerful ⓐ 명랑한 · contented ⓐ 만족하는
- distinctive ⓐ 특이한 · greedily ⓐd 탐욕스럽게
- swallow ⓥ 삼키다 · dusk ⓝ 해질 무렵[황혼]
- bamboo ⓝ 대나무 · tempt ⓥ 유혹하다 · blossom ⓝ 꽃
- seek ⓥ 찾다, 추구하다 · distant ⓐ 먼 · reveal ⓥ 밝히다
- unintended ⓐ 의도치 않은 · encounter ⓝ 접촉, 만남
- remarkably ⓐd 매우, 정말 · chat ⓥ 수다를 떨다
- enthusiastically ⓐd 신나게, 열정적으로 · exclaim ⓥ 외치다
- glance ⓥ 흘긋 보다 · imitate ⓥ 모방하다 · genuine ⓐ 진정한

(A) 옛날에 히말라야 산맥 깊숙한 곳에 작은 판다가 살았다. 그는 다른 모든 판다들만큼 평범했다. 그는 머리부터 발끝까지 전부 하얬다. 그의 두 개의 큰 귀, 네 개의 털 많은 발, 그리고 귀여운 둥근 코는 모두 서리처럼 하얘서 (a) 그가 평범하고 슬프게 느끼게 하였다. 그의 주위에 있는 명랑하고 만족스러운 판다들과 달리 그는 특이하고 특별하며 독특해지기를 갈망했다.

(C) 독특함에 대한 열망에 사로잡혀 작은 판다는 (c) 그의 먼 사촌인 멋진 검은 반점으로 뒤덮인 거대한 흰 판다로부터 영감을 찾으려 했다. 그러나 사촌은 그 반점이 진흙과 의도치 않게 접촉한 결과이며, 그는 그것(반점)을 싫어한다고 밝혔다. 실망한 채로 작은 판다는 집으로 걸어갔다. 가는 길에 그는 붉은 깃털을 가진 공작새를 만났는데 그 공작새는 (d) 그가 야생 베리를 먹어서 붉게 변했다고 설명했다.

(B) 작은 판다는 경로를 바꾸어 가장 가까운 베리 덤불로 서둘러 가서, 탐욕스럽게 한입 가득 즙이 많은 빨간 베리를 먹었다. 하지만 그것들은 너무 써서 그는 한 개도 삼킬 수 없었다. 해질 무렵 그는 마침내 집에 도착했고 그가 가장 좋아하는 대나무에 천천히 올라갔다. 그곳에서 (b) 그가 그것의 모든 꽃을 먹도록 유혹하는 달콤한 향기를 가진 기묘한 검고 붉은 꽃을 발견하였다.

(D) 다음 날 아침 맑은 하늘 아래에서 작은 판다는 기분이 매우 좋아졌다. 아침 식사 중에 그는 다른 판다들이 신나게 수다를 떨고 있는 것을 발견하고 이유를 물어보았다. 그늘은 웃음을 터뜨리며 "네 자신을 좀 봐!"라고 외쳤다. 아래를 흘긋 보고, 그는 한때 하얬던 자신의 털이 이제 새까맣고 빛나는 붉은색으로 얼룩져 있다는 것을 발견했다. 그는 매우 기뻤고 (e) 그의 소원이 남들을 모방하기보다는 예상치 못한 곳과 진정한 경험으로부터 실현될 수 있음을 깨달았다.

왜 2등급? 내용 일치 문제에서 사건의 순서와 구체적인 행동을 꼼꼼히 파악해야 정답과 오답을 가려낼 수 있는 2등급 대비 문제이다. 판다가 집에 돌아갈 때 만난 것과 집에 도착해서 발견한 것은 명확히 다르다.

43 정답 ②

주어진 글 (A)에 이어질 내용을 순서에 맞게 배열한 것으로 가장 적절한 것은?

① (B) — (D) — (C)
② (C) — (B) — (D)
③ (C) — (D) — (B)
④ (D) — (B) — (C)
⑤ (D) — (C) — (B)

왜 정답·오답? ★★★ [정답률 79%]

- **(A):** 평범한 작은 판다가 살았는데 그는 온몸이 새하얘서 자신을 특별하지 않다고 느꼈고, 독특해지기를 갈망했다.
→ 독특해지기를 갈망했던 작은 판다가 겪는 일이 이어질 것이다.

(B): 그는 가까운 베리 덤불로 가서 빨간 베리를 먹었지만 너무 써서 삼킬 수 없었다. 집으로 돌아와 대나무에 올랐는데, 그곳에서 달콤한 향을 풍기는 검고 붉은 꽃을 발견했다.

➡ 베리 덤불로 가서 베리를 먹은 이유가 앞에 나와야 하고, 검고 붉은 꽃을 발견하고 어떤 행동을 했는지가 뒤에 이어져야 한다.

(C): 그는 독특해지기 위해 검은 반점을 가진 사촌을 찾아갔으나, 정작 그는 자신의 반점을 싫어한다고 말하여 작은 판다는 실망했다. 집에 가던 길에 붉은 깃털의 공작새를 만나, 그가 야생 베리를 먹고 붉게 변했다는 이야기를 들었다.

➡ 독특해지기를 갈망하여 사촌을 찾아간 것이므로 (A)에 이어지는 내용이다. 집에 가던 길에 붉은 깃털의 공작새를 만나 야생 베리에 대한 이야기를 들었으므로 (B)가 (C) 뒤에 이어진다.

(D): 다음 날 아침, 작은 판다는 자신의 털이 검고 붉게 변한 것을 발견하고는 기뻐했고 특별함은 남을 따라 하는 것이 아니라, 예상치 못한 경험에서 얻어진다는 깨달음을 얻었다.

➡ 작은 판다의 털이 검고 붉게 변하게 된 이유가 나오는 (B)에 이어지는 내용이다. 작은 판다가 자신만의 특별한 색깔을 가지게 되어 기뻐하며 깨달음을 얻는 것으로 글이 마무리된다. ▶ 글의 순서는 ② (C) — (B) — (D)임

44 정답 ④

밑줄 친 (a)~(e) 중에서 가리키는 대상이 나머지 넷과 <u>다른</u> 것은?

① (a)   ② (b)   ③ (c)   ④(d)   ⑤ (e)
= the little panda = the little panda = the little panda's = the peacock = the little panda's

〉왜 정답? ✱✱✽ [정답률 77%]

④ (d) he: 야생 베리를 먹고 붉게 변했다고 말하는 동물 ▶ the peacock

〉왜 오답?

① (a) him: 자신이 너무 하얘서 평범함과 슬픔을 느낀 동물 ▶ the little panda
② (b) him : 검고 붉은 꽃을 발견하고 그것을 먹도록 유혹당한 동물
   ▶ the little panda
③ (c) his : 검은 반점을 가진 거대한 흰 판다와 먼 사촌 관계인 동물
   ▶ the little panda's
⑤ (e) his : 소원이 예상치 못한 경험으로부터 실현될 수 있음을 깨달은 동물
   ▶ the little panda's

45 정답 ③

윗글의 'little panda'에 관한 내용으로 적절하지 <u>않은</u> 것은?
① 다른 판다들과는 달리 특별해지기를 갈망했다.
   Unlike ~ pandas around him, he desired to be distinctive ~.
② 베리가 너무 써서 한 개도 삼킬 수 없었다.
   they were so bitter he couldn't swallow even one
③ 집에 돌아오는 길에 검고 붉은 꽃을 발견하였다.
   he finally got home ~ discovered a strange black and red flower
④ 그의 사촌은 자신의 검은 반점을 싫어했다. he disliked them
⑤ 다른 판다들이 왜 신나게 수다를 떠는지 물어보았다.
   he found the other pandas chatting enthusiastically and asked why

〉왜 정답? ✱✱✽ [정답률 46%]

작은 판다가 집에 도착한 후 대나무에서 검고 붉은 꽃을 발견한 것이므로 집에 돌아오는 길에 검고 붉은 꽃을 발견했다는 ③은 적절하지 않다.

〉왜 오답?

① 다른 판다들과는 달리 특별해지기를 갈망했다. (Unlike ~ pandas around him, he desired to be distinctive, special, and unique.)
② 베리가 너무 써서 한 개도 삼킬 수 없었다. (they were so bitter he couldn't swallow even one)
④ 그의 사촌은 자신의 검은 반점을 싫어했다. (the cousin revealed the patches were from an unintended encounter with mud, and he disliked them)
⑤ 다른 판다들이 왜 신나게 수다를 떠는지 물어보았다. (he found the other pandas chatting enthusiastically and asked why)

10회 Dictation
문제 p. 190

01 our mid-term exam / electronic devices / regarded as cheating / wish you all

02 aware of the risks / potentially / criminal purposes / For real

03 captures attention / creates interest / surprising statistic / with a boring introduction

04 doggy daycare center / star-patterned tunnel / bone-shaped / three food dispensers

05 better understanding of the moves / with a camera / could you do that / immediately

06 your needs / sleep disorder / for sensitive skin / valid

07 caught a cold / new hiking sticks / applied for / pre-training program

08 explore the life and times / his birthplace / senior-year priority / afford that

09 opening ceremony / three-legged / importantly / A half-price discount

10 manual grinder / automatic / storage capacity / adjustability setting

11 Definitely / on my family trip

12 delivery status / has arrived

13 digesting food / prescribed / relieve your stomach problems / instead of relying on medicine

14 tipping culture / quite puzzled / while complaining / Romans do

15 advanced math / creative / got a good grade / doubting herself

[16~17] AI technology / personalized responses / significantly reduces / contract analysis / years of practice / potential

10회 어휘 Review Test
문제 p. 194

01 특성	15 be willing to	29 considerable
02 자동의	16 broad	30 pretend
03 인문학	17 electronic	31 anticipation
04 전념	18 mutual	32 psychologically
05 발현	19 constraint	33 fundamental
06 scent	20 ambiguous	34 substances
07 valid	21 testimony	35 enthusiastically
08 digest	22 sanitation	36 strategy
09 priority	23 identification	37 reinforces
10 potentially	24 encounter	38 manipulated
11 result in	25 passive	39 reconstruct
12 contribute to	26 exceed	40 instantly
13 engage in	27 demonstrate	
14 afford to	28 dedicate	

01 정답 ② *컨벤션 센터의 안내 로봇 서비스 소개

[Chime bell rings.]
[차임벨이 울린다.]

M : Hello, visitors.
남 : 안녕하세요, 방문객 여러분.

This is Scott Wolfman from the Edison Convention Center management office.
저는 Edison 컨벤션 센터 관리소의 Scott Wolfman입니다.

We're doing our best to make sure (부사적 용법(~하도록)) that visitors have a wonderful experience in our convention center.
저희는 방문객들이 저희 컨벤션 센터에서 멋진 경험을 하도록 최선을 다하고 있습니다.

As ('~로서') part of our effort, our center provides a robot guide service. [단서] 방문객을 위해 안내 로봇 서비스를 제공한다고 소개함
노력의 일부로서, 우리 센터는 안내 로봇 서비스를 제공합니다.

The robot offers guided-tours of our exhibitions.
로봇은 전시회의 가이드 투어를 제공합니다.

Foreign languages (복수 주어), such as Chinese and Spanish, are (복수 동사) available.
중국어나 스페인어와 같은 외국어도 이용할 수 있습니다.

And if you lose your way, the robot will accompany you to where (선행사(the place)가 생략된 관계부사) you want to go.
그리고 여러분이 길을 잃으면, 로봇은 여러분이 가고자 하는 곳으로 동행할 것입니다.

So, please feel free to ask our friendly robot guide, and (명령문, and ...: ~해라, 그러면 …할 것이다.) it'll kindly help you.
그러니, 저희의 친절한 안내 로봇에게 자유롭게 물어보시면, 친절하게 당신을 도울 것입니다.

I hope this service makes your experience even (비교급 강조 부사) better.
저는 이 서비스가 여러분의 경험을 훨씬 더 좋게 만들기를 바랍니다.

Thank you.
감사합니다.

• exhibition ⓝ 전시회 • accompany ⓥ 동행하다

다음을 듣고, 남자가 하는 말의 목적으로 가장 적절한 것을 고르시오.
① 로봇 프로그램 만족도 조사 참여를 독려하려고 만족도 조사는 언급하지 않음
②관람객을 위한 안내 로봇 서비스를 소개하려고 로봇은 가이드 투어, 길 안내 등의 서비스를 제공함
③ 전시 작품 해설 서비스 중단을 안내하려고 서비스를 소개하고 있음
④ 오디오 가이드 대여 장소를 공지하려고 오디오 가이드 대여는 언급하지 않음
⑤ 전시관 온라인 예약 방법을 설명하려고 온라인 예약 방법은 언급하지 않음

왜 정답? ✽❀❀ [정답률 96%]

Edison 컨벤션 센터에서는 방문객을 위해 안내 로봇 서비스를 제공하고 있으며, 구체적으로 전시회의 가이드 투어나 길 안내 등의 서비스를 제공할 것이라고 소개하고 있으므로 정답은 ②이다.

왜 오답?

① 로봇을 자유롭게 사용하라는 안내였으나 만족도 조사는 언급하지 않았다. 함정
③ 서비스의 중단을 알리는 것이 아닌, 새로운 서비스를 소개하고 있다.
④ 오디오 가이드 대여 장소는 언급하지 않았다.
⑤ 전시관 온라인 예약 방법은 언급하지 않았다.

02 정답 ① *번역 프로그램으로 편지를 쓰고 있는 Kevin

W : Kevin, what are you doing?
여 : Kevin, 무엇을 하고 있니?

M : Mom, I'm writing a letter to my sponsored (과거분사(child 수식)) child in Congo.
남 : 엄마, 저는 콩고에 있는 제 후원 아동에게 편지를 쓰고 있어요.

W : That's why (That's why + 결과: 그래서 ~하다) you're writing in French. Your French has gotten (현재완료(완료)) better and better.
여 : 그래서 네가 프랑스어로 쓰고 있구나. 네 프랑스어가 점점 더 나아졌어.

M : Actually, I got help from a translation program.
남 : 사실, 저는 번역 프로그램의 도움을 받았어요.

W : I see. [Pause] Did you check the translated (과거분사(text 수식)) text before copying it?
여 : 그렇구나. [잠시 후] 너는 번역된 글을 복사하기 전에 확인해 봤니?

M : No, I didn't. Do you think I have to?
남 : 아니요. 제가 그렇게 해야 할까요?

W : Yes. You'd better check (had better + 동사원형: ~하는 편이 낫다) the translation.
여 : 응. 번역을 확인하는 편이 나을 거야.

M : Well, I think the translation program does a better job than I can.
남 : 글쎄요, 전 번역 프로그램이 제가 할 수 있는 것보다 더 잘한다고 생각해요.

W : Not exactly. The translation could have meanings different from what (선행사를 포함하는 관계대명사) you intended. [단서 1] 번역 프로그램을 사용한 번역문은 의도와 다른 의미를 나타낼 수 있다고 경고함
여 : 그렇진 않아. 번역은 네가 의도했던 것과는 다른 의미를 지닐 수도 있어.

M : Hmm, you may be right. The translated text often loses the meaning of my original writing.
남 : 음, 맞는 것 같아요. 번역된 글은 종종 제 원래 글의 의미를 잃어요.

W : See? When translating a text with a translation program, you need to check the results. [단서 2] 번역 프로그램으로 번역한 결과물은 확인할 필요가 있음
여 : 그렇지? 번역 프로그램으로 글을 번역할 때, 넌 결과물을 확인할 필요가 있어.

M : Okay. Thanks for your advice.
남 : 좋아요. 조언 감사합니다.

• sponsor ⓥ 후원하다 • translation ⓝ 번역 • intend ⓥ 의도하다
• original ⓐ 원래의

대화를 듣고, 여자의 의견으로 가장 적절한 것을 고르시오.
①번역 프로그램으로 번역한 글은 검토가 필요하다.
② 읽기 학습을 통해 쓰기 능력을 향상시킬 수 있다. 쓰기 능력 향상에 대한 언급은 없음
③ 글을 인용할 때는 출처를 명확히 밝혀야 한다. 글의 인용에 관한 내용은 언급하지 않음
④ 예상 독자를 고려하여 글을 작성해야 한다. 글 작성 방법에 대해서는 언급하지 않음
⑤ 번역기 사용은 외국어 학습에 효과적이다. 번역기를 사용할 때 주의할 점을 조언함

왜 정답? ✽❀❀ [정답률 96%]

남자는 프랑스어로 편지를 쓰기 위해 번역 프로그램을 사용하고 있고, 여자는 남자에게 번역된 글을 그대로 복사하기 전에 확인할 필요가 있다고 조언하고 있으므로 정답은 ①이다.

왜 오답?

② 쓰기 능력 향상에 대한 언급은 없었다.
③ 글의 인용에 관한 내용은 언급하지 않았다.
④ 예상 독자를 고려한 글 쓰기에 관한 내용은 언급하지 않았다.
⑤ 번역기를 사용할 때 주의할 점을 조언했으나, 그것이 외국어 학습에 효과적이라는 내용은 언급하지 않았다.

03 정답 ⑤　＊여자의 중고 에어컨을 구매하려는 남자

[Cell phone rings.]
[휴대 전화가 울린다.]

M : Hello. This is Johnny. We**'ve been messaging** *(현재완료진행)* each other on the online marketplace.
남 : 안녕하세요. 저는 Johnny입니다. 우리는 온라인 시장에서 서로 메시지를 해오고 있었어요.

W : Oh, hi. You have more questions about the air conditioner, right?
여 : 오, 안녕하세요. 당신은 에어컨에 관해 질문이 더 있는 것이 맞죠?

M : Yes. Could you tell me how long you**'ve been using** *(현재완료진행)* it?
남 : 네. 당신이 그것을 얼마나 오랫동안 사용해 왔는지 말해줄 수 있나요?

W : I bought it a year ago. It works well and is like new as you can see from the photo.
여 : 저는 그걸 1년 전에 샀습니다. 그건 잘 작동하고, 사진에서 볼 수 있듯이 새것 같아요.

M : Then why do you want to sell it?
남 : 그러면 당신은 그것을 왜 팔고자 합니까?

W : Because I don't need it anymore. I**'m moving** *(현재진행(예정된 가까운 미래))* to a place with a built-in air conditioner. **단서 1** 여자는 에어컨이 필요 없어서 팔려고 함
여 : 왜냐하면 전 그게 더 이상 필요하지 않아서요. 저는 빌트인 에어컨이 있는 곳으로 이사를 갑니다.

M : I see. I**'d like** *(would like = want)* to buy it, then. It's $400, correct? **단서 2** 남자는 여자가 사용하던 에어컨을 구매하고자 함
남 : 알겠습니다. 그러면 전 그걸 사고 싶어요. 400달러 맞죠?

W : That's right. When can you pick it up?
여 : 맞습니다. 언제 가지러 오실 수 있나요?

M : Maybe tomorrow. I need to find a truck **to load** *(형용사적 용법(a truck 수식))* it on first.
남 : 아마 내일이요. 전 우선 그걸 실을 트럭을 찾아봐야 합니다.

W : Okay. Let me know when you're ready.
여 : 좋아요. 준비되면 알려주세요.

M : Thanks. I'll call you again.
남 : 감사합니다. 다시 연락드릴게요.

- marketplace ⓝ 시장, 장터 ・ move ⓥ 이사를 가다
- pick up ~을 가져가다 ・ load ⓥ (짐을) 싣다

> 대화를 듣고, 두 사람의 관계를 가장 잘 나타낸 것을 고르시오.
> ① 광고 제작자 – 사진작가 광고와 관련된 내용이 아님
> ② 이사업체 직원 – 의뢰인 여자는 이사가 예정되어 있지만 남자는 이사업체 직원이 아님
> ③ 고객 – 에어컨 설치 기사 에어컨 설치에 관한 내용이 아니라 판매에 관한 내용임
> ④ 트럭 운전사 – 물류 창고 직원 물류 창고에 관련된 내용은 언급되지 않음
> ⑤ 구매자 – 중고 물품 개인 판매자 여자가 중고 에어컨을 팔려고 하자 남자가 구매하고자 함

> **왜 정답 ?** ✽✽✽ [정답률 87%]

여자는 곧 에어컨이 갖춰진 집으로 이사 갈 예정이라 중고 에어컨을 팔고자 한다. 남자는 온라인에서 여자의 에어컨 사진을 보고 메시지를 보내 에어컨을 구매하고 싶다는 의사를 밝혔다. 따라서 두 사람의 관계는 ⑤이다.

> **왜 오답 ?**

① 광고와 관련된 내용은 언급되지 않았다.
② 남자는 여자의 이사를 돕는 업체 직원이 아니라, 여자가 이사하기 전에 처분할 에어컨을 구매할 사람이다.
③ 에어컨 설치에 관한 내용이 아니라 중고 에어컨 판매에 관한 내용이다.
④ 남자는 중고 에어컨을 실을 트럭을 따로 알아보고 여자에게 연락하겠다고 했을 뿐, 트럭 운전사가 아니다.

04 정답 ④　＊학생 라운지 디자인

W : Hi, Benjamin. Did you finish your work for the student lounge design contest?
여 : 안녕, Benjamin. 학생 라운지 디자인 대회를 위한 작업을 끝냈니?

M : Yes. I'm confident that I'm going to win. Here's my design for it.
남 : 네. 전 제가 우승할 것이라 확신해요. 여기 제 디자인이 있어요.

W : Awesome. Is that a hanging plant in front of the window? **①의 단서** 창문 앞에 걸어놓는 식물이 있음
여 : 훌륭해. 창문 앞에 저건 걸어놓는 식물이니?

M : Yes. The plant will give a fresh feel to the lounge. What do you think about the banner on the wall?
남 : 네. 식물은 라운지에 신선한 느낌을 줄 거예요. 벽에 있는 현수막에 대해서는 어떻게 생각하세요?

W : I love it. The slogan "TO THE WORLD" **goes well with** *('~와 잘 어울리다')* the world map. **②의 단서** 세계 지도에 "세계로"라는 슬로건이 있음
여 : 맘에 들어. "세계로"라는 슬로건은 세계 지도와 잘 어울려.

M : I hope this place **helps students dream** *(준사역동사 help + 목적어 + (to) 동사원형)* big.
남 : 전 이 장소가 학생들이 크게 꿈을 꾸도록 돕기를 바라요.

W : That's cool. And the two cushions on the sofa **make the atmosphere cozier.** *(사역동사 / 목적어 / 목적격 보어)* **③의 단서** 소파 위에 쿠션 두 개가 있음
여 : 그거 멋지구나. 그리고 소파 위에 쿠션 두 개는 분위기를 더 아늑하게 만들어주네.

M : You're right. Check out the square-shaped table as well. **④의 단서** 사각형 테이블이 아니라 원형 테이블이 있음
남 : 맞아요. 사각형 테이블도 한 번 보세요.

W : Good. It can be useful. Most of all, students will love the vending machine under the clock. **⑤의 단서** 시계 아래 자판기가 있음
여 : 좋아. 그거 유용하겠네. 무엇보다, 학생들이 시계 아래 자판기를 좋아할 거야.

M : You bet!
남 : 당연하죠!

- confident ⓐ 자신감 있는, 확신하는 ・ atmosphere ⓝ 분위기
- cozy ⓐ 아늑한, 편안한 ・ vending machine 자판기

> 대화를 듣고, 그림에서 대화의 내용과 일치하지 않는 것을 고르시오.

세계 지도에 "세계로"라는 슬로건이 있음 ②
창문 앞에 걸어놓는 식물이 있음 ①
시계 아래 자판기가 있음 ⑤
소파 위에 쿠션 두 개가 있음 ③
사각형 테이블이 아니라 원형 테이블이 있음 ④

> **왜 정답 ?** ✽✽✽ [정답률 93%]

남자는 여자에게 사각형 테이블도 확인해 보라고 했지만, 그림에는 원형 테이블이 놓여 있으므로 대화의 내용과 일치하지 않는 것은 ④이다.

> **왜 오답 ?**

① 창문 앞에 걸어놓는 식물이 있다.
② 세계 지도에 "세계로"라는 슬로건이 있다.
③ 소파 위에 쿠션 두 개가 있다.
⑤ 시계 아래 자판기가 있다.

M : Ms. Kim, Empty Your Plate Day is coming. How's the preparation going?
남 : Kim 선생님, '식판 비우기의 날'이 다가와요. 준비는 어떻게 되고 있나요?

W : I've finally decided on the lunch menu for that day. ③의 함정
여 : 전 마침내 그날을 위한 점심 메뉴를 결정했어요.

M : You did! How did you do that?
남 : 그랬군요! 그걸 어떻게 했나요?

W : I did a survey of students' favorite foods. ④의 함정
여 : 전 학생들이 가장 좋아하는 음식에 관한 설문 조사를 했어요.

M : Good idea! Can I help you with anything?
남 : 좋은 생각이에요! 제가 도울 일이 있을까요?

W : Actually, Mr. Han, I'm not sure how to motivate students to participate.
여 : 실은, Han 선생님, 전 어떻게 학생들이 참여하도록 동기 부여를 해야 할지 모르겠어요.

M : How about an award for the class with the fewest leftovers?
남 : 잔반이 가장 적은 학급에 상을 주는 건 어때요? ⑤의 함정

W : Sounds great. But how will we find that class?
여 : 좋아요. 하지만 그 학급을 우리가 어떻게 찾죠?

M : You could give a sticker to the students who leave nothing on their plates. And then, you can find the class with the most stickers.
남 : 식판에 아무것도 남기지 않은 학생들에게 스티커를 줄 수 있어요. 그러면, 당신은 가장 많은 스티커를 가진 학급을 찾을 수 있어요. 단서 1 여자는 남자에게 스티커를 준비해달라고 부탁함

W : Excellent. Could you prepare some stickers for me?
여 : 훌륭해요. 저를 위해 스티커를 좀 준비해 줄 수 있으신가요?

M : Sure. I'll do that for you. 단서 2 남자는 여자의 부탁을 들어주겠다고 함
남 : 물론이죠. 제가 그것을 해 드릴게요.

W : Thanks. Then I'll put a notice on the bulletin board. ②의 함정
여 : 감사합니다. 그러면 제가 게시판에 안내문을 게시할게요.

• motivate ⓥ 동기 부여를 하다 • participate ⓥ 참여하다
• leftover ⓝ 잔반 • notice ⓝ 안내문 • bulletin board 게시판

> 대화를 듣고, 남자가 할 일로 가장 적절한 것을 고르시오.

① 스티커 준비하기 여자는 남자에게 스티커를 준비해달라고 부탁함
② 안내문 게시하기 여자가 할 일임
③ 급식 메뉴 선정하기 여자가 이미 급식 메뉴를 선정함
④ 설문 조사 실시하기 여자가 이미 설문 조사를 실시함
⑤ 우수 학급 시상하기 우수 학급 시상은 '식판 비우기의 날' 이후에 진행될 예정임

> 왜 정답? ＊＊＊ [정답률 96%]

여자와 남자는 '식판 비우기의 날'을 준비하면서 학생들을 어떻게 참여시킬지 논의하고 있다. 남자는 식판에 아무것도 남기지 않은 학생들에게 스티커를 주자고 제안했고, 여자는 그 제안에 동의하며 남자에게 스티커 준비를 부탁하고 있으므로 정답은 ①이다.

> 왜 오답?

② 여자가 안내문을 게시하겠다고 했다.
③ 여자가 이미 급식 메뉴를 선정했다.
④ 여자가 이미 설문 조사를 실시했다.
⑤ 우수 학급 시상은 '식판 비우기의 날' 이후에 진행될 예정이다.

W : Welcome to Boom Telecom. How can I help you?
여 : Boom Telecom에 오신 걸 환영합니다. 무엇을 도와드릴까요?

M : Hi. I'm thinking of changing my internet provider. What service plans do you have?
남 : 안녕하세요. 전 제 인터넷 서비스 제공 업체를 바꾸려고 생각 중입니다. 무슨 요금제가 있나요?

W : Okay. We have the Economic plan that's $20 per month. And the Supreme plan, which is faster, is $30 per month.
여 : 좋습니다. 저희는 한 달에 20달러인 알뜰 요금제가 있습니다. 그리고 수프림 요금제는 더 빠르고, 한 달에 30달러입니다. 단서 1 수프림 요금제는 한 달에 30달러임

M : I prefer the faster one.
남 : 전 더 빠른 것을 선호합니다.

W : Alright. We also have an OTT service for an extra $10 per month. What do you think? 단서 2 OTT 서비스는 한 달에 추가 10달러임
여 : 좋습니다. 저희는 또한 매달 추가 10달러에 OTT 서비스를 드립니다. 어떠세요?

M : Awesome. I'd like that as well.
남 : 훌륭합니다. 전 그것도 원해요.

W : Excellent choice. Then you'll have the Supreme plan with the OTT service, right? 단서 3 수프림 요금제와 OTT 서비스를 선택함
여 : 훌륭한 선택입니다. 그러면 OTT 서비스와 수프림 요금제를 고르시는 게 맞죠?

M : Correct. Can I get a discount?
남 : 맞습니다. 제가 할인을 받을 수 있나요?

W : I'm afraid that the 10% discount promotion is over. 단서 4 10% 할인 행사는 종료되어 할인을 받을 수 없음
여 : 10% 할인 행사가 종료되어 안타깝습니다.

M : That's a shame. But I'll take it anyway.
남 : 그거 아쉽군요. 하지만 어쨌든 그걸로 하겠습니다.

W : Thank you. Please fill in this paper with your payment information.
여 : 감사합니다. 이 서류에 결제 정보를 작성해 주세요.

M : Okay. [Writing sound] Here you are. 남 : 네. [적는 소리] 여기 있습니다.

• service plan 요금제 • prefer ⓥ 선호하다 • discount ⓝ 할인
• promotion ⓝ 판매 촉진 • fill in (서식을) 작성하다

> 대화를 듣고, 남자가 매달 지불할 금액을 고르시오.
① $20 ② $27 ③ $30 ④ $36 ⑤ $40
$30(수프림 요금제) + $10(OTT 서비스)

> 왜 정답? ＊＊＊ [정답률 71%]

남자는 속도가 더 빠른 월 30달러짜리 수프림 요금제를 선택했고, 매달 10달러의 추가 비용으로 제공되는 OTT 서비스도 신청했으므로, 남자가 지불할 금액은 ⑤ '40달러'이다.

[Cell phone rings.] [휴대 전화가 울린다.]

M : Hi, Isabella. 남 : 안녕, Isabella.

W : Hi, Lorenzo. Did you finish your part-time job? ②의 함정
여 : 안녕, Lorenzo. 넌 아르바이트를 끝냈니?

M : Yes. I'm on my way to a meeting for a chemistry project. What's up? ④의 함정
남 : 응. 난 화학 프로젝트를 위한 모임에 가는 중이야. 무슨 일이야?

W : Your favorite talk show is *The Alice Mitchell Show*, right?
여 : 네가 가장 좋아하는 토크 쇼는 The Alice Mitchell Show가 맞지?

M : Yeah, I'm a big fan of hers. I even went to her book signing event. ③의 함정
남 : 맞아, 난 그녀의 엄청난 팬이야. 난 심지어 그녀의 책 사인회도 갔어.

W : I knew it! I got two tickets for her talk show. It's next Saturday evening.

여 : 역시! 내가 그녀의 토크 쇼 티켓을 두 장 얻었어. 다음 주 토요일 저녁이야.

M : Whoa! Can you please take me with you?

남 : 와! 나를 데려가 줄 수 있어?

W : Actually, I'm not available that day. The tickets are all yours.

여 : 사실, 난 그날 갈 수 없어. 그 티켓은 다 네 거야.

M : Wait, why can't you go? Is it **because of** the family gathering you mentioned before? ①의 함정
  because of+명사

남 : 잠깐, 너는 왜 못 가? 네가 예전에 언급했던 가족 모임 때문이야?

W : No, that's in two weeks. Next Saturday I have to attend my friend's wedding. 단서 여자는 다음 주 토요일에 친구의 결혼식에 참석해야 함

여 : 아니, 그건 2주 뒤야. 다음 주 토요일에 나는 내 친구의 결혼식에 참석해야 해.

M : Oh, I see. Then I'll take the tickets with pleasure. Thank you so much.

남 : 오, 알겠어. 그러면 내가 기쁜 마음으로 그 티켓을 받을게. 정말 고마워.

- chemistry ⓝ 화학 - signing event 사인회 - gathering ⓝ 모임
- mention ⓥ 언급하다

대화를 듣고, 여자가 토크 쇼를 방청하러 갈 수 없는 이유를 고르시오.

① 가족 모임에 가야 해서 여자의 가족 모임은 2주 뒤에 있음
② 아르바이트를 해야 해서 남자가 아르바이트를 끝냈다는 언급으로 만든 오답
③ 책 사인회를 준비해야 해서 남자가 책 사인회에 간 적이 있다는 언급으로 만든 오답
④ 화학 프로젝트를 해야 해서 남자가 화학 프로젝트를 위한 모임에 가는 중이라는 언급으로 만든 오답
⑤ 친구 결혼식에 참석해야 해서 여자는 다음 주 토요일에 친구 결혼식에 참석해야 함

왜 정답? ✽✽✽ [정답률 96%]

여자는 다음 주 토요일에 친구의 결혼식에 참석해야 해서 토크 쇼에 갈 수 없다고 했으므로 정답은 ⑤이다.

왜 오답?

① 여자의 가족 모임은 다음 주 토요일이 아니라 2주 뒤에 있다. 주의
② 남자가 아르바이트를 끝냈다는 것으로 만든 오답이다.
③ 책 사인회에 간 적이 있다는 것으로 만든 오답이다.
④ 화학 프로젝트를 위한 모임에 가는 중이라는 것으로 만든 오답이다.

---

08 정답 ④ ✽북극금 수영 대회

W : Michael, look at this poster. The Polar Bear Swim **will be held** soon. 미래시제 수동태

여 : Michael, 이 포스터를 봐. '북극금 수영 대회'가 곧 열릴 거야.

M : I know! **I've been** really **looking** forward to it. [Pause] It's on December 23rd. ①의 단서 행사 날짜
  현재완료진행

남 : 그러니까! 난 그거 정말로 기대하고 있었어. [잠시 후] 12월 23일이구나.

W : Yeah. We can enjoy winter sea-swimming.

여 : 맞아. 우리는 겨울 바다 수영을 즐길 수 있어.

M : How nice! **To join** this event, we must hand in a medical check-up paper. ②의 단서 제출 서류
  부사적 용법(목적)

남 : 멋지다! 이 이벤트에 참가하려면 우리는 건강 검진 결과지를 제출해야 해.

W : I think it's a good policy for everyone's health since the water is icy cold.

여 : 물이 얼음장처럼 차갑기 때문에 난 그건 모든 사람의 건강을 위해 좋은 정책이라고 생각해.

M : I agree. By the way, it says that there's a limit of 100 people.

남 : 동의해. 그런데, 인원이 100명으로 제한된다고 하네. ③의 단서 최대 참가 인원

W : Oh, we must hurry. Look! Registration starts this Saturday.

여 : 오, 우리는 서둘러야겠어. 봐! 등록이 이번 주 토요일에 시작이야.

M : I'll set a reminder on my phone.

남 : 내가 내 핸드폰에 리마인더를 설정해 둘게.

W : Great idea. And the entry fee is just $15. ⑤의 단서 참가비

여 : 좋은 생각이야. 그리고 참가비는 겨우 15달러야.

M : Yes. And all entry fees will be donated to charity.

남 : 맞아. 그리고 모든 참가비는 자선단체에 기부될 거야.

W : Cool. Let's have some icy fun **while doing** a good deed.
  사이에 주어와 be동사 생략

여 : 멋지다. 좋은 일을 하면서 물놀이를 즐기자.

- hand in ~을 제출하다 - medical check-up 건강 검진
- policy ⓝ 정책 - registration ⓝ 등록 - entry fee 참가비
- donate ⓥ 기부하다 - deed ⓝ 행위, 행동

대화를 듣고, Polar Bear Swim에 관해 언급되지 않은 것을 고르시오.

① 행사 날짜 It's on December 23rd.
② 제출 서류 we must hand in a medical check-up paper
③ 최대 참가 인원 there's a limit of 100 people
④ 기념품 언급되지 않음
⑤ 참가비 the entry fee is just $15

왜 정답? ✽✽✽ [정답률 94%]

북극금 수영 대회의 행사 날짜, 제출 서류, 최대 참가 인원, 참가비는 언급되었지만, 기념품은 언급되지 않았으므로 정답은 ④이다.

왜 오답?

① 행사 날짜는 12월 23일이라고 했다.
② 제출 서류는 건강 검진 결과라고 했다.
③ 최대 참가 인원은 100명이라고 했다.
⑤ 참가비는 15달러라고 했다.

---

09 정답 ③ ✽당일치기 여행 프로그램 Walk in the Snow

W : Hello, listeners! Are you **a winter person**?
  a ~ person: ~을 좋아하는 사람(a cat person: 고양이를 좋아하는 사람)

여 : 안녕하세요, 청취자 여러분! 여러분은 겨울을 좋아하시나요?

Then, Walk in the Snow might just be the adventure for you.
그러면, '눈 속 걷기'는 딱 당신을 위한 모험일지도 모릅니다.

It's a one-day tour program at Great White Mountain.
그것은 Great White 산에서의 1일 투어 프로그램입니다. ①의 단서

Regardless of hiking experience, anyone **who** is interested in hiking can participate in the tour. ②의 단서
  주격 관계대명사
하이킹 경험과 관계없이, 하이킹에 관심이 있는 누구나 투어에 참여할 수 있습니다.

Participants are required to bring their own snowshoes and poles.
참가자들은 각자의 설피(눈신)와 폴대를 가져와야 합니다.

But equipment is also available to rent for a small fee. ③의 단서 장비는 무료가 아니라 적은 요금을 지불하고 대여할 수 있음
하지만 장비는 적은 요금으로 대여할 수도 있습니다.

The registration fee is $10, and we offer discounts to students. ④의 단서
등록비는 10달러이고, 학생들에게는 할인을 제공합니다.

Don't forget **that** you must register in advance **to participate**.
  목적어절 접속사 *부사적 용법(목적)*
참여하기 위해서는 사전에 등록해야 한다는 것을 잊지 마세요. ⑤의 단서

For more information, please visit our website, www.walkinthesnow.com.
더 많은 정보를 보시려면, 저희의 웹사이트 www.walkinthesnow.com에 방문해 주세요.

Thank you.
감사합니다.

- adventure ⓝ 모험 - regardless of ~와 관계없이
- participant ⓝ 참가자 - equipment ⓝ 장비 - in advance 미리

Walk in the Snow에 관한 다음 내용을 듣고, 일치하지 <u>않는</u> 것을 고르시오.

① 1일 투어 프로그램이다. It's a one-day tour program at Great White Mountain.
② 하이킹에 관심이 있는 누구든 참여할 수 있다. anyone who is interested in hiking can participate in the tour
③ 장비를 무료로 대여할 수 있다. equipment is also available to rent for a small fee
④ 학생에게 등록비 할인을 해 준다. we offer discounts to students
⑤ 참여하려면 사전에 등록해야 한다. you must register in advance to participate

왜 정답? ✱✱✱ [정답률 92%]

장비는 적은 금액을 지불하고 대여할 수 있다고(equipment is also available to rent for a small fee) 했으므로 장비를 무료로 대여할 수 있다고 한 ③은 일치하지 않는다.

왜 오답?

① Great White 산에서 열리는 1일 투어 프로그램이라고 했다.
② 하이킹 경험과 관계없이, 하이킹에 관심이 있는 누구든 참여할 수 있다고 했다.
④ 등록비는 10달러이고, 학생에게 등록비 할인을 해 준다고 했다.
⑤ 참여하려면 사전에 등록해야 한다고 했다.

---

10 정답 ③ ✱ 새로운 달력을 고르는 부부

M : Honey, what are you looking at?
남 : 여보, 무엇을 보고 있나요?

W : It's a brochure for a new calendar. Why don't we choose one together?
why don't we 동사원형: ~하는 게 어때?
여 : 이건 새로운 달력에 대한 안내서예요. 같이 하나 골라보는 건 어때요?

M : Great. How much do you want to spend?
남 : 좋아요. 당신은 얼마를 지출하고 싶으요?

W : I think more than $20 is not reasonable.
여 : 전 20달러 이상은 합리적이지 않다고 생각해요. 단서 1 20달러가 넘지 않아야 함 (⑤ 제외)

M : Agreed. How about trying a new format instead of a wall calendar? We've only used wall calendars so far.
how about -ing: ~하는 게 어때?   현재완료
남 : 동의해요. 벽걸이 달력 대신에 새로운 형태를 도전해 보는 건 어때요? 우리는 지금까지 벽걸이 달력만 써왔어요. 단서 2 책상에 세워 두는 형태를 고르고자 함 (④ 제외)

W : Good idea. Let's pick the standing desk format, then.
여 : 좋은 생각이에요. 그러면 책상에 세워 두는 형태를 골라요. 단서 3 재활용 가능한 종이로 만들어진 것을 선호함 (① 제외)

M : Okay. And I prefer one that's made of recyclable paper.
주격 관계대명사
남 : 좋아요. 그리고 전 재활용 가능한 종이로 만들어진 것을 선호해요.

W : Me, too. It's more eco-friendly than those that cannot be recycled.
= calendars 주격 관계대명사
여 : 저도요. 그건 재활용될 수 없는 것들보다 더 친환경적이에요.

M : Then, let's cross this out. Now, we have two options left.
과거분사(options 수식)
Which one do you prefer?
남 : 그러면, 이건 지웁시다. 이제 두 옵션이 남았어요. 어느 것을 선호하나요?

W : I think the classic art theme doesn't match our interior design. 단서 4 고전 예술 테마는 실내 장식과 어울리지 않는다고 생각함 (② 제외)
여 : 전 고전 예술 테마는 우리의 실내 장식과 어울리지 않는다고 생각해요.

M : Good point. Then, let's choose this one.
남 : 좋은 지적이에요. 그러면, 이걸 고릅시다.

- brochure ⓝ 안내서   • reasonable ⓐ 합리적인
- format ⓝ 형식, 형태   • instead of ~ 대신에   • so far 지금까지
- recyclable ⓐ 재활용 가능한   • eco-friendly ⓐ 친환경의
- cross out 선을 그어 지우다   • match ⓥ 어울리다

다음 표를 보면서 대화를 듣고, 두 사람이 선택할 달력을 고르시오.

Calendar 달력   재활용 가능한 종이가 아님

	Model 제품	Price 가격	Format 형태	Recyclable Paper 재활용 가능한 종이	Theme 테마
①	A	$8	standing desk 책상에 세워 두는 형태	×	modern art 현대 예술
②	B	$10	standing desk	○	classic art 고전 예술
③	C	$12	standing desk	○	movie
④	D	$16	wall 벽에 거는 형태	○	nature 자연
⑤	E	$22	wall	×	animal 동물

20달러가 넘음   고전 예술 테마임

왜 정답? ✱✱✱ [정답률 81%]

부부는 새로운 달력을 고르면서 20달러를 넘지 않고(⑤ 제외), 책상에 세워 두는 형태이며(④ 제외), 재활용 가능한 종이로 만들어지고(① 제외), 고전 예술 테마가 아닌 것(② 제외)을 선택했으므로 정답은 ③이다.

왜 오답?

① 재활용 가능한 종이가 아니다.
② 고전 예술 테마이다.
④ 벽에 거는 형태이다.
⑤ 20달러가 넘는다.

---

11 정답 ① ✱ 국회에서 연설하게 된 Lucas

W : Congratulations, Lucas! I heard you were invited to speak at the National Assembly.
여 : 축하해, Lucas! 난 네가 국회에서 연설하도록 초청받았다고 들었어.

M : Thanks. It's a real honor. I think the article I wrote in the newspaper made a strong impression.
앞에 목적격 관계대명사가 생략됨   단서 1 남자는 신문에 썼던 기사로 강한 인상을 남겨서 국회에 초청받음
남 : 고마워. 그건 정말 영광이야. 난 내가 신문에 썼던 기사가 강한 인상을 남겼다고 생각해.

W : I'm so proud of you. What did you mostly write about?
여 : 난 네가 정말 자랑스러워. 넌 주로 무엇에 대해 썼어? 단서 2 여자는 남자에게 그 기사의 내용이 무엇인지 물어봄

M : **I covered the worrying state of marine life.**
남 : 난 해양 생물의 걱정스러운 상태를 보도했어.

- National Assembly 국회   • honor ⓝ 영광
- impression ⓝ 인상   • mostly ⓐⓓ 주로   • cover ⓥ 보도하다
- state ⓝ 상태   • marine ⓐ 해양의   • biology ⓝ 생물학

대화를 듣고, 여자의 마지막 말에 대한 남자의 응답으로 가장 적절한 것을 고르시오.

① I covered the worrying state of marine life. 남자가 쓴 신문 기사의 내용을 물었음
  난 해양 생물의 걱정스러운 상태를 보도했어.
② I sent an article to the biology department. 기사를 어디에 보냈는지를 물어본 것이 아님
  난 생물학 부서에 기사를 보냈어.
③ Whatever you did, let's not speak about it. 대화의 흐름에 어울리지 않음
  네가 무엇을 했건 간에, 그것에 대해 이야기하지 말자.
④ I spent lots of time preparing the speech. 남자의 연설 준비 과정을 물어본 것이 아님
  난 연설을 준비하는 데 많은 시간을 썼어.
⑤ The article was mainly read by students. 기사의 대상 독자를 물어본 것이 아님
  기사는 주로 학생들이 읽어.

왜 정답? ✱✱✱ [정답률 54%]

남자는 자신이 썼던 신문 기사 덕분에 국회에 초청을 받아 연설을 하게 되었다. 여자는 남자를 자랑스러워하며, 남자가 무엇에 관해 신문 기사를 썼는지를 물어보고 있다. 따라서 남자는 ① '난 해양 생물의 걱정스러운 상태를 보도했어.'라고 응답하는 것이 적절하다.

왜 오답?

② 기사를 어디에 보냈는지를 물어보는 상황이 아니다.
③ 신문 기사가 무엇인지 물어보는 대화 내용에 어울리지 않는 응답이다.
④ 남자의 연설 준비 과정을 물어보는 상황이 아니다.
⑤ 기사의 대상 독자를 물어보는 상황이 아니다.

12 정답 ② *셔틀버스의 운영을 몰랐던 Claire

M : Claire, why are you sweating? It's pretty cold outside.
남 : Claire, 왜 땀을 흘리고 있니? 밖은 꽤 추운데.

W : Hey, Jamie. I ran to be in time for class. It's too far to walk from the subway station to our college, don't you think?
여 : Jamie야. 난 수업을 제시간에 오기 위해 뛰었어. 지하철역에서 우리 대학교까지 걷는 건 너무 멀어, 그렇게 생각하지 않니?

M : Yes, but the shuttle bus began running last week. You can take it instead. 단서 남자는 여자에게 지난주부터 셔틀버스가 운영하기 시작했다고 알려줌
남 : 맞아, 하지만 셔틀버스가 지난주부터 운영하기 시작했어. 넌 대신 그걸 탈 수 있어.

W : **Good news. Thanks for letting me know.**
여 : 좋은 소식이야. 알려줘서 고마워.

- sweat ⓥ 땀을 흘리다   - in time 제시간에

대화를 듣고, 남자의 마지막 말에 대한 여자의 응답으로 가장 적절한 것을 고르시오.
① Take care. The weather is freezing cold. 날씨에 관한 대화가 아님
조심해. 날씨가 엄청 추워.
②Good news. Thanks for letting me know.
좋은 소식이야. 알려줘서 고마워.   남자는 여자가 모르고 있었던 셔틀버스 운영에 대해 알려줌
③Hurry up. The bus is leaving very soon.
서둘러. 버스는 금방 떠날 거야.   버스를 타고자 하는 상황이 아님
④Seriously? I'd better try walking, then.
정말로? 난 그러면 걸어보는 게 좋겠네.   여자는 먼 거리를 걷는 것을 힘들어함
⑤Really? I was on the shuttle bus, too.
정말로? 나도 셔틀버스를 타고 있었어.   여자는 셔틀버스 운영에 대해 모르고 있음

왜 정답? **✱✱** [정답률 74%]
여자는 수업에 늦지 않기 위해 지하철역에서 대학교까지 뛰어왔다. 남자는 여자에게 셔틀버스가 지난주부터 운영하기 시작했다고 말하며, 그걸 탈 수 있다고 알려주었다. 따라서 남자의 말에 여자는 ② '좋은 소식이야. 알려줘서 고마워.'라고 응답하는 것이 적절하다.

왜 오답?
① 남자와 여자가 날씨에 관한 대화를 하는 상황이 아니다.
③ 남자와 여자가 서둘러 버스를 타고자 하는 상황이 아니다.
④ 여자가 먼 거리를 걷는 것을 힘들어하자, 남자가 셔틀버스를 알려주는 상황이다.
⑤ 여자는 셔틀버스 운영에 대해 모르고 있었다.

13 정답 ④ *무료 체험 기간이 만료된 파일 읽기 앱

W : Good morning, Pablo.
여 : 좋은 아침이야, Pablo.

M : Hi, Eva. Look at my new tablet PC.
남 : 안녕, Eva. 내 새로운 태블릿 PC를 봐.

W : Wow. How do you like it?
여 : 와. 어때?

M : It's opened a brand new world to me. But I have a small problem.
남 : 그건 나에게 완전히 새로운 세상을 열어주었어. 하지만 작은 문제가 있어.

W : What is it? Maybe I can be of help.
여 : 뭐야? 아마 내가 도울 수 있을 거야.

M : This file works well on my laptop, but it won't open on my tablet.
남 : 이 파일은 내 노트북에서는 잘 작동하지만, 내 태블릿에서는 열리지 않아.

W : Did you install a file-reading app? You need one to open the file on a tablet.
여 : 넌 파일 읽기 앱을 설치했어? 넌 태블릿에서 파일을 열려면 하나 필요할 거야.

M : I already did that a week ago.
남 : 난 이미 일주일 전에 그렇게 했어.

W : Then, I'll check a few things. [Tapping sound] I got it. The free trial period of this app is over. 단서 1 파일 읽기 앱의 무료 체험 기간이 끝남
여 : 그러면, 내가 몇 가지 확인해 볼게. [두드리는 소리] 알겠다. 이 앱의 무료 체험 기간이 끝났어.

M : Oh, that's why it doesn't work. Do you think I should pay for this app?
남 : 오, 그래서 그것이 작동하지 않았구나. 내가 이 앱에 돈을 내야 한다고 생각해?

W : Well, it depends on you. You can consider it if you need this app. 단서 2 남자에게 앱이 필요하다면 구매를 고려해 볼 수 있다고 조언함
여 : 글쎄, 그건 너에게 달렸지. 네가 이 앱이 필요하다면 그걸 고려해 볼 수 있어.

M : **I see. I'll give it some thought before buying this app.**
남 : 알겠어. 이 앱을 구매하기 전에 생각을 좀 해볼게.

- install ⓥ 설치하다   - trial ⓐ 체험의   - depend on ~에 달려 있다
- alphabetical ⓐ 알파벳순의
- give it some thought 그것에 대해 좀 생각해 보다

대화를 듣고, 여자의 마지막 말에 대한 남자의 응답으로 가장 적절한 것을 고르시오. [3점]
Man: _____
① Definitely. That's why I got a refund for the app.
확실해. 그래서 내가 앱을 환불받았어.   남자는 파일 읽기 앱을 구매한 적이 없음
② Sorry. I should have repaired my tablet PC earlier.
미안해. 내가 태블릿 PC를 더 일찍 고쳤어야 했는데.
③ Exactly. Documents were filed in alphabetical order.
정확해. 문서들은 알파벳 순서로 정리되어 있었어.   파일을 찾지 못하는 것이 문제가 아님
④I see. I'll give it some thought before buying this app.
알겠어. 이 앱을 구매하기 전에 생각을 좀 해볼게.   앱이 필요하다면 구매를 고려해보라고 조언함
⑤Don't worry. I still have a few more days for the free trial.
걱정하지 마. 난 아직 무료 체험이 며칠 더 있어.   파일 읽기 앱의 무료 체험 기간은 이미 만료됨
태블릿 PC가 고장 난 것이 아니라 파일이 열리지 않는 것이 문제임

왜 정답? **✱✱** [정답률 87%]
남자는 새로운 태블릿 PC에서 파일이 열리지 않는 문제를 겪자, 여자는 파일 읽기 앱의 무료 체험 기간이 끝났다는 것을 알려주었다. 남자가 앱에 돈을 내야 할지 고민하자, 여자는 앱이 필요하다고 생각하면 구매를 고려해 볼 수 있다고 조언했다. 따라서 이에 대한 응답으로 ④ '알겠어. 이 앱을 구매하기 전에 생각을 좀 해볼게.'가 가장 적절하다.

왜 오답?   주의
① 남자는 파일 읽기 앱을 구매한 적이 없으므로 환불받았다는 것은 적절하지 않다.
② 태블릿 PC가 고장 난 것이 아니라 파일이 열리지 않는 것이 문제이다.
③ 파일을 정리하지 못하거나 찾지 못하는 것이 문제가 아니다.
⑤ 파일 읽기 앱의 무료 체험 기간은 이미 만료되었다.

14 정답 ③ *노트 필기 자원봉사에 가입하고자 하는 Naomi

M : Hi, Naomi. What are you up to?
남 : 안녕, Naomi. 지금 무엇을 하고 있어?

W : Hi. I'm looking for volunteer work. Didn't you say you're volunteering?
여 : 안녕. 난 자원봉사 일을 찾고 있어. 너 자원봉사를 하고 있다고 말하지 않았어?

M : Yes. I'm working as a note-taker.
남 : 맞아. 난 노트 필기하는 사람으로 일하고 있어.

W : You mean helping students with hearing difficulties?
여 : 청각 장애가 있는 학생들을 돕는다는 뜻이지?

M : Right. It helps deaf students understand the class better.
남 : 맞아. 그건 농인 학생들이 수업을 더 잘 이해할 수 있도록 도와줘.

W : Interesting. Could you tell me more?
여 : 흥미롭다. 나에게 좀 더 말해 줄 수 있어?

M : I type everything during class, even jokes. The more detailed, the more understandable.
남 : 나는 수업 동안 모든 내용, 심지어 농담까지도 받아 적어. 더 자세할수록 더 이해하기 쉬워.

W : It sounds like a unique and valuable experience.
여 : 그건 특별하고 가치 있는 경험인 것 같아.

M : Yeah. Are you thinking about joining?
남 : 맞아. 너도 가입할 생각이 있니? 단서 1 여자는 학기 중에 자원봉사에 가입할 수 있을지 물어봄

W : Absolutely. But can I join in the middle of the semester?
여 : 물론이지. 하지만 내가 학기 중간에 가입할 수 있을까?

M : It could be possible. I heard **one member quit a few days** 앞에 명사절 접속사 that 생략
ago. 단서 1 남자는 한 부원이 며칠 전에 그만뒀다고 들었기 때문에 가능할 수도 있다고 답함
남 : 가능할 수도 있어. 나는 한 부원이 며칠 전에 그만뒀다고 들었어.

W : Lucky me. Is the position still available?
여 : 행운이다. 그 자리는 아직 공석이지? 단서 3 남자는 그 자리가 아직 공석인지에 대해 직접 문의해 보라고 여자에게 조언함

M : Hmm, I'm not sure, but if you ask the student volunteer center, you'll get an answer immediately.
남 : 음, 확실하지 않지만, 네가 학생 봉사 센터에 문의하면 즉시 답을 받을 거야.

W : **Okay. Wish me luck in getting this volunteer work.**
여 : 좋아. 이 자원봉사 일을 구하도록 나에게 행운을 빌어줘.

· hearing difficulty 청각 장애   · deaf ⓐ 귀가 먹은, 농인의
· in the middle of ~의 도중에[중간에]   · immediately ⓐⅾ 즉시
· sign language 수어

대화를 듣고, 남자의 마지막 말에 대한 여자의 응답으로 가장 적절한 것을 고르시오. [3점]

Woman : _____

① Good idea. Let's learn how to read sign language.
좋은 생각이야. 수어를 어떻게 읽는지 배우자.   수어에 관한 언급은 없음
② You're right. That's because I wanted to help him.
네가 맞아. 그건 내가 그를 돕고 싶었기 때문이야.   여자는 아직 자원봉사 동아리에 가입하지 않음
③Okay. Wish me luck in getting this volunteer work.   여자는
좋아. 이 자원봉사 일을 구하도록 나에게 행운을 빌어줘.   자원봉사에 공석이 있는지 확인해 보고자 함
④ Trust me. I bet you'll be selected as a note-taker.
나를 믿어. 난 네가 노트 필기하는 사람으로 뽑힐 것이라 확신해.
⑤ Wonderful. Thank you for taking notes for me in class.
훌륭해. 수업 중 나를 위해 노트 필기를 해줘서 고마워.   남자가 여자를 위해 노트
노트 필기하는 사람으로 새로 지원할 사람은 여자임   필기를 해준 것이 아님

왜 정답 ? ✿✿✿ [정답률 90%]

봉사활동을 찾고 있는 여자에게 남자는 노트 필기 자원봉사를 소개했다. 여자가 학기 중에도 가입할 수 있는지 묻자, 남자는 마침 부원 한 명이 며칠 전에 그만두어서 가능할 수도 있다고 했다. 이어서 남자는 그 자리가 아직 공석인지에 대해 학생 봉사 센터에 직접 문의해 보라고 여자에게 조언하고 있다. 따라서 남자의 마지막 말에 대한 여자의 적절한 응답은 ③ '좋아. 이 자원봉사 일을 구하도록 나에게 행운을 빌어줘.'이다.

왜 오답 ?

① 청력에 어려움이 있는 학생들을 위해 노트 필기를 하는 봉사활동으로, 수어에 관한 언급은 없었다.
② 여자는 아직 자원봉사 동아리에 가입하지 않았으므로 누군가를 돕고 싶었기 때문이었다는 말은 적절하지 않다.
④ 남자는 이미 노트 필기하는 사람으로 활동하고 있으므로, 상대방이 뽑힐 것이라고 확신한다는 것은 적절하지 않다. ─ 주의
⑤ 남자가 여자를 위해 노트 필기를 하는 것이 아니라 노트 필기 자원봉사에 대해 이야기하는 중이다.

---

15 정답 ⑤ ＊방문할 빵집의 목록을 작성하는 Tony와 Kate

M : Tony and Kate are members of the bread lovers club.
남 : Tony와 Kate는 빵을 사랑하는 사람들의 모임 회원이다.

They plan to go on a bakery tour every month.
그들은 매달 빵집 투어를 가기로 계획한다.
부사적 용법(목적)
To make a list of places to visit, they're sharing their ideas about must-visit bakeries.
방문할 장소의 목록을 만들기 위해, 그들은 꼭 방문해야 할 빵집에 관한 아이디어를 나누고 있다.

Kate proposes a bakery **whose** bread **she thinks** is super 소유격 관계대명사   삽입절
delicious.
Kate는 그녀가 생각하기에 빵이 엄청 맛있는 빵집을 제안한다.

However, Tony finds out that the baker there quit and since 현재완료
then there **have been** lots of reviews **complaining** about **the**   reviews 수식
동명사의 의미상 주어   동명사(전치사 about의 목적어)   단서 1 Kate가 제안한 빵집이
bread quality getting worse.   혹평받고 있다는 것을 알게 됨
그러나, Tony는 그곳의 제빵사가 그만두었고, 그때부터 빵의 질이 나빠지고 있다는 것을 알게 된다. 불평하는 후기들이 많이 있다는 것을 알게 된다.
목적어절 접속사
So, he wants to suggest **that** they choose a better bakery for
their where-to-go list.   단서 2 그래서 Tony는 Kate에게 다른 빵집을 고르자고
제안하고 싶음
그래서, 그는 가야 할 곳 목록을 위해 더 나은 빵집을 골라야 한다고 제안하기를 원한다.

In this situation, what would Tony most likely say to Kate?
이 상황에서, Tony가 Kate에게 할 말로 가장 적절한 것은 무엇인가?

Tony: **How about finding a different bakery for the list?**
Tony: 목록을 위해 다른 빵집을 찾는 게 어때?

＊상황 요약: Tony는 Kate가 추천한 빵집에 불만스러운 후기가 많아진 것을 발견했고, Kate에게 다른 빵집을 고르자고 제안하고자 함

· must-visit ⓐ 꼭 방문해야 할   · propose ⓥ 제안하다
· review ⓝ 후기   · complain ⓥ 불평하다

다음 상황 설명을 듣고, Tony가 Kate에게 할 말로 가장 적절한 것을 고르시오. [3점]

Tony : _____

① Why don't we post a review of this bakery?   후기를 적는 게 아니라
이 빵집에 대한 후기를 게시하는 게 어때?   방문할 빵집의 목록을 정하고 있음
② Let's give her the baker of the month award.
그녀에게 이달의 제빵사 상을 주자.   상을 주는 것에 관한 언급은 없음
③ We'd better check if we're on the waiting list.
우리가 대기 목록에 있는지 확인하는 편이 좋아.   실제로 대기하는 중이 아님
④ We should come later when the repairs are done.
우리는 나중에 수리가 끝나면 와야 해.   수리에 관한 언급은 없음
⑤How about finding a different bakery for the list?
목록을 위해 다른 빵집을 찾는 게 어때?   다른 빵집을 고르자고 제안함

왜 정답 ? ✿✿✿ [정답률 77%]

Tony와 Kate는 함께 방문할 빵집의 목록을 고르고 있다. Kate는 본인이 생각하기에 엄청 맛있는 빵집을 추천했으나, Tony는 그곳의 제빵사가 그만둔 후로 불만스러운 후기들이 많아진 것을 발견했다. 이에 Tony는 목록에 넣을 다른 빵집을 고르자고 Kate에게 제안하고 싶어 하므로, ⑤ '목록을 위해 다른 빵집을 찾는 게 어때?'라고 말하는 것이 적절하다.

왜 오답 ?

① Tony와 Kate는 이미 빵집을 방문하고 후기를 적는 것이 아니다. (✖ 이유: 이미 작성된 후기를 보고 더 나은 빵집을 고르려고 하는 것이다.)
② 이달의 제빵사 상에 관한 언급은 없다.
③ Tony와 Kate는 실제로 예약했거나, 대기하는 중이 아니다.
④ 빵집이 수리 중이라 다른 장소를 찾으려는 것이 아니다.

16~17 ＊개에게 해로운 과일들

W : Hello, students. //
여 : 안녕하세요, 학생 여러분 //
가주어   의미상 주어 진주어
Last time, / we learned / why **it**'s good **for us to eat** fruits and veggies. //
지난번에 / 우리는 배웠습니다 / 우리가 왜 과일과 채소를 먹는 것이 좋은지를 //
not always(부분 부정): 항상 ~한 것은 아니다
But what's good for us / **isn't always** good for animals. //
하지만 우리에게 좋은 것이 / 항상 동물들에게 좋은 것은 아닙니다 //
의문사 what + to부정사: 무엇을 ~할지
Today, / let's find out **what** fruits **to avoid** / when feeding dogs. // 16번 단서: 개에게 먹이를 줄 때 피해야 할 과일에 대해 이야기할 것임
오늘 / 무슨 과일을 피할지 알아봅시다 / 개에게 먹이를 줄 때 //
17번①   be known to 동사원형: ~하다고 알려져 있다
First, / **grapes** **are known** / to be highly toxic to dogs. //
먼저 / 포도는 알려져 있습니다 / 개에게 매우 독성이 강하다고 //

You should be careful / because even a single grape can cause / severe health damage. //
여러분은 조심해야 합니다 / 한 알의 포도조차 일으킬 수 있기에 / 심각한 건강 피해를 //

Now, let's take a look at cherries. //
이제 체리를 봅시다 //
17번 ②

If a dog swallows their seeds, / the dog is likely to **have difficulties breathing**. //
have difficulty(difficulties) -ing: ~하는 데 어려움을 겪다
개가 그것의 씨앗을 삼키면 / 개는 숨 쉬는 데 어려움을 겪을 것입니다 //

Next, if your dog doesn't eat avocados, / it would be for the best. //
17번 ③
다음으로 여러분의 개가 아보카도를 먹지 않는다면 / 그것은 최선일 것입니다 //

동명사 주어
That's because **eating** large amounts of avocados / can make **your dog sick**. //
make의 목적어와 목적격 보어(형용사)
많은 양의 아보카도를 먹는 것은 / 여러분의 개를 아프게 만들 수 있기 때문입니다 //

let의 목적어와 목적격 보어(원형부정사)
Finally, don't let **your dog snack** on grapefruits. //
마지막으로 여러분의 개가 자몽을 간식으로 먹도록 두지 마세요 //
17번 ④

so... that S can ~ 구문: 너무 …해서 ~할 수 있다
The fruit contains **so** much acid / **that some dogs can** develop stomach problems. //
그 과일은 너무 많은 산을 함유해서 / 몇몇 개들은 위장 문제를 일으킬 수 있습니다 //

Now, you may understand / why some fruits are said to be harmful to dogs. //
이제 여러분은 이해했을 겁니다 / 왜 몇몇 과일이 개들에게 해롭다고 이야기되는지 //

앞에 명사절 접속사 that 생략
I hope / **this information will help** / you and your dog / in living a happy life. //
저는 바랍니다 / 이 정보가 돕기를 / 여러분과 여러분의 개가 / 행복한 삶을 사는 것을 //

- veggie ⓝ 채소   - feed ⓥ 먹이를 주다
- toxic ⓐ 독성이 있는   - severe ⓐ 심각한   - swallow ⓥ 삼키다
- breathe ⓥ 숨을 쉬다   - snack on ~을 간식으로 먹다
- grapefruit ⓝ 자몽   - contain ⓥ 포함하다, 함유하다
- acid ⓝ (화학) 산   - pose ⓥ (문제를) 일으키다

여 : 안녕하세요, 학생 여러분. 지난번에 우리는 우리가 왜 과일과 채소를 먹는 것이 좋은지를 배웠습니다. 하지만 우리에게 좋은 것이 항상 동물들에게 좋은 것은 아닙니다. 오늘, 개에게 먹이를 줄 때 무슨 과일을 피할지 알아봅시다. 먼저, 포도는 개에게 매우 독성이 강하다고 알려져 있습니다. 한 알의 포도조차 심각한 건강 피해를 일으킬 수 있기에 여러분은 조심해야 합니다. 이제 체리를 봅시다. 개가 그것의 씨앗을 삼키면 개는 숨 쉬는 데 어려움을 겪을 것입니다. 다음으로 여러분의 개가 아보카도를 먹지 않는다면, 그것은 최선일 것입니다. 많은 양의 아보카도를 먹는 것은 여러분의 개를 아프게 만들 수 있기 때문입니다. 마지막으로 여러분의 개가 자몽을 간식으로 먹도록 두지 마세요. 그 과일은 너무 많은 산을 함유해서 몇몇 개들은 위장 문제를 일으킬 수 있습니다. 이제 여러분은 왜 몇몇 과일이 개들에게 해롭다고 이야기되는지 이해했을 겁니다. 저는 이 정보가 여러분과 여러분의 개가 행복한 삶을 사는 것을 돕기를 바랍니다.

16 정답 ①

여자가 하는 말의 주제로 가장 적절한 것은?
① fruits that can pose a risk to dogs' health
개의 건강에 위험을 주는 과일들 / 개에게 먹이면 건강 문제를 일으키는 과일들을 소개함
② ways to help dogs develop a taste for fruits
개가 과일에 대한 입맛을 키우도록 돕는 방법들 / 개의 입맛에 관한 언급은 없음
③ tips for protecting garden fruits from animals
동물로부터 정원 과일들을 지키는 팁들 / 동물이 과일에게 피해를 입히는 내용이 아님
④ reasons fruits should be included in dogs' diets
과일이 개의 식단에 포함되어야 할 이유들 / 과일이 식단에 포함되면 위험한 과일들에 관한 내용임
⑤ stories that use fruits and vegetables as characters
과일과 채소를 등장인물로 사용하는 이야기들 / 과일과 채소가 등장하는 이야기에 관한 언급은 없음

왜 정답? ✽※※ [정답률 93%]
개에게 먹이를 줄 때 피해야 할 과일들로 포도, 체리, 아보카도, 자몽을 소개하고 있다. 따라서 여자가 하는 말의 주제로 가장 적절한 것은 ① '개의 건강에 위험을 주는 과일들'이다.

왜 오답?
② 개의 입맛을 키우는 것에 관한 언급은 없다.
③ 과일이 동물의 건강에 해를 입히는 내용이지, 동물이 과일에 해를 입히는 내용이 아니다.
④ 개의 식단에 포함되면 위험한 과일들을 소개하고 있으므로 반대 내용이다.
⑤ 과일과 채소가 등장하는 이야기에 관한 언급은 없다.

17 정답 ⑤

언급된 과일이 아닌 것은?
① grapes 포도는 개에게 매우 독성이 강함
포도
② cherries 체리의 씨앗은 개가 숨 쉬는 것을 어렵게 함
체리
③ avocados 아보카도는 개를 아프게 만듦
아보카도
④ grapefruits 자몽은 위장 문제를 일으킴
자몽
⑤ cranberries 크랜베리는 언급되지 않음
크랜베리

왜 정답? ✽※※ [정답률 95%]
개의 건강에 위협을 주는 과일로 포도, 체리, 아보카도, 자몽은 언급했지만 ⑤ '크랜베리'는 언급하지 않았다.

왜 오답?
① 포도는 개에게 매우 독성이 강하기 때문에 한 알조차 조심해야 한다.
② 체리의 씨앗은 개가 숨 쉬는 것을 어렵게 한다.
③ 아보카도를 먹는 것은 개를 아프게 만든다.
④ 자몽은 너무 많은 산을 함유해서 위장 문제를 일으킨다.

18 정답 ⑤ ✽ 새로운 의류 매장의 판매직에 지원하는 Grace

Dear Ms. MacAlpine, / 친애하는 MacAlpine 씨께 /
명사절 접속사
I was so excited to hear / **that** your brand is opening a new shop / on Bruns Street next month. //
저는 듣고 매우 들떴습니다 / 당신의 브랜드가 새 매장을 연다는 것을 / 다음 달에 Bruns 거리에 //

현재완료(계속)   helps의 목적어와 목적격 보어(to부정사)
I **have always appreciated** / the way your brand helps / **women to feel** more stylish and confident. //
저는 항상 높이 평가해 왔습니다 / 당신의 브랜드가 도와주는 방식 / 여성들이 더 멋지고 자신감 있게 느끼도록 //

단서 1 구인 광고에 대한 응답으로 편지를 쓰고 있음
I am writing / in response to your ad / in the Bruns Journal. //
저는 편지를 쓰고 있습니다 / 당신의 광고에 대한 응답으로 / Bruns Journal에 있는 //

I graduated from the Meline School of Fashion / and **have worked** as a sales assistant / at LoganMart for the last five years. //
현재완료(계속)
저는 Meline 패션 학교를 졸업했고 / 판매 보조원으로 일해 왔습니다 / 지난 5년간 LoganMart에서 //

현재완료(계속)
During that time, / I've developed strong customer service and sales skills, / and now I **would like** to apply for the sales position / in your clothing store. // **단서 2** 판매원으로서의 자질을 소개하며 판매직에 지원하고자 함
= want
그 기간 동안 / 저는 뛰어난 고객 서비스 및 판매 기술을 발달시켜 왔고 / 이제 판매직에 지원하고 싶습니다 / 당신의 의류 매장의 //

I am available for an interview / at your earliest convenience. //
저는 인터뷰가 가능합니다 / 당신이 편한 가장 빠른 시간에 //

I look forward to hearing from you. //
당신으로부터 대답을 듣게 되기를 기대합니다 //

Thank you for reading my letter. //
저의 편지를 읽어 주셔서 감사드립니다 //

Yours sincerely, Grace Braddock / Grace Braddock 드림 /

- appreciate ⓥ 감사하다   - confident ⓐ 자신감 있는
- in response to ~에 대한 응답으로   - ad(= advertisement) ⓝ 광고
- graduate ⓥ 졸업하다   - at one's convenience 편한 때에

친애하는 MacAlpine 씨께,

저는 당신의 브랜드가 다음 달에 Bruns 거리에 새 매장을 연다는 것을 듣고 매우 들떴습니다. 저는 당신의 브랜드가 여성들이 더 멋지고 자신감 있게 느끼도록 도와주는 방식을 항상 높이 평가해 왔습니다. 저는 Bruns Journal에 있는 당신의 광고에 대한 응답으로 편지를 쓰고 있습니다. 저는 Meline 패션 학교를 졸업했고 지난 5년간 LoganMart에서 판매 보조원으로 일해 왔습니다. 그 기간 동안 저는 뛰어난 고객 서비스 및 판매 기술을 발달시켜 왔고, 이제 당신의 의류 매장의 판매직에 지원하고 싶습니다. 저는 당신이 편한 가장 빠른 시간에 인터뷰가 가능합니다. 당신으로부터 대답을 듣게 되기를 기대합니다. 저의 편지를 읽어 주셔서 감사드립니다.
Grace Braddock 드림

다음 글의 목적으로 가장 적절한 것은?

① 영업 시작일을 문의하려고 영업이 다음 달에 시작한다는 것을 이미 알고 있음
② 인터뷰 일정을 변경하려고 구직 인터뷰를 요청하고 있음
③ 디자인 공모전에 참가하려고 디자인 공모전에 관한 언급은 없음
④ 제품 관련 문의에 답변하려고 특정 제품과 관련된 언급은 없음
⑤ 의류 매장 판매직에 지원하려고 새로 오픈하는 의류 매장의 판매직에 지원하고자 함

왜 정답? ✱✱✱ [정답률 92%]

브랜드가 새 매장을 연다는 소식을 듣고, 자신의 패션 관련 학력과 경력을 소개하며 의류 매장의 판매직에 지원하고자 하므로 정답은 ⑤이다.

왜 오답?

① 영업은 다음 달에 시작한다고 제시되었다.
② 구직 인터뷰를 요청하고 있으므로, 일정을 변경한다는 것은 옳지 않다. 주의
③ 디자인 공모전에 관한 언급은 없었다.
④ 특정 제품과 관련된 언급은 없었다.

19 정답 ① ✱ 신혼여행에서 결혼 반지를 잃어버린 부부

I had never seen a beach / with such white sand or water / that was such a beautiful shade of blue. //
나는 해변을 한 번도 본 적이 없었다 / 그렇게 하얀 모래나 바다를 가진 / 그렇게 아름다운 푸른 색조의 //

Jane and I set up a blanket on the sand / while looking forward to our ten days of honeymooning / on an exotic island. //
Jane과 나는 모래 위에 담요를 깔았다 / 열흘간의 신혼여행을 기대하면서 / 이국적인 섬에서의 //
단서 1 Jane과 나는 이국적인 섬에서의 아름다운 신혼여행에 들떠 기대하고 있음

"Look!" // Jane waved her hand / to point at the beautiful scene before us / — and her gold wedding ring / went flying off her hand. //
단서 2 아내가 손을 흔들 때 결혼반지가 빠져버림
"저기 좀 봐" / Jane이 그녀의 손을 흔들어 / 우리 앞의 아름다운 풍경을 가리켰다 / 그러자 그녀의 금으로 된 결혼반지가 / 그녀의 손에서 빠져 날아갔다 //

I tried to see / where it went, / but the sun hit my eyes / and I lost track of it. //
나는 보려고 노력했지만 / 그것이 날아간 곳을 / 햇빛이 눈에 들어와 / 그것이 가던 방향을 놓쳤다 //

I didn't want to lose her wedding ring, / so I started looking in the area / where I thought it had landed. //
나는 그녀의 결혼반지를 잃어버리고 싶지 않아서 / 장소를 들여다보기 시작했다 / 내가 생각하기에 그것이 떨어졌을 //

However, the sand was so fine / and I realized / that anything heavy, like gold, / would quickly sink / and might never be found again. // 단서 3 해변에서 결혼반지를 찾을 수 없을 것임을 깨달음
하지만 모래가 너무 고왔고 / 나는 깨달았다 / 금처럼 무거운 것은 / 빨리 가라앉아 / 다시는 발견되지 않을 수도 있겠다는 것을 //

- shade ⓝ 색조 • honeymoon ⓥ 신혼여행을 하다
- exotic ⓐ 이국적인 • track ⓝ (이동하는) 길[방향]
- land ⓥ (땅에) 떨어지다 • fine ⓐ 고운

나는 그렇게 하얀 모래나 그렇게 아름다운 푸른 색조의 바다를 가진 해변을 한 번도 본 적이 없었다. 이국적인 섬에서의 열흘간의 신혼여행을 기대하면서 Jane과 나는 모래 위에 담요를 깔았다. "저기 좀 봐!" Jane이 그녀의 손을 흔들어 우리 앞의 아름다운 풍경을 가리켰다. 그러자 그녀의 금으로 된 결혼반지가 그녀의 손에서 빠져 날아갔다. 나는 그것이 날아간 곳을 보려고 노력했지만, 햇빛이 눈에 들어와 그것의 가던 방향을 놓쳤다. 나는 그녀의 결혼반지를 잃어버리고 싶지 않아서 내가 생각하기에 그것이 떨어졌을 장소를 들여다보기 시작했다. 하지만 모래가 너무 고왔고 나는 금처럼 무거운 것은 빨리 가라앉아 다시는 발견되지 않을 수도 있겠다는 것을 깨달았다.

다음 글에 드러난 'I'의 심경 변화로 가장 적절한 것은?

① excited → frustrated
들뜬 → 좌절한 처음에는 신혼여행으로 들떠있었지만, 결혼반지를 잃어버려 좌절함
② pleased → jealous 처음에는 기뻤지만, 결혼반지를 잃어버려 좌절함
기쁜 → 질투하는
③ nervous → confident 처음에는 신혼여행에 기뻐하므로 긴장될 상황이 아님
긴장된 → 자신감 있는
④ annoyed → grateful 마지막에 결혼반지를 찾지 못했으므로 감사할 상황이 아님
성가신 → 감사하는
⑤ relaxed → indifferent 마지막에 결혼반지를 잃어버렸으므로 무관심한 상황이 아님
편안한 → 무관심한

왜 정답? ✱✱✱ [정답률 88%]

전반부: 이국적이고 아름다운 섬의 해변에서 앞으로 열흘간의 신혼여행을 기대하고 있음 ▶ '들뜬', '기쁜', 또는 '편안한'
후반부: 아내가 손을 흔들 때 결혼반지가 빠졌고, 해변에서 반지를 찾지는 못할 것을 깨달음 ▶ '좌절한'
따라서 I의 심경 변화는 ① '들뜬 → 좌절한'이다.

왜 오답?

② 마지막에 결혼반지를 잃어버려 좌절했으므로, 질투하는 상황이 아니다.
③ 처음에는 신혼여행에 대한 기대를 하고 있으므로, 긴장될 상황이 아니다.
④ 마지막에 결혼반지를 찾지 못했으므로, 감사할 상황이 아니다.
⑤ 마지막에 결혼반지를 잃어버렸으므로, 무관심한 상황이 아니다. 주의

20 정답 ④ ✱ 졸업 이후에도 자발적인 성장 이루기

Unfortunately, / many people don't take personal responsibility / for their own growth. //
안타깝게도 / 많은 사람들이 개인적인 책임을 지지 않는다 / 그들 자신의 성장에 대해 //

Instead, / they simply run the race / laid out for them. //
대신 / 그들은 단지 경주를 한다 / 그들에게 놓인 //
단서 1 사람들은 학교를 다닐 때는 발전을 계속 함

They do well / enough in school to keep advancing. //
그들은 제법 잘한다 / 학교에서 계속 발전할 만큼 //

Maybe / they manage to get a good job / at a well-run company. //
아마도 / 그들은 좋은 일자리를 얻는 것을 해낸다 / 잘 운영되는 회사에서 //

But so many think and act / as if their learning journey ends / with college. //
하지만 아주 많은 사람들이 생각하고 행동한다 / 마치 그들의 배움의 여정이 끝나는 것처럼 / 대학으로 //

They have checked all the boxes in the life / that was laid out for them / and now lack a road map / describing the right ways / to move forward and continue to grow. //
그들은 삶의 모든 사항을 체크했고 / 그들에게 놓인 / 이제는 로드 맵이 없다 / 올바른 방법을 설명해 주는 / 앞으로 나아가고 계속 성장할 수 있는 //

In truth, / that's when the journey really begins. //
사실 / 그때가 여정이 진정으로 시작되는 때이다 //

When school is finished, / your growth becomes voluntary. //
학교 교육이 끝나면 / 여러분의 성장은 자발적이게 된다 //
단서 2 학교 졸업 후에 성장은 자발적으로 이루어짐

Like healthy eating habits or a regular exercise program, / you need to commit to it / and devote thought, time, and energy to it. // 단서 3 성장을 위해 자발적으로 에너지를 투자해야 함
건강한 식습관이나 규칙적인 운동 프로그램처럼 / 여러분은 그것에 전념하고 / 그것에 생각, 시간, 그리고 에너지를 쏟을 필요가 있다 //

Otherwise, it simply won't happen / — and your life and career
are likely to **stop progressing** / as a result. //
「stop + -ing」 ~하는 것을 멈추다
그렇지 않으면 그것은 그냥 일어나지 않을 것이고 / 여러분의 삶과 경력이 진전을 멈출
가능성이 있다 / 결과적으로 //

- take responsibility for ~에 책임을 지다   • advance ⓥ 발전하다
- manage to (간신히) 해내다   • well-run ⓐ 잘 운영되는
- commit to ~에 전념하다   • devote ~ to … ~을 …에 쏟다[바치다]
- otherwise ⓐⓓ 그렇지 않으면   • career ⓝ 경력

안타깝게도 많은 사람들이 그들 자신의 성장에 대해 개인적인 책임을 지지 않는
다. 대신, 그들은 단지 그들에게 놓인 경주를 한다. 그들은 학교에서 계속 발전
할 만큼 제법 잘한다. 아마도 그들은 잘 운영되는 회사에서 좋은 일자리를 얻는
것을 해낸다. 하지만 아주 많은 사람들이 마치 그들의 배움의 여정이 대학으로
끝나는 것처럼 생각하고 행동한다. 그들은 그들에게 놓인 삶의 모든 사항을 체
크했고 이제는 앞으로 나아가고 계속 성장할 수 있는 올바른 방법을 설명해 주
는 로드 맵이 없다. 사실, 그때가 여정이 진정으로 시작되는 때이다. 학교 교육
이 끝나면, 여러분의 성장은 자발적이게 된다. 건강한 식습관이나 규칙적인 운
동 프로그램처럼 여러분은 그것에 전념하고 그것에 생각, 시간, 그리고 에너지
를 쏟을 필요가 있다. 그렇지 않으면 그것은 그냥 일어나지 않을 것이고, 결과
적으로 여러분의 삶과 경력이 진전을 멈출 가능성이 있다.

> 다음 글에서 필자가 주장하는 바로 가장 적절한 것은?
> ① 성공 경험을 위해 달성 가능한 목표를 수립해야 한다. 달성 가능한 목표 수립은 언급되지 않음
> ② 체계적인 경력 관리를 위해 전문가의 도움을 받아야 한다. 경력 관리를 위해 전문가의 도움을 받는 내용은 언급되지 않음
> ③ 건강을 위해 꾸준한 운동과 식습관 관리를 병행해야 한다. 꾸준한 운동과 식습관 관리처럼 졸업 후에도 자발적인 성장에 전념하라는 내용임
> ④ 졸업 이후 성장을 위해 자발적으로 배움을 실천해야 한다. 졸업 후에도 자발적으로 배움을 위해 노력해야 한다는 내용임
> ⑤ 적성에 맞는 직업을 찾기 위해 학교 교육에 충실해야 한다. 학교 교육 이후의 성장에 관한 내용임

> **왜 정답?** ★★※ [정답률 85%]

사람들은 학교에 다니는 동안은 끊임없이 발전하지만, 졸업 후에는 성장을 멈춘다고
한다. 졸업 후의 성장은 온전히 개인의 책임이며, 이를 위해 자발적으로 에너지를
쏟아야 한다고 주장하고 있으므로 정답은 ④이다.

> **왜 오답?**

① 달성 가능한 목표 수립은 언급되지 않았다.
② 경력 관리를 위해 전문가의 도움을 받는 내용은 언급되지 않았다.
③ 꾸준한 운동과 식습관 관리를 병행하라는 내용이 아니라, 그러한 것들과
  마찬가지로 졸업 후에도 자발적인 성장에 전념하라는 내용이다. 함정
⑤ 학교 교육 이후의 성장에 관한 내용이다.

---

21 정답 ④ ⭐2등급 대비 [정답률 56%]

*객관적이면서도 주관적인 색 인지

Many people take the commonsense view / **that** color is an
동격절 접속사
objective property / of things, / or of the light **that** bounces off
주격 관계대명사(선행사 light)
= things
them. // 단서 1 색은 사물, 또는 사물의 빛 반사로 인한 객관적인 속성이라는 견해가 있음
많은 사람들이 상식적인 견해를 취한다 / 색은 객관적인 속성이라는 / 사물의 / 또는
사물로부터 튕겨 나오는 빛의 //
뒤에 목적어절 접속사 that이 생략됨
They say a tree's leaves are green / because they reflect green
주격 관계대명사   원급 비교
light / — a greenness **that** is just **as** real **as** the leaves. //
그들은 나뭇잎이 녹색이라고 말한다 / 녹색 빛을 반사하기 때문에 / (정확히 나뭇잎만큼
진짜인 녹색) //
명사절 접속사   타동사
Others argue / **that** color doesn't **inhabit** the physical world at
all / but exists only in the eye or mind of the viewer. //
다른 사람들은 주장한다 / 색이 물리적인 세계에 전혀 존재하지 않고 / 보는 사람의 눈이나
정신 안에만 존재한다고 / 단서 2 색은 사람의 눈과 정신에 의한 주관적인 속성이라는 견해가 있음
명사절 접속사
They maintain / **that** if a tree fell in a forest / and no one was
형용사적 용법(no one 수식)
there **to see** it, / its leaves would be colorless / — and **so would**
so가 앞으로 가면서 주어와 동사가 도치됨
everything else. // 그들은 주장한다 / 만약 나무가 숲에서 쓰러지고 / 그것을 볼 사람이
아무도 거기에 없다면 / 그것의 잎은 색이 없을 것이고 / 다른 모든 것들도 그럴 것이라고 //

뒤에 목적어절 접속사 that이 생략됨
They say / there is no such *thing* as color; / there are only the
주격 관계대명사
people **who** see it. //
그들은 말한다 / 색 같은 '것'은 없고 / 그것을 보는 사람들만 있다고 //
Both positions are, / in a way, correct. // 단서 3 색이 객관적이라는 견해와
주관적이라는 견해는 어떤 면에서는 모두 옳음
두 가지 입장 모두 / 어떤 면에서는 옳다 //
Color is objective *and* subjective / — "the place," **as Paul Cézanne**
관계부사   삽입절
put it, / "**where** our brain and the universe meet." //
색은 객관적이고 '동시에' 주관적이며 / Paul Cézanne이 말했듯이 장소이다 / '우리의 뇌와
우주가 만나는' // 단서 4 색은 객관적인 세상의 빛이 주관적인
부사절 접속사   뇌에 의해 해석될 때 만들어짐
Color is created / **when** light from the world / is registered by
the eyes / and interpreted by the brain. //
색은 만들어진다 / 세상으로부터의 빛이 / 눈에 의해 등록되고 / 뇌에 의해 해석될 때 //

- commonsense ⓐ 상식적인   • objective ⓐ 객관적인
- property ⓝ 속성, 성질   • bounce off 튕겨 나오다
- reflect ⓥ 반사하다   • inhabit ⓥ ~에 살다[존재하다]
- physical ⓐ 물리적인   • subjective ⓐ 주관적인

많은 사람들이 색은 사물 또는 사물로부터 튕겨 나오는 빛의 객관적인 속성이
라는 상식적인 견해를 취한다. 그들은 나뭇잎이 녹색 빛(정확히 나뭇잎만큼 진
짜인 녹색)을 반사하기 때문에 녹색이라고 말한다. 다른 사람들은 색이 물리적
인 세계에 전혀 존재하지 않고 보는 사람의 눈이나 정신 안에만 존재한다고 주
장한다. 그들은 만약 나무가 숲에서 쓰러지고 그것을 볼 사람이 아무도 거기에
없다면, 그것의 잎은 색이 없을 것이고, 다른 모든 것들도 그럴 것이라고 주장
한다. 그들은 색 같은 '것'은 없고 그것을 보는 사람만 있다고 말한다. 두 가
지 입장 모두 어떤 면에서는 옳다. 색은 객관적이고 '동시에' 주관적이며, Paul
Cézanne이 말했듯이 '우리의 뇌와 우주가 만나는 곳'이다. 색은 세상으로부터
의 빛이 눈에 의해 등록되고 뇌에 의해 해석될 때 만들어진다.

> 밑줄 친 our brain and the universe meet가 다음 글에서 의미하는
> 바로 가장 적절한 것은? [3점] our brain은 나의 관점을 가리키지만, the universe는
> 다른 이들의 관점이 아닌 객관적인 빛의 반사를 가리킴
> ① we see things beyond the range of perception 객관적인 빛의 반사를
> 우리는 인식의 범위를 넘어서 사물을 본다   인식하기 때문에 인식의 범위를 넘어설 수 없음
> ② objects appear different by the change of light
> 사물들은 빛의 변화에 의해 다르게 나타난다   주관적인 해석에 관한 내용이 빠져 있음
> ③ your perspectives and others' reach an agreement
> 당신의 관점과 다른 이들의 관점이 합의를 이룬다
> ④ our mind and physical reality interact with each other
> 우리의 정신과 물리적 현실이 서로 상호작용한다
> ⑤ structures of the human brain and the universe are
> similar 인간의 뇌와 우주 구조의 유사성은 언급되지 않음
> 인간 뇌와 우주의 구조는 유사하다
> 객관적인 현실과 주관적인 해석이 상호작용하여 색을 인식함

> **왜 2등급?** 지문에 등장한 단어들이 선택지 곳곳에 배치되어 있어 정답을 단번에
> 찾기 어려운 2등급 대비 문제이다. 대립하는 두 가지 주장에 해당하는 단어들을 잘
> 정리하여 밑줄 친 부분의 단어들과 비교하며 의미를 파악해야 한다.

| 문제 풀이 순서 |

1st 밑줄 친 부분이 포함된 문장을 읽고, 그 의미가 무엇일지 예상한다.

> 색은 객관적이고 '동시에' 주관적이며, Paul Cézanne이 말했듯이 '우리의
> 뇌와 우주가 만나는 곳'이다.

➡ 색이 객관적인 동시에 주관적이라고 했다. 이 사실에 관하여 '우리의 뇌'와 '우주'가
각각 무엇을 나타내는지, 그 둘이 '만나는' 것이 무엇을 의미하는지 파악해야 한다.

2nd 글의 나머지 부분에서 색에 관하여 대립하는 주장을 파악하고 정답을 찾는다.

- **주장 1:** 색은 사물, 또는 사물의 빛 반사로 인한 객관적인 속성이라는 견해가
  있다. 단서 1
- **주장 2:** 색은 사람의 눈과 정신에 의한 주관적인 속성이라는 견해도 있다. 단서 2
- **결론:** 색이 객관적이라는 견해와 주관적이라는 견해는 어떤 면에서는 모두 옳다.
  단서 3

➡ '우리의 뇌와 우주가 만나는'이라는 뜻은 세상의 빛이 반사되어 만들어 낸 색(물리적
현실, 객관적)이 우리의 눈과 뇌에서 해석되는 것(우리의 정신, 주관적)으로
인식된다는 것을 의미한다.

▶ 따라서 정답은 ④ '우리의 정신과 물리적 현실이 서로 상호작용한다'이다.

① **we see things beyond the range of perception**
우리는 인식의 범위를 넘어서 사물을 본다
객관적인 빛의 반사를 인식하기 때문에 시각은 인식의 범위를 넘어설 수 없다.

② **objects appear different by the change of light**
사물들은 빛의 변화에 의해 다르게 나타난다
객관적인 빛의 반사와 주관적인 해석을 모두 언급해야 하는데, 주관적인 해석에 관한 내용이 빠져있다.

③ **your perspectives and others' reach an agreement**
당신의 관점과 다른 이들의 관점이 합의에 이른다
your perspective와 others' (perspective) 모두 주관적인 관점에 해당하므로, 객관적인 현실에 관한 내용이 빠져있다.

④ **our mind and physical reality interact with each other**
우리의 정신과 물리적 현실이 서로 상호작용한다
주관적인 해석(our mind)과 객관적인 현실(physical reality)이 서로 상호작용하여 색을 인식한다는 내용이다.

⑤ **structures of the human brain and the universe are similar**
인간 뇌와 우주의 구조는 유사하다
인간의 뇌와 우주 구조의 유사성은 언급되지 않았다.

---

22 정답 ⑤ ★ 소설의 세부 사항은 무엇을 담아야 하는가

사이에 주어와 be동사 생략
When writing a novel, / research for information needs to be done. // **단서1** 소설을 쓸 때는 정보 조사를 해야 함
소설을 쓸 때 / 정보를 위한 조사가 행해질 필요가 있다 //

주격 보어절 접속사
The thing is / **that** some kinds of fiction / demand a higher level of detail: / crime fiction, for example, or scientific thrillers. //
문제는 / 어떤 종류의 소설은 / 더 높은 수준의 세부 사항을 요구한다는 것이다 / 예를 들어 범죄 소설이나 과학 스릴러와 같은 //

부사적 용법(형용사 hard 수식)
The information is never hard **to find**; / one website for authors
부사절 접속사(~하도록)
/ even organizes trips to police stations, / **so that** crime writers can get it right. //
정보는 찾기에 결코 어렵지 않다 / 작가들을 위한 한 웹사이트는 / 심지어 경찰서로의 견학을 계획하기도 한다 / 범죄물 작가들이 정보를 제대로 얻을 수 있도록 //

간접목적어 직접목적어 형용사적 용법
Often, / a polite letter will earn **you permission** / **to visit** a
병렬 구조
particular location / and **record** all the details **that** you need. //
목적격 관계대명사
종종 / 정중한 편지는 여러분에게 허가를 얻어 줄 것이다 / 특정한 장소를 방문하고 / 필요한 모든 세부 사항을 기록할 수 있는 //

명사절 접속사 부사절 접속사(조건)
But remember / **that** you will drive your readers to boredom / **if**
명사절 접속사 앞에 목적격 관계대명사 생략
you think / **that** you need to pack everything **you discover** into your work. // **단서2** 조사한 모든 세부 사항을 소설에 담으면 지루해짐
하지만 기억하라 / 여러분은 독자들을 지루하게 만들 것이라는 것을 / 만약 여러분이 생각할 경우 / 발견한 모든 것을 작품에 담아야 한다고 //

주격 관계대명사 문장의 본동사 주격 관계대명사
The details **that** matter / **are** those **that** reveal the human experience. // **단서3** 중요한 세부 사항은 인간의 경험을 드러내는 것임
중요한 세부 사항은 / 인간의 경험을 드러내는 것이다 //

분사구문을 이끎
The crucial thing is / telling a story, / **finding** the characters, the tension, and the conflict / — not the train timetable or the building blueprint. // **단서4** 중요한 세부 사항은 인물, 긴장, 갈등 등 인간의 이야기임
중요한 것은 / 이야기를 말하는 것이다 / 인물, 긴장, 그리고 갈등을 찾아가며 / 기차 시간표나 건물 청사진이 아니라 //

- **demand** ⓥ 요구하다 · **crime fiction** 범죄 소설
- **organize** ⓥ 계획하다, 준비하다 · **get it right** 제대로 이해하다
- **permission** ⓝ 허가 · **drive ~ to …** ⓥ ~을 …하게 만들다
- **boredom** ⓝ 지루함 · **reveal** ⓥ 드러내다 · **crucial** ⓐ 중요한
- **tension** ⓝ 긴장 · **conflict** ⓝ 갈등 · **blueprint** ⓝ 청사진

소설을 쓸 때 정보를 위한 조사가 행해질 필요가 있다. 문제는 예를 들어 범죄 소설이나 과학 스릴러와 같은 어떤 종류의 소설은 더 높은 수준의 세부 사항을 요구한다는 것이다. 정보는 찾기에 결코 어렵지 않다. 작가들을 위한 한 웹사이트는 범죄물 작가들이 정보를 제대로 얻을 수 있도록 심지어 경찰서로의 탐방을 조직하기도 한다. 종종 정중한 편지는 여러분에게 특정한 장소를 방문하고 필요한 모든 세부 사항을 기록할 수 있는 허가를 얻어 줄 것이다. 하지만 만약 여러분이 발견한 모든 것을 작품에 담아야 한다고 생각할 경우 여러분은 독자들을 지루하게 만들 것이라는 것을 기억하라. 중요한 세부 사항은 인간의 경험을 드러내는 것이다. 중요한 것은 기차 시간표나 건물 청사진이 아니라 인물, 긴장, 그리고 갈등을 찾아가며 이야기를 말하는 것이다.

다음 글의 요지로 가장 적절한 것은?
① 작품의 완성도는 작가의 경험의 양에 비례한다.
경험의 양이 아니라 세부 사항에 비례함
② 작가의 상상력은 가장 훌륭한 이야기 재료이다. 작가의 상상력은 언급되지 않음
③ 소설에서 사건 전개에 대한 묘사는 구체적일수록 좋다.
묘사를 구체적으로 하기보다는 인간의 경험을 중심으로 해야 한다고 설명함
④ 소설을 쓸 때 독자의 관심사를 먼저 고려하는 것이 중요하다. 독자의 관심사는 언급되지 않음
⑤ 소설에 포함될 세부 사항은 인간의 경험을 드러내는 것이어야 한다.
소설의 세부 사항은 인간의 경험을 드러내는 것이어야 함

>왜 정답? ★★❀ [정답률 71%]
작가가 조사한 모든 세부 사항을 소설에 담게 되면 소설은 지루해진다고 설명하고 있다. 글쓴이는 중요한 세부 사항은 인간의 경험을 드러내는 것으로, 인물, 긴장, 갈등을 찾아가며 이야기를 말해야 한다고 설명했으므로, 글의 요지로 가장 적절한 것은 ⑤이다.

>왜 오답?
① 작품의 완성도는 작가의 경험의 양이 아니라 인간의 경험과 관련된 세부 사항에 비례한다.
② 작가의 상상력은 언급되지 않았다.
③ 묘사를 구체적으로 하는 것이 아니라, 인간의 경험을 중심으로 해야 한다고 설명했다. (▶◀ 이유: in detail이 '구체적으로 묘사하는 것'을 떠올리도록 만든 오답이다.)
④ 독자의 관심사는 언급되지 않았다.

---

23 정답 ④ ★ 구강 건강의 중요성과 영향력

부사적 용법(목적)
Nearly everything has to go through your mouth / **to get** to the
from A to B: A에서 B까지
rest of you, / **from** food and air **to** bacteria and viruses. //
거의 모든 것이 여러분의 입을 거쳐야 한다 / 여러분의 나머지 부분에 도달하기 위해 / 음식과 공기에서부터 박테리아와 바이러스까지 //

선행사를 포함한 관계대명사
A healthy mouth can help your body / get **what** it needs and prevent it from harm / **단서1** 입은 몸의 영양을 공급하고 피해를 막아줌
건강한 입은 몸을 도와줄 수 있다 / 여러분의 몸이 필요한 것을 얻고, 피해로부터 지키도록 //

to부정사의 의미상 주어
— with adequate space **for air** to travel to your lungs, / and
주격 관계대명사
healthy teeth and gums / **that prevent** harmful microorganisms
prevent A from -ing: A가 ~하는 것을 막다
from entering your bloodstream. //
공기가 폐로 이동할 수 있는 적당한 공간 / 그리고 건강한 치아와 잇몸으로 / 해로운 미생물이 혈류로 들어가는 것을 막는 //

every + 단수 명사
From the moment you are created, / oral health affects **every aspect** of your life. // **단서2** 구강 건강은 삶의 모든 측면에 영향을 미침
여러분이 생겨난 순간부터 / 구강 건강은 여러분의 삶의 모든 측면에 영향을 미친다 //

선행사를 포함한 관계대명사(주어절을 이끎)
What happens in the mouth / is usually just **the tip of the iceberg**
병렬 구조
/ and **a reflection** / of **what** is happening in other parts of the body. //
선행사를 포함하는 관계대명사(전치사의 목적어절을 이끎)
입안에서 일어나는 일은 / 대개 빙산의 일각일 뿐이며 / 반영이다 / 신체의 다른 부분에서 일어나고 있는 일의 //

주격 관계대명사
Poor oral health can be a cause of a disease / **that** affects the entire body. // **단서3** 나쁜 구강 건강은 신체 질병의 원인이 될 수 있음
나쁜 구강 건강은 질병의 원인일 수 있다 / 전체 몸에 영향을 끼치는 //

The microorganisms / in an unhealthy mouth / can enter the
bloodstream / and travel anywhere in the body, / posing serious
health risks. //
_{병렬 구조}
_{분사구문을 이룸}
건강하지 않은 입안의 미생물은 / 혈류로 들어가고 / 신체의 어느 곳이든 이동하여 / 심각한
건강상의 위험을 초래할 수 있다 //

- • nearly @ 거의   • go through ~을 거쳐가다   • adequate @ 적당한
- • lung ⓝ 폐   • gum ⓝ 잇몸   • harmful @ 해로운
- • bloodstream ⓝ 혈류   • oral @ 구강의   • affect ⓥ 영향을 미치다
- • aspect ⓝ 측면   • tip of the iceberg 빙산의 일각
- • reflection ⓝ 반영, 반사   • entire @ 전체의
- • pose ⓥ ~을 초래하다, 제기하다   • immune system 면역 체계

음식과 공기에서부터 박테리아와 바이러스까지 거의 모든 것이 여러분의 나머
지 부분에 도달하기 위해 여러분의 입을 거쳐야 한다. 건강한 입은 공기가 폐로
이동할 수 있는 적당한 공간, 그리고 해로운 미생물이 혈류로 들어가는 것을 막
는 건강한 치아와 잇몸으로 여러분의 몸이 필요한 것을 얻고, 피해로부터 몸을
지키도록 도와줄 수 있다. 여러분이 생겨난 순간부터 구강 건강은 여러분의 삶
의 모든 측면에 영향을 미친다. 입안에서 일어나는 일은 대개 빙산의 일각일 뿐
이며 신체의 다른 부분에서 일어나고 있는 일의 반영이다. 나쁜 구강 건강은 전
체 몸에 영향을 끼치는 질병의 원인일 수 있다. 건강하지 않은 입안의 미생물은
혈류로 들어가고 신체의 어느 곳이든 이동하여 심각한 건강상의 위험을 초래할
수 있다.

다음 글의 주제로 가장 적절한 것은?
① the way the immune system fights viruses
면역 체계가 바이러스와 싸우는 방법   면역 체계는 언급되지 않음
② the effect of unhealthy eating habits on the body
건강하지 않은 식습관이 몸에 미치는 영향   식습관은 언급되지 않음
③ the difficulty in raising awareness about oral health
구강 건강에 관한 인식을 높이는 것의 어려움   구강 건강에 관한 인식 제고는 언급되지 않음
④ the importance of oral health and its impact on the body
구강 건강의 중요성과 몸에 미치는 영향   구강 건강의 중요성과 영향력에 관한 내용임
⑤ the relationship between oral health and emotional
well-being   정서적 행복은 언급되지 않음
구강 건강과 정서적 행복 간의 관계

왜 정답? ✽✽✽ [정답률 86%]

도입: 거의 모든 것은 인간의 입을 통하고, 입은 몸의 영양을 공급하고 피해를
막아줌 **단서 1**

주제: 구강 건강은 삶의 모든 면에 영향을 미치며, 특히 나쁜 구강 건강은 질병을
일으킬 수 있음 **단서 2**, **단서 3**

➡ 공기부터 박테리아까지 거의 모든 것이 인간의 입을 통하고, 구강 건강은 우리 삶의
모든 면에 영향을 미침
▶ 따라서 글의 주제로는 ④ '구강 건강의 중요성과 몸에 미치는 영향'이 가장
적절하다.

왜 오답?
① 면역 체계는 언급되지 않았다.
② 식습관은 언급되지 않았다.
③ 구강 건강에 관한 인식 제고는 언급되지 않았다. (▶◀ 이유: 구강 건강의 중요성에
관한 내용이지, 사람들의 인식 제고는 언급되지 않았다.)
⑤ 정서적 행복에 관한 언급은 없었다.

24 정답 ② ＊인간이 지루함을 느끼는 이유

Kids tire of their toys, / college students get sick of cafeteria
food, / and sooner or later most of us / lose interest in our
favorite TV shows. //
아이들은 자기들의 장난감에 지루해하고 / 대학생들은 카페테리아 음식에 싫증을 내고 /
머지않아 우리 중 대부분은 / 우리가 가장 좋아하는 TV 쇼에 흥미를 잃는다 //
The bottom line is / that we humans are easily bored. //
_{명사절 접속사}
_{과거분사(주격 보어)}
요점은 / 우리 인간이 쉽게 지루해한다는 것이다 //   **단서 1** 인간은 쉽게 지루함을 느낌

But why should this be true? //
그런데 왜 이것이 사실이어야 할까 //
The answer lies buried deep in our nerve cells, / which are
_{과거분사(주격 보어)}   _{주격 관계대명사}
designed to reduce / their initial excited response to stimuli /
each time they occur. // **단서 2** 인간은 신경학적으로 같은 자극이 반복될 때마다 반응이
약해지도록 설계됨
답은 우리의 신경 세포 내에 깊이 숨어 있다 / 약화하도록 설계된 / 그것에 대한 초기의 흥분된
반응을 / 자극이 일어날 때마다 //

At the same time, / these neurons enhance their responses / to
things that change / — especially things that change quickly. //
_{주격 관계대명사}   _{주격 관계대명사}
동시에 / 이 뉴런들은 반응을 강화한다 / 변화하는 것들에 대한 / 특히 빠르게 변화하는 것들에 //

We probably evolved this way / because our ancestors got more
survival value, / for example, from attending to / what was
_{선행사를 포함한 관계대명사}   _{강조 용법의 재귀대명사}
moving in a tree / (such as a puma) / than to the tree itself. //
우리는 아마도 이런 방식으로 진화했을 것이다 / 우리의 조상이 더 많은 생존 가치를 얻었기
때문에 / 예를 들면 주의를 기울이는 것으로부터 / 나무에서 움직이는 것에 / (퓨마처럼) / 나무
그 자체보다 //
단서 3 인간은 변하지 않는 환경에 지루함을 느끼고,
새로운 자극을 두드러지게 느끼는 것이 생존에 유리했음
Boredom in reaction to an unchanging environment / turns
down the level of neural excitation / so that new stimuli / (like
our ancestor's hypothetical puma threat) / stand out more. //
변하지 않는 환경에 대한 반응으로의 지루함은 / 신경 흥분의 수준을 낮춰 / 새로운 자극이 /
(우리 조상이 가정한 퓨마의 위협과 같은) / 더 두드러지게 한다 //

It's the neural equivalent / of turning off a front door light / to
_{부사적 용법(목적)}
see the fireflies. //
이것은 신경적 대응물이다 / 앞문의 불을 끄는 것의 / 반딧불이를 보기 위해 //

- • tire of ~에 질리다[싫증이 나다]   • get sick of ~에 싫증이 나다
- • cafeteria ⓝ 구내식당, 카페테리아   • sooner or later 머지않아
- • the bottom line is ~ 요점은 ~이다   • be designed to ~하도록 설계되다
- • initial @ 초기의   • response ⓝ 반응
- • stimulus ⓝ 자극(pl. stimuli)   • occur ⓥ 발생하다
- • enhance ⓥ 강화하다   • especially @ 특히   • value ⓝ 가치
- • threat ⓝ 위협   • firefly ⓝ 반딧불이   • brilliant @ 영특한
- • detect ⓥ 감지하다   • destruction ⓝ 파괴

아이들은 자기들의 장난감에 지루해하고, 대학생들은 카페테리아 음식에 싫증
을 내고, 머지않아 우리 중 대부분은 우리가 가장 좋아하는 TV 쇼에 흥미를 잃
는다. 요점은 우리 인간이 쉽게 지루해한다는 것이다. 그런데 왜 이것이 사실이
어야 할까? 답은 자극이 일어날 때마다 그것에 대한 초기의 흥분된 반응을 약화
하도록 설계된 우리의 신경 세포 내에 깊이 숨어 있다. 동시에 이 뉴런들은 변
화하는 것들, 특히 빠르게 변화하는 것들에 대한 반응을 강화한다. 예를 들면
우리는 아마도 우리의 조상이 나무 그 자체보다 (퓨마처럼) 나무에서 움직이는
것에 주의를 기울이는 것으로부터 더 많은 생존 가치를 얻었기 때문에 이런 방
식으로 진화했을 것이다. 변하지 않는 환경에 대한 반응으로의 지루함은 신경
흥분의 수준을 낮춰 (우리 조상이 가정한 퓨마의 위협과 같은) 새로운 자극이
더 두드러지게 한다. 이것은 반딧불이를 보기 위해 앞문의 불을 끄는 것의 신경
적 대응물이다.

다음 글의 제목으로 가장 적절한 것은?
① The Brain's Brilliant Trick to Overcome Fear
두려움을 극복하기 위한 뇌의 영특한 속임수   puma threat이 언급된 것으로 만든 오답
② Boredom: Neural Mechanism for Detecting Change   지루함을
지루함: 변화를 감지하기 위한 신경학적 메커니즘   느낌으로써 변화하는 환경을 더욱 잘 감지하게 됨
③ Humans' Endless Desire to Pursue Familiar Experiences
익숙한 경험을 추구하고자 하는 인간의 끊임없는 욕구
④ The Destruction of Nature in Exchange for Human
Survival   자연 파괴에 관한 내용은 언급되지 않음
인간의 생존과 맞교환한 자연 파괴
⑤ How Humans Changed the Environment to Their
Advantage   인간은 환경을 바꾼 것이 아니라 생존에 유리한 방식으로 진화했다고 함
인간이 자신의 이익을 위해 환경을 바꾼 방법
인간이 익숙한 경험을 추구한다는 내용은 언급되지 않음

현상: 인간은 쉽게 지루함을 느낌 단서 1

이유: 인간은 신경학적으로 같은 자극이 반복될 때마다 반응이 약해지도록 설계됨 단서 2

근거: 인간은 변하지 않는 환경에 지루함을 느끼고, 새로운 자극을 두드러지게 느끼는 것이 생존에 유리했음 단서 3

예시: 움직이지 않는 나무에 주의를 기울이는 것보다, 나무에서 움직이는 퓨마에 주의를 기울이는 것이 생존에 유리함

➡ 인간은 변하지 않는 상황에 쉽게 지루함을 느끼고, 변화하는 상황에 빠르고 강렬하게 반응한다. 그것이 생존에 더 유리했기 때문에 인간은 그러한 방식으로 진화했다고 설명하고 있다.

▶ 따라서 글의 제목으로 가장 적절한 것은 ② '지루함: 변화를 감지하기 위한 신경학적 메커니즘'이다.

왜 오답?

① 두려움을 극복하기 위한 전략이 아니라, 변화를 빠르게 감지하기 위한 전략이 주된 내용이다.

③ 인간이 익숙한 경험을 추구한다는 내용이 아니라, 오히려 싫증을 낸다는 내용이다. 주의

④ 자연 파괴에 관한 내용은 언급되지 않았다.

⑤ 인간은 환경을 바꾼 것이 아니라 생존에 유리한 방식으로 진화했다고 했다.

다음 도표의 내용과 일치하지 않는 것은?

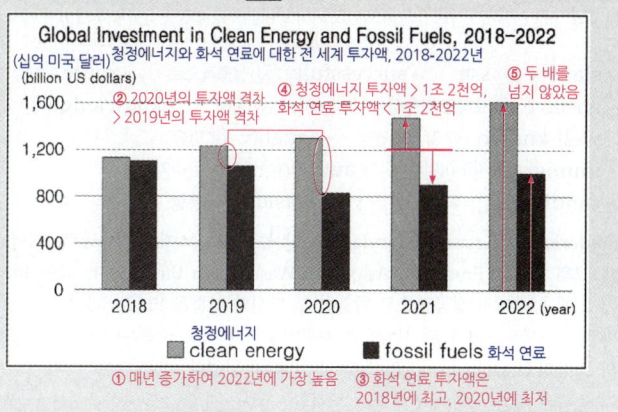

Global Investment in Clean Energy and Fossil Fuels, 2018-2022
(십억 미국 달러) 청정에너지와 화석 연료에 대한 전 세계 투자액, 2018-2022년

① 매년 증가하여 2022년에 가장 높음
② 2020년의 투자액 격차 > 2019년의 투자액 격차
④ 청정에너지 투자액 > 1조 2천억, 화석 연료 투자액 < 1조 2천억
⑤ 두 배를 넘지 않았음
③ 화석 연료 투자액은 2018년에 최고, 2020년에 최저

■ clean energy 청정에너지
■ fossil fuels 화석 연료

왜 정답? ✿✿✿ [정답률 88%]

2022년 청정에너지 투자액은 약 1조 6천억 달러이고, 화석 연료 투자액은 약 1조 달러로, 청정에너지 투자액이 화석 연료 투자액의 두 배를 넘지 않는다. 따라서 도표의 내용과 일치하지 않는 것은 ⑤이다.

왜 오답?

① 청정에너지 투자액은 매년 증가하여 2022년에 가장 높았다.

② 2020년 청정에너지와 화석 연료 사이의 투자액 격차는 4천억 달러 이상으로, 2019년의 투자액 격차보다 크다.

③ 화석 연료 투자액은 2018년에 약 1조 1천억 달러로 최고이며, 2020년에 약 8천억 달러로 최저이다.

④ 2021년 청정에너지 투자액은 1조 2천억 달러를 넘었고, 화석 연료 투자액은 넘지 않았다.

---

25 정답 ⑤ ✱청정에너지와 화석 연료에 대한 전 세계 투자액 ─

The above graph shows / global energy investment / in clean energy and in fossil fuels / between 2018 and 2022. //
위의 그래프는 보여 준다 / 전 세계 에너지 투자액을 / 청정에너지와 화석 연료에 대한 / 2018년과 2022년 사이에 //

① Since 2018 / global energy investment in clean energy / continued to rise, / reaching its highest level in 2022. //
청정에너지 투자액은 매년 증가하여 2022년에 가장 높았음
2018년 이후로 / 청정에너지에 대한 전 세계 투자액은 / 계속해서 상승했으며 / 2022년에 가장 높은 수준에 도달했다 //

② The investment gap / between clean energy and fossil fuels / 투자액 격차는 2020년이 2019년보다 더 큼
in 2020 / was larger than that in 2019. //
= the investment gap between clean energy and fossil fuels
투자액 격차는 / 청정에너지와 화석 연료 사이 / 2020년의 / 2019년의 그것보다 컸다 //

③ Investment in fossil fuels / was highest in 2018 / and lowest in 2020. // 화석 연료 투자액은 2018년이 최고이고, 2020년이 최저임
화석 연료에 대한 투자액은 / 2018년에 가장 높았고 / 2020년에 가장 낮았다 //

④ In 2021, / investment in clean energy / exceeded 1,200 billion dollars, / while investment in fossil fuels did not. //
2021년에는 / 청정에너지에 대한 투자액이 / 1조 2000억 달러를 넘은 반면 / 화석 연료에 대한 투자액은 그러지 않았다 //
2021년 청정에너지 투자액은 1조 2,000억 이상, 화석 연료 투자액은 1조 2,000억 미만임

⑤ In 2022, / the global investment in clean energy / was more
= the global investment
(→ less) than double / that of fossil fuels. //
2022년에는 / 청정에너지에 대한 전 세계 투자액이 / 두 배 이상이었다(→ 미만이었다) / 화석 연료의 그것의 //
단서 2022년 청정에너지 투자액은 약 1조 6천억 달러, 화석 연료 투자액은 약 1조 달러로, 두 배를 넘지 않았음

• investment ⓝ 투자, 투자액 • fossil fuel 화석 연료 • gap ⓝ 차이

위의 그래프는 2018년과 2022년 사이에 청정에너지와 화석 연료에 대한 전 세계 에너지 투자액을 보여 준다. ① 2018년 이후로 청정에너지에 대한 전 세계 투자액은 계속해서 상승했으며, 2022년에 가장 높은 수준에 도달했다. ② 2020년의 청정에너지와 화석 연료 사이 투자액 격차는 2019년의 그것보다 컸다. ③ 화석 연료에 대한 투자액은 2018년에 가장 높았고 2020년에 가장 낮았다. ④ 2021년에는 청정에너지에 대한 투자액이 1조 2천억 달러를 넘은 반면, 화석 연료에 대한 투자액은 그러지 않았다. ⑤ 2022년에는 청정에너지에 대한 전 세계 투자액이 화석 연료의 그것의 두 배 이상이었다(→ 두 배를 넘지 않았다).

---

26 정답 ③ ✱Frederick Douglass의 생애

Frederick Douglass was born / into slavery at a farm in Maryland. // ①의 단서 Maryland에서 노예로 태어남
Frederick Douglass는 태어났다 / Maryland의 한 농장에서 노예로 //

His full name at birth / was Frederick Augustus Washington Bailey. //
태어났을 때 그의 성명은 / Frederick Augustus Washington Bailey였다 //

He changed his name to Frederick Douglass / after he successfully escaped from slavery in 1838. //
그는 자신의 이름을 Frederick Douglass로 바꿨다 / 1838년에 노예 상태에서 성공적으로 탈출한 후 //

He became a leader of the Underground Railroad / — a network of people, places, and routes / that helped enslaved people 주격 관계대명사 과거분사 (people 수식)
escape to the north. // ②의 단서 노예들이 탈출하는 것을 돕는 조직의 리더가 됨
그는 Underground Railroad의 리더가 되었다 / 사람, 장소, 경로의 조직인 / 노예가 된 사람들을 북쪽으로 탈출하도록 돕는 //

He assisted other runaway slaves / until they could safely get to other areas in the north. //
그는 다른 도망친 노예들을 도왔다 / 그들이 북쪽의 다른 지역에 안전하게 도착할 수 있을 때까지 //
③의 단서 다른 노예들로부터 읽고 쓰는 법을 배운 것이 아니라, 독학하고 다른 노예들에게도 가르침을 전파함
간접목적어(재귀대명사)
As a slave, / he had taught himself to read and write / and he 과거완료(대과거) 직접목적어(to부정사)
spread that knowledge to other slaves as well. //
노예로서 / 그는 읽고 쓰는 것을 독학했고 / 그 지식을 다른 노예들에게도 전파했다 //
사이에 주어와 be동사 생략
Once free, / he became a well-known abolitionist / and strong believer in equality / for all people including Blacks, Native Americans, women, and recent immigrants. //
자유로워지고 난 뒤 / 그는 유명한 노예제 폐지론자이자 / 평등에 대한 강한 신봉자가 되었다 / 흑인, 아메리카 원주민, 여성, 그리고 최근 이민자들을 포함한 모든 사람들을 위한 //
현재분사(autobiographies 수식)
He wrote several autobiographies / describing his experiences as a slave. // ④의 단서 노예로서의 자신의 경험을 묘사한 자서전을 씀
그는 몇 권의 자서전을 썼다 / 노예로서의 자신의 경험을 묘사한 //

In addition to all this, / he became the first African-American candidate for vice president of the United States. //
이 모든 것에 더하여 / 그는 미국의 첫 아프리카계 미국인 부통령 후보가 되었다 //
⑤의 단서 미국의 첫 아프리카계 미국인 부통령 후보가 됨

- slavery ⓝ 노예　　　· successfully ⓐ 성공적으로　　　· route ⓝ 길
- enslave ⓥ 노예로 만들다　　· assist ⓥ 돕다　　　· knowledge ⓝ 지식
- well-known ⓐ 잘 알려진　　· equality ⓝ 평등
- immigrant ⓝ 이민자　　· autobiography ⓝ 자서전
- candidate ⓝ 후보자　　· vice president 부통령

Frederick Douglass는 Maryland의 한 농장에서 노예로 태어났다. 태어났을 때 그의 성명은 Frederick Augustus Washington Bailey였다. 그는 1838년에 노예 상태에서 성공적으로 탈출한 후 자신의 이름을 Frederick Douglass로 바꿨다. 그는 노예가 된 사람들을 북쪽으로 탈출하도록 돕는 사람, 장소, 경로의 조직인 Underground Railroad의 리더가 되었다. 그는 다른 도망친 노예들이 북쪽의 다른 지역에 안전하게 도착할 수 있을 때까지 그들을 도왔다. 노예로서 그는 읽고 쓰는 것을 독학했고, 그 지식을 다른 노예들에게도 전파했다. 자유로워지고 난 뒤 그는 유명한 노예제 폐지론자이자 흑인, 아메리카 원주민, 여성, 그리고 최근 이민자들을 포함한 모든 사람들을 위한 평등에 대한 강한 신봉자가 되었다. 그는 노예로서의 자신의 경험을 묘사한 몇 권의 자서전을 썼다. 이 모든 것에 더하여 그는 미국의 첫 아프리카계 미국인 부통령 후보가 되었다.

> **Frederick Douglass에 관한 다음 글의 내용과 일치하지 않는 것은?**
> ① Maryland에서 노예로 태어났다.
> Frederick Douglass was born into slavery ~ in Maryland.
> ② 노예들이 탈출하는 것을 돕는 조직의 리더가 되었다.
> became a leader of ~ a network ~ that helped enslaved people escape
> ③ 다른 노예들로부터 읽고 쓰는 법을 배웠다.
> he had taught himself to read and write
> ④ 노예로서의 자신의 경험을 묘사한 자서전을 썼다.
> wrote several autobiographies describing his experiences as a slave
> ⑤ 미국의 첫 아프리카계 미국인 부통령 후보가 되었다.
> became the first African-American candidate for vice president of the United States

왜 정답? ✱✱✱ [정답률 93%]

Frederick Douglass는 읽고 쓰는 법을 독학했다고 (he had taught himself to read and write) 했으므로 다른 노예들로부터 읽고 쓰는 법을 배웠다고 한 ③은 글의 내용과 일치하지 않는다.

왜 오답?

① Maryland에서 노예로 태어났다. (Frederick Douglass was born into slavery ~ in Maryland.)
② 노예들이 탈출하는 것을 돕는 조직인 Underground Railroad의 리더가 되었다. (became a leader of ~ a network ~ that helped enslaved people escape)
④ 노예로서의 자신의 경험을 묘사한 자서전을 썼다. (wrote several autobiographies describing his experiences as a slave)
⑤ 미국의 첫 아프리카계 미국인 부통령 후보가 되었다. (became the first African-American candidate for vice president of the United States)

---

27 정답 ⑤ ✱2023 오스트레일리아 게이트볼 챔피언십 안내

2023 Australian Gateball Championships /
2023 오스트레일리아 게이트볼 챔피언십 /
The Diamond Coast is getting set / to welcome the Australian
　　　　　　　　　　　　　부사적 용법(목적)
Gateball Championships. //
Diamond Coast는 준비를 하고 있습니다 / 오스트레일리아 게이트볼 챔피언십을 환영할 //
Join this great outdoor competition / and be the winner this
　　　　　　　　　병렬 구조
year! //
이 멋진 야외 대회에 참여해서 / 올해 우승자가 되세요 //

When & Where / 언제 & 어디서 /
- December 19 – 22, 2023 / **①의 단서** 4일 동안 진행됨
2023년 12월 19일부터 22일까지 /
- Diamond Coast Performance Centre /
Diamond Coast 공연 센터 /

Schedule of Matches / 경기 일정 /
- Doubles matches (9 a.m. – 11 a.m.) / **②의 단서** 복식 경기는 오전에 열림
복식 경기 (오전 9시부터 오전 11시까지) /
- Team matches (1 p.m. – 3 p.m.) /
단체 경기 (오후 1시부터 오후 3시까지) /
Prizes / 상 /
- Every participant will receive / a certificate for entry. //
모든 참가자는 받을 것입니다 / 참가 증서를 **③의 단서** 모든 참가자는 참가 증서를 받음
수동태 동사
- Champions are awarded a medal. //
우승자들은 메달을 받습니다 //
Note / 참고 /
- Participation is free. // **④의 단서** 참가비는 무료임
참가비는 무료입니다 //
- Visit www.australiangateball.com for registration. //
등록을 위해 www.australiangateball.com을 방문하십시오 //
(Registration on site is not available.) //
(현장 등록은 불가합니다) // **⑤의 단서** 현장에서 등록하는 것은 불가함

- get set 준비하다　　· competition ⓝ 대회, 경기
- doubles match 복식 경기　　· participant ⓝ 참가자
- certificate ⓝ 증서　　· award ⓥ (상을) 주다

2023 오스트레일리아 게이트볼 챔피언십
Diamond Coast는 오스트레일리아 게이트볼 챔피언십을 환영할 준비를 하고 있습니다. 이 멋진 야외 대회에 참여해서 올해 우승자가 되세요!
언제 & 어디서
- 2023년 12월 19일부터 22일까지
- Diamond Coast 공연 센터
경기 일정
- 복식 경기 (오전 9시부터 오전 11시까지)
- 단체 경기 (오후 1시부터 오후 3시까지)
상
- 모든 참가자는 참가 증서를 받을 것입니다.
- 우승자들은 메달을 받습니다.
참고
- 참가비는 무료입니다.
- 등록을 위해 www.australiangateball.com을 방문하십시오.
  (현장 등록은 불가합니다.)

> **2023 Australian Gateball Championships에 관한 다음 안내문의 내용과 일치하지 않는 것은?**
> ① 4일 동안 진행된다. December 19 – 22, 2023
> ② 복식 경기는 오전에 열린다. Doubles matches (9 a.m. – 11 a.m.)
> ③ 모든 참가자는 참가 증서를 받는다.
> Every participant will receive a certificate for entry.
> ④ 참가비는 무료이다. Participation is free.
> ⑤ 현장에서 등록하는 것이 가능하다. Registration on site is not available.

왜 정답? ✱✱✱ [정답률 90%]

등록은 웹사이트를 통해 해야 하며, 현장에서 등록하는 것은 불가능하다고 (Registration on site is not available.) 했으므로 현장에서 등록하는 것이 가능하다고 한 ⑤는 안내문의 내용과 일치하지 않는다.

왜 오답?

① 4일 동안 진행된다. (December 19 – 22, 2023)
② 복식 경기는 오전에 열린다. (Doubles matches (9 a.m. – 11 a.m.))
③ 모든 참가자는 참가 증서를 받는다. (Every participant will receive a certificate for entry.)
④ 참가비는 무료이다. (Participation is free.)

28 정답 ⑤ ＊도시 어드벤처 탐색 행사 안내

The Amazing Urban Adventure Quest / 놀라운 도시 어드벤처 탐색 /

Explore Central Park / **while solving** clues and completing
〈사이에 주어와 be동사 생략〉
challenges! //
Central Park를 탐험하세요 / 단서를 해결하고 도전을 완수하면서 //
①의 단서 참여하는 동안 스마트폰의 안내를 받아야 함

Guided by your smartphone, / make your way / among the
〈분사구문〉
well-known places in the park. //
스마트폰의 안내를 받으면서 / 자신의 길을 만들어 보세요 / 공원의 명소들 속 //

When & How / 언제 & 어떻게 /

• Available 365 days a year (from sunrise to sunset) /
1년 365일 이용 가능 (일출부터 일몰까지) / ②의 단서 일 년 내내 일몰까지만 참여할 수 있음

• Start when you want. // 여러분이 원할 때 시작하세요 //

• Get a stamp at each checkpoint. //
각 체크포인트에서 스탬프를 받으세요 //

Adventure Courses / 어드벤처 코스 /

• East Side: Starts at Twilight Gardens (no age limit) /
동편: Twilight Gardens에서 시작합니다 (나이 제한 없음) /

• West Side: Starts at Strawberry Castle (over 15 years old) /
서편: Strawberry Castle에서 시작합니다 (15세 초과) / ③의 단서 서편 코스는 15세 초과라는 나이 제한이 있음

Registration & Cost / 등록 & 비용 /

• Sign up online at www.urbanquest.com. //
www.urbanquest.com에서 온라인으로 등록하세요 //

• $40 for a team of 2 – 5 people /
2-5명으로 구성된 팀당 $40 / ④의 단서 1인당이 아니라 팀당 40달러의 요금이 듦

• Save 20% with discount code: / CENTRALQUEST //
할인 코드로 20%를 절약하세요 / CENTRALQUEST // ⑤의 단서 할인 코드는 CENTRALQUEST임

• urban ⓐ 도시의 • clue ⓝ 단서 • registration ⓝ 등록
• sign up 등록하다 • save ⓥ ~을 절약하다[아끼다]
• discount ⓝ 할인

놀라운 도시 어드벤처 탐색

단서를 해결하고 도전을 완수하면서 Central Park를 탐험하세요! 스마트폰의 안내를 받으면서 공원의 명소들 속 자신의 길을 만들어 보세요.
언제 & 어떻게
• 1년 365일 이용 가능 (일출부터 일몰까지)
• 여러분이 원할 때 시작하세요.
• 각 체크포인트에서 스탬프를 받으세요.
어드벤처 코스
• 동편: Twilight Gardens에서 시작합니다. (나이 제한 없음)
• 서편: Strawberry Castle에서 시작합니다. (15세 초과)
등록 & 비용
• www.urbanquest.com에서 온라인으로 등록하세요.
• 2-5명으로 구성된 팀당 $40
• 할인 코드 CENTRALQUEST로 20%를 절약하세요.

The Amazing Urban Adventure Quest에 관한 다음 안내문의 내용과 일치하는 것은?
① 참여하는 동안 스마트폰 사용은 금지된다. Guided by your smartphone
② 일 년 내내 일몰 후 참여할 수 있다.
　Available 365 days a year (from sunrise to sunset)
③ 서편 코스는 나이 제한이 없다.
　West Side: Starts at Strawberry Castle (over 15 years old)
④ 1인당 40달러의 요금이 든다. $40 for a team of 2 – 5 people
⑤ 할인받을 수 있는 코드가 있다.
　Save 20% with discount code: CENTRALQUEST

〉왜 정답 ? ＊❋❋ [정답률 90%]

20% 할인을 받을 수 있는 코드를 소개했으므로 (Save 20% with discount code: CENTRALQUEST) 안내문의 내용과 일치하는 것은 ⑤이다.

〉왜 오답 ?

① 참여하는 동안 스마트폰의 안내를 받는다. (Guided by your smartphone)
② 일 년 내내 일몰까지만 참여할 수 있다. (Available 365 days a year (from sunrise to sunset))
③ 서편 코스는 15세 초과라는 나이 제한이 있다. (West Side: Starts at Strawberry Castle (over 15 years old))
④ 1인당이 아니라 2-5명으로 구성된 팀당 40달러의 요금이 든다. ($40 for a team of 2 — 5 people)

29 정답 ④ ＊장기 이식자의 뇌사 판정 기준

다음 글의 밑줄 친 부분 중, 어법상 틀린 것은? [3점]

Some countries **have proposed** tougher guidelines / for
〈현재완료〉
determining brain death / when transplantation — transferring
organs to others — / is under consideration. //
일부 국가는 더 엄격한 지침을 제안했다 / 뇌사를 결정하는 것에 대한 / 장기 이식, 즉 다른 사람에게 장기를 전달하는 것을 / 고려 중일 때 //

In several European countries, / there are legal requirements /
which specify /
〈주격 관계대명사〉
몇몇 유럽 국가에는 / 법적 요건들이 있다 / 명시하는 /
〈명사절 접속사〉
① **that** a whole team of doctors must agree / over the diagnosis
of death / in the case of a potential donor. //
의사 팀 전체가 동의해야 한다고 / 사망 진단에 / 잠재적 기증자의 경우 //

The reason for these strict regulations / for diagnosing brain
〈단수 주어〉
death in potential organ donors /
이러한 엄격한 규정들의 이유는 / 잠재적인 장기 기증자의 뇌사 진단에 대한 /
〈단수 동사〉 〈명사적 용법(주격 보어)〉
② **is**, no doubt, **to ease** public fears / of a premature diagnosis of
brain death / for the purpose of obtaining organs. //
의심할 바 없이 대중의 두려움을 완화하기 위한 것이다 / 너무 이른 뇌사 진단에 대한 / 장기 확보를 위한 //

But **it** is questionable / **whether** these requirements reduce
〈가주어〉   〈진주어〉
public suspicions / as much as they create ③ **them**. //
= public suspicions
하지만 의문이다 / 이러한 요건들이 대중의 의심을 줄여 주는지 / 그것을 만들어 내는 만큼 //

They certainly maintain mistaken beliefs / **that** diagnosing brain
〈동격절 접속사〉
death / is an unreliable process ④ **lack(→lacking)** precision. //
그것들은 확실히 잘못된 믿음을 유지시킨다 / 뇌사 진단이 / 정확성이 결여된 신뢰하기 어려운 과정이라는 //
단서 명사 process를 수식하는 현재분사 자리임

As a matter of consistency, at least, / criteria for diagnosing the
deaths of organ donors / should be exactly the same / as for
those for ⑤ **whom** immediate burial or cremation is intended. //
〈목적격 관계대명사〉
적어도 일관성의 이유로 / 장기 기증자의 사망 진단 기준은 / 정확히 동일해야 한다 / 즉각적인 매장 또는 화장이 예정된 사람들에 대한 그것과 //

• propose ⓥ 제안하다 • tough ⓐ 엄격한, 힘든
• transplantation ⓝ 이식 • transfer ⓥ 전달하다, 옮기다
• legal requirement 법적 요건 • specify ⓥ 명시하다
• potential ⓐ 잠재적인 • regulation ⓝ 규정, 규제
• no doubt 의심할 바 없이, 틀림없는 • ease ⓥ 완화하다
• premature ⓐ 너무 이른 • obtain ⓥ 확보하다
• suspicion ⓝ 의심 • belief ⓝ 믿음, 신념
• unreliable ⓐ 믿을 수 없는 • precision ⓝ 정확성
• consistency ⓝ 일관성 • criterion ⓝ 기준(pl. criteria)
• burial ⓝ 매장

일부 국가는 장기 이식, 즉 다른 사람에게 장기를 전달하는 것을 고려 중일 때 뇌사를 결정하는 것에 대한 더 엄격한 지침을 제안했다. 몇몇 유럽 국가에는 잠재적 기증자의 경우 의사 팀 전체가 사망 진단에 동의해야 한다고 명시하는 법적 요건들이 있다. 잠재적인 장기 기증자의 뇌사 진단에 대한 이러한 엄격한 규정들의 이유는 의심할 바 없이 장기 확보를 위한 너무 이른 뇌사 진단에 대한

대중의 두려움을 완화하기 위한 것이다. 하지만 이러한 요건들이 대중의 의심을 만들어 내는 만큼 그것을 줄여 주는지는 의문이다. 그것들은 뇌사 진단이 정확성이 결여된 신뢰하기 어려운 과정이라는 잘못된 믿음을 확실히 유지시킨다. 적어도 일관성의 이유로 장기 기증자의 사망 진단 기준은 즉각적인 매장 또는 화장이 예정된 사람들에 대한 그것과 정확히 동일해야 한다.

⟩**왜** 정답 ? ★★★ [정답률 53%]

④ 하나의 절은 하나의 동사만 가진다!

┌ They certainly maintain mistaken beliefs / **that** [diagnosing
│　　　　　　　　　　　　　　　　　동격절 접속사　　주어
│ brain death **is** an unreliable process ④ ~~lack~~(→ lacking)
│　　　　동사　　　　　　　　　　　　　　명사 process를 수식하는 현재분사로 바뀌어야 함
└ precision.]//

(단서) 밑줄이 동사 lack에 있고, that절에 포함되어 있으므로

(발상) 동사 lack이 that절에서 유일한 동사의 역할을 하는지 확인해야 한다.

(해결) that절의 주어는 diagnosing brain death이고 동사는 is이므로, lack은 동사로 쓰일 수 없다. 문맥상 lack은 '정확성이 부족한 절차'라는 의미로 바로 앞의 명사 process를 수식하고 있다.
따라서 동사가 아니라 현재분사 lacking으로 고쳐야 어법상 적절하다.

(개념) 모든 절에는 하나의 동사만 있어야 하며, 본동사 외의 동사는 의미에 따라 준동사(동명사, to부정사, 분사)로 고쳐야 한다.

⟩**왜** 오답 ?

① 접속사 that 뒤에는 완전한 절이 온다.

전치사구: 제외하고 생각하기
┌ In several European countries, / there are legal requirements /
│　　　　　　　　　　　　　　　　　　　　　　　　　which의 선행사
│ which specify / ① **that** a whole team of doctors must agree /
│주격 관계대명사　명사절 접속사(specify의 목적어 역할)
│　　　　　　　　관계사절의 동사　　　　완전한 1형식 문장
└ over the diagnosis of death / in the case of a potential donor. //

명사절 접속사 that은 완전한 문장을 이끌고, 문장에서 명사(주어, 목적어, 보어)의 역할을 한다. (개념)
관계사절 안에서 that은 목적어 역할을 하는 명사절을 이끌며, 주어와 동사로 이루어진 완전한 1형식 문장으로 이루어져 있다. (단서)
명사절 접속사로 that이 알맞게 쓰였다.

② 동사는 주어에 그 수를 일치시킨다.

문장의 주어
┌ The reason for these strict regulations / for diagnosing brain
│　　　　　　수식어구(제외하고 생각하기)
│ death in potential organ donors / ② **is**, no doubt, to ease
│　　　　　　　　　　　　　　　　　동사　　　　　　명사적 용법(주격 보어)
│ public fears / of a premature diagnosis of brain death / for the
│　　　　　수식어구(제외하고 생각하기)
└ purpose of obtaining organs. //

주어를 꾸미는 수식어구와 상관없이 핵심 주어의 수에 동사의 수를 일치시킨다. (개념)
문장의 핵심 주어는 단수 명사인 The reason이므로, be동사의 단수형인 is가 알맞게 쓰였다.

③ 대명사는 앞에서 반복되는 명사를 찾아 수를 일치시킨다.

가주어
┌ But **it** is questionable / **whether** these requirements reduce
│　　　　　　　　　　　　　진주어(whether 절)
│　　　　　　　　　　　　　= these requirements　주어＋동사＋목적어
└ public suspicions / as much as they create ③ **them**. //
　　　　　　　　　　　　　　　　　　　　　= public suspicions

대명사는 앞에서 언급된 명사를 반복하며, 반복되는 명사와 수를 일치시킨다. (개념)
문맥상 복수 대명사 them이 가리키는 것은 복수 명사인 public suspicions이다.
앞에 언급된 복수 명사를 받는 복수 대명사 them이 알맞게 쓰였다.

⑤ 목적격 관계대명사는 전치사의 목적어로도 쓰인다.

┌ As a matter of consistency, at least, / criteria for diagnosing the
│
│ deaths of organ donors / should be exactly the same / as for
│　선행사　　　　목적격 관계대명사　　　　　　　be intended for: ~이 예정되다
└ those for ⑤ **whom** immediate burial or cremation is intended. //

관계대명사는 전치사의 목적어로 쓰일 수 있다. (개념)
목적격 관계대명사 whom이 전치사 for의 목적어로 쓰였다. (단서)
전치사와 선행사를 관계사절 뒤로 옮기면 원래의 문장인 immediate burial or cremation is intended for those가 완성된다.
전치사 for의 목적어로 목적격 관계대명사 whom이 알맞게 쓰였다.

30 정답 ④ ＊미니멀리즘의 진정한 의미

다음 글의 밑줄 친 부분 중, 문맥상 낱말의 쓰임이 적절하지 않은 것은?

The term minimalism gives a negative impression / to some
　　　　　　　　　　　　　　　　　주격 관계대명사　명사절 접속사
people / **who** think **that** it is all about sacrificing valuable
possessions. //
미니멀리즘이라는 용어는 부정적인 인상을 준다 / 일부 사람들에게 / 그것을 소중한 소유물을 희생하는 것에 관한 것으로만 생각하는 //

This insecurity naturally stems from / their ① **attachment** to
their possessions. //
이러한 불안은 자연스럽게 비롯된다 / 자신의 소유물에 대한 애착에서 //
　가주어　　　　진주어　　　재귀적 용법　　　　　　주격 관계대명사
It is difficult **to distance oneself** / from something **that** has been
around for quite some time. //
자신을 멀리 두는 것은 어렵다 / 꽤 오랫동안 곁에 있어 왔던 것으로부터 //
분사구문
Being an emotional animal, / human beings give meaning / to
the things around them. //
감정의 동물이기 때문에 / 인간은 의미를 부여한다 / 그들의 곁에 있는 물건에 //
　　　　　　　현재분사　　　　　　명사절 접속사
So, the question **arising** here / is **that** if minimalism will ② **hurt**
one's emotions, / why become a minimalist? //
그래서 여기서 생기는 질문은 / 미니멀리즘이 사람의 감정을 상하게 한다면 / 왜 미니멀리스트가 되느냐는 것이다 //

The answer is very simple; / the assumption of the question is
fundamentally ③ **wrong**. //
대답은 매우 간단하다 / 그 질문의 가정은 근본적으로 틀리다 //

Minimalism does not hurt emotions. // (단서) 미니멀리즘은 감정을 상하게 하지
미니멀리즘은 감정을 상하게 하지 않는다 // 않으므로, 당장의 슬픈 감정은 머지않아 극복될 것임
　　　　　　　　　　　　　　사이에 주어와 be동사 생략
You might feel a bit sad / **while getting** rid of a useless item /
but sooner than later, / this feeling will be ④ **maintained**
(→ overcome) / by the joy of clarity. //
여러분은 조금 슬퍼할 수도 있다 / 쓸모없는 물건을 치우면서 / 하지만 머지않아 / 이 느낌은 유지될(→ 극복될) 것이다 / 명료함의 기쁨으로 //
　　　　　　　　　　　　　　명사절 접속사
Minimalists never argue / **that** you should leave / every
convenience of the modern era. //
미니멀리스트는 주장하지 않는다 / 여러분이 버려야 한다고 / 현대의 모든 편의를 //
　　　　　　　　　　　　동격절 접속사
They are of the view / **that** you only need to ⑤ **eliminate** stuff
　주격 관계대명사
/ **that** is unused / or not going to be used in the near future. //
그들은 견해를 가지고 있다 / 여러분이 물건을 없애기만 하면 된다는 / 사용되지 않거나 / 가까운 미래에 사용되지 않을 //

- term ⓝ 용어　　　• impression ⓝ 인상　　　• sacrifice ⓥ 희생하다
- possession ⓝ 소유물　　• insecurity ⓝ 불안
- stem from ~에서 비롯되다　　• attachment ⓝ 애착
- distance … from ~ …을 ~로부터 멀리 두다　　• hurt ⓥ 상하게 하다
- assumption ⓝ 가정　　• fundamentally (ad) 근본적으로
- get rid of ~을 제거하다　　　• sooner than later 머지않아
- clarity ⓝ 명료함　　• convenience ⓝ 편의　　　• modern era 현대
- be of the view that ~라는 견해를 갖다　　• eliminate ⓥ 없애다

미니멀리즘이라는 용어는 그것을 소중한 소유물을 희생하는 것에 관한 것으로만 생각하는 일부 사람들에게 부정적인 인상을 준다. 이러한 불안은 자신의 소유물에 대한 ① 애착에서 자연스럽게 비롯된다. 꽤 오랫동안 곁에 있어 왔던 것으로부터 자신을 멀리 두는 것은 어렵다. 감정의 동물이기 때문에, 인간은 그들

의 곁에 있는 물건에 의미를 부여한다. 그래서 여기서 생기는 질문은 미니멀리즘이 사람의 감정을 ② 상하게 한다면 왜 미니멀리스트가 되느냐는 것이다. 대답은 매우 간단하다. 그 질문의 가정은 근본적으로 ③ 틀리다. 미니멀리즘은 감정을 상하게 하지 않는다. 여러분은 쓸모없는 물건을 치우면서 조금 슬퍼할 수도 있지만 머지않아 이 느낌은 명료함의 기쁨으로 ④ 유지될(→ 극복될) 것이다. 미니멀리스트는 여러분이 현대의 모든 편의를 버려야 한다고 주장하지 않는다. 그들은 여러분이 사용되지 않거나 가까운 미래에 사용되지 않을 물건을 ⑤ 없애기만 하면 된다는 견해를 가지고 있다.

>왜 정답? **✻✻✺** [정답률 68%]

④ maintained 유지되다

[여러분은 쓸모없는 물건을 치우면서 조금 슬퍼할 수도 있지만 머지않아 이 느낌은 명료함의 기쁨으로 ④ ~~유지될~~ 극복될 것이다.

➡ 미니멀리즘은 감정을 상하게 하지 않는다고 했으므로, 물건을 치우는 동안은 조금 슬플 수도 있지만, 그 감정이 '유지될' 것이라는 표현은 문맥상 적절하지 않다.
  ▶ maintained를 overcome(극복될)과 같은 말로 바꿔야 함

>왜 오답?

① attachment 애착

[이러한 불안은 자신의 소유물에 대한 ① 애착에서 자연스럽게 비롯된다.

➡ 곁에 있어 왔던 것을 멀리하는 것은 어렵다고 했으므로, 불안이 소유물에 대한 '애착에서 비롯된다'는 표현은 적절하다. ▶ attachment는 문맥에 맞음

② hurt 상하게 하다

[그래서 여기서 생기는 질문은 미니멀리즘이 사람의 감정을 ② 상하게 한다면 왜 미니멀리스트가 되느냐는 것이다.

➡ 미니멀리즘은 소중한 것을 희생시킨다는 부정적인 인상, 즉 불안을 일으킨다고 설명했으므로, 미니멀리즘은 감정을 '상하게 한다'라고 가정하는 표현은 적절하다.
  ▶ hurt는 문맥에 맞음

③ wrong 틀린

[그 질문의 가정은 근본적으로 ③ 틀리다.

➡ 미니멀리즘은 사람의 감정을 상하게 한다고 인식되지만, 사실은 그렇지 않다는 내용이 이어지고 있으므로, 그 가정이 '틀리다'라는 표현은 적절하다.
  ▶ wrong은 문맥에 맞음

⑤ eliminate 없애다

[그들은 여러분이 사용되지 않거나 가까운 미래에 사용되지 않을 물건을 ⑤ 없애기만 하면 된다는 견해를 가지고 있다.

➡ 미니멀리즘은 자신에게 필요하지 않은 물건을 비우는 행위이므로, '없애다'라는 표현은 적절하다. ▶ eliminate는 문맥에 맞음

---

31 정답 ① ✱시각의 적응력 ─────

A remarkable characteristic of the visual system / is **that** it has the ability of **adapting itself**. //
명사절 접속사
시각 체계의 두드러진 특징은 / 스스로 적응하는 능력이 있다는 것이다 //

Psychologist George M. Stratton made **this clear** / in an impressive self-experiment. //
목적어 목적격 보어
심리학자 George M. Stratton은 이것을 분명히 했다 / 인상적인 자가 실험에서 //

Stratton wore reversing glasses for several days, / **which** literally turned the world upside down for him. //
계속적 용법의 주격 관계대명사
Stratton은 며칠 동안 반전 안경을 착용했는데 / 그 안경은 말 그대로 그에게 세상을 뒤집어 놓았다 //

In the beginning, / this caused him great difficulties: / just **putting** food in his mouth with a fork / **was** a challenge for him. //
동명사 주어   단수 동사
처음에 이것은 그에게 큰 어려움을 초래하였다 / 포크로 음식을 입에 넣는 것조차 / 그에게는 도전이었다 //

With time, however, / his visual system adjusted to the new stimuli from reality, / and he was able to act normally / in his environment again, /
그러나 시간이 지나면서 / 그의 시각 체계는 현실의 새로운 자극에 적응했고 / 정상적으로 행동할 수 있었다 / 다시 자신의 환경에서 /
분사구문
even **seeing it upright** / when he concentrated. //
심지어 똑바로 보면서 / 그가 집중했을 때는 //
단서 1 반전 안경을 낀 환경에 적응하며 정상적으로 행동함

As he took off his reversing glasses, / he was again confronted with problems: /
반전 안경을 벗었을 때 / 그는 다시 문제에 직면했다 /

he used the wrong hand / when he wanted to reach for something, / for example. //
그는 반대 손을 사용했다 / 그가 무언가를 잡기를 원할 때 / 예를 들어 //
단서 2 반전 안경을 벗고 나서도 금세 적응하여 정상으로 돌아옴

Fortunately, / Stratton could reverse the perception, / and he did not have to wear reversing glasses / for the rest of his life. //
다행히 / Stratton은 지각을 뒤집을 수 있었고 / 반전 안경을 착용하지 않아도 되었다 / 평생 //

For him, / everything returned to normal / after one day. //
그에게 / 모든 것이 정상으로 돌아왔다 / 하루 만에 //

- remarkable ⓐ 두드러진 · characteristic ⓝ 특징
- visual system 시각 체계 · adapt ⓥ 적응하다
- psychologist ⓝ 심리학자 · self-experiment ⓝ 자가 실험
- literally ⓐⓓ 말 그대로 · upside down 거꾸로
- difficulty ⓝ 어려움 · challenge ⓝ 도전
- stimulus ⓝ 자극 (pl. stimuli) · concentrate ⓥ 집중하다
- be confronted with ~에 직면하다 · fortunately ⓐⓓ 다행히
- perception ⓝ 지각

시각 체계의 두드러진 특징은 **스스로 적응하는** 능력이 있다는 것이다. 심리학자 George M. Stratton은 인상적인 자가 실험에서 이것을 분명히 했다. Stratton은 며칠 동안 반전 안경을 착용했는데 그 안경은 말 그대로 그에게 세상을 뒤집어 놓았다. 처음에 이것은 그에게 큰 어려움을 초래하였다. 포크로 음식을 입에 넣는 것조차 그에게는 도전이었다. 그러나 시간이 지나면서 그의 시각 체계는 현실의 새로운 자극에 적응했고, 그가 집중했을 때는 심지어 똑바로 보면서, 다시 자신의 환경에서 정상적으로 행동할 수 있었다. 반전 안경을 벗었을 때 그는 다시 문제에 직면했다. 예를 들어 그가 무언가를 잡기를 원할 때 그는 반대 손을 사용했다. 다행히 Stratton은 지각을 뒤집을 수 있었고 평생 반전 안경을 착용하지 않아도 되었다. 그에게 하루 만에 모든 것이 정상으로 돌아왔다.

다음 빈칸에 들어갈 말로 가장 적절한 것을 고르시오.

①adapting itself 시각은 스스로 적응하는 능력이 있음
  스스로 적응하는
② visualizing ideas 생각을 시각화하는 내용이 아님
  생각을 시각화하는
③ assessing distances 거리를 가늠하는 것과 관련 없음
  거리를 가늠하는
④ functioning irregularly 불규칙적으로 기능한다는 언급은 없음
  불규칙적으로 기능하는
⑤ operating independently 독립적으로 작동한다는 내용이 아님
  독립적으로 작동하는

>왜 정답? **✻✻✺** [정답률 68%]

빈칸 문장	시각 체계의 두드러진 특징은 _____ 능력이 있다는 것이다.

➡ **빈칸 문장:** 시각 체계는 '무엇'할 수 있는 능력이 있다.

빈칸 문장 뒤 예시	반전 안경 실험 • 반전 안경을 낀 환경에 시간이 흐르며 적응함 **단서 1** • 반전 안경을 벗고 나서도 금세 적응하여 정상으로 돌아옴 **단서 2**

➡ 반전 안경 실험을 통해 시각에 변화를 주었을 때, 초반에는 어려움을 겪었지만 시간이 흐르면서 새로운 자극에 적응했다는 내용임
  ▶ 시각은 그 자극에 변화를 주더라도 스스로 적응하는 능력이 있다는 내용이므로, 정답은 ① '스스로 적응하는'이다.

2023.11 11회

32 정답 ② ★정보 접근성과 지적 자신감의 상관관계

Participants in a study were asked / to answer questions / like
"Why does the moon have phases?" //
한 연구의 참가자들이 요청받았다 / 질문들에 답하도록 / '달은 왜 상을 가지고 있을까'와 같은 //

Half the participants were told / to search for the answers on
the internet, / while the other half weren't allowed / to do so. //
참가자의 절반은 말을 들었고 / 인터넷에서 답을 검색하라는 / 나머지 절반은 허용되지 않았다
/ 그렇게 하도록 //

Then, in the second part of the study, / all of the participants
were presented / with a new set of questions, / such as "Why
does Swiss cheese have holes?" //
그다음, 연구의 두 번째 단계에서 / 모든 참가자는 제시받았다 / 일련의 새로운 질문들을 /
'스위스 치즈에는 왜 구멍이 있을까'와 같은 //

These questions were unrelated / to the ones asked during the
first part of the study, / so participants who used the internet /
had absolutely no advantage / over those who hadn't. //
이 질문들은 관련이 없어서 / 연구의 첫 번째 단계에서 질문받았던 것들과는 / 인터넷을
사용한 참가자들은 / 이점이 전혀 없었다 / 그러지 않은 참가자들보다 //

You would think / that both sets of participants would be
equally sure or unsure / about how well they could answer the
new questions. //
여러분은 생각할 것이다 / 두 집단의 참가자들이 동일한 정도로 확신하거나 확신하지 못할
것으로 / 새로운 질문들에 얼마나 잘 대답할 수 있을지에 대해 //

But those who used the internet in the first part of the study /
rated themselves as more knowledgeable / than those who
hadn't, / even about questions / they hadn't searched online for. //
그러나 연구의 첫 번째 단계에서 인터넷을 사용했던 참가자들은 / 스스로가 더 많이 알고
있다고 평가했다 / 그러지 않았던 참가자들보다 / 질문들에 대해서조차 / 자신이 온라인에서
검색하지 않았던 //

The study suggests / that having access to unrelated information
/ was enough to pump up their intellectual confidence. //
이 연구는 시사한다 / 관련 없는 정보에 접근하는 것이 / 그들의 지적 자신감을 부풀리기에
충분했다는 것을 //

- participant ⓝ 참가자 - be allowed to ~하도록 허용되다
- be unrelated to ~와 연관되지 않다 - absolutely ⓐⓓ 절대적으로
- equally ⓐⓓ 동등하게 - rate ⓥ 평가하다
- knowledgeable ⓐ 유식한 - suggest ⓥ 시사하다
- have access to ~에 접근하다 - judgment ⓝ 판단
- pump up 부풀리다, 증대하다 - intellectual ⓐ 지능의
- confidence ⓝ 자신감 - endure ⓥ 견디다
- challenging ⓐ 힘든 - collaboration ⓝ 협동
- motivate ⓥ 동기를 부여하다 - pursue ⓥ 추구하다
- in-depth ⓐ 심도 있는, 면밀한

한 연구의 참가자들이 '달은 왜 상을 가지고 있을까'와 같은 질문들에 답하도록
요청받았다. 참가자의 절반은 인터넷에서 답을 검색하라는 말을 들었고 나머지
절반은 그렇게 하도록 허용되지 않았다. 그다음, 연구의 두 번째 단계에서 모든
참가자는 '스위스 치즈에는 왜 구멍이 있을까'와 같은 일련의 새로운 질문들을
제시받았다. 이 질문들은 연구의 첫 번째 단계에서 질문받았던 것들과는 관련이
없어서 인터넷을 사용한 참가자들은 그러지 않은 참가자들보다 이점이 전혀 없
었다. 여러분은 두 집단의 참가자들이 새로운 질문들에 얼마나 잘 대답할 수 있
을지에 대해 동일한 정도로 확신하거나 확신하지 못할 것으로 생각할 것이다.

그러나 연구의 첫 번째 단계에서 인터넷을 사용했던 참가자들은 자신이 온라
인에서 검색하지 않았던 질문들에 대해서조차 그러지 않았던 참가자들보다 스
로가 더 많이 알고 있다고 평가했다. 이 연구는 관련 없는 정보에 접근하는 것
이 그들의 지적 자신감을 부풀리기에 충분했다는 것을 시사한다.

다음 빈칸에 들어갈 말로 가장 적절한 것을 고르시오.

① improve their judgment skills 참가자들은 오히려 비이성적인 판단을 하고 있음
판단 능력을 향상하기에
② pump up their intellectual confidence 이전에 관련 없는 정보를 검색했던
그들의 지적 자신감을 부풀리기에 경험만으로도 스스로를 더 많이 알고 있다고 평가함
③ make them endure challenging situations
그들이 어려운 상황을 견디도록 만들기에 참가자들이 어려운 상황을 견디는 내용은 언급되지 않음
④ lead to a collaboration among the participants
참가자들 사이에 협동을 이끌기에 참가자들 사이에 협동은 언급되지 않음
⑤ motivate them to pursue in-depth knowledge
그들이 심도 있는 지식을 추구하도록 동기를 부여하기에
심도 있는 지식을 추구한 것이 아니라 오히려 근거 없는 자신감을 비치게 됨

> **왜 정답** ? ★★★ [정답률 52%]

빈칸 문장	이 연구는 관련 없는 정보에 접근하는 것이 _____ 충분했다는 것을 시사한다.

➡ 관련 없는 정보에 접근한 것만으로도 참가자들은 '무엇을' 하기에 충분했다고
했으므로, 단서
정보 접근과 참가자들의 특성이 연결된 연구가 앞에 제시되었을 것이다. 발상

➡ 참가자들은 두 가지 질문을 받음
질문 1: '달은 왜 상을 가지고 있을까'
질문 2: '스위스 치즈에는 왜 구멍이 있을까'
질문 1에서 참가자 절반은 인터넷 검색을 했고, 절반은 하지 못함
질문 2는 질문 1과 전혀 관련이 없기 때문에, 질문 1에서 인터넷 검색을 했던
사람도 질문 2를 답변할 때 이점이 없었음 단서 1
하지만 연구 결과, 질문 1에서 인터넷을 검색했던 참가자들은 질문 2의 답조차도
본인들이 더 많이 알고 있다고 평가함 단서 2

➡ 우리는 관련 없는 정보에 접근했더라도 스스로를 더 많이 알고 있다고 평가한다는
것이다.
▶ 즉, 관련 없는 정보를 검색한 것만으로도 ② '그들의 지적 자신감을 부풀리기에'
충분했다.

> **왜 오답** ?

① 참가자들은 오히려 관련 없는 정보를 보고도 자신이 더 지식이 많다는 비이성적인
판단을 하고 있다.
③ 참가자들이 어려운 상황을 견디는 내용은 언급되지 않았다.
④ 참가자들 사이에 협동은 언급되지 않았다.
⑤ 참가자들은 심도 있는 지식을 추구한 것이 아니라 오히려 근거 없는 자신감을
비치게 되었다. 함정

33 정답 ④ ★한 번에 하나의 관점만 취하며 세상을 이해하는 경향

Anthropologist Gregory Bateson suggests / that we tend to
understand the world / by focusing in on particular features
within it. //
인류학자 Gregory Bateson은 제안한다 / 우리가 세상을 이해하는 경향이 있다고 / 세상
안의 특정한 특징에 초점을 맞춤으로써 //

Take platypuses. //
오리너구리를 예로 들어보자 //

We might zoom in so closely to their fur / that each hair appears
different. //
우리가 그들의 털을 매우 가까이 확대하면 / 각 가닥이 다르게 보인다 //

We might also zoom out / to the extent where it appears as a
single, uniform object. //
우리는 또한 축소할 수도 있다 / 그것이 하나의 동일한 개체로 보이는 정도까지 //

We might take the platypus as an individual, / or we might treat it as part of a larger unit / such as a species or an ecosystem. //
우리는 오리너구리를 개체로 취급할 수도 있고 / 더 큰 단위의 일부로 취급할 수도 있다 / 종 또는 생태계와 같이
가주어 **진주어**
단서1 오리너구리를 어떻게 보는지에 따라 다르게 취급할 수 있음
It's possible to move between many of these perspectives, /
이러한 많은 관점 사이를 이동하는 것은 가능하다 /
단서2 많은 관점 사이를 이동하며 초점을 달리 맞추는 것이 가능함
although we may need some additional tools and skills / to
부사적 용법(목적)
zoom in on individual pieces of hair / or zoom out to entire ecosystems. //
비록 몇 가지 추가 도구와 기술이 필요할지도 모르지만 / 개별 머리카락을 확대하거나 / 전체 생태계로 축소하기 위해 //

Crucially, however, / we can only take up one perspective at a time. //
그러나 결정적으로 / 우리는 한 번에 하나의 관점만 취할 수 있다 //

We can pay attention to the varied behavior of individual
과거분사
선행사를 포함한 관계대명사
animals, / look at what unites them into a single species, / or
병렬 구조
look at them as part of bigger ecological patterns. //
우리는 개별 동물의 다양한 행동에 주의를 기울일 수 있고 / 그들을 단일 종으로 통합하는 것을 살펴볼 수도 있고 / 더 큰 생태학적 패턴의 일부로서 그들을 살펴볼 수도 있다 //

Every possible perspective involves / emphasizing certain aspects and ignoring others. //
가능한 모든 관점은 포함한다 / 특정 측면을 강조하고 다른 측면을 외면하는 것을 //
단서3 우리가 무언가를 볼 때, 특정 측면을 강조하고 다른 측면은 외면함

- tend to ~하는 경향이 있다 · fur ⓝ 털
- to the extent where ~할 정도까지 · uniform ⓐ 동일한, 획일적인
- object ⓝ 개체 · unit ⓝ 단위 · species ⓝ 종(種)
- ecosystem ⓝ 생태계 · perspective ⓝ 관점
- additional ⓐ 추가적인 · individual ⓐ 개별의
- entire ⓐ 전체의 · crucially ⓐⓓ 결정적으로 · varied ⓐ 다양한
- behavior ⓝ 행동 · unite ⓥ 통합하다
- ecological ⓐ 생태학적인 · emphasize ⓥ 강조하다
- aspect ⓝ 측면 · ignore ⓥ 무시하다, 외면하다 · framework ⓝ 틀

인류학자 Gregory Bateson은 우리가 **세상 안의 특정한 특징에 초점을 맞춤으로써** 세상을 이해하는 경향이 있다고 제안한다. 오리너구리를 예로 들어보자. 우리가 그들의 털을 매우 가까이 확대하면 각 가닥이 다르게 보인다. 우리는 또한 그것이 하나의 동일한 개체로 보이는 정도까지 축소할 수도 있다. 우리는 오리너구리를 개체로 취급할 수도 있고 종 또는 생태계와 같이 더 큰 단위의 일부로 취급할 수도 있다. 비록 개별 머리카락을 확대하거나 전체 생태계로 축소하기 위해 몇 가지 추가 도구와 기술이 필요할지도 모르지만, 이러한 많은 관점 사이를 이동하는 것은 가능하다. 그러나 결정적으로 우리는 한 번에 하나의 관점만 취할 수 있다. 우리는 개별 동물의 다양한 행동에 주의를 기울일 수 있고, 그들을 단일 종으로 통합하는 것을 살펴볼 수도 있고, 더 큰 생태학적 패턴의 일부로서 그들을 살펴볼 수도 있다. 가능한 모든 관점은 특정 측면을 강조하고 다른 측면을 외면하는 것을 포함한다.

다음 빈칸에 들어갈 말로 가장 적절한 것을 고르시오. [3점]
① using our experiences as a guide 우리의 경험에 관한 언급은 없음
우리의 경험을 안내서로 사용함으로써
② breaking the framework of old ideas 오래된 생각의 틀을 깬다는 언급은 없음
오래된 생각의 틀을 깸으로써
③ adding new information to what we know 새로운 정보를 더한다는 내용은 없음
우리가 아는 것에 새로운 정보를 더함으로써
④ focusing in on particular features within it 특정한 특징에 초점을
세상 안의 특정한 특징에 초점을 맞추는 것으로써 두고 이에 맞는 관점을 가지며 세상을 이해함
⑤ considering both bright and dark sides of it
그것의 밝은 면과 어두운 면을 둘 다 고려함으로써 밝은 면과 어두운 면을 고려한다는 내용은 없음

왜 정답? ❋❋❋ [정답률 68%]

| 빈칸 문장 | 인류학자 Gregory Bateson은 우리가 _____ 세상을 이해하는 경향이 있다고 제안한다. |

→ **빈칸 문장**: 우리가 세상을 '어떻게' 이해하는 경향이 있는지가 핵심이다.
→ **Gregory Bateson의 연구 결과**:
예시: 오리너구리를 확대하면 모든 털이 달라 보이고, 축소하면 동일한 하나의 개체로 보임 **단서1**
적용: 대상을 하나의 개체로 볼지, 더 큰 단위의 일부로 볼지 등 여러 관점 사이를 이동하는 것은 가능함 **단서2**
결론: 우리가 세상을 이해할 때도 하나의 관점을 취해 특정 측면을 강조하고 다른 측면은 외면하며 초점을 맞춤 **단서3**
▶ 인간이 세상을 바라보는 방식은 특정한 특징에 초점을 맞추어 여러 관점 중 하나를 택하는 것이므로, 우리는 세상을 ④ '세상 안의 특정한 특징에 초점을 맞춤으로써' 이해한다.

왜 오답?
① 우리의 경험에 관한 언급은 없었다.
② 오래된 생각의 틀을 깬다는 언급은 없었다.
③ 새로운 정보를 더한다는 내용은 없었다.
⑤ 밝은 면과 어두운 면을 고려한다는 내용은 없었다.

2023.11 11회

34 정답 ④ ＊플라톤이 실재론을 설명한 방식

Plato's realism includes all aspects of experience / but is most easily explained / by considering the nature of mathematical
'~함으로써'
and geometrical objects / such as circles. //
플라톤의 실재론은 경험의 모든 측면을 포함하지만 / 가장 쉽게 설명된다 / 수학적이고 기하학적인 대상의 특성을 고려함으로써 / 원과 같은 //

He asked the question, / what is a circle? //
그는 질문을 했다 / '원이란 무엇인가'라는 //

You might indicate a particular example / carved into stone or
병렬 구조(example 수식)
drawn in the sand. //
여러분은 특정한 예를 가리킬 수 있다 / 돌에 새겨져 있거나 모래에 그려진 //
단서1 플라톤은 세상에 물리적으로 나타나는 어떠한 원도 완벽하지 않다고 지적함

However, Plato would point out / that, if you looked closely
가정법 과거
enough, / you would see / that neither it, nor indeed any
neither A nor B: A와 B 둘 다 아닌
physical circle, was perfect. //
그러나 플라톤은 지적할 것이다 / 여러분이 충분히 면밀히 관찰한다면 / 여러분이 알게 될 것이라고 / 그 어느 것도, 진정 어떤 물리적인 원도 완벽하지 않다는 것을 //

They all possessed flaws, / and all were subject to change / and decayed with time. //
그것들 모두는 결함을 가지고 있었고 / 모두 변화의 영향을 받고 / 시간이 지남에 따라 쇠하였다 //

So how can we talk about perfect circles / if we cannot actually see or touch them? //
단서2 플라톤은 우리가 보는 모든 원이 완벽하지 않은데, 완벽한 원을 어떻게 논할 수 있을지 고민함
그렇다면, 우리가 완벽한 원에 대해 어떻게 이야기할 수 있을까 / 그것을 실제로 보거나 만질 수 없다면 //

Plato's extraordinary answer / was that the world we see
앞에 목적격 관계대명사가 생략됨
is a poor reflection / of a deeper unseen reality of *Forms*, or
universals, / 단서3 플라톤은 우리가 보는 세상이 실재를 불충분하게 반영한다고 설명함
플라톤의 비범한 대답은 / 우리가 보는 세상이 불충분한 반영물이라는 것이다 / 더 깊은 보이지 않는 '형상' 또는 '보편자'라는 실재의 /
관계부사
where perfect cats chase perfect mice / in perfect circles around perfect rocks. //
완벽한 고양이가 완벽한 쥐를 쫓는 / 완벽한 암석 주변에서 완벽한 원을 그리며 //

Plato believed / that the *Forms* or *universals* are the true reality /
주격 관계대명사
that exists in **an invisible but perfect world beyond our senses**. //
플라톤은 믿었다 / '형상' 또는 '보편자'가 진정한 실재라고 / 보이지 않지만 우리의 감각을 넘어선 완벽한 세계에 존재하는 //

- realism ⓝ 실재론 · geometrical ⓐ 기하학적인
- nature ⓝ 본성 · indicate ⓥ 가리키다 · carve ⓥ 조각하다, 새기다
- point out 지적하다 · indeed ⓐ 진실로, 진정
- physical ⓐ 물리적인 · flaw ⓝ 결함
- be subject to ~에 영향을 받다 · decay ⓥ 부패하다, 쇠하다
- extraordinary ⓐ 비범한 · reflection ⓝ 반영, 반영물
- unseen ⓐ 보이지 않는 · exist ⓥ 존재하다
- observable ⓐ 관찰 가능한 · overlap ⓥ 겹치다 · sense ⓝ 감각
- stereotype ⓝ 고정관념 · generalization ⓝ 일반화

플라톤의 실재론은 경험의 모든 측면을 포함하지만, 원과 같은 수학적이고 기하학적인 대상의 특성을 고려함으로써 가장 쉽게 설명된다. 그는 '원이란 무엇인가'라는 질문을 했다. 여러분은 돌에 새겨져 있거나 모래에 그려진 특정한 예를 가리킬 수 있다. 그러나 플라톤은 여러분이 충분히 면밀히 관찰한다면, 여러분이 그 어느 것도, 진정 어떤 물리적인 원도 완벽하지 않다는 것을 알게 될 것이라고 지적할 것이다. 그것들 모두는 결함을 가지고 있었고, 모두 변화의 영향을 받고 시간이 지남에 따라 쇠하였다. 그렇다면, 우리가 완벽한 원을 실제로 보거나 만질 수 없다면, 그것에 대해 어떻게 이야기할 수 있을까? 플라톤의 비범한 대답은 우리가 보는 세상이 완벽한 고양이가 완벽한 암석 주변에서 완벽한 원을 그리며 완벽한 쥐를 쫓는 '형상' 또는 '보편자'라는 더 깊은 보이지 않는 실재의 불충분한 반영물이라는 것이다. 플라톤은 '형상' 또는 '보편자'가 **보이지 않지만 우리의 감각을 넘어선 완벽한 세계**에 존재하는 진정한 실재라고 믿었다.

다음 빈칸에 들어갈 말로 가장 적절한 것을 고르시오. [3점]
① observable phenomena of the physical world
물리적 세상의 관찰 가능한 현상들 `플라톤은 물리적 세상의 관찰 가능한 현상들은 모두 '형상' 또는 '보편자'가 이 세상에 불완전하게 반영된 것이라 주장함`
② our experiences shaped by external influences
외부의 영향으로 형성된 우리의 경험 `우리의 경험에 관한 언급은 없음`
③ an overlapping area between emotion and reason
감정과 이성 사이의 중첩되는 영역 `감정과 이성에 관한 언급은 없음`
④ an invisible but perfect world beyond our senses
보이지 않지만 우리의 감각을 넘어선 완벽한 세계
⑤ our perception affected by stereotype or generalization
고정관념이나 일반화에 영향을 받은 우리의 인식 `고정관념과 일반화에 관한 언급은 없음`
`플라톤은 '형상' 또는 '보편자'가 우리가 볼 수 없는 완벽한 세계에 존재한다고 주장함`

왜 정답? ★★★ [정답률 57%]

빈칸 문장	플라톤은 '형상' 또는 '보편자'가 ＿＿＿＿＿＿＿에 존재하는 진정한 실재라고 믿었다.

➡ **빈칸 문장:** 플라톤은 '형상' 또는 '보편자'의 개념이 '여기'에 존재하는 진정한 실재라고 주장함

➡ **Plato의 실재론:**
비유: 세상에 물리적으로 나타나는 어떠한 원도 완벽하지 않음 `단서1`
적용: 우리가 세상에서 보는 모든 원이 완벽하지 않고 구체적인 형상이 없는데, 완벽한 원을 어떻게 논할 수 있을지 고민함 `단서2`
결론: 우리가 볼 수 없는 더 깊은 '형상' 또는 '보편자'에 완벽한 실재가 존재하며, 우리가 세상에서 보는 모든 것은 그 실재가 이 세상에 불완전하게 반영된 것이라 설명함 `단서3`

▶ 플라톤은 우리가 볼 수 없는 더 깊은 세계에 '형상' 또는 '보편자'라는 완벽한 실재가 있으며, 그것이 불완전하게 반영된 것이 우리가 보는 세상이라고 설명했다. 따라서 플라톤이 생각했던 '형상' 또는 '보편자'의 개념이 존재하는 곳은 ④ '보이지 않지만 우리의 감각을 넘어선 완벽한 세계'이다.

왜 오답?
① 플라톤은 물리적 세상의 관찰 가능한 현상들은 모두 '형상' 또는 '보편자'가 이 세상에 불완전하게 반영된 것이라 주장했으므로, 빈칸의 내용과 상반된 보기이다. `함정`
② 우리의 경험에 관한 언급은 없었다.
③ 감정과 이성에 관한 언급은 없었다.
⑤ 고정관념과 일반화에 관한 언급은 없었다.

---

35 정답 ③ ＊대수의 법칙의 정의와 활용

다음 글에서 전체 흐름과 관계 <u>없는</u> 문장은?

In statistics, / the law of large numbers / describes a situation / 관계부사 동명사 주어 단수 동사 **where having** more data **is** better for making predictions. //
통계학에서 / 대수의 법칙은 / 상황을 설명한다 / 더 많은 데이터를 갖는 것이 예측하는 데 더 좋은 //

According to it, / **the more often** an experiment is conducted, / 「the 비교급 ~, the 비교급 …」: ~할수록 더 …하다 **the closer** the average of the results can be expected to match / the true state of the world. // `단서1` 대수의 법칙에 따르면, 실험이 자주 수행될수록 그 결과를 현실과 더 가깝게 예측할 수 있음
그것에 따르면 / 실험이 더 자주 수행될수록 / 그 결과의 평균이 더 맞춰지는 것으로 예상될 수 있다 / 세상의 실제 상태에 //

① For instance, / on your first encounter with the game of roulette, / you may have beginner's luck / after betting on 7. //
예를 들어 / 룰렛 게임을 처음 접했을 때 / 여러분은 초보자의 운이 있을 수 있다 / 7에 베팅한 후 //

② But **the more often** you repeat this bet, / **the closer** the relative 「the 비교급 ~, the 비교급 …」: ~할수록 더 …하다 frequency of wins and losses is expected to approach / the true chance of winning, /
하지만 당신이 이 베팅을 더 자주 반복할수록 / 승패의 상대적인 빈도가 더 가까워질 것으로 예상되는데 / 진짜 승률에 /
분사구문을 이끄는 현재분사 **meaning** that your luck will at some point fade away. //
이는 당신의 운이 어느 순간 사라진다는 것을 의미한다 // `단서2` 룰렛 게임을 더 자주 반복할수록 승패의 상대적인 빈도를 예측하기 쉬워짐

③ Each number's symbolic meanings / **can be** interpreted 병렬 구조 주격 관계대명사 in various ways / and **are** promising in situations / **that** may change unexpectedly. //
(각 숫자의 상징적인 의미는 / 다양한 방식으로 해석될 수 있으며 / 상황에서 유망하다 / 예상치 못하게 바뀔 수 있는 //) `단서3` 마찬가지로 자동차 보험사도 더 많은 데이터를 수집해서 사고의 패턴을 예측하고자 함

④ Similarly, / car insurers collect large amounts of data / 부사적 용법(목적) 동격절 접속사 **to figure out** the chances / **that** drivers will cause accidents, / ~에 따라 **depending on** their age, region, or car brand. //
마찬가지로 / 자동차 보험사는 많은 양의 데이터를 수집한다 / 확률을 파악하기 위해 / 운전자가 사고를 일으킬 / 그들의 연령, 지역 또는 자동차 브랜드에 따라 //

⑤ Both casinos and insurance industries / rely on the law of 부사적 용법(목적) large numbers / **to balance** individual losses. //
카지노와 보험 산업 모두 / 대수의 법칙에 의존한다 / 개별 손실의 균형을 맞추기 위해 // `단서4` 카지노(룰렛 게임)와 자동차 보험 산업 모두 대수의 법칙에 의존함

- statistics ⓝ 통계학 · law of large numbers 대수의 법칙
- describe ⓥ 설명하다 · prediction ⓝ 예측
- conduct ⓥ 수행하다 · average ⓝ 평균 · state ⓝ 상태
- encounter ⓝ 만남, 접함 · relative ⓐ 상대적인
- frequency ⓝ 빈도 · approach ⓥ 접근하다
- fade away 사라지다 · symbolic ⓐ 상징적인
- interpret ⓥ 해석하다 · unexpectedly ⓐ 예상치 못하게
- insurer ⓝ 보험사 · figure out ~을 알아내다
- balance ⓥ 균형을 맞추다

통계학에서 대수의 법칙은 더 많은 데이터를 갖는 것이 예측하는 데 좋은 상황을 설명한다. 그것에 따르면 실험이 더 자주 수행될수록 그 결과의 평균이 세상의 실제 상태에 더 맞춰지는 것으로 예상될 수 있다. ① 예를 들어 룰렛 게임을 처음 접했을 때 7에 베팅한 후 여러분은 초보자의 운이 있을 수 있다. ② 하지만 당신이 이 베팅을 더 자주 반복할수록 승패의 상대적인 빈도가 진짜 승률에 더 가까워질 것으로 예상되는데 이는 당신의 운이 어느 순간 사라진다는 것을 의미한다. (③ 각 숫자의 상징적인 의미는 다양한 방식으로 해석될 수 있으며 예상치 못하게 바뀔 수 있는 상황에서 유망하다.) ④ 마찬가지로 자동차 보험사는 운전자가 그들의 연령, 지역 또는 자동차 브랜드에 따라 사고를 일으킬 확률을 파악하기 위해 많은 양의 데이터를 수집한다. ⑤ 카지노와 보험 산업 모두 개별 손실의 균형을 맞추기 위해 대수의 법칙에 의존한다.

글의 앞부분: 통계학에서 대수의 법칙은 더 많은 데이터를 갖는 것이 예측하는 데 더 좋은 상황을 설명한다. 그것에 따르면 실험이 더 자주 수행될수록 그 결과의 평균이 세상의 실제 상태에 더 맞춰지는 것으로 예상될 수 있다.

➡ 대수의 법칙을 정의하고, 이것이 실제로 적용되는 곳을 설명하는 글이다.

① 예를 들어(For instance) 룰렛 게임을 처음 접했을 때 7에 베팅한 후 여러분은 초보자의 운이 있을 수 있다.

➡ 대수의 법칙의 예시로서 룰렛 게임을 들며, 처음 게임을 할 때는 데이터가 매우 적으므로 그 확률이 실제 상태와는 다를 수 있고, 누군가에게는 운이 따를 수도 있다고 설명한다. ▶ ①은 무관한 문장이 아님

② 하지만(But) 당신이 이 베팅을 더 자주 반복할수록 승패의 상대적인 빈도가 진짜 승률에 더 가까워질 것으로 예상되는데 이는 당신의 운이 어느 순간 사라진다는 것을 의미한다.

➡ 초보자의 운과 반대되는 내용을 But으로 연결하며, 룰렛 게임을 반복할수록 그 확률이 실제와 가까워지는, 즉 운이 사라진다는 설명이 이어진다.
▶ ②은 무관한 문장이 아님

③ 각 숫자의 상징적인 의미는 다양한 방식으로 해석될 수 있으며 예상치 못하게 바뀔 수 있는 상황에서 유망하다.

➡ 대수의 법칙을 설명하는 중에 숫자의 상징적인 의미가 다양하게 해석될 수 있다는 내용은 앞 문장과의 흐름에 맞지 않는다. ▶ ③이 무관한 문장임

④ 마찬가지로(Similarly) 자동차 보험사는 운전자가 그들의 연령, 지역 또는 자동차 브랜드에 따라 사고를 일으킬 확률을 파악하기 위해 많은 양의 데이터를 수집한다.

➡ Similarly로 룰렛과 마찬가지인 자동차 보험사의 예시를 들며, 자동차 보험사는 더 많은 데이터를 수집해서 사고의 패턴을 예측하고자 한다고 설명한다.
▶ ④은 무관한 문장이 아님

⑤ 카지노와 보험 산업 모두 개별 손실의 균형을 맞추기 위해 대수의 법칙에 의존한다.

➡ 카지노(룰렛 게임)와 자동차 보험 산업 모두 대수의 법칙에 의존한다고 정리하며 글을 마무리하고 있다. ▶ ⑤은 무관한 문장이 아님

＊ 글의 흐름

도입	대수의 법칙에 따르면, 실험이 자주 수행될수록 그 결과를 현실과 더 가깝게 예측할 수 있음
예시 ①	카지노에서는 룰렛 게임이 반복될수록 베팅의 결과는 실제 확률과 가까워짐
예시 ②	자동차 보험사에서는 더 많은 데이터를 수집할수록 사고의 패턴을 예측하기 쉬움
결론	카지노(룰렛 게임)와 자동차 보험 산업 모두 대수의 법칙에 의존하고 있음

36 정답 ④ ＊청소년이 그릇된 결정을 내릴 확률이 높은 이유 —

The adolescent brain is not fully developed / until its early twenties. //
청소년기의 뇌는 완전히 발달하지 않는다 / 20대 초반까지는 //
뒤에 목적어절을 이끄는 접속사 that 생략
This means / the way / the adolescents' decision-making circuits integrate and process information / may put them at a disadvantage. // 단서1 청소년의 불완전한 뇌 발달은 의사 결정 시 청소년을 불리하게 만듦
이것은 의미한다 / 방식이 / 청소년의 의사 결정 회로가 정보를 통합하고 처리하는 / 그들을 불리하게 만들 수 있음을 //

단서2 (C)와 상반되는 내용이 On the other hand로 연결됨
(A) On the other hand, / the limbic system matures earlier, /
분사구문을 이끄는 현재분사
playing a central role / in processing emotional responses. //
반면 / 대뇌변연계는 더 일찍 성숙하여 / 중심적인 역할을 한다 / 정서적 반응을 처리하는 데 //
Because of its earlier development, / it is more likely to influence decision-making. //
그것의 더 이른 발달로 인해 / 그것이 의사 결정에 영향을 미칠 가능성이 더 높다 //
수동태 동사
Decision-making in the adolescent brain / is led by emotional factors / more than the perception of consequences. //
청소년기의 뇌에서 의사 결정은 / 감정적인 요인에 의해 이끌어진다 / 결과의 인식보다 //

(B) Due to these differences, / there is an imbalance /
이러한 차이점 때문에 / 불균형이 존재한다 단서3 (C)와 (A)에서 청소년기의 뇌가 얼마나 다른지에 대한 설명이 언급된 후에 나와야 함
between feeling-based decision-making / ruled by the more
between A and B 구문 과거분사
mature limbic system / and logical-based decision-making / by the not-yet-mature prefrontal cortex. //
감정 기반 의사 결정과 / 더 성숙한 대뇌변연계에 의해 지배되는 / 논리 기반 의사 결정 사이에는 / 아직 성숙하지 않은 전전두엽 피질에 의한 //
간접의문문(의문사+주어+동사)
This may explain / why some teens are more likely to make bad decisions. // 단서4 주어진 글에 이어서 뇌 영역 중 나중에 발달하는 영역을 먼저 언급함
이것은 설명해 줄 수 있다 / 왜 일부 십 대들이 그릇된 결정을 내릴 가능성이 더 높은지를 //
주격 관계대명사
(C) One of their brain regions / that matures later / is the
prefrontal cortex, / which is the control center, / tasked with
과거분사 (the prefrontal cortex 수식)
thinking ahead and evaluating consequences. //
뇌 영역 중 하나는 / 나중에 성숙하는 / 전전두엽 피질이며 / 통제 센터인 / 그것은 미리 생각하고 결과를 평가하는 임무를 맡고 있다 //
prevent A from -ing: A가 ~하는 것을 막다
It is the area of the brain / responsible for preventing you from
병렬 구조
sending off an initial angry text / and modifying it with kinder words. //
그것은 뇌의 영역이다 / 당신이 초기의 화가 난 문자를 보내는 것을 막고 / 그것을 더 친절한 단어로 수정하게 하는 역할을 하는 //

- adolescent ⓐ 청소년기의 · decision-making ⓝ 의사결정
- circuit ⓝ 회로 · process ⓥ 처리하다
- put ~ at a disadvantage ~을 불리하게 만들다
- on the other hand 반면에 · mature ⓥ 성숙해지다 ⓐ 성숙한
- influence ⓥ 영향을 미치다 · factor ⓝ 요인
- imbalance ⓝ 불균형 · feeling-based ⓐ 감정에 기반한
- rule ⓥ 지배하다 · logical-based ⓐ 논리에 기반한
- evaluate ⓥ 평가하다 · initial ⓐ 초기의 · modify ⓥ 수정하다

청소년기의 뇌는 20대 초반까지는 완전히 발달하지 않는다. 이것은 청소년의 의사 결정 회로가 정보를 통합하고 처리하는 방식이 그들을 불리하게 만들 수 있음을 의미한다. (C) 나중에 성숙하는 뇌 영역 중 하나는 통제 센터인 전전두엽 피질이며, 그것은 미리 생각하고 결과를 평가하는 임무를 맡고 있다. 그것은 당신이 초기의 화가 난 문자를 보내는 것을 막고 그것을 더 친절한 단어로 수정하게 하는 역할을 하는 뇌의 영역이다. (A) 반면 대뇌변연계는 더 일찍 성숙하여 정서적 반응을 처리하는 데 중심적인 역할을 한다. 그것의 더 이른 발달로 인해 그것이 의사 결정에 영향을 미칠 가능성이 더 높다. 청소년기의 뇌에서 의사 결정은 결과의 인식보다 감정적인 요인에 의해 이끌어진다. (B) 이러한 차이점 때문에 더 성숙한 대뇌변연계에 의해 지배되는 감정 기반 의사 결정과 아직 성숙하지 않은 전전두엽 피질에 의한 논리 기반 의사 결정 사이에는 불균형이 존재한다. 이것은 왜 일부 십 대들이 그릇된 결정을 내릴 가능성이 더 높은지를 설명해 줄 수 있다.

주어진 글 다음에 이어질 글의 순서로 가장 적절한 것을 고르시오. [3점]

① (A) — (C) — (B) (A)는 주어진 글과 상반되는 (On the other hand) 내용이 아님
② (B) — (A) — (C)
③ (B) — (C) — (A) 주어진 글에는 (B)의 차이점을 가리킬 만한 내용이 없음
④ (C) — (A) — (B) (C) 청소년의 뇌에서 늦게 발달하는 영역이 있음 → (A) 반면, 청소년의 뇌에서 빨리 발달하는 영역이 있음 → (B) 이러한 차이점 때문에 청소년은 그릇된 결정을 내릴 가능성이 높아짐
⑤ (C) — (B) — (A)
(A)에서 발달 속도가 다른 뇌의 영역을 모두 소개한 후, (B)에서 그 차이로 인한 결과를 설명해야 함

1st 각 문단의 내용을 파악하고, 글의 논리적인 순서를 추론한다.

주어진 글: 청소년기의 뇌는 20대 초반까지는 완전히 발달하지 않는다. 이것은 청소년의 의사 결정 회로가 정보를 통합하고 처리하는 방식이 그들을 불리하게 만들 수 있음을 의미한다. **단서**

➡ **주어진 글 뒤:** 청소년기에 뇌가 어떻게 발달하는지, 그리고 그것이 그들을 왜 불리하게 만드는지에 관한 자세한 설명이 이어질 것이다. **발상**

(A): 반면(On the other hand) 대뇌변연계는 더 일찍 성숙하여 정서적 반응을 처리하는 데 중심적인 역할을 한다. 그것의 더 이른 발달로 인해 그것이 의사 결정에 영향을 미칠 가능성이 더 높다. 청소년기의 뇌에서 의사 결정은 결과의 인식보다 감정적인 요인에 의해 이끌어진다.

➡ **(A) 앞:** 역접의 연결어 On the other hand로 청소년기에 일찍 발달하는 뇌의 영역을 설명하고 있으므로, 앞에는 청소년기보다 늦게 발달하는 뇌의 영역을 언급해야 한다. ▶ 주어진 글 바로 뒤에 (A)가 올 수 없음

(A) 뒤: 청소년기에 뇌의 특정 영역의 발달 시기가 달라짐으로써 어떤 결과를 가져오는지에 대한 내용이 이어질 것이다.

(B): 이러한 차이점 때문에(Due to these differences) 더 성숙한 대뇌변연계에 의해 지배되는 감정 기반 의사 결정과 아직 성숙하지 않은 전전두엽 피질에 의한 논리 기반 의사 결정 사이에는 불균형이 존재한다. 이것은 왜 일부 십 대들이 그릇된 결정을 내릴 가능성이 더 높은지를 설명해 줄 수 있다.

➡ **(B) 앞:** 대뇌변연계는 이미 (A)에서 언급되었고 (A)의 앞에 청소년기보다 늦게 발달하는 뇌의 영역을 언급해야 하는데, (B)에 나타난 전전두엽 피질이 이에 해당한다는 것을 유추할 수 있다. 전전두엽 피질과 대뇌변연계를 순서대로 설명한 뒤에 이들을 종합하는 (B)가 이어지는 흐름이므로, 대뇌변연계가 언급된 (A)가 앞에 와야 한다. ▶ (A)에 이어지는 내용임 (순서: (A) ➡ (B))

(B) 뒤: 의사 결정 사이의 불균형은 십 대들이 그릇된 결정을 내릴 가능성이 높은 이유라고 언급하며 글을 마무리한다.

(C): 나중에 성숙하는 뇌 영역 중 하나는 통제 센터인 전전두엽 피질이며, 그것은 미리 생각하고 결과를 평가하는 임무를 맡고 있다. 그것은 당신이 초기의 화가 난 문자를 보내는 것을 막고 그것을 더 친절한 단어로 수정하게 하는 역할을 하는 뇌의 영역이다.

➡ **(C) 앞:** 청소년기보다 나중에 발달하는 뇌의 영역이 있다는 내용을 언급해야 한다. ▶ 주어진 글에 이어지는 내용임 (순서: 주어진 글 ➡ (C))

(C) 뒤: 반대로 청소년기보다 오히려 빨리 발달하는 뇌의 영역인 대뇌변연계가 언급된 (A)가 이어질 것이다. ▶ (C) 뒤에 (A)가 이어져야 함 (순서: 주어진 글 ➡ (C) ➡ (A) ➡ (B))

2nd 글이 한눈에 들어오도록 정리하여 정답을 확인한다.

주어진 글: 청소년기에는 뇌가 완전히 발달하지 않아서 의사 결정 시 불리할 수 있다.
→ **(C):** 결과를 미리 평가하는 전전두엽 피질은 청소년기보다 늦게 발달한다.
→ **(A):** 반면, 정서적인 반응을 다루는 대뇌변연계는 청소년기에 빨리 발달한다.
→ **(B):** 이러한 차이점 때문에 청소년기는 감정에 기반한 그릇된 결정을 내릴 가능성이 높다.
▶ 주어진 글 다음에 이어질 글의 순서는 (C) ➡ (A) ➡ (B)이므로 정답은 ④임

37 정답 ③ ＊딥 러닝 얼굴 인식 접근법의 한계와 극복 방안

Despite the remarkable progress / in deep-learning based facial recognition approaches / in recent years, / **in terms of** identification performance, / they still have limitations. //
눈에 띄는 발전에도 불구하고 / 딥 러닝 기반의 얼굴 인식 접근법의 / 최근 몇 년 동안 / 식별 성능 측면에서 / 여전히 그것은 한계를 가지고 있다 //

These limitations relate / to the database **used** in the learning stage. // **단서 1** 딥 러닝 얼굴 인식 접근법의 한계는 딥 러닝이 학습하는 데이터베이스와 관련 있음
이러한 한계는 관련이 있다 / 학습 단계에서 사용되는 데이터베이스와 //

(A) **단서 2** (B)와 (C)에서 언급된 시간에 따라 사람의 얼굴이 바뀐다는 문제를 가리킴
To counteract this problem, / researchers **have developed** models / for face aging or digital de-aging. //
이 문제에 대응하기 위해 / 연구자들은 모델을 개발했다 / 얼굴 노화나 디지털 노화 완화의 //

It **is used to compensate** for the differences / in facial characteristics, / **which** appear over a given time period. //
그것은 차이를 보완하는 데 사용된다 / 얼굴 특성의 / 주어진 기간 동안 나타나는 //

(B) If the **selected** database / does not contain enough instances, / the result may be systematically affected. //
선택된 데이터베이스가 / 충분한 사례를 포함하지 않으면 / 그 결과가 시스템적으로 영향을 받을 수 있다 // **단서 3** 주어진 글에서 딥 러닝이 학습하는 데이터베이스 때문에 문제가 발생한다는 내용 뒤에 이어짐

For example, / the performance of a facial biometric system may decrease / if the person **to be identified** / was enrolled over 10 years ago. //
예를 들어 / 안면 생체 측정 시스템의 성능이 저하될 수 있다 / 식별될 사람이 / 10년도 더 전에 등록된 경우 // **단서 4** (B)에서 언급된 '오래된 데이터'를 구체적으로 설명하고 있음

(C) The factor **to consider** / is **that** this person may experience changes / in the texture of the face, / particularly with the appearance of wrinkles and sagging skin. //
고려해야 할 요인은 / 이 사람이 변화를 경험할 수 있다는 것이다 / 얼굴의 질감 / 특히 주름과 처진 피부가 나타나는 것을 동반한 //

These changes may be highlighted / by weight gain or loss. //
이러한 변화는 두드러질 수 있다 / 체중 증가 또는 감소에 의해 //

- **remarkable** ⓐ 눈에 띄는, 두드러진 - **progress** ⓝ 발전, 진전
- **facial** ⓐ 얼굴의 - **recognition** ⓝ 인식 - **identification** ⓝ 식별
- **performance** ⓝ 성능 - **limitation** ⓝ 한계
- **relate to** ~와 관련이 있다 - **counteract** ⓥ 대응하다
- **compensate for** ~을 보완하다 - **characteristic** ⓝ 특징
- **instance** ⓝ 사례, 예시 - **systematically** ⓐⓓ 체계적으로
- **enroll** ⓥ 등록하다 - **factor** ⓝ 요인 - **texture** ⓝ 질감
- **particularly** ⓐⓓ 특히 - **appearance** ⓝ 발현, 나타나는 것
- **wrinkle** ⓝ 주름 - **highlight** ⓥ 강조하다

최근 몇 년 동안 딥 러닝 기반의 얼굴 인식 접근법의 눈에 띄는 발전에도 불구하고, 식별 성능 측면에서 여전히 그것은 한계를 가지고 있다. 이러한 한계는 학습 단계에서 사용되는 데이터베이스와 관련이 있다. (B) 선택된 데이터베이스가 충분한 사례를 포함하지 않으면 그 결과가 시스템적으로 영향을 받을 수 있다. 예를 들어 식별될 사람이 10년도 더 전에 등록된 경우 안면 생체 측정 시스템의 성능이 저하될 수 있다. (C) 고려해야 할 요인은 이 사람이 특히 주름과 처진 피부가 나타나는 것을 동반한 얼굴의 질감 변화를 경험할 수 있다는 것이다. 이러한 변화는 체중 증가 또는 감소에 의해 두드러질 수 있다. (A) 이 문제에 대응하기 위해 연구자들은 얼굴 노화나 디지털 노화 완화의 모델을 개발했다. 그것은 주어진 기간 동안 나타나는 얼굴 특성의 차이를 보완하는 데 사용된다.

주어진 글 다음에 이어질 글의 순서로 가장 적절한 것을 고르시오.

① (A) — (C) — (B) 주어진 글에는 (A)의 '문제를 가리킬 만한 내용이 구체화되지 않음
② (B) — (A) — (C) (A)의 '문제'는 (B)와 (A)의 내용을 모두 포함함
③ (B) — (C) — (A) (B) 데이터베이스가 너무 적거나 오래된 경우 성능이 저하됨 — (C) 사람은 시간이 지나며 체중이 바뀌면서 얼굴의 질감에 변화가 일어남 — (A) 이 문제에 대응하기 위해 연구자들은 새로운 모델을 개발해 노화의 차이를 보완함
④ (C) — (A) — (B)
⑤ (C) — (B) — (A) (C)는 (B)에서 언급된 '오래 전에 등록된 데이터'를 구체적으로 설명하고 있으므로 (B) 뒤에 이어져야 함

1st 각 문단의 내용을 파악하고, 글의 논리적인 순서를 추론한다.

주어진 글: 최근 몇 년 동안 딥 러닝 기반의 얼굴 인식 접근법의 눈에 띄는 발전에도 불구하고, 식별 성능 측면에서 여전히 그것은 한계를 가지고 있다. 이러한 한계는 학습 단계에서 사용되는 데이터베이스와 관련이 있다. **단서**

➡ **주어진 글 뒤:** 딥 러닝이 학습하는 데이터베이스에 어떤 한계가 있는지 설명할 것이다. **발상**

─(A): 이 문제(this problem)에 대응하기 위해 연구자들은 얼굴 노화나 디지털 노화 완화의 모델을 개발했다. 그것은 주어진 기간 동안 나타나는 얼굴 특성의 차이를 보완하는 데 사용된다.

→ **(A) 앞**: '이 문제'라고 했으므로 앞에 구체적인 문제가 언급되어야 한다.
▶ 주어진 글 바로 뒤에 (A)가 올 수 없음
(A) 뒤: 앞에서 언급된 문제에 대응하기 위해 연구자들은 새로운 모델을 개발해 노화의 차이를 보완했다고 설명하므로, (A)가 글의 결론일 것이다.
▶ (A)가 마지막에 올 확률이 높음

─(B): 선택된 데이터베이스가 충분한 사례를 포함하지 않으면 그 결과가 시스템적으로 영향을 받을 수 있다. 예를 들어 식별될 사람이 10년도 더 전에 등록된 경우 안면 생체 측정 시스템의 성능이 저하될 수 있다.

→ **(B) 앞**: 선택된 데이터베이스가 너무 적거나 오래되었을 때 문제가 발생할 수 있다고 설명하고 있으므로, 주어진 글에서 말한 데이터베이스의 한계를 소개하고 있다. ▶ 주어진 글에 이어지는 내용임 (순서: 주어진 글 → (B))
(B) 뒤: 이러한 데이터베이스의 한계를 고려할 때 무엇을 염두에 두어야 하는지를 구체적으로 설명할 것이다. ▶ (C)가 이어질 확률이 높음

─(C): 고려해야 할 요인은 이 사람(this person)이 특히 주름과 처진 피부가 나타나는 것을 동반한 얼굴의 질감 변화를 경험할 수 있다는 것이다. 이러한 변화는 체중 증가 또는 감소에 의해 두드러질 수 있다.

→ **(C) 앞**: (B)에서 예시로 언급한 '식별될 사람'이 (C)에서 this person으로 다시 언급되었다. 사람은 체중이 변하면서 얼굴도 변할 수 있다고 설명하고 있으므로, (B)에서 언급한 '오래된 데이터베이스'를 구체적으로 설명하고 있다.
▶ (B)에 이어지는 내용임 (순서: 주어진 글 → (B) → (C))
(C) 뒤: 데이터베이스가 이러한 문제를 지닐 때, 이를 어떻게 해결할지에 대한 내용이 소개될 것이다.
▶ (A)가 이어져야 함 (순서: 주어진 글 → (B) → (C) → (A))

2nd 글이 한눈에 들어오도록 정리하여 정답을 확인한다.

주어진 글: 딥 러닝 얼굴 인식 접근법의 한계는 데이터베이스와 관련 있다.
→ **(B)**: 데이터베이스가 너무 적거나 오래된 경우, 시스템의 성능이 저하될 수 있다.
→ **(C)**: 사람은 시간이 지나고 체중이 바뀌면서 얼굴의 질감에 변화가 일어난다.
→ **(A)**: 이 문제에 대응하기 위해 연구자들은 새로운 모델을 개발해 노화의 차이를 보완했다.
▶ 주어진 글 다음에 이어질 글의 순서는 (B) → (C) → (A)이므로 정답은 ③임

38 정답 ⑤ *초생산적인 종 재배의 명암

글의 흐름으로 보아, 주어진 문장이 들어가기에 가장 적절한 곳을 고르시오.

분사구문을 이끄는 현재분사
Leaving the contribution of that strategy to one side, / the
명사절 접속사
danger of creating more uniform crops / is that they are more
'~에 관해서는'
at risk / when it comes to disasters. //
그 전략의 기여를 차치하고 / 더 획일적인 작물을 만드는 것의 위험은 / 그것들이 더 큰
위험에 처한다는 것이다 / 재앙과 관련해 // **단서 1** 앞에는 획일적인 작물이 전략에 기여한 긍정적인
측면이, 뒤에는 재앙과 관련한 위험성이 나와야 함

The decline in the diversity of our food / is an entirely human-
made process. //
우리 음식의 다양성의 감소는 / 전적으로 인간이 만든 과정이다 //
주격 관계대명사
The biggest loss of crop diversity / came in the decades / that
followed the Second World War. //
농작물 다양성의 가장 큰 손실은 / 수십 년 동안 나타났다 / 제2차 세계 대전 이후 //
'~하려는 시도에서'
(①) In an attempt to save millions from extreme hunger, / crop
형용사적 용법(ways 수식)
scientists found ways / to produce grains such as rice and wheat /
on an enormous scale. //
수백만 명의 사람들을 극도의 배고픔에서 구하고자 하는 시도에서 / 작물 과학자들이 방법을
발견했다 / 쌀과 밀과 같은 곡물을 생산하는 / 엄청난 규모로 //

(②) And thousands of traditional varieties / were replaced / by
= varieties
a small number of new super-productive ones. //
그리고 수천 개의 전통적인 종들은 / 대체되었다 / 소수의 새로운 초(超)생산적인 종들로 //

(③) The strategy worked spectacularly well, / at least to begin
with. //
그 전략은 굉장히 잘 작동했다 / 적어도 처음에는 //

(④) Because of it, / grain production tripled, / and between
1970 and 2020 / the human population more than doubled. //
그것 때문에 / 곡물 생산량은 세 배가 되었다 / 1970년과 2020년 사이에 / 인구는 두 배 이상
증가했다 // **단서 2** 소수의 초생산적인 종을 만드는 전략은 성공적이었다는 내용이 앞에서부터 이어짐

단수 주어   주격 관계대명사
(⑤) Specifically, / a global food system / that depends on just
단수 동사   동명사의 부정
a narrow selection of plants / has a greater chance / of not being
able to survive / diseases, pests and climate extremes. //
특히 / 세계적인 식량 시스템은 / 농작물의 좁은 선택에만 의존하는 / 더 높은 가능성을 가진다
/ 생존하지 못할 / 질병, 해충 및 기후 위기로부터 // **단서 3** 농작물의 선택지가 좁으면 질병, 해충,
기후 위기에서 살아남기 어렵다는 점을 언급함

- leave A to one side A를 보류하다 · contribution ⓝ 기여
- strategy ⓝ 전략 · be at risk 위험에 처하다 · disaster ⓝ 재앙
- decline ⓝ 감소 · diversity ⓝ 다양성 · entirely ⓐⓓ 전적으로
- process ⓝ 과정 · extreme ⓐ 극심한 · hunger ⓝ 배고픔
- grain ⓝ 곡물 · enormous ⓐ 거대한 · scale ⓝ 규모
- traditional ⓐ 전통적인 · variety ⓝ 품종
- super-productive ⓐ 초생산적인
- spectacularly ⓐⓓ 극적으로, 굉장히 · specifically ⓐⓓ 특히
- depend on ~에 의존하다 · climate extreme 기후 위기

우리 음식의 다양성의 감소는 전적으로 인간이 만든 과정이다. 농작물 다양성의 가장 큰 손실은 제2차 세계 대전 이후 수십 년 동안 나타났다. (①) 수백만 명의 사람들을 극도의 배고픔에서 구하고자 하는 시도에서 작물 과학자들이 쌀과 밀과 같은 곡물을 엄청난 규모로 생산하는 방법을 발견했다. (②) 그리고 수천 개의 전통적인 종들은 소수의 새로운 초(超)생산적인 종들로 대체되었다. (③) 그 전략은 적어도 처음에는 굉장히 잘 작동했다. (④) 그것 때문에 곡물 생산량은 세 배가 되었고 1970년과 2020년 사이에 인구는 두 배 이상 증가했다. (⑤ **그 전략의 기여를 차치하고, 더 획일적인 작물을 만드는 것의 위험은 그것들이 재앙과 관련해 더 큰 위험에 처한다는 것이다.**) 특히 농작물의 좁은 선택에만 의존하는 세계적인 식량 시스템은 질병, 해충 및 기후 위기로부터 생존하지 못할 더 높은 가능성을 가진다.

| 문제 풀이 순서 | ★★★ [정답률 43%]

1st 주어진 문장을 해석하고, 연결어, 지시어 등을 확인한다.

─Leaving the contribution of that strategy to one side, the
danger of creating more uniform crops is that they are more
at risk when it comes to disasters.
그 전략의 기여를 차치하고, 더 획일적인 작물을 만드는 것의 위험은 그것들이 재앙과
관련해 더 큰 위험에 처한다는 것이다.

→ **주어진 문장 앞**: '그 전략의 기여'라고 했으므로 **단서**
앞에는 획일적인 작물을 만드는 것이 전략에 기여한 긍정적인 측면이 언급되어야
한다. **발상**

→ **주어진 문장 뒤**: '더 큰 위험에' 처한다라고 했으므로 **단서**
뒤에는 획일적인 작물을 만드는 것이 재앙과 관련하여 어떻게 위험한지 언급되어야
한다. **발상**

2nd 찾은 단서를 생각하며 각 선택지의 앞뒤 흐름이 매끄러운지 확인한다.

- **①의 앞 문장과 뒤 문장**

앞 문장: 농작물 다양성의 가장 큰 손실은 제2차 세계 대전 이후 수십 년 동안 나타났다.
뒤 문장: 수백만 명의 사람들을 극도의 배고픔에서 구하고자 하는 시도에서 작물 과학자들이 쌀과 밀과 같은 곡물을 엄청난 규모로 생산하는 방법을 발견했다.

→ 농작물의 다양성이 손실된 과정을 설명할 뿐, 그것이 전략에 어떤 기여를 했는지는 구체적으로 언급되지 않았다. ▶ 주어진 문장이 ①에 들어갈 수 없음

- **②의 앞 문장과 뒤 문장**
  - 앞 문장: ①의 뒤 문장과 같음
  - 뒤 문장: 그리고 수천 개의 전통적인 종들은 소수의 새로운 초(超)생산적인 종들로 대체되었다.
  - ➡ 앞 문장에서 언급했듯이, 전쟁 후 배고픔을 해소하고자 초 생산적인 종들을 재배하게 되었다는 내용이 이어지고 있다. ▶ 주어진 문장이 ②에 들어갈 수 없음

- **③의 앞 문장과 뒤 문장**
  - 앞 문장: ②의 뒤 문장과 같음
  - 뒤 문장: 그 전략은 적어도 처음에는 굉장히 잘 작동했다.
  - ➡ 작물의 선택지를 줄이는 '전략이 긍정적인 결과를 낳았다는 내용이 이어지고 있다.
  - ▶ 주어진 문장이 ③에 들어갈 수 없음

- **④의 앞 문장과 뒤 문장**
  - 앞 문장: ③의 뒤 문장과 같음
  - 뒤 문장: 그것 때문에 곡물 생산량은 세 배가 되었고 1970년과 2020년 사이에 인구는 두 배 이상 증가했다.
  - ➡ 그 전략이 성공하여 곡물 생산량과 인구가 증가했다는 내용이 이어지고 있다.
  - ▶ 주어진 문장이 ④에 들어갈 수 없음

- **⑤의 앞 문장과 뒤 문장**
  - 앞 문장: ④의 뒤 문장과 같음
  - 뒤 문장: 특히 농작물의 좁은 선택에만 의존하는 세계적인 식량 시스템은 질병, 해충 및 기후 위기로부터 생존하지 못할 더 높은 가능성을 가진다.
  - ➡ 앞 문장에서 농작물의 좁은 선택지 전략이 성공했던 과정을 설명했고, 뒤 문장에서는 농작물의 좁은 선택지 전략이 위험성을 지니고 있다는 내용이 이어지고 있다. 따라서 초 생산적인 종을 재배하는 것이 긍정적으로 기여했다는 내용에서 위험성에 관한 내용으로 옮겨가는 주어진 문장은 ⑤에 오는 것이 적절하다.
  - ▶ 주어진 문장이 ⑤에 들어가야 함

3rd 글이 한눈에 들어오도록 정리하여 정답을 확인한다.

음식의 다양성 감소는 2차 세계대전 이후 수십 년간 나타났다.
(①) 사람들을 배고픔에서 구하기 위해 작물 과학자들은 대규모 곡물 생산법을 발견했다.
(②) 이 과정에서 수천 개의 전통적인 종들은 소수의 초 생산적인 종으로 대체되었다.
(③) 이 전략은 처음에는 잘 작동했다.
(④) 이 전략으로 곡물 생산량과 인구가 증가했다.
(⑤ 그 전략의 기여를 차치하고, 획일적인 작물을 만드는 것은 재앙과 관련해 위험하다.)
농작물의 좁은 선택지에 의존하는 시스템은 질병, 해충, 기후 위기에서 생존하지 못할 가능성이 커진다.

39 정답 ④ ＊전통을 버리고 쇠퇴하기 시작한 쿠바 야구팀 —

글의 흐름으로 보아, 주어진 문장이 들어가기에 가장 적절한 곳을 고르시오.

A few years ago, / Cuba altered that uniform style, /
modernizing it / and perhaps **conforming** to other countries'
style; /
병렬 구조
몇 년 전 / 쿠바는 그 유니폼 스타일을 바꿨다 / 유니폼을 현대화하고 / 아마도 다른 나라의 스타일에 맞추면서 /

interestingly, / the national team **has declined** / since that
time. //
현재완료(계속)
단서 1 쿠바팀이 유니폼을 바꾼 후부터 쇠퇴하기 시작했다는 내용이 시작됨
흥미롭게도 / 국가 대표 팀은 쇠퇴해 왔다 / 그 시기부터 //

Between 1940 and 2000, / Cuba ruled the world baseball scene. //
1940년과 2000년 사이에 / 쿠바는 세계 야구계를 지배했다 //

They won / 25 of the first 28 World Cups / and 3 of 5 Olympic
Games. //
그들은 이겼다 / 첫 28회의 월드컵 중 25회와 / 5회의 올림픽 게임 중 3회를 //
be known for ~: ~로 알려지다
(①) The Cubans **were known / for** wearing uniforms covered in
red / from head to toe, / a strong contrast to the more conservative
현재분사(style 수식)
North American style / **featuring** grey or white pants. //
쿠바인들은 알려져 있었는데 / 빨간색으로 뒤덮인 유니폼을 입는 것으로 / 머리부터 발끝까지 / 이것은 더 보수적인 북미 스타일과 강한 대조를 이룬다 / 회색이나 흰색 바지를 특징으로 하는 //
부정어가 앞에 오면서 주어와 동사가 도치됨
(②) Not only **were their athletic talents** superior, / the Cubans
비교급 강조
appeared **even** stronger / from just the colour of their uniforms. //
쿠바인들의 운동 재능이 뛰어났을 뿐만 아니라 / 그들은 훨씬 더 강하게 보였다 / 그들의 유니폼의 색깔만으로도 //

(③) A game would not even start / and the opposing team
would already be scared. // **단서 2** 쿠바팀은 유니폼만으로 상대방의 기선을 제압하는 등 승승장구했음
경기가 시작하지 않았는데도 / 상대 팀은 이미 겁에 질리곤 했다 //
주격 관계대명사
(④) The country **that** ruled international baseball for decades /
현재완료
has not been on top since that uniform change. //
수십 년 동안 국제 야구를 지배했던 그 나라는 / 그 유니폼 교체 이후로 정상에 오른 적이 없었다 //
단서 3 승승장구했던 쿠바는 유니폼을 교체한 후로 정상에 오른 적 없음

(⑤) Traditions are important for a team; /
전통은 팀에게 중요하다 /
부사적 용법(목적)
while a team brand or image can adjust / **to keep up with**
present times, / if it abandons or neglects its roots, / negative
effects can surface. //
팀 브랜드나 이미지는 조정될 수 있지만 / 현시대를 따르기 위해 / 팀이 그들의 뿌리를 버리거나 무시하면 / 부정적인 영향이 표면화될 수 있다 //

- -

- alter ⓥ 바꾸다 · modernize ⓥ 현대화하다
- conform to ~에 순응하다 · interestingly ⒜ 흥미롭게도
- decline ⓥ 쇠퇴하다 · rule ⓥ 지배하다 · contrast ⓝ 대조
- feature ⓥ ~을 특징으로 하다 · athletic ⓐ 운동의
- opposing team 상대 팀 · tradition ⓝ 전통 · adjust ⓥ 조정하다
- keep up with ~에 따르다 · abandon ⓥ 버리다
- neglect ⓥ 무시하다 · root ⓝ 뿌리, 기원 · effect ⓝ 영향

1940년과 2000년 사이에 쿠바는 세계 야구계를 지배했다. 그들은 첫 28회의 월드컵 중 25회와 5회의 올림픽 게임 중 3회를 이겼다. (①) 쿠바인들은 머리부터 발끝까지 빨간색으로 뒤덮인 유니폼을 입는 것으로 알려져 있었는데, 이것은 회색이나 흰색 바지를 특징으로 하는 더 보수적인 북미 스타일과 강한 대조를 이룬다. (②) 쿠바인들의 운동 재능이 뛰어났을 뿐만 아니라 그들은 그들의 유니폼의 색깔만으로도 훨씬 더 강하게 보였다. (③) 경기가 시작하지 않았는데도 상대 팀은 이미 겁에 질리곤 했다. (④ 몇 년 전 쿠바는 유니폼을 현대화하고 아마도 다른 나라의 스타일에 맞추면서 그 유니폼 스타일을 바꿨다. 흥미롭게도 국가 대표 팀은 그 시기부터 쇠퇴해 왔다.) 수십 년 동안 국제 야구를 지배했던 그 나라는 그 유니폼 교체 이후로 정상에 오른 적이 없었다. (⑤) 전통은 팀에게 중요하다. 팀 브랜드나 이미지는 현시대를 따르기 위해 조정될 수 있지만 팀이 그들의 뿌리를 버리거나 무시하면 부정적인 영향이 표면화될 수 있다.

| 문제 풀이 순서 | ★★★ [정답률 54%]

1st 주어진 문장을 해석하고, 연결어, 지시어 등을 확인한다.

A few years ago, Cuba altered that uniform style,
modernizing it and perhaps conforming to other countries'
style; interestingly, the national team has declined since that
time.
몇 년 전 쿠바는 유니폼을 현대화하고 아마도 다른 나라의 스타일에 맞추면서 그 유니폼 스타일을 바꿨다. 흥미롭게도 국가 대표 팀은 그 시기부터 쇠퇴해 왔다.

2nd 찾은 단서를 생각하며 각 선택지의 앞뒤 흐름이 매끄러운지 확인한다.

- ①의 앞 문장과 뒤 문장

앞 문장: 1940년과 2000년 사이에 쿠바는 세계 야구계를 지배했다. 그들은 첫 28회의 월드컵 중 25회와 5회의 올림픽 게임 중 3회을 이겼다.
뒤 문장: 쿠바인들은 머리부터 발끝까지 빨간색으로 뒤덮인 유니폼을 입는 것으로 알려져 있었는데, 이것은 회색이나 흰색 바지를 특징으로 하는 더 보수적인 북미 스타일과 강한 대조를 이룬다.

➡ 쿠바가 20세기에 세계 야구계를 지배했던 역사와 그들만의 유니폼의 특징을 이어서 소개하고 있다. ▶ 주어진 문장이 ①에 들어갈 수 없음

- ②의 앞 문장과 뒤 문장

앞 문장: ①의 뒤 문장과 같음
뒤 문장: 쿠바인들의 운동 재능이 뛰어났을 뿐만 아니라 그들은 그들의 유니폼의 색깔만으로도 훨씬 더 강하게 보였다.

➡ 앞에서 쿠바가 야구계를 지배했던 역사와 독특한 유니폼의 특성을 설명하고, 뒤에서 그 독특한 유니폼 색깔이 그들이 강력해 보였던 이유라 설명하고 있다.
▶ 주어진 문장이 ②에 들어갈 수 없음

- ③의 앞 문장과 뒤 문장

앞 문장: ②의 뒤 문장과 같음
뒤 문장: 경기가 시작하지 않았는데도 상대 팀은 이미 겁에 질리곤 했다.

➡ 앞에서 쿠바만의 유니폼 색깔이 그들을 강력하게 보이도록 해주었다고 설명했고, 뒤에서 구체적으로 유니폼만으로 상대 팀을 겁에 질리게 했던 모습을 소개하고 있다. ▶ 주어진 문장이 ③에 들어갈 수 없음

- ④의 앞 문장과 뒤 문장

앞 문장: ③의 뒤 문장과 같음
뒤 문장: 수십 년 동안 국제 야구를 지배했던 그 나라는 그 유니폼 교체 이후로 정상에 오른 적이 없었다.

➡ 앞에서 쿠바만의 독특한 유니폼 색깔 덕분에 승승장구할 수 있었던 역사를 소개했으나, 뒤에서는 쿠바팀이 유니폼을 교체한 후로 정상에 오른 적이 없다는 내용이 이어지고 있다. 따라서 쿠바팀이 유니폼 덕분에 강력한 팀으로 자리매김했다가 유니폼을 바꾼 후 쇠퇴했다는 내용으로 전환되기에, 주어진 문장은 ④에 오는 것이 적절하다. ▶ 주어진 문장이 ④에 들어가야 함

- ⑤의 앞 문장과 뒤 문장

앞 문장: ④의 뒤 문장과 같음
뒤 문장: 전통은 팀에게 중요하다. 팀 브랜드나 이미지는 현시대를 따르기 위해 조정될 수 있지만 팀이 그들의 뿌리를 버리거나 무시하면 부정적인 영향이 표면화될 수 있다.

➡ 앞에서 전통적인 유니폼을 바꾼 후 정상에 오른 적이 없었다고 소개했고, 뒤에서는 쿠바팀의 사례를 통해 팀의 전통과 뿌리를 무시하면 부정적인 영향이 나타날 수 있다고 하며 글을 마무리했다.
▶ 주어진 문장이 ⑤에 들어갈 수 없음

3rd 글이 한눈에 들어오도록 정리하여 정답을 확인한다.

쿠바는 20세기에 세계 야구계를 지배했다.
(①) 쿠바팀은 보수적인 북미 스타일과는 대조되는 독특한 유니폼으로 유명했다.
(②) 쿠바의 이러한 독특한 유니폼 스타일은 그들을 더욱 강하게 보이게 해주었다.
(③) 경기가 시작하기 전에도 상대 팀은 쿠바팀의 유니폼만으로 겁에 질리곤 했다.
(④ 몇 년 전 쿠바는 유니폼 스타일을 바꿨고, 흥미롭게도 쿠바팀은 그때부터 쇠퇴했다.)
쿠바는 유니폼을 교체한 후로 정상에 오른 적이 없었다.
(⑤) 전통은 팀에게 중요하며, 전통이 일부 조정될 수는 있지만 그 뿌리를 버리면 부정적인 영향력이 나타난다.

40 정답 ① ＊초기 문화 진화 모델과 수정된 버전

Many of the first models of cultural evolution / drew noticeable connections / between culture and genes /
문화 진화의 많은 초기 모델들은 / 주목할 만한 접점을 이끌어냈다 / 문화와 유전자 사이의 /
by **using** concepts from theoretical population genetics / and
applying them to culture. // [병렬 구조] [단서 1] 초기 문화 진화 모델은 문화와 유전자 사이의 접점을 끌어내 두 개념을 유사하게 설명함
이론 집단 유전학의 개념을 사용함으로써 / 그리고 그것들을 문화에 적용함으로써 //

Cultural patterns of transmission, innovation, and selection / are conceptually likened / to genetic processes of transmission, mutation, and selection. //
전파, 혁신, 선택의 문화적 방식은 / 개념적으로 유사하다 / 전달, 돌연변이, 선택의 유전적 과정과 //

However, these approaches had to be modified / **to account for** [부사적 용법(목적)] the differences / between genetic and cultural transmission. //
그러나 이러한 접근법은 수정되어야만 했다 / 차이점을 설명하기 위해 / 유전자의 전달과 문화 전파 사이의 // [단서 2] 하지만 이러한 접근법은 유전자의 전달과 문화 전파 사이의 차이점을 설명하려면 수정되어야 했음
For example, / we do not **expect** / **the cultural transmission** / to [5형식 동사] [목적어] [목적격 보어(to부정사)] **follow** the rules of genetic transmission strictly. //
예를 들어 / 우리는 예상하지 않는다 / 문화 전파가 / 유전자 전달의 규칙을 엄격하게 따를 것이라고 //

If two biological parents / have different forms of a cultural trait, / their child is **not necessarily** equally likely to acquire / the ['반드시 ~한 것은 아니다(부분 부정)'] mother's or father's form of that trait. //
만약 두 명의 생물학적인 부모가 / 서로 다른 문화적인 특성의 형태를 가진다면 / 그들의 자녀는 반드시 동일하게 획득하지 않을 수 있다 / 엄마 혹은 아빠의 그 특성의 형태를 //
Further, a child can acquire cultural traits / **not only** from its [not only A but also B: A뿐만 아니라 B도] parents / **but also** from nonparental adults and peers; /
더욱이 아이는 문화적인 특성을 얻을 수 있다 / 부모로부터뿐만 아니라 / 부모가 아닌 성인이나 또래로부터도 / [단서 3] 문화적인 특성은 부모가 아닌 성인이나 또래 등 다양한 요인에서 얻을 수 있음
thus, the frequency of a cultural trait in the population / is relevant / beyond just the probability / **that** an individual's [동격절 접속사] parents had that trait. //
따라서 집단의 문화적인 특성의 빈도는 / 유의미하다 / 단지 확률을 넘어서 / 한 개인의 부모가 그 특성을 가졌을 //

> → Early cultural evolution models / **used** the (A) **similarity** / between culture and genes / [병렬 구조]
> 초기의 문화 진화 모델들은 / 유사성을 사용했다 / 문화와 유전자 사이의 / [부사절 접속사(이유)]
> but **had to** be revised / **since** cultural transmission / allows for more (B) **diverse** factors / than genetic transmission. //
> 그러나 수정되어야만 했다 / 문화 전파가 / 더 다양한 요인을 허용하기 때문에 / 유전자의 전달보다 //

- evolution ⓝ 진화 - draw ⓥ 이끌어내다
- noticeable ⓐ 주목할 만한 - connection ⓝ 접점, 연결
- gene ⓝ 유전자 - concept ⓝ 개념
- theoretical population genetics 이론 집단 유전학

- apply ⓥ 적용하다 • transmission ⓝ 전파
- innovation ⓝ 혁신 • selection ⓝ 선택
- conceptually ⓐⓓ 개념적으로 • liken to ~와 유사하다
- mutation ⓝ 돌연변이 • modify ⓥ 수정하다
- account for ~을 설명하다 • strictly ⓐⓓ 엄격하게 • trait ⓝ 특성
- acquire ⓥ 습득하다 • further ⓐⓓ 더욱이
- nonparental ⓐ 부모가 아닌 • peer ⓝ 동료 • frequency ⓝ 빈도
- probability ⓝ 개연성, 확률 • revise ⓥ 수정하다, 개정하다
- credible ⓐ 믿을 만한

문화 진화의 많은 초기 모델들은 이론 집단 유전학의 개념을 사용함으로써 그리고 그것들을 문화에 적용함으로써 문화와 유전자 사이의 주목할 만한 접점을 이끌어냈다. 전파, 혁신, 선택의 문화적 방식은 전달, 돌연변이, 선택의 유전적 과정과 개념적으로 유사하다. 그러나 이러한 접근법은 유전자의 전달과 문화 전파 사이의 차이점을 설명하기 위해 수정되어야만 했다. 예를 들어, 우리는 문화 전파가 유전자 전달의 규칙을 엄격하게 따를 것이라고 예상하지 않는다. 만약 두 명의 생물학적인 부모가 서로 다른 문화적인 특성의 형태를 가진다면, 그들의 자녀는 반드시 엄마 혹은 아빠의 그 특성의 형태를 동일하게 획득하지 않을 수 있다. 더욱이 아이는 문화적인 특성을 부모로부터뿐만 아니라 부모가 아닌 성인이나 또래로부터도 얻을 수 있다. 따라서 집단의 문화적인 특성의 빈도는 단지 한 개인의 부모가 그 특성을 가졌을 확률을 넘어서 유의미하다.
→ 초기의 문화 진화 모델들은 문화와 유전자 사이의 (A) 유사성을 사용했지만, 문화 전파가 유전자의 전달보다 더 (B) 다양한 요인을 허용하기 때문에 수정되어야만 했다.

다음 글의 내용을 한 문장으로 요약하고자 한다. 빈칸 (A), (B)에 들어갈 말로 가장 적절한 것은? [3점]

(A)	(B)	
① similarity 유사성	— diverse 다양한	초기 모델에서는 문화와 유전의 유사성을 활용했지만, 문화 전파가 더 다양한 요인에 영향을 받기 때문에 수정됨
② similarity 유사성	— limited 제한된	문화 전파는 더 제한된 요인이 아니라 다양한 요인에 영향을 받음
③ difference 차이점	— flexible 유연한	초기 모델에서는 문화와 유전의 차이점이 아닌 유사성을 활용함
④ difference 차이점	— complicated 복잡한	초기 모델에서는 문화와 유전의 차이점이 아닌 유사성을 활용함
⑤ interaction 상호작용	— credible 믿을 만한	문화 전파가 더 믿을 만한 요인을 허용한다는 것은 언급되지 않음

| 문제 풀이 순서 | ✿✿✿ [정답률 61%]

1st 요약문을 통해 글에서 무엇을 찾아야 하는지 확인한다.

요약문	초기의 문화 진화 모델들은 문화와 유전자 사이의 (A) _____ 을 사용했지만, 문화 전파가 유전자의 전달보다 더 (B) _____ 요인을 허용하기 때문에 수정되어야만 했다.

➡ 글에서 찾아야 하는 것
(A): 초기 문화 진화 모델들은 문화와 유전 사이의 유사성, 차이점, 상호작용을 사용했는지
(B): 후에 문화 전파가 유전자의 전달보다 더 다양한, 제한된, 유연한, 복잡한, 믿을 만한 요인을 허용하는 것이 밝혀졌는지

2nd 글의 내용을 파악하여 요약문을 완성한다.

초기 문화 진화 모델의 특징: 문화와 유전자 사이의 접점을 끌어내 두 개념을 설명했고, 문화의 방식과 유전의 과정을 개념적으로 유사하게 보았음 단서1
내용 전환: 하지만 이러한 접근법은 유전자의 전달과 문화 전파 사이의 차이점을 설명하려면 수정되어야 함 단서2
수정된 모델의 특징: 유전적인 특성은 부모에게서만 얻을 수 있지만, 문화적인 특성은 부모가 아닌 성인이나 또래 등 다양한 요인에서 얻을 수 있음 단서3

➡ 초기 문화 진화 모델은 문화와 유전의 유사성을 활용하여 두 개념을 설명했지만, 문화 전파가 유전자 전달보다 훨씬 다양한 요인에 영향을 받는다는 것을 설명하기 위해 이 모델은 수정되어야 했다.

▶ (A)에는 similarity(유사성)가, (B)에는 diverse(다양한)가 들어가야 하므로 정답은 ①임

초기 문화 진화 모델	문화와 유전의 접점을 활용하여 둘을 개념적으로 유사하게 설명했다.
내용 전환	유전자의 전달과 문화 전파 사이의 차이점을 설명하려면 초기 모델은 수정되어야 했다.
수정된 모델	유전적인 특성은 부모에게서만 얻을 수 있지만, 문화적인 특성은 부모가 아닌 성인이나 또래 등 다양한 요인에서 얻을 수 있다.

➡ 초기의 문화 진화 모델들은 문화와 유전자 사이의 (A) 유사성을 사용했지만, 문화 전파가 유전자의 전달보다 더 (B) 다양한 요인을 허용하기 때문에 수정되어야만 했다.

| 선택지 분석 |

① **similarity — diverse** 유사성 - 다양한
초기 모델에서는 문화와 유전의 유사성을 활용했지만, 문화 전파가 더 다양한 요인에 영향을 받기 때문에 수정되었다.

② **similarity — limited** 유사성 - 제한된
문화 전파는 더 제한된 요인이 아니라 다양한 요인에 영향을 받는다.

③ **difference — flexible** 차이점 - 유연한
초기 모델에서는 문화와 유전의 차이점이 아닌 유사성을 활용했다.

④ **difference — complicated** 차이점 - 복잡한
초기 모델에서는 문화와 유전의 차이점이 아닌 유사성을 활용했다.

⑤ **interaction — credible** 상호작용 - 믿을 만한
문화 전파가 더 믿을 만한 요인을 허용한다는 것은 언급되지 않았다.

---

41 ~ 42 ＊그룹 행동에서 드러나는 인간의 본성

A ball thrown into the air / is acted upon by the initial force given it, / persisting as inertia of movement / and tending to carry it in the same straight line, /
공중으로 던져진 공은 / 초기에 그것에 주어진 힘에 의해 움직여지는데 / 운동의 관성으로 지속하며 / 같은 직선으로 나아가려는 경향을 보이고 /

and by the constant pull of gravity downward, / as well as by the resistance of the air. //
아래로 지속적으로 당기는 중력에 의해서도 움직여진다 / 공기의 저항뿐만 아니라 //

It moves, accordingly, / in a (a) curved path. //
그에 맞춰 공은 움직인다 / 곡선의 경로로 //

Now the path does not represent / the working of any particular force; /
이제 그 경로는 나타내지는 않는다 / 어떤 특정한 힘의 작동을 /

there is simply the (b) combination / of the three elementary forces mentioned; /
결합이 존재할 뿐이다 / 언급된 세 가지 기본적인 힘의 /

but in a real sense, / there is something in the total action / besides the isolated action of three forces, / namely, their joint action. //
41번 단서1: 공의 움직임은 세 가지 힘의 각각의 작용 외에도 공동 작용으로 일어남
42번 단서1: 개별적인 힘에만 집중하면 볼 수 없는 공동 작용이 존재함
하지만 사실은 / 전체적인 작용에 무언가가 있는데 / 세 가지 힘의 고립된 작용 외에 / 이름하여 그들의 공동 작용이다 //

In the same way, / when two or more human individuals are together, / their mutual relationships and their arrangement into a group /
같은 방식으로 / 두 명 혹은 그 이상의 인간 개인이 같이 있을 때 / 그들의 상호 관계와 그들의 집단으로의 배치는 /

are things which would not be (c) concealed(→ revealed) / if we confined our attention to each individual separately. //
감춰지지(→ 드러나지) 않을 것이다 / 만약 우리가 관심을 개별적으로 각각의 개인에게 국한시킨다면 //

The significance of group behavior / is greatly (d) <u>increased</u> in the case of human beings / by the fact /
그룹 행동의 중요성이 / 인간의 경우 크게 증가된다 / 사실로 인해 /
<u>동격절 접속사</u>
<mark>that</mark> some of the tendencies to action of the individual / are related definitely to other persons, / and could not be aroused /
<u>현재분사(other persons 수식)</u>
except by other persons <mark>acting</mark> as stimuli. //
개인 행동의 몇몇 경향은 / 명백하게 다른 사람들과 관련이 있고 / 유발되지 않을 수 있다는 / 자극으로 작동하는 다른 사람들 없이는 // **42번** 단서 2: 고립된 인간은 자신의 본성을 드러내지 않으며, 다른 사람들과의 관계 속에서만 본성이 드러남
An individual in complete (e) <u>isolation</u> / would not reveal / their competitive tendencies, / their tendencies towards the opposite sex, / their protective tendencies towards children. //
완전한 고립 속의 개인은 / 드러내지 않을 것이다 / 그들의 경쟁적인 성향 / 이성에 대한 그들의 성향 / 아이에 대한 그들의 보호적 성향을 //
<u>명사절 접속사</u>
This shows / <mark>that</mark> the traits of human nature do not fully appear / until the individual is brought into relationships with other individuals. // **41번** 단서 2: 마찬가지로, 인간의 본성은 다른 개인과의 관계 속에서 완전히 드러남
이것은 보여 준다 / 인간 본성의 특성이 완전히 나타나지 않는다는 것을 / 개인이 다른 개인과의 관계에 관여될 때까지는 //

- persist ⓥ 지속하다
- constant ⓐ 지속적인
- resistance ⓝ 저항
- represent ⓥ 나타내다
- elementary ⓐ 기본적인
- isolated ⓐ 고립된
- arrangement ⓝ 배치
- confine ⓥ 제한하다, 국한하다
- separately ⓐⓓ 개별적으로
- tendency ⓝ 경향
- stimulus ⓝ 자극 (pl. stimuli)
- human nature 인간 본성
- tend to ~하는 경향이 있다
- downward ⓐⓓ 아래로
- accordingly ⓐⓓ 그에 따라
- combination ⓝ 결합
- besides prep ~ 외에
- joint ⓐ 공동의
- mutual ⓐ 상호의
- conceal ⓥ 감추다, 숨기다
- attention ⓝ 관심
- significance ⓝ 중요성
- definitely ⓐⓓ 명백히
- competitive ⓐ 경쟁적인

공중으로 던져진 공은 초기에 그것에 주어진 힘에 의해 움직여지는데, 운동의 관성으로 지속하며 같은 직선으로 나아가려는 경향을 보이고, 공기의 저항뿐만 아니라 아래로 지속적으로 당기는 중력에 의해서도 움직여진다. 그에 맞춰 공은 (a) 곡선의 경로로 움직인다. 이제 그 경로는 어떤 특정한 힘의 작동을 나타내지는 않는다. 언급된 세 가지 기본적인 힘의 (b) 결합이 존재할 뿐이다. 하지만 사실은 세 가지 힘의 고립된 작용 외에 전체적인 작용에 무언가가 있는데, 이름하여 그들의 공동 작용이다. 같은 방식으로, 두 명 혹은 그 이상의 인간 개인이 같이 있을 때 그들의 상호 관계와 그들의 집단으로의 배치는 만약 우리가 관심을 개별적으로 각각의 개인에게 국한시킨다면 (c) 감춰지지(→ 드러나지) 않을 것들이다. 개인 행동의 몇몇 경향은 명백하게 다른 사람들과 관련이 있고 자극으로 작동하는 다른 사람들 없이는 유발되지 않을 수 있다는 사실로 인해 그룹 행동의 중요성이 인간의 경우 크게 (d) 증가된다. 완전한 (e) 고립 속의 개인은 그들의 경쟁적인 성향, 이성에 대한 그들의 성향, 아이에 대한 그들의 보호적 성향을 드러내지 않을 것이다. 이것은 개인이 다른 개인과의 관계에 관여될 때까지는 인간 본성의 특성이 완전히 나타나지 않는다는 것을 보여 준다.

41 정답 ⑤

윗글의 제목으로 가장 적절한 것은?
① Common Misunderstandings in Physics
물리학의 흔한 오해들 물리학에 비유하여 인간의 그룹 행동을 설명한 글임
② Collaboration: A Key to Success in Relationships
협력: 관계에서의 성공의 열쇠 협력에 대한 언급은 없음
③ Interpersonal Traits and Their Impact on Science
대인관계의 특성과 그들이 과학에 미치는 영향 특성이 과학에 미치는 영향은 언급되지 않음 대인관계의
④ Unbalanced Forces Causing Objects to Accelerate
물체의 가속을 일으키는 불균형한 힘들
⑤ Human Traits Uncovered by Interpersonal Relationships
대인관계로 드러나는 인간의 특성들 인간이 다른 사람들과 관계를 맺으며 드러나는 특성들을 설명한 글임
물체에 가해지는 힘은 인간의 그룹 행동을 설명하기 위한 비유일 뿐이었음

왜 정답? ★★★ [정답률 53%]
- 공의 움직임은 세 가지 힘의 각각의 작용 외에도 공동 작용으로 일어남 **41번 단서 1**
- 마찬가지로, 인간의 본성은 다른 개인과의 관계 속에서 완전히 드러남 **41번 단서 2**

➡ **그룹 행동에서 드러나는 인간의 본성**
비유: 공을 하늘에 던졌을 때 개별적으로 작용하는 힘 외에도 그 힘들이 합쳐져서 공동 작용이 발생함
주제: 인간의 본성도 이와 마찬가지로, 고립될 때는 드러나지 않던 본성들이 다른 사람들과의 관계 속에서 드러남
▶ 따라서 제목으로 가장 적절한 것은 ⑤ '대인관계로 드러나는 인간의 특성들'이다.

왜 오답?
① 물리학에 비유하여 그룹 속에서의 인간의 특성을 설명한 글이다.
② 협력에 대한 언급은 없다.
③ 대인관계의 특성이 과학에 미치는 영향에 대한 언급은 없다.
④ 물체의 가속을 일으키는 힘들에 관한 글이 아니다. (▶ 이유: 물체에 가해지는 힘은 그룹 속에서의 인간의 행동을 설명하기 위한 비유일 뿐이다.)

42 정답 ③

밑줄 친 (a)~(e) 중에서 문맥상 낱말의 쓰임이 적절하지 <u>않은</u> 것은? [3점]
① (a) 곡선의 공중으로 던져진 공은 직선으로 나아가다가 아래로 떨어지므로 곡선으로 움직임
② (b) 결합 운동의 관성, 공기의 저항, 중력이 결합하여 운동을 만들어냄
③ (c) 감춰지다 개인에게만 초점을 맞추면 그 특성이 드러나지 않음
④ (d) 증가된다 인간에게는 그룹 행동의 중요성이 증가됨
⑤ (e) 고립 인간은 고립 상태에서는 그들의 본성을 드러내지 않음

왜 정답? ★★★ [정답률 45%]
③ (c) concealed 감춰지다

같은 방식으로(In the same way), 두 명 혹은 그 이상의 인간 개인이 같이 있을 때 그들의 상호 관계와 그들의 집단으로의 배치는 만약 우리가 관심을 개별적으로 각각의 개인에게 국한시킨다면 (c) ~~감춰지지~~ 않을 것들이다. 드러나지

➡ 앞서 공에 가해지는 힘의 비유에서 개별적인 힘들 외에도 공동 작용이 존재한다고 설명했으므로, 인간도 개인에게만 초점을 맞추면 그 특성이 '드러나지' 않을 것이라고 해야 흐름이 자연스럽다.
▶ concealed를 revealed(드러나다)와 같은 반의어로 바꿔야 함

왜 오답?
① (a) curved 곡선의
그에 맞춰 공은 (a) 곡선의 경로로 움직인다.
➡ 공중으로 던져진 공은 운동의 관성에 의해 직선으로 나아가다가 공기의 저항, 아래로 당기는 중력 등이 작용하여 땅으로 떨어지게 되므로 '곡선의' 경로로 움직인다. ▶ curved는 문맥에 맞음

② (b) combination 결합
언급된 세 가지 기본적인 힘의 (b) 결합이 존재할 뿐이다.
➡ 공이 곡선의 경로로 움직이는 것은 운동의 관성, 공기의 저항, 중력이 각각 작용한 것이 아니라 세 힘이 '결합'하여 운동을 만들어낸 것이다.
▶ combination은 문맥에 맞음

④ (d) increased 증가된다
개인 행동의 몇몇 경향은 명백하게 다른 사람들과 관련이 있고 자극으로 작동하는 다른 사람들 없이 유발되지 않을 수 있다는 사실로 인해 그룹 행동의 중요성이 인간의 경우 크게 (d) 증가된다.
➡ 인간도 그룹 속에서 다른 사람들과 관계를 맺을 때 개인의 행동 경향이 드러나게 되므로, 인간에게는 그룹 행동의 중요성이 '증가된다'는 내용이다.
▶ increased는 문맥에 맞음

⑤ (e) isolation 고립

[완전한 (e) 고립 속의 개인은 그들의 경쟁적인 성향, 이성에 대한 그들의
성향, 아이에 대한 그들의 보호적 성향을 드러내지 않을 것이다.

➡ 인간이 다른 사람들과 관계를 전혀 맺지 않고 있는 완전한 '고립' 상태에서는 그들의
본성을 드러내지 않을 것이라는 내용이다. ▶ isolation은 문맥에 맞음

43~45 ＊성자가 준 깨달음

주격 관계대명사
(A) There once lived a man in a village / who was not happy
with his life. //
옛날 어느 마을에 한 남자가 살았다 / 자신의 삶이 행복하지 않은 //

He was always troubled / by one problem or another. //
그는 항상 어려움을 겪었다 / 하나 혹은 또 다른 문제로 //

One day, a saint with his guards / stopped by his village. //
어느 날 한 성자가 그의 경호인들과 함께 / 그의 마을에 들렀다 //

Many people heard the news / and started going to him / with
their problems. // 45번① 많은 사람들이 자신들의 문제를 가지고 성자에게 갔음
많은 사람들이 그 소식을 듣고 / 그에게 가기 시작했다 / 그들의 문제를 가지고 //

The man also decided to visit the saint. //
그 남자 역시 성자를 방문하기로 결정했다 //

= a man
Even after reaching the saint's place in the morning, / (a) he
형용사적 용법(opportunity 수식)
didn't get the opportunity / to meet him till evening. //
아침에 성자가 있는 곳에 도착하고 난 후에도 / 그는 기회를 얻지 못했다 / 저녁 때까지 그를
만날 // 43번 단서 1: 남자는 저녁까지 성자를 기다림

＊(A) 문단 요약: 한 남자는 자신의 문제를 해결하기 위해 성자를 기다림
명사절 접속사
(B) But the saint also asked / if the man could do a small job for
him. // 43번 단서 2, 45번② 성자는 남자에게 작은 일을 부탁함
그런데 성자는 또한 물었다 / 그 남자가 그를 위해 작은 일을 해 줄 수 있는지 //

He told the man / to take care of a hundred camels in his group
that night, / saying "When all hundred camels sit down, / you
can go to sleep." // 45번③ 성자는 남자가 낙타를 모두 재우는 것이 아니라 앉히면 잠을 자러
가도 좋다고 했음
성자는 그 남자에게 말했다 / 그날 밤에 그의 일행에 있는 백 마리 낙타를 돌봐 달라고 / "백
마리 낙타 모두가 자리에 앉으면 / 당신은 자러 가도 좋습니다"라고 말하면서 //

The man agreed. //
그 남자는 동의했다 //

명사절 접속사
The next morning when the saint met that man, / (b) he asked if
과거완료(대과거)   **= a saint**
the man had slept well. //
다음 날 아침에 성자가 그 남자를 만났을 때 / 그는 남자가 잠을 잘 잤는지 물어보았다 //
Being이 생략된 분사구문
Tired and sad, / the man replied / that he couldn't sleep even
for a moment. //
피곤해하고 슬퍼하면서 / 남자는 대답했다 / 한순간도 잠을 자지 못했다고 //

＊(B) 문단 요약: 성자는 낙타 백 마리가 모두 앉았을 때 잠에 들라고 부탁함

(C) In fact, the man tried very hard / but couldn't make all the
사역동사 + 목적어 + 목적격 보어(원형부정사)
camels sit at the same time / because every time (c) he made one
= a man
camel sit, / another would stand up. //
사실 그 남자는 아주 열심히 노력했지만 / 모든 낙타를 동시에 앉게 할 수 없었다 / 그가 낙타
한 마리를 앉힐 때마다 / 다른 낙타 한 마리가 일어섰기 때문에 //

'아무리 ~하더라도'
The saint told him, / "You realized / that no matter how hard
사역동사 + 목적어 + 목적격 보어(원형부정사)
you try, / you can't make all the camels sit down. //
그 성자는 그에게 말했다 / "당신이 깨달았습니다 / 아무리 열심히 노력하더라도 / 모든 낙타를
앉게 만들 수는 없다는 것을 //
수동태 동사
If one problem is solved, / for some reason, / another will arise /
like the camels did. // 43번 단서 3: 성자는 남자에게 문제들이 낙타와 같다는 깨달음을 전해줌
만약 한 가지 문제가 해결되면 / 어떤 이유로 / 또 다른 문제가 일어날 것입니다 / 낙타가 그런
것처럼 //
45번④ 성자는 문제가 있어도 인생을 즐겨야 한다고 말했음
So, humans should enjoy life / despite these problems." //
그래서 인간은 삶을 즐겨야 합니다 / 이러한 문제에도 불구하고"라고 //

＊(C) 문단 요약: 한숨도 자지 못한 남자에게 성자는 문제들이 낙타와 같다는 깨달음을
전해줌

43번 단서 4: 남자가 마침내 성자를 만남   = a man   명사절 접속사
(D) When the man got to meet the saint, / (d) he confessed / that
he was very unhappy with life /
마침내 그가 성자를 만났을 때 / 그는 고백했다 / 삶이 매우 불행하다고 /

because problems always surrounded him, / like workplace
tension or worries about his health. //
항상 문제가 자기를 둘러싸고 있어서 / 직장 내 긴장이나 건강에 대한 걱정과 같이 //
= A man
(e) He said, / "Please give me a solution / so that all the problems
in my life will end / and I can live peacefully." //
그는 말했다 / "제발 해결책을 주세요 / 나의 삶의 모든 문제들이 끝나고 / 제가 평화롭게 살 수
있도록"이라고 //
명사절 접속사
The saint smiled and said / that he would answer the request
the next day. // 43번 단서 5, 45번⑤ 성자는 남자에게 다음 날 요청에 답을 주겠다고 함
성자는 미소 지으면서 말했다 / 그가 다음 날 그 요청에 답해 주겠다고 //

＊(D) 문단 요약: 그 남자는 해결책을 요구했고, 성자는 다음 날에 답을 주기로 함

- saint ⓝ 성자 · guard ⓝ 경호인 · opportunity ⓝ 기회
- camel ⓝ 낙타 · reply ⓥ 답하다 · in fact 사실
- arise ⓥ 일어나다 · despite prep ~에도 불구하고
- confess ⓥ 고백하다 · surround ⓥ 둘러싸다 · tension ⓝ 긴장
- solution ⓝ 해결책 · request ⓝ 요청

(A) 옛날 어느 마을에 자신의 삶이 행복하지 않은 한 남자가 살았다. 그는 항상
하나 혹은 또 다른 문제로 어려움을 겪었다. 어느 날 한 성자가 그의 경호인들
과 함께 그의 마을에 들렀다. 많은 사람들이 그 소식을 듣고 그들의 문제를 가
지고 그에게 가기 시작했다. 그 남자 역시 성자를 방문하기로 결정했다. 아침에
성자가 있는 곳에 도착하고 난 후에도 (a) 그는 저녁 때까지 그를 만날 기회를
얻지 못했다.
(D) 마침내 그가 성자를 만났을 때 (d) 그는 직장 내 긴장이나 건강에 대한 걱정
과 같이 항상 문제가 자기를 둘러싸고 있어서 삶이 매우 불행하다고 고백했다.
(e) 그는 "나의 삶의 모든 문제가 끝나고 제가 평화롭게 살 수 있도록 제발 해결
책을 주세요."라고 말했다. 성자는 미소 지으면서 그가 다음 날 그 요청에 답해
주겠다고 말했다.
(B) 그런데 성자는 또한 그 남자가 그를 위해 작은 일을 해 줄 수 있는지 물었
다. 성자는 그 남자에게 "백 마리 낙타 모두가 자리에 앉으면 당신은 자러 가도
좋습니다."라고 말하면서 그날 밤에 그의 일행에 있는 백 마리 낙타를 돌봐 달
라고 말했다. 그 남자는 동의했다. 다음 날 아침에 성자가 그 남자를 만났을 때
(b) 그는 남자가 잠을 잘 잤는지 물어보았다. 피곤해하고 슬퍼하면서 남자는 한
순간도 잠을 자지 못했다고 대답했다.
(C) 사실 그 남자는 아주 열심히 노력했지만 (c) 그가 낙타 한 마리를 앉힐 때마
다 다른 낙타 한 마리가 일어섰기 때문에 모든 낙타를 동시에 앉게 할 수 없었
다. 그 성자는 그에게 "당신이 아무리 열심히 노력하더라도 모든 낙타를 앉게
만들 수는 없다는 것을 깨달았습니다. 만약 한 가지 문제가 해결되면 낙타가 그
런 것처럼 어떤 이유로 또 다른 문제가 일어날 것입니다. 그래서 인간은 이러한
문제에도 불구하고 삶을 즐겨야 합니다."라고 말했다.

43 정답 ④

주어진 글 (A)에 이어질 내용을 순서에 맞게 배열한 것으로 가장 적절한
것은?
① (B) — (D) — (C) 저녁까지 성자를 기다렸다는 (A)에 이어 마침내 남자가 성자를 만났다는
(D)가 가장 먼저 와야 함
② (C) — (B) — (D) ┐
┘ 성자가 부탁하는 (B) 뒤에 깨달음을 주는 (C)가 와야 함
③ (C) — (D) — (B) ┐
(D) 그 남자는 성자를 만나 문제의 해결책을 요구했고, 성자는 다음
④ (D) — (B) — (C) 날에 답을 주겠다고 함 - (B) 성자는 밤에 낙타 백 마리를 돌보면서
모든 낙타가 앉았을 때 잠에 들라고 부탁함 - (C) 한숨도 자지 못한
⑤ (D) — (C) — (B) 남자에게 성자는 문제들이 낙타와 같다는 깨달음을 전해줌
성자가 남자에게 낙타와 관련된 깨달음을 주는 (C)가 가장 마지막에 와야 함

> **왜 정답·오답?** ✿ ❀ ❀ [정답률 86%]

[(A): 한 남자는 성자가 마을을 방문한다는 소식을 듣고, 자신의 문제를
해결하기 위해 성자를 기다렸다.

➡ 남자가 성자를 만나 깨달음을 얻는 이야기가 이어질 것이다.

[B]: 성자는 밤에 낙타 백 마리를 돌보면서 모든 낙타가 앉았을 때 잠에
들라고 부탁했다.
→ 남자가 성자와 만난 내용이 앞에 나와야 하고, 성자가 낙타를 부탁한 후 벌어지는
일이 뒤에 이어져야 한다.
[C]: 한숨도 자지 못한 남자에게 성자는 문제들이 낙타와 같다는 깨달음을
전해주었다.
→ 성자가 밤새 남자에게 낙타를 부탁했던 [B]에 이어지는 내용이고, 이 부탁을 통해
문제들이 낙타와 같다는 깨달음을 전해주는 글의 마무리 부분이다.
[D]: 그 남자는 성자를 만나 문제의 해결책을 요구했고, 성자는 다음 날에
답을 주겠다고 했다.
→ 남자가 성자를 기다렸다는 (A)에 이어지는 내용이고, 뒤에는 남자가 성자를 통해
문제의 해결책을 얻어가는 과정이 이어져야 한다.
▶ (A) 성자가 마을을 방문한다는 소식을 듣고 한 남자가 밤가지 그를 기다림 → (D)
그 남자는 성자를 만나 문제의 해결책을 요구했고, 성자는 다음 날에 답을 주겠다고
함 → (B) 성자는 밤에 낙타 백 마리를 돌보면서 모든 낙타가 앉았을 때 잠에 들 것을
부탁함 → (C) 한숨도 자지 못한 남자에게 성자는 문제들이 낙타와 같다는 깨달음을
전해줌
▶ 글의 순서는 ④ (D) — (B) — (C)임

44 정답 ②

밑줄 친 (a)~(e) 중에서 가리키는 대상이 나머지 넷과 다른 것은?
① (a) = a man ②(b) = a saint ③ (c) = a man ④ (d) = a man ⑤ (e) = A man

왜 정답? ✱✱❀ [정답률 80%]
② (b) he: 남자에게 잘 잤는지 물어본 사람 ▶ a saint

왜 오답?
① (a) he: 저녁까지 성자를 만날 기회를 얻지 못한 사람 ▶ a man
③ (c) he: 밤새 낙타를 한 마리씩 앉히려고 노력했던 사람 ▶ a man
④ (d) he: 성자를 만나 삶이 여러 문제로 불행하다고 고백했던 사람 ▶ a man
⑤ (e) He: 성자에게 자신이 평화롭게 살도록 해결책을 요청했던 사람 ▶ A man

45 정답 ③

윗글에 관한 내용으로 적절하지 않은 것은?
① 많은 사람들이 자신들의 문제를 가지고 성자에게 갔다.
Many people heard the news and started going to him with their problems.
② 성자는 자신을 위해 작은 일을 해 줄 수 있는지 남자에게 물었다.
But the saint also asked if the man could do a small job for him.
③ 성자는 남자가 낙타를 모두 재우면 잠을 자러 가도 좋다고 했다.
When all hundred camels sit down, you can go to sleep.
④ 성자는 문제가 있어도 인생을 즐겨야 한다고 말했다.
So, humans should enjoy life despite these problems.
⑤ 성자는 남자의 요청에 대한 답을 다음 날 말해 주기로 했다.
The saint smiled and said that he would answer the request the next day.

왜 정답? ✱✱❀ [정답률 70%]
성자는 남자에게 낙타를 앉히고 나면 잠을 자러 가도 좋다고(When all hundred
camels sit down, you can go to sleep.) 했으므로, ③은 적절하지 않다.

왜 오답?
① 많은 사람들이 자신들의 문제를 가지고 성자에게 갔다. (Many people heard
the news and started going to him with their problems.)
② 성자는 자신을 위해 작은 일을 해 줄 수 있는지 남자에게 물었다. (But the saint
also asked if the man could do a small job for him.)
④ 성자는 문제가 있어도 인생을 즐겨야 한다고 말했다. (So, humans should
enjoy life despite these problems.)
⑤ 성자는 남자의 요청에 대한 답을 다음 날 말해 주기로 했다. (The saint smiled
and said that he would answer the request the next day.)

11회 Dictation
문제 p. 208

01 doing our best to / As part of our effort / exhibitions /
lose your way / it'll kindly
02 sponsored / gotten better and better / You'd better check /
with a translation program
03 We've been messaging / how long you've been /
don't need it anymore / load it on first
04 Did you finish / in front of the window /
helps students dream big / love the vending machine
05 I've finally decided / a survey of / help you with anything /
how will we find / bulletin
06 Economic / per month / get a discount / fill in this paper
07 chemistry / I even went to / take me with you /
you mentioned before
08 looking forward to it / we must hand in / Registration /
donated to charity
09 Regardless of hiking experience / equipment /
in advance to participate
10 brochure / Why don't we choose / instead of a wall calendar /
made of recyclable paper / let's cross this out
11 I heard you were invited / Assembly / the article I wrote /
did you mostly
12 sweating / too far to walk / take it instead
13 It's opened / can be of help / install / check a few things /
trial period / that's why
14 looking for volunteer work / Could you / valuable / join in /
quit a few days ago / get an answer immediately
15 To make a list / proposes / lots of reviews /
quality getting worse
[16~17] veggies / highly toxic / cause severe health damage /
have difficulties breathing / snack on grapefruits /
develop stomach problems / said to be harmful

11회 어휘 Review Test
문제 p. 212

01 후원하다
02 전시회
03 동행하다
04 번역
05 장비
06 format
07 load
08 confident
09 atmosphere
10 trial
11 account for
12 be subject to
13 regardless of
14 hand in

15 conform to
16 transmission
17 significance
18 regulation
19 commonsense
20 extraordinary
21 recognition
22 assumption
23 premature
24 difficulty
25 geometrical
26 alter
27 integrate
28 assist

29 enhance
30 inhabit
31 combination
32 frequency
33 adjust
34 diversity
35 insurance
36 Crucially
37 guidelines
38 perception
39 advantage
40 permission

01 정답 ① ＊폭설로 인한 등산로 폐쇄 공지

[Chime bell rings.]
[차임벨이 울린다.]

M : Good morning.
남 : 안녕하세요.

This is Ethan Cooper from the Reindeer Mountain maintenance office.
저는 Reindeer Mountain 관리 사무소의 Ethan Cooper입니다.

Last night, we had 20cm of heavy snow.
지난밤에, 20cm의 폭설이 내렸습니다.

Most of the snow melted away with the sun out in the morning, but some of **it** froze in the shade.
= the snow
아침에 해가 뜨면서 대부분의 눈이 녹았지만, 일부는 그늘에서 얼어붙었습니다.
앞에 주격 관계대명사와 be동사가 생략됨

For hikers' safety, we've closed some of the trails **covered** with ice. **단서 1** 얼음으로 뒤덮인 등산로 일부를 폐쇄함
등산객들의 안전을 위해, 저희는 얼음으로 뒤덮인 등산로 일부를 폐쇄했습니다.

At this moment, Sunrise Trail and Lakeview Trail are unavailable for hikers.
현재, Sunrise Trail과 Lakeview Trail은 등산객들이 이용하실 수 없습니다.

I'll make an announcement later when the trails are ready **to be reopened.**
to부정사의 수동태
등산로가 다시 개방될 준비가 되면 나중에 공지하겠습니다.

Until then, keep in mind that Sunrise Trail and Lakeview Trail are closed. **단서 2** 공지 전까지 Sunrise Trail과 Lakeview Trail은 폐쇄됨
그때까지는, Sunrise Trail과 Lakeview Trail이 폐쇄된다는 것을 명심하세요.

Thank you.
감사합니다.

- **maintenance** ⓝ 보수, 관리   • **melt** ⓥ 녹다   • **freeze** ⓥ 얼다
- **shade** ⓝ 그늘   • **hiker** ⓝ 등산객   • **trail** ⓝ 산길, 자국
- **unavailable** ⓐ 이용할 수 없는   • **announcement** ⓝ 공고, 발표
- **keep in mind** 명심하다

다음을 듣고, 남자가 하는 말의 목적으로 가장 적절한 것을 고르시오.
① 얼음으로 덮인 일부 등산로 폐쇄를 공지하려고
　폭설로 얼어붙은 등산로 일부를 폐쇄했다고 했음
② 등산객에게 야간 산행의 위험성을 경고하려고
　야간 산행에 대한 언급은 없음
③ 겨울 산행을 위한 안전 장비를 안내하려고
　안전 장비에 대한 내용은 없음
④ 긴급 제설에 필요한 작업자를 모집하려고
　폭설이 내렸다는 것으로 만든 오답
⑤ 일출 명소인 전망대를 소개하려고
　아침에 해가 떴다는 것으로 만든 함정

＞왜 정답 ？ ✽✽✽ [정답률 91%]

지난밤에 폭설이 내려 일부 등산로가 얼어붙었음을 알리며, 등산객들의 안전을 위해 등산로 일부를 폐쇄했다고 공지하고 있으므로 정답은 ①이다.

＞왜 오답 ？

② 밤에 폭설이 내렸다고 했을 뿐, 야간 산행에 대해서는 언급하지 않았다.
③ 눈 내린 등산로를 위한 안전 장비를 안내하는 내용이 아니다.
④ 폭설이 내렸다는 것으로 만든 오답으로, 긴급 제설이나 작업자 모집에 대한 내용이 아니다. 함정
⑤ 일출 명소를 소개하는 내용이 아니다.

02 정답 ① ＊조리법은 꼭 따라야 할까?

M : Honey, what are you doing?
남 : 여보, 뭐 하고 있어요?

W : I'm looking for the measuring spoons. Do you know **where they are**?
목적어 역할을 하는 간접의문문
여 : 계량스푼을 찾고 있어요. 그게 어디 있는지 알아요?

M : They're in the first drawer. Why do you need them?
남 : 그것들은 첫 번째 서랍에 있어요. 당신은 그게 왜 필요해요?

W : The recipe **says** four teaspoons of sugar.
'~라고 쓰여 있다'
여 : 조리법에 설탕 네 티스푼이라고 쓰여 있어요.

M : Dear, you don't have to follow the recipe as it is.
남 : 여보, 조리법을 그대로 따를 필요는 없어요. **단서 1** 남자는 조리법을 있는 그대로 따를 필요는 없다고 함

W : What do you mean?
여 : 무슨 뜻이에요?

M : A recipe is just an example. You don't need to add the same amount of ingredients as stated in the recipe. **단서 2** 조리법과 같은 양의 재료를 첨가할 필요는 없다고 함
남 : 조리법은 그냥 예시일 뿐이에요. 당신은 조리법에 명시된 것과 같은 양의 재료를 첨가할 필요는 없어요.

W : Hmm. Right. Sometimes the food is too sweet when I cook **based on** the recipe instructions.
'~에 따라'
여 : 음. 맞아요. 조리법 설명에 따라 요리하면 가끔 음식이 너무 달아요.

M : See? You don't need to stick to the recipe.
남 : 맞죠? 당신은 조리법을 고수할 필요는 없어요. **단서 3** 남자는 조리법을 그대로 따를 필요는 없다고 반복해서 주장함

W : Okay. I'll remember that.
여 : 알았어요. 그걸 기억할게요.

- **measuring spoon** 계량스푼   • **drawer** ⓝ 서랍
- **recipe** ⓝ 조리법   • **ingredient** ⓝ 재료   • **state** ⓥ 말하다, 명시하다
- **instruction** ⓝ 설명, 지시   • **stick to** ~을 고수하다

대화를 듣고, 남자의 의견으로 가장 적절한 것을 고르시오.
① 조리법을 있는 그대로 따를 필요는 없다.
　조리법과 같은 양의 재료를 넣을 필요는 없다고 했음
② 요리 도구를 정기적으로 소독해야 한다.
　요리 도구 소독에 대한 내용은 없음
③ 설탕 섭취는 단기 기억력을 향상시킨다.
　설탕 섭취를 권장하는 내용이 아님
④ 열량이 높은 음식은 건강에 좋지 않다.
　음식이 너무 달다는 말을 이용한 오답
⑤ 신선한 재료는 요리의 풍미를 높인다.
　재료의 신선도는 언급되지 않음

＞왜 정답 ？ ✽✽✽ [정답률 97%]

계량스푼을 찾으며 조리법대로 설탕을 넣으려고 하는 여자에게 남자는 조리법은 예시일 뿐이라서 그대로 따를 필요는 없다고 했다. 따라서 남자의 의견으로 가장 적절한 것은 ①이다.

＞왜 오답 ？

② 요리 도구인 계량스푼이 언급되기는 했지만, 이를 소독하라는 내용은 나오지 않았다.
③ 설탕에 대한 언급은 있지만, 기억력과 관련된 대화는 하지 않았다.
④ 음식이 너무 달다는 말을 이용한 오답으로, 열량이 높은 음식과 건강의 관계에 대한 내용은 아니다.
⑤ 대화에서 재료의 신선도는 언급되지 않았다.

03 정답 ② ＊게임에 넣을 음악 제작 요청

[Door knocks.]
[문 두드리는 소리]

W : Can I come in?
여 : 들어가도 될까요?

M : Yes. Oh, Ms. Smith. Did you read the email I sent?
　　 앞에 목적격 관계대명사가 생략됨
남 : 네. 오, Smith 씨. 제가 보낸 이메일 읽어보셨나요?

W : I did. I liked your game scenario. The characters <u>exploring</u>
　　The characters를 수식하는 현재분사구
　　<u>space</u> were very mysterious. How did you create the
　　characters? **단서 1** 남자는 게임 시나리오와 등장인물들을 만드는 사람임
여 : 읽었습니다. 저는 당신의 게임 시나리오가 마음에 들었어요. 우주를 탐험하는
　　등장인물들이 매우 신비로웠습니다. 어떻게 등장인물들을 만드셨나요?

M : Actually, old science fiction movies inspired me <u>to design</u>
　　명사적 용법(목적격 보어)
　　those characters.
남 : 사실, 오래된 공상과학 영화들이 제가 그 등장인물들을 만드는 데 영감을 주었습니다.

W : Interesting. Now, could you describe the main character
　　more specifically? It'll be helpful <u>when</u> I compose the theme
　　부사절 접속사
　　song for the character. **단서 2** 여자는 주제곡을 작곡하는 사람임
여 : 흥미롭군요. 자, 주인공에 대해 더 구체적으로 설명해 주시겠어요? 그것은 제가
　　등장인물에 대한 주제곡을 작곡할 때 도움이 될 것입니다.

M : Well, he's a thrill seeker. So, a strong, bold, and rhythmic
　　sound would suit him.
남 : 음, 그는 스릴을 추구하는 사람입니다. 그래서, 강하고, 대담하고, 리듬감 있는 소리가
　　그에게 어울릴 것 같아요.

W : Okay. Do you need anything else?
여 : 알겠습니다. 더 필요한 것이 있으세요?

M : I also want you <u>to make</u> some background music.
　　명사적 용법(목적격 보어)
남 : 저는 당신이 배경음악도 좀 만들어 주셨으면 합니다. **단서 3** 남자가 여자에게 배경음악을
　　만들어 달라고 부탁함

W : Of course. When do you need them?
여 : 물론이죠. 언제 그것들이 필요하신가요?

M : By December 21st. I'd like to start putting the music into the
　　game by then.
남 : 12월 21일까지요. 저는 그때까지 게임에 그 음악을 넣고 싶습니다.

W : All right. Then I'll talk to you later.
여 : 좋습니다. 나중에 말씀드리겠습니다.

- character ⓝ 등장인물　　· explore ⓥ 탐험하다
- mysterious ⓐ 신비한　　· science fiction 공상과학
- inspire ⓥ 영감을 주다　　· specifically ⓐd 구체적으로
- compose ⓥ 작곡하다　　· theme song 주제곡　　· bold ⓐ 대담한
- rhythmic ⓐ 리듬감 있는　　· suit ⓥ 어울리다
- background music 배경음악

대화를 듣고, 두 사람의 관계를 가장 잘 나타낸 것을 고르시오.

① 음악 평론가 – 방송 연출가　theme song, background music을 이용한 오답
② 작곡가 – 게임 제작자
　　남자는 게임 시나리오와 등장인물들을 만들고 여자는 주제곡과 배경음악을 작곡함
③ 독자 – 웹툰 작가
　　등장인물(character)을 이용한 함정
④ 삽화가 – 소설가
　　삽화를 그리는 것에 대한 언급은 없음
⑤ 영화감독 – 배우
　　시나리오가 나왔지만, 게임 시나리오임

〉왜 정답 ? ✿✿✿ [정답률 93%]

여자는 남자의 게임 시나리오가 마음에 들었다고 하면서 등장인물을 위한 주제곡을
작곡할 때 도움이 될 수 있도록 주인공에 대해 더 설명해달라고 요청했다.
더 필요한 것을 묻는 여자에게 남자는 배경음악을 만들어 줄 것을 부탁하고 있으므로
두 사람의 관계로 가장 적절한 것은 ②이다.

〉왜 오답 ?

① theme song, background music 등을 이용한 오답으로, 음악에 대해
　 평론하고 있는 대화가 아니다.
③ 웹툰을 그리거나 읽는 것에 대한 내용이 아니다.
④ 소설을 쓰거나 삽화를 그리는 것에 대한 언급은 없다. (▶이유: 소설의 삽화가
　 아니라 시나리오의 음악과 관련된 대화이다.)
⑤ 게임 시나리오이므로 영화감독과 배우의 관계라고 할 수 없다.

---

04 정답 ④ ＊Chelsea가 꿈꾸는 방

M : Hi, Chelsea. Did you finish your art assignment?
남 : 안녕, Chelsea. 너 미술 과제 다 했어?

W : Oh, my dream room drawing? Yes. Here's the picture.
여 : 오, 내가 꿈꾸는 방 그리기 말이야? 응. 여기 그림이 있어.

M : Wow, it's so creative. There is a staircase next to the door.
남 : 와, 정말 창의적이야. 문 옆에 계단이 있네. **①의 단서** 문 옆에 계단이 있음

W : Yes. I'<u>ve</u> always <u>dreamed</u> of a room with two floors. Look at
　　현재완료(계속)
　　the three light bulbs above the staircase. **②의 단서** 계단 위에 세 개의
　　전구가 있음
여 : 응. 나는 항상 2층짜리 방을 꿈꿔왔어. 계단 위에 있는 세 개의 전구를 봐.

M : They look very stylish. And I like the flower picture above
　　 =the flower picture
　　the sofa. <u>It</u>'ll bring warmth to your room. **③의 단서** 소파 위에
　　꽃 그림이 있음
남 : 그것들은 아주 멋져 보여. 그리고 나는 소파 위에 있는 꽃 그림이 좋아. 그게 네 방에
　　따뜻함을 가져올 거야.

W : Thanks. Check out the square-shaped rug on the floor.
　　④의 단서 바닥에는 사각형이 아니라 원형 깔개가 있음
여 : 고마워. 바닥에 있는 사각형 모양의 깔개를 봐.

M : It <u>goes well with</u> this place. Oh, there is a bookshelf by the
　　'~와 잘 어울리다'
　　sofa. **⑤의 단서** 소파 옆에 책장이 있음
남 : 이 장소랑 잘 어울리네. 오, 소파 옆에 책장이 있네.

W : You're right. I want to keep my favorite books nearby.
여 : 맞아. 내가 좋아하는 책들을 근처에 두고 싶거든.

M : That's a good idea.
남 : 그거 좋은 생각이야.

- assignment ⓝ 과제　　· creative ⓐ 창의적인　　· staircase ⓝ 계단
- floor ⓝ 바닥, 층　　· light bulb 전구　　· stylish ⓐ 멋진
- warmth ⓝ 온기, 따뜻함　　· check out ~을 확인하다[보다]
- square ⓝ 사각형　　· rug ⓝ 깔개　　· bookshelf ⓝ 책장

대화를 듣고, 그림에서 대화의 내용과 일치하지 않는 것을 고르시오.

계단 위에 세 개의 전구가 있음
소파 위에 꽃 그림이 있음
소파 옆에 책장이 있음
문 옆에 계단이 있음
비닥에는 사각형이 아니라 원형 깔개가 있음

〉왜 정답 ? ✿✿✿ [정답률 89%]

여자는 남자에게 바닥에 있는 사각형 모양의 깔개를 보라고 했지만, 그림에는 원형
깔개가 있으므로 ④이 대화의 내용과 일치하지 않는다.

〉왜 오답 ?

① 문 옆에 계단이 있다.
② 계단 위에 세 개의 전구가 있다.
③ 소파 위에 꽃 그림이 있다.
⑤ 소파 옆에 책장이 있다.

2022.11
12회

05 정답 ⑤ ＊만화가와의 토크쇼 준비 ─────

W : Jamie, is the cartoon artist on her way?
여 : Jamie, 그 만화가는 오고 계신가요?

M : Yes. She'll arrive at our studio in an hour.
남 : 네. 그녀는 한 시간 후에 우리 스튜디오에 도착할 겁니다.

W : Perfect. Let's check if we have everything ready for our talk show.
여 : 좋아요. 우리의 토크쇼를 위한 준비가 다 되었는지 확인해 봅시다.

M : Okay. I **set** up a chair for our guest yesterday. ③의 함정
 ('set-set-set')
남 : 알겠습니다. 제가 어제 우리의 게스트를 위해 의자를 설치해 놓았습니다.

W : Great. And I bought a drink and **put** it on the table. ①의 함정
 ('put-put-put')
여 : 좋아요. 그리고 제가 음료를 사서 탁자 위에 놓았어요.

M : Good. Did you prepare a pencil? The artist said she'll draw
 (뒤에 목적어절 접속사 that이 생략됨)
 caricatures of us during the live show.
남 : 좋습니다. 연필은 준비하셨나요? 그 만화가가 생방송 중에 우리의 캐리커처를 그려주신다고 하셨어요.

W : Oh, she told me **that** she'll bring her own pencil.
 (직접목적어절 접속사)
여 : 오, 그녀는 저에게 본인의 연필을 가져올 거라고 하셨어요.

M : She did? Then we don't need it.
남 : 그러셨어요? 그럼 그건 필요 없겠네요.

W : Yeah. **By the way**, where's the sketchbook?
 ('그런데, 그나저나')
여 : 네. 그런데, 스케치북은 어디 있나요?

M : Oops. I left **it** in my car. I'll go get it right now.
 (= the sketchbook)   단서 남자는 차에 두고 온 스케치북을 가지러 갈 것임
남 : 이런. 제가 차에 두고 왔어요. 제가 지금 바로 그것을 가져올게요.

W : Fine. Then I'll check the microphones. ④의 함정
여 : 좋아요. 그러면 저는 마이크를 점검해 볼게요.

M : Thanks.
남 : 고맙습니다.

- cartoon artist 만화가 • on one's way 가고[오고] 있는
- set up 준비하다, 설치하다 • caricature ⓝ 캐리커처

┌─────────────────────────────────────┐
│ 대화를 듣고, 남자가 할 일로 가장 적절한 것을 고르시오. │
│ ① 음료 구매하기 여자가 이미 구매해 놓음 │
│ ② 연필 준비하기 연필은 만화가가 직접 가져오기로 함 │
│ ③ 의자 설치하기 의자는 남자가 어제 설치해 놓음 │
│ ④ 마이크 점검하기 마이크는 여자가 점검하기로 함 │
│ ⑤ 스케치북 가져오기 남자가 차에 두고 온 것을 가져올 것임 │
└─────────────────────────────────────┘

▶왜 정답? ✱✱✱ [정답률 96%]
만화가와의 토크쇼 준비가 다 되었는지 확인하는 상황이다. 여자가 남자에게 스케치북이 어디 있냐고 묻자, 남자는 차에 두고 왔다고 하면서 바로 가져오겠다고 했으므로 정답은 ⑤이다.

▶왜 오답?
① 음료는 여자가 이미 구매해 놓았다.
② 연필은 만화가가 직접 가져오기로 했다.
③ 의자는 남자가 어제 설치해 놓았다.
④ 마이크는 남자가 아니라 여자가 점검할 것이라고 했다. 함정

06 정답 ④ ＊Crispy Fried Chicken에서 주문하기 ─────

M : Welcome to Crispy Fried Chicken. What would you like to order?
남 : Crispy Fried Chicken에 오신 것을 환영합니다. 무엇을 주문하시겠습니까?

W : What kind of chicken do you have?
여 : 어떤 종류의 치킨이 있나요?

M : We only have two kinds. Fried chicken is $15 and barbecue chicken is $20.
남 : 두 종류만 있습니다. 프라이드치킨은 15달러이고 바비큐치킨은 20달러입니다.

W : I'll have one fried and one barbecue chicken.
여 : 프라이드치킨 하나와 바비큐치킨 하나 주세요. 단서 1 15달러인 프라이드치킨 하나와 20달러인 바비큐치킨 하나를 구매함

M : Okay. Would you like some potato chips with your order?
 (최상급 비교)
 They're our **most popular** side dish.
 (= potato chips)
남 : 알겠습니다. 감자칩도 함께 주문하시겠어요? 저희의 가장 인기 있는 사이드 메뉴입니다.

W : How much are **they**?
여 : 그건 얼마인가요?

M : One basket of potato chips is $2.
남 : 감자칩 한 상자에 2달러입니다.

W : Then I'll get one basket. 단서 2 2달러인 감자칩 한 상자를 구매함
여 : 그럼 한 상자 주세요.

M : Will that be all?
남 : 그것이 전부인가요?

W : Yes. And can I use this coupon for a free soda?
여 : 네. 그리고 무료 탄산음료 쿠폰을 사용할 수 있을까요?

M : Of course. You can grab any soda from the fridge.
남 : 물론이죠. 냉장고에서 탄산음료를 아무거나 가져가셔도 됩니다.

W : Great. Here's my credit card.
여 : 좋아요. 여기 제 신용카드가 있습니다.

- basket ⓝ 상자, 바구니 • soda ⓝ 탄산음료 • fridge ⓝ 냉장고

┌─────────────────────────────────────┐
│ 대화를 듣고, 여자가 지불할 금액을 고르시오. [3점] │
│ ① $17 ② $22 ③ $35 ④$37 ⑤ $39 │
│ $15(프라이드치킨 하나)+$20(바비큐치킨 하나)+$2(감자칩 한 상자) │
└─────────────────────────────────────┘

▶왜 정답? ✱✱✳ [정답률 70%]
여자는 하나에 15달러인 프라이드치킨 하나와 20달러인 바비큐치킨 하나를 주문했고, 사이드 메뉴로 2달러인 감자칩 한 상자를 구매했다. 따라서 여자가 지불할 금액은 ④ '37달러'이다.

07 정답 ① ＊얼음낚시에 갈 수 없는 Leo ─────

[Cell phone rings.]
[휴대 전화가 울린다.]

W : Leo, I'm sorry I missed your call. What's up?
여 : Leo, 네 전화를 못 받아서 미안해. 무슨 일이야?

M : Well, I just called to tell you **that** I can't go ice fishing with
 (직접목적어절 접속사)
 you this weekend.
남 : 음, 이번 주말에 너랑 얼음낚시하러 갈 수 없다고 말하려고 전화했어.

W : Oh, no. I **heard** the weather will be perfect this weekend. ④의 함정
 (뒤에 목적어절 접속사 that이 생략됨)
여 : 아, 안 돼. 이번 주말에 날씨가 완벽할 거라고 들었어.

M : I'm sorry. I really **wish I could go**.
 (I wish+가정법 과거: ~라면 좋을 텐데)
남 : 미안해. 나도 정말 갈 수 있으면 좋겠어.

W : **Didn't you say** you're off from work this weekend? ③의 함정
 (뒤에 목적어절 접속사 that이 생략)
여 : 너 이번 주말에 일 쉰다고 하지 않았어?

M : I am. It's not because of work. Actually, I hurt my wrist.
남 : 맞아. 일 때문이 아니야. 사실, 나는 손목을 다쳤어. 단서 손목을 다쳐서 얼음낚시를 갈 수 없음

W : That's terrible. Are you okay?
여 : 저런. 너 괜찮아?

M : Don't worry. I'll be fine.
남 : 걱정하지 마. 괜찮아질 거야.

W : How did you get injured?
여 : 어쩌다 다쳤어?

M : I **was** playing basketball with a friend and **sprained** my
 (병렬 구조)
 wrist. ⑤의 함정
남 : 나는 친구와 농구를 하다가 손목을 삐었어.

W : Did you go to the hospital? ②의 함정
여 : 병원에는 갔어?

M : I did. The doctor told me 직접목적어절 접속사 that it'll be better in a month.
남 : 갔지. 의사 선생님이 한 달 후면 나을 거라고 했어.

W : That's good. I hope you feel better soon.
여 : 잘됐네. 나는 네가 곧 나아지길 바라.

- -

• miss ⓥ 놓치다　• off ⓐ 쉬는　• wrist ⓝ 손목
• injure ⓥ 부상을 입다　• sprain ⓥ (특히 손목·발목을) 삐다

대화를 듣고, 남자가 얼음낚시를 갈 수 없는 이유를 고르시오.

① 손목을 다쳐서 농구를 하다가 손목을 다쳐서 얼음낚시를 갈 수 없다고 했음
② 병원에 입원해야 해서 병원에는 이미 다녀왔음
③ 직장에 출근해야 해서 주말에 일을 쉰다고 했음
④ 기상 여건이 나빠져서 주말에 날씨가 좋다고 했음
⑤ 친구와 농구를 해야 해서 친구와 농구를 하다가 다쳤다는 내용으로 만든 오답

>왜 정답? ✽❀❀ [정답률 90%]

남자는 여자에게 이번 주말에 얼음낚시를 갈 수 없다고 하면서 친구와 농구를 하다가 손목을 다쳤다고 했다. 따라서 남자가 얼음낚시를 갈 수 없는 이유로 가장 적절한 것은 ①이다.

>왜 오답?

② 남자는 병원에 이미 다녀왔다고 했다.
③ 남자는 주말에 일을 쉰다고 했다.
④ 주말에 오히려 날씨가 좋을 거라고 했다.
⑤ 남자가 친구와 농구를 하다가 다쳤다는 내용으로 만든 오답이다. 함정

---

08 정답 ③ ＊어린이 도기기 수업 등록하기

M : Honey, look at this flyer about Kids' Pottery Class.
남 : 여보, 어린이 도기기 수업에 관한 이 전단지 좀 봐요.

W : Okay. Let's take a look.
여 : 알았어요. 어디 한번 봅시다.

뒤에 목적어절 접속사 that이 생략됨
M : I think our little Austin would love to make his own cereal bowl.
남 : 내 생각에 우리 아이 Austin이 자신의 시리얼 그릇을 만들고 싶어 할 것 같아요.

W : I think so, too. It says that the class is held on October 8th. We can take him there on that day. ①의 단서 날짜
여 : 저도 그렇게 생각해요. 전단지에 수업이 10월 8일에 있다고 적혀 있어요. 우리는 아이를 그날 거기로 데려갈 수 있어요.

M : Great. And it's held in Pottery Village. It's a 10-minute drive from our home. ②의 단서 장소
남 : 좋아요. 그리고 그건 도기기 마을에서 하네요. 우리 집에서 차로 10분 거리에 있어요.

W : That's so close. And check out the price. The class costs only $15. ④의 단서 수강료
여 : 정말 가깝네요. 그리고 가격을 봐요. 수업은 단돈 15달러예요.

M : That's reasonable. We should sign up. How can we register for the class?
남 : 적당하네요. 우리는 등록해야겠어요. 어떻게 수업을 등록할 수 있나요?

뒤에 목적어절 접속사 that이 생략됨　부사적 용법(목적)
W : It says you can simply scan the QR code to register online. ⑤의 단서 등록 방법
여 : 온라인으로 등록하려면 그냥 QR코드를 스캔하면 된다고 적혀있어요.

M : Okay. Let's do it right away.
남 : 알았어요. 지금 바로 합시다.

- -

• flyer ⓝ 전단지　• pottery ⓝ 도기기　• bowl ⓝ 그릇
• cost ⓥ (비용이) ~이다　• reasonable ⓐ 적당한, 합리적인
• sign up 참가하다, 등록하다　• register ⓥ 등록하다

대화를 듣고, Kids' Pottery Class에 관해 언급되지 <u>않은</u> 것을 고르시오.

① 날짜 It says that the class is held on October 8th.
② 장소 it's held in Pottery Village
③ 수강 인원 언급되지 않음
④ 수강료 The class costs only $15.
⑤ 등록 방법 It says you can simply scan the QR code to register online.

>왜 정답? ✽❀❀ [정답률 93%]

Kids' Pottery Class의 날짜, 장소, 수강료, 등록 방법은 언급되었지만, 수강 인원에 대해서는 언급되지 않았으므로 정답은 ③이다.

>왜 오답?

① 10월 8일에 수업이 있다고 했다.
② 도기기 마을에서 수업한다고 했다.
④ 수강료는 15달러라고 했다.
⑤ QR코드를 스캔해서 온라인으로 등록할 수 있다고 했다.

---

09 정답 ④ ＊2022 온라인 휘파람 불기 선수권 대회 ────

W : Hello, listeners. The most interesting music competition is back!
여 : 안녕하세요, 청취자 여러분. 가장 흥미로운 음악 경연대회가 돌아왔습니다!

You can now sign up for the 2022 Online Whistling Championship. ①의 단서 좋아하는 어떤 노래든 선택할 수 있음
여러분은 지금 2022 온라인 휘파람 불기 선수권 대회에 참가할 수 있습니다.

목적격 관계대명사　목적어절 접속사
You can select any song that you like, but note that the length of your whistling video is limited to three minutes.
여러분은 여러분이 원하는 어떤 노래든 선택할 수 있지만, 여러분의 휘파람 동영상의 길이는 3분으로 제한된다는 것에 주의하세요.

부사적 용법(목적)
To enter the competition, you must upload your video on our website by December 4th. ②의 단서 12월 4일까지 동영상을 업로드해야 함
대회에 참가하기 위해서는, 12월 4일까지 저희 웹사이트에 여러분의 동영상을 업로드하셔야 합니다.

접속사가 생략되지 않은 분사구문
When recording your whistling, be sure to turn off the echo effect on the microphone. ③의 단서 녹음 시 마이크의 에코 효과를 반드시 꺼야 함
휘파람 소리를 녹음할 때는, 반드시 마이크의 에코 효과를 끄십시오.

Winners will be decided by public online voting. ④의 단서 수상자는 공개 온라인 투표로 결정됨
수상자는 공개 온라인 투표로 결정될 것입니다.

The result will be announced on our website. ⑤의 단서 결과는 웹사이트에 발표될 것임
결과는 저희 웹사이트에 발표될 것입니다.

We look forward to your enthusiastic participation.
여러분의 열정적인 참여를 기대합니다.

- -

• competition ⓝ (경연)대회　• sign up for ~에 참가하다
• whistling ⓝ 휘파람, 휘파람 불기　• championship ⓝ 선수권 대회
• note ⓥ 주목[주의]하다　• echo ⓝ (소리의) 울림
• look forward to ~을 기대하다　• enthusiastic ⓐ 열렬한

2022 Online Whistling Championship에 관한 다음 내용을 듣고, 일치하지 <u>않는</u> 것을 고르시오.

① 좋아하는 어떤 노래든 선택할 수 있다. You can select any song that you like
② 12월 4일까지 동영상을 업로드해야 한다.
you must upload your video on our website by December 4th
③ 녹음 시 마이크의 에코 효과를 반드시 꺼야 한다.
When recording your whistling, be sure to turn off the echo effect on the microphone.
④ 운영진의 심사에 의해 수상자들이 결정될 것이다.
Winners will be decided by public online voting.
⑤ 결과는 웹사이트에 발표될 것이다.
The result will be announced on our website.

왜 정답? ❋❋❋ [정답률 86%]

수상자는 공개 온라인 투표로 결정될 것이라고(Winners will be decided by public online voting.) 했으므로 운영진의 심사에 의해 수상자들이 결정될 것이라고 한 ④이 일치하지 않는다.

왜 오답?

① 어떤 노래든 선택할 수 있다고 했다.
② 12월 4일까지 웹사이트에 동영상을 업로드하라고 했다.
③ 녹음할 때는 반드시 마이크의 에코 효과를 끄라고 했다.
⑤ 결과는 웹사이트에 발표될 것이라고 했다.

10 정답 ② ＊침실 커튼 선택하기

M : Honey, I'm looking at a shopping site to choose curtains for [부사적 용법(목적)] our bedroom. But there are too many options to consider. [형용사적 용법(options 수식)]

남 : 여보, 나는 우리의 침실에 쓸 커튼을 고르려고 쇼핑 사이트를 보고 있어요. 하지만 고려할 선택지가 너무 많아요.

W : Okay. Let's pick one together.

여 : 알았어요. 같이 하나를 골라봐요.

M : I don't think we should spend more than $100. [단서 1] 100달러가 넘지 않아야 함(⑤ 제외)

남 : 나는 우리가 100달러 이상을 써야 한다고 생각하지 않아요.

W : I agree. Let's drop this one. And some of them are machine washable at home.

여 : 동의해요. 이것은 제외합시다. 그리고 그것들 중 일부는 집에서 기계 세탁을 할 수 있어요.

M : Fantastic. We won't have to pay for dry cleaning all the time. [단서 2] 기계 세탁이 가능한 것을 구매하려고 함(③ 제외)

남 : 좋아요. 우리는 항상 드라이클리닝 비용을 지불할 필요는 없겠어요.

W : Good for us. Let's cross out this one then. What about a blackout option?

여 : 잘됐네요. 그럼 이건 지워요. 암막 옵션은 어떤가요? [단서 3] 빛 차단이 되는 것을 구매하려고 함(① 제외)

M : We definitely need it. It'll completely block sunlight, so we won't be disturbed. And which color do you like? [수동태의 미래시제]

남 : 우리는 그것이 꼭 필요해요. 그것이 햇빛을 완전히 차단해서, 우리는 방해받지 않을 거예요. 그리고 당신은 어떤 색이 좋아요?

W : I don't mind any color except for gray.

여 : 회색을 제외하면 어떤 색도 상관없어요. [단서 4] 회색이 아닌 것을 구매하려고 함(④ 제외)

M : Okay. Then we narrowed it down to one.

남 : 알았어요. 그러면 우리는 하나로 좁혔네요.

W : Well then, let's choose this one.

여 : 자 그러면, 이것으로 선택해요.

- option ⓝ 선택(권) · consider ⓥ 고려하다
- machine washable 기계 세탁할 수 있는
- cross out (줄을 그어) 지우다 · blackout ⓝ (창문에 치는) 암막, 빛 차단
- disturb ⓥ 방해하다 · except for ~을 제외하고는
- narrow ⓥ 좁히다

다음 표를 보면서 대화를 듣고, 두 사람이 선택할 커튼을 고르시오.

Curtains 커튼

	Product 제품	Price 가격	Care Instruction 관리 지침	Blackout 암막	Color 색상
①	A	$70	machine washable 기계 세탁할 수 있는	×	navy 남색
②	B	$80	machine washable	○	brown 갈색
③	C	$90	dry cleaning only 드라이클리닝만 가능한	○	ivory 상아색
④	D	$95	machine washable	○	gray 회색
⑤	E	$110	dry cleaning only	×	white 흰색

암막 기능이 없음
100달러가 넘음 · 기계 세탁이 불가능함 · 회색은 제외함

왜 정답? ❋❋❋ [정답률 73%]

남자와 여자는 100달러가 넘지 않고(⑤ 제외) 기계 세탁을 할 수 있으며(③ 제외) 암막 기능이 있는 것 중(① 제외) 회색이 아닌(④ 제외) 커튼을 선택했으므로 정답은 ②이다.

왜 오답?

① 암막 기능이 있어야 한다.
③ 기계 세탁이 불가능하다.
④ 회색은 제외한다고 했다.
⑤ 100달러 이상 쓰고 싶지 않다고 했다.

11 정답 ① ＊롤러코스터 탑승 기다리기

M : Excuse me. Is this really the line for the rollercoaster?

남 : 실례합니다. 이게 정말 롤러코스터 줄인가요?

W : Yes. This is the line for the ride.

여 : 네. 여기가 그 놀이기구 줄이에요.

M : Oh, no. I can't believe it. There are so many people standing in line. How long have you been waiting here? [앞에 주격 관계대명사와 be동사가 생략됨][현재완료 진행시제]

남 : 아, 안 돼. 믿을 수가 없네요. 정말 많은 사람들이 줄을 서고 있네요. 당신은 여기에서 얼마나 기다리셨나요? [단서] 남자는 여자에게 얼마나 오래 기다리고 있는지 물었음

W : **I've been waiting for 30 minutes.**

여 : 저는 30분 동안 기다리고 있어요.

- ride ⓝ 놀이기구 · construction ⓝ 건설, 공사

대화를 듣고, 남자의 마지막 말에 대한 여자의 응답으로 가장 적절한 것을 고르시오.

① I've been waiting for 30 minutes. 얼마나 오래 기다리고 있는지에 대한 대답
저는 30분 동안 기다리고 있어요.
② I've enjoyed this ride very much. 놀이기구가 재밌었는지 묻지 않음
저는 이 놀이기구를 매우 즐겼어요.
③ You're standing in the correct line. 맞는 줄에 있는지를 물어본 것이 아님
당신은 맞는 줄에 있어요.
④ I have enough time to wait for you. 기다려 달라고 부탁한 것이 아님
저는 당신을 기다릴 충분한 시간이 있어요.
⑤ You may end the construction in a year. 공사와 관련된 대화가 아님
당신은 1년 안에 공사를 끝낼 수 있습니다.

왜 정답? ❋❋❋ [정답률 94%]

많은 사람들이 롤러코스터를 타려고 줄을 서 있는 것을 알게 된 남자가 여자에게 얼마나 오래 기다리고 있는지를 물었다. 따라서 여자는 ① '저는 30분 동안 기다리고 있어요.'라고 응답하는 것이 가장 적절하다.

왜 오답?

② 놀이기구가 재밌었는지를 물어본 것이 아니다.
③ 맞는 줄에 서 있는 것은 이미 확인했다.
④ 기다려 달라고 부탁하지 않았으므로 적절한 응답이 아니다.
⑤ 공사와 관련한 내용은 전혀 나오지 않았다.

12 정답 ② ＊울고 있는 아이를 본 Chris

W : Chris, what are you looking at?

여 : Chris, 뭘 보고 있어요?

M : A little boy is crying and wandering around the park. He's all by himself. [병렬 구조]

남 : 한 어린 소년이 울면서 공원을 돌아다니고 있어요. 그 아이는 혼자예요.

W : Oh, I see him, too. We should ask him if he's lost. [직접목적어절 접속사]

여 : 아, 저도 그 아이를 봤어요. 우리는 그 아이가 길을 잃었는지 물어봐야겠어요.

M : **Okay. Let's see if he needs our help.** [단서] 울고 있는 아이에게 길을 잃어버린 것인지 물어보려고 함

남 : 그래요. 그 아이가 우리의 도움이 필요한지 확인해 봅시다.

- wander ⓥ 돌아다니다, 헤매다 · all by oneself (다른 사람 없이) 혼자

대화를 듣고, 여자의 마지막 말에 대한 남자의 응답으로 가장 적절한 것을 고르시오.

① No way. I don't know who's lost. 길을 잃은 사람이 누구인지 묻지 않음
아니에요. 저는 누가 길을 잃었는지 몰라요.

②Okay. Let's see if he needs our help.
그래요. 그 아이가 우리의 도움이 필요한지 확인해 봅시다.

③ Exactly. Just stop crying like a child. 여자가 울고 있는 것이 아님
맞아요. 아이처럼 우는 것을 그냥 멈추세요.

④ Sure. He loves walking around the park.
물론이에요. 그는 공원을 산책하는 것을 좋아해요. 공원을 돌아다닌다는 것으로 만든 오답

⑤ Thanks. We were worried about our son.
고마워요. 우리는 우리의 아들이 걱정됐어요. 아이의 부모가 하게 될 응답임

• 울고 있는 아이에게 길을 잃어버린 것인지 물어보자고 하는 말에 적절한 응답임

▷왜 정답 ? ✽✿✿ [정답률 88%]

Chris가 울면서 혼자 공원을 돌아다니는 어린 소년을 봤다고 하자 여자는 아이가 길을 잃어버린 것인지 물어보자고 했으므로 ② '그래요. 그 아이가 우리의 도움이 필요한지 확인해 봅시다.'라고 말하는 것이 남자의 응답으로 가장 적절하다.

▷왜 오답 ?

① 길을 잃은 사람이 누구인지 물어본 것이 아니므로 적절한 응답이 아니다.
(▶ 이유: 소년이 누구인지 궁금해하는 상황이 아니다.)

③ 여자가 울고 있는 것이 아니므로 부적절하다.

④ 공원을 돌아다닌다는 것으로 만든 오답으로, 아이가 공원을 산책하는 것을 좋아하는지 물어본 것이 아니다.

⑤ 아이를 찾아주었을 때 부모가 하게 될 응답일 것이다. 주의

13 정답 ③ ✽ 면접을 준비 중인 Samuel

M : Hi, Ava.
남 : 안녕, Ava.

W : Hi, Samuel. Are you all set for the job interview?
여 : 안녕, Samuel. 면접 준비는 다 됐어? 단서 1 남자는 면접 준비를 하고 있음

M : I'm still working on it. I've come up with a list of questions 앞에 목적격 관계대명사 생략
the interviewer might ask.
남 : 아직 하는 중이야. 면접관이 물어볼 수 있는 질문 목록을 생각해 놓았어. 동명사구 주어(단수 취급)

W : Good job. Preparing answers to those questions will help you for the interview.
여 : 잘했네. 그 질문들에 대한 답변을 준비하는 것은 면접에 도움이 될 거야.

M : But I think I'm not ready.
남 : 하지만 나는 준비가 안 된 것 같아.

W : Hmm. Have you thought about how you'll make a good 간접의문문(의문사+주어+동사)
first impression?
여 : 음. 너는 어떻게 좋은 첫인상을 남길지 생각해 봤어?

M : Could you be more specific?
남 : 좀 더 구체적으로 말해줄래?

W : You know a smile makes you look confident. Also, people 뒤에 목적어절 접속사 that이 생략됨 원형부사(makes의 목적격 보어)
usually dress up to give a favorable impression. 부사적 용법(목적)
여 : 미소가 자신감 있어 보이도록 해주는거 알잖아. 또, 사람들은 호의적인 인상을 주기 위해서 보통 옷을 갖춰 입지. 단서 2 여자가 남자에게 미소와 복장과 관련된 조언을 함

M : That's a good point.
남 : 그거 좋은 지적이야.

W : I believe you'll get a good interview result with a proper presentation of yourself.
여 : 네가 적절한 자기소개를 하면 좋은 면접 결과를 얻을 수 있을 거라고 나는 믿어.

M : Okay. Then I'm going to practice smiling and look for my best suit. 단서 3 남자는 웃는 연습을 하고 좋은 정장을 찾아보겠다고 함
남 : 알았어. 그럼 나는 웃는 연습을 하고 내 최고의 정장을 찾을 거야.

W : **Good. Your effort will give a good impression on the interviewer.**
여 : 좋아. 너의 노력이 면접관에게 좋은 인상을 줄 거야.

• come up with ~을 생각해 내다[찾아내다]　• impression ⓝ 인상
• specific ⓐ 구체적인　• confident ⓐ 자신감 있는

• dress up 옷을 갖춰 입다　• favorable ⓐ 호의적인
• presentation ⓝ 소개, 발표　• previous ⓐ 이전의
• candidate ⓝ 후보자, 지원자　• upcoming ⓐ 다가오는, 곧 있을

대화를 듣고, 남자의 마지막 말에 대한 여자의 응답으로 가장 적절한 것을 고르시오. [3점]

Woman: _____

① Great. I believe my previous offer will benefit your company. 회사 관계자에게 할 만한 응답임
좋습니다. 제가 전에 한 제안이 귀사에 도움이 될 것이라고 믿습니다.

② I'm sorry. Your interview has been delayed to next Wednesday. 면접관이 할 수 있는 말임
죄송합니다. 귀하의 면접이 다음 주 수요일로 연기되었습니다.

③Good. Your effort will give a good impression on the interviewer. 여자의 조언에 따르겠다고 함
좋아. 너의 노력이 면접관에게 좋은 인상을 줄 거야.

④ Excellent. The second candidate's work experience caught my eye. 면접관이 하게 될 만한 응답임
훌륭해요. 두 번째 후보자의 업무 경험이 제 눈길을 끄네요.

⑤ No worries. You can purchase nice clothes for the upcoming party. best suit를 이용한 오답
걱정하지 마. 너는 다가오는 파티를 위해 멋진 옷을 구입할 수 있어.

▷왜 정답 ? ✽✿✿ [정답률 93%]

면접을 준비 중인 Samuel은 미소를 짓고 옷을 갖춰 입는 게 좋겠다는 Ava의 조언에 따라 면접을 위해 웃는 연습을 하고, 좋은 정장을 입을 것이라고 했다.
따라서 이에 대한 여자의 응답으로 가장 적절한 것은 ③ '좋아. 너의 노력이 면접관에게 좋은 인상을 줄 거야.'이다.

▷왜 오답 ?

① 회사의 관계자에게 할 만한 응답으로, 면접을 준비하고 있는 사람에게는 부적절한 응답이다.

② Ava가 Samuel의 면접을 보고 있는 것이 아니다.

④ 면접관이 하게 될 만한 응답으로, 여자는 면접으로 면접을 보고 있는 상황이 아니므로 적절하지 않다. 함정

⑤ best suit가 언급된 것으로 만든 오답으로, 파티를 준비하는 내용이 아니다.

14 정답 ① ✽ 초록색 신발 구매하기

W : Excuse me.
여 : 실례합니다.

M : Yes, ma'am. How can I help you?
남 : 네, 사모님. 무엇을 도와드릴까요?

W : How much are those shoes?
여 : 저 신발은 얼마인가요?

M : They're $60. But today only, we're offering a 30% discount. 현재진행 시제
남 : 60달러입니다. 하지만 오늘만 30퍼센트 할인을 제공해 드립니다.

W : That's a good price. Do you have a size six?
여 : 좋은 가격이네요. 6 사이즈가 있나요?

M : Sure. Here they are. Take a seat here and try them on. 병렬 구조
남 : 물론입니다. 여기 있습니다. 여기 앉아서 신어보세요.

W : Thank you. [Pause] Well, these shoes are a little tight for me. Can I get a size six and a half?
여 : 감사합니다. [잠시 휴] 음, 이 신발은 제게 좀 꽉 끼네요. 6.5 사이즈를 주시겠어요?

M : I'm sorry. That size in this color is sold out.
남 : 죄송합니다. 이 색상의 그 사이즈는 품절입니다.

W : Do you have these shoes in a different color?
여 : 이 신발의 다른 색상은 있나요?

M : Let me check. [Typing sounds] We have red and green in storage. 단서 1 빨간색과 초록색 신발은 재고가 있음
남 : 확인해 보겠습니다. [타자 치는 소리] 창고에 빨간색과 초록색이 있습니다.

W : A green pair sounds good. I want to try them on.
여 : 초록색이 좋을 것 같아요. 신어보고 싶어요. 단서 2 여자는 초록색 신발을 신어보고 싶다고 함

M : **Please wait. I'll be back with the shoes in a minute.**
남 : 잠시만 기다리세요. 금방 신발을 가지고 오겠습니다.

- try on ~을 입어[신어]보다　　• tight ⓐ 꽉 끼는　　• storage ⓝ 창고, 저장
- refund ⓝ 환불

- psychology ⓝ 심리학　　• expert ⓝ 전문가　　• field ⓝ 분야
- renowned ⓐ 유명한, 명성 있는　　• manage to 간신히 ~하다
- set up 마련하다, 준비하다　　• severe ⓐ 심한
- stomachache ⓝ 복통　　• extend ⓥ 연장하다
- assignment ⓝ 과제　　• appointment ⓝ 약속
- checkup 건강 진단

대화를 듣고, 여자의 마지막 말에 대한 남자의 응답으로 가장 적절한 것을 고르시오.

Man: _____

　　　　　　　　　　　　　　　　　　창고에 있는 신발을 여자가 신어보고 싶다고 함
① Please wait. I'll be back with the shoes in a minute.
잠시만 기다리세요. 금방 신발을 가지고 오겠습니다.
② Hurry up. You don't have enough time to do this.
서두르세요. 당신은 이것을 할 충분한 시간이 없어요.　　여자가 서둘러야 할 상황이 아님
③ Of course. You can get a refund for these shoes.
물론입니다. 이 신발을 환불받으실 수 있습니다.　　여자가 신발을 환불하는 상황이 아님
④ Don't worry. The color doesn't matter to me.
걱정하지 마세요. 색상은 저에게 중요하지 않습니다.
⑤ Sorry. The red ones are already sold out.
죄송합니다. 빨간색은 이미 품절입니다.　　빨간색은 창고에 있다고 했음
종업원인 남자가 색상이 자신에게 중요하지 않다고 답하는 것은 부적절함

왜 정답 ? ✸✸✸ [정답률 92%]

신발을 신어본 여자가 좀 더 큰 사이즈의 신발을 요청하자 남자는 동일한 색상의 신발은 품절이라고 하면서 빨간색과 초록색 신발은 창고에 재고가 있다고 했다. 이에 여자는 초록색 신발을 신어보고 싶다고 했으므로 남자는 ① '잠시만 기다리세요. 금방 신발을 가지고 오겠습니다.'라고 응답하는 것이 가장 적절하다.

왜 오답 ?

② 여자가 서둘러야 할 상황이 아니므로 적절하지 않다.
③ 여자는 신발의 환불이 아니라 구매를 위해 방문했다.
④ 종업원인 남자가 색상이 자신에게는 중요하지 않다고 하는 것은 적절하지 않다.
⑤ 빨간색 신발은 재고가 있다고 했다.

15 정답 ② ✸ Jacob 교수와의 약속을 변경하려는 Amelia

M : Amelia is a high school student.
남 : Amelia는 고등학생이다.

She is working on a psychology project.
그녀는 심리학 프로젝트를 하고 있다.

목적어절 접속사　　　　　　　　비교급 강조 부사
She thinks that an interview with an expert in the field will make her project even better.
그녀는 그 분야의 전문가와의 인터뷰가 그녀의 프로젝트를 훨씬 더 좋게 만들 것이라고 생각한다.

계속적 용법의 주격 관계대명사
She emails Professor Jacob, who is a renowned psychology professor.
그녀는 Jacob 교수에게 이메일을 보내는데, 그는 유명한 심리학 교수이다.

부사절 접속사(양보)
Even though he's busy, she manages to set up an interview with him.
그는 바쁘지만, 그녀는 가까스로 그와의 인터뷰 자리를 마련했다.

Unfortunately, on that morning, she eats a sandwich and feels sick.
　　　　　　　　　　　병렬 구조
불행하게도, 그날 아침, 그녀는 샌드위치를 먹고 속이 안 좋아진다.

뒤에 목적어절 접속사 that이 생략됨
She knows this interview is important, and difficult to set up again.
그녀는 이 인터뷰가 중요하고, 다시 자리를 마련하기 어렵다는 것을 안다.

But she can't go meet him because of a severe stomachache.
하지만 그녀는 심한 복통 때문에 그를 만나러 갈 수 없다.　　단서 1 Amelia는 복통 때문에 Jacob 교수를 만나러 갈 수 없음

So she wants to ask him if he can reschedule their meeting.
그래서 그녀는 그가 만남을 재조정할 수 있는지 묻기를 원한다.　　단서 2 Amelia는 일정을 재조정하는 것이 가능한지 묻기를 원함

In this situation, what would Amelia most likely say to Professor Jacob?
이 상황에서, Amelia가 Jacob 교수에게 할 말로 가장 적절한 것은 무엇인가?

Amelia: **Would it be possible to change our appointment?**
Amelia: 저희의 약속을 변경하는 것이 가능할까요?

*상황 요약: Amelia는 심리학 프로젝트를 위해 유명한 심리학 교수인 Jacob 교수와의 인터뷰 자리를 마련했지만, 복통 때문에 일정을 재조정하고 싶음

다음 상황 설명을 듣고, Amelia가 Jacob 교수에게 할 말로 가장 적절한 것을 고르시오. [3점]

Amelia: _____

① Could you extend the deadline for the assignment?
과제의 마감일을 연장해 주실 수 있나요?　　Jacob 교수가 내준 과제를 하는 상황이 아님
② Would it be possible to change our appointment?
저희의 약속을 변경하는 것이 가능할까요?　　만남 일정을 재조정할 수 있는지 묻기를 원함
③ Why don't you join my final psychology project?
제 마지막 심리학 프로젝트에 참여하시는 게 어떤가요?　　이미 Jacob 교수와 약속을 잡은 상황임
④ Do you want to meet at the information center?
안내센터에서 만나기를 원하시나요?　　모임 장소를 정하려는 것이 아님
⑤ How about visiting the doctor for a checkup?
진찰을 받으러 병원에 가시는 게 어떤가요?　　Jacob 교수가 아픈 것이 아님

왜 정답 ? ✸✸✸ [정답률 78%]

Amelia는 자신의 심리학 프로젝트를 위해 유명한 심리학 교수인 Jacob 교수와 어렵게 인터뷰 약속을 잡았지만, 심한 복통 때문에 갈 수 없게 되었다. 일정을 재조정할 수 있는지 Jacob 교수에게 묻기를 원한다고 했으므로 ② '저희의 약속을 변경하는 것이 가능할까요?'라고 말하는 것이 가장 적절하다.

왜 오답 ?

① Jacob 교수가 내준 과제를 하는 상황이 아니다. **주의**
③ 이미 Jacob 교수와 약속을 잡은 상황에 프로젝트에 참여해달라는 부탁은 적절하지 않다.
④ 모임 장소를 정하려는 것이 아니므로 어디서 만나기를 원하는지 묻는 것은 적절하지 않다.
⑤ Jacob 교수가 아픈 것이 아니므로 의사의 진찰을 권하는 것은 어색하다.

16~17 ✸ 메시지를 전달한 과거의 방법들

W : Good morning, students. //
여 : 좋은 아침입니다, 학생 여러분 //

These days / we can easily send messages to each other / using phones or computers. //
　　　　　　　　　　　　　　　　분사구문
요즘 / 우리는 서로에게 쉽게 메시지를 보낼 수 있습니다 / 전화나 컴퓨터를 사용하여 //

원급 비교
However, / communication has not always been as simple / as it is today. //
그러나 / 통신이 항상 간단했던 것은 아닙니다 / 오늘날 그런 것처럼 //

부사적 용법(목적)
Here are a few ways / people in the past / used to carry their messages. // 16번 단서: 과거의 사람들이 메시지를 전달하기 위해 사용했던 몇 가지 방법들을 소개함
여기 몇 가지 방법이 있습니다 / 과거의 사람들이 / 그들의 메시지를 전달하기 위해 사용했던 //

17번 ①
First, / some tribes used a special drum. //
먼저 / 몇몇 부족들은 특별한 북을 사용했습니다 //

They were able to send warnings or important information / by varying the pitch or beat. //
by v-ing: ~함으로써
그들은 경고나 중요한 정보를 보낼 수 있었습니다 / 음정이나 박자를 다르게 해서 //

부사적 용법(목적)
Next, / other people used smoke / to send messages over long distances. //　　17번 ②
다음으로 / 다른 사람들은 연기를 사용했습니다 / 먼 거리로 메시지를 보내기 위해 //

부사적 용법(목적)
For example, / our ancestors used smoke / to signal attacks from enemies. //
예를 들어 / 우리의 조상들은 연기를 사용했습니다 / 적들로부터의 공격을 알리기 위해 //

17번 ③
Third, / a pigeon was a reliable means of communication. //
셋째 / 비둘기는 믿을 수 있는 통신의 수단이었습니다 //

It always found its way home / with messages attached to its legs. //

with+(대)명사+분사: ~가 …한[된] 채로

그것은 항상 집을 찾아왔습니다 / 그것의 다리에 메시지를 부착한 채로 //

Finally, / a horse was one of the most efficient ways / to communicate. // 17번⑤

형용사적 용법(ways 수식)

마지막으로 / 말은 가장 효율적인 방법 중 하나였습니다 / 통신을 하는 //

핵심 주어

The horse / with a messenger on its back / delivered mail more quickly / than runners. //

동사

말은 / 전달자를 그것의 등에 태운 / 우편물을 더 빨리 배달했습니다 / 달리는 사람보다 //

Now / you may understand / the ways of sending messages / back in the old days. //

이제 / 여러분은 이해할 수 있을 것입니다 / 메시지를 보내는 방법을 / 옛날에 //

Then let's take a look in detail / at each communication method. //

그럼 자세히 알아보겠습니다 / 각 통신 방법에 대해 //

- tribe ⓝ 부족 • warning ⓝ 경고 • vary ⓥ 다르게 하다
- pitch ⓝ 음정 • beat ⓝ 박자 • distance ⓝ 거리
- ancestor ⓝ 조상 • signal ⓥ 알리다 • reliable ⓐ 믿을 수 있는
- means ⓝ 수단 • attach ⓥ 붙이다 • efficient ⓐ 효율적인
- deliver ⓥ 전달하다 • in detail 상세하게 • spread ⓝ 확산
- prehistoric ⓐ 선사 시대의

여 : 좋은 아침입니다, 학생 여러분. 요즘 우리는 전화나 컴퓨터를 사용하여 서로에게 쉽게 메시지를 보낼 수 있습니다. 그러나, 오늘날 그런 것처럼 통신이 항상 간단했던 것은 아닙니다. 여기 과거의 사람들이 그들의 메시지를 전달하기 위해 사용했던 몇 가지 방법들이 있습니다. 먼저, 몇몇 부족들은 특별한 북을 사용했습니다. 그들은 음정이나 박자를 다르게 해서 경고나 중요한 정보를 보낼 수 있었습니다. 다음으로, 다른 사람들은 먼 거리로 메시지를 보내기 위해 연기를 사용했습니다. 예를 들어, 우리 조상들은 적들로부터의 공격을 알리기 위해 연기를 사용했습니다. 셋째, 비둘기는 믿을 수 있는 통신의 수단이었습니다. 비둘기는 다리에 메시지를 부착한 채로 항상 집을 찾아왔습니다. 마지막으로, 말은 통신을 하는 가장 효율적인 방법 중 하나였습니다. 전달자를 등에 태운 말은 달리는 사람보다 우편물을 더 빨리 배달했습니다. 이제 여러분은 옛날에 메시지를 보내는 방법을 이해할 수 있을 것입니다. 그럼, 각 통신 방법에 대해 자세히 알아보겠습니다.

16 정답 ②

여자가 하는 말의 주제로 가장 적절한 것은?

① ways to stop the spread of false information
허위 정보의 확산을 막는 방법들   허위 정보 확산과 관련된 내용은 언급되지 않음
②methods of delivering messages in the past
과거에 메시지를 전달한 방법들   과거의 다양한 통신 수단에 대한 내용
③ modes of communication in modern times
현대의 통신 방식들   과거의 통신 방식에 대한 담화임
④ types of speeches according to purposes
목적에 따른 담화의 종류들   목적에 따라 담화가 달라진다는 내용이 아님
⑤ means to survive in prehistoric times
선사 시대에 생존하기 위한 수단들   생존 수단에 대한 내용이 아님

왜 정답? ✽✽✽ [정답률 90%]

요즘은 전화나 컴퓨터를 사용해서 메시지를 쉽게 전달하지만, 과거에는 오늘날처럼 쉽지 않았다고 하면서 북, 연기, 비둘기, 말을 소개하고 있다. 따라서 여자가 하는 말의 주제로 가장 적절한 것은 ② '과거에 메시지를 전달한 방법들'이다.

왜 오답?

① 허위 정보에 관한 내용은 언급되지 않았다.
③ 현대의 통신 방식은 도입부에 잠깐 언급되었을 뿐이다. (☞ 이유: 현대가 아니라 과거의 통신 수단을 이야기했다.)
④ 목적에 따라 담화가 달라진다는 내용이 아니다.
⑤ 선사 시대의 생존 수단에 대한 언급은 없다.

17 정답 ④

언급된 수단이 아닌 것은?

① drum First, some tribes used a special drum.
북
② smoke Next, other people used smoke to send messages over long distances.
연기
③ pigeon Third, a pigeon was a reliable means of communication.
비둘기
④ flag 언급되지 않음
깃발
⑤ horse Finally, a horse was one of the most efficient ways to communicate.
말

왜 정답? ✽✽✽ [정답률 93%]

메시지를 전달한 과거의 방식으로 북, 연기, 비둘기, 말을 소개했지만 ④ '깃발'은 언급하지 않았다.

왜 오답?

① 어떤 부족들은 과거에 메시지를 전달하는 수단으로 특별한 북을 이용했다고 했다.
② 어떤 사람들은 과거에 장거리의 메시지를 전달하는 수단으로 연기를 사용했다고 했다.
③ 비둘기는 과거에 믿을 만한 통신 수단이었다고 했다.
⑤ 말은 과거에 가장 효율적인 통신 수단 중 하나였다고 했다.

18 정답 ② ✱ 성과를 반영한 급여 인상 요청

Dear Mr. Krull, /
친애하는 Krull 씨께 /

동명사를 목적어로 취하는 동사

I have greatly enjoyed working / at Trincom Enterprises / as a sales manager. //

저는 일하는 것을 매우 즐겨 왔습니다 / Trincom Enterprises에서 / 영업 매니저로 //

Since I joined in 2015, / I have been a loyal and essential member of this company, / and have developed innovative ways / to contribute to the company. //

병렬 구조

2015년에 입사한 이후 / 저는 이 회사의 충성스럽고 필수적인 구성원이었고 / 혁신적인 방법들을 개발해 왔습니다 / 회사에 기여할 //

Moreover, / in the last year alone, / I have brought in two new major clients to the company, / increasing the company's total sales by 5%. //

분사구문(결과)

게다가 / 작년 한 해에만 / 저는 두 개의 주요 고객사를 회사에 새로 유치했습니다 / 회사의 총매출을 5퍼센트 증가시키면서 //

Also, / I have voluntarily trained 5 new members of staff, / totaling 35 hours. //

분사구문(결과)

또한 / 저는 신규 직원 5명을 자발적으로 교육해 왔습니다 / 합계가 35시간이 되도록 //

I would therefore request your consideration / in raising my salary, / which I believe reflects my performance / as well as the industry average. // 단서 자신의 성과를 반영하여 급여를 인상하는 것에 대한 고려를 요청함

계속적 용법의 주격 관계대명사   삽입절

따라서 저는 당신의 고려를 요청합니다 / 제 급여를 인상하는 것에 대한 / 그리고 저는 이것이 제 성과를 반영한다고 믿습니다 / 업계 평균뿐만 아니라 //

look forward to v-ing: ~을 기대하다

I look forward to speaking with you soon. //

저는 당신과 곧 이야기하기를 기대합니다 //

Kimberly Morss /
Kimberly Morss /

- loyal ⓐ 충성스러운, 충실한 • essential ⓐ 필수적인
- innovative ⓐ 혁신적인 • contribute ⓥ 기여하다
- voluntarily ⓐ𝖽 자발적으로, 자원해서 • total ⓥ 합계가 ~이 되다
- request ⓥ 요청하다 • consideration ⓝ 고려
- reflect ⓥ 반영하다 • performance ⓝ 성과

친애하는 Krull 씨께,

저는 Trincom Enterprises에서 영업 매니저로 일하는 것을 매우 즐겨 왔습니다. 2015년에 입사한 이후, 저는 이 회사의 충성스럽고 필수적인 구성원이었고, 회사에 기여할 혁신적인 방법들을 개발해 왔습니다. 게다가, 저는 작년 한 해만 두 개의 주요 고객사를 회사에 새로 유치하여 회사의 총매출을 5퍼센트 증가시켰습니다. 또한 저는 신규 직원 5명을 자발적으로 교육해 왔고, 그 합계가 35시간이 되었습니다. 따라서 저는 제 급여를 인상하는 것에 대한 당신의 고려를 요청하고, 이것이 업계 평균뿐만 아니라 제 성과도 반영한다고 믿습니다. 저는 당신과 곧 이야기하기를 기대합니다.

Kimberly Morss

다음 글의 목적으로 가장 적절한 것은?

① 부서 이동을 신청하려고 부서 이동에 대한 언급은 없음
②급여 인상을 요청하려고 급여를 인상하는 것에 대한 고려를 요청하는 내용
③ 근무 시간 조정을 요구하려고 신규 직원 교육 누적 시간이 35시간이라는 것으로 만든 오답
④ 기업 혁신 방안을 제안하려고 회사에 기여할 혁신적 방법들을 개발했다는 내용으로 만든 오답
⑤ 신입 사원 연수에 대해 문의하려고 신규 직원을 교육했다고 언급했을 뿐임

왜 정답? ✿❀❀ [정답률 87%]

영업 매니저로 일하면서 회사에 기여할 혁신적인 방법들을 개발해 왔다고 하면서, 매출 증가나 직원 교육 등의 성과를 언급했다. 이러한 이유로 급여 인상에 대한 고려를 요청한다고 했으므로 글의 목적으로 가장 적절한 것은 ②이다.

왜 오답?

① 영업 매니저로 일했다는 내용은 있지만, 부서 이동에 대한 언급은 없다.
③ 신규 직원을 교육한 시간이 35시간인 것이지 근무 시간 조정을 요청한 것이 아니다.
④ 회사에 기여할 혁신적 방법들을 개발했다는 내용은 있지만, 기업 혁신 방안을 제안하고 있지는 않다. (✄ 이유: 기업 혁신 방안은 급여 인상에 참고할 만한 성과일 뿐이다.)
⑤ 신규 직원을 교육했다고 했지 신입 사원 연수에 대해 문의하는 것이 아니다.

19 정답 ② ＊휴가 중 받게 된 부재중 전화

On one beautiful spring day, / I was fully enjoying my day off. //
어느 아름다운 봄날 / 나는 휴가를 충분히 즐기고 있었다 //

I arrived at the nail salon, / and muted my cellphone / so that ~하기 위해서, ~하도록
I would be disconnected for the hour / and feel calm and peaceful. //
나는 네일 샵에 도착했다 / 그리고 나의 휴대 전화를 음 소거했다 / 그 시간 동안 단절되도록 / 그리고 차분하고 평화롭게 느낄 수 있도록 //
단서1 네일 샵에서 매니큐어를 받으면서 편안함을 느낌

I was so comfortable / while I got a manicure. //
나는 아주 편안했다 / 매니큐어를 받는 동안 //
병렬 구조
As I left the place, / I checked my cellphone / and saw four missed calls / from a strange number. //
내가 그 장소를 떠날 때 / 나는 나의 휴대 전화를 확인했다 / 그리고 네 통의 부재중 전화를 봤다 / 낯선 번호에서 온 //

I knew immediately / that something bad was coming, and I called back. //
목적어절 접속사
나는 즉시 알았다 / 나쁜 어떤 일이 생겼다는 것을 / 그리고 다시 전화했다 //
목적어절 접속사
A young woman answered and said / that my father had fallen over a stone / and was injured, / now seated on a bench. //
한 젊은 여성이 전화를 받아 말했다 / 나의 아버지가 돌에 걸려 넘어졌고 / 그리고 다쳐서 / 지금 벤치에 앉아 있다고 //
단서2 아버지가 넘어져서 다쳤다는 전화를 받음
부사절 접속사(이유)
I was really concerned / since he had just recovered from his knee surgery. // 단서3 무릎 수술을 한 지 얼마 되지 않은 아버지가 걱정됨
나는 정말 걱정되었다 / 그가 무릎 수술에서 막 회복했기 때문에 //

I rushed getting into my car / to go see him. //
나는 급히 차에 올랐다 / 그를 보러 가기 위해 //

- day off (근무를) 쉬는 날 • mute ⓥ (소리를) 작게 하다, 음 소거하다
- disconnect ⓥ 단절하다 • calm ⓐ 침착한, 차분한
- immediately ⓐⓓ 즉시 • fall over ~에 걸려 넘어지다
- injured ⓐ 다친, 부상을 입은 • concerned ⓐ 걱정되는
- recover ⓥ 회복하다 • surgery ⓝ 수술
- indifferent ⓐ 무관심한 • annoyed ⓐ 화난

어느 아름다운 봄날, 나는 휴가를 충분히 즐기고 있었다. 나는 네일 샵에 도착해서 그 시간 동안 단절되어 차분하고 평화롭게 느낄 수 있도록 나의 휴대 전화를 음 소거했다. 나는 매니큐어를 받는 동안 아주 편안했다. 내가 그 장소를 떠날 때, 나는 나의 휴대 전화를 확인했고 낯선 번호에서 걸려 온 네 통의 부재중 전화를 봤다. 나는 나쁜 어떤 일이 생겼다는 것을 즉시 알고 다시 전화했다. 한 젊은 여성이 전화를 받아 나의 아버지가 돌에 걸려 넘어져 다쳤고 지금 벤치에 앉아 있다고 말했다. 그가 무릎 수술에서 막 회복했기 때문에 나는 정말 걱정되었다. 나는 그를 보러 가기 위해 급히 차에 올랐다.

다음 글에 드러난 'I'의 심경 변화로 가장 적절한 것은?

① nervous → confident 자신감을 느끼는 내용은 나오지 않음
   긴장한   자신감 있는
②relaxed → worried 편안하게 휴가를 즐기던 중 아버지가 다쳤다는 연락을 받고 걱정함
   편안한   걱정하는
③ excited → indifferent 아버지가 다친 것을 알고 걱정했으므로 무관심한 것이 아님
   신이 난   무관심한
④ pleased → jealous 질투하는 내용은 언급되지 않음
   기쁜   질투하는
⑤ annoyed → grateful 화를 내거나 감사하는 내용은 없음
   화난   감사하는

왜 정답? ✿❀❀ [정답률 89%]

전반부: 아름다운 봄날에 휴가를 즐기면서 매니큐어를 받음 ▶ '편안한', '신이 난', '기쁜'
후반부: 아버지가 다치셨다는 것을 알게 됨 ▶ '걱정하는'
따라서 I의 심경 변화는 ② '편안한 → 걱정하는'이다.

왜 오답?

① 글에 자신감을 느끼는 것과 관련된 내용은 언급되지 않았다.
③ 후반부에 아버지가 다친 것을 알고 걱정하는 내용이 나오므로 무관심하다고 볼 수 없다.
④ 질투하는 것과 관련된 내용은 나오지 않았다.
⑤ 화를 내거나 감사하는 내용은 모두 언급되지 않았다.

20 정답 ⑤ ＊상업용 블로그가 성공하기 위한 방법

You already have a business / and you're about to launch your be about to-v: 막 ~하려고 하다
blog / so that you can sell your product. // ~하도록
여러분은 이미 사업체를 가지고 있다 / 그리고 여러분은 여러분의 블로그를 시작하려는 참이다 / 여러분의 제품을 팔 수 있도록 //
관계부사
Unfortunately, / here is where a 'business mind' can be a bad thing. //
유감스럽게도 / 여기가 '비즈니스 정신'이 나쁜 것이 될 수 있는 지점이다 //
목적어절 접속사
Most people believe / that to have a successful business blog / 현재분사(blog 수식)
promoting a product, / they have to stay strictly 'on the topic.' //
대부분의 사람들은 믿는다 / 성공적인 상업용 블로그를 가지기 위해서 / 제품을 홍보하는 / 그들이 엄격하게 '그 주제에' 머물러야 한다고 //
핵심 주어(단수)   단수 동사
If all you're doing / is shamelessly promoting your product, / then who is going to want to read / the latest thing you're writing about? //
만일 여러분이 하는 일의 전부가 / 뻔뻔스럽게 여러분의 제품을 홍보하는 것이라면 / 그러면 누가 읽고 싶어 할까 / 여러분이 쓰고 있는 최신의 것을 //

Instead, / you need to give some useful or entertaining information away / for free / so that people have a reason / to ~하도록
형용사적 용법(reason 수식)
keep coming back. // 단서1 블로그에서 무료로 유용하고 재미있는 정보를 제공해 사람들이 다시 방문할 이유를 만들어야 함
대신에 / 여러분은 어떤 유용하거나 재미있는 정보를 줄 필요가 있다 / 무료로 / 사람들이 이유를 가지도록 / 계속해서 다시 방문할 //

Only by doing this / can you create an interested audience / **that**
you will then be able to sell to. //
이렇게 해야만 / 여러분은 관심 있는 독자를 만들 수 있다 / 여러분이 그다음에 판매를 할 수
있게 될 //
So, / **the best way** to be successful / with a business blog / **is to**
write about things / that your audience will be interested in. //
따라서, / 성공하기 위한 가장 좋은 방법은 / 상업용 블로그로 / (어떤) 것들에 관해 쓰는 것이다
/ 여러분의 독자가 관심을 가질 //

- launch ⓥ (새로운 일을) 시작하다[개시하다] • promote ⓥ 홍보하다
- strictly ⓐⒹ 엄격하게 • shamelessly ⓐⒹ 뻔뻔스럽게
- give ~ away ~을 나누어 주다 • entertaining ⓐ 재미있는, 즐거움을 주는
- audience ⓝ 청중, 독자

여러분은 이미 사업체를 가지고 있고 여러분의 제품을 팔 수 있도록 여러분의
블로그를 시작하려는 참이다. 유감스럽게도, 여기가 '비즈니스 정신'이 나쁜
것이 될 수 있는 지점이다. 대부분의 사람들은 제품을 홍보하는 성공적인
상업용 블로그를 가지기 위해서 그들이 엄격하게 '그 주제에' 머물러야 한다고
믿는다. 만일 여러분이 하는 일의 전부가 뻔뻔스럽게 여러분의 제품을 홍보하는
것이라면, 그렇다면 누가 여러분이 쓰고 있는 최신의 것을 읽고 싶어 할까?
대신에, 사람들이 계속해서 다시 방문할 이유를 가지도록 여러분은 어떤
유용하거나 재미있는 정보를 무료로 줄 필요가 있다. 이렇게 해야만 여러분은
여러분이 그다음에 판매를 할 수 있게 될 관심 있는 독자를 만들 수 있다.
따라서, 상업용 블로그로 성공하기 위한 가장 좋은 방법은 여러분의 독자가
관심을 가질 만한 것들에 관해 쓰는 것이다.

다음 글에서 필자가 주장하는 바로 가장 적절한 것은?

① 인터넷 게시물에 대한 윤리적 기준을 세워야 한다.
② 블로그를 전문적으로 관리할 인력을 마련해야 한다.
③ 신제품 개발을 위해 상업용 블로그를 적극 활용해야 한다.
④ 상품에 대한 고객들의 반응을 정기적으로 분석할 필요가 있다.
⑤ 상업용 블로그는 사람들이 흥미 있어 할 정보를 제공해야 한다.

▶ **왜 정답?** ✱✱✱ [정답률 93%]

- **문제점**: 상업용 블로그에 제품 홍보 글만 쓴다면 사람들은 읽고 싶지 않을 것임
- **해결책**: 유용하고 재미있는 정보를 무료로 주고, 사람들이 관심을 가질 만한 것에
  관해 쓰기
  ▶ 상업용 블로그는 사람들이 흥미 있어 할 정보를 제공해서 블로그에 다시
  방문하도록 해야 한다는 주장이므로 정답은 ⑤이다.

▶ **왜 오답?**

① 인터넷 게시물의 윤리적 기준에 대한 내용은 언급되지 않았다.
② 블로그를 관리할 전문적인 인력을 마련해야 한다는 글이 아니다.
③ 신제품 개발과 관련된 내용은 나오지 않았고, 블로그의 활용 목적이 아니라 활용
  방안과 관련된 내용이다. ◀주의
④ 고객의 반응을 분석해야 한다는 내용은 언급되지 않았다.

21 정답 ③ ✱중요한 것은 힘들게 얻는다는 잘못된 생각

Our language helps / to reveal our deeper assumptions. //
우리의 언어는 돕는다 / 우리의 더 깊은 전제를 드러내는 것을 //
Think of these revealing phrases: / When we accomplish
something important, / **we say** / it took "blood, sweat, and
tears." //
이것을 잘 드러내는 다음과 같은 문구들을 생각해 보라 / 우리가 중요한 무언가를 성취할 때 /
우리는 말한다 / 그것이 '피, 땀, 그리고 눈물'을 필요로 했다고 /
We say / important achievements are "hard-earned." //
우리는 말한다 / 중요한 성과는 '힘들게 얻은' 것이라고 //
We recommend a "hard day's work" / when "day's work"
would be enough. //
우리는 '힘든 하루 동안의 일'이라는 말을 권한다 / '하루 동안의 일'이라는 말로도 충분할 때 //

When we talk of "easy money," / **we are implying** / it was
obtained / through illegal or questionable means. //
우리가 '쉬운 돈'이라는 말을 할 때 / 우리는 넌지시 드러내고 있다 / 그것이 얻어졌다는 것을 /
불법적이거나 의심스러운 수단을 통해 //
We use the phrase "That's easy **for you** to say" / as a criticism,
/ usually when we are seeking to invalidate / someone's
opinion. //
우리는 '말은 쉽지'라는 문구를 사용한다 / 비판으로 / 우리가 보통 틀렸음을 입증하려고 할 때
/ 누군가의 의견이 //
It's like we all automatically accept / **that** the "right" way is,
inevitably, the harder one. //
이는 마치 우리가 모두 자동적으로 받아들이는 것과 같다 / '올바른' 방법은 반드시 더 어려운
방법이라는 것을 //
In my experience / this is hardly ever questioned. //
나의 경험상 / 이것은 거의 한 번도 의문이 제기되지 않는다 //
What would happen / if you **do** challenge this sacred cow? //
무슨 일이 일어날까 / 만약 여러분이 정말로 이 신성한 소에 맞선다면 //
We don't even pause to consider / that **something important**
and valuable / could be made easy. //
우리는 잠시 멈춰 생각해 보지도 않는다 / 중요하고 가치 있는 무언가가 / 쉬운 것으로
만들어질 수 있다고 //
What if / the biggest thing / **keeping us from doing what matters**
/ is the false assumption / **that** it has to take huge effort? //
만약 ~라면 어떨까 / 가장 큰 것이 / 우리가 중요한 일을 하지 못하게 하는 / 잘못된 전제라면 /
그것은 엄청난 노력을 필요로 한다는 //

- reveal ⓥ 드러내다 • assumption ⓝ 추정, 전제
- accomplish ⓥ 성취하다 • achievement ⓝ 성취, 성과
- imply ⓥ 암시하다, 넌지시 나타내다 • obtain ⓥ 얻다
- illegal ⓐ 불법적인 • questionable ⓐ 의심스러운
- means ⓝ 수단 • criticism ⓝ 비판, 비평
- automatically ⓐⒹ 자동으로, 무의식적으로
- inevitably ⓐⒹ 반드시, 불가피하게
- challenge ⓥ 도전하다, 의문을 제기하다 • sacred ⓐ 신성한
- pause ⓥ 잠시 멈추다 • valuable ⓐ 가치 있는
- matter ⓥ 중요하다 • false ⓐ 잘못된 • tendency ⓝ 경향
- hardship ⓝ 고난 • solid ⓐ 확고한 • abandon ⓥ 버리다
- notion ⓝ 개념, 생각 • superstition ⓝ 미신

우리의 언어는 우리의 더 깊은 전제를 드러내는 것을 돕는다. 이것을 잘
드러내는 다음과 같은 문구들을 생각해 보라. 우리가 중요한 무언가를 성취할
때, 우리는 그것이 '피, 땀, 그리고 눈물'을 필요로 했다고 말한다. 우리는
중요한 성과는 '힘들게 얻은' 것이라고 말한다. 우리는 '하루 동안의 일'이라는
말로도 충분할 때 '힘든 하루 동안의 일'이라는 말을 권한다. 우리가 '쉬운
돈'이라는 말을 할 때, 우리는 그것이 불법적이거나 의심스러운 수단을 통해
얻어졌다는 것을 넌지시 드러내고 있다. 우리는 보통 누군가의 의견이 틀렸음을
입증하려고 할 때, '말은 쉽지'라는 문구를 비판으로 사용한다. 이는 마치
우리가 모두 '올바른' 방법은 반드시 더 어려운 방법이라는 것을 자동적으로
받아들이는 것과 같다. 나의 경험상 이것은 거의 한 번도 의문이 제기되지
않는다. 만약 여러분이 정말로 이 신성한 소에 맞선다면 무슨 일이 일어날까?
우리는 중요하고 가치 있는 무언가를 쉬운 것으로 만들 수 있다고 잠시 멈춰
생각해 보지도 않는다. 만약 우리가 중요한 일을 하지 못하게 하는 가장 큰
것이 중요한 일은 엄청난 노력을 필요로 한다는 잘못된 전제라면 어떨까?

밑줄 친 challenge this sacred cow가 다음 글에서 의미하는 바로 가장 적절한 것은? [3점]

① resist the tendency to avoid any hardship
  어떤 고난도 피하려는 경향에 저항하다
② escape from the pressure of using formal language
  격식 있는 언어 사용에 대한 압박에서 벗어나다
③ doubt the solid belief that only hard work is worthy
  노력(힘든 일)만이 가치가 있다는 확고한 믿음을 의심하다
④ abandon the old notion that money always comes first
  돈이 항상 우선이라는 오래된 생각을 버리다
⑤ break the superstition that holy animals bring good luck
  신성한 동물들이 행운을 가져다준다는 미신을 깨다

- 우리는 중요한 무언가를 성취할 때, 그것이 '피, 땀, 그리고 눈물'을 필요로 했다고 말하고, 중요한 성과는 힘들게 얻어진다고 말함 단서1
- 우리는 올바른 방법은 어려운 방법이라고 믿으며 이것에 의문을 제기하지 않음 단서2

➡ 중요한 성과는 힘들게 얻어지며, 올바른 방법은 어려운 방법이라고 믿는 것
= this sacred cow
▶ '이 신성한 소(this sacred cow)에 맞서는' 것은 ③ '노력(힘든 일)만이 가치가 있다는 확고한 믿음을 의심하다'를 의미한다.

≫왜 오답?

① '어떤 고난도 피하려는 경향이 아니라 '노력해야만 중요한 성취를 이룬다는 생각'이므로 의미하는 바와 반대되는 내용이다.
② 격식 있는 언어에 대한 언급은 없으므로 정답이 될 수 없다.
④ 돈을 가장 중시한다는 내용은 나오지 않았다.
⑤ sacred cow를 이용해서 만든 오답으로, 동물에 관한 내용이 아니다. 함정

---

22 정답 ① ★문제 대처를 막는 두려움을 주는 뉴스

The old saying is that "knowledge is power," / but when it comes to scary, threatening news, / research suggests the exact opposite. //
오래된 격언에 따르면 '아는 것이 힘이다'라고 한다 / 하지만 무섭고 위협적인 뉴스에 관한 한 / 연구는 정반대를 시사한다 //

Frightening news can actually rob people / of their inner sense of control, / making them less likely to take care of themselves and other people. // 단서1 두려움을 주는 뉴스는 사람들로부터 내면의 통제력을 빼앗음
두려움을 주는 뉴스는 실제로 사람들로부터 빼앗을 수 있다 / 내면의 통제력을 / 그들이 스스로와 다른 사람들을 돌볼 가능성을 더 낮게 만들면서 //

Public health research shows / that when the news presents health-related information / in a pessimistic way, /
공중 보건 연구는 보여준다 / 뉴스가 건강과 관련된 정보를 제시할 때 / 비관적인 방식으로 /

people are actually less likely to take steps / to protect themselves from illness / as a result. //
사람들이 조치를 취할 가능성이 실제로 더 낮다는 것을 / 질병으로부터 자신을 보호하기 위해 / 결과적으로 //

A news article / that's intended to warn people / about increasing cancer rates, / for example, / can result in fewer people choosing to get screened / for the disease /
뉴스 기사는 / 사람들에게 경고하려 하는 / 증가하는 암 발생률에 대해 / 예를 들어 / 더 적은 사람들이 검사받도록 선택하는 결과를 가져올 수 있다 / 그 병에 대해 /

because they're so terrified / of what they might find. //
그들이 너무 두려워하기 때문에 / 그들이 발견할지도 모를 것에 대해 //

This is also true / for issues such as climate change. //
이것은 또한 사실이다 / 기후 변화와 같은 문제에도 // 단서2 두려움을 주는 뉴스는 사람들을 우울하게 해서 그들이 조치를 덜 취하게 함

When a news story is all doom and gloom, / people feel depressed / and become less interested / in taking small, personal steps / to fight ecological collapse. //
뉴스가 온통 파멸과 암울한 상황일 때 / 사람들은 우울하게 느낀다 / 그리고 흥미를 덜 느끼게 된다 / 작고 개인적인 조치를 취하는 것에 / 생태학적 붕괴와 싸우기 위한 //

- saying ⓝ 속담, 격언 · threatening ⓐ 위협적인
- opposite ⓝ 반대 · frightening ⓐ 두려움을 주는
- inner ⓐ 내면의 · pessimistic ⓐ 비관적인
- take a step 조치를 취하다 · intend ⓥ 의도하다 · rate ⓝ 비율

- screen ⓥ (특정 질병이 있는지) 검진하다 · terrified ⓐ 두려워하는, 겁이 난
- be true for ~에 해당되다 · climate ⓝ 기후
- doom ⓝ 파멸, (불행한) 운명 · gloom ⓝ 우울, 어둠
- depressed ⓐ 우울한 · ecological ⓐ 생태학적인
- collapse ⓝ 붕괴

오래된 격언에 따르면 '아는 것이 힘이다'라고 하지만, 무섭고 위협적인 뉴스에 관한 한, 연구는 정반대를 시사한다. 두려움을 주는 뉴스는 실제로 사람들로부터 내면의 통제력을 빼앗을 수 있어서, 그들이 스스로와 다른 사람들을 돌볼 가능성을 더 낮게 만든다. 공중 보건 연구는 뉴스가 건강과 관련된 정보를 비관적인 방식으로 제시할 때, 결과적으로 사람들이 질병으로부터 자신을 보호하기 위한 조치를 취할 가능성이 실제로 더 낮다는 것을 보여준다. 예를 들어, 증가하는 암 발생률에 대해 사람들에게 경고하려 하는 뉴스 기사는 그들이 발견할지도 모를 것에 대해 너무 두려워하기 때문에 더 적은 사람들이 그 병에 대해 검사받는 것을 선택하는 결과를 가져올 수 있다. 이것은 기후 변화와 같은 문제에도 해당된다. 뉴스가 온통 파멸과 암울한 상황일 때, 사람들은 우울하게 느끼고 생태학적 붕괴와 싸우기 위한 작고 개인적인 조치를 취하는 것에 흥미를 덜 느끼게 된다.

다음 글의 요지로 가장 적절한 것은?

① 두려움을 주는 뉴스는 사람들이 문제에 덜 대처하게 할 수 있다.
　두려움을 주는 뉴스는 사람들을 우울하게 만들어서 조치를 덜 취하게 한다고 했음
② 정보를 전달하는 시기에 따라 뉴스의 영향력이 달라질 수 있다.
　정보 전달 시기에 대해서는 언급하지 않았음
③ 지속적인 환경 문제 보도가 사람들의 인식 변화를 이끈다.
　환경 문제 보도는 두려움을 주는 뉴스에 대한 하나의 예시로 언급된 것임
④ 정보 제공의 지연은 정확한 문제 인식에 방해가 될 수 있다.
　정보 제공이 늦어지면 안 된다는 내용이 아님
⑤ 출처가 불분명한 건강 정보는 사람들에게 유익하지 않다.
　출처의 명확성에 대한 내용은 없음

≫왜 정답? ★★☆ [정답률 79%]

'아는 것이 힘'이지만, 무섭고 위협적인 뉴스에는 적용되지 않는다.
➡ 사람들 내면의 통제력을 빼앗아 스스로와 주변을 덜 돌보게 함 단서1
➡ 사람들은 작고 개인적인 조치조차 덜 취함 단서2
▶ 두려움을 주는 뉴스는 사람들이 문제에 덜 대처하게 한다는 것이므로 정답은 ①이다.

≫왜 오답?

② 정보를 전달하는 '시기'에 대한 언급은 없다.
③ 환경 문제 보도는 하나의 예시로 언급된 것으로 글 전체를 포괄할 수 없다. 주의
④ 빠른 정보의 제공을 권장하는 글이 아니다.
⑤ 건강 정보의 출처와 그 명확성에 대한 내용은 없다.

---

23 정답 ⑤ ★녹는 얼음과 해수면 상승이 미치는 영향

The most remarkable and unbelievable consequence / of melting ice and rising seas / is that together they are a kind of time machine, /
가장 놀랍고 믿을 수 없는 결과는 / 녹는 얼음과 상승하는 바다의 / 그것들이 합쳐서 일종의 타임머신이라는 것이다 / 단서1 녹는 얼음과 상승하는 바다는 하루의 기간을 바꾸고 있음

so real that they are altering the duration of our day. //
(이것은) 너무나 현실적이어서 그것들이 우리 하루의 기간을 바꾸고 있다 //

It works like this: / As the glaciers melt and the seas rise, / gravity forces more water / toward the equator. //
그것은 이처럼 작동한다 / 빙하가 녹고 바다가 높아지면서 / 중력이 더 많은 물을 밀어 넣는다 / 적도를 향해 //

This changes the shape of the Earth / ever so slightly, / making it fatter around the middle, /
이것은 지구의 모양을 변화시킨다 / 아주 약간 / 가운데 주변으로 그것을 더 불룩하게 만들면서 /

계속적 용법의 주격 관계대명사
which in turns slows the rotation of the planet / similarly to the
관계부사절
way / a ballet dancer slows her spin / by spreading out her arms. //
그리고 그것은 결과적으로 행성의 회전을 늦춘다 / 방식과 유사하게 / 발레 무용수가 그녀의
회전을 늦추는 / 양팔을 뻗어서 //

The slowdown isn't much, / just a few thousandths of a second
each year, / but like the barely noticeable jump of rising seas
= the slowdown
every year, / it adds up. // **단서 3** 감속은 점점 쌓임
이 감속은 크지 않다 / 매년 단지 몇천분의 1초로 / 하지만 해마다 상승하는 바다의
알아차리기 힘든 증가처럼 / 그것은 쌓인다 //

When dinosaurs lived on the Earth, / a day lasted only about
twenty-three hours. //
공룡들이 지구에 살았을 때 / 하루는 약 23시간만 지속되었다 //

- remarkable ⓐ 놀라운, 주목할 만한 · unbelievable ⓐ 믿을 수 없는
- consequence ⓝ 결과 · alter ⓥ 바꾸다, 고치다
- duration ⓝ (지속되는) 기간 · glacier ⓝ 빙하 · gravity ⓝ 중력
- equator ⓝ (지구의) 적도 · rotation ⓝ 회전
- spread out (몸을) 뻗다 · barely ⓐd 간신히, 거의 ~ 아니게
- noticeable ⓐ 알아차릴 수 있는, 뚜렷한 · add up 누적되다, 쌓이다
- dinosaur ⓝ 공룡 · last ⓥ 지속하다 · temperature ⓝ 온도
- principle ⓝ 원리 · maintain ⓥ 유지하다
- biodiversity ⓝ (균형 잡힌 환경을 위한) 생물의 다양성

녹는 얼음과 상승하는 바다의 가장 놀랍고 믿을 수 없는 결과는 그것들이
합쳐서 일종의 타임머신이라는 것이고, 이것은 너무나 현실적이어서 그것들이
우리 하루의 기간을 바꾸고 있다. 그것은 이처럼 작동한다. 빙하가 녹고 바다가
높아지면서 중력이 적도를 향해 더 많은 물을 밀어 넣는다. 이것은 지구의
모양을 아주 약간 변화시켜 가운데 주변으로 그것을 더 불룩하게 만들고,
이것은 결과적으로 발레 무용수가 양팔을 뻗어서 그녀의 회전을 늦추는 방식과
유사한 방식으로 행성의 회전을 늦춘다. 이 감속이 매년 단지 몇천분의 1초로
크지는 않지만, 해마다 상승하는 바다의 알아차리기 힘든 증가처럼, 그것은
쌓인다. 공룡들이 지구에 살았을 때, 하루는 약 23시간만 지속되었다.

다음 글의 주제로 가장 적절한 것은?
① cause of rising temperatures on the Earth
지구의 기온 상승의 원인   지구의 기온이 오르는 원인은 설명하지 않음
② principles of planets maintaining their shapes
행성이 그들의 모양을 유지하는 원리   행성의 모양이 변화한다고 했음
③ implications of melting ice on marine biodiversity
녹는 얼음이 해양 생물의 다양성에 미치는 영향   해양 생물에 관한 내용은 없음
④ way to keep track of time without using any device
장치를 사용하지 않고 시간을 기록하는 방법   마지막 문장에 시간을 언급한 것으로 만든 오답
⑤ impact of melting ice and rising seas on the length of
a day   빙하가 녹고 바다가 높아지면서 행성의 회전을 늦춰서 하루의 기간을 바꾸고 있다고 했음
녹는 얼음과 해수면 상승이 하루의 길이에 미치는 영향

>왜 정답? ✱✱✽ [정답률 79%]

얼음이 녹아 해수면이 상승하는 것은 하루의 기간을 바꾸고 있다. **단서 1**
1 빙하가 녹으면서 중력이 적도로 더 많은 물을 보냄
2 지구의 모양이 가운데가 더 불룩한 모양으로 바뀜
3 행성의 회전을 늦춤 **단서 2**
4 감속은 크지 않지만 누적됨 **단서 3**

→ 얼음이 녹는 것이 하루의 기간을 바꾸는 과정을 순서대로 설명함
▶ 따라서 글의 주제는 ⑤ '녹는 얼음과 해수면 상승이 하루의 길이에 미치는
영향'이 가장 적절하다.

>왜 오답?

① 얼음이 녹는다고는 했지만, 지구의 기온이 상승하는 이유에 대해서는 나오지
않았다.
② 빙하가 녹고 바다가 높아지면서 지구의 모양이 변한다고 했으므로 적절하지 않다.
③ 해양 생물의 다양성에 관한 글이 아니다.
④ 공룡이 지구에 살았을 때 하루는 약 23시간이었다고 했을 뿐, 시간을 기록하는
방법에 대한 글이 아니다. 감속이 크지 않지만 시간이 결국 **꿀**팁
변할 수도 있음을 설명하는 대목

---

24 정답 ④ ＊옳다는 것이 새로운 가능성을 막는다

Have you ever brought up an idea or suggestion / to someone
지각동사+목적어+원형부사어
/ and heard them immediately say / "No, that won't work."? //
아이디어나 제안을 내놓은 적이 있는가 / 누군가에게 / 그리고 그들이 즉시 말한 것을 들은
적이 있는가 / "아니, 그건 안 될 거야"라고 //

You may have thought, / "He/she didn't even give it a chance. //
How do they know it won't work?" //
여러분은 아마도 생각했을지도 모른다 / "그 사람은 기회조차 주지 않았어 // 어떻게 그들은
그것이 안 될 것이라는 것을 알지"라고 // **단서 1** 어떤 일에 대해 옳을 때, 다른
관점이나 기회를 닫게 됨
When you are right about something, / you close off the
possibility / of another viewpoint or opportunity. //
여러분이 어떤 일에 대해 옳다면 / 여러분은 가능성을 닫는다 / 다른 관점이나 기회의 //
동명사 주어(단수 취급)   단수 동사
Being right about something means / that "it is the way it is,
period." //
어떤 일에 대해 옳다는 것은 의미한다 / "그것은 원래 그런 거야, 끝"이라는 것을 //

You may be correct. //
여러분이 맞을 수도 있다 //

Your particular way of seeing it / may be true with the facts. //
여러분이 그것을 보는 특정한 방법이 / 사실에 부합할 수도 있다 //
동명사 주어
However, / considering the other option or the other person's
point of view / can be beneficial. // **단서 2** 다른 관점을 고려하는 것이 이로울 수 있음
하지만 / 다른 선택이나 다른 사람의 관점을 고려하는 것은 / 이로울 수 있다 //

If you see their side, / you will see something new / or, at worse,
전치사의 목적어(간접의문문)
learn something / about how the other person looks at life. //
만약 여러분이 그들의 관점을 안다면 / 여러분은 새로운 것을 보거나 / 그것보다는 나쁘더라도
무언가를 배울 것이다 / 상대방이 삶을 바라보는 방식에 대해 //
뒤에 목적어절 접속사 that이 생략됨
Why would you think / everyone sees and experiences life / the
way you do? //
왜 여러분은 생각하는가 / 모두가 삶을 보거나 경험할 것이라고 / 여러분이 하는 방식대로 //
'~ 외에'
Besides how boring that would be, / it would eliminate all new
opportunities, ideas, invention, and creativity. //
그것이 얼마나 지루할지는 제외하고라도 / 그것은 모든 새로운 기회, 아이디어, 발명, 그리고
창의성을 없앨 것이다 // **단서 3** 자신이 옳다고 생각하면 새로운 기회나 창의성이 없어질 수 있음

- bring up (화제를) 꺼내다 · suggestion ⓝ 제안
- immediately ⓐd 즉시 · close off ~을 차단하다[막다]
- possibility ⓝ 가능성 · viewpoint ⓝ 관점
- period ⓝ 마침표, 끝 · consider ⓥ 고려하다 · option ⓝ 선택(지)
- point of view 관점 · beneficial ⓐ 유익한, 이로운
- eliminate ⓥ 제거하다, 없애다 · invention ⓝ 발명
- honest ⓐ 정직한 · filter out (액체·빛 등에서) ~을 걸러내다
- block ⓥ 막다, 차단하다

누군가에게 아이디어나 제안을 내놓고, 그들이 즉시 "아니, 그건 안 될
거야."라고 말한 것을 들은 적이 있는가? 여러분은 아마도 "그 사람은
기회조차 주지 않았어. 어떻게 그들은 그것이 안 될 것이라는 것을 알지?"라고
생각했을지도 모른다. 여러분이 어떤 일에 대해 옳다면, 여러분은 다른
관점이나 기회의 가능성을 닫아 버린다. 어떤 일에 대해 옳다는 것은 "그것은
원래 그런 거야, 끝."이라고 하는 것을 의미한다. 여러분이 맞을 수도 있다.
여러분이 그것을 보는 특정한 방법이 사실에 부합할 수도 있다. 하지만 다른
선택이나 다른 사람의 관점을 고려하는 것은 이로울 수 있다. 만약 여러분이
그들의 관점을 안다면, 여러분이 새로운 것을 보거나 그것보다는 나쁘더라도
다른 사람이 삶을 바라보는 방식에 대한 무언가를 배울 것이다. 왜 모두가
여러분이 하는 방식대로 삶을 보거나 경험할 것이라고 생각하는가? 그것이
얼마나 지루할지는 제외하고라도, 그것은 모든 새로운 기회, 아이디어, 발명,
그리고 창의성을 없앨 것이다.

자신이 옳다고만 생각하면 창의성이나 기회가 없어질 수 있다는 내용

다음 글의 제목으로 가장 적절한 것은?

① The Value of Being Honest 옳은 것의 안 좋은 점에 대해 말하는 내용임
정직한 것의 가치
② Filter Out Negative Points of View
부정적인 관점을 걸러내라 다른 사람의 관점도 고려해야 한다고 했음
③ Keeping Your Word: A Road to Success
약속 지키기: 성공으로 가는 길 약속을 지키는 것에 대한 언급은 없음
④ Being Right Can Block New Possibilities
옳다는 것이 새로운 가능성을 차단할 수 있다
⑤ Look Back When Everyone Looks Forward
모두가 앞을 볼 때 뒤를 돌아보라 남들과 다르게 생각해야 한다는 내용이 아님

| 문제 풀이 순서 | ★★★ [정답률 57%]

1st 글의 앞부분을 읽으며 이어질 내용을 예상한다.

누군가에게 아이디어나 제안을 내놓고, 그들이 즉시 "아니, 그건 안 될 거야."라고 말한 것을 들은 적이 있는가? 여러분은 아마도 "그 사람은 기회조차 주지 않았어. 어떻게 그들은 그것이 안 될 것이라는 것을 알지?"라고 생각했을 것이다. 여러분이 어떤 일에 대해 옳다면, 여러분은 다른 관점이나 기회의 가능성을 닫아 버린다. 단서 1

➡ 다른 사람에게 제안을 한 뒤 부정적인 반응을 들은 적이 있는지 질문을 던지면서, 어떤 일에 대해 옳을 때, 다른 관점이나 기회를 닫게 된다고 했다. 단서

➡ 자신만이 옳다고 생각하면 새로운 기회를 얻지 못한다는 내용의 글일 것이다. 발상

2nd 글의 나머지 부분에서 내용을 파악하고 정답을 찾는다.

• 여러분이 어떤 일에 대해 옳다면, 여러분은 다른 관점이나 기회의 가능성을 닫아 버린다. 단서 2

• 왜 모두가 여러분이 하는 방식대로 삶을 보거나 경험할 것이라고 생각하는가? 그것이 얼마나 지루할지는 제외하고라도, 그것은 모든 새로운 기회, 아이디어, 발명, 그리고 창의성을 없앨 것이다. 단서 3

➡ 자신이 옳다고 생각하는 것은 다른 관점의 가능성을 닫고, 새로운 기회나 아이디어, 창의성 등을 없앨 것이라고 했다.

▶ 따라서 ④ '옳다는 것이 새로운 가능성을 차단할 수 있다'가 글의 제목으로 가장 적절하다.

| 선택지 분석 |

① The Value of Being Honest
정직한 것의 가치
옳다고 생각하는 것의 안 좋은 점에 대해 말하는 글로 정직함의 가치와는 관련이 없다.

② Filter Out Negative Points of View
부정적인 관점을 걸러내라
다른 사람의 관점도 걸러내지 말고 고려해야 한다고 했다.

③ Keeping Your Word: A Road to Success
약속 지키기: 성공으로 가는 길
약속을 지키라고 조언하는 글이 아니다.

④ Being Right Can Block New Possibilities
옳다는 것이 새로운 가능성을 차단할 수 있다
자신이 옳다고만 생각하면 여러 기회가 없어질 수 있다고 했다.

⑤ Look Back When Everyone Looks Forward
모두가 앞을 볼 때 뒤를 돌아보라
다른 사람의 관점도 받아들이라고 했지 남들과 다르게 생각해야 한다는 내용이 아니다.

---

25 정답 ④ ＊고기를 덜 먹거나 안 먹는 이유 ——————

The graph above shows / the survey results on reasons / for
앞에 주격 관계대명사가 be동사가 생략됨   = people
people interested in eating less meat / and those eating no meat
/ in the UK in 2018. //
위의 그래프는 보여 준다 / 이유에 대한 조사 결과를 / 고기를 덜 먹는 것에 관심 있는 사람들에 대한 / 그리고 고기를 먹지 않는 사람들(에 대한) / 영국에서 2018년에 //

주격 관계대명사
① For the group of people / who are interested in eating less
meat, / health is the strongest motivator / for doing so. //
사람들의 집단에게 / 고기를 덜 먹는 것에 관심이 있는 / 건강은 가장 강력한 동기이다 / 그렇게 하는 // 고기를 덜 먹는 것에 관심 있는 사람들에게 건강이 49퍼센트로 가장 높음

② For the group of non-meat eaters, / animal welfare accounts
for the largest percentage / among all reasons, / followed by
environment, health, and taste. // 고기를 먹지 않는 사람들: 동물 복지(52%) > 환경(32%) > 건강(31%) > 맛(30%)
고기를 먹지 않는 사람들의 집단의 경우 / 동물 복지가 가장 큰 비율을 차지한다 / 모든 이유 중에서 / 환경, 건강, 그리고 맛이 그 뒤를 따른다 //

핵심 주어(단수)
③ The largest percentage point difference / between the two
단수 동사
groups / is in animal welfare, / whereas the smallest difference
is in environment. // 가장 큰 차이: 동물 복지(52%-22%=30%) / 가장 작은 차이: 환경(32%-22%=10%)
가장 큰 퍼센트포인트 차이는 / 두 집단 사이의 / 동물 복지에 있는 반면 // 단서 맛 때문에 고기를 먹지 않는 사람들은 30퍼센트이고, 고기를 덜 먹는 것에 관심 있는 사람들은 10퍼센트이므로 3배임

④ The percentage of non-meat eaters / citing taste / is four(→
= the percentage
three) times higher / than that of people / interested in reducing
their meat consumption / citing taste. //
고기를 먹지 않는 사람들의 비율은 / 맛을 언급하면서 / 4(→ 3)배 높다 / 사람들의 비율보다 / 고기 섭취를 줄이는 데 관심이 있는 / 맛을 언급하면서 //

주격 관계대명사
⑤ Weight management ranks the lowest / for people who don't
eat meat, / with less than 10 percent. // 고기를 먹지 않는 사람들에게 체중 관리는 9퍼센트로 가장 낮음
체중 관리는 가장 낮은 순위를 차지한다 / 고기를 먹지 않는 사람들에게 / 10퍼센트 미만으로 //

• motivator ⓝ 동기 (요인) • welfare ⓝ 복지
• account for (부분·비율을) 차지하다 • cite ⓥ 언급하다
• consumption ⓝ 섭취, 소비 • management ⓝ 관리
• rank ⓥ (순위를) 차지하다

위의 그래프는 고기를 덜 먹는 것에 관심 있는 사람들과 고기를 먹지 않는 사람들의 이유에 대한 2018년 영국에서의 조사 결과를 보여 준다. ① 고기를 덜 먹는 것에 관심이 있는 사람들의 집단에게, 건강은 그렇게 하는 가장 강력한 동기이다. ② 고기를 먹지 않는 사람들의 집단의 경우, 모든 이유 중에서 동물 복지가 가장 큰 비율을 차지하고 있고, 환경, 건강, 그리고 맛이 그 뒤를 따른다. ③ 두 집단 사이의 가장 큰 퍼센트포인트 차이는 동물 복지에 있는 반면, 가장 작은 차이는 환경에 있다. ④ 맛을 언급하는 고기를 먹지 않는 사람들의 비율은 맛을 언급하는 고기 섭취를 줄이는 데 관심이 있는 사람들의 비율보다 4(→ 3)배 높다. ⑤ 체중 관리는 고기를 먹지 않는 사람들에게 10퍼센트 미만으로 가장 낮은 순위를 차지한다.

다음 도표의 내용과 일치하지 않는 것은?
영국에서 고기를 덜 먹는 것에 관심 있는 사람들과 고기를 먹지 않는 사람들의 이유 (2018년)

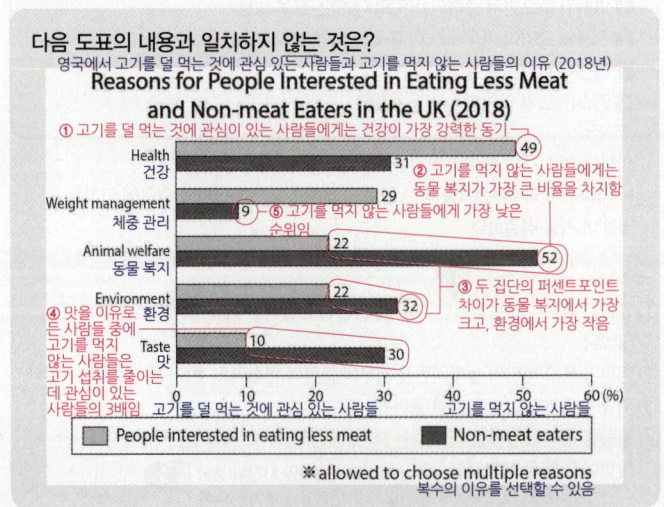

Reasons for People Interested in Eating Less Meat and Non-meat Eaters in the UK (2018)

① 고기를 덜 먹는 것에 관심이 있는 사람들에게는 건강이 가장 강력한 동기
② 고기를 먹지 않는 사람들에게는 동물 복지가 가장 큰 비율을 차지함
⑤ 고기를 먹지 않는 사람들에게 가장 낮은 순위임
③ 두 집단의 퍼센트포인트 차이가 동물 복지에서 가장 크고, 환경에서 가장 작음
④ 맛을 이유로 든 사람들 중에 고기를 먹지 않는 사람들은 고기 섭취를 줄이는 데 관심이 있는 사람들의 3배임

Health 건강: 49, 31
Weight management 체중 관리: 29, 9
Animal welfare 동물 복지: 22, 52
Environment 환경: 22, 32
Taste 맛: 10, 30

고기를 덜 먹는 것에 관심 있는 사람들 고기를 먹지 않는 사람들

☐ People interested in eating less meat ■ Non-meat eaters

※ allowed to choose multiple reasons
복수의 이유를 선택할 수 있음

맛 때문에 고기를 먹지 않는 사람들의 비율은 30퍼센트로, 맛 때문에 고기 섭취를 줄이는 데 관심이 있는 사람들의 비율인 10퍼센트의 4배가 아니라 3배이다. 따라서 ④이 도표의 내용과 일치하지 않는다.

＞왜 오답 ?

① 고기를 덜 먹는 것에 관심이 있는 사람들에게는 건강이 49퍼센트로 가장 강력한 동기이다.
② 고기를 먹지 않는 사람의 경우 동물 복지가 52퍼센트로 가장 큰 비율을 차지하고, 환경, 건강, 맛이 그 뒤에 이어진다.
③ 두 집단의 퍼센트포인트 차이는 동물 복지가 가장 크고(52퍼센트와 22퍼센트로 30퍼센트포인트 차이), 환경이 가장 작다(32퍼센트와 22퍼센트로 10퍼센트포인트 차이).
⑤ 고기를 먹지 않는 사람에게 체중 관리는 9퍼센트로 가장 낮은 순위를 차지한다.

26 정답 ③ ＊Margaret Knight의 생애

Margaret Knight was an exceptionally prolific inventor / in the late 19th century; / journalists occasionally compared her to
①의 단서 기자들이 '여자 Edison'이라는 별명을 지어 주었음
compare A to B : A를 B에 비교하다
Thomas Edison / by nicknaming her "a woman Edison." //
Margaret Knight는 특출나게 다작한 발명가였다 / 19세기 후반에 / 기자들은 가끔 그녀를 Thomas Edison과 비교했다 / 그녀에게 '여자 Edison'이라는 별명을 지어 주어 //

From a young age, / she built toys for her older brothers. //
어린 나이부터 / 그녀는 오빠들을 위해 장난감을 만들었다 //

After her father died, / Knight's family moved to Manchester. //
그녀의 아버지가 돌아가신 후 / Knight의 가족은 Manchester로 이사했다 //

Knight left school in 1850, / at age 12, / to earn money for her
계속적 용법의 관계부사
부사적 용법(목적)
family / at a nearby textile factory, / where she witnessed a
②의 단서 가족을 위해 돈을
fellow worker injured / by faulty equipment. // 벌려고 학교를 그만두었음
Knight는 1850년에 학교를 그만두었다 / 12세의 나이에 / 가족을 위해 돈을 벌기 위해 / 가까이에 있는 직물 공장에서 / 그곳에서 그녀는 동료 노동자가 부상을 당하는 것을 목격했다 / 결함이 있는 장비에 의해 //

That led her to create her first invention, / a safety device for textile equipment, / but she never earned money from the invention. // **③의 단서** 직물 장비에 쓰이는 안전장치를 발명했지만, 돈을 벌지는 못했음
그것은 그녀가 자신의 첫 번째 발명품을 만들도록 이끌었다 / 직물 장비에 쓰이는 안전장치를 / 하지만 그녀는 결코 그 발명품으로 돈을 벌지 못했다 //

She also invented a machine / that cut, folded and glued flat-
병렬 구조
bottomed paper bags / and was awarded her first patent / in
1871 / for it. // **④의 단서** 밑이 평평한 종이 가방을 자르고 접고 붙이는 기계를 발명했음
그녀는 또한 기계를 발명했다 / 밑이 평평한 종이 가방을 자르고, 접고, 붙이는 / 그리고 자신의 첫 특허를 받았다 / 1871년에 / 그것으로 //

It eliminated the need / for workers to assemble them / slowly
to assemble의 의미상 주어
by hand. //
그것은 필요를 없앴다 / 작업자들이 그것들을 조립할 / 손으로 천천히 //

Knight received 27 patents in her lifetime / and entered the
병렬 구조
National Inventors Hall of Fame / in 2006. //
Knight는 자신의 일생 동안 27개의 특허를 받았다 / 그리고 국립 발명가 명예의 전당에 입성했다 / 2006년에 // **⑤의 단서** 2006년에 국립 발명가 명예의 전당에 입성했음

- exceptionally [ad] 유난히, 특출나게 - inventor [n] 발명가
- journalist [n] 기자, 언론인 - occasionally [ad] 가끔
- nickname [v] 별명을 붙이다 - textile [n] 직물
- witness [v] 목격하다 - faulty [a] 결함이 있는
- equipment [n] 장비, 설비 - device [n] 장치
- flat-bottomed [a] 바닥이 평평한 - eliminate [v] 제거하다, 없애다
- assemble [v] 조립하다

Margaret Knight는 19세기 후반에 특출나게 다작한 발명가였고, 기자들은 그녀에게 '여자 Edison'이라는 별명을 지어 주어 가끔 Thomas Edison과 비교했다. 어린 나이부터, 그녀는 오빠들을 위해 장난감을 만들었다. 그녀의

아버지가 돌아가신 후, Knight의 가족은 Manchester로 이사했다. Knight는 가족을 위해 가까이에 있는 직물 공장에서 돈을 벌기 위해 1850년, 12세의 나이에 학교를 그만두었는데, 그곳에서 그녀는 동료 노동자가 결함이 있는 장비에 의해 부상을 당하는 것을 목격했다. 그것은 그녀가 자신의 첫 번째 발명품, 즉 직물 장비에 쓰이는 안전장치를 만들도록 이끌었지만, 그녀는 결코 그 발명품으로 돈을 벌지 못했다. 그녀는 또한 밑이 평평한 종이 가방을 자르고, 접고, 붙이는 기계를 발명했고 1871년에 그것으로 자신의 첫 특허를 받았다. 그것은 작업자들이 손으로 그것들을 천천히 조립할 필요를 없앴다. Knight는 자신의 일생 동안 27개의 특허를 받았고, 2006년에 국립 발명가 명예의 전당에 입성했다.

Margaret Knight에 관한 다음 글의 내용과 일치하지 않는 것은?
① 기자들이 '여자 Edison'이라는 별명을 지어 주었다.
by nicknaming her "a woman Edison."
② 가족을 위해 돈을 벌려고 학교를 그만두었다.
Knight left school in 1850, at age 12, to earn money for her family
③ 직물 장비에 쓰이는 안전장치를 발명하여 많은 돈을 벌었다.
but she never earned money from the invention
④ 밑이 평평한 종이 가방을 자르고 접고 붙이는 기계를 발명했다.
She also invented a machine that cut, folded and glued flat-bottomed paper bags
⑤ 2006년에 국립 발명가 명예의 전당에 입성했다.
entered the National Inventors Hall of Fame in 2006

＞왜 정답 ? ✿✾✾ [정답률 90%]

Margaret Knight는 직물 장비에 쓰이는 안전장치를 발명했지만, 그 발명품으로 돈은 벌지 못했다고 했다. (That led her to create her first invention, a safety device for textile equipment, but she never earned money from the invention.) 따라서 ③이 글의 내용과 일치하지 않는다.

＞왜 오답 ?

① 기자들이 그녀에게 '여자 Edison'이라는 별명을 지어 주어 Thomas Edison과 비교했다고 했다. (journalists occasionally compared her to Thomas Edison by nicknaming her "a woman Edison.")
② 가족을 위해 돈을 벌려고 1850년에 12세의 나이에 학교를 그만두었다고 했다. (Knight left school in 1850, at age 12, to earn money for her family)
④ 밑이 평평한 종이 가방을 자르고 접고 붙이는 기계를 발명했다고 했다. (She also invented a machine that cut, folded and glued flat-bottomed paper bags)
⑤ 2006년에 국립 발명가 명예의 전당에 입성했다고 했다. (entered the National Inventors Hall of Fame in 2006)

27 정답 ⑤ ＊전자 폐기물 재활용의 날

E-Waste Recycling Day /
전자 폐기물 재활용의 날 /

E-Waste Recycling Day / is an annual event in our city. //
전자 폐기물 재활용의 날은 / 우리 시의 연례행사입니다 //
명령문
Bring your used electronics / such as cell phones, tablets, and laptops / to recycle. //
여러분의 중고 전자 제품을 가져오세요 / 휴대 전화, 태블릿, 노트북과 같이 / 재활용할 //

Go green! // 친환경적으로 행동해요 //

When / 언제 /

Saturday, December 17, 2022 / 2022년 12월 17일 토요일 /

8:00 a.m. – 11:00 a.m. / **①의 단서** 3시간 동안 진행됨
오전 8시부터 오전 11시까지 /

Where / 어디서 /

Lincoln Sports Center / **②의 단서** Lincoln 스포츠 센터에서 열림
Lincoln 스포츠 센터 /

Notes / 주의 사항 /

- Items NOT accepted: / light bulbs, batteries, and microwaves /
허용되지 않는 품목들 / 전구, 건전지, 전자레인지 / **③의 단서** 전자레인지는 허용되지 않는 품목임
조동사가 포함된 수동태
- All personal data on the devices / must be wiped out in advance. // **④의 단서** 기기 속 모든 개인 정보는 미리 삭제되어야 함
기기 속 모든 개인 정보는 / 미리 삭제되어야 합니다 //

- This event is free / but open only to local residents. //
이 행사는 무료입니다 / 하지만 지역 주민에게만 개방됩니다 // ⑤의 단서 행사는 무료이지만 지역 주민에게만 개방됨

Please contact us at 986-571-0204 / for more information. //
986-571-0204로 연락주세요 / 더 많은 정보를 원하시면 //

- e-waste ⓝ 전자 폐기물
- annual ⓐ 해마다의, 연례의
- electronics ⓝ 전자 제품
- accept ⓥ 받아들이다, 허용하다
- light bulb 전구
- microwave ⓝ 전자레인지
- wipe out ~을 완전히 없애다[삭제하다]
- in advance 사전에, 미리
- resident ⓝ 거주자, 주민

전자 폐기물 재활용의 날

전자 폐기물 재활용의 날은 우리 시의 연례행사입니다. 휴대 전화, 태블릿, 노트북과 같이 재활용할 중고 전자 제품을 가져오세요. 친환경적으로 행동해요!

언제
2022년 12월 17일 토요일
오전 8시부터 오전 11시까지

어디서
Lincoln 스포츠 센터

주의 사항
- 허용되지 않는 품목들: 전구, 건전지, 전자레인지
- 기기 속 모든 개인 정보는 미리 삭제되어야 합니다.
- 이 행사는 무료이나 지역 주민에게만 개방됩니다.
더 많은 정보를 원하시면 986-571-0204로 연락주세요.

E-Waste Recycling Day에 관한 다음 안내문의 내용과 일치하지 않는 것은?

① 3시간 동안 진행된다. 8:00 a.m.-11:00 a.m.
② Lincoln 스포츠 센터에서 열린다. Lincoln Sports Center
③ 전자레인지는 허용되지 않는 품목이다.
Items NOT accepted: light bulbs, batteries, and microwaves
④ 기기 속 모든 개인 정보는 미리 삭제되어야 한다.
All personal data on the devices must be wiped out in advance.
⑤ 거주 지역에 상관없이 참가할 수 있다.
This event is free but open only to local residents.

왜 정답? ✽✽✽ [정답률 92%]

행사는 무료이지만 지역 주민에게만 개방된다고(This event is free but open only to local residents.) 했으므로 거주 지역에 상관없이 참가할 수 있다고 한 ⑤은 안내문의 내용과 일치하지 않는다.

왜 오답?

① 행사는 오전 8시부터 오전 11시까지 3시간 동안 진행된다. (8:00 a.m.–11:00 a.m.)
② Lincoln 스포츠 센터에서 열린다. (Lincoln Sports Center)
③ 전구, 건전지, 전자레인지는 허용되지 않는 품목이다. (Items NOT accepted: light bulbs, batteries, and microwaves)
④ 기기 속 모든 개인 정보는 미리 삭제해야 한다. (All personal data on the devices must be wiped out in advance.)

28 정답 ③ ＊해저 걷기 활동

Undersea Walking Activity /
해저 걷기 활동 /

Enjoy a fascinating underwater walk / on the ocean floor. //
매력적인 수중 걷기를 즐기세요 / 해양 바닥에서 //

Witness wonderful marine life / on foot! // '걸어서, 도보로'
멋진 바다 생물을 직접 보세요 / 걸어 다니며 //

Age Requirement / 연령 요건 /
10 years or older / 10세 이상 /

Operating Hours / 영업시간 /
from Tuesday to Sunday / ①의 단서 월요일은 운영하지 않음
화요일부터 일요일까지 /

9:00 a.m. – 4:00 p.m. / 오전 9시부터 오후 4시까지 /

Price / 가격 /
$30 (insurance fee included) / ②의 단서 가격에 보험료 포함됨
30달러 (보험료 포함) /

What to Bring / 가져올 것 /
swim suit and towel / 수영복과 수건 /

Notes / 주의 사항 /
- Experienced lifeguards accompany you / throughout the activity. // ③의 단서 숙련된 안전 요원이 활동 내내 동행함
숙련된 안전 요원이 여러분과 동행합니다 / 활동 내내 //
- With a special underwater helmet, / you can wear glasses / during the activity. // ④의 단서 특수 수중 헬멧을 착용하면 안경을 쓸 수 있음
특수 수중 헬멧 착용 시 / 여러분은 안경을 쓸 수 있습니다 / 활동 중에 //
- Reservations can be made / on-site or online at www.seawalkwonder.com. // ⑤의 단서 현장 또는 온라인으로 예약할 수 있음 조동사가 포함된 수동태
예약은 할 수 있습니다 / 현장 또는 www.seawalkwonder.com에서 온라인으로 //

- fascinating ⓐ 매력적인, 대단히 흥미로운
- witness ⓥ 목격하다
- marine life 해양 생물
- requirement ⓝ 요건, 필요조건
- insurance ⓝ 보험
- experienced ⓐ 경험 있는, 숙련된
- accompany ⓥ 동반하다, 동행하다
- underwater ⓐ 수중의

해저 걷기 활동

해양 바닥에서 매력적인 수중 걷기를 즐기세요. 걸어 다니며 멋진 바다 생물을 직접 보세요!

연령 요건
10세 이상

영업시간
화요일부터 일요일까지
오전 9시부터 오후 4시까지

가격
30달러 (보험료 포함)

가져올 것
수영복과 수건

주의 사항
- 숙련된 안전 요원이 활동 내내 여러분과 동행합니다.
- 특수 수중 헬멧 착용 시 여러분은 활동 중에 안경을 쓸 수 있습니다.
- 예약은 현장 또는 www.seawalkwonder.com에서 온라인으로 할 수 있습니다.

Undersea Walking Activity에 관한 다음 안내문의 내용과 일치하는 것은?

① 연중무휴로 운영된다. from Tuesday to Sunday
② 가격에 보험료는 포함되어 있지 않다. $30 (insurance fee included)
③ 숙련된 안전 요원이 활동 내내 동행한다.
Experienced lifeguards accompany you throughout the activity.
④ 특수 수중 헬멧 착용 시 안경을 쓸 수 없다.
With a special underwater helmet, you can wear glasses during the activity.
⑤ 현장 예약은 불가능하다.
Reservations can be made on-site or online at www.seawalkwonder.com.

왜 정답? ✽✽✽ [정답률 87%]

숙련된 안전 요원이 활동 내내 동행한다고(Experienced lifeguards accompany you throughout the activity.) 했으므로 안내문의 내용과 일치하는 것은 ③이다.

왜 오답?

① 화요일부터 일요일까지 운영한다고 했으므로 월요일은 운영하지 않음을 알 수 있다. (from Tuesday to Sunday)
② 가격은 보험료 포함 30달러라고 했다. ($30 (insurance fee included))
④ 특수 수중 헬멧 착용 시 활동 중에도 안경을 쓸 수 있다고 했다. (With a special underwater helmet, you can wear glasses during the activity.)
⑤ 예약은 현장과 온라인으로 할 수 있다고 했다. (Reservations can be made on-site or online at www.seawalkwonder.com.)

29 정답 ④ ＊학습이 가능한 인공 지능

다음 글의 밑줄 친 부분 중, 어법상 틀린 것은? [3점]

You may have seen headlines / in the news / about **some of the things** / machines **powered by artificial intelligence** can do. //
> 뒤에 목적격 관계대명사 생략
> 과거분사구(machines 수식)

여러분은 헤드라인들을 본 적이 있을 것이다 / 뉴스에서 / 몇 가지 일에 대해 / 인공 지능으로 구동되는 기계가 할 수 있는 //

However, / if you were to consider all the tasks / ① **that** AI-powered machines could actually perform, / it would be quite mind-blowing! //
> 목적격 관계대명사

하지만 / 당신이 모든 작업을 고려한다면 / AI로 구동되는 기계가 실제로 수행할 수 있는 / 그것은 꽤 놀라울 것이다 //

One of the key features of artificial intelligence / ② **is** that it enables machines to learn new things, / rather than requiring programming / specific to new tasks. //
> 핵심 주어(단수)
> 단수 동사

인공 지능의 핵심 특징 중 하나는 / 그것이 기계들이 새로운 것을 학습할 수 있게 한다는 것이다 / 프로그래밍을 필요로 하기보다는 / 새로운 작업에 특화된 //

Therefore, / the core difference / between computers of the future and ③ **those** of the past / is that future computers will be able to learn and self-improve. //
> 복수 지시대명사(= computers)
> 주격 보어절 접속사

그러므로 / 핵심적인 차이점은 / 미래의 컴퓨터들과 과거의 그것들 간에 / 미래의 컴퓨터는 학습하고 스스로 개선할 수 있을 것이라는 점이다 //

In the near future, / smart virtual assistants will know more about you / than your closest friends and family members ④ **are(→ do)**. // **단서** 일반동사인 know를 대신해야 하므로 be동사 are는 쓸 수 없음

가까운 미래에 / 스마트 가상 비서는 여러분에 대해 더 많이 알게 될 것이다 / 여러분의 가장 가까운 친구나 가족이 아는 것보다 //

Can you imagine / **how that might change** our lives? //
> 간접의문문(의문사+주어+동사)

여러분은 상상할 수 있는가 / 그것이 우리의 삶을 어떻게 변화시킬지 //

These kinds of changes are exactly / why **it** is so important ⑤ **to recognize** the implications / **that** new technologies will have for our world. //
> 가주어
> 진주어
> 목적격 관계대명사

이러한 종류의 변화들은 정확히 ~이다 / 영향을 인식하는 것이 매우 중요한 이유 / 새로운 기술들이 우리 세계에 미칠 //

- **power** ⓥ 작동시키다, 동력을 공급하다
- **artificial intelligence** 인공 지능(AI) ・ **task** ⓝ 과업, 작업
- **perform** ⓥ 수행하다 ・ **mind-blowing** ⓐ 놀라운, 감동적인
- **feature** ⓝ 특징, 특색 ・ **core** ⓐ 핵심적인 ・ **virtual** ⓐ 가상의
- **assistant** ⓝ 조수, 비서 ・ **recognize** ⓥ 인식하다
- **implication** ⓝ 영향, 결과

여러분은 인공 지능으로 구동되는 기계가 할 수 있는 몇 가지 일에 대한 헤드라인들을 뉴스에서 본 적이 있을 것이다. 하지만, AI로 구동되는 기계가 실제로 수행할 수 있는 모든 작업을 고려한다면, 그것은 꽤 놀라울 것이다! 인공 지능의 핵심 특징들 중 하나인 그것이 새로운 작업에 특화된 프로그래밍을 필요로 하기보다는 기계들이 새로운 것을 학습할 수 있게 한다는 것이다. 그러므로, 미래의 컴퓨터들과 과거의 컴퓨터들 사이의 핵심적인 차이점은 미래의 컴퓨터가 학습하고 스스로 개선할 수 있을 것이라는 점이다. 가까운 미래에, 스마트 가상 비서는 여러분에 대해 여러분의 가장 가까운 친구나 가족이 아는 것보다 더 많이 알게 될 것이다. 그것이 우리의 삶을 어떻게 변화시킬지 상상할 수 있는가? 이러한 종류의 변화들은 정확히 새로운 기술들이 우리 세계에 미칠 영향을 인식하는 것이 매우 중요한 이유이다.

왜 정답? ★★★ [정답률 51%]

④ know를 대신하는 대동사로 are가 쓰였다!

In the near future, / smart virtual assistants **will know** more about you / **than** your closest friends and family members ④ ~~are~~(→ do). //
> 주어 / 일반동사
> 접속사
> 일반동사를 대신해야 함 / 주어

단서 밑줄이 be동사인 are에 있으므로

발상 be동사가 쓰일 자리가 맞는지 확인해야 한다.

해결 의미상 스마트 가상 비서는 친구나 가족이 '아는' 것보다 더 많이 알게 될 것이라고 해석되어야 하므로 are는 앞에 나온 일반동사 know의 반복적인 사용을 대신하는 대동사로 쓰였음을 알 수 있다.
일반동사를 대신하는 대동사는 be동사가 아니라 do동사이므로, 복수 주어 your closest friends and family members에 맞는 복수 동사 do로 고쳐야 한다.

개념 앞에 나온 동사가 일반동사일 때는 do동사가, be동사일 때는 be동사가 대동사로 쓰인다.

왜 오답?

① 목적격 관계대명사는 목적어가 없는 불완전한 절을 이끈다.

However, / if you were to consider all the **tasks** / [① **that** AI-powered machines **could** actually **perform**], / it would be quite mind-blowing! //
> 선행사
> 주어 / 동사 / 목적격 관계대명사

단서 밑줄이 that에 있으므로

발상 명사절 접속사, 관계대명사, 관계부사 등 중에서 어느 것으로 쓰였는지를 확인해야 한다.

해결 that 뒤에 동사 could perform의 목적어가 없는 불완전한 절이 이어지므로 tasks를 수식하는 목적격 관계대명사로 that은 적절하게 쓰였다.

개념 관계대명사 that은 주어나 목적어가 빠진 불완전한 절을 이끈다.

② 동사는 주어에 그 수를 일치시킨다.

One of the key features of artificial intelligence / ② **is** that it enables machines to learn new things, / rather than requiring programming / specific to new tasks. //
> 핵심 주어(단수) / 수식어구 / 단수 동사
> 주격 보어절 접속사
> 제외하고 생각하기

단서 동사 is에 밑줄이 있으므로

발상 주어를 찾아 수 일치 여부를 확인한다.

해결 문장의 핵심 주어는 One으로 단수 명사이므로 동사도 단수 동사인 is가 알맞게 쓰였다.

개념 주어를 꾸미는 수식어구와 상관없이 핵심 주어의 수에 동사의 수를 일치시킨다.

③ 지시대명사는 그것이 가리키는 것에 수를 일치시킨다.

Therefore, / the core difference / between **computers** of the future and ③ **those** of the past / **is** that future computers will be able to learn and self-improve. //
> 핵심 주어(단수)
> 단수 동사
> 지시대명사

단서 밑줄이 지시대명사 those에 있으므로

발상 those가 가리키는 대상을 찾아 그 수가 일치하는지 확인한다.

해결 문맥상 미래의 컴퓨터들과 과거의 '컴퓨터들' 간에 핵심적인 차이점을 이야기하는 것이므로 those가 지칭하는 대상은 computers로 복수이다. 따라서 복수대명사 those는 어법상 적절하게 쓰였다.

개념 앞에 나온 명사의 반복을 피하기 위해 단수는 지시대명사 that을, 복수는 지시대명사 those를 쓴다.

2022. 11
12회

⑤ 명사적 용법의 to부정사가 쓰였다.

> 주격 보어절을 이끄는 의문사 가주어
> These kinds of changes are exactly / why it is so important
> 진주어
> ⑤ to recognize the implications / that new technologies
> will have for our world. //

(단서) 밑줄이 to recognize에 있으므로

(발상) to recognize가 문장에 명사, 형용사, 부사 중에 어떤 역할을 하는지 확인한 후,
쓰임새에 맞게 쓰였는지 확인해야 한다.

(해결) '영향을 인식하는 것'을 의미하는 to부정사구는 문장의 진주어이다.
형식적인 주어 자리에 가주어 it이 쓰인 문장으로 to recognize는 명사적
용법으로 적절하게 사용되었다.

(개념) to부정사는 명사처럼 주어, 목적어, 보어 역할을 할 수 있다.

---

30 정답 ④ * 옥신이 좌우하는 식물의 성장

다음 글의 밑줄 친 부분 중, 문맥상 낱말의 쓰임이 적절하지 않은 것은?
[3점]

Plant growth is controlled / by a group of hormones called
앞에 주격 관계대명사와 be동사가 생략됨
auxins / found at the tips of stems and roots of plants. //
식물의 성장은 조절된다 / 옥신이라고 불리는 호르몬 그룹에 의해 / 식물의 줄기와 뿌리의
끝에서 발견되는 //
앞에 주격 관계대명사와 be동사가 생략됨
Auxins produced at the tips of stems / tend to accumulate on the
주격 관계대명사
side of the stem / that is in the shade. //
줄기의 끝에서 생산된 옥신은 / 줄기의 옆면에 축적되는 경향이 있다 / 그늘진 곳에 있는 //

Accordingly, / the auxins ① stimulate growth / on the shaded
side of the plant. //
따라서 / 옥신은 성장을 자극한다 / 식물의 그늘진 면에서의 //

Therefore, / the shaded side grows faster / than the side facing
the sunlight. //
그러므로 / 그늘진 면은 더 빨리 자란다 / 햇빛을 마주하는 면보다 //
명사적 용법(목적격 보어)
This phenomenon causes the stem to bend and appear / to be
growing ② towards the light. //
이 현상은 줄기가 휘어지게 하고 보이게 한다 / 빛을 향하여 성장하는 것처럼 //

Auxins have the ③ opposite effect / on the roots of plants. //
옥신은 반대의 효과를 가진다 / 식물의 뿌리에서는 //

Auxins in the tips of roots / tend to limit growth. //
뿌리 끝에 있는 옥신은 / 성장을 억제하는 경향이 있다 //
부사절 접속사(조건)
If a root is horizontal in the soil, / the auxins will accumulate on
the lower side / and interfere with its development. //
만약 하나의 뿌리가 토양 속에서 수평이라면 / 옥신은 아래쪽에 축적될 것이다 / 그리고
그것의 발달을 방해할 것이다 // (단서) 옥신이 뿌리 아래쪽에 축적되면 뿌리 아래쪽의 발달을 방해함

Therefore, / the lower side of the root will grow ④ faster(→
slower) / than the upper side. //
그러므로 / 뿌리의 아래쪽은 더 빠르게(→ 더 느리게) 자라게 된다 / 위쪽보다 //

This will, in turn, cause the root to bend ⑤ downwards, / with
with+(대)명사+분사: 부대상황(~하면서)
the tip of the root growing in that direction. //
이것은 결과적으로 뿌리가 아래로 휘어지게 한다 / 뿌리의 끝부분은 그 방향으로 자라면서 //

- tip ⓝ 끝 (부분) • stem ⓝ (식물의) 줄기 • accumulate ⓥ 축적하다
- shade ⓝ 그늘 • accordingly ⓐⓓ 따라서, 그래서
- stimulate ⓥ 자극하다 • face ⓥ 직면하다, 마주하다
- phenomenon ⓝ 현상 • bend ⓥ 구부러지다, 휘어지다
- opposite ⓐ 반대의 • limit ⓥ 제한하다 • horizontal ⓐ 수평의
- soil ⓝ 토양 • interfere with ~을 방해하다
- development ⓝ 발달 • in turn 결국, 결과적으로

식물의 성장은 식물의 줄기와 뿌리의 끝에서 발견되는 옥신이라고 불리는
호르몬 그룹에 의해 조절된다. 줄기의 끝에서 생산된 옥신은 그늘진 곳에
있는 줄기의 옆면에 축적되는 경향이 있다. 따라서, 옥신은 식물의 그늘진
면에서의 성장을 ① 자극한다. 그러므로 그늘진 면은 햇빛을 마주하는 면보다
더 빨리 자란다. 이 현상은 줄기가 휘어지게 하고 빛을 ② 향하여 성장하는
것처럼 보이게 한다. 옥신은 식물의 뿌리에서는 ③ 반대의 효과를 가진다.
뿌리 끝에 있는 옥신은 성장을 억제하는 경향이 있다. 만약 하나의 뿌리가 토양
속에서 수평이라면, 옥신은 아래쪽에 축적되어 그것의 발달을 방해할 것이다.
그러므로 뿌리의 아래쪽은 위쪽보다 ④ 더 빠르게(→ 더 느리게) 자라게 된다.
이것은 결과적으로 뿌리가 ⑤ 아래로 휘어지게 하고 뿌리의 끝부분은 그
방향으로 자란다.

〉왜 정답? ★★★ [정답률 53%]
④ faster 더 빠르게

> 만약 하나의 뿌리가 토양 속에서 수평이라면, 옥신은 아래쪽에
> 축적되어 그것의 발달을 방해할 것이다. 그러므로 뿌리의 아래쪽은
> 위쪽보다 ④ 더 빠르게 자라게 된다.
> 　　　　더 느리게

➡ 뿌리 끝에 있는 옥신은 성장을 억제하는 경향이 있어서 옥신이 뿌리 아래쪽에
축적되면 뿌리의 발달을 방해한다고 했다. 그러므로 뿌리 아래쪽은 위쪽보다 '더
빠르게' 자란다는 것은 문맥에 맞지 않는다.
▶ faster를 slower(더 느리게)와 같은 반의어로 바꿔야 함

〉왜 오답?
① stimulate 자극하다

> 따라서, 옥신은 식물의 그늘진 면에서의 성장을 ① 자극한다. 그러므로
> 그늘진 면은 햇빛을 마주하는 면보다 더 빨리 자란다.

➡ 이어지는 문장에서 그늘진 면이 햇빛을 마주하는 면보다 더 빨리 자란다고
했으므로, 옥신은 식물의 그늘진 부분에서의 성장을 '자극할' 것이다.
▶ stimulate는 문맥에 맞음

② towards 향하여

> 이 현상은 줄기가 휘어지게 하고 빛을 ② 향하여 성장하는 것처럼
> 보이게 한다.

➡ 그늘진 면이 햇빛을 마주하는 면보다 더 빨리 자라서 줄기가 휘어진다고 했으므로
빛을 '향하여' 자라는 것처럼 보일 것이다.
▶ towards는 문맥에 맞음

③ opposite 반대의

> 옥신은 식물의 뿌리에서는 ③ 반대의 효과를 가진다. 뿌리 끝에 있는
> 옥신은 성장을 억제하는 경향이 있다.

➡ 앞에서는 옥신이 줄기의 성장을 자극한다고 했는데, 이어지는 문장에서 뿌리
끝에서는 옥신이 성장을 억제한다고 했으므로 '반대의' 효과임을 알 수 있다.
▶ opposite은 문맥에 맞음

⑤ downwards 아래로

> 이것은 결과적으로 뿌리가 ⑤ 아래로 휘어지게 하고 뿌리의 끝부분은
> 그 방향으로 자란다.

➡ 앞에서 뿌리 아래쪽의 발달을 방해한다고 했으므로 '아래로' 휘어지게 할 것이다.
▶ downwards는 문맥에 맞음

31 정답 ③ ＊성과를 향상하는 자유의 제한

부사적 용법(목적)
To demonstrate / how best to defeat the habit of delaying, /
설명하기 위해 / 미루는 습관을 가장 잘 무너뜨리는 방법을 /

Dan Ariely, **a professor of psychology and behavioral economics**, / performed an experiment on students / in three of his classes at MIT. //
심리학 및 행동경제학 교수인 Dan Ariely는 / 학생들을 대상으로 실험을 수행했다 / MIT에서의 자신의 수업 중 세 개에서 //

간접목적어　　직접목적어
He assigned **all classes three reports** / over the course of the semester. //
그는 모든 수업에 세 개의 보고서를 과제로 부여했다 / 학기 과정 동안 //

The first class had to choose / three due dates / for themselves, / up to and including the last day of class. //
첫 번째 수업(의 학생들)은 선택해야 했다 / 세 개의 마감일을 / 스스로 / 종강일을 포함한 날짜까지 //

The second had no deadlines / — all three papers just had to be submitted / by the last day of class. //
두 번째는 마감일이 없었고 / 세 개의 보고서가 모두 제출되기만 하면 되었다 / 종강일까지 //

간접목적어　　직접목적어
In his third class, / he gave **students three set deadlines** / over the course of the semester. //
그의 세 번째 수업에서 / 그는 학생들에게 세 개의 정해진 마감일을 주었다 / 학기 과정 동안 //

목적어절 접속사
At the end of the semester, / he found / **that** students with set deadlines received the best grades, /
학기 말에 / 그는 알아냈다 / 마감일이 정해진 학생들이 최고의 성적을 받았다는 것을 /

= students
the students with no deadlines had the worst, / and **those** who could choose their own deadlines / fell somewhere in the middle. // **단서 1** 과제의 마감일이 정해질수록 학생들의 성적이 좋음
마감일이 없는 학생들은 최하의 성적을 받았고 / 자신의 마감일을 선택할 수 있었던 학생들은 / 그 중간 어디쯤의 위치에 있었다(는 것을) //

목적어절 접속사　　**단서 2** 자기 통제와 성과를 향상함
Ariely concludes / **that restricting freedom** / — whether by the professor / or by students **who** recognize their own tendencies to delay things / — improves self-control and performance. //
주격 관계대명사
Ariely는 결론짓는다 / 자유를 제한하는 것은 / 교수에 의해서든 / 혹은 학생에 의해서든 / 일을 미루는 자신의 성향을 인식한 / 자기 통제와 성과를 향상한다고 //

- demonstrate ⓥ 보여주다, 설명하다　• defeat ⓥ 패배시키다, 이기다
- delay ⓥ 미루다　• behavioral ⓐ 행동의, 행동에 관한
- assign ⓥ 맡기다, 배정하다　• due date 마감일, 만기일
- for oneself 스스로　• submit ⓥ 제출하다
- conclude ⓥ 결론을 내리다　• restrict ⓥ 제한하다
- recognize ⓥ 인식하다　• tendency ⓝ 경향, 성향
- performance ⓝ 수행, 성과　• reward ⓝ 보상
- obstacle ⓝ 장애물　• assignment ⓝ 과제
- competition ⓝ 경쟁

미루는 습관을 가장 잘 무너뜨리는 방법을 설명하기 위해, 심리학 및 행동경제학 교수인 Dan Ariely는 MIT의 자신의 수업 중 세 개에서 학생들을 대상으로 실험을 수행했다. 그는 학기 과정 동안 모든 수업에 세 개의 보고서를 과제로 부여했다. 첫 번째 수업의 학생들은 종강일까지 포함해서 세 개의 마감일을 스스로 선택해야 했다. 두 번째는 마감일이 없었고, 세 개의 보고서 모두 종강일까지 제출되기만 하면 되었다. 그의 세 번째 수업에서, 그는 학기 과정 동안 학생들에게 세 개의 정해진 마감일을 주었다. 학기 말에, 그는 마감일이 정해진 학생들이 최고의 성적을 받았고, 마감일이 없는 학생들은 최하의 성적을 받았으며, 자신의 마감일을 선택할 수 있었던 학생들은 그 중간 어디쯤의 위치에 있었다는 것을 알아냈다. Ariely는, 교수에 의해서든 혹은 일을 미루는 자신의 성향을 인식한 학생들에 의해서든, **자유를 제한하는 것**은 자기 통제와 성과를 향상한다고 결론짓는다.

다음 빈칸에 들어갈 말로 가장 적절한 것을 고르시오.

① offering rewards 과제에 대한 보상은 언급되지 않음
　보상을 제공하는 것
② removing obstacles 장애물을 제거하라는 내용이 아님
　장애물을 제거하는 것
③ restricting freedom 마감일을 주는 것은 자유를 제한하는 것임
　자유를 제한하는 것
④ increasing assignments 과제의 양은 늘리지 않았음
　과제를 늘리는 것
⑤ encouraging competition 각 그룹의 학생들이 경쟁하는 것이 아님
　경쟁을 권장하는 것

왜 정답? ＊＊❀ [정답률 66%]

빈칸 문장	Ariely는, 교수에 의해서든 혹은 일을 미루는 자신의 성향을 인식한 학생들에 의해서든, _____은 자기 통제와 성과를 향상한다고 결론짓는다.

➡ 빈칸 문장: Ariely는 '무엇이' 자기 통제와 성과를 향상한다고 결론지었다.
➡ Ariely의 실험 결과:
　그룹 **1**: 과제의 마감일을 스스로 선택함 ➡ 중간 정도의 성적
　그룹 **2**: 과제의 마감일이 없음 ➡ 최하의 성적
　그룹 **3**: 과제마다 마감일이 정해져 있음 ➡ 최고의 성적
　▶ '마감일'이 존재한다는 것은 '자유가 제한'된다는 것이므로 자기 통제와 성과를 향상하는 것은 ③ '자유를 제한하는 것'이다.

왜 오답?

① 주어진 과제에 서로 다른 보상을 제공하는 실험을 한 것이 아니다.
② 오히려 장애물이라고 할 수 있는 마감일을 부여하는 것에 대해 긍정적으로 말하고 있다. (➤ 이유: 마감일이 정해지면 자유로운 과제 수행에 제한이 생기므로 장애물이라고 볼 수 있다.)
④ 모든 수업에서 과제의 양을 늘리거나 줄이지 않았으므로 적절하지 않다.
⑤ 세 그룹의 학생들이 서로 경쟁하도록 한 것이 아니다.

2022.11

12회

32 정답 ② ＊삶을 바꾼 상호 의존

「전치사+관계대명사」
The best way / **in which** innovation changes our lives / is by **enabling people to work for each other**. //
최고의 방법은 / 혁신이 우리의 삶을 바꾸는 / 사람들이 서로를 위해 일할 수 있도록 함으로써이다 /

주격 보어절 접속사
The main theme of human history / is **that** we become steadily more specialized / in **what** we produce, / and steadily more diversified / in what we consume: /
선행사를 포함하는 관계대명사
인류 역사의 주요한 주제는 / 우리가 꾸준히 더 전문화된다는 것이다 / 우리가 생산하는 것에 / 그리고 꾸준히 더 다양화된다(는 것이다) / 우리가 소비하는 것에 /

we move away / from unstable self-sufficiency / to safer mutual interdependence. // **단서 1** 우리는 불안정한 자급자족에서 서로 간의 상호 의존으로 옮겨감
즉, 우리는 옮겨간다 / 불안정한 자급자족에서 / 더 안전한 서로 간의 상호 의존으로 //

by v-ing: ~함으로써
By concentrating on serving other people's needs / for forty hours a week / — which we call a job /
다른 사람들의 필요를 충족시키는 것에 집중함으로써 / 일주일에 40시간 동안 / 그것을 우리는 직업이라고 부르는데 /

— you can spend the other seventy-two hours / (not counting fifty-six hours in bed) / relying on the services / **provided** to you by other people. // **단서 2** 우리는 타인의 필요를 충족시키기 위해 일하고,
앞에 주격 관계대명사와 be동사가 생략됨　　남은 시간에는 다른 사람들이 제공하는 서비스에 의지함
여러분은 나머지 72시간을 보낼 수 있다 / (잠자는 56시간은 계산에 넣지 않고) / 서비스에 의지하여 / 다른 사람들에 의해 여러분에게 제공되는 /

가목적어　　진목적어
Innovation has made **it** possible **to work** for a fraction of a second / in order to be able to afford / to turn on an electric lamp / for an hour, / **단서 3** 혁신을 통해 우리가 일하는 시간이 짧아짐
혁신은 아주 짧은 시간 동안 일하는 것을 가능하게 했다 / 여유를 가질 수 있게 하기 위해 / 전등을 켜는 / 한 시간 동안 /

분사구문을 이끄는 현재분사 　주격 관계대명사
providing the quantity of light / **that** would have required a
whole day's work / if you had to make it yourself /
빛의 양을 제공하면서 / 하루 종일의 노동을 필요로 했었을 / 여러분이 그것을 스스로
만들어야 했다면 /
　　　　　　　　　　　　　　　　　　　　　　　부사적 용법(목적)
by collecting and refining sesame oil or lamb fat / **to burn** in a
simple lamp, / as much of humanity did / in the not so distant
past. //
참기름이나 양의 지방을 모으고 정제함으로써 / 간단한 등을 켜기 위해 / 많은 인류가 그랬던
것처럼 / 그리 멀지 않은 과거에 //

- innovation ⓝ 혁신　・ theme ⓝ 주제　・ steadily ⓐ๋d 꾸준히
- specialized ⓐ 전문화된　・ diversified ⓐ 다양화된, 여러 가지의
- unstable ⓐ 불안정한　・ self-sufficiency ⓝ 자급자족
- mutual ⓐ 서로의, 상호간의　・ interdependence ⓝ 상호 의존
- concentrate ⓥ 집중하다　・ rely ⓥ 의존하다, 믿다
- afford ⓥ (금전적·시간적) 여유[형편]가 되다　・ sesame oil 참기름
- lamb ⓝ 어린 양　・ humanity ⓝ 인류　・ creatively ⓐ๋d 창의적으로
- personalized ⓐ 개인화된　・ commercialize ⓥ 상품화하다

혁신이 우리의 삶을 바꾸는 최고의 방법은 **사람들이 서로를 위해 일할 수 있도록 함**으로써이다. 인류 역사의 주요한 주제는 우리가 생산하는 데 꾸준히 더 전문화되고 소비하는 데 꾸준히 더 다양화되는 것이다. 즉, 우리는 불안정한 자급자족에서 더 안전한 서로 간의 상호 의존으로 옮겨간다는 것이다. 일주일에 40시간 동안 사람들의 필요를 충족시키는 것, 즉 우리가 직업이라고 부르는 것에 집중함으로써, 여러분은 다른 사람들에 의해 여러분에게 제공되는 서비스에 의지하여 나머지 72시간(잠자는 56시간은 계산에 넣지 않고)을 보낼 수 있다. 혁신은 전등을 한 시간 동안 켜는 여유를 가질 수 있게 하기 위해 아주 짧은 시간 동안 일하는 것을 가능하게 했고, 그것은 만약 여러분이 그리 멀지 않은 과거에 많은 인류가 했던 것처럼 단순한 등을 켜기 위해 참기름이나 양의 지방을 모으고 정제함으로써 그것을 스스로 만들어야 했다면 하루 종일의 노동을 필요로 했었을 빛의 양을 제공했다.

다음 빈칸에 들어갈 말로 가장 적절한 것을 고르시오. [3점]
① respecting the values of the old days
　지난날의 가치를 존중함　　　　　　　　혁신으로 과거보다 효율적으로 일하게 됨
②enabling people to work for each other
　사람들이 서로를 위해 일할 수 있도록 함　자급자족에서 상호 의존으로 옮겨간다고 했음
③ providing opportunities to think creatively
　창의적으로 생각하는 기회를 제공함　　　창의적인 생각을 강조하는 내용이 아님
④ satisfying customers with personalized services
　개인화된 서비스로 고객을 만족시킴　　　개인화가 아니라 서로 의존한다고 함
⑤ introducing and commercializing unusual products
　이색적인 상품을 소개하고 상품화함　　　이색적인 상품에 관한 글이 아님

| 문제 풀이 순서 | ★★★ [정답률 45%]

1st 먼저 빈칸 문장을 읽고, 빈칸에 들어갈 말을 예측한다.

| 빈칸 문장 | 혁신이 우리의 삶을 바꾸는 최고의 방법은 ＿＿＿으로써이다. |

➡ '무엇을 함으로써' 우리의 삶이 바뀌었다고 했으므로, (단서)
혁신이 어떻게 우리의 삶을 바꿨는지에 대해 설명할 것이다. (발상)

2nd 글의 나머지 부분을 읽고, 혁신이 의미하는 바가 무엇인지 찾는다.

- 우리의 생산은 전문화되고 소비는 다양화됨(불안정한 자급자족 → 서로 간의 상호 의존) (단서1)　이것이 바로 혁신! (꿀팁)
- 일주일에 40시간은 다른 사람을 위해 일하고, 나머지 72시간은 다른 사람이 제공하는 서비스에 의지함 (단서2)

➡ 이를 통해 인류는 과거와는 달리 짧은 시간에 효율적으로 일할 수 있게 되었다. (단서3)
▶ 즉, 혁신은 ②'사람들이 서로를 위해 일할 수 있도록 함'으로써 우리의 삶을 바꿨다.

| 선택지 분석 |

① **respecting the values of the old days**
　지난날의 가치를 존중함
과거보다 전문화되고 다양화된 것을 긍정적으로 말하는 글이다.

② **enabling people to work for each other**
　사람들이 서로를 위해 일할 수 있도록 함
자급자족하던 과거의 삶에서 벗어나 서로의 서비스에 의존하게 됐다고 했다.

③ **providing opportunities to think creatively**
　창의적으로 생각하는 기회를 제공함
창의적인 생각을 강조하는 내용은 없었다.

④ **satisfying customers with personalized services**
　개인화된 서비스로 고객을 만족시킴
개인화가 아니라 전문화되었다고 했으며, 고객 만족은 언급되지 않았다.

⑤ **introducing and commercializing unusual products**
　이색적인 상품을 소개하고 상품화함
상품을 소개하고 상품화하는 것과 관련된 내용이 아니다.

33 정답 ③ ＊스스로 유혹 차단하기

If you've ever made a poor choice, / you might be interested / in
　　　　　how to-v: ~하는 법
learning **how to break** that habit. //
여러분이 한 번이라도 좋지 못한 선택을 한 적이 있다면 / 여러분은 관심이 있을지도 모른다 /
그 습관을 깨는 방법을 배우는 데 /
　　　　　　형용사적 용법(way 수식)　　　　　　명사적 용법(주격 보어)
One great way / **to trick** your brain into doing so / is **to sign** a
"Ulysses Contract." //
한 가지 좋은 방법은 / 그렇게 하도록 여러분의 뇌를 속이는 / 'Ulysses 계약'에 서명하는
것이다 //

The name of this life tip / comes from the Greek myth about
　　　　　　　동격
Ulysses, / a captain whose ship sailed past the island of **the**
　　　　　소유격 관계대명사
Sirens, / a tribe of dangerous women /
　　　　　동격
이러한 인생 조언의 이름은 / Ulysses에 관한 그리스 신화에서 유래되었다 / 사이렌의 섬을
자신의 배로 항해해 지나갔던 선장인 / 위험한 여성 부족인 /
주격 관계대명사
who lured victims to their death / with their irresistible songs. //
희생자들을 죽음으로 유혹한 / 저항할 수 없는 노래로 //

Knowing that he would otherwise be unable to resist, /
그가 그렇게 하지 않으면 저항할 수 없다는 것을 알고 /

Ulysses instructed his crew / **to stuff** their ears with cotton / and
　　　　　　　　　　　　　　　　　병렬 구조
tie him to the ship's mast / **to prevent** him from turning their
　　　　　　　　　　　　　　부사적 용법(목적)
ship / towards the Sirens. // (단서1) Ulysses는 사이렌의 유혹을 이겨 내기 위해
스스로 배에 묶었음
Ulysses는 자신의 선원들을 지시했다 / 그들의 귀를 솜으로 막으라고 / 그리고 그를 배의
돛대에 묶으라고 / 그가 배를 돌리는 것을 막기 위해 / 사이렌에게로 //

It worked for him / and you can do the same thing / by **locking
yourself** / **out of your temptations**. //
그것은 그에게 효과가 있었다 / 그리고 여러분은 같은 일을 할 수 있다 / 스스로를
차단함으로써 / 여러분의 유혹으로부터 //　(단서2) 휴대 전화를 어떻게 멀리할
수 있을지를 예시로 제시함
For example, / if you want to stay off your cellphone / and
　　　　　　　　　　　　　　　　　　　　주격 관계대명사
concentrate on your work, / **delete** the apps **that** distract you /
　　　　　　　　　　　　　병렬 구조
or **ask** a friend to change your password! //
예를 들어 / 만약 여러분이 휴대 전화를 멀리하고 싶다면 / 그리고 여러분의 일에 집중하고
(싶다면) / 여러분의 주의를 산만하게 하는 앱들을 삭제하라 / 또는 친구에게 여러분의
비밀번호를 바꿔 달라고 요청하라 //

- trick ⓥ 속이다　・ contract ⓝ 계약　・ myth ⓝ 신화
- tribe ⓝ 부족　・ victim ⓝ 희생자　・ irresistible ⓐ 저항할 수 없는
- otherwise ⓐ๋d 그렇지 않으면　・ resist ⓥ 저항하다
- instruct ⓥ 지시하다　・ crew ⓝ (배·비행기의) 선원[승무원]
- stuff ⓥ 채워 넣다　・ temptation ⓝ 유혹
- concentrate ⓥ 집중하다　・ distract ⓥ 주의를 산만하게 하다
- mindset ⓝ 사고방식　・ track ⓥ 추적하다　・ progress ⓝ 과정

여러분이 한 번이라도 좋지 못한 선택을 한 적이 있다면, 여러분은 그 습관을 깨는 방법을 배우는 데 관심이 있을지도 모른다. 그렇게 하도록 여러분의 뇌를 속이는 한 가지 좋은 방법은 'Ulysses 계약'에 서명하는 것이다. 이러한 인생 조언의 이름은 저항할 수 없는 노래로 희생자들을 죽음으로 유혹한 위험한 여성 부족인 사이렌의 섬을 자신의 배로 항해해 지나갔던 선장 Ulysses에 관한 그리스 신화에서 유래되었다. 그렇게 하지 않으면 저항할 수 없다는 것을 알고, Ulysses는 자신이 배를 사이렌에게로 돌리는 것을 막기 위해 자신의 선원들이 그들의 귀를 솜으로 막고 그를 배의 돛대에 묶으라고 지시했다. 그것은 그에게 효과가 있었고 여러분은 **여러분의 유혹으로부터 스스로를 차단함**으로써 같은 일을 할 수 있다. 예를 들어, 만약 여러분이 휴대 전화를 멀리하고 여러분의 일에 집중하고 싶다면, 여러분의 주의를 산만하게 하는 앱들을 삭제하거나 친구에게 여러분의 비밀번호를 바꿔 달라고 요청하라!

다음 빈칸에 들어갈 말로 가장 적절한 것을 고르시오.

① letting go of all-or-nothing mindset
모 아니면 도라는 사고방식을 버림 │ 극단적인 사고방식을 버리라는 내용이 아님
② finding reasons why you want to change
여러분이 변하고싶은 이유를 찾음 │ 이유를 찾아야 한다는 내용은 언급되지 않음
③ locking yourself out of your temptations
여러분의 유혹으로부터 스스로를 차단함 │ 스스로 유혹을 차단하기 위한 노력을 하라고 함
④ building a plan and tracking your progress
계획을 수립하고 여러분의 진행 과정을 추적함 │ 계획 수립과 진행 과정에 대한 내용이 아님
⑤ focusing on breaking one bad habit at a time
한 번에 나쁜 습관 하나씩 깨는 데 집중함 │ 한 번에 하나씩 해결하라는 내용이 아님

왜 정답? ❋❋❋ [정답률 61%]

빈칸 문장	그것은 그에게 효과가 있었고 여러분은 _____으로써 같은 일을 할 수 있다.
빈칸 문장 앞 예시	그렇게 하지 않으면 저항할 수 없다는 것을 알고 Ulysses는 자신이 배를 사이렌으로 돌리는 것을 막기 위해 자신의 선원들이 그들의 귀를 솜으로 막고 그를 배의 돛대에 묶으라고 지시했다. 단서 1

➡ 빈칸 문장: 그에게 그것이 효과가 있었듯, 여러분도 '무엇을 함'으로써 같은 일을 할 수 있다. 단서
▶ '그'가 누구이고, '그것'은 무엇인지를 확인해야 한다. 발상

➡ 빈칸 문장 앞 예시: Ulysses(= 그)는 사이렌에게 유혹되지 않기 위해 스스로 배에 묶였다(= 그것).

| 빈칸 문장 뒤 예시 | 예를 들어(For example), 만약 여러분이 휴대 전화를 멀리하고 여러분의 일에 집중하고 싶다면, 여러분의 주의를 산만하게 하는 앱들을 삭제하거나 친구에게 여러분의 비밀번호를 바꿔 달라고 요청하라! 단서 2 |

➡ 빈칸 문장 뒤 예시: Ulysses가 스스로를 사이렌에게서 차단했듯, 휴대 전화의 앱들을 삭제하거나 비밀번호를 바꿈으로써 휴대 전화를 멀리할 수 있다.
▶ 따라서 ③ '여러분의 유혹으로부터 스스로를 차단함'으로써 여러분도 Ulysses와 같은 일을 할 수 있다는 것이다.

왜 오답?
① 극단적인 사고방식을 버리라는 글이 아니다.
② 변하고자 하는 이유를 찾는 것이 중요하다는 내용이 아니다.
④ 계획 수립과 그 진행 과정에 대한 내용이 아니다. 함정
⑤ 첫 문장에 나온 break, habit을 넣어 만든 오답으로, 나쁜 습관을 한 번에 하나씩 해결하라고 조언하는 내용이 아니다.

---

34 정답 ③ ✱실내 생활이 진화를 만든다?

단서 1 집은 실내 생활에 적응된 종을 수용하고 새로운 방향으로 진화하게 함

Our homes aren't just ecosystems, / they're unique ones, / hosting species / that are adapted to indoor environments / and pushing evolution in new directions. //
└병렬구조┘
우리의 집은 단순한 생태계가 아니다 / 그것들은 독특한 곳이다 / 종들을 수용하고 / 실내 환경에 적응된 / 새로운 방향으로 진화를 밀어붙이면서 //

단서 2 살충제와 독 등에 대한 내성을 키우며 진화했음

Indoor microbes, insects, and rats have all evolved / the ability to survive our chemical attacks, / developing resistance to antibacterials, insecticides, and poisons. //
형용사적 용법(ability 수식) 주어 분사구문
실내 미생물, 곤충, 그리고 쥐들은 모두 진화시켜 왔다 / 우리의 화학적 공격에서 살아남을 수 있는 능력을 / 항균제, 살충제, 그리고 독에 대한 내성을 키우면서 //

German cockroaches are known / to have developed a distaste for glucose, / which is commonly used as bait / in roach traps. //
계속적 용법의 주격 관계대명사
독일 바퀴벌레는 알려져 있다 / 포도당에 대한 혐오감을 발달시켜 왔다고 / 그리고 그것은 미끼로 흔히 사용된다 / 바퀴벌레 덫에 //

Some indoor insects, / which have fewer opportunities to feed / than their outdoor counterparts, / seem to have developed the ability to survive / when food is limited. //
주어 계속적 용법의 주격 관계대명사 본동사
일부 실내 곤충들은 / 먹이를 잡아먹을 더 적은 기회를 가지는데 / 야외(에 사는) 상대방에 비해 / 생존할 수 있는 능력을 발달시켜 온 것으로 보인다 / 먹이가 제한적일 때 //

Dunn and other ecologists have suggested / that as the planet becomes more developed and more urban, / more species will evolve the traits / they need to thrive indoors. //
목적어절 접속사 앞에 목적격 관계대명사 생략
Dunn과 다른 생태학자들은 말해 왔다 / 지구가 점점 더 발전되고 도시화되면서 / 더 많은 종들이 특성들을 진화시킬 것이라고 / 실내에서 번성하기 위해 그들이 필요로 하는 //

단서 3 실내 생활은 우리도 진화하게 만들었음

Over a long enough time period, / indoor living could drive our evolution, too. //
충분히 긴 시간에 걸쳐 / 실내 생활은 또한 우리의 진화를 이끌 수 있었다 //

Perhaps my indoorsy self / represents the future of humanity. //
아마도 실내 생활을 좋아하는 내 모습은 / 인류의 미래를 대변할 것이다 //

- ecosystem ⓝ 생태계 · adapt ⓥ 적응하다 · evolution ⓝ 진화
- microbe ⓝ 미생물 · evolve ⓥ 진화하다
- resistance ⓝ 저항(력), 내성 · antibacterial ⓝ 항균제
- insecticide ⓝ 살충제 · cockroach ⓝ 바퀴벌레(= roach)
- distaste ⓝ 혐오감, 불쾌감 · counterpart ⓝ 상대(방)
- ecologist ⓝ 생태학자 · urban ⓐ 도시의 · trait ⓝ 특성, 속성
- thrive ⓥ 번성하다, 번창하다 · indoorsy ⓐ 실내 생활을 좋아하는
- humanity ⓝ 인류 · extinct ⓐ 멸종된 · habitat ⓝ 서식지

우리의 집은 단순한 생태계가 아니라 독특한 곳이며, 실내 환경에 적응된 종들을 수용하고 새로운 방향으로 진화를 밀어붙인다. 실내 미생물, 곤충, 그리고 쥐들은 모두 항균제, 살충제, 독에 대한 내성을 키우면서 우리의 화학적 공격에서 살아남을 수 있는 능력을 진화시켜 왔다. 독일 바퀴벌레는 바퀴벌레 덫에서 미끼로 흔히 사용되는 포도당에 대한 혐오감을 발달시켜 온 것으로 알려져 있다. 야외(에 사는) 상대방에 비해 먹이를 잡아먹을 더 적은 기회를 가지는 일부 실내 곤충은 먹이가 제한적일 때 생존할 수 있는 능력을 발달시켜 온 것으로 보인다. Dunn과 다른 생태학자들은 지구가 점점 더 발전되고 도시화되면서, 더 많은 종들이 **실내에서 번성하기 위해 그들이 필요로 하는 특성들을 진화시킬** 것이라고 말해 왔다. 충분히 긴 시간에 걸쳐, 실내 생활은 또한 우리의 진화를 이끌 수 있었다. 아마도 실내 생활을 좋아하는 내 모습은 인류의 미래를 대변할 것이다.

다음 빈칸에 들어갈 말로 가장 적절한 것을 고르시오. [3점]

① produce chemicals to protect themselves
자신을 보호하기 위해 화학 물질을 생산하다 │ 화학 물질을 생산하는 종에 대한 언급은 없음
② become extinct with the destroyed habitats
파괴된 서식지와 함께 멸종하다 │ 서식지 파괴, 종의 멸종과 관련된 내용이 아님
③ evolve the traits they need to thrive indoors
실내에서 번성하기 위해 그들이 필요로 하는 특성들을 진화시키다 │ 실내 생활에 적응하기 위해 진화했음
④ compete with outside organisms to find their prey
먹이를 찾기 위해 외부 유기체와 경쟁하다 │ 외부 유기체와 경쟁한다는 내용이 아님
⑤ break the boundaries between wildlife and humans
야생 동물과 인간 사이의 경계를 허물다 │ 야생 동물과 인간과의 경계에 대한 글이 아님

2022.11

12회

1st 먼저 빈칸 문장을 읽고, 빈칸에 들어갈 말을 예측한다.

| 빈칸 문장 | Dunn과 다른 생태학자들은 지구가 점점 더 발전되고 도시화되면서, 더 많은 종들이 ＿＿＿＿＿＿＿ 것이라고 말해 왔다. |

➡ 지구가 발전하면서 더 많은 종들이 '어떠할' 것이라고 했으므로, **단서** 도시화에 따라 생물들이 '어떻게' 되었는지 파악해야 한다. **발상**

2nd 글의 나머지 부분을 확인해서 정답을 찾는다.

| 글의 앞부분 | • 우리의 집은 단순한 생태계가 아니라 독특한 곳이며, 실내 환경에 적응된 종들을 수용하고 새로운 방향으로 진화를 밀어붙인다. **단서 1**
• 실내 미생물, 곤충, 그리고 쥐들은 모두 항균제, 살충제, 독에 대한 내성을 키우면서 우리의 화학적 공격에서 살아남을 수 있는 능력을 진화시켜 왔다. **단서 2** |

➡ 집은 미생물, 곤충, 쥐 등에게 화학적 공격을 가하지만, 동시에 그들이 내성을 키워 살아남도록 하는 새로운 방향의 진화를 이끈다.
▶ 빈칸 문장의 species의 예시로 실내 미생물, 곤충, 쥐를 제시함

| 글의 뒷부분 | • 충분히 긴 시간에 걸쳐, 실내 생활은 또한 우리의 진화를 이끌 수 있었다. **단서 3**
• 아마도 실내 생활을 좋아하는 내 모습은 인류의 미래를 대변할 것이다. |

➡ 실내 생활은 앞서 언급한 생물뿐 아니라 인류의 진화도 이끌었다.
▶ 즉, 지구가 발전하면서 더 많은 종들이 ③ '실내에서 번성하기 위해 그들이 필요로 하는 특성들을 진화시킬' 것이다.

| 선택지 분석 |

① **produce chemicals to protect themselves**
자신을 보호하기 위해 화학 물질을 생산하다
화학적 공격에서 살아남을 수 있는 능력을 진화시켜 온 종들에 대한 언급은 있지만, 화학 물질을 생산하는 종에 대해서는 언급되지 않았다.

② **become extinct with the destroyed habitats**
파괴된 서식지와 함께 멸종하다
파괴된 서식지나 종의 멸종과 관련된 내용은 언급하지 않았다.

③ **evolve the traits they need to thrive indoors**
실내에서 번성하기 위해 그들이 필요로 하는 특성들을 진화시키다
예시를 통해 여러 종이 실내 환경에 적응하기 위해 진화했음을 설명했다.

④ **compete with outside organisms to find their prey**
먹이를 찾기 위해 외부 유기체와 경쟁하다
먹이를 잡아먹을 기회가 적은 일부 실내 곤충이 진화했다고 한 것은 하나의 예시이다.

⑤ **break the boundaries between wildlife and humans**
야생 동물과 인간 사이의 경계를 허물다
야생 동물과 인간이 가까워진다는 내용이라고 볼 수 없다.

35 정답 ④ *시가 주는 이점

다음 글에서 전체 흐름과 관계 없는 문장은?

동명사 주어(단수 취급) 단수 동사
Developing a personal engagement with poetry / brings a number of benefits to you / as an individual, / in both a personal and a professional capacity. // 핵심문장, 단서 1 시는 개인에게 많은 이점을 가져다줌
시와의 개인적 관계를 발전시키는 것은 / 여러분에게 많은 이점을 가져다준다 / 한 개인으로서 / 개인적인 능력과 전문적인 능력 모두에서 //

① Writing poetry has been shown / to have physical and mental benefits, /
시를 쓰는 것은 보여져 왔다 / 신체적, 정신적 이점을 지닌 것으로 /
with+(대명사)+분사: ~하면서
with expressive writing found / to improve immune system and
to부정사의 병렬 구조
lung function, / diminish psychological distress, / and enhance relationships.
표현적 글쓰기가 밝혀지면서 / 면역 체계와 폐 기능을 향상하고 / 심리적 고통을 줄이고 / 관계를 증진하는 것으로 //

② Poetry has long been used / to aid different mental health
to부정사의 병렬 구조
needs, / develop empathy, / and reconsider our relationship / with both natural and built environments. //
시는 오랫동안 사용되어 왔다 / 여러 정신 건강에 필요한 것들을 돕기 위해 / 공감 능력을 개발하기 위해 / 그리고 우리의 관계를 재고하기 위해 / 자연적 환경과 만들어진 환경 모두와의 //

③ Poetry is also an incredibly effective way / of actively targeting the cognitive development period, / improving your
분사구문
productivity and scientific creativity / in the process. //
시는 또한 믿을 수 없을 정도로 효과적인 방법이다 / 인지 발달 시기를 적극적으로 겨냥하는 / 여러분의 생산성과 과학적 창의력을 향상하면서 / 그 과정에서 //

④ Poetry is considered / to be an easy and useful means of expressing emotions, / but you fall into frustration / when you
부사절 접속사
realize its complexity. //)
(시는 여겨진다 / 감정을 표현하는 쉽고 유용한 수단으로 / 하지만 여러분은 좌절감에 빠진다 / 여러분이 그것의 복잡성을 깨달을 때 //)

⑤ In short, / poetry has a lot to offer, / if you give it the
형용사적 용법(opportunity 수식)
opportunity to do so. // 단서 2 시는 개인에게 제공할 많은 것을 가지고 있음
간단히 말해서 / 시는 제공할 많은 것을 가지고 있다 / 만약 여러분이 시에게 그렇게 할 기회를 준다면 //

- engagement ⓝ 관계 ・ poetry ⓝ (집합적으로) 시
- benefit ⓝ 이점, 혜택 ・ professional ⓐ 전문적인
- capacity ⓝ 능력, 용량 ・ expressive ⓐ 표현의, 표현적인
- immune ⓐ 면역의 ・ lung ⓝ 폐, 허파 ・ function ⓝ 기능
- diminish ⓥ 줄이다, 약화하다 ・ psychological ⓐ 심리적인
- distress ⓝ 고통 ・ enhance ⓥ (질을) 높이다, 향상하다
- aid ⓥ 지원하다, 돕다 ・ empathy ⓝ 공감 (능력)
- incredibly ⓐⓓ 믿을 수 없을 정도로 ・ target ⓥ 목표로 삼다, 겨냥하다
- productivity ⓝ 생산성 ・ frustration ⓝ 좌절감

시와의 개인적 관계를 발전시키는 것은 개인적인 능력과 전문적인 능력 모두에서 한 개인으로서의 여러분에게 많은 이점을 가져다준다. ① 표현적 글쓰기가 면역 체계와 폐 기능을 향상하고, 심리적 고통을 줄이고, 관계를 증진하는 것으로 밝혀지면서, 시를 쓰는 것은 신체적, 정신적 이점을 지닌 것으로 보여져 왔다. ② 시는 여러 정신 건강에 필요한 것들을 지원하고, 공감 능력을 개발하고, 자연적 환경과 만들어진 환경 둘 다와의 관계를 재고하기 위해 오랫동안 사용되어 왔다. ③ 시는 또한 인지 발달 시기를 적극적으로 겨냥하는 믿을 수 없을 정도로 효과적인 방법이며, 그 과정에서 여러분의 생산성과 과학적 창의력을 향상한다. (④ 시는 감정을 표현하는 쉽고 유용한 수단으로 여겨지지만, 여러분이 그것의 복잡성을 깨달았을 때 여러분은 좌절감에 빠진다.) ⑤ 간단히 말해서, 만약 여러분이 시에게 그렇게 할 기회를 준다면, 시는 제공할 많은 것을 가지고 있다.

첫 문장: 시와의 개인적 관계를 발전시키는 것은 개인적인 능력과 전문적인 능력 모두에서 한 개인으로서의 여러분에게 많은 이점을 가져다준다.

➡ 시가 개인의 여러 능력에 미치는 긍정적인 영향을 이야기하는 글이다.

① 표현적 글쓰기가 면역 체계와 폐 기능을 향상하고, 심리적 고통을 줄이고, 관계를 증진하는 것으로 밝혀지면서, 시를 쓰는 것은 신체적, 정신적 이점을 지닌 것으로 보여져 왔다.

➡ 시가 가져다주는 이점의 예시로 면역 체계 및 폐 기능 향상, 심리적 고통 감소, 관계 개선 등이 자연스럽게 이어진다.
▶ ①은 무관한 문장이 아님

② 시는 여러 정신 건강에 필요한 것들을 지원하고, 공감 능력을 개발하고, 자연적 환경과 만들어진 환경 둘 다와의 관계를 재고하기 위해 오랫동안 사용되어 왔다.

➡ 정신 건강 및 공감 능력의 향상, 환경과의 관계 개선에 활용되었다는 등 시의 이점이 앞 문장에 계속 이어진다.
▶ ②은 무관한 문장이 아님

③ 시는 또한(also) 인지 발달 시기를 적극적으로 겨냥하는 믿을 수 없을 정도로 효과적인 방법이며, 그 과정에서 여러분의 생산성과 과학적 창의력을 향상시킨다.

➡ 시의 또 다른 이점인 인지 발달 촉진, 생산성 및 창의력 향상이 연결어 also로 이어지는 자연스러운 흐름이다.
▶ ③은 무관한 문장이 아님

④ 시는 감정을 표현하는 쉽고 유용한 수단으로 여겨지지만, 여러분이 그것의 복잡성을 깨달았을 때 여러분은 좌절감에 빠진다.

➡ 계속 시의 긍정적인 효과에 관해 이야기하다가 시의 복잡성을 깨달으면 좌절하게 된다는 부정적인 내용이 이어지므로, 전체 글의 흐름에 맞지 않는다.
▶ ④이 무관한 문장임

⑤ 간단히 말해서(In short), 만약 여러분이 시에게 그렇게 할 기회를 준다면, 시는 제공할 많은 것을 가지고 있다.

➡ In short는 앞에 나온 내용을 요약하는 연결어이다. ③까지 이어진 시의 이점을 잘 활용하면 많은 이득을 얻을 수 있다면서 글을 마무리하고 있다.
▶ ⑤은 무관한 문장이 아님

＊ 글의 흐름

도입	시는 개인에게 많은 이점을 가져다줌
예시 ①	신체적, 정신적 이점을 지닌 시는 오랫동안 사용되어 옴
예시 ②	시는 생산성과 과학적 창의력을 향상함
결론	시에게 기회를 준다면 시는 우리에게 많은 것을 제공할 것임

---

36 정답 ③ ＊자동화로 대체되는 일자리

Things are changing. //
상황이 변화하고 있다 // **단서 1** 캐나다와 미국의 일자리가 자동화로 인해 위기에 처할 것임
<u>It</u> has been reported / <u>that</u> 42 percent of jobs in Canada are at risk, / and 62 percent of jobs in America / will be in danger / due to advances in automation. //
~이 보도되어 왔다 / 캐나다의 일자리 중 42퍼센트가 위기에 처해 있다고 / 그리고 미국의 일자리 중 62퍼센트가 / 위기에 처할 것이라고 / 자동화의 발전으로 인해 //

(A) However, / <u>what</u>'s difficult to automate / is the ability to creatively solve problems. // **단서 2** 앞에 자동화하기 어려운 것과 반대되는 내용이 나와야 함
하지만 / 자동화하기 어려운 것은 / 창의적으로 문제들을 해결하는 능력이다 //

Whereas workers in "doing" roles / can be replaced by robots, / <u>the role</u> of creatively solving problems / <u>is</u> more dependent on an irreplaceable individual. //
반면에 '(기계적인 일을) 하는' 역할의 노동자들은 / 로봇들에 의해 대체될 수 있다 / 창의적으로 문제를 해결하는 역할은 / 대체 불가능한 개인에 더 의존한다 //

(B) You might say / <u>that</u> the numbers seem a bit unrealistic, / but the threat is real. // **단서 3** '그 숫자들'은 주어진 글에 나온 퍼센트를 가리킴
여러분은 말할지 모른다 / 그 숫자들이 약간 비현실적으로 보인다고 / 하지만 그 위협은 현실이다 //

One fast food franchise has a robot / <u>that</u> can flip a burger in ten seconds. //
한 패스트푸드 체인점은 로봇을 가지고 있다 / 10초 안에 버거 하나를 뒤집을 수 있는 //

It is just a simple task / but the robot could replace an entire crew. // 그것은 단지 단순한 일일 뿐이다 / 하지만 그 로봇은 전체 직원을 대체할 수도 있다 //
(C) Highly skilled jobs / are also at risk. // **단서 4** 앞에 위기에 처한 다른 직업들에 대한 내용이 와야 함
고도로 숙련된 직업들 / 또한 위기에 처해 있다 //

A supercomputer, / for instance, / can suggest available treatments for specific illnesses / in an automated way, / <u>drawing on the body of medical research and data</u> / on diseases. //
슈퍼컴퓨터는 / 예를 들면 / 특정한 질병들에 대해 이용 가능한 치료법을 제안할 수 있다 / 자동화된 방식으로 / 방대한 양의 의학 연구와 데이터를 이용하여 / 질병에 대한 //

- at risk 위험에 처한
- advance ⓝ 발전, 진전
- automation ⓝ 자동화
- automate ⓥ 자동화하다
- dependent ⓐ 의존하는
- irreplaceable ⓐ 대체할 수 없는
- unrealistic ⓐ 비현실적인
- threat ⓝ 위협
- flip ⓥ (휙) 뒤집다
- task ⓝ (해야 할) 일, 업무
- draw on ~을 이용하다

상황이 변화하고 있다. 캐나다의 일자리 중 42퍼센트가 위기에 처해 있고, 미국의 일자리 중 62퍼센트가 자동화의 발전으로 인해 위기에 처할 것이라고 보도되어 왔다. (B) 여러분은 그 숫자들이 약간 비현실적으로 보인다고 말할지 모르지만, 그 위협은 현실이다. 한 패스트푸드 체인점은 10초 안에 버거 하나를 뒤집을 수 있는 로봇을 가지고 있다. 그것은 단지 단순한 일일 뿐이지만 그 로봇은 전체 직원을 대체할 수도 있다. (C) 고도로 숙련된 직업들 또한 위기에 처해 있다. 예를 들면, 슈퍼컴퓨터는 질병에 대한 방대한 양의 의학 연구와 데이터를 이용하여 특정한 질병들에 대해 이용 가능한 치료법을 자동화된 방식으로 제안할 수 있다. (A) 하지만, 자동화하기 어려운 것은 창의적으로 문제들을 해결하는 능력이다. '(기계적인 일을) 하는' 역할의 노동자들은 로봇들에 의해 대체될 수 있는 반면에, 창의적으로 문제를 해결하는 역할은 대체 불가능한 개인에 더 의존한다.

주어진 글 다음에 이어질 글의 순서로 가장 적절한 것을 고르시오.

① (A) — (C) — (B) (B)의 the numbers(그 숫자들)는 주어진 글에 나온 퍼센트를 가리킴
② (B) — (A) — (C) (A) 앞에는 자동화하기 어려운 것과 반대되는 내용이 나와야 함
③ (B) — (C) — (A) 많은 일자리가 자동화의 발전으로 위기에 처함 — (B) 단순한 일을 하는 로봇이 전체 직원을 대체할 수도 있음 — (C) 고도로 숙련된 직업들도 위기에 처함 — (A) 창의적으로 문제를 해결하는 역할은 자동화할 수 없음
④ (C) — (A) — (B)
⑤ (C) — (B) — (A) (C)에서 고도로 숙련된 직업들 '또한' 위기에 처해 있다고 했는데 주어진 글에는 위기에 처한 다른 직업이 없음

1st 각 문단의 내용을 파악하고, 글의 논리적인 순서를 추론한다.

> **주어진 글:** 상황이 변화하고 있다. 캐나다의 일자리 중 42퍼센트가 위기에 처해 있고, 미국의 일자리 중 62퍼센트가 자동화의 발전으로 인해 위기에 처할 것이라고 보도되어 왔다. (단서)

➡ **주어진 글 뒤:** 자동화로 인해 사라지는 일자리와 사라지지 않는 일자리에는 어떤 것들이 있는지 설명하는 내용이 이어질 것이다. (발상)

> **(A):** 하지만(However), 자동화하기 어려운 것은 창의적으로 문제들을 해결하는 능력이다. '(기계적인 일을) 하는' 역할의 노동자들은 로봇들에 의해 대체될 수 있는 반면에, 창의적으로 문제를 해결하는 역할은 대체 불가능한 개인에 더 의존한다.

➡ **(A) 앞:** 역접의 연결어 However로 자동화하기 어려운 직업의 특성을 언급하고 있으므로, 앞에는 이와 대조되는 자동화가 가능한 직업들이 언급되어야 한다.
▶ 주어진 글 바로 뒤에 (A)가 올 수 없음
(A) 뒤: 기계적으로 작업하는 직업은 대체되고 창의적으로 문제를 해결하는 직업은 대체되기 어렵다는 문장으로 마무리했다.
▶ (A)가 마지막에 올 확률이 높음

> **(B):** 여러분은 그 숫자들(the numbers)이 약간 비현실적으로 보인다고 말할지 모르지만, 그 위협은 현실이다. 한 패스트푸드 체인점은 10초 안에 버거 하나를 뒤집을 수 있는 로봇을 가지고 있다. 그것은 단지 단순한 일일 뿐이지만 그 로봇은 전체 직원을 대체할 수도 있다.

➡ **(B) 앞:** **1** '그 숫자들(the numbers)'이 가리키는 대상이 앞에 나와야 한다.
2 자동화로 인해 사라지는 캐나다와 미국 내 직업의 비율이 주어진 글에 있다.
▶ (B) 앞에 주어진 글이 와야 함 (순서: 주어진 글 → (B))
(B) 뒤: 단순노동을 하는 직업이 자동화될 수 있다고 했으므로, 반대로 자동화되지 않을 직업에 관한 내용이 이어질 것이다.

> **(C):** 고도로 숙련된 직업들 또한(also) 위기에 처해 있다. 예를 들면, 슈퍼컴퓨터는 질병에 대한 방대한 양의 의학 연구와 데이터를 이용하여 특정한 질병들에 대해 이용 가능한 치료법을 자동화된 방식으로 제안할 수 있다.

➡ **(C) 앞:** also라고 했으므로 앞에 자동화될 수 있는 또 다른 직업의 예시가 나와야 한다.
▶ 버거를 뒤집는 단순한 노동의 일자리가 자동화될 수 있다고 한 (B)가 (C) 앞에 와야 함 (순서: 주어진 글 → (B) → (C))
(C) 뒤: 고도로 숙련된 슈퍼컴퓨터마저 자동화될 수 있음을 시사했으므로, 자동화되기 어려운 직업에 관해 이야기한 (A)가 올 것이다.
▶ (C) 뒤에 (A)가 이어져야 함 (순서: 주어진 글 → (B) → (C) → (A))

2nd 글이 한눈에 들어오도록 정리하여 정답을 확인한다.

주어진 글: 세계적으로 자동화로 인해 사라지는 일자리가 상당히 많다.
→ **(B):** 그 수치가 비현실적으로 느껴지겠지만, 실제로 한 패스트푸드 체인점에서 도입한 로봇이 햄버거 조리라는 단순한 업무를 하는 인력을 대거 대체할 수도 있다.
→ **(C):** 슈퍼컴퓨터가 데이터를 이용하여 질병 치료법을 제안할 수 있는 것처럼, 고도로 숙련된 직업들 역시 자동화될 위기에 처해 있다.
→ **(A):** 하지만 단순한 기계적 업무가 아닌 창의적인 문제 해결 능력을 요구하는 업무는 로봇에 의해 대체되기 어렵다.
▶ 주어진 글 다음에 이어질 글의 순서는 (B) → (C) → (A)이므로 정답은 ③임

---

37 정답 ⑤ *도움을 주고받는 너도밤나무

Each beech tree grows in a particular location / and soil conditions can vary greatly / in just a few yards. //
각각의 너도밤나무는 고유한 장소에서 자란다 / 그리고 토양의 조건들은 크게 달라질 수 있다 / 단 몇 야드 안에서도 //
단서 1 너도밤나무가 자라는 토양의 조건은 가까운 거리 내에서도 크게 달라질 수 있음

The soil can have a great deal of water / or almost no water. //
토양은 다량의 물을 가질 수 있고 / 또는 거의 물이 없을 수도 있다 //

It can be full of nutrients or not. //
그것은 영양분이 가득할 수도 아닐 수도 있다 //

단서 2 This는 (B)의 마지막에 언급한, 나무들 사이의 당 차이를 균등하게 한다는 내용을 가리킴
(A) This is taking place underground / through the roots. //
복합관계대명사
이것은 지하에서 일어나고 있다 / 뿌리들을 통해 //

복합관계대명사
Whoever has an abundance of sugar / hands some over; / **whoever** is running short / gets help. //
풍부한 당을 가진 나무는 어떤 나무라도 / 일부를 건네준다 / 부족해지는 나무는 어떤 나무라도 / 도움을 받는다 //

형용사적 용법(system 수식)
Their network acts as a system / **to make sure** that no trees fall too far behind. //
그들의 연결망은 시스템으로서 역할을 한다 / 그 어떤 나무도 너무 뒤처지지 않는 것을 확실히 하기 위한 //

(B) However, / the rate is the same. //
그러나 / 그 정도는 동일하다 // **단서 3** 앞에 정도가 동일하다는 것과 반대되는 내용이 나와야 함

whether A or B: A이든 B이든
Whether they are thick **or** thin, / all the trees of the same species are using light / **to produce** the same amount of sugar per leaf. //
부사적 용법(결과)
그들이 굵든 가늘든 / 같은 종의 모든 나무들은 빛을 사용한다 / 그래서 이파리당 같은 양의 당을 생산한다 //

Some trees have plenty of sugar / and some have less, / but the trees equalize this difference between them / **by transferring** sugar. //
by v-ing: ~함으로써
어떤 나무들은 충분한 당을 지니고 / 어떤 것들은 더 적게 지닌다 / 하지만 나무들은 그들 사이의 이 차이를 균등하게 한다 / 당을 전달함으로써 //
단서 4 주어진 글에서 말한 너도밤나무의 토양의 조건들이 다른 것에 따른 결과임

병렬 구조
(C) Accordingly, / each tree **grows** more quickly or more slowly / and **produces** more or less sugar, / and thus you would expect / every tree to be photosynthesizing / at a different rate. //
이에 따라 / 각 나무는 더 빨리 혹은 더 느리게 자라고 / 더 많거나 더 적은 당을 생산한다 / 그래서 여러분은 기대할 것이다 / 모든 나무가 광합성을 할 것이라고 / 다른 정도로 //

- beech tree 너도밤나무
- soil ⓝ 흙, 토양
- vary ⓥ (상황에 따라) 달라지다
- nutrient ⓝ 영양분
- underground ⓐⓓ 지하에서
- abundance ⓝ 풍부(함)
- run short (~이) 부족하다
- plenty of 풍부한, 많은
- equalize ⓥ 균등하게 하다
- transfer ⓥ 전달하다, 옮기다
- accordingly ⓐⓓ 따라서, 그에 따라
- rate ⓝ 정도, 비율

각각의 너도밤나무는 고유한 장소에서 자라고 토양의 조건들은 단 몇 야드 안에서도 크게 달라질 수 있다. 토양은 다량의 물을 가지거나 거의 물이 없을 수도 있다. 그것은 영양분이 가득할 수도 아닐 수도 있다. (C) 이에 따라, 각 나무는 더 빨리 혹은 더 느리게 자라고 더 많은 혹은 더 적은 당을 생산하는데, 그래서 여러분은 모든 나무가 다른 정도로 광합성을 할 것이라고 기대할 것이다. (B) 그러나 그 정도는 동일하다. 그들이 굵든 가늘든 간에, 같은 종의 모든 나무들은 빛을 사용하여 이파리당 같은 양의 당을 생산한다. 어떤 나무들은 충분한 당을 지니고 어떤 것들은 더 적게 지니지만, 나무들은 당을 전달함으로써 그들 사이의 이 차이를 균등하게 한다. (A) 이것은 뿌리들을 통해 지하에서 일어나고 있다. 풍부한 당을 가진 나무가 누구든 간에 일부를 건네주고, 부족해지는 나무는 누구든 간에 도움을 받는다. 그들의 연결망은 그 어떤 나무도 너무 뒤처지지 않는 것을 확실히 하기 위한 시스템으로서 역할을 한다.

주어진 글 다음에 이어질 글의 순서로 가장 적절한 것을 고르시오. [3점]

① (A) — (C) — (B) (C)는 주어진 글의 결과이므로 주어진 글에 이어져야 함
② (B) — (A) — (C)
③ (B) — (C) — (A) However(그러나)로 시작하는 (B)와 상반된 내용이 주어진 글에 없음
④ (C) — (A) — (B) (A)의 This가 가리키는 것은 (B)의 마지막에 언급됨
⑤ (C) — (B) — (A) 너도밤나무가 자라는 토양의 조건은 서로 다름 — (C) 너도밤나무가 자라는 속도와 생산하는 당이 다름 — (B) 그러나 각 나무들은 같은 양의 당을 생산함 — (A) 뿌리를 통해 나무들은 당을 주고받으며 균등하게 함

| 문제 풀이 순서 | ✳✳✳ [정답률 60%]

1st 각 문단의 내용을 파악하고, 글의 논리적인 순서를 추론한다.

> **주어진 글:** 각각의 너도밤나무는 고유한 장소에서 자라고 토양의 조건들은 단 몇 야드 안에서도 크게 달라질 수 있다. 토양은 다량의 물을 가지거나 거의 물이 없을 수도 있다. 그것은 영양분이 가득할 수도 아닐 수도 있다. (단서)

➡ **주어진 글 뒤:** 서로 다른 토양에서 너도밤나무가 어떻게 다르게 자라는지를 설명하는 내용이 이어질 것이다. (발상)

> **(A):** 이것(This)은 뿌리들을 통해 지하에서 일어나고 있다. 풍부한 당을 가진 나무가 누구든 간에 일부를 건네주고, 부족해지는 나무는 누구든 간에 도움을 받는다. 그들의 연결망은 그 어떤 나무도 너무 뒤처지지 않는 것을 확실히 하기 위한 시스템으로서 역할을 한다.

➡ **(A) 앞:** '이것(This)'이 무엇인지 설명하는 내용이 앞에 와야 한다.
▶ (A) 앞에 주어진 글이 올 수 없음
(A) 뒤: 서로 다른 조건의 토양에서 자랄지라도 어떤 나무도 뒤처지지 않게 한다는 것은 글의 결말일 가능성이 크다.
▶ (A)가 마지막에 올 확률이 높음

> **(B):** 그러나(However) 그 정도(the rate)는 동일하다. 그들이 굵든 가늘든 간에, 같은 종의 모든 나무들은 빛을 사용하여 이파리당 같은 양의 당을 생산한다. 어떤 나무들은 충분한 당을 지니고 어떤 것들은 더 적게 지니지만, 나무들은 당을 전달함으로써 그들 사이의 이 차이를 균등하게 한다.

➡ **(B) 앞:** **1** 어떤 '정도(rate)'를 말하는 것인지 언급되어야 하고,
2 역접의 연결어 However로 연결되므로 앞에는 반대되는 내용(정도가 다르다는 내용)이 와야 한다.
▶ 주어진 글과 (A)에는 해당 내용이 없으므로 (C)가 올 확률이 높음
(B) 뒤: 나무들은 서로 당을 전달함으로써 그들 사이의 격차를 줄인다는 것을 (A)에서 This로 설명했다.
▶ (A)가 (B) 뒤에 와야 함 (순서: (B) ➡ (A))

> **(C):** 이에 따라(Accordingly), 각 나무는 더 빨리 혹은 더 느리게 자라고 더 많은 혹은 더 적은 당을 생산하는데, 그래서 여러분은 모든 나무가 다른 정도로 광합성을 할 것이라고 기대할 것이다.

➡ **(C) 앞:** 앞서 예상한 것처럼 주어진 글에 이어지는 내용으로, 서로 다른 토양에서 너도밤나무가 어떻게 다르게 자랄 것인지 예상하는 내용이 이어졌다.
▶ 주어진 글에 이어지는 내용임 (순서: 주어진 글 ➡ (C))
(C) 뒤: 광합성의 정도가 다를 것이라고 예상한 것과 달리 '그 정도'는 동일하다고 한 (B)가 이어져야 한다.
▶ (C) 뒤에 (B)가 이어져야 함 (순서: 주어진 글 ➡ (C) ➡ (B) ➡ (A))

2nd 글이 한눈에 들어오도록 정리하여 정답을 확인한다.

주어진 글: 너도밤나무가 자라는 토양의 조건은 가까이에서도 크게 달라질 수 있다.
➡ **(C):** 이에 따라 각 나무가 광합성을 하는 정도는 모두 다를 것이다.
➡ **(B):** 하지만 나무들은 서로 당을 주고받음으로써 그 차이를 균등하게 만든다.
➡ **(A):** 이것은 뿌리에서 일어나며 이 연결망으로 어떤 나무도 뒤처지지 않게 한다.
▶ 주어진 글 다음에 이어질 글의 순서는 (C) ➡ (B) ➡ (A)이므로 정답은 ⑤임

38 정답 ⑤ ✳언어를 바라보는 서로 다른 견해

글의 흐름으로 보아, 주어진 문장이 들어가기에 가장 적절한 곳을 고르시오. [3점]

2022.11
12회

단서 1 앞에 언어가 인간의 삶에서 매우 중요하다는 것과 반대되는 내용이 나와야 함
Nevertheless, / language is enormously important in human
병렬 구조
life / and contributes largely to our ability / to cooperate with
형용사적 용법(ability 수식)
each other / in dealing with the world. //
그럼에도 불구하고 / 언어는 인간의 삶에서 매우 중요하다 / 그리고 우리의 능력에 상당히 기여한다 / 서로 협력하는 / 세계를 다루는 데 있어서 //

부사적 용법(목적)
Should we use / language to understand mind / or mind to
부사적 용법(목적)
understand language? //
우리는 사용해야 하는가 / 사고를 이해하기 위해 언어를 / 아니면 언어를 이해하기 위해 사고를 //

(①) Analytic philosophy historically assumes / that language
목적어절 접속사의 병렬 구조
is basic / and that mind would make sense / if proper use of
language was appreciated. //
분석 철학은 역사적으로 가정한다 / 언어가 기본이라고 / 그리고 사고가 이치에 맞을 것이라고 / 적절한 언어 사용이 제대로 인식된다면 //

(②) Modern cognitive science, / however, / rightly judges /
목적어절 접속사
that language is just one aspect of mind of great importance / in
human beings / but not fundamental to all kinds of thinking. //
현대 인지 과학은 / 그러나 / 당연히 판단한다 / 언어가 매우 중요한 사고의 한 측면일 뿐이고 / 인간에게 / 모든 종류의 사고에 근본적이지는 않다고 //

(③) Countless species of animals / manage to navigate the
world, solve problems, and learn / without using language, /
수많은 종의 동물들이 / 세계를 항해하고, 문제를 해결하고, 학습해 낸다 / 언어를 사용하지 않고 /
주격 관계대명사
through brain mechanisms / that are largely preserved in the
minds of humans. //
두뇌의 메커니즘을 통해 / 인간의 사고 속에 대체로 보존된 //
목적어절 접속사
(④) There is no reason to assume / that language is fundamental
to mental operations. // **단서 2** 언어가 정신 작용의 기본이 아니라고 함
가정할 이유는 없다 / 언어가 정신 작용의 기본이라고 //

(⑤) Our species *homo sapiens* / has been astonishingly
계속적 용법의 주격 관계대명사
successful, / which depended in part on language, /
우리 종족, '호모 사피엔스'는 / 놀라운 성공을 거두어 왔다 / 그리고 그것은 언어에 부분적으로
의존했다 / **단서 3** 언어가 호모 사피엔스의 성공에 영향을 미침

first as an effective contributor / to collaborative problem
병렬 구조(~로서)
solving / and much later, / as collective memory / through
written records. //
처음에는 효과적인 기여 요소로서 / 협력적인 문제 해결에 / 그리고 훨씬 나중에는 / 집단 기억으로서의 / 글로 쓰인 기록을 통한 //

- enormously ⓐⓓ 엄청나게, 대단히　　• contribute ⓥ 기여하다
- cooperate ⓥ 협력하다　　• deal with ~을 다루다
- analytic philosophy 분석 철학　　• assume ⓥ 가정하다
- cognitive science 인지 과학　　• rightly ⓐⓓ 당연히
- judge ⓥ 판단하다　　• aspect ⓝ 측면
- fundamental ⓐ 근본적인, 기본적인　　• countless ⓐ 셀 수 없이 많은
- navigate ⓥ 항해하다, 길을 찾다　　• preserve ⓥ 보존하다
- operation ⓝ 작용, 작동　　• astonishingly ⓐⓓ 놀라운 정도로
- contributor ⓝ 기여 요소, 원인 제공자
- collaborative ⓐ 협력적인, 공동의　　• collective ⓐ 협력적인

우리는 사고를 이해하기 위해 언어를 사용해야 하는가 아니면 언어를 이해하기 위해 사고를 사용해야 하는가? (①) 분석 철학은 언어가 기본이고 적절한 언어 사용이 제대로 인식된다면 그 사고가 이치에 맞을 것이라고 역사적으로 가정한다. (②) 그러나 현대 인지 과학은 언어가 인간에게 매우 중요한 사고의 한 측면일 뿐 모든 종류의 사고에 근본적이지는 않다고 당연히 판단한다. (③) 수많은 종의 동물들이 인간의 사고 속에 대체로 보존된 두뇌의 메커니즘을 통해 언어를 사용하지 않고 세계를 항해하고, 문제를 해결하고, 학습해 낸다. (④) 언어가 정신 작용의 기본이라고 가정할 이유는 없다. (⑤ 그럼에도 불구하고, 언어는 인간의 삶에서 매우 중요하며 세계를 다루는 데 있어서 서로 협력하는 우리의 능력에 상당히 기여한다.) 우리 종족, '호모 사피엔스'는 놀라운 성공을 거두어 왔는데, 이것은 처음에는 협력적인 문제 해결에 효과적인 기여 요소로서, 그리고 훨씬 나중에는 글로 쓰인 기록을 통한 집단 기억으로서의 언어에 부분적으로 의존했다.

| 문제 풀이 순서 | ★★★ [정답률 50%]

1st 주어진 문장을 해석하고, 연결어, 지시어 등을 확인한다.

> Nevertheless, language is enormously important in human life and contributes largely to our ability to cooperate with each other in dealing with the world.
> 그럼에도 불구하고, 언어는 인간의 삶에서 매우 중요하며 세계를 다루는 데 있어서 서로 협력하는 우리의 능력에 상당히 기여한다.

➡ 주어진 문장 앞: 'Nevertheless(그럼에도 불구하고)'라고 했으므로 [단서] 앞에는 언어가 인간의 삶에서 중요하지 않다는 내용이 와야 한다. [발상]

2nd 찾은 단서를 생각하며 각 선택지의 앞뒤 흐름이 매끄러운지 확인한다.

- ①의 앞 문장과 뒤 문장

> **앞 문장:** 우리는 사고를 이해하기 위해 언어를 사용해야 하는가 아니면 언어를 이해하기 위해 사고를 사용해야 하는가?
> **뒤 문장:** 분석 철학은 언어가 기본이고 적절한 언어 사용이 제대로 인식된다면 그 사고가 이치에 맞을 것이라고 역사적으로 가정한다.

➡ 앞 문장에서 던진 질문에 대한 답을 뒤 문장에서 말하고 있다.
　▶ 주어진 문장이 ①에 들어갈 수 없음

- ②의 앞 문장과 뒤 문장

> **앞 문장:** ①의 뒤 문장과 같음
> **뒤 문장:** 그러나(however) 현대 인지 과학은 언어가 인간에게 매우 중요한 사고의 한 측면일 뿐 모든 종류의 사고에 근본적이지는 않다고 당연히 판단한다.

➡ 앞 문장의 '분석 철학'의 관점과 다른 '현대 인지 과학'의 관점을 역접의 연결어 however로 이어간다.
　▶ 주어진 문장이 ②에 들어갈 수 없음

- ③의 앞 문장과 뒤 문장

> **앞 문장:** ②의 뒤 문장과 같음
> **뒤 문장:** 수많은 종의 동물들이 인간의 사고 속에 대체로 보존된 두뇌의 메커니즘을 통해 언어를 사용하지 않고 세계를 항해하고, 문제를 해결하고, 학습해낸다.

➡ '언어가 모든 종류의 사고에 근본적이지는 않다'라는 앞 문장의 주장을 뒷받침하는 설명을 이어간다.
　▶ 주어진 문장이 ③에 들어갈 수 없음

- ④의 앞 문장과 뒤 문장

> **앞 문장:** ③의 뒤 문장과 같음
> **뒤 문장:** 언어가 정신 작용의 기본이라고 가정할 이유는 없다.

➡ 앞 문장의 견해와 동일한 주장을 반복한다.
　▶ 주어진 문장이 ④에 들어갈 수 없음

- ⑤의 앞 문장과 뒤 문장

> **앞 문장:** ④의 뒤 문장과 같음
> **뒤 문장:** 우리 종족, '호모 사피엔스'는 놀라운 성공을 거두어 왔는데, 이것은 처음에는 협력적인 문제 해결에 효과적인 기여 요소로서, 그리고 훨씬 나중에는 글로 쓰인 기록을 통한 집단 기억으로서의 언어에 부분적으로 의존했다.

➡ 앞에서는 언어가 정신 작용의 기본이라고 가정할 이유는 없다면서 부정적인 견해를 말했는데, 뒤에서는 언어가 문제 해결에 효과적인 기여 요소라고 하며 상반된 견해를 말하고 있다.
　따라서 '그럼에도 불구하고' 언어가 서로 협력하는 우리의 능력에 상당히 기여한다고 한 주어진 문장이 ⑤에 오는 것이 적절하다.
　▶ 주어진 문장이 ⑤에 들어가야 함

3rd 글이 한눈에 들어오도록 정리하여 정답을 확인한다.

사고를 이해하기 위해 언어를 사용해야 할까, 언어를 이해하기 위해 사고를 사용해야 할까?
(①) 분석 철학은 언어 사용이 제대로 인식된다면, 그 사고가 이치에 맞을 것이라고 가정한다.
(②) 그러나 현대 인지 과학은 언어가 모든 사고에 근본적이지는 않다고 판단한다.
(③) 수많은 종의 동물들이 두뇌의 메커니즘을 통해 언어의 사용 없이 문제를 해결한다.
(④) 언어가 정신 작용의 기본이라고 가정할 이유는 없다.
(⑤ 그럼에도 불구하고, 언어는 서로 협력하는 우리의 능력에 기여한다.)
'호모 사피엔스'는 처음에는 협력적인 문제 해결에 기여 요소로서, 나중에는 기록을 통한 집단 기억으로서의 언어에 부분적으로 의존했다.

글의 흐름으로 보아, 주어진 문장이 들어가기에 가장 적절한 곳을 고르시오.

뒤에 목적어절 접속사 that이 생략됨
If we could magically remove the glasses, / we would find the two water bodies would not mix well. //
만약 우리가 마법처럼 그 유리잔들을 없앨 수 있다면 / 우리는 두 액체가 잘 섞이지 않는다는 것을 알게 될 것이다 //
단서 1 the glasses(그 유리잔들) 안에 든 액체들이 섞이지 않을 상황이 앞에 나와야 함

Take two glasses of water. //
물 두 잔을 가져와라 //

'둘 중 하나'
Put a little bit of orange juice / into one / and a little bit of lemon juice / into the other. //
'나머지 하나'
약간의 오렌지주스를 넣어라 / 하나의 잔에는 / 그리고 약간의 레몬주스를 (넣어라) / 나머지 잔에는 //

선행사를 포함하는 관계대명사   주격 보어가 복수이므로 복수 동사가 옴
(①) What you have / are essentially two glasses of water / but with a completely different chemical makeup. //
여러분이 가지고 있는 것은 / 본질적으로 두 잔의 물이다 / 하지만 완전히 다른 화학적 성질을 지닌 //

병렬 구조
(②) If we take the glass / containing orange juice / and heat it, /
만약 우리가 잔을 가져와 / 오렌지주스가 든 / 그것을 가열한다면 /

we will still have two different glasses of water / with different chemical makeups, / but now they will also have different temperatures. //
단서 2 오렌지주스가 든 잔을 가열하면, 온도와 화학적 성질이 다른 두 잔의 물이 됨
우리는 여전히 다른 두 잔의 물을 가지고 있을 것이다 / 다른 화학적 성질을 지닌 / 하지만 이제 그것들은 또한 다른 온도를 가질 것이다 //
단서 3 액체들은 만나면 조금은 섞이지만 분리된 채로 남을 것임 관계부사
(③) Perhaps they would mix a little / where they met; / however, / they would remain separate / because of their different chemical makeups and temperatures. //
전치사
어쩌면 그것들은 조금 섞일 것이다 / 그것들이 만났던 곳에서 / 하지만 / 그것들은 분리된 상태로 남아 있을 것이다 / 그것들의 다른 화학적 성질과 온도 때문에 //

(④) The warmer water would float / on the surface of the cold water / because of its lighter weight. //
전치사
더 따뜻한 물은 떠 있을 것이다 / 찬물의 표면에 / 그것의 더 가벼운 무게 때문에 //

주격 관계대명사
(⑤) In the ocean / we have bodies of water / that differ in temperature and salt content; / for this reason, / they do not mix. //
바다에서 / 우리는 액체들을 가지고 있다 / 온도와 염분에서 다른 / 이러한 이유로 / 그것들은 섞이지 않는다 //

- **magically** ad 마법처럼 · **remove** ⓥ 제거하다, 없애다
- **essentially** ad 본질적으로 · **completely** ad 완전히
- **chemical** ⓐ 화학적인 · **makeup** ⓝ 성질, 구성
- **contain** ⓥ ~이 들어 있다 · **temperature** ⓝ 온도
- **separate** ⓐ 분리된, 따로 떨어진 · **float** ⓥ (물이나 공기 위에) 떠 있다
- **differ** ⓥ 다르다 · **salt content** 염분

물 두 잔을 가져와라. 하나의 잔에는 약간의 오렌지주스를 넣고 다른 잔에는 약간의 레몬주스를 넣어라. (①) 여러분이 가지고 있는 것은 본질적으로 두 잔의 물이지만 완전히 다른 화학적 성질을 지닌 것들이다. (②) 만약 우리가 오렌지주스가 든 잔을 가져와 그것을 가열한다면, 우리는 여전히 다른 화학적 성질을 지닌 다른 두 잔의 물을 가지고 있을 것이지만, 이제 그것들은 또한 다른 온도를 가질 것이다. (③ 만약 우리가 마법처럼 그 유리잔들을 없앨 수 있다면, 우리는 두 액체가 잘 섞이지 않는다는 것을 알게 될 것이다.) 어쩌면 그것들은 그것들이 만났던 곳에서 조금 섞일 것이다. 하지만, 그것들의 다른 화학적 성질과 온도 때문에 그것들은 분리된 상태로 남아 있을 것이다. (④) 더 따뜻한 물은 그것의 더 가벼운 무게 때문에 찬물의 표면에 떠 있을 것이다. (⑤) 바다에서 우리는 온도와 염분에서 다른 액체들을 가지고 있다. 이러한 이유로, 그것들은 섞이지 않는다.

| 문제 풀이 순서 | ★★★ [정답률 55%]

1st 주어진 문장을 해석하고, 연결어, 지시어 등을 확인한다.

> If we could magically remove the glasses, we would find the two water bodies would not mix well.
> 만약 우리가 마법처럼 그 유리잔들을 없앨 수 있다면, 우리는 두 액체가 잘 섞이지 않는다는 것을 알게 될 것이다.

➡ **주어진 문장 앞:** '그 유리잔들(the glasses)'이라고 했으므로 **단서** 앞에 섞이지 않을 두 액체를 담은 유리잔에 대한 언급이 있어야 한다. **발상**

2nd 찾은 단서를 생각하여 각 선택지의 앞뒤 흐름이 매끄러운지 확인한다.

- ①의 앞 문장과 뒤 문장

> **앞 문장:** 물 두 잔을 가져와라. 하나의 잔에는 약간의 오렌지주스를 넣고 다른 잔에는 약간의 레몬주스를 넣어라.
> **뒤 문장:** 여러분이 가지고 있는 것은 본질적으로 두 잔의 물이지만 완전히 다른 화학적 성질을 지닌 것들이다.

➡ 앞 문장에서 언급한 물 두 잔을 뒤 문장에서 부연 설명한다.
▶ 주어진 문장이 ①에 들어갈 수 없음

- ②의 앞 문장과 뒤 문장

> **앞 문장:** ①의 뒤 문장과 같음
> **뒤 문장:** 만약(If) 우리가 오렌지주스가 든 잔을 가져와 그것을 가열한다면, 우리는 여전히 다른 화학적 성질을 지닌 다른 두 잔의 물을 가지고 있을 것이지만, 이제 그것들은 또한 다른 온도를 가질 것이다.

➡ 앞에서 언급한 오렌지주스를 가열하는 상황을 If로 가정한다.
▶ 주어진 문장이 ②에 들어갈 수 없음

- ③의 앞 문장과 뒤 문장

> **앞 문장:** ②의 뒤 문장과 같음
> **뒤 문장:** 어쩌면 그것들은 그것들이 만났던 곳에서 조금 섞일 것이다. 하지만, 그것들의 다른 화학적 성질과 온도 때문에 그것들은 분리된 상태로 남아 있을 것이다.

➡ 앞에서 이야기하고 있는 두 잔의 물이 어떻게 만나게 됐는지가 빠져있다. 따라서 유리잔들을 없애는 상황을 가정한 주어진 문장이 ③에 와야 한다.
▶ 주어진 문장이 ③에 들어가야 함

- ④의 앞 문장과 뒤 문장

> **앞 문장:** ③의 뒤 문장과 같음
> **뒤 문장:** 더 따뜻한 물은 그것의 더 가벼운 무게 때문에 찬물의 표면에 떠 있을 것이다.

➡ 앞에서 분리된 상태로 남아 있을 것이라고 한 물이 어떻게 분리된 상태인지를 부연 설명한다.
▶ 주어진 문장이 ④에 들어갈 수 없음

2022.11
12회

> **앞 문장:** ④의 뒤 문장과 같음
> **뒤 문장:** 바다에서 우리는 온도와 염분에서 다른 액체들을 가지고 있다. 이러한 이유로, 그것들은 섞이지 않는다.

➡ 앞에서 설명한 이유로 바다에 있는 온도와 염분이 다른 액체들은 섞이지 않는다며 글을 마무리한다.

▶ 주어진 문장이 ⑤에 들어갈 수 없음

3rd 글이 한눈에 들어오도록 정리하여 정답을 확인한다.

각각 오렌지주스와 레몬주스가 들어있는 물 두 잔이 있다.
(①) 그것들은 완전히 다른 화학적 성질을 지닌 두 잔의 물이다.
(②) 만약 오렌지주스가 든 잔을 가열한다면, 두 잔의 물은 이제 서로 다른 화학적 성질에 더불어 서로 다른 온도를 가진다.
(③ 만약 유리잔들을 없앤다면, 두 액체는 잘 섞이지 않을 것이다.)
서로 만난 부분에서는 조금 섞일지라도 서로 다른 화학적 성질과 온도 때문에 분리된 채로 남을 것이다.
(④) 따뜻한 물은 무게가 가벼워 찬물 위에 떠 있을 것이다.
(⑤) 이것이 바다에서 온도와 염분이 다른 액체들이 섞이지 않는 이유이다.

40 정답 ② ＊성찰적 일기 쓰기의 역할

One of the most powerful tools / **to find** meaning in our lives /
(핵심 주어(단수)) (형용사적 용법(tools 수식))
is reflective journaling / — thinking back on and writing about
(단수 동사)
what has happened to us. //
가장 강력한 도구들 중 하나는 / 우리의 삶에서 의미를 찾기 위한 / 성찰적 일기 쓰기이다 / 즉 우리에게 일어난 일을 돌아보고 그것에 대해 쓰는 것이다 //

In the 1990s, / Stanford University researchers asked
undergraduate students / on spring break / **to journal** about
(명사적 용법(목적격 보어))
their most important personal values and their daily activities; /
1990년대에 / Stanford University 연구자들이 학부생들에게 요청했다 / 봄방학에 / 그들의 가장 중요한 개인적인 가치와 그들의 하루의 활동들에 대해 쓰도록 /
others **were asked** / to write about only the good things / **that**
(수동태 동사) (주격 관계대명사)
happened to them in the day. //
다른 사람들은 요청받았다 / 좋은 일만 쓰도록 / 그날 그들에게 일어난 /
Three weeks later, / **the students** / **who** had written about their
(복수 주어) (주격 관계대명사)
values / **were** happier, healthier, and more confident / about
(복수 동사)
their ability to handle stress /
3주 후에 / 학생들은 / 자신의 가치에 관해 썼던 / 더 행복하고, 더 건강하고, 더 자신 있었다 / 스트레스를 다루는 그들의 능력에 대해 /
than the **ones** / **who** had only focused on the good stuff, //
(= students) (주격 관계대명사)
학생들보다 / 좋은 것에만 초점을 맞췄던 //
단서 1 '가치'에 관해 일기를 쓴 학생들이 더 행복했음
(전치사의 목적어(간접의문문))
By reflecting / on how their daily activities supported their
values, / students had gained a new perspective / on those
activities and choices. //
단서 2 하루의 활동이 '가치'를 뒷받침하는 방식을 성찰하면서 새로운 관점을 얻었음
성찰함으로써 / 어떻게 그들의 하루의 활동들이 그들의 가치를 뒷받침하는지에 대해 / 학생들은 새로운 관점을 얻었다 / 그 활동들과 선택들에 대해 //

Little stresses and hassles / were now demonstrations of their
values / in action. //
작은 스트레스와 귀찮은 일들은 / 이제 그들의 가치를 보여주는 것이었다 / 행동에서 //

Suddenly, / their lives were full of meaningful activities. //
갑자기 / 그들의 삶은 의미 있는 활동으로 가득 찼다 //
(앞에 to가 생략됨)
And all they had to do / was **reflect and write** about it / —
positively reframing their experiences / with their personal
values. //
단서 3 개인적인 가치로 그들의 경험을 '재구성함'
그리고 그들이 해야 했던 모든 일은 / 그것에 대해 돌아보고 쓰는 것이었다 / 그들의 경험을 긍정적으로 재구성하면서 / 개인적인 가치로 //

→ Journaling about daily activities / based on what we
(사역동사+목적어+목적격 보어(원형부정사))
believe to be (A) **worthwhile** / can **make us feel** / that our life
is meaningful /
일상의 활동에 대해 일기를 쓰는 것은 / 우리가 가치 있다고 믿는 것에 근거하여 / 우리가 느끼게 만들 수 있다 / 우리의 삶이 의미 있다는 것을 /
by (B) **rethinking** our experiences in a new way. //
새로운 방식으로 자신의 경험들을 다시 생각함으로써 //

··

- reflective ⓐ 성찰적인 · journaling ⓝ 일기 쓰기
- think back on ~을 돌이켜 보다 · undergraduate ⓝ (대학) 학부생
- value ⓝ 가치 · handle ⓥ 다루다 · reflect ⓥ 성찰하다, 숙고하다
- support ⓥ 뒷받침하다 · perspective ⓝ 관점
- demonstration ⓝ 입증, (분명히) 보여줌 · reframe ⓥ 재구성하다
- worthwhile ⓐ 가치 있는

우리의 삶에서 의미를 찾기 위한 가장 강력한 도구들 중 하나는 성찰적 일기 쓰기, 즉 우리에게 일어난 일을 돌아보고 그것에 대해 쓰는 것이다. 1990년대에 Stanford University 연구자들이 봄방학에 학부생들에게 그들의 가장 중요한 개인적인 가치와 그들의 하루의 활동들에 대해 쓰도록 요청했다. 다른 사람들은 그날 그들에게 일어난 좋은 일만 쓰도록 요청받았다. 3주 후에, 자신의 가치에 관해 썼던 학생들은 좋은 것에만 초점을 맞췄던 학생들보다 더 행복하고, 더 건강하고, 스트레스를 다루는 자신의 능력에 대해 더 자신 있었다. 어떻게 그들의 하루의 활동들이 그들의 가치를 뒷받침하는지에 대해 성찰함으로써, 학생들은 그 활동들과 선택들에 대해 새로운 관점을 얻었다. 작은 스트레스와 귀찮은 일들은 이제 행동에서 그들의 가치를 보여주는 것이었다. 갑자기, 그들의 삶은 의미 있는 활동으로 가득 찼다. 그리고 그들이 해야 했던 모든 일은 그들의 경험을 개인적인 가치로 긍정적으로 재구성하면서 그것에 대해 돌아보고 쓰는 것이었다.
→ 우리가 (A) 가치 있다고 믿는 것에 근거하여 일상의 활동에 대해 일기를 쓰는 것은 새로운 방식으로 자신의 경험들을 (B) 다시 생각함으로써 우리가 자신의 삶이 의미 있다는 것을 느끼게 만들 수 있다.

> 다음 글의 내용을 한 문장으로 요약하고자 한다. 빈칸 (A), (B)에 들어갈 말로 가장 적절한 것은?
>
> | | (A) | | (B) | |
> |---|---|---|---|---|
> | ① | factual
사실에 기반을 둔 | — | rethinking
다시 생각하기 | 사실만 일기로 쓴 것이 아님 |
> | ② | worthwhile
가치 있는 | — | rethinking
다시 생각하기 | 자신의 경험을 돌아보면서 개인적인 가치로 재구성하여 썼음 |
> | ③ | outdated
진부한 | — | generalizing
일반화하기 | 진부하다고 믿는 것을 일기로 일반화한 것이 아님 |
> | ④ | objective
객관적인 | — | generalizing
일반화하기 | 자신의 경험을 객관화한 것이 아님 |
> | ⑤ | demanding
힘든 | — | describing
묘사하기 | 힘들었던 활동을 묘사한 것이 아님 |

| 문제 풀이 순서 | ★★★ [정답률 63%]

1st 요약문을 통해 글에서 무엇을 찾아야 하는지 확인한다.

요약문	우리가 (A) _____ 고 믿는 것에 근거하여 일상의 활동에 대해 일기를 쓰는 것은 새로운 방식으로 자신의 경험들을 (B) _____ 으로써 우리가 자신의 삶이 의미 있다는 것을 느끼게 만들 수 있다.

➡ 글에서 찾아야 하는 것
(A): 우리가 사실에 기반을 뒀다고, 가치 있다고, 진부하다고, 객관적이라고, 힘들다고 믿는 것에 근거하여 일상의 활동에 대해 일기를 쓰는 것이
(B): 새로운 방식으로 경험들을 다시 생각함으로써, 일반화함으로써, 묘사함으로써 삶의 의미를 느끼게 만드는지

- 3주 후에, 자신의 가치에 관해 썼던 학생들은 좋은 것에만 초점을 맞췄던 학생들보다 더 행복하고, 더 건강하고, 스트레스를 다루는 자신의 능력에 대해 더 자신 있었다. **단서 1**
- 어떻게 그들의 하루의 활동들이 그들의 가치를 뒷받침하는지에 대해 성찰함으로써, 학생들은 그 활동들과 선택들에 대해 새로운 관점을 얻었다. **단서 2**

➡ 개인적으로 중요한 가치와 하루의 활동을 일기로 쓴 학부생들: 긍정적 결과
하루에 일어난 좋은 일만 일기로 쓴 학부생들: 부정적 결과
▶ '가치 있다'고 믿는 것에 근거하여 성찰함으로써 새로운 관점을 얻은 것이므로 (A)에는 ② worthwhile이 들어가야 함

- 갑자기, 그들의 삶은 의미 있는 활동으로 가득 찼다. 그리고 그들이 해야 했던 모든 일은 그들의 경험을 개인적인 가치로 긍정적으로 재구성하면서 그것에 대해 돌아보고 쓰는 것이었다. **단서 3**

➡ 개인적인 가치로 그들의 경험을 긍정적으로 '돌아보고 재구성함으로써' 삶이 의미 있는 활동으로 가득하게 됐다.
▶ (B)에는 ①, ② rethinking이 들어가야 함

연구 내용	개인이 중시하는 가치와 일상의 활동들을 성찰하며 일기를 쓰는 것과 하루에 일어난 좋은 일만 일기로 쓰는 것의 효과를 비교하는 연구를 진행했다.
연구 결과 ①	좋은 일에 대해서만 일기를 쓰는 것보다 본인에게 중요한 가치를 근거로 일상의 활동들을 성찰하는 일기를 쓰는 것이 행복감, 건강, 자신감 면에서 더 긍정적으로 작용했다.
연구 결과 ②	본인에게 중요한 가치를 염두에 두고 일기를 쓰는 것이 일상의 활동들을 새로운 관점으로 바라보게 했다.
결론	자신이 중시하는 가치를 바탕으로 일상의 활동들에 대해 다시 생각할 때, 모든 선택과 경험이 새롭고 의미 있게 느껴진다.

➡ 우리가 (A) 가치 있다고 믿는 것에 근거하여 일상의 활동에 대해 일기를 쓰는 것은 새로운 방식으로 자신의 경험들을 (B) 다시 생각함으로써 우리가 자신의 삶이 의미 있다는 것을 느끼게 만들 수 있다.

| 선택지 분석 |

① factual — rethinking
사실에 기반을 둔 — 다시 생각하기
사실에 근거하여 일기를 쓰라고 하는 글이 아니다.

② worthwhile — rethinking
가치 있는 — 다시 생각하기
가치를 바탕으로 일상을 되돌아보는 것은 삶의 의미를 느낄 수 있게 한다고 했다.

③ outdated — generalizing
진부한 — 일반화하기
진부하다고 믿는 것을 일기로 씀으로써 일반화한 것이 아니다.

④ objective — generalizing
객관적인 — 일반화하기
일상을 객관적인 시각에서 바라보라는 내용이 아니다.

⑤ demanding — describing
힘든 — 묘사하기
힘들었던 활동을 일기에 묘사하라는 내용은 언급되지 않았다.

41~42 ✽ 눈과 뇌의 협력의 결과인 시각

Mike May lost his sight / at the age of three. //
Mike May는 자신의 시력을 잃었다 / 세 살 때 //

Because he had spent the majority of his life / adapting to being blind / — and even cultivating a skiing career in this state — /
그는 자신의 인생의 대부분을 보냈기 때문에 / 보이지 않는 것에 적응하는 데 / 그리고 심지어 이 상태에서 스키 경력을 쌓는 데 (보냈기 때문에) /
병렬 구조
by v-ing: ~함으로써

his other senses compensated / by growing (a) stronger. //
그의 다른 감각들은 보충되었다 / 더 강해지는 것을 통해 //
42번 단서 1: 시력이 회복되었을 때 전반적 인식이 방해받았음

However, / when his sight was restored through a surgery / in his forties, / his entire perception of reality was (b) disrupted. //
그러나 / 그의 시력이 수술을 통해 회복되었을 때 / 40대에 / 그의 현실에 대한 전반적 인식은 방해받았다 /
41번 단서 1: 시력이 회복된 후 뇌에 과부하가 걸려서 세상은 두려운 장소가 되었음

Instead of being thrilled that he could see now, / as he'd expected, / his brain was so overloaded with new visual stimuli / that the world became a frightening and overwhelming place. //
동명사의 수동태
so ~ that ... : 너무 ~해서 ...하다
이제 볼 수 있다는 것에 감격하는 대신 / 그가 예상했던 것처럼 / 그의 뇌가 새로운 시각적 자극으로 너무 과부하가 걸려서 / 세상은 두렵고 압도적인 장소가 되었다 //

After he'd learned to know his family / through touch and smell, / he found that he couldn't recognize his children / with his eyes, / and this left him puzzled. //
목적어절 접속사
그가 자신의 가족을 아는 것을 배운 후 / 만지는 것과 냄새를 통해 / 그는 자신의 아이들을 알아볼 수 없다는 것을 알게 되었다 / 자신의 눈으로 / 그리고 이것은 그를 혼란스러운 상태로 남겨 두었다 //

Skiing also became a lot harder / as he struggled to adapt / to the visual stimulation. //
비교급 강조 부사
스키 또한 훨씬 더 어려워졌다 / 그가 적응하려고 힘쓰면서 / 시각적인 자극에 //
41번 **42번** 단서 2: 시력을 회복하고 오히려 스키가 어려워짐

This (c) confusion occurred / because his brain hadn't yet learned to see. //
이 혼란은 일어났다 / 그의 뇌가 아직 보는 것을 배우지 못했기 때문에 //

Though we often tend to assume / our eyes function as video cameras / which relay information to our brain, /
부사절 접속사(양보)
주격 관계대명사
비록 우리는 종종 가정하는 경향이 있지만 / 우리의 눈이 비디오카메라로서 기능한다고 / 우리의 뇌에 정보를 전달하는 /

advances in neuroscientific research have proven / that this is actually not the case. //
목적어절 접속사
신경 과학 연구의 발전은 증명했다 / 이것이 실제로 그렇지 않다는 것을 //
41번 **42번** 단서 3: 시력은 우리의 눈과 뇌 사이의 협력적인 노력임

Instead, / sight is a collaborative effort / between our eyes and our brains, / and the way we process (d) visual reality / depends on the way these two communicate. //
핵심 주어(단수)
단수 동사 ✽
대신 / 시력은 협력적인 노력이다 / 우리의 눈과 뇌 사이의 / 그리고 우리가 시각적 현실을 처리하는 방법은 / 이 두 가지가 소통하는 방식에 달려 있다 //

If communication between our eyes and our brains is disturbed, / our perception of reality is altered accordingly. //
만약 우리의 눈과 뇌 사이의 의사소통이 방해된다면 / 현실에 대한 우리의 인식은 그에 따라 바뀐다 //

And because other areas of May's brain had adapted / to process information / primarily through his other senses, /
그리고 May의 뇌의 다른 부분들은 적응했었기 때문에 / 정보를 처리하는 것에 / 주로 그의 다른 감각을 통해 /

the process of learning how to see / was (e) easier(→ harder) / than he'd anticipated. //
how to-v: ~하는 방법
보는 방법을 배우는 과정은 / 더 쉬웠다(→ 더 어려웠다) / 그가 예상했던 것보다 //

- majority ⓝ 대다수, 대부분 · adapt ⓥ 적응하다
- cultivate ⓥ 경작하다, (관계를) 쌓다 · state ⓝ 상태
- compensate ⓥ 보상하다, 보충되다 · entire ⓐ 전체의
- perception ⓝ 인식 · disrupt ⓥ 방해하다
- thrilled ⓐ 감격한, 짜릿한
- overload ⓥ (짐을) 너무 많이 싣다, 과부하가 걸리게 하다
- stimulus ⓝ 자극(pl. stimuli) · overwhelming ⓐ 압도적인
- recognize ⓥ 알아보다, 인식하다 · puzzled ⓐ 혼란스러워하는
- stimulation ⓝ 자극 · confusion ⓝ 혼란, 혼동
- assume ⓥ 가정하다 · function ⓥ 기능하다
- relay ⓥ 전달하다 · neuroscientific ⓐ 신경 과학의
- collaborative ⓐ 협력적인, 공동 작업의 · alter ⓥ 바꾸다, 고치다
- accordingly ⓐⓓ 그에 따라 · anticipate ⓥ 예상하다, 기대하다

Mike May는 세 살 때 자신의 시력을 잃었다. 그는 자신의 인생의 대부분을 보이지 않는 것에 적응하는 데, 그리고 심지어 이 상태에서 스키 경력을 쌓는 데도 보냈기 때문에, 자신의 다른 감각들은 (a) 더 강해지는 것을 통해 보충되었다. 그러나 그의 시력이 40대에 수술을 통해 회복되었을 때, 그의 현실에 대한 전반적 인식은 (b) 방해받았다. 그가 예상했던 것처럼 이제 볼 수 있다는 것에 감격하는 대신, 자신의 뇌가 새로운 시각적 자극으로 너무 과부하가 걸려 세상은 두렵고 압도적인 장소가 되었다. 그가 만지는 것과 냄새를 통해 자신의 가족을 아는 것을 배운 후, 그는 자신의 눈으로 자신의 아이들을 알아볼 수 없다는 것을 알게 되었고 이것은 그를 혼란스러운 상태로 남겨 두었다. 스키 또한 그가 시각적인 자극에 적응하려고 힘쓰면서 훨씬 더 어려워졌다.

이 (c) 혼란은 그의 뇌가 아직 보는 것을 배우지 못했기 때문에 일어났다. 비록 우리는 종종 우리의 눈이 우리의 뇌에 정보를 전달하는 비디오카메라로서 기능한다고 가정하는 경향이 있지만, 신경 과학 연구의 발전은 이것이 실제로 그렇지 않다는 것을 증명했다. 대신, 시력은 우리의 눈과 뇌 사이의 협력적인 노력이며, 우리가 (d) 시각적 현실을 처리하는 방법은 이 두 가지가 소통하는 방식에 달려 있다. 만약 우리의 눈과 뇌 사이의 의사소통이 방해된다면, 현실에 대한 우리의 인식은 그에 따라 바뀐다. 그리고 May의 뇌의 다른 부분들은 주로 그의 다른 감각을 통해 정보를 처리하는 것에 적응했었기 때문에, 보는 방법을 배우는 과정은 그가 예상했던 것보다 (e) 더 쉬웠다(→ 더 어려웠다).

41 정답 ①

윗글의 제목으로 가장 적절한 것은?
① Eyes and Brain Working Together for Sight
  시력을 위해 함께 일하는 눈과 뇌 — 시력은 눈과 뇌 사이의 협력적인 노력임
② Visualization: A Useful Tool for Learning
  시각화: 학습을 위한 유용한 도구 — 학습을 위해 시각화하는 것에 대한 내용이 아님
③ Collaboration Between Vision and Sound
  시각과 소리의 협업 — 시각과 소리가 아니라 눈과 뇌의 협업에 대한 내용임
④ How to Ignore New Visual Stimuli
  새로운 시각적 자극을 무시하는 방법 — 시각적 자극을 무시하라는 내용이 아님
⑤ You See What You Believe
  당신은 당신이 믿는 것을 본다 — 믿는 대로 보게 된다는 내용이 아님

| 문제 풀이 순서 | ★★❀ [정답률 75%]

1st 글의 앞부분을 읽으며 이어질 내용을 예상한다.

| 글의 앞부분 | Mike May는 세 살 때 자신의 시력을 잃었다. 그는 자신의 인생의 대부분을 보이지 않는 것에 적응하는 데, 그리고 심지어 이 상태에서 스키 경력을 쌓는 데도 보냈기 때문에, 자신의 다른 감각들은 (a) 더 강해지는 것을 통해 보충되었다. |

➡ 어렸을 때 시력을 잃은 Mike May는 보이지 않는 것에 적응하며 스키 경력을 쌓았는데, 이는 다른 감각들이 더 강해져 시각을 보충했기 때문이다. **단서**
따라서 시각을 보충하는 다른 감각들과 관련된 내용일 것이다. **발상**

2nd **1st** 에서 발상한 것을 토대로 글을 읽고, 내용을 파악한다.

- 시력이 회복됐을 때 현실에 대한 인식은 방해받았다. → 세상은 두렵고 압도적인 장소가 되었다. **41번 단서 1**
- 시각적 자극에 적응하려 하자 스키도 어려워졌다. **41번 단서 2**

➡ 그의 시력은 회복되었지만, 뇌가 전에는 없던 새로운 시각적 자극으로 과부하가 걸려 세상은 두려워졌고 스키를 타는 것도 어려워졌다.
▶ 즉, 시각은 눈과 뇌가 함께 작용하는 것임

3rd 글의 주제에 알맞은 제목을 고른다.

시력은 눈과 뇌 사이의 협력적인 노력이며, 이들이 소통하는 방식에 시각적 현실 처리 방법이 달라진다. **41번 단서 3**

➡ 시력은 눈과 뇌 사이의 협력적인 노력이며, 그 소통을 통해 현실을 인식하게 된다고 말하는 글이다.
▶ 따라서 글의 제목으로 가장 적절한 것은 ① '시력을 위해 함께 일하는 눈과 뇌'이다.

| 선택지 분석 |

① **Eyes and Brain Working Together for Sight**
  시력을 위해 함께 일하는 눈과 뇌
  시력은 눈과 뇌 사이의 협력적인 노력이라고 했다.

② **Visualization: A Useful Tool for Learning**
  시각화: 학습을 위한 유용한 도구
  학습을 위해 시각화를 활용하라고 말하는 글이 아니다.

③ **Collaboration Between Vision and Sound**
  시각과 소리의 협업
  시각과 소리가 아니라 눈과 뇌의 협업에 관해 설명하는 글이다.

④ **How to Ignore New Visual Stimuli**
  새로운 시각적 자극을 무시하는 방법
  Mike May가 시각적 자극 때문에 과부하가 걸렸다고 했지, 이를 무시하라는 내용이 아니다.

⑤ **You See What You Believe**
  당신은 당신이 믿는 것을 본다
  믿는 대로 보게 된다는 것은 언급되지 않았다.

42 정답 ⑤

밑줄 친 (a)~(e) 중에서 문맥상 낱말의 쓰임이 적절하지 않은 것은?
① (a) 시력을 잃은 상태로 스키를 타면 다른 감각들은 더 강해질 것임
  더 강한
② (b) 시력이 회복된 후 뇌에 과부하가 생겼으므로 인식이 방해받은 것임
  방해받다
③ (c) 시력을 회복하고 혼란스러워졌다고 했음
  혼란
④ (d) 시각적 인식을 위해 눈과 뇌가 협력해야 함
  시각적인
⑤ (e) 시력을 되찾은 후 스키 타는 것이 더 어려워졌다고 했음
  더 쉬운

❯왜 정답 ? ★★❀ [정답률 64%]

⑤ (e) easier 더 쉬운

그리고 May의 뇌의 다른 부분들은 주로 그의 다른 감각을 통해 정보를 처리하는 것에 적응했었기 때문에, 보는 방법을 배우는 과정은 그가 예상했던 것보다 (e) 더 쉬웠다.
더 어려웠다

➡ May가 시력을 되찾은 후에도 시각이 아닌 감각들로 정보를 처리하는 것에 익숙했다고 했으므로 보는 방법을 배우는 과정이 '더 쉬웠다'고 하는 것은 문맥에 맞지 않는다.
▶ easier를 harder(더 어려운)와 같은 반의어로 바꿔야 함

왜 오답?

① (a) stronger 더 강한

> 그는 자신의 인생의 대부분을 보이지 않는 것에 적응하는 데, 그리고 심지어 이 상태에서 스키 경력을 쌓는 데도 보냈기 때문에, 자신의 다른 감각들은 (a) 더 강해지는 것을 통해 보충되었다.

➡ 시력이 없는 상태로 스키 경력을 쌓는 데 인생의 대부분을 보냈다고 했으므로 다른 감각들은 '더 강해'졌을 것이다.

▶ stronger는 문맥에 맞음

② (b) disrupted 방해받다

> 그러나 그의 시력이 40대에 수술을 통해 회복되었을 때, 그의 현실에 대한 전반적 인식은 (b) 방해받았다.
> 그가 예상했던 것처럼 이제 볼 수 있다는 것에 감격하는 대신, 자신의 뇌가 새로운 시각적 자극으로 너무 과부하가 걸려 세상은 두렵고 압도적인 장소가 되었다.

➡ 시력이 회복된 후 뇌에 과부하가 생겼다고 했으므로 현실에 대한 인식은 '방해받은' 것이라고 할 수 있다.

▶ disrupted는 문맥에 맞음

③ (c) confusion 혼란

> 그가 만지는 것과 냄새를 통해 자신의 가족을 아는 것을 배운 후, 그는 자신의 눈으로 자신의 아이들을 알아볼 수 없다는 것을 알게 되었고 이것은 그를 혼란스러운 상태로 남겨 두었다. 스키 또한 그가 시각적인 자극에 적응하려고 힘쓰면서 훨씬 더 어려워졌다.
> 이 (c) 혼란은 그의 뇌가 아직 보는 것을 배우지 못했기 때문에 일어났다.

➡ 시력을 회복한 후 눈으로 아이들을 알아볼 수 없고 스키도 훨씬 더 어려워졌기 때문에 '혼란'이 생겼다고 했다.

▶ confusion은 문맥에 맞음

④ (d) visual 시각적인

> 대신, 시력은 우리의 눈과 뇌 사이의 협력적인 노력이며, 우리가 (d) 시각적 현실을 처리하는 방법은 이 두 가지가 소통하는 방식에 달려 있다.

➡ 시력은 눈과 뇌 사이의 협력적인 노력이라고 했으므로 '시각적' 현실을 처리하는 방법은 눈과 뇌의 소통 방식에 달려 있을 것이다.

▶ visual은 문맥에 맞음

─── 어법 특강 ───

＊ 주어-동사 수 일치

– 문장의 주어가 명사구 혹은 명사절일 때 항상 단수 취급한다. to부정사구, 동명사구나 의문사절, that절, whether절 등과 같은 명사절이 주어로 오는 경우 동사와 멀어질 수 있기 때문에 수 일치 여부를 쉽게 판단하기 힘들다. 따라서 항상 문장을 전체적으로 파악해야 한다.

• **Whether he will accept my offer is** not certain yet.
  명사절 주어 / 단수 동사
  (그가 나의 제안을 받아들일 지는 아직 확실하지 않다.)

• **To overcome my emotional problems is** difficult.
  to부정사구 주어 / 단수 동사
  (나의 감정적인 문제들을 극복하는 것은 어렵다.)

43~45 ＊테디 베어를 양보한 Marie

(A) On my daughter Marie's 8th birthday, / she received a bunch of presents / from her friends at school. //
나의 딸 Marie의 8번째 생일에 / 그녀는 많은 선물을 받았다 / 학교에서 친구들로부터 //

That evening, / with her favorite present, a teddy bear, in her arms, / we went to a restaurant / **to celebrate** her birthday. //
부사적 용법(목적) ＊
그날 저녁 / 그녀가 가장 좋아하는 선물인 테디 베어를 팔에 안고 / 우리는 식당에 갔다 / 그녀의 생일을 축하하기 위해 //
45번 ① 테디 베어를 팔에 안고 생일을 축하하기 위해 식당에 갔음

Our server, a friendly woman, / noticed my daughter holding the teddy bear / and said, / "My daughter loves teddy bears, too." //
동격
다정한 여성인 우리의 종업원은 / 나의 딸이 테디 베어를 안고 있다는 것을 알아차렸다 / 그리고 말했다 / "나의 딸도 테디 베어를 좋아해요"라고 //

Then, / we started chatting / about (a) her family. //
= our server's
그리고 나서 / 우리는 담소를 나누기 시작했다 / 그녀의 가족에 대해 //
43번 단서 1: Marie의 가족은 종업원의 가족에 대해 담소를 나누기 시작했음

★(A) 문단 요약: Marie의 생일에 간 식당에서 종업원이 자신의 딸도 테디 베어를 좋아한다고 말했음

(B) **When** Marie came back out, / I asked her / what she **had been doing**. //
부사절 접속사 / 과거완료 진행형
43번 단서 2: 식당으로 다시 뛰어 들어갔다가 돌아온 Marie에게 무엇을 했는지 물었음
Marie가 돌아왔을 때 / 나는 그녀에게 물었다 / 무엇을 하고 있었냐고 //

She said / **that** she gave her teddy bear to our server / **so that** she could give it to (b) her daughter. //
목적어절 접속사 / = our server's / '(그래서) ~하도록'
그녀는 말했다 / 자신의 테디 베어를 우리의 종업원에게 주었다고 / 그녀가 자신의 딸에게 그것을 줄 수 있도록 //

I was surprised at her sudden action / because I could see / how much she loved that bear already. //
45번 ② T는 Marie의 갑작스러운 행동에 놀랐음
나는 그녀의 갑작스러운 행동에 놀랐다 / 알 수 있었기 때문에 / 이미 그녀가 그 테디 베어를 얼마나 좋아하는지 //

(c) She **must have seen** the look on my face, / because she said, /
= Marie must have p.p.: ~했음에 틀림없다
그녀는 내 얼굴의 표정을 봤음에 틀림없다 / 왜냐하면 그녀가 말했기 때문이다 /

"I can't imagine being stuck in a hospital bed. // I just want her to get better soon." //
"저는 병원 침대에 갇혀 있는 것을 상상할 수 없어요 // 전 그저 그녀가 빨리 낫기를 바랄 뿐이에요"라고 //

★(B) 문단 요약: Marie는 자신이 정말 좋아하는 테디 베어를 종업원에게 주며 그녀의 딸에게 주라고 했음

(C) I felt moved by Marie's words / **as** we walked toward the car. //
부사절 접속사(시간)
43번 단서 3: Marie가 종업원의 딸이 빨리 낫기를 바란다고 말한 것에 감동했음
나는 Marie의 말에 감동받았다 / 우리가 차를 향해 걸어갈 때 //

Then, / our server **ran** out to our car / and **thanked** Marie for her generosity. //
병렬 구조
45번 ③ 종업원은 Marie의 관대함에 고마워했음
그때 / 우리의 종업원이 우리 차로 달려 나왔다 / 그리고 Marie의 관대함에 고마워했다 //

The server said / **that** (d) she had never had anyone / doing anything like that / for her family before. //
목적어절 접속사 / = our server
종업원은 말했다 / 어떤 사람도 가진 적이 없었다고 / 그런 일을 해 준 / 이전에 자신의 가족을 위해 //

Later, Marie said / it was her best birthday ever. //
나중에 Marie는 말했다 / 그날이 그녀의 최고의 생일이었다고 //

I was so proud of her empathy and warmth, / and this was an unforgettable experience / for our family. //
나는 그녀의 공감과 따뜻함이 너무 자랑스러웠다 / 그리고 이것은 잊을 수 없는 경험이었다 / 우리 가족에게 //

★(C) 문단 요약: 종업원이 Marie에게 고마워했고 Marie의 가족에게도 잊을 수 없는 경험이었음

43번 단서 4, 45번 ④ 종업원은 자신의 딸이 다리가 부러져서 병원에 있다고 말했음

(D) The server mentioned / during the conversation / **that** her daughter was in the hospital / with a broken leg. //
목적어절 접속사
그 종업원은 말했다 / 대화 중에 / 자신의 딸이 병원에 있다고 / 다리가 부러져 //

2022.11
12회

= Our server · 목적어절 접속사

(e) <u>She</u> also said / <u>that</u> Marie looked about the same age / as her daughter. //

그녀는 또한 말했다 / Marie가 나이가 거의 똑같아 보인다고 / 자신의 딸과 //

She was so kind and attentive all evening, / and even gave

간접목적어 · 직접목적어

<u>Marie cookies</u> for free. // **45번 ⑤** 종업원은 Marie에게 쿠키를 무료로 주었음

그녀는 저녁 내내 매우 친절하고 세심했다 / 그리고 심지어 Marie에게 쿠키를 무료로 주었다 //

After we finished our meal, / we paid the bill / and began to

walk to our car / when unexpectedly Marie <u>asked</u> me to wait /

병렬 구조

and <u>ran</u> back into the restaurant. //

우리가 식사를 마친 후 / 우리는 요금을 지불하고 / 우리 차로 걸어가기 시작했다 / 그때 갑자기 Marie가 나에게 기다려 달라고 부탁했다 / 그리고 식당으로 다시 뛰어 들어갔다 //

*(D) 문단 요약: 종업원의 딸은 Marie와 나이가 비슷한데 지금 병원에 있다고 했고, 식사 후에 Marie가 식당으로 다시 들어갔음

• a bunch of 다수의, 많은   • notice ⓥ 알아차리다
• chat ⓥ 담소를 나누다   • sudden ⓐ 갑작스러운
• be stuck in ~에 갇히다   • generosity ⓝ 관대함, 너그러움
• empathy ⓝ 공감 (능력)   • unforgettable ⓐ 잊을 수 없는
• mention ⓥ 언급하다, 말하다   • conversation ⓝ 대화
• attentive ⓐ 주의를 기울이는, 세심한
• unexpectedly ⓐⓓ 예상치 못하게, 갑자기

(A) 나의 딸 Marie의 8번째 생일에, 그녀는 학교에서 친구들로부터 많은 선물을 받았다. 그날 저녁, 그녀가 가장 좋아하는 선물인 테디 베어를 팔에 안고 우리는 그녀의 생일을 축하하기 위해 식당에 갔다. 다정한 여성인 우리의 종업원은 나의 딸이 테디 베어를 안고 있다는 것을 알아차렸고, "나의 딸도 테디 베어를 좋아해요."라고 말했다. 그리고 나서, 우리는 (a) <u>그녀의</u> 가족에 대해 담소를 나누기 시작했다.

(D) 그 종업원은 대화 중에 자신의 딸이 다리가 부러져 병원에 있다고 말했다. (e) 그녀는 또한 Marie가 자신의 딸과 나이가 거의 똑같아 보인다고 말했다. 그녀는 저녁 내내 매우 친절하고 세심했고, 심지어 Marie에게 쿠키를 무료로 주었다. 우리가 식사를 마친 후, 우리는 요금을 지불하고 우리 차로 걸어가기 시작했는데 그때 갑자기 Marie가 나에게 기다려 달라고 부탁하고 식당으로 다시 뛰어 들어갔다.

(B) Marie가 돌아왔을 때 나는 그녀에게 무엇을 하고 있었느냐고 물었다. 그녀는 자신의 테디 베어를 우리의 종업원에게 주어서 그녀가 (b) <u>자신의</u> 딸에게 그것을 줄 수 있도록 했다고 말했다. 나는 이미 그녀가 그 테디 베어를 얼마나 좋아하는지 알 수 있었기 때문에 그녀의 갑작스러운 행동에 놀랐다. (c) <u>그녀는</u> 내 얼굴의 표정을 분명히 봤을 것인데, 왜냐하면 그녀가 "저는 병원 침대에 갇혀 있는 것을 상상할 수 없어요. 전 그저 그녀가 빨리 낫기를 바랄 뿐이에요."라고 말했기 때문이다.

(C) 우리가 차를 향해 걸어갈 때 나는 Marie의 말에 감동했다. 그때 우리의 종업원이 우리 차로 달려 나와 Marie의 관대함에 고마워했다. (d) <u>그녀는</u> 이전에 자신의 가족을 위해 그런 일을 해 준 어떤 사람도 가진 적이 없었다고 종업원은 말했다. 나중에 Marie는 그날이 그녀의 최고의 생일이었다고 말했다. 나는 그녀의 공감과 따뜻함이 너무 자랑스러웠고, 이것은 우리 가족에게 잊을 수 없는 경험이었다.

---

43 정답 ④

주어진 글 (A)에 이어질 내용을 순서에 맞게 배열한 것으로 가장 적절한 것은?

① (B) — (D) — (C)
테디 베어를 종업원에게 주는 (B)보다 종업원의 딸이 병원에 있다고 하는 (D)가 먼저 와야 함
② (C) — (B) — (D)
(C)는 Marie의 행동에 감동하는 마무리 부분이므로 마지막에 와야 함
③ (C) — (D) — (B)
④ (D) — (B) — (C)
(D) 식사 후에 Marie가 식당으로 다시 들어감 — (B) Marie는 테디 베어를 종업원에게 주고 그녀의 딸에게 주라고 했음 — (C) Marie의 가족에게도 잊을 수 없는 경험이었음
⑤ (D) — (C) — (B)
(B)에서 한 Marie의 행동에 대해 (C)에서 감동하는 순서가 되어야 함

> **왜** 정답 · 오답**?** ✱✿✿ [정답률 82%]

(A): 나의 딸 Marie는 생일 선물로 받은 테디 베어를 팔에 안고 식당에 갔는데, 이를 본 종업원이 자신의 딸도 테디 베어를 좋아한다고 말했고 우리는 대화를 하기 시작했다.

⇒ 어떤 대화를 나눴는지가 이어질 것이다.

(B): 돌아온 Marie에게 무엇을 했는지 묻자, 자신의 테디 베어를 종업원의 딸에게 줄 수 있도록 그녀에게 주었다고 했다. 나는 Marie가 테디 베어를 얼마나 좋아하는지 알았기 때문에 놀랐다.

⇒ Marie가 돌아오기 전에 어딘가로 갔다는 내용이 앞에 있어야 하고, 뒤에는 테디 베어를 받은 종업원의 행동이 이어질 것이다.

(C): 그때 종업원이 달려 나와 Marie에게 고마워했고, Marie의 가족에게도 잊을 수 없는 경험이었다.

⇒ Marie와 그녀의 가족에게 잊을 수 없는 경험이었다며 글을 마무리했다.

(D): 종업원은 그녀의 딸이 Marie와 나이가 같아 보인다고 하며, 다리가 부러져 병원에 있다고 했다. 식사를 마친 후 차로 걸어가던 중 Marie가 갑자기 식당으로 뛰어 들어갔다.

⇒ 대화를 시작했다는 (A)에 이어지는 내용이고 뒤에는 Marie가 어딘가에서 돌아왔다는 (B)가 이어져야 한다.
▶ (D) 식사 후 Marie가 식당으로 다시 들어감 ➡ (B) 돌아온 Marie는 테디 베어를 종업원에게 주며 그녀의 딸에게 주라고 했음 ➡ (C) 종업원은 Marie에게 고마워했고, Marie의 가족에게도 잊을 수 없는 경험이었음
▶ 글의 순서는 ④ (D) ➡ (B) ➡ (C)임

---

44 정답 ③

밑줄 친 (a)~(e) 중에서 가리키는 대상이 나머지 넷과 <u>다른</u> 것은?
① (a)   ② (b)   ③(c)   ④ (d)   ⑤ (e)
= our server's   = our server's   = Marie   = our server   = Our server

> **왜** 정답 **?** ✱✿✿ [정답률 71%]

③ (c) She: 'I'의 표정을 보고 종업원의 딸이 빨리 낫기를 바란다는 말을 한 사람
▶ Marie

> **왜** 오답 **?**

① (a) her: Marie의 가족이 담소를 나누기 시작한 대상 ▶ our server's
② (b) her: Marie가 테디 베어를 준 대상 ▶ our server's
④ (d) she: 자신의 가족을 위해 관대함을 베풀어 준 사람이 없었다고 말한 사람
▶ our server
⑤ (e) She: 자신의 딸과 Marie의 나이가 비슷해 보인다고 말한 사람 ▶ Our server

---

45 정답 ④

윗글에 관한 내용으로 적절하지 <u>않은</u> 것은?
① Marie는 테디 베어를 팔에 안고 식당에 갔다.
with her favorite present, a teddy bear, in her arms, we went to a restaurant
② 'I'는 Marie의 갑작스러운 행동에 놀랐다.
I was surprised at her sudden action
③ 종업원은 Marie의 관대함에 고마워했다.
our server ~ thanked Marie for her generosity
④ 종업원은 자신의 딸이 팔이 부러져서 병원에 있다고 말했다.
The server mentioned ~ that her daughter was in the hospital with a broken leg.
⑤ 종업원은 Marie에게 쿠키를 무료로 주었다.
even gave Marie cookies for free

종업원은 자신의 딸이 다리가 부러져 병원에 있다고(The server mentioned during the conversation that her daughter was in the hospital with a broken leg.) 했다. 따라서 팔이 부러져서 병원에 있다고 한 ④은 적절하지 않다.

왜 오답 ?

① Marie는 테디 베어를 팔에 안고 생일을 축하하기 위해 식당에 갔다고 했다. (That evening, with her favorite present, a teddy bear, in her arms, we went to a restaurant to celebrate her birthday.)

② 'I'는 Marie의 갑작스러운 행동에 놀랐다고 했다. (I was surprised at her sudden action)

③ 종업원이 차로 달려와서 Marie의 관대함에 고마워했다고 했다. (Then, our server ran out to our car and thanked Marie for her generosity.)

⑤ 종업원은 Marie에게 쿠키를 무료로 주었다고 했다. (She was so kind and attentive all evening, and even gave Marie cookies for free.)

어법 특강

＊ to부정사의 명사적 용법

– to부정사가 명사로 쓰여 '~ 하는 것'을 의미하며 주어, 목적어, 보어 역할을 한다.

• I need <u>to ask</u> myself what I really like.
　　　　　목적어
(나는 내가 정말 무엇을 좋아하는지 스스로에게 물어볼 필요가 있다.)

• The doctor's plan is <u>to go</u> to Nepal to help the sick.
　　　　　　　　　　보어
(그 의사의 계획은 아픈 사람들을 돕기 위해 네팔에 가는 것이다.)

＊ to부정사의 형용사적 용법

– to부정사가 형용사처럼 쓰여 명사를 수식한다.

• Women have the chance <u>to reach</u> their potential as athletes.
　　　　　　　　　　the chance 수식
(여성들이 운동선수로서 자신의 잠재력을 발휘할 수 있는 기회를 가진다.)

– 「be + to부정사」 형태로 주어를 보충 설명(예정, 의무, 가능, 운명, 의도)한다.

• This train is <u>to leave</u> at 10:00.
　　　　　　　예정
(이 기차는 10시에 출발할 예정이다.)

＊ to부정사의 부사적 용법

– to부정사의 부사적 용법에는 목적, 감정의 원인, 결과, 이유, 판단의 근거, 형용사 수식의 쓰임이 있다.

• Hundreds of millions of people have died <u>to defend</u> their country.
　　　　　　　　　　　　　　　　　　목적
(수억 명의 사람들이 그들의 나라를 지키기 위해 죽었다.)

• It's an honor <u>to meet</u> you.
　　　　　　감정의 원인
(당신을 만나다니 영광입니다.)

12회 Dictation
문제 p. 226

01 melted away with the sun out / we've closed some of the trails / unavailable for hikers

02 They're in the first drawer / the same amount of ingredients / stick to the recipe

03 The characters exploring space / inspired me to design / the theme song / start putting the music into the game

04 the three light bulbs above the staircase / rug on the floor / keep my favorite books nearby

05 set up a chair for our guest / she'll draw caricatures of us / I left it in my car

06 some potato chips with your order / Will that be all / any soda from the fridge

07 you're off from work / sprained my wrist / it'll be better in a month

08 make his own cereal bowl / It's a 10-minute drive / simply scan the QR code

09 the length of your whistling video / be sure to turn off the echo effect / by public online voting

10 are machine washable at home / so we won't be disturbed / any color except for gray

11 How long have you been waiting here

12 crying and wandering around the park

13 a list of questions / to give a favorable impression / practice smiling and look for my best suit

14 are a little tight for me / these shoes in a different color / red and green in storage

15 renowned psychology professor / a severe stomachache / if he can reschedule their meeting

[16~17] used to carry their messages / by varying the pitch or beat / to signal attacks from enemies / quickly than runners

---

12회 어휘 Review Test
문제 p. 230

01 언급하다	**15** manage to	**29** extend
02 부족	**16** collective	**30** signal
03 적도	**17** empathy	**31** attentive
04 면역의	**18** reflective	**32** means
05 유혹	**19** experienced	**33** accumulate
06 severe	**20** motivator	**34** illegal
07 superstition	**21** unstable	**35** abundance
08 favorable	**22** consequence	**36** irreplaceable
09 witness	**23** distaste	**37** loyal
10 maintenance	**24** textile	**38** function
11 draw on	**25** renowned	**39** perspective
12 interfere with	**26** eliminate	**40** engagement
13 wipe out	**27** equalize	
14 keep track of	**28** navigate